TRAVELING WITH YOUR PET

THE AAA PETBOOK®

The AAA guide to more than 10,000 pet-friendly, AAA-RATED® lodgings across the United States & Canada

2nd Edition

AAA

President & CEO: Robert Darbelnet

Executive Vice President, Publishing and Administration: Rick Rinner

Managing Director, Publishing: Alan Borne

Managing Director, GIS/Cartography and Administration: Bob Hopkins

Director, GIS/Publishing Development and Support: Ramin Kalhor

Director, Product Development: Bill Wood

Director, Publishing Operations: Susan Sears

Director, Tourism Information Development: Michael Petrone

Director, Travel Information: Jeff Zimmerman

Manager, Electronic Media Design: Mike McCrary

Manager, Graphic Communication Services: Yvonne Macklin

Manager, Prepress, Quality Services and Photography Services: Tim Johnson

Manager, Product Support: Linda Indolfi

Manager, Publishing Communications and Marketing: Josette Constantino

Manager, GIS/Publishing Development and Support: Robert D. Miller

Manager, Travel Information Operations: Brenda Daniels

Manager, Travel Store Operations: Sharon Edwards

National Sales Manager: Robert Foley

Regional Managers, Tourism Information Development: Todd Cronson, Larry Hamilton, Michel Mousseau, Stacy Mower, Patrick Schardin, Bob Sheron

Data Processing: Kelly Giewont, Melinda Ragland, Jan Roza, Andrea Tlumacki

Designers: Michele Deitsch, Tim Reilly

Development Editor: Greg Weekes

Electronic Pagination: Christine Carter

Photo Research: Patricia Nasser, Diane Norden

Product Manager: Cynthia Psarakis

Programming: James Cothrine

AAA Publishing wishes to acknowledge the following organizations for their assistance:

American Boarding Kennels Association, American Veterinary Medical Association, Humane Society of the United States, National Association of Professional Pet Sitters, Pet Sitters International, U.S. Dept. of Agriculture-Animal & Plant Health Inspection Service

Cover photos

Front: John Lawlor/FPG International
Spine: Telegraph-FPG International
Back: P. Wallick/H. Armstrong Roberts

Please send any comments to:
Product Manager, AAA PetBook, AAA Publishing, Mail Stop 66, 1000 AAA Dr., Heathrow, FL 32746

ISBN 1-56251-320-6
Stock # 5522

Second Edition

Printed in Canada by Quebecor Printing, L'Eclaireur, Québec.

TABLE OF CONTENTS

ABOUT THIS BOOK

Welcome to the 2nd edition of **Traveling With Your Pet—The AAA PetBook**®. Traveling With Your Pet is a must for the traveler who's also an animal lover. This comprehensive book provides all the information you need to know about taking a four-legged friend on the road. Will Spot be a good car passenger? Is it safe to take Snowball on a plane? What are the important rules of pet etiquette? Is pet insurance a good idea? *Traveling With Your Pet* answers all of these questions and more. Here are just some of the features covered:

- An extensive roundup of animal clinics compiled by the Veterinary Emergency & Critical Care Society (VECCS). Names, addresses and phone numbers offer an at-your-fingertips way to plan for unexpected or emergency situations, both en route and at your destination.

- Listings of national public lands in the United States and Canada, with recreation information.

- Border crossing procedures and tips for travelers—both entering Canada from the United States and vice versa.

- Policies pertaining to service animals.

Traveling With Your Pet lists more than 10,000 AAA-RATED® lodgings. And the listings show AAA's trustworthy diamond ratings, the traveler's assurance of quality. Other handy features include:

- Informative highway directions.

- Specific information about lodgings' pet policies: deposits and fees, housekeeping service, designated rooms and other stipulations relating to travelers with pets.

- Additional details about the lodgings themselves, including icons for amenities, recreation, dining and accessibility.

- Icons designating AAA's member discount programs.

All of this valuable information is packaged in a contemporary, easy-to-read format, making *Traveling With Your Pet—The AAA PetBook*® as indispensable an on-the-road companion as Spot's water dish or Snowball's litter box. Don't leave home without it, and remember: It always pays to *Travel With Someone You Trust*®.

More and more, people are viewing their pets as full-fledged members of the family. Spot and Snowball often have their own beds, premium-quality foods, a basketful of toys and a special place in their humans' hearts.

Until it's time to go on vacation, that is. Then the family dog or cat is consigned to "watching the fort" at home while everyone else experiences the joy of traveling. Many pet lovers hesitate to take their animals with them because they don't think they'll be able to find accommodations that accept four-legged guests. Others aren't sure how — or if — their furry friends will adapt.

The truth is, including a pet in the family vacation is fairly easy, so long as you plan ahead. Most pets respond well to travel, a fact that isn't lost on the tourism industry. More than 10,000 AAA-RATED® hotels and motels from coast to coast are pet-friendly, and airline bookings for pet passengers are on the rise. Great companions at home, pets are earning their stripes on the road, too.

So if you've been longing to hit the trail with a canine or feline companion, read the tips on the following pages. You may find that a getaway can be far more enjoyable with than without your pet.

Should Your Pet Travel?

Before you make reservations, determine if your pet should travel. Most animals can and do make the most of the experience, but a small percentage simply are not cut out for traveling. Illness, physical condition and temperament are important factors, as is your pet's ability to adjust to such stresses as changes to his environment and routine. When in doubt, check with your veterinarian. If you feel your pet isn't up to the trip, it's better for everyone if he stays home.

❖ **Rule #1: Pets who are very young, very old, pregnant, sick, injured, prone to biting or excessive vocalizing, or who cannot follow basic obedience commands should not travel.**

Even if Spot and Snowball are seasoned travelers, take into account the type of vacation and activities you have planned. No pet is going to be happy (or safe) cooped up in a car or hotel room. Likewise, the family dog may love camping and hiking, but the family cat may not. Putting a little thought toward your animal's needs and safety will pay off in a more enjoyable vacation for everyone.

❖ **Rule #2: If your pet can't actively participate in the trip, she should stay home.**

Most of the information in this guide pertains to cats and dogs. If your traveling companion is a bird, hamster, pig, ferret, lizard or other exotic creature, remember that unusual animals are not always accepted as readily as more conventional pets. Always specify the type of pet you have when making arrangements.

Also check states' animal policies. **Hawaii** imposes 30- and 120-day quarantines for all imported carnivorous animals to prevent the importation of rabies. Guide dogs (but not other service animals) are exempt from the quarantine, although they still must undergo vaccinations, serum antibody testing and microchip identification. For additional details, obtain the brochure "Animal Quarantine Station" from the Hawaii Department of Agriculture, Animal Quarantine Station, 99-951 Halawa Valley St., Aiea, HI 96701-3246; phone (808) 483-7151. Guide dog owners should request information on the certified guide exemption program.

North Carolina has stringent restrictions regarding pets in lodgings. Make certain you understand an accommodation's specific policies before making reservations.

❖ **Rule #3: Be specific when making travel plans that include your pet. Nobody wants unpleasant surprises on vacation.**

If Spot and Snowball stay behind, leave them in good hands while you're gone. **Family, friends and neighbors** make good sitters (provided they're willing), especially if they know your pet and can care for him in your home. Provide detailed instructions for feeding, exercise and medication, as well as phone numbers for your destination, your veterinarian and your local animal emergency clinic.

Professional pet sitters offer a range of services, from feeding and walking your pet daily to full-time house sitting while you are gone. Interview several candidates, and always check credentials and references. For additional information, contact the National Association of

Professional Pet Sitters or Pet Sitters International. *(See sidebars below and on p. 7.)*

Kennels board many animals simultaneously and generally are run by professionals who will provide food and exercise according to your instructions. Pets usually are kept in a run (dogs) or cage (cats and small dogs) and may not get the same level of human interaction as at home. **Veterinary clinics** also board pets and may be the best choice if yours is sick, injured or needs special medical care. For further information on how to select a kennel, contact the American Boarding Kennels Association. *(See sidebars below and on p. 7.)*

Veterinarians, fellow pet owners and professional associations are a good source of referrals for sitters and kennels.

🐾 **Rule #4: Never leave your pet with someone you don't trust.**

Choosing a Pet Sitter

Before hiring a pet sitter, ask:
- Are they insured (for commercial liability) and bonded?
- What is included in the fee?
- Do they require current vaccinations?
- What kind of animals do they typically care for?
- How will they handle a medical, weather or home emergency?
- Do they fully understand your pet's medical or dietary needs?
- How much time will they spend with your pet?

The pet sitter should:
- Have a polished, professional attitude.
- Provide references.
- Have a standard contract outlining terms of service.
- Have experience in caring for animals.
- Insist on current vaccinations.
- Ask about your pet's health, temperament, schedule and needs.
- Visit and interact with your pet before you leave.
- Devote time and attention to your pet.
- Be affiliated with pet care organizations.

Be sure you:
- Explain your pet's personality — favorite toys, good and bad habits, hiding spots, general health, etc.
- Leave care instructions, keys, food and water dishes, extra supplies (food, medication, etc.) and phone numbers for your veterinarian and an emergency contact.
- Bring pets inside before leaving.

Choosing a Kennel

Before reserving a kennel, ask:
- What is included in the fee?
- Do they require current vaccinations?
- What kind of animals do they board?
- How will they handle a medical or weather emergency?
- Will your pet be kept in a cage or run?
- Will your pet receive daily exercise?
- Do they fully understand your pet's medical or dietary needs?
- How and how often will they interact with your pet?

The kennel should:
- Require proof of current vaccinations.
- Be clean, well-ventilated and offer adequate protection from the elements.
- Have separate areas for dogs, cats and other animals, with secure fencing and caging.
- Clean and disinfect facilities daily.
- Give your pet his regular food on his regular schedule.
- Provide soft bedding in runs/cages.
- Understand your pet's medical needs.
- Provide or obtain veterinary care if necessary.
- Offer sufficient supervision.
- Have a friendly, animal-loving staff.

Be sure you:
- Notify staff of behavior quirks (dislike of other animals, children, etc.).
- Provide food and medication.
- Leave a familiar object with your pet.
- Leave phone numbers for your veterinarian and an emergency contact.
- Spend time with your pet before boarding him.

Travelers Who Have Disabilities

Individuals with disabilities who own service animals to assist them with everyday activities undoubtedly face challenges, but traveling should not be one of them. Service animals (the accepted term for animals trained to help people with disabilities) are not pets and thus are not subject to many of the laws or policies pertaining to pets.

The Americans With Disabilities Act (ADA) defines a service animal as "any guide dog, signal dog or other animal individually trained to provide assistance to an individual with a disability." ADA regulations stipulate that public accommodations are required to modify policies, practices and procedures to permit the use of a service animal by an individual with a disability.

The purpose of these regulations is to provide equal access opportunities for people with disabilities and to ensure that they are not separated from their service animals. A tow truck operator, for example, must allow a service animal to ride in the truck with her owner rather than in the towed vehicle.

Public accommodations may charge a fee or deposit to an individual who has a disability — provided that fee or deposit is required of all customers — but no fees or deposits may be charged for the service animal, even those normally charged for pets.

The handler (the animal's owner) is responsible for her care and behavior; if she creates an altercation or poses a direct threat, the handler may be required to remove the animal from the premises and pay for any resulting damages.

The **Delta Society,** an organization devoted to companion and service animals, has information about laws that affect people and service animals in public accommodations. Phone (800) 869-6898 for a catalog, or visit Delta's web site: http://www.deltasociety.org.

Preparing Your Pet for Travel

Happily, many vacations can be planned to include fun activities for pets. Trips to parks, nature trails, the ocean or lakes offer exposure to the world beyond the window or fence at home, as well as the chance to explore new

CONTACT INFORMATION

The following organizations offer information, tips, brochures and other travel materials designed to help you and your pet enjoy a happy and safe vacation.

American Animal Hospital Association
12575 W. Bayaud Ave.
Lakewood, CO 80228
(800) 883-6301
http://www.healthypet.com/

American Boarding Kennels Association
4575 Galley Rd., Ste. 400A
Colorado Springs, CO 80915
(719) 591-1113
http://www.abka.com/

American Society for the Prevention of Cruelty to Animals
424 E. 92nd St.
New York, NY 10128
(212) 876-7700
http://www.aspca.org/

American Veterinary Medical Association
1931 N. Meacham Rd., Ste. 100
Schaumburg, IL 60173
(847) 925-8070
http://www.avma.org/

Humane Society of the United States
2100 L St. NW
Washington, DC 20037
(202) 452-1100
http://www.hsus.org/

National Association of Professional Pet Sitters
1030 15th St. NW, Ste. 870
Washington, DC 20005
(202) 393-3317
http://www.petsitters.org/

Pet Sitters International
418 E. King St.
King, NC 27021-9163
(336) 983-9222
http://www.petsit.com/

USDA-APHIS
Deputy Administrator
USDA-APHIS-Animal Care
4700 River Rd., Unit 84
Riverdale, MD 20737-1234
(301) 734-4981
http://www.aphis.usda.gov/

sights and sounds. Even the streets of an unfamiliar city can provide a smorgasbord of discoveries for your animal friend to enjoy.

Once you decide Spot and Snowball are ready to hit the road, plan accordingly:

✤ Get a clean bill of health from the veterinarian. Update your pet's vaccinations, check his general physical condition and obtain a health certificate showing proof of up-to-date inoculations, particularly rabies, distemper and kennel cough. Such documentation will be necessary if you cross state or country lines, and also may come in handy in the unlikely event your pet gets lost and must be retrieved from the local shelter. Don't forget to ask the doctor about potential health risks at your destination (Lyme disease, heartworm infection) and the necessary preventive measures.

If your pet is taking prescribed medicine pack a sufficient supply, plus a few days' extra. Also take the prescription in case you need a refill. Be prepared for emergencies by getting the names and numbers of clinics or doctors at your destination from your veterinarian or the American Animal Hospital Association *(see sidebar, p. 7)*. **Hint:** Obtain these references before you leave and keep them handy throughout the trip.

Make sure your pet is in good physical shape overall, especially if you are planning an active vacation. If your animal is primarily sedentary or overweight, he may not be up to lengthy hikes through the woods.

Note: Some owners believe a sedated animal will travel more easily than one that is fully aware, but this is rarely the case. In fact, tranquilizing an animal can make travel much more stressful. Always consult a veterinarian about what is best for your pet, and administer sedatives only under the doctor's direction. In addition, never give an animal medication that is specifically prescribed for humans. The dosage may be too high for an animal's much smaller body mass, or may cause dangerous side effects.

✤ Acclimate your pet to car travel. Even if you're flying, your pet will have to ride in the car to get to the airport or terminal, and you don't want any unpleasant surprises before departure.

Some animals are used to riding in the car and even enjoy it. But most associate the inside of the carrier or the car with one thing only: the annual visit to the V-E-T. Considering that these visits usually end with a jab from a sharp needle, it's no wonder that some pets forget their training and act up in the car. If this is your situation, you will have to re-train your animal to view a drive as a reward, not a punishment. Even older pets can be trained to be excellent automobile companions.

Begin by allowing your pet to become used to the car without actually going anywhere. Then take short trips to places that are fun for animals, such as the park or the drive-through window at a fast-food restaurant. (Keep those indulgent snacks to a minimum!) Be sure to praise her for good behavior with words, petting and healthy treats. It shouldn't take long before you and your furry friend are enjoying leisurely drives without incident. *(See "Traveling by Car," p. 11.)*

✤ Brush up on behavior. Will Snowball make a good travel companion? Or will he be an absolute terror on the road? Don't wait until the vacation is already under way to find out; review general behavioral guidelines with respect to your animal, keeping in mind that the unfamiliarity of travel situations may test the temperament of even the most well-behaved pet.

It's a good idea to socialize Spot by exposing her to other people and animals (especially if she normally stays inside). You're likely to encounter both on your trip, and it is important that she learns to behave properly in the company of strangers. Make her introduction to the outside world gradual, such as a walk in a new neighborhood or taking her along while you run errands. Exposure to new situations will help reduce fear of the unknown and result in more socially acceptable behavior.

Is your pet housebroken? How is he around children? Does he obey vocal commands? Be honest about your animal's ability to cope in unfamiliar surroundings. Depending on the length and nature of the trip and your pet's level of command response, an obedience refresher course might be a good idea.

✤ Learn about your destination. Check into quarantines or other restrictions well in advance, and make follow-up calls as your departure date approaches. Find out what types of documentation will be required — not just en route, but on the way home as well.

Be aware of potential safety or health risks where you're going, and plan accordingly. For example, the southeastern United States — particularly Florida — has alligators and heartworm-carrying mosquitoes, and many mountainous and wooded areas may harbor ticks that transmit Lyme disease.

Confirm all travel plans within a few days of your departure, especially with lodgings and airlines; their policies may have changed after you made the reservations. If you plan to visit state parks or attractions that accept pets on the premises, obtain their animal regulations in advance.

❧ **Determine the best mode of transportation.** Most people traveling with pets drive. Many airlines do accept animals in the passenger cabin or cargo hold, and as more people choose to fly with their pet these airlines are becoming more pet-conscious. Restrictions vary as to the type and number of pets an airline will carry, however, so inquire about animal shipping and welfare policies before making reservations. If your pet must travel in the cargo hold, heed the cautionary advice in the "Traveling by Air" section of this book. *(See p. 11.)*

Flying is really the only major option to car travel. Amtrak, as well as Greyhound and other interstate bus lines, do not accept pets. Local rail and bus companies may allow pets in small carriers, but this is an exception rather than a rule. The only cruise ship that permits pets is the *Queen Elizabeth 2* (on trans-Atlantic crossings), and animals are restricted to the cargo area.

Note: Seeing-eye dogs and other service animals are exempt from the regulations prohibiting pets on Amtrak and interstate bus lines.

A word of advice: Never try to sneak your pet onto any mode of public transportation where she is not permitted. You may face legal action or fines, and the animal may be confiscated if discovered.

❧ **Pack as carefully for your pet as you do for yourself.** *(See checklist, below.)* Make sure she has a collar with a license tag and ID tag(s) listing her name and yours, along with your address and phone number. As an added pre-

What To Take

- ☐ Carrier or crate. *(See "Selecting a Carrier or Crate," p. 10, for specifications.)*
- ☐ Nylon or leather collar or harness, license tag, ID tag(s) and leash. All should be sturdy and should fit your pet properly.
- ☐ Food and water dishes.
- ☐ Can opener and spoon (for canned food).
- ☐ An ample supply of food, plus a few days' extra.
- ☐ Bottled water from home. (Many animals are finicky about their drinking water.)
- ☐ Cooler with ice.
- ☐ Healthy treats.
- ☐ Medications, if necessary.
- ☐ Health certificate and other required documents.
- ☐ A blanket or other bedding. (If your pet is used to sleeping on the furniture, bring an old blanket or sheet to place on top of the hotel's bedding.)
- ☐ Litter supplies (for cats or other small animals), a scooper and plastic bags (for dogs).
- ☐ Favorite toys.
- ☐ Carpet deodorizer.
- ☐ Chewing preventative.

- ☐ A recent photograph and a written description including name, breed, gender, height, weight, coloring and distinctive markings.
- ☐ Grooming supplies:
  comb/brush
  nail clippers
  shampoo
  towels
  cotton balls/tissues
  paper towels
- ☐ First-aid kit:
  gauze
  bandages and adhesive tape
  towels
  hydrogen peroxide
  rubbing alcohol
  ointment
  muzzle
  scissors
  tweezers (for removing ticks, burrs, splinters, etc.)
  local emergency phone numbers
  first-aid guide (such as "Pet First Aid: Cats & Dogs," published by The Humane Society of the United States and the American Red Cross)

caution, some owners outfit their dog with a second tag listing the name and number of a contact person at home. Popular backup identification methods are to have your animal tattooed with an ID number (usually a social security number) or to implant a microchip under her skin.

If your pet requires medication, make sure that is specified on his tag. This helps others understand your animal's needs and also may prevent people from keeping a found pet or from stealing one to sell.

Note: Choke chains, collars that tighten when they are pulled, may be useful during training sessions, but they do not make good full-time collars. If the chain catches on something, your pet could choke herself trying to pull free. For regular wear, use a harness or a conventional collar made of nylon or leather.

Selecting a Carrier or Crate

This is one of the most important steps in ensuring your pet's safety when traveling. A good-quality carrier not only contains your pet during transit, it also gives him a safe, reassuring place to stay when confinement is necessary at your destination. Acclimate the animal before the trip so he views the crate as a cozy den, not a place of exile.

If you plan to travel by car, a carrier will confine your pet en route, and also may come in handy if Spot or Snowball must stay in the room unsupervised. A secured crate will prevent your pet from escaping from the room when the cleaning staff arrives, or at night if camping in the open. *(See "At Your Destination," p. 15.)*

Some airlines allow small pets to travel in the passenger cabin as carry-on luggage. There are no laws dictating the type of carrier to use, but remember that it must be small enough to fit under a standard airplane seat, usually **13″ W x 9″ H x 23″ D or 10″ W x 16″ H x 24″ D.** If your pet will be flying in the cargo hold, you must use a carrier that meets U.S. Department of Agriculture Animal and Plant Health Inspection Service (USDA-APHIS) specifications. *(See "Traveling by Air," p. 11.)*

Crates are available at pet supply stores; some airlines also sell carriers. Soft-sided travel bags are handy for flyers with small pets. The Sherpa Bags sold by Sherpa's Pet Trading Co. are approved by most major airlines and are available for 6-, 16- and 22-lb. animals; phone (800) 743-7723 for information.

Even if you never take to the skies, these common-sense guidelines provide a good rule of thumb in selecting a crate for other uses. USDA-APHIS rules stipulate the following:

🐾 The crate must be enclosed, but with ventilation openings occupying at least 14 percent of total wall space, at least one-third of which must be located on the top half of the kennel. A 3/4″ lip or rim must surround the exterior to prevent air holes from being blocked.

🐾 The crate must open easily, but must be sufficiently strong to hold up during normal cargo transit procedures (loading, unloading, etc.).

🐾 The floor must be solid and leakproof, and must be covered with an absorbent lining or material (such as an old towel or litter).

🐾 The crate must be just large enough to allow the animal to turn freely while standing, and to have a full range of normal movement while standing or lying down.

🐾 The crate must offer exterior grips or handles so that handlers do not have to place their hands or fingers inside.

🐾 If the carrier has wheels, they must be removed or immobilized prior to loading.

🐾 One inch-high lettering stating "Live Animal" or "Wild Animal" must be placed visibly on the exterior, and must be accompanied by directional arrows showing the crate's proper orientation. It also is a good idea to label the crate with your name, home address and home phone number, as well as an address and phone number where you can be reached during the trip. (Hint: Use an adhesive label or an indelible marker and write directly on the crate, as paper may be ripped off accidentally in transit.)

🐾 Attach a list of care instructions (feeding, watering, etc.) for a 24-hour period to the exterior of the carrier. This will help airport workers care for your pet if he is sent to the wrong destination.

☙ If you are traveling with multiple pets, note that crates may contain only one animal whose weight exceeds 20 pounds. Smaller animals may travel together under the following guidelines: one species to a crate, except compatible dogs and cats of similar size; 2 puppies or kittens under 6 months of age; 15 guinea pigs or rabbits; 50 hamsters. **Note:** These are federal limits; airlines may impose more stringent regulations.

Traveling by Car

The first step in ensuring your pet's well-being during a vacation is to train her to ride in the car. For safety reasons, pets should be confined to the back seat, either in a carrier or a harness attached to the car's seat belt. This keeps the animal from interfering with or distracting the driver, and also may save her life in the event of an accident. And a restrained animal will not be able to break free and run away the second the car door is opened.

To help prevent car sickness, feed your pet a light meal 4-6 hours before departing. Do not give an animal food or water in a moving vehicle.

Never allow your pet to ride in the bed of a pickup truck. It's illegal in some states; he also can jump out or be thrown, endangering himself and others on the road. Harnessing or leashing him to the truck bed is not advisable either: If he tries to jump out, he could be dragged along the road or the restraint could become a noose. Avoid placing animals in campers or trailers as well. **If your pet cannot ride in the car with you, leave him at home.**

Don't let your dog stick her head out the window, no matter how enjoyable it seems. Road debris and other flying objects can injure delicate eyes and ears, and the animal is at greater risk for severe injury if the vehicle should stop suddenly or be struck. If it is hot outside, run the air conditioner instead of opening the windows, and be sure that the air flow is reaching your pet.

AAA recommends that drivers stop every 2 hours to stretch their legs and take a quick break from driving. Your pet will appreciate the same break. Plan to visit a rest stop every 4 hours or so to let him have a drink and a chance to answer the call of nature. (Cat owners should bring along a litter box; dog owners should clean up afterward.)

Be sure your pet is leashed before opening the car door. This is not merely a courtesy to fellow travelers; it will prevent her from unexpectedly breaking free and running away. Keep in mind that even the most obedient pet may become disoriented during travel or in strange places and set off for home. **Hint:** If your pet is not used to traveling, use a harness instead of a collar; it is more difficult for an animal to wriggle out of a harness.

NEVER leave an animal in a parked car, even if the windows are partially open. Even on pleasant days the temperature inside a car can soar to well over 100 degrees in less than 10 minutes, placing your pet at risk for heatstroke and possibly death. On very cold days, hypothermia is a risk. Also, animals left unattended in parked cars frequently are stolen.

Traveling by Air

(Service animals are normally exempt from most of the regulations and fees specified in this section. Check policies with your airline when making reservations.)

Opinion is divided as to whether air travel is truly safe for pets. Statistically, it is less dangerous than being a passenger in a car, but some experts warn of potentially deadly conditions for animals. The truth lies somewhere in between: Most pets arrive at their destination in fine condition, but death or injury is always a possibility. Before you decide to fly, know the risk factors and the necessary precautions to keep your pet safe.

☙ **Determine whether your pet is fit to fly.** The Animal Welfare Act (AWA), administered by USDA-APHIS, specifies that dogs and cats must be at least 8 weeks old and weaned at least 5 days before air travel. Animals that are very young, very old, pregnant, ill or injured should not fly at all. Cats, snub-nosed dogs (pugs, boxers, etc.) and long-nosed dogs (shelties, collies, etc.) are prone to severe respiratory difficulties in an airplane's poorly ventilated cargo hold and should travel only in the passenger cabin (if size allows) with their owner.

Also find out whether your pet is allowed to fly. Most major airlines permit only dogs, cats and birds in the cabin but will transport additional species in the hold.

HEATSTROKE AND HYPOTHERMIA

The best way to treat heatstroke or hypothermia is to prevent it. Do not leave pets unattended in a car, even if only for a few minutes. Also heed airlines' restrictions on pet travel, and carefully investigate animal welfare policies to make certain the airline has safeguards to protect your pet from both conditions.

Other preventive measures are to avoid strenuous exercise — including such activities as hiking and "fetch" — when the sun is strongest (10 a.m.-2 p.m.), and to provide your pet access to clean, fresh drinking water at all times.

Following are the warning signs and basic first aid for heatstroke and hypothermia. Always be alert to your pet's physical condition and watch for symptoms — immediate attention to the situation may mean the difference between life and death. If your pet is struck with either disorder, take him to an animal hospital or veterinarian as fast as safely possible.

HEATSTROKE:

Symptoms
- rapid, shallow breathing
- excessive salivation
- heavy panting
- hot to the touch
- glazed eyes
- unsteadiness, dizziness
- deep red or purple tongue or gums
- vomiting
- body temperature of 104 F or higher

First Aid
- place pet in the shade
- quickly dampen with cool water, especially on the head and neck
- give small amounts of water

HYPOTHERMIA:

Symptoms
- shivering
- weakness
- lethargy
- cold to the touch
- body temperature of 95 F or lower

First Aid
- place in a warm area
- wrap in towels or a blanket
- quickly warm by gently massaging the head, chest and extremities

❧ **Decide where your pet will fly.** Most animals fly in the hold as checked baggage when traveling with their owners, or as cargo when they are unaccompanied. The AWA was enacted to ensure animals traveling in this manner are treated humanely and are not subjected to dangerous or life-threatening conditions. For specific requirements pertaining to your animal, check with the airline in advance.

Items classified as "dangerous goods" (dry ice or toxic chemicals, for example) must be transported in a different part of the hold from where live animals are carried. Some planes are designed to have separate hold areas, but so-called "people mover" airlines that are primarily interested in getting human passengers from one point to another as quickly as possible may not give priority to this feature. Check your airline's specific baggage policies so you know exactly where in the hold your pet will be traveling.

Small pets may be taken into the passenger cabin with you as carry-on luggage. This places the animal's welfare squarely in your hands but is feasible only if he is very well-behaved and fits comfortably in a container that meets standard carry-on regulations. *(See "Selecting a Carrier or Crate," p. 10.)* Keep in mind that the carrier — with the animal inside — must be kept under the seat in front of you throughout the flight. **Note:** AWA regulations do not apply to animals traveling in the cabin.

❧ **Do your homework.** Investigate the airline's animal transport and welfare policies, especially if you are flying with a small or commuter airline. All airlines are subject to the basic regulations of the AWA, but specific standards of care vary greatly from one company to another. Do your research well in advance and confirm the information 24-48 hours before departing.

The more information an airline provides, the better care your pet is likely to receive. Beware of companies that have vague animal welfare guidelines, or none at all. Also talk to fellow travelers and pet owners about their experiences. Some airlines have excellent reputations for caring for pets; others have very poor track records. Finally, keep in mind that airlines are not required to transport live animals and can refuse to carry them for any reason.

❧ **Protect your investment.** Most people think of their pets as part of the family, but the legal system assigns them the same value as a piece of luggage. Inquire about insurance — an airline that won't insure animals in its care may not be the right one for your pet. (Always read the fine print before purchasing any insurance policy.) Also ask if the airline's workers are trained to handle animals. Few are, but it doesn't hurt to check. Remember, it's up to you to choose an airline that values pets and will treat yours with care.

❧ **Understand the potential hazards.** Because a plane's cargo hold is neither cooled nor heated until takeoff, the most dangerous time for your pet is that spent on the ground in this unventilated compartment. In summer the space absorbs heat while the plane sits on the tarmac; the reverse is true in winter, when it is no warmer inside the hold than outside. Both instances expose pets to the possibility of serious injury or death from heatstroke or hypothermia. **Note:** The latter also may be a concern during flight if the hold's heater is disabled or turned off, allowing the temperature to drop to near-freezing levels.

❧ To minimize these risks, USDA-APHIS rules prohibit animals from being kept in the hold or on the tarmac for more than 45 minutes when temperatures are above 85 F or below 45 F. Some airlines impose even tighter temperature restrictions and may not permit animals to fly on planes going to cities where the ground temperatures may exceed these limits. (Exceptions may be made for animals whose veterinarians certify they are acclimated to colder temperatures, but never warmer.)

❧ **Make stress-free travel arrangements.** Once you decide to fly, reserve space for Spot or Snowball when you arrange your own tickets, preferably well in advance of your travel date. Airlines accept only a limited number of animals per flight — usually two to four in the passenger cabin and one pet per passenger — on a first-come, first-served basis. More animals are generally allowed in the cargo hold.

Prepare to pay an additional fee, about $50 each way. (Unfortunately, pets are not eligible for frequent flyer miles.) Always reconfirm your reservations and flight information 24-48 hours before departure.

If your pet will be flying in the hold, travel on the same plane and reserve a nonstop flight. This not only reduces the danger of heatstroke or hypothermia during layovers, it also eliminates the possibility that she will be placed on the wrong connecting flight. In summer, fly during the early morning or late evening when temperatures are cooler. Because of large crowds and the chance of heavy air traffic causing delays, avoid holiday travel whenever possible.

Additional precautions may be necessary when traveling outside the United States and Canada. Other countries may impose lengthy quarantines, and airline workers outside North America may not be bound by animal welfare laws. *(See "International Travel," p. 18.)*

❧ **Play an active role in your pet's well-being.** Flying safely with your pet requires careful planning and attention to his welfare. See the veterinarian within 10 days of departure for a health certificate (required by most airlines) and a pre-flight check-up.

Address any concerns you have about your pet traveling by air, especially if you are considering tranquilization. Sedation usually is not recommended for cats and dogs, regardless of whether they fly in the cabin or in the hold. Exposure to increased altitude pressure can create respiratory and cardiovascular problems; animals with short, wide heads are particularly susceptible to disorientation and possible injury. Sedation should never be administered without your veterinarian's approval.

Obtain an airline-approved carrier and acclimate your pet to its presence by leaving it open with a familiar object inside. A sturdy, well-ventilated crate adds an additional measure of protection. *(See "Preparing Your Pet for Travel," p. 7, and "Selecting a Carrier or Crate," p. 10.)*

Because animals are classified as luggage, they may be loaded on the plane via conveyor belt. If the crate falls off the belt, your pet could be injured or released. Ask that she be hand-carried on and off the plane, and that you be permitted to watch both procedures. Also ask about "counter-to-counter" shipping, in which the animal is loaded immediately before departure and unloaded immediately after arrival. There usually is an additional fee for this service.

Make sure you will have access to your pet if there is a lengthy layover or delay. Think twice about flying on an airline that won't allow you to check on your animal under such circumstances.

❧ **Prepare for the flight.** Exercise your pet before the flight, and arrive at least 1 but not more than 4 hours before departure. If he is traveling as carry-on luggage, check-in is normally at the passenger terminal; if he is traveling as checked baggage or as cargo in the cargo hold, proceed to the airline's cargo terminal, which is often in a different location. Find this out when making reservations and again when confirming flight information.

Airline Contact Information

Following is a list of the major North American airlines and their toll-free telephone numbers.

Web site addresses have been given for those airline web sites that include information about flying with animals. Hint: Look under links for baggage, cargo or programs and services, or do a site search for "pets."

Air Canada . . . . (800) 776-3000
http://www.aircanada.ca

Alaska Airlines . . . . (800) 426-0333
http://www.alaska-air.com

America West Airlines. . . (800) 235-9292
http://www.americawest.com/

(Accepts carry-on animals only, except America West Express flights.)

American Airlines . . . . . . (800) 433-7300
http://www.americanair.com/

Canadian Airlines . . . . . .(800) 426-7000

Continental Airlines. . . . . (800) 525-0280
http://www.flycontinental.com/

Delta Airlines. . . . . (800) 221-1212
http://www.delta-air.com/

Northwest Airlines. . . . . . (800) 225-2525
http://www.nwa.com/

Southwest Airlines . . . . . (800) 435-9792
http://www.iflyswa.com/

(Accepts service animals only.)

TWA. . . . . (800) 221-2000
http://www.twa.com/

United Airlines . . . . (800) 241-6522
http://www.ual.com/

US Airways . . . . (800) 428-4322
http://www.usair.com/

Make sure your animal's crate is properly labeled and secured, but do not lock it in case airline personnel have to provide emergency care. Include an ice pack for extra comfort on a hot day, a hot water bottle on a cold one. **Hint:** Wrap in a towel to prevent leaking.

Do not feed your pet less than 4 hours before departure, but provide water up to boarding. **Hint:** Freeze water in the bowl so that it melts throughout the trip, providing a constant drinking source.

Spot or Snowball should wear a sturdy collar (breakaway collars are recommended for cats) and two identification tags marked with your name, home address and phone number, and travel address and phone number. It's also a good idea to clip your pet's nails before departure so they won't accidentally get caught on any part of the carrier.

Note: You may be required to take your pet out of the carrier as you pass through security on your way to the gate. Make sure the animal is wearing a collar and leash or harness.

Attach food and water dishes inside the carrier so that airline workers can reach them without opening the door. If the trip will take longer than 12 hours, also attach a plastic bag with at least one meal's worth of dry food. Animals under 16 weeks of age must be fed every 12 hours, adult animals every 24 hours. Water must be provided at least every 12 hours, regardless of the animal's age.

Allow your pet to answer the call of nature before boarding, but do not take her out of the carrier while in the terminal. As a courtesy, wait until you are outside and away from fellow travelers. Keep her leash with you — do not leave it inside or attached to the kennel.

If your pet is traveling as carry-on luggage, let the passenger sitting next to you know. Someone with allergies may want to change seats.

Perhaps the most important precaution is to alert the flight crew and the captain that your pet is aboard. The pilot must activate the heater for the cargo hold; make sure this is done once you are in the air. If there are layovers or delays, ask the flight crew to be sure your pet has adequate shelter and/or ventilation; better yet, ask them to allow you to check in person.

If you have arranged to watch your pet being unloaded, ask a flight attendant to call the baggage handlers and let them know you are on the way. Above all, do not hesitate to voice any concerns you have for your pet's welfare — it is your responsibility to do so.

🐾 **Be prepared for emergencies.** In the unlikely event your pet gets lost en route, contact the airline, local humane shelters, animal control agencies or USDA-APHIS. Many airlines can trace a pet that was transferred to the wrong flight. If your pet is injured in transit, proceed to the nearest animal hospital; register any complaints with USDA-APHIS. **Hint:** Carry a list of emergency contact numbers and a current photograph of your pet in your wallet or purse, just in case.

At Your Destination

How well you and your companion behave on the road directly affects the way future furry travelers will be treated. Always clean up after your pet and keep him under your control. This is not only a courtesy to fellow human travelers; it's the surest way to enjoy a safe and happy vacation.

Inquire about pet policies before making lodging reservations. Properties may impose restrictions on the type or size of pet allowed, or they may designate only certain rooms, such as smoking rooms, for travelers with animals. If you have a dog, get a room on the first floor with direct access outside, preferably near a walking area; keep her leashed on any excursion.

Lodgings may have supervision policies requiring that pets be crated when unattended or that they may not be left alone at all. Allow your pet only in designated exercise or animal-approved areas; never take him into such off-limits places as the lobby, pool, patio or restaurant. Prepare to receive limited housekeeping service, or none at all.

Expect to pay some type of additional charge, which may be per room or per pet and may include any of the following: refundable deposit, nonrefundable deposit, daily fee, weekly fee.

If staying with friends or relatives, make certain your pet is a welcome guest. Know and respect their "house rules," especially if they have small children or pets of their own.

Once in the room, check for such hazards as chemically treated toilet water, hiding spaces and electrical cords before freeing your pet. Give her time to adjust to her new surroundings under your supervision.

Above all, practice good "petiquette":

🐾 Try not to leave your pet alone, but if you must, crate or otherwise confine her.

🐾 Crate at night as well.

🐾 To keep your pet and the housekeeper from having an unexpected encounter, leave the "Do Not Disturb" sign on the door when you go out without him.

🐾 Barking dogs make poor hotel neighbors — keep your pet quiet.

🐾 Don't allow your pet on the furniture. If she insists on sleeping on the bed, bring a bedspread or sheet from home and place that on top of the hotel bedding.

🐾 Clean up after your pet immediately — inside the room and out — and leave no trace of him behind when checking out.

🐾 Dispose of litter and other "accidents" properly — check with housekeeping.

🐾 Notify the management immediately if something is damaged, and be ready to pay for repairs.

🐾 Add a little extra to the housekeeping tip.

🐾 When you take your pet out of the room, keep her leashed, especially in wilderness areas and around small children. No matter how obedient she is at home, new stimuli and distractions may cause her to forget or ignore vocal commands. Know and obey animal policies at parks, beaches and other public areas. Check before arriving to make certain animals still are welcome, even if you've been there before — the rules may have changed.

🐾 Look for outdoor cafes when selecting restaurants. For health reasons, pets are not permitted inside eating establishments, but many restaurants allow animals to sit quietly with their owners at outdoor tables. Drive-through restaurants are another alternative.

In Case of Emergency

Be prepared for any turn of events by knowing how to get to the nearest animal hospital. *(See "Animal Clinics," p. 30.)* Also have the name and number of a local animal shelter and a local veterinarian handy — ask your veterinarian for a recommendation. Take first-aid supplies with you and know how to use them. An animal in pain may become aggressive, so exercise caution at all times.

Emergency evacuation shelters do not accept pets, and domesticated animals do not fare well if left to weather an emergency on their own, especially when far from home. Avert a potential tragedy by planning in advance where you will go with your pet in case of evacuation. Use the listings in this guide to find other lodgings willing to take you and your pet. Above all, don't wait for disaster to strike. Leave as soon as the evacuation order is announced, and take your animal with you.

The Great Outdoors

Travelers planning an active or camping vacation should make some additional preparations. Check in advance to be sure your pet is permitted at campgrounds, parks, beaches, trails and anywhere else you will be visiting. If there are restrictions — and there usually are — follow them. Remember that pets other than service animals usually are not allowed in public buildings.

Note: It is not advisable to take animals other than dogs into wilderness areas. For example, bringing a pet is not recommended at some national parks in Alaska. Also keep in mind that rural areas often have few veterinarians and even fewer boarding kennels.

Use common sense. Clean up after your pet, do not allow excessive vocalizing and keep her under your control. If the property requires your pet to be leashed or crated at all times, do so. Few parks or natural areas will allow a pet to be unattended, even when chained — the risk of disagreeable encounters with other travelers or wildlife is too great. The National Park Service may confiscate pets that harm wildlife or other visitors.

If camping, crate your pet at night to protect him from the elements and predators. (Chaining confines the animal but won't keep him from becoming a midnight snack.)

When hiking, stick to the trail and keep your pet on a short leash. It is all too easy for an unleashed pet to wander off and get lost or fall prey to a larger animal. Keep an eye out for such wildlife as alligators, bears, big cats, porcupines and skunks, and avoid other dogs and small children. Be aware of indigenous poisonous plants, such as English ivy and oleander, or those causing physical injury, such as cactus, poison ivy or stinging nettle. Your veterinarian or local poison control center should be able to give you a full list of hazardous flora.

Before setting out on the trail, make sure both of you are in good physical shape. An animal that rarely exercises at home will not suddenly be ready for a 10-mile trek across uneven terrain. Plan a hike well within the limits of your pet's endurance, and don't push — remember, if Spot gets too tired to make it back on her own, you'll have to carry her.

Carry basic first-aid supplies (including a first-aid guide) and fresh drinking water for both of you — "found" water may contain harmful germs or toxins. Drink often, not just when thirst strikes, and have your pet do the same. Watch for signs of dehydration, leg or foot injuries, heat exhaustion or heatstroke. Stop immediately and return home or to camp if any of these occur. *(See "Heatstroke and Hypothermia" sidebar, p. 12.)*

Note: Dogs can carry their own backpacks (check your local pet store for specially designed packs), but should never carry more than one-third of their body weight. Train the dog to accept the pack beforehand, and only use it with a strong, healthy animal in excellent physical condition.

No matter where or how you spend your vacation, visit the veterinarian when you return home to check for injuries, parasites and general health.

Note: Most campgrounds accept pets; call ahead to be sure. AAA CampBooks®, a series of 11 regional titles, contain extensive listings of public (run by state, provincial and national parks or local governments) and privately owned campgrounds in the United States and Canada.

Traveling Between the United States and Canada

Traveling across the international border with your pet — either from the United States into Canada or from Canada into the United States — should prove largely hassle-free, although some basic regulations need to be kept in mind.

Passports to enter Canada or return to the United States are not required for native-born citizens of either country. Proof of citizenship is required; a birth or baptismal certificate and a photo ID (a driver's license, which also establishes proof of residence) normally are sufficient. Naturalized citizens should carry their naturalization certificate, and U.S. resident aliens must have an Alien Registration Receipt Card (Green Card).

U.S. Customs grants returning U.S. citizens who stay in Canada more than 48 hours an individual $400 exemption (if not used within the prior 30 days). Any amount over the $400 exemption is subject to duty.

The exemption is based on fair retail value and applies to goods acquired for personal or household use or as gifts but not intended for sale. All items for which the exemption is claimed must accompany you upon return. A $200 exemption is granted for stays of less than 48 hours.

A 7 percent Goods and Service Tax (GST) is levied on most items sold and most services rendered in Canada. In Nova Scotia, New Brunswick and Newfoundland, a Harmonized Sales Tax (HST) of 15 percent (which includes the GST) is charged on goods and services. Rebates can be claimed on some items. Brochures that explain the GST and contain a rebate form are available at tourist information centers, customs offices and duty free shops at the border and in airports.

U.S. citizens taking pet cats and dogs into Canada must carry a health certificate signed by a licensed veterinarian that describes the animal and provides proof of rabies vaccination within the past 36 months. Collar tags are not sufficient proof of immunization. The certificate also is needed to bring a pet back into the United States; make sure the vaccination doesn't expire while you're in Canada.

Service animals are exempt from these rules. Also exempt are up to two puppies or kittens under 3 months old; obtain a certificate of health from your veterinarian indicating that the animal is too young to vaccinate. **Note:** Pets entering Canada through Newfoundland require a certificate and entry permit, which must be obtained in advance. For details, contact the Canadian Embassy; 501 Pennsylvania Ave. N.W., Washington, DC 20001; phone (202) 682-1740.

Canadian Food Inspection Agency (CFIA) Import Service Centers provide additional pet information: in eastern Canada, (905) 612-6282; in western Canada, (604) 541-3370. If you need assistance while in Canada, contact the U.S. Embassy, 490 Sussex Dr., Ottawa, ON, Canada K1N 1G8; phone (613) 238-5335.

Canadian Customs allows Canadian citizens to bring back from the United States, duty and tax free, goods valued up to $200 any number of times per year, provided the visit is 48 hours or more. A $50 exemption, excluding alcoholic beverages and tobacco products, may be claimed if the visit is 24 hours or more and no other exemption is being used. If returning from a visit of 7 days or more (not counting the day of departure from Canada), the exemption goes up to $500.

Canadian travelers may take pet cats and dogs into the United States with no restrictions, but U.S. Customs requires that dogs have proof of rabies vaccination no less than 30 days before arrival. For additional information on U.S. regulations, contact the Veterinary Services department of the USDA-APHIS National Center for Import and Export,

PET INSURANCE

Just like their owners, pets can experience major medical problems at some point in their lifetime—even those that live indoors. And if illness strikes while you're on the road, it may be necessary to obtain care quickly. As a result, more and more people who travel with their devoted companion are considering pet health insurance.

Insurance plans run the gamut from basic coverage and routine care for illness and injury to comprehensive health maintenance, vaccinations and exams. Annual premiums range from less than $100 to more than $350, depending on the type of pet and plan. When choosing your plan, consider the following:

- What are the enrollment guidelines (age, breed, specific restrictions, etc.)?
- Which expenses are covered and which are excluded?
- What is the plan's policy concerning existing health problems?
- Does the plan allow you to use your own veterinarian?
- How are veterinary fees paid?
- Is a multiple pet discount offered?

If you're thinking about pet insurance for your dog or cat, contact AAA Insurance Services for more information; phone (407) 444-8608.

(301) 734-8383. **Note:** North Carolina lodgings have stringent regulations regarding pets; obtain information about an individual property's policies before making reservations.

International Travel

If you plan to travel abroad with Spot or Snowball, prepare for a lengthy flight and at least a short quarantine period. Be aware that airline and animal workers in other countries may not be bound by the same animal welfare laws that exist in the United States and Canada. Before you make firm plans, contact the embassy or consulate at your destination for information about documentation and quarantine requirements, animal control laws and animal welfare regulations. *(See "Traveling by Air," p. 11.)*

As with any trip, have your pet checked by your regular veterinarian within 10 days of departure to obtain a health certificate showing proof of rabies and other inoculations. If you are traveling with an animal other than a domesticated dog or cat, check with USDA-APHIS for restrictions or additional documentation required.

The leaflet "Pets, Wildlife and U.S. Customs" has general information about traveling abroad with animals; write U.S. Customs Service, P.O. Box 7407, Washington, DC 20044.

Note: Many island nations, such as Australia and the United Kingdom, are rabies-free and impose a quarantine on animals brought in from the United States and Canada. Hawaii imposes 30- and 120-day quarantines for all imported animals except guide dogs. *(See "Should Your Pet Travel?", p. 5.)*

Loss Prevention Tips

Desperately searching the woods or an unfamiliar town for a missing pet is a heartbreaking way to spend your vacation. Fortunately, this scenario is easily prevented by following these helpful tips:

🐾 Have your pet wear a sturdy nylon or leather collar with current ID and rabies tags firmly attached. Be sure the ID tag includes the phone number of an emergency contact.

🐾 Keep your pet on a leash or harness at all times. Even highly trained animals can become agitated or disoriented in unfamiliar surroundings and fail to obey vocal commands.

🐾 Attach the leash or harness while your pet is still inside the closed car or crate.

🐾 Do not leave your pet unattended at any time, anywhere. A stolen pet is extremely difficult to recover.

🐾 Escape-proof your hotel room by crating your pet and asking hotel management to make certain no one enters your room while you are gone. (Inform the property that you're traveling with an animal when making reservations.)

🐾 Take along a recent picture and a detailed written description of your pet.

If the unthinkable happens and your pet gets lost, the following steps will help improve your chances of recovering him:

🐾 If your pet is lost in transit, contact the airline immediately. Ask to trace her via the automated baggage tracking system, which most airlines have.

🐾 Contact local police, animal control, animal shelters, humane organizations and veterinary clinics immediately and provide them with a description and a recent photograph. Stay in contact with them until your pet is found, and provide a phone number where you can be reached, at your destination and at home.

🐾 Post signs and place an ad in the local newspaper so that anyone who comes across your pet knows she is lost and how to reach you.

Many pets are found within a week, but it can take longer. There are extraordinary true stories of animals reunited with their families many weeks or months after they were lost. The important thing is to keep looking and not give up.

The Last Word

You are ultimately responsible for your pet's welfare and behavior while traveling. Since animals cannot speak for themselves, it is up to you to focus on your pet's well-being every step of the way. It also is important to make sure he conducts himself properly so that other pets will be welcome visitors in the future. Following the common-sense information in this book will help ensure that both you and your animal companion have a safe and happy trip.

PET-FRIENDLY PLACES

National Public Lands
Animal Clinics

The National Public Lands listed below permit pets on a leash. Keep in mind that animals may be prohibited from entering public buildings and even some areas outdoors, particularly those that are ecologically sensitive. Specific pet policies vary from park to park and are subject to change. Always check in advance regarding any applicable regulations and to confirm that pets are still permitted where you are going.

Never leave your pet unattended. Keep him leashed or crated at all times. Follow park guidelines faithfully, and monitor your pet's behavior; the National Park Service may confiscate pets that harm wildlife or other visitors. *For additional information on outdoor vacations, see "The Great Outdoors," p. 16.*

United States

Alabama

Conecuh National Forest
On the Alabama-Florida border.
(334) 222-2555

Horseshoe Bend National Military Park
12 mi. north of Dadeville on SR 49.
(256) 234-7111

Talladega National Forest
In central Alabama.
(205) 926-9765

Tuskegee National Forest
Northeast of Tuskegee.
(334) 727-2652

William B. Bankhead National Forest
In northwestern Alabama.
(205) 489-5111

Alaska

Chugach National Forest
Along the Gulf of Alaska from Cape Suckling to Seward.
(907) 271-2500

Denali National Park and Preserve
In south-central Alaska.
(907) 683-2294

Glacier Bay National Park and Preserve
North of Cross Sound to the Canadian border.
(907) 697-2230

Kenai Fjords National Park
Southeastern side of the Kenai Peninsula.
(907) 224-3175

Tongass National Forest
In southeastern Alaska.
(907) 586-8751 or 228-6220

Wrangell-St. Elias National Park and Preserve
In southeastern Alaska, northwest of Tongass National Forest.
(907) 822-5234

Arizona

Apache-Sitgreaves National Forests
In east-central Arizona.
(520) 333-4301

Coconino National Forest
In northern Arizona.
(520) 527-3600

Coronado National Forest
In southeastern Arizona and southwestern New Mexico.
(520) 670-4552

Glen Canyon National Recreation Area
In north-central Arizona.
(520) 608-6404

Grand Canyon National Park
In northwestern Arizona.
(520) 638-7888
🅰 🏍 ⛱ 👪 🍴

Kaibab National Forest
In north-central Arizona.
(520) 635-4061 or (800) 863-0546
🅰 🏍 ⛱ 👪 🍴

Lake Mead National Recreation Area
In northwestern Arizona.
(702) 293-8906
🅰 🏍 ⛱ 🏊 👪 🍴

Petrified Forest National Park
In east-central Arizona, east of Holbrook.
(520) 524-6228
🏍 ⛱ 👪 🍴

Prescott National Forest
In central Arizona.
(520) 771-4700
🅰 🏍 ⛱ 🍴

Saguaro National Park
Two districts, 15 mi. east and west of Tucson.
(520) 733-5153
🚲 🅰 🏍 ⛱ 👪

Tonto National Forest
In central Arizona.
(602) 225-5200
🚲 🅰 🏍 ⛱ 🏊 🍴

Arkansas

Buffalo National River
In northwestern Arkansas.
(870) 741-5443 or 449-4311
🅰 🏍 ⛱ 🏊 👪 🍴

Felsenthal National Wildlife Refuge
7 mi. west of Crossett on US 82.
(870) 364-3168
🅰 🏍 ⛱ 👪

Hot Springs National Park
In western Arkansas.
(501) 624-3383
🅰 🏍 ⛱ 👪

Ouachita National Forest
In west-central Arkansas and southeastern Oklahoma.
(501) 321-5202
🚲 🅰 🏍 ⛱ 🏊 👪 🍴

Ozark National Forest
In northwestern Arkansas.
(501) 968-2354
🚲 🅰 🏍 ⛱ 🏊 👪

St. Francis National Forest
In east-central Arkansas.
(870) 295-5278
🅰 🏍 ⛱ 🏊

California

Angeles National Forest
In southern California.
(626) 574-5200
🚲 🅰 🏍 ⛱ 🏊 👪 🍴

Cleveland National Forest
In southwestern California.
(858) 674-2901
🚲 🅰 🏍 ⛱ 👪 🍴

Death Valley National Park
Along the Nevada border in east-central California.
(760) 786-2331
🅰 🏍 ⛱ 🏊 👪 🍴

Eldorado National Forest
In central California.
(530) 644-6048
🚲 🅰 🏍 ⛱ 🏊 👪 🍴

Golden Gate National Recreation Area
North of the Golden Gate Bridge and in northern and western San Francisco.
(415) 556-0560
🚲 🅰 🏍 ⛱ 🏊 👪 🍴

Inyo National Forest
In central California.
(760) 873-2400
🚲 🅰 🏍 ⛱ 🏊 👪 🍴

Joshua Tree National Park
East of Desert Hot Springs.
(760) 367-5500
🅰 🏍 ⛱ 👪

King Range National Conservation Area
On the northern California coast west of Garberville.
(707) 825-2322
🚲 🅰 🏍 ⛱ 🏊 👪 🍴

Klamath National Forest
In northern California.
(530) 842-6131
🚲 🅰 🏍 ⛱ 🏊 👪

Lassen National Forest
In northern California.
(530) 257-2151
🚲 🅰 🏍 ⛱ 🏊 👪 🍴

Lassen Volcanic National Park
In northeastern California.
(530) 595-4444
🅰 🏍 ⛱ 🏊 👪 🍴

🚲 Bicycling　🅰 Camping　🏍 Hiking　⛱ Picnicking
🏊 Swimming　👪 Visitor center　🍴 Food service

Los Padres National Forest
In southern California.
(805) 683-6711
🦽 🔺 🐎 🏕 🛶

Mendocino National Forest
In northwestern California.
(530) 934-2350 or 934-3316
🦽 🔺 🐎 🏕 🛶 🎣 🍴

Modoc National Forest
In northeastern California.
(530) 233-5811
🦽 🔺 🐎 🏕 🛶 🎣

Mojave National Preserve
Between I-15 and I-40 in southeastern California.
(760) 733-4040
🔺 🐎 🏕 🎣 🍴

Plumas National Forest
In northern California.
(530) 283-2050
🦽 🔺 🐎 🏕 🛶 🎣 🍴

Point Reyes National Seashore
Along the California coast just north of San Francisco.
(415) 663-1092
🦽 🔺 🐎 🏕 🎣 🍴

Redwood National Park
On the northern California coast.
(707) 464-6101, ext. 5064 or 5265
🦽 🔺 🐎 🏕 🛶 🎣 🍴

San Bernardino National Forest
In southern California.
(909) 383-5588
🦽 🔺 🐎 🏕 🛶 🎣 🍴

Santa Monica Mountains National Recreation Area
West from Griffith Park in Los Angeles to the Ventura
County line.
(818) 597-9192 or (805) 370-2300 in Calif.
🦽 🔺 🐎 🏕 🛶 🎣 🍴

Sequoia and Kings Canyon National Parks
In east-central California.
(559) 565-3341
🔺 🐎 🏕 🎣 🍴

Sequoia National Forest
In south-central California.
(559) 784-1500
🦽 🔺 🐎 🏕 🛶 🎣 🍴

Shasta-Trinity National Forests
In northern California.
(530) 246-5222
🔺 🐎 🏕 🛶 🎣 🍴

Sierra National Forest
In central California.
(559) 297-0706
🦽 🔺 🐎 🏕 🛶 🎣 🍴

Six Rivers National Forest
In northwestern California.
(707) 441-3523
🦽 🔺 🐎 🏕 🛶 🎣 🍴

Smith River National Recreation Area
Within Six Rivers National Forest in northwestern
California.
(707) 441-3523
🦽 🔺 🐎 🏕 🛶

Stanislaus National Forest
In central California.
(209) 532-3671
🦽 🔺 🐎 🏕 🛶 🍴

Tahoe National Forest
In north-central California.
(530) 265-4531
🔺 🐎 🏕 🛶 🎣 🍴

**Whiskeytown-Shasta-Trinity National Recreation
Area**
North and west of Redding.
(530) 241-6584
🦽 🔺 🐎 🏕 🛶 🎣 🍴

Yosemite National Park
In central California.
(209) 372-0200
🦽 🔺 🐎 🏕 🛶 🎣 🍴

Colorado

Arapaho National Forest
In north-central Colorado.
(970) 498-2770 or TDD 498-2707
🦽 🔺 🐎 🏕 🛶 🎣

Arapaho National Recreation Area
In north-central Colorado.
(970) 887-4100 or TDD 887-4101
🦽 🔺 🐎 🏕 🛶

Black Canyon of the Gunnison National Park
In western Colorado.
(970) 240-5300 or 249-1915, ext. 23
🔺 🐎 🏕 🎣 🍴

Curecanti National Recreation Area
In south-central Colorado between Gunnison and
Montrose, paralleling US 50.
(970) 641-2337, ext. 9
🔺 🐎 🏕 🛶 🎣 🍴

**Grand Mesa-Uncompahgre-Gunnison National
Forests**
In west-central Colorado.
(970) 874-6600
🦽 🔺 🐎 🏕 🍴

Mesa Verde National Park
In southwestern Colorado.
(970) 529-4465
🔺 🐎 🏕 🎣 🍴

Pike National Forest
In central Colorado.
(719) 545-8737
🚲 ⛺ 🥾 🏕 🏨 🍽

Rio Grande National Forest
In south-central Colorado.
(719) 852-5941
🚲 ⛺ 🥾 🏕 🏨

Rocky Mountain National Park
In north-central Colorado.
(970) 586-1206 or 586-1333
⛺ 🥾 🏕 🏨 🍽

Roosevelt National Forest
In north-central Colorado.
(970) 498-2770
🚲 ⛺ 🥾 🏕 🏊

Routt National Forest
In northwestern Colorado.
(970) 879-1870
🚲 ⛺ 🥾 🏕 🏊 🏨

San Isabel National Forest
In south-central Colorado.
(719) 545-8737
⛺ 🥾 🏕 🏨 🍽

San Juan National Forest
In southwestern Colorado.
(970) 247-4874
🚲 ⛺ 🥾 🏕 🏊 🏨 🍽

White River National Forest
In west-central Colorado.
(970) 945-2521
🚲 ⛺ 🥾 🏕 🏊 🏨 🍽

Florida

Ocala National Forest
In north-central Florida.
(352) 625-2520
⛺ 🥾 🏕 🏊 🏨 🍽

Georgia

Chattahoochee and Oconee National Forests
In central and northern Georgia.
(770) 536-0541
⛺ 🥾 🏕 🏊 🏨

Chattahoochee River National Recreation Area
North of Atlanta.
(770) 399-8070
🚲 🥾 🏕 🍽

Idaho

Boise National Forest
In south-central Idaho.
(208) 373-4007
🚲 ⛺ 🥾 🏕 🏊 🏨 🍽

Caribou National Forest
In southeastern Idaho.
(208) 236-7500
⛺ 🥾 🏕 🏊

Clearwater National Forest
In northeastern Idaho.
(208) 476-4541
⛺ 🥾 🏕 🏊 🏨

Hells Canyon National Recreation Area
In western Idaho and northeastern Oregon.
(509) 758-0616 or 758-1957
🚲 ⛺ 🥾 🏕 🏨

Idaho Panhandle National Forest
In northern and northwestern Idaho.
(208) 765-7223
🚲 ⛺ 🥾 🏕 🏊

Nez Perce National Forest
In north-central Idaho.
(208) 983-1950
🚲 ⛺ 🥾 🏕 🏊 🏨

Payette National Forest
In west-central Idaho.
(208) 634-0700
🚲 ⛺ 🥾 🏕 🏊 🏨

Salmon-Challis National Forest
In east-central Idaho.
(208) 756-5100
⛺ 🥾 🏕 🏊 🍽

Sawtooth National Forest
In south-central Idaho.
(208) 737-3200
🚲 ⛺ 🥾 🏕 🏊 🏨 🍽

Sawtooth National Recreation Area
In south-central Idaho.
(208) 727-5013 or (800) 260-5970
🚲 ⛺ 🥾 🏕 🏊 🏨 🍽

Targhee National Forest
In southeastern Idaho.
(208) 624-3151
⛺ 🥾 🏕 🏊 🍽

🚲 Bicycling   ⛺ Camping   🥾 Hiking   🏕 Picnicking
🏊 Swimming   🏨 Visitor center   🍽 Food service

Illinois

Shawnee National Forest
In southern Illinois.
(618) 253-7114 or (800) 699-6637
[A] [兩] [⛺] [⚓]

Indiana

Hoosier National Forest
In southern Indiana.
(812) 275-5987
[♿] [A] [兩] [⛺] [⚓] [👫]

Indiana Dunes National Lakeshore
On the southern shore of Lake Michigan.
(219) 926-7561, ext. 225
[♿] [A] [兩] [⛺] [⚓] [👫]

Kentucky

Big South Fork National River and Recreation Area
In southeastern Kentucky and northeastern Tennessee.
(931) 879-3625
[♿] [A] [兩] [⛺] [⚓] [👫]

Daniel Boone National Forest
In eastern Kentucky.
(606) 745-3100
[A] [兩] [⛺] [⚓] [👫]

Daniel Boone National Forest (Laurel River Lake)
In southeastern Kentucky west of Corbin.
(606) 745-3100
[A] [兩] [⛺] [⚓]

Daniel Boone National Forest (Rockcastle)
In southeastern Kentucky 22 mi. southwest of London via SR 192/3497.
(606) 745-3100
[A] [兩] [⛺] [⚓]

Land Between the Lakes National Recreation Area
In western Kentucky and Tennessee.
(270) 924-2000 or (800) 525-5077
[♿] [A] [兩] [⛺] [👫]

Mammoth Cave National Park
In south-central Kentucky 8 mi. west of Cave City.
(270) 758-2328
[♿] [A] [兩] [⛺] [👫] [🍽]

Louisiana

Kisatchie National Forest
In central and northern Louisiana.
(318) 473-7160
[A] [兩] [⛺] [⚓]

Maine

Acadia National Park
Along the Atlantic coast southeast of Bangor.
(207) 288-3338
[♿] [A] [兩] [⛺] [⚓] [👫] [🍽]

Maryland

Assateague Island National Seashore
In southeastern Maryland south of Ocean City.
(410) 641-1441 or 641-3030
[♿] [A] [兩] [⛺] [⚓] [👫]

Michigan

Hiawatha National Forest
In Michigan's Upper Peninsula.
(906) 786-4062
[♿] [A] [兩] [⛺] [⚓] [👫]

Huron-Manistee National Forests
In the northern part of the Lower Peninsula.
(231) 775-2421 or (800) 821-6263
[♿] [A] [兩] [⛺] [⚓] [👫]

Ottawa National Forest
In Michigan's Upper Peninsula.
(906) 932-1330
[♿] [A] [兩] [⛺] [⚓] [👫]

Pictured Rocks National Lakeshore
Along Lake Superior in Michigan's Upper Peninsula.
(906) 387-3700
[A] [兩] [⛺] [⚓] [👫]

Sleeping Bear Dunes National Lakeshore
Along Lake Michigan in the northwestern part of the Lower Peninsula.
(231) 326-5134
[A] [兩] [⛺] [⚓] [👫]

Minnesota

Chippewa National Forest
In north-central Minnesota.
(218) 335-8600 or TDD 335-8632
[♿] [A] [兩] [⛺] [⚓] [👫] [🍽]

Superior National Forest
In northeastern Minnesota.
(218) 626-4300
[♿] [A] [兩] [⛺] [⚓] [👫] [🍽]

Mississippi

Bienville National Forest
In central Mississippi.
(601) 469-3811
[A] [兩] [⛺] [⚓] [👫]

Gulf Islands National Seashore
Along the Gulf of Mexico in southern Mississippi.
(228) 875-9057
[A] [⛺] [⚓] [👫] [🍽]

Missouri

Mark Twain National Forest
In southern Missouri.
(573) 364-4621
🚴 🅰 🥾 🌲 🏊

Mark Twain National Forest (Big Bay)
1 mi. southeast of Shell Knob on SR 39, then 3 mi.
southeast on CR YY.
(573) 364-4621
🅰 🌲 🏊

Mark Twain National Forest (Crane Lake)
12 mi. south of Ironton off SR 49 and CR E.
(573) 364-4621
🚴 🥾 🌲

Mark Twain National Forest (Fourche Lake)
18 mi. west of Doniphan on SR 160.
(573) 364-4621
🥾 🌲

Mark Twain National Forest (Noblett Lake)
8 mi. west of Willow Springs on SR 76, then 1.5 mi.
south on SR 181, 3 mi. southeast on CR AP and 1
mi. southwest on FR 857.
(573) 364-4621
🚴 🅰 🥾 🌲

Mark Twain National Forest (Pinewoods Lake)
7 mi. north of Ellsinore on SR 67, then 2 mi. west on
CR 60.
(573) 364-4621
🚴 🥾 🌲 🏊

Mark Twain National Forest (Red Bluff)
1 mi. east of Davisville on CR V, then 1 mi. north on
FR 2011.
(573) 364-4621
🅰 🥾 🌲 🏊

Ozark National Scenic Riverways
In southeastern Missouri.
(573) 323-4236
🅰 🥾 🌲 🏊 🏠 🍽

Montana

Beaverhead-Deerlodge National Forest Area
In southwestern Montana.
(406) 683-3900
🚴 🅰 🥾 🌲 🏊

Bighorn Canyon National Recreation Area
In southern Montana and northern Wyoming.
(406) 666-2412
🅰 🥾 🌲 🏊 🏠 🍽

Bitterroot National Forest
In western Montana.
(406) 363-7161
🅰 🥾 🌲 🏊 🏠

Custer National Forest/Dakota Prairie Grasslands
In southeastern Montana.
(406) 248-9885
🚴 🅰 🥾 🌲 🏊 🍽

Flathead National Forest
In northwestern Montana.
(406) 758-5204
🚴 🅰 🥾 🌲 🏊 🏠

Gallatin National Forest
In south-central Montana.
(406) 522-2520
🚴 🅰 🥾 🌲 🏊 🏠 🍽

Glacier National Park
In northwestern Montana.
(406) 888-7800
🅰 🥾 🌲 🏊 🏠 🍽

Helena National Forest
In west-central Montana.
(406) 449-5201
🅰 🥾 🌲 🏊

Kootenai National Forest
In northwestern Montana.
(406) 293-6211
🚴 🅰 🥾 🌲 🏊 🏠 🍽

Lewis and Clark National Forest
In central Montana.
(406) 791-7700
🅰 🥾 🌲 🏊

Nebraska

Nebraska National Forest
In central and northwestern Nebraska.
(308) 432-0300 or TDD 432-0304
🚴 🅰 🥾 🌲 🏊

Oglala National Grassland
In northwestern Nebraska, 17 mi. north of Crawford
via SR 2.
(308) 432-0300
🅰 🥾 🌲 🏠

Nevada

Great Basin National Park
In central Nevada, 5 mi. west of Baker near the
Nevada-Utah border.
(775) 234-7331
🅰 🥾 🌲 🏠 🍽

🚴 Bicycling   🅰 Camping   🥾 Hiking   🌲 Picnicking
🏊 Swimming   🏠 Visitor center   🍽 Food service

Humboldt-Toiyabe National Forest
In central, western, northern and southern Nevada and eastern California.
(775) 331-6444
[symbols]

New Hampshire

White Mountain National Forest
In northern New Hampshire.
(603) 528-8721 or TDD 528-8722
[symbols]

New Jersey

Gateway National Recreation Area
In northeastern New Jersey (Sandy Hook Unit).
(732) 872-5970
[symbols]

New Mexico

Carson National Forest
In north-central New Mexico.
(505) 758-6200
[symbols]

Chaco Culture National Park
In northwestern New Mexico.
(505) 786-7014
[symbols]

Cibola National Forest
In central New Mexico.
(505) 281-3304
[symbols]

Gila National Forest
In southwestern New Mexico.
(505) 388-8201
[symbols]

Lincoln National Forest
In south-central New Mexico.
(505) 434-7200
[symbols]

Santa Fe National Forest
In north-central New Mexico between the San Pedro Mountains and the Sangre de Cristo Mountains.
(505) 438-7840
[symbols]

New York

Finger Lakes National Forest
In north-central New York on a ridge between Seneca and Cayuga lakes, via I-90, I-81 and SR 17.
(607) 546-4470
[symbols]

Fire Island National Seashore
In southeastern New York on Fire Island, off the south shore of Long Island.
(631) 289-4810
[symbols]

Gateway National Recreation Area (Jamaica Bay District)
On Brooklyn and Queens boroughs in New York City.
(718) 338-3687 or 338-3688
[symbols]

Gateway National Recreation Area (Staten Island Unit)
On Staten Island borough in New York City.
(718) 338-3687 or 338-3688
[symbols]

North Carolina

Cape Hatteras National Seashore
In eastern North Carolina along the Outer Banks.
(252) 473-2111 or 441-5711
[symbols]

Croatan National Forest
In southeastern North Carolina.
(252) 638-5628
[symbols]

Great Smoky Mountains National Park
In western North Carolina.
(423) 436-1200
[symbols]

Nantahala National Forest
At North Carolina's southwestern tip.
(704) 257-4200
[symbols]

Nantahala National Forest (Hanging Dog)
5 mi. northwest of Murphy on SR 1326.
(704) 257-4200
[symbols]

Nantahala National Forest (Jackrabbit Mountain)
10 mi. northeast of Hayesville via US 64, SR 175 and SR 1155.
(704) 257-4200
[symbols]

Nantahala National Forest (Standing Indian Mountain)
12 mi. west of Franklin on US 64, then 2 mi. east on old US 64 and 2 mi. south on FR 67.
(704) 257-4200
[symbols]

Pisgah National Forest
In western North Carolina.
(704) 257-4200
[symbols]

Pisgah National Forest (Lake Powhatan)
7 mi. southwest of Asheville on SR 191 and FR 3484.
(704) 257-4200
(Bicycling) (Camping) (Hiking) (Picnicking) (Swimming)

Pisgah National Forest (Rocky Bluff)
3 mi. south of Hot Springs on SR 209.
(704) 257-4200
(Camping) (Hiking) (Picnicking)

Uwharrie National Forest
In central North Carolina.
(910) 576-6391
(Camping) (Hiking) (Picnicking) (Swimming)

North Dakota

Theodore Roosevelt National Park (North Unit)
In western North Dakota.
(701) 623-4466
(Camping) (Hiking) (Picnicking) (Visitor center)

Theodore Roosevelt National Park (South Unit)
In western North Dakota.
(701) 623-4466
(Camping) (Hiking) (Picnicking) (Visitor center)

Ohio

Cuyahoga Valley National Recreation Area
In northeastern Ohio.
(216) 524-1497
(Bicycling) (Hiking) (Picnicking) (Visitor center)

Oklahoma

Chickasaw National Recreation Area
In southern Oklahoma.
(580) 622-3165
(Camping) (Hiking) (Picnicking) (Swimming) (Visitor center)

Ouachita National Forest
In southeastern Oklahoma and west-central Arkansas.
(501) 321-5202
(Bicycling) (Camping) (Hiking) (Picnicking) (Swimming) (Visitor center) (Food service)

Oregon

Crater Lake National Park
On the crest of the Cascade Range off SR 62.
(541) 594-2211, ext. 402
(Bicycling) (Camping) (Hiking) (Picnicking) (Visitor center) (Food service)

Deschutes National Forest
In central Oregon 6 mi. south of Bend via US 97.
(541) 388-2715 or 388-5664
(Bicycling) (Camping) (Hiking) (Picnicking) (Swimming) (Visitor center) (Food service)

Fremont National Forest
In south-central Oregon.
(541) 947-2151
(Bicycling) (Camping) (Hiking) (Picnicking) (Swimming)

Hells Canyon National Recreation Area
In northeastern Oregon and western Idaho.
(541) 523-3356 or (800) 523-1235
(Camping) (Hiking) (Picnicking) (Visitor center)

Malheur National Forest
In eastern Oregon.
(541) 575-3000
(Bicycling) (Camping) (Hiking) (Picnicking) (Swimming)

Mount Hood National Forest
In northwestern Oregon.
(888) 622-4822
(Bicycling) (Camping) (Hiking) (Picnicking) (Swimming) (Visitor center) (Food service)

Ochoco National Forest
In central Oregon off US 26.
(541) 416-6500
(Bicycling) (Camping) (Hiking) (Picnicking) (Swimming)

Oregon Dunes National Recreation Area
Between North Bend and Florence.
(541) 271-3611
(Camping) (Hiking) (Picnicking) (Swimming) (Visitor center)

Rogue River National Forest
In southwestern Oregon off I-5 from Medford.
(541) 858-2200
(Bicycling) (Camping) (Hiking) (Picnicking) (Swimming) (Food service)

Siskiyou National Forest
In southwestern Oregon.
(541) 471-6500
(Bicycling) (Camping) (Hiking) (Picnicking) (Swimming) (Visitor center)

Siuslaw National Forest
In western Oregon.
(541) 750-7000
(Bicycling) (Camping) (Hiking) (Picnicking) (Swimming) (Visitor center)

Umatilla National Forest
In northeastern Oregon.
(541) 278-3716
(Bicycling) (Camping) (Hiking) (Picnicking) (Swimming) (Visitor center)

Umpqua National Forest
In southwestern Oregon 33 mi. east of Roseburg on SR 138.
(541) 672-6601 or TDD (541) 957-3459
(Bicycling) (Camping) (Hiking) (Picnicking) (Swimming) (Visitor center) (Food service)

Wallowa-Whitman National Forest
In northeastern Oregon.
(541) 523-1205
(Camping) (Hiking) (Picnicking) (Swimming)

(Bicycling) Bicycling (Camping) Camping (Hiking) Hiking (Picnicking) Picnicking
(Swimming) Swimming (Visitor center) Visitor center (Food service) Food service

Willamette National Forest
In western Oregon.
(541) 465-6521
[icons]

Winema National Forest
In south-central Oregon off US 97N or 140W from
Klamath Falls.
(541) 883-6714
[icons]

Pennsylvania

Allegheny National Forest
In northwestern Pennsylvania.
(814) 723-5150 or TDD 726-2710
[icons]

Delaware Water Gap National Recreation Area
In eastern Pennsylvania and northwestern New
Jersey.
(570) 588-2451
[icons]

South Carolina

Francis Marion National Forest
On the Coastal Plain north of Charleston.
(843) 561-4000
[icons]

Sumter National Forest
In western South Carolina.
(803) 561-4000
[icons]

South Dakota

Badlands National Park
In southwestern South Dakota.
(605) 433-5361, ext. 100
[icons]

Black Hills National Forest
In southwestern South Dakota.
(605) 673-2251 or TDD 673-4954
[icons]

Custer National Forest/Dakota Prairie Grasslands
In northwestern South Dakota.
(605) 797-4432
[icons]

Wind Cave National Park
In southwestern South Dakota.
(605) 745-4600
[icons]

Tennessee

**Big South Fork National River National Recreation
Area**
In northeastern Tennessee and southeastern Kentucky.
(931) 879-3625
[icons]

Cherokee National Forest
In eastern Tennessee.
(423) 476-9700
[icons]

Great Smoky Mountains National Park
In eastern Tennessee.
(423) 436-1200
[icons]

Land Between the Lakes National Recreation Area
In western Kentucky and Tennessee.
(270) 924-2000 or (800) 525-7077
[icons]

Texas

Amistad National Recreation Area
Northwest of Del Rio via US 90.
(830) 775-7491
[icons]

Angelina National Forest
In east Texas.
(409) 639-8620
[icons]

Big Bend National Park
Southeast of Alpine on SR 118 and US 385.
(915) 477-2251
[icons]

Davy Crockett National Forest
In east Texas.
(409) 655-2299 or 831-2246
[icons]

Guadalupe Mountains National Park
110 mi. east of El Paso on US 62/180.
(915) 828-3251
[icons]

Lake Meredith National Recreation Area
45 mi. northeast of Amarillo and 9 mi. west of Borger
via SR 136.
(806) 857-3151
[icons]

Padre Island National Seashore
On Padre Island paralleling the Texas coast between
Port Isabel and Corpus Christi.
(361) 949-8068
[icons]

Sabine National Forest
In east Texas.
(409) 787-3870 or 275-2632
[icons]

Sam Houston National Forest
40 mi. north of Houston in east Texas.
(281) 344-6205
[icons]

Utah

Arches National Park
5 mi. northwest of Moab on US 191.
(435) 259-8161 or TTY 259-5279
[A] [林] [⊞] [†∩]

Ashley National Forest
In northeastern Utah.
(435) 789-1181
[占] [A] [林] [⊞] [土] [†∩] [◉]

Bryce Canyon National Park
26 mi. southeast of Panguitch via US 89 and SRs 12 and 63.
(435) 834-5322
[A] [林] [⊞] [†∩] [◉]

Canyonlands National Park
In southeastern Utah.
(435) 259-7164
[A] [林] [⊞] [†∩]

Capitol Reef National Park
5 mi. east of Torrey on SR 24.
(435) 425-3791
[占] [A] [林] [⊞] [†∩]

Dixie National Forest
In southwestern Utah.
(435) 865-3700
[占] [A] [林] [⊞] [土] [†∩] [◉]

Fishlake National Forest
In south-central Utah.
(435) 896-9233
[占] [A] [林] [⊞] [†∩] [◉]

Flaming Gorge National Recreation Area
In northeastern Utah.
(435) 784-3445
[占] [A] [林] [⊞] [土] [†∩] [◉]

Glen Canyon National Recreation Area
In south-central Utah.
(520) 608-6404 or 608-6200
[A] [林] [⊞] [土] [†∩] [◉]

Manti-La Sal National Forest
In southeastern Utah.
(435) 637-2817
[A] [林] [⊞] [◉]

Uinta National Forest
In central Utah.
(801) 377-5780
[占] [A] [林] [⊞] [土] [†∩]

Wasatch-Cache National Forest
In north-central and northeastern Utah.
(801) 524-3900
[占] [A] [林] [⊞] [土]

Zion National Park
In southwestern Utah.
(435) 772-3256
[A] [林] [⊞] [†∩] [◉]

Vermont

Green Mountain National Forest
In south-central Vermont.
(802) 747-6700
[A] [林] [⊞] [土]

Virginia

George Washington and Jefferson National Forests
In western Virginia and the eastern edge of West Virginia.
(888) 265-0019
[占] [A] [林] [⊞] [土] [†∩]

Mount Rogers National Recreation Area
In southwestern Virginia.
(540) 783-5196 or (800) 628-7202
[占] [A] [林] [⊞] [土] [†∩]

Shenandoah National Park
In western Virginia.
(540) 999-3500
[A] [林] [⊞] [†∩] [◉]

Washington

Gifford Pinchot National Forest
In southwestern Washington.
(360) 891-5000
[占] [A] [林] [⊞] [土] [†∩] [◉]

Lake Roosevelt National Recreation Area
In northeastern Washington.
(509) 633-9441
[A] [⊞] [土] [†∩] [◉]

Mount Baker-Snoqualmie National Forest (Douglas Fir)
2 mi. east of Glacier on SR 542.
(425) 775-9702 or (800) 627-0062
[A] [林] [⊞]

Mount Baker-Snoqualmie National Forest (Horseshoe Cove)
14 mi. north of Concrete on Baker Lake.
(425) 775-9702 or (800) 627-0062
[A] [林] [土]

Mount Baker-Snoqualmie National Forest (Shannon Creek)
24 mi. north of Concrete on Baker Lake.
(425) 775-9702 or (800) 627-0062
[A] [林] [⊞] [土]

[占] Bicycling   [A] Camping   [林] Hiking   [⊞] Picnicking
[土] Swimming   [†∩] Visitor center   [◉] Food service

Olympic National Forest
In northwestern Washington.
(360) 956-2400
[♿] [⛺] [🚶] [🏕] [🚣] [🛏] [🍴]

West Virginia

Monongahela National Forest
In eastern West Virginia.
(304) 636-1800 (voice and TDD)
[⛺] [🚶] [🏕] [🚣] [🛏]

New River Gorge National River
Between Fayetteville and Hinton.
(304) 465-0508
[🚶] [🏕] [🚣] [🛏]

Spruce Knob-Seneca Rocks National Recreation Area
In east-central West Virginia.
(304) 567-2827
[⛺] [🚶] [🏕] [🚣] [🛏]

Wisconsin

Apostle Islands National Lakeshore
Off northern Wisconsin's Bayfield Peninsula in Lake Superior.
(715) 779-3397
[⛺] [🚶] [🏕] [🚣] [🛏]

Chequamegon National Forest
In north-central Wisconsin.
(715) 762-2461 or TDD 762-5701
[♿] [⛺] [🚶] [🏕] [🚣] [🍴]

Nicolet National Forest
In northeastern Wisconsin.
(715) 362-1300
[♿] [⛺] [🚶] [🏕] [🚣]

St. Croix National Riverway
Running 252 mi. from Cable to Prescott.
(715) 483-3284
[⛺] [🚶] [🏕] [🚣] [🛏]

Wyoming

Bighorn Canyon National Recreation Area
In Montana and northern Wyoming.
(406) 666-2412
[⛺] [🚶] [🏕] [🚣] [🛏] [🍴]

Bighorn National Forest
In north-central Wyoming.
(307) 672-0751
[⛺] [🚶] [🏕] [🍴]

Devils Tower National Monument
Between Sundance and Hulett.
(307) 467-5283
[⛺] [🚶] [🏕] [🚣] [🛏]

Flaming Gorge National Recreation Area
On the Wyoming-Utah border.
(435) 784-3445
[♿] [⛺] [🚶] [🏕] [🚣] [🛏] [🍴]

Fossil Butte National Monument
14 mi. west of Kemmerer on US 30.
(307) 877-4455
[🚶] [🏕] [🛏]

Grand Teton National Park
In northwestern Wyoming.
(307) 739-3410
[♿] [⛺] [🚶] [🏕] [🚣] [🛏] [🍴]

Medicine Bow National Forest
In eastern Wyoming.
(307) 745-2300
[♿] [⛺] [🚶] [🏕] [🚣] [🛏]

Shoshone National Forest
In northwestern Wyoming.
(307) 527-6241
[♿] [⛺] [🚶] [🏕] [🚣] [🛏] [🍴]

Yellowstone National Park
In northwestern Wyoming.
(307) 344-7381
[⛺] [🚶] [🏕] [🛏] [🍴]

Canada

Alberta

Elk Island National Park
In central Alberta, east of Edmonton.
(780) 992-2950
[⛺] [🚶] [🏕] [🛏] [🍴]

Jasper National Park
In west-central Alberta along the British Columbia border.
(780) 852-6161
[♿] [⛺] [🚶] [🏕] [🚣] [🛏] [🍴]

Waterton Lakes National Park
In Alberta's southwestern corner.
(403) 859-5133
[⛺] [🚶] [🏕] [🚣] [🛏] [🍴]

British Columbia

Glacier National Park
In southeastern British Columbia.
(250) 837-7500
[⛺] [🚶] [🏕] [🛏] [🍴]

Kootenay National Park
In southeastern British Columbia.
(250) 347-9615 or (800) 748-7275
🚲 🅰 🕺 🏕 🏊 🛉 🍽

Mount Revelstoke National Park
In southeastern British Columbia.
(250) 837-7500
🕺 🏕

Pacific Rim National Park Reserve
On the southwestern coast of Vancouver Island.
(250) 726-7721 or 726-4212
🅰 🕺 🏕 🏊

Yoho National Park
On the British Columbia-Alberta border.
(250) 343-6783
🚲 🅰 🕺 🏕 🛉 🍽

Manitoba

Riding Mountain National Park
In western Manitoba.
(204) 848-7275 or (800) 707-8480
🚲 🅰 🕺 🏕 🏊 🛉 🍽

New Brunswick

Fundy National Park
On Hwy. 114, 130 km. southwest of Moncton.
(506) 887-6000
🅰 🕺 🏕 🏊 🛉 🍽

Kouchibouguac National Park
On Hwy. 134, north of Moncton.
(506) 876-2443 or TDD 876-4205
🚲 🅰 🕺 🏕 🏊 🛉 🍽

Newfoundland

Gros Morne National Park
On Newfoundland's western coast.
(709) 458-2417, 458-2066 or TDD 458-2996
🅰 🕺 🏕 🏊 🛉

Terra Nova National Park
In eastern Newfoundland.
(709) 533-2801
🅰 🕺 🏕 🏊 🛉 🍽

Northwest Territories

Nahanni National Park Reserve
145 km. west of Fort Simpson in western Northwest
Territories.
(867) 695-3151
🅰 🕺 🏕 🏊 🛉

Wood Buffalo National Park
On the Northwest Territories-Alberta border.
(867) 872-2349
🅰 🕺 🏕 🏊 🛉

Nova Scotia

Cape Breton Highlands National Park
5 km. northeast of Chéticamp on Cabot Tr.
(902) 224-2306 or (888) 773-8888
🅰 🕺 🏕 🏊 🛉 🍽

Kejimkujik National Park
In southwestern Nova Scotia off Hwy. 8 at Maitland
Bridge.
(902) 682-2772
🅰 🕺 🏕 🏊 🛉 🍽

Ontario

Bruce Peninsula National Park
In southwestern Ontario.
(519) 596-2233
🅰 🕺 🏕 🏊 🛉

Prince Edward Island

Prince Edward Island National Park
Along the island's northern shore.
(902) 566-7050
🚲 🅰 🕺 🏕 🏊 🛉 🍽

Quebec

Forillon National Park
20 km. northeast of Gaspé via Hwy. 132.
(418) 368-5505 or (800) 463-6769
🚲 🅰 🕺 🏕 🏊 🛉 🍽

La Mauricie National Park
North of Trois Rivières via Hwy. 55.
(819) 536-2638
🚲 🅰 🕺 🏕 🏊 🛉 🍽

Saskatchewan

Grasslands National Park
Between Val Marie and Killdeer in southern
Saskatchewan.
(306) 298-2257
🅰 🕺 🏕 🛉

Prince Albert National Park
In central Saskatchewan.
(306) 663-5322
🚲 🅰 🕺 🏕 🏊 🛉 🍽

🚲 Bicycling 🅰 Camping 🕺 Hiking 🏕 Picnicking
🏊 Swimming 🛉 Visitor center 🍽 Food service

This list of animal clinics in the United States and Canada is provided by the Veterinary Emergency & Critical Care Society as a service to the community for information purposes only. This is not to be construed as a certification or an endorsement of any clinic listed.

If you are traveling to an area not covered in this list, be prepared for an emergency by asking your regular veterinarian to recommend a clinic or veterinarian at your destination. The American Animal Hospital Association also provides a veterinary locator service to clinics that meet the association's high standards for veterinary care. Contact the association at (800) 883-6301 or online at http://www.healthypet.com *(see sidebar, p. 7)*.

United States

Alabama

Village Veterinary Clinic
403 Opelika Rd., Auburn
(334) 821-7730

Emergency Pet Care
4524 Southlake Pkwy., Birmingham
(205) 988-5988

Kent's Animal Hospital
3222 6th Ave. S., Birmingham
(205) 323-1536

Emergency Clinic of North Alabama
2306-A Memorial Pkwy. SW, Huntsville
(256) 533-7600

Rehm Animal Clinic
951 Hillcrest Rd., Mobile
(334) 639-9120

Carriage Hills Animal Clinic
3200 E. Bypass, Montgomery
(334) 277-2867

Alaska

Pet Emergency Treatment Inc.
3315 Fairbanks St., Anchorage
(907) 274-5636

Arizona

East Valley Veterinary Hospital
1721 E. University Dr., Mesa
(602) 890-8283

Mesa Veterinary Hospital
858 N. Country Club Dr., Mesa
(602) 833-7330

Emergency Animal Clinic
2260 West Glendale Ave., Phoenix
(602) 995-3757

Palo Verde Animal Hospital
1215 E. Northern Ave., Phoenix
(602) 944-9661

Emergency Animal Clinic
7901 E. McDowell Rd., Scottsdale
(602) 949-8001

Paradise Valley Emergency Animal Clinic
10614 N. 71st Pl., Scottsdale
(602) 991-1845

Animal Emergency Clinic
2661 N. First Ave., Tucson
(602) 293-5470

Animal Emergency Service
4832 E. Speedway St., Tucson
(602) 327-5624

Animal Emergency West
1675 West Grant Rd., Tucson
(602) 792-1858

Arkansas

Animal Emergency Clinic
801 John Barrow Rd., #6, Little Rock
(501) 224-3784

California

Animal Hospital of Antioch
2204 A St., Antioch
(925) 754-6700

Antioch Veterinary Hospital
1432 West 10th St., Antioch
(925) 757-2233

Central Coast Pet Emergency Clinic
1558 W. Branch St., Arroyo Grande
(805) 489-6573

Kern Animal Emergency Clinic
4300 Easton Dr., #1, Bakersfield
(805) 322-6019

Pet Emergency Treatment Service Inc.
1048 University Ave., Berkeley
(510) 841-7387

United Emergency Animal Clinic
1657 S. Bascom Ave., Campbell
(408) 371-6282

AKA Sacramento Animal Medical Group
4990 Manzanita Ave., Carmichael
(916) 331-2059

Acacia Veterinary Hospital
479 East Ave., Chico
(530) 345-1338

Contra Costa Veterinary Emergency Clinic
1410 Monument Blvd., Concord
(925) 798-2900

Solano Pet Emergency Clinic
4437 Central Pl., Cordelia
(707) 864-1444

East Valley Emergency Pet Clinic
938 N. Diamond Bar Blvd., Diamond Bar
(909) 861-5737

Tri-Valley Veterinary Emergency Clinic
6743 Dublin Blvd., Dublin
(925) 828-0654

Vet Care
7660 Amador Valley Blvd., Dublin
(925) 556-1299

Emergency Pet Clinic of San Gabriel Valley
3254 Santa Anita Ave., El Monte
(626) 579-4550

Greenback Veterinary Hospital
8311 Greenback Ln., Fair Oaks
(916) 725-1541

All Care Animal Referral Center
18440 E. Amistad St., Fountain Valley
(714) 963-0909

Central Veterinary Hospital & Emergency Service
5245 Central Ave., Fremont
(510) 797-7387

Veterinary Emergency Services
1639 N. Fresno St., Fresno
(559) 486-0520

Orange County Emergency Pet Clinic
12750 Garden Grove Blvd., Garden Grove
(714) 537-3032

Chatoak Pet Clinic
17659 Chatsworth St., Granada Hills
(818) 363-7444

Animal Emergency Clinic
12022 La Crosse Ave., Grand Terrace
(903) 825-9350

Animal Emergency Clinic of Victor Valley
17085 Main St., Hesperia
(619) 948-2868

North Orange County Pet Clinic
1474 S. Harbor Blvd., La Habra
(714) 537-3032

Pet Emergency Clinic of East County
5232 Jackson Dr., #105, La Mesa
(619) 462-4800

Animal Emergency Hospital
1055 W. Ave. M, #101, Lancaster
(805) 723-3959

Loomis Basin Veterinary Clinic
3901 Sierra College Blvd., Loomis
(916) 652-5816

Adobe Animal Hospital
396 First St., Los Altos
(650) 948-9661

Animal Emergency Facility
1736 South Sepulveda Blvd., #A, Los Angeles
(310) 473-1561

Eagle Rock Emergency Pet Clinic
4252 Eagle Rock Blvd., Los Angeles
(323) 254-7382

West Los Angeles Animal Hospital
1818 South Sepulveda Blvd., Los Angeles
(310) 473-2951

Animal Urgent Care
28085 Hillcrest, Mission Viejo
(949) 364-6228

Veterinary Emergency Clinic
1800 Prescott Rd., #E, Modesto
(209) 825-9350

Monterey Peninsula/Salinas Veterinary Emergency Clinic
2 Harris Ct., #A1, Monterey
(831) 489-6573

Central Orange County Emergency Animal Clinic
3720 Campus Dr., Newport Beach
(949) 261-7979

Animal Emergency & Trauma Center
11057 E. Rosencrans Ave., Norwalk
(562) 863-2522

South Peninsula Veterinary Emergency Clinic
3045 Middlefield Rd., Palo Alto
(650) 494-1461

Animal Emergency Clinic of Pasadena
2121 Foothill Blvd., Pasadena
(626) 564-0704

McClave Vet Hospital
6950 Reseda Blvd., Reseda
(818) 881-5102

Rimforest Animal Hospital
1299 Bearsprings Rd., Rimforest
(909) 337-8587

Animal Care Center of Sonoma County
6620 Redwood Dr., Rohnert Park
(707) 584-4343

Emergency Animal Clinic of Sacramento
9700 Business Park Dr., #404, Sacramento
(916) 362-3111

Sacramento Emergency Veterinary Clinic
2201 El Camino Ave., Sacramento
(916) 922-3425

San Clemente Veterinary Hospital
1833 South El Camino Real, San Clemente
(949) 492-5777

Animal Emergency Clinic
246 W. Washington St., San Diego
(619) 748-7387

Animal Emergency Clinic
13240 Evening Creek Dr., San Diego
(619) 748-7387

Emergency Animal Hospital & Referral Center
2317 Hotel Cir. South, San Diego
(619) 299-2400

All Animals Emergency Hospital
1333 9th Ave., San Francisco
(415) 566-0531

Mission Pet Hospital
720 Valencia St., San Francisco
(415) 552-1969

Emergency Animal Clinic of San Jose
5440 Thornwood Dr., San Jose
(408) 578-5623

Alameda County Emergency Pet Clinic
14790 Washington Ave., San Leandro
(510) 352-6080

Northern Peninsula Veterinary Emergency Clinic
227 N. Amphlett Blvd., San Mateo
(650) 348-2575

Marin County Veterinary Emergency Clinic
4240 Redwood Hwy., San Rafael
(415) 472-2266

Santa Cruz Veterinary Hospital
2585 Soquel Dr., Santa Cruz
(831) 475-5400

North Bay Animal Emergency Hospital
1304 Wilshire Blvd., Santa Monica
(310) 451-8962

Pet Care Veterinary Hospital
1370 Fulton Rd., Santa Rosa
(707) 579-5900

Beverly Oaks Animal Hospital
14302 Ventura Blvd., Sherman Oaks
(818) 788-2022

Emergency Animal Clinic
5152 Sepulveda Blvd., #A, Sherman Oaks
(818) 788-7860

American Veterinary Hospital
2109 Tapo St., #3, Simi Valley
(805) 581-9111

Rancho Sequoia Veterinary Hospital
3380 Los Angeles Ave., Simi Valley
(805) 522-7476

Associated Veterinary Emergency Services
3008 E. Hammer Ln., #115, Stockton
(209) 952-8387

Animal Emergency Center
11740 Ventura Blvd., Studio City
(818) 760-3882

Emergency Pet Clinic of the Inland Empire
27443 Jefferson Ave., Temecula
(909) 695-5044

Pet Emergency Clinic of Thousand Oaks
2967 North Moorpark Rd., Thousand Oaks
(805) 492-2436

Animal Emergency Clinic of the Desert
72-374 Ramon Rd., Thousand Palms
(760) 343-3438

Emergency Pet Clinic of South Bay
2325 Torrance Blvd., Torrance
(310) 320-8300

Central Veterinary Hospital
281 North Central Ave., Upland
(909) 981-2855

Pet Emergency Clinic of Ventura
2301 S. Victoria Ave., Ventura
(805) 642-8562

North County Emergency Animal Clinic
100 N. Rancho Santa Fe Rd., #133, Vista
(760) 734-4433

Washington Blvd. Animal Hospital
12116 East Washington Blvd., Whittier
(562) 693-8233

Colorado

All Pets Veterinary Clinic
5290 Manhattan Cir., Boulder
(303) 499-5335

Boulder Emergency Pet Clinic
1658 30th St., Boulder
(303) 440-7722

Animal Emergency Care
5752 North Academy Blvd., Colorado Springs
(719) 260-7141

Animal Emergency Center
2812 East Pikes Peak Ave., Colorado Springs
(719) 578-9300

Animal Emergency Room
9870 E. Alameda Ave., Denver
(303) 366-3527

Central Veterinary Emergency Services
2401 S. Downing St., Denver
(303) 733-2440

Animal Hospital Center
250 W. Lehow Ave., Englewood
(303) 794-2024

Veterinary Teaching Hospital
300 W. Drake Rd., Fort Collins
(970) 221-4535

Animal Emergency Service, Inc.
9797 West Colfax Ave., Lakewood
(303) 232-6227

Centennial Veterinary Clinic
2731 W. Belleview Ave., Littleton
(303) 795-0130

Wheat Ridge Animal Hospital
3695 Kipling St., Wheat Ridge
(303) 424-3325

Connecticut

East of the River Veterinary Emergency Clinic
222 Boston Tpk., Bolton
(860) 646-6134

New Haven Central Hospital
843 State St., New Haven
(203) 865-0878

Animal Emergency and Critical Care
41 Prospect Ave., West Hartford
(860) 233-8387

Florida

Emergency Animal Services
4525 Ulmerton Rd., Clearwater
(813) 572-4310

Animal Emergency Clinic
103 N. Powerline Rd., Deerfield Beach
(954) 428-9888

Pet Emergency Center
921 E. Cypress Creek Rd., Fort Lauderdale
(954) 772-0420

Animal Emergency and Referral Center
3984 S. US 1, Fort Pierce
(561) 466-3441

AA Pet Emergency Services
4000-B Newberry Rd., Gainesville
(352) 373-4444

Animal Clinic of Jupiter West
6779 W. Indiantown Rd., Jupiter
(561) 743-0153

Veterinary Emergency Clinic
3609 Hwy. 98 S., Lakeland
(863) 665-3199

Lantana Animal Clinic
3530 Lantana Rd., Lantana
(561) 439-0694

Promenade Animal Hospital
4424 N. University Dr., Lauderhill
(954) 748-9600

Animal Emergency Clinic South
8429 S.W. 132nd St., Miami
(305) 251-2096

Knowles Emergency Clinic
1000 N.W. 27th Ave., Miami
(305) 649-1234

Snapper Creek Emergency Clinic
9933 Sunset Dr., Miami
(305) 279-2323

Emergency Pet Hospital of Collier County
1217 Airport Rd. S., Naples
(941) 263-8010

Emergency Veterinary Clinic Okaloosa/Walton
210 A Government St., Niceville
(850) 729-3335

Veterinary Emergency Clinic
9500 Satellite Blvd., Orlando
(407) 644-4449

Pet Emergency & Critical Care Clinic
3816 Northlake Blvd., Palm Beach Gardens
(561) 691-9999

After Hours Emergency Animal Clinic of Hollywood
6602 Pines Blvd., Pembroke Pines
(305) 962-0300

West Florida Animal Medical Center
8560 N. Davis Hwy., Pensacola
(850) 479-9484

Animal Emergency Clinic of Pasco
8740 US Hwy. 19 N., Port Richey
(727) 841-6575

Emergency Veterinary Clinic of Sarasota
7517 S. Tamiami Tr., #107, Sarasota
(941) 923-7260

Animal Emergency of Hernando
3496 Deltona Blvd., Spring Hill
(352) 666-0904

Animal Emergency Clinic of St. Petersburg
3165 22nd Ave. N., St. Petersburg
(727) 323-1311

Allied Veterinary Emergency
401 9th Ave., Tallahassee
(850) 222-0123

Northwood Animal Hospital
1881-B North Martin Luther King Jr. Blvd., Tallahassee
(850) 385-8181

Murphy Animal Hospital
6845 N. Dale Mabry, Tampa
(813) 879-6090

Tampa Bay Veterinary Emergency Service
1501 S. Belcher Rd., Tampa
(813) 531-5752

Animal Emergency Clinic
3425 Forest Hill Blvd., West Palm Beach
(561) 433-2244

Summit Boulevard Animal Hospital
1000 S. Military Tr., #B and C, West Palm Beach
(561) 439-7900

Veterinary Emergency Clinic
882 Jackson Ave., Winter Park
(407) 644-4449

Georgia

Animal Emergency Clinic
228 Sandy Springs Pl., Atlanta
(404) 252-7881

Animal Emergency Clinic of Greater Augusta
2401 Washington Rd., #B, Augusta
(706) 733-7458

Animal Emergency Care
2009 Mercer University Dr., Macon
(912) 750-0911

Cobb Emergency Veterinary Clinic
630 Cobb Pkwy. N., Marietta
(770) 424-9157

Peachtree Corners Animal Clinic
4020 Holcomb Bridge Rd., Norcross
(770) 448-0700

Animal Emergency Center of North Fulton
900 Mansell Rd., #19, Roswell
(770) 594-2266

Chattahoochee Animal Clinic
1176 Alpharetta St., Roswell
(770) 993-6329

Savannah Veterinary Emergency Clinic
604 E. 67th St., Savannah
(912) 355-6113

Animal Emergency Clinic of Gwinnett
2090-A Lawrenceville-Suwanee Rd., Suwanee
(770) 277-3220

Illinois

Chicago Veterinary Emergency Services, Assoc.
3123 N. Clybourn Ave., Chicago
(312) 281-7110

Animal Emergency Center
2005 Mall St., Collinsville
(618) 346-1843

Emergency Veterinary Care South
13815 S. Cicero Ave., Crestwood
(708) 388-3771

All Creatures Emergency
1806 Belvidere Rd., Grayslake
(708) 548-5347

Emergency Veterinary Service
820 Ogden Ave., Lisle
(630) 960-2900

Animal Emergency and Critical Care Center
1810 Frontage Rd., Northbrook
(847) 564-5775

Animal Emergency Clinic
1211 11th St., Rockford
(815) 961-0255

Emergency Pet Care Center
530 Dunham Rd., St. Charles
(708) 377-2102

Animal 911
9851 Gross Point Rd., Skokie
(708) 328-9110

Animal Emergency of Lake County
131 Townline Rd., Vernon Hills
(847) 680-8600

Indiana

Emergency Animal Clinic
1313 Broadway, Fort Wayne
(219) 426-1062

Animal Emergency Clinic
8250 Bash St., Indianapolis
(317) 595-0414

Indianapolis Spay-Neuter 24-Hr. Animal Care Center
4030 W. 86th St., Indianapolis
(317) 872-0200

Indianapolis Vet Emergency Clinic
5245 Victory Dr., Indianapolis
(317) 782-4418

Newburgh Plaza Veterinary Clinic
5044 State Rte. 261, Newburgh
(812) 422-3300

New Carlisle Animal Clinic
8935 East US 20, New Carlisle
(219) 654-3129

Calumet Emergency Veterinary Clinic
216 W. Lincoln Hwy., Schererville
(219) 865-0970

Arbor View Animal Hospital
244 W. US Hwy. 6, Valparaiso
(219) 762-6586

Purdue Veterinary Teaching Hospital-Purdue University
1249 Lynn Hall, West Lafayette
(317) 494-1107

Iowa

Animal Emergency Clinic
1330 2nd Ave., Des Moines
(515) 280-3051

Kansas

Mission Medvet
5501 Johnson Dr., Mission
(913) 722-5566

Emergency Veterinary Clinic
10333 Metcalf, Overland Park
(913) 649-6850

Wichita Emergency Veterinary Clinic
737 S. Washington, Wichita
(316) 262-5321

Kentucky

Northern Kentucky Emergency & Specialty
5042 Old Taylor Mill Rd., Covington
(606) 261-9900

Colonial Animal Clinic
1601 Argillite Rd., Flatwoods
(606) 836-8112

AA Small Animal Emergency Service
423 Southland Dr., Lexington
(606) 276-2505

Hagyard Davidson McGee Veterinarians
4250 Ironworks Pike, Lexington
(606) 255-8741

Jefferson Animal & Emergency Hospital
4504 Outer Loop, Louisville
(502) 966-4104

Paducah Veterinary Clinic
3205 Central Ave., Paducah
(502) 443-8835

Louisiana

West Bank Pet Emergency Clinic
2417 Lapalco Blvd., Gretna
(504) 392-1932

Animal Emergency Clinic
1955 Veterans Memorial Blvd., Metairie
(504) 271-1234

Magnolia Pet Hospital
9954 Lake Forest Blvd., New Orleans
(504) 244-8550

Maine

Norway Veterinary Hospital
Route 26, Lower Main St., Norway
(207) 743-6384

Animal Emergency Clinic
352 Warren Ave., Portland
(207) 878-3121

Maryland

Anne Arundel Veterinary Emergency Clinic, Inc.
2138 B Generals Hwy., Annapolis
(410) 224-0331

Harford Veterinary Emergency Service
2105 Laurel Bush Rd., Bel Air
(410) 836-5173

Emergency Veterinary Clinic
32 Mellor Ave., Catonsville
(410) 788-7040

Emergency Animal Center, Inc.
1896 Urbana Pike, Ste. 23, Clarksburg
(301) 831-1088

Veterinary Referral Associates, Inc.
15021 Dufief Mill Rd., Gaithersburg
(301) 340-3129

Beltway Emergency Hospital
11660 Annapolis Rd., Rt. 450, Glenn Dale
(301) 721-1886

Emergency Animal Center, Inc.
1896 Urbana Pike, #23, Hyattstown
(201) 831-1088

Metropolitan Emergency Animal Clinic
12213 Nebel St., Rockville
(301) 770-5227

Animal Emergency Clinic
1711 York Rd., Timonium
(410) 252-8387

Veterinary Emergency Treatment Service
3 Rockefeller Ct., Waldorf
(301) 638-0988

Westminster Veterinary Hospital — Emergency Trauma Center
269 W. Main St., Westminster
(410) 848-3363

Massachusetts

Angell Memorial Animal Hospital
350 S. Huntington Ave., Boston
(617) 522-7282

Roberts Animal Hospital
516 Washington St., Hanover
(617) 826-2306

Holyoke Animal Hospital
320 Easthampton Rd., Holyoke
(413) 538-8700

Animal Health Care Associates
Martha's Vineyard Airport, Martha's Vineyard
(508) 693-6515

Veterinary Emergency Center
1299 Highland Ave., Needham
(617) 453-0143

Tufts University School Of Veterinary Medicine
200 Westboro Rd., North Grafton
(508) 839-5395

South Deerfield Veterinary Clinic
I-91 (Elm Street Exit), South Deerfield
(413) 665-3626

Veterinary Associates of Cape Cod
16 Commonwealth Ave., South Yarmouth
(508) 394-3566

Rowley Memorial Animal Hospital
53 Bliss St., Springfield
(413) 785-1221

Animal Extra Care
19 Main St., Wakefield
(617) 245-0045

Animal Emergency Center
595 West Center St., West Bridgewater
(508) 583-4220

Michigan

Oakland Veterinary Emergency Center
44136 Westminster Way, Canton
(313) 334-1555

Allied Veterinary Emergency Service
24400 Ford Rd., Dearborn Heights
(313) 274-3300

Animal Emergency Clinic
1007 S. Ballenger Hwy., Flint
(313) 238-7557

Animal Emergency Clinic of Kent Co.
422 College Ave. NE, Grand Rapids
(616) 774-7163

Lansing Veterinary Urgent Care
5133 S. Martin Luther King Jr. Blvd., Lansing
(517) 393-9200

Veterinary Medical Center
243 N. Jebauy Dr., Ludington
(616) 845-0385

Veterinary Emergency Service & Critical Care
28223 John R Rd., Madison Heights
(248) 547-4677

Oakland Veterinary Emergency
1843 Orchard Lake Rd., Silvan Lake
(313) 334-1555

Michigan Veterinary Specialist
21600 West 11 Mile Rd., Southfield
(810) 354-0303

Affiliated Veterinary Emergency Clinic
14085 Northline Rd., Southgate
(734) 284-1700

Union Lake Veterinary Hospital
6545 Looley Lake Rd., Waterford
(313) 363-1508

Minnesota

South Metro Animal Emergency Clinic
14520 Pennock Ave., Apple Valley
(612) 953-3737

Coon Rapids Clinic
1616 Coon Rapids Blvd., Coon Rapids
(317) 754-9434

Emergency Veterinary Service
4708 Olson Memorial Hwy., Golden Valley
(612) 529-1755

Animal Emergency Clinic, P.A.
301 University Ave., St. Paul
(612) 293-1800

Mississippi

Animal Emergency Hospital
10395 Old Hwy. 49, Gulfport
(601) 831-1397

Bienville Medical Center
1524 US 90 East, Ocean Springs
(601) 872-1231

Missouri

Animal Emergency Clinic
12501 Natural Bridge Rd., Bridgeton
(314) 739-1500

Animal Emergency Clinic
334 Fort Zumwalt Sq., O'Fallon
(314) 240-5496

Animal Emergency Clinic South
9937 Big Bend Blvd., St. Louis
(314) 822-7600

Montana

Animal Medical Clinic
5100 9th Ave. South, Great Falls
(406) 761-8183

Nebraska

VCA-Rohrig Animal Hospital
8022 W. Dodge Rd., Omaha
(402) 399-8100

Nevada

Carson Tahoe Veterinary Hospital
3389 S. Carson St., Carson City
(702) 883-8238

Animal Emergency Center
1914 E. Sahara Ave., Las Vegas
(702) 457-8050

Lake Mead Animal Hospital
4805 E. Lake Mead Blvd., Las Vegas
(702) 453-5906

Painted Desert Animal Hospital
4601 N. Rancho Dr., Las Vegas
(702) 645-2543

Animal Emergency Center
6427 S. Virginia St., Reno
(775) 851-3600

New Hampshire

Animal Emergency Clinic
2626 Brown Ave., Pine Island Plaza, Manchester
(603) 666-6677

State Line Veterinary Hospital
325 S. Daniel Webster Hwy., Nashua
(603) 888-2751

Animal Medical Center
1550 Woodbury Ave., Portsmouth
(603) 436-4922

Emergency Veterinary Clinic of the Seacoast
300 Gosling Rd., Portsmouth
(603) 436-5941

New Jersey

Jersey Shore Veterinary Emergency Service
505 Union Ave., Brielle
(908) 363-3200

Associated Veterinary Emergency Service
210 White Horse Pike, Clementon
(609) 784-2304

Central Jersey Veterinary Service
643 Route 27, Iselin
(908) 283-3535

Ocean County Veterinary Hospital
838 River Ave., Lakewood
(908) 363-7202

Oradell Animal Hospital
481 Kinderkamack Rd., Oradell
(201) 262-0010

Alliance Emergency Veterinary Clinic
540 Route 10 West, Randolph
(201) 328-8553

Garden State Veterinary Specialist
1 Pine St., Tinton Falls
(908) 922-0011

Shrewsbury Referral Group & Emergency Service
1008 Shrewsbury Ave., Tinton Falls
(908) 542-0014

Animal Emergency Group
647 Bloomfield Ave., West Caldwell
(201) 226-3282

New Mexico

Albuquerque Animal Emergency Clinic
5005 Prospect Ave. N.E., Albuquerque
(505) 884-3433

Animal Medical Hospital
2901 North Prince St., Clovis
(505) 762-3769

Great Plains Veterinary Clinic
2720 Lovington Hwy., Hobbs
(505) 392-5513

Ruidoso Animal Clinic
160 Sudderth, Ruidoso
(505) 257-4027

Emergency Veterinary Clinic of Santa Fe
1911 St. Michael's Dr., Santa Fe
(505) 984-0625

New York

Central Veterinary Hospital
388 Central Ave., Albany
(518) 434-2115

Greater Buffalo Veterinary Services
4949 Main St., Amherst
(716) 839-4043

Bayside Animal Clinic
36-43 Bell Blvd., Bayside
(718) 224-4451

Bellerose Animal Hospital
242-01 Jamaica Ave., Bellerose
(718) 347-1057

Brooklyn Veterinary Emergency Service
453 Bay Bridge Ave., Brooklyn
(718) 748-5180

Capital District Animal Emergency Clinic
1086 New London Rd., Cohoes
(518) 785-1094

Crawford Far Rockaway Animal Hospital
708 Beach-19th St., Far Rockaway
(718) 327-0256

Boulevard Animal Clinic
112-49 Queens Blvd., Forest Hills
(718) 261-1231

Great Neck Animal Clinic
501 Great Neck Rd., Great Neck
(516) 466-9191

Homer/Tully Animal Clinics
66 S. West St., Homer
(607) 749-7223

Queens Veterinary Emergency Clinic
187-11 Hillside Ave., Jamaica
(718) 454-4141

Hilton Hospital for Animals
120 Merrick Rd., Lynbrook
(516) 887-2914

Animal Medical Center
510 East 62nd St., New York
(212) 838-8100

Manhattan Veterinary Group
240 East 80th St., New York
(212) 988-1000

West End Veterinary Emergency Center
250 West 100th St., New York
(212) 666-7387

Orchard Park Veterinary Medical Center
3507 Orchard Park Rd., Orchard Park
(716) 622-6660

Animal Emergency Clinic of Hudson Valley
328 Manchester Rd., Poughkeepsie
(914) 471-8242

Animal Emergency Clinic of Rochester
241 Norris Dr., Rochester
(716) 271-2111

Animal Emergency Service
280-L Middle Country Rd., Selden
(516) 698-2225

Emergency Veterinary Group
5 Boone St., Staten Island
(718) 494-0050

Veterinary Emergency Center
1293 Clove Rd., Staten Island
(718) 720-4211

Animal Emergency Clinic
2612 Erie Blvd. East, Syracuse
(315) 446-7933

Valley Cottage Animal Hospital
202 Route 303, Valley Cottage
(915) 268-9263

Central Veterinary Associates
73 W. Merrick Rd., Valley Stream
(516) 825-3066

Animal Care Hospital
4535 Old Vestal Rd., Vestal
(607) 770-9999

Schroon River Animal Hospital
Horicon Avenue, Warrensburg
(518) 623-3181

Nassau Animal Emergency Group
740 Old County Rd., Westbury
(516) 665-6263

North Carolina

Animal Emergency Clinic, P.A.
500 Long Shoals Rd., Arden
(704) 687-0509

Emergency Veterinary Clinic
1500 Elizabeth Ave., Charlotte
(704) 376-9622

Freedom Animal Hospital
3055 Freedom Dr., Charlotte
(704) 399-6534

Triangle Pet Emergency Treatment Service
3319 Chapel Hill Blvd., Durham
(919) 489-0615

Veterinary Emergency Clinic of Gaston County
728 E. Franklin Blvd., Gastonia
(704) 866-7918

Animal Emergency Clinic of Pitt County
101 S.E. Greenville Blvd., Greenville
(919) 355-3825

Cabarrow Emergency Veterinary Clinic
1317 S. Cannon Blvd., Kannapolis
(704) 932-1182

After Hours Small Animal Emergency Clinic
409 Vick Ave., Raleigh
(919) 781-5145

Animal Emergency Clinic at Tryon Hills
3535 South Wilmington St., Raleigh
(919) 662-5559

Wilmington Animal Emergency Clinic
5739 Oleander Dr., Wilmington
(919) 791-7387

Forsyth After Hours Veterinary Emergency Clinic
7781 Northpoint Blvd., Winston-Salem
(336) 896-0902

Ohio

County Animal Hospital
11605 Stablewatch Ct., Cincinnati
(513) 398-8000

Emergency Veterinary Clinic of Cincinnati
4779 Red Bank Rd., Cincinnati
(513) 561-5688

Cleveland Animal Emergency & Specialty Clinic
5320 West 140th St., Cleveland
(216) 362-6000

Columbus Veterinary Emergency Service
5747 Cleveland Ave., Columbus
(614) 890-2545

Dayton Emergency Vet Clinic
2714 Springboro West, Dayton
(937) 293-2714

Animal Medical & Emergency Hospital
3859 West Dublin-Granville Rd., Dublin
(614) 889-2556

Lorain County Animal Emergency Center
1909 North Ridge Rd., Lorain
(440) 240-1400

Aaron Animal Clinic and Emergency Hospital
6210 Broadview Rd., Parma
(216) 459-0606

Oklahoma

Midtown Animal Hospital
1101 S.W. Park Ave., Lawton
(405) 353-3438

Veterinary Emergency and Critical Care Hospital
1800 W. Memorial Rd., Oklahoma City
(405) 749-6989

Animal Emergency Center
7220 E. 41st St., Tulsa
(918) 665-0508

Oregon

Willamette Veterinary Clinic
650 S.W. Third St., Corvallis
(503) 753-2223

Dove Lewis Emergency Animal Hospital
1984 N.W. Pettygrove St., Portland
(503) 228-7281

Parkway Animal Hospital
2655 N.W. Broad St., Roseburg
(503) 672-1621

Salem Veterinary Emergency Clinic
450 Pine St. N.E., Salem
(503) 588-8082

Emergency Veterinary Clinic of Tualatin
19314 S.W. Mohave Ct., Tualatin
(503) 691-7922

Pennsylvania

Providence Veterinary Hospital
24th and Providence Ave., Chester
(215) 872-4000

Valley Central Emergency Veterinary Hospital
210 Fullerton Ave., Fullerton
(215) 435-5588

Animal Emergency & Critical Care Service
1900 W. Old Lincoln Hwy., Langhorne
(610) 750-2774

Langdon & Leveto Veterinary Hospital & Emergency Center
316 Conneaut Lake Rd., Meadville
(814) 337-3271

Animal Emergency Clinic of Bucks County
4016 Fox Hill Ln., Newtown Square
(215) 946-8668

Animal Emergency Clinic of Bucks County
7029 Bristol Pike, Oakford
(215) 355-9317

After Hours Animal Emergency Hospital
560 McNeilly Rd., Pittsburgh
(412) 344-6888

Allegheny Veterinary Emergency Association
1835 Rte. 286, Pittsburgh
(724) 325-1881

Castle Shannon Veterinary Hospital
3610 Library Rd., Pittsburgh
(412) 885-2500

Tri-County Veterinary Emergency Service
2250 Old Bethlehem Pike, Quakertown
(215) 536-6245

Metropolitan Veterinary Emergency Service
915 Trouper Rd., Valley Forge
(610) 666-0995

Animal Emergency Clinic
3256 Susquehanna Tr., York
(717) 767-5355

Rhode Island

North Kingstown Animal Hospital
3637 Quaker Ln., North Kingstown
(401) 295-9777

Animal Care Services
135 Meadow St., Warwick
(401) 738-6695

Warwick Animal Hospital
1950 Elmwood Ave., Warwick
(401) 785-2222

South Carolina

Animal Emergency Center
132 Stonemark Ln., Columbia
(843) 744-3372

Animal Hospital of North Myrtle Beach
2501 Hwy. 17 S., North Myrtle Beach
(803) 272-8121

Veterinary Emergency Clinic of Spartanburg
1291 Ashville Hwy., Spartanburg
(803) 591-1923

Tennessee

Keith Street Animal Clinic
1990 Keith St., Cleveland
(615) 476-1804

After Hours Pet Emergency Clinic
215 Center Park Dr., Knoxville
(423) 966-3888

Knoxville Pet Emergency Hospital
1819 Ailor Ave., Knoxville
(423) 637-1114

Memphis Pet Emergency Hospital
5650 Mt. Moriah, Memphis
(901) 365-9690

Texas

I-20 Animal Medical Center
5750 I-20 West, Arlington
(817) 478-9238

Animal Emergency Hospital of Austin
4106 N. Lamar Blvd., Austin
(512) 459-4336

Emergency Animal Hospital of Austin
4544 S. Lamar Blvd., #760, Austin
(512) 899-0955

Emergency Animal Hospital of Austin
12034 Research Blvd., Austin
(512) 331-6121

North Texas Emergency Pet Center
1445 MacArthur, #246, Carrollton
(214) 323-1310

Cove Animal Clinic
2515 E. Hwy. 190, Copperas Cove
(817) 547-0355

Emergency Animal Clinic
12101 Greenville Ave., #118, Dallas
(214) 994-9110

Whiterock Animal Hospital
11414 East Northwest Hwy., Dallas
(214) 328-3255

El Paso Animal Emergency Center
2101 Texas Ave., El Paso
(915) 545-1148

Airport Freeway Animal Emerency Clinic
209 N. Main St., Euless
(817) 571-2088

Ridgmar Animal Hospital
2020 S. Las Vegas Tr., Fort Worth
(817) 246-6005

Animal Emergency Clinic
8921 Katy Frwy., Houston
(713) 932-9589

Animal Emergency Clinic
1111 West Loop S., Houston
(713) 888-0666

Animal Emergency Clinic Southeast
10331 Gulf Frwy., Houston
(713) 941-8460

Steeplechase Animal Hospital
9609 F.M. 1960 Rd. West, Houston
(713) 890-8875

Animal Emergency Clinic Southeast
1100 Gulf Frwy. S., #104, League City
(713) 332-1678

Safari Animal Care Centers
2450 E. Main St., #D, League City
(713) 332-5612

Lake Olympia Animal Hospital
3603 Glenn Lakes Ln., Missouri City
(713) 499-7242

Permian Basin Emergency Veterinary Clinic
13528 W. US Hwy. 80, Odessa
(915) 561-8301

Emergency Pet Clinic
8503 Broadway, #101, San Antonio
(210) 822-2873

Southwest Freeway Animal Hospital & Emergency Center
15575 Southwest Frwy., Sugarland
(281) 491-8387

Utah

Animal Medical Services
469 W. Center St., Orem
(801) 225-3346

Central Valley Emergency Animal Clinic
55 E. Miller Ave., Salt Lake City
(801) 487-1325

Vermont

Lamoille Valley Veterinary Services
278 Vermont Route 15 East, Hyde Park
(802) 888-7911

Virginia

Virginia-Maryland Veterinary Emergency Service
2660 Duke St., Alexandria
(703) 823-3601

Albemarle Veterinary Hospital
445 Westfield Rd., Charlottesville
(804) 973-6146

Veterinary Emergency Treatment Service
370 Greenbriar Dr., #A2, Charlottesville
(804) 973-3519

Animal Emergency Clinic
1210 Snowden St., Fredericksburg
(703) 371-1282

Animal Emergency Hospital
2 Cardinal Park Dr., #101B, Leesburg
(703) 777-5755

Animal Emergency Clinic of Central Virginia
1000 Miller Park Sq., Lynchburg
(804) 846-1504

Veterinary Referral of Northern Virginia
610 Centreville Rd., Manassas
(703) 631-1030

Veterinary Emergency Center
3312 W. Gary St., Richmond
(804) 353-9000

Springfield Emergency Veterinary Hospital
6651-F Backlick Rd., Springfield
(703) 451-8900

Animal Emergency Care
1060 Lynnhaven Pkwy., Virginia Beach
(757) 468-0071

Tidewater Veterinary Emergency Clinic
5425 Virginia Beach Blvd., Virginia Beach
(757) 499-5463

Silver Spring Veterinary Hospital
241 Garber Ln., Winchester
(540) 662-2301

Washington

Auburn Veterinary Hospital
718 Auburn Way N., Auburn
(206) 833-4510

Aerowood Animal Hospital
2975 156th St. S.E., Bellevue
(425) 746-6557

Mid-Columbia Pet Emergency Service
8300 Gage Blvd., Bldg. 6, Kennewick
(509) 783-1991

Vista Veterinary Hospital
5603 W. Canal Dr., Kennewick
(509) 783-2131

Animal Emergency & Referral Center
19511 24th Ave. W., Lynnwood
(425) 745-6745

Animal Emergency/Trauma Center
19689 7th Ave., #325, Poulsbo
(206) 697-7771

Emergency Animal Hospital
10310 Central Valley Rd., Poulsbo
(206) 692-6162

Emerald City Emergency Clinic
4102 Stone Way N., Seattle
(206) 634-9000

Five Corners Veterinary Hospital
15707 1st Ave. S., Seattle
(206) 243-2982

Pet Emergency Clinic
21 Mission Ave. E., Spokane
(509) 326-6620

Emergency Veterinary Service
6818 E. 4th Plain Blvd., #C, Vancouver
(206) 694-3007

West Virginia

Middletown Animal Clinic
Route 5, Fairmont
(304) 366-6130

Kanawha Valley Animal Emergency Clinic
5304 MacCorkle Ave. S.W., South Charleston
(304) 768-2911

Wisconsin

Fox Valley Animal Referral Center
842 Westhill Blvd., Appleton
(414) 993-9193

Animal Emergency Center
2100 W. Silver Spring Ave., Glendale
(414) 540-6710

Emergency Clinic for Animals
229 W. Beltline Hwy., Madison
(608) 274-7772

Animal Clinic & Hospital
2734 Calumet Dr., Sheboygan
(414) 565-2125

Emergency Veterinary Service
752 Westmount Dr., #L1, Waukesha
(414) 542-3241

Canada

British Columbia

Animal Emergency Clinic
#103-6337 198th St., Langley
(604) 514-1711

Animal Emergency Clinic
1590 West 4th Ave., Vancouver
(604) 734-5104

Ontario

Park Animal Hospital
1958 Burnham Thorpe Rd. E., Mississauga
(905) 625-5222

Niagara Veterinary Emergency Clinic
210 Glendale Ave., St. Catherines
(905) 641-3185

Animal Emergency Clinic of Durham
1912 Dundas St. E., Whitby
(905) 576-3031

Pet-Friendly
Accommodations

How to Use the Listings
U.S. Lodgings
Canadian Lodgings

How to Use the Listings

Some 10,000 AAA-RATED® properties across North America accept traveling pets. This guide provides listings for those lodgings in the United States and Canada that roll out the welcome mat for pets as well as the people who love them.

For the purpose of this book, "pets" are domestic cats or dogs. If you are planning to travel with any other kind of animal — particularly such exotic pets as birds or reptiles — check with the property before making definite plans. If you are taking a nontraditional pet, expect to keep her crated at all times.

Note: Always inform the management that you are traveling with an animal; you may be fined if you do not declare your pet. Many properties require guests with pets to sign a waiver or release form and to pay for the room with a credit card. Of course, whether you pay in cash or by credit card, you will be held liable for any damages caused by your pet, even if the property does not charge a deposit or pet fee. It is not a good idea to leave your pet unattended in the room, but if you must, crate him and notify the management. When in public areas, keep your pet leashed and do not allow him to disturb other guests.

About the Listings

Geographic listings are used for accuracy and consistency; lodgings are listed under the city or town in which they physically are located — or in some cases under the nearest recognized city or town. For a complete list of all cities within a state or province, see the comprehensive City Index at the beginning of the corresponding section.

U.S. properties are given first, followed by Canadian properties. Most listings are alphabetically organized by state or province, city and establishment name. Reflecting contemporary travel patterns, properties in some cities or towns may instead be listed within destination cities or areas. Such "vicinity cities" and their listings will be shown alphabetically in the destination city or area, and the vicinity city also will appear in alphabetical order in the City Index, along with the page number on which the listings begin.

Each listing provides the following information (see sample listing, next page):

❶ Symbol denoting Official Appointment (OA) properties. The OA program permits properties to display and advertise the 4- or 5-diamond emblem. OAs have a special interest in serving AAA/CAA members. Ask if they offer special member amenities such as free breakfast, early check-in/late check-out, free room upgrade, free local phone calls, etc.

❷ Diamond rating.

❸ Property name.

❹ Lodging classification.

❺ Special amenities offered. These properties provide an additional benefit to pets, such as treats, toys or gifts, pet sitting and/or walking, a pet menu, food/water dishes, pet sheets or pillows, pet beds or other extras.

❻ Telephone number.

❼ Two-person, two-bed (2P/2B) rate for the peak season and cancellation notice validity period (if more than 48 hrs.). Rates may be lower at other times of the year. Rates listed are usually daily, but weekly rates also may be listed. **Note:** Most properties accept any or all of the major credit cards, including American Express, MasterCard and VISA. If a property accepts only cash, the phrase "(no credit cards)" follows the rates.

❽ Physical address and highway directions. If no physical address was available, the phrase "call for directions" appears.

❾ Exterior or interior corridors.

❿ Pet policies. If the phrase "Pets accepted" appears, the property does accept pets but specific information was unavailable at press time. Otherwise, pet-specific policies are denoted as follows:

Size. "Very small" denotes pets weighing up to 10 lbs.; "small," up to 25 lbs.; "medium," up to 50 lbs.; and "large," up to 100 lbs. If no size is specified, the property accepts pets of all sizes.

Species. "Other" indicates the property accepts animals other than dogs and cats. Always call ahead and specify the type of pet you plan to bring.

Deposits and fees. Includes the dollar amount, the type of charge (refundable deposit or nonrefundable fee), the frequency of the charge and whether the charge is per pet or per room.

Designated rooms. Guests with pets are placed in certain rooms, often smoking rooms or those on the ground floor.

Housekeeping service. The phrase "service with restrictions" denotes properties that require the pet to be crated, removed or attended by the owner during housekeeping service.

Supervision. The pet is required to be supervised at all times.

Crate. The pet must be crated when the owner is not present. If this policy applies only to cats, the phrase "(cats only)" will follow.

❶ Property discounts and amenities:

🅢🅐🅥🅔 Minimum 10% discount.

🅢🅤🅑 SYC&S chain partners.

🅐🅢🅚 May offer discount.

🅢🅩 Senior discount.

🆇 Non-smoking rooms.

🅕 Semi-accessible or 🅛 fully accessible.

🅐 Hearing impaired.

🅢 Roll-in showers.

🅔 Refrigerator.

🖳 Coffee maker.

🅣 Restaurant on premises.

🅐 Outdoor pool.

🅐 Indoor pool.

🅐 Indoor/outdoor pool.

🆇 Recreation facilities.

🅚 No air conditioning.

🅒🅣🅥 No cable TV.

🆀 No telephones.

It is important to remember that animal policies do change; always confirm policies, restrictions and fees with the lodging when making reservations and again 1-2 days before departure.

Listing information is subject to change. All listing information was accurate at press time. However, lodging rates and policies change and the publisher cannot be held liable for changes occurring after publication.

AAA DIAMOND RATINGS

Before a property is listed by AAA, it must satisfy a set of minimum standards regarding basic lodging needs as identified by AAA members. If a property meets those requirements, it is assigned a diamond rating reflecting the overall quality of the establishment.

AAA ratings range from one to five diamonds and indicate the property's physical and service standards as measured against the standards of each diamond level. The rating process takes into account the property's classification; i.e., its physical structure and style of operation.

◆ Properties meet all Listing Requirements. They are clean and well-maintained.

◆◆ Properties maintain the attributes offered at the 1-diamond level while showing noticeable enhancements in room decor and quality of furnishings.

(Continued next page)

Sample Listing

❶ ❷ ❸ ❹❺

🅐🅐🅐 ◆◆◆ **Pet-Friendly Inn** 🅗 🐾 ❼   ❽   ❾

(000) 123-4567. **$55-$135, 7 days notice.** 105 Doggy Lane, I-99 exit 55. Ext corridors. **Pets:** Small, dogs only. $50 deposit/room, $25 one-time fee/pet, $5.50 daily fee/pet. Designated rooms, service w/restrictions, supervision, crate. ❿

🅢🅐🅥🅔 🅢🅩 🆇 🅕 🅐 🅢 🅔 🖳 🅣 🅐 🆇

❻   ⓫

◆◆◆ Properties show a marked upgrade in physical attributes, services and comfort. Additional amenities, services and facilities may be offered.

◆◆◆◆ Properties reflect an exceptional degree of hospitality, service and attention to detail while offering upscale facilities and a variety of amenities.

◆◆◆◆◆ Property facilities and operations exemplify an impeccable standard of excellence while exceeding guest expectations in hospitality and service. These renowned properties are both striking and luxurious, offering many extra amenities.

Lodging Classifications

A Apartment: Establishments that primarily offer transient guest accommodations with one or more bedrooms, a living room, a full kitchen and an eating area. Studio-type apartments may combine the sleeping and living areas into one room.

BB Bed & Breakfast: Usually smaller establishments emphasizing a more personal relationship between operators and guests, leading to an "at home" feeling. Guest units tend to be individually decorated. Rooms may not include some modern amenities such as televisions and telephones, and may have a shared bathroom. Usually owner-operated, with a common room or parlor separate from the innkeeper's living quarters, where guests and operators can interact during evening and breakfast hours. Evening office closures are normal. A continental or full, hot breakfast is served and is included in the room rate.

X Complex: A combination of two or more types of lodging classifications.

CO Condominium: Establishments that primarily offer guest accommodations that are privately owned by individuals and available for rent. These can include apartment-style units or homes. A variety of room styles and decor treatments as well as limited housekeeping service is typical. May have off-site registration.

C Cottage: Establishments that primarily provide individual housing units that may offer one or more separate sleeping rooms, a living room and cooking facilities. Usually incorporate rustic decor treatments and are geared to vacationers.

CI Country Inn: Although similar in definition to a bed and breakfast, country inns are usually larger in size, provide more spacious public areas and offer a dining facility that serves at least breakfast and dinner. May be located in a rural setting or downtown area.

H Hotel: Usually high-rise establishments offering a full range of on-premises food and beverage service, cocktail lounge, entertainment, conference facilities, business services, shops and recreational activities. Wide range of services provided by uniformed staff on duty 24 hours. Parking arrangements vary.

L Lodge: Typically two or more stories with all facilities in one building, rustic decor. Located in vacation, ski, fishing areas, etc. Usually has food and beverage service.

M Motel: Low-rise or multistory establishment offering limited public and recreational facilities.

MI Motor Inn: Single or multistory establishment offering on-premises food and beverage service. Meeting and banquet facilities and some recreational activities. Usually complimentary on-site parking.

RA Ranch: Often offers rustic decor treatments and food and beverage facilities. Entertainment and recreational activities are geared to a Western-style adventure vacation. May provide some meeting facilities.

R Resort: Geared to vacation travelers. It is a destination offering varied food and beverage outlets, specialty shops, meeting or conference facilities, entertainment and extensive recreational facilities for special interests such as golf, tennis, skiing, fishing and water sports. Assorted social and recreational programs are typically offered in season, and a variety of package plans are usually available, including meal plans incorporated into the rates. Larger resorts may offer a variety of guest accommodations.

U.S. Lodgings

ALABAMA

ANDALUSIA

◆ **Days Inn** Ⓜ ☆
(334) 427-0050. **$50-$56, 7 days notice.** 1604 E Bypass Hwy 84. Just s of US 84. Ext corridors. **Pets:** Other. $6 daily fee/room. Supervision.
ⒶⓈⓀ ☒ 🛢 🖥 ☕

ARDMORE

ⒶⒶⒶ ◆◆ **Econo Lodge** Ⓜ
(256) 423-6699. **$37-$47.** 28555 Boyds Chapel Rd. I-65 exit 365. Ext corridors. **Pets:** Small. No service, supervision, crate.
ⓈⒶⓋⒺ Ⓢ☒ 🛢 🖥

ATHENS

ⒶⒶⒶ ◆◆◆ **Best Western Inn** Ⓜ ☆
(256) 233-4030. **$49-$74, 7 days notice.** 1329 Hwy 72 E. I-65 exit 351. Ext corridors. **Pets:** Very small, dogs only. $8 daily fee/pet, $8 one-time fee/pet. Designated rooms, no service, supervision, crate.
ⓈⒶⓋⒺ ☒ 🛢 🖥 ☕

BIRMINGHAM METROPOLITAN AREA

BIRMINGHAM

◆◆ **Baymont Inn & Suites-Birmingham** Ⓜ
(205) 995-9990. **$56-$56.** 513 Cahaba Park Cir. I-459 exit 19, 1.5 mi s off US 280. Int corridors. **Pets:** Supervision.
Ⓢ☒ 🛢 🖥 ⒸⓉⓋ

ⒶⒶⒶ ◆◆◆ **Best Suites of America** Ⓜ
(205) 940-9990. **$75-$135.** 140 State Farm Pkwy. I-65 exit 255, 0.5 mi nw. Int corridors. **Pets:** Designated rooms, no service, supervision, crate.
ⓈⒶⓋⒺ ☒ 🏊 ⓢ 🛢 🖥 ☕

ⒶⒶⒶ ◆◆◆ **Embassy Suites Birmingham** Ⓗ
(205) 879-7400. **$119-$149.** 2300 Woodcrest Place. Just n of jct US 31 and 280, exit 21st Ave (southbound), then 0.3 mi s. Int corridors. **Pets:** No service, supervision, crate.
ⓈⒶⓋⒺ Ⓢ☒ 🏊 🛢 🖥 🍽 ☕

◆◆ **Holiday Inn Express** Ⓜ
(205) 956-8211. **$52-$63.** 7941 Crestwood Blvd. I-20 exit 132, just e on US 78. Ext corridors. **Pets:** Medium. Designated rooms, no service, supervision, crate.
ⒶⓈⓀ ☒ 🏊 🛢 ☕

◆◆◆ **La Quinta Inn & Suites-Birmingham Homewood** Ⓜ ☆
(205) 290-0150. **$79-$119.** 60 State Farm Pkwy. I-65 exit 255, 0.9 mi nw frontage road. Int corridors. **Pets:** Small, other. No service, supervision, crate.
ⒶⓈⓀ ☒ ⓢ 🛢 🖥 ☕

◆◆◆ **La Quinta Inn-Birmingham** Ⓜ
(205) 324-4510. **$59-$89.** 905 11th Ct W. I-59/20 exit 123, just nw. Ext corridors. **Pets:** Designated rooms, supervision.
ⒶⓈⓀ ☒ 🛢 🖥 ☕

ⒶⒶⒶ ◆◆ **Motel Birmingham Garden Courtyards** Ⓜ ☆
(205) 956-4440. **$59-$110.** 7905 Crestwood Blvd. I-20 exit 132, just e on US 78. Ext corridors. **Pets:** Medium. $20 one-time fee/room. Designated rooms, no service, supervision, crate.
ⓈⒶⓋⒺ ☒ 🛢 🖥 ☕ ☒

ⒶⒶⒶ ◆◆◆ **Pickwick Hotel** Ⓗ
(205) 933-9555. **$89-$129.** 1023 20th St S. At Five Points, 1.5 mi s of downtown. Int corridors. **Pets:** Very small. Designated rooms, no service, supervision, crate.
ⓈⒶⓋⒺ Ⓢ☒ 🛢 🖥

◆◆◆ **Redmont Hotel** Ⓗ ☆
(205) 324-2101. **$129.** 2101 Fifth Ave N. Downtown, corner Fifth Ave and 21st St; I-65, 22nd St exit, then s. Int corridors. **Pets:** Medium. $75 deposit/pet. No service, supervision, crate.
ⒶⓈⓀ ☒ 🛢 🖥 🍽

◆◆◆ **Residence Inn By Marriott** 🅰 ❀
(205) 991-8686. **$89-$89.** 3 Green Hill Pkwy at US 280. 2 mi s of jct I-459 and US 280. Ext corridors. **Pets:** Other. $100 one-time fee/room. Supervision.
(ASK) (S/D) (X) (🖪) (💻) (🖼) (X)

◆◆◆ **Residence Inn by Marriott** 🅼
(205) 943-0044. **$139, 30 days notice.** 50 State Farm Pkwy. 1 mi nw, from I-65 exit 255. Int corridors. **Pets:** Medium. Supervision.
(ASK) (S/D) (X) (🖪) (💻) (🖼)

🐾🐾 ◆◆◆ **The Tutwiler, A Wyndham Grand Heritage Hotel** 🅷
(205) 322-2100. **$140.** Park Pl at 21st St N. Downtown. Int corridors. **Pets:** No service, supervision, crate.
(SAVE) (S/D) (X) (🖪) (💻) (🍴)

CALERA

◆◆◆ **Holiday Inn Express** 🅼
(205) 668-3641. **$59-$79.** 357 Hwy 304. I-65 exit 231, just se. Ext corridors. **Pets:** Small. Designated rooms, supervision.
(ASK) (S/D) (X) (🖼) (🖼)

HOMEWOOD

◆◆◆ **Holiday Inn Homewood** 🅼🅸 ❀
(205) 942-2041. **$89-$89.** 260 Oxmoor Rd. I-65 northbound exit 256; southbound 256A, just w. Int corridors. **Pets:** Small. Supervision.
(S/D) (X) (🖪) (💻) (🍴) (🖼) (X)

◆◆ **Microtel** 🅼
(205) 945-5550. **$38-$38.** 251 Summit Pkwy. I-65 exit 256, 0.3 mi w. Int corridors. **Pets:** Medium. Designated rooms, no service, supervision, crate.
(X) (🖼)

◆◆◆ **The Mountain Brook Inn** 🅼🅸 ❀
(205) 870-3100. **$115-$115.** 2800 Hwy 280. 5 mi se on US 280. Int corridors. **Pets:** Small. $25 one-time fee/room. Designated rooms, no service, supervision, crate.
(X) (🖪) (💻) (🍴) (🖼) (X)

🐾🐾 ◆◆ **Red Roof Inn** 🅼 ❀
(205) 942-9414. **$46-$64.** 151 Vulcan Rd. I-65 exit 256 northbound; exit 256A southbound, just nw. Ext corridors. **Pets:** Other. Designated rooms, no service, supervision, crate.
(SAVE) (X) (CTV)

HOOVER

🐾🐾 ◆◆◆ **AmeriSuites** 🅼 ❀
(205) 988-8444. **$94-$114.** 2980 Hwy 150. Jct I-459 and US 31; 0.5 mi s on US 31, 0.8 mi w on SR 150. Int corridors. **Pets:** Small. No service, supervision, crate.
(SAVE) (X) (🖼) (🖪) (💻) (🖼) (CTV)

◆◆◆ **La Quinta Inn & Suites-Birmingham Hoover** 🅼 ❀
(205) 403-0096. **$69-$99.** 120 Riverchase Pkwy E. I-65 and Valleydale Rd (exit 247). Int corridors. **Pets:** Other. No service, supervision, crate.
(ASK) (X) (🖼) (🖪) (💻) (🖼)

LEEDS

🐾🐾 ◆◆ **Days Inn of Leeds** 🅼 ❀
(205) 699-9833. **$50-$80.** 1835 Ashville Rd. On US 411; 0.3 mi s of I-20, exit 144 eastbound. Ext corridors. **Pets:** Small. $5 daily fee/pet. Designated rooms, no service, supervision, crate.
(SAVE) (X) (🖪) (🖼)

MOODY

◆◆ **Super 8 Motel** 🅼 ❀
(205) 640-7091. **$42-$50, 30 days notice.** 2451 Moody Pkwy. On US 411; 1 mi n of I-20, westbound exit 144; eastbound 144B. Ext corridors. **Pets:** Small, other. Supervision.
(ASK) (S/D) (X)

PELHAM

◆◆ **Best Western Oak Mountain Inn** 🅼
(205) 982-1113. **$59-$69.** 100 Bishop Cir. I-65 exit 246, just sw; just s on State Park Rd. Int corridors. **Pets:** Medium. Supervision.
(ASK) (X) (🖼) (🖪) (🖼)

◆◆ **Comfort Inn-Pelham** 🅼 ❀
(205) 444-9200. **$59-$89.** 110 Cahaba Valley Pkwy. On SR 119, 0.3 mi w of jct I-65, exit 246. Ext corridors. **Pets:** Other. Supervision.
(ASK) (X) (🖪) (🖼)

RIVERSIDE

🐾🐾 ◆◆ **Best Western Riverside Inn** 🅼🅸 ❀
(205) 338-3381. **$59-$69.** 11900 Hwy 78. On US 78 at jct I-20, exit 162, just se. Ext corridors. **Pets:** Small. Supervision.
(SAVE) (X) (🖪) (🍴) (🖼) (X)

VESTAVIA HILLS

◆◆◆ **Hampton Inn South** 🅼 ❀
(205) 822-2224. **$69-$82, 30 days notice.** 1466 Montgomery Hwy. I-65 exit 252, US 31, 0.5 mi e. Ext corridors. **Pets:** Small, dogs only. Supervision.
(ASK) (S/D) (X) (💻) (🖼)

🐾🐾 ◆◆◆ **Holiday Inn-South On The Lake** 🅼🅸
(205) 822-4350. **$71-$81.** 1548 Montgomery Hwy. US 31, 0.3 mi w of I-65, exit 252. Ext corridors. **Pets:** Medium. Designated rooms, no service, supervision, crate.
(SAVE) (S/D) (X) (🖼) (🖪) (💻) (🍴) (🖼) (X)

❀ **END METROPOLITAN AREA** ❀

BOAZ

◆◆ Best Western Boaz Outlet Center **M** ❀
(256) 593-8410. **Call for rates.** 751 Hwy 431 S. SR 431, at Outlet Center. Ext/int corridors. **Pets:** Small, other. No service, supervision, crate.
[ASK] [✕] [☒]

AAA ◆◆ Key West Inn **M** ❀
(256) 593-0800. **$50-$65, 30 days notice.** 10535 SR 168. 0.5 mi w of jct US 431. Ext corridors. **Pets:** $5 daily fee/pet, $5 one-time fee/pet. Supervision.
[SAVE] [S⚡] [✕] [☎] [💻]

CLANTON

AAA ◆◆◆ Best Western Inn **M**
(205) 280-1006. **$48-$68, 5 days notice.** 801 Bradberry Ln. I-65 exit 205, 0.5 mi e. Ext corridors. **Pets:** Small. Supervision.
[SAVE] [✕] [⚡] [☎] [☒]

◆◆ Days Inn **MI**
(205) 755-0510. **$40-$55.** 2000 Holiday Inn Dr. I-65 exit 205, just ne on US 31 and SR 22. Ext corridors. **Pets:** Small. Designated rooms, no service, supervision, crate.
[ASK] [S⚡] [✕] [🍴] [☒]

◆◆ Key West Inn **M** ❀
(205) 755-8500. **$44-$70.** 2045 7th St S. I-65 exit 205, just w on US 31 and SR 22. Ext corridors. **Pets:** $5 daily fee/pet, $5 one-time fee/pet. Designated rooms, no service, supervision, crate.
[ASK] [✕] [☎] [💻]

◆◆ Shoney's Inn **MI** ❀
(205) 280-0306. **$37-$50.** 946 Lake Mitchell Rd. I-65 exit 208, just w. Ext corridors. **Pets:** Medium. $20 deposit/room. No service, supervision, crate.
[ASK] [✕] [🍴] [☒]

CULLMAN

AAA ◆◆◆ Best Western Fairwinds Inn **M** ❀
(256) 737-5009. **$49-$79.** 1917 Commerce Ave NW. I-65 exit 310, just e. Ext corridors. **Pets:** Small. $5 daily fee/pet. Designated rooms, no service, supervision, crate.
[SAVE] [✕] [☎] [💻] [☒]

◆◆ Days Inn **MI** ❀
(256) 739-3800. **$44-$58.** 1841 4th St SW. I-65 exit 308, Hwy 278. Ext corridors. **Pets:** Medium. $4 one-time fee/room. Supervision.
[ASK] [✕] [☎] [🍴] [☒]

DALEVILLE

◆◆ Econo Lodge **M**
(334) 598-6304. **$36-$51, 5 days notice.** 444 N Daleville Ave. 1 mi n jct US 84 and SR 85. Ext corridors. **Pets:** Medium. No service, supervision, crate.
[ASK] [✕] [☎] [💻] [☒]

AAA ◆ Green House Inn & Lodge **M** ❀
(334) 598-1475. **$33-$40, 3 days notice.** 761 S Daleville Ave. At jct US 84 and SR 85. Ext corridors. **Pets:** Medium, other. $5 daily fee/pet. Supervision.
[✕] [☎] [☒]

DECATUR

AAA ◆◆◆ Key West Inn & Suites **M**
(256) 355-1999. **$79-$88.** 2212 Danville Rd. SR 67, at intersection with Beltline. Int corridors. **Pets:** Medium. Supervision.
[SAVE] [S⚡] [✕] [⚡] [☎] [💻] [☒]

◆◆ Ramada Limited **M**
(256) 353-0333. **$47-$52.** 1317 E Hwy 67. On SR 67, 4 mi nw of I-65, exit 334, 0.3 mi e jct US 31. Ext corridors. **Pets:** Medium. No service, supervision, crate.
[ASK] [S⚡] [✕] [☎] [☒] [✕]

DEMOPOLIS

◆◆ Riverview Inn **M** ❀
(334) 289-0690. **$45-$55.** 110 Yacht Basin Dr. On US 43, 1.5 mi n of jct US 80. Ext corridors. **Pets:** No service, supervision, crate.
[✕] [☎]

DOTHAN

AAA ◆◆◆ Comfort Inn **M** ❀
(334) 793-9090. **$70-$76.** 3593 Ross Clark Cir. 3 mi nw on US 231. Int corridors. **Pets:** Other. No service, supervision, crate.
[SAVE] [✕] [☎] [💻] [☒]

AAA ◆◆ Days Inn **M** ❀
(334) 793-2550. **$38-$48, 3 days notice.** 2841 Ross Clark Cir. 2 mi sw on US 231. Ext corridors. **Pets:** Medium, other. $5 daily fee/pet, $15 one-time fee/pet. Supervision.
[SAVE] [✕] [☎] [💻] [☒]

AAA ◆◆◆ Econo Lodge **M** ❀
(334) 673-8000. **$46-$55, 7 days notice.** 2910 Ross Clark Cir. 2 mi sw on US 231 bypass. Ext corridors. **Pets:** Very small, dogs only. $100 deposit/room, $5 daily fee/pet, $10 one-time fee/pet. No service, supervision, crate.
[SAVE] [✕] [♿] [⚡] [☎] [☒]

AAA ◆◆◆ Hampton Inn **M** ❀
(334) 671-3700. **$56-$56.** 3071 Ross Clark Cir. On US 231 bypass; at jct US 84W. Ext corridors. **Pets:** Other. Supervision.
[SAVE] [✕] [🏠] [📷] [☎] [💻]

◆◆◆ Holiday Inn-South **MI**
(334) 794-8711. **$61-$76.** 2195 Ross Clark Cir SE. 2 mi s on US 231; jct US 84W. Ext corridors. **Pets:** No service, supervision, crate.
[ASK] [S⚡] [✕] [☎] [💻] [🍴] [☒]

ENTERPRISE

◆◆◆ Ramada Inn **MI**
(334) 347-6262. **$52-$67.** 630 Glover Ave. On SR 248, 0.5 mi w of US 84 bypass. Ext corridors. **Pets:** Very small. No service, supervision, crate.
[ASK] [✕] [📷] [⚡] [☎] [💻] [🍴] [☒]

EUFAULA

AAA ◆◆ Best Western Eufaula Inn **M**
(334) 687-3900. **$38-$55, 3 days notice.** 1375 Hwy 431 S.
1.3 mi s of jct US 82. Ext corridors. **Pets:** Medium. No
service, supervision, crate.
[SAVE] [X] [▪] [▣]

◆◆ Ramada Inn **M** ❀
(334) 687-2021. **$49-$65, 7 days notice.** 631 E Barbour St.
On US 82; 0.5 mi e of jct US 431. Ext corridors.
Pets: Small, other. No service, supervision, crate.
[ASK] [X] [▪] [▣] [¶] [▣]

EVERGREEN

AAA ◆◆◆ Comfort Inn **M** ❀
(334) 578-4701. **$45-$78.** I-65/Bates Rd. I-65, exit 96 and
SR 83, on sw service road. Ext corridors. **Pets:** Medium. $5
daily fee/pet. No service, supervision, crate.
[SAVE] [X] [▱] [▪] [▣]

◆◆ Days Inn of Evergreen **M** ❀
(334) 578-2100. **$39-$44.** Rt 2 Box 389. I-65 exit 96, on SR
83. Ext corridors. **Pets:** Other. $5 daily fee/pet. Supervision.
[ASK] [▣] [X] [▪]

FLORENCE

◆◆ Best Western Executive Inn **M**
(256) 766-2331. **$49-$54.** 504 S Court St. On US 43 and
72 at jct SR 17 and 157. Ext corridors. **Pets:** Medium.
Designated rooms, no service, supervision, crate.
[ASK] [▣] [X] [▪] [▣] [¶] [▣]

◆ Days Inn-Florence **M** ❀
(256) 766-2620. **$50-$65, 3 days notice.** 1915 Florence
Blvd. US 72. Ext corridors. **Pets:** Medium, other. $50
deposit/room. No service, supervision, crate.
[ASK] [▣] [X] [▪] [▣]

AAA ◆ Super 8 Motel **M** ❀
(256) 757-2167. **$42-$52.** 101 Hwy 72 & 43E. E on US 72,
0.3 mi w of jct US 43. Ext corridors. **Pets:** $20 deposit/pet,
$7 daily fee/pet. Designated rooms, no service, supervision,
crate.
[SAVE] [X] [▪] [▣] [X]

FOLEY

◆◆ Key West Inn **M** ❀
(334) 943-1241. **$80-$90, 7 days notice.** 2520 S McKenzie
St. On SR 59, 1.8 mi s of jct US 98. Ext corridors. **Pets:** $5
daily fee/pet, $5 one-time fee/pet. Designated rooms, no
service, supervision, crate.
[ASK] [X] [▪] [▣] [▣]

FORT PAYNE

◆◆ Travelodge **M** ❀
(256) 845-0481. **$35-$65.** 1828 Gault Ave N. I-59, exit 222,
1.8 mi s on US 11. Ext corridors. **Pets:** Other. $10 daily
fee/pet. Supervision.
[ASK] [X] [▪] [¶] [▣]

GADSDEN

AAA ◆◆ Red Roof Inn **M** ❀
(256) 543-1105. **$51-$78.** 1600 Rainbow Dr. I-59 exit 182, 4
mi e on I-759, exit 4A, just s on US 411. Ext corridors.
Pets: Medium, other. No service, supervision, crate.
[SAVE] [X] [▱] [▪] [▣]

GREENVILLE

AAA ◆◆◆ Best Western Inn **M** ❀
(334) 382-9200. **$50-$65.** 106 Cahaba Rd. I-65 exit 130,
just w of SR-185. Ext corridors. **Pets:** Other. $10 one-time
fee/room. No service, supervision, crate.
[SAVE] [▣] [X] [▪] [▣]

AAA ◆◆ Econo Lodge **M**
(334) 382-3118. **$50-$55.** 946 Fort Dale Rd. I-65 exit 130,
just ne. Ext corridors. **Pets:** Small. No service, supervision,
crate.
[SAVE] [▣] [X] [▪] [▣]

◆◆◆ Hampton Inn-Greenville **M** ❀
(334) 382-9631. **$67-$79, 7 days notice.** 219 Interstate Dr.
I-65 exit 130, 0.5 mi nw. Int corridors. **Pets:** Medium. Supervision.
[ASK] [▣] [X] [♿] [▪] [▣] [▣]

◆◆ Ramada Inn **M**
(334) 382-2651. **$48-$48.** 941 Fort Dale Rd. I-65 exit 130,
just e. Ext corridors. **Pets:** Medium. No service, supervision,
crate.
[ASK] [▣] [X] [▪] [▣] [¶] [▣]

GUNTERSVILLE

◆◆ Days Inn **M** ❀
(256) 582-3200. **$54-$80, 5 days notice.** 14040 Hwy 431
S. 2.3 mi s from jct SR 69. Ext corridors. **Pets:** $5 daily
fee/pet. No service, supervision, crate.
[ASK] [X] [▪] [▣]

AAA ◆◆ Super 8 Motel-Guntersville **M**
(256) 582-8444. **$48-$60, 7 days notice.** 14347 Hwy 431S.
2 mi s from jct SR 69. Ext corridors. **Pets:** No service,
supervision, crate.
[SAVE] [▣] [X] [▪]

HAMILTON

◆◆ Best Western Hamilton **M** ❀
(205) 921-7831. **Call for rates.** 2031 Military St S. From
Hwy 78 exit 14. Ext corridors. **Pets:** Small. $25 deposit/
room. No service, supervision, crate.
[X] [▣] [¶] [▣]

◆◆ Days Inn **M** ❀
(205) 921-1790. **$59-$70** (no credit cards), 3 days notice.
1849 Military St. Hwy 78 exit 14, 1.1 mi ne Hwy 43. Ext
corridors. **Pets:** $5 daily fee/pet. No service, supervision,
crate.
[ASK] [▣] [X] [▪] [▣] [▣]

HEFLIN

◆ Howard Johnson Express Inn **M**
(256) 463-2900. **Call for rates.** 1957 Almon St. I-20 exit
199, on SR 9, just ne. Ext corridors. **Pets:** Supervision.
[ASK] [X] [▪]

HUNTSVILLE

◆◆ **Baymont Inn & Suites-Huntsville** Ⓜ ✿
(256) 830-8999. **$54-$59.** 4890 University Dr. US 72, 5 mi w of jct US 231/431. Int corridors. **Pets:** Small, other. Designated rooms, supervision.
🗙 🖥 💻 🔄

◆◆◆ **Holiday Inn Express** Ⓜ ✿
(256) 721-1000. **$59-$65.** 3808 University Dr. US 72, 2 mi w of jct US 231/431. Ext/int corridors. **Pets:** Other. $50 deposit/room. Supervision.
ⒶⓈⓀ 🗙 🖥

◆◆◆ **Holiday Inn-Space Center** ⓂⒾ ✿
(256) 837-7171. **$62-$68.** 3810 University Dr. US 72, 2 mi w of jct US 231/431. Ext/int corridors. **Pets:** Small. $50 deposit/room. No service, supervision, crate.
ⒶⓈⓀ 🗙 🖥 💻 🍴 🔄

◆◆◆ **Huntsville Hilton** Ⓗ
(256) 533-1400. **$99-$125.** 401 Williams Ave. Downtown across from Von Braun Center. Int corridors. **Pets:** Very small. No service, supervision, crate.
ⒶⓈⓀ 🗙 🖥 💻 🍴 🔄

◆◆◆ **La Quinta Inn-Huntsville Research Pk** Ⓜ
(256) 830-2070. **$49-$79.** 4870 University Dr. US 72, 5 mi w of US 231. Ext corridors. **Pets:** Small. Designated rooms, no service, supervision, crate.
ⒶⓈⓀ 🗙 🖥 💻 🔄

◆◆◆ **La Quinta Inn-Huntsville Space
Center** Ⓜ ✿
(256) 533-0756. **$49-$79.** 3141 University Dr. US 72, 1.3 mi w of jct US 231/431. Ext corridors. **Pets:** Small. No service, supervision, crate.
ⒶⓈⓀ 🗙 🖥 💻 🔄

MADISON

◆◆ **Days Inn-Huntsville Airport** Ⓜ ✿
(256) 772-9550. **$46-$57.** 102 Arlington Dr. I-565 exit 8, 0.5 mi nw SR20. Ext corridors. **Pets:** Very small. $10 daily fee/pet. Supervision.
ⒶⓈⓀ 🗙 🖥 💻 🔄

🆎 ◆ **Motel 6-1087** Ⓜ
(256) 772-7479. **$38-$54.** 8995 Madison Blvd. I-565 exit 8, just w. Ext corridors. **Pets:** Medium. No service, supervision, crate.
🗙 👟 🔄

MOBILE

🆎 ◆◆ **Best Inns of America** Ⓜ
(334) 343-4911. **$49-$79.** 156 Beltline Hwy S. I-65 exit 4, 0.5 mi s on w frontage road. Int corridors. **Pets:** Medium. Supervision.
ⓈⓐⓥⒺ Ⓢ🗙 👟 🖥 🔄

🆎 ◆◆◆ **Best Suites of America** Ⓜ
(334) 343-4949. **$67-$97.** 150 Beltline Hwy S. I-65 exit 4, 0.5 mi s on w frontage road. Int corridors. **Pets:** Small. Supervision.
ⓈⓐⓥⒺ Ⓢ🗙 🖥 💻 🔄

🆎 ◆◆◆ **The Clarion Hotel At Bel Air** Ⓗ ✿
(334) 476-6400. **$50-$90.** 3101 Airport Blvd. I-65 exit 3, 0.8 mi e. Int corridors. **Pets:** Other. $25 one-time fee/room. Supervision.
ⓈⓐⓥⒺ Ⓢ🗙 🖥 💻 🔄 📺

◆ **Days Inn of Mobile** Ⓜ ✿
(334) 661-8181. **$45-$45.** 5480 Inn Rd. I-10 exit 15B at jct US 90. Ext corridors. **Pets:** Medium. $8 daily fee/pet. No service, supervision, crate.
ⒶⓈⓀ 🗙 👟 🖥 🔄 📺

◆◆◆ **Drury Inn** Ⓜ
(334) 344-7700. **$59-$75.** 824 S Beltline Hwy. 0.3 mi sw of jct I-65 and Airport Blvd on service road. Int corridors. **Pets:** Supervision.
🗙 🖥 💻 🔄

◆◆ **GuestHouse Inn** Ⓜ ✿
(334) 471-2402. **$40-$55, 7 days notice.** 3132 Government Blvd. I-65 exit 1, just ne on US 90. Int corridors. **Pets:** Large, other. $20 deposit/room. Supervision.
ⒶⓈⓀ 🗙 🖥 🔄 🗙

◆◆◆ **Holiday Inn-Bellingrath Gardens** ⓂⒾ
(334) 666-5600. **$59-$85.** 6527 Hwy 90 W. I-10 exit 15B, just ne. Int corridors. **Pets:** Supervision.
🗙 👟 🖥 💻 🍴 🔄

◆◆◆ **Holiday Inn Downtown Historic District** Ⓗ
(334) 694-0100. **$135-$155, 3 days notice.** 301 Government St. Downtown. Int corridors. **Pets:** Small. Supervision.
ⒶⓈⓀ 🗙 🖥 💻 🍴 🔄

◆◆ **Holiday Inn-I-65** ⓂⒾ
(334) 342-3220. **$62-$80.** 850 S Beltline Hwy. I-65 exit 3, 0.5 mi sw on w service road. Ext corridors. **Pets:** Small. No service, supervision, crate.
ⒶⓈⓀ 🗙 🖥 💻 🍴 🔄

◆◆◆ **La Quinta Inn-Mobile** Ⓜ ✿
(334) 343-4051. **$62-$82.** 816 Beltline Hwy S. On service road sw of jct I-65, exit 3B and Airport Blvd. Ext corridors. **Pets:** Small. No service, supervision, crate.
ⒶⓈⓀ 🗙 🖥 💻 🔄

🆎 ◆ **Olsson Motel** Ⓜ ✿
(334) 661-5331. **$29-$35.** 4137 Government Blvd. I-65 exit 1, 2 mi w on US 90. Ext corridors. **Pets:** Very small, dogs only. $5 daily fee/room, $5 one-time fee/room. No service, supervision, crate.
🗙 🖥

◆◆◆ **Radisson Admiral Semmes Hotel** Ⓗ
(334) 432-8000. **$140-$260.** 251 Government St. Downtown. Int corridors. **Pets:** Supervision.
ⒶⓈⓀ 🗙 👟 🖥 💻 🍴 🔄 📺

🆎 ◆◆ **Red Roof Inn-North** Ⓜ
(334) 476-2004. **$41-$68.** 33 S Beltline Hwy. I-65 exit 4, just se. Ext corridors. **Pets:** Small. Supervision.
ⓈⓐⓥⒺ 🗙

🆎 ◆◆ **Red Roof Inn-South** Ⓜ ✿
(334) 666-1044. **$37-$47.** 5450 Coca Cola Rd. I-10 exit 15B, 0.3 mi e on US 90. Ext corridors. **Pets:** Small, other. Supervision.
ⓈⓐⓥⒺ 🗙 👟 📺

(AAA) ◆◆ Shoney's Inn of Mobile 🅜 ❖
(334) 660-1520. **$49-$64.** 5472A Inn Rd. I-10 exit 15B, at jct US 90. Ext corridors. **Pets:** Other. $25 deposit/room. Designated rooms, supervision.
SAVE ⊠ ❘❙ 💻 � 🏖

MONTGOMERY

◆◆ Baymont Inn & Suites-Montgomery 🅜
(334) 277-6000. **$47-$47.** 5225 Carmichael Rd. I-85, exit 6 at East Blvd. Int corridors. **Pets:** Medium. Designated rooms, no service, supervision, crate.
⊠ ❘❙ 💻 🏖

(AAA) ◆◆ Best Inns of America-Montgomery 🅜 ❖
(334) 270-9199. **$49-$62.** 5135 Carmichael Rd. I-85 exit 6, just sw. Int corridors. **Pets:** Small, other. $30 one-time fee/room. No service, supervision, crate.
SAVE S🔟 ⊠ 🔦 ❘❙ 💻 🏖

◆◆ Econo Lodge 🅜 ❖
(334) 284-3400. **$40-$58.** 4135 Troy Hwy. On US 82 and 231, 0.5 mi se of jct South and East blvds. Ext corridors. **Pets:** Very small. $8 deposit/pet, $8 daily fee/pet, $8 one-time fee/pet. Designated rooms, no service, supervision, crate.
ASK ⊠ ❘❙ 💻

(AAA) ◆◆◆ Holiday Inn-East 🅜 ❖
(334) 272-0370. **$69-$119.** 1185 Eastern Bypass. I-85 exit 6, just ne on US 80 and 231. Ext/int corridors. **Pets:** Small, other. $25 one-time fee/room. Supervision.
SAVE ⊠ 🎣 ❘❙ 💻 � 🏖

◆◆◆ La Quinta Inn-Montgomery 🅜
(334) 271-1620. **$59-$79.** 1280 East Blvd. I-85 exit 6. Ext corridors. **Pets:** Medium. No service, supervision, crate.
ASK ⊠ ❘❙ 💻 🏖

◆◆◆ Residence Inn by Marriott 🅐
(334) 270-3300. **$99-$99.** 1200 Hilmar Ct. I-85 exit 6, 0.3 mi se on Carmichael Rd. Int corridors. **Pets:** No service, supervision, crate.
ASK ⊠ ❘❙ 💻 🏖 ⊠

NORTHPORT

(AAA) ◆◆ Best Western Catalina Inn 🅜 ❖
(205) 339-5200. **$40-$50.** 2015 McFarland Blvd. I-59/20 exit 71, to 359/SR 69, n to US 82, just w. Ext corridors. **Pets:** Medium. $10 daily fee/room, $10 one-time fee/room. Supervision.
SAVE S🔟 ⊠ ❘❙ 💻 🏖

OPELIKA

(AAA) ◆◆ Best Western Mariner Inn 🅜
(334) 749-1461. **$35-$99.** 1002 Columbus Pkwy. I-85 exit 62, just w. Ext corridors. **Pets:** Designated rooms, supervision.
SAVE S🔟 ⊠ ❘❙ 🏖

OXFORD

(AAA) ◆ Econo Lodge–Anniston/Oxford 🅜 ❖
(256) 831-9480. **$32-$47.** 25 Elm St. I-20 exit 185, just sw on SR 21. Ext corridors. **Pets:** Small. $7 daily fee/room. Supervision.
SAVE ⊠ ❘❙ 💻 🏖

(AAA) ◆◆◆ Holiday Inn-Anniston/Oxford 🅜 ❖
(256) 831-3410. **$59-$69.** US 78 & SR 21. I-20 exit 185, just n. Ext corridors. **Pets:** Designated rooms, supervision.
SAVE ⊠ ❘❙ 💻 � 🏖 ⊠

◆◆ Sleep Inn 🅜 ❖
(256) 831-2191. **$52-$65.** 88 Colonial Dr. I-20 exit 188. Int corridors. **Pets:** Medium, dogs only. Supervision.
ASK ⊠ ❘❙ 💻 🏖

OZARK

(AAA) ◆◆◆ Best Western Ozark Inn 🅜 ❖
(334) 774-5166. **$44-$52, 3 days notice.** Deese Rd, US 231S. 0.5 mi s of jct US 231 and SR 249; on US 231 at Deese Rd. Ext corridors. **Pets:** Very small. No service, supervision, crate.
SAVE S🔟 ⊠ 💻 🏖

◆◆◆ Holiday Inn-Ozark, Ft Rucker 🅜
(334) 774-7300. **$48-$48.** 151 Hwy 231N. On US 231, 0.3 mi n of jct SR 249. Ext corridors. **Pets:** No service, supervision, crate.
ASK ⊠ ❘❙ 💻 � 🏖

PRATTVILLE

◆◆◆ Holiday Inn-Prattville 🅜 ❖
(334) 285-3420. **$57-$65.** 2598 Cobbs Ford Rd. I-652 exit 179. Ext corridors. **Pets:** Other. No service, supervision, crate.
ASK S🔟 ⊠ 💻 � 🏖

SELMA

◆◆ Holiday Inn 🅜 ❖
(334) 872-0461. **$55-$65, 3 days notice.** 1710 W Highland Ave. 2.3 mi w on US 80. Ext corridors. **Pets:** Other. Supervision.
ASK ⊠ ❘❙ 💻 � 🏖

STEVENSON

(AAA) ◆ Budget Inn 🅜
(256) 437-2215. **$40-$45.** 42973 US 72. Ext corridors. **Pets:** Designated rooms, no service, supervision, crate.
SAVE ⊠ ❘❙ 💻

THOMASVILLE

(AAA) ◆◆ Best Western Inn 🅜
(334) 636-0614. **$42-$54.** 1400 Mosely Dr. On US 43. Ext corridors. **Pets:** Supervision.
SAVE ⊠ ❘❙ 🏖

TROY

◆◆◆ Holiday Inn Express M
(334) 670-0012. **$50-$50.** Hwy 231, US 29. 0.3 mi n of jct US 29. Ext corridors. **Pets:** Medium. No service, supervision, crate.
ASK ⊠ 🖬 🖵

◆◆◆ Holiday Inn-of Troy MI
(334) 566-1150. **$53-$64.** Hwy 231 at Hwy 29. Just n of jct US 29. Ext corridors. **Pets:** Very small. Designated rooms, no service, supervision, crate.
ASK S🖬 ⊠ 🖬 🖵 🍴 ☎

TUSCALOOSA

AAA ◆◆ Key West Inn M ☸
(205) 556-3232. **$55.** 4700 Doris Pate Dr. I-59/20 exit 76, just n. Int corridors. **Pets:** Medium, other. $5 daily fee/pet. Supervision.
SAVE S🖬 ⊠ 🖬 🖵 ☎

◆◆◆ La Quinta Inn-Tuscaloosa M
(205) 349-3270. **$49-$79.** 4122 McFarland Blvd E. I-20/59 exit 73, just sw on US 82. Ext corridors. **Pets:** Medium. No service, supervision, crate.
ASK ⊠ 🖬 🖵 ☎

◆ Masters Economy Inn M ☸
(205) 556-2010. **$34-$48.** 3600 McFarland Blvd. I-59/20 exit 73, just nw on US 82. Ext corridors. **Pets:** Medium, other. $6 daily fee/room. Supervision.
S🖬 ⊠ 🖬 ☎

AAA ◆◆ Ramada Inn M ☸
(205) 759-4431. **$45-$60.** 631 Skyland Blvd E. I-20/59 exit 73, to McFarland Blvd (US 82), just w. Ext/int corridors. **Pets:** Other. Designated rooms, no service, supervision, crate.
SAVE ⊠ 🖾 🖬 🖵 ☎

YORK

◆◆ Days Inn-York M ☸
(205) 392-9675. **$50-$70.** 17700 SR 17. 0.3 mi s of I-59/20, exit 8. Ext corridors. **Pets:** Other. $10 one-time fee/room. No service, supervision, crate.
ASK ⊠ 🖬 🖵

ALASKA

ANCHORAGE

◆◆◆ Aurora Winds Resort BB
(907) 346-2533. **$105-$250, 3 days notice.** 7501 Upper O'Malley Rd. 6.5 mi s on US 1 (New Seward Hwy), 4 mi e on O'Malley Rd, just n on Hillside Dr, just e. Int corridors. **Pets:** No service, supervision, crate.
SAVE ✕ 🖥 💻 📶 CTV

◆◆◆ Best Western Barratt Inn MI ❀
(907) 243-3131. **$139-$167.** 4616 Spenard Rd. 4 mi sw, 0.4 mi n on Jewel Lake Rd. Ext/int corridors. **Pets:** Other. $50 deposit/room, $5 daily fee/room. No service, supervision, crate.
SAVE S✕ 🖥 🐾 🖥 💻 🍽

◆◆ Comfort Inn Ship Creek M
(907) 277-6887. **$179-$219.** 111 W Ship Creek Ave. From downtown, 3rd and E sts, 0.3 mi n on E St, across the railway, just e on Ship Creek Ave (formerly Warehouse Ave). Int corridors. **Pets:** Small. No service, supervision, crate.
ASK S✕ 🐾 🖥 💻 🏊 ✕ 📶

◆◆ Days Inn MI
(907) 276-7226. **$155-$250.** 321 E 5th Ave. Downtown at Cordova. Ext/int corridors. **Pets:** Supervision.
SAVE ✕ 🐾 ♿ 🖥 💻 🍽

◆◆◆ Hilton Anchorage H
(907) 272-7411. **$209-$229.** 500 W 3rd Ave. Downtown at E St. Int corridors. **Pets:** Designated rooms, no service, supervision, crate.
✕ 🐾 ♿ 🖥 💻 🏊

◆◆◆ Holiday Inn Express Anchorage Airport M ❀
(907) 248-8848. **$129-$129, 3 days notice.** 4411 Spenard Rd. 4 mi sw, 0.5 mi n on Jewell Lake Rd. Int corridors. **Pets:** Dogs only. $10 deposit/room. Designated rooms, supervision.
ASK S✕ ♿ 📶 🖥 💻 🏊

◆◆ Merrill Field Inn M ❀
(907) 276-4547. **$100-$125.** 420 Sitka St. 1 mi e via US 1 (Glenn Hwy). Directly opposite Merrill Field Airstrip. Ext corridors. **Pets:** Other. $7 daily fee/pet. Supervision.
S✕ 🖥 📶

◆◆ Microtel Inn & Suites M ❀
(907) 245-5002. **$129-$149.** 5205 Northwood Dr. From jct International Airport Rd and Spenard Rd, 0.5 mi e on Frontage Rd, just n. Int corridors. **Pets:** $50 deposit/room. Designated rooms, no service, supervision, crate.
ASK S✕ 🖥 💻

◆ Parkwood Inn M
(907) 563-3590. **$115-$115.** 4455 Juneau St. From International Airport Rd, 0.4 mi n on Old Seward Hwy, just e on 45th St. Ext corridors. **Pets:** Other. $50 deposit/room, $5 one-time fee/pet. Designated rooms, supervision.
SAVE S✕ 🖥 💻 📶

◆◆◆ Regal Alaskan Hotel H ❀
(907) 243-2300. **$260-$300.** 4800 Spenard Rd. 4 mi sw, just n on Jewel Lake Rd. Int corridors. **Pets:** Other. $50 deposit/pet. Supervision.
SAVE S✕ 🐾 📶 🖥 💻 🍽 ✕

◆ Super 8 Motel-Anchorage M
(907) 276-8884. **$169-$1889.** 3501 Minnesota Dr. At 36th Ave, just n of Spenard Rd. Int corridors. **Pets:** Small. No service, supervision, crate.
ASK S✕ ✕

◆◆ Westmark Inn Anchorage M ❀
(907) 272-7561. **$109-$109.** 115 E Third Ave. Downtown e, at Barrow St. Ext/int corridors. **Pets:** Other. No service, supervision, crate.
SAVE ✕ 🍽 📶

CANTWELL

◆◆ Backwoods Lodge M ❀
(907) 768-2232. **$110-$120, 7 days notice.** From George Parks Hwy, milepost 210, just e on Denali Hwy. Ext corridors. **Pets:** Other. $50 deposit/room. No service, supervision, crate.
✕ 🖥 💻 ✕ 📶

EAGLE RIVER

◆ Eagle River Motel M ❀
(907) 694-5000. **$75-$89.** 11111 Old Eagle River Rd. From Glenn Hwy, Eagle River exit, just e; in town centre. Ext corridors. **Pets:** $7 daily fee/room. No service, supervision, crate.
✕ 🖥 📶

FAIRBANKS

◆◆◆ Comfort Inn-Chena River M ❀
(907) 479-8080. **$139-$209.** 1908 Chena Landings Loop. From Airport Way, just n on Pegger Rd, just e on Phillips Field Rd, follow signs in wooded area s of road.. Int corridors. **Pets:** Other. $50 deposit/room. Supervision.
ASK S✕ ♿ 📶 🖥 🏊

◆◆ Regency Fairbanks Hotel MI
(907) 452-3200. **$165-$175.** 95 Tenth Ave. Center; just w of US 2 (Steese Expwy). Int corridors. **Pets:** Small. No service, supervision, crate.
✕ 🖥 🍽 CTV

HAINES

♠♠ ◆◆ Captain's Choice Inc Motel **M** 🐾
(907) 766-3111. **$94-$145.** 108 2nd Ave N. 2nd and Dalton sts. Ext corridors. **Pets:** Other. $10 one-time fee/room. Supervision.
[SAVE] [⊠] [🛏] [💻] [🅰]

HOMER

♠♠ ◆◆ Best Western Bidarka Inn **MI** 🐾
(907) 235-8148. **$125-$146.** 575 Sterling Hwy. 0.3 mi n on SR 1. Ext/int corridors. **Pets:** Other. $10 daily fee/pet. Supervision.
[SAVE] [🆓] [⊠] [🛏] [💻] [🍽] [🔀] [🅰]

KETCHIKAN

♠♠ ◆◆ Best Western Landing **MI** 🐾
(907) 225-5166. **$120-$155.** 3434 Tongass Ave. Across from the Alaska Marine Hwy Ferry Terminal. Ext/int corridors. **Pets:** Other. $50 deposit/pet, $10 daily fee/room, $10 one-time fee/room. Designated rooms, no service, supervision, crate.
[SAVE] [🆓] [⊠] [🛏] [💻] [🍽] [🔀] [🅰]

KODIAK

♠♠ ◆◆ Best Western Kodiak Inn **MI** 🐾
(907) 486-5712. **$139-$149.** 236 W Rezanof Dr. Center; 0.3 mi w of ferry terminal. Ext/int corridors. **Pets:** $50 deposit/room, $25 one-time fee/room. Designated rooms, no service, supervision, crate.
[SAVE] [⊠] [🌀] [🛏] [💻] [🍽] [🅰]

◆◆ Buskin River Inn **MI** 🐾
(907) 487-2700. **Call for rates.** 1395 Airport Way. Opposite to Kodiak Airport. Int corridors. **Pets:** $15 daily fee/pet. Designated rooms, no service, supervision, crate.
[ASK] [⊠] [🛏] [💻] [🍽] [🅰]

SKAGWAY

♠♠ ◆◆ Westmark Inn Skagway **MI**
(907) 983-6000. **$119-$119.** Just off center; at 3rd and Spring sts. Ext/int corridors. **Pets:** Designated rooms, no service, supervision, crate.
[SAVE] [⊠] [🍽] [🅰]

TOK

♠♠ ◆◆ Cleft of the Rock Bed & Breakfast **X** 🐾
(907) 883-4219. **$80-$125, 3 days notice.** Mile .5 Sundog Tr. From jct SR 1 and 2, 3 mi w on SR 2 to Sundog Tr, 0.5 mi n. Ext/int corridors. **Pets:** Other. $25 deposit/pet. No service, supervision, crate.
[SAVE] [⊠] [🛏] [💻] [🔀] [🅰] [CTV]

♠♠ ◆◆ Westmark Tok **MI** 🐾
(907) 883-5174. **$129-$129.** On SR 1 at jct SR 2. Ext corridors. **Pets:** Medium, dogs only. Designated rooms, no service, supervision, crate.
[SAVE] [⊠] [🍽] [🅰] [CTV]

VALDEZ

♠♠ ◆◆ Westmark Valdez **MI**
(907) 835-4391. **$99-$99.** 100 Fidalgo Dr. At small boat harbor. Int corridors. **Pets:** Designated rooms, no service, supervision, crate.
[SAVE] [⊠] [🌀] [🚬] [🍽] [🔀] [🅰]

WASILLA

◆◆ Kozey Cabins **C** 🐾
(907) 376-3190. **$85-$100, 7 days notice.** 351 E Spruce Ave. 1.4 mi n on Parks Hwy, 1.4 mi e on Lucille St, just s. Ext corridors. **Pets:** Dogs only. $50 deposit/room, $10 daily fee/pet. Designated rooms, supervision.
[ASK] [⊠] [🛏] [💻] [🅰] [CTV]

CITY INDEX

AJO

◆ **La Siesta Motel** M
(520) 387-6569. **$36-$58, 3 days notice.** 2561 N Ajo-Gila Bend Hwy. 1.8 mi n on SR 85. Ext corridors. **Pets:** No service, supervision, crate.
⊠ 🛢 💻 ⊠

AAA ◆ **Marine Motel** M 🐾
(520) 387-7626. **$44-$65.** 1966 N 2nd Ave. 1 mi n on SR 85. Ext corridors. **Pets:** Dogs only. Supervision.
SAVE S🔊 ⊠ 🛢

BENSON

AAA ◆◆◆ **Best Western Quail Hollow Inn** M
(520) 586-3646. **$40-$70, 7 days notice.** 699 N Ocotillo St. Adjacent to I-10, exit 304. Ext corridors. **Pets:** Supervision.
SAVE S🔊 ⊠ 🛢 💻 🍃

AAA ◆◆◆ **Holiday Inn Express** M 🐾
(520) 586-8800. **$69-$89.** 630 S Village Loop. SR 90, at jct I-80, exit 302. Int corridors. **Pets:** Small, dogs only. $50 deposit/room. Designated rooms, no service, supervision, crate.
SAVE S🔊 ⊠ ⚿ 📶 🛢 💻 🍃

◆◆ **Super 8 Motel** M 🐾
(520) 586-1530. **$43-$45.** 855 N Ocotillo Rd. Just n of I-10, exit 304. Ext corridors. **Pets:** Other. $10 deposit/pet. Designated rooms, supervision.
ASK S🔊 ⊠ 🛢 🍃

BISBEE

AAA ◆◆ **San Jose Lodge** M 🐾
(520) 432-5761. **$49-$75.** 1002 Naco Hwy. Jct SR 92 and 80, take SR 92 2.5 mi sw, 1.5 mi s on Naco Hwy. Ext corridors. **Pets:** Other. $125 deposit/pet, $10 daily fee/pet. Designated rooms, no service, supervision, crate.
SAVE S🔊 ⊠ 🛢 🍴 🍃

BULLHEAD CITY

AAA ◆◆◆ **Best Western Bullhead City Inn** M 🐾
(520) 754-3000. **$45-$69.** 1126 Hwy 95. 1.8 mi s of Laughlin Bridge on SR 95, then just e on 3rd St. Ext corridors. **Pets:** $25 deposit/room, $5 one-time fee/room. Supervision.
SAVE S🔊 ⊠ 🛢 🍃

◆ **First Choice Inn** M
(520) 758-1711. **$50-$250.** 2200 Rancho Colorado. 3.5 mi s of Laughlin Bridge on SR 95, then just e. Int corridors. **Pets:** Supervision.
⊠ 🛢 🍃

AAA ◆ **Lake Mohave Resort** R 🐾
(520) 754-3245. **$100, 72 days notice.** Katherine Landing. 3 mi n of SR 68 and Davis Dam, in Lake Mead National Recreation Area. Ext corridors. **Pets:** $25 deposit/pet, $5 daily fee/pet. Supervision.
SAVE 🛢 💻 🍴 ⊠ CTV

◆◆ **Lodge on The River** M
(520) 758-8080. **Call for rates.** 1717 Hwy 95. On SR 95, 3.8 mi s of Laughlin Bridge. Ext corridors. **Pets:** Medium. No service, supervision, crate.
⊠ 🖾 🛢 💻 🍃

◆◆ **Shangri-la Lodge/Villager Lodge** M
(520) 758-1117. **$30-$60, 3 days notice.** 1767 Georgia Ln. 2 mi s of Laughlin Bridge. Ext corridors. **Pets:** No service, supervision, crate.
ASK ⊠ 🛢

AAA ◆◆◆ **Sunridge Hotel & Conference Center** MI 🐾
(520) 754-4700. **$49-$89.** 839 Landon Dr. 3 mi n on SR 95, 1.3 mi e on SR 68, just s on Landon Dr. Ext corridors. **Pets:** $100 deposit/pet. Supervision.
SAVE S🔊 ⊠ 🛢 🍃

CAMP VERDE

(AAA) ◆◆◆ Comfort Inn M ❀
(520) 567-9000. **$49-$79.** 340 N Industrial Dr. Adjacent to I-17, exit 287. Int corridors. **Pets:** Other. $15 one-time fee/room. No service, supervision, crate.
[SAVE] [S🐾] [✕] [🐾] [🖊] [🛏] [💻] [🌊]

(AAA) ◆◆ Microtel Inn & Suites of Camp Verde M ❀
(520) 567-3700. **$49-$84.** 504 Industrial Dr. Adjacent to I-17, exit 287. Int corridors. **Pets:** Other. $10 daily fee/room. No service, supervision, crate.
[SAVE] [S🐾] [✕] [🖊] [🛏] [💻] [🌊]

CASA GRANDE

◆◆◆ Best Western Casa Grande Suites M
(520) 836-1600. **$62-$110, 3 days notice.** 665 Via Del Cielo. On SR 287, 1 mi w of jct I-10, exit 194. Ext corridors. **Pets:** No service, supervision, crate.
[ASK] [S🐾] [✕] [🛏] [💻] [🌊]

◆◆◆ Holiday Inn M ❀
(520) 426-3500. **$74-$87.** 777 N Pinal Ave. Center of town, at jct SR 84 and 287. Int corridors. **Pets:** Other. Supervision.
[✕] [🛏] [💻] [🍴] [🌊]

(AAA) ◆ Motel 6–1263 M
(520) 836-3323. **$44-$60.** 4965 N Sunland Gin Rd. Adjacent to I-10, exit 200. Ext corridors. **Pets:** Supervision.
[S🐾] [✕] [🌊] [CTV]

CHAMBERS

(AAA) ◆◆ Best Western Chieftain M
(520) 688-2754. **$56-$65.** Adjacent to I-40, exit 333, at jct US 191. Ext corridors. **Pets:** Supervision.
[SAVE] [S🐾] [✕] [🍴] [🌊]

COTTONWOOD

(AAA) ◆◆◆ Best Western Cottonwood Inn M
(520) 634-5575. **$69-$99.** 993 S Main. On SR 89A at jct SR 260. Ext corridors. **Pets:** Designated rooms, no service, supervision, crate.
[SAVE] [S🐾] [✕] [🛏] [💻] [🍴] [🌊]

◆ Cottonwood Pines Motel M
(520) 634-9975. **$35-$52.** 920 S Camino Real. 0.9 mi s of jct SR 89, just w of Main St. Ext corridors. **Pets:** Very small. Designated rooms, supervision.
[ASK] [✕] [🛏]

(AAA) ◆ The View Motel M ❀
(520) 634-7581. **$34-$48.** 818 S Main St. Just w of jct SR 260/SR 89A. Ext corridors. **Pets:** Other. $25 deposit/room, $5 daily fee/pet. Supervision.
[SAVE] [✕] [🌊] [CTV]

EAGAR

◆◆◆ Best Western Sunrise Inn M ❀
(520) 333-2540. **$53-$99.** 128 N Main St. Just n of SR 260, 1.5 mi s of Springerville and US 60. Ext corridors. **Pets:** Medium, other. Designated rooms, supervision.
[ASK] [S🐾] [✕] [🐾] [🛏] [💻]

EHRENBERG

(AAA) ◆◆ Best Western Flying J Motel M ❀
(520) 923-9711. **$79-$109.** Adjacent to I-10, exit 1. Int corridors. **Pets:** Large, other. $20 deposit/room. No service, supervision, crate.
[SAVE] [S🐾] [✕] [🛏] [🍴] [🌊] [CTV]

ELOY

(AAA) ◆ Super 8 Motel M ❀
(520) 466-7804. **$55-$60.** 3945 W Houser Rd. Adjacent to I-10 at Toltec Rd; 4 mi se of jct I-8. Ext corridors. **Pets:** Other. $5 one-time fee/pet. Supervision.
[SAVE] [S🐾] [✕] [🛏] [🌊]

FLAGSTAFF

(AAA) ◆◆◆ AmeriSuites M ❀
(520) 774-8042. **$89-$159.** 2455 S Beulah Blvd. Nw of jct I-17 and I-40; from I-40 exit 195B, just n to Forest Meadows, w to Beulah Blvd, then just s on Beulah Blvd. Int corridors. **Pets:** Medium. No service, supervision, crate.
[SAVE] [S🐾] [✕] [🐾] [🛏] [💻] [🌊]

(AAA) ◆◆ Best Western Kings House Motel M ❀
(520) 774-7186. **$60-$80.** 1560 E Route 66. On US 89, 180 and I-40 business loop; from I-40 exit 198, 1 mi n to Route 66. Ext corridors. **Pets:** Designated rooms, no service, supervision, crate.
[SAVE] [S🐾] [✕] [🛏] [🌊]

(AAA) ◆ Canyon Inn M
(520) 774-7301. **$60-$100.** 500 S Milton Rd. Just e jct Milton Rd and US 66. Ext corridors. **Pets:** Medium. Supervision.
[SAVE] [S🐾] [✕]

(AAA) ◆◆ Comfort Inn M ❀
(520) 774-7326. **$49-$109.** 914 S Milton Rd. 1.2 mi n of jct I-17 and I-40; from I-40, exit 195B. Ext corridors. **Pets:** Other. Designated rooms, no service, supervision, crate.
[SAVE] [S🐾] [✕] [🛏]

(AAA) ◆◆ Crystal Inn M
(520) 774-4581. **$60-$95.** 602 W Rt 66. 1.5 mi n of jct I-17 and I-40, exit 195B, just w of Milton Rd. Ext corridors. **Pets:** Small. Supervision.
[SAVE] [S🐾] [✕] [🌊]

(AAA) ◆◆ Days Inn Flagstaff Hwy 66 M ❀
(520) 774-5221. **$59-$119, 3 days notice.** 1000 W Hwy 66. From I-40, exit 195B, 1.5 n, then just w on Rt 66. Ext corridors. **Pets:** Other. $10 daily fee/room, $10 one-time fee/room. No service, supervision, crate.
[SAVE] [S🐾] [✕] [🐾] [🍴] [🌊]

(AAA) ◆◆ Days Inn-I-40 M ❀
(520) 779-1575. **$49-$109, 7 days notice.** 2735 S Woodlands Village Blvd. NW of jct I-40 and I-17; from I-40 exit 195B, just n to Forest Meadows, w to Beulah Blvd, then just s on Woodlands Village Blvd.. Int corridors. **Pets:** Other. Supervision.
[SAVE] [S🐾] [✕] [🛏]

◆◆ Econo Lodge I-40 & I-17 🅼 ✿
(520) 774-2225. **$60-$120.** 2355 S Beulah Blvd. Nw of jct I-40 and I-17; from I-40 exit 195B, 0.2 mi n to Forest Meadows, then w 1 blk.. Int corridors. **Pets:** Medium. $5 daily fee/pet. No service, supervision, crate.
🆂🅰🆅🅴 ✕ 🛢 🖳 🕹

◆◆ Econo Lodge Lucky Lane 🅼
(520) 774-7701. **$49-$99.** 2480 E Lucky Ln. N side of I-40, Butler Ave exit 198; e on Lucky Ln. Int corridors. **Pets:** No service, supervision, crate.
🆂🅰🆅🅴 🆂🅳 ✕ 🛢 🖳 🕹

◆◆◆ Embassy Suites/Flagstaff-Grand Canyon Gateway 🅼 ✿
(520) 774-4333. **$114-$209.** 706 S Milton Rd. 1.5 mi n of jct I-17 and I-40, exit 195B. Int corridors. **Pets:** Medium, other. $25 one-time fee/room. Supervision.
🅰🆂🅺 🆂🅳 ✕ 🕹 🛢 🖳 🕹

◆◆◆ Holiday Inn Flagstaff/Grand Canyon 🅼🅸
(520) 526-1150. **$70-$100.** 2320 E Lucky Ln. N side of I-40, Butler Ave exit 198. Int corridors. **Pets:** Small. Supervision.
🅰🆂🅺 🆂🅳 ✕ 🕹 🛢 🖳 🕹 🕹

◆◆ Howard Johnson Hotel 🅼🅸 ✿
(520) 779-6944. **$69-$129.** 2200 E Butler Ave. Just nw of I-40, exit 198. Int corridors. **Pets:** $10 one-time fee/pet. Designated rooms, no service, supervision, crate.
🆂🅰🆅🅴 🆂🅳 ✕ 🛢 🖳 🕹 🕹

◆◆ Howard Johnson Inn 🅼🅸 ✿
(520) 526-1826. **$49-$69.** 3300 E Rt 66. I-40, exit 201, then 1.7 mi w. Ext corridors. **Pets:** Other. No service, supervision, crate.
🆂🅰🆅🅴 🆂🅳 ✕ 🖳 🕹

◆◆ Inn Suites Hotel 🅼
(520) 774-7356. **$67-$195.** 1008 E Route 66. On US 89, 180 and I-40 business loop; from I-40 exit 198, 1 mi n to Rte 66. Ext corridors. **Pets:** Medium. No service, supervision, crate.
🆂🅰🆅🅴 ✕ 🛢 🖳 🕹 ✕

◆◆◆ La Quinta Inn & Suites 🅼 ✿
(520) 556-8666. **$65-$85.** 2015 S Beulah Blvd. Nw of jct I-40 and I-17, from I-40 exit 195B, just n to Forest Meadow, then just w. Int corridors. **Pets:** Small, other. $25 deposit/room. Designated rooms, no service, supervision, crate.
🆂🅰🆅🅴 ✕ 🕹 🛢 🖳 🕹

◆◆◆ Ramada Limited 🅼 ✿
(520) 773-1111. **$69-$89, 30 days notice.** 2755 Woodlands Village Blvd. Nw of jct I-40 and I-17. From I-40 exit 195B, just n to Forest Meadows St, then w to Beulah Rd, then just s. Ext corridors. **Pets:** Other. $10 daily fee/room. Designated rooms, supervision.
🅰🆂🅺 🆂🅳 ✕ 🕹 🛢 🖳 🕹

◆◆ Ramada Limited-Lucky Lane 🅼 ✿
(520) 779-3614. **$59-$75.** 2350 E Lucky Ln. Adjacent to I-40, exit 198. Ext corridors. **Pets:** Small, other. Supervision.
🆂🅰🆅🅴 🆂🅳 ✕ 🕹 🛢 🕹

◆◆ Red Roof Inn 🅼
(520) 779-5121. **$39-$74.** 2520 E Lucky Ln. I-40 exit 198, just e on Lucky Ln. Ext corridors. **Pets:** Supervision.
🆂🅰🆅🅴 🆂🅳 ✕ 🛢 🖳 🕹

◆◆◆ Residence Inn by Marriott 🅰 ✿
(520) 526-5555. **$160-$160.** 3440 N Country Club Dr. Just s of I-40, exit 201. Ext corridors. **Pets:** Large, other. $10 daily fee/room. Designated rooms, supervision.
🅰🆂🅺 🆂🅳 ✕ 🕹 🛢 🖳 🕹 ✕

◆◆ Super 8 Motel 🅼 ✿
(520) 526-0818. **$54-$74.** 3725 N Kasper Ave. US 180, 89 and I-40 Business Loop, 0.5 mi w of jct I-40, exit 201. Int corridors. **Pets:** Other. Supervision.
🅰🆂🅺 🆂🅳 ✕ 🕹

◆ University/Grand Canyon Travelodge 🅼 ✿
(520) 774-3381. **$45-$80.** 801 W Highway 66. I-40 exit 191 then 2 mi e. Ext corridors. **Pets:** Other. $25 deposit/room. Supervision.
🆂🅰🆅🅴 🆂🅳 ✕ 🕹 🛢 🖳

FLORENCE

◆◆ Rancho Sonora Inn 🅼 ✿
(520) 868-8000. **$69-$74, 7 days notice.** 9198 N Hwy 79. On SR 79, 5 mi s of SR 287. Ext corridors. **Pets:** Medium, other. $10 one-time fee/room. Designated rooms, supervision.
✕ 🕹 ✕ 🅲🆃🆅

FOREST LAKES

◆◆ Forest Lakes Lodge 🅼
(520) 535-4727. **$41-$69.** SR 260, 16 mi w of Heber. Ext corridors. **Pets:** No service, supervision, crate.
🆂🅰🆅🅴 🆂🅳 ✕ 🛢 🕸

GILA BEND

◆◆◆ Best Western Space Age Lodge 🅼🅸 ✿
(520) 683-2273. **$64-$79.** 401 E Pima St. Business Loop I-8, in center of town. Ext corridors. **Pets:** Other. Supervision.
🆂🅰🆅🅴 🆂🅳 ✕ 🛢 🖳 🕹 🕹

◆ Super 8 Motel 🅼
(520) 683-6311. **$59-$62.** 2888 Butterfield Tr. Just w of I-8, exit 119. Int corridors. **Pets:** Medium. Designated rooms, no service, supervision, crate.
🅰🆂🅺 🆂🅳 ✕ 🕹

GLOBE

◆◆ Comfort Inn 🅼
(520) 425-7575. **Call for rates.** 1515 South St. 1 mi e on US 60. Ext corridors. **Pets:** Supervision.
🅰🆂🅺 🆂🅳 ✕ 🛢 🕹

◆◆ Holiday Inn Express-Globe 🅼 ✿
(520) 425-7008. **$68-$68.** 2119 Hwy 60. 4 mi w on US 60. Int corridors. **Pets:** Small. Supervision.
🅰🆂🅺 🆂🅳 ✕ 🛢

◆◆◆ Ramada Limited 🅼
(520) 425-5741. **$47-$75.** 1699 E Ash St. 1.3 mi e on US 60. Ext/int corridors. **Pets:** Medium. Designated rooms, supervision.
🆂🅰🆅🅴 🆂🅳 ✕ 🛢 🕹

GRAND CANYON

(AAA) ◆◆ Rodeway Inn-Red Feather Lodge M ❀
(520) 638-2414. **$79-$119.** On SR 64 in Tusayan; 9 mi s of Grand Canyon Village, outside Park Boundary. Ext/int corridors. **Pets:** Other. $45 deposit/room, $5 one-time fee/pet. No service, supervision, crate.

[SAVE] [S.D] [X] [I] [P] [ᗧ]

HEBER

(AAA) ◆◆◆ Best Western Sawmill Inn M ❀
(520) 535-5053. **$60-$68.** 1877 Hwy 260. 0.5 mi e on SR 260. Ext corridors. **Pets:** Medium. $25 deposit/room, $10 daily fee/pet. No service, supervision, crate.

[SAVE] [S.D] [X] [I] [P]

HOLBROOK

(AAA) ◆◆ Best Western Adobe Inn M
(520) 524-3948. **$45-$55.** 615 W Hopi Dr. On US 180, 1 mi e of jct I-40, exit 285. Ext corridors. **Pets:** Designated rooms, no service, supervision, crate.

[SAVE] [S.D] [X] [ᗧ]

(AAA) ◆◆◆ Best Western Arizonian Inn MI ❀
(520) 524-2611. **$52-$70.** 2508 E Navajo Blvd. I-40, exit 289, then 0.5 mi w. Ext corridors. **Pets:** Small, other. Supervision.

[SAVE] [S.D] [X] [I] [ᗧ]

(AAA) ◆ Budget Host Holbrook Inn M ❀
(520) 524-3809. **$22-$30.** 235 W Hopi Dr. On US 180, just w of downtown; from I-40 use exit 285. Ext corridors. **Pets:** Other. $10 deposit/room. No service, supervision, crate.

[SAVE] [S.D] [X] [I]

◆◆◆ Comfort Inn MI
(520) 524-6131. **$46-$70.** 2602 E Navajo Blvd. Just w of I-40, exit 289. Ext corridors. **Pets:** Supervision.

[ASK] [S.D] [X] [I] [P] [ᗧ]

◆◆ Econo Lodge M ❀
(520) 524-1448. **$30-$55.** 2596 E Navajo Blvd. Just w of I-40, exit 289. Ext corridors. **Pets:** $25 deposit/room. No service, supervision, crate.

[ASK] [S.D] [X] [I] [P] [ᗧ]

◆◆◆ Holbrook Holiday Inn Express M ❀
(520) 524-1466. **$67-$67.** 1308 E Navajo Blvd. Just n of I-40, exit 286. Int corridors. **Pets:** Other. $5 daily fee/room. Designated rooms, no service, supervision, crate.

[ASK] [S.D] [X] [I] [P] [ᗧ]

◆◆◆ Ramada Limited M ❀
(520) 524-2566. **$50-$59.** 2608 E Navajo Blvd. Just w of I-40, exit 289. Ext corridors. **Pets:** $5 deposit/pet. Designated rooms, no service, supervision, crate.

[ASK] [S.D] [X] [I] [ᗧ]

◆◆ Relax Inn M
(520) 524-6815. **$35-$40.** 2418 E Navajo Blvd. I-40, exit 289; 0.4 mi w. Ext corridors. **Pets:** Medium. No service, supervision, crate.

[ASK] [S.D] [X] [I]

KINGMAN

(AAA) ◆◆◆ Best Western A Wayfarer's Inn M
(520) 753-6271. **$56-$72.** 2815 E Andy Devine. On I-40 business loop; 0.5 mi sw of I-40, exit 53. Ext corridors. **Pets:** Supervision.

[SAVE] [S.D] [X] [I] [P] [ᗧ]

(AAA) ◆◆◆ Best Western King's Inn M ❀
(520) 753-6101. **$57-$72, 7 days notice.** 2930 E Andy Devine. On I-40 business loop; 0.3 mi sw of jct I-40, exit 53. Ext corridors. **Pets:** Other. Supervision.

[SAVE] [S.D] [X] [ᗧ'] [I] [P] [ᗧ]

(AAA) ◆◆ Brunswick Hotel H ❀
(520) 718-1800. **$25-$60.** 315 E Andy Devine. Downtown Historic district on Rt 66. Int corridors. **Pets:** Small. $25 deposit/pet, $10 daily fee/pet. No service, supervision, crate.

[SAVE] [S.D] [X] [ᗧ'] [I] [II]

(AAA) ◆◆ Days Inn East M
(520) 757-7337. **$35-$75, 3 days notice.** 3381 E Andy Devine. SR 66; 0.5 mi ne of jct I-40, exit 53. **Pets:** Medium. Designated rooms, supervision.

[SAVE] [S.D] [X] [I] [ᗧ]

(AAA) ◆◆◆ Days Inn West M
(520) 753-7500. **$45-$75, 3 days notice.** 3023 E Andy Devine. On I-40 business loop, just sw of jct I-40, exit 53. Ext corridors. **Pets:** Designated rooms, supervision.

[SAVE] [S.D] [X] [I] [ᗧ]

(AAA) ◆ High Desert Inn M ❀
(520) 753-2935. **$25-$75.** 2803 E Andy Devine. On I-40 business loop; 0.5 mi sw of jct I-40, exit 53. Ext corridors. **Pets:** Other. Supervision.

[SAVE] [S.D] [X]

(AAA) ◆ Hill Top Motel M
(520) 753-2198. **$24-$48, 3 days notice.** 1901 E Andy Devine. On I-40 business loop; 2 mi sw of I-40, exit 53; 2.3 mi e, exit 48. Ext corridors. **Pets:** Supervision.

[SAVE] [X] [I] [ᗧ]

◆◆ Holiday Inn MI
(520) 753-6262. **$39-$99, 3 days notice.** 3100 E Andy Devine. On I-40 business loop; 0.3 mi w of I-40, exit 53. Ext corridors. **Pets:** Supervision.

[ASK] [S.D] [X] [P] [II] [ᗧ]

(AAA) ◆ Motel 6–1114 M ❀
(520) 753-9222. **$42-$58.** 424 W Beale St. Just s of I-40, exit 48. Ext corridors. **Pets:** Small, other. Supervision.

[S.D] [X] [ᗧ'] [ᗧ]

(AAA) ◆◆ Quality Inn M
(520) 753-4747. **$50-$90.** 1400 E Andy Devine. On I-40 business loop; 2.3 mi sw of I-40, exit 53; 2 mi e of exit 48. Ext corridors. **Pets:** Supervision.

[SAVE] [S.D] [X] [I] [P] [ᗧ]

(AAA) ◆◆ Super 8 Motel M
(520) 757-4808. **$36-$59, 3 days notice.** 3401 E Andy Devine. On SR 66, 0.3 mi ne of jct I-40, exit 53. Int corridors. **Pets:** Small. Supervision.

[SAVE] [S.D] [X] [I]

LAKE HAVASU CITY

◆◆ Best Western Lake Place Inn **M**
(520) 855-2146. **$50-$90.** 31 Wing's Loop. 1 mi e of SR 95 via Swanson Ave. Ext corridors. **Pets:** Supervision.
[SAVE] [S🐾] [⊠] [📞] [🔲] [🖼]

◆◆◆ Holiday Inn **M** ❀
(520) 855-4071. **$60-$80.** 245 London Bridge Rd. 0.5 mi n of London Bridge. Ext/int corridors. **Pets:** $10 daily fee/room. Supervision.
[ASK] [S🐾] [⊠] [🏊] [👟] [📞] [🔲] [🍽] [🖼]

◆◆◆ Island Inn Hotel **M** ❀
(520) 680-0606. **$65-$90.** 1300 W McCulloch Blvd. 0.5 mi sw of SR 95, over London Bridge. Int corridors. **Pets:** Other. $10 one-time fee/pet. Supervision.
[SAVE] [S🐾] [⊠] [🖼]

◆ Lake Havasu City Super 8 **M** ❀
(520) 855-8844. **$36-$56, 4 days notice.** 305 London Bridge Rd. Just w of SR 95, exit Palo Verde. Int corridors. **Pets:** Medium, other. $50 deposit/room. Designated rooms, supervision.
[⊠] [🖼]

MIAMI

◆◆ Copper Hills Inn & Suites **M**
(520) 425-7151. **$42-$45.** 4805 E Hwy 60. US 60; 0.3 mi w of jct SR 88. Ext corridors. **Pets:** No service, supervision, crate.
[ASK] [S🐾] [⊠] [📞] [🍽] [🖼]

MUNDS PARK

◆◆ Motel In The Pines **M** ❀
(520) 286-9699. **$40-$65.** 80 W Pinewood Rd. Just e of I-17, exit 322. 17 mi s of Flagstaff. Ext corridors. **Pets:** Small, other. $30 deposit/room, $3 daily fee/pet, $3 one-time fee/pet. Designated rooms, no service, supervision, crate.
[SAVE] [S🐾] [⊠] [📞] [🔲]

NOGALES

◆ Americana Motor Hotel **M** ❀
(520) 287-7211. **$45-$63, 3 days notice.** 639 N Grand Ave. 1 mi n of International Border on I-19 business loop, 0.6 mi s of jct SR 82. Int corridors. **Pets:** Very small, dogs only. $5 daily fee/pet, $5 one-time fee/pet. Designated rooms, no service, supervision, crate.
[SAVE] [S🐾] [⊠] [📞] [🍽] [🖼]

◆◆ Best Western Siesta Motel **M** ❀
(520) 287-4671. **$70-$90.** 673 N Grand Ave. 1 mi n of International Border on Business Loop 19, 0.6 mi s of jct SR 82. Ext corridors. **Pets:** Small, other. Supervision.
[SAVE] [S🐾] [⊠] [📞] [🖼]

◆◆ Super 8 Motel **M**
(520) 281-2242. **Call for rates.** 547 W Mariposa Rd. Just e of I-19, exit 4, Mariposa Rd. Ext/int corridors. **Pets:** Small. No service, supervision, crate.
[⊠] [📞] [🔲] [🍽] [🖼]

◆◆ Travelodge **M**
(520) 287-4627. **$40-$54.** 921 N Grand Ave. 1.3 mi n of International Border on Business Loop 19, just s of jct SR 82. Ext corridors. **Pets:** Supervision.
[ASK] [S🐾] [⊠] [🖼]

PAGE

◆◆◆ Best Western Arizonainn **M** ❀
(520) 645-2466. **Call for rates.** 716 Rimview Dr. 0.7 mi e of US 89 via SR 89L, Lake Powell Blvd. Int corridors. **Pets:** Medium. $10 daily fee/pet, $10 one-time fee/pet. Supervision.
[⊠] [📞] [🖼]

◆ Econo Lodge **M** ❀
(520) 645-2488. **$55-$69, 3 days notice.** 121 S Lake Powell Blvd. 1.3 mi e on Lake Powell Blvd from US 89/SR 89L. Ext corridors. **Pets:** Small. $5 one-time fee/pet. Designated rooms, no service, supervision, crate.
[SAVE] [S🐾] [⊠] [🖼]

◆◆◆ Lake Powell Days Inn & Suites **M**
(520) 645-2800. **$79-$99.** 961 N Hwy 89. On US 89. Int corridors. **Pets:** Supervision.
[ASK] [S🐾] [🏊] [👟] [📞] [🖼]

◆ Lake Powell Motel **M** ❀
(520) 645-2433. **$79-$99, 3 days notice.** US 89. On US 89; 4 mi n of Glen Canyon Dam, 3 mi w of Wahweap Marina, at north entrance to marina. Ext corridors. **Pets:** Other. Designated rooms, supervision.
[SAVE] [S🐾] [⊠] [🖼]

◆◆ Motel 6–Page/Lake Powell–4013 **M** ❀
(520) 645-5888. **$55-$70, 3 days notice.** 637 S Lake Powell Blvd. Just e of SR 89, on Business Loop 89A (Lake Powell Blvd). Int corridors. **Pets:** Medium, other. No service, supervision, crate.
[ASK] [S🐾] [⊠] [👟] [🖼]

◆◆◆ Ramada Inn Page/Lake Powell **M** ❀
(520) 645-8851. **$69-$99.** 287 N Lake Powell Blvd. US 89/SR 89L, 0.8 mi e on Lake Powell Blvd. Int corridors. **Pets:** Supervision.
[SAVE] [S🐾] [⊠] [📞] [🍽] [🖼]

◆◆◆ Wahweap Lodge **R** ❀
(520) 645-2433. **$169-$189, 3 days notice.** 100 Lakeshore Dr. 4 mi n of Glen Canyon Dam via US 89 and Lakeshore Dr. Int corridors. **Pets:** Other. Designated rooms, supervision.
[SAVE] [S🐾] [⊠] [🏊] [📞] [🔲] [🍽] [🖼] [⊠]

PARKER

◆◆◆ Best Western Parker Inn **M** ❀
(520) 669-6060. **$59-$99.** 1012 Geronimo Ave. E of US 95. Int corridors. **Pets:** Very small, other. Designated rooms, supervision.
[SAVE] [S🐾] [⊠] [👟] [📞] [🖼]

PAYSON

⬤⬤ ◆◆◆ **Best Western Paysonglo Lodge M**
(520) 474-2382. **$75-$140.** 1005 S Beeline Hwy. On SR 87, 1 mi s of jct SR 260. Ext corridors. **Pets:** Designated rooms, no service, supervision, crate.
⬤⬤ ⊠ ⬛ ⬛

⬤⬤ ◆◆◆ **Days Inn & Suites M**
(520) 474-9800. **$69-$149, 24 days notice.** 301 A S Beeline Hwy. On SR 87 just s of jct SR 260. Int corridors. **Pets:** Medium. No service, supervision, crate.
⬛ ⬤⬤ ⬛ ⬛ ⬛ ⬛ ⬛

⬤⬤ ◆◆◆ **Holiday Inn Express M** ❀
(520) 472-7484. **$79-$149.** 206 S BeeLine. SR 87, just s of jct SR 260. Int corridors. **Pets:** Medium. $15 deposit/room, $10 one-time fee/room. Designated rooms, no service, supervision, crate.
⬛ ⊠ ⬛ ⬛ ⬛ ⬛

◆◆◆ **Inn of Payson M** ❀
(520) 474-3241. **$89-$89.** 801 N Beeline Hwy. .3 mi n of SR 260 on SR 87. Ext corridors. **Pets:** $10 daily fee/room. Supervision.
⬛ ⬤⬤ ⊠ ⬛ ⬛ ⬛ ⬛ ⬛ ⬛ ⬛ ⬛

◆◆◆ **Majestic Mountain Inn M** ❀
(520) 474-0185. **$56-$99.** 602 E Hwy 260. On SR 260. 0.5 mi e of jct SR 87. Ext corridors. **Pets:** Medium. Supervision.
⊠ ⬛ ⬛ ⬛

⬤⬤ ◆◆◆ **Payson Pueblo Inn M**
(520) 474-5241. **$54-$159.** 809 E Hwy 260. On SR 260; 0.8 mi e of SR 87. Ext corridors. **Pets:** Small. Supervision.
⬛ ⊠ ⬛ ⬛

◆◆ **Rim Country Inn M**
(520) 474-4526. **$39-$89.** 101 West Phoenix St. SR 87, 1.3 mi s of jct SR 260. Int corridors. **Pets:** Large. No service, supervision, crate.
⬛ ⬤⬤ ⊠ ⬛

⬤⬤ ◆ **Trails End Motel M** ❀
(520) 474-2283. **$39-$99.** 811 S Beeline Hwy. 0.5 mi s of jct SR 260 and SR 87. Ext/int corridors. **Pets:** Medium, other. $5 daily fee/room, $5 one-time fee/room. Supervision.
⬛ ⬤⬤ ⊠ ⬛ ⬛

PHOENIX METROPOLITAN AREA

APACHE JUNCTION

⬤⬤ ◆ **Apache Junction Motel M** ❀
(480) 982-7702. **$54-$66, 7 days notice.** 1680 W Apache Tr. 2 mi n of US 60, exit Ironwood Dr, just w of Ironwood Dr. Ext corridors. **Pets:** Small, dogs only. $20 one-time fee/pet. Designated rooms, no service, supervision, crate.
⬛ ⊠ ⬛

◆◆ **Apache Junction Super 8 M** ❀
(480) 288-8888. **$74-$88.** 251 E 29th Ave. From US 60 exit Idaho Rd 0.3 mi ne. Ext/int corridors. **Pets:** Very small, dogs only. $25 deposit/room. Supervision.
⬛ ⊠ ⬛ ⬛

CAREFREE

⬤⬤ ◆◆◆◆◆ **The Boulders Resort R** ❀
(480) 488-9009. **$545-$545, 21 days notice.** 34631 N Tom Darlington Rd. Scottsdale. on Scottsdale Rd 11 mi n of Bell Rd to Carefree Hwy, then just n; 12.7 mi e of jct I-17 and SR 74, then just n. Ext corridors. **Pets:** Other. $100 deposit/ room. Supervision.
⬤⬤ ⊠ ⬛ ⬛ ⬛ ⊠

CHANDLER

◆◆◆ **Hawthorn Suites Ltd M** ❀
(480) 705-8881. **$99-$109.** 5858 W Chandler Blvd. I-10 exit 160 (Chandler Blvd), 1.5 mi e. Int corridors. **Pets:** Other. $100 one-time fee/room. No service, supervision, crate.
⊠ ⬛ ⬛ ⬛

◆◆◆ **Holiday Inn Express Hotel &**
Suites M ❀
(480) 785-8500. **$99-$119.** 15221 S 50th St. Just w of I-10, exit 160 (Chandler Blvd). Int corridors. **Pets:** Other. $5 one-time fee/pet. Supervision.
⬛ ⬤⬤ ⊠ ⬛ ⬛ ⬛

◆◆◆ **Homewood Suites M** ❀
(480) 753-6200. **$159-$209.** 7373 W Detroit St. From I-10, exit 160 (Chandler Blvd), 0.4 mi e, n on 54th. Int corridors. **Pets:** Small, dogs only. $100 one-time fee/pet. No service, supervision, crate.
⬛ ⬤⬤ ⊠ ⬛ ⬛ ⬛

◆ **Microtel Inn M** ❀
(480) 705-8882. **$59-$69, 3 days notice.** 255 N Kyrene. I-10 exit 160 (Chandler Blvd), 1.5 mi e, just n. Int corridors. **Pets:** Other. No service, supervision, crate.
⬛ ⬤⬤ ⊠ ⬛

⬤⬤ ◆◆ **Red Roof Inn-Chandler M** ❀
(480) 857-4969. **$50-$85.** 7400 W Boston St. I-10 exit 160 (Chandler Blvd), 0.4 mi e, s on Southgate. Int corridors. **Pets:** Small, other. Supervision.
⬛ ⊠ ⬛

⬤⬤ ◆◆◆ **Sheraton San Marcos Resort H** ❀
(480) 963-6655. **$99-$199.** 1 San Marcos Pl. Just s of Chandler Blvd on Arizona Ave. Ext corridors. **Pets:** Medium, other. $50 deposit/room. No service, supervision, crate.
⬛ ⬤⬤ ⊠ ⬛ ⬛ ⬛ ⬛ ⬛

⬤⬤ ◆◆◆ **Windmill Inn of Chandler M** ❀
(480) 812-9600. **$116-$134.** 3535 W Chandler Blvd. I-10 exit 160 (Chandler Blvd), 3.9 mi e, corner of Country Club Way. Int corridors. **Pets:** Other. Supervision.
⬛ ⬤⬤ ⊠ ⬛ ⬛ ⊠

GLENDALE

◆◆◆ Holiday Inn Express Arrowhead [M] ❧
(623) 412-2000. **$89-$109, 3 days notice.** 7885 W Arrow-head Towne Ctr Dr. Just n of Bell on 79th Ave, on the grounds of Arrowhead Towne Mall. Ext corridors. **Pets:** Small, other. $25 one-time fee/room. Designated rooms, no service, supervision, crate.

[ASK] [S🐾] [✕] [⌂] [🛏] [💻] [🍽]

GOODYEAR

⑭ ◆◆ Best Western Phoenix Goodyear Inn [M]
(623) 932-3210. **$89-$89.** 55 N Litchfield Rd. I-10, exit 128; 0.8 mi s. Ext/int corridors. **Pets:** Supervision.

[SAVE] [S🐾] [✕] [🛏] [💻] [🍽] [🍽]

◆◆◆ Holiday Inn Express [M] ❧
(623) 535-1313. **$129-$149, 3 days notice.** 1313 Litchfield Rd. Just n of I-10, exit 128, Litchfield Rd. Int corridors. **Pets:** Medium. $25 deposit/room. Supervision.

[ASK] [S🐾] [✕] [🛏] [🍽]

LITCHFIELD PARK

◆◆◆◆ The Wigwam Resort [R]
(623) 935-3811. **$330-$475.** 300 Wigwam Blvd. I-10 west; exit Litchfield Rd; 2 mi n. Ext corridors. **Pets:** Medium. No service, supervision, crate.

[ASK] [S🐾] [✕] [🍽] [🛏] [🍽] [🍽] [✕]

MESA

⑭ ◆◆◆ Arizona Golf Resort & Conference Center [R] ❧
(480) 832-3202. **$149-$169.** 425 S Power Rd. 1.3 mi n of US 60 (Superstition Frwy) exit Power Rd; se corner of Broadway and Power rds, entrance on Broadway Rd. Ext corridors. **Pets:** Other. Supervision.

[SAVE] [✕] [🛏] [💻] [🍽] [🍽] [✕]

⑭ ◆◆ Best Western Mesa Inn [M] ❧
(480) 964-8000. **$70-$99.** 1625 E Main St. 2 mi n of US 60 (Superstition Frwy) Stapley Dr exit; 0.5 mi e on Main St. Ext corridors. **Pets:** $5 one-time fee/pet. No service, supervision, crate.

[SAVE] [S🐾] [✕] [🛏] [💻] [🍽]

◆◆◆ Best Western Superstition Springs Inn & Suites [M]
(480) 641-1164. **$65-$135, 3 days notice.** 1342 S Power Rd. Just n of US 60 (Superstition Frwy) Power Rd exit, on the nw corner of Power Rd and Hampton Ave at Superstition Springs Mall. Ext corridors. **Pets:** No service, supervision, crate.

[ASK] [S🐾] [✕] [⚷] [⌂] [🛏] [💻] [🍽]

◆ Days Inn [M] ❧
(480) 844-8900. **$86-$106.** 333 W Juanita. 0.5 mi se of US 60, exit Country Club Dr. Int corridors. **Pets:** Small, other. $25 deposit/pet. No service, supervision, crate.

[ASK] [S🐾] [✕] [🛏] [💻] [🍽]

◆◆ Holiday Inn Hotel & Suites [M]
(480) 964-7000. **$99-$99.** 1600 S Country Club Dr. US 60, Superstition Frwy, Country Club Dr exit. Ext/int corridors. **Pets:** No service, supervision, crate.

[✕] [🛏] [💻] [🍽] [🍽]

◆◆◆ Homestead Village [M] ❧
(480) 752-2266. **$59-$59.** 1920 W Isabella. Just s of US 60, Dobson Rd exit. Ext corridors. **Pets:** Small. $75 one-time fee/room. Supervision.

[✕] [🛏] [💻]

⑭ ◆◆◆ La Quinta Inn & Suites-Mesa [M] ❧
(480) 844-8747. **$95-$115.** 902 W Grove Ave. US 60 Alma School Rd exit , 0.5 mi n to Southern Ave, 0.5 mi e to Extension Rd, then just s to Grove Ave. Int corridors. **Pets:** Small. Supervision.

[SAVE] [✕] [🛏] [💻] [🍽]

⑭ ◆◆◆ La Quinta Inn & Suites-Superstition Springs [M]
(480) 654-1970. **$95-$115.** 6530 E Superstition Springs Blvd. Just s US 60 Power Rd exit. Int corridors. **Pets:** Small. Supervision.

[SAVE] [✕] [🛏] [💻] [🍽]

⑭ ◆ Motel 6–1030 [M]
(480) 834-0066. **$42-$61.** 1511 S Country Club Dr. SR 60, exit 179 (Country Club Dr), just n. Ext corridors. **Pets:** Medium. Designated rooms, no service, supervision, crate.

[S🐾] [✕] [🛏] [🍽]

◆◆◆ Residence Inn by Marriott Mesa [M] ❧
(480) 610-0100. **$149.** 941 W Grove Ave. Int corridors. **Pets:** Other. $10 daily fee/room, $50 one-time fee/room. Supervision.

[ASK] [✕] [🛏] [💻] [🍽] [✕]

⑭ ◆ Sleep Inn of Mesa [M] ❧
(480) 807-7760. **$39-$109, 7 days notice.** 6347 E Southern Ave. Int corridors. **Pets:** Medium. $50 deposit/room. Designated rooms, no service, supervision, crate.

[SAVE] [S🐾] [✕] [🛏] [💻] [🍽]

◆◆ Travelodge Suites Mesa [M]
(480) 832-5961. **$84-$124.** 4244 E Main St. From I-60, exit Greenfield Rd, 2 mi n, just w. Ext corridors. **Pets:** Small. Designated rooms, no service, supervision, crate.

[ASK] [S🐾] [✕] [🛏] [💻] [🍽]

PEORIA

◆◆◆ Comfort Suites of Peoria [M]
(623) 334-3993. **$99-$134.** 8473 W Paradise Ln. Loop 101, Bell Rd exit, then se. Int corridors. **Pets:** Medium. No service, supervision, crate.

[ASK] [S🐾] [✕] [🛏] [💻] [🍽]

⑭ ◆◆◆ La Quinta Inn & Suites [M] ❧
(623) 487-1900. **$99-$119.** 16321 N 83 Ave. Loop 101, Bell Rd exit, then se. Int corridors. **Pets:** Medium. $5 daily fee/room. Supervision.

[SAVE] [✕] [🛏] [💻] [🍽]

◆◆◆ Residence Inn by Marriott [M] ❧
(623) 979-2074. **$219.** 8435 W Paradise Ln. Loop 101, Bell Rd exit, then just e. Int corridors. **Pets:** Other. $100 one-time fee/room. No service, supervision, crate.

[ASK] [S🐾] [✕] [🍽]

PHOENIX

AAA ◆◆◆ **AmeriSuites-Phoenix Metro Center** **M**
(602) 997-8800. **$89-$126.** 10838 N 25th Ave. Int corridors. **Pets:** Small. Designated rooms, supervision.
[SAVE] [S🐾] [✕] [📠] [💻] [🐾]

AAA ◆◆ **Best Western Airport Inn** **MI**
(602) 273-7251. **$99-$119.** 2425 S 24th St. Just s of I-10 airport exit (24th St); eastbound travel to University Dr, re-enter I-10 westbound. Ext/int corridors. **Pets:** Medium. No service, supervision, crate.
[SAVE] [S🐾] [✕] [🐾] [📠] [🍴] [🐾]

AAA ◆◆◆ **Best Western Bell Hotel** **M** 🐾
(602) 993-8300. **$93-$109.** 17211 N Black Canyon Hwy. Adjacent to I-17, exit Bell Rd E, just n on frontage road. Ext corridors. **Pets:** Small, dogs only. $25 one-time fee/room. Designated rooms, no service, supervision, crate.
[SAVE] [S🐾] [✕] [🐾] [📠] [💻] [🐾]

AAA ◆◆ **Comfort Inn Black Canyon** **M**
(602) 242-8011. **$76-$109.** 5050 N Black Canyon Hwy. W side of I-17, Camelback Rd exit. Ext corridors. **Pets:** Medium. Designated rooms, supervision.
[SAVE] [S🐾] [✕] [📠] [💻] [🐾]

◆◆◆ **Comfort Suites** **M**
(602) 861-3900. **$99-$109, 7 days notice.** 10210 N 26th Dr. I-17, Peoria Ave exit. Int corridors. **Pets:** Very small. Designated rooms, supervision.
[ASK] [S🐾] [✕] [📠] [💻] [🐾]

AAA ◆◆◆ **Crowne Plaza Phoenix-Metrocenter** **H**
(602) 943-2341. **$119.** 2532 W Peoria Ave. Adjacent to I-17, exit Peoria Ave, ne corner. Int corridors. **Pets:** Medium. Designated rooms, no service, supervision, crate.
[SAVE] [S🐾] [✕] [♿] [🐾] [🐾] [📠] [💻] [🍴] [🐾] [✕]

AAA ◆◆ **Days Inn-Airport** **M** 🐾
(602) 244-8244. **$72-$105.** 3333 E Van Buren. I-10 exit Washington, e to 32nd St, n to Van Buren just e. Ext/int corridors. **Pets:** Medium. $25 deposit/room. Supervision.
[SAVE] [S🐾] [✕] [📠] [💻] [🍴] [🐾]

AAA ◆ **Days Inn-I-17 & Thomas** **M** 🐾
(602) 257-0801. **$73-$99.** 2420 W Thomas Rd. I-17, Thomas Rd exit, at ne corner of junction. Int corridors. **Pets:** Medium. $25 daily fee/pet, $25 one-time fee/pet. No service, supervision, crate.
[SAVE] [S🐾] [✕] [🐾] [📠] [💻] [🐾]

AAA ◆◆◆ **Embassy Suites-Biltmore** **H** 🐾
(602) 955-3992. **$239-$239.** 2630 E Camelback Rd. Just n of Camelback Rd on 24th St, adjacent to Biltmore Fashion Park. Int corridors. **Pets:** Small, other. $25 one-time fee/room. Supervision.
[SAVE] [S🐾] [✕] [🐾] [📠] [💻] [🐾]

◆◆◆ **Embassy Suites Hotel Airport West** **H** 🐾
(602) 957-1910. **$149-$180.** 2333 E Thomas Rd. Just w of 24th St. Ext corridors. **Pets:** $10 daily fee/room. Supervision.
[ASK] [S🐾] [✕] [🐾] [📠] [💻] [🍴] [🐾]

◆◆◆ **Hampton Inn I-17** **M** 🐾
(602) 864-6233. **$94, 48 days notice.** 8101 Black Canyon Hwy. Adjacent to I-17, Northern Ave exit. Ext corridors. **Pets:** Other. $25 one-time fee/room. Supervision.
[ASK] [S🐾] [✕] [🐾] [📠] [💻] [🐾]

◆◆◆ **Hilton Suites-Phoenix** **H** 🐾
(602) 222-1111. **$157-$157.** 10 E Thomas Rd. On Thomas Rd just e of Central Ave, in Phoenix Plaza. Int corridors. **Pets:** Small. $150 deposit/pet. Supervision.
[ASK] [S🐾] [✕] [🐾] [♿] [📠] [💻] [🍴] [🐾]

◆◆◆ **Holiday Inn Express Hotel & Suites** **MI**
(602) 453-9900. **$109-$189.** 3401 E University Dr. Adjacent to I-10, University Dr exit. Int corridors. **Pets:** Very small. Designated rooms, no service, supervision, crate.
[ASK] [S🐾] [✕] [📠] [💻] [🐾]

◆◆◆ **Holiday Inn Express Hotel and Suites** **M** 🐾
(602) 452-2020. **$149-$199, 21 days notice.** 620 N 6th St. 0.5 mi s of I-10, exit 7th St. Int corridors. **Pets:** Small. Supervision.
[ASK] [S🐾] [✕] [📠] [💻] [🐾] [✕]

AAA ◆◆◆ **Holiday Inn-Select Airport** **H** 🐾
(602) 273-7778. **$99-$149.** 4300 E Washington St. Nw corner of Washington and 44th Sts. Int corridors. **Pets:** Small. $25 deposit/pet. No service, supervision, crate.
[SAVE] [✕] [🐾] [📠] [💻] [🍴] [🐾]

AAA ◆◆◆ **Holiday Inn West** **H** 🐾
(602) 484-9009. **$99-$129.** 1500 N 51st Ave. Adjacent to n side of I-10 W, exit 51st Ave. Int corridors. **Pets:** Small, other. $25 one-time fee/room. No service, supervision, crate.
[SAVE] [S🐾] [✕] [♿] [🐾] [📠] [💻] [🍴] [🐾]

◆◆◆ **Homestead Village/Guest Suites/Phoenix Metro** **M** 🐾
(602) 944-7828. **$59-$59.** 2102 W Dunlap Ave. 0.6 mi e of I-17, exit Dunlap Ave. Ext corridors. **Pets:** Other. $100 one-time fee/room. Supervision.
[✕]

◆◆◆ **Homestead Village North/Deer Valley** **M** 🐾
(602) 843-1151. **$59-$59.** 18405 N 27th Ave. W side of I-17, Union Hills Dr exit. Ext corridors. **Pets:** Other. $100 one-time fee/room. Supervision.
[✕]

◆◆◆ **Homewood Suites Hotel** **M** 🐾
(602) 674-8900. **$99.** 2536 W Beryl Ave. E side of I-17, Peoria Ave exit. Int corridors. **Pets:** Medium, other. $200 deposit/room, $50 one-time fee/room. Supervision.
[ASK] [S🐾] [✕] [💻] [🐾]

AAA ◆◆ **Howard Johnson-Grand Ave** **M** 🐾
(602) 264-9164. **$109-$109.** 3400 Grand Ave. **Pets:** Medium. $100 deposit/room. No service, supervision, crate.
[SAVE] [S🐾] [✕] [📠] [🐾]

AAA ◆◆◆ **La Quinta Inn & Suites-Chandler** **M** 🐾
(480) 961-7700. **$85-$105.** 15241 S 50th St. Just w of I-10, exit 160, Chandler Blvd. Int corridors. **Pets:** Supervision.
[SAVE] [✕] [📠] [💻] [🐾]

⚠️ ◆◆◆ La Quinta Inn-Coliseum Ⓜ
(602) 258-6271. **$69-$89.** 2725 N Black Canyon Hwy. Adjacent to I-17, Thomas Rd exit. Ext corridors. **Pets:** Small. Designated rooms, no service, supervision, crate.
SAVE ✕ 🛏 💻 🖼

⚠️ ◆◆◆ La Quinta Phoenix North Ⓜ
(602) 993-0800. **$79-$99.** 2510 W Greenway Rd. Adjacent to I-17, exit Greenway Rd. Ext corridors. **Pets:** Designated rooms, no service, supervision, crate.
SAVE ✕ 🐾 🛏 🖼 ✕

⚠️ ◆◆◆ Lexington Hotel at City Square Ⓗ
(602) 279-9811. **$99-$139.** 100 W Clarendon Ave. Just w of Central Ave, 0.3 mi s of Indian School Rd, on the n side of Clarendon Ave. Int corridors. **Pets:** Very small. Designated rooms, no service, supervision, crate.
SAVE 🆔 ✕ 🛏 💻 🍴 🖼

◆◆ Los Olivos Hotel & Suites Ⓜ
(602) 528-9100. **$99-$129.** 202 E McDowell Rd. Just e of Central Ave, on n side of McDowell Rd. Int corridors. **Pets:** Designated rooms, no service, supervision, crate.
ASK 🆔 ✕ 🛏 💻 🍴 🖼

⚠️ ◆◆ Premier Inns Ⓜ 🐾
(602) 943-2371. **$50-$100.** 10402 N Black Canyon Hwy. I-17, exit 208, w to 28th Dr, 0.5 mi to Metro Pkwy, e to 27th Ave, then n. Ext corridors. **Pets:** Designated rooms, no service, supervision, crate.
SAVE 🆔 ✕ 🛏 💻 🖼

⚠️ ◆◆ Quality Hotel & Resort Ⓜ
(602) 248-0222. **$109-$129.** 3600 N 2nd Ave. On 2nd Ave just n of Osborn Rd; 0.5 mi s of Indian School. Int corridors. **Pets:** Medium. Supervision.
SAVE 🆔 ✕ 🐾 🛋 🛏 💻 🍴 🖼 ✕

◆◆◆ Quality Inn-South Mountain Ⓜ 🐾
(480) 893-3900. **$99-$119.** 5121 E La Puente Ave. Just w of I-10, exit 157, Elliot Rd. Ext corridors. **Pets:** Medium. $25 one-time fee/room. No service, supervision, crate.
ASK 🆔 ✕ 🛏 💻 🍴 🖼

⚠️ ◆◆◆ Ramada Limited Suites Ⓜ 🐾
(602) 957-1350. **$99-$109, 7 days notice.** 3211 E Pinchot. Just n of Thomas. Ext corridors. **Pets:** Very small, dogs only. $25 one-time fee/room. Supervision.
SAVE 🆔 ✕ 🐾 🛏 💻 🖼

⚠️ ◆◆ Red Roof Inn Ⓜ 🐾
(602) 233-8004. **$50-$85.** 5215 W Willetta. I-10, 51st Ave exit, just n. Int corridors. **Pets:** Other. No service, supervision, crate.
SAVE ✕ 🛏 💻 🖼

⚠️ ◆◆ Red Roof Inn-Phoenix Ⓜ
(602) 866-1049. **$50-$85.** 17222 N Black Cyn Fwy. I-17 at Bell Rd, exit 212 N on Frontage Rd w side. Int corridors. **Pets:** Small. Supervision.
SAVE ✕ 🐾 🛋 🖼

⚠️ ◆◆◆ Residence Inn By Marriott Ⓜ 🐾
(602) 864-1900. **$119-$139.** 8242 N Black Canyon Hwy. W side of I-17; exit Dunlap Ave, 0.5 mi s. Ext/int corridors. **Pets:** Medium. $200 deposit/room, $50 one-time fee/room. No service, supervision, crate.
SAVE 🆔 ✕ 🐾 🛋 🛏 💻 🖼 ✕

◆◆◆◆ Sheraton Crescent Hotel Ⓗ
(602) 943-8200. **$119-$250.** 2620 W Dunlap Ave. Adjacent to I-17, exit Dunlap Ave, ne corner of intersection. Int corridors. **Pets:** Small. No service, supervision, crate.
✕ 🛋 🐾 🛋 🛏 💻 🍴 🖼 ✕

◆◆ Sleep Inn Sky Harbor Airport Ⓜ 🐾
(480) 967-7100. **$89-$129.** 2621 S 47th Pl. 0.7 mi n of I-10, southbound exit 153, westbound exit 153A; just nw of University Dr exit on 48th St/SR 143 (Hohokam Expressway). Int corridors. **Pets:** Medium. $25 one-time fee/room. Supervision.
ASK 🆔 ✕ 🛏 💻 🖼

⚠️ ◆ Super 8-Airport Ⓜ
(602) 244-1627. **$89.** 3401 E Van Buren. Ext/int corridors. **Pets:** Designated rooms, no service, supervision, crate.
SAVE 🆔 ✕ 🖼

◆◆◆ Super 8 Motel Ⓜ 🐾
(602) 415-0888. **$70-$85.** 1242 N 53rd Ave. Adjacent to I-10, exit 51st Ave. Int corridors. **Pets:** Large, other. $50 deposit/room. No service, supervision, crate.
ASK 🆔 ✕ 🛏 🖼

◆◆◆ TownePlace Suites-Phoenix Ⓜ
(602) 943-9510. **$39-$85.** 9425-B N Black Canyon Hwy. Adjacent to e side of I-17, Dunlap Ave exit, just n of intersection. Int corridors. **Pets:** Small. Supervision.
ASK 🆔 ✕ 🖼

⚠️ ◆ Travelodge-Fairgrounds Ⓜ 🐾
(602) 269-6281. **$50-$70.** 1624 N Black Canyon Hwy. Adj to I-17, just n of jct I-10 & I-17. Ext corridors. **Pets:** Small. $25 deposit/room. Designated rooms, no service, supervision, crate.
SAVE 🆔 ✕ 💻 🖼

⚠️ ◆◆◆ Wellesley Inn & Suites Phoenix Airport Ⓜ
(602) 225-2998. **$80-$100.** 4357 E Oak St. 0.4 mi s of Thomas Rd on 44th St. Ext corridors. **Pets:** No service, supervision, crate.
SAVE 🆔 ✕

⚠️ ◆◆ Wellesley Inn & Suites Phoenix/Chandler Ⓜ
(480) 753-6700. **$99-$109.** 5035 E Chandler Blvd. Just w of I-10, exit 160, Chandler Blvd. Ext corridors. **Pets:** Very small. Designated rooms, no service, supervision, crate.
SAVE 🆔 ✕ 🛏 💻 🖼

⚠️ ◆◆◆ Wellesley Inn & Suites Phoenix/Metrocenter Ⓜ
(602) 870-2999. **$65-$110.** 11211 N Black Canyon Hwy. Just n of Peoria Ave on e side of I-17. Ext corridors. **Pets:** Supervision.
SAVE 🆔 ✕ 🖼

⚠️ ◆◆◆ Wellesley Inn & Suites Phoenix/Park Central Ⓜ 🐾
(602) 279-9000. **$100-$100.** 217 W Osborn Rd. 0.7 mi s of Indian School Rd. Int corridors. **Pets:** $50 deposit/room, $75 one-time fee/room. No service, supervision, crate.
SAVE 🆔 ✕ 🖼

SCOTTSDALE

◆◆◆ AmeriSuites-Scottsdale/Civic Center 🅗 ❖
(480) 423-9944. **$125-$179.** 7300 E Third Ave. 0.2 mi e of Scottsdale Rd. Int corridors. **Pets:** Small, other. Designated rooms, supervision.
SAVE 🔊 ✕ 🖥 💻 🖨

◆◆◆ Country Inn & Suites By Carlson Ⓜ
(480) 314-1200. **$109-$129.** 10801 N 89th Pl. Just n of Shea Blvd, just e of Pima Rd. Int corridors. **Pets:** Supervision.
ASK 🔊 ✕ 🖥 💻 🖨

◆◆◆ Doubletree La Posada Resort–Scottsdale 🆁 ❖
(480) 952-0420. **$210-$210, 3 days notice.** 4949 E Lincoln Dr. Se corner of Lincoln Dr and Tatum Blvd, enter from Lincoln Dr. Ext corridors. **Pets:** Other. $25 deposit/room. Supervision.
SAVE ✕ 🎰 💻 🍴 🖨 ✕

◆◆◆ Gainey Suites Hotel Ⓜ ❖
(480) 922-6969. **$139-$212.** 7300 E Gainey Suites Dr. Just e of Scottsdale and DoubleTree Ranch rds. Int corridors. **Pets:** Other. $150 one-time fee/room. Supervision.
ASK 🔊 ✕ 🖥 💻 🖨 ✕

◆◆◆ Hampton Inn-Oldtown Scottsdale Ⓜ
(480) 941-9400. **$89-$109.** 4415 N Civic Center Plaza. 0.2 mi e of Scottsdale Rd and just s of Camelback Rd, via 75th St. Ext/int corridors. **Pets:** Supervision.
ASK ✕ 🖥 💻 🖨

◆◆◆ Holiday Inn Hotel & Suites Ⓜ ❖
(480) 951-4000. **$159-$169.** 7515 E Butherus Dr. At Scottsdale Municipal Airport; 0.8 mi n of Thunderbird Rd, 0.5 mi e of Scottsdale Rd, on the s side of Butherus Dr. Ext corridors. **Pets:** Small. $25 deposit/room. No service, supervision, crate.
SAVE 🔊 ✕ 🎰 🖥 💻 🍴 🖨

◆◆◆ Holiday Inn Old Town Scottsdale Ⓜ
(480) 994-9203. **$130-$145.** 7353 E Indian School Rd. Just e of Scottsdale Rd, on s side of Indian School Rd. Ext corridors. **Pets:** Small. Supervision.
SAVE ✕ 🎰 🖥 💻 🍴 🖨 ✕

◆◆ Homestead Village Ⓜ
(480) 994-0297. **$85-$100.** 3560 N Marshall Way. Just w of Scottsdale Rd, just s of Goldwater. Ext corridors. **Pets:** Very small. Designated rooms, no service, supervision, crate.
ASK ✕ 🖥 🖨

◆◆◆ Homewood Suites Hotel Phoenix/Scottsdale Ⓜ ❖
(480) 368-8705. **$130-$130.** 9880 N Scottsdale Rd. 0.5 mi s of Shea Blvd. Int corridors. **Pets:** Medium, other. $150 one-time fee/pet. Supervision.
ASK 🔊 ✕ 🖥 💻 🖨

◆◆◆ Hospitality Suite Resort Ⓜ ❖
(480) 949-5115. **$129-$159.** 409 N Scottsdale Rd. Just n of McKellips, on e side of Scottsdale Rd. Ext corridors. **Pets:** Medium. $100 deposit/room. Supervision.
SAVE 🔊 ✕ 💻 🍴 🖨 ✕

◆◆ InnSuites Hotel Scottsdale Ⓜ ❖
(480) 941-1202. **$79-$99.** 7707 E McDowell Rd. Just w of Hayden Rd, on s side of McDowell Rd. Ext corridors. **Pets:** $25 deposit/pet, $25 one-time fee/pet. Supervision.
ASK 🔊 ✕ 🖥 💻 🍴 🖨 ✕

◆◆◆ La Quinta Inn & Suites Ⓜ
(480) 614-5300. **$99-$125.** 8888 E Shea Blvd. Just e of Pima Rd. Int corridors. **Pets:** Medium. Supervision.
SAVE ✕ 🎰 🎲 🖥 💻 🖨

◆◆◆◆◆ Marriott's Camelback Inn Resort, Golf Club & Spa 🆁
(480) 948-1700. **$255-$469.** 5402 E Lincoln Dr. 0.5 mi e of Tatum Blvd, on n side of Lincoln Dr. Ext corridors. **Pets:** Medium. No service, supervision, crate.
SAVE 🔊 ✕ 🎰 🎲 🖥 💻 🍴 🖨 ✕

◆◆◆ Marriott's Mountain Shadows Resort and Golf Club 🆁 ❖
(480) 948-7111. **$199-$229, 5 days notice.** 5641 E Lincoln Dr. 1 mi e of Tatum Blvd, on s side of Lincoln Dr. Ext corridors. **Pets:** Very small, dogs only. Supervision.
ASK 🔊 ✕ 🎰 🎲 🎲 🖥 💻 🍴 🖨 ✕

◆◆◆◆ The Phoenician 🆁 ❖
(480) 941-8200. **$525-$655, 7 days notice.** 6000 E Camelback Rd. 0.5 mi w of 64th St. Int corridors. **Pets:** Very small, other. Supervision.
✕ 🎲 🎲 🖥 💻 🍴 🖨 ✕

◆◆◆ Quality Inn and Suites Ⓜ ❖
(480) 675-7665. **$119-$139.** 3131 N Scottsdale Rd. Ne corner of Scottsdale Rd and Earll Dr. Int corridors. **Pets:** Medium. Designated rooms, supervision.
ASK 🔊 ✕ 🖥 💻 🖨

◆◆ Ramada Valley Ho Resort Ⓜ
(480) 945-6321. **$99-$129, 3 days notice.** 6850 Main St. 0.4 mi w of Scottsdale Rd, just s of Indian School Rd, on n side of Main St. Ext corridors. **Pets:** Medium. No service, supervision, crate.
✕ 🖥 💻 🍴 🖨 ✕

◆◆◆ Renaissance Cottonwoods Resort 🆁 ❖
(480) 991-1414. **$149-$279.** 6160 N Scottsdale Rd. Just n of McDonald Dr, on w side of Scottsdale Rd. Ext corridors. **Pets:** Medium. $50 deposit/room. Supervision.
SAVE 🔊 ✕ 🎲 💻 🍴 🖨 ✕

◆◆◆ Residence Inn by Marriott Ⓜ ❖
(480) 948-8666. **$149-$179.** 6040 N Scottsdale Rd. Nw corner Scottsdale Rd and McDonald Dr. Ext/int corridors. **Pets:** Small. $6 daily fee/pet, $50 one-time fee/room. Designated rooms, no service, supervision, crate.
ASK 🔊 ✕ 🎲 🎰 🖥 💻 🖨 ✕

◆◆ Scottsdale Pima Inn & Suites Ⓜ ❖
(480) 948-3800. **$99-$154.** 7330 N Pima Rd. 0.4 mi n of Indian Bend Rd, on w side of Pima Rd. Ext/int corridors. **Pets:** Other. $100 deposit/room. No service, supervision, crate.
SAVE 🔊 ✕ 🖥 💻 🖨

AAA ◆◆ **Sleep Inn** M ❀
(480) 998-9211. **$85-$103.** 16630 N Scottsdale Rd. Just s of Bell Rd. Int corridors. **Pets:** Small. $50 deposit/pet. Supervision.
SAVE S6 ✕ 🛢 💻 🖘

◆◆◆ **Summerfield Suites Hotel** M
(480) 946-7700. **$159-$189, 3 days notice.** 4245 N Civic Center Blvd. 0.3 mi e of Scottsdale Rd. Ext corridors. **Pets:** Small. Designated rooms, supervision.
ASK S6 ✕ 🛢 💻 🖘

SUN CITY/SUN CITY WEST

AAA ◆◆◆ **Best Western Inn & Suites of Sun City** M ❀
(623) 933-8211. **$80-$95.** 11201 Grand Ave. Sw side of Grand Ave (US 60), just nw of 111th Ave. Ext/int corridors. **Pets:** Medium, other. Designated rooms, supervision.
SAVE S6 ✕ 🐾 🛢 💻 🖘

SURPRISE

◆◆◆ **Quality Inn & Suites** M ❀
(623) 583-3500. **$99-$119.** 16741 N Greasewood St. 1 mi e of US 60 (Grand Ave). Int corridors. **Pets:** Small. $5 daily fee/pet. Designated rooms, no service, supervision, crate.
ASK S6 ✕ 🛢 💻 🖘

AAA ◆◆◆ **Windmill Inn at Sun City West** M ❀
(623) 583-0133. **$149.** 12545 W Bell Rd. 0.6 mi e of Dysart Rd, on s side of Bell Rd. Int corridors. **Pets:** Other. Supervision.
SAVE S6 ✕ 🐾 🛢 💻 🖘 ✕

TEMPE

AAA ◆◆◆ **AmeriSuites/Arizona Mills Mall** M ❀
(480) 831-9800. **$99-$129.** 1520 W Baseline Rd. From I-10 exit 155 (Baseline Rd), 0.4 mi e, nw corner Priest Dr. Int corridors. **Pets:** Other. Supervision.
SAVE S6 ✕ 🥾 🛢 💻 🖘

AAA ◆◆◆ **Best Western Inn of Tempe** M ❀
(480) 784-2233. **$112-$132.** 670 N Scottsdale Rd. Adjacent to s side of SR 202 Loop (Red Mountain Frwy), exit 7 (Scottsdale Rd). Int corridors. **Pets:** Medium, other. Designated rooms, supervision.
SAVE S6 ✕ 🛢 💻 🍴

◆◆ **Country Inn & Suites By Carlson** M ❀
(480) 345-8585. **$59-$109.** 1660 W Elliot Rd. Just e of I-10, exit Elliot Rd, on n side of Elliot Rd. Ext corridors. **Pets:** $250 deposit/room. Supervision.
ASK S6 ✕ 🐾 🛢 💻 🖘

AAA ◆◆◆ **Fiesta Inn** M ❀
(480) 967-1441. **$165-$185.** 2100 S Priest Dr. 0.5 mi e of I-10, at the sw corner of Priest Dr and Broadway Rd, enter from Priest Dr. Ext corridors. **Pets:** No service, supervision, crate.
SAVE S6 ✕ 🐾 🛢 💻 🍴 🖘 ✕

◆◆◆ **Hampton Inn & Suites** M ❀
(480) 675-9799. **$105-$125.** 1429 N Scottsdale Rd. Just s of McKellips Rd e side of Scottsdale Rd; 0.6 mi n of SR 202 (Red Mountain Frwy). Ext corridors. **Pets:** Small. $50 one-time fee/room. Supervision.
ASK S6 ✕ 🐾 🥾 🛢 💻 🖘 ✕

◆◆◆ **Holiday Inn** M ❀
(480) 968-3451. **$154-$164.** 915 E Apache Blvd. Se corner Apache Blvd and Rural Rd. Int corridors. **Pets:** Other. Supervision.
ASK S6 ✕ 🐾 🛢 💻 🍴 🖘

◆◆ **Holiday Inn Express/Tempe** M
(480) 820-7500. **$99-$129.** 5300 S Priest Dr. I-10 exit 155 (Baseline Rd), 0.4 mi e, just s on Priest Dr. Int corridors. **Pets:** Medium. No service, supervision, crate.
ASK S6 ✕ 🛢 💻 🖘

◆◆ **Homestead Village** M
(602) 414-4470. **$59-$59.** 4909 S Wendler Dr. From I-10 exit 155 (Baseline Rd), 0.4 mi nw. Ext corridors. **Pets:** Very small. No service, supervision, crate.
✕ 🛢 💻

◆◆ **Howard Johnson Express** M
(480) 736-1700. **$80-$90.** 1915 E Apache Blvd. 0.4 mi e of McClintock. Ext corridors. **Pets:** Supervision.
ASK S6 ✕ 🛢 💻 🖘

AAA ◆◆◆ **InnSuites Tempe/Phoenix Airport** M ❀
(480) 897-7900. **$99-$109.** 1651 W Baseline Rd. From I-10 exit 155 (Baseline Rd), just e. Ext corridors. **Pets:** Other. $25 one-time fee/room. Supervision.
SAVE S6 ✕ 🛢 💻 🍴 🖘 ✕

AAA ◆◆◆ **La Quinta Inn** M ❀
(480) 967-4465. **$89-$109.** 911 S 48th St. 0.8 mi n of I-10, eastbound exit 153 (SR 143), westbound exit 153A (SR 143); exit University Dr, on s side of University Dr and e side of SR 143 (Hohokam Expwy). Ext corridors. **Pets:** Medium. Supervision.
SAVE ✕ 🐾 🛢 💻 🖘 ✕

AAA ◆◆◆ **Mainstay Suites-Tempe** M ❀
(480) 557-8880. **$110-$130.** 2165 W 15th St. 0.3 mi ne of I-10, exit 153, Broadway Rd; then just nw on S 52nd St. Int corridors. **Pets:** Small. $100 deposit/room. Supervision.
SAVE S6 ✕ 🛢 🖘

◆◆ **Microtel Inn & Suites** M ❀
(480) 774-2500. **$59-$89, 3 days notice.** 1375 E University Dr. 0.5 mi e of Rural Rd. Int corridors. **Pets:** Medium. $50 one-time fee/room. Supervision.
ASK S6 ✕ 🛢 💻 🖘

AAA ◆◆ **Red Roof Inn Phoenix Airport** M
(480) 449-3205. **$49-$84.** 2135 W 15th St. 0.3 mi ne of I-10, exit 153, Broadway Rd, just nw on s 52nd St. Int corridors. **Pets:** Small. No service, supervision, crate.
SAVE ✕ 🛢 🖘

◆◆◆ **Residence Inn by Marriott** M ❀
(480) 756-2122. **$99-$179.** 5075 S Priest Dr. I-10 exit 155 (Baseline Rd), 0.4 mi e, just n on Priest Dr. Ext/int corridors. **Pets:** Small, other. $200 deposit/room, $6 daily fee/room, $50 one-time fee/room. Supervision.
ASK S6 ✕ 🛢 💻 🖘 ✕

(AAA) ◆◆ **Rodeway Inn Phoenix Airport East** [M]
(480) 967-3000. **$59-$79.** 1550 S 52nd St. 0.3 mi ne of I-10; exit 153, Broadway Rd. Ext corridors. **Pets:** Designated rooms, no service, supervision, crate.

[SAVE] [S] [X] [Ⓩ] [🗝] [💻] [🖼]

◆◆◆ **Tempe Mission Palms Hotel** [H]
(480) 894-1400. **$209-$299.** 60 E Fifth St. Just e of Mill Ave and 0.3 mi n of University Dr. Int corridors. **Pets:** Small. Designated rooms, no service, supervision, crate.

[ASK] [S] [X] [Ⓩ] [🗝] [🗝] [💻] [🍴] [🖼] [🖾]

◆◆ **Tempe Super 8** [M] ❀
(480) 967-8891. **$69-$99.** 1020 E Apache Blvd. Just e of Rural Rd. Ext corridors. **Pets:** Medium. $15 one-time fee/room. Designated rooms, no service, supervision, crate.

[ASK] [S] [X] [🗝] [🖼]

(AAA) ◆◆ **Tempe/University Travelodge** [M] ❀
(480) 968-7871. **$69-$89.** 1005 E Apache Blvd. Just e of Rural Rd, on s side of Apache Blvd. Ext corridors. **Pets:** Small. $4 daily fee/room. Designated rooms, no service, supervision, crate.

[SAVE] [S] [X] [Ⓩ] [🗝] [💻] [🖼]

❀   **END METROPOLITAN AREA**   ❀

PINETOP LAKESIDE

◆◆◆ **Bartram's White Mountain Bed & Breakfast** [BB]
(520) 367-1408. **Call for rates** (no credit cards). 1916 W Woodlake Lake Rd. 1.8 mi s of SR 260, via Woodland and Woodland Lake rds w. Int corridors. **Pets:** Designated rooms, supervision.

[X] [🔔] [CTV] [Ⓩ]

(AAA) ◆◆◆ **Holiday Inn Express** [M] ❀
(520) 367-6077. **$79-$109.** 431 E White Mountain Blvd. Int corridors. **Pets:** Small. No service, supervision, crate.

[SAVE] [X] [🗝] [💻]

◆◆ **Lazy Oaks Resort** [C] ❀
(520) 368-6203. **$62-$78** (no credit cards), 21 days notice. 1075 Larson Rd. 0.8 mi nw of Lakeside via SR 260, 1.3 mi s on Rainbow Lake Dr, then Larson Rd. Ext corridors. **Pets:** Medium. No service, supervision, crate.

[🗝] [🖾] [🔔] [Ⓩ]

◆◆◆ **Northwoods Resort** [C] ❀
(520) 367-2966. **$69-$139.** 165 E White Mountain Blvd. On SR 260. Ext corridors. **Pets:** $12 daily fee/pet, $12 one-time fee/pet. No service, supervision, crate.

[X] [🗝] [💻] [🖾] [🔔] [Ⓩ]

(AAA) ◆◆ **Woodland Inn & Suites** [M] ❀
(520) 367-3636. **$55-$109.** 458 E White Mountain Blvd. On SR 260. Ext corridors. **Pets:** Small, other. Designated rooms, no service, supervision, crate.

[SAVE] [S] [X] [🗝] [💻]

TOLLESON

(AAA) ◆◆ **Econo Lodge** [M]
(623) 936-4667. **$80-$90.** 1520 N 84th Dr. Adjacent and just n of I-10, at exit 135(83rd Ave); 0.5 mi n via McDowell St. Int corridors. **Pets:** Medium. Designated rooms, supervision.

[SAVE] [S] [X] [🗝] [Ⓩ] [🗝] [💻] [🖼]

YOUNGTOWN

(AAA) ◆ **Motel 6-22** [M]
(623) 977-1318. **$56-$72.** 11133 Grand Ave. Just w of 111th Ave on Grand Ave (US 60). Ext corridors. **Pets:** Supervision.

[S] [X] [🖼]

PRESCOTT

◆◆ **Best Western Prescottonian Motel** [MI] ❀
(520) 445-3096. **$59-$89.** 1317 E Gurley St. On SR 89 (Gurley St) 1.2 mi e of Montezuma St. Ext corridors. **Pets:** Small. Designated rooms, no service, supervision, crate.

[ASK] [S] [X] [Ⓩ] [🗝] [💻] [🍴]

◆◆ **Lynx Creek Farm Bed & Breakfast** [BB] ❀
(520) 778-9573. **$85-$155.** 5555 Onyx Dr. 5.5 mi e on SR 69 from jct SR 69 and SR 89 to Onyx Dr, then 0.5 mi (dirt/gravel road). Ext corridors. **Pets:** Other. $10 daily fee/pet. No service, supervision, crate.

[X] [💻] [CTV] [Ⓩ]

(AAA) ◆ **Motel 6-166** [M]
(520) 776-0160. **$42-$58.** 1111 E Sheldon St. 0.5 mi e of Montezuma St. Ext corridors. **Pets:** Supervision.

[S] [X] [🖾] [🖼]

◆◆ **Prescott Super 8 Motel** [M] ❀
(520) 776-1282. **$49-$69.** 1105 E Sheldon St. E end of town off Gurley. Int corridors. **Pets:** Dogs only. $10 daily fee/room. Supervision.

[ASK] [S] [X] [Ⓩ] [🗝] [🖼]

PRESCOTT VALLEY

(AAA) ◆◆ **Days Inn/Prescott Valley** [M] ❀
(520) 772-8600. **$59-$95.** 7875 E Hwy 69. 0.3 mi w of Robert Rd. Ext corridors. **Pets:** Other. $50 deposit/room. Supervision.

[SAVE] [S] [X] [🗝] [🖼]

RIO RICO

⟨AAA⟩ ◆◆◆◆ Rio Rico Resort & Country Club [R]
(520) 281-1901. **$165-$185.** 1069 Camino Caralampi. 8 mi n of Nogales on I-19, exit 17, Rio Rico Dr; then 0.5 mi w. Ext corridors. **Pets:** No service, supervision, crate.
[SAVE] [S⊄] [✕] [⟨⟩] [⟨⟩] [🖥] [🖳] [¶] [🛏] [✕]

SAFFORD

⟨AAA⟩ ◆◆ Best Western Desert Inn [M] ✿
(520) 428-0521. **$53-$59.** 1391 W Thatcher Blvd. US 70, 1 mi w of jct US 191. Ext corridors. **Pets:** Medium. No service, supervision, crate.
[SAVE] [S⊄] [✕] [🖥] [🖳] [🛏]

◆◆ Comfort Inn [M] ✿
(520) 428-5851. **$46-$78.** 1578 W Thatcher Blvd. On US 70, 1.3 mi w of jct US 191. Ext corridors. **Pets:** Medium. No service, supervision, crate.
[ASK] [S⊄] [✕] [🖥] [🖳] [🛏]

◆◆◆ Days Inn [M]
(520) 428-5000. **$65-$120.** 520 E Hwy 70. 0.5 mi e on US 70 and US 171. Ext corridors. **Pets:** Small. Designated rooms, no service, supervision, crate.
[ASK] [S⊄] [✕] [⟨⟩] [⟨⟩] [⟨⟩] [🖥] [🖳] [🛏]

◆◆◆ Ramada Inn-Spa Resort [MI]
(520) 428-3200. **$80-$150.** 420 E Hwy 70. 0.5 mi e on US 70 and US 191. Ext/int corridors. **Pets:** Small. Designated rooms, no service, supervision, crate.
[ASK] [S⊄] [✕] [⟨⟩] [⟨⟩] [🖥] [🖳] [🛏]

SEDONA

⟨AAA⟩ ◆◆◆ Best Western Inn of Sedona [M] ✿
(520) 282-3072. **$125-$125.** 1200 W Hwy 89A. 1.2 mi w of SR 179. Ext corridors. **Pets:** Other. $10 one-time fee/room. Designated rooms, no service, supervision, crate.
[SAVE] [S⊄] [✕] [🖥] [🖳] [🛏]

⟨AAA⟩ ◆◆◆ Desert Quail Inn [M]
(520) 284-1433. **$64-$149.** 6626 Hwy 179. 6.5 mi w of SR 179. Ext corridors. **Pets:** Small. Supervision.
[SAVE] [S⊄] [✕] [🖥] [🖳] [🛏]

⟨AAA⟩ ◆◆◆ Hawthorn Suites Ltd Bell Rock inn [MI]
(520) 282-4161. **$59-$139.** 6246 Hwy 179. 6 mi s of SR 89A, in Village of Oak Creek. Ext/int corridors. **Pets:** Small. Designated rooms, no service, supervision, crate.
[SAVE] [S⊄] [✕] [🖥] [🖳] [¶] [🛏]

⟨AAA⟩ ◆◆◆ Matterhorn Lodge [M] ✿
(520) 282-7176. **$74-$104, 48 days notice.** 230 Apple Ave. Just w of SR 89A in the Uptown Sedona shopping area. Ext corridors. **Pets:** Other. Designated rooms, no service, supervision, crate.
[✕] [🖥] [🖳] [🛏]

⟨AAA⟩ ◆◆◆ Quality Inn-King's Ransom [MI]
(520) 282-7151. **$79-$149.** 771 Hwy 179. 0.8 mi s of SR 89A. Ext/int corridors. **Pets:** Medium. No service, supervision, crate.
[SAVE] [S⊄] [✕] [🖥] [🖳] [¶] [🛏]

⟨AAA⟩ ◆◆◆ Sky Ranch Lodge [M] ✿
(520) 282-6400. **$75-$180.** Airport Rd. 1 mi w of jct SR 89A and SR 179, 1 mi s on Airport Rd, on w side. Ext corridors. **Pets:** Medium. $10 daily fee/pet. Designated rooms, no service, supervision, crate.
[✕] [🖥] [🖳] [🛏]

⟨AAA⟩ ◆◆ Village Lodge [M] ✿
(520) 284-3626. **$45-$49, 3 days notice.** 78 Bell Rock Blvd. 6 mi s on SR 179, just w on Bell Rock Blvd; in Village of Oak Creek. Ext/int corridors. **Pets:** Medium, other. Supervision.
[SAVE] [S⊄] [✕] [🖥] [🖳]

SELIGMAN

◆ Historic Route 66 Motel [M] ✿
(520) 422-3204. **$47-$67.** 500 W Hwy 66. I-40, exit 121. Ext corridors. **Pets:** $25 deposit/room. Designated rooms, no service, supervision, crate.
[ASK] [S⊄] [✕] [🖳]

SHOW LOW

⟨AAA⟩ ◆◆ Days Inn [M] ✿
(520) 537-4356. **$57-$65.** 480 W Deuce of Clubs Ave. 1.3 mi w on US 60 and SR 260. Ext/int corridors. **Pets:** Small. $5 daily fee/pet. No service, supervision, crate.
[SAVE] [S⊄] [✕] [⟨⟩] [🖥] [¶] [🛏]

⟨AAA⟩ ◆◆ Kiva Motel [M]
(520) 537-4542. **$40-$59.** 261 E Deuce of Clubs Ave. 0.5 mi w on US 60 and SR 260. Ext corridors. **Pets:** Small. No service, supervision, crate.
[SAVE] [S⊄] [✕] [🖥] [🖳]

◆ Motel 6 [M]
(520) 537-7694. **$46-$62.** 1941 E Deuce of Clubs Ave. US 60, 0.5 mi e of jct SR 260. Ext corridors. **Pets:** Medium. No service, supervision, crate.
[S⊄] [✕] [🖥]

⟨AAA⟩ ◆ Snowy River Motel [M] ✿
(520) 537-2926. **$34-$39.** 1640 E Deuce of Clubs Ave. US 60, just e of jct SR 260. Ext corridors. **Pets:** Small, dogs only. $5 daily fee/pet, $5 one-time fee/pet. Supervision.
[S⊄] [✕] [🖳]

SIERRA VISTA

⟨AAA⟩ ◆◆◆ Best Western Mission Inn [M] ✿
(520) 458-8500. **$57-$77.** 3460 E Fry Blvd. Just w of jct SR 90 and 92. Ext corridors. **Pets:** Medium, other. No service, supervision, crate.
[SAVE] [S⊄] [✕] [⟨⟩] [🖥] [🖳] [🛏]

◆◆◆ Sierra Suites [M] ✿
(520) 459-4221. **$79-$79.** 391 E Fry Blvd. 2.5 mi w of jct SR 90 and SR 92. Ext corridors. **Pets:** $25 one-time fee/room. Supervision.
[ASK] [S⊄] [✕] [🖥] [🛏]

◆◆ Super 8 Motel [M]
(520) 459-5380. **$49-$69.** 100 Fab Ave. Just e of main entrance to Fort Huachuca. Ext corridors. **Pets:** Designated rooms, no service, supervision, crate.
[ASK] [S⊄] [✕] [⟨⟩] [🖥] [🛏]

(AAA) ◆◆◆ Thunder Mountain Inn **M** ❀
(520) 458-7900. **$55-$75.** 1631 S Hwy 92. SR 92, 1 mi s of jct SR 90. Int corridors. **Pets:** Other. Supervision.
[SAVE] [⛽] [✕] [🛏] [📺] [☕]

(AAA) ◆◆◆ Windemere Hotel & Conference Center **M** ❀
(520) 459-5900. **$78-$86, 3 days notice.** 2047 S Hwy 92. SR 92, 1.5 mi s of jct SR 90. Int corridors. **Pets:** Other. $50 deposit/room. Supervision.
[SAVE] [⛽] [✕] [🛏] [📺] [☕]

SPRINGERVILLE

(AAA) ◆ Super 8 Motel **M** ❀
(520) 333-2655. **$37-$60.** 138 W Main St. Just w on Main St (US 60/180). Ext corridors. **Pets:** Other. $5 one-time fee/room. No service, supervision, crate.
[SAVE] [⛽] [✕] [🛏] [📺]

ST. JOHNS

(AAA) ◆◆ Super 8 **M** ❀
(520) 337-2990. **$36-$44, 7 days notice.** 75 E Commercial. Downtown. Ext corridors. **Pets:** Other. $25 deposit/room. Designated rooms, no service, supervision, crate.
[SAVE] [✕] [🛏]

TAYLOR

(AAA) ◆◆ Silver Creek Inn **M** ❀
(520) 536-2600. **$46-$65.** 825 N Main St. 0.6 mi n on SR 77. Ext corridors. **Pets:** Small. $20 one-time fee/room. Designated rooms, no service, supervision, crate.
[SAVE] [⛽] [✕] [🛏] [📺]

TOMBSTONE

◆ Tombstone Motel **M** ❀
(520) 457-3478. **$45-$70.** 502 E Fremont St. On SR 80, in center of town. Ext corridors. **Pets:** Medium. $25 deposit/ pet. Supervision.
[ASK] [✕] [🛏]

(AAA) ◆◆ Trail Riders Inn **M**
(520) 457-3573. **$35-$45.** 13 N 7th St. Ext corridors. **Pets:** Small. Designated rooms, supervision.
[✕]

TUBA CITY

◆◆ Quality Inn Tuba City **M** ❀
(520) 283-4545. **$85-$135.** Main & Moenave. On Main St (US 160), 1 mi n of jct US 160 and SR 264, adjacent to historic Tuba Trading Post. Int corridors. **Pets:** Medium. $25 deposit/pet. Designated rooms, no service, supervision, crate.
[ASK] [⛽] [✕] [🛏] [📺] [🍴]

TUBAC

◆◆◆ Tubac Golf Resort **R** ❀
(520) 398-2211. **$135-$145, 7 days notice.** 1 Otero Rd. E of I-19 between exits 34 and 40. Ext corridors. **Pets:** Medium. $15 daily fee/pet. Designated rooms, supervision.
[✕] [🛏] [📺] [☕] [✕] [CTV]

TUCSON METROPOLITAN AREA

GREEN VALLEY

(AAA) ◆◆◆ Best Western Green Valley **M**
(520) 625-2250. **$79-$129.** 111 S La Canada Dr. 0.5 mi sw of I-19, exit 65, Esperanza Rd. Int corridors. **Pets:** Supervision.
[SAVE] [⛽] [✕] [🛏] [📺] [🍴] [☕]

◆◆ Holiday Inn Express **M**
(520) 625-0900. **$119-$139, 5 days notice.** 19200 S I-19 Frontage Rd. Adjacent to I-19, exit 69, Duval Mine Rd. Int corridors. **Pets:** Medium. Supervision.
[ASK] [✕] [🛏] [📺] [☕]

TUCSON

◆◆◆ Baymont Inn **M**
(520) 624-3200. **$84-$90, 7 days notice.** 1560 W Grant Rd. Just w of I-10, exit 256 (Grant Rd). Int corridors. **Pets:** Medium. Supervision.
[ASK] [⛽] [✕] [🛏] [📺] [☕]

◆◆ Baymont Inn & Suites-Tucson Airport **M** ❀
(520) 889-6600. **$70-$110.** 2548 E Medina Rd. Just n of entrance to Tucson International Airport. Int corridors. **Pets:** Small. $20 deposit/room, $5 daily fee/room. Supervision.
[ASK] [⛽] [✕] [♿] [❓] [🛏] [📺] [☕]

◆◆ Best Western Executive Inn **M** ❀
(520) 791-7551. **$65-$85.** 333 W Drachman St. I-10,Speedway Blvd exit; 0.5 mi e to Main St, then 0.3 mi n. Int corridors. **Pets:** Designated rooms, supervision.
[ASK] [⛽] [✕] [🛏] [🍴] [☕]

(AAA) ◆◆◆ Best Western InnSuites-Catalina **M** ❀
(520) 297-8111. **$119-$189.** 6201 N Oracle Rd. On Oracle Rd (SR 77), just s of Orange Grove Rd. Ext corridors. **Pets:** Small. $25 deposit/room. No service, supervision, crate.
[SAVE] [⛽] [✕] [🛏] [📺] [☕] [✕]

◆ Candlelight Suites **M** ❀
(520) 747-1440. **$65-$70.** 1440 S Craycroft Rd. Just s of 22nd St. Ext corridors. **Pets:** Small. $50 deposit/room. No service, supervision, crate.
[ASK] [⛽] [✕] [🛏] [☕]

◆◆◆ Clarion Santa Rita Hotel & Suites **M** ❀
(520) 622-4000. **$99-$159, 7 days notice.** 88 E Broadway. Downtown, 0.6 mi e of I-10, Broadway/Congress exit 258. Int corridors. **Pets:** Medium. $50 one-time fee/room. No service, supervision, crate.
[ASK] [⛽] [✕] [🛏] [📺] [☕]

◆◆◆ **Comfort Suites** Ⓜ ❖
(520) 888-6676. **$130.** 515 W Auto Mall Dr. Just w of SR 77 (Oracle Rd) and Tucson Mall. Int corridors. **Pets:** Medium, other. $10 one-time fee/room. No service, supervision, crate.

ASK Ⓢ ✕ 🖃 💻 🕭

◆◆◆ **DoubleTree Guest Suites-Tucson** Ⓜ❗ ❖
(520) 721-7100. **$127-$127.** 6555 E Speedway Blvd. Just e of Wilmot Rd. Ext corridors. **Pets:** Small, other. $25 one-time fee/room. No service, supervision, crate.

✕ 🖃 💻 🍴 🕭

◆◆◆ **Doubletree Hotel at Reid Park** Ⓗ ❖
(520) 881-4200. **$119-$139.** 445 S Alvernon Way. Just s of Broadway Blvd. Ext/int corridors. **Pets:** Medium, other. $50 deposit/room. Supervision.

ASK Ⓢ ✕ ⟳ 🖃 💻 🍴 🕭 ✕

Ⓐ ◆◆◆ **Embassy Suites Hotel-Broadway** Ⓜ
(520) 745-2700. **$109-$159.** 5335 E Broadway. Ext corridors. **Pets:** Medium. No service, supervision, crate.

SAVE Ⓢ ✕ 🖃 💻 🕭

◆◆◆ **Four Points Hotel By Sheraton** Ⓜ❗
(520) 622-6611. **$89-$99, 5 days notice.** 350 S Freeway. Adjacent to I-10, exit 258 (Congress St). Ext/int corridors. **Pets:** Small. No service, supervision, crate.

ASK Ⓢ ✕ ⟳ ⟳ ⌂ 🖃 💻 🍴 🕭

Ⓐ ◆◆ **Ghost Ranch Lodge** Ⓜ❗ ❖
(520) 791-7565. **$69-$99.** 801 W Miracle Mile. 1 mi e of I-10, exit 255, Miracle Mile; just w of Oracle Rd (SR77). Ext corridors. **Pets:** Other. Supervision.

SAVE Ⓢ ✕ 🖃 💻 🍴 🕭

Ⓐ ◆◆◆◆ **The Golf Villas at Oro Valley** ⒸⓄ ❖
(520) 498-0098. **$489.** 10950 N La Canada. I-10, exit Ina Rd E, 4 mi to La Canada, then 4.5 mi n. Ext corridors. **Pets:** Medium, other. No service, supervision, crate.

SAVE Ⓢ ✕ 🖃 💻 🕭

Ⓐ ◆◆◆ **Hampton Inn North** Ⓜ ❖
(520) 206-0602. **$69-$130.** 1375 W Grant Rd. Grant Rd, just w of I-10, exit 256. Int corridors. **Pets:** Medium, other. No service, supervision, crate.

SAVE Ⓢ ✕ ⌂ ⟳ 🖃 💻 🕭

◆◆◆ **Hawthorn Suites LTD** Ⓜ ❖
(520) 298-2300. **$99-$139.** 7007 E Tanque Verde Rd. Just w of Sabino Canyon Rd. Ext corridors. **Pets:** Small. $25 one-time fee/pet. No service, supervision, crate.

ASK Ⓢ ✕ 🖃 💻 🕭

◆◆◆ **Holiday Inn-City Center** Ⓗ
(520) 624-8711. **$107-$127.** 181 W Broadway. Just e of I-10, Congress St/Broadway exit 258. Int corridors. **Pets:** No service, supervision, crate.

ASK Ⓢ ✕ 🖃 💻 🍴 🕭

◆◆ **Inn Suites Hotel & Resort** Ⓜ❗ ❖
(520) 622-3000. **$75-$125.** 475 N Granada Ave. Adjacent and just e of I-10, St Mary's Rd exit. Ext/int corridors. **Pets:** Other. $50 deposit/room. Supervision.

ASK Ⓢ ✕ 🖃 💻 🍴 🕭 ✕

Ⓐ ◆ **Knights Inn** Ⓜ
(520) 624-8291. **$99-$119.** 720 W 29th St. W side I-10, exit 22nd St (exit 259) then 0.5 mi s, then just w on 29th St. Ext corridors. **Pets:** Small. No service, supervision, crate.

SAVE Ⓢ ✕ 🕭

Ⓐ ◆◆◆ **La Quinta Inn & Suites Airport** Ⓜ ❖
(520) 573-3333. **$89-$109.** 7001 S Tucson Blvd. Just n of Tucson International Airport. Int corridors. **Pets:** Medium, other. Supervision.

SAVE ✕ ⌂ ⟳ 🖃 💻 🕭

Ⓐ ◆◆◆ **La Quinta Inn-East** Ⓜ ❖
(520) 747-1414. **$75-$95.** 6404 E Broadway. Just e of Wilmot Rd. Ext corridors. **Pets:** Small, other. No service, supervision, crate.

SAVE Ⓢ ✕ 🖃 💻 🕭

Ⓐ ◆◆ **La Quinta Inn-West** Ⓜ
(520) 622-6491. **$79-$99.** 665 N Frwy. W side of I-10, St Mary's Rd exit. Ext corridors. **Pets:** Large. Supervision.

SAVE ✕ 🖃 💻 🕭

Ⓐ ◆◆ **Red Roof Inn Tucson North** Ⓜ
(520) 744-8199. **$66-$91.** 4940 W Ina Rd. Just w of I-10, Ina Rd exit 248. Int corridors. **Pets:** Small. Supervision.

SAVE ✕ ⟳ 🕭

Ⓐ ◆◆ **Red Roof Inn-Tucson South** Ⓜ❗ ❖
(520) 571-1400. **$66-$91.** 3700 E Irvington Rd. 5 mi se on I-10, exit Palo Verde Rd; westbound exit 264, eastbound exit 264B, just e of Palo Verde Rd. Ext corridors. **Pets:** Small, other. Supervision.

SAVE ✕ 🖃 🕭

◆◆◆ **Residence Inn By Marriott** Ⓐ
(520) 721-0991. **$149-$189.** 6477 E Speedway Blvd. Just e of Wilmot Rd. Ext corridors. **Pets:** Small. No service, supervision, crate.

ASK Ⓢ ✕ ⟳ 🖃 💻 🕭 ✕

Ⓐ ◆◆ **Rodeway Inn I-10 & Grant Rd** Ⓜ❗ ❖
(520) 622-7791. **$50-$89.** 1365 W Grant Rd. Just w of I-10, Grant Rd exit 256. Ext corridors. **Pets:** Large, other. $10 one-time fee/room. Supervision.

SAVE Ⓢ ✕ ⟳ 🖃 💻 🍴 🕭

Ⓐ ◆ **Rodeway Inn-Park Ave at I-10** Ⓜ ❖
(520) 884-5800. **$99-$120.** 810 E Benson Hwy. Just s of I-10, Park Ave/Benson Hwy exit 262. Ext corridors. **Pets:** Medium, other. $25 deposit/room. Supervision.

SAVE Ⓢ ✕ 🖃 💻 🕭

Ⓐ ◆◆◆ **Sheraton El Conquistador** Ⓡ
(520) 544-5000. **$354-$469, 7 days notice.** 10000 N Oracle Rd. SR 77, 3.5 mi n of Ina Rd. Ext/int corridors. **Pets:** Small. No service, supervision, crate.

SAVE Ⓢ ✕ 🖃 💻 🍴 🕭 ✕

Ⓐ ◆◆ **Studio 6** Ⓜ ❖
(520) 746-0030. **Call for rates.** 4950 S Outlet Center Rd. Adjacent to I-10; exit 264 eastbound, exit 264B; just w of Palo Vere Rd and s of Irvington Rd. Ext corridors. **Pets:** Small. $25 one-time fee/pet. No service, supervision, crate.

✕ 🖃 💻 🕭

AAA ◆◆◆ Wayward Winds Lodge M ❖
(520) 791-7526. **$69-$99, 3 days notice.** 707 W Miracle Mile. 1.2 mi e of I-10, exit 255, Miracle Mile; just w of Oracle Rd (SR 77). Ext corridors. **Pets:** Medium. $25 deposit/room, $5 one-time fee/pet. Designated rooms, supervision.
SAVE 🔊 ✕ 🔒 💻 🖼

AAA ◆◆◆◆ Westward Look Resort R
(520) 297-1151. **$200-$299, 7 days notice.** 245 E Ina Rd. 0.5 mi e on Ina Rd from Oracle Rd (SR 77), just n on Westward Look Dr. Ext corridors. **Pets:** Designated rooms, no service, supervision, crate.
SAVE 🔊 ✕ ✏ ♿ 🔒 💻 🍴 🖼 ✕

AAA ◆◆◆ Windmill Inn at St. Philip's Plaza M
(520) 577-0007. **$145.** 4250 N Campbell Ave. Se corner Campbell Ave and River Rd. Int corridors. **Pets:** Designated rooms, no service, supervision, crate.
SAVE 🔊 ✕ ♿ 🔒 🖼 ✕

❖ **End Metropolitan Area** ❖

WICKENBURG

AAA ◆◆ Best Western Rancho Grande M ❖
(520) 684-5445. **$66-$101.** 293 E Wickenburg Way. Center on Wickenburg Way (US 60). Ext corridors. **Pets:** Other. Supervision.
SAVE 🔊 ✕ 🔒 💻 🖼 ✕

◆◆ Super 8 Motel M ❖
(520) 684-0808. **$55-$75, 3 days notice.** 925 N Tegner. 1 mi n of US 60, on Hwy 93. Ext/int corridors. **Pets:** Other. $5 daily fee/pet. Designated rooms, supervision.
ASK 🔊 ✕ 🔒 💻

WILLCOX

AAA ◆◆◆ Best Western Plaza Inn M
(520) 384-3556. **$59-$59.** 1100 W Rex Allen Dr. Just s of I-10, exit 340. Ext corridors. **Pets:** Designated rooms, no service, supervision, crate.
SAVE 🔊 ✕ ♿ 🔒 💻 🍴 🖼

AAA ◆◆ Days Inn M ❖
(520) 384-4222. **$40-$55.** 724 N Bisbee Ave. Adjacent to I-10, exit 340. Ext corridors. **Pets:** Medium, other. $5 daily fee/room, $5 one-time fee/pet. Supervision.
SAVE 🔊 ✕ 🔒 🖼

WILLIAMS

AAA ◆ Arizona Welcome Inn & Suites M
(520) 635-9127. **$45-$59.** 750 N Grand Canyon Blvd. Just s of I-40, exit 163. Int corridors. **Pets:** Small. Designated rooms, supervision.
SAVE 🔊 ✕ 🔒

AAA ◆ Budget Host Inn M ❖
(520) 635-4415. **$30-$48.** 620 W Route 66. On I-40 Business Loop; 1 mi e of I-40 exit 161. Ext corridors. **Pets:** Very small. $5 daily fee/pet, $5 one-time fee/pet. Designated rooms, no service, supervision, crate.
SAVE 🔊 ✕ 🔒

AAA ◆◆ El Rancho Motel M
(520) 635-2552. **$52-$72.** 617 E Rt 66. On I-40 business loop, from I-40 exit 163, 0.8 mi s, then just e on Rt 66. Ext corridors. **Pets:** Supervision.
SAVE 🔊 ✕ 🔒 💻 🖼

AAA ◆ Highlander Motel M ❖
(520) 635-2541. **$40-$45.** 533 W Route 66. On I-40 business loop; 1.2 mi e of I-40, exit 161. Ext corridors. **Pets:** Medium, other. $5 daily fee/pet, $5 one-time fee/pet. No service, supervision, crate.
SAVE 🔊 ✕

AAA ◆◆◆ Holiday Inn M ❖
(520) 635-4114. **$79-$119.** 950 N Grand Canyon Blvd. Adjacent to I-40, exit 163. Int corridors. **Pets:** Other. Supervision.
SAVE ✕ ♿ ✏ ♿ 🔒 💻 🍴 🖼

◆◆ Motel 6 Countryside M
(520) 635-4464. **$36-$67.** 710 W Route 66. On I-40 business loop; 1.2 mi e of I-40 exit 161. Int corridors. **Pets:** Medium. No service, supervision, crate.
ASK 🔊 ✕ 🔒

◆◆ Motel 6-4010 M
(520) 635-9000. **$38-$69.** 831 W Rt 66 Ave. On I-40 business loop, 1 mi e of I-40 exit 161. Int corridors. **Pets:** No service, supervision, crate.
ASK 🔊 ✕ 🖼

◆◆◆ Mountain Side Inn M
(520) 635-4431. **$76-$86.** 642 E RT 66. On I-40 business loop, from I-40 exit 163, 0.6 mi s, then just e on Rt 66. Ext corridors. **Pets:** No service, supervision, crate.
ASK 🔊 ✕ 💻 🍴 🖼 ✕

AAA ◆◆◆ Quality Inn-Mountain Ranch M ❖
(520) 635-2693. **$89-$109.** 6701 E Mountain Ranch Rd. 8 mi e, adjacent to I-40, Deer Farm Rd, exit 171. Ext corridors. **Pets:** Other. $20 one-time fee/room. Designated rooms, no service, supervision, crate.
SAVE 🔊 ✕ 🔒 💻 🍴 🖼 ✕

AAA ◆ Route 66 Inn M ❖
(520) 635-4791. **$40-$70.** 128 E Route 66. I-40 exit 163, then .5 mi to Route 66, then .1 mi e. Ext corridors. **Pets:** Small, dogs only. $5 one-time fee/room. No service, supervision, crate.
SAVE 🔊 ✕ 🔒

◆◆ Super 8 Motel M
(520) 635-4045. **$59-$89.** 911 W RT 66 Ave. On w side of I-40 business loop; 1 mi e of I-40 exit 161. Int corridors. **Pets:** Designated rooms, no service, supervision, crate.
ASK 🔊 ✕ 🔒 💻 🖼

◆ The Westerner Motel
(520) 635-4312. **$38-$48.** 530 W Rt 66. On I-40 business loop; 1.3 mi e of I-40, exit 161. Ext corridors. **Pets:** Small, other. $20 deposit/room. No service, supervision, crate.
☐☐☐☐

WINDOW ROCK

◆◆ Navajo Nation Inn
(520) 871-4108. **$57-$62.** 48 W Hwy 264. 34 mi e of SR 191 on SR 264. Ext corridors. **Pets:** Small. No service, supervision, crate.
☐☐☐

WINSLOW

◆◆◆ Best Western Adobe Inn
(520) 289-4638. **$50-$67.** 1701 North Park Dr. Adjacent to I-40, exit 253. Int corridors. **Pets:** Small, other. Supervision.
☐☐☐☐☐☐☐

◆◆◆ Days Inn
(520) 289-1010. **$39-$95.** 2035 W Hwy 66. Just s of I-40, exit 252. Int corridors. **Pets:** Small. $20 deposit/room. No service, supervision, crate.
☐☐☐☐

◆ Econo Lodge
(520) 289-4687. **$45-$79, 5 days notice.** 1706 N Park Dr. Adjacent to I-40, exit 253. Ext corridors. **Pets:** Small, other. $5 one-time fee/room. Supervision.
☐☐☐☐☐☐☐

◆◆ Holiday Inn Express
(520) 289-2960. **Call for rates.** 816 Transcon Ln. From I-40 n side at exit 255. Int corridors. **Pets:** Other. Supervision.
☐☐☐☐

◆◆◆ La Posada Hotel
(520) 289-4366. **$69-$99, 7 days notice.** 303 E 2nd St. I-40, exit 252, s to Rt 66 (2nd St), then 0.5 mi e at jct SR 87 and Historic Rt 66. Int corridors. **Pets:** No service, supervision, crate.
☐☐☐☐☐☐

◆◆ Motel 6 Winslow
(520) 289-9581. **$40-$50.** 520 W Desmond St. Just w on North Park Dr, just s of I-40, exit 253. Int corridors. **Pets:** Small. Supervision.
☐☐☐☐☐☐

◆◆ Super 8 Motel
(520) 289-4606. **$46-$58.** 1916 W Third St. Just e of I-40, exit 252. Int corridors. **Pets:** Other. $15 deposit/room. Designated rooms, no service, supervision, crate.
☐☐☐

◆◆ Town House Lodge
(520) 289-4611. **Call for rates.** 1914 W Third St. 0.5 mi e of I-40 exit 252. Ext corridors. **Pets:** Medium. Supervision.
☐☐☐☐☐

YUMA

◆◆ Airport Travelodge
(520) 726-4721. **$54-$84.** 711 E 32nd St. I-8 Business Loop; 2.3 mi se of jct US 95. Ext corridors. **Pets:** No service, supervision, crate.
☐☐☐☐☐☐

◆◆◆ Best Western Coronado
(520) 783-4453. **$72-$150, 7 days notice.** 233 4th Ave. I-8 business loop; From I-8, eastbound exit 4th Ave, 0.5 mi s; westbound exit 1 (Giss Pkwy), 0.5 mi w. Ext corridors. **Pets:** No service, supervision, crate.
☐☐☐☐☐☐☐

◆◆◆ Best Western InnSuites Hotel & Suites
(520) 783-8341. **$99-$99.** 1450 Castle Dome Ave. Just ne of I-8, at jct SR 95 (16th St). Ext corridors. **Pets:** Small. $25 deposit/room. No service, supervision, crate.
☐☐☐☐☐☐☐☐

◆◆◆ Comfort Inn
(520) 782-1200. **$70-$99.** 1691 S Riley Ave. 0.5 mi w of I-8, exit US 95 (16th St). Int corridors. **Pets:** Medium. Supervision.
☐☐☐☐☐☐☐

◆◆◆ Holiday Inn Express
(520) 344-1420. **$72-$82.** 3181 S 4th Ave. On I-8 business loop, 2 mi s of jct US 95, at 32nd St. Ext corridors. **Pets:** Medium. No service, supervision, crate.
☐☐☐☐☐

◆◆◆ Radisson Suites Inn Yuma
(520) 726-4830. **$119-$179.** 2600 S 4th Ave. I-8 business loop; 1.2 mi s of jct US 95. Ext corridors. **Pets:** Medium. No service, supervision, crate.
☐☐☐☐☐

◆◆◆ Shilo Conference Hotel
(520) 782-9511. **$79-$150.** 1550 S Castle Dome Ave. Just ne of I-8, at jct SR 95 (16th St). Int corridors. **Pets:** Medium. $10 daily fee/pet, $10 one-time fee/pet. Designated rooms, no service, supervision, crate.
☐☐☐☐☐☐☐

◆◆ Yuma Cabana Motel
(520) 783-8311. **$56-$74.** 2151 S 4th Ave. I-8 business loop; 0.6 mi s of jct US 95. Int corridors. **Pets:** Medium. Designated rooms, no service, supervision, crate.
☐☐☐☐☐

◆◆ Yuma Super 8 Motel
(520) 782-2000. **$73-$93.** 1688 S Riley Ave. Just w of I-8, exit US 95 (16th St). Int corridors. **Pets:** Supervision.
☐☐☐☐☐☐

ARKADELPHIA

AAA ◆◆◆ Best Western-Continental Inn M ☼
(870) 246-5592. **$65-$65.** 136 Valley Rd. I-30, exit 78. Ext corridors. **Pets:** Large, other. No service, supervision, crate.
[SAVE] [S☐] [✕] [✍] [🖥] [💻] [🖨] [✕]

BATESVILLE

◆◆◆ Ramada Inn of Batesville MI ☼
(870) 698-1800. **$62-$68.** 1325 N St Louis St. 1 mi n on US 67/167. Ext corridors. **Pets:** Medium. $20 deposit/room. No service, supervision, crate.
[ASK] [S☐] [✕] [🖥] [💻] [🍴] [🖨]

BENTON

◆◆◆ Best Western Inn M
(501) 778-9695. **$46-$70.** 17036 I-30. I-30, exit 117, on w service road. Ext/int corridors. **Pets:** No service, supervision, crate.
[ASK] [S☐] [✕] [🖥] [💻] [🖨]

◆◆ Days Inn M
(501) 776-3200. **$50-$55.** 17701 I-30. I-30, exit 118, on e service road. Ext corridors. **Pets:** Supervision.
[ASK] [S☐] [✕] [✍] [🖥] [💻] [🖨]

AAA ◆◆ Econo Lodge M ☼
(501) 776-1515. **$32-$40.** 1221 Hot Springs Rd. I-30, exit 117. Int corridors. **Pets:** Medium. $5 daily fee/pet. Designated rooms, no service, supervision, crate.
[SAVE] [S☐] [✕] [🖥] [💻]

AAA ◆◆◆ Ramada Inn MI ☼
(501) 776-1900. **$44-$59, 7 days notice.** 16732 I-30. I-30, exit 117. Ext corridors. **Pets:** Small. $6 daily fee/pet, $6 one-time fee/pet. No service, supervision, crate.
[SAVE] [S☐] [✕] [✍] [🖥] [🍴] [🖨]

AAA ◆ Scottish Inn M
(501) 778-4591. **$32-$38, 7 days notice.** 17900 I-30. I-30, exit 118, 0.5 mi on n frontage road. Ext corridors. **Pets:** Designated rooms, no service, supervision, crate.
[SAVE] [S☐] [✕] [🖥] [🖨]

AAA ◆ Troutt Motel M
(501) 778-3633. **$27-$38, 7 days notice.** 15438 Interstate 30. Just s of jct I-30, exit 116, on w service road. Ext corridors. **Pets:** Designated rooms, no service, supervision, crate.
[SAVE] [S☐] [✕] [🖥]

BLYTHEVILLE

◆◆◆ Comfort Inn of Blytheville M ☼
(870) 763-7081. **$60-$66.** 1520 E Main. I-55, exit 67. Ext corridors. **Pets:** Small, other. Designated rooms, supervision.
[ASK] [S☐] [✕] [🖥] [🍴] [🖨]

◆◆ Drury Inn M ☼
(870) 763-2300. **$55-$71.** 201 Access Rd. I-55, exit 67. Int corridors. **Pets:** Large, other. Designated rooms, supervision.
[✕] [✍] [🖥] [💻]

◆◆◆ Holiday Inn MI ☼
(870) 763-5800. **$68-$85.** 1121 E Main. I-55, exit 67. Ext/int corridors. **Pets:** Small. $25 deposit/pet. Designated rooms, no service, supervision, crate.
[ASK] [S☐] [✕] [🖥] [💻] [🍴] [🖨]

BRINKLEY

◆◆ Best Western Brinkley MI ☼
(870) 734-1650. **$39-$69, 4 days notice.** 1306 Hwy 17 N. I-40, exit 216. Ext corridors. **Pets:** Small. Designated rooms, supervision.
[ASK] [S☐] [✕] [💻] [🍴] [🖨] [✕]

AAA ◆◆◆ Super 8 Motel MI ☼
(870) 734-4680. **$44-$49, 7 days notice.** I-40 & Hwy 49 N. I-40, exit 216. Ext corridors. **Pets:** Large, other. Supervision.
[SAVE] [S☐] [✕] [🍴] [🖨]

CARLISLE

AAA ◆◆ Best Western-Interstate Inn Carlisle M
(870) 552-7566. **$44-$70, 3 days notice.** I-40, exit 183. Ext corridors. **Pets:** Small. Supervision.
[SAVE] [S☐] [✕] [🖨]

CLARKSVILLE

AAA ◆◆◆ Best Western Sherwood Motor Inn M ☼
(501) 754-7900. **$39-$59.** 1203 S Rogers St. I-40, exit 58. Ext corridors. **Pets:** Other. Supervision.
[SAVE] [S☐] [✕] [🖥] [💻] [🖨]

CONWAY

🆔 ◆◆◆ Comfort Inn 🅼 ☙
(501) 329-0300. **$45-$70.** 150 Hwy 65 N. I-40, exit 125. Ext corridors. **Pets:** Supervision.
🆂🅰🆅🅴 🆂🅾 ⊠ 🕖 🅱 🖵 🕿

◆◆ Howard Johnson Inn 🅼
(501) 329-2961. **$45-$75, 3 days notice.** Hwy 65 N & I-40. I-40, exit 125, just w. Ext/int corridors. **Pets:** Small. Designated rooms, no service, supervision, crate.
🅰🆂🅺 🆂🅾 ⊠ 🅱 🍴 🕿

🆔 ◆ Motel 6 🅼
(501) 327-6623. **$35-$48.** 1105 Hwy 65 N. I-40, exit 125, 0.3 mi e. Ext corridors. **Pets:** Small. No service, supervision, crate.
🆂🅾 ⊠ 🕖 🖵 🕿

🆔 ◆◆ Ramada Inn 🅼 ☙
(501) 329-8392. **$52-$64, 30 days notice.** 815 E Oak St. I-40, exit 127. Ext corridors. **Pets:** Medium, other. $10 one-time fee/room. Supervision.
🆂🅰🆅🅴 🆂🅾 ⊠ 🕖 🅱 🖵 🍴 🕿

DARDANELLE

🆔 ◆◆ Western Frontier Motel 🅼 ☙
(501) 229-4118. **$36-$46.** I-40, exit 81, 7 mi s on US 7; at jct Hwy 7, 22 and 27. Ext corridors. **Pets:** Small. $10 daily fee/pet, $10 one-time fee/pet. Designated rooms, no service, supervision, crate.
🆂🅰🆅🅴 🆂🅾 ⊠ 🅱 🍴 🕿

EL DORADO

🆔 ◆◆ Comfort Inn 🅼 ☙
(870) 863-6677. **$64-$71.** 2303 Junction City Rd. On US 167, 0.5 mi n of US 82 bypass, at jct US 82B. Ext/int corridors. **Pets:** Small, dogs only. No service, supervision, crate.
🆂🅰🆅🅴 🆂🅾 ⊠ 🕖 🕿

EUREKA SPRINGS

◆◆◆ A Cliff Cottage, The Place Next Door, A Bed & Breakfast Inn 🅱🅱
(501) 253-7409. **$120-$195.** 42 Armstrong St. Downtown, via SR 23 N, 0.5 mi n of jct US 62, then ne. Int corridors. **Pets:** Medium. Designated rooms, no service, supervision, crate.
⊠ 🅱 🖵 🆉

◆ Basin Park Hotel 🅷 ☙
(501) 253-7837. **$72-$109, 3 days notice.** 12 Spring St. Downtown, 0.7 mi n of jct US 62, via SR 23 N. Int corridors. **Pets:** Small. No service, supervision, crate.
🅰🆂🅺 🆂🅾 🅱 🖵 🍴

🆔 ◆◆◆ Best Western Inn of the Ozarks 🅼 ☙
(501) 253-9768. **$49-$89.** 0.5 mi w of jct US 62B and SR 23 on US 62. Ext corridors. **Pets:** No service, supervision, crate.
🆂🅰🆅🅴 🆂🅾 ⊠ 🕖 🅲 🅱 🖵 🕿 🖂

🆔 ◆◆ Colonial Mansion Inn 🅼 ☙
(501) 253-7300. **$32-$68.** 154 Huntsville. On SR 23, s of jct US 62. Ext/int corridors. **Pets:** Small. Designated rooms, no service, supervision, crate.
🆂🅰🆅🅴 🆂🅾 ⊠ 🅱 🖵 🕿

◆◆ Days Inn 🅼
(501) 253-8863. **$59-$120.** 120 W Van Buren. On US 62, just w of jct SR 23 N. Ext corridors. **Pets:** Small. No service, supervision, crate.
🅰🆂🅺 🆂🅾 ⊠ 🖵 🕿

◆◆ Dogwood Inn 🅼 ☙
(501) 253-7200. **$48-$58, 3 days notice.** 170 Huntsville Rd. 0.3 mi s of jct US 62 on SR 23. Ext corridors. **Pets:** Small. $10 one-time fee/pet. Designated rooms, no service, supervision, crate.
⊠ 🅱 🖵 🕿 🖂

🆔 ◆◆◆ Howard Johnson Express 🅼
(501) 253-6665. **$58-$99, 3 days notice.** 4042 E Van Buren. On US 62, 1.8 mi e of jct SR 23. Ext corridors. **Pets:** Supervision.
🆂🅰🆅🅴 🆂🅾 ⊠ 🖵 🕿

◆◆◆ Lazee Daze Log Cabin Resort 🅲 ☙
(501) 253-7026. **$105-$135.** 5432 Hwy 23 S. On SR 23, 6.3 mi s of jct US 62. Ext corridors. **Pets:** Dogs only. $50 deposit/pet, $20 one-time fee/pet. No service, supervision, crate.
⊠ 🅱 🖵 🖂 🅲🆃🆅 🆉

◆ Road Runner Inn 🅼
(501) 253-8166. **$33-$44, 3 days notice.** 3034 Mundell Rd. 4 mi s of jct US 62 on SR 187, 3 mi se. Ext corridors. **Pets:** Medium. Designated rooms, no service, supervision, crate.
🅱 🖵 🅲🆃🆅 🆉

🆔 ◆◆ Travelers Inn 🅼
(501) 253-8386. **$38-$58, 3 days notice.** 2044 E Van Buren St. On US 62, 0.3 mi e of jct SR 23. Ext corridors. **Pets:** Very small. Supervision.
🆂🅰🆅🅴 🆂🅾 ⊠ 🅱 🖵 🕿 🖂

FAYETTEVILLE

◆◆◆ Best Western Windsor Suites 🅼
(501) 587-1400. **$70-$85.** 1122 S Futrall Dr. US 71, exit 62. Ext corridors. **Pets:** Designated rooms, supervision.
🅰🆂🅺 🆂🅾 ⊠ 🅲 🅱 🖵 🕿

🆔 ◆◆ Days Inn 🅼
(501) 443-4323. **$69-$100.** 2402 N College Ave. 1.5 mi n on US 71B. Ext corridors. **Pets:** Small. Designated rooms, supervision.
🆂🅰🆅🅴 🆂🅾 ⊠ 🕿

◆◆◆ Fayetteville Hilton 🅷 ☙
(501) 442-5555. **$80-$160, 7 days notice.** 70 N East Ave. Just w of US 71B and SR 471, downtown. Int corridors. **Pets:** Small. Supervision.
🅰🆂🅺 🆂🅾 ⊠ 🅲 🅱 🕿

◆◆◆ Holiday Inn Express 🅼
(501) 444-6006. **$70-$95.** 1251 N Shiloh Dr. US 71, exit 64. Int corridors. **Pets:** Supervision.
🅰🆂🅺 🆂🅾 ⊠ 🅱 🖵

◆◆ Quality Inn M ❀
(501) 444-9800. **$60-$100.** 523 S Shiloh Dr. US 71, exit 62. Ext corridors. **Pets:** Medium. $15 one-time fee/room. Designated rooms, no service, supervision, crate.

ASK S X ⟨⟩ ❚ ▣ ⌂

◆◆ Ramada Inn M
(501) 443-3431. **$55-$78, 5 days notice.** 3901 N College Ave. On US 71B at jct Joyce Blvd, 0.4 mi s of Northwest Arkansas Mall. Ext/int corridors. **Pets:** Small. Designated rooms, supervision.

ASK S X ⌂ X

◆◆ Sleep Inn M ❀
(501) 587-8700. **$54-$99.** 728 Milsap Rd. US 71, exit 67, 1 mi e to US 71B, just s. Int corridors. **Pets:** Small. $10 deposit/room. No service, supervision, crate.

ASK S X ⟨⟩ ❚ ▣

FORREST CITY

ⓐ ◆◆ Best Western Colony Inn M
(870) 633-0870. **$70-$100, 7 days notice.** 2333 N Washington. I-40, exit 241A. Ext corridors. **Pets:** Supervision.

SAVE S X ❚ ▣ ⌂

◆◆◆ Holiday Inn M ❀
(870) 633-6300. **$65-$68.** 200 Holiday Dr. I-40, exit 241B. Ext corridors. **Pets:** Small. Supervision.

ASK S X ▣ ⌐ ⌂ X

◆◆ Luxury Inn M
(870) 633-8990. **$32-$39, 3 days notice.** 315 Barrowhill Rd. I-40, exit 241B, 0.5 mi n on Hwy 1. Ext corridors. **Pets:** Medium. Designated rooms, supervision.

ASK S X

FORT SMITH

◆◆ Baymont Inn & Suites M
(501) 484-5770. **$46-$53.** 2123 Burnham Rd. Off SR 22, just w of jct I-540 (Rogers Ave), exit 8A. Int corridors. **Pets:** Supervision.

S X ⟨⟩ ⌐ ❚ ▣ ⌂

ⓐ ◆◆ Best Western-Fort Smith M ❀
(501) 785-4121. **$48-$58.** 101 N 11th St. On US 64 and 71B, just n of jct SR 22. Ext/int corridors. **Pets:** Other. $50 deposit/room. Supervision.

SAVE S X ⌐ ❚ ▣ ⌂

ⓐ ◆◆ Best Western Kings Row Inn M ❀
(501) 452-4200. **$39-$73.** 5801 Rogers Ave. Just w of I-540 (Rogers Ave), exit 8A on SR 22. Ext corridors. **Pets:** Very small. No service, supervision, crate.

SAVE S X ⌐ ❚ ▣ ⌂

ⓐ ◆◆ Days Inn M
(501) 783-0548. **$36-$50.** 1021 Garrison Ave. Center. Ext corridors. **Pets:** Supervision.

SAVE S X ⟨⟩ ❚ ⌂

◆◆ Fifth Season Inn M
(501) 452-4880. **$59-$79.** 2219 S Waldron Rd. I-540, exit 8A (Rogers Ave W), just s of Rogers and Waldron. Ext/int corridors. **Pets:** Medium. Supervision.

ASK S ❚ ▣ ⌐ ⌂

◆◆◆ Holiday Inn Fort Smith Civic Center H ❀
(501) 783-1000. **$89-$109.** 700 Rogers Ave. Just s of Garrison Ave, US 64; downtown. Int corridors. **Pets:** Other. $25 one-time fee/room. No service, supervision, crate.

ASK S X ⟨⟩ ❚ ▣ ⌐ ⌂

◆◆ Ramada Inn M
(501) 646-2931. **$47-$59.** 5103 Towson Ave. 3 mi s on US 71B. Int corridors. **Pets:** No service, supervision, crate.

ASK S X ⟨⟩ ❚ ⌐ ⌂

HARRISON

ⓐ ◆◆ Family Budget Inn M ❀
(870) 743-1000. **$30-$37.** 401 S Main Hwy 65B S. 1 mi s on US 65B from jct of SR 7. Ext corridors. **Pets:** Small, dogs only. $50 deposit/room, $3 daily fee/room, $3 one-time fee/room. Designated rooms, no service, supervision, crate.

SAVE S X ❚ ⌂ X

◆◆ Harrison Hotel & Suites M
(870) 741-2391. **$52-$61.** 816 N Main. Off US 62/65, on business route. Ext/int corridors. **Pets:** Small. Supervision.

ASK S X ❚ ▣ ⌐ ⌂

◆◆ Super 8 Motel M
(870) 741-1741. **$45-$57.** 1330 Hwy 62/65 N. 5 mi n on US 62/65. Int corridors. **Pets:** Designated rooms, supervision.

ASK S X ❚ ▣ ⌂

HOPE

ⓐ ◆◆◆ Best Western of Hope M ❀
(870) 777-9222. **$50-$63, 7 days notice.** I-30 & US 278. Jct I-30, exit 30. Ext corridors. **Pets:** Other. Supervision.

SAVE S X ❚ ▣ ⌂

◆◆◆ Holiday Inn Express M
(870) 722-6262. **$61-$70.** 2600 North Hervey. I-30, exit 30. Int corridors. **Pets:** Small. Supervision.

ASK S X ⟨⟩ ⌐ ❚ ▣ ⌂

ⓐ ◆◆ Quality Inn M
(870) 777-0777. **$40-$49, 7 days notice.** I-30 & SR 29. I-30, exit 31, just n on SR 29. Ext corridors. **Pets:** Supervision.

SAVE S X ❚ ▣ ⌂

◆◆ Super 8 Motel M ❀
(870) 777-8601. **$29-$39.** I-30 & Hwy 4. I-30, exit 30, just ne on frontage road. Ext corridors. **Pets:** Other. No service, supervision, crate.

ASK S X ❚ ▣ ⌂ X

HOT SPRINGS

◆◆ Super 8 Motel M ❀
(501) 525-0188. **$56-$79.** 4726 Central Ave. On SR 7, 5 mi s of jct US 270. Int corridors. **Pets:** Small. $25 one-time fee/room. Designated rooms, no service, supervision, crate.

ASK S X ❚

HOT SPRINGS NATIONAL PARK

◆◆◆ Clarion Resort 🅼 ❀
(501) 525-1391. **$70-$149, 3 days notice.** 4813 Central Ave. 5.5 mi s on SR 7. Int corridors. **Pets:** Small. $10 daily fee/room. Supervision.

⬛⬛⬛⬛⬛⬛⬛⬛⬛

◆◆◆ Lake Hamilton Resort 🅷 ❀
(501) 767-5511. **$99-$150.** 2803 Albert Pike Rd. 5 mi w on US 270. Int corridors. **Pets:** $10 daily fee/pet. Supervision.

⬛⬛⬛⬛⬛⬛⬛⬛⬛

◆ Margarete Motel 🅼 ❀
(501) 623-1192. **$33-$48.** 217 Fountain St. Just off SR 7, near bathhouse row. Ext corridors. **Pets:** Medium. $50 deposit/room, $5 one-time fee/room. No service, supervision, crate.

⬛⬛⬛

◆◆ The Park Hotel 🅲🅸
(501) 624-5323. **$65-$125.** 211 Fountain St. Off SR 7, just w near bathhouse row. Int corridors. **Pets:** Medium. Supervision.

⬛⬛⬛⬛

◆◆ Quality Inn 🅼🅸
(501) 624-3321. **$64-$89.** 1125 E Grand Ave. On US 70, 1.3 mi e of jct US 270. Ext corridors. **Pets:** Small. Designated rooms, supervision.

⬛⬛⬛⬛⬛⬛⬛⬛

◆◆ Ramada Inn Towers 🅷
(501) 623-3311. **$63-$73.** 218 Park Ave. Center; on US 70B and SR 7. Int corridors. **Pets:** Small. Designated rooms, supervision.

⬛⬛⬛⬛⬛

◆ Travelier Inn 🅼🅸 ❀
(501) 624-4681. **$29-$52.** 1045 E Grand Ave. On US 70, 1.2 mi e SR 7. Ext corridors. **Pets:** Other. Supervision.

⬛⬛⬛⬛⬛⬛

JACKSONVILLE

◆◆ Days Inn 🅼 ❀
(501) 982-1543. **$46-$55, 7 days notice.** 1414 John Hardin Dr. US 67/167, exit 10B southbound; exit 11 northbound. Ext/int corridors. **Pets:** Medium. $5 daily fee/pet, $5 one-time fee/pet. No service, supervision, crate.

⬛⬛⬛⬛

JONESBORO

◆◆◆ Holiday Inn of Jonesboro 🅼🅸 ❀
(870) 935-2030. **Call for rates.** 3006 S Caraway Rd. US 63, Caraway Rd exit, just n. Ext/int corridors. **Pets:** Small. No service, supervision, crate.

⬛⬛⬛⬛⬛

◆◆ Jonesboro Best Western 🅼 ❀
(870) 932-6600. **$46-$57, 7 days notice.** 2901 Phillips Dr. US 63, Stadium/Caraway exit, just n on Stadium. Ext corridors. **Pets:** Other. Supervision.

⬛⬛⬛⬛⬛

◆◆ Ramada Limited 🅼 ❀
(870) 932-5757. **$54-$64, 3 days notice.** 3000 Apache Dr. US 63, Stadium/Caraway exit, just n on Stadium. Ext/int corridors. **Pets:** Other. $10 deposit/room. Designated rooms, supervision.

⬛⬛⬛⬛⬛

◆◆ Super 8 Motel 🅼
(870) 972-0849. **$30-$35.** 2500 S Caraway Rd. US 63, Caraway Rd exit, 0.5 mi n. Int corridors. **Pets:** Supervision.

⬛⬛⬛

LITTLE ROCK

◆◆◆ AmeriSuites/Financial Center 🅼
(501) 225-1075. **$89-$119.** 10920 Financial Center Pkwy. Jct I-430 and I-630, Shackleford Rd exit. Int corridors. **Pets:** Supervision.

⬛⬛⬛⬛⬛

◆◆ Baymont Inn & Suites-Little Rock West 🅼
(501) 225-7007. **$56-$63.** 1010 Breckenridge Rd. I-430, exit 8, just e to Breckenridge Rd, just s. Int corridors. **Pets:** Supervision.

⬛⬛⬛⬛⬛

◆◆◆ Hampton Inn Little Rock I-30 🅼 ❀
(501) 562-6667. **$57-$75.** 6100 Mitchell Dr. I-30, exit 133. Int corridors. **Pets:** No service, supervision, crate.

⬛⬛⬛⬛⬛⬛

◆◆◆ Holiday Inn Select 🅼🅸
(501) 223-3000. **$98, 3 days notice.** 201 S Shackleford. Jct of I-430 and 630. Ext/int corridors. **Pets:** No service, supervision, crate.

⬛⬛⬛⬛⬛⬛

◆◆ Knights Inn 🅼 ❀
(501) 568-6800. **$33-$40.** 9709 I-30. I-30, exit 131 on s service road. Ext corridors. **Pets:** Small. $5 daily fee/pet, $5 one-time fee/pet. No service, supervision, crate.

⬛⬛⬛⬛⬛

◆◆◆ La Quinta Inn-Fair Park 🅼
(501) 664-7000. **$59-$75.** 901 Fair Park Blvd. I-630, exit 4. Ext corridors. **Pets:** No service, supervision, crate.

⬛⬛⬛⬛⬛⬛⬛

◆◆◆ La Quinta Inn-Otter Creek 🅼🅸
(501) 455-2300. **$65-$82.** 11701 I-30. I-30, exit 128. Ext corridors. **Pets:** Designated rooms, supervision.

⬛⬛⬛⬛⬛

◆◆◆ La Quinta Inn-South 🅼 ❀
(501) 568-1030. **$59-$76.** 2401 W 65th St. I-30, exit 135. Ext corridors. **Pets:** Small. Supervision.

⬛⬛⬛⬛

◆◆ Red Roof Inn 🅼 ❀
(501) 562-2694. **$38-$47.** 7900 Scott Hamilton Dr. I-30, exit 134. Ext corridors. **Pets:** Small. No service, supervision, crate.

⬛⬛

◆◆◆ Residence Inn 🄰 ❀
(501) 312-0200. **$139.** 1401 S Shackleford Rd. I-430, exit 5, just n. Int corridors. **Pets:** Medium, other. $8 daily fee/pet. Supervision.

⬛⬛⬛⬛⬛⬛⬛⬛⬛

MAGNOLIA

◆◆ **Best Western-Coachman's Inn** Ⓜ 🐾
(870) 234-6122. **$69, 3 days notice.** 420 E Main St. Just e of square on Business Rt 82B. Ext corridors. **Pets:** Small, other. No service, supervision, crate.

🅰️🆂 ⊠ 🖥 💻 🍴 🔷

MARION

◆◆ **Best Western-Regency Motor Inn** Ⓜ 🐾
(870) 739-3278. **$48-$60, 7 days notice.** 3635 I-55. I-55, exit 10, via western service road. Ext corridors. **Pets:** Small, other. No service, supervision, crate.

🅰️🆂 🆂 ⊠ 🖊️ 🔷

MAUMELLE

◆◆◆ **Comfort Suites** Ⓜ 🐾
(501) 851-8444. **$62-$69.** 14322 Frontier Dr. I-40, exit 142. Int corridors. **Pets:** $20 one-time fee/room. No service, supervision, crate.

🅰️🆂 🆂 ⊠ 🖊️ ✴️ 🖥 💻 🔷

MENA

🔷 ◆ **Ozark Inn of Mena** Ⓜ 🐾
(501) 394-1100. **$28-$35.** 2102 US 71 S. 2 mi s on US 71. Ext corridors. **Pets:** Medium, other. No service, supervision, crate.

⊠ 🔷

MOUNTAIN HOME

◆◆ **Best Western-Carriage Inn** Ⓜ 🐾
(870) 425-6001. **$45-$85.** 963 US 62 E. 1.3 mi e. Ext corridors. **Pets:** Very small. $20 deposit/pet. No service, supervision, crate.

🅰️🆂 🆂 ⊠ 🖥 🔷

◆ **Buzzard Roost Inn** 🅻
(870) 492-5187. **$39-$39, 30 days notice.** 4271 Buzzard Roost Rd. SR 178, 2.2 mi se of jct US 62. Ext corridors. **Pets:** Small. Supervision.

🖥 💻 🍴 ⊠ ✔️

🔷 ◆◆◆ **Teal Point Resort** 🅲 🐾
(870) 492-5145. **$66-$90, 45 days notice.** 715 Teal Point Rd. 7 mi e on US 62, 0.6 mi n following signs on CR 406. Ext corridors. **Pets:** $7 daily fee/pet. Designated rooms, no service, supervision, crate.

🖥 💻 🔷 ⊠ ✔️

NEWPORT

◆ **Days Inn Newport** Ⓜ
(870) 523-6411. **$50-$65.** 101 Olivia Dr. US 67, exit 83, 1 mi w. Ext corridors. **Pets:** Medium. Designated rooms, supervision.

🅰️🆂 🆂 ⊠ 🔷

◆◆ **Park Inn International** Ⓜ 🐾
(870) 523-5851. **$47-$62.** 901 Hwy 367 N. US 67, exit 83, 1 mi w, 0.3 mi n. Ext corridors. **Pets:** Other. No service, supervision, crate.

🅰️🆂 🆂 ⊠ 🖥 🍴 🔷

NORTH LITTLE ROCK

◆◆ **Baymont Inn & Suites-North Little Rock** Ⓜ
(501) 758-8888. **$59-$66.** 4311 Warden Rd. US 67/167, exit 1B northbound; exit 1 southbound. Int corridors. **Pets:** Medium. Supervision.

🆂 ⊠ 🖊️ ✴️ 🖥 💻 🔷

◆◆ **Days Inn** Ⓜ
(501) 945-4100. **Call for rates.** 5800 Pritchard Dr. I-40, exit 157. Ext corridors. **Pets:** Supervision.

🅰️🆂 ⊠

◆◆◆ **Days Inn** Ⓜ 🐾
(501) 851-3297. **$45-$55.** 7200 Bicentennial Rd. I-40, exit 142. Ext corridors. **Pets:** Small, dogs only. $25 deposit/pet, $10 daily fee/pet, $10 one-time fee/pet. Designated rooms, no service, supervision, crate.

🅰️🆂 🆂 ⊠ 🖕 🖊️ ✴️ 🖥

◆◆◆ **Hampton Inn** Ⓜ 🐾
(501) 771-2090. **$59-$65, 3 days notice.** 500 W 29th St. I-40, exit 152. Int corridors. **Pets:** No service, supervision, crate.

🆂 ⊠ 🖊️ 💻 🔷

◆◆ **Howard Johnson Inn** Ⓜ 🐾
(501) 758-1440. **$59-$69.** 111 W Pershing Blvd. I-40, exit 152. Ext/int corridors. **Pets:** Small. $10 daily fee/pet. Designated rooms, no service, supervision, crate.

🅰️🆂 🆂 ⊠ 🖊️ 🖥 💻 🍴 🔷

🔷 ◆◆◆ **La Quinta North** Ⓜ 🐾
(501) 945-0808. **$62-$82.** 4100 E McCain Blvd. At jct US 67/167, exit 1A northbound; exit 1 southbound. Ext corridors. **Pets:** Other. No service, supervision, crate.

🆂🅰️🆅🅴 ⊠ 🖊️ 🖥 💻 🔷

◆ **Masters Inn** Ⓜ 🐾
(501) 945-4167. **$30-$34.** 2508 Jacksonville Hwy. I-40, exit 157. Ext corridors. **Pets:** Small, other. $5 daily fee/room. Supervision.

🅰️🆂 🆂 ⊠ 🖊️ 🖥 🔷

🔷 ◆◆ **Super 8 North** Ⓜ
(501) 945-0141. **$40-$48.** 1 Gray Rd. I-40, exit 157. Ext/int corridors. **Pets:** Small. Designated rooms, no service, supervision, crate.

🆂🅰️🆅🅴 🆂 ⊠ 🍴 🔷

OSCEOLA

🔷 ◆◆◆ **Best Western Inn** Ⓜ
(870) 563-3222. **$50-$66, 7 days notice.** 4635 W Keiser. I-55, exit 48. Ext corridors. **Pets:** Very small. No service, supervision, crate.

🆂🅰️🆅🅴 🆂 ⊠ 🖥 🍴 🔷

OZARK

◆◆ **Oxford Inn** Ⓜ 🐾
(501) 667-1131. **$34-$41.** 305 N 18th St. On SR 23, just n of jct US 64; 3 mi s of jct I-40, exit 35. Ext corridors. **Pets:** Small. $5 daily fee/pet, $5 one-time fee/pet. No service, supervision, crate.

⊠ 🔷

PINE BLUFF

◆◆ **Best Western Pines** Ⓜ
(870) 535-8640. **$53-$63.** 2700 E Harding. 2.5 mi se on US 65B. Ext corridors. **Pets:** No service, supervision, crate.
(ASK) (S🐾) (✕) (🍴) (🖾)

◆◆◆ **Hampton Inn Pine Bluff** Ⓜ 🐾
(870) 850-0444. **$60-$70.** 3103 E Market St. US 65 bypass, next to The Pines Mall. Int corridors. **Pets:** Dogs only. Supervision.
(✕) (👤) (🕖) (🖉) (🖥) (🖾)

RUSSELLVILLE

⚠ ◆◆◆ **Best Western Inn** Ⓜ 🐾
(501) 967-1000. **$44-$56, 7 days notice.** 2326 N Arkansas Ave. I-40, exit 81. Ext corridors. **Pets:** Very small, dogs only. Designated rooms, no service, supervision, crate.
(SAVE) (S🐾) (✕) (🖥) (🖾)

◆◆◆ **Holiday Inn** Ⓜ
(501) 968-4300. **$65-$70.** 2407 N Arkansas Ave. I-40, exit 81. Ext corridors. **Pets:** Supervision.
(ASK) (S🐾) (✕) (🖥) (🖾)

◆ **Park Motel** Ⓜ
(501) 968-4862. **$26-$36.** 2615 W Main St. I-40, exit 81, 2 mi s on SR 7, 1.6 mi w on US 64. Ext corridors. **Pets:** Very small. No service, supervision, crate.
(ASK) (S🐾) (✕) (🖥) (🖾)

SEARCY

◆◆ **Comfort Inn** Ⓜ
(501) 279-9100. **Call for rates.** 107 N Rand St. US 67, exit 46. Ext corridors. **Pets:** Designated rooms, no service, supervision, crate.
(✕) (🖾)

⚠ ◆ **Royal Inn** Ⓜ 🐾
(501) 268-3511. **$30-$45, 3 days notice.** 2203 E Race Ave. US 67/167, exit 46, 1.1 mi w. Ext corridors. **Pets:** Dogs only. Designated rooms, no service, supervision, crate.
(✕) (🖥)

◆◆◆ **Searcy Hampton Inn** Ⓜ
(501) 268-0654. **$59-$74.** 3204 E Race Ave. US 67, exit 46. Ext/int corridors. **Pets:** Medium. Designated rooms, no service, supervision, crate.
(ASK) (✕) (🕖) (🖥) (🖾)

SILOAM SPRINGS

◆◆ **Super 8 Motel** Ⓜ
(501) 524-8898. **$60-$65.** 1800 Hwy 412 W. On US 412, 0.3 mi e. Ext corridors. **Pets:** Designated rooms, supervision.
(ASK) (S🐾) (✕) (🖾) (🖥) (🖾)

SPRINGDALE

◆◆◆ **Baymont Inn & Suites-Springdale** Ⓜ
(501) 751-2626. **$51-$57.** 1300 S 48th St. US 71, exit 52, just e at jct US 412. Int corridors. **Pets:** Very small. Designated rooms, supervision.
(S🐾) (✕) (👤) (🕖) (🖾) (🖥) (🖥) (🖾)

◆◆◆ **Hampton Inn & Suites** Ⓜ 🐾
(501) 756-3500. **$79-$99.** 1700 S 48th St. US 71, exit 52. Int corridors. **Pets:** Small, other. Designated rooms, supervision.
(ASK) (S🐾) (✕) (👤) (🕖) (🖾) (🖥) (🖥) (🖾)

◆◆◆ **Holiday Inn Northwest AR Hotel & Convention Center** Ⓗ 🐾
(501) 751-8300. **$160.** 1500 S 48th St. US 71, exit 72, just e on US 412. Int corridors. **Pets:** Medium, other. $20 deposit/room. Supervision.
(ASK) (S🐾) (✕) (🕖) (🖾) (🖥) (🖥) (🍴) (🖾)

TEXARKANA

◆◆ **Baymont Inn & Suites-Texarkana** Ⓜ 🐾
(870) 773-1000. **$50-$55.** 5102 N State Line Ave. Jct I-30, US 59 and 71, exit 223B. Int corridors. **Pets:** Medium, other. Supervision.
(S🐾) (✕) (🖥) (🖥) (🖾)

⚠ ◆◆ **Best Western Kings Row Inn & Suites** Ⓜ 🐾
(870) 774-3851. **$50-$58.** 4200 N State Line Ave. I-30, exit 223A, 0.3 mi s on US 71 and 59. Ext/int corridors. **Pets:** Very small. Supervision.
(SAVE) (S🐾) (✕) (🖥) (🍴) (🖾)

◆◆◆ **Holiday Inn Texarkana** Ⓜ 🐾
(870) 774-3521. **$68-$78.** 5100 N State Line Ave. Jct I-30, US 59 and 71, exit 223B. Int corridors. **Pets:** Other. $25 one-time fee/room. Supervision.
(ASK) (S🐾) (✕) (🖾) (🖥) (🖥) (🍴) (🖾)

⚠ ◆◆◆ **Shoney's Inn** Ⓜ
(870) 772-0070. **$65-$75.** 5210 N State Line Ave. US 71 and 59, ne of I-30, exit 223B. Ext corridors. **Pets:** Medium. Supervision.
(SAVE) (S🐾) (✕) (🖥) (🖾)

VAN BUREN

◆◆◆ **Comfort Inn** Ⓜ 🐾
(501) 474-2223. **$50-$89, 3 days notice.** 3131 Cloverleaf. I-40 to I-540, exit 2A. Int corridors. **Pets:** Very small. $25 deposit/pet. Supervision.
(ASK) (S🐾) (✕) (🖥) (🖾)

◆◆◆ **Holiday Inn Express** Ⓜ
(501) 474-8100. **$69.** 1903 N 6th St. I-40, exit 5. Ext corridors. **Pets:** No service, supervision, crate.
(ASK) (S🐾) (✕) (🖾) (🖥) (🖾)

⚠ ◆ **Motel 6–1264** Ⓜ
(501) 474-8001. **$36-$52.** 1716 Fayetteville Rd. I-40, exit 5, just s. Ext corridors. **Pets:** No service, supervision, crate.
(S🐾) (✕) (🕖) (🖾) (🖾)

◆◆ **Super 8 Motel** Ⓜ 🐾
(501) 471-8888. **Call for rates.** 106 North Plaza Ct. I-40, exit 5, s of jct US 59. Ext/int corridors. **Pets:** Other. $25 deposit/room. Supervision.
(✕) (🖥) (🖾)

WEST HELENA

◆◆◆ Best Western Inn 🅜 ❀
(870) 572-2592. **$50-$65.** 1053 Hwy 49 W. US 49, 3 mi w. Ext corridors. **Pets:** Very small. Designated rooms, supervision.

🄰🄺 🗐 ⨂ 🈲 🖵 🖾

WEST MEMPHIS

◆◆◆ Comfort Inn 🅜
(870) 732-0044. **$58-$65, 3 days notice.** 1300 Ingram Blvd. I-40 and I-55, exit 279A. Ext corridors. **Pets:** Small. Designated rooms, no service, supervision, crate.

🄰🄺 🗐 ⨂ 🔖 🎤 🈯 🈲 🖵 🖾

◆◆ Econo Lodge 🅜
(870) 732-2830. **$45-$49.** 2315 S Service Rd. I-40 and I-55, exit 279A. Ext corridors. **Pets:** Supervision.

🄰🄺 🗐 ⨂ 🎤 🈲 🖵

◆◆ West Memphis Super 8 🅜 ❀
(870) 735-8818. **$59-$68, 3 days notice.** 901 Martin Luther King Jr Dr. I-40, exit 280 (Club Rd); I-55, exit 4. Int corridors. **Pets:** Medium. $15 one-time fee/room. No service, supervision, crate.

🄰🄺 🗐 ⨂ 🈯

WHEATLEY

⨺ ◆◆ Ramada Limited 🅜
(870) 457-2202. **$46-$55, 7 days notice.** 129 Lawson Rd. I-40, exit 221. Ext corridors. **Pets:** Small. No service, supervision, crate.

🅢🄰🅅🄴 🗐 ⨂ 🈲 🖾

CALIFORNIA

CITY INDEX

CITY INDEX (continued)

ALTURAS

(AAA) ◆◆ Best Western Trailside Inn M ☆
(530) 233-4111. **$55-$60, 7 days notice.** 343 N Main St. On US 395. Ext corridors. **Pets:** Small, dogs only. $10 one-time fee/pet. No service, supervision, crate.

[SAVE] [S☐] [✕] [☐] [☐]

(AAA) ◆◆ Super 8 Motel M
(530) 233-3545. **$54-$62, 3 days notice.** 511 N Main St. On US 395. Ext corridors. **Pets:** No service, supervision, crate.

[S☐] [✕]

ANAHEIM

(AAA) ◆◆◆ Anaheim Marriott Hotel H
(714) 750-8000. **$125-$270.** 700 W Convention Way. Just w of Harbor Blvd. Int corridors. **Pets:** Supervision.

[✕] [☐] [☐] [☐] [☐]

**(AAA) ◆◆ Best Western Anaheim
   Stardust M ☆**
(714) 774-7600. **$48-$89, 3 days notice.** 1057 W Ball Rd. Just w of I-5. Ext corridors. **Pets:** Small. $50 deposit/pet. No service, supervision, crate.

[SAVE] [S☐] [✕] [☐] [☐]

◆◆◆ Hawthorn Suites, Ltd M
(714) 535-7773. **$79-$89, 3 days notice.** 1752 S Clementine St. Just n of Katella Ave. Int corridors. **Pets:** Medium. Supervision.

[ASK] [S☐] [✕] [☐] [☐] [☐]

(AAA) ◆◆◆ Hilton Anaheim H ☆
(714) 750-4321. **$88-$189, 7 days notice.** 777 Convention Way. Just s of Katella Ave. Int corridors. **Pets:** Other. Supervision.

[SAVE] [✕] [☐] [☐] [☐] [☐] [☐]

(AAA) ◆◆◆ Quality Hotel Maingate M
(714) 750-3131. **$99-$150.** 616 Convention Way at Harbor Blvd. Just s of Katella Ave. Int corridors. **Pets:** No service, supervision, crate.

[SAVE] [S☐] [✕] [☐] [☐] [☐] [☐]

(AAA) ◆◆ Red Roof Inn M
(714) 635-6461. **$51-$77.** 1251 N Harbor Blvd. Just s of SR 91. Ext corridors. **Pets:** Small. Designated rooms, no service, supervision, crate.

[SAVE] [✕] [☐] [☐]

◆◆◆ Residence Inn By Marriott A ☆
(714) 533-3555. **$178-$239.** 1700 S Clementine St at Freedman Way. Just sw of I-5, exit Katella Ave. Ext corridors. **Pets:** Small, other. $10 daily fee/pet, $60 one-time fee/room. Designated rooms, supervision.

[ASK] [S☐] [✕] [☐] [☐] [☐] [✕]

ANAHEIM HILLS

(AAA) ◆◆◆ Best Western Anaheim Hills M
(714) 779-0252. **$89-$109.** 5710 E La Palma Ave. 0.3 mi n of SR 91; exit Imperial Hwy. Ext/int corridors. **Pets:** Medium. Supervision.

[SAVE] [S☐] [✕] [☐] [☐] [☐]

ANDERSON

(AAA) ◆◆◆ AmeriHost Inn-Anderson M ☆
(530) 365-6100. **$59-$139.** 2040 Factory Outlet Dr. W of I-5, exit Factory Outlet Dr. Int corridors. **Pets:** No service, supervision, crate.

[SAVE] [✕] [♿] [☐] [☐] [☐] [☐]

(AAA) ◆◆ Anderson Valley Inn M ☆
(530) 365-2566. **$45-$65.** 2861 Mc Murry Dr. E of I-5, exit Central Anderson. Ext corridors. **Pets:** $5 daily fee/pet, $5 one-time fee/pet. No service, supervision, crate.

[✕] [☐]

(AAA) ◆◆ Best Western Knights Inn M
(530) 365-2753. **$50-$60.** 2688 Gateway Dr. E of I-5 exit Central Anderson, Lassen Park exit. Ext corridors. **Pets:** Supervision.

[SAVE] [S☐] [✕] [☐] [☐] [☐]

ANTIOCH

◆◆ Ramada Inn M ☆
(925) 754-6600. **$89-$125.** 2436 Mahogany Way. At Hwy 4 and Somersville Rd. Ext corridors. **Pets:** Small. $30 one-time fee/pet. No service, supervision, crate.

[ASK] [S☐] [✕] [♿] [☐] [☐] [☐]

ARCATA

AAA ◆◆ **Arcata Super 8** **M** ✼
(707) 822-8888. **$49-$59.** 4887 Valley West Blvd. 2 mi n, e of US 101, exit Guintoli Ln E. Int corridors. **Pets:** Designated rooms, supervision.

[SAVE] [S🐾] [✕] [🖥]

AAA ◆◆◆ **Best Western Arcata Inn** **M** ✼
(707) 826-0313. **$83-$87.** 4827 Valley West Blvd. 2 mi n, e of US 101, exit Guintoli Rd. Ext corridors. **Pets:** Small, dogs only. $10 one-time fee/pet. Designated rooms, no service, supervision, crate.

[SAVE] [S🐾] [✕] [🖊] [🎱] [🛏] [🖥] [🌊]

AAA ◆◆◆ **Comfort Inn** **M** ✼
(707) 826-2827. **$65-$120.** 4701 Valley West Blvd. 2 mi n, e of US 101, exit Guintoli Ln. Ext corridors. **Pets:** Small, dogs only. $25 deposit/room. No service, supervision, crate.

[SAVE] [S🐾] [✕] [🎣] [🎱] [🛏] [🌊]

AAA ◆ **Hotel Arcata** **H** ✼
(707) 826-0217. **$72-$138.** 708 9th St. At Central Plaza. Int corridors. **Pets:** Other. $50 deposit/pet, $5 daily fee/pet. Supervision.

[SAVE] [S🐾] [✕] [🖥] [🍽] [📶]

◆◆ **North Coast Inn** **M** ✼
(707) 822-4861. **$105-$140.** 4975 Valley West Blvd. 2 mi n, e of US 101 Guintoli Ln. Int corridors. **Pets:** Small, other. $50 deposit/room, $20 one-time fee/room. Designated rooms, no service, supervision, crate.

[ASK] [S🐾] [✕] [🍽] [🌊] [📶]

ATASCADERO

AAA ◆ **Super 8 Motel** **M**
(805) 466-0794. **$49-$125.** 6505 Morro Rd. On SR 41, just w of jct US 101. Ext corridors. **Pets:** Supervision.

[SAVE] [S🐾] [✕] [🛏]

AUBURN

AAA ◆◆◆ **Best Western Golden Key Motel** **M** ✼
(530) 885-8611. **$68-$72.** 13450 Lincoln Way. Off and adjacent to I-80; via Foresthill Rd. Ext corridors. **Pets:** Medium. $10 one-time fee/pet. Designated rooms, supervision.

[SAVE] [S🐾] [✕] [🖥] [🌊]

◆◆◆ **Holiday Inn-Auburn** **MI**
(530) 887-8787. **$109.** 120 Grass Valley Hwy. Jct I-80 and SR 49. Int corridors. **Pets:** Small. Designated rooms, no service, supervision, crate.

[ASK] [S🐾] [✕] [🎱] [🖥] [🌊]

BADGER

◆◆ **Badger Inn Motel** **M** ✼
(559) 337-0022. **$75-$85, 3 days notice.** 49496 Hwy 245. On SR 245, 12 mi s of entrance to Kings Canyon National Park. Ext corridors. **Pets:** Other. Supervision.

[S🐾] [✕] [🍽] [🌊] [✕] [🎱] [CTV] [📼]

BAKERSFIELD

AAA ◆ **Best Inn** **M** ✼
(661) 764-5221. **$40-$54.** 200 Trask St. 15 mi w of Bakersfield at jct I-5 and Stockdale Hwy. Ext corridors. **Pets:** Small. $5 daily fee/room, $5 one-time fee/room. No service, supervision, crate.

[SAVE] [S🐾] [✕] [🌊]

AAA ◆◆◆ **Best Western Heritage Inn-Buttonwillow** **M** ✼
(661) 764-6268. **$49-$60, 4 days notice.** 253 Trask St. 15 mi w of Bakersfield, at jct I-5 and Stockdale Hwy. Ext corridors. **Pets:** Small. $5 daily fee/room. No service, supervision, crate.

[SAVE] [S🐾] [✕] [🎱] [🌊]

AAA ◆◆◆ **Best Western Hill House** **MI** ✼
(661) 327-4064. **$49-$75.** 700 Truxtun Ave St. 2 mi e of SR 99, California Ave exit to Chester Ave, n to Truxtun Ave. Int corridors. **Pets:** $5 daily fee/pet, $5 one-time fee/pet. No service, supervision, crate.

[SAVE] [S🐾] [✕] [🛏] [🍽] [🌊]

AAA ◆◆ **Best Western Inn-Bakersfield** **MI**
(661) 327-9651. **$49-$79.** 2620 Buck Owens Blvd. E side of SR 99, northbound exit Buck Owens Blvd, southbound exit Rosedale Hwy. Int corridors. **Pets:** Medium. No service, supervision, crate.

[S🐾] [✕] [🛏] [🖥] [🍽] [🌊]

AAA ◆ **Comfort Inn-Central** **M** ✼
(661) 831-1922. **$36-$55.** 830 Wible Rd. Adjacent to SR 99; 0.8 mi ne of Ming Ave exit. Ext corridors. **Pets:** Medium. $5 daily fee/pet, $5 one-time fee/pet. No service, supervision, crate.

[SAVE] [S🐾] [✕] [🎱] [🛏] [🌊]

AAA ◆◆◆ **Doubletree Hotel** **H**
(661) 323-7111. **$99-$175.** 3100 Camino Del Rio Ct. On SR 58, just w of jct SR 99, Rosedale Hwy exit. Int corridors. **Pets:** Small. No service, supervision, crate.

[SAVE] [S🐾] [✕] [🎣] [🖊] [🛏] [🖥] [🍽] [🌊]

AAA ◆◆◆ **La Quinta Inn** **M**
(661) 325-7400. **$59-$79.** 3232 Riverside Dr. E side of SR 99, southbound exit Rosedale Hwy, northbound exit Buck Owens Blvd, just n of Rosedale Hwy. Ext corridors. **Pets:** Supervision.

[SAVE] [✕] [🌊]

◆◆ **Oxford Inn & Suites** **M**
(661) 324-5555. **$44-$60.** 4500 Buck Owens Blvd. Just e of SR 99, 1 mi n of Rosedale Hwy. From SR 99, southbound exit Rosedale Hwy, northbound Buck Owens Blvd. Ext corridors. **Pets:** Designated rooms, no service, supervision, crate.

[ASK] [✕] [🌊]

AAA ◆◆ **Parkway Inn** **MI**
(661) 327-0681. **$45-$75.** 3535 Rosedale Hwy. West side of SR 99, exit SR 58 Rosedale Hwy, just s on Camino Del Real Ct. Ext/int corridors. **Pets:** No service, supervision, crate.

[SAVE] [S🐾] [✕] [🛏] [🍽] [🌊]

♦♦♦ Quality Inn Ⓜ ❀
(661) 325-0772. **$46-$61.** 1011 Oak St. E side of SR 99, exit California Ave, just s. Ext/int corridors. **Pets:** Medium. $10 one-time fee/pet. Supervision.

[SAVE] [Sₒ] [✕] [❚] [▣] [☎]

♦♦♦ Residence Inn by Marriott Ⓐ ❀
(661) 321-9800. **$115-$165.** 4241 Chester Ln. Just w of SR 99, exit California Ave, just n. Ext corridors. **Pets:** Other. $6 daily fee/pet, $60 one-time fee/room. Supervision.

[ASK] [Sₒ] [✕] [⌂] [▣] [☎] [✕]

♦♦♦ Rio Bravo Resort Ⓡ ❀
(661) 872-5000. **Call for rates.** 11200 Lake Ming Rd. 12 mi e on SR 178, 2.5 mi n on Alfred Harrell Hwy. Int corridors. **Pets:** Small, other. $50 deposit/room. No service, supervision, crate.

[SAVE] [✕] [▣] [⑪] [☎] [✕]

♦♦ Royal Oak Inn Ⓜ
(661) 324-9686. **$38-$52.** 889 Oak St. E side of SR 99, exit California Ave, then just s. Ext corridors. **Pets:** No service, supervision, crate.

[ASK] [Sₒ] [✕] [❚] [▣] [☎]

♦♦ Travelodge Hotel & Entertainment Center Ⓜ
(661) 324-6666. **$59-$99, 7 days notice.** 818 Real Rd. W side of SR 99, exit California Ave, then s. Ext/int corridors. **Pets:** Supervision.

[ASK] [Sₒ] [✕] [✎] [▣] [⑪] [☎]

BANNING

♦♦ Banning Travelodge Ⓜ
(951) 849-1000. **$47-$63.** 1700 W Ramsey St. Adjacent to I-10, exit 22nd St, 0.5 mi e. Ext corridors. **Pets:** Supervision.

[SAVE] [Sₒ] [✕] [☎]

♦♦ Super 8 Motel Ⓜ
(951) 849-6887. **$48-$69.** 1690 W Ramsey St. Adjacent to I-10, 22nd St exit, 0.5 mi e. Int corridors. **Pets:** Very small. Supervision.

[SAVE] [Sₒ] [✕] [❚] [☎]

BARSTOW

♦♦ Barstow-Super 8 Motel Ⓜ ❀
(760) 256-8443. **$52-$66.** 170 Coolwater Ln. I-15, exit Main St, 0.3 mi w, then s. Ext corridors. **Pets:** $3 daily fee/pet, $3 one-time fee/pet. No service, supervision, crate.

[SAVE] [Sₒ] [✕] [❚] [▣] [☎]

♦ Best Motel Ⓜ ❀
(760) 256-6836. **$30-$34.** 1281 E Main St. O.5 mi w of I-15; from I-15 and westbound I-40, E Main St exit. Ext corridors. **Pets:** Small. Designated rooms, supervision.

[SAVE] [Sₒ] [✕] [❚] [☎]

♦ Econolodge Ⓜ ❀
(760) 256-2133. **$38-$55.** 1230 E Main St. 0.8 mi w of I-15; from I-15 and westbound I-40, E Main St exits. Ext corridors. **Pets:** Other. $5 daily fee/room, $5 one-time fee/room. No service, supervision, crate.

[ASK] [Sₒ] [✕] [❚] [▣] [☎]

♦ Executive Inn Ⓜ
(760) 256-7581. **$28-$50.** 1261 E Main St. 0.8 mi w of I-15; from I-15 and westbound I-40, E Main St exits. Ext corridors. **Pets:** Designated rooms, no service, supervision, crate.

[SAVE] [Sₒ] [✕] [❚] [☎]

♦ Good Nite Inn Ⓜ
(760) 253-2121. **$51-$85.** 2551 Commerce Pkwy. 8 mi s on I-15. Ext corridors. **Pets:** Supervision.

[SAVE] [Sₒ] [✕] [❚] [☎]

♦♦♦ Holiday Inn Express Ⓜ ❀
(760) 256-1300. **$69-$109.** 1861 W Main St. 0.8 mi ne of I-15, exit W Main St. Int corridors. **Pets:** Other. $20 deposit/room. No service, supervision, crate.

[ASK] [Sₒ] [✕] [❚] [☎]

♦♦ Quality Inn Ⓜ
(760) 256-6891. **Call for rates, 7 days notice.** 1520 E Main St. 0.3 mi w of I-15; from I-15 and I-40 westbound, E Main St exit. Ext corridors. **Pets:** Small. Designated rooms, no service, supervision, crate.

[ASK] [Sₒ] [✕] [▣] [⑪] [☎]

♦ Stardust Inn Ⓜ ❀
(760) 256-7116. **$30-$45.** 901 E Main St. I-15, Barstow Rd exit, 0.8 mi n, then 0.4 mi e. Ext corridors. **Pets:** Very small, dogs only. $5 deposit/pet, $5 one-time fee/pet. Designated rooms, no service, supervision, crate.

[SAVE] [Sₒ] [✕] [❚] [☎]

BEAUMONT

♦ Budget Host Inn Ⓜ ❀
(909) 845-2185. **$36-$50.** 625 E 5th St. Adjacent to I-10, exit Beaumont Ave; just e. Ext corridors. **Pets:** Medium. $2 daily fee/pet, $2 one-time fee/pet. No service, supervision, crate.

[SAVE] [Sₒ] [✕] [☎] [CTV]

♦ Windsor Motel Ⓜ
(909) 845-1436. **$34-$44.** 1265 E 6th St. From I-10, westbound exit Pennsylvania Ave, 1 blk n, then e; eastbound take first Beaumont exit, 2 mi e. Ext corridors. **Pets:** Medium. No service, supervision, crate.

[SAVE] [Sₒ] [✕] [❚] [☎]

BENICIA

♦♦♦ Best Western Heritage Inn Ⓜ ❀
(707) 746-0401. **$70-$105, 7 days notice.** 1955 E 2nd St. E off I-780, exit Central Benicia/E 2nd St. Int corridors. **Pets:** Medium. $25 one-time fee/room. No service, supervision, crate.

[SAVE] [Sₒ] [✕] [❚] [▣] [☎]

BERRY CREEK

♦♦♦ Lake Oroville Bed & Breakfast Ⓑⓑ ❀
(530) 589-0700. **$105-$155, 5 days notice.** 240 Sunday Dr. Exit SR 70 at SR 162, 15 mi e on SR 162 to Bell Ranch Rd, 0.5 mi w to Sunday Dr. Int corridors. **Pets:** Other. $10 one-time fee/pet. Designated rooms, supervision.

[ASK] [Sₒ] [✕] [CTV]

BIG BEAR LAKE

⚠ ◆◆ Alpine Village Suites Lodge M ❀
(909) 866-5460. **$109-$145.** 546 Pine Knot Ave. In the Village area; on SR 18 Business Rt. Ext/int corridors. **Pets:** Medium, other. $100 deposit/room. Supervision.

SAVE S6 ✕ ✗ ✗

⚠ ◆ Bear Claw Cabins C
(909) 866-7633. **Call for rates, 3 days notice.** 586 Main St. Just e on SR 18 & S on Main St. Ext corridors. **Pets:** Very small. Supervision.

SAVE ✗

⚠ ◆ Big Bear Lake Inn M ❀
(909) 866-3477. **$79-$99, 3 days notice.** 39471 Big Bear Blvd. 2.3 mi w on SR 18. Ext corridors. **Pets:** Medium. $50 deposit/pet, $20 daily fee/pet. Designated rooms, no service, supervision, crate.

SAVE S6 ✕ ✗ ✗

⚠ ◆◆ Cozy Hollow Lodge C ❀
(909) 866-8886. **Call for rates.** 40409 Big Bear Blvd. 0.8 mi w on SR 18. Ext corridors. **Pets:** Other. $50 deposit/room, $5 daily fee/pet. No service, supervision, crate.

SAVE ✗ ✗ ✗

◆◆ Eagle's Nest Bed & Breakfast BB
(909) 866-6465. **$85-$150, 5 days notice.** 41675 Big Bear Blvd. 1 mi e on SR 18. Ext/int corridors. **Pets:** Medium. Designated rooms, no service, supervision, crate.

ASK ✕ ✗ ✗ ✗

⚠ ◆ Edgewater Inn M
(909) 866-4161. **$89-$99.** 40570 Simonds Dr. Just n of SR 18. Ext corridors. **Pets:** Small. No service, supervision, crate.

SAVE S6 ✗ ✗ ✗

⚠ ◆◆ Frontier Lodge & Motel C ❀
(909) 866-5888. **$79-$290.** 40472 Big Bear Blvd. 0.5 mi w on SR 18. Ext corridors. **Pets:** Other. $10 daily fee/pet. No service, supervision, crate.

SAVE S6 ✗ ✗ ✗

⚠ ◆◆ Golden Bear Cottages C ❀
(909) 866-2010. **$69-$119.** 39367 Big Bear Blvd. 2 mi w on SR 18. Ext corridors. **Pets:** Other. $10 daily fee/pet. No service, supervision, crate.

SAVE ✗ ✗ ✗ ✗ ✗

⚠ ◆◆◆ Grey Squirrel Resort C ❀
(909) 866-4335. **$68-$95.** 39372 Big Bear Blvd. 2.5 mi e of dam on SR 18. Ext corridors. **Pets:** Other. $100 deposit/room, $10 daily fee/pet, $10 one-time fee/pet. Designated rooms, supervision.

SAVE S6 ✕ ✗ ✗ ✗ ✗

⚠ ◆ Happy Bear Village Resort C
(909) 866-2415. **$65-$165, 30 days notice.** 40154 Big Bear Lodge. 1 mi w on SR 18. Ext corridors. **Pets:** Small. Designated rooms, supervision.

SAVE S6 ✕ ✗ ✗ ✗ ✗

⚠ ◆◆◆ Holiday Inn-Big Bear Chateau H ❀
(909) 866-6666. **$119-$169, 3 days notice.** 42200 Moonridge Rd. 1.5 mi e on SR 18, just s. Int corridors. **Pets:** Medium. $25 one-time fee/pet. Designated rooms, no service, supervision, crate.

SAVE S6 ✕ ✗ ✗ ✗

⚠ ◆◆ Honey Bear Lodge M
(909) 866-7825. **$49-$119, 7 days notice.** 40994 Pennsylvania Ave. Just e of SR 18 Business Rt (Pine Knot Ave). Ext corridors. **Pets:** Medium. Designated rooms, no service, supervision, crate.

SAVE ✕ ✗ ✗ ✗

◆ Quail Cove Lakeside Lodge C ❀
(909) 866-5957. **$89-$229.** 39117 N Shore Dr. Just sw of Fawnskin on SR 38. Ext corridors. **Pets:** Dogs only. $100 deposit/room, $10 daily fee/pet. No service, supervision, crate.

ASK S6 ✗ ✗

⚠ ◆◆ Robinhood Inn MI
(909) 866-4643. **$54-$279, 7 days notice.** 40797 Lakeview Dr. SR 18, Lakeview Dr at Pine Knot Ave. Ext corridors. **Pets:** Medium. No service, supervision, crate.

SAVE S6 ✕ ✗ ✗ ✗ ✗

⚠ ◆◆ Shore Acres Lodge C
(909) 866-8200. **$95-$350.** 40090 Lakeview Dr. 0.8 mi w of village. Ext corridors. **Pets:** Supervision.

SAVE ✗ ✗ ✗

⚠ ◆◆ Stage Coach Lodge C ❀
(909) 878-3008. **$84-$125.** 652 Jeffries. 0.5 mi e on SR 18, just s. Ext corridors. **Pets:** Other. $75 deposit/room, $10 daily fee/pet. No service, supervision, crate.

SAVE S6 ✗ ✗

⚠ ◆◆ Timber Haven Lodge C ❀
(909) 866-3568. **$49-$179.** 877 Tulip Ln. 1.8 mi w on SR 18, 0.3 mi s. Ext corridors. **Pets:** Dogs only. $100 deposit/room, $10 daily fee/pet. Supervision.

SAVE S6 ✕ ✗ ✗

⚠ ◆◆◆ Timberline Lodge C ❀
(909) 866-4141. **$71-$200.** 39921 Big Bear Blvd. 1.5 mi w on SR 18. Ext corridors. **Pets:** $10 daily fee/pet. Supervision.

S6 ✗ ✗ ✗ ✗ ✗

⚠ ◆◆ Wildwood Resort C
(909) 878-2178. **$66-$148, 30 days notice.** 40210 Big Bear Blvd. 0.8 mi w of village on SR 18. Ext/int corridors. **Pets:** Supervision.

SAVE S6 ✕ ✗ ✗ ✗

⚠ ◆◆ Wishing Well Motel M ❀
(909) 866-3505. **$69-$99, 3 days notice.** 540 Pine Knot Blvd. SR 18 Business Rt. Ext corridors. **Pets:** Other. $2 one-time fee/pet. Supervision.

SAVE S6 ✕ ✗

BIG PINE

◆◆ Big Pine Motel M ❀
(760) 938-2282. **$30-$46.** 370 S Main. On US 395. Ext corridors. **Pets:** Medium. $4 daily fee/pet. Supervision.
[X][B][P]

◆ Bristlecone Motel M ❀
(760) 938-2067. **Call for rates.** 101 N Main. On US 395. Ext corridors. **Pets:** Other. Supervision.
[SAVE][X][B]

BISHOP

◆◆◆ Best Western Bishop Holiday Spa Lodge M ❀
(760) 873-3543. **$65-$99.** 1025 N Main St. 0.8 mi n on US 395. Ext corridors. **Pets:** Small, other. Designated rooms, supervision.
[SAVE][S][X][B][P][≈]

◆◆◆ Best Western Creekside Inn M ❀
(760) 872-3044. **$99-$151.** 725 N Main St. Just n of downtown on US 395. Int corridors. **Pets:** Medium. Supervision.
[SAVE][S][X][≋][≈]

◆◆◆ Comfort Inn M
(760) 873-4284. **$59-$99.** 805 N Main St. 0.5 mi n on US 395. Ext corridors. **Pets:** Supervision.
[SAVE][S][X][B][P][≈]

◆◆ Motel 6-4094 ❀
(760) 873-8426. **$39-$89.** 1005 N Main St. 0.8 mi n on US 395. Ext corridors. **Pets:** Small, other. Designated rooms, no service, supervision, crate.
[S][X][B][≈]

◆◆ Rodeway Inn M
(760) 873-3564. **$60-$90.** 150 E Elm St. Just n of Downtown, and e of US 395. Ext/int corridors. **Pets:** Supervision.
[SAVE][S][X][B][≈]

◆◆ Super 8 Motel M ❀
(760) 872-1386. **$60-$65.** 535 S Main St. 0.3 mi s on US 395. Ext corridors. **Pets:** Other. Supervision.
[SAVE][S][X][P][≈]

◆ Thunderbird Motel M
(760) 873-4215. **$50-$99.** 190 W Pine St. Downtown, just w of US 395. Ext corridors. **Pets:** Supervision.
[SAVE][S][X][B][P]

◆◆ Vagabond Inn M ❀
(760) 873-6351. **$67-$78.** 1030 N Main St. 0.8 mi n on US 395. Ext corridors. **Pets:** Large, other. $5 daily fee/pet. Supervision.
[SAVE][S][X][B][P][≈]

BLYTHE

◆◆ Best Western Sahara Motel M ❀
(760) 922-7105. **$75-$110.** 825 W Hobsonway. Just n of I-10, Lovekin Blvd exit. Ext corridors. **Pets:** Medium. No service, supervision, crate.
[SAVE][S][X][B][P][≈]

◆◆ Comfort Inn M
(760) 922-4146. **$75-$95.** 903 W Hobsonway. Just n of I-10, exit Lovekin Blvd. Ext corridors. **Pets:** Small. Designated rooms, supervision.
[SAVE][S][X][B][P][≈]

◆◆◆ Hampton Inn M ❀
(760) 922-9000. **$75-$110, 3 days notice.** 900 W Hobsonway. Just nw of I-10; exit Lovekin Blvd. Ext corridors. **Pets:** Small, other. $25 deposit/room, $10 one-time fee/room. Designated rooms, no service, supervision, crate.
[SAVE][S][X][B][≈]

◆◆ Holiday Inn Express M ❀
(760) 921-2300. **$79-$119, 7 days notice.** 600 W Donlon St. Adjacent to s side of I-10, Lovekin Blvd exit. Ext corridors. **Pets:** Medium. $10 daily fee/pet. No service, supervision, crate.
[SAVE][S][X][B][≈]

◆◆ Tropics Inn & Suites M
(760) 922-5101. **$50-$85.** 9274 E Hobsonway. From I-10, exit Intake Blvd, just n, then 0.3 mi w. Ext corridors. **Pets:** Small. No service, supervision, crate.
[SAVE][S][X][B][≈]

BODEGA BAY

◆◆◆ Bodega Coast Inn M ❀
(707) 875-2217. **$129-$189.** 521 SR 1 N. 2 blks s on SR 1. Ext corridors. **Pets:** Other. Supervision.
[S][X][B][P][K]

BRAWLEY

◆◆ Town House Lodge M ❀
(760) 344-5120. **Call for rates.** 135 Main St. At jct SR 78 and 86. Ext corridors. **Pets:** Other. Supervision.
[SAVE][S][X][B][P][≈]

BRIDGEPORT

◆◆◆ Best Western Ruby Inn M
(760) 932-7241. **$85-$170.** 333 Main St. Center on US 395, just n of courthouse. Ext corridors. **Pets:** Supervision.
[SAVE][S][X][B][P]

◆ Redwood Motel M ❀
(760) 932-7060. **$60-$90.** 425 Main St. N side of town, on US 395. Ext corridors. **Pets:** Medium, other. $5 one-time fee/pet. Designated rooms, no service, supervision, crate.
[X][≋][P]

◆ Silver Maple Inn M ❀
(760) 932-7383. **$55-$80.** 310 Main St. Center; on US 395, next to the courthouse. Ext corridors. **Pets:** Other. No service, supervision, crate.
[SAVE][S][X][P][K]

◆◆◆ Walker River Lodge M ❀
(760) 932-7021. **$70-$140, 3 days notice.** 100 Main St. South end of town, on US 395. Ext corridors. **Pets:** Supervision.
[X][♪][B][P][≈][X]

BUELLTON

◆ **Econo Lodge** Ⓜ ❀
(805) 688-0022. **$45-$99.** 630 Ave of Flags. Adjacent to US 101; southbound first Buellton exit; northbound Frontage Rd exit, just w over the frwy. Ext/int corridors. **Pets:** Medium, dogs only. No service, supervision, crate.
(ASK) (S✿) (✕) (🖥) (CTV)

BUENA PARK

⚫ ◆ ◆ **Innsuites Hotels Buena Park Suite Hotel** Ⓜ ❀
(714) 522-7360. **$99-$109, 7 days notice.** 7555 Beach Blvd. Just s of SR 91. Ext corridors. **Pets:** Small. $25 deposit/room. Supervision.
(SAVE) (S✿) (✕) (🖥) (🖥) (🖥)

BURNEY

⚫ ◆ **Charm Motel** Ⓜ ❀
(530) 335-2254. **$47-$64.** 37363 Main St. 0.8 mi e on SR 299. Ext corridors. **Pets:** Dogs only. $10 one-time fee/pet. No service, supervision, crate.
(SAVE) (S✿) (✕) (🖥) (🖥)

⚫ ◆ **Green Gables Motel** Ⓜ
(530) 335-2264. **$47-$65.** 37385 Main St. 0.8 mi e on SR 299. Ext corridors. **Pets:** No service, supervision, crate.
(SAVE) (S✿) (✕) (🖥) (🖥) (🖥)

⚫ ◆ ◆ **Shasta Pines Motel** Ⓜ ❀
(530) 335-2201. **$35-$69, 4 days notice.** 37386 Main St. 0.8 mi e on SR 299. Ext corridors. **Pets:** Very small, dogs only. $50 deposit/pet, $6 daily fee/pet, $6 one-time fee/pet. Supervision.
(S✿) (✕) (🖥) (🖥) (🖥)

BUTTONWILLOW

⚫ ◆ **Good Nite Inn** Ⓜ
(661) 764-5121. **Call for rates.** 20645 Tracy Road. Adjacent to I-5 at jct SR 58. Ext corridors. **Pets:** Small. Designated rooms, no service, supervision, crate.
(SAVE) (S✿) (✕) (🖥) (🖥)

⚫ ◆ **Super 8 Motel** Ⓜ
(661) 764-5117. **$37-$49, 3 days notice.** 20681 Tracy Ave. Adjacent to I-5, exit SR 58. Ext corridors. **Pets:** Small. No service, supervision, crate.
(SAVE) (S✿) (✕) (🖥) (🖥) (🖥)

CALIMESA

⚫ ◆ ◆ **Calimesa Inn Motel** Ⓜ ❀
(909) 795-2536. **$45-$60.** 1205 Calimesa Blvd. Just n of I-10, exit Calimesa Blvd. Ext corridors. **Pets:** Small. $6 daily fee/pet, $6 one-time fee/pet. Supervision.
(SAVE) (S✿) (✕) (🖥) (🖥)

CALIPATRIA

⚫ ◆ ◆ ◆ **Calipatria Inn** Ⓜ
(760) 348-7348. **$59-$74.** 700 N Sorenson. 0.5 mi n on SR 111. Ext corridors. **Pets:** Large. Designated rooms, no service, supervision, crate.
(SAVE) (S✿) (✕) (🖥) (🖥) (🖥)

CAMARILLO

⚫ ◆ ◆ **Good Nite Inn** Ⓜ ❀
(805) 388-5644. **$45-$50, 7 days notice.** 1100 Ventura Blvd. Adj to US 101, exit Carmen Dr. Ext corridors. **Pets:** Medium, other. Designated rooms, no service, supervision, crate.
(SAVE) (✕) (🖥) (🖥) (🖥)

CAMBRIA

⚫ ◆ ◆ **Cambria Shores Inn** Ⓜ
(805) 927-8644. **$65-$135, 3 days notice.** 6276 Moonstone Beach Dr. 2 mi n, adjacent to SR 1. Ext corridors. **Pets:** Medium. Supervision.
(SAVE) (✕) (🖥) (🖥) (🖥)

CAMERON PARK

⚫ ◆ ◆ ◆ **Best Western Cameron Park Inn** Ⓜ
(530) 677-2203. **Call for rates.** 3361 Coach Ln. 12 mi w of Placerville on US 50, exit Cameron Park Dr. Ext corridors. **Pets:** Medium. No service, supervision, crate.
(SAVE) (✕) (🖥) (🖥)

CAMPBELL

◆ ◆ ◆ **Residence Inn By Marriott-San Jose** Ⓜ ❀
(408) 559-1551. **$159-$159.** 2761 S Bascom Ave. Exit SR 17 via Camden Ave E; then n. Ext corridors. **Pets:** Other. $10 daily fee/pet, $75 one-time fee/pet. No service, supervision, crate.
(✕) (🖥)

CAPITOLA

◆ ◆ ◆ **Capitola Inn** Ⓜ ❀
(831) 462-3004. **$75-$175.** 822 Bay Ave. Just w of SR 1, Bay Ave exit. Ext/int corridors. **Pets:** Other. $20 daily fee/pet, $20 one-time fee/pet. Supervision.
(ASK) (S✿) (✕) (🖥) (🖥) (🖥)

CARLSBAD

◆ ◆ ◆ ◆ ◆ **Four Seasons Resort Aviara** ⓡ
(760) 603-6800. **$415-$525, 3 days notice.** 7100 Four Seasons Point. 2 mi se of I-5 on Batiquitos Lagoon, exit Poinsettia Ln/Aviara Pkwy. **Pets:** No service, supervision, crate.
(ASK) (✕) (🖥) (🍴) (🖥) (✕)

⚫ ◆ ◆ **Inns of America** Ⓜ ❀
(760) 931-1185. **$80-$90.** 751 Raintree Dr. Adjacent to I-5, Poinsettia Ln exit; just w to Ave Encinas, just n. Ext corridors. **Pets:** Medium. $10 one-time fee/room. No service, supervision, crate.
(SAVE) (S✿) (✕) (🖥) (🍴) (🖥)

⚫ ◆ **Motel 6-1021** Ⓜ ❀
(760) 434-7135. **$40-$61.** 1006 Carlsbad Village Dr. Just w of I-5. Ext corridors. **Pets:** Medium, other. No service, supervision, crate.
(S✿) (✕)

CASTAIC

⟨AAA⟩ ◆◆ Comfort Inn 🅼 ❖
(661) 295-1100. **$64-$89.** 31558 Castaic Rd. I-5, northbound exit Parker Rd, 0.3 mi ne, southbound exit Lake Hughes Rd, 0.5 mi se. Ext corridors. **Pets:** Medium. $10 one-time fee/room. Designated rooms, supervision.

🆂🅰🆅🅴 🆂🅳 ⊠ 🗝 🖥 🈁

CATHEDRAL CITY

⟨AAA⟩ ◆◆ Days Inn Suites 🅼 ❖
(760) 324-5939. **$220.** 69-151 E Palm Canyon Dr. SR 111 just e of Date Palm Rd. Ext corridors. **Pets:** Medium. $50 deposit/room, $10 daily fee/pet. Designated rooms, no service, supervision, crate.

🆂🅰🆅🅴 🆂🅳 ⊠ 🖥 🈁

⟨AAA⟩ ◆◆◆ Doral Palm Springs Resort 🆁 ❖
(760) 322-7000. **$169-$330, 3 days notice.** 67-967 Vista Chino. 1.8 mi sw of I-10, exit Date Palm Dr. Int corridors. **Pets:** Small. $50 one-time fee/room. Supervision.

🆂🅰🆅🅴 ⊠ 🗝 🖥 🈁 🆗

CAYUCOS

⟨AAA⟩ ◆ Cypress Tree Motel 🅼 ❖
(805) 995-3917. **$50-$90.** 125 S Ocean Ave. On SR 1 business route. Ext corridors. **Pets:** Other. $10 one-time fee/room. Supervision.

🆂🅰🆅🅴 🆂🅳 ⊠ 🖥 🈁

⟨AAA⟩ ◆ Dolphin Inn 🅼 ❖
(805) 995-3810. **$45-$95, 3 days notice.** 399 S Ocean Ave. SR 1 business route. Ext corridors. **Pets:** $10 deposit/pet, $10 one-time fee/room. Supervision.

🆂🅰🆅🅴 🆂🅳 ⊠ 🗝 🖥 🈁

⟨AAA⟩ ◆ Estero Bay Motel 🅼 ❖
(805) 995-3614. **$72-$125, 3 days notice.** 25 S Ocean Ave. SR 1 business route. Ext corridors. **Pets:** Dogs only. $15 one-time fee/room. No service, supervision, crate.

🆂🅰🆅🅴 🆂🅳 ⊠ 🗝 🖥 🈁

⟨AAA⟩ ◆ Shoreline Inn 🅼 ❖
(805) 995-3681. **$80-$160.** #1 N Ocean Ave. Ext corridors. **Pets:** $15 one-time fee/pet. Supervision.

🆂🅰🆅🅴 ⊠ 🗝 🖥 🈁

CEDARVILLE

⟨AAA⟩ ◆ Sunrise Motel 🅼 ❖
(530) 279-2161. **$35-$50.** 54889 Hwy 299. 0.5 mi w on Hwy 299. Ext corridors. **Pets:** Small. $25 deposit/pet, $10 daily fee/pet, $10 one-time fee/pet. Designated rooms, no service, supervision, crate.

🆂🅰🆅🅴 ⊠ 🗝 🖥

CHICO

⟨AAA⟩ ◆ Deluxe Inn 🅼 ❖
(530) 342-8386. **$39-$53.** 2507 Esplanade. 2 mi n on SR 99 business route. Ext corridors. **Pets:** Other. $4 daily fee/pet, $4 one-time fee/pet. No service, supervision, crate.

🆂🅰🆅🅴 🆂🅳 ⊠ 🗝 🈁

◆◆◆ Holiday Inn of Chico 🅼🅸 ❖
(530) 345-2491. **Call for rates.** 685 Manzanita Ct. Just w of SR 99, via Cohasset Rd. Int corridors. **Pets:** Medium, other. $25 one-time fee/room. No service, supervision, crate.

🅰🆂🅺 🆂🅳 ⊠ 🗝 🖥 🈁 🈁

◆◆◆ Oxford Suites 🅼🅸 ❖
(530) 899-9090. **$85-$159.** 2035 Business Ln. SR 99, exit 20th St e. Int corridors. **Pets:** Small. $15 one-time fee/room. No service, supervision, crate.

🅰🆂🅺 🆂🅳 ⊠ 🗝 🈁

⟨AAA⟩ ◆ Safari Garden Motel 🅼 ❖
(530) 343-3201. **$45-$50.** 2352 Esplanade. 2 mi n on SR 99 business rt. Ext corridors. **Pets:** Medium, dogs only. $25 deposit/room. Designated rooms, no service, supervision, crate.

🆂🅰🆅🅴 🆂🅳 ⊠ 🗝 🖥 🈁

⟨AAA⟩ ◆ Super 8 Motel 🅼
(530) 345-2533. **$45-$75.** 655 Manzanita Ct. Just w of SR 99, via Cohasset Rd. Int corridors. **Pets:** Supervision.

🆂🅰🆅🅴 🆂🅳 ⊠ 🗝 🈁

COALINGA

⟨AAA⟩ ◆◆ Big Country Inn 🅼 ❖
(559) 935-0866. **$52-$86.** 25020 W Dorris Ave. W of and adjacent to I-5, at SR 198, Hanford-Lemoore off-ramp. Ext corridors. **Pets:** Small. $5 daily fee/pet, $5 one-time fee/pet. No service, supervision, crate.

🆂🅰🆅🅴 🆂🅳 ⊠ 🗝 🖥 🈁

⟨AAA⟩ ◆◆◆ The Inn at Harris Ranch 🅼🅸 ❖
(559) 935-0717. **$100-$110.** 24505 W Doris Ave. E side and adjacent to I-5; at SR 198, Hanford-Lemoore off-ramp. Ext/int corridors. **Pets:** Other. $10 one-time fee/pet. Designated rooms, no service, supervision, crate.

🆂🅰🆅🅴 🆂🅳 ⊠ 🅭 🖥 🈁 🈁

COLUMBIA

◆ Columbia Gem Motel 🅲
(209) 532-4508. **$50-$150.** 22131 Parrotts Ferry Rd. 3 mi n of Sonora, on Parrotts Ferry Rd; 1 mi from Columbia State Historic Park. Ext corridors. **Pets:** No service, supervision, crate.

⊠ 🗝 🖥 🈁

CONCORD

◆◆ Concord Inn 🅼🅸
(925) 687-5500. **$99-$109.** 1050 Burnett Ave. Exit I-680 E Concord Ave; Diamond Ave S; Burnett Ave W. Ext/int corridors. **Pets:** Supervision.

🅰🆂🅺 🆂🅳 ⊠ 🗝 🖥 🈁 🈁

⟨AAA⟩ ◆◆◆◆ Sheraton Concord Hotel 🅼🅸
(925) 825-7700. **$89-$139.** 45 John Glenn Dr. E off I-680 exit Concord Ave. Int corridors. **Pets:** Small. Designated rooms, no service, supervision, crate.

🆂🅰🆅🅴 🆂🅳 ⊠ 🅭 🗝 🖥 🈁 🈁 🆗

CORNING

+++ Amerihost Inn-Corning 🅼 ❀
(530) 824-5200. **$55-$75.** 910 Hwy 99 W. I-5, exit Solano St, e of and adjacent. Int corridors. **Pets:** Other. Supervision.

(SAVE) (S💲) (X) (👣) (🖐) (🛏) (💻) (🔜)

+++ Best Western Inn-Corning 🅼
(530) 824-2468. **$54-$79.** 2165 Solano St. Exit I-5 e via Corning exit, 1 blk e. Ext corridors. **Pets:** Designated rooms, no service, supervision, crate.

(X) (🛏) (💻) (🔜)

++ Days Inn 🅼 🐾
(530) 824-2000. **$42-$50, 7 days notice.** 3475 Hwy 99W. Exit I-5 at South Ave, 0.3 mi s. Int corridors. **Pets:** Other. $5 one-time fee/pet. No service, supervision, crate.

(ASK) (S💲) (X) (🔜)

+++ Shilo Inn 🅼
(530) 824 2940. **$55-$109.** 3350 Sunrise Way. 1 mi s; e and adjacent to I-5, exit South Ave. Int corridors. **Pets:** No service, supervision, crate.

(ASK) (S💲) (X) (🛏) (🔜)

CORONA

+++ Dynasty Suites-Corona 🅼
(909) 371-7185. **$48-$54.** 1805 W 6th St. S side of SR 91, eastbound exit 6th St; westbound exit Maple St. Ext corridors. **Pets:** Small. Designated rooms, no service, supervision, crate.

(S💲) (X) (🛏) (🔜)

COSTA MESA

+++ Doubletree Hotel/Orange County Airport 🅷
(714) 540-7000. **$89-$154.** 3050 Bristol St. Just s of I-405, exit Bristol St. Int corridors. **Pets:** Supervision.

(SAVE) (S💲) (X) (🛏) (💻) (🍴) (🔜)

+++ La Quinta Inn 🅼 ❀
(714) 957-5841. **$59-$79.** 1515 South Coast Dr. Just nw of I-405, Harbor Blvd exit. Ext corridors. **Pets:** Small. Designated rooms, no service, supervision, crate.

(SAVE) (X) (🛏) (💻) (🔜)

++ Ramada Limited 🅼 ❀
(949) 645-2221. **$82-$112.** 1680 Superior Ave at 17th St. Just w of SR 55, Newport Blvd. Ext corridors. **Pets:** Small, other. $50 deposit/room.

(ASK) (S💲) (X) (🛏) (💻) (🔜) (CTV)

+++ Residence Inn by Marriott 🅰 ❀
(714) 241-8800. **$129.** 881 W Baker St. Adjacent to s side of SR 73, Bear St exit; from SR 55, Baker St exit. Ext corridors. **Pets:** Other. $6 daily fee/room, $60 one-time fee/room. Supervision.

(ASK) (S💲) (X) (💻) (🔜) (X)

++ Vagabond Inn 🅼 ❀
(714) 557-8360. **$60-$70.** 3205 Harbor Blvd. Just s of I-405, Harbor Blvd exit (entrance from Gisler, just w of Harbor). Ext corridors. **Pets:** Other. $5 daily fee/pet. Supervision.

(SAVE) (S💲) (X) (🛏) (💻) (🔜)

+++ The Westin South Coast Plaza Hotel 🅷 ❀
(714) 540-2500. **$115-$175.** 686 Anton Blvd. Just n of I-405, Bristol St exit. Int corridors. **Pets:** Small. No service, supervision, crate.

(SAVE) (S💲) (X) (💻) (🔜) (X)

+++ Wyndham Garden Hotel 🅷 ❀
(714) 751-5100. **$79-$125.** 3350 Ave of the Arts. I-405, exit Bristol St, n to Anton Blvd, 2 blks e, just n. Int corridors. **Pets:** Small, other. $25 one-time fee/pet. Supervision.

(SAVE) (S💲) (X) (🖊) (🛏) (💻) (🍴) (🔜)

CRESCENT CITY

++ Best Value Pacific Motor Hotel 🅼
(707) 464-4141. **Call for rates.** 440 Hwy 101N. On US 101. Ext corridors. **Pets:** No service, supervision, crate.

(X) (🛏) (💻) (X)

++ Super 8 🅼 ❀
(707) 464-4111. **$56-$79.** 685 Hwy 101 S. E of US 101S, opposite harbor. Ext corridors. **Pets:** Small, dogs only. $5 daily fee/pet, $5 one-time fee/pet. Designated rooms, no service, supervision, crate.

(SAVE) (S💲) (X) (💻) (X)

DANA POINT

+++ Holiday Inn Express Dana Point Edgewater 🅼
(949) 240-0150. **Call for rates.** 34744 Pacific Coast Hwy. I-5, southbound exit Pacific Coast Hwy, northbound exit Beach Cities; then exit Coast Hwy s from Transition Rd, 0.8 mi. Ext corridors. **Pets:** Medium. No service, supervision, crate.

(ASK) (S💲) (X) (🛏)

DANVILLE

++ Danville Inn 🅼
(925) 838-8080. **$65-$80.** 803 Camino Ramon. E of and adjacent to I-680; exit via Sycamore Valley Rd. Ext/int corridors. **Pets:** Supervision.

(S💲) (X) (💻) (🔜)

DAVIS

++ Best Western University Lodge 🅼 ❀
(530) 756-7890. **$75-$99.** 123 B St. Just e of U of C campus. Ext corridors. **Pets:** Small, other. $15 daily fee/room. No service, supervision, crate.

(SAVE) (S💲) (X) (🛏) (💻) (X)

+++ Howard Johnson Hotel 🅼 ❀
(530) 792-0800. **$79-$105.** 4100 Chiles Rd. I-80, exit at Mace Blvd, just s, then 0.3 mi w. Int corridors. **Pets:** Medium, other. $10 one-time fee/pet. Supervision.

(SAVE) (S💲) (X) (🏠) (🛏) (💻) (🔜)

DELANO

+ Comfort Inn 🅼 ❀
(661) 725-1022. **$52-$60.** 2211 Girard St. Just e of SR 99; County Line exit. Ext corridors. **Pets:** Small. $5 daily fee/room, $5 one-time fee/room. No service, supervision, crate.

(SAVE) (S💲) (X) (🔜)

◆◆ Shilo Inn 🅼
(661) 725-7551. **$45-$69.** 2231 Girard St. Just e of SR 99;
County Line exit. Int corridors. **Pets:** Medium. No service,
supervision, crate.
ASK SD ✕ 🖵 🌊

DESERT HOT SPRINGS

🅰 ◆ Stardust Motel 🅼 ❀
(760) 329-5443. **$48-$63.** 66634 5th St. 0.5 mi n, just e of
Palm Dr. Ext corridors. **Pets:** Other. Supervision.
SAVE ✕ 🖬 🌊 🔲

DINUBA

🅰 ◆◆◆ Best Western Americana Inn 🅼 ❀
(559) 595-8401. **$50-$70.** 1450 S Alta Ave. 0.6 mi sw of
downtown. Int corridors. **Pets:** Small, dogs only. $50
deposit/room. No service, supervision, crate.
SAVE SD ✕ 🐾 🖬 🖵 🌊

DIXON

🅰 ◆◆◆ Best Western Inn 🅼 ❀
(707) 678-1400. **$68-$99, 7 days notice.** 1345 Commercial
Way. Adjacent to I-80, exit Pitt School Road, 8 mi west of
U.C. Davis Campus. Ext corridors. **Pets:** $50 deposit/room,
$10 one-time fee/room. Designated rooms, no service,
supervision, crate.
SAVE SD ✕ 🖬 🖵 🌊

DUNNIGAN

🅰 ◆◆◆ Best Western Country 🅼 ❀
(530) 724-3471. **$52-$79.** 3930 Road 89. I-5, Dunnigan
exit. Ext corridors. **Pets:** No service, supervision, crate.
SAVE SD ✕ 🐾 🖬 🌊

🅰 ◆◆ Value Lodge 🅼 ❀
(530) 724-3333. **$46-$58.** 3930 Road 89. I-5, Dunnigan
exit. Int corridors. **Pets:** No service, supervision, crate.
SAVE SD ✕ 🖬 🌊

DUNSMUIR

🅰 ◆◆◆ Caboose Motel-Railroad Park
Resort 🅼 ❀
(530) 235-4440. **$60-$90.** 100 Railroad Park Rd. 1 mi s exit
I-5, Railroad Park Rd. **Pets:** $10 daily fee/pet. Supervision.
✕ 🖬 🖵 🌊

🅰 ◆◆ Cedar Lodge Motel 🅼 ❀
(530) 235-4331. **$36-$48, 4 days notice.** 4201 Dunsmuir
Ave. Exit I-5 at Dunsmuir/Siskiyou; w 0.5 mi. Ext corridors.
Pets: Dogs only. $5 daily fee/pet. Supervision.
SAVE ✕ 🖵

EL CENTRO

🅰 ◆◆◆ Barbara Worth Golf Resort &
Convention Center 🆁 ❀
(760) 356-2806. **$64-$80.** 2050 Country Club Dr. 9 mi e of
El Centro; 2.3 mi w of Holtville; from I-8, take Bowker Rd 2
mi n, then 3 mi e on CRS-80. Ext/int corridors.
Pets: Medium. $100 deposit/room. No service, supervision,
crate.
SAVE SD ✕ 🖬 🖵 🍴 🌊 🔲

🅰 ◆◆ Brunner's 🅼
(760) 352-6431. **$65-$73.** 215 N Imperial Ave. 1 mi n of I-8,
exit Imperial Ave. Ext corridors. **Pets:** Designated rooms, no
service, supervision, crate.
SAVE SD ✕ 🖬 🖵 🍴 🌊

🅰 ◆◆ Days Inn 🅼
(760) 352-5511. **$50-$70.** 1425 Adams Ave. On SR 86 and
I-8 Business Loop, just e of Imperial Ave. Ext corridors.
Pets: No service, supervision, crate.
SAVE SD ✕ 🖬 🌊

🅰 ◆◆◆ Ramada Inn 🅼
(760) 352-5152. **$56-$67, 7 days notice.** 1455 Ocotillo Dr.
Adjacent to I-8, exit Imperial Ave. Ext/int corridors.
Pets: Small. No service, supervision, crate.
SAVE ✕ 🖬 🍴 🌊

🅰 ◆◆ Super 8-El Centro 🅼
(760) 352-0715. **$50-$70.** 611 N Imperial Ave. 1 mi n.
Pets: Very small. Supervision.
SAVE SD ✕ 🖬 🌊

EL PORTAL

🅰 ◆◆◆ Yosemite View Lodge 🅼 ❀
(209) 379-2681. **$109-$159, 7 days notice.** 11136 Hwy
140. Just w of Y N P West Gate. Ext corridors. **Pets:** Other.
$6 daily fee/pet. Supervision.
✕ ♿ 🐕 🐾 🖵 🌊 ✕

ENCINITAS

🅰 ◆◆ Days Inn 🅼 ❀
(760) 944-0260. **$69-$99.** 133 Encinitas Blvd. Just w of I-5.
Ext corridors. **Pets:** Medium. $25 one-time fee/room. Des-
ignated rooms, supervision.
SAVE SD ✕ 🖬 🌊

ESCONDIDO

🅰 ◆ Rodeway Inn 🅼
(760) 746-0441. **$49-$65.** 250 W El Norte. 1 mi e of I-15,
exit El Norte to Centre City Pkwy. Ext corridors. **Pets:** No
service, supervision, crate.
SAVE SD ✕ 🖬 🖵

🅰 ◆◆◆ The Sheridan Inn 🅼
(760) 743-8338. **$59-$99.** 1341 N Escondido Blvd. 1 mi e of
I-15; Exit El Norte, just e of Centre City Pkwy. Ext corridors.
Pets: Supervision.
SAVE SD ✕ 🖬 🖵 🌊

🅰 ◆◆◆ Welk Resort Center 🆁
(760) 749-3000. **$139-$190, 3 days notice.** 8860 Lawrence
Welk Dr. 9 mi n on I-15, between Deer Springs and Old
Castle Rd exits. Ext corridors. **Pets:** Very small. Designated
rooms, no service, supervision, crate.
SAVE ✕ 🖬 🖵 🍴 🌊 ✕

EUREKA

🅰 ◆◆◆ Best Western Bayshore Inn 🅼 ❀
(707) 268-8005. **$70-$135.** 3500 Broadway. On US 101, s
of Bayshore Mall. Ext corridors. **Pets:** Other. $50 deposit/
room. No service, supervision, crate.
SAVE SD ✕ 🖬 🖵 🍴 🌊

◆◆◆ Eureka Inn 🅷
(707) 442-6441. **$88-$157.** 518 7th St. E of US 101 N. Int corridors. **Pets:** Supervision.
SAVE Sᴅ ⊠ 🔋 🕆 🐾

◆◆ Eureka Ramada Limited 🅼 ❀
(707) 443-2206. **$65-$85.** 270 5th St. On US 101 northbound. Int corridors. **Pets:** Small. $25 deposit/room, $8 daily fee/pet. Designated rooms, supervision.
SAVE Sᴅ ⊠ 🔋 💻 🐾

◆ Eureka Town House Motel 🅼 ❀
(707) 443-4536. **$42-$58.** 933 4th St. US 101 southbound, corner 4th and K sts. Ext corridors. **Pets:** Medium, dogs only. $5 one-time fee/room. Designated rooms, no service, supervision, crate.
SAVE Sᴅ ⊠ 🔋 💻 🐾

◆◆◆ Quality Inn 🅼
(707) 443-1601. **$68-$120.** 1209 4th St. On US 101 southbound, between M and N sts;. Ext corridors. **Pets:** Supervision.
SAVE Sᴅ ⊠ 🔋 💻 🐾

◆◆◆ Red Lion Hotel 🅼🅸 ❀
(707) 445-0844. **$82-$92.** 1929 4th St. US 101 southbound between T and V sts. Int corridors. **Pets:** Other. $15 one-time fee/pet. Supervision.
SAVE Sᴅ ⊠ 🐾 🔋 💻 🕆 🐾

◆◆ Sunrise Inn & Suites 🅼 ❀
(707) 443-9751. **$45-$59.** 129 4th St. US 101 southbound at C St, northbound exit C St West. Ext corridors. **Pets:** Very small, other. $4 daily fee/pet, $4 one-time fee/pet. No service, supervision, crate.
SAVE Sᴅ ⊠ 🐾

FALL RIVER MILLS

◆ Hi-Mont Motel 🅼 ❀
(530) 336-5541. **$50-$71.** 43021 Bridge St.. 1 mi w on Hwy 299 at Bridge St.. Ext corridors. **Pets:** Other. $10 one-time fee/pet. Supervision.
SAVE Sᴅ ⊠ 🐾 🔋 💻

◆ Lava Creek Lodge 🆇 ❀
(530) 336-6288. **$75-$130.** One Island Rd. 12 mi n of SR 299 via Glenburn Rd, e on Brown Rd and n on CR A19, bear right on Island Rd to gravel driveway. Ext corridors. **Pets:** Other. $12 daily fee/pet. Supervision.
⊠ 🕆 🐾 🐾 CTV 🐾

FALLBROOK

◆◆ Best Western Franciscan Inn 🅼 ❀
(760) 728-6174. **$62-$82.** 1635 S Mission Rd. 1 mi s on CR S-13. Ext corridors. **Pets:** Small. $10 one-time fee/room. Designated rooms, no service, supervision, crate.
Sᴅ ⊠ 🔋 💻 🐾

◆◆◆ La Estancia Inn 🅼
(760) 723-2888. **$65-$105.** 3135 S Old Hwy 395. Adjacent to I-15, exit Pala Rd and SR 76, 0.3 mi n. Ext/int corridors. **Pets:** Supervision.
ASK Sᴅ ⊠ 🔋 🐾

FISH CAMP

◆◆ The Narrow Gauge Inn 🅼🅸
(559) 683-7720. **$140, 4 days notice.** 48571 Hwy 41. 4 mi from South Gate to YNP. Ext corridors. **Pets:** Supervision.
⊠ 💻 🕆 🐾 🐾

◆◆◆◆ Tenaya Lodge at Yosemite 🅷
(559) 683-6555. **$169-$294.** 1122 Hwy 41. 2 mi from south gate to YNP. Int corridors. **Pets:** Small. Designated rooms, supervision.
⊠ 🐾 🐾 🔋 💻 🕆 🐾 🐾

FORT BRAGG

◆◆ Beachcomber Motel 🅼 ❀
(707) 964-2402. **$79-$119.** 1111 N Main St. 1 mi n on SR 1. Ext corridors. **Pets:** $10 daily fee/pet. Supervision.
⊠ 🔋 💻 🐾 🐾

◆◆ Cleone Gardens Inn 🅼 ❀
(707) 964-2788. **$77-$150, 3 days notice.** 24600 N Hwy 1. 3 mi n on SR 1. Ext corridors. **Pets:** Medium, dogs only. $5 daily fee/pet. Designated rooms, no service, supervision, crate.
⊠ 🐾

FORTUNA

◆◆◆ Best Western Country Inn 🅼 ❀
(707) 725-6822. **$78-$83.** 2025 Riverwalk Dr. W of US 101, exit Kenmar Rd/Riverwalk. Ext corridors. **Pets:** Other. No service, supervision, crate.
SAVE Sᴅ ⊠ 🐾 🐾 🐾 🔋 💻 🐾

◆◆ Fortuna Super 8 🅼 ❀
(707) 725-2888. **$54-$79.** 1805 Alamar Way. w of US 101 exit Kenmar Rd/Riverwalk. Ext corridors. **Pets:** Small, dogs only. $20 deposit/room, $6 daily fee/pet, $6 one-time fee/pet. No service, supervision, crate.
SAVE ⊠ 🐾 🔋 💻

◆◆◆ Holiday Inn Express 🅼 ❀
(707) 725-5500. **$95-$125, 3 days notice.** 1859 Alamar Way. W of US 101, exit Kenmar Rd/Riverwalk. Ext corridors. **Pets:** Small, dogs only. $20 deposit/room. No service, supervision, crate.
SAVE Sᴅ ⊠ 🔋 🐾

FOUNTAIN VALLEY

◆◆ Ramada Limited-Huntington Beach/ Fountain Valley 🅼 ❀
(714) 847-3388. **$79-$79.** 9125 Recreation Cir. Adj to I-405; northbound exit Warner Ave W, southbound exit Magnolia just e. Ext corridors. **Pets:** Medium, other. $25 deposit/room, $20 daily fee/pet, $20 one-time fee/pet. Designated rooms, supervision.
SAVE Sᴅ ⊠ 🔋 🐾

◆◆◆ Residence Inn by Marriott 🅰 ❀
(714) 965-8000. **$94-$169.** 9930 Slater Ave. Just n of I-405, exit Brookhurst St. Ext corridors. **Pets:** Other. $6 daily fee/room, $40 one-time fee/room. Supervision.
ASK Sᴅ ⊠ 🔋 💻 🐾 🐾

FREMONT

▲▲▲ ◆◆◆ Best Western Garden Court Inn 🅜
(510) 792-4300. **$139-$149, 3 days notice.** 5400 Mowry
Ave. E of I-880 exit Ave E Mowry Ave. Int corridors.
Pets: Small. Designated rooms, no service, supervision,
crate.

[SAVE] [S6] [✕] [📵] [💻] [🐾]

◆ Good Nite Inn 🅜
(510) 656-9307. **Call for rates.** 4135 Cushing Pkwy. W of
I-880 exit Fremont Blvd/Cushing Pkwy. Ext corridors.
Pets: Small. Supervision.

[✕] [📵] [🐾]

◆◆ Homestead Village Guest Studios 🅜 🐾
(510) 353-1664. **$109-$134.** 46080 Fremont Blvd. W of
I-880 exit Fremont Blvd/Cushing Pkwy. Int corridors.
Pets: Small. $75 one-time fee/room. Supervision.

[ASK] [✕] [💷] [CTV]

◆◆◆ La Quinta Inn & Suites 🅜 🐾
(510) 445-0808. **$109-$139.** 46200 Landing Pkwy. W of
I-880, exit Fremont Blvd/Cushing Pkwy. Int corridors.
Pets: Small, other. No service, supervision, crate.

[✕] [💷] [📵] [💻] [🐾]

◆◆◆ Residence Inn By Marriott 🅜 🐾
(510) 794-5900. **$189-$209.** 5400 Farwell Pl. E of I-880,
exit Mowry Ave. Ext corridors. **Pets:** Other. $10 daily fee/
pet, $75 one-time fee/room. Supervision.

[ASK] [S6] [✕] [🐾] [✕]

FRESNO

▲▲▲ ◆◆◆ Best Western Garden Court
Inn 🅜 🐾
(559) 237-1881. **$49-$89, 5 days notice.** 2141 N Parkway
Dr. Just w of SR 99, Clinton Ave exit, just s. Ext corridors.
Pets: Medium, other. $50 deposit/pet, $10 daily fee/pet. No
service, supervision, crate.

[SAVE] [S6] [✕] [🔊] [📵] [💻] [🍴] [🐾]

◆◆ Days Inn-Parkway 🅜 🐾
(559) 268-6211. **$39-$69.** 1101 N Parkway Dr. W of SR 99,
Olive St exit. Ext corridors. **Pets:** Small. $5 daily fee/pet, $5
one-time fee/pet. No service, supervision, crate.

[ASK] [S6] [✕] [📵] [🐾] [✕]

▲▲▲ ◆◆◆ Holiday Inn Express-Barcus 🅜 🐾
(559) 277-5700. **$105.** 5046 N Barcus. Just e of SR 99,
Shaw Ave exit. Int corridors. **Pets:** Small. $20 one-time
fee/room. No service, supervision, crate.

[SAVE] [S6] [✕] [📵] [🔊] [📵] [💻] [🐾]

▲▲▲ ◆ Knights Inn 🅜 🐾
(559) 275-7766. **$49-$69.** 3093 N Parkway. Just w of SR
99, Shields Ave exit from S Clinton exit from n. Ext corridors. **Pets:** $25 deposit/pet, $5 daily fee/pet, $5 one-time
fee/pet. No service, supervision, crate.

[SAVE] [S6] [✕] [📵] [📵] [💻] [🐾]

▲▲▲ ◆◆◆ La Quinta Inn 🅜 🐾
(559) 442-1110. **$59-$79.** 2926 Tulare St. Just w of SR 41,
Tulare St exit. Ext corridors. **Pets:** Medium. No service,
supervision, crate.

[SAVE] [✕] [📵] [🔊] [📵] [💻] [🐾]

◆◆◆ Radisson Hotel 🅷
(559) 268-1000. **$90-$90.** 2233 Ventura St. E of SR 99,
Ventura St exit; adjacent to Convention Center. Int corridors.
Pets: Designated rooms, no service, supervision, crate.

[ASK] [S6] [✕] [📵] [🔊] [💷] [📵] [💻] [🍴] [🐾]

◆◆ Ramada Inn-Ashlan 🅜 🐾
(559) 275-2727. **$59-$85, 3 days notice.** 4278 W Ashlan
Ave. Just w of SR 99 Ashlan Ave exit. Ext corridors.
Pets: Supervision.

[ASK] [S6] [✕] [📵] [🐾]

▲▲▲ ◆ Ramada Limited 🅜
(559) 442-1082. **$45-$60, 3 days notice.** 1804 W Olive
Ave. 0.2 mi w of SR 99, Olive Ave exit. Ext corridors.
Pets: Supervision.

[S6] [✕] [📵] [🐾]

◆◆◆ Residence Inn by Marriott 🅜 🐾
(559) 222-8900. **$124.** 5322 N Diana Ave. 0.3 mi w of SR
41, Shaw Ave exit, n on Blackstone and e on Barstow. Int
corridors. **Pets:** Other. $6 daily fee/pet, $75 one-time fee/
room. Supervision.

[ASK] [S6] [✕] [📵] [🔊] [💷] [💻] [🐾]

◆ Rodeway Inn 🅜
(559) 268-0363. **$32-$40.** 949 N Parkway Dr. SR 99 exit
Olive Ave; w to Parkway Dr. Ext corridors. **Pets:** Small.
Supervision.

[ASK] [S6] [✕] [📵] [🐾]

▲▲▲ ◆ Super 8-Downtown 🅜 🐾
(559) 268-0621. **$45-$55, 3 days notice.** 2127 Inyo St. 0.5
mi e of SR 99, Ventura St exit. Ext corridors. **Pets:** $5 daily
fee/pet. No service, supervision, crate.

[SAVE] [S6] [✕] [🔊] [📵] [🐾]

◆◆ Super 8-Parkway 🅜 🐾
(559) 268-0741. **$49-$89.** 1087 N Parkway Dr. Just w of
SR 99; Olive Ave exit. Ext corridors. **Pets:** Other. $50
deposit/pet, $10 daily fee/pet. No service, supervision,
crate.

[ASK] [S6] [✕] [📵] [💻] [🐾]

▲▲▲ ◆ Super 8-University 🅜
(559) 294-0224. **$52-$61.** 2655 E Shaw Ave. 8 mi e of SR
99, Shaw Ave exit. Ext corridors. **Pets:** Designated rooms,
no service, supervision, crate.

[SAVE] [S6] [✕] [📵] [🐾]

▲▲▲ ◆◆ Travelodge 🅜 🐾
(559) 276-7745. **$49-$69.** 3093 N Parkway. Just w of SR
99, Sheilds Ave exit. Ext corridors. **Pets:** $25 deposit/pet,
$5 daily fee/pet, $5 one-time fee/pet. No service, supervision, crate.

[SAVE] [S6] [✕] [📵] [💻] [🐾]

◆◆ Travelodge Blackstone 🅜 🐾
(559) 229-9840. **$45.** 3876 N Blackstone Ave. 0.3 mi w of
SR 41, Shields Ave exit. Ext corridors. **Pets:** Other. $5 daily
fee/pet. No service, supervision, crate.

[ASK] [S6] [✕] [📵] [💻] [🐾]

GARBERVILLE

AAA ◆◆◆ **Best Western Humboldt House Inn** M
(707) 923-2771. **$85-$95.** 701 Redwood Dr. US 101 1st exit. Ext corridors. **Pets:** Other. Designated rooms, no service, supervision, crate.
SAVE

AAA ◆◆ **Motel Garberville** M
(707) 923-2422. **$49-$69.** 948 Redwood Dr. On US 101 business rt. Ext corridors. **Pets:** Small. No service, supervision, crate.
SAVE

AAA ◆◆ **Sherwood Forest Motel** M
(707) 923-2721. **$60-$94.** 814 Redwood Dr. North and southbound US 101 1st exit. Ext corridors. **Pets:** Small. No service, supervision, crate.

GARDEN GROVE

◆◆◆ **Candlewood Suites Anaheim-South** M
(714) 539-4200. **Call for rates** (no credit cards). 12901 Garden Grove Blvd. Just w of Haster St; from SR 22, exit Haster St. Int corridors. **Pets:** Medium. $200 one-time fee/room. No service, supervision, crate.

GILROY

AAA ◆◆ **Leavesley Inn** M
(408) 847-5500. **$50-$73.** 8430 Murray Ave. Just w of US 101; Leavesley Rd exit. Ext corridors. **Pets:** Small. $10 one-time fee/pet. Designated rooms, no service, supervision, crate.
SAVE

AAA ◆◆ **Rodeway Inn** M
(408) 847-0688. **$52-$92.** 611 Leavesley Rd. Just e of US 101, Leavesley Rd exit. Ext corridors. **Pets:** Small, other. $50 deposit/room. Designated rooms, no service, supervision, crate.
SAVE

GLENNVILLE

◆ **The Bunkhouse Motel** M
(661) 536-9100. **$65-$95, 3 days notice.** 12044 Hwy 15S. ON SR 155 at jct Granite Rd. Ext corridors. **Pets:** $20 deposit/room. Supervision.
A$K CTV

GRASS VALLEY

◆◆ **Alta Sierra Village Inn** M
(530) 273-9102. **$49-$160.** 11858 Tammy Way. 6 mi s; e 1.1 mi on Alta Sierra Dr; s 0.8 mi on Norlene; e 0.5 mi on Tammy; follow signs to Alta Sierra Country Club. Ext corridors. **Pets:** $10 one-time fee/room. Supervision.

AAA ◆◆ **Best Western Gold Country Inn** M
(530) 273-1393. **$70-$95.** 11972 Sutton Way. 1 mi e; off and adjacent to SR 20 and 49; midway between Grass Valley and Nevada City; exit Brunswick Rd. Ext corridors. **Pets:** Medium, other. $10 one-time fee/pet. No service, supervision, crate.
SAVE

AAA ◆ **Coach N' Four Motel** M
(530) 273-8009. **$48-$80, 3 days notice.** 628 S Auburn St. SR 49, exit E Empire St, 0.3 mi e. Ext corridors. **Pets:** Other. $50 deposit/pet, $10 one-time fee/pet. Designated rooms, no service, supervision, crate.
CTV

AAA ◆◆ **Golden Chain Resort Motel** M
(530) 273-7279. **$48-$88, 3 days notice.** 13363 SR 49. 2.5 mi s on SR 49. Ext corridors. **Pets:** Small. $10 daily fee/pet. Designated rooms, no service, supervision, crate.
CTV

AAA ◆ **Holiday Lodge** M
(530) 273-4406. **$48-$60.** 1221 E Main St. 1.3 mi e; 0.8 mi e on Old Hwy 20 and 49; exit SR 49 Frwy via Idaho-Maryland Rd exits. Ext corridors. **Pets:** Small, dogs only. $20 deposit/pet. No service, supervision, crate.
SAVE

GRIDLEY

AAA ◆◆ **Pacific Motel** M
(530) 846-4580. **$37-$58.** 1308 Hwy 99. 1 mi s on SR 99. Ext corridors. **Pets:** $3 one-time fee/room. No service, supervision, crate.

GROVELAND

AAA ◆◆ **Groveland Hotel** CI
(209) 962-4000. **$125-$145.** 18767 Main St. Center. **Pets:** Other. No service, supervision, crate.
SAVE CTV

AAA ◆◆ **Yosemite Westgate Motel** M
(209) 962-5281. **$69-$149, 3 days notice.** 7633 Hwy 120. 12 mi e on SR 120. Ext corridors. **Pets:** $10 daily fee/pet. No service, supervision, crate.
SAVE CTV

GUALALA

AAA ◆◆ **Gualala Country Inn** M
(707) 884-4343. **$89-$165.** 47955 Center St. E side of SR 1. Ext/int corridors. **Pets:** Other. $10 one-time fee/pet. Supervision.
AC

AAA ◆ **Surf Motel** M
(707) 884-3571. **$89-$175.** 39170 Hwy 1. W side of Hwy SR 1. Ext corridors. **Pets:** Small. Designated rooms, no service, supervision, crate.
AC

HANFORD

(AAA) ◆◆◆ Sequoia Inn M
(559) 582-0338. **$66-$76.** 1655 Mall Dr. Exit SR 198 at 12th
Ave, n to Mall Dr. Int corridors. **Pets:** Small. Designated
rooms, no service, supervision, crate.
[SAVE] [S] [X] [■] [▣] [≋]

HAYWARD

(AAA) ◆ Phoenix Lodge M ☼
(510) 786-0417. **$45-$80.** 500 West A St. W of I-880, A St
exit. Int corridors. **Pets:** Small, other. $25 deposit/pet, $10
daily fee/room. No service, supervision, crate.
[SAVE] [S] [X] [⚿] [■]

HEALDSBURG

(AAA) ◆◆ Best Western Dry Creek Inn M ☼
(707) 433-0300. **$84-$159.** 198 Dry Creek Rd. just e of US
101, Dry Creek Rd exit. Ext corridors. **Pets:** Medium, other.
$15 daily fee/pet. No service, supervision, crate.
[X] [⊡] [■] [▣] [≋]

(AAA) ◆◆ Fairview Motel M ☼
(707) 433-5548. **$65-$95, 4 days notice.** 74 Healdsburg
Ave. Just e of US 101; central Healdsburg exit. Ext corridors. **Pets:** Small, dogs only. $50 deposit/room, $10 one-
time fee/pet. Designated rooms, no service, supervision,
crate.
[S] [X] [■] [≋] [X]

HEMET

(AAA) ◆◆ Best Western Hemet Motor Inn M ☼
(909) 925-6605. **$40-$58.** 2625 W Florida Ave. 1.3 mi w on
SR 74 and 79. Ext corridors. **Pets:** Small. $10 one-time
fee/room. Designated rooms, no service, supervision, crate.
[SAVE] [S] [X] [■] [▣] [≋]

(AAA) ◆ Coach Light Motel M ☼
(909) 658-3237. **$32-$44.** 1640 W Florida Ave. 1 mi w on
SR 74 and SR 79. Ext corridors. **Pets:** Small, other. $7
one-time fee/room. Supervision.
[SAVE] [S] [X] [■] [≋] [CTV]

(AAA) ◆◆ Hemet Inn M ☼
(909) 929-6366. **$36-$46.** 800 W Florida Ave. 0.7 mi w on
SR 74 and 79. Ext corridors. **Pets:** Small, dogs only. $10
one-time fee/pet. Designated rooms, no service, supervision, crate.
[SAVE] [S] [X] [⚿] [■] [▣] [≋]

◆◆ Hemet Travelodge M ☼
(909) 766-1902. **$75-$85.** 1201 W Florida Ave. 0.8 mi w on
SR 74 and 79. Ext corridors. **Pets:** Other. $10 daily fee/pet.
No service, supervision, crate.
[ASK] [S] [X] [■] [≋]

(AAA) ◆◆ Ramada Inn M
(909) 929-8900. **$46-$54.** 3885 W Florida Ave. 2 mi w on
SR 74 and 79. Ext corridors. **Pets:** No service, supervision,
crate.
[SAVE] [S] [X] [■] [≋]

HESPERIA

(AAA) ◆ Days Inn Suites M ☼
(760) 948-0600. **$55-$64.** 14865 Bear Valley Rd. Just e of
I-15, exit Bear Valley Rd; 0.5 mi e of Victor Valley Mall. Ext
corridors. **Pets:** Supervision.
[SAVE] [S] [X] [■]

HOPE VALLEY

(AAA) ◆◆ Sorensen's R ☼
(530) 694-2203. **$80-$450.** 14255 Hwy 88. On Hwy 88, 1
mi e of jct 89. Ext corridors. **Pets:** Other. Designated rooms,
supervision.
[X] [■] [⑪] [X] [K] [CTV] [Z]

IDYLLWILD

(AAA) ◆◆ Fireside Inn C ☼
(909) 659-2966. **$55-$110.** 54540 N Circle Dr. 0.3 mi ne of
SR 243 and Village Center. Ext corridors. **Pets:** Other. $10
one-time fee/room. No service, supervision, crate.
[X] [■] [≋] [Z]

IMPERIAL

(AAA) ◆◆ Best Western Imperial Valley Inn MI
(760) 355-4500. **$48-$87, 3 days notice.** 1093 Airport Blvd.
On SR 86, 2.5 mi n of El Centro. Ext corridors. **Pets:** No
service, supervision, crate.
[SAVE] [S] [X] [■] [▣] [⑪] [≋]

INDEPENDENCE

(AAA) ◆ Ray's Den Motel M ☼
(760) 878-2122. **$43-$56.** 405 N Edwards. On US 395. Ext
corridors. **Pets:** Other. $6 daily fee/room. No service, super-
vision, crate.
[SAVE] [S] [X] [■]

INDIAN WELLS

(AAA) ◆◆◆◆ Miramonte Resort H ☼
(760) 341-2200. **$259-$339, 3 days notice.** 76-477 Hwy
111. SR 111. Ext/int corridors. **Pets:** Small. $50 one-time
fee/room. Supervision.
[SAVE] [S] [X] [■] [▣] [⑪] [≋]

INDIO

(AAA) ◆◆◆ Best Western Date Tree Hotel M
(760) 347-3421. **$59-$129.** 81-909 Indio Blvd. 0.5 mi s of
I-10, westbound Monroe St exit; eastbound Indio Blvd exit.
Pets: Small. Supervision.
[SAVE] [S] [X] [■] [≋] [X]

(AAA) ◆◆ Comfort Inn M ☼
(760) 347-4044. **$59-$129.** 43-505 Monroe St. 0.5 mi s of
I-10; exit Monroe St. Int corridors. **Pets:** $25 deposit/room,
$10 one-time fee/room. No service, supervision, crate.
[SAVE] [S] [X] [■] [≋]

(AAA) ◆◆ Palm Shadow Inn M ☼
(760) 347-3476. **$84-$144, 7 days notice.** 80-761 Hwy 111.
SR 111, 0.8 mi e of Jefferson Ave. Ext corridors.
Pets: Medium, other. $300 deposit/pet, $10 daily fee/pet,
$10 one-time fee/pet. Designated rooms, supervision.
[SAVE] [S] [X] [■] [▣] [≋]

ⒶⒶⒶ ◆◆ **Royal Plaza Inn** 🅜 ✿
(760) 347-0911. **$64-$119, 3 days notice.** 82-347 Hwy 111. SR 111, 0.4 mi e of Monroe St. Int corridors. **Pets:** Designated rooms, no service, supervision, crate.

[SAVE] [✕] [🔌] [🍴] [🏊]

ⒶⒶⒶ ◆◆ **Super 8 Motel** 🅜 ✿
(760) 342-0264. **$79-$104, 7 days notice.** 81753 Hwy 111. Just s of SR 111 and w of Monroe. Ext corridors. **Pets:** $25 deposit/room, $5 daily fee/pet, $5 one-time fee/pet. Designated rooms, no service, supervision, crate.

[SAVE] [S🔒] [✕] [🏊]

IRVINE

ⒶⒶⒶ ◆◆◆ **Atrium Hotel at Orange County**
    Airport 🄷
(949) 833-2770. **$148-$179.** 18700 MacArthur Blvd. 0.5 mi s of I-405. Int corridors. **Pets:** Small. No service, supervision, crate.

[SAVE] [S🔒] [✕] [🔌] [🖥] [🍴] [🏊]

ⒶⒶⒶ ◆◆◆ **Hilton Irvine/Orange County**
    Airport 🄷
(949) 833-9999. **$169-$224.** 18800 MacArthur Blvd. 0.5 mi s of I-405. Int corridors. **Pets:** No service, supervision, crate.

[SAVE] [S🔒] [✕] [🔌] [🖥] [🍴] [🏊] [✕]

◆◆◆ **Homestead Village** 🅜
(949) 727-4228. **$69-$79.** 30 Technology Dr. E side of I-5, exit Alton Pkwy. Ext corridors. **Pets:** Small. Supervision.

[✕]

◆◆◆ **Irvine Marriott Hotel** 🄷 ✿
(949) 553-0100. **Call for rates.** 18000 Von Karman Ave. Adjacent to I-405, exit Jamboree Rd; s to Michelson Dr, w to Von Karman Ave. Int corridors. **Pets:** Medium. No service, supervision, crate.

[ASK] [S🔒] [✕] [🔌] [🖥] [🍴] [🏊] [✕]

◆◆◆ **Residence Inn by Marriott-Irvine**
    Spectrum 🄰 ✿
(949) 380-3000. **Call for rates.** 10 Morgan at Alton Pkwy. 2 mi e of I-5, exit Alton Pkwy. Ext corridors. **Pets:** Other. $6 daily fee/pet, $40 one-time fee/room. Supervision.

[✕] [🏊] [✕]

JACKSON

ⒶⒶⒶ ◆ **Amador Motel** 🅜 ✿
(209) 223-0970. **$35-$65.** 12408 Kennedy Flat Rd. 1.5 mi n at jct SR 49 and 88 on Frontage Rd. Ext corridors. **Pets:** Other. No service, supervision, crate.

[S🔒] [✕] [🔌] [🖥] [🏊] [CTV]

ⒶⒶⒶ ◆◆ **El Campo Casa Resort Motel** 🅜 ✿
(209) 223-0100. **$46-$85.** 12548 Kennedy Flat Rd. 1.5 mi w in Martell, at jct SR 49 and 88 on Frontage Rd; approach off SR 88. Ext corridors. **Pets:** Medium, other. Supervision.

[SAVE] [✕] [🖥] [🏊] [✕] [CTV] [✕]

ⒶⒶⒶ ◆◆ **Jackson Gold Lodge** 🅜
(209) 223-0486. **$54-$80.** 850 N SR 49/88. 0.5 mi w on SR 49 and 88. Ext corridors. **Pets:** No service, supervision, crate.

[SAVE] [S🔒] [✕] [🖥] [🏊]

JENNER

◆◆ **Jenner Inn & Cottages** 🄲
(707) 865-2377. **$75-$235, 7 days notice.** 10400 Hwy 1. Ext corridors. **Pets:** Supervision.

[ASK] [✕] [🔌] [🖥] [🍴] [✕] [CTV]

JULIAN

ⒶⒶⒶ ◆◆ **Apple Tree Inn** 🅜 ✿
(760) 765-0222. **$77-$87.** 4360 Hwy 78. 3 mi w on SR 78 and 79. Ext corridors. **Pets:** $50 deposit/pet, $10 daily fee/pet. No service, supervision, crate.

[SAVE] [S🔒] [✕] [🖥] [🏊]

JUNE LAKE

◆ **Gull Lake Lodge** 🄰 ✿
(760) 648-7516. **$50-$95, 21 days notice.** 132 Leonard Ave. In the village area just N of SR 158, via Knoll and Bruce sts.. Ext corridors. **Pets:** Other. $6 daily fee/room. Designated rooms, no service, supervision, crate.

[✕] [🖥] [✕] [✕]

ⒶⒶⒶ ◆◆ **June Lake Motel & Cabins** 🅜 ✿
(760) 648-7547. **$60-$150.** 2716 Boulder Dr. SR 158, in center of village. Ext corridors. **Pets:** $10 daily fee/pet, $10 one-time fee/pet. Designated rooms, supervision.

[✕] [🔌] [🖥] [✕]

ⒶⒶⒶ ◆◆ **June Lake Villager** 🅜
(760) 648-7712. **$25-$75, 30 days notice.** 85 Boulder Dr. Center of village, on SR 158. Ext corridors. **Pets:** Designated rooms, no service, supervision, crate.

[✕] [🖥] [✕]

KELSEYVILLE

◆ **Bell Haven Resort** 🄲 ✿
(707) 279-4329. **$470-$470.** 3415 White Oak Way. 6 mi e of SR 29, just no of Soda Bay Rd. Ext corridors. **Pets:** Other. $10 daily fee/pet. Supervision.

[ASK] [S🔒] [✕] [🖥] [✕] [✕] [✕]

KERNVILLE

ⒶⒶⒶ ◆ **Hi-Ho Resort Lodge** 🅜 ✿
(760) 376-2671. **$65-$85, 5 days notice.** 11901 Sierra Hwy. 1.2 mi s on Sierra Way. Ext corridors. **Pets:** $10 daily fee/pet, $10 one-time fee/pet. Supervision.

[S🔒] [✕] [🏊] [✕] [✕]

ⒶⒶⒶ ◆ **River View Lodge** 🅜
(760) 376-6019. **$55-$95.** 2 Sirretta St. In center of town, on Kernville Rd, at the bridge. Ext corridors. **Pets:** Small. No service, supervision, crate.

[SAVE] [S🔒] [✕] [🔌] [✕] [✕]

KETTLEMAN CITY

ⒶⒶⒶ ◆◆ **Best Western Inn** 🅜
(559) 386-0804. **$61-$91, 7 days notice.** 33410 Powers DR. East of and adjacent to I-5, exit SR 41 n, 0.3 mi to Bernard, n 0.3 mi. Ext corridors. **Pets:** Medium. Designated rooms, no service, supervision, crate.

[SAVE] [S🔒] [✕] [🔌] [🖥] [🏊] [CTV]

⬤ ◆◆ Super 8 M 🐾
(559) 386-9530. **$43-$69.** 33415 Powers Dr. 2 mi sw; 0.5 blk e off I-5, jct SR 41; exit Kettleman City-Paso Robles. Ext corridors. **Pets:** Medium, other. $40 deposit/room, $10 one-time fee/room. No service, supervision, crate.

🆂 🆂 ⊠ ⊡ 🖼 CTV

KING CITY

⬤ ◆◆ Courtesy Inn M 🐾
(831) 385-4646. **$42-$150.** 4 Broadway Cir. Just w of US 101; Broadway exit. Ext corridors. **Pets:** Other. $10 daily fee/pet. Designated rooms, no service, supervision, crate.

🆂 ⊠ 🏠 📖 ⊡ 🖥 📺 🖼

KINGSBURG

⬤ ◆◆ Swedish Inn M 🐾
(559) 897-1022. **$48-$58.** 401 Conejo St. Just w of SR 99, Conejo exit. Ext corridors. **Pets:** Other. $25 deposit/room. Supervision.

🆂 ⊠ ⊡ 🖥 🖼

LAGUNA BEACH

◆◆◆ The Carriage House-Bed & Breakfast BB 🐾
(949) 494-8945. **$140-$160, 3 days notice.** 1322 Catalina St. 1 mi s; just e of SR 1, via Cress St. Ext corridors. **Pets:** Medium. $10 daily fee/pet. No service, supervision, crate.

⊠ ⊡ 🖥 🖼 ☎

LAKE TAHOE METROPOLITAN AREA

KINGS BEACH

⬤ ◆ Stevenson's Holliday Inn M
(530) 546-2269. **$59-$129, 5 days notice.** 8742 N Lake Blvd. SR 28, 1 mi e of SR 267. Ext corridors. **Pets:** Medium. No service, supervision, crate.

🆂 🆂 ⊠ ⊡ 🖼 🖥

SOUTH LAKE TAHOE

⬤ ◆◆ Alder Inn M 🐾
(530) 544-4485. **$42-$125.** 1072 Ski Run Blvd. 2 1/2 blks s off US 50 on Ski Run Blvd; 0.8 mi below Heavenly Valley ski lift terminal. Ext corridors. **Pets:** $10 daily fee/pet. Supervision.

🆂 🆂 ⊠ ⊡ 🖥 🖼 🖥

⬤ ◆◆ Alpenrose Inn M
(530) 544-2985. **$49-$99, 3 days notice.** 4074 Pine Blvd. 0.3 mi n of US 50 via Park Ave. Ext corridors. **Pets:** Small. Designated rooms, no service, supervision, crate.

🆂 🆂 ⊠ ⊡ 🖥 🖼

◆ Beachside Inn, Suites, Spas & Coppuccino Bar M 🐾
(530) 544-2400. **$35-$79.** 930 Park Av. 3 blks from casino center. Ext corridors. **Pets:** Other. Supervision.

⊡ 🖥 🖼

⬤ ◆◆ Casa Laguna Inn BB 🐾
(949) 494-2996. **$89-$249, 3 days notice.** 2510 S Coast Hwy. 1.3 mi se on SR 1. Ext corridors. **Pets:** Other. $5 daily fee/pet. Supervision.

⊠ ⊡ 🖼 🖥

LAKE ARROWHEAD

⬤ ◆◆◆ Arrowhead Saddleback Inn CI 🐾
(909) 336-3571. **$79-$170, 7 days notice.** SR 173, at jct SR 189, across from entrance to Lake Arrowhead Village. Ext/int corridors. **Pets:** Small. $10 daily fee/pet. Designated rooms, supervision.

🆂 🆂 ⊠ ⊡ 🍽

⬤ ◆◆ Arrowhead Tree Top Lodge M 🐾
(909) 337-2311. **$59-$173, 7 days notice.** 27992 Rainbow Dr. SR 173, 0.3 mi s of Lake Arrowhead Village. Ext corridors. **Pets:** Medium. $10 daily fee/pet. Designated rooms, supervision.

🆂 🆂 ⊡ 🖼 🖥 ☎

⬤ ◆◆ Blue Jay Lodge M 🐾
(530) 544-5232. **$59-$129.** 4133 Cedar Ave. 2 blks from casino center. Ext corridors. **Pets:** Small. $25 deposit/room, $10 daily fee/room. Designated rooms, supervision.

🆂 🆂 ⊠ ⊡ 🖥 🖼 🖥

⬤ ◆◆ Days Inn-Casino Area/South Lake Tahoe M 🐾
(530) 541-4800. **$67-$115, 3 days notice.** 968 Park Ave. 3 blks w of casino center; 1 blk n off US 50 toward lake at Park and Cedar aves. Int corridors. **Pets:** $25 deposit/room, $5 daily fee/pet. Designated rooms, supervision.

🆂 🆂 ⊠ 🖥 🖼

⬤ ◆ Econo Lodge M 🐾
(530) 544-2036. **$45-$125, 3 days notice.** 3536 Lake Tahoe Blvd. US 50, 1.5 mi w of Casino Center. Ext corridors. **Pets:** Medium, other. Supervision.

🆂 🆂 ⊠ 🖼 🖥

⬤ ◆◆ High Country Lodge M
(530) 541-0508. **$25-$150, 5 days notice.** 1227 Emerald Bay Rd. 0.5 mi n of airport; on US 50. Ext corridors. **Pets:** Small. Designated rooms, no service, supervision, crate.

🆂 🆂 ⊠ ⊡ 🖥

(AAA) ◆◆ Lakepark Lodge M ❀
(530) 541-5004. **$45-$85.** 4081 Cedar Ave. Just off Hwy 50, near Stateline Casinos. Ext corridors. **Pets:** Medium, dogs only. $40 deposit/room, $10 one-time fee/room. No service, supervision, crate.
[SAVE] [✕] [🔧] [▭]

(AAA) ◆◆ Lampliter Motel M ❀
(530) 544-2936. **Call for rates, 3 days notice.** 4143 Cedar Ave. 2 blks n of US 50, adjacent to Casino Center. Ext corridors. **Pets:** Medium. $100 deposit/room, $8 one-time fee/room. Designated rooms, no service, supervision, crate.
[SAVE] [✕] [▭] [🐾]

(AAA) ◆ Ridgewood Inn M ❀
(530) 541-8589. **$40-$78, 3 days notice.** 1341 Emerald Bay Rd. US 50, 0.5 mi n of airport. Ext corridors. **Pets:** $25 deposit/room. No service, supervision, crate.
[S🐾] [✕] [🐾]

(AAA) ◆ Rodeway Inn M ❀
(530) 541-7900. **$29-$99, 3 days notice.** 4082 Lake Tahoe Blvd. US 50, 1 blk w of casino center. Ext corridors. **Pets:** Other. $10 deposit/room, $10 daily fee/room, $10 one-time fee/room. Designated rooms, no service, supervision, crate.
[SAVE] [S🐾] [✕] [▭] [🐾] [🐾]

(AAA) ◆◆◆ Tahoe Keys Resort X
(530) 544-5397. **$108-$440.** 599 Tahoe Keys Blvd. Exit US 50 at Tahoe Keys Blvd, 1 mi w. Ext corridors. **Pets:** Small. No service, supervision, crate.
[SAVE] [S🐾] [✕] [▭] [🐾] [✕] [🐾]

(AAA) ◆◆◆ Tahoe Lakeshore Lodge and Spa M ❀
(530) 541-2180. **$129-$500.** 930 Bal BiJou Rd. On lake, 1.5 mi w of casino center; off US 50. Ext/int corridors. **Pets:** Small. Supervision.
[✕] [▭] [🐾] [✕] [🐾]

(AAA) ◆ Tahoe Sundowner Motel M
(530) 541-2282. **$30-$140, 5 days notice.** 1211 Emerald Bay Rd. On US 50, 0.5 mi n of airport. Ext corridors. **Pets:** Very small. Designated rooms, no service, supervision, crate.
[S🐾] [✕] [🐾]

(AAA) ◆ Tahoe Sunset Lodge M ❀
(530) 541-2940. **$25-$110, 7 days notice.** 1171 Emerald Bay Rd. US 50, 0.5 mi n of airport. Ext corridors. **Pets:** Other. Supervision.
[SAVE] [S🐾] [🔧] [▭]

(AAA) ◆◆ Tahoe Valley Lodge M
(530) 541-0353. **$95-$195, 7 days notice.** 2241 Lake Tahoe Blvd. 0.5 mi e of jct US 50 and SR 89, at Tahoe Keys Blvd. Ext corridors. **Pets:** Small. Designated rooms, no service, supervision, crate.
[SAVE] [S🐾] [✕] [🔧] [▭] [🐾]

TAHOMA

◆◆ Norfolk Woods Inn & Restaurant C
(530) 525-5000. **$100-$170.** 6941 West Lake Blvd. On SR 89, 9 mi s of Tahoe City. Ext/int corridors. **Pets:** Medium. Designated rooms, no service, supervision, crate.
[✕] [🍴] [🐾] [🐾]

TRUCKEE

◆◆ The Inn at Truckee M ❀
(530) 587-8888. **$89-$139.** 11506 Deerfield Dr. Exit I-80 at SR 89, just s. Int corridors. **Pets:** $11 daily fee/pet. No service, supervision, crate.
[ASK] [S🐾] [✕] [CTV]

❀ **END METROPOLITAN AREA** ❀

LANCASTER

(AAA) ◆◆ Best Western Antelope Valley Inn M
(661) 948-4651. **$69-$91.** 44055 N Sierra Hwy. 2.3 mi e of SR 14 and 138, Ave K exit. Ext/int corridors. **Pets:** Small. Supervision.
[SAVE] [✕] [🔧] [🍴] [🐾]

◆◆ Oxford Inn & Suites M ❀
(661) 949-3423. **$55-$70, 3 days notice.** 1651 West Avenue K. Adjacent to SR 14, exit Ave K, then just w. Int corridors. **Pets:** Other. $15 one-time fee/room. No service, supervision, crate.
[ASK] [S🐾] [✕] [🔧] [▭] [🐾]

LATHROP

(AAA) ◆◆ Days Inn M ❀
(209) 982-1959. **$58-$68, 5 days notice.** 14750 S Harlan Rd. Exit I-5 at Lathrop Rd. Int corridors. **Pets:** Medium. $10 daily fee/pet. Supervision.
[SAVE] [✕] [♿] [🔧] [🐾]

LEBEC

◆◆ Best Rest Inn M ❀
(661) 248-2700. **$49-$59.** 42810 Frazier Mtn Park Rd. Just w of I-5; exit Frazier Park. Int corridors. **Pets:** Other. $10 daily fee/pet, $10 one-time fee/pet. Designated rooms, supervision.
[ASK] [S🐾] [✕] [♿] [🔧] [🍴] [🐾]

LEE VINING

(AAA) ◆◆ Murphey's Motel M ❀
(760) 647-6316. **$68-$98.** On US 395. Ext corridors. **Pets:** Small. $5 daily fee/pet, $5 one-time fee/pet. Supervision.
[🐾] [CTV]

LEMOORE

(AAA) ◆◆ Best Western Vineyard Inn M ❀
(559) 924-1261. **$60-$75.** 877 East D St. 0.8 mi nw of SR 198, Houston St exit eastbound; D St exit westbound. Ext corridors. **Pets:** Supervision.
[S🐾] [✕] [🔧] [▭] [🐾]

LEWISTON

◆ Old Lewiston Inn BB
(530) 778-3385. $75-$85, 7 days notice. Deadwood Rd. Ext/int corridors. Pets: Designated rooms, no service, supervision, crate.
ASK

LINDSAY

ⒶⒶⒶ ◆◆ Olive Tree Inn M ❤
(559) 562-5188. $47-$57. 390 N Hwy 65. On SR 65. Ext corridors. Pets: Medium. $10 daily fee/pet, $10 one-time fee/pet. Supervision.
❌ 🛈 🖼

LITTLE RIVER

ⒶⒶⒶ ◆◆ The Inn at Schoolhouse Creek BB ❤
(707) 937-5525. $115-$225. 7051 N Hwy 1. 3 mi s of Mendocino; e of Coast Hwy. Ext corridors. Pets: $5 daily fee/pet, $15 one-time fee/room. Designated rooms, no service, supervision, crate.
❌ 🖵 🕷

LIVERMORE

◆◆◆ Hampton Inn M
(925) 606-6400. $94, 7 days notice. 2850 Constitution Dr. Exit I-580 Airway/Collier Canyon Rd N. Int corridors. Pets: Designated rooms, no service, supervision, crate.
ASK ❌ 🛈 🖵 🖼

◆◆◆ Residence Inn By Marriott M
(925) 373-1800. Call for rates. 1000 Airway Blvd. Exit I-580 Airway/Collier Canyon Rd N. Ext corridors. Pets: No service, supervision, crate.
❌ 🖼 🗶 CTV

LODI

ⒶⒶⒶ ◆◆ Comfort Inn M ❤
(209) 367-4848. $65-$69. 118 N Cherokee Ln. 0.3 mi n on business Rt SR 99. Ext corridors. Pets: $10 daily fee/pet, $10 one-time fee/pet. Designated rooms, no service, supervision, crate.
SAVE S🔊 ❌ 🛈 🖵 🖼

LOMPOC

ⒶⒶⒶ ◆◆◆ Best Western Vandenberg Inn M ❤
(805) 735-7731. $70-$100, 7 days notice. 940 E Ocean Ave. 1 mi e on SR 1 and 246. Ext corridors. Pets: Other. $20 one-time fee/room. No service, supervision, crate.
SAVE S🔊 ❌ 🛈 🖵 🍴 🖼

ⒶⒶⒶ ◆◆◆ Inn of Lompoc M ❤
(805) 735-7744. $69-$89. 1122 North H St. 1.2 mi n on SR 1. Ext/int corridors. Pets: Other. $15 one-time fee/room. Supervision.
SAVE S🔊 ❌ 🛈 🖵 🖼

ⒶⒶⒶ ◆◆◆ Quality Inn & Executive Suites M ❤
(805) 735-8555. $79-$99. 1621 North H St. 1.8 mi n on SR 1. Int corridors. Pets: Medium. $25 one-time fee/room. Designated rooms, no service, supervision, crate.
SAVE S🔊 ❌ 🛈 🖵 🖼

ⒶⒶⒶ ◆ Tally Ho Motor Inn M ❤
(805) 735-6444. $39-$65. 1020 E Ocean Ave. 1 mi e on SR 1 and 246. Ext corridors. Pets: Small, other. $10 daily fee/room. Designated rooms, no service, supervision, crate.
SAVE S🔊 ❌ 🛈 🖵

LONE PINE

ⒶⒶⒶ ◆◆◆ Alabama Hills Inn M ❤
(760) 876-8700. $53-$78. 1920 S Main St. 1.5 mi s on US 395. Int corridors. Pets: Small. $5 daily fee/pet, $5 one-time fee/pet. Supervision.
SAVE S🔊 ❌ 🛈 🖼

ⒶⒶⒶ ◆◆◆ Best Western Frontier Motel M
(760) 876-5571. $50-$94. 1008 S Main St. 0.5 mi s on US 395. Ext corridors. Pets: No service, supervision, crate.
SAVE S🔊 ❌ 🛈 🖵 🖼

ⒶⒶⒶ ◆◆◆ Dow Villa Motel M ❤
(760) 876-5521. $75-$105. 310 S Main St. US 395. Ext corridors. Pets: Other. Designated rooms, no service, supervision, crate.
SAVE S🔊 ❌ 🗭 🛈 🖵 🖼

ⒶⒶⒶ ◆ National 9 Trails Motel M
(760) 876-5555. $45-$89. 633 S Main St. 0.3 mi s on US 395. Ext corridors. Pets: No service, supervision, crate.
❌ 🛈 🖵 🖼

Los Angeles Metropolitan Area

ARCADIA

◆◆◆ Residence Inn by Marriott A ❤
(626) 446-6500. Call for rates. 321 E Huntington Dr. 0.5 mi w of I-210, exit Huntington Dr. Ext corridors. Pets: Other. $6 daily fee/pet, $50 one-time fee/room. Supervision.
❌ 🖵 🖼 🗶

BALDWIN PARK

◆◆◆ Radisson Hotel-San Gabriel Valley H ❤
(626) 962-6000. $94-$109. 14635 Baldwin Park Towne Center. N side of I-10, exit Puente Ave. Int corridors. Pets: Medium, other. Supervision.
ASK S🔊 ❌ 🛈 🖵 🍴 🖼

BEVERLY HILLS

(AAA) ♦♦♦♦ **Beverly Hilton** 🅷 ❀
(310) 274-7777. **$270-$330.** 9876 Wilshire at Santa Monica Blvd. Int corridors. **Pets:** Small, other. Supervision.
[SAVE] [✕] [☎] [🖳] [🍴] [🏊]

♦♦♦♦ **L'Ermitage Beverly Hills** 🅷 ❀
(310) 278-3344. **$418-$448, 3 days notice.** 9291 Burton Way. Ext corridors. **Pets:** Medium, other. $150 deposit/room, $10 one-time fee/room. Supervision.
[ASK] [✕] [♿] [🐾] [🍴] [🏊]

♦♦♦♦ **Regent Beverly Wilshire** 🅷 ❀
(310) 275-5200. **$350-$580.** 9500 Wilshire Blvd at Rodeo Dr. Int corridors. **Pets:** No service, supervision, crate.
[✕] [🍴] [🏊]

BREA

♦♦♦ **Homestead Village** 🅼
(714) 528-2500. **$59-$94.** 3050 E Imperial Blvd. 1 mi e of SR 57 at Saturn St. Ext corridors. **Pets:** Supervision.
[✕]

(AAA) ♦ **Hyland Motel** 🅼
(714) 990-6867. **$45-$50.** 727 S Brea Blvd. 0.8 mi ne of Bastanchury Rd. Ext corridors. **Pets:** Supervision.
[SAVE] [✕] [☎] [🖳]

♦♦♦ **Woodfin Suite Hotel-Brea** 🅼
(714) 579-3200. **$159-$199.** 3100 E Imperial Hwy. 1.8 mi e of SR 57, exit Imperial Hwy. Ext corridors. **Pets:** Supervision.
[ASK] [S✓] [✕] [🖳] [🏊]

BURBANK

(AAA) ♦♦♦ **Burbank Airport Hilton & Convention Center** 🅷 ❀
(818) 843-6000. **$110-$270.** 2500 Hollywood Way. 1 mi s of I-5, exit Hollywood Way. Int corridors. **Pets:** Medium, other. No service, supervision, crate.
[SAVE] [S✓] [✕] [☎] [🖳] [🍴] [🏊]

♦♦♦ **Holiday Inn-Burbank** 🅷
(818) 841-4770. **$123-$133.** 150 E Angeleno. Just e of I-5; northbound exit Olive Ave, southbound exit Verdugo Ave. Int corridors. **Pets:** Medium. Designated rooms, no service, supervision, crate.
[ASK] [✕] [♿] [🐾] [☎] [🖳] [🍴] [🏊]

CALABASAS

(AAA) ♦ **Good Nite Inn** 🅼🅸 ❀
(818) 880-6000. **$55-$70.** 26557 Agoura Rd. US 101, exit Lost Hills Rd, just s, then 0.4 mi e. Ext corridors. **Pets:** Small, dogs only. No service, supervision, crate.
[SAVE] [S✓] [✕] [☎] [🖳] [🏊]

CERRITOS

♦♦♦ **Sheraton Cerritos Hotel at Towne Center** 🅷
(562) 809-1500. **Call for rates.** 12725 Center Court Dr. Just s of SR 91; westbound exit Artesia/Bloomfield, eastbound exit Shoemaker Rd. Int corridors. **Pets:** No service, supervision, crate.
[S✓] [✕] [🏠] [☎] [🖳] [🍴] [🏊]

CHATSWORTH

♦ **Ramada Inn** 🅼 ❀
(818) 998-5289. **$65-$79, 3 days notice.** 21340 Devonshire St. SR 118, De Soto Ave exit; 1.5 mi e, then 0.5 mi n. Int corridors. **Pets:** Small. $50 deposit/room, $10 daily fee/pet, $10 one-time fee/pet. Designated rooms, no service, supervision, crate.
[ASK] [S✓] [✕] [☎] [🖳] [🍴] [🏊]

♦♦♦ **Summerfield Suites Hotel** 🅼 ❀
(818) 773-0707. **$130-$160.** 21902 Lassen St. Just e of Topanga Canyon Blvd. Ext corridors. **Pets:** Large. $10 daily fee/pet, $150 one-time fee/room. Supervision.
[ASK] [S✓] [✕] [☎] [🖳] [🏊] [✕]

COMMERCE

♦♦ **Ramada Inn** 🅼
(562) 806-4777. **Call for rates.** 7272 Gage Ave. Just sw of I-5, exit Slauson Ave. Int corridors. **Pets:** Small. Supervision.
[✕] [☎] [🖳] [🏊]

♦♦♦ **Wyndham Garden Hotel** 🅷 ❀
(323) 887-8100. **$79-$129.** 5757 Telegraph Rd. Adjacent e side of I-5, between Washington Blvd and Atlantic Ave off ramps. Int corridors. **Pets:** Supervision.
[ASK] [S✓] [✕] [☎] [🖳] [🏊]

CULVER CITY

(AAA) ♦♦♦ **Radisson Hotel-LA Westside** 🅷
(310) 649-1776. **$99-$119.** 6161 Centinela Ave. Adjacent to I-405, Jefferson Blvd exit. Int corridors. **Pets:** Supervision.
[✕] [☎] [🖳] [🍴] [🏊]

CYPRESS

♦♦♦ **Woodfin Suite Hotel-Cypress** 🅼
(714) 828-4000. **Call for rates.** 5905 Corporate Ave. Just s of Cerritos Ave and just w of Valley View. Int corridors. **Pets:** Small. No service, supervision, crate.
[ASK] [✕] [☎] [🖳] [🏊]

DIAMOND BAR

(AAA) ♦♦ **Best Western Diamond Bar** 🅼 ❀
(909) 860-3700. **$60-$80.** 259 Gentle Spring Ln. Adj to jct SR 60 and 57; just w of Diamond Bar Blvd. Ext corridors. **Pets:** Small. Supervision.
[SAVE] [S✓] [✕] [🆗] [☎] [🏊]

DOWNEY

(AAA) ♦♦♦ **Embassy Suites Hotel** 🅷
(562) 861-1900. **$144-$154.** 8425 Firestone Blvd. 2 mi w of I-605, exit Firestone Blvd. Int corridors. **Pets:** Small. Designated rooms, supervision.
[SAVE] [S✓] [✕] [☎] [🖳] [🍴] [🏊]

EL SEGUNDO

(AAA) ♦♦♦ **Embassy Suites-LAX South** 🅼🅸 ❀
(310) 640-3600. **$164-$164.** 1440 E Imperial Ave. 1 blk w of Sepulveda Blvd. Int corridors. **Pets:** Small, other. $25 daily fee/pet. Supervision.
[SAVE] [S✓] [✕] [☎] [🖳] [🍴] [🏊]

◆◆◆ Homestead Village **M**
(310) 607-4000. **$413-$453.** 1910 E Mariposa Ave. Just e of SR 1 (Sepulveda Blvd). Ext corridors. **Pets:** Very small. Designated rooms, supervision.
[ASK] [S̸o] [X]

◆◆◆ Summerfield Suites Hotel-El
Segundo/LAX **H**
(310) 725-0100. **$220-$260.** 810 S Douglas Ave. Just w of Aviation Blvd at Rosecrans. Ext/int corridors. **Pets:** Designated rooms, no service, supervision, crate.
[ASK] [S̸o] [X] [▣] [▧] [X]

FULLERTON

ⓐⓐⓐ ◆◆ Fullerton Inn **M** ✤
(714) 773-4900. **$45-$55.** 2601 W Orangethorpe Ave. 0.3 mi ne of SR 91, Riverside Frwy, exit Magnolia Ave. Ext corridors. **Pets:** Very small. $5 daily fee/pet. No service, supervision, crate.
[SAVE] [S̸o] [X] [▤] [▧]

◆◆◆ Fullerton Marriott Hotel at California State
Univ **M**
(714) 738-7300. **$124-$164.** 2701 E Nutwood Ave. Adjacent w side of SR 57. Int corridors. **Pets:** Small. Supervision.
[X] [♿] [⚐] [▤] [▣] [¶¶] [▧]

GLENDALE

ⓐⓐⓐ ◆ Vagabond Inn **M**
(818) 240-1700. **$72-$81.** 120 W Colorado St. 1 mi s of SR 134, Brand Blvd exit. Ext corridors. **Pets:** Small. No service, supervision, crate.
[SAVE] [S̸o] [X] [▤] [▣] [▧]

HOLLYWOOD

ⓐⓐⓐ ◆◆◆ Best Western Hollywood
Hills **M** ✤
(323) 464-5181. **$89-$129.** 6141 Franklin Ave. Just e of Vine St. Ext/int corridors. **Pets:** Small. Supervision.
[S̸o] [X] [▤] [▣] [¶¶] [▧]

INGLEWOOD

ⓐⓐⓐ ◆◆◆ Hampton Inn-Los Angeles International
Airport **M**
(310) 846-3200. **$75-$99, 3 days notice.** 10300 La Cienega Blvd. Just w of I-405, exit Century Blvd, 1.5 mi e of LAX. Int corridors. **Pets:** Small. No service, supervision, crate.
[SAVE] [S̸o] [X] [▣]

LA MIRADA

◆◆◆ Residence Inn by Marriott **M** ✤
(714) 523-2800. **$119-$149.** 14419 Firestone Blvd. E side of I-5, exit Valley View, 0.5 mi se on Firestone Blvd. Ext corridors. **Pets:** Small. $6 daily fee/pet, $75 one-time fee/ room. No service, supervision, crate.
[ASK] [X] [▤] [▣] [▧] [X]

LONG BEACH

ⓐⓐⓐ ◆◆ Best Western of Long Beach **M** ✤
(562) 599-5555. **$59-$106, 7 days notice.** 1725 Long Beach Blvd. Just s of SR 1 (Pacific Coast Hwy). Int corridors. **Pets:** Supervision.
[SAVE] [S̸o] [X] [▤] [▧]

ⓐⓐⓐ ◆◆ Comfort Inn Downtown **M** ✤
(562) 590-8858. **$69-$129, 3 days notice.** 1133 Atlantic Ave. 1 mi n of Ocean Blvd. Int corridors. **Pets:** Medium, other. Supervision.
[SAVE] [S̸o] [X] [♿] [▤] [▣] [¶¶] [▧]

ⓐⓐⓐ ◆◆ Days Inn- City Center **M** ✤
(562) 591-0088. **$50-$65** (no credit cards). 1500 E Pacific Coast Hwy. Across from Long Beach City College, on Sr 1. Ext corridors. **Pets:** Small. $10 daily fee/pet. Designated rooms, no service, supervision, crate.
[SAVE] [S̸o] [X] [▤] [▣]

ⓐⓐⓐ ◆◆◆ GuestHouse Hotel **M** ✤
(562) 597-1341. **$68-$68, 48 days notice.** 5325 E Pacific Coast Hwy. On SR 1. Ext corridors. **Pets:** Other. $10 one-time fee/room. Designated rooms, supervision.
[SAVE] [X] [▤] [▣] [¶¶] [▧]

ⓐⓐⓐ ◆◆◆◆ Hilton Long Beach **H**
(562) 983-3400. **$129-$350.** Two World Trade Center. Downtown area, just e of I-710, exit Broadway. Int corridors. **Pets:** No service, supervision, crate.
[SAVE] [S̸o] [X] [▣] [¶¶] [▧]

LOS ANGELES

ⓐⓐⓐ ◆ Beverly Laurel Motor Hotel **M** ✤
(323) 651-2441. **$69-$83.** 8018 Beverly Blvd. Just w of Fairfax Ave. Ext corridors. **Pets:** Medium. $100 deposit/ room, $5 daily fee/pet, $5 one-time fee/pet. No service, supervision, crate.
[S̸o] [X] [▤] [¶¶] [▧]

ⓐⓐⓐ ◆◆◆◆ Century Plaza Hotel &
Tower **H** ✤
(310) 277-2000. **$325-$475.** 2025 Avenue of the Stars. Century City. Int corridors. **Pets:** Other. Supervision.
[SAVE] [S̸o] [X] [♿] [⚐] [▨] [▣] [¶¶] [▧]

ⓐⓐⓐ ◆◆◆◆ Four Seasons Hotel **H**
(310) 273-2222. **$345-$1300.** 300 S Doheny Dr. Corner of Burton Way. Int corridors. **Pets:** Supervision.
[SAVE] [S̸o] [X] [▣] [¶¶] [▧]

ⓐⓐⓐ ◆◆◆ Holiday Inn City Center **H**
(213) 748-1291. **$90-$170, 3 days notice.** 1020 S Figueroa St at Olympic Blvd. Int corridors. **Pets:** Supervision.
[SAVE] [S̸o] [X] [▤] [▣] [¶¶] [▧]

ⓐⓐⓐ ◆◆◆ Holiday Inn-Downtown **H**
(213) 628-9900. **$129-$169.** 750 Garland Ave. Just w of SR 110 at 8th St. Int corridors. **Pets:** Supervision.
[SAVE] [X] [▤] [▣] [¶¶] [▧]

◆◆◆ Hotel Inter-Continental Los Angeles at California Plaza 🅗 ❀
(213) 617-3300. **$260-$316.** 251 S Olive St. Just n of 4th St. Int corridors. **Pets:** Small, other. $100 one-time fee/room. Supervision.

🅰🆂🅚 ☒ 🄳 🄴 🄸 🄰

◆◆◆◆ Hotel Sofitel 🅗 ❀
(310) 278-5444. **$229-$344.** 8555 Beverly Blvd. 2.5 mi n of I-10, exit La Cienega Blvd; across from Beverly Center. Int corridors. **Pets:** Small, other. $50 deposit/room. Supervision.

🅰🆂🅚 🆂 ☒ 🄸 🄰

◆◆ Kawada Hotel 🅗
(213) 621-4455. **$99-$129.** 200 S Hill St. S on SR 110, exit Hill St, then 1.5 mi s; n on SR 110, exit 9th St, just e to Figueroa St, then 0.8 mi n to 2nd St, just e, corner of Hill and 2nd St. Int corridors. **Pets:** Small. No service, supervision, crate.

🅰🆂🅚 🆂 ☒ 🄳 🄴 🄸

⚑ ◆◆◆ Los Angeles Airport Hilton & Towers 🅗
(310) 410-4000. **$148-$168.** 5711 W Century Blvd. 0.8 mi e of airport. Int corridors. **Pets:** No service, supervision, crate.

🆂🄰🆅🄴 ☒ 🄳 🄴 🄸 🄰

◆◆◆ Los Angeles Airport Marriott Hotel 🅗
(310) 641-5700. **$99-$159.** 5855 W Century Blvd. 0.5 mi e of airport. Int corridors. **Pets:** Supervision.

☒ 🄶 🄺 🄳 🄴 🄸 🄰

⚑ ◆◆◆ Quality Hotel-Los Angeles Airport 🅗 ❀
(310) 645-2200. **$80-$100.** 5249 W Century Blvd. 1.5 blks w of I-405. Int corridors. **Pets:** Medium. $25 daily fee/pet. No service, supervision, crate.

🆂🄰🆅🄴 🆂 ☒ 🄳 🄴 🄸 🄰

⚑ ◆◆◆ Radisson Wilshire Plaza Hotel 🅗
(213) 381-7411. **$125-$145.** 3515 Wilshire Blvd. On Wilshire Blvd at Normandie Ave. Int corridors. **Pets:** Supervision.

🆂🄰🆅🄴 🆂 ☒ 🄳 🄴 🄸 🄰

◆◆◆ Residence Inn by Marriott-Beverly Hills 🅐 ❀
(310) 277-4427. **$149-$149.** 1177 S Beverly Dr. At Pico Blvd. Int corridors. **Pets:** Medium, other. $250 deposit/room, $10 daily fee/pet, $80 one-time fee/room. Supervision.

🅰🆂🅚 🆂 ☒ 🄳 🄴

⚑ ◆◆◆ Travelodge Hotel at Lax 🅜 ❀
(310) 649-4000. **$69-$109.** 5547 W Century Blvd. 1 mi e of airport at Aviation Blvd. Ext/int corridors. **Pets:** Other. $8 daily fee/pet. No service, supervision, crate.

🆂🄰🆅🄴 🆂 ☒ 🄳 🄴 🄸 🄰

⚑ ◆ Vagabond Inn Figueroa 🅜
(213) 746-1531. **$78-$88.** 3101 S Figueroa St. 0.5 mi sw of SR 110, Adams Blvd exit. Ext corridors. **Pets:** Small. Designated rooms, no service, supervision, crate.

🆂🄰🆅🄴 🆂 ☒ 🄳 🄴 🄰

◆◆◆ The Westin Hotel-Los Angeles Airport 🅗 ❀
(310) 216-5858. **$169-$179.** 5400 W Century Blvd. Int corridors. **Pets:** Small, other. $100 deposit/room. Supervision.

🅰🆂🅚 🆂 ☒ 🄴 🄸 🄰

◆◆◆◆ W Los Angeles 🅗
(310) 208-8765. **$279-$419.** 930 Hilgard Ave. Westwood Village, just n of Wilshire Blvd. Int corridors. **Pets:** Small. No service, supervision, crate.

🅰🆂🅚 🆂 ☒ 🄸 🄰

MANHATTAN BEACH

⚑ ◆◆◆ Barnabey's Hotel 🅗
(310) 545-8466. **$109-$169, 3 days notice.** 3501 N Sepulveda Blvd. On SR 1, just s of Rosecrans Ave. Int corridors. **Pets:** Small. Designated rooms, no service, supervision, crate.

🆂🄰🆅🄴 🆂 ☒ 🄳 🄴 🄸 🄰 🄓

◆◆◆ Residence Inn by Marriott 🅐 ❀
(310) 546-7627. **$145-$208.** 1700 N Sepulveda Blvd. On SR 1, 1 mi s of Rosecrans Ave. Ext corridors. **Pets:** Medium, other. $8 daily fee/pet, $75 one-time fee/room. Supervision.

🅰🆂🅚 🆂 ☒ 🄳 🄴 🄰 🄓

MISSION HILLS

⚑ ◆◆ Best Western Mission Hills Inn 🅜 ❀
(818) 891-1771. **$68-$80.** 10621 Sepulveda Blvd. Just s of SR 118, 0.3 mi e of I-405. Ext/int corridors. **Pets:** Small. $50 deposit/room. Designated rooms, no service, supervision, crate.

🆂🄰🆅🄴 🆂 ☒ 🄶 🄳 🄴 🄰

MONROVIA

◆◆◆ Holiday Inn 🅗 ❀
(626) 357-1900. **$95-$275.** 924 W Huntington Dr. Adjacent to I-210, exit Huntington Dr. Int corridors. **Pets:** Small. $50 deposit/room. No service, supervision, crate.

🅰🆂🅚 🆂 ☒ 🄵 🄴 🄸 🄰

◆◆◆ Homestead Village 🅜
(626) 256-6999. **$79-$99.** 930 S Fifth Ave. S side of I-210, exit Huntington Dr. Int corridors. **Pets:** Small. No service, supervision, crate.

🅰🆂🅚 🆂 ☒ 🄵 🄺 🄴

PASADENA

⚑ ◆◆◆ Quality Inn Pasadena 🅜 ❀
(626) 796-9291. **$65-$79.** 3321 E Colorado Blvd. Just SW of I-210, exit Madre St. Ext corridors. **Pets:** Other. $200 deposit/room, $10 daily fee/pet. Designated rooms, no service, supervision, crate.

🆂🄰🆅🄴 🆂 ☒ 🄳 🄴 🄰

⚑ ◆◆ Vagabond Inn 🅜 ❀
(626) 449-3170. **$58-$71.** 1203 E Colorado Blvd. 0.3 mi s of I-210, exit Hill St. Ext/int corridors. **Pets:** Small. $5 daily fee/pet. Designated rooms, no service, supervision, crate.

🆂🄰🆅🄴 🆂 ☒ 🄳 🄴 🄰

PICO RIVERA

(AAA) ◆◆ Pico Rivera Travelodge **M**
(562) 949-6648. **$45-$55, 7 days notice.** 7222 Rosemead Blvd. On SR 19; 1.6 mi n of I-5. Ext corridors. **Pets:** Designated rooms, no service, supervision, crate.
(SAVE) (S) (X) (H) (🖼) (CTV)

POMONA

◆◆◆ Sheraton Suites Fairplex **H** ❧
(909) 622-2220. **$139-$189.** 601 W McKinley Ave. N of I-10; eastbound exit White Ave, westbound exit Fairplex Dr. Int corridors. **Pets:** Medium, other. $75 deposit/room, $25 one-time fee/room. No service, supervision, crate.
(ASK) (S) (X) (H) (🖵) (🍴) (🖼)

◆◆◆ Shilo Hotel-Pomona **MI** ❧
(909) 598-0073. **$79-$129.** 3200 Temple Ave. Adjacent to SR 57, Temple Ave exit. Int corridors. **Pets:** Other. $10 daily fee/room. Supervision.
(ASK) (S) (X) (H) (🍴) (🖼)

REDONDO BEACH

(AAA) ◆ Vagabond Inn **M**
(310) 378-8555. **$65-$90.** 6226 Pacific Coast Hwy. 1.5 mi se on SR 1. **Pets:** Designated rooms, no service, supervision, crate.
(SAVE) (S) (X) (H) (🖵) (🖼)

SAN DIMAS

(AAA) ◆◆ Red Roof Inn **M** ❧
(909) 599-2362. **$56-$82.** 204 N Village Ct. E side of I-210, exit Arrow Hwy. Ext corridors. **Pets:** Medium, other. Supervision.
(SAVE) (X) (🦽) (📠) (🖼)

SAN PEDRO

(AAA) ◆ Vagabond Inn **M**
(310) 831-8911. **$55-$65.** 215 S Gaffey. Just s of I-110. Ext corridors. **Pets:** Supervision.
(SAVE) (S) (X) (H) (🖼)

SANTA MONICA

(AAA) ◆◆◆ The Georgian **H** ❧
(310) 395-6333. **$212-$257.** 1415 Ocean Ave. Int corridors. **Pets:** Small, other. $250 deposit/room, $100 one-time fee/room. Supervision.
(SAVE) (S) (X) (H) (🖵) (🍴)

(AAA) ◆◆◆ Holiday Inn-Santa Monica
Beach **H** ❧
(310) 451-0676. **$175-$275, 3 days notice.** 120 Colorado Blvd. Int corridors. **Pets:** Medium. $50 daily fee/pet. Designated rooms, no service, supervision, crate.
(SAVE) (S) (X) (H) (🖵) (🍴) (🖼) (X)

(AAA) ◆◆◆◆ Loews Santa Monica Beach
Hotel **H** ❧
(310) 458-6700. **$290-$435.** 1700 Ocean Ave. Int corridors. **Pets:** Small. $500 deposit/pet, $5 daily fee/room. Designated rooms, supervision.
(S) (X) (🍴) (🖼) (X)

SEAL BEACH

◆◆◆ Radisson Inn of Seal Beach **M**
(562) 493-7501. **$110-$120.** 600 Marina Dr. Just s of SR 1, Pacific Coast Hwy. Ext/int corridors. **Pets:** Small. Supervision.
(ASK) (S) (X) (🖵) (🖼) (X)

SHERMAN OAKS

(AAA) ◆◆◆ Best Western Carriage Inn **MI** ❧
(818) 787-2300. **$99-$150.** 5525 Sepulveda Blvd. Adjacent to I-405, Burbank Blvd exit. Ext/int corridors. **Pets:** Medium. $50 deposit/pet. Designated rooms, no service, supervision, crate.
(SAVE) (S) (X) (✈) (H) (🖵) (🍴) (🖼)

SYLMAR

(AAA) ◆ Good Nite Inn **M** ❧
(818) 362-8899. **$45-$65, 30 days notice.** 12835 Enicinitas Ave. I-5 exit Roxford St, just e to Encinitas Ave, then just s. **Pets:** Small. No service, supervision, crate.
(SAVE) (S) (X) (🖼)

TORRANCE

◆◆◆ Residence Inn by Marriott **A** ❧
(310) 543-4566. **$178-$178.** 3701 Torrance Blvd. Just e of Hawthorne Blvd. Ext corridors. **Pets:** Small. $200 deposit/pet, $6 daily fee/pet, $40 one-time fee/room. Supervision.
(ASK) (S) (X) (H) (🖵) (🖼) (X)

◆◆◆ Summerfield Suites Hotel **M** ❧
(310) 371-8525. **$198-$228.** 19901 Prairie Ave. Between 190th St and Del Amo Blvd. Ext/int corridors. **Pets:** Very small. $10 daily fee/room, $150 one-time fee/room. No service, supervision, crate.
(ASK) (S) (X) (H) (🖵) (🖼) (X)

WEST COVINA

(AAA) ◆◆◆ Comfort Inn **M**
(626) 915-6077. **$59-$85.** 2804 E Garvey Ave S. S side of I-10 between Barranca and Citrus Ave exits. Ext/int corridors. **Pets:** Small. No service, supervision, crate.
(SAVE) (S) (X) (H) (🖼)

◆◆◆ Hampton Inn **M** ❧
(626) 967-5800. **Call for rates.** 3145 E Garvey Ave N. Adjacent to I-10, exit Barranca St. Int corridors. **Pets:** $25 deposit/room. No service, supervision, crate.
(S) (X) (🖵) (🖼)

(AAA) ◆◆◆ Holiday Inn-West Covina **MI** ❧
(626) 966-8311. **$79-$79.** 3223 E Garvey Ave N. Adjacent to I-10, exit Barranca St. Int corridors. **Pets:** Small, other. $25 deposit/room. No service, supervision, crate.
(SAVE) (S) (X) (H) (🖵) (🍴) (🖼)

WEST HOLLYWOOD

◆◆◆ The Argyle **H** ❧
(323) 654-7100. **Call for rates, 3 days notice.** 8358 Sunset Blvd. Just e of La Cienega Blvd. Int corridors. **Pets:** Very small, dogs only. $700 deposit/pet. Supervision.
(ASK) (X) (🍴) (🖼)

◆◆◆ Le Montrose Suite Hotel De Gran
  Luxe 🅷 ❖
(310) 855-1115. **$480.** 900 Hammond St at Cynthia. Just s
of Sunset Blvd, just e of Doheny. Int corridors. **Pets:** Small.
$75 one-time fee/room. Supervision.
🄰🅂🄺 ⊠ 🛏 💻 🍴 ⊠

◆◆◆ Le Parc Suite Hotel 🄼🄸 ❖
(310) 855-8888. **$195-$285.** 733 N West Knoll Dr. Just n of
Melrose Ave and just w of La Cienega Blvd. Int corridors.
Pets: Other. $75 one-time fee/pet. Supervision.
🄰🅂🄺 🅂🄳 ⊠ 🛏 💻 🍴 🖂 ⊠

◆◆◆ Summerfield Suites Hotel 🄼🄸 ❖
(310) 657-7400. **Call for rates.** 1000 Westmount Dr. 3 blks
s of Sunset Blvd, just n of Santa Monica Blvd. Int corridors.
Pets: Large. $250 deposit/room, $10 daily fee/pet, $75 one-
time fee/room. Supervision.
⊠ 💻 🖂

◆◆◆◆ Sunset Marquis Hotel & Villas 🄼🄸
(310) 657-1333. **$315-$1200.** 1200 N Alta Loma Rd. Just s
of Sunset Blvd. Int corridors. **Pets:** Small. No service,
supervision, crate.
⊠ 🛏 💻 🍴 🖂

❖ **END METROPOLITAN AREA** ❖

LOS BANOS

🄰🄰🄰 ◆◆ Best Western John Jay Inn 🄼🄸 ❖
(209) 827-0954. **$45-$105.** 301 W Pacheco Blvd. On SR
152. Int corridors. **Pets:** Small. $15 one-time fee/pet. Des-
ignated rooms, no service, supervision, crate.
🅂🄰🅅🄴 🅂🄳 ⊠ 🖐 🖐 🛏 💻 🖂

🄰🄰🄰 ◆ Regency Inn 🄼🄸 ❖
(209) 826-3871. **$37-$48, 5 days notice.** 349 W Pacheco
Blvd. On SR 152. Ext corridors. **Pets:** Medium, other. $20
deposit/room, $4 daily fee/pet, $4 one-time fee/pet. No
service, supervision, crate.
🅂🄰🅅🄴 ⊠ 🛏 🖂

LOS GATOS

🄰🄰🄰 ◆◆◆ Los Gatos Lodge 🄼🄸 ❖
(408) 354-3300. **$119-$169.** 50 Los Gatos-Saratoga Rd.
Just e of SR 17, E Los Gatos exit. Ext/int corridors.
Pets: Small. No service, supervision, crate.
🅂🄰🅅🄴 🅂🄳 ⊠ 🖐 🖐 🛏 💻 🍴 🖂 ⊠

MADERA

🄰🄰🄰 ◆◆◆ Best Western Madera Valley
  Inn 🄼🄸 ❖
(559) 673-5164. **$67-$75.** 317 North G St. Just e of SR 99,
Central Madera exit. Int corridors. **Pets:** Supervision.
🅂🄰🅅🄴 🅂🄳 ⊠ 🛏 💻 🍴 🖂

🄰🄰🄰 ◆◆ Liberty Inn 🄼
(559) 675-8697. **$45-$65, 3 days notice.** 22683 Ave 18
1/2. 5 min n; just w of SR 99, Ave 18 1/2 exit. Int corridors.
Pets: No service, supervision, crate.
🅂🄰🅅🄴 ⊠ 🖐 🛏 🖂

WHITTIER

🄰🄰🄰 ◆◆ Vagabond Inn 🄼 ❖
(562) 698-9701. **$60-$70.** 14125 E Whittier Blvd. 2 mi e of
I-605. Ext corridors. **Pets:** Small, other. $10 daily fee/pet.
Designated rooms, no service, supervision, crate.
🅂🄰🅅🄴 🅂🄳 ⊠ 🛏 💻 🖂

WOODLAND HILLS

🄰🄰🄰 ◆◆◆ Holiday Inn-Woodland Hills 🄼🄸 ❖
(818) 883-6110. **$99-$109.** 21101 Ventura Blvd. Adjacent to
US 101, DeSoto St exit. Int corridors. **Pets:** Medium, other.
$25 one-time fee/room. No service, supervision, crate.
🅂🄰🅅🄴 🅂🄳 ⊠ 🛏 💻 🍴 🖂

🄰🄰🄰 ◆◆ Vagabond Inn 🄼🄸
(818) 347-8080. **$65-$77.** 20157 Ventura Blvd. Adjacent to
US 101, Winnetka Ave exit. Ext corridors. **Pets:** No service,
supervision, crate.
🅂🄰🅅🄴 🅂🄳 ⊠ 🛏 💻 🖂

◆ Super 8 🄼 ❖
(559) 661-1131. **$46-$70.** 1855 W Cleveland Ave. Just w of
SR 99, Cleveland Ave exit. Ext corridors. **Pets:** $3 daily
fee/pet. No service, supervision, crate.
🄰🅂🄺 🅂🄳 ⊠ 🛏 🖂

MAMMOTH LAKES

🄰🄰🄰 ◆◆ Austria Hof Lodge 🄻 ❖
(760) 934-2764. **$80-$120.** 924 Canyon Blvd. Old Mammoth Rd, take SR 203 1.2 mi w, then 1 mi w on Canyon
Blvd. Int corridors. **Pets:** $100 deposit/room, $10 daily fee/
pet. Designated rooms, supervision.
🅂🄰🅅🄴 ⊠ 🛏 💻 🍴 ⊠ 🐾

🄰🄰🄰 ◆◆ Econolodge Wildwood Inn 🄼
(760) 934-6855. **$59-$109, 7 days notice.** 3626 Main St.
On SR 203, 0.7 mi W of Old Mammoth Rd. Ext corridors.
Pets: Designated rooms, supervision.
🅂🄰🅅🄴 🅂🄳 ⊠ 🛏 💻 🖂 🐾

🄰🄰🄰 ◆◆ Executive Inn 🄼
(760) 934-8892. **$59-$109, 7 days notice.** 54 Sierra Blvd.
Just n of SR 203 (Main St); 0.6 mi w of Old Mammoth Rd.
Int corridors. **Pets:** Supervision.
🅂🄰🅅🄴 🅂🄳 ⊠ 💻 🐾

◆◆◆ Holiday Inn Hotel & Suites 🄼🄸
(760) 924-1234. **Call for rates.** 3236 Main St. ON SR 203,
just w of jct Old Mammoth Rd. Int corridors. **Pets:** Medium.
Designated rooms, no service, supervision, crate.
⊠ 🖐 🖐 💻 🖂

🄰🄰🄰 ◆◆ Royal Pines Resort 🄼 ❖
(760) 934-2306. **$65-$95, 7 days notice.** 3814 View Point
Rd. On SR 203, 0.5 mi W of Old Mammoth Rd. Ext/int
corridors. **Pets:** Dogs only. $5 daily fee/pet. Designated
rooms, supervision.
⊠ 💻 🐾

◆◆◆ **Shilo Inn** **M**
(760) 934-4500. **$85-$150.** 2963 Main St. On SR 203, just
e of Old Mammoth Rd. Int corridors. **Pets:** No service,
supervision, crate.

[ASK] [S6] [✕] [🛏] [🍴] [💻] [🏊]

(AAA) ◆◆ **Sierra Nevada Rodeway Inn** **MI** ❀
(760) 934-2515. **$99-$159, 7 days notice.** 164 Old Mammoth Rd. Just s of SR 203. Ext/int corridors. **Pets:** $25
deposit/pet. No service, supervision, crate.

[SAVE] [S6] [✕] [🛏] [💻] [🍴] [🏊] [🎾]

MARIPOSA

(AAA) ◆◆ **Best Western Yosemite Way**
          Station **M** ❀
(209) 966-7545. **$79-$85.** 4999 Hwy 140. SR 140 at SR
49S. Ext corridors. **Pets:** Medium, other. $5 daily fee/pet.
Supervision.

[✕] [🛏] [🏊] [🏊]

(AAA) ◆ **E. C. Yosemite Motel** **M** ❀
(209) 742-6800. **$59-$64.** 5180 Jones St. Jct SR 49 and
140 N. Ext corridors. **Pets:** Small. $50 deposit/pet, $10
daily fee/pet, $10 one-time fee/pet. Designated rooms, no
service, supervision, crate.

[✕] [🏊]

(AAA) ◆◆ **Mariposa Lodge** **M** ❀
(209) 966-3607. **$60-$85.** 5052 Hwy 140. Center. Ext corridors. **Pets:** Medium, other. $10 daily fee/pet. Supervision.

[✕] [🛏] [💻] [🏊]

(AAA) ◆◆ **Miners Inn** **M** ❀
(209) 742-7777. **$59-$159.** 5181 Hwy 49 N. SR 49, n at SR
140. Ext/int corridors. **Pets:** Other. $5 daily fee/pet. No serv-
ice, supervision, crate.

[S6] [✕] [🛏] [💻] [🍴] [🏊]

MARYSVILLE

(AAA) ◆ **Marysville Motor Lodge** **M** ❀
(530) 743-1531. **$30-$50.** 904 E Street. Jct SR 70 and SR
20. Ext corridors. **Pets:** Medium, dogs only. $5 daily fee/pet,
$5 one-time fee/pet. No service, supervision, crate.

[SAVE] [S6] [✕] [🛏] [💻] [🏊]

MENDOCINO

(AAA) ◆◆ **Blackberry Inn** **M** ❀
(707) 937-5281. **$90-$145.** 44951 Larkin Rd. Just e of SR
1, Larkin Rd exit. Ext corridors. **Pets:** Medium, other. $10
daily fee/pet. Designated rooms, supervision.

[✕] [🛏] [💻] [🎾]

(AAA) ◆◆◆ **Mendocino Seaside Cottages** **BB** ❀
(707) 485-0239. **$100-$561** (no credit cards). 10940 Lansing St. 0.6 mi nw of SR 1, Little Lake Rd or Lansing St
exit. Ext/int corridors. **Pets:** Other. $80 deposit/room. Des-
ignated rooms, no service, supervision, crate.

[SAVE] [S6] [✕] [🛏] [💻] [✕] [🎾] [🎾]

(AAA) ◆◆◆◆ **Stanford Inn by the Sea** **X** ❀
(707) 937-5615. **$215-$275, 7 days notice.** 44850
Comptche-Ukiah Rd. 0.5 mi e of SR 1, Comptche-Ukiah Rd
exit. Ext corridors. **Pets:** Other. $25 one-time fee/pet.
Supervision.

[SAVE] [✕] [🛏] [🎾] [🍴] [💻] [🍴] [🏊] [✕] [🎾]

MERCED

(AAA) ◆◆◆ **Best Western Sequoia Inn** **MI** ❀
(209) 723-3711. **$54-$90.** 1213 V St. Just w of SR 99,
Gustine-Sonora exit. Ext corridors. **Pets:** Other. $10
deposit/room. No service, supervision, crate.

[SAVE] [S6] [✕] [🛏] [💻] [🏊]

(AAA) ◆◆ **Days Inn** **M** ❀
(209) 722-2726. **$68-$95.** 1199 Motel Dr. Just e of SR 99,
Childs Ave or SR 140 exit. Ext corridors. **Pets:** Small. $100
deposit/room, $10 one-time fee/room. Designated rooms,
no service, supervision, crate.

[SAVE] [S6] [✕] [🛏] [💻] [🏊]

(AAA) ◆◆ **Merced-Yosemite Traveldoge** **M**
(209) 722-6224. **$55-$75.** 1260 Yosemite Pkwy. 0.2 mi e of
SR 99, SR 140 exit. Ext corridors. **Pets:** Small. No service,
supervision, crate.

[SAVE] [S6] [✕] [🛏] [🎾] [🛏] [💻] [🏊]

(AAA) ◆◆ **Super 8** **M**
(209) 384-1303. **$49-$69.** 1983 E Childs Ave. Just e of SR
99, Childs Ave exit. Int corridors. **Pets:** Small. No service,
supervision, crate.

[SAVE] [S6] [✕] [🛏] [🎾] [🛏] [🏊]

MI WUK VILLAGE

(AAA) ◆◆ **Mi-Wuk Motor Lodge** **M**
(209) 586-3031. **$50-$117, 5 days notice.** 24680 SR 108.
15 mi e of Sonora on SR 108. Ext corridors. **Pets:** No
service, supervision, crate.

[SAVE] [S6] [✕] [💻] [🏊]

MILPITAS

(AAA) ◆◆ **Best Western Brookside Inn** **M**
(408) 263-5566. **$99-$119.** 400 Valley Way. E of I-880, exit
Calaveras Blvd/SR 237 N Abbott Ave. Int corridors.
Pets: Supervision.

[SAVE] [S6] [✕] [🎾] [🛏] [💻] [🏊]

◆◆◆ **Candlewood Suites-Milipitas** **M** ❀
(408) 719-1212. **$159-$179.** 40 Ranch Dr. Ne quadrant
I-880 and SR 237, exit SR 237 (McCarthy Ranch Rd). Int
corridors. **Pets:** Small. $10 daily fee/pet, $75 one-time fee/
pet. Supervision.

[ASK] [S6] [✕]

(AAA) ◆◆ **Inns of America** **M**
(408) 946-8889. **$94-$95.** 270 S Abbott Ave. Exit I-880 at
Calaveras Blvd; adjacent to Serra Shopping Center. Ext
corridors. **Pets:** Medium. No service, supervision, crate.

[SAVE] [S6] [✕] [🛏] [🏊]

◆◆◆ **Residence Inn By Marriott** **M** ❀
(408) 941-9222. **$129-$209.** 1501 California Cr. I-880, exit
Dixon Landing Rd E, just s. Int corridors. **Pets:** Medium,
other. $15 daily fee/pet, $100 one-time fee/room. Supervision.

[ASK] [S6] [✕] [🎾] [🏊]

MODESTO

AAA ◆ ◆ **Best Western Town House**
Lodge
(209) 524-7261. **$57-$73.** 909 16th St. 1 mi e off Frwy 99; exit via Central Modesto at I St. Ext corridors. **Pets:** Other. No service, supervision, crate.

[SAVE] [S6] [X] [H] [E] [S]

AAA ◆ **Chalet Motel** [M] ❀
(209) 529-4370. **$38-$52.** 115 Downey Ave. 0.5 mi ne on SR 108. Ext/int corridors. **Pets:** Small. $20 deposit/room, $5 one-time fee/room. Designated rooms, no service, supervision, crate.

[SAVE] [S6] [X] [H] [S]

◆ ◆ ◆ **DoubleTree** [H] ❀
(209) 526-6000. **$99-$129.** 1150 9th St. SR 99 northbound exit central Modesto; southbound exit Maze Blvd; at Convention Center Plaza. Int corridors. **Pets:** Medium. $50 deposit/room. No service, supervision, crate.

[ASK] [S6] [X] [🌙] [H] [E] [🍴] [S]

AAA ◆ ◆ **Howard Johnson Express Inn** [M] ❀
(209) 537-4821. **$55-$80.** 1672 Herndon Rd. Exit SR 99 Hatch Rd; s on Herndon. Ext corridors. **Pets:** Small. No service, supervision, crate.

[SAVE] [S6] [X] [H] [S]

◆ **Travelodge** [M] ❀
(209) 524-3251. **$49-$65.** 722 Kansas Ave. Exit SR 99 (Kansas Ave), w. Ext corridors. **Pets:** Small, dogs only. $15 deposit/room, $10 daily fee/room, $10 one-time fee/room. No service, supervision, crate.

[ASK] [S6] [X] [E] [S]

AAA ◆ **Vagabond Inn** [M] ❀
(209) 521-6340. **$64-$78.** 1525 McHenry Ave. 2 mi n on SR 108; from SR 99, Briggsmore Ave exit; 2.3 mi e to McHenry Ave, then just s. Ext corridors. **Pets:** Small, other. $5 one-time fee/pet. Supervision.

[SAVE] [S6] [X] [E] [S]

MOJAVE

AAA ◆ **Desert Inn** [M] ❀
(661) 824-2518. **$35-$44.** 1954 Hwy 58. On SR 58, just e of jct SR 14. Ext corridors. **Pets:** Other. Supervision.

[S6] [X] [H]

AAA ◆ **Econo Lodge** [M] ❀
(661) 824-2463. **$36-$46.** 2145 Hwy 58. SR 58, just e of SR 14. Ext corridors. **Pets:** Other. $5 daily fee/pet, $5 one-time fee/pet. No service, supervision, crate.

[SAVE] [S6] [X] [H] [S]

AAA ◆ **Scottish Inns** [M] ❀
(661) 824-9317. **$35-$60.** 16352 Sierra Hwy. On SR 14 and 58. Ext corridors. **Pets:** Medium. $10 daily fee/pet. No service, supervision, crate.

[X] [H] [S]

MONTEREY PENINSULA METROPOLITAN AREA

CARMEL VALLEY

AAA ◆ ◆ ◆ **Carmel Valley Lodge** [X] ❀
(831) 659-2261. **$139-$309, 7 days notice.** 8 Ford Rd. 11.5 mi e of SR 1; Carmel Valley Rd, at Ford Rd. Ext corridors. **Pets:** Dogs only. $10 daily fee/pet. No service, supervision, crate.

[SAVE] [S6] [X] [🌙] [H] [E] [S] [K]

CARMEL BY THE SEA

AAA ◆ ◆ ◆ **Best Western Carmel Mission**
Inn [M] ❀
(831) 624-1841. **$129-$239.** 3665 Rio Rd. 1 mi s on SR 1, at Rio Rd. Ext/int corridors. **Pets:** $25 one-time fee/room. Designated rooms, supervision.

[SAVE] [S6] [X] [H] [E] [🍴] [S]

AAA ◆ ◆ ◆ **Carmel Country Inn** [BB]
(831) 625-3263. **$95-$205, 7 days notice.** 4 blks n of Ocean Ave; at Dolores and 3rd Ave. Ext corridors. **Pets:** Medium. No service, supervision, crate.

[SAVE] [S6] [H] [E] [K]

AAA ◆ ◆ ◆ **Carmel Garden Court** [BB]
(831) 624-6926. **$170-$265, 7 days notice.** 3 blks n off Ocean Ave, at 4th Ave and Torres St. Ext corridors. **Pets:** No service, supervision, crate.

[SAVE] [H] [E] [K]

AAA ◆ ◆ **Carmel River Inn** [X]
(831) 624-1575. **$100-$180, 3 days notice.** 1 mi s on SR 1; n of Carmel River Bridge at Oliver Rd. Ext corridors. **Pets:** Medium. Supervision.

[S6] [X] [H] [E] [S] [K]

◆ ◆ **Carmel Tradewinds Inn** [M] ❀
(831) 624-2776. **Call for rates.** 4 blks n off Ocean Ave at Mission St and 3rd Ave. Ext corridors. **Pets:** Medium. $25 daily fee/pet, $25 one-time fee/pet. No service, supervision, crate.

[H] [E] [S] [K]

AAA ◆ ◆ ◆ ◆ **Carmel Valley Ranch** [R] ❀
(831) 625-9500. **$255-$615.** One Old Ranch Rd. 6.3 mi e of SR 1 via Carmel Valley Rd, exit at Robinson Canyon Rd and follow signs. Ext corridors. **Pets:** $200 deposit/room, $75 one-time fee/room. Designated rooms, supervision.

[SAVE] [S6] [X] [H] [E] [🍴] [S] [X]

AAA ◆ ◆ ◆ **Coachman's Inn** [M] ❀
(831) 624-6421. **$95-$275, 3 days notice.** Just s of Ocean Ave, San Carlos St between 7th and 8th aves. Ext corridors. **Pets:** Medium, dogs only. $15 daily fee/pet. Designated rooms, no service, supervision, crate.

[SAVE] [S6] [H] [E] [K]

AAA ◆ ◆ ◆ **Cypress Inn** [H] ❀
(831) 624-3871. **$175-$225.** Just s off Ocean Ave; at Lincoln St and 7th Ave. Ext/int corridors. **Pets:** $20 daily fee/pet. No service, supervision, crate.

[X] [H] [K]

◆◆◆◆ Highlands Inn, A Park Hyatt Hotel 🅜 ❀
(831) 624-3801. **$305-$330, 3 days notice.** 4 mi s on SR 1, in Carmel Highlands. Ext corridors. **Pets:** Other. Supervision.

[SAVE] [✕] [✍] [🛏] [💻] [🍴] [⌂] [✕] [🐾]

◆◆◆◆ Quail Lodge Resort & Golf Club 🆁
(831) 624-2888. **$295-$550, 3 days notice.** 8205 Valley Greens Dr. 3.5 mi e of SR 1, via Carmel Valley Rd. Ext corridors. **Pets:** Medium. Designated rooms, no service, supervision, crate.

[SAVE] [✕] [✍] [✍] [🛏] [💻] [🍴] [⌂] [✕] [🐾]

◆◆◆ Sunset House 🅱🅱 ❀
(831) 624-4884. **$140-$190.** Just s off Ocean on Camino Real. Ext/int corridors. **Pets:** Dogs only. $25 daily fee/pet, $25 one-time fee/room. Designated rooms, supervision.

[SAVE] [🛏] [🐾]

◆◆◆ Wayside Inn 🅜 ❀
(831) 624-5336. **$129-$189, 3 days notice.** 1 blk s off Ocean Ave, at Mission St and 7th Ave. Ext corridors. **Pets:** Other. Designated rooms, no service, supervision, crate.

[SAVE] [✕] [🛏] [💻] [🐾]

MARINA

◆◆ Monterey/Marina Beach Travelodge 🅜 ❀
(831) 883-0300. **$99-$235, 3 days notice.** 3290 Dunes Dr. Just w of SR 1, Reservation Rd exit. Ext corridors. **Pets:** Small, other. Supervision.

[SAVE] [S₀] [✕] [🛏] [💻] [✕]

MONTEREY

◆◆◆ Bay Park Hotel 🅜 ❀
(831) 649-1020. **$99-$170.** 1425 Munras Ave. Just w of SR 1, Munras Ave exit. Int corridors. **Pets:** Small, other. $10 daily fee/pet. Supervision.

[✕] [✍] [✍] [🛏] [💻] [🍴] [⌂]

◆◆◆ Best Western Victorian Inn 🅜 ❀
(831) 373-8000. **$159-$399.** 487 Foam St. 3.4 mi w of SR 1, Monterey exit. Ext/int corridors. **Pets:** $100 deposit/room, $25 one-time fee/room. Designated rooms, supervision.

[SAVE] [S₀] [✕] [✍] [✍] [✍] [🛏] [💻] [🐾]

◆◆ Carmel Hill Lodge 🅜
(831) 373-3252. **$69-$189, 3 days notice.** 1374 Munras Ave. Just w of SR 1, Munras Ave exit. **Pets:** Medium. Supervision.

[SAVE] [✕] [✍] [⌂] [🐾]

◆◆ Cypress Gardens Motel 🅜 ❀
(831) 373-2761. **$105-$139, 3 days notice.** 1150 Munras Ave. 0.5 mi w of SR 1, Munras Ave exit. Ext corridors. **Pets:** $10 daily fee/room. Designated rooms, no service, supervision, crate.

[SAVE] [✕] [✍] [🛏] [💻] [⌂] [🐾]

◆◆ El Adobe Inn 🅜 ❀
(831) 372-5409. **$49-$179, 3 days notice.** 936 Munras Ave. 0.6 mi w of SR 1, Munras Ave exit. Ext corridors. **Pets:** Medium, other. $10 deposit/room, $10 daily fee/room. Supervision.

[SAVE] [S₀] [✕] [✍] [🛏] [💻] [🐾]

◆◆◆ Hyatt Regency-Monterey Resort & Conference Center 🆇
(831) 372-1234. **$175-$200.** 1 Old Golf Course Rd. Just e of SR 1; northbound exit Aguajito Rd; southbound Monterey exit. Int corridors. **Pets:** Small. Designated rooms, no service, supervision, crate.

[SAVE] [✕] [♿] [✍] [✍] [🛏] [💻] [🍴] [⌂] [✕] [🐾]

◆◆ Monterey Bay Lodge 🅜 ❀
(831) 372-8057. **$89-$179.** 55 Camino Aguajito. Just w of SR 1, Aguajito Rd exit. Ext corridors. **Pets:** Medium. $100 deposit/room, $10 daily fee/pet. No service, supervision, crate.

[SAVE] [S₀] [✕] [🛏] [💻] [⌂] [🐾]

◆◆◆ Monterey Beach Hotel-Best Western 🅜 ❀
(831) 394-3321. **$129-$249, 3 days notice.** 2600 Sand Dunes Dr. Just w of SR 1, Del Rey oaks exit. Ext corridors. **Pets:** Other. $25 daily fee/room. Designated rooms, no service, supervision, crate.

[SAVE] [S₀] [✕] [🛏] [💻] [🍴] [⌂]

◆◆◆ Monterey Marriott 🅷 ❀
(831) 649-4234. **$229-$289.** 350 Calle Principal. 2 mi w of SR 1, Del Monte Ave or Munras Ave exits; opposit conference center. Int corridors. **Pets:** Medium, dogs only. Supervision.

[ASK] [S₀] [✕] [♿] [✍] [✍] [🛏] [💻] [🍴] [⌂]

◆◆ Munras Lodge 🅜 ❀
(831) 646-9696. **$69-$199.** 1010 Munras Ave. 0.7 mi w of SR 1, Soledad Dr/Munras Ave exits. Int corridors. **Pets:** Large, other. Supervision.

[SAVE] [✕] [🛏] [🐾]

PACIFIC GROVE

◆◆ Lighthouse Lodge & Suites 🅜 ❀
(831) 655-2111. **$129-$179, 3 days notice.** 1150 Lighthouse Ave. 0.5 mi w of 17 Mile Dr. Ext corridors. **Pets:** Medium, dogs only. $25 daily fee/pet. Designated rooms, supervision.

[ASK] [S₀] [✕] [✍] [✍] [🛏] [💻] [⌂] [🐾]

◆◆◆ Old St. Angela Inn 🅱🅱 ❀
(831) 372-3246. **$110-$225, 3 days notice.** 321 Central Ave. Center at Forest Ave. Ext/int corridors. **Pets:** Small. Supervision.

[S₀] [✕] [🐾] [CTV]

PEBBLE BEACH

◆◆◆◆ The Lodge at Pebble Beach 🆇 ❀
(831) 624-3811. **$395-$1925, 3 days notice.** 17 Mile Dr. Off SR 1, on 17 Mile Dr. Ext/int corridors. **Pets:** Small, dogs only. Supervision.

[✕] [♿] [✍] [✍] [🛏] [🍴] [⌂] [✕] [🐾]

❀ **End Metropolitan Area** ❀

MORGAN HILL

◆◆◆ Best Western Country Inn Ⓜ ✿
(408) 779-0447. **$70-$95.** 16525 Condit Rd. Just e of US 101; Tennant Ave, or E Dunne Ave exit. Int corridors. **Pets:** Designated rooms, supervision.
(SAVE) (Sᴅ) (✕) (🛏) (▣) (🞠)

MORRO BAY

◆◆ Best Western El Rancho Ⓜ ✿
(805) 772-2212. **$59-$119.** 2460 Main St. East side of SR 1, northbound exit SR 41, southbound exit San Jacinto St. Ext corridors. **Pets:** Other. $10 one-time fee/pet. Supervision.
(SAVE) (Sᴅ) (✕) (🛏) (▣) (🍽) (🞠) (ᴋ)

◆◆ Best Western Tradewinds Motel Ⓜ ✿
(805) 772-7376. **$79-$149.** 225 Beach St & Market Ave. Ext corridors. **Pets:** Small, other. Supervision.
(SAVE) (Sᴅ) (✕) (🛏) (▣)

◆◆ Days Inn Ⓜ
(805) 772-2711. **$49-$145, 3 days notice.** 1095 Main St. Just n of Morro Bay Blvd. Ext corridors. **Pets:** Small. Designated rooms, supervision.
(SAVE) (Sᴅ) (✕) (🛏) (▣) (ᴋ)

◆ Morro Crest Inn Ⓜ ✿
(805) 772-7740. **$35-$115, 7 days notice.** 670 Main St. Just s of Morro Bay Blvd. Ext corridors. **Pets:** Medium, dogs only. $20 deposit/pet, $5 daily fee/pet. Designated rooms, supervision.
(✕) (🛏) (▣) (ᴋ)

◆◆ Sundown Motel Ⓜ
(805) 772-7381. **$38-$95.** 640 Main St. Just s of Morro Bay Blvd. Ext corridors. **Pets:** Supervision.
(✕) (🛏) (ᴋ)

◆◆ Villager Motel Ⓜ
(805) 772-1235. **$35-$145, 3 days notice.** 1098 Main St. Just n of Morro Bay Blvd. Ext corridors. **Pets:** Small. Supervision.
(SAVE) (Sᴅ) (✕) (🛏) (▣) (ᴋ)

MOUNT SHASTA

◆◆◆ Best Western Tree House Motor Inn Ⓜ
(530) 926-3101. **$78-$100.** 111 Morgan Way. E off and adjacent to I-5; exit Central Mt Shasta, 2nd exit. Ext/int corridors. **Pets:** Small. No service, supervision, crate.
(SAVE) (Sᴅ) (✕) (🞉) (🛏) (🍽) (🞠)

◆◆ Econo Lodge Ⓜ ✿
(530) 926-3145. **$45-$69, 48 days notice.** 908 S Mt Shasta Blvd. e of I-5 exit Central, 0.5 mi then s 0.5 mi. Ext corridors. **Pets:** Small. $20 deposit/pet, $8 one-time fee/pet. No service, supervision, crate.
(SAVE) (Sᴅ) (✕) (🛏) (▣) (🞠)

◆◆ Evergreen Lodge Ⓜ ✿
(530) 926-2143. **$39-$59, 3 days notice.** 1312 S Mount Shasta Blvd. Exit I-5 central, 0.5 mi s 1 mi s. Ext corridors. **Pets:** Small. $6 daily fee/pet, $6 one-time fee/pet. Designated rooms, no service, supervision, crate.
(SAVE) (Sᴅ) (✕) (🞠)

◆◆ Mountain Air Lodge Ⓜ ✿
(530) 926-3411. **$42-$48.** 1121 S Mount Shasta Blvd. e off I-5 exit Central, 0.5 mi e then s 0.5 mi. Ext corridors. **Pets:** Other. $5 daily fee/pet. No service, supervision, crate.
(Sᴅ) (✕)

◆◆ Pine Needles Motel Ⓜ ✿
(530) 926-4811. **$39-$59, 3 days notice.** 1340 S Mt Shasta Blvd. Exit I-5 central, 0.5 mi e then 1 mi s. Ext corridors. **Pets:** Small. $6 daily fee/pet. Designated rooms, no service, supervision, crate.
(SAVE) (Sᴅ) (✕) (🛏) (🞠)

◆◆ Swiss Holiday Lodge Ⓜ ✿
(530) 926-3446. **$36-$48, 3 days notice.** 2400 S Mt. Shasta Blvd. E of I-5 at McCloud/SR 89 exit, just n at first left. Ext corridors. **Pets:** Small. $5 daily fee/pet, $5 one-time fee/pet. No service, supervision, crate.
(Sᴅ) (✕) (🛏) (🞠)

MOUNTAIN VIEW

◆◆ Best Western Tropicana Lodge Ⓜ ✿
(650) 961-0220. **$90-$105.** 1720 El Camino Real W. Exit US 101 Shoreline S, 2 mi to SR 82, then 0.3 mi w. Ext/int corridors. **Pets:** Designated rooms, no service, supervision, crate.
(SAVE) (Sᴅ) (✕) (🛏) (▣) (🞠)

◆◆◆ Residence Inn By Marriott Ⓜ ✿
(650) 940-1300. **Call for rates.** 1854 El Camino Real. US 101, exit S Rengstorff; e on El Camino Real. Ext corridors. **Pets:** Other. $10 daily fee/pet, $75 one-time fee/room. Supervision.
(✕) (🞠)

NAPA

◆ Napa Valley Budget Inn Ⓜ ✿
(707) 257-6111. **$70-$120.** 3380 Solano Ave. Just w off SR 29 via Redwood Rd, just s. Ext corridors. **Pets:** $10 one-time fee/room. No service, supervision, crate.
(✕) (🛏) (🞠) (CTV)

NEEDLES

◆◆◆ Best Western Colorado River Inn Ⓜ ✿
(760) 326-4552. **$65-$80, 5 days notice.** 2371 W Broadway. 0.3 mi e of I-40, W Broadway/River Rd exit. Ext corridors. **Pets:** Small, other. Designated rooms, no service, supervision, crate.
(SAVE) (Sᴅ) (✕) (🛏) (▣) (🞠)

◆◆◆ Best Western Royal Inn Ⓜ ✿
(760) 326-5660. **$60-$75, 5 days notice.** 1111 Pashard St. Adjacent to I-40, W Broadway/River Rd exit. Ext corridors. **Pets:** Medium, other. $30 deposit/room. Designated rooms, no service, supervision, crate.
(SAVE) (Sᴅ) (✕) (🛏) (🞠)

◆◆◆ Days Inn & Suites Ⓜ
(760) 326-5836. **$35-$75.** 1215 Hospitality Ln. From I-40 at J St exit. Ext corridors. **Pets:** Supervision.
(ASK) (Sᴅ) (✕) (🞗) (🛏) (🞠)

(AAA) ◆ Imperial 400 Motor Inn M
(760) 326-2145. **$23-$32.** 644 W Broadway. I-40, eastbound exit J St, westbound exit E Broadway. Ext corridors. **Pets:** Supervision.

[SAVE] [Sₒ] [✕] [🛈] [⊟]

◆ Overland Inn MI
(760) 326-8808. **$25-$30.** 712 W Broadway. On business loop I-40; exit J St eastbound; exit E Broadway westbound. Ext corridors. **Pets:** Supervision.

[ASK] [Sₒ] [✕] [🛈] [⊟]

(AAA) ◆ River Valley Motor Lodge M 🐾
(760) 326-3839. **$22-$30.** 1707 W Needles Hwy. 1 mi nw on I-40 business loop; from I-40 eastbound exit J St, eastbound exit W Broadway. Ext corridors. **Pets:** Small. Designated rooms, no service, supervision, crate.

[SAVE] [✕] [🛈] [⊟]

◆◆ Super 8 Motel of Needles M
(760) 326-4501. **$38-$55.** 1102 E Broadway. Adjacent to I-40 exit US 95, E Broadway. Ext corridors. **Pets:** Designated rooms, no service, supervision, crate.

[ASK] [Sₒ] [✕] [⊟]

NEVADA CITY

◆ Outside Inn M
(530) 265-2233. **$55-$120.** 575 E Broad St. In the historic district. Ext corridors. **Pets:** Supervision.

[ASK] [✕] [🛈] [⊡] [⊟]

NEWPORT BEACH

(AAA) ◆◆◆◆◆ Four Seasons Hotel Newport Beach H 🐾
(949) 759-0808. **$265-$375.** 690 Newport Center Dr. In Newport Center; 1 mi e of SR 1. Int corridors. **Pets:** Very small. Designated rooms, no service, supervision, crate.

[SAVE] [✕] [⊟] [✕]

(AAA) ◆◆◆ Hyatt Newporter H
(949) 729-1234. **$159-$184.** 1107 Jamboree Rd. 0.5 mi n of SR 1. Ext/int corridors. **Pets:** Small. No service, supervision, crate.

[SAVE] [✕] [🛈] [⊡] [⊤] [⊟] [✕]

◆◆◆ Newport Beach Marriott Hotel & Tennis Club H
(949) 640-4000. **Call for rates.** 900 Newport Center Dr. 0.5 mi e of SR 1, in Newport Center. Ext/int corridors. **Pets:** Small. No service, supervision, crate.

[✕] [🛈] [⊡] [⊤] [⊟] [✕]

◆◆◆ Newport Beach Marriott Suites H 🐾
(949) 854-4500. **Call for rates.** 500 Bayview Circle. At intersection of Jamboree Rd and Bayview Way. Int corridors. **Pets:** Medium, other. $10 daily fee/pet. No service, supervision, crate.

[✕] [🛈] [⊡] [⊤] [⊟]

NOVATO

(AAA) ◆◆ Inn Marin M 🐾
(415) 883-5952. **$89-$109.** 250 Entrada Dr. Just w of US 101 at Ignacio Blvd exit, then just n on Enfrente Rd. Ext corridors. **Pets:** Other. $20 one-time fee/room. Supervision.

[SAVE] [✕] [🛈] [⊟]

OAKHURST

(AAA) ◆◆◆ Best Western Yosemite Gateway Inn MI
(559) 683-2378. **$79-$96.** 40530 Hwy 41. 0.8 mi n of jct SR 49. Ext corridors. **Pets:** Small. Designated rooms, no service, supervision, crate.

[SAVE] [Sₒ] [✕] [⊘] [🛈] [⊡] [⊟] [✕]

(AAA) ◆◆ Comfort Inn-Oakhurst M 🐾
(559) 683-8282. **$89-$89.** 40489 Hwy 41. 0.5 mi n of jct SR 49. Ext corridors. **Pets:** Small, other. $5 daily fee/pet. Designated rooms, no service, supervision, crate.

[SAVE] [✕] [⊘] [🛈] [⊡] [⊟]

OAKLAND

◆◆ Clarion Suites Lake Merritt Hotel H 🐾
(510) 832-2300. **$139-$159.** 1800 Madison St. I-880, exit at Broadway, 0.8 mi e to 17th St, then just s. **Pets:** Large. $75 deposit/room, $75 one-time fee/room. Supervision.

[ASK] [Sₒ] [✕] [🛈] [⊡] [⊤] [🐾]

(AAA) ◆◆◆ Oakland Airport Hilton MI
(510) 635-5000. **$114-$249.** 1 Hegenberger Rd. 1.3 mi e of Oakland Airport; w of I-880, exit Hegenberger Rd 1 mi. Int corridors. **Pets:** Medium. No service, supervision, crate.

[SAVE] [Sₒ] [✕] [⊗] [🛈] [⊡] [⊤] [⊟]

OCCIDENTAL

(AAA) ◆◆ Occidental Lodge M 🐾
(707) 874-3623. **$45-$98, 3 days notice.** 3610 Bohemian Hwy. In the village. Ext corridors. **Pets:** Medium. $8 daily fee/pet. No service, supervision, crate.

[✕] [⊟] [🐾]

OCEANSIDE

(AAA) ◆◆ Ramada Limited Oceanside M
(760) 967-4100. **$69-$99.** 1440 Mission Ave. Ext corridors. **Pets:** Supervision.

[SAVE] [Sₒ] [✕] [🛈] [⊡]

OJAI

(AAA) ◆◆ Best Western Casa Ojai M 🐾
(805) 646-8175. **$70-$120, 48 days notice.** 1302 E Ojai Ave. 0.8 mi e on SR 150. Ext corridors. **Pets:** Small. $50 deposit/room. No service, supervision, crate.

[SAVE] [Sₒ] [✕] [⊡] [⊟]

◆◆◆ Blue Iguana Inn M 🐾
(805) 646-5277. **$99-$145, 7 days notice.** 11794 N Ventura Ave. 2.5 mi w on SR 33. Ext corridors. **Pets:** Medium, dogs only. $20 daily fee/pet, $100 one-time fee/pet. No service, supervision, crate.

[ASK] [Sₒ] [✕] [🛈] [⊡] [⊟]

(AAA) ◆◆ Oakridge Inn M 🐾
(805) 649-4018. **$45-$95.** 780 N Ventura Ave. In Oak View, 4 mi s on SR 33, 2 mi e of Lake Casitas. Ext corridors. **Pets:** Small. $50 deposit/pet, $15 daily fee/pet, $15 one-time fee/pet. No service, supervision, crate.

[SAVE] [Sₒ] [✕] [🛈] [⊡]

◆◆◆ **Ojai Valley Inn & Spa** 🄡 🐾
(805) 646-5511. **$245-$390, 3 days notice.** 905 Country Club Rd. 1 mi w on SR 150, 0.3 mi s. Ext/int corridors. **Pets:** Small. $35 daily fee/room, $35 one-time fee/room. Designated rooms, supervision.
🄰🄢🄺 🖥 ⊠ 🛢 🖵 🍴 🕿 ⊠

ONTARIO

🄰🄰🄰 ◆◆ **Good Nite Inn** 🄼 🐾
(909) 983-3604. **$55-$70.** 1801 East G St. Adjacent to I-10, exit Vineyard Ave, just s, then just w. Ext/int corridors. **Pets:** Medium, other. Supervision.
🆂🄰🆅🄴 🖥 ⊠ 🍴 🕿

🄰🄰🄰 ◆◆◆ **Holiday Inn Hotel & Suites** 🄼 🐾
(909) 466-9600. **$105-$125.** 3400 Shelby St. Adjacent to I-10, exit Haven Ave, just n, then w. Ext corridors. **Pets:** Medium. $50 deposit/pet, $25 one-time fee/pet. No service, supervision, crate.
🆂🄰🆅🄴 🖥 ⊠ 🛢 🖵 🍴 🕿 ⊠

◆◆◆ **La Quinta Inn & Suites** 🄼
(909) 476-1112. **$79-$99.** 3555 Inland Empire Blvd. Just n of I-10, exit Haven Ave, 1.3 mi ne of airport. Int corridors. **Pets:** Supervision.
🄰🄢🄺 ⊠ 🕭 🖋 🛢 🖵 🕿

🄰🄰🄰 ◆◆ **Red Roof Inn-Ontario Airport** 🄼 🐾
(909) 988-8466. **$60-$105.** 1818 E Holt Blvd. 1.8 mi s of I-10, Vineyard Ave exit. Int corridors. **Pets:** Small, other. $10 one-time fee/room. No service, supervision, crate.
🆂🄰🆅🄴 ⊠ 🛢 🕿

◆◆◆ **Residence Inn by Marriott** 🄼
(909) 937-6788. **$125-$154.** 2025 Convention Center Way. From I-10 exit Vineyard Ave, just s then 1 blk e. Ext corridors. **Pets:** Small. Supervision.
🄰🄢🄺 🖥 ⊠ 🛢 🖵 🕿 ⊠

ORANGE

🄰🄰🄰 ◆◆◆ **Hilton Suites**
Anaheim/Orange 🄷 🐾
(714) 938-1111. **$115-$205, 3 days notice.** 400 North State College Blvd. Just e of I-5; southbound exit State College Blvd, northbound Chapman Ave. Int corridors. **Pets:** Supervision.
🆂🄰🆅🄴 🖥 ⊠ 🛢 🖵 🍴 🕿

🄰🄰🄰 ◆◆◆ **Residence Inn by Marriott** 🄰 🐾
(714) 978-7700. **$92-$114.** 201 N State College Blvd. Adjacent to I-5, just n of Chapman Ave. Ext corridors. **Pets:** Small, other. $10 daily fee/pet, $100 one-time fee/room. Supervision.
⊠ 🖵 🕿 ⊠

ORLAND

🄰🄰🄰 ◆◆ **Amber Light Inn Motel** 🄼 🐾
(530) 865-7655. **$36-$42, 7 days notice.** 828 Newville Rd. Exit I-5 via Chico, SR 32 off-ramp, then 0.3 mi e. Ext corridors. **Pets:** Very small, other. $10 deposit/pet, $10 one-time fee/room. Designated rooms, no service, supervision, crate.
🖥 ⊠ 🕿

🄰🄰🄰 ◆◆ **Orland Inn** 🄼 🐾
(530) 865-7632. **$35-$48.** 1052 South St. 0.5 mi s; northbound exit I-5E via Orland-Fairgrounds, southbound exit I-5E via CR 16; adjacent to I-5 in Stony Creek Shopping Center. Ext corridors. **Pets:** Other. No service, supervision, crate.
🆂🄰🆅🄴 🖥 ⊠ 🕭 🕿

OROVILLE

🄰🄰🄰 ◆◆◆ **Best Inn & Suites** 🄼 🐾
(530) 533-9673. **$69-$85.** 1470 Feather River Blvd. SR 70 exit E Montgomery. Int corridors. **Pets:** $100 deposit/room. No service, supervision, crate.
🆂🄰🆅🄴 🖥 ⊠ 🖋 🛢 🕿

◆ **Days Inn-Oroville** 🄼
(530) 533-3297. **$45-$99.** 1745 Feather River Blvd. SR 70 exit E Montgomery St, just e to Feather River Blvd, 0.5 mi s. Ext corridors. **Pets:** Supervision.
🄰🄢🄺 🖥 ⊠ 🛢 🖵 🕿

🄰🄰🄰 ◆◆ **Oroville Travelodge** 🄼 🐾
(530) 533-7070. **$45-$60.** 580 Oro Dam Blvd. Exit SR 70 at Oro Dam Blvd, 0.3 mi e. Ext corridors. **Pets:** Other. No service, supervision, crate.
🆂🄰🆅🄴 🖥 ⊠ 🛢 🖵 🕿

OXNARD

🄰🄰🄰 ◆◆◆ **Best Western Oxnard Inn** 🄼 🐾
(805) 483-9581. **$69-$99.** 1156 S Oxnard Blvd. 3 mi s of US 101, northbound exit Vineyard Ave, then left to Oxnard Rd; southbound exit Oxnard Blvd. Ext corridors. **Pets:** Small. $10 one-time fee/room. No service, supervision, crate.
🆂🄰🆅🄴 🖥 ⊠ 🛢 🖵 🕿

🄰🄰🄰 ◆◆ **Casa Sirena Hotel & Marina** 🄼 🐾
(805) 985-6311. **$79-$99, 3 days notice.** 3605 Peninsula Rd. 0.5 mi w of Victoria Blvd via Channel Islands Blvd at Channel Islands Harbor. Ext/int corridors. **Pets:** $50 one-time fee/room. Designated rooms, no service, supervision, crate.
🆂🄰🆅🄴 ⊠ 🛢 🖵 🍴 🕿 ⊠

◆◆◆ **Radisson Hotel-Oxnard** 🄷 🐾
(805) 485-9666. **$89-$89.** 600 Esplanade Dr. Just s of US 101 exit Vineyard Ave. Int corridors. **Pets:** Small, dogs only. $50 one-time fee/pet. No service, supervision, crate.
🄰🄢🄺 🖥 ⊠ 🕝 🍺 🖋 🛢 🖵 🍴 🕿

◆◆◆ **Residence Inn At River Ridge** 🄰 🐾
(805) 278-2200. **$114-$114.** 2101 W Vineyard Ave. 1.8 mi sw of US 101, exit Vineyard Ave. Ext corridors. **Pets:** Very small. $250 deposit/pet, $5 daily fee/room, $100 one-time fee/room. No service, supervision, crate.
🄰🄢🄺 ⊠ 🍺 🛢 🕿 ⊠

🄰🄰🄰 ◆ **Vagabond Inn** 🄼 🐾
(805) 983-0251. **$52-$69.** 1245 N Oxnard Bl. 1.5 mi s of US 101 on SR 1, northbound exit Vineyard, southbound exit Oxnard Bl. Ext corridors. **Pets:** Other. $5 daily fee/pet. Supervision.
🆂🄰🆅🄴 🖥 ⊠ 🛢 🖵 🕿 ⊠

PALM DESERT

◆◆ Casa Larrea Resort 🅼 🐾
(760) 568-0311. **$64-$104, 30 days notice.** 73-771 Larrea St. Just s of SR 111, between San Luis Rey and Portola Ave. Ext corridors. **Pets:** Small, dogs only. $100 deposit/pet. No service, supervision, crate.
🗙 🛢 💻 🐾

◆◆ Desert Patch Inn 🅼 🐾
(760) 346-9161. **$56-$98, 7 days notice.** 73758 Shadow Mountain Dr. Just s of SR 111 between San Luis Rey and Portola Ave. Ext corridors. **Pets:** Medium, other. $25 deposit/room. Supervision.
🗙 🛢 💻 🐾 🗶

🆎 ◆◆ The Inn at Deep Canyon 🅼 🐾
(760) 346-8061. **$99-$179, 3 days notice.** 74470 Abronia Tr. Just s of SR 111 via Deep Canyon Rd. Ext corridors. **Pets:** Medium, other. Designated rooms, supervision.
🆂🅰🆅🅴 🗙 🛢 💻 🐾

🆎 ◆◆◆ Residence Inn by Marriott 🅰 🐾
(760) 776-0050. **$199-$325, 7 days notice.** 38-305 Cook St. 1 mi s of I-10, exit Cook St. Ext corridors. **Pets:** Small. $5 daily fee/pet, $200 one-time fee/room. No service, supervision, crate.
🆂🅰🆅🅴 🛅 🗙 💻 🐾 🗶

PALM SPRINGS

◆◆ Casa Cody Country Inn 🅼
(760) 320-9346. **Call for rates, 3 days notice.** 175 S Cahuilla Rd. Just w of SR 111, just s of Tahquitz Canyon Way. Ext corridors. **Pets:** Medium. Supervision.
🐾

◆◆◆ Comfort Inn 🅼
(760) 778-3699. **$59-$119.** 390 S Indian Canyon Dr. Ext corridors. **Pets:** Medium. Supervision.
🆎🆂🅺 🛅 🗙 💻 🐾

🆎 ◆◆◆ Estrella Inn & Villas 🆇 🐾
(760) 320-4117. **$165-$265, 7 days notice.** 415 S Belardo Rd. Downtown, just w of Palm Canyon Dr. Ext/int corridors. **Pets:** Medium, dogs only. $25 daily fee/pet. Designated rooms, no service, supervision, crate.
🛅 🗙 💻 🐾

🆎 ◆◆ Hotel California 🅼 🐾
(760) 322-8855. **$69-$135, 3 days notice.** 424 E Palm Canyon Dr. 1.5 mi s. Ext corridors. **Pets:** Small, dogs only. $5 daily fee/pet, $50 one-time fee/pet. No service, supervision, crate.
🆂🅰🆅🅴 🗙 🛢 💻 🐾

◆◆◆ Palm Springs Hilton Resort 🅷
(760) 320-6868. **$175-$185, 3 days notice.** 400 E Tahquitz Canyon Way. Just e of Indian Canyon Dr. Int corridors. **Pets:** Small. Designated rooms, no service, supervision, crate.
🆎🆂🅺 🗙 🛢 💻 🍴 🐾 🗶

◆◆◆ Palm Springs Riviera Resort 🅷 🐾
(760) 327-8311. **$149-$149.** 1600 N Indian Canyon Dr. 1.5 mi n. Int corridors. **Pets:** Dogs only. $200 deposit/room. Supervision.
🆎🆂🅺 🗙 🖋 🛢 💻 🍴 🐾 🗶

🆎 ◆◆◆ Quality Inn Resort 🅼
(760) 323-2775. **$99-$129.** 1269 E Palm Canyon Dr. 2.3 mi se on Palm Canyon Dr. Ext corridors. **Pets:** Small. Supervision.
🆂🅰🆅🅴 🛅 🗙 🛢 💻 🐾

◆◆◆ Ramada Resort Inn & Conference Center 🅼🅸
(760) 323-1711. **$109-$199, 3 days notice.** 1800 E Palm Canyon Dr. 2.5 mi se on Palm Canyon Dr. Ext/int corridors. **Pets:** $50 deposit/room. Supervision.
🆎🆂🅺 🛅 🗙 🛢 💻 🍴 🐾

🆎 ◆◆ Royal Sun Inn 🅼 🐾
(760) 327-1564. **$69-$99.** 1700 S Palm Canyon Dr. 1.5 mi se on Palm Canyon Dr. Ext corridors. **Pets:** Other. Supervision.
🆂🅰🆅🅴 🛅 🗙 🛢 💻 🐾

◆◆ San Marino Hotel 🅼 🐾
(760) 325-6902. **$109-$169, 72 days notice.** 225 W Baristo Rd. Just w of downtown area. Ext corridors. **Pets:** Small, dogs only. $50 deposit/room, $10 daily fee/room. Supervision.
🗙 🐾

◆ Super 8 Lodge 🅼 🐾
(760) 322-3757. **$66-$86.** 1900 N Palm Canyon Dr. 1.5 mi n. Ext corridors. **Pets:** Medium, dogs only. $10 daily fee/room. No service, supervision, crate.
🆎🆂🅺 🛅 🗙 🛢 🐾

◆◆ Villa Rosa Inn 🅼 🐾
(760) 327-5915. **$75-$135, 3 days notice.** 1577 S Indian Tr. 2 mi se on Palm Canyon Dr, just n. Ext corridors. **Pets:** Very small. Supervision.
🗙 🛢 🐾

🆎 ◆◆ Ville Orleans Resort Hotel 🅼
(760) 864-6200. **$69-$225.** 269 Chuckwalla Rd. 1.5 mi n of downtown; just e of Indian Canyon Dr. Ext corridors. **Pets:** Supervision.
🆂🅰🆅🅴 🗙 🛢 💻 🐾

PALO ALTO

◆◆◆ Crowne Plaza Cabana Hotel 🅷 🐾
(650) 857-0787. **$195-$195.** 4290 El Camino Real. On SR 82, US 101 exit San Antonio Rd; 0.4 mi n on El Camino. Ext/int corridors. **Pets:** Small. $100 deposit/room, $25 one-time fee/room. No service, supervision, crate.
🆎🆂🅺 🛅 🗙 🖋 📷 🖋 🛢 💻 🍴 🐾

◆◆◆ Sheraton Palo Alto Hotel 🅼🅸 🐾
(650) 328-2800. **$209-$279.** 625 El Camino Real. Exit US 101 Embarcadero W, to SR 82, 0.5 mi n, opposite Stanford University. Int corridors. **Pets:** Medium, other. $50 daily fee/pet. No service, supervision, crate.
🆎🆂🅺 🗙 🛢 💻 🍴 🐾

PARADISE

🆎 ◆◆◆ Best Inn & Suites 🅼
(530) 876-0191. **$59-$88.** 5475 Clark Rd. On SR 191, 0.5 mi s of Pearson Rd. Int corridors. **Pets:** Medium. Supervision.
🆂🅰🆅🅴 🛅 🗙 🖋 🖋 🛢 💻 🐾

⚫⚫ ◆◆ **Paradise Inn** 🅜 ❀
(530) 877-2127. **$42-$55.** 5423 Skyway. 1.5 mi w. Ext corridors. **Pets:** $25 deposit/pet, $5 daily fee/pet, $5 one-time fee/pet. No service, supervision, crate.

⚫⚫ ◆◆◆ **Ponderosa Gardens Motel** 🅜 ❀
(530) 872-9094. **$58-$85.** 7010 Skyway. Center; 2 blks e. Ext corridors. **Pets:** $6 daily fee/pet. Supervision.

PASO ROBLES

⚫⚫ ◆ **Travelodge Paso Robles** 🅜
(805) 238-0078. **$45-$72.** 2701 Spring St. 0.5 mi w of US 101, exit Spring St. Ext corridors. **Pets:** Small. No service, supervision, crate.

PISMO BEACH

⚫⚫ ◆◆◆ **Oxford Suites Resort** 🅜 ❀
(805) 773-3773. **$89-$129.** 651 Five Cities Dr. Adjacent to US 101, exit 4th St. Ext corridors. **Pets:** Medium, other. $10 one-time fee/pet. No service, supervision, crate.

◆◆ **Shell Beach Motel** 🅜
(805) 773-4373. **Call for rates.** 653 Shell Beach Rd. 2 mi n in Shell Beach; adj to US 101 and SR 1. Ext corridors. **Pets:** Supervision.

PLACERVILLE

⚫⚫ ◆◆ **Mother Lode Motel** 🅜 ❀
(530) 622-0895. **Call for rates, 3 days notice.** 1940 Broadway. 2 mi e; adjacent to US 50; exit Point View Dr. Ext corridors. **Pets:** Small. $50 deposit/room, $10 daily fee/pet, $10 one-time fee/pet. Designated rooms, no service, supervision, crate.

PLEASANT HILL

◆◆◆ **Residence Inn By Marriott-Pleasant Hill** 🅜 ❀
(925) 689-1010. **$159-$199.** 700 Ellinwood Way. Exit I-680 Willow Pass Rd, to Taylor W; s Contra Costa Blvd, e on Ellinwood Dr, n on Ellinwood Way. Ext/int corridors. **Pets:** Other. $6 daily fee/pet, $75 one-time fee/room. Supervision.

PLEASANTON

◆◆◆ **Candlewood Suites** 🅜 ❀
(925) 463-1212. **$119-$129.** 5535 Johnson Dr. I-580, Hopyard S exit, w on Owen. Int corridors. **Pets:** Medium, other. $10 daily fee/pet, $75 one-time fee/room. No service, supervision, crate.

◆◆◆ **Crowne Plaza-Pleasanton** 🄷 ❀
(925) 847-6000. **$69-$165.** 11950 Dublin Canyon Rd. Exit I-580 at Foothill Rd, 0.3 mi s. Int corridors. **Pets:** Medium. Supervision.

◆◆◆◆ **Hilton Pleasanton at the Club** 🄷
(925) 463-8000. **$69-$234.** 7050 Johnson Dr. In se quadrant at jct I-580 and I-680. Int corridors. **Pets:** No service, supervision, crate.

◆◆ **Super 8 Lodge** 🅜 ❀
(925) 463-1300. **$70-$95.** 5375 Owens Ct. Exit I-580 at Hopyard Rd, 2 blks s. Ext corridors. **Pets:** Other. $100 deposit/room. No service, supervision, crate.

POLLOCK PINES

⚫⚫ ◆◆◆ **Stagecoach Motor Inn** 🅜
(530) 644-2029. **$58-$78, 3 days notice.** 5940 Pony Express Tr. 12 mi e of Placerville; eastbound exit US 50 at Pollock Pines, 1 mi e on Pony Express Tr, westbound exit Sly Park, 1 mi on Pony Express Tr. **Pets:** Large. Supervision.

RAMONA

⚫⚫ ◆◆ **Ramona Valley Inn** 🅜 ❀
(760) 789-6433. **$50-$77.** 416 Main St. On SR 78, 0.5 mi NE of jct SR 67. Ext corridors. **Pets:** Small, dogs only. Designated rooms, supervision.

RANCHO CORDOVA

⚫⚫ ◆◆◆ **AmeriSuites** 🄼
(916) 635-4799. **$69-$126.** 10744 Gold Center Dr. Exit US 50 at Zinfandel Dr, just s. Int corridors. **Pets:** Medium. Designated rooms, supervision.

⚫⚫ ◆◆◆ **Best Western Heritage Inn** 🄼
(916) 635-4040. **Call for rates.** 11269 Point East Dr. 12 mi e of Sacramento; exit US 50 Sunrise Blvd S. Int corridors. **Pets:** Small. Designated rooms, no service, supervision, crate.

⚫⚫ ◆◆ **Inns of America** 🅜 ❀
(916) 351-1213. **$52-$59.** 12249 Folsom Blvd. Exit Hwy 50 at Hazel Ave, then just s. Ext corridors. **Pets:** Small, other. $10 one-time fee/room. No service, supervision, crate.

◆◆ **Mather Inn** 🅜 ❀
(916) 363-3344. **Call for rates.** 3240 Mather Field Rd. 9 mi e of Sacramento, exit US 50 at Mather Field Rd. Ext corridors. **Pets:** Medium, other. $25 deposit/room. Supervision.

RANCHO MIRAGE

⚫⚫ ◆◆◆◆ **The Westin Mission Hills Resort** 🄷 ❀
(760) 328-5955. **$215-$239, 7 days notice.** 71-333 Dinah Shore Dr. 2 mi sw of I-10, exit Bob Hope Dr. Ext corridors. **Pets:** Supervision.

RED BLUFF

◆ Cinderella Riverview Motel M
(530) 527-5490. **$32-$48, 7 days notice.** 600 Rio St. Exit I-5 at SR 36W, central district; 0.4 mi w on Antelope Blvd. Ext corridors. **Pets:** Small. Designated rooms, no service, supervision, crate.

◆◆ Days Inn & Suites M ❀
(530) 527-6130. **$30-$100.** 5 John Sutter St. I-5, exit at S Main St. Ext corridors. **Pets:** Other. $5 daily fee/pet. Supervision.

◆◆ Red Bluff Inn M ❀
(530) 529-2028. **$37-$52, 7 days notice.** 30 Gilmore Rd. Exit I-5, SR 36W-Central District; just s on Gilmore Rd. Ext corridors. **Pets:** Small, other. $6 daily fee/room. Designated rooms, no service, supervision, crate.

◆ Relax Inn M ❀
(530) 527-3545. **$25-$46.** 250 S Main St. Exit I-5 at SR 36W (Central District), 0.5 mi w on Antelope Blvd, 0.7 mi s. Ext corridors. **Pets:** Other. $5 daily fee/pet, $5 one-time fee/pet. Designated rooms, no service, supervision, crate.

◆ Sportsman Lodge M ❀
(530) 527-2888. **$33-$55, 3 days notice.** 768 Antelope Blvd. Exit I-5 at SR 36E, Susanville/Lassen Park exit, 1.5 mi e. Ext corridors. **Pets:** $20 deposit/pet, $5 daily fee/pet. Designated rooms, no service, supervision, crate.

◆◆ Super 8 Motel M ❀
(530) 527-8882. **$39-$55.** 203 Antelope Blvd. Exit I-5 at SR 36 E, Susanville/Lassen Park exit. Int corridors. **Pets:** $20 deposit/room. Supervision.

◆◆ Travelodge Red Bluff M ❀
(530) 527-6020. **$39-$59.** 38 Antelope Blvd. Exit I-5 at SR 36W (Central District), 0.2 mi w on Antelope Blvd. Ext corridors. **Pets:** $15 deposit/pet, $5 daily fee/pet. Designated rooms, no service, supervision, crate.

REDCREST

◆◆ Redcrest Resort C ❀
(707) 722-4208. **$47-$85, 3 days notice.** 26459 Avenue of the Giants. Exit US 101 at Redcrest, just n. Ext corridors. **Pets:** $5 daily fee/pet. No service, supervision, crate.

REDDING

◆◆ Best Western Hospitality House M ❀
(530) 241-6464. **$50-$70.** 532 N Market St. W of I-5; northbound exit Lake Blvd 0.5 mi to Market, 0.5 mi s; southbound exit Market St, 2 mi s. Ext corridors. **Pets:** Small. $25 deposit/pet, $6 daily fee/room. Designated rooms, supervision.

◆◆ Best Western Ponderosa Inn M
(530) 241-6300. **$44-$59.** 2220 Pine St. 1.5 mi w of I-5, Cypress Ave exit. Ext corridors. **Pets:** Small. Designated rooms, supervision.

◆◆ Comfort Inn M ❀
(530) 221-6530. **$49-$64.** 2059 Hilltop Dr. Exit I-5 Cypress Ave E; 0.3 mi n. Ext corridors. **Pets:** Medium. $100 deposit/ room. No service, supervision, crate.

◆◆ Holiday Inn Express M
(530) 241-5500. **$89-$120.** 1080 Twin View Blvd. W of I-5, exit Twin View Blvd. Int corridors. **Pets:** Supervision.

◆◆◆ La Quinta Inn M
(530) 221-8200. **$69-$89.** 2180 Hilltop Dr. Exit I-5 Cypress Ave E, 0.5 mi n. Int corridors. **Pets:** Small. Designated rooms, no service, supervision, crate.

◆◆◆ Oxford Suites M ❀
(530) 221-0100. **$69-$69.** 1967 Hilltop Dr. Exit I-5 Cypress E, 0.5 mi n. Ext/int corridors. **Pets:** Small. $15 one-time fee/room. Supervision.

◆◆◆ Ramada Limited M ❀
(530) 246-2222. **$79-$99, 7 days notice.** 1286 Twin View Blvd. I-5, Twin View Blvd E, just n. Int corridors. **Pets:** $15 one-time fee/pet. No service, supervision, crate.

◆◆ River Inn M ❀
(530) 241-9500. **$46-$60.** 1835 Park Marina Dr. Exit I-5 at SR 299 W, 1 mi w, exit at Park Marina Dr. Ext corridors. **Pets:** Large, other. $6 daily fee/pet. Supervision.

◆◆ Vagabond Inn M ❀
(530) 223-1600. **$55-$65.** 536 E Cypress Ave. W off I-5 via Cypress Ave. Ext corridors. **Pets:** Small. $6 daily fee/pet. Designated rooms, no service, supervision, crate.

REDLANDS

◆◆ Best Western Sandman Motel M
(909) 793-2001. **$45-$95.** 1120 W Colton Ave. Adjacent to I-10, exit Tennessee St, just s, then e. Ext corridors. **Pets:** Designated rooms, no service, supervision, crate.

◆ Good Nite Inn M
(909) 793-3723. **$40-$70.** 1675 Industrial Park Ave. South side of I-10, just w of Alabama St exit. Ext corridors. **Pets:** Small. No service, supervision, crate.

REDWOOD CITY

◆◆◆ Hotel Sofitel San Francisco Bay at Redwood Shores 🖪 ❀

(650) 598-9000. **$119-$309.** 223 Twin Dolphin Dr. Exit US 101 at Marine World Pkwy E, 0.5 mi s on Twin Dolphin Dr. Int corridors. **Pets:** Medium. $25 one-time fee/room. Supervision.

(ASK) (S☎) (✕) (Ψ) (☎)

REEDLEY

◆◆◆ Edgewater Inn 🖿 ❀

(559) 637-7777. **$51-$66.** 1977 W Manning Ave. 12 mi e of SR 99 via Manning Hwy. Ext corridors. **Pets:** Dogs only. $7 daily fee/pet. No service, supervision, crate.

(SAVE) (S☎) (✕) (🖿) (☎) (☎) (CTV)

RIALTO

◆◆◆ Best Western Empire Inn 🖿 ❀

(909) 877-0690. **$59-$119.** 475 W Valley Blvd. I-10, exit Riverside Ave, n to Valley Blvd, 0.5 mi w. Ext corridors. **Pets:** Medium. $5 one-time fee/pet. No service, supervision, crate.

(SAVE) (S☎) (✕) (Ψ) (☎)

RIDGECREST

◆◆◆ Best Western China Lake Inn 🖿 ❀

(760) 371-2300. **$60-$80.** 400 S China Lake Blvd. 0.4 mi s of Ridgecrest Blvd, on US 395 business route. Ext corridors. **Pets:** Small. No service, supervision, crate.

(SAVE) (S☎) (✕) (🖿) (☎) (☎)

◆◆ Econo Lodge 🖿 ❀

(760) 446-2551. **$44-$54.** 201 Inyokern Rd. On SR 178 and US 395 business route, just w of China Lake Blvd. Ext corridors. **Pets:** Small, dogs only. No service, supervision, crate.

(SAVE) (S☎) (✕) (🖿) (☎) (☎)

◆◆◆ Heritage Inn & Suites 🖿 ❀

(760) 446-7951. **$69-$75, 7 days notice.** 1050 N Norma. On Norma St, just n of Drummond Ave. Int corridors. **Pets:** $100 deposit/room. No service, supervision, crate.

(SAVE) (✕) (🖿) (☎) (Ψ) (☎)

◆◆ Quality Inn 🖿 ❀

(760) 375-9731. **$45-$59.** 507 S China Lake Blvd. 0.5 mi s of Ridgecrest Blvd, on US 395 business route. Ext corridors. **Pets:** Small. $8 daily fee/pet, $8 one-time fee/pet. Designated rooms, no service, supervision, crate.

(SAVE) (S☎) (✕) (🖿) (☎)

RIO DELL

◆ Humboldt Gables Motel 🖿 ❀

(707) 764-5609. **$40-$65.** 40 W Davis St. Exit US 101 Rio Dell/Davis St W. Ext corridors. **Pets:** Other. $100 deposit/ pet. No service, supervision, crate.

(S☎) (✕) (🖿) (☎) (M)

RIVERSIDE

◆◆ Best Western of Riverside 🖿 ❀

(909) 359-0770. **$59-$129, 7 days notice.** 10518 Magnolia Ave. 7 mi sw on SR 91, exit Tyler St, 2 blks n, then 0.3 mi w. Ext corridors. **Pets:** Small, other. $100 deposit/room. Designated rooms, no service, supervision, crate.

(SAVE) (S☎) (✕) (🖿) (☎) (CTV)

◆◆◆ Dynasty Suites-Riverside 🖿

(909) 369-8200. **$48-$54.** 3735 Iowa Ave. Just sw of SR 60, exit University Ave; n on Iowa Ave. Ext corridors. **Pets:** Supervision.

(S☎) (✕) (🖿) (☎) (☎)

ROCKLIN

◆◆◆ First Choice Inn 🖿 ❀

(916) 624-4500. **$88-$100.** 4420 Rocklin Rd. US 80 e exit Rocklin Rd; westbound exit Rocklin. Int corridors. **Pets:** Small, other. $100 deposit/room, $20 one-time fee/ room. Supervision.

(SAVE) (S☎) (✕) (♿) (🗲) (🐾) (🖿) (☎)

ROHNERT PARK

◆◆◆◆ Doubletree Hotel-Sonoma County 🖪 ❀

(707) 584-5466. **$149-$219.** One Doubletree Dr. 3 mi s of Santa Rosa; exit US 101, Golf Course Dr. Int corridors. **Pets:** Medium, other. Supervision.

(ASK) (S☎) (✕) (🖿) (☎) (Ψ) (☎) (✕)

◆ Good Nite Inn 🖿

(707) 584-8180. **$39-$70.** 5040 Redwood Dr. Just w of US 101, exit Golf Course Dr. Ext corridors. **Pets:** Very small. No service, supervision, crate.

(ASK) (S☎) (✕) (🖿) (☎)

◆ Ramada Limited 🖿

(707) 584-1600. **Call for rates.** 6288 Redwood Dr. Exit US 101 via W Rohnert Park Expwy. Ext corridors. **Pets:** No service, supervision, crate.

(✕) (☎)

ROSAMOND

◆ Devonshire Inn Motel 🖿

(661) 256-3454. **$54-$54.** 2076 Rosamond Blvd. Just e of SR 14, exit Edwards/Rosamond. Ext corridors. **Pets:** Supervision.

(SAVE) (S☎) (✕) (🖿) (☎)

ROSEVILLE

◆◆ Best Western Roseville Inn 🖿

(916) 782-4434. **$68-$95.** 220 Harding Blvd. Exit w off I-80 via Douglas, just n. Ext corridors. **Pets:** Small. No service, supervision, crate.

(SAVE) (S☎) (✕) (🖿) (☎)

◆◆◆ Oxford Suites 🖿 ❀

(916) 784-2222. **$79-$99.** 130 N Sunrise Ave. Exit e off I-80 via Douglas Blvd, 0.3 mi n. Ext corridors. **Pets:** Other. $15 one-time fee/room. Supervision.

(ASK) (S☎) (✕) (🖿) (☎)

◆◆◆ Residence Inn 🅼 ✤
(916) 772-5500. **$129-$129.** 1930 Taylor Rd. I-80, Eureka Taylor Rd exit, just s. Int corridors. **Pets:** $10 daily fee/room, $100 one-time fee/room. No service, supervision, crate.

(A$K) (S🅾) (✕) (▣) (▣) (✕)

SACRAMENTO

⦿ ◆◆ Best Western Expo Inn 🅼 ✤
(916) 922-9833. **$70-$100.** 1413 Howe Ave. 2.5 mi n of jct SR 16 and US 50, exit Howe Ave. Int corridors. **Pets:** Medium, other. $100 deposit/room. Designated rooms, no service, supervision, crate.

(SAVE) (S🅾) (✕) (🅷) (▣) (🎴)

⦿ ◆◆◆ Best Western Harbor Inn & Suites 🅼 ✤
(916) 371-2100. **$79-$89.** 1250 Halyard Dr. 4 mi w; exit Business Loop 80 via Harbor Blvd. Ext/int corridors. **Pets:** Small. $10 daily fee/pet, $10 one-time fee/pet. No service, supervision, crate.

(SAVE) (S🅾) (✕) (🅷) (▣) (🎴)

◆◆◆ Candlewood Suites 🅼 ✤
(916) 646-1212. **$69-$120.** 555 Howe Ave. US 50, exit Howe Ave, 1.5 mi n. Int corridors. **Pets:** Other. $10 daily fee/room, $75 one-time fee/room. Supervision.

(A$K) (S🅾) (✕) (♿) (🎴) (🅷) (▣)

⦿ ◆◆ Canterbury Inn 🅼
(916) 927-0927. **$69-$74.** 1900 Canterbury Rd. 3 mi e of Capitol via SR 160, 16th St extension. Ext corridors. **Pets:** Small. Supervision.

(SAVE) (✕) (♿) (🎴) (▣) (🍴) (🎴)

⦿ ◆◆ Clarion Hotel 🅷 ✤
(916) 444-8000. **$114-$139.** 700 16th St. On SR 160; 1.3 mi n of Business Loop 80, 16th St exit. Int corridors. **Pets:** Other. $35 one-time fee/room. Supervision.

(SAVE) (S🅾) (✕) (🎴) (🅷) (▣) (🍴) (🎴) (CTV)

◆◆◆ Days Inn-Discovery Park 🅼
(916) 442-6971. **$69-$79.** 350 Bercut Dr. 2.3 mi nw of Business Loop 80; off I-5 exit, E Richards Blvd. Ext corridors. **Pets:** Medium. No service, supervision, crate.

(A$K) (S🅾) (✕) (🅷) (▣) (🎴) (CTV)

◆◆◆ Doubletree Hotel 🅷 ✤
(916) 929-8855. **$149-$219.** 2001 Point West Way. 3.n mi e; 1 blk off Business Loop 80; exit via Arden Way. Int corridors. **Pets:** Small, other. $50 deposit/room, $25 one-time fee/room. Designated rooms, no service, supervision, crate.

(A$K) (S🅾) (✕) (🅷) (▣) (▣) (🍴) (🎴)

⦿ ◆ Econo Lodge 🅼 🐾
(916) 443-6631. **$45-$82.** 711 16th St. SR 160, 1 mi n of Business Loop 80, I-80 business loop eastbound exit 15th St, westbound 16th St, I-5 exit J St. Ext corridors. **Pets:** Other. $6 daily fee/pet. Designated rooms, supervision.

(SAVE) (S🅾) (✕) (♿) (🎴) (🅷) (CTV)

◆◆ Heritage Hotel 🅼 ✤
(916) 929-7900. **Call for rates.** 1780 Tribute Rd. W off Business Loop 80 via Exposition Blvd. Int corridors. **Pets:** Other. Supervision.

(✕) (🅷) (🍴) (🎴)

◆◆ Homestead Guest Studios 🅼
(916) 564-7500. **$59-$64.** 2810 Gateway Oaks Dr. I-5 exit at W El Camino Ave, just w, then 0.4 mi n. Ext corridors. **Pets:** Medium. Designated rooms, supervision.

(✕)

⦿ ◆◆ Host Airport Hotel 🅼
(916) 922-8071. **$75-$115.** 6945 Airport Blvd. 11 mi nw from capitol; 6 mi nw of I-80, off I-5 at the Sacramento Metropolitan Airport. Ext corridors. **Pets:** Medium. No service, supervision, crate.

(SAVE) (S🅾) (✕)

⦿ ◆◆ Inns of America 🅼
(916) 386-8408. **$49-$58.** 25 Howe Ave. Sw corner of jct SR 50 and Howe Ave. Ext corridors. **Pets:** Medium. Designated rooms, no service, supervision, crate.

(SAVE) (S🅾) (✕) (🎴)

◆◆◆ La Quinta Inn 🅼
(916) 348-0900. **$75-$95.** 4604 Madison Ave. 9 mi e; exit I-80 at Madison Ave. Ext corridors. **Pets:** Supervision.

(A$K) (✕) (▣) (🎴)

◆◆◆ La Quinta Inn-Sacramento Downtown 🅼
(916) 448-8100. **$79-$99.** 200 Jibboom St. 2.3 mi nw of Business Loop 80; off I-5 exit Richards Blvd W. Ext corridors. **Pets:** Designated rooms, no service, supervision, crate.

(A$K) (✕) (🅷) (▣) (🎴)

◆◆◆ Marriott Residence Inn 🅼 ✤
(916) 920-9111. **$139-$139.** 1530 Howe Ave. 2.5 mi n of jct SR 16 and US 50, Howe Ave eixt. Ext corridors. **Pets:** Medium, other. $100 deposit/room, $100 one-time fee/room. No service, supervision, crate.

(A$K) (S🅾) (✕) (♿) (🎴) (🅷) (▣) (🎴)

◆◆◆ Radisson Hotel 🅷 ✤
(916) 922-2020. **$79-$139.** 500 Leisure Ln. Exit Business Route 80 at Exposition Blvd, 0.4 mi w. Ext corridors. **Pets:** Medium, other. $100 deposit/pet. Supervision.

(A$K) (S🅾) (✕) (🎴) (▣) (🍴) (🎴) (✕)

⦿ ◆◆ Ramada Inn 🅼 ✤
(916) 487-7600. **$63-$89.** 2600 Auburn Blvd. Exit Business route 80 at Fulton Ave. Int corridors. **Pets:** Medium, other. $75 deposit/room. No service, supervision, crate.

(S🅾) (✕) (🅷) (▣) (🍴) (🎴)

◆◆◆ Red Lion's Sacramento Inn 🅼
(916) 922-8041. **$115-$168.** 1401 Arden Way. Exit Business Loop 80 via Arden Way; in Arden Fair Shopping Plaza lot. Ext/int corridors. **Pets:** No service, supervision, crate.

(A$K) (S🅾) (✕) (🅷) (▣) (🍴) (🎴) (✕)

⦿ ◆◆ Vagabond Inn 🅼 ✤
(916) 446-1481. **$80-$90.** 909 3rd St. 8 blks w of Capitol; adjacent to Chinese Cultural Center and Old Sacramento Historic Quarter; exit J St. Ext corridors. **Pets:** Small. $20 daily fee/pet. Designated rooms, no service, supervision, crate.

(SAVE) (S🅾) (✕) (🎴) (🅷) (🎴)

SALINAS

◆◆◆ **Barlocker's Rustling Oaks Ranch** 🅁🄰 🐾
(831) 675-9121. **$75-$150, 7 days notice.** 25252 Limeklin Rd. 6 mi w of US 101, Chualar exit; w on River Rd, s (left) after bridge, to Limekiln, right at sign. Ext/int corridors. **Pets:** Other. $100 deposit/pet. Supervision.

☒ ☒ 🄺 🄲🅃🅅 ☎

🄐🄐🄐 ◆ **El Dorado Motel** 🅼
(831) 449-2442. **$36-$79.** 1351 N Main St. 1 mi ne of US 101, N Main St exit. Ext corridors. **Pets:** Medium. No service, supervision, crate.

🆂🄰🆅🄴 🆂🗗 ☒ 🄱 🄺

🄐🄐🄐 ◆◆ **Vagabond Inn** 🅼 🐾
(831) 758-4693. **$75-$80.** 131 Kern St. Just e of US 101, Market St exit. Ext corridors. **Pets:** Medium, other. $5 daily fee/pet. Designated rooms, supervision.

🆂🄰🆅🄴 🆂🗗 ☒ 🗈 🄱 🄵 ☎

SAN BERNARDINO

🄐🄐🄐 ◆◆ **Days Inn** 🅼 🐾
(909) 881-1702. **$39-$99.** 1386 E Highland Ave. 1.2 mi w of SR 30, exit Highland Ave. Ext corridors. **Pets:** Very small. $10 daily fee/pet, $10 one-time fee/pet. Designated rooms, no service, supervision, crate.

🆂🄰🆅🄴 🆂🗗 ☒ ☎

◆◆◆ **La Quinta Inn** 🅼
(909) 888-7571. **$69-$89.** 205 E Hospitality Ln. Just nw of I-10, Waterman Ave exit. Ext corridors. **Pets:** Supervision.

🄰🆂🄺 ☒ 🄱 🄻 ☎

SAN CLEMENTE

◆◆◆ **Holiday Inn-San Clemente Resort** 🅼🄸 🐾
(949) 361-3000. **$129-$149.** 111 S Avenida de Estrella. I-5 S exit Ave Palizada; I-5 N exit Ave Presidio, 0.5 mi se. Int corridors. **Pets:** Other. $10 daily fee/pet, $10 one-time fee/pet. Supervision.

🄰🆂🄺 ☒ 🄱 ☎

SAN DIEGO METROPOLITAN AREA

CHULA VISTA

🄐🄐🄐 ◆ **Chula Vista Travel Inn** 🅼 🐾
(619) 420-6600. **$45-$89.** 394 Broadway at G St. 0.8 mi e of I-5, exit E St. Ext corridors. **Pets:** Very small. $50 deposit/pet. Designated rooms, no service, supervision, crate.

🆂🄰🆅🄴 🆂🗗 ☒ 🄱 🄻 ☎

🄐🄐🄐 ◆◆◆ **La Quinta Inn** 🅼 🐾
(619) 691-1211. **$79-$99.** 150 Bonita Rd. Just w of I-805, E St and Bonita Rd exit. Ext corridors. **Pets:** Small, other. Supervision.

🆂🄰🆅🄴 ☒ ☎

🄐🄐🄐 ◆◆ **Palomar Inn** 🅼 🐾
(619) 423-8889. **$79-$149.** 801 Palomar St. Adjacent to I-5, exit Palomar St. Ext corridors. **Pets:** Very small, dogs only. Supervision.

🆂🄰🆅🄴 ☒ 🄱 🄻

CORONADO

◆◆ **Crown City Inn** 🅼🄸 🐾
(619) 435-3116. **$105-$135.** 520 Orange Ave. Ext corridors. **Pets:** Medium, other. $8 daily fee/pet. Supervision.

☒ 🄱 🄻 🍽 ☎ ☒

🄐🄐🄐 ◆◆◆◆ **Loews Coronado Bay Resort** 🄷 🐾
(619) 424-4000. **$195-$195.** 4000 Coronado Bay Rd. 5.8 mi s of Coronado Bridge, via Silver Strand Blvd. Int corridors. **Pets:** Small, other. Supervision.

🆂🗗 ☒ 🄱 🍽 ☎ ☒

DEL MAR

◆◆◆ **Del Mar Inn, A Clarion Carriage House** 🅼 🐾
(858) 755-9765. **$109-$189, 3 days notice.** 720 Camino Del Mar. From I-5, Del Mar Heights Rd exit 1 mi w, 0.3 mi n. Int corridors. **Pets:** Very small, other. $25 deposit/room, $25 daily fee/room, $25 one-time fee/room. Designated rooms, no service, supervision, crate.

🄰🆂🄺 🆂🗗 ☒ 🄱 ☎

IMPERIAL BEACH

🄐🄐🄐 ◆◆ **Hawaiian Gardens Suite-Hotel** 🄰
(619) 429-5303. **$79-$175.** 1031 Imperial Beach Blvd. 2 mi w of I-5, Coronado Ave exit. Ext corridors. **Pets:** Supervision.

☒ ☎ 🄺

LA JOLLA

🄐🄐🄐 ◆◆ **Andrea Villa Inn** 🅼 🐾
(858) 459-3311. **$109-$155, 3 days notice.** 2402 Torrey Pines Rd. 1.5 mi n of town. Ext/int corridors. **Pets:** Small. $25 one-time fee/pet. Supervision.

🆂🄰🆅🄴 🆂🗗 ☒ 🄱 ☎

🄐🄐🄐 ◆◆◆◆ **Hilton La Jolla/Torrey Pines** 🄷 🐾
(858) 558-1500. **$185-$300.** 10950 N Torrey Pines Rd. 1.5 mi nw of I-5, exit Genesee Ave; adjacent to Torrey Pines Municipal Golf Course. Int corridors. **Pets:** Small. Supervision.

🆂🄰🆅🄴 ☒ 🄱 🍽 ☎ ☒

🄐🄐🄐 ◆◆◆◆ **Hyatt Regency La Jolla** 🄷 🐾
(858) 552-1234. **$189.** 3777 La Jolla Village Dr. Just e of I-5; exit La Jolla Village Dr. Int corridors. **Pets:** $100 deposit/room. Supervision.

🆂🄰🆅🄴 ☒ 🄱 🄻 🍽 ☎ ☒

◆◆◆ **La Jolla Marriott** 🅷
(858) 587-1414. **$219.** 4240 La Jolla Village Dr. 0.5 mi e of I-5, corner of Regents Rd. Int corridors. **Pets:** No service, supervision, crate.

🅰🆂🅺 ⊠ 🔋 💻 🍽 🕿

◆◆◆ **Residence Inn by Marriott** 🅼
(858) 587-1770. **$189.** 8901 Gilman Dr. 1.5 mi nw of I-5, exit Gilman Dr. Ext corridors. **Pets:** Supervision.

🅰🆂🅺 ⊠ 💻 🕿

NATIONAL CITY

🔺🔺🔺 ◆◆ **Holiday Inn-South Bay** 🅼🅸 ☙
(619) 474-2800. **$79-$79.** 700 National City Blvd. Just e of I-5, southbound exit 8th St, northbound exit Plaza Blvd. Ext corridors. **Pets:** Medium. $25 deposit/pet. No service, supervision, crate.

🆂🅰🆅🅴 ⊠ 🔋 🍽 🕿

🔺🔺🔺 ◆◆◆ **Radisson Suites-National City** 🅼 ☙
(619) 336-1100. **$89-$89.** 801 National City Blvd. Just e of I-5, southbound exit 8th St, northbound exit Plaza Blvd. Ext corridors. **Pets:** Medium. $25 deposit/pet. No service, supervision, crate.

🆂🅰🆅🅴 ⊠ 🔋 💻

POWAY

🔺🔺🔺 ◆◆ **Poway Country Inn** 🅼 ☙
(858) 748-6320. **$55-$79.** 13845 Poway Rd. 1 mi e of Pomerado Rd. Ext corridors. **Pets:** Small. Supervision.

🆂🅰🆅🅴 🆂🟦 ⊠ 🔋 💻 🕿

RANCHO BERNARDO

🔺🔺🔺 ◆◆◆ **La Quinta Inn** 🅼 ☙
(858) 484-8800. **$69-$89.** 10185 Paseo Montril. Adjacent to I-15; exit Rancho Penasquitos Blvd/Poway Rd. Ext corridors. **Pets:** Small, other. No service, supervision, crate.

🆂🅰🆅🅴 ⊠ 🏠 🔋 💻 🕿

🔺🔺🔺 ◆◆◆ **Radisson Suite Hotel** 🅼🅸 ☙
(858) 451-6600. **$119-$119.** 11520 W Bernardo Ct. 0.5 mi sw of I-15 exit Rancho Bernardo Rd. Ext corridors. **Pets:** Small, dogs only. Designated rooms, no service, supervision, crate.

🆂🅰🆅🅴 🆂🟦 ⊠ 🏠 🔋 💻 🍽 🕿

◆◆ **Rancho Bernardo Travelodge** 🅼 ☙
(858) 487-0445. **$60-$80.** 16929 W Bernardo Dr. From I-15, exit Rancho Bernardo Rd, 1 blk w, just s. Ext corridors. **Pets:** Small. $25 deposit/pet, $10 daily fee/pet. No service, supervision, crate.

🅰🆂🅺 🆂🟦 ⊠ 🔋 💻 🕿

◆◆◆ **Residence Inn by Marriott** 🅼 ☙
(858) 673-1900. **$209.** 11002 Rancho Carmel Dr. Just e of I-15, exit Carmel Mountain Rd. Ext/int corridors. **Pets:** Other. $6 daily fee/pet, $150 one-time fee/room. Supervision.

🅰🆂🅺 🆂🟦 ⊠ 💻 🕿 ⊠

RANCHO SANTA FE

◆◆◆ **The Inn at Rancho Santa Fe** 🆇
(858) 756-1131. **$130-$250, 3 days notice.** Linea del Cielo at Paseo. In village area; from I-5, exit Lomas Sante Fe Dr, 4 mi e on CR S-8 (Lomas Santa Fe Dr and Linea del Cielo). Ext/int corridors. **Pets:** Designated rooms, no service, supervision, crate.

🅰🆂🅺 🆂🟦 🔋 💻 🍽 🕿 ⊠

◆◆◆◆ **Rancho Valencia Resort** 🆁 ☙
(858) 756-1123. **$700, 7 days notice.** 5921 Valencia Cir. From I-5, take Via De La Valle 1.3 mi e, 0.5 mi s on El Camino Real, 2.5 mi e on San Dieguito Rd, 1 mi nw on Rancho Diegueno Rd and Rancho Valencia. Ext corridors. **Pets:** Dogs only. $75 daily fee/pet. Supervision.

🅰🆂🅺 ⊠ 💻 🍽 🕿 ⊠

SAN DIEGO

🔺🔺🔺 ◆◆ **Beach Haven Inn** 🅼 ☙
(858) 272-3812. **$90-$120, 3 days notice.** 4740 Mission Blvd. In Pacific Beach area. Ext corridors. **Pets:** Small, other. $5 daily fee/pet. No service, supervision, crate.

🆂🅰🆅🅴 🆂🟦 ⊠ 🕿

🔺🔺🔺 ◆◆◆ **Crown Point View Suite-Hotel** 🅰
(858) 272-0676. **$115-$250.** 4088 Crown Point Dr. 0.3 blk s of Pacific Beach Dr. Ext corridors. **Pets:** $50 one-time fee/ room. Supervision.

⊠ 🔋 💻 🅺

🔺🔺🔺 ◆◆ **Diamond Head Inn** 🅼 ☙
(858) 273-1900. **$109-$169, 3 days notice.** 605 Diamond St. Just w of Mission Blvd, Pacific Beach area. Ext corridors. **Pets:** Medium. $5 daily fee/room, $25 one-time fee/ room. Supervision.

🆂🅰🆅🅴 🆂🟦 ⊠ 💻 🅺

🔺🔺🔺 ◆◆◆ **Doubletree Hotel-San Diego Mission Valley** 🅷 ☙
(619) 297-5466. **$139-$159.** 7450 Hazard Center Dr. Adjacent to SR 163, exit Friars Rd. Int corridors. **Pets:** Other. Supervision.

🆂🅰🆅🅴 🆂🟦 ⊠ 🔋 💻 🍽 🕿 ⊠

◆◆◆ **Four Points Hotel By Sheraton** 🅼🅸
(858) 277-8888. **$115-$115.** 8110 Aero Dr. From SR 163, southbound exit Balboa Ave, 1 mi se via Kearny Villa Rd, northbound exit Kearny Villa Rd, 0.8 mi ne. Int corridors. **Pets:** Very small. Designated rooms, no service, supervision, crate.

🅰🆂🅺 ⊠ 🔋 💻 🍽 🕿 ⊠

🔺🔺🔺 ◆◆ **Goodnite Inn Near Sea World** 🅼 ☙
(619) 543-9944. **$47-$59.** 3880 Greenwood St. Adjacent to I-5 and I-8; Sports Arena area. Ext/int corridors. **Pets:** Small, other. No service, supervision, crate.

🆂🅰🆅🅴 🆂🟦 ⊠ 🔋

◆◆◆ **Hanalei Hotel** 🅷 ☙
(619) 297-1101. **$94-$104.** 2270 Hotel Cir. N side of I-8. Ext corridors. **Pets:** Other. $50 one-time fee/room. Supervision.

⊠ 💻 🍽 🕿

AAA ◆◆◆ Hilton San Diego Mission Valley H ☙
(619) 543-9000. **$134-$219.** 901 Camino del Rio S. Adjacent to I-8, exit Mission Center Rd. Int corridors. **Pets:** Very small, dogs only. $100 deposit/pet, $50 one-time fee/room. Designated rooms, no service, supervision, crate.
[SAVE] [⊠] [▣] [¶¶]

AAA ◆◆◆◆ Hilton San Diego Resort R ☙
(619) 276-4010. **$130-$359.** 1775 E Mission Bay Dr. Adjacent to I-5; 0.5 mi n of Sea World Dr exit. Ext/int corridors. **Pets:** $50 one-time fee/room. Supervision.
[SAVE] [⅗▢] [⊠] [▤] [▣] [¶¶] [▧] [⊠]

◆◆◆ Holiday Inn on the Bay H
(619) 232-3861. **$149-$189.** 1355 N Harbor Dr at Ash St. Int corridors. **Pets:** Supervision.
[⊠] [▤] [▣] [¶¶] [▧]

AAA ◆ Lamplighter Inn & Suites M ☙
(619) 582-3088. **$65-$100.** 6474 El Cajon Blvd. 1 mi sw of I-8; exit 70th St. Ext corridors. **Pets:** Medium. $5 daily fee/pet. Supervision.
[⊠] [▧]

AAA ◆ Old Town Inn M ☙
(619) 260-8024. **$55-$95.** 4444 Pacific Hwy. From jct I-5 and I-8, exit Morena Blvd; 0.6 mi s. Ext corridors. **Pets:** Medium. $5 daily fee/pet. Supervision.
[⊠]

AAA ◆ Pacific Inn Hotel & Suites-By the Bay M ☙
(619) 232-6391. **$59-$89.** 1655 Pacific Hwy. Ext corridors. **Pets:** Medium, other. $10 daily fee/pet. No service, supervision, crate.
[SAVE] [⅗▢] [⊠] [▤] [▧]

AAA ◆◆ Premier Inns M ☙
(619) 291-8252. **$39-$89, 7 days notice.** 2484 Hotel Circle Pl. Adjacent to I-8, exit Taylor St. Ext corridors. **Pets:** Small. Designated rooms, supervision.
[SAVE] [⅗▢] [⊠] [▧]

◆◆◆ Residence Inn by Marriott-San Diego A ☙
(858) 278-2100. **$147.** 5400 Kearny Mesa Rd. Adjacent to SR 163, exit Clairemont Mesa. Ext corridors. **Pets:** Small, other. $6 daily fee/pet, $50 one-time fee/room. Supervision.
[ASK] [⊠] [▤] [▣] [▧] [⊠]

◆◆◆ Residence Inn by Marriott-San Diego Downtown A ☙
(619) 338-8200. **$150.** 1747 Pacific Hwy. Just s of Grape St; from I-5 southbound exit Front St, northbound exit Hawthorn St. Int corridors. **Pets:** $6 daily fee/pet, $50 one-time fee/room. Designated rooms, supervision.
[ASK] [⊠] [▤] [▣] [▧]

AAA ◆◆◆◆ San Diego Marriott Hotel & Marina H ☙
(619) 234-1500. **$275-$300.** 333 W Harbor Dr. Adjacent to Seaport Village and San Diego Convention Center. Int corridors. **Pets:** Other. Supervision.
[SAVE] [⅗▢] [⊠] [▣] [¶¶] [▧] [⊠]

◆◆◆ San Diego Marriott Mission Valley H
(619) 692-3800. **$189.** 8757 Rio San Diego Dr. Just n of I-8, exit Qualcomm Way. Int corridors. **Pets:** Medium. Supervision.
[ASK] [⊠] [▣] [¶¶] [▧] [⊠]

◆◆◆ San Diego Marriott Suites-Downtown H ☙
(619) 696-9800. **$130-$130.** 701 A St corner 7th Ave. Adjacent to Symphony Hall. Int corridors. **Pets:** Other. $50 one-time fee/pet. No service, supervision, crate.
[⊠] [▣] [¶¶] [▧]

AAA ◆◆◆ San Diego Paradise Point Resort R ☙
(858) 274-4630. **$190-$350.** 1404 W Vacation Rd. In Mission Bay Park at W Vacation Rd and Ingraham St. Ext corridors. **Pets:** Supervision.
[SAVE] [⊠] [▤] [▣] [¶¶] [▧] [⊠]

AAA ◆◆ Vagabond Inn Mission Bay M
(858) 274-7888. **$67-$87.** 4540 Mission Bay Dr. Northbound, 0.5 mi nw of I-5, exit Grand Ave/Garnet Ave; southbound, 0.3 mi sw, exit Balboa Ave. Int corridors. **Pets:** No service, supervision, crate.
[SAVE] [⅗▢] [⊠] [▤] [▧]

AAA ◆◆ Vagabond Inn-Mission Valley M ☙
(619) 297-1691. **$73-$88.** 625 Hotel Circle South. S side of I-8. Ext corridors. **Pets:** Other. $10 daily fee/room. No service, supervision, crate.
[SAVE] [⅗▢] [⊠] [▤] [▣] [▧]

AAA ◆ Vagabond Inn-Point Loma M ☙
(619) 224-3371. **$64-$78.** 1325 Scott St. Just sw of Harbor Dr. Ext corridors. **Pets:** Medium. $10 daily fee/pet. Supervision.
[SAVE] [⅗▢] [⊠] [▤] [▣] [▧]

SAN YSIDRO

AAA ◆◆ International Motor Inn M ☙
(619) 428-4486. **$65-$75.** 190 E Calle Primera. Adjacent to I-5, exit Via de San Ysidro, then just se. Ext corridors. **Pets:** Small, other. No service, supervision, crate.
[SAVE] [⅗▢] [⊠] [▤] [▣] [▧]

☙ **END METROPOLITAN AREA** ☙

SAN FRANCISCO METROPOLITAN AREA

BURLINGAME

◆◆◆◆ Embassy Suites-SFO 🅷 ❀
(650) 342-4600. **$139-$234.** 150 Anza Blvd. Just e of US 101; Broadway-Burlingame or Anza Blvd exits. Int corridors. **Pets:** Medium. $50 one-time fee/pet. No service, supervision, crate.

(A$K) ⊠ 🐾 🗐 🌀 🗎 🖳 🍴 🌊

⏺ ◆◆ Red Roof Inn 🅼 ❀
(650) 342-7772. **$110-$150.** 777 Airport Blvd. Just s of airport; US 101, Broadway-Burlingame or E Anza Blvd exits. Ext corridors. **Pets:** Small, other. No service, supervision, crate.

(SAVE) ⊠ 🗐 🌀 🌊

◆◆◆◆ San Francisco Airport Marriott 🅷
(650) 692-9100. **$199-$219.** 1800 Old Bayshore Hwy. Just e of US 101; Millbrae Ave exit. Int corridors. **Pets:** Small. No service, supervision, crate.

⊠ 🐾 🗐 🌀 🗎 🖳 🍴 🌊

⏺ ◆◆ Vagabond Inn-Airport 🅼
(650) 692-4040. **$89-$99.** 1640 Bayshore Hwy. Just e of US 101; Millbrae Ave exit. Ext corridors. **Pets:** Small. Designated rooms, no service, supervision, crate.

(SAVE) (S🔒) ⊠ 🗎 🖳

MILLBRAE

◆◆◆ The Westin Hotel-San Francisco Airport 🅷
(650) 692-3500. **Call for rates.** 1 Old Bayshore Hwy. Just e of US 101, Millbrae Ave exit. Int corridors. **Pets:** Small. $400 deposit/room. Designated rooms, no service, supervision, crate.

⊠ ♿ 🗐 🌀 🖳 🍴 🌊 ⊠

SAN BRUNO

◆◆◆ Summerfield Suites Hotel 🅼 ❀
(650) 588-0770. **$300.** 1350 Huntington Ave. 380 exit El Camino N, e on Sneath Lane. Ext corridors. **Pets:** Large, other. $10 daily fee/pet, $50 one-time fee/room. No service, supervision, crate.

(A$K) (S🔒) ⊠ 🗎 🖳 🌊 ⊠

SAN CARLOS

◆◆ Homestead Guest Studios 🅼
(650) 368-2600. **$518-$623.** 3 Circle Star Way. W of US 101 exit Whipple Ave, W to Industrial, just n. Int corridors. **Pets:** No service, supervision, crate.

⊠ 🌀

⏺ ◆◆◆ Inns of America 🅼
(650) 631-0777. **$129-$139.** 555 Skyway Rd. US 101, exit Holly St/Redwood Shores, e to Airport Blvd, then just s. Int corridors. **Pets:** Large. Supervision.

(SAVE) ⊠ 🌀 🗎 🌊

SAN FRANCISCO

⏺ ◆◆◆ Beresford Arms 🅷
(415) 673-2600. **$105-$125.** 701 Post St. 3 blks w of Union Sq. Int corridors. **Pets:** Small. Designated rooms, supervision.

(SAVE) (S🔒) ⊠ 🗎 🃁 (CTV)

⏺ ◆◆◆ Best Western Tuscan Inn at Fisherman's Wharf 🅷
(415) 561-1100. **$189-$208.** 425 Northpoint St. Just s of the wharf at Mason St. Int corridors. **Pets:** Supervision.

⊠ 🌀 🗎 🖳 🍴

◆◆◆◆ Campton Place Hotel 🅷 ❀
(415) 781-5555. **$325-$445.** 340 Stockton St. Just n of Union Square. Int corridors. **Pets:** Small, other. $35 daily fee/room. Supervision.

(A$K) ⊠ 🍴

⏺ ◆◆◆ Holiday Inn-Civic Center 🅼 ❀
(415) 626-6103. **$179-$199, 3 days notice.** 50 8th St. 2 blks from Civic Auditorium; just s Market St and BART Station. Int corridors. **Pets:** Small. $100 deposit/pet, $10 daily fee/pet. Designated rooms, no service, supervision, crate.

(SAVE) (S🔒) ⊠ 🐾 🌀 🖳 🍴 🌊

⏺ ◆◆◆ Holiday Inn-Financial District 🅷 ❀
(415) 433-6600. **$229-$249, 3 days notice.** 750 Kearny St. 1 blk from Chinatown. Int corridors. **Pets:** Small. Designated rooms, no service, supervision, crate.

(SAVE) (S🔒) ⊠ 🍴 🌊

⏺ ◆◆ Hotel Beresford 🅷
(415) 673-9900. **$99-$115.** 635 Sutter St. 1 blk nw of Union Square (at Mason St). Int corridors. **Pets:** Very small. Supervision.

(SAVE) (S🔒) ⊠ 🗎 🍴 🃁

⏺ ◆◆◆◆ Hotel Monaco 🅷 ❀
(415) 292-0100. **$219-$219.** 501 Geary St. Just w of Union Square at Taylor St. Int corridors. **Pets:** Other. Designated rooms, no service, supervision, crate.

⊠ 🖳 🍴

⏺ ◆◆◆◆ Hotel Nikko 🅷
(415) 394-1111. **$315-$385.** 222 Mason St. 3 blks w of Union Square. Int corridors. **Pets:** Small. Designated rooms, no service, supervision, crate.

(SAVE) ⊠ ♿ 🌀 🖳 🍴 🌊

⏺ ◆◆ The Laurel Inn 🅼 ❀
(415) 567-8467. **$99-$149.** 444 Presidio Ave. 1 mi w of US 101 (Van Ness Ave), 1 mi e of Park Presidio Blvd (SR 1) at California St. Int corridors. **Pets:** Other. Supervision.

(SAVE) (S🔒) ⊠ 🌀 🃁

⏺ ◆◆ Pacific Heights Inn 🅼
(415) 776-3310. **$85-$130.** 1555 Union St. Just w of US 101 (Van Ness Ave). Ext corridors. **Pets:** Very small. Supervision.

(S🔒) ⊠ 🗎 🖳 🃁

◆◆◆◆ **The Pan Pacific Hotel** 🏨
(415) 771-8600. **$440.** 500 Post St. Just w of Union Square at Mason St. Int corridors. **Pets:** Small. Designated rooms, no service, supervision, crate.

(ASK) (S🐾) (✕) (🍴)

🔶 ◆◆◆ **The Prescott Hotel** 🏨 🐾
(415) 563-0303. **$190-$225.** 545 Post St. Just w of Union Square. Int corridors. **Pets:** Other. $500 deposit/room. No service, supervision, crate.

(SAVE) (✕) (🍴)

◆◆◆◆ **San Francisco Marriott** 🏨
(415) 896-1600. **$279-$279.** 55 Fourth St. 2 blks s of Union Square; 1 blk n of Moscone Center. Int corridors. **Pets:** Small. Designated rooms, no service, supervision, crate.

(✕) (🍴) (🛎)

◆◆◆ **San Francisco Marriott Fisherman's Wharf** 🏨 🐾
(415) 775-7555. **$289.** 1250 Columbus Ave. Just s of the wharf at Bay St. Int corridors. **Pets:** Small. $5 daily fee/room, $50 one-time fee/room. No service, supervision, crate.

(S🐾) (✕) (👨‍🦽) (🐾) (👣) (🛏) (💻) (🍴)

◆◆ **Travelodge By The Bay** 🅼
(415) 673-0691. **$130-$160.** 1450 Lombard St. On US 101. Ext corridors. **Pets:** Supervision.

(ASK) (S🐾) (✕) (👤) (👣) (🛏) (💻) (CTV)

🔶 ◆◆◆◆ **The Westin St. Francis** 🏨 🐾
(415) 397-7000. **$229-$279.** 335 Powell St. On Union Square. **Pets:** Small. $25 deposit/room. Designated rooms, supervision.

(SAVE) (S🐾) (✕) (💻) (🍴)

SAN MATEO

🔶 ◆◆ **Best Western San Mateo Los Prados Inn** 🅼
(650) 341-3300. **$109-$149.** 2940 S Norfolk St. E of and adjacent to US 101. Ext/int corridors. **Pets:** Small. No service, supervision, crate.

(SAVE) (S🐾) (✕) (🛏) (💻)

◆◆ **Homestead Guest Studios** 🅼
(650) 574-1744. **$518-$658.** 1830 Gateway Dr. S of SR 92, exit Foster City Blvd, w on Metro Center. Ext corridors. **Pets:** Supervision.

(✕)

◆◆◆ **Residence Inn by Marriott** 🅼 🐾
(650) 574-4700. **$109-$219.** 2000 Winward Way. 0.8 mi se from jct US 101 and SR 92; exit SR 92 via Edgewater Blvd. Ext corridors. **Pets:** Medium, other. $6 daily fee/pet, $75 one-time fee/room. Supervision.

(✕) (🛎) (🐾)

◆◆ **Villa Hotel Airport South** 🅼🅸 🐾
(650) 341-0966. **$89-$129.** 4000 S El Camino Real. 8 mi s of San Francisco International Airport, exit US 101 W Hillsdale Blvd, 0.5 mi s on SR 82. Ext/int corridors. **Pets:** Other. $100 deposit/room. No service, supervision, crate.

(ASK) (S🐾) (✕) (🛏) (💻) (🍴) (🛎)

SAN RAFAEL

◆◆ **Villa Inn** 🅼 🐾
(415) 456-4975. **$70-$99.** 1600 Lincoln Ave. Off US 101, southbound Lincoln Ave off-ramp; northbound Central San Rafael exit, 0.3 mi w on Fourth St, 0.5 mi n. Ext corridors. **Pets:** Medium, dogs only. $20 deposit/room. No service, supervision, crate.

(ASK) (S🐾) (✕) (🛏) (💻) (🍴) (🛎)

SOUTH SAN FRANCISCO

◆◆◆ **La Quinta Inn** 🅼 🐾
(650) 583-2223. **$105-$125.** 20 Airport Blvd. Just W of US 101 at S Airport Blvd exit. Int corridors. **Pets:** Large, other. No service, supervision, crate.

(ASK) (✕) (👣) (🛏) (💻) (🛎)

🐾 **END METROPOLITAN AREA** 🐾

SAN JACINTO

🔶 ◆ **Crown Motel** 🅼
(909) 654-7133. **$37-$43.** 138 S Ramona Blvd. Just n on SR 79. Ext corridors. **Pets:** Small. No service, supervision, crate.

(SAVE) (✕) (🛏) (🛎)

SAN JOSE

🔶 ◆◆◆◆ **Doubletree Hotel** 🏨 🐾
(408) 453-4000. **$239-$239.** 2050 Gateway Pl. 0.3 mi e of San Jose International Airport; via airport blvd w of and adjacent to US 101 exit N 1st St; northbound, exit Brokaw Rd.. Int corridors. **Pets:** Other. $100 deposit/room. Designated rooms, no service, supervision, crate.

(SAVE) (S🐾) (✕) (🛏) (💻) (🍴) (🛎)

◆◆ **Homestead Guest Studios** 🅼 🐾
(408) 573-0648. **$89-$124.** 1560 N First St. 1 mi e of San Jose International Airport; s off US 101; exit via N 1st St. Int corridors. **Pets:** Small, other. $75 one-time fee/pet. Designated rooms, supervision.

(ASK) (S🐾) (✕) (💻)

◆◆◆ **Homewood Suites** 🅼 🐾
(408) 428-9900. **$189-$354.** 10 W Trimble Rd. Exit US 101 Trimble Rd, 1.3 mi e, 2 mi ne San Jose Int'l Airport. Ext/int corridors. **Pets:** Small, other. $200 deposit/pet, $75 one-time fee/pet. No service, supervision, crate.

(ASK) (S🐾) (✕) (👨‍🦽) (🐾) (🛎) (🐾)

◆◆◆ **San Jose Hilton & Towers** 🏨
(408) 287-2100. **$139-$240.** 300 Almaden Blvd. Int corridors. **Pets:** No service, supervision, crate.

(✕) (🛏) (💻) (🍴) (🛎)

◆◆◆ Summerfield Suites Hotel M ✿
(408) 436-1600. **$99-$299.** 1602 Crane Ct. US 101 exit Brokaw E, 0.4 mi to Bering S, 0.5 mi. Ext corridors. **Pets:** Small. $75 deposit/pet, $75 one-time fee/pet. Supervision.

(ASK) ⊠ 🛢 💻 🏊

SAN JUAN BAUTISTA

(AAA) ◆◆ San Juan Inn M ✿
(831) 623-4380. **$60-$99, 3 days notice.** 410 Alameda. Jct SR 156. Ext corridors. **Pets:** Medium. $10 daily fee/pet, $10 one-time fee/pet. Supervision.

(S6) ⊠ 🛢 💻 🏊

SAN JUAN CAPISTRANO

(AAA) ◆◆◆ Best Western Capistrano Inn M ✿
(949) 493-5661. **$69-$119, 3 days notice.** 27174 Ortega Hwy. On SR 74, just e of I-5. **Pets:** Small, other. $25 one-time fee/room. Supervision.

(SAVE) (S6) ⊠ 🛢 💻 🏊

SAN LUIS OBISPO

(AAA) ◆◆ Best Western Olive Tree Inn M ✿
(805) 544-2800. **$79-$159.** 1000 Olive St. Just w of US 101 at jct SR 1; US 101 northbound Morro Bay exit, southbound Santa Rosa exit. Ext corridors. **Pets:** Small, dogs only. $25 deposit/room, $10 daily fee/pet, $10 one-time fee/room. Designated rooms, no service, supervision, crate.

(SAVE) (S6) ⊠ 🛢 🏊

(AAA) ◆◆◆ Best Western Royal Oak Hotel M
(805) 544-4410. **$79-$99.** 214 Madonna Rd. Just s of US 101, Madonna Rd exit. Ext/int corridors. **Pets:** Small. Supervision.

(SAVE) ⊠ 🛢 💻 🏊 (K)

(AAA) ◆◆◆ Days Inn M ✿
(805) 549-9911. **$49-$145.** 2050 Garfield St. Just se of US 101, exit Monterey St. Ext corridors. **Pets:** Small, dogs only. $50 deposit/pet, $10 daily fee/pet. Designated rooms, no service, supervision, crate.

(SAVE) (S6) ⊠ 🛢 🏊

(AAA) ◆◆ Heritage Inn Bed & Breakfast BB
(805) 544-7440. **$65-$150, 7 days notice.** 978 Olive St. Just w of US 101, at jct SR 1; Santa Rosa exit southbound, Morro Bay exit northbound. Int corridors. **Pets:** Supervision.

⊠ (K) (CTV) (Z)

(AAA) ◆◆◆ Sands Suites & Motel M ✿
(805) 544-0500. **$89-$139.** 1930 Monterey St. Just s of jct US 101, Monterey St exit. Ext corridors. **Pets:** $5 one-time fee/room. Supervision.

(SAVE) ⊠ 🛢 🏊

(AAA) ◆ San Luis Obispo Travelodge M ✿
(805) 543-5110. **$79-$149.** 1825 Monterey St. Just s of jct US 101; exit Grand Ave. Ext corridors. **Pets:** Supervision.

(SAVE) (S6) ⊠ 🛢 💻 🏊

(AAA) ◆◆ Vagabond Inn M ✿
(805) 544-4710. **$69-$84.** 210 Madonna Rd. Just s of US 101, Madonna Rd exit. Ext corridors. **Pets:** Other. $5 daily fee/pet. Supervision.

(SAVE) (S6) ⊠ 🛢 💻 🏊

SAN MARCOS

◆◆◆ Quails Inn at Lake San Marcos Resort MI
(760) 744-0120. **$99-$199.** 1025 La Bonita Dr. 2 mi s of SR 78, Rancho Santa Fe Rd exit, 0.5 mi e via Lake San Marcos Dr and San Marino Dr; at Lake San Marcos. Ext/int corridors. **Pets:** Supervision.

(ASK) (S6) ⊠ 🛢 💻 🍴 🏊 ⊠

SAN RAMON

◆◆◆ Residence Inn by Marriott M ✿
(925) 277-9292. **$159.** 1071 Market Pl. E of I-680, exit Bollinger Canyon Rd. Ext corridors. **Pets:** Other. $5 daily fee/pet, $75 one-time fee/room. Supervision.

⊠ 🏊 ⊠

◆◆◆ San Ramon Marriott at Bishop Ranch H ✿
(925) 867-9200. **$169-$169.** 2600 Bishop Dr. I-680, exit Bollinger Canyon e, n on Sunset, just w. Int corridors. **Pets:** Medium, other. Supervision.

⊠ 🛢 💻 🍴 🏊

SAN SIMEON

(AAA) ◆◆ Motel 6 Premiere–1212 MI
(805) 927-8691. **$66-$95.** 9070 Castillo Dr. SR 1. Int corridors. **Pets:** Small. No service, supervision, crate.

(S6) ⊠ 🍴 🏊

(AAA) ◆◆ Silver Surf Motel M ✿
(805) 927-4661. **$69-$119.** 9390 Castillo Dr. On SR 1. Ext corridors. **Pets:** $5 daily fee/pet. Designated rooms, no service, supervision, crate.

(SAVE) (S6) ⊠ 🏊 (K)

SANGER

(AAA) ◆ Town House Motel M ✿
(559) 875-5531. **$40-$45.** 1308 Church Ave. 0.7 mi n, 1.3 mi s of SR 180 at Academy Ave. Ext corridors. **Pets:** Supervision.

(SAVE) (S6) ⊠ 🏊

SANTA ANA

(AAA) ◆ GuestHouse Inn & Suites M ✿
(714) 558-2772. **$49-$79.** 2151 E First St. E of I-5, exit First St. Ext corridors. **Pets:** Medium. $50 deposit/pet, $5 daily fee/pet. Designated rooms, no service, supervision, crate.

(SAVE) (S6) ⊠ 💻 🏊

(AAA) ◆◆ Red Roof Inn M
(714) 542-0311. **$56-$82.** 2600 N Main St. 0.3 mi n of I-5, exit Main St. Ext/int corridors. **Pets:** Supervision.

(SAVE) ⊠ 🛢 🏊

SANTA BARBARA

(AAA) ◆◆◆ Beachcomber Inn M ✿
(805) 965-4577. **$65-$355.** 202 W Cabrillo Blvd. Just s of US 101, between Bath St and Chapala. Ext corridors. **Pets:** Small. $10 daily fee/room. Designated rooms, no service, supervision, crate.

(SAVE) (S6) ⊠ 🛢 🏊 (K)

◆ Blue Sands Motel ▣ ✿
(805) 965-1624. **$75-$185, 3 days notice.** 421 S Milpas St. 0.3 mi s of US 101. Ext corridors. **Pets:** Small. $5 daily fee/pet. Designated rooms, supervision.
⊠ 🖬 ⬛ 🕭 🕅

◆◆◆ Fess Parker's Doubletree Resort ▣ ✿
(805) 564-4333. **$195-$289, 3 days notice.** 633 E Cabrillo Blvd. Just s of US 101 via Milpas St. Ext/int corridors. **Pets:** Designated rooms, supervision.
⊠ ⬛ 🍴 🕭 🕅

◆◆◆ Four Seasons Biltmore ▣
(805) 969-2261. **$290-$650, 3 days notice.** 1260 Channel Dr. 0.3 mi s of US 101, in Montecito area, exit Olive Mill Rd. Ext/int corridors. **Pets:** Medium. Supervision.
🔑 ⊠ ⬛ 🍴 🕭 🕅 🕅

◆◆◆ Holiday Inn-Santa Barbara/Goleta ▣ ✿
(805) 964-6241. **$120-$160.** 5650 Calle Real. 7 mi nw adjacent to US 101; between Patterson and Fairview Ave exits. Ext corridors. **Pets:** Medium. $25 one-time fee/room. Supervision.
🔑 🕭 ⊠ 🖬 ⬛ 🍴 🕭

◆◆ Ocean Palms Beach Resort ▣
(805) 966-9133. **$65-$355.** 232 W Cabrillo Blvd. 0.3 mi e of Castillo St. Ext/int corridors. **Pets:** Small. Designated rooms, supervision.
🕭 🕭 ⊠ 🖬 ⬛ 🕭 🕅

◆◆◆ Pacifica Suites ▣
(805) 683-6722. **$125-$185.** 5490 Hollister Ave. From US 101, exit Patterson Ave, 0.5 mi s, then 0.5 mi w on Hollister Ave. Ext/int corridors. **Pets:** No service, supervision, crate.
🕭 🕭 ⊠ 🖬 ⬛ 🕭

SANTA CATALINA ISLAND

◆◆◆ Best Western Catalina Canyon Resort & Spa ▣
(310) 510-0325. **$159-$250, 3 days notice.** 888 Country Club Dr. In Avalon, 0.5 mi from the harbor. Ext corridors. **Pets:** Small. No service, supervision, crate.
🕭 🕭 ⊠ ⬛ 🍴 🕭

SANTA CLARA

◆◆ GuestHouse Inn & Suites-Silicon Valley USA ▣ ✿
(408) 241-3010. **$109-$220.** 2930 El Camino Real. SR 82, 0.5 mi w of San Tomas Expwy; US 101 exit s Bowers Ave. Ext corridors. **Pets:** $10 daily fee/pet. Supervision.
🕭 🕭 ⊠ 🖬 ⬛ 🕭

◆◆◆ Santa Clara Marriott Hotel ▣
(408) 988-1500. **$89-$265, 3 days notice.** 2700 Mission College. 0.5 mi e off US 101; exit Great America Pkwy; 0.8 mi s of Great America Theme Park. Int corridors. **Pets:** Supervision.
🔑 🕭 ⊠ 🖬 ⬛ 🍴 🕭 🕅

◆◆ The Vagabond Inn ▣ ✿
(408) 241-0771. **$89-$99.** 3580 El Camino Real. On SR 82; se corner of Lawrence Expwy cloverleaf. Ext corridors. **Pets:** Small. $5 daily fee/pet. Designated rooms, no service, supervision, crate.
🕭 🕭 ⊠ 🖬 ⬛ 🕭

◆◆◆ The Westin Hotel-Santa Clara ▣ ✿
(408) 986-0700. **$280-$325.** 5101 Great America Pkwy. 0.8 mi e off US 101, exit Great America Pkwy; at Santa Clara Convention Center. Int corridors. **Pets:** Very small. No service, supervision, crate.
🔑 🕭 ⊠ 🕭 🕅 🖬 ⬛ 🍴 🕭 🕅

SANTA CRUZ

◆◆◆ Ocean Pacific Lodge ▣ ✿
(831) 457-1234. **$110-$130.** 120 Washington. 6 blks se of SR 1. Ext corridors. **Pets:** Small. $20 one-time fee/room. Designated rooms, supervision.
🕭 🕭 ⊠ 🖬 🕭

◆◆ Pacific Inn ▣ ✿
(831) 425-3722. **$59-$199, 3 days notice.** 330 Ocean St. 1 mi from jct SR 1 and 17. Int corridors. **Pets:** Other. $10 daily fee/pet, $20 one-time fee/pet. Supervision.
⊠ 🖬 ⬛ 🕭

◆ Santa Cruz Riviera Travelodge ▣ ✿
(831) 423-9515. **$94-$189.** 619 Riverside Ave. 3 blks from beach. Ext corridors. **Pets:** Small, other. $10 daily fee/pet. No service, supervision, crate.
🕭 🕭 ⊠ ⬛ 🕭 🕅 📺

SANTA MARIA

◆◆◆ Best Western Big America ▣ ✿
(805) 922-5200. **$69-$99.** 1725 N Broadway. On SR 135, 0.5 mi sw of jct US 101, exit Broadway. Ext corridors. **Pets:** Medium. No service, supervision, crate.
🕭 🕭 ⊠ 🖬 🍴 🕭

◆◆ Comfort Inn ▣
(805) 922-5891. **$69-$89.** 210 S Nicholson Ave. 0.5 blk e of US 101, Main St exit. Int corridors. **Pets:** No service, supervision, crate.
🔑 🕭 ⊠ 🖬 🕭 🕅

◆◆◆ Historic Santa Maria Inn ▣ ✿
(805) 928-7777. **$99-$139.** 801 S Broadway. From US 101, take Main St 1 mi w, then 0.5 mi s on Broadway. Int corridors. **Pets:** Small. $50 one-time fee/room. No service, supervision, crate.
🔑 🕭 ⊠ 🖬 ⬛ 🍴 🕭

SANTA NELLA

◆◆ Best Western Andersen's Inn ▣ ✿
(209) 826-5534. **$66-$79.** 12367 Hwy 33S. E off and adjacent to I-5; 4 mi n of SR 152, Pacheco Pass Rd; exit I-5 via Santa Nella-Gustine SR 33. Ext corridors. **Pets:** Other. Designated rooms, no service, supervision, crate.
🕭 🕭 ⊠ 🕭

◆◆◆ Holiday Inn Express ▣ ✿
(209) 826-8282. **$59-$75.** 28976 W Plaza Dr. 2 blk e of I-5; SR 33 exit. Ext corridors. **Pets:** Designated rooms, supervision.
🕭 🕭 ⊠ 🖬 ⬛ 🕭

◆◆ Ramada Inn Mission de Oro 🅼 ☺
(209) 826-4444. **$50-$85.** 13070 Hwy 33S. Adjacent to Jct I-5 and SR 33; 4 mi n of SR 152. Ext/int corridors. **Pets:** Medium. $10 daily fee/room. No service, supervision, crate.

[ASK] [🆂🅾] [✕] [🛏] [🍴] [🖙] [✕]

SANTA ROSA

🆔 ◆◆◆ Best Western Garden Inn 🅼 ☺
(707) 546-4031. **$85-$110.** 1500 Santa Rosa Ave. US 101; northbound exit Baker Ave; southbound exit Corby Ave. Ext corridors. **Pets:** Medium, dogs only. $10 one-time fee/pet. Designated rooms, no service, supervision, crate.

[SAVE] [🆂🅾] [✕] [🛏] [🖙] [🍴] [🖙]

🆔 ◆◆◆ Hillside Inn Motel 🅼
(707) 546-9353. **$58-$68.** 2901 4th St. 2.5 mi e off US 101 on SR 12, at Farmers Ln and 4th St. Ext corridors. **Pets:** No service, supervision, crate.

[✕] [🖙] [🍴] [🖙]

◆◆◆ Holiday Inn Express 🅼
(707) 545-9000. **Call for rates.** 870 Hopper Ave. Exit US 101 at Mendocino/Hopper Ave exit, just w of US 101. Ext corridors. **Pets:** Designated rooms, no service, supervision, crate.

[🆂🅾] [✕] [🛏] [🖙] [🖙]

🆔 ◆◆◆ Los Robles Lodge 🅼 ☺
(707) 545-6330. **$78-$118.** 1985 Cleveland Ave. 1 mi n off US 101; exit via Steele Ln. Ext corridors. **Pets:** $10 daily fee/pet. Designated rooms, supervision.

[SAVE] [🆂🅾] [✕] [🖙] [🖙] [🛏] [🖙] [🍴] [🖙]

🆔 ◆◆ Santa Rosa Travelodge 🅼
(707) 542-3472. **$55-$90.** 1815 Santa Rosa Ave. 1.5 mi s on US 101 business route, northbound exit US 101 via Baker Ave; southbound Santa Rosa Ave-Corby. Ext corridors. **Pets:** Large. Supervision.

[SAVE] [🆂🅾] [✕] [🛏] [🖙] [🖙]

SELMA

🆔 ◆◆ Best Western John Jay Inn 🅼 ☺
(559) 891-0300. **$55-$87.** 2799 Floral Ave. 10 mi s of Fresno exit Floral Ave; 2 blks e. Int corridors. **Pets:** Small. $15 one-time fee/room. No service, supervision, crate.

[SAVE] [🆂🅾] [✕] [🖙] [🖙] [🛏] [🖙] [🖙]

🆔 ◆ Super 8 Motel 🅼
(559) 896-2800. **$45-$75.** 3142 S Highland Ave. SR 99, Floral Ave exit. Int corridors. **Pets:** Medium. Supervision.

[SAVE] [🆂🅾] [✕] [🖙]

SHASTA LAKE

🆔 ◆◆ Bridge Bay Resort 🅼 ☺
(530) 275-3021. **$89-$89, 3 days notice.** on Lake Shasta exit I-5; at Bridge Bay Rd; 12 mi n of Redding. Ext corridors. **Pets:** Other. $25 deposit/pet, $6 daily fee/pet. Designated rooms, no service, supervision, crate.

[SAVE] [🆂🅾] [✕] [🍴] [🖙] [✕]

🆔 ◆◆ Fawndale Lodge & RV Resort 🅼
(530) 275-8000. **$43-$75.** 1 mi s of Shasta Lake. E of I-5, exit Fawndale Rd.(10 mi n of Redding). Ext corridors. **Pets:** Medium. No service, supervision, crate.

[🆂🅾] [✕] [🛏] [🖙] [🖙]

SIERRA CITY

🆔 ◆◆ Herrington's Sierra Pines 🅼 ☺
(530) 862-1151. **$49-$73.** 100 Main St. 0.5 mi w on SR 49. Ext corridors. **Pets:** Other. No service, supervision, crate.

[SAVE] [🆂🅾] [🖙] [🍴] [🎵] [🖙]

SIMI VALLEY

◆◆◆ Radisson-Simi Valley 🅷
(805) 583-2000. **$99-$99.** 999 Enchanted Way. Adjacent to SR 118; exit 1st St. Int corridors. **Pets:** No service, supervision, crate.

[✕] [🛏] [🖙] [🍴] [🖙]

SMITH RIVER

◆◆ Best Western Ship Ashore Motel 🅼 ☺
(707) 487-3141. **$58-$88.** 12340 Hwy 101. 2.8 mi n on US 101; 3 mi s of OR-CA stateline. Ext corridors. **Pets:** Very small. No service, supervision, crate.

[🆂🅾] [✕] [🛏] [🖙] [🍴] [✕] [🎵]

SOLVANG

🆔 ◆ Viking Motel 🅼 ☺
(805) 688-1337. **$38-$125.** 1506 Mission Dr. Just w on SR 246. Ext corridors. **Pets:** Small. $10 one-time fee/pet. Designated rooms, no service, supervision, crate.

[SAVE] [🆂🅾] [✕] [🛏]

SONOMA

🆔 ◆◆◆ Best Western Sonoma Valley
Inn 🅼 ☺
(707) 938-9200. **$129-$369, 3 days notice.** 550 2nd St W. 1 blk w of Town Plaza. Ext corridors. **Pets:** $15 daily fee/room. Designated rooms, supervision.

[✕] [🛏] [🖙] [🖙]

SONORA

🆔 ◆◆ Aladdin Motor Inn 🅼 ☺
(209) 533-4971. **$68-$76.** 14260 Mono (Hwy 108) Way. 3.5 mi e on SR 108. Ext/int corridors. **Pets:** Medium, other. $5 one-time fee/pet. Designated rooms, no service, supervision, crate.

[✕] [🛏] [🖙] [🖙]

🆔 ◆◆◆ Best Western Sonora Oaks Motor
Hotel 🅼 ☺
(209) 533-4400. **$89-$109.** 19551 Hess Ave. 3.5 mi e on SR 108; corner of Hess Ave. Ext/int corridors. **Pets:** Large, other. $10 one-time fee/pet. Supervision.

[SAVE] [🆂🅾] [✕] [🎵] [🖙] [🖙]

🆔 ◆ Miners Motel 🅼
(209) 532-7850. **$45-$75.** 18740 SR 108. 1 mi e of Jamestown on SR 108 and SR 49. Ext corridors. **Pets:** No service, supervision, crate.

[SAVE] [✕] [🛏] [🖙] [🖙]

🆔 ◆◆ Sonora Days Inn 🅼 ☺
(209) 532-2400. **$71-$145.** 160 S Washington St. Downtown. Ext/int corridors. **Pets:** Other. $10 daily fee/room. Designated rooms, no service, supervision, crate.

[SAVE] [🆂🅾] [✕] [🛏] [🖙] [🍴] [🖙]

AAA ◆ **Sonora Gold Lodge** M ❖
(209) 532-3952. **$44-$74.** 480 Stockton St. 0.5 mi sw on SR 108 business route and 49. Ext corridors. **Pets:** Other. $10 one-time fee/room. Designated rooms, supervision.
SAVE S❍ ✕ ❐ ☕

◆◆ **Sonora Quality Inn** M
(209) 984-0315. **$49-$99.** 18730 Hwy 108. 1 mi e of Jamestown on SR 108 & 49. Ext corridors. **Pets:** Medium. Designated rooms, no service, supervision, crate.
ASK S❍ ✕ ❐ ☕

ST. HELENA

◆◆ **El Bonita Motel** M ❖
(707) 963-3216. **$120-$250, 3 days notice.** 195 Main St. 0.8 mi s on SR 29. Ext corridors. **Pets:** Other. $5 daily fee/pet, $5 one-time fee/room. Supervision.
✕ ✎ ❒ ❐ ☕ CTV

◆◆◆ **Harvest Inn** MI
(707) 963-9463. **Call for rates.** One Main St. 1.5 mi s on SR 29. Ext corridors. **Pets:** Supervision.
✕ ❒ ❐ ☕ ✕

STOCKTON

AAA ◆◆ **Best Western Inn** M
(209) 948-0321. **$50-$65.** 550 W Charter Way. Exit I-5A at Charter Way, 0.3 mi e; 3 mi w of SR 99. Ext corridors. **Pets:** Small. Designated rooms, no service, supervision, crate.
SAVE S❍ ✕ ❒ ❐ ☕

◆◆ **City Center Days Inn** M
(209) 948-6151. **$42-$60.** 33 N Center St. 1 blk n; w off El Dorado St via Weber; southbound SR 99 traffic exit Wilson Way, northbound w via Mariposa Rd to Charter Way; I-5 exit Downtown. Ext corridors. **Pets:** No service, supervision, crate.
ASK S❍ ✕ ☕ CTV

AAA ◆ **Econo Lodge of Stockton** M ❖
(209) 466-5741. **$44-$56.** 2210 S Manthey Rd. Exit I-5 w 8th St off ramp; 0.3 mi s of jct SR 4. Int corridors. **Pets:** Small, dogs only. $25 deposit/room. Designated rooms, no service, supervision, crate.
SAVE S❍ ✕ ❒ ☕

◆◆ **Holiday Inn** MI ❖
(209) 474-3301. **$69-$199.** 111 E March Ln. Exit I-5 March Ln 2 mi e, corner El Dorado St. Int corridors. **Pets:** Small, dogs only. Supervision.
✕ ❐ ⊓ ☕

◆◆◆ **La Quinta Inn** M
(209) 952-7800. **$69-$89.** 2710 W March Ln. Just w of I-5 at March Ln exit. Ext corridors. **Pets:** Medium. No service, supervision, crate.
ASK ✕ ❐ ☕

◆◆◆ **Residence Inn by Marriott** MI
(209) 472-9800. **$119-$139, 3 days notice.** 3240 W March Lane. Exit I-5; at March Ln, 0.5 mi w. Int corridors. **Pets:** Small. Designated rooms, no service, supervision, crate.
✕ ❐ ☕

SUN CITY

AAA ◆ **Travelodge** M
(909) 679-1133. **$45-$65.** 27955 Encanto DR. Just e of I-215, exit McCall Blvd. Ext corridors. **Pets:** Supervision.
SAVE S❍ ✕ ❐ ☕

SUNNYVALE

◆◆ **Homestead Village** M ❖
(408) 734-3431. **$99-$134.** 1255 Orleans Dr. N of Hwy 237; exit Mathilda then e on Moffett Park Dr to Orleans Dr. Ext corridors. **Pets:** Small. $75 one-time fee/pet. No service, supervision, crate.
✕ ❐

◆◆◆ **Residence Inn by Marriott** M ❖
(408) 720-1000. **$199-$239.** 750 Lakeway Dr. Exit US 101 Lawrence Expwy S, then e on Oakmead. Ext corridors. **Pets:** Medium, other. $10 daily fee/room, $75 one-time fee/room. No service, supervision, crate.
ASK ✕ ☕ ✕

◆◆◆ **Residence Inn by Marriott** M ❖
(408) 720-8893. **$199-$239.** 1080 Stewart Dr. US 101 exit Lawrence Expwy S, Duane Ave W, Stewart Dr S. Ext corridors. **Pets:** $10 daily fee/pet, $75 one-time fee/room. Supervision.
ASK ✕ ❒ ❐ ☕ ✕

◆◆◆ **Summerfield Suites Hotel** M ❖
(408) 745-1515. **$160-$190.** 900 Hamlin Ct. Exit SR 237 at Mathilda Ave S, w on Ross. Ext corridors. **Pets:** Medium. $10 daily fee/room, $200 one-time fee/room. No service, supervision, crate.
ASK S❍ ✕ ❒ ❐ ☕ ✕

AAA ◆ **The Vagabond Inn** M ❖
(408) 734-4607. **$65-$75.** 816 Ahwanee Ave. S off US 101; exit via Mathilda Ave S. Ext corridors. **Pets:** Small. $5 daily fee/pet. Designated rooms, no service, supervision, crate.
SAVE S❍ ✕ ❐ ☕

SUSANVILLE

AAA ◆◆ **River Inn** M
(530) 257-6051. **$46-$54.** 1710 Main St. 0.8 mi e on SR 36. Ext corridors. **Pets:** Medium. Designated rooms, no service, supervision, crate.
S❍ ✕ ❒ ☕

AAA ◆◆ **Super 8 Motel** M ❖
(530) 257-2782. **$48-$62.** 2975 Johnstonville Rd. 1.8 mi e; off SR 36. Ext corridors. **Pets:** Medium, other. $5 daily fee/pet, $5 one-time fee/pet. No service, supervision, crate.
SAVE S❍ ✕ ❒

TEHACHAPI

AAA ◆◆◆ **Best Western Mountain Inn** M ❖
(661) 822-5591. **$55-$60.** 416 W Tehachapi Blvd. SR 58, exit SR 202, then 1 mi e. Ext corridors. **Pets:** Other. Supervision.
SAVE S❍ ✕ ❒ ❐ ☕

◍ ◆◆◆ **Tehachapi Summit**
Travelodge  🐾
(661) 823-8000. **$46-$60.** 500 Steuber Rd. Adjacent to SR 58 eastbound exit Monolith; westbound exit Tehachapi. Int corridors. **Pets:** Other. $5 one-time fee/room. Supervision.
🅂🄰🆅🄴 🆂 ⊗ 🄱 🄻 🍴 🅿

TEMECULA

◍ ◆◆ **Comfort Inn**  🐾
(909) 699-5888. **$47-$67.** 27338 Jefferson Ave. West side of I-15, exit Winchester Rd; just n. Ext corridors. **Pets:** Other. $10 daily fee/room. No service, supervision, crate.
🅂🄰🆅🄴 🆂 ⊗ 🄱 🅿

◍ ◆◆◆ **Temecula Valley Inn**  🐾
(909) 699-2444. **$109-$119, 3 days notice.** 27660 Jefferson Ave. Int corridors. **Pets:** Supervision.
🆂 ⊗ 🄱 🄻 🅿

THOUSAND OAKS

◆◆◆ **Thousand Oaks Inn**  🐾
(805) 497-3701. **$72-$95.** 75 W Thousand Oaks Blvd. Adjacent to US 101, exit Moorpark Rd, 0.3 mi w. Ext corridors. **Pets:** Small, other. $75 one-time fee/pet. Designated rooms, no service, supervision, crate.
🄰🅂🄺 🆂 ⊗ 🄱 🄻 🅿

◆ **Thousand Oaks Village Inn**
(805) 496-0102. **Call for rates.** 1425 Thousand Oaks Blvd. Just ne of US 101, exit Rancho Rd; from SR 23 exit I-10 and Sand Oaks Blvd. Ext corridors. **Pets:** Small. No service, supervision, crate.
⊗ 🄱 🅿

THREE RIVERS

◍ ◆◆◆ **Best Western Holiday Lodge** 🄼
(559) 561-4119. **$79-$93.** 40105 Sierra Drive. 2 mi sw on SR 198. Ext corridors. **Pets:** Small. Designated rooms, no service, supervision, crate.
🅂🄰🆅🄴 🆂 ⊗ 🄱 🄻 🅿 ⊗

◍ ◆◆◆ **Buckeye Tree Lodge** 🄼 🐾
(559) 561-5900. **$73-$103, 3 days notice.** 46000 Sierra Dr. 6 mi ne on SR 198, 0.5 mi sw of entrance to Sequoia National Park. Ext corridors. **Pets:** $4 daily fee/pet. Supervision.
🅂🄰🆅🄴 🆂 ⊗ 🄱 🄻 🅿 ⊗

◍ ◆◆◆ **Lazy J Ranch Motel** 🄼 🐾
(559) 561-4449. **$60-$95, 3 days notice.** 39625 Sierra Dr. 2.5 mi sw on SR 198. Ext corridors. **Pets:** Dogs only. $5 one-time fee/room. Supervision.
🅂🄰🆅🄴 🆂 ⊗ 🄱 🄻 🅿 ⊗

◍ ◆◆ **The River Inn** 🄼 🐾
(559) 561-4367. **$55-$59, 3 days notice.** 45176 Sierra Dr. 5 mi ne on SR 198, 1.5 mi sw of entrance to Sequoia National Park. Ext corridors. **Pets:** Other. $5 daily fee/pet, $5 one-time fee/pet. Supervision.
⊗ 🄱 🆉

◍ ◆◆ **Sequoia Village Inn** 🄲
(559) 561-3652. **Call for rates, 7 days notice.** 45971 Sierra Dr. 6 mi ne on SR 198; 0.5 mi sw of entrance to Sequoia National Park. Ext corridors. **Pets:** Supervision.
🅂🄰🆅🄴 🆂 🄱 🄻 🅿 🆉

◍ ◆◆ **Sierra Lodge** 🄼 🐾
(559) 561-3681. **$40-$95, 3 days notice.** 43175 Sierra Dr. SR 198, 3 mi sw of entrance to Sequoia National Park. Ext corridors. **Pets:** Other. $20 deposit/room, $5 daily fee/pet. Designated rooms, supervision.
🅂🄰🆅🄴 🆂 ⊗ 🄱 🄻 🅿

TRINIDAD

◍ ◆◆ **Bishop Pine Lodge** 🄲 🐾
(707) 677-3314. **$70-$80, 7 days notice.** 1481 Patricks Point Dr. W of US 101; northbound exit Trinidad, then 2 mi n on Patricks Point Dr; southbound exit Seawood, then 1 mi s on Patricks Point Dr. Ext/int corridors. **Pets:** Other. $10 daily fee/pet. No service, supervision, crate.
🄱 🅿 🄺

TULARE

◍ ◆◆◆ **Best Western Town & Country**
Lodge 🄼 🐾
(559) 688-7537. **$60-$66.** 1051 N Blackstone. Just w of SR 99, Prosperity Ave exit. Int corridors. **Pets:** $10 one-time fee/room. Supervision.
🅂🄰🆅🄴 ⊗ 🄴 🄱 🅿

◍ ◆◆◆ **Green Gable Inn** 🄼 🐾
(559) 686-3432. **$53-$58.** 1010 E Prosperity Ave. Just e of SR 99, Prosperity Ave exit. Int corridors. **Pets:** Small, dogs only. No service, supervision, crate.
🅂🄰🆅🄴 🆂 ⊗ 🄴 🄱 🅿

◍ ◆ **Inns of America** 🄼
(559) 686-0985. **$49-$54.** 1183 N Blackstone St. Just w of SR 99, Prosperity Ave exit. Ext corridors. **Pets:** Small. No service, supervision, crate.
🅂🄰🆅🄴 🆂 ⊗ 🅿

TURLOCK

◆◆◆ **Best Western The Gardens Motor**
Inn 🄼 🐾
(209) 634-9351. **$65-$78.** 1119 Pedras Rd. Exit SR 99 at Fulkerth Rd, 1 mi e to N Golden State Blvd, just n to Pedras Rd, then right. Ext corridors. **Pets:** $20 deposit/pet. No service, supervision, crate.
🄰🅂🄺 🆂 ⊗ 🄱 🅿

◍ ◆◆ **The Tree Inn** 🄼 🐾
(209) 668-3400. **$49-$75.** 200 W Glenwood Ave. Exit Hwy 99, Lander exit. Ext corridors. **Pets:** Small. $20 deposit/ room. Designated rooms, supervision.
🅂🄰🆅🄴 ⊗ 🄺 🄱 🄻 🅿

TWAIN HARTE

◍ ◆ **Eldorado Motel** 🄼 🐾
(209) 586-4479. **$42-$65.** 22678 Blackhawk Dr. Exit SR 108 via Twain Harte; corner Twain Harte and Blackhawk drs, opposite golf course. Ext corridors. **Pets:** Other. $10 daily fee/pet, $10 one-time fee/pet. Supervision.
🅂🄰🆅🄴 🆂 ⊗ 🄱 🄻 🄺 🆉

TWENTYNINE PALMS

◆◆ Circle 'C' M
(760) 367-7615. **$70-$85.** 6340 El Rey Ave. 1.5 mi w on SR 62, just n. Ext corridors. **Pets:** No service, supervision, crate.

(A$K) (S̄ō) (✕) (⌂)

UKIAH

◆◆ Days Inn M ❀
(707) 462-7584. **$55-$105, 7 days notice.** 950 N State St. Exit US 101 at N State St, 0.5 mi s on N State St. Ext corridors. **Pets:** Small. $5 daily fee/pet, $5 one-time fee/pet. Designated rooms, no service, supervision, crate.

(SAVE) (S̄ō) (✕) (⌂)

◆ Rodeway Inn M ❀
(707) 462-2906. **$40-$69.** 1050 S State St. Exit US 101 at Talmage Rd off-ramp, 0.5 mi w. Ext corridors. **Pets:** Dogs only. $10 daily fee/pet, $10 one-time fee/pet. Designated rooms, no service, supervision, crate.

(SAVE) (S̄ō) (✕) (⌂)

◆ Super 8 Motel M ❀
(707) 462-6657. **$40-$95.** 1070 S State St. Exit US 101 at Talmage exit, 1 mi w. Ext corridors. **Pets:** Medium. $5 one-time fee/pet. Designated rooms, supervision.

(SAVE) (S̄ō) (✕) (⌂)

◆◆ Western Traveler Motel M
(707) 468-9167. **$45-$65.** 693 S Orchard Ave. Exit US 101 via Gobbi St W. Ext corridors. **Pets:** Designated rooms, no service, supervision, crate.

(SAVE) (S̄ō) (✕) (⌂)

VACAVILLE

◆◆ Best Western Heritage Inn M
(707) 448-8453. **$70-$115.** 1420 E Monte Vista Ave. Exit I-80 Monte Vista N. Ext corridors. **Pets:** Supervision.

(SAVE) (S̄ō) (✕) (⌂)

◆◆ Vacaville Super 8 M
(707) 449-8884. **$49-$69.** 101 Allison Ct. N of and adjacent to I-80, exit Monte Vista Ave. Int corridors. **Pets:** Small. No service, supervision, crate.

(A$K) (S̄ō) (✕) (⌂) (CTV)

VALLEJO

◆◆ Best Western Inn at Marine World M
(707) 554-9655. **$89-$159.** 1596 Fairgrounds Dr. Exit I-80 at SR 37 N, 0.3 mi w. Int corridors. **Pets:** Supervision.

(A$K) (S̄ō) (✕) (⌂) (⌂)

◆◆◆ Holiday Inn at Six Flags Marine World M ❀
(707) 644-1200. **$109-$129.** 1000 Fairgrounds Dr. N of I-80, exit Marine World Pkwy, SR 37 0.3 mi. Int corridors. **Pets:** Medium, other. $5 daily fee/pet. No service, supervision, crate.

(A$K) (S̄ō) (✕) (⌂) (⌂) (⌂) (⌂)

◆◆ Quality Inn M ❀
(707) 643-1061. **$49-$109.** 44 Admiral Callaghan Ln. E off and adjacent to I-80; exit via Tennessee St-Mare Island. Ext corridors. **Pets:** Other. $10 daily fee/pet. Designated rooms, no service, supervision, crate.

(SAVE) (S̄ō) (✕) (⌂) (⌂) (⌂) (⌂)

◆ Ramada Inn M
(707) 643-2700. **$70-$145.** 1000 Admiral Callaghan Ln. Exit I-80 s at Columbus Pkwy; 0.5 mi w on Admiral Callaghan Ln. Ext corridors. **Pets:** Designated rooms, no service, supervision, crate.

(A$K) (S̄ō) (✕) (⌂) (⌂) (⌂)

VENTURA

◆◆ Best Western Inn of Ventura M ❀
(805) 648-3101. **$99-$119.** 708 E Thompson Blvd. Just e of California St; from US 101, northbound exit California St, southbound exit Ventura Ave. Ext corridors. **Pets:** Other. $25 deposit/room, $25 one-time fee/room. No service, supervision, crate.

(SAVE) (✕) (⌂) (⌂)

◆◆◆ La Quinta Inn M
(805) 658-6200. **$59-$79.** 5818 Valentine Rd. Just s of US 101; exit Victoria Ave. Ext/int corridors. **Pets:** Medium. Supervision.

(SAVE) (✕) (⌂) (⌂) (⌂) (⌂) (⌂)

◆◆ Vagabond Inn MI
(805) 648-5371. **$66-$85.** 756 E Thompson Blvd. 0.3 mi e on US 101 business rt; from US 101 northbound exit California St, southbound exit Ventura Ave. Ext corridors. **Pets:** Small. Designated rooms, no service, supervision, crate.

(SAVE) (S̄ō) (✕) (⌂) (⌂) (⌂) (⌂)

VICTORVILLE

◆ Budget Inn M ❀
(760) 241-8010. **$32-$44.** 14153 Kentwood Blvd. Just w of I-15, exit SR 18W; Palmdale Rd. Ext corridors. **Pets:** $10 deposit/room. No service, supervision, crate.

(SAVE) (S̄ō) (✕) (⌂)

◆◆◆ Ramada Inn H
(760) 245-6565. **$79-$86, 3 days notice.** 15494 Palmdale Rd. Just w of I-15, exit SR 18W, Palmdale Rd. Int corridors. **Pets:** Small. Designated rooms, no service, supervision, crate.

(SAVE) (S̄ō) (✕) (⌂) (⌂)

◆◆ Red Roof Inn M ❀
(760) 241-1577. **$51-$77.** 13409 Mariposa Rd. E Side of I-15, between Bear Valley Rd and Palmdale Rd exits. Ext corridors. **Pets:** Medium. $10 one-time fee/room. Supervision.

(SAVE) (✕) (⌂) (⌂)

VISALIA

◆◆ Best Western Visalia Inn M ❀
(559) 732-4561. **$76-$80.** 623 W Main St. Just w of downtown and n of SR 198. Ext corridors. **Pets:** Small. $6 daily fee/pet, $6 one-time fee/pet. No service, supervision, crate.

(SAVE) (✕) (⌂) (⌂)

☎ ◆◆◆ John Jay Inn & Suites M ☥
(559) 651-3700. **$60-$156.** 9300 W Airport Dr. Just e of SR 99, adjacent to SR 198, exit Plaza Dr. Int corridors. **Pets:** Small. $100 deposit/room. Designated rooms, no service, supervision, crate.

SAVE ☑ ☒ ☐ ☐ ☐

VISTA

☎ ◆◆◆ La Quinta Inn M
(760) 727-8180. **$65-$85.** 630 Sycamore Ave at Thibodo Rd. Adjacent to SR 78, exit Sycamore Ave. Ext/int corridors. **Pets:** Medium. Designated rooms, no service, supervision, crate.

SAVE ☒ ☐ ☐ ☐

WALNUT CREEK

◆◆◆◆ Embassy Suites Hotel H ☥
(925) 934-2500. **$149-$199.** 1345 Treat Blvd. E of and adjacent to I-680, northbound exit Treat Blvd, southbound exit Oak Park Blvd at Pleasant Hill Bart Station. Int corridors. **Pets:** Large, other. $10 daily fee/pet, $75 one-time fee/pet. Supervision.

ASK ☑ ☒ ☐ ☐ ☐ ☐

☎ ◆◆◆ Holiday Inn of Walnut Creek M
(925) 932-3332. **$124.** 2730 N Main St. I-680 exit N Main St, n. Int corridors. **Pets:** No service, supervision, crate.

SAVE ☑ ☒ ☐ ☐ ☐ ☐

☎ ◆◆ Walnut Creek Motor Lodge M ☥
(925) 932-2811. **$65-$80.** 1960 N Main St. Just e off I-680 and SR 24; northbound exit e via Ygnacio Valley Rd, southbound exit e via N Main St. Ext corridors. **Pets:** Very small, dogs only. No service, supervision, crate.

☑ ☒ ☐ ☐

WATSONVILLE

☎ ◆◆ Best Western Inn M ☥
(831) 724-3367. **$67-$130.** 740 Freedom Blvd. On SR 152. Ext corridors. **Pets:** Dogs only. $50 deposit/room, $5 daily fee/pet. Supervision.

SAVE ☑ ☒ ☐ ☐ ☐

◆◆ Red Roof Inn M ☥
(831) 740-4520. **$65-$96.** 1620 W Beach St. Just w of SR 1; exit Riverside DR (SR 129). Int corridors. **Pets:** Medium. $50 deposit/room. Designated rooms, supervision.

ASK ☒ ☐ ☐

WEAVERVILLE

☎ ◆◆◆ Best Western Weaverville Victorian Inn M
(530) 623-4432. **$55-$95.** 1709 Main St. On SR 299. Ext corridors. **Pets:** Small. No service, supervision, crate.

SAVE ☑ ☒ ☐ ☐ ☐

☎ ◆◆ 49er Gold Country Inn M ☥
(530) 623-4937. **$34-$79.** 718 Main St. On SR 299. Ext corridors. **Pets:** Other. Supervision.

SAVE ☒ ☐ ☐ ☐

☎ ◆ Motel Trinity M ☥
(530) 623-2129. **$49-$79, 4 days notice.** 1112 Main St. Ext corridors. **Pets:** Medium. $10 deposit/room. Designated rooms, no service, supervision, crate.

SAVE ☑ ☒ ☐ ☐

◆ Red Hill Motel C ☥
(530) 623-4331. **$30-$75.** Red Hill Rd. On SR 299, just w of SR 3. Ext corridors. **Pets:** Other. Supervision.

☐ ☒

WEED

☎ ◆◆◆ Best Inn & Suites-Grand Manor M ☥
(530) 938-1982. **$69-$96.** 1844 Shastina Dr. E of I-5 at S Weed exit. Int corridors. **Pets:** Medium, other. $100 deposit/room. Supervision.

SAVE ☑ ☒ ☐ ☐ ☐ ☐

☎ ◆◆◆ Holiday Inn Express M
(530) 938-1308. **$69-$77.** 1830 Black Butte Dr. I-5 exit s Weed. Int corridors. **Pets:** Designated rooms, supervision.

SAVE ☑ ☒

☎ ◆◆ Sis-Q-Inn Motel M ☥
(530) 938-4194. **$46-$66.** 1825 Shastina Dr. Exit I-5, s Weed. Int corridors. **Pets:** Medium. $5 daily fee/pet. Designated rooms, no service, supervision, crate.

SAVE ☑ ☒ ☐

WESTLEY

☎ ◆ Days Inn M ☥
(209) 894-5500. **$45-$60.** 7144 McKraken Rd. Off and adjacent to I-5, exit Westley. Ext corridors. **Pets:** Medium, other. $10 one-time fee/room. No service, supervision, crate.

SAVE ☑ ☒ ☐ CTV

WILLIAMS

☎ ◆◆◆ Granzella's Inn M ☥
(530) 473-3310. **$60-$95.** 391 6th St. Exit I-5 at main Williams exit, 0.5 mi w. Int corridors. **Pets:** Other. $10 one-time fee/room. No service, supervision, crate.

SAVE ☑ ☒ ☐ ☐ ☐ ☐

☎ ◆ Stage Stop Motel M
(530) 473-2281. **$33-$45.** 330 N 7th St. Exit I-5 via SR 20 business route, 3 blks w. Ext corridors. **Pets:** Small. Designated rooms, no service, supervision, crate.

SAVE ☑ ☒ ☐ ☐

☎ ◆◆ Woodcrest Inn M ☥
(530) 473-2381. **Call for rates.** 400 C St. Exit I-5 at Williams, just w on E St , just n on 4th St. Ext corridors. **Pets:** Medium. $5 daily fee/pet, $5 one-time fee/pet. Designated rooms, no service, supervision, crate.

☒ ☐ ☐

WILLITS

[AAA] ◆◆◆ **Baechtel Creek Inn** [M] 🐾
(707) 459-9063. **$59-$108.** 101 Gregory Ln. US 101; west on Gregory Ln. Ext corridors. **Pets:** Small, dogs only. $10 daily fee/pet. Designated rooms, no service, supervision, crate.
[SAVE] [SD] ⊠ ▣ 🏊

WILLOWS

[AAA] ◆◆◆ **Best Western Golden Pheasant Inn** [MI] 🐾
(530) 934-4603. **$59-$109.** 249 N Humboldt Ave. E side of I-5; exit frwy via Willow-Elk Creek-Glenn Rd. Ext corridors. **Pets:** Other. $10 daily fee/pet. No service, supervision, crate.
[SAVE] [SD] ⊠ ☕ 🏊

[AAA] ◆ **Cross Roads West Inn** [M] 🐾
(530) 934-7026. **$39-$59.** 452 N Humboldt Ave. E side of I-5; exit via Willow-Elk Creek-Glenn Rd. Ext corridors. **Pets:** Small, other. Designated rooms, no service, supervision, crate.
⊠ 🏊

◆◆ **Super 8 Motel** [M] 🐾
(530) 934-2871. **$44-$54.** 457 Humboldt Ave. Exit I-5 via Willow- Elk Creek- Glenn Rd. Int corridors. **Pets:** Other. $100 deposit/room. Supervision.
[ASK] [SD] ⊠ ▣ 🏊

WOODLAND

[AAA] ◆ **Cinderella Motel** [M] 🐾
(530) 662-1091. **$42-$68, 3 days notice.** 99 W Main St. 0.8 mi w on I-5 business loop; northbound I-5 exit Main St 2 mi w, southbound exit West St, 1.5 mi s to Main St, 1 blk w. Ext corridors. **Pets:** Small. Supervision.
[SAVE] [SD] ⊠ ▣ 🏊

YOSEMITE NATIONAL PARK

◆◆ **The Redwoods In Yosemite** [C] 🐾
(209) 375-6666. **$101-$500.** 8038 Chilnualna Falls Rd. In Wawona, 6 mi inside the southern entrance via SR 41 and Chilnualna Falls Rd. Ext corridors. **Pets:** Other. $15 one-time fee/pet. Supervision.
⊠ 🍴 [CTV]

YOUNTVILLE

[AAA] ◆◆◆◆ **Vintage Inn** [MI]
(707) 944-1112. **$225-$300, 7 days notice.** 6541 Washington St. Center; SR 29 exit Yountville. Ext corridors. **Pets:** Medium. Supervision.
[SAVE] [SD] ⊠ ▣ ☕ 🏊 🍴

YREKA

[AAA] ◆◆◆ **AmeriHost Inn-Yreka** [M]
(530) 841-1300. **$62-$72.** 148 Moonlit Oaks Ave. Exit I-5 at SR 3/Fort Jones. Int corridors. **Pets:** Designated rooms, supervision.
[SAVE] [SD] ⊠ ♿ ▣ ☕ 🏊

[AAA] ◆◆◆ **Best Western Miner's Inn** [M] 🐾
(530) 842-4355. **$59-$69.** 122 E Miner St. Just w off I-5 via Central Yreka. Ext corridors. **Pets:** No service, supervision, crate.
[SD] ⊠ ♿ ▣ ☕ 🍴

[AAA] ◆◆ **Days Inn** [M] 🐾
(530) 842-1612. **$46-$75.** 1806B Fort Jones Rd. Exit I-5 at jct SR 3. Int corridors. **Pets:** Medium, other. $20 deposit/room, $8 daily fee/room, $8 one-time fee/room. Designated rooms, supervision.
[SAVE] [SD] ⊠ ▣ 🏊

[AAA] ◆ **Rodeway Inn** [M] 🐾
(530) 842-4404. **$34-$55.** 526 S Main St. 0.3 mi s; I-5 via Central Yreka exit. Ext corridors. **Pets:** Other. $5 daily fee/pet, $5 one-time fee/pet. Designated rooms, supervision.
[SAVE] ⊠ ▣ 🏊

◆ **Super 8-Yreka** [M] 🐾
(530) 842-5781. **$48-$54.** 136 Montague Rd. W of I-5, exit Montague Rd. Ext corridors. **Pets:** Medium. $5 daily fee/pet, $5 one-time fee/pet. Designated rooms, no service, supervision, crate.
[ASK] [SD] ⊠ ▣ 🏊

[AAA] ◆◆ **Wayside Inn** [M]
(530) 842-4412. **$45-$78.** 1235 S Main St. Northbound exit I-5 Ft Jones, 1 mi n; southbound exit Central Yreka, 1 mi s. Ext corridors. **Pets:** No service, supervision, crate.
[SAVE] ⊠ ▣ 🏊

YUBA CITY

◆◆ **Days Inn** [M] 🐾
(530) 674-1711. **$42-$64.** 700 N Palora Ave. Exit SR 99 at Bridge St, 0.5 mi s of SR 20. Ext corridors. **Pets:** Medium. $25 deposit/pet, $5 daily fee/pet. No service, supervision, crate.
[ASK] [SD] ⊠ 🏋 ♿ ▣ 🏊

◆◆ **Motel Orleans** [M]
(530) 674-1592. **$34-$62.** 730 Palora Ave. E of and adjacent to SR 99, 0.5 mi s of jct SR 20, exit SR 99 at Bridge St. Int corridors. **Pets:** Medium. No service, supervision, crate.
[ASK] [SD] ⊠ ▣ 🏊

YUCCA VALLEY

[AAA] ◆◆◆ **Oasis of Eden Inn & Suites** [M] 🐾
(760) 365-6321. **$49-$106.** 56377 Twentynine Palms Hwy. 1 mi w of Jct SR 62 and SR 247. Ext corridors. **Pets:** Medium. $25 deposit/pet, $10 daily fee/pet. Designated rooms, supervision.
[SD] ⊠ ▣ ☕ 🏊

[AAA] ◆◆ **Super 8 Motel** [M] 🐾
(760) 228-1773. **$44-$78.** 57096 29 Palms Hwy. SR 62, 0.3 mi w of jct SR 247. Int corridors. **Pets:** $20 deposit/room, $3 daily fee/pet, $3 one-time fee/pet. No service, supervision, crate.
[SAVE] [SD] ⊠ ▣ 🏊

COLORADO

ALAMOSA

AAA ◆◆ **Best Western Alamosa Inn** Ⓜ ❖
(719) 589-2567. **$65-$99.** 1919 Main St. 1 mi w on US 160 and 285. Ext corridors. **Pets:** Small. $10 one-time fee/room. No service, supervision, crate.
[SAVE] [S📶] [✕] [💻] [▯] [⌑]

AAA ◆◆◆ **Comfort Inn of Alamosa** Ⓜ ❖
(719) 587-9000. **$65-$90, 7 days notice.** 6301 Rd 107S. 2.3 mi w on US 160. Int corridors. **Pets:** Small. $15 one-time fee/room. Supervision.
[SAVE] [✕]

AAA ◆◆◆ **Holiday Inn** Ⓜ ❖
(719) 589-5833. **$92.** 333 Sante Fe Ave. Just e of jct SR 17 on US 160. Int corridors. **Pets:** Other. No service, supervision, crate.
[SAVE] [S📶] [✕] [🛏] [🐾] [💻] [▯] [⌑]

ASPEN

AAA ◆◆◆ **The Aspen Club Lodge** Ⓛ ❖
(970) 925-6760. **$220-$495, 30 days notice.** 709 E Durant. At base of Aspen Mountain. Ext/int corridors. **Pets:** Other. Designated rooms, supervision.
[SAVE] [S📶] [✕] [🛏] [💻] [▯] [⌑] [✕]

◆◆ **Hotel Aspen** Ⓜ ❖
(970) 925-3441. **$99-$329, 30 days notice.** 110 W Main St. Just w on SR 82. Ext/int corridors. **Pets:** Dogs only. $20 daily fee/room. Designated rooms, supervision.
[ASK] [S📶] [✕] [🛏] [💻] [⌑]

AAA ◆◆◆◆ **Hotel Jerome** Ⓗ
(970) 920-1000. **$710-$2400, 30 days notice.** 330 E Main St. Downtown on SR 82. Int corridors. **Pets:** Designated rooms, no service, supervision, crate.
[SAVE] [S📶] [✕] [▯] [⌑]

◆◆◆ **Hotel Lenado** ⒷⒷ ❖
(970) 925-6246. **$119-$429, 30 days notice.** 200 S Aspen St. Just s of SR 82 via Aspen St at jct of Hopkins St. Ext/int corridors. **Pets:** Medium. $500 deposit/room. Supervision.
[🔒]

AAA ◆◆◆ **Limelite Lodge** Ⓜ ❖
(970) 925-3025. **$185-$375, 45 days notice.** 228 E Cooper St. Just s of SR 82 at Monarch and Cooper sts; opposite Wagner Park. Ext corridors. **Pets:** Other. Designated rooms, no service, supervision, crate.
[SAVE] [S📶] [✕] [🐾] [🦴] [🔒] [⌑]

AAA ◆◆◆◆◆ **The Little Nell** Ⓗ ❖
(970) 920-4600. **$3900, 30 days notice.** 675 E Durant Ave. Beside the gondola at the base of Aspen Mountain. Int corridors. **Pets:** Other. Supervision.
[S📶] [🔒] [▯] [⌑] [✕]

◆◆◆◆ **The St. Regis Aspen** Ⓗ
(970) 920-3300. **$339-$709.** 315 E Dean St. From SR 82, s on Monarch, then just e. Int corridors. **Pets:** Supervision.
[ASK] [S📶] [✕] [🐾] [▯] [✕]

BEAVER CREEK

◆◆◆ **Comfort Inn-Vail/Beaver Creek** Ⓜ ❖
(970) 949-5511. **$75-$259, 7 days notice.** 0161 W Beaver Creek Blvd. S of I-70, exit 167. Int corridors. **Pets:** Small. $15 one-time fee/room. Supervision.
[ASK] [S📶] [✕] [🐾] [⌑]

BOULDER

◆◆◆ **The Broker Inn** Ⓜ ❖
(303) 444-3330. **$128-$138.** 555 30th St. US 36, Baseline Rd exit, 0.3 mi e to 30th, then just s. Int corridors. **Pets:** Other. Designated rooms, no service, supervision, crate.
[ASK] [S📶] [✕] [🛏] [💻] [▯] [⌑] [✕]

◆◆◆ Days Inn Boulder [M] 🐾
(303) 499-4422. **$94-$104.** 5397 S Boulder Rd. US 36, Boulder Rd exit, just e. Int corridors. **Pets:** Medium. Designated rooms, no service, supervision, crate.
[A$K] ☒ ▣ 🏊

[AAA] **◆◆ Foot of The Mountain Motel** [C] 🐾
(303) 442-5688. **$60-$75.** 200 Arapahoe Ave. 1.8 mi w of US 36. Ext corridors. **Pets:** $5 daily fee/pet. No service, supervision, crate.
▣ ⚒ [AC]

[AAA] **◆◆ Holiday Inn** [MI]
(303) 443-3322. **$94-$109.** 800 28th St. US 36, Baseline exit via Frontage Rd; opposite Colorado University campus.. Ext/int corridors. **Pets:** Designated rooms, no service, supervision, crate.
[SD] ☒ 🦻 ▣ ☕ 🍴 🏊

◆◆◆ Homewood Suites [M] 🐾
(303) 499-9922. **$149-$210.** 4950 Baseline Rd. 0.3 mi e of US 36 on Baseline Rd, behind Meadows Shopping Center; or Baseline exit off Foothills Pkwy (Hwy 157), just w; entry off Baseline Rd. Ext/int corridors. **Pets:** Other. $50 one-time fee/room. Supervision.
[A$K] [SD] ☒ 🦻 ▣ ☕ 🏊 ⚒

◆◆◆ Residence Inn by Marriott [A]
(303) 449-5545. **$199.** 3030 Center Green Dr. 0.5 mi e of US 36; on Valmont Rd at corner of Foothills Pkwy. Ext corridors. **Pets:** No service, supervision, crate.
[A$K] [SD] ☒ 🦻 ♿ ▣ ☕ 🏊 ⚒

◆◆◆ Super 8 of Boulder [M]
(303) 443-7800. **$85-$125.** 970 28th St. US 36 frontage road; opposite Colorado University campus. Ext corridors. **Pets:** Medium. No service, supervision, crate.
☒ ♿ ▣ 🏊

BRUSH

[AAA] **◆◆◆ Best Western Brush** [M] 🐾
(970) 842-5146. **$60-$78.** 1208 N Colorado Ave. N of I-76, exit 90B. Ext/int corridors. **Pets:** Small. $5 one-time fee/room. No service, supervision, crate.
[SAVE] [SD] ☒ ☕ 🏊

◆ Budget Host Empire Motel [M] 🐾
(970) 842-2876. **$30-$42.** 1408 Edison St. I-76, exit 90A (SR 71), to US 34, 0.9 mi w. Ext corridors. **Pets:** Medium. $2 daily fee/pet. No service, supervision, crate.
[A$K] [SD] ☒

BUENA VISTA

[AAA] **◆◆◆ Vista Inn** [M] 🐾
(719) 395-8009. **$75-$95.** 733 US Hwy 24 N. 0.5 mi n on US 24. Int corridors. **Pets:** Small, dogs only. $50 deposit/room, $7 daily fee/pet. Designated rooms, no service, supervision, crate.
☒

BURLINGTON

◆◆◆ Burlington Comfort Inn [M] 🐾
(719) 346-7676. **$59-$89, 3 days notice.** 282 S Lincoln St. I-70, exit 437, on US 385. Int corridors. **Pets:** $50 deposit/room, $10 daily fee/room, $10 one-time fee/room. Designated rooms, no service, supervision, crate.
[A$K] [SD] ☒ ♿ ☕ 🏊

[AAA] **◆◆ Chapparal Budget Host** [M]
(719) 346-5361. **$35-$55.** 405 S Lincoln. I-70, exit 437 at jct US 385. Ext corridors. **Pets:** Supervision.
[SAVE] [SD] ☒ ☕ 🏊

[AAA] **◆◆ Sloans Motel** [M] 🐾
(719) 346-5333. **$34-$44, 3 days notice.** 1901 Rose Ave. 0.5 mi n of I-70 E, exit 437, on US 385, just e on US 24; I-70 W, exit 438, then 1 mi w on US 24. Ext corridors. **Pets:** Medium. Designated rooms, supervision.
[SAVE] ☒ 🚶 ♿ ▣ ☕

CANON CITY

[AAA] **◆◆◆ Best Western Royal Gorge Motel** [MI] 🐾
(719) 275-3377. **$69-$89.** 1925 Fremont Dr. 0.8 mi e on US 50. Ext/int corridors. **Pets:** Small, other. $10 one-time fee/pet. Designated rooms, supervision.
[SAVE] [SD] ☒ ▣ ☕ 🍴 🏊 ⚒

[AAA] **◆◆◆ Canon Inn** [MI] 🐾
(719) 275-8676. **$68-$84.** 3075 E Hwy 50. 2 mi e jct SR 115 and US 50. Int corridors. **Pets:** Other. $25 deposit/room. Supervision.
☒ ▣ 🍴 🏊

CASTLE ROCK

[AAA] **◆◆◆ Best Western Inn & Suites** [M] 🐾
(303) 814-8800. **$84-$99.** 595 Genoa Way. I-25, exit 184, just w to Castleton, then left. Int corridors. **Pets:** Medium, other. $10 daily fee/pet. Designated rooms, no service, supervision, crate.
[SAVE] [SD] ☒ ♿ ▣ ☕ 🏊

◆◆ Comfort Inn [M]
(303) 660-2222. **$59-$145, 7 days notice.** 200 Wolfensberger Rd. I-25, exit 182. Int corridors. **Pets:** Supervision.
[A$K] [SD] ☒ 🦻 ♿ ▣ 🏊

◆◆◆ Holiday Inn Express [M] 🐾
(303) 660-9733. **$89-$109.** 884 Park St. I-25, exit 182, just w. Int corridors. **Pets:** $10 daily fee/pet. No service, supervision, crate.
[A$K] [SD] ☒ ♿ ▣ 🏊

CEDAREDGE

[AAA] **◆◆◆ Super 8 of Cedaredge** [M]
(970) 856-7824. **$62-$103, 30 days notice.** 530 S Grand Mesa Dr. Just s on Rt 65. Int corridors. **Pets:** Designated rooms, no service, supervision, crate.
[SAVE] ☒ ♿ ▣ 🏊

COLORADO SPRINGS METROPOLITAN AREA

COLORADO SPRINGS

🛆🛆 ◆◆ The Alikar Gardens Resort Ⓐ
(719) 475-2564. **$109-$169, 7 days notice.** 1123 Verde Dr. 2 mi ne of I-25, exit 138 on Circle Dr. Ext corridors. **Pets:** Supervision.
🆂🅰🆅🅴 🆂👁 🗙 🔋 💻 🍽

🛆🛆🛆 ◆◆◆ Antlers Adam's Mark Ⓗ
(719) 473-5600. **$205-$220.** 4 S Cascade Ave. I-25, exit 142, just e on Bijou, then just s. Int corridors. **Pets:** Small. Designated rooms, supervision.
🆂🅰🆅🅴 🆂👁 🗙 🔋 🔥 🗲 🔋 💻 🍽 🖼

🛆🛆 ◆◆ Apollo Park Executive Suites Ⓐ ❄
(719) 634-0286. **$69-$99, 3 days notice.** 805 S Circle Dr, 2-B. 2.5 mi e and n of I-25, exit 138 via Circle Dr. Int corridors. **Pets:** Medium. $10 daily fee/room. Designated rooms, supervision.
🆂🅰🆅🅴 🆂👁 🗙 💻 🖼

🛆🛆 ◆◆◆ Best Western Le Baron
Hotel-Downtown Ⓜ ❄
(719) 471-8680. **$85-$95.** 314 W Bijou St. I-25, exit 142, nw corner. Int corridors. **Pets:** Medium, other. $50 deposit/room. Supervision.
🆂🅰🆅🅴 🗙 🔥 🔋 💻 🍽 🖼

◆◆ The Best Western Palmer House Ⓜ ❄
(719) 636-5201. **$79-$89.** 3010 N Chestnut. Nw of I-25, exit 145. Ext corridors. **Pets:** Small, other. $10 daily fee/pet. Designated rooms, supervision.
🅰🆂🅺 🆂👁 🗙 🔋 💻 🍽 🖼 🗙

🛆🛆 ◆ Chief Motel Ⓜ ❄
(719) 473-5228. **$45-$70.** 1624 S Nevada Ave. I-25, exit 140A northbound; 140B southbound. Ext corridors. **Pets:** Dogs only. $10 deposit/room, $5 daily fee/pet, $5 one-time fee/pet. Designated rooms, no service, supervision, crate.
🆂🅰🆅🅴 🆂👁 🗙 🔋

🛆🛆 ◆◆◆ Comfort Suites Ⓜ ❄
(719) 536-0731. **$89-$149.** 1055 Kelly Johnson Blvd. I-25, exit 150, just s on Academy to Kelly Johnson Blvd, then w. Int corridors. **Pets:** Medium, other. $50 deposit/room. Designated rooms, no service, supervision, crate.
🆂🅰🆅🅴 🆂👁 🗙 🔥 🗲 🔋 💻 🖼

◆◆◆ Doubletree Hotel Colorado Springs, World
Arena Ⓗ ❄
(719) 576-8900. **$99-$149.** 1775 E Cheyenne Mtn Blvd. I-25, exit 138, just w, entry on E Cheyenne Mtn Blvd. Int corridors. **Pets:** Other. $10 daily fee/pet. Supervision.
🅰🆂🅺 🆂👁 🗙 🔥 🔥 🗲 🔋 💻 🍽 🖼 📺

◆◆◆ Drury Inn-Pikes Peak Ⓜ ❄
(719) 598-2500. **$74-$99.** 8155 N Academy Blvd. E of I-25, exit 150. Int corridors. **Pets:** Other. Supervision.
🗙 🗲 🔋 💻 🖼

◆◆◆ Hampton Inn-North Ⓜ ❄
(719) 593-9700. **Call for rates.** 7245 Commerce Center Dr. Nw of I-25, exit 149, then just w and n. Int corridors. **Pets:** Other. $25 one-time fee/room. Supervision.
🗙 🗲 🔋 💻 🖼 📺

🛆🛆 ◆◆◆ Holiday Inn Garden of the Gods Ⓜ
(719) 598-7656. **$89-$99.** 505 Pope's Bluff Tr. Just sw of I-25, exit 146. Int corridors. **Pets:** Medium. Supervision.
🆂🅰🆅🅴 🗙 🔥 🗲 🔋 💻 🍽 🖼 🗙

🛆🛆 ◆◆ Howard Johnson Express Inn Ⓜ ❄
(719) 634-1545. **$50-$90.** 1231 S Nevada Ave. Just n of I-25, exit 140A northbound; exit 140B southbound. Ext corridors. **Pets:** Very small. $10 deposit/pet, $5 daily fee/pet. Designated rooms, no service, supervision, crate.
🆂🅰🆅🅴 🆂👁 🗙 🔋 💻 🖼

🛆🛆 ◆◆◆ La Quinta Inn Garden of the
Gods Ⓜ ❄
(719) 528-5060. **$75-$105.** 4385 Sinton Rd. Just e of I-25, exit 146. Ext corridors. **Pets:** Small. Designated rooms, no service, supervision, crate.
🆂🅰🆅🅴 🗙 🗲 🔋 💻 🖼

🛆🛆 ◆◆ Motel 6–35 Ⓜ
(719) 520-5400. **$50-$76.** 3228 N Chestnut. I-25, exit 145 (Fillmore St), from n take U-turn with caution onto Chestnut, just n. Ext corridors. **Pets:** Small. Supervision.
🆂👁 🗙 🔥 🖼 📺

🛆🛆 ◆◆ Quality Inn-Garden of the Gods Ⓜ ❄
(719) 593-9119. **$81-$111, 3 days notice.** 555 W Garden of the Gods Rd. I-25, exit 146, just w. Int corridors. **Pets:** Other. $50 deposit/pet. Supervision.
🆂🅰🆅🅴 🆂👁 🗙 🔥 🔋 💻 🖼

🛆🛆 ◆◆◆ Radisson Inn & Suites Ⓜ ❄
(719) 597-7000. **$129-$129.** 1645 N Newport Rd. I-25, exit 139, 4 mi e on US 24 bypass (Fountain Blvd). Int corridors. **Pets:** Medium. $100 deposit/room. Supervision.
🆂🅰🆅🅴 🆂👁 🗙 🔥 🔥 🗲 🔋 💻 🍽 🖼

🛆🛆 ◆◆◆ Radisson Inn Colorado Springs
North Ⓜ ❄
(719) 598-5770. **$109-$140, 5 days notice.** 8110 N Academy Blvd. E of I-25, exit 150. Int corridors. **Pets:** Small, dogs only. $50 deposit/pet. No service, supervision, crate.
🗙 🔥 🗲 🔋 💻 🖼

🛆🛆 ◆◆ Ramada Inn-Garden of the Gods Ⓜ
(719) 633-5541. **$59-$89, 5 days notice.** 3125 Sinton Rd. Just ne of I-25, exit 145. Ext/int corridors. **Pets:** Medium. Supervision.
🆂🅰🆅🅴 🆂👁 🗙 🗲 🗲 🔋 🍽 🖼

◆◆◆ Residence Inn by Marriott-North Ⓐ ❄
(719) 574-0370. **Call for rates.** 3880 N Academy Blvd. I-25, exit 146, 6 mi e on Austin Bluffs Pkwy to Academy (SR 83), 0.3 mi s. Ext corridors. **Pets:** Other. $15 daily fee/pet. Supervision.
🗙 🗲 🔋 💻 🖼 🗙

◆◆◆ Residence Inn by Marriott-South Ⓜ ❄
(719) 576-0101. **$169.** 2765 Geyser Dr. I-25, exit 138 (Circle Blvd), just w to E Cheyenne Mountain Blvd, then just s. Int corridors. **Pets:** Other. $5 daily fee/room, $50 one-time fee/room. Supervision.
🅰🆂🅺 🆂👁 🗙 🔥 🗲 🔋 💻 🖼 🗙

◆◆ **Rodeway Inn** Ⓜ
(719) 471-0990. **$75-$85, 3 days notice.** 2409 E Pikes Peak Ave. I-25, exit 143, e on Uintah to Union, s to Pikes Peak, then e; I-25, exit 135, ne on Academy to Pikes Peak, then w. Ext corridors. **Pets:** Small. No service, supervision, crate.

(ASK) (S🐾) ⊠ 🗋 🖵 🕿

🛆 ◆◆ **Sleep Inn** Ⓜ ❀
(719) 260-6969. **$84-$104.** 1075 Kelly Johnson Blvd. I-25, exit 150, just s on Academy to Kelly Johnson Blvd, then w. Int corridors. **Pets:** Medium, other. $50 deposit/room. Designated rooms, no service, supervision, crate.

(SAVE) (S🐾) ⊠ (🏠) (🔥) 🖵

🛆 ◆ **Stagecoach Motel** Ⓜ ❀
(719) 633-3894. **$45-$69, 3 days notice.** 1647 S Nevada Ave. I-25, exit 140A or 140B, just s. Ext corridors. **Pets:** Small. $5 daily fee/pet. Designated rooms, supervision.

(SAVE) (S🐾) ⊠ 🗋

🛆 ◆◆ **Travelodge** Ⓜ ❀
(719) 632-4600. **$199-$285.** 2625 Ore Mill Rd. 2.3 mi nw of I-25, exit 141; on US 24, entry via 26th St. Int corridors. **Pets:** Medium, other. $20 one-time fee/room. No service, supervision, crate.

(SAVE) (S🐾) ⊠ 🖵 🕿

MANITOU SPRINGS

🛆 ◆ **Red Wing Motel** Ⓜ ❀
(719) 685-5656. **$49-$64.** 56 El Paso Blvd. 4 mi w on US 24, from I-25 exit 141, exit Manitou Ave, just e to Beckers Ln, then n. Ext corridors. **Pets:** Other. $7 daily fee/room, $7 one-time fee/room. No service, supervision, crate.

(SAVE) (S🐾) ⊠ 🗋 🖵 🕿 ⊠

❀ **End Metropolitan Area** 🐾

CORTEZ

🛆 ◆◆ **Anasazi Motor Inn** Ⓜ❘ ❀
(970) 565-3773. **$57-$71.** 640 S Broadway. 1 mi sw on US 160 and 666. Ext corridors. **Pets:** Other. $50 deposit/room. Supervision.

(SAVE) (S🐾) ⊠ (🔥) 🗋 🖵 🍴 🕿

🛆 ◆◆◆ **Best Western Turquoise Inn &**
       Suites Ⓜ ❀
(970) 565-3778. **$89-$119.** 535 E Main St. On US 160. Ext corridors. **Pets:** Other. $10 one-time fee/room. Designated rooms, supervision.

(SAVE) (S🐾) ⊠ (🔥) 🗋 🖵 🕿

🛆 ◆◆ **Budget Host Inn** Ⓜ ❀
(970) 565-3738. **$52-$78.** 2040 E Main St. 1.3 mi e on US 160, w of jct SR 145. Ext corridors. **Pets:** Other. $5 daily fee/pet, $5 one-time fee/pet. No service, supervision, crate.

(SAVE) ⊠ 🕿

🛆 ◆◆◆ **Comfort Inn** Ⓜ
(970) 565-3400. **$79-$99.** 2321 E Main. 1.3 mi e on US 160. Ext/int corridors. **Pets:** Designated rooms, no service, supervision, crate.

(SAVE) (S🐾) ⊠ 🕿

🛆 ◆◆ **Days Inn** Ⓜ❘
(970) 565-8577. **$64-$89.** Hwy 160 & Jct 145. 1.5 mi e, on US 160, at jct SR 145. Ext/int corridors. **Pets:** Supervision.

(SAVE) (S🐾) ⊠ 🍴 🕿

🛆 ◆◆ **Econo Lodge** Ⓜ ❀
(970) 565-3474. **$55-$99, 5 days notice.** 2020 E Main St. 1.3 mi e on US 160. Ext corridors. **Pets:** Other. $20 deposit/room. Designated rooms, no service, supervision, crate.

(SAVE) (S🐾) ⊠ 🗋 🖵 🕿

◆◆◆ **Holiday Inn Express** Ⓜ ❀
(970) 565-6000. **$99-$137.** 2121 E Main St. 1.3 mi e on US 160. Int corridors. **Pets:** $10 deposit/room. Designated rooms, no service, supervision, crate.

(ASK) (S🐾) ⊠ (🐾) 🗋 🕿

🛆 ◆◆ **Tomahawk Lodge** Ⓜ ❀
(970) 565-8521. **$43-$69.** 728 S Broadway. 0.5 mi sw on US 160/666. Ext corridors. **Pets:** Dogs only. $25 deposit/pet. Designated rooms, no service, supervision, crate.

(SAVE) (S🐾) ⊠ 🕿

🛆 ◆◆ **Travelodge** Ⓜ ❀
(970) 565-7778. **$49-$79.** 440 S Broadway. 0.8 mi sw on US 160/666. Ext corridors. **Pets:** Medium. $25 deposit/room, $5 one-time fee/pet. No service, supervision, crate.

(SAVE) (S🐾) ⊠ 🖵 🕿

CRAIG

◆◆ **Best Western Inn of Craig** Ⓜ ❀
(970) 824-8101. **$59-$89.** 755 E Victory Way. 0.5 mi e on US 40. Ext corridors. **Pets:** Designated rooms, no service, supervision, crate.

(S🐾) ⊠ 🗋 🖵

🛆 ◆ **Craig Motel** Ⓜ ❀
(970) 824-4491. **$30-$58.** 894 Yampa Ave. 0.4 mi n of US 40, on SR 13 (Yampa Ave). Ext corridors. **Pets:** Other. $4 daily fee/pet. Supervision.

(SAVE) (S🐾) ⊠ 🗋 🖵

◆◆ **Holiday Inn & Suites** Ⓜ❘
(970) 824-4000. **$82-$102.** 300 S Hwy 13. 0.3 mi s on SR 13 from jct US 40. Int corridors. **Pets:** Small. Designated rooms, supervision.

(ASK) (S🐾) ⊠ 🗋 🖵 🍴 🕿

🛆 ◆◆◆ **Ramada Limited** Ⓜ
(970) 824-9282. **$65-$119.** 262 Commerce St. 0.3 mi s on SR 13 from jct US 40. Int corridors. **Pets:** Supervision.

(SAVE) (S🐾) ⊠ (🏠) (🐾) 🗋 🖵 🕿

CRESTED BUTTE

⚠ ◆◆◆ **Sheraton Crested Butte**
        Resort 🅷 **❀**
(970) 349-8000. **$218-$240, 45 days notice.** 6 Emmons
Rd. 2.5 mi n on SR 135; at Mt Crested Butte ski area. Int
corridors. **Pets:** $30 daily fee/room. Designated rooms, no
service, supervision, crate.
[SAVE] [S🔴] [✕] [🕯] [🖬] [🖥] [¶] [🔍] [✕] [🎿]

DELTA

⚠ ◆◆ **Best Western Sundance** 🅼 **❀**
(970) 874-9781. **$60-$70, 7 days notice.** 903 Main St. 0.5
mi s on US 50. Ext corridors. **Pets:** Medium, other. $5 daily
fee/room. No service, supervision, crate.
[SAVE] [S🔴] [✕] [🖬] [🖥] [¶] [🔍]

⚠ ◆◆ **Budget Host Southgate Inn** 🅼
(970) 874-9726. **$45-$60.** 2124 S Main St. 1.5 mi s on US
50. Ext corridors. **Pets:** Small. No service, supervision,
crate.
[S🔴] [✕] [🖬] [🔍]

DENVER METROPOLITAN AREA

AURORA

⚠ ◆◆◆ **AmeriSuites** 🅼 **❀**
(303) 371-0700. **$119-$119.** 16250 E 40th Ave. I-70, exit
283 (Chambers Rd), just n, then 0.5 mi e. Int corridors.
Pets: $25 one-time fee/room. Supervision.
[SAVE] [S🔴] [✕] [🕯] [🖉] [🖬] [🖥] [🔍]

◆◆◆ **Doubletree Hotel Denver**
        Southeast 🅷 **❀**
(303) 337-2800. **$65-$102.** 13696 Iliff Pl. Just w of I-225,
exit 5. Int corridors. **Pets:** Other. Supervision.
[ASK] [S🔴] [✕] [🕯] [🖉] [🖬] [🖥] [¶] [🔍]

◆◆◆ **Hampton Inn Aurora** 🅼
(303) 369-8400. **$69-$79.** 1500 S Abilene St. Just e and 1
mi n from I-225, exit 5 (Iliff Ave). Int corridors.
Pets: Medium. No service, supervision, crate.
[ASK] [S🔴] [✕] [🕯] [🖬] [🖥] [🔍]

⚠ ◆◆ **Holiday Inn Denver International**
        Airport 🅼 **❀**
(303) 371-9494. **$80, 30 days notice.** 15500 E 40th Ave.
I-70, exit 283 (Chambers Rd). Int corridors. **Pets:** Other.
$20 one-time fee/room. No service, supervision, crate.
[SAVE] [S🔴] [✕] [🕯] [🖉] [🖬] [🖥] [¶] [🔍]

◆◆◆ **La Quinta Inn-Aurora** 🅼
(303) 337-0206. **$69-$89.** 1011 S Abilene. E of I-225, exit 7.
Ext corridors. **Pets:** Supervision.
[ASK] [✕] [🕯] [🖉] [🖬] [🖥] [🔍]

⚠ ◆◆ **Sleep Inn Denver Airport** 🅼 **❀**
(303) 373-1616. **$72-$81.** 15900 E 40th Ave. From airport,
Pena Blvd s to 40th Ave W; I-70, exit 283 (Chambers Rd),
just n and e. Int corridors. **Pets:** Other. $25 one-time fee/
room. Supervision.
[SAVE] [S🔴] [✕] [🕯] [🖉] [🖬] [🔍]

DENVER

⚠ ◆◆◆ **Adam's Mark Hotel** 🅷 **❀**
(303) 893-3333. **$169-$184.** 1550 Court Pl. I-25, Colfax Ave
exit, just beyond US Mint, just n. Int corridors. **Pets:** Supervision.
[SAVE] [S🔴] [✕] [🕯] [🖉] [🖬] [🖥] [¶] [🔍]

⚠ ◆◆◆ **Best Western Executive Hotel** 🅼
(303) 373-5730. **$82-$82, 7 days notice.** 4411 Peoria St.
Just n of I-70, exit 281. Int corridors. **Pets:** Small. Designated rooms, no service, supervision, crate.
[SAVE] [S🔴] [✕] [🕯] [🖉] [🖬] [🖥] [¶] [🔍]

⚠ ◆◆ **Best Western Landmark Hotel** 🅼 **❀**
(303) 388-5561. **$99-$109.** 455 S Colorado Blvd. I-25, exit
204, 1 mi n. Int corridors. **Pets:** Medium, other. $25 deposit/
pet. No service, supervision, crate.
[SAVE] [S🔴] [✕] [🖬] [🖥] [¶] [🔍] [✕]

◆◆◆ **Denver Marriott Hotel City Center** 🅷
(303) 297-1300. **$169-$169.** 1701 California St at 17th St.
I-25, E Colfax exit, to Welton 0.5 mi ne and left on 18th,
then 1 blk. Int corridors. **Pets:** Medium. Designated rooms,
no service, supervision, crate.
[ASK] [S🔴] [✕] [🕯] [🖬] [🖥] [¶] [🔍]

◆◆◆ **Denver Marriott Southeast Hotel** 🅷
(303) 758-7000. **$139-$169.** 6363 E Hampden Ave. Just e
of I-25, exit 201. Ext/int corridors. **Pets:** No service, supervision, crate.
[ASK] [S🔴] [✕] [🕯] [🖉] [🖉] [🖬] [🖥] [🔍]

◆◆◆ **Denver Marriott Tech Center** 🅷 **❀**
(303) 779-1100. **$169-$169, 7 days notice.** 4900 S Syracuse St. I-25, exit 199 (Belleview Ave), e to S Syracuse,
just n. Int corridors. **Pets:** Small. $100 deposit/room. No
service, supervision, crate.
[✕] [🕯] [🖉] [🖉] [🖬] [🖥] [¶] [🔍]

◆◆◆ **DoubleTree Hotel Denver** 🅷 **❀**
(303) 321-3333. **$69-$89.** 3203 Quebec St. 0.5 mi s of I-70,
exit 278. Int corridors. **Pets:** Other. $50 deposit/room. No
service, supervision, crate.
[ASK] [S🔴] [✕] [🖉] [🖉] [🖬] [🖥] [¶] [🔍]

◆◆◆ **Drury Inn-Denver** 🅼 **❀**
(303) 373-1983. **$67-$92.** 4400 E Peoria St. I-70, exit 281,
just n. Int corridors. **Pets:** Medium. No service, supervision,
crate.
[✕] [🖉] [🖬] [🖥] [🔍]

⚠ ◆◆◆ **Embassy Suites-Denver International**
        Airport 🅷
(303) 375-0400. **$107-$112.** 4444 N Havana. N of I-70, exit
280. Int corridors. **Pets:** No service, supervision, crate.
[SAVE] [S🔴] [✕] [🕯] [🖉] [🖬] [🖥] [¶] [🔍]

◆◆◆ Hawthorn Suites Ⓜ

(303) 804-9900. **$149.** 5001 S Ulster. I-25, exit 199 (Belleview), to Ulster, then just n. Int corridors. **Pets:** Medium. No service, supervision, crate.

🅰🆂🅺 Ⓢ🅙 ✕ 🄳 🄴 🄴 🄱 💻 🕿 ⊠

ⒶⒶⒶ ◆◆◆ Holiday Chalet A Victorian Hotel Bed & Breakfast 🅱🅱 ❀

(303) 321-9975. **$99-$160.** 1820 E Colfax Ave. 1.3 mi e on US 40. Int corridors. **Pets:** Small, dogs only. $50 deposit/room, $5 daily fee/room. Designated rooms, no service, supervision, crate.

🆂🅰🆅🅴 ✕ 🄱 💻 🄲🅣🅥

◆◆◆ Holiday Inn Central Airport Area Ⓜ ❀

(303) 321-6666. **$79-$99.** 4040 Quebec St. I-70, exit 278, to Smith Rd exit, just e. Ext/int corridors. **Pets:** Other. Supervision.

🅰🆂🅺 Ⓢ🅙 ✕ 🄴 🄱 💻 🕿 🕿

ⒶⒶⒶ ◆◆◆ Hotel Monaco 🄷 ❀

(303) 296-1717. **$170-$205.** 1717 Champa St. Downtown at 17th and Champa sts. Int corridors. **Pets:** Other. Designated rooms, no service, supervision, crate.

🆂🅰🆅🅴 Ⓢ🅙 ✕ 🄵 🄳 🄴 💻 🕿

◆◆◆ La Quinta Inn-Cherry Creek Ⓜ ❀

(303) 758-8886. **$85-$105.** 1975 S Colorado Blvd. Just s of I-25, exit 204. Ext corridors. **Pets:** Medium. No service, supervision, crate.

🅰🆂🅺 ✕ 🄳 🄱 💻 🕿

◆◆◆ La Quinta Inn-Downtown Ⓜ

(303) 458-1222. **$75-$95.** 3500 Park Ave W. I-25, exit 213, 38th Ave, just s. Ext/int corridors. **Pets:** Small. No service, supervision, crate.

🅰🆂🅺 ✕ 🄵 🄳 💻 🕿

ⒶⒶⒶ ◆◆◆◆ Loews Giorgio Hotel 🄷 ❀

(303) 782-9300. **$79-$259.** 4150 E Mississippi. I-25, exit 204, 1 mi n on Colorado Blvd, just e. Int corridors. **Pets:** Supervision.

🆂🅰🆅🅴 Ⓢ🅙 ✕ 🄵 🄳 🄱 💻 🕿

ⒶⒶⒶ ◆◆ Motel 6-312 Ⓜ

(303) 371-1980. **$40-$61.** 12020 E 39th Ave. Exit 281 off I-70, (eastbound); westbound, take Peoria exit, just s. Ext corridors. **Pets:** Small. Supervision.

Ⓢ🅙 ✕ 🄳 🄴 🄱 🕿 🄲🅣🅥

ⒶⒶⒶ ◆◆◆ Quality Inn & Suites I-70 East Ⓜ ❀

(303) 320-0260. **$74-$79.** 4590 Quebec St. Just n of I-70, exit 278. Int corridors. **Pets:** Medium, other. Supervision.

🆂🅰🆅🅴 Ⓢ🅙 ✕ 🄵 🄴 🄱 💻 🕿 🕿

ⒶⒶⒶ ◆◆◆ Quality Inn South-DTC Ⓜ ❀

(303) 758-2211. **$66-$98.** 6300 E Hampden Ave. E of I-25, exit 201. Ext/int corridors. **Pets:** Small. $6 daily fee/pet. No service, supervision, crate.

🆂🅰🆅🅴 Ⓢ🅙 ✕ 🄵 🄳 🄴 🄱 💻 🕿 🕿

ⒶⒶⒶ ◆◆ Ramada Inn Airport Ⓜ ❀

(303) 388-6161. **$58-$58.** 3737 Quebec St. S of I-70, exit 278. Int corridors. **Pets:** $50 deposit/pet. Supervision.

🆂🅰🆅🅴 Ⓢ🅙 ✕ 🄱 💻 🕿 🕿

ⒶⒶⒶ ◆◆◆ Ramada Inn-Downtown West Ⓜ

(303) 433-8331. **$102-$114.** 1975 Bryant St. W of I-25, exit 210B. Int corridors. **Pets:** Supervision.

🆂🅰🆅🅴 Ⓢ🅙 ✕ 💻 🕿 🕿

ⒶⒶⒶ ◆◆◆ Red Roof Inn & Suites Ⓜ ❀

(303) 371-5300. **$45-$72.** 6890 Tower Rd. 4.2 mi n on I-70, exit 286, 0.8 mi s of Pena Blvd. Int corridors. **Pets:** Small. Supervision.

🆂🅰🆅🅴 Ⓢ🅙 ✕ 🄵 🄴 🄱

◆◆◆ Residence Inn by Marriott Denver Downtown 🄰 ❀

(303) 458-5318. **$135.** 2777 Zuni St. Just w of I-25, exit 212B. Ext corridors. **Pets:** Other. $15 one-time fee/pet. Supervision.

🅰🆂🅺 Ⓢ🅙 ✕ 🄳 🄱 💻 🕿

ⒶⒶⒶ ◆◆ Super 8 Denver-Central Ⓜ ❀

(303) 393-7666. **$60-$75, 7 days notice.** 7201 E 36th Ave. 0.3 mi s of I-70, exit 278. Int corridors. **Pets:** $5 daily fee/pet. No service, supervision, crate.

🆂🅰🆅🅴 Ⓢ🅙 ✕ 🄱 🕿

◆◆◆ TownePlace Suites by Marriott-Denver Southeast Ⓜ ❀

(303) 759-9393. **$69-$119.** 3699 S Monaco St Pkwy. I-25, exit 201, just e, just s. Int corridors. **Pets:** Medium. $10 daily fee/room. Supervision.

🅰🆂🅺 Ⓢ🅙 ✕ 🄴 🄱 🕿

◆◆◆◆ The Westin Tabor Center Denver 🄷 ❀

(303) 572-9100. **$135-$140.** 1672 Lawrence St. I-25, Auraria Pkwy exit, across Speer to 14th, then 2 blks s, then e. Int corridors. **Pets:** Other. Supervision.

✕ 🄳 🄳 🄴 💻 🕿 🕿 ⊠

ENGLEWOOD

◆◆◆ Hampton Inn Southeast Ⓜ ❀

(303) 792-9999. **Call for rates.** 9231 E Arapahoe Rd. E of I-25, exit 197. Int corridors. **Pets:** Small, other. No service, supervision, crate.

✕ 🄵 🄳 🄱 💻 🕿

◆◆◆ Holtze Executive Village 🄰 ❀

(303) 290-1100. **$69-$69.** 6380 S Boston St. Just e of I-25, exit 197, just n. Ext corridors. **Pets:** $100 one-time fee/pet. Supervision.

🅰🆂🅺 Ⓢ🅙 ✕ 🄱 💻 🕿 ⊠

ⒶⒶⒶ ◆◆◆ MainStay Suites Denver Tech Center Ⓜ ❀

(303) 858-1669. **$79-$99.** I-25, exit 197 (Arapahoe Rd), se on Clinton to Costilla, then w. Int corridors. **Pets:** Small. $50 one-time fee/room. Supervision.

🆂🅰🆅🅴 Ⓢ🅙 ✕ 🄳 🄳 🄴 🄱 💻

◆◆◆ Quality Suites Englewood Ⓜ ❀

(303) 858-0700. **$89-$109.** 7374 S Clinton St. I-25 to Dry Creek Rd, just e. Int corridors. **Pets:** $5 daily fee/pet, $50 one-time fee/pet. Designated rooms, supervision.

🅰🆂🅺 Ⓢ🅙 ✕ 🄵 🄳 🄱 💻 🕿

◆◆◆ Residence Inn by Marriott-Denver South 🅼 🐾
(303) 740-7177. **$130-$130.** 6565 S Yosemite St. Just w of I-25, exit 197 (Arapahoe Rd), then n. Ext corridors. **Pets:** Other. $5 daily fee/room, $50 one-time fee/room. Supervision.

🄰🅂🄺 🖪 ☒ 🗗 ⚙ 🞉 💻 🕿 ⊠

🅐🅐🅐 ◆◆ Sleep Inn Denver Tech Center 🅼 🐾
(303) 662-9950. **$45-$69.** 9257 Costilla Ave. I-25, exit 197 (Araphoe), just se on Clinton Ave to Costilla Ave, then w. Int corridors. **Pets:** Small. $25 one-time fee/room. Supervision.

🅂🄰🅅🄴 🖪 ☒ 🖑 🗗 ⚙ 🞉

◆◆◆ Summerfield Suites Denver South 🅼 🐾
(303) 706-1945. **$169-$260, 21 days notice.** 9280 E Costilla Ave. I-25, exit 197 (Arapahoe), just se on Clinton. Int corridors. **Pets:** Small, other. $10 daily fee/room, $150 one-time fee/room. Supervision.

🄰🅂🄺 🖪 ☒ 🗗 ⚙ 🞉 💻 🕿

◆◆◆ Woodfield Suites Denver Tech Center 🅼 🐾
(303) 799-4555. **$129.** 9009 E Arapahoe Rd. E of I-25, exit 197. Int corridors. **Pets:** No service, supervision, crate.

🄰🅂🄺 🖪 ☒ 🖑 🗗 ⚙ 🞉 💻 🕿

GOLDEN

◆◆◆ Days Inn Denver West 🅼🅸 🐾
(303) 277-0200. **$79-$99.** 15059 W Colfax Ave. E of I-70, exit 262. Int corridors. **Pets:** Small, other. $6 daily fee/pet. Designated rooms, supervision.

🄰🅂🄺 🖪 ☒ 🗗 ⚙ 🞉 💻 🕽 🕿

◆◆◆ Denver Marriott West 🅷
(303) 279-9100. **Call for rates.** 1717 Denver West Blvd. N of I-70, exit 263. Int corridors. **Pets:** Supervision.

☒ 🞉 🗗 ⚙ 🞉 💻 🕽 🕿

◆◆◆ Holiday Inn Denver West Village 🅼🅸 🐾
(303) 279-7611. **$95-$125.** 14707 W Colfax Ave. I-70, exit 262, just e. Ext/int corridors. **Pets:** Medium. $50 deposit/room. Supervision.

🄰🅂🄺 🖪 ☒ 🞉 🗗 🞉 🞉 💻 🕽 🕿 ⊠

◆◆◆ La Quinta Inn-Golden 🅼 🐾
(303) 279-5565. **$75-$95.** 3301 Youngfield Service Rd. I-70, exit 264 (32nd Ave), then 32nd Ave to Youngfield Service Rd. Ext corridors. **Pets:** Supervision.

🄰🅂🄺 🖪 ☒ 💻 🕿

◆◆◆ Quality Suites 🅼 🐾
(303) 526-2000. **$99-$136.** 29300 US Hwy 40. I-70 (Evergreen Pkwy), exit 252, on w side of El Rancho Restaurant. Int corridors. **Pets:** Very small, dogs only. $200 deposit/pet. No service, supervision, crate.

🄰🅂🄺 🖪 ☒ 🗗 💻 🕿

GREENWOOD VILLAGE

🅐🅐🅐 ◆◆ Wellesley Inn & Suites 🅼 🐾
(303) 220-8448. **$84-$84, 3 days notice.** 5200 S Quebec St. I-25, exit 199 (Bellview Ave), just w to S Quebec, just s. Ext corridors. **Pets:** Other. $50 deposit/pet. No service, supervision, crate.

🅂🄰🅅🄴 🖪 ☒ 🞉 ⚙ 🗗 💻

HIGHLANDS RANCH

◆◆◆ Residence Inn Denver South Highlands Ranch 🅼 🐾
(303) 683-5500. **$116-$153, 30 days notice.** 93 W Centennial Blvd. C-470, Broadway exit, just s on Broadway, then w. Int corridors. **Pets:** Other. $100 one-time fee/room. No service, supervision, crate.

🄰🅂🄺 🖪 ☒ 🖑 🗗 ⚙ 🞉 💻 🕿 ⊠

LAKEWOOD

◆◆ Best Western-Denver West 🅼🅸
(303) 238-7751. **$59-$79.** 11595 W 6th Ave. US 6, Simms-Union exit, just n; I-70 E, exit 261, 3 mi e on US 6; I-70 W, exit s to US 6, then 6 mi w. Ext/int corridors. **Pets:** Medium. Supervision.

🄰🅂🄺 🖪 ☒ 🗗 💻 🕽 🕿

🅐🅐🅐 ◆◆◆ Comfort Inn & Suites-SW Denver 🅼
(303) 989-5500. **$49-$99.** 3440 S Vance St. Just ne of jct US 285 (Hampden Ave) and S Wadsworth Blvd, e on Girton Dr, then just s. Int corridors. **Pets:** No service, supervision, crate.

🅂🄰🅅🄴 🖪 ☒ 🗗 💻 🕿

🅐🅐🅐 ◆◆ Ramada Inn-Denver West 🅼🅸
(303) 238-1251. **$69-$79.** 7150 W Colfax. 3 blks e of jct Wadsworth and Colfax. Ext corridors. **Pets:** No service, supervision, crate.

🅂🄰🅅🄴 ☒ ⚙ 🗗 💻 🕽

◆◆◆ Residence Inn by Marriott Denver SW/Lakewood 🅼
(303) 985-7676. **$99-$159.** 7050 W Hampden Ave. Just se of jct US 285 (W Hampden Ave) and Wadsworth Blvd, then e on Jefferson and n on frontage road. Int corridors. **Pets:** Small. No service, supervision, crate.

🄰🅂🄺 🖪 ☒ 🗗 ⚙ 🞉 💻 🕿 ⊠

◆◆◆ TownePlace Suites by Marriott-Lakewood 🅼 🐾
(303) 232-7790. **$49-$99.** 800 Tabor St. US 6, Simms/Union exit, just n to 8th, then w. Int corridors. **Pets:** Other. $10 daily fee/room. Supervision.

🄰🅂🄺 🖪 ☒ 🖑 🗗 🞉 💻 🕿

NORTHGLENN

◆◆◆ Holiday Inn Denver-Northglenn 🅼🅸
(303) 452-4100. **$89-$99.** 10 E 120th Ave. E of I-25, exit 223. Int corridors. **Pets:** Supervision.

🄰🅂🄺 🖪 ☒ 🖑 🗗 ⚙ 🞉 💻 🕽 🕿

WESTMINSTER

🅐🅐🅐 ◆◆◆ Hawthorn Inn & Suites 🅼 🐾
(303) 438-5800. **$85-$112.** 10179 Church Ranch Way. US 36 (Boulder Tpke), 104th Church Ranch Blvd exit, just s to 103rd Pl, then e. Int corridors. **Pets:** Small. $50 deposit/room. Designated rooms, no service, supervision, crate.

🅂🄰🅅🄴 🖪 ☒ 🖑 🗗 🞉 💻

◆◆◆ La Quinta Inn-Denver North 🅼 🐾
(303) 252-9800. **$69-$89.** 345 W 120th Ave. W of I-25, exit 223. Ext corridors. **Pets:** Small. Supervision.

🄰🅂🄺 ☒ 🗗 🞉 💻 🕿

◆◆◆ La Quinta Inn-Westminster Mall M
(303) 425-9099. **$79-$99.** 8701 Turnpike Dr. US 36 (Boulder Tpke), Sheridan Ave exit, just s on Sheridan, left on Turnpike Dr at 87th. Ext corridors. **Pets:** Small. Supervision.

[ASK] [✕] [🛏] [🎧] [▯] [💻] [🏊]

WHEAT RIDGE

◆◆◆ Holiday Inn Express Denver West M ❀
(303) 423-4000. **Call for rates.** 4700 Kipling St. Just s of I-70, exit 267. Int corridors. **Pets:** $20 one-time fee/room. No service, supervision, crate.

[✕] [🛏] [🎧] [▯] [🏊]

❀ **END METROPOLITAN AREA** ❀

DILLON

⍟ ◆◆◆ Best Western Ptarmigan Lodge M
(970) 468-2341. **$65-$123, 30 days notice.** 652 Lake Dillon Dr. 1.3 mi se of I-70 exit 205 on US 6, then 0.3 mi s on Lake Dillon Dr; opposite Lake Dillon. Ext/int corridors. **Pets:** No service, supervision, crate.

[SAVE] [🛏] [✕] [▯] [💻] [▯] [🎧]

DURANGO

⍟ ◆◆ Alpine Motel M ❀
(970) 247-4042. **$50-$84.** 3515 N Main Ave. 2.7 mi n of jct US 160 W and US 550, on US 550. Ext corridors. **Pets:** Other. No service, supervision, crate.

[SAVE] [✕] [▯]

⍟ ◆ Caboose Motel M ❀
(970) 247-1191. **$48-$68.** 3363 Main Ave. 2.5 mi n of jct US 550 and US 160. Ext corridors. **Pets:** Medium, dogs only. $5 one-time fee/room. Designated rooms, no service, supervision, crate.

[SAVE] [🛏] [✕] [▯]

◆◆ Days Inn Durango M ❀
(970) 259-1430. **$79-$104.** 1700 CR 203. 4.5 mi n on US 550; entry just s of establishment, then w on CR 203. Int corridors. **Pets:** No service, supervision, crate.

[ASK] [🛏] [✕] [🏊]

⍟ ◆◆◆ DoubleTree Hotel Durango H ❀
(970) 259-6580. **$154-$171, 7 days notice.** 501 Camino Del Rio. At jct of US 160 and 550. Int corridors. **Pets:** Other. $10 daily fee/pet. No service, supervision, crate.

[✕] [🛏] [🎧] [🌡] [▯] [💻] [▯] [🏊] [✕]

⍟ ◆◆ Holiday Inn M
(970) 247-5393. **$100-$140.** 800 Camino Del Rio. Just n of jct US 160 W and 550. Ext corridors. **Pets:** No service, supervision, crate.

[SAVE] [🛏] [✕] [🎧] [💻] [▯] [🏊]

⍟ ◆◆ Iron Horse Inn M ❀
(970) 259-1010. **$99-$119.** 5800 N Main Ave. 4.5 mi n on US 550. Ext corridors. **Pets:** Other. $50 deposit/pet. Designated rooms, no service, supervision, crate.

[SAVE] [🛏] [✕] [▯] [💻] [▯] [🏊]

◆◆◆ Quality Inn Denver West M ❀
(303) 467-2400. **$49-$89.** 12100 W 44th Ave. I-70, exit Ward Rd and W 44th Ave, 0.3 mi se. Int corridors. **Pets:** Medium. $50 deposit/pet. Supervision.

[ASK] [🛏] [✕] [▯] [💻] [▯] [✕]

◆◆◆ Quality Inn & Suites M ❀
(970) 259-7900. **Call for rates.** 455 S Camino Del Rio. 1.5 mi e on US 160. Int corridors. **Pets:** Other. $50 deposit/ room. Designated rooms, supervision.

[✕] [🛏] [🎧] [▯] [💻] [🏊]

◆◆◆ Residence Inn by Marriott M ❀
(970) 259-6200. **$169-$220.** 21691 Hwy 160 W. Just w on US 160. Int corridors. **Pets:** Small. $20 daily fee/pet. No service, supervision, crate.

[ASK] [🛏] [✕] [🎧] [▯] [💻] [🏊] [✕]

◆◆◆ The Rochester Hotel B ❀
(970) 385-1920. **$149-$199.** 726 E Second Ave. Just e of Main via 7th St and just n. Int corridors. **Pets:** Medium, other. $15 daily fee/pet. Designated rooms, no service, supervision, crate.

[ASK] [🛏] [✕] [▯] [💻]

⍟ ◆◆ Rodeway Inn M ❀
(970) 259-2540. **$79-$109.** 2701 Main Ave. 2 mi n jct US 160 W and US 550, on US 550. Ext corridors. **Pets:** Dogs only. $5 daily fee/pet. No service, supervision, crate.

[SAVE] [🛏] [✕] [▯] [💻] [🏊]

⍟ ◆◆ Travelodge M ❀
(970) 247-1741. **$72-$98.** 2970 Main Ave. 2.2 mi n jct US 160 and 550, on US 550. Ext corridors. **Pets:** Other. $8 daily fee/pet, $8 one-time fee/pet. No service, supervision, crate.

[SAVE] [🛏] [✕] [▯] [💻]

EAGLE

⍟ ◆◆◆ Best Western Eagle Lodge & Suites M ❀
(970) 328-6316. **$67-$128.** 200 Loren Ln. S of I-70, exit 147. Int corridors. **Pets:** Dogs only. $50 deposit/pet. Supervision.

[SAVE] [🛏] [✕] [🎧] [▯] [💻] [🏊]

EDWARDS

◆◆◆ The Inn at Riverwalk M ❀
(970) 926-0606. **$160-$290, 30 days notice.** 27 Main St. I-70, exit 163, 0.5 mi s. Int corridors. **Pets:** Other. $25 one-time fee/pet. Supervision.

[ASK] [🛏] [✕] [🎧] [▯] [🏊]

ESTES PARK

⚫ ◆◆ Castle Mountain Lodge 🄲 ❀
(970) 586-3664. **$110-$185, 30 days notice.** 1520 Fall River Rd. 1 mi w on US 34, on Fall River. Ext corridors. **Pets:** Dogs only. $15 daily fee/pet. Designated rooms, supervision.
🄷 ⌧ 🄺 🄩

⚫ ◆ Four Winds Motor Lodge Ⓜ ❀
(970) 586-3313. **$66-$85, 3 days notice.** 1120 Big Thompson Ave. 1 mi w on US 34. Ext corridors. **Pets:** $15 daily fee/pet. No service, supervision, crate.
🆂🅰🆅🅴 ⌧ 🄷 🄬 🄐 🄺

⚫ ◆◆ Timber Creek Chalets 🄲
(970) 586-8803. **$95-$185, 30 days notice.** 2115 Fall River Rd. 2.9 mi w of jct US 34 and US 36 on US 34 (Fall River Rd). Ext corridors. **Pets:** Small. No service, supervision, crate.
🆂🅱 ⌧ 🄷 🄬 🄐 🄺

EVANS

⚫ ◆◆ Sleep Inn Ⓜ ❀
(970) 356-2180. **$75, 3 days notice.** 3025 8th Ave. Just sw of jct US 34 and US 85 bypass. Int corridors. **Pets:** Medium, other. $20 one-time fee/room. Supervision.
🆂🅰🆅🅴 🆂🅱 ⌧ 🄵 🄍 🄳 🄷 🄐

FAIRPLAY

⚫ ◆◆ The Western Inn Ⓜ ❀
(719) 836-2026. **$55-$70.** 490 Hwy 285. US 285, 0.3 mi n of jct SR 9. Ext corridors. **Pets:** Other. $25 deposit/pet, $5 one-time fee/pet. No service, supervision, crate.
🆂🅰🆅🅴 🆂🅱 ⌧ 🄷 🄺

FORT COLLINS

◆◆◆ Fort Collins Comfort Suites Ⓜ ❀
(970) 206-4597. **$75-$100.** 1415 Oak Ridge Dr. I-25, exit 265 (Harmony Rd), 3 mi w to McMurray Dr, just s, then w. Int corridors. **Pets:** $15 daily fee/room, $15 one-time fee/room. Designated rooms, no service, supervision, crate.
🄰🆂🄺 🆂🅱 ⌧ 🄍 🄳 🄷 🄬 🄐

◆◆◆ Holiday Inn I-25 Holidome Ⓜ❶ ❀
(970) 484-4660. **Call for rates.** 3836 E Mulberry St. Just nw of I-25 exit 269B. Ext/int corridors. **Pets:** $50 deposit/pet. Designated rooms, no service, supervision, crate.
🄰🆂🄺 ⌧ 🄷 🄬 🄌 🄐

◆◆ Sleep Inn Ⓜ
(970) 484-5515. **$69-$89.** 3808 E Mulberry St. I-25, exit 269B, just nw. Int corridors. **Pets:** Medium. Designated rooms, no service, supervision, crate.
🄰🆂🄺 🆂🅱 ⌧ 🄳 🄬

◆◆ Super 8 Motel Ⓜ
(970) 493-7701. **$51-$81.** 409 Centro Way. I-25, exit 269B, just w. Int corridors. **Pets:** Supervision.
⌧ 🄷

◆◆◆ University Park Holiday Inn 🄷 ❀
(970) 482-2626. **$89-$119.** 425 W Prospect Rd. 1 mi s on US 287, just w. Int corridors. **Pets:** Other. Supervision.
🄰🆂🄺 🆂🅱 ⌧ 🄍 🄳 🄷 🄬 🄐 🄌 🄐

FORT MORGAN

◆◆ Best Western Park Terrace Inn Ⓜ❶
(970) 867-8256. **$52-$78.** 725 Main St. 0.5 mi s of I-76, exit 80. Ext corridors. **Pets:** No service, supervision, crate.
🄰🆂🄺 🆂🅱 ⌧ 🄷 🄐 🄌 🄐

⚫ ◆◆ Central Motel Ⓜ ❀
(970) 867-2401. **$39-$56.** 201 W Platte Ave. 0.4 mi s of I-76, exit 80, just w on US 34. Ext corridors. **Pets:** Other. $5 one-time fee/room. No service, supervision, crate.
🆂🅰🆅🅴 🆂🅱 ⌧ 🄷

◆◆ Econo Lodge Ⓜ❶
(970) 867-9481. **$50.** 1409 Barlow Rd. Just n of I-76, exit 82. Ext/int corridors. **Pets:** No service, supervision, crate.
🄰🆂🄺 🆂🅱 ⌧ 🄷 🄌 🄐

FRISCO

⚫ ◆◆ Best Western Lake Dillon Lodge Ⓜ❶ ❀
(970) 668-5094. **$119-$159, 7 days notice.** 1202 Summit Blvd. S of I-70, exit 203. Int corridors. **Pets:** Other. $50 deposit/room. Designated rooms, supervision.
🆂🅱 ⌧ 🄷 🄬 🄌 🄐

⚫ ◆◆ New Summit Inn Ⓜ ❀
(970) 668-3220. **$105-$140.** 1205 N Summit Blvd. S of I-70, exit 203. Int corridors. **Pets:** Other. $20 deposit/pet, $5 one-time fee/pet. No service, supervision, crate.
⌧ 🄷

⚫ ◆◆ Snowshoe Motel Ⓜ
(970) 668-3444. **$80-$115.** 521 Main St. I-70, exit 203 westbound, 1 mi s to Main St, just w; I 70, exit 201, eastbound. Ext corridors. **Pets:** Small. Supervision.
⌧ 🄷 🄺

FRUITA

⚫ ◆ H-Motel Ⓜ
(970) 858-7198. **$35-$55, 3 days notice.** 333 Hwy 6 & 50. I-70 (use caution), exit 19, 0.5 mi e on Hwy 6. Ext corridors. **Pets:** Large. Designated rooms, no service, supervision, crate.
🆂🅰🆅🅴 ⌧ 🄷

⚫ ◆◆◆ Super 8 Motel Ⓜ ❀
(970) 858-0808. **$55-$60.** 399 Jurassic Ave. I-70 (use caution) exit 19, 0.3 mi s, just e of Dinosaur Discovery Museum. Int corridors. **Pets:** $20 deposit/pet, $5 daily fee/pet. Designated rooms, no service, supervision, crate.
🆂🅰🆅🅴 🆂🅱 ⌧ 🄦 🄍 🄌 🄐

GEORGETOWN

⚫ ◆ Georgetown Motor Inn Ⓜ ❀
(303) 569-3201. **$54-$60.** 1100 Rose. Exit 228 off I-70, just s and 0.3 mi w. Ext corridors. **Pets:** Large. $10 one-time fee/room. Designated rooms, no service, supervision, crate.
🆂🅰🆅🅴 🆂🅱 ⌧ 🄷 🄐 🄺

GLENWOOD SPRINGS

⚫ ◆◆ Best Western Caravan Inn Ⓜ ❀
(970) 945-7451. **$75-$99.** 1826 Grand Ave. I-70, exit 116, 1.3 mi s on SR 82. Ext corridors. **Pets:** Other. $50 deposit/room, $5 daily fee/pet. Designated rooms, no service, supervision, crate.
🆂🅰🆅🅴 🆂🅱 ⌧ 🄐 🄧

△△△ ◆◆◆ **Ramada Inn & Suites** Ⓜ
(970) 945-2500. **$90-$130.** 124 W 6th St. Just w of I-70, exit 116. Ext/int corridors. **Pets:** Designated rooms, no service, supervision, crate.
(SAVE) (S2) (×) (🔒) (🖵) (🍴) (🏊)

△△△ ◆◆ **Silver Spruce Motel** Ⓜ
(970) 945-5458. **$55-$100.** 162 W 6th St. Off I-70, exit 116, just w on frontage road. Ext corridors. **Pets:** Designated rooms, no service, supervision, crate.
(SAVE) (S2) (×) (🔒)

GRANBY

△△△ ◆◆◆ **The Inn at Silver Creek** Ⓡ ❀
(970) 887-2131. **$89-$189, 31 days notice.** 62927 Hwy 40. 2 mi se on US 40. Int corridors. **Pets:** $12 one-time fee/room. No service, supervision, crate.
(SAVE) (S2) (×) (🔒) (🖵) (🍴) (🏊) (🐕) (🎾)

GRAND JUNCTION

△△△ ◆◆◆ **Adam's Mark Hotel-Grand Junction** Ⓗ ❀
(970) 241-8888. **$79-$79.** 743 Horizon Dr. I-70, exit 31, just s. Int corridors. **Pets:** Supervision.
(SAVE) (S2) (×) (🚲) (🔒) (🖵) (🍴) (🏊) (🎾)

△△△ ◆◆◆ **Best Western Clifton Inn** Ⓜ
(970) 434-3400. **$59-$89.** 3228 I-70 business loop. I-70, exit 37, on I-70 business loop at jct SR 141. Ext corridors. **Pets:** Supervision.
(SAVE) (S2) (×) (🔒) (🏊)

△△△ ◆◆ **Best Western Horizon Inn** Ⓜ ❀
(970) 245-1410. **$55-$74.** 754 Horizon Dr. 0.3 mi n of I-70, exit 31. Ext corridors. **Pets:** Medium, other. No service, supervision, crate.
(SAVE) (S2) (×) (🐱) (🚲) (🔒) (🖵) (🏊) (🎾)

△△△ ◆◆ **Days Inn of Grand Junction** Ⓜ ❀
(970) 245-7200. **$60-$71.** 733 Horizon Dr. I-70, exit 31. Int corridors. **Pets:** Medium. $50 deposit/room. Designated rooms, supervision.
(SAVE) (S2) (×) (🔒) (🖵) (🍴) (🏊)

△△△ ◆◆ **Grand Junction Super 8** Ⓜ
(970) 248-8080. **$50-$60.** 728 Horizon Dr. I-70, exit 31, s. Int corridors. **Pets:** Medium. Designated rooms, no service, supervision, crate.
(SAVE) (S2) (×) (🏊)

△△△ ◆◆◆ **Grand Vista Hotel** Ⓜ
(970) 241-8411. **$72-$99.** 2790 Crossroads Blvd. I-70, exit 31, 0.3 mi n. Int corridors. **Pets:** Designated rooms, supervision.
(SAVE) (S2) (×) (🔒) (🍴) (🏊)

△△△ ◆◆◆ **Holiday Inn** Ⓜ ❀
(970) 243-6790. **$79-$84.** 755 Horizon Dr. I-70, exit 31, nw corner. Ext/int corridors. **Pets:** Small, dogs only. No service, supervision, crate.
(SAVE) (S2) (×) (🚲) (🔒) (🖵) (🍴) (🏊) (🎾)

△△△ ◆◆◆ **La Quinta Inns & Suites** Ⓜ ❀
(970) 241-2929. **$75-$95.** 2761 Crossroads Blvd. I-70, exit 31, n to Crossroads, just w. Int corridors. **Pets:** Medium. Supervision.
(SAVE) (×) (♿) (🚲) (🚲) (🔒) (🖵) (🏊)

△△△ ◆◆ **West Gate Inn** Ⓜ ❀
(970) 241-3020. **$49-$69.** 2210 Hwys 6 & 50. I-70, exit 26, then 0.3 mi se. Ext corridors. **Pets:** Other. $50 deposit/room. Designated rooms, no service, supervision, crate.
(SAVE) (×) (🍴) (🏊)

GREAT SAND DUNES NATIONAL MONUMENT

△△△ ◆◆ **Great Sand Dunes Lodge** Ⓜ ❀
(719) 378-2900. **$70-$80.** 7900 Hwy 150 N. From Alamosa, 16 mi e on US 160, 16 mi n on SR 150, at entrance to Great Sand Dunes National Monument. Ext corridors. **Pets:** Medium. $10 one-time fee/room. Supervision.
(×) (🖵) (🏊) (CTV)

GREELEY

◆◆◆ **Best Western Ramkota Inn** Ⓜ
(970) 353-8444. **$59-$105.** 701 8th St. Downtown; on US 85 business route. Int corridors. **Pets:** No service, supervision, crate.
(ASK) (S2) (×) (🐱) (🚲) (🚲) (🔒) (🖵) (🍴) (🏊)

◆◆◆ **Holiday Inn Express** Ⓜ
(970) 330-7495. **$65-$90.** 2563 W 29th St. Just sw of US 34 bypass at 23rd Ave exit. Int corridors. **Pets:** Medium. Supervision.
(×) (🐱) (🚲) (🚲) (🔒) (🏊)

◆◆ **Microtel Inn & Suites** Ⓜ ❀
(970) 392-1530. **$53-$64.** 5630 W 10th St. 5 mi w on US 34 Business Rt. Int corridors. **Pets:** Other. $50 deposit/pet, $5 daily fee/pet. Supervision.
(ASK) (S2) (×) (🐱) (🚲) (🚲) (🔒) (🖵)

GUNNISON

△△△ ◆◆ **ABC Motel** Ⓜ ❀
(970) 641-2400. **$56-$69.** 212 E Tomichi Ave. US 50, near Western State College. Ext corridors. **Pets:** $5 daily fee/room, $5 one-time fee/room. No service, supervision, crate.
(SAVE) (S2) (×) (🔒)

△△△ ◆◆ **Hylander Inn** Ⓜ ❀
(970) 641-0700. **$58-$82.** 412 E Tomichi Ave. US 50, near Western State College, opposite Legion Park. Ext corridors. **Pets:** Other. $5 one-time fee/room. No service, supervision, crate.
(×)

HOT SULPHUR SPRINGS

△△△ ◆ **Canyon Motel** Ⓜ
(970) 725-3395. **$42-$70.** 221 Byers Ave. On US 40. Ext corridors. **Pets:** Small. Designated rooms, no service, supervision, crate.
(SAVE) (S2) (×) (🔒) (🎾)

△△△ ◆◆ **Stagecoach Country Inn** Ⓑⓑ
(970) 725-3910. **$45-$74.** 412 Nevava St. 0.3 mi off SR 40, going n on Aspen. Int corridors. **Pets:** Designated rooms, supervision.
(SAVE) (×) (🎾) (CTV) (Ⓩ)

HOTCHKISS

⊛ ◆◆ Hotchkiss Inn M ❖
(970) 872-2200. **$39-$59.** 406 Hwy 133. 0.3 mi e jct SR 92/133. Ext corridors. **Pets:** Large. $5 one-time fee/room. Supervision.
[SAVE] [S6] [⊠]

IDAHO SPRINGS

⊛ ◆◆ H & H Motor Lodge M ❖
(303) 567-2838. **$54-$84.** 2445 Colorado Blvd. 0.5 mi w of I-70, exit 241A, opposite Argo Gold Mill. Ext/int corridors. **Pets:** Small. $5 daily fee/pet. Designated rooms, no service, supervision, crate.
[SAVE] [⊠] [🖥]

⊛ ◆ Peoriana Motel M ❖
(303) 567-2021. **$38-$65.** 2901 Colorado Blvd. 0.3 mi w of I-70, exit 241A. Ext corridors. **Pets:** Small, dogs only. Designated rooms, no service, supervision, crate.
[SAVE] [⊠] [ℳ] [☎]

⊛ ◆ 6 & 40 Motel M
(303) 567-2691. **$45-$95.** 2920 Colorado Blvd. W of I-70, exit 241A. Ext corridors. **Pets:** No service, supervision, crate.
[SAVE] [S6] [⊠] [🖥] [⊠] [ℳ]

JULESBURG

⊛ ◆ Platte Valley Inn Ⓜ
(970) 474-3336. **$45-$58.** 15225 Hwy 385 & I-76. N of I-76, exit 180. Ext corridors. **Pets:** Small. No service, supervision, crate.
[SAVE] [S6] [⊠] [🖵] [¶] [☁]

LA JUNTA

⊛ ◆◆◆ Holiday Inn Express M
(719) 384-2900. **$74-$84.** 27994 US Hwy 50 Frontage Rd. 0.8 mi w on US 50. Int corridors. **Pets:** Supervision.
[SAVE] [S6] [⊠] [🗐] [🖥] [☁]

⊛ ◆◆ Stagecoach Motel Ⓜ
(719) 384-5476. **$40-$50.** 905 W 3rd St. US 50 and 350. Ext corridors. **Pets:** Small. No service, supervision, crate.
[SAVE] [⊠] [🖥] [☁]

⊛ ◆ Travel Inn M ❖
(719) 384-2504. **$34-$42.** 110 E First St. On US 50. Ext corridors. **Pets:** $10 deposit/pet, $20 one-time fee/pet. Designated rooms, no service, supervision, crate.
[SAVE] [⊠] [🖥]

LAMAR

⊛ ◆◆◆ Best Western Cow Palace Inn Ⓜ ❖
(719) 336-7753. **$81-$90.** 1301 N Main St. 0.8 mi n on US 50 and 287. Ext/int corridors. **Pets:** Small, other. Supervision.
[SAVE] [S6] [⊠] [☎] [🖥] [🖵] [¶] [☁]

⊛ ◆◆ Blue Spruce Motel Ⓜ
(719) 336-7454. **$30-$37.** 1801 S Main St. 1.3 mi s on US 287 and 385. Ext corridors. **Pets:** Small. No service, supervision, crate.
[SAVE] [S6] [⊠] [🖥] [☁]

⊛ ◆ Passport Inn Ⓜ ❖
(719) 336-7746. **$32-$47.** 113 N Main St. Jct US 50 and 385, just e. Ext corridors. **Pets:** Medium, dogs only. $5 daily fee/pet, $5 one-time fee/pet. No service, supervision, crate.
[SAVE] [S6] [⊠] [🖥]

LEADVILLE

⊛ ◆ Alps Motel Ⓜ ❖
(719) 486-1223. **$43-$64.** 207 Elm St. Just s on US 24. Int corridors. **Pets:** Medium. $7 daily fee/pet. Designated rooms, no service, supervision, crate.
[⊠] [🖥] [ℳ]

LIMON

⊛ ◆◆◆ Best Western Limon Inn Ⓜ ❖
(719) 775-0277. **$65-$85, 5 days notice.** 925 T Ave. I-70, exit 359. Int corridors. **Pets:** $10 one-time fee/room. No service, supervision, crate.
[SAVE] [S6] [⊠] [☁]

◆◆◆ Holiday Inn Express Ⓜ ❖
(719) 775-0700. **$85-$85.** 2505 6th St. I-70, exit 359, s to 6th St. Int corridors. **Pets:** $15 daily fee/pet. Designated rooms, no service, supervision, crate.
[ASK] [S6] [⊠] [♨] [🖥] [☁]

⊛ ◆◆ Preferred Motor Inn Ⓜ ❖
(719) 775-2385. **$38-$60.** 158 E Main St. W of I-70, exit 361. Ext/int corridors. **Pets:** Small. $4 daily fee/pet. Designated rooms, no service, supervision, crate.
[SAVE] [S6] [⊠] [🖥] [☁] [⊠]

⊛ ◆◆ Safari Motel Ⓜ
(719) 775-2363. **$44-$62.** 637 Main St. 0.8 mi w of I-70, exit 361. Ext corridors. **Pets:** Small. Designated rooms, no service, supervision, crate.
[SAVE] [S6] [⊠] [☁] [⊠]

⊛ ◆◆ Super 8 Motel Ⓜ ❖
(719) 775-2889. **$52-$65.** 937 Hwy 24. I-70, exit 359. Int corridors. **Pets:** $10 one-time fee/pet. No service, supervision, crate.
[SAVE] [S6] [⊠] [☁]

LONGMONT

◆◆◆ Raintree Plaza Hotel Suites Conference Center Ⓜ ❖
(303) 776-2000. **$144-$184.** 1900 Ken Pratt Blvd. 1 mi s on US 287, 1.3 mi sw on SR 119. Int corridors. **Pets:** No service, supervision, crate.
[ASK] [S6] [⊠] [♨] [☁] [🖥] [🖵] [¶] [☁]

◆◆ Super 8 Motel Ⓜ ❖
(303) 772-0888. **$62-$86.** 10805 Turner Blvd. Exit 240 off I-25 at jct with SR 119; or 7 mi e of town on SR 119. Int corridors. **Pets:** Other. No service, supervision, crate.
[ASK] [S6] [⊠]

LOUISVILLE

⊛ ◆◆◆ Comfort Inn of Boulder County Ⓜ
(303) 604-0181. **$99-$139.** 1196 Dillon Rd. US 36 (Boulder Tpke), Louisville/Superior exit (SR 170), just n on McCaslin Blvd, then w on Dillon Rd, next to cinemas. Int corridors. **Pets:** Medium. Designated rooms, supervision.
[SAVE] [S6] [⊠] [🚶] [☁] [🖥]

LOVELAND

♦ Budget Host Exit 254 Inn M ✿
(970) 667-5202. **$38-$69.** 2716 SE Frontage Rd. E of I-25, exit 254. Ext corridors. **Pets:** Small. Supervision.

MARBLE

♦♦♦ Ute Meadows Inn Bed & Breakfast BB ✿
(970) 963-7088. **$120-$150.** 2880 CR 3. From SR 133, 3 mi toward Marble. Int corridors. **Pets:** Dogs only. $15 daily fee/pet, $15 one-time fee/pet. Designated rooms, supervision.

MESA VERDE NATIONAL PARK

♦♦ Far View Lodge in Mesa Verde M ✿
(970) 529-4421. **$98-$98.** 10 mi e of Cortez; 8 mi w of Mancos on US 160; then 15 mi within the park; near park visitors center. Ext corridors. **Pets:** Medium. $50 deposit/room. Designated rooms, no service, supervision, crate.

MONTE VISTA

♦♦♦ Best Western Movie Manor Motor Inn M
(719) 852-5921. **$80-$100, 7 days notice.** 2830 W Hwy 160. 2 mi w on US 160. Ext corridors. **Pets:** Medium. Designated rooms, no service, supervision, crate.

♦♦♦ Comfort Inn M ✿
(719) 852-0612. **$55-$90.** 1519 Grande Ave. 0.3 mi e on US 160. Int corridors. **Pets:** Medium. Supervision.

MONTROSE

♦♦ Black Canyon Motel M ✿
(970) 249-3495. **$50-$95.** 1605 E Main St. 1 mi e on US 50. Ext corridors. **Pets:** Other. Supervision.

♦♦♦ Comfort Inn M
(970) 240-8000. **$41-$75.** 2100 E Main St. 1.3 mi e on US 50. Int corridors. **Pets:** Very small. Designated rooms, no service, supervision, crate.

♦♦♦ Holiday Inn Express Hotel & Suites H ✿
(970) 240-1800. **$99-$139.** 1391 S Townsend Ave. 1 mi s on US 550, turn e on Niagara Ave. Int corridors. **Pets:** Other. Designated rooms, no service, supervision, crate.

♦♦ San Juan Inn M ✿
(970) 249-6644. **$48-$70.** 1480 S Townsend. 1 mi s on US 550. Ext corridors. **Pets:** Small. $6 one-time fee/pet. Designated rooms, no service, supervision, crate.

♦♦ Super 8 Motel M
(970) 249-9294. **$50-$66.** 1705 E Main St. 1 mi e on US 50. Int corridors. **Pets:** Small. Designated rooms, supervision.

♦♦ Uncompahgre Bed & Breakfast BB ✿
(970) 240-4000. **$70-$95.** 21049 Uncompahgre Rd. 8 mi s on US 550. Int corridors. **Pets:** Medium, dogs only. $2 daily fee/room. No service, supervision, crate.

♦♦ Western Motel M ✿
(970) 249-3481. **$38-$46.** 1200 E Main St. 0.8 mi e on US 50. Ext corridors. **Pets:** Dogs only. $25 deposit/room, $5 daily fee/pet. No service, supervision, crate.

OURAY

♦♦♦ Ouray Victorian Inn & Resort Accommodations M
(970) 325-7222. **$84-$190.** 50 3rd Ave. Just w of US 550 via 3rd Ave. Ext corridors. **Pets:** Designated rooms, no service, supervision, crate.

♦♦ Rivers Edge Motel M ✿
(970) 325-4621. **$55-$90.** 110 7th Ave. Just w of US 550 (Main St) via 7th Ave. Ext corridors. **Pets:** Dogs only. $5 daily fee/room. Supervision.

PAGOSA SPRINGS

♦♦ Fireside Inn C ✿
(970) 264-9204. **$94-$139.** 1600 E Hwy 160. 1.3 mi e on US 160. Ext corridors. **Pets:** Other. $25 deposit/room, $5 daily fee/pet. No service, supervision, crate.

♦♦ Pagosa High Country Lodge M ✿
(970) 264-4181. **$66-$100, 30 days notice.** 3821 E Hwy 160. 3 mi e on US 160. Ext/int corridors. **Pets:** Other. $15 one-time fee/room. No service, supervision, crate.

PUEBLO

♦♦ Best Western Town House Motel M
(719) 543-6530. **$55-$75.** 8th St & N Santa Fe Ave. Just w and 0.4 mi n of I-25, exit 99B. Ext corridors. **Pets:** Designated rooms, no service, supervision, crate.

♦♦♦ Hampton Inn M ✿
(719) 544-4700. **$79-$89.** 4703 N Frwy. I-25, exit 102, just w. Ext corridors. **Pets:** Other. $15 one-time fee/room. Designated rooms, supervision.

♦♦ Holiday Inn M ✿
(719) 543-8050. **$69-$79.** 4001 N Elizabeth. I-25, exit 101 (US 50 W), 0.3 mi n on service road. Ext/int corridors. **Pets:** Medium. Designated rooms, no service, supervision, crate.

♦ Motel 6–1186 M ✿
(719) 543-8900. **$39-$61.** 960 Hwy 50 W. I-25, exit 101, 0.3 mi w. Ext corridors. **Pets:** Small. Supervision.

◆◆◆ Ramada Inn 🅜🅸
(719) 542-3750. **Call for rates.** 2001 N Hudson. 0.5 mi e of I-25, exit 100A. Ext/int corridors. **Pets:** Medium. Designated rooms, no service, supervision, crate.

[×] [🛏] [▣] [🍽] [🛉]

PURGATORY

⊕⊕⊕ ◆◆◆ Best Western Lodge at Purgatory 🅜🅸
(970) 247-9669. **$89-$149, 3 days notice.** 49617 US 550N. US 550, at base of Purgatory ski area. Int corridors. **Pets:** Medium. No service, supervision, crate.

[SAVE] [Sö] [×] [🛏] [▣] [🍽] [🛉] [×] [🐾]

⊕⊕⊕ ◆◆◆ Sheraton Tamarron Resort 🆁 🐾
(970) 259-2000. **$129-$449.** 40292 US Hwy 550 N. 9 mi s on US 550. Ext/int corridors. **Pets:** Large, dogs only. $15 daily fee/room. Designated rooms, supervision.

[SAVE] [×] [🐝] [🛏] [▣] [🍽] [🛉] [×]

RIDGWAY

⊕⊕⊕ ◆◆◆ Ridgway-Telluride Super 8 Lodge 🅜
(970) 626-5444. **$73-$80.** 373 Palomino Tr. On US 550, at jct with SR 62. Int corridors. **Pets:** Designated rooms, supervision.

[SAVE] [×] [🛉]

SALIDA

⊕⊕⊕ ◆◆ Aspen Leaf Lodge 🅜 🐾
(719) 539-6733. **$39-$69, 3 days notice.** 7350 Hwy 50W. US 50, just w of Hot Springs Pool. Ext corridors. **Pets:** Medium. $100 deposit/room, $5 daily fee/pet. Designated rooms, no service, supervision, crate.

[SAVE] [Sö] [×] [🛏]

⊕⊕⊕ ◆ Circle R Motel 🅜 🐾
(719) 539-6296. **$40-$62.** 304 E Rainbow Blvd. US 50. Ext corridors. **Pets:** Large, other. $3 one-time fee/room. No service, supervision, crate.

[SAVE] [×] [🛏]

⊕⊕⊕ ◆◆◆ Holiday Inn Express 🅜
(719) 539-8500. **$85-$125.** 7400 US Hwy 50 W. US 50 W, 0.3 mi w of Hot Springs pool. Int corridors. **Pets:** Small. Supervision.

[SAVE] [Sö] [×] [🛏] [🛉]

⊕⊕⊕ ◆◆ Rainbow Inn 🅜 🐾
(719) 539-4444. **$50-$75.** 105 E Hwy 50. US 50. Ext corridors. **Pets:** No service, supervision, crate.

[SAVE] [×] [🛏]

⊕⊕⊕ ◆◆ Silver Ridge Lodge 🅜 🐾
(719) 539-2553. **$55-$75.** 545 W Rainbow Blvd. US 50, just w of Chamber of Commerce and opposite Hot Springs pool. Ext corridors. **Pets:** Other. $5 one-time fee/pet. Supervision.

[SAVE] [Sö] [×] [🛏] [▣] [🛉]

◆◆ Super 8 Motel 🅜 🐾
(719) 539-6689. **$55-$89.** 525 W Rainbow Blvd. On US 50, opposite Hot Springs Pool. Ext corridors. **Pets:** Medium. No service, supervision, crate.

[ASK] [Sö] [×] [🛏] [▣] [🛉] [×]

⊕⊕⊕ ◆◆◆ Travelodge 🅜
(719) 539-2528. **$65-$85, 7 days notice.** 7310 Hwy 50. US 50 W. Ext corridors. **Pets:** Large. No service, supervision, crate.

[SAVE] [Sö] [×] [🛏] [🛉]

⊕⊕⊕ ◆◆ Woodland Motel 🅜 🐾
(719) 539-4980. **$41-$82.** 903 W 1st. US 50 westbound, 1.5 mi on SR 291; US 50 eastbound, 1 mi ne on G St, then 6 blks w on SR 291; US 285 southbound, take SR 291 8 mi s and e. Ext corridors. **Pets:** Other. Supervision.

[×] [🛏]

SILVERTON

⊕⊕⊕ ◆◆ Alma House B&B 🅱🅱
(970) 387-5336. **$65-$110.** 220 E 10th St. From SR 110 off US 550 to 10th, then just SE. Int corridors. **Pets:** Supervision.

[SAVE] [×] [▣] [🛉] [🐝]

⊕⊕⊕ ◆◆ Villa Dallavalle B & B 🅱🅱
(970) 387-5555. **$60-$95.** 1257 Blair. SR 110, off US 550 se on 12th to Blair, just n. Int corridors. **Pets:** Small. Supervision.

[×] [🛉]

⊕⊕⊕ ◆◆◆ The Wyman Hotel & Inn 🅱🅱 🐾
(970) 387-5372. **$85-$170.** 1371 Greene (Main) St. Ne corner of Greene (Main) St and 14th St. Int corridors. **Pets:** Other. $15 daily fee/pet. Designated rooms, supervision.

[×] [🛏] [🛉]

SNOWMASS VILLAGE

◆◆◆ Silvertree Hotel 🅷 🐾
(970) 923-3520. **Call for rates, 30 days notice.** 100 Elbert Ln. 4 mi sw of SR 82 via Brush Creek and Snowmelt Rd, lot 8; in Upper Village. Int corridors. **Pets:** No service, supervision, crate.

[×] [🐝] [🛏] [▣] [🍽] [🛉] [×] [🛉]

⊕⊕⊕ ◆◆◆ Snowmass Mountain Chalet 🅻 🐾
(970) 923-3900. **$130-$310, 45 days notice.** 115 Daly Lane. 4 mi sw of SR 82 via Lower Village Rd; Lot 5. Ext/int corridors. **Pets:** Other. $100 deposit/room. No service, supervision, crate.

[SAVE] [Sö] [×] [🛏] [🛉] [🛉]

SOUTH FORK

⊕⊕⊕ ◆ Budget Host/Ute Bluff Lodge 🅜 🐾
(719) 873-5000. 27680 W Hwy 160. 2 mi e of jct US 160 and SR 149. Ext corridors. **Pets:** Medium, dogs only. $5 one-time fee/pet. No service, supervision, crate.

[SAVE] [×] [🛏] [▣] [🛉] [CTV]

⊕⊕⊕ ◆◆◆ Comfort Inn 🅜 🐾
(719) 873-5600. **$59-$150.** 0182 E Frontage Rd. On US 160. Int corridors. **Pets:** Large, other. $20 deposit/room. No service, supervision, crate.

[SAVE] [Sö] [×] [🛏] [▣] [🛉]

⊕⊕⊕ ◆◆ Wolf Creek Ski Lodge 🅜🅸 🐾
(719) 873-5547. **$50-$68.** 31042 Hwy W 160. On US 160. Ext corridors. **Pets:** No service, supervision, crate.

[SAVE] [Sö] [×] [🛏] [×] [🛉]

STEAMBOAT SPRINGS

◆◆◆ **Holiday Inn Steamboat** Ⓜ ❀
(970) 879-2250. **$90-$170, 21 days notice.** 3190 S Lincoln Ave. 3 mi e on US 40. Int corridors. **Pets:** $25 deposit/room. Supervision.

(ASK) (S⅙) (✕) (⅙) (⌀) (⌀) (⌀) (⌀) (⍔) (⍨) (⍨)

🅐 ◆◆ **Rabbit Ears Motel** Ⓜ ❀
(970) 879-1150. **$129-$169, 3 days notice.** 201 Lincoln Ave. Just e on US 40, opposite Municipal Hot Springs Pool and adjacent to Yampa River Park. Ext corridors. **Pets:** Supervision.

(SAVE) (S⅙) (✕) (⌀) (⍔) (✕)

◆◆◆ **Sheraton Steamboat Resort** Ⓡ ❀
(970) 879-2220. **$79-$369, 45 days notice.** 2200 Village Inn Court. 2.3 mi e on US 40, 1 mi n on Mt. Werner Rd; at ski area. Int corridors. **Pets:** Large, other. Supervision.

(✕) (⌀) (⅙) (⌀) (⍨) (⍔) (⍨) (✕)

🅐 ◆◆ **Super 8 Motel** Ⓜ ❀
(970) 879-5230. **$72-$89.** 3195 S Lincoln Ave. 3 mi e on US 40. Int corridors. **Pets:** Medium, dogs only. $20 deposit/room. Designated rooms, no service, supervision, crate.

(SAVE) (S⅙) (✕)

STERLING

◆◆◆ **Best Western Sundowner** Ⓜ ❀
(970) 522-6265. **$74-$105.** 125 Overland Trail St. Just w of I-76, exit 125. Ext/int corridors. **Pets:** Medium. $10 one-time fee/pet. Designated rooms, no service, supervision, crate.

(ASK) (S⅙) (✕) (⍨)

🅐 ◆ **Colonial Motel** Ⓜ ❀
(970) 522-3382. **$33-$38.** 915 S Division. Exit 125, US Rt 6 W to 2nd traffic light (4th St), s on US Rt 6 0.7 mi. Ext corridors. **Pets:** Dogs only. $5 daily fee/pet. No service, supervision, crate.

(SAVE) (✕) (⌀) (⍔)

◆◆ **Ramada Inn** Ⓜ
(970) 522-2625. **$85-$105.** I-76 & Hwy 6 E. On US 6, exit 125 off I-76. Ext/int corridors. **Pets:** No service, supervision, crate.

(ASK) (S⅙) (✕) (⌀) (⌀) (⍔) (⍨) (⍨)

STRATTON

🅐 ◆◆◆ **Best Western Golden Prairie Inn** Ⓜ
(719) 348-5311. **$49-$85.** 700 Colorado Ave. N of I-70, exit 419. Ext corridors. **Pets:** Small. Designated rooms, no service, supervision, crate.

(SAVE) (S⅙) (✕) (⌀) (⍨) (⍨)

TELLURIDE

◆◆◆ **Hotel Columbia Telluride** Ⓗ ❀
(970) 728-0660. **$395, 45 days notice.** 300 W San Juan Ave. Just s of SR 145 Spur at Aspen and San Juan sts; opposite gondola. Int corridors. **Pets:** Dogs only. $15 daily fee/room. Supervision.

(ASK) (S⅙) (✕) (⌀) (⍨) (✕) (⍗)

TRINIDAD

🅐 ◆◆ **Best Western Trinidad Inn** Ⓜ
(719) 846-2215. **$79-$99.** 900 W Adams. I-25, exit 13A, then straight uphill and across bridge. Ext corridors. **Pets:** No service, supervision, crate.

(SAVE) (S⅙) (✕) (⌀) (⍨) (⍨)

🅐 ◆◆ **Budget Host Derrick Motel** Ⓜ ❀
(719) 846-3307. **$53-$70.** 10301 Santa Fe Trail Dr. I-25, exit 11, just ne. Ext corridors. **Pets:** $5 daily fee/pet, $5 one-time fee/pet. No service, supervision, crate.

(SAVE) (S⅙) (✕) (⌀) (⍔)

🅐 ◆◆ **Budget Summit Inn** Ⓜ ❀
(719) 846-2251. **$44-$119, 3 days notice.** 9800 Santa Fe Trail Dr. I-25, exit 11, just se. Ext/int corridors. **Pets:** Large. $10 one-time fee/room. Designated rooms, no service, supervision, crate.

(✕) (⌀) (⅙) (⌀) (⍨) (✕)

🅐 ◆◆ **Days Inn** Ⓜ ❀
(719) 846-2271. **$59-$99.** 702 W Main St. I-25, exit 13B. Ext corridors. **Pets:** Large. $5 daily fee/pet. Supervision.

(SAVE) (✕) (⌀) (⍔) (⍨) (⍨)

◆◆◆ **Holiday Inn** Ⓜ ❀
(719) 846-4491. **$129.** 3125 Toupal Dr. I-25, exit 11. Int corridors. **Pets:** Medium, other. Designated rooms, supervision.

(ASK) (S⅙) (✕) (⌀) (⍔) (⍨) (⍨)

◆◆ **Super 8 Motel** Ⓜ ❀
(719) 846-8280. **$52-$90.** 1924 Freedom Rd. I-25, exit 15. Int corridors. **Pets:** Medium. $10 one-time fee/room. No service, supervision, crate.

(ASK) (S⅙) (✕) (⌀) (⍔)

VAIL

🅐 ◆◆◆ **Antlers at Vail** Ⓒ⚬ ❀
(970) 476-2471. **$160-$370, 60 days notice.** 680 W Lionshead Pl. 0.5 mi w of I-70, exit 176, just s on Lionshead Cir at Lionshead Pl at Vail Ski area. Ext corridors. **Pets:** Other. $15 daily fee/pet. Designated rooms, supervision.

(✕) (⌀) (⌀) (⍨) (⍗)

VICTOR

◆◆ **Victor Hotel** Ⓗ
(719) 689-3553. **Call for rates.** 397 Victor Ave. Downtown at 4th and Victor (on SR 67). Int corridors. **Pets:** Small. No service, supervision, crate.

(ASK) (✕) (⍨) (⍗)

WALSENBURG

🅐 ◆◆ **Best Western Rambler** Ⓜ
(719) 738-1121. **$65-$89.** 457 US Hwy 85-87. I-25, exit 52. Ext corridors. **Pets:** No service, supervision, crate.

(SAVE) (S⅙) (✕) (⍨) (⍨)

🅐 ◆ **Country Host Motel** Ⓜ
(719) 738-3800. **$48-$64** (no credit cards). 553 US 85 & 87. I-25, exit 52, 0.4 mi w. Ext corridors. **Pets:** Medium. No service, supervision, crate.

(SAVE) (S⅙) (✕) (✕)

WINTER PARK

🅐 ◆◆◆ **The Vintage Hotel** Ⓜ ❀
(970) 726-8801. **$485, 30 days notice.** 100 Winter Park Dr. 2.5 mi se on US 40, near ski area. Int corridors. **Pets:** Designated rooms, no service, supervision, crate.

(SAVE) (✕) (⌀) (⍔) (⍨) (⍨) (✕) (⍗)

CITY INDEX

BRANFORD

♦♦ Motel 6–1279 🅼 🐾
(203) 483-5828. **$46-$62.** 320 E Main St (US 1). I-95, exit 55, 0.3 mi n on US 1. Int corridors. **Pets:** Small, other. Supervision.

BRIDGEPORT

♦♦♦ Bridgeport Holiday Inn 🅷
(203) 334-1234. **$119-$159.** 1070 Main St. SR 8 N, exit 2, 0.7 mi se; SR 8 S, exit 2, just s, then e. Int corridors. **Pets:** Medium. Supervision.

BROOKFIELD

♦♦ Twin Tree Inn 🅼 🐾
(203) 775-0220. **$75-$95.** 1030 Federal Rd (Rt 7 & 202). From jct SR 25 and US 202, 1 mi n. Ext/int corridors. **Pets:** $10 one-time fee/room. Supervision.

DANBURY

♦♦♦ Danbury Hilton & Towers 🅷 🐾
(203) 794-0600. **$95-$176, 7 days notice.** 18 Old Ridgebury Rd. I-84, eastbound exit 2; westbound exit 2A. Int corridors. **Pets:** Small. $50 deposit/room. Designated rooms, no service, supervision, crate.

♦♦♦ Holiday Inn 🅼 🐾
(203) 792-4000. **$121-$125.** 80 Newtown Rd. I-84, exit 8, 0.5 mi s on US 6 W. Int corridors. **Pets:** Other. Supervision.

♦♦ Ramada Inn 🅼 🐾
(203) 792-3800. **$69-$125.** 116 Newtown Rd. I-84, exit 8 (Newtown Rd), ne corner. Int corridors. **Pets:** Other. No service, supervision, crate.

♦♦♦ Residence Inn by Marriott 🅼
(203) 797-1256. **$129-$149.** 22 Segar St. I-84, exit 4, just n. **Pets:** Medium. Supervision.

ESSEX

♦♦♦ Griswold Inn 🅒🅘
(860) 767-1776. **$90-$195.** 36 Main St. 2.3 mi e of SR 9, exit 3. Int corridors. **Pets:** Medium. No service, supervision, crate.

GROTON

♦♦♦ Morgan Inn & Suites 🅼 🐾
(860) 448-3000. **$85-$150.** 135 Gold Star Hwy. I-95, exit 86, 0.5 mi ne on SR 184. Int corridors. **Pets:** Medium, other. $10 daily fee/room. Designated rooms, no service, supervision, crate.

HARTFORD METROPOLITAN AREA

AVON

♦♦♦ Avon Old Farms Hotel 🅼🅘
(860) 677-1651. **$180-$180.** 279 Avon Mountain Rd. Jct US 44 and SR 10. Ext/int corridors. **Pets:** Designated rooms, supervision.

CROMWELL

♦♦♦ Comfort Inn 🅼 🐾
(860) 635-4100. **$89-$94.** 111 Berlin Rd (Rt 372). I-91, exit 21, just e on SR 372. Int corridors. **Pets:** $15 daily fee/room. No service, supervision, crate.

♦♦ Super 8 Motel 🅼
(860) 632-8888. **$56-$65, 3 days notice.** 1 Industrial Park Rd. I-91, exit 21, just w. Int corridors. **Pets:** Small. No service, supervision, crate.

EAST HARTFORD

♦♦♦ Holiday Inn 🅼🅘
(860) 528-9611. **$119-$129.** 363 Roberts St. I-84, exit 58, then w. Int corridors. **Pets:** Designated rooms, supervision.

Wellesley Inn & Suites M ❀
(860) 289-4950. **$79-$110, 3 days notice.** 333 Roberts St. I-84, exit 58, then w. Int corridors. **Pets:** Small. Designated rooms, no service, supervision, crate.
[SAVE] [S] [X] [🔲] [🖥]

EAST WINDSOR

Best Western Colonial Inn MI
(860) 623-9411. **$85-$225, 30 days notice.** 161 Bridge St. I-91, exit 45, just w. Int corridors. **Pets:** Designated rooms, supervision.
[SAVE] [S] [X] [🔲] [🖥] [🍴] [🏊]

ENFIELD

Red Roof Inn M ❀
(860) 741-2571. **$50-$107.** 5 Hazard Ave. I-91, exit 47 E. Ext corridors. **Pets:** Other. Supervision.
[SAVE] [X] [🔲] [🖥] [🔲]

Super 8 Motel-Enfield M ❀
(860) 741-3636. **$45-$115.** 1543 King St. I-91, exit 46, 0.3 mi n on US 5. Ext corridors. **Pets:** Dogs only. $10 daily fee/room, $10 one-time fee/room. No service, supervision, crate.
[SAVE] [X] [🔲]

FARMINGTON

Centennial Inn Suites M ❀
(860) 677-4647. **$129-$179.** 5 Spring Ln. From US 6, 0.3 mi e of jct SR 177. Ext/int corridors. **Pets:** Other. $10 daily fee/pet. Supervision.
[ASK] [S] [X] [🔲] [🔲] [🖥] [🏊]

HARTFORD

Crowne Plaza H
(860) 549-2400. **$79-$219.** 50 Morgan St. I-91, exit 32B; I-84, eastbound exit 50; westbound exit 52. Int corridors. **Pets:** Designated rooms, supervision.
[ASK] [S] [X] [🔲] [🔲] [🔲] [🔲] [🖥] [🍴] [🏊]

Goodwin Hotel H
(860) 246-7500. **Call for rates.** 1 Haynes St. Downtown; across from Civic Center (Asylum St). Int corridors. **Pets:** Small. Designated rooms, no service, supervision, crate.
[ASK] [X] [🔲] [🔲] [🔲]

Red Roof Inn M
(860) 724-0222. **$56-$93.** 100 Weston St. Just w of jct I-91, exit 33. Ext corridors. **Pets:** Designated rooms, supervision.
[SAVE] [X] [🔲] [🔲] [🔲]

Super 8 Motel M ❀
(860) 246-8888. **$54-$63, 3 days notice.** 57 W Service Rd. I-91, exit 33, 0.8 mi se. Int corridors. **Pets:** Designated rooms, no service, supervision, crate.
[ASK] [S] [X] [🔲]

SIMSBURY

The Ironhorse Inn M ❀
(860) 658-2216. **$79-$89, 4 days notice.** 969 Hopmeadow St. On US 202 and SR 10. Int corridors. **Pets:** Other. No service, supervision, crate.
[SAVE] [X] [🔲] [🏊]

WINDSOR

The Residence Inn by Marriott Hartford-Windsor A ❀
(860) 688-7474. **$128-$128.** 100 Dunfey Ln. I-91, exit 37 (Windsor-Bloomfield Ave), just w on SR 305 to Dunfey Ln, 0.3 mi n. Ext corridors. **Pets:** Other. $100 one-time fee/room. Supervision.
[ASK] [S] [X] [🔲] [🔲] [🖥] [🏊] [🔲]

WINDSOR LOCKS

Baymont Inn & Suites-Hartford/Airport M
(860) 623-3336. **$77-$87.** 64 Ella Grasso Tpke. On SR 75, just n of jct SR 20. Int corridors. **Pets:** Medium. Supervision.
[S] [X] [🔲] [🔲] [🔲] [🖥]

Homewood Suites Hartford-Windsor Locks M
(860) 627-8463. **$159-$179.** 65 Ella T Grasso Tpke. On SR 75, 0.3 mi n of jct SR 20. Ext/int corridors. **Pets:** Small. No service, supervision, crate.
[ASK] [S] [X] [🔲] [🔲] [🔲] [🔲] [🖥] [🏊] [🔲]

❀ END METROPOLITAN AREA ❀

LAKEVILLE

Inn at Iron Masters MI ❀
(860) 435-9844. **$95-$145.** 229 Main St. 0.5 mi ne on US 44 and SR 41. Ext corridors. **Pets:** Large, dogs only. Designated rooms, supervision.
[SAVE] [X] [🔲] [🖥] [🏊]

Interlaken Inn Resort and Conference Center X ❀
(860) 435-9878. **$149-$189, 7 days notice.** 74 Interlaken Rd. On SR 112, 0.5 mi w of jct SR 41. Int corridors. **Pets:** Other. $10 deposit/room, $10 one-time fee/room. Designated rooms, supervision.
[X] [🔲] [🔲] [🖥] [🍴] [🏊] [🔲]

LEDYARD

◆◆ **The Mare's Inn B & B** BB
(860) 572-7556. **$100-$175.** 333 Colonel Ledyard Hwy. I-95, exit 89, 1 mi n to Gold Star Hwy, 0.6 mi w, then 0.7 mi n. Int corridors. **Pets:** Small. Supervision.

⊠ 🛢 🖳

MERIDEN

🏵 ◆◆◆ **Ramada Plaza Hotel** H ❀
(203) 238-2380. **$79-$169.** 275 Research Pkwy. I-91, exit 17 southbound; exit 16 northbound, 0.5 mi e, then s. Int corridors. **Pets:** Small. No service, supervision, crate.

SAVE S🛢 ⊠ 🛏 🎢 🖳 🍴 🖼

◆◆◆ **Residence Inn by Marriott** M ❀
(203) 634-7770. **$174.** 390 Bee St. I-91, exit 16 northbound; exit 176 southbound, 0.5 mi e. Ext/int corridors. **Pets:** Other. $200 one-time fee/room. Supervision.

ASK S🛢 ⊠ 🛢 🖳 🖼 ⊠

MYSTIC

🏵 ◆◆◆ **AmeriSuites (Mystic/I-95 &**
Seaport) M ❀
(860) 536-9997. **$99-$209.** 224 Greenmanville Ave. I-95, exit 90, just se. Int corridors. **Pets:** Very small, other. $50 deposit/room. No service, supervision, crate.

SAVE S🛢 ⊠ 🎽 🛢 🖳 🖼

NEW HAVEN

◆◆◆ **Residence Inn by Marriott** A
(203) 777-5337. **$145-$180.** 3 Long Wharf Dr. I-95, exit 46, 0.6 mi nw. Ext corridors. **Pets:** Small. No service, supervision, crate.

ASK S🛢 ⊠ 🎢 🛢 🖳 🖼 ⊠

NEW LONDON

🏵 ◆◆ **Red Roof Inn** M ❀
(860) 444-0001. **$60-$100.** 707 Colman St. I-95, northbound exit 82A; southbound exit 83, just n. Ext corridors. **Pets:** Other. Designated rooms, no service, supervision, crate.

SAVE ⊠ 🎢

NORFOLK

◆◆ **Blackberry River Inn** BB
(860) 542-5100. **$95-$195.** 536 Greenwoods Rd W. On US 44, 3 mi w of jct SR 272. Int corridors. **Pets:** Small. Designated rooms, supervision.

⊠ 🛢 🖼 🎽

NORTH HAVEN

🏵 ◆◆◆ **Holiday Inn** MI
(203) 239-4225. **$79-$129.** 201 Washington Ave. On US 5; at I-91, exit 12. Int corridors. **Pets:** Designated rooms, no service, supervision, crate.

SAVE S🛢 ⊠ 🛏 🛢 🖳 🍴 🖼

NORWALK

◆◆ **Homestead Guest Studios** M
(203) 847-6888. **Call for rates.** 400 Main Ave. Merritt Pkwy (US 15), exit 40B, just n. Int corridors. **Pets:** Large. No service, supervision, crate.

⊠ 🎢 🎽 🛢 🖳

OLD LYME

🏵 ◆◆◆ **Old Lyme Inn** CI
(860) 434-2600. **$99-$175.** 85 Lyme St. I-95, exit 70, n on SR 156, right on US 1 for 0.5 mi, then left. Int corridors. **Pets:** Large. Designated rooms, no service, supervision, crate.

⊠ 🛢

OLD SAYBROOK

🏵 ◆◆ **Sandpiper Inn** M ❀
(860) 399-7973. **$65-$135.** 1750 Boston Post Rd. I-95, exit 66, just s of jct SR 166 on US 1. Ext/int corridors. **Pets:** Small. $20 deposit/room, $10 one-time fee/room. Designated rooms, supervision.

SAVE S🛢 ⊠ 🛢 🖼

RIVERSIDE

◆◆ **Howard Johnson Hotel** M ❀
(203) 637-3691. **$89-$119, 7 days notice.** 1114 Boston Post Rd. I-95, exit 5, just s on US 1 (Boston Post Rd). Ext corridors. **Pets:** Medium, other. Supervision.

ASK S🛢 ⊠ 🎢 🛢 🖳 🍴 🖼

RIVERTON

◆◆ **Old Riverton Inn** CI
(860) 379-8678. **$55-$130.** 436 E River Rd (SR 20). Center. Int corridors. **Pets:** Medium. Supervision.

⊠ 🛢

SHELTON

🏵 ◆◆◆ **AmeriSuites** M ❀
(203) 925-5900. **$154-$154.** 695 Bridgeport Ave. SR 8, exit 12, just w, then 0.4 mi s. Int corridors. **Pets:** Very small. $25 deposit/pet. No service, supervision, crate.

SAVE S🛢 ⊠ 🛢 🖳 🖼

🏵 ◆◆◆ **Ramada Plaza Hotel** H
(203) 929-1500. **$69-$155.** 780 Bridgeport Ave. SR 8, exit 12, 0.8 mi sw. Int corridors. **Pets:** Small. Supervision.

SAVE S🛢 ⊠ 🛢 🖳 🍴 🖼

◆◆◆ **Residence Inn by Marriott** A ❀
(203) 926-9000. **Call for rates.** 1001 Bridgeport Ave. SR 8, exit 11, 0.3 mi w. Ext corridors. **Pets:** Other. $20 daily fee/room, $350 one-time fee/room. No service, supervision, crate.

⊠ 🛢 🖳 🖼 ⊠

SOUTHBURY

◆◆◆ **Southbury Hilton** H ❀
(203) 598-7600. **$136-$151.** 1284 Strongtown Rd. I-84, exit 16. Int corridors. **Pets:** $100 deposit/room. Designated rooms, no service, supervision, crate.

ASK ⊠ 🛢 🖳 🍴 🖼

STAMFORD

◆◆◆ Holiday Inn Select  ❀
(203) 358-8400. **$209.** 700 Main St. Downtown; I-95 S, exit 8, then w; I-95 N, exit 7, just w, then n. Int corridors. **Pets:** Medium. $150 deposit/room, $75 one-time fee/room. Supervision.

(ASK) (S) (X) (⌂) (🐾) (🔲) (💻) (🍴) (🏊)

STRATFORD

◆◆ Ramada Inn Stratford
(203) 375-8866. **Call for rates.** 225 Lordship Blvd. I-95, exit 30, just s. Int corridors. **Pets:** Medium. Designated rooms, no service, supervision, crate.

(ASK) (X) (🔲) (💻) (🍴) (🏊)

TORRINGTON

⚠ ◆◆ Days Inn  ❀
(860) 496-8808. **$69-$79, 3 days notice.** 395 Winsted Rd. SR 8 N, exit 45, just w, then 0.6 mi s. Ext corridors. **Pets:** $15 daily fee/room, $15 one-time fee/pet. Supervision.

(SAVE) (S)

WATERBURY

◆◆◆ House on the Hill (BB) ❀
(203) 757-9901. **$125-$165, 7 days notice.** 92 Woodlawn Terr. I-84, exit 21, 0.6 mi n on Meadow and Willow sts, 0.4 mi ne on Pine St. Int corridors. **Pets:** Dogs only. No service, supervision, crate.

(X) (🔲) (💻)

◆◆◆ Sheraton Waterbury Hotel (H)
(203) 573-1000. **$139.** 3580 E Main St. I-84, westbound exit 26; eastbound exit 25A, 1st left and 1st right. Int corridors. **Pets:** Small. No service, supervision, crate.

(ASK) (S) (X) (⌂) (🔲) (💻) (🍴) (🏊) (X)

WATERFORD

⚠ ◆◆ Lamplighter Motel  ❀
(860) 442-7227. **$60-$110.** 211 Waterford Pkwy N. I-95, exit 81, then s. Ext corridors. **Pets:** Medium. $50 deposit/pet. No service, supervision, crate.

(🔲) (🏊)

WESTBROOK

⚠ ◆◆ Maples Motel  ❀
(860) 399-9345. **$55-$75.** 1935 Boston Post Rd. On US 1, 1.5 mi e of jct SR 153, I-95, exit 65. Ext corridors. **Pets:** Other. Designated rooms, no service, supervision, crate.

(SAVE) (S) (X) (🔲) (💻) (🏊) (Z)

DELAWARE

CLAYMONT

◆◆◆ Hilton Wilmington North
(302) 792-2700. **$59-$99.** 630 Naamans Rd. SR 92, just w of I-95, exit 11 northbound; exit 11 southbound; onto I-495, exit 6 (Naamans Rd). Int corridors. **Pets:** Supervision.

DEWEY BEACH

◆◆◆ Atlantic Oceanside Motel
(302) 227-8811. **$89-$229, 7 days notice.** 1700 Hwy 1. Jct of US 1 and McKinley St. Ext corridors. **Pets:** No pets Memorial Day weekend - Labor Day. $25 deposit/room, $5 daily fee/pet. Supervision.

◆◆ Bellbuoy Motel
(302) 227-6000. **$65-$165.** 21 Van Dyke St. SR 1, on oceanside blk of Van Dyke St. Ext corridors. **Pets:** Medium, dogs only. $6 daily fee/pet. Designated rooms, no service, supervision, crate.

◆◆◆ Best Western-Gold Leaf Hotel
(302) 226-1100. **$99-$199, 3 days notice.** 1400 Hwy 1. On Hwy 1. Int corridors. **Pets:** Medium. $15 daily fee/pet. Designated rooms, no service, supervision, crate.

◆ Sea-Esta Motel I
(302) 227-7666. **$49-$139, 3 days notice.** 2306 Hwy 1. Hwy 1 at Houston St. Ext corridors. **Pets:** Other. $6 daily fee/pet. Supervision.

◆◆ Sea Esta Motel III
(302) 227-4343. **$55-$179, 3 days notice.** 1409 Hwy 1. Jct Hwy 1 and Rodney St. Ext corridors. **Pets:** Other. $6 daily fee/pet. Supervision.

FENWICK ISLAND

◆◆ Atlantic Budget Inn
(302) 539-7673. **$79-$129, 5 days notice.** Rt 54 & Ocean Hwy. Jct of US 1 and SR 54. Ext corridors. **Pets:** Designated rooms, supervision.

MILLSBORO

◆◆ Atlantic Budget Inn-Millsboro
(302) 934-6711. **$99-$189.** 210 W DuPont Hwy. US 113. Ext corridors. **Pets:** Small. $15 deposit/room, $10 one-time fee/room. Designated rooms, no service, supervision, crate.

NEW CASTLE

◆◆ New Castle Travelodge
(302) 654-5544. **$48-$48.** 1213 West Ave. 0.3 mi n of jct I-295 and SR 9. Ext corridors. **Pets:** Medium. Supervision.

◆◆ Quality Inn Skyways
(302) 328-6666. **$84-$119.** 147 N DuPont Hwy. US 13, 40 and 301, from I-95, exit 5A; 0.6 mi s on Rt 141 to exit 1B. Ext corridors. **Pets:** Supervision.

◆◆ Rodeway Inn
(302) 328-6246. **$59-$74.** 111 S DuPont Hwy. US 13, 40 and 301, 2.5 mi s of jct I-295. Ext corridors. **Pets:** Other. Supervision.

NEWARK

◆◆◆ Homestead Village Guest Studios
(302) 283-0800. **$73-$78.** 333 Continental Dr. SR 58 (Churchman's Rd), 0.3 mi n of I-95, exit 4B; at rear of Christiana Executive Campus. Int corridors. **Pets:** Small. $135 one-time fee/pet. Supervision.

◆◆ Red Roof Inn-Wilmington
(302) 292-2870. **$57-$73.** 415 Stanton Christiana Rd. SR 7, 0.5 mi n of I-95, exit 4B. Ext corridors. **Pets:** Medium, other. Supervision.

◆◆◆ Residence Inn by Marriott
(302) 453-9200. **$88-$179.** 240 Chapman Rd. I-95, exit 3, 0.3 mi e on SR 273E, 0.5 mi n. Ext corridors. **Pets:** Small. No service, supervision, crate.

REHOBOTH BEACH

◆◆ Atlantic Budget Inn-Downtown
(302) 227-9446. **$89-$149, 7 days notice.** 154 Rehoboth Ave. Downtown at Rehoboth Ave and 2nd St. Ext corridors. **Pets:** No service, supervision, crate.

SEAFORD

AAA ◆◆◆ Best Western Seaford Inn **M** ☸
(302) 629-8385. **$69-$89.** 225 N Dual Hwy. 0.8 mi n on US 13 from SR 20. Ext corridors. **Pets:** Small. $10 one-time fee/room. Designated rooms, supervision.
[SAVE] [S] [X] [⌀] [🛏] [💻] [📶]

WILMINGTON

AAA ◆◆◆ Best Western Brandywine Valley
Inn **M** ☸
(302) 656-9436. **$72-$132.** 1807 Concord Pike. US 202, 0.5 mi n of jct I-95, exit 8. Ext corridors. **Pets:** Other. Supervision.
[S] [X] [⌀] [🛏] [💻] [📶]

WASHINGTON

Best Western-New Hampshire Suites Hotel
(202) 457-0565. **$169-$239.** 1121 New Hampshire Ave NW. Just ne of 22nd and L St nw. Int corridors. **Pets:** Small, other. Designated rooms, no service, supervision, crate.

Doubletree Guest Suites-New Hampshire Avenue
(202) 785-2000. **$109-$179.** 801 New Hampshire Ave NW. Just sw of I St NW; just sw of Washington Ave. Int corridors. **Pets:** $15 daily fee/pet. Designated rooms, no service, supervision, crate.

Doubletree Guest Suites-Pennsylvania Avenue
(202) 333-8060. **$199-$199.** 2500 Pennsylvania Ave NW. L and 25th sts NW; 2 blks from Foggy Bottom Metro Station. Int corridors. **Pets:** Small, other. $12 daily fee/pet. Designated rooms, supervision.

Four Seasons Hotel Washington
(202) 342-0444. **$350-$565.** 2800 Pennsylvania Ave NW. In Georgetown. Int corridors. **Pets:** Small, other. Designated rooms, no service, supervision, crate.

Georgetown Suites-Harbour Building
(202) 298-1600. **$165-$210.** 1000 29th St NW. In Georgetown; at jct of K and 29th sts. Int corridors. **Pets:** Small. Supervision.

The Hay-Adams Hotel
(202) 638-6600. **$300-$420.** 1 Lafayette Sq. NW. 16th and H sts NW, just n of the White House. Int corridors. **Pets:** Medium. Designated rooms, no service, supervision, crate.

Hilton Washington & Towers
(202) 483-3000. **$209-$399.** 1919 Connecticut Ave NW. Just n of Dupont Cir, at T St NW. Int corridors. **Pets:** Large. Supervision.

Holiday Inn-Central
(202) 483-2000. **$99-$199, 30 days notice.** 1501 Rhode Island Ave NW. Just e of Scott Circle. Int corridors. **Pets:** Small. No service, supervision, crate.

Holiday Inn Select
(202) 737-1200. **$149-$189, 3 days notice.** 1155 14th St NW. Massachusetts Ave, at Thomas Cir NW. Int corridors. **Pets:** Small. $25 one-time fee/room. No service, supervision, crate.

Hotel Sofitel Washington DC
(202) 797-2000. **$199-$239.** 1914 Connecticut Ave NW. Just n of Dupont Circle. Int corridors. **Pets:** Medium. Designated rooms, supervision.

Hotel Washington
(202) 638-5900. **$185-$260.** 515 15th St NW. Just e of the White House, at Pennsylvania Ave and 15th St NW; 2 blks from Metro Center Metro Station. Int corridors. **Pets:** Supervision.

The Jefferson Hotel
(202) 347-2200. **Call for rates.** 1200 16th St NW. 16th and M sts NW. Int corridors. **Pets:** Small. No service, supervision, crate.

Lincoln Suites Downtown
(202) 223-4320. **$149-$179.** 1823 L St NW. Between 18th and 19th sts NW. Int corridors. **Pets:** Supervision.

Loews L'Enfant Plaza Hotel
(202) 484-1000. **$189-$259.** 480 L'Enfant Plaza SW. Maine Ave exit, off I-395. Int corridors. **Pets:** Other. Supervision.

The Madison
(202) 862-1600. **$350-$400, 3 days notice.** 1177 15th St NW. 15th and M sts NW. Int corridors. **Pets:** Small. Designated rooms, no service, supervision, crate.

Marriott Wardman Park Hotel
(202) 328-2000. **$289-$289.** 2660 Woodley Rd NW at Connecti Ave. Just w of Connecticut Ave; at Woodley Park/Zoo Metro Station. Int corridors. **Pets:** Small. No service, supervision, crate.

Omni Shoreham Hotel
(202) 234-0700. **$189-$309.** 2500 Calvert St NW. Just w of Connecticut Ave; adjacent to Rock Creek Park. Int corridors. **Pets:** No service, supervision, crate.

Park Hyatt Washington D.C.
(202) 789-1234. **$300-$325.** 1201 24th St NW. 24th and M sts NW. Int corridors. **Pets:** Medium. Supervision.

Renaissance Mayflower Hotel
(202) 347-3000. **$149-$365.** 1127 Connecticut Ave NW. Just n of K St NW. Int corridors. **Pets:** Supervision.

The River Inn
(202) 337-7600. **$109-$160.** 924 25th St NW. Between K and I sts NW. Int corridors. **Pets:** Small. $50 one-time fee/room. No service, supervision, crate.

◆◆ **The Savoy Suites Georgetown** 🅷 🐾
(202) 337-9700. **$79-$199.** 2505 Wisconsin Ave NW. In upper Georgetown area; 0.3 mi s of Massachusetts Ave NW. Int corridors. **Pets:** Supervision.
(ASK) (S🐾) (✕) (🝱) (🅗) (💻) (🍽)

◆◆◆◆ **Swissotel Washington, The**
Watergate 🅷 🐾
(202) 965-2300. **$325-$325.** 2650 Virginia Ave NW. Adjacent to The Kennedy Center. Int corridors. **Pets:** No service, supervision, crate.
(ASK) (✕) (🝱) (🐾) (🅗) (💻) (✕🐾)

(AAA) ◆◆◆◆ **The Washington Monarch Hotel** 🅷
(202) 429-2400. **$298-$298.** 2401 M St NW. 24th and M sts NW. Int corridors. **Pets:** Small. No service, supervision, crate.
(SAVE) (S🐾) (✕) (🝱) (🍽)

(AAA) ◆◆◆◆ **The Westin Fairfax** 🅷 🐾
(202) 293-2100. **$155-$325.** 2100 Massachusetts Ave NW. At 21st St. Int corridors. **Pets:** $100 one-time fee/room. Supervision.
(S🐾) (✕) (🝱) (💻)

◆◆◆◆ **The Willard Inter-Continental** 🅷
(202) 628-9100. **$395-$510.** 1401 Pennsylvania Ave NW. Just e of The White House. Int corridors. **Pets:** Small. No service, supervision, crate.
(✕) (🝱) (🐾) (💻) (🍽)

◆◆◆ **Wyndham Washington DC** 🅷
(202) 429-1700. **$219.** 1400 M St NW. At Thomas Cir. Int corridors. **Pets:** No service, supervision, crate.
(ASK) (S🐾) (✕) (🝱) (💻) (🍽)

CITY INDEX

ALACHUA

AAA ◆◆ Comfort Inn **M** ❀
(904) 462-2414. **$55-$125, 7 days notice.** 15405 Martin Luther King Blvd. I-75 exit 78, just e on US 441. Ext corridors. **Pets:** Small, dogs only. $10 daily fee/pet, $10 one-time fee/pet. Designated rooms, no service, supervision, crate.

SAVE S🅓 ✕ 🔲 🖾

APALACHICOLA

AAA ◆◆◆ The Gibson Inn **CI** ❀
(850) 653-2191. **$75-$120.** Market St & Ave C. On US 98 at w end of bridge. Int corridors. **Pets:** Large. $5 one-time fee/room. Supervision.

SAVE S🅓 ✕

AAA ◆◆ Rancho Inn **M** ❀
(850) 653-9435. **$47-$73.** 240 Hwy 98. 0n US 98, 1 mi w. Ext corridors. **Pets:** Other. $6 daily fee/pet. No service, supervision, crate.

SAVE ✕ 🖳

ARCADIA

◆◆◆ Best Western Arcadia Inn **M** ❀
(863) 494-4884. **$79-$119.** 504 S Brevard Ave. 0.6 mi s of SR 70 on US 17. Ext corridors. **Pets:** Small, other. $15 one-time fee/pet. Supervision.

ASK ✕ 🔲 🖾

BOCA RATON

(AAA) ◆◆◆ Boca Raton Radisson Suite Hotel Ⓜ ❀
(561) 483-3600. **$199-$245.** 7920 Glades Rd. SR 808, facing Florida Tpke exit 75; in Arvida Parkway Center. Int corridors. **Pets:** Medium, other. $100 one-time fee/room. Supervision.

(SAVE) (S₆) (✕) (≋) (🛉) (💻) (☎)

◆◆◆ Doubletree Guest Suites-Boca Raton Ⓜ
(561) 997-9500. **$139-$259.** 701 NW 53rd St. In Arvida Corp Park; just w of jct I-95, exit 40 (Yamato Rd). Ext corridors. **Pets:** Supervision.

(ASK) (✕) (≋) (🛉) (💻) (🍴) (☎)

(AAA) ◆◆◆ Ramada Inn Ⓜ ❀
(561) 395-6850. **$105-$135.** 2901 N Federal Hwy. US 1, 1 mi n of jct SR 808 (Glades Rd). Ext corridors. **Pets:** Medium. $100 deposit/room, $10 daily fee/pet. Designated rooms, no service, supervision, crate.

(SAVE) (✕) (≋) (🛉) (💻) (🍴) (☎)

◆◆◆ Residence Inn-By Marriott-Boca Raton Ⓐ
(561) 994-3222. **$159-$229.** 525 NW 77th St. Jct I-95, just w of Congress Ave, exit 40C. Ext corridors. **Pets:** No service, supervision, crate.

(ASK) (S₆) (✕) (≋) (🛉) (💻) (☎) (✕)

BONIFAY

(AAA) ◆◆ Best Western-Tivoli Inn Ⓜ
(850) 547-4251. **$50-$60.** 2004 S Waukesha St. SR 79, 0.5 mi n of I-10, exit 17. Ext corridors. **Pets:** Small. No service, supervision, crate.

(SAVE) (✕) (☎) (✕)

BRADENTON

(AAA) ◆◆ Econo Lodge Ⓜ
(941) 758-7199. **$59-$95.** 6727 14th St W (US 41 S). US 41, 2 mi s of jct SR 70. Ext corridors. **Pets:** Supervision.

(SAVE) (✕) (🛉) (☎)

(AAA) ◆◆ Howard Johnson Express Inn Ⓜ ❀
(941) 756-8399. **$55-$89, 7 days notice.** 6511 14th (US 41) St W. US 41, 1.5 mi s of jct SR 70. Ext corridors. **Pets:** Medium. $5 daily fee/pet, $5 one-time fee/pet. No service, supervision, crate.

(SAVE) (✕) (🛉) (💻) (☎)

(AAA) ◆◆◆ Park Inn Club & Breakfast Ⓜ ❀
(941) 795-4633. **$104-$134.** 4450 47th St W. 2 mi w of jct US 41 and SR 684 (Cortez Rd), just s. Int corridors. **Pets:** Medium. $5 daily fee/room. No service, supervision, crate.

(SAVE) (✕) (≋) (🛉) (☎)

(AAA) ◆◆ Super 8 Motel Ⓜ
(941) 756-6656. **$50-$74.** 6516 14th St W. US 41, 1.5 mi s of jct SR 70. Ext corridors. **Pets:** Designated rooms, no service, supervision, crate.

(SAVE) (S₆) (✕) (🛉) (☎)

BRADENTON BEACH

◆◆◆ Tortuga Inn Ⓜ ❀
(941) 778-6611. **$100-$230, 3 days notice.** 1325 Gulf Dr N. SR 789, 0.3 mi n of jct SR 684. Ext corridors. **Pets:** Small, other. $25 one-time fee/room. Designated rooms, supervision.

(✕) (🛉) (☎) (✕)

(AAA) ◆◆◆ Tradewinds Resort Ⓐ ❀
(941) 779-0010. **$116-$263.** 1603 Gulf Dr N. SR 789, 0.5 mi n of jct SR 684. Ext corridors. **Pets:** Medium. $25 one-time fee/room. Designated rooms, supervision.

(✕) (🛉) (💻) (☎) (✕)

BROOKSVILLE

◆◆ Holiday Inn Ⓜ
(352) 796-9481. **Call for rates.** 30307 Cortez Blvd. I-75 exit 61, just w on SR 50. Ext corridors. **Pets:** Designated rooms, supervision.

(ASK) (✕) (✎) (🛉) (💻) (🍴) (☎) (✕)

BUNNELL

(AAA) ◆◆◆ Best Western Plantation Inn Ⓜ
(904) 437-3737. **$50-$50.** 2251 S Old Dixie Hwy. At I-95, exit 90. Ext corridors. **Pets:** No service, supervision, crate.

(SAVE) (S₆) (✕) (🍴) (☎)

BUSHNELL

(AAA) ◆◆ Best Western Guest House Inn Ⓜ ❀
(352) 793-5010. **$49-$79.** 2224 W SR 48. I-75, just e. Ext corridors. **Pets:** Small. $10 daily fee/pet. No service, supervision, crate.

(SAVE) (✕) (≋) (🛉) (☎) (✕)

CAPE CORAL

(AAA) ◆ Quality Inn-Nautilus Ⓜ ❀
(941) 542-2121. **$90-$110, 7 days notice.** 1538 Cape Coral Pkwy. Jct Del Prado Blvd. Int corridors. **Pets:** Other. $10 daily fee/pet. Designated rooms, supervision.

(SAVE) (✕) (≋) (🛉) (💻) (☎)

CARRABELLE

◆◆◆ The Moorings At Carrabelle Ⓜ ❀
(850) 697-2800. **$85-$85.** 1000 US 98. US 98 just e of bridge. Ext corridors. **Pets:** Other. $50 deposit/pet, $10 daily fee/pet. Supervision.

(ASK) (S₆) (🛉) (💻) (☎) (✕)

CEDAR KEY

(AAA) ◆◆ Park Place Motel & Condominiums Ⓒ ❀
(352) 543-5737. **$65-$80.** 211 2nd St. 2nd St at A St. Ext corridors. **Pets:** Other. $7 daily fee/pet. Designated rooms, supervision.

(SAVE) (✕) (🛉) (💻)

CHARLOTTE HARBOR

◆◆ **Banana Bay Waterfront Motel** Ⓜ ✿
(941) 743-4441. **$49-$72, 3 days notice.** 23285 Bayshore Rd. At jct US 41. Ext corridors. **Pets:** Small. $15 one-time fee/room. No service, supervision, crate.

⟨ASK⟩ ⟨S⟩ ⟨✕⟩ 🛏 💻 ⟨✕⟩

CHIEFLAND

⚠ ◆◆ **Best Western Suwannee Valley**
     Inn Ⓜ ✿
(352) 493-0663. **$50-$75.** 1125 N Young Blvd. On US 19/98; just n of jct US 129. Ext corridors. **Pets:** Medium. $6 daily fee/pet, $6 one-time fee/pet. Designated rooms, no service, supervision, crate.

⟨SAVE⟩ ⟨✕⟩ 🛏 ⟨⌂⟩

CHIPLEY

◆◆ **Super 8 Motel** Ⓜ
(850) 638-8530. **$40-$45.** 1700 Main St. I-10, exit 18; nw corner. Ext corridors. **Pets:** No service, supervision, crate.

⟨ASK⟩ ⟨S⟩ ⟨✕⟩

COCOA

⚠ ◆◆ **Best Western Cocoa Inn** Ⓜ
(321) 632-1065. **$69-$89, 7 days notice.** 4225 W King St. SR 520, 0.3 mi e of jct I-95, exit 75. Ext corridors. **Pets:** Small. Supervision.

⟨SAVE⟩ ⟨✕⟩ ⟨♪⟩ ⟨⌂⟩ 🛏 ⟨⌂⟩

⚠ ◆◆ **Econo Lodge-Space Center** Ⓜ
(321) 632-4561. **$45-$95.** 3220 N Cocoa Blvd. US 1, just n of jct SR 528. Ext corridors. **Pets:** No service, supervision, crate.

⟨SAVE⟩ ⟨S⟩ ⟨✕⟩ 🛏 💻 ⟨⌂⟩ ⟨⌂⟩

⚠ ◆◆ **Ramada Inn Cocoa-Kennedy Space**
     Center Ⓜ ✿
(321) 631-1210. **$89-$99.** 900 Friday Rd. SR 524, w of jct I-95, exit 76. Ext corridors. **Pets:** Small, other. $25 deposit/room. No service, supervision, crate.

⟨SAVE⟩ ⟨✕⟩ 🛏 ⟨⌂⟩ ⟨⌂⟩ ⟨✕⟩

⚠ ◆◆ **Super 8 Motel** Ⓜ ✿
(321) 631-1212. **$69-$79.** 900 Friday Rd. US I-95 exit 76; 0.5 mi sw. Ext corridors. **Pets:** Small, other. $25 deposit/room. No service, supervision, crate.

⟨SAVE⟩ ⟨✕⟩ 🛏 ⟨⌂⟩ ⟨✕⟩

COCOA BEACH

⚠ ◆◆◆ **Best Western Ocean Inn** Ⓜ ✿
(321) 784-2550. **$89-$169.** 5500 N Atlantic Ave. SR A1A, 0.8 mi n of jct SR 520. Ext corridors. **Pets:** Very small. No service, supervision, crate.

⟨SAVE⟩ ⟨✕⟩ ⟨♪⟩ 🛏 💻 ⟨⌂⟩

⚠ ◆◆◆ **Days Inn Oceanfront** Ⓜ ✿
(321) 783-7621. **$89-$199.** 5600 N Atlantic Ave. SR A1A, 0.8 mi n of jct SR 520. Ext/int corridors. **Pets:** Small. Designated rooms, no service, supervision, crate.

⟨SAVE⟩ ⟨✕⟩ ⟨⌂⟩ ⟨♪⟩ ⟨⌂⟩ 🛏 💻 ⟨⌂⟩ ⟨✕⟩

⚠ ◆◆ **Econo Lodge Resort of Cocoa**
     Beach Ⓜ ✿
(321) 783-2252. **$45-$125.** 1275 N Atlantic Ave. 1.7 mi s of SR 520 on A1A. Ext corridors. **Pets:** Other. Designated rooms, supervision.

⟨SAVE⟩ ⟨✕⟩ 🛏 💻 ⟨⌂⟩ ⟨⌂⟩

⚠ ◆◆ **South Beach Inn** Ⓜ
(321) 784-3333. **$80-$130.** 1701 S Atlantic Ave. SR A1A northbound, 5 mi s of jct SR 520 at Indian Village Tr, 1.5 mi n of Patrick AFB. Ext corridors. **Pets:** Small. No service, supervision, crate.

⟨SAVE⟩ ⟨✕⟩

⚠ ◆◆ **Surf Studio Beach Resort** Ⓜ ✿
(321) 783-7100. **$80-$145, 7 days notice.** 1801 S Atlantic Ave. SR A1A northbound, 5 mi s of jct SR 520 at Francis St, 1.3 mi n of Partrick AFB. Ext corridors. **Pets:** $20 daily fee/pet. No service, supervision, crate.

🛏 💻 ⟨⌂⟩ ⟨✕⟩

CRESCENT CITY

◆◆ **Lake View Motel** Ⓜ ✿
(904) 698-1090. **$38-$50.** 1004 N Summit St. 1 mi n on US 17. Ext corridors. **Pets:** Small, other. No service, supervision, crate.

⟨✕⟩ 🛏 💻 ⟨⌂⟩

CRESTVIEW

◆◆ **Holiday Inn** Ⓜ ✿
(850) 682-6111. **$64-$70.** 4050 S Ferdon Blvd. SR 85, 0.5 mi s of I-10, exit 12. Ext corridors. **Pets:** Small. $25 deposit/room. No service, supervision, crate.

⟨ASK⟩ ⟨S⟩ ⟨✕⟩ ⟨⌂⟩ 💻 ⟨⌂⟩ ⟨⌂⟩

⚠ ◆◆ **Super 8 Motel** Ⓜ ✿
(850) 682-9649. **$38-$63.** 3925 S Ferdon Blvd. I-10, exit 12; 0.3 mi s. Ext corridors. **Pets:** Other. $5 one-time fee/room. No service, supervision, crate.

⟨SAVE⟩ ⟨S⟩ ⟨✕⟩ 🛏

CROSS CITY

⚠ ◆◆ **Carriage Inn** Ⓜ ✿
(352) 498-0001. **$29-$45.** 280 E Main (US 19/98/27A). 0.5 mi s on US 19, 27A and 98. Ext corridors. **Pets:** Other. $5 daily fee/pet. Supervision.

⟨SAVE⟩ ⟨✕⟩ ⟨⌂⟩ ⟨⌂⟩

CRYSTAL RIVER

⚠ ◆◆ **Best Western Crystal River**
     Resort Ⓡ ✿
(352) 795-3171. **$75-$105.** 614 NW Hwy 19. On US 19/98, 0.8 mi n of jct SR 44. Ext corridors. **Pets:** Small, other. $3 daily fee/pet. Supervision.

⟨SAVE⟩ ⟨✕⟩ ⟨♪⟩ ⟨⌂⟩ 🛏 ⟨⌂⟩ ⟨✕⟩

DANIA

◆◆◆ Sheraton Fort Lauderdale Airport
Hotel 🅗 ❀

(954) 920-3500. **$139-$179.** 1825 Griffin Rd. Adjoining Design Center of the Americas at jct I-95, exit 26. Int corridors. **Pets:** Small. $50 one-time fee/room. No service, supervision, crate.

A$K ⊠ ⑁ ⑂ 🄴 🄱 🄻 🄸 🄰 ⊠

DAYTONA BEACH

◉◉ ◆◆ Breakers Beach Oceanfront
Motel 🅜 ❀

(904) 252-0863. **$45-$91, 21 days notice.** 27 S Ocean Ave. Ext corridors. **Pets:** Medium, dogs only. $10 daily fee/room. Supervision.

SAVE 🆂 ⊠ 🄱 🄻 🄰

⊕⊕⊕ ◆ Budget Host Inn, The Candlelight 🅜

(904) 252-1142. **$32-$42.** 1305 S Ridgewood Ave. US 1, 0.5 mi n of SR 400. Ext corridors. **Pets:** Small. No service, supervision, crate.

SAVE ⊠ 🄱 🄻

◆ Cardinal Motel 🅜 ❀

(904) 252-1035. **$50-$70, 21 days notice.** 738 N Atlantic Ave. Hwy US 92E to Atlantic Ave, 1.5 mi n. Ext/int corridors. **Pets:** Small. $100 deposit/pet, $10 daily fee/pet. No service, supervision, crate.

A$K 🄱 🄰

◉◉◉ ◆◆◆ The Plaza Resort & Spa 🅗

(904) 255-4471. **$149-$189.** 600 N Atlantic Ave. SR A1A, 1 mi n of US 92. Int corridors. **Pets:** Designated rooms, supervision.

SAVE ⊠ ⑂ 🄱 🄻 🄸 🄰 ⊠

◆◆◆ Radisson Resort 🅗 ❀

(904) 239-9800. **$109-$169.** 640 N Atlantic Ave. SR A1A, 1 mi n of jct SR 90. Int corridors. **Pets:** Small. $25 one-time fee/pet. No service, supervision, crate.

A$K 🆂 ⊠ ⑁ ⑂ 🄴 🄱 🄻 🄸 🄰 ⊠

⊕⊕⊕ ◆◆ Ramada Inn Speedway 🅜 ❀

(904) 255-2422. **$79-$99.** 1798 W International Speedway Blvd. 3 mi w on US 92, 2 mi e of I-95, exit 87. Ext corridors. **Pets:** Small, other. $25 one-time fee/room. Supervision.

SAVE ⊠ ⑂ 🄱 🄸 🄰

⊕⊕⊕ ◆ Scottish Inn 🅜 ❀

(904) 258-5742. **$95-$120.** 1515 S Ridgewood Ave. US 1, just n of SR 400. Ext corridors. **Pets:** Very small, dogs only. $25 deposit/pet, $5 daily fee/pet. Designated rooms, supervision.

SAVE ⊠ 🄱 🄰

DAYTONA BEACH SHORES

⊕⊕⊕ ◆◆ Atlantic Ocean Palm Inn 🅜 ❀

(904) 761-8450. **$60-$190, 21 days notice.** 3247 S Atlantic Ave. SR A1A, 5 mi s of jct US 92. Ext corridors. **Pets:** Small, dogs only. $15 one-time fee/room. Designated rooms, no service, supervision, crate.

SAVE ⊠ 🄱 🄰

⊕⊕⊕ ◆◆◆ Quality Inn Ocean Palms 🅜 ❀

(904) 255-0476. **$120-$279.** 2323 S Atlantic Ave. SR A1A, 2.5 mi s of jct US 92. Ext corridors. **Pets:** Other. $50 deposit/room. Supervision.

SAVE 🆂 ⊠ ⑁ ⑂ 🄴 🄱 🄻 🄸 🄰 ⊠

DE FUNIAK SPRINGS

◆◆ Best Western Crossroads Inn 🅜 ❀

(850) 892-5111. **$59-$69, 7 days notice.** 2343 Freeport Rd. Jct US 331 and I-10, exit 14. Ext/int corridors. **Pets:** Medium, other. Designated rooms, supervision.

A$K 🆂 ⊠ 🄸 🄰

⊕⊕⊕ ◆◆ Days Inn 🅜 ❀

(850) 892-6115. **$50-$85.** 472 Hugh Adams Rd. Jct I-10, exit 14 and US 331. Ext corridors. **Pets:** Medium. $10 daily fee/pet, $10 one-time fee/pet. Designated rooms, supervision.

SAVE ⊠ 🄱

DELAND

◆◆◆ Holiday Inn 🅜 ❀

(904) 738-5200. **$85-$109.** 350 E International Speedway Blvd. 0.3 mi ne on US 92 from jct US 17. Int corridors. **Pets:** $10 daily fee/pet. Supervision.

A$K ⊠ 🄱 🄻 🄸 🄰

DELRAY BEACH

◆◆ The Colony Hotel & Cabana Club 🅗 ❀

(561) 276-4123. **$69-$119, 3 days notice.** 525 E Atlantic Ave. Center; on SR 806 at jct US 1 northbound. Int corridors. **Pets:** Other. $25 daily fee/pet. Supervision.

⊠ 🄸 ⊠

ELKTON

⊕⊕⊕ ◆◆ Comfort Inn St. Augustine 🅜 ❀

(904) 829-3435. **$49-$149.** 2625 SR 207. I-95, exit 94, just w. Ext corridors. **Pets:** Other. $10 daily fee/room. Supervision.

SAVE ⊠ 🄰 CTV

ELLENTON

◆◆◆ Best Western Inn 🅜 ❀

(941) 729-8505. **$80-$110.** 5218 17th St E. I-75, exit 43; 0.3 mi w on US 301, just n on 51st Ave E, just e. Ext corridors. **Pets:** Small, other. $10 one-time fee/room. Supervision.

A$K 🆂 ⊠ 🄱 🄰

◆◆◆ Shoney's Inn Lakeside 🅜 ❀

(941) 729-0600. **Call for rates.** 4915 17th St E. I-75, exit 43; 0.3 mi w on US 301, just n on 51st Ave E, just w. Ext corridors. **Pets:** Small. $10 one-time fee/room. No service, supervision, crate.

⊠ ⑁ 🄴 🄱 🄰

FLAGLER BEACH

⊕⊕⊕ ◆◆ Beach Front Motel 🅜 ❀

(904) 439-0089. **$45-$50.** 1544 S A1A. On SR A1A, 1 mi s of SR 100. Ext corridors. **Pets:** Medium. $20 one-time fee/room. No service, supervision, crate.

SAVE ⊠ 🄱 🄻 ⊠

FORT LAUDERDALE METROPOLITAN AREA

CORAL SPRINGS

◆◆◆ La Quinta Inn 🅼 ❀
(954) 753-9000. **$105-$135.** 3701 University Dr. SR 817; just n of jct Sample Rd (SR 834). Int corridors. **Pets:** Small, other. No service, supervision, crate.

(A$K) (✕) (🛇) (🏃) (🐾) (📶) (💻) (🛏)

🆔 ◆◆◆ Radisson Resort Coral Springs 🅼🅸 ❀
(954) 753-5598. **$169-$189** (no credit cards). 11775 Heron Bay Blvd. From Sawgrass Expwy/SR 869 exit Coral Ridge Dr n for 0.3 mi then left onto Heron Bay Blvd then first right. Int corridors. **Pets:** Small, other. $100 deposit/room, $50 one-time fee/room. Designated rooms, no service, supervision, crate.

(SAVE) (S🔒) (✕) (🛇) (🏃) (💻) (🍴) (🛏) (✕)

🆔 ◆◆ Wellesley Inn & Suites 🅼
(954) 344-2200. **$84-$109.** 3100 N University Dr. SR 817; just s of jct Sample Rd (SR 834). Int corridors. **Pets:** Small. No service, supervision, crate.

(SAVE) (✕) (🛇) (🐾) (🏃) (💻) (🛏)

DAVIE

◆◆ Homestead Village Guest Studios
    Davie/Plantation 🅼
(954) 476-1211. **Call for rates.** 7550 SR 84 E. I-595 exit University Dr/SR 817, to SR 84E, then 0.3 mi. Ext corridors. **Pets:** Designated rooms, supervision.

(✕) (🛇) (🛇) (🐾) (🏃) (💻)

DEERFIELD BEACH

🆔 ◆◆ Comfort Inn-Oceanside 🅼 ❀
(954) 428-0650. **$89-$199.** 50 SE 20th Ave. SR A1A, at jct SR 810 (Hillsboro Blvd). Int corridors. **Pets:** Small, other. $25 one-time fee/pet. No service, supervision, crate.

(SAVE) (S🔒) (✕) (🛇) (🏃) (💻) (🍴) (🛏)

🆔 ◆◆◆ Comfort Suites 🅼 ❀
(954) 570-8887. **$119-$189.** 1040 E Newport Center Dr. Jct I-95, exit 36C, SW 10th St. Ext corridors. **Pets:** Dogs only. Supervision.

(SAVE) (S🔒) (✕) (🛇) (🏃) (🛏)

◆◆◆ La Quinta Inn 🅼 ❀
(954) 421-1004. **$99-$115.** 351 W Hillsboro Blvd. SR 810, 0.3 mi e of jct I-95, exit 37. Ext corridors. **Pets:** Small, other. No service, supervision, crate.

(A$K) (✕) (🛇) (🛇) (💻) (🛏)

🆔 ◆◆◆ Quality Suites 🅼🅸 ❀
(954) 570-8888. **$129-$199.** 1050 E Newport Center Dr. Jct I-95, exit 36C, SW 10th St. Ext corridors. **Pets:** Dogs only. Supervision.

(SAVE) (S🔒) (✕) (🛇) (🏃) (💻) (🍴) (🛏) (✕)

FORT LAUDERDALE

🆔 ◆◆◆ AmeriSuites Fort Lauderdale/17th
    Street 🅼
(954) 763-7670. **$174.** 1851 SE Tenth Ave. From A1A/17th St Cswy, just s. Int corridors. **Pets:** Small. No service, supervision, crate.

(SAVE) (✕) (🛇) (🛇) (🐾) (🏃) (💻) (🛏)

◆◆ Birch Patio Motel 🅼 ❀
(954) 563-9540. **$35-$95.** 617 N Birch Rd. 0.4 mi s on SR A1A from jct SR 838 (Sunrise Blvd), w on Aurumar St. Ext corridors. **Pets:** $10 daily fee/pet. Designated rooms, supervision.

(A$K) (S🔒) (✕) (🏃) (💻) (🛏)

◆◆◆ The Doubletree Guest Suites/Galleria/
    Intracoastal Waterway 🅷
(954) 565-3800. **$239.** 2670 E Sunrise Blvd. Intracoastal Bridge on Sunrise Blvd (SR 838); 3 blks w of jct A1A. Int corridors. **Pets:** Supervision.

(A$K) (S🔒) (✕) (🛇) (🏃) (💻) (🍴) (🛏) (✕)

◆◆◆ DoubleTree Oceanfront Hotel 🅼🅸 ❀
(954) 524-8733. **Call for rates.** 440 Seabreeze Blvd. Just s of Las Olas Blvd, on SR A1A. Int corridors. **Pets:** Small, other. Supervision.

(✕) (🛇) (🏃) (💻) (🍴) (🛏)

◆◆◆ La Quinta Inn-Cypress Creek 🅼
(954) 491-7666. **$99-$119.** 999 W Cypress Creek Rd. 0.8 mi w of jct I-95, exit 33 (33B northbound) at Powerline Rd. Int corridors. **Pets:** Small. No service, supervision, crate.

(A$K) (✕) (🛇) (🏃) (💻) (🛏)

🆔 ◆ Motel 6–55 🅼 ❀
(954) 760-7999. **$56-$72.** 1801 SR 84. I-95, exit 54 (SR 84E); just e, then U-turn at light. **Pets:** Small. No service, supervision, crate.

(✕) (🛇) (🛏)

🆔 ◆◆ Red Roof Inn 🅼
(954) 776-6333. **$90-$101.** 4800 NW 9th Ave (Powerline Rd). On Powerline Rd; just sw of jct Commercial Blvd and I-95, exit 32. Int corridors. **Pets:** Medium. Supervision.

(SAVE) (✕) (🛇) (🐾) (🛏)

🆔 ◆◆◆ The Westin, Fort Lauderdale 🅷
(954) 772-1331. **$129-$209.** 400 Corporate Dr. Just e of I-95, exit 33; in Radice Corporate Park. Int corridors. **Pets:** Small. Supervision.

(✕) (🛇) (🐾) (💻) (🍴) (🛏) (✕)

HOLLYWOOD

🆔 ◆◆◆ Clarion Hotel Hollywood Beach 🅷
(954) 458-1900. **$90-$229.** 4000 S Ocean Dr. SR A1A, at jct SR 858 (Hallandale Beach Blvd). Int corridors. **Pets:** Designated rooms, no service, supervision, crate.

(SAVE) (✕) (🛇) (🐾) (🏃) (💻) (🍴) (🛏) (✕)

🆔 ◆◆◆ Comfort Inn-Ft. Lauderdale/Hollywood
    Airport 🅼
(954) 922-1600. **$54-$129, 7 days notice.** 2520 Stirling Rd. Just e of jct I-95, exit 25, 2 mi s of airport; 4 mi sw of airport entrance. Ext corridors. **Pets:** No service, supervision, crate.

(SAVE) (✕) (🛇) (🛇) (🐾) (💻) (🛏)

◆◆◆ Days Inn Fort Lauderdale/Hollywood Airport South Ⓜ ❀

(954) 923-7300. **$69-$159.** 2601 N 29th Ave. SR 822 (Sheridan St), just nw of I-95, exit 24. Int corridors. **Pets:** $10 one-time fee/pet. Designated rooms, supervision.

ⒶⓈⓀ ⊠ 🕮 🖬 🔄

◆◆◆ La Quinta Inn & Suites Ⓜ

(954) 922-2295. **$109-$119.** 2620 N 26th Ave. I-95, exit 24 Sheridan St (SR 822), just e to Oakwood, then just left. Int corridors. **Pets:** Small. No service, supervision, crate.

ⒶⓈⓀ ⊠ 🕭 🕮 🕹 🖬 🖃 🔄 ⊠

LAUDERDALE BY THE SEA

ⓐⓐⓐ ◆◆◆ Courtyard Villa Ⓜ ❀

(954) 776-1164. **$120-$120, 30 days notice.** 4312 El Mar Dr. From Commerical Blvd (SR 870) just s. Ext corridors. **Pets:** Small. $100 deposit/room. No service, supervision, crate.

ⓈⒶⓋⒺ ⊠ 🖬 🖃 🔄 ⊠

PEMBROKE PINES

◆◆◆ Grand Palms Golf & Country Club Resort Ⓡ ❀

(954) 431-8800. **$135-$155.** 110 Grand Palms Dr. SR 820, 0.4 mi w of jct I-75, exit 5B (Pines Blvd). Ext corridors. **Pets:** Small. Supervision.

ⒶⓈⓀ Ⓢₒ ⊠ 🖬 🖃 🎢 🔄 ⊠

PLANTATION

ⓐⓐⓐ ◆◆◆ AmeriSuites Plantation Ⓜ

(954) 370-2220. **$116-$134.** 8530 W Broward Blvd. I-595, exit 5 and Pine Island Rd; 1.3 mi n, behind the Westside Corporate Center. Int corridors. **Pets:** Small. No service, supervision, crate.

ⓈⒶⓋⒺ ⊠ 🕭 🕮 🕹 🖬 🖃 🔄

ⓐⓐⓐ ◆◆◆ Holiday Inn Plantation Ⓜ ❀

(954) 472-5600. **$159.** 1711 N University Dr. SR 817, just s of jct SR 838, Sunrise Blvd. Ext/int corridors. **Pets:** $10 daily fee/room. Supervision.

ⓈⒶⓋⒺ ⊠ 🕮 🕹 🖬 🖃 🎢 🔄

◆◆◆ La Quinta Inn & Suites Ⓜ

(954) 476-6047. **$85-$129** (no credit cards). 8101 Peters Rd. From I-595 exit 6, University Dr (SR 817 N), just w of University (SR 817); in the Crossroad Office Park. Int corridors. **Pets:** Supervision.

ⒶⓈⓀ ⊠ 🕭 🕮 🕹 🖬 🖃 🔄

◆◆◆ Residence Inn by Marriott-Plantation Ⓐ

(954) 723-0300. **$169.** 130 N University Dr. University Dr (SR 817), just n of jct Broward Blvd (SR 842). Int corridors. **Pets:** Supervision.

ⒶⓈⓀ ⊠ 🕭 🕮 🕹 🖬 🖃 🔄 ⊠

ⓐⓐⓐ ◆◆◆ Wellesley Inn & Suites Ⓜ

(954) 473-8257. **$110-$110.** 7901 SW 6th St. 0.3 mi w of University Dr (SR 817), at s edge of Broward Blvd (SR 842). Int corridors. **Pets:** Small. Designated rooms, no service, supervision, crate.

ⓈⒶⓋⒺ ⊠ 🕮 🕹 🖬 🖃 🔄

POMPANO BEACH

ⓐⓐⓐ ◆◆ Sea Castle Resort Inn Ⓜ ❀

(954) 941-2570. **$91-$169.** 730 N Ocean Blvd. On SR A1A; 1 mi n of jct SR 814 (Atlantic Blvd). Ext corridors. **Pets:** Other. $15 daily fee/room. Supervision.

ⓈⒶⓋⒺ ⊠ 🖬 🖃 🔄 ⊠

ⓐⓐⓐ ◆◆◆ Wellesley Inn & Suites Ⓜ

(954) 783-1050. **$119-$129.** 1401 SW 15th St. From I-95 exit 33B Cypress Creek Rd to Andrews Ave, just s, then turn left onto McNab St. Int corridors. **Pets:** Small. Designated rooms, supervision.

ⓈⒶⓋⒺ Ⓢₒ ⊠ 🕮 🕹 🖬 🖃 🔄

SUNRISE

◆◆◆ Baymont Inn-Sunrise/Sawgrass Ⓜ

(954) 846-1200. **$96-$106.** 13651 NW 2nd St. SW 136th Ave, 0.3 mi n of Jct I-595, exit 1 and SR 84; 0.5 mi e of jct I-75 and Sawgrass Expwy; adjoining the Blockbuster Family Entertainment Park. Int corridors. **Pets:** Medium. Designated rooms, no service, supervision, crate.

⊠ 🕮 🕹 🖬 🖃 🔄

ⓐⓐⓐ ◆◆◆ Wellesley Inn & Suites Ⓜ

(954) 845-9929. **$110-$110.** 13600 NW 2nd St. SW 136th Ave, 0.3 mi n of jct I-595, exit 1 and SR 84; 0.5 mi e of jct I-75 and Sawgrass Expwy; adjoining Blockbuster Family Entertainment Park. Int corridors. **Pets:** Very small. Supervision.

ⓈⒶⓋⒺ ⊠ 🕮 🕹 🖬 🖃 🔄

TAMARAC

◆◆ Baymont Inn & Suites-Fort Lauderdale Ⓜ

(954) 485-7900. **$86-$86.** 3800 W Commercial Blvd. SR 870 (Commercial Blvd); 0.8 mi e of Florida Tpke, exit 62, just e of jct SR 7 and US 441. Int corridors. **Pets:** Supervision.

⊠ 🖬 🖃 🔄

◆◆ Homestead Village Guest Studios-Fort Lauderdale Ⓜ

(954) 733-6644. **$62-$110, 7 days notice.** 3873 W Commercial Blvd. SR 870 (Commercial Blvd), 0.7 mi e of Florida Tpke, exit 62, then just e of jct SR 7 and US 441. Ext corridors. **Pets:** Small. Supervision.

⊠ 🕮 🕹 🖬 🖃 ⒸⓉⓋ

ⓐⓐⓐ ◆◆ Wellesley Inn & Suites Ⓜ

(954) 484-6909. **$95-$95.** 5070 N SR 7. SR 7 and US 441; just n of jct SR 870 (Commercial Blvd); 0.5 mi e of Florida Tpke exit 62. Int corridors. **Pets:** Medium. Designated rooms, no service, supervision, crate.

ⓈⒶⓋⒺ Ⓢₒ ⊠ 🕮 🕹 🖬 🖃 🔄

❀ **END METROPOLITAN AREA** ❀

FORT MYERS

◆◆ Baymont Inn M
(941) 275-3500. **$98-$98, 30 days notice.** 2717 Colonial Blvd. I-75, exit 22, 4 mi w on SR 884. Ext corridors. **Pets:** Small. Supervision.

(A$K) (S₆) (X) (∅) (⊟) (⊑) (⌂)

⊕ ◆◆ Best Western Springs Resort MI ☙
(941) 267-7900. **$99-$120.** 18051 S Tamiami Tr. On US 41 at jct Constitution Blvd. Ext corridors. **Pets:** Small, dogs only. $100 deposit/pet, $10 daily fee/pet, $10 one-time fee/pet. Supervision.

(SAVE) (S₆) (X) (⊟) (¶) (⌂)

⊕ ◆◆◆ Comfort Suites Airport M ☙
(941) 768-0005. **$119-$149.** 13651A Indian Paint Ln. I-75 exit 21; just w. Int corridors. **Pets:** Medium, other. $10 daily fee/room. Supervision.

(SAVE) (X) (∅) (⊟) (⊑) (⌂)

◆◆ Days Inn Fort Myers South M ☙
(941) 936-1311. **$38-$114.** 11435 Cleveland Ave S. On US 41, 1.6 mi n of jct Daniels Pkwy. Ext corridors. **Pets:** Other. Supervision.

(A$K) (X) (∅) (⊟) (⌂)

◆◆◆ La Quinta Inn M
(941) 275-3300. **$75-$92.** 4850 S Cleveland Ave. US 41, 0.5 mi s of jct SR 884 (Colonial Blvd). Ext corridors. **Pets:** Small. No service, supervision, crate.

(A$K) (X) (∩) (∅) (⊟) (⌂)

⊕ ◆◆◆ Quality Inn Historic District MI ☙
(941) 332-3232. **$89-$159.** 2431 Cleveland Ave. US 41, just n of Lee Memorial Hospital. Int corridors. **Pets:** Dogs only. Supervision.

(SAVE) (X) (⊟) (⊑) (¶) (⌂)

⊕ ◆◆ Radisson Inn Sanibel Gateway MI ☙
(941) 466-1200. **$75-$119, 3 days notice.** 20091 Summerlin Rd SW. 3 mi e of Sanibel Cswy on SR 869. Ext corridors. **Pets:** Small. $50 one-time fee/room. No service, supervision, crate.

(SAVE) (S₆) (X) (∅) (⊙) (⊟) (⊑) (¶) (⌂) (⋈)

◆◆◆ Residence Inn by Marriott A
(941) 936-0110. **Call for rates.** 2960 Colonial Blvd. I-75, exit 22, 3.5 mi w on SR 884. Int corridors. **Pets:** Supervision.

(A$K) (X) (∅) (⊟) (⊑) (⌂) (⋈)

◆◆ Sleep Inn Airport M ☙
(941) 561-1117. **$99-$99.** 13651 Indian Paint Ln. I-75 exit 21 (Daniels Pkwy) just w. Int corridors. **Pets:** Medium, other. $10 daily fee/room. Supervision.

(A$K) (S₆) (X) (∅) (⊙) (⊑) (⌂)

⊕ ◆◆ Ta Ki-Ki Motel M ☙
(941) 334-2135. **$58-$80, 7 days notice.** 2631 1st St. I-75, exit 25; 4.5 mi w on SR 80. Ext corridors. **Pets:** Other. No service, supervision, crate.

(SAVE) (X) (⊟) (⊑) (⌂) (⋈)

⊕ ◆◆ Wellesley Inn & Suites M ☙
(941) 278-3949. **$95-$115.** 4400 Ford St Extension. I-75, exit 22; 3.7 mi w on SR 884. Int corridors. **Pets:** Other. $10 one-time fee/room. Supervision.

(SAVE) (X) (∅) (⊟) (⊑) (⌂)

FORT MYERS BEACH

⊕ ◆◆ Best Western Beach Resort M ☙
(941) 463-6000. **$99-$269, 7 days notice.** 684 Estero Blvd. 0.5 mi nw. Ext corridors. **Pets:** Small. $10 daily fee/pet. Designated rooms, no service, supervision, crate.

(SAVE) (X) (∅) (⊙) (⊟) (⊑) (⌂) (⋈)

⊕ ◆◆◆ Casa Playa Beach Resort M ☙
(941) 765-0510. **$199-$305, 60 days notice.** 510 Estero Blvd. 0.5 mi n of Matanzas Pass Bridge via 5th St. Ext corridors. **Pets:** $10 daily fee/pet. Designated rooms, supervision.

(SAVE) (X) (⊟) (⊑) (⌂)

FORT PIERCE

⊕ ◆◆ Days Inn M ☙
(561) 466-4066. **$59-$94.** 6651 Darter Ct. US I-95, exit 65. Ext corridors. **Pets:** Small. $10 one-time fee/room. Supervision.

(SAVE) (X) (∅) (⊟) (⊑) (⌂)

⊕ ◆◆◆ Holiday Inn Express M
(561) 464-5000. **$82.** 7151 Okeechobee Rd. SR 70 at tpke exit 152; 0.7 mi w of jct I-95, exit 65. Ext corridors. **Pets:** Small. Supervision.

(SAVE) (S₆) (X) (∅) (⊑) (⌂)

⊕ ◆ Royal Inn M ☙
(561) 464-0405. **$59-$79.** 222 Hernando St. 2.5 mi e on SR A1A, southbound to Hernando St, just s. Ext corridors. **Pets:** Medium, dogs only. $15 one-time fee/pet. Designated rooms, no service, supervision, crate.

(SAVE) (S₆) (X) (⊟)

FORT WALTON BEACH

◆ Best Inn M ☙
(850) 244-0121. **$62-$125.** 100 Miracle Strip Pkwy. 0.5 mi w on US 98. Ext corridors. **Pets:** Dogs only. $10 one-time fee/room. Designated rooms, no service, supervision, crate.

(A$K) (S₆) (X) (⊟)

⊕ ◆◆ Days Inn M
(850) 244-6184. **$62-$66.** 135 Miracle Strip Pkwy. 1.3 mi w on US 98. Ext corridors. **Pets:** Medium. Supervision.

(SAVE) (S₆) (X) (⌂)

⊕ ◆ Marina Motel & Efficiencies M ☙
(850) 244-1129. **$70-$80.** 1345 Miracle Strip Pkwy E. 1 mi e on US 98. Ext/int corridors. **Pets:** Medium. $100 deposit/room, $9 daily fee/pet. Supervision.

(SAVE) (X) (⊟) (⊑) (⌂) (⋈)

GAINESVILLE

◆◆◆ **La Quinta Inn** 🅼
(352) 332-6466. **$69-$99.** 920 NW 69th Terrace. SR 26, ne of jct I-75, exit 76; behind Red Lobster. Ext corridors. **Pets:** Medium. No service, supervision, crate.

🔠 ⊠ 🐾 🛢 🖵 🛍

🅰🅰 ◆◆ **Red Roof Inn-Gainesville** 🅼
(352) 336-3311. **$59-$75.** 3500 SW 42nd St. I-75, exit 75, just ne. Int corridors. **Pets:** Small. No service, supervision, crate.

🆂🅰🆅🅴 ⊠ 👣 🛢 🛍

HAINES CITY

🅰🅰 ◆◆◆ **Best Western Lake Hamilton** 🅼 🐾
(863) 421-6929. **$81-$81.** 605 B Moore Rd. On US 27, just s of jct SR 544, 2 mi s of jct US 17/92. Ext corridors. **Pets:** Other. $3 daily fee/room. No service, supervision, crate.

🆂🅰🆅🅴 ⊠ 🏠 🛢 🖵 🛍 ⊠

🅰🅰 ◆◆ **Howard Johnson Inn** 🅼 🐾
(863) 422-8621. **$49-$89, 7 days notice.** 1504 US 27S. US 27; 1.8 mi s of jct US 17/92. Ext corridors. **Pets:** Other. $5 daily fee/room, $10 one-time fee/room. Supervision.

🆂🅰🆅🅴 🆂🅳 ⊠ 🛢 🖵 🍽 🛍

HERNANDO

◆◆◆ **Best Western Citrus Hills Lodge** 🅼 🐾
(352) 527-0015. **$85-$105.** 350 E Norvell Bryant Hwy. On CR 486 at jct Citrus Hills Blvd. Ext corridors. **Pets:** Small. $10 daily fee/room, $10 one-time fee/room. Designated rooms, supervision.

🔠 🆂🅳 ⊠ 👣 🐾 🛢 🖵 🍽 🛍

INDIALANTIC

🅰🅰 ◆◆ **Budget Inn of Indialantic** 🅼 🐾
(321) 779-9994. **$39-$140, 3 days notice.** 2900 N A1A Hwy. On SR A1A, 0.4 mi s of SR 518 (Eau Gallie Causeway). Ext corridors. **Pets:** Very small. $25 deposit/room, $10 daily fee/room, $15 one-time fee/room. Designated rooms, supervision.

⊠ 🛢 🍽 🛍

◆◆ **Casablanca Inn** 🅼 🐾
(321) 728-7188. **$60-$80, 3 days notice.** 1805 N Hwy A1A. SR A1A, 1.8 mi s of SR 518 (Eau Gallie Cswy). Ext corridors. **Pets:** Small, dogs only. $5 daily fee/pet. Supervision.

🔠 ⊠ 🛢 🖵 🛍

◆◆◆ **Melbourne Oceanfront Quality Suites Hotel** 🅼 🐾
(321) 723-4222. **$159-$199.** 1665 N SR A1A. SR A1A, 1.5 mi n of jct US 192. Ext corridors. **Pets:** $25 deposit/pet, $10 daily fee/pet. Designated rooms, no service, supervision, crate.

🔠 🆂🅳 ⊠ 🐾 🖵 🍽 ⊠

◆◆◆ **Oceanfront Cottages** 🅲 🐾
(321) 725-8474. **$99-$125, 60 days notice.** 612 Wavecrest Ave. Just s of e end of US 192. Ext corridors. **Pets:** Small. $100 deposit/room, $15 daily fee/pet. No service, supervision, crate.

⊠ 🛢 🖵 🛍 ⊠

INVERNESS

◆◆ **The Crown Hotel** 🅲🅸 🐾
(352) 344-5555. **$50-$85.** 109 N Seminole Ave. Center, just n of jct US41/SR44. Int corridors. **Pets:** Small. $5 daily fee/pet, $10 one-time fee/pet. Supervision.

🔠 ⊠ 🍽 🛍

ISLAMORADA

🅰🅰 ◆◆ **Sands of Islamorada** 🅼 🐾
(305) 664-2791. **$150-$240.** 80051 Overseas Hwy. US 1, MM80. Ext corridors. **Pets:** Other. $10 daily fee/pet. Supervision.

👣 🛢 🖵 🛍 ⊠

◆◆ **White Gate Court** 🅼 🐾
(305) 664-4136. **$98-$200.** 76010 Overseas Hwy. On US 1, just s of MM77, s side of the road. Ext corridors. **Pets:** Other. $8 daily fee/pet. Supervision.

⊠ 🛢 ⊠

JACKSONVILLE METROPOLITAN AREA

AMELIA CITY

🅰🅰 ◆◆◆◆◆ **The Ritz-Carlton, Amelia Island** 🆁
(904) 277-1100. **$229-$429, 7 days notice.** 4750 Amelia Island Pkwy. On SR A1A in Summer Beach. Int corridors. **Pets:** Supervision.

⊠ 🐾 🍽 🛍 ⊠

BALDWIN

🅰🅰 ◆◆ **Best Western Inn Baldwin** 🅼 🐾
(904) 266-9759. **$45-$95.** 1088 US 301 & I-10. I-10, exit 50, just s. Ext corridors. **Pets:** Medium. $8 daily fee/pet, $8 one-time fee/pet. No service, supervision, crate.

🆂🅰🆅🅴 ⊠ 🛍

FERNANDINA BEACH

🅰🅰 ◆◆◆ **Florida House Inn** 🅲🅸 🐾
(904) 261-3300. **$70-$160, 7 days notice.** 22 S 3rd St. In Fernandina Beach Historic District. Ext/int corridors. **Pets:** Dogs only. $10 daily fee/pet, $10 one-time fee/pet. Supervision.

🆂🅰🆅🅴 ⊠ ⊠

◆◆ **The Inn at Fernandina Beach** 🅼🅸
(904) 277-2300. **$69-$94.** 2707 Sadler Rd. Just w of US A1A. Ext corridors. **Pets:** Designated rooms, no service, supervision, crate.

🔠 🆂🅳 ⊠ 🛢 🖵 🍽 🛍

JACKSONVILLE

◆◆◆ AmeriSuites/BayMeadows M ❖
(904) 737-4477. **$109.** 8277 Western Way Cir. Just e of I-95, exit 100, off Baymeadows Rd. Int corridors. **Pets:** Medium, other. $10 daily fee/room. Supervision.

SAVE ⊠ 🐾 🛇 🖪 🖃 🕿

◆◆ Baymont Inn & Suites-Jacksonville M
(904) 268-9999. **$54-$63.** 3199 Hartley Rd. I-295, exit 2A northbound; exit 2 southbound, at SR 13. Int corridors. **Pets:** Small. Designated rooms, no service, supervision, crate.

⊠ 🐾 🖪 🖃 🕿

◆◆ Best Inns of America M
(904) 739-3323. **$47-$58.** 8220 Dix Ellis Tr. Sw off Baymeadows Rd, w of jct I-95, exit 100. Ext corridors. **Pets:** Supervision.

SAVE 🐾 ⊠ 🐾 🕿

◆◆◆ Comfort Suites Hotel
Baymeadows M
(904) 739-1155. **$60-$130.** 8333 Dix Ellis Tr. I-95, exit 100, sw off Baymeadows Rd. Ext corridors. **Pets:** Designated rooms, no service, supervision, crate.

SAVE ⊠ 🐾 🖪 🖃 🕿

◆◆◆ Hampton Inn M ❖
(904) 741-4980. **$89-$99.** 1170 Airport Entrance Rd. I-95, exit 127, jct Airport Rd. Ext corridors. **Pets:** Other. Supervision.

ASK ⊠ 🐾 🕿

◆◆◆ Holiday Inn Baymeadows MI ❖
(904) 737-1700. **$59-$79.** 9150 Baymeadows Rd. 0.3 mi e of jct I-95, exit 100. Ext/int corridors. **Pets:** Small. $35 deposit/room. No service, supervision, crate.

⊠ 🐾 🖪 🖃 🍴 🕿

◆◆◆ Holiday Inn Express Hotel and
Suites M ❖
(904) 332-9500. **$59-$120.** 4675 Salisbury Rd. I-95, exit 101, just e, then s. Int corridors. **Pets:** Small, other. $10 daily fee/pet. Designated rooms, no service, supervision, crate.

SAVE ⊠ 🐾 🛇 🖪 🖃 🕿

◆◆◆ Holiday Inn I-95 North MI ❖
(904) 741-4404. **Call for rates.** 14670 Duval Rd. Jct Airport Rd and I-95, exit 127. Ext/int corridors. **Pets:** Small. Supervision.

ASK ⊠ 🐾 🛇 🖪 🍴 🕿 ⊠

◆◆ Homestead Village Guest Studios M
(904) 642-9911. **$59-$79.** 10020 Skinner Lake Dr. I-95, exit 101, 3.5 mi on JTB to Gate Pkwy, just ne. Ext corridors. **Pets:** Medium. Designated rooms, supervision.

⊠ 🐾 🛇 🖪 🖃

◆◆◆ Homestead Village Guest
Studios-Baymeadows M ❖
(904) 739-1881. **$49-$69.** 8300 Western Way. I-95, exit 100, just e to Western Way, just s. Int corridors. **Pets:** Small, other. $75 one-time fee/pet. No service, supervision, crate.

⊠ 🛇 🖃

◆◆◆ Homewood Suites M ❖
(904) 733-9299. **$139-$175.** 8737 Baymeadows Rd. I-95, exit 100, 0.3 mi w. Ext/int corridors. **Pets:** Other. $75 one-time fee/room. Supervision.

ASK 🐾 ⊠ 🖪 🖃 🕿 ⊠

◆◆ Inns of America M ❖
(904) 281-0198. **$55-$55.** 4300 Salisbury Rd N. 0.5 mi n of jct Butler Blvd and I-95, exit 101. Ext corridors. **Pets:** Other. Supervision.

SAVE ⊠ 🖪 🕿

◆◆◆ La Quinta Inn M
(904) 296-0703. **$65-$105.** 4868 Lenoir Ave S. I-95, exit 101, nw corner. Int corridors. **Pets:** Small. No service, supervision, crate.

ASK ⊠ 🐾 🐾 🛇 🖪 🖃 🕿

◆◆◆ La Quinta Inn-Baymeadows M
(904) 731-9940. **$59-$99.** 8255 Dix Ellis Tr. I-95, exit 100 (Baymeadows Rd), sw corner. Ext corridors. **Pets:** Small. Designated rooms, supervision.

ASK ⊠ 🖪 🖃 🕿

◆◆◆ La Quinta Inn-Jacksonville/Orange
Park M ❖
(904) 778-9539. **$59-$86.** 8555 Blanding Blvd. At jct SR 21 and I-295, exit 4. Ext corridors. **Pets:** Medium, other. $50 deposit/room. Supervision.

ASK ⊠ 🐾 🕿

◆◆◆ La Quinta Inn-North M
(904) 751-6960. **$59-$89.** 812 Dunn Ave. Jct Dunn Ave and I-95, exit 125. Ext corridors. **Pets:** Small. Supervision.

ASK ⊠ 🐾 🖪 🕿 ⊠

◆◆◆ Quality Hotel Southpoint MI ❖
(904) 281-0900. **$59-$119, 5 days notice.** 4660 Salisbury Rd. I-95, exit 101 (J T Butler Blvd), just e. Int corridors. **Pets:** Small. $25 deposit/pet, $10 daily fee/pet. Designated rooms, supervision.

SAVE ⊠ 🐾 🖪 🖃 🍴 🕿

◆◆ Ramada Inn & Suites M ❖
(904) 786-0500. **$70-$80.** 510 S Lane Ave. I-10, exit 54, just n. Ext corridors. **Pets:** Small, dogs only. Supervision.

SAVE 🖪 🖃 🍴 🕿

◆◆◆ Ramada Inn Conference Center MI ❖
(904) 268-8080. **$70-$80.** 3130 Hartley Rd. I-295, exit 2A northbound; exit 2 southbound, just n on SR 13. Ext corridors. **Pets:** Medium. $10 daily fee/room. No service, supervision, crate.

⊠ 🐾 🖃 🍴 🕿

◆◆◆ Red Roof Inn M ❖
(904) 296-1006. **$50-$71.** 6969 Lenoir Ave E. I-95, exit 101, nw corner. Int corridors. **Pets:** Small, other. Supervision.

SAVE ⊠ 🐾 🛇 🖪 🖃 🕿

◆◆ Red Roof Inn-Airport M ❖
(904) 741-4488. **$40-$73.** 14701 Airport Entrance Rd. Jct Airport Rd and I-95, exit 127. Ext corridors. **Pets:** Small, other. Supervision.

SAVE ⊠

◆◆ **Red Roof Inn-South** Ⓜ ☙
(904) 777-1000. **$44-$57.** 6099 Youngerman Cir. Jct SR 21 and I-295, exit 4. Ext corridors. **Pets:** Medium, other. Supervision.
(SAVE) (✕)

◆◆◆ **Residence Inn by Marriott** Ⓐ ☙
(904) 733-8088. **$79-$119.** 8365 Dix Ellis Tr. I-95, exit 100, sw off Baymeadows Rd. Ext corridors. **Pets:** $75 one-time fee/room. Supervision.
(A$K) (✕) (🔊) (▣) (🖼) (✕)

JACKSONVILLE BEACH

⚎ ◆◆ **Days Inn Oceanfront Resort** Ⓜ ☙
(904) 249-7231. **$79-$129.** 1031 S 1st St. On 1st St at 11th Ave S. Ext corridors. **Pets:** Small, dogs only. $25 one-time fee/pet. No service, supervision, crate.
(SAVE) (🔊) (✕) (🖥) (▣) (🎁) (🖼) (✕)

☙ **END METROPOLITAN AREA** ☙

JENSEN BEACH

◆◆◆ **River Palm Cottages** Ⓒ ☙
(561) 334-0401. **$125-$199.** 2325 NE Indian River Dr. On SR 707 (NE Indian River Dr) s of jct 732 (Jensen Cswy). Ext corridors. **Pets:** Other. $10 daily fee/room. Supervision.
(A$K) (✕) (🖼) (✕) (☎)

JUNO BEACH

◆◆ **Holiday Inn Express-North Palm Beach** Ⓜ ☙
(561) 622-4366. **$79-$199.** 13950 US Hwy 1. US 1, at jct Donald Ross Rd. Int corridors. **Pets:** $25 one-time fee/pet. No service, supervision, crate.
(A$K) (✕) (🔊) (🖥) (▣) (🖼)

KEY LARGO

⚎ ◆◆ **Howard Johnson Resort Key Largo** Ⓜ
(305) 451-1400. **$139-$349, 7 days notice.** 10245 Overseas Hwy. US 1, at MM102. Int corridors. **Pets:** Designated rooms, supervision.
(SAVE) (🔊) (✕) (🔊) (🖥) (▣) (🍴) (🖼) (✕)

KEY WEST

⚎ ◆◆ **Alexander Palms Court** Ⓜ ☙
(305) 296-6413. **$145-$395.** 715 South St. Just 2 n of Duval St. Ext corridors. **Pets:** Other. $25 one-time fee/room. Supervision.
(SAVE) (🖥) (▣) (🖼)

⚎ ◆◆◆ **Center Court Historic Inn & Cottages** ⒷⒷ ☙
(305) 296-9292. **$178-$338.** 916 Center St. In Old Town; 0.5 mi n of jct US 1, between Duval and Simonton sts. Ext/int corridors. **Pets:** Other. $10 daily fee/pet. Supervision.
(✕) (🖥) (🖼)

⚎ ◆◆◆ **Chelsea House** ⒷⒷ ☙
(305) 296-2211. **$130-$210.** 707 Truman Ave. At the corner of Elizabeth St and Truman Ave. **Pets:** $10 daily fee/pet. Designated rooms, supervision.
(SAVE) (✕) (🖥) (▣) (🖼)

ORANGE PARK

◆◆◆ **Comfort Inn** Ⓜ ☙
(904) 264-3297. **$69-$69.** 341 Park Ave. I-295, exit 3, just s on US 17. Ext corridors. **Pets:** Other. $25 one-time fee/room. Supervision.
(A$K) (🔊) (✕) (🖥) (▣) (🖼) (✕)

◆◆ **Days Inn** Ⓜ ☙
(904) 269-8887. **$54-$66.** 4280 Eldridge Loop. I-295, exit 3, just s on US 17. Int corridors. **Pets:** Other. $25 one-time fee/room. Supervision.
(✕) (🖥) (▣)

⚎ ◆◆ **Courtney's Place Historic Guest Cottages and Inn** Ⓒ ☙
(305) 294-3480. **$109-$189, 21 days notice.** 720 Whitmarsh Ln. In Old Town; just e from jct Petronia and Simonton sts. Ext corridors. **Pets:** Other. Designated rooms, supervision.
(SAVE) (🖥) (▣) (🖼)

⚎ ◆◆◆ **The Cuban Club Suites** Ⓐ ☙
(305) 296-0465. **$249-$399.** 1102-1108 Duval St. In Old Town; corner of Duval and Amelia sts Registration at La Casa de Luces on Amelia St. Int corridors. **Pets:** Small, dogs only. $200 deposit/room, $10 daily fee/pet. Supervision.
(✕) (🖥)

◆◆◆ **Curry Mansion Inn** ⒷⒷ ☙
(305) 294-5349. **$180-$325.** 511 Caroline St. In Old Town; just n of jct Duval St. Ext/int corridors. **Pets:** Small. No service, supervision, crate.
(✕) (🖥) (🖼)

⚎ ◆◆◆ **Frances St Bottle Inn** ⒷⒷ ☙
(305) 294-8530. **$135-$165.** 535 Frances St. From US 1/Roosevelt Blvd, right onto White St, then left onto Southard St at corner of Frances and Southard sts. Int corridors. **Pets:** Other. Designated rooms, supervision.
(✕) (🖥) (☎)

⚎ ◆◆ **The Palms Hotel** ⒷⒷ ☙
(305) 294-3146. **$140-$185, 7 days notice.** 820 White St. Just w of Truman. Ext corridors. **Pets:** Other. No service, supervision, crate.
(SAVE) (🔊) (🖼) (✕)

◆◆◆ **The Travelers Palm Garden Cottage** Ⓒ
(305) 294-9560. **$105-$350, 21 days notice.** 815 Catherine St. Just e of Duval St. Ext corridors. **Pets:** Designated rooms, no service, supervision, crate.
(✕) (🖥) (▣) (🖼) (✕)

LAKE CITY

⬤⬤⬤ ◆◆◆ Best Western Inn M ❀
(904) 752-3801. **$40-$80.** 4720 US 90 W. I-75, exit 82, just w. Ext corridors. **Pets:** Small. $5 daily fee/pet. Designated rooms, supervision.
[SAVE] [S🐾] [✕] [🛢] [🖾] [🖾]

◆◆ Days Inn I-10 M
(904) 758-4224. **$45-$65.** US 441. I-10, exit 44, just s. Ext corridors. **Pets:** Designated rooms, supervision.
[A$K] [✕] [🛢] [🖾] [🖾]

⬤⬤⬤ ◆◆ Driftwood Motel M ❀
(904) 755-3545. **$29-$32.** 4380 US Hwy 90 W. I-75 exit 82, 0.7 mi e. Ext corridors. **Pets:** Small, dogs only. $5 daily fee/pet. Designated rooms, no service, supervision, crate.
[SAVE] [✕]

⬤⬤⬤ ◆◆ Dynasty Inn & Suites M
(904) 752-6262. **$45-$50.** 4670 W US Hwy 90. I-75 exit 82, just se. Ext/int corridors. **Pets:** Medium. Designated rooms, no service, supervision, crate.
[SAVE] [S🐾] [✕] [🛢] [🖾] [🖾] [🖾]

⬤⬤⬤ ◆◆ Econo Lodge South M ❀
(904) 755-9311. **$39-$46.** Rt 2, Box 6008. I-75, exit 80, at US 441. Ext corridors. **Pets:** Small. $10 deposit/room. Designated rooms, no service, supervision, crate.
[SAVE] [✕] [🖾] [🖾]

⬤⬤⬤ ◆ Knights Inn M ❀
(904) 752-7720. **$33-$48.** Rt 13, Box 201. I-75, exit 82, ne corner. Ext corridors. **Pets:** Other. $5 one-time fee/pet. Supervision.
[SAVE] [S🐾] [✕] [🖾]

⬤⬤⬤ ◆◆ Scottish Inn M ❀
(904) 755-0230. **$29-$39.** 4450 US 90 W. I-75, exit 82, 0.6 mi e. Ext corridors. **Pets:** Small. $5 daily fee/pet. Designated rooms, supervision.
[SAVE] [✕]

LAKE WORTH

⬤⬤⬤ ◆◆ Lago Motor Inn M ❀
(561) 585-5246. **$58-$68, 7 days notice.** 714 S Dixie Hwy. US 1, just s of jct 6th Ave S; from jct I-95, exit 47, 0.7 mi e and just s on US 1. Ext corridors. **Pets:** $20 deposit/room, $9 daily fee/pet, $9 one-time fee/pet. Supervision.
[SAVE] [✕] [🛢] [🖾]

⬤⬤⬤ ◆ Martinique Motor Lodge M ❀
(561) 585-2502. **$45-$75, 7 days notice.** 801 S Dixie Hwy. US 1, just s of jct 6th Ave S, 0.5 mi e of jct I-95 exit 47. Ext corridors. **Pets:** Small, dogs only. $7 daily fee/room, $7 one-time fee/room. Designated rooms, no service, supervision, crate.
[SAVE] [S🐾] [🛢] [🖾]

⬤⬤⬤ ◆ White Manor Motel M
(561) 582-7437. **$50-$62.** 1618 S Federal Hwy. 1 mi e of I-95, exit 47, 0.8 mi s on SR 5 (Federal Hwy). Ext corridors. **Pets:** Small. Designated rooms, no service, supervision, crate.
[SAVE] [🛢] [🖾]

LAKELAND

⬤⬤⬤ ◆◆◆ AmeriSuites Lakeland Center M ❀
(863) 413-1122. **$109-$129.** 525 W Orange St. At the Lakeland Center. Int corridors. **Pets:** Small, other. No service, supervision, crate.
[SAVE] [✕] [⬥] [🖉] [🖳] [🛢] [🖵] [🖾]

◆◆◆ Baymont Inn & Suites-Lakeland M
(863) 815-0606. **$74-$81.** 4315 Lakeland Park Dr. Just nw of jct SR 33 and I-4, exit 19. Int corridors. **Pets:** No service, supervision, crate.
[✕] [⬥] [🖉] [🖳] [🛢] [🖵] [🖾]

⬤⬤⬤ ◆◆◆ Comfort Inn M
(863) 688-9221. **$65-$80.** 1817 E Memorial Blvd. 2 mi e of jct US 98 and US 92. Ext corridors. **Pets:** Supervision.
[SAVE] [✕] [🛢] [🖾]

◆◆◆ La Quinta Inn & Suites M ❀
(863) 859-2866. **$105-$119.** 1024 Crevasse St. I-4, exit 18, just n on US 98. Int corridors. **Pets:** Small. $25 deposit/pet. Supervision.
[A$K] [✕] [⬥] [🖉] [🖳] [🛢] [🖵] [🖾]

⬤⬤⬤ ◆◆ Royalty Inn M ❀
(863) 858-4481. **$55-$95.** 3425 Hwy 98N. I-4, exit 18, ne corner. Int corridors. **Pets:** $10 daily fee/room. No service, supervision, crate.
[SAVE] [✕] [🛢] [🖾]

⬤⬤⬤ ◆◆◆ Wellesley Inn & Suites M ❀
(863) 859-3399. **$105-$125.** 3520 N Hwy US 98. I-4, exit 18, 0.3 mi w on US 98, at Lakeland Square Mall. Int corridors. **Pets:** Very small. Supervision.
[SAVE] [✕] [⬥] [🖉] [🖳] [🛢] [🖵] [🖾]

LIVE OAK

⬤⬤⬤ ◆◆ Econo Lodge M
(904) 362-7459. **$50-$65.** I-10, exit 40, just s on US 129. Ext corridors. **Pets:** Supervision.
[SAVE] [✕] [🛢] [🖵] [🖾]

⬤⬤⬤ ◆◆ Suwannee River Best Western Inn M ❀
(904) 362-6000. **$42-$85, 7 days notice.** 6819 US 129. I-10, exit 40, 0.3 mi s. Ext corridors. **Pets:** Small. $10 daily fee/pet. No service, supervision, crate.
[SAVE] [✕] [🛢] [🖾]

LONGBOAT KEY

◆◆ Riviera Beach Motel ▲ ❀
(941) 383-2552. **$800-$1100, 30 days notice.** 5451 Gulf of Mexico Dr. SR 789; 5 mi s of jct SR 684 (Cortez Rd). Ext corridors. **Pets:** Small, dogs only. $100 deposit/pet, $10 daily fee/pet. Supervision.
[🛢] [🖵] [🖾]

MACCLENNY

⬤⬤⬤ ◆◆ Econo Lodge M ❀
(904) 259-3000. **$50-$65.** I-10, exit 48, just s of jct SR 121. Ext corridors. **Pets:** Small, other. Supervision.
[SAVE] [S🐾] [✕] [🛢] [🖵] [🖾]

MARIANNA

(AAA) ◆◆ Best Western Marianna Inn 🅼 ☼
(850) 526-5666. **$46-$60.** 2086 Hwy 71. SR 71, 0.3 mi s of jct I-10, exit 21. Ext corridors. **Pets:** Designated rooms, supervision.
[SAVE] [S🄳] [⊠] [❚] [🖼]

(AAA) ◆◆◆ Comfort Inn 🅼 ☼
(850) 526-5600. **$46-$65, 7 days notice.** 2175 Hwy 71. At jct I-10, exit 21 and SR 71, just nw. Ext corridors. **Pets:** Small. $20 one-time fee/room. Designated rooms, supervision.
[SAVE] [⊠] [❚] [▣] [🖼]

MELBOURNE

◆◆◆ Baymont Inn & Suites-Melbourne 🅼
(321) 242-9400. **$72-$79.** 7200 George T Edwards Dr. SR 509, just w of I-95, exit 73. Int corridors. **Pets:** Medium. Designated rooms, no service, supervision, crate.
[⊠] [🎵] [♿] [❚] [▣] [🖼]

◆◆◆ Best Western Harborview 🅼
(321) 724-4422. **$59-$69.** 964 S Harbor City Blvd. 2 mi n of SR 192 on US 1 at jct Nasa Blvd. Int corridors. **Pets:** No service, supervision, crate.
[SAVE] [⊠] [❚] [▣] [🍴] [🖼]

(AAA) ◆◆ Super 8 🅼 ☼
(321) 723-4430. **$60-$60.** 1515 S Harbor City Blvd. I-95, exit 71, 7 mi e to US 1 on SR 192, then 0.5 mi n. Int corridors. **Pets:** Other. $20 deposit/room. Supervision.
[SAVE] [S🄳] [⊠] [♿] [♿]

MIAMI METROPOLITAN AREA

COCONUT GROVE

(AAA) ◆◆◆◆ Mayfair House Hotel 🅷 ☼
(305) 441-0000. **$199-$649.** 3000 Florida Ave. Center; adjoining Mayfair shops at Florida Ave and Virginia St. Ext/int corridors. **Pets:** Small, dogs only. $20 daily fee/room. Supervision.
[SAVE] [S🄳] [⊠] [🎵] [❚] [🍴]

CUTLER RIDGE

◆◆◆ Baymont Inn-Miami (Cutler Ridge) 🅼
(305) 278-0001. **$75-$80.** 10821 Caribbean Blvd. Florida Tpke exit 12 (US 1), nw corner. Int corridors. **Pets:** No service, supervision, crate.
[⊠] [♿] [🎵] [♿] [❚] [▣] [🖼]

FLORIDA CITY

(AAA) ◆◆ Coral Roc Motel 🅼 ☼
(305) 246-2888. **$45-$78.** 1100 N Krome Ave. On SR 997; just w of US 1, 0.5 mi s of Homestead. Ext corridors. **Pets:** Small. $5 one-time fee/pet. No service, supervision, crate.
[SAVE] [❚] [🖼]

◆◆◆ Hampton Inn 🅼
(305) 247-8833. **$99-$99.** 124 E Palm Dr. On US 1, 0.3 mi s of Florida Tpke terminus. Ext corridors. **Pets:** Supervision.
[S🄳] [⊠] [🎵] [❚] [▣] [🖼]

HOMESTEAD

(AAA) ◆ Everglades Motel 🅼 ☼
(305) 247-4117. **$39-$68.** 605 S Krome Ave. Just w of US 1 between Lucy and 6th sts; on SR 997, 0.5 mi s of center of town. Ext corridors. **Pets:** Small. $5 one-time fee/pet. No service, supervision, crate.
[SAVE] [⊠] [❚] [🖼]

◆◆ Homestead Days Inn 🅼
(305) 245-1260. **Call for rates, 3 days notice.** 51 S Homestead Blvd. On US 1; 1.2 mi n of Florida Tpke, 320 St SW and US 1. Ext corridors. **Pets:** Small. No service, supervision, crate.
[⊠] [❚] [🖼]

KENDALL

(AAA) ◆◆◆ AmeriSuites 🅼 ☼
(305) 279-8688. **$129-$179.** 11520 SW 88th St. Florida Tpke, exit 20 (SW 88th (Kendall Dr)), just e on SR 94, behind McDonalds 0.3 mi s. Int corridors. **Pets:** Small. Supervision.
[SAVE] [⊠] [♿] [🎵] [♿] [❚] [▣] [🖼]

MIAMI

◆◆◆ Club Hotel by Doubletree 🅼
(305) 266-0000. **$112-$112.** 1101 NW 57th Ave. 2.5 mi sw of airport entrance on Red Rd and jct SR 836 Dolphin Expwy. Int corridors. **Pets:** Supervision.
[A$K] [⊠] [🎵] [❚] [▣] [🍴] [🖼]

◆◆ Hampton Inn-Downtown 🅼
(305) 854-2070. **$100-$120.** 2500 Brickell Ave. 2 mi s at entrance to Rickenbacher Cswy; Key Biscayne exit off I-95. Ext/int corridors. **Pets:** No service, supervision, crate.
[⊠] [🎵] [▣] [🖼]

◆◆◆ Hampton Inn-Miami Airport West 🅼 ☼
(305) 513-0777. **$109-$139.** 3620 NW 79th Ave. From Palmetto Expwy (SR 826), exit NW 58th St, just s of jct NW 58th St and NW 79th Ave. Int corridors. **Pets:** Small. $25 one-time fee/room. No service, supervision, crate.
[A$K] [⊠] [♿] [🎵] [♿] [❚] [▣] [🖼]

(AAA) ◆◆ Holiday Inn-Downtown 🅼
(305) 374-3000. **$109-$149.** 200 SE 2nd Ave. Just s of Flagler St on US 1 and 41, 0.8 mi e of I-95 exit 3. Int corridors. **Pets:** Small. Supervision.
[SAVE] [S🄳] [⊠] [🎵] [❚] [▣] [🍴] [🖼]

◆◆ Homestead Village Guest Studios Miami Airport/Doral **M**

(305) 436-1811. **Call for rates.** 8720 NW 33rd St. SR 826 (Palmetto Expwy), 0.8 mi w on NW 36th St, then s on 87th St, 0.6 mi on right in the Westpoint Office Park. Ext corridors. **Pets:** Designated rooms, supervision.

⊠ 🔊 🛗 🔲 📺

◆◆◆ La Quinta Inn & Suites-Miami Airport West **M**

(305) 436-0830. **$99-$129.** 8730 NW 27th St. From SR 836 (Dolphin Expwy), just n or 87th NW Ave. Int corridors. **Pets:** Small. No service, supervision, crate.

(ASK) 🔊 ⊠ 🛗 🔊 📺 🛗 🔲 📺

◆◆◆ La Quinta Inn Miami Airport North **M** 🐾

(305) 599-9902. **$85-$105.** 7401 NW 36th St. NW 36th St, just e of jct SR 826, Palmetto Expwy. Ext corridors. **Pets:** Medium. Supervision.

(ASK) ⊠ 🔊 🛗 🔲 📺

◆◆◆ Quality Inn-South **M** 🐾

(305) 251-2000. **$81-$104.** 14501 S Dixie Hwy (US 1). US 1 at SW 145th St. Ext corridors. **Pets:** Other. Supervision.

(SAVE) ⊠ 🔊 🛗 🔲 📺 ‖ 📺

MIAMI BEACH

◆◆ Breakwater Hotel **H** 🐾

(305) 532-1220. **$149-$239, 3 days notice.** 940 Ocean Dr. E of SR A1A, between 9th and 10th sts. Int corridors. **Pets:** Small, other. Supervision.

(ASK) ⊠ ‖

◆◆◆ Comfort Inn Oceanside **M** 🐾

(305) 868-1200. **$85-$155.** 6261 Collins Ave. A1A/Collins Ave at 63rd St. Int corridors. **Pets:** Small. $10 daily fee/pet, $25 one-time fee/pet. No service, supervision, crate.

(SAVE) 🔊 ⊠ 🔊 🛗 🔲 📺 ‖

◆◆ Days Inn Art Deco/Convention Center **M**

(305) 538-6631. **$109-$159, 7 days notice.** 100 21st St. SR A1A (Collins Ave) at 21st St. Ext/int corridors. **Pets:** Small. $100 deposit/room. No service, supervision, crate.

(SAVE) 🔊 ⊠ 🔊 🛗 🔲 📺 ‖ 📺

◆◆◆ Fontainebleau Hilton Resort & Towers **H** 🐾

(305) 538-2000. **$239-$269, 5 days notice.** 4441 Collins Ave. On SR A1A. Int corridors. **Pets:** Small, dogs only. No service, supervision, crate.

(ASK) ⊠ 🔊 🛗 🔲 📺 ‖ 📺

◆◆◆◆ Loews Miami Beach Hotel **H**

(305) 604-1601. **$329-$419, 3 days notice.** 1601 Collins Ave. On SR A1A, at Collins Ave and 16th Ave. Int corridors. **Pets:** Supervision.

(ASK) 🔊 ⊠ 🔊 🛗 🔲 📺 ‖ 📺

◆◆ The Regal Hotel on South Beach **M**

(305) 532-7093. **$95-$155, 3 days notice.** 436 Ocean Dr. Just e of Collins Ave (A1A) between 4th and 5th sts. Int corridors. **Pets:** Small. Designated rooms, no service, supervision, crate.

(SAVE) 🔊 ⊠ 🛗 ‖ 📺

MIAMI SPRINGS

◆◆◆ Baymont Inn & Suites-Miami Airport **M**

(305) 871-1777. **$99-$109.** 3501 NW Le Jeune Rd. SR 953, (Le Jeune Rd) at jct SR 112. Int corridors. **Pets:** No service, supervision, crate.

⊠ 🔊 🛗 🔲 📺

◆◆◆ Clarion Hotel-Miami International Airport **MI**

(305) 871-1000. **$120-$145.** 5301 NW 36th St. Between Le Jeune Rd and SR 828 (Palmetto Expwy). Int corridors. **Pets:** No service, supervision, crate.

(SAVE) ⊠ 🔊 🛗 🔲 📺 ⊠

◆◆◆ Comfort Inn Airport East **M** 🐾

(305) 887-2153. **$116-$136.** 5125 NW 36th St. Between Le Jeune Rd and SR 826 (Palmetto Expwy). Int corridors. **Pets:** $25 one-time fee/room. Supervision.

(SAVE) ⊠ 🔊 🛗

◆◆◆ Comfort Inn & Suites-Miami International Airport **M** 🐾

(305) 871-6000. **$110-$135.** 5301 NW 36th St. Between Le Jeune Rd and SR 828 (Palmetto Expwy). Int corridors. **Pets:** Medium, other. $25 daily fee/pet. No service, supervision, crate.

(SAVE) ⊠ 🔊 🛗 🔲 📺 ⊠

◆◆◆ MainStay Suites-Miami Springs **M** 🐾

(305) 870-0448. **$65-$75.** 101 Fairway Dr. I-95 to SR 112W, exit NW 36th St, then w, right on Palmeto Dr, then w, behind the Clarion Hotel. Between LeJeune Rd and SR 826 (Palmetto Expwy). Int corridors. **Pets:** Medium. $100 deposit/room, $10 daily fee/room. Supervision.

(SAVE) 🔊 ⊠ 🔊 🛗 📺

◆◆ Red Roof Inn Miami Airport **M** 🐾

(305) 871-4221. **$70-$100.** 3401 NW LeJeune Rd. 0.5 mi n of airport entrance; on SR 953 at jct SR 112. Int corridors. **Pets:** Small, other. No service, supervision, crate.

(SAVE) ⊠ 📺

◆◆ Sleep Inn-Miami Airport **M**

(305) 871-7553. **$116-$136.** 105 Fairway Dr. I-95 to SR 112W, exit NW 36th St, then w, right on Palmeto Dr, then w; behind the Clarion Hotel, between LeJeune Rd and SR 826 (Palmetto Expwy). Int corridors. **Pets:** Small. No service, supervision, crate.

(SAVE) ⊠ 🔊 🛗 📺

SUNNY ISLES

◆◆◆ Newport Beachside Hotel & Resort **H** 🐾

(305) 949-1300. **$149-$209, 3 days notice.** 16701 Collins Ave. SR A1A, at jct SR 826, Sunny Isles Blvd. Int corridors. **Pets:** Small. Supervision.

(SAVE) ⊠ 🔊 🛗 🔲 ‖ 📺 ⊠

🐾   **END METROPOLITAN AREA**   🐾

NAPLES

◆◆◆ Baymont Inn & Suites Naples M ❀
(941) 352-8400. **$84-$102.** 185 Bedzel Cir. I-75, exit 15, just w. Int corridors. **Pets:** Small, other. $10 deposit/room. Designated rooms, no service, supervision, crate.

[X] [∩] [∅] [≪] [⊟] [▣] [≋]

◆◆ Fairfield Inn and Suites M
(941) 262-6181. **$95-$150.** 221 9th St S. US 41, just s of Central Ave. Ext corridors. **Pets:** Small. Designated rooms, no service, supervision, crate.

[SAVE] [X] [⊟] [▣] [↿↾] [≋] [X]

◆◆ Red Roof Inn M ❀
(941) 774-3117. **$100-$140.** 1925 Davis Blvd. SR 84, just e of jct US 41. Ext corridors. **Pets:** Medium, other. $100 deposit/room. No service, supervision, crate.

[SAVE] [X] [≪] [⊟] [▣] [≋]

◆◆◆ Waterside Villas A
(941) 732-2007. **$525-$740** (no credit cards). 2864 Gulfview Dr. 0.5 mi w of jct US 41 at jct Gulfview Dr. Ext corridors. **Pets:** No service, supervision, crate.

[X] [⊟] [▣] [≋] [X]

◆◆◆ Wellesley Inn & Suites M ❀
(941) 793-4646. **$99-$149.** 1555 5th Ave S. 1 mi s on US 41, at jct SR 84. Int corridors. **Pets:** Other. $10 daily fee/pet. Supervision.

[SAVE] [S⚬] [X] [∅] [⊟] [▣] [≋]

NAVARRE

◆◆◆ Comfort Inn & Conference Center M ❀
(850) 939-1761. **$89-$113.** 8700 Navarre Pkwy. US 98, 0.3 mi n of Navarre Beach Bridge. Ext corridors. **Pets:** Other. $10 daily fee/pet. Supervision.

[ASK] [S⚬] [X] [⊟] [▣] [≋]

NEW SMYRNA BEACH

◆ Smyrna Motel M ❀
(904) 428-2495. **$45-$75, 7 days notice.** 1050 N Dixie Frwy. 1.2 mi n on US 1. Ext corridors. **Pets:** Medium, other. Supervision.

[SAVE] [X] [⊟] [▣]

NORTH FORT MYERS

◆◆ Econo Lodge M ❀
(941) 995-0571. **$65-$70, 30 days notice.** 13301 N Cleveland Ave. US 41, 1.1 mi n of Caloosahatchee Bridge. Ext corridors. **Pets:** Medium. Designated rooms, no service, supervision, crate.

[SAVE] [X] [⊟] [▣] [≋]

OCALA

◆ Budget Host Inn M ❀
(352) 732-6940. **$36-$62.** 4013 NW Blitchton Rd. I-75, exit 70, 0.3 mi n on US 27. Ext corridors. **Pets:** $4 daily fee/pet. No service, supervision, crate.

[SAVE] [X] [⊟]

◆◆ Comfort Inn M ❀
(352) 629-8850. **$55-$75.** 4040 W Silver Springs Blvd. I-75, exit 69, just w on SR 40. Ext corridors. **Pets:** Medium. $5 daily fee/pet. No service, supervision, crate.

[SAVE] [X] [⊟] [≋]

◆ Days Inn M ❀
(352) 629-7041. **$55-$75.** 3811 NW Blitchton Rd. US 27, just n of I-75, exit 70. Ext/int corridors. **Pets:** Other. $5 daily fee/pet, $5 one-time fee/pet. No service, supervision, crate.

[SAVE] [X] [⊟] [≋] [X]

◆◆ Holiday Inn Ocala M ❀
(352) 629-0381. **$109, 5 days notice.** 3621 W Silver Springs Blvd. I-75, exit 69, just e. Ext corridors. **Pets:** Other. $20 one-time fee/room. Designated rooms, supervision.

[SAVE] [S⚬] [X] [⊟] [▣] [↿↾] [≋]

◆◆◆ La Quinta Inn & Suites M
(352) 861-1137. **$75-$109.** 3530 SW 36th Ave. I-75 exit 68, just e. Int corridors. **Pets:** Supervision.

[ASK] [X] [≪] [⊟] [≋]

◆◆ Ramada Inn & Conference Center M ❀
(352) 732-3131. **$55-$79.** 3810 NW Blitchton Rd. US 27, just w of jct I-75, exit 70. Ext corridors. **Pets:** Small. $50 deposit/room, $5 daily fee/room, $5 one-time fee/room. Designated rooms, no service, supervision, crate.

[ASK] [X] [≪] [⊟] [↿↾] [≋] [X]

OKEECHOBEE

◆◆ Budget Inn M ❀
(863) 763-3185. **$59-$89.** 201 S Parrott Ave. US 98 and 441, just s of jct SR 70. Ext corridors. **Pets:** Small, dogs only. $7 daily fee/pet. Designated rooms, no service, supervision, crate.

[SAVE] [S⚬] [X] [⊟] [≋]

◆◆ Economy Inn M ❀
(863) 763-1148. **$45-$79, 3 days notice.** 507 N Parrott Ave. US 441, 0.3 mi n of jct SR 70. Ext corridors. **Pets:** Small. $5 daily fee/pet, $5 one-time fee/pet. No service, supervision, crate.

[SAVE] [X] [⊟]

◆◆◆ Holiday Inn Express M ❀
(863) 357-3529. **$79-$135.** 3975 Hwy 441 S. US 98 and 441, 3 mi s of jct SR 70, 0.3 mi n of Lake Okeechobee and jct SR 78. Ext corridors. **Pets:** Small, dogs only. Designated rooms, no service, supervision, crate.

[ASK] [X] [∩] [∅] [⊟] [≋]

OLD TOWN

◆◆ Suwannee Gables Motel M ❀
(352) 542-7752. **$48-$115, 7 days notice.** HC 3 Box 208. US 19, 98 and 27A; 2 mi s of jct SR 349. Ext corridors. **Pets:** Small, other. $60 deposit/pet, $8 daily fee/pet, $8 one-time fee/pet. No service, supervision, crate.

[X] [⊟] [≋] [X]

ORLANDO METROPOLITAN AREA

ALTAMONTE SPRINGS

◆◆◆ **Embassy Suites Orlando North** 🅷
(407) 834-2400. **$109-$134.** 225 E Altamonte Dr. Jct I-4, exit 48, 0.3 mi e on SR 436, 0.3 mi n on North Lake Blvd. Int corridors. **Pets:** Designated rooms, no service, supervision, crate.

A$K 🌡 ⊠ 🛅 🍽 ⬛ 🖥 💻 🍴 🏊

🏾 ◆◆◆ **Hampton Inn** 🅼 🐾
(407) 869-9000. **$85.** 151 N Douglas Ave. Just nw of jct SR 436 and I-4, exit 48. Ext corridors. **Pets:** $60 one-time fee/room. No service, supervision, crate.

SAVE ⊠ ♿ 🍽 ⬛ 🖥 💻 🏊

◆◆◆ **La Quinta Inn-Orlando North** 🅼
(407) 788-1411. **$89-$109.** 150 S Westmonte Dr. Just s of SR 436; 0.3 mi w of jct I-4, exit 48. Ext corridors. **Pets:** Medium. Supervision.

A$K ⊠ 🍽 🖥 ⬛ 💻 🏊

◆◆◆ **Residence Inn by Marriott** 🅰
(407) 788-7991. **$128-$159.** 270 Douglas Ave. Jct I-4, exit 48; just w on SR 436, just n. Ext corridors. **Pets:** Small. Designated rooms, no service, supervision, crate.

A$K ⊠ 🍽 ⬛ 💻 🏊 ⊠

APOPKA

◆◆◆ **Crosby's Motor Inn** 🅼 🐾
(407) 886-3220. **$50-$60, 7 days notice.** 1440 W Orange Blossom Tr Hwy 441. 1.8 mi nw on US 441. Ext corridors. **Pets:** $10 daily fee/pet. Supervision.

⊠ ⬛ 💻 🏊 CTV

CLERMONT

◆◆ **Mulberry Inn B&B** 🅲 🐾
(352) 242-0670. **$70-$95, 7 days notice.** 915 W Montrose St. 1.6 mi w of US 27 on SR 50, 0.3 mi on 8th St, just w. Ext/int corridors. **Pets:** Small, other. $10 one-time fee/pet. Designated rooms, supervision.

⊠ ⬛ 💻 🍴 ⊠

DAVENPORT

🏾 ◆◆◆ **Days Inn-South of Disney** 🅼
(863) 424-2596. **$49-$159.** 2425 Frontage Rd. On US 27; just s of jct I-4, exit 23. Ext corridors. **Pets:** Supervision.

SAVE ⊠ 🛅 ⬛ 🏊

◆◆◆ **Super 8 Motel Maingate South** 🅼 🐾
(863) 420-8888. **$39-$79.** 5620 US Hwy 27 N. 0.5 mi n of jct I-4, exit 23. Ext corridors. **Pets:** Medium, other. Supervision.

A$K ⊠ 🖥 ⬛ 🏊

KISSIMMEE

🏾 ◆◆ **Best Western-Eastgate** 🅼 🐾
(407) 396-0707. **$49-$159.** 5565 W Irlo Bronson Memorial Hwy. On US 192, 2 mi e of jct I-4, exit 25A. Ext corridors. **Pets:** Other. $10 daily fee/room. Designated rooms, no service, supervision, crate.

SAVE ⊠ 🍽 ⬛ 🍴 🏊 ⊠

🏾 ◆◆◆ **Comfort Suites Main Gate Resort** 🅼 🐾
(407) 390-9888. **$59-$150.** 7888 W Irlo Bronson Hwy. 3.5 mi w of jct I-4 exit 25; on US 192. Ext corridors. **Pets:** Small, other. Supervision.

SAVE ⊠ ♿ 🍽 ⬛ 🖥 💻 🏊

🏾 ◆◆ **Days Suites/Main Gate East of Walt Disney World Resort** 🅼 🐾
(407) 396-7900. **$259-$399, 3 days notice.** 5820 W Irlo Bronson Memorial Hwy. US 192, 1.5 mi e of I-4, exit 25A. Ext corridors. **Pets:** Small, dogs only. $10 deposit/pet. Designated rooms, no service, supervision, crate.

SAVE ⊠ 🍽 ⬛ 🏊

🏾 ◆◆ **Flamingo Inn** 🅼 🐾
(407) 846-1935. **$24-$39, 3 days notice.** 801 E Vine St. US 192, 0.3 mi e of jct 441 and 192. Ext corridors. **Pets:** Small, dogs only. $8 daily fee/pet. No service, supervision, crate.

SAVE 🌡 ⊠ 🖥 ⬛ 💻 🏊

◆◆◆ **Holiday Inn Hotel & Suites Main Gate East** 🅼🅸 🐾
(407) 396-4488. **$89-$109.** 5678 W Irlo Bronson Memorial Hwy. On US 192; 2 mi e of jct I-4 exit 25A. Ext corridors. **Pets:** Small, other. Supervision.

A$K 🌡 ⊠ ♿ 🍽 🖥 ⬛ 💻 🍴 🏊 ⊠

🏾 ◆◆ **Holiday Inn Kissimmee Downtown** 🅼🅸
(407) 846-2713. **$145-$165, 3 days notice.** 2009 W Vine St. I-4, 8 mi e at exit 25A; on US 192 1.3 mi w of jct US 17-92 and 441. Ext corridors. **Pets:** Small. Supervision.

SAVE 🌡 ⊠ ⬛ 💻 🍴 🏊 ⊠

🏾 ◆◆◆ **Holiday Inn Maingate West** 🅼🅸 🐾
(407) 396-1100. **$89-$189, 3 days notice.** 7601 Black Lake Rd. Just n of US 192, 2.8 mi w of I-4, exit 25B; 1 mi w of Disney main gate access road. Ext corridors. **Pets:** Small. $100 deposit/room, $50 one-time fee/room. No service, supervision, crate.

SAVE 🌡 ⊠ 🍽 🖥 ⬛ 💻 🍴 🏊 ⊠

🏾 ◆◆◆ **Holiday Inn-Nikki Bird Resort-Maingate** 🅼🅸
(407) 396-7300. **$80-$225.** 7300 W Irlo Bronson Memorial Hwy. US 192, 2.3 mi w of jct I-4 exit 25B; 1 mi w of Disney World main gate. Ext corridors. **Pets:** Small. Supervision.

SAVE ⊠ ♿ 🍽 🖥 ⬛ 💻 🍴 🏊 ⊠

◆◆◆ **Homewood Suites Maingate at the Parkway** 🅼
(407) 396-2229. **$139.** 3100 Parkway Blvd. 0.3 mi e of I-4 exit 25A; 0.5 mi n of US 192. Ext/int corridors. **Pets:** Medium. Supervision.

A$K ⊠ ⬛ 💻 🏊 ⊠

🏾 ◆◆ **Larson's Inn & Family Suites** 🅼🅸 🐾
(407) 396-6100. **$69-$99, 3 days notice.** 6075 W Irlo Bronson Memorial Hwy. On US 192, 1 mi e of jct I-4 exit 25A. Ext corridors. **Pets:** Medium. $150 deposit/pet, $10 daily fee/pet. Supervision.

SAVE ⊠ ⬛ 💻 🍴 🏊 ⊠

⚫⚫⚫ ◆◆ Magic Castle Inn & Suites
Eastgate M ☼
(407) 396-1212. **$34-$58.** 4559 W Hwy 192. 4.5 mi w of US 17-92 and 441; 6.5 mi e of Disney/Epcot entrance. Ext corridors. **Pets:** $25 deposit/room, $6 daily fee/pet. Designated rooms, supervision.

⊞ ⓢ ⊠ ⊟ ⊡ ⊜ ⊠

⚫⚫⚫ ◆◆ Magic Castle Inn & Suites
Maingate M ☼
(407) 396-2212. **$36-$60.** 5055 W Irlo Bronson Memorial Hwy. US 192; 3.2 mi e of jct I-4. Ext corridors. **Pets:** Small. $25 deposit/pet, $6 daily fee/pet. Designated rooms, supervision.

⊞ ⊠ ⊟ ⊜ ⊠

⚫⚫⚫ ◆◆ Masters Inn-Kissimmee M
(407) 396-4020. **$59-$79.** 5367 W Irlo Bronson Hwy. US 192, 2.5 mi e of jct I-4, exit 25. Ext corridors. **Pets:** Small. No service, supervision, crate.

⊞ ⓢ ⊠ ⊟ ⊡

⚫⚫⚫ ◆◆ Masters Inn-Main Gate M
(407) 396-7743. **$59-$79.** 2945 Entry Point Blvd. On US 192; 2.5 mi w of jct I-4 exit 25; 1 mi w of Disney World main gate. Ext corridors. **Pets:** Small. Supervision.

⊞ ⓢ ⊠ ⊟ ⊜

⚫⚫⚫ ◆◆ Motel 6-464 M 🐾
(407) 396-6333. **$30-$56.** 5731 W Irlo Bronson Hwy. 2 mi e of I-4, exit 25. Ext corridors. **Pets:** Medium. No service, supervision, crate.

⊠ ♿ ⊘ ⊡ ⊟ ⊜

⚫⚫⚫ ◆◆ Motel 6-436 M
(407) 396-6422. **$40-$56.** 7455 W Irlo Bronson Hwy. US 192, 2 mi w of Jct I-4, exit 25; 1 mi w of Disney World main gate. Ext corridors. **Pets:** Small. No service, supervision, crate.

⊠ ⓕ ⊘ ⊡ ⊜

⚫⚫⚫ ◆◆◆ Ramada Inn Resort Maingate Ⓜ ☼
(407) 396-4466. **$89-$189, 3 days notice.** 2950 Reedy Creek Blvd. On US 192; 2 mi w of jct I-4, 1 mi w of Disney World access road. Ext corridors. **Pets:** Small. $75 one-time fee/room. Supervision.

⊞ ⓢ ⊠ ♿ ⊘ ⊡ ⊟ ⊡ ⊡ ⊜ ⊠

⚫⚫⚫ ◆◆ Red Roof Inn M
(407) 396-0065. **$41-$68.** 4970 Kyngs Heath Rd. 3.2 mi se I-4, exit 27. Ext corridors. **Pets:** Supervision.

⊞ ⊠ ⊟ ⊜

⚫⚫⚫ ◆◆◆ Summerfield Resort ▲ ☼
(407) 847-7222. **$250-$299.** 2422 Summerfield Pl. SR 423 (Bermuda Ave), 1 mi n of US 192, Florida Tpke exit 249; 2.5 mi w and 2.5 mi s. Ext corridors. **Pets:** Other. $25 one-time fee/pet. Supervision.

⊞ ⊠ ⊘ ⊡ ⊜ ⊠

⚫⚫⚫ ◆◆ Travelodge Hotel 🅷 🐾
(407) 846-1530. **$39-$79.** 201 Simpson Rd. Florida Tpke exit 244; 0.3 mi w on US 192, just n. Ext corridors. **Pets:** Small, other. $5 daily fee/room, $5 one-time fee/room. Supervision.

⊞ ⊠ ⊟ ⊡ ⊡ ⊜

LAKE BUENA VISTA

⚫⚫⚫ ◆◆ Comfort Inn At Lake Buena
Vista Ⓜ ☼
(407) 239-7200. **$99.** 8442 Palm Pkwy. 0.5 mi n on CR 535 from jct I-4, exit 27, 0.5 mi e. Ext corridors. **Pets:** Medium, other. $50 deposit/room, $6 daily fee/pet. No service, supervision, crate.

⊞ ⊠ ♿ ⊘ ⓕ ⊟ ⊡ ⊜

⚫⚫⚫ ◆◆ Days Inn Lake Buena Vista
Hotel Ⓜ ☼
(407) 239-4441. **$73-$180.** 12799 Apopka-Vineland Rd. CR 535 at jct I-4, exit 27. Int corridors. **Pets:** Small, other. Supervision.

⊞ ⊠ ⊘ ⊡ ⊜ ⊠

⚫⚫⚫ ◆◆◆ Holiday Inn-SunSpree Resort-Lake
Buena Vista 🅷 ☼
(407) 239-4500. **$68-$189.** 13351 SR 535. SR 535; 0.3 mi se of I-4, exit 27. Ext corridors. **Pets:** Small, other. $25 one-time fee/room. Supervision.

⊞ ⓢ ⊠ ⊘ ⊟ ⊡ ⊡ ⊜ ⊠

⚫⚫⚫ ◆◆◆ Residence Inn by Marriott, Lake Buena
Vista ▲ ☼
(407) 239-7700. **$219-$289.** 8800 Meadow Creek Dr. 0.5 mi se of jct I-4 exit 27, on SR 535, 0.8 mi s at sign. Ext corridors. **Pets:** Other. $100 deposit/room, $50 one-time fee/room. No service, supervision, crate.

⊞ ⓢ ⊠ ⓕ ⊡ ⊡ ⊜ ⊠

LAKE MARY

◆◆◆ La Quinta Inn & Suites M ☼
(407) 805-9901. **$99-$125.** 1060 Greenwood Blvd. Just se of I-4, exit 50 via Lake Mary Blvd. Int corridors. **Pets:** Small, other. No service, supervision, crate.

ⒶⓈⓀ ♿ ⊘ ⓕ ⊟ ⊡ ⊜

⚫⚫⚫ ◆◆◆ MainStay Suites M ☼
(407) 829-2332. **$80, 7 days notice.** 1040 Greenwood Blvd. I-4, exit 50, 0.5 mi s on Lake Emma Rd; in Commerce Park. Int corridors. **Pets:** Small. $100 deposit/room, $10 daily fee/pet. No service, supervision, crate.

⊞ ⓢ ⊠ ♿ ⊘ ⓕ ⊟ ⊡

LEESBURG

⚫⚫⚫ ◆◆ Shoney's Inn Meeting & Conference
Center M
(352) 787-1210. **$49-$55.** 1308 N 14th St. At jct US 27 and 441. Ext corridors. **Pets:** Supervision.

⊞ ⓢ ⊠ ⊜

◆◆ Super 8 Motel M ☼
(352) 787-6363. **Call for rates.** 1392 North Blvd W. At jct US 27 and 441. Int corridors. **Pets:** Small. No service, supervision, crate.

⊠ ⓕ ⊘ ⊟ ⊜

LONGWOOD

◆◆ Ramada Inn North-Orlando 🅼 ❖

(407) 862-4000. **$64-$68.** 2025 W SR 434. SR 434 at jct I-4, exit 49. Ext corridors. **Pets:** Medium. No service, supervision, crate.

(ASK) (S🔒) (✕) (🖥) (🍴) (🌊)

MAITLAND

◆◆◆ Wellesley Inn & Suites 🅼

(407) 659-0066. **$89-$129.** 1951 Summit Tower Blvd. I-4, exit 47, 1 mi w. Int corridors. **Pets:** No service, supervision, crate.

(SAVE) (✕) (♿) (🐾) (📋) (🖥) (💻) (🌊)

ORLANDO

◆◆◆ AmeriSuites Orlando Airport 🅼 ❖

(407) 240-3939. **$99-$109.** 7500 Augusta National Dr. 2 mi n of airport terminal via SR 436 and TG Lee Blvd. Int corridors. **Pets:** Small, other. Supervision.

(SAVE) (✕) (🐾) (📋) (🖥) (💻) (🌊)

◆◆◆ AmeriSuites (Orlando/Convention Center) 🅼 ❖

(407) 370-4720. **$89-$129.** 8741 International Dr. 0.7 mi s of SR 482 (Sandlake Rd), just e of I-4, exit 29A. Int corridors. **Pets:** Small, other. Supervision.

(SAVE) (✕) (🐾) (📋) (🖥) (💻) (🌊)

◆◆◆ Baymont Inn & Suites-Orlando South 🅼

(407) 240-0500. **$64-$64.** 2051 Consulate Dr. US 17-92 and 441, just s of SR 528 (Bee Line Expwy), off Florida Tpke, exit 254. Int corridors. **Pets:** No service, supervision, crate.

(✕) (🐾) (🖥) (💻) (🌊)

◆◆ Best Western Orlando West 🅼 ❖

(407) 841-8600. **$69-$99, 3 days notice.** 2014 W Colonial Dr. SR 50, 1.5 mi w of I-4; 0.4 mi e of jct SR 423. Int corridors. **Pets:** Small. $25 deposit/room, $5 daily fee/room. Designated rooms, no service, supervision, crate.

(SAVE) (✕) (🖥) (💻) (🍴) (🌊)

◆◆◆ Comfort Inn-North 🅼 ❖

(407) 629-4000. **$79-$125.** 830 Lee Rd. SR 423; 0.4 mi w of jct I-4, exit 46 (Lee Rd). Int corridors. **Pets:** Medium. $10 daily fee/pet, $25 one-time fee/room. Designated rooms, no service, supervision, crate.

(SAVE) (✕) (🐾) (📋) (🖥) (💻) (🌊)

◆◆ Days Inn-Convention Center/Sea World 🅼 ❖

(407) 352-8700. **$59-$118.** 9990 International Dr. I-4, exit 28, then just e to International Dr; Bee Line Expwy (SR 528), exit 1, then just n. Ext corridors. **Pets:** Medium. Supervision.

(SAVE) (✕) (🐾) (🍴) (🌊) (✕)

◆◆ Days Inn East of Universal Studios 🅼 ❖

(407) 351-3800. **$89-$119, 3 days notice.** 5827 Caravan Ct. 0.3 mi e of SR 435 (Kirkman Rd); 0.8 mi ne of I-4, exit 30B. Ext corridors. **Pets:** Medium, other. $10 daily fee/pet. Supervision.

(SAVE) (S🔒) (✕) (🏠) (🐾) (📋) (🍴) (🌊)

◆ Econo Lodge-Central 🅼 ❖

(407) 293-7221. **$46-$85, 5 days notice.** 3300 W Colonial Dr. SR 50, 2 mi w of jct I-4, 1.2 mi w of jct US 17-92 and 441. Ext corridors. **Pets:** Medium, other. $6 daily fee/room. Designated rooms, no service, supervision, crate.

(SAVE) (✕) (🌊)

◆◆◆ Holiday Inn Express 🅼

(407) 351-4430. **$89-$189, 3 days notice.** 6323 International Dr. From I-4, exit 30A, to 1st light, then just right. Int corridors. **Pets:** Medium. Designated rooms, no service, supervision, crate.

(SAVE) (S🔒) (✕) (♿) (🐾) (📋) (🖥) (💻) (🌊)

◆◆◆ Holiday Inn Hotel & Suites At Universal Studios 🅼 ❖

(407) 351-3333. **$89-$109, 3 days notice.** 5905 S Kirkman Rd. On SR 435 (Kirkman Rd); 0.5 mi n of I-4, exit 30B. Int corridors. **Pets:** Medium. $50 one-time fee/pet. No service, supervision, crate.

(ASK) (✕) (♿) (🐾) (📋) (🖥) (💻) (🍴) (🌊)

◆◆◆ Holiday Inn-International Drive Resort 🅼 ❖

(407) 351-3500. **$89-$225.** 6515 International Dr. I-4, exit 29, just e on Sand Lake Rd, then 0.5 mi n. Ext/int corridors. **Pets:** Small, other. $75 deposit/pet, $25 one-time fee/pet. No service, supervision, crate.

(SAVE) (✕) (🏠) (🐾) (📋) (🖥) (💻) (🍴) (🌊) (✕)

◆◆◆ Holiday Inn Orlando North-Winter Park 🅼

(407) 645-5600. **$79-$109.** 626 Lee Rd. SR 438, just w of I-4, exit 46 (Lee Rd). Int corridors. **Pets:** Small. No service, supervision, crate.

(S🔒) (✕) (🐾) (📋) (🖥) (💻) (🍴) (🌊)

◆◆ Howard Johnson Plaza Resort Universal Gateway 🅼

(407) 351-2000. **$64-$102, 3 days notice.** 7050 Kirkman Rd. On SR 435, 0.8 mi s of jct I-4, exit 30A. **Pets:** Small. No service, supervision, crate.

(SAVE) (S🔒) (✕) (🖥) (🍴) (🌊) (✕)

◆◆◆ La Quinta Inn Airport 🅼 ❖

(407) 857-9215. **$85-$105.** 7931 Daetwyler Dr. Bee Line Expwy (SR 528); at Trade Port exit 9, via McCoy Rd. Int corridors. **Pets:** Small, other. Designated rooms, supervision.

(ASK) (✕) (🐾) (📋) (🖥) (💻) (🌊)

◆◆◆ La Quinta Inn & Suites Orlando Airport North 🅼 ❖

(407) 240-5000. **$102-$122.** 7160 N Frontage Rd. Just w of SR 436, just n of SR 528 (Bee Line Expwy). Int corridors. **Pets:** Small. No service, supervision, crate.

(ASK) (✕) (🐾) (📋) (🖥) (💻) (🌊)

◆◆◆ La Quinta Inn-Orlando International Drive 🅼 ❖

(407) 351-1660. **$75-$105.** 8300 Jamaican Ct. I-4, exit 29, just e on Sand Lake Rd, then just s on International Dr. Ext corridors. **Pets:** Small, other. Supervision.

(ASK) (✕) (♿) (🐾) (📋) (🖥) (💻) (🌊) (✕)

⬥⬥ Masters Inn International Drive M ❀
(407) 345-1172. **$69-$89.** 8222 Jamaican Ct. I-4, exit 29, just e on Sand Lake Rd, then just s on International Dr. Ext corridors. **Pets:** Other. No service, supervision, crate.
[SAVE] [✕] [🖉] [🛏] [🔲]

⬥⬥ Quality Inn International MI
(407) 996-1600. **$39-$99.** 7600 International Dr. I-4, exit 29, just e on Sand Lake Rd, then just n. Ext corridors. **Pets:** Medium. Designated rooms, no service, supervision, crate.
[ASK] [S🔲] [✕] [🍴] [🔲]

⬥⬥⬥ Quality Inn-Plaza MI ❀
(407) 996-8585. **$39-$99.** 9000 International Dr. I-4, exit 29, just e on Sand Lake Rd, then 1 mi s (SR 482). Ext corridors. **Pets:** Medium, other. $50 deposit/room, $6 daily fee/pet. No service, supervision, crate.
[ASK] [✕] [🔲] [🖉] [🔲] [🍴] [🔲]

⬤⬤⬤ ⬥⬥ Red Roof Inn M ❀
(407) 352-1507. **$50-$100.** 9922 Hawaiian Ct. I-4, exit 28, then just e to International Dr; Bee Line Expwy (SR 528), exit 1, then just n. Ext corridors. **Pets:** Small. No service, supervision, crate.
[SAVE] [✕] [🔲] [🛏] [🔲]

⬥⬥⬥ Residence Inn by Marriott-Orlando International Dr A
(407) 345-0117. **$109-$249.** 7975 Canada Ave. I-4,exit 29; then just e on Sand Lake Rd (SR 482). Ext corridors. **Pets:** Medium. Supervision.
[ASK] [S🔲] [✕] [🖉] [🔲] [🛏] [🔲] [🔲]

⬥⬥ Rodeway Inn International M ❀
(407) 996-4444. **$39-$95.** 6327 International Dr. I-4 exit 30A, 1st light, right 0.5 mi. Ext/int corridors. **Pets:** Medium, other. $50 deposit/room, $6 daily fee/pet. No service, supervision, crate.
[ASK] [✕] [🔲] [🖉] [🔲] [🔲] [🍴] [🔲]

⬤⬤⬤ ⬥ Travelodge Orlando Centroplex M ❀
(407) 423-1671. **$45-$80.** 409 N Magnolia Ave. Corner of Magnolia Ave, Rosalind Ave and Livingston St. Ext/int corridors. **Pets:** Medium, other. Supervision.
[SAVE] [S🔲] [✕] [🔲] [🔲]

⬥⬥⬥ Wellesley Inn & Suites M
(407) 345-0026. **$69-$99.** 5635 Windhover Dr. Just e of SR 435 (Kirkman Rd); 1 mi n of I-4 exit 30B. Int corridors. **Pets:** Designated rooms, supervision.
[SAVE] [✕] [🔲] [🖉] [🔲] [🛏] [🔲] [🔲]

⬥⬥ Wellesley Inn & Suites M
(407) 248-8010. **$95-$115.** 8687 Commodity Cir. Just w SR 423 (John Young Pkwy), just s of SR 482 (Sandlake Rd), in Southpark development. Int corridors. **Pets:** Supervision.
[SAVE] [S🔲] [✕] [🖉] [🔲] [🛏] [🔲] [🔲]

SANFORD

⬥⬥ Marina Hotel & Conference Center MI ❀
(407) 323-1910. **$49-$59.** 530 N Palmetto Ave. 4.5 mi se of I-4, exit 51 (SR 46); 0.3 mi n. Ext corridors. **Pets:** Very small. $20 one-time fee/room. No service, supervision, crate.
[ASK] [✕] [🔲] [🔲] [🍴] [🔲] [✕]

⬥ Super 8 Motel M ❀
(407) 323-3445. **$45-$85.** 4750 SR 46 W. Jct I-4 and exit 51. Ext corridors. **Pets:** Other. $50 deposit/room. Supervision.
[ASK] [✕] [🔲] [🔲]

TAVARES

⬤⬤⬤ ⬥ Budget Inn M
(352) 343-4666. **$65-$79.** 101 W Burleigh Blvd. On US 441, 0.3 mi e of jct SR 19 S. Ext corridors. **Pets:** Designated rooms, supervision.
[✕] [🔲] [🔲]

⬤⬤⬤ ⬥⬥⬥ Inn On The Green M ❀
(352) 343-6373. **$56-$74.** 700 E Burleigh Blvd. On US 441, 1 mi e of jct SR 19. Ext corridors. **Pets:** Small, other. $50 deposit/room. Designated rooms, supervision.
[SAVE] [✕] [🔲] [🔲] [🔲] [✕]

❀ **END METROPOLITAN AREA** ❀

ORMOND BEACH

⬤⬤⬤ ⬥⬥⬥ Comfort Inn Interstate M ❀
(904) 672-8621. **$79-$150, 30 days notice.** 1567 N US 1 & I-95. On US 1 at jct I-95 exit 89. Ext corridors. **Pets:** Supervision.
[SAVE] [✕] [🖉] [🔲]

⬤⬤⬤ ⬥⬥ Comfort Inn On The Beach M ❀
(904) 677-8550. **$60-$145.** 507 S Atlantic Ave. SR A1A; 1 mi s of jct SR 40. Ext corridors. **Pets:** Very small. $5 daily fee/pet. No service, supervision, crate.
[SAVE] [✕] [🔲] [🔲]

⬤⬤⬤ ⬥⬥ Days Inn Ormond Beach I-95 M ❀
(904) 672-7341. **$40-$90.** 1608 N US 1 & I-95. On US 1, just nw of jct I-95 exit 89. Ext corridors. **Pets:** Other. $5 daily fee/room. Supervision.
[SAVE] [S🔲] [✕] [🔲]

⬤⬤⬤ ⬥⬥ Driftwood Beach Motel M
(904) 677-1331. **$45-$63.** 657 S Atlantic Ave. On SR A1A; 1.5 mi s of jct SR 40. Ext corridors. **Pets:** Very small. Designated rooms, no service, supervision, crate.
[SAVE] [🔲] [🔲]

PALM BEACH

⬤⬤⬤ ⬥⬥⬥ The Chesterfield Hotel H
(561) 659-5800. **$229-$450, 7 days notice.** 363 Cocoanut Row. Just w of SR A1A at Australian Ave and Cocoanut Row. Int corridors. **Pets:** Small. Designated rooms, no service, supervision, crate.
[SAVE] [✕] [🖉] [🔲] [🍴] [🔲]

ⒶⒶⒶ ◆◆◆◆◆ The Four Seasons Resort, Palm Beach 🅷 ☙
(561) 582-2800. **$385-$660, 7 days notice.** 2800 S Ocean Blvd. SR A1A, 0.3 mi n of jct SR 802. Int corridors. **Pets:** Very small. Designated rooms, supervision.
ⓈⒶⓋⒺ ⊠ 🐾 ⑪ 🍽 ⊠

◆◆◆ Heart of Palm Beach Hotel 🅼🅸
(561) 655-5600. **$149-$259.** 160 Royal Palm Way. Center; just e of SR A1A. Int corridors. **Pets:** Medium. Designated rooms, no service, supervision, crate.
ⒶⓈⓀ ⊠ 🐾 🅱 ⑪ 🍽 ⊠

ⒶⒶⒶ ◆◆◆ Plaza Inn 🅱🅱 ☙
(561) 832-8666. **$195-$250, 3 days notice.** 215 Brazilian Ave. Center; at Brazilian Ave and SR A1A (s County Rd). Int corridors. **Pets:** Medium. Supervision.
ⓈⒶⓋⒺ ⊠ 🐾 🅱 🍽

PALM BEACH GARDENS
ⒶⒶⒶ ◆◆ Inns of America 🅼
(561) 626-4918. **$81-$81.** 4123 Northlake Blvd. Jct I-95 exit 56. Ext corridors. **Pets:** No service, supervision, crate.
ⓈⒶⓋⒺ ⊠ 🅱 🍽

PALM BEACH SHORES
ⒶⒶⒶ ◆◆ Best Western Seaspray Inn 🅼🅸 ☙
(561) 844-0233. **$100-$170.** 123 S Ocean Ave. On Singer Island; 0.5 mi s of SR A1A. Int corridors. **Pets:** Medium. $15 daily fee/pet. Supervision.
ⓈⒶⓋⒺ ⊠ 🅱 🖵 🍽 ⊠

PALM COAST
ⒶⒶⒶ ◆◆ Palm Coast Villas 🅼 ☙
(904) 445-3525. **$45-$45, 30 days notice.** 5454 N Oceanshore Blvd. I-95 exit 91C; 2.8 mi e to SR A1A, 1.8 mi n. Ext corridors. **Pets:** Other. No service, supervision, crate.
ⓈⒶⓋⒺ 🍽

PANAMA CITY
ⒶⒶⒶ ◆◆ Best Western Bayside Inn 🅼🅸 ☙
(850) 763-4622. **$68-$130, 3 days notice.** 711 W Beach Dr. Business Rt US 98; 0.5 mi w of jct US 231. Ext corridors. **Pets:** Other. $10 one-time fee/room. Designated rooms, supervision.
ⓈⒶⓋⒺ Ⓢ🄳 ⊠ 🅱 🖵 ⑪ 🍽 ⊠

◆◆◆ La Quinta Inn and Suites 🅼 ☙
(850) 914-0022. **$72-$95.** 1030 E 23rd St. Jct US 231 and CR 390A. Int corridors. **Pets:** Small. No service, supervision, crate.
ⒶⓈⓀ ⊠ 🄻 🄴 🅱 🖵 🍽

◆ Super 8 Motel 🅼
(850) 784-1988. **Call for rates, 7 days notice.** 207 Hwy 231 N. Just n of jct US 98. Ext/int corridors. **Pets:** Small. No service, supervision, crate.
⊠ 🅱 🍽

PENSACOLA
ⒶⒶⒶ ◆◆ Comfort Inn-NAS Corry 🅼 ☙
(850) 455-3233. **$79-$89.** 3 New Warrington Rd. Just n of jct US 98 and SR 292. Ext corridors. **Pets:** Other. $25 one-time fee/pet. Supervision.
ⓈⒶⓋⒺ Ⓢ🄳 ⊠ 🅱 🖵 🍽

◆◆ Days Inn North 🅼 ☙
(850) 476-9090. **$49-$89, 7 days notice.** 7051 Pensacola Blvd. I-10, exit 3A, 0.3 mi s on US 29. Int corridors. **Pets:** Medium. $10 daily fee/pet, $10 one-time fee/pet. No service, supervision, crate.
ⒶⓈⓀ ⊠ 🅱 🍽

◆◆◆ La Quinta Inn 🅼 ☙
(850) 474-0411. **$69-$95.** 7750 N Davis Hwy. I-10, exit 5; just n on SR 291. Ext corridors. **Pets:** Medium. Supervision.
ⒶⓈⓀ ⊠ 🄴 🅱 🖵 🍽 ⒸⓉⓋ

◆◆◆ The Pensacola Grand Hotel 🅷 ☙
(850) 433-3336. **$90-$100, 3 days notice.** 200 E Gregory St. Jct I-110 and US 98. Int corridors. **Pets:** Small. $50 one-time fee/room. Supervision.
ⒶⓈⓀ Ⓢ🄳 ⊠ 🅱 🖵 ⑪ 🍽

ⒶⒶⒶ ◆◆◆ Ramada Inn Bayview 🅼🅸 ☙
(850) 477-7155. **$72-$78, 3 days notice.** 7601 Scenic Hwy. US 90, sw of I-10 exit 6. Int corridors. **Pets:** Small, other. Supervision.
ⓈⒶⓋⒺ Ⓢ🄳 ⊠ 🅱 🖵 ⑪ 🍽

◆◆ Ramada Limited 🅼 ☙
(850) 944-0333. **$52-$58.** 8060 Lavalle Way. I-10, exit 2, just sw. Ext corridors. **Pets:** Medium. $25 one-time fee/room. Supervision.
ⒶⓈⓀ Ⓢ🄳 ⊠ 🅱 🖵 🍽

◆◆ Red Roof Inn 🅼 ☙
(850) 478-4499. **$44-$93.** 6919 Pensacola Blvd. I-10 exit 3A, 0.5 mi s. Int corridors. **Pets:** Other. Supervision.
ⒶⓈⓀ ⊠ 🅱 🍽

ⒶⒶⒶ ◆◆ Red Roof Inn 🅼 ☙
(850) 476-7960. **$46-$60.** 7340 Plantation Rd. I-10, exit 5, just s University Mall entrance. Ext corridors. **Pets:** Small. No service, supervision, crate.
ⓈⒶⓋⒺ ⊠ ⒸⓉⓋ

ⒶⒶⒶ ◆◆◆ Shoney's Inn & Suites 🅼 ☙
(850) 484-8070. **$67-$67, 3 days notice.** 8080 N Davis Hwy. I-10, exit 5, just n on SR 291. Int corridors. **Pets:** Other. $17 one-time fee/room. No service, supervision, crate.
ⓈⒶⓋⒺ Ⓢ🄳 ⊠ 🅱 🖵 🍽

PERRY
ⒶⒶⒶ ◆◆ Best Budget Inn 🅼 ☙
(850) 584-6231. **$38-$43.** 2220 US 19 S. US 19 and 98, 0.4 mi s jct US 221. Ext corridors. **Pets:** $2 daily fee/room, $3 one-time fee/room. Supervision.
ⓈⒶⓋⒺ ⊠ 🍽

PORT CHARLOTTE

◆◆◆ Days Inn of Port Charlotte M
(941) 627-8900. **$79-$109.** 1941 Tamiami Tr. On US 41. Ext corridors. **Pets:** Supervision.

[ASK] [✕] [🖊] [🛏] [🖼]

▲▲▲ ◆◆◆ Quality Inn Downtown M
(941) 625-4181. **$85-$100.** 3400 Tamiami Tr. Center on US 41, just s of jct Harbor Blvd. Ext/int corridors. **Pets:** Small. Designated rooms, no service, supervision, crate.

[SAVE] [✕] [🛏] [💻] [🖼]

PUNTA GORDA

▲▲▲ ◆◆◆ Best Western Waterfront Inn MI ❖
(941) 639-1165. **$89-$109.** 300 Retta Esplanade. US 41 southbound, just s of Peace River Bridge. Int corridors. **Pets:** Other. $25 one-time fee/pet. Supervision.

[SAVE] [✕] [🖊] [🛏] [💻] [🍴] [🖼] [✕]

QUINCY

◆◆ Allison House Inn BB ❖
(850) 875-2511. **$80-$95.** 215 N Madison St. Just e of town center. Int corridors. **Pets:** Small, dogs only. Supervision.

[ASK] [🔊] [✕] [✕] [✉]

SANIBEL

▲▲▲ ◆◆ Waterside Inn on the Beach M ❖
(941) 472-1345. **$184-$270** (no credit cards), 30 days notice. 3033 W Gulf Dr. From causeway, Periwinkle Way 4 mi w to Tarpon Bay Rd, 1 mi s, then 1 mi w. Ext corridors. **Pets:** Small. $5 one-time fee/pet. Designated rooms, supervision.

[✕] [🛏] [💻] [🖼] [✕]

SARASOTA

▲▲▲ ◆◆ The Calais Motel-Apartments A
(941) 921-5797. **$79-$98, 3 days notice.** 1735 Stickney Point Rd. On SR 72, 0.3 mi sw of jct US 41. Ext corridors. **Pets:** Designated rooms, no service, supervision, crate.

[SAVE] [✕] [🛏] [💻] [🖼]

▲▲▲ ◆◆◆ Comfort Inn M
(941) 921-7750. **$79-$129.** 5778 Clark Rd. I-75 exit 37, just w on SR 72. Int corridors. **Pets:** No service, supervision, crate.

[SAVE] [✕] [🖊] [🖋] [🛏] [🖼]

▲▲▲ ◆◆◆ Coquina on the Beach
Resort M ❖
(941) 388-2141. **$169-$199.** 1008 Ben Franklin Dr. St Armands Key, on Lido Beach, 0.9 mi s of St Armands Cir. Ext corridors. **Pets:** Other. $25 one-time fee/room. Supervision.

[SAVE] [🛏] [💻] [🖼]

◆◆ Days Inn-Airport MI ❖
(941) 355-9721. **$72-$110.** 4900 N Tamiami Tr. US 41, just s of jct University Pkwy. Ext corridors. **Pets:** Other. $6 daily fee/room. Supervision.

[ASK] [✕] [🖊] [🛏] [💻] [🍴] [🖼] [✕]

◆◆◆ Holiday Inn Express Sarasota Siesta
Key M
(941) 924-4900. **$124.** 6600 S Tamiami Tr. On US 41, just s of jct SR 72. Ext corridors. **Pets:** Supervision.

[🔊] [✕] [🖊] [🖋] [🛏] [💻] [🖼]

◆◆ Ramada Limited M ❖
(941) 921-7812. **$100-$130** (no credit cards), 7 days notice. 5774 Clark Rd. I-75 exit 37, just w on SR 76. Int corridors. **Pets:** Medium. $10 daily fee/pet. Designated rooms, no service, supervision, crate.

[ASK] [✕] [🖊] [🖋] [🛏] [💻] [🖼]

▲▲▲ ◆◆◆ Wellesley Inn & Suites M ❖
(941) 366-5128. **$100-$130.** 1803 N Tamiami Tr. US 41, 1 mi n of jct SR 780. Int corridors. **Pets:** Very small, other. $10 one-time fee/room. Designated rooms, no service, supervision, crate.

[SAVE] [🔊] [✕] [🖊] [🖊] [🖋] [🛏] [💻] [🖼]

SATELLITE BEACH

▲▲▲ ◆◆ Days Inn M ❖
(321) 777-3552. **$69-$100.** 180 SR A1A. SR A1A, 0.3 mi s of jct SR 404. Ext corridors. **Pets:** Medium, other. Supervision.

[SAVE] [✕] [🖋] [🛏] [🖼]

SEBRING

▲▲▲ ◆◆◆ Inn On The Lakes MI ❖
(863) 471-9400. **$65-$82, 3 days notice.** 3100 Golfview Rd. US 27, 1.5 mi n of jct SR 17. Ext/int corridors. **Pets:** Small, other. $40 one-time fee/room. Designated rooms, supervision.

[SAVE] [✕] [🛏] [💻] [🍴] [🖼] [✕]

SIESTA KEY

◆◆ Gulf Terrace Vacation Apartments A ❖
(941) 349-4444. **$620-$755, 30 days notice.** 1105 Point of Rocks Rd. 0.5 mi s of jct SR 72 (Stickney Point Rd) on Midnight Pass Rd, just w. Ext corridors. **Pets:** Dogs only. $10 daily fee/room. Designated rooms, supervision.

[ASK] [✕] [🛏] [💻] [🖼]

◆◆ Miramar Beach Apartments of Siesta
Key A ❖
(941) 349-6800. **$100-$150, 45 days notice.** 92 Avenida Messina. In Siesta Village, just w of Ocean Blvd. Ext corridors. **Pets:** $100 one-time fee/room. Supervision.

[ASK] [🔊] [✕] [🛏] [🖼]

▲▲▲ ◆◆ Tropical Breeze Inn A ❖
(941) 349-1125. **$375-$1500, 7 days notice.** 140 Columbus Blvd. In Siesta Key Village; just w of Ocean Blvd. Ext corridors. **Pets:** Small, other. $40 one-time fee/room. Designated rooms, no service, supervision, crate.

[SAVE] [🔊] [✕] [🛏] [💻] [🖼]

▲▲▲ ◆◆◆ Turtle Beach Resort A ❖
(941) 349-4554. **$1400-$2035.** 9049 Midnight Pass Rd. 2.8 mi s of jct SR 72 (Stickney Pt). Ext corridors. **Pets:** Other. Supervision.

[✕] [🛏] [💻] [🖼] [✕]

SILVER SPRINGS

◆◆ Holiday Inn-Silver Springs [MI] ❀
(352) 236-2575. **$55-$79, 3 days notice.** 5751 E Silver Springs Blvd. SR 40 across from Silver Springs entrance. Ext corridors. **Pets:** Small, dogs only. $50 deposit/room. Supervision.
[⊗] [📱] [💻] [🍴] [🛬]

◉◉◉ ◆ Sun Plaza Motel [MI] ❀
(352) 236-2343. **$35-$55.** 5461 E Silver Springs Blvd. SR 40 at jct CR 35. Ext corridors. **Pets:** $10 one-time fee/room. Supervision.
[SAVE] [⊗] [📱] [🛬] [⊠]

SOUTH DAYTONA

◉◉◉ ◆ Red Carpet Inn [M]
(904) 767-6681. **$150.** 1855 S Ridgewood Ave. US 1, 0.5 mi s of SR 400. Ext corridors. **Pets:** No service, supervision, crate.
[SAVE] [S₀] [📱] [🛬]

SOUTH PALM BEACH

◆◆ Palm Beach Hawaiian Ocean Inn [MI]
(561) 582-5631. **$140-$310, 3 days notice.** 3550 S Ocean Blvd. On SR A1A, 1.5 mi s of jct SR 802. Ext corridors. **Pets:** Medium. Designated rooms, no service, supervision, crate.
[ASK] [⊗] [📱] [💻] [🍴] [🛬] [⊠]

ST. AUGUSTINE

◉◉◉ ◆◆ Best Western Inn [M] ❀
(904) 829-1999. **$39-$120.** 2445 SR 16. I-95, exit 95; sw corner. Ext corridors. **Pets:** Small, dogs only. $8 daily fee/pet. Designated rooms, no service, supervision, crate.
[SAVE] [⊗] [🛬]

◉◉◉ ◆◆◆ Days Inn Historic [M] ❀
(904) 829-6581. **$41-$115.** 2800 N Ponce de Leon Blvd. US 1 at SR 16. Ext corridors. **Pets:** Medium. $10 daily fee/pet. Supervision.
[SAVE] [⊗] [🎷] [📱] [🍴] [🛬] [CTV]

◆◆ Days Inn-West [MI] ❀
(904) 824-4341. **$49-$89.** 2560 SR 16. Jct I-95, exit 95; on SR 16. Ext corridors. **Pets:** Large, dogs only. $10 daily fee/pet. Designated rooms, supervision.
[ASK] [S₀] [⊗] [📱] [💻] [🍴] [🛬]

◉◉◉ ◆◆ Ramada Limited St Augustine [M]
(904) 829-5643. **$54-$59.** 2535 SR 16. SR 16, 0.3 mi w of jct I-95, exit 95. Ext corridors. **Pets:** No service, supervision, crate.
[SAVE] [S₀] [⊗] [💻] [🛬]

◉◉◉ ◆◆ Scottish Inns [M]
(904) 824-2871. **$40-$75.** 110 San Marco Ave. Center, Old Mission and San Marco aves, across from Mission of Nombre De Dios. Ext corridors. **Pets:** Medium. Supervision.
[SAVE] [⊗] [🛬]

ST. AUGUSTINE BEACH

◉◉◉ ◆◆◆ Best Western Ocean Inn [M] ❀
(904) 471-8010. **$69-$159.** 3955 A1A S. SR A1A, just s of southern jct SR 3. Ext corridors. **Pets:** $15 daily fee/pet. Designated rooms, no service, supervision, crate.
[SAVE] [S₀] [⊗] [🛬]

**◉◉◉ ◆◆◆ Holiday Inn-St Augustine
Beach** [M] ❀
(904) 471-2555. **$110-$130.** 860 A1A Beach Blvd. 5.8 mi s of bridge on SR A1A. Ext/int corridors. **Pets:** Small, dogs only. $10 daily fee/room. Designated rooms, supervision.
[SAVE] [⊗] [🎷] [💻] [🍴] [🛬] [⊠]

STARKE

◉◉◉ ◆◆ Best Western Motor Inn [M] ❀
(904) 964-6744. **$40-$65, 30 days notice.** 1290 N Temple Ave. 1 mi n on US 301 from jct SR 100. Ext corridors. **Pets:** Very small. $25 deposit/room, $10 one-time fee/room. Designated rooms, no service, supervision, crate.
[SAVE] [⊗] [📱] [🛬]

STEINHATCHEE

◉◉◉ ◆◆◆ Steinhatchee Landing Resort [C] ❀
(352) 498-3513. **$140-$367.** SR 51 N. SR 51, 8 mi w of jct US 19/98. Ext corridors. **Pets:** Small, dogs only. $250 deposit/room, $25 one-time fee/pet. Designated rooms, supervision.
[SAVE] [⊗] [📱] [💻] [🍴] [🛬] [⊠]

◆◆ Steinhatchee River Inn [M] ❀
(352) 498-4049. **$60-$70** (no credit cards). 1111 Riverside Dr. Center of town. Ext corridors. **Pets:** Small, dogs only. $5 daily fee/pet. No service, supervision, crate.
[⊗] [📱] [💻] [🛬]

**◉◉◉ ◆◆◆ The Sunset Place Resort
Motel** [M] ❀
(352) 498-0860. **$85-$95.** 115 1st St SW. SR 51, 12 mi w of jct US 98. Ext corridors. **Pets:** Other. $5 daily fee/pet. Supervision.
[⊗] [📱] [💻] [🛬] [⊠]

STUART

◆◆◆ Indian River Plantation Marriott Resort [R]
(561) 225-3700. **$179-$250, 3 days notice.** 555 NE Ocean Blvd. 4 mi ne on SR A1A, on s end of Hutchinson Island at e end of causeway. Ext/int corridors. **Pets:** Small. Designated rooms, no service, supervision, crate.
[ASK] [S₀] [⊗] [🎷] [🌀] [📱] [💻] [🍴] [🛬] [⊠]

◉◉◉ ◆◆ Pirates Cove Resort & Marina [MI] ❀
(561) 287-2500. **$145-$195.** 4307 SE Bayview St. 0.3 mi e of CR A1A via Bayview St. Ext corridors. **Pets:** Other. $100 one-time fee/room. Designated rooms, supervision.
[SAVE] [S₀] [⊗] [📱] [💻] [🛬] [⊠]

TALLAHASSEE

◉◉◉ ◆◆ Best Inns of America [M]
(850) 562-2378. **$42-$63.** 2738 Graves Rd. I-10, exit 29; n side. Ext corridors. **Pets:** Designated rooms, supervision.
[SAVE] [S₀] [⊗] [📱] [🛬]

◆◆ Econo Lodge M 🐾
(850) 385-6155. **$45-$60.** 2681 N Monroe St. I-10, exit 29, 0.5 mi s. Ext corridors. **Pets:** Small, other. Designated rooms, supervision.

◆◆◆ La Quinta Inn-North M 🐾
(850) 385-7172. **$59-$92.** 2905 N Monroe St (US 27). I-10, exit 29, s side. Ext corridors. **Pets:** Medium, other. Supervision.

◆◆◆ La Quinta Inn-Tallahassee South M
(850) 878-5099. **$59-$89.** 2850 Apalachee Pkwy. 3 mi se on US 27. Ext corridors. **Pets:** No service, supervision, crate.

◆ Motel 6–420 M
(850) 668-2600. **$40-$56.** 1481 Timberlane Dr. I-10, exit 30, 0.3 mi n, w on Timberlane, next to Market Square Shopping Center. Ext corridors. **Pets:** Small. No service, supervision, crate.

◆◆ Red Roof Inn M 🐾
(850) 385-7884. **$47-$62.** 2930 Hospitality St. I-10, exit 29, s side, just off US 27. Ext corridors. **Pets:** Small, other. Supervision.

◆◆◆ Shoney's Inn M 🐾
(850) 386-8286. **$65-$73.** 2801 N Monroe St. I-10, exit 29, s side. Ext corridors. **Pets:** Other. $10 one-time fee/room. No service, supervision, crate.

Tampa Bay Metropolitan Area

APOLLO BEACH

◆◆ Ramada Bayside Inn & Resort MI 🐾
(813) 641-2700. **$85-$105, 3 days notice.** 6414 Surfside Blvd. I-75, exit 47; 1.8 mi w on CR 672; US 41, 1.8 mi s to Apollo Beach Blvd, 2.4 mi w to Surfside Blvd. Ext corridors. **Pets:** Small. $15 daily fee/pet. No service, supervision, crate.

BRANDON

◆◆◆ Behind the Fence Bed & Breakfast BB 🐾
(813) 685-8201. **$79-$99** (no credit cards), 7 days notice. 1400 Viola Dr. I-75, exit 49; just s on US 301 (northbound), 1.5 mi s on US 301 (southbound); 2.5 mi e on Bloomingdale Ave, just n on CountrySide St at jct Viola Dr. Ext/int corridors. **Pets:** Supervision.

◆◆◆ La Quinta Inn & Suites M
(813) 643-0574. **$95-$125.** 310 Grand Regency Blvd. I-75, exit 51, just e on SR 60, 0.4 mi n; in Regency Park. Int corridors. **Pets:** Small. No service, supervision, crate.

CLEARWATER

◆◆◆ Homestead Village Guest Studios A
(727) 572-4800. **$109.** 2311 Ulmerton Rd. I-275 southbound exit 18; northbound exit 16, 1.5 mi w on SR 688. Ext corridors. **Pets:** Small. Supervision.

◆◆◆ La Quinta Inn Clearwater-Airport M
(727) 572-7222. **$69-$109.** 3301 Ulmerton Rd. I-275 southbound exit 18; northbound exit 16, 1.7 mi w on SR 688. Int corridors. **Pets:** Supervision.

◆◆◆ Residence Inn by Marriott A 🐾
(727) 573-4444. **Call for rates.** 5050 Ulmerton Rd. 1 mi e of jct US 19; on SR 688. Ext corridors. **Pets:** Other. $150 one-time fee/pet. Supervision.

HOLIDAY

◆◆ Best Western-Tahitian Resort MI 🐾
(727) 937-4121. **$69-$99, 3 days notice.** 2337 US 19. US 19, 3 mi n of jct SR 582, 1.5 mi s of SR 54. Ext corridors. **Pets:** Other. $5 daily fee/room. No service, supervision, crate.

NEW PORT RICHEY

◆◆ Econo Lodge M 🐾
(727) 845-4990. **$60-$95, 5 days notice.** 7631 US 19. On US 19, 0.8 mi n of jct Main St. Ext corridors. **Pets:** $10 daily fee/room. Designated rooms, no service, supervision, crate.

PALM HARBOR

◆◆ Knights Inn-Clearwater/Palm Harbor M 🐾
(727) 789-2002. **$79.** 34106 US 19N. US 19, 1.8 mi n of CR 752 (Tampa Rd). Ext corridors. **Pets:** Other. $150 deposit/room, $10 daily fee/pet. Designated rooms, supervision.

◆◆◆ Red Roof Inn M 🐾
(727) 786-2529. **$69-$76** (no credit cards), 7 days notice. 32000 US 19 N. On US 19, 0.4 mi s of jct Tampa Rd. Ext corridors. **Pets:** Medium. $10 daily fee/pet. Supervision.

PINELLAS PARK

◆◆ La Mark Charles Motel M ❀
(727) 527-7334. **$75-$120, 30 days notice.** 6200 34th St
N. I-275, exit 15; 1.4 mi w on Gandy Blvd (SR 694) 0.8 mi
s on US 19. Ext corridors. **Pets:** Very small. $25 deposit/
pet, $10 one-time fee/room. Designated rooms, no service,
supervision, crate.

◆◆◆ La Quinta Inn-Pinellas Park M
(727) 545-5611. **$75-$105.** 7500 US Hwy 19N. I-275, exit
15; 1.4 mi s on Gandy Blvd (SR 694), just n. Ext corridors.
Pets: Small. Supervision.

PLANT CITY

◆◆ Days Inn Plant City MI ❀
(813) 752-0570. **$70-$85, 3 days notice.** 301 S Frontage
Rd. I-4, exit 13A westbound; exit 14 (eastbound), just e. Ext
corridors. **Pets:** Other. $10 one-time fee/pet. Supervision.

PORT RICHEY

◆◆◆ Comfort Inn M ❀
(727) 863-3336. **$65-$80.** 11810 US 19. US 19, just s of jct
SR 52. Ext corridors. **Pets:** Medium, other. $6 daily fee/pet.
No service, supervision, crate.

RUSKIN

◆◆◆ Bahia Beach Island Resort & Marina R
(813) 645-3291. **$89-$109, 3 days notice.** 611 Destiny Dr.
3.5 mi w of US 41 via Shell Point Rd following signs. Ext/int
corridors. **Pets:** No service, supervision, crate.

◆◆◆ Southern Comfort Bed &
    Breakfast BB ❀
(813) 645-6361. **$95-$95, 3 days notice.** 2409 Ravine Dr.
From jct US 41 just e on 14 Ave se, 1.1 mi sw on 1st St,
just w, on 24th Ave sw, just s. Int corridors. **Pets:** Medium.
Supervision.

SAFETY HARBOR

◆◆◆ Safety Harbor Resort and
    Spa R ❀
(727) 726-1161. **$139-$199, 7 days notice.** 105 N Bayshore Dr. 1.8 mi e on Main St from jct SR 611. Int corridors.
Pets: Small, other. $30 one-time fee/room. Supervision.

ST. PETE BEACH

◆◆ Bay Street Villas & Resort Marina A ❀
(727) 360-5591. **$90-$140, 30 days notice.** 7201 Bay St.
0.3 mi e on 73rd Ave from jct Gulf Blvd, just s. Ext corridors.
Pets: Small. $5 daily fee/pet. No service, supervision, crate.

◆◆ Ritz Motel A ❀
(727) 360-7642. **$59-$80.** 4237 Gulf Blvd. SR 699, 0.5 mi n
of Pinellas Bayway. Ext corridors. **Pets:** Other. $20 one-
time fee/pet. Supervision.

ST. PETERSBURG

◆◆◆ La Quinta Inn M ❀
(727) 527-8421. **$69-$95.** 4999 34th St N. I-275, exit 14
(54th Ave N); 0.3 mi w, just s on US 19 (34th St). Ext
corridors. **Pets:** Small, other. No service, supervision, crate.

◆◆◆ St. Petersburg Bayfront Hilton H
(727) 894-5000. **$145-$205, 3 days notice.** 333 1st St S.
I-275, exit 9; e to 1st St and just n, across from Al Lang
Stadium. Int corridors. **Pets:** Supervision.

SUN CITY CENTER

◆◆ Sun City Center MI ❀
(813) 634-3331. **$79-$79.** 1335 Rickenbacker Dr. I-75, exit
46 northbound; exit 46B southbound, 2.1 mi e on SR 674.
Ext corridors. **Pets:** $8 one-time fee/room. No service,
supervision, crate.

TAMPA

◆◆◆ AmeriSuites Near Busch
    Gardens M ❀
(813) 979-1922. **$89-$119.** 11408 N 30th St. I-75, exit 54,
4.5 mi w, just s on N 30th St from jct Fowler Ave; I-275, exit
34, 1.8 mi e, just s. Int corridors. **Pets:** Very small. $25
one-time fee/pet. Designated rooms, no service, supervision, crate.

◆◆◆ Amerisuites-Tampa Airport M ❀
(813) 282-1037. **$139-$199.** 4811 W Main St. I-275, exit 21
southbound, 0.5 mi w on Westshore; exit 20A northbound,
1 mi n on Kennedy Blvd, 1 mi w on Westshore. Int corridors. **Pets:** Very small. Supervision.

◆◆◆ Baymont Inn & Suites M ❀
(813) 930-6900. **$79-$79.** 9202 N 30th St. I-275, exit 33, 2
mi w of Busch Gardens maingate. Ext corridors.
Pets: Medium. Designated rooms, no service, supervision,
crate.

◆◆◆ Baymont Inn-Tampa Fairgrounds M
(813) 626-0885. **$69-$76.** 4811 US 301 N. I-4, exit 6 westbound (exit 6A eastbound); just se on US 301. Int corridors.
Pets: Supervision.

◆◆◆ Baymont Inn-Tampa Southeast M ❀
(813) 684-4007. **$85-$92.** 602 S Falkenburg Rd. I-75, exit
51, just w at jct SR 60 and S Falkenburg Rd. Int corridors.
Pets: Small. Designated rooms, supervision.

AAA ◆◆◆ Best Western All Suites Hotel Behind Busch Gardens **M** ❀
(813) 971-8930. **$109-$129.** 3001 University Center Dr. I-75, exit 54, 4.5 mi w, 0.5 mi s of Fowler Ave on 30th St; 1.8 mi e of I-275 Fowler Ave exit 34, 0.5 mi s on 30th St. Ext corridors. **Pets:** Large. $10 daily fee/pet. Supervision.
(SAVE) (⊠) (🖉) (🖥) (💻) (🍴) (🌊)

AAA ◆◆ Days Inn Airport Stadium **M**
(813) 877-6181. **$79-$105, 7 days notice.** 2522 N Dale Mabry. I-275 exit 23A, 0.5 mi n. Ext corridors. **Pets:** Medium. Designated rooms, supervision.
(SAVE) (🔊) (⊠) (🖉) (🖥) (🖥) (🌊)

◆◆ Days Inn-Tampa North **M** ❀
(813) 977-1550. **$58-$88.** 701 E Fletcher Ave. Just e of I-275, exit 35. Ext corridors. **Pets:** Other. $6 daily fee/pet. Supervision.
(ASK) (⊠) (🖉) (🖥) (💻) (🌊)

◆◆◆ Four Points Hotel by Sheraton Tampa East **H** ❀
(813) 626-0999. **$149-$149, 3 days notice.** 7401 E Hills-borough Ave. I-4 exit 5 eastbound; exit 6 westbound, 0.4 mi n. Ext/int corridors. **Pets:** $45 one-time fee/room. Designated rooms, no service, supervision, crate.
(ASK) (⊠) (🖉) (🖥) (🖥) (💻) (🍴) (🌊)

◆◆◆ Holiday Inn Express **M** ❀
(813) 961-1000. **$79-$79.** 400 E Bears Ave. I-275, exit 36, just w. Ext corridors. **Pets:** Small, other. $10 one-time fee/room. Designated rooms, no service, supervision, crate.
(ASK) (🔊) (⊠) (🖥) (🖥) (💻) (🌊)

◆◆◆ Holiday Inn Express Hotel & Suites Stadium/Airport **M**
(813) 877-6061. **$95-$105.** 4732 N Dale Mabry. I-275 Dale Mabry exit 23A, 2 mi n. Ext corridors. **Pets:** No service, supervision, crate.
(ASK) (🔊) (⊠) (🖥) (🖉) (🖥) (💻) (🌊)

◆◆◆ Holiday Inn Tampa **M**
(813) 971-4710. **$72-$130.** 2701 E Fowler Ave. I-275 exit 34, 1.5 mi e on SR 582. Ext/int corridors. **Pets:** Designated rooms, no service, supervision, crate.
(ASK) (⊠) (🖥) (🖉) (🖥) (🖥) (💻) (🍴) (🌊)

AAA ◆ Howard Johnson Airport-Stadium **M** ❀
(813) 875-8818. **$64-$74.** 2055 N Dale Mabry. I-275 exit 23A, 0.8 mi n. Ext corridors. **Pets:** Other. Supervision.
(SAVE) (🔊) (⊠) (🖉) (🖥) (💻) (🍴) (🌊)

◆◆◆ La Quinta Inn Airport **M** ❀
(813) 287-0440. **$79-$109.** 4730 Spruce St. I-275 exit 21, southbound; exit 20A northbound Westshore Dr, exit 0.8 mi w, then just w. Ext corridors. **Pets:** Small. Supervision.
(ASK) (⊠) (🖉) (🖥) (💻) (🌊)

◆◆◆ La Quinta Inn & Suites USF **M** ❀
(813) 910-7500. **$79-$129.** 3701 E Fowler. I-75 exit 54, 4.8 mi w. Int corridors. **Pets:** Medium. No service, supervision, crate.
(ASK) (⊠) (🖥) (🖉) (🖥) (🖥) (💻) (🌊)

◆◆◆ La Quinta Inn State Fair **M**
(813) 623-3591. **$50-$75.** 2904 Melbourne Blvd. I-4, exit 3, just n. Ext/int corridors. **Pets:** Small. No service, supervision, crate.
(ASK) (⊠) (🖥) (🖉) (🖥) (💻) (🌊)

AAA ◆◆ Motel 6–483 **M**
(813) 932-4948. **$40-$61.** 333 E Fowler Ave. I-275 exit 34 just w. Ext corridors. **Pets:** Medium. No service, supervision, crate.
(⊠) (🌊)

AAA ◆◆ Motel 6 Tampa East–1192 **M** ❀
(813) 628-0888. **$40-$56.** 6510 N US 301. I-4, exit 6 westbound; exit 6A (eastbound), 0.7 mi n. Ext corridors. **Pets:** Small, other. No service, supervision, crate.
(⊠) (🖥) (🌊)

AAA ◆◆ Ramada Airport Inn & Conference Center **H** ❀
(813) 289-1950. **$129-$129.** 5303 W Kennedy Blvd. I-275, exit 21, southbound 0.4 mi e on Westshore; 0.5 mi s on W Kennedy Blvd exit 20B northbound just e. Ext/int corridors. **Pets:** Other. $25 deposit/room. Designated rooms, no service, supervision, crate.
(SAVE) (⊠) (🖉) (🖥) (🖥) (💻) (🍴) (🌊)

AAA ◆◆ Red Roof Inn **M** ❀
(813) 932-0073. **$66-$88.** 2307 E Busch Blvd. I-275 exit 33, 1.7 mi w. Ext corridors. **Pets:** Medium, other. Supervision.
(SAVE) (⊠) (🌊)

AAA ◆◆ Red Roof Inn-Brandon **M**
(813) 681-8484. **$66-$89.** 10121 Horace Ave. I-75, exit 51; just w to S Falkenberg Rd, just n. Ext corridors. **Pets:** No service, supervision, crate.
(SAVE) (⊠) (🖉)

AAA ◆◆ Red Roof Inn-Fairgrounds **M**
(813) 623-5245. **$64-$96.** 5001 N US 301. I-4, exit 6 westbound; exit 6A eastbound, just se. Ext corridors. **Pets:** Small. No service, supervision, crate.
(SAVE) (⊠) (🖉)

AAA ◆◆◆ Wellesley Inn & Suites **M** ❀
(813) 637-8990. **$139-$169.** 1805 N Westshore Blvd. I-275 exit 21 (southbound); exit 20A (northbound), 1 mi n on Kennedy Blvd, 1.3 mi w. Int corridors. **Pets:** Small. $15 daily fee/pet, $100 one-time fee/room. Designated rooms, no service, supervision, crate.
(SAVE) (⊠) (🖥) (🖉) (🖥) (🖥) (💻) (🌊)

TARPON SPRINGS

◆◆ Days Inn Hotel & Suites **M**
(727) 938-8000. **$67-$77.** 40050 US Hwy 19 N. On US 19, 0.8 mi s of jct Tarpon Ave. Ext corridors. **Pets:** Designated rooms, supervision.
(ASK) (🔊) (⊠) (🖥) (💻) (🍴) (🌊)

TEMPLE TERRACE

◆◆◆ Residence Inn by Marriott Tampa North **M** ❀
(813) 972-4400. **$139-$179.** 13420 N Telecom Pkwy. I-75, exit 55, 1.1 mi w on Fletcher Ave; in Tampa Telecom Park. Int corridors. **Pets:** Small, other. $100 one-time fee/pet. No service, supervision, crate.
(ASK) (⊠) (🖥) (🖉) (🖥) (🖥) (💻) (🌊) (⊠)

WESLEY CHAPEL

(AAA) ◆◆◆ **Comfort Inn** 🅼 ❀
(813) 991-4600. **$55-$75.** 5642 Oakley Blvd. I-75, exit 58, just w. Int corridors. **Pets:** $9 daily fee/pet. Designated rooms, supervision.
(SAVE) (X) (🏠) (🍽) (💺) (🔋) (🍴) (🏊)

(AAA) ◆ **Masters Inn Tampa North** 🅼
(813) 973-0155. **$49-$69.** 27807 SR 54W. I-75 exit 58, just w. Ext corridors. **Pets:** Very small. No service, supervision, crate.
(SAVE) (🏋) (X) (🍽) (🔋) (🍴) (🏊)

❀ **END METROPOLITAN AREA** ❀

TITUSVILLE

(AAA) ◆◆◆ **Best Western Space Shuttle Inn** 🅼 ❀
(321) 269-9100. **$89-$119.** 3455 Cheney Hwy. SR 50, just e of jct I-95, exit 79. Ext corridors. **Pets:** Other. $5 one-time fee/pet. Designated rooms, supervision.
(SAVE) (X) (🔋) (🍴) (🏊) (X)

(AAA) ◆◆ **Days Inn-Kennedy Space Center** 🅼 ❀
(321) 269-4480. **$59-$135.** 3755 Cheney Hwy. SR 50; at jct I-95, exit 79. Ext corridors. **Pets:** Other. $10 one-time fee/pet. Designated rooms, supervision.
(SAVE) (X) (🔋) (💺) (🍴) (🏊)

(AAA) ◆◆◆ **Holiday Inn-Kennedy Space Center** 🅼
(321) 269-2121. **$79-$129, 7 days notice.** 4951 S Washington Ave. US 1; 0.5 mi s of jct SR 50, 1.7 mi n of jct SR 405. Ext corridors. **Pets:** No service, supervision, crate.
(SAVE) (X) (🍽) (🔋) (💺) (🍴) (🏊) (X)

VENICE

(AAA) ◆◆◆ **Days Inn** 🅼 ❀
(941) 493-4558. **$94-$110.** 1710 S Tamiami Tr. I-75, exit 35; 0.8 mi w on Jacaranda Blvd, 3.6 mi sw on Venice Ave; 2 mi s on US 41. Ext corridors. **Pets:** $30 one-time fee/room. No service, supervision, crate.
(SAVE) (🏋) (X) (🔋) (🍴) (🏊)

(AAA) ◆◆◆ **Inn at the Beach Resort** 🅼 ❀
(941) 484-8471. **$165-$359.** 725 W Venice Ave. On Venice Beach at jct the Esplande. Ext corridors. **Pets:** Medium. Supervision.
(SAVE) (X) (🔋) (💺) (🏊)

(AAA) ◆◆ **Motel 6–364** 🅼
(941) 485-8255. **$56-$72.** 281 US 41 Bypass N. I-75, exit 35, 0.8 mi w on Jacaranda Blvd, 3 mi sw on Venice Ave, just n. Ext corridors. **Pets:** Medium. No service, supervision, crate.
(X) (🍽) (💺) (🏊) (CTV)

VERO BEACH

(AAA) ◆◆ **Days Inn** 🅼
(561) 562-9991. **$64-$79.** 8800 20th St. SR 60, 0.5 mi e of jct I-95, exit 68. Ext corridors. **Pets:** Small. Designated rooms, supervision.
(SAVE) (X) (🍴) (🏊)

WEEKI WACHEE

◆◆◆ **Best Western Weeki Wachee Resort** 🅼 ❀
(352) 596-2007. **$69-$79.** 6172 Commercial Way. US 19 at jct SR 50 (Cortez Blvd). Ext corridors. **Pets:** Other. Supervision.
(ASK) (X) (🍽) (🔋) (🏊)

◆◆◆ **Comfort Inn** 🅼 ❀
(352) 596-9000. **$55-$90.** 9373 Cortez Blvd. SR 50, 0.3 mi e of jct US 19. Int corridors. **Pets:** Medium, other. $10 daily fee/pet. No service, supervision, crate.
(ASK) (🏋) (X) (🍽) (💺) (🔋) (🏊)

WEST MELBOURNE

◆◆ **Howard Johnson** 🅼 ❀
(321) 768-8439. **$75-$89.** 4431 W New Haven Ave. I-95, exit 71, just e on SR 192. Ext corridors. **Pets:** Medium, other. $20 one-time fee/room. Designated rooms, supervision.
(ASK) (🏋) (🔋) (💺) (🏊)

WEST PALM BEACH

(AAA) ◆◆◆ **Comfort Inn-on Palm Beach Lakes** 🅼 ❀
(561) 689-6100. **$109-$179.** 1901 Palm Beach Lakes Blvd. Just w of jct I-95, exit 53. Int corridors. **Pets:** Medium, other. $25 daily fee/pet. Designated rooms, no service, supervision, crate.
(SAVE) (🏋) (X) (🍽) (🔋) (💺) (🍴) (🏊)

◆◆ **Days Inn-West Palm Beach/Airport North** 🅼 ❀
(561) 689-0450. **$59-$129.** 2300 45th St. On SR 702, (45th St) at jct I-95, exit 54. Ext corridors. **Pets:** $10 daily fee/pet. No service, supervision, crate.
(ASK) (X) (🍽) (💺) (🔋) (🍴) (🏊) (X)

◆◆◆ **Hibiscus House Bed & Breakfast** 🅱🅱 ❀
(561) 863-5633. **$95-$240.** 501 30th St. 1.2 mi n on Flagler Dr from jct Palm Beach Lakes Blvd, 0.3 mi w. Int corridors. **Pets:** Supervision.
(ASK) (X) (🔋) (🏊)

(AAA) ◆◆ **Red Roof Inn-West Palm Beach** 🅼 ❀
(561) 697-7710. **$70-$102.** 2421 Metro Center Blvd E. On CR 702, just w of jct I-95 exit 54 (45th St); in the Metrocentre Corporate Park. Ext/int corridors. **Pets:** Small. Designated rooms, no service, supervision, crate.
(SAVE) (X) (♿) (🍽) (💺) (🔋) (🏊)

 ◆◆◆ Wellesley Inn & Suites Ⓜ ❀
(561) 689-8540. **$64-$134.** 1910 Palm Beach Lakes Blvd. Just w of jct I-95 exit 53. Int corridors. **Pets:** Small. $50 one-time fee/pet. No service, supervision, crate.

WILLISTON

◆ Williston Motor Inn Ⓜ
(352) 528-4801. **$32-$34.** 606 W Noble Ave. 0.5 mi n on US 27 Alt. Ext corridors. **Pets:** No service, supervision, crate.

WINTER HAVEN

◆◆◆ Best Western Admiral's Inn Ⓜ ❀
(863) 324-5950. **$82-$112.** 5665 Cypress Gardens Blvd. SR 540, 3 mi e of jct US 17 (at entrance to Cypress Gardens). Ext/int corridors. **Pets:** Small, other. $10 deposit/room. Supervision.

◆◆ Cypress Motel Ⓜ ❀
(863) 324-5867. **$60-$65, 7 days notice.** 5651 Cypress Gardens Rd. 6 mi e of jct US 17; 1.8 mi w of jct US 27 on SR 540, 0.5 mi n on SR 540A. Ext corridors. **Pets:** Other. $10 one-time fee/room. Designated rooms, no service, supervision, crate.

◆◆ Howard Johnson Inn Ⓜ
(863) 294-7321. **$80-$109.** 1300 Third St SW. 0.8 mi s on US 17. Int corridors. **Pets:** No service, supervision, crate.

ADAIRSVILLE

◆◆ Comfort Inn M 🐾
(770) 773-2886. **$45-$95.** 107 Princeton Blvd. I-75 exit 128, just w. Ext corridors. **Pets:** $5 one-time fee/pet. No service, supervision, crate.

◆◆◆ Ramada Limited M
(770) 769-9726. **$36-$50.** 500 Georgia North Cir. I-75 exit 128, 0.3 mi w. Ext corridors. **Pets:** Small. No service, supervision, crate.

ADEL

◆◆ Days Inn I-75 M 🐾
(912) 896-4574. **$36-$44.** 1200 W 4th St. I-75 exit 10, nw corner. Ext corridors. **Pets:** Medium. $5 daily fee/pet. Designated rooms, supervision.

◆◆◆ Hampton Inn M 🐾
(912) 896-3099. **$57-$65, 7 days notice.** 1500 W 4th St. I-75 exit 10, nw corner. Int corridors. **Pets:** $5 daily fee/ room. Supervision.

◆◆ Howard Johnson Express Inn M 🐾
(912) 896-2244. **$34-$39.** 1103 W 4th St. I-75 exit 10, se corner. Ext corridors. **Pets:** Medium. $5 daily fee/pet. Designated rooms, supervision.

ALBANY

◆◆ Days Inn M 🐾
(912) 888-2632. **$40-$45.** 422 W Oglethorpe Blvd. 1 mi e on US 19 business route and 82. Ext corridors. **Pets:** Small. $10 one-time fee/room. Designated rooms, no service, supervision, crate.

◆◆◆ Holiday Inn Albany Mall M 🐾
(912) 883-8100. **$89.** 2701 Dawson Rd. 7 mi w on Dawson Rd, 0.5 mi s of jct US 82 and SR 520; opposite Albany Mall. Ext/int corridors. **Pets:** Medium. $25 one-time fee/pet. Supervision.

◆◆ Ramada Inn M
(912) 883-3211. **$50-$57.** 2505 N Slappey Blvd. 4 mi nw on US 19 business route at jct US 19 and 82. Ext/int corridors. **Pets:** Supervision.

AMERICUS

◆◆◆ 1906 Pathway Inn Bed & Breakfast BB 🐾
(912) 928-2078. **$65-$125.** 501 S Lee St. SR 280 0.5 mi s SR 377. Int corridors. **Pets:** Small, other. $50 deposit/room, $20 one-time fee/room. No service, supervision, crate.

◆◆◆ Ramada Inn M
(912) 924-4431. **Call for rates.** 1205 Martin Luther King Jr Blvd. 1 mi w of downtown on US 19 S. Ext corridors. **Pets:** Supervision.

ASHBURN

◆◆ Days Inn M 🐾
(912) 567-3346. **$32-$45.** 823 E Washington Ave. I-75 exit 28, just w. Ext corridors. **Pets:** Medium. $5 daily fee/pet, $5 one-time fee/pet. Designated rooms, supervision.

ATHENS

⚫⚫⚫ ◆◆◆ **Best Western-Colonial Inn** 🅜 ❀
(706) 546-7311. **$49-$79, 7 days notice.** 170 N Milledge
Ave. 0.5 mi w; on SR 15 at jct US Business Rt 78 (Broad
St). Ext corridors. **Pets:** Other. $10 daily fee/room, $25
one-time fee/room. Supervision.
🆂🅰🆅🅴 ⊠ 🔲 🕿

◆◆◆ **Holiday Inn Express** 🅜
(706) 546-8122. **Call for rates.** 513 W Broad St. Downtown
on US 78. Int corridors. **Pets:** Supervision.
🅐🆂🅺 ⊠ 🔲 🔲 🕿

ATLANTA METROPOLITAN AREA

ACWORTH

◆◆ **Best Western Frontier Inn** 🅜
(770) 974-0116. **$50-$65.** 3530 Cherokee. I-75 exit 120, just
nw. Ext corridors. **Pets:** Medium. Designated rooms, supervision.
🅐🆂🅺 ⊠ 🔲 🔲 🕿 ⊠

⚫⚫⚫ ◆◆ **Days Inn** 🅜
(770) 974-1700. **$35-$75.** 5035 Cowan Rd. I-75 exit 120,
just sw. Ext corridors. **Pets:** Supervision.
🆂🅰🆅🅴 ⊠ 🕿

⚫⚫⚫ ◆◆◆ **Quality Inn** 🅜
(770) 974-1922. **$40-$60.** 4980 Cowan Rd. I-75 exit 120,
just sw. Ext corridors. **Pets:** Medium. Supervision.
🆂🅰🆅🅴 ⊠ 🔲 🔲 🕿

⚫⚫⚫ ◆◆ **Red Roof Inn** 🅜 ❀
(770) 974-5400. **$40-$45, 7 days notice.** 5320 Glade Rd.
I-75 exit 121, just sw. Ext corridors. **Pets:** Small. $10 one-
time fee/pet. Designated rooms, no service, supervision,
crate.
🆂🅰🆅🅴 ⊠ 🔲 🕿

⚫⚫⚫ ◆◆◆ **Super 8 Motel** 🅜 ❀
(770) 966-9700. **$42-$65.** 4970 Cowan Rd. I-75 exit 120,
just sw. Ext corridors. **Pets:** Small. $8 daily fee/room. Des-
ignated rooms, no service, supervision, crate.
🆂🅰🆅🅴 ⊠ 🖉 🔲 🕿

ALPHARETTA

⚫⚫⚫ ◆◆◆
AmeriSuites-Atlanta/Windward 🅜 ❀
(770) 343-9566. **$109-$149.** 5595 Windward. SR 400 exit
11, just w. Int corridors. **Pets:** Small. $25 deposit/room. No
service, supervision, crate.
🆂🅰🆅🅴 ⊠ 🏠 🖉 🅵 🔲 🔲 🕿

⚫⚫⚫ ◆◆◆ **Homewood Suites** 🄰 ❀
(770) 998-1622. **$98-$161.** 10775 Davis Dr. SR 400 exit 8,
nw corner. Int corridors. **Pets:** Medium, other. $50 one-time
fee/pet. Supervision.
🆂🅰🆅🅴 ⊠ 🏠 🅵 🔲 🔲 🕿

⚫⚫⚫ ◆◆◆ **La Quinta Inn & Suites** 🅜 ❀
(770) 754-7800. **$59-$129.** 1350 North Point Dr. SR 400
exit 9, 0.5 mi e. Int corridors. **Pets:** Small, other. No service,
supervision, crate.
🆂🅰🆅🅴 ⊠ 🏠 🖉 🅵 🔲 🔲 🕿

◆◆◆ **Residence Inn by Marriott** 🄰 ❀
(770) 664-0664. **$149.** 5465 Windward Pkwy W. SR 400
exit 11, 0.5 mi w. Ext/int corridors. **Pets:** Other. $100 one-
time fee/room. Supervision.
🅐🆂🅺 ⊠ 🖉 🔲 🔲 🕿 ⊠

◆◆◆ **Staybridge Suites** 🅜 ❀
(770) 569-7200. **Call for rates.** 3980 North Point Pkwy. SR
400 exit 10, 0.5 mi e. Int corridors. **Pets:** Medium, other.
$75 one-time fee/room. No service, supervision, crate.
⊠ 🏠 🅵 🔲 🔲 🕿 ⊠

ATLANTA

⚫⚫⚫ ◆◆◆ **AmeriSuites-Atlanta/Perimeter
Center** 🅜 ❀
(770) 730-9300. **$85-$85.** 1005 Crestline Pkwy. SR 400 exit
5A (Dunwoody), 0.3 mi e. Int corridors. **Pets:** Small. No
service, supervision, crate.
🆂🅰🆅🅴 🆂🅳 ⊠ 🏠 🖉 🅵 🔲 🔲 🕿

⚫⚫⚫ ◆◆ **Ansley Inn** 🅱🅱 ❀
(404) 872-9000. **$109-$169, 3 days notice.** 253 15th St.
I-75/85, exit 14th St; just e to Peachtree St, just n to 15th
St, then just e. Ext/int corridors. **Pets:** Small. Supervision.
🆂🅰🆅🅴 ⊠ 🔲

◆◆ **Baymont Inn & Suites-Atlanta Lenox** 🅜
(404) 321-0999. **$57-$57.** 2535 Chantilly Dr NE. On e side
of I-85 at southbound, exit 30; northbound exit 28, 2 mi on
Buford Hwy to Lenox Rd, just e under hwy. Int corridors.
Pets: Medium. Designated rooms, no service, supervision,
crate.
⊠ 🖉 🔲 🔲

⚫⚫⚫ ◆◆◆ **Best Western Granada Suite
Hotel** 🅜
(404) 876-6100. **$89-$159.** 1302 W Peachtree St. I-75S exit
102 (14th St), just e on 14th, just n on W Peachtree to 16th
St; I-75/85N exit 101, just e on 10th St to W Peachtree, 0.6
mi n. Int corridors. **Pets:** Medium. No service, supervision,
crate.
🆂🅰🆅🅴 🆂🅳 🔲 🔲

⚫⚫⚫ ◆◆◆ **Best Western Inn at the
Peachtrees** 🅜 ❀
(404) 577-6970. **$79-$129.** 330 W Peachtree St. I-75/85;
exit International Blvd northbound, exit Williams St southbound. Ext/int corridors. **Pets:** Small. $25 one-time fee/
room. Supervision.
🆂🅰🆅🅴 ⊠ 🔲 🔲

◆◆◆ **Crowne Plaza-Atlanta Powers Ferry** ⌗
(770) 955-1700. **$69-$164.** 6345 Powers Ferry Rd NW.
I-285 exit 15, se corner. Int corridors. **Pets:** Small. Designated rooms, no service, supervision, crate.

ASK ☒ 🏠 ✆ 🗄 💻 🍴 🏊

⚑ ◆◆◆ **Emory Inn** ⓜ
(404) 712-6700. **$89.** 1641 Clifton Rd. I-85 exit 31, 2 mi s
on SR 42, then 0.8 mi e on Clifton Rd; next to Emory
University. Ext corridors. **Pets:** Medium. Designated rooms,
no service, supervision, crate.

SAVE ☒ 🏠 🗄 💻 🍴 🏊

◆◆◆◆◆ **Four Seasons Hotel**
Atlanta ⌗ 🐾
(404) 881-9898. **$235-$1055.** 75 14th St. Midtown I-75/85,
exit 14th St, 0.3 mi e. Int corridors. **Pets:** Supervision.

☒ 🏠 🐶 🍴 🏊

◆◆◆ **Hawthorn Suites-Atlanta NW** Ⓐ
(770) 952-9595. **$119-$179.** 1500 Parkwood Cir. I-75 exit
110, (Windy Hill) 0.5 mi e, 0.3 mi s on Powers Ferry Rd. Ext
corridors. **Pets:** Small. Designated rooms, no service,
supervision, crate.

ASK ☒ 🖾 🗄 💻 🏊 ☒

◆◆◆ **Holiday Inn Select Atlanta**
Perimeter ⓜ 🐾
(770) 457-6363. **$59-$149.** 4386 Chamblee-Dunwoody Rd.
I-285 exit 22, eastbound sw corner; westbound follow
access road 1.3 mi to Chamblee-Dunwoody Rd, just s; ne
corner. Int corridors. **Pets:** Other. $100 deposit/room, $25
one-time fee/room. No service, supervision, crate.

ASK ☒ 🐶 🖾 🗄 💻 🍴 🏊

◆◆◆ **Homestead Village Guest Studios** ⓜ
(770) 522-0025. **Call for rates.** 1050 Hammond Dr. I-285
exit 18 (eastbound) 0.5 mi n to Hammond Dr, 0.5 mi e;
I-285 exit 20 (westbound) just n, then just w. Ext corridors.
Pets: Small. Supervision.

🗄 💻

◆◆◆ **Homestead Village Guest Studios-Executive**
Park ⓜ
(404) 325-1223. **Call for rates.** 1339 Executive Park Dr
NE. I-85 exit 31, just e to Executive Park Dr, just s. Ext
corridors. **Pets:** Small. Supervision.

☒ 🐶 🖾 🗄 💻

◆◆◆ **Homewood Suites-Cumberland** ⓜ 🐾
(770) 988-9449. **Call for rates.** 3200 Cobb Pkwy SW.
I-285, eastbound exit 13; westbound exit 14, 0.7 mi se on
US 41 (Cobb Pkwy). Ext/int corridors. **Pets:** Other. $75
one-time fee/room. No service, supervision, crate.

☒ 🐶 🗄 💻 🏊 ☒

⚑ ◆◆◆ **La Quinta Inn & Suites** ⓜ
(770) 801-9002. **$59-$99.** 2415 Paces Ferry Rd SE. I-285
exit 12, just w. Int corridors. **Pets:** Small. No service, supervision, crate.

SAVE ☒ 🏠 🐶 🖾 🗄 💻 🏊

⚑ ◆◆◆ **La Quinta Inn & Suites** ⓜ 🐾
(770) 350-6177. **$59-$129.** 6260 Peachtree-Dunwoody.
I-285E exit 18, 0.5 mi n, 0.7 mi e on Hammond Dr to
Peachtree-Dunwoody, 0.5 mi n; I-285W exit 20, 0.8 mi n. Int
corridors. **Pets:** Small, other. Supervision.

SAVE ☒ 🏠 🖾 🗄 💻 🏊

⚑ ◆ **Masters Inn Six Flags** ⓜ
(404) 696-4690. **$59-$73.** 4120 Fulton Industrial Blvd. I-20
exit 14, just n. Ext corridors. **Pets:** Supervision.

SAVE 🐶 ☒ 🗄 🍴 🏊

⚑ ◆◆ **Red Roof Inn-Druid Hills** ⓜ
(404) 321-1653. **$50-$64.** 1960 N Druid Hills Rd. I-85 exit
31, just w. Ext corridors. **Pets:** Small. No service, supervision, crate.

SAVE ☒ 🗄

⚑ ◆◆ **Red Roof Inn-Six Flags** ⓜ 🐾
(404) 696-4391. **$56-$83.** 4265 Shirley Dr SW. I-20 exit 14,
se corner. Ext corridors. **Pets:** Small. No service, supervision, crate.

SAVE ☒

◆◆◆ **Residence Inn-Buckhead/Lenox** Ⓐ 🐾
(404) 467-1660. **$134.** 2220 Lake Blvd. I-85 exit 31, 1.6 mi
w on N Druid Hills which becomes E Roxboro, just n on
Lenox Park Blvd. Int corridors. **Pets:** Medium. $150 one-
time fee/room. No service, supervision, crate.

ASK 🐶 ☒ 🏠 🖾 🗄 💻 🏊

◆◆◆ **Residence Inn by Marriott-Atlanta**
Downtown Ⓐ 🐾
(404) 522-0950. **$185.** 134 Peachtree St NW. I-75/85
(northbound) exit 94 (Dobbs), 1 mi w. Int corridors.
Pets: Other. Supervision.

ASK ☒ 🖾 🗄 💻

◆◆◆ **Residence Inn by Marriott Atlanta**
Dunwoody Ⓐ
(770) 455-4446. **$69-$119.** 1901 Savoy Dr. I-285 exit 22,
just e on Savoy Drive. Ext corridors. **Pets:** Small. Supervision.

ASK ☒ 🗄 💻 🏊 ☒

◆◆◆ **Residence Inn by Marriott-Buckhead** Ⓐ
(404) 239-0677. **Call for rates.** 2960 Piedmont Rd NE. I-85
exit 28, 1.5 mi n. Ext corridors. **Pets:** Supervision.

ASK ☒ 🐶 🗄 💻 🏊 ☒

◆◆◆ **Residence Inn by Marriott Midtown** Ⓐ
(404) 872-8885. **$114.** 1041 W Peachtree St. Midtown; I-75/
I-85 10th St exit, just e to W Peachtree St, just n. Int
corridors. **Pets:** No service, supervision, crate.

ASK 🐶 ☒ 🏠 🖾 🗄 💻

◆◆◆ **Residence Inn by Marriott-Perimeter**
West Ⓐ 🐾
(404) 252-5066. **$115-$166.** 6096 Barfield Rd. I-285 E exit
18, 0.5 mi n on Glenridge to Hammond, 0.3 mi e to Barfield
Rd; I-285 W exit 20 Peachtree-Dunwoody Rd, 0.5 mi n to
Hammond Dr, just w. Ext corridors. **Pets:** Other. $75 one-
time fee/room. Supervision.

ASK ☒ 🗄 💻 🏊 ☒

◆◆◆ **Summerfield Suites Hotel** Ⓐ 🐾
(404) 250-0110. **$99-$195.** 760 Mt Vernon Hwy NE. From
I-285, exit 17, 0.8 mi w on Roswell Rd and 1 mi e. Ext/int
corridors. **Pets:** Small. $150 one-time fee/room. No service,
supervision, crate.

ASK 🐶 ☒ 🏠 🖾 🗄 💻 🏊

◆◆◆ **Summerfield Suites Hotel Buckhead** Ⓐ
(404) 262-7880. **$259, 5 days notice.** 505 Pharr Rd. Pharr
Rd and Maple Dr, just w of Piedmont. Ext/int corridors.
Pets: Designated rooms, supervision.

ASK ☒ 🗄 💻 🏊

◉ ◆◆ University Inn at Emory M ✿
(404) 634-7327. **$84-$134, 3 days notice.** 1767 N Decatur Rd. I-85 exit 32, 3.8 mi s on Clairmont Rd to N Decatur Rd; then 0.8 mi w; opposite Emory Med Complex. Ext/int corridors. **Pets:** Other. $15 daily fee/room. Supervision.
⟦SAVE⟧ ⟦✕⟧ ⟦⌘⟧ ⟦✦⟧ ⟦🗎⟧ ⟦💻⟧ ⟦⊿⟧

◆◆◆ W Atlanta H
(770) 396-6800. **$119-$209.** 111 Perimeter Center W. I-285 exit 21, (Ashford-Dunwoody), 0.5 mi n to Perimeter Center W, opposite Perimeter Mall. Int corridors. **Pets:** Small. Designated rooms, no service, supervision, crate.
⟦✕⟧ ⟦⌂⟧ ⟦✦⟧ ⟦🗎⟧ ⟦💻⟧ ⟦†⟧ ⟦⊿⟧

◉ ◆◆◆ Wellesley Inn & Suites M
(770) 226-0242. **$85-$105** (no credit cards). 2225 Interstate N Pkwy West SE. I-75 exit 110. Int corridors. **Pets:** Small. No service, supervision, crate.
⟦SAVE⟧ ⟦So⟧ ⟦✕⟧ ⟦⌂⟧ ⟦⌘⟧ ⟦✦⟧ ⟦🗎⟧ ⟦💻⟧ ⟦⊿⟧

◆◆◆ The Westin Atlanta North H ✿
(770) 395-3900. **$99-$119.** 7 Concourse Pkwy. I-285W exit 20; I-285E, exit 18 (Glenridge Dr) just n to Hammond Dr, just e. Int corridors. **Pets:** Small. Supervision.
⟦ASK⟧ ⟦✕⟧ ⟦⌘⟧ ⟦🗎⟧ ⟦💻⟧ ⟦†⟧ ⟦⊿⟧ ⟦✕⟧

◆◆◆ Wyndham Garden Hotel at Vinings H
(770) 432-5555. **$125.** 2857 Paces Ferry Rd. I-285 exit 12, 0.6 mi e. Int corridors. **Pets:** Small. Supervision.
⟦ASK⟧ ⟦So⟧ ⟦✕⟧ ⟦⌘⟧ ⟦🗎⟧ ⟦💻⟧ ⟦†⟧ ⟦⊿⟧ ⟦✕⟧

AUSTELL

◉ ◆◆◆ La Quinta-Atlanta West/Six
　　　　　　　　Flags M ✿
(770) 944-2110. **$79-$109.** 7377 Six Flags Dr. I-20 exit 13B westbound; exit 13 eastbound, just n. Ext/int corridors. **Pets:** Small, other. Supervision.
⟦SAVE⟧ ⟦✕⟧ ⟦⌘⟧ ⟦🗎⟧ ⟦💻⟧ ⟦⊿⟧

COLLEGE PARK

◉ ◆◆ Baymont Inn-Atlanta Airport M
(404) 766-0000. **$59-$88.** 2480 Old National Pkwy. I-85S exit 16; I-285 exit 1; se corner. Int corridors. **Pets:** Small. Supervision.
⟦SAVE⟧ ⟦✕⟧ ⟦🗎⟧ ⟦💻⟧

◉ ◆◆◆ La Quinta Inn Airport M ✿
(404) 768-1241. **$49-$69.** 4874 Old National Hwy. I-85 exit 16, I-285 exit 1, ne corner. Ext corridors. **Pets:** Small. $25 deposit/room. Designated rooms, no service, supervision, crate.
⟦SAVE⟧ ⟦✕⟧ ⟦💻⟧ ⟦⊿⟧

◆◆◆ Marriott Atlanta Airport H ✿
(404) 766-7900. **$139-$174.** 4711 Best Rd. I-85 exit 18; just w, se on access road to Best Rd, just s. Int corridors. **Pets:** Small, dogs only. $50 one-time fee/room. Supervision.
⟦✕⟧ ⟦⌂⟧ ⟦⌘⟧ ⟦✦⟧ ⟦🗎⟧ ⟦💻⟧ ⟦†⟧ ⟦⊿⟧ ⟦✕⟧

◆◆ Ramada Hotel Atlanta Airport South M
(404) 996-4321. **Call for rates.** 1551 Phoenix Blvd. I-285 exit 43, just sw. Ext/int corridors. **Pets:** Designated rooms, no service, supervision, crate.
⟦✕⟧ ⟦⌘⟧ ⟦✦⟧ ⟦🗎⟧ ⟦💻⟧ ⟦†⟧ ⟦⊿⟧

◉ ◆◆ Red Roof Inn Airport M ✿
(404) 761-9701. **$46-$73.** 2471 Old National Pkwy. I-85 exit 16; I-285 exit 1, just s. Ext corridors. **Pets:** Small. No service, supervision, crate.
⟦SAVE⟧ ⟦✕⟧

DECATUR

◆◆ Holiday Inn Express I-20 East M
(770) 981-5670. **Call for rates.** 4300 Snapfinger Woods Dr. I-20 exit 36, just ne. Ext corridors. **Pets:** Small. Designated rooms, no service, supervision, crate.
⟦ASK⟧ ⟦✕⟧ ⟦✦⟧ ⟦⊿⟧

DORAVILLE

◆◆ Howard Johnson Hotel M ✿
(770) 448-7220. **Call for rates.** 4422 Northeast Expwy. I-85 exit 36, just sw; 1.3 mi n of I-285; from 285 E to I-85, exit Pleasantdale Rd. Ext corridors. **Pets:** Small. $10 daily fee/pet. Designated rooms, no service, supervision, crate.
⟦ASK⟧ ⟦✕⟧ ⟦✦⟧ ⟦🗎⟧ ⟦💻⟧ ⟦⊿⟧

◉ ◆ Masters Inn M
(770) 454-8373. **$45-$59.** 3092 Presidential Pkwy. I-85 exit 34, just e, then n. Ext corridors. **Pets:** Small. No service, supervision, crate.
⟦SAVE⟧ ⟦✕⟧ ⟦🗎⟧ ⟦⊿⟧

DULUTH

◉ ◆◆◆ Amerisuites/Gwinnett Mall M
(770) 623-6800. **$99-$149.** 3390 Venture Pkwy. I-85 exit 40, just w to Venture Pkwy, just n. Int corridors. **Pets:** Supervision.
⟦SAVE⟧ ⟦✕⟧ ⟦⌂⟧ ⟦⌘⟧ ⟦🗎⟧ ⟦💻⟧ ⟦⊿⟧

◉ ◆◆◆ AmeriSuites-John's Creek M
(770) 622-5858. **$105-$145.** 11505 Medlock Bridge Rd. Jct of SR 141 (Medlock Bridge Rd) and Findley Rd. Int corridors. **Pets:** Small. No service, supervision, crate.
⟦SAVE⟧ ⟦✕⟧ ⟦⌂⟧ ⟦⌘⟧ ⟦✦⟧ ⟦🗎⟧ ⟦💻⟧ ⟦⊿⟧

◉ ◆◆◆ Hampton Inn &
　　　　　　Suites-Gwinnett M ✿
(770) 931-9800. **$109.** 1725 Pineland Rd. I-85 exit 40, just 0.3 mi e to Crestwood, just s. Int corridors. **Pets:** Other. $75 one-time fee/room. Supervision.
⟦So⟧ ⟦✕⟧ ⟦⌂⟧ ⟦✦⟧ ⟦🗎⟧ ⟦💻⟧ ⟦⊿⟧

◆◆◆ Homestead Village Guest Studios-Gwinnett
　　　　Place M
(770) 931-3113. **$79.** 3525 Breckenridge Blvd. I-85 exit 40, just n to Breckenridge Blvd, just e. Ext corridors. **Pets:** Small. Supervision.
⟦✕⟧ ⟦⌂⟧ ⟦✦⟧ ⟦🗎⟧ ⟦💻⟧

EAST POINT

◆◆◆ Clarion Hotel Atlanta Airport M
(404) 762-5566. **$69-$79, 30 days notice.** 3601 N Desert Dr. I-285 exit 3, just ne. Int corridors. **Pets:** Small. Designated rooms, no service, supervision, crate.
⟦ASK⟧ ⟦So⟧ ⟦✕⟧ ⟦🗎⟧ ⟦💻⟧ ⟦†⟧ ⟦⊿⟧

◆◆◆ **Crowne Plaza Atlanta Airport** 🅷 ❀
(404) 768-6660. **$79-$179.** 1325 Virginia Ave. I-85 exit 19, southbound exit 19A; northbound, just w. Int corridors. **Pets:** Other. $100 deposit/room, $25 one-time fee/room. Supervision.
(ASK) ⊠ 🛈 🗐 📺 🍴 🍽

◆◆◆ **Drury Inn & Suites Atlanta Airport** Ⓜ ❀
(404) 761-4900. **$79-$99.** 1270 Virginia Ave. I-85 exit 19 (Virginia Ave), just e. Int corridors. **Pets:** Other. Supervision.
⊠ 🛈 🗐 📺 🍽

FOREST PARK

◆◆ **Motel 6** Ⓜ ❀
(404) 363-6429. **$44-$56.** 5060 Frontage Rd. I-75 exit 78, just e, then just s. Int corridors. **Pets:** Other. No service, supervision, crate.
⊠

ⒶⒶⒶ ◆◆ **Super 8 Motel** Ⓜ ❀
(404) 363-8811. **$50-$70, 7 days notice.** 410 Old Dixie Way. I-75 exit 77, just e. Ext corridors. **Pets:** Small, other. $5 one-time fee/pet. No service, supervision, crate.
(SAVE) Ⓢ ⊠ 🗐 🍽

JONESBORO

ⒶⒶⒶ ◆◆◆ **Holiday Inn-Atlanta South** Ⓜ ❀
(770) 968-4300. **$69-$119.** 6288 Old Dixie Hwy. I-75 exit 77, just w. Int corridors. **Pets:** Other. $25 one-time fee/ room. Supervision.
(SAVE) ⊠ 🛈 🗐 🍴 🍽 ⊠

ⒶⒶⒶ ◆◆ **Shoneys Inn-Atlanta South** Ⓜ
(770) 968-5018. **$49-$63.** 6358 Old Dixie Rd. I-75 exit 77, just w. Ext corridors. **Pets:** No service, supervision, crate.
(SAVE) ⊠ 🗐 📺 🍽

KENNESAW

◆◆ **Best Western of Kennesaw** Ⓜ ❀
(770) 424-7666. **$54-$74.** 3375 Busbee Dr. I-75 exit 117, just e. Ext corridors. **Pets:** Medium, other. $6 daily fee/pet. Designated rooms, supervision.
(ASK) ⊠ 🗐 🍽 ⊠

◆◆◆ **Country Inn & Suites By Carlson** Ⓜ
(770) 423-7105. **Call for rates.** 3192 Barrett Lakes Blvd. I-75 exit 117, just w to Barrett Lakes Blvd, just s. Int corridors. **Pets:** Designated rooms, supervision.
⊠ 🛈 🗐 🗐 📺 🍽

ⒶⒶⒶ ◆◆ **Red Roof Inn-Town Center Mall** Ⓜ
(770) 429-0323. **$50-$60.** 520 Roberts Ct NW. I-75, exit 116, se corner. Ext corridors. **Pets:** Supervision.
(SAVE) ⊠

ⒶⒶⒶ ◆◆ **Rodeway Inn** Ⓜ
(770) 590-0519. **$37-$55.** 1460 George Busbee Pkwy. I-75 exit 118, just e. Ext corridors. **Pets:** Small. No service, supervision, crate.
(SAVE) Ⓢ ⊠ 🗐 🍽

LITHONIA

ⒶⒶⒶ ◆◆◆ **La Quinta Inn Panola Road** Ⓜ ❀
(770) 981-6411. **$49-$79.** 2859 Panola Rd. I-20 exit 37, just n. Ext/int corridors. **Pets:** Medium, other. Supervision.
(SAVE) ⊠ 🗐 📺 🍽

MARIETTA

ⒶⒶⒶ ◆◆ **Best Inns of America** Ⓜ ❀
(770) 955-0004. **$46-$65.** 1255 Franklin Rd. I-75 exit 111, 0.3 mi w to Franklin Rd; just s. Int corridors. **Pets:** Other. $20 deposit/room. No service, supervision, crate.
(SAVE) Ⓢ ⊠ 🗐 🍽

◆◆◆ **Drury Inn & Suites-Atlanta Northwest** Ⓜ
(770) 612-0900. **$67-$87.** 1170 Powers Ferry Pl. I-75 exit 111 (Delk Rd), just e. Int corridors. **Pets:** Medium. Designated rooms, no service, supervision, crate.
⊠ 🛈 🗐 🗐 📺 🍽

ⒶⒶⒶ ◆◆ **Econo Lodge Northwest** Ⓜ ❀
(770) 952-0052. **$44-$49, 7 days notice.** 1940 Leland Dr. I-75 exit 110 (Windy Hill), just e, 0.3 mi n. Ext/int corridors. **Pets:** Other. Supervision.
(SAVE) ⊠ 🗐

ⒶⒶⒶ ◆◆◆ **Holiday Inn Hotel & Suites
Marietta** Ⓜ
(770) 952-7581. **$92-$102.** 2265 Kingston Ct. I-75 exit 111, 0.3 mi w. Int corridors. **Pets:** No service, supervision, crate.
(SAVE) ⊠ 🛈 🗐 🗐 📺 🍴 🍽

ⒶⒶⒶ ◆◆◆ **La Quinta Inn Marietta** Ⓜ
(770) 951-0026. **$49-$95.** 2170 Delk Rd. I-75 exit 111, 0.3 mi w. Ext/int corridors. **Pets:** Small. No service, supervision, crate.
(SAVE) ⊠ 🗐 📺 🍽

ⒶⒶⒶ ◆ **Masters Inn Marietta** Ⓜ
(770) 951-2005. **$39-$53.** 2682 Windy Hill Rd. I-75 exit 110, just w, Circle 75, just w. Ext corridors. **Pets:** Very small. No service, supervision, crate.
(SAVE) Ⓢ ⊠ 🗐

ⒶⒶⒶ ◆◆ **Motel 6–749** Ⓜ
(770) 952-8161. **$38-$55.** 2360 Delk Rd. I-75 exit 111, just e. Ext corridors. **Pets:** Medium. No service, supervision, crate.
⊠ 🗐 🍽

◆◆ **Ramada Inn-Atlanta North** Ⓜ
(770) 952-3251. **$65-$69.** 2767 Windy Hill Rd. I-75 exit 110, just e. Ext corridors. **Pets:** Supervision.
(ASK) Ⓢ ⊠ 🛈 🗐 🗐 📺 🍴 🍽

ⒶⒶⒶ ◆◆◆ **Ramada Limited Suites** Ⓜ ❀
(770) 919-7878. **$55-$85, 7 days notice.** 630 Franklin Rd. I-75 exit 112, 0.3 mi w to Franklin Rd, 0.3 mi s. Ext corridors. **Pets:** Medium. $6 daily fee/pet, $6 one-time fee/pet. Supervision.
(SAVE) ⊠ 🗐 🗐 📺 🍽

ⒶⒶⒶ ◆◆◆ **Super 8 Motel** Ⓜ ❀
(770) 919-2340. **$45-$60, 7 days notice.** 610 Franklin Rd. I-75 exit 112, 0.3 mi w to Franklin Rd, then 0.3 mi s. Ext corridors. **Pets:** $5 daily fee/pet, $5 one-time fee/pet. Supervision.
(SAVE) ⊠ 🗐 🍽

MORROW

◆◆ Best Western Southlake Inn M ❧
(770) 961-6300. **$50-$99.** 6437 Jonesboro Rd. I-75 exit 76, just e. Ext corridors. **Pets:** Medium, other. No service, supervision, crate.

[SAVE] [⊠] [🖥] [🕿]

◆◆◆ Drury Inn & Suites M ❧
(770) 960-0500. **$68-$88.** 6520 S Lee St. I-75 exit 76, just e. Int corridors. **Pets:** Other. No service, supervision, crate.

[⊠] [🏠] [🕹] [🖥] [💻] [🕿]

◆◆◆ Quality Inn M ❧
(770) 960-1957. **$45-$79, 7 days notice.** 6597 Hwy 54. I-75 exit 76, just w. Ext corridors. **Pets:** Medium, other. $5 one-time fee/pet. No service, supervision, crate.

[SAVE] [So] [⊠] [🖥] [💻] [🕿]

◆◆ Red Roof Inn-South M ❧
(770) 968-1483. **$49-$51.** 1348 Southlake Plaza Dr. I-75 exit 76, just e to Southlake Plaza Dr, then just n. Ext corridors. **Pets:** Small, other. Supervision.

[SAVE] [⊠]

◆◆ Sleep Inn M ❧
(770) 472-9800. **$49-$89, 7 days notice.** 2185 Mt Zion Pkwy. I-75 exit 75A, just w to Mt Zion Pkwy, just s. Int corridors. **Pets:** Medium. $50 deposit/pet, $5 daily fee/pet. Designated rooms, no service, supervision, crate.

[SAVE] [⊠] [🏠] [🖥] [🕿]

NORCROSS

◆◆◆ Amberley Suite Hotel MI ❧
(770) 263-0515. **$59-$99.** 5885 Oakbrook Pkwy. I-85 exit 37; 0.5 mi e to Live Oak Pkwy, 0.8 mi n and w. Int corridors. **Pets:** Large. $50 one-time fee/room. Supervision.

[⊠] [🕹] [🖥] [💻] [🍴] [🕿]

◆◆◆ AmeriSuites Atlanta/Peachtree Corners M
(770) 416-7655. **$119-$129, 3 days notice.** 5600 Peachtree Pkwy. I-285 exit 23, 5.8 mi n on SR 141; I-85 exit 37, 4 mi n, w on Holcomb Bridge Rd, 1.8 mi n. Int corridors. **Pets:** Small. No service, supervision, crate.

[SAVE] [⊠] [🏠] [🕹] [🕹] [🖥] [💻] [🕿]

◆◆◆ Drury Inn & Suites M ❧
(770) 729-0060. **$67-$87.** 5655 Jimmy Carter Blvd. I-85 exit 37, just w. Int corridors. **Pets:** Small. No service, supervision, crate.

[⊠] [🏠] [🕹] [🕹] [🖥] [💻] [🕿]

◆◆◆ Homestead Village Guest Studios-Peachtree Corners M
(770) 449-9966. **Call for rates.** 7049 Jimmy Carter Blvd. I-285 exit 23B, 4 mi n; I-85 exit 37, 4 mi n. Ext corridors. **Pets:** Small. Supervision.

[⊠] [🏠] [🕹] [🖥] [💻]

◆◆◆ Homewood Suites-Norcross A
(770) 448-4663. **$195.** 450 Technology Pkwy. I-85N exit 37, 4 mi w to Peachtree Industrial Blvd, 0.4 mi n, w on Holcomb Bridge Rd, 2 blks n on Peachtree Pkwy; I-285 exit 23B, 5 mi n on SR 141. Ext/int corridors. **Pets:** Medium. Designated rooms, no service, supervision, crate.

[⊠] [🏠] [🕹] [🖥] [💻] [🕿] [⊠]

◆◆◆ La Quinta Inn-Jimmy Carter M ❧
(770) 448-8686. **$45-$79.** 6187 Dawson Blvd. I-85 exit 37, just e to McDonough Dr, just s. Ext corridors. **Pets:** Small. $25 daily fee/room, $25 one-time fee/room. No service, supervision, crate.

[SAVE] [⊠] [🖥] [💻] [🕿]

◆◆◆ La Quinta-Peachtree M ❧
(770) 449-5144. **$45-$75.** 5375 Peachtree Industrial Blvd. I-285 exit 23B, 5.5 mi n; I-85 exit 37, 4 mi w to Peachtree Industrial Blvd, 1.5 mi n. Ext corridors. **Pets:** Medium, other. Supervision.

[SAVE] [⊠] [🕹] [🖥] [💻] [🕿]

◆◆◆ Northeast Atlanta Hilton 🔲 ❧
(770) 447-4747. **Call for rates.** 5993 Peachtree Industrial Blvd. I-285 exit 23B, 4.5 mi ne. Int corridors. **Pets:** Small, other. Supervision.

[⊠] [🏠] [🕹] [🖥] [💻] [🍴] [🕿]

◆◆ Quality Inn-Norcross M ❧
(770) 449-7322. **$39-$59.** 6045 Oakbrook Pkwy. I-85 exit 37, just e to Live Oak Pkwy, 1 mi n and w. Ext/int corridors. **Pets:** Small, other. $15 one-time fee/room. Supervision.

[ASK] [⊠] [🖥] [💻] [🕿]

◆◆ Ramada Limited and Suites M
(770) 446-2882. **$50-$55.** 5395 Peachtree Industrial Blvd. I-285 exit 23B, 5.5 mi n; I-85 exit 37, 4 mi w to Peachtree Industrial Blvd, 1.5 mi n. Int corridors. **Pets:** Supervision.

[ASK] [⊠] [🏠] [🕹] [🖥] [💻] [🕿]

◆◆ Red Roof Inn-Indian Trail M ❧
(770) 448-8944. **$47-$53.** 5171 Brook Hollow Pkwy. I-85 exit 38, just w to Brook Hollow Pkwy, just s. Ext corridors. **Pets:** Medium, other. Supervision.

[SAVE] [⊠]

ROSWELL

◆◆ Baymont Inn & Suites-Atlanta Roswell M ❧
(770) 552-0200. **$61-$61.** 575 Old Holcomb Bridge Rd. SR 400 exit 7B, just w. Int corridors. **Pets:** Medium. $50 deposit/room. No service, supervision, crate.

[⊠] [🕹] [🖥] [💻] [🕿]

◆◆◆ Hampton Inn M ❧
(770) 587-5161. **$69-$89, 3 days notice.** 9995 Old Dogwood Rd. SR 400 exit 7B, just w to Old Dogwood Rd, just n. Ext corridors. **Pets:** $25 deposit/room. Supervision.

[⊠] [🏠] [🕹] [💻] [🕿]

◆◆◆ Homestead Village Guest Studios-Roswell M
(770) 992-9449. **Call for rates.** 9955 Old Dogwood Rd. SR 400 exit 7B, just w. Ext corridors. **Pets:** Small. Supervision.

[⊠] [🏠] [🕹] [🕹] [🖥] [💻]

SMYRNA

◆◆◆ AmeriHost Inn-Smyrna M
(404) 794-1600. **$68-$84, 7 days notice.** 5130 S Cobb Dr. I-285 exit 10, 0.3 mi w. Int corridors. **Pets:** Small. Supervision.

[SAVE] [So] [⊠] [🏠] [🕹] [🕹] [🖥] [💻] [🕿]

◆◆◆ Homestead Village Guest
    Studios-Cumberland **M**
(770) 432-4000. **Call for rates.** 3103 Sports Ave. I-285 exit
14 westbound; exit 13 eastbound, just n to Spring Rd, 0.3
mi w. Ext corridors. **Pets:** Small. Supervision.

🅧 🏠 🔥 🔋 💻

AAA ◆◆ Red Roof Inn-North **M** 🐾
(770) 952-6966. **$46-$67.** 2200 Corporate Plaza. I-75 exit
110, just w to Corporate Plaza, just s. Ext corridors.
Pets: Small, other. No service, supervision, crate.

SAVE 🅧

SUWANEE

AAA ◆◆◆ Holiday Inn **MI** 🐾
(770) 945-4921. **$79-$109.** 2955 Hwy 317. I-85 exit 44. Ext
corridors. **Pets:** Small. $25 one-time fee/room. No service,
supervision, crate.

SAVE 🅧 🔋 🍴 🔄 🅧

TUCKER

◆◆◆ Homestead Village Guest
    Studios-Northlake **M**
(770) 934-4040. **Call for rates.** 1795 Crescent Center Blvd.
I-285 exit 28, just e to Northlake Pkwy, just s to Crescent
Center Blvd, then 0.6 mi s. Ext corridors. **Pets:** Designated
rooms, supervision.

🅧 🏠 🔥 🔋 💻

🐾 **END METROPOLITAN AREA** 🐾

AUGUSTA

AAA ◆◆◆ AmeriSuites **M** 🐾
(706) 733-4656. **$71.** 1062 Claussen Rd. I-20, exit 66 (Riv-
erwatch Pkwy), just nw. Int corridors. **Pets:** Other. $30 one-
time fee/room. Supervision.

SAVE 🅧 🔥 🔋 💻 🔄

AAA ◆◆◆ Comfort Inn Medical Center **M**
(706) 722-2224. **$56-$65.** 1455 Walton Way. 1 mi w. Int
corridors. **Pets:** Small. Designated rooms, no service,
supervision, crate.

SAVE 🅧 🔥 🔋 💻 🔄

◆◆◆ Holiday Inn Gordon Highway at Bobby
    Jones **MI**
(706) 737-2300. **$78-$96.** 2155 Gordon Hwy. On SR 78
and 278 at jct I-520E, exit 4A. Ext corridors. **Pets:** Medium.
Supervision.

ASK 🅧 🔋 💻 🍴 🔄

AAA ◆◆◆ Holiday Inn West **MI** 🐾
(706) 738-8811. **$59-$79.** 1075 Stevens Creek Rd. I-20 exit
65, just ne on service road. Ext corridors. **Pets:** Medium,
other. No service, supervision, crate.

SAVE 🔊 🅧 🔥 🔋 💻 🍴 🔄

AAA ◆◆◆ La Quinta Inn **M**
(706) 733-2660. **$45-$79.** 3020 Washington Rd. I-20 exit 65
(Washington Rd), just n. Ext/int corridors. **Pets:** Medium.
Designated rooms, no service, supervision, crate.

SAVE 🅧 🏠 🎵 🔋 💻 🔄

AAA ◆◆◆ La Quinta Atlanta Stone Mountain **M**
(770) 496-1317. **$55-$89.** 1819 Mountain Industrial Blvd.
I-285 exit 30B, 3.5 mi e to Mountain Industrial Blvd, ne
corner. Ext corridors. **Pets:** Medium. Designated rooms,
supervision.

SAVE 🅧 💻 🔄

AAA ◆ Masters Inn Tucker **M** 🐾
(770) 938-3552. **$39-$53.** 1435 Montreal Rd. I-285 exit 29,
just w. Ext corridors. **Pets:** Very small. $10 one-time fee/
room. No service, supervision, crate.

SAVE 🔊 🅧 🔋 🔄

AAA ◆◆ Red Roof Inn-Atlanta (Tucker NE) **M**
(770) 496-1311. **$46-$73.** 2810 Lawrenceville Hwy. I-285
exit 29, just w. Ext corridors. **Pets:** Designated rooms,
supervision.

SAVE 🅧 🎵

◆◆◆ The Partridge Inn **H** 🐾
(706) 737-8888. **$89-$89.** 2110 Walton Way. 1.3 mi w off
15th St. Int corridors. **Pets:** Other. $25 one-time fee/room.
Supervision.

ASK 🅧 🔋 💻 🍴 🔄

AAA ◆◆◆ Radisson Riverwalk Hotel **H** 🐾
(706) 722-8900. **$104-$114, 7 days notice.** 2 10th St.
Downtown, on Riverwalk at 10th and Reynolds. Int corridors. **Pets:** Medium. $25 deposit/room. No service, super-
vision, crate.

🅧 🏠 🎵 🔋 💻 🍴 🔄

AAA ◆◆◆ Radisson Suites Inn **MI** 🐾
(706) 868-1800. **$79-$99.** 3038 Washington Rd. I-20, exit
65, 0.3 mi n. Ext corridors. **Pets:** Medium. $25 one-time
fee/room. No service, supervision, crate.

SAVE 🅧 🔋 💻 🍴 🔄

AAA ◆◆◆ Sheraton Augusta Hotel **H** 🐾
(706) 855-8100. **$84-$94.** 2651 Perimeter Pkwy. Jct I-520,
exit 2 and Wheeler Rd; entrance 0.3 mi w at Perimeter
Pkwy. Int corridors. **Pets:** Small, other. No service, supervision, crate.

SAVE 🔊 🅧 🏠 🔋 💻 🍴 🔄

BLAIRSVILLE

AAA ◆◆ Misty Mountain Inn & Cottages **BB** 🐾
(706) 745-4786. **$50-$85, 3 days notice.** 4376 Misty Mountain Ln. 2.7 mi s on US 19/129, 3.7 mi e on Town Creek
Rd. Ext/int corridors. **Pets:** Other. Designated rooms, supervision.

SAVE 🔋 💻 🅧 🎵

▲▲ ◆◆ Nottely Dam Guest House & World Class
    Horse Facility 🅱🅱
(706) 745-7939. **$55-$85** (no credit cards), 7 days notice.
2266 Nottely Dam Rd. 8 mi w on US 76/SR 515, 4 mi n on
CR 325. Int corridors. **Pets:** Small. No service, supervision,
crate.
[SAVE] [✕] [✕] [CTV] [☎]

BLUE RIDGE

▲▲ ◆◆ Days Inn 🅼 ❀
(706) 632-2100. **$50-$80.** SR 515 Connector 76. On SR
515 and US 76. Ext corridors. **Pets:** Designated rooms,
supervision.
[SAVE] [✕] [🛏] [🖾]

BREMEN

▲▲ ◆◆ Days Inn Bremen 🅼
(770) 537-4646. **$45-$50.** 35 Price Creek Rd. I-20 exit 3.
Ext corridors. **Pets:** Small. Designated rooms, supervision.
[SAVE] [🖬] [✕] [🛏] [🖾]

BRUNSWICK

◆◆ Baymont Inn & Suites-Brunswick 🅼
(912) 265-7725. **$49-$54.** 105 Tourist Dr. I-95 exit 7A, 0.3
mi se. Int corridors. **Pets:** Medium. Designated rooms, no
service, supervision, crate.
[✕] [🖉] [🛏] [🖳] [🖾]

▲▲ ◆◆ Best Western Brunswick Inn 🅼 ❀
(912) 264-0144. **$51-$66.** 5323 New Jesup Hwy. I-95 exit
7B, just w on US 341. Ext corridors. **Pets:** Other. Supervision.
[SAVE] [✕] [🛏] [🖾]

▲▲ ◆◆◆ Comfort Inn 🅼🄸 ❀
(912) 264-6540. **$59-$89.** 5308 New Jesup Hwy. I-95 exit
7B, just w on US 25 and 341. Int corridors. **Pets:** Other. $5
daily fee/pet, $5 one-time fee/pet. Supervision.
[SAVE] [✕] [🖉] [🖳] [🛏] [🖳] [🍴] [🖾]

▲▲ ◆◆◆ Embassy Suites 🄷 ❀
(912) 264-6100. **$89-$109.** 500 Mall Blvd. I-95 exit 8, 1.5 mi
s on SR 25; in Glynn Place Mall. Int corridors. **Pets:** Other.
$10 daily fee/room. No service, supervision, crate.
[SAVE] [✕] [🛏] [🖳] [🖾]

▲▲ ◆◆◆ Holiday Inn I-95 🅼🄸 ❀
(912) 264-4033. **$59-$89.** 5252 New Jesup Hwy. I-95 exit
7B, nw corner, on US 341. Ext corridors. **Pets:** Other. $10
daily fee/room. Supervision.
[SAVE] [✕] [🖳] [🖳] [🍴] [🖾] [✕]

◆◆◆ Ramada Inn I-95 🅼🄸 ❀
(912) 264-3621. **$52-$60.** 3040 Scarlet St. I-95 exit 7A, just
e on US 341 and 25. Ext corridors. **Pets:** Small, other. $10
one-time fee/room. Designated rooms, no service, supervision, crate.
[ASK] [✕] [🛏] [🖳] [🍴] [🖾]

▲▲ ◆◆ Sleep Inn 🅼 ❀
(912) 261-0670. **$39-$89, 7 days notice.** 5272 New Jesup
Hwy. I-95 exit 7B, just w on US 25 and 341. Int corridors.
Pets: $5 one-time fee/pet. No service, supervision, crate.
[SAVE] [✕] [🖚] [🖉] [🖳] [🖾]

◆◆ Super 8 Motel 🅼 ❀
(912) 264-8800. **$50-$99, 7 days notice.** 5280 New Jesup
Hwy. I-95 exit 7B, just w. Int corridors. **Pets:** Other. $10
one-time fee/pet. No service, supervision, crate.
[ASK] [🖬] [✕] [🖳]

BYRON

▲▲ ◆◆◆ Best Western Inn and Suites 🅼 ❀
(912) 956-3056. **$56-$56.** 101 Dunbar Rd at Hwy 49. I-75
exit 46, se corner. Ext corridors. **Pets:** Medium. $10 one-
time fee/room. No service, supervision, crate.
[SAVE] [✕] [🖉] [🛏] [🖾]

CAIRO

▲▲ ◆◆ Best Western Executive Inn 🅼🄸
(912) 377-8000. **$55-$75.** 2800 US 84E. 1 mi e on US 84.
Ext corridors. **Pets:** No service, supervision, crate.
[SAVE] [✕] [🍴] [🖾]

CALHOUN

▲▲ ◆◆ Budget Host Shepherd Motel 🅼🄸 ❀
(706) 629-8644. **$33-$42.** 3900 Hwy 53 E. I-75 exit 129,
just e. Ext corridors. **Pets:** Other. Supervision.
[SAVE] [✕] [🖉] [🛏] [🖾]

▲▲ ◆ Duffy's Motel North 🅼🄸 ❀
(706) 629-4436. **$23-$28.** 1441 US 41N. I-75 exit 132, just
w. Ext corridors. **Pets:** No service, supervision, crate.
[SAVE] [✕]

▲▲ ◆ Econo Lodge 🅼 ❀
(706) 625-5421. **$30-$40.** 1438 US Hwy 41N. I-75 exit 132,
just w. Ext corridors. **Pets:** Small. $5 daily fee/pet. Desig-
nated rooms, no service, supervision, crate.
[SAVE] [✕] [🖳] [🖾]

▲▲ ◆◆ Howard Johnson 🅼🄸 ❀
(706) 629-9191. **$40-$45, 3 days notice.** 1220 Red Bud
Rd. I-75 exit 130, just w. Ext corridors. **Pets:** Other. $5 daily
fee/pet. No service, supervision, crate.
[SAVE] [✕] [🍴] [🖾]

▲▲ ◆◆ Knights Inn of Calhoun 🅼 ❀
(706) 629-4521. **$37-$49.** 2261 US 41 NE. I-75 exit 132,
just e. Ext corridors. **Pets:** Medium. $4 daily fee/pet. No
service, supervision, crate.
[SAVE] [✕] [🖾]

▲▲ ◆◆◆ Quality Inn-Calhoun 🅼 ❀
(706) 629-9501. **$45-$60.** 915 Hwy 53 East SE. I-75 exit
129, just e. Ext corridors. **Pets:** Small, dogs only. $5 daily
fee/pet. Supervision.
[SAVE] [✕] [🛏] [🖳] [🍴] [🖾]

▲▲ ◆◆ Ramada Limited 🅼 ❀
(706) 629-9207. **$44-$49.** 1204 Red Bud Rd NE. I-75 exit
130, just w. Ext corridors. **Pets:** Small. $10 deposit/pet, $5
daily fee/pet, $5 one-time fee/pet. No service, supervision,
crate.
[SAVE] [✕] [🖾]

CARROLLTON

◆◆ Crossroads Hotel Center M
(770) 832-2611. **Call for rates.** 1202 S Park St. Jct US 27 and SR 166. Ext corridors. **Pets:** Medium. Designated rooms, supervision.

⊠ 🔋 📶 🍴 🕿

CARTERSVILLE

❀ ◆◆ Comfort Inn M ❖
(770) 387-1800. **$34-$48.** 28 SR 20 Spur. I-75 exit 125, 0.3 mi se. Ext corridors. **Pets:** $5 daily fee/pet, $5 one-time fee/pet. No service, supervision, crate.

(SAVE) (S) ⊠ 🔋 🕿

❀ ◆◆ Days Inn-Cartersville M ❖
(770) 382-1824. **$42-$88.** 5618 Hwy 20 SE. I-75 exit 125, just w. Ext corridors. **Pets:** Small, other. $10 daily fee/pet, $10 one-time fee/pet. Supervision.

(SAVE) ⊠ 🔋 🕿

❀ ◆◆◆ Holiday Inn M
(770) 386-0830. **$69-$69.** 2336 Hwy 411 NE. I-75 exit 126, sw corner. Int corridors. **Pets:** Supervision.

(SAVE) ⊠ 📶 🔋 📶 🍴 🕿

❀ ◆◆ Howard Johnson Express M
(770) 386-0700. **$50-$80.** 25 Carson Loop NW. I-75 exit 127, nw corner. Ext corridors. **Pets:** Supervision.

(SAVE) (S) ⊠ 📶 🕿 ⊠

❀ ◆◆ Knights Inn M ❖
(770) 386-7263. **$40-$75.** 420 E Church St. I-75 exit 124, 1.5 mi w. Ext corridors. **Pets:** Small. $10 daily fee/room, $10 one-time fee/room. No service, supervision, crate.

(SAVE) ⊠ 🔋

◆◆ Motel 6–4046 M ❖
(770) 386-1449. **$34-$50.** 5657 Hwy 20 NE. I-75 exit 125, 0.3 mi e. Ext corridors. **Pets:** Other. Supervision.

⊠ 🕿

◆◆ Super 8 Motel M ❖
(770) 382-8881. **Call for rates.** 41 SR 20 Spur SE. I-75 exit 125, 0.3 mi w. Int corridors. **Pets:** Medium. $10 daily fee/pet, $10 one-time fee/pet. No service, supervision, crate.

⊠ 🔋 📶

◆◆ Travelodge M
(770) 387-2696. **$40-$45.** 35 Carson Loop Dr. I-75 exit 127, just w. Ext corridors. **Pets:** Medium. Supervision.

(ASK) ⊠ 🔋 📶 🕿

CHATSWORTH

❀ ◆◆ Key West Inn M ❖
(706) 517-1155. **$45-$60, 30 days notice.** 501 GI Maddox Pkwy. Jct SR 76 and US 411. Ext corridors. **Pets:** Medium. $5 daily fee/pet, $5 one-time fee/pet. Designated rooms, no service, supervision, crate.

(SAVE) (S) ⊠ 🔋

CLAYTON

❀ ◆◆◆ Shoney's Inn & Suites M
(706) 782-2214. **$89-$109, 7 days notice.** US 441 S. 1 mi s on US 441S. Ext corridors. **Pets:** Small. No service, supervision, crate.

(SAVE) ⊠ 🔋 📶 🕿

COLUMBUS

◆◆ Baymont Inn & Suites-Columbus M ❖
(706) 323-4344. **$54-$59.** 2919 Warm Springs Rd. I-185 southbound exit 5; northbound exit 5A, just e. Int corridors. **Pets:** Other. $50 deposit/room. Supervision.

⊠ 📶 🔋 📶 🕿

◆◆◆ Days Inn M ❖
(706) 561-4400. **Call for rates.** 3452 Macon Rd. I-185 exit 4, just e. Ext corridors. **Pets:** Medium, other. Supervision.

(ASK) ⊠ 🔋 📶 🕿

❀ ◆◆◆ Holiday Inn-Columbus Airport M
(706) 324-0231. **$59-$89.** 2800 Manchester Expwy. I-185, southbound exit 5; northbound exit 5B, just w. Int corridors. **Pets:** Small. Supervision.

(SAVE) ⊠ 📶 🔋 📶 🍴 🕿

◆◆◆ Howard Johnson Express M ❖
(706) 322-6641. **$55-$74.** 1011 Veterans Pkwy. Downtown. Ext corridors. **Pets:** $25 one-time fee/room. No service, supervision, crate.

(ASK) ⊠ 📶 🔋 📶 🍴 🕿

❀ ◆◆◆ La Quinta Inn M
(706) 568-1740. **$62-$82.** 3201 Macon Rd. I-185 exit 4, just w. Ext corridors. **Pets:** Supervision.

(SAVE) ⊠ 📶 🔋 📶 🕿

❀ ◆ Motel 6 #058 M ❖
(706) 687-7214. **$35-$44.** 3050 Victory Dr. On US 280. Ext corridors. **Pets:** Small, other. No service, supervision, crate.

⊠ 🕿 (CTV)

◆◆ Super 8 Motel of Columbus M ❖
(706) 322-6580. **Call for rates.** 2935 Warm Springs Rd. I-185 southbound exit 5; northbound exit 5A, just e. Int corridors. **Pets:** Small, other. $25 deposit/room. No service, supervision, crate.

⊠ 📶

COMMERCE

◆ GuestHouse Inn-Banks Crossing M
(706) 335-5147. **$39-$99.** 30934 US 441S. I-85 exit 53, 0.3 mi e. Ext corridors. **Pets:** Medium. No service, supervision, crate.

(ASK) (S) ⊠ 🕿

❀ ◆◆ Holiday Inn Express M
(706) 335-5183. **$52-$76.** 30747 US 441S. I-85 exit 53, just se. Ext corridors. **Pets:** Supervision.

(SAVE) ⊠ 🔋 🕿

CONYERS

[AAA] ◆◆◆ **Comfort Inn** [M] 🐾
(770) 760-0300. **$69-$89.** 1363 Klondike Rd. I-20 exit 41. Int corridors. **Pets:** Very small. $15 one-time fee/room. No service, supervision, crate.
[SAVE] [SD] 🚭 ▣ 📺 🏊

[AAA] ◆◆◆ **La Quinta Inn & Suites** [M]
(770) 918-0092. **$79-$109.** 1184 Dogwood Dr. I-20 exit 42, just n. Int corridors. **Pets:** Small. Supervision.
[SAVE] 🚭 ♿ ▣ 📺 🏊

[AAA] ◆◆ **Ramada Limited** [M] 🐾
(770) 760-0777. **$64-$99, 7 days notice.** 1070 Dogwood Dr. I-20 exit 42, just n Hwy 138, 0.5 mi w. Ext corridors. **Pets:** Medium. $25 daily fee/pet, $20 one-time fee/pet. Designated rooms, no service, supervision, crate.
[SAVE] [SD] 🚭 ▣ 🏊

CORDELE

[AAA] ◆◆◆ **Best Western Colonial Inn** [M] 🐾
(912) 273-5420. **$38-$49.** 1706 16th Ave E. I-75 exit 33, just w. Ext/int corridors. **Pets:** Medium, other. $10 deposit/room. Supervision.
[SD] 🚭 ▣ 🏊 🏋

[AAA] ◆◆◆ **Cordele Conference Center** [MI]
(912) 273-4117. **$45-$45, 7 days notice.** 1711 E 16th Ave. Jct I-75 exit 33 and US 280. Ext corridors. **Pets:** Medium. Supervision.
[SAVE] 🚭 📺 🏊

◆◆ **Days Inn** [M] 🐾
(912) 273-1123. **$45-$50.** 2115 16th Ave E. Jct I-75 exit 33 and US 280. Ext corridors. **Pets:** Small. $10 one-time fee/room. No service, supervision, crate.
[A$K] [SD] 🚭 ▣ 🏊

[AAA] ◆ **Economy Inn** [M] 🐾
(912) 273-2456. **$27-$50.** 1618 E 16th Ave. I-75 exit 33, 0.3 mi w. Ext corridors. **Pets:** Other. No service, supervision, crate.
[SAVE] [SD] 🚭 ▣

[AAA] ◆◆◆ **Ramada Inn** [MI] 🐾
(912) 273-5000. **$48-$53, 3 days notice.** 2016 16th Ave E. Jct I-75 exit 33 and US 280. Ext corridors. **Pets:** Medium. $5 daily fee/room. No service, supervision, crate.
[SAVE] 🚭 ▣ 🍴 🏊

COVINGTON

[AAA] ◆◆◆ **Holiday Inn Express** [M] 🐾
(770) 787-4900. **$70-$75.** 10111 Alcovy Rd. I-20 exit 45A. Ext corridors. **Pets:** Small, dogs only. $25 one-time fee/room. No service, supervision, crate.
[SAVE] [SD] 🚭 ♿ ▣ 📺 🏊

DALTON

[AAA] ◆◆ **Best Inns of America** [M] 🐾
(706) 226-1100. **$55-$69.** 1529 W Walnut Ave. I-75 exit 136, just e. Ext corridors. **Pets:** Medium, other. $25 deposit/room. Supervision.
[SAVE] [SD] 🚭 🏊

[AAA] ◆◆ **Best Western Inn of Dalton** [MI] 🐾
(706) 226-5022. **$37-$53.** 2106 Chattanooga Rd. I-75 exit 137, just w. Ext corridors. **Pets:** Very small, dogs only. Supervision.
[SAVE] 🚭 ▣ 🍴 🏊 🏋

[AAA] ◆◆◆ **Holiday Inn** [MI] 🐾
(706) 278-0500. **$59-$79, 7 days notice.** 515 Holiday Dr. I-75 exit 136, nw corner. Ext corridors. **Pets:** Medium. Designated rooms, supervision.
[SAVE] 🚭 👂 📺 🍴 🏊

DARIEN

[AAA] ◆◆◆ **Holiday Inn Express** [M] 🐾
(912) 437-5373. **$58-$63.** I-95 & SR 251 Magnolia Bluff. I-95 exit 10, just w. Int corridors. **Pets:** Other. $10 one-time fee/pet. Supervision.
[SAVE] 🚭 👂 ▣ 🏊

DAWSONVILLE

[AAA] ◆◆◆ **Days Inn** [M]
(706) 216-4410. **$59-$110.** 76 N Georgia Ave. 0.5 mi s of jct SR 400 and 53. Int corridors. **Pets:** Supervision.
[SAVE] 🚭 🚶 ♿ ▣ 🏊

DILLARD

[AAA] ◆◆◆ **The Dillard House** [MI] 🐾
(706) 746-5348. **$49-$119.** US 441, 0.3 mi e via Old Dillard Rd. Ext corridors. **Pets:** Small, dogs only. $5 one-time fee/room. Supervision.
🚭 ▣ 📺 🍴 🏊 🏋

DUBLIN

◆◆◆ **Holiday Inn Hotel & Suites** [MI]
(912) 272-7862. **$58.** 2190 Hwy 441 S. I-16 exit 14, ne corner. Ext corridors. **Pets:** Small. Designated rooms, no service, supervision, crate.
[A$K] [SD] 🚭 ♿ 👂 ▣ 📺 🍴 🏊 🏋

FORSYTH

[AAA] ◆◆ **Best Western Hilltop Inn** [M] 🐾
(912) 994-9260. **$36-$46.** 951 Hwy 42 N. On SR 42; e of I-75, exit 63. Ext corridors. **Pets:** Small. $25 deposit/pet. Supervision.
[SAVE] 🚭 🏊

◆◆◆ **Hampton Inn** [M] 🐾
(912) 994-9697. **$59-$64.** 520 Holiday Cir. I-75 exit 61, Tift College Dr and Juliette Rd. Int corridors. **Pets:** Other. Supervision.
[A$K] 🚭 🚶

◆◆◆ **Holiday Inn Forsyth** [MI]
(912) 994-5691. **Call for rates.** 480 Holiday Cir. I-75 exit 61, sw corner. Ext corridors. **Pets:** Medium. Designated rooms, supervision.
🚭 👂 ▣ 📺 🍴 🏊

GARDEN CITY

♦♦ Masters Inn Garden City Ⓜ ❀
(912) 964-4344. **$45-$59.** 4200 Hwy 21N; Augusta Rd. On SR 21N, 0.3 mi nw of terminus, I-516. Int corridors. **Pets:** Very small. $6 one-time fee/room. No service, supervision, crate.

ⓈAVE 🐾 ☒ ⓐ 🖥 🍴 ⌬

GLENNVILLE

♦♦ Cheeri-O Motel Ⓜ ❀
(912) 654-2176. **$33-$40.** 0.8 mi s on US 25 and 301. Ext corridors. **Pets:** Small. $5 daily fee/pet, $5 one-time fee/pet. No service, supervision, crate.

ⓈAVE ☒ 🖥 🖳

GOLDEN ISLES METROPOLITAN AREA

JEKYLL ISLAND

♦♦♦ Clarion Resort Buccaneer Ⓜ
(912) 635-2261. **$99-$179.** 85 S Beachview Dr. 0.5 mi s of jct SR 520. Ext/int corridors. **Pets:** Medium. Designated rooms, supervision.

ⓈAVE 🐾 ☒ ⓐ 🖳 🍴 ⌬ ☒

♦♦ Comfort Inn Island Suites Ⓜ ❀
(912) 635-2211. **$99-$179, 3 days notice.** 711 N Beachview Dr. 1.5 mi n from jct SR 520 (Ben Fortson Pkwy) and N Beachview Dr. Ext corridors. **Pets:** Medium, other. $10 daily fee/pet, $10 one-time fee/pet. Supervision.

ⓈAVE ☒ 👆 🖥 🖳 🍴 ⌬ ☒

♦♦♦ Jekyll Inn Ⓜ ❀
(912) 635-2332. **$99-$129, 3 days notice.** 975 N Beachview Dr. From jct SR 520 (Ben Fortson Pkwy) and Beachview Dr, 3 mi n. Ext corridors. **Pets:** Small, other. $10 daily fee/room. Supervision.

ⓈAVE 🖥 🖳 🍴 ⌬ ☒

♦♦ Seafarer Inn & Suites Ⓜ ❀
(912) 635-2202. **$49-$99.** 700 N Beachview Dr. From jct SR 520 (Ben Fortson Pkwy) and Beachview Dr, 1.5 mi n. Ext corridors. **Pets:** Other. $5 daily fee/pet. No service, supervision, crate.

ⓈAVE 🐾 ☒ 🖥 ⌬ ☒

❀ END METROPOLITAN AREA ❀

HELEN

♦♦ The Helendorf River Inn & Towers Ⓜ ❀
(706) 878-2271. **$74-$99.** 33 Munichstrasse. Center on SR 17 and 75. Ext corridors. **Pets:** Other. $10 daily fee/pet. Designated rooms, supervision.

🖥 🖳 ⌬ ☒

HOGANSVILLE

♦♦ Key West Inn Ⓜ ❀
(706) 637-9395. **$48-$60.** 1888 E Main St. I-85 exit 6, just w. Ext corridors. **Pets:** Very small, dogs only. $10 deposit/pet, $5 daily fee/pet, $5 one-time fee/pet. Designated rooms, no service, supervision, crate.

ⓈAVE ☒ 🖥 🖳 ⌬

JEFFERSONVILLE

♦♦ Days Inn Jeffersonville Ⓜ
(912) 945-3785. **$58-$64.** 6996 Exit 8 on I-16. I-16 exit 8, just sw. Ext corridors. **Pets:** Designated rooms, no service, supervision, crate.

ⒶSK ☒ ⌬

KINGSLAND

♦♦♦ Best Western Kings Bay Inn Ⓜ ❀
(912) 729-7666. **$55-$69.** 1353 Hwy 40 E. I-95 exit 2, 0.3 mi e. Ext corridors. **Pets:** $30 deposit/room. Supervision.

ⓈAVE ☒ ⓐ 🖥 🖳 ⌬ ☒

♦♦ Econo Lodge Ⓜ ❀
(912) 673-7336. **$48-$88.** 1135 E King Ave. I-95 exit 2. Ext corridors. **Pets:** Other. $25 deposit/room. No service, supervision, crate.

ⒶSK ☒ ♿ ⓐ ⒸE 🖥 🖳 ⌬

♦♦♦ Holiday Inn Kingsland Ⓜ
(912) 729-3000. **$69-$99.** 930 US Hwy 40 E. I-95 exit 2, nw corner. Ext corridors. **Pets:** Supervision.

ⓈAVE 🐾 ☒ 🖥 🖳 🍴 ⌬

♦♦ Super 8 Motel Ⓜ ❀
(912) 729-6888. **$39-$48.** 120 Edenfield Dr. I-95 exit 2, se corner. **Pets:** Small. $5 daily fee/pet, $5 one-time fee/pet. No service, supervision, crate.

ⓈAVE ☒ 🖥 🖳

LAGRANGE

♦♦ Days Inn-La Grange/Callaway Gardens Ⓜ ❀
(706) 882-8881. **$45-$75.** 2606 Whitesville Rd. I-85 exit 2, just e. Ext corridors. **Pets:** $6 daily fee/pet, $6 one-time fee/pet. Supervision.

ⓈAVE 🐾 ☒ ⒸE 🖥 🖳 ⌬

LAKE PARK

♦♦♦ Days Inn Ⓜ ❀
(912) 559-0229. **$36-$47.** 4913 Timber Dr. I-75 exit 2. Ext corridors. **Pets:** Other. Supervision.

ⒶSK ☒ 🖳 ⌬

♦♦ Holiday Inn Express Ⓜ
(912) 559-5181. **$40-$70.** 1198 Lake Blvd. I-75 exit 2. Ext corridors. **Pets:** Small. Supervision.

ⒶSK 🐾 ☒ ⌬

ⓐⓐ ◆◆ Super 8 Motel Ⓜ ✿
(912) 559-8111. **$42-$44.** 4907 Timber Dr. I-75, exit 2, ne corner. Ext corridors. **Pets:** Very small. $20 deposit/pet, $10 daily fee/pet, $10 one-time fee/pet. Designated rooms, no service, supervision, crate.
SAVE ✕ ▤

ⓐⓐ ◆◆ Travelodge Ⓜ ✿
(912) 559-0110. **$36-$42.** 4912 Timber Dr. I-75 exit 2, just w, just n. Int corridors. **Pets:** Medium. No service, supervision, crate.
SAVE ✕ 🏠 ▤ 💻

LOCUST GROVE

◆◆ Executive Inn Ⓜ ✿
(770) 957-2671. **$29-$40.** 4854 Hampton Rd. I-75 exit 68, just e. Ext corridors. **Pets:** Small, dogs only. $10 deposit/pet, $5 daily fee/pet, $15 one-time fee/pet. No service, supervision, crate.
ASK 🛏 ✕ ▤ 🖼

ⓐⓐ ◆◆ Super 8 Motel Ⓜ
(770) 957-2936. **$40-$50.** 4605 Bill Gardner Pkwy. I-75 exit 68, just w. Ext corridors. **Pets:** Small. Designated rooms, no service, supervision, crate.
SAVE ✕ ▤ 🖼

LOUISVILLE

ⓐⓐ ◆◆ Louisville Motor Lodge Ⓜ
(912) 625-7168. **$49.** 308 Hwy 1 Bypass. 1 mi ne on US 1 bypass. Ext corridors. **Pets:** Small. No service, supervision, crate.
SAVE 🛏 ✕ ▤

MACON

ⓐⓐ ◆◆◆ Best Western Inn & Suites Ⓜ ✿
(912) 781-5300. **$56-$56.** 4681 Chambers Rd. I-475 exit 1, se corner. Ext corridors. **Pets:** Medium. $10 one-time fee/room. No service, supervision, crate.
SAVE ✕ 🖼 ▤ 🖼

ⓐⓐ ◆◆◆ Comfort Inn-North Ⓜ ✿
(912) 746-8855. **$54-$69, 3 days notice.** 2690 Riverside Dr. I-75 exit 54. Ext/int corridors. **Pets:** $50 deposit/room. Designated rooms, no service, supervision, crate.
SAVE ✕ 🏠 ▤ 💻 🖼

◆◆ Days Inn North Ⓜ ✿
(912) 745-8521. **Call for rates.** 2737 Sheraton Dr. I-75 exit 54, Pierce Ave; 0.5 mi ne via Sheraton Dr. Ext corridors. **Pets:** Other. $5 one-time fee/pet. Supervision.
✕ ▤ 🖼

◆◆◆ Hampton Inn Ⓜ
(912) 471-0660. **$69-$69, 30 days notice.** 3680 Riverside Dr. I-75 exit 55A, sw corner. Ext corridors. **Pets:** Small. No service, supervision, crate.
✕ ▤ 💻 🖼

◆◆◆ Holiday Inn Express Ⓜ
(912) 474-0600. **Call for rates.** 2720 Riverside Dr. I-75 exit 54, just nw. Int corridors. **Pets:** Designated rooms, no service, supervision, crate.
✕ 🏠 🖼 ▤ 💻 🖼

◆◆◆ Holiday Inn Macon Conference Center Ⓜ🅸
(912) 474-2610. **Call for rates.** 3590 Riverside Dr. I-75 exit 55A. Ext corridors. **Pets:** Small. Supervision.
ASK ✕ ▤ 💻 🍴 🖼

ⓐⓐ ◆◆ Knights Inn-Macon Ⓜ ✿
(912) 471-1230. **$32-$48.** 4952 Romiser Rd. I-475 at jct US 80, exit 1. Ext corridors. **Pets:** Small. $5 daily fee/pet. Designated rooms, no service, supervision, crate.
SAVE ✕ ▤ 🖼

ⓐⓐ ◆◆◆ La Quinta Inn & Suites Ⓜ ✿
(912) 475-0206. **$59-$89.** 3944 River Place Dr. I-75 exit 55A, se corner. Int corridors. **Pets:** Small, other. No service, supervision, crate.
SAVE ✕ 🏠 🖼 ▤ 💻 🖼

ⓐⓐ ◆◆ Masters Inn Ⓜ
(912) 788-8910. **$29-$43.** 4295 Pio Nono Ave. 0.3 mi s on Pio Nono Ave; jct I-75S exit 49A, I-75N exit 49. Ext corridors. **Pets:** Supervision.
SAVE ✕ 🏠 🎵 🖼 ▤ 🖼

ⓐⓐ ◆◆◆ Quality Inn Ⓜ
(912) 781-7000. **$45-$45, 5 days notice.** 4630 Chambers Rd. I-475 exit 1, just se. Ext corridors. **Pets:** Supervision.
SAVE ✕ ▤ 💻 🖼

◆ Ramada Inn and Conference Center Ⓜ🅸
(912) 474-0871. **$52-$71, 3 days notice.** 5009 Harrison Rd. I-475 and exit 1, nw corner. Ext corridors. **Pets:** Supervision.
ASK ✕ ▤ 💻 🍴 🖼

ⓐⓐ ◆◆ Red Roof Inn Ⓜ ✿
(912) 477-7477. **$40-$64.** 3950 River Place Dr. I-75 at Arkwright Rd exit 55A. Int corridors. **Pets:** Medium, other. Supervision.
SAVE ✕ 🖼 ▤ 🖼

ⓐⓐ ◆◆◆ Rodeway Inn Ⓜ ✿
(912) 781-4343. **$45-$45.** 4999 Eisenhower Pkwy. I-475 exit 1, 0.3 mi e on US 80. Ext corridors. **Pets:** Medium. $20 deposit/room. No service, supervision, crate.
SAVE ✕ ▤ 💻 🖼

ⓐⓐ ◆◆◆ Super 8 North Macon Ⓜ
(912) 757-8688. **$55-$75, 7 days notice.** 3935 Arkwright Rd. I-75 exit 55A. Int corridors. **Pets:** Small. Designated rooms, no service, supervision, crate.
SAVE 🛏 ✕ ▤ 🖼

MADISON

ⓐⓐ ◆◆ Ramada Inn-Antebellum Ⓜ🅸
(706) 342-2121. **$44-$65.** I-20 & US 441. I-20 exit 51, just s. Ext corridors. **Pets:** Small. No service, supervision, crate.
SAVE 🛏 ✕ ▤ 💻 🍴 🖼

MCDONOUGH

◆◆ Brittany American Inn Ⓜ
(770) 957-5821. **$35-$42, 7 days notice.** 1171 Hwy 20 & 81. I-75 exit 70, se corner. Ext corridors. **Pets:** No service, supervision, crate.
ASK ✕ 🖼

Days Inn ◆◆ 🐾
(770) 957-5261. **$47-$59.** 744 SR 155S & I-75. I-75 exit 69, just e. Ext corridors. **Pets:** Small. $5 daily fee/pet, $5 one-time fee/pet. No service, supervision, crate.

Holiday Inn McDonough ◆◆◆ 🐾
(770) 957-5291. **$69-$79.** 930 Hwy 155 S. I-75 exit 69, just w. Ext corridors. **Pets:** Supervision.

MILLEDGEVILLE

Holiday Inn ◆◆◆
(912) 452-3502. **$56-$69.** 2627 N Columbia St. 4 mi nw on US 441 and SR 24. Ext corridors. **Pets:** Small. No service, supervision, crate.

NEWNAN

Best Western-Shenandoah Inn ◆◆ 🐾
(770) 304-9700. **$60-$70, 7 days notice.** 620 Hwy 34E. I-85 exit 9, just w. Ext corridors. **Pets:** Medium. $10 daily fee/room. Designated rooms, no service, supervision, crate.

Holiday Inn Express ◆◆ 🐾
(770) 251-2828. **$61-$65, 3 days notice.** 6 Herring Rd. I-85 exit 9, just w. Ext corridors. **Pets:** Supervision.

PERRY

Best Inn & Suites ◆◆ 🐾
(912) 987-2585. **$36-$50** (no credit cards), 3 days notice. 202 Valley Dr. I-75 exit 43, sw corner. Ext corridors. **Pets:** Other. $15 deposit/room, $5 daily fee/room, $15 one-time fee/room. No service, supervision, crate.

Comfort Inn ◆◆◆ 🐾
(912) 987-7710. **$45-$65.** 1602 Sam Nunn Blvd. I-75 exit 43, just w. Ext corridors. **Pets:** Small, other. $10 one-time fee/room. Designated rooms, no service, supervision, crate.

Hampton Inn ◆◆◆ 🐾
(912) 987-7681. **Call for rates.** 102 Hampton Ct. I-75 exit 43, se corner. Int corridors. **Pets:** $65 one-time fee/room. Designated rooms, no service, supervision, crate.

New Perry Hotel-Motel ◆◆
(912) 987-1000. **$30-$51.** 800 Main St. On US 341, just off US 41; from I-75 exit 43, then 0.8 mi se. Ext/int corridors. **Pets:** Small. No service, supervision, crate.

Quality Inn ◆◆◆ 🐾
(912) 987-1345. **$50-$75.** 1504 Sam Nunn Blvd. I-75 exit 43. Ext corridors. **Pets:** $5 daily fee/room. No service, supervision, crate.

Super 8 Motel ◆◆◆
(912) 987-0999. **$45-$55.** 102 Plaza Dr. I-75 exit 43, 0.3 mi e. Ext corridors. **Pets:** Supervision.

PINE MOUNTAIN

White Columns Motel ◆
(706) 663-2312. **$55-$55.** 19727 S US 27. 1 mi s on US 27. Ext corridors. **Pets:** Small. No service, supervision, crate.

RICHMOND HILL

Econo Lodge ◆◆ 🐾
(912) 756-3312. **$45-$100, 7 days notice.** 4701 US 17 S. On US 17 at I-95, exit 14. Ext corridors. **Pets:** $5 daily fee/pet, $5 one-time fee/pet. Designated rooms, no service, supervision, crate.

RINGGOLD

Super 8 Motel ◆◆ 🐾
(706) 965-7080. **Call for rates.** 5400 Alabama Hwy. I-75 exit 140, just e. Ext corridors. **Pets:** Other. Supervision.

ROME

Holiday Inn-Sky Top Center ◆◆◆ 🐾
(706) 295-1100. **$59-$65.** 20 US 411E. 2 mi e on US 411. Ext corridors. **Pets:** Supervision.

SAVANNAH

Baymont Inn & Suites-Savannah ◆◆ 🐾
(912) 927-7660. **$59-$66.** 8484 Abercorn St. 6.3 mi sw of historic district on SR 204. Int corridors. **Pets:** Medium, other. $50 deposit/room. Designated rooms, no service, supervision, crate.

Best Western Central ◆◆
(912) 355-1000. **$49-$79, 3 days notice.** 45 Eisenhower Dr. 5.8 mi sw of historic district on SR 204. Ext corridors. **Pets:** Very small. No service, supervision, crate.

East Bay Inn ◆◆◆
(912) 238-1225. **$129-$189.** 225 E Bay St. Historic district, corner of Bay and Lincoln sts. Int corridors. **Pets:** Designated rooms, supervision.

Econo Lodge Gateway ◆◆ 🐾
(912) 925-2280. **$75-$120, 3 days notice.** 7 Gateway Blvd W. I-95 exit 16, just w on SR 204. Ext corridors. **Pets:** Small. $25 deposit/room, $5 daily fee/pet. Designated rooms, no service, supervision, crate.

Holiday Inn I-95 South ◆◆◆ 🐾
(912) 925-2770. **$67-$75.** I-95 & SR 204. I-95 exit 16, se corner. Ext corridors. **Pets:** Small. Designated rooms, no service, supervision, crate.

◆◆ **Joan's on Jones B & B** 🆑 ❀
(912) 234-3863. **$135-$150** (no credit cards), 7 days notice.
17 W Jones St. Se corner Jones and Whitaker sts. Ext
corridors. **Pets:** Medium, dogs only. $50 one-time fee/room.
Designated rooms, supervision.
⊠ 🖵

🆑 ◆◆◆ **La Quinta Inn** 🅼 ❀
(912) 355-3004. **$65-$95.** 6805 Abercorn St. 5.5 mi sw of
historic district, via SR 204. Ext corridors. **Pets:** Medium.
Supervision.
🆂🅰🆅🅴 ⊠ 🐾 🔒 🖵 🖫

🆑 ◆◆◆ **La Quinta Inn-Savannah I-95** 🅼 ❀
(912) 925-9505. **$59-$85.** 6 Gateway Blvd S. I-95 exit 16,
just e off SR 204. Ext corridors. **Pets:** Medium. Supervision.
🆂🅰🆅🅴 ⊠ 🐾 🐾 🖋 🖵 🖫

🆑 ◆◆◆ **Olde Harbour Inn** 🅱🅱 ❀
(912) 234-4100. **$139-$249.** 508 E Factors Walk. Historical
Riverfront District on Factors Walk; Lincoln St ramp off E
Bay St. Ext corridors. **Pets:** Small, other. $35 one-time
fee/pet. Designated rooms, no service, supervision, crate.
🆂🅰🆅🅴 ⊠ 🔒 🖵

◆◆◆ **Savannah Residence Inn by**
Marriott 🅼 ❀
(912) 356-3266. **$117-$159.** 5710 White Bluff Rd. 5.5 mi s
of historic district. Int corridors. **Pets:** Other. $100 one-time
fee/room. Supervision.
🅰🆂🅺 ⊠ 🖋 🖵 🖫

🆑 ◆◆ **Shoney's Inn** 🅼
(912) 925-7050. **$72.** 17003 Abercorn St. I-95 exit 16, SR
204, ne corner. Ext corridors. **Pets:** Medium. Designated
rooms, no service, supervision, crate.
🆂🅰🆅🅴 🆂🅳 ⊠ 🔒 🖫

ST. MARYS

◆◆ **Goodbread House Bed & Breakfast** 🅱🅱
(912) 882-7490. **Call for rates** (no credit cards). 209
Osborne St. I-95 exit 2, 9 mi e on SR 40. Int corridors.
Pets: Medium. Supervision.
⊠

◆◆ **GuestHouse Inn & Suites** 🅼🅸 ❀
(912) 882-6250. **$39, 3 days notice.** 2710 Osborne Rd. Jct
US 40 and Spur 40. Ext corridors. **Pets:** Very small. $25
deposit/room, $5 one-time fee/room. No service, supervi-
sion, crate.
🅰🆂🅺 🆂🅳 ⊠ 🔒 🖵 🖫 ⊠

STATESBORO

◆◆◆ **Statesboro Inn & Restaurant** 🅲🅸 ❀
(912) 489-8628. **$85-$125.** 106 S Main St. Downtown; just
s of town center on US 301/25. Ext/int corridors.
Pets: Small, other. $25 deposit/room, $10 daily fee/room.
Designated rooms, no service, supervision, crate.
🅰🆂🅺 🆂🅳 ⊠ 🔒 🖵

◆◆ **Super 8 Motel** 🅼 ❀
(912) 764-5631. **Call for rates, 20 days notice.** 109 N
Main St. Downtown, w of center. Ext corridors. **Pets:** Other.
$10 deposit/room. No service, supervision, crate.
🅰🆂🅺 ⊠ 🔒

STOCKBRIDGE

🆑 ◆ **Motel 6-1117** 🅼 ❀
(770) 389-1142. **$40-$56.** 7233 Davidson Pkwy. I-675 exit
1, ne corner. Ext corridors. **Pets:** Medium. No service,
supervision, crate.
⊠ 🐾 🖋 🖫 📺

🆑 ◆◆ **Super 8 Motel Atlanta South** 🅼 ❀
(770) 474-5758. **$45-$65, 7 days notice.** 1451 Hudson
Bridge Rd. I-75 exit 73, just w. Ext corridors. **Pets:** Small.
Supervision.
🆂🅰🆅🅴 ⊠ 🔒 🖵 🖫

SWAINSBORO

🆑 ◆◆ **Bradford Inn** 🅼
(912) 237-2400. **$46-$46.** 2.2 mi s of jct US
80, SR 26 and US 1. Ext corridors. **Pets:** Small. Designated rooms, no service, supervision, crate.
🆂🅰🆅🅴 🆂🅳 ⊠ 🔒 🖵

THOMASTON

◆◆◆ **Days Inn** 🅼 ❀
(706) 648-9260. **$56-$64.** 1211 Hwy 19 N. 2.5 mi n of
center. Ext corridors. **Pets:** Small. $50 deposit/room, $10
daily fee/pet. No service, supervision, crate.
🅰🆂🅺 ⊠ 🖋 🔒 🖵 🖫

THOMASVILLE

◆◆◆ **GuestHouse Inns & Suites** 🅼🅸
(912) 226-7111. **$59-$69.** 15138 US Hwy 19S. 0.3 mi s of
US 319. Ext corridors. **Pets:** Supervision.
🅰🆂🅺 ⊠ 🐾 🐾 🔒 🖵 🍴 🖫

THOMSON

🆑 ◆◆◆ **Best Western White Columns**
Inn 🅼🅸 ❀
(706) 595-8000. **$53-$66.** 1890 Washington Rd. I-20 exit
59. Ext corridors. **Pets:** Other. $10 daily fee/pet. Supervi-
sion.
🆂🅰🆅🅴 ⊠ 🔒 🖵 🖫

🆑 ◆ **Days Inn** 🅼
(706) 595-2262. **$45-$55.** 2658 Cobb Ham Rd. I-20 exit 60,
ne corner. Ext corridors. **Pets:** Medium. Supervision.
🆂🅰🆅🅴 🆂🅳 ⊠ 🔒 📺

TIFTON

◆◆◆ **Hampton Inn** 🅼 ❀
(912) 382-8800. **$59-$71, 3 days notice.** 720 Hwy 319S.
On US 319 at jct I-75, exit 18. Ext corridors. **Pets:** Medium,
other. $5 one-time fee/pet. Supervision.
⊠ 🖵 🖫

◆◆◆ **Holiday Inn** 🅼🅸 ❀
(912) 382-6687. **$60-$65.** 1208 Hwy 82 W. At jct I-75, US
82 and 319, exit 18. Ext corridors. **Pets:** Other. Supervision.
🅰🆂🅺 🆂🅳 ⊠ 🔒 🖵

🆑 ◆◆ **Howard Johnson Inn** 🅼🅸
(912) 386-2100. **$42-$55.** 1103 King Rd. Jct I-75, exit 19
(W 2nd St). Ext corridors. **Pets:** Supervision.
🆂🅰🆅🅴 🆂🅳 ⊠ 🔒 🖵 🍴 🖫

▲▲ ◆◆ Masters Inn-Tifton M
(912) 382-8100. **$29-$43.** 901 7th St W. At jct I-75, US 82 and 319. Ext corridors. **Pets:** No service, supervision, crate.
SAVE ⊠ 🖥 🕿

◆◆ Super 8 Motel M
(912) 382-9500. **Call for rates.** I-75 exit 19 (W 2nd St), se corner. Ext corridors. **Pets:** Medium. Designated rooms, no service, supervision, crate.
ASK ⊠ 🕿

VALDOSTA

▲▲ ◆◆◆ Best Western King of the Road M
(912) 244-7600. **$49-$59.** 1403 N St. Augustine Rd. I-75 exit 5 (SR 94), nw corner. Ext corridors. **Pets:** Designated rooms, no service, supervision, crate.
SAVE ⊠ 🖉 🖥 🍴 🕿

▲▲ ◆◆◆ Comfort Inn M ❖
(912) 242-1212. **$53-$65, 7 days notice.** 2101 W Hill. I-75 exit 4, sw corner. Ext/int corridors. **Pets:** Medium. Designated rooms, no service, supervision, crate.
SAVE S⊘ ⊠ 🖥 🖵 🍴 🕿

◆◆ Days Inn I-75 North M ❖
(912) 244-4460. **$36-$42.** 4598 N Valdosta Rd. I-75 exit 6, nw corner. Ext corridors. **Pets:** Medium, other. $5 daily fee/pet. Designated rooms, supervision.
ASK S⊘ ⊠ 🕿

◆◆ Days Inn I-75 South M ❖
(912) 249-8800. **$38-$45.** 1827 W Hill Ave. I-75 exit 4, se corner on US 84. Ext corridors. **Pets:** Medium. $5 daily fee/pet. Designated rooms, supervision.
ASK S⊘ ⊠ 🖑 🖉 🖥 🕿

▲▲ ◆◆◆ Holiday Inn M ❖
(912) 242-3881. **$57.** 1309 St Augustine Rd. I-75 exit 5, just e on SR 94. Ext corridors. **Pets:** Small. $10 one-time fee/room. Supervision.
SAVE ⊠ 🖥 🖵 🍴 🕿

▲▲ ◆ Motel 6 #421 M
(912) 333-0047. **$28-$44.** 2003 W Hill Ave. I-75 exit 4, US 84, se corner. Ext corridors. **Pets:** Small. No service, supervision, crate.
⊠ 🖉 🕿 CTV

▲▲ ◆◆◆ Quality Inn North M
(912) 244-8510. **$55-$65.** 1209 St. Augustine Rd. I-75 exit 5, 0.3 mi e on SR 94. Ext corridors. **Pets:** Supervision.
SAVE ⊠ 🖥 🖵 🕿 🗙

◆◆ Quality Inn South M ❖
(912) 244-4520. **$35-$50.** 1902 W Hill Ave. I-75 exit 4, just e on US 84. Ext corridors. **Pets:** Medium. Supervision.
ASK ⊠ 🖵 🕿 🗙

◆◆◆ Ramada Limited M ❖
(912) 242-1225. **$49-$99.** 2008 W Hill Ave. I-75 exit 4, just e on US 84. Ext corridors. **Pets:** Other. $5 one-time fee/room. Supervision.
ASK S⊘ ⊠ 🖥 🕿

◆◆ Super 8 Motel I-75 M ❖
(912) 249-8000. **$36-$44.** 1825 W Hill Ave. I-75 exit 4, se corner on US 84. Int corridors. **Pets:** Medium. $5 daily fee/pet. Designated rooms, supervision.
ASK S⊘ ⊠ 🖉

VIDALIA

▲▲ ◆◆ Days Inn M ❖
(912) 537-9251. **$40-$50.** 1503 Lyons Hwy, 280E. 1 mi e on US 280. Ext corridors. **Pets:** Small. $10 daily fee/pet, $10 one-time fee/pet. No service, supervision, crate.
SAVE S⊘ ⊠ 🖥 🖵 🕿

◆◆◆ Holiday Inn Express M
(912) 537-9000. **$50-$67.** 2619 E First St. 2.3 mi e on US 280. Ext corridors. **Pets:** Medium. Designated rooms, no service, supervision, crate.
ASK ⊠ 🖥 🕿 🗙

WARNER ROBINS

▲▲ ◆◆ Best Western Peach Inn M ❖
(912) 953-3800. **$45-$57.** 2739 Watson Blvd. I-75 exit 45, 4.1 mi e. Ext corridors. **Pets:** Small. $10 deposit/pet, $5 daily fee/pet, $5 one-time fee/pet. No service, supervision, crate.
SAVE S⊘ ⊠ 🖉 🖥 🕿

▲▲ ◆◆◆ Comfort Inn M
(912) 922-7555. **$50-$61.** 95 S Hwy 247. Jct US 129/SR 247 and Russell Pkwy on nw corner; I-75 exit 45 Rt 247 Connector; 1.3 mi e to SR 247/US 129, then 1.6 mi s. Ext/int corridors. **Pets:** Supervision.
SAVE ⊠ 🖉 🖉 🖥 🕿

◆ Super 8 Motel M ❖
(912) 923-8600. **$58-$177, 7 days notice.** 105 Woodcrest Blvd. From SR 129, 6 mi e (Watson Blvd) to Woodcrest Blvd. Int corridors. **Pets:** Other. $5 daily fee/room, $25 one-time fee/room. Supervision.
ASK S⊘ ⊠ 🖥

WAYCROSS

▲▲ ◆◆ Days Inn M
(912) 285-4700. **$32-$54.** 2016 Memorial Dr. 2 mi se on US 1 and 23. Ext corridors. **Pets:** Supervision.
SAVE ⊠ 🖥 🕿

▲▲ ◆◆◆ Holiday Inn M ❖
(912) 283-4490. **$60-$67, 3 days notice.** 1725 Memorial Dr. At jct US 82 and 1. Ext corridors. **Pets:** Medium, other. Designated rooms, supervision.
SAVE ⊠ 🖥 🖵 🕿 🗙

◆◆◆ Jameson Inn M
(912) 283-3800. **$54-$66.** 950 City Blvd. Just e US 1. Ext corridors. **Pets:** Medium. Designated rooms, supervision.
ASK S⊘ ⊠ 🖑 🖥 🕿

Note: Hawaii imposes 30- and 120-day quarantines for all imported animals to prevent the presence and spread of rabies. Guide dogs (but not other service animals) are exempt from the quarantine, although they still must undergo vaccinations, microchip identification and a blood test on arrival in Hawaii. The quarantine does not apply to resident animals. For additional information, contact the Hawaii Department of Agriculture, Animal Quarantine Station, 99-951 Halawa Valley St., Aiea, HI 96701-3246; phone (808) 483-7151. Guide dog owners should request information on the certified guide exemption program.

KAUPULEHU

🔺🔺🔺🔺🔺 **Four Seasons Resort Hualalai at Historic Ka'upulehu** 🆁 🐾
(808) 325-8000. **$450-$650.** Off SR 19; 6 mi n of Kona International Airport. Ext corridors. **Pets:** Very small. Supervision.
🔀 ⓕ 🎵 🎬 💻 🍴 🛄 🔀

WAILEA

🔺🔺🔺🔺🔺 **Four Seasons Resort, Maui at Wailea** 🆁 🐾
(808) 874-8000. **$305-$595.** 3900 Wailea Alanui Dr. In resort area; off SR 31. Ext/int corridors. **Pets:** Other. Supervision.
🔀 ⓕ 🎵 🎬 💻 🍴 🛄 🔀

IDAHO

ASHTON

◆◆ Super 8 M
(208) 652-7885. **$55-$57.** 164 White Pine Dr. Just off US 20. Int corridors. **Pets:** Large. No service, supervision, crate.

BLACKFOOT

◆◆◆ Best Western Blackfoot Inn M 🐾
(208) 785-4144. **$50-$90, 30 days notice.** 750 Jensen Grove Dr. I-15, exit 93, just e on Bergener, 0.4 mi n on Parkway. Int corridors. **Pets:** Other. No service, supervision, crate.

BLISS

◆◆ Amber Inn Motel M
(208) 352-4441. **$33-$39.** 17286 US Hwy 30. Just s of I-84, exit 141. Int corridors. **Pets:** Medium. Supervision.

BOISE

◆◆◆ AmeriSuites M 🐾
(208) 375-1200. **$99-$99.** 925 N Milwaukee St. I-84, exit 49 (Franklin St), just w on Franklin St, 0.5 mi s. Int corridors. **Pets:** Small, other. $20 deposit/room. Supervision.

◆◆ BestRest Inn M
(208) 322-4404. **$50-$50.** 8002 Overland Rd. Just sw of I-84, exit 50A eastbound; exit 50A westbound, just s on Cole, just w. Ext corridors. **Pets:** Medium. Supervision.

◆◆ Boise Super 8 Lodge M 🐾
(208) 344-8871. **$53-$68.** 2773 Elder St. Just n of I-84, exit 53. Int corridors. **Pets:** $25 deposit/room. No service, supervision, crate.

◆◆◆ Cavanaughs ParkCenter Suites M
(208) 342-1044. **Call for rates.** 424 E Parkcenter Blvd. 2.3 mi n of I-84, exit 54, just e on Beacon and Parkcenter Blvd. Int corridors. **Pets:** Small. No service, supervision, crate.

◆◆◆ DoubleTree Hotel Boise Downtown M
(208) 344-7691. **$129-$129.** 1800 Fairview Ave. 1 mi n of I-184, Fairview Ave exit. Int corridors. **Pets:** Medium. Designated rooms, supervision.

◆◆◆ DoubleTree Hotel Riverside M 🐾
(208) 343-1871. **$99-$158.** 2900 Chinden Blvd. Just n of I-184, Fairview Ave exit, just w on Garden. Int corridors. **Pets:** Large, other. No service, supervision, crate.

◆◆ Econo Lodge Boise M 🐾
(208) 344-4030. **$42-$52.** 4060 Fairview Ave. Just n of I-184, Fairview Ave exit. Int corridors. **Pets:** Small, dogs only. $25 deposit/pet, $10 one-time fee/pet. No service, supervision, crate.

◆◆◆ Hampton Inn M 🐾
(208) 331-5600. **$64-$84, 30 days notice.** 3270 S Shoshone St. Just n of I-84, exit 53. Int corridors. **Pets:** $25 deposit/room. Designated rooms, no service, supervision, crate.

◆◆◆ Holiday Inn M 🐾
(208) 344-8365. **$99-$109.** 3300 Vista Ave. Just n of I-84, exit 53. Int corridors. **Pets:** Other. Designated rooms, supervision.

◆◆◆ Owyhee Plaza Hotel M 🐾
(208) 343-4611. **$74-$138.** 1109 Main St. City center; at 11th and Main sts. Ext/int corridors. **Pets:** Small. $25 deposit/room. Designated rooms, no service, supervision, crate.

◆◆◆ Quality Inn Airport Suites M 🐾
(208) 343-7505. **$59-$74.** 2717 Vista Ave. 0.5 mi n of I-84, exit 53. Ext corridors. **Pets:** Medium, dogs only. $5 daily fee/pet. Designated rooms, no service, supervision, crate.

◆◆ Rodeway Inn of Boise M
(208) 376-2700. **$70-$100.** 1115 N Curtis Rd. Just sw of I-184, Curtis Rd exit. Ext/int corridors. **Pets:** Designated rooms, no service, supervision, crate.

◆◆◆ Shilo Inn-Boise Airport 🅼 ☙

(208) 343-7662. **$79-$129.** 4111 Broadway Ave. Just sw of I-84, exit 54. Int corridors. **Pets:** Medium. $10 daily fee/pet. Designated rooms, no service, supervision, crate.

[ASK] [S⬤] [✕] [🖊] [✑] [🔲] [💻] [🐾]

◆◆ Shilo Inn-Boise Riverside 🅼

(208) 344-3521. **$65-$115.** 3031 Main St. I-184, Fairview Ave exit, 0.5 mi n, just w on S 30th St. Int corridors. **Pets:** Designated rooms, no service, supervision, crate.

[ASK] [S⬤] [✕] [🔲] [🐾] [✕]

BONNERS FERRY

⊕ ◆◆◆ Best Western Kootenai River Inn 🅼

(208) 267-8511. **$90-$105, 7 days notice.** 7160 Plaza St. City center; on US 95. Int corridors. **Pets:** Medium. No service, supervision, crate.

[SAVE] [✕] [🔲] [💻] [🍴] [🐾]

BURLEY

⊕ ◆◆◆ Best Western Burley Inn & Convention Center 🅼

(208) 678-3501. **$54-$70.** 800 N Overland Ave. Just s of I-84, exit 208. Ext/int corridors. **Pets:** Medium. Designated rooms, supervision.

[SAVE] [S⬤] [✕] [🖊] [✑] [🔲] [🍴] [🐾] [✕]

◆◆ Budget Motel of Burley 🅼

(208) 678-2200. **$44-$60.** 900 N Overland Ave. Just s of I-84, exit 208. Ext corridors. **Pets:** Designated rooms, no service, supervision, crate.

[ASK] [S⬤] [✕] [🖊] [✑] [🐾]

CALDWELL

⊕ ◆◆◆ Best Inn & Suites 🅼 ☙

(208) 454-2222. **$59-$121.** 901 Specht. Just s of I-84, exit 29. Int corridors. **Pets:** Other. Supervision.

[SAVE] [S⬤] [✕] [🔲] [💻] [🐾] [CTV]

◆◆◆ Best Western Caldwell Inn & Suites 🅼 ☙

(208) 454-7225. **$59-$140.** 908 Specht Ave. Just s of I-84, exit 29. Int corridors. **Pets:** Small, dogs only. $50 deposit/pet. No service, supervision, crate.

[ASK] [S⬤] [✕] [✑] [🔲] [💻] [🐾]

COEUR D'ALENE

⊕ ◆◆◆ Best Inn & Suites 🅼 ☙

(208) 765-5500. **$69-$99.** 280 W Appleway. Just ne of I-90, exit 12. Int corridors. **Pets:** Other. Supervision.

[SAVE] [✕] [🔲] [💻] [🐾] [✕]

⊕ ◆◆◆ Coeur d'Alene Inn & Conference Center 🅼

(208) 765-3200. **$115-$139.** W 414 Appleway. Just n of I-90, exit 12. Int corridors. **Pets:** Medium. Designated rooms, supervision.

[SAVE] [S⬤] [✕] [🖊] [✑] [🔲] [💻] [🍴] [🐾]

◆◆◆◆ The Coeur d'Alene Resort 🆁 ☙

(208) 765-4000. **$179-$509, 7 days notice.** 115 S 2nd Ave. 2 mi s of I-90, exit 11. Ext/int corridors. **Pets:** Medium. Supervision.

[ASK] [S⬤] [✕] [💻] [🍴] [🐾] [✕]

◆◆ Days Inn-Coeur D'Alene 🅼 ☙

(208) 667-8668. **$55-$82.** 2200 NW Blvd. Just se of I-90, exit 11. Int corridors. **Pets:** Other. $25 deposit/pet. No service, supervision, crate.

[ASK] [S⬤] [✕] [🖐] [🖊] [✑] [🔲] [💻]

⊕ ◆◆◆ Hawthorn Inn & Suites 🅼 ☙

(208) 667-6777. **$99-$129, 3 days notice.** 2209 E Sherman Ave. Just s of I-90, exit 15. Int corridors. **Pets:** Other. Designated rooms, no service, supervision, crate.

[SAVE] [S⬤] [✕] [🖐] [🔲] [💻] [🐾]

⊕ ◆◆ Rodeway Inn Pines Resort Motel 🅼 ☙

(208) 664-8244. **$53-$89.** 1422 N West Blvd. 0.8 mi s of I-90, exit 11. Ext corridors. **Pets:** No service, supervision, crate.

[SAVE] [S⬤] [✕] [🖐] [🖊] [✑] [🔲] [💻] [🐾]

◆◆◆ Shilo Inn 🅼 ☙

(208) 664-2300. **$69-$179.** 702 W Appleway. Just n of I-90, exit 12, just w. Int corridors. **Pets:** Other. $10 one-time fee/room. Supervision.

[ASK] [S⬤] [✕] [🖐] [🖊] [✑] [🔲] [💻] [🐾]

DRIGGS

⊕ ◆◆ Best Western Teton West Motel 🅼 ☙

(208) 354-2363. **$70-$85.** 476 S Main St. 0.7 mi n on SR 33. Int corridors. **Pets:** Medium. $25 deposit/pet. No service, supervision, crate.

[S⬤] [✕] [💻] [🐾]

GRANGEVILLE

◆ Monty's Motel 🅼 ☙

(208) 983-2500. **$35-$46.** W 700 Main. Jct SR 13 and US 95. Ext corridors. **Pets:** Medium. No service, supervision, crate.

[✕] [🔲] [🐾]

HAGERMAN

⊕ ◆◆ Hagerman Valley Inn 🅼 ☙

(208) 837-6196. **$48.** 661 Frog's Landing. S end of town on US 30. Ext/int corridors. **Pets:** Small. $25 deposit/room, $5 daily fee/room. No service, supervision, crate.

[SAVE] [S⬤] [✕]

HAILEY

⊕ ◆◆ Airport Inn 🅼

(208) 788-2477. **$65-$90, 7 days notice.** 820 4th Ave S. Just n of Hwy 75 at 4th Ave, near airport. Ext corridors. **Pets:** Large. Supervision.

[✕] [🔲] [💻]

IDAHO FALLS

⊕ ◆◆◆ Best Western CottonTree Inn 🅼 ☙

(208) 523-6000. **$86-$130.** 900 Lindsay Blvd. I-15, exit 119, just e. Int corridors. **Pets:** Small, other. $25 deposit/room. No service, supervision, crate.

[SAVE] [S⬤] [✕] [🔲] [💻] [🐾]

◆◆◆ Best Western Driftwood Motel 🄼 🐾
(208) 523-2242. **$75-$110.** 575 River Pkwy. I-15, exit 118, 0.5 mi e on Broadway, 0.3 mi n. Ext corridors. **Pets:** Medium, other. $10 deposit/pet, $10 one-time fee/pet. No service, supervision, crate.

🆂🄰🆅🖪 ⊠ 🄱 🖥 🖵 🏊 ⊠

◆◆◆ Cavanaughs on the Falls 🄼🄸
(208) 523-8000. **$68-$88.** 475 River Pkwy. I-15, exit 118, 0.5 mi e on Broadway, then just n. Ext/int corridors. **Pets:** Medium. Designated rooms, no service, supervision, crate.

🄴🖥 🄱 🖵 🍴 🏊

◆◆◆ Shilo Conference Hotel 🄼🄸 🐾
(208) 523-0088. **$79-$149.** 780 Lindsay Blvd. I-15, exit 119, just se. Int corridors. **Pets:** Other. $10 daily fee/room. Designated rooms, no service, supervision, crate.

🄰🆂🄺 🆂🄰🆅🖪 ⊠ 🄱 🖵 🍴 🏊

JEROME

◆◆◆ Best Western Sawtooth Inn and Suites 🄼 🐾
(208) 324-9200. **$59-$89.** 2653 S Lincoln. I-84, exit 168, just n on SR 79. Int corridors. **Pets:** Other. $50 deposit/pet. Designated rooms, no service, supervision, crate.

🆂🄰🆅🖪 🆂🄰🆅🖪 ⊠ 🄴🖥 🄱 🖵 🏊

KAMIAH

◆◆ Lewis Clark Resort & Motel 🄼🄸 🐾
(208) 935-2556. **$32-$47.** 1.5 mi e on US 12. Ext corridors. **Pets:** No service, supervision, crate.

🄰🆂🄺 🆂🄰🆅🖪 ⊠ 🄴🖥 🄱 🖵 🍴 🏊

KELLOGG

◆ Silverhorn Motor Inn 🄼🄸 🐾
(208) 783-1151. **$51-$61.** 699 W Cameron Ave. Just ne of I-90, exit 49. Int corridors. **Pets:** Other. Designated rooms, supervision.

⊠ 🍴

◆◆ Super 8 Motel-Kellogg 🄼 🐾
(208) 783-1234. **$53-$65.** 601 Bunker Ave. 0.5 mi s of I-90, exit 49. Int corridors. **Pets:** Other. $20 deposit/room. No service, supervision, crate.

🆂🄰🆅🖪 🆂🄰🆅🖪 ⊠ 🄲 🄱 🏊

KETCHUM

◆◆◆ Best Western Tyrolean Lodge 🄼 🐾
(208) 726-5336. **$70-$135, 3 days notice.** 260 Cottonwood. S end of town, just w of SR 75 on Rivers St, just s on 3rd Ave. Int corridors. **Pets:** Small. $5 daily fee/pet. Designated rooms, supervision.

🆂🄰🆅🖪 🆂🄰🆅🖪 ⊠ 🄱 🏊 ⊠ 🄺

◆◆ Christiania Motor Lodge 🄼
(208) 726-3351. **$89-$105, 3 days notice.** 651 Sun Valley Rd. Just ne on Sun Valley Rd from jct of SR 75. Ext corridors. **Pets:** Medium. Supervision.

🄰🆂🄺 🆂🄰🆅🖪 ⊠ 🄱 🏊 🄺

◆◆◆ Clarion Inn of Sun Valley 🄼 🐾
(208) 726-5900. **$85-$250, 7 days notice.** 600 N Main St. N end of downtown on SR 75 (Main St), corner of 6th and Main sts. Ext/int corridors. **Pets:** Other. $25 deposit/room. Supervision.

🆂🄰🆅🖪 🆂🄰🆅🖪 ⊠ 🄴🖥 🄱 🖵 🏊

◆◆◆ Heidelberg Inn 🄼 🐾
(208) 726-5361. **$85-$130.** 1908 Warm Springs Rd. 1.3 mi w on Warm Springs Rd from jct of SR 75 (Main St). Ext corridors. **Pets:** Medium. $10 daily fee/pet. Designated rooms, supervision.

🆂🄰🆅🖪 ⊠ 🄴🖥 🄱 🖵 🏊 ⊠ 🄺

LEWISTON

◆◆◆ Comfort Inn 🄼 🐾
(208) 798-8090. **$63-$122.** 2128 8th Ave. 1.2 mi s on US 12 from jct US 95, just s on 21st. Int corridors. **Pets:** Other. $10 daily fee/room. No service, supervision, crate.

🄰🆂🄺 🆂🄰🆅🖪 ⊠ 🄵 🄽 🄴🖥 🄱 🖵 🏊

◆◆ Howard Johnson Express 🄼 🐾
(208) 743-9526. **$52-$102.** 1716 Main St. 1.6 mi s on US 12 from jct US 95. Ext corridors. **Pets:** Other. $25 deposit/room. No service, supervision, crate.

🆂🄰🆅🖪 🆂🄰🆅🖪 ⊠ 🄱 🖵 🏊

◆◆ Red Lion Hotel 🄼🄸
(208) 799-1000. **$69-$79.** 621 21st St. 1.2 mi s on US 12 from jct US 95, just s. Int corridors. **Pets:** Small. Supervision.

🄰🆂🄺 🆂🄰🆅🖪 ⊠ 🄱 🖵 🍴 🏊

◆◆ Riverview Inn 🄼 🐾
(208) 746-3311. **$38-$47.** 1325 Main St. Downtown. Int corridors. **Pets:** Other. No service, supervision, crate.

🄰🆂🄺 🆂🄰🆅🖪 ⊠ 🄱 🖵 🏊

◆◆ Sacajawea Select Inn 🄼🄸
(208) 746-1393. **$48-$58.** 1824 Main St. 1.5 mi s on US 12 from jct US 95. Ext/int corridors. **Pets:** No service, supervision, crate.

🆂🄰🆅🖪 🆂🄰🆅🖪 ⊠ 🄵 🄴🖥 🄱 🍴 🏊

◆◆ Super 8 Motel 🄼 🐾
(208) 743-8808. **Call for rates.** 3120 North & South Hwy. Just e on US 12 from jct US 95. Int corridors. **Pets:** Other. $25 deposit/room. Supervision.

🄰🆂🄺 ⊠ 🄱

MACKAY

◆ Wagon Wheel Motel 🄼 🐾
(208) 588-3331. **$35-$70.** 809 W Custer. 0.3 mi n on Hwy 93. Ext corridors. **Pets:** $5 one-time fee/room. No service, supervision, crate.

🆂🄰🆅🖪 🆂🄰🆅🖪 🄱 🖵 ⊠ 🄺

MCCALL

◆◆◆ Best Western McCall 🄼 🐾
(208) 634-6300. **$70-$90.** 415 3rd St. SR 55, just s of jct of Lake St and SR 55. Ext/int corridors. **Pets:** Other. No service, supervision, crate.

🆂🄰🆅🖪 🆂🄰🆅🖪 ⊠ 🄵 🄴🖥 🄱 🏊

❖❖ McCall Super 8 Lodge M ❖
(208) 634-4637. **$60-$65.** 303 S 3rd. S end of town on SR 55. Int corridors. **Pets:** Other. $20 deposit/room, $4 daily fee/pet, $4 one-time fee/pet. Designated rooms, supervision.
[SAVE] [S₀] [✕] [🏠] [♨] [📺]

❖ Scandia Inn Motel M ❖
(208) 634-7394. **$50-$54.** 401 N 3rd St. SR 55, just s of jct of Lake St and SR 55. Ext corridors. **Pets:** Small, dogs only. Designated rooms, no service, supervision, crate.
[✕] [📺] [📡] [🐾]

MONTPELIER

❀❖❖❖ Best Western Clover Creek Inn M ❖
(208) 847-1782. **$56-$72, 3 days notice.** 243 N 4th St. Just n on US 30 from jct of US 89S. Ext corridors. **Pets:** Small, other. No service, supervision, crate.
[SAVE] [S₀] [✕] [📺] [♨]

❀ ❖❖ The Fisher Inn M ❖
(208) 847-1772. **$35-$45.** 601 N 4th. 0.8 mi n on US 30 jct of US 89S. Ext corridors. **Pets:** Small. $5 one-time fee/room. Designated rooms, no service, supervision, crate.
[✕] [📡] [🐾]

MOSCOW

❀ ❖❖❖ Best Western University Inn M ❖
(208) 882-0550. **$65-$100.** 1516 Pullman Rd. 1 mi w on SR 8 from jct of US 95. Int corridors. **Pets:** Medium. $10 daily fee/room. Designated rooms, no service, supervision, crate.
[SAVE] [S₀] [✕] [♿] [🅿] [📺] [📡] [🍴] [🏊]

❀ ❖❖ Mark IV Motor Inn M ❖
(208) 882-7557. **$49-$129.** 414 N Main St. 0.4 mi n on US 95 from jct of SR 8. Ext/int corridors. **Pets:** Other. $5 daily fee/pet. No service, supervision, crate.
[SAVE] [S₀] [✕] [📺] [🍴] [🏊]

MOUNTAIN HOME

❀ ❖❖❖ Best Western Foothills Motor Inn M ❖
(208) 587-8477. **$59-$89.** 1080 Hwy 20. Just n of I-84, exit 95. Ext corridors. **Pets:** Other. $50 deposit/pet. Supervision.
[SAVE] [S₀] [✕] [♨] [📺] [📡] [🏊]

❖ Motel Thunderbird M ❖
(208) 587-7927. **$34-$42.** 910 Sunset Strip. I-84, exit 90, 3.3 mi se. Ext corridors. **Pets:** Medium. $5 daily fee/pet. No service, supervision, crate.
[✕] [📺] [🏊]

❖❖ Sleep Inn M ❖
(208) 587-9743. **$59-$69.** 1180 Hwy 20. I-84, exit 95, just n on US 20. Int corridors. **Pets:** Other. $50 deposit/pet. Supervision.
[ASK] [S₀] [✕] [📺] [📡] [🍴]

NAMPA

❖❖ Shilo Inn-Nampa Boulevard M
(208) 466-8993. **$45-$85.** 617 Nampa Blvd. Just sw of I-84, exit 35. Int corridors. **Pets:** Supervision.
[✕] [📡] [📺]

❖❖❖ Shilo Inn Nampa Suites M
(208) 465-3250. **$59-$109.** 1401 Shilo Dr. I-84, exit 36, just nw. Int corridors. **Pets:** No service, supervision, crate.
[ASK] [S₀] [✕] [📡] [📺] [♨] [🍴] [🏊]

❖❖ Sleep Inn-Nampa M ❖
(208) 463-6300. **$54-$105.** 1315 Industrial Rd. Just s of I-84, exit 36. Int corridors. **Pets:** Other. $25 deposit/pet, $10 one-time fee/room. No service, supervision, crate.
[ASK] [S₀] [✕] [♿] [📡] [♨] [📺] [📺] [🏊]

NEW MEADOWS

❀ ❖❖ Hartland Inn & Motel M ❖
(208) 347-2114. **$44-$115.** 211 Norris St. US 95, just n of jct of SR 55. Ext/int corridors. **Pets:** Medium. $5 one-time fee/room. Designated rooms, no service, supervision, crate.
[SAVE] [S₀] [✕] [📺] [📡] [🐾]

OROFINO

❀ ❖❖ Konkolville Motel M ❖
(208) 476-5584. **$40-$47.** 2000 Konkolville Rd. 2.7 mi e on Michigan Ave from jct US 12 and SR 7 (Bridge). Ext corridors. **Pets:** Other. $5 daily fee/room. Designated rooms, no service, supervision, crate.
[SAVE] [✕] [📺] [📡] [🏊]

POCATELLO

❀ ❖❖❖ Best Western CottonTree Inn M ❖
(208) 237-7650. **$75.** 1415 Bench Rd. Just e of I-15, exit 71. Int corridors. **Pets:** Other. $50 deposit/room. No service, supervision, crate.
[SAVE] [S₀] [✕] [📺] [🍴] [🏊] [🐾]

❀ ❖❖❖ Cavanaughs Pocatello Hotel M
(208) 233-2200. **$62-$72.** 1555 Pocatello Creek Rd. Just e of I-15, exit 71. Int corridors. **Pets:** Designated rooms, no service, supervision, crate.
[SAVE] [S₀] [✕] [📺] [📺] [🍴] [🏊]

❖❖❖ Comfort Inn M ❖
(208) 237-8155. **$69-$119.** 1333 Bench Rd. Just e of I-15, exit 71. Int corridors. **Pets:** Small, dogs only. Designated rooms, no service, supervision, crate.
[ASK] [S₀] [✕] [📡] [📺] [🏊]

❖❖ Econo Lodge-University M ❖
(208) 233-0451. **$45-$59.** 835 S 5th Ave. 1.8 mi n of I-15, exit 67; across from Idaho State University. Int corridors. **Pets:** Other. $20 deposit/room. Designated rooms, no service, supervision, crate.
[ASK] [S₀] [✕] [📺] [📺] [🍴]

❀ ❖❖❖ Holiday Inn-Pocatello M ❖
(208) 237-1400. **$69-$79.** 1399 Bench Rd. Just e of I-15, exit 71. Ext/int corridors. **Pets:** Medium, other. Supervision.
[SAVE] [S₀] [✕] [📡] [♨] [📺] [📺] [🍴] [🏊] [🐾]

❀ ❖❖ Super 8 Motel M ❖
(208) 234-0888. **$48-$64.** 1330 Bench Rd. Just e of I-15, exit 71. Int corridors. **Pets:** Other. $2 one-time fee/room. Designated rooms, supervision.
[SAVE] [S₀] [✕] [♨] [📺]

◆ **Thunderbird Motel**
(208) 232-6330. **$36-$50.** 1415 S 5th Ave. I-15, exit 67, 1.3 mi n, just s of Idaho State University. Ext corridors. **Pets:** Small. No service, supervision, crate.

POST FALLS

◆◆◆ **Best Western Cavanaugh Templin's Resort** M ❖
(208) 773-1611. **$90-$115.** 414 E First Ave. I-90 E, exit 5, just s to First Ave; I-90 W, exit 6, 1 mi w on Seltice Way to Spokane St, 0.5 mi s. Int corridors. **Pets:** Large, other. $5 daily fee/pet. Designated rooms, supervision.

◆◆ **Howard Johnson Express** M ❖
(208) 773-4541. **$49-$84.** W 3705 5th Ave. Just ne of I-90, exit 2. Int corridors. **Pets:** Medium. $5 daily fee/pet. Designated rooms, supervision.

◆◆ **Sleep Inn** M
(208) 777-9394. **$60-$70.** 100 N Pleasant View Rd. Just s of I-90, exit 2. Int corridors. **Pets:** Supervision.

REXBURG

◆◆◆ **Best Western CottonTree Inn** MI ❖
(208) 356-4646. **$72-$92.** 450 W 4th S. 1 mi e of US 20, S Rexburg exit. Int corridors. **Pets:** Small. Designated rooms, no service, supervision, crate.

◆◆◆ **Comfort Inn** M ❖
(208) 359-1311. **$45-$100, 30 days notice.** 1565 W Main St. Just e of jct of US 20, Salmon/Rexburg exit and SR 33. Int corridors. **Pets:** Other. No service, supervision, crate.

◆◆ **Days Inn** M ❖
(208) 356-9222. **$52-$62.** 271 S 2nd W. US 20, S Rexburg exit, 1.8 mi e, just n. Ext corridors. **Pets:** Small. Designated rooms, no service, supervision, crate.

RIGGINS

◆ **Pinehurst Resort Cottages** C ❖
(208) 628-3323. **$35-$60.** MM 182 on US 95. 13 mi s on US 95. Ext corridors. **Pets:** Dogs only. $3 daily fee/pet. No service, supervision, crate.

SAGLE

◆◆ **Bottle Bay Resort & Marina** C ❖
(208) 263-5916. **$85-$135, 30 days notice.** 115 Resort Rd. 8.3 mi e on Bottle Bay Rd from US 95. Ext corridors. **Pets:** $5 daily fee/pet. No service, supervision, crate.

SALMON

◆ **Motel DeLuxe** M ❖
(208) 756-2231. **$30-$55, 7 days notice.** 112 S Church St. Downtown, just s of Main St. Ext corridors. **Pets:** Other. No service, supervision, crate.

SANDPOINT

◆◆◆ **Hawthorn Inn & Suites** MI
(208) 263-9581. **$89-$109.** 415 Cedar St. Downtown, US 95 S at Fourth and Cedar sts. Ext/int corridors. **Pets:** Designated rooms, supervision.

◆◆ **Lakeside Inn** M ❖
(208) 263-3717. **$64-$99.** 106 Bridge St. Downtown, just e of US 95 N. Ext corridors. **Pets:** Medium, dogs only. $5 daily fee/pet. Designated rooms, no service, supervision, crate.

◆◆ **Monarch Inn** M ❖
(208) 263-1222. **$39-$52.** Bonner Mall, Hwy 95 N. 0.5 mi n on US 95 N from jct SR 200. Int corridors. **Pets:** $5 one-time fee/pet. No service, supervision, crate.

◆◆ **Quality Inn Sandpoint** MI
(208) 263-2111. **$54-$89.** 807 N 5th. US 2/95, just s of jct SR 200. Int corridors. **Pets:** Designated rooms, no service, supervision, crate.

◆◆ **Sandpoint Microtel Inn** M ❖
(208) 263-5383. **$50-$80.** 477255 Hwy 95 N. Int corridors. **Pets:** Small, other. Designated rooms, supervision.

◆◆ **Super 8 Motel** M ❖
(208) 263-2210. **$45-$60.** 476841 Hwy 95 N. 0.7 mi n on US 95 from jct SR 200. Int corridors. **Pets:** Other. $25 one-time fee/room. No service, supervision, crate.

SODA SPRINGS

◆ **J-R Inn** M
(208) 547-3366. **$44.** 179 W 2nd S. US 30. Ext corridors. **Pets:** Small. No service, supervision, crate.

STANLEY

◆◆ **Jerry's Country Store & Motel** M ❖
(208) 774-3566. **$55-$65, 5 days notice.** 1 mi n on SR 75 from jct of SR 21. Ext corridors. **Pets:** Other. $5 daily fee/pet, $5 one-time fee/pet. No service, supervision, crate.

◆◆ **Mountain Village Lodge** MI ❖
(208) 774-3661. **$74-$74.** Corner US 75 & SR 21, #1. Jct US 75 and SR 21. Ext corridors. **Pets:** Medium. $25 deposit/room, $10 daily fee/pet. Designated rooms, supervision.

SUN VALLEY

◆◆◆ **Sun Valley's Elkhorn Resort** 🅇
(208) 622-4511. **$88-$208.** 100 Elkhorn Rd. 0.7 mi e on Dollar Rd, 1.7 mi s. Int corridors. **Pets:** Small. Designated rooms, no service, supervision, crate.
🄰🅂🄺 🅂🄳 🗙 🔋 🍽 🖼 🗙 🐾

TETONIA

🔱 ◆◆ **Teton Mountain View Lodge** 🅼 🐾
(208) 456-2741. **$59-$79.** 510 Egbert Ave. On Hwy 33. Ext corridors. **Pets:** Other. $10 daily fee/pet. No service, supervision, crate.
🅂🄰🅅🄴 🅂🄳 🗙

TWIN FALLS

🔱 ◆◆◆ **Best Western Apollo Motor Inn** 🅼 🐾
(208) 733-2010. **$50-$66.** 296 Addison Ave W. I-84, exit 173, 6.5 mi s on US 93, 1.2 mi w. Ext corridors. **Pets:** Medium. No service, supervision, crate.
🅂🄰🅅🄴 🅂🄳 🗙 🖼

🔱 ◆◆◆ **Best Western Cavanaughs Canyon Springs Inn** 🅼
(208) 734-5000. **$83-$100.** 1357 Blue Lakes Blvd N. I-84, exit 173, 0.4 mi s on US 93. Int corridors. **Pets:** Small. No service, supervision, crate.
🅂🄰🅅🄴 🅂🄳 🗙 🖉 💻 🍽 🖼

◆◆◆ **Comfort Inn** 🅼
(208) 734-7494. **$59-$109, 7 days notice.** 1893 Canyon Springs Rd. I-84, exit 173, 3.5 mi s on US 93. Int corridors. **Pets:** No service, supervision, crate.
🄰🅂🄺 🅂🄳 🗙 🔋 🖼

◆◆◆ **Shilo Inn** 🅼
(208) 733-7545. **$89-$159.** 1586 Blue Lakes Blvd N. I-84, exit 173, 3.7 mi s on US 93. Int corridors. **Pets:** Medium. Designated rooms, no service, supervision, crate.
🄰🅂🄺 🅂🄳 🗙 🦽 🖉 🖉 🔋 💻 🖼

◆◆ **Sleep Inn** 🅼
(208) 324-6400. **$42-$45.** 1200 Centennial Spur. I-84 exit 173, just n on US 93. Int corridors. **Pets:** Supervision.
🗙 🖉 🔋

WALLACE

🔱 ◆◆◆ **Best Western Wallace Inn** 🅼 🐾
(208) 752-1252. **$70-$86.** 100 Front St. Just s of I-90, exit 61. Int corridors. **Pets:** Other. $20 daily fee/room, $20 one-time fee/room. Designated rooms, supervision.
🅂🄰🅅🄴 🅂🄳 🗙 🖈 🖉 🔋 🍽 🖼

ILLINOIS

CITY INDEX

ALTAMONT

AAA ◆◆ Best Western Carriage Inn Ⓜ ❀
(618) 483-6101. **$42-$69, 7 days notice.** 1304 S Main St.
Just n from jct I-70 and SR 128, exit 82. Ext corridors.
Pets: Other. $5 daily fee/pet, $5 one-time fee/pet. No service, supervision, crate.
[SAVE] [S₀] [✕] [🎾] [🖥] [💻] [¶] [🌊]

◆◆ Super 8 Motel Ⓜ
(618) 483-6300. **$40-$90, 30 days notice.** SR 26 S. Just s
from jct I-70 and SR 128, exit 82. Ext corridors.
Pets: Medium. Designated rooms, no service, supervision, crate.
[ASK] [S₀] [✕] [✕]

ALTON

AAA ◆◆◆ Comfort Inn Ⓜ
(618) 465-9999. **$49-$120.** 11 Crossroads Ct. Jct SR 140;
off Hwy 3. Int corridors. **Pets:** Designated rooms, no service, supervision, crate.
[SAVE] [S₀] [✕] [♿] [🎾] [🔧] [🖥] [💻] [🌊]

◆◆◆ Holiday Inn Alton Ⓜ ❀
(618) 462-1220. **$92.** 3800 Homer Adams Pkwy. Jct SR
140; off Hwy 3. Int corridors. **Pets:** Other. $15 one-time fee/room. Designated rooms, supervision.
[ASK] [S₀] [✕] [🎾] [🖥] [💻] [¶] [🌊]

◆◆ Super 8 Motel Ⓜ ❀
(618) 465-8885. **$42-$79.** 1800 Homer Adams Pkwy. On
SR 111, 1.8 mi e of jct SR 67. Int corridors. **Pets:** Other. No service, supervision, crate.
[ASK] [S₀] [✕] [🏠] [🖥] [💻]

ATLANTA

◆◆ I-55 Motel Ⓜ
(217) 648-2322. **Call for rates.** 103 Empire St. Just nw of
I-55, exit 140. Int corridors. **Pets:** Medium. No service, supervision, crate.
[✕]

BEARDSTOWN

◆◆ Super 8 Motel Ⓜ ❀
(217) 323-5858. **$40-$55.** 1903 Grand Ave. US 67, just w
from SR 125. Int corridors. **Pets:** Other. $25 deposit/room.
No service, supervision, crate.
[ASK] [S₀] [✕] [🖥] [🌊]

BELLEVILLE

◆◆ Super 8 Motel Ⓜ
(618) 234-9670. **Call for rates.** 600 E Main St. 0.4 mi e
from SR 159. Ext corridors. **Pets:** Designated rooms, supervision.
[ASK] [✕] [🖥]

BLOOMINGTON

◆◆◆ Country Inn & Suites By Carlson [M] ❀
(309) 828-7177. **$74-$86.** 923 Maple Hill Rd. From I-55/74, exit 160B, 0.3 mi w to Wiley Dr, just n, then just e. Int corridors. **Pets:** Medium. Designated rooms, no service, supervision, crate.
(ASK) 🔊 ⊠ 💺 👟 🔋 💻 ➿

◆◆◆ GuestHouse Inn [M] ❀
(309) 663-1361. **$61-$81.** 1803 E Empire St. SR 9, just e of I-55 business route, Veterans Pkwy. Int corridors. **Pets:** Medium. $6 daily fee/pet. Supervision.
(ASK) 🔊 ⊠ 🕗 🔋 💻

❀ ◆◆◆◆ Jumer's Chateau [M]
(309) 662-2020. **$103-$173.** 1601 Jumer Dr. I-55 business route (Veterans Pkwy), 1.3 mi n of jct SR 9, 1 mi s of jct I-55. Int corridors. **Pets:** Small. Designated rooms, no service, supervision, crate.
(SAVE) 🔊 ⊠ 🕗 🔋 💻 ➿

◆◆◆ Radisson Hotel & Conference Center-Bloomington [M]
(309) 664-6446. **$89-$119.** 10 Brickyard Dr. On US Business 55 (Veterans Pkwy), just n from US 150. Int corridors. **Pets:** Medium. No service, supervision, crate.
(ASK) 🔊 ⊠ 🕗 👟 🔋 💻 🍴 ➿

CARBON CLIFF

◆◆ Super 8 Motel-East Moline [M] ❀
(309) 796-1999. **Call for rates.** 2201 John Deere Expwy. I-80, exit 4A, 5 mi w on SR 5 (John Deere Rd); from I-74, exit 4B, 5 mi e on SR 5 (John Deere Rd). Int corridors. **Pets:** Small. $25 deposit/pet. Designated rooms, no service, supervision, crate.
(ASK) ⊠ 🔋

CARBONDALE

❀ ◆◆ Best Inns [M] ❀
(618) 529-4801. **$57.** 1345 E Main St. 1.3 mi e on SR 13, next to University Mall. Ext corridors. **Pets:** Small, other. Designated rooms, supervision.
(SAVE) 🔊 ⊠ 🔋 ➿

◆◆◆ Holiday Inn Carbondale [M]
(618) 529-1100. **$69-$83, 7 days notice.** 800 E Main St. 1 mi e on SR 13. Int corridors. **Pets:** No service, supervision, crate.
(ASK) 🔊 ⊠ 🕗 🔋 💻 🍴 ➿

◆◆ Super 8 Motel [M] ❀
(618) 457-8822. **$42-$79.** 1180 E Main St. 1 mi e on SR 13. Int corridors. **Pets:** No service, supervision, crate.
(ASK) 🔊 ⊠ 🕗 🔋 💻

CARLINVILLE

◆◆ Carlin Villa Motel [M]
(217) 854-3201. **$37-$68.** 18891 Rt 4. 0.5 mi s from jct SR 108 and 4. Ext/int corridors. **Pets:** Supervision.
⊠ 🔋 💻 ➿

CASEYVILLE

❀ ◆◆ Best Inns of America [M]
(618) 397-3300. **$38-$60.** 2423 Old Country Inn Dr. Just s from jct I-64 and Rt 157, exit 9. Int corridors. **Pets:** Small. Supervision.
(SAVE) 🔊 ⊠ 🕗 👟 🔋 ➿

CENTRALIA

◆◆ Bell Tower Inn [M]
(618) 533-1300. **$46-$63.** 200 E Noleman St. Jct US 51 S and SR 161. Int corridors. **Pets:** Medium. No service, supervision, crate.
(ASK) ⊠ 🕗 🔋 💻 ➿ ⊠

CHAMPAIGN

◆◆◆ Baymont Inn [M] ❀
(217) 356-8900. **$65, 3 days notice.** 302 W Anthony Dr. I-74, exit 182, just n on Neil St, just w. Int corridors. **Pets:** Other. Designated rooms, no service, supervision, crate.
(ASK) 🔊 ⊠ 🕗 🔋 💻

◆◆◆ Drury Inn & Suites [M]
(217) 398-0030. **$85-$87.** 905 W Anthony Dr. Just n from I-74, exit 181. Int corridors. **Pets:** Supervision.
⊠ 💺 🕗 👟 🔋 💻 ➿

◆◆◆ La Quinta Inn [M]
(217) 356-4000. **$65-$85.** 1900 Center Dr. From jct I-74 and Neil St (exit 182B), just n. Int corridors. **Pets:** Designated rooms, supervision.
(ASK) ⊠ 🎦 🕗 🔋 💻 ➿

❀ ◆◆ Red Roof Inn #170 [M] ❀
(217) 352-0101. **$40-$50.** 212 W Anthony Dr. From jct I-74 and Neil St (exit 182B), just n to Anthony Dr, then just w. Ext corridors. **Pets:** Medium, other. Supervision.
(SAVE) ⊠ 🕗

CHARLESTON

❀ ◆◆ Best Western Worthington Inn [M] ❀
(217) 348-8161. **$56-$76.** 920 W Lincoln Ave. 2.5 mi w on SR 16 (Lincoln Hwy). Ext corridors. **Pets:** Small. $50 deposit/pet. No service, supervision, crate.
(SAVE) 🔊 ⊠ 🔋 💻 🍴 ➿

CHICAGO METROPOLITAN AREA

ALSIP

◆◆◆ Baymont Inn-Chicago SW 🅼 ❀
(708) 597-3900. **$140.** 12801 S Cicero. At I-294, Cicero Ave
S exit. Int corridors. **Pets:** Medium. $50 deposit/room. Designated rooms, no service, supervision, crate.

(A$K) (S🐾) (✕) (♿) (🐾) (✆) (📋) (📺)

🅐🅐🅐 ◆◆◆ Radisson Hotel-Alsip 🅼🛈 ❀
(708) 371-7300. **$139-$149.** 5000 W 127th St at Cicero
Ave. I-294, Cicero S exit, just w. Int corridors. **Pets:** Large.
No service, supervision, crate.

(SAVE) (S🐾) (✕) (♿) (✆) (📋) (📺) (🛎) (🏊)

ANTIOCH

🅐🅐🅐 ◆◆ Best Western Regency Inn 🅼 ❀
(847) 395-3606. **$90-$145.** 350 Rt 173. SR 173, 0.5 mi w of
jct SR 83. Int corridors. **Pets:** Small. $25 deposit/room. No
service, supervision, crate.

(SAVE) (S🐾) (✕) (✆) (🏊)

ARLINGTON HEIGHTS

🅐🅐🅐 ◆◆◆ AmeriSuites 🅼 ❀
(847) 956-1400. **$109-$139.** 2111 S Arlington Heights Rd.
I-90, Arlington Heights Rd exit, 0.6 mi n. Int corridors.
Pets: Very small. Designated rooms, supervision.

(SAVE) (S🐾) (✕) (📋) (🏊)

🅐🅐🅐 ◆◆ Best Western Arlington Inn 🅼🛈
(847) 255-2900. **$60-$86.** 948 E Northwest Hwy. US 14,
just e of Arlington Heights Rd. Ext/int corridors. **Pets:** No
service, supervision, crate.

(SAVE) (S🐾) (✕) (🐾) (✆) (📋) (📺) (🛎) (🏊)

◆◆◆ La Quinta Inn-Arlington Heights 🅼 ❀
(847) 253-8777. **$89-$109.** 1415 W Dundee Rd. SR 53, exit
Dundee Rd, just e. Int corridors. **Pets:** Small. No service,
supervision, crate.

(A$K) (✕) (🐾) (📋) (🏊)

🅐🅐🅐 ◆◆ Motel 6–1048 🅼
(847) 806-1230. **$47-$62.** 441 W Algonquin Rd. I-90, exit
Arlington Heights Rd, just n on Arlington Heights Rd, 0.5 mi
w. Int corridors. **Pets:** Supervision.

(S🐾) (✕) (🐾) (🐾)

🅐🅐🅐 ◆◆◆ Radisson Hotel Arlington Heights 🅼🛈
(847) 364-7600. **$159-$169, 7 days notice.** 75 W Algonquin Rd. I-90, exit Arlington Heights Rd, just n. Int corridors.
Pets: Designated rooms, supervision.

(SAVE) (✕) (🐾) (✆) (📋) (📺) (🛎) (🏊)

🅐🅐🅐 ◆◆ Red Roof Inn #102 🅼 ❀
(847) 228-6650. **$66-$95.** 22 W Algonquin Rd. I-90, exit
Arlington Heights Rd, 0.5 mi n. Ext corridors.
Pets: Medium, other. Designated rooms, no service, supervision, crate.

(SAVE) (✕) (📺)

◆◆◆ Sheraton Arlington Park 🄷
(847) 394-2000. **$229.** 3400 W Euclid Ave. At Arlington
Park Race Track, jct Euclid Ave E and SR 53. Int corridors.
Pets: No service, supervision, crate.

(A$K) (S🐾) (✕) (🐾) (✆) (📋) (📺) (🛎) (🏊)

BANNOCKBURN

◆◆◆ Woodfield Suites 🅼
(847) 317-7300. **$89-$139, 3 days notice.** 2000 Lakeside
Dr. I-94, Halfday Rd exit e. Int corridors. **Pets:** Supervision.

(A$K) (S🐾) (✕) (♿) (🐾) (📋) (✆) (📋) (📺) (🏊)

BOLINGBROOK

◆◆◆ Holiday Inn Hotel & Suites 🅼🛈 ❀
(630) 679-1600. **$116.** 205 Remington Blvd. I-55, exit 267,
just n to Remington Blvd, 0.4 mi sw. Int corridors.
Pets: Small, other. Supervision.

(A$K) (✕) (🐾) (📋) (✆) (📋) (📺) (🛎) (🏊)

BRIDGEVIEW

🅐🅐🅐 ◆◆ Exel Inn of Bridgeview 🅼
(708) 430-1818. **$56-$87.** 9625 S 76th Ave. I-294, exit 95th
St, just s. Int corridors. **Pets:** No service, supervision, crate.

(S🐾) (✕) (✆) (📋)

CALUMET PARK

◆◆ Super 8 Motel Chicago Southwest 🅼 ❀
(708) 385-9100. **$62-$88, 3 days notice.** 12808 S Ashland
Ave. I-57, exit 353, just e. Int corridors. **Pets:** Other. $20
deposit/room. Supervision.

(A$K) (S🐾) (✕) (♿) (🐾) (📋)

CHICAGO

🅐🅐🅐 ◆◆◆◆ The Ambassador West, A Wyndham
            Grand Heritage Hotel 🄷 ❀
(312) 787-3700. **$215.** 1300 N State Pkwy. Corner of
Goethe St and State Pkwy. Int corridors. **Pets:** Medium.
$25 deposit/room. Supervision.

(SAVE) (S🐾) (✕) (🐾) (📋) (🛎)

🅐🅐🅐 ◆◆◆◆ Chicago Hilton & Towers 🄷 ❀
(312) 922-4400. **$159.** 720 S Michigan Ave. Overlooking
Lake Michigan and Grant Park, s of I-290 (Congress Pkwy).
Int corridors. **Pets:** Other. No service, supervision, crate.

(SAVE) (✕) (🐾) (📋) (✆) (📋) (🛎) (🏊) (📺)

🅐🅐🅐 ◆◆◆ Claridge Hotel 🄷 ❀
(312) 787-4980. **$139-$225.** 1244 N Dearborn Pkwy. Just s
of Goethe St. Int corridors. **Pets:** Medium, other. No service, supervision, crate.

(SAVE) (S🐾) (✕) (📋) (🛎)

🅐🅐🅐 ◆◆◆ Fairmont Hotel-At Grant Park 🄷
(312) 565-8000. **$199-$339, 3 days notice.** 200 N Columbus Dr. Just e of jct Michigan Ave and Wacker Dr. Int
corridors. **Pets:** Small. Supervision.

(SAVE) (S🐾) (✕) (🐾) (🛎) (🏊)

♦♦♦♦♦ Four Seasons Hotel
Chicago 🅗 ✿
(312) 280-8800. **$360-$3500.** 120 E Delaware. At jct Michigan Ave. Int corridors. **Pets:** Small, other. No service, supervision, crate.

♦♦♦ Hilton Chicago O'Hare
Airport 🅗 ✿
(773) 686-8000. **$146-$146.** Opposite and connected to terminal bldgs at O'Hare Airport, accessed via I-190. Int corridors. **Pets:** Other. Supervision.

♦♦♦ Holiday Inn Chicago Mart Plaza 🅗 ✿
(312) 836-5000. **$245-$295.** 350 N Orleans. 14th thru 23rd floors, atop the Apparel Center, at the Merchandise Mart. Int corridors. **Pets:** Medium. No service, supervision, crate.

♦♦♦ House of Blues, A Loews Hotel 🅗 ✿
(312) 245-0333. **$179-$289.** 333 N Dearborn St. On Chicago River between Dearborn and State sts. Int corridors. **Pets:** Large, other. Supervision.

♦♦♦♦ The Palmer House Hilton 🅗 ✿
(312) 726-7500. **$189-$374.** 17 E Monroe St. Between State and Wabash aves. Int corridors. **Pets:** Large. $250 deposit/pet. No service, supervision, crate.

♦♦♦ Radisson Hotel & Suites Chicago 🅗
(312) 787-2900. **$129-$129.** 160 E Huron St. Just e of N Michigan Ave. Int corridors. **Pets:** Small. Designated rooms, no service, supervision, crate.

♦♦♦♦ Renaissance Chicago
Hotel 🅗 ✿
(312) 372-7200. **$219-$239, 7 days notice.** 1 W Wacker Dr. State St and Wacker Dr. Int corridors. **Pets:** Very small. $45 one-time fee/room. No service, supervision, crate.

♦♦♦ Residence Inn by Marriott Chicago
Downtown 🅐
(312) 943-9800. **$269.** 201 E Walton St. Corner Walton and Miesvan der Rohe. Int corridors. **Pets:** Medium. Supervision.

♦♦♦♦♦ The Ritz-Carlton, Chicago (A Four Seasons Hotel) 🅗
(312) 266-1000. **$425-$485.** 160 E Pearson St. Jct N Michigan Ave and E Pearson St; in Water Tower Place. Int corridors. **Pets:** Small. Designated rooms, no service, supervision, crate.

♦♦♦♦ The Sutton Place Hotel 🅗
(312) 266-2100. **$275-$795.** 21 E Bellevue Pl. Jct of Rush St. Int corridors. **Pets:** Small. Designated rooms, no service, supervision, crate.

♦♦♦ The Westin Michigan Avenue
Chicago 🅗 ✿
(312) 943-7200. **$129-$324.** 909 N Michigan Ave. Across from John Hancock Center. Int corridors. **Pets:** Small, other. No service, supervision, crate.

CRYSTAL LAKE

♦♦ Super 8 Motel 🅜
(815) 455-2388. **Call for rates.** 577 Crystal Point Dr. On US 14; 1 mi w of jct SR 31. Int corridors. **Pets:** No service, supervision, crate.

DEERFIELD

♦♦♦ Marriott Suites Deerfield 🅗
(847) 405-9666. **$149-$179.** 2 Parkway Blvd N. I-94, exit Deerfield Rd northbound, just w in Parkway North Center, or off Saunders Rd between Lake Cook and Deerfield rds. Int corridors. **Pets:** Large. Supervision.

♦♦♦ Residence Inn by Marriott 🅐 ✿
(847) 940-4644. **Call for rates.** 530 Lake Cook Rd. I-94, exit Lake Cook Rd, 1.8 mi e, 3 blks n on Corporate 500 Dr Access Rd. Ext corridors. **Pets:** Large, other. $15 daily fee/pet. Supervision.

DES PLAINES

♦♦ Travelodge Chicago O'Hare 🅜 ✿
(847) 296-5541. **$84-$169.** 3003 Mannheim Rd. US 12 and 45, n of jct SR 72. Ext/int corridors. **Pets:** Medium, other. $25 deposit/room. No service, supervision, crate.

DOWNERS GROVE

♦♦♦ Marriott Suites Downers Grove 🅜🅘
(630) 852-1500. **$179.** 1500 Opus Pl. I-355, exit Butterfield Rd, 0.3 mi e, 0.3 mi s on Finley Rd. Int corridors. **Pets:** Small. No service, supervision, crate.

♦♦ Red Roof Inn 🅜
(630) 963-4205. **$51-$76.** 1113 Butterfield Rd. On frontage road, 0.8 mi e of I-355, Butterfield Rd, (SR 56) exit; just w of Highland Ave N exit off I-88. Ext corridors. **Pets:** Supervision.

ELGIN

♦♦♦ Baymont Inn 🅜 ✿
(847) 931-4800. **$76-$96.** 500 Toll Gate Rd. I-90, exit 31N, just n. Int corridors. **Pets:** Other. Supervision.

♦♦ Days Inn Elgin 🅜
(847) 695-2100. **$60-$81, 3 days notice.** 1585 W Dundee Ave. I-90, exit SR 25, 0.5 mi n. Ext/int corridors. **Pets:** Large. No service, supervision, crate.

ELK GROVE VILLAGE

◆◆ Exel Inn of Elk Grove Village M ❀
(847) 895-2085. **$61-$84.** 1000 W Devon Ave. Thorndale Ave exit, off I-290 (SR 53), 0.5 mi w to Rohlwing Rd, 0.5 mi n to Devon Ave, 0.3 mi e. Int corridors. **Pets:** Small, other. Designated rooms, no service, supervision, crate.

🌀 ⊠ 🎱 🖬 💻

◆◆ Exel Inn of O'Hare M
(847) 803-9400. **$69-$88.** 2881 Touhy Ave. Jct SR 83 and SR 72, 1.5 mi e on SR 72, Higgins/Touhy Ave. Int corridors. **Pets:** No service, supervision, crate.

🌀 ⊠ 🎱 🖬 💻

◆◆◆ Holiday Inn of Elk Grove M
(847) 437-6010. **Call for rates.** 1000 Busse Rd. SR 83 (Busse Rd), 0.3 mi s of jct Higgins Rd (SR 72). Int corridors. **Pets:** Small. No service, supervision, crate.

⊠ 🎱 🖬 💻 🍴 🍽

◆◆◆ La Quinta Inn O'Hare Airport M
(847) 439-6767. **$89-$99.** 1900 Oakton St. Jct of Higgins Rd, Oakton St and Busse Rd. Int corridors. **Pets:** Supervision.

⊠ 🖬 💻 🍽

◆◆◆ Sheraton Suites Elk Grove/O'Hare H
(847) 290-1600. **$89-$219.** 121 Northwest Point Blvd. S on Arlington Heights Blvd off I-90 exit in Northwest Point Corp Park. Int corridors. **Pets:** Medium. Designated rooms, supervision.

🆂🅰🆅🅴 🌀 ⊠ 🎱 🎱 🖬 💻 🍴 🍽 ⊠

ELMHURST

◆◆ Holiday Inn Chicago-Elmhurst M ❀
(630) 279-1100. **$114-$134.** 624 N York Rd. I-290, exit 12, just n. Int corridors. **Pets:** Other. No service, supervision, crate.

🅰🆂🅺 🌀 ⊠ 🎱 💻 🍴 🍽 ⊠

GLEN ELLYN

◆◆◆ Holiday Inn M
(630) 629-6000. **$89-$129.** 1250 Roosevelt Rd. SR 38; 0.8 mi e of I-355, Roosevelt Rd exit. Int corridors. **Pets:** Medium. No service, supervision, crate.

🅰🆂🅺 🌀 ⊠ 🎱 🎱 🎱 🖬 💻 🍴 🍽

GLENVIEW

◆◆ Baymont Inn & Suites-Chicago NW (Glenview) M ❀
(847) 635-8300. **$71-$76.** 1625 Milwaukee Ave. I-294, exit Willow Rd, just w to Sanders Rd, 0.5 mi s to SR 21 (Milwaukee Ave), 0.5 mi se to Lake Ave. Int corridors. **Pets:** $50 deposit/room. Designated rooms, no service, supervision, crate.

🌀 ⊠ 🎱 🖬 💻

◆ Motel 6-1040 M ❀
(847) 390-7200. **$45-$61.** 1535 Milwaukee Ave. From I-294, exit Willow Rd, just w to Sanders Rd, 0.5 mi s to Milwaukee Ave (SR 21), 0.5 mi se. Int corridors. **Pets:** Small, other. No service, supervision, crate.

🌀 ⊠ 🎱

GURNEE

◆◆◆ Baymont Inn & Suites Chicago North M ❀
(847) 662-7600. **$100-$125.** 5688 N Ridge Rd. I-94, exit SR 132, just e via service road. Int corridors. **Pets:** Medium, other. Designated rooms, no service, supervision, crate.

🌀 ⊠ 🎱 🎱 🎱 🖬 💻

◆◆ Comfort Inn M
(847) 855-8866. **$112-$135.** 6080 Gurnee Mills Blvd E. I-94, exit SR 132 W. Int corridors. **Pets:** Medium. Supervision.

🅰🆂🅺 🌀 ⊠ 🎱 🎱 🖬 💻 🍽

HARVARD

◆◆◆ AmeriHost Inn-Harvard M
(815) 943-0700. **$63-$73.** 1701 S Division St. Jct US 14 and SR 23. Int corridors. **Pets:** Small. Supervision.

🆂🅰🆅🅴 🌀 ⊠ 🎱 🎱 🖬 💻 🍽

HOFFMAN ESTATES

◆◆◆ AmeriSuites M ❀
(847) 839-1800. **$129-$139.** 2750 Greenspoint Pkwy. Just off Barrington Rd, 0.3 mi s of jct I-90, just n of SR 72 (Higgins Rd). Int corridors. **Pets:** Very small. No service, supervision, crate.

🆂🅰🆅🅴 🌀 ⊠ 🎱 🎱 🖬 💻 🍽

◆◆ Baymont Inn & Suites-Chicago NW (Hoffman Estates) M
(847) 882-8848. **$73-$80.** 2075 Barrington Rd. 0.3 mi s of I-90, 0.3 mi n of SR 72 (Higgins Rd). Int corridors. **Pets:** Medium. Designated rooms, no service, supervision, crate.

🌀 ⊠ 🎱 🖬 💻

◆◆◆ La Quinta Inn M ❀
(847) 882-3312. **$85-$109.** 2280 Barrington Rd. Corner Barrington Rd and SR 72 (Higgins Rd), 0.3 mi s of I-90. Int corridors. **Pets:** Small, other. Designated rooms, supervision, crate.

🅰🆂🅺 ⊠ 🎱 🎱 🖬 💻 🍽

◆◆ Red Roof Inn M
(847) 885-7877. **$56-$69.** 2500 Hassell Rd. Just off Barrington Rd, 0.3 mi s of jct I-90, 0.3 mi n of SR 72 (Higgins Rd). Ext corridors. **Pets:** No service, supervision, crate.

🆂🅰🆅🅴 ⊠ 🎱 🖬

JOLIET

◆◆◆ Comfort Inn-Joliet South M
(815) 744-1770. **$42-$66, 7 days notice.** 135 S Larkin Ave. I-80, exit 130B, 0.5 mi n. Int corridors. **Pets:** Small. Designated rooms, no service, supervision, crate.

🅰🆂🅺 🌀 ⊠ 🎱 🖬 🍽

◆◆◆ Comfort Inn North M ❀
(815) 436-5141. **$52-$74, 7 days notice.** 3235 Norman Ave. I-55, exit 257, just e. Int corridors. **Pets:** Medium. Designated rooms, no service, supervision, crate.

🅰🆂🅺 🌀 ⊠ 🎱 🖬 🍽

◆◆◆ **Holiday Inn Express-Joliet** 🅜 ❀
(815) 729-2000. **$69-$119.** 411 S Larkin Ave. I-80, exit 130B. Int corridors. **Pets:** Small, dogs only. $10 daily fee/pet. Designated rooms, no service, supervision, crate.

🄰🅂🄺 ⊠ 🛏 🔥 🚫 ⊡

🆎🆎🆎 ◆ **Motel 6 Joliet I-80–694** 🅜
(815) 729-2800. **$40-$56.** 1850 McDonough St. I-80, exit 130B, 0.3 mi n Rt 7, just w. Ext corridors. **Pets:** Small. No service, supervision, crate.

🅂🄳 ⊠ 🔥 🔥 🄲🅃🅅

🆎🆎🆎 ◆◆ **Motel 6 Joliet I-55–1296** 🅜
(815) 439-1332. **$40-$61.** 3551 Mall Loop Dr. I-55, exit 257, 0.4 mi e Rt 30, 0.4 mi s. Int corridors. **Pets:** Small. No service, supervision, crate.

🅂🄳 ⊠ 🛏 🔥 🔥

🆎🆎🆎 ◆◆ **Red Roof Inn** 🅜
(815) 741-2304. **$38-$64.** 1750 McDonough St. I-80, exit 130B at jct SR 7. Ext corridors. **Pets:** Designated rooms, supervision.

🆂🅰🆅🅴 ⊠ 🔥 🚫

LANSING

🆎🆎🆎 ◆◆ **Red Roof Inn** 🅜
(708) 895-9570. **$56-$71.** 2450 E 173rd St. I-80/94, exit 161B, just n. Ext corridors. **Pets:** Designated rooms, supervision.

🆂🅰🆅🅴 ⊠ 🔥

LIBERTYVILLE

🆎🆎🆎 ◆◆ **Best Inns of America** 🅜
(847) 816-8006. **$62-$89.** 1809 N Milwaukee Ave. Jct SR 137 and 21. Int corridors. **Pets:** Medium. Supervision.

🆂🅰🆅🅴 🅂🄳 ⊠ 🔥 🚫 ⊡

◆◆◆ **Candlewood Suites** 🅜 ❀
(847) 247-9900. **$119-$139.** 1100 N US Rte 45. I-94, exit Buckley Rd (SR 137), 5.6 mi w to US 45, 1.4 mi s. Int corridors. **Pets:** $150 one-time fee/room. No service, supervision, crate.

🄰🅂🄺 🅂🄳 ⊠ 🛏 🔥 🚫 🖥

LINCOLNSHIRE

🆎🆎🆎 ◆◆◆◆ **Marriott's Lincolnshire Resort** 🅡 ❀
(847) 634-0100. **$99-$204.** 10 Marriott Dr. I-94, exit Halfday Rd, 2 mi w to jct US 45, SR 21 & 22, just s. Ext/int corridors. **Pets:** Small. $25 one-time fee/pet. No service, supervision, crate.

⊠ 🔥 🔥 🔥 🚫 🖥 🍴 🚫 ⊠

LISLE

◆◆◆ **Radisson Hotel Lisle-Naperville** 🅷
(630) 505-1000. **$169-$199.** 3000 Warrenville Rd. From I-88 Naperville Rd exit, just n on Naperville Rd, 0.3 mi e. Int corridors. **Pets:** Small. Supervision.

🄰🅂🄺 🅂🄳 ⊠ 🚫 🍴 ⊠ ⊠

LOMBARD

◆◆◆ **Homestead Village Guest Studios** 🅜 ❀
(630) 928-0202. **Call for rates.** 2701 Technology Dr. I-88, exit Highland Ave N, just n, 0.6 mi e on Butterfield Rd, just s. Int corridors. **Pets:** Small. $75 one-time fee/room. Designated rooms, no service, supervision, crate.

⊠ 🔥 🔥 🔥 🚫 🖥

◆◆◆ **Residence Inn by Marriott-Lombard** 🄰
(630) 629-7800. **$139-$139.** 2001 S Highland Ave. From I-88, exit Highland Ave, 1 mi n to jct 22nd St. Ext corridors. **Pets:** Designated rooms, no service, supervision, crate.

🄰🅂🄺 🅂🄳 ⊠ 🔥 🔥 🚫 🖥 ⊠ ⊠

MATTESON

◆◆◆ **Baymont Inn & Suites-Chicago (Matteson)** 🅜 ❀
(708) 503-0999. **$67-$87.** 5210 W Southwick Dr. 0.3 mi e of jct US 30 and I-57 on US 30; entrance 0.3˝ mi s on Cicero Ave. Int corridors. **Pets:** Medium, other. $50 deposit/room. Designated rooms, no service, supervision, crate.

🅂🄳 ⊠ 🔥 🚫 🖥

NAPERVILLE

🆎🆎🆎 ◆◆ **Chicago/Naperville Travelodge** 🅜 ❀
(630) 505-0200. **$49-$59.** 1617 N Naperville/Wheaton Rd. I-88, Naperville Rd exit, 0.3 mi s. Ext/int corridors. **Pets:** Medium. $25 one-time fee/room. No service, supervision, crate.

🆂🅰🆅🅴 🅂🄳 ⊠ 🔥 🚫 🖥

◆◆◆ **Country Inn & Suites By Carlson** 🅜 ❀
(630) 548-0966. **$89-$109, 7 days notice.** 1847 W Diehl Rd. I-88, SR 59 exit, just s. Int corridors. **Pets:** Small, other. $5 daily fee/room. Designated rooms, no service, supervision, crate.

🄰🅂🄺 🅂🄳 ⊠ 🛏 🔥 🔥 🚫 🖥 ⊠

🆎🆎🆎 ◆◆ **Exel Inn of Naperville** 🅜 ❀
(630) 357-0022. **$57-$85.** 1585 N Naperville Rd/Wheaton Rd. I-88, Naperville Rd exit, 0.5 mi s. Int corridors. **Pets:** Small, other. Designated rooms, no service, supervision, crate.

🅂🄳 ⊠ 🚫 🖥

◆◆◆ **Hawthorn Suites-Naperville** 🅜
(630) 548-0881. **$99-$179.** 1843 W Diehl Rd. I-88, exit SR 59, just s to Diehl Rd, then just w. Int corridors. **Pets:** No service, supervision, crate.

🄰🅂🄺 🅂🄳 ⊠ 🔥 🔥 🚫 🖥 ⊠ ⊠

◆◆◆ **Homestead Village Guest Studios** 🅜
(630) 577-0200. **$69-$95.** 1827 Centre Point Cir. I-88, Naperville Rd S exit, 0.8 mi w on Diehl Rd. Int corridors. **Pets:** Medium. No service, supervision, crate.

🄰🅂🄺 🅂🄳 ⊠ 🔥 🔥 🔥 🚫 🖥

🆎🆎🆎 ◆◆ **Red Roof Inn** 🅜 ❀
(630) 369-2500. **$71-$81.** 1698 W Diehl Rd. I-88, SR 59 exit, just s. Ext corridors. **Pets:** Other. No service, supervision, crate.

🆂🅰🆅🅴 ⊠

NORTHBROOK

◆◆◆ Radisson Hotel & Conference Center ☑ ☀
(847) 298-2525. **$69-$89, 3 days notice.** 2875 N Milwaukee Ave. On SR 21, 0.5 mi s of jct US 45. Int corridors. **Pets:** No service, supervision, crate.

⟨ASK⟩ ⟨S⟩ ⟨✕⟩ ⟨∕⟩ ⟨❚⟩ ⟨▣⟩ ⟨�︘⟩ ⟨⬗⟩

ⓐⓐⓐ ◆◆ Red Roof Inn ☑ ☀
(847) 205-1755. **$70-$88.** 340 Waukegan Rd. Jct I-94 and SR 43 (Waukegan Rd). Ext corridors. **Pets:** Other. $100 deposit/pet. No service, supervision, crate.

⟨SAVE⟩ ⟨✕⟩

OAKBROOK TERRACE

◆◆◆ Hilton Suite Oakbrook Terrace ☐
(630) 941-0100. **$139-$139.** 10 Drury Ln. Just se of jct SR 83 (Kingery Hwy) and SR 38 (Roosevelt Rd). Int corridors. **Pets:** No service, supervision, crate.

⟨ASK⟩ ⟨S⟩ ⟨✕⟩ ⟨✸⟩ ⟨❚⟩ ⟨▣⟩ ⟨�︘⟩ ⟨⬗⟩

◆◆◆ La Quinta Inn-Oakbrook Terrace ☑
(630) 495-4600. **$85-$105.** 1 S 666 Midwest Rd. Just n of 22nd St/Cermak Rd. Int corridors. **Pets:** Small. Supervision.

⟨ASK⟩ ⟨✕⟩ ⟨∕⟩ ⟨▣⟩ ⟨⬗⟩

PALATINE

ⓐⓐⓐ ◆◆ Motel 6-1039 ☑
(847) 359-0046. **$44-$66.** 1450 E Dundee Rd. On SR 68, just w of jct SR 53, Dundee Rd exit. Int corridors. **Pets:** Small. No service, supervision, crate.

⟨S⟩ ⟨✕⟩ ⟨∕⟩ ⟨✸⟩ ⟨CTV⟩

PROSPECT HEIGHTS

ⓐⓐⓐ ◆◆ Exel Inn of Prospect Heights ☑ ☀
(847) 459-0545. **$42-$66.** 540 Milwaukee Ave. Jct SR 21 and US 45. Int corridors. **Pets:** Small. Designated rooms, no service, supervision, crate.

⟨S⟩ ⟨✕⟩ ⟨∕⟩ ⟨❚⟩ ⟨▣⟩

ROSEMONT

ⓐⓐⓐ ◆◆◆ Holiday Inn O'Hare International ☐
(847) 671-6350. **$149-$159.** 5440 N River Rd. I-190, exit 1B, just s. Int corridors. **Pets:** No service, supervision, crate.

⟨SAVE⟩ ⟨S⟩ ⟨✕⟩ ⟨�an⟩ ⟨∕⟩ ⟨✸⟩ ⟨❚⟩ ⟨▣⟩ ⟨�︘⟩ ⟨⬗⟩

ⓐⓐⓐ ◆◆◆ Hotel Sofitel-Chicago O'Hare ☐ ☀
(847) 678-4488. **$235-$275.** 5550 N River Rd. I-190, exit 1B, just s. Int corridors. **Pets:** $100 deposit/room, $25 one-time fee/room. Supervision.

⟨SAVE⟩ ⟨S⟩ ⟨✕⟩ ⟨∕⟩ ⟨❚⟩ ⟨�︘⟩ ⟨⬗⟩

◆◆◆◆ Marriott Suites Chicago O'Hare ☐
(847) 696-4400. **$139-$224.** 6155 N River Rd. I-190, exit River Rd, then n. Int corridors. **Pets:** Small. Designated rooms, no service, supervision, crate.

⟨✕⟩ ⟨an⟩ ⟨∕⟩ ⟨❚⟩ ⟨▣⟩ ⟨�︘⟩ ⟨⬗⟩

SCHAUMBURG

ⓐⓐⓐ ◆◆◆ AmeriSuites (Chicago/Schaumburg) ☑ ☀
(847) 330-1060. **$89-$154.** 1851 McConnor Pkwy. I-290, exit 1A (Woodfield/Golf Rd) northbound, just n to Golf Rd, just w to McConner Pkwy, just n; exit 1B (Woodfield/Golf Rd) southbound. Int corridors. **Pets:** Very small, other. $20 one-time fee/room. Designated rooms, no service, supervision, crate.

⟨SAVE⟩ ⟨S⟩ ⟨✕⟩ ⟨✥⟩ ⟨∕⟩ ⟨✸⟩ ⟨❚⟩ ⟨▣⟩ ⟨⬗⟩

◆◆◆ Chicago Marriott Schaumburg ☐ ☀
(847) 240-0100. **$82-$199.** 50 N Martingale Rd. Higgins Rd W (SR 72) exit of I-290 and SR 53, 0.5 mi s of SR 72. Int corridors. **Pets:** Medium. $25 one-time fee/room. Designated rooms, no service, supervision, crate.

⟨✕⟩ ⟨an⟩ ⟨∕⟩ ⟨✸⟩ ⟨▣⟩ ⟨�︘⟩ ⟨⬗⟩

◆◆◆ Drury Inn ☑ ☀
(847) 517-7737. **$81-$99.** 600 N Martingale Rd. I-290, Higgins Rd W (SR 72) exit. Int corridors. **Pets:** Small, other. Supervision.

⟨✕⟩ ⟨∕⟩ ⟨❚⟩ ⟨▣⟩ ⟨⬗⟩

◆◆◆ Homestead Village Guest Studios-Schaumburg ☑
(847) 882-6900. **$89-$94.** 51 E State Pkwy. I-90 exit Roselle Rd, 0.8 mi s, then just e. Int corridors. **Pets:** Supervision.

⟨✕⟩ ⟨an⟩ ⟨∕⟩ ⟨✸⟩ ⟨❚⟩ ⟨▣⟩

◆◆◆ Homewood Suites Schaumburg ☑
(847) 605-0400. **$79-$169.** 815 E American Ln. From jct I-290 and SR 53, 0.5 mi w on Higgins, 0.8 mi n on Meacham, 0.8 mi w. Ext/int corridors. **Pets:** No service, supervision, crate.

⟨ASK⟩ ⟨S⟩ ⟨✕⟩ ⟨an⟩ ⟨∕⟩ ⟨❚⟩ ⟨▣⟩ ⟨⬗⟩

◆◆◆ La Quinta Inn ☑
(847) 517-8484. **$85-$105.** 1730 E Higgins Rd. I-290, exit Higgins Rd W (SR 72). Int corridors. **Pets:** Medium. Designated rooms, no service, supervision, crate.

⟨ASK⟩ ⟨✕⟩ ⟨∕⟩ ⟨▣⟩ ⟨⬗⟩

◆◆◆ Summerfield Suites Hotel ☑
(847) 619-6677. **$79-$169.** 901 E Woodfield Office Ct. 1.5 w on SR 72(Higgins Rd) from jct SR 53, then 0.3 mi n on Plum Grove Rd. Ext/int corridors. **Pets:** Small. Supervision.

⟨ASK⟩ ⟨✕⟩ ⟨∕⟩ ⟨❚⟩ ⟨▣⟩ ⟨⬗⟩ ⟨✕⟩

SCHILLER PARK

◆◆◆ Residence Inn by Marriott-O'Hare Schiller Park ☑
(847) 725-2210. **$169.** 9450 W Lawrence Ave. 0.5 mi e of US 12 and 45. Int corridors. **Pets:** No service, supervision, crate.

⟨ASK⟩ ⟨✕⟩ ⟨❚⟩ ⟨▣⟩ ⟨✕⟩

SKOKIE

◆◆◆ Holiday Inn Northshore ☑
(847) 679 8900. **$119-$129, 30 days notice.** 5300 W Touhy Ave. I-94 exit 39A, 0.5 mi w. Ext/int corridors. **Pets:** Supervision.

⟨✕⟩ ⟨∕⟩ ⟨✸⟩ ⟨❚⟩ ⟨▣⟩ ⟨�︘⟩ ⟨⬗⟩

◆◆◆ **Howard Johnson Hotel-Skokie** Ⓜ
(847) 679-4200. **$107-$149.** 9333 Skokie Blvd. On US 41, just n of Gross Point Rd. Int corridors. **Pets:** Medium. Supervision.

[SAVE] [S&] [X] [⌖] [📖] [💻] [🍴] [🖼]

SOUTH HOLLAND

 ◆◆ **Red Roof Inn** Ⓜ
(708) 331-1621. **$48-$66.** 17301 S Halsted Rd. N of I-80 and I-294, exit Halsted St N. Ext corridors. **Pets:** Small. Supervision.

[SAVE] [X]

TINLEY PARK

◆◆◆ **Baymont Inn & Suites-Chicago (Tinley Park)** Ⓜ
(708) 633-1200. **$68-$92.** 7255 W 183rd St. I-80, exit 148B, just n. Int corridors. **Pets:** Supervision.

[S&] [X] [⌖] [🔖] [⌖] [📖] [💻] [🖼]

VERNON HILLS

 ◆◆◆ **AmeriSuites Vernon Hills/Chicago** Ⓜ
(847) 918-1400. **$87-$114.** 450 N Milwaukee Ave. SR 21, 0.3 mi s of jct SR 60. Int corridors. **Pets:** Supervision.

[SAVE] [S&] [X] [🔖] [🔖] [⌖] [📖] [💻] [🖼]

◆◆◆ **Homestead Village Guest Studios** Ⓜ ✿
(847) 955-1111. **$50-$74.** 675 Woodlands Pkwy. I-94, exit SR 60 (Town Line Rd), 2.1 mi w to Milwaukee Ave (SR 21), 1.9 mi s to Woodlands Pkwy, then just w. Int corridors. **Pets:** Medium, other. $10 daily fee/room. No service, supervision, crate.

[X] [🔖] [🔖] [⌖] [📖] [💻]

WARRENVILLE

 ◆◆◆ **AmeriSuites/Warrenville** Ⓜ
(630) 393-0400. **$79-$169.** 4305 Weaver Pkwy. Just s of I-88, Winfield Rd exit. Int corridors. **Pets:** No service, supervision, crate.

[SAVE] [S&] [X] [🔖] [🔖] [⌖] [📖] [💻] [🖼]

WAUKEGAN

 ◆◆ **Best Inns of America** Ⓜ ✿
(847) 336-9000. **$52-$68.** 31 N Green Bay Rd. I-94, exit SR 132 E (Grand Ave), 3.5 mi e to SR 131, 0.7 mi s. Int corridors. **Pets:** Small. $10 daily fee/pet. No service, supervision, crate.

[SAVE] [X] [⌖] [📖] [🖼]

WESTMONT

◆◆◆ **Homestead Village Guest Studios** Ⓜ ✿
(630) 323-9292. **Call for rates.** 855 Pasquinelli Dr. SR 83 exit Ogden Ave (Rt 34), just w to Pasquinelli Dr, 0.5 mi n. Int corridors. **Pets:** Other. $75 one-time fee/room. Supervision.

[X] [🔖] [🔖] [⌖] [⌖] [📖]

WILLOWBROOK

 ◆◆ **Red Roof Inn** Ⓜ ✿
(630) 323-8811. **$67-$79.** 7535 Robert Kingery Hwy. I-55, exit 274, 0.5 mi n on SR 83. Ext corridors. **Pets:** No service, supervision, crate.

[SAVE] [X] [🔖] [⌖]

WINTHROP HARBOR

◆◆ **Sandpiper Inn** Ⓜ
(847) 746-7380. **$69-$109.** 301 Sheridan Rd. 0.5 mi n on Sheridan Rd (SR 137). Int corridors. **Pets:** Supervision.

[ASK] [S&] [X] [⌖] [💻]

 ✿ **END METROPOLITAN AREA** ✿

CHILLICOTHE

◆◆ **Super 8 Motel** Ⓜ ✿
(309) 274-2568. **$46-$64, 3 days notice.** 615 S 4th St. 1.1 mi s on SR 29. Int corridors. **Pets:** $50 deposit/room. No service, supervision, crate.

[ASK] [S&] [X] [⌖]

CLINTON

◆◆ **Days Inn-Clinton** Ⓜ
(217) 935-4140. **Call for rates.** 1101 Kleeman Dr. US 51 bypass and Kleeman Dr. Int corridors. **Pets:** Very small. No service, supervision, crate.

[X] [⌖] [⌖] [💻] [X]

COLLINSVILLE

◆◆◆ **Drury Inn Collinsville** Ⓜ
(618) 345-7700. **$66-$88.** 602 N Bluff Rd. Just n of jct I-55, I-70 and SR 157, exit 11. Int corridors. **Pets:** Small. No service, supervision, crate.

[X] [🔖] [🔖] [⌖] [💻] [🖼]

 ◆◆ **Motel 6-1133** Ⓜ
(618) 345-2100. **$42-$58.** 295A N Bluff Rd. Just s of jct I-70/55 and SR 157 (Bluff Rd). Int corridors. **Pets:** Small. No service, supervision, crate.

[S&] [X] [🔖] [⌖] [🖼]

◆◆◆ **Pear Tree Inn by Drury** Ⓜ ✿
(618) 345-9500. **$58-$78.** 552 Ramada Blvd. At jct I-55/70, exit 11 and SR 157. Ext corridors. **Pets:** Small, other. No service, supervision, crate.

[X] [🔖] [🔖] [⌖] [💻] [🖼]

◆◆ **Super 8 Motel** Ⓜ
(618) 345-8008. **$42-$79.** 2 Gateway Dr. Just n of jct I-70, I-55 and SR 157, exit 11 (N Bluff Rd). Int corridors. **Pets:** Small. Supervision.

ⒶⓈⓀ ⓈⒹ ⓧ 🄴 🄻🄳

DANVILLE

🄰🄰🄰 ◆◆◆ **Best Western Regency Inn** Ⓜ ❖
(217) 446-2111. **$52-$64.** 360 Eastgate Dr. At jct Lynch Rd and I-74, exit 220. Ext/int corridors. **Pets:** Small. $10 daily fee/pet. Designated rooms, no service, supervision, crate.

Ⓢ🄰🄫🄴 ⓈⒹ ⓧ 🄴 🄰🄴

🄰🄰🄰 ◆◆◆ **Best Western Riverside** Ⓜ ❖
(217) 431-0020. **$60-$75, 3 days notice.** 57 S Gilbert St. On US 150 and SR 1, 0.8 mi n of I-74, exit 215. Ext/int corridors. **Pets:** Medium. $10 daily fee/pet. Designated rooms, no service, supervision, crate.

Ⓢ🄰🄫🄴 ⓈⒹ ⓧ 🄴 🄰🄴

◆◆ **Comfort Inn** Ⓜ
(217) 443-8004. **$42-$61, 7 days notice.** 383 Lynch Dr. Jct I-74 and Lynch Dr (exit 220). Int corridors. **Pets:** Medium. Designated rooms, supervision.

ⒶⓈⓀ ⓈⒹ ⓧ 🄐 🄴 🄻🄳 🄰🄴

◆◆ **Super 8-Danville** Ⓜ
(217) 443-4499. **$59, 7 days notice.** 377 Lynch Dr. I-74 and Lynch Dr (exit 220). Int corridors. **Pets:** Medium. Designated rooms, supervision.

ⒶⓈⓀ ⓈⒹ ⓧ 🄴 🄻🄳

DE KALB

🄰🄰🄰 ◆◆◆ **Best Western DeKalb Inn & Suites** Ⓜ ❖
(815) 758-8661. **$69-$69.** 1212 W Lincoln Hwy. I-88, exit Annie Glidden Rd, 2 mi n to W Lincoln Hwy, just w. Ext/int corridors. **Pets:** Medium. $10 daily fee/room. Designated rooms, no service, supervision, crate.

Ⓢ🄰🄫🄴 ⓈⒹ ⓧ 🄐 🄴 🄻🄳 🄰🄴

DECATUR

◆◆ **Baymont Inn-Decatur** Ⓜ
(217) 875-5800. **$60-$65.** 5100 Hickory Pt Frontage Rd. Just n from jct I-72 and US 51, exit 141B, then s. Int corridors. **Pets:** Supervision.

ⓈⒹ ⓧ 🄐 🄴 🄻🄳

◆◆◆ **Country Inn & Suites By Carlson** Ⓜ
(217) 872-2402. **$73-$79.** 5150 Hickory Pt Frontage Rd. Just n from jct I-72 and US 51, exit 141B, then s. Int corridors. **Pets:** Medium. Supervision.

ⓈⒹ ⓧ 🄐 🄐 🄴 🄻🄳 🄰🄴

◆◆◆ **Holiday Inn Select Conference Hotel** Ⓜ
(217) 422-8800. **$95-$110.** 4191 W Hwy 36. US 36, 1 mi e of jct I-72 and US 51, exit 133A. Int corridors. **Pets:** Medium. Designated rooms, supervision.

ⒶⓈⓀ ⓈⒹ ⓧ 🄑 🄐 🄒 🄴 🄻🄳 🄰🄴 🄧

◆ **Super 8 Motel-Decatur** Ⓜ
(217) 877-8888. **Call for rates.** 3141 N Water St. 1.8 mi s of jct I-72 & US 51 (exit 141A). Int corridors. **Pets:** Small. Designated rooms, no service, supervision, crate.

ⓧ 🄻🄳

DIXON

◆◆◆ **Best Western Brandywine Lodge** Ⓜ ❖
(815) 284-1890. **$59-$70.** 443 Illinois Rt 2. SR 2, 3.6 mi w of jct SR 26. Int corridors. **Pets:** Other. $25 deposit/room. No service, supervision, crate.

ⓈⒹ ⓧ 🄴 🄣 🄰🄴

EAST PEORIA

◆◆ **Super 8 Motel** Ⓜ ❖
(309) 698-8889. **$42-$79.** 725 Taylor St. Just e from I-74, exit 96. Int corridors. **Pets:** Medium, other. Designated rooms, no service, supervision, crate.

ⒶⓈⓀ ⓈⒹ ⓧ 🄴 🄻🄳

EFFINGHAM

◆◆◆ **Baymont Inn** Ⓜ ❖
(217) 342-2525. **$54-$69.** 1103 Ave of Mid-America. Just n from jct I-57/70 and SR 32/33, exit 160. Int corridors. **Pets:** Small. $10 one-time fee/room. No service, supervision, crate.

ⒶⓈⓀ ⓈⒹ ⓧ 🄐 🄴 🄻🄳 🄰🄴

🄰🄰🄰 ◆◆ **Best Inns of America** Ⓜ
(217) 347-5141. **$38-$55.** 1209 N Keller Dr. 0.5 mi w on SR 32/33 from jct I-70/57, exit 160. Ext corridors. **Pets:** Supervision.

Ⓢ🄰🄫🄴 ⓈⒹ ⓧ 🄐 🄰🄴

🄰🄰🄰 ◆◆ **Best Western Raintree Inn** Ⓜ
(217) 342-4121. **$40-$57.** 1811 W Fayette Ave. Jct I-57/70, exit 159. Ext/int corridors. **Pets:** Medium. Designated rooms, supervision.

Ⓢ🄰🄫🄴 ⓈⒹ ⓧ 🄴 🄣 🄰🄴

🄰🄰🄰 ◆◆◆ **Comfort Inn** Ⓜ
(217) 347-5050. **$64-$125.** 1304 W Evergreen Dr. Just e of I-57, exit 160, just n. Int corridors. **Pets:** Supervision.

Ⓢ🄰🄫🄴 ⓈⒹ ⓧ 🄓 🄒 🄴 🄻🄳 🄰🄴

◆◆◆ **Comfort Suites** Ⓜ
(217) 342-3151. **$55-$68.** 1310 W Fayette Rd. 0.4 mi e from I-57/70, exit 159. Int corridors. **Pets:** Medium. No service, supervision, crate.

ⒶⓈⓀ ⓧ 🄓 🄒 🄴 🄻🄳 🄰🄴

🄰🄰🄰 ◆◆ **Days Inn** Ⓜ ❖
(217) 342-9271. **$34-$47.** 1412 W Fayette Ave. Just e of I-57 and I-70, exit 159. Ext corridors. **Pets:** Other. No service, supervision, crate.

Ⓢ🄰🄫🄴 ⓈⒹ ⓧ 🄴 🄻🄳 🄰🄴

◆ **Econo Lodge** Ⓜ ❖
(217) 347-7131. **$40-$50.** 1205 N Keller Dr. Just n from I-57 and 70, exit 160. Ext/int corridors. **Pets:** Medium, other. $5 deposit/pet. No service, supervision, crate.

ⒶⓈⓀ ⓈⒹ ⓧ 🄴 🄻🄳 🄰🄴 🄧

◆◆◆ **Hampton Inn** Ⓜ ❖
(217) 342-4499. **$62-$88, 3 days notice.** 1509 Hampton Dr. Just s from jct I-57/I-70 and SR 32/33, exit 160. Int corridors. **Pets:** Designated rooms, supervision.

ⒶⓈⓀ ⓈⒹ ⓧ 🄓 🄒 🄴 🄻🄳 🄰🄴

◆◆ **Quality Inn** M
(217) 342-4161. **$40-$50.** 1600 W Fayette Ave. Just e of I-57/70, exit 159. Ext corridors. **Pets:** Supervision.

⟨ASK⟩ ⟨Sₒ⟩ ⟨✕⟩ ⟨⌖⟩ ⟨▣⟩ ⟨⊿⟩

◆◆◆ **Ramada Inn** MI
(217) 342-2131. **$62-$90, 3 days notice.** 1201 N Keller Dr. Just ne from jct I-57 and I-70, exit 160. Ext/int corridors. **Pets:** Medium. Designated rooms, supervision.

⟨ASK⟩ ⟨Sₒ⟩ ⟨✕⟩ ⟨▤⟩ ⟨▣⟩ ⟨⊿⟩ ⟨✕⟩

◆◆ **Super 8 Motel** M
(217) 342-6888. **$42-$79.** 1400 Thelma Keller Ave. 0.5 mi n on SR 32/33 from jct I-70 and I-57, exit 160. Int corridors. **Pets:** Designated rooms, no service, supervision, crate.

⟨ASK⟩ ⟨Sₒ⟩ ⟨✕⟩ ⟨⌖⟩ ⟨▤⟩ ⟨▣⟩

FAIRVIEW HEIGHTS

◆◆◆ **Drury Inn** M
(618) 398-8530. **$65-$85.** 12 Ludwig Dr. Jct I-64 and SR 159, exit 12. Int corridors. **Pets:** Small. Supervision.

⟨✕⟩ ⟨▤⟩ ⟨▣⟩ ⟨⊿⟩

⟨AAA⟩ ◆◆◆ **Ramada Inn Fairview Heights** MI ❀
(618) 632-4747. **$69-$79.** 6900 N Illinois Ave. Just n of jct I-64 and SR 159, exit 12. Int corridors. **Pets:** Small, other. $10 one-time fee/room. No service, supervision, crate.

⟨SAVE⟩ ⟨Sₒ⟩ ⟨✕⟩ ⟨▤⟩ ⟨▣⟩ ⟨❀⟩ ⟨⊿⟩ ⟨CTV⟩

◆◆ **Super 8 Motel** M
(618) 398-8338. **$42-$79.** 45 Ludwig Dr. Jct I-64 and SR 159, exit 12. Int corridors. **Pets:** Supervision.

⟨ASK⟩ ⟨Sₒ⟩ ⟨✕⟩ ⟨⌖⟩ ⟨▤⟩ ⟨▣⟩

FORSYTH

◆◆ **Comfort Inn of Forsyth** M
(217) 875-1166. **$52-$69, 7 days notice.** 134 Barnett Ave. 0.5 mi n from jct I-72 and US 51, exit 141B. Int corridors. **Pets:** Supervision.

⟨ASK⟩ ⟨Sₒ⟩ ⟨✕⟩ ⟨⌖⟩ ⟨▤⟩ ⟨▣⟩ ⟨⊿⟩

◆◆◆ **Hampton Inn** M ❀
(217) 877-5577. **$62-$77, 7 days notice.** 1429 Hickory Point Dr. 0.5 mi n of jct I-7 & US 51, exit 141B. Int corridors. **Pets:** Other. Supervision.

⟨Sₒ⟩ ⟨✕⟩ ⟨⌂⟩ ⟨⌖⟩ ⟨▤⟩ ⟨▣⟩ ⟨⊿⟩

GALENA

⟨AAA⟩ ◆◆◆ **Best Western Quiet House
        Suites** M ❀
(815) 777-2577. **$91-$190.** 9923 US 20 W. On US 20, 1 mi e. Ext/int corridors. **Pets:** $15 one-time fee/pet. Designated rooms, no service, supervision, crate.

⟨SAVE⟩ ⟨Sₒ⟩ ⟨✕⟩ ⟨▤⟩ ⟨⊿⟩

GALESBURG

◆◆◆ **Comfort Inn** M ❀
(309) 344-5445. **$54-$119, 7 days notice.** 907 W Carl Sandburg Dr. From US 34 exit at US 150 E, to Carl Sandburg Dr. Int corridors. **Pets:** $15 one-time fee/room. Designated rooms, no service, supervision, crate.

⟨ASK⟩ ⟨Sₒ⟩ ⟨✕⟩ ⟨⌂⟩ ⟨⌖⟩ ⟨▤⟩ ⟨▣⟩

◆◆◆ **Holiday Inn Express** M ❀
(309) 343-7100. **$60-$127.** 2285 Washington St. Jct I-74 and US 150, exit 48A, just w to Michigan Ave, just s to Washington St, then just e. Int corridors. **Pets:** Designated rooms, supervision.

⟨ASK⟩ ⟨Sₒ⟩ ⟨✕⟩ ⟨⌖⟩ ⟨⌖⟩ ⟨▤⟩ ⟨▣⟩ ⟨⊿⟩

⟨AAA⟩ ◆◆◆ **Jumer's Continental Inn** MI
(309) 343-7151. **$63-$80.** 260 S Soangetaha Rd. From I-74, exit 48, just e on Main St, then s. Int corridors. **Pets:** Small. No service, supervision, crate.

⟨SAVE⟩ ⟨Sₒ⟩ ⟨✕⟩ ⟨⌖⟩ ⟨▤⟩ ⟨▣⟩ ⟨❀⟩ ⟨⊿⟩ ⟨✕⟩

◆◆ **Ramada Inn** H ❀
(309) 343-9161. **$50-$60.** 29 Public Sq. On Main St (US 150), downtown. Int corridors. **Pets:** Medium, other. $20 daily fee/room, $20 one-time fee/room. No service, supervision, crate.

⟨ASK⟩ ⟨Sₒ⟩ ⟨✕⟩ ⟨▤⟩ ⟨▣⟩ ⟨❀⟩ ⟨⊿⟩

GILMAN

◆◆ **Days Inn** M ❀
(815) 265-7283. **$45-$60.** 834 Hwy 24 W. I-57, exit 283, just e. Ext/int corridors. **Pets:** $5 daily fee/pet. Designated rooms, no service, supervision, crate.

⟨ASK⟩ ⟨✕⟩ ⟨⊿⟩

⟨AAA⟩ ◆◆ **Super 8 of Gilman** M ❀
(815) 265-7000. **$49-$63.** 1301 S Crescent St. I-57, exit 283, 0.3 mi e. Int corridors. **Pets:** Small, other. No service, supervision, crate.

⟨SAVE⟩ ⟨Sₒ⟩ ⟨✕⟩ ⟨⌖⟩

JACKSONVILLE

⟨AAA⟩ ◆◆ **Star Lite Motel** M ❀
(217) 245-7184. **$38-$48.** 1910 W Morton Ave. 1.8 mi w on US 67 and SR 104 W. Ext corridors. **Pets:** Medium. $5 one-time fee/room. Supervision.

⟨SAVE⟩ ⟨Sₒ⟩ ⟨✕⟩ ⟨▤⟩ ⟨✕⟩

KEWANEE

⟨AAA⟩ ◆◆ **Kewanee Motor Lodge** M ❀
(309) 853-4000. **$45-$50.** 400 S Main St. SR 78, 0.8 mi s of US 36. Ext corridors. **Pets:** Other. $10 deposit/room, $5 daily fee/pet. No service, supervision, crate.

⟨SAVE⟩ ⟨Sₒ⟩ ⟨✕⟩ ⟨▤⟩

KNOXVILLE

◆◆ **Super 8 Galesburg/Knoxville** M ❀
(309) 289-2100. **$49-$68.** 737 Knox Hwy 10. I-74, exit 51, just w to Knox Hwy 10, then just n. Int corridors. **Pets:** Medium. $25 deposit/pet, $7 daily fee/pet. Designated rooms, no service, supervision, crate.

⟨ASK⟩ ⟨Sₒ⟩ ⟨✕⟩ ⟨▤⟩ ⟨⊿⟩

LINCOLN

◆◆◆ **Comfort Inn** M
(217) 735-3960. **$55-$100, 3 days notice.** 2811 Woodlawn Rd. 0.3 mi e from I-55, exit 126. Int corridors. **Pets:** Small. No service, supervision, crate.

⟨ASK⟩ ⟨Sₒ⟩ ⟨✕⟩ ⟨⌖⟩ ⟨▤⟩ ⟨▣⟩ ⟨⊿⟩

◆◆◆ Holiday Inn Express M ❖
(217) 735-5800. **$68-$68.** 130 Olson Rd. I-55, exit 126, just s to Heitman Dr, just w to Olson Dr, then just n. Int corridors. **Pets:** Other. Designated rooms, supervision.

ASK S⅄ ✕ ☐ ⊡ ⌂

MARION

◆◆ Best Inns of America M
(618) 997-9421. **$37-$50.** 2700 W DeYoung. Just w from jct I-57 and SR 13, exit 54B. Ext corridors. **Pets:** No service, supervision, crate.

SAVE S⅄ ✕ ☐ ⌂

◆ Days Inn-Marion M ❖
(618) 997-1351. **$55-$65.** 1802 Bittle Pl. Jct I-57 & SR 13 (exit 54A), 0.5 mi e. Ext/int corridors. **Pets:** Other. $5 daily fee/pet, $5 one-time fee/pet. No service, supervision, crate.

ASK S⅄ ✕

◆◆◆ Drury Inn M
(618) 997-9600. **$55-$73.** 2706 W DeYoung. 0.5 mi w of jct I-57 and SR 13, exit 54. Int corridors. **Pets:** No service, supervision, crate.

✕ ⌖ ⌯ ⌘ ☐ ⊡ ⌂

◆◆ Super 8 Motel M
(618) 993-5577. **$42-$79.** 2601 W De Young St. Just w from jct I-57 and SR 13, exit 54B. Int corridors. **Pets:** No service, supervision, crate.

ASK S⅄ ✕ ⌯ ☐ ⊡

MATTOON

◆◆◆ Ramada Inn & Conference
Center MI ❖
(217) 235-0313. **$56-$77.** 300 Broadway Ave E. 1.5 mi e on SR 16, 1 mi w of jct I-57, exit 190B. Ext/int corridors. **Pets:** Medium, other. Supervision.

SAVE S⅄ ✕ ☐ ⊡ ⑪ ⌂

MCLEAN

◆◆ Super 8 Motel M ❖
(309) 874-2366. **$44-$95.** RR 1 Box 85. Just w from I-55, exit 145. Int corridors. **Pets:** Small. $50 deposit/room, $3 daily fee/pet. Designated rooms, no service, supervision, crate.

ASK S⅄ ✕ ⌂

METROPOLIS

◆◆◆ Best Inns Of America M ❖
(618) 524-8200. **$41-$61.** 2055 E 5th St. Just w from I-24, exit 37. Int corridors. **Pets:** Small. Supervision.

SAVE ✕ ⌯ ⌘ ☐ ⌂

◆◆◆ Comfort Inn M ❖
(618) 524-7227. **$48-$57.** 2118 E 5th St. Off I-24, exit 37, 0.3 mi e of 5th St, follow signs. Int corridors. **Pets:** Medium. $10 daily fee/pet, $10 one-time fee/pet. Designated rooms, no service, supervision, crate.

ASK S⅄ ✕ ☐ ⌂

◆◆◆ Isle of View Bed & Breakfast BB ❖
(618) 524-5838. **$43-$125, 7 days notice.** 205 Metropolis St. 0.3 mi s of US 45, 3 mi w of I-24 exit 37. Int corridors. **Pets:** Medium, other. No service, supervision, crate.

ASK

◆◆◆ Players AmeriHost Inn M ❖
(618) 524-5678. **$70-$82.** 203 E Front St. I-24, exit 37, just s from downtown. Int corridors. **Pets:** Medium. Supervision.

SAVE S⅄ ✕ ⌯ ⌖ ☐ ⊡ ⌂

MOLINE

◆◆◆ Comfort Inn M
(309) 762-7000. **$64-$95, 7 days notice.** 2600 52nd Ave. In Moline, IL; I-280 and 74, exit 5B or 18A, just s to "T", 0.5 mi nw on 27th St. Int corridors. **Pets:** Small. No service, supervision, crate.

ASK S⅄ ✕ ☐ ⊡ ⌂

◆◆ Exel Inn of Moline M
(309) 797-5580. **$42-$59.** 2501 52nd Ave. In Moline, IL; from I-280 and I-74, exit 5B, just s on US 6 and 150, 1 mi nw on 27th St. Int corridors. **Pets:** Small. Supervision.

S⅄ ✕ ☐ ⊡

◆◆◆ Hampton Inn-Airport M ❖
(309) 762-1711. **$71-$85.** 6920 27th St. In Moline, IL; from I-280 and I-74, exit 5B, just s on US 6, nw on 27th St; 0.3 mi e of Quad City Airport entrance. Int corridors. **Pets:** Other. No service, supervision, crate.

ASK S⅄ ✕ ⌯ ☐ ⊡ ⌂

◆◆◆ Holiday Inn-Airport Convention
Center MI ❖
(309) 762-8811. **$70.** 6902 27th St. In Moline, IL; from I-280, exit 18A eastbound; I-74, exit 58 westbound, just s on US 6 and 150, just nw. Int corridors. **Pets:** Medium, other. No service, supervision, crate.

ASK S⅄ ✕ ⌯ ☐ ⊡ ⑪ ⌂ ✕

◆◆◆ Holiday Inn Express-Moline
Airport M ❖
(309) 762-8300. **$59-$75.** 6910 27th St. In Moline, IL; from I-280 E (exit 18A); I-74 W (exit 58), just s on US 6 and 150, just nw. Int corridors. **Pets:** No service, supervision, crate.

ASK S⅄ ✕ ☐

◆◆◆ La Quinta Inn M ❖
(309) 762-9008. **$65-$85.** 5450 27th St. In Moline, IL; from I-280, exit 18A eastbound; I-74, exit 5B westbound, just s on US 6 and 150, just nw on 27th St; 0.3 mi e of Quad City Airport entrance. Int corridors. **Pets:** Small, other. Designated rooms, supervision.

ASK ✕ ☐ ⊡ ⌂

MORRIS

◆◆ Comfort Inn M ❖
(815) 942-1433. **$57-$76.** 70 Gore Rd W. I-80, exit 112, 0.3 mi nw. Int corridors. **Pets:** Other. Designated rooms, supervision.

ASK S⅄ ✕ ☐ ⌂

◆◆ Holiday Inn MI ❖
(815) 942-6600. **Call for rates.** 200 Gore Rd. I-80, exit 112, 0.3 mi nw. Int corridors. **Pets:** Designated rooms, no service, supervision, crate.

✕ ⌖ ☐ ⊡ ⑪ ⌂

MORTON

◆◆◆ Comfort Inn M
(309) 266-8888. **$55-$90, 7 days notice.** 210 E Ashland St. 0.4 mi ne of I-74, exit 102. Int corridors. **Pets:** Medium. Designated rooms, no service, supervision, crate.
(ASK) (S6) (X) (H) (≈)

MOUNT VERNON

(AAA) ◆◆ Best Inns of America M
(618) 244-4343. **$34-$50.** 222 S 44th. Jct I-57/64 and SR 15, just e to 44th, then just s. Ext corridors. **Pets:** Supervision.
(SAVE) (S6) (X) (≈) (≈)

◆◆◆ Drury Inn M
(618) 244-4550. **$55-$75.** 145 N 44th St. Jct I-57/64 and SR 15 (exit 95), just e, then just n (entry through restaurant parking lot). Int corridors. **Pets:** Medium. No service, supervision, crate.
(X) (≈) (H) (≈) (≈)

(AAA) ◆◆ Econo Lodge & Suites MI ❀
(618) 242-6370. **$43-$53.** 120 N 44th St. Jct I-57/64 and SR 15, just e to 44th St, then just n. Ext/int corridors. **Pets:** Very small. $7 daily fee/room, $7 one-time fee/room. Designated rooms, no service, supervision, crate.
(SAVE) (S6) (X) (H) (≈) (H) (≈)

◆◆◆ Holiday Inn H ❀
(618) 244-7100. **$75-$75, 3 days notice.** 222 Potomac Blvd. Jct I-57, I-64 and SR 15, exit 59, just w to Potomac, then just n. Int corridors. **Pets:** Medium. No service, supervision, crate.
(ASK) (S6) (X) (♁) (≈) (H) (≈) (H) (≈)

◆◆ Super 8 Motel M ❀
(618) 242-8800. **$42-$79.** 401 S 44th St. Jct I-57/64 and SR 15, just e, then just s. Int corridors. **Pets:** Medium, other. No service, supervision, crate.
(ASK) (S6) (X) (H) (≈)

◆◆ Thrifty Inn M
(618) 244-7750. **$44-$62.** 100 N 44th St. Jct I-57/64 and SR 15, exit 95, just e. Ext corridors. **Pets:** Medium. No service, supervision, crate.
(X) (≈)

NASHVILLE

(AAA) ◆◆ Best Western U S Inn M
(618) 478-5341. **$38-$59, 5 days notice.** 11640 SR 127. 0.3 mi s from jct I-64 and SR 127, exit 50. Int corridors. **Pets:** Small. No service, supervision, crate.
(SAVE) (S6) (X) (♁) (≈) (H) (≈) (≈)

NORMAL

(AAA) ◆◆◆ Best Western University Inn M ❀
(309) 454-4070. **$59-$89.** 6 Trader Cir. US 51, just s of jct I-55, exit 165A. Int corridors. **Pets:** No service, supervision, crate.
(SAVE) (S6) (X) (≈) (H) (≈)

◆◆◆ Comfort Suites M
(309) 452-8588. **$57-$74, 7 days notice.** 310 B Greenbriar Dr. I-55 business route (Veterans Pkwy), at Fort Jesse Rd intersection, 1.3 mi s of jct I-55, exit 167. Int corridors. **Pets:** Supervision.
(ASK) (S6) (X) (♁) (≈) (H) (≈) (≈)

◆◆◆ Holiday Inn Bloomington-Normal MI
(309) 452-8300. **$100, 3 days notice.** 8 Traders Cir. I-55, exit 165A, 0.5 mi e, return on service road. Int corridors. **Pets:** Small. No service, supervision, crate.
(ASK) (S6) (X) (♁) (H) (≈) (H) (H) (≈)

O'FALLON

(AAA) ◆◆◆ Comfort Inn M ❀
(618) 624-6060. **$60-$75, 3 days notice.** 1100 Eastgate Dr. I-64, exit 19B, 0.5 mi n on SR 158, just sw. **Pets:** Other. $50 deposit/room. Supervision.
(SAVE) (S6) (X) (H) (≈) (≈)

◆◆ Econo Lodge M ❀
(618) 628-8895. **$59-$59.** 1409 W Hwy 50. US 50, 0.4 mi w from I-64, exit 14. Int corridors. **Pets:** Other. Supervision.
(ASK) (S6) (X) (♁) (H) (≈) (≈)

OGLESBY

◆◆◆ Holiday Inn Express M
(815) 883-3535. **Call for rates.** 900 Holiday St. Just e of I-39, exit 54. Int corridors. **Pets:** No service, supervision, crate.
(X) (H) (≈) (≈)

OKAWVILLE

◆ Okawville Super 8 Motel M ❀
(618) 243-6525. **$40-$50.** 812 N Henhouse Rd. Just s from I-64, exit 41. Int corridors. **Pets:** $5 one-time fee/room. Supervision.
(ASK) (S6) (X) (≈) (H)

OTTAWA

◆◆◆ Holiday Inn Express M ❀
(815) 433-0029. **$63-$72.** 120 W Stevenson Rd. SR 23 just n of I-80, exit 90. Int corridors. **Pets:** Other. Designated rooms, supervision.
(ASK) (S6) (X) (H) (≈) (≈)

PARIS

(AAA) ◆◆ Pinnell Motor Inn M
(217) 465-6441. **$45-$70.** 11639 Hwy 1. 2 mi n on US 150 and SR 1. Ext corridors. **Pets:** Medium. Supervision.
(SAVE) (S6) (X)

PEKIN

(AAA) ◆◆◆ Best Western Pekin Inn M
(309) 347-5533. **$53-$68.** 2801 E Court St. 2.5 mi e on SR 9 from jct SR 29. Ext corridors. **Pets:** Medium. Designated rooms, supervision.
(SAVE) (X) (♁) (H) (≈) (≈)

◆◆◆ Comfort Inn M
(309) 353-4047. **$100.** 3240 Vandever Ave. Just n of SR 9, 3 mi e from jct SR 29. Int corridors. **Pets:** Supervision.
(ASK) (S6) (X) (≈) (H) (≈) (≈)

PEORIA

◆◆◆ Comfort Suites M
(309) 688-3800. **$55-$74, 7 days notice.** 4021 War Memorial Dr. Jct I-74 and US 150 E, exit 89. Int corridors. **Pets:** Small. Designated rooms, no service, supervision, crate.

(ASK) (S⧄) (✕) (🐾) (🛏) (🖥) (🍽)

◆◆◆ Holiday Inn-Brandywine MI ❀
(309) 686-8000. **$90-$95.** 4400 N Brandywine Dr. Jct I-74 and US 150 W, exit 89. Int corridors. **Pets:** Other. $25 deposit/room. No service, supervision, crate.

(ASK) (S⧄) (✕) (🐾) (🛏) (🖥) (🍴) (🍽)

◆◆◆ Holiday Inn City Centre H
(309) 674-2500. **$98-$138, 7 days notice.** 500 Hamilton Blvd. Center. Int corridors. **Pets:** Medium. Supervision.

(ASK) (S⧄) (✕) (🛏) (🖥) (🍴) (🍽)

⊕ ◆◆◆ Jumer's Castle Lodge H
(309) 673-8040. **$79-$95.** 117 N Western Ave. I-74, exit 91 (University South), 1 mi s to Moss, 0.3 mi w to Western Ave. Int corridors. **Pets:** Medium. Supervision.

(SAVE) (S⧄) (✕) (🐾) (🛏) (🖥) (🍴) (🍽)

◆◆◆ Mark Twain Hotel H
(309) 676-3600. **$85-$85.** 225 NE Adams St. Just w of I-74, exit 98B westbound; exit 93 eastbound. Int corridors. **Pets:** Designated rooms, supervision.

(ASK) (S⧄) (✕) (🛏) (🖥) (🍴)

⊕ ◆◆ Red Roof Inn M
(309) 685-3911. **$46-$56.** 4031 N War Memorial Dr. Jct I-74 and US 150 E, exit 89. Ext corridors. **Pets:** Medium. Supervision.

(SAVE) (✕) (🐾) (🛏)

◆◆◆ Residence Inn by Marriott M ❀
(309) 681-9000. **$130-$140, 7 days notice.** 4201 N War Memorial Dr. Jct I-74 and War Memorial Dr, exit 89, just n, enter through Northlands Mall. Int corridors. **Pets:** Medium, other. $10 daily fee/room, $25 one-time fee/room. No service, supervision, crate.

(ASK) (S⧄) (✕) (🐾) (🛏) (🖥) (🍽) (🗙)

◆◆ Super 8 Motel of Peoria M ❀
(309) 688-8074. **$42-$79.** 4025 War Memorial Dr. Jct I-74 and US 150 E, exit 89. Int corridors. **Pets:** Other. Designated rooms, no service, supervision, crate.

(ASK) (S⧄) (🐾) (🛏) (🖥)

PERU

◆◆◆ Ramada Limited M ❀
(815) 224-9000. **$63-$69.** 4389 Venture Dr. Jct I-80 and SR 251, exit 75, 0.5 mi s to Venture Dr, then 0.9 mi nw. Int corridors. **Pets:** Medium. Designated rooms, no service, supervision, crate.

(ASK) (S⧄) (✕) (🛏) (🖥) (🍽)

PONTOON BEACH

⊕ ◆◆ Best Western Camelot Inn M
(618) 931-2262. **$49-$69, 3 days notice.** 1240 E Old Chain of Rocks Rd. From jct I-270 and SR 111 (exit 6B), just n on SR 111 (E Old Chain of Rocks Rd). Int corridors. **Pets:** Supervision.

(SAVE) (S⧄) (✕) (🛏) (🍽)

PRINCETON

◆ Princeton Motor Lodge M ❀
(815) 875-1121. **$36-$44.** 1844 N Main St. SR 26; 0.3 mi s of jct I-80, exit 56. Ext corridors. **Pets:** Other. No service, supervision, crate.

(S⧄) (✕)

QUINCY

◆◆◆ Comfort Inn M ❀
(217) 228-2700. **$49-$78.** 4100 Broadway. 1.3 mi w of jct I-175 and SR 104, exit 14. Int corridors. **Pets:** Other. $10 one-time fee/room. No service, supervision, crate.

(ASK) (S⧄) (✕) (🛏) (🖥) (🍽)

◆◆ Super 8 Motel M ❀
(217) 228-8808. **$43-$51.** 224 N 36th St. 1.8 mi w from jct I-175 and SR 104, exit 14, just s. Int corridors. **Pets:** No service, supervision, crate.

(ASK) (S⧄) (✕) (🍴) (🛏)

RANTOUL

◆◆◆ Best Western Heritage Inn M ❀
(217) 892-9292. **$50-$58.** 420 S Murray Rd. Jct I-57 and US 136, exit 250), 0.5 mi e to Murray Rd, then just s. Ext corridors. **Pets:** Other. Supervision.

(ASK) (S⧄) (✕) (🛏) (🖥) (🍽)

RAYMOND

◆◆◆ Holiday Inn-Carlinville MI ❀
(217) 324-2100. **$62-$70.** 19067 W Frontage Rd. Jct I-55 and SR 108 (exit 60), just w. Int corridors. **Pets:** Other. $10 one-time fee/room. Supervision.

(ASK) (S⧄) (✕) (🍴) (🛏) (🖥) (🍴) (🍽) (🗙)

ROBINSON

◆◆◆ Best Western Robinson Inn M ❀
(618) 544-8448. **$48-$95.** 1500 W Main St. 1 mi w on SR 33. Int corridors. **Pets:** Other. $5 daily fee/pet. Supervision.

(ASK) (S⧄) (✕) (🐾) (🛏) (🖥)

ROCK FALLS

◆ Rock Falls Super 8 M ❀
(815) 626-8800. **$46-$60.** 2100 1st Ave. Jct I-88 and SR 40 (exit 41), 1.3 mi n on 1st Ave, just w on W 21st St. Int corridors. **Pets:** Medium. No service, supervision, crate.

(ASK) (S⧄) (✕) (🛏)

ROCKFORD

⊕ ◆◆◆ Best Suites of America M ❀
(815) 227-1300. **$65-$93.** 7401 Walton Ave. From I-90, MM 63 1/2, just w to Bell School Rd, then just s. Int corridors. **Pets:** Small. $25 one-time fee/pet. No service, supervision, crate.

(SAVE) (S⧄) (✕) (🖥) (🛏) (🖥) (🍽)

⊕ ◆◆◆ Best Western Colonial Inn Motor Lodge M
(815) 398-5050. **$78-$98.** 4850 E State St. 3.5 mi w of I-90 on US 20 business route from exit MM 63 1/2. Int corridors. **Pets:** Small. Designated rooms, no service, supervision, crate.

(SAVE) (S⧄) (✕) (🐾) (🛏) (🍽)

◆◆ **Comfort Inn of Rockford** Ⓜ ✿
(815) 398-7061. **$59-$79.** 7392 Argus Dr. From jct I-90 and US 20 business route, 0.4 mi w to Bell School Rd, just n to Argus Dr, just w. Int corridors. **Pets:** Small. $10 one-time fee/pet. Designated rooms, no service, supervision, crate.

(A$K) (S☐) (✕) (✍) (🖥) (💻) (🌐)

ⓐⓐⓐ ◆◆ **Exel Inn of Rockford** Ⓜ
(815) 332-4915. **$42-$64.** 220 S Lyford Rd. Just se of I-90 at US business route exit, MM 63 1/2. Int corridors. **Pets:** Medium. No service, supervision, crate.

(S☐) (✕) (🖥) (💻)

ⓐⓐⓐ ◆◆ **Red Roof Inn** Ⓜ ✿
(815) 398-9750. **$63-$76.** 7434 E State St. Just w of I-90, US 20 business route exit at MM 63 1/2. Ext corridors. **Pets:** Other. Supervision.

(SAVE) (✕) (✍) (🖥)

◆◆◆ **Residence Inn by Marriott** Ⓐ
(815) 227-0013. **$89-$129.** 7542 Colosseum Dr. Just w of I-90, US 20 business route exit; MM 63 1/2. Int corridors. **Pets:** Small. Designated rooms, no service, supervision, crate.

(A$K) (S☐) (✕) (🏠) (✍) (🐾) (🖥) (💻) (🌐) (✕)

ⓐⓐⓐ ◆◆ **Sweden House Lodge** Ⓜ ✿
(815) 398-4130. **$40-$70.** 4605 E State St. Just 4 mi w of I-90, US 20 business route exit (State St; MM 63 1/2). Ext/int corridors. **Pets:** Medium. $10 daily fee/room. Designated rooms, no service, supervision, crate.

(SAVE) (S☐) (✕) (🖥) (🌐)

SALEM

ⓐⓐⓐ ◆ **Continental Motel** Ⓜ ✿
(618) 548-3090. **$28-$36.** 1600 E Main St. 2.3 mi e from jct I-57 and US 50, exit 116. Ext corridors. **Pets:** Designated rooms, supervision.

(SAVE) (✕) (💻)

◆◆◆ **Holiday Inn** Ⓜ ✿
(618) 548-4212. **$56-$61.** 1812 W Main St. Jct I-57 and US 50, exit 116. Ext corridors. **Pets:** Medium. Designated rooms, no service, supervision, crate.

(A$K) (S☐) (✕) (🖥) (🍴) (🌐)

◆◆ **Super 8 Motel of Salem** Ⓜ ✿
(618) 548-5882. **$42-$79.** 118 N Paragon Rd. Jct I-57 and US 50, exit 116. Ext/int corridors. **Pets:** No service, supervision, crate.

(A$K) (S☐) (✕) (🏠) (✍) (🖥) (💻)

SAVOY

ⓐⓐⓐ ◆◆ **Best Western Paradise Inn Motel** Ⓜ ✿
(217) 356-1824. **$50-$70.** 1001 N Dunlap. From jct I-74 and Neil St (exit 182), 5 mi s on US 45; or from I-57, exit 229, 1 mi e to US 45, then 2.5 mi n. Ext corridors. **Pets:** Small. $5 daily fee/pet. Designated rooms, no service, supervision, crate.

(SAVE) (S☐) (✕) (🖥) (💻) (🌐) (✕)

SHEFFIELD

ⓐⓐⓐ ◆◆ **Days Inn** Ⓜ
(815) 454-2361. **$40-$65, 24 days notice.** 16733 Hwy 40. Jct I-80 and SR 40, exit 45. Int corridors. **Pets:** Small. No service, supervision, crate.

(SAVE) (S☐) (✕) (🍴)

SPRINGFIELD

◆◆◆ **Baymont Inn** Ⓜ ✿
(217) 529-6655. **$65-$72.** 5871 S 6th St. Just ne from I-55, exit 90. Int corridors. **Pets:** Very small, dogs only. Designated rooms, no service, supervision, crate.

(A$K) (S☐) (✕) (🏠) (✍) (🖥) (💻) (🌐)

ⓐⓐⓐ ◆◆ **Best Inns of America** Ⓜ
(217) 522-1100. **$55-$85.** 500 N 1st St. Just n of capitol; at 1st St and Carpenter. Int corridors. **Pets:** No service, supervision, crate.

(SAVE) (S☐) (✕) (✍) (🌐)

◆◆◆ **Comfort Inn** Ⓜ ✿
(217) 787-2250. **$58-$82, 7 days notice.** 3442 Freedom Dr. Just n of jct US 36 and Rt 4, exit 93. Int corridors. **Pets:** Dogs only. No service, supervision, crate.

(A$K) (S☐) (✕) (✍) (🖥) (💻) (🌐)

◆◆ **Days Inn** Ⓜ ✿
(217) 529-0171. **$54-$84.** 3000 Stevenson Dr. Just w of jct I-55, exit 94 (Stevenson Dr). Ext corridors. **Pets:** Other. $5 daily fee/room. Supervision.

(A$K) (S☐) (✕) (✍) (🖥) (🌐)

◆◆◆ **Drury Inn & Suites** Ⓜ
(217) 529-3900. **$65-$85.** 3180 S Dirksen Pkwy. Just w of jct I-55 exit 94 and Stevenson Dr. Int corridors. **Pets:** Very small. Designated rooms, no service, supervision, crate.

(✕) (🐾) (✍) (✍) (🖥) (💻) (🌐)

◆◆◆ **Hampton Inn of Springfield** Ⓜ ✿
(217) 529-1100. **$66-$76.** 3185 S Dirksen Pkwy. From jct I-55, exit 94, just w on Stevenson Dr. Int corridors. **Pets:** Other. Supervision.

(S☐) (✕) (🏠) (✍) (🖥) (💻) (🌐)

◆◆◆ **Hilton Springfield** Ⓗ ✿
(217) 789-1530. **$79-$149.** 700 E Adams St. Just e of the Old Capitol Building at 7th and Adams sts. Int corridors. **Pets:** Other. Supervision.

(A$K) (S☐) (✕) (🐾) (🖥) (💻) (🍴) (🌐)

◆◆ **Holiday Inn-East Hotel & Conference Center** Ⓜ
(217) 529-7171. **$71-$81.** 3100 S Dirksen Pkwy. 0.3 mi nw of jct I-55, exit 94 and Stevenson Dr. Int corridors. **Pets:** Supervision.

(A$K) (S☐) (✕) (✍) (🖥) (💻) (🍴) (🌐) (✕)

◆◆ **Pear Tree Inn by Drury** Ⓜ
(217) 529-9100. **$46-$65.** 3190 S Dirksen Pkwy. Just w of jct I-55, exit 94 Stevenson Dr. Int corridors. **Pets:** Medium. Designated rooms, no service, supervision, crate.

(✕) (🐾)

◆◆ **Ramada Limited (South)** M ❀
(217) 529-1410. **$49-$69.** 5970 S 6th St. 0.3 mi e from I-55, exit 90. Int corridors. **Pets:** Very small. $10 deposit/room, $10 daily fee/room, $10 one-time fee/room. Designated rooms, no service, supervision, crate.

(ASK) (S✆) (✕) (🐾)

(AAA) ◆◆ **Red Roof Inn** M ❀
(217) 753-4302. **$50-$68.** 3200 Singer Ave. Just w of I-55, exit 96B. Ext corridors. **Pets:** Supervision.

(SAVE) (✕) (🔊)

◆◆ **Sleep Inn** M
(217) 787-6200. **$45-$60, 7 days notice.** 3470 Freedom Dr. Jct Rt 36 and 4, exit 93. Int corridors. **Pets:** Supervision.

(ASK) (S✆) (✕) (🔊) (🐾) (🏋) (💻)

◆◆ **Super 8 Springfield South** M
(217) 529-8898. **$42-$57, 7 days notice.** 3675 S Sixth St. Jct I-55 and Business US 55, (exit 92A), just n to Hazel Bell, just w to Access Rd, just n. Int corridors. **Pets:** Designated rooms, no service, supervision, crate.

(ASK) (S✆) (✕) (🏋)

STAUNTON

◆◆ **Staunton Super 8** M 🐾
(618) 635-5353. **Call for rates.** 1527 Herman Rd. Off I-55, 0.3 mi w from exit 41. Int corridors. **Pets:** Other. No service, supervision, crate.

(ASK) (✕) (🔊) (🏋)

TUSCOLA

◆◆◆ **Holiday Inn Express** M ❀
(217) 253-6363. **$70-$88.** 1201 Tuscola Blvd. Jct I-57 and US 36 (exit 212), 0.3 mi w to Progress Blvd, just s to Tuscola Blvd, then 0.4 mi se. Int corridors. **Pets:** Other. Designated rooms, no service, supervision, crate.

(ASK) (S✆) (✕) (🏋) (🏋) (💻) (🐾)

◆◆ **Super 8 Motel-Tuscola** M
(217) 253-5488. **$47-$65.** 1007 E Hwy 36. Jct I-57 and US 36, exit 212, 0.4 mi w. Int corridors. **Pets:** Supervision.

(ASK) (S✆) (✕)

ULLIN

(AAA) ◆◆ **Best Western Cheekwood Inn** M ❀
(618) 845-3700. **$48-$68.** 128 Cheekwood Ln. Jct I-57 and Ullin Rd, exit 18. Int corridors. **Pets:** Large, other. Supervision.

(SAVE) (S✆) (✕) (🐾)

URBANA

◆◆◆ **Ramada**
Limited-Urbana/Champaign M ❀
(217) 328-4400. **$50-$95.** 902 W Killarney St. From jct I-74 and Lincoln Ave (exit 183), just s to Killarney St, then just w. Int corridors. **Pets:** Small, dogs only. $50 deposit/pet. No service, supervision, crate.

(✕) (🏋) (💻) (🐾)

◆◆ **Sleep Inn** M ❀
(217) 367-6000. **$48-$89, 7 days notice.** 1908 N Lincoln Ave. From jct I-74 and Lincoln Ave (exit 183), 0.5 mi s. Int corridors. **Pets:** $50 deposit/room, $4 one-time fee/room. No service, supervision, crate.

(ASK) (S✆) (✕) (🔊) (🏋) (💻) (🐾)

VANDALIA

(AAA) ◆◆ **Days Inn** M ❀
(618) 283-4400. **$52-$58.** 1920 Kennedy Blvd. US 51, 0.6 mi n from I-70, exit 63 (US 51 exit, Vandalia). Ext corridors. **Pets:** Other. $10 deposit/room. Designated rooms, supervision.

(SAVE) (✕) (🏋) (💻) (🐾)

(AAA) ◆◆ **Jay's Inn** M ❀
(618) 283-1200. **$34-$52.** 720 Gochenour St. Just s of jct I-70 and US 51, exit 63. Ext corridors. **Pets:** Other. Supervision.

(SAVE) (S✆) (✕) (💻)

(AAA) ◆◆◆ **Ramada Limited Vandalia** M ❀
(618) 283-1400. **$50-$62.** 2707 Veterans Ave. Just s of I-70, exit 61. Int corridors. **Pets:** Other. $10 deposit/pet. Designated rooms, supervision.

(SAVE) (S✆) (✕) (🏋) (💻) (🐾)

(AAA) ◆◆ **Travelodge of Vandalia** M ❀
(618) 283-2363. **$37-$59, 5 days notice.** 1500 N 6th St. Just s of jct I-70 and US 51, exit 63. Ext corridors. **Pets:** Dogs only. $3 daily fee/pet. No service, supervision, crate.

(SAVE) (S✆) (✕) (🏋) (💻) (🐾) (✕)

WASHINGTON

◆◆ **Super 8 Motel** M ❀
(309) 444-8881. **$31-$54, 7 days notice.** 1884 Washington Rd. On Business SR 24, 1.5 mi w. Int corridors. **Pets:** Medium. $10 one-time fee/room. Designated rooms, no service, supervision, crate.

(ASK) (S✆) (✕) (🔊) (🏋)

WATSEKA

(AAA) ◆ **Carousel Inn Motel** M ❀
(815) 432-4966. **$33-$40.** 1120 E Walnut St. 1 mi e on US 24. Ext corridors. **Pets:** Medium. $20 deposit/room. No service, supervision, crate.

(SAVE) (S✆) (✕) (🏋)

(AAA) ◆◆ **Super 8 Motel** M ❀
(815) 432-6000. **$52-$67, 7 days notice.** 710 W Walnut. On US 24. Int corridors. **Pets:** Other. $3 daily fee/room. Designated rooms, no service, supervision, crate.

(SAVE) (S✆) (✕) (🏋)

WENONA

◆◆ **Super 8 Motel** M ❀
(815) 853-4371. **Call for rates.** 5 Cavalry Dr. Just e from I-39, exit 35. Int corridors. **Pets:** Other. $50 deposit/pet. Supervision.

(ASK) (✕) (🏋)

WEST CITY

ⒶⒶⒶ ◆◆ Days Inn Benton Ⓜ 🐾
(618) 439-3183. **$45-$54.** 711 W Main St. Just e of I-57, exit 71. Int corridors. **Pets:** Medium. Designated rooms, supervision.
Ⓢⓐⓥⓔ Ⓢ🐾 ☒ ☗ 🔲 📺 🍴

◆◆ Super 8 Motel of Benton/West City Ⓜ 🐾
(618) 438-8205. **Call for rates.** 711 1/2 W Main. Just e from jct I-57 and SR 14, exit 71. Int corridors. **Pets:** Medium. Designated rooms, supervision.
ⒶⓈⓀ ☒ 🐾 ☗

AUBURN

◆◆◆ Holiday Inn Express  ✿
(219) 925-1900. **Call for rates.** 404 Touring Dr. Off SR 8, just e of I-69, exit 129. Int corridors. **Pets:** Designated rooms, no service, supervision, crate.

BLOOMINGTON

◆◆ Bloomington Super 8 M
(812) 323-8000. **$52-$67, 3 days notice.** 1000 W SR 46 bypass. 0.5 mi e of jct US 37 and SR 45/46 bypass. Int corridors. **Pets:** Designated rooms, supervision.

◆◆◆ Hampton Inn M ✿
(812) 334-2100. **$69-$87.** 2100 N Walnut St. 1 mi e of jct SR 37 on SR 45 and 46 bypass, just s on College Ave/ Walnut St.. Int corridors. **Pets:** Small, other. Supervision.

◆◆ Travelodge M ✿
(812) 339-6191. **$55-$95.** 2615 E 3rd St. Jct E 3rd St and SR 46. Ext/int corridors. **Pets:** Small. $20 deposit/pet, $5 daily fee/pet, $5 one-time fee/pet. No service, supervision, crate.

BLUFFTON

◆ Budget Inn M ✿
(219) 824-0820. **$35-$45.** 1420 N Main St. SR 1 and 116. Ext corridors. **Pets:** Medium. $7 daily fee/pet, $7 one-time fee/pet. Designated rooms, supervision.

BRAZIL

◆◆ Howard Johnson Express M ✿
(812) 446-2345. **$55-$100, 7 days notice.** 935 W SR 42. Jct I-70 and SR 59, exit 23, just s to SR 42, then just e. Ext corridors. **Pets:** Other. $5 daily fee/pet. Supervision.

CLARKSVILLE

◆◆◆ Best Western Green Tree Inn M ✿
(812) 288-9281. **$59-$69.** 1425 Broadway. I-65, exit 4, just w. Ext corridors. **Pets:** Medium, dogs only. Supervision.

CLOVERDALE

◆◆◆ Holiday Inn Express M ✿
(765) 795-5050. **$69-$99.** 1017 N Main St. I-70, exit 41. Int corridors. **Pets:** Other. $25 deposit/room. No service, supervision, crate.

COLUMBUS

◆◆◆ Holiday Inn Columbus-Conference Center MI
(812) 372-1541. **$79-$99.** 2480 Jonathan Moore Pike. I-65, exit 68, just e on SR 46. Ext/int corridors. **Pets:** Supervision.

CRAWFORDSVILLE

◆◆◆ Holiday Inn MI ✿
(765) 362-8700. **$81.** 2500 N Lafayette Rd. On US 231, 0.3 mi s of jct I-74, exit 34. Ext corridors. **Pets:** Small. Supervision.

DALE

◆◆◆ Baymont Inn & Suites M ✿
(812) 937-7000. **$69-$99.** 20857 N US 231. Jct I-64 and US 231, just s. Int corridors. **Pets:** Small, other. $20 deposit/room. Designated rooms, no service, supervision, crate.

DECATUR

🚗 ◆◆ Days Inn Ⓜ 🐾
(219) 728-2196. **$49-$60.** 1033 N 13th St. On US 27 and 33, 0.5 mi n of jct US 224. Ext/int corridors. **Pets:** Dogs only. $5 daily fee/pet. Supervision.

〔SAVE〕 Ⓢ ✖ 🖥 🖵

ELKHART

🚗 ◆ Diplomat Motel Ⓜ
(219) 264-4118. **$34-$45, 7 days notice.** 3300 Cassopolis Rd. I-80/90, exit 92. Ext corridors. **Pets:** Small. No service, supervision, crate.

〔SAVE〕 ✖ 🖥

◆ Econo Lodge Ⓜ 🐾
(219) 262-0540. **$37-$69, 5 days notice.** 3440 Cassopolis St. I-80/90, exit 92, 0.3 mi n. Ext corridors. **Pets:** Medium. $10 deposit/room. Supervision.

〔ASK〕 Ⓢ ✖ 🖵

◆◆ The Fairway Inn Ⓜ 🐾
(219) 266-1940. **Call for rates.** 115 N Pointe Blvd. I-80/90, exit 92, just n. Int corridors. **Pets:** Other. No service, supervision, crate.

〔ASK〕 ✖ 🖥 🖵

◆◆ Ramada Inn Ⓜ
(219) 262-1581. **Call for rates.** 3011 Belvedere Rd. I-80/90, exit 92, 0.3 mi s. Int corridors. **Pets:** Small. Supervision.

〔ASK〕 ✖ 🖥 🖵 🍴 🕿 ✖

🚗 ◆◆ Red Roof Inn-Elkhart Ⓜ 🐾
(219) 262-3691. **$51-$73.** 2902 Cassopolis St. I-80/90, exit 92, 0.5 mi s. Ext corridors. **Pets:** Other. No service, supervision, crate.

〔SAVE〕 ✖ 🗊 🖧 🖥 〔CTV〕

◆ Super 8 Motel-Elkhart Ⓜ 🐾
(219) 264-4457. **$54-$68.** 345 Windsor Ave. I-80/90, exit 92, just s. Int corridors. **Pets:** Medium, other. $5 daily fee/ room. Supervision.

〔ASK〕 Ⓢ ✖ 🖵

🚗 ◆◆ Turnpike Motel Ⓜ 🐾
(219) 264-1108. **$34-$46, 7 days notice.** 3500 Cassopolis St. I-80/90, exit 92, 0.3 mi n. Ext corridors. **Pets:** Small, other. $3 daily fee/pet, $3 one-time fee/pet. Designated rooms, no service, supervision, crate.

〔SAVE〕 Ⓢ ✖ 🖥 🖵

EVANSVILLE

◆◆◆ Comfort Inn Ⓜ 🐾
(812) 477-2211. **$65-$80.** 5006 Morgan Ave. SR 62 E (Morgan Ave), 1.5 mi w of jct I-164 and SR 62, exit 9. Int corridors. **Pets:** Small, other. Supervision.

〔ASK〕 Ⓢ ✖ 🗊 🖥 🖵 🕿

🚗 ◆◆◆ Days Inn-East Ⓜ 🐾
(812) 473-7944. **$45-$88.** 4819 Tecumseh Ln. Off Green River Rd at jct SR 66, (Lloyd Expwy), just s. Int corridors. **Pets:** Medium. $5 one-time fee/pet. No service, supervision, crate.

〔SAVE〕 Ⓢ ✖ 🖧 🖨 🕿

◆◆◆ Drury Inn & Suites Evansville East Ⓜ 🐾
(812) 471-3400. **$59-$81.** 100 Cross Pointe Blvd. Jct I-164 and SR 66 (Lloyd Expwy), exit 7B, 0.5 mi w. Int corridors. **Pets:** Small. Supervision.

✖ 🖧 🗊 🖨 🖥 🖵 🕿

◆◆◆ Drury Inn-Evansville North Ⓜ 🐾
(812) 423-5818. **$59-$81.** 3901 US 41 N. On US 41, 2.5 mi n of jct SR 62 and 66, (Lloyd Expwy), 3.3 mi sw of Regional Airport entrance. Int corridors. **Pets:** Other. No service, supervision, crate.

✖ 🖥 🖵 🕿

◆◆◆ Lees Inn Ⓜ 🐾
(812) 477-6663. **$69-$169.** 5538 E Indiana St. On SR 66 (Lloyd Expwy), 1.5 mi w of jct I-164, exit 7B; adjoining Village Commons Shops. Int corridors. **Pets:** Other. No service, supervision, crate.

Ⓢ ✖ 🗊 🖥 🖵

◆◆◆ Red Roof Inn Evansville Ⓜ 🐾
(812) 476-3600. **$50-$55.** 8331 E Walnut St. Jct I-164 and SR 66 (Lloyd Expwy), exit 76, 0.5 mi w to Eagle Crest Blvd, 0.3 mi se to Fuquay, just s to Walnut, then 0.4 mi e. Int corridors. **Pets:** Small. No service, supervision, crate.

〔ASK〕 ✖ 🖧 🗊 🖨 🖥 🕿

◆◆◆ Residence Inn by Marriott 🅐 🐾
(812) 471-7191. **$96-$96.** 8283 E Walnut St. Jct I-164 and SR 66 (Lloyd Expwy), exit 7B, 0.5 mi w to Eagle Crest Blvd, 0.3 mi se to Fuquay St, then 0.3 mi e. Int corridors. **Pets:** Other. $200 one-time fee/room. Supervision.

〔ASK〕 ✖ 🖧 🗊 🖨 🖥 🖵 🕿 ✖

◆◆ Super 8 Motel Ⓜ 🐾
(812) 476-4008. **$49-$63, 5 days notice.** 4600 Morgan Ave. SR 62 E (Morgan Ave), 1.7 mi w of jct I-164 and SR 62, exit 9. Int corridors. **Pets:** Designated rooms, supervision.

〔ASK〕 Ⓢ ✖ 🖥

FORT WAYNE

◆◆◆ Baymont Inn Ⓜ
(219) 489-2220. **$54-$109, 7 days notice.** 1005 W Washington Center Rd. Jct I-69, exit 111B, 0.5 mi e. Int corridors. **Pets:** Supervision.

〔ASK〕 Ⓢ ✖ 🗊 🖥 🖵

🚗 ◆◆ Best Inns of America Ⓜ 🐾
(219) 483-0091. **$41-$55, 7 days notice.** 3017 W Coliseum Blvd. I-69, exit 109A, just s, just w. Int corridors. **Pets:** Other. Supervision.

〔SAVE〕 Ⓢ ✖ 🖥

🚗 ◆ Days Inn East Downtown Ⓜ 🐾
(219) 424-1980. **$40-$90.** 3730 E Washington Blvd. US 24, at jct Business Rt 930. Ext corridors. **Pets:** Medium. $5 daily fee/pet. Supervision.

〔SAVE〕 Ⓢ ✖ 🖥 🍴 🕿

◆◆ Econo Lodge Ⓜ 🐾
(219) 484-6262. **$45-$69.** 2908 Goshen Rd. I-69, exit 109A, 0.5 mi s of jct US 30 and 33. Int corridors. **Pets:** $25 deposit/room. No service, supervision, crate.

〔ASK〕 Ⓢ ✖ 🖥 🕿

◆◆◆ **Fort Wayne Marriott** 🅷
(219) 484-0411. **$130-$140.** 305 E Washington Center Rd. Jct I-69, exit 112A (Coldwater Rd). Int corridors. **Pets:** Medium. Supervision.
(ASK) (×) 🔒 💻 🍴 🛄 (×)

◆◆◆ **Hampton Inn & Suites** 🎗
(219) 489-0908. **$99.** 5702 Challenger Pkwy. I-69, exit 111B, off Washington Center Rd. Int corridors. **Pets:** Supervision.
(ASK) 🛄 (×) 🔧 🐾 🖌 🔒 💻 🛄

◆◆◆ **Lees Inn** 🎗
(219) 489-8888. **$69-$160.** 5707 Challenger Pkwy. I-69, exit 111B. Int corridors. **Pets:** No service, supervision, crate.
🛄 (×) 🔒 💻

🎗 ◆◆ **Red Roof Inn-Fort Wayne** 🎗
(219) 484-8641. **$47-$62.** 2920 Goshen Rd. I-69, exit 109A, at jct US 30 bypass. Ext corridors. **Pets:** Medium. Supervision.
(SAVE) (×) 🖌

◆◆◆ **Residence Inn by Marriott** 🅰 🐾
(219) 484-4700. **Call for rates.** 4919 Lima Rd. I-69, exit 111A, just s. Ext corridors. **Pets:** $100 one-time fee/room. No service, supervision, crate.
(×) 🔒 💻 🛄 (×)

FRANKFORT

◆◆◆ **Holiday Inn Express** 🎗
(765) 659-4400. **$61-$92, 5 days notice.** 592 S Co Rd 200 W. I-65, exit 158, 6.1 mi e or from jct US 421/SR 38/SR 39, 1.8 mi w. Int corridors. **Pets:** Very small. No service, supervision, crate.
(ASK) 🛄 (×) 🐾 🖌 🔒 💻 🛄

FRENCH LICK

◆◆ **The Pines at Patoka Lake Village** 🅲 🐾
(812) 936-9854. **$79-$89.** 7900 W CR 1025S. 11 mi s on SR 145, 0.5 mi e on Lake Village Dr. Ext corridors. **Pets:** No service, supervision, crate.
🔒 💻 (×) (TV) 🅩

GOSHEN

🎗 ◆◆ **Best Western Inn** 🎗 🐾
(219) 533-0408. **$56-$64.** 900 Lincolnway E. 1 mi se on US 33. Ext corridors. **Pets:** Designated rooms, no service, supervision, crate.
(SAVE) 🛄 (×)

GREENCASTLE

🎗 ◆ **College Inn** 🎗
(765) 653-4167. **$28-$48.** 315 Bloomington St. US 231, 8 mi n of jct I-70, exit 41. Ext corridors. **Pets:** Medium. Supervision.
(SAVE) 🛄 (×) 🔒

GREENSBURG

🎗 ◆◆◆ **Best Western Pines Inn** 🎗 🐾
(812) 663-6055. **$64-$95.** 2317 N SR 3. I-74, exit 134A. Int corridors. **Pets:** Medium, other. $5 daily fee/pet. Supervision.
(SAVE) 🛄 (×) 🐾 🔒 💻 🛄

◆◆ **Lees Inn** 🎗
(812) 663-9998. **$59-$160.** 2211 N SR 3. I-74, exit 134A. Int corridors. **Pets:** Designated rooms, supervision.
🛄 (×) 🐾 🔒 💻

HAMMOND

◆◆ **Holiday Inn Chicago Southeast/Hammond** 🎗 🐾
(219) 844-2140. **$96.** 3830 179th St. I-80/94, exit Cline Ave S, just s. Int corridors. **Pets:** Small, other. $50 deposit/room. No service, supervision, crate.
(ASK) 🛄 (×) 🐾 💻 🍴 🛄

◆◆◆ **Residence Inn by Marriott** 🅰
(219) 844-8440. **$109.** 7740 Corinne. I-80/94, Kennedy Ave S exit. Int corridors. **Pets:** Supervision.
🛄 (×) 🔧 🐾 🖌 🔒 💻 🛄 (×)

HOBART

◆◆◆ **Comfort Inn** 🎗
(219) 947-7677. **$80-$90.** 1915 S Mississippi St. I-65, exit 255 (61st St), then just e. Int corridors. **Pets:** Small. Supervision.
(ASK) 🛄 (×) 🕮 🐾 🖌 💻 🛄

HOWE

🎗 ◆◆ **Super 8 Motel** 🎗 🐾
(219) 562-2828. **$60-$72, 20 days notice.** 7333 N SR 9. 0.5 mi s of jct I-80 and 90, exit 121. Int corridors. **Pets:** Other. No service, supervision, crate.
(SAVE) 🛄 (×) 🔧 🐾 🖌 🔒 (TV)

INDIANAPOLIS METROPOLITAN AREA

ANDERSON

🎗 ◆◆ **Best Inns** 🎗
(765) 644-2000. **$47-$57.** 5706 Scatterfield Rd. I-69, exit 26, on SR 9. Int corridors. **Pets:** Designated rooms, no service, supervision, crate.
(SAVE) 🛄 (×) 🐾

◆◆ **Comfort Inn-Anderson** 🎗
(765) 644-4422. **$45-$62, 7 days notice.** 2205 E 59th St. I-69, exit 26 on SR 109. Int corridors. **Pets:** Small. No service, supervision, crate.
(ASK) 🛄 (×) 🐾 🔒 🛄

◆◆◆ **Lees Inn** 🎗
(765) 649-2500. **$59-$159.** 2114 E 59th St. I-69, exit 26, on SR 109. Int corridors. **Pets:** Supervision.
🛄 (×) 💻

CHESTERFIELD

◆◆ Super 8 Motel 🅼 🐾
(765) 378-0888. **$43-$56.** I-69, exit 34. Ext/int corridors. **Pets:** Other. $25 deposit/room. No service, supervision, crate.

(A$K) (S🔥) (✕)

EDINBURGH

🆎 ◆◆ Best Western Horizon Inn 🅼 🐾
(812) 526-9883. **$39-$135, 3 days notice.** 11780 N US Hwy 31. US 31, n of jct I-65, exit 76B. Int corridors. **Pets:** Medium, other. $10 deposit/room, $7 daily fee/room, $7 one-time fee/room. No service, supervision, crate.

(SAVE) (S🔥) (✕) (🖼)

FISHERS

◆◆◆ Frederick-Talbott Inn 🅱🅱 🐾
(317) 578-3600. **$99-$199, 7 days notice.** 13805 Allisonville Rd. From I-465 and Allisonville Rd, exit 35, 6.2 mi n; from I-69, exit 5, 1.5 mi w on 116th St to Allisonville Rd, 2 mi n. Int corridors. **Pets:** Dogs only. No service, supervision, crate.

(A$K) (S🔥) (✕)

◆◆◆ Holiday Inn Express-Indianapolis Northeast 🅼 🐾
(317) 578-2000. **Call for rates.** 9790 North by Northeast Blvd. I-69, exit 3, just ne. Int corridors. **Pets:** Medium, other. No service, supervision, crate.

(A$K) (✕) (♿) (🐾) (📶) (📷) (📺) (🖼) (📺)

◆◆◆ Holiday Inn-Indianapolis Northeast 🅼🅸 🐾
(317) 578-9000. **$84-$96.** 9780 North by Northeast Blvd. I-69, exit 3, just ne. Int corridors. **Pets:** Small, other. No service, supervision, crate.

(A$K) (S🔥) (✕) (♿) (🐾) (📷) (📷) (🖼) (🍴) (🖼)

GREENFIELD

◆◆ Budget Motel 🅼 🐾
(317) 462-4493. **$34-$52.** 1310 W Main St. 1 mi w on US 40, 4 mi sw of I-70, exit 104. Ext corridors. **Pets:** Small. $10 daily fee/pet, $10 one-time fee/pet. No service, supervision, crate.

(A$K) (S🔥) (✕) (📷) (📷)

◆◆◆ Lees Inn 🅼
(317) 462-7112. **$59-$160.** 2270 N State St. Jct I-70 and SR 9, exit 104. Int corridors. **Pets:** Supervision.

(S🔥) (✕) (🐾) (📷) (📷)

GREENWOOD

◆◆ Comfort Inn Greenwood 🅼
(317) 887-1515. **Call for rates.** 110 Sheek Rd. I-65, exit 99. Ext corridors. **Pets:** No service, supervision, crate.

(✕) (📷) (📷) (🖼)

INDIANAPOLIS

🆎 ◆◆◆ AmeriSuites/Keystone Crossing 🅼
(317) 843-0064. **$99-$109.** 9104 Keystone Crossing. I-465, exit 33, 0.5 mi s on SR 431, just e on 86th St, then 0.5 mi n. Int corridors. **Pets:** Small. No service, supervision, crate.

(SAVE) (S🔥) (✕) (🐾) (📷) (📷) (📷) (🖼)

◆◆ Baymont Inn & Suites-Indianapolis Airport 🅼
(317) 244-8100. **$70-$75.** 2650 Executive Dr. I-465, exit 11, 0.3 mi e. Int corridors. **Pets:** Medium. Designated rooms, no service, supervision, crate.

(S🔥) (✕) (🐾) (📷) (📷)

◆◆◆ Baymont Inn & Suites Indy East 🅼
(317) 897-2300. **$60-$65, 6 days notice.** 2349 Post Dr. I-70 and Post Rd, exit 91. Int corridors. **Pets:** Supervision.

(S🔥) (✕) (♿) (🐾) (📷) (📷) (📷)

◆◆◆ Comfort Inn-Indianapolis Downtown 🅼 🐾
(317) 631-9000. **$98-$108.** 530 S Capitol Ave. Just s of South St; across from RCA Dome. Int corridors. **Pets:** Other. No service, supervision, crate.

(A$K) (S🔥) (✕) (♿) (🐾) (📷) (🖼)

◆◆◆ Comfort Inn-North 🅼
(317) 872-3100. **$45-$74, 7 days notice.** 3880 W 92nd St. I-465, exit 27, just s. Int corridors. **Pets:** Designated rooms, supervision.

(A$K) (S🔥) (✕) (📷) (📷) (🖼)

◆◆◆ Days Inn & Suites Castleton 🅼
(317) 841-9700. **Call for rates.** 8275 Craig St. I-69, exit 1, 0.5 mi w to Craig St, just n. Int corridors. **Pets:** No service, supervision, crate.

(✕) (🐾) (📷) (📷)

◆◆◆ Drury Inn 🅼
(317) 876-9777. **$58-$80.** 9320 N Michigan Rd. I-465, exit 27, just s. Int corridors. **Pets:** Medium. No service, supervision, crate.

(✕) (🐾) (📷) (📷) (🖼)

🆎 ◆◆ Econo Lodge Downtown 🅼
(317) 634-6100. **$49-$170, 3 days notice.** 1530 N Meridian St. On US 31 (Meridian St) between 15th and 16th sts. Int corridors. **Pets:** Small. Supervision.

(SAVE) (S🔥) (✕) (🖼) (📺)

◆◆◆ Four Points by Sheraton-Indianapolis East 🅼🅸 🐾
(317) 897-4000. **$79-$109, 3 days notice.** 7701 E 42nd St. I-465, exit 42 (Pendleton Pike). Int corridors. **Pets:** Supervision.

(A$K) (S🔥) (✕) (📷) (📷) (📷) (🍴) (🖼)

◆◆◆ Hampton Inn-Northwest 🅼 🐾
(317) 290-1212. **$77-$92.** 7220 Woodland Dr. I-465, exit 21. Int corridors. **Pets:** Large. Supervision.

(A$K) (S🔥) (✕) (🐾) (📷) (🖼)

🆎 ◆◆◆ Holiday Inn East 🅷
(317) 359-5341. **$89-$89.** 6990 E 21st St. I-70 and Shadeland Ave, exit 89, 0.5 mi w of jct I-465. Int corridors. **Pets:** Medium. Supervision.

(SAVE) (S🔥) (✕) (🐾) (📷) (🍴) (🖼)

◆◆◆ Holiday Inn-Southeast 🅼🅸
(317) 783-7751. **$109.** 5120 Victory Dr. I-465 and I-74, exit 52 (Emerson Ave). Int corridors. **Pets:** Medium. Supervision.

(A$K) (S🔥) (✕) (📷) (📷) (🍴) (🖼)

◆◆◆ **Homewood Suites-At The Crossing** Ⓜ
(317) 253-1919. **Call for rates.** 2501 E 86th St. I-465, exit 33, 0.5 mi s on SR 431, then 0.3 mi w. Ext/int corridors. **Pets:** No service, supervision, crate.

⊠ 🚭 🅱 💻 🕿 ⊠

◆◆ **Howard Johnson Express Inn & Suites** Ⓜ
(317) 841-8585. **$69-$77.** 7202 E 82nd St. I-69, exit 1, 0.3 mi e to Clear Vista, just n, then just w on Clear Vista Ln. Ext corridors. **Pets:** Supervision.

(ASK) 🚭 ⊠ 🖊 🅱 💻 🕿

ⒶⒶⒶ ◆◆◆◆ **Indianapolis Marriott** 🏨 ✿
(317) 352-1231. **$89-$139.** 7202 E 21st St. I-70, exit 89, 0.3 mi se, 0.5 mi w of jct I-465. Int corridors. **Pets:** Other. Supervision.

🚭 ⊠ 🖊 🅱 💻 🍴 🕿

◆◆◆ **La Quinta Inn-Airport** Ⓜ ✿
(317) 247-4281. **$59-$79.** 5316 W Southern Ave. I-465, exit 11A, 0.5 mi e on Airport Expwy to Lynhurst Dr exit. Int corridors. **Pets:** Small, other. Designated rooms, no service, supervision, crate.

(ASK) ⊠ 🖊 💻 🕿

◆◆◆ **La Quinta Inn-East** Ⓜ ✿
(317) 359-1021. **$75-$95.** 7304 E 21st St. I-70 and Shadeland Ave, exit 89, just s to 21st St, just e. Int corridors. **Pets:** Medium, other. Supervision.

(ASK) ⊠ 🅱 💻 🕿

◆◆ **Lees Inn** Ⓜ
(317) 297-8880. **$69-$209.** 5011 N Lafayette Rd. I-65, exit 121 (Lafayette Rd), 0.3 mi n. Int corridors. **Pets:** No service, supervision, crate.

🚭 ⊠ 💻

ⒶⒶⒶ ◆◆◆ **MainStay Suites-Indianapolis** Ⓜ ✿
(317) 334-7829. **$75-$100.** 8520 Northwest Blvd. I-465, exit 23 (W 86th), just e. Int corridors. **Pets:** Medium. $10 daily fee/room. Supervision.

(SAVE) 🚭 ⊠ ♿ 🖊 ⒸⒻ 🅱 💻 🕿

ⒶⒶⒶ ◆◆◆◆ **Omni Indianapolis North Hotel** 🏨
(317) 849-6668. **$175-$195.** 8181 N Shadeland Ave. I-69, exit 1, just e. Int corridors. **Pets:** Small. Supervision.

(SAVE) 🚭 ⊠ 🖊 ⒸⒻ 🅱 💻 🍴 🕿

ⒶⒶⒶ ◆◆◆◆ **Omni Severin Hotel** 🏨
(317) 634-6664. **$119-$249.** 40 W Jackson Pl. Opposite Union Station. Int corridors. **Pets:** Designated rooms, supervision.

(SAVE) 🚭 ⊠ 🖊 ⒸⒻ 🅱 💻 🍴 🕿

ⒶⒶⒶ ◆◆ **Pickwick Farms Airport** Ⓐ ✿
(317) 240-3567. **$78-$85, 3 days notice.** 25 Beachway Dr. Ne of I-465, exit 13A. Ext corridors. **Pets:** Other. $100 deposit/pet, $10 daily fee/pet, $50 one-time fee/pet. Supervision.

(SAVE) 🚭 ⊠ 🅱 💻 🕿

ⒶⒶⒶ ◆◆ **Pickwick Farms Short-Term Furnished Apartments** Ⓐ
(317) 872-6506. **$35-$85, 3 days notice.** 9300 N Ditch Rd. I-465, exit 31, just s to 96th St, 1.5 mi w to N Ditch Rd, just s. Ext corridors. **Pets:** No service, supervision, crate.

(SAVE) 🅱 💻 🕿 ⊠

ⒶⒶⒶ ◆◆◆ **Quality Inn & Suites At The Pyramids** Ⓜ ✿
(317) 875-7676. **$49-$250.** 9090 Wesleyan Rd. I-465, exit 27, just s to DePauw Blvd, just e, then just s. Int corridors. **Pets:** Medium, other. Supervision.

(SAVE) 🚭 ⊠ 🅱 💻 🕿

◆◆ **Quality Inn I-70 East** Ⓜ ✿
(317) 897-2000. **$49-$94.** 2141 N Post Rd. I-70 and Post Rd, exit 91, just s. Int corridors. **Pets:** Medium. $5 daily fee/pet, $20 one-time fee/pet. Designated rooms, no service, supervision, crate.

(ASK) 🚭 ⊠ 🅱 💻 🍴 🕿 ⊠

ⒶⒶⒶ ◆◆◆ **Quality Inn South** Ⓜ
(317) 787-8341. **$69-$150.** 520 E Thompson Rd. I-465 and 74, exit 2B, just s. Ext/int corridors. **Pets:** Large. Supervision.

(SAVE) 🚭 ⊠ 💻 🍴 🕿

ⒶⒶⒶ ◆◆ **Red Roof Inn-South** Ⓜ ✿
(317) 788-9551. **$40-$56.** 5221 Victory Dr. At jct I-465 and I-74, exit 52 (Emerson Ave). Ext corridors. **Pets:** No service, supervision, crate.

(SAVE) ⊠ 🖊 ⒸⒻ ⒸⓉⓋ

◆◆ **Red Roof Inn-Southside** Ⓜ ✿
(317) 788-0811. **Call for rates.** 450 Bixler Rd. I-465 and 74, exit 2B. Int corridors. **Pets:** Medium. $5 daily fee/pet, $5 one-time fee/pet. No service, supervision, crate.

(ASK) ⊠ 🕿

ⒶⒶⒶ ◆◆ **Red Roof Inn-Speedway** Ⓜ ✿
(317) 293-6881. **$45-$67.** 6415 Debonair Ln. Just se of jct US 136, I-74 and I-465, exit 16A. Ext corridors. **Pets:** Other. Supervision.

(SAVE) ⊠ 🖊 🅱

◆◆◆ **Residence Inn by Marriott** Ⓐ
(317) 872-0462. **Call for rates.** 3553 Founders Rd. I-465, exit 27, 1 mi s. Ext corridors. **Pets:** No service, supervision, crate.

(ASK) ⊠ 🖊 🅱 💻 🕿 ⊠

◆◆◆ **Residence Inn by Marriott/Indianapolis Airport** Ⓐ
(317) 244-1500. **$109-$179.** 5224 W Southern Ave. I-465, exit 11A, 0.5 mi e on Airport Expwy to Lynhurst Dr exit. Int corridors. **Pets:** Medium. No service, supervision, crate.

(ASK) ⊠ 🖊 ⒸⒻ 🅱 💻 🕿 ⊠

◆◆◆ **Residence Inn by Marriott Indianapolis/Fishers** Ⓐ
(317) 842-1111. **$119-$159.** 9765 Crosspoint Blvd. I-69, exit 3, just nw. Int corridors. **Pets:** Designated rooms, supervision.

(ASK) 🚭 ⊠ 🏠 🖊 ⒸⒻ 🅱 💻 🕿 ⊠

◆◆◆ **Residence Inn Indianapolis on the Canal** Ⓐ ✿
(317) 822-0840. **$149-$239.** 350 W New York St. At New York and Senate. Int corridors. **Pets:** Small. $5 daily fee/pet, $50 one-time fee/pet. No service, supervision, crate.

(ASK) 🚭 ⊠ ♿ 🖊 ⒸⒻ 🅱 💻 🕿

◆◆◆ **Sheraton Indianapolis North** 🏨 ✿
(317) 846-2700. **$89-$139.** 8787 Keystone Crossing. I-465, exit 33; connected to the Fashion Mall. Int corridors. **Pets:** Small. $75 deposit/room. No service, supervision, crate.

(ASK) 🚭 ⊠ 🖊 ⒸⒻ 💻 🍴 🕿

◆◆◆ Wellesley Inn & Suites 🅜 ❀
(317) 471-0700. **$89-$89.** 9370 Waldemar Rd. I-465, exit 27, just s to 92nd St, just w to Waldemar Rd, 0.3 mi n. Int corridors. **Pets:** Very small, other. Supervision.

◆◆◆ Wellesley Inn & Suites 🅜
(317) 241-0700. **$89-$99.** 5350 W Southern Ave. I-465, exit 11A, just e to Lynhurst, just s, then just w. Int corridors. **Pets:** No service, supervision, crate.

◆◆◆ The Westin Suites Indianapolis North 🅜🅘
(317) 574-6770. **$99-$159.** 8787 Keystone Crossing. I-465, exit 33, connected to the fashion mall. Int corridors. **Pets:** Very small. No service, supervision, crate.

LEBANON

◆◆◆ Comfort Inn 🅜
(765) 482-4800. **$66-$205.** 210 Sam Ralston Rd. SR 32 at jct I-65, exit 140. Int corridors. **Pets:** Designated rooms, no service, supervision, crate.

◆◆◆ Holiday Inn Central Indiana Conference Center 🅜🅘
(765) 482-0500. **$79-$79.** 505 S SR 39. On SR 39 at jct I-65, exit 139. Ext/int corridors. **Pets:** Small. Designated rooms, no service, supervision, crate.

◆◆ Lees Inn 🅜 ❀
(765) 482-9611. **$59-$139.** 1245 SR 32 W. I-65 at jct SR 32, exit 140. Int corridors. **Pets:** Other. No service, supervision, crate.

◆◆ Super 8 Motel 🅜
(765) 482-9999. **Call for rates.** 405 N Mount Zion Rd. I-65, exit 140. Int corridors. **Pets:** Designated rooms, no service, supervision, crate.

MARTINSVILLE

◆◆◆ Lees Inn 🅜
(765) 342-1842. **$59-$159.** 50 Bill's Blvd. Jct SR 37 and Ohio St, just w. Int corridors. **Pets:** No service, supervision, crate.

PLAINFIELD

◆◆◆ Lees Inn & Suites 🅜 ❀
(317) 837-9000. **$69-$199.** 6010 Gateway Dr. N of I-70, exit 66. Int corridors. **Pets:** Other. No service, supervision, crate.

SHELBYVILLE

◆◆◆ Lees Inn 🅜 ❀
(317) 392-2299. **$59-$139.** 111 Lee Blvd. Jct I-74 and SR 44, exit 116. Int corridors. **Pets:** Small, other. Designated rooms, no service, supervision, crate.

❀ **END METROPOLITAN AREA** ❀

JASPER

◆◆ Days Inn Jasper 🅜🅘
(812) 482-6000. **$65-$84.** 272 Brucke Strasse. On SR 162 and 164, 0.5 mi e of jct US 231. Ext/int corridors. **Pets:** Supervision.

KOKOMO

◆◆ Comfort Inn 🅜 ❀
(765) 452-5050. **$62-$82, 7 days notice.** 522 Essex Dr. On US 31, just n of jct US 35. Int corridors. **Pets:** Large. $15 deposit/room, $15 one-time fee/room. Designated rooms, no service, supervision, crate.

◆◆◆ Hampton Inn & Suites 🅜 ❀
(765) 455-2900. **$79-$99.** 2920 S Reed Rd. On US 31, 2 mi s of jct US 35. Int corridors. **Pets:** Large. Supervision.

◆◆ Super 8 Motel 🅜
(765) 455-3288. **$48-$65.** 5110 Clinton Dr. Off US 31, 2.8 mi s of jct US 35. Int corridors. **Pets:** Small. No service, supervision, crate.

LA PORTE

◆◆ Ramada Inn 🅜🅘 ❀
(219) 362-4585. **$69-$129, 30 days notice.** 444 Pine Lake Ave. 1.5 mi n on US 35. Int corridors. **Pets:** Medium. $25 one-time fee/room. Supervision.

LAFAYETTE

◆◆◆ Comfort Suites 🅜 ❀
(765) 447-0016. **$74-$150.** 31 Frontage Rd. I-65, exit 172 (SR 26), just e. Int corridors. **Pets:** Other. $10 one-time fee/room. Designated rooms, supervision.

◆◆◆ Holiday Inn Express 🅜 ❀
(765) 449-4808. **$75-$85, 30 days notice.** 201 Frontage Rd. I-65, exit 172. Int corridors. **Pets:** Other. No service, supervision, crate.

◆◆◆ Homewood Suites 🅜 ❀
(765) 448-9700. **$92-$152.** 3939 SR 26 E. I-65, exit 172 (SR 26), 0.8 mi w. Ext/int corridors. **Pets:** Large, other. $10 daily fee/pet. No service, supervision, crate.

◆ **Knights Inn** 🅼 ❀
(765) 447-5611. **$149.** 4110 SR 26 E. I-65, exit 172, 0.3 mi w. Ext corridors. **Pets:** Other. Supervision.

[ASK] [S🔥] [✕] [📱] [💻] [🖼]

🆔 ◆◆◆ **Radisson Inn-Lafayette** 🅼🅸 ❀
(765) 447-0575. **$99, 3 days notice.** 4343 SR 26 E. I-65, exit 172 (SR 26), 0.3 mi n. Int corridors. **Pets:** Small, other. $10 one-time fee/pet. Designated rooms, no service, supervision, crate.

[SAVE] [S🔥] [✕] [📱] [🖱] [📱] [💻] [🍴] [🖼]

🆔 ◆◆ **Ramada Inn-Lafayette** 🅼🅸
(765) 447-9460. **$70-$100, 7 days notice.** 4221 SR 26 E. SR 26, 0.3 mi w on I-65, exit 172. Int corridors. **Pets:** Designated rooms, supervision.

[SAVE] [S🔥] [✕] [📱] [📱] [💻] [🍴] [🖼]

🆔 ◆◆ **Red Roof Inn-Lafayette** 🅼
(765) 448-4671. **$48-$62.** 4201 SR 26 E. I-65, exit 72, 0.3 mi w. Ext corridors. **Pets:** Large. No service, supervision, crate.

[SAVE] [✕]

LOGANSPORT

◆◆◆ **Holiday Inn** 🅼🅸 ❀
(219) 753-6351. **$150, 3 days notice.** 3550 E Market St. 2.5 mi e on US 24. Int corridors. **Pets:** Medium. Supervision.

[ASK] [S🔥] [✕] [📱] [💻] [🍴] [🖼]

MARION

🆔 ◆◆◆ **Comfort Suites** 🅼 ❀
(765) 651-1006. **$89-$99.** 1345 N Baldwin Ave. On SR 9, 1.5 mi n of jct SR 18. Int corridors. **Pets:** Medium. $10 daily fee/room. Designated rooms, no service, supervision, crate.

[SAVE] [S🔥] [✕] [📱] [🖱] [📱] [💻] [🖼]

◆◆◆ **Holiday Inn-Marion** 🅼🅸 ❀
(765) 668-8801. **$69-$89, 30 days notice.** 501 E 4th St. On SR 18, at corner of 4th and Shunk sts. Int corridors. **Pets:** Other. $25 one-time fee/room. No service, supervision, crate.

[ASK] [S🔥] [✕] [📱] [💻] [🍴] [🖼]

MERRILLVILLE

🆔 ◆ **Knights Inn** 🅼 ❀
(219) 736-5100. **$39-$59, 3 days notice.** 8250 Louisiana St. 0.5 mi se of jct US 30 and I-65, exit 253A. Ext corridors. **Pets:** Large. Designated rooms, no service, supervision, crate.

[SAVE] [S🔥] [✕] [📱] [🖼] [CTV]

◆◆◆ **La Quinta Inn** 🅼
(219) 738-2870. **$65-$85** (no credit cards). 8210 Louisiana St. Off US 30, 0.3 mi se of jct I-65, exit 253A. Int corridors. **Pets:** Medium. Supervision.

[ASK] [✕] [📱] [💻] [🖼]

🆔 ◆ **Motel 6–1254** 🅼 ❀
(219) 738-2701. **$36-$52.** 8290 Louisiana St. 0.5 mi se of jct US and I-65, exit 253A. Int corridors. **Pets:** Small, other. Supervision.

[S🔥] [✕] [🖱] [🖼]

🆔 ◆◆◆ **Radisson Hotel at Star Plaza** 🅷
(219) 769-6311. **$99-$159.** 800 E 81st Ave. I-65, exit 253B. Int corridors. **Pets:** Medium. Supervision.

[SAVE] [S🔥] [✕] [🖱] [📱] [💻] [🍴] [🖼] [✕]

🆔 ◆◆ **Red Roof Inn-Merrillville** 🅼
(219) 738-2430. **$51-$71.** 8290 Georgia St. US 30, 0.3 mi sw of jct I-65, exit 253B. Ext corridors. **Pets:** Medium. Supervision.

[SAVE] [✕] [🖱] [🖱]

◆◆◆ **Residence Inn by Marriott** 🅰
(219) 791-9000. **$119.** 8018 Delaware Place. Just off US 30 at I-65, exit 253B. Int corridors. **Pets:** Small. No service, supervision, crate.

[ASK] [✕] [🖱] [🖱] [🖱] [📱] [💻] [🖼] [✕]

◆◆ **Super 8 Motel** 🅼
(219) 736-8383. **$43-$58.** 8300 Louisiana St. Off US 30, 0.5 mi se of jct I-65, exit 253A. Int corridors. **Pets:** No service, supervision, crate.

[ASK] [S🔥] [✕] [🖱] [🖱] [📱]

MICHIGAN CITY

◆ **Knights Inn** 🅼 ❀
(219) 874-9500. **$55-$99.** 201 W Kieffer Rd. I-94, exit 34B, 0.3 mi n on US 421. Ext corridors. **Pets:** $50 deposit/room, $10 one-time fee/room. Designated rooms, supervision.

[ASK] [S🔥] [✕] [📱] [💻] [🖼]

🆔 ◆◆ **Red Roof Inn-Michigan City** 🅼
(219) 874-5251. **$57-$78.** 110 W Kieffer Rd. I-94, exit 34B, 0.3 mi n on US 421. Ext corridors. **Pets:** No service, supervision, crate.

[SAVE] [✕] [🖱] [📱] [CTV]

MISHAWAKA

◆◆ **Super 8 Motel** 🅼
(219) 247-0888. **Call for rates.** 535 W University Dr. I-80/90, exit 83 to SR 23, 1.6 mi to Main St, just s on Main St to University Dr, just w. Int corridors. **Pets:** Small. Designated rooms, no service, supervision, crate.

[✕]

MONTGOMERY

◆◆ **Red Roof Inn** 🅼
(812) 486-2600. **$45-$53, 7 days notice.** Box 60, CR 650 E. From jct US 50 & First St, 0.9 mi n to CR 650 e then 0.3 mi e. Int corridors. **Pets:** Small. Supervision.

[ASK] [S🔥] [✕] [🖱] [📱] [✕]

MOUNT VERNON

◆◆◆ **Four Seasons Motel** 🅼
(812) 838-4821. **$50-$89.** 2400 W 4th St. SR 62, 1.8 mi w of jct SR 69 N. Ext corridors. **Pets:** Medium. Supervision.

[ASK] [S🔥] [✕] [📱] [💻] [🖼]

◆◆ **Super 8 Motel** 🅼
(812) 838-8888. **$44-$55.** 6225 Hwy 69 S. On SR 69 bypass just n from SR 62. Int corridors. **Pets:** Large. Supervision.

[ASK] [S🔥] [✕] [📱] [🖼]

MUNCIE

◆◆ Comfort Inn M
(765) 282-6666. **$54-$74, 7 days notice.** 4011 W Bethel Ave. I-69, exit 41, 6.3 mi e on SR 332 (W McGalliard), just n. Int corridors. **Pets:** Medium. No service, supervision, crate.
ASK S× X 🔒 🍽

◆◆ Lees Inn M ❀
(765) 282-7557. **$69-$179.** 3302 Everbrook Ln. I-69, exit 41, 6 mi e on SR 332 (W McGalliard). Int corridors. **Pets:** Other. No service, supervision, crate.
S× X ⌆ 🔒 🍽

◆◆ Muncie Days Inn M
(765) 288-2311. **$53-$63, 7 days notice.** 3509 N Everbrook Ln. I-69, exit 41, 6.3 mi e on SR 332, just n. Int corridors. **Pets:** Medium. No service, supervision, crate.
ASK S× X 🔒

⊕ ◆◆◆ Radisson Hotel Roberts H ❀
(765) 741-7777. **$65-$109, 30 days notice.** 420 S High St. Corner of High St. Int corridors. **Pets:** Small. $25 deposit/room. No service, supervision, crate.
SAVE S× X 🔒 🍽 🍴 🍽

◆ Super 8 Motel M ❀
(765) 286-4333. **$46-$55.** 3601 W Fox Ridge Ln. I-69, exit 41, 6 mi e on SR 332. Int corridors. **Pets:** $25 deposit/pet. Supervision.
ASK S× X 🔒

NEW ALBANY

◆◆◆ Holiday Inn Express Louisville Northwest M ❀
(812) 945-2771. **$99.** 411 W Spring St. I-64, exit 123. Int corridors. **Pets:** No service, supervision, crate.
ASK S× X ⌆ 🔒 🍽 🍽

NEW CASTLE

⊕ ◆◆ Best Western Raintree Inn M ❀
(765) 521-0100. **$56-$69.** 2836 S SR 3. SR 3, 2.5 mi n of jct I-70, exit 123. Ext/int corridors. **Pets:** Small, other. $20 deposit/pet. Supervision.
S× X ⌆ 🔒 🍽 🍴 🍽

NEW HAVEN

◆ Hometown Inn M ❀
(219) 749-5058. **$37-$62.** 6910 US 30 E. 4 mi e on Business Rt 930. Ext corridors. **Pets:** Small. $25 deposit/room. No service, supervision, crate.
ASK S× X 🔒

PLYMOUTH

◆◆ Days Inn M
(219) 935-4276. **$39-$45, 3 days notice.** 2229 N Michigan St. SR 17, just s of jct US 30. Ext corridors. **Pets:** No service, supervision, crate.
ASK S× X

◆◆ Ramada Inn M
(219) 936-4013. **$73-$90.** 2550 N Michigan St. 0.5 mi n on SR 17 from jct US 30. Ext corridors. **Pets:** Small. Supervision.
ASK S× X 🍽 🍴 🍽

⊕ ◆◆ Super 8 Motel M ❀
(219) 936-8856. **$50-$130, 7 days notice.** 2160 N Oak Rd. Just off US 30. Int corridors. **Pets:** Small. No service, supervision, crate.
SAVE S× X 🍽

PORTAGE

◆◆ Comfort Inn M
(219) 763-7177. **$99-$99.** 2300 Willow Creek. At I-80/ 90 (Indiana Toll Rd), exit 23, 1.5 mi s of I-94, exit 19. Int corridors. **Pets:** Supervision.
ASK S× X

◆◆◆ Hampton Inn-Portage M ❀
(219) 764-1919. **$64-$99.** 6353 Melton Rd. I-94, exit 19, 0.3 mi s, just e on US 20. Int corridors. **Pets:** Supervision.
ASK S× X ⌆ ⌆ ⌆ 🔒 🍽 🍽

PORTLAND

⊕ ◆◆ Hoosier Inn M ❀
(219) 726-7113. **$38-$50.** 1620 Maridian St. 0.5 mi n on US 27. Ext corridors. **Pets:** Dogs only. $4 daily fee/pet. No service, supervision, crate.
SAVE S× X 🔒 🍽

RICHMOND

⊕ ◆◆ Best Western Imperial Motor Lodge M ❀
(765) 966-1505. **$36-$66.** 3020 E Main St. I-70, exit 156A, 2 mi w. Ext corridors. **Pets:** Medium, other. $5 daily fee/pet, $5 one-time fee/pet. Supervision.
SAVE X 🔒 🍽

⊕ ◆ Days Inn M ❀
(765) 966-7591. **$45-$75, 7 days notice.** 540 W Eaton Pike. Jct I-70, exit 156A. Ext corridors. **Pets:** Small. $5 daily fee/pet, $5 one-time fee/pet. No service, supervision, crate.
SAVE S× X 🍽

◆◆◆ Holiday Inn-Richmond H ❀
(765) 966-7511. **$86-$150.** 5501 National Rd E. I-70, exit 156A, 0.3 mi w. Int corridors. **Pets:** Large. $10 daily fee/room. No service, supervision, crate.
ASK S× X ⌆ ⌆ ⌆ 🔒 🍽 🍴 🍽

⊕ ◆◆ Super 8 Motel-Richmond M
(765) 962-7576. **$48-$75.** 2525 Chester Blvd. I-70, exit 151A. Int corridors. **Pets:** Designated rooms, no service, supervision, crate.
SAVE S× X 🍽

ROCKVILLE

⊕ ◆◆◆ Billie Creek Village & Inn M ❀
(765) 569-3430. **$69-$79, 3 days notice.** Billie Creek Dr. 1.4 mi e on US 36. Int corridors. **Pets:** Other. Supervision.
SAVE X ⌆ 🔒 🍽

ROSELAND

⊕ ◆◆ Best Inns of America/South Bend M
(219) 277-7700. **$54-$61.** 425 Dixie Hwy N. I-80/90, exit 77, 0.8 mi n on US 933. Int corridors. **Pets:** Designated rooms, no service, supervision, crate.
SAVE S× X

ⓐ ◆◆ Days Inn-South Bend/Notre Dame Ⓜ
(219) 277-0510. **$59-$79.** 52757 US 31 N. I-80/90, exit 77, 1 mi n. Ext corridors. **Pets:** Medium. Supervision.
[SAVE] [⑥] [✕] [⌂]

◆◆ Holiday Inn-University Area Ⓜ ❀
(219) 272-6600. **$81-$99, 3 days notice.** On US 31 and 33, 0.8 mi n of I-90 and I-80, exit 77. Ext/int corridors. **Pets:** Other. $25 deposit/room. No service, supervision, crate.
[ASK] [⑥] [✕] [✎] [▣] [¶] [⌂] [✕]

SCOTTSBURG

ⓐ ◆◆◆ Best Western Scottsburg Inn Ⓜ
(812) 752-2212. **$60-$95, 30 days notice.** 1525 West McClain St. I-65, exit 29. Int corridors. **Pets:** Medium. Supervision.
[SAVE] [⑥] [✕] [✎] [▣] [¶] [⌂] [✕]

ⓐ ◆◆ Mariann Travel Inn Ⓜ
(812) 752-3396. **$39-$58.** SR 56. I-65, exit 29. Ext corridors. **Pets:** Medium. Supervision.
[SAVE] [⑥] [✕] [▣] [¶] [⌂] [✕]

SHIPSHEWANA

◆◆ Super 8 Ⓜ ❀
(219) 768-4004. **$60-$79.** 470 S Van Buren. 1 mi s on SR 5. Int corridors. **Pets:** $8 daily fee/pet. No service, supervision, crate.
[✕] [✎]

SOUTH BEND

◆◆◆ Residence Inn by Marriott Ⓐ
(219) 289-5555. **$99-$119.** 716 N Niles Ave. N Michigan Ave (US 33), just e on Northshore Ave, 0.4 mi s. Ext corridors. **Pets:** Supervision.
[ASK] [✕] [▣] [▣] [⌂] [✕]

TAYLORSVILLE

◆◆ Comfort Inn Ⓜ
(812) 526-9747. **$58-$109.** 10330 US 31. I-65, exit 76A, just s. Ext corridors. **Pets:** Supervision.
[ASK] [⑥] [✕] [▣] [▣] [⌂]

TELL CITY

◆◆◆ Ramada Limited Ⓜ
(812) 547-3234. **$59-$73.** 235 Orchard Hill Dr. Just off SR 66, 1.7 mi se of jct SR 37. Int corridors. **Pets:** Medium. Designated rooms, no service, supervision, crate.
[ASK] [⑥] [✕] [♿] [✎] [▣] [▣]

TERRE HAUTE

◆◆◆ Comfort Suites Ⓜ
(812) 235-1770. **$58-$75, 7 days notice.** 501 E Margaret Ave. Just ne from I-70, exit 7. Int corridors. **Pets:** Small. Designated rooms, supervision.
[ASK] [⑥] [✕] [♿] [✎] [▣] [▣] [⌂]

◆◆◆ Drury Inn Ⓜ ❀
(812) 238-1206. **$62-$78.** 3040 Hwy 41 S. US 41 and 150 at jct I-70, exit 7. Int corridors. **Pets:** Small, other. No service, supervision, crate.
[✕] [♿] [✎] [▣] [▣] [⌂]

ⓐ ◆◆◆ Holiday Inn Ⓜ ❀
(812) 232-6081. **$89-$89, 3 days notice.** 3300 US 41 S. Just s of jct I-70 and US 41/150, exit 7. Ext/int corridors. **Pets:** Other. Supervision.
[SAVE] [⑥] [✕] [✎] [▣] [▣] [¶] [⌂]

◆◆ Knights Inn Ⓜ
(812) 234-9931. **$53.** 401 E Margaret Dr. Just ne of US 41 and 150, from jct I-70, exit 7.. Ext corridors. **Pets:** No service, supervision, crate.
[ASK] [⑥] [✕] [▣] [▣] [⌂]

◆◆◆ Pear Tree Inn by Drury Ⓜ ❀
(812) 234-4268. **$55-$71.** 3050 US 41 S. US 41 and 150 at jct I-70, exit 7. Int corridors. **Pets:** Medium, other. No service, supervision, crate.
[✕] [✎]

◆◆ Super 8 Lodge Ⓜ ❀
(812) 232-4890. **$75-$90.** 3089 S 1st St. Just nw of US 41 and 150 from jct I-70, exit 7.. Int corridors. **Pets:** Medium, other. No service, supervision, crate.
[✕]

VINCENNES

ⓐ ◆◆◆ Holiday Inn Ⓜ
(812) 886-9900. **$49-$74.** 600 Wheatland Rd. US Hwy 50, 41 and 150, exit 6. Ext/int corridors. **Pets:** Medium. No service, supervision, crate.
[SAVE] [⑥] [✕] [▣] [▣] [¶] [⌂]

WARSAW

◆◆◆ Ramada Plaza Hotel of Warsaw Ⓜ
(219) 269-2323. **$82-$88, 7 days notice.** 2519 E Center St. At jct US 30 E. Int corridors. **Pets:** Designated rooms, supervision.
[ASK] [⑥] [✕] [▣] [▣] [¶] [⌂]

◆◆ Super 8 Motel Ⓜ ❀
(219) 268-2888. **Call for rates.** 3014 Frontage Rd. Off US 30. Int corridors. **Pets:** Other. Supervision.
[✕] [🛏] [✎] [⌂]

WASHINGTON

◆◆◆ Baymont Inn & Suites Ⓜ ❀
(812) 254-7000. **$54-$91.** 7 Cumberland Dr. Just ne jct US 50 and SR 57. Int corridors. **Pets:** Other. Supervision.
[ASK] [⑥] [✕] [✎] [▣] [▣] [⌂] [✕]

WEST LAFAYETTE

ⓐ ◆◆ Holiday Inn Ⓜ ❀
(765) 567-2131. **$58-$99.** 5600 SR 43 N. I-65, exit 178. Int corridors. **Pets:** Other. Supervision.
[SAVE] [✕] [▣] [▣] [¶] [⌂]

◆◆ Super 8 Motel-West Lafayette Ⓜ ❀
(765) 567-7100. **$56-$79.** 2030 Northgate Dr. I-65, exit 178, just n on SR 43. Int corridors. **Pets:** Small. $50 deposit/room. Designated rooms, no service, supervision, crate.
[ASK] [⑥] [✕] [🛏] [✎] [▣] [▣]

ADAIR

◆ Adair Budget Inn M ☼
(515) 742-5553. **$33-$50.** 100 S 5th St. I-80, exit 76. Ext corridors. **Pets:** $25 deposit/room. Designated rooms, no service, supervision, crate.
S X

◆◆ Super 8 Motel M ☼
(515) 742-5251. **$40-$60.** 111 S 5th St. N of I-80, exit 76. Int corridors. **Pets:** Very small. $20 deposit/room. Designated rooms, no service, supervision, crate.
ASK S X

ALBIA

◆ Indian Hills Inn MI ☼
(515) 932-7181. **$44-$66.** 100 Hwy 34 E. Just e of jct US 34 and SR 5. Ext corridors. **Pets:** Medium. $25 deposit/pet, $8 daily fee/pet. Designated rooms, no service, supervision, crate.
X ⚘ ⓘ ☎

AMANA

◆◆◆ Amana Holiday Inn MI ☼
(319) 668-1175. **$84-$90.** I-80, exit 225 and US 151; in Little Amana complex. Int corridors. **Pets:** No service, supervision, crate.
ASK S X ⚘ ⓘ ☎ ⓘ ☎ X

◆◆◆ Comfort Inn Amana Colonies M
(319) 668-2700. **$62-$100.** 2185 U Ave. Just n of jct I-80 and exit 225 (US 151). Int corridors. **Pets:** No service, supervision, crate.
SAVE X ⚘ ⓘ ☎

AMES

◆◆◆ Best Western Starlite Village MI ☼
(515) 232-9260. **$56-$76, 30 days notice.** 2601 E 13th St. 0.5 mi w of I-35, exit 113. Int corridors. **Pets:** Small, dogs only. No service, supervision, crate.
SAVE X ⚘ ⓘ ☎ ⓘ ☎

◆◆ Comfort Inn-Ames M ☼
(515) 232-0689. **$55-$85.** 1605 S Dayton Ave. Just nw of jct I-35 and US 30. Int corridors. **Pets:** Small, other. $5 daily fee/pet. Designated rooms, no service, supervision, crate.
ASK S X ⓘ ☎ ☎

◆◆◆ Holiday Inn-Gateway Center MI ☼
(515) 292-8600. **$95-$125.** 2100 Greenhills Dr. 3.5 mi w on US 30 from jct I-35. Int corridors. **Pets:** Designated rooms, no service, supervision, crate.
ASK S X ⚘ ⚘ ⚘ ⓘ ☎ ⓘ ☎ X

◆◆ Howard Johnson Express Inn M
(515) 232-8363. **$55-$68, 7 days notice.** 1709 S Duff. Just n of jct US 30 and exit 148 (Duff Ave). Ext corridors. **Pets:** Very small. Designated rooms, no service, supervision, crate.
SAVE S X ⓘ ☎ ☎

◆◆ University Inn M ☼
(515) 232-0280. **$55-$85, 3 days notice.** 229 S Duff Ave. 1 mi n of jct US 30 and Duff Ave. Int corridors. **Pets:** Medium. $20 one-time fee/room. Supervision.
SAVE S X ⓘ

ANKENY

◆◆ Best Western Starlite Village of Ankeny MI ☼
(515) 964-1717. **$55-$75.** 133 SE Delaware Ave. I-35, exit 92, just w. Int corridors. **Pets:** Designated rooms, supervision.
S X ⓘ ☎ ⓘ ☎

ARNOLDS PARK

◆◆ Fillenwarth Beach R
(712) 332-5646. **$96-$528** (no credit cards), 21 days notice. 87 Lake Shore Dr. West Lake Okoboji; just w of US 71. Ext corridors. **Pets:** No service, supervision, crate.
ⓘ ☎ ☎ X

ATLANTIC

◆◆ Econo Lodge **M** ❀
(712) 243-4067. **$50-$60.** 0.5 mi s of jct I-80 and US 71 (exit 60). Int corridors. **Pets:** Other. Designated rooms, supervision.

ASK S⊘ ✕ ⮑ ⌂ CTV

BETTENDORF

⊛ ◆◆ Econo Lodge **M**
(319) 355-6471. **$50-$65.** 2205 Kimberly Rd. In Bettendorf, IA; 0.3 mi w of I-74, exit 3, 0.5 mi n; from I-74, exit 2, 0.3 mi w and 0.8 mi s. Ext corridors. **Pets:** No service, supervision, crate.

SAVE S⊘ ✕ ⊟ ⮑ ⌂

◆◆◆ Holiday Inn-Bettendorf Quad Cities **M**
(319) 355-4761. **Call for rates.** 909 Middle Rd. In Bettendorf, IA; jct I-74 and US 67, exit 3, just w. Int corridors. **Pets:** No service, supervision, crate.

ASK ✕ ⛽ ⊟ ⮑ ⌖ ⌂

⊛ ◆◆◆ Jumer's Castle
    Lodge-Bettendorf **H** ❀
(319) 359-7141. **$78-$146, 30 days notice.** 900 Spruce Hills Dr. In Bettendorf, IA; just e of jct I-74, exit 2, 3 mi s of jct I-74 and 80. Int corridors. **Pets:** $25 deposit/room. Supervision.

SAVE S⊘ ✕ 🖊 ⊟ ⮑ ⌂ ✕

BURLINGTON

⊛ ◆◆◆ Best Western Pzazz Motor
    Inn **M** ❀
(319) 753-2223. **$57-$72.** 3001 Winegard Dr. Just n of jct US 61 and 34. Int corridors. **Pets:** Other. Supervision.

SAVE S⊘ ✕ 🖊 ⛽ ⊟ ⮑ ⌖ ⌂

CARROLL

◆◆ Nice Stay Inn **M**
(712) 792-9214. **$30-$43.** 1507 Radiant Rd. US 30, 0.3 mi w of jct US 30 and 71. Ext corridors. **Pets:** Supervision.

ASK S⊘ ✕ ⊟ ⮑

CEDAR FALLS

◆◆◆ Holiday Inn University Plaza **M**
(319) 277-2230. **Call for rates.** 5826 University Ave. 3 mi w of US 218. Ext/int corridors. **Pets:** Supervision.

✕ ⊟ ⮑ ⌖ ⌂

◆◆ Midwest Lodge **M**
(319) 277-1550. **Call for rates.** 4410 University Ave. 3 mi w of US 63. Int corridors. **Pets:** No service, supervision, crate.

ASK ✕ 🖊 ⊟ ⮑ ⌂

◆◆ University Inn **M** ❀
(319) 277-1412. **$36-$53.** 4711 University Ave. 2 mi w of US 63. Ext/int corridors. **Pets:** $35 deposit/pet. Supervision.

S⊘ ✕ ⊟ ⮑

CEDAR RAPIDS

◆◆ Best Inn **M** ❀
(319) 363-9999. **$56-$59, 5 days notice.** 3233 Southridge Dr SW. Just nw of jct I-380, exit 17 (33rd Ave SW). Int corridors. **Pets:** $10 one-time fee/room. Designated rooms, no service, supervision, crate.

ASK S⊘ ✕ ⌂ 🖊 ⊟ ⮑

⊛ ◆◆ Best Western Cooper's Mill Hotel &
    Restaurant **M** ❀
(319) 366-5323. **$59-$79.** 100 F Ave NW. Just w of I-380; northbound exit 19C, right at end of exit, make an immediate U-turn and go under I-380; southbound exit 20A, cross river, right on 1st St NW. Int corridors. **Pets:** Small, other. $50 deposit/room. Supervision.

S⊘ ✕ ⊟ ⌖ ⮑

⊛ ◆◆◆ Best Western Longbranch Hotel &
    Convention Center **M** ❀
(319) 377-6386. **$60-$90.** 90 Twixt Town Rd. US 151 business route, just ne of jct SR 100; from jct I-380, 2.8 mi e on SR 100 (Collins Rd), just ne on US 151 business route. Int corridors. **Pets:** Other. $5 daily fee/pet. No service, supervision, crate.

S⊘ ✕ ⮑ ⌖ ⌂ ✕

◆◆◆ Collins Plaza Hotel & Convention
    Center **H**
(319) 393-6600. **$109-$119.** 1200 Collins Rd NE. On SR 100, 1 mi e of jct I-380, exit 24 (Collins Rd). Int corridors. **Pets:** Small. Designated rooms, no service, supervision, crate.

ASK S⊘ ✕ 🖊 ⊟ ⮑ ⌖ ⌂

◆◆◆ Comfort Inn of Cedar Rapids
    North **M** ❀
(319) 393-8247. **$60-$85, 7 days notice.** 5055 Rockwell Dr. SR 100, 1.3 mi e of jct I-380, exit 24 (Collins Rd). Int corridors. **Pets:** Small. Designated rooms, no service, supervision, crate.

ASK S⊘ ✕ 🖊 ⊟ ⮑

◆◆ Comfort Inn-South **M**
(319) 363-7934. **$42-$64, 7 days notice.** 390 33rd Ave SW. Just w of jct I-380, exit 17 (33rd Ave SW). Int corridors. **Pets:** No service, supervision, crate.

ASK S⊘ ✕ ⊟ ⮑

◆◆◆ Days Inn of Cedar Rapids **M** ❀
(319) 365-4339. **$39-$58, 7 days notice.** 3245 Southgate Pl SW. Just w of jct I-380, exit 17 (33rd Ave SW). Int corridors. **Pets:** Other. $10 daily fee/room. Designated rooms, supervision.

ASK S⊘ ✕ 🖊 ⊟ ⮑

⊛ ◆◆ Exel Inn of Cedar Rapids **M**
(319) 366-2475. **$35-$60.** 616 33rd Ave SW. 0.3 mi w of jct I-380, exit 17 (33rd Ave SW). Int corridors. **Pets:** Small. Designated rooms, supervision.

S⊘ ✕ ⊟ ⮑

⊛ ◆◆ Red Roof Inn **M**
(319) 366-7523. **$36-$68.** 3325 Southgate Ct SW. Just sw of jct I-380, exit 17 (33rd Ave SW). Ext corridors. **Pets:** Medium. Supervision.

SAVE ✕ ⌂ 🖊

◆◆◆ Residence Inn 🅜 ❀
(319) 395-0111. **$84-$159.** 1900 Dodge Rd NE. Just e of jct I-380 and exit 24A (Collins Rd exit). Int corridors. **Pets:** Medium, other. $5 daily fee/room, $50 one-time fee/room. Supervision.

⊠ 🕭 📶 🐾 📶 🕒 🐾 ⊠

◆◆◆ Sheraton Four Points Hotel 🄷 ❀
(319) 366-8671. **$90-$100.** 525 33rd Ave SW. Just w of jct I-380, exit 17 (33rd Ave SW). Int corridors. **Pets:** $50 deposit/room. Supervision.

🄰🅂🄺 🕭 ⊠ 📶 🕒 🐾 🕕 🐾

◆◆ Super 8 Motel 🅜 ❀
(319) 363-1755. **Call for rates.** 400 33rd Ave SW. Just w of jct I-380 and exit 17. Int corridors. **Pets:** Small, dogs only. $10 daily fee/pet, $10 one-time fee/pet. Designated rooms, supervision.

⊠ 📶 🕒

CLEAR LAKE

◆◆ Best Western Holiday Lodge 🅜🄸 ❀
(515) 357-5253. **$56-$80.** 2023 US Hwy 18. 0.3 mi w of jct I-35 and US 18. Ext/int corridors. **Pets:** Other. No service, supervision, crate.

🄰🅂🄺 🕭 ⊠ 📶 🕒 🐾 🕒 🕕 🐾

🄰🄰🄰 ◆◆ Budget Inn Motel 🅜
(515) 357-8700. **$43-$54.** 1306 N 25th St. Just nw of jct I-35 and US 18. Int corridors. **Pets:** Small. Designated rooms, supervision.

🆂🄰🆅🄴 🕭 ⊠ 🐾 ⊠

◆ Lake Country Inn 🅜 ❀
(515) 357-2184. **$30-$40.** 518 Hwy 18 W. 2 mi w on Hwy 18 from jct I-35. Ext corridors. **Pets:** Other. No service, supervision, crate.

🄰🅂🄺 ⊠ 📶 🄲🅃🅅

CLINTON

🄰🄰🄰 ◆◆◆ Best Western-Frontier Motor Inn 🅜🄸
(319) 242-7112. **$54-$99.** 2300 Lincolnway. 3.5 mi w on US 30 and 67. Ext/int corridors. **Pets:** Supervision.

🆂🄰🆅🄴 🕭 ⊠ 📶 🕒 🐾 🕕 🐾

◆◆◆ Country Inn & Suites By Carlson 🅜
(319) 244-9922. **$69-$109.** 2224 Lincolnway. 3.5 mi w on US 30 and 67. Int corridors. **Pets:** Supervision.

🄰🅂🄺 🕭 ⊠ 🕭 📶 🕒 🐾 🕒 🐾

◆◆ Super 8 Motel-Clinton 🅜 ❀
(319) 242-8870. **$50-$69.** 1711 Lincolnway. 2.8 mi w on US 30 and 67. Int corridors. **Pets:** Small. $25 deposit/room. No service, supervision, crate.

🄰🅂🄺 ⊠ 📶

CLIVE

◆◆◆ Baymont Inn & Suites-DesMoines 🅜
(515) 221-9200. **$67-$74.** 1390 NW 118th St. I-80 and 35, exit 124 (University Ave). Int corridors. **Pets:** Designated rooms, no service, supervision, crate.

🆂🄰 ⊠ 🕭 📶 🕒 🐾 🕒 🐾 🄲🅃🅅

🄰🄰🄰 ◆◆◆ Four Points Hotel by Sheraton 🅜🄸
(515) 278-5575. **$69-$69.** 11040 Hickman Rd. I-35 and I-80, exit 125, 0.3 mi e. Int corridors. **Pets:** Supervision.

🆂🄰🆅🄴 ⊠ 🕭 📶 🕒 🐾 🕒 🐾 🕕 🐾

◆◆◆ Residence Inn by Marriott 🅜
(515) 223-7700. **$109-$139.** 11428 Forest Ave. Jct I-80/35, exit 124 (University Ave), just ne. Ext corridors. **Pets:** No service, supervision, crate.

🄰🅂🄺 🆂🄰 ⊠ 📶 🕭 📶 🕒 🐾 🕒 🐾 ⊠

COLUMBUS JUNCTION

◆◆ Columbus Motel 🅜
(319) 728-8080. **$39-$46.** SR 92 E. 0.5 mi e on SR 92. Int corridors. **Pets:** Small. No service, supervision, crate.

⊠ 📶 🕒

CORALVILLE

🄰🄰🄰 ◆◆◆ Best Western-Cantebury Inn & Suites 🅜🄸
(319) 351-0400. **$70-$140.** 704 1st Ave. Just s of jct I-80, exit 242. Int corridors. **Pets:** Small. Supervision.

🆂🄰🆅🄴 🆂🄰 ⊠ 📶 🕭 📶 🕒 🐾 🕒 🐾

◆◆◆ Comfort Inn of Coralville 🅜 ❀
(319) 351-8144. **$60-$105, 7 days notice.** 209 W 9th St. Just s of jct I-80, exit 242. Int corridors. **Pets:** Designated rooms, no service, supervision, crate.

🄰🅂🄺 🆂🄰 ⊠ 📶 🕒 🐾 🕒 🐾

◆◆ Ramada Westfield Inn 🅜🄸
(319) 354-7770. **$60-$90.** 2530 Holiday Rd. SR 965, 0.3 mi n of jct I-80, exit 240. Ext/int corridors. **Pets:** Small. Supervision.

🄰🅂🄺 🆂🄰 ⊠ 📶 🕕 🐾 ⊠

COUNCIL BLUFFS

🄰🄰🄰 ◆◆ Best Western Crossroads of the Bluffs 🅜🄸
(712) 322-3150. **$74-$74.** 2216 27th Ave. I-80, exit 1B (24th St). Int corridors. **Pets:** Medium. Designated rooms, no service, supervision, crate.

🆂🄰🆅🄴 🆂🄰 ⊠ 📶 🕕 🐾

🄰🄰🄰 ◆◆◆ Best Western Metro Inn & Suites 🅜 ❀
(712) 328-3171. **$55-$74, 7 days notice.** 3537 W Broadway. Just e of I-29 on US 6; I-29, 9th Ave exit, just e, just n to Broadway, just w. Ext/int corridors. **Pets:** Medium. Designated rooms, no service, supervision, crate.

🆂🄰🆅🄴 🆂🄰 ⊠ 📶 🕭 📶 🕒 🐾

◆◆◆ Comfort Suites 🅜 ❀
(712) 323-9760. **$100-$159.** 1801 S 35th St. I-29, exit 52, Nebraska Ave E. Int corridors. **Pets:** Other. $10 one-time fee/room. Designated rooms, no service, supervision, crate.

🄰🅂🄺 🆂🄰 ⊠ 🕭 📶 🕭 📶 🕒 🐾

◆◆ Days Inn 🅜 ❀
(712) 323-2200. **$54-$70.** 3619 9th Ave. I-29, exit 53A. Int corridors. **Pets:** Other. $10 deposit/room. Designated rooms, no service, supervision, crate.

🄰🅂🄺 🆂🄰 ⊠ 📶 🕒

◆◆ **Econo Lodge** 🅜
(712) 366-9699. **$56-$96.** 3208 S 7th St. I-80, exit 3, just s. Int corridors. **Pets:** Designated rooms, supervision.
🅐🅢🅚 🅢🅓 ✕ 🅑 🖭

◆ **Super 8 Motel** 🅜 🐾
(712) 322-2888. **$50-$60.** 2712 S 24th St. Jct I-80 and exit 1B (24th St). Int corridors. **Pets:** Other. Designated rooms, no service, supervision, crate.
🅐🅢🅚 🅢🅓 ✕

◆◆ **Travelodge** 🅜🅘 🐾
(712) 328-3881. **$64-$70, 7 days notice.** 2325 Ave N. Just se of jct I-29 and exit 55 (25th St). Int corridors. **Pets:** Medium, dogs only. $5 daily fee/pet. Supervision.
🅐🅢🅚 🅢🅓 ✕ 🍴 🖾

CRESCO

🅐🅐🅐 ◆ **Cresco Motel** 🅜 🐾
(319) 547-2240. **$35-$61.** 620 2nd Ave SE. On SR 9 on the e side of town. Ext corridors. **Pets:** Other. $10 daily fee/room. No service, supervision, crate.
🆂🅰🆅🅴 🅢🅓 ✕ 🅕

DAVENPORT

◆◆◆ **Baymont Inn & Suites-Davenport** 🅜 🐾
(319) 386-1600. **$59-$59.** 400 Jason Way Ct. In Davenport, IA; I-80, exit 295A S, left at 65th St, 0.5 mi n on frontage road. Int corridors. **Pets:** Medium. $50 deposit/room. Designated rooms, supervision.
🅢🅓 ✕ 🕖 🅕 🅑 🖭 🖾

🅐🅐🅐 ◆◆◆ **Best Western SteepleGate Inn** 🅜🅘 🐾
(319) 386-6900. **$79-$99.** 100 W 76th St. In Davenport, IA; on US 61; at jct I-80, exit 295A, entrance 0.5 mi s via 65th St and Frontage Rd. Int corridors. **Pets:** Medium. $5 daily fee/pet. No service, supervision, crate.
🆂🅰🆅🅴 🅢🅓 ✕ 🕖 🅑 🖭 🍴 🖾

◆◆◆ **Country Inn & Suites By Carlson** 🅜 🐾
(319) 388-6444. **$78, 7 days notice.** 140 E 55th St. In Davenport, IA; jct I-80 and US 61, exit 295, 1.4 mi s. Int corridors. **Pets:** Medium. Designated rooms, supervision.
🅐🅢🅚 🅢🅓 ✕ 🅖 🅕 🅑 🖭 🖾

◆◆ **Days Inn of Davenport** 🅜 🐾
(319) 355-1190. **$45-$64.** 3202 E Kimberly Rd. In Davenport, IA; jct I-74, exit 2. Int corridors. **Pets:** Medium, other. $5 one-time fee/pet. No service, supervision, crate.
🅐🅢🅚 🅢🅓 ✕ 🕖 🅑 🖭 🖾

🅐🅐🅐 ◆◆ **Exel Inn of Davenport** 🅜
(319) 386-6350. **$39-$62.** 6310 N Brady St. In Davenport, IA; US 61, 0.5 mi s of jct I-80, exit 295A. Int corridors. **Pets:** No service, supervision, crate.
🅢🅓 ✕ 🕖 🅑 🖭

◆◆◆ **Hampton Inn-Davenport** 🅜 🐾
(319) 359-3921. **$79, 3 days notice.** 3330 E Kimberly Rd. In Davenport, IA; 0.3 mi w of jct I-74, exit 2, 0.3 mi s. Int corridors. **Pets:** Medium. Designated rooms, supervision.
🅐🅢🅚 🅢🅓 ✕ 🅑 🖭 🖾

◆◆◆ **Residence Inn** 🅜 🐾
(319) 391-8877. **$99-$109.** 120 E 55th St. In Davenport, IA; jct I-80 and US 61, exit 295, 1.4 mi s. Int corridors. **Pets:** Medium, other. $100 one-time fee/room. No service, supervision, crate.
🅐🅢🅚 🅢🅓 ✕ 🅕 🅑 🖭 🖾 🖾

DENISON

◆◆◆ **Best Western Denison's Inn** 🅜
(712) 263-5081. **Call for rates.** 502 Boyer Valley Rd. 0.3 mi sw of jct US 30, 59 and SR 141. Int corridors. **Pets:** Designated rooms, no service, supervision, crate.
🖾

DES MOINES

🅐🅐🅐 ◆◆◆ **Best Inns of America** 🅜 🐾
(515) 270-1111. **$64-$94.** 5050 Merle Hay Rd. Jct I-80, 35 and exit 131, just n. Int corridors. **Pets:** Medium, other. No service, supervision, crate.
🆂🅰🆅🅴 🅢🅓 ✕ 🕖 🗀 🅑 🖭 🖾

◆◆ **Best Western Bavarian Inn** 🅜🅘 🐾
(515) 265-5611. **$64-$89, 7 days notice.** 5220 NE 14th St. Hwy 69 N, 0.3 mi n of jct I-80/Hwy 69, exit 136. Int corridors. **Pets:** Small, other. $25 deposit/room. Designated rooms, no service, supervision, crate.
🅐🅢🅚 🅢🅓 ✕ 🅑 🖭 🍴 🖾 🖾

🅐🅐🅐 ◆◆ **Best Western Colonial** 🅜 🐾
(515) 265-7511. **$43-$61.** 5020 NE 14th St. US 69, n of I-35 and 80, exit 136. Ext/int corridors. **Pets:** Designated rooms, no service, supervision, crate.
🆂🅰🆅🅴 🅢🅓 ✕

◆◆ **Best Western Starlite Village** 🅜🅘
(515) 282-5251. **$70-$95, 30 days notice.** 929 3rd St. Westbound on I-235, exit 3rd St downtown; eastbound exit 3rd St, across from Veterans Auditorium. Int corridors. **Pets:** No service, supervision, crate.
🅐🅢🅚 🅢🅓 ✕ 🕖 🅑 🍴 🖾

◆◆ **Comfort Inn** 🅜
(515) 287-3434. **$60-$99.** 5231 Fleur Dr. Across from airport. Int corridors. **Pets:** No service, supervision, crate.
🅐🅢🅚 🅢🅓 ✕ 🗀 🕖 🅑 🖭 🖾

◆◆◆◆ **Des Moines Marriott Downtown** 🅷 🐾
(515) 245-5500. **$74-$174.** 700 Grand Ave. Grand Ave and 7th St; just s of I-235. Int corridors. **Pets:** Supervision.
✕ 🗀 🕖 🅖 🅑 🖭 🍴 🖾

🅐🅐🅐 ◆ **Hickman Motor Lodge** 🅜 🐾
(515) 276-8591. **$40-$55.** 6500 Hickman Rd. I-35 and 80, exit 125, 2.5 mi e. Ext corridors. **Pets:** Designated rooms, no service, supervision, crate.
🆂🅰🆅🅴 🅢🅓 ✕ 🅑 🖭

◆◆◆ **Holiday Inn-Merle Hay** 🅜🅘 🐾
(515) 278-0271. **$79, 7 days notice.** 5000 Merle Hay Rd. S of I-35 and I-80, exit 131. Ext/int corridors. **Pets:** Other. No service, supervision, crate.
🅐🅢🅚 🅢🅓 ✕ 🗀 🅑 🖭 🍴 🖾

◍ ◆◆ Motel 6–30 **M** ❀
(515) 287-6364. **$40-$56.** 4817 Fleur Dr. From jct I-35 and SR 5, 5 mi e on Army Post Rd, then 0.5 mi n. Ext corridors. **Pets:** Small. No service, supervision, crate.
⬛ ⊠ 🖫 ᴄᴛᴠ

◆◆◆ Savery Hotel and Spa **H** ❀
(515) 244-2151. **$139-$169, 3 days notice.** 401 Locust St. Downtown. Int corridors. **Pets:** $25 one-time fee/room. No service, supervision, crate.
ᴀsᴋ ⬛ ⊠ 🛈 🖫 🔲 💻 🔲 ᴀ

◆◆ Super 8 Lodge **M**
(515) 278-8858. **Call for rates.** 4755 Merle Hay Rd. S of I-80 and 35, exit 131. Int corridors. **Pets:** Medium. No service, supervision, crate.
⊠ 🔲 💻

DUBUQUE

◍ ◆◆◆ Best Western Dubuque Inn **M**
(319) 556-7760. **$59-$99.** 3434 Dodge St. US 20, 3 mi w of jct US 52, 61, 151 and Mississippi Bridge. Int corridors. **Pets:** Small. Supervision.
sᴀᴠᴇ ⬛ ⊠ 🖉 🔲 💻 🔲 ᴀ

◍ ◆◆◆ Best Western Midway Hotel **M** ❀
(319) 557-8000. **$79-$109.** 3100 Dodge St. US 20, 2.3 mi w of jct US 52, 61, 151 and Mississippi Bridge. Int corridors. **Pets:** Medium. Supervision.
sᴀᴠᴇ ⬛ ⊠ 🖉 🔲 💻 ᴀ

◆◆◆ Comfort Inn of Dubuque **M** ❀
(319) 556-3006. **$59-$99, 7 days notice.** 4055 McDonald Dr. US 20, 3.8 mi w of jct US 52, 61, 151 and Mississippi Bridge. Int corridors. **Pets:** Other. $15 deposit/room. No service, supervision, crate.
ᴀsᴋ ⬛ ⊠ 🖉 🔲 💻 ᴀ

◆◆ Days Inn-Dubuque **M** ❀
(319) 583-3297. **$49-$69.** 1111 Dodge St. US 20, 0.8 mi w of jct US 52, 61, 151 and Mississippi Bridge, Hill/Bryant exit. Ext corridors. **Pets:** Medium, other. Designated rooms, no service, supervision, crate.
ᴀsᴋ ⊠ 🔲 💻 🔲 ᴀ

◆◆◆ Holiday Inn Dubuque Five Flags **H** ❀
(319) 556-2000. **$84, 7 days notice.** 450 Main St. Downtown; at Main and 4th St W; facing the Five Flags Theater. Int corridors. **Pets:** Large, other. $75 deposit/room. Designated rooms, no service, supervision, crate.
ᴀsᴋ ⬛ ⊠ 🛈 🖫 🔲 💻 🔲 ᴀ

EVANSDALE

◍ ◆◆ Ramada Limited **M** ❀
(319) 235-1111. **$55-$90, 7 days notice.** 450 Evansdale Dr. Just n of jct I-380 and exit 68. Int corridors. **Pets:** $25 deposit/room. Designated rooms, no service, supervision, crate.
sᴀᴠᴇ ⬛ ⊠ 🛈 🔲 ᴀ

FAIRFIELD

◆◆ Best Western Fairfield Inn **M** ❀
(515) 472-2200. **$57-$74.** 2200 W Burlington Ave. On US 34, 1 mi w of jct SR 1. Int corridors. **Pets:** Small, other. No service, supervision, crate.
⬛ ⊠ 🔲 🔲 ᴀ

FORT DODGE

◆◆◆ Comfort Inn **M** ❀
(515) 573-3731. **Call for rates.** 2938 5th Ave S. 6 mi n of jct US 20 and exit 124 (Coalville), on Hwy P59; 2 mi w on 5th Ave, Business US 20. Int corridors. **Pets:** Medium, other. $10 one-time fee/room. Designated rooms, no service, supervision, crate.
⊠ 🛈 🖉 🔲 💻 ᴀ

FORT MADISON

◍ ◆◆ The Madison Inn Motel **M** ❀
(319) 372-7740. **$42-$52, 7 days notice.** 3440 Ave L. US 2 and 61, 2 mi w. Ext corridors. **Pets:** Small, dogs only. $5 daily fee/room, $5 one-time fee/room. Designated rooms, no service, supervision, crate.
sᴀᴠᴇ ⊠ 🔲

GLENWOOD

◍ ◆ Bluff View Motel **M** ❀
(712) 622-8191. **$38-$42.** 57902 190 St. W of I-29, exit 35 at jct US 34, adjacent to interstate. Int corridors. **Pets:** $5 daily fee/pet. Designated rooms, no service, supervision, crate.
sᴀᴠᴇ ⬛ ⊠ 🔲

GRINNELL

◍ ◆◆ Econo Lodge **M** ❀
(515) 236-6116. **$48-$62, 3 days notice.** 2210 West St S. I-80 and SR 146, exit 182. Ext/int corridors. **Pets:** Large. Designated rooms, no service, supervision, crate.
sᴀᴠᴇ ⬛ ⊠ 🔲

HAMPTON

◆◆◆ AmericInn Motel & Suites **M** ❀
(515) 456-5559. **$75-$130.** 702 Central Ave W. Near downtown. Int corridors. **Pets:** Small, other. $100 deposit/room. No service, supervision, crate.
ᴀsᴋ ⬛ ⊠ 🖉 🖫 🔲 💻 ᴀ

IDA GROVE

◆ Delux Motel **M** ❀
(712) 364-3317. **$35-$50.** 5981 US 175. Jct US 59 S and 175. Ext corridors. **Pets:** Large. Designated rooms, no service, supervision, crate.
⊠ 🔲

INDEPENDENCE

◆◆ Super 8 Motel **M**
(319) 334-7041. **$45-$60.** 2000 1st St W. Jct US 20, exit 252, 1.4 mi n. Int corridors. **Pets:** Small. Supervision.
ᴀsᴋ ⬛ ⊠ 🛈 🔲

IOWA CITY

◍ ◆◆◆ Sheraton Iowa City Plaza Hotel **H** ❀
(319) 337-4058. **$69-$149.** 210 S Dubuque St. Downtown; Dubuque and Burlington sts (SR 1). Int corridors. **Pets:** Small. Supervision.
sᴀᴠᴇ ⬛ ⊠ 🛈 🖉 🔲 💻 🔲 ᴀ

JEFFERSON

AAA ◆ **Redwood Motel M**
(515) 386-3116. **$33-$45, 3 days notice.** 209 E US 30. US 30, just e of jct US 30 and SR 4. Ext corridors. **Pets:** Medium. Designated rooms, no service, supervision, crate.

[SAVE] [S🐾] [✕] [CTV]

JOHNSTON

AAA ◆◆◆ **The Inn & Conference Center at Merle Hay M**
(515) 276-5411. **$69-$79.** 5055 Merle Hay Rd. Just n of jct I-80 and 35, exit 131 (Merle Hay Rd). Int corridors. **Pets:** Supervision.

[SAVE] [S🐾] [✕] [🗨] [🖬] [🖳] [🖾]

KEOKUK

AAA ◆ **Econo Lodge M** 🐾
(319) 524-3252. **$39-$59.** 3764 Main Street Rd. 2.8 mi nw on US 218. Ext corridors. **Pets:** Other. $5 daily fee/room. No service, supervision, crate.

[SAVE] [S🐾] [✕] [🖪] [🖬] [🖾]

LE CLAIRE

◆◆◆ **Comfort Inn Riverview M** 🐾
(319) 289-4747. **$70-$80.** 902 Mississippi View Ct. Jct I-80 and US 67, exit 306, 0.5 mi n to Eagle Ridge Rd, then 0.3 mi sw. Int corridors. **Pets:** Medium, dogs only. $25 one-time fee/pet. No service, supervision, crate.

[ASK] [S🐾] [✕] [🖪] [🖬] [🖳] [🖾]

◆◆◆ **Super 8 of Le Claire M**
(319) 289-5888. **Call for rates.** 1522 Welcome Center Dr. Jct I-80 and US 67, exit 306, 0.5 mi n to Eagle Ridge Rd, then 0.3 mi sw to Mississippi View Ct. Int corridors. **Pets:** Medium. Designated rooms, no service, supervision, crate.

[✕] [🖪] [🖪] [🖬] [🖳]

LE MARS

◆ **Amber Inn Motel M**
(712) 546-7066. **$40-$45.** 635 Eighth Ave SW. US 75, 0.7 mi s of jct SR 3, s end of town. Ext/int corridors. **Pets:** Designated rooms, no service, supervision, crate.

[✕] [🖬]

MANCHESTER

◆◆ **Super 8 of Manchester M**
(319) 927-2533. **$50-$96.** 1020 W Main. Jct US 20 and SR 13, exit 275, 1.5 mi n, then 0.3 mi e. Int corridors. **Pets:** Large. Supervision.

[ASK] [S🐾] [✕] [🖪] [🖬] [🖳]

MARQUETTE

◆ **The Frontier Motel M**
(319) 873-3497. **$40-$85.** 101 S 1st St. US 18 and SR 76. Ext corridors. **Pets:** Small. Designated rooms, no service, supervision, crate.

[✕] [🖾]

MARSHALLTOWN

AAA ◆◆◆ **Best Western Regency Inn M** 🐾
(515) 752-6321. **$64-$101.** 3303 S Center St. Jct US 30 and SR 14. Int corridors. **Pets:** Small, dogs only. $10 one-time fee/room. No service, supervision, crate.

[SAVE] [S🐾] [✕] [🗨] [🖪] [🖬] [🖳] [🍽] [🖾]

◆◆◆ **Comfort Inn M** 🐾
(515) 752-6000. **$50-$85.** 2613 S Center St. SR 14, 0.5 mi n of jct US 30 and SR 14. Int corridors. **Pets:** Small, other. $10 one-time fee/room. No service, supervision, crate.

[ASK] [S🐾] [✕] [🖪] [🗨] [🖪] [🖬] [🖳] [🖾]

MASON CITY

◆◆ **Days Inn Mason City M** 🐾
(515) 424-0210. **$40-$76.** 2301 4th St SW. On US 18, 6 mi e of jct I-35 and US 18, exit 194. Int corridors. **Pets:** Other. No service, supervision, crate.

[ASK] [S🐾] [✕] [🖪] [🖬] [🖳]

◆◆◆ **Holiday Inn M** 🐾
(515) 423-1640. **$69-$73.** 2101 4th St SW (US 18). 1.5 mi w of jct US 18 and 65, on US 18; 8 mi e of jct I-35 and US 18. Ext/int corridors. **Pets:** $10 daily fee/room. Supervision.

[ASK] [S🐾] [✕] [🖬] [🖳] [🍽] [🖾]

AAA ◆◆ **Thriftlodge M**
(515) 424-2910. **$43-$62, 3 days notice.** 24 5th St SW. Just w of jct US 18 and 65. Ext/int corridors. **Pets:** Supervision.

[SAVE] [S🐾] [✕] [🖬] [🖾]

NEWTON

◆◆ **Days Inn of Newton M** 🐾
(515) 792-2330. **$40-$70.** 1605 W 19th St S. N of I-80, exit 164. Int corridors. **Pets:** Other. $7 one-time fee/room. Supervision.

[ASK] [S🐾] [✕] [🖪] [🖳]

AAA ◆◆◆ **Radisson Inn Newton M** 🐾
(515) 792-3333. **$74-$82.** 208 W 4th St N. Downtown. Int corridors. **Pets:** Small. No service, supervision, crate.

[SAVE] [✕] [🖪] [🖪] [🖬] [🖳] [🍽] [🖾]

AAA ◆◆ **Ramada Limited M** 🐾
(515) 792-8100. **$50-$65.** 1405 W 19th St S. Just n of jct I-80 and SR 14, exit 164. Int corridors. **Pets:** Medium. $10 daily fee/pet, $10 one-time fee/pet. Designated rooms, no service, supervision, crate.

[SAVE] [S🐾] [✕]

OKOBOJI

AAA ◆◆ **Country Club Motel M** 🐾
(712) 332-5617. **$65-$97, 3 days notice.** 1107 Sanborn Ave. Just w of jct US 71 and Sanborn Ave. Ext corridors. **Pets:** Supervision.

[SAVE] [S🐾] [✕] [🖬] [🖾]

◆◆◆ **Village East Resort R**
(712) 332-2161. **$149-$159, 7 days notice.** 1405 US 71. 3 mi s from jct SR 9 and US 71. Ext/int corridors. **Pets:** Small. Supervision.

[✕] [🖪] [🗨] [🖪] [🖬] [🖳] [🍽] [🖾] [✕]

OSCEOLA

◆◆◆ AmericInn Motel & Suites Ⓜ
(515) 342-9400. **$137.** 111 Ariel Cir. Jct I-35 and exit 33, just w. Int corridors. **Pets:** Medium. No service, supervision, crate.

A$K S🔒 ⊠ 🏠 ⌨ 🔌 🖥 🏊

OSKALOOSA

◆◆ Traveler Budget Inn Ⓜ
(515) 673-8333. **Call for rates.** 1210 A Ave E. On SR 92, e side of town. Ext corridors. **Pets:** Small. No service, supervision, crate.

⊠ 🔌 🖥

OTTUMWA

◆ Colonial Motor Inn Ⓜ ❀
(515) 683-1661. **$33-$43.** 1534 Albia Rd. W on US 34, s at Quincy St, 0.5 mi to Albia Rd, just w. Ext/int corridors. **Pets:** Other. $10 one-time fee/room. Supervision.

A$K S🔒 ⊠ 🔌

◆◆ Days Inn of Ottumwa Ⓜ
(515) 682-8131. **$50-$56.** 206 Church St. 0.5 mi s on US 34, at jct US 63; business exit. Ext corridors. **Pets:** Small. No service, supervision, crate.

A$K S🔒 ⊠ 🔌 🖥 🍴 🏊

SIBLEY

◆◆ Super 8 Motel Ⓜ
(712) 754-3603. **Call for rates.** 1108 2nd Ave. On SR 60. Int corridors. **Pets:** Medium. No service, supervision, crate.

⊠ 🔌 🖥

SIOUX CITY

◆◆◆ Baymont Inn Ⓜ
(712) 233-2302. **$56-$66.** 3101 Singing Hills Blvd. Jct I-29 and exit 143, just e. Int corridors. **Pets:** Medium. Designated rooms, supervision.

A$K S🔒 ⊠ 🏠 ⌨ 🔌 🖥 🏊

◆◆◆ Best Western City Centre Ⓜ ❀
(712) 277-1550. **$55-$75.** 130 Nebraska St. Just w of US 20 and I-29 business district exit. Int corridors. **Pets:** $50 deposit/room. No service, supervision, crate.

A$K S🔒 ⊠ 🔌 🏊

◆◆◆ Comfort Inn Ⓜ
(712) 274-1300. **$69-$89.** 4202 S Lakeport St. 0.3 mi s of jct US 20 and Lakeport St; do not use Business US 20. Int corridors. **Pets:** Supervision.

A$K S🔒 ⊠ 🐾 🔌 🖥 🏊

◆◆◆ Hamilton Inn Ⓜ ❀
(712) 277-3211. **Call for rates.** 1401 Zenith Dr. I-29, exit 149 (Hamilton Blvd). Int corridors. **Pets:** Supervision.

A$K ⊠ 🐾 🔌 🖥 🍴 🏊

ⒶⒶⒶ ◆◆◆ Hilton Sioux City Ⓗ
(712) 277-4101. **$79-$79.** 707 4th St. Downtown. Int corridors. **Pets:** Small. Supervision.

SAVE ⊠ 🔌 🖥 🍴 🏊

◆◆◆ Holiday Inn Ⓜ
(712) 277-9400. **$65-$95.** 701 Gordon Dr. I-29, exit 147B. Int corridors. **Pets:** Small. Supervision.

A$K S🔒 ⊠ ⌨ 🔌 🖥 🍴 🏊

◆ Motel 6–45 Ⓜ
(712) 277-3131. **$37-$53.** 6166 Harbor Dr. Just w of jct I-29 and exit 141. Int corridors. **Pets:** Designated rooms, no service, supervision, crate.

S🔒 ⊠ ⌨ CTV

◆◆ Super 8 Motel Ⓜ
(712) 274-1520. **$50-$70, 7 days notice.** 4307 Stone Ave. Gordon Dr, 3 mi e of jct I-29, exit 147B. Int corridors. **Pets:** Medium. No service, supervision, crate.

A$K S🔒 ⊠ 🏠

SLOAN

◆◆ Winna Vegas Inn Ⓜ
(712) 428-4280. **$48-$58, 7 days notice.** 1862 Hwy 141. Just e of jct I-29 and exit 127. Int corridors. **Pets:** No service, supervision, crate.

A$K S🔒 ⊠ 🏠 ⌨ 🖥

SPIRIT LAKE

◆ Oaks Motel Ⓜ ❀
(712) 336-2940. **$79-$79.** 1701 Chicago. Just e on SR 9 and US 71. Ext corridors. **Pets:** Other. $20 deposit/room. Designated rooms, supervision.

⊠ 🔌 🐾

STORY CITY

◆◆ Super 8 Motel Ⓜ
(515) 733-5281. **$44-$60.** 515 Factory Outlet Dr. Just w of jct I-35 and exit 124. Int corridors. **Pets:** No service, supervision, crate.

A$K S🔒 ⊠ 🏠 🔌

ⒶⒶⒶ ◆◆ Viking Motor Inn Ⓜ ❀
(515) 733-4306. **$45-$60.** 1520 Broad St. Just w of I-35, exit 124. Int corridors. **Pets:** Other. No service, supervision, crate.

SAVE S🔒 ⊠ 🔌 🏊 🐾

STUART

◆◆ Super 8 Motel Ⓜ
(515) 523-2888. **$39-$59.** 203 SE 7th St. At jct I-80 and exit 93. Int corridors. **Pets:** Designated rooms, no service, supervision, crate.

A$K S🔒 ⊠ 🏠

TOLEDO

◆◆ Super 8 Motel Ⓜ ❀
(515) 484-5888. **$42-$64.** 207 Hwy 30 W. Just w of jct US 30 and 63. Ext/int corridors. **Pets:** Other. No service, supervision, crate.

A$K S🔒 ⊠ 🏠 🔌

URBANDALE

⚫⚫⚫ ◆◆◆ Comfort Inn of Urbandale M ❀
(515) 270-1037. **$70-$90, 3 days notice.** 5900 Sutton Dr.
I-80, exit 131, just s and w. Int corridors. **Pets:** Medium,
other. $5 daily fee/pet, $5 one-time fee/pet. No service,
supervision, crate.
SAVE S⬚ ⊠ ⬚ ⬚ 💻 🔲

⚫⚫⚫ ◆◆ Days Inn-West M
(515) 278-2811. **$55-$79.** 10841 Douglas Ave. I-35 and 80,
exit 126, 0.3 mi e. Ext corridors. **Pets:** Large. Supervision.
SAVE S⬚ ⊠ ⬚ ⬚ 💻 🔲

WALNUT

⚫⚫⚫ ◆ Red Carpet Inn M
(712) 784-2233. **$49-$79.** 33246 Antique City Dr. Just s of
jct I-80 and exit 46. Int corridors. **Pets:** Designated rooms,
supervision.
SAVE S⬚ ⊠ ⬚

◆◆◆ Super 8 Motel M
(712) 784-2221. **$39-$59.** 2109 Antique City Dr. N of I-80,
exit 46. Int corridors. **Pets:** No service, supervision, crate.
ASK S⬚ ⊠ ⬚ ⬚ 🔲

WASHINGTON

◆◆ Super 8 Motel-Washington M ❀
(319) 653-6621. **Call for rates.** 119 Westview Dr. 1.5 mi w
on SR 1 and 92. Int corridors. **Pets:** $25 deposit/pet. Des-
ignated rooms, no service, supervision, crate.
⊠ ⬚ ⊠

WATERLOO

◆◆◆ Comfort Inn of Waterloo M ❀
(319) 234-7411. **$65-$80, 7 days notice.** 1945 La Porte
Rd. At jct I-380 N, exit 72. Int corridors. **Pets:** Designated
rooms, no service, supervision, crate.
ASK S⬚ ⊠ ⬚ ⬚ 💻 🔲

⚫⚫⚫ ◆◆ Exel Inn of Waterloo M
(319) 235-2165. **$37-$57.** 3350 University Ave. 2 mi w of
US 63. Int corridors. **Pets:** Small. Designated rooms, supervision.
S⬚ ⊠ ⬚ ⬚ 💻

◆◆◆ Holiday Inn Convention Center 🅷
(319) 233-7560. **$79-$79.** 205 W 4th St. Downtown; 4th
and Commercial sts. Int corridors. **Pets:** Small. Supervision.
⊠ ⬚ ⬚ ⬚ 💻 ⬚ 🔲

◆◆◆ Holiday Inn Express M ❀
(319) 233-9191. **$55-$71.** 2141 La Porte Rd. I-380, exit 72.
Int corridors. **Pets:** Supervision.
ASK S⬚ ⊠ ⬚ 🔲

⚫⚫⚫ ◆◆◆ Motel 6-4081 M ❀
(319) 236-3238. **$40-$48.** 2343 Logan Ave. On US 63, 2 mi
n of jct US 218 and 63. Int corridors. **Pets:** Other. Designated rooms, no service, supervision, crate.
SAVE ⊠ ⬚ ⬚ 💻 🔲

⚫⚫⚫ ◆◆◆ Quality Inn & Suites M ❀
(319) 235-0301. **$54-$230.** 226 W Fifth St. Downtown. Int
corridors. **Pets:** Other. Supervision.
SAVE ⊠ ⬚ ⬚ ⬚ 💻

WAVERLY

⚫⚫⚫ ◆◆◆ Best Western Red Fox Inn Resort &
            Conference Center MI ❀
(319) 352-5330. **$59-$69, 3 days notice.** 1900 Heritage
Way. 2 mi w on SR 3. Ext/int corridors. **Pets:** Other. Supervision.
SAVE S⬚ ⊠ ⬚ ⬚ 💻 ⬚ 🔲 ⊠

WEBSTER CITY

◆◆ The Executive Inn M
(515) 832-3631. **$53-$69.** 1700 Superior St. 0.5 mi n on SR
17 and Hwy 20. Int corridors. **Pets:** Supervision.
ASK S⬚ ⊠ ⬚ 💻 🔲

WEST BURLINGTON

◆◆◆ AmericInn Motel & Suites M ❀
(319) 758-9000. **$66-$106.** 628 S Gear Ave. Just ne of jct
US 34 and exit 260 (Gear Ave). Int corridors.
Pets: Medium, other. $50 deposit/room. Designated rooms,
no service, supervision, crate.
⊠ ⬚ ⬚ ⬚ ⬚ 💻 🔲

WEST DES MOINES

◆◆◆ Candlewood Suites-West Des
           Moines M ❀
(515) 221-0001. **$85-$85.** 7625 Office Plaza Dr N. Just sw
of jct I-80 and exit 121 (74th St). Int corridors. **Pets:** Other.
Designated rooms, no service, supervision, crate.
ASK S⬚ ⊠ ⬚ ⬚ ⬚ 💻

◆◆◆ Holiday Inn-University Park MI ❀
(515) 223-1800. **$79-$129.** 1800 50th St. At jct I-80 and 35,
exit 124 (University Ave). Int corridors. **Pets:** Small. $50
deposit/room, $25 daily fee/room. Int corridors. **Pets:** no
service, supervision, crate.
ASK S⬚ ⊠ ⬚ ⬚ ⬚ ⬚ 💻 🔲 ⬚

⚫⚫⚫ ◆◆ Motel 6-1408 M
(515) 267-8885. **$40-$56.** 7655 Office Plaza Dr N. Just sw
of jct I-80 and exit 121 (74th St). Int corridors.
Pets: Medium. Designated rooms, no service, supervision,
crate.
S⬚ ⊠ ⬚ ⬚ ⬚ 🔲 CTV

WILLIAMS

◆◆ Best Western Norseman Inn M ❀
(515) 854-2281. **$40-$58.** 3086 220th St. Just e of jct I-35
and exit 144. Int corridors. **Pets:** Medium, other. Designated
rooms, no service, supervision, crate.
S⬚ ⊠

WILLIAMSBURG

⚫⚫⚫ ◆◆◆ Best Western Quiet House
            Suites M ❀
(319) 668-9777. **$76-$155.** 1708 N Highland St. I-80, exit
220, 0.8 mi n; across from Tanger Outlet Mall. Int corridors.
Pets: Medium. $15 daily fee/pet. Designated rooms, no
service, supervision, crate.
SAVE S⬚ ⊠ ⬚ ⬚ 💻 🔲

◆◆◆ Crest Motel **M** ✿
(319) 668-1522. **$45-$70.** 340 W Evans St. I-80, exit 220, 0.3 mi w; across from Tanger Factory Outlet Mall. Ext corridors. **Pets:** Medium. $5 daily fee/pet. Designated rooms, no service, supervision, crate.

◆◆◆ Ramada Limited **M**
(319) 668-1000. **Call for rates.** 120 Hawkeye Dr. Just s of jct I-80 and exit 220, on Hwy 149. Ext corridors. **Pets:** No service, supervision, crate.

🅰🅰🅰 ◆◆◆ Super 8 Motel **M**
(319) 668-9718. **$59-$79.** 1708 N Highland St. I-80, exit 220, 0.8 mi n; across from Tanger Outlet Mall. Ext/int corridors. **Pets:** Medium. Designated rooms, no service, supervision, crate.

[SAVE] [S🅓] [✕] [🖋]

WINTERSET

◆◆ Super 8 Motel **M**
(515) 462-4888. **Call for rates.** 1312 N 10th St. SR 92, 0.5 mi e of jct US 169 and SR 92. Int corridors. **Pets:** Small. No service, supervision, crate.

[✕] [🏠] [💻] [CTV]

◆ Village View Motel **M** ✿
(515) 462-1218. **$34-$48.** 711 SR 92 E. 0.3 mi e on SR 92 from jct N US Hwy 169 and SR 92. Int corridors. **Pets:** Small. $5 one-time fee/pet. Supervision.

[✕] [CTV]

KANSAS

ABILENE

(AAA) ◆◆◆ Best Western Abilene's Pride **M**
(785) 263-2800. **$49-$69.** 1709 N Buckeye. I-70, exit 275, 0.5 mi s. Ext/int corridors. **Pets:** No service, supervision, crate.
[SAVE] ⊠ 🔊 🔋 🖳 🍴 ⌨

(AAA) ◆◆ Best Western President's Inn **M** ❀
(785) 263-2050. **$36-$51.** 2210 N Buckeye. At jct I-70 and SR 15, exit 275. Ext corridors. **Pets:** Other. Supervision.
[SAVE] [S🔊] ⊠ 🌫 🔋 🖳 🍴 ⌨

(AAA) ◆◆ Diamond Motel **M** ❀
(785) 263-2360. **$25-$40.** 1407 NW 3rd St. 1.3 mi s of I-70, exit 275, then 1 mi w. Ext corridors. **Pets:** Small, dogs only. No service, supervision, crate.
[SAVE] ⊠ 🔋

ARKANSAS CITY

◆◆ Best Western Hallmark Motor Inn **M** ❀
(316) 442-1400. **$44-$54.** 1617 N Summit St. 2 mi n on US 77. Ext corridors. **Pets:** Other. $5 one-time fee/pet. Supervision.
[ASK] [S🔊] ⊠ 🔋 🖳 ⌨

BAXTER SPRINGS

(AAA) ◆◆ Baxter Inn-4-Less **M**
(316) 856-2106. **$36-$42.** 2451 Military Ave. On US 69 Alt; 1.5 mi s from jct US 166. Int corridors. **Pets:** Small. Supervision.
[SAVE] ⊠

BELOIT

◆◆ Super 8 Motel-Beloit **M** ❀
(785) 738-4300. **$47-$66, 7 days notice.** 205 W Hwy 24. Just e of jct SR 14. Int corridors. **Pets:** Other. Supervision.
[ASK] [S🔊] ⊠ 🏠 🔊 🌫 🔋

BURLINGTON

◆◆ Country Haven Inn **M**
(316) 364-8260. **$49-$64, 3 days notice.** 207 Cross St. Just e of US 75, 1 mi n of center. Int corridors. **Pets:** No service, supervision, crate.
[ASK] [S🔊] ⊠ 🔋

CHANUTE

(AAA) ◆ Chanute Safari Inn **M**
(316) 431-9460. **$35-$49.** 3428 S Santa Fe. 2.5 mi s on S Sante Fe, 1.5 mi e of US 169, exit 35th St. Ext corridors. **Pets:** Designated rooms, no service, supervision, crate.
[SAVE] [S🔊] ⊠ 🔋 🖳 ⌨

(AAA) ◆ Guest House Motor Inn **M** ❀
(316) 431-0600. **$27-$36.** 1814 S Santa Fe. 1.5 mi s on S Sante Fe, 2.5 mi ne of US 169, exit 35th St. Ext corridors. **Pets:** Small. Supervision.
[SAVE] [S🔊] ⊠ 🖳 ⌨

CLAY CENTER

(AAA) ◆◆ Cedar Court Motel **M** ❀
(785) 632-2148. **$30-$55.** 905 Crawford. 0.5 mi e on US 24. Ext corridors. **Pets:** Small. Designated rooms, no service, supervision, crate.
[SAVE] ⊠ 🌫 🔋 🍴 ⌨

COLBY

(AAA) ◆◆ Best Western Crown Motel **M**
(785) 462-3943. **$50-$79.** 2320 S Range. I-70, exit 53, just s on SR 25. Ext/int corridors. **Pets:** Designated rooms, supervision.
[S🔊] ⊠ 🖳 ⌨

(AAA) ◆◆◆ Comfort Inn **M** ❀
(785) 462-3833. **$54-$99.** 2225 S Range. I-70, exit 53. Int corridors. **Pets:** Other. $5 daily fee/room, $5 one-time fee/room. Designated rooms, supervision.
[SAVE] [S🔊] ⊠ 🔊 🔋 🖳 ⌨

AAA ◆◆ **Days Inn** **M** ☀
(785) 462-8691. **$48-$65.** 1925 S Range. I-70, exit 53, 0.3 mi n on SR 25. Int corridors. **Pets:** Small. $5 one-time fee/pet. Designated rooms, no service, supervision, crate.
SAVE S6 ⊠ 🖥 💻 🖼

◆◆◆ **Holiday Inn Express** **M**
(785) 462-8787. **Call for rates.** 645 W Willow. I-70, exit 53, just n. Int corridors. **Pets:** Designated rooms, supervision.
⊠ 🗐 🕹 🖥 💻 🖼

COTTONWOOD FALLS

AAA ◆◆◆◆ **The Grand Central Hotel** **CI** ☀
(316) 273-6763. **$129-$179, 4 days notice.** 215 Broadway. Center, just w of US 177. Int corridors. **Pets:** Very small, dogs only. No service, supervision, crate.
SAVE S6 ⊠ 🕹 💻 🍴 🖾

COUNCIL GROVE

AAA ◆◆ **The Cottage House Hotel & Motel** **M**
(316) 767-6828. **$50-$90, 7 days notice.** 25 N Neosho. Downtown; just n of Main St. Ext/int corridors. **Pets:** Supervision.
SAVE S6 ⊠ 🖥 💻

DODGE CITY

◆◆ **Best Western Silver Spur Lodge** **MI** ☀
(316) 227-2125. **$45-$62.** 1510 W Wyatt Earp Blvd. 1.2 mi w on US 50 business route. Ext/int corridors. **Pets:** Small. $5 deposit/room. No service, supervision, crate.
ASK S6 ⊠ 🖥 🍴 🖼

◆◆◆ **Holiday Inn Express** **M**
(316) 227-5000. **$85-$120, 3 days notice.** 2320 W Wyatt Earp. 1.4 mi w on US 50 business route. Int corridors. **Pets:** Supervision.
ASK S6 ⊠ 🗐 🕹 🖥 💻 🖼

◆◆ **Super 8** **M** ☀
(316) 225-3924. **$57-$76, 3 days notice.** 1708 W Wyatt Earp. 1.3 mi w on US 50 business route. Int corridors. **Pets:** Small. Supervision.
ASK S6 ⊠ 🗐 🖥 💻 🖼

EL DORADO

AAA ◆◆ **Best Western Red Coach Inn** **MI**
(316) 321-6900. **$49-$99, 7 days notice.** 2525 W Central Ave. On SR 196 and 254, 0.8 mi e of turnpike, exit 71. Ext corridors. **Pets:** Supervision.
SAVE S6 ⊠ 🗐 🖥 🍴 🖼

AAA ◆ **Heritage Inn** **M**
(316) 321-6800. **$34-$54.** 2515 W Central. On SR 196 and 254; 0.8 mi e of turnpike, exit 71. Ext corridors. **Pets:** Supervision.
SAVE S6 ⊠ 🖥

ELLSWORTH

◆◆ **Best Western Garden Prairie Inn** **M** ☀
(785) 472-3116. **$54-$69.** 1400 N Hwy 156. 1 mi ne, on SR 140 at jct SR 156. Ext/int corridors. **Pets:** Medium, dogs only. $6 daily fee/pet, $6 one-time fee/pet. Designated rooms, no service, supervision, crate.
ASK S6 ⊠ 🖼

EMPORIA

AAA ◆ **Budget Host Inn** **M** ☀
(316) 343-6922. **$29-$48.** 1830 E Hwy 50. 0.5 mi w of I-35, exit 133. Ext corridors. **Pets:** Supervision.
SAVE S6 ⊠

◆◆ **Days Inn** **M** ☀
(316) 342-1787. **$48-$66, 3 days notice.** 3032 Hwy 50 W. On US 50, 0.3 mi e of turnpike gate city route. Ext/int corridors. **Pets:** Other. Supervision.
ASK S6 ⊠ 🗐 🖥 💻 🖼

AAA ◆ **Econo Lodge** **M** ☀
(316) 343-7750. **$40-$54.** 2511 W 18th. Off I-35, exit 128 (Industrial St). Int corridors. **Pets:** Small. $25 deposit/pet, $5 daily fee/pet, $5 one-time fee/pet. Designated rooms, no service, supervision, crate.
SAVE S6 ⊠ 🖥 💻 🖼

◆◆ **Ramada Inn & Conference Center** **MI** ☀
(316) 343-2200. **$55-$90.** 2700 W 18th. I-35, exit 128 (Industrial St). Ext/int corridors. **Pets:** $10 deposit/room. Designated rooms, no service, supervision, crate.
ASK S6 ⊠ 🖥 💻 🍴 🖼

FORT SCOTT

◆◆ **Best Western Fort Scott Inn** **MI** ☀
(316) 223-0100. **$58-$65.** 101 State St. On US 69 bypass, southbound US 54 exit; northbound 3rd St exit. Ext/int corridors. **Pets:** $5 one-time fee/room. Supervision.
ASK S6 ⊠ 🖥 🍴 🖼

◆ **1st Interstate Inn** **M**
(316) 223-5330. **$54-$74, 7 days notice.** 2222 S Main. On US 69, 2.5 mi s of US 54. Int corridors. **Pets:** No service, supervision, crate.
ASK S6 ⊠ 🗐

GARDEN CITY

AAA ◆◆ **Best Western Red Baron Hotel** **H** ☀
(316) 275-4164. **$46-$60.** 2205 E Hwy 50. 2.3 mi e on US 50 city route, at US 83 bypass. Ext corridors. **Pets:** Large, other. Supervision.
SAVE S6 ⊠ 🗐 🖥 🖼 🖾

AAA ◆◆ **Best Western Wheat Lands Hotel &**
  Conference Center **H** ☀
(316) 276-2387. **$48-$75.** 1311 E Fulton. 1 mi e on US 50 city route. Ext corridors. **Pets:** Medium. Supervision.
SAVE S6 ⊠ 🗐 🖥 💻 🖼 🖾

◆◆ **Days Inn** **M** ☀
(316) 275-5095. **$60-$81, 3 days notice.** 1818 Commanche Dr. W of US 50 and 83 bypass on SR 156. Ext corridors. **Pets:** Other. Supervision.
ASK S6 ⊠ 🗐 🕹 🖥 🖼

◆◆ **Garden City Inn** **M**
(316) 276-7608. **$59-$79.** 1202 W Kansas Ave. At jct Business Rts US 50 W and 83 N. Int corridors. **Pets:** Supervision.
ASK S6 ⊠ 🕹 🖥 🖼

◆◆ **Garden City Plaza Inn** Ⓜ
(316) 275-7471. **$60-$70.** 1911 E Kansas. 0.5 mi w of US 50 and 83 bypass, on SR 156. Int corridors. **Pets:** Medium. No service, supervision, crate.

(ASK) (S) (✕) (🛏) 🗄 (¶) 🖼

◆◆◆ **Holiday Inn Express Hotel & Suites** Ⓜ
(316) 275-5900. **$85-$120, 3 days notice.** 2502 E Kansas Ave. At jct US 50, SR 83 and 156. Int corridors. **Pets:** Medium. No service, supervision, crate.

(ASK) (S) (✕) (🗝) (🛏) 🗄 🖥 🖼

🅐🅐🅐 ◆◆ **National 9 Inn** Ⓜ 🐾
(316) 275-0677. **$44-$59.** 123 Honey Bee Ct. 2.3 mi e on US 50 city route, at US 83 bypass. Ext corridors. **Pets:** Other. Supervision.

(SAVE) (S) (✕) 🗄 🖼

GOODLAND

🅐🅐🅐 ◆◆ **Best Western Buffalo Inn** Ⓜ 🐾
(785) 899-3621. **$62-$69.** 830 W Hwy 24. I-70, exit 17 or 19, n to jct US 24 and SR 27. Ext corridors. **Pets:** Other. $10 deposit/room. Designated rooms, supervision.

(SAVE) (S) (✕) 🖼 (✕)

◆◆◆ **Comfort Inn** Ⓜ
(785) 899-7181. **$59-$99.** 2519 Enterprise Rd. I-70, exit 17. Int corridors. **Pets:** Small. Designated rooms, no service, supervision, crate.

(ASK) (S) (✕) (♿) (♿) 🗄

GREAT BEND

🅐🅐🅐 ◆◆ **Best Western Angus Inn** Ⓜ 🐾
(316) 792-3541. **$49-$79.** 2920 10th St. 0.8 mi w on US 56, 156 and SR 96. Ext/int corridors. **Pets:** Medium, other. No service, supervision, crate.

(SAVE) (S) (✕) (🗝) 🗄 🖥 (¶) 🖼

◆◆◆ **Holiday Inn** Ⓜ 🐾
(316) 792-2431. **$67-$67.** 3017 10th St. 1 mi w on US 56, 156 and SR 96. Ext/int corridors. **Pets:** Medium, other. No service, supervision, crate.

(ASK) (S) (✕) (🗝) 🖥 (¶) 🗄 (✕)

🅐🅐🅐 ◆◆ **Travelers Budget Inn** Ⓜ
(316) 793-5448. **$33-$53.** 4200 W 10th St. 2 mi w on US 56, 156 and SR 96. Ext corridors. **Pets:** Medium. Designated rooms, no service, supervision, crate.

(SAVE) (S) (✕) 🗄

GREENSBURG

◆◆ **Best Western J-Hawk Motel** Ⓜ 🐾
(316) 723-2121. **$45-$65.** 515 W Kansas Ave. 0.3 mi w on US 54. Ext corridors. **Pets:** Designated rooms, no service, supervision, crate.

(ASK) (S) (✕) 🗄 🖥 🖼

HAYS

◆◆◆ **Best Western Vagabond Motel** Ⓜ 🐾
(785) 625-2511. **$52-$68.** 2524 Vine St. On US 183, 1 mi s of jct I-70, exit 159. Ext corridors. **Pets:** Medium. No service, supervision, crate.

(ASK) (S) (✕) (🗝) 🗄 🖥 🖼

🅐🅐🅐 ◆◆ **Budget Host Villa** Ⓜ
(785) 625-2563. **$30-$52.** 810 E 8th. On US 183, 2 mi s of jct I-70, exit 159. Ext corridors. **Pets:** Small. Designated rooms, supervision.

(SAVE) (✕) 🗄 🖥 🖼

◆◆◆ **Hampton Inn-Hays** Ⓜ 🐾
(785) 625-8103. **$65-$85.** 3801 Vine St. Off I-70, exit 159. Ext corridors. **Pets:** Other. Supervision.

(ASK) (S) (✕) (🗝) 🖼

◆◆◆ **Holiday Inn-Hays** Ⓜ
(785) 625-7371. **$74.** 3603 Vine St. On US 183, just s of I-70, exit 159. Ext/int corridors. **Pets:** Supervision.

(ASK) (S) (✕) (🗝) 🗄 🖼 (✕)

HAYSVILLE

🅐🅐🅐 ◆◆ **Haysville Inn** Ⓜ 🐾
(316) 522-1000. **$36-$40.** 301 E 71st S. I-35, exit 39, just w. Ext corridors. **Pets:** Small. No service, supervision, crate.

(SAVE) (S) (✕) (🗝)

HUTCHINSON

🅐🅐🅐 ◆ **Astro Motel** Ⓜ
(316) 663-1151. **$30-$60, 7 days notice.** 15 E 4th. Downtown; just e of Main St. Ext corridors. **Pets:** Designated rooms, supervision.

(SAVE) (✕) 🗄 🖼

◆◆ **Comfort Inn** Ⓜ 🐾
(316) 663-7822. **$67-$88, 3 days notice.** 1621 Super Plaza. 3 mi ne, just w of jct SR 61 and N 17th Ave. Int corridors. **Pets:** No service, supervision, crate.

(ASK) (S) (✕) (🗝) (♿) 🗄 🖥 🖼

◆◆◆ **Holiday Inn Express Hotel and Suites** Ⓜ 🐾
(316) 669-5200. **$85-$120, 3 days notice.** 1601 Super Plaza. 3 mi ne, just w of SR 61. Int corridors. **Pets:** Small, dogs only. No service, supervision, crate.

(ASK) (S) (✕) (♿) 🗄 🖼

◆◆ **Quality Inn City Center** Ⓜ
(316) 663-1211. **$45-$69.** 15 W 4th St. Just e of SR 96, downtown. Ext corridors. **Pets:** Supervision.

(ASK) (S) (✕) (🗝) 🗄 🖥 🖼

◆◆ **Ramada Inn** Ⓜ 🐾
(316) 669-9311. **Call for rates.** 1400 N Lorraine St. 2.5 mi ne at jct SR 61 and N 11th Ave. Ext/int corridors. **Pets:** Supervision.

(✕) (🗝) 🗄 🖥 (¶) 🖼

INDEPENDENCE

◆◆◆ **Appletree Inn** Ⓜ 🐾
(316) 331-5500. **$54-$65.** 201 N 8th St. 8th and Laurel sts. Ext/int corridors. **Pets:** Other. No service, supervision, crate.

(✕) 🗄 🖼

IOLA

🅐🅐🅐 ◆◆◆ **Best Western Inn** Ⓜ 🐾
(316) 365-5161. **$45-$53.** 1315 N State. 1 mi n on US 169. Ext corridors. **Pets:** Small. Supervision.

(SAVE) (S) (✕) (🗝) (🗝) 🗄 🖥 (¶) 🖼

JUNCTION CITY

⚠️ ◆◆ Days Inn 🅼 ☘
(785) 762-2727. **$59-$65.** 1024 S Washington St. Just n of I-70, exit 296. Ext/int corridors. **Pets:** Other. Designated rooms, no service, supervision, crate.
[SAVE] [S📶] [✕] [🔌] [🛏] [🖥] [🌊]

⚠️ ◆◆ Econo Lodge 🅼
(785) 238-8181. **$28-$72.** 211 Flint Hills Blvd. I-70, exit 299 (Grandview Plaza). Int corridors. **Pets:** Supervision.
[SAVE] [S📶] [✕] [🛏] [🖥]

◆◆◆ Holiday Inn Express 🅼 ☘
(785) 762-4200. **$74-$74, 7 days notice.** 120 N East St. I-70, exit 298, just nw. Int corridors. **Pets:** $5 daily fee/pet, $5 one-time fee/pet. No service, supervision, crate.
[ASK] [S📶] [✕] [🔌] [🛏] [🖥] [🌊]

⚠️ ◆◆ Ramada Limited 🅼 ☘
(785) 238-1141. **$57.** 1133 S Washington St. I-70, exit 296. Ext corridors. **Pets:** Small, dogs only. $10 deposit/room, $5 one-time fee/room. Designated rooms, no service, supervision, crate.
[SAVE] [S📶] [✕] [🛏]

KANSAS CITY METROPOLITAN AREA

KANSAS CITY

⚠️ ◆◆◆ Best Western Inn and Conference Center 🅼 ☘
(913) 677-3060. **$79-$89.** 501 Southwest Blvd. On US 169; just s of 7th St and I-35, exit 234. Int corridors. **Pets:** Designated rooms, no service, supervision, crate.
[SAVE] [S📶] [✕] [🛏] [🌊]

LENEXA

◆◆◆ La Quinta Inn 🅼
(913) 492-5500. **$65-$85.** 9461 Lenexa Dr. I-35, exit 224 (95th St), just ne; entrance left on Monrovia Rd off 95th St. Int corridors. **Pets:** Supervision.
[ASK] [✕] [🐾] [🛏] [🖥] [🌊]

⚠️ ◆◆◆ Wellesley Inn & Suites 🅼
(913) 894-5550. **$79-$109.** 8015 Lenexa Dr. From jct I-35 and exit 227, 1 mi s on e frontage road. Ext corridors. **Pets:** No service, supervision, crate.
[SAVE] [S📶] [✕] [🔌] [🐾] [🛏] [🖥] [🌊]

MERRIAM

◆◆◆ Drury Inn Shawnee Mission/Merriam 🅼 ☘
(913) 236-9200. **$60-$80.** 9009 Shawnee Mission Pkwy. I-35, exit 228B (Shawnee Mission Pkwy). Int corridors. **Pets:** Small. Designated rooms, no service, supervision, crate.
[✕] [🔌] [🛏] [🖥] [🌊]

◆◆◆ Homestead Village Guest Studios 🅼 ☘
(913) 236-6006. **$79.** 6451 E Frontage Rd. Just se of jct I-35 and exit 228B. **Pets:** Small, other. Supervision.
[✕] [♿] [🔌] [🐾] [🛏] [🖥]

OVERLAND PARK

⚠️ ◆◆◆ AmeriSuites 🅷 ☘
(913) 451-2553. **$82-$127.** 6801 W 112th St. From jct I-435 and exit 79, 0.6 mi s on Metcalf Ave, to 112th St, then just e. Int corridors. **Pets:** Small. No service, supervision, crate.
[SAVE] [S📶] [✕] [♿] [🔌] [🐾] [🛏] [🖥] [🌊]

⚠️ ◆◆◆ Doubletree Hotel 🅷 ☘
(913) 451-6100. **$74-$149.** 10100 College Blvd. Just s of jct I-435 and US 69; College Blvd E exit off US 69. Int corridors. **Pets:** Other. $150 one-time fee/room. Supervision.
[SAVE] [✕] [🛏] [🖥] [🍴] [🌊]

◆◆◆ Drury Inn-Overland Park 🅼
(913) 345-1500. **$68-$88.** 10951 Metcalf Ave. S of I-435, US 169 (Metcalf Ave) and exit 79. Int corridors. **Pets:** Medium. No service, supervision, crate.
[✕] [🐾] [🔌] [🛏] [🖥] [🌊]

◆◆◆ Holiday Inn of Mission-Overland Park 🅼
(913) 262-3010. **$72-$85.** 7240 W 63rd St. 1 mi e of I-35 and Shawnee Mission Pkwy, exit 228B. Ext/int corridors. **Pets:** Small. No service, supervision, crate.
[ASK] [S📶] [✕] [🐾] [🔌] [♿] [🛏] [🖥] [🍴] [🌊] [✕]

◆◆◆ Holtze Executive Village 🅼 ☘
(913) 344-8800. **$109-$149, 3 days notice.** 11400 College Blvd. From jct I-435 & exit 82 (Quivira Rd), 0.3 mi s, then just e. Int corridors. **Pets:** Small, dogs only. $75 deposit/room. Designated rooms, supervision.
[ASK] [S📶] [✕] [🔌] [♿] [🛏] [🖥] [🌊] [✕]

◆◆◆ Homestead Village Guest Studios 🅼 ☘
(913) 661-7111. **$59-$80, 3 days notice.** 5401 W 110th St. Just s of jct I-435 and exit 77B (Nall Ave). Int corridors. **Pets:** Small. $75 one-time fee/room. Supervision.
[✕] [♿] [🔌] [🛏] [🖥]

⚠️ ◆◆ Red Roof Inn-Overland Park 🅼 ☘
(913) 341-0100. **$51-$71.** 6800 W 108th St. I-435 and US 169-Metcalf Ave, exit 79. Ext corridors. **Pets:** Other. Designated rooms, supervision.
[SAVE] [✕] [🐾]

◆◆ White Haven Motor Lodge 🅼 ☘
(913) 649-8200. **$44-$54.** 8039 Metcalf Ave. On US 169 (Metcalf Ave) at 81st St; 3.5 mi n of I-435, exit 79 (US 169). Ext corridors. **Pets:** Small. No service, supervision, crate.
[✕] [🛏] [🌊]

☘ END METROPOLITAN AREA ☘

LANSING

(AAA) ◆◆ Econo Lodge M ❀
(913) 727-2777. **$42-$60.** 504 N Main. On US 73 and SR 7, 10 mi n from jct I-70, Leavenworth exit. Int corridors. **Pets:** Small, other. $25 deposit/room. No service, supervision, crate.

[SAVE] [S⊘] [✕] [📶] [📺]

◆◆◆ Holiday Inn Express Hotel & Suites M ❀
(913) 250-1000. **$83-$103, 3 days notice.** 120 Express Dr. Downtown on SR 7, just s of jct SR 5. Int corridors. **Pets:** Other. $50 deposit/room. No service, supervision, crate.

[ASK] [S⊘] [✕] [♿] [☕] [📶] [📺] [≋]

LARNED

◆◆ Best Western Townsman Inn M
(316) 285-3114. **$50-$60.** 123 E 14th. At jct US 56 and SR 156. Ext corridors. **Pets:** Medium. Designated rooms, no service, supervision, crate.

[ASK] [S⊘] [✕] [📶] [♿] [☕] [📺] [≋]

LAWRENCE

(AAA) ◆◆ Best Western Hallmark Inn M ❀
(785) 841-6500. **$54-$80, 7 days notice.** 730 Iowa St. 1 mi w on US 59, 1 mi s of W Lawrence Tpke exit. Ext corridors. **Pets:** $100 deposit/room, $10 one-time fee/room. Designated rooms, no service, supervision, crate.

[SAVE] [S⊘] [✕] [📺] [≋]

(AAA) ◆◆◆ Days Inn M ❀
(785) 843-9100. **$71-$95.** 2309 Iowa St. On US 59 at jct SR 10. Ext/int corridors. **Pets:** Other. $20 deposit/room. Designated rooms, no service, supervision, crate.

[SAVE] [S⊘] [✕] [♿] [☕] [📶] [📺] [≋]

(AAA) ◆◆◆ Holiday Inn M ❀
(785) 841-7077. **$99-$109.** 200 McDonald Dr. On SR 59, 0.5 mi s of I-70, W Lawrence exit. Ext/int corridors. **Pets:** Other. $25 deposit/room. Supervision.

[SAVE] [S⊘] [✕] [☕] [📶] [📺] [🍴] [≋] [✕]

◆◆◆ Ramada Inn M
(785) 842-7030. **$58-$82.** 2222 W 6th St. 1 mi s of I-70 Tpke, exit 202. Int corridors. **Pets:** Small. No service, supervision, crate.

[ASK] [S⊘] [✕] [☕] [📶] [📺] [🍴] [≋]

(AAA) ◆◆ Westminster Inn M
(785) 841-8410. **$50-$62, 3 days notice.** 2525 W 6th St. W on US 40, 0.3 mi w of turnpike exit 202. Ext corridors. **Pets:** Small. Designated rooms, no service, supervision, crate.

[SAVE] [✕] [≋]

LEAVENWORTH

(AAA) ◆◆ Best Western Hallmark Inn M ❀
(913) 651-6000. **$52-$64.** 3211 S 4th St. On US 73 and SR 7. Ext corridors. **Pets:** Medium, other. Designated rooms, no service, supervision, crate.

[SAVE] [S⊘] [✕] [📶] [📺] [≋]

LIBERAL

(AAA) ◆◆ Best Western LaFonda Motel & Restaurant M ❀
(316) 624-5601. **$38-$61.** 229 W Pancake Blvd. On US 54. Ext corridors. **Pets:** Small. No service, supervision, crate.

[SAVE] [S⊘] [✕] [☕] [📶] [📺] [🍴] [≋]

(AAA) ◆ Cimarron Inn M
(316) 624-6203. **$33-$45, 3 days notice.** 564 E Pancake Blvd. On US 54, 0.7 mi e of jct US 83 business route, 0.8 mi w of US 83 bypass. Ext corridors. **Pets:** Designated rooms, no service, supervision, crate.

[SAVE] [S⊘] [✕] [📺]

(AAA) ◆◆ Liberal Inn M ❀
(316) 624-7254. **$45-$67.** 603 E Pancake Blvd. On US 54, 0.5 mi w of US 83. Int corridors. **Pets:** No service, supervision, crate.

[SAVE] [S⊘] [✕] [📶] [📺] [≋]

(AAA) ◆ Thunderbird Inn M ❀
(316) 624-7271. **$30-$38, 3 days notice.** 2100 N Kansas Ave. 2 mi n of US 54. Ext corridors. **Pets:** $25 deposit/room, $25 one-time fee/room. No service, supervision, crate.

[SAVE] [✕] [📶] [≋]

LYONS

◆ Lyons Inn M
(316) 257-5185. **$36-$50.** 817 W Main. 1 mi w on SR 56 and 96. Int corridors. **Pets:** No service, supervision, crate.

[ASK] [S⊘] [✕] [📶]

MANHATTAN

◆◆◆ Hampton Inn M
(785) 539-5000. **$62-$74.** 501 E Poyntz. From SR 177, 0.3 mi e on US 24. Int corridors. **Pets:** Medium. Designated rooms, no service, supervision, crate.

[ASK] [S⊘] [✕] [☕] [📶] [📺] [≋]

(AAA) ◆◆◆ Holiday Inn/Holidome M
(785) 539-5311. **$83.** 530 Richards Dr. 2.5 mi sw on SR 18, 0.3 mi e of jct SR 113. Ext/int corridors. **Pets:** Designated rooms, supervision.

[SAVE] [S⊘] [✕] [☕] [📶] [📺] [🍴] [≋] [✕]

(AAA) ◆ Motel 6–152 M
(785) 537-1022. **$38-$54.** 510 Tuttle Creek Blvd. 0.3 mi ne on US 24 and SR 177. Ext corridors. **Pets:** Supervision.

[S⊘] [✕] [☕] [♿] [≋]

◆◆◆ Ramada Plaza Hotel M ❀
(785) 539-7531. **$85-$139, 7 days notice.** 17th & Anderson. 1 mi n of SR 18; opposite Kansas State University. Int corridors. **Pets:** $10 one-time fee/room. No service, supervision, crate.

[ASK] [S⊘] [✕] [📶] [📺] [🍴] [≋]

MARYSVILLE

◆◆ Best Western Surf Motel M ❀
(785) 562-2354. **$49-$54.** 2105 Center St. 1 mi e on US 36. Ext/int corridors. **Pets:** Medium, other. $5 deposit/pet. Supervision.

[ASK] [S⊘] [✕] [☕] [📶] [📺]

◆◆ **Oak Tree Inn-Marysville** Ⓜ ❖
(785) 562-1234. **$54.** 1127 Pony Express Hwy. 1.6 mi e on (Pony Express Hwy) US 36. Int corridors. **Pets:** $10 one-time fee/room. Supervision.

(A$K) (S▵) (✕) (🛄)

◆◆ **Super 8 Motel** Ⓜ ❖
(785) 562-5588. **Call for rates.** 1155 Pony Express Hwy. 2 mi e on US 36. Int corridors. **Pets:** Other. $5 deposit/room. Designated rooms, no service, supervision, crate.

(A$K) (✕) (🛄)

MCPHERSON

◆◆ **Best Western Holiday Manor Motel** Ⓜ ❖
(316) 241-5343. **$52-$62.** 2211 E Kansas Ave. I-135, exit 60. Ext/int corridors. **Pets:** Small. $10 daily fee/pet. No service, supervision, crate.

(A$K) (S▵) (✕) (🏊) (🛄) (🍴) (🍽)

🆔 ◆ **Red Coach Inn** Ⓜ ❖
(316) 241-6960. **$47-$59.** 2111 E Kansas Ave. I-135, exit 60, just w. Ext/int corridors. **Pets:** Other. $15 one-time fee/room. Designated rooms, no service, supervision, crate.

(SAVE) (S▵) (✕) (🛄) (🍴) (🍽) (✕)

MEADE

🆔 ◆ **Dalton's Bedpost Motel** Ⓜ ❖
(316) 873-2131. **$34-$40, 3 days notice.** 519 Carthage. On US 54. Ext corridors. **Pets:** Other. No service, supervision, crate.

(SAVE) (S▵) (✕)

MEDICINE LODGE

🆔 ◆ **Copa Motel** Ⓜ ❖
(316) 886-5673. **$33-$42, 3 days notice.** 401 W Fowler. Just e of jct 281 N and US 160. Ext corridors. **Pets:** Small. Designated rooms, no service, supervision, crate.

(SAVE) (S▵) (✕) (🖥) (🍽)

NEWTON

🆔 ◆◆ **Best Western Red Coach Inn** 🅷 ❖
(316) 283-9120. **$51-$109.** 1301 E 1st St. I-135, exit 31. Ext/int corridors. **Pets:** Other. No service, supervision, crate.

(SAVE) (S▵) (✕) (🏊) (🛄) (🖥) (🍽)

◆◆ **Days Inn Newton** Ⓜ ❖
(316) 283-3330. **$55-$59.** 105 Manchester. I-135, exit 31. Int corridors. **Pets:** Supervision.

(A$K) (S▵) (✕) (🛄) (🖥) (🍽)

NORTON

🆔 ◆◆ **Hillcrest Motel** Ⓜ
(785) 877-3343. **$40-$48.** Hwy 36 W. On US 36 and 383, 0.3 mi w of jct US 283. Ext corridors. **Pets:** Small. No service, supervision, crate.

(SAVE) (✕) (🍽) (✕)

OAKLEY

🆔 ◆ **Annie Oakley Motel** Ⓜ ❖
(785) 672-3223. **$33-$44.** 428 Center Ave. Center. Ext corridors. **Pets:** Small. No service, supervision, crate.

(SAVE) (S▵)

◆◆ **Best Western Golden Plains Motel** Ⓜ ❖
(785) 672-3254. **$49-$69, 7 days notice.** 3506 US 40. I-70, exit 76, 1.7 mi w. Ext corridors. **Pets:** Small, other. No service, supervision, crate.

(A$K) (S▵) (✕) (🖥) (🍽)

🆔 ◆ **1st Travel Inn** Ⓜ
(785) 672-3226. **$33-$49.** 708 Center Ave. Center. Ext corridors. **Pets:** Small. No service, supervision, crate.

(SAVE) (S▵) (✕) (🍴) (🍽)

🆔 ◆◆ **Kansas Kountry Inn** Ⓜ ❖
(785) 672-3131. **$40-$66.** 3538 US 40. Off I-70, exit 76, 1.5 mi w. Ext corridors. **Pets:** Designated rooms, no service, supervision, crate.

(SAVE) (S▵) (✕) (🖥) (🍽)

OBERLIN

🆔 ◆ **Frontier Motel** Ⓜ
(785) 475-2203. **$31-$49.** 207 E Frontier Pkwy. On US 36, 0.5 mi e of jct US 83. Ext corridors. **Pets:** Small. No service, supervision, crate.

(SAVE) (S▵) (✕) (🛄) (🍴) (🍽)

OTTAWA

🆔 ◆◆ **Best Western Hallmark Inn** Ⓜ ❖
(785) 242-7000. **$49-$79.** 2209 S Princeton Rd. At jct I-35 and US 59, exit 183B. Ext corridors. **Pets:** Medium. $50 deposit/room, $10 one-time fee/pet. Designated rooms, no service, supervision, crate.

(SAVE) (S▵) (✕) (🛄) (🖥) (🍽)

🆔 ◆◆ **Days Inn** Ⓜ ❖
(785) 242-4842. **$45-$80, 7 days notice.** 1641 S Main. On US 59, 1.5 mi n of I-35, exit 183B. Ext corridors. **Pets:** Small, dogs only. $25 deposit/room. Designated rooms, no service, supervision, crate.

(SAVE) (S▵) (✕) (🛁) (🛄) (🖥) (🍽)

🆔 ◆◆ **Econo Lodge** Ⓜ
(785) 242-3400. **$42-$80, 7 days notice.** 2331 S Cedar Rd. At jct I-35 and US 59, exit 183B. Int corridors. **Pets:** Supervision.

(SAVE) (S▵) (✕) (🛄) (🖥) (🍽)

🆔 ◆◆◆ **Holiday Inn Express** Ⓜ ❖
(785) 242-2224. **$50-$90, 5 days notice.** 606 E 23rd St. Off I-35, exit 183B. Ext corridors. **Pets:** Small. $25 deposit/room. Designated rooms, no service, supervision, crate.

(SAVE) (S▵) (✕) (🛁) (🛄) (🖥) (🍽)

PHILLIPSBURG

◆◆ **Cottonwood Inn** Ⓜ
(785) 543-2125. **$47-$87, 7 days notice.** 1200 State St. 2.1 mi e on US 36. Ext corridors. **Pets:** Medium. No service, supervision, crate.

(A$K) (S▵) (✕) (🍽)

PRATT

🆔 ◆◆ **Best Western Hillcrest Motel** Ⓜ
(316) 672-6407. **$35-$65, 3 days notice.** 1336 E 1st St. 1 mi e on US 54. Ext corridors. **Pets:** Designated rooms, supervision.

(SAVE) (S▵) (✕) (🛄) (🍽)

♦♦ Days Inn M ☻
(316) 672-9465. **$42-$65.** 1901 E 1st. 1.7 mi e on US 54. Ext corridors. **Pets:** Medium. $20 deposit/room, $5 daily fee/room, $5 one-time fee/room. No service, supervision, crate.
[SAVE] [S] [X] [日] [🖼]

♦ Economy Inn M ☻
(316) 672-5588. **$26-$65.** 1401 E First St. 1 mi e on US 54. Ext corridors. **Pets:** Medium. $5 daily fee/room, $5 one-time fee/room. Supervision.
[SAVE] [S] [X] [日] [🖼]

♦ Evergreen Inn M ☻
(316) 672-6431. **$23-$32, 3 days notice.** 20001 W US Hwy 54. 3 mi w on US 54. Ext corridors. **Pets:** Other. Designated rooms, supervision.
[ASK] [S] [X] [日] [🖼]

♦♦♦ Holiday Inn Express M
(316) 672-9433. **$65-$82, 3 days notice.** 1401 W Hwy 54. 2 mi w on US 54. Int corridors. **Pets:** Supervision.
[ASK] [S] [X] [🏵] [日] [🖳] [🖼]

♦♦ Pratt Super 8 M ☻
(316) 672-5945. **Call for rates.** 1906 E 1st St. 1.7 mi e on US 54. Int corridors. **Pets:** Small, other. Supervision.
[X]

QUINTER

♦ Budget Host "Q" Motel M ☻
(785) 754-3337. **$40-$50, 5 days notice.** On SR 212 at jct I-70, exit 107. Ext corridors. **Pets:** Other. Supervision.
[X] [𝍐]

RUSSELL

♦♦ Days Inn M ☻
(785) 483-6660. **$40-$62.** 1225 S Fossil St. Off I-70, exit 184, just n. Ext corridors. **Pets:** Other. $25 deposit/room, $3 daily fee/pet, $3 one-time fee/pet. Designated rooms, no service, supervision, crate.
[ASK] [S] [X] [日] [🖼]

SABETHA

♦♦ Sabetha Country Inn M
(785) 284-2300. **Call for rates.** 1423 S 75 Hwy. Just s on US 75. Int corridors. **Pets:** No service, supervision, crate.
[X] [日]

SALINA

♦♦♦ Best Western Mid-America Inn M ☻
(785) 827-0356. **$47-$62.** 1846 N 9th St. I-70, exit 252, just s. Ext corridors. **Pets:** Other. Supervision.
[S] [X] [𝍐] [𝍐] [🖼]

♦♦ Comfort Inn M ☻
(785) 826-1711. **$40-$70.** 1820 W Crawford. I-135, exit 92, 0.3 mi e. Int corridors. **Pets:** Other. $5 daily fee/pet. Designated rooms, no service, supervision, crate.
[ASK] [S] [X] [🏵] [日] [🖳] [🖼]

♦♦♦ Holiday Inn of Salina M
(785) 823-1739. **$59-$75.** 1616 W Crawford St. I-135, exit 92, 0.5 mi e. Int corridors. **Pets:** Small. Designated rooms, no service, supervision, crate.
[ASK] [S] [X] [🏵] [日] [🖳] [𝍐] [🖼] [X]

♦♦ Ramada Inn M ☻
(785) 825-8211. **$72-$72.** 1949 N 9th St. I-70, exit 252, just s. Ext corridors. **Pets:** Other. $10 deposit/room. Supervision.
[ASK] [S] [X] [🖼]

♦♦ Red Coach Inn M ☻
(785) 825-2111. **$59-$75.** 2020 W Crawford. 2 mi s on I-135 from jct I-70; I-135, exit 92, just w. Ext/int corridors. **Pets:** $15 one-time fee/room. Designated rooms, no service, supervision, crate.
[SAVE] [S] [X] [🏵] [𝍐] [日] [🖼] [X]

♦♦ Salina Super 8 Motel M ☻
(785) 823-9215. **$45-$75, 30 days notice.** 1640 W Crawford. 2 mi s on I-135 from jct I-70; I-135, exit 92, just e. Int corridors. **Pets:** Other. No service, supervision, crate.
[ASK] [S] [X]

♦♦ Super 8 I-70 M ☻
(785) 823-8808. **$56-$78.** 120 E Diamond Dr. I-70, exit 252, just n. Int corridors. **Pets:** Medium. $6 daily fee/pet. No service, supervision, crate.
[SAVE] [S] [X] [𝍐] [日] [🖼]

SHARON SPRINGS

♦♦ Oak Tree Inn M ☻
(785) 852-4664. **$55-$73.** At jct US 40 and SR 27. Ext/int corridors. **Pets:** $20 deposit/room. No service, supervision, crate.
[ASK] [S] [X] [🏵] [𝍐] [日] [𝍐]

TOPEKA

♦♦ Best Western Meadow Acres Motel M ☻
(785) 267-1681. **$50-$90, 7 days notice.** 2950 S Topeka Blvd. Eastbound I-470 exit 6; westbound US 177, 1.5 mi n. Ext corridors. **Pets:** Small. $8 one-time fee/pet. Designated rooms, no service, supervision, crate.
[SAVE] [S] [X] [日] [🖳] [🖼]

♦♦♦ Capitol Plaza Hotel H
(785) 431-7200. **$107-$119.** 1717 Topeka Blvd. I-70, exit SE 8th Ave, 0.5 mi s to Topeka Blvd, 1.1 mi s; I-470, exit Topeka Blvd, 2.9 mi n. Int corridors. **Pets:** Designated rooms, no service, supervision, crate.
[ASK] [S] [X] [🏵] [𝍐] [日] [🖳] [𝍐] [🖼]

♦♦ Comfort Inn M ☻
(785) 273-5365. **$64-$109.** 1518 SW Wanamaker Rd. I-470, exit 1 and Wanamaker Rd. Int corridors. **Pets:** Small. Designated rooms, no service, supervision, crate.
[ASK] [S] [X] [日] [🖳] [🖼]

♦♦♦ Days Inn Capital Centre M ☻
(785) 232-7721. **$54-$69.** 914 SE Madison. I-70 E, exit 362-B (8th Ave), just e to 10th Ave, just n; I-70 W, exit 362-C, 10th Ave and Madison, just w. Int corridors. **Pets:** Supervision.
[ASK] [S] [X] [🏵] [日] [🖳] [𝍐] [🖼]

◆◆ Ramada Inn Downtown 🏨 🐾

(785) 234-5400. **$85-$95.** 420 SE Sixth St. I-70, exit 362B, just e. Int corridors. **Pets:** Small. Designated rooms, supervision.

(A$K) 🔊 ⊠ 🖥 💻 🍴 🕾

◆◆◆ Residence Inn 🅰

(785) 271-8903. **$99.** 1620 SW Westport Dr. Off I-470, exit 1 (Wanamaker Rd). Int corridors. **Pets:** No service, supervision, crate.

(A$K) 🔊 ⊠ 🕿 🖋 🖥 💻 🕾 ⊠

ULYSSES

🔺 ◆◆◆ Single Tree Inn 🅼 🐾

(316) 356-1500. **$60-$75, 3 days notice.** 2033 W Oklahoma St. 1.5 mi w on US 160. Int corridors. **Pets:** Medium, other. $25 deposit/room. Designated rooms, supervision.

(SAVE) 🔊 ⊠ 🕿 🖥 💻

WAMEGO

🔺 ◆ Simmer Motel 🅼

(785) 456-2304. **$30-$42.** 1215 Hwy 24 W. 0.5 mi w on US 24 from jct SR 99. Ext corridors. **Pets:** Small. Designated rooms, no service, supervision, crate.

(SAVE) ⊠ 🖥 💻 🕾 ⊠

WICHITA

🔺 ◆◆◆ Best Western Airport Red Coach Inn 🅼 🐾

(316) 942-5600. **$82-$86.** 6815 W Kellogg. Off I-235, exit 7A or 7B, 0.3 mi w on US 54. Int corridors. **Pets:** Small, other. $25 deposit/room, $25 one-time fee/room. No service, supervision, crate.

(SAVE) 🔊 ⊠ 🖋 🖥 🍴 🕾 ⊠

🔺 ◆◆ Best Western Red Coach Inn 🅼 🐾

(316) 832-9387. **$64-$69.** 915 E 53rd St N. I-135, exit 13. Ext/int corridors. **Pets:** Small, dogs only. $15 daily fee/pet, $25 one-time fee/pet. Supervision.

(SAVE) 🔊 ⊠ 🕿 🖥 🍴 🕾 ⊠

◆◆◆ Comfort Inn 🅼 🐾

(316) 686-2844. **$69-$89.** 9525 E Corporate Hills. 6 mi e, just n of jct US 54, SR 96 and turnpike exit 50. Int corridors. **Pets:** Medium. $20 one-time fee/room. Designated rooms, no service, supervision, crate.

(A$K) 🔊 ⊠ 👵 🕿 🖋 🖥 💻 🕾

🔺 ◆◆ Comfort Inn 🅼 🐾

(316) 522-1800. **$60-$86.** 4849 S Laura. I-135, exit 1AB (47th St S), just e. Int corridors. **Pets:** Other. $10 deposit/room, $10 daily fee/room. No service, supervision, crate.

(SAVE) 🔊 ⊠ 🕿 🖋 🖥 💻 🕾

🔺 ◆◆◆ Comfort Suites Airport 🅼 🐾

(316) 945-2600. **$79-$159.** 658 Westdale. Jct US 54 and I-235, adjacent to Towne West Square. Int corridors. **Pets:** Small, other. No service, supervision, crate.

(SAVE) 🔊 ⊠ 🕿 🖥 💻 🕾

◆◆ Four Points Hotel Wichita 🏨

(316) 686-7131. **$65-$65.** 549 S Rock Rd. On US 54 and SR 96, 0.5 mi w of turnpike, exit 50. Ext/int corridors. **Pets:** Supervision.

(A$K) 🔊 ⊠ 🏠 🕿 🖋 🖥 💻 🍴 🕾

◆◆◆ Hampton Inn 🅼

(316) 686-3576. **$74-$99.** 9449 E Corporate Hills. 6 mi e, just n of jct US 54, SR 96 and turnpike exit 50. Int corridors. **Pets:** Supervision.

(A$K) 🔊 ⊠ 👵 🕿 🖋 🖥 💻 🕾

◆◆◆ Hawthorn Suites at Reflection Ridge 🅼 🐾

(316) 729-5700. **$100-$170, 3 days notice.** 2405 N Ridge Rd. I-235, exit 10, 2 mi w on Zoo Blvd/21st St N, then just n. Int corridors. **Pets:** Small, other. $50 one-time fee/room. No service, supervision, crate.

(A$K) 🔊 ⊠ 🏠 🖋 🖥 💻

🔺 ◆◆◆ Holiday Inn Wichita/Airport 🅼 🐾

(316) 943-2181. **$79-$89.** 5500 W Kellogg. On US 54, jct I-235. Int corridors. **Pets:** Small. No service, supervision, crate.

(SAVE) ⊠ 🕿 🖋 🖥 💻 🍴 🕾

🔺 ◆◆◆ The Kansas Inn 🅼 🐾

(316) 269-9999. **$55-$65.** 1011 N Topeka Ave. Off I-135, exit 8 (13th St), 0.7 mi w, then 0.3 mi s. Int corridors. **Pets:** Other. $5 daily fee/room. Designated rooms, supervision.

(SAVE) 🔊 ⊠ 🕿 🖋 🖥

◆◆◆ La Quinta Inn 🅼 🐾

(316) 681-2881. **$65-$85.** 7700 E Kellogg. On US 54 and SR 96, 0.5 mi w of turnpike exit 50; adjacent to Towne East Shopping Mall; nw corner of Kellogg and Rock rds. Int corridors. **Pets:** Small, dogs only. No service, supervision, crate.

(A$K) ⊠ 🕿 🖋 🖥 💻 🕾

🔺 ◆◆ Quality Inn-Airport 🅼 🐾

(316) 722-8730. **$45-$55.** 600 S Holland. 0.5 mi w of I-235, exit 7 on US 54. Int corridors. **Pets:** Medium. $20 deposit/room. No service, supervision, crate.

(SAVE) 🔊 ⊠ 🕿 🖥 💻 🕾

◆◆ Red Carpet Inn 🅼

(316) 264-2323. **$38-$44, 5 days notice.** 925 N Broadway. Off I-135, exit 8 (13th St), 0.8 mi w, then 0.5 mi s. Ext corridors. **Pets:** Small. Supervision.

🔊 ⊠ 🖥

🔺 ◆◆ Red Carpet Inn 🅼 🐾

(316) 529-4100. **$48-$55.** 607 E 47th St S. I-135, exit 1B (47th St S), 0.3 mi w. Ext corridors. **Pets:** Small. $5 daily fee/pet, $5 one-time fee/pet. No service, supervision, crate.

(SAVE) 🔊 ⊠ 🖥

YATES CENTER

◆ Star Motel 🅼 🐾

(316) 625-2175. **$25-$33.** 206 S Fry. On US 54 at jct US 75. Ext corridors. **Pets:** Other. No service, supervision, crate.

⊠

ASHLAND

⁴⁴⁴ ◆◆◆ Days Inn M ❅
(606) 928-3600. **$47-$68.** 12700 SR 180. I-64, exit 185, 0.8 mi n. Int corridors. **Pets:** Medium, other. $5 daily fee/pet. No service, supervision, crate.

[SAVE] [S⁄] [✕] [🛏] [💻] [🏊]

⁴⁴⁴ ◆◆ Knights Inn M ❅
(606) 928-9501. **$38-$48, 7 days notice.** 7216 US Rt 60. 5 mi sw on US 60; 4.8 mi n of jct I-64, exit 185. Ext corridors. **Pets:** Small, other. $5 daily fee/room. Designated rooms, no service, supervision, crate.

[SAVE] [S⁄] [✕] [🛏] [🏊]

BARDSTOWN

⁴⁴⁴ ◆◆ Bardstown-Parkview Motel MI ❅
(502) 348-5983. **$60-$70.** 418 E Stephen Foster Ave. 0.5 mi e on US 150; e of jct US 62. Ext corridors. **Pets:** Small. No service, supervision, crate.

[SAVE] [S⁄] [✕] [🛏] [🍽] [🏊] [✕]

⁴⁴⁴ ◆◆◆ Hampton Inn M ❅
(502) 349-0100. **$65-$80.** 985 Chambers Blvd. Just s of US 245. Int corridors. **Pets:** Other. Supervision.

[SAVE] [✕] [♿] [🐾] [🖥] [🛏] [💻] [🏊]

⁴⁴⁴ ◆◆◆ Holiday Inn Convention Center MI ❅
(502) 348-9253. **$59-$74.** 1875 New Haven Rd. Blue Grass Pkwy, exit 21. Ext corridors. **Pets:** Medium. Supervision.

[SAVE] [S⁄] [✕] [🛏] [💻] [🍽] [🏊] [✕]

⁴⁴⁴ ◆ Old Kentucky Home Motel M ❅
(502) 348-5979. **$60-$65.** 414 W Stephen Foster Ave. 0.5 mi w on US 62. Ext corridors. **Pets:** Other. $20 deposit/room. No service, supervision, crate.

[✕] [🛏] [💻] [🏊]

◆◆◆ Ramada Inn M ❅
(502) 349-0363. **$55-$180.** 523 N Third St. 0.5 mi n on US 150. Ext corridors. **Pets:** $10 one-time fee/room. No service, supervision, crate.

[ASK] [S⁄] [✕] [🛏] [💻] [🏊]

BEREA

⁴⁴⁴ ◆◆◆ Boone Tavern Hotel-Berea College H
(606) 986-9358. **$60-$90.** 100 Main St. I-75, exit 76, 1.5 mi ne on SR 21. Int corridors. **Pets:** No service, supervision, crate.

[SAVE] [S⁄] [✕] [🐾]

◆◆ Days Inn M
(606) 986-7373. **$40-$45.** 1202 Walnut Meadow Rd. W of I-75, exit 77. Ext corridors. **Pets:** No service, supervision, crate.

[ASK] [S⁄] [✕] [🛏] [🛏] [🏊] [✕] [CTV]

⁴⁴⁴ ◆◆◆ Holiday Motel M ❅
(606) 986-9311. **$45-$65.** 100 Jane St. Jct I-75, exit 76, just e. Ext corridors. **Pets:** Small. $5 daily fee/room, $5 one-time fee/room. Designated rooms, no service, supervision, crate.

[✕] [🐾] [🛏] [🏊]

⁴⁴⁴ ◆◆ Knights Inn Berea M ❅
(606) 986-2384. **$38-$60.** 715 Chestnut St. I-75, exit 76, 0.3 mi e. Ext corridors. **Pets:** Other. $5 daily fee/pet, $5 one-time fee/pet. Supervision.

[SAVE] [S⁄] [✕] [🛏]

⁴⁴⁴ ◆◆ Super 8 Motel M ❅
(606) 986-8426. **$39-$60.** 196 Prince Royal Dr. I-75, exit 76, 0.3 mi e. Ext corridors. **Pets:** No service, supervision, crate.

[SAVE] [S⁄] [✕] [🛏] [🏊]

BOWLING GREEN

◆◆ Days Inn M ❅
(270) 781-6470. **$38-$65, 7 days notice.** 4617 Scottsville Rd. 0.3 mi e of I-65, exit 22. Int corridors. **Pets:** $10 one-time fee/pet. Supervision.

[ASK] [S⁄] [✕] [🐾] [🏊]

◆◆◆ Drury Inn-Bowling Green M ❅
(270) 842-7100. **$62-$82.** 3250 Scottsville Rd. I-65, exit 22 (Scottsville Rd), just w. Int corridors. **Pets:** Small, other. No service, supervision, crate.

[✕] [🖥] [🛏] [🏊]

◆◆◆ **Holiday Inn** [MI] 🐾
(270) 781-1500. **$40-$90.** 3240 Scottsville Rd. I-65, exit 22 (Scottsville Rd). Ext corridors. **Pets:** Medium, other. No service, supervision, crate.
[ASK] [SD] 🚭 🦻 ☎ ☕ 🍴 🏊

[AAA] ◆◆◆ **News Inn of Bowling Green** [M] 🐾
(270) 781-3460. **$42-$65, 3 days notice.** 3160 Scottsville Rd. I-65, exit 22 (Scottsville Rd). Ext corridors. **Pets:** Small. $5 daily fee/room. Designated rooms, no service, supervision, crate.
[SAVE] [SD] 🚭 ☎ 🏊

◆◆ **Ramada Inn** [MI] 🐾
(270) 781-3000. **$58-$65.** 4767 Scottsville Rd. I-65, exit 22 (Scottsville Rd), 0.3 mi e. Int corridors. **Pets:** Medium. No service, supervision, crate.
[ASK] 🚭 🦻 ☎ ☕ 🍴 🏊 🏋

[AAA] ◆◆ **Super 8 Motel** [M]
(270) 781-9594. **$39-$54, 5 days notice.** 250 Cumberland Trace Rd. I-65, exit 22 (Scottsville Rd), just ne. Int corridors. **Pets:** Supervision.
[SAVE] [SD] 🚭 ☎ 🏊

BURKESVILLE

◆◆ **Riverfront Lodge** [M] 🐾
(270) 864-3300. **$39-$48.** 305 Keen St. 0.5 mi e on SR 90. Ext corridors. **Pets:** $5 daily fee/room. Supervision.
[SD] 🚭 🏊 🏋

CADIZ

◆◆◆ **Holiday Inn Express** [M]
(270) 522-3700. **$64-$85, 3 days notice.** 153 Broad Bent Blvd. I-24, exit 65, just s. Int corridors. **Pets:** Medium. Designated rooms, supervision.
[ASK] [SD] 🚭 ☎ 🏊

◆◆◆ **Super 8 Motel** [M]
(270) 522-7007. **$43-$63, 3 days notice.** 154 Hospitality Ln. I-24, exit 65. Ext corridors. **Pets:** Designated rooms, no service, supervision, crate.
[ASK] [SD] 🚭 ☕ 🏊

CAMPBELLSVILLE

◆◆ **Best Western Campbellsville Lodge** [M] 🐾
(270) 465-7001. **$54-$59.** 1400 E Broadway. 1 mi e on US 68 and SR 55. Int corridors. **Pets:** Very small. Supervision.
[ASK] [SD] 🚭 ☎ 🏊

CARROLLTON

[AAA] ◆◆ **Days Inn Carrollton** [MI] 🐾
(502) 732-9301. **$55-$59, 3 days notice.** 61 Inn Rd. I-71, exit 44. Int corridors. **Pets:** Small. No service, supervision, crate.
[SAVE] [SD] 🚭 ☎ 🏊

◆◆ **Holiday Inn Express** [M] 🐾
(502) 732-6661. **$59-$65, 3 days notice.** 141 Inn Rd. I-71, exit 44. Int corridors. **Pets:** Small. $20 deposit/room. No service, supervision, crate.
[ASK] [SD] 🚭 ☎

◆◆ **Super 8 Carrollton** [M] 🐾
(502) 732-0252. **$49-$55, 3 days notice.** 130 Slumber Ln. At jct SR 227 and I-71, exit 44. Int corridors. **Pets:** Small. No service, supervision, crate.
[ASK] [SD] 🚭 ☎

CAVE CITY

◆◆ **Best Western Kentucky Inn** [M] 🐾
(270) 773-3161. **$44-$74.** 1009 Doyle Ave. Se of I-65, exit 53. Ext corridors. **Pets:** $5 daily fee/room, $5 one-time fee/room. No service, supervision, crate.
[ASK] [SD] 🚭 🏊

[AAA] ◆◆◆ **Comfort Inn** [M] 🐾
(270) 773-2030. **$40-$80.** 801 Mammoth Cave St. I-65, exit 53; just ne. Ext corridors. **Pets:** Very small. $5 one-time fee/pet. Designated rooms, no service, supervision, crate.
[SAVE] [SD] 🚭 🚿 ☎ ☕ 🏊 🏋

◆◆ **Days Inn Cave City** [M]
(270) 773-2151. **$56-$76.** 822 Mammoth Cave Rd. I-65, exit 53, just e. Ext/int corridors. **Pets:** Supervision.
[ASK] [SD] 🚭 🦻 ☎ 🏊

[AAA] ◆◆◆ **Holiday Inn Express** [M] 🐾
(270) 773-3101. **$64-$79.** 102 Happy Valley Rd. I-65 exit 53. Ext corridors. **Pets:** Small. $7 daily fee/room. No service, supervision, crate.
[SAVE] [SD] 🚭 🦻 ☎ ☕ 🏊

◆◆ **Quality Inn** [M]
(270) 773-2181. **$49-$79.** 1006 A Doyle Ave. I-65, exit 53, just se. Ext corridors. **Pets:** No service, supervision, crate.
[ASK] [SD] 🚭 🦻 ☎ ☕ 🏊 🏋

[AAA] ◆◆◆ **Super 8 Motel** [M]
(270) 773-2500. **$49-$85.** 799 Mammoth Cave St. I-65, exit 53 (US 90) 0.5 mi e to SR 70 n, just n. Ext corridors. **Pets:** Small. Designated rooms, no service, supervision, crate.
[SAVE] [SD] 🚭 ♿ 🚿 ☎ 🏊

CORBIN

◆◆◆ **Baymont Inn & Suites** [M] 🐾
(606) 523-9040. **$40-$65.** 174 Adams Rd. I-75, exit 29. Int corridors. **Pets:** Small. Designated rooms, no service, supervision, crate.
[ASK] [SD] 🚭 ♿ 🚿 ☎ ☕ 🏊

COVINGTON

[AAA] ◆◆◆ **Clarion Hotel Riverview** [H]
(606) 491-1200. **$104-$114, 5 days notice.** 668 W 5th St. Jct I-71 and 75, exit 192 (5th St). Int corridors. **Pets:** Designated rooms, supervision.
[SAVE] [SD] 🚭 🛗 🦻 🚿 ☎ ☕ 🍴 🏊

◆◆◆ **Embassy Suites Cincinnati Rivercenter** [H]
(606) 261-8400. **$139-$189.** 10 E River Center Blvd. I-75, exit 192, 0.8 mi e on 5th Ave, 0.3 mi n on Madison. Int corridors. **Pets:** Designated rooms, supervision.
🚭 🛗 🦻 ☎ ☕ 🍴 🏊

◆◆◆ Sandford House Bed & Breakfast 🅱🅱
(606) 291-9133. **$50-$100.** 1026 Russell St. I-71 and I-75, exit 192, 0.5 mi e on 5th St, 0.5 mi s. Int corridors. **Pets:** Medium. No service, supervision, crate.

❌ 🖥 💻

DANVILLE

◆◆ Super 8 Motel M ❀
(606) 236-8881. **$42-$65, 7 days notice.** 3663 Hwy 150/127 bypass. 2.5 mi s on US 150 E bypass, 0.5 mi e of jct US 127. Int corridors. **Pets:** Other. $25 deposit/pet, $6 daily fee/pet, $6 one-time fee/pet. No service, supervision, crate.

ASK 🔟 ❌ 🗒 🖥

DRY RIDGE

◆◆◆ Holiday Inn Express M ❀
(606) 824-7161. **$69-$75.** 1050 Fashion Ridge Rd. I-75, exit 159. Int corridors. **Pets:** Small. $20 deposit/room, $10 one-time fee/room. No service, supervision, crate.

ASK 🔟 ❌ 🖥

EDDYVILLE

◆◆◆ Eddy Bay Lodging M ❀
(270) 388-9960. **$64-$125, 30 days notice.** 75 Forest Glen Dr. On SR 93, 3.6 mi s of I-24, exit 45. Ext corridors. **Pets:** Dogs only. $20 deposit/pet, $3 daily fee/pet. No service, supervision, crate.

🖥 💻 ❌ 📺 ✆

◆◆ Holiday Hills Townhouses M
(270) 388-7236. **$140, 30 days notice.** 5631 Kentucky 93 S. I-24, exit 45, 2 mi s on SR 93. Ext corridors. **Pets:** Designated rooms, supervision.

🖥 💻 🖼 ❌ ✆

ELIZABETHTOWN

◆◆ Best Western Cardinal Inn M ❀
(270) 765-6139. **$59-$79, 4 days notice.** 642 E Dixie Ave. US 31W, 0.3 mi nw of I-65, exit 91. Ext/int corridors. **Pets:** $5 daily fee/pet, $5 one-time fee/pet. No service, supervision, crate.

ASK 🔟 ❌ 💻 🖼 ❌

◆◆ Comfort Inn Atrium Gardens M ❀
(270) 769-3030. **$64-$129, 4 days notice.** 1043 Executive Dr. I-65, exit 94. Int corridors. **Pets:** Supervision.

ASK 🔟 ❌ 🖥 💻 🖼

🅰🅰🅰 ◆◆ Days Inn M ❀
(270) 769-5522. **$48-$54.** 2010 N Mulberry. I-65, exit 94. Ext corridors. **Pets:** Very small. $5 daily fee/pet, $5 one-time fee/pet. Designated rooms, no service, supervision, crate.

SAVE 🔟 ❌ 🖥 🖼 ❌

◆◆ Red Roof Inn M ❀
(270) 765-4166. **$41-$68.** 2009 N Mulberry St. I-65, exit 94. Int corridors. **Pets:** Small. Designated rooms, no service, supervision, crate.

❌ 🗒 🖥 💻 🖼

◆◆ Super 8 Motel M ❀
(270) 737-1088. **$45-$99.** 2028 N Mulberry St. I-65, exit 94. Int corridors. **Pets:** Medium. $7 daily fee/pet, $7 one-time fee/pet. No service, supervision, crate.

ASK 🔟 ❌ 🗒 🗒 🖥 🖼

ERLANGER

◆◆◆ Baymont Inn & Suites M ❀
(606) 746-0300. **$60-$105.** 1805 Airport Exchange Blvd. I-275, exit 2. Int corridors. **Pets:** Large. $50 deposit/room. No service, supervision, crate.

ASK 🔟 ❌ 🗒 🗒 🖥 💻 🖼

◆◆ Comfort Inn-Cincinnati Airport MI
(606) 727-3400. **$62-$69.** 630 Donaldson Rd. Off SR 236, w of jct I-71 and I-75, southbound exit 184; northbound exit 184B. Int corridors. **Pets:** Designated rooms, supervision.

ASK 🔟 ❌ 💻 🍴 🖼

◆◆◆ Residence Inn by Marriott, Cincinatti Airport 🅰 ❀
(606) 282-7400. **$159.** 2811 Circleport Dr. I-275, exit 2. Int corridors. **Pets:** Other. $100 one-time fee/pet. Supervision.

ASK 🔟 ❌ 🗒 🗒 🖥 💻 🖼 ❌

FLORENCE

🅰🅰🅰 ◆◆◆ AmeriSuites (Cincinnati Airport) M ❀
(606) 647-1170. **$89-$139.** 300 Meijer Dr. I-75, exit 182. Int corridors. **Pets:** Medium, other. No service, supervision, crate.

SAVE 🔟 ❌ 🗒 🗒 🗒 🖥 💻 🖼

◆◆◆ Best Western Inn Florence M ❀
(606) 525-0090. **$70-$90.** 7821 Commerce Dr. I-75, exit 181. Int corridors. **Pets:** $6 daily fee/pet, $6 one-time fee/pet. No service, supervision, crate.

ASK 🔟 ❌ 🗒 🗒 🖥 🖼

🅰🅰🅰 ◆◆ Knights Inn Florence M ❀
(606) 371-9711. **$47-$60.** 8049 Dream St. I-71 and I-75, exit 180, just e on US 42, then just n. Ext corridors. **Pets:** $10 daily fee/pet, $10 one-time fee/pet. Designated rooms, supervision.

SAVE 🔟 ❌ 🖥 🖼

🅰🅰🅰 ◆◆ Super 8 Motel M
(606) 283-1221. **$52-$58.** 7928 Dream St. I-75, exit 180, just e on US 42, just n. Int corridors. **Pets:** Supervision.

SAVE 🔟 ❌ 🖥

FRANKFORT

🅰🅰🅰 ◆◆ Bluegrass Inn M
(502) 695-1800. **$40-$58, 7 days notice.** 635 Versailles Rd. 4 mi e on US 60 and 421; 1 mi n on US 60 from jct I-64, exit 58. Ext corridors. **Pets:** No service, supervision, crate.

SAVE 🔟 ❌ 🖥 🖼

FRANKLIN

🅰🅰🅰 ◆◆ Comfort Inn M
(270) 586-6100. **$40-$50.** 3794 Nashville Rd. I-65, exit 2. Ext corridors. **Pets:** Small. Supervision.

SAVE 🔟 ❌ 🗒 🖥 🖼

◆◆◆ Days Inn 🅜 ✿
(270) 598-0163. **$40-$50.** 103 Trotter Ln. I-65, exit 6, just w. Ext corridors. **Pets:** $5 daily fee/pet, $5 one-time fee/pet. Supervision.
[SAVE] [S🔽] [✕] [🐾] [🖫] [🖫] [🖾]

◆◆ Holiday Inn Express 🅜
(270) 586-5090. **$60-$70.** 3811 Nashville Rd. I-65, exit 2, just w. Ext corridors. **Pets:** Very small. Designated rooms, supervision.
[SAVE] [S🔽] [✕] [🐾] [🖫] [🖾]

◆◆ Quality Inn 🅜 ✿
(270) 586-3291. **$36-$50, 3 days notice.** 3894 Nashville Rd. I-65, exit 2, just w. Ext corridors. **Pets:** $6 daily fee/pet. No service, supervision, crate.
[SAVE] [S🔽] [✕] [🖫] [🖾] [CTV]

GEORGETOWN

◆◆ Days Inn of Georgetown 🅜 ✿
(502) 863-5000. **$35-$50.** 385 Cherry Blossom Way. I-75, exit 129. Ext corridors. **Pets:** $5 daily fee/pet. No service, supervision, crate.
[SAVE] [S🔽] [✕] [🐾] [🖫] [🖫] [🖾] [✕]

◆◆ Shoney's Inn-Georgetown 🅜 ✿
(502) 868-9800. **$54-$63, 5 days notice.** 200 Shoney Dr. Jct I-75 and US 62, exit 126. Ext corridors. **Pets:** Medium. $5 daily fee/pet. Supervision.
[SAVE] [S🔽] [✕] [🖾]

◆◆ Super 8 Motel 🅜 ✿
(502) 863-4888. **$37-$52.** 250 Shoney Dr. Jct I-75 and US 62, exit 126. Ext/int corridors. **Pets:** $3 daily fee/room. Supervision.
[ASK] [S🔽] [✕] [🐾] [🖫] [🖾]

GLASGOW

◆◆ Comfort Inn 🅜 ✿
(270) 651-9099. **$44-$49.** 210 Calvary Dr. Cumberland Pkwy, exit 11, just n. Ext corridors. **Pets:** Other. $5 daily fee/room. No service, supervision, crate.
[SAVE] [S🔽] [✕] [🐾] [🖫] [🖫] [🖾]

◆◆ Family Budget Inn 🅜
(270) 651-5191. **$33-$60.** 1003 W Main. At jct US 31 E bypass and US 68. Ext corridors. **Pets:** Small. No service, supervision, crate.
[ASK] [S🔽] [✕] [🖫] [🖾]

GRAND RIVERS

◆◆◆ Best Western Kentucky-Barkley Lakes Inn 🅜 ✿
(270) 928-2700. **$52-$87.** 720 Complex Dr. I-24, exit 31. Ext/int corridors. **Pets:** Small, other. $5 daily fee/room. Designated rooms, supervision.
[SAVE] [S🔽] [✕] [🖫] [🖫] [🖾]

HARLAN

◆◆◆ Best Western Harlan 🅜 ✿
(606) 573-3385. **$69-$85.** 2608 S Hwy 421. 1.7 mi s on US 421. Int corridors. **Pets:** Small. Supervision.
[SAVE] [S🔽] [✕] [🖉] [🐾] [🖾]

HEBRON

◆◆◆ Radisson Inn-Cincinnati Airport 🅜
(606) 371-6166. **$115-$129.** Cincinnati N KY Airport. At Greater Cincinnati Airport; 4 mi w of I-71 and I-75 via I-275, exit 4B from I-275 (SR 212), 1.3 mi w on SR 212. Int corridors. **Pets:** Designated rooms, supervision.
[ASK] [S🔽] [✕] [🖉] [🖫] [🖵] [🍴] [🖾]

HENDERSON

◆ Scottish Inns 🅜 ✿
(270) 827-1806. **$38-$55, 7 days notice.** 2820 US 41 N. 2 mi n on US 41. Ext corridors. **Pets:** Small. $5 one-time fee/room. Designated rooms, no service, supervision, crate.
[SAVE] [S🔽] [✕] [🖫] [🖾]

◆◆ Super 8 Motel: Henderson, KY-So Evansville, IN 🅜
(270) 827-5611. **$46-$70, 7 days notice.** 2030 Hwy 41 N. 1 mi n on US 41. Ext corridors. **Pets:** Designated rooms, no service, supervision, crate.
[SAVE] [S🔽] [✕] [🖫] [🖾]

HOPKINSVILLE

◆◆◆ Holiday Inn 🅜 ✿
(270) 886-4413. **$69-$69.** 2910 Fort Campbell Blvd. Pennyrile Pkwy, exit 7A, 0.6 mi n on 41A. Int corridors. **Pets:** Other. Supervision.
[ASK] [S🔽] [✕] [🖫] [🖵] [🍴] [🖾]

◆◆◆ Hopkinsville Best Western 🅜
(270) 886-9000. **Call for rates.** 4101 Fort Campbell Blvd. US 41A, jct Pennyrile Pkwy. Int corridors. **Pets:** Supervision.
[✕] [🖫] [🖵] [🖾]

HORSE CAVE

◆◆ Budget Host Inn 🅜 ✿
(270) 786-2165. **$37-$47.** I-65 & SR 218. I-65, exit 58. Ext corridors. **Pets:** Small, other. $5 daily fee/pet, $5 one-time fee/pet. Designated rooms, no service, supervision, crate.
[SAVE] [✕] [🖫] [🍴] [🖾]

KUTTAWA

◆◆ Days Inn 🅜 ✿
(270) 388-4060. **$59-$67.** 139 Days Inn Dr. I-24, exit 40, just s. Ext corridors. **Pets:** Medium. $10 one-time fee/pet. Supervision.
[ASK] [S🔽] [✕] [🐾] [🐾] [🖾]

LEBANON

◆◆ Country Hearth Inn 🅜
(270) 692-4445. **$46-$56, 3 days notice.** 720 W Main St. SR 55 and US 68. Int corridors. **Pets:** Supervision.
[SAVE] [S🔽] [✕] [🐾] [🖫] [🖵]

LEXINGTON

◆◆◆ Best Western Regency/Lexington 🅜
(606) 293-2202. **$69-$104.** 2241 Elkhorn Dr. I-75, exit 110. Ext/int corridors. **Pets:** Small. Supervision.
[SAVE] [S🔽] [✕] [🐾] [🖫] [🖵] [🖾]

◆◆◆ Hilton Garden Inn Ⓜ ❀
(606) 543-8300. **$99-$149.** 1973 Plaudit Pl. I-75, exit 108, just w. Int corridors. **Pets:** $10 daily fee/room. No service, supervision, crate.

(ASK) (S🐾) (✕) (♿) (🔥) (🏖) (🛏) (💻) (🍴) (🌅)

◆◆◆ Holiday Inn-Lexington North Ⓜ ❀
(606) 233-0512. **$85-$105.** 1950 Newtown Pike. SR 922 at jct I-64 and I-75, exit 115. Ext/int corridors. **Pets:** Medium, other. $75 deposit/room. Designated rooms, no service, supervision, crate.

(ASK) (S🐾) (✕) (♿) (🔥) (🛏) (💻) (🍴) (🌅) (✕)

◆◆◆ Holiday Inn Lexington South Ⓜ ❀
(606) 263-5241. **$65-$99, 7 days notice.** 5532 Athens-Boonesboro Rd. I-75, exit 104. Int corridors. **Pets:** Small. Supervision.

(ASK) (S🐾) (✕) (🔥) (🛏) (💻) (🍴) (🌅) (✕)

⟨AAA⟩ ◆◆◆ La Quinta Inn Ⓜ
(606) 231-7551. **$99.** 1919 Stanton Way. Off SR 922 at jct I-64 and I-75, exit 115. Int corridors. **Pets:** Medium. Designated rooms, no service, supervision, crate.

(SAVE) (✕) (🛏) (💻) (🌅)

⟨AAA⟩ ◆◆◆◆ Marriott's Griffin Gate Resort Ⓡ
(606) 231-5100. **$139-$159.** 1800 Newtown Pike. At I-64 and 75, exit 115, jct SR 922. Int corridors. **Pets:** Medium. Designated rooms, no service, supervision, crate.

(S🐾) (✕) (♿) (🔥) (🛏) (💻) (🍴) (🌅) (✕)

⟨AAA⟩ ◆◆◆ Quality Inn Northwest Ⓜ ❀
(606) 233-0561. **$40-$80.** 1050 Newtown Pike. I-75 and 64, exit 115, 1 mi s on SR 922. Ext corridors. **Pets:** Medium. $10 deposit/room. Supervision.

(SAVE) (S🐾) (✕) (🛏) (💻) (🌅)

⟨AAA⟩ ◆◆◆ Radisson Plaza Hotel Lexington Ⓗ
(606) 231-9000. **$159-$179.** 369 W Vine St. Corner of Vine and Broadway. Int corridors. **Pets:** Medium. No service, supervision, crate.

(SAVE) (S🐾) (✕) (🔥) (🏖) (📺) (🛏) (💻) (🍴) (🌅)

⟨AAA⟩ ◆◆ Red Roof Inn-North Ⓜ ❀
(606) 293-2626. **$46-$68.** 1980 Haggard Ct. I-75 and I-64, exit 113, 0.3 mi sw. Ext corridors. **Pets:** Large, other. Supervision.

(SAVE) (✕)

⟨AAA⟩ ◆◆ Red Roof Inn South Ⓜ
(606) 277-9400. **$44-$82.** 2651 Wilhite Dr. Jct US 27 and SR 4. Ext corridors. **Pets:** Supervision.

(SAVE) (✕) (🔥) (🛏)

◆◆◆ Residence Inn by Marriott Ⓐ
(606) 231-6191. **$134.** 1080 Newtown Pike. I-75 and I-64, exit 115, 1 mi s on SR 922. Ext corridors. **Pets:** Designated rooms, no service, supervision, crate.

(ASK) (S🐾) (✕) (🛏) (💻) (🌅) (✕)

⟨AAA⟩ ◆◆ Shoney's Inn-Lexington Ⓜ ❀
(606) 269-4999. **$53-$71, 7 days notice.** 2753 Richmond Rd. I-75, exit 104, 5 mi w on US 25 (Richmond Rd). Ext corridors. **Pets:** Small. $5 daily fee/pet. Supervision.

(SAVE) (S🐾) (✕) (🛏) (🌅)

◆◆ Super 8 Motel Ⓜ ❀
(606) 299-6241. **$48-$72.** 2351 Buena Vista Rd. At I-75, exit 110. Int corridors. **Pets:** Small. $10 one-time fee/pet. Supervision.

(ASK) (S🐾) (✕) (🔥) (🛏)

LIBERTY

⟨AAA⟩ ◆◆ The Brown Motel Ⓜ
(606) 787-6224. **$49-$58.** 579 Wallace Wilkinson Blvd. 1 mi n on US 127; 0.5 mi n of jct SR 70. Ext corridors. **Pets:** No service, supervision, crate.

(SAVE) (S🐾) (🛏) (🌅) (✕)

LONDON

⟨AAA⟩ ◆◆ Budget Host Westgate Inn Ⓜ ❀
(606) 878-7330. **$36-$49.** 254 W Daniel Boone Pkwy. SR 80, w of jct I-75, exit 41. Ext/int corridors. **Pets:** Small, other. No service, supervision, crate.

(SAVE) (S🐾) (✕) (♿) (🔥) (🛏) (🌅) (✕)

◆◆◆ Red Roof Inn Ⓜ ❀
(606) 862-8844. **$41-$68.** 110 Melcon Ln. I-75, exit 41. Int corridors. **Pets:** Other. $6 daily fee/pet. Supervision.

(✕) (🔥) (🛏) (💻) (🌅)

Lᴏᴜɪsᴠɪʟʟᴇ Mᴇᴛʀᴏᴘᴏʟɪᴛᴀɴ Aʀᴇᴀ

HURSTBOURNE

⟨AAA⟩ ◆◆ Red Roof Inn-East Ⓜ ❀
(502) 426-7621. **$46-$68.** 9330 Blairwood Rd. 0.3 mi nw of jct I-64 and Hurstbourne Ln. Ext corridors. **Pets:** Small. No service, supervision, crate.

(SAVE) (✕) (🔥)

◆◆ Travelodge Louisville-Hurstbourne Ⓜ
(502) 425-8010. **$42-$134, 7 days notice.** 9340 Blairwood Rd. 0.3 mi nw of jct I-64 and Hurstbourne Ln, exit 15. Ext/int corridors. **Pets:** Supervision.

(ASK) (S🐾) (✕) (🛏) (💻) (🌅)

JEFFERSONTOWN

⟨AAA⟩ ◆◆◆ AmeriSuites Ⓜ
(502) 426-0119. **$79-$129.** 701 S Hurstbourne Pkwy. I-64, exit 15, 1 mi n. Int corridors. **Pets:** Supervision.

(SAVE) (S🐾) (✕) (🔥) (🛏) (💻) (🌅)

⟨AAA⟩ ◆◆ Days Inn-Southeast Ⓜ
(502) 491-1040. **$39-$70.** 1850 Embassy Square Blvd. I-64, exit 15, 0.5 mi se on Hurstbourne Rd and Embassy Sq Blvd. Ext corridors. **Pets:** Small. Designated rooms, no service, supervision, crate.

(SAVE) (S🐾) (✕) (🌅)

⊕ ◆◆◆ Doubletree Club Hotel & Conference Center H
(502) 491-4830. **$89-$89, 60 days notice.** 9700 Bluegrass Pkwy. 0.5 mi se of jct I-64 and Hurstbourne Ln. Int corridors. **Pets:** Supervision.

[SAVE] [S] [X] [⊘] [🛇] [💻] [🍴] [🏊]

⊕ ◆◆◆ Holiday Inn-Hurstbourne MI ☸
(502) 426-2600. **$125.** 1325 S Hurstbourne Pkwy. Jct I-64, exit 15 (Hurstbourne Ln). Int corridors. **Pets:** Other. $25 one-time fee/room. Supervision.

[SAVE] [S] [X] [⊘] [🛇] [💻] [🍴] [🏊]

◆◆◆ Residence Inn By Marriott A
(502) 425-1821. **Call for rates, 7 days notice.** 120 N Hurstbourne Pkwy. 1.8 mi n of jct I-64, exit 15. Ext corridors. **Pets:** Supervision.

[X] [🛇] [💻] [🏊] [X]

◆◆ Sleep Inn East MI ☸
(502) 266-6776. **$59-$89.** 1850 Priority Way. I-64, exit 17, 0.5 mi s of Blankenbaker Rd. Int corridors. **Pets:** Other. $10 daily fee/pet. No service, supervision, crate.

[ASK] [S] [X] [⊘] [⊘] [🛇] [💻]

LOUISVILLE

◆◆◆ Aleksander House Bed & Breakfast BB ☸
(502) 637-4985. **$80-$150.** 1213 S First St. I-65, exit 135 (St Catherine St), just s. Int corridors. **Pets:** $20 deposit/ room, $10 daily fee/pet. No service, supervision, crate.

[ASK] [S] [X] [🛇] [💻]

◆◆◆ Breckinridge Inn MI ☸
(502) 456-5050. **$59-$75.** 2800 Breckinridge Ln. Just s of I-264, exit 18A. Int corridors. **Pets:** $50 one-time fee/pet. No service, supervision, crate.

[ASK] [S] [X] [🛇] [💻] [🍴] [🏊] [X]

⊕ ◆◆ Days Inn East MI ☸
(502) 896-8871. **$58-$88, 30 days notice.** 4621 Shelbyville Rd. On US 60, 0.5 mi w of jct I-264, exit 20B. Ext/int corridors. **Pets:** Other. $25 one-time fee/room. Supervision.

[SAVE] [S] [X] [🛇] [💻] [🏊] [X]

◆◆◆ Executive West H
(502) 367-2251. **$68-$104.** 830 Phillips Ln. At Fairgrounds/ Expo Center Main Gate exit off I-264, exit 11. Int corridors. **Pets:** No service, supervision, crate.

[ASK] [S] [X] [⊘] [🛇] [💻] [🍴] [🏊]

◆◆◆ Holiday Inn Airport East MI ☸
(502) 452-6361. **$103-$134, 21 days notice.** 1465 Gardiner Ln. I-264, at Newburg Rd S exit 15B westbound; exit 15 eastbound. Int corridors. **Pets:** Small. No service, supervision, crate.

[ASK] [S] [X] [⊘] [💻] [🍴] [🏊] [X]

⊕ ◆◆◆ Holiday Inn Louisville (Downtown) H ☸
(502) 582-2241. **$96-$116.** 120 W Broadway. Just w on US 60 business route and US 150. Int corridors. **Pets:** Medium. No service, supervision, crate.

[SAVE] [S] [X] [⊘] [⊘] [🛇] [💻] [🍴] [🏊]

◆◆◆ Holiday Inn South-Airport MI ☸
(502) 964-3311. **Call for rates.** 3317 Fern Valley Rd. I-65, exit 128, at jct Fern Valley Rd. Int corridors. **Pets:** Medium. $30 one-time fee/room. Designated rooms, no service, supervision, crate.

[ASK] [X] [⊘] [⊘] [⊘] [🛇] [🍴] [🏊] [X]

⊕ ◆◆ Holiday Inn-Southeast MI
(502) 454-0451. **$80-$99, 7 days notice.** 3255 Bardstown Rd. S on US 31 E and 150 at jct I-264, exit 16 (Bardstown Rd). Ext/int corridors. **Pets:** Medium. Designated rooms, no service, supervision, crate.

[SAVE] [S] [X] [⊘] [🛇] [🍴] [🏊]

⊕ ◆◆◆ MainStay Suites MI ☸
(502) 267-4454. **$89-$250.** 1650 Alliant Ave. I-64, exit 17, just s. Int corridors. **Pets:** Medium, other. $100 deposit/ room, $10 daily fee/room. No service, supervision, crate.

[SAVE] [X] [⊘] [⊘] [🛇] [💻] [🏊]

◆◆◆ Old Louisville Inn BB
(502) 635-1574. **$85-$195.** 1359 S 3rd St. I-65, exit 135 (St Catherine St), 0.4 mi w on St Catherine St, 0.4 mi s. Int corridors. **Pets:** Small. No service, supervision, crate.

[ASK] [CTV] [⊘]

⊕ ◆◆ Red Roof Inn-Airport-Fairgrounds M
(502) 968-0151. **$45-$157.** 4704 Preston Hwy. I-65, exit 130. Ext corridors. **Pets:** Designated rooms, supervision.

[SAVE] [X]

⊕ ◆◆ Red Roof Inn-Southeast-Fairgrounds M ☸
(502) 456-2993. **$50-$83.** 3322 Red Roof Inn Pl. 0.3 mi s of I-264, exit 15B westbound; I-264, exit 15 eastbound. Ext corridors. **Pets:** Small, other. No service, supervision, crate.

[SAVE] [X]

⊕ ◆◆◆◆ The Seelbach Hilton Louisville's Grand Hotel H ☸
(502) 585-3200. **$179-$274.** 500 Fourth Ave. I-65, exit 136C (Muhammad Ali), 0.3 mi w on Muhammad Ali Blvd, just s. Int corridors. **Pets:** Other. $50 deposit/room. Supervision.

[SAVE] [S] [X] [⊘] [⊘] [⊘] [💻] [🍴]

⊕ ◆◆ Sleep Inn Fairgrounds MI ☸
(502) 368-9597. **$69-$89.** 3330 Preston Hwy. I-264, Fairgrounds and Expo Main Gate exit, 0.5 e on Phillips, just n. Int corridors. **Pets:** Small. $25 one-time fee/room. No service, supervision, crate.

[SAVE] [S] [X] [⊘] [💻]

SHEPHERDSVILLE

⊕ ◆◆◆ Best Western South MI ☸
(502) 543-7097. **$53-$63, 30 days notice.** 211 S Lakeview Dr. I-65, exit 117. Int corridors. **Pets:** Small. Supervision.

[SAVE] [S] [X] [🍴] [🏊]

MADISONVILLE

◆◆◆ Days Inn Madisonville Ⓜ
(270) 821-8620. **$59-$71.** 1900 Lantaff Blvd. Pennyrile Pkwy, exit 44. Int corridors. **Pets:** Small. Designated rooms, no service, supervision, crate.

Ⓐ Ⓢ Ⓧ ⓐ 🔲 🔲 🔲 🔲

MAYFIELD

◆◆ Super 8 Motel Ⓜ
(270) 247-8899. **$43-$49, 3 days notice.** 1100 Links Ln. Purchase Pkwy, just s on SR 121 (exit 24). Int corridors. **Pets:** No service, supervision, crate.

Ⓐ Ⓢ Ⓧ 🔲

MORTONS GAP

◆◆◆ Best Western Pennyrile Inn Ⓜ ☀
(270) 258-5201. **$44-$54.** White City Rd. Pennyrile Pkwy, exit 37 (US 41). Ext corridors. **Pets:** Medium, other. $15 deposit/room. Supervision.

Ⓢ Ⓢ Ⓧ 🔲 🔲 🔲

MOUNT VERNON

◆◆ Kastle Inn Motel Ⓜ ☀
(606) 256-5156. **$46-$60.** I-75, exit 59, jct US 25. Ext corridors. **Pets:** Medium, other. No service, supervision, crate.

Ⓢ Ⓢ Ⓧ 🔲 🔲

MULDRAUGH

◆◆ Golden Manor Motel Ⓜ ☀
(502) 942-2800. **$41-$51.** 116 S Dixie Hwy. Center; on Hwy 31 W. Ext corridors. **Pets:** Small. $10 daily fee/pet, $10 one-time fee/pet. No service, supervision, crate.

Ⓧ 🔲 🔲 🔲

MURRAY

◆ Murray Plaza Court Ⓜ ☀
(270) 753-2682. **$33-$39.** S 12th St. 1 mi s on US 641. Ext corridors. **Pets:** Other. No service, supervision, crate.

Ⓧ 🔲

NEWPORT

◆◆◆ Comfort Suites Riverfront Ⓜ ☀
(606) 291-6700. **$93-$98.** 420 Riverboat Row. I-471, exit 5, just e on SR 8. Int corridors. **Pets:** Supervision.

Ⓢ Ⓢ Ⓧ ⓐ 🔲 🔲

OAK GROVE

◆◆◆ Baymont Inn Ⓜ ☀
(270) 439-0022. **Call for rates.** 12759 Ft Campbell Blvd. I-24, exit 86, 41A. Int corridors. **Pets:** $50 deposit/room, $5 one-time fee/pet. No service, supervision, crate.

Ⓐ Ⓧ Ⓛ ⓐ 🔲 🔲 🔲

◆◆◆ Days Inn Ft. Campbell Ⓜ
(270) 640-3888. **$49-$69.** 212 Auburn St. I-24, exit 86, just s. Ext corridors. **Pets:** Medium. Designated rooms, no service, supervision, crate.

Ⓐ Ⓢ Ⓧ ⓐ ⓐ 🔲 🔲

OWENSBORO

ⒶⒶⒶ ◆◆◆ Holiday Inn Ⓜ ☀
(270) 685-3941. **$79.** 3136 W 2nd St. 2 mi w on US 60. Ext/int corridors. **Pets:** Other. Supervision.

Ⓢ Ⓢ Ⓧ ⓐ ⓐ 🔲 🔲 🔲 🔲 🔲

◆◆ Owensboro Super 8 Motel Ⓜ ☀
(270) 685-3388. **$46-$56.** 1027 Goetz Dr. US 60 bypass, exit 4 at jct US 431. Int corridors. **Pets:** Other. Supervision.

Ⓐ Ⓢ Ⓧ ⓐ 🔲

◆◆◆ WeatherBerry Bed & Breakfast Ⓑ ☀
(270) 684-8760. **$65-$80.** 2731 W 2nd St. US 60, 1 mi e of US 60 bypass, just n on Ewing St, then just w. Int corridors. **Pets:** No service, supervision, crate.

Ⓐ Ⓢ Ⓧ Ⓒ

PADUCAH

◆◆◆ Baymont Inn & Suites Ⓜ ☀
(270) 443-4343. **$46-$57.** 5300 Old Cairo Rd. Just w from I-24, exit 3. Int corridors. **Pets:** Small. $50 deposit/room. No service, supervision, crate.

Ⓐ Ⓢ Ⓧ ⓐ Ⓛ 🔲 🔲

ⒶⒶⒶ ◆◆ Best Inns of America Ⓜ ☀
(270) 442-3334. **$45-$62.** 5001 Hinkleville Rd. Just w from I-24, exit 4. Ext corridors. **Pets:** Small. No service, supervision, crate.

Ⓢ Ⓢ Ⓧ ⓐ ⓐ

◆◆◆ Drury Inn Ⓜ ☀
(270) 443-3313. **$59-$79.** 3975 Hinkleville Rd. I-24, exit 4, just e. Int corridors. **Pets:** Small. No service, supervision, crate.

Ⓧ Ⓛ 🔲 🔲 🔲

◆◆◆ Drury Suites-Paducah Ⓜ ☀
(270) 441-0024. **$69-$85.** 120 McBride Ln. I-24 at US 60, exit 4. Int corridors. **Pets:** Medium, other. No service, supervision, crate.

Ⓧ Ⓛ Ⓛ 🔲 🔲 🔲

◆◆◆ Hampton Inn-Paducah Ⓜ ☀
(270) 442-4500. **$61-$79.** 4930 Hinkleville Rd. Just w from I-24, exit 4. Int corridors. **Pets:** Other. No service, supervision, crate.

Ⓧ ⓐ ⓐ 🔲 🔲

◆◆ Pear Tree Inn-Paducah Ⓜ ☀
(270) 444-7200. **$39-$66.** 4910 Hinkleville Rd. I-24, exit 4; just w. Ext corridors. **Pets:** Medium, other. No service, supervision, crate.

Ⓧ 🔲 🔲

◆◆ Quality Inn Ⓜ
(270) 443-8751. **$40-$47.** 1380 Irvin Cobb Dr. I-24, exit 7, 3.5 mi e on US 62. Ext corridors. **Pets:** No service, supervision, crate.

Ⓐ Ⓢ Ⓧ 🔲 🔲 🔲

◆◆◆ Ramada Limited Suites Ⓜ ☀
(270) 442-4191. **$49-$56.** 5135 Cairo Rd. Just e from I-24, exit 3. Int corridors. **Pets:** Other. Supervision.

Ⓐ Ⓢ Ⓧ Ⓛ Ⓛ 🔲

PAINTSVILLE

⚐ ◆◆ Days Inn Paintsville M ❀
(606) 789-3551. **$50-$90.** 512 S Mayo Tr. Jct US 23, 1.9 mi s on SR 321. Ext corridors. **Pets:** Medium. $5 daily fee/pet. Designated rooms, no service, supervision, crate.

[SAVE] [S⬤] [✕] [🛏] [🖼]

RADCLIFF

⚐ ◆◆ Super 8 Motel M ❀
(270) 352-1888. **$49-$60.** 395 Redmar Blvd. 0.8 mi n on US 31 W, then e. Int corridors. **Pets:** Other. $25 deposit/pet. No service, supervision, crate.

[SAVE] [S⬤] [✕] [♿] [🛏]

RICHMOND

⚐ ◆◆◆ Best Western Roadstar Inn M ❀
(606) 623-9121. **$69-$89.** 1751 Lexington Rd. I-75, exit 90 northbound; I-75, exit 90A southbound. Int corridors. **Pets:** Small. Supervision.

[SAVE] [S⬤] [✕] [🏊] [🛏] [🖥] [🖼]

◆◆ Days Inn M ❀
(606) 624-5769. **$53-$58.** 2109 Belmont Dr. I-75, exit 90 northbound; I-75, exit 90B southbound. Ext corridors. **Pets:** Small, other. $10 one-time fee/room. Supervision.

[ASK] [✕] [🛏] [🖼]

◆ Travelodge M
(606) 623-0881. **$30-$40, 3 days notice.** 1698 Northgate Dr. I-75, exit 90 northbound; I-75, exit 90A southbound. Ext corridors. **Pets:** Small. No service, supervision, crate.

[ASK] [S⬤] [✕] [♿] [🛏] [🖼]

SHELBYVILLE

⚐ ◆◆◆ Best Western Shelbyville Lodge M ❀
(502) 633-4400. **$49-$79, 7 days notice.** 115 Isaac Shelby Dr. 0.5 mi n on SR 55 from jct I-64, exit 32. Int corridors. **Pets:** Small. No service, supervision, crate.

[SAVE] [S⬤] [✕] [🛏] [🖥] [🖼]

SMITHS GROVE

⚐ ◆◆ Bryce Inn M ❀
(270) 563-5141. **$39-$53.** 592 S Main St. I-65, exit 38, 0.3 mi w. Ext corridors. **Pets:** Very small, dogs only. $5 one-time fee/room. Supervision.

[SAVE] [S⬤] [✕] [🛏] [🖥] [🖼] [✕]

VERSAILLES

◆◆◆ 1823 Historic Rose Hill Inn BB ❀
(606) 873-5957. **$69-$140.** 233 Rose Hill. Just s on SR 33 (S Main St), then just w. Ext/int corridors. **Pets:** Dogs only. $10 one-time fee/room. Designated rooms, no service, supervision, crate.

[ASK] [S⬤] [✕] [🛏] [🖥] [CTV]

WILLIAMSTOWN

⚐ ◆◆ Days Inn M
(606) 824-5025. **$42-$55, 7 days notice.** 211 SR 36 W. I-75, exit 154, just n. Ext corridors. **Pets:** Very small. Supervision.

[SAVE] [S⬤] [✕] [🛏] [🖥] [🖼]

ALEXANDRIA

⚫ ◆◆ Best Western Inn & Suites Conference Center M
(318) 445-5530. **$60-$72.** 2720 W MacArthur Dr. 0.9 mi n of jct SR 28 and US 71/165 (MacArthur Dr). Ext/int corridors. **Pets:** Very small. Designated rooms, no service, supervision, crate.

◆◆◆ La Quinta Inn & Suites-Alexandria M 🐾
(318) 442-3700. **$59-$99.** 6116 West Calhoun Dr. I-49 exit 90 (Airbase Rd). Int corridors. **Pets:** Small, other. Supervision.

⚫ ◆◆ Rodeway Inn M 🐾
(318) 448-1611. **$36-$46.** 742 MacArthur Dr. 0.4 mi s jct US 71/165 (MacArthur Dr) and SR 28. Ext corridors. **Pets:** Other. $25 deposit/room. Supervision.

BATON ROUGE

⚫ ◆◆◆ AmeriSuites-Baton Rouge East M
(225) 769-4400. **$79-$149.** 6080 Bluebonnet Blvd. I-10 exit 162. Int corridors. **Pets:** Very small. Designated rooms, no service, supervision, crate.

◆◆ Baymont Inn & Suites-Baton Rouge M 🐾
(225) 291-6600. **$49-$54.** 10555 Rieger Rd. Just n of I-10, exit 163 (Siegen Ln). Int corridors. **Pets:** Very small, other. $50 deposit/room. Designated rooms, no service, supervision, crate.

⚫ ◆◆ Comfort Inn M 🐾
(225) 927-5790. **$69-$89.** 2445 S Acadian Thrwy. 0.5 mi n of jct I-10, exit 157B. Int corridors. **Pets:** Very small, other. $10 daily fee/room. No service, supervision, crate.

◆◆◆ La Quinta Inn-Baton Rouge M
(225) 924-9600. **$69-$95.** 2333 S Acadian Thrwy. I-10 at Acadian Thrwy, exit 157B. Ext corridors. **Pets:** Large. Designated rooms, supervision.

⚫ ◆◆ Red Roof Inn M
(225) 275-6600. **$44-$51.** 11314 Boardwalk Dr. Just n of I-10, exit 4 (Sherwood Forest). Ext corridors. **Pets:** Medium. Supervision.

◆◆◆ Residence Inn by Marriott ▲
(225) 927-5630. **$105-$135.** 5522 Corporate Blvd. I-10 exit 158, 0.5 mi ne. Ext corridors. **Pets:** Small. Designated rooms, no service, supervision, crate.

⚫ ◆◆ Shoney's Inn and Suites of Baton Rouge M 🐾
(225) 925-8399. **$55-$63.** 9919 Gwenadele Dr. Just n of I-12 exit 2B, on US 61. Ext corridors. **Pets:** Small. $25 deposit/room. Supervision.

BOSSIER CITY

◆◆◆ La Quinta Inn M 🐾
(318) 747-4400. **$69-$95.** 309 Preston Blvd. I-20 exit 21, just w. Ext corridors. **Pets:** Small. Supervision.

◆◆◆ Residence Inn by Marriott-Shreveport/Bossier City ▲ 🐾
(318) 747-6220. **$134.** 1001 Gould Dr. I-20 exit 21. Ext corridors. **Pets:** Medium. $150 one-time fee/room. Supervision.

BREAUX BRIDGE

⚫ ◆◆◆ Best Western Breaux Bridge M 🐾
(337) 332-1114. **$65-$80, 7 days notice.** 2088-B Rees St. I-10 exit 109 (Rees St). Ext corridors. **Pets:** Other. $10 one-time fee/pet. Supervision.

CROWLEY

⚫ ◆◆◆ Best Western-Crowley M
(337) 783-2378. **$65-$80, 7 days notice.** 9571 Egan Hwy. Off I-10 exit 80. Ext corridors. **Pets:** No service, supervision, crate.

DARROW

⚜️ ◆◆ Tezcuco Plantation B & B 🅱️🅱️ ❀
(225) 562-3929. **$65-$165, 3 days notice.** 3138 Hwy 44.
I-10 exit 179, 5.5 mi s. Ext/int corridors. **Pets:** Medium. $25
deposit/room. Supervision.
🆂🅰️🆅🅴 ✕ 🈁 📟 🍴 📺

DELHI

◆◆ Best Western Delhi Inn Ⓜ️
(318) 878-5126. **$42-$68.** 35 Snider Rd. I-20 exit 153, on s
frontage road. Ext corridors. **Pets:** No service, supervision,
crate.
🅰️🆂🅺 🆂🅰️ ✕ 🈁 📟 🔄

◆◆ Days Inn Ⓜ️ ❀
(318) 878-9000. **$40-$50.** 13 Snider Rd. I-20 exit 153. Ext
corridors. **Pets:** Large, other. $10 one-time fee/room. Des-
ignated rooms, supervision.
🅰️🆂🅺 ✕ 🈁 📟 🔄

HOUMA

◆◆◆ Hampton Inn Ⓜ️
(504) 873-3140. **$67-$77.** 1728 Martin Luther King Blvd. 0.9
mi n of jct S Hollywood Rd and Martin Luther King Blvd. Int
corridors. **Pets:** Designated rooms, no service, supervision,
crate.
🅰️🆂🅺 ✕ 📟 🔄

KINDER

◆◆◆ Holiday Inn Express Ⓜ️ ❀
(337) 738-3381. **$99.** 11750 US Hwy 165. N jct US 190/
165, 5.1 mi on US 165. Ext/int corridors. **Pets:** Small.
Supervision.
🅰️🆂🅺 🆂🅰️ ✕ 🏃 🔄 🈁 📟

LAFAYETTE

◆◆◆ Comfort Inn Lafayette Ⓜ️ ❀
(337) 232-9000. **$74-$79.** 1421 SE Evangeline Thrwy. Just
se, jct Pinhook Rd (SR 182). Int corridors. **Pets:** Other. No
service, supervision, crate.
🅰️🆂🅺 ✕ 🔄 🈁 📟 🍴 🔄

◆◆◆ La Quinta Inn-Lafayette Ⓜ️ ❀
(337) 233-5610. **$69-$99.** 2100 NE Evangeline Thrwy. On
US 167; 0.3 mi s of I-10 exit 103A. Ext corridors.
Pets: Medium. Supervision.
🅰️🆂🅺 ✕ 🔄 🈁 📟 🔄

⚜️ ◆◆ Red Roof Inn Ⓜ️ ❀
(337) 233-3339. **$51-$67.** 1718 N University Ave (SR 182).
Just n of I-10 exit 101. Ext corridors. **Pets:** Medium, other.
No service, supervision, crate.
🆂🅰️🆅🅴 ✕

LAKE CHARLES

⚜️ ◆◆◆ Best Suites of America Ⓜ️
(337) 439-2444. **$69-$150.** 401 Lakeshore Dr. Eastbound
I-10 exit 29 (business district/tourist bureau); westbound exit
30B (Ryan St business district), just s. Int corridors.
Pets: Designated rooms, no service, supervision, crate.
🆂🅰️🆅🅴 🆂🅰️ ✕ 🔄 🔄 🈁 📟 🔄

LIVONIA

◆ Oak Tree Inn Ⓜ️
(225) 637-2590. **$59-$69.** 7875 Airline Hwy. Jct SR 77 and
US 190, 0.3 mi w. Ext corridors. **Pets:** Supervision.
🅰️🆂🅺 🆂🅰️ ✕ 🔄

MANSFIELD

⚜️ ◆ Mansfield Inn Ⓜ️
(318) 872-5034. **$39-$48.** 1055 Washington Ave. On US
84; 1 mi w of jct US 171. Ext corridors. **Pets:** Medium.
Supervision.
🆂🅰️🆅🅴 🆂🅰️ ✕ 🈁 🔄

MINDEN

⚜️ ◆◆◆ Best Western Ⓜ️ ❀
(318) 377-1001. **$55-$65.** 1411 Sibley Rd. I-20 exit 47, just
n. Ext corridors. **Pets:** Medium. $5 one-time fee/room. Des-
ignated rooms, no service, supervision, crate.
🆂🅰️🆅🅴 ✕ 🔄 🔄 🈁 🔄

MONROE

⚜️ ◆◆ Days Inn Ⓜ️ ❀
(318) 345-2220. **$45-$53.** 5650 Frontage Rd. Just s of I-20,
exit 120; 0.5 mi e on s service road; opposite Pecan Land
Shopping Mall. Ext corridors. **Pets:** No service, supervision,
crate.
🆂🅰️🆅🅴 🆂🅰️ ✕ 🈁 🔄

◆◆◆ La Quinta Inn-Monroe Ⓜ️ ❀
(318) 322-3900. **$59-$79.** 1035 US 165 bypass S. Just ne
of I-20 exit 118B, on US 165 service road. Ext corridors.
Pets: Small. $50 deposit/pet. No service, supervision, crate.
🅰️🆂🅺 ✕ 🔄 📟

MORGAN CITY

⚜️ ◆◆◆ Holiday Inn-Morgan City Ⓜ️ ❀
(504) 385-2200. **$69-$85.** 520 Roderick St. 1.5 mi s of jct
US 90 and SR 70. Ext corridors. **Pets:** Medium, other. $50
one-time fee/room. Supervision.
🆂🅰️🆅🅴 🆂🅰️ ✕ 🔄 🈁 📟 🍴 🔄

NEW IBERIA

⚜️ ◆◆◆ Best Western Inn & Suites Ⓜ️ ❀
(337) 364-3030. **$58-$64, 30 days notice.** 2714 Hwy 14.
On SR 14, 0.3 mi e of jct US 90. Ext/int corridors.
Pets: Large. $50 deposit/room. Supervision.
🆂🅰️🆅🅴 🆂🅰️ ✕ 🈁 📟 🍴 🔄

NEW ORLEANS METROPOLITAN AREA

GRETNA

◆◆◆ La Quinta Inn-New Orleans West Bank 🅜 ✿

(504) 368-5600. **$79-$99.** 50 Terry Pkwy. S US 90 business route, exit 9A (Terry Pkwy), N US 90 (Westbank Expwy), exit 9 (Terry Pkwy/General DeGaulle). Ext corridors. **Pets:** Small, other. Supervision.

(ASK) ⊠ 🖾 🛢 💻 🖾

KENNER

⚠ ◆◆◆ Hilton New Orleans Airport 🅷 ✿

(504) 469-5000. **$110-$212, 7 days notice.** 901 Airline Dr. On US 61 (Airline Dr). Int corridors. **Pets:** Medium. $25 one-time fee/room. No service, supervision, crate.

(SAVE) 🖾 ⊠ 🖾 🛢 💻 🍴 🖾 🖾

◆◆◆ La Quinta Inn-New Orleans Airport 🅜

(504) 466-1401. **$85-$119.** 2610 Williams Blvd. I-10 exit 223A, 0.3 mi s. Int corridors. **Pets:** Very small. Designated rooms, no service, supervision, crate.

(ASK) ⊠ 🛢 💻 🖾

LA PLACE

⚠ ◆◆◆ Best Western of La Place 🅜 ✿

(504) 651-4000. **$179, 3 days notice.** 4289 Main St. I-10 exit 209, just s. Ext corridors. **Pets:** Very small. Supervision.

(SAVE) 🖾 ⊠ 🖾 🛢 💻 🖾

METAIRIE

◆◆◆ La Quinta Inn-New Orleans Causeway 🅜

(504) 835-8511. **$79-$105.** 3100 I-10 Service Rd. I-10 exit 228 (Causeway Blvd). Ext corridors. **Pets:** Medium. Supervision.

(ASK) ⊠ 🖾 🖾 🛢 💻 🖾

◆◆◆ La Quinta Inn-New Orleans Veterans 🅜

(504) 456-0003. **$79-$99.** 5900 Veterans Memorial Blvd. Just off I-10, exit 225. Ext/int corridors. **Pets:** Supervision.

(ASK) ⊠ 🖾 🖾 🛢 💻 🖾

NEW ORLEANS

⚠ ◆◆◆ The Ambassador Hotel 🅷 ✿

(504) 527-5271. **$59-$189, 3 days notice.** 535 Tchoupitoulas. Between Poydras and Lafayette sts. Int corridors. **Pets:** Medium. $75 deposit/room. No service, supervision, crate.

(SAVE) ⊠ 🖾 💻 🍴

◆◆◆ The Fairmont Hotel 🅷

(504) 529-7111. **Call for rates.** 123 Baronne St. Downtown between Canal and University sts. Int corridors. **Pets:** Medium. Supervision.

⊠ 🖾 🖾 🛢 🍴 🖾 🖾 (CTV)

⚠ ◆◆◆ French Quarter Courtyard Hotel 🅜

(504) 522-7333. **$59-$189, 3 days notice.** 1101 N Rampart St. On the northern edge of the French Quarter, between Ursulines and Governor Nicholls sts. Ext/int corridors. **Pets:** Designated rooms, no service, supervision, crate.

(SAVE) ⊠ 🖾 💻 🖾

⚠ ◆◆◆ Hilton New Orleans Riverside 🅷

(504) 561-0500. **$119-$234, 3 days notice.** 2 Poydras St. Poydras St, at the Mississippi River. Int corridors. **Pets:** Very small. Designated rooms, no service, supervision, crate.

(SAVE) ⊠ 🖾 🖾 🛢 💻 🍴 🖾 🖾

◆◆◆ La Quinta Inn-New Orleans Bullard 🅜 ✿

(504) 246-3003. **$69-$89.** 12001 I-10 Service Rd. Off I-10 exit 245, Bullard Rd. Ext corridors. **Pets:** Small, other. No service, supervision, crate.

(ASK) ⊠ 🖾 🛢 💻 🖾

◆◆◆ La Quinta Inn-New Orleans Crowder 🅜 ✿

(504) 246-5800. **$69-$89.** 8400 I-10 Service Rd. 7 mi e at Crowder Blvd, exit 242 off I-10. Ext corridors. **Pets:** Small. No service, supervision, crate.

(ASK) ⊠ 🖾 🛢 💻 🖾

⚠ ◆◆◆◆ Le Meridien Hotel New Orleans 🅷 ✿

(504) 525-6500. **$270-$285.** 614 Canal St. Registration and parking on Common St. Int corridors. **Pets:** Very small, dogs only. $100 deposit/pet. No service, supervision, crate.

(SAVE) ⊠ 🖾 🛢 💻 🍴 🖾

⚠ ◆◆◆◆ Royal Sonesta Hotel New Orleans 🅷 ✿

(504) 586-0300. **$185-$360.** 300 Bourbon St. Garage entrance on Conti or Bienville sts. Int corridors. **Pets:** Very small. $50 one-time fee/pet. Designated rooms, no service, supervision, crate.

(SAVE) ⊠ 🖾 🖾 🛢 🍴 🖾

⚠ ◆◆◆◆ Windsor Court Hotel 🅷 ✿

(504) 523-6000. **$275-$320.** 300 Gravier St. Between Magazine and Tchoucitoulas sts. Int corridors. **Pets:** Small, other. $150 deposit/room, $150 daily fee/room. No service, supervision, crate.

(SAVE) ⊠ 🖾 🛢 🖾

SLIDELL

⚠ ◆◆ Econo Lodge 🅜 ✿

(504) 641-2153. **$45-$100.** 58512 Tyler Rd. At jct I-10 and US 190, exit 266, just e. Ext corridors. **Pets:** Small, other. Supervision.

(SAVE) 🖾 ⊠ 🛢 💻

✿ END METROPOLITAN AREA ✿

OPELOUSAS

 ◆◆◆ **Best Western Opelousas** Ⓜ ❖
(337) 942-5540. **$65-$80, 7 days notice.** 5791 I-49 Service Rd S. From I-49, exit 18 (Creswell Lane), on w service road. Ext corridors. **Pets:** Other. $10 one-time fee/pet. Supervision.
SAVE ⊠ ☒

RAYVILLE

⚫ ◆◆ **Cottonland Inn** Ⓜ ❖
(318) 728-5985. **$45.** 116 Cottonland. I-20 and Hwy 137 (exit 138). Ext corridors. **Pets:** Medium, other. Supervision.
SAVE ⊠ ☒ ☒ ☒

RUSTON

◆◆ **Holiday Inn** Ⓜ
(318) 255-5901. **$49-$49, 3 days notice.** 401 N Service Rd. I-20 exit 85 on Frontage Rd, e of US 167. Ext corridors. **Pets:** Medium. Supervision.
ASK ☒ ⊠ ☒ ☒ ☒ ☒ ☒

◆◆◆ **Ramada Limited of Ruston** Ⓜ ❖
(318) 242-0070. **$65-$85, 7 days notice.** 1951 N Service Rd E. I-20 exit 86. Int corridors. **Pets:** Small. $10 deposit/room. No service, supervision, crate.
ASK ⊠ ☒ ☒ ☒ ☒ ☒

SHREVEPORT

⚫ ◆◆◆ **Holiday Inn-Financial Plaza** Ⓜ ❖
(318) 688-3000. **$85-$110, 5 days notice.** 5555 Financial Plaza. From I-20, exit 10 (Pines Rd); s on Pines Rd, 1 mi e on frontage road. Int corridors. **Pets:** Medium, other. Supervision.
SAVE ⊠ ☒ ☒ ☒ ☒ ☒

◆◆◆ **La Quinta Inn & Suites-Shreveport** Ⓜ ❖
(318) 671-1100. **$89-$109.** 6700 Financial Cir. I-20 exit 10. Int corridors. **Pets:** Small. Supervision.
ASK ⊠ ☒ ☒ ☒ ☒

⚫ ◆◆ **Red Roof Inn** Ⓜ
(318) 938-5342. **$46-$68.** 7296 Greenwood Rd. I-20 and Greenwood Rd, exit 8. Ext corridors. **Pets:** Supervision.
SAVE ⊠

ST. FRANCISVILLE

◆◆ **Green Springs Bed & Breakfast** 𝐁𝐁 ❖
(225) 635-4232. **$95-$195.** 7463 Tunica Trace. US 61, 4 mi n jct US 61 and SR 10, to SR 66, 0.9 mi w. Ext/int corridors. **Pets:** Medium. No service, supervision, crate.
⊠ ☒ ☒ ☒ ☒

SULPHUR

◆◆◆ **La Quinta Inn-Sulphur/Lake Charles** Ⓜ
(337) 527-8303. **$59-$89.** 2600 S Ruth St. At jct SR 27 and I-10, exit 20. Ext corridors. **Pets:** Supervision.
ASK ⊠ ☒ ☒ ☒ ☒

WEST MONROE

⚫ ◆◆ **Red Roof Inn** Ⓜ
(318) 388-2420. **$40-$50.** 102 Constitution Dr. Jct I-20 and Thomas Rd, exit 114. Ext corridors. **Pets:** Medium. No service, supervision, crate.
SAVE ⊠

MAINE

CITY INDEX

AUGUSTA

◆◆◆ Best Western Senator Inn M ☙
(207) 622-5804. **$89-$149.** 284 Western Ave. On US 202, SR 11 and 100; off I-95 and Maine Tpke, exit 30A southbound; northbound exit 30. Ext/int corridors. **Pets:** Other. $50 deposit/room, $9 daily fee/pet. Designated rooms, no service, supervision, crate.

◆◆ Motel 6–1270 M
(207) 622-0000. **$42-$58.** 18 Edison Dr. On US 202, SR 11 and 100; off I-95 and Maine Tpke, exit 30A southbound, exit 30 northbound. Int corridors. **Pets:** Medium. No service, supervision, crate.

◆◆ Travelodge Hotel M ☙
(207) 622-6371. **$70-$70.** 390 Western Ave. On US 202, SR 11 and 100, at I-95 and Maine Tpke, exit 30B southbound. Ext corridors. **Pets:** Supervision.

BAILEY ISLAND

◆◆◆ Log Cabin Lodging & Fine Food CI ☙
(207) 833-5546. **$120-$210, 21 days notice.** Rt 24. After Crossing Bailey Island Bridge, 0.5 mi s on SR 24. Ext/int corridors. **Pets:** Medium, dogs only. Supervision.

BANGOR

◆◆ Best Inn M ☙
(207) 947-0566. **$75-$90.** 570 Main St. At jct I-395 and Main St. Int corridors. **Pets:** No service, supervision, crate.

◆◆◆ Best Western White House M ☙
(207) 862-3737. **$85-$100.** 155 Littlefield Ave. From I-95, Coldbrook Rd exit 44, 5.5 mi s of downtown Bangor. Ext/int corridors. **Pets:** Other. No service, supervision, crate.

◆◆ Comfort Inn M ☙
(207) 942-7899. **Call for rates.** 750 Hogan Rd. I-95, exit 49, northbound, left turn on Hogan Rd; southbound right turn, 0.5 mi. Int corridors. **Pets:** Other. Supervision.

◆◆ Country Inn at The Mall M
(207) 941-0200. **$60-$80.** 936 Stillwater Ave. I-95, exit 49; northbound, left turn on Hogan Rd; southbound right turn, 0.5 mi. Int corridors. **Pets:** Designated rooms, no service, supervision, crate.

◆◆ Days Inn M ☙
(207) 942-8272. **Call for rates.** 250 Odlin Rd. I-95, exit 45B; 0.3 mi e on US 2 and SR 100. Int corridors. **Pets:** Other. $6 one-time fee/room. No service, supervision, crate.

◆ Econo Lodge M ☙
(207) 945-0111. **$45-$89.** 327 Odlin Rd. I-95, exit 45B, just e on US 2 and SR 100. Int corridors. **Pets:** Other. $6 one-time fee/room. No service, supervision, crate.

◆◆◆ Holiday Inn-Bangor M ☙
(207) 947-0101. **Call for rates.** 404 Odlin Rd. I-95, exit 45B, at jct Odlin Rd and I-395. Int corridors. **Pets:** Other. Designated rooms, supervision.

◆◆ Holiday Inn Bangor-Civic Center M
(207) 947-8651. **$75-$90, 3 days notice.** 500 Main St. Center. Int corridors. **Pets:** Supervision.

◆ Main Street Inn M ☙
(207) 942-5282. **$52-$62.** 480 Main St. I-95, exit 45A, to I-395 exit 3B. Ext/int corridors. **Pets:** Supervision.

◆◆ The Phenix Inn at West Market Square BB
(207) 947-0411. **$90-$159.** 20 Broad St. Center. Int corridors. **Pets:** Designated rooms, no service, supervision, crate.

◆◆◆ **Ramada Inn** Ⓜ ✿
(207) 947-6961. **$49-$99, 3 days notice.** 357 Odlin Rd.
I-95, exit 45B, at jct Odlin Rd and I-395. Int corridors.
Pets: No service, supervision, crate.
ⒶⓈⓀ Ⓢ ⊠ ▤ ▣ ▥ ⌂

◆◆ **Riverside Inn** Ⓜ
(207) 947-3800. **Call for rates.** 495 State St. Adjacent to
Eastern Maine Medical Center. Int corridors. **Pets:** Supervision.
⊠ ▤ ▣

⍟ ◆ **Rodeway Inn** Ⓜ
(207) 942-6301. **$40-$80.** 482 Odlin Rd. I-95, exit 45B, left
of Odlin Rd. Ext corridors. **Pets:** Designated rooms, no
service, supervision, crate.
ⓈⒶ Ⓢ ⊠ ▤ ▥

BAR HARBOR

⍟ ◆◆◆◆ **Balance Rock Inn 1903** Ⓑ ✿
(207) 288-2610. **$225-$525.** 21 Albert Meadow. Center of
town, s on Main St and just e. Ext/int corridors.
Pets: Medium. $15 daily fee/pet. Designated rooms, supervision.
⊠ ▤ ⌂

⍟ ◆◆◆ **Best Western Inn** Ⓜ ✿
(207) 288-5823. **$98-$105.** SR 3. 4.8 mi w. Ext corridors.
Pets: Medium. Designated rooms, supervision.
ⓈⒶ Ⓢ ⊠ ▤ ⌂

⍟ ◆◆ **Days Inn** Ⓜ ✿
(207) 288-3321. **$145.** 120 Eden St. 1 mi w on SR 3. Ext
corridors. **Pets:** Other. No service, supervision, crate.
ⓈⒶ ⊠ ▤ ⒸⓉⓋ

◆ **Hutchin's Mountain View Cottages** Ⓒ ✿
(207) 288-4833. **$58-$84, 7 days notice.** 4 mi w on SR 3.
Ext corridors. **Pets:** Other. Supervision.
⌂ Ⓚ Ⓩ

⍟ ◆◆◆ **The Ledgelawn Inn** Ⓑ ✿
(207) 288-4596. **$95-$275.** 66 Mt. Desert St. Center. Ext/int
corridors. **Pets:** Medium. $15 daily fee/pet. Designated
rooms, supervision.
⊠ ⌂

BATH

◆◆◆ **Holiday Inn Bath/Brunswick** Ⓜ ✿
(207) 443-9741. **$89-$134.** 139 Richardson St. 0.3 mi s on
US 1. Int corridors. **Pets:** No service, supervision, crate.
ⒶⓈⓀ Ⓢ ⊠ Ⓓ ▤ ▣ ▥ ⌂

BELFAST

⍟ ◆ **Admiral's Ocean Inn** Ⓜ ✿
(207) 338-4260. **$48-$75.** 2 mi n on US 1. Ext corridors.
Pets: $20 deposit/room. Designated rooms, no service,
supervision, crate.
ⓈⒶ Ⓢ ⊠ ⌂

⍟ ◆◆◆ **Belfast Bay Meadows Inn** Ⓑ ✿
(207) 338-5715. **$85-$165.** l92 Northport Ave (US 1). US 1,
2 mi s from jct SR 3. Ext/int corridors. **Pets:** Other. $15
daily fee/pet. No service, supervision, crate.
⊠ ▤ ⊠

◆◆ **Belfast Harbor Inn** Ⓜ ✿
(207) 338-2740. **$59-$119.** RR 5, Box 5230. 1 mi n on US
1. Ext/int corridors. **Pets:** $10 daily fee/pet, $10 one-time
fee/pet. Designated rooms, no service, supervision, crate.
ⒶⓈⓀ ⊠ ⌂

⍟ ◆◆◆ **Comfort Inn** Ⓜ ✿
(207) 338-2090. **$129-$159.** Rt 1 Box 35. 2 mi n from jct
SR 3. Int corridors. **Pets:** $10 daily fee/room. Designated
rooms, no service, supervision, crate.
ⓈⒶ Ⓢ ⊠ Ⓚ Ⓓ Ⓚ ▤ ▣ ⌂

⍟ ◆◆ **Gull Motel** Ⓜ ✿
(207) 338-4030. **$65-$79, 3 days notice.** RR 5 Box 5377.
On US 1, 3 mi n from jct SR 3. Ext corridors. **Pets:** Dogs
only. $10 daily fee/pet. Designated rooms, supervision.
ⓈⒶ ⊠

⍟ ◆◆ **Seascape Motel & Cottages** Ⓜ
(207) 338-2130. **$75-$99, 3 days notice.** Rt 1. 2 mi n on
US 1. **Pets:** No service, supervision, crate.
ⓈⒶ Ⓢ ⊠ ▤

BETHEL

◆ **Bethel Inn & Country Club** Ⓧ
(207) 824-2175. **Call for rates.** 1 Bethel Inn Dr. Center of
village on SR 5; just s of US 2 and SR 26. Int corridors.
Pets: Supervision.
⊠ Ⓚ Ⓚ ▤ ▣ ⌂ ⊠

◆◆ **The Inn At the Rostay** Ⓜ
(207) 824-3111. **$45-$108.** 186 Mayville Rd (US 2). 2 mi e
on US 2. Ext corridors. **Pets:** Small. No service, supervision, crate.
⊠ ▤ ▥

⍟ ◆◆ **L'Auberge Country Inn** Ⓒ
(207) 824-2774. **$79-$129.** Mill Hill Rd. Center of village;
adjacent to Village Common. Int corridors. **Pets:** Medium.
Supervision.
ⓈⒶ ⊠ ▥ Ⓚ ⒸⓉⓋ Ⓩ

BOOTHBAY

◆◆ **Hillside Acres Cabins & Motel** Ⓧ ✿
(207) 633-3411. **$55-$75.** Adams Pond Rd. 9 mi s on SR
27 from US 1, then just w. Ext/int corridors. **Pets:** Supervision.
⊠ ▤ ▣ ⌂ Ⓚ Ⓩ

⍟ ◆◆ **White Anchor Motel** Ⓜ ✿
(207) 633-3788. **$39-$75.** SR 27. US 1 to SR 27, 7.5 mi s.
Ext/int corridors. **Pets:** Other. $50 deposit/pet. Designated
rooms, no service, supervision, crate.
⊠ Ⓩ

BOOTHBAY HARBOR

⍟ ◆◆ **The Pines Motel** Ⓜ ✿
(207) 633-4555. **$70-$90.** Sunset Rd. 1 mi on e side of
harbor. Ext corridors. **Pets:** Other. No service, supervision,
crate.
ⓈⒶ Ⓢ ▤ ⌂ ⊠ Ⓚ

♦♦♦ Welch House Inn BB
(207) 633-3431. $80-$155, 7 days notice. 56 McKown St. Center. Ext/int corridors. Pets: Small. Designated rooms, no service, supervision, crate.

⊠ 🖪 🖅

BREWER

♦ Brewer Motor Inn M ❀
(207) 989-4476. $49-$59. 359 Wilson St. I-95, exit 45A to I-395, exit 4, n on Rt 15 to Rt 1A, then 0.5 mi e. Ext/int corridors. Pets: Designated rooms, supervision.

SAVE S⊘ ⊠

BRUNSWICK

♦ Maineline Motel M ❀
(207) 725-8761. $70-$100. 133 Pleasant St. Center; 0.5 mi s on US 1; from I-95, exit 22, 1 mi n on US 1. Ext corridors. Pets: $5 daily fee/pet. No service, supervision, crate.

SAVE S⊘ ⊠ 🖪 🖵 🖄

♦♦ Viking Motor Inn M ❀
(207) 729-6661. $64-$89. 287 Bath Rd. US 1, Cooks Corner exit; left on Bath Rd then 1 mi. Ext/int corridors. Pets: Medium, dogs only. $5 daily fee/pet. No service, supervision, crate.

⊠ 🖪 🖄

BUCKSPORT

♦♦ Best Western Jed Prouty Motor Inn M
(207) 469-3113. $79-$99, 7 days notice. Center, on SR 15. Int corridors. Pets: No service, supervision, crate.

S⊘ ⊠

CALAIS

♦♦ Calais Motor Inn MI
(207) 454-7111. $69-$74. 293 Main St. 0.5 mi s on US 1. Ext/int corridors. Pets: Small. Supervision.

S⊘ ⊠ 🍴 🖄

♦♦ International Motel M ❀
(207) 454-7515. $45-$120. 276 Main St. 0.5 mi s on US 1. Ext corridors. Pets: Designated rooms, no service, supervision, crate.

SAVE S⊘ ⊠ 🖪 🖵

CAMDEN

♦♦♦ Blue Harbor House, A Village Inn GI ❀
(207) 236-3196. $95-$175. 67 Elm St. Center; on US 1. Ext/int corridors. Pets: Designated rooms, supervision.

⊠ 🍴

♦♦♦ Camden Harbour Inn GI ❀
(207) 236-4200. $195-$255, 7 days notice. 83 Bayview St. Center; off US 1, 0.3 mi e. Int corridors. Pets: Dogs only. $20 one-time fee/pet. Designated rooms, no service, supervision, crate.

🖪 🍴 🎵 CTV

CAPE ELIZABETH

♦♦♦♦ Inn By The Sea MI ❀
(207) 799-3134. $269-$549. 40 Bowery Beach (SR 77) Rd. 7 mi s on SR 77. Ext/int corridors. Pets: Other. Designated rooms, supervision.

SAVE S⊘ ⊠ 🖪 🖵 🍴 🖄 🎵 🎵

CARIBOU

♦♦♦ Caribou Inn & Convention
Center MI ❀
(207) 498-3733. $60-$78. Rt 3. 3 mi s on US 1. Int corridors. Pets: Other. Supervision.

SAVE S⊘ ⊠ 🖪 🖄

CASTINE

♦♦ Pentagoet Inn BB
(207) 326-8616. $99-$150. Main St. Center. Int corridors. Pets: Supervision.

⊠ 🎵 CTV 🖅

CORNISH

♦♦♦ Midway Motel M ❀
(207) 625-8835. $49-$74, 7 days notice. S Hiram Rd. 0.7 mi w on SR 25, just past corner of SR 25 and S Hiram Rd. Ext/int corridors. Pets: Large, dogs only. $5 daily fee/pet. No service, supervision, crate.

⊠ 🖪 🖵

DAMARISCOTTA

♦ County Fair Motel M ❀
(207) 563-3769. $64-$71. 1 mi n of center on US 1 (business), from jct SR 129/130. Ext corridors. Pets: Designated rooms, no service, supervision, crate.

SAVE S⊘ ⊠ 🎵

EAGLE LAKE

♦♦ Overlook Motel M ❀
(207) 444-4535. $94. N Main St. Center on Rt 11. Ext/int corridors. Pets: Other. Supervision.

🖪

EAST BOOTHBAY

♦♦ Smuggler's Cove Motor Inn M
(207) 633-2800. $89-$159. 4 mi e on SR 96 from jct SR 27. Ext corridors. Pets: No service, supervision, crate.

SAVE 🖪 🖵 🖄 🎵 🎵

EDGECOMB

♦♦ Sheepscot River Inn & Restaurant MI ❀
(207) 882-6343. $80-$120. 306 Eddy Rd. 1 mi w on US 1; on e side of Davies Bridge, 1 mi e of Wiscasset. Ext/int corridors. Pets: Other. Designated rooms, supervision.

ASK ⊠ 🖪 🖵 🖄

ELLSWORTH

◆◆ Colonial Travelodge M ❀
(207) 667-5548. **$84-$108.** 321 High St. 1.3 mi e on SR 3. Int corridors. **Pets:** Medium. $25 deposit/room. Designated rooms, no service, supervision, crate.

(A$K) (S/6) (✕) (💰) (🛏) (💻) (🍴) (🏊)

◆◆◆ Comfort Inn M ❀
(207) 667-1345. **$129-$139, 7 days notice.** 130 High St. Center. Int corridors. **Pets:** Other. $25 deposit/room, $5 daily fee/room. No service, supervision, crate.

(A$K) (S/6) (✕) (♿) (💰) (🛏)

◆◆◆ Holiday Inn M ❀
(207) 667-9341. **$130-$170.** 215 High St. Jct US 1, 1A and SR 3. Int corridors. **Pets:** Other. Designated rooms, no service, supervision, crate.

(A$K) (S/6) (✕) (♿) (💻) (🍴) (🏊) (✕)

(AAA) ◆◆ Jasper's Motel M ❀
(207) 667-5318. **$66-$82, 3 days notice.** 200 High St. 1 mi e on US 1 and SR 3. Ext corridors. **Pets:** $10 one-time fee/room. Supervision.

(SAVE) (S/6) (✕)

(AAA) ◆◆ Twilite Motel M ❀
(207) 667-8165. **$66-$86.** 147 Bucksport Rd. 1.5 mi w from jct US 1, 1A and SR 3; on US 1 and SR 3. Ext corridors. **Pets:** Dogs only. $10 one-time fee/room. Designated rooms, no service, supervision, crate.

(SAVE) (S/6) (✕) (🛏) (💻)

(AAA) ◆ The White Birches M ❀
(207) 667-3621. **$90-$100.** US 1, 1.5 mi n from jct SR 3. Ext corridors. **Pets:** Other. Supervision.

(SAVE) (✕) (🛏) (✕)

FARMINGTON

(AAA) ◆ Mount Blue Motel M ❀
(207) 778-6004. **$40-$45.** Wilton Rd. 2 mi w on US 2 and SR 4. Ext corridors. **Pets:** $7 one-time fee/pet. Supervision.

(SAVE) (✕)

FREEPORT

(AAA) ◆◆ Eagle Motel M
(207) 865-4088. **$84-$94.** 215 US Rt 1S. I-95, exit 19 southbound; 1.8 mi s on US 1; exit 17 northbound; 1.5 mi n of US 1. Ext corridors. **Pets:** Designated rooms, no service, supervision, crate.

(SAVE) (✕) (🛏)

(AAA) ◆◆◆ Freeport Inn M ❀
(207) 865-3106. **$100-$120.** 335 US 1S. From I-95, exit 17, 1 mi n on US 1. Ext/int corridors. **Pets:** Other. Designated rooms, supervision.

(✕) (🛏) (💻) (🍴) (🏊) (✕)

(AAA) ◆◆◆ Isaac Randall House BB ❀
(207) 865-9295. **$105-$145, 7 days notice.** 5 Independence Dr. I-95, exit 19, 0.5 mi n on US 1, Independence Dr parallels US 1 on the w side. Ext/int corridors. **Pets:** Other. Supervision.

(SAVE) (✕) (🛏) (✕)

◆◆ Super 8 Motel M ❀
(207) 865-1408. **$42-$110.** 262 US Rt 1S. From I-95, exit 19; 0.3 mi s on US 1. Int corridors. **Pets:** Other. Supervision.

(A$K) (S/6) (✕) (🔒)

GRAND LAKE STREAM

◆◆ Leen's Lodge C
(207) 796-5575. **$90-$180, 45 days notice.** 10 mi w off US Rt 1, 2 mi n on gravel entry road. Ext corridors. **Pets:** Designated rooms, no service, supervision, crate.

(A$K) (S/6) (🛏) (🍴) (✕) (🐾) (CTV) (✈)

GREENVILLE

(AAA) ◆◆ Greenwood Motel M ❀
(207) 695-3321. **$54-$75.** 3 mi w on SR 6 and 15 in Greenville Jct. Ext corridors. **Pets:** $5 daily fee/pet. Designated rooms, no service, supervision, crate.

(SAVE) (S/6) (✕) (🛏) (🏊) (✕)

(AAA) ◆◆ Kineo View Motor Lodge M ❀
(207) 695-4470. **$69-$79.** SR 15. 2.5 mi s. Ext corridors. **Pets:** $5 daily fee/room. Designated rooms, supervision.

(SAVE) (S/6) (✕) (✕) (🐾) (CTV)

HOULTON

(AAA) ◆ Scottish Inns M ❀
(207) 532-2236. **$40-$60.** 239 Bangor St. I-95, exit 62, 1 mi s on US 1, 1 mi sw on US 2A. Ext/int corridors. **Pets:** Other. $9 daily fee/pet, $9 one-time fee/pet. Designated rooms, no service, supervision, crate.

(SAVE) (S/6) (✕) (🛏)

JACKMAN

(AAA) ◆◆ Sky Lodge Motel & Cabins X
(207) 668-2171. **$49-$165.** PO Box 428. 1 mi n, on US 201. Ext corridors. **Pets:** Medium. No service, supervision, crate.

(SAVE) (✕) (🐾)

KENNEBUNK

(AAA) ◆◆ The Lodge at Kennebunk M ❀
(207) 985-9010. **$69-$99.** 95 Alewive Rd. I-95 (Maine Tpke), exit 3, just n on SR 35. Ext corridors. **Pets:** Small. $10 daily fee/pet. Designated rooms, no service, supervision, crate.

(S/6) (✕) (🛏) (💻) (🏊)

KENNEBUNKPORT

(AAA) ◆◆◆ The Colony Hotel H ❀
(207) 967-3331. **$175-$425, 3 days notice.** 140 Ocean Ave. From Dock Square, 1 mi s. Int corridors. **Pets:** Other. $25 daily fee/pet. Supervision.

(✕) (🍴) (🏊) (✕) (🐾)

(AAA) ◆◆◆ Lodge At Turbat's Creek M ❀
(207) 967-8700. **$95-$139.** Turbat's Creek Rd. From Dock Square, 0.5 mi e on Maine St, 0.6 mi ne on Wildes, then just se. Ext corridors. **Pets:** Dogs only. No service, supervision, crate.

(SAVE) (✕) (🏊)

KITTERY

◆◆ **Enchanted Nights Bed & Breakfast** 🅱🅱 🐾
(207) 439-1489. **$58-$132.** 29 Wentworth St. I-95, exit 2
(Kittery), 1 mi s on SR 236, just w on SR 103. Ext/int
corridors. **Pets:** Other. Supervision.
⊠ 🅩

LEWISTON

🔺 ◆◆ **Motel 6–1223** M
(207) 782-6558. **$43-$59.** 516 Pleasant St. Maine Tpke,
exit 13, follow sign for Lisbon, just w. Ext/int corridors.
Pets: Small. Supervision.
🅢 ⊠ 🅩 🄲

LINCOLNVILLE

◆◆ **Pine Grove Cottages** 🅲 🐾
(207) 236-2929. **$65-$125, 5 days notice.** RR 3. 2 mi s on
US 1. Ext corridors. **Pets:** Other. $7 daily fee/pet, $7 one-
time fee/pet. No service, supervision, crate.
🄳 ⊠

LUBEC

🔺 ◆◆ **The Eastland Motel** M 🐾
(207) 733-5501. **$38-$60.** From jct US 1 and SR 189, 8 mi
e on SR 189. Ext/int corridors. **Pets:** Medium. $5 daily
fee/pet. Designated rooms, supervision.
⊠

MACHIAS

🔺 ◆◆ **The Bluebird Motel** M
(207) 255-3332. **$54-$60.** 1 mi s on US 1. Ext corridors.
Pets: Small. Designated rooms, no service, supervision,
crate.
🆂🅰🆅🅴 🅢 ⊠ 🄵 🄳

🔺 ◆◆ **Machias Motor Inn** M 🐾
(207) 255-4861. **$60-$65.** 26 E Main St. 0.5 mi e on US 1.
Ext corridors. **Pets:** Dogs only. $5 daily fee/pet. Supervi-
sion.
🆂🅰🆅🅴 ⊠ 🔁

◆ **Maineland Motel** M 🐾
(207) 255-3334. **$35-$53.** 1 mi e on US 1. Ext corridors.
Pets: Small. $5 daily fee/pet, $5 one-time fee/pet. Designated rooms, supervision.
⊠ 🔲

MEDWAY

◆◆◆ **Gateway Inn** M 🐾
(207) 746-3193. **$45-$100.** Rt 157. I-95, exit 56, 0.3 mi w.
Ext/int corridors. **Pets:** Other. Supervision.
🄰 🅢 ⊠ 🔁

◆ **Katahdin Shadows Motel** M
(207) 746-5162. **Call for rates, 7 days notice.** I-95, exit 56,
1.5 mi w on SR 157. Ext corridors. **Pets:** Supervision.
🔁 ⊠

MILFORD

◆◆ **Milford Motel** M 🐾
(207) 827-3200. **$54-$59.** PO Box 850. 0.5 mi n on Rt 2.
Ext corridors. **Pets:** No service, supervision, crate.
⊠

MILLINOCKET

◆◆ **Best Western Heritage Motor Inn** Ⓜ️🅸 🐾
(207) 723-9777. **$79-$99.** 935 Central St. 0.8 mi e on SR
11 and 157. Int corridors. **Pets:** Small. Supervision.
🄰 🅢 ⊠ 🄵

NAPLES

◆◆ **Augustus Bove House** 🅱🅱 🐾
(207) 693-6365. **$79-$175.** Corner SR 302 and 114. Int
corridors. **Pets:** $10 one-time fee/room. Designated rooms,
supervision.
🄰 🅢 ⊠ 🔲

NEWPORT

🔺 ◆◆ **Lovley's Motel** M 🐾
(207) 368-4311. **$30-$90.** At jct I-95, US 2, SR 11 and 100;
exit 39. Ext corridors. **Pets:** Supervision.
🆂🅰🆅🅴 🅢 ⊠ 🔲 🔁 🅧 🄲🅣🅥

OGUNQUIT

🔺 ◆◆◆ **The Captain Thomas Resort Motel** Ⓜ️🅸
(207) 646-4600. **$129-$179, 7 days notice.** 305 US 1. 0.8
mi n on US 1. Ext corridors. **Pets:** Small. Designated
rooms, no service, supervision, crate.
🅢 ⊠ 🄳 🔲 🄵 🔁

◆◆ **Studio East Motor Inn** M
(207) 646-7297. **$109-$129, 5 days notice.** 43 Main St.
Center; on US 1. Ext corridors. **Pets:** Small. No service,
supervision, crate.
⊠ 🄳 🄵

🔺 ◆◆ **White Rose Inn** 🅧
(207) 646-3432. **$95-$150.** 89 Rt 1. Just s. Ext/int corridors.
Pets: Supervision.
⊠ 🄳 🅩

OLD ORCHARD BEACH

🔺 ◆◆ **Beau Rivage Motel** M 🐾
(207) 934-4668. **$99-$160.** 54 E Grand Ave. 0.3 mi e of
Orchard St. Ext corridors. **Pets:** Medium. $25 deposit/pet,
$10 daily fee/pet. Designated rooms, no service, supervi-
sion, crate.
🆂🅰🆅🅴 ⊠ 🄲 🄳 🔲 🔁

◆ **The Crest Motel** M 🐾
(207) 934-4060. **$128-$162, 7 days notice.** 35 E Grand
Ave. Just e of Old Orchard St. Ext corridors. **Pets:** Small,
other; no pets Memorial Day - Labor Day. $100 deposit/
room, $10 daily fee/room. Designated rooms, no service,
supervision, crate.
🅢 🄳 🔁 ⊠

◆ **Flagship Motel** M ❖
(207) 934-4866. **$69-$109, 7 days notice.** 54 W Grand Ave. 0.5 mi w on SR 9. Ext corridors. **Pets:** Small, dogs only. $10 daily fee/room, $10 one-time fee/room. Designated rooms, no service, supervision, crate.
⊠ 🖥 ⌨

🏨 ◆◆ **Old Colonial Motel** M ❖
(207) 934-9862. **$105-$175.** 61 W Grand Ave. 0.5 mi w on SR 9 (W Grand Ave). Ext corridors. **Pets:** Medium, other. Supervision.
⊠ 🖥 💻 ⌨ ⊠

🏨 ◆◆ **Sea View Motel** M ❖
(207) 934-4180. **$70-$190, 3 days notice.** 65 W Grand Ave. 0.5 mi w on SR 9 (W Grand Ave). Ext corridors. **Pets:** Medium. $100 deposit/room. Supervision.
⌨ ⊠ 🖥 💻 ⌨ ⊠

🏨 ◆◆ **Waves Oceanfront Resort** M ❖
(207) 934-4949. **$100-$159, 3 days notice.** 87 W Grand Ave. 0.5 mi w on SR 9 (W Grand Ave). Ext corridors. **Pets:** Small. Designated rooms, no service, supervision, crate.
⊠ 🖥 💻 ⌨ ⌨ ⊠

ORONO

◆◆◆ **Best Western Black Bear Inn & Conference Center** M ❖
(207) 866-7120. **$70-$110.** 4 Godfrey Dr. Jct I-95 and Stillwater Ave, exit 51. Int corridors. **Pets:** Other. $3 daily fee/room. No service, supervision, crate.
⌨ ⌨ ⊠ ⌨ ⌨

◆◆ **University Motor Inn** M ❖
(207) 866-4921. **$45-$65.** 5 College Ave. 0.4 mi n on US 2, 8 mi n of Bangor; I-95, exit 50-51. Int corridors. **Pets:** Medium, other. Designated rooms, supervision.
⊠ ⌨

PORTLAND

◆◆ **Back Cove Inn** BB ❖
(207) 772-2557. **$100-$100.** 575 Forest Ave. I-295, exit 6B, 0.7 mi w. Int corridors. **Pets:** Designated rooms, supervision.
⌨ ⊠ ⌨

◆◆◆ **Doubletree Hotel** MI ❖
(207) 774-5611. **$153-$153.** 1230 Congress St. I-295, exit 5 northbound, reverse direction on SR 22; exit 5B southbound. Int corridors. **Pets:** $50 deposit/room. Designated rooms, supervision.
⊠ ⌨ ⌨ 🖥 💻 ⌨ ⌨

🏨 ◆◆◆ **Holiday Inn-West** MI ❖
(207) 774-5601. **$114-$143.** 81 Riverside St. At Maine Tpke, exit 8. Int corridors. **Pets:** Other. Designated rooms, supervision.
⌨ ⌨ ⊠ ⌨ ⌨ 🖥 💻 ⌨ ⌨

🏨 ◆◆ **Howard Johnson Hotel** MI ❖
(207) 774-5861. **$99-$135.** 155 Riverside St. I-95 (Maine Tpke), exit 8, jct SR 25. Ext/int corridors. **Pets:** $50 deposit/room. Supervision.
⌨ ⌨ ⊠ 🖥 💻 ⌨ ⌨ ⌨

PRESQUE ISLE

🏨 ◆◆ **Country View Hotel & Convention Center** MI
(207) 764-3321. **$60-$120.** 1 mi s on US 1. Int corridors. **Pets:** Designated rooms, no service, supervision, crate.
⌨ ⌨ ⊠ ⌨ ⌨

ROCKLAND

🏨 ◆ **Navigator Motor Inn** MI ❖
(207) 594-2131. **$75-$110, 3 days notice.** 520 Main St. On US 1. Ext corridors. **Pets:** Designated rooms, no service, supervision, crate.
⌨ ⊠ 🖥 ⌨

🏨 ◆◆ **Trade Winds Motor Inn** MI ❖
(207) 596-6661. **$69-$139.** 2 Park Dr. Center; on US 1. Ext/int corridors. **Pets:** Designated rooms, supervision.
⌨ ⌨ ⊠ 🖥 ⌨ ⌨

RUMFORD

🏨 ◆◆ **Linnell Motel & RestInn Conference Center** M ❖
(207) 364-4511. **$50-$75.** US 2. 2 mi w. Ext/int corridors. **Pets:** Other. $5 daily fee/room. No service, supervision, crate.
⌨ ⌨ ⊠ 🖥

◆◆ **The Madison Motor Inn** MI ❖
(207) 364-7973. **$55-$125.** US 2. 4 mi w. Ext corridors. **Pets:** Large, other. Designated rooms, supervision.
⌨ ⌨ ⊠ 🖥 💻 ⌨ ⊠

SACO

◆ **Saco Motel** M ❖
(207) 284-6952. **$45-$70.** 473 Main St. I-95, exit 5, to US 1, 0.5 mi s on US 1. Ext corridors. **Pets:** Medium, dogs only. Designated rooms, supervision.
⌨ ⊠ 🖥 ⌨

◆◆ **Tourist Haven Motel** M
(207) 284-7251. **Call for rates.** 757 Portland Rd. 2.5 mi n on US 1. Ext corridors. **Pets:** Medium. Supervision.
🖥

SANFORD

🏨 ◆ **Bar-H Motel** M ❖
(207) 324-4662. **$45-$89, 3 days notice.** 581 Main St, Rt 109. 3 mi s. Ext corridors. **Pets:** $25 deposit/pet, $10 daily fee/pet, $10 one-time fee/pet. Designated rooms, no service, supervision, crate.
⌨ ⊠ 🖥 ⌨

SCARBOROUGH

◆ **Pride Motel & Cottages** X ❖
(207) 883-4816. **$60-$105.** 677 US 1. I-95 (Maine Tpke), exit 5, 0.5 mi e to US 1, 4.5 mi n. Ext corridors. **Pets:** Other. $5 daily fee/room. No service, supervision, crate.
⊠ 🖥 💻 ⌨

SKOWHEGAN

(AAA) ◆ Breezy Acres Motel M
(207) 474-2703. **$40-$68, 7 days notice.** 1.5 mi s on US 201. Ext corridors. **Pets:** Medium. Designated rooms, supervision.
(SAVE) (S🐾) (✕) (📶) (🏊) (✕)

SOUTH PORTLAND

(AAA) ◆◆◆ AmeriSuites M
(207) 775-3900. **$99-$159.** 303 Sable Oaks Dr. I-95 (Maine Tpke), exit 7, n on Maine Mall Rd, then w on Running Hill Rd. Int corridors. **Pets:** Supervision.
(SAVE) (S🐾) (✕) (♿) (🏋) (📶) (📺) (🏊)

(AAA) ◆◆◆ Best Western Merry Manor Inn M ☆
(207) 774-6151. **$119-$149.** 700 Main St. I-95 (Maine Tpke), exit 7, 3 mi e to US 1 jct exit 7 spur road and US 1. Ext/int corridors. **Pets:** Other. No service, supervision, crate.
(S🐾) (✕) (♿) (🏋) (📶) (📺) (🍽) (🏊)

(AAA) ◆◆◆ Howard Johnson Hotel M ☆
(207) 775-5343. **$94-$159.** 675 Main St. Jct of US 1 and Maine Tpke access road; 1.3 mi e of Maine Tpk, exit 7. Int corridors. **Pets:** Other. Designated rooms, no service, supervision, crate.
(SAVE) (S🐾) (✕) (📶) (📺) (🍽) (🏊)

◆◆◆ Portland Marriott Hotel H
(207) 871-8000. **$189-$189.** 200 Sable Oaks Dr. I-95 (Maine Tpke), exit 7 n on Maine Mall Rd, then w on Running Hill Rd to Sable Oaks Dr. Int corridors. **Pets:** Small. Designated rooms, no service, supervision, crate.
(ASK) (S🐾) (✕) (🛎) (🏌) (📶) (📺) (🍽) (🏊) (✕)

SOUTHPORT

(AAA) ◆◆ The Lawnmeer Inn X ☆
(207) 633-2544. **$95-$150, 7 days notice.** 2 mi s on Boothbay Harbor on SR 27, just s of bridge to Southport Island. Ext/int corridors. **Pets:** Medium. $10 daily fee/pet. Designated rooms, no service, supervision, crate.
(SAVE) (✕) (🍽) (✕)

SPRUCE HEAD

◆◆ The Craignair Inn at Clark Island CI ☆
(207) 594-7644. **$48-$120.** 533 Clark Island Rd. 2.5 mi w on SR 73, 1.5 mi s. Ext/int corridors. **Pets:** Medium, dogs only. $9 daily fee/room. No service, supervision, crate.
(✕) (🐾) (📺)

WATERVILLE

(AAA) ◆◆◆ Best Western Waterville MI ☆
(207) 873-3335. **$95-$140, 5 days notice.** 356 Main St. I-95, exit 34 (Main St). Int corridors. **Pets:** No service, supervision, crate.
(SAVE) (S🐾) (✕) (📶) (🍽) (🏊)

(AAA) ◆ Budget Host Airport Inn MI ☆
(207) 873-3366. **$60-$100, 3 days notice.** 400 Kennedy Memorial Dr. I-95, exit 33, 0.3 mi e on SR 11 (Kennedy Memorial Dr). Ext/int corridors. **Pets:** Other. $10 one-time fee/pet. No service, supervision, crate.
(SAVE) (✕) (📶) (🍽)

(AAA) ◆◆ Econo Lodge M ☆
(207) 872-5577. **$65-$80.** 455 Kennedy Memorial Dr. SR 11, at Waterville-Oakland I-95, exit 33. Ext/int corridors. **Pets:** $5 daily fee/pet. Supervision.
(SAVE) (S🐾) (✕) (🏊)

◆◆◆ Holiday Inn MI ☆
(207) 873-0111. **Call for rates.** 375 Main St. On SR 104 at I-95 Main St, exit 34. Int corridors. **Pets:** Other. Supervision.
(✕) (📶) (📺) (🍽) (🏊)

WELLS

(AAA) ◆◆ Ne'r Beach Motel M
(207) 646-2636. **$44-$109.** US 1, 0.8 mi s of jct SR 9B. Ext corridors. **Pets:** Designated rooms, supervision.
(✕) (📶) (📺) (🏊) (✕)

WILTON

(AAA) ◆◆ Whispering Pines Motel M ☆
(207) 645-3721. **$51-$91, 3 days notice.** 183 Lake Rd. SR 2, 1 mi w of jct SR 4. Ext corridors. **Pets:** Large, other. $3 daily fee/pet. Designated rooms, no service, supervision, crate.
(SAVE) (S🐾) (✕) (📶) (📺) (✕)

YARMOUTH

(AAA) ◆◆ Down-East Village Motel MI ☆
(207) 846-5161. **$89-$99.** 705 US Rt 1. On US 1; from I-95, northbound exit 16; southbound exit 17. Ext corridors. **Pets:** $5 daily fee/pet. No service, supervision, crate.
(SAVE) (S🐾) (✕) (📶) (📺) (🏊)

YORK

(AAA) ◆◆ York Commons Inn M ☆
(207) 363-8903. **$100-$110, 3 days notice.** 362 US 1. I-95, York Ogunquit exit, 1 mi s. Int corridors. **Pets:** Medium, other. Designated rooms, supervision.
(SAVE) (S🐾) (✕) (🏌) (📶) (🏊)

CITY INDEX

BALTIMORE METROPOLITAN AREA

ABERDEEN

(AAA) ◆◆◆ **Four Points Sheraton Hotel** Ⓜ ❀
(410) 273-6300. **$79-$99.** 980 Hospitality Way. SR 22, just
e of I-95, exit 85. Int corridors. **Pets:** Other. Supervision.
SAVE 🛇 ✖ 🖹 🔋 💻 🍴 🌊

(AAA) ◆◆◆ **Holiday Inn Chesapeake
House** Ⓜ ❀
(410) 272-8100. **$95-$125.** 1007 Beards Hill Rd. SR 22,
just e of I-95, exit 85. Int corridors. **Pets:** Small. No service,
supervision, crate.
SAVE 🛇 ✖ 🖹 🔋 💻 🍴 🌊

(AAA) ◆◆ **Red Roof Inn** Ⓜ
(410) 273-7800. **$35-$72.** 988 Hospitality Way. SR 22, e of
I-95, exit 85. Ext corridors. **Pets:** Supervision.
SAVE ✖ 🖹 🔋

ANNAPOLIS

(AAA) ◆◆◆◆ **Loews Annapolis Hotel** Ⓗ ❀
(410) 263-7777. **$135-$185.** 126 West St. US 50 and 301;
exit 24 eastbound, exit 24A westbound; 1.4 mi s on SR 70
(Rowe Blvd), just sw on Calvert St, just w. Int corridors.
Pets: Other. Supervision.
SAVE 🛇 ✖ 🖹 🔌 🔋 💻 🌊

(AAA) ◆◆ **MainStay Suites** Ⓜ ❀
(410) 571-6600. **$59-$125.** 120 Admiral Cochrane Dr. US
50 to Admiral Cochrane Dr S. Int corridors. **Pets:** Medium,
other. $100 deposit/room, $10 daily fee/room. No service,
supervision, crate.
SAVE 🛇 ✖ 🖹 🔌 🔋 💻 🌊 CTV

(AAA) ◆◆◆ **Radisson Hotel Annapolis** Ⓜ
(410) 224-3150. **$69-$119.** 210 Holiday Ct. 2.3 mi sw on
US 50 and 301, exit 22 to Riva Rd, then 0.3 mi n on Riva
Rd. Int corridors. **Pets:** Medium. No service, supervision,
crate.
SAVE ✖ 🖹 🔌 🔋 🍴 🌊

◆◆◆ **Residence Inn by Marriott** Ⓐ
(410) 573-0300. **$160-$160.** 170 Admiral Cochrane Dr. 2.3
mi sw on US 50 and 301, exit 22 to Riva Rd, just s on Riva
Rd, then just e. Ext corridors. **Pets:** Large. Supervision.
ASK 🛇 ✖ 🖹 🔋 💻 🌊 ✖

BALTIMORE

◆◆◆ **Admiral Fell Inn** Ⓒ ❀
(410) 522-7377. **$139-$219.** 888 S Broadway. Facing the
waterfront in historic Fells Point; corner Broadway and
Thames sts. Int corridors. **Pets:** Dogs only. $35 daily fee/
room. Designated rooms, no service, supervision, crate.
ASK 🛇 ✖ 🔌 🔋 🍴

◆◆◆ **Doubletree Inn At The Colonnade** Ⓗ ❀
(410) 235-5400. **$119-$119.** 4 W University Pkwy. 5 mi n on
I-83, exit 9A, 0.5 mi e on Cold Springs Ln to Roland Ave/
University Pkwy, then 1 mi s. Int corridors. **Pets:** Small.
Supervision.
ASK 🛇 ✖ 🖹 💻 🌊

(AAA) ◆◆◆ **Holiday Inn-Security/Belmont** Ⓜ ❀
(410) 265-1400. **$77-$77.** 1800 Belmont Ave. I-695, exit 17,
0.3 mi n. Ext corridors. **Pets:** Small. Supervision.
SAVE 🛇 ✖ 🖹 🔋 💻 🍴 🌊

◆◆◆ **The Tremont Hotel** Ⓐ
(410) 576-1200. **$115-$115.** 8 E Pleasant St. Just s of US
40E, off Charles St. Int corridors. **Pets:** Designated rooms,
no service, supervision, crate.
✖ 🖹 🔌 🔋 💻 🍴

◆◆◆ **Tremont Plaza Hotel** Ⓐ ❀
(410) 727-2222. **$115-$115.** 222 St Paul Pl. At St Paul Pl
and Saratoga St. Int corridors. **Pets:** Medium, other. $50
deposit/room, $5 daily fee/room. No service, supervision,
crate.
✖ 🖹 🔌 🔋 💻 🍴 🌊

COLUMBIA

(AAA) ◆◆◆ **Wellesley Inn & Suites** **M** ☆
(410) 872-2994. **$79-$125.** 8890 Stanford Blvd. I-95, exit 41B, 1.3 mi w on SR 175, 0.5 mi s on Snowden River Pkwy, just w on McGaw Rd, 0.3 mi nw. Int corridors. **Pets:** Very small. $150 deposit/room, $100 one-time fee/room. No service, supervision, crate.

[SAVE] [S6] [X] [H] [IMG] [☆]

EDGEWOOD

(AAA) ◆◆◆ **Best Western Invitation Inn** **M** ☆
(410) 679-9700. **$59-$99.** 1709 Edgewood Rd. Just e of jct I-95 and SR 24, exit 77. Ext corridors. **Pets:** Other. $50 deposit/pet. Designated rooms, no service, supervision, crate.

[SAVE] [S6] [X] [⌂] [K] [H] [☆]

(AAA) ◆◆ **Days Inn-Edgewood** **M** ☆
(410) 671-9990. **$63-$84.** 2116 Emmorton Park Rd. Jct I-95 and SR 24, exit 77A. Ext corridors. **Pets:** Small, dogs only. $10 daily fee/pet. Designated rooms, no service, supervision, crate.

[SAVE] [S6] [X] [K] [H]

GLEN BURNIE

(AAA) ◆ **Days Inn-Glen Burnie** **M** ☆
(410) 761-8300. **$89-$109, 3 days notice.** 6600 Ritchie Hwy. SR 2, 0.5 mi s off I-695, exit 3B eastbound; exit 2 westbound. Ext corridors. **Pets:** $10 daily fee/room. No service, supervision, crate.

[SAVE] [S6] [X] [⌂] [K] [H] [☆]

(AAA) ◆◆◆ **Holiday Inn-Baltimore South** **M**
(410) 636-4300. **$99.** 6323 Ritchie Hwy. Jct SR 2 and I-695, eastbound exit 3A, westbound exit 2. Int corridors. **Pets:** Small. Supervision.

[SAVE] [S6] [X] [⌂] [H] [YI] [☆]

HANOVER

(AAA) ◆◆◆ **Holiday Inn Express-BWI Airport** **M**
(410) 684-3388. **$89-$150.** 7481 Ridge Rd. Just e of jct SR 176 and SR 713, 1 mi e of SR 295, exit SR 100E, then exit 10B. Int corridors. **Pets:** Small. Supervision.

[SAVE] [X] [⌂] [H] [IMG] [YI] [☆]

(AAA) ◆◆ **Red Roof Inn-BWI Parkway** **M**
(410) 712-4070. **$55-$81.** 7306 Parkway Dr S. 0.7 mi w of SR 295, exit 100 w to exit 8 (Coca-Cola Dr), 0.5 mi se. Ext corridors. **Pets:** Supervision.

[SAVE] [X] [⌂] [H] [CTV]

HUNT VALLEY

(AAA) ◆◆◆ **Embassy Suites Hotel** **H** ☆
(410) 584-1400. **$99-$189.** 213 International Cir. I-83, exit 20A (Shawan Rd). Int corridors. **Pets:** Medium. $50 one-time fee/room. Designated rooms, no service, supervision, crate.

[SAVE] [S6] [X] [⌂] [K] [H] [IMG] [YI] [☆]

◆◆◆ **Residence Inn by Marriott** **A** ☆
(410) 584-7370. **Call for rates.** 10710 Beaver Dam Rd. I-83, exit 20A (Shawan Rd) southbound, 0.3 mi e on Shawan Rd, 1.5 mi s on McCormick St; northbound I-83, exit 18, 0.3 mi e, then just n. Ext corridors. **Pets:** Other. $50 deposit/pet. Designated rooms, no service, supervision, crate.

[X] [⌂] [H] [IMG] [☆] [X]

JESSUP

(AAA) ◆◆ **Red Roof Inn-Columbia/Jessup** **M**
(410) 796-0380. **$58-$71.** 8000 Washington Blvd. US 1, 0.3 mi s of jct SR 175; 0.5 mi e of I-95, exit 41A. Ext corridors. **Pets:** No service, supervision, crate.

[SAVE] [X] [⌂] [CTV]

LINTHICUM HEIGHTS

(AAA) ◆◆◆ **AmeriSuites Baltimore/BWI**
        Airport **M** ☆
(410) 859-3366. **$99-$209.** 940 International Dr. I-695, exit 7A, 1 mi s on SR 295 (Baltimore-Washington Pkwy), just e on W Nursery Rd. Int corridors. **Pets:** Very small. Designated rooms, no service, supervision, crate.

[SAVE] [S6] [X] [&] [K] [H] [IMG] [☆]

(AAA) ◆◆◆ **Comfort Inn Airport** **M** ☆
(410) 789-9100. **$89-$129.** 6921 Baltimore Annapolis Blvd. Jct SR 170 and 648, 0.3 mi n of jct I-695; exit 6A eastbound, exit 5 westbound. Int corridors. **Pets:** Large, other. Supervision.

[SAVE] [S6] [X] [⌂] [⌂] [K] [H] [IMG]

(AAA) ◆◆◆ **Comfort Suites-BWI Airport** **M** ☆
(410) 691-1000. **$79-$139.** 815 Elkridge Landing Rd. I-695, exit 7A, 1 mi s on SR 295 (Baltimore-Washington Pkwy), 1.3 mi e on W Nursery Rd. Int corridors. **Pets:** Other. $25 one-time fee/pet. No service, supervision, crate.

[SAVE] [S6] [X] [&] [K] [H] [IMG]

◆◆◆ **Doubletree Guest Suites Hotel BWI** **H**
(410) 850-0747. **$89-$189.** 1300 Concourse Dr. I-695, exit 7A, 1 mi s on SR 295 then 0.7 mi e on W Nursery Rd, then 0.5 mi w on Winterson. Int corridors. **Pets:** Medium. No service, supervision, crate.

[ASK] [S6] [X] [⌂] [H] [IMG] [YI] [☆] [X] [CTV]

◆◆◆ **Hampton Inn BWI Airport** **M**
(410) 850-0600. **$99-$119.** 829 Elkridge Landing Rd. I-95, exit off SR 295, 1 mi n to SR 170 n, then 0.6 mi w. Int corridors. **Pets:** Small. No service, supervision, crate.

[ASK] [S6] [X] [⌂] [H] [IMG]

(AAA) ◆◆◆ **Holiday Inn-BWI Airport** **M**
(410) 859-8400. **$143-$143.** 890 Elkridge Landing Rd. I-195 exit, off SR 295, 1 mi n to SR 170 n, then 0.8 mi w. Int corridors. **Pets:** Small. Designated rooms, supervision.

[SAVE] [S6] [X] [⌂] [⌂] [H] [IMG] [YI] [☆]

◆◆ **Homestead Village Guest**
        Studios-BWI **M** ☆
(410) 691-2500. **$72-$84, 7 days notice.** 939 International Dr. I-695, exit 7A, 1 mi s on SR 295 (Baltimore-Washington Pkwy), just e on W Nursery Rd. Ext corridors. **Pets:** Very small, other. $75 one-time fee/room. No service, supervision, crate.

[X] [&] [⌂] [K] [H] [IMG]

◆◆◆ **Homewood Suites Hotel-BWI Airport** Ⓐ
(410) 684-6100. **$139-$174.** 1181 Winterson Rd. I-695, exit
7A; 1 mi s on SR 295, 0.7 mi e on W Nursery Rd, just n. Int
corridors. **Pets:** Supervision.
Ⓐ$Ⓚ Ⓢⓓ ⓧ ⓛ ⓓ ⓔ ⬛ ⬛ ⬛

⚙⚙ ◆◆ **Red Roof Inn-BWI Airport** Ⓜ
(410) 850-7600. **$66-$93.** 827 Elkridge Landing Rd. I-195
exit, off SR 295, 1 mi n to SR 170 n, then 0.5 mi w. Ext
corridors. **Pets:** Small. No service, supervision, crate.
Ⓢ Ⓐ Ⓥ Ⓔ Ⓒ Ⓣ Ⓥ

◆◆◆ **Sheraton International Hotel On BWI
    Airport** Ⓜ
(410) 859-3300. **$125-$198.** 7032 Elm Rd. I-195, exit 1A
(SR 170), 0.5 mi n on SR 170, just e. Int corridors.
Pets: Medium. No service, supervision, crate.
Ⓐ$Ⓚ Ⓢⓓ ⓧ ⓓ ⬛ ⬛ ⬛ Ⓒ Ⓣ Ⓥ

TIMONIUM

⚙⚙ ◆◆ **Red Roof Inn-Timonium** Ⓜ ❋
(410) 666-0380. **$60-$78.** 111 W Timonium Rd. I-83, exit
16A northbound, exit 16 southbound. Ext corridors.
Pets: Other. Supervision.
Ⓢ Ⓐ Ⓥ Ⓔ Ⓒ Ⓣ Ⓥ

TOWSON

⚙⚙ ◆◆ **Days Inn-Baltimore East** Ⓜ ❋
(410) 882-0900. **$64-$139, 7 days notice.** 8801 Loch
Raven Blvd. I-695, exit 29B. Int corridors. **Pets:** Medium,
other. $15 one-time fee/room. Supervision.
Ⓢ Ⓐ Ⓥ Ⓔ Ⓓ Ⓔ ⬛ ⬛

❋   **END METROPOLITAN AREA**   ❋

CUMBERLAND

◆◆◆ **Holiday Inn** Ⓜ
(301) 724-8800. **$89-$109, 3 days notice.** 100 S George
St. I-68, exit 43C, just n. Int corridors. **Pets:** Medium. No
service, supervision, crate.
Ⓐ$Ⓚ Ⓢⓓ ⓧ ⬛ ⬛ ⬛ ⬛ ⬛

DISTRICT OF COLUMBIA
METROPOLITAN AREA

BELTSVILLE

◆◆◆ **Sheraton-College Park** Ⓜ
(301) 937-4422. **$149.** 4095 Powder Mill Rd. Jct I-95 and
SR 212 W, exit 29B; 2 mi n of I-495 (Capital Beltway). Int
corridors. **Pets:** Supervision.
Ⓐ$Ⓚ Ⓢⓓ ⓧ ⓓ Ⓒ ⬛ ⬛ ⬛ ⬛ ⬛

BETHESDA

◆◆◆ **Residence Inn by Marriott-Bethesda** Ⓐ
(301) 718-0200. **$209-$209.** 7335 Wisconsin Ave. I-495,
exit 34; 2.5 mi s on SR 355; entrance on Waverly St. Int
corridors. **Pets:** Medium. No service, supervision, crate.
Ⓐ$Ⓚ Ⓢⓓ ⓧ ⓓ ⬛ ⬛ ⬛

⚙⚙ ◆◆ **Holiday Inn-Cromwell Bridge** Ⓜ ❋
(410) 823-4410. **$80-$109.** 1100 Cromwell Bridge Rd. Jct
I-695, exit 29A. Int corridors. **Pets:** Small. No service,
supervision, crate.
Ⓢ Ⓢⓓ ⓧ ⓓ ⬛ ⬛ ⬛ ⬛

WESTMINSTER

◆ **The Boston Inn** Ⓜ ❋
(410) 848-9095. **$36-$70.** 533 Baltimore Blvd. 0.9 mi se on
SR 97/140 from jct SR 27. Ext corridors. **Pets:** Dogs only.
$50 deposit/room. No service, supervision, crate.
Ⓐ$Ⓚ Ⓢⓓ ⓧ ⬛ ⬛

◆◆◆ **Comfort Inn-Westminster** Ⓜ
(410) 857-1900. **$49-$89.** 451 WMC Dr. 1.7 mi w on SR
140 from jct SR 27, adjacent to Western Maryland College.
Int corridors. **Pets:** Large. Designated rooms, supervision.
Ⓐ$Ⓚ Ⓢⓓ ⓧ ⓓ ⬛ ⬛ ⬛

⚙⚙ ◆◆ **Days Inn-Westminster** Ⓜ ❋
(410) 857-0500. **$46-$84.** 25 S Cranberry Rd. 0.4 mi se on
SR 97/140 from jct SR 27, just n. Int corridors.
Pets: Medium, other. No service, supervision, crate.
Ⓢ Ⓢⓓ ⓧ ⓓ ⬛ ⬛ ⬛

CHEVY CHASE

◆◆◆ **Holiday Inn Chevy Chase** Ⓗ
(301) 656-1500. **$139-$139, 3 days notice.** 5520 Wisconsin Ave. 0.8 mi s on SR 355, from jct SR 191. Int corridors.
Pets: Large. Supervision.
Ⓢⓓ ⓧ ⓓ ⬛ ⬛ ⬛ ⬛

GAITHERSBURG

⚙⚙ ◆◆ **Comfort Inn Shady Grove** Ⓜ ❋
(301) 330-0023. **$49-$119.** 16216 Frederick Rd. Jct SR 355
and Shady Grove Rd, exit 8 off I-270, 1 mi e on Shady
Grove Rd. Int corridors. **Pets:** Supervision.
Ⓢ Ⓢⓓ ⓧ ⓓ ⬛ ⬛ ⬛

⟐ ◆◆◆ Hilton Gaithersburg 🅷
(301) 977-8900. **$79-$109.** 620 Perry Pkwy. Jct I-270 and SR 124; exit 11 northbound, exit 11A southbound. Int corridors. **Pets:** Medium. No service, supervision, crate.

SAVE ✕ 🕭 🕭 ▣ 🍴 🖾

◆◆◆ Holiday Inn-Gaithersburg 🅼
(301) 948-8900. **$69-$89.** 2 Montgomery Village Ave. 0.3 mi e of I-270; exit 11 northbound, exit 11A southbound. Int corridors. **Pets:** Very small. No service, supervision, crate.

✕ 🕭 🕭 🖥 ▣ 🍴 🖾

⟐ ◆◆ Red Roof Inn-Gaithersburg 🅼
(301) 977-3311. **$70-$95.** 497 Quince Orchard Rd. 0.3 mi w of I-270, Quince Orchard Rd exit; northbound exit 10, southbound exit 11B. Ext corridors. **Pets:** Designated rooms, no service, supervision, crate.

SAVE ✕ 🕭 CTV

◆◆◆ Residence Inn by Marriott-Gaithersburg 🅰 ❀
(301) 590-3003. **$194.** 9721 Washingtonian Blvd. I-270, exit 9B, 0.9 mi s on Fields Rd, just ne. Int corridors. **Pets:** $6 daily fee/pet, $100 one-time fee/room. No service, supervision, crate.

ASK 🕭 ✕ 🕭 🕭 🕭 🖥 ▣ 🖾 ✕

◆◆◆ Summerfield Suites Hotel-Gaithersburg 🅰 ❀
(301) 527-6000. **$150.** 200 Skidmore Blvd. Off SR 355 via S Westland Rd, just n on SR 355 from jct I-370. Ext corridors. **Pets:** Medium, other. $15 daily fee/room, $200 one-time fee/room. Supervision.

🕭 ✕ 🕭 🕭 🕭 🖥 ▣ 🖾 ✕

◆◆◆ TownePlace Suites by Marriott-Gaithersburg 🅼
(301) 590-2300. **$59-$109.** 212 Perry Pkwy. I-270 exit 11, northbound; exit 11A southbound, just e or SR 214 to SR 355, 0.3 mi s on SR 355, then 0.5 mi sw. Int corridors. **Pets:** Medium. No service, supervision, crate.

ASK 🕭 ✕ 🕭 🕭 🕭 🖥 ▣ 🖾

GERMANTOWN

◆◆ Homestead Village Guest Studios 🅼
(301) 515-4500. **$69-$104.** 20141 Century Blvd. I-270, exit 15B, just w to Aircraft Dr, then n. Ext corridors. **Pets:** Medium. Supervision.

✕ 🕭 🕭 🕭 🖥 ▣

LANHAM

⟐ ◆ Red Roof Inn-Lanham 🅼
(301) 731-8830. **$57-$77.** 9050 Lanham Severn Rd. 0.3 mi ne of jct I-95/I-495 and SR 450E, exit 20A. Ext corridors. **Pets:** No service, supervision, crate.

SAVE ✕ 🖥 CTV

LAUREL

⟐ ◆◆◆ Comfort Suites Hotel at Laurel Lakes 🅼 ❀
(301) 206-2600. **$79-$125.** 14402 Laurel Pl. 1.4 mi s on US 1, from jct SR 198; adjacent to Laurel Lakes Mall. Int corridors. **Pets:** Medium, other. $50 deposit/room. Supervision.

SAVE ✕ 🕭 🖥 ▣ 🖾

⟐ ◆◆ Red Roof Inn-Laurel 🅼
(301) 498-8811. **$56-$66.** 12525 Laurel Bowie Rd. SR 197, 0.3 mi w of SR 295 (Baltimore-Washington Pkwy), exit SR 197 (Laurel Bowie Rd). Ext corridors. **Pets:** Small. No service, supervision, crate.

SAVE ✕ 🕭

OXON HILL

⟐ ◆ Red Roof Inn-Oxon Hill 🅼
(301) 567-8030. **$56-$83.** 6170 Oxon Hill Rd. SR 414, 0.5 mi sw of I-95/I-495, exit 4A. Ext corridors. **Pets:** Small. Supervision.

SAVE ✕ 🕭 CTV

ROCKVILLE

⟐ ◆◆ Best Western Washington Gateway Hotel 🅼 ❀
(301) 424-4940. **$79-$149, 3 days notice.** 1251 W Montgomery Ave. SR 28, just w of jct I-270, exit 6 to exit 6B. Int corridors. **Pets:** Medium, other. $10 one-time fee. Designated rooms, no service, supervision, crate.

SAVE 🕭 ✕ 🕭 🖥 🍴 🖾

⟐ ◆◆◆ Quality Suites-Shady Grove 🅼 ❀
(301) 840-0200. **$70-$170.** 3 Research Ct. Just sw of I-270, exit 8 (Shady Grove Rd). Int corridors. **Pets:** Other. $100 one-time fee/pet. Designated rooms, supervision.

SAVE 🕭 ✕ 🕭 🕭 🖥 ▣ 🖾

◆◆ Red Roof Inn-Rockville 🅼
(301) 987-0965. **$90-$120.** 16001 Shady Grove Rd. I-270, exit 8, 0.5 mi e. Ext corridors. **Pets:** Small. No service, supervision, crate.

✕ 🕭 🕭 🕭 🍴 🖾

◆◆◆ Woodfin Suites Hotel 🅼 ❀
(301) 590-9880. **$124-$124.** 1380 Piccard Dr. 0.3 mi s of I-270, exit 8 (Shady Grove Rd); 1 mi w of SR 355 via Redland Rd. Ext corridors. **Pets:** Other. $5 daily fee/room, $50 one-time fee/room. No service, supervision, crate.

🕭 ✕ 🕭 🕭 🖥 ▣ 🖾

UPPER MARLBORO

⟐ ◆ Forest Hills Motel 🅼 ❀
(301) 627-3969. **$45-$55.** 2901 Crain Hwy. 2.6 mi n on US 301, from jct SR 4. Ext corridors. **Pets:** $10 deposit/room, $10 daily fee/room, $10 one-time fee/room. No service, supervision, crate.

SAVE 🕭 ▣ CTV

❀ **END METROPOLITAN AREA** ❀

EASTON

◆◆◆ Days Inn 🅼 ☼
(410) 822-4600. **$86-$115.** 7018 Ocean Gateway. US 50, 2 mi s of jct SR 331. Ext corridors. **Pets:** Medium. $10 daily fee/pet. Supervision.

[ASK] [S🐾] [✕] [🐾] [🛏] [💻] [🏖]

FREDERICK

🅐🅐🅐 ◆◆ Comfort Inn 🅼
(301) 695-6200. **$69-$89.** 420 Prospect Blvd. US 15, Jefferson St,·just se. Int corridors. **Pets:** Small. No service, supervision, crate.

[SAVE] [S🐾] [✕] [🐾] [🛏] [💻] [🏖]

🅐🅐🅐 ◆ Econo Lodge 🅼 ☼
(301) 698-0555. **$45-$65.** 6005 Urbana Pike. Jct SR 85 & 355. Ext corridors. **Pets:** Small. $10 daily fee/pet. Designated rooms, no service, supervision, crate.

[SAVE] [S🐾] [✕] [🛏] [💻] [🏖]

🅐🅐🅐 ◆◆◆ Hampton Inn 🅼🛈
(301) 698-2500. **$89-$89.** 5311 Buckeystown Pike (SR 85). I-270, exit 31B, 0.6 mi w via SR 85. Int corridors. **Pets:** Small. No service, supervision, crate.

[SAVE] [✕] [🐾] [🛏] [💻] [🍴] [🏖]

◆◆ Holiday Inn Express-FSK Mall 🅼 ☼
(301) 695-2881. **$72.** 5579 Spectrum Dr. I-270, exit 31A, just e on SR 85. Int corridors. **Pets:** Other. $25 deposit/room. No service, supervision, crate.

[ASK] [S🐾] [✕] [🔓] [🐾] [🛏] [💻]

◆◆◆ Holiday Inn-Francis Scott Key Mall 🅼🛈
(301) 694-7500. **$79-$99.** 5400 Holiday Dr. I-270, exit 31A, just se on SR 85. Int corridors. **Pets:** No service, supervision, crate.

[✕] [🐾] [🛏] [💻] [🍴] [🏖] [✕]

🅐🅐🅐 ◆◆◆ Holiday Inn Frederick/Ft. Detrick 🅼🛈 ☼
(301) 662-5141. **$70-$85, 7 days notice.** 999 W Patrick St. I-70, exit 48, 2.7 mi e on US 40; at jct US 15. Ext corridors. **Pets:** Other. Supervision.

[SAVE] [S🐾] [✕] [🐾] [🛏] [💻] [🍴] [🏖]

🅐🅐🅐 ◆◆ Red Horse Motor Inn 🅼🛈 ☼
(301) 662-0281. **$44-$67, 7 days notice.** 998 W Patrick St. US 40, w of jct US 15. Int corridors. **Pets:** Other. No service, supervision, crate.

[SAVE] [S🐾] [✕] [🔓] [🛏] [🍴]

FROSTBURG

◆◆ Comfort Inn 🅼 ☼
(301) 689-2050. **$56-$83.** 11100 New Georges Creek Rd. I-68, exit 34, 1 mi n on SR 36. Int corridors. **Pets:** Other. $10 one-time fee/room. Supervision.

[ASK] [S🐾] [✕] [🐾] [💻]

GRANTSVILLE

◆◆◆ Holiday Inn 🅼🛈
(301) 895-5993. **$49-$79, 3 days notice.** 2541 Chestnut Ridge Rd N. I-68, exit 22, just s, on US 249. Int corridors. **Pets:** No service, supervision, crate.

[ASK] [S🐾] [✕] [🍴] [🏖]

◆◆ Walnut Ridge Bed & Breakfast [BB] ☼
(301) 895-4248. **$65-$75, 5 days notice.** 92 Main St. I-68, exit 19, just n on SR 495, then 0.5 mi w on US 40. Ext/int corridors. **Pets:** $10 daily fee/room, $10 one-time fee/room. Designated rooms, no service, supervision, crate.

[ASK] [S🐾] [✕] [🛏] [💻]

HAGERSTOWN

🅐🅐🅐 ◆◆◆ Comfort Suites 🅼 ☼
(301) 791-8100. **$69-$99.** 1801 Dual Hwy. I-70, exit 32B, 0.8 mi w on US 40. Int corridors. **Pets:** Small. Supervision.

[SAVE] [S🐾] [✕] [🔓] [🛏] [💻] [🏖]

🅐🅐🅐 ◆◆ Econo Lodge 🅼
(301) 791-3560. **$55-$65.** 18221 Mason Dixon Rd. I-81, exit 1 (in Pennsylvania), just sw on SR 163, at MD-PA state line. Int corridors. **Pets:** Small. No service, supervision, crate.

[SAVE] [S🐾] [✕] [💻]

🅐🅐🅐 ◆◆◆ Four Points Hotel by Sheraton 🅼 ☼
(301) 790-3010. **$69-$69.** 1910 Dual Hwy. I-70, exit 32B, 0.5 mi n. Int corridors. **Pets:** Medium. $75 deposit/room. No service, supervision, crate.

[SAVE] [S🐾] [✕] [🛏] [🏖]

🅐🅐🅐 ◆◆ Motel 6–1259 🅼 ☼
(301) 582-4445. **$44-$60.** 11321 Massey Blvd. I-81, exit 5, 0.5 mi e, 0.5 mi n of jct I-81 and I-70. Ext corridors. **Pets:** Small, other. No service, supervision, crate.

[S🐾] [✕] [🔓] [🏖]

◆◆ Quality Inn 🅼 ☼
(301) 733-2700. **$55-$60.** 1101 Dual Hwy. I-70 exit 32B, 2.2 mi w on US 40. Int corridors. **Pets:** $10 daily fee/pet. Designated rooms, no service, supervision, crate.

[ASK] [S🐾] [✕] [🛏] [💻]

🅐🅐🅐 ◆ State Line Motel 🅼
(301) 733-8262. **$32-$42.** 18221 Mason Dixon Rd. I-81, exit 1 (in Pennsylvania), just sw on SR 163; at MD-PA state line. Ext corridors. **Pets:** No service, supervision, crate.

[S🐾] [✕]

◆◆ Super 8 🅼
(301) 739-5800. **$42-$55.** 1220 Dual Hwy. I-70, exit 32B, 2.1 mi nw on US 40. Int corridors. **Pets:** Supervision.

[ASK] [S🐾] [✕]

◆◆ Venice Inn 🅼🛈 ☼
(301) 733-0830. **$65-$74, 7 days notice.** 431 Dual Hwy. I-70, exit 32B, 2.8 mi w on US 40. Ext/int corridors. **Pets:** Other. Supervision.

[ASK] [S🐾] [✕] [🛏] [🍴] [🏖]

JOPPA

◆ Super 8 Motel 🅼
(410) 676-2700. **$60-$76.** 1015 Pulaski Hwy. I-95, exit 74, 1 mi s on SR 152, just w on US 40. Int corridors. **Pets:** Large. No service, supervision, crate.

[ASK] [S🐾] [✕] [🔓] [CTV]

MCHENRY

◆◆ Comfort Inn **M** ❖
(301) 387-4200. **$60-$100.** 2704 Deep Creek Dr. I-68, exit 14A, 15 mi s on SR 219. Int corridors. **Pets:** Other. $10 one-time fee/room. Supervision.
🄰🄢🄺 🆂🄸 ⊠ 🖬

◆◆ Wisp Mountain Resort/Hotel & Conference Center **R**
(301) 387-5581. **$79-$169, 7 days notice.** 290 Marsh Hill Rd. 1 mi s on US 219 from jct SR 42, just w on Sang Run Rd, 0.3 mi s. Int corridors. **Pets:** Small. Supervision.
🄰🄢🄺 ⊠ 🖉 🖬 🖳 🍴 🕋 🕱

NORTH EAST

◆◆◆ Crystal Inn **M**
(410) 287-7100. **$89-$89.** 1 Center Dr. I-95, exit 100, 0.3 mi se on SR 272. Int corridors. **Pets:** Designated rooms, no service, supervision, crate.
🄰🄢🄺 🆂🄸 ⊠ 🖉 🖲 🖬 🕋

OCEAN CITY

🄰🄐🄐 ◆◆ Fenwick Inn **MI** ❖
(410) 250-1100. **$119-$189, 3 days notice.** 13801 Coastal Hwy. 138th and Coastal Hwy. Int corridors. **Pets:** Small. $10 daily fee/room. Designated rooms, supervision.
🆂🄰🅅🄴 🆂🄸 ⊠ 🖉 🖬 🖳 🍴 🕋

🄰🄐🄐 ◆◆◆ Sheraton Fontainebleau Hotel **H**
(410) 524-3535. **$239-$299, 3 days notice.** 10100 Coastal Hwy. 101st St E Coastal Hwy. Int corridors. **Pets:** No service, supervision, crate.
🆂🄰🅅🄴 ⊠ 🖉 🖬 🖳 🍴 🕋 🕱

PERRYVILLE

🄰🄐🄐 ◆◆◆ Comfort Inn **M**
(410) 642-2866. **$55-$76.** 61 Heather Ln. I-95, exit 93. Ext corridors. **Pets:** Medium. Supervision.
🆂🄰🅅🄴 🆂🄸 ⊠ 🖉 🖬

POCOMOKE CITY

🄰🄐🄐 ◆◆ Quality Inn of Pocomoke **M**
(410) 957-1300. **$60-$90, 7 days notice.** 825 Ocean Hwy. 2.5 mi s on US 13. Ext corridors. **Pets:** Medium. Designated rooms, no service, supervision, crate.
🆂🄰🅅🄴 🆂🄸 ⊠ 🖉 🖬 🖳 🕋

PRINCESS ANNE

◆ Econo Lodge **M**
(410) 651-9400. **$54-$89.** 10936 Market Ln. 2 mi s on US 13. Ext corridors. **Pets:** Supervision.
🄰🄢🄺 🆂🄸 ⊠ 🖬 🖳 🕋

◆◆◆ Waterloo Country Inn **CI** ❖
(410) 651-0883. **$100-$225, 7 days notice.** 28822 Mt Vernon Rd. 3.3 mi w on SR 362 from jct US 13. Int corridors. **Pets:** Other. Designated rooms, no service, supervision, crate.
⊠ 🖳 🍴 🕋 🕱

RAWLINGS

🄰🄐🄐 ◆ Diplomat Motel **M** ❖
(301) 729-2311. **$35-$48.** 17012 McMullen Hwy. US 220, 0.4 mi s of jct SR 956. Ext corridors. **Pets:** Medium. $5 daily fee/pet, $5 one-time fee/pet. Designated rooms, no service, supervision, crate.
🆂🄰🅅🄴 🆂🄸 ⊠ 🖬

ROCK HALL

🄰🄐🄐 ◆◆◆ Huntingfield Manor Bed & Breakfast **BB** ❖
(410) 639-7779. **$90-$140, 7 days notice.** 4928 Eastern Neck Rd. 1.8 mi s on SR 445 from jct SR 20. Ext/int corridors. **Pets:** Supervision.
🆂🄰🅅🄴 ⊠ 🖬 🖳 🕱 🄲🅃🅅 🖉

◆ Mariners Motel **M** ❖
(410) 639-2291. **$60-$70.** 5681 S Hawthorne Ave. 0.3 mi e of SR 20. Ext corridors. **Pets:** Other. No service, supervision, crate.
⊠ 🖬 🖳 🕋 🕱

SALISBURY

🄰🄐🄐 ◆◆◆ Best Western Salisbury Plaza **M** ❖
(410) 546-1300. **$98-$119, 3 days notice.** 1735 N Salisbury Blvd. US 13 business route, 1.5 mi n of US 50. Ext corridors. **Pets:** $10 daily fee/room. Supervision.
🆂🄰🅅🄴 ⊠ 🖬 🖳 🕋

🄰🄐🄐 ◆◆◆ Comfort Inn **M** ❖
(410) 543-4666. **$53-$120.** 2701 N Salisbury Blvd. US 13, 0.5 mi n of jct US 13 business route and bypass. Int corridors. **Pets:** Other. Supervision.
🆂🄰🅅🄴 🆂🄸 ⊠ 🖉 🖬 🖳

🄰🄐🄐 ◆◆ Howard Johnson Inn-Salisbury **MI** ❖
(410) 742-7194. **$66-$120.** 2625 N Salisbury Blvd. US 13, 0.5 mi n of jct US 13 business route and bypass. Ext corridors. **Pets:** Other. Supervision.
🆂🄰🅅🄴 🆂🄸 ⊠ 🖉 🖬 🖳 🍴 🕋

SNOW HILL

◆◆◆ River House Inn **BB**
(410) 632-2722. **$99-$195, 7 days notice.** 201 E Market St. 1 mi w on SR 394 from jct SR 113. Ext/int corridors. **Pets:** Supervision.
🄰🄢🄺 🆂🄸 ⊠ 🖬 🖳 🕱 🖉

SOLOMONS

🄰🄐🄐 ◆◆◆ Holiday Inn Select Solomons Hotel **H** ❖
(410) 326-6311. **$94-$109.** 155 Holiday Dr. Center; SR 2-4. Int corridors. **Pets:** Other. Supervision.
🆂🄰🅅🄴 🆂🄸 ⊠ 🖉 🖬 🖳 🍴 🕋 🕱

THURMONT

🄰🄐🄐 ◆◆ Rambler Inn **M** ❖
(301) 271-2424. **$42-$62, 7 days notice.** 426 W Church St. US 15 at SR 550. Ext/int corridors. **Pets:** Small. No service, supervision, crate.
⊠ 🖬

WALDORF

◆ **Days Inn of Waldorf**
(301) 932-9200. **$65-$85.** 11370 Days Court. 0.5 mi s on US 301 from jct SR 228. Int corridors. **Pets:** Small. Designated rooms, supervision.

🅰 🆂 ⊠ 🔳 🖵

AAA ◆ **Econo Lodge of Waldorf** Ⓜ
(301) 645-0022. **$55-$65.** 11770 Business Park Dr. 1 mi n on US 301 from jct 228. Int corridors. **Pets:** Small. No service, supervision, crate.

🆂🅰🆅🅴 ⊠ 🐾 🔳 🖵

WILLIAMSPORT

AAA ◆◆ **Red Roof Inn** Ⓜ 🐾
(301) 582-3500. **$42-$49.** 310 E Potomac St. I-81, exit 2; 0.3 mi sw on US 11. Ext corridors. **Pets:** Small. Designated rooms, no service, supervision, crate.

🆂🅰🆅🅴 🆂 ⊠ 🐾 🔳 🖾

MASSACHUSETTS

CITY INDEX

AMHERST

◆◆ University Lodge 🅜 ❀
(413) 256-8111. **$55-$105.** 345 N Pleasant St. 0.9 mi n of center. Ext corridors. **Pets:** Medium. Designated rooms, no service, supervision, crate.
🅐🆂🅺 🆂🅱 ⊠ ▣

BARRE

⨀ ◆◆◆ Jenkins Inn 🄲🄸 ❀
(978) 355-6444. **$110-$150.** 7 West St. Ne end of town green on SR 122 and 32. Int corridors. **Pets:** Other. $5 daily fee/pet. No service, supervision, crate.
🆂🅰🆅🅴 🆂🅱 ⊠ ▣ 🍴 🄲🅣🅥

BOSTON METROPOLITAN AREA

ANDOVER

◆◆ Andover Inn 🄲🄸 ❀
(978) 475-5903. **$99-$115.** 1 Chapel Ave. 2.3 mi s of I-495, exit 41A via SR 28; at Phillips Academy Campus. Int corridors. **Pets:** Other. Supervision.
⊠ 🄲🅣🅥

◆◆◆ Wyndham Andover 🄷
(978) 975-3600. **$155.** 123 Old River Rd. 4.5 mi w at jct I-93 and River Rd; just e of I-93, exit 45; behind office park. Int corridors. **Pets:** Medium. Supervision.
🅐🆂🅺 🆂🅱 ⊠ 🎢 🖥 🍴 🕿

BEDFORD

◆◆◆ Renaissance Bedford Hotel 🄷
(781) 275-5500. **$194-$204.** 44 Middlesex Tpke. 2.5 mi n of I-95 (SR 128), exit 32B via Middlesex Tpke. Int corridors. **Pets:** Supervision.
🅐🆂🅺 🆂🅱 ⊠ 🎢 ✆ 🕿 ⊠

BOSTON

◆◆◆◆ Boston Harbor Hotel 🄷 ❀
(617) 439-7000. **Call for rates.** 70 Rowes Wharf. At Rowes Wharf. Int corridors. **Pets:** Other. Supervision.
⊠ 🎢 🕿 ⊠

◆◆◆◆ The Eliot Suite Hotel 🄷 ❀
(617) 267-1607. **$275-$395.** 370 Commonwealth Ave. Corner Commonwealth (SR 2) and Massachusetts (SR 2A) aves. Int corridors. **Pets:** Other. No service, supervision, crate.
🅐🆂🅺 ⊠ 🖧

◆◆◆◆ Fairmont Copley Plaza 🄷
(617) 267-5300. **$219-$379.** 138 St. James Ave. At Copley Sq. Int corridors. **Pets:** Medium. No service, supervision, crate.
🅐🆂🅺 🆂🅱 ⊠ 🎢 🖧 🍴

**⨀ ◆◆◆◆◆ Four Seasons Hotel
Boston** 🄷 ❀
(617) 338-4400. **$465-$595.** 200 Boylston St. At Boylston St and Park Sq. Int corridors. **Pets:** Very small, other. Designated rooms, no service, supervision, crate.
⊠ 🛎 🎢 🕿

◆◆◆ Hilton Boston Back Bay 🄷
(617) 236-1100. **Call for rates.** 40 Dalton St. Adjacent to Copley Place; at Dalton and Belvedere sts. Int corridors. **Pets:** Supervision.
⊠ 🎢 🖥 🖥 🍴 🕿

◆◆◆◆ Hotel Le Meridien 🄷
(617) 451-1900. **$333.** 250 Franklin St. Center; on Post Office Sq. Int corridors. **Pets:** Medium. Supervision.
⊠ 🎢 🖧 ▣ 🍴 🕿

⊕ ◆ Howard Johnson Hotel-Kenmore 🅷
(617) 267-3100. **$135-$135, 3 days notice.** 575 Commonwealth Ave. Just w of Kenmore Sq, 2 blks n of Fenway Park. Int corridors. **Pets:** Supervision.

[SAVE] [✕] [▯] [▭] [⌂]

⊕ ◆◆ Howard Johnson Lodge Fenway 🅼
(617) 267-8300. **$115-$115, 3 days notice.** 1271 Boylston St. Backing on to Fenway Park. Int corridors. **Pets:** Supervision.

[SAVE] [✕] [▯] [▭] [⑊] [⌂]

◆◆◆ Regal Bostonian Hotel 🅷
(617) 523-3600. **$305-$470, 3 days notice.** Faneuil Hall Marketplace. Int corridors. **Pets:** Supervision.

[ASK] [S▯] [✕] [⌕] [🎜] [⑊]

⊕ ◆◆◆◆ The Ritz-Carlton, Boston 🅷 ❀
(617) 536-5700. **$455-$2500.** 15 Arlington St. Overlooking the Public Gardens; Arlington and Newbury sts. Int corridors. **Pets:** $30 daily fee/room. Supervision.

[✕] [🎜] [⑊]

◆◆◆ Seaport Hotel 🅷
(617) 385-4000. **$259-$349.** 1 Seaport Ln. At World Trade Center/Commonwealth Pier. Int corridors. **Pets:** Supervision.

[ASK] [S▯] [✕] [🎜] [⌗] [▭] [⑊]

⊕ ◆◆◆ Sheraton-Boston Hotel 🅷
(617) 236-2000. **$259-$259.** 39 Dalton St. Prudential Center, turnpike exit 22. Int corridors. **Pets:** Supervision.

[✕] [♿] [🎜] [⌗] [▯] [▭] [⑊] [⌂]

⊕ ◆◆◆◆ Swissotel Boston 🅷 ❀
(617) 451-2600. **$379-$449.** One Ave de Lafayette. Center; just e of Boston Common at Lafayette Pl. Int corridors. **Pets:** Small. Supervision.

[SAVE] [S▯] [✕] [⌕] [🎜] [▭] [⑊] [⌂]

◆◆◆ The Westin Hotel, Copley Place Boston 🅷 ❀
(617) 262-9600. **Call for rates.** 10 Huntington Ave. I-90 (Massachusetts Tpke), exit 22; at Copley Sq. Int corridors. **Pets:** Other. Supervision.

[✕] [🎜] [⌗] [▭] [⑊] [⌂]

BRAINTREE

⊕ ◆◆ Days Inn-Braintree 🅼
(781) 848-1260. **$99-$115.** 190 Wood Rd. Just n of jct I-93 and SR 128 on SR 37, 0.5 mi w. Int corridors. **Pets:** Very small. Supervision.

[SAVE] [✕] [▯] [CTV]

BURLINGTON

◆◆ Homestead Village Guest Studios 🅼 ❀
(781) 359-9099. **Call for rates.** 40 South St. Just n of I-95, exit 32A; in Northwest Park opposite Burlington Mall. Int corridors. **Pets:** Small, other. $75 one-time fee/room. Supervision.

[✕] [🎜] [⌗] [▯] [▭]

◆◆◆ Summerfield Suites Hotel 🅼 ❀
(781) 270-0800. **$109-$199.** 2 Van de Graaf Dr. I-95, exit 33A, just s on US 3, then 0.5 mi w on Wayside Rd. Int corridors. **Pets:** Medium. $10 daily fee/room, $150 one-time fee/room. No service, supervision, crate.

[ASK] [S▯] [✕] [🎜] [⌗] [▯] [▭] [⌂] [⊠]

CAMBRIDGE

◆◆◆ The Charles Hotel in Harvard Square 🅷 ❀
(617) 864-1200. **$240-$430.** 1 Bennett St. Just s from Harvard Square; corner Eliot and Bennett sts. Int corridors. **Pets:** No service, supervision, crate.

[ASK] [S▯] [✕] [⌕] [🎜] [⑊] [⌂]

⊕ ◆ Howard Johnson Hotel Cambridge 🅷
(617) 492-7777. **$135-$135, 3 days notice.** 777 Memorial Dr. On US 3 and SR 2; 3 blks from I-90 (Massachusetts Tpke), exit 18, via River St Bridge. Int corridors. **Pets:** Supervision.

[SAVE] [✕] [▯] [▭] [⑊] [⌂]

◆◆◆ Residence Inn by Marriott Cambridge 🅼 ❀
(617) 349-0700. **Call for rates.** 6 Cambridge Center. Corner of 6th and Broadway. Int corridors. **Pets:** Other. $10 daily fee/pet, $100 one-time fee/room. Supervision.

[✕] [🎜] [⌗] [▯] [▭] [⌂]

CONCORD

◆◆ Best Western at Historic Concord 🅼
(978) 369-6100. **$94-$129.** 740 Elm St. 1.8 mi w just off SR 2 and 2A. Int corridors. **Pets:** Supervision.

[ASK] [S▯] [✕] [▯] [⌂]

DANVERS

◆◆◆ Residence Inn by Marriott 🅼 ❀
(978) 777-7171. **$148-$148.** 51 Newbury St (Rt 1). On US 1 N, just s of jct SR 114; entrance via T.G.I. Friday's parking lot. Ext corridors. **Pets:** $10 daily fee/pet, $50 one-time fee/pet. No service, supervision, crate.

[ASK] [S▯] [✕] [⌗] [▯] [▭] [⌂] [⊠]

DEDHAM

◆◆◆ Hilton Dedham Place 🅷
(781) 329-7900. **$224-$239.** 25 Allied Dr. Just e of jct I-95 and SR 128, exit 14. Int corridors. **Pets:** Supervision.

[ASK] [S▯] [✕] [🎜] [▭] [⑊] [⌂] [⊠]

FRAMINGHAM

⊕ ◆◆ Red Roof Inn 🅼 ❀
(508) 872-4499. **$65-$105.** 650 Cochituate Rd. On SR 30 at jct I-90 (Massachusetts Tpke), exit 13; from SR 9 in Natick, 0.8 mi n on Speen St, then w on SR 30, following signs for Massachusetts Tpke. Ext corridors. **Pets:** Supervision.

[SAVE] [✕] [▯] [▭] [CTV]

GLOUCESTER

⬤ ◆◆ Cape Ann Motor Inn 🅼 ☙
(978) 281-2900. **$115-$130, 7 days notice.** 33 Rockport Rd. 2 mi n of the terminus of SR 128 via SR 127A. Ext corridors. **Pets:** Other. No service, supervision, crate.

🔲 ⊠ 🐾

⬤ ◆ The Manor Inn 🆇 ☙
(978) 283-0614. **$89-$139.** 141 Essex Ave. On SR 133, 2.3 mi e of exit 14, SR 128. Ext/int corridors. **Pets:** Medium. $25 deposit/pet, $10 daily fee/pet. Designated rooms, no service, supervision, crate.

🆂🅰🆅🅴 🆂 ⊠ 🆅

LAWRENCE

◆◆◆ Hampton Inn Boston/North Andover 🅼
(978) 975-4050. **$79-$99.** 224 Winthrop Ave. At jct I-495, exit 42A and SR 114. Int corridors. **Pets:** Designated rooms, no service, supervision, crate.

🅰🆂🅺 🆂 ⊠ 🐾 🔲

LEXINGTON

◆ Battle Green Motor Inn 🅼 ☙
(781) 862-6100. **$99-$109.** 1720 Massachusetts Ave. Center; on SR 4 and 225, 2 mi s of I-95 and SR 128, exit 31A. Int corridors. **Pets:** Supervision.

⊠ 🔲 🛟

MALDEN

◆ New Englander Motor Court 🅼
(781) 321-0505. **$69-$89.** 551 Broadway. On SR 99; 1.5 mi ne of Malden. Ext corridors. **Pets:** Supervision.

🅰🆂🅺 🆂 ⊠ 🔲

MARLBOROUGH

◆◆◆ Embassy Suites Boston Marlborough 🅼
(508) 485-5900. **$174.** 123 Boston Post Rd W. Just off US 20, 0.5 mi w of I-495, exit 24B. Int corridors. **Pets:** Very small. Designated rooms, no service, supervision, crate.

🅰🆂🅺 🆂 ⊠ 🔲 🐾 🌀 🔲 🔲 🍴 🛟

◆◆ Homestead Village Guest Studios 🅼 ☙
(508) 490-9911. **$99-$114.** 19 Northborough Rd. On US 20, just w of I-495, exit 24B. Int corridors. **Pets:** Small, other. $75 one-time fee/pet. Supervision.

⊠ 🐾 🔲 🔲 🔲

NEPONSET

⬤ ◆◆ Susse Chalet Boston Hotel 🅼 ☙
(617) 287-9100. **$120-$165.** 800 Morrissey Blvd. I-93 and SR 3, 0.5 mi sw; northbound, exit 13; southbound exit 12, follow signs to Morrissey Blvd. Ext/int corridors. **Pets:** $50 deposit/room. Designated rooms, no service, supervision, crate.

🆂🅰🆅🅴 🆂 ⊠ 🔲 🛟

NEWTON

◆◆◆ Sheraton Newton Hotel 🅷
(617) 969-3010. **Call for rates.** 320 Washington St. I-90 (Massachusetts Tpke) exit 17 and jct SR 16. Int corridors. **Pets:** Supervision.

⊠ 🐾 🔲 🔲 🍴 🛟

NORTH CHELMSFORD

◆◆◆ Hawthorne Suites, LTD 🅼 ☙
(978) 256-5151. **$139.** 25 Research Pl. From SR 3, exit 32, 0.3 mi ne on SR 4. Int corridors. **Pets:** Medium, other. $10 daily fee/room, $50 one-time fee/room. Designated rooms, no service, supervision, crate.

🅰🆂🅺 🆂 ⊠ 🔲 🔲 🔲 🔲 🛟

PEABODY

⬤ ◆◆ MainStay Suites 🅼🅸 ☙
(978) 531-6632. **$109-$139.** 200 Jubilee Dr. SR 128, exit 28, just s to Centenial Dr, w to the end, n to Jubilee Dr, then 1.1 mi e. Int corridors. **Pets:** Other. $100 deposit/room, $10 daily fee/room. Supervision.

🆂🅰🆅🅴 🆂 ⊠ 🔲 🔲 🛟

QUINCY

◆ Presidents' City Inn 🅼
(617) 479-6500. **$95-$110.** 845 Hancock St. On SR 3A (Hancock St); 2.2 mi se of I-93, exit 12. Ext corridors. **Pets:** Small. Designated rooms, supervision.

🅰🆂🅺 🆂 ⊠

ROCKPORT

⬤ ◆◆ Sandy Bay Motor Inn 🅼
(978) 546-7155. **$102-$150, 7 days notice.** 173 Main St. 0.5 mi s on SR 127. Ext/int corridors. **Pets:** Medium. No service, supervision, crate.

⊠ 🔲 🍴 🛟 ⊠

SALEM

◆◆◆ Hawthorne Hotel 🅷 ☙
(978) 744-4080. **$140-$189, 3 days notice.** 18 Washington Sq W. On SR 1A; adjoining the historical district and facing the Salem Witch Museum. Int corridors. **Pets:** $15 one-time fee/room. Supervision.

🅰🆂🅺 🆂 ⊠ 🔲 🔲 🍴

⬤ ◆◆◆ The Salem Inn 🅱🅱 ☙
(978) 741-0680. **$160-$290, 7 days notice.** 7 Summer St. On SR 114 at jct Essex St; 3 mi e of jct SR 128, exit 25A. Int corridors. **Pets:** Other. $15 one-time fee/pet. Designated rooms, no service, supervision, crate.

🆂🅰🆅🅴 ⊠ 🔲

TEWKSBURY

◆◆◆ Residence Inn by Marriott-Boston/Tewksbury 🅼
(978) 640-1003. **$129-$169.** 1775 Andover St. On SR 133; from I-495, exit 39, 0.3 mi w. Ext corridors. **Pets:** No service, supervision, crate.

🅰🆂🅺 🆂 ⊠ 🔲 🐾 🔲 🔲 🔲 🛟 ⊠

WALTHAM

◆◆ Homestead Village Guest Studios 🅼 ☙
(781) 890-1333. **$99-$114.** 52 Fourth Ave. Just se of I-95 and SR 128, exit 27A; behind the Westin Hotel. Int corridors. **Pets:** Medium, other. $75 one-time fee/room. No service, supervision, crate.

🅰🆂🅺 🆂 ⊠ 🔲 🔲 🔲

◆◆◆ Summerfield Suites Hotel Ⓜ ❀
(781) 290-0026. **$139-$249.** 54 Fourth Ave. Just e of I-95
and SR 128, exit 27A; behind the Westin Hotel. Int corridors. **Pets:** Medium. $10 daily fee/room, $150 one-time
fee/room. No service, supervision, crate.
🅐🅢🅚 🆂🐾 ⊠ 🖆 🗂 🅒 🅗 💻 �

◆◆◆ The Westin Hotel, Waltham Ⓗ ❀
(781) 290-5600. **Call for rates.** 70 Third Ave. Just se of jct
I-95 and SR 128, exit 27A. Int corridors. **Pets:** Supervision.
⊠ 🖆 🅒 💻 🍴 �

WOBURN

◆◆ Hampton Inn Boston-Woburn Ⓜ ❀
(781) 935-7666. **Call for rates.** 315 Mishawum Rd. N side
of I-95 and SR 128, exit 36, southbound at exit, northbound
just n, just w; opposite Woburn Mall. Int corridors.
Pets: Medium. Supervision.
⊠ 🖆 🖆 🅒 🍴

◆◆ Ramada Inn Ⓜ
(781) 935-8760. **$149-$199.** 15 Middlesex Canal Park Rd.
S of exit 35 of I-95 and SR 128 via SR 38. Int corridors.
Pets: Very small. No service, supervision, crate.
🅐🅢🅚 🆂🐾 ⊠ 🖆 🅒 🅒 💻 🍴 �

❀ **END METROPOLITAN AREA** ❀

CAPE COD METROPOLITAN AREA

BUZZARDS BAY

🅐🅐🅐 ◆◆ Bay Motor Inn Ⓒ ❀
(508) 759-3989. **$79-$99.** 223 Main St. 0.5 mi w of the
Bourne Rotary, exit 2 from SR 25. Ext corridors. **Pets:** $5
daily fee/room. No service, supervision, crate.
🆂🅰🆅🅴 🆂🐾 💻 🌻

CENTERVILLE

🅐🅐🅐 ◆◆ Centerville Corners Motor
    Lodge Ⓜ ❀
(508) 775-7223. **$115-$130, 7 days notice.** 369 S Main St.
1 mi s of SR 28 at jct S Main St and Craigville Beach Rd.
Ext corridors. **Pets:** Medium, other. $5 daily fee/pet. Desig-
nated rooms, supervision.
⊠ 🅒 💻 🌻

FALMOUTH

◆◆◆ Holiday Inn-Falmouth Cape Cod Ⓜ ❀
(508) 540-2000. **$160-$250.** 291 Jones Rd. 0.5 mi e of SR
28 on Jones Rd, just e of jct Jones and Gillford sts. Int
corridors. **Pets:** Supervision.
🅐🅢🅚 🆂🐾 ⊠ 🅒 💻 🍴 🌻

🅐🅐🅐 ◆◆ Mariner Motel Ⓜ
(508) 548-1331. **$69-$99.** 555 Main St. 0.5 mi e on SR 28.
Ext corridors. **Pets:** Small. Supervision.
⊠ 🅒 🌻 ⊠

HYANNIS

◆◆ Comfort Inn Ⓜ ❀
(508) 771-4804. **$109-$175.** 1470 Rt 132. US 6, exit 6, 1.3
mi se on SR 132. Ext/int corridors. **Pets:** Other. $50
deposit/room, $5 daily fee/pet. No service, supervision,
crate.
🅐🅢🅚 🆂🐾 ⊠ 🖆 🅒 🌻

HYANNIS PORT

🅐🅐🅐 ◆◆ Harbor Village Ⓒ
(508) 775-7581. **Call for rates** (no credit cards), 30 days
notice. 160 Marstons Ave. From Hyannis, 1 mi w on Main
St, 0.3 mi sw on Scudder Ave, 0.5 mi s on Greenwood Ave.
Ext corridors. **Pets:** Small. Designated rooms, no service,
supervision, crate.
🆂🅰🆅🅴 💻 ⊠

ORLEANS

🅐🅐🅐 ◆◆◆ Skaket Beach Motel Ⓜ ❀
(508) 255-1020. **$91-$164.** 203 Cranberry Hwy, Rt 6A. At
jct US 6, exit 12. Ext corridors. **Pets:** $9 daily fee/pet.
Supervision.
⊠ 🅒 💻 🌻

PROVINCETOWN

◆◆◆ Bayshore Ⓜ ❀
(508) 487-9133. **$950-$1995, 30 days notice.** 493 Commercial St. 0.8 mi e of Town Hall. Ext corridors. **Pets:** $15
daily fee/room. Supervision.
🅒 💻 ⊠

◆◆◆ Best Inn Ⓜ ❀
(508) 487-1711. **$154-$169, 3 days notice.** 698 Commercial St. 1.5 mi se on SR 6A. Ext corridors. **Pets:** Other.
Supervision.
🅐🅢🅚 🆂🐾 ⊠ 🖆 🅒 💻 🍴 🌻

🅐🅐🅐 ◆◆ Surfside Inn Ⓜ
(508) 487-1726. **$129-$189, 21 days notice.** 543 Commercial St. 1 mi e of Town Hall. Ext/int corridors. **Pets:** Supervision.
🅒 💻 🍴 🌻 ⊠

◆◆ **White Wind Inn** 🆑 ❀
(508) 487-1526. **$160-$225.** 174 Commercial St. Just w of town hall. Int corridors. **Pets:** Medium, dogs only. $50 deposit/room, $10 daily fee/room. Designated rooms, supervision.
🗙 🔌 ▭

SANDWICH

◆◆ **The Earl of Sandwich Motel** 🅼
(508) 888-1415. **$85-$109, 7 days notice.** 378 Rt 6A. At MM 5.1. Ext corridors. **Pets:** Medium. Designated rooms, supervision.
🗙 🔌 🗙

🅰 ◆ **Sandwich Lodge & Resort** 🅼 ❀
(508) 888-2275. **$110-$170, 7 days notice.** 54 Rt 6A. 1 mi w. Ext/int corridors. **Pets:** Other. $15 one-time fee/room. Supervision.
🆂🅰🆅🅴 🆂🅳 🗙 🔌 🖻

SOUTH YARMOUTH

🅰 ◆◆ **Motel 6-4042** 🅼 ❀
(508) 394-4000. **$75-$85.** 1314 Rt 28. 0.3 mi w of Bass River Bridge. Int corridors. **Pets:** Small. Supervision.
🆂🅰🆅🅴 🆂🅳 🗙 🔌 🖻

❀ END METROPOLITAN AREA ❀

CHICOPEE

🅰 ◆◆ **Super 8-Chicopee Motor Lodge** 🅼
(413) 592-6171. **$57-$75, 3 days notice.** 463 Memorial Dr (Rt 33). I-90 (Massachusetts Tpke), exit 5. Int corridors. **Pets:** Medium. No service, supervision, crate.
🆂🅰🆅🅴 🆂🅳 🗙 🖻

GREENFIELD

🅰 ◆◆◆ **The Brandt House** 🆑 ❀
(413) 774-3329. **$125-$195.** 29 Highland Ave. From I-91, exit 26, 1.8 mi e on SR 2A and se via Cresent St. Int corridors. **Pets:** Medium, dogs only. $20 one-time fee/pet. Supervision.
🆂🅰🆅🅴 🗙 🔌 🗙

HADLEY

◆◆◆ **Howard Johnson** 🅼
(413) 586-0114. **$75-$145.** 401 Russell St. On SR 9 at jct SR 116 N. Int corridors. **Pets:** Medium. Designated rooms, supervision.
🅰🆂🅺 🆂🅳 🗙 🔌 ▭ 🖻

HANCOCK

🅰 ◆◆◆ **Jericho Valley Inn** 🅼
(413) 458-9511. **$68-$138.** 2541 Hancock Rd. On SR 43, 5 mi s of jct US 7. Ext/int corridors. **Pets:** Supervision.
🆂🅰🆅🅴 🆂🅳 🗙 🔌 ▭ 🖻 🗙

KINGSTON

🅰 ◆◆ **The Inn At Plymouth Bay** 🅼 ❀
(781) 585-3831. **$99-$130.** 149 Main St. On SR 3A at jct SR 3, exit 9, 3.5 mi n of jct US 44/SR 3A.. Int corridors. **Pets:** Supervision.
🆂🅰🆅🅴 🆂🅳 🗙 🔌 🖻

LANESBORO

🅰 ◆ **Mt View Motel** 🅼 ❀
(413) 442-1009. **$48-$125, 3 days notice.** 499 S Main St. 1 mi s on US 7. Ext corridors. **Pets:** Medium. $25 deposit/pet, $7 daily fee/pet, $7 one-time fee/pet. Designated rooms, no service, supervision, crate.
🆂🅰🆅🅴 🆂🅳 🗙 🔌

🅰 ◆ **The Weathervane Motel** 🅼
(413) 443-3230. **$35-$125.** 475 S Main St. 1.3 mi s on US 7. Ext corridors. **Pets:** Small. Designated rooms, supervision.
🆂🅰🆅🅴 🆂🅳 🗙 🔌

LENOX

◆◆◆ **Seven Hills Country Inn & Restaurant** 🅲🅸
(413) 637-0060. **$85-$325, 30 days notice.** 40 Plunkett St. From jct US 7/20, 0.6 mi e on US 20, then 0.8 mi s. Ext/int corridors. **Pets:** Supervision.
🅰🆂🅺 🆂🅳 🗙 🍴 🖻 🗙

MANSFIELD

🅰 ◆◆ **Motel 6-1248** 🅼
(508) 339-2323. **$54-$70.** 60 Forbes Blvd. From I-95, exit 7A, 1.3 mi n of jct I-495, exit 12, just off SR 140; in Cabot Business Park. Int corridors. **Pets:** Small. Supervision.
🆂🅳 🗙 🖿 🖻

MIDDLEBORO

◆◆ **Days Inn-Plymouth/Middleboro** 🅼 ❀
(508) 946-4400. **$77-$95.** 30 E Clark St. I-495, exit 4, at SR 105. Int corridors. **Pets:** Other. $3 daily fee/room. No service, supervision, crate.
🅰🆂🅺 🆂🅳 🗙 🖿 🖻

ORANGE

🅰 ◆ **Executive Inn** 🅼 ❀
(978) 544-8864. **$45-$65, 7 days notice.** 110 Daniel Shay Hwy. US 202, just n of jct SR 2, exit 16. Ext/int corridors. **Pets:** Very small, dogs only. Designated rooms, supervision.
🆂🅰🆅🅴 🆂🅳 🗙 🔌

RAYNHAM

◆◆ **Days Inn Taunton** 🅼 ❀
(508) 824-8647. **$69-$99.** 164 New State Hwy. On US 44, 0.8 mi w of SR 24, exit 13B. Ext/int corridors. **Pets:** Other. No service, supervision, crate.
🅰🆂🅺 🆂🅳 🗙 🖿 🖻

REHOBOTH

◆◆◆ Five Bridge Inn Bed & Breakfast `BB` ❀
(508) 252-3190. **$78-$125.** 154 Pine St. 1.6 mi n of US 44, 3.3 mi w of jct US 118; from US 44 n on Blanding, e on Broad, n on Salisbury, then w. Int corridors. **Pets:** Other. $10 daily fee/room. Supervision.
⬛⬛⬛⬛⬛⬛⬛⬛

ROCKLAND

◆◆ Holiday Inn
　　Express-Boston/Rockland `M` ❀
(781) 871-5660. **$114-$129.** 909 Hingham St. On SR 228, 0.3 mi sw of SR 3, exit 14. Ext/int corridors. **Pets:** Other. $50 deposit/room, $6 daily fee/pet. Supervision.
⬛⬛⬛⬛

◆◆◆ Ramada Inn-Rockland `MI` ❀
(781) 871-0545. **$149-$189.** 929 Hingham St. On SR 228, 0.3 mi sw of SR 3, exit 14. Int corridors. **Pets:** Small. Supervision.
⬛⬛⬛⬛⬛⬛⬛⬛

SEEKONK

⬛ ◆◆ Motel 6–1289 `M` ❀
(508) 336-7800. **$56-$71.** 821 Fall River Ave. On SR 114A, just n of I-195, exit 1. Int corridors. **Pets:** Supervision.
⬛⬛

SOMERSET

◆◆ Quality Inn-Fall River/Somerset `M` ❀
(508) 678-4545. **$75-$125.** 1878 Wilbur Ave. At jct SR 103 and I-195, eastbound exit 4; westbound exit 4A. Int corridors. **Pets:** Other. No service, supervision, crate.
⬛⬛⬛⬛⬛⬛

SOUTHBOROUGH

⬛ ◆◆ Red Roof Inn `M` ❀
(508) 481-3904. **$64-$104.** 367 Turnpike Rd. On SR 9 at jct I-495, exit 23A. Ext corridors. **Pets:** Other. Supervision.
⬛⬛⬛

SPRINGFIELD

⬛ ◆◆◆ Holiday Inn `H` ❀
(413) 781-0900. **$129-$149.** 711 Dwight St. I-291, exit 2B westbound; exit 2A (Chestnut St) eastbound. Int corridors. **Pets:** Small, dogs only. Supervision.
⬛⬛⬛⬛⬛⬛⬛⬛

STURBRIDGE

⬛ ◆◆ American Motor Lodge-Best
　　Western `MI` ❀
(508) 347-9121. **$75-$95.** 350 Main St. On US 20 at jct SR 131. Int corridors. **Pets:** Medium. No service, supervision, crate.
⬛⬛⬛⬛⬛

⬛ ◆◆◆ Comfort Inn & Suites at Pistol
　　Pond `M` ❀
(508) 347-3306. **$90-$110.** US 20. 0.5 mi e of jct I-90 (Massachusetts Tpke), exit 9 and I-84, exit 3A. Ext corridors. **Pets:** Medium. Designated rooms, no service, supervision, crate.
⬛⬛⬛⬛⬛⬛⬛

⬛ ◆◆ Days Inn `M` ❀
(508) 347-3391. **$75-$120, 7 days notice.** 66-68 Old Route 15, Haynes St. I-84, exit 2, following signs to SR 131, on I-84 service road. Ext/int corridors. **Pets:** Medium. $7 daily fee/room. No service, supervision, crate.
⬛⬛⬛⬛⬛

⬛ ◆◆ Green Acres Motel `M` ❀
(508) 347-3496. **$55-$95.** 2 Shepard Rd, Rt 131. Just off SR 131, 1.4 mi s of jct US 20. Ext corridors. **Pets:** Medium. $5 daily fee/pet, $5 one-time fee/pet. Designated rooms, no service, supervision, crate.
⬛⬛⬛⬛⬛

⬛ ◆◆ Publick House Historic Inn & County Motor
　　Lodge `X`
(508) 347-3313. **$100-$170.** 295 Main St. On the Common; SR 131, 0.5 mi s of jct US 20 on SR 131; I-90, exit 9; I-84, exit 3B. Ext/int corridors. **Pets:** Medium. No service, supervision, crate.
⬛⬛⬛⬛⬛

⬛ ◆◆ Rodeway Inn `M` ❀
(508) 347-9673. **$60-$120.** 172 Main St. On SR 131, 1.4 mi s of jct US 20 and SR 131. Ext corridors. **Pets:** $10 daily fee/pet. Designated rooms, no service, supervision, crate.
⬛⬛⬛⬛⬛

◆◆◆ Sturbridge Host Hotel and Conference Center
　　on Cedar Lake `MI`
(508) 347-7393. **$119-$179.** 366 Main St. US 20, just w of I-90 (Massachusetts Tpke), exit 9; I-84, exit 3B. Int corridors. **Pets:** Medium. No service, supervision, crate.
⬛⬛⬛⬛⬛⬛⬛⬛

WEST SPRINGFIELD

⬛ ◆◆ Red Roof Inns `M` ❀
(413) 731-1010. **$56-$93.** 1254 Riverdale (US 5) St. I-91, exit 13A (US 5 N). Ext corridors. **Pets:** Supervision.
⬛⬛⬛⬛

WEST STOCKBRIDGE

⬛ ◆◆ Pleasant Valley Motel `M` ❀
(413) 232-8511. **$55-$165.** Rt 102. I-90, exit B3 eastbound, 0.5 mi s on SR 22 and 3.5 mi e Rt 102; exit 1 westbound, 0.4 mi e. Ext corridors. **Pets:** Medium. $10 daily fee/pet, $10 one-time fee/pet. Designated rooms, no service, supervision, crate.
⬛⬛⬛⬛

WESTBOROUGH

◆◆◆ Residence Inn by Marriott
　　Boston/Westborough `M` ❀
(508) 366-7700. **$89-$199.** 25 Connector Rd. 0.3 mi s of SR 9, Computer Dr/Research Dr exit, just w of jct I-495, exit 23B. Ext/int corridors. **Pets:** Medium, other. $100 one-time fee/room. No service, supervision, crate.
⬛⬛⬛⬛⬛⬛⬛⬛⬛⬛

◆◆◆ **Wyndham Westborough Hotel** 🅼
(508) 366-5511. **Call for rates.** 5400 Computer Dr. Computer/Research Dr exit from SR 9, just w of I-495, exit 23B. Int corridors. **Pets:** Small. Supervision.

WILLIAMSTOWN

◆◆ **Cozy Corner Motel** 🅼 🐾
(413) 458-8006. **$70-$105.** 284 Sand Springs Rd & US 7. On US 7, 1.5 mi n of jct SR 2. Ext corridors. **Pets:** Other. $25 deposit/room, $5 daily fee/pet. No service, supervision, crate.

🆇 🔧

🆀🆀🆀 ◆◆ **The Villager Motel** 🅼 🐾
(413) 458-4046. **$65-$95.** 953 Simonds Rd. On US 7, 1.7 n of jct SR 2. Ext corridors. **Pets:** Medium. $10 daily fee/pet. Designated rooms, no service, supervision, crate.

🆇 🔧

WORCESTER

🆀🆀🆀 ◆◆ **The Regency Suites** 🅷 🐾
(508) 753-3512. **$95-$125.** 70 Southbridge St. I-290, exit 13, 0.5 mi n on SR 122. Int corridors. **Pets:** Medium, other. $50 deposit/room. Supervision.

SAVE 🆂🅾 🆇 🔧 💻 🍽 🛎

CITY INDEX

ALBION

◆◆ **Best Western Adams Arms Motel**
(517) 629-3966. **Call for rates.** 400 B Dr N. I-94, exit 121, just e on service road. Ext corridors. **Pets:** No service, supervision, crate.
⊠ ▱

ALGONAC

◆◆ **Linda's Lighthouse Inn** 🅱🅱
(810) 794-2992. **$70-$135, 7 days notice.** 5965 Pte. Tremble Rd. I-94, exit 243, 14 mi e on M-29. Int corridors. **Pets:** Supervision.
⊠ ⊠ CTV

ALPENA

◆◆◆ **Holiday Inn** 🅼🅸 ❁
(517) 356-2151. **$84-$114.** 1000 Hwy 23 N. 1 mi n on US 23. Int corridors. **Pets:** Supervision.
A$K S⊙ ⊠ ▱ ⑪ ▱ ⊠

ANN ARBOR

◆◆◆ **Holiday Inn North Campus** 🅼🅸
(734) 769-9800. **$112-$136.** 3600 Plymouth Rd. US 23, exit 41 (Plymouth Rd), just sw. Int corridors. **Pets:** Medium. Designated rooms, no service, supervision, crate.
A$K S⊙ ⊠ ⑂ ⏃ ▤ ▱ ⑪ ▱ ⊠

◈ ◆ **Motel 6–1247** 🅼
(734) 665-9900. **$50-$66.** 3764 S State St. I-94, exit 177 (State St), just s, then just w on Airport Rd. Ext corridors. **Pets:** Small. No service, supervision, crate.
S⊙ ⊠ ⟨ ▱

◈ ◆◆ **Red Roof Inn** 🅼 ❁
(734) 996-5800. **$59-$79.** 3621 Plymouth Rd. US 23, exit 41 (Plymouth Rd), just nw. Ext corridors. **Pets:** Other. No service, supervision, crate.
SAVE ⊠ ⑦ CTV

◆◆◆ **Residence Inn by Marriott** 🅰 ❁
(734) 996-5666. **$99-$169.** 800 Victors Way. I-94, exit 177 (State St), just ne. Ext corridors. **Pets:** Other. $160 one-time fee/room. No service, supervision, crate.
A$K S⊙ ⊠ ⑦ ⟨ ▤ ▱ ▱ ⊠

AU GRES

◈ ◆◆ **Best Western Pinewood Lodge** 🅼
(517) 876-4060. **$79-$109.** 510 W US 23. Just w on US 23. Int corridors. **Pets:** Designated rooms, supervision.
SAVE S⊙ ⊠ ▤ ▱ ▱

BARAGA

◆ **Carla's Lake Shore Motel & Restaurant** 🅼 ❁
(906) 353-6256. **$45-$52.** 6 mi n on US 41. Ext corridors. **Pets:** Other. $5 daily fee/pet. No service, supervision, crate.
A$K S⊙ ⊠ ▤ ⑪ 🆇 CTV

◆ **Super 8 Motel** M
(906) 353-6680. **$46-$53, 7 days notice.** 790 Michigan Ave. 1 mi w on SR 38. Int corridors. **Pets:** Small. Designated rooms, supervision.
(ASK) (S⊕) (X) (X⊗)

BATTLE CREEK

◆◆◆ **Battle Creek Inn** MI ❀
(616) 979-1100. **$62-$82.** 5050 Beckley Rd. I-94, exit 97 (Capital Ave). Ext/int corridors. **Pets:** Other. No service, supervision, crate.
(SAVE) (S⊕) (X) (⊟) (⊡) (⊞) (⊜) (X)

◆◆◆ **Baymont Inn & Suites-Battle Creek** M ❀
(616) 979-5400. **$63-$87.** 4725 Beckley Rd. I-94, exit 97 (Capitol Ave S), just w. Int corridors. **Pets:** $50 deposit/room. Designated rooms, supervision.
(ASK) (S⊕) (X) (⊘) (⊡) (⊟) (⊡) (⊜) (CTV)

◆◆ **Days Inn** M
(616) 979-3561. **$50-$100.** 4786 Beckley Rd. I-94, exit 97 (Capital Ave). Ext corridors. **Pets:** Designated rooms, no service, supervision, crate.
(ASK) (S⊕) (X) (⊓) (⊟)

◆◆◆ **Hampton Inn** M
(616) 979-5577. **$68-$83.** 1150 Riverside Dr. I-94, exit 97, 0.3 mi e on Beckley Rd. Int corridors. **Pets:** No service, supervision, crate.
(ASK) (S⊕) (X) (⊓) (⊘) (⊟) (⊜)

◆ **Knights Inn** M ❀
(616) 964-2600. **$39-$60.** 2595 Capital Ave SW. I-94, exit 97, 0.3 mi n. Ext corridors. **Pets:** Very small, other. $25 deposit/room. Designated rooms, no service, supervision, crate.
(SAVE) (S⊕) (X) (⊟) (⊜)

◆◆◆◆ **McCamly Plaza Hotel** H
(616) 963-7050. **$129-$139.** 50 Capital Ave SW. Center. Int corridors. **Pets:** No service, supervision, crate.
(SAVE) (S⊕) (X) (⊓) (⊘) (⊡) (⊟) (⊜)

◆ **Motel 6–1149** M ❀
(616) 979-1141. **$32-$58.** 4775 Beckley Rd. I-94 and Capital Ave, exit 97. Ext corridors. **Pets:** Small. No service, supervision, crate.
(S⊕) (X) (⊓) (⊡) (⊜) (CTV)

◆◆ **Super 8 Motel** M ❀
(616) 979-1828. **$47-$61.** 5395 Beckley Rd. I-94, exit 97, 0.3 mi e. Int corridors. **Pets:** Other. $25 deposit/room. Supervision.
(ASK) (S⊕) (X) (⊓) (⊟)

BAY CITY

◆◆◆ **AmericInn of Bay City** M ❀
(517) 671-0071. **$59-$134.** 3915 Three Mile Rd. Jct I-75 and Wilder Rd, exit 164. Int corridors. **Pets:** Other. No service, supervision, crate.
(SAVE) (S⊕) (X) (⊘) (⊟) (⊜)

◆ **Delta Motel** M ❀
(517) 684-4490. **$27-$40, 7 days notice.** 1000 S Euclid Ave. From jct I-75 and US 10, 1.8 mi e on SR 25, 0.8 mi s on SR 13. Ext corridors. **Pets:** Very small, dogs only. $25 deposit/room. Designated rooms, no service, supervision, crate.
(S⊕) (X) (⊟)

◆◆◆ **Holiday Inn** MI
(517) 892-3501. **$80-$90.** 501 Saginaw St. Center line on I-75 business loop, SR 15 and 25. Int corridors. **Pets:** Medium. Designated rooms, no service, supervision, crate.
(ASK) (S⊕) (X) (⊛) (⊡) (⊞) (⊜)

BAY VIEW

◆◆ **Comfort Inn** M ❀
(231) 347-3220. **$48-$225.** 1314 US 31 N. At jct US 31 and SR 119. Int corridors. **Pets:** Other. Supervision.
(SAVE) (S⊕) (X) (⊟) (⊡)

BENTON HARBOR

◆◆ **Days Inn** MI ❀
(616) 925-7021. **$50-$105.** 2699 Michigan Hwy M-139. I-94, exit 28 (M-139). Int corridors. **Pets:** $10 daily fee/pet. Designated rooms, no service, supervision, crate.
(SAVE) (S⊕) (X) (⊟) (⊞) (⊜)

◆ **Motel 6** M
(616) 925-5100. **$40-$56** (no credit cards). 2063 Pipestone Rd. I-94, exit 29, just ne. Ext corridors. **Pets:** Designated rooms, no service, supervision, crate.
(S⊕) (X) (⊛) (⊜)

◆◆ **Ramada Inn** MI ❀
(616) 927-1172. **$69-$109.** 798 Ferguson Dr. I-94, exit 28 (M-139). Int corridors. **Pets:** Other. $5 daily fee/pet. Designated rooms, supervision.
(ASK) (S⊕) (X) (⊟) (⊡) (⊞) (⊜)

◆◆ **Red Roof Inn** M
(616) 927-2484. **$53-$81.** 1630 Mall Dr. I-94, exit 29 (Pipestone Rd). Ext corridors. **Pets:** Supervision.
(SAVE) (X) (⊓) (⊘) (⊟)

BEULAH

◆ **Pine Knot Resort** M
(231) 882-7751. **$80-$110.** 171 N Center St. 1 mi ne on US 31 from jct SR 115. Ext corridors. **Pets:** No service, supervision, crate.
(S⊕) (⊟) (⊡) (X⊗)

BIRCH RUN

◆◆ **Super 8 Motel** M ❀
(517) 624-4440. **Call for rates.** 9235 E Birch Run Rd. I-75, exit 136, just e. Int corridors. **Pets:** No service, supervision, crate.
(ASK) (X) (⊟)

BREVORT

◆ **Chapel Hill Motel** Ⓜ ❀
(906) 292-5534. **$44-$54, 3 days notice.** 4422 W US 2.
Center on US 2. Ext/int corridors. **Pets:** Small, dogs only.
$5 one-time fee/pet. Supervision.

⊠ 🛏 💻 🖼 ⊠ 📺

BRIDGEPORT

◆◆ **Baymont Inn-Saginaw (Bridgeport)** Ⓜ ❀
(517) 777-3000. **Call for rates.** 6460 Dixie Hwy. I-75, exit
144A. Int corridors. **Pets:** Medium. Supervision.

⊠ 🖋 🛏 💻

🅰🅰🅰 ◆◆ **Motel 6–1255** Ⓜ
(517) 777-2582. **$33-$49.** 6361 Dixie Hwy. I-75, exit 144B.
Ext corridors. **Pets:** Small. Supervision.

🆂 ⊠ 🖋 🛏

CADILLAC

◆ **Cadillac Sands Resort** Ⓜ
(231) 775-2407. **$75-$95, 3 days notice.** 6319 E M115. Jct
SR 115 and 55. Ext/int corridors. **Pets:** Supervision.

🅰🆂🔑 🆂 ⊠ 🛏 🍴 🖼 ⊠

🅰🅰🅰 ◆ **Econo Lodge** Ⓜ ❀
(231) 775-6700. **$65-$120.** 2501 Sunnyside Dr. Jct SR 55
and 115. Ext/int corridors. **Pets:** Medium, other. No service,
supervision, crate.

🆂🅰🆅🅴 🆂 ⊠ 🛏 💻 ⊠

🅰🅰🅰 ◆◆◆ **McGuires Resort & Conference**
Center Ⓡ ❀
(231) 775-9947. **$89-$129, 7 days notice.** 7880 Mackinaw
Tr. 0.5 mi w of US 131. Ext/int corridors. **Pets:** Other. $15
one-time fee/room. Designated rooms, supervision.

🆂🅰🆅🅴 ⊠ 🖋 🔑 🛏 🍴 🖼 ⊠

◆ **Pine Chata Resort** Ⓜ
(231) 775-4677. **$50-$60.** 5936 E M 55. SR 55, 0.3 mi w of
jct SR 115. Ext corridors. **Pets:** Supervision.

🆂 ⊠ 🛏 ⊠

◆ **Pine Knoll Motel** Ⓜ ❀
(231) 775-9471. **$35-$65.** 8072 Mackinaw Tr. 0.8 mi w of
US 131. Ext corridors. **Pets:** Medium. $15 deposit/pet. Des-
ignated rooms, no service, supervision, crate.

🆂 ⊠ 🖼 ⊠

◆ **Sun'n Snow Motel** Ⓜ
(231) 775-9961. **$49-$64.** 301 S Lake Mitchell Dr. Jct SR
115 and 55. Ext corridors. **Pets:** Medium. Supervision.

🆂 ⊠ 🛏 ⊠

CASCADE

◆◆◆ **Country Inn & Suites By Carlson** Ⓜ
(616) 977-0909. **$74-$98.** 5399 28th St. I-96, exit 43B, just
e on SR 11. Int corridors. **Pets:** Medium. No service, supervision, crate.

🅰🆂🔑 🆂 ⊠ 🔑 🌀 🖋 🛏 💻 🖼

🅰🅰🅰 ◆◆ **Exel Inn of Grand Rapids** Ⓜ
(616) 957-3000. **$45-$70.** 4855 28th St SE. On SR 11, 0.5
mi w of jct I-96, exit 43A. Int corridors. **Pets:** Small. Designated rooms, no service, supervision, crate.

🆂 ⊠ 🛏

🅰🅰🅰 ◆◆ **Hampton Inn** Ⓜ ❀
(616) 956-9304. **$65-$94.** 4981 28th St SE. I-96, exit 43A,
0.5 mi w on SR 11. Int corridors. **Pets:** Small. No service,
supervision, crate.

🅰🆂🔑 🆂 ⊠ 🌀 🛏 💻 🖼

🅰🅰🅰 ◆◆ **Red Roof Inn** Ⓜ
(616) 942-0800. **$59-$78.** 5131 28th St SE. I-96, exit 43A,
0.3 mi w on SR 11. Ext corridors. **Pets:** Supervision.

🆂🅰🆅🅴 ⊠ 🖋

CEDARVILLE

◆◆◆ **Comfort Inn** Ⓜ ❀
(906) 484-2266. **$80-$160.** 106 W M-134. On SR 134, just
w of SR 129. Int corridors. **Pets:** Medium, dogs only. Designated rooms, no service, supervision, crate.

🅰🆂🔑 🆂 ⊠ 💻 🖼 ⊠

CHARLEVOIX

◆◆ **Sleep Inn** Ⓜ ❀
(231) 547-0300. **$49-$133.** 800 Petoskey Ave. 1 mi n on
US 31. Int corridors. **Pets:** Medium. $25 deposit/room. Des-
ignated rooms, no service, supervision, crate.

🅰🆂🔑 ⊠ 🖋 🖼

CHARLOTTE

🅰🅰🅰 ◆◆ **Super 8 Motel** Ⓜ
(517) 543-8288. **$54-$63.** 828 E Shepherd St. I-69, exit 60,
just w on SR 50. Int corridors. **Pets:** Medium. Supervision.

🆂🅰🆅🅴 🆂 ⊠ 🛏

CHEBOYGAN

🅰🅰🅰 ◆ **Birch Haus Motel** Ⓜ ❀
(231) 627-5862. **$30-$55.** 1301 Mackinaw Ave. On US 23,
0.8 mi nw. Ext corridors. **Pets:** Medium, dogs only. $5 daily
fee/pet. No service, supervision, crate.

🆂🅰🆅🅴 ⊠ 🛏

🅰🅰🅰 ◆ **Pine River Motel** Ⓜ ❀
(231) 627-5119. **$40-$50, 3 days notice.** 102 Lafayette. 0.5
mi e on US 23. Ext corridors. **Pets:** Dogs only. $10 daily
fee/pet, $10 one-time fee/pet. Designated rooms, no serv-
ice, supervision, crate.

🆂🅰🆅🅴 🆂 ⊠ ⊠

CLARE

🅰🅰🅰 ◆ **Budget Inn** Ⓜ ❀
(517) 386-7201. **$34-$100.** 1110 N McEwan St. Just n of
US 27 business route. Ext corridors. **Pets:** Very small. $10
deposit/room. No service, supervision, crate.

🆂🅰🆅🅴 🆂 ⊠ 🛏 🖼

COLDWATER

🅰🅰🅰 ◆◆◆ **Quality Inn Convention**
Center Ⓜ ❀
(517) 278-2017. **$72-$94.** 1000 Orleans Blvd. I-69 and US
12, exit 13, just n, then just e. Int corridors. **Pets:** Designated rooms, supervision.

🆂🅰🆅🅴 🆂 ⊠ 🛏 💻 🍴 🖼

(AAA) ◆◆ Super 8 Motel **M** ❀
(517) 278-8833. **$55-$70.** 600 Orleans Blvd. 0.3 mi w of jct
I-69 and US 12 exit 13, just n, then just e. Int corridors.
Pets: Other. No service, supervision, crate.
[SAVE] [S] [X] [&] [&'] [🔲]

COMSTOCK PARK

(AAA) ◆ Swan Inn **M** ❀
(616) 784-1224. **$45-$80.** 5182 Alpine Ave. From I-96 and
Alpine Ave, 3 mi n on SR 37. Ext corridors. **Pets:** Medium,
other. No service, supervision, crate.
[SAVE] [X] [🔲] [↑↑] [🔄]

COPPER HARBOR

(AAA) ◆ Lake Fanny Hooe Resort **M** ❀
(906) 289-4451. **$58-$68, 7 days notice.** 505 Second St.
Just s on Manganese Rd. Ext corridors. **Pets:** Other. $3
daily fee/pet. Supervision.
[SAVE] [🔲] [X] [K'] [Z]

(AAA) ◆ Norland Motel **M** ❀
(906) 289-4815. **$36-$64** (no credit cards), 7 days notice.
US 41, F #172. 2 mi e on US 41; beyond entrance to Fort
Wilkins State Park. Ext corridors. **Pets:** Other. $5 daily fee/
pet. No service, supervision, crate.
[X] [🔲] [💻] [X] [K'] [Z]

DETROIT METROPOLITAN AREA

ALLEN PARK

(AAA) ◆◆◆ Best Western Greenfield Inn **M**
(313) 271-1600. **$89-$114.** 3000 Enterprise Dr. At jct I-94
and Oakwood Blvd, 2 mi from Greenfield Village. Int corridors. **Pets:** Designated rooms, supervision.
[X] [S] [🔲] [💻] [↑↑] [🔄]

AUBURN HILLS

(AAA) ◆◆◆ AmeriSuites **M**
(248) 475-9393. **$69-$129.** 1545 Opdyke Road. I-75, exit
79 (University Dr), w then n. Int corridors. **Pets:** Supervision.
[SAVE] [S] [X] [S] [&'] [🔲] [💻] [🔄]

◆◆◆ Hilton Suites Auburn Hills **H** ❀
(248) 334-2222. **$125-$125.** 2300 Featherstone Rd. I-75,
exit 79, w on University Dr, then 0.5 mi s on Opdyke Rd,
just e. Int corridors. **Pets:** Other. Supervision.
[ASK] [S] [X] [S] [&'] [🔲] [💻] [↑↑] [🔄]

◆◆ Homestead Village Guest Studios **A**
(248) 340-8888. **Call for rates.** 3315 University Dr. I-75,
exit 79, 0.9 mi e. Int corridors. **Pets:** Small. Supervision.
[🔲] [💻]

(AAA) ◆ Motel 6 -1065 **M** ❀
(248) 373-8440. **$50-$66.** 1471 Opdyke Rd. I-75, exit 79,
0.3 mi w. Ext corridors. **Pets:** Medium. No service, supervision, crate.
[S] [X] [&'] [CTV]

(AAA) ◆◆◆ Wellesley Inn & Suites **M** ❀
(248) 335-5200. **$69-$139.** 2100 Feather Stone Rd. I-75,
exit 79, w on University Dr, then 0.5 mi s on Opdyke Rd,
just e. Int corridors. **Pets:** Small. $50 deposit/pet. No serv-
ice, supervision, crate.
[SAVE] [S] [X] [🔲] [💻] [🔄]

BELLEVILLE

(AAA) ◆◆ Red Roof Inn Metro Airport **M** ❀
(734) 697-2244. **$67-$84.** 44501 I-94 N Expwy, Service Dr.
At jct I-94 and Belleville Rd, exit 190. Ext corridors.
Pets: Other. Supervision.
[SAVE] [X] [S] [🔲]

◆◆ Super 8 Motel **M**
(734) 699-1888. **Call for rates.** 45707 I-94 Service Dr. I-94,
exit 190 (Belleville Rd), just s. Int corridors. **Pets:** No service, supervision, crate.
[X] [🔲] [💻]

BIRMINGHAM

◆◆◆ Holiday Inn Express Birmingham **M**
(248) 646-7300. **Call for rates.** 34952 Woodward Ave.
Center on SR 1; Woodward and Maple Rd. Ext/int corridors. **Pets:** Designated rooms, no service, supervision,
crate.
[X] [&'] [🔲] [💻]

CANTON

◆◆◆ Baymont Inn & Suites-Detroit West **M**
(734) 981-1808. **$70-$77.** 41211 Ford Rd. At jct Ford Rd
and I-275, exit 25. Int corridors. **Pets:** Supervision.
[S] [X] [S] [🔲] [💻]

(AAA) ◆ Motel 6–1070 **M**
(734) 981-5000. **$45-$61.** 41216 Ford Rd. At jct Ford Rd
and I-275, exit 25. Ext corridors. **Pets:** Designated rooms,
no service, supervision, crate.
[S] [X] [&'] [🔄]

◆◆ Super 8 Motel-Canton **M**
(734) 722-8880. **$55-$67.** 3933 Lotz Rd. Jct I-275 and SR
12, exit 22. Int corridors. **Pets:** Supervision.
[S] [X] [S] [🔲]

DEARBORN

(AAA) ◆◆ Red Roof Inn-Dearborn **M** ❀
(313) 278-9732. **$66-$82.** 24130 Michigan Ave. Jct US 12
and 24. Ext corridors. **Pets:** Medium, other. No service,
supervision, crate.
[SAVE] [X] [S] [CTV]

(AAA) ◆◆◆◆ The Ritz-Carlton **H**
(313) 441-2000. **$225-$1500.** 300 Town Center Dr.
Between Ford Rd and Michigan Ave exits, on Service Dr,
off SR 39 (Southfield Frwy). Int corridors. **Pets:** No service,
supervision, crate.
[SAVE] [X] [S] [💻] [↑↑] [🔄]

DETROIT

◆◆◆ **Detroit Marriott Renaissance Center** 🅷 ❀
(313) 568-8000. **$159-$209.** Renaissance Center. Downtown. Int corridors. **Pets:** Small, dogs only. Supervision.
⊠ 🔊 🄴 🔒 🍴

◆◆◆ **Hotel St. Regis** 🅷
(313) 873-3000. **$116, 30 days notice.** 3071 W Grand Blvd. W Grand Blvd and Cass. Int corridors. **Pets:** Supervision.
⊠ 🔒 🍴

🆀 ◆◆◆ **Omni Detroit Riverplace** 🅼🄸
(313) 259-9500. **Call for rates.** 1000 River Pl. Downtown on E Jefferson 1.5 mi, s on McDougall 4 blks. Int corridors. **Pets:** Supervision.
🆂🅰🆅🅴 ⊠ 🖥 🔊 🚫

◆◆◆ **Residence Inn By Marriott-Dearborn** 🅰 ❀
(313) 441-1700. **$159.** 5777 Southfield Service Dr. Just n of Southfield Frwy at jct Ford Rd. Ext corridors. **Pets:** Other. $7 daily fee/room, $100 one-time fee/room. No service, supervision, crate.
🅰🆂🅺 🆂🄳 ⊠ 🔊 🔒 🖥 🔊 🚫

FARMINGTON HILLS

🆀 ◆◆ **Red Roof Inn-Farmington Hills** 🅼
(248) 478-8640. **$57-$75.** 24300 Sinacola Ct. I-96/275 and M-5, Grand River Ave exit 165. Ext corridors. **Pets:** Supervision.
🆂🅰🆅🅴 ⊠ 🔊

HAZEL PARK

◆◆ **Quality Inn** 🅼🄸 ❀
(248) 399-5800. **$90, 30 days notice.** 1 W 9 Mile Rd. I-75, exit 9 Mile Rd, exit 60. Int corridors. **Pets:** Other. Supervision.
🅰🆂🅺 🆂🄳 ⊠ 🔒 🖥 🍴 🔊

LIVONIA

🆀 ◆◆◆ **AmeriSuites-Detroit/Livonia** 🅼
(734) 953-9224. **$95-$113.** 19300 Haggerty Rd. I-275, exit 169, just w on 7 Mile Rd. Int corridors. **Pets:** Designated rooms, no service, supervision, crate.
🆂🅰🆅🅴 🆂🄳 ⊠ 🄴 🔒 🖥 🔊

◆◆◆ **Residence Inn Detroit-Livonia** 🅰 ❀
(734) 462-4201. **$139.** 17250 Fox Dr. Jct I-275, exit 170 (6 Mile Rd), just nw. Int corridors. **Pets:** Other. $100 one-time fee/room. Supervision.
🅰🆂🅺 ⊠ 🔊 🔊 🄴 🔒 🖥 🔊 🚫

MADISON HEIGHTS

🆀 ◆◆ **Red Roof Inn** 🅼
(248) 583-4700. **$56-$78.** 32511 Concord Dr. I-75, exit 65A, at 14 Mile Rd. Ext corridors. **Pets:** Designated rooms, supervision.
🆂🅰🆅🅴 ⊠ 🔊

◆◆◆ **Residence Inn by Marriott-Madison Heights** 🅼
(248) 583-4322. **Call for rates.** 32650 Stephenson Hwy. Stephenson Hwy at 14 Mile Rd, just w of I-75, exit 65. Ext corridors. **Pets:** No service, supervision, crate.
⊠ 🔊 🔒 🖥 🔊 🚫

NEW BALTIMORE

◆ **Lodgekeeper** 🅼
(810) 949-4520. **Call for rates.** 29101 23 Mile Rd. At jct I-94 and SR 29, exit 243. Ext/int corridors. **Pets:** Medium. Designated rooms, no service, supervision, crate.
🅰🆂🅺 ⊠ 🔒

PLYMOUTH

🆀 ◆◆ **Red Roof Inn-Plymouth** 🅼
(734) 459-3300. **$60-$77.** 39700 Ann Arbor Rd. At jct I-275 and Ann Arbor Rd, exit 28. Ext corridors. **Pets:** Supervision.
🆂🅰🆅🅴 ⊠ 🔊 🄴

PONTIAC

◆◆◆ **Residence Inn by Marriott Detroit/Pontiac** 🅰
(248) 858-8664. **$89-$199.** 3333 Centerpoint Pkwy. I-75, exit 75 (Square Lake Rd), w via Opdyke Rd. Int corridors. **Pets:** Medium. No service, supervision, crate.
🅰🆂🅺 🆂🄳 ⊠ 🔊 🄴 🔒 🖥 🔊 🚫

ROCHESTER HILLS

🆀 ◆◆ **Red Roof Inn** 🅼 ❀
(248) 853-6400. **$57-$75.** 2580 Crooks Rd. Jct M-59 and Crooks Rd. Ext corridors. **Pets:** Other. No service, supervision, crate.
🆂🅰🆅🅴 ⊠ 🔊 📺

ROMULUS

◆◆◆ **Baymont Inn & Suites-Detroit/Airport** 🅼
(734) 722-6000. **$75-$80.** 9000 Wickham Rd. I-94, exit 198 (Merriman Rd). Int corridors. **Pets:** Large. No service, supervision, crate.
🆂🄳 ⊠ 🔊 🔒 🖥

◆◆◆ **Detroit Airport Marriott Hotel** 🅷
(734) 941-9400. **Call for rates.** Detroit Metro Airport. I-94, exit 198 (Metro Airport). Int corridors. **Pets:** No service, supervision, crate.
⊠ ♿ 🔊 🄴 🔒 🖥

◆◆◆ **Romulus Marriott At Detroit Airport** 🅷
(734) 729-7555. **Call for rates.** 30559 Flynn Dr. Off I-94, Merriman Rd, exit 198. Int corridors. **Pets:** Supervision.
⊠ 🏠 🔊 🖥 🍴 🔊

ROSEVILLE

◆◆◆ **Baymont Inn & Suites-Detroit(Roseville)** 🅼 ❀
(810) 296-6910. **$67-$84.** 20675 13 Mile Rd. Jct I-94 and Little Mack Rd, exit 232. Int corridors. **Pets:** Medium. $50 deposit/pet. Designated rooms, no service, supervision, crate.
🆂🄳 ⊠ 🔊 🔒 🖥

◆◆◆ Georgian Inn M ❖
(810) 294-0400. **$69-$90.** 31327 Gratiot Ave. On SR 3, n of 13 Mile Rd; just w of I-94, eastbound Gratiot Ave exit 27; westbound Little Mack Rd, exit 232. Ext corridors. **Pets:** Small, dogs only. No service, supervision, crate.

[SAVE] [S+] [X] [🛏] [🍴] [🏊]

◆◆ Red Roof Inn-Roseville M
(810) 296-0310. **$52-$70.** 31800 Little Mack Rd. At jct I-94 and Little Mack Rd, exit 232. Ext corridors. **Pets:** No service, supervision, crate.

[SAVE] [X] [🔷] [🔷] [🛏] [CTV]

SOUTHFIELD

◆◆◆ Hilton Inn-Southfield M
(248) 357-1100. **$99-$99.** 26000 American Dr. US 10 NW (Northwestern Hwy) W Beck Rd, 0.3 mi s on Franklin Rd. Int corridors. **Pets:** No service, supervision, crate.

[X] [🔷] [💷] [🍴] [🏊]

◆◆◆ Holiday Inn-Southfield M ❖
(248) 353-7700. **$116-$116.** 26555 Telegraph Rd. 14 mi nw on US 24 at jct I-696. Int corridors. **Pets:** Small. $50 deposit/pet. No service, supervision, crate.

[X] [🔷] [🔷] [💷] [🍴] [🏊]

◆◆◆ Homestead Guest Studios-Southfield M
(248) 213-4500. **Call for rates.** 28500 Northwestern Hwy. Just nw of jct US 24 (Telegraph Rd) and I-696, exit 9, on service road. Int corridors. **Pets:** Small. Supervision.

[X] [🔷] [🔷] [💷] [🛏]

◆◆◆ Red Roof Inn-Southfield M
(248) 353-7200. **$60-$73.** 27660 Northwestern Hwy. Just nw of jct Telegraph Rd and I-696, exit 9. Ext corridors. **Pets:** Medium. Supervision.

[SAVE] [X]

◆◆◆ Residence Inn by Marriott A
(248) 352-8900. **Call for rates.** 26700 Central Park Blvd. I-696, exit 11 (Evergreen), sw corner of 11 mile and Evergreen. Ext corridors. **Pets:** Supervision.

[ASK] [X] [🔷] [🛏] [💷] [🏊] [X]

SOUTHGATE

◆◆◆ Baymont Inn &
　　Suites-Detroit(Southgate) M ❖
(734) 374-3000. **$67-$74.** 12888 Reeck Rd. Jct I-75 and Northline Rd, exit 37. Int corridors. **Pets:** Small, other. $50 deposit/room. No service, supervision, crate.

[S+] [X] [🔷] [🛏] [💷]

STERLING HEIGHTS

◆◆ Knights Inn-Detroit/Sterling Heights M
(810) 268-0600. **$50-$70.** 7887 17 Mile Rd. 17 mi n, on SR 53, jct Van Dyke and 17 Mile Rd. Ext corridors. **Pets:** Small. No service, supervision, crate.

[SAVE] [S+] [X] [🛏]

◆◆ Sterling Heights Super 8 Motel M
(810) 795-8800. **Call for rates.** 34550 Van Dyke Ave. M-53 (Van Dyke Ave), between 12 Mile and 15 Mile rds. Int corridors. **Pets:** Supervision.

[X] [🔷] [🛏]

TAYLOR

◆◆ Red Roof Inn-Taylor M
(734) 374-1150. **$60-$75.** 21230 Eureka Rd. Jct I-75 and Eureka Rd, exit 36. Ext corridors. **Pets:** No service, supervision, crate.

[SAVE] [X] [CTV]

◆◆ Super 8 Motel-Taylor M
(734) 283-8830. **Call for rates.** 15101 Huron St. At jct I-75 and Eureka Rd, exit 36. Int corridors. **Pets:** No service, supervision, crate.

[X] [🛏] [💷] [CTV]

TROY

◆◆◆ Drury Inn M ❖
(248) 528-3330. **$86-$106.** 575 W Big Beaver Rd. 0.3 mi e of jct I-75 and Big Beaver Rd, exit 69. Int corridors. **Pets:** Other. Designated rooms, no service, supervision, crate.

[X] [🔷] [🛏] [💷] [🍴] [🏊]

◆◆◆ Holiday Inn-Troy M ❖
(248) 689-7500. **$135.** 2537 Rochester Ct. I-75, exit 67, 0.3 mi sw on Rochester Rd (SR 150), just n. Int corridors. **Pets:** Other. $10 one-time fee/room. No service, supervision, crate.

[ASK] [S+] [X] [🛏] [💷] [🍴] [🏊]

◆◆◆ Northfield Hilton M
(248) 879-2100. **$189-$204, 3 days notice.** 5500 Crooks Rd. At jct I-75 and Crooks Rd, exit 72. Int corridors. **Pets:** Supervision.

[SAVE] [S+] [X] [🔷] [🔷] [🛏] [💷] [🍴] [🏊]

◆◆ Red Roof Inn-Troy M ❖
(248) 689-4391. **$57-$72.** 2350 Rochester Ct. I-75, exit 67, 0.3 mi sw. Ext corridors. **Pets:** Other. No service, supervision, crate.

[SAVE] [X] [🔷]

◆◆◆ Residence Inn by Marriott A ❖
(248) 689-6856. **Call for rates.** 2600 Livernois Rd. 0.5 mi e of jct I-75 and Big Beaver Rd, exit 69, 0.5 mi s. Ext corridors. **Pets:** Other. $6 daily fee/room, $240 one-time fee/pet. Supervision.

[X] [🔷] [🛏] [💷] [🏊] [X]

UTICA

◆◆◆ Baymont Inn & Suites-Detroit (Utica) M
(810) 731-4700. **$89-$96.** 45311 Park Ave. At jct of Van Dyke (M-53) and Hall Rd (M-59). Int corridors. **Pets:** Medium. Designated rooms, no service, supervision, crate.

[S+] [X] [🔷] [🔷] [🛏] [💷] [🏊]

WARREN

◆◆◆ Baymont Inn & Suites-Detroit (Warren) M
(810) 574-0550. **$67-$74.** 30900 Van Dyke Rd. 12.5 mi n on SR 53; 2 mi n of jct I-696, exit 23. Int corridors. **Pets:** Medium. Designated rooms, no service, supervision, crate.

[S+] [X] [🔷] [🛏] [💷]

⚅ ◆◆ Quality Inn M ❀
(810) 264-0100. **$69-$79.** 32035 Van Dyke Ave. I-696, exit 23, 2.7 mi n. Int corridors. **Pets:** Medium. $20 daily fee/pet. Designated rooms, no service, supervision, crate.

⚅ ◆◆ Red Roof Inn-Warren M ❀
(810) 573-4300. **$51-$73.** 26300 Dequindre Rd. Just ne of jct I-696, exit 20. Ext corridors. **Pets:** Supervision.

◆◆◆ Residence Inn by Marriott M ❀
(810) 558-8050. **Call for rates.** 30120 Civic Center Blvd. I-696, exit 23, 2 mi n on Van Dyke. Ext/int corridors. **Pets:** Other. $75 one-time fee/room. No service, supervision, crate.

❀ **END METROPOLITAN AREA** ❀

EAGLE HARBOR

⚅ ◆ Shoreline Resort M
(906) 289-4441. **$52-$72.** 201 Front St, F #2015. On SR 26. Ext corridors. **Pets:** No service, supervision, crate.

EAST LANSING

◆◆◆ Residence Inn by Marriott A
(517) 332-7711. **$124, 3 days notice.** 1600 E Grand River Ave. US 127, Grand River Ave exit, 2.6 mi se on SR 43. Ext corridors. **Pets:** No service, supervision, crate.

ELK RAPIDS

⚅ ◆ Camelot Inn M ❀
(231) 264-8473. **$53-$88, 3 days notice.** 10962 Hwy 31 S. 2 mi s on US 31. Ext corridors. **Pets:** Medium, dogs only. Designated rooms, no service, supervision, crate.

ESCANABA

⚅ ◆◆ Bay View Motel M
(906) 786-2843. **$45-$60.** 4.5 mi n on US 2/41/SR 35. Ext/int corridors. **Pets:** Designated rooms, no service, supervision, crate.

⚅ ◆ Hiawatha Motel M ❀
(906) 786-1341. **$32-$48.** 2400 Ludington St. 0.5 mi w on US 2/41. Ext corridors. **Pets:** Supervision.

FLINT

◆◆◆ Holiday Inn Express M ❀
(810) 238-7744. **$99-$169.** 1150 Robert T Longway Blvd. I-475, exit 8A. Int corridors. **Pets:** Small, dogs only. $50 deposit/room. Designated rooms, no service, supervision, crate.

⚅ ◆ Howard Johnson Lodge M ❀
(810) 733-5910. **$40-$65.** G-3277 Miller Rd. I-75, exit 117 southbound; exit 117B northbound, just w. Ext corridors. **Pets:** Other. $10 daily fee/pet. Supervision.

⚅ ◆◆ Red Roof Inn M ❀
(810) 733-1660. **$46-$68.** G-3219 Miller Rd. I-75, exit 117 southbound; exit 117B northbound, just w. Ext corridors. **Pets:** Other. Supervision.

◆◆ Super 8 Motel-Flint M
(810) 230-7888. **$49-$56, 7 days notice.** 3033 Claude Ave. Just w of I-75, exit 117 southbound, exit 117B northbound and Miller Rd. Int corridors. **Pets:** Small. Supervision.

FRANKENMUTH

◆◆◆ Drury Inn M ❀
(517) 652-2800. **$60-$110.** 260 S Main St. Center; in SR 83. Int corridors. **Pets:** Small. No service, supervision, crate.

GAYLORD

⚅ ◆◆◆ Best Western Royal Crest Motel M ❀
(517) 732-6451. **$59-$99, 3 days notice.** 803 S Otsego Ave. I-75, exit 279, 2.3 mi ne on I-75 business loop. Int corridors. **Pets:** Medium. No service, supervision, crate.

⚅ ◆ Downtown Motel M
(517) 732-5010. **$42-$68.** 208 S Otsego Ave. I-75, exit 282, 0.5 mi e and 0.3 mi s on I-75 business loop. Ext corridors. **Pets:** Small. No service, supervision, crate.

◆ Econo Lodge M
(517) 732-5133. **Call for rates.** 2880 S Otsego. Just ne of I-75 and Old US 27, exit 279. Ext corridors. **Pets:** Designated rooms, no service, supervision, crate.

◆◆ Holiday Inn M ❀
(517) 732-2431. **$70-$97.** 833 W Main St. I-75, exit 282, 0.3 mi e on SR 32. Ext/int corridors. **Pets:** Other. No service, supervision, crate.

⚅ ◆◆ Super 8 Motel M ❀
(517) 732-5193. **$45-$135.** 1042 W Main. Just w of jct I-75 and SR 32, exit 282. Ext/int corridors. **Pets:** $50 deposit/pet. Designated rooms, no service, supervision, crate.

◆ **Timberly Motel** M ❖
(517) 732-5166. **$40-$64.** 881 S Otsego Ave. I-75, exit 279, 2.5 mi n on I-75 business loop (Old US 27). Ext corridors. **Pets:** Medium. Designated rooms, no service, supervision, crate.
SAVE S X X

GRAND MARAIS

◆ **Alverson Motel** M ❖
(906) 494-2681. **$47-$54, 3 days notice.** Randolph Rd. Just e of SR 77. Ext corridors. **Pets:** Other. Supervision.
X B X K Z

◆◆ **Voyageur's Motel** M
(906) 494-2389. **$50-$71.** E Wilson St. 0.5 mi e of SR 77. Ext corridors. **Pets:** Small. Designated rooms, supervision.

GRAND RAPIDS

◆◆◆ **Days Inn-Downtown** H ❖
(616) 235-7611. **$65-$98, 3 days notice.** 310 Pearl St NW. US 131, Pearl St exit. Int corridors. **Pets:** Medium, other. $10 daily fee/room. No service, supervision, crate.
ASK S X B B T

◆◆ **Holiday Inn-North** MI ❖
(616) 363-9001. **$75-$85.** 270 Ann St NW. US 131, exit 88, 1.8 mi n. Int corridors. **Pets:** $10 one-time fee/room. Designated rooms, supervision.
X B B T

◆◆◆ **Homewood Suites Hotel** M ❖
(616) 285-7100. **$94-$150.** 3925 28th St SE. I-96, exit 43B (28th St SW), 1.5 mi w to E Paris Ave, then just n. Int corridors. **Pets:** Other. $5 daily fee/room, $80 one-time fee/room. Supervision.
ASK S X L P B P

GRAYLING

◆◆◆ **Holiday Inn** MI ❖
(517) 348-7611. **$109-$129.** 2650 S Business Loop. I-75 business loop, 0.8 mi s. Ext/int corridors. **Pets:** Other. Supervision.
SAVE S X T L B P T X

◆ **North Country Lodge** M
(517) 348-8471. **$50-$160.** 617 N I-75 Business Loop. 1 mi n. Ext corridors. **Pets:** Small. Designated rooms, no service, supervision, crate.
SAVE X B X

◆◆ **Super 8 Motel** M ❖
(517) 348-8888. **$60-$75.** 5828 Nelson A Miles Pkwy. I-75, exit 251. Int corridors. **Pets:** Other. $50 deposit/room. Supervision.
ASK X L X X

HANCOCK

◆◆ **Best Western Copper Crown Motel** M ❖
(906) 482-6111. **$50-$60, 7 days notice.** 235 Hancock Ave. On US 41S. Ext/int corridors. **Pets:** Other. Designated rooms, no service, supervision, crate.
ASK S X P X X

HARBOR SPRINGS

◆ **Harbor Springs Cottage Inn** M ❖
(231) 526-5431. **$90-$100.** 145 Zoll St. 4 blks se; just s of SR 119, following signs. Ext corridors. **Pets:** Other. $5 daily fee/room. Supervision.
S X B P X

HART

◆ **Budget Host Hart Motel** M ❖
(231) 873-2151. **$52-$89.** 715 State. Center. Ext corridors. **Pets:** Small, dogs only. $20 deposit/room. Designated rooms, no service, supervision, crate.
SAVE S X

◆◆◆ **Comfort Inn** M ❖
(231) 873-3456. **$79-$119.** 2248 N Comfort Dr. US 31, exit Mears/Hart, just e on US 31 business route. Int corridors. **Pets:** Other. $10 daily fee/room. Supervision.
SAVE X X B P X

HONOR

◆ **Sunny Woods Resort** M
(231) 325-3952. **$67-$89.** 14065 Honor Hwy. 3 mi e on US 31. Ext corridors. **Pets:** Small. Supervision.
SAVE X B P X

HOUGHTON

◆◆ **Best Western-Franklin Square Inn** MI
(906) 487-1700. **$89-$149.** 820 Shelden Ave. Center. Int corridors. **Pets:** Small. No service, supervision, crate.
ASK S X B P T X X

◆◆ **Best Western King's Inn** M
(906) 482-5000. **$63-$108.** 215 Shelden Ave. Center; on US 41. Int corridors. **Pets:** Small. No service, supervision, crate.
ASK S X P X X

HOUGHTON LAKE

◆ **Hillside Motel** M ❖
(517) 366-5711. **$48-$56, 3 days notice.** 3419 W Houghton Lake Dr. On SR 55, 6 mi e of US 27; 10 mi w of I-75. Ext corridors. **Pets:** Dogs only. No service, supervision, crate.
X B X

◆ **Holiday On The Lake** MI ❖
(517) 422-5195. **$60-$85, 7 days notice.** 100 Clearview Rd. On Old US 27, 0.5 mi n of SR 55. Ext corridors. **Pets:** Other. $15 daily fee/pet. No service, supervision, crate.
SAVE S B P T X

◆◆ **Quality Inn** MI
(517) 422-5175. **$60-$90.** 9285 W Houghton Lake Dr. At jct US 27 and SR 55. Int corridors. **Pets:** Supervision.
SAVE S X B P T X

HOWELL

(AAA) ◆◆◆ **Best Western Howell** **M** ❀
(517) 548-2900. **$69-$100, 7 days notice.** 1500 Pinckney
Rd. I-96, exit 137, just s on CR (D-19). Ext corridors.
Pets: Very small, dogs only. $10 deposit/pet, $10 daily fee/
pet. Designated rooms, no service, supervision, crate.
(SAVE) (S̄) (✕) (🖥) (🏊)

IMLAY CITY

(AAA) ◆◆◆ **Days Inn** **M** ❀
(810) 724-8005. **$60-$63.** 6692 Newark Rd. I-69, exit 168,
0.3 mi n, then w. Int corridors. **Pets:** Other. $50 deposit/pet,
$8 daily fee/pet. No service, supervision, crate.
(SAVE) (S̄) (✕) (📶) (🖥) (🏊)

◆◆ **Super 8 Motel-Imlay City** **M** ❀
(810) 724-8700. **$49-$80.** 6951 Newark Rd. I-69, exit 168,
just n to Newark Rd, just e. Int corridors. **Pets:** Other. $50
deposit/room, $8 daily fee/pet, $8 one-time fee/pet. No
service, supervision, crate.
(ASK) (S̄) (✕) (📶) (🖥)

INDIAN RIVER

(AAA) ◆ **Star Gate Motel** **M** ❀
(231) 238-7371. **$32-$46, 3 days notice.** 4646 S Straits
Hwy. I-75, exit 310, 0.3 mi w, then 1.8 mi s on Old US 27.
Ext corridors. **Pets:** Medium, other. $5 daily fee/room, $5
one-time fee/room. Designated rooms, no service, supervision, crate.
(SAVE) (S̄) (✕) (🖥) (🏊)

IONIA

(AAA) ◆◆ **Super 8 Motel** **M**
(616) 527-2828. **$51-$109.** 7245 S State Rd. Jct I-96 and
SR 66, exit 67. Int corridors. **Pets:** Designated rooms,
supervision.
(SAVE) (✕) (🏠) (📶) (🖥)

IRON MOUNTAIN

(AAA) ◆◆ **Best Western Executives Inn** **M**
(906) 774-2040. **$53-$69.** 1518 S Stephenson Ave. 0.8 mi e
on US 2. Int corridors. **Pets:** No service, supervision, crate.
(SAVE) (S̄) (✕) (🖥) (🏊)

(AAA) ◆ **Budget Host-Lake Antoine Motel** **M** ❀
(906) 774-6797. **$35-$52.** 1663 N Stephenson Ave. 1.5 mi
nw on US 2 and 141. Ext corridors. **Pets:** Medium. $5 daily
fee/pet, $5 one-time fee/pet. Designated rooms, supervi-
sion.
(SAVE) (S̄) (✕) (🖥) (🏊) (🏊)

◆◆ **Days Inn** **M**
(906) 774-2181. **$50-$85.** W8176 S US 2. 1.8 mi e on US
2. Ext/int corridors. **Pets:** No service, supervision, crate.
(ASK) (S̄) (✕) (🖥) (🏊) (🏊)

IRONWOOD

(AAA) ◆ **Crestview Motel** **M**
(906) 932-4845. **$32-$60.** 424 W Cloverland Dr. W edge on
US 2. Ext corridors. **Pets:** No service, supervision, crate.
(SAVE) (✕) (🖥) (🖥) (🏊)

(AAA) ◆ **Royal Motel** **M**
(906) 932-4230. **$31-$41, 7 days notice.** 715 W Cloverland
Dr. 1 mi w on US 2. Ext corridors. **Pets:** Medium. Designated rooms, supervision.
(SAVE) (✕) (🏊)

◆ **Super 8 Motel** **M** ❀
(906) 932-3395. **$66-$84, 3 days notice.** 160 E Cloverland
Dr. Jct US 2 and US 2 business route. Int corridors. **Pets:**
$25 deposit/pet. Designated rooms, supervision.
(ASK) (S̄) (✕) (🖥) (🖥) (🏊)

ISHPEMING

(AAA) ◆◆ **Best Western Country Inn** **MI** ❀
(906) 485-6345. **$71-$81.** 850 US 41 W. On US 41, just n
of town. Int corridors. **Pets:** Other. Designated rooms, no
service, supervision, crate.
(SAVE) (S̄) (✕) (🍴) (🏊) (🏊)

JACKSON

◆◆◆ **Baymont Inn-Jackson** **M** ❀
(517) 789-6000. **$62-$90.** 2035 Service Dr. I-94, exit 138,
just n. Int corridors. **Pets:** Small, other. Supervision.
(S̄) (✕) (📶) (🖥) (🖥)

◆◆◆ **Holiday Inn** **MI** ❀
(517) 783-2681. **$94-$99.** 2000 Holiday Inn Dr. I-94, exit
138, just n. Ext/int corridors. **Pets:** Medium. $20 one-time
fee/room. No service, supervision, crate.
(ASK) (S̄) (✕) (📶) (🎱) (🖥) (🖥) (🍴) (🏊) (🏊)

(AAA) ◆ **Motel 6–1088** **M**
(517) 789-7186. **$42-$86.** 830 Royal Dr. I-94, exit 138, just
s. Ext corridors. **Pets:** Very small. No service, supervision,
crate.
(S̄) (✕) (📶) (🎱) (🏊)

◆◆ **Super 8 Motel** **M** ❀
(517) 788-8780. **$49-$65.** 2001 Shirley Dr. I-94, exit 138,
just n. Int corridors. **Pets:** Very small. No service, supervision, crate.
(ASK) (S̄) (✕) (📶) (🖥)

KALAMAZOO

◆◆◆ **Baymont Inn & Suites-Kalamazoo** **M**
(616) 372-7999. **$50-$75.** 2203 S 11th St. US 131, exit 36B
(Stadium Dr), just w. Int corridors. **Pets:** Medium. Supervision.
(S̄) (✕) (🖥) (🖥)

(AAA) ◆◆ **Comfort Inn** **M** ❀
(616) 381-7000. **$79-$79** (no credit cards). 3820 Sprinkle
Rd. I-94, exit 80, just s. Int corridors. **Pets:** Small. $25
deposit/room. Designated rooms, supervision.
(SAVE) (S̄) (✕) (🏠) (🖥) (🖥) (🏊) (CTV)

◆◆◆ **Holiday Inn-Airport** **MI**
(616) 381-7070. **Call for rates.** 3522 Sprinkle Rd. I-94, exit
80, just s. Int corridors. **Pets:** No service, supervision, crate.
(ASK) (✕) (📶) (🖥) (🖥) (🏊)

◆◆◆ **Holiday Inn-West** **MI**
(616) 375-6000. **$79-$99.** 2747 S 11th St. US 131, exit
Stadium Dr, just w. Int corridors. **Pets:** No service, supervision, crate.
(ASK) (S̄) (✕) (🏠) (📶) (🖥) (🍴) (🏊) (🏊)

◆◆◆ Quality Inn & Suites 🅼 ❅
(616) 388-3551. **$50-$70** (no credit cards). 3750 Easy St. I-94, exit 80, just sw. Int corridors. **Pets:** Other. No service, supervision, crate.

🄰🅂🄺 🅂🄳 ⊠ 🖉 🎁 🖼

🄰🄰🄰 ◆◆ Red Roof Inn-East 🅼 ❅
(616) 382-6350. **$50-$83.** 3701 E Cork St. Nw of jct I-94 and Sprinkle Rd, exit 80. Ext corridors. **Pets:** Supervision.

🆂🅰🆅🅴 ⊠ 🐾 🖉 📺

🄰🄰🄰 ◆◆ Red Roof Inn-West 🅼
(616) 375-7400. **$50-$80.** 5425 W Michigan Ave. US 131, exit 36B (Stadium Dr), just nw. Ext corridors. **Pets:** Medium. Designated rooms, no service, supervision, crate.

🆂🅰🆅🅴 ⊠

◆◆◆ Residence Inn by Marriott 🄰 ❅
(616) 349-0855. **Call for rates.** 1500 E Kilgore. I-94, exit 78, just w. Ext/int corridors. **Pets:** Other. $6 daily fee/pet, $125 one-time fee/room. No service, supervision, crate.

⊠ 🖉 🎁 📖 🖼 🐾

KENTWOOD

◆◆◆ Residence Inn by Marriott 🄰
(616) 957-8111. **$99-$99.** 2701 E Beltline. Jct SR 11 and E Beltline (SR 37). Ext corridors. **Pets:** Small. Designated rooms, no service, supervision, crate.

🄰🅂🄺 🅂🄳 ⊠ 🖉 🎁 📖 🖼 🐾

LAKE CITY

🄰🄰🄰 ◆ Northcrest Motel 🅼
(231) 839-2075. **$49-$62.** 1341 S Lakeshore. 1 mi s on SR 55 and 66. Ext corridors. **Pets:** Supervision.

🆂🅰🆅🅴 🅂🄳 📖 🖼 🐾

LAKESIDE

◆◆◆ White Rabbit Inn 🄱🄱 ❅
(616) 469-4620. **$95-$200, 7 days notice.** 14634 Red Arrow Hwy. I-94, exit 6, w on Townline Rd 1.5 mi, then 2 mi n. Ext corridors. **Pets:** No service, supervision, crate.

⊠ 🎁 📖 📺 🔌

LANSING

◆◆ Best Western Governor's Inn Conference Center 🅼
(517) 393-5500. **$69-$110.** 6133 S Pennsylvania Ave. I-96, Cedar/Holt exit 104, just n of interstate. Int corridors. **Pets:** Supervision.

🄰🅂🄺 🅂🄳 ⊠ 🎁 🍴 🖼 🐾

🄰🄰🄰 ◆◆ Best Western Midway Hotel 🅼🅸 ❅
(517) 627-8471. **$79-$99.** 7711 W Saginaw Hwy. I-96 and SR 43, exit 93B, just e. Int corridors. **Pets:** Other. Designated rooms, supervision.

🆂🅰🆅🅴 🅂🄳 ⊠ 🎁 📖 🍴 🖼

◆◆◆ Hawthorn Suites Ltd 🅼 ❅
(517) 886-0600. **$99.** 901 Delta Commerce Dr. I-96 and SR 43, exit 93B, 0.8 mi e on Saginaw St. Int corridors. **Pets:** $125 one-time fee/room. No service, supervision, crate.

🄰🅂🄺 🅂🄳 ⊠ 🎁 📖

🄰🄰🄰 ◆◆ Red Roof Inn-East 🅼 ❅
(517) 332-2575. **$50-$82.** 3615 Dunckel Rd. Just e of jct I-496 and US 127, Jolly Rd exit 11. Ext corridors. **Pets:** Other. Supervision.

🆂🅰🆅🅴 ⊠ 🖉

🄰🄰🄰 ◆◆ Red Roof Inn-West 🅼 ❅
(517) 321-7246. **$52-$73.** 7412 W Saginaw Hwy. Jct I-96 and W Saginaw Hwy, exit 93B. Ext corridors. **Pets:** Other. Supervision.

🆂🅰🆅🅴 ⊠

◆◆◆ Residence Inn 🄰 ❅
(517) 886-5030. **$84-$145.** 922 Delta Commerce Dr. I-96 and SR 43, exit 93B, 0.8 mi e on Saginaw St. Int corridors. **Pets:** Large, other. $10 daily fee/room, $100 one-time fee/room. No service, supervision, crate.

⊠ 🎁 📖 🖼 🐾

LUDINGTON

◆◆◆ Holiday Inn Express 🅼 ❅
(231) 845-7004. **Call for rates.** 5323 W US 10. 1.4 mi w of jct US 10 and 31. Int corridors. **Pets:** Other. $10 one-time fee/room. Designated rooms, no service, supervision, crate.

⊠ 🐾 🎁 🖼

MACKINAW CITY

◆◆◆ Baymont Inn Suites 🅼 ❅
(231) 436-7737. **$99-$129.** 109 S Nicolet St. I-75, exit 338. Int corridors. **Pets:** Medium. $50 deposit/room. Designated rooms, supervision.

🄰🅂🄺 🅂🄳 ⊠ 🐾 🎁 📖 🖼 🐾

🄰🄰🄰 ◆ Beachcomber Motel on the Water 🅼 ❅
(231) 436-8451. **$59-$125, 3 days notice.** 1011 S Huron Dr. 1 mi s on US 23. Ext corridors. **Pets:** Small. $5 daily fee/pet, $5 one-time fee/pet. No service, supervision, crate.

🆂🅰🆅🅴 🅂🄳 ⊠ 🎁 🐾

🄰🄰🄰 ◆ The Beach House 🄲
(231) 436-5353. **$57-$135.** 11490 W US 23 St. 1.3 mi s on US 23. Ext corridors. **Pets:** Very small. Designated rooms, no service, supervision, crate.

🆂🅰🆅🅴 🎁 🖼 🐾 🔌

🄰🄰🄰 ◆◆ Budget Host Mackinaw City 🅼
(231) 436-5543. **$62-$138, 3 days notice.** 517 N Huron St. Just n. Ext corridors. **Pets:** Supervision.

🆂🅰🆅🅴 🅂🄳 ⊠ 🖼 🐾

🄰🄰🄰 ◆ Capri Motel 🅼 ❅
(231) 436-5498. **$45-$75.** 801 S Nicolet St. 0.5 mi s, across from information center. Ext corridors. **Pets:** Medium. $5 daily fee/room, $5 one-time fee/room. No service, supervision, crate.

🆂🅰🆅🅴 ⊠ 🖼 🐾

🄰🄰🄰 ◆◆ Econo Lodge at the Bridge 🅼
(231) 436-5026. **$69-$159.** 412 Nicolet St. I-75, exit 339. Ext corridors. **Pets:** No service, supervision, crate.

🆂🅰🆅🅴 🅂🄳 ⊠ 🎁 📖

◆◆ **The Grand Mackinaw** 🅜 ❀
(231) 436-8831. **$68-$135, 3 days notice.** 907 S Huron St.
0.8 mi se on US 23. Ext corridors. **Pets:** Very small, dogs
only. $50 deposit/room, $10 daily fee/pet. Designated
rooms, no service, supervision, crate.

⟨ASK⟩ 🆂 ⊠ 🛢 🖵 🕿 ⊠

🅐🅐🅐 ◆◆◆ **Holiday Inn Express Hotel** 🅜 ❀
(231) 436-7100. **$42-$159.** 364 Louvingney. At bridge, I-75,
exit 339. Int corridors. **Pets:** Small. Supervision.

⟨SAVE⟩ 🆂 ⊠ 🛢 🕿 ⊠

🅐🅐🅐 ◆ **Kings Inn** 🅜 ❀
(231) 436-5322. **$40-$98, 3 days notice.** 1020 S Nicolet
St. I-75 N, exit 337, 0.5 mi n; I-75 S, exit 338, 0.5 mi s. Ext
corridors. **Pets:** Small, dogs only. $10 daily fee/pet, $10
one-time fee/pet. Designated rooms, supervision.

⟨SAVE⟩ 🆂 ⊠ 🛢 🕿 ⊠

🅐🅐🅐 ◆◆ **La Mirage' Motel** 🅜
(231) 436-5304. **$48-$122, 3 days notice.** 699 N Huron St.
I-75, exit 339. Ext corridors. **Pets:** Large. Supervision.

⟨SAVE⟩ 🆂 ⊠ 🛢 🕿

🅐🅐🅐 ◆◆ **Motel 6–4011** 🅜 ❀
(231) 436-8961. **$49-$149.** 206 N Nicolet St. At bridge I-75,
exit 339. Ext/int corridors. **Pets:** Large, dogs only. $50
deposit/room. No service, supervision, crate.

⟨SAVE⟩ 🆂 ⊠ 🛢 🕿

🅐🅐🅐 ◆◆ **Quality Inn Beachfront** 🅜 ❀
(231) 436-5051. **$69-$219.** 917 S Huron St. 1 mi se on US
23. Ext corridors. **Pets:** Small, dogs only. $10 daily fee/pet.
Designated rooms, no service, supervision, crate.

⟨SAVE⟩ 🆂 ⊠ 🛢 🖵 🕿 ⊠

🅐🅐🅐 ◆◆ **Ramada Inn Convention Center** 🅜 ❀
(231) 436-5535. **$59-$159.** 450 S Nicolet. I-75, exit 338. Int
corridors. **Pets:** Large, dogs only. $50 deposit/room. No
service, supervision, crate.

⟨SAVE⟩ 🆂 ⊠ 🛢 🍴 🕿 ⊠

🅐🅐🅐 ◆ **Starlite Budget Inns** 🅜 ❀
(231) 436-5959. **$42-$79, 3 days notice.** 116 Old US 31.
I-75 S, exit 338, 0.3 mi e; I-75 N, exit 337, just ne. Ext
corridors. **Pets:** Small, dogs only. $10 daily fee/pet. Super-
vision.

⟨SAVE⟩ 🆂 ⊠ 🛢 🕿 ⊠

🅐🅐🅐 ◆◆ **Super 8 Motel** 🅜 ❀
(231) 436-5252. **$55-$155.** 601 N Huron Ave. I-75 N, exit
339 (Nicolet St), just n, then just e. Ext/int corridors.
Pets: Large, dogs only. $50 deposit/room. No service,
supervision, crate.

⟨SAVE⟩ 🆂 ⊠ 🛢 🕿 ⊠

◆ **Val-Ru Motel** 🅜 ❀
(231) 436-7691. **$39-$59, 3 days notice.** 14394 N Mackinaw Hwy. I-75 N, exit 337; I-75 S, exit 338, s on SR 108.
Ext corridors. **Pets:** $70 deposit/pet, $7 daily fee/pet, $7
one-time fee/pet. No service, supervision, crate.

⊠ 🕿 ⊠

🅐🅐🅐 ◆◆ **Vindel Motel** 🅜
(231) 436-5273. **$59-$89.** 223 W Central Ave. 0.3 mi w. Ext
corridors. **Pets:** Designated rooms, supervision.

⟨SAVE⟩ 🆂 ⊠ 🛢 🖵 🕿 ⊠

MANISTEE

🅐🅐🅐 ◆ **Hillside Motel** 🅜 ❀
(231) 723-2584. **$50-$110.** 1675 US 31 S. 1.5 mi s on US
31. Ext corridors. **Pets:** Medium, dogs only. $8 daily fee/pet.
Designated rooms, supervision.

⊠ 🛢 🖵 🕿 ⊠

MANISTIQUE

🅐🅐🅐 ◆◆◆ **Comfort Inn** 🅜 ❀
(906) 341-6981. **$89-$119.** 726 E Lakeshore Dr. 0.5 mi e
on US 2. Int corridors. **Pets:** Other. $6 daily fee/pet, $6
one-time fee/pet. No service, supervision, crate.

⟨SAVE⟩ 🆂 ⊠ 🛢 🖵 ⊠

MARQUETTE

🅐🅐🅐 ◆ **Birchmont Motel** 🅜 ❀
(906) 228-7538. **$38-$52.** 2090 US 41 S. 4.3 mi s on US
41 and SR 28. Ext corridors. **Pets:** $6 one-time fee/room.
Designated rooms, no service, supervision, crate.

⟨SAVE⟩ ⊠ 🛢 🕿 🐾

🅐🅐🅐 ◆◆ **Holiday Inn** 🅜 ❀
(906) 225-1351. **$79-$79.** 1951 US 41 W. 1.8 mi w on US
41 and SR 28. Int corridors. **Pets:** Other. Designated
rooms, no service, supervision, crate.

⟨SAVE⟩ 🆂 ⊠ 🛢 🍴 🕿

🅐🅐🅐 ◆◆ **Ramada Inn** 🅜 ❀
(906) 228-6000. **$94-$99.** 412 W Washington St. 0.5 w on
US 41 business route. Int corridors. **Pets:** Other. Supervision.

⟨SAVE⟩ 🆂 ⊠ 🍴 🕿

🅐🅐🅐 ◆◆ **Tiroler Hof Inn** 🅜
(906) 226-7516. **$44-$60.** 1880 US 41 S. 1.8 mi se on US
41 and SR 28. Ext corridors. **Pets:** Small. Designated
rooms, no service, supervision, crate.

🆂 ⊠ 🛢 ⊠

🅐🅐🅐 ◆ **Travelodge** 🅜 ❀
(906) 249-1712. **$52-$69.** 1010 M-28 E. Jct US 41 S and
SR 28 E. Int corridors. **Pets:** Other. $5 daily fee/pet. Des-
ignated rooms, no service, supervision, crate.

⟨SAVE⟩ 🆂 ⊠ 🛢 🖵 🕿 ⊠

MARSHALL

🅐🅐🅐 ◆ **Arbor Inn-Historic Marshall** 🅜
(616) 781-7772. **$52-$64.** 15435 W Michigan Ave. I-69 and
Michigan Ave, exit 36, just w. Ext corridors. **Pets:** Very
small. Designated rooms, no service, supervision, crate.

⟨SAVE⟩ ⊠ 🛢 🕿

MENOMINEE

🅐🅐🅐 ◆ **Howard Johnson Express** 🅜 ❀
(906) 863-4431. **$45-$70.** 2516 10th St. 1 mi n on US 41.
Int corridors. **Pets:** No service, supervision, crate.

⟨SAVE⟩ 🆂 ⊠ 🛢 🖵

MIDLAND

◆◆ Best Western Valley Plaza Resort Ⓜ ☀
(517) 496-2700. **$62-$82.** 5221 Bay City Rd. US 10 W, Midland/Bay City Rd exit; US 10 E, Waldo Rd exit, 2.5 mi s on Waldo Rd, 1 mi e. Int corridors. **Pets:** Medium, other. $25 deposit/room. No service, supervision, crate.

(ASK) Ⓢ ⊠ 🛏 🖥 🍴 🍽 ⊠

🅰 ◆◆ Fairview Inn Ⓜ
(517) 631-0070. **$62-$89.** 2200 W Wackerly St. Jct US 10 and Eastman Rd. Int corridors. **Pets:** Small. No service, supervision, crate.

(SAVE) Ⓢ ⊠ 🛏 🍽

🅰 ◆◆◆ Holiday Inn Ⓜ ☀
(517) 631-4220. **$79-$99.** 1500 W Wackerly. Jct US 10 and Eastman Rd. Ext/int corridors. **Pets:** Large, other. Designated rooms, supervision.

(SAVE) Ⓢ ⊠ 🛏 🖥 🍴 🍽 ⊠

🅰 ◆◆ Sleep Inn of Midland Ⓜ ☀
(517) 837-1010. **$55-$84.** 2100 W Wackerly. Jct US 10 and Eastman Rd. Int corridors. **Pets:** Other. Supervision.

(SAVE) Ⓢ ⊠ 🛏 🖥 🍽

MONROE

🅰 ◆◆◆ Comfort Inn Ⓜ ☀
(734) 384-1500. **$64-$84.** 6500 E Albain Rd. At jct I-75 and La Plaisance Rd, exit 11, just w. Int corridors. **Pets:** Other. $10 daily fee/room. Designated rooms, supervision.

(SAVE) Ⓢ ⊠ 🛏 🖥 🍽

🅰 ◆ Hometown Inn Ⓜ ☀
(734) 289-1080. **$40-$55.** 1885 Welcome Way. Jct I-75 and SR 50, exit 15. Ext corridors. **Pets:** Other. $25 deposit/room, $5 one-time fee/room. No service, supervision, crate.

(SAVE) Ⓢ ⊠ 🛏

MOUNT PLEASANT

🅰 ◆◆◆ Comfort Inn Ⓜ
(517) 772-4000. **$69-$129.** 2424 S Mission St. 2 mi s on US 27 business route; close to CMU. Int corridors. **Pets:** Designated rooms, supervision.

(SAVE) Ⓢ ⊠ 🛏 🖥 🍽

◆◆◆ Holiday Inn Ⓜ
(517) 772-2905. **$79-$169, 3 days notice.** 5665 E Pickard Ave. Jct US 27 and SR 20 E. Ext/int corridors. **Pets:** Medium. No service, supervision, crate.

(ASK) Ⓢ ⊠ 🛏 🖥 🍴 🍽 ⊠

◆◆ Super 8 Motel Ⓜ ☀
(517) 773-8888. **Call for rates.** 2323 S Mission. 1.8 mi s on US 27 business route. Int corridors. **Pets:** Other. Designated rooms, supervision.

⊠ 🛏 🖥

MUNISING

🅰 ◆ Alger Falls Motel Ⓜ
(906) 387-3536. **$48-$65.** E9427 E State Hwy M28. 2 mi e on SR 28 and 94. Ext corridors. **Pets:** Small. Supervision.

(SAVE) Ⓢ ⊠ 🛏 ⊠

◆◆ Best Western Ⓜ
(906) 387-4864. **Call for rates.** M28. 3 mi e on SR 28. Ext/int corridors. **Pets:** Supervision.

⊠ 🛏 🍴 🍽 ⊠

◆◆◆ Comfort Inn Ⓜ ☀
(906) 387-5292. **$65-$98, 3 days notice.** M-28 E. 1.5 mi e on SR 28. Int corridors. **Pets:** Designated rooms, no service, supervision, crate.

(ASK) Ⓢ ⊠ 🍽 ⊠

🅰 ◆ Star-Lite Motel Ⓜ
(906) 387-2291. **$32-$38.** 500 M-28 E. 0.5 mi e on SR 28. Ext corridors. **Pets:** Supervision.

⊠ 🐾

🅰 ◆ Sunset Motel Ⓜ ☀
(906) 387-4574. **$48-$52.** 1315 Bay St. 1 mi e on E Munising Ave (CR 58). Ext corridors. **Pets:** Medium, dogs only. $5 daily fee/pet. Designated rooms, no service, supervision, crate.

⊠ 🛏 ⊠ 🐾 🍽

🅰 ◆ Terrace Motel Ⓜ ☀
(906) 387-2735. **$48-$64, 3 days notice.** 420 Prospect. 0.5 mi e, just off SR 28. Ext corridors. **Pets:** Medium. $3 daily fee/room. Designated rooms, no service, supervision, crate.

(SAVE) Ⓢ ⊠ 🛏 ⊠ 🐾 🍽

NORTON SHORES

🅰 ◆ Bel Aire Motel Ⓜ ☀
(231) 733-2196. **$56-$72.** 4240 Airline Rd. At jct Business US 31 and I-96; northbound US 31, exit Business US 31; exit 1A Airline Rd, southbound US 31 exit Airline Rd, westbound I-96 exit 1A Airline Rd. Ext corridors. **Pets:** Small, dogs only. $25 deposit/room. Supervision.

(SAVE) ⊠

🅰 ◆ Seaway Motel Ⓜ ☀
(231) 733-1220. **$60-$90, 7 days notice.** 631 W Norton Ave. From US 31 S exit, 2.5 mi nw on US 31 business route. Ext corridors. **Pets:** Very small, dogs only. $25 deposit/room. No service, supervision, crate.

Ⓢ ⊠ 🛏 🍽

ONTONAGON

🅰 ◆ Scott's Superior Inn & Cabins Ⓜ ☀
(906) 884-4866. **$39-$49.** 277 Lakeshore Rd. 1.5 mi sw on SR 64. Ext/int corridors. **Pets:** $5 daily fee/pet, $5 one-time fee/room. Designated rooms, no service, supervision, crate.

(SAVE) ⊠ 🛏 ⊠

PAW PAW

🅰 ◆◆◆ Quality Inn & Suites Ⓜ ☀
(616) 655-0303. **$67-$110, 3 days notice.** 153 Ampey Rd. I-94, exit 60, just nw. Int corridors. **Pets:** $25 deposit/pet. Designated rooms, no service, supervision, crate.

(SAVE) Ⓢ ⊠ 🦽 🐾 🍳 🛏 🖥 🍽

PERRY

◆ **Heb's Inn Motel** Ⓜ ❖
(517) 625-7500. **$43-$55.** 2811 Lansing Rd. Just se of jct I-69 and SR 52. Ext corridors. **Pets:** Small. $2 daily fee/room, $5 one-time fee/room. No service, supervision, crate.
Ⓐ$Ⓚ Ⓢ✖

PLAINWELL

Ⓐ ◆◆◆ **Comfort Inn** Ⓜ ❖
(616) 685-9891. **$67-$180.** 622 Allegan St. US 131, exit 49A. Int corridors. **Pets:** Medium, other. $30 deposit/room. No service, supervision, crate.
Ⓢ Ⓢ ✖ 🅱 🖵 🖼

PORT HURON

Ⓐ ◆ **MainStreet Lodge** Ⓜ ❖
(810) 984-3166. **$58-$68.** 514 Huron Ave. I-94, exit 271; I-69, exit 199, 5 mi e on Business 69, 2 mi n on Military St via Huron Ave. Int corridors. **Pets:** $5 daily fee/room. No service, supervision, crate.
Ⓢ Ⓢ ✖ 🅱 🖵

PORTLAND

Ⓐ ◆◆◆ **Best Western American Heritage Inn** Ⓜ ❖
(517) 647-2200. **$58-$77.** 1681 Grand River Ave. I-96, exit 77, just n. Int corridors. **Pets:** Small, other. Designated rooms, no service, supervision, crate.
Ⓢ Ⓢ ✖ Ⓚ 🅱 🖵 🖼

PRUDENVILLE

Ⓐ ◆ **Shea's Lake Front Lodge** Ⓛ
(517) 366-5910. **$48-$52.** 125 Pine St. I-75, exit 227, 8 mi w on SR 55. Ext/int corridors. **Pets:** Medium. Designated rooms, no service, supervision, crate.
Ⓢ 🅱 🖵 ✖ Ⓚ 🆉

SAGINAW

◆◆◆ **Four Points Hotel by Sheraton** Ⓜ ❖
(517) 790-5050. **$78-$78.** 4960 Towne Centre Rd. I-675, exit 6, just w on Tittabawassee Rd. Int corridors. **Pets:** Small. $100 deposit/pet, $50 one-time fee/room. No service, supervision, crate.
Ⓐ$Ⓚ Ⓢ ✖ 🅱 🖵 🍽 🖼

Ⓐ ◆◆ **Holiday Inn Saginaw I-75/Frankenmuth Area** Ⓜ
(517) 755-0461. **$81-$92.** 1408 S Outer Dr. Jct I-75 and SR 46, exit 149B. Int corridors. **Pets:** Medium. Supervision.
Ⓢ Ⓢ ✖ 🅱 🖵 🍽 🖼 ✖

Ⓐ ◆ **Knights Inn-Saginaw South** Ⓜ ❖
(517) 754-9200. **$43-$47, 5 days notice.** 1415 S Outer Dr. Jct I-75 and SR 46, exit 149B. Ext corridors. **Pets:** Small. Supervision.
Ⓢ Ⓢ ✖ 🅱 🖵 🖼

Ⓐ ◆◆ **Red Roof Inn** Ⓜ ❖
(517) 754-8414. **$44-$57.** 966 S Outer Dr. Jct I-75 and SR 46, exit 149B. Ext corridors. **Pets:** Medium, other. Supervision.
Ⓢ ✖

Ⓐ ◆ **Rodeway Inn** Ⓜ
(517) 753-2461. **$50-$80.** 3425 Holland Rd. At jct I-75 and SR 46, exit 149B. Ext corridors. **Pets:** Large. No service, supervision, crate.
Ⓢ Ⓢ ✖ 🅱 🍽

SAULT STE. MARIE

◆ **Bavarian Economy Inn** Ⓜ ❖
(906) 632-6864. **$52-$69.** 2006 Ashmun St. I-75, exit 392, 2 mi ne on I-75 business spur. Ext/int corridors. **Pets:** Small, dogs only. $5 one-time fee/pet. No service, supervision, crate.
Ⓐ$Ⓚ Ⓢ ✖ 🅱

Ⓐ ◆ **Budget Host Crestview Inn** Ⓜ ❖
(906) 635-5213. **$49-$79.** 1200 Ashmun St. I-75, exit 392, 2.8 mi ne on I-75 business spur. Ext corridors. **Pets:** Other. $5 daily fee/room, $5 one-time fee/room. Designated rooms, supervision.
Ⓢ Ⓢ ✖ 🅱

◆ **Grand Motel** Ⓜ ❖
(906) 632-2141. **$36-$84, 3 days notice.** 1100 E Portage Ave. 0.8 mi e at end of I-75 business spur. Ext/int corridors. **Pets:** Other. Supervision.
Ⓐ$Ⓚ Ⓢ ✖ 🖼

Ⓐ ◆◆ **Mid-City Motel** Ⓜ ❖
(906) 632-6832. **$44-$54.** 304 E Portage Ave. Just e at end of I-75 business spur. Ext corridors. **Pets:** Small. Supervision.
✖

◆ **Royal Motel** Ⓜ ❖
(906) 632-6323. **$48-$48.** 1707 Ashmun St. I-75, exit 392, 2 mi ne on I-75 business spur. Ext corridors. **Pets:** Small, dogs only. Designated rooms, no service, supervision, crate.
Ⓐ$Ⓚ Ⓢ ✖ 🖵 ✖

Ⓐ ◆◆ **Super 8 Motel** Ⓜ ❖
(906) 632-8882. **$65-$74.** 3826 I-75 Business Spur. I-75, exit 392, 0.5 mi ne. Int corridors. **Pets:** Other. Designated rooms, no service, supervision, crate.
Ⓢ ✖ Ⓚ ✖

SILVER CITY

Ⓐ ◆◆◆ **Best Western Porcupine Mountain Lodge** Ⓜ ❖
(906) 885-5311. **$79-$89, 3 days notice.** 120 Lincoln Ave. On SR 107, 0.3 mi w of SR 64. Int corridors. **Pets:** Small, dogs only. $10 daily fee/room. Supervision.
Ⓢ Ⓢ ✖ 🍽 🖼 ✖

Ⓐ ◆◆ **Tomlinson's Rainbow Lodging** Ⓜ ❖
(906) 885-5348. **$60-$68, 30 days notice.** 2900 M-64. SR 64, just e of jct SR 107. Ext corridors. **Pets:** Medium, dogs only. $50 deposit/room, $10 one-time fee/room. Designated rooms, no service, supervision, crate.
Ⓢ Ⓢ ✖ 🅱 🖵 ✖

ST. IGNACE

◆ **Bay View Motel**
(906) 643-9444. **$52-$72.** 1133 N State St. 3 mi n of bridge
tollgate; on I-75 business route. Ext corridors. **Pets:** Other.
$5 daily fee/room, $5 one-time fee/room. Designated
rooms, no service, supervision, crate.

⊠ ☎

◆◆ **Budget Host Inn** M 🐾
(906) 643-9666. **$58-$98.** 700 N State St. 1.8 mi n of bridge
tollgate on I-75 business route. Ext/int corridors.
Pets: Other. $20 deposit/room. No service, supervision,
crate.

⊠ 🛏 🍽 ⊠

◆◆ **Howard Johnson Express Inn** M 🐾
(906) 643-9700. **$79-$89, 3 days notice.** 913 Boulevard Dr.
At jct I-75 and US 2 W. Int corridors. **Pets:** Dogs only. $8
daily fee/pet. Designated rooms, no service, supervision,
crate.

ASK S⃝ ⊠ 🍽 🍽 ⊠

◆ **Wayside Motel** M
(906) 643-8944. **$45-$70.** 751 N State St. 2 mi n of bridge
tollgate on I-75 business route. Ext corridors. **Pets:** Small.
Supervision.

SAVE S⃝ ⊠ 🍽 ⊠

STEVENSVILLE

◆◆◆ **Baymont Inn & Suites-Stevensville** M
(616) 428-9111. **$62-$67, 30 days notice.** 2601 W Marquette Woods Rd. I-94, exit 23. Int corridors. **Pets:** No service,
supervision, crate.

S⃝ ⊠ 🏠 🎲 🗝 🛏 🍽

◆◆ **Park Inn International** M 🐾
(616) 429-3218. **$65-$90.** 4290 Red Arrow Hwy. I-94, exit
23 (Stevensville exit), 0.5 mi n. Ext/int corridors.
Pets: Other. No service, supervision, crate.

SAVE S⃝ ⊠ 🗝 🛏 🍽 🍴 🍽

STURGIS

◆◆◆ **Comfort Inn** M 🐾
(616) 651-7881. **$50-$50.** 1301 S Centerville Rd. 1 mi s on
SR 66 from jct US 12, 1.8 mi n of Indiana Toll Rd, exit 121.
Int corridors. **Pets:** Medium, other. $15 one-time fee/room.
Designated rooms, no service, supervision, crate.

SAVE S⃝ ⊠ 🎲 🗝 🛏 🍽 🍽

◆ **Green Briar Motor Inn** M 🐾
(616) 651-2361. **$38-$55.** 71381 S Centerville Rd. 0.3 mi s
on SR 66, n of Indiana Toll Rd, exit 121. Ext corridors.
Pets: Very small, dogs only. $5 daily fee/pet, $5 one-time
fee/pet. Designated rooms, no service, supervision, crate.

SAVE S⃝ ⊠ 🍽 CTV

SUTTONS BAY

◆ **Red Lion Motor Lodge** M
(231) 271-6694. **Call for rates.** 4290 S West Bay Shore
Rd. 5 mi s on SR 22. Ext corridors. **Pets:** Designated
rooms, no service, supervision, crate.

⊠ 🛏 🍽 ☎

TAWAS CITY

◆ **Tawas Motel-Resort** M 🐾
(517) 362-3822. **$50-$80, 3 days notice.** 1124 US 23S. 1.3
mi s on US 23. Ext corridors. **Pets:** Large. Supervision.

SAVE S⃝ ⊠ 🛏 🍽 ⊠

TECUMSEH

◆◆ **Tecumseh Inn Motel** M 🐾
(517) 423-7401. **$45-$65.** 1445 W Chicago Blvd. 1.5 mi w
of city on SR 50, 15 mi w of US 23, Dundee exit. Ext
corridors. **Pets:** $25 deposit/room. Designated rooms,
supervision.

⊠ 🛏 🍽

THREE RIVERS

◆◆ **Three Rivers Inn** M 🐾
(616) 273-9521. **$43-$73.** 1200 W Broadway. 2 mi sw on
US 131 and SR 60. Int corridors. **Pets:** $10 one-time fee/
pet. No service, supervision, crate.

⊠ 🍴 🍽

TRAVERSE CITY

◆◆◆ **Holiday Inn** M
(231) 947-3700. **Call for rates.** 615 E Front St. 0.5 mi e on
US 31. Int corridors. **Pets:** Designated rooms, no service,
supervision, crate.

⊠ 🎲 🛏 🍽 🍴 🍽 ⊠

◆◆ **Main Street Inns U.S.A.** M 🐾
(231) 929-0410. **$60-$150.** 618 E Front St. 0.5 mi e on US
31/SR 72/37. Ext corridors. **Pets:** Other. Designated rooms,
no service, supervision, crate.

ASK S⃝ ⊠ 🛏 🍽

◆◆ **Motel 6–4065** M 🐾
(231) 938-3002. **Call for rates.** 1582 US 31 N. 4.3 mi e on
US 31. Int corridors. **Pets:** Small. $6 daily fee/pet. Desig-
nated rooms, no service, supervision, crate.

⊠ 🏠 🍽

TROUT LAKE

◆ **McGowan's Family Motel &
Restaurant** M 🐾
(906) 569-3366. **$45-$48.** M-123. Center, on SR 123. Ext
corridors. **Pets:** Small, dogs only. No service, supervision,
crate.

🛏 🍴 ⊠ 🎿 ☎

WALKER

◆ **Riviera Motel** M 🐾
(616) 453-2404. **$39-$45.** 4350 Remembrance Rd. I-96,
exit 26, just s, 0.6 mi w on 3 Mile Rd, 0.4 mi s on Wilson
Ave, then just e. Ext corridors. **Pets:** Small, dogs only.
Designated rooms, no service, supervision, crate.

SAVE S⃝ ⊠ 🛏

WEST BRANCH

◆ **La Hacienda Motel** M
(517) 345-2345. **$44-$63.** 969 W Houghton Ave. I-75, exit
215, 1.5 mi e on I-75 business loop. Ext corridors.
Pets: Very small. No service, supervision, crate.

SAVE S⃝ ⊠ 🛏 ⊠

◆◆ Super 8 Motel **M** ❖
(517) 345-8488. **$58-$64.** 2596 Austin's Way. I-75, exit 212, Cook Rd. Int corridors. **Pets:** Medium. $25 deposit/room. No service, supervision, crate.
SAVE Sᴅ ⊠

WHITEHALL

◆ Lake Land Motel **M** ❖
(231) 894-5644. **$60-$65.** 1002 E Colby St. US 31, Colby Rd exit, 0.8 mi w on US 31 business route. Ext corridors. **Pets:** Other. $5 one-time fee/room. Supervision.
⊠

WYOMING

◆ Super 8 Motel **M** ❖
(616) 530-8588. **$53-$65.** 727 44th St SW. US 131, exit 79. Int corridors. **Pets:** Medium, other. $5 one-time fee/pet. Designated rooms, no service, supervision, crate.
ASK Sᴅ ⊠ 🖥

MINNESOTA

CITY INDEX

AITKIN

◆◆ 40 Club Inn M ❀
(218) 927-2903. **$76.** 950 2nd St NW. On SR 210, 1 mi w of jct US 169. Int corridors. **Pets:** Other. $5 daily fee/pet. Designated rooms, no service, supervision, crate.
ASK ✕ 🐾 🛏 💻 🏊

◆◆ Ripple River Motel M ❀
(218) 927-3734. **$36-$75.** 701 Minnesota Ave S. On US 169, 0.8 mi s of jct SR 210. Ext corridors. **Pets:** $10 one-time fee/pet. Designated rooms, supervision.
✕ 🛏

ALBERT LEA

◆◆ Albert Lea Countryside Inn
Motel M ❀
(507) 373-2446. **$34-$65, 3 days notice.** 2102 E Main St. 1.3 mi w on CR 46 from jct I-35, exit 11. Ext/int corridors. **Pets:** Medium. $3 daily fee/pet. No service, supervision, crate.
SAVE ✕ 🛏

◆ Bel Aire Motor Inn M ❀
(507) 373-3983. **$35-$100.** 700 Hwy 69 S. US 69, 3.4 mi s of jct I-90 and US 69, exit 154. Ext corridors. **Pets:** Medium. $3 daily fee/pet. Designated rooms, no service, supervision, crate.
SAVE 🐾 ✕ 🛏 🏊

◆◆◆ Best Western Albert Lea Inn M ❀
(507) 373-8291. **$55-$75, 3 days notice.** 2301 E Main St. 1 mi w on CR 46 from jct I-35, exit 11. Int corridors. **Pets:** Medium, other. $8 daily fee/pet. Designated rooms, no service, supervision, crate.
SAVE 🐾 ✕ 🐾 🛏 💻 🍴 🏊

ALEXANDRIA

◆◆◆ AmericInn Motel M ❀
(320) 763-6808. **$50-$100.** 4520 SR 29 S. 0.3 mi n of I-94, exit 103. Int corridors. **Pets:** Small, other. Supervision.
ASK 🐾 ✕ 🐾 🛏 💻

◆◆◆ Arrowwood-A Radisson Resort R ❀
(320) 762-1124. **$129-$129, 30 days notice.** 2100 Arrow-wood Ln. 3 mi n of I-94, exit 103, 0.8 mi w on CR 82, 2.5 mi n on CR 22. Int corridors. **Pets:** Small, dogs only. $50 deposit/room. Designated rooms, no service, supervision, crate.
ASK 🐾 ✕ 🐕 🛏 💻 🏊 ✕

◆◆◆ Country Inn & Suites By Carlson Ⓜ

(320) 763-9900. **$69-$129.** 5304 Hwy 29 S. Just sw of I-94, exit 103. Int corridors. **Pets:** No service, supervision, crate.

🅰🆂🅺 🆂▱ ✕ 🏠 🗐 🖾 🖬 🖵 🖻

◆◆ Super 8 Motel Ⓜ ♣

(320) 763-6552. **$44-$60.** 4620 SR 29 S. I-94, exit 103, 0.3 mi n. Int corridors. **Pets:** $25 deposit/room. No service, supervision, crate.

🅰🆂🅺 🆂▱ ✕

AUSTIN

ⓐⓐⓐ ◆◆ Country Side Inn Ⓜ

(507) 437-7774. **$39-$62.** 3303 Oakland Ave W. Just nw of I-90, exit 175 (Oakland Ave). Int corridors. **Pets:** Small. No service, supervision, crate.

🆂🅰🆅🅴 🆂▱ ✕ 🖬 🖵

◆◆ Days Inn Ⓜ ♣

(507) 433-8600. **$64-$64.** 700 16th Ave NW. Just nw of I-90, exit 178A (4th St NW). Int corridors. **Pets:** Other. $20 deposit/pet. Designated rooms, no service, supervision, crate.

🅰🆂🅺 🆂▱ ✕ 🖉

◆◆◆ Holiday Inn Holidome & Austin Conference Center Ⓜ ♣

(507) 433-1000. **Call for rates.** 1701 4th St NW. Just nw of I-90, exit 178A (4th St NW). Int corridors. **Pets:** Other. $20 deposit/pet. Designated rooms, no service, supervision, crate.

✕ 🏠 🖉 🖬 🖵 🖻 🥄 🖻 🖾

BABBITT

◆◆◆ Timber Bay Lodge & Houseboats Ⓒ ♣

(218) 827-3682. **$745-$1245, 60 days notice.** 8347 Timber Bay Rd. 2.8 mi e of jct CR 21 via CR 70 and CR 623. Ext corridors. **Pets:** $10 daily fee/pet. Supervision.

🖬 🖵 🖾 🅇 🆃🆅 🗷

BAUDETTE

◆◆◆ AmericInn Motel & Suites Ⓜ ♣

(218) 634-3200. **$60-$72.** 0.5 mi w on SR 11. Int corridors. **Pets:** Dogs only. Supervision.

🅰🆂🅺 🆂▱ ✕ 🖕 🖉 🖉 🖬 🖵 🖻

BAXTER

◆◆◆ Country Inn By Carlson Ⓜ ♣

(218) 828-2161. **$79-$89.** 1220 Dellwood Dr N. On SR 371, 1 mi n, jct SR 371 and 210. Int corridors. **Pets:** Small, dogs only. No service, supervision, crate.

🅰🆂🅺 🆂▱ ✕ 🏠 🖉 🖾 🖬 🖵 🖻

BEMIDJI

◆ Bel Air Motel Ⓜ

(218) 751-3222. **$28-$62.** 1350 Paul Bunyan Dr NW. 0.5 mi e of the nw jct of US 2, 71 and SR 197. Ext corridors. **Pets:** Designated rooms, no service, supervision, crate.

✕ 🖬 🖵

ⓐⓐⓐ ◆◆ Best Western Bemidji Ⓜ ♣

(218) 751-0390. **$45-$75.** 2420 Paul Bunyan Dr. Intersection of jct US 2, 71 and SR 197, exit 71. Int corridors. **Pets:** Other. Designated rooms, no service, supervision, crate.

🆂🅰🆅🅴 🆂▱ ✕ 🖾 🖬 🖵 🖻

ⓐⓐⓐ ◆◆◆ Comfort Inn Ⓜ

(218) 751-7700. **$55-$110.** 3500 Comfort Dr NW. 1 mi w of jct US 2, 71 and SR 197. Int corridors. **Pets:** Small. Designated rooms, no service, supervision, crate.

🆂🅰🆅🅴 🆂▱ ✕ 🖬 🖵 🖻

ⓐⓐⓐ ◆ Edgewater Inn Ⓜ ♣

(218) 751-3600. **$45-$84.** 1015 Paul Bunyan Dr NE. 0.8 mi se on SR 197 (Paul Bunyan Dr). Ext/int corridors. **Pets:** Small. $5 daily fee/pet. No service, supervision, crate.

🆂🅰🆅🅴 🆂▱ ✕ 🖬 🖵 🖾

◆◆◆ Holiday Inn Express Ⓜ ♣

(218) 751-2487. **$55-$75.** 2422 Ridgeway Ave NW. 0.5 mi e of jct US 2, 71 and SR 197. Int corridors. **Pets:** Small, other. No service, supervision, crate.

🅰🆂🅺 🆂▱ ✕ 🏠 🖉 🖵 🖻

ⓐⓐⓐ ◆◆◆ Ruttger's Birchmont Lodge Ⓡ ♣

(218) 751-1630. **$48-$309, 30 days notice.** 530 Birchmont Beach Rd. 3.6 mi n on CR 21 (Bemidji Ave N) from jct SR 197 (Paul Bunyan Dr NW). Ext/int corridors. **Pets:** Other. $8 daily fee/pet. Designated rooms, supervision.

🆂🅰🆅🅴 🆂▱ 🖬 🖵 🥄 🖻 🖾

BLACKDUCK

◆◆◆ AmericInn Motel Ⓜ ♣

(218) 835-4500. **$45-$95.** 81 Brandl Dr NW. 0.3 mi s of jct US 71 and SR 72 on US 71. Int corridors. **Pets:** Designated rooms, no service, supervision, crate.

🅰🆂🅺 🆂▱ ✕ 🖉 🖉 🖬 🖵 🖻

BLUE EARTH

◆◆◆ AmericInn of Blue Earth Ⓜ ♣

(507) 526-4215. **$57-$71.** 1495 Domes Dr. Just s of jct I-90 and exit 119. Int corridors. **Pets:** $5 one-time fee/room. Designated rooms, no service, supervision, crate.

✕ 🏠 🖉 🖬 🖵 🖻

◆◆ Super 8 Motel of Blue Earth Ⓜ ♣

(507) 526-7376. **$44-$58, 4 days notice.** 1120 N Grove St. Just s of jct I-90 and exit 119. Int corridors. **Pets:** Other. $5 daily fee/room, $5 one-time fee/room. Designated rooms, supervision.

🅰🆂🅺 ✕ 🖬

BRAINERD

◆ Days Inn Ⓜ

(218) 829-0391. **$59-$79.** 1630 Fairview Rd N. On SR 210 and 371, adjacent to the Paul Bunyan Amusement Center. Int corridors. **Pets:** Medium. Designated rooms, no service, supervision, crate.

🅰🆂🅺 🆂▱ ✕

◆◆◆ Holiday Inn Ⓜ ♣

(218) 829-1441. **Call for rates.** 2115 S 6th St. On SR 371, 1.8 mi s of jct SR 210. Ext/int corridors. **Pets:** Supervision.

✕ 🖉 🖬 🖵 🥄 🖻 🖾

BRECKENRIDGE

🚗 ◆◆ South Haven Inn M 🐾
(218) 643-3125. **$30-$50.** 1120 Buffalo Ave. 1 mi s on jct US 75 and Minnesota Ave. Ext corridors. **Pets:** Other. Designated rooms, no service, supervision, crate.

CLOQUET

◆◆ Super 8 Motel M 🐾
(218) 879-1250. **$53-$75.** 121 Big Lake Rd. 1.3 mi n of jct I-35 on SR 33, exit 237. Int corridors. **Pets:** Medium. $5 one-time fee/pet. Designated rooms, supervision.

CROOKSTON

◆◆ Northland Inn of Crookston M
(218) 281-5210. **Call for rates.** 2200 University Ave. 1.5 mi n on US 2 W and 75 N. Int corridors. **Pets:** Designated rooms, no service, supervision, crate.

ASK ✕ 🍴 🏊

DETROIT LAKES

🚗 ◆◆◆ Best Western Holland House & Suites M
(218) 847-4483. **$89-$109, 3 days notice.** 615 Hwy 10 E. 1.3 mi se on US 10. Ext/int corridors. **Pets:** Supervision.

SAVE ✕ 🦴 💻 🏊

🚗 ◆◆ Budget Host Inn M 🐾
(218) 847-4454. **$40-$80.** 895 Hwy 10 E. 1.5 mi se on Hwy 10 E. Ext corridors. **Pets:** Other. $10 daily fee/room. Supervision.

✕ 🦴 💻

🚗 ◆◆ Castaway Inn & Resort X
(218) 847-4449. **$59-$89, 3 days notice.** 1226 E Shore Dr. 3 mi se on US 10. Ext corridors. **Pets:** Small. Designated rooms, no service, supervision, crate.

SAVE ✕ 🦴 💻 ✕

◆◆◆ Country Inn & Suites By Carlson M 🐾
(218) 847-2000. **$65-$80.** 1330 Hwy 10 E. Just e of jct CR 53 E and US 10. Int corridors. **Pets:** Small. $25 deposit/room. Designated rooms, no service, supervision, crate.

ASK 🦸 ✕ 🛏 🦴 💻 🏊

◆◆◆ Holiday Inn Lakeside M
(218) 847-2121. **$80-$120.** Hwy 10 E. 2 mi se on US 10. Int corridors. **Pets:** Small. Designated rooms, no service, supervision, crate.

ASK 🦸 ✕ 🦴 💻 🍴 🏊 ✕

DILWORTH

◆◆◆ Howard Johnson Inn of Fargo/Moorhead M
(218) 287-1212. **Call for rates.** 701 Center Ave E. 0.5 mi e on US 10. Int corridors. **Pets:** Medium. Designated rooms, no service, supervision, crate.

✕ 🦴 💻 🍴

DULUTH

◆◆◆ AmericInn Motel & Suites of Duluth/Proctor M 🐾
(218) 624-1026. **$70-$155.** 185 US Hwy 2. Jct US 2 and I-35, 0.8 mi n. Int corridors. **Pets:** Other. $25 deposit/room. Designated rooms, no service, supervision, crate.

ASK 🦸 ✕ 🐾 🦾 🦴 💻 🍴 🏊

🚗 ◆◆ Best Western Downtown Motel M
(218) 727-6851. **$55-$90.** 131 W 2nd St. Center, 2nd St at 2nd Ave W. Ext/int corridors. **Pets:** Supervision.

SAVE 🦸 ✕ 🦴

🚗 ◆◆◆ Best Western Edgewater Motel M
(218) 728-3601. **$69-$139.** 2400 London Rd. Northside, just nw of I-35, exit 258 (21st Ave E). Ext/int corridors. **Pets:** No service, supervision, crate.

SAVE 🦸 ✕ 🐾 🦴 💻 🏊 ✕

◆◆◆ Days Inn-Duluth M 🐾
(218) 727-3110. **$59-$129.** 909 Cottonwood Ave. SR 194, just n of jct US 53. Int corridors. **Pets:** Other. Supervision.

ASK 🦸 ✕ 🦾 🦴

🚗 ◆◆◆ Hawthorn Suites at Waterfront Plaza 🅷 🐾
(218) 727-4663. **$119-$239.** 325 Lake Ave S. In Canal Park area. Int corridors. **Pets:** Very small, other. $75 deposit/room. Designated rooms, no service, supervision, crate.

SAVE 🦸 ✕ 🛏 🐾 🦾 🦴 💻 🍴 🏊

◆◆◆ Manor On The Creek Country Inn Bed & Breakfast 🅱🅱 🐾
(218) 728-3189. **$129-$199, 8 days notice.** 2215 E Second St. I-35, exit 21st Ave E, 0.4 mi w, just n. Ext/int corridors. **Pets:** Dogs only. $10 one-time fee/room. No service, supervision, crate.

ASK 🦸 ✕ 🦴 💻

◆◆◆ Radisson Hotel Duluth-Harborview 🅷 🐾
(218) 727-8981. **$79-$119.** 505 W Superior St. Center; Superior St at 5th Ave W. Int corridors. **Pets:** Small. $50 deposit/room, $10 daily fee/room. Designated rooms, supervision.

✕ 🦴 💻 🏊

◆◆ Voyageur Lakewalk Inn M 🐾
(218) 722-3911. **$45-$70.** 333 E Superior St. I-35, exit Superior St, just n at jct 4th Ave e and Superior St. Ext corridors. **Pets:** Other. $10 deposit/pet. No service, supervision, crate.

✕ 🦴 💻

EAST GRAND FORKS

◆◆◆ Comfort Inn M 🐾
(218) 773-9545. **$39-$99.** 1400 Gateway Dr NE. US 2, 1 mi e. Int corridors. **Pets:** Designated rooms, no service, supervision, crate.

ASK 🦸 ✕ 🦴 💻 🏊

ELY

◆ **Motel Ely-Budget Host** M ❀
(218) 365-3237. **$49-$75, 30 days notice.** 1047 E Sheridan St. US 1 and SR 169. Ext corridors. **Pets:** Medium.
$10 one-time fee/room. Designated rooms, no service,
supervision, crate.
[S🐾] [✕] [▭]

◆◆ **Silver Rapids Lodge Resort** 🅇 ❀
(218) 365-4877. **$50-$180, 60 days notice.** 3 mi e on SR
169, from jct CR 21, 3 mi s on CR 58 and 16. Ext corridors.
Pets: $50 deposit/room, $10 daily fee/pet. Designated
rooms, no service, supervision, crate.
[🔒] [▭] [✕] [CTV]

FAIRMONT

◆◆◆ **Comfort Inn** M ❀
(507) 238-5444. **$59-$84.** 2225 N State St. Jct SR 15 and
I-90, exit 102. Int corridors. **Pets:** Other. Designated rooms,
no service, supervision, crate.
[ASK] [S🐾] [✕] [🐾] [▭] [🔁]

◆◆◆ **Holiday Inn** Ⓜ❀
(507) 238-4771. **$89-$159.** 1201 Torgerson Dr. Jct SR 15
and I-90, exit 102. Int corridors. **Pets:** Other. Designated
rooms, no service, supervision, crate.
[ASK] [✕] [🔒] [▭] [🔁] [✕]

◆◆ **Super 8 Motel** Ⓜ ❀
(507) 238-9444. **$54-$59.** 1200 Torgerson Dr. Jct SR 15
and I-90, exit 102. Int corridors. **Pets:** Other. Designated
rooms, no service, supervision, crate.
[ASK] [S🐾] [✕]

FARIBAULT

◆◆◆ **AmericInn Motel** M
(507) 334-9464. **$69-$85, 7 days notice.** 1801 Lavender
Dr. 0.3 mi e on SR 21 from jct I-35, exit 59. Int corridors.
Pets: Medium. Supervision.
[ASK] [S🐾] [✕] [🔁] [🐾] [🔒] [▭] [🔁]

⚑ ◆◆ **Select Inn** M ❀
(507) 334-2051. **$37-$53.** 4040 SR 60 W. On SR 60, just w
of jct I-35, exit 56. Int corridors. **Pets:** Other. $25 deposit/
room. Supervision.
[SAVE] [S🐾] [✕] [🐾] [🔒] [▭] [🔁]

FERGUS FALLS

⚑ ◆◆◆ **AmericInn Motel** M ❀
(218) 739-3900. **$57-$114.** 526 Western Ave N. Just se of
jct of I-94 and SR 210, exit 54. Int corridors. **Pets:** $50
deposit/room. Designated rooms, no service, supervision,
crate.
[SAVE] [S🐾] [✕] [🐾] [🔁] [🐾] [🔒] [🔁]

◆◆ **Days Inn** M
(218) 739-3311. **$38-$61, 3 days notice.** 610 Western Ave.
Just ne of jct I-94 and SR 210, exit 54. Int corridors.
Pets: Designated rooms, no service, supervision, crate.
[ASK] [S🐾] [✕] [🔁]

Motel 7 M

◆ **Motel 7** M
(218) 736-2554. **$32-$45, 4 days notice.** 616 Frontier Dr.
Just ne of jct I-94 and SR 210. Int corridors. **Pets:** Small.
No service, supervision, crate.
[✕] [🔒]

FINLAYSON

◆◆ **Super 8 Motel** M
(320) 245-5284. **Call for rates.** 2811 SR 23. I-35, exit 195
(SR 23). Int corridors. **Pets:** Medium. No service, supervision, crate.
[✕] [CTV]

FOSSTON

◆◆ **Super 8 Motel** M ❀
(218) 435-1088. **$41-$49.** 108 S Amber. 0.5 mi e on US 2.
Int corridors. **Pets:** Medium, dogs only. $10 deposit/room.
No service, supervision, crate.
[ASK] [S🐾] [✕] [🔒]

GARRISON

◆◆◆ **Country Inn & Suites By Carlson** M ❀
(320) 692-4050. **$105-$129, 7 days notice.** On SR 169,
just s of jct SR 18. Int corridors. **Pets:** Large, other. Supervision.
[ASK] [S🐾] [✕] [🔒] [▭] [🔁]

GAYLORD

◆◆ **Gold Leaf Inn & Suites** M ❀
(507) 237-5860. **$45-$65.** 330 Main Ave E. 1.5 mi e. Int
corridors. **Pets:** Medium. Designated rooms, no service,
supervision, crate.
[✕] [🐾] [🔒]

GRAND MARAIS

⚑ ◆◆◆ **Aspen Lodge** M
(218) 387-2500. **$65-$110, 3 days notice.** 310 E Hwy 61.
SR 61, just ne of center. Ext/int corridors. **Pets:** No service,
supervision, crate.
[SAVE] [S🐾] [✕] [🐾] [🐾] [🔒] [🔁]

⚑ ◆◆◆ **Best Western Superior Inn &
Suites** M
(218) 387-2240. **$99-$139, 3 days notice.** 104 1st Ave E.
SR 61, just ne of center. Ext/int corridors. **Pets:** Supervi-
sion.
[SAVE] [✕] [🔁] [🐾] [🔒] [▭]

◆◆◆ **Gunflint Lodge** 🆁 ❀
(218) 388-2294. **$165-$362, 60 days notice.** 143 S Gunflint
Lake. 43 mi n of Grand Marais, 0.8 mi e of jct Hwy 12
(Gunflint Tr) and CR 50. Ext corridors. **Pets:** $10 daily
fee/pet. Supervision.
[🔒] [▭] [📺] [✕] [🐾] [CTV] [🔁]

⚑ ◆◆ **Nor'Wester Lodge and Outfitter** 🅲 ❀
(218) 388-2252. **$498-$1249.** 7778 Gunflint Tr. 30 mi nw on
CR 12, Gunflint Tr from jct SR 61. Ext corridors.
Pets: Other. $10 daily fee/pet. No service, supervision,
crate.
[🔒] [▭] [✕] [🐾] [CTV] [🔁]

Super 8 Motel M
(218) 387-2448. **$69-$99, 3 days notice.** 1711 W Hwy 61. 1 mi sw on SR 61. Ext/int corridors. **Pets:** Small. Supervision.
[SAVE] [icons]

Tomteboda Motel M
(218) 387-1585. **$59-$79, 7 days notice.** 1800 W Hwy 61. SR 61, 1 mi sw. Ext corridors. **Pets:** Small. No service, supervision, crate.
[icons]

Wedgewood Motel M
(218) 387-2944. **$30-$42.** 1663 E Hwy 61. SR 61, 2.5 mi ne. Ext corridors. **Pets:** Dogs only. No service, supervision, crate.
[icons]

GRAND RAPIDS

Best Western Rainbow Inn MI
(218) 326-9655. **$56-$71.** 1300 US 169 E. US 169 N, 0.5 mi ne of jct US 2 E. Int corridors. **Pets:** Other. $50 deposit/room. Supervision.
[SAVE] [icons]

Country Inn By Carlson M
(218) 327-4960. **$68-$106, 30 days notice.** 2601 Hwy 169 S. US 169 S, 2 mi s of jct US 2. Int corridors. **Pets:** Medium, dogs only. No service, supervision, crate.
[SAVE] [icons]

Days Inn M
(218) 326-3457. **$45-$75.** 311 E Hwy 2. US 2 E, at jct US 169 N. Ext/int corridors. **Pets:** Small, dogs only. Designated rooms, no service, supervision, crate.
[SAVE] [icons]

Sawmill Inn MI
(218) 326-8501. **$57-$85.** 2301 S Pokegama Ave. On US 169, 2 mi s of jct US 2. Ext/int corridors. **Pets:** Large, other. Supervision.
[SAVE] [icons]

GRANITE FALLS

Granite Falls Super 8 Motel M
(320) 564-4075. **$45-$52.** 845 W SR 212. 0.5 mi w of jct SR 23 and 212. Int corridors. **Pets:** Small. $5 daily fee/pet. No service, supervision, crate.
[ASK] [icons]

HARMONY

Country Lodge Motel M
(507) 886-2515. **$45-$80.** 525 Main Ave N. 0.4 mi n on US 52. Int corridors. **Pets:** Large. No service, supervision, crate.
[SAVE] [icons]

HIBBING

Days Inn M
(218) 263-8306. **Call for rates.** 1520 SR 37 E. On SR 37, 0.3 mi e of jct US 169. Int corridors. **Pets:** Small. No service, supervision, crate.
[icons]

Hibbing Park Hotel MI
(218) 262-3481. **$70-$75.** 1402 E Howard St. On US 169 and SR 73, facing the Paulucci Space Theatre. Int corridors. **Pets:** Other. $50 deposit/room. Designated rooms, supervision.
[ASK] [icons]

HINCKLEY

Hinckley Gold Pine Inn M
(320) 384-6112. **$49-$75.** 325 Fire Monument. Just w of jct I-35 and SR 48. Ext/int corridors. **Pets:** $5 daily fee/room. No service, supervision, crate.
[SAVE] [icons]

Holiday Inn Express M
(320) 384-7171. **$51-$79.** 604 Weber Ave. Just se of jct I-35 and SR 48. Int corridors. **Pets:** Small. $10 one-time fee/room. Supervision.
[ASK] [icons]

HUTCHINSON

Best Western Victorian Inn MI
(320) 587-6030. **$58-$82.** 1000 Hwy 7 W. 1 mi w of jct SR 15 on SR 7. Int corridors. **Pets:** Supervision.
[SAVE] [icons]

INTERNATIONAL FALLS

Hilltop Motel M
(218) 283-2505. **$35-$59.** 2002 2nd Ave W. US 53, 1 mi s of jct US 11 and 53. Ext corridors. **Pets:** Small, dogs only. $10 one-time fee/pet. No service, supervision, crate.
[ASK] [icons]

Holiday Inn MI
(218) 283-8000. **$84-$94, 3 days notice.** 1500 Hwy 71 W. 1.5 mi w on US 71 and SR 11 W. Int corridors. **Pets:** Other. Designated rooms, no service, supervision, crate.
[ASK] [icons]

Thunderbird Lodge X
(218) 286-3151. **$65-$89.** 2170 CR 139. 10.5 mi e on SR 11 from jct US 53, 0.3 mi n. Ext/int corridors. **Pets:** Supervision.
[SAVE] [icons]

JACKSON

Prairie Winds Budget Host Inn M
(507) 847-2020. **$29-$48.** 950 US 71. US 71, 0.4 mi s of jct I-90 and US 71, exit 73. Ext corridors. **Pets:** Other. $5 one-time fee/pet. Designated rooms, no service, supervision, crate.
[SAVE] [icons]

Super 8 of Jackson M
(507) 847-3498. **$54-$65, 7 days notice.** 2025 Hwy 71 N. Just n of jct I-90 and US Hwy 71 N, exit 73. Int corridors. **Pets:** $6 daily fee/pet. Designated rooms, no service, supervision, crate.
[ASK] [icons]

LITCHFIELD

⚑ ◆◆ ScotWood Motel **M** 🐾
(320) 693-2496. **$58-$89, 30 days notice.** 1017 E Frontage Rd. On US 12. Int corridors. **Pets:** Small. No service, supervision, crate.
SAVE 🔊 ✕ ⊟ 🖾

LITTLE FALLS

⚑ ◆◆◆ Country Inn & Suites By
Carlson **M** 🐾
(320) 632-1000. **$59-$69.** 209 16th St NE. Just ne of jct SR 10 and 27. Int corridors. **Pets:** Small. Designated rooms, no service, supervision, crate.
SAVE 🔊 ✕ ⅙ 🗲 ⊟ 🖳 🖾

LONG PRAIRIE

⚑ ◆◆ Budget Host Inn **M** 🐾
(320) 732-6118. **$40-$49, 3 days notice.** 417 Lake St. On US 71/SR 27, just s of jct SR 287. Ext corridors. **Pets:** Designated rooms, no service, supervision, crate.
SAVE 🔊 ✕ ⊟ 🖳

LUTSEN

⚑ ◆◆◆ The Mountain Inn at Lutsen **M** 🐾
(218) 663-7244. **$69-$129, 45 days notice.** Ski Hill Rd. CR 36, 1.3 mi n of jct SR 61, on road to Lutsen Mountain Ski Area. Int corridors. **Pets:** Other. $15 one-time fee/room. Designated rooms, supervision.
SAVE 🔊 ✕ ⊟ 🖾 CTV

⚑ ◆◆ Solbakken Resort **X** 🐾
(218) 663-7566. **$39-$230.** 4874 W Hwy 61. SR 61, 1.3 mi n of jct CR 4, Caribou Tr. Ext corridors. **Pets:** Other. $5 daily fee/pet. Designated rooms, no service, supervision, crate.
SAVE ✕ 🗲 ⊟ 🖳 🖾 🎾 CTV

MANKATO

◆◆◆ Comfort Inn of Mankato **M**
(507) 388-5107. **$59-$89.** 131 Apache Pl. Just s of jct US 14 and SR 22 S. Int corridors. **Pets:** Small. No service, supervision, crate.
ASK 🔊 ✕ 🗲 ⊟ 🖾

◆◆◆ Days Inn **M** 🐾
(507) 387-3332. **$50-$90.** 1285 Range St. US 169, 0.3 mi s of jct US 14. Int corridors. **Pets:** Other. $5 daily fee/room. Designated rooms, no service, supervision, crate.
ASK 🔊 ✕ ⅙ 🗲 ⊟ 🖳 🖾

◆◆◆ Econo Lodge **M** 🐾
(507) 345-8800. **Call for rates.** 111 W Lind Ct. US 169, 0.3 mi s of jct US 14. Int corridors. **Pets:** Other. Supervision.
✕ ⅙ 🗲 ⊟ 🖳

◆◆◆ Holiday Inn-Downtown **MI** 🐾
(507) 345-1234. **$105.** 101 E Main St. Main St at Riverfront Dr. Int corridors. **Pets:** Supervision.
ASK 🔊 ✕ ⅙ 🗲 🗲 ⊟ 🖳 🖾 ✕

MARSHALL

⚑ ◆◆◆ Best Western Marshall Inn **MI** 🐾
(507) 532-3221. **$64-$105.** 1500 E College Dr. SR 19, just w of jct SR 23. Int corridors. **Pets:** Dogs only. $25 deposit/room, $5 one-time fee/room. Designated rooms, no service, supervision, crate.
SAVE 🔊 ✕ ⊟ 🖳 🍽 🖾

◆◆◆ Comfort Inn **M** 🐾
(507) 532-3070. **$59-$77.** 1511 E College Dr. SR 19, w of jct SR 23. Int corridors. **Pets:** Other. No service, supervision, crate.
ASK 🔊 ✕ ⅙ 🗲 🗲 ⊟ 🖳 🖾

◆◆ Super 8 Motel **M** 🐾
(507) 537-1461. **$50-$60, 3 days notice.** 1106 E Main St. 0.3 mi se on US 59 from jct SR 23. Int corridors. **Pets:** Other. $50 deposit/room. No service, supervision, crate.
ASK 🔊 ✕ 🗲 ⊟

MCGREGOR

◆◆ Country Meadows Inn **M**
(218) 768-7378. **$60-$74.** PO Box 428. Jct SR 65 and 210. Int corridors. **Pets:** No service, supervision, crate.
✕ 🗲 ⊟ 🖳 🖾

MILACA

⚑ ◆◆ Super 8 Motel **M**
(320) 983-2660. **$52-$60.** 215 10th Ave SE. Jct of Hwys 23 and 169. Int corridors. **Pets:** Designated rooms, no service, supervision, crate.
SAVE 🔊 ✕ ⅙ 🗲 🖳 CTV

MINNEAPOLIS-ST. PAUL METROPOLITAN AREA

BLOOMINGTON

⚑ ◆◆◆ AmeriSuites **H** 🐾
(612) 854-0700. **$79-$149.** 7800 International Dr. Just sw of I-494, at 34th Ave exit. Int corridors. **Pets:** Very small. Designated rooms, no service, supervision, crate.
SAVE 🔊 ✕ ⅙ 🗲 ⊟ 🖳 🖾

◆◆ Baymont Inn **M**
(612) 881-7311. **$74-$90.** 7815 Nicollet Ave S. Just s of I-494, exit 4A (Nicollet Ave). Int corridors. **Pets:** Small. Designated rooms, no service, supervision, crate.
🔊 ✕ 🗲 ⊟ 🖳

♠♠♠ **Best Western Thunderbird Hotel** M ❄
(612) 854-3411. **$97-$180.** 2201 E 78th St. Just s of I-494, exit 2A (24th Ave). Int corridors. **Pets:** Designated rooms, no service, supervision, crate.

SAVE S❄ ✕ 🛅 🎧 🍴 🍽

♦♦♦ **Clarion Hotel Minneapolis** M
(612) 830-1300. **$99-$99.** 8151 Bridge Rd. Just se of jct I-494 and SR 100, exit France Ave from I-494, 1 mi w on frontage road. Int corridors. **Pets:** Supervision.

SAVE S❄ ✕ 🎧 🛅 🍽 🍴 🍽

♦♦ **Exel Inn of Minneapolis** M
(612) 854-7200. **$61-$85.** 2701 E 78th St. Just se of I-494, exit 2A (24th Ave). Int corridors. **Pets:** Small. Designated rooms, no service, supervision, crate.

S❄ ✕ 🎧 🛅 🍽

♦♦♦ **Hilton Minneapolis-St. Paul Airport** H ❄
(612) 854-2100. **$105-$105.** 3800 E 80th St. I-494, 34th Ave exit, just se. Int corridors. **Pets:** Small, dogs only. $25 deposit/pet. No service, supervision, crate.

ASK ✕ 🛅 🍽 🍴 🍽

♦♦♦♦ **Hotel Sofitel** H
(612) 835-1900. **$95-$125.** 5601 W 78th St. Just nw of jct I-494 and SR 100, access via SR 100 and Industrial Blvd. Int corridors. **Pets:** Designated rooms, no service, supervision, crate.

✕ 🎧 🛅 🍴

♦♦♦ **Minneapolis Airport Marriott** M ❄
(612) 854-7441. **$149-$149.** 2020 E 79th St. Just sw of I-494, exit 2A (24th Ave). Int corridors. **Pets:** Small. Supervision.

ASK S❄ ✕ 🎧 🛅 🍽 🍴 🍽

♠♠♠ **Radisson Hotel South & Plaza Tower** H
(612) 835-7800. **$159-$179.** 7800 Normandale Blvd. Jct I-494 and SR 100. Int corridors. **Pets:** Designated rooms, supervision.

SAVE S❄ ✕ 🎧 🛅 🍽 🍴 🍽

BROOKLYN CENTER

♦♦ **Baymont Inn & Suites-Minneapolis North** M
(612) 561-8400. **$74-$89.** 6415 James Cir N. Jct I-94/694 and Shingle Creek Pkwy, exit 34. Int corridors. **Pets:** Supervision.

S❄ ✕ 🎧 🛅 🍽

♠♠♠ **Hilton Minneapolis North** H ❄
(612) 566-8000. **$79-$79, 3 days notice.** 2200 Freeway Blvd. Jct I-94/694 and Shingle Creek Pkwy, exit 34. Int corridors. **Pets:** Small, other. $20 deposit/room. No service, supervision, crate.

SAVE ✕ 🎧 🛅 🍽 🍴 🍽 🍽

BROOKLYN PARK

♠♠ **Northwest Inn & Conference Center** M ❄
(612) 566-8855. **$79-$89, 3 days notice.** 6900 Lakeland Ave N. Jct of I-94 exit 31, on CR 81. Int corridors. **Pets:** Medium, other. $75 deposit/room, $50 one-time fee/ room. No service, supervision, crate.

SAVE S❄ ✕ 🎧 🛅 🍽 🍴 🍽 🍽

♠♠ **Sleep Inn** M ❄
(612) 971-8000. **$69-$109.** 7011 Northland Cir. I-94, exit 30 (Boone Ave). Int corridors. **Pets:** Medium, other. $50 deposit/room. Supervision.

SAVE S❄ ✕ 🎧 🍽 🍽 CTV

BURNSVILLE

♠♠♠ **Country Inn By Carlson** M ❄
(612) 892-1900. **$64-$74.** 14331 Nicollet Ct. 0.5 mi se of jct I-35 W and CR 42 off Nicollet Ave. Int corridors. **Pets:** $11 one-time fee/pet. Supervision.

SAVE S❄ ✕ 🎧 🛅 🍽

♦♦♦ **Hampton Inn** M ❄
(612) 435-6366. **Call for rates.** 14400 Nicollet Ct. 0.5 mi se of jct I-35 W and CR 42, off Nicollet Ave. Int corridors. **Pets:** Designated rooms, no service, supervision, crate.

✕ 🎧 🛅 🍽

♠♠ **Red Roof Inn-Burnsville** M ❄
(612) 890-1420. **$58-$68.** 12920 Aldrich Ave S. Just sw of I-35 W, exit 2 (Burnsville Pkwy). Ext corridors. **Pets:** No service, supervision, crate.

SAVE ✕ 🎧

♦♦ **Super 8 Motel** M ❄
(612) 894-3400. **Call for rates.** 1101 Burnsville Pkwy. Just w of I-35 W. Int corridors. **Pets:** Small, dogs only. $10 daily fee/room. No service, supervision, crate.

✕

CHISAGO CITY

♦♦ **Super 8 Motel-Chisago City/Lindstrom** M
(651) 257-8088. **Call for rates.** 11650 Lake Blvd. 1.3 mi ne on US 8. Int corridors. **Pets:** Large. No service, supervision, crate.

✕ 🛅

CLEARWATER

♦♦ **Budget Inn** M
(320) 558-2221. **Call for rates.** 945 SR 24. Just n of I-94, exit 178. Int corridors. **Pets:** Designated rooms, supervision.

✕ 🎧 🛅 CTV

COON RAPIDS

♠♠♠ **Country Suites By Carlson** M ❄
(612) 780-3797. **$90-$111.** 155 Coon Rapids Blvd. 0.5 mi e of SR 610. Int corridors. **Pets:** Medium, other. $100 deposit/ room, $3 daily fee/pet. No service, supervision, crate.

SAVE S❄ ✕ 🎧 🎧 🛅 🍽 🍽

🅐 ◆◆◆ Holiday Inn Express Hotel &
Suites M ❄
(612) 792-9292. **$85-$85.** 9333 Springbrook Dr. 0.5 mi e of
SR 610. Int corridors. **Pets:** Other. Supervision.
[SAVE] [S] [L] [C] [B] [P] [A]

EAGAN

◆◆◆ Holiday Inn Express Hotel & Suites
Eagan-Mall of America M ❄
(651) 681-9266. **$110-$110.** 1950 Rahncliff Ct. Jct I-35 E
and Cliff Rd, exit 93, just w on Cliff Rd, then just s. Int
corridors. **Pets:** Medium. $25 deposit/room, $10 daily fee/
pet. Designated rooms, no service, supervision, crate.
[ASK] [S] [X] [B] [P] [C] [B] [P] [A]

◆◆◆ Homestead Village Guest Studios M ❄
(651) 905-1778. **Call for rates.** 3015 Denmark Ave. Just se
of I-35 E, exit 98 (Lone Oak Rd). Int corridors. **Pets:** Small,
other. $75 one-time fee/room. No service, supervision,
crate.
[X] [P] [C] [B]

◆◆◆ Residence Inn by Marriott-Mpls/St. Paul
Airport A ❄
(651) 829-0033. **Call for rates.** 3040 Eagandale Pl. Just sw
of I-35 E, exit 98 (Lone Oak Rd); behind Lone Oak Plaza.
Ext corridors. **Pets:** Other. $5 daily fee/room, $100 one-time
fee/room. Supervision.
[X] [P] [P] [A] [X]

EDEN PRAIRIE

◆◆◆ Homestead Village Guest Studios M ❄
(612) 942-6818. **$72-$87.** 11905 Technology Dr. Just sw of
jct I-494 and US 212. Int corridors. **Pets:** $75 one-time
fee/room. Supervision.
[ASK] [X] [L] [C] [B] [P]

◆◆◆ The Residence Inn by Marriott-Minneapolis
SW A
(612) 829-0033. **$135-$135.** 7780 Flying Cloud Dr. On US
169 S and 212 (Flying Cloud Dr), at jct I-494. Int corridors.
Pets: Supervision.
[ASK] [S] [X] [B] [P] [A] [X]

EDINA

🅐 ◆◆◆ Hawthorn Suites Hotel H
(612) 893-9300. **$125-$125.** 3400 Edinborough Way. I-494,
France Ave exit, 0.3 mi n to Minnesota Dr, just e. Int corridors. **Pets:** Small. Designated rooms, no service, supervision, crate.
[SAVE] [X] [B] [P] [A]

ELK RIVER

◆◆ AmericInn Motel M ❄
(612) 441-8554. **$60-$120.** 17432 Hwy 10. 1.5 mi se on US
10/169. Int corridors. **Pets:** $100 deposit/room, $10 daily
fee/pet. No service, supervision, crate.
[ASK] [X] [C] [B] [P] [A]

FRIDLEY

◆◆◆ Best Western Kelly Inn MI
(612) 571-9440. **$79-$99.** 5201 Central Ave NE. 0.3 mi s of
I-694, exit 38 (Central Ave/SR 65). Ext/int corridors.
Pets: Very small. Supervision.
[ASK] [S] [X] [C] [B] [A]

INVER GROVE HEIGHTS

◆◆◆ AmericInn Hotel & Suites M ❄
(651) 450-7511. **Call for rates.** 5861 Blaine Ave E. Just se
of US 52 at Upper 55th St. Int corridors. **Pets:** Medium,
other. $100 deposit/room. No service, supervision, crate.
[ASK] [X] [L] [C] [B] [P] [A]

LAKEVILLE

◆◆◆ Comfort Inn M ❄
(612) 898-3700. **$80-$87, 7 days notice.** 10935 176th St
W. Just se of jct I-35 and SR 50 (exit 85). Int corridors.
Pets: $10 one-time fee/pet. Designated rooms, no service,
supervision, crate.
[ASK] [S] [X] [L] [C] [B] [P] [A]

◆◆ Friendly Host Inn-Lakeville M
(612) 435-7191. **$59-$79.** 17296 Kenrick Ave. On frontage
road at jct I-35 and SR 50 (exit 85). Ext/int corridors.
Pets: Small. Designated rooms, no service, supervision,
crate.
[ASK] [X] [B] [A] [X]

🅐 ◆◆ Super 8 Motel MI ❄
(612) 469-1134. **$58-$76.** 20800 Kenrick Ave. Just e of I-35
on CR 70. Int corridors. **Pets:** Other. No service, supervision, crate.
[SAVE] [S] [X] [C] [B] [T] [A]

MAPLEWOOD

🅐 ◆◆◆ Best Western Maplewood Inn MI ❄
(651) 770-2811. **$99-$129.** 1780 E CR D. I-694, exit 50, 0.5
mi sw (White Bear Ave), adjacent to nw corner of Maplewood Mall. Int corridors. **Pets:** $10 daily fee/pet. Designated
rooms, no service, supervision, crate.
[SAVE] [S] [X] [P] [B] [P] [T] [A]

MINNEAPOLIS

◆◆◆ Best Western Normandy Inn M ❄
(612) 370-1400. **$69-$109.** 405 S 8th St. S 8th St at S 4th
Ave. Int corridors. **Pets:** Very small. Supervision.
[X] [P] [A]

◆◆◆ Crowne Plaza Northstar Hotel H ❄
(612) 338-2288. **$89-$139.** 618 S 2nd Ave. S 2nd Ave at S
7th St. Int corridors. **Pets:** Large, other. $50 deposit/room.
Supervision.
[ASK] [S] [X] [P] [C] [B] [P] [T]

🅐 ◆◆◆◆ Hilton Minneapolis H
(612) 376-1000. **$125-$305.** 1001 Marquette Ave. Between
S 10th and S 11th St. Int corridors. **Pets:** Medium. No
service, supervision, crate.
[SAVE] [X] [P] [C] [B] [P] [T] [A]

(AAA) ◆◆◆ Holiday Inn Metrodome 🅷 🐾
(612) 333-4646. **$118-$159.** 1500 Washington Ave S. Washington at S 15th Ave. Int corridors. **Pets:** Other. $25 deposit/room, $25 one-time fee/room. No service, supervision, crate.

SAVE 🔟 ❌ 🗐 🎦 🔒 🔲 🍴 🕸

(AAA) ◆◆◆ Hyatt Whitney 🅷 🐾
(612) 339-9300. **$165-$190.** 150 Portland Ave. Portland Ave at 2nd St S. Int corridors. **Pets:** Supervision.

SAVE ❌ 🍴

(AAA) ◆◆◆◆ The Marquette Hotel 🅷 🐾
(612) 333-4545. **$79-$259.** 710 Marquette Ave. Marquette at S 7th St. Int corridors. **Pets:** Medium, other. $200 deposit/room. No service, supervision, crate.

SAVE ❌ 🎦 🔲 🍴

◆◆◆ Minneapolis Marriott City Center 🅷 🐾
(612) 349-4000. **Call for rates.** 30 S 7th St. Between Hennepin and Nicollet; in City Center shopping complex. Int corridors. **Pets:** $100 deposit/room. No service, supervision, crate.

❌ 🔒 🎦 🔒 🔲 🍴

(AAA) ◆◆◆ Radisson Hotel Metrodome 🅷 🐾
(612) 379-8888. **$129-$159.** 615 Washington Ave SE. 1 mi n of I-94, exit 235B U of M exit via Fulton, Oak St SE and Washington Ave SE. Int corridors. **Pets:** No service, supervision, crate.

SAVE 🔟 ❌ 🎦 🔒 🔲 🍴

(AAA) ◆◆◆◆ Radisson Plaza Hotel Minneapolis 🅷
(612) 339-4900. **$89-$239.** 35 S 7th St. Between Nicollet and Hennepin aves; in Radisson-Dayton shopping complex. Int corridors. **Pets:** Small. Supervision.

❌ 🔒 🎦 🔒 🔲 🍴

◆◆◆ Regal Minneapolis Hotel 🅷 🐾
(612) 332-6000. **$99-$199.** 1313 Nicollet Mall. Jct of Nicollet and Grant sts. Int corridors. **Pets:** Supervision.

ASK 🔟 ❌ 🔒 🔒 🔲 🍴 🕸

MINNETONKA

◆◆◆ Minneapolis Marriott-Southwest 🅷
(612) 935-5500. **Call for rates.** 5801 Opus Pkwy. Just nw of jct Cross Town Hwy 62 and US 169, Bren Rd exit off US 169. Int corridors. **Pets:** Supervision.

ASK ❌ 🎦 🔒 🔲 🕸

◆◆◆ Ramada Plaza Hotel Minneapolis 🅼
(612) 593-0000. **$124-$124.** 12201 Ridgedale Dr. 0.3 mi s of I-394, exit 1C (Ridgedale Dr). Int corridors. **Pets:** Designated rooms, no service, supervision, crate.

ASK 🔟 ❌ 🔒 🔲 🍴 🕸

MONTICELLO

◆◆ Best Western Silver Fox Inn 🅼
(612) 295-4000. **$59-$120.** 1114 Cedar St. 0.3 mi se of I-94, exit 193. Int corridors. **Pets:** Small. No service, supervision, crate.

ASK 🔟 ❌ 🔒 🍴 🕸 📺

(AAA) ◆◆◆ Days Inn 🅼 🐾
(612) 295-1111. **$55-$95.** 200 E Oakwood Dr. 0.3 mi se of I-94, exit 193. Int corridors. **Pets:** $5 daily fee/pet, $5 one-time fee/pet. Designated rooms, no service, supervision, crate.

SAVE 🔟 ❌ 🔒 🔲

PLYMOUTH

(AAA) ◆◆◆ Best Western Kelly Inn 🅼 🐾
(612) 553-1600. **$79-$94.** 2705 N Annapolis Ln. Just e of I-494, exit 22 (SR 55). Int corridors. **Pets:** Other. $20 deposit/room. Designated rooms, supervision.

SAVE 🔟 ❌ 🔒 🔒 🔲 🍴 🕸

◆◆◆ Radisson Hotel & Conference Center 🅷 🐾
(612) 559-6600. **$79-$119.** 3131 Campus Dr. 0.8 mi nw of jct SR 55 and CR 61. Int corridors. **Pets:** $50 deposit/room. Designated rooms, supervision.

ASK ❌ 🎦 🔒 🔲 🍴 🕸 ❌

(AAA) ◆◆ Red Roof Inn 🅼 🐾
(612) 553-1751. **$50-$66.** 2600 Annapolis Ln N. Just e of I-494, exit 22, SR 55. Ext corridors. **Pets:** Other. Designated rooms, supervision.

SAVE ❌

RICHFIELD

◆◆◆ Candlewood Suites 🅼 🐾
(612) 869-7704. **$59-$120.** 351 W 77th St. Just ne of I-495, exit Lyndale Ave. Int corridors. **Pets:** Other. Supervision.

ASK 🔟 ❌ 🔒 🎦 🔒

ROGERS

◆◆ AmericInn Motel 🅼 🐾
(612) 428-4346. **$56-$115.** 21800 Industrial Blvd. At jct SR 101 and I-94, exit 207. Int corridors. **Pets:** Medium. $6 daily fee/room. Designated rooms, no service, supervision, crate.

ASK 🔟 ❌ 🔒 🔒 🕸 📺

SAVAGE

◆◆ Comfort Inn 🅼 🐾
(612) 894-6124. **Call for rates.** 4601 SR 13 W. Just e on SR 13 at CR 31. Int corridors. **Pets:** Medium, other. $25 deposit/room, $25 one-time fee/room. Designated rooms, supervision.

❌ 🔒 🕸

ST. LOUIS PARK

(AAA) ◆ Lakeland Motel 🅼 🐾
(612) 926-6575. **$50-$65.** 4025 Hwy 7. On SR 7, 0.5 mi e of SR 100. Int corridors. **Pets:** $10 deposit/pet, $5 daily fee/pet, $5 one-time fee/pet. Designated rooms, supervision.

🔟 ❌ 🔒

ST. PAUL

AAA ◆◆◆ **Best Western Kelly Inn-State Capitol** Ⓜ ❄
(651) 227-8711. **$94-$114.** 161 St. Anthony Ave. At jct I-35 E and I-94; near state capitol. Int corridors. **Pets:** No service, supervision, crate.

ⓈⒶⓋⒺ 🅢🄳 ⊠ 🄺 🄱 🄷 ⌘

AAA ◆◆ **Exel Inn of St. Paul** Ⓜ
(651) 771-5566. **$52-$84.** 1739 Old Hudson Rd. Just nw of I-94, exit White Bear Ave. Int corridors. **Pets:** Medium. No service, supervision, crate.

🅢🄳 ⊠ 🄐 🄱 🄾

◆◆ **Holiday Inn RiverCentre** Ⓜ ❄
(651) 292-8929. **$97-$97.** 175 W 7th St. Jct Kellogg Blvd and 7th St, across from St. Paul Civic Center. Int corridors. **Pets:** Small. $100 deposit/room. Designated rooms, no service, supervision, crate.

🄰🅂🄺 🅢🄳 ⊠ 🄐 🄱 🄾 🄲🅃🅅

◆◆◆ **Holiday Inn St. Paul East-3M Area** Ⓜ❄
(651) 731-2220. **$85-$125.** 2201 Burns Ave. Just sw of I-94, exit McNight Rd. Int corridors. **Pets:** Small. Designated rooms, no service, supervision, crate.

🄰🅂🄺 🅢🄳 ⊠ 🄐 🄱 🄾 🄷 ⌘

AAA ◆◆ **Ramada Inn & Conference Center** Ⓜ
(651) 735-2333. **$74-$74.** 1870 Old Hudson Rd. Just ne of I-94, White Bear Ave exit. Int corridors. **Pets:** Medium. Designated rooms, no service, supervision, crate.

ⓈⒶⓋⒺ 🅢🄳 ⊠ 🄱 🄾 🄷 ⌘

AAA ◆◆ **Travelodge** Ⓜ ❄
(651) 735-2337. **$71-$71.** 1870 Old Hudson Rd. Just ne of I-94, White Bear Ave exit. Int corridors. **Pets:** Very small, dogs only. $25 deposit/room. Designated rooms, no service, supervision, crate.

ⓈⒶⓋⒺ 🅢🄳 ⊠ 🄾 🄷 ⌘

STILLWATER

AAA ◆◆◆ **Best Western Stillwater Inn** Ⓜ
(651) 430-1300. **$58-$79.** 1750 Frontage Rd W. 3 mi sw on SR 36 at Washington Ave. Int corridors. **Pets:** No service, supervision, crate.

ⓈⒶⓋⒺ 🅢🄳 ⊠ 🄺 🄱

TAYLORS FALLS

AAA ◆◆ **The Springs Country Inn** Ⓜ ❄
(651) 465-6565. **$45-$95, 5 days notice.** 361 Government St. Just w of jct US 8 and SR 95. Ext corridors. **Pets:** Other. $7 one-time fee/room. Designated rooms, supervision.

ⓈⒶⓋⒺ 🅢🄳 ⊠ 🄱

WOODBURY

◆◆◆ **Hampton Inn** Ⓜ
(651) 578-2822. **$69-$99.** 1450 Weir Dr. Just nw of I-494, exit 59 (Valley Creek Rd). Int corridors. **Pets:** Medium. Designated rooms, no service, supervision, crate.

🄰🅂🄺 🅢🄳 ⊠ 🄻 🄐 🄺 🄱 🄾 ⌘

AAA ◆◆ **Red Roof Inn** Ⓜ ❄
(651) 738-7160. **$60-$76.** 1806 Wooddale Dr. Just se of I-494, exit 59 (Valley Creek Rd). Ext corridors. **Pets:** Other. Supervision.

ⓈⒶⓋⒺ ⊠ 🄐

❄ **END METROPOLITAN AREA** ❄

MONTEVIDEO

◆◆◆ **Country Inn & Suites By Carlson** Ⓜ ❄
(320) 269-8000. **$63-$81.** 1805 E SR 7. On SR 7. Int corridors. **Pets:** Other. $200 deposit/room. No service, supervision, crate.

🄰🅂🄺 🅢🄳 ⊠ 🄱 🄾 ⌘

MOORHEAD

◆◆ **Best Western Red River Inn & Conference Center** Ⓜ
(218) 233-6171. **$54-$62.** 600 30th Ave S. Sw jct of I-94 and US 75, exit 1A. Int corridors. **Pets:** No service, supervision, crate.

🄰🅂🄺 🅢🄳 ⊠ 🄷 ⌘

AAA ◆◆ **Motel 75** Ⓜ ❄
(218) 233-7501. **$35-$48.** 810 Belsly Blvd. 0.5 mi s on US 75 from jct I-94, exit 1A. Int corridors. **Pets:** Designated rooms, supervision.

ⓈⒶⓋⒺ 🅢🄳 ⊠

MORA

◆◆◆ **AmericInn Motel & Suites** Ⓜ ❄
(320) 679-5700. **$62-$112, 7 days notice.** 1877 Frontage Rd. Just s on SR 65. Int corridors. **Pets:** Dogs only. $50 deposit/room, $10 daily fee/pet, $10 one-time fee/room. Designated rooms, no service, supervision, crate.

⊠ 🄵 🄺 🄱 🄾 ⌘

AAA ◆◆ **Ann River Swedish Motel** Ⓜ
(320) 679-2972. **$31-$60.** 1819 S Hwy 65. 0.3 mi s on SR 65 from jct 23 W. Ext corridors. **Pets:** Designated rooms, no service, supervision, crate.

ⓈⒶⓋⒺ 🅢🄳 ⊠ 🄱 🄾

◆◆ **Motel Mora** Ⓜ ❄
(320) 679-3262. **$32-$44.** 301 SR 65 S. Just s on SR 65 from jct SR 23 E. Ext corridors. **Pets:** Medium. $5 daily fee/room. No service, supervision, crate.

⊠ 🄱

MORRIS

AAA ◆◆ **Best Western Prairie Inn** Ⓜ
(320) 589-3030. **$36-$76.** 200 SR 28 E. Just sw of jct US 59 and SR 28. Int corridors. **Pets:** Medium. Supervision.
[SAVE] [S🐾] [✕] [📶] [❚❘] [🛍]

NEW ULM

◆◆◆ **Holiday Inn** Ⓜ ❀
(507) 359-2941. **$94-$144.** 2101 S Broadway. 1.8 mi se on SR 15/68. Int corridors. **Pets:** Small, other. Designated rooms, no service, supervision, crate.
[✕] [📶] [💻] [🛍]

◆◆ **Super 8 Motel-New Ulm** Ⓜ
(507) 359-2400. **$48-$72.** 1901 S Broadway. 1.5 mi se on SR 15/68 at jct 20th St S. Int corridors. **Pets:** Designated rooms, supervision.
[ASK] [S🐾] [✕] [👶] [🐾] [📶]

NISSWA

◆◆ **Days Inn** Ⓜ ❀
(218) 963-3500. **$63-$96.** 45 N Smiley Rd. SR 371, 1.5 mi s of jct CR 18, at n jct CR 77. Int corridors. **Pets:** $25 deposit/pet. No service, supervision, crate.
[ASK] [S🐾] [✕] [👶] [📶] [🛍]

◆ **Nisswa Motel** Ⓜ ❀
(218) 963-7611. **$61-$75, 4 days notice.** 1426 Merrill Ave. Center; just s of Main St. Ext corridors. **Pets:** Medium, dogs only. $3 one-time fee/pet. Designated rooms, supervision.
[ASK] [✕] [📶] [💻]

OLIVIA

◆◆ **The Sheep Shedde Inn** Ⓜ ❀
(320) 523-5000. **$50-$65.** 2425 W Lincoln Ave. Just e of jct US 71 and 212. Int corridors. **Pets:** Dogs only. $10 one-time fee/room. No service, supervision, crate.
[✕] [📶] [💻] [❚❘]

ONAMIA

◆◆ **Econo Lodge of Mille Lacs Lake** Ⓜ
(320) 532-3838. **Call for rates.** 40993 US 169. 6 mi n on US 169. Int corridors. **Pets:** No service, supervision, crate.
[✕] [👶] [📶] [✕]

◆◆◆ **Eddy's Lake Mille Lacs Resort** Ⓜ
(320) 532-3657. **$69-$79.** 41334 Shakopee Lake Rd. 6 mi n on US 169 at jct SR 26 (Shakopee Lake Rd). Int corridors. **Pets:** Medium. Designated rooms, no service, supervision, crate.
[ASK] [S🐾] [✕] [👶] [📶] [💻] [❚❘] [🛍] [✕] [CTV]

ORR

◆◆ **North Country Inn** Ⓜ ❀
(218) 757-3778. **$46-$55.** 4483 Hwy 53. 0.3 mi s. Int corridors. **Pets:** Other. $11 one-time fee/pet. No service, supervision, crate.
[✕] [👶] [CTV]

OWATONNA

◆◆ **Budget Host Inn** Ⓜ
(507) 451-8712. **$40-$59.** 745 State Ave. 0.3 mi e of I-35, exit 42A. Ext corridors. **Pets:** Small. No service, supervision, crate.
[ASK] [S🐾] [✕] [📶]

◆◆◆ **Country Inn & Suites By Carlson** Ⓜ ❀
(507) 455-9295. **$69-$99.** 130 Allen Ave SW. Just se of I-35, exit 41 (Bridge St). Int corridors. **Pets:** Small, other. $10 daily fee/room. Designated rooms, no service, supervision, crate.
[ASK] [S🐾] [✕] [👶] [🐾] [👶] [📶] [💻] [🛍]

AAA ◆◆ **Oakdale Motel** Ⓜ ❀
(507) 451-5480. **$30-$69, 7 days notice.** 1418 S Oak Ave. I-35, exit 40, 1 mi e on US 14 and 218, then 0.5 mi n on CR 45. Ext corridors. **Pets:** $50 deposit/pet, $10 one-time fee/pet. Designated rooms, no service, supervision, crate.
[SAVE] [S🐾] [✕] [📶]

◆◆ **Ramada Inn** Ⓜ ❀
(507) 455-0606. **$54-$74, 7 days notice.** 1212 N I-35. 0.3 mi nw I-35, exit 42B. Int corridors. **Pets:** Other. Supervision.
[ASK] [S🐾] [✕] [📶] [❚❘] [🛍]

PINE RIVER

◆◆ **Travelodge** Ⓜ ❀
(218) 587-4499. **$74-$79.** 2684 SR 371 SW. 1 mi s. Ext corridors. **Pets:** No service, supervision, crate.
[ASK] [S🐾] [✕] [💻]

PRINCETON

◆◆ **Rum River Motel** Ⓜ ❀
(612) 389-3120. **$36-$45.** 510 19th Ave N. Just w of jct US 169 and SR 95. Int corridors. **Pets:** Small, dogs only. Supervision.
[✕] [📶] [CTV]

RED WING

AAA ◆◆◆ **Best Western Quiet House & Suites** Ⓜ
(651) 388-1577. **$96-$179.** 752 Withers Harbor Dr. 1.5 mi n on US 61, at Withers Harbour Dr, opposite side of US 61 from Pottery Mall. Ext/int corridors. **Pets:** Small. Designated rooms, no service, supervision, crate.
[SAVE] [S🐾] [✕] [👶] [👶] [📶] [🛍]

◆◆◆ **Days Inn** Ⓜ ❀
(651) 388-3568. **$40-$85.** 955 E 7th St. 1.7 mi se on US 61/63. Ext corridors. **Pets:** Other. $7 daily fee/pet. Designated rooms, supervision.
[ASK] [S🐾] [✕] [📶] [💻] [🛍]

◆◆ **Super 8 Motel** Ⓜ
(651) 388-0491. **$42-$89.** 232 Withers Harbor Dr. 1.5 mi nw on US 61, exit Withers Harbor Dr. Int corridors. **Pets:** Designated rooms, no service, supervision, crate.
[ASK] [S🐾] [✕] [👶] [👶] [📶] [🛍] [CTV]

ROCHESTER

◆◆◆ **Country Inn & Suites By Carlson** Ⓜ
(507) 285-3335. **$79-$109.** 4323 US Hwy 52. US Hwy 52, 41st St NW exit. Int corridors. **Pets:** Small. Designated rooms, no service, supervision, crate.
🅰🆂🅺 🆂🔟 ⊠ 🔗 🔧 ⬛ 💻 🐾

◆◆ **Days Inn-South** Ⓜ
(507) 286-1001. **$44-$59.** 111 28th St SE. 0.5 mi n of jct US 52 and US 63 (Broadway). Int corridors. **Pets:** Medium. No service, supervision, crate.
🅰🆂🅺 🆂🔟 ⊠ 🔗 🔧

🅐🅐🅐 ◆◆ **Daystop** Ⓜ 🐾
(507) 282-2733. **$36-$65.** 11 17th Ave SW. Just nw of US 52, exit 2nd St SW. Ext/int corridors. **Pets:** Small, other. Supervision.
🆂🅰🆅🅴 🆂🔟 ⊠ 🔧 🔧

◆◆ **Econo Lodge** Ⓜ 🐾
(507) 288-1855. **$44-$59.** 519 3rd Ave SW. Just s of Mayo Clinic, 3rd Ave SW at 5th St SW. Ext corridors. **Pets:** Small. Designated rooms, supervision.
🅰🆂🅺 🆂🔟 ⊠ 💻

◆◆ **Econo Lodge-South** Ⓜ
(507) 282-9905. **$44-$59.** 1850 S Broadway. 1 mi s of jct US 14 and US 63 (Broadway). Int corridors. **Pets:** Designated rooms, no service, supervision, crate.
🅰🆂🅺 🆂🔟 ⊠ 🔧 🔧 💻

🅐🅐🅐 ◆◆ **Executive Suites Hotel and Economy Inn by Kahler** Ⓜ 🐾
(507) 289-8646. **$80-$80.** 9 NW 3rd Ave. Just n of Mayo Clinic; across from Methodist Hospital. Int corridors. **Pets:** Designated rooms, no service, supervision, crate.
⊠ 🔗 🔧 🔧 ⬛ 💻 🍴 🐾

◆◆◆ **Holiday Inn South** Ⓜ
(507) 288-1844. **$69-$99.** 1630 S Broadway. On US 63 (Broadway), 0.5 mi s of jct US 14. Ext/int corridors. **Pets:** Small. Designated rooms, supervision.
🅰🆂🅺 🆂🔟 ⊠ 🔧 🔧 ⬛ 🍴 🐾

🅐🅐🅐 ◆◆◆ **The Kahler Grand Hotel** 🅷 🐾
(507) 282-2581. **$99-$99.** 20 2nd Ave SW. Opposite Mayo Clinic and Methodist Hospital. Int corridors. **Pets:** Medium, other. Designated rooms, no service, supervision, crate.
🆂🔟 ⊠ 🔗 🔧 🔧 ⬛ 💻 🍴 🐾

🅐🅐🅐 ◆◆◆ **Marriott Hotel** 🅷
(507) 280-6000. **$189-$199.** 101 1st Ave SW. Just e of Mayo Clinic. Int corridors. **Pets:** No service, supervision, crate.
⊠ 🔗 🔧 🔧 ⬛ 💻 🍴 🐾

◆◆ **Microtel Inn and Suites** Ⓜ 🐾
(507) 286-8780. **$46-$73.** 4210 Hwy 52N. SR 52, 41st St NW. Int corridors. **Pets:** Other. $5 daily fee/room. No service, supervision, crate.
🅰🆂🅺 ⊠ 🔧 🔗 🔧 🔧 💻

🅐🅐🅐 ◆◆◆ **Quality Inn & Suites** Ⓜ 🐾
(507) 282-8091. **$89-$89.** 1620 1st Ave SE. On US 63 (Broadway), 0.5 mi s of jct US 14. Ext/int corridors. **Pets:** Other. $5 daily fee/pet. Designated rooms, no service, supervision, crate.
🆂🅰🆅🅴 🆂🔟 ⊠ 💻

🅐🅐🅐 ◆◆◆◆ **Radisson Plaza Hotel** 🅷 🐾
(507) 281-8000. **$109-$109.** 150 S Broadway. On US 63. Int corridors. **Pets:** No service, supervision, crate.
🆂🅰🆅🅴 ⊠ 🔗 🔧 ⬛ 💻 🍴 🐾

◆◆ **Ramada Limited** Ⓜ 🐾
(507) 288-9090. **$69-$99, 3 days notice.** 435 16th Ave NW. Just se of jct US 14 and 52, Civic Center Dr exit. Int corridors. **Pets:** Medium, other. Designated rooms, no service, supervision, crate.
🅰🆂🅺 🆂🔟 ⊠ 🔧 🔧 ⬛ 💻 🐾

◆◆ **Super 8 Motel-South** Ⓜ
(507) 288-8288. **$49-$69.** 1230 S Broadway. Jct of US 63 and 14. Int corridors. **Pets:** Designated rooms, supervision.
🅰🆂🅺 🆂🔟 ⊠ 🔗 🔧 🔧 💻 🐾

◆◆ **Super 8 Motel-West** Ⓜ
(507) 281-5100. **$44-$69.** 1608 2nd St SW. Just e of US 52, exit 2nd St SW, just w of St Mary's Hospital. Int corridors. **Pets:** Small. Supervision.
🅰🆂🅺 🆂🔟 ⊠ 🔧 🔧

◆◆ **Travelodge Downtown** Ⓜ
(507) 289-4095. **$44-$69.** 426 2nd St SW. Just w of Mayo Clinic. Int corridors. **Pets:** Medium. No service, supervision, crate.
🅰🆂🅺 🆂🔟 ⊠ 🔗 🔧 💻

ROSEAU

◆◆ **AmericInn** Ⓜ
(218) 463-1045. **$49-$62.** 1090 3rd St NW. 1 mi w on SR 11. Int corridors. **Pets:** Designated rooms, supervision.
🆂🔟 ⊠ 🔧 🔗 🔧 🐾 ⊠

◆◆◆ **North Country Inn** Ⓜ 🐾
(218) 463-9444. **$48-$68, 3 days notice.** 902 3rd St NW. 0.8 mi w on SR 11. Int corridors. **Pets:** $50 deposit/room, $25 one-time fee/room. No service, supervision, crate.
🅰🆂🅺 🆂🔟 ⊠ 🔗 🔧 🐾

SAUK CENTRE

🅐🅐🅐 ◆◆◆ **AmericInn Motel & Suites** Ⓜ 🐾
(320) 352-2800. **$50-$103.** 1230 Timberlane Dr. Just ne of I-94. Int corridors. **Pets:** $50 deposit/room. Designated rooms, no service, supervision, crate.
🆂🅰🆅🅴 ⊠ 🔗 🔧 🐾

◆ **Hillcrest Motel** Ⓜ
(320) 352-2215. **$24-$32.** 965 S Main St. 0.5 mi n of I-94, exit 127, on SR 71. Ext/int corridors. **Pets:** Medium. No service, supervision, crate.
⊠ 💻

SILVER BAY

🅐🅐🅐 ◆◆ **Mariner Motel** Ⓜ 🐾
(218) 226-4488. **$40-$70, 3 days notice.** 46 Outer Dr. Just w off SR 61, at traffic signal. Ext corridors. **Pets:** Dogs only. Designated rooms, no service, supervision, crate.
🆂🅰🆅🅴 ⊠ 🔧 🔧 💻 🆇

SLEEPY EYE

◆◆◆ Best Western Inn of Seven Gables **M**
(507) 794-5390. **$59-$76.** 1100 E Main St. US 14, 0.8 mi e of jct CR 4 and US 14. Int corridors. **Pets:** No service, supervision, crate.
S **X** **H** **≈**

ST. CLOUD

◆◆◆ AmericInn Motel & Suites **M**
(320) 253-6337. **$79-$89.** 4385 Clearwater Rd. Just ne of I-94, exit 171 (CR 75). Int corridors. **Pets:** Medium. Designated rooms, no service, supervision, crate.
ASK **S** **X** **f** **G** **H** **■** **≈**

◆◆◆ Best Western Americanna Inn & Conference Center **M** 🐾
(320) 252-8700. **$50-$121.** 520 S US Hwy 10. 0.3 mi s on US 10 from jct SR 23. Ext/int corridors. **Pets:** Medium, other. $10 daily fee/pet. Designated rooms, supervision.
SAVE **S** **X** **f** **G** **H** **■** **¶¶** **≈**

◆◆◆ Best Western Kelly Inn **M** 🐾
(320) 253-0606. **$64-$109.** 1 Sunwood Dr. Center; SR 23 at 4th Ave S. Int corridors. **Pets:** Other. No service, supervision, crate.
SAVE **S** **X** **f** **G** **H** **■** **¶¶** **≈**

◆◆ Days Inn **M**
(320) 253-0500. **$49-$79.** 420 SE US 10. 0.3 mi s on US 10, e on frontage road, from jct SR 23. Int corridors. **Pets:** Small. No service, supervision, crate.
SAVE **S** **X** **≈**

◆◆◆ Holiday Inn Express **M** 🐾
(320) 240-8000. **$54-$72.** 4322 Clearwater Rd. Just ne of I-94, exit 171 (CR 75). Int corridors. **Pets:** Other. No service, supervision, crate.
ASK **S** **X** **&** **f** **G** **H** **■** **≈**

◆◆◆ Holiday Inn Hotel & Suites **M** 🐾
(320) 253-9000. **$70-$200.** 75 37th Ave S. At jct SR 15 and 23. Int corridors. **Pets:** Small, other. No service, supervision, crate.
ASK **S** **X** **f** **H** **■** **¶¶** **≈** **X**

◆◆ Quality Inn **M** 🐾
(320) 253-4444. **$49-$149.** 70 S 37th Ave. Just e of jct SR 15 and 23. Int corridors. **Pets:** $50 deposit/room. Designated rooms, supervision.
SAVE **S** **X** **f** **f** **G** **H** **■**

◆◆◆ Ramada Limited & Suites **M** 🐾
(320) 253-3200. **$60-$80.** 121 Park Ave S. Just w of jct SR 15 and 23. Int corridors. **Pets:** Small, dogs only. Designated rooms, no service, supervision, crate.
ASK **S** **X** **&** **f** **H** **■** **≈**

◆ Thrifty Motel **M**
(320) 253-6320. **$32-$38.** 130 14th Ave NE. 0.3 mi e of jct US 10 and SR 23. Int corridors. **Pets:** Supervision.
X **G** **H**

◆◆ Travelodge **M** 🐾
(320) 253-3338. **$50-$67, 5 days notice.** 3820 Roosevelt Rd. 1 mi n of I-94, exit 171 (CR 75). Int corridors. **Pets:** Large, other. Supervision.
SAVE **S** **X** **G** **H** **■**

STAPLES

◆◆ Super 8 Motel **M**
(218) 894-3585. **$38-$57.** 109 2nd Ave W. US 10, 0.5 mi w of jct SR 210S. Int corridors. **Pets:** Small. No service, supervision, crate.
ASK **S** **X**

THIEF RIVER FALLS

◆◆ Best Western Inn of Thief River Falls **M** 🐾
(218) 681-7555. **$54-$69.** 1060 Hwy 32 S. 1 mi s on SR 32. Int corridors. **Pets:** Medium. $75 deposit/room. No service, supervision, crate.
SAVE **S** **X** **H** **■** **¶¶** **≈**

◆◆◆ C'mon Inn **M**
(218) 681-3000. **$49-$69.** 1586 Hwy 59 SE. 1 mi se on US 59. Int corridors. **Pets:** Medium. Supervision.
ASK **S** **X** **H** **≈**

◆ Hartwood Motel **M** 🐾
(218) 681-2640. **$29-$40.** 1010 N Main Ave. 0.5 mi n on SR 32, from jct US 59. Ext/int corridors. **Pets:** Other. Designated rooms, no service, supervision, crate.
SAVE **X** **■**

◆◆ Super 8 Motel **M** 🐾
(218) 681-6205. **Call for rates.** 1915 Hwy 59 SE. 2 mi se on US 59. Int corridors. **Pets:** $25 deposit/room. No service, supervision, crate.
X

TOFTE

◆◆◆ AmericInn-Motel & Suites **M** 🐾
(218) 663-7899. **$79-$165, 7 days notice.** 7261 W Hwy 61. On Hwy 61. Int corridors. **Pets:** Other. $10 one-time fee/room. Designated rooms, no service, supervision, crate.
SAVE **S** **X** **G** **H** **≈** **CTV**

◆◆◆ Best Western Cliff Dweller Motel **M** 🐾
(218) 663-7273. **$70-$100, 3 days notice.** 6452 W Hwy 61. Between Tofte and Lutsen on SR 61, 0.3 mi n of MM 86. Ext corridors. **Pets:** Other. $25 one-time fee/room. Designated rooms, no service, supervision, crate.
ASK **S** **X** **G** **AC** **CTV**

◆◆◆ Bluefin Bay on Lake Superior **C** 🐾
(218) 663-7296. **$95-$495, 7 days notice.** SR 61. Ext corridors. **Pets:** Other. $12 one-time fee/room. Designated rooms, no service, supervision, crate.
X **H** **■** **¶¶** **≈** **X** **AC**

TWO HARBORS

◆◆◆ AmericInn Lodge and Suites **M** 🐾
(218) 834-3000. **$77-$136, 3 days notice.** 1088 Hwy 61. 0.7 mi s, on SR 61. Int corridors. **Pets:** Other. Supervision.
ASK **S** **X** **&** **G** **H** **■** **≈** **X**

◆◆◆ Country Inn By Carlson **M** 🐾
(218) 834-5557. **$54-$129, 7 days notice.** 1204 7th Ave. On SR 61, 0.5 mi s of Center. Int corridors. **Pets:** Small. Supervision.
ASK **S** **X** **f** **f** **H** **■** **≈**

◆◆◆ Superior Shores Resort ⊠ ❀
(218) 834-5671. **$119.** 1521 Superior Shores Dr. 1.5 mi n on SR 61. Ext/int corridors. **Pets:** Other. $25 deposit/room. Designated rooms, no service, supervision, crate.
🏠⊠🛅🖳🛏🍴🐾⊠

VIRGINIA

◆◆◆ AmericInn Motel & Suites Ⓜ
(218) 741-7839. **$67-$75.** 5480 18th Ave W. On US 53, just s of jct US 169. Int corridors. **Pets:** Small. Designated rooms, supervision.
⊠🏠🖉🛅🖳🛏

◆ Lakeshor Motor Inn Downtown Ⓜ ❀
(218) 741-3360. **$39-$62.** 404 N 6th Ave. Center; just n of Chestnut St. Ext corridors. **Pets:** Supervision.
🏠⊠🛅🖳

◆ Ski-View Motel Ⓜ
(218) 741-8918. **$30-$44.** 903 N 17th St N. 0.5 mi n on Hwy 53; from jct US 53 and 169, 0.5 mi e on 9th St N, just n on 9th Ave W. Ext/int corridors. **Pets:** Supervision.
⊠🖳

WARROAD

◆◆ Can-Am Motel Ⓜ
(218) 386-3807. **$38-$69.** 406 Main Ave NE. 1 mi w on SR 11, on the n side of railway tracks. Int corridors. **Pets:** No service, supervision, crate.
🅰🏠⊠

◆◆ The Patch Motel Ⓜ
(218) 386-2723. **$38-$69.** Hwy 11 W. 1 mi w on SR 11. Int corridors. **Pets:** Medium. No service, supervision, crate.
🅰🏠⊠🖉🛏

WILLMAR

◆◆◆ Comfort Inn Ⓜ ❀
(320) 231-2601. **$72-$99.** 2200 E US 12. 1.8 mi e on US 12. Int corridors. **Pets:** Designated rooms, no service, supervision, crate.
🅰🏠⊠🖉🛅🛏

◆◆ Days Inn-Willmar Ⓜ ❀
(320) 231-1275. **$51-$81.** 225 28th St SE. 2.3 mi e on US 12. Int corridors. **Pets:** Designated rooms, no service, supervision, crate.
🅰🏠⊠🖉🖳

**◆◆◆ Holiday Inn & Willmar Conference
   Center** Ⓜ ❀
(320) 235-6060. **$92-$109.** 2100 US 12E. 1.8 mi e on US 12. Int corridors. **Pets:** Designated rooms, no service, supervision, crate.
🅰🏠⊠🖉🖳🍴🛏

WINDOM

◆◆ Super 8 of Windom Ⓜ ❀
(507) 831-1120. **$40-$59.** 222 3rd Ave S. Just n of jct US 71 and SR 60. Int corridors. **Pets:** Other. $6 one-time fee/pet. Designated rooms, supervision.
🅰🏠⊠🛅🖳

WINONA

**◆◆◆ Best Western Riverport Inn &
   Suites** Ⓜ ❀
(507) 452-0606. **$59-$89.** 900 Bruski Dr. Jct US 14/61 and SR 43. Int corridors. **Pets:** Small, other. $11 daily fee/pet. Designated rooms, no service, supervision, crate.
🅰🏠⊠🛅🖳🍴🛏

◆◆ Quality Inn Ⓜ
(507) 454-4390. **$69-$90.** 956 Mankato Ave. Jct US 14/61 and SR 43. Ext/int corridors. **Pets:** Medium. Designated rooms, no service, supervision, crate.
🆂🅰🆅🏠⊠🛅🖳🍴🛏

◆◆ Super 8 Motel Ⓜ ❀
(507) 454-6066. **Call for rates.** 1025 Sugar Loaf Rd. Jct US 14/61 and SR 43. Int corridors. **Pets:** Medium. $10 daily fee/pet, $10 one-time fee/pet. Designated rooms, supervision.
⊠

WORTHINGTON

◆◆◆ AmericInn Motel Ⓜ ❀
(507) 376-4500. **Call for rates.** 1475 Darling Dr. Jct US 59 and I-90, exit 43, just s. Int corridors. **Pets:** Other. Designated rooms, no service, supervision, crate.
⊠🏠🖉🖉🛅🖳🛏

◆◆ Best Western Worthington Motel Ⓜ
(507) 376-4146. **$55-$60.** 1923 Dover St. 0.5 mi s of I-90, exit 45, at jct US 59 and SR 60. Ext/int corridors. **Pets:** Designated rooms, no service, supervision, crate.
🆂🅰🏠⊠🛅⊠

◆◆ Days Inn Ⓜ ❀
(507) 376-6155. **$54-$79.** 207 Oxford St. On SR 266, 1 mi se of I-90, exit 42 and SR 266. Ext/int corridors. **Pets:** Other. $6 daily fee/pet. No service, supervision, crate.
🅰🏠⊠🖉🖉🛅🖳🛏

◆◆◆ Ramada Inn of Worthington Ⓜ
(507) 372-2991. **$62-$69, 3 days notice.** 2015 Humiston Ave. Just n of jct I-90 and US 59 (exit 43). Int corridors. **Pets:** Designated rooms, supervision.
🅰🏠⊠🛅🖳🍴🛏

MISSISSIPPI

ABERDEEN

AAA ◆◆◆ **Best Western Aberdeen Inn** M 🐾
(662) 369-4343. **$46-$62.** 801 E Commerce St. At jct US 45 and Hwy 25. Ext corridors. **Pets:** Small, other. No service, supervision, crate.
SAVE ✕ 🔋 🍴 🏊

BATESVILLE

◆◆ **Comfort Inn** M
(662) 563-1188. **$55-$67.** 290 Power Dr. Jct I-55, exit 243B, on SR 6. Ext corridors. **Pets:** Supervision.
ASK ✕ 🔋 💻 🏊

◆◆ **Ramada Limited** M
(662) 563-4528. **Call for rates.** 695 Hwy 6E. 0.5 mi w of I-55, exit 243B. Ext corridors. **Pets:** Large. Designated rooms, supervision.
ASK ✕ 🔋 🏊

BAY ST. LOUIS

AAA ◆◆ **Key West Inn** M 🐾
(228) 466-0444. **$62-$80, 3 days notice.** 1000 Hwy 90. On US 90, 2.5 mi e of jct SR 603. Ext corridors. **Pets:** Small. $5 daily fee/pet. Supervision.
SAVE 🐾 ✕ 🔋 💻

BILOXI

◆◆◆ **Holiday Inn-Coliseum** M 🐾
(228) 388-3551. **$66-$135.** 2400 W Beach Blvd. 5 mi w on US 90. Ext corridors. **Pets:** Small. $100 deposit/room, $25 one-time fee/room. No service, supervision, crate.
ASK 🐾 ✕ 🏊 🔋 💻 🍴 🏊

◆◆◆ **Holiday Inn Express** M 🐾
(228) 388-1000. **$75-$108.** 2416 Beach Blvd. 5.5 mi w on US 90. Ext corridors. **Pets:** Small. $100 deposit/room, $25 one-time fee/room. No service, supervision, crate.
ASK 🐾 ✕ 💳 🏊

AAA ◆◆◆ **Lofty Oaks Inn B & B** BB
(228) 392-6722. **$99-$150, 5 days notice.** 17288 Hwy 67. I-10 exit 41, 6.2 mi n on SR 67. Ext/int corridors. **Pets:** Designated rooms, supervision.
SAVE 🐾 🔋 💻 🏊

AAA ◆ **Motel 6–1113** M
(228) 388-5130. **$50-$66.** 2476 Beach Blvd. US 90, 5 mi w. Ext corridors. **Pets:** Medium. No service, supervision, crate.
✕ 💳 🏊

FOREST

AAA ◆◆◆ **Best Western Forest Inn** M 🐾
(601) 469-2640. **$54-$60.** At jct I-20 and SR 35, exit 88. Ext corridors. **Pets:** Supervision.
SAVE ✕ 🍴 🏊

AAA ◆◆◆ **Comfort Inn** M
(601) 469-2100. **$55-$70.** 1250 Hwy 35S. On SR 35, 0.3 mi n of I-20, exit 88. Ext corridors. **Pets:** Medium. No service, supervision, crate.
SAVE ✕ 🔋 🏊

GREENVILLE

◆◆ **Ramada Inn** M 🐾
(662) 332-4411. **$50-$60.** 2700 Hwy 82E. 3 mi e on US 82. Ext corridors. **Pets:** Medium. No service, supervision, crate.
🐾 ✕ 🔋 💻 🍴 🏊 ✕

GRENADA

◆◆◆ **Holiday Inn** M 🐾
(662) 226-2851. **$57-$57.** 1796 Sunset Dr. At jct I-55, exit 206 and SR 7 and 8; on frontage road. Ext/int corridors. **Pets:** Other. Supervision.
✕ 🔋 💻 🍴 🏊

GULFPORT

◆◆◆ **Holiday Inn I-10/Airport** M 🐾
(228) 868-8200. **$55-$85.** 9415 Hwy 49N. I-10 exit 34A, just s on US 49. Ext corridors. **Pets:** Small. Designated rooms, no service, supervision, crate.
ASK ✕ 🍴 🏊

HATTIESBURG

AAA ◆◆◆ **Baymont Inn & Suites** M
(601) 264-8380. **$65-$80** (no credit cards). 123 Plaza Dr. I-59 exit 65, just nw. Int corridors. **Pets:** Medium. No service, supervision, crate.
SAVE ✕ 💳 🔋 💻 🏊

◆◆◆ **Comfort Inn** M 🐾
(601) 268-2170. **$59-$120.** 6595 Hwy 49N. On US 49, near jct I-59, exit 67A. Ext corridors. **Pets:** Medium. $25 one-time fee/room. No service, supervision, crate.
ASK 🐾 ✕ 🔋 🍴 🏊

AAA ◆◆◆ **Hampton Inn of Hattiesburg** M 🐾
(601) 264-8080. **$59-$69.** 4301 Hardy St. I-59 exit 65, just nw. Ext/int corridors. **Pets:** Small, other. Supervision.
SAVE ✕ 💳 🔋 💻 🏊 CTV

JACKSON

⚫⚫⚫ ◆◆◆ Best Suites of America-Jackson Ⓜ
(601) 899-9000. **$74-$125.** 5411 I-55 N. I-55 exit 102A
northbound; exit 102 southbound, s on w service road. Int
corridors. **Pets:** No service, supervision, crate.

[SAVE] [S] [X] [🐾] [ℰ] [🛏] [💻] [🍽]

◆◆◆ Crowne Plaza-Jackson Ⓗ ⚘
(601) 969-5100. **$110-$145.** 200 E Amite St. Center. Int
corridors. **Pets:** Small. $125 deposit/room. Supervision.

[ASK] [X] [🐾] [ℰ] [🛏] [💻] [🍽] [🍴] [🐾]

◆◆◆ Holiday Inn Hotel & Suites Ⓗ
(601) 366-9411. **$85-$115.** 5075 I-55 N. I-55, exit 102 s on
frontage road. Ext/int corridors. **Pets:** Medium. No service,
supervision, crate.

[ASK] [X] [ℰ] [🛏] [💻] [🍴] [🐾] [CTV]

◆◆◆ Holiday Inn-Southwest Ⓜ ⚘
(601) 355-3472. **$78.** 2649 Hwy 80 West. I-20 exit 42B, just
nw. Ext/int corridors. **Pets:** Small. $8 deposit/room. Super-
vision.

[S] [X] [ℰ] [🛏] [💻] [🍴] [🐾] [CTV]

◆◆◆ La Quinta Inn-Jackson North Ⓜ
(601) 957-1741. **$55-$85.** 616 Briarwood Dr. I-55 exit 102,
just ne. Ext corridors. **Pets:** Small. Supervision.

[ASK] [X] [🛏] [💻] [🐾] [CTV]

◆◆◆ La Quinta Inn-Jackson South Ⓜ
(601) 373-6110. **$52-$69.** 150 Angle St. I-20 exit 43A, just
w of Terry Rd. Ext corridors. **Pets:** Small. Supervision.

[ASK] [X] [🛏] [💻] [🐾]

⚫⚫⚫ ◆◆ Red Roof Inn Coliseum Ⓜ ⚘
(601) 969-5006. **$49-$58.** 700 Larson St. I-55N exit 96B,
just w. Ext corridors. **Pets:** Small, other. No service, supervision, crate.

[SAVE] [X] [🐾] [CTV]

⚫⚫⚫ ◆◆ Red Roof Inn Ridgeland Ⓜ ⚘
(601) 956-7707. **$51-$78.** 810 Adcock Dr. I-55N exit 103,
just ne on Frontage Rd. Ext corridors. **Pets:** Large. No
service, supervision, crate.

[SAVE] [X] [CTV]

◆◆◆ Residence Inn by Marriott Ⓐ ⚘
(601) 355-3599. **$99-$129.** 881 E River Pl. I-55 exit 96C,
just e. Ext corridors. **Pets:** Supervision.

[ASK] [S] [X] [🐾] [🛏] [💻] [🐾] [X]

⚫⚫⚫ ◆◆ Shoney's Inn of Jackson Ⓜ ⚘
(601) 956-6203. **$58-$72, 3 days notice.** I-55N exit 103,
just ne on County Line Rd. Ext corridors. **Pets:** Other. $25
deposit/room. Supervision.

[SAVE] [X] [🛏] [💻] [🐾]

◆◆ Super 8 Motel Ⓜ ⚘
(601) 372-1006. **$42-$55, 5 days notice.** 2655 I-55S. At jct
I-55 and 20, McDowell Rd northbound; exit 92A southbound. Int corridors. **Pets:** Small, other. $25 deposit/room.
Supervision.

[ASK] [S] [X] [🐾]

KOSCIUSKO

⚫⚫⚫ ◆◆ Best Western Parkway Inn Ⓜ ⚘
(662) 289-6252. **$46-$62, 7 days notice.** 1052 Veterans
Memorial Dr. At jct SR 35 and Natchez Trace Pkwy. Ext
corridors. **Pets:** Small. $5 daily fee/pet, $5 one-time fee/pet.
No service, supervision, crate.

[SAVE] [X] [🛏] [🐾]

MCCOMB

⚫⚫⚫ ◆◆◆ Days Inn McComb Ⓜ ⚘
(601) 684-5566. **$69-$99.** 2298 Delaware Ave. I-55 exit 17,
just nw. Ext corridors. **Pets:** Small. $8 one-time fee/room.
Supervision.

[SAVE] [X] [🛏] [💻] [🍴] [🐾]

MERIDIAN

◆◆ Baymont Inn & Suites-Meridian Ⓜ
(601) 693-2300. **$39-$39.** 1400 Roebuck Dr. I-59 and 20
exit 153, US 45S. Int corridors. **Pets:** Large. No service,
supervision, crate.

[X] [🛏] [💻] [🐾]

◆◆ Econo Lodge Ⓜ
(601) 693-9393. **$40-$55, 7 days notice.** 2405 S Frontage
Rd. I-20 and 59 exit 153, 0.5 mi w. Ext corridors.
Pets: Medium. No service, supervision, crate.

[ASK] [X]

◆◆◆ Holiday Inn Express Ⓜ ⚘
(601) 693-4521. **$65-$90.** 1401 Roebuck Dr. I-20 and 59
exit 153, just s. Ext corridors. **Pets:** Medium. Supervision.

[ASK] [X] [ℰ] [💻] [🐾]

MOSS POINT

◆◆◆ Holiday Inn Express Ⓜ ⚘
(228) 474-2100. **$49-$79.** 4800 Amoco Dr. I-10 exit 69, just
sw. Int corridors. **Pets:** Small. Supervision.

[X] [🏠] [🐾] [ℰ] [🛏] [💻] [🐾]

◆◆◆ Shular Inn Ⓜ ⚘
(228) 475-8444. **$49-$54.** 6623 Hwy 63. I-10 exit 69, just s.
Ext corridors. **Pets:** Small. $3 daily fee/pet, $3 one-time
fee/pet. No service, supervision, crate.

[X] [🛏]

NATCHEZ

◆◆◆ Cedar Grove Plantation Ⓑⓑ ⚘
(601) 445-0585. **$100-$145, 7 days notice.** 617 Kingston
Rd. US 61, 3.5 mi s from jct US 84 and 98, 6.5 mi e. Int
corridors. **Pets:** No service, supervision, crate.

[X] [🐾] [X] [CTV] [🐾]

⚫⚫⚫ ◆◆◆ The Guest House Historic Inn Ⓒⓘ
(601) 442-1054. **$94-$127.** 201 N Pearl St. Corner of
Franklin St. Ext/int corridors. **Pets:** Supervision.

[SAVE] [X] [💻] [🍴]

◆◆ Ramada Inn Hilltop Ⓜ ⚘
(601) 446-6311. **$60-$70, 30 days notice.** 130 John R
Junkin Dr. On US 84 and 98 at Mississippi River Bridge.
Ext/int corridors. **Pets:** Other. Supervision.

[S] [X] [🛏] [💻] [🍴] [🐾]

NEWTON

(AAA) ◆◆ Days Inn M 🐾
(601) 683-3361. **$45-$53.** 261 Eastside Dr. I-20 exit 109, 0.3 mi s on SR 15. Ext corridors. **Pets:** Medium, other. $8 daily fee/pet. No service, supervision, crate.
[SAVE] [S📶] [✕] [🖻]

OCEAN SPRINGS

(AAA) ◆◆◆ Holiday Inn Express M 🐾
(228) 875-7555. **$89.** 7304 Washington Ave. I-10 exit 50, 0.4 mi s on SR 609. Ext corridors. **Pets:** Supervision.
[SAVE] [✕] [🖘] [🖴] [🖻]

OXFORD

◆◆ Downtown Inn-Oxford MI
(662) 234-3031. **$70-$95.** 400 N Lamar Ave. SR 6, downtown Oxford Lamar Blvd exit, just n of Town Square. Ext corridors. **Pets:** Medium. Supervision.
[ASK] [S📶] [✕] [🖴] [🖵] [🖾] [🖻]

PASCAGOULA

(AAA) ◆◆ La Font Inn MI
(228) 762-7111. **$61-$73.** 2703 Denny Ave. 1 mi e on US 90, from I-10 exit 69, 3.5 mi s on SR 63, 2 mi w on US 90. Ext/int corridors. **Pets:** Medium. Supervision.
[SAVE] [S📶] [✕] [🖴] [🖵] [🖻] [✕]

PHILADELPHIA

(AAA) ◆◆ Key West Inn M 🐾
(601) 656-0052. **$59-$79.** 1004 Central Dr. At jct of SR 15 and 16. Ext corridors. **Pets:** Medium. $5 daily fee/pet, $5 one-time fee/pet. No service, supervision, crate.
[SAVE] [S📶] [✕] [🖴] [🖵] [🖻]

RICHLAND

(AAA) ◆◆ Days Inn M 🐾
(601) 932-5553. **$55-$80, 7 days notice.** 1035 US Hwy 49 S. On US 49, 4 mi s of I-20, exit 47A. Ext corridors. **Pets:** $5 daily fee/pet. No service, supervision, crate.
[SAVE] [S📶] [✕] [🖴] [CTV]

ROBINSONVILLE

◆ Key West Inn M
(662) 363-0021. **$50-$50.** US 61. On US 61, 0.3 mi n of SR 304. Ext corridors. **Pets:** Medium. Designated rooms, no service, supervision, crate.
[ASK] [✕] [🖴] [🖵]

SOUTHAVEN

(AAA) ◆◆ Best Western Inn M 🐾
(662) 393-4174. **$55-$139.** 8945 Hamilton Rd. Just e of I-55, exit 291. Ext corridors. **Pets:** Medium. $25 deposit/room. Designated rooms, no service, supervision, crate.
[SAVE] [S📶] [✕] [🖴] [🖵] [🖻]

STARKVILLE

◆◆◆ Ramada Inn University Center MI
(662) 323-6161. **$59-$65.** 403 Hwy 12 E. On SR 12, 1.3 mi sw of jct US 82. Ext corridors. **Pets:** Small. No service, supervision, crate.
[ASK] [S📶] [✕] [🖙] [🖴] [🖵] [🖾] [🖻]

TUPELO

◆◆◆ Executive Inn MI
(662) 841-2222. **$64-$77, 7 days notice.** 1011 N Gloster St. From jct US 78 and 45, 1.3 mi s to McCullough Blvd; then w. Int corridors. **Pets:** Medium. Supervision.
[ASK] [✕] [🖴] [🖵] [🖾] [🖻]

◆◆◆ The Mockingbird Inn Bed & Breakfast BB
(662) 841-0286. **$65-$125, 3 days notice.** 305 N Gloster. On Old US 45, just n of jct SR 6. Int corridors. **Pets:** Very small. Designated rooms, supervision.
[ASK] [S📶] [✕]

(AAA) ◆◆ Red Roof Inn Tupelo M
(662) 844-1904. **$46-$73.** 1500 McCullough Blvd. On SR 178, just w of jct SR 145 (Gloster St). Ext corridors. **Pets:** Supervision.
[SAVE] [✕] [🖙] [🖴] [🖻]

◆◆ Super 8 Motel M 🐾
(662) 842-0448. **$42-$54** (no credit cards). 3898 McCullough Blvd. Hwy 78 exit Belden, just ne. Ext corridors. **Pets:** Small. $5 daily fee/pet. Designated rooms, no service, supervision, crate.
[ASK] [✕] [🖴]

VICKSBURG

(AAA) ◆◆ Battlefield Inn MI 🐾
(601) 638-5811. **$59-$75.** 4137 I-20 N Frontage Rd. 1 mi e, I-20, exit 4B. Ext/int corridors. **Pets:** Medium, other. $5 daily fee/pet. Supervision.
[SAVE] [✕] [🖴] [🖾] [🖻] [✕]

(AAA) ◆◆◆ The Corners Bed & Breakfast Inn BB 🐾
(601) 636-7421. **$75-$125, 3 days notice.** 601 Klein St. I-20 exit 1A, 2.3 mi n on Washington, just w. Ext/int corridors. **Pets:** Other. Supervision.
[SAVE] [✕] [🖴] [🖵]

◆◆ Super 8 Motel M 🐾
(601) 638-5077. **$40-$56.** 4127 I-20 Frontage Rd. I-20 exit 4B, just ne on Frontage Rd; adjacent to national battlefield. Int corridors. **Pets:** Small. $25 deposit/room. No service, supervision, crate.
[ASK] [✕] [🖴] [🖻]

CITY INDEX

ARNOLD

◆◆◆ Drury Inn-St Louis South
(636) 296-9600. **$63-$86.** 1201 Drury Ln. 0.3 mi e from jct I-55 and SR 141, exit 191. Int corridors. **Pets:** Small. Supervision.

BETHANY

⚑⚑⚑ ◆◆ Family Budget Inn
(660) 425-7915. **$39-$49.** 4014 Millen. Jct I-35, exit 92. Int corridors. **Pets:** Medium. No service, supervision, crate.

BOLIVAR

⚑⚑⚑ ◆ Welcome Inn
(417) 326-5268. **$25-$40.** 4710 S 128th Rd, S Hwy 13 S. On Frontage Rd, 0.3 mi s of jct SR 13, SR 83 and SR 15 business route. Ext corridors. **Pets:** Other. $25 deposit/room, $5 daily fee/pet. No service, supervision, crate.

BOURBON

⚑⚑⚑ ◆ Budget Inn Motel
(573) 732-4080. **$35-$40, 5 days notice.** 55 Hwy C. I-44, exit 218. Ext corridors. **Pets:** Small, dogs only. $15 deposit/pet, $5 daily fee/pet, $5 one-time fee/pet. Designated rooms, no service, supervision, crate.

BRANSON

◆◆◆ Baymont Inn & Suites
(417) 336-6161. **$73-$145.** 2375 Green Mountain Dr. 2.5 mi w jct US 65 and SR 76, just s. Int corridors. **Pets:** Small. $50 deposit/pet, $3 daily fee/room. Designated rooms, no service, supervision, crate.

⚑⚑⚑ ◆◆ Best Western Branson Rustic Oak
(417) 334-6464. **$50-$75.** 403 W Hwy 76. 0.3 mi e from SR 76 and US 65 on SR 76. Ext corridors. **Pets:** Designated rooms, no service, supervision, crate.

◆◆◆ Branson Grand Ramada
(417) 336-6646. **$89-$89.** 245 N Wildwood. From jct US 65, 3 mi w on SR 76, then 0.5 mi n. Int corridors. **Pets:** Small. Supervision.

⚑⚑⚑ ◆◆◆ Branson Inn
(417) 334-5121. **$55-$61.** 448 SR 248. On SR 248, 0.3 mi w of jct US 65. Int corridors. **Pets:** $5 daily fee/pet. Supervision.

◆◆ The Branson Lodge
(417) 334-3105. **$49-$79.** 2456 State Hwy 165. On SR 165, 3.2 mi s of jct SR 76. Ext corridors. **Pets:** No service, supervision, crate.

✦✦✦✦ Chateau on the Lake Resort Hotel & Convention Center 🏨 🐾
(417) 334-1161. **$169-$269, 3 days notice.** 415 N State Hwy 265. Just n of jct Hwys 165 and 265. Int corridors. **Pets:** Small. Designated rooms, no service, supervision, crate.
[SAVE] 🚫 ♿ 🍽 🎬 🛗 💻 🍴 🛍 🚫

✦✦✦ Days Inn of Branson Ⓜ 🐾
(417) 334-5544. **$59-$100.** 3524 Keeter St. From jct SR 376, 0.5 mi e on SR 76, then 0.3 mi w. Ext corridors. **Pets:** Small, other. $10 daily fee/pet. Supervision.
[SAVE] [SO] 🚫 🎬 🎬 🛗 🍴 🛍 🚫

✦✦ 1st Inn Gold Ⓜ 🐾
(417) 334-7000. **Call for rates.** 2719 W Hwy 76. 2.5 mi w of jct US 65. Ext/int corridors. **Pets:** Small. $10 one-time fee/room. Designated rooms, no service, supervision, crate.
[SAVE] 🚫 🛗 🛍

✦✦ Hall of Fame Hotel Ⓜ 🐾
(417) 334-5161. **$50-$65.** 3005 W Hwy 76. 2.5 mi w on SR 76. Ext/int corridors. **Pets:** $15 one-time fee/pet. Designated rooms, no service, supervision, crate.
[ASK] [SO] 🚫 🎬 🛗 💻 🛍

✦✦ Harmony Place Ⓜ
(417) 334-5510. **Call for rates.** 3514 W Hwy 76. 0.5 mi e of jct US 76 and Shepherd of the Hills Expwy. Ext corridors. **Pets:** No service, supervision, crate.
[ASK] 🚫 🛗 🛍

✦✦✦ Hotel Grand Victorian Ⓜ
(417) 336-2935. **$99-$99.** 2325 W Hwy 76. On SR 76, 2.6 mi w of US 65. Int corridors. **Pets:** Small. Designated rooms, no service, supervision, crate.
[SAVE] [SO] 🚫 🎬 🛗 💻 🛍

✦✦✦ Howard Johnson Ⓜ 🐾
(417) 336-5151. **$59-$150.** 3027-A W Hwy 76. On SR 76, 3.5 mi w of jct US 65. Ext corridors. **Pets:** Medium. $10 daily fee/pet. Supervision.
[SAVE] [SO] 🚫 🎬 🛗 💻 🍴 🛍 🚫

✦✦ Lakeshore Resort 🆑 🐾
(417) 334-6262. **$80-$150, 21 days notice.** 1773 Lakeshore Dr. From US 65, 2 mi e on SR 76 to Lake Rd 76-3, then 1.7 mi n. Ext corridors. **Pets:** Medium. $25 deposit/pet, $15 one-time fee/pet. Supervision.
🚫 🛗 💻 🛍 🚫

✦✦ MidTown Inn Ⓜ
(417) 334-7474. **$49-$54, 3 days notice.** 2330 W Hwy 76. 2.6 mi w of jct US 65 and SR 76. Ext corridors. **Pets:** Supervision.
[SAVE] [SO] 🚫 🎬 💻 🛍

✦✦ Motel 6–4027 Ⓜ 🐾
(417) 336-6088. **$49-$54.** 2651 Shepherd of the Hills Expw. From jct SR 76, 1 mi e. Int corridors. **Pets:** Medium, other. Supervision.
[ASK] [SO] 🚫 🎬 🛍

✦✦ Peach Tree Inn Ⓜ 🐾
(417) 335-5900. **$79-$79.** 2450 Green Mountain Dr. From jct US 65, 1.5 mi w on SR 76, then just s. Ext corridors. **Pets:** Small. $25 deposit/room. Designated rooms, supervision.
[SAVE] [SO] 🚫 🛗 💻 🛍

✦✦✦ Ramada Limited Ⓜ 🐾
(417) 337-5207. **$70-$90.** 2316 Shephard of the Hills Expw. From jct SR 76, 1.3 mi e. Int corridors. **Pets:** Other. $5 daily fee/room. No service, supervision, crate.
[ASK] [SO] 🚫 🎬 🛗 💻 🛍

✦✦✦ Red Roof Inn #502 Ⓜ 🐾
(417) 335-4500. **$59-$102.** 220 S Wildwood Dr. 2 mi w on SR 76, just s. Int corridors. **Pets:** Small, dogs only. $10 daily fee/pet. No service, supervision, crate.
🚫 🎬 🛗

✦✦✦ Residence Inn by Marriott 🅰 🐾
(417) 336-4077. **$89-$94.** 280 Wildwood Dr S. 2 mi w on US 76, just s. Int corridors. **Pets:** Other. $5 daily fee/room, $25 one-time fee/room. Supervision.
[ASK] [SO] 🚫 🛗 🎬 🎬 🛗 💻 🛍

✦✦ Rock View Resort Ⓜ 🐾
(417) 334-4678. **$54-$79, 30 days notice.** 1049 Parkview Dr. From jct US 65, 4 mi w on SR 165, then 0.3 mi s via Dale Dr, then 0.7 mi w. Ext corridors. **Pets:** Small. $50 deposit/room, $7 daily fee/pet. No service, supervision, crate.
[SO] 🛗 💻 🛍 🚫 🗑

✦✦✦ Settle Inn Resort & Conference Center Ⓜ🅘 🐾
(417) 335-4700. **$49-$95.** 3050 Green Mountain Dr. 3 mi w on Hwy 76 from jct US 65 and 76, 0.8 mi s. Int corridors. **Pets:** Other. $8 daily fee/pet. No service, supervision, crate.
[SAVE] [SO] 🚫 🎬 🛗 🛗 🍴 🛍

✦✦ Shady Acre Motel Ⓜ 🐾
(417) 338-2316. **$32-$38** (no credit cards). On SR 76, 1.1 mi w of jct SR 265. Ext corridors. **Pets:** Small, other. $10 one-time fee/pet. Designated rooms, supervision.
🚫 🛗 🛍 🚫

✦✦ Taney Motel Ⓜ
(417) 334-3143. **$26-$43, 3 days notice.** 311 Hwy 65 N Business Rt. Just n SR 65 business route, from jct SR 76. Ext corridors. **Pets:** Medium. Designated rooms, no service, supervision, crate.
[SAVE] [SO] 🚫 🛗 🛍

✦✦✦ Welk Resort Center Ⓜ🅘
(417) 336-3575. **$94-$99, 3 days notice.** 1984 SR 165. On SR 165, 2.9 mi s of jct SR 76. Int corridors. **Pets:** Medium. Supervision.
[SAVE] [SO] 🚫 🎬 🛗 💻 🍴 🛍

BRANSON WEST

✦✦ Colonial Mountain Inn Ⓜ 🐾
(417) 272-8414. **$40-$45.** On SR 76, 0.3 mi e of jct SR 13. Ext corridors. **Pets:** Small, dogs only. $5 daily fee/pet. Designated rooms, supervision.
🚫 🛍 🚫

BUFFALO

✦✦ Goodnite Inn Ⓜ 🐾
(417) 345-3245. **$25-$43.** 642 S Ash. US 65. **Pets:** Medium. $25 deposit/room, $5 daily fee/room. No service, supervision, crate.
[SAVE] [SO] 🚫 🛍

BUTLER

◆◆ Super 8 Motel–Butler 🐾
(660) 679-6183. **$41-$60.** 1114 W Fort Scott St. At jct US 71 and SR 52 W, Amoret and Butler exit. Ext corridors. **Pets:** $5 daily fee/pet, $50 one-time fee/pet. Supervision.
ASK S✗

CAMERON

🆎 ◆◆◆ Best Western Acorn Inn  🐾
(816) 632-2187. **$51-$75.** On US 36, 0.3 mi e of jct I-35 and exit 54. Ext corridors. **Pets:** Medium, other. No service, supervision, crate.
SAVE S✗

◆◆◆ Comfort Inn M 🐾
(816) 632-5655. **$59-$74, 7 days notice.** 1803 Comfort Ln. Just e of jct I-35 and exit 54. Int corridors. **Pets:** Medium. $75 deposit/room. No service, supervision, crate.
ASK S✗

🆎 ◆◆ Days Inn M 🐾
(816) 632-6623. **$35-$55.** 501 Northland Dr. Just off US 69, just s of jct US 36 and US 69. Int corridors. **Pets:** Other. $3 daily fee/pet. Supervision.
SAVE S✗

🆎 ◆◆ Econo Lodge M
(816) 632-6571. **$32-$55, 7 days notice.** 220 E Grand. From I-35, exit 54, 0.5 mi w on US 36, then just s on US 36. Ext corridors. **Pets:** Medium. No service, supervision, crate.
SAVE S✗

CAPE GIRARDEAU

◆◆◆ Drury Lodge M
(573) 334-7151. **$60-$77.** 104 S Vantage Dr. At jct I-55 and exit 96. Ext/int corridors. **Pets:** Small. No service, supervision, crate.
✗

◆◆◆ Drury Suites-Cape Girardeau M
(573) 339-9500. **$79-$95.** 3303 Campster Dr. I-55, exit 96. Int corridors. **Pets:** Small. No service, supervision, crate.
✗

◆◆◆ Hampton Inn M
(573) 651-3000. **$68-$83.** 103 Cape W Pkwy. 0.3 mi sw of I-55, exit 96. Int corridors. **Pets:** Supervision.
✗

◆◆◆ Holiday Inn of Cape Girardeau M
(573) 334-4491. **$89-$185.** 3257 William St. At jct I-55 and exit 96. Ext/int corridors. **Pets:** Small. No service, supervision, crate.
ASK S✗

◆◆ Pear Tree Inn by Drury M
(573) 334-3000. **$48-$65.** 3248 William St. At jct I-55 and exit 96. Int corridors. **Pets:** Supervision.
✗

◆◆◆ Victorian Inn of Cape Girardeau M 🐾
(573) 651-4486. **$62-$82.** 3265 William St. At jct I-55 and exit 96. Ext/int corridors. **Pets:** Small. No service, supervision, crate.
ASK S✗

CARTHAGE

🆎 ◆◆ Days Inn M 🐾
(417) 358-2499. **$42-$53.** 2244 Grand Ave. Just off SR 571, 3 mi ne of jct US 71, Garrison Ave exit northbound 0.7 mi e; 0.6 mi n from jct US 71 exit SR HH southbound.. Ext corridors. **Pets:** Very small, other. $10 one-time fee/pet. Designated rooms, no service, supervision, crate.
SAVE S✗

🆎 ◆◆◆ Econo Lodge M 🐾
(417) 358-3900. **$48-$70.** 1441 W Central. On SR 96, at jct US 71. Ext/int corridors. **Pets:** Other. $5 daily fee/pet. Designated rooms, supervision.
SAVE S✗

CASSVILLE

🆎 ◆◆ Budget Inn M 🐾
(417) 847-4196. **$34-$58, 3 days notice.** Downtown, on SR 76, 86 and 112, just e of jct SR 248. Ext corridors. **Pets:** Small. $10 deposit/room. No service, supervision, crate.
SAVE S✗

◆ IMA Holiday Motel and RV Park M 🐾
(417) 847-3163. **$30-$46.** 85 S Main. Just w of downtown; on SR 37 business route, 76, 86 and 112. Ext corridors. **Pets:** Small, dogs only. $5 one-time fee/room. Supervision.
ASK S✗

◆◆ Super 8 Motel M
(417) 847-4888. **$44-$56.** 101 S Hwy 37. Just s of jct 76, 86 and 37 business route. Int corridors. **Pets:** Small. Designated rooms, no service, supervision, crate.
ASK S✗

CHILLICOTHE

🆎 ◆◆ Best Western Inn M
(660) 646-0572. **$50-$80.** 1020 S Washington St. At jct US 36 and 65. Ext/int corridors. **Pets:** Small. No service, supervision, crate.
SAVE S✗

◆◆ Chillicothe Super 8 Motel M 🐾
(660) 646-7888. **$45-$51.** 580 Old Hwy 36 E. 0.8 mi e of jct US 36 and 65. Int corridors. **Pets:** Medium. No service, supervision, crate.
ASK S✗

🆎 ◆◆◆ Grand River Inn M 🐾
(660) 646-6590. **$53-$58.** 606 W Business 36. On Old US 36, just e of jct US 65. Ext/int corridors. **Pets:** Other. No service, supervision, crate.
SAVE S✗

CLINTON

◆◆◆ Days Inn of Clinton M
(660) 885-6901. **$60-$70.** Hwy 7 & Rives Rd. Northern jct of Hwys 7 and 13. Int corridors. **Pets:** Small. Designated rooms, no service, supervision, crate.
ASK S✗

🆎 ◆ Safari Motel M
(660) 885-3395. **$28-$50.** 1505 N 2nd St. At n jct SR 13 and 7. Ext corridors. **Pets:** Supervision.
 S✗

COLUMBIA

◆◆ **Baymont Inn & Suites-Columbia** M ❀
(573) 445-1899. **$59-$67.** 2500 I-70 Dr SW. Just w of jct I-70 and Stadium Blvd, exit 124, on Frontage Rd. Int corridors. **Pets:** No service, supervision, crate.
⟨S₀⟩⟨✕⟩⟨∅⟩⟨🛢⟩⟨▢⟩

AAA ◆◆ **Days Inn Conference Center** M
(573) 445-8511. **$59-$89.** 1900 I-70 Dr SW. Just e of jct I-70 and Stadium Blvd, exit 124 on frontage road. Ext corridors. **Pets:** Designated rooms, no service, supervision, crate.
⟨SAVE⟩⟨S₀⟩⟨✕⟩⟨∅⟩⟨🛢⟩⟨▢⟩⟨¶⟩⟨📶⟩

◆◆◆ **Drury Inn** M ❀
(573) 445-1800. **$64-$84.** 1000 Knipp St. Just s of jct I-70 and Stadium Blvd, exit 124. Int corridors. **Pets:** Small, other. Supervision.
⟨✕⟩⟨∅⟩⟨🛢⟩⟨▢⟩⟨📶⟩

AAA ◆◆ **Econo Lodge-Columbia** M
(573) 442-1191. **$45-$79, 7 days notice.** 900 I-70 Dr SW. On I-70 business loop at jct I-70 (West Blvd), exit 125. Int corridors. **Pets:** Supervision.
⟨SAVE⟩⟨S₀⟩⟨✕⟩⟨🛢⟩⟨▢⟩⟨📶⟩⟨✕⟩

◆◆◆ **Holiday Inn East-Holidome** M ❀
(573) 449-2491. **Call for rates.** 1612 N Providence Rd. At jct I-70 (Providence Rd), exit 126. Ext/int corridors. **Pets:** Other. Designated rooms, no service, supervision, crate.
⟨✕⟩⟨🛏⟩⟨🛢⟩⟨▢⟩⟨¶⟩⟨📶⟩

◆◆◆ **Holiday Inn Express** M
(573) 449-4422. **$75-$100, 7 days notice.** 801 Keene St. Just se of jct I-70 and exit 128A. Int corridors. **Pets:** Small. No service, supervision, crate.
⟨ASK⟩⟨S₀⟩⟨✕⟩⟨♿⟩⟨∅⟩⟨🛢⟩⟨▢⟩⟨📶⟩

◆◆◆ **Holiday Inn Select Executive
Center** M ❀
(573) 445-8531. **$85.** 2200 I-70 Dr SW. Just w of jct I-70 and Stadium Blvd, exit 124. Int corridors. **Pets:** Other. $75 deposit/room. Supervision.
⟨ASK⟩⟨S₀⟩⟨✕⟩⟨🛏⟩⟨∅⟩⟨🛢⟩⟨▢⟩⟨¶⟩⟨📶⟩

◆◆◆ **Ramada Inn & Conference Center** M ❀
(573) 449-0051. **$69-$99, 30 days notice.** 1100 Vandiver Dr. On US 63 at jct I-70, exit 127. Ext/int corridors. **Pets:** Other. $20 deposit/room. Supervision.
⟨ASK⟩⟨S₀⟩⟨✕⟩⟨♿⟩⟨∅⟩⟨🛏⟩⟨🛢⟩⟨▢⟩⟨¶⟩⟨📶⟩

AAA ◆◆ **Red Roof Inn-Columbia** M ❀
(573) 442-0145. **$47-$62.** 201 E Texas Ave. I-70, exit 126 (Providence Rd). Ext corridors. **Pets:** Small. Designated rooms, no service, supervision, crate.
⟨SAVE⟩⟨✕⟩⟨CTV⟩

AAA ◆◆ **Travelodge** M ❀
(573) 449-1065. **$50-$76.** 900 Vandiver Dr. Just n of jct I-70 and exit 127 (US Hwy 63). Ext corridors. **Pets:** Medium. $10 one-time fee/pet. Designated rooms, no service, supervision, crate.
⟨SAVE⟩⟨S₀⟩⟨✕⟩⟨🛢⟩⟨▢⟩⟨📶⟩

CONCORDIA

◆◆ **Best Western Heidelberg Inn** M ❀
(660) 463-2114. **$45-$70.** 406 NW 2nd St. 0.3 mi sw of jct I-70 and SR 23, exit 58. Int corridors. **Pets:** Other. $20 deposit/room, $3 daily fee/pet. Designated rooms, no service, supervision, crate.
⟨ASK⟩⟨S₀⟩⟨✕⟩⟨∅⟩⟨🛢⟩⟨📶⟩⟨✕⟩

AAA ◆◆ **Days Inn of Concordia** M ❀
(660) 463-7987. **$40-$69.** 301 NW 3rd St. At I-70, exit 58 and SR 23. Ext/int corridors. **Pets:** Small. $20 deposit/room, $10 daily fee/room. Designated rooms, no service, supervision, crate.
⟨SAVE⟩⟨S₀⟩⟨✕⟩⟨🛢⟩⟨📶⟩

CUBA

AAA ◆◆ **Best Western Cuba Inn** M ❀
(573) 885-7707. **$38-$52.** 246 Hwy P. Jct I-44, exit 208. Ext corridors. **Pets:** Small, dogs only. $10 daily fee/pet, $10 one-time fee/pet. Designated rooms, no service, supervision, crate.
⟨SAVE⟩⟨S₀⟩⟨✕⟩⟨▢⟩⟨📶⟩

DONIPHAN

◆◆◆ **Days Inn Doniphan** M ❀
(573) 996-2400. **$50-$99.** 100 Oaktree Village. Just e of jct US 160 and 142. Ext corridors. **Pets:** Medium. $10 one-time fee/pet. Designated rooms, supervision.
⟨ASK⟩⟨S₀⟩⟨✕⟩⟨🛢⟩⟨▢⟩⟨📶⟩⟨✕⟩

ELLINGTON

◆◆ **Scenic Rivers Motel** M ❀
(573) 663-7722. **$38-$43.** 231 N 2nd St. Jct Hwys 21 and 106. Ext corridors. **Pets:** Medium, other. No service, supervision, crate.

FESTUS

◆◆◆ **Baymont Inn** M ❀
(636) 937-2888. **$60-$65.** 1303 Veterans Blvd. Just w of I-55, exit 175. Int corridors. **Pets:** Other. $50 deposit/room. No service, supervision, crate.
⟨ASK⟩⟨S₀⟩⟨✕⟩⟨🛢⟩⟨▢⟩

◆◆◆ **Drury Inn Festus** M
(636) 933-2400. **$60-$85.** 1001 Veterans Blvd. I-55, exit 175, just e. Int corridors. **Pets:** Small. No service, supervision, crate.
⟨✕⟩⟨🛢⟩⟨▢⟩⟨📶⟩

GRAY SUMMIT

AAA ◆◆ **Best Western Diamond Inn Motel** M
(636) 742-3501. **$99-$109.** 2875 Hwy 100. I-44, exit 253. Ext corridors. **Pets:** Designated rooms, no service, supervision, crate.
⟨SAVE⟩⟨S₀⟩⟨✕⟩⟨∅⟩⟨📶⟩⟨✕⟩

HANNIBAL

AAA ◆◆ **Days Inn** M
(573) 248-1700. **$46-$75.** 4070 Market St. At jct US 61S and 61 business route. Ext corridors. **Pets:** Designated rooms, no service, supervision, crate.
⟨SAVE⟩⟨✕⟩⟨📶⟩

◆◆◆ Hannibal Inn **M**
(573) 221-6610. **$70-$75, 3 days notice.** 4141 Market St. 2 mi s of jct US 36 and 61; on US 61. Ext/int corridors. **Pets:** Designated rooms, no service, supervision, crate.
(ASK) (S&D) (X) (🛏) (🍴) (📺) (🍴) (🔲) (X)

M ◆◆ Hannibal Travelodge **M** ❖
(573) 221-4100. **$56-$70.** 500 Mark Twain Ave. 1 mi e of jct US 61 and 36 on US 36; just w of Mississippi River. Ext corridors. **Pets:** Designated rooms, no service, supervision, crate.
(SAVE) (X) (🛏) (🔲) (📺)

HARRISONVILLE

M ◆◆ Best Western Harrisonville **M**
(816) 884-3200. **$45-$76.** 2201 N Rockhaven Rd. On SR 291, just n of jct US 71. Ext corridors. **Pets:** Medium. No service, supervision, crate.
(SAVE) (S&D) (X) (🛏) (📺) (X)

M ◆ Budget Host Caravan Motel **M** ❖
(816) 884-4100. **$31-$49, 7 days notice.** 1705 Hwy 291 N. 0.3 mi n of jct US 71. Ext corridors. **Pets:** Medium. $10 deposit/room. No service, supervision, crate.
(SAVE) (X) (🛏) (CTV)

M ◆ Slumber Inn Motel **M**
(816) 884-3100. **$32-$44, 3 days notice.** 21400 E 275th St. Just w of jct US 71 and SR 7 S. Ext corridors. **Pets:** Supervision.
(SAVE) (S&D) (X) (🛏) (📺)

HAYTI

◆◆ Pear Tree Inn **M** ❖
(573) 359-2702. **$50-$70.** 1317 Hwy 84. I-55, exit 19. Ext/int corridors. **Pets:** Large, other. Designated rooms, supervision.
(X) (🍴) (📺)

HIGGINSVILLE

◆◆ Best Western Camelot Inn **M**
(660) 584-3646. **$50-$70, 7 days notice.** 6683 S Hwy 13. I-70 and SR 13, exit 49. Ext/int corridors. **Pets:** Large. No service, supervision, crate.
(S&D) (X) (🍴) (📺) (CTV)

◆◆ Super 8 Motel-Higginsville **M**
(660) 584-7781. **$47-$54.** Just se of jct, I-70 and exit 49 (SR 13). Int corridors. **Pets:** Designated rooms, no service, supervision, crate.
(ASK) (S&D) (X) (CTV)

HOLTS SUMMIT

◆◆ Summit Plaza Hotel **M** ❖
(573) 896-8787. **$49-$66.** 150 City Plaza. US 54 and CR 00. Int corridors. **Pets:** Very small. $6 daily fee/pet. Designated rooms, no service, supervision, crate.
(ASK) (S&D) (X) (🍴)

HOUSTON

M ◆◆ Southern Inn Motel **M** ❖
(417) 967-4591. **$37-$46.** 1493 S Hwy 63. 1.3 mi s on US 63. Ext corridors. **Pets:** Medium. $6 daily fee/pet. No service, supervision, crate.
(SAVE) (S&D) (X)

JACKSON

◆◆◆ Drury Inn & Suites **M** ❖
(573) 243-9200. **$56-$75.** 225 Drury Ln. Off I-55, exit 105 (Fruitland), 0.3 mi w on SR 61. Int corridors. **Pets:** Small, other. No service, supervision, crate.
(X) (🍴) (🔲) (🛏) (🔲) (📺)

JEFFERSON CITY

◆◆◆ Capitol Plaza Hotel & Convention
    Center **H** ❖
(573) 635-1234. **$79-$117.** 415 W McCarty St. On US 50 and 63 S, just e of jct US 54. Int corridors. **Pets:** Small, other. Supervision.
(ASK) (S&D) (X) (🔲) (🛏) (🔲) (📺) (🍴) (📺)

◆◆ Hotel De Ville **M**
(573) 636-5231. **$69-$79.** 319 W Miller St. On US 50 E and 63 S, just e of jct US 54. Int corridors. **Pets:** Small. No service, supervision, crate.
(ASK) (S&D) (X) (🛏) (🔲) (🍴) (📺)

M ◆◆ Ramada Inn-Jefferson City **M** 🐾
(573) 635-7171. **$57-$62, 7 days notice.** 1510 Jefferson St. US 54, 0.5 m nw of Ellis Blvd exit. Ext/int corridors. **Pets:** Other. $10 daily fee/room. Designated rooms, supervision.
(SAVE) (S&D) (X) (🔲) (🛏) (🔲) (📺) (🍴) (📺)

JOPLIN

M ◆◆ Best Western Hallmark Inn **M** ❖
(417) 624-8400. **$47-$57.** 3600 Range Line Rd. On US 71, at jct I-44, exit 8B. Ext corridors. **Pets:** Medium, other. $10 deposit/room. Designated rooms, supervision.
(SAVE) (S&D) (X) (🛏) (📺)

M ◆◆ Best Western Sands Inn **M** ❖
(417) 624-8300. **$40-$59, 3 days notice.** 1611 Range Line Rd. I-44, exit 8B (US 71B), 2 mi n. Ext corridors. **Pets:** Small. Designated rooms, no service, supervision, crate.
(SAVE) (S&D) (X) (📺)

◆◆◆ Drury Inn **M** ❖
(417) 781-8000. **$64-$84.** 3601 Range Line Rd. I-44, exit 8B. Int corridors. **Pets:** Medium. Designated rooms, no service, supervision, crate.
(X) (🍴) (🛏) (📺)

M ◆◆◆ Holiday Inn **H** ❖
(417) 782-1000. **$79-$94, 3 days notice.** 3615 Range Line Rd. I-44, exit 8, (US 71B). Int corridors. **Pets:** Small. $25 deposit/room. Designated rooms, no service, supervision, crate.
(SAVE) (S&D) (X) (🍴) (🛏) (🔲) (📺) (🍴) (📺)

◆◆ **Microtel Inn & Suites Joplin** Ⓜ ❀
(417) 626-8282. **$40-$44.** 4101 Richard Joseph Blvd. I-44,
exit 8A. Int corridors. **Pets:** Small, other. Supervision.
Ⓐ$Ⓚ Ⓢ6 ☒ 🗐 Ⓒ 🔓 🖳 🐾

Ⓐ ◆ **Motel 6–427** Ⓜ
(417) 781-6400. **$36-$52.** 3031 S Range Line Rd. From jct
I-44 and exit 8B (Range Line Rd), 1 mi n. Ext corridors.
Pets: Small. No service, supervision, crate.
Ⓢ6 ☒ Ⓒ 🐾

Ⓐ ◆◆ **Sleep Inn** Ⓜ
(417) 782-1212. **$54-$59.** I-44 & State Hwy 43 S. Just s of
jct I-44, exit 4. Int corridors. **Pets:** Designated rooms,
no service, supervision, crate.
Ⓢ🅰🆅🅴 Ⓢ6 ☒ Ⓒ 🖳

◆◆ **Super 8 Motel-Joplin** Ⓜ ❀
(417) 782-8765. **$38-$71, 5 days notice.** 2830 E 36th St.
I-44, exit 8B (US 71B). Int corridors. **Pets:** Other. No service, supervision, crate.
Ⓐ$Ⓚ Ⓢ6 ☒ 🔓

◆ **Westwood Motel** Ⓜ ❀
(417) 782-7212. **$33-$39.** 1700 W 30th St. From I-44, exit
6, 1.3 mi n to 32nd St, 1 mi w, 0.3 mi n on McClelland Blvd;
adjacent to St. John's Medical Center. Ext corridors.
Pets: Other. $20 deposit/room, $5 one-time fee/room. Designated rooms, supervision.
☒ Ⓒ 🔓 🖳 🐾

KANSAS CITY METROPOLITAN AREA

GRAIN VALLEY

Ⓐ ◆◆ **Travelodge** Ⓜ ❀
(816) 224-3420. **$50-$80.** 105 Sunny Lane Dr. N of jct I-70
and exit 24. Ext corridors. **Pets:** Medium. $5 one-time fee/
pet. No service, supervision, crate.
Ⓢ🅰🆅🅴 Ⓢ6 ☒ Ⓒ 🔓 🖳 🐾

INDEPENDENCE

Ⓐ ◆◆◆ **Howard Johnson Hotel** Ⓜ ❀
(816) 373-8856. **$79-$129.** 4200 S Noland Rd. I-70, exit 12.
Int corridors. **Pets:** Other. $25 deposit/room. Supervision.
Ⓢ🅰🆅🅴 Ⓢ6 ☒ 🗐 Ⓒ 🔓 🖳 🐾 ☒

Ⓐ ◆◆ **Red Roof Inn-Independence** Ⓜ ❀
(816) 373-2800. **$48-$60.** 13712 E 42nd Terr. Just sw of jct
I-70 and exit 12 (Noland Rd). Ext corridors. **Pets:** Medium,
other. Designated rooms, no service, supervision, crate.
Ⓢ🅰🆅🅴 ☒ 🗐 Ⓒ 🅲🆃🆅

KANSAS CITY

◆◆◆ **Baymont Inn & Suites-KC South** Ⓜ ❀
(816) 822-7000. **$61-$68.** 8601 Hillcrest Rd. I-435 and 87th
St, exit 69. Int corridors. **Pets:** Other. Supervision.
Ⓢ6 ☒ Ⓒ 🗐 Ⓒ 🔓

◆◆ **Baymont Inn & Suites-North Kansas
City** Ⓜ ❀
(816) 221-1200. **$61-$68.** 2214 Taney Rd. At jct I-35, I-29
and exit 6A. Int corridors. **Pets:** Small. $20 deposit/room.
Designated rooms, no service, supervision, crate.
Ⓢ6 ☒ 🗐 🔓 🖳

◆◆◆ **Drury Inn & Suites** Ⓜ ❀
(816) 880-9700. **$64-$84.** 7900 NW Tiffany Springs Pkwy.
Just w of jct I-29 and exit 10. Int corridors. **Pets:** Small,
dogs only. No service, supervision, crate.
☒ Ⓒ Ⓒ 🔓 🖳 🐾

◆◆◆ **Drury Inn-Stadium** Ⓜ
(816) 923-3000. **$69-$95.** 3830 Blue Ridge Cutoff. N of I-70
and exit 9; across from Truman Sports Complex. Int corridors. **Pets:** Supervision.
☒ 🗐 🗐 🔓 🖳 🐾

Ⓐ ◆◆ **Econo Lodge KCI Airport** Ⓜ
(816) 464-5082. **$40-$80, 5 days notice.** 11300 NW Prairie
View Rd. At jct I-29 and 112th St NW, exit 12. Int corridors.
Pets: Small. Supervision.
Ⓢ🅰🆅🅴 Ⓢ6 ☒ 🖳

◆◆◆ **Embassy Suites Hotel KCI Airport** Ⓗ
(816) 891-7788. **$109-$119.** 7640 NW Tiffany Springs
Pkwy. E of jct I-29 and exit 10. Int corridors. **Pets:** Small.
Designated rooms, no service, supervision, crate.
Ⓐ$Ⓚ Ⓢ6 ☒ 🗐 🗐 Ⓒ 🔓 🖳 🗐 🐾

◆◆◆ **Historic Suites of America** Ⓜ
(816) 842-6544. **$170-$245.** 612 Central Ave. Just s of I-70,
US 24 and 40, Broadway exit (downtown). Int corridors.
Pets: Small. Designated rooms, supervision.
Ⓐ$Ⓚ Ⓢ6 ☒ Ⓒ 🔓 🖳 🐾

◆◆◆ **Holiday Inn Kansas City South** Ⓜ ❀
(816) 765-4100. **$89-$100, 30 days notice.** 5701 Longview
Rd. 1 mi s of jct I-435 and US 71, on US 71. Int corridors.
Pets: Large, other. $15 one-time fee/room. Supervision.
Ⓐ$Ⓚ ☒ 🔓 🖳 🗐 🐾

◆◆◆ **Homestead Village Guest Studios** Ⓜ ❀
(816) 531-2212. **$80-$99.** 4535 Main St. Just ne of Country
Club Plaza. Int corridors. **Pets:** Small, other. $75 one-time
fee/room. Supervision.
☒ Ⓒ Ⓒ 🖳

◆◆◆ **Kansas City Airport Marriott Hotel** Ⓗ
(816) 464-2200. **$79-$139.** 775 Brasilia Ave. On KCI Airport; I-29 and exit 13, 1 mi w on Airport exit to Bern St. Int
corridors. **Pets:** Medium. No service, supervision, crate.
☒ Ⓒ 🗐 Ⓒ 🔓 🖳 🗐 🐾

◆◆◆ **Kansas City Marriott Downtown** Ⓗ
(816) 421-6800. **$92-$169.** 200 W 12th St. Just s of I-70,
US 24 and 40. Int corridors. **Pets:** Small. Designated
rooms, no service, supervision, crate.
☒ Ⓒ 🖳 🗐 🐾

Ⓐ ◆◆◆ **MainStay Suites** Ⓜ
(816) 891-8500. **$65-$100.** 9701 N Shannon Dr. I-29 and
Tiffany Springs Rd (exit 10). Int corridors. **Pets:** Medium.
Designated rooms, no service, supervision, crate.
Ⓢ🅰🆅🅴 Ⓢ6 ☒ Ⓒ 🗐 Ⓒ 🔓 🖳 🐾

◆◆ **Motel 6–1170**
(816) 333-4468. **$45-$61.** 6400 E 87th St. Just e of jct I-435 and exit 69. Ext corridors. **Pets:** Small. No service, supervision, crate.

🛇 ⊠ 🖾 🖾

◆◆◆ **Ramada Inn**
(816) 741-9500. **$69-$69.** 7301 NW Tiffany Springs Rd. Jct I-29 and exit 10, 1 mi s on frontage road. Int corridors. **Pets:** Medium. No service, supervision, crate.

🆂🅰🆅🅴 🛇 ⊠ 📷 🍴 🖾 🖾 🖾

◆◆ **Red Roof Inn-North** 🎹
(816) 452-8585. **$59-$77.** 3636 NE Randolph Rd. Just e of I-435 and SR 210, exit 55B northbound; exit 55 southbound. Ext corridors. **Pets:** Small. No service, supervision, crate.

🆂🅰🆅🅴 ⊠

◆◆◆ **The Residence Inn By Marriott**
 KCI 🅰 ❀
(816) 891-9009. **$129-$129.** 9900 NW Prairie View Rd. I-29, exit 10. Ext corridors. **Pets:** Small, other. $5 daily fee/room, $50 one-time fee/room. No service, supervision, crate.

🆂🅰🆂🅺 ⊠ 🖾 🖾 🍴 🖾 🖾 🖾 🖾

◆◆◆ **Residence Inn by Marriott Union**
 Hill 🅰 ❀
(816) 561-3000. **$144-$144.** 2975 Main St. 1.8 mi s. Ext corridors. **Pets:** Small. $50 deposit/pet, $5 daily fee/pet, $50 one-time fee/pet. Supervision.

🆂🅰🆂🅺 🛇 ⊠ 🖾 🍴 🖾 🖾

◆◆◆◆ **The Ritz-Carlton Kansas City** 🅷
(816) 756-1500. **$250.** 401 Ward Pkwy. In Country Club Plaza. Int corridors. **Pets:** Small. No service, supervision, crate.

⊠ 🖾 🍴 🖾

◆◆◆ **Sleep Inn** 🎹 ❀
(816) 891-0111. **$60-$65.** 7611 NW 97th Terrace. Just sw of jct I-29 and exit 10. Int corridors. **Pets:** Other. $15 one-time fee/room. No service, supervision, crate.

🆂🅰🆅🅴 🛇 ⊠ 🖾 🖾 🖾 🍴 🖾 🖾

◆◆ **Super 8 Motel-NW Kansas City** 🎹
(816) 587-0808. **$48-$67, 3 days notice.** 6900 NW 83rd Terr. Just sw of jct I-29 and exit 8. Int corridors. **Pets:** Small. Designated rooms, supervision.

🆂🅰🆂🅺 🛇 ⊠ 🍴

◆◆◆ **Westin Crown Center** 🅷 ❀
(816) 474-4400. **$110-$110.** 1 Pershing Rd. 0.5 mi s. Int corridors. **Pets:** Medium, other. $25 one-time fee/pet. No service, supervision, crate.

🆂🅰🆂🅺 🛇 ⊠ 📷 🖾 🍴 🖾 🖾 🍴 🖾 🖾

KEARNEY

◆◆ **Kearney Super 8 Motel** 🎹
(816) 628-6800. **$50-$55, 7 days notice.** 210 Platte Clay Way. Jct I-35 and exit 26, just ne. Int corridors. **Pets:** Designated rooms, supervision.

🆂🅰🆂🅺 🛇 ⊠

LEE'S SUMMIT

◆◆◆ **Comfort Inn of Lee's Summit** 🎹 ❀
(816) 524-8181. **$69-$99.** 607 SE Oldham Pkwy. Jct of US 50 and SR 291 N. Int corridors. **Pets:** $10 one-time fee/pet. Designated rooms, no service, supervision, crate.

🆂🅰🆂🅺 🛇 ⊠ 🖾 🍴 🖾

◆◆◆ **Lee's Summit Holiday Inn Express** 🎹 ❀
(816) 795-6400. **$84-$109.** 4825 NE Lakewood Way. Just se of jct I-470 and exit 14. Int corridors. **Pets:** Medium. Supervision.

🆂🅰🆂🅺 🛇 ⊠ 🖾 🖾 🍴 🖾

LIBERTY

◆◆ **Best Western Hallmark**
 Inn-North 🎹 ❀
(816) 781-8770. **$61-$75.** 209 N 291 Hwy. I-35, exit 16 and SR 152, 0.8 mi e on SR 152, just n. Ext corridors. **Pets:** Small, other. $20 one-time fee/room. No service, supervision, crate.

🆂🅰🆅🅴 ⊠ 🍴 🖾 🖾 📺

NORTH KANSAS CITY

◆◆◆ **Harrah's North Kansas City Casino and**
 Hotel 🅷
(816) 472-7777. **$119-$149.** One Riverboat Dr. From jct of I-35 and exit 6A, 1mi e on SR 210 (Armour Rd). Int corridors. **Pets:** Small. Designated rooms, no service, supervision, crate.

🆂🅰🆂🅺 🛇 ⊠ 🖾 🖾 🍴 🖾 🖾

PLATTE CITY

◆◆◆ **Comfort Inn-KCI** 🎹 ❀
(816) 858-5430. **$59-$99.** 1200 Hwy 92. I-29, exit 18, 1 mi w. Int corridors. **Pets:** Small. No service, supervision, crate.

🆂🅰🆅🅴 🛇 ⊠ 🖾 🖾 🍴 🖾

❀   **END METROPOLITAN AREA**   ❀

KENNETT

◆◆ **Cambridge Inn** 🎹 ❀
(573) 888-9860. **$65-$85.** 110 Independence. Hwy 412 and 25. Ext corridors. **Pets:** $10 daily fee/pet. No service, supervision, crate.

🆂🅰🆂🅺 🛇 ⊠ 🍴 🖾 🖾

KIMBERLING CITY

◆◆◆ **Kimberling Arms Resort** 🎹 ❀
(417) 739-2461. **$64-$79.** 1 S Hwy 13. On US 13; at the Kimberling City Bridge. Ext corridors. **Pets:** Small. No service, supervision, crate.

🆂🅰🆅🅴 🛇 ⊠ 🍴 🖾 🖾 🖾

⊕⊕ ◆◆ Kimberling Heights Resort Motel Ⓜ
(417) 779-4158. **$44-$59.** 1.5 mi s on US 13. Ext corridors.
Pets: Supervision.
🆂🅰🆅🅴 🆂🅰 🗐 🔲 🔁 ⌧ 🔁

⊕⊕ ◆◆ Kimberling Inn Resort & Conference
Center Ⓧ ❀
(417) 739-4311. **$70-$160, 3 days notice.** Hwy 13. Hwy
13; adjacent to Kimberling City Shopping Center. Ext corridors. **Pets:** Small, other. $100 deposit/room. Supervision.
🆂🅰🆅🅴 ⌧ 🗐 🔲 🍴 🔁 ⌧

KIRKSVILLE

⊕⊕ ◆◆◆ Best Western Shamrock Inn Ⓜ
(660) 665-8352. **$48-$56, 3 days notice.** 2501 S Business
63. 0.3 mi w jct US 63 and Business 63. Ext corridors.
Pets: Medium. No service, supervision, crate.
🆂🅰🆅🅴 ⌧ 🗐 🔁 ⌧

⊕⊕ ◆◆ Budget Host Village Inn Ⓜ ❀
(660) 563-3000. **$40-$47.** 1304 S Baltimore. US 63 S. Ext
corridors. **Pets:** Small, other. $5 daily fee/pet. Supervision.
🆂🅰🆅🅴 🆂🅰 ⌧ 🗐

◆◆ Comfort Inn Ⓜ ❀
(660) 665-2205. **$60-$75.** 2209 N Baltimore. US 63 N. Int
corridors. **Pets:** Designated rooms, supervision.
🅰🆂🅺 🆂🅰 ⌧ 🔓 🔁 🗐 🔲

KNOB NOSTER

◆◆ Whiteman Inn Ⓜ
(660) 563-0000. **$44-$75.** 2340 W Irish Ln. Jct US 50 and
SR 23. Ext/int corridors. **Pets:** Small. No service, supervision, crate.
🅰🆂🅺 🆂🅰 ⌧ 🔁 🗐 🔲 🔁

LAKE OZARK

◆◆◆ Holiday Inn Resort & Conference
Center Ⓜ ❀
(573) 365-2334. **$120-$130.** Business Hwy 54. 2.6 mi s of
Bagnell Dam on US 54 business route. Ext/int corridors.
Pets: Other. $50 deposit/room, $5 daily fee/room, $5 one-
time fee/room. Supervision.
🅰🆂🅺 🆂🅰 ⌧ 🔁 🔁 🔁 🗐 🔲 🍴 🔁 ⌧

LAMAR

◆◆ Best Western Blue Top Inn Ⓜ ❀
(417) 682-3333. **$35-$47, 3 days notice.** 65 SE 1st Ln. On
US 160, just se of jct US 71. Ext corridors. **Pets:** Other. No
service, supervision, crate.
🆂🅰 ⌧ 🔁

LEBANON

⊕⊕ ◆◆ Best Western Wyota Inn Ⓜ ❀
(417) 532-6171. **$38-$54.** 1225 Milk Creek Rd. I-44, exit
130. Ext corridors. **Pets:** Very small. $25 deposit/pet. Des-
ignated rooms, no service, supervision, crate.
🆂🅰🆅🅴 🆂🅰 ⌧ 🗐 🔲 🔁

◆ Brentwood Motel Ⓜ ❀
(417) 532-6131. **$29-$41.** 1320 S Jefferson. I-44, exit 129,
just s. Ext corridors. **Pets:** $50 deposit/room. Designated
rooms, no service, supervision, crate.
🅰🆂🅺 🆂🅰 ⌧ 🗐

◆◆ Econo Lodge Ⓜ
(417) 588-3226. **$39-$50.** 2073 W Elm. I-44 and exit 127,
just n. Ext corridors. **Pets:** Small. Designated rooms, no
service, supervision, crate.
🅰🆂🅺 🆂🅰 ⌧

◆◆ Quality Inn Ⓜ
(417) 532-7111. **$49-$60.** 2071 W Elm. I-44, exit 127. Ext
corridors. **Pets:** Designated rooms, supervision.
🅰🆂🅺 🆂🅰 ⌧ 🔲 🍴 🔁

LOUISIANA

⊕⊕ ◆◆ River's Edge Motel Ⓜ ❀
(573) 754-4522. **$33-$48.** 201 Mansion St. On US 54 at
Champ Clark Bridge. Ext corridors. **Pets:** Small, dogs only.
$20 deposit/room. No service, supervision, crate.
🆂🅰🆅🅴 ⌧ 🗐 🔲

MACON

◆◆ Best Western Inn Ⓜ ❀
(660) 385-2125. **$43-$51, 3 days notice.** 28933 Sunset Dr.
On Outer Rd S at US 36 and Long Branch Lake exit. Ext
corridors. **Pets:** Other. $20 deposit/room. Supervision.
🅰🆂🅺 🆂🅰 ⌧ 🗐 🔲 🔁

◆◆ Super 8 Motel Ⓜ
(660) 385-5788. **$41-$43.** 203 E Briggs Dr. Jct US 63 and
36. Int corridors. **Pets:** Small. No service, supervision,
crate.
🅰🆂🅺 🆂🅰 ⌧ 🗐

MARSHFIELD

◆◆◆ Holiday Inn Express Ⓜ
(417) 859-6000. **$69-$69.** 1301 Banning St. I-44 exit 100,
se corner. Int corridors. **Pets:** Small. No service, supervision, crate.
🅰🆂🅺 🆂🅰 ⌧ 🔓 🔁

MARSTON

◆◆ Super 8 Motel Ⓜ ❀
(573) 643-9888. **$45-$60, 7 days notice.** 501 SE Outer Rd.
I-55, exit 40. Int corridors. **Pets:** Other. $25 deposit/room.
Supervision.
🅰🆂🅺 🆂🅰 ⌧

MARYVILLE

◆◆ Super 8 Motel-Maryville Ⓜ ❀
(660) 582-8088. **$42-$51, 7 days notice.** Hwy 71S. 2 mi s
on US 71. Int corridors. **Pets:** Other. $10 deposit/room. No
service, supervision, crate.
🅰🆂🅺 🆂🅰 ⌧ 🗐 🔲

MEXICO

Best Western Inn
(573) 581-1440. **$38-$75.** 1010 E Liberty St. 0.5 mi e on US 54. Ext corridors. **Pets:** Designated rooms, no service, supervision, crate.

◆ Villa Inn
(573) 581-8350. **$29-$40, 3 days notice.** 4224 S Clark, Hwy 54 S Business. From jct US 54 and 54 S Business, 0.8 mi n. Ext corridors. **Pets:** Other. $3 deposit/pet, $3 daily fee/pet, $3 one-time fee/pet. Supervision.

MOBERLY

◆◆◆ Ramada Inn of Moberly
(660) 263-6540. **$53-$87.** US 24 & 63. At jct US 24 and 63. Ext/int corridors. **Pets:** Small. $30 deposit/pet. Supervision.

MONETT

◆◆ Oxford Inn
(417) 235-8039. **$45-$53.** 868 Hwy 60. On US 60, 1.3 mi e of jct SR 37. Ext corridors. **Pets:** Small. No service, supervision, crate.

MONROE CITY

◆◆ Monroe City Inn
(573) 735-4200. **$37-$50.** 3 Gateway Sq. US 24 and 36. Int corridors. **Pets:** Medium. $5 deposit/pet, $5 one-time fee/pet. No service, supervision, crate.

MOUNT VERNON

◆◆ Bel-Aire Motor Inn
(417) 466-2111. **$38-$50.** 900 E Mt Vernon Blvd. I-44, exit 46, just n. Ext/int corridors. **Pets:** Large, other. Supervision.

◆◆ Budget Host Ranch Motel
(417) 466-2125. **$40-$52.** 1015 E Mount Vernon Blvd. I-44, exit 46. Ext corridors. **Pets:** Small. $5 daily fee/pet. Supervision.

MOUNTAIN GROVE

◆◆ Best Western Ranch House Inn
(417) 926-3152. **$38-$54.** 111 E 17th St. At jct US 60 and 95, just s. Ext corridors. **Pets:** Small. No service, supervision, crate.

◆◆ Days Inn of Mountain Grove
(417) 926-5555. **$36-$52.** 300 E 19th St. At jct of US 60 and 95. Ext corridors. **Pets:** Supervision.

NEOSHO

◆◆ Super 8 Motel
(417) 455-1888. **$48-$63.** 3085 Gardner/Edgewood Dr. US 71, just s of jct US 60 and 71. Int corridors. **Pets:** Very small. $10 daily fee/pet. No service, supervision, crate.

NEVADA

◆◆ Best Western Rambler Motel
(417) 667-3351. **$36-$55.** 1401 E Austin St. On US 71 business route, just e of jct US 54, 1 mi w of jct US 71, Camp Clark and Nevada exit. Ext corridors. **Pets:** Small, other. No service, supervision, crate.

◆◆ Comfort Inn
(417) 667-6777. **$50-$55.** 2345 Marvel Dr. On US 71 business route, just w of jct US 71, Camp Clark and Nevada exit. Ext/int corridors. **Pets:** Small. Designated rooms, no service, supervision, crate.

OSAGE BEACH

◆◆ Lake Chateau Resort
(573) 348-2791. **$74-$89.** 5066 Hwy 54. Just s of Grand Glaize Bridge. Ext corridors. **Pets:** $10 one-time fee/pet. Designated rooms, no service, supervision, crate.

◆ Scottish Inns
(573) 348-3123. **$43-$59.** 5404 Hwy 54. 1 mi w of Grand Glaize Bridge. Ext corridors. **Pets:** Small. $5 daily fee/pet. Designated rooms, supervision.

OZARK

◆◆◆ Comfort Inn
(417) 485-6688. **$63-$69.** 1900 W Evangel St. US 65, exit SR 14, sw corner. Int corridors. **Pets:** Medium. $10 one-time fee/pet. Supervision.

PACIFIC

◆◆◆ Holiday Inn Express
(636) 257-8400. **$100-$149, 5 days notice.** 1400 W Osage St. I-44, exit 257. Ext/int corridors. **Pets:** Small, other. Supervision.

PERRYVILLE

◆◆ Best Western Colonial Inn
(573) 547-1091. **$57-$68.** 1500 Liberty St. I-55 and US 51 S, exit 129. Int corridors. **Pets:** Small, other. Supervision.

POPLAR BLUFF

◆◆◆ Comfort Inn
(573) 686-5200. **$54-$66, 7 days notice.** 2582 N West-wood Blvd. 3 mi n on US 60 and 67. Int corridors. **Pets:** Medium. $10 one-time fee/room. Designated rooms, supervision.

◆◆◆ Drury Inn M
(573) 686-2451. **$62-$82.** 2220 N Westwood Blvd. 3 mi n on US 60 and 67. Int corridors. **Pets:** No service, supervision, crate.

◆◆ Pear Tree Inn-Poplar Bluff M
(573) 785-7100. **$50-$69.** 2218 N Westwood Blvd. 3 mi n on US 60 and 67. Ext corridors. **Pets:** Small. No service, supervision, crate.

◆◆ Ramada Inn MI
(573) 785-7711. **Call for rates.** 2115 N Westwood Blvd. 3 mi n on US 60 and 67. Ext corridors. **Pets:** Small. No service, supervision, crate.

PORTAGEVILLE

◆ TeRoy Motel M
(573) 379-5461. **$32-$38.** 903 N Hwy 61. I-55, exit 32, 1.2 mi w, following signs. Ext corridors. **Pets:** Small. No service, supervision, crate.

RICH HILL

◆ Apache Motel M
(417) 395-2161. **$32-$38.** On Hwy B, just e of jct US 71. Ext corridors. **Pets:** No service, supervision, crate.

ROLLA

◆ Bestway Inn M
(573) 341-2158. **$26-$46.** 1631 Martin Springs Dr. I-44, exit 184. Ext corridors. **Pets:** Small. $5 deposit/pet. Designated rooms, no service, supervision, crate.

◆◆◆ Best Western Coachlight M
(573) 341-2511. **$65-$71.** 1403 Martin Springs Dr. At jct I-44 and Business Rt 44 S, exit 184. Ext corridors. **Pets:** Other. Designated rooms, no service, supervision, crate.

◆◆ Days Inn M
(573) 341-3700. **$45-$75.** 1207 Kingshighway. Just s of jct I-44, exit 184. Ext corridors. **Pets:** Other. Supervision.

◆◆◆ Drury Inn M
(573) 364-4000. **$40-$66.** 2006 N Bishop. Off I-44, exit 186, Hwy 63. Ext/int corridors. **Pets:** Small. No service, supervision, crate.

◆◆ Econo Lodge M
(573) 341-3130. **$37-$57, 7 days notice.** 1417 Martin Springs Dr. I-44, exit 184. Ext corridors. **Pets:** Other. Designated rooms, no service, supervision, crate.

◆◆◆ Holiday Inn Express M
(573) 364-8200. **$60-$90.** 1507 Martin Springs Dr. I-44, exit 184. Int corridors. **Pets:** Small, other. No service, supervision, crate.

◆◆◆ Howard Johnson Inn MI
(573) 364-7111. **$49-$75.** 127 H J Dr. I-44, exit 184. Ext/int corridors. **Pets:** Small. $10 one-time fee/pet. No service, supervision, crate.

◆◆ Ramada Inn Rolla MI
(573) 364-7977. **Call for rates.** 1701 Martin Spring Dr. I-44, exit 184. Ext corridors. **Pets:** Small. $25 deposit/pet. Designated rooms, no service, supervision, crate.

◆◆ Western Inn M
(573) 341-3050. **$33-$48.** 1605 Martin Springs Dr. I-44, exit 184. Ext/int corridors. **Pets:** Other. No service, supervision, crate.

SIKESTON

◆◆◆ Best Western Coach House Inn & Suites MI
(573) 471-9700. **$59-$69.** 220 S Interstate Dr. I-55, exit 67, just e, 0.5 mi s on Interstate Dr (Frontage Rd). Int corridors. **Pets:** Medium, other. $25 deposit/room. Designated rooms, supervision.

◆◆◆ Drury Inn M
(573) 471-4100. **$65-$89.** 2602 E Malone. I-55, exit 67. Int corridors. **Pets:** Other. Supervision.

◆◆◆ Pear Tree Inn by Drury M
(573) 471-8660. **$45-$65.** 2602 Rear East Malone. I-55, exit 67. Ext corridors. **Pets:** No service, supervision, crate.

SPRINGFIELD

◆◆◆ Baymont Inn & Suites M
(417) 889-8188. **$54-$69.** 3776 S Glenstone Ave. US 60. Int corridors. **Pets:** Small. Designated rooms, no service, supervision, crate.

◆◆ Best Western Coach House Inn MI
(417) 862-0701. **$44-$59.** 2535 N Glenstone Ave. I-44, exit 80A. Ext corridors. **Pets:** No service, supervision, crate.

Best Western Route 66 Rail Haven M
(417) 866-1963. **$35-$75.** 203 S Glenstone Ave. I-44, exit 80A, 3 mi s. Ext corridors. **Pets:** Other. Supervision.

Clarion Hotel H
(417) 883-6550. **$69-$89.** 3333 S Glenstone Ave. US 60, 0.5 mi n. Int corridors. **Pets:** $10 daily fee/pet. Designated rooms, no service, supervision, crate.

Comfort Suites M
(417) 886-5090. **$79-$95, 21 days notice.** 1260 E Independence St. US 60 (James River Expwy), exit National Ave. Ext corridors. **Pets:** Other. $10 one-time fee/pet. Supervision.

Days Inn M
(417) 862-0153. **$69-$150, 21 days notice.** 621 W Sunshine. US 160 and 60, 0.5 mi w. Int corridors. **Pets:** Medium. $10 daily fee/pet. No service, supervision, crate.

Drury Inn & Suites-Springfield M
(417) 863-8400. **$66-$86.** 2715 N Glenstone Ave. I-44, exit 80A, just s. Int corridors. **Pets:** Other. No service, supervision, crate.

GuestHouse Suites Plus A
(417) 520-7300. **$89.** 1550 E Raynell Pl. US 65, exit Battlefield Rd, 2.3 mi w, just s on Delaware, then just w. Ext corridors. **Pets:** Small. $75 deposit/room, $25 one-time fee/room. Supervision.

Holiday Inn University Plaza Hotel H
(417) 864-7333. **$99.** 333 John Q Hammons Pkwy. 0.5 mi e on St Louis St. Int corridors. **Pets:** Supervision.

Motel 6-1190 M
(417) 833-0880. **$34-$50.** 3114 Kentwood N. I-44, exit 80B. Ext corridors. **Pets:** Small. No service, supervision, crate.

Pear Tree Inn M
(417) 869-0001. **$44-$64.** 2745 N Glenstone Ave. I-44, exit 80A, just s. Ext/int corridors. **Pets:** Other. Supervision.

Ramada Inn MI
(417) 869-3900. **$54-$74.** 2820 N Glenstone. I-44, exit 80A, se. Ext/int corridors. **Pets:** Medium. $25 deposit/pet. Designated rooms, no service, supervision, crate.

Ramada Limited M
(417) 882-2220. **$59-$69, 3 days notice.** 3404 E Ridgeview. US 65, Battlefield Rd exit. Int corridors. **Pets:** Other. $10 daily fee/room. Supervision.

Red Roof Inn M
(417) 831-2100. **$36-$57.** 2655 N Glenstone Ave. I-44, exit 80A, just s. Ext corridors. **Pets:** Other. Supervision.

Sleep Inn of Springfield M
(417) 886-2464. **$64-$79, 7 days notice.** 233 E Camino Alto. US 60, Campbell Ave exit. Int corridors. **Pets:** Small. $10 one-time fee/room. Supervision.

Solar Inn M
(417) 866-6776. **$36-$55.** 2355 N Glenstone Ave. I-44, exit 80A. Ext corridors. **Pets:** Small. $25 deposit/room. Supervision.

ST. CLAIR

Budget Lodging M
(636) 629-1000. **$45-$69.** 866 S Outer Rd W. At jct I-44 and exit 240, then w. Ext/int corridors. **Pets:** Other. $5 daily fee/pet. Designated rooms, supervision.

ST. JAMES

Comfort Inn M
(573) 265-5005. **$59-$89, 7 days notice.** 110 N Outer Rd. I-44, exit 195, sw corner. Ext/int corridors. **Pets:** Small, dogs only. Designated rooms, no service, supervision, crate.

ST. JOSEPH

Drury Inn M
(816) 364-4700. **$59-$79.** 4213 Frederick Blvd. At jct I-29 and SR 6, exit 47. Int corridors. **Pets:** Small, other. No service, supervision, crate.

Holiday Inn MI
(816) 279-8000. **$82-$82.** 102 S Third St. Off I-229, Edmond St exit northbound; Felix St southbound; in the downtown area. Int corridors. **Pets:** Medium. Supervision.

Ramada Inn MI
(816) 233-6192. **$70-$80.** 4016 Frederick Ave. I-29, exit 47. Int corridors. **Pets:** Designated rooms, supervision.

ST. LOUIS METROPOLITAN AREA

BRIDGETON

AAA ◆◆ Red Roof Inn-Bridgeton **M** ❀
(314) 291-3350. **$57-$75.** 3470 Hollenberg Dr. 0.4 mi w
from jct I-270, exit 20B. Ext corridors. **Pets:** Designated
rooms, no service, supervision, crate.

SAVE ⊠ CTV

CLAYTON

◆◆◆ The Daniele Hotel **H**
(314) 721-0101. **$139.** 216 N Meramec Ave. 1.5 mi n of
I-64/US 40, exit 31 on Brentwood, e on Maryland, then just
n; from I-170, Ladue exit 1F, 0.8 mi e on Maryland, then just
n. Int corridors. **Pets:** Supervision.

ASK SAVE ⊠ 🛢 🖾

CREVE COEUR

◆◆◆ Drury Inn & Suites-Creve Coeur **M** ❀
(314) 989-1100. **$85-$105.** 11980 Olive Blvd. I-270, exit 14.
Int corridors. **Pets:** Other. No service, supervision, crate.

⊠ ♿ 🖉 🖾 🛢 🖳 🖾

EDMUNDSON

◆◆◆ Drury Inn-St. Louis Airport **M**
(314) 423-7700. **$76-$101.** 10490 Natural Bridge Rd. I-70,
Lambert exit 236, just se. Int corridors. **Pets:** Small. Designated rooms, no service, supervision, crate.

⊠ ♿ 🖉 🖾 🛢 🖳 🖾

EUREKA

AAA ◆◆◆ Ramada Inn at Six Flags **MI**
(636) 938-6661. **$129-$219.** 4901 Allenton Rd. Jct I-44 and
Allenton Rd, exit 261. Ext/int corridors. **Pets:** Small. No
service, supervision, crate.

SAVE SAVE ⊠ 🛢 🖳 🖾 🖾 CTV

AAA ◆◆ Red Carpet Inn **M** ❀
(636) 938-5348. **$60-$76.** 1725 W 5th St. 0.8 mi ne from jct
I-44 and Allenton Rd. Ext corridors. **Pets:** Medium. $20
deposit/pet. Designated rooms, no service, supervision,
crate.

SAVE SAVE ⊠ 🛢 🖾 🖾 CTV

FENTON

◆◆◆ Drury Inn & Suites Fenton **M** ❀
(636) 343-7822. **$68-$89.** 1088 S Hwy Dr. Jct I-44 and
Bowles Ave, exit 274. Int corridors. **Pets:** Small, other. No
service, supervision, crate.

⊠ 🖉 🛢 🖳 🖾

◆◆ Pear Tree Inn Fenton **M** ❀
(636) 343-8820. **$49-$75.** 1100 S Hwy Dr. Jct I-44 and
Bowles Ave, exit 274. Int corridors. **Pets:** Other. Supervision.

⊠ 🖉 🛢 🖾

FLORISSANT

AAA ◆◆ Red Roof Inn-Florissant **M** ❀
(314) 831-7900. **$53-$73.** 307 Dunn Rd. From I-270, eastbound exit 26B at Graham/Hanley rds, just n; westbound
exit at Florissant Rd (exit 27), 1 mi w on service road (Dunn
Rd). Ext corridors. **Pets:** Medium. Designated rooms, no
service, supervision, crate.

SAVE ⊠ 🖉 🖾

FORISTELL

AAA ◆◆ Best Western West 70 Inn **M** ❀
(636) 673-2900. **$50-$65.** 12 Hwy W. Jct exit I-70/US 40
and CR W (exit 203). Int corridors. **Pets:** Medium, other.
$10 one-time fee/pet. Designated rooms, supervision.

SAVE SAVE ⊠ 🖾

HAZELWOOD

◆◆◆ La Quinta Inn-Airport **M** ❀
(314) 731-3881. **$62-$82.** 5781 Campus Ct. Jct I-270 and
McDonnell Blvd, exit 23, just s. Int corridors. **Pets:** Small.
Designated rooms, no service, supervision, crate.

ASK ⊠ 🖉 🛢 🖳 🖾

KIRKWOOD

AAA ◆◆◆ Best Western Kirkwood Inn **H** ❀
(314) 821-3950. **$73-$88.** 1200 S Kirkwood Rd. Just n from
jct I-44 and Lindbergh Blvd, exit 277B. Int corridors.
Pets: Medium, other. $10 daily fee/room. No service, super-
vision, crate.

SAVE SAVE ⊠ 🖉 🛢 🖳 🍽 🖾

MARYLAND HEIGHTS

◆◆◆ Baymont Inn & Suites-St.Louis
    (Westport) **M**
(314) 878-1212. **$66-$73.** 12330 Dorsett Rd. Just w from jct
I-270 and Dorsett Rd, exit 17. Int corridors. **Pets:** Medium.
Designated rooms, no service, supervision, crate.

SAVE ⊠ 🛢 🖳

AAA ◆◆◆ Best Western Westport Park
    Hotel **MI** ❀
(314) 291-8700. **$79-$89, 7 days notice.** 2434 Old Dorsett
Rd. Just ne from jct I-270 and Dorsett Rd, exit 17. Int
corridors. **Pets:** Small. No service, supervision, crate.

SAVE ⊠ 🖉 🖾 🛢 🖳 🍽 🖾

AAA ◆◆◆ Comfort Inn Westport **MI**
(314) 878-1400. **$76-$100.** 12031 Lackland Rd. 1.3 mi se
from jct I-270 and Page Ave, exit 16A. Int corridors.
Pets: Medium. No service, supervision, crate.

SAVE ⊠ 🖉 🖾 🛢 🖳 🖾

◆◆◆ Drury Inn-Westport **M** ❀
(314) 576-9966. **$69-$89.** 12220 Dorsett Rd. I-270, exit 17,
just se. Int corridors. **Pets:** Medium. No service, supervision, crate.

⊠ 🖉 🛢 🖳 🖾

◆◆◆ **Harrah's Hotel at Riverport Casino
Center**
(314) 770-8100. **Call for rates.** 777 Casino Center Dr. Off
I-70 from Earth City Expwy, exit 231, 1 mi s to Casino
Center Dr, 1.2 mi nw. Int corridors. **Pets:** No service, super-
vision, crate.

⊠ ♿ 🛏 🔲 📺

◆◆ **Homestead Village Guest Studios** 🅼
(314) 878-8777. **$59.** 12161 Lackland Rd. Jct I-270 and
Page Ave, exit 16A, just e to Lackland Rd, then 0.3 mi w.
Int corridors. **Pets:** Small. Supervision.

⊠ 🛏 🔲

◆◆◆ **La Quinta Inn & Suites St. Louis
Westport** 🅼 ☙
(314) 991-3262. **$65-$85.** 11805 Lackland Rd. 1.5 mi se
from jct I-270 and Page Ave, exit 16A. Int corridors.
Pets: Small, other. Designated rooms, no service, supervision, crate.

🅰🆂🅺 ⊠ ♿ 📶 📺 🛏 🔲 📺

🆀🆀🆀 ◆◆ **Red Roof Inn-Westport** 🅼 ☙
(314) 991-4900. **$49-$62.** 11837 Lackland Rd. 1.5 mi se
from jct I-270 and Page Ave, exit 16A E. Ext corridors.
Pets: Other. Supervision.

🆂🅰🆅🅴 ⊠ 📶 📶

◆◆◆ **Summerfield Suites Hotel** 🅼 ☙
(314) 878-1555. **$109-$149.** 1855 Craigshire Rd. 1.8 mi sw
from jct I-270 and Page Ave, exit 16A. Ext/int corridors.
Pets: Medium. $10 daily fee/room, $150 one-time fee/room.
No service, supervision, crate.

🅰🆂🅺 📶 ⊠ 📶 🛏 🔲 📺 ⊠

MEHLVILLE

◆◆◆ **Best Western 55 South Inn** 🅼
(314) 416-7639. **$75-$135.** 6224 Heimos Industrial Park Dr.
I-55, exit 193, just e to Heimos Industrial Park Dr, then just
n. Int corridors. **Pets:** Medium. Designated rooms, no service, supervision, crate.

🅰🆂🅺 📶 ⊠ 📶 🛏 🔲 📺

◆◆◆ **Holiday Inn-South I-55 & Butler Hill
Rd** 🅼🅸 ☙
(314) 894-0700. **$85-$105.** 4234 Butler Hill Rd. Jct of I-55
and Butler Hill Rd, exit 195. Ext/int corridors. **Pets:** Other.
$100 deposit/room, $5 daily fee/room. No service, supervision, crate.

🅰🆂🅺 📶 ⊠ 📶 🛏 🔲 📶 📺

🆀🆀🆀 ◆◆ **Motel 6–1138** 🅼
(314) 892-3664. **$46-$62.** 6500 S Lindbergh Blvd. I-55 and
US 67 (Lindbergh Blvd), exit 197. Ext corridors.
Pets: Small. No service, supervision, crate.

📶 ⊠ 📶 📺 📺

RICHMOND HEIGHTS

◆◆◆ **Residence Inn By Marriott-St. Louis
Galleria** 🅰 ☙
(314) 862-1900. **$70-$129.** 1100 McMorrow Ave. I-170 N,
exit 1C; I-170 S, exit Brentwood Ave, 0.5 mi e of Galleria
via Galleria Pkwy. Ext corridors. **Pets:** Other. $10 daily fee/
pet, $25 one-time fee/pet. Supervision.

🅰🆂🅺 📶 ⊠ ♿ 📶 📺 🛏 🔲 📺 ⊠

ST. ANN

◆◆◆ **Hampton Inn-St. Louis Airport** 🅼
(314) 427-3400. **$75-$100.** 10800 Pear Tree Ln. Just sw of
I-70, exit 236. Int corridors. **Pets:** Designated rooms, no
service, supervision, crate.

⊠ 🛏 🔲 📺

ST. CHARLES

◆◆◆ **Baymont Inn St. Charles** 🅼 ☙
(636) 946-6936. **$59-$59.** 1425 S 5th St. 0.3 mi w of Missouri River Bridge on I-70 at Fifth St (exit 229B). Int corridors. **Pets:** Other. $5 daily fee/room. Supervision.

🅰🆂🅺 📶 ⊠ 📶 🛏 🔲 📶 📺

🆀🆀🆀 ◆◆ **Red Roof Inn-St Charles** 🅼
(636) 947-7770. **$57-$67.** 2010 Zumbehl Rd. Jct I-70 and
Zumbehl Rd, exit 227. Ext corridors. **Pets:** Small. Supervision.

🆂🅰🆅🅴 ⊠ 📶

ST. LOUIS

◆◆◆ **Drury Inn Convention Center** 🅼🅸
(314) 231-8100. **$75-$100.** 711 N Broadway. From I-70 exit
at Convention Center, just s. Int corridors. **Pets:** Supervision.

⊠ 🛏 🔲 📶 📺

◆◆◆ **Drury Inn Union Station** 🅼🅸
(314) 231-3900. **$106-$131.** 201 S 20th St. Just e of Jefferson Ave; between Market St and Clark Ave. Int corridors.
Pets: Small. Supervision.

⊠ 📶 🛏 🔲 📶 📺

◆◆◆ **Hampton Inn Union Station** 🅷
(314) 241-3200. **$95-$120.** 2211 Market St. From I-64/US
40, exit 39 just n on Jefferson, then just e. Int corridors.
Pets: Medium. Designated rooms, no service, supervision,
crate.

⊠ 🛏 🔲 📶 📺

◆◆◆ **Holiday Inn Downtown Select** 🅷 ☙
(314) 421-4000. **$89-$119.** 811 N 9th St. I-70, exit 250, just
w of Convention Center. Int corridors. **Pets:** Small. $100
deposit/room. No service, supervision, crate.

⊠ 📶 🛏 🔲 📶 📺

◆◆◆ **Omni Majestic Hotel** 🅷 ☙
(314) 436-2355. **$99-$169.** 1019 Pine St. Between 10th
and 11th. Int corridors. **Pets:** Other. Supervision.

🅰🆂🅺 📶 ⊠ 📶 🛏 🔲 📶

🆀🆀🆀 ◆◆ **Red Roof Inn-Hampton** 🅼 ☙
(314) 645-0101. **$76-$100.** 5823 Wilson Ave. 0.3 mi se
from jct I-44 and Hampton Ave, exit 286. Ext corridors.
Pets: Other. Supervision.

🆂🅰🆅🅴 ⊠ 📶

🆀🆀🆀 ◆◆◆ **Regal Riverfront Hotel** 🅷 ☙
(314) 241-9500. **$109-$119.** 200 S Fourth St. Between
Spruce and Walnut sts. Int corridors. **Pets:** Small. Supervision.

🆂🅰🆅🅴 ⊠ 📶 🛏 🔲 📶 📺

ST. PETERS

◆◆◆ Drury Inn-St. Charles/St. Peters 🅼 ❀
(636) 397-9700. **$65-$86.** 80 Mid Rivers Mall Drive. I-70 at exit 222. Int corridors. **Pets:** Other. No service, supervision, crate.

⊠ ♿ 🐾 🖺 🛏 🖵 🖨

◆◆◆ Holiday Inn Select of St. Peters/St.
    Charles 🅼📶
(636) 928-1500. **$70-$90.** 4221 S Outer Rd. I-70, Cave Springs exit 225, 0.5 mi w. Int corridors. **Pets:** Small. Designated rooms, supervision.

A$K �ᵈ ⊠ 🛏 🖵 🍴 🖨

WENTZVILLE

◆◆◆ Holiday Inn-Wentzville 🅼📶
(636) 327-7001. **$79-$94.** 900 Corporate Pkwy. I-70 exit 212A, 0.3 mi w on SR Service Rd. Int corridors. **Pets:** Very small. Designated rooms, no service, supervision, crate.

A$K 🖬 ⊠ 🐾 🛏 🍴 🖨

❀ **END METROPOLITAN AREA** ❀

ST. ROBERT

🆔 ◆◆◆ Best Western Montis Inn 🅼 ❀
(573) 336-4299. **$45-$65, 3 days notice.** 14086 Hwy Z. I-44, exit 163. Ext corridors. **Pets:** Other. No service, supervision, crate.

SAVE 🖬 ⊠ 🛏 🖨

🆔 ◆◆◆ Days Inn 🅼 ❀
(573) 336-5556. **$47-$67.** 14125 Hwy Z. I-44 exit 163. Ext corridors. **Pets:** Medium. $5 daily fee/pet. Designated rooms, no service, supervision, crate.

SAVE 🖬 ⊠ 🛏 🖨

🆔 ◆◆ Econo Lodge 🅼 ❀
(573) 336-7272. **$50-$70.** I-44 and exit 161. Ext corridors. **Pets:** Small. No service, supervision, crate.

SAVE 🖬 ⊠ 🛏 🖵 🖨

◆◆ Ramada Inn-Fort Leonard Wood 🅼📶
(573) 336-3121. **$51-$59.** I-44, eastbound exit 161; westbound exit 161A. Ext/int corridors. **Pets:** No service, supervision, crate.

A$K 🖬 ⊠ 🐾 🛏 🖵 🍴 🖨 🖾

STE. GENEVIEVE

🆔 ◆◆ Family Budget Inn 🅼 ❀
(573) 543-2272. **$40-$60.** 17030 New Bremen Rd. Just w on SR M from jct I-55, exit 143. Ext/int corridors. **Pets:** $20 deposit/room, $3 one-time fee/room. Designated rooms, no service, supervision.

SAVE 🖬 ⊠ 🛏 🖨

STOCKTON

🆔 ◆ Holliday Motel 🅼 ❀
(417) 276-4443. **$37-$45.** 400 Hwy 32 E. SR 32, just e of jct SR 39. Ext corridors. **Pets:** Other. $5 one-time fee/pet. Supervision.

SAVE 🖬 ⊠ 🖨

🆔 ◆◆ Super 8 Motel-Wentzville 🅼 ❀
(636) 327-5300. **$40-$53, 7 days notice.** 4 Pantera Dr. I-70/US 40, exit 208 (Pearce Blvd), on S Outer Rd. Int corridors. **Pets:** Dogs only. $50 deposit/pet. No service, supervision, crate.

SAVE 🖬 ⊠ 🐾 🖨

🆔 ◆ Villager Lodge 🅼
(636) 327-6263. **$35-$55.** 404 N Business Rt 61. I-70, exit 210B, 0.5 mi n to Pitman Ave, just w to Business Rt 61, then 0.4 mi n. Ext corridors. **Pets:** Small. Supervision.

SAVE 🖬 ⊠ 🛏

STRAFFORD

◆◆ Super 8 Motel 🅼
(417) 736-3883. **$35-$46.** 315 E Chestnut St. I-44, exit 88, se corner. Int corridors. **Pets:** Supervision.

⊠

SULLIVAN

🆔 ◆◆ Best Western-Sullivan 🅼 ❀
(573) 468-3136. **$45-$60.** 307 N Service Rd. I-44, exit 225. Ext corridors. **Pets:** $5 daily fee/pet. No service, supervision, crate.

SAVE 🖬 ⊠ 🛏 🖵 🖨

🆔 ◆◆ Family Motor Inn 🅼 ❀
(573) 468-4119. **$45-$65.** 209 N Service Rd W. I-44, exit 225. Ext corridors. **Pets:** Dogs only. $3 daily fee/room. Supervision.

SAVE 🖬 ⊠ 🛏 🖨 🖾

◆◆ Ramada Inn 🅼📶 ❀
(573) 468-4172. **$45-$60, 7 days notice.** 309 N Service Rd. I-44, exit 225. Ext corridors. **Pets:** Small. $25 deposit/room. No service, supervision, crate.

A$K 🖬 ⊠ 🍴 🖨

SWEET SPRINGS

🆔 ◆◆ People's Choice Motel 🅼 ❀
(660) 335-6315. **$29-$41.** 1001 N Locust St. Jct I-70 and SR 127, exit 66. Ext corridors. **Pets:** $20 deposit/room. No service, supervision, crate.

SAVE 🖬 ⊠

TIPTON

◆ Twin Pine Motel 🅼 ❀
(660) 433-5525. **$29-$42.** 452 Hwy 50 W. On US 50 and SR 5; w of town. Ext corridors. **Pets:** Very small, other. $5 daily fee/pet. No service, supervision, crate.

A$K 🖬 ⊠ 🛏

WAPPAPELLO

◆◆◆ Millers Motor Lodge
(573) 222-8579. **$48-$89, 7 days notice.** Rt 2, Box 2900. 2 mi s of Wappapello Dam, on Hwy T. Ext corridors. **Pets:** Small. $10 one-time fee/room. No service, supervision, crate.

WARRENSBURG

⬤⬤⬤ ◆◆ University Inn Conference Center Ⓜ
(660) 747-5125. **$49-$64.** Jct Hwys 13 & 50. Jct US 50 and SR 13. Ext corridors. **Pets:** Medium. No service, supervision, crate.
SAVE S✆ ✕ ⊟ ❚❙ ⌂

WEST PLAINS

◆◆ Ramada Inn Ⓜ
(417) 256-8191. **$50-$59.** 1301 Preacher Roe Blvd. 2 mi sw at jct US 160 and 63 bypass. Ext/int corridors. **Pets:** Other. $10 daily fee/room. Supervision.

BELGRADE

AAA ◆◆◆ Holiday Inn Express **M** 🐾
(406) 388-0800. **$74-$74.** 6261 Jackrabbit Ln. I-90, exit 298, just s on SR 85. Int corridors. **Pets:** Other. No service, supervision, crate.
[SAVE] [S🐾] [✕] [🔔] [🖥] [💻] [🍴]

BIG SKY

AAA ◆◆◆ Best Western Buck's T-4
Lodge **M** 🐾
(406) 995-4111. **$119-$169, 7 days notice.** 46625 Gallatin Rd. US 191, 1 mi s of Big Sky entrance. Ext/int corridors. **Pets:** Medium, other. $5 daily fee/pet. No service, supervision, crate.
[SAVE] [S🐾] [✕] [💻] [🖥] [💻] [🍴] [✕]

AAA ◆◆◆ Comfort Inn at Big Sky **M**
(406) 995-2333. **$99-$129, 30 days notice.** 47214 Gallatin Rd. US 191, 0.7 mi s of Big Sky entrance. Int corridors. **Pets:** Small. No service, supervision, crate.
[SAVE] [S🐾] [✕] [💻] [🖥] [💻] [🖥] [✕] [CTV]

◆◆◆ 320 Guest Ranch **RA** 🐾
(406) 995-4283. **$125-$319, 30 days notice.** 205 Buffalo Horn. US 191, 11.8 mi s of Big Sky. Ext corridors. **Pets:** Other. $10 daily fee/pet. No service, supervision, crate.
[ASK] [S🐾] [✕] [🖥] [💻] [🍴] [✕] [🎿]

BIG TIMBER

◆◆◆ Big Timber Super 8 Motel **M** 🐾
(406) 932-8888. **$57-$74.** Hwy 10. I-90, exit 367. Int corridors. **Pets:** Supervision.
[ASK] [S🐾] [✕] [🔔]

BIGFORK

AAA ◆◆ Timbers Motel **M** 🐾
(406) 837-6200. **$32-$78, 7 days notice.** 8540 Hwy 35. Just n on SR 35 from jct of SR 209. Ext corridors. **Pets:** $25 deposit/room, $5 daily fee/pet. No service, supervision, crate.
[✕] [🔔] [💻] [🖥]

BILLINGS

AAA ◆◆◆ Best Western Billings **M** 🐾
(406) 248-9800. **$68-$89.** 5610 S Frontage Rd. I-90, exit 446, just s. Ext/int corridors. **Pets:** Medium, other. Designated rooms, no service, supervision, crate.
[SAVE] [S🐾] [✕] [🔔] [🖥] [🖥] [💻]

AAA ◆◆◆ Best Western Ponderosa Inn **M**
(406) 259-5511. **$55-$80.** 2511 1st Ave N. Downtown, I-90 business loop. Ext/int corridors. **Pets:** Designated rooms, supervision.
[SAVE] [S🐾] [✕] [🔔] [🖥] [💻] [🍴] [🖥]

AAA ◆◆◆ The Billings Inn **M** 🐾
(406) 252-6800. **$49-$65.** 880 N 29th St. I-90, exit 27th St, 2 mi n on 27th St, just w on 9th Ave; across from Deaconess Hospital. Int corridors. **Pets:** Other. $5 daily fee/room. Designated rooms, no service, supervision, crate.
[SAVE] [S🐾] [✕] [🔔]

◆◆ Billings Super 8 Lodge **M** 🐾
(406) 248-8842. **$45-$65, 30 days notice.** 5400 Southgate Dr. I-90, exit 447, just n on S Billings Blvd, 0.8 mi w on King Ave, just s on Parkway Ln. Int corridors. **Pets:** Other. $20 deposit/room. No service, supervision, crate.
[ASK] [S🐾] [✕] [🔔] [🖥] [🔔]

AAA ◆◆◆ Cherry Tree Inn **M** 🐾
(406) 252-5603. **$35-$50.** 823 N Broadway. I-90, exit 450, 2 mi n on 27th St, just w on 9th Ave; opposite Deaconess Hospital. Int corridors. **Pets:** Other. No service, supervision, crate.
[✕] [🔔] [💻]

◆◆◆ Comfort Inn of Billings **M**
(406) 652-5200. **$70-$80.** 2030 Overland Ave. I-90, exit 446, n on King Ave W, just s on Overland Ave, 1st stoplight. Int corridors. **Pets:** Supervision.
[ASK] [S🐾] [✕] [🔔] [🖥] [💻] [🖥]

◆◆ Days Inn **M**
(406) 252-4007. **Call for rates.** 843 Parkway Ln. I-90, exit 447, just n on S Billings Blvd, 0.8 mi s on Parkway Ln, just s; I-90, exit 446; following signs eastbound. Int corridors. **Pets:** Designated rooms, no service, supervision, crate.
[✕] [🔔] [🖥] [💻]

AAA ◆◆◆ Hilltop Inn **M** ☆
(406) 245-5000. **$51-$65.** 1116 N 28th St. I-90, exit 27th St, 2 mi n on 27th St, just w on 11th Ave, just n; adjacent to St Vincent Hospital. Int corridors. **Pets:** Other. $5 daily fee/room. Designated rooms, no service, supervision, crate.
SAVE S✆ ✕ ⌂ ⬛

◆◆◆ Holiday Inn Grand Montana Billings **H**
(406) 248-7701. **$79-$99.** 5500 Midland Rd. I-90, exit 446. Int corridors. **Pets:** Medium. Designated rooms, supervision.
ASK S✆ ✕ ♿ ▨ ⬯ ⬛ ▣ ⊓ ⌲

◆◆◆ Howard Johnson Express Inn **M**
(406) 248-4656. **$69-$79, 7 days notice.** 1001 S 27th St. I-90, exit 450, just n on SR 3 (S 27th St). Int corridors. **Pets:** No service, supervision, crate.
ASK S✆ ✕ ⌂ ⬯ ⬛ ▣

AAA ◆◆ Kelly Inn **M** ☆
(406) 252-2700. **$46-$76, 7 days notice.** 5425 Midland Rd. I-90, exit 446, 0.5 mi se. Ext/int corridors. **Pets:** Medium, other. Designated rooms, no service, supervision, crate.
SAVE S✆ ✕ ⬯ ⬛ ▣ ⌲

◆◆◆ Quality Inn Homestead **M** ☆
(406) 652-1320. **$56-$81.** 2036 Overland Ave. I-90, exit 446, n on King Ave W, 2 blks s, 1st stoplight. Int corridors. **Pets:** $25 deposit/room. Supervision.
ASK S✆ ✕ ⬛ ▣ ⌲

AAA ◆◆◆ Radisson Northern Hotel **H**
(406) 245-5121. **$89-$109.** 19 N 28th St. Downtown. Int corridors. **Pets:** Medium. Designated rooms, supervision.
SAVE S✆ ✕ ▨ ⬛ ▣ ⊓

◆◆ Ramada Limited **M** ☆
(406) 252-2584. **$60-$80.** 1345 Mullowney Ln. I-90, exit 446, just s. Int corridors. **Pets:** Other. $20 deposit/room. No service, supervision, crate.
ASK S✆ ✕ ▨ ⬯ ⬛ ⌲

AAA ◆◆ Rimview Inn **M**
(406) 248-2622. **$47-$58.** 1025 N 27th St. I-90, exit 450, 2 mi n. Ext/int corridors. **Pets:** Small. Designated rooms, supervision.
SAVE S✆ ✕ ⬛

◆◆◆ Sheraton Billings Hotel **H** ☆
(406) 252-7400. **$85-$99.** 27 N 27th St. I-90 business loop and SR 3. Int corridors. **Pets:** Medium. Supervision.
ASK ✕ ⬯ ⬛ ▣ ⊓ ⌲

BOZEMAN

◆◆◆ Bozeman Days Inn and Conference Center **M** ☆
(406) 587-5251. **$58-$99.** 1321 N 7th. I-90, exit 306, just s. Int corridors. **Pets:** $25 deposit/room. Designated rooms, no service, supervision, crate.
ASK S✆ ✕ ⬯ ⬛ ▣

AAA ◆◆ The Bozeman Inn **M**
(406) 587-3176. **$57-$79.** 1235 N 7th Ave. I-90, exit 306, just s. Ext corridors. **Pets:** Designated rooms, no service, supervision, crate.
SAVE S✆ ✕ ⬛ ▣ ⌲

◆◆ Bozeman Super 8 **M** ☆
(406) 586-1521. **$55-$75.** 800 Wheat Dr. I-90, exit 306, just n, just w. Int corridors. **Pets:** Medium, other. $5 daily fee/pet. Designated rooms, no service, supervision, crate.
ASK S✆ ✕ ⬛

AAA ◆◆◆ Bozeman's Western Heritage Inn **M** ☆
(406) 586-8534. **$58-$83.** 1200 E Main St. I-90 business loop, 0.5 mi w of jct I-90, exit 309. Int corridors. **Pets:** $25 deposit/room, $5 daily fee/pet. No service, supervision, crate.
SAVE S✆ ✕

◆◆◆ Bridger Mountains Highland House **BB**
(406) 587-0904. **$82-$90.** 1540 Nelson Rd. I-90, exit 305, just n, just s on Springhill Rd, w on SR 205 0.9 mi, then n on Nelson Rd 1.5 mi. Int corridors. **Pets:** Medium. No service, supervision, crate.
✕ ⬛ K CTV ☎

AAA ◆◆◆ Holiday Inn **M** ☆
(406) 587-4561. **$99-$99.** 5 Baxter Ln. I-90 business loop, just s of jct I-90, exit 306. Int corridors. **Pets:** Other. Supervision.
SAVE S✆ ✕ ⬯ ⬛ ▣ ⊓ ⌲

AAA ◆ Rainbow Motel **M** ☆
(406) 587-4201. **$50-$70.** 510 N 7th Ave. I-90 business loop, 0.8 mi s of jct I-90, exit 306. Ext corridors. **Pets:** Small. $5 one-time fee/room. Designated rooms, no service, supervision, crate.
SAVE ✕ ⬛ ▣ ⌲

◆◆ Ramada Limited **M** ☆
(406) 585-2626. **$59-$119.** 2020 Wheat Dr. I-90, exit 306, just n, just w. Ext/int corridors. **Pets:** Other. Supervision.
ASK S✆ ✕ ⌲

AAA ◆◆ Royal "7" Budget Inn **M** ☆
(406) 587-3103. **$48-$58.** 310 N 7th Ave. I-90 business loop, 0.8 mi s of jct I-90, exit 306. Ext corridors. **Pets:** Other. Designated rooms, no service, supervision, crate.
✕ ⬛ ⊠

◆◆ Sleep Inn **M** ☆
(406) 585-7888. **$79-$99.** 817 Wheat Dr. I-90, exit 306, just n. Int corridors. **Pets:** Dogs only. Supervision.
ASK S✆ ✕ ⌂ ⬯ ⬛ ▣ ⌲

AAA ◆◆ TLC Inn **M** ☆
(406) 587-2100. **$60-$69.** 805 Wheat Dr. I-90, exit 306, just n and just w. Int corridors. **Pets:** $5 daily fee/room. No service, supervision, crate.
SAVE S✆ ✕ ⬛

BUTTE

AAA ◆◆◆ Best Western Butte Plaza Inn **M** ☆
(406) 494-3500. **$89-$109, 3 days notice.** 2900 Harrison Ave. I-90, exit 127 (Harrison Ave). Int corridors. **Pets:** Medium. $50 deposit/room. Designated rooms, supervision.
SAVE S✆ ✕ ⬛ ▣ ⊓ ⌲

✦✦✦ Comfort Inn of Butte M ✿
(406) 494-8850. **$59-$94.** 2777 Harrison Ave. Just s off I-90 and I-15, exit 127. Int corridors. **Pets:** Medium. $5 daily fee/room. No service, supervision, crate.

✦✦✦ Days Inn M ✿
(406) 494-7000. **$58-$109.** 2700 Harrison Ave. I-15, exit 127, just n on Harrison Ave, e on Cornell St. Int corridors. **Pets:** Medium. Designated rooms, no service, supervision, crate.

✦✦✦ Ramada Inn Copper King MI ✿
(406) 494-6666. **$89-$109.** 4655 Harrison Ave S. I-15 and 90, exit 127A, 2 mi s on SR 2 (Harrison Ave). Int corridors. **Pets:** Other. $10 daily fee/room. Designated rooms, supervision.

✦✦ Rocker Inn M ✿
(406) 723-5464. **$38-$48.** 122001 W Brown's Gulch Rd. I-15 and I-90, exit 122 (Rocker). Int corridors. **Pets:** Medium. Designated rooms, supervision.

✦✦ Super 8 Motel of Butte M ✿
(406) 494-6000. **$60-$80, 5 days notice.** 2929 Harrison Ave. I-15 and 90, exit 127, just s. Int corridors. **Pets:** Medium, other. $50 deposit/room, $5 daily fee/pet. Designated rooms, supervision.

✦✦ War Bonnet Inn MI ✿
(406) 494-7800. **$69-$99, 5 days notice.** 2100 Cornell Ave. I-15 and I-90, exit 127B, just n on Harrison Ave, just e. Int corridors. **Pets:** Other. $10 one-time fee/pet. Designated rooms, supervision.

CHINOOK

✦✦ Chinook Motor Inn MI
(406) 357-2248. **$44-$58, 5 days notice.** 100 Indiana St. US 2. Int corridors. **Pets:** Designated rooms, no service, supervision, crate.

CHOTEAU

✦ Big Sky Motel M ✿
(406) 466-5318. **$38-$55.** 209 S Main. US 89 from city center. Ext corridors. **Pets:** Other. $5 one-time fee/pet. Designated rooms, no service, supervision, crate.

COLSTRIP

✦✦ Super 8 Motel of Colstrip LLC M
(406) 748-3400. **$49-$53.** 6227 Main St. SR 39. Int corridors. **Pets:** No service, supervision, crate.

COLUMBIA FALLS

✦✦ Glacier Park Super 8 M
(406) 892-0888. **$63-$78.** 7336 US 2 E. Just n on US 2 from jct of SR 40/206. Ext/int corridors. **Pets:** Supervision.

✦✦✦ Meadow Lake Resort X ✿
(406) 892-7601. **$89-$459, 30 days notice.** 100 St Andrews Dr. Jct US 2 and SR 40, 1.4 mi e on US 2, 1.1 mi n on Meadow Lake Blvd. Ext/int corridors. **Pets:** $15 daily fee/pet. Designated rooms, no service, supervision, crate.

COLUMBUS

✦✦ Super 8 of Columbus M ✿
(406) 322-4101. **$49-$74.** 602 8th Ave N. SR 78, just s jct I-90, exit 408. Int corridors. **Pets:** Other. $5 one-time fee/room. Supervision.

CONRAD

✦✦ Super 8 of Conrad M ✿
(406) 278-7676. **$49-$74.** 215 N Main. I-15, exit 339, just w. Int corridors. **Pets:** Other. $50 deposit/room, $5 daily fee/pet. No service, supervision, crate.

COOKE CITY

✦ Soda Butte Lodge MI
(406) 838-2251. **$65-$70, 3 days notice.** 209 US 212. Center; on US 212. Int corridors. **Pets:** Supervision.

CUT BANK

✦✦ Glacier Gateway Inn M
(406) 873-5544. **$46-$57.** 1121 E Railroad St. US 2, just e from city center. Int corridors. **Pets:** Supervision.

DEER LODGE

✦✦✦ Coleman Fee Mansion Bed & Breakfast BB ✿
(406) 846-2922. **$65-$150, 7 days notice.** 500 Missouri Ave. City center. Ext/int corridors. **Pets:** Small, dogs only. $10 daily fee/pet, $10 one-time fee/pet. No service, supervision, crate.

✦✦ Scharf's Motor Inn M ✿
(406) 846-2810. **$30-$50.** 819 Main St. Downtown; on I-90 business loop. Ext corridors. **Pets:** Other. No service, supervision, crate.

✦✦ Super 8 Motel M ✿
(406) 846-2370. **$54-$79.** 1150 N Main St. I-90, exit 184, 0.3 mi s. Int corridors. **Pets:** Medium, other. $5 one-time fee/pet. Designated rooms, no service, supervision, crate.

DILLON

✦✦✦ Best Western Paradise Inn M ✿
(406) 683-4214. **$51-$71.** 650 N Montana St. I-15, exit 63, 0.3 mi s on SR 41. Ext corridors. **Pets:** No service, supervision, crate.

⚠️ ◆◆◆ Comfort Inn of Dillon M 🐾
(406) 683-6831. **$55-$74.** 450 N Interchange. I-15, exit 63 (N Dillon). Int corridors. **Pets:** Other. $5 daily fee/pet. No service, supervision, crate.
[SAVE] [S🐾] [✕] [🔔] [🍴] [💻] [🏊]

⚠️ ◆◆◆ GuestHouse Inns & Suites M 🐾
(406) 683-3636. **$65-$75.** 580 Sinclair. I-15, exit 63 (N Dillon). Int corridors. **Pets:** Other. $10 one-time fee/room. Supervision.
[S🐾] [✕] [♿] [🍴] [🔔] [💻] [🏊]

⚠️ ◆◆ Sundowner Motel M 🐾
(406) 683-2375. **$43-$50.** 500 N Montana St. I-15, exit 63, just s. Ext corridors. **Pets:** Other. Designated rooms, no service, supervision, crate.
[SAVE] [✕] [🍴]

◆◆ Super 8 Motel M
(406) 683-4288. **Call for rates.** 550 N Montana St. I-15, exit 63, just n on US 91. Int corridors. **Pets:** Supervision.
[✕] [🔔]

EAST GLACIER PARK

⚠️ ◆ Dancing Bears Inn M
(406) 226-4402. **$55-$75, 7 days notice.** 147 Montana St. Center; just off US 2, following signs. Ext/int corridors. **Pets:** No service, supervision, crate.
[SAVE] [✕] [🔔]

ENNIS

⚠️ ◆◆◆ El Western Resort 🅲 🐾
(406) 682-4217. **$65-$185, 3 days notice.** US Hwy 287 S. 0.8 mi s on US 287. Ext corridors. **Pets:** $5 daily fee/pet. No service, supervision, crate.
[SAVE] [✕] [🔔] [💻] [🍴] [🎵]

⚠️ ◆◆ Fan Mountain Inn M 🐾
(406) 682-5200. **$40-$65.** 204 N Main. US 287, just nw of city center. Ext corridors. **Pets:** Dogs only. $5 daily fee/room, $5 one-time fee/room. No service, supervision, crate.
[✕] [🔔] [🔔] [🍴]

⚠️ ◆ Riverside Motel M 🐾
(406) 682-4240. **$40-$60.** 346 Main St. US 287, e of town. Ext corridors. **Pets:** Other. $3 one-time fee/pet. Designated rooms, no service, supervision, crate.
[SAVE] [S🐾] [✕] [🔔] [💻] [🎵]

⚠️ ◆ Sportsman Lodge M 🐾
(406) 682-4242. **$45-$65.** 310 US Hwy 287 N. US 287, just nw of city center. Ext corridors. **Pets:** $5 daily fee/pet, $5 one-time fee/pet. Designated rooms, no service, supervision, crate.
[SAVE] [✕] [🔔] [🔔] [🎵]

FORSYTH

⚠️ ◆◆ Best Western Sundowner Inn M 🐾
(406) 356-2115. **$55-$55.** 1018 Front St. I-94, exit 95, 0.5 mi nw on N Frontage Rd. Ext corridors. **Pets:** $3 daily fee/pet, no service, supervision, crate.
[S🐾] [✕] [🔔] [💻]

⚠️ ◆◆ Rails Inn Motel M 🐾
(406) 356-2242. **$45-$55, 3 days notice.** 3rd & Front sts. I-90, exit 93, just n, 0.5 mi e on Frontage Rd. Int corridors. **Pets:** Other. No service, supervision, crate.
[SAVE] [S🐾] [✕] [🔔] [🔔]

⚠️ ◆ Restwel Motel M 🐾
(406) 356-2771. **$34-$40.** 810 Front St. I-94, exit 95, 0.8 mi nw on N Frontage Rd. Ext corridors. **Pets:** Small. Designated rooms, no service, supervision, crate.
[SAVE] [S🐾] [✕] [🔔]

⚠️ ◆ Westwind Motor Inn M 🐾
(406) 356-2038. **$36-$39.** 225 Westwind Lane. 0.3 mi n of I-94, exit 93 (W Main St). Int corridors. **Pets:** $2 daily fee/pet, $2 one-time fee/pet. No service, supervision, crate.
[SAVE] [S🐾] [✕]

GALLATIN GATEWAY

◆◆ Millers of Montana Bed & Breakfast BB
(406) 763-4102. **$50-$75** (no credit cards), 7 days notice. 1.4 mi n on US 191, 0.7 mi e, veer just s, turn right, continue to end of drive. Int corridors. **Pets:** Very small. Supervision.
[ASK] [S🐾] [✕] [🎵] [🎵] [📺] [🎵]

GARDINER

⚠️ ◆◆◆ Best Western by Mammoth Hot Springs M
(406) 848-7311. **$85-$109.** S Hwy 89. 0.5 mi n on US 89. Ext/int corridors. **Pets:** Designated rooms, no service, supervision, crate.
[S🐾] [✕] [♿] [🔔] [💻] [🏊] [🎵]

⚠️ ◆ Yellowstone River Motel M
(406) 848-7303. **$55-$75.** 14 E Park St. Just e of US 89. Ext corridors. **Pets:** Medium. Designated rooms, supervision.
[SAVE] [S🐾] [✕] [🏠] [🔔] [🎵]

◆◆ Yellowstone Super 8-Gardiner M
(406) 848-7401. **$94-$94.** Hwy 89. On US 89. Int corridors. **Pets:** No service, supervision, crate.
[ASK] [S🐾] [✕] [🔔] [💻] [🏊] [📺]

GLASGOW

◆◆◆ Cottonwood Inn M 🐾
(406) 228-8213. **$48-$66.** 45 1st Ave NE. 0.5 mi e on US 2. Int corridors. **Pets:** Designated rooms, supervision.
[ASK] [S🐾] [✕] [🔔] [🔔] [🏊]

GLENDIVE

⚠️ ◆◆ Best Western Jordan Inn M 🐾
(406) 377-5655. **$55-$81, 7 days notice.** 222 N Kendrick Ave. Downtown, on I-94 business loop, from I-94, exit 215 (city center). Ext/int corridors. **Pets:** Small. $5 one-time fee/pet. Designated rooms, supervision.
[SAVE] [S🐾] [✕] [🔔] [🔔] [🏊]

⚠️ ◆◆ Budget Host Riverside Inn M 🐾
(406) 377-2349. **$37-$48.** 44 Hwy 16. I-94, exit 213, just s. Ext corridors. **Pets:** Medium, other. $10 deposit/pet. No service, supervision, crate.
[SAVE] [✕]

[AAA] ◆ **El Centro Motel** [M] 🐾
(406) 365-5211. **$24-$35.** 112 S Kendrick Ave. I-94, exit 215, 1.4 mi w on Merril Way, just n on Bell St, just w. Ext corridors. **Pets:** Other. Designated rooms, supervision.
[S/D] ⊠ ▣

GREAT FALLS

[AAA] ◆◆◆ **Best Western Heritage Inn** [MI] 🐾
(406) 761-1900. **$99.** 1700 Fox Farm Rd. Just s of I-15 business loop, US 89 and SR 200, 0.8 mi e of I-15, exit 278 (10th Ave S). Int corridors. **Pets:** Small, other. Designated rooms, supervision.
[SAVE] [S/D] ⊠ 🦻 ▣ ☕ 🍴 🏊

[AAA] ◆◆◆ **Best Western Ponderosa Inn** [MI] 🐾
(406) 761-3410. **$54-$69.** 220 Central Ave. Downtown. Ext/int corridors. **Pets:** $10 one-time fee/room. Designated rooms, no service, supervision, crate.
[SAVE] [S/D] ⊠ ▣ 🍴 🏊

[AAA] ◆◆ **Central Motel** [M] 🐾
(406) 453-0161. **$35-$70.** 715 Central Ave W. 1 mi e of I-15, exit 280 (Central Ave). Ext corridors. **Pets:** Medium. $15 deposit/pet, $10 daily fee/room, $10 one-time fee/room. Designated rooms, no service, supervision, crate.
[SAVE] [S/D] ⊠ ▣ ☕

◆◆◆ **Comfort Inn Great Falls** [M] 🐾
(406) 454-2727. **$70-$85.** 1120 9th St S. I-15, exit 278, 3 mi e on SR 200, just s on 9th St, 3.3 mi w on SR 200, just s. Int corridors. **Pets:** Other. $5 daily fee/pet. Designated rooms, supervision.
[A$K] [S/D] ⊠ 🚹 🦻 ▣ ☕ 🏊

◆◆ **Days Inn of Great Falls** [M] 🐾
(406) 727-6565. **$63-$76.** 101 14th Ave NW. I-15, exit 280, 1.3 mi e on Central Ave, 0.8 mi n 3rd St NW, just w. Int corridors. **Pets:** Dogs only. $5 one-time fee/room. No service, supervision, crate.
[A$K] [S/D] ⊠

[AAA] ◆◆◆ **The Great Falls Inn** [M] 🐾
(406) 453-6000. **$49-$63.** 1400 28th St S. US 87 and 89, to 26th St S, s 0.3 mi to 15th Ave S, just e. Int corridors. **Pets:** Other. $5 daily fee/pet. Designated rooms, no service, supervision, crate.
[SAVE] [S/D] ⊠ 🚹 ♿ ▣ ☕

◆◆ **Great Falls Super 8 Lodge** [M] 🐾
(406) 727-7600. **$46-$70.** 1214 13th St S. I-15 exit 278, e on 10th Ave S, 2.7 mi, just s. Int corridors. **Pets:** Other. No service, supervision, crate.
[A$K] [S/D] ☕

[AAA] ◆◆◆ **Holiday Inn Great Falls** [MI] 🐾
(406) 727-7200. **$65-$85.** 400 10th Ave S. Just s of US 89 and SR 200, 2 mi e of I-15, exit 278 (10th Ave S). Int corridors. **Pets:** Very small. $25 deposit/room. No service, supervision, crate.
[SAVE] [S/D] ⊠ 🦻 ▣ ☕ 🍴 🏊

[AAA] ◆◆ **Plaza Inn** [M] 🐾
(406) 452-9594. **$36-$65, 7 days notice.** 1224 10th Ave S. I-15 business loop, US 89 and SR 200. Ext corridors. **Pets:** Medium. $10 daily fee/room, $10 one-time fee/room. Designated rooms, no service, supervision, crate.
[SAVE] [S/D] ⊠

[AAA] ◆◆ **Ski's Western Motel** [M] 🐾
(406) 453-3281. **$35-$70.** 2420 10th Ave S. 2 mi se on I-15 business loop, US 89 and SR 200. Ext corridors. **Pets:** Medium. $15 deposit/room, $10 daily fee/room, $10 one-time fee/room. Designated rooms, no service, supervision, crate.
[SAVE] [S/D] ⊠ ▣

[AAA] ◆◆◆ **TownHouse Inn of Great Falls** [MI] 🐾
(406) 761-4600. **$80-$80.** 1411 10th Ave S. SR 200 and 15th St. Int corridors. **Pets:** Other. $5 daily fee/pet, $5 one-time fee/pet. No service, supervision, crate.
[SAVE] [S/D] ⊠ 🦻 ▣ ☕ 🍴 🏊

HAMILTON

[AAA] ◆◆ **Comfort Inn of Hamilton** [M] 🐾
(406) 363-6600. **$59-$84.** 1113 N First St. N of city center on US 93. Int corridors. **Pets:** Other. $4 daily fee/pet. No service, supervision, crate.
[SAVE] [S/D] ⊠ 🦻 ♿ ▣ ☕

HARDIN

[AAA] ◆◆ **American Inn of Hardin** [MI]
(406) 665-1870. **$45-$79.** 1324 N Crawford Ave. I-90, exit 495, just s on SR 47. Ext corridors. **Pets:** Small. Designated rooms, supervision.
⊠ 🦻 ▣ 🍴 🏊

◆◆ **Western Motel** [M] 🐾
(406) 665-2296. **$45-$70.** 830 W 3rd St. I-90 E, exit 495, 1.3 mi s on SR 47 and Rt 313, just e; I-90 W, exit 497, 0.3 mi w on I-90 business loop, continue straight on 3rd St 0.7 mi. Ext corridors. **Pets:** Other. $3 daily fee/pet. No service, supervision, crate.
⊠ ▣

HARLOWTON

◆ **Corral Motel** [M] 🐾
(406) 632-4331. **$35-$45.** 0.5 mi e at jct US 12 and 191. Ext corridors. **Pets:** No service, supervision, crate.
⊠ ▣

◆ **Countryside Inn** [M] 🐾
(406) 632-4119. **$38-$57.** 309 3rd St NE. US 12E. Ext corridors. **Pets:** Small. Designated rooms, no service, supervision, crate.
[A$K] [S/D] ⊠ ▣

HAVRE

[AAA] ◆◆ **TownHouse Inn of Havre** [M]
(406) 265-6711. **$59-$84.** 601 W 1st St. Just w on US 2. Int corridors. **Pets:** No service, supervision, crate.
[SAVE] [S/D] ⊠ 🦻 ▣ ☕ 🏊

HELENA

◆◆◆ **Appleton Inn Bed & Breakfast** [BB] 🐾
(406) 449-7492. **$85-$150, 7 days notice.** 1999 Euclid Ave. I-15, exit 193, 1.3 mi w on Cedar St, 1.7 mi w at jct US 12 W (Lyndale Ave). Int corridors. **Pets:** Small. No service, supervision, crate.
⊠

◆◆◆ **Barrister Bed & Breakfast** 🅱🅱 ❀
(406) 443-7330. **$90-$105.** 416 N Ewing. 0.4 mi from Last
Chance Gulch, 0.9 mi w of State Capitol on 6th Ave, just n.
Int corridors. **Pets:** Other. Supervision.
A$K ⊠ ☎

◆◆◆ **Comfort Inn of Helena** 🅼 ❀
(406) 443-1000. **$60-$70.** 750 N Fee St. I-15, exit 192, just
n. Int corridors. **Pets:** Small, other. $10 one-time fee/room.
Designated rooms, supervision.
A$K S🄳 ⊠ 🛆 🖥 💻 🍽

◆◆ **Days Inn Helena** 🅼 ❀
(406) 442-3280. **$49-$90.** 2001 Prospect Ave. I-15, exit
192, just w. Int corridors. **Pets:** Medium, other. $25 deposit/
room. No service, supervision, crate.
A$K S🄳 ⊠ 🛆 📷 🖉 🖥

◆◆◆ **Elkhorn Mountain Inn** 🅼 ❀
(406) 442-6625. **$60-$67.** 1 Jackson Creek. 5 mi s, I-15,
exit 187 (Montana City), just w. Int corridors. **Pets:** Other.
$5 daily fee/pet. Supervision.
SAVE S🄳 ⊠ 🖐 🖉 🖥 💻

◆ **Lamplighter Motel** 🄲
(406) 442-9200. **$42-$53.** 1006 Madison. Hwy 12W, just s
of Lundy Shopping Center. Ext corridors. **Pets:** Medium.
Designated rooms, no service, supervision, crate.
SAVE S🄳 ⊠ 🖉 🖥

◆◆ **Shilo Inn** 🅼 ❀
(406) 442-0320. **$69-$99.** 2020 Prospect Ave. 2 mi e, just w
of I-15 interchange, enter from e on Prospect Ave; I-15, exit
192 (Capital). Int corridors. **Pets:** Other. $10 daily fee/room.
Supervision.
SAVE S🄳 ⊠ 🖥 💻 🍽

◆◆ **Super 8 Motel** 🅼 ❀
(406) 443-2450. **$56-$78.** 2200 11th Ave. I-15 S, Capitol
(area) exit; I-15 N, exit w business district on US 12. Int
corridors. **Pets:** Medium. $25 deposit/room, $5 daily fee/
room. Designated rooms, no service, supervision, crate.
A$K S🄳 ⊠ 📷 🖉 💻

HUNGRY HORSE

◆◆ **Mini Golden Inns Motel** 🅼 ❀
(406) 387-4313. **$80-$86, 30 days notice.** 8955 US 2E. E
end of town. Ext corridors. **Pets:** Small. No service, supervision, crate.
SAVE ⊠ 🖐 🖉 🖥 💻

KALISPELL

◆◆ **Aero Inn** 🅼 ❀
(406) 755-3798. **$34-$74.** 1830 US 93S. 1 mi s on US 93
from jct of US 2. Int corridors. **Pets:** $10 deposit/room.
Designated rooms, no service, supervision, crate.
SAVE S🄳 ⊠ 🖉 🖥 🍽

◆◆◆ **Best Western Cavanaughs Outlaw
        Hotel** 🅼� ❀
(406) 755-6100. **$95-$95.** 1701 Hwy 93 S. 1.4 mi s on US
93 from jct US 2. Int corridors. **Pets:** Supervision.
SAVE S🄳 ⊠ 🖥 💻 🍽 🍽 🗡

◆◆◆ **Cavanaughs at Kalispell Center** 🅼🄸
(406) 752-6660. **$95-$95.** 20 N Main. Just s on US 93 from
jct of US 2, e end of Kalispell Center. Int corridors.
Pets: Medium. Supervision.
SAVE S🄳 ⊠ 🛆 🖥 💻 🍽 🍽

◆◆ **Days Inn Kalispell** 🅼 ❀
(406) 756-3222. **$64-$74.** 1550 Hwy 93 N. 1.3 mi n on US
93 from jct of US 2. Int corridors. **Pets:** Medium. No service, supervision, crate.
A$K S🄳 ⊠

◆◆ **Four Seasons Motor Inn** 🅼🄸 ❀
(406) 755-6123. **$58-$79.** 350 N Main St. On US 93, just n
of jct US 2. Ext/int corridors. **Pets:** Medium. $5 one-time
fee/room. Designated rooms, supervision.
SAVE S🄳 ⊠ 🍽

◆ **Glacier Gateway Motel** 🅼
(406) 755-3330. **$45-$75.** 264 N Main St. Nw corner of jct
US 2 and 93. Ext corridors. **Pets:** Supervision.
SAVE S🄳 🖥 💻

◆◆ **Kalispell Grand Hotel** 🄷 ❀
(406) 755-8100. **$71-$78.** 100 Main St. Downtown; on US
93. Int corridors. **Pets:** Supervision.
SAVE S🄳 ⊠ 🍽

◆ **Motel 6 Kalispell–290** 🅼 ❀
(406) 752-6355. **$66-$82.** 1540 Hwy 93 S. 1.2 mi s on US
93 from jct of US 2. Ext corridors. **Pets:** Small, other. No
service, supervision, crate.
S🄳 ⊠ 🛆 🖉 🍽

◆◆ **Red Lion Inn Kalispell** 🅼🄸 ❀
(406) 755-6700. **$49-$79.** 1330 Hwy 2 W. 1 mi w on US 2
from jct of US 93. Int corridors. **Pets:** Medium, other. $15
one-time fee/room. Designated rooms, no service, supervision, crate.
SAVE ⊠ 💻 🍽 🍽

◆◆ **Super 8 Motel-Kalispell** 🅼 ❀
(406) 755-1888. **$62-$76, 30 days notice.** 1341 1st Ave E.
1.2 mi s on US 93 from jct of US 2. Int corridors. **Pets:** $25
deposit/pet. No service, supervision, crate.
A$K S🄳 ⊠ 🛆 📷 💻

◆ **White Birch Motel** 🅼 ❀
(406) 752-4008. **$42-$47.** 17 Shady Ln. 0.4 mi e on SR 35
from jct US 2, just s. Ext corridors. **Pets:** Dogs only. No
service, supervision, crate.
S🄳 🖥 💻 🗡 ☎

LAKESIDE

◆◆ **Sunrise Vista Inn** 🅼 ❀
(406) 844-3864. **$68-$88, 3 days notice.** 7005 US 93. N
edge of town on US 93. Ext corridors. **Pets:** Medium. $10
deposit/room, $10 one-time fee/room. Designated rooms,
no service, supervision, crate.
A$K ⊠ 🖥 💻 🗡

LEWISTOWN

◆ **B & B Motel** 🅼
(406) 538-5496. **$39-$48.** 520 E Main St. Downtown. Ext
corridors. **Pets:** Designated rooms, supervision.
SAVE S🄳 ⊠ 🖥

LIBBY

AAA ◆◆ **Super 8 Motel** M ❀
(406) 293-2771. **$49-$77.** 448 US 2 W. Just w on US 2 from jct SR 37. Int corridors. **Pets:** Other. $5 one-time fee/room. Designated rooms, no service, supervision, crate.
SAVE S X 🖾

LINCOLN

AAA ◆◆ **Leeper's Motel** M ❀
(406) 362-4333. **$39-$50.** Hwy 200 & 1st Ave. Just w on SR 200. Ext corridors. **Pets:** Small. $5 one-time fee/pet. No service, supervision, crate.
SAVE S X 🖬 🗷

LIVINGSTON

AAA ◆ **Budget Host Parkway Motel** M ❀
(406) 222-3840. **$52-$72, 3 days notice.** 1124 W Park. US 89, 0.5 mi n jct I-90, exit 333. Ext corridors. **Pets:** Other. $4 one-time fee/pet. Designated rooms, no service, supervision, crate.
SAVE S X 🖬 🖫 🖾

AAA ◆◆ **Del Mar Motel Inc** M
(406) 222-3120. **$49-$70.** Just w of jct US 89, on I-90 business loop. Ext corridors. **Pets:** No service, supervision, crate.
SAVE S X 🖬 🖫 🖾 X

AAA ◆◆◆ **Econo Lodge** M ❀
(406) 222-0555. **$46-$89.** 111 Rogers Ln. I-90 exit 333, just n on US 89, then just w. Int corridors. **Pets:** Other. $5 daily fee/room. Designated rooms, no service, supervision, crate.
SAVE S X 🖢 🕭 🖫 🖬 🖫 🖾

AAA ◆◆ **Paradise Inn** M
(406) 222-6320. **$79-$89.** Park Rd & Rogers Ln. US 89, n of jct I-90 and US 191, exit 333. Ext/int corridors. **Pets:** No service, supervision, crate.
SAVE S X 🖬 🖩 🖾

MILES CITY

AAA ◆◆◆ **Best Western War Bonnet Inn** M ❀
(406) 232-4560. **$60-$75.** 1015 S Haynes Ave. SR 59, 0.3 mi n jct I-94, exit 138 (Broadus). Ext corridors. **Pets:** Other. Supervision.
SAVE S X 🖬 🖾

AAA ◆◆ **Days Inn** M ❀
(406) 232-3550. **$35-$60.** 1006 S Haynes Ave. SR 59, 0.3 mi n jct I-94, exit 138 (Broadus). Ext corridors. **Pets:** Other. $5 one-time fee/room. Supervision.
SAVE S X 🖫 🖫 🖾

MISSOULA

◆◆ **Best Inn North** M ❀
(406) 542-7550. **$63-$71.** 4953 N Reserve St. W on I-90, exit 101, just s. Int corridors. **Pets:** Other. $6 daily fee/room. Supervision.
ASK S X 🖫 🖬

◆◆ **Best Inn South** M ❀
(406) 251-2665. **$63-$71.** 3803 Brooks St. I-90, exit 101, to Reserve St, 5 mi s to Hwy 93, just w. Int corridors. **Pets:** Other. $6 daily fee/room. Supervision.
SAVE S X 🖫 🖬 🖫

AAA ◆◆ **Best Western Executive Inn** M ❀
(406) 543-7221. **$50-$70.** 201 E Main St. I-90, exit 104 (Orange St), 0.5 mi s to Broadway, 0.5 mi e to Washington, just s to Main St, just w. Ext corridors. **Pets:** Large, other. $25 deposit/room. No service, supervision, crate.
SAVE S X 🖬 🖫 🖩 🖾

AAA ◆◆◆ **Best Western Grant Creek Inn** M ❀
(406) 543-0700. **$89-$149.** 5280 Grant Creek Rd. Just n of I-90, exit 101. Int corridors. **Pets:** Medium. $25 deposit/room. Designated rooms, no service, supervision, crate.
SAVE S X 🕭 🖫 🖬 🖫 🖾

◆◆ **Campus Inn** M ❀
(406) 549-5134. **Call for rates.** 744 E Broadway. I-90, exit 105 (Van Buren St), just s to Broadway, just w. Ext/int corridors. **Pets:** Other. $6 daily fee/pet. No service, supervision, crate.
X 🖫 🖬 🖾

◆◆◆ **Comfort Inn** M ❀
(406) 542-0888. **$74-$150.** 4545 N Reserve St. 0.5 mi s of I-90, exit 101. Int corridors. **Pets:** Medium. $10 daily fee/room. No service, supervision, crate.
ASK S X 🕭 🖫 🖬 🖫 🖾

AAA ◆◆ **The Creekside Inn** M ❀
(406) 549-2387. **$45-$65.** 630 E Broadway. I-90, exit 105 (Van Buren St), just s to Broadway, then w. Ext corridors. **Pets:** Large, other. $25 deposit/room. No service, supervision, crate.
SAVE S X 🖾

AAA ◆◆◆ **Days Inn/Westgate** M ❀
(406) 721-9776. **$66-$71.** 8600 Truck Stop Rd. Just n of I-90, exit 96. Int corridors. **Pets:** $5 daily fee/pet, $5 one-time fee/pet. Supervision.
SAVE S X

AAA ◆◆ **Doubletree Hotel Missoula/Edgewater** M
(406) 728-3100. **$105-$135.** 100 Madison. I-90, exit 105 (Van Buren St), just s, then w on Front St. Int corridors. **Pets:** Designated rooms, no service, supervision, crate.
X 🕭 🕭 🖫 🖬 🖫 🖩 🖾

AAA ◆ **Downtown Motel** M ❀
(406) 549-5191. **$37-$45.** 502 E Broadway. I-90, just w of exit 105 (Van Buren St). Ext corridors. **Pets:** $6 one-time fee/pet. Designated rooms, supervision.
SAVE X 🖬 🖫

◆◆◆ **Hampton Inn** M ❀
(406) 549-1800. **$75-$89.** 4805 N Reserve St. Just s of I-90, exit 101. Int corridors. **Pets:** $10 one-time fee/room. Designated rooms, supervision.
X 🕭 🕭 🖫 🖫 🖾

(AAA) ◆◆◆ Holiday Inn Missoula-Parkside 🅷
(406) 721-8550. **$89-$89.** 200 S Pattee St. I-90, Orange St exit, 0.5 mi s to Broadway, just e to Pattee St, just s. Int corridors. **Pets:** Medium. Designated rooms, no service, supervision, crate.
[SAVE] [S💲] [✕] [🌀] [🛏] [🍴] [🏊]

(AAA) ◆ Hubbard's Ponderosa Lodge Ⓜ
(406) 543-3102. **$47-$60.** 800 E Broadway. I-90, exit 105 (Van Buren St), just s to Broadway, then w. Ext/int corridors. **Pets:** Designated rooms, supervision.
[SAVE] [S💲] [✕] [🛏]

(AAA) ◆◆◆ Orange Street Budget Motor Inn Ⓜ 🐾
(406) 721-3610. **$43-$49.** 801 N Orange St. Just s of I-90, exit 104. Int corridors. **Pets:** $5 one-time fee/room. Designated rooms, no service, supervision, crate.
[✕] [🛏]

(AAA) ◆◆◆ Red Lion Inn Ⓜ 🐾
(406) 728-3300. **$125-$125.** 700 W Broadway. I-90, Orange St exit, just w. Ext corridors. **Pets:** Medium. $5 daily fee/room. Designated rooms, no service, supervision, crate.
[SAVE] [S💲] [✕] [💻] [🏊]

(AAA) ◆◆ Redwood Lodge Ⓜ
(406) 721-2110. **$54-$64.** 8060 Hwy 93 N. Just s of I-90, exit 96. Ext corridors. **Pets:** Supervision.
[SAVE] [S💲] [✕] [🛏]

(AAA) ◆ Royal Motel Ⓜ 🐾
(406) 542-2184. **$40-$48.** 338 Washington St. I-90, exit 105, just s on Van Buren, 0.5 mi w on Broadway. Ext corridors. **Pets:** Other. $20 deposit/pet, $4 daily fee/pet, $4 one-time fee/pet. Designated rooms, no service, supervision, crate.
[✕] [🛏]

(AAA) ◆◆◆ Ruby's Inn & Convention Center Ⓜ 🐾
(406) 721-0990. **$69-$89.** 4825 N Reserve St. Just s of I-90, exit 101. Ext/int corridors. **Pets:** Other. $10 one-time fee/room. No service, supervision, crate.
[SAVE] [S💲] [✕] [🦽] [🌀] [🔥] [🛏] [💻] [🍴] [🏊]

◆◆ Sleep Inn Ⓜ
(406) 543-5883. **$58-$68.** 3425 Dore Ln. I-90, exit 101, 5 mi on Reserve St, just e on Brooks St. Int corridors. **Pets:** Medium. Designated rooms, no service, supervision, crate.
[ASK] [S💲] [✕] [🏠] [🌀] [🔥] [🛏] [🏊]

◆◆ Super 8-Brooks St Ⓜ 🐾
(406) 251-2255. **$51-$61.** 3901 Brooks St. 5 mi s of I-90, exit 101, just w. Int corridors. **Pets:** Small, dogs only. $4 daily fee/pet. Supervision.
[ASK] [S💲] [✕]

(AAA) ◆ Travelers Inn Motel Ⓜ 🐾
(406) 728-8330. **$55-$65.** 4850 N Reserve St. W on I-90, exit 101 (Reserve St), just s. Ext corridors. **Pets:** Small, dogs only. $2 daily fee/pet. Designated rooms, no service, supervision, crate.
[SAVE] [S💲] [✕] [🛏]

OVANDO

(AAA) ◆◆◆ Lake Upsata Guest Ranch 🆁🅰
(406) 793-5890. **$220** (no credit cards), 90 days notice. 135 Lake Upsata Rd. 7.5 mi w on SR 200 to MM 38, 3.4 mi n on Woodworth Rd, 1 mi e. Ext corridors. **Pets:** No service, supervision, crate.
[✕] [🛏] [💻] [✕] [🅰] [CTV] [🏊]

POLSON

◆◆ Days Inn Ⓜ
(406) 883-3120. **$70-$75.** 914 Hwy 93. S of downtown on US 93. Ext corridors. **Pets:** Medium. Designated rooms, no service, supervision, crate.
[ASK] [S💲] [✕]

RED LODGE

◆◆ Best Western Lu Pine Inn Ⓜ
(406) 446-1321. **$49-$79.** 702 S Hauser. 0.4 mi s, just w of US 212. Int corridors. **Pets:** Designated rooms, no service, supervision, crate.
[S💲] [✕] [🛏] [🏊]

◆◆◆ Comfort Inn of Red Lodge Ⓜ
(406) 446-4469. **$80-$150.** 612 N Broadway. Jct US 212 and SR 78, n entrance. Int corridors. **Pets:** Supervision.
[ASK] [S💲] [✕] [🦽] [🔥] [🛏] [💻] [🏊]

(AAA) ◆◆ Super 8 of Red Lodge Ⓜ
(406) 446-2288. **$65-$120.** 1223 S Broadway Ave. Just s on US 212. Ext/int corridors. **Pets:** Small. Supervision.
[SAVE] [S💲] [✕] [🛏] [💻] [🏊]

(AAA) ◆◆ Yodeler Motel Ⓜ 🐾
(406) 446-1435. **$48-$68.** 601 S Broadway. Just s on US 212. Ext corridors. **Pets:** Dogs only. Designated rooms, no service, supervision, crate.
[SAVE] [S💲] [✕] [🛏] [💻]

RONAN

◆ Starlite Motel Ⓜ 🐾
(406) 676-7000. **$52-$67.** 18 Main St SW. Just w of intersection of US 93 and Main. Ext corridors. **Pets:** $20 deposit/pet, $7 daily fee/pet. Designated rooms, no service, supervision, crate.
[✕] [🛏] [💻]

SEELEY LAKE

(AAA) ◆◆◆ The Emily A 🅱🅱
(406) 677-3474. **$115-$115, 7 days notice.** SR 83 N, MM20. 5 mi n on SR 83, just n of MM20. Int corridors. **Pets:** Supervision.
[✕] [✕] [🅰] [CTV] [🏊]

(AAA) ◆◆ Wilderness Gateway Inn Ⓜ
(406) 677-2095. **$53-$59.** SR 83. S end of town on SR 83. Ext corridors. **Pets:** Small. No service, supervision, crate.
[SAVE] [S💲] [✕] [🅰]

SHELBY

AAA ◆◆◆ **Comfort Inn of Shelby** **M** ✿
(406) 434-2212. **$59-$84.** 50 Frontage Rd. I-15, exit 363, just w, just s on McKinley Ave; from US 2, just s on McKinley Ave. Int corridors. **Pets:** $50 deposit/pet, $5 daily fee/pet. Supervision.
[SAVE] [S] [X] [🛏] [🍴] [📶]

AAA ◆◆◆ **Crossroads Inn** **M** ✿
(406) 434-5134. **$41-$53.** US 2. Int corridors. **Pets:** $5 daily fee/pet. Supervision.
[SAVE] [S] [X] [🛏] [🍴] [📶]

AAA ◆◆ **O'Haire Manor Motel** **M** ✿
(406) 434-5555. **Call for rates.** 204 2nd St S. Just s of Main St via Maple St. Ext/int corridors. **Pets:** Medium. $5 daily fee/room. Designated rooms, supervision.
[SAVE] [X] [🍴]

ST. IGNATIUS

AAA ◆◆ **Stoneheart Inn** **BB** ✿
(406) 745-4999. **$40-$60.** 26 N Main. US 93 s on Main. Int corridors. **Pets:** Supervision.
[SAVE] [S] [X] [CTV] [📶]

AAA ◆ **Sunset Motel** **M** ✿
(406) 745-3900. **$54-$63, 3 days notice.** 32670 Hwy 93. Just s of downtown exit on US 93. **Pets:** Medium, dogs only. $5 one-time fee/room. No service, supervision, crate.
[SAVE] [S] [X] [🍴] [📶]

SUPERIOR

AAA ◆◆ **Budget Host Big Sky Motel** **M**
(406) 822-4831. **$44-$54.** 103 4th Ave E. Just n of I-90, exit 47. Ext corridors. **Pets:** No service, supervision, crate.
[SAVE] [S] [X]

THOMPSON FALLS

◆◆ **The Riverfront** **M** ✿
(406) 827-3460. **$49-$89, 21 days notice.** 4907 Scenic SR 200 W. 1 mi w of city center. Ext corridors. **Pets:** Other. $5 daily fee/pet. No service, supervision, crate.
[X] [🍴] [📶] [X] [CTV]

THREE FORKS

AAA ◆◆ **Broken Spur Motel** **M** ✿
(406) 285-3237. **$44-$52.** 124 West Elm. I-90, exit 278 westbound, 1.3 mi sw on SR 2; exit 274 eastbound, 1 mi s on Hwy 287 to jct Hwy 2, 3 mi se on SR 2. Ext corridors. **Pets:** Other. $5 daily fee/pet, $5 one-time fee/pet. No service, supervision, crate.
[SAVE] [S] [X] [🍴]

◆◆ **Fort Three Forks Motel Inc** **M** ✿
(406) 285-3233. **$36-$65.** 10776 Hwy 287. I-90, exit 274 and Hwy 287. Ext corridors. **Pets:** Medium. $5 daily fee/pet, $5 one-time fee/pet. Designated rooms, no service, supervision, crate.
[X] [🍴] [X]

WEST YELLOWSTONE

AAA ◆◆◆ **Best Western Cross Winds Motor Inn** **M** ✿
(406) 646-9557. **$75-$120, 3 days notice.** 201 Firehole Ave. Just w of US 191 and 287, on US 20 at Dunraven St and Firehole Ave; at end of city park. Ext corridors. **Pets:** No service, supervision, crate.
[S] [X] [🍴] [📶]

AAA ◆◆◆ **Best Western Desert Inn** **M** ✿
(406) 646-7376. **$75-$139, 3 days notice.** 133 Canyon Ave. US 191 at jct US 20, corner of Canyon and Firehole aves. Int corridors. **Pets:** No service, supervision, crate.
[S] [X] [🛏] [🍴] [📶]

◆◆◆ **Best Western Weston Inn** **M**
(406) 646-7373. **$50-$110, 3 days notice.** 103 Gibbon St. US 191 at corner of Canyon Ave and Gibbon St. Ext/int corridors. **Pets:** Supervision.
[S] [X] [🍴] [📶] [📶]

AAA ◆◆ **Big Western Pine Motel** **M** ✿
(406) 646-7622. **$25-$89, 3 days notice.** 234 Firehole Ave. Just w of Canyon Ave, corner Firehole Ave and Electric St, on US 20 and 191. Ext/int corridors. **Pets:** Other. $5 daily fee/pet, $5 one-time fee/pet. Designated rooms, no service, supervision, crate.
[X] [🍴] [📶] [📶]

AAA ◆ **Buckboard Motel** **M**
(406) 646-9020. **$60-$88.** 119 Electric St. Just nw of park entrance, w off US 191 at Electric St and Madison Ave. Ext corridors. **Pets:** Supervision.
[SAVE] [X]

AAA ◆◆◆ **Days Inn West Yellowstone** **M** ✿
(406) 646-7656. **$99-$145.** 304 Madison St. Just nw of park entrance, w off US 191. Ext/int corridors. **Pets:** Medium. $8 daily fee/pet. Designated rooms, supervision.
[SAVE] [X] [🛏] [🍴] [📶] [📶] [X]

AAA ◆ **Evergreen Motel** **M** ✿
(406) 646-7655. **$29-$79, 3 days notice.** 229 Firehole Ave. Just w of Canyon, on US 20 and 191. Ext corridors. **Pets:** Other. Supervision.
[X] [CTV]

AAA ◆◆◆ **Kelly Inn** **M** ✿
(406) 646-4544. **$79-$139.** 104 S Canyon St. Just w of Yellowstone Park entrance, s of jct US 191, 287 and 20. Ext/int corridors. **Pets:** Other. No service, supervision, crate.
[SAVE] [S] [X] [🛏] [🍴] [📶]

AAA ◆ **One Horse Motel** **M** ✿
(406) 646-7677. **$29-$79, 3 days notice.** 216 Dunraven St. Just w of US 191 and 287, on US 20 at Dunraven St and Firehole Ave; at end of city park. Ext corridors. **Pets:** Small, other. Supervision.
[X] [🍴] [CTV]

AAA ◆◆◆ **Three Bear Lodge Annex** **M**
(406) 646-7353. **$60-$70.** 24 Dunraven St. Just w of park entrance. Ext corridors. **Pets:** No service, supervision, crate.
[SAVE] [X] [📶]

(AAA) ◆◆◆ Three Bear Motor Lodge **M**
(406) 646-7353. **$70-$80.** 217 Yellowstone Ave. Just w of park entrance. Ext/int corridors. **Pets:** No service, supervision, crate.
[SAVE] [X] [B] [≈]

(AAA) ◆◆◆ Travelers Lodge **M**
(406) 646-9561. **$70-$90.** 225 Yellowstone Ave. Just w of park entrance. Ext corridors. **Pets:** Very small. No service, supervision, crate.
[SAVE] [X] [🐾] [B] [≈] [X]

◆◆◆ Yellowstone Lodge **M** 🐾
(406) 646-0020. **$99-$149** (no credit cards). 251 Electric St. Just w of Yellowstone National Park entrance. Int corridors. **Pets:** Medium. $25 deposit/room, $5 one-time fee/pet. Designated rooms, no service, supervision, crate.
[ASK] [S6] [X] [🐾] [B] [▣] [≈]

WHITE SULPHUR SPRINGS

◆◆◆ All Seasons Super 8 Motel **M** 🐾
(406) 547-8888. **$48-$58.** 808 3rd Ave SW. On US 89, s end of town. Int corridors. **Pets:** Dogs only. $20 deposit/room. No service, supervision, crate.
[ASK] [S6] [X] [B]

WHITEFISH

(AAA) ◆◆ Alpinglow Inn **CO** 🐾
(406) 862-6966. **$75-$122, 30 days notice.** 3900 Big Mountain Rd. Jct of US 93 and SR 487, 2.4 mi n on SR 487, 5.2 mi n at flashing light. Int corridors. **Pets:** Medium, dogs only. $10 one-time fee/room. Designated rooms, no service, supervision, crate.
[SAVE] [S6] [X] [🍴] [X]

(AAA) ◆◆◆ Best Western Rocky Mountain
Lodge **M** 🐾
(406) 862-2569. **$119-$129.** 6510 Hwy 93S. 1.3 mi s on US 93 from jct of SR 487. Ext/int corridors. **Pets:** Other. $10 daily fee/room. Designated rooms, no service, supervision, crate.
[SAVE] [S6] [X] [🐾] [B] [▣] [≈]

(AAA) ◆◆ Chalet Motel **M** 🐾
(406) 862-5581. **$37-$84.** 6430 US 93S. 1 mi n on US 93 from jct SR 40. Ext corridors. **Pets:** $5 daily fee/pet. Designated rooms, no service, supervision, crate.
[SAVE] [S6] [X] [B] [▣] [≈]

(AAA) ◆◆◆ Quality Inn Pine Lodge **M** 🐾
(406) 862-7600. **$60-$130, 7 days notice.** 920 Spokane Ave. 1 mi s on US 93. Int corridors. **Pets:** No service, supervision, crate.
[SAVE] [S6] [X] [🐾] [🐾] [B] [≈]

(AAA) ◆◆ Super 8 Motel **M** 🐾
(406) 862-8255. **$78-$83.** 800 Spokane Ave. 1 mi s on US 93 from jct of SR 487. Int corridors. **Pets:** Medium. $5 daily fee/pet. Designated rooms, no service, supervision, crate.
[SAVE] [S6]

AINSWORTH

🅰️ ◆◆◆ Comfort Inn M ❖
(402) 387-1050. **$45-$60.** 1124 E 4th St. 0.5 mi e on US 20. Int corridors. **Pets:** $10 daily fee/pet. Supervision.
🆂🅰🆅🅴 🆂🅾 ⊠ 🎣 🐾 🎿 ☎ 💻 🏊

◆ Super 8 Motel M
(402) 387-0700. **$38-$49.** 1025 E 4th St. 0.5 mi e on US 20. Int corridors. **Pets:** Small. No service, supervision, crate.
🅰🆂🅺 🆂🅾 ⊠

ALLIANCE

◆ Sunset Motel M ❖
(308) 762-8660. **$40-$49.** 1210 E Hwy 2. 1 mi e on SR 2 from jct US 385. Ext/int corridors. **Pets:** Other. $5 daily fee/pet. Designated rooms, no service, supervision, crate.
🆂🅾 ⊠ ☎ 💻 🏊

🅰️ ◆◆ West Way Motel M
(308) 762-4040. **$39-$54.** 1207 W 3rd, Hwy 2 & 385. 1 mi w on US 385 and SR 2. Ext corridors. **Pets:** Supervision.
🆂🅰🆅🅴 🆂🅾 ⊠ ☎ 🍴

AURORA

🅰️ ◆◆ Budget Host, Ken's Motel M
(402) 694-3141. **$30-$38.** 1515 11th St. On US 34, 0.5 mi w of jct SR 14. Ext corridors. **Pets:** Designated rooms, no service, supervision, crate.
🆂🅰🆅🅴 ⊠ ☎

BELLEVUE

🅰️ ◆◆ American Family Inn M ❖
(402) 291-0804. **$42-$58.** 1110 Fort Crook Rd S. US 75, 0.3 mi n of jct SR 370 and Fort Crook Rd. Ext corridors. **Pets:** Medium, other. $25 deposit/room, $7 one-time fee/room. No service, supervision, crate.
🆂🅰🆅🅴 🆂🅾 ⊠ 🐾 🎿 🎣 ☎ 🏊 ⊠

CHADRON

🅰️ ◆◆ Best Western West Hills Inn M ❖
(308) 432-3305. **$59-$79, 7 days notice.** 1100 W 10th St. Jct US 385 and 20. Ext/int corridors. **Pets:** Supervision.
🆂🅰🆅🅴 🆂🅾 ⊠ ☎ 💻 🏊

◆ Westerner Motel M ❖
(308) 432-5577. **$35-$50.** 300 Oak St. On US 20, 0.5 mi e of jct US 385 and SR 87. Ext corridors. **Pets:** Other. No service, supervision, crate.
🆂🅰🆅🅴 🆂🅾 ⊠ ☎

COLUMBUS

🅰️ ◆◆ Days Inn M
(402) 564-2527. **$42-$55.** 371 33rd Ave. 1 mi s from n jct of US 30 and 81. Int corridors. **Pets:** Designated rooms, supervision.
🆂🅰🆅🅴 🆂🅾 ⊠ ☎

🅰️ ◆◆ Sleep Inn M ❖
(402) 562-5200. **$48-$82.** 303 23rd St. On US 30, 2 mi e of jct US 30 and 81, e side of town. Int corridors. **Pets:** Small, other. $10 daily fee/pet, $10 one-time fee/pet. Designated rooms, no service, supervision, crate.
🆂🅰🆅🅴 🆂🅾 ⊠ 🐾 🎿 🎣 ☎ 💻 🏊

COZAD

🅰️ ◆◆ Budget Host Circle S Motel M ❖
(308) 784-2290. **$30-$38.** 440 S Meridian. I-80, exit 222, 0.3 mi n. Ext corridors. **Pets:** Other. No service, supervision, crate.
🆂🅰🆅🅴 ⊠ ☎ 🍴 🏊

◆◆ Motel 6-Cozad–4091 M ❖
(308) 784-4900. **$41-$45.** 809 S Meridian. I-80, exit 222. Int corridors. **Pets:** Very small, other. Supervision.
🆂🅾 ⊠ ☎

FAIRBURY

🅰️ ◆◆ Capri Motel M ❖
(402) 729-3317. **$28-$40.** 1100 14th St. On US 136 at jct SR 15. Ext corridors. **Pets:** Small, dogs only. $25 one-time fee/pet. Designated rooms, no service, supervision, crate.
⊠ ☎

FREMONT

◆◆ Comfort Inn M
(402) 721-1109. **$55-$89.** 1649 E 23rd Ave. 2 mi e on US 30, just e of Business US 275. Int corridors. **Pets:** No service, supervision, crate.
🅰🆂🅺 🆂🅾 ⊠ ☎ 💻 🏊

◆◆◆ Holiday Lodge M ❦
(402) 727-1110. **$55-$78, 7 days notice.** 1220 E 23rd St. US 30 at jct Business US 275 and 30. Ext/int corridors. **Pets:** $25 deposit/room. Designated rooms, supervision.
🆂🅰🆅🅴 SD ✕ 🖵 🍴 ⌸

◆◆ Super 8 Motel-Fremont M
(402) 727-4445. **Call for rates.** 1250 E 23rd St. On US 30, 1 mi w of jct US 275. Int corridors. **Pets:** Small. Designated rooms, no service, supervision, crate.
✕ 🗋

FULLERTON

◆◆ The Fullerton Inn M ❦
(308) 536-2699. **$43-$58.** S Hwy 14. On SR 14, just s of center. Int corridors. **Pets:** Medium. $25 deposit/room, $5 daily fee/room. Designated rooms, no service, supervision, crate.
🅰🆂🅺 SD ✕ 🏠

GOTHENBURG

◆◆ Gothenburg Super 8 M ❦
(308) 537-2684. **$47-$68.** 401 Platte River Dr. Just n of I-80, exit 211. Int corridors. **Pets:** Supervision.
SD ✕ 🗄 🖵 ⌸

GRAND ISLAND

◆◆ Best Western Riverside Inn M
(308) 384-5150. **$64-$76.** 3333 Ramada Rd. I-80, exit 312, 5 mi n to US 34, 2 mi e to Locust St; I-80, exit 318, 3 mi n to US 34, 5 mi w to Locust St. Ext/int corridors. **Pets:** Designated rooms, no service, supervision, crate.
🅰🆂🅺 SD ✕ 🗄 🖵 🍴 ⌸

◆◆◆ Holiday Inn-Interstate 80 M ❦
(308) 384-7770. **$49-$84.** 7838 S US Hwy 281. On US 281, at jct I-80, Grand Island-Hastings, exit 312. Int corridors. **Pets:** Other. Designated rooms, no service, supervision, crate.
✕ 🗋 🗅 🖵 🍴 ⌸

◆ Oak Grove Inn M ❦
(308) 384-1333. **$25-$45.** 3205 S Locust St. I-80, exit 312, 5 mi n to US 34, 2 mi e to Locust St at jct; I-80, exit 318, 3 mi n to US 34, then 5 mi w to Locust St at jct. Int corridors. **Pets:** Other. $10 daily fee/room, $10 one-time fee/pet. Designated rooms, no service, supervision, crate.
🅰🆂🅺 SD ✕

◆◆ Super 8 M ❦
(308) 384-4380. **Call for rates.** 2603 S Locust. I-80, exit 312, 5 mi n to US 34, 2 mi e to Locust St, 0.5 mi n; I-80, exit 318, 3 mi n to US 34, 5 mi w to Locust St, then 0.5 mi n. Int corridors. **Pets:** No service, supervision, crate.
✕ 🗄 ⌸

◆◆ USA Inns of America M ❦
(308) 381-0111. **$40-$50.** 7000 S Nine Bridge Rd. US 281 at jct I-80, Grand Island-Hastings, exit 312. Ext/int corridors. **Pets:** Small. $5 daily fee/pet, $5 one-time fee/pet. Supervision.
🅰🆂🅺 ✕ 🗄 🖵

HASTINGS

◆◆ Holiday Inn M ❦
(402) 463-6721. **$70-$80.** 2205 Osborne Dr E. 2 mi n on US 34 and 281. Ext/int corridors. **Pets:** Other. No service, supervision, crate.
🅰🆂🅺 SD ✕ 🏠 🗋 🗅 🗄 🖵 ⌸

◆◆ Midlands Lodge M ❦
(402) 463-2428. **$30-$56, 7 days notice.** 910 West J St. At jct US 6, 34 and 281. Ext corridors. **Pets:** Other. Designated rooms, no service, supervision, crate.
🆂🅰🆅🅴 SD ✕ 🗄 ⌸

◆ Rainbow Motel M
(402) 463-2989. **$29-$40.** 1000 West J St. On US 6, just w of jct US 34 and 281. Ext corridors. **Pets:** Supervision.
🆂🅰🆅🅴 ✕ 🗄 🖵

◆◆ Super 8 M ❦
(402) 463-8888. **$52-$62.** 2200 N Kansas Ave. 2 mi n on US 34/281. Int corridors. **Pets:** Other. No service, supervision, crate.
🅰🆂🅺 SD ✕ 🗋 🗅 🗄 🖵

◆◆ USA Inns M ❦
(402) 463-1422. **$34-$44.** 2424 E Osborne Dr. 2 mi n on US 34/281. Ext/int corridors. **Pets:** Medium, dogs only. No service, supervision, crate.
🅰🆂🅺 SD ✕ 🗄 🖵

KEARNEY

◆◆◆ Best Western Inn of Kearney M ❦
(308) 237-5185. **$49-$79.** 1010 3rd Ave. SR 44, 1 mi n of I-80, exit 272. Ext/int corridors. **Pets:** No service, supervision, crate.
🆂🅰🆅🅴 SD ✕ 🗋 🖵 🍴 ⌸

◆ Budget Motel South M ❦
(308) 237-5991. **$38-$62.** 411 S 2nd Ave. SR 44, 0.7 mi n of I-80, exit 272. Ext/int corridors. **Pets:** Large, dogs only. $5 daily fee/pet, $5 one-time fee/pet. Designated rooms, no service, supervision, crate.
🆂🅰🆅🅴 SD ✕ ⌸

◆ Western Inn South M ❦
(308) 234-1876. **$39-$56, 5 days notice.** 510 Third Ave. On SR 44, 0.6 mi n of I-80, exit 272. Ext/int corridors. **Pets:** Other. $5 daily fee/room. No service, supervision, crate.
🆂🅰🆅🅴 ✕ 🗄 🖵 ⌸

KIMBALL

◆◆ Days Inn-Kimball M
(308) 235-4671. **Call for rates.** 611 E 3rd St. 0.5 mi e on US 30, 1.5 mi ne of jct SR 71 and I-80, exit 20. Ext corridors. **Pets:** Designated rooms, no service, supervision, crate.
✕ 🗄 ⌸

◆ 1st Interstate Inn M ❦
(308) 235-4601. **Call for rates.** Rt 1, Box 136. Jct I-80 and US 71, exit 20. Ext corridors. **Pets:** Very small. $5 one-time fee/pet. Designated rooms, no service, supervision, crate.
🅰🆂🅺 ✕ 🗄

LEXINGTON

AAA ◆ **Budget Host Minute Man Motel** M ❀
(308) 324-5544. **$34-$48.** 801 S Plum Creek Pkwy. 2 mi n on US 283 from jct I-80, exit 237. Ext corridors. **Pets:** Medium, dogs only. $5 one-time fee/room. Designated rooms, no service, supervision, crate.
SAVE S🛇 ☒

LINCOLN

AAA ◆◆ **Best Western Airport Inn** MI
(402) 475-9541. **$54-$72.** 3200 NW 12th. I-80 airport exit 399. Int corridors. **Pets:** Supervision.
SAVE S🛇 ☒ ⑪ ⌂

AAA ◆◆◆ **Best Western Villager Courtyard & Gardens Hotel** MI ❀
(402) 464-9111. **$79-$99.** 5200 O St. 3 mi e on US 6 city route and 34. Ext corridors. **Pets:** Other. $25 deposit/room. Supervision.
SAVE S🛇 ☒ ⌂ ⬠ ⬡ ⬛ ⬜ ⑪ ⌂

◆◆◆ **Chase Suite Hotel by Woodfin** A
(402) 483-4900. **$79-$200.** 200 S 68th Pl. 4.3 mi e on US 34, just s of jct 68th St. Ext corridors. **Pets:** Designated rooms, no service, supervision, crate.
ASK S🛇 ☒ ⌂ ⬠ ⬡ ⬛ ⬜ ⌂ ☒

◆◆ **Comfort Inn of Lincoln** M ❀
(402) 475-2200. **$55-$99.** 2940 NW 12th St. I-80, exit 399, airport exit; enter at Perkins Restaurant. Int corridors. **Pets:** Other. $5 daily fee/room. Designated rooms, supervision.
ASK S🛇 ☒ ⬛

◆◆◆ **Comfort Suites** M ❀
(402) 476-8080. **$69-$119.** 4231 Industrial Ave. 2 mi s I-80, exit 403. Int corridors. **Pets:** Other. $10 daily fee/room, $10 one-time fee/room. No service, supervision, crate.
ASK S🛇 ☒ ⬠ ⬡ ⬛ ⬜ ⌂

◆◆ **Days Inn South** M ❀
(402) 423-7111. **$50-$70.** 1140 Calvert St. 2.5 mi s on SR 2. Ext/int corridors. **Pets:** $10 daily fee/pet. No service, supervision, crate.
ASK S🛇 ☒

◆◆◆ **Hawthorn Suites Ltd** M
(402) 464-4400. **$89-$115.** 216 N 48th St. 2.5 mi e on US 6 city route and 34; just ne of 48th and O sts. Int corridors. **Pets:** Supervision.
ASK S🛇 ☒ ⬡ ⬛ ⬜ ⌂

◆◆◆ **Holiday Inn Express** M ❀
(402) 474-1417. **$75-$75, 30 days notice.** 1010 W Bond St. Just w of I-80, exit 399. Int corridors. **Pets:** Other. Supervision.
ASK S🛇 ☒ ⬡ ⬛ ⌂

◆◆ **Microtel Inn & Suites** M
(402) 476-2591. **$49-$59.** 2505 Fairfield St. I-80, exit 403, 2.2 mi s, then just w. Int corridors. **Pets:** No service, supervision, crate.
ASK S🛇 ☒ ⌂ ⬡ ⬛ ⬜

AAA ◆◆◆ **Ramada Inn** M
(402) 475-4971. **$55-$82.** 1101 W Bond St. I-80, exit 399. Int corridors. **Pets:** Designated rooms, supervision.
SAVE S🛇 ☒ ⬡ ⬡ ⬛ ⬜ ⌂

◆◆◆ **Red Roof Inn & Suites** M ❀
(402) 438-4700. **$65-$70.** 6501 N 28th St. 0.3 mi s of I-80, exit 403. Int corridors. **Pets:** Other. $10 deposit/room. Supervision.
ASK ☒ ⬡ ⬛ ⬜ ⌂

◆◆ **Sleep Inn** M ❀
(402) 475-1550. **$58-$65, 5 days notice.** 3400 NW 12th St. I-80, exit 399 (airport exit). Int corridors. **Pets:** Other. $25 deposit/room. Supervision.
ASK S🛇 ☒ ⌂ ⬡ ⬛ ⬜ ⌂

AAA ◆◆ **Town House Motel** A ❀
(402) 475-3000. **$65-$80, 7 days notice.** 1744 M St. Downtown. Int corridors. **Pets:** Other. Supervision.
SAVE S🛇 ☒ ⬡ ⬛ ⬜

MCCOOK

◆◆◆ **Holiday Inn Express** M
(308) 345-4505. **$58-$70.** 1 Holiday Bison Dr. On US 83, 0.3 mi n of jct US 6 and 34. Int corridors. **Pets:** Supervision.
ASK S🛇 ☒ ⌂ ⬡ ⬛

◆ **Super 8 Motel** M ❀
(308) 345-1141. **$40-$50.** 1103 E B St. 0.5 mi e on US 6/34. Ext corridors. **Pets:** Small, other. Designated rooms, no service, supervision, crate.
ASK S🛇 ☒

MORRILL

◆◆ **Oak Tree Inn** MI ❀
(308) 247-2111. **$45-$60.** 80700 Hwy 26. 0.5 mi e. Ext/int corridors. **Pets:** Other. $5 one-time fee/pet. No service, supervision, crate.
ASK S🛇 ☒ ⌂ ⬛ ⬜ ⑪

NEBRASKA CITY

AAA ◆◆ **Apple Inn** M ❀
(402) 873-5959. **$40-$50, 3 days notice.** 502 S 11th. Center. Ext/int corridors. **Pets:** Small, dogs only. $5 daily fee/room. Designated rooms, supervision.
SAVE S🛇 ☒ ⬡ ⬛ ⬜ ⌂

NORFOLK

AAA ◆◆ **Norfolk Country Inn** MI ❀
(402) 371-4430. **$52-$58.** 1201 S 13th St. At jct US 275 bypass and US 81. Ext corridors. **Pets:** Designated rooms, supervision.
SAVE S🛇 ☒ ⬛ ⬜ ⑪ ⌂

AAA ◆◆ **White House Inn** M ❀
(402) 371-3133. **$50-$50.** 2206 Market Ln. On US 275 bypass, 1 mi w of US 81. Int corridors. **Pets:** Other. $20 deposit/room. No service, supervision, crate.
SAVE S🛇 ☒ ⬡ ⬜ ⬛

NORTH PLATTE

(AAA) ◆◆ **Best Western Chalet Lodge** [M] ❀
(308) 532-2313. **$59-$70.** 920 N Jeffers St. US 83 and 30, 2 mi n of jct I-80, exit 177. Ext corridors. **Pets:** Other. $3 daily fee/pet. Supervision.
[SAVE] [S♂] [✕] [🔌] [💻] [🍴]

(AAA) ◆◆◆ **Holiday Inn Express** [M] ❀
(308) 532-9500. **$76.** 300 Holiday Frontage Rd. Just s of I-80, exit 177. Int corridors. **Pets:** $10 one-time fee/room. Supervision.
[SAVE] [S♂] [✕] [🐾] [🔌] [🔌] [💻] [🍴]

(AAA) ◆◆◆ **Quality Inn & Suites** [M] ❀
(308) 532-9090. **$75-$160.** 2102 S Jeffers. Jct I-80, exit 177, 0.8 mi n on US 83. Ext/int corridors. **Pets:** Other. $25 deposit/room, $5 one-time fee/room. Supervision.
[SAVE] [S♂] [✕] [🐾] [🐾] [🔌] [🔌] [💻] [🍴] [🍴] [✕]

(AAA) ◆◆ **Ramada Limited** [M] ❀
(308) 534-3120. **$57-$100, 30 days notice.** 3201 S Jeffers. 0.3 mi s of I-80, exit 177. Int corridors. **Pets:** Small. $5 daily fee/pet, $5 one-time fee/pet. No service, supervision, crate.
[SAVE] [S♂] [✕] [🍴] [🍴]

(AAA) ◆◆ **Travelers Inn** [M] ❀
(308) 534-4020. **$30-$38.** 602 E 4th St. I-80, exit 177; US 83, 1.5 mi n to E US 30, just e on US 30. Ext corridors. **Pets:** Other. Designated rooms, no service, supervision, crate.
[SAVE] [S♂] [✕] [🔌] [🍴]

O'NEILL

(AAA) ◆ **Elms Motel** [M] ❀
(402) 336-3800. **$28-$36.** 414 E Hwy 20. 1 mi se on US 20/275. Ext corridors. **Pets:** Other. Designated rooms, supervision.
[SAVE] [S♂] [✕] [✕]

(AAA) ◆ **Golden Hotel** [H] ❀
(402) 336-4436. **$29-$45.** 406 E Douglas. Center; jct US 20/275/281. Ext/int corridors. **Pets:** Supervision.
[SAVE] [S♂] [✕] [🔌] [💻]

OGALLALA

(AAA) ◆◆ **Days Inn** [M] ❀
(308) 284-6365. **$60-$70.** 601 Stagecoach Tr. Just ne of I-80, exit 126, on frontage road. Int corridors. **Pets:** Other. $6 daily fee/room, $6 one-time fee/room. Designated rooms, supervision.
[SAVE] [S♂] [✕] [🔌]

(AAA) ◆ **Econo Lodge** [M] ❀
(308) 284-2056. **$39-$65.** 108 Prospector Dr. I-80, exit 126, just se. Ext corridors. **Pets:** Medium. $5 daily fee/pet, $5 one-time fee/pet. No service, supervision, crate.
[SAVE] [S♂] [✕] [🍴]

◆◆◆ **Holiday Inn Express** [M]
(308) 284-2266. **$72-$80.** 501 Stagecoach Rd. I-80, exit 126, just n, then e on service road. Ext/int corridors. **Pets:** Small. Designated rooms, no service, supervision, crate.
[ASK] [S♂] [✕] [🐾] [🔌] [🔌]

◆◆ **Ramada Limited** [MI]
(308) 284-3623. **$55-$72.** 201 Chuckwagon Rd. I-80, exit 126, just nw. Ext/int corridors. **Pets:** Supervision.
[ASK] [S♂] [✕] [💻] [🍴] [🍴]

OMAHA

◆◆◆ **Baymont Inn-Omaha** [M]
(402) 592-5200. **$55-$62.** 10760 M St. I-80, exit 445, 0.3 mi e on L St, entry off 108th St. Int corridors. **Pets:** No service, supervision, crate.
[S♂] [✕] [🐾] [🔌] [💻]

(AAA) ◆ **Ben Franklin Motel** [M] ❀
(402) 895-2200. **$46-$56.** 10308 Sapp Bros Dr. SR 50, exit 440, 0.3 mi via service road. Ext corridors. **Pets:** Medium. $5 daily fee/room. Supervision.
[SAVE] [S♂] [✕] [🔌] [💻] [🍴]

◆◆ **Best Inn** [M]
(402) 895-2555. **$47-$55.** 9305 S 145th St. On SR 50 at I-80, exit 440, n to 1st stoplight, just w. Int corridors. **Pets:** Supervision.
[ASK] [S♂] [✕] [🔌]

(AAA) ◆◆◆ **Best Western Central-Executive Center** [MI]
(402) 397-3700. **$79-$89.** 3650 S 72nd St at I-80. At jct 72nd St and I-80, exit 449. Int corridors. **Pets:** Small. Designated rooms, no service, supervision, crate.
[SAVE] [S♂] [✕] [🐾] [🐾] [🔌] [🔌] [💻] [🍴] [🍴]

◆◆◆ **Crowne Plaza Omaha-Old Mill** [MI]
(402) 496-0850. **$139.** 655 N 108th Av St. I-680, Dodge St exit 3, 108th St to 108th Ave and N Old Mill Rd exit, just n. Int corridors. **Pets:** Medium. No service, supervision, crate.
[ASK] [S♂] [🔌] [💻] [🍴] [🍴]

(AAA) ◆◆◆ **Four Points by ITT Sheraton** [MI] ❀
(402) 895-1000. **$75-$75.** 4888 S 118th St. US 275 and SR 92, 0.3 mi w of jct I-80, exit 445 (L St w). Int corridors. **Pets:** Small, other. $10 daily fee/room. Designated rooms, no service, supervision, crate.
[SAVE] [✕] [🐾] [🔌] [🔌] [💻] [🍴] [🍴]

◆◆◆ **Hampton Inn-Southwest** [M]
(402) 593-2380. **Call for rates.** 10728 L St. I-80, exit 445, 0.3 mi e. Int corridors. **Pets:** Small. No service, supervision, crate.
[ASK] [✕] [🐾] [🔌] [💻] [🍴]

◆◆◆ **Hawthorn Suites** [M] ❀
(402) 331-0101. **$93-$105.** 11025 M St. I-80, exit 445, 0.3 mi e on L St, entry off 108th St. Ext corridors. **Pets:** Small. $6 daily fee/pet, $6 one-time fee/pet. Supervision.
[ASK] [S♂] [✕] [🐾] [🔌] [🔌] [💻] [🍴] [✕]

◆◆◆ **Holiday Inn Central** [MI] ❀
(402) 393-3950. **$85-$125.** 3321 S 72nd St. Just n of jct I-80 and exit 449 (72nd St). Int corridors. **Pets:** Small. $125 deposit/room, $25 one-time fee/room. No service, supervision, crate.
[ASK] [S♂] [✕] [🐾] [🐾] [🔌] [🔌] [💻] [🍴] [🍴] [✕]

◆◆◆ Homewood Suites 🅼 🐾
(402) 397-7500. **$86-$96.** 7010 Hascall St. I-80, exit 449 (72nd S), just e on Hascall. Ext/int corridors. **Pets:** Small. $100 deposit/room, $50 one-time fee/room. No service, supervision, crate.

◆◆◆ La Quinta Inn 🅼
(402) 493-1900. **$59-$79.** 3330 N 104th Ave. At jct I-680 and Maple St, exit 4, w to 108th St, right to Bedford, right to 104th Ave. Int corridors. **Pets:** Medium. Designated rooms, no service, supervision, crate.

◆ Motel 6–161 🅼 🐾
(402) 331-3161. **$40-$56.** 10708 M St. I-80, exit 445, 0.4 mi e on L St, entry on 108th St. Ext corridors. **Pets:** Small, other. No service, supervision, crate.

🆎 ◆◆◆◆ Omaha Marriott Hotel 🅼🅸
(402) 399-9000. **$74-$175.** 10220 Regency Cir. Just se of jct I-680 and US 6 (exit 3, Dodge Street). Int corridors. **Pets:** Medium. Designated rooms, no service, supervision, crate.

◆◆◆ Ramada Inn Central 🄷
(402) 397-7030. **$95-$105.** 7007 Grover St. I-80, exit 449 (72nd St). Int corridors. **Pets:** Medium. Supervision.

◆◆ Ramada Limited 🅼 🐾
(402) 896-9500. **$65-$75, 5 days notice.** 9505 S 142nd St. Jct I-80 and exit 440. Int corridors. **Pets:** Very small, dogs only. $5 daily fee/pet. No service, supervision, crate.

🆎 ◆◆ Satellite Motel 🅼
(402) 733-7373. **$36-$48.** 6006 L St. On US 275 and SR 92, 0.8 mi s of I-80, exit 450 (60th St). Ext/int corridors. **Pets:** Medium. Supervision.

OSHKOSH

🆎 ◆ Shady Rest Motel 🅼 🐾
(308) 772-4115. **$32-$38.** 102 Main St. On US 26, jct Main St. Ext corridors. **Pets:** No service, supervision, crate.

PAXTON

🆎 ◆◆ Paxton Days Inn 🅼 🐾
(308) 239-4510. **$50-$65, 3 days notice.** 851 Paxton Rd. Just n of I-80, exit 145. Ext corridors. **Pets:** $10 one-time fee/room. Designated rooms, no service, supervision, crate.

SCOTTSBLUFF

🆎 ◆◆ Best Western Scottsbluff Inn 🅼🅸 🐾
(308) 635-3111. **$55-$72.** 1901 21st Ave. 1.8 mi e on US 26. Int corridors. **Pets:** Other. $6 daily fee/room. Supervision.

🆎 ◆ Capri Motel 🅼 🐾
(308) 635-2057. **$32-$40.** 2424 Ave I. 1.5 mi nw, just s of 27th St on Ave I. Ext corridors. **Pets:** Other. $3 daily fee/room. Supervision.

🆎 ◆ Lamplighter American Inn 🅼 🐾
(308) 632-7108. **$35-$44, 5 days notice.** 606 E 27th St. US 26 business route, 0.5 mi e of jct SR 71. Int corridors. **Pets:** Small, dogs only. $50 deposit/room, $5 daily fee/pet, $10 one-time fee/pet. Designated rooms, no service, supervision, crate.

🆎 ◆ Sands Motel 🅼 🐾
(308) 632-6191. **$29-$38.** 814 W 27th St. 1.5 mi nw, on Business Rts US 26 and 71. Ext corridors. **Pets:** Small. $4 daily fee/pet. Supervision.

SEWARD

◆◆ Seward Super 8 🅼
(402) 643-3388. **$46-$56.** 1329 Progressive Rd. Hwy 15, 3 mi n of jct I-80 and Hwy 15. Ext/int corridors. **Pets:** Small. Designated rooms, supervision.

SIDNEY

◆◆◆ Holiday Inn & Conference Center 🅼🅸 🐾
(308) 254-2000. **$89-$89.** 664 Chase Blvd. Just s of I-80, exit 59. Int corridors. **Pets:** Other. $10 deposit/pet, $10 daily fee/pet, $10 one-time fee/pet. Supervision.

🆎 ◆ Sidney Motor Lodge 🅼 🐾
(308) 254-4581. **$38-$55.** 2031 Illinois St. On US 30, w edge of town. Ext corridors. **Pets:** Other. Designated rooms, no service, supervision, crate.

SOUTH SIOUX CITY

◆ Flamingo Inn & Suites 🅼
(402) 494-8874. **$39-$59, 5 days notice.** 2829 Dakota Ave. 2 mi s of jct I-29 and Dakota Ave exit. Ext/int corridors. **Pets:** Small. Designated rooms, no service, supervision, crate.

◆◆◆ Marina Inn Conference Center 🅼🅸
(402) 494-4000. **$69-$109, 3 days notice.** 4th & B. I-29, exit 148; on banks of Missouri River (turn e at stoplight by Nebraska side of bridge). Int corridors. **Pets:** Small. Supervision.

🆎 ◆ Park Plaza Motel 🅼
(402) 494-2021. **$38-$55.** 1201 1st Ave. 1 mi s of I-29, exit 148 (Dakota Ave). Ext corridors. **Pets:** Small. Designated rooms, no service, supervision, crate.

THEDFORD

⊕ ◆◆◆ Rodeway Inn M ☙
(308) 645-2284. **$46-$67.** HC 58 Box 1D. 1 mi e on SR 2, just w of US 83. Int corridors. **Pets:** Other. $25 deposit/ room, $5 daily fee/room. Supervision.
SAVE 🆂 ☒ 🖉 📷 🖵

VALENTINE

⊕ ◆◆ Motel Raine M
(402) 376-2030. **$30-$48.** US 20 W. 0.5 mi sw on US 20. Ext corridors. **Pets:** No service, supervision, crate.
SAVE ☒ 🖵

⊕ ◆◆ Trade Winds Lodge M ☙
(402) 376-1600. **$38-$61.** E Hwy 20 & 83. 1 mi se on US 20/83. Ext corridors. **Pets:** Other. Supervision.
SAVE 🆂 ☒ 📷 🖾

YORK

⊕ ◆◆ Best Western Palmer Inn M
(402) 362-5585. **$39-$69.** 2426 S Lincoln Ave. 1 mi n on US 81 from jct I-80, exit 353. Ext corridors. **Pets:** Small. Designated rooms, no service, supervision, crate.
SAVE 🆂 ☒ 🖵 🖾 ☒

AMARGOSA VALLEY

◆◆◆ Longstreet Inn, Casino RV Park & Golf Club Ⓜ ❖

(775) 372-1777. **$69-$99.** 373 Stateline. 7 mi n of jct SR 127 and SR 190 (Death Valley Jct) on SR 373; 15 mi s of jct SR 95 and SR 373 on SR 373. Int corridors. **Pets:** Medium. $50 deposit/room. Supervision.

⊠ ⑪ ☎

BATTLE MOUNTAIN

ⒶⒶⒶ ◆◆ Best Western Big Chief Motel Ⓜ ❖

(775) 635-2416. **$40-$55.** 434 W Front St. Just n of I-80; exit 229 or 233. Ext corridors. **Pets:** Medium, other. $5 daily fee/pet. Designated rooms, no service, supervision, crate.

SAVE Ⓢ ⊠ 🐾 ⊟

ⒶⒶⒶ ◆◆ Comfort Inn Ⓜ

(775) 635-5880. **$49-$59.** 521 E Front St. Just N of I-80, exit 229 or 233. Int corridors. **Pets:** Supervision.

SAVE Ⓢ ⊠ 🐾 ⊟

BEATTY

◆ Burro Inn Ⓜ ❖

(775) 553-2225. **$37-$42.** Third St & Hwy 95. 4 blks s on SR 95. Ext corridors. **Pets:** $25 deposit/room, $5 daily fee/pet. Supervision.

⊠ 🐾 ⑪

CARLIN

ⒶⒶⒶ ◆◆ Best Inn & Suites Ⓜ

(775) 754-6110. **$49-$84.** 1018 Fir St. Just s of I-80, exit 280. Int corridors. **Pets:** Supervision.

SAVE Ⓢ ⊠ 🛏 🐾 ⓖ ⊟ ▣

CARSON CITY

ⒶⒶⒶ ◆◆ Best Value Ⓜ ❖

(775) 882-2007. **$33-$47.** 2731 S Carson St. 1.3 mi s on US 50 and 395. Ext corridors. **Pets:** Other. $30 deposit/room. Supervision.

Ⓢ ⊠ ⊟ ☎

◆◆ Best Western Trailside Inn Ⓜ ❖

(775) 883-7300. **Call for rates.** 1300 N Carson St. 0.5 mi n on US 395. Ext corridors. **Pets:** Medium. $100 deposit/room, $6 daily fee/pet, $6 one-time fee/pet. No service, supervision, crate.

ASK Ⓢ ⊠ ⊟ ▣ ☎

◆ Carson City Super 8 Ⓜ ❖

(775) 883-7800. **$46-$82.** 2829 S Carson. South end of town. Int corridors. **Pets:** Small. $25 deposit/room, $8 daily fee/pet, $8 one-time fee/pet. Designated rooms, no service, supervision, crate.

ASK Ⓢ ⊠ ⊟ CTV

ⒶⒶⒶ ◆◆ Days Inn Ⓜ

(775) 883-3343. **$36-$95.** 3103 N Carson St. US 395N, n end of city. Ext corridors. **Pets:** Supervision.

SAVE Ⓢ ⊠ ⊟

ELKO

ⒶⒶⒶ ◆◆◆ Best Western Elko Inn Express Ⓜ

(775) 738-7261. **$54-$79.** 837 Idaho St. 1 mi s of I-80, exit 301 or 303. Ext corridors. **Pets:** No service, supervision, crate.

Ⓢ ⊠ 🐾 ⊟

ⒶⒶⒶ ◆◆◆ Best Western Gold Country Motor Inn Ⓜ ❖

(775) 738-8421. **$69-$109.** 2050 Idaho St. Just s of I-80 exit 303. Ext corridors. **Pets:** Medium, other. $15 one-time fee/room. No service, supervision, crate.

SAVE Ⓢ ⊠ 🛏 🐾 ⓖ ⊟ ▣ ⑪

ⒶⒶⒶ ◆◆◆ High Desert Inn Ⓜ ❖

(775) 738-8425. **$59-$99.** 3015 Idaho St. Just s of I-80 exit 303. Ext/int corridors. **Pets:** Other. $10 one-time fee/room. Supervision.

SAVE Ⓢ ⊠ 🐾 ⊟ ▣ ⑪ ☎

ⒶⒶⒶ ◆◆◆ Red Lion Inn & Casino Ⓜ ❖

(775) 738-2111. **$79-$109.** 2065 Idaho St. Just s of I-80 exit 303. Int corridors. **Pets:** Medium, other. $15 one-time fee/room. No service, supervision, crate.

SAVE Ⓢ ⊠ 🛏 🐾 ▣ ⑪

◆◆◆ Shilo Inn Ⓜ

(775) 738-5522. **$69-$129.** 2401 Mountain City Hwy. Just N of I-80, exit 301. Int corridors. **Pets:** Very small. No service, supervision, crate.

ASK Ⓢ ⊠ 🐾 ⊟ ☎

ⒶⒶⒶ ◆◆ Thunderbird Motel Ⓜ ❖

(775) 738-7115. **$49-$79.** 345 Idaho St. 1 mi s of I-80, exit 301 or 303. Ext corridors. **Pets:** Small, other. $25 deposit/room. No service, supervision, crate.

SAVE Ⓢ ⊠ 🐾 ⊟

ELY

Ⓐ ◆ Fireside Inn Ⓜ ☙
(775) 289-3765. **$38-$43.** McGill Hwy. 2 mi n on US 93. Ext corridors. **Pets:** Medium. No service, supervision, crate.
〔SAVE〕〔S🐾〕✕ 🖪 💻

Ⓐ ◆◆◆ Ramada Inn-Copper Queen Casino Ⓧ ☙
(775) 289-4884. **$60-$85.** 805 Great Basin Blvd. 0.3 mi s of jct 6, 50 and 93. Ext/int corridors. **Pets:** Supervision.
〔SAVE〕✕ 🖪 💻 🍴 ➰

FALLON

Ⓐ ◆ Budget Inn of Fallon Ⓜ ☙
(775) 423-2277. **$40-$46.** 1705 S Taylor St. 0.5 mi s of US 50. Ext corridors. **Pets:** Very small, other. $25 deposit/room. No service, supervision, crate.
〔SAVE〕✕ 🖪 💻

Ⓐ ◆◆ Western Motel Ⓜ ☙
(775) 423-5118. **$37-$43.** 125 S Carson St. Just e of US 95. Ext corridors. **Pets:** Other. $5 daily fee/pet. Supervision.
〔SAVE〕〔S🐾〕✕ 🖪 ➰

FERNLEY

Ⓐ ◆◆ Best Western Fernley Inn Ⓜ
(775) 575-6776. **Call for rates.** 1405 E Newlands Dr. Just s of I-80, exit 48. Ext corridors. **Pets:** Designated rooms, supervision.
〔SAVE〕✕ 🛋 🐾 🖪 ➰

GARDNERVILLE

Ⓐ ◆◆ Westerner Motel Ⓜ ☙
(775) 782-3602. **$35-$40.** 1353 US 395 N. US 395S, south end of town. Ext corridors. **Pets:** Dogs only. Designated rooms, no service, supervision, crate.
✕ 🖪 ➰

JACKPOT

Ⓐ ◆◆◆ Horseshu Hotel & Casino Ⓜ
(775) 755-7777. **$42-$67.** 1385 Hwy 93. On SR 93. Int corridors. **Pets:** Very small. No service, supervision, crate.
〔SAVE〕〔S🐾〕✕ 💻 🍴 ✂

LAKE TAHOE METROPOLITAN AREA

STATELINE

◆◆◆◆ Harrah's Hotel & Casino Ⓗ
(775) 588-6611. **Call for rates.** In Casino area. In casino area. Int corridors. **Pets:** Designated rooms, no service, supervision, crate.
〔ASK〕✕ 🍴 ➰

☙ END METROPOLITAN AREA ☙

LAS VEGAS METROPOLITAN AREA

BOULDER CITY

◆ Super 8 Motel Ⓜ
(702) 294-8888. **$50-$300.** 704 Nevada Hwy. On US 93. Ext corridors. **Pets:** Medium. Supervision.
〔ASK〕〔S🐾〕✕ 🖪 ➰

ECHO BAY

Ⓐ ◆◆ Echo Bay Resort Ⓜ!
(702) 394-4000. **$90-$100, 3 days notice.** On Lake Mead; 4 mi e of SR 167. Int corridors. **Pets:** No service, supervision, crate.
〔SAVE〕🍴 ✂ 〔CTV〕

INDIAN SPRINGS

Ⓐ ◆ Indian Springs Motor Hotel Ⓜ ☙
(702) 879-3700. **$33-$49.** 300 Tonopah Hwy. On US 95, 45 mi n of Las Vegas. Int corridors. **Pets:** Small, other. $5 daily fee/pet. Supervision.
〔SAVE〕〔S🐾〕✕ 🖪 🍴 〔CTV〕

LAS VEGAS

Ⓐ ◆◆◆ AmeriSuites Las Vegas Ⓜ ☙
(702) 369-3366. **$69-$129.** 4520 Paradise Ave. Cross sts Harmon & Paradise, e of the strip. Int corridors. **Pets:** Very small. Supervision.
〔SAVE〕〔S🐾〕✕ 🐾 🖫 🖪 💻 ➰

◆◆◆ Best Inn & Suites Ⓜ ☙
(702) 632-0229. **$59-$99.** 4288 N Nellis Blvd. From I-15 at Craig exit e to N Las Vegas Blvd. Int corridors. **Pets:** Other. $50 deposit/room, $5 daily fee/pet. No service, supervision, crate.
〔ASK〕〔S🐾〕✕ 🐾 🖫 🖪 💻

Ⓐ ◆◆ Best Western Main Street Inn Ⓜ! ☙
(702) 382-3455. **$39-$125.** 1000 N Main St. I-15N, exit 43E; I-15S, exit 44E. Ext corridors. **Pets:** Other. $8 daily fee/pet. No service, supervision, crate.
〔S🐾〕✕ 🖪 🍴 ➰

Best Western Nellis Motor Inn M ❖❖ ☀
(702) 643-6111. **$49-$150.** 5330 E Craig Rd. 7 mi ne; 0.3 mi from Nellis AFB; I-15, exit 48 e. Ext corridors. **Pets:** $50 deposit/room, $10 daily fee/pet. No service, supervision, crate.

SAVE 🚭 ❌ 🔲 💻 🛍 🚷

Best Western Parkview Inn M ❖❖ ☀
(702) 385-1213. **$49-$125.** 921 Las Vegas Blvd N. 8 blks n on US 91 and 93. Ext corridors. **Pets:** Other. $8 daily fee/pet. No service, supervision, crate.

❌ 🛍

Comfort Inn M ❖❖❖ ☀
(702) 399-1500. **$80-$80.** 910 E Cheyenne Ave. I-15 exit 46 Cheyenne West. Int corridors. **Pets:** $5 daily fee/pet. Designated rooms, no service, supervision, crate.

SAVE 🚭 ❌ 🛋 🔲 💻 🛍

Crowne Plaza MI ❖❖❖ ☀
(702) 369-4400. **$125-$185, 30 days notice.** 4255 S Paradise Rd. Exit I-15 Flamingo, e 0.5 mi to Paradise, s 0.3 mi. Int corridors. **Pets:** $200 deposit/room. Designated rooms, supervision.

SAVE 🚭 ❌ 🛋 🍴 🔲 💻 🍽 🛍

Emerald Springs-Holiday Inn MI ❖❖❖
(702) 732-9100. **$79-$99.** 325 E Flamingo Rd. I-15 exit E Flamingo Rd. Int corridors. **Pets:** No service, supervision, crate.

SAVE 🚭 ❌ 🔲 💻 🍽 🛍

Four Seasons Hotel Las Vegas H ❖❖❖❖❖ ☀
(702) 632-5000. **$200-$400.** 3960 Las Vegas Blvd S. I-15, E Tropicana exit, s on the strip. Int corridors. **Pets:** Small. No service, supervision, crate.

❌ 🛋 🔲 💻 🍽 🛍 🚷

Hawthorn Inn & Suites M ❖❖❖ ☀
(702) 798-7736. **$79-$129.** 4975 S Valley View Blvd. I-15, exit Tropicana Ave W, 0.025 mi. Int corridors. **Pets:** Medium. $18 one-time fee/pet. Designated rooms, no service, supervision, crate.

SAVE 🚭 ❌ 🛋 🔲 💻 🛍

Hawthorn Suites–Las Vegas M ❖❖❖ ☀
(702) 739-7000. **$115-$195.** 5051 Duke Ellington Way. Exit I-15, at E Tropicana Ave, 0.8 mi e to Duke Ellington Way, just s. Ext corridors. **Pets:** Other. Supervision.

ASK 🚭 ❌ 🍴 🛋 🔲 💻 🛍 🚷

Holiday Inn Express M ❖❖❖ ☀
(702) 256-3766. **$89-$175.** 8669 W Sahara Ave. Exit I-15 at Sahara, 6.5 mi w. Int corridors. **Pets:** Medium. $20 one-time fee/room. Supervision.

SAVE 🚭 ❌ 🛋 🔲 💻 🛍

Howard Johnson Las Vegas Strip M ❖❖ ☀
(702) 388-0301. **$49-$79.** 1401 Las Vegas Blvd. From I-15 exit Sahara E to Las Vegas Blvd, then n. Ext/int corridors. **Pets:** Very small. $10 deposit/pet, $10 one-time fee/room. No service, supervision, crate.

SAVE 🚭 ❌ 🔲 💻 🍽 🛍

La Quinta Inn M ❖❖❖ ☀
(702) 739-7457. **$69-$99.** 3782 Las Vegas Blvd S. 5.5 mi s on the Strip. Ext corridors. **Pets:** Small. Supervision.

SAVE ❌

Residence Inn Las Vegas Convention Center H ❖❖❖ ☀
(702) 796-9300. **$95-$145.** 3225 Paradise Rd. Opposite Convention Center. Ext corridors. **Pets:** Small, other. $10 daily fee/room, $50 one-time fee/room. Supervision.

❌ 🛋 🔲 💻 🛍 🚷

Super 8 Motel Las Vegas Strip MI ❖❖ ☀
(702) 794-0888. **$50-$72.** 4250 S Koval Ln. From I-15 at Flamingo Rd E Koval exit, then s. Int corridors. **Pets:** Large, other. $25 deposit/pet, $10 daily fee/pet. Designated rooms, no service, supervision, crate.

ASK 🚭 ❌ 🍴 🛋 🔲 🛍

Wellesley Inn & Suites M ❖❖❖ ☀
(702) 731-3111. **$50-$80.** 1550 E Flamingo Rd. From I-15, Flamingo Rd E exit, then 2 mi. Int corridors. **Pets:** Other. $50 deposit/room. No service, supervision, crate.

SAVE 🚭 ❌ 🍴 🛋 🔲 💻 🛍

LAUGHLIN

Don Laughlin's Riverside Resort Hotel & Casino H ❖❖❖ ☀
(702) 298-2535. **$25-$109.** 1650 S Casino Dr. 2 mi s of Davis Dam. Int corridors. **Pets:** Small. $100 deposit/room, $8 daily fee/room. Designated rooms, supervision.

ASK 🚭 ❌ 🍴 🛋 🔲 🍽 🛍

MESQUITE

Budget Inn & Suites M ❖❖ ☀
(702) 346-7444. **$35-$55.** 390 N Sandhill. At exit 122. Ext corridors. **Pets:** Medium, other. $10 daily fee/room. Designated rooms, no service, supervision, crate.

ASK 🚭 ❌ 🛋 🔲 🛍

Virgin River Hotel Casino Bingo MI ❖❖ ☀
(702) 346-7777. **$19-$50.** 100 Pioneer Blvd. W of and adjacent to I-15, exit 122. Ext corridors. **Pets:** Medium, other. $25 deposit/room. No service, supervision, crate.

❌ 🔲 💻 🍽 🛍

PAHRUMP

Saddle West Hotel & Casino MI ❖❖ ☀
(775) 727-1111. **$37-$52.** 1220 S Hwy 160. Downtown. Ext corridors. **Pets:** Medium. Supervision.

SAVE 🚭 ❌ 🛋 🔲 💻 🍽 🛍

☀ **END METROPOLITAN AREA** ☀

LOVELOCK

◆◆◆ **Ramada Inn-Sturgeon's Casino** Ⓜ ❖
(775) 273-2971. **$49-$69.** 1420 Cornell Ave. Just N of I-80; exits #105 or 107. Ext corridors. **Pets:** Large, other. $100 deposit/room. Designated rooms, no service, supervision, crate.

(ASK) (S↕) (✕) (♪) (▤) (▣) (Ⅱ) (⌂)

MILL CITY

🆎 ◆ **Super 8 Motel** Ⓜ ❖
(775) 538-7311. **$39-$49, 7 days notice.** 6000 E Frontage Rd. Just n of I-80, exits 149 or 151. Int corridors. **Pets:** Other. $20 deposit/room, $5 daily fee/pet. No service, supervision, crate.

(SAVE) (S↕) (✕)

MINDEN

🆎 ◆◆◆ **Best Western Minden** Ⓜ
(775) 782-7766. **$65-$125.** 1795 Ironwood DR. US 395 exit Ironwood Drive w; 0.5 mi n of jct US 395 and SR 88. Ext corridors. **Pets:** Supervision.

(SAVE) (S↕) (✕) (▤) (⌂)

🆎 ◆◆ **Holiday Lodge** Ⓜ ❖
(775) 782-2288. **$32-$48.** 1591 US 395N. Center, on US 395N. Ext corridors. **Pets:** Medium, dogs only. $20 deposit/pet, $4 daily fee/pet. No service, supervision, crate.

(✕) (▤) (⌂)

OVERTON

◆◆◆ **Best Western North Shore Inn at Lake Mead** Ⓜ ❖
(702) 397-6000. **$55-$65.** 520 N Moapa Valley Blvd. From I-15, exit 93 on SR 169. Int corridors. **Pets:** Medium, other. $50 deposit/room. Designated rooms, no service, supervision, crate.

(ASK) (S↕) (✕) (▤) (▣) (⌂) (✕)

RENO

◆◆◆ **Holiday Inn-Downtown** Ⓗ ❖
(775) 786-5151. **$79-$109.** 1000 E 6th St. 12 blks e; I-80 via Wells. Int corridors. **Pets:** Other. $50 deposit/room. No service, supervision, crate.

(ASK) (S↕) (✕) (♪) (▤) (▣) (Ⅱ) (⌂)

◆◆◆ **La Quinta Inn** Ⓜ
(775) 348-6100. **$65-$85.** 4001 Market St. US 395 northbound exit airport, southbound exit Villanova Dr. Ext corridors. **Pets:** Medium. Designated rooms, no service, supervision, crate.

(ASK) (✕) (♿) (♪) (▤) (▣) (⌂)

◆ **Miner's Inn** Ⓜ
(775) 329-3464. **$39-$53.** 1651 N Virginia St. Opposite University of Nevada. Ext corridors. **Pets:** Designated rooms, supervision.

(ASK) (S↕) (✕) (▤) (⌂)

🆎 ◆ **Reno Downtown Travelodge** Ⓜ ❖
(775) 329-3451. **$49-$75.** 655 W 4th St. From I-80 at Keystone exit, just e. Ext corridors. **Pets:** $8 daily fee/pet, $8 one-time fee/pet. Designated rooms, no service, supervision, crate.

(S↕) (✕) (▤) (▣) (⌂)

◆◆◆ **Residence Inn by Marriott** Ⓜ ❖
(775) 853-8800. **$112-$148.** 9845 Gateway Dr. 5 mi s; exit US 395 at S Meadows Pkwy; e to Gateway Dr. Int corridors. **Pets:** Small. $6 daily fee/pet, $75 one-time fee/room. Supervision.

(✕) (⌂)

🆎 ◆◆ **Super 8 Motel at Meadow Wood Courtyard** Ⓜ ❖
(775) 825-2940. **$45-$65.** 5851 S Virginia St. US 395 at S McCarran Blvd. Ext corridors. **Pets:** Other. $10 daily fee/pet. Supervision.

(SAVE) (S↕) (✕) (⌂) (♪) (▤) (▣) (Ⅱ)

🆎 ◆◆ **Travelodge Reno Central** Ⓜ ❖
(775) 786-2500. **$53-$81.** 2050 Market St. US 395 exit W Mill St. Int corridors. **Pets:** Small, other. $200 deposit/pet, $8 daily fee/pet. Designated rooms, no service, supervision, crate.

(SAVE) (S↕) (✕) (⌂)

🆎 ◆ **Vagabond Inn** Ⓜ
(775) 825-7134. **$65-$70.** 3131 S Virginia St. 2.5 mi s on US 395. Ext corridors. **Pets:** No service, supervision, crate.

(SAVE) (S↕) (✕) (▤) (▣) (⌂)

TONOPAH

🆎 ◆◆◆ **Best Western Hi Desert Inn** Ⓜ ❖
(775) 482-3511. **$49-$69.** 320 Main St. On US 6 and 95. Int corridors. **Pets:** Dogs only. Supervision.

(S↕) (✕) (♪) (▤) (⌂)

🆎 ◆◆ **Jim Butler Motel** Ⓜ ❖
(775) 482-3577. **$34-$40.** 100 S Main St. On US 6 and 95. Ext corridors. **Pets:** Small, dogs only. Designated rooms, supervision.

(S↕) (✕) (▤)

TOPAZ LAKE

🆎 ◆◆ **Topaz Lodge** Ⓜ ❖
(775) 266-3338. **$39-$53.** 1979 US 395S. US 395S at Topaz Lake, 22 mi s of Gardervile, NV. Ext corridors. **Pets:** Dogs only. $5 daily fee/room, $5 one-time fee/room. Designated rooms, supervision.

(✕) (Ⅱ) (⌂) (✕)

WELLS

🆎 ◆◆ **Best Western Sage Inn** Ⓜ
(775) 752-3353. **$46-$59.** 576 6th St. 0.5 mi n of I-80 exit 352. Int corridors. **Pets:** No service, supervision, crate.

(SAVE) (S↕) (✕) (▤)

◆◆ **Super 8 Motel** Ⓜ ❖
(775) 752-3384. **$60-$85.** 930 6th St. 0.5 mi w of jct US 93, I 80 exit 352. Ext corridors. **Pets:** Medium, other. $20 deposit/pet, $5 daily fee/pet, $5 one-time fee/pet. Designated rooms, no service, supervision, crate.

(✕) (▤)

WINNEMUCCA

🆎 ◆◆◆ **Best Western Gold Country Inn** Ⓜ
(775) 623-6999. **$79-$119.** 921 W Winnemucca Blvd. Just S of I-80; exit 176 or 178. Int corridors. **Pets:** Supervision.

(SAVE) (S↕) (✕) (▤) (▣)

◆◆◆ Best Western Holiday Motel Ⓜ ❀
(775) 623-3684. **$59-$89.** 670 W Winnemucca Blvd. Just S of I-80; exit 176 or 178. Ext corridors. **Pets:** Other. Designated rooms, supervision.
[SAVE] [S♂] [✕] [🛏] [▦]

◆◆◆ Days Inn Ⓜ ❀
(775) 623-3661. **$64-$84.** 511 W Winnemucca Blvd. Just S of I-80; exit 176 or 178. Ext corridors. **Pets:** Other. $10 one-time fee/room. No service, supervision, crate.
[SAVE] [S♂] [✕] [🛏] [▦]

◆ Economy Inn Ⓜ
(775) 623-5281. **$38-$75, 4 days notice.** 635 W Winnemucca Blvd. 0.5 mi w on I-80 (Business Rt), exit 176 or 178. Ext corridors. **Pets:** Medium. No service, supervision, crate.
[S♂] [✕] [🛏] [▦] [🖼]

◆◆ Holiday Inn Express Ⓜ ❀
(775) 625-3100. **Call for rates.** 1987 W Winnemucca Blvd. Just s of I-80, exit 176. Int corridors. **Pets:** Other. $50 deposit/room, $10 one-time fee/room. Designated rooms, no service, supervision, crate.
[✕] [♿] [⟁] [⟁] [🛏] [🖼]

◆◆ Ramada Limited Ⓜ ❀
(775) 623-1119. **$59-$85.** 1620 W Winnemucca Blvd. Just s of I-80, exit 176; 0.3 mi e. Ext corridors. **Pets:** Other. $5 one-time fee/pet. Supervision.
[S♂] [✕] [🛏] [🖼]

◆◆◆ Red Lion Inn & Casino Ⓜ ❀
(775) 623-2565. **$79-$119.** 741 W Winnemucca Blvd. Just S of I-80; exit 176 or 178. Int corridors. **Pets:** Other. Supervision.
[SAVE] [S♂] [✕] [⟁] [🛏] [▦] [🍴]

◆◆ Val-U Inn Ⓜ
(775) 623-5248. **$62-$62.** 125 E Winnemucca Blvd. Just s of I-80, exit 176 or 178. Int corridors. **Pets:** Small. Designated rooms, no service, supervision, crate.
[SAVE] [S♂] [✕] [🛏] [🖼]

NEW HAMPSHIRE

CITY INDEX

BARTLETT

[AAA] ◆◆◆ **The Villager Motel** [M] 🐾
(603) 374-2742. **$69-$119.** Rt 302. 1 mi e on US 302; 1.3 mi w of Attitash Ski Area. Ext corridors. **Pets:** Medium. $7 daily fee/pet. Designated rooms, no service, supervision, crate.
[SD] ⊠ ▣ ☕ 🏊 ✂

BERLIN

[AAA] ◆ **Traveler Motel** [M]
(603) 752-2500. **$39-$99.** 25 Pleasant St. Center. Ext corridors. **Pets:** Small. Designated rooms, no service, supervision, crate.
[SAVE] [SD] ⊠ ▣ ☕

CAMPTON

[AAA] ◆◆ **Plymouth White Mountain Hotel** [MI] 🐾
(603) 536-3520. **$76-$125.** Rt 3. I-93, exit 27, just ne. Int corridors. **Pets:** Other. $50 deposit/room. Designated rooms, supervision.
[SAVE] [SD] ⊠ 🍴 🏊

CENTER HARBOR

◆ **The Meadows Lakeside Lodging** [M]
(603) 253-4347. **$65-$110, 7 days notice.** Center, on SR 25. Int corridors. **Pets:** No service, supervision, crate.
[A$K] ⊠ ▣ ✂ [CTV]

CHESTERFIELD

◆◆◆ **Chesterfield Inn** [CI] 🐾
(603) 256-3211. **$105-$225, 5 days notice.** 399 Cross Rd. On SR 9, 2 mi e of I-91, exit 3. Ext/int corridors. **Pets:** No service, supervision, crate.
⊠ ▣ ☕

CLAREMONT

[AAA] ◆◆ **Best Budget Inn** [M] 🐾
(603) 542-9567. **$38-$65.** 24 Sullivan St. In center of city, just n of jct SR 11/12/103/120. Ext corridors. **Pets:** Medium, dogs only. $12 daily fee/pet. Designated rooms, no service, supervision, crate.
[SAVE] [SD] ⊠ ▣

COLEBROOK

[AAA] ◆◆ **Northern Comfort Motel** [M]
(603) 237-4440. **$48-$72, 3 days notice.** 1.3 mi s on US 3. Ext corridors. **Pets:** Medium. No service, supervision, crate.
⊠ ▣ ☕ 🏊 ✂

CONCORD

◆◆◆ **Concord Comfort Inn** [M] 🐾
(603) 226-4100. **$165.** 71 Hall St. I-93, exit 13, n on Main St, then 0.3 mi w. Int corridors. **Pets:** Other. $10 daily fee/room. Supervision.
[A$K] [SD] ⊠ 🚶 ♿ ▣ ☕ 🏊

◆◆◆ **Holiday Inn** [MI] 🐾
(603) 224-9534. **$79-$149.** 172 N Main St. I-93, exit 14, jct US 3 and 4. Int corridors. **Pets:** Supervision.
[A$K] [SD] ⊠ 🚶 ♿ ▣ ☕ 🍴 🏊

CONWAY

◆◆ **White Deer Motel** [M]
(603) 447-5366. **$49-$119, 7 days notice.** 379 White Mountain Hwy. 2.1 mi s of jct US 302, 0.5 m n of Village Center on SR 16. Ext/int corridors. **Pets:** Designated rooms, no service, supervision, crate.
[A$K] [SD] ⊠ ☕ ☎

DOVER

◆◆ **Days Inn** [M] 🐾
(603) 742-0400. **$80-$140.** 481 Central Ave. Downtown Dover; from Spaulding Tpke, exit 7, 2 mi n on SR 108. Ext/int corridors. **Pets:** $50 deposit/room. No service, supervision, crate.
[A$K] [SD] ⊠ ▣ ☕ 🏊

DURHAM

◆◆ **Hickory Pond Inn & Golf Course** [BB] 🐾
(603) 659-2227. **Call for rates, 3 days notice.** 1 Stagecoach Rd. 2.8 mi s on SR 108. Int corridors. **Pets:** Designated rooms, supervision.
⊠ ▣ ✂

EXETER

◆◆ Best Western Hearthside Motor Inn
(603) 772-3794. **$60-$110.** 137 Portsmouth Ave. I-95, exit 2, 3 mi w on SR 101 to SR 108, 0.3 mi s on SR 108; center; 0.4 mi e on High St, 0.3 mi n on SR 108. Int corridors. **Pets:** Designated rooms, supervision.
⬜⬜⬜⬜

FITZWILLIAM

◆◆ The Unique Yankee Bed & Breakfast 🆇 🐾
(603) 242-6706. **$60-$130, 7 days notice.** 354 Upper Troy Rd. Rt 12, 1 mi w on Bowkerville Rd to Upper Troy Rd, just s. Int corridors. **Pets:** $50 deposit/room. No service, supervision, crate.
⬜⬜⬜

FRANCONIA

⬤⬤⬤ ◆◆ Gale River Motel 🅼 🐾
(603) 823-5655. **$82-$120, 7 days notice.** 1 Main St. Jct I-93, exit 38, 0.8 mi n on SR 18. Ext corridors. **Pets:** Dogs only. $5 daily fee/room, $5 one-time fee/room. Designated rooms, supervision.
⬜⬜⬜⬜⬜⬜⬜⬜

GILMANTON

⬤⬤⬤ ◆◆◆ Temperance Tavern 🆇 🐾
(603) 267-7349. **$75-$125.** Old Province Rd. Jct SR 140 and 107; in Gilmanton Historic District. Int corridors. **Pets:** No service, supervision, crate.
⬜⬜⬜⬜⬜

GORHAM

◆ Colonial Comfort Inn 🅼 🐾
(603) 466-2732. **$42-$125.** 370 Main St. Jct US 2 and SR 16. Ext corridors. **Pets:** No service, supervision, crate.
⬜⬜⬜

◆ Moose Brook Motel 🅼 🐾
(603) 466-5400. **$39-$69, 5 days notice.** 65 Lancaster Rd. US 2, 0.5 mi w of jct SR 16. Ext corridors. **Pets:** $5 daily fee/room. Designated rooms, no service, supervision, crate.
⬜⬜⬜

◆◆◆ Royalty Inn 🅼 🐾
(603) 466-3312. **$57-$88.** 130 Main St. Center; on US 2 and SR 16. Ext/int corridors. **Pets:** Other. $5 daily fee/room, $5 one-time fee/room. Designated rooms, supervision.
⬜⬜⬜⬜⬜⬜⬜

⬤⬤⬤ ◆◆ Top Notch Motor Inn 🅼 🐾
(603) 466-5496. **$69-$142.** 265 Main St. Center; on US 2 and SR 16. Ext corridors. **Pets:** Small, dogs only. Designated rooms, no service, supervision, crate.
⬜⬜⬜⬜⬜⬜⬜

◆◆ Town & Country Motor Inn 🅼 🐾
(603) 466-3315. **$48-$94.** US Rt 2. US 2, 0.5 mi e of jct SR 16. Ext/int corridors. **Pets:** $6 daily fee/room. Designated rooms, no service, supervision, crate.
⬜⬜⬜

HAMPTON FALLS

◆◆◆ Hampton Falls Inn 🅼 🐾
(603) 926-9545. **$99-$169, 3 days notice.** 11 Lafayette Rd (US 1). I-95, exit 1, 0.5 mi e on SR 107, 1 mi n on US 1. Int corridors. **Pets:** Medium, dogs only. $50 deposit/room. Designated rooms, no service, supervision, crate.
⬜⬜⬜⬜⬜

HENNIKER

⬤⬤⬤ ◆◆ Henniker Motel 🅼 🐾
(603) 428-3536. **$49-$74, 3 days notice.** Craney Pond Rd. Jct I-89, exit 5, 6.5 mi w on SR 9 and 202, to jct SR 114, 3 mi s on SR 114 to Flanders Rd, 0.5 mi w via signs. Ext/int corridors. **Pets:** $3 one-time fee/room. No service, supervision, crate.
⬜⬜⬜⬜⬜⬜

JACKSON

⬤⬤⬤ ◆◆ Dana Place Inn 🆑 🐾
(603) 383-6822. **$99-$155.** Jct SR 16A and 16B at covered bridge, 5 mi n on SR 16. Ext/int corridors. **Pets:** Dogs only. Designated rooms, no service, supervision, crate.
⬜⬜⬜⬜⬜

⬤⬤⬤ ◆◆ Whitneys' Inn-Jackson 🆑 🐾
(603) 383-8916. **$135-$155.** Rt 16B. 1.7 mi n. Ext/int corridors. **Pets:** $25 one-time fee/room. Designated rooms, supervision.
⬜⬜⬜⬜⬜⬜

KEENE

◆◆◆ Best Western Sovereign Hotel 🅼 🐾
(603) 357-3038. **$103-$150.** 401 Winchester St. On SR 10, just s of jct SR 12 and 101. Int corridors. **Pets:** Other. No service, supervision, crate.
⬜⬜⬜⬜⬜⬜⬜

⬤⬤⬤ ◆◆◆ Days Inn 🅼 🐾
(603) 352-7616. **$125-$155.** 175 Key Rd. SR 101, just n, via Winchester St, then 0.3 mi w. Int corridors. **Pets:** Designated rooms, supervision.
⬜⬜⬜⬜⬜⬜⬜

LEBANON

◆◆◆ Holiday Inn Express 🅼
(603) 448-5070. **$129-$155, 30 days notice.** 135 SR 120. I-89, exit 18, 0.8 mi n. Ext/int corridors. **Pets:** Supervision.
⬜⬜⬜

LINCOLN

⬤⬤⬤ ◆◆ Parker's Motel 🅼 🐾
(603) 745-8341. **$54-$89, 3 days notice.** US 3. 2 mi ne of I-93, exit 33. Ext corridors. **Pets:** $25 deposit/room, $5 daily fee/room. Designated rooms, no service, supervision, crate.
⬜⬜⬜⬜⬜

LISBON

◆◆ Ammonoosuc Inn 🆑 🐾
(603) 838-6118. **$60-$130.** 641 Bishop Rd. Rt 302 & 10, 1.5 mi w. **Pets:** Very small. Designated rooms, no service, supervision, crate.
⬜⬜⬜⬜⬜⬜⬜⬜

LITTLETON

AAA ◆◆ Eastgate Motor Inn **M**
(603) 444-3971. **$64-$70.** 335 Cottage St. US 302 and SR 116, at jct I-93, exit 41. Ext/int corridors. **Pets:** No service, supervision, crate.

⊠ 🖼 ⊠

LOUDON

◆◆◆ Lovejoy Farm Bed & Breakfast **BB** 🐾
(603) 783-4007. **$69-$87.** 268 Lovejoy Rd. Jct SR 106 and 129, just w on SR 129, then nw on Village Rd, 1.2 mi n. Int corridors. **Pets:** Medium, dogs only. No service, supervision, crate.

⊠ ⊠ 🏍 🖳 ☎

MANCHESTER

◆◆◆ Center of New Hampshire-Holiday Inn **H**
(603) 625-1000. **Call for rates.** 700 Elm St. Downtown; at jct Granite St. Int corridors. **Pets:** Small. Designated rooms, supervision.

🔑 ⊠ 🗞 🖰 🍴 🖳

AAA ◆◆ Econo Lodge **M**
(603) 624-0111. **$55-$120.** 75 W Hancock St. I-293, exit 4, just nw. Int corridors. **Pets:** Small. No service, supervision, crate.

🕊 🖫 ⊠ 🖰 🖳

MERRIMACK

◆◆◆ Merrimack Hotel and Conference
      Center **M**
(603) 424-8000. **$89-$149.** 4 Executive Park Dr. Everett Tpke, exit 11, just w. Int corridors. **Pets:** Small. No service, supervision, crate.

🔑 🖫 ⊠ 🗞 🖰 🖳 🍴 🖳

◆◆◆ Residence Inn by Marriott **A** 🐾
(603) 424-8100. **Call for rates.** 246 Daniel Webster Hwy. Everett Tpke, exit 11, just e, then 0.6 mi s on SR 3. Ext/int corridors. **Pets:** Other. $5 daily fee/pet, $50 one-time fee/room. Designated rooms, supervision.

⊠ 🏠 🗞 🖱 🖰 🖳 🖼 ⊠

MOULTONBOROUGH

AAA ◆◆ Matterhorn Motor Lodge **M** 🐾
(603) 253-4314. **$95-$125, 7 days notice.** 340 Rt 25. 3 mi w on SR 25. Ext corridors. **Pets:** Medium, other. $10 daily fee/pet. Designated rooms, no service, supervision, crate.

🕊 ⊠ 🖼 ⊠

MOUNT SUNAPEE

AAA ◆◆◆ Best Western Sunapee Lake
            Lodge **M**
(603) 763-2010. **$89-$149.** 1403 Rt 103. Just e of jct SR 103B. Int corridors. **Pets:** Supervision.

🕊 ⊠ 🖱 🖰 🖼

NASHUA

AAA ◆ Motel 6–1062 **M** 🐾
(603) 889-4151. **$48-$64.** 2 Progress Ave. US 3, exit 5 W, just w on SR 111, just sw via Main Vunstable Rd. Ext/int corridors. **Pets:** Medium, other. No service, supervision, crate.

🖫 ⊠ 🗞 🖼 🖳

◆◆◆ Nashua Marriott Hotel **M** 🐾
(603) 880-9100. **$85-$125.** 2200 Southwood Dr. US 3, exit 8, just w in Southwood Corporate Park. Int corridors. **Pets:** Other. Supervision.

🔑 ⊠ 🏠 🗞 🖰 🖳 🍴 🖼

AAA ◆◆ Red Roof Inn **M** 🐾
(603) 888-1893. **$59-$89.** 77 Spitbrook Rd. US 3, exit 1, just e. Ext corridors. **Pets:** Other. No service, supervision, crate.

🕊 ⊠ 🏠 🗞 🖰

NORTH CONWAY

AAA ◆◆◆ Isaac E Merrill House Inn **BB**
(603) 356-9041. **$59-$179.** 720 Kearsarge Rd. From lights at town center, onto Kearsarge Rd, to hilltop, left turn, 1 mi. Int corridors. **Pets:** Very small. No service, supervision, crate.

🕊 🖫 ⊠ 🖰 🖳 ⊠

◆◆ Mt Washington Valley Motor Lodge **M** 🐾
(603) 356-5486. **$69-$149, 3 days notice.** 1567 White Mountain Hwy. Center; 2 mi s on US 302 and SR 16. Int corridors. **Pets:** Small, dogs only. $50 deposit/pet. Supervision.

⊠ 🖰 🖳 🍴 🖼 ⊠

AAA ◆◆◆ North Conway Mountain Inn **M** 🐾
(603) 356-2803. **$69-$169, 3 days notice.** White Mountain Hwy. 1 mi s from center on SR 16 and US 302. Ext corridors. **Pets:** Supervision.

🕊 🖫 ⊠

PITTSBURG

◆ The Glen **L** 🐾
(603) 538-6500. **$77-$192** (no credit cards), 7 days notice. 77 The Glen Rd. 8.5 mi n on US 3, follow signs. Ext/int corridors. **Pets:** No service, supervision, crate.

🖰 🖳 🍴 ⊠ 🏍 🖳 ☎

PORTSMOUTH

◆◆◆ Residence Inn by Marriott **M** 🐾
(603) 436-8880. **$169-$199.** 1 International Dr. SR 4/16, exit 1, just s. Int corridors. **Pets:** Other. $250 one-time fee/room. Designated rooms, no service, supervision, crate.

🔑 🖫 ⊠ 🖐 🖰 🖳 🖼 ⊠

ROCHESTER

AAA ◆◆ Anchorage Inn **M** 🐾
(603) 332-3350. **$59-$89.** 80 Main. Exit 12, jct Spaulding Tpke and SR 125. Ext corridors. **Pets:** Large, other. $5 daily fee/pet, $5 one-time fee/pet. Supervision.

🖫 ⊠ 🖰 🖼

SALEM

◆◆◆ **Holiday Inn-Salem New Hampshire** [MI] ❁
(603) 893-5511. **$129-$149.** 1 Keewaydin Dr. I-93, exit 2, just sw. Int corridors. **Pets:** Medium, other. Supervision.

[ASK] [S&] [✕] [🔑] [🔲] [💻] [🍴] [🛎]

[AAA] ◆◆ **Red Roof Inn** [M] ❁
(603) 898-6422. **$76-$86.** 15 Red Roof Ln. I-93, exit 2, just se. Ext corridors. **Pets:** Other. Supervision.

[SAVE] [✕] [🔑]

SUGAR HILL

◆◆◆ **The Hilltop Inn** [BB] ❁
(603) 823-5695. **$125-$155, 8 days notice.** 1348 Main St. I-93, exit 38, 0.5 mi n on SR 18, 2.8 mi w on SR 117. Int corridors. **Pets:** Dogs only. $10 daily fee/room. Supervision.

[✕] [🔲] [✕] [🎿] [CTV]

SUNAPEE

◆ **The Burkehaven Motel** [M] ❁
(603) 763-2788. **$69-$84.** 179 Burkehaven Hill Rd. Just e on SR 11 from jct SR 103B, then 0.5 mi e to Sunapee Harbor, then 0.8 mi s (Burkehave Hill Rd). Ext corridors. **Pets:** No service, supervision, crate.

[✕] [🔲] [💻] [🛎] [✕] [🎿] [CTV] [☎]

◆◆◆ **Dexter's Inn** [CI] ❁
(603) 763-5571. **$95-$180.** 258 Stagecoach Rd. Jct SR 103B and Rt 11, 0.4 mi w on SR 11, 1.75 mi s (Winn Hill Rd). Ext/int corridors. **Pets:** Other. $10 daily fee/room. Supervision.

[✕] [🔲] [💻] [🍴] [🛎] [✕] [CTV] [☎]

SWANZEY

◆◆ **Loafer Inn at the 1792 Whitecomb House B & B** [BB] ❁
(603) 357-6624. **Call for rates.** 27 Main St. 4 mi s of Keene on Rt 10. Int corridors. **Pets:** Small. $25 deposit/room. No service, supervision, crate.

[✕] [💻] [🎿] [CTV] [☎]

TAMWORTH

[AAA] ◆◆◆ **The Tamworth Inn** [CI]
(603) 323-7721. **$140-$220.** 15 Cleveland Hill Rd. Jct SR 16 and 113, 3 mi w on SR 113; center of Tamworth Village. Int corridors. **Pets:** Supervision.

[SAVE] [✕] [🛎] [✕] [CTV] [☎]

WENTWORTH

◆◆ **Hilltop Acres** [BB] ❁
(603) 764-5896. **$100-$125.** Eastside & Buffalo rds. From jct SR 25, 25A and 118, e on SR 25.3 mi, 0.3 mi n. Ext/int corridors. **Pets:** Other. $10 daily fee/pet, $10 one-time fee/pet. Designated rooms, supervision.

[✕] [🔲] [💻] [🎿] [CTV] [☎]

WEST LEBANON

[AAA] ◆◆◆ **Airport Economy Inn** [M]
(603) 298-8888. **$50-$95.** 45 Airport Rd. Jct I-89, exit 20 and SR 12A, just s on SR 12A, then just e. Int corridors. **Pets:** Small. Designated rooms, no service, supervision, crate.

[✕] [🔑] [🔲] [🛎]

WOLFEBORO

◆◆◆ **The Lake Motel** [M]
(603) 569-1100. **$100-$110, 30 days notice.** 280 S Main St. 0.5 mi se on SR 28. Ext/int corridors. **Pets:** Designated rooms, no service, supervision, crate.

[🔲] [💻] [✕]

WOODSVILLE

[AAA] ◆ **All Seasons Motel** [M]
(603) 747-2157. **$50-$75, 3 days notice.** 36 Smith St. Jct SR 10, 0.4 mi w on US 302, then 0.3 mi se. Ext corridors. **Pets:** Small. Designated rooms, no service, supervision, crate.

[SAVE] [S&] [✕] [🔲] [🛎] [✕]

[AAA] ◆◆ **Nootka Lodge** [M]
(603) 747-2418. **$50-$110, 3 days notice.** 36 Smith St. Jct SR 10 and US 302. Ext corridors. **Pets:** Designated rooms, no service, supervision, crate.

[SAVE] [S&] [✕] [🔲] [🛎] [✕]

CITY INDEX

ATLANTIC CITY METROPOLITAN AREA

ABSECON

◆◆ Days Inn-Absecon/Atlantic City M ✿
(609) 652-2200. **$60-$175, 7 days notice.** 224 E White Horse Pike (US 30). Garden State Pkwy, exit 40 southbound; northbound U-turn through Atlantic City Service Plaza, s to exit 40, 0.4 mi e on US 30. Ext corridors. **Pets:** $20 daily fee/room. Designated rooms, no service, supervision, crate.

SOMERS POINT

◆◆◆ Residence Inn by Marriott at Greate Bay Golf Club A ✿
(609) 927-6400. **$149-$199, 7 days notice.** 900 Mays Landing Rd. 1 mi e of Garden State Pkwy, exit 30 southbound; 1 mi e of Garden State Pkwy, exit 29 northbound. Ext corridors. **Pets:** Other. $75 one-time fee/room. Supervision.

✿ END METROPOLITAN AREA ✿

BEACH HAVEN

◆◆ Engleside Inn M ✿
(609) 492-1251. **$170-$255, 30 days notice.** 30 Engleside Ave. 6.9 mi s of SR 72 Cswy to Engleside Ave, just e. Ext corridors. **Pets:** Other. $10 daily fee/pet. Supervision.

CAPE MAY

◆◆ Marquis de Lafayette Hotel M ✿
(609) 884-3500. **$219-$359.** 501 Beach Ave. Between Decatur and Ocean sts. Ext/int corridors. **Pets:** Other. $50 deposit/pet, $20 daily fee/pet. Designated rooms, supervision.

COLESVILLE

◆ High Point Country Inn M ✿
(973) 702-1860. **$64-$85.** 1328 SR 23 N. 1 mi n of town center. Ext corridors. **Pets:** Other. $5 daily fee/pet, $5 one-time fee/pet. Supervision.

EAST BRUNSWICK

◆◆◆ Hilton East Brunswick H ✿
(732) 828-2000. **$89-$119.** 3 Tower Center Blvd. New Jersey Tpke, exit 9, SR 18 N, first right on service road. Int corridors. **Pets:** Medium. Designated rooms, supervision.

EAST HANOVER

◆◆◆ Ramada Inn & Conference Center M ✿
(973) 386-5622. **$60-$159, 90 days notice.** 130 Rt 10 W. I-287, exit 39, 4 mi e. Int corridors. **Pets:** Other. Designated rooms, no service, supervision, crate.

EAST RUTHERFORD

◆◆ Homestead Guest Studios M ✿
(201) 939-8866. **Call for rates.** 300 SR 3 E. New Jersey Tpke, exit 16W (from western spur), sports complex right after toll (3E). Int corridors. **Pets:** Medium. $75 one-time fee/room. Designated rooms, no service, supervision, crate.

◆◆◆ **Sheraton Meadowlands** 🄷
(201) 896-0500. **Call for rates.** 2 Meadowlands Plaza. New Jersey Tpke, exit 16W (from western spur), sports complex 1st right after toll (3E) to Sheraton Plaza Dr. Int corridors. **Pets:** No service, supervision, crate.

EAST WINDSOR

◆◆ **Days Inn** Ⓜ 🐾
(609) 448-3200. **$89-$124.** 460 Rt 33 E. New Jersey Tpke, exit 8, just e. Int corridors. **Pets:** Other. Supervision.

EDISON

◆◆ **Ramada Plaza Hotel** 🄷
(732) 661-1000. **$89-$99, 7 days notice.** 3050 Woodbridge Ave. New Jersey Tpke, exit 10, 0.6 mi w on US 514, toward Raritan Center. Int corridors. **Pets:** Medium. Designated rooms, no service, supervision, crate.

⑅◈🛢💻🍴🌊

🆎 ◆◆ **Red Roof Inn** Ⓜ 🐾
(732) 248-9300. **$69-$88.** 860 New Durham Rd. I-287 N, exit 2A, 0.5 mi w via Bridge St, then left; I-287 S, exit 3, just w. Ext corridors. **Pets:** Medium. No service, supervision, crate.

SAVE ◈ 🏠 🌀

◆◆◆ **Sheraton Edison** 🄷
(732) 225-8300. **$199-$199.** 125 Raritan Center Pkwy. 0.5 mi se of New Jersey Tpke, exit 10, on CR 514 keep right after tolls. Int corridors. **Pets:** Supervision.

ASK 🛢◈🌀🔳🛢💻🍴🌊

🆎 ◆◆ **Wellesley Inn & Suites** Ⓜ 🐾
(732) 287-0171. **$99-$149.** 831 US 1 S. 1 mi s of I-287. Int corridors. **Pets:** Medium. $10 daily fee/pet, $10 one-time fee/pet. Supervision.

SAVE 🛢◈🌀🛢💻

ELIZABETH

🆎 ◆◆◆ **Hilton Newark Airport** 🄷 🐾
(908) 351-3900. **$99-$239.** 1170 Spring St. New Jersey Tpke, exit 13A, on US 1 and 9 N, U-turn on McClellan St. Int corridors. **Pets:** Medium, other. No service, supervision, crate.

SAVE ◈ 🏠 🌀 🛢 💻 🍴 🌊

ENGLEWOOD

◆◆ **Radisson Hotel Englewood** 🄷
(201) 871-2020. **$209-$239.** 401 S Van Brunt St. SR 4 W, Van Brunt exit; SR 4 E, Grand Ave/Englewood exit, just n. Int corridors. **Pets:** Medium. No service, supervision, crate.

ASK 🛢◈🌀🔳🛢💻🍴🌊

FAIR LAWN

🆎 ◆◆◆ **AmeriSuites** Ⓜ 🐾
(201) 475-3888. **$134-$170.** 41-01 Broadway (Rt 4 W). On SR 4, 0.7 mi w of jct Garden State Pkwy, exit 161 northbound; exit 163 southbound. Int corridors. **Pets:** Small, dogs only. Designated rooms, supervision.

SAVE 🛢◈🏠🌀🔳🛢💻🌊

FLEMINGTON

◆◆ **The Ramada Inn** Ⓜ 🐾
(908) 782-7472. **$89-$102.** 250 Hwy 202 & SR 31. 0.5 mi s of the circle. Ext corridors. **Pets:** Medium. $50 deposit/room, $10 daily fee/pet. Supervision.

ASK 🛢◈🌀🛢💻🍴🌊

HASBROUCK HEIGHTS

🆎 ◆◆◆ **Hilton Hasbrouck Heights** 🄷 🐾
(201) 288-6100. **$99-$189.** 650 Terrace Ave. I-80 E local lanes, exit 64B westbound; exit 64 eastbound, just s on SR 17 S. Int corridors. **Pets:** Small, dogs only. Supervision.

SAVE 🛢◈🌀🔳🛢💻🍴🌊

HAZLET

🆎 ◆◆ **Wellesley Inn & Suites** Ⓜ 🐾
(732) 888-2800. **$99-$159.** 3215 SR 35 N. Garden State Pkwy, exit 117, 1.5 mi s on SR 35, U-turn Hazlet Ave. Int corridors. **Pets:** Medium. $5 daily fee/pet. No service, supervision, crate.

SAVE 🛢◈🦽🌀🔳🛢

LAWRENCEVILLE

🆎 ◆◆ **Red Roof Inn-Princeton** Ⓜ 🐾
(609) 896-3388. **$66-$98.** 3203 Brunswick Pike (US 1). I-295, exit 67A, just n. Ext corridors. **Pets:** Other. Supervision.

SAVE ◈🌀🔳

MAHWAH

🆎 ◆◆◆ **Sheraton Crossroads Hotel** 🄷
(201) 529-1660. **$199-$219.** 1 International Blvd, Rt 17. At jct SR 17 N and exit 66 off I-287. Int corridors. **Pets:** Medium. Designated rooms, no service, supervision, crate.

SAVE ◈🌀💻🍴🌊◈

MIDDLETOWN

🆎 ◆◆ **Howard Johnson Inn** Ⓜ 🐾
(732) 671-3400. **$86-$150.** 750 Hwy 35 S. Garden State Pkwy, exit 114, to SR 35 via Red Hill Rd and King's Hwy, 0.3 mi s. Int corridors. **Pets:** Other. $6 daily fee/room. Supervision.

SAVE 🛢◈🌀🛢💻🌊

MONMOUTH JUNCTION

🆎 ◆◆ **Red Roof Inn/North Princeton** Ⓜ
(732) 821-8800. **$56-$88.** 208 New Rd. On US 1 S at New Rd. Ext corridors. **Pets:** Medium. Designated rooms, no service, supervision, crate.

SAVE ◈🌀

◆◆◆ **Residence Inns by Marriott** Ⓜ 🐾
(732) 329-9600. **Call for rates.** 4225 Rt 1. 0.5 mi s of Raymond Rd. Int corridors. **Pets:** Other. $175 one-time fee/room. Designated rooms, supervision.

◈🌀🛢💻🌊◈

MOUNT ARLINGTON

◆◆◆ Four Points Hotel Sheraton ⬛
(973) 770-2000. **$85-$85.** 15 Howard Blvd. I-80, exit 30, just n. Int corridors. **Pets:** Small. No service, supervision, crate.

⬛ ⬛ ⬛ ⬛ ⬛ ⬛ ⬛

NEWARK

◆◆ Sheraton Hotel Newark Airport ⬛
(973) 690-5500. **$206-$206.** 128 Frontage Rd. New Jersey Tpke, exit 14, via frontage road, 2nd right after toll booth. Int corridors. **Pets:** Small. Supervision.

⬛ ⬛ ⬛ ⬛ ⬛ ⬛

OCEAN CITY

◆◆ Crossings Motor Inn ⬛ ❖
(609) 398-4433. **$95-$170, 7 days notice.** 3420 Haven Ave. Garden State Pkwy, exit 25, 3 mi e; 0.3 mi w of ocean beaches on the s end of town. Ext corridors. **Pets:** Other. $100 deposit/room, $15 daily fee/pet. Designated rooms, supervision.

⬛ ⬛ ⬛ ⬛

PARAMUS

◆◆ Radisson Inn Paramus ⬛
(201) 262-6900. **$160-$160.** 601 From Rd. On service road (From Rd) w of Garden State Pkwy, exit 165; northbound Ridgewood exit (shopping center), southbound Oradell (shopping center). Int corridors. **Pets:** Small. Supervision.

⬛ ⬛ ⬛ ⬛ ⬛ ⬛ ⬛ ⬛

PARSIPPANY

◆◆◆ Hilton Parsippany ⬛ ❖
(973) 267-7373. **$79-$199.** 1 Hilton Court. In Hilton Court; I-287, northbound exit 39; southbound exit 39B, 1.3 mi w on SR 10. Int corridors. **Pets:** Small. $50 deposit/room. No service, supervision, crate.

⬛ ⬛ ⬛ ⬛ ⬛ ⬛ ⬛ ⬛ ⬛ ⬛

◆◆ Ramada Limited ⬛ ❖
(973) 263-0404. **$95-$120.** 949 Rt 46 E. I-80, exit 47 westbound; exit 45 eastbound, 0.5 mi e. Int corridors. **Pets:** $200 deposit/room. Supervision.

⬛ ⬛ ⬛ ⬛ ⬛ ⬛ ⬛

◆◆ Red Roof Inn ⬛ ❖
(732) 334-3737. **$80-$90.** 855 US 46 E. I-80 W, exit 47; I-80 E, exit 45, then 0.5 mi e. Ext corridors. **Pets:** Medium. $20 deposit/room. No service, supervision, crate.

⬛ ⬛ ⬛ ⬛ ⬛

PHILADELPHIA METROPOLITAN AREA

BORDENTOWN

◆ Days Inn-Bordentown ⬛ ❖
(609) 298-6100. **$80-$94.** 1073 US 206 N. New Jersey Tpke, exit 7, 0.8 mi n. Ext corridors. **Pets:** Other. Designated rooms, no service, supervision, crate.

⬛ ⬛ ⬛ ⬛ ⬛ ⬛

CHERRY HILL

◆◆ Holiday Inn-Cherry Hill ⬛
(856) 663-5300. **$94-$94.** Rt 70 & Sayer Ave. I-295, exit 34B, 2.5 mi w; opposite Garden State Race Track. Int corridors. **Pets:** Medium. No service, supervision, crate.

⬛ ⬛ ⬛ ⬛ ⬛ ⬛ ⬛ ⬛

◆◆◆ Residence Inn by Marriott ⬛
(856) 429-6111. **$150.** 1821 Old Cuthbert Rd. I-295, exit 34A, just e to Marlkress Rd jughandle, then back to Old Cuthbert Rd, just n. Ext corridors. **Pets:** Large. Supervision.

⬛ ⬛ ⬛ ⬛ ⬛ ⬛ ⬛

MOUNT HOLLY

◆◆◆ Best Western Burlington Inn ⬛ ❖
(609) 261-3800. **$86-$122.** Box 2020 Rt 541, RD 1. New Jersey Tpke, exit 5, just n. Int corridors. **Pets:** Small. $20 deposit/room, $10 daily fee/pet. Designated rooms, no service, supervision, crate.

⬛ ⬛ ⬛ ⬛ ⬛

MOUNT LAUREL

◆◆◆ Red Roof Inn ⬛
(856) 234-5589. **$51-$83.** 603 Fellowship Rd. New Jersey Tpke, exit 4, just nw on SR 73 to Fellowship Rd just s; I-295, exit 36A, just se on SR 73 to Fellowship Rd, just s. Ext corridors. **Pets:** Medium. No service, supervision, crate.

⬛ ⬛ ⬛

◆◆◆ Summerfield Suites Hotel ⬛ ❖
(856) 222-1313. **$179.** 3000 Crawford Pl. I-295, exit 36A, SR 73 S 1.5 mi; New Jersey Tpke, exit 4, 1 mi on Rt 73 S. Ext/int corridors. **Pets:** Small. $150 one-time fee/room. No service, supervision, crate.

⬛ ⬛ ⬛ ⬛ ⬛ ⬛ ⬛ ⬛ ⬛

PENNS GROVE

◆◆◆ Wellesley Inns & Suites ⬛ ❖
(856) 299-3800. **$50-$150.** 517 S Pennsville-Auburn Rd. 1 mi e of Delaware Memorial Bridge; jct US 40 and New Jersey Tpke, exit 1; I-295, exit 2B. Int corridors. **Pets:** Small, other. $10 deposit/room. Designated rooms, no service, supervision, crate.

⬛ ⬛ ⬛ ⬛ ⬛ ⬛ ⬛ ⬛ ⬛

RUNNEMEDE

(AAA) ◆◆◆ Holiday Inn-Runnemede M
(856) 939-4200. **$99-$120, 7 days notice.** 109 9th Ave. New Jersey Tpke, exit 3, 0.3 mi se to 9th Ave just e; I-295, exit 28, 1.3 mi se to 9th Ave. Int corridors. **Pets:** Medium. No service, supervision, crate.
[SAVE] [S] [X] [&] [B] [C] [T] [A]

VOORHEES

◆◆◆ Hampton Inn M
(856) 346-4500. **$99-$99.** 121 Laurel Oak Rd. I-295, exit 32, 2.3 mi e on Haddonfield-Berlin Rd, s on White Horse Rd, 0.3 mi to Laurel Oak Rd; in Voorhees Corporate Center. Int corridors. **Pets:** Medium, other. Supervision.
[ASK] [S] [X] [&] [D] [B] [C] [A]

WINSLOW

(AAA) ◆◆ Knights Inn M
(609) 561-6200. **$40-$99.** 530 Rt 73. Atlantic City Expwy, exit 31 westbound or exit 33 eastbound, just nw. Ext corridors. **Pets:** Small, dogs only. $10 deposit/room. No service, supervision, crate.
[SAVE] [S] [X] [B] [C]

❋   END METROPOLITAN AREA   ❋

PISCATAWAY

◆◆◆ Embassy Suites Hotel H
(732) 980-0500. **$99-$225.** 121 Centennial Ave. I-287, exit 9 (SR 18), just s on Highland Park to Centennial Ave; in Office Park. Int corridors. **Pets:** Small, other. $250 deposit/room, $250 one-time fee/room. No service, supervision, crate.
[ASK] [S] [X] [D] [B] [C] [T] [A]

PRINCETON

(AAA) ◆◆◆ AmeriSuites H
(609) 720-0200. **$175-$200, 7 days notice.** 3565 US 1 S. 1.5 mi s of jct CR 526 and 571. Int corridors. **Pets:** $50 deposit/room. No service, supervision, crate.
[SAVE] [S] [X] [&] [D] [C] [B] [A]

(AAA) ◆◆ Novotel Princeton Hotel M
(609) 520-1200. **$89-$169.** 100 Independence Way. On US 1; I-295, exit 67, 3 mi n of jct CR 526 and 571; in Princeton Corporate Center. Int corridors. **Pets:** Small, other. Supervision.
[SAVE] [S] [X] [D] [B] [C] [T] [A]

RAMSEY

(AAA) ◆◆ The Inn at Ramsey M
(201) 327-6700. **$60-$150.** 1315 SR 17 S. Jct I-287 and SR 17 S, then 3 mi s. Int corridors. **Pets:** $100 deposit/room, $10 daily fee/room. No service, supervision, crate.
[SAVE] [S] [X] [B] [T]

(AAA) ◆◆ Wellesley Inn & Suites M
(201) 934-9250. **$59-$124.** 946 Rt 17 N. Jct Airmont Rd. Int corridors. **Pets:** Medium. $5 daily fee/room. Designated rooms, supervision.
[SAVE] [S] [X] [&] [D] [C] [B] [C]

SECAUCUS

(AAA) ◆◆◆ AmeriSuites M
(201) 422-9480. **$159-$269.** 575 Park Plaza Dr. New Jersey Tpke, exits 16E, 17 or 16W via SR 3 to Harmon Meadow Blvd, then just w. Int corridors. **Pets:** Very small. No service, supervision.
[SAVE] [S] [X] [&] [D] [C] [B] [C]

◆◆◆ Meadowlands Crowne Plaza H
(201) 348-6900. **$129-$229.** 2 Harmon Plaza. Between eastern and western spurs of New Jersey Tpke, exits 16E, 17 or 16W via SR 3 exit Meadowlands Pkwy. Int corridors. **Pets:** Small. Designated rooms, no service, supervision, crate.
[ASK] [S] [X] [D] [B] [C] [T] [A] [X]

(AAA) ◆◆◆ Radisson Suite Hotel Meadowlands H
(201) 863-8700. **$119-$209, 30 days notice.** 350 Rt 3 W, Mill Creek Dr. In Mill Creek Mall; between eastern and western spurs of New Jersey Tpke, exits 16E, 17 or 16W via SR 3 and Harmon Meadow Blvd. Int corridors. **Pets:** Medium. $25 one-time fee/pet. Designated rooms, no service, supervision, crate.
[SAVE] [S] [X] [D] [B] [C] [T] [A]

(AAA) ◆◆ Red Roof Inn-Meadowlands M
(201) 319-1000. **$70-$142.** 15 Meadowland Pkwy. Between eastern and western spurs of New Jersey Tpke, exits 16E, 17 or 16W via SR 3 exit Meadowland Pkwy. Ext corridors. **Pets:** Medium. No service, supervision, crate.
[SAVE] [X] [D] [X]

SOMERSET

(AAA) ◆◆ Holiday Inn-Somerset H
(732) 356-1700. **$149-$149.** 195 Davidson Ave. I-287, exit 10, (direction Bound Brook) just n on CR 527, 0.5 mi sw. Int corridors. **Pets:** Small. $50 deposit/room. No service, supervision, crate.
[SAVE] [S] [X] [B] [C] [T] [A]

(AAA) ◆◆◆ Quality Inn-Somerset M
(732) 469-5050. **$64-$125.** 1850 Easton Ave. Just s of I-287, exit 10 (direction New Brunswick) on CR 527. Ext/int corridors. **Pets:** No service, supervision, crate.
[SAVE] [S] [X] [D] [B] [C] [T] [A]

◆◆◆ Summerfield Suites Hotel M
(732) 356-8000. **Call for rates.** 260 Davidson Ave. I-287, exit 10 (direction Bound Brook), just n on CR 527 to Davidson Ave, 0.8 mi sw. Ext/int corridors. **Pets:** Small. $10 daily fee/pet, $200 one-time fee/room. Supervision.
[ASK] [X] [D] [B] [C] [A] [X]

SOUTH PLAINFIELD

◆◆ **Holiday Inn** [MI] 🐾
(908) 753-5500. **$69-$129.** 4701 Stelton Rd. I-287, exit 5, just n; adjacent to Middlesex Mall. Int corridors. **Pets:** Other. Supervision.
[A$K] [S/D] ⊠ 👂 ▣ 📺 🍴 🏊

SPRINGFIELD

◆◆ **Holiday Inn Springfield** [MI] 🐾
(973) 376-9400. **$125.** 304 Rt 22 W. 4 mi w of Garden State Pkwy, northbound exit 140; southbound exit 140A. Int corridors. **Pets:** Supervision.
[A$K] [S/D] ⊠ 👂 ▣ 📺 🍴 🏊

TINTON FALLS

[AAA] ◆◆ **Red Roof Inn** [M] 🐾
(732) 389-4646. **$56-$83.** 11 Centre Plaza. Garden State Pkwy, exit 105, just right at 1st light after toll. Ext corridors. **Pets:** No service, supervision, crate.
[SAVE] ⊠ ♿ 👂 ☎ 📺

◆◆◆ **Residence Inn by Marriott** [M] 🐾
(732) 389-8100. **$109-$149.** 90 Park Rd. Garden State Pkwy, exit 105, 1st jughandle after toll, immediate left before Courtyard by Marriott, just n, then e. Ext corridors. **Pets:** Medium, other. $175 one-time fee/room. Supervision.
[A$K] [S/D] ⊠ 👂 ▣ 📺 🏊 🏋

◆◆ **Sunrise Suites Hotel** [M] 🐾
(732) 389-4800. **$209.** 3 Centre Plaza. Garden State Pkwy, exit 105, 1st right at Hope Rd after toll. Ext/int corridors. **Pets:** Small, other. $10 daily fee/pet. No service, supervision, crate.
⊠ 👂 ▣ 📺 🏊

TOMS RIVER

◆◆ **Holiday Inn** [MI] 🐾
(732) 244-4000. **Call for rates.** 290 Hwy 37 E. Garden State Pkwy, exit 82, 1.5 mi e. Int corridors. **Pets:** Other. No service, supervision, crate.
⊠ ▣ 📺 🍴 🏊

[AAA] ◆◆ **Howard Johnson Hotel-Toms River** [MI]
(732) 244-1000. **$110-$189, 3 days notice.** 955 Hooper Ave. Garden State Pkwy, exit 82, 1 mi e on SR 37. Int corridors. **Pets:** Medium. Supervision.
[SAVE] [S/D] ⊠ 👂 ▣ 📺 🍴 🏊

WARREN

◆◆◆ **Somerset Hills Hotel** [H] 🐾
(908) 647-6700. **$115-$235.** 200 Liberty Corner Rd. I-78, exit 33, just n CR 525. Int corridors. **Pets:** Other. $25 daily fee/room. Designated rooms, no service, supervision, crate.
[A$K] [S/D] ⊠ 👂 ☎ ▣ 📺 🍴 🏊

WEEHAWKEN

[AAA] ◆◆◆ **Sheraton Suites at Lincoln Harbor** [H]
(201) 617-5600. **$289-$319.** 500 Harbor Blvd. 0.4 mi e off US 495. Int corridors. **Pets:** Very small. Designated rooms, no service, supervision, crate.
[SAVE] [S/D] ⊠ 👂 ☎ ▣ 📺 🍴 🏊

WHIPPANY

◆◆◆ **Homestead Village Guest Studios** [M] 🐾
(973) 463-1999. **$99-$99.** 125 Rt 10 E. I-287, exit 10E, 3.6 mi e. Int corridors. **Pets:** Small, other. $75 one-time fee/room. Supervision.
[A$K] [S/D] ⊠ 👂 ☎ ▣ 📺

[AAA] ◆◆ **Howard Johnson Inn** [MI] 🐾
(973) 539-8350. **$59-$125.** 1255 Rt 10 E. I-287, exit 39B southbound; exit 39 northbound, just w. Int corridors. **Pets:** Medium, other. $20 deposit/pet. No service, supervision, crate.
[SAVE] [S/D] ⊠ 👂 ☎ ▣ 📺 🏊

◆◆◆ **Summerfield Suites-Hanover** [M]
(973) 605-1001. **Call for rates.** 1 Ridgedale Ave. I-287, exit 39 (Rt 10 W), just nw. Int corridors. **Pets:** Small. Supervision.
⊠ ♿ 👂 ☎ ▣ 📺 🏊

WOODBRIDGE

◆◆ **Homestead Village Guest Studios** [M] 🐾
(732) 442-8333. **$99.** 1 Hoover Way. New Jersey Tpke, exit 11, 1.4 mi to US 9 N, just w on King George Post Rd. Int corridors. **Pets:** Medium, other. $75 one-time fee/pet. No service, supervision, crate.
[A$K] [S/D] ⊠ ♿ 👂 ☎ ▣ 📺

WOODCLIFF LAKE

[AAA] ◆◆◆ **Hilton Woodcliff Lake** [H]
(201) 391-3600. **$186-$206.** 200 Tice Blvd. Northbound Garden State Pkwy, exit 171, left on Glen Rd from exit ramp, right on Chestnut Ridge Road, 0.5 mi to Tice Blvd, just left. Int corridors. **Pets:** Designated rooms, no service, supervision, crate.
[SAVE] [S/D] ⊠ 👂 ☎ ▣ 📺 🍴 🏊 🏋

NEW MEXICO

CITY INDEX

ALAMOGORDO

◆◆ All American Inn M
(505) 437-1850. **$30-$38.** 508 S White Sands Blvd. 1 mi s on US 54, 70 and 82. Ext corridors. **Pets:** No service, supervision, crate.

◆◆◆ Best Western Desert Aire Motor Hotel M ❀
(505) 437-2110. **$57-$62, 3 days notice.** 1021 S White Sands Blvd. 1.5 mi s on US 54, 70 and 82. Ext corridors. **Pets:** Other. $50 deposit/pet. Supervision.

◆◆◆ Holiday Inn Express-Alamogordo M
(505) 437-7100. **$65-$65.** 1401 S White Sands Blvd. US 70, 0.6 mi n of jct US 70, 54 and 82. Int corridors. **Pets:** Small. Designated rooms, no service, supervision, crate.

◆◆ Motel 6–368 M
(505) 434-5970. **$34-$60.** 251 Panorama Blvd. US 70, 0.6 mi n of jct US 70, 54 and 82. Ext corridors. **Pets:** Medium. No service, supervision, crate.

◆◆ Super 8 Motel M ❀
(505) 434-4205. **Call for rates.** 3204 N White Sands Blvd. US 54, 70 and 82, 2 mi n. Int corridors. **Pets:** Designated rooms, no service, supervision, crate.

ALBUQUERQUE

◆◆◆ Albuquerque Holiday Inn Express M
(505) 247-1500. **$79-$89.** 2331 Centre Ave SE. I-25, exit 222A, 1 mi e to Yale Blvd, just n, then just e. Int corridors. **Pets:** Small. No service, supervision, crate.

◆◆◆ Amberley Suite Hotel M ❀
(505) 823-1300. **$89-$99.** 7620 Pan American Frwy NE. I-25, exit 231, 0.8 mi n on frontage road. Int corridors. **Pets:** Medium, dogs only. $15 one-time fee/room. Designated rooms, no service, supervision, crate.

◆◆◆ AmeriSuites M ❀
(505) 242-9300. **$85-$107.** 1400 Sunport Place SE. I-25, exit 221, 0.3 mi e to University Blvd exit, just n to Woodward Rd. Int corridors. **Pets:** Very small. No service, supervision, crate.

◆◆◆ AmeriSuites M ❀
(505) 872-9000. **$69-$107.** 6901 Arvada Ave NE. I-40, exit 162 westbound; exit 162B eastbound, 0.7 mi n. Int corridors. **Pets:** Very small. No service, supervision, crate.

◆◆◆ Baymont Inn Airport M
(505) 242-1555. **$65-$75.** 1511 Gibson Blvd SE. I-25, exit 222 (Gibson Blvd) northbound; exit 222A southbound, just e. Int corridors. **Pets:** Supervision.

◆◆◆ Baymont Inn & Suites Albuquerque North M
(505) 345-7500. **$61-$66.** 7439 Pan American Frwy NE. I-25, exit 231, just w. Int corridors. **Pets:** Medium. Supervision.

◆◆◆ Best Western Airport Inn M ❀
(505) 242-7022. **$79-$99.** 2400 Yale Blvd SE. I-25, exit 222 (Gibson Blvd) northbound; exit 222A southbound, 1 mi e, just s. Int corridors. **Pets:** $10 daily fee/room. Designated rooms, supervision.

◆◆◆ Best Western American Motor Inn & RV Park M
(505) 298-7426. **$69-$99.** 12999 Central Ave NE. I-40, exit 167, 0.3 mi w on Central Ave westbound; exit 166 right on Juan Tabo, left on Central Ave, then 0.5 mi eastbound. Ext corridors. **Pets:** Supervision.

◆◆◆ Brittania & W E Mauger Estate Bed & Breakfast BB ❀
(505) 242-8755. **$89-$199.** 701 Roma Ave NW. I-25, exit 225 (Lomas Ave), 1 mi w, just s on 7th Ave. Int corridors. **Pets:** Dogs only. $30 one-time fee/room. Supervision.

◆◆◆ ClubHouse Inn & Suites [M] 🐾
(505) 345-0010. **$89-$133.** 1315 Menaul Blvd NE. I-25, exit 227A, just e to University Blvd, 0.5 mi s to Menual Blvd, 0.5 mi w. Int corridors. **Pets:** No service, supervision, crate.
[ASK] [SD] ⊠ 🦯 🦻 ☎ 🖥 🏊

[AAA] **◆◆◆ Comfort Inn-Airport** [M] 🐾
(505) 243-2244. **$55-$95.** 2300 Yale Blvd SE. I-25, exit 222A (Gibson Blvd) southbound; exit 222 northbound, 1 mi n, just s. Ext/int corridors. **Pets:** Medium, other. $10 one-time fee/room. Designated rooms, supervision.
[SAVE] [SD] ⊠ 🦻 🚿 🏊

◆◆◆ Comfort Inn & Suites [M]
(505) 822-1090. **$65-$89.** 5811 Signal Ave NE. I-25, exit 233, just e via Alaneda. Int corridors. **Pets:** Small. No service, supervision, crate.
[ASK] [SD] ⊠ ♿ 🦻 🚿 ☎ 🖥 🏊

[AAA] **◆◆◆ Comfort Inn East** [MI] 🐾
(505) 294-1800. **$49-$61.** 13031 Central Ave NE. I-40, exit 167, just w. Ext corridors. **Pets:** Other. $3 daily fee/room. Supervision.
[SAVE] [SD] ⊠ ♿ 🦻 🚿 ☎ 🖥 🍴 🏊

[AAA] **◆◆ Days Inn-East** [M]
(505) 294-3297. **$50-$65.** 13317 Central Ave NE. I-40, exit 167, just s. Ext corridors. **Pets:** Small. Supervision.
[SAVE] [SD] ⊠ 🏊

◆◆◆ Days Inn Eubank [M]
(505) 275-3297. **$45-$70.** 10321 Hotel Cir NE. I-40, exit 165, just n on Eubank Ave. Ext corridors. **Pets:** Supervision.
[ASK] [SD] ⊠ 🏊

◆◆◆ Days Inn West [M]
(505) 836-3297. **Call for rates.** 6031 Iliff Rd NW. I-40, exit 155, just s on Coors Rd, just w. Ext corridors. **Pets:** Medium. Designated rooms, supervision.
⊠ ♿ 🦻 🚿 🏊

[AAA] **◆◆ Econo Lodge** [M] 🐾
(505) 292-7600. **$55-$76, 5 days notice.** 13211 Central Ave NE. I-40, exit 167, just s. Ext corridors. **Pets:** Medium. $5 one-time fee/pet. Designated rooms, no service, supervision, crate.
[SAVE] [SD] ⊠ 🖥

[AAA] **◆◆◆ Econo Lodge Old Town** [M] 🐾
(505) 243-8475. **$50-$95.** 2321 Central Ave NW. I-40, exit 157A, 0.6 mi s on Rio Grande Blvd, 0.4 mi w. Ext corridors. **Pets:** Medium. $10 daily fee/room, $10 one-time fee/room. Designated rooms, no service, supervision, crate.
[SAVE] [SD] ⊠ ☎ 🖥 🏊

[AAA] **◆◆◆ Hampton Inn-North** [M] 🐾
(505) 344-1555. **$60-$110.** 5101 Ellison NE. I-25, exit 231, just w. Ext corridors. **Pets:** Other. No service, supervision, crate.
⊠ 🦯 🦻 ☎ 🖥 🏊

◆◆◆ Holiday Inn Express [M] 🐾
(505) 275-8900. **$95-$100, 30 days notice.** 10330 Hotel Ave NE. I-40, exit 165, 2 blks n on Eubank Ave. Ext corridors. **Pets:** Small. $5 daily fee/pet, $5 one-time fee/pet. No service, supervision, crate.
[ASK] [SD] ⊠ 🦻 🚿 ☎ 🖥 🏊

◆◆◆ Holiday Inn-Mountain View [MI]
(505) 884-2511. **$90-$119.** 2020 Menaul Blvd NE. I-40, exit 160 (Carlisle Blvd), 0.3 mi n to Menaul Blvd, 1 mi w. Int corridors. **Pets:** Medium. Supervision.
[ASK] [SD] ⊠ 🦯 🦻 🚿 ☎ 🖥 🍴 🏊

◆◆ Homestead Village Guest Studios [A]
(505) 883-8888. **$59, 30 days notice.** 2401 Wellsley Dr NE. I-40, exit 160, just n to Menaul Blvd, just w, just s. Ext corridors. **Pets:** Small. Supervision.
⊠ 🚿 ☎ 🖥

[AAA] **◆◆◆ Howard Johnson Express Inn** [M] 🐾
(505) 828-1600. **$55-$69.** 7630 Pan American Frwy. I-25, exit 231, 0.8 mi n on Frontage Rd. Int corridors. **Pets:** Medium, other. $5 daily fee/room, $5 one-time fee/room. Supervision.
[SAVE] [SD] ⊠ 🦻 🚿 🖥 🏊 ✂

◆◆◆ La Quinta Inn-Airport [M] 🐾
(505) 243-5500. **$75-$95.** 2116 Yale Blvd SE. I-25, exit 222A (Gibson Blvd) southbound; exit 222 (Gibson Blvd) northbound, 1 mi e. Ext/int corridors. **Pets:** Very small. No service, supervision, crate.
[ASK] ⊠ ♿ 🦻 🚿 ☎ 🖥 🏊

◆◆◆ La Quinta Inn North [M]
(505) 821-9000. **$69-$89.** 5241 San Antonio Dr NE. I-25, exit 231, just e. Ext corridors. **Pets:** Medium. No service, supervision, crate.
[ASK] ⊠ ♿ 🦻 🚿 ☎ 🖥 🏊

◆◆◆ La Quinta Inn San Mateo [M]
(505) 884-3591. **$65-$85.** 2424 San Mateo Blvd NE. I-40, exit 161 westbound; exit 161B eastbound, just n. Ext corridors. **Pets:** Small. Supervision.
[ASK] ⊠ 🦻 🚿 ☎ 🖥 🏊

[AAA] **◆◆ Motel 6–1349** [M] 🐾
(505) 243-8017. **$38-$54.** 1000 Avenida Cesar Chavez. I-25, exit 223, just w. Ext corridors. **Pets:** Medium, other. Supervision.
[SD] ⊠ 🦯 🚿 🏊

[AAA] **◆◆ Motel 6 Premiere–741** [M]
(505) 831-3400. **$34-$50.** 6015 Iliff Rd NW. I-40, exit 155, just s on Coors Blvd, just w. Ext corridors. **Pets:** Medium. No service, supervision, crate.
[SD] ⊠ 🦯 🦻 🚿 ☎ 🏊

◆◆◆ Plaza Inn Albuquerque [MI] 🐾
(505) 243-5693. **$80-$92.** 900 Medical Arts NE. I-25, exit 225, just e. Int corridors. **Pets:** Medium. $25 deposit/pet. No service, supervision, crate.
[ASK] [SD] ⊠ ☎ 🖥 🍴 🏊

[AAA] **◆◆◆ Radisson Hotel & Conference Center** [H] 🐾
(505) 888-3311. **$99-$99.** 2500 Carlisle Blvd NE. I-40, exit 160, just n. Ext/int corridors. **Pets:** $50 deposit/room. Designated rooms, supervision.
[SAVE] [SD] ⊠ ♿ 🦻 🚿 ☎ 🖥 🍴 🏊

◆◆◆ Ramada Inn Mountainview [MI]
(505) 271-1000. **$55-$105.** 25 Hotel Cir NE. I-40, exit 165, just n via Hotel Cir. Ext/int corridors. **Pets:** Medium. Designated rooms, no service, supervision, crate.
[ASK] ⊠ 🦻 🚿 ☎ 🖥 🍴 🏊

◆◆◆ Residence Inn by Marriott Ⓐ ❀
(505) 881-2661. **$126.** 3300 Prospect NE. I-40, exit 160, just n to Menaul Blvd, just w, just s on Wellesley Dr NE. Ext corridors. **Pets:** Other. $10 daily fee/room, $50 one-time fee/room. Supervision.

(ASK) (S☉) (✕) (🐾) (🖥) (💻) (🍽) (✕)

◆◆ Super 8 Motel East Ⓜ ❀
(505) 271-4807. **$45-$50.** 450 Paisano NE. I-40, exit 166, just n to Cooper, just s. Int corridors. **Pets:** $5 daily fee/pet. No service, supervision, crate.

(ASK) (S☉) (✕) (🐾)

◆◆ Super 8 Motel of Albuquerque Ⓜ ❀
(505) 888-4884. **$45-$50.** 2500 University Blvd NE. I-25, exit 227A, just s. Int corridors. **Pets:** $5 daily fee/pet. No service, supervision, crate.

(ASK) (S☉) (✕) (🐾) (🖥) (🍽)

ⒶⒶⒶ ◆◆◆ Wyndham Hotel Ⓗ ❀
(505) 843-7000. **$59-$99.** 2910 Yale Blvd SE. I-25, exit 222 (Gibson Blvd) northbound; exit 222A southbound, 1 mi e on Gibson Blvd, 0.5 mi s. Int corridors. **Pets:** Small, other. Supervision.

(SAVE) (S☉) (✕) (🐾) (🖥) (🍽) (💻) (🍽) (✕) (✕)

ALTO

◆◆ High Country Lodge Ⓒ ❀
(505) 336-4321. **$79-$139, 7 days notice.** Hwy 48. Center. Ext corridors. **Pets:** Small, dogs only. $10 one-time fee/pet. Supervision.

(🍽) (💻) (✕) (✕)

ANGEL FIRE

◆◆ Angel Fire Resort Ⓡ ❀
(505) 377-6401. **$195-$315.** 1 N Angel Fire Rd. From US 64, 2.6 mi s on SR 434, then 0.4 mi. Int corridors. **Pets:** Supervision.

(ASK) (S☉) (✕) (🍽) (💻) (🍽) (✕) (✕) (🍸)

ARROYO SECO

◆◆◆ Adobe and Stars B & B ⒷⒷ ❀
(505) 776-2776. **$105-$180.** 584 SR 150. 1.1 mi ne on SR 150 at Valdez Rd. Ext/int corridors. **Pets:** Medium. $50 deposit/pet, $20 one-time fee/pet. Designated rooms, no service, supervision, crate.

(ASK) (S☉) (✕) (🍽) (🍸) (CTV)

ARTESIA

ⒶⒶⒶ ◆◆ Artesia Inn Ⓜ ❀
(505) 746-9801. **$38-$55, 3 days notice.** 1820 S 1st St. 1.5 mi s on US 285. Ext corridors. **Pets:** Medium. $10 one-time fee/room. Supervision.

(SAVE) (S☉) (✕) (🍽) (💻) (✕)

BELEN

◆◆◆ Best Western Ⓜ ❀
(505) 861-3181. **$59-$74.** 2111 Sosimo Padilla Blvd. I-25, exit 191, just w of jct. Ext/int corridors. **Pets:** Medium, other. $20 deposit/room, $5 one-time fee/pet. No service, supervision, crate.

(ASK) (S☉) (✕) (🍸) (🍽) (💻) (✕)

BLOOMFIELD

◆◆ Super 8 Motel Ⓜ ❀
(505) 632-8886. **$40-$44.** 525 W Broadway Blvd. Jct of US 64 and SR 44. Int corridors. **Pets:** Medium. $10 deposit/room, $10 one-time fee/pet. No service, supervision, crate.

(ASK) (S☉) (✕) (🐾) (🍽)

CARLSBAD

ⒶⒶⒶ ◆◆◆ Best Western Motel Stevens ⓂⒾ ❀
(505) 887-2851. **$54-$59, 3 days notice.** 1829 S Canal St. 1 mi s on US 62, 180 and 285. Ext corridors. **Pets:** Small. Designated rooms, no service, supervision, crate.

(SAVE) (S☉) (✕) (🐾) (🍽) (💻) (🍽) (✕) (✕)

ⒶⒶⒶ ◆◆ Carlsbad Inn Ⓜ
(505) 887-1171. **$32-$45.** 2019 S Canal St. 1.5 mi s on US 62, 180 and 285. Ext corridors. **Pets:** Medium. Supervision.

(SAVE) (S☉) (✕) (🍽) (✕) (✕)

◆◆ Continental Inn Ⓜ ❀
(505) 887-0341. **$35-$55.** 3820 National Parks Hwy. 3.5 mi sw on US 62 and 180. Ext corridors. **Pets:** Dogs only. $10 deposit/pet. Supervision.

(ASK) (S☉) (✕) (🍽) (💻) (✕)

ⒶⒶⒶ ◆◆◆ Days Inn of Carlsbad Ⓜ
(505) 887-7800. **$50-$62, 7 days notice.** 3910 National Parks Hwy. 3.5 mi sw on US 62 and 180. Ext corridors. **Pets:** Medium. No service, supervision, crate.

(SAVE) (S☉) (✕) (🐾) (🍸) (🍽) (💻) (✕)

ⒶⒶⒶ ◆◆◆ Holiday Inn Carlsbad ⓂⒾ
(505) 885-8500. **$80-$104.** 601 S Canal. Center on US 62, 180 and 285, Canal St at Lee St. Ext corridors. **Pets:** Small. Supervision.

(SAVE) (S☉) (✕) (🐾) (🍸) (🐾) (🍽) (💻) (🍽) (✕) (✕)

ⒶⒶⒶ ◆◆◆ Quality Inn ⓂⒾ ❀
(505) 887-2861. **$49-$69, 7 days notice.** 3706 National Park Hwy. 3 mi sw on US 62 and 180. Ext corridors. **Pets:** Other. Designated rooms, no service, supervision, crate.

(SAVE) (✕) (🐾) (🍽) (💻) (🍽) (✕)

ⒶⒶⒶ ◆ Stagecoach Inn Ⓜ ❀
(505) 887-1148. **$36-$46.** 1819 S Canal. 1 mi s on US 62, 180 and 285. Ext corridors. **Pets:** Other. Designated rooms, no service, supervision, crate.

(SAVE) (S☉) (✕) (🍽) (✕) (✕)

CHAMA

ⒶⒶⒶ ◆◆ River Bend Lodge Ⓜ ❀
(505) 756-2264. **$63-$78.** 2625 Hwy 64/84. 0.5 mi s of SR 17. Ext corridors. **Pets:** Medium. $10 one-time fee/room. No service, supervision, crate.

(SAVE) (S☉) (✕) (🍽) (💻)

CLAYTON

ⒶⒶⒶ ◆◆◆ Best Western Kokopelli Lodge Ⓜ ❀
(505) 374-2589. **$59-$89.** 702 S 1st St. US 87, 0.5 mi se of jct US 56 and 64. Ext corridors. **Pets:** $5 daily fee/pet, $5 one-time fee/pet. Supervision.

(SAVE) (S☉) (✕) (🍽) (💻) (✕)

◆◆ **Super 8 Motel** M
(505) 374-8127. **$50-$65.** 1425 S 1st St. US 87, 1 mi se of jct US 56 and 64. Int corridors. **Pets:** No service, supervision, crate.
(ASK) (S) (X) (🐾)

CLOVIS

(AAA) ◆◆ **Comfort Inn** M
(505) 762-4591. **$40-$65.** 1616 Mabry Dr. 1 mi e on US 60, 70 and 84. Ext corridors. **Pets:** Small. No service, supervision, crate.
(SAVE) (S) (X) (📞) (🐾)

◆◆ **Days Inn** M ✿
(505) 762-2971. **$39-$53, 7 days notice.** 1720 Mabry Dr. 1 mi e on US 60, 70 and 84. Ext corridors. **Pets:** $10 deposit/room. No service, supervision, crate.
(ASK) (S) (X) (📞) (🐾) (X)

◆◆◆ **Holiday Inn** M ✿
(505) 762-4491. **$55-$105, 7 days notice.** 2700 Mabry Dr. 1.5 mi e on US 60, 70 and 84. Ext corridors. **Pets:** Small, other. No service, supervision, crate.
(ASK) (S) (X) (🍴) (🐾) (🖊) (📞) (📠) (🍴) (🐾) (X)

DEMING

(AAA) ◆◆ **Anselment's Butterfield Stage Motel** M
(505) 544-0011. **$29-$38, 3 days notice.** 309 W Pine. Center. Ext corridors. **Pets:** Supervision.
(SAVE) (S) (X) (📞) (🐾)

(AAA) ◆◆◆ **Best Western Mimbres Valley Inn** M ✿
(505) 546-4544. **$39-$49, 7 days notice.** 1500 W Pine. I-10, exit 81. Ext corridors. **Pets:** Small, other. $25 deposit/room, $7 daily fee/pet, $7 one-time fee/pet. Supervision.
(SAVE) (S) (X) (📞) (🐾)

(AAA) ◆◆◆ **Days Inn** M ✿
(505) 546-8813. **$36-$48.** 1601 E Pine St. 1.3 mi e on US 70 and 80 city route and I-10 business loop. Ext corridors. **Pets:** Medium. $5 daily fee/pet. No service, supervision, crate.
(SAVE) (S) (X) (🐾)

(AAA) ◆◆ **The Deming Motel** M ✿
(505) 546-2737. **$28-$38.** 500 W Pine St. I-10, exit 82, 4 blks w on Motel Dr/Pine St. Ext corridors. **Pets:** Small, other. $4 daily fee/pet. Designated rooms, no service, supervision, crate.
(SAVE) (S) (X) (📞) (🐾)

(AAA) ◆◆◆ **Grand Motor Inn** M
(505) 546-2632. **$38.** 1721 E Spruce St. 1.3 mi e on US 70 and 80 city route and I-10 business loop. Ext corridors. **Pets:** Medium. No service, supervision, crate.
(SAVE) (S) (X) (📞) (🐾)

◆◆◆ **Holiday Inn** M ✿
(505) 546-2661. **$50-$60.** I-10, exit 85. Ext corridors. **Pets:** Supervision.
(X) (🐾) (🖊) (📞) (📠) (🍴) (🐾)

(AAA) ◆◆ **Motel 6—285** M
(505) 546-2623. **$34-$50.** I-10 and Country Club Dr. Ext corridors. **Pets:** Medium. No service, supervision, crate.
(S) (X) (📞) (📠) (🐾)

(AAA) ◆ **Wagon Wheel Motel** M ✿
(505) 546-2681. **$24-$29.** 1109 W Pine St. 1 mi w on US 70 and 80 city route, just e of exit 81, off I-10. Ext corridors. **Pets:** Medium. No service, supervision, crate.
(SAVE) (S) (X) (📞)

ELEPHANT BUTTE

(AAA) ◆◆◆ **Quality Inn** M ✿
(505) 744-5431. **$75-$85.** SR 195. I-25, exit 83, 4 mi e. Ext corridors. **Pets:** Medium. $20 daily fee/pet. No service, supervision, crate.
(SAVE) (S) (X) (📞) (📠) (🍴) (🐾) (X)

ESPANOLA

(AAA) ◆◆◆ **Comfort Inn** M
(505) 753-2419. **$58-$68.** 604-B S Riverside Dr. US 84 and 285, just s of jct SR 68. Int corridors. **Pets:** Supervision.
(SAVE) (S) (X) (📞) (📠) (🐾)

FARMINGTON

(AAA) ◆◆◆ **Best Western Inn & Suites** M ✿
(505) 327-5221. **$79-$109.** 700 Scott Ave. 0.8 mi e on US 64 at Bloomfield Blvd and Scott Ave. Int corridors. **Pets:** Other. $10 one-time fee/pet. Designated rooms, no service, supervision, crate.
(SAVE) (S) (X) (🐾) (📞) (📠) (🍴) (🐾)

(AAA) ◆◆◆ **Comfort Inn** M
(505) 325-2626. **$50-$70.** 555 Scott Ave. 0.8 mi e on US 64 (Bloomfield Blvd), just n. Int corridors. **Pets:** Medium. No service, supervision, crate.
(SAVE) (X) (📞) (📠) (🐾)

◆◆◆ **Holiday Inn Express** M ✿
(505) 325-2545. **$69-$75.** 2110 Bloomfield Blvd. 1.6 mi e on US 64. Int corridors. **Pets:** $50 deposit/room. No service, supervision, crate.
(ASK) (S) (X) (🍴) (🐾) (🖊) (📞) (📠) (🐾)

◆◆◆ **Holiday Inn of Farmington** M ✿
(505) 327-9811. **$75-$81.** 600 E Broadway. 0.8 mi e on US 64 at Bloomfield Blvd and Scott Ave. Int corridors. **Pets:** Other. $50 deposit/room. Supervision.
(ASK) (S) (X) (🐾) (📞) (📠) (🍴) (🐾)

◆◆◆ **La Quinta Inn** M
(505) 327-4706. **$69-$89.** 675 Scott Ave. 0.8 mi e on US 64 at Bloomfield Blvd and Scott Ave. Ext corridors. **Pets:** No service, supervision, crate.
(ASK) (X) (🍴) (🐾) (📞) (📠) (🐾)

(AAA) ◆◆ **Super 8 Motel** M ✿
(505) 325-1813. **$48-$64, 3 days notice.** 1601 E Broadway. Just n of jct SR 44. Int corridors. **Pets:** Medium, dogs only. $5 daily fee/pet, $5 one-time fee/pet. No service, supervision, crate.
(SAVE) (S) (X) (🖊) (📞)

GALLUP

◆ Ambassador Motel M
(505) 722-3843. **$25-$31.** 1601 W Hwy 66. I-40, exit 20, 0.5 mi s to US 66, just w. Ext corridors. **Pets:** Supervision.
⊠ 🚗 ⊠

◆◆◆ Best Western Inn & Suites M
(505) 722-2221. **$69-$99.** 3009 US 66 W. I-40, exit 16, 1 mi e. Int corridors. **Pets:** Medium. No service, supervision, crate.
SAVE 🔊 ⊠ 🛈 💻 🍴 🚗

◆ Blue Spruce Lodge M
(505) 863-5211. **$24-$32, 3 days notice.** 1119 US 66E. I-40, exit 22, just s to US 66, then just e. Ext corridors. **Pets:** Supervision.
SAVE 🔊 ⊠

◆ Budget Inn M 🐾
(505) 722-6631. **$26-$49.** 3150 US 66 W. I-40, exit 16, 0.8 mi e. Ext corridors. **Pets:** Small. Designated rooms, no service, supervision, crate.
SAVE 🔊 ⊠

◆◆◆ Comfort Inn M 🐾
(505) 722-0982. **$46-$62.** 3208 US 66 W. I-40, exit 16, 0.3 mi e. Int corridors. **Pets:** Medium, other. $5 daily fee/pet. Supervision.
SAVE 🔊 ⊠ 🛈 💻 🚗

◆◆◆ Days Inn West M
(505) 863-6889. **$45-$65.** 3201 W Hwy 66. I-40, exit 16, 0.3 mi e. Ext corridors. **Pets:** Small. No service, supervision, crate.
SAVE 🔊 ⊠ 🛈 🚗

◆ Economy Inn M 🐾
(505) 863-9301. **$20-$29.** 1709 US 66 W. I-40, exit 20, s to US 66, 0.5 mi w. Ext corridors. **Pets:** Medium. $20 deposit/room. No service, supervision, crate.
SAVE 🔊 ⊠ 🛈

◆◆◆ Gallup Travelodge M
(505) 722-2100. **$35-$60.** 3275 US 66 W. I-40, exit 16, just e. Int corridors. **Pets:** Small. No service, supervision, crate.
SAVE 🔊 ⊠ 🛈 🖾 💻 🚗

◆◆◆ Holiday Inn Express-Gallup M 🐾
(505) 726-1000. **$70-$150.** 1500 W Maloney Ave. I-40, exit 20, just n on Munoz Dr, just w. Ext/int corridors. **Pets:** Other. Supervision.
SAVE 🔊 ⊠ 🛈 🖾 🛈 💻 🚗

◆◆◆ Holiday Inn Holidome M
(505) 722-2201. **$65-$105.** 2915 US 66 W. I-40, exit 16, s to US 66, then 1 mi e. Ext/int corridors. **Pets:** Small. Supervision.
SAVE 🔊 ⊠ 🛈 💻 🍴 🚗 ⊠

◆ Road Runner Motel M 🐾
(505) 863-3804. **$26-$36, 3 days notice.** 3012 Hwy 66 E. I-40, exit 16, 1 mi w o. Ext corridors. **Pets:** $10 daily fee/pet, $10 one-time fee/pet. Designated rooms, no service, supervision, crate.
⊠ 🛈 🍴 🚗

◆ Roseway Inn M
(505) 863-9385. **$29-$39, 3 days notice.** 2003 US 66 W. I-40, exit 20, 1 mi w. Int corridors. **Pets:** Small. No service, supervision, crate.
SAVE 🔊 ⊠ 🛈 🍴 🚗

◆◆ Sleep Inn M 🐾
(505) 863-3535. **$53-$65.** 3820 E US 66. I-40, exit 26, just e. Int corridors. **Pets:** $5 daily fee/pet. No service, supervision, crate.
SAVE ⊠ 🖾 🖾 🛈 🚗

GLENWOOD

◆◆ Los Olmos Guest Ranch C 🐾
(505) 539-2311. **$60-$103, 4 days notice.** 1 Los Olmos Rd. US 180. Ext corridors. **Pets:** Other. $5 daily fee/pet. Supervision.
⊠ 🍴 🚗 ⊠ 📺 📺 🆎

GRANTS

◆◆◆ Best Western Inn & Suites of Grants M 🐾
(505) 287-7901. **$59-$89.** 1501 E Santa Fe Ave. I-40, exit 85. Int corridors. **Pets:** Small, other. Supervision.
SAVE 🔊 ⊠ 📀 🛈 💻 🍴 🚗

◆◆◆ Days Inn M 🐾
(505) 287-8883. **$50-$90.** 1504 E Santa Fe Ave. I-40, exit 85, 0.3 mi n of e interchange. Ext corridors. **Pets:** Small. No service, supervision, crate.
SAVE 🔊 ⊠

◆◆◆ Grants Travelodge M
(505) 287-7800. **$35-$60.** 1608 E Santa Fe Ave. I-40, exit 85. Ext corridors. **Pets:** Supervision.
SAVE 🔊 ⊠ 🖾 🖾 💻 🚗

◆◆◆ Holiday Inn Express M 🐾
(505) 285-4676. **$59-$79, 7 days notice.** 1496 E Sante Fe Ave. I-40, exit 85, 0.3 mi n of e interchange. Ext/int corridors. **Pets:** Other. Supervision.
SAVE 🔊 ⊠ 🚗

◆◆ Leisure Lodge M 🐾
(505) 287-2991. **$28-$32.** 1204 E Santa Fe Ave. I-40, exit 85, 0.8 mi w on Business Loop 40. Ext corridors. **Pets:** Other. No service, supervision, crate.
SAVE 🔊 ⊠ 🛈 🚗

◆◆ Sands Motel M 🐾
(505) 287-2996. **$35-$50.** 112 McArthur St. I-40, exit 85, 1.5 mi w on Business Loop 40. Ext corridors. **Pets:** $10 one-time fee/pet. Designated rooms, no service, supervision, crate.
SAVE 🔊 ⊠ 🛈

HERNANDEZ

◆◆◆ Casa del Rio BB 🐾
(505) 753-2035. **$95-$125, 21 days notice.** Hwy 84, MM 199.46. 2.3 mi n from jct US 285, then just e on gated drive. Ext/int corridors. **Pets:** Other. Supervision.
⊠ 🖾 🛈 📺 📺 🆎

HOBBS

AAA ◆◆ Best Inn M
(505) 397-3251. **$42-$47, 3 days notice.** 501 N Marland Blvd. 2.5 mi e on US 62 and 180. Ext/int corridors. **Pets:** Small. Designated rooms, no service, supervision, crate.
SAVE SD X H ⌨ ⌂

AAA ◆◆ Days Inn M ☀
(505) 397-6541. **$32-$45.** 211 N Marland Blvd. 2 mi e on US 62 and 180. Ext corridors. **Pets:** Very small. $10 deposit/room. No service, supervision, crate.
SAVE SD X 🖉 H ⌂

AAA ◆◆ Econo Lodge M
(505) 397-3591. **$28-$43.** 619 N Marland Blvd. 2.5 mi e on US 62 and 180. Ext corridors. **Pets:** Designated rooms, no service, supervision, crate.
SAVE SD X H ⌨ ⌂

◆◆ Innkeepers M ☀
(505) 397-7171. **$40-$50.** 309 N Marland Blvd. 2 mi e on US 62 and 180. Ext corridors. **Pets:** Other. $20 deposit/room. No service, supervision, crate.
ASK SD X H ⌨ ⌂

AAA ◆◆ Travelodge Hobbs M
(505) 393-4101. **$40-$70.** 1301 E Broadway. 2 mi e on US 62 and 180. Ext corridors. **Pets:** Small. Designated rooms, no service, supervision, crate.
SAVE SD X H ⌨ ⌂

LAS CRUCES

◆◆◆ Baymont Inn & Suites Las Cruces M ☀
(505) 523-0100. **$38-$43.** 1500 Hickory Dr. I-10, exit 140, just se of jct I-25 and Avenida de Mesilla. Int corridors. **Pets:** Medium. $50 deposit/room. Designated rooms, no service, supervision, crate.
SD X ⌰ 🖉 H ⌨ ⌂

AAA ◆◆◆ Best Western Mesilla Valley Inn M ☀
(505) 524-8603. **$59-$79.** 901 Avenida de Mesilla. I-10, exit 140 (Mesilla). Ext corridors. **Pets:** Medium, other. Supervision.
SAVE SD X 🖉 H ⌨ ⌑ ⌂

AAA ◆◆◆ Best Western Mission Inn M
(505) 524-8591. **$45-$65.** 1765 S Main St. I-10, exit 142, 1 mi n. Ext corridors. **Pets:** Small. Supervision.
SAVE SD X H ⌑ ⌂ X

◆◆◆ Comfort Suites M ☀
(505) 522-1300. **$59-$79.** 2101 S Triviz. I-25, exit 1. Int corridors. **Pets:** Small, dogs only. $15 daily fee/room. Designated rooms, no service, supervision, crate.
ASK SD X ⌰ 🖉 🖉 H ⌨ ⌂

AAA ◆◆◆ Days Inn M ☀
(505) 526-4441. **$55-$60.** 2600 S Valley Dr. I-10, exit 142 (University Ave). Int corridors. **Pets:** Other. Supervision.
SAVE SD X 🖉 H ⌨ ⌑ ⌂

AAA ◆ Desert Lodge Motel M ☀
(505) 524-1925. **$24-$32.** 1900 W Picacho St. I-10, exit 139, 1 mi n, 0.8 mi e on Picacho St (I-10 business route); I-25, exit 6A, 2 mi sw on (US 70 W), 2 mi w. Ext corridors. **Pets:** Small. $10 deposit/pet, $10 one-time fee/pet. Supervision.
SD X

◆◆◆ Hampton Inn M
(505) 526-8311. **$52-$69.** 755 Avenida de Mesilla. I-10, exit 140 (Mesilla). Ext corridors. **Pets:** Small. No service, supervision, crate.
ASK SD X H ⌨ ⌂

◆◆◆ Hilltop Hacienda B & B BB
(505) 382-3556. **$75-$85.** 2600 Westmoreland St. I-25, exit 6A, just e to Del Rey St, 3 mi n to Westmoreland St, then 1 mi e. Int corridors. **Pets:** No service, supervision, crate.
ASK SD X X CTV

AAA ◆◆◆ Holiday Inn de Las Cruces M ☀
(505) 526-4411. **$49-$65.** 201 E University Ave. 2.8 mi s on US 80, 85 and 180 at jct I-10, exit 142. Int corridors. **Pets:** Other. $30 deposit/pet. No service, supervision, crate.
SAVE SD X ⌰ 🖉 🖉 H ⌨ ⌑ ⌂

◆◆◆ Holiday Inn Express M ☀
(505) 527-9947. **Call for rates.** 2200 S Valley Dr. I-10, exit 142, then 2 blks w. Ext corridors. **Pets:** Small. No service, supervision, crate.
ASK X ⌰ 🖉 H ⌨ ⌂

◆◆◆ La Quinta Inn-Las Cruces M ☀
(505) 524-0331. **$59-$79.** 790 Avenida de Mesilla. I-10, exit 140 (Mesilla). Int corridors. **Pets:** Other. Supervision.
ASK X ⌰ 🖉 H ⌨ ⌂

◆◆◆ Las Cruces Hilton Inn H ☀
(505) 522-4300. **$77-$77.** 705 S Telshor Blvd. I-25, exit 3 (Lohman Dr). Int corridors. **Pets:** Small. $50 deposit/pet. Designated rooms, supervision.
ASK SD X ⌰ 🖉 H ⌨ ⌑ ⌂

◆◆◆ Lundeen's Inn of the Arts BB ☀
(505) 526-3326. **$53-$150, 3 days notice.** 618 S Alameda Blvd. Center. Int corridors. **Pets:** Medium. $15 one-time fee/room. No service, supervision, crate.
ASK X

AAA ◆◆ Motel 6-363 M
(505) 525-1010. **$36-$52.** 235 La Posada Ln. 2.8 mi s on US 80, 85 and 180 at jct I-10 exit 142. Ext corridors. **Pets:** Small. No service, supervision, crate.
SD X ⌂ CTV

AAA ◆◆ Royal Host Motel M ☀
(505) 524-8536. **$27-$38.** 2146 W Picacho St. I-10, exit 139, 1 mi n, then 0.5 mi e on Picacho St (I-10 business route). Ext corridors. **Pets:** Large. $5 one-time fee/room. No service, supervision, crate.
SAVE X ⌂

◆◆◆ Sleep Inn M ☀
(505) 522-1700. **$49-$69.** 2121 S Triviz. I-25, exit 1. Int corridors. **Pets:** Supervision.
ASK SD X ⌰ 🖉 🖉 H ⌨ ⌂

◆◆ **Super 8 Motel** 🅜 ❖
(505) 523-8695. **$34-$34.** 245 La Posada Ln. 2.8 mi s on US 80, 85 and 180 at jct I-10, exit 142. Int corridors. **Pets:** Medium, other. $25 one-time fee/room. Supervision.
(ASK) (✕) (■)

◆◆◆ **TRH Smith Bed & Breakfast** 🅱🅱 ❖
(505) 525-2525. **$56-$132.** 909 N Alameda Blvd. Center. Int corridors. **Pets:** Small. $15 daily fee/pet. Supervision.
(✕) (CTV)

LAS VEGAS

🆔 ◆◆◆ **Comfort Inn** 🅜 ❖
(505) 425-1100. **$65-$75.** 2500 N Grand Ave. US 85 and I-25 business route, just sw of jct I-25, exit 347. Int corridors. **Pets:** Designated rooms, no service, supervision, crate.
(SAVE) (S🐾) (✕) (☎)

🆔 ◆ **El Camino Motel** 🅜 ❖
(505) 425-5994. **$40-$60.** 1152 N Grand Ave. US 85 and I-25 business route, 0.3 mi w of jct I-25, exit 345; SR 65, 0.5 mi n. Ext corridors. **Pets:** Very small. $20 deposit/pet, $6 daily fee/pet. Designated rooms, no service, supervision, crate.
(SAVE) (S🐾) (✕) (🍴)

🆔 ◆◆ **Inn on the Santa Fe Trail** 🅜 ❖
(505) 425-6791. **$64-$79.** 1133 N Grand Ave. I-25 business route and US 84, 0.3 mi w from jct; I-25, exit 345, 0.5 mi n. Ext corridors. **Pets:** $5 daily fee/room. No service, supervision, crate.
(SAVE) (S🐾) (✕) (■) (🍴) (☎)

🆔 ◆◆◆ **Plaza Hotel** 🅷 ❖
(505) 425-3591. **$63-$97.** 230 Plaza. I-25, exit 343; w following signs to Old Town Plaza. Int corridors. **Pets:** Other. $10 daily fee/pet, $10 one-time fee/pet. Supervision.
(SAVE) (S🐾) (✕) (■) (💻)

LORDSBURG

🆔 ◆◆◆ **Best Western American Motor Inn** 🅜
(505) 542-3591. **$39-$44.** 944 E Motel Dr. 1.5 mi e on US 70 and 80, 1 mi w of exit 24 off I-10. Ext corridors. **Pets:** Medium. Supervision.
(SAVE) (S🐾) (✕) (■) (🍴) (☎) (✕)

◆◆◆ **Best Western Western Skies** 🅜
(505) 542-8807. **$53-$58.** 1303 S Main St. I-10, exit 22. Ext corridors. **Pets:** Small. Supervision.
(ASK) (S🐾) (✕) (■) (🍴) (☎)

◆◆◆ **Days Inn** 🅜 ❖
(505) 542-3600. **$55-$75.** 1100 W Motel Dr. I-10, exit 20. **Pets:** Other. $7 deposit/room. Supervision.
(ASK) (S🐾) (✕) (🍴) (☎) (■) (☎)

◆◆◆ **Holiday Inn Express** 🅜
(505) 542-3666. **$59-$59.** 1408 S Main. I-10, exit 22. Int corridors. **Pets:** Medium. No service, supervision, crate.
(ASK) (S🐾) (✕) (♿) (📠) (■) (💻) (☎)

MILAN

◆ **Crossroads Motel** 🅜
(505) 287-9264. **$24-$27.** 1600 W US 66. I-40, exit 79. Ext corridors. **Pets:** Small. No service, supervision, crate.
(ASK) (✕) (■) (☎)

MORIARTY

🆔 ◆◆ **Days Inn** 🅜 ❖
(505) 832-4451. **$43-$59.** US 66 W & I-40. I-40, exit 194. Int corridors. **Pets:** Other. $5 daily fee/pet, $5 one-time fee/pet. No service, supervision, crate.
(SAVE) (S🐾) (✕) (■)

◆◆ **Motel 6** 🅜 ❖
(505) 832-6666. **$40-$56.** 109 Rt 66 E. 0.5 mi e on US 66, 1 mi e of I-40, exit 197. Int corridors. **Pets:** Medium, other. Supervision.
(✕) (♿) (📠) (🐾) (☎)

🆔 ◆◆ **Sunset Motel** 🅜 ❖
(505) 832-4234. **$39-$47.** 501 Old Rt 66. 0.5 mi e on US 66, 1 mi w of e interchange I-40, exit 197. Ext corridors. **Pets:** Other. $5 daily fee/pet. Supervision.
(SAVE) (S🐾) (✕) (■)

🆔 ◆◆ **Super 8 Motel** 🅜
(505) 832-6730. **$50-$70.** 1611 W Old Rt 66. I-40, exit 194, then 0.5 mi e on Central Ave. Int corridors. **Pets:** Small. Designated rooms, no service, supervision, crate.
(SAVE) (S🐾) (✕) (♿) (■)

PLACITAS

◆◆◆ **Hacienda de Placitas Inn of the Arts** 🅱🅱
(505) 867-0082. **$99-$199.** 491 Hwy 165. I-25, exit 242, 4.9 mi ne. Ext corridors. **Pets:** No service, supervision, crate.
(✕) (■) (💻) (☎)

RANCHOS DE TAOS

🆔 ◆ **The Taos Motel** 🅜 ❖
(505) 758-2524. **$39-$55** (no credit cards). 1798 Paseo Del Pueblo Sur Ave. Center, on SR 68. Ext corridors. **Pets:** Other. Designated rooms, supervision.
(SAVE) (S🐾) (✕)

RATON

🆔 ◆ **Budget Host Melody Lane Motel** 🅜 ❖
(505) 445-3655. **$44-$49.** 136 Canyon Dr. I-25, exit 454, 0.8 mi s on I-25 business loop. Ext corridors. **Pets:** Medium. Supervision.
(SAVE) (S🐾) (✕) (📠)

◆ **Raton Super 8** 🅜
(505) 445-2355. **$48-$58.** 1610 Cedar. I-25, exit 451. Int corridors. **Pets:** Medium. Supervision.
(ASK) (S🐾) (✕) (📠) (■)

RIO RANCHO

🆔 ◆◆◆ **Best Western Inn at Rio Rancho** 🅜
(505) 892-1700. **$79-$129.** 1465 Rio Rancho Blvd. I-25, exit 233, 6.5 mi w on Alameda Blvd; I-40, exit 155, 10 mi n on Coors Rd/Coors Bypass to Hwy 528, 1 mi n. Ext corridors. **Pets:** No service, supervision, crate.
(SAVE) (S🐾) (✕) (📠) (💻) (🍴) (☎)

⚛ ◆◆ **Days Inn** Ⓜ ❀
(505) 892-8800. **$75-$90.** 4200 Crestview Dr. I-25, exit 233 (Alameda Blvd), then 8 mi w on NM 528; I-40, exit 155, then 8 mi n on Coors Rd (NM 448). Ext corridors. **Pets:** Medium, other. $20 deposit/room, $5 one-time fee/ room. Designated rooms, supervision.
ⓈⒶⓋⒺ 🆂 ⊠ 🔋 📶

◆◆◆ **Ramada Limited Hotel** Ⓜ
(505) 892-5998. **$45-$50, 3 days notice.** 4081 High Resort Blvd. I-25, exit 233, then 8 mi w on Alameda Blvd (NM 528); I-40, exit 155, 8 mi n on Coors Rd (NM 448). Int corridors. **Pets:** Designated rooms, no service, supervision, crate.
Ⓐ🆂🅺 🆂 ⊠ 🔋 📶

◆◆ **Rio Rancho Super 8 Motel** Ⓜ
(505) 896-8888. **Call for rates.** 4100 Barbara Loop. I-25, exit 233, 0.5 mi w on Alameda Blvd, 3.8 mi nw on 528, just e. Int corridors. **Pets:** Medium. No service, supervision, crate.
⊠ 🔋

⚛ ◆◆◆ **Wellesley Inn & Suites** Ⓜ ❀
(505) 892-7900. **$49-$99.** 2221 Rio Rancho Blvd. I-25, exit 233 6 mi w on Alameda Blvd, turns into Rio Rancho Blvd/SR 528. Int corridors. **Pets:** Very small, other. No service, supervision, crate.
ⓈⒶⓋⒺ ⊠ 🎵 🔋 📺 📶

ROSWELL

⚛ ◆◆ **Best Western El Rancho Palacio Motor Lodge** Ⓜ ❀
(505) 622-2721. **$42-$65.** 2205 N Main St. 1.8 mi n on US 70 and 285. Ext corridors. **Pets:** Other. Supervision.
ⓈⒶⓋⒺ 🆂 ⊠ 🔋 📶

⚛ ◆◆◆ **Best Western Sally Port Inn & Suites** ⓂⓁ ❀
(505) 622-6430. **$69-$99.** 2000 N Main St. 1.5 mi n on US 70 and 285. Int corridors. **Pets:** Other. $10 one-time fee/ room. Designated rooms, no service, supervision, crate.
ⓈⒶⓋⒺ 🆂 ⊠ 🔋 📺 🍴 📶 ⊠

⚛ ◆◆ **Budget Inn-North** Ⓜ ❀
(505) 623-6050. **$30-$50.** 2101 N Main St. 1.8 mi n on US 70 and 285. Ext corridors. **Pets:** Small, dogs only. $2 daily fee/pet, $2 one-time fee/pet. No service, supervision, crate.
ⓈⒶⓋⒺ 🆂 ⊠ 🔋 📶

⚛ ◆◆ **Budget Inn West** Ⓜ ❀
(505) 623-3811. **$27-$48.** 2200 W 2nd St. 2 mi w on US 70 and 380. Ext corridors. **Pets:** Small, dogs only. $2 daily fee/pet. No service, supervision, crate.
ⓈⒶⓋⒺ 🆂 ⊠ 🔋 📶

⚛ ◆◆ **Days Inn** ⓂⓁ ❀
(505) 623-4021. **$44-$65.** 1310 N Main St. 0.8 mi n on US 70 and 285. Ext corridors. **Pets:** Other. No service, supervision, crate.
ⓈⒶⓋⒺ 🆂 ⊠ 🔋 📺 🍴 📶

⚛ ◆◆ **Frontier Motel** Ⓜ ❀
(505) 622-1400. **$28-$48.** 3010 N Main St. 2.5 mi n on US 70 and 285. Ext corridors. **Pets:** Other. Supervision.
⊠ 🔋 📶

⚛ ◆◆ **Leisure Inn** Ⓜ ❀
(505) 622-2575. **$32-$46.** 2700 W 2nd St. 2.5 mi w on US 70 and 380. Ext corridors. **Pets:** Small, dogs only. $4 daily fee/pet, $4 one-time fee/pet. No service, supervision, crate.
ⓈⒶⓋⒺ ⊠ 🔋 📶 ⊠

◆◆ **Motel 6 of Roswell–4075** Ⓜ
(505) 625-6666. **Call for rates.** 3307 N Main St. Int corridors. **Pets:** Designated rooms, supervision.
⊠ 🎵 🔋 📶

⚛ ◆◆ **National 9 Inn** Ⓜ ❀
(505) 622-0110. **$29-$38.** 2001 N Main St. 1.5 mi n on US 285 and 70. Ext corridors. **Pets:** Medium, dogs only. No service, supervision, crate.
ⓈⒶⓋⒺ 🆂 ⊠ 🔋 📶

⚛ ◆◆◆ **Ramada Inn** ⓂⓁ ❀
(505) 623-9440. **$64-$78.** 2803 W 2nd. 2.5 mi w on US 70 and 380. Ext/int corridors. **Pets:** Other. $50 deposit/room. Designated rooms, supervision.
ⓈⒶⓋⒺ 🆂 ⊠ 🍴 📶

RUIDOSO

◆◆◆ **Village Lodge** Ⓐ
(505) 258-5442. **$79-$129, 7 days notice.** 1000 Mechem Dr. 2 mi n on SR 48. Ext corridors. **Pets:** Supervision.
⊠ 🔋 📺

RUIDOSO DOWNS

⚛ ◆◆ **Bestway Inn** Ⓜ
(505) 378-8000. **$110-$185.** US 70, 0.5 mi e of jct US 70 and SR 48. Ext corridors. **Pets:** Small. Designated rooms, supervision.
ⓈⒶⓋⒺ 🆂 ⊠ 🔋

SANTA FE

⚛ ◆◆◆ **Alexander's Inn** ⒷⒷ ❀
(505) 986-1431. **$90-$160.** 529 E Palace Ave. 6 blks e of Plaza. Ext/int corridors. **Pets:** Other. $20 one-time fee/pet. Supervision.
⊠ 🔋 📺 🎿

◆◆◆ **Best Western of Santa Fe** Ⓜ ❀
(505) 438-3822. **$65-$125.** 3650 Cerrillos Rd. I-25, exit 278B, 2.8 mi n. Int corridors. **Pets:** Other. No service, supervision, crate.
⊠ 🎵 🔋 📶

⚛ ◆ **Cactus Lodge Motel** Ⓜ ❀
(505) 471-7699. **$48-$88.** 2864 Cerrillos Rd. 3.8 mi sw on US 85. Ext corridors. **Pets:** Dogs only. No service, supervision, crate.
ⓈⒶⓋⒺ 🆂 ⊠ 🔋

◆◆◆ **Casapueblo Inn** ⒷⒷ ❀
(505) 988-4455. **$159-$269, 3 days notice.** 138 Park Ave. Center intersection Guadalupe and Park. Ext corridors. **Pets:** Supervision.
Ⓐ🆂🅺 🆂 ⊠ 🎵 🔋 📺

◆◆◆ **Cerrillos Road Travelodge** Ⓜ ❀
(505) 471-4000. **$79-$119.** 3450 Cerrillos Rd. I-25, exit 278, then 3 mi n. Int corridors. **Pets:** Small. $10 daily fee/room. Designated rooms, supervision.
Ⓐ🆂🅺 ⊠ 🐾 🎵 🔋 📺 📶

◆◆◆ **Cities of Gold Casino Hotel** 🅼🅸
(505) 455-0515. **$85-$85** (no credit cards). Rt 11 Box 21B. 15 mi n on US 84/285. Int corridors. **Pets:** Small. No service, supervision, crate.
🅰🆂🅺 ⊠ 🅕 🅳 🅗 🖳 🍴

🆎🅰🅰 ◆◆◆ **Comfort Inn** 🅼
(505) 474-7330. **$75-$125.** 4312 Cerrillos Rd. I-25, exit 278, 1.6 mi n. Int corridors. **Pets:** Supervision.
🆂🅰🆅🅴 🆂🅾 ⊠ 🅐 🅳 🅗 🖳 🏊

◆◆ **Days Inn of Santa Fe** 🅼
(505) 424-3297. **$69-$85.** 2900 Cerrillos Rd. I-25, exit 278, 4 mi n at Siler Rd. Ext corridors. **Pets:** Supervision.
🅰🆂🅺 🆂🅾 ⊠ 🅗 🏊

🆎🅰🅰 ◆◆◆◆ **Eldorado Hotel** 🅷
(505) 988-4455. **$239-$269, 3 days notice.** 309 W San Francisco. Just w of The Plaza, at Sandoval St. Int corridors. **Pets:** No service, supervision, crate.
🆂🅰🆅🅴 🆂🅾 ⊠ 🅐 🖳 🍴 🏊

🆎🅰🅰 ◆◆◆ **El Paradero Bed & Breakfast** 🅱🅱 ☙
(505) 988-1177. **$65-$125.** 220 W Manhattan Ave. 0.3 mi s on Cerrillos Rd, 1/2 blk on E Manhattan Ave. Ext/int corridors. **Pets:** Dogs only. $10 daily fee/pet. No service, supervision, crate.
⊠ 🅳 🅗 🖳

◆◆◆ **Hacienda Nicholas** 🅱🅱
(505) 986-1431. **$160, 30 days notice.** 320 E Marcy St. 4 blks e of the Plaza. Ext/int corridors. **Pets:** No service, supervision, crate.
⊠

🆎🅰🅰 ◆◆◆ **Holiday Inn** 🅷
(505) 473-4646. **$129, 3 days notice.** 4048 Cerrillos Rd. I-25, exit 278B, 2.3 mi n just n of Rodeo Dr. Int corridors. **Pets:** Small. No service, supervision, crate.
🆂🅰🆅🅴 ⊠ 🅕 🅐 🅳 🖳 🍴 🏊

🆎🅰🅰 ◆◆◆ **Hotel Santa Fe** 🅷 ☙
(505) 982-1200. **$169-$259.** 1501 Paseo de Peralta. At Cerrillos Rd, 0.6 mi s of the Plaza. Int corridors. **Pets:** Dogs only. $15 daily fee/pet. Supervision.
🆂🅰🆅🅴 🆂🅾 ⊠ 🅐 🅳 🍴 🏊

◆◆◆◆ **Inn of the Anasazi** 🅷 ☙
(505) 988-3030. **$265-$415, 3 days notice.** 113 Washington Ave. Just ne of The Plaza. Int corridors. **Pets:** $50 one-time fee/pet. No service, supervision, crate.
⊠ 🅐 🅳 🖳 🍴

🆎🅰🅰 ◆◆◆ **Inn On The Alameda** 🅼 ☙
(505) 984-2121. **$147-$342, 3 days notice.** 303 E Alameda Blvd. 4 blks e of The Plaza. Ext/int corridors. **Pets:** Other. $20 daily fee/room. Supervision.
🆂🅰🆅🅴 🆂🅾 ⊠ 🅐 🅳 🅗

🆎🅰🅰 ◆◆◆ **La Quinta Inn** 🅼 ☙
(505) 471-1142. **$95-$115.** 4298 Cerrillos Rd. I-25, Cerrillos Rd exit, 1.8 mi n. Ext corridors. **Pets:** Medium. No service, supervision, crate.
🆂🅰🆅🅴 ⊠ 🅐 🅳 🅗 🖳 🏊

◆◆◆ **Las Palomas** 🅼
(505) 988-4455. **Call for rates, 3 days notice.** 119 Park Ave. 4 blks w of the Plaza. Ext corridors. **Pets:** Supervision.
⊠ 🅐 🅳 🅗 🖳

◆◆ **The Madeleine** 🅱🅱 ☙
(505) 982-3465. **$80-$160** (no credit cards). 106 Faithway. 3 blks e of the Plaza (Palace to Faithway). Ext/int corridors. **Pets:** Other. $20 one-time fee/pet. Supervision.
⊠ 🅳 🖳 🅚

🆎🅰🅰 ◆ **Motel 6–150** 🅼
(505) 473-1380. **$52-$68.** 3007 Cerrillos Rd. I-25, exit 278, 3.8 mi n. Ext corridors. **Pets:** Medium. No service, supervision, crate.
🆂🅾 ⊠ 🅳 🏊

🆎🅰🅰 ◆◆◆ **Quality Inn** 🅼🅸 ☙
(505) 471-1211. **$95-$105.** 3011 Cerrillos Rd. I-25, exit 278B, 3.8 mi n. Int corridors. **Pets:** Supervision.
🆂🅰🆅🅴 ⊠ 🅳 🖳 🍴 🏊

◆◆◆ **Residence Inn by Marriott** 🅰
(505) 988-7300. **Call for rates.** 1698 Galisteo St. I-25, exit 282, 1 mi n on St Francis Dr to St Michaels Dr, just e. Ext corridors. **Pets:** Supervision.
⊠ 🅐 🅳 🖳 🏊 ⊠

◆◆◆ **RIO VISTA SUITES** 🅲🅾
(505) 982-6636. **$135-$165, 3 days notice.** 320 Artist Rd. 527 E Alameda St, 0.5 mi e of center. Ext corridors. **Pets:** Supervision.
🅰🆂🅺 🆂🅾 ⊠ 🅳 🖳

SANTA ROSA

🆎🅰🅰 ◆◆ **Best Western Adobe Inn** 🅼 ☙
(505) 472-3446. **$45-$65.** 1501 Will Rogers Dr. I-40, exit 275. Ext corridors. **Pets:** Small, other. No service, supervision, crate.
🆂🅰🆅🅴 🆂🅾 ⊠ 🏊

🆎🅰🅰 ◆◆◆ **Best Western Santa Rosa Inn** 🅼 ☙
(505) 472-5877. **$50-$65.** 3022 Will Rogers Dr. I-40, exit 277, 0.5 mi w on Will Rogers Dr (US 66). Ext corridors. **Pets:** Small, other. $25 deposit/room. Designated rooms, no service, supervision, crate.
🆂🅰🆅🅴 🆂🅾 ⊠ 🅳 🏊

◆◆◆ **Comfort Inn** 🅼 ☙
(505) 472-5570. **$56-$99.** 3343 E Will Rogers Dr. US 84, just w of I-40, exit 277. Ext corridors. **Pets:** Other. $10 daily fee/room, $10 one-time fee/pet. No service, supervision, crate.
🅰🆂🅺 🆂🅾 ⊠ 🖳 🏊

🆎🅰🅰 ◆◆ **Days Inn of Santa Rosa** 🅼
(505) 472-5985. **$45-$55.** 1830 Will Rogers Dr. I-40, exit 275, then 2 blks e. Ext corridors. **Pets:** Small. Supervision.
🆂🅰🆅🅴 🆂🅾 ⊠

🆎🅰🅰 ◆◆◆ **Holiday Inn Express** 🅼 ☙
(505) 472-5411. **$45-$70, 5 days notice.** 3300 Will Rogers Dr. I-40, exit 277, then 0.3 mi w on Will Rogers Dr (US 66). Int corridors. **Pets:** Small. Designated rooms, no service, supervision, crate.
🆂🅰🆅🅴 🆂🅾 ⊠ 🖳 🏊

🆎🅰🅰 ◆ **Motel 6–273** 🅼
(505) 472-3045. **$42-$58.** 3400 Will Rogers Dr. I-40, exit 277, then 0.3 mi w on Will Rogers Dr (US 66). Ext corridors. **Pets:** Medium. No service, supervision, crate.
🆂🅾 ⊠ 🅐 🅳 🏊

◆◆ Ramada Limited Ⓜ
(505) 472-4800. **$50-$80.** 1701 Will Rogers Dr. I-40, exit 275, just e. Int corridors. **Pets:** Designated rooms, no service, supervision, crate.
⟦SAVE⟧ ⟦S🐾⟧ ⟦✕⟧ ⟦🛏⟧ ⟦🖼⟧

◆◆ Super 8 Motel-Santa Rosa Ⓜ
(505) 472-5388. **Call for rates.** 1201 Will Rogers Dr. I-40, exit 275, 2 blks w. Int corridors. **Pets:** Medium. No service, supervision, crate.
⟦✕⟧

SILVER CITY

◆◆◆ Copper Manor Motel Ⓜ
(505) 538-5392. **$43-$58.** 710 Silver Heights Blvd. 1.3 mi ne on US 180 and SR 90. Ext corridors. **Pets:** Small. No service, supervision, crate.
⟦SAVE⟧ ⟦S🐾⟧ ⟦✕⟧ ⟦🛏⟧ ⟦🍴⟧ ⟦🖼⟧

◆◆ The Drifter Motel Ⓜ
(505) 538-2916. **$41-$50.** 711 Silver Heights Blvd. 1.3 mi ne on US 180 and SR 90. Ext corridors. **Pets:** Small. No service, supervision, crate.
⟦SAVE⟧ ⟦S🐾⟧ ⟦✕⟧ ⟦🛏⟧ ⟦🍴⟧ ⟦🖼⟧

◆◆ Econolodge Silver City Ⓜ 🐾
(505) 534-1111. **$40-$70, 7 days notice.** 1120 Hwy 180 E. 1.5 mi ne on US 180 and SR 90. Int corridors. **Pets:** $30 deposit/room. No service, supervision, crate.
⟦SAVE⟧ ⟦S🐾⟧ ⟦✕⟧ ⟦🖐⟧ ⟦🛏⟧ ⟦🖼⟧

◆◆ Holiday Motor Hotel Ⓜ 🐾
(505) 538-3711. **$47-$59.** 3420 Hwy 180E. 2 mi ne on jct SR 180 and 90. Ext corridors. **Pets:** Other. Supervision.
⟦ASK⟧ ⟦S🐾⟧ ⟦✕⟧ ⟦🎯⟧ ⟦🛏⟧ ⟦🍴⟧ ⟦🖼⟧

◆◆ Super 8 Motel Ⓜ
(505) 388-1983. **$39-$60.** 1040 E Hwy 180. 1.5 mi ne on US 180 and SR 90. Int corridors. **Pets:** Designated rooms, no service, supervision, crate.
⟦SAVE⟧ ⟦S🐾⟧ ⟦✕⟧ ⟦🛏⟧ ⟦💻⟧

SOCORRO

◆◆◆ Econo Lodge Ⓜ 🐾
(505) 835-1500. **$32-$58.** 713 California Ave NW. 1 mi s of I-25, exit 150. Ext corridors. **Pets:** Small. $5 one-time fee/pet. Designated rooms, no service, supervision, crate.
⟦SAVE⟧ ⟦S🐾⟧ ⟦✕⟧ ⟦🛏⟧ ⟦💻⟧ ⟦🖼⟧

◆◆◆ Holiday Inn Express Ⓜ
(505) 838-0556. **$79-$104.** 1100 California Ave NE. Center. Ext/int corridors. **Pets:** No service, supervision, crate.
⟦ASK⟧ ⟦S🐾⟧ ⟦✕⟧ ⟦🖐⟧ ⟦🎯⟧ ⟦🖐⟧ ⟦🛏⟧ ⟦🖼⟧

◆◆ Motel 6 Ⓜ
(505) 835-4300. **$36-$52.** 807 S US 85. Exit 147. Ext corridors. **Pets:** Small. No service, supervision, crate.
⟦S🐾⟧ ⟦✕⟧ ⟦🖐⟧ ⟦🎯⟧ ⟦🖐⟧ ⟦🛏⟧ ⟦🖼⟧

TAOS

◆◆ El Pueblo Lodge Ⓜ 🐾
(505) 758-8700. **$50-$125, 7 days notice.** 412 Paseo del Pueblo Norte. US 64, 0.5 mi n of jct SR 68 and Taos Plaza. Ext corridors. **Pets:** Other. $10 daily fee/pet. Designated rooms, supervision.
⟦SAVE⟧ ⟦S🐾⟧ ⟦✕⟧ ⟦🎯⟧ ⟦🖐⟧ ⟦🛏⟧ ⟦💻⟧ ⟦🖼⟧

◆◆◆ Fechin Inn Ⓜ 🐾
(505) 751-1000. **$109-$169, 3 days notice.** 227 Paseo Del Pueblo Norte. Center; just n on US 64 of jct SR 68 and Taos Plaza. Int corridors. **Pets:** Medium, other. $20 daily fee/pet. Supervision.
⟦SAVE⟧ ⟦S🐾⟧ ⟦✕⟧ ⟦🖐⟧ ⟦🖐⟧ ⟦🛏⟧

◆◆◆ Holiday Inn Don Fernando de Taos Ⓜ
(505) 758-4444. **$100-$130.** 1005 Paseo del Pueblo Sur. SR 68, 1.8 mi sw of jct US 64 and Taos Plaza. Ext corridors. **Pets:** No service, supervision, crate.
⟦SAVE⟧ ⟦S🐾⟧ ⟦✕⟧ ⟦🎯⟧ ⟦🛏⟧ ⟦💻⟧ ⟦🍴⟧ ⟦🖼⟧ ⟦✕⟧

◆◆◆ Inn On The Rio Ⓜ 🐾
(505) 758-7199. **$69-$129.** 910 E Kit Carson Rd. US 64, 1.5 mi e of jct SR 68 and Taos Plaza. Ext corridors. **Pets:** Other. Supervision.
⟦SAVE⟧ ⟦S🐾⟧ ⟦✕⟧ ⟦🖼⟧ ⟦✕⟧ ⟦🐾⟧

◆◆◆ Quality Inn Ⓜ 🐾
(505) 758-2200. **$59-$99, 3 days notice.** 1043 Paseo del Pueblo Sur. SR 68, 2 mi sw of jct US 64 and Taos Plaza. Ext/int corridors. **Pets:** Other. $7 daily fee/pet. Designated rooms, no service, supervision, crate.
⟦SAVE⟧ ⟦S🐾⟧ ⟦✕⟧ ⟦🎯⟧ ⟦🛏⟧ ⟦💻⟧ ⟦🍴⟧ ⟦🖼⟧

◆◆◆ Ramada Inn de Taos Ⓜ 🐾
(505) 758-2900. **$79-$120.** 615 Paseo del Pueblo Sur. SR 68, 1 mi sw of jct US 64 and Taos Plaza. Ext corridors. **Pets:** Small. $10 deposit/room, $10 daily fee/room, $10 one-time fee/room. Designated rooms, supervision.
⟦ASK⟧ ⟦S🐾⟧ ⟦✕⟧ ⟦🛏⟧ ⟦💻⟧ ⟦🍴⟧ ⟦🖼⟧

◆◆ Sagebrush Inn Ⓜ 🐾
(505) 758-2254. **$85-$115, 3 days notice.** 1508 Paseo del Pueblo Sur. SR 68, 3 mi sw of jct US 64 and Taos Plaza. Ext corridors. **Pets:** Other. Designated rooms, supervision.
⟦SAVE⟧ ⟦S🐾⟧ ⟦✕⟧ ⟦🎯⟧ ⟦🛏⟧ ⟦💻⟧ ⟦🍴⟧ ⟦🖼⟧

◆◆ Sun God Lodge Ⓜ 🐾
(505) 758-3162. **$75-$105, 3 days notice.** 919 Paseo del Pueblo Sur. SR 68, 1.8 mi sw of jct US 64 and Taos Plaza. Ext corridors. **Pets:** Small. $50 deposit/pet, $10 one-time fee/room. Designated rooms, no service, supervision, crate.
⟦SAVE⟧ ⟦S🐾⟧ ⟦✕⟧ ⟦🛏⟧ ⟦💻⟧

◆◆◆ Touchstone Bed & Breakfast ⒷⒷ 🐾
(505) 758-0192. **$90-$250.** 110 Mabel Dodge Ln. N from jct US 64 and 68 (center of town) 1.1 mi, on e side of road, follow signs. Ext/int corridors. **Pets:** Very small, dogs only. $50 deposit/pet. No service, supervision, crate.
⟦SAVE⟧ ⟦S🐾⟧ ⟦✕⟧ ⟦💻⟧ ⟦🐾⟧

TRUTH OR CONSEQUENCES

◆◆◆ Best Western Hot Spring Motor Inn Ⓜ
(505) 894-6665. **$55-$60.** 2270 N Date St. I-25, exit 79. Ext corridors. **Pets:** Supervision.
⟦SAVE⟧ ⟦S🐾⟧ ⟦✕⟧ ⟦🛏⟧ ⟦🍴⟧ ⟦🖼⟧

◆◆ Super 8 Motel Ⓜ 🐾
(505) 894-7888. **$50-$61.** 2151 N Date St. I-25, exit 79, just s. Int corridors. **Pets:** Other. $15 deposit/pet. Supervision.
⟦SAVE⟧ ⟦✕⟧

TUCUMCARI

◆ Americana Motel Ⓜ ❀
(505) 461-0431. **$24-$42.** 406 E Tucumcari Blvd. I-40, exit 332, 1.5 mi n on SR 18, 0.5 mi e on US 66. Ext corridors. **Pets:** Medium, other. Designated rooms, no service, supervision, crate.
[SAVE] [✕]

◆◆◆ Best Western Discovery Inn Ⓜ ❀
(505) 461-4884. **$69-$74.** 200 E Estrella. I-40, exit 332. Ext corridors. **Pets:** Other. $5 daily fee/room. Designated rooms, supervision.
[SAVE] [S🔒] [✕] [📖] [🍴] [🖙]

◆◆ Best Western Pow Wow Inn Ⓜ ❀
(505) 461-0500. **$46-$79, 7 days notice.** 801 W Tucumcari Blvd. I-40, exit 332, 1.5 mi n on SR 18, 0.5 mi w on US 66. Ext corridors. **Pets:** Other. $10 deposit/room. No service, supervision, crate.
[SAVE] [S🔒] [✕] [🐾] [📖] [🍴] [🖙] [✕]

◆◆◆ Comfort Inn Ⓜ ❀
(505) 461-4094. **$59-$89, 7 days notice.** 2800 E Tucumcari Blvd. I-40, exit 335, then 0.5 mi w. Ext corridors. **Pets:** Medium. No service, supervision, crate.
[ASK] [S🔒] [✕] [📖] [🖙]

◆◆◆ Holiday Inn Ⓜ ❀
(505) 461-3780. **$65-$95.** 3716 E Tucumcari Blvd. I-40, exit 335, 0.3 mi w on US 66. Ext corridors. **Pets:** Small. $6 daily fee/room. Designated rooms, supervision.
[SAVE] [S🔒] [✕] [🐾] [📖] [📖] [🍴] [🖙] [✕]

◆◆ Howard Johnson Ⓜ
(505) 461-2747. **$40-$70.** 3604 E Tucumcari Blvd. I-40, exit 335, then 0.5 mi w. Int corridors. **Pets:** Small. Supervision.
[SAVE] [S🔒] [✕] [📖]

◆◆ Microtel Inn Ⓜ
(505) 461-0600. **$40-$56.** 2420 S First St. I-40, exit 332, just n. Int corridors. **Pets:** Supervision.
[SAVE] [S🔒] [✕] [📖] [🖙]

◆◆ Rodeway Inn East Ⓜ ❀
(505) 461-0360. **$24-$68.** 1023 E Tucumcari Blvd. I-40, exit 333 to Tucumcari Blvd, 0.6 mi w. Ext corridors. **Pets:** Medium, other. Supervision.
[SAVE] [S🔒] [✕] [📖] [📖] [🖙]

◆◆ Safari Motel Ⓜ
(505) 461-3642. **$26-$40.** 722 E Tucumcari Blvd. I-40, exit 332; 1.5 mi n on 1st St, 0.4 mi e on US 66. Ext corridors. **Pets:** Small. Designated rooms, no service, supervision, crate.
[SAVE] [S🔒] [✕] [🖙]

◆◆ Super 8 Motel Ⓜ
(505) 461-4444. **$40-$69.** 4001 E Tucumcari Blvd. I-40, exit 335, just w. Int corridors. **Pets:** Designated rooms, no service, supervision, crate.
[ASK] [S🔒] [✕] [🖙]

◆◆ Tucumcari Travelodge Ⓜ
(505) 461-1401. **$30-$50.** 1214 E Tucumcari Blvd. I-40, exit 333, 1.5 mi n on Mountain Rd, then 0.5 mi w. Ext corridors. **Pets:** Medium. No service, supervision, crate.
[SAVE] [S🔒] [✕] [📖] [🖙]

VAUGHN

◆◆ Bel-Air Motel Ⓜ ❀
(505) 584-2241. **$30-$40.** 1 mi e on US 54, 60 and 285. Ext corridors. **Pets:** Small. No service, supervision, crate.
[✕] [📖]

WHITE ROCK

◆◆ Bandelier Inn Ⓜ ❀
(505) 672-3838. **$62-$69.** 132 SR 4. Ext corridors. **Pets:** Other. $7 daily fee/pet. Designated rooms, supervision.
[SAVE] [S🔒] [✕] [📖]

WHITES CITY

◆◆◆ Best Western Cavern Inn Ⓜ ❀
(505) 785-2291. **$65-$85.** 17 Carlsbad Caverns Hwy. US 62 and 180 at jct SR 7. Ext corridors. **Pets:** Medium. $10 daily fee/room. No service, supervision, crate.
[SAVE] [S🔒] [✕] [🐾] [🖙] [✕]

CITY INDEX

ALBANY

AAA ◆◆◆ Albany Mansion Hill Inn & Restaurant BB ☙
(518) 465-2038. **$125-$165, 5 days notice.** 115 Philip St at Park Ave. From I-90 to I-787 s to Madison Ave exit (US 20 W), to Philip St, then s; from I-87 to I-787 to downtown exit (US 20 W), Madison to Philip St, then s. Ext/int corridors. **Pets:** Other. Supervision.

SAVE Sᴅ ⊠ 🛏 🖵 ¶

AAA ◆◆ Albany Ramada Inn MI ☙
(518) 489-2981. **$92-$125.** 1228 Western Ave. 5 mi w on US 20; 0.7 mi se of I-87, exit 24; or 0.7 mi s of I-90 exit 2 (Fuller Rd) westbound; following signs to US 20. Int corridors. **Pets:** $10 one-time fee/pet. No service, supervision, crate.

SAVE Sᴅ ⊠ 🐾 🐾 🛏 🖵 ¶ 🏊

AAA ◆◆◆ Crowne Plaza Albany H ☙
(518) 462-6611. **$89.** State & Lodge sts. Center; at Ten Eyck Plaza. Int corridors. **Pets:** Medium. Supervision.

SAVE Sᴅ ⊠ 🐾 🛏 🖵 ¶ 🏊

ALEXANDRIA BAY

AAA ◆◆◆◆ Riveredge Resort & Hotel R ☙
(315) 482-9917. **$218-$298.** 17 Holland St. I-81, exit 50 N, n on SR 12, just ne. Int corridors. **Pets:** Very small. $10 daily fee/pet. No service, supervision, crate.

SAVE ⊠ 🐾 🛏 ¶ 🏊 ⊠

ANGELICA

◆◆◆ Angelica Inn Bed & Breakfast BB ☙
(716) 466-3295. **$60-$100.** 64 W Main St. SR 17, exit 31, 0.5 mi w. Int corridors. **Pets:** Small. $25 deposit/pet, $10 daily fee/pet, $10 one-time fee/room. Designated rooms, no service, supervision, crate.

ASK Sᴅ ⊠ 🛏 🖵 🗷

AUBURN

◆◆◆ Holiday Inn MI ☙
(315) 253-4531. **$89-$139.** 75 North St. SR 34, n of SR 5 and US 20. Int corridors. **Pets:** Medium, other. Designated rooms, no service, supervision, crate.

ASK Sᴅ ⊠ 🛏 🖵 ¶ 🏊

AVOCA

AAA ◆ Caboose Motel M ☙
(607) 566-2216. **$37-$51, 3 days notice.** 8620 SR 415. I-390, exit 1, 2.2 mi n on SR 415. Ext corridors. **Pets:** Medium. No service, supervision, crate.

⊠ 🛏 🖵 🏊 ⊠

BATAVIA

AAA ◆◆ Best Western Batavia Inn MI ☙
(716) 343-1000. **$74-$109.** 8204 Park Rd. Just sw from jct I-90 and SR 98. Int corridors. **Pets:** No service, supervision, crate.

SAVE ⊠ ¶ 🏊

◆◆ Crown Inn M ❀
(716) 343-2311. **$56-$89.** 8212 Park Rd. I-90, exit 48, just
sw. Int corridors. **Pets:** Small, other. Designated rooms, no
service, supervision, crate.
(SAVE) (S⬤) (✕) (▣)

BATH

◆◆ Days Inn MI ❀
(607) 776-7644. **$60-$95.** 330 W Morris St. SR 17, exit 38,
just n. Int corridors. **Pets:** Medium. No service, supervision,
crate.
(ASK) (S⬤) (✕) (▣) (💻) (🍽) (🏊)

BELLPORT

◆◆◆ The Great South Bay Inn BB ❀
(631) 286-8588. **$105-$125, 7 days notice.** 160 S Country
Rd. Downtown; on Main St (S Country Rd). Int corridors.
Pets: Small. $15 daily fee/pet. Supervision.
(✕) (🎁)

BERLIN

◆◆ The Sedgwick Inn CI
(518) 658-2334. **Call for rates.** 17971 Rt 22. 1 mi s on Rt
22. Ext/int corridors. **Pets:** Small. Designated rooms, supervision.
(✕) (▣) (💻) (🐾)

BINGHAMTON

◆◆ Comfort Inn M ❀
(607) 722-5353. **$55-$125.** 1156 Front St. I-81, exit 6, just n
of Broome Community College. Int corridors. **Pets:** Other.
Designated rooms, no service, supervision, crate.
(SAVE) (S⬤) (✕) (▣) (💻)

◆◆◆ Days Inn M
(607) 724-3297. **$85-$95, 90 days notice.** 1000 Front St.
I-81 S, exit 6, 2 mi s on Rt 11; I-81 N, exit 5 (Front St), 1 mi
n on Rt 11. Int corridors. **Pets:** Small. Supervision.
(ASK) (S⬤) (✕) (🐾) (▣) (🏊)

◆◆◆ Holiday Inn Arena H ❀
(607) 722-1212. **$90-$90.** 2-8 Hawley St. Downtown. Int
corridors. **Pets:** $25 one-time fee/room. Supervision.
(ASK) (S⬤) (✕) (🐾) (▣) (💻) (🍽) (🏊)

◆◆ Motel 6–1222 M
(607) 771-0400. **$39-$55.** 1012 Front St. I-81 S, exit 6, 2 mi
s on Rt 11; I-81 N, exit 5 (Front St), 1 mi n on Rt 11. Int
corridors. **Pets:** Designated rooms, supervision.
(S⬤) (✕) (🐾) (📼)

◆◆ Ramada Inn MI ❀
(607) 724-2412. **$82-$102.** 65 Front St. I-81, exit 5; SR 17
E, exit 72, 1 mi s. Int corridors. **Pets:** Small. $25 deposit/
room. No service, supervision, crate.
(SAVE) (S⬤) (✕) (💻) (🍽) (🏊)

◆◆ Super 8 Motel-Binghamton M ❀
(607) 773-8111. **$35-$105.** 650 Old Front St. I-81, exit 5 to
access road. Int corridors. **Pets:** Other. No service, supervision, crate.
(ASK) (S⬤) (✕)

◆ Super 8 Upper Court Street MI ❀
(607) 775-3443. **$42-$60.** 771 Upper Court St. I-81 S, exit
3; I-81 N, exit 2 W; SR 17 W, exit 75. Ext corridors.
Pets: Small, other. Supervision.
(ASK) (S⬤) (✕) (🐾) (🍽) (🏊)

BOONVILLE

◆◆ Headwaters Motor Lodge M
(315) 942-4493. **$45-$65.** 13524 Rt 12. SR 12, 0.7 mi n of
jct US 12 and 120. Int corridors. **Pets:** Small. No service,
supervision, crate.
(SAVE) (S⬤) (✕) (🐾)

BRIGHTON

◆◆◆ Hampton Inn-South M ❀
(716) 272-7800. **$99-$99.** 717 E Henrietta Rd. I-390, exit
16B (Henrietta Rd) southbound; exit 16 northbound. Int corridors. **Pets:** Medium, other. Supervision.
(ASK) (S⬤) (✕) (🎁) (🐾) (💻)

◆◆ Wellesley Inn & Suites M ❀
(716) 427-0130. **$60-$105.** 797 E Henrietta Rd. SR 15A, at
I-390, exit 16 northbound; exit 16B southbound. Int corridors. **Pets:** Small, other. Supervision.
(SAVE) (S⬤) (✕) (🎁) (📼) (🐾) (💻)

BROCKPORT

◆◆ Econo Lodge of Brockport M ❀
(716) 637-3157. **$50-$90.** 6575 4th Section Rd. Just w on
SR 31 from jct SR 19. Ext corridors. **Pets:** Other. No service, supervision, crate.
(SAVE) (S⬤) (✕) (🐾) (▣) (🏊) (✕)

BUFFALO METROPOLITAN AREA

AMHERST

◆◆◆ Buffalo Marriott-Niagara H
(716) 689-6900. **$99-$159.** 1340 Millersport Hwy. I-290, exit
5B, 0.5 mi n on SR 263 (Millersport Hwy). Int corridors.
Pets: Supervision.
(SAVE) (S⬤) (✕) (🎁) (🐾) (▣) (💻) (🍽) (🏊)

◆◆ Lord Amherst Motor Hotel MI ❀
(716) 839-2200. **$59-$85.** 5000 Main St. SR 5, just w of jct
I-290, exit 7A. Ext/int corridors. **Pets:** Supervision.
(SAVE) (S⬤) (✕) (🐾) (🐾) (▣) (💻) (🍽) (🏊)

◆◆ Red Roof Inn M ❀
(716) 689-7474. **$70-$90.** 42 Flint Rd. I-290, exit 5B, 0.5 mi
n on SR 263 (Millersport Hwy). Ext corridors. **Pets:** Other.
Supervision.
(SAVE) (✕) (🐾) (🐾)

BOWMANSVILLE

❀❀ ◆◆ Red Roof Inn-Buffalo Airport **M**
(716) 633-1100. **$63-$87.** 146 Maple Dr. Just e of SR 78, just n of entrance to I-90 (New York Thruway), exit 49; behind Bob Evans Restaurant. Ext corridors. **Pets:** Small. No service, supervision, crate.

SAVE ✕ 🖉 📱

BUFFALO

❀❀ ◆◆ Best Western Inn-On The
Avenue **M** 🐾
(716) 886-8333. **$99-$125.** 510 Delaware Ave. Downtown; between Virginia and Allen sts. Int corridors. **Pets:** Small, dogs only. $100 deposit/room. Designated rooms, supervision.

SAVE 🌡 ✕ 📱

❀❀ ◆◆ Holiday Inn-Downtown 🅷
(716) 886-2121. **$109-$119, 3 days notice.** 620 Delaware Ave. Downtown; between Allen and North sts. Int corridors. **Pets:** No service, supervision, crate.

SAVE 🌡 ✕ 📱 💻 🍴 🍽

CHEEKTOWAGA

◆◆◆ Homewood Suites Hotel **M** 🐾
(716) 685-0700. **$109-$149.** 760 Dick Rd. 0.3 mi sw jct of SR 33, Dick Rd exit. Int corridors. **Pets:** Small. $85 one-time fee/room. No service, supervision, crate.

✕ 📱 💻 🍽

❀❀ ◆◆ Wellesley Inn & Suites **M** 🐾
(716) 631-8966. **$85-$115.** 4630 Genesee St. SR 33, 1 mi w of jct SR 78. Int corridors. **Pets:** $5 daily fee/room. Designated rooms, no service, supervision, crate.

SAVE 🌡 ✕ 🈀 🍳 📱 💻

GRAND ISLAND

◆◆ Cinderella Motel **M** 🐾
(716) 773-2872. **$35-$69, 3 days notice.** 2797 Grand Island Blvd. I-190 N, exit 19, 1.3 mi w on SR 324; I-190 S, exit 20B, just e on SR 324. Ext corridors. **Pets:** Small. No service, supervision, crate.

✕ 📱 🄵

HAMBURG

◆◆ Penny Wise Inn **M**
(716) 648-2000. **$32-$95.** 5245 Camp Rd. SR 75, just nw of jct I-90, exit 57. Ext corridors. **Pets:** Small. No service, supervision, crate.

ASK 🌡 ✕ 📱 🍽

❀❀ ◆◆ Red Roof Inn **M** 🐾
(716) 648-7222. **$44-$71.** 5370 Camp Rd. SR 75, just se of jct I-90, exit 57. Ext corridors. **Pets:** Other. Supervision.

SAVE ✕ 🖉

TONAWANDA

◆◆ Microtel-Tonawanda **M** 🐾
(716) 693-8100. **$45-$71.** 1 Hospitality Centre Way. Just n on SR 384 (Delaware St) from jct I-290, exit 1, 0.5 mi e on Crestmount Ave. Int corridors. **Pets:** Other. $10 deposit/room. Supervision.

ASK 🌡 ✕ 🈀 📱

WILLIAMSVILLE

◆◆ Microtel-Lancaster **M**
(716) 633-6200. **$45-$50.** 50 Freeman Rd. Just e on Frontage Rd from jct SR 78; 0.3 mi n of jct I-90 (New York Thruway), exit 49. Int corridors. **Pets:** Supervision.

✕

◆◆◆ Residence Inn by Marriott
Buffalo/Amherst 🅰 🐾
(716) 632-6622. **$120-$150.** 100 Maple Rd. Just e on Maple Rd from jct SR 263 (Millersport Hwy). Ext corridors. **Pets:** $6 daily fee/pet. Supervision.

ASK 🌡 ✕ 🈀 🖉 📱 💻 🍽 ✕

❀ END METROPOLITAN AREA ❀

CAMBRIDGE

◆ Cambridge Inn Bed & Breakfast 🅱🅱 🐾
(518) 677-5741. **$48-$75** (no credit cards), 3 days notice. 16 W Main St. 0.3 mi w of jct rts 22 and 372. Ext/int corridors. **Pets:** Dogs only. Supervision.

ASK 📱 💻

CANANDAIGUA

❀❀ ◆◆◆ Canandaigua Inn on the
Lake **M1** 🐾
(716) 394-7800. **$104-$144.** 770 S Main St. Just s of jct SR 332, US 20 and SR 5. Int corridors. **Pets:** Small, dogs only. $20 one-time fee/room. No service, supervision, crate.

SAVE ✕ 🄳 🖉 🍳 📱 💻 🍴 🍽 ✕

❀❀ ◆◆ Econo Lodge Canandaigua **M** 🐾
(716) 394-9000. **$61-$75.** 170 Eastern Blvd. 0.5 mi e of jct SR 332, SR 5 and US 20. Int corridors. **Pets:** Other. No service, supervision, crate.

SAVE 🌡 ✕ 📱 💻

CANASTOTA

◆◆ Days Inn **M** 🐾
(315) 697-3309. **$59-$89.** N Peterboro St. On SR 13, at jct New York Thruway exit 34. Int corridors. **Pets:** Other. Supervision.

ASK 🌡 ✕

CANTON

◆◆ Best Western University Inn M
(315) 386-8522. **$78-$88.** 90 E Main St. 1 mi e on US 11, at jct US 11, 68 and 310. Int corridors. **Pets:** Small. Supervision.

ASK ⛽ ✕ ✎ 🛏 💻 🍴 🖼

CLIFTON PARK

◆◆◆ Comfort Inn M ❀
(518) 373-0222. **$119-$149.** 41 Fire Rd. Just n of Rt 146; I-87, northbound exit 9; southbound exit 9 E. Int corridors. **Pets:** Other. Supervision.

SAVE ⛽ ✕ 🛏 💻 🖼

CLINTON

◆◆ The Hedges BB ❀
(315) 853-3031. **$65-$125, 7 days notice.** 180 Sanford Ave. College St, 0.3 mi n Elm St to Sanford Ave. Int corridors. **Pets:** Small, other. $6 daily fee/room. No service, supervision, crate.

ASK ✕ 🛏 💻 🖼

COBLESKILL

◆◆ Best Western of Cobleskill M ❀
(518) 234-4321. **$126-$149.** 12 Campus Dr Extension. On SR 7, 0.8 mi e of jct SR 10; from I-88, exit 22 westbound; exit 21 eastbound. Int corridors. **Pets:** Other. $20 deposit/room. Designated rooms, supervision.

SAVE ⛽ ✕ 🛁 🍽 🛏 💻 🍴 🖼

COLONIE

◆◆◆ Albany Marriott H
(518) 458-8444. **Call for rates.** 189 Wolf Rd. 0.3 mi se of I-87 Northway, exit 4. Int corridors. **Pets:** Designated rooms, no service, supervision, crate.

✕ 🛁 🍽 🛏 💻 🍴 🖼

◆◆ Ambassador Motor Inn M ❀
(518) 456-8982. **$55-$88.** 1600 Central Ave. 5.4 mi w on SR 5; 0.8 mi w I-87, exit 2 W. Ext corridors. **Pets:** Other. $50 deposit/room. Designated rooms, no service, supervision, crate.

SAVE ✕

◆◆ Days Inn Airport M
(518) 459-3600. **Call for rates.** 16 Wolf Rd. Just n of jct SR 5 and I-87 Northway, exit 2 E; opposite Colonie Shopping Mall. Int corridors. **Pets:** Medium. Supervision.

✕ 🍽 🛏 🖼

◆◆ Econo Lodge Albany M ❀
(518) 456-8811. **$68-$75.** 1632 Central Ave. 0.8 mi w of I-87 Northway, exit 2 W, just off SR 5. Int corridors. **Pets:** Small. Supervision.

SAVE ⛽ ✕ 🛁 🛏 💻

◆◆ Red Roof Inn M ❀
(518) 459-1971. **$58-$88.** 188 Wolf Rd. I-87 Northway, exit 4, 0.3 mi e. Ext corridors. **Pets:** Medium, dogs only. No service, supervision, crate.

SAVE ✕ 🛁

COOPERS PLAINS

◆◆ Stiles Motel M ❀
(607) 962-5221. **$42-$52.** 9239 Victory Hwy. SR 17, exit 42, 0.3 mi s to Victory Hwy (CR 415), then 0.3 mi n. Ext corridors. **Pets:** Other. $5 daily fee/pet. Supervision.

SAVE ⛽ ✕ 🛏 🖼

CORNING

◆◆◆ Radisson Hotel Corning H
(607) 962-5000. **$109-$165.** 125 Denison Pkwy E. Center; on SR 17. Int corridors. **Pets:** Small. No service, supervision, crate.

✕ 🛏 💻 🍴 🖼

CORTLAND

◆◆◆ Comfort Inn M
(607) 753-7721. **$79-$129, 7 days notice.** 2 1/2 Locust Ave. Just e of I-81, exit 11. Int corridors. **Pets:** Medium. Designated rooms, supervision.

ASK ⛽ ✕ 🛏 🍴

◆◆ Holiday Inn Cortland M
(607) 756-4431. **$79-$109.** 2 River St. I-81, exit 11. Int corridors. **Pets:** Medium. No service, supervision, crate.

ASK ⛽ ✕ 💻 🍴 🖼

◆◆ Super 8 Motel-Cortland M ❀
(607) 756-5622. **$58-$98, 7 days notice.** 188 Clinton Ave Extension. SR 13 at I-81, exit 11. Int corridors. **Pets:** Medium, other. $10 one-time fee/room. Designated rooms, no service, supervision, crate.

ASK ⛽ ✕

CUBA

◆◆ Cuba Coachlight Motel M ❀
(716) 968-1992. **$39-$55.** 1 N Branch Rd. New York Rt 17, exit 28, n to N Branch Rd, then e. Int corridors. **Pets:** Other. $5 daily fee/room. No service, supervision, crate.

SAVE ⛽ ✕ 🛏

DELHI

◆◆ Buena Vista Motel M ❀
(607) 746-2135. **$42-$82, 7 days notice.** Rt 28, Andes Rd. SR 28, 0.8 mi e of jct SR 10. Ext corridors. **Pets:** No service, supervision, crate.

✕ 🛏 💻

DIAMOND POINT

◆◆ Diamond Cove Cottages C ❀
(518) 668-5787. **$595-$1650, 30 days notice.** 3648 Lake Shore Dr. 3.3 mi n on SR 9 N from I-87, exit 22. Ext corridors. **Pets:** Small. $50 deposit/pet. No service, supervision, crate.

🛏 🖼 ✂

DOVER PLAINS

◆◆◆ Old Drovers Inn CI ❀
(914) 832-9311. **$150-$395.** Old Rt 22. 3 mi s of village, 0.7 mi n e off SR 22 via signs. Int corridors. **Pets:** Other. Supervision.

CTV 📠

DUNKIRK

AAA ◆◆◆ Comfort Inn **M** ☸
(716) 672-4450. **$70-$80.** 3925 Vineyard Dr. Just w of jct
SR 60 and I-90, exit 59. Int corridors. **Pets:** Large. $10
one-time fee/pet. Supervision.
[SAVE] [S🐾] [✕] [🛏] [🔌] [💻]

AAA ◆◆ Days Inn **M** ☸
(716) 673-1351. **$61-$81.** 10455 Bennett Rd. SR 60, just s
of jct I-90, exit 59. Ext/int corridors. **Pets:** Other. Designated
rooms, no service, supervision, crate.
[SAVE] [S🐾] [✕] [🔌] [💻]

◆◆◆ Four Points Sheraton Harborfront
    Hotel **M** ☸
(716) 366-8350. **$69-$199.** 30 Lake Shore Dr E. SR 5, 0.3
mi w of jct SR 60. Int corridors. **Pets:** Medium, other. $10
daily fee/room. Designated rooms, no service, supervision,
crate.
[ASK] [S🐾] [✕] [🔊] [🔌] [💻] [🍴] [🏊]

◆ Southshore Motor Lodge **X** ☸
(716) 366-2822. **$49-$98, 21 days notice.** 5040 W Lake
Rd (Rt 5). SR 5, 4 mi w of jct SR 60. Ext corridors.
Pets: Dogs only. Designated rooms, supervision.
[🔌] [💻] [🏊] [🎱]

◆◆ The Vineyard Motel & Restaurant **M**
(716) 366-4400. **$50-$70.** 3929 Vineyard Dr. Just w of jct
SR 60 and I-90, exit 59. Ext corridors. **Pets:** Designated
rooms, no service, supervision, crate.
[ASK] [S🐾] [✕] [🍴] [🏊] [✕]

EAST HAMPTON

AAA ◆◆ Dutch Motel **M** ☸
(631) 324-4550. **$115-$150, 60 days notice.** 488 Montauk
Hwy. 1.3 mi e on SR 27 E (Montauk Hwy). Ext corridors.
Pets: Small, dogs only. $10 daily fee/pet, $10 one-time
fee/pet. Designated rooms, no service, supervision, crate.
[SAVE] [🔌] [🏊]

EAST SYRACUSE

◆◆ East Syracuse Super 8 **M** ☸
(315) 432-5612. **$45-$66.** 6620 Old Collamer Rd. I-90, exit
35 (Carrier Cir), just e on SR 298, just n. Int corridors.
Pets: Small, other. $10 daily fee/room. No service, supervi-
sion, crate.
[ASK] [S🐾] [✕] [🛏] [🔊] [🔌]

AAA ◆◆◆ Holiday Inn East-Carrier Circle **M**
(315) 437-2761. **$94-$109.** 6555 Old Collamer Rd. I-90, exit
35 (Carrier Cir), to SR 298 E to College Pl. Ext/int corridors.
Pets: No service, supervision, crate.
[SAVE] [S🐾] [✕] [🔊] [🔌] [💻] [🍴] [🏊]

◆◆ Microtel Inn Syracuse **M** ☸
(315) 437-3500. **$44-$59.** 6608 Old Collamer Rd. I-90, exit
35 (Carrier Cir) to SR 298 E. Int corridors. **Pets:** $5 one-
time fee/room. Supervision.
[✕] [🔊] [🔊] [🔌]

◆◆◆ Residence Inn By Marriott **A**
(315) 432-4488. **$115-$131.** 6420 Yorktown Cir. I-90, exit
35; at Carrier Cir. Ext corridors. **Pets:** Designated rooms,
no service, supervision, crate.
[ASK] [S🐾] [✕] [🛏] [🔊] [🔌] [💻] [🏊] [✕]

ELLICOTTVILLE

AAA ◆◆ The Jefferson Inn **BB** ☸
(716) 699-5869. **$110-$145, 30 days notice.** 3 Jefferson
St. Just n of jct US 219 and SR 242; center. Int corridors.
Pets: Dogs only. $10 deposit/pet. Supervision.
[✕] [🔌] [💻]

ELMIRA

◆◆◆ Holiday Inn-Elmira Riverview
    Downtown **M**
(607) 734-4211. **$129.** 760 E Water St. SR 17, exit 56
(Water St), just s on Church St, 0.4 mi e on Judson, just s;
SR 17, exit 57, 0.5 mi s. Ext/int corridors. **Pets:** No service,
supervision, crate.
[ASK] [S🐾] [✕] [🔌] [💻] [🍴] [🏊]

FAIRPORT

AAA ◆ Trail Break Motor Inn **M** ☸
(716) 223-1710. **$35-$69.** 7340 Pittsford-Palmyra Rd. 1.5
mi e of SR 250 on SR 31. Ext corridors. **Pets:** Other. $5
daily fee/pet, $5 one-time fee/pet. No service, supervision,
crate.
[S🐾] [✕] [🔌]

FALCONER

AAA ◆◆ Motel 6–1215 **M**
(716) 665-3670. **$48-$64.** 1980 E Main St. SR 17, exit 13,
just w on SR 394. Int corridors. **Pets:** Small. No service,
supervision, crate.
[S🐾] [✕] [🔊] [🔌]

FARMINGTON

AAA ◆◆ Budget Inn **M** ☸
(716) 924-5020. **$36-$70.** 6001 Rt 96. SR 96 at jct SR 332,
1 mi s of I-90, exit 44. Ext corridors. **Pets:** Small. $5 daily
fee/pet, $5 one-time fee/pet. Supervision.
[SAVE] [S🐾] [✕] [🔌]

FISHKILL

AAA ◆◆◆ MainStay Suites Fishkill **M** ☸
(914) 897-2800. **$125-$135.** 25 Merritt Blvd. I-84, exit 13,
just n. Int corridors. **Pets:** Medium, other. $100 deposit/
room, $5 one-time fee/pet. Supervision.
[SAVE] [S🐾] [✕] [🔊] [🔊] [🔌] [💻] [✕]

◆◆◆ Residence Inn by Marriott **A**
(914) 896-5210. **$139-$159.** 2481 Rt 9. On US 9, just n of
jct I-84, exit 13. Ext corridors. **Pets:** Small. Supervision.
[ASK] [S🐾] [✕] [🔊] [🔌] [💻] [🏊] [✕]

AAA ◆◆ Wellesley Inn & Suites **M**
(914) 896-4995. **$75-$150.** 2477 Rt 9. Just n of I-84, exit
13. Int corridors. **Pets:** Small. Designated rooms, no service, supervision, crate.
[SAVE] [S🐾] [✕] [🔊] [🔊] [🔌] [💻]

GATES

⊕⊕ ◆◆ **Comfort Inn Central** Ⓜ ❀
(716) 436-4400. **$64-$79, 7 days notice.** 395 Buell Rd. SR 204, 0.3 mi w of jct I-390, exit 18B; opposite entrance to Rochester-Monroe County Airport. Int corridors. **Pets:** $25 deposit/pet. Designated rooms, no service, supervision, crate.
[SAVE] [S⊘] [✕] [🖉] [🖥] [💻]

◆◆◆ **Holiday Inn-Airport** Ⓜ❚ ❀
(716) 328-6000. **$115-$115.** 911 Brooks Ave. SR 204 at jct I-390, exit 18A. Int corridors. **Pets:** Small, other. $50 deposit/room. Designated rooms, no service, supervision, crate.
[ASK] [S⊘] [✕] [🖉] [🖥] [💻] [🍴] [🏊]

GENEVA

⊕⊕ ◆◆ **Motel 6-1216** Ⓜ ❀
(315) 789-4050. **$50-$66.** 485 Hamilton St. 1.5 mi w on US 20 and SR 5. Int corridors. **Pets:** Very small. No service, supervision, crate.
[S⊘] [✕]

◆◆◆ **Ramada Inn Geneva Lakefront** Ⓜ❚ ❀
(315) 789-0400. **$99-$149.** 41 Lakefront Dr. I-90, exit 42, 8 mi s on SR 14. Int corridors. **Pets:** Other. $10 daily fee/pet. No service, supervision, crate.
[ASK] [S⊘] [✕] [🖉] [🖥] [💻] [🍴] [🏊]

GREAT NECK

◆◆◆ **Inn at Great Neck** ❚
(516) 773-2000. **$195-$240.** 30 Cutter Mill Rd. From jct Middleneck Rd, just w. Int corridors. **Pets:** Designated rooms, supervision.
[ASK] [✕] [🖉] [🖉] [🖥] [💻] [🍴]

GREECE

⊕⊕ ◆◆◆ **Comfort Inn-West** Ⓜ ❀
(716) 621-5700. **$74-$89, 7 days notice.** 1501 W Ridge Rd. SR 104, 0.5 mi e of jct SR 390 and 104 (Ridge Rd). Int corridors. **Pets:** Other. $10 one-time fee/room. Designated rooms, no service, supervision, crate.
[SAVE] [S⊘] [✕] [🖥] [💻]

◆◆◆ **Hampton Inn-Rochester North** Ⓜ ❀
(716) 663-6070. **$78-$96.** 500 Center Place Dr. I-390, Ridge Rd E exit, just e on Rt 104, just n on Buckman Rd to Center Place Dr. Int corridors. **Pets:** Small, other. No service, supervision, crate.
[✕] [🖉] [🖉] [🖥] [💻]

◆◆◆ **Residence Inn by Marriott-West** Ⓜ ❀
(716) 865-2090. **$84-$169.** 500 Paddy Creek Cir. I-390, exit 24, just e on SR 104 (Ridge Rd), just s on Hoover Dr, just w. Int corridors. **Pets:** Other. $10 daily fee/room, $150 one-time fee/room. No service, supervision, crate.
[ASK] [S⊘] [✕] [🖉] [🖥] [💻] [🏊] [🏊]

⊕⊕ ◆◆ **Wellesley Inn & Suites** Ⓜ ❀
(716) 621-2060. **$60-$105.** 1635 W Ridge Rd. SR 104, just e of I-390. Int corridors. **Pets:** Other. Designated rooms, supervision.
[SAVE] [S⊘] [✕] [🖉] [🖉] [🖉] [🖥] [💻]

HAMLIN

◆◆ **Sandy Creek Manor House** [BB] ❀
(716) 964-7528. **$60-$95.** 1960 Redman Rd. 0.3 mi n of SR 18, 2 mi w of SR 19. Int corridors. **Pets:** Other. $5 daily fee/pet. No service, supervision, crate.
[S⊘] [✕] [🖉] [🖉]

HANCOCK

⊕⊕ ◆◆ **Smiths Colonial Motel** Ⓜ ❀
(607) 637-2989. **$45-$75.** RR 1, Box 172D, Rt 97. SR 17, exit 87; or 87A to Rt 97 S. Ext corridors. **Pets:** Supervision.
[SAVE] [✕]

HARTWICK SEMINARY

⊕⊕ ◆◆◆ **Best Western Cooperstown Inn & Suites** Ⓜ
(607) 547-9439. **$140-$210.** 50 Commons Dr, Rt 28. Center; on SR 28. Int corridors. **Pets:** Supervision.
[SAVE] [S⊘] [✕] [🖉] [🖉] [🖉] [🖥] [🏊]

HAUPPAUGE

◆◆◆ **Wyndham Wind Watch Hotel & Hamlet Golf Club** ❚
(631) 232-9800. **$185.** 1717 Vanderbilt Motor Pkwy. I-495, exit 57, just n to Motor Pkwy, 1.3 mi ne. Int corridors. **Pets:** No service, supervision, crate.
[ASK] [S⊘] [✕] [🖉] [🖥] [💻] [🍴] [🏊] [✕]

HENRIETTA

⊕⊕ ◆◆ **Econo Lodge-Rochester South** Ⓜ ❀
(716) 427-2700. **$64-$79, 7 days notice.** 940 Jefferson Rd. Just w on SR 252, I-390, exit 14A. Int corridors. **Pets:** Other. Supervision.
[SAVE] [S⊘] [✕] [🖥] [💻]

◆◆ **Microtel** Ⓜ ❀
(716) 334-3400. **Call for rates.** 905 Lehigh Station Rd. SR 253, 0.3 mi e of jct SR 15; I-390, northbound exit 12; southbound exit 12A, just n on SR 253. Int corridors. **Pets:** Other. No service, supervision, crate.
[✕] [🖥]

⊕⊕ ◆◆ **Red Roof Inn-Henrietta** Ⓜ ❀
(716) 359-1100. **$48-$83.** 4820 W Henrietta Rd. US 15, just s of jct SR 253. Ext corridors. **Pets:** Other. No service, supervision, crate.
[SAVE] [✕]

◆◆◆ **Residence Inn by Marriott** Ⓐ ❀
(716) 272-8850. **$97-$130.** 1300 Jefferson Rd. I-390, exit 14A, 0.5 mi e. Ext corridors. **Pets:** $6 daily fee/room, $125 one-time fee/room. Supervision.
[✕] [🖉] [🖥] [💻] [🏊] [✕]

HERKIMER

⊕⊕ ◆◆ **Herkimer Motel** Ⓜ ❀
(315) 866-0490. **$46-$68.** 100 Marginal Rd. Jct SR 28 and I-90 (New York Thruway), exit 30. Ext/int corridors. **Pets:** No service, supervision, crate.
[SAVE] [S⊘] [✕] [🖉] [🖥] [🏊]

▲▲▲ ◆ Inn Towne Motel [M] ❀
(315) 866-1101. **$36-$58.** 227 N Washington St. I-90, exit 30, 1 mi n on Rt 28, just w. Ext corridors. **Pets:** Small. $10 one-time fee/room. Designated rooms, no service, supervision, crate.
[SAVE] [✕] [🔋]

HIGHLAND FALLS

▲▲▲ ◆◆ Best Western Palisade Motel [M] ❀
(914) 446-9400. **$80-$120.** 17 Main St. SR 218, at jct US 9 W, 2.5 mi s of US Military Academy s gate. Ext corridors. **Pets:** $25 deposit/room. No service, supervision, crate.
[SAVE] [S🔋] [🔋]

HORSEHEADS

▲▲▲ ◆◆ Motel 6 Horseheads–1217 [M] ❀
(607) 739-2525. **$42-$58.** 4133 Rt 17. S side of Hwy 17, 0.5 mi w of jct Rt 17 and 13. Ext/int corridors. **Pets:** Small, other. No service, supervision, crate.
[S🔋] [✕] [🏠]

HUDSON

◆◆◆ St. Charles Hotel [H] ❀
(518) 822-9900. **$79-$109.** 16-18 Park Pl. Center; on SR 9 (Park Pl), n of jct SR 9G. Int corridors. **Pets:** Other. $75 deposit/room. Supervision.
[✕] [🏠] [&] [🍽]

HUNTER

◆◆◆ Hunter Inn [CI]
(518) 263-3777. **$80-$195.** Rt 23A. On Rt 23A. Int corridors. **Pets:** Supervision.
[✕] [🍽]

ITHACA

▲▲▲ ◆◆◆ Holiday Inn-Executive Tower [M] ❀
(607) 272-1000. **$99-$159, 30 days notice.** 222 S Cayuga St. Just n from SR 96B. Ext/int corridors. **Pets:** Other. $50 deposit/room. No service, supervision, crate.
[SAVE] [S🔋] [✕] [🔋] [🔋] [🍽] [🏠]

◆◆◆ La Tourelle Country Inn [CI] ❀
(607) 273-2734. **$79-$299.** 1150 Danby Rd. 3 mi s on SR 96B from Ithaca. Int corridors. **Pets:** Other. $50 deposit/room. Designated rooms, no service, supervision, crate.
[A$K] [S🔋] [✕] [🔋] [🔋] [✕]

▲▲▲ ◆◆ Meadow Court Inn [M] ❀
(607) 273-3885. **$75-$150.** 529 S Meadow St. 1.5 mi s on SR 13 and 96. Ext/int corridors. **Pets:** Other. $10 daily fee/pet. Supervision.
[✕] [🏠] [🔋] [🍽]

JAMESTOWN

▲▲▲ ◆◆◆ Comfort Inn [M]
(716) 664-5920. **$99-$149.** 2800 N Main St Extension. SR 17, exit 12 (SR 60). Int corridors. **Pets:** Supervision.
[SAVE] [S🔋] [✕] [🔋] [🔋]

JOHNSON CITY

▲▲▲ ◆◆◆ Best Western of Johnson City [M] ❀
(607) 729-9194. **$54-$67.** 569 Harry L Dr. 0.3 mi n of SR 17, exit 70 N; opposite Oakdale Mall. Int corridors. **Pets:** Other. Designated rooms, supervision.
[SAVE] [S🔋] [✕] [🔋]

▲▲▲ ◆◆ Red Roof Inn-Binghamton [M] ❀
(607) 729-8940. **$56-$73.** 590 Fairview St. 0.3 mi n of SR 17, exit 70 N. Ext corridors. **Pets:** Other. Supervision.
[SAVE] [✕]

JOHNSTOWN

◆◆◆ Holiday Inn [M]
(518) 762-4686. **Call for rates.** 308 N Comrie Ave. 2 mi n on SR 30A. Ext/int corridors. **Pets:** No service, supervision, crate.
[✕] [🔋] [🔋] [🍽] [🏠]

KINGSTON

▲▲▲ ◆◆◆ Holiday Inn [M] ❀
(914) 338-0400. **$119-$159.** 503 Washington Ave. I-87, exit 19, just e of traffic circle. Int corridors. **Pets:** Other. No service, supervision, crate.
[SAVE] [S🔋] [✕] [🔋] [🔋] [🍽] [🏠]

LAKE GEORGE

◆◆ Balmoral Motel [M] ❀
(518) 668-2673. **$59-$99.** 444 Canada St. 0.3 mi n on SR 9, at jct Rt 9 and 9 N. Ext corridors. **Pets:** Small, dogs only. $50 deposit/pet, $10 daily fee/pet. Supervision.
[A$K] [S🔋] [✕] [🔋] [🏠]

◆◆ Green Haven [M]
(518) 668-2489. **$64-$114.** 3136 Lake Shore Dr. 1.8 mi n on SR 9 N, 0.8 mi n of I-87, exit 22. Ext corridors. **Pets:** Designated rooms, no service, supervision, crate.
[A$K] [S🔋] [✕] [🔋] [🔋] [🏠] [✕]

▲▲▲ ◆◆ Lyn Aire Motel [M]
(518) 668-4612. **$99-$149.** 1872 SR 9. I-87, exit 21, 1 mi s. Ext corridors. **Pets:** Small. Designated rooms, supervision.
[SAVE] [🔋] [🏠] [✕]

LAKE LUZERNE

▲▲▲ ◆ Luzerne Court [M] ❀
(518) 696-2734. **$50-$90.** 508 Lake Ave. 1.1 mi ne on SR 9 N; from I-87, exit 21, 8.7 mi sw on Rt 9N. Ext corridors. **Pets:** Other. Supervision.
[🔋] [🍽] [🏠] [🔋]

LAKE PLACID

▲▲▲ ◆◆ Art Devlin's Olympic Motor Inn, Inc [M] ❀
(518) 523-3700. **$58-$118.** 350 Main St. 0.5 mi s on SR 86. Ext corridors. **Pets:** Other. Supervision.
[✕] [🔋] [🏠]

Best Western-Golden Arrow Hotel 🏨 🐾
(518) 523-3353. **$79-$169, 7 days notice.** 150 Main St. Center. Int corridors. **Pets:** $25 one-time fee/pet. Designated rooms, no service, supervision, crate.

Edge of the Lake Motel 🏨 🐾
(518) 523-9430. **$61-$109.** 56 Saranac Ave. 0.5 mi w on SR 86. Ext/int corridors. **Pets:** Medium. $5 daily fee/pet. No service, supervision, crate.

Hilton Lake Placid Resort 🏨 🐾
(518) 523-4411. **$119-$199, 7 days notice.** 1 Mirror Lake Dr. 0.3 mi w on SR 86. Int corridors. **Pets:** $50 deposit/pet, $25 one-time fee/pet. No service, supervision, crate.

Howard Johnson Resort Inn 🏨 🐾
(518) 523-9555. **$70-$130, 3 days notice.** 90 Saranac Ave. Ext/int corridors. **Pets:** Other. Supervision.

Lake Placid Ramada Inn 🏨 🐾
(518) 523-2587. **$59-$140, 3 days notice.** 8-12 Saranac Ave. 0.3 mi w on SR 86. Ext/int corridors. **Pets:** Other. No service, supervision, crate.

Lake Placid Resort/Holiday Inn 🏨 🐾
(518) 523-2556. **$69-$229, 7 days notice.** 1 Olympic Dr. Center. Int corridors. **Pets:** $75 deposit/pet. Supervision.

Swiss Acres Inn & Restaurant 🏨
(518) 523-3040. **$50-$85, 7 days notice.** 189 Saranac Ave. 1 mi w on SR 86. Ext/int corridors. **Pets:** Supervision.

LANSING

Econo Lodge 🏨 🐾
(607) 257-1400. **$46-$125, 7 days notice.** 2303 N Triphammer Rd. 3.5 mi n on SR 13, Triphammer Rd exit; adjoining Cayuga Mall. Int corridors. **Pets:** Small, other. $10 daily fee/pet. No service, supervision, crate.

Ramada Inn-Airport 🏨
(607) 257-3100. **$95-$179.** 2310 N Triphammer Rd. Jct SR 13 and 34, 3.5 mi n on SR 13, Triphammer Rd exit, just w. Int corridors. **Pets:** No service, supervision, crate.

LATHAM

Century House Restaurant & Hotel 🏨 🐾
(518) 785-0931. **$109-$129.** 997 New Loudon Rd. 9 mi n on US 9; 1.5 mi n of jct SR 7. Int corridors. **Pets:** Medium, dogs only. Supervision.

Hampton Inn-Latham 🏨 🐾
(518) 785-0000. **$109-$134.** US 9, just n of jct Rt 7 and I-87, exit 7. Int corridors. **Pets:** Small. $75 deposit/room. Designated rooms, supervision.

Microtel Inn 🏨 🐾
(518) 782-9161. **$47-$80, 7 days notice.** 7 Rensselaer Ave. Just w of I-87, exit 6. Int corridors. **Pets:** Other. Supervision.

Residence Inn by Marriott Albany Airport 🅰
(518) 783-0600. **$155-$205.** 1 Residence Inn Dr. On SR 7, 2 mi w of jct I-87, exit 6. Ext corridors. **Pets:** Small. Supervision.

LIBERTY

Days Inn Liberty 🏨
(914) 292-7600. **$52-$95.** 25 Sullivan Ave. SR 17, exit 100, 0.3 mi e. Int corridors. **Pets:** No service, supervision, crate.

Ramada Limited 🏨 🐾
(914) 292-7171. **$99-$120.** 7 Rt 52 E. SR 17, exit 100, just e. Int corridors. **Pets:** Other. $5 daily fee/pet, $5 one-time fee/pet. Supervision.

LITTLE FALLS

Best Western Little Falls Motor Inn 🏨 🐾
(315) 823-4954. **$60-$75.** 20 Albany St. On SR 5 and 167. Int corridors. **Pets:** Other. $10 deposit/room. Supervision.

LIVERPOOL

Days Inn-North 🏨
(315) 451-1511. **$69-$210, 5 days notice.** 400 7th North St. 4 mi n, w of I-81, exit 7th North St, at jct I-90 (New York Thruway), exit 36 and I-81. Ext/int corridors. **Pets:** No service, supervision, crate.

Hampton Inn 🏨 🐾
(315) 457-9900. **$67-$105.** 417 7th N St. I-81, exit 7th North St at jct I-90 (New York Thruway), exit 36. Int corridors. **Pets:** Other. Supervision.

Holiday Inn Syracuse/Liverpool 🏨
(315) 457-1122. **$120-$150.** 441 Electronics Pkwy. I-90 (New York Thruway), exit 37, 1.3 mi w of I-81, exit 25, 7th N St at Electronics Pkwy. Int corridors. **Pets:** Designated rooms, no service, supervision, crate.

Homewood Suites 🏨 🐾
(315) 451-3800. **$199, 7 days notice.** 275 Elwood Davis Rd. 1 mi w of jct I-81, exit 7th N St. Int corridors. **Pets:** Small. $75 one-time fee/pet. No service, supervision, crate.

Knights Inn M ✿
(315) 453-6330. **$35-$99.** 430 Electronics Pkwy. Just s of I-90 (New York Thruway), exit 37 (Electronics Pkwy). Ext corridors. **Pets:** Very small. Supervision.
SAVE Sₐ ✕ 🖬

LIVINGSTON MANOR

The Magical Land of Oz B & B BB
(914) 438-3418. **$75-$85.** 455 Shandelee Rd. SR 17, exit 96, 4 mi s following signs. Int corridors. **Pets:** Medium. Designated rooms, no service, supervision, crate.
ASK ✕ AC CTV ✆

LONG LAKE

Journey's End Cottages C ✿
(518) 624-5381. **$625-$700, 60 days notice.** Deerland Rd, Rt 30. 1 mi s on SR 30 and 28 N. Ext corridors. **Pets:** Medium. Supervision.
🖬 ✕ AC ✆

Long View Lodge CI ✿
(518) 624-2862. **$65-$85, 7 days notice.** Rt 28 N & 30. 2.3 mi s on SR 30 and 28 N. Int corridors. **Pets:** Designated rooms, supervision.
✕ 🖬 ⑪ ✕ AC

LOWMAN

Red Jacket Motor Inn MI ✿
(607) 734-1616. **$39-$75, 3 days notice.** Rt 17. SR 17, just e from CR 8 (between MM 195 and 196). Ext corridors. **Pets:** Dogs only. $10 daily fee/pet, $10 one-time fee/pet. Supervision.
SAVE Sₐ ✕ 🖬 ⑪ 🖾 ✕

MALONE

Four Seasons Motel M
(518) 483-3490. **$45-$59.** 236 W Main St. 1 mi w on SR 11. Ext corridors. **Pets:** Medium. Supervision.
SAVE Sₐ ✕ 🖬 🖾

Super 8 Motel at Jons M ✿
(518) 483-8123. **$60-$66, 5 days notice.** Finny Blvd, Rt 30. SR 30 S, just s of jct SR 11 and 30. Int corridors. **Pets:** Medium. Designated rooms, no service, supervision, crate.
SAVE Sₐ ✕ ⑪ 🖬

MCGRAW

Econo Lodge of Cortland M ✿
(607) 753-7594. **$54-$95, 30 days notice.** 3775 US Rt 11. I-81, exit 10. Int corridors. **Pets:** Very small, dogs only. $10 daily fee/pet, $10 one-time fee/pet. Designated rooms, no service, supervision, crate.
SAVE Sₐ ✕

MIDDLETOWN

Middletown Motel M ✿
(914) 342-2535. **$50-$90, 7 days notice.** 501 Rt 211 E. At jct SR 17, exit 120 and SR 211. Ext/int corridors. **Pets:** Designated rooms, no service, supervision, crate.
✕ ⑪ 🖬 🖾

Super 8 Motel M
(914) 692-5828. **$65-$95.** 563 Rt 211 E. SR 211, 0.3 mi e of jct SR 17, exit 120; 0.5 mi n of I-84, exit 4 W. Int corridors. **Pets:** Supervision.
ASK Sₐ ✕ CTV

MONTOUR FALLS

Falls Motel M ✿
(607) 535-7262. **$65-$125.** 239 N Genesee St. SR 14 S, just w; SR 14 N, just w, then just e. Ext corridors. **Pets:** Small. Supervision.
ASK ✕ 🖬

Relax Inn M ✿
(607) 535-7183. **$44-$89, 3 days notice.** 100 Clawson Blvd. Jct SR 14 and 224. Ext corridors. **Pets:** Small, dogs only. $10 deposit/pet, $10 daily fee/pet, $10 one-time fee/pet. Designated rooms, no service, supervision, crate.
SAVE Sₐ ✕ 🖬

NEW HAMPTON

Days Inn-Middletown M ✿
(914) 374-2411. **$49-$89.** Rt 17M. On US 6 and SR 17M, 0.8 mi s of jct I-84, exit 3 E. Ext/int corridors. **Pets:** Supervision.
ASK Sₐ ✕ 🖬 🖾

NEW HARTFORD

Holiday Inn Utica MI ✿
(315) 797-2131. **$89-$159.** 1777 Burrstone Rd. I-90 (New York Thruway), exit 31, 4.5 mi w on SR 5 W, exit on Burrstone Rd, 1 mi nw. Int corridors. **Pets:** Medium, dogs only. $25 deposit/room. No service, supervision, crate.
ASK Sₐ ✕ ✆ 🖬 ▣ ⑪ 🖾

NEW YORK METROPOLITAN AREA

ELMSFORD

Hampton Inn White Plains/Tarrytown M ✿
(914) 592-5680. **$117-$129.** 200 Tarrytown Rd. SR 119 W (Tarrytown Rd); I-287, exit 1; I-87, exit 8, just s. Int corridors. **Pets:** Other. No service, supervision, crate.
ASK Sₐ ✕ 🚹 ✆ 🚭 🖬 ▣ 🖾

MOUNT KISCO

Holiday Inn MI ✿
(914) 241-2600. **$160.** 1 Holiday Inn Dr. Sawmill Pkwy, exit 37, just e. Int corridors. **Pets:** Medium. $5 one-time fee/room. No service, supervision, crate.
SAVE Sₐ ✕ ✆ 🚭 🖬 ▣ ⑪ 🖾

NEW YORK

◆◆◆◆ The Carlyle 🅷
(212) 744-1600. **Call for rates.** 35 E 76th St. At Madison Ave. Int corridors. **Pets:** No service, supervision, crate.

◆◆◆ Courtyard by Marriott/Manhattan-Times Square South 🅼
(212) 391-0088. **Call for rates.** 114 W 40th St. Between Broadway and 6th Ave. Int corridors. **Pets:** Small. No service, supervision, crate.

◆◆◆ Crowne Plaza Manhattan 🅷
(212) 977-4000. **Call for rates.** 1605 Broadway. 49th and Broadway. Int corridors. **Pets:** No service, supervision, crate.

◆◆◆ Dumont Plaza Suite Hotel 🅷 🐾
(212) 481-7600. **$321-$351.** 150 E 34th. Between Lexington and 3rd Ave. Int corridors. **Pets:** Very small, dogs only. $200 deposit/room. Designated rooms, no service, supervision, crate.

◆◆◆◆ The Essex House-A Westin Hotel 🅷 🐾
(212) 247-0300. **Call for rates.** 160 Central Park S. Between 6th (Ave of the Americas) and 7th aves. Int corridors. **Pets:** Medium. Supervision.

◆◆◆◆◆ Four Seasons Hotel, New York 🅷 🐾
(212) 758-5700. **$535-$665, 3 days notice.** 57 E 57th St. Between Park and Madison. Int corridors. **Pets:** Very small. Supervision.

◆◆◆ Holiday Inn Broadway 🅼
(212) 736-3800. **$269-$399.** 49 W 32nd St. Corner of Broadway and 32nd St. Int corridors. **Pets:** Medium. No service, supervision, crate.

◆◆◆ Holiday Inn Wall Street Hotel 🅷 🐾
(212) 232-7700. **$219-$219, 21 days notice.** 15 Gold St. Corner of Gold and Platt sts. Int corridors. **Pets:** Medium. $100 deposit/room. Supervision.

◆◆◆◆ Hotel Plaza Athenee 🅷 🐾
(212) 734-9100. **$430-$620.** 37 E 64th St. Between Madison and Park aves. Int corridors. **Pets:** Medium. Supervision.

◆◆◆ La Guardia Marriott Hotel 🅷 🐾
(718) 565-8900. **$239.** 102-05 Ditmars Blvd. 0.3 mi e of 94th St exit of Grand Central Pkwy. Int corridors. **Pets:** Very small. Supervision.

Ⓐ◆◆◆◆ Le Parker Meridien New York 🅷 🐾
(212) 245-5000. **$365-$435.** 118 W 57th St. Between 6th and 7th aves, (vehicle entrance on 56th St). Int corridors. **Pets:** Other. Supervision.

◆◆◆ Loews New York Hotel 🅷 🐾
(212) 752-7000. **$319.** 569 Lexington Ave. Lexington Ave at E 51st St. Int corridors. **Pets:** Small, other. No service, supervision, crate.

◆◆◆◆ The Lowell Hotel 🅷
(212) 838-1400. **Call for rates.** 28 E 63rd St. Between Park and Madison aves. Int corridors. **Pets:** Designated rooms, no service, supervision, crate.

Ⓐ◆◆ The Mayflower Hotel On The Park 🅷 🐾
(212) 265-0060. **$190-$250.** 15 Central Park W. At 61st St. Int corridors. **Pets:** Other. Designated rooms, supervision.

◆◆◆ Millennium Broadway 🅷 🐾
(212) 768-4400. **$290-$410.** 145 W 44th St. Between 6th and 7th aves. Int corridors. **Pets:** Medium. Supervision.

Ⓐ◆◆◆ New York Marriott Marquis 🅷
(212) 398-1900. **$335-$520.** 1535 Broadway. Between 45th and 46th sts, motor entrance on 46th St. Int corridors. **Pets:** Small. Designated rooms, no service, supervision, crate.

Ⓐ◆◆◆◆ The New York Palace 🅷 🐾
(212) 888-7000. **$540-$690.** 455 Madison Ave. Between 50th and 51st (valet parking access on 50th). Int corridors. **Pets:** Very small. No service, supervision, crate.

◆◆ Novotel New York 🅷
(212) 315-0100. **$119-$249.** 226 W 52nd St. At Broadway; motor access on 52nd. Int corridors. **Pets:** Small. Designated rooms, no service, supervision, crate.

◆◆◆◆ The Peninsula New York 🅷 🐾
(212) 956-2888. **$550-$1750.** 700 5th Ave. 5th Ave at 55th St. Int corridors. **Pets:** Small, dogs only. Supervision.

◆◆◆◆ The Pierre 🅷 🐾
(212) 838-8000. **Call for rates.** 2 E 61st St. At 5th Ave. Int corridors. **Pets:** Very small, other. Supervision.

◆◆◆ The Regency Hotel 🅷
(212) 759-4100. **Call for rates.** 540 Park Ave. At 61st. Int corridors. **Pets:** Very small. Supervision.

AAA ◆◆◆◆ Renaissance New York Hotel **H** ❀
(212) 765-7676. **$299-$415.** 714 7th Ave at 48th St. Times Square, Broadway and 7th Ave; auto access from 7th Ave. Int corridors. **Pets:** Medium, dogs only. $50 one-time fee/room. Supervision.

◆◆◆ Sheraton Manhattan Hotel **H**
(212) 581-3300. **Call for rates.** 790 7th Ave. Between 51st and 52nd sts. Int corridors. **Pets:** No service, supervision, crate.
🗙 ♿ 🐾 📠 🍴

◆◆◆ Sheraton New York Hotel & Towers **H**
(212) 581-1000. **Call for rates.** 811 7th Ave. At 52nd St. Int corridors. **Pets:** No service, supervision, crate.
🗙 ♿ 🐾 📠 🍴

◆◆◆ Southgate Tower Suite Hotel **H**
(212) 563-1800. **$278-$308.** 371 7th Ave. At 31st St. Int corridors. **Pets:** Supervision.
ASK 🗙 🐾 📠 🍴

◆◆◆ Surrey Hotel **H** ❀
(212) 288-3700. **$450-$480.** 20 E 76th. 76th and Madison. Int corridors. **Pets:** Supervision.
ASK 🗙 🐾 📠

◆◆◆ Swissotel New York-The Drake **H**
(212) 421-0900. **Call for rates.** 440 Park Ave. At 56th St, between Park and Madison aves. Int corridors. **Pets:** Supervision.
🗙 🐾 📠 🍴

AAA ◆◆◆ The Warwick New York **H**
(212) 247-2700. **$245-$260.** 65 W 54th St. Corner of 54th St and 6th Ave. Int corridors. **Pets:** Designated rooms, supervision.
🗙 🐾 📠

PEEKSKILL

AAA ◆◆ Peekskill Inn **M** ❀
(914) 739-1500. **$95-$120.** 634 Main St. Rt 9 and jct Rt 6, e to top of Main St. Ext corridors. **Pets:** Small. No service, supervision, crate.
🗙 🍴

SUFFERN

AAA ◆◆ Wellesley Inn & Suites **M** ❀
(914) 368-1900. **$71-$103.** 17 N Airmont Rd. I-87 (287), exit 14B, just s. Int corridors. **Pets:** Small. $25 deposit/room. Designated rooms, no service, supervision, crate.
🗙 🐾 📠

TARRYTOWN

AAA ◆◆◆ Hilton of Tarrytown **M** ❀
(914) 631-5700. **$109-$279.** 455 S Broadway. US 9 S thruway, I-287/87, exit 9. Int corridors. **Pets:** Medium. No service, supervision, crate.
🗙 🐾 📠 🍴 🗙

❀   **END METROPOLITAN AREA**   ❀

NIAGARA FALLS METROPOLITAN AREA

NEWFANE

◆◆ Lake Ontario Motel **M** ❀
(716) 778-5004. **$37-$84, 5 days notice.** 3330 Lockport-Olcott Rd. 2.2 mi n of jct SR 104 on SR 78. Int corridors. **Pets:** No service, supervision, crate.
ASK 🗙 📠

NIAGARA FALLS

AAA ◆◆◆ Best Western Inn on the River **M**
(716) 283-7612. **$89-$169.** 7001 Buffalo Ave. I-190, exit 21, just s on SR 384. Int corridors. **Pets:** Small. No service, supervision, crate.
🗙 📠 🍴 🗙

AAA ◆◆◆ Best Western Summit Inn **M** ❀
(716) 297-5050. **$89-$139.** 9500 Niagara Falls Blvd. I-190, exit 22, 2.1 mi e on US 62. Int corridors. **Pets:** No service, supervision, crate.
🗙 📠

AAA ◆◆ Knights Inn **M** ❀
(716) 297-3647. **$68-$89, 7 days notice.** 9900 Niagara Falls Blvd. I-190, exit 22, 2.5 mi s on US 62 (Niagara Falls Blvd); I-290, exit 3, 10 mi n on US 62 (Niagara Falls Blvd). Ext corridors. **Pets:** Other. $100 deposit/room. Designated rooms, no service, supervision, crate.
🗙 📠

◆◆ Ramada Inn at the Falls **M** ❀
(716) 282-1212. **$65-$145.** 240 Rainbow Blvd N. Downtown; adjoining Rainbow Shopping Center. Int corridors. **Pets:** $25 deposit/room. No service, supervision, crate.
ASK 🗙 🐾 📠 🍴

AAA ◆ Travelers Budget Inn **M** ❀
(716) 297-3228. **$29-$109, 3 days notice.** 9001 Niagara Falls Blvd. I-190 exit 22, 1.7 mi e on US 62. Ext corridors. **Pets:** Other. $10 daily fee/room, $10 one-time fee/room. Designated rooms, no service, supervision, crate.
🗙 📠

❀   **END METROPOLITAN AREA**   ❀

NORTH SYRACUSE

◆◆◆ The Club Hotel by DoubleTree Airport
Area ▥ ❀
(315) 457-4000. **$99-$99, 3 days notice.** 6701 Buckley Rd.
0.8 mi w of jct I-81 (7th North St) and I-90, exit 36. Int
corridors. **Pets:** $20 deposit/room. Supervision.
🅰🅢 ⬚ ⊠ ⬚ ⬚ ⬚ ⬚ ⬚

NORWICH

◆◆ Howard Johnson Hotel ▥ ❀
(607) 334-2200. **$99-$159, 3 days notice.** 75 N Broad St.
Downtown, on SR 12. Int corridors. **Pets:** Other. $5 one-
time fee/room. Designated rooms, no service, supervision,
crate.
🅰🅢 ⬚ ⊠ ⬚ ⬚ ⬚ ⬚

OGDENSBURG

◆◆ Days Inn-Ogdensburg ▥ ❀
(315) 393-3200. **$48-$75.** 1200 Patterson St. At jct Rt 68
and 37. Ext corridors. **Pets:** Other. $7 one-time fee/pet. No
service, supervision, crate.
🅰🅢 ⬚ ⊠ ⬚ ⬚

◆◆◆ The Stonefence Hotel, Motel ▥ ❀
(315) 393-1545. **$63-$119.** 7191 St Hwy 37. On SR 37, 0.5
mi w of Western jct SR 68. Ext/int corridors. **Pets:** Medium,
dogs only. $13 one-time fee/room. Designated rooms, no
service, supervision, crate.
⊠ ⬚ ⬚ ⬚ ⬚

OLD FORGE

◆◆◆ Best Western Sunset Inn ▥
(315) 369-6836. **$99-$189, 7 days notice.** Rt 28. 0.3 mi s.
Ext/int corridors. **Pets:** Designated rooms, no service,
supervision, crate.
⬚ ⊠ ⬚ ⬚ ⬚

OLEAN

◆◆◆ Hampton Inn ▥
(716) 375-1000. **Call for rates.** 101-109 Main St. Downtown; on Main St at Union St (SR 16). Int corridors.
Pets: No service, supervision, crate.
⊠ ⬚ ⬚ ⬚ ⬚

ONEONTA

◆◆◆ Holiday Inn Oneonta/Cooperstown
Area ▥
(607) 433-2250. **$199.** Rt 23 Southside. On SR 23, 1.5 mi e
of jct I-88, exit 15. Int corridors. **Pets:** No service, supervision, crate.
⬚ ⬚ ⊠ ⬚ ⬚ ⬚ ⬚ ⬚ ⬚

◆◆ Super 8 Motel ▥ ❀
(607) 432-9505. **Call for rates.** 4973 SR 23. SR 23, 0.3 mi
e of I-88, exit 15. Int corridors. **Pets:** Medium. Designated
rooms, supervision.
⊠ ⬚ ⬚

OWEGO

◆◆ Sunrise Motel ▥ ❀
(607) 687-5667. **$43-$49.** 3778 Waverly Rd. SR 17, exit 64,
SR 96 across river w to 17C, then 2 mi on left. Ext corridors. **Pets:** Small. $5 daily fee/room. No service, supervi-
sion, crate.
⬚ ⬚ ⊠

PAINTED POST

◆◆◆ Best Western Lodge on the
Green ▥ ❀
(607) 962-2456. **$80-$80.** 3171 Canada Rd. SR 17, exit 44,
s to Gang Mills exit, then n. Ext corridors. **Pets:** Other. No
service, supervision, crate.
⬚ ⬚ ⊠ ⬚ ⬚ ⬚ ⬚

PARKSVILLE

◆◆◆ Best Western Paramount ▥
(914) 292-6700. **$45-$220.** Tanzman Rd. 0.3 mi n following
signs, SR 17, exit 98. Int corridors. **Pets:** Supervision.
⬚ ⬚ ⬚ ⬚ ⬚ ⬚

PEMBROKE

◆◆ Darien Lakes Econolodge ▥ ❀
(716) 599-4681. **$60-$80.** 8493 SR 77. On SR 77, 0.3 mi s
of I-90, exit 48A. Int corridors. **Pets:** Other. No service,
supervision, crate.
🅰🅢 ⬚ ⊠ ⬚ ⬚

PINE VALLEY

◆◆◆ Best Western Marshall
Manor ▥ ❀
(607) 739-3891. **$57-$71.** 3527 Watkins Rd. SR 14, 5 mi n
of jct SR 17, exit 52. Ext corridors. **Pets:** $4 daily fee/pet.
No service, supervision, crate.
⬚ ⬚ ⊠ ⬚ ⬚ ⬚

PLAINVIEW

◆◆◆ Residence Inn by Marriott ▥ ❀
(516) 433-6200. **$189-$199.** 9 Gerhard Rd. Off Old Country
Rd, opposite Central General Hospital; I-495 (Long Island
Expwy), exit 44 S, exit 10, just e. Int corridors.
Pets: Medium, other. $20 daily fee/pet, $100 one-time fee/
room. No service, supervision, crate.
⊠ ⬚ ⬚ ⬚ ⬚ ⬚ ⬚

PLATTSBURGH

◆◆◆ Baymont Inn & Suites-Plattsburgh ▥ ❀
(518) 562-4000. **$67-$77.** 16 Plaza Blvd. I-87, exit 37. Int
corridors. **Pets:** Medium. Designated rooms, no service,
supervision, crate.
⬚ ⊠ ⬚ ⬚ ⬚ ⬚ ⬚

◆◆ The Inn at Smithfield by Best
Western ▥ ❀
(518) 561-7750. **$79-$99.** 446 Rt 3. Jct I-87 Northway, exit
37. Int corridors. **Pets:** Other. Supervision.
⬚ ⬚ ⊠ ⬚ ⬚ ⬚ ⬚

PORT JERVIS

[AAA] ◆◆◆ **Comfort Inn** [MI] 🐾
(914) 856-6611. **$69-$119.** 40 Greenville Tpke. I-84, exit 1, follow signs. Int corridors. **Pets:** Medium. $50 deposit/pet. Designated rooms, no service, supervision, crate.
[SAVE] [S/D] ⊠ ⬛ 📺 🍴 🏊

POUGHKEEPSIE

◆◆◆ **Holiday Inn Express** [MI]
(914) 473-1151. **$109-$169.** 341 South Rd. US 9, 1.8 mi s of jct US 44 and SR 55. Int corridors. **Pets:** No service, supervision, crate.
[ASK] [S/D] ⊠ 👂 ♿ ⬛ 🏊

RIPLEY

[AAA] ◆ **Budget Host Colonial Squire** [M] 🐾
(716) 736-8000. **$49-$55, 7 days notice.** 6151 Shortman Rd. I-90, exit 61. Ext corridors. **Pets:** Supervision.
[SAVE] [S/D] ⊠ 🏊

RIVERHEAD

◆◆◆ **Ramada Inn-East End** [MI] 🐾
(631) 369-2200. **$149-$189.** 1830 SR 25. I-495, exit 72 (SR 25 E). Int corridors. **Pets:** $100 deposit/room. No service, supervision, crate.
[ASK] [S/D] ⊠ ⬛ 🍴 🏊

ROCHESTER

[AAA] ◆◆◆ **Crowne Plaza Rochester** [H] 🐾
(716) 546-3450. **$89-$129.** 70 State St. Downtown. Int corridors. **Pets:** Small, other. Supervision.
[SAVE] [S/D] ⊠ 👂 ⬛ 📺 🍴 🏊

ROCKVILLE CENTRE

[AAA] ◆◆◆ **Holiday Inn** [MI] 🐾
(516) 678-1300. **$155-$165.** 173 Sunrise Hwy. On SR 27. Ext corridors. **Pets:** Other. $15 daily fee/pet, $15 one-time fee/pet. Supervision.
[SAVE] [S/D] ⊠ 🚶 ⬛ 📺 🍴 🏊

ROME

◆ **Adirondack Thirteen Pines Motel** [M] 🐾
(315) 337-4930. **$40-$50, 3 days notice.** 7353 River Rd. SR 365 E, 0.5 mi e of jct Hwy 49. Ext corridors. **Pets:** Small, dogs only. No service, supervision, crate.
⬛ 🏊 ✂

[AAA] ◆ **American Heritage Motor Inn** [M]
(315) 339-3610. **$35-$55.** 799 Lower Lawrence St. Hwy 49, 69 and 26, Lawrence St exit. Ext corridors. **Pets:** Supervision.
[SAVE] [S/D] ⊠ ⬛

[AAA] ◆◆ **Beeches-Paul Revere Motor Lodge** [MI] 🐾
(315) 336-1776. **$56-$69.** 7900 Turin Rd. SR 26, 2 mi n of jct SR 46. Ext corridors. **Pets:** Other. $5 daily fee/room. Supervision.
[SAVE] [S/D] ⊠ ⬛ 🍴 🏊

ROSCOE

[AAA] ◆◆ **Roscoe Motel** [M]
(607) 498-5220. **$45-$65.** Old Rt 17. SR 17, exit 94, 0.5 mi n on SR 206, just w. Ext corridors. **Pets:** Supervision.
⬛ 🏊 ☎

ROTTERDAM

◆◆ **Super 8 Schenectady** [M] 🐾
(518) 355-2190. **Call for rates.** 3083 Carman Rd. At jct Curry and Carman rds; I-90, exit 25. Int corridors. **Pets:** Supervision.
⊠ ⬛

SARANAC LAKE

[AAA] ◆◆◆ **Adirondack Comfort Inn** [MI] 🐾
(518) 891-1970. **$75-$120.** 148 Lake Flower Ave. 0.8 mi e on SR 86. Int corridors. **Pets:** $20 one-time fee/room. Designated rooms, no service, supervision, crate.
[SAVE] [S/D] ⊠ 🍴 🏊

[AAA] ◆ **Adirondack Motel** [M] 🐾
(518) 891-2116. **$50-$135, 7 days notice.** 23 Lake Flower Ave. 0.5 mi e on SR 86. Ext corridors. **Pets:** Dogs only. $5 daily fee/pet. No service, supervision, crate.
⊠ ⬛ ✂

[AAA] ◆◆◆ **The Hotel Saranac of Paul Smith's College** [MI] 🐾
(518) 891-2200. **$75-$105, 3 days notice.** 101 Main St. Center. Int corridors. **Pets:** Other. $5 daily fee/pet. Supervision.
[SAVE] [S/D] ⊠ 👂 ⬛ 📺

◆ **Lake Flower Inn** [M] 🐾
(518) 891-2310. **$68-$92.** 15 Lake Flower Ave. 0.6 mi se on SR 86. Ext corridors. **Pets:** Dogs only. Designated rooms, supervision.
⊠ 🏊 ✂

[AAA] ◆◆ **Lake Side Motel** [M]
(518) 891-4333. **$49-$99, 3 days notice.** 27 Lake Flower Ave. 0.5 mi se on SR 86. Ext corridors. **Pets:** Supervision.
[SAVE] [S/D] ⊠ ⬛ 🏊 ✂

SARATOGA SPRINGS

◆◆◆ **Holiday Inn** [MI] 🐾
(518) 584-4550. **$219-$279, 3 days notice.** 232 Broadway, Rt 9. Just s on US 9, at jct SR 50. Int corridors. **Pets:** Other. Supervision.
[ASK] [S/D] ⊠ 👂 ⬛ 📺 🍴 🏊

[AAA] ◆◆◆ **Union Gables Bed & Breakfast** [BB]
(518) 584-1558. **$240-$300.** 55 Union Ave. I-87 Northway, exit 14, 1.8 mi s. Int corridors. **Pets:** No service, supervision, crate.
⊠ ⬛ ✂

SCHENECTADY

◆◆ **Days Inn** [M] 🐾
(518) 370-3297. **$79-$99.** 167 Nott Terr. 2 blks n of jct State St (SR 5) and Nott Terr. Int corridors. **Pets:** Other. $15 daily fee/pet. Designated rooms, no service, supervision, crate.
[ASK] [S/D] ⊠ 👂 ⬛ 📺

◆◆◆ **Holiday Inn-Downtown Schenectady** 🅼
(518) 393-4141. **$89-$129.** 100 Nott Terr. Center; 2 blks n of jct Nott Terr. and State St (SR 5). Int corridors. **Pets:** Supervision.
🄰🅂🄺 🆂🛏 ⊠ 🛢 📟 ▥ 🍴 ⌖ ⊠

SCHROON LAKE

🆊 ◆ **Blue Ridge Motel** 🅼
(518) 532-7521. **$55-$75.** 6 mi n on US 9, exit 28, 4 mi n on US 9. Ext/int corridors. **Pets:** Supervision.
🆂🄰🅅🄴 🆂🛏 ⊠ 📟 ⌖ ⊠ 🄲🅅 ▤

SOUTH WORCESTER

◆◆ **Charlotte Valley Inn Bed & Breakfast** 🅱🅱 ❀
(607) 397-8164. **$115-$125, 7 days notice.** 480 CR 40. SR 23, 0.5 mi n on Deleware CR 9/40. Int corridors. **Pets:** Medium, dogs only. $25 one-time fee/pet. Designated rooms, supervision.
🄰🅂🄺 🆂🛏 ⊠ 🄺 🄲🅅

SOUTHPORT

🆊 ◆◆ **Coachman Motor Lodge** 🅼 ❀
(607) 733-5526. **$55-$90.** SR 17, exit 56, follow signs 1.8 mi s on SR 14. Ext corridors. **Pets:** Medium. No service, supervision, crate.
🆂🄰🅅🄴 🆂🛏 🛢 📟

SYRACUSE

◆◆ **Days Inn Syracuse East** 🅼 ❀
(315) 437-5998. **$55-$85, 7 days notice.** 6609 Thompson Rd. I-90, exit 35, at Carrier Cir. Int corridors. **Pets:** $10 daily fee/pet. Designated rooms, no service, supervision, crate.
🄰🅂🄺 🆂🛏 ⊠ 🛢

🆊 ◆◆◆ **Holiday Inn/Farrell Road** 🅼 ❀
(315) 457-8700. **$89-$89.** 100 Farrell Rd. Exit 39 Thruway to I-690 E to John Glenn Blvd exit. Int corridors. **Pets:** Supervision.
🆂🄰🅅🄴 🆂🛏 ⊠ ♿ 🐾 🛢 🛢 📟 🍴 ⌖

🆊 ◆◆ **Ramada Limited-University/Carrier Circle** 🅼 ❀
(315) 463-0202. **$59-$99.** 6590 Thompson Rd. I-90, exit 35 (Carrier Cir), just w. Int corridors. **Pets:** Other. $10 one-time fee/room. Supervision.
🆂🄰🅅🄴 🆂🛏 ⊠ 🛢

🆊 ◆◆ **Red Roof Inn** 🅼
(315) 437-3309. **$56-$73.** 6614 N Thompson Rd. At Thruway exit 35 (Carrier Cir). Ext corridors. **Pets:** Supervision.
🆂🄰🅅🄴 ⊠ 🐾

TICONDEROGA

🆊 ◆ **Circle Court Motel** 🅼
(518) 585-7660. **$54-$64.** 440 Montcalm St. SR 9 N; at Liberty Monument traffic circle. Ext corridors. **Pets:** Medium. Supervision.
🆂🄰🅅🄴 🆂🛏 🛢

UNIONDALE

◆◆◆ **Long Island Marriott Hotel & Conference Center** 🄷
(516) 794-3800. **$179-$215.** 101 James Doolittle Blvd. Meadowbrook Pkwy, exit M4 (follow signs to coliseum), exit Hempstead Tpke W; adjacent to Nassau Coliseum. Int corridors. **Pets:** Medium. No service, supervision, crate.
⊠ 🐾 🛢 📟 🍴 ⌖ ⊠

UTICA

🆊 ◆ **A-1 Motel** 🅼 ❀
(315) 735-6698. **$50-$60, 5 days notice.** 238 N Genesee St. Just s of Thruway, exit 31. Int corridors. **Pets:** Medium, dogs only. Supervision.
🆂🄰🅅🄴 🆂🛏 ⊠ 🛢

◆◆◆ **Best Western Gateway Adirondack Inn** 🅼 ❀
(315) 732-4121. **$75-$170.** 175 N Genesee St. 0.5 mi s of I-90 Thruway, exit 31. Int corridors. **Pets:** Supervision.
🄰🅂🄺 🆂🛏 ⊠ 🐾 🛢 📟

◆◆◆ **Radisson Hotel-Utica Centre** 🄷 ❀
(315) 797-8010. **$119-$159.** 200 Genesee St. Downtown. Int corridors. **Pets:** $30 deposit/room, $10 one-time fee/room. No service, supervision, crate.
🄰🅂🄺 🆂🛏 ⊠ 🛢 📟 🍴 ⌖

🆊 ◆◆ **Red Roof Inn** 🅼 ❀
(315) 724-7128. **$65-$105.** 20 Weaver St. I-90, exit 31. Ext corridors. **Pets:** Medium, other. Supervision.
🆂🄰🅅🄴 ⊠ 🐾

VALATIE

🆊 ◆◆ **Blue Spruce Inn & Suites** 🅼 ❀
(518) 758-9711. **$55-$80, 7 days notice.** 3093 Route 9. 1 mi n. Ext corridors. **Pets:** No service, supervision, crate.
🆂🄰🅅🄴 ⊠ 🛢 🍴 ⌖

VESTAL

◆◆ **Howard Johnson Express Inn (Suny)** 🅼 ❀
(607) 729-6181. **$45-$90, 3 days notice.** 3601 Vestal Pkwy E. SR 17, exit 70 S, 1 mi s on Rt 201 S, 0.5 mi w on Rt 434 W. Int corridors. **Pets:** Dogs only. $10 daily fee/room. Designated rooms, supervision.
🄰🅂🄺 🆂🛏 ⊠ 🛢 📟 ⌖

🆊 ◆ **Parkway Motel** 🅼 ❀
(607) 785-3311. **$30-$68, 3 days notice.** 900 Vestal Pkwy E 434. SR 17, exit 67 S to SR 434, then e. Ext corridors. **Pets:** Small. $20 deposit/room. No service, supervision, crate.
🆂🄰🅅🄴 🆂🛏 ⊠ 🛢 ⌖

◆◆◆ **Residence Inn by Marriott** 🄰
(607) 770-8500. **$99-$150.** 4610 Vestal Pkwy. SR 17, exit 70 S, 2.5 mi s on US 201, 1 mi e on SR 434 E, right on Plaza Dr to access road. Ext corridors. **Pets:** Small. No service, supervision, crate.
🄰🅂🄺 🆂🛏 ⊠ 🛢 📟 ⌖ ⊠

VICTOR

⚠️ ◆◆ Microtel  ❅
(716) 924-9240. **$54-$64, 7 days notice.** 7498 Main St Fishers. Just off SR 96, s of I-90, exit 45. Int corridors. **Pets:** Other. Supervision.
[SAVE] [S] [✕] [✎] [☐] [▣]

WATERLOO

⚠️ ◆◆◆ Holiday Inn Waterloo-Seneca Falls
(315) 539-5011. **$119-$139.** 2468 SR 414. SR 414, 0.5 mi n at jct US 20 and 5, 4 mi s of I-90, exit 41. Int corridors. **Pets:** Small. Designated rooms, no service, supervision, crate.
[SAVE] [S] [✕] [☐] [▣] [🍴] [🔲] [✕]

WATERTOWN

◆◆ The Inn  ❅
(315) 788-6800. **$50-$70.** 1190 Arsenal St. I-81, exit 45, 0.3 mi e. Int corridors. **Pets:** Other. Supervision.
[ASK] [S] [✕] [▣] [🔲]

WATKINS GLEN

⚠️ ◆ Chieftain Motel ❅
(607) 535-4759. **$49-$69, 5 days notice.** 3815 SR 14. 3 mi n on SR 14, at jct SR 14A. Ext corridors. **Pets:** Other. $25 deposit/pet. Designated rooms, no service, supervision, crate.
[SAVE] [☐] [🔲]

WEEDSPORT

◆◆ Best Western Weedsport Inn  ❅
(315) 834-6623. **$59-$110.** 2709 Erie Dr. 0.3 mi w on SR 31 from jct SR 34; 0.5 mi sw of I-90, exit 40. Ext corridors. **Pets:** Other. Supervision.
[ASK] [S] [✕] [☐] [▣] [🔲]

WESTMORELAND

⚠️ ◆ Carriage Motor Inn 🅼 ❅
(315) 853-3561. **$38-$48, 5 days notice.** SR 233. SR 233, just n at exit 32, I-90 Thruway. Ext corridors. **Pets:** Small, dogs only. Supervision.
[SAVE] [S] [✕]

WILMINGTON

⚠️ ◆ Grand View Motel 🅼 ❅
(518) 946-2209. **$62-$89.** SR 86. 1 mi e. Ext corridors. **Pets:** Small. Designated rooms, no service, supervision, crate.
[SAVE] [S] [✕] [🔲] [✕]

⚠️ ◆◆ Hungry Trout Motor Inn 🅼
(518) 946-2217. **$69-$139, 7 days notice.** SR 86. 2 mi w. Ext corridors. **Pets:** Small. Supervision.
[SAVE] [S] [✕] [☐] [▣] [🔲] [✕]

⚠️ ◆◆ Ledge Rock at Whiteface Mountain 🅼 ❅
(518) 946-2379. **$79-$120.** Placid Rd, SR 86. 3 mi sw on SR 86. Ext corridors. **Pets:** $50 deposit/room. Designated rooms, no service, supervision, crate.
[SAVE] [S] [✕] [☐] [▣] [🔲] [✕]

⚠️ ◆◆ North Pole Motor Inn 🅼 ❅
(518) 946-7733. **$59-$79, 7 days notice.** SR 86. 1 mi sw. Ext corridors. **Pets:** Dogs only. $5 one-time fee/room. Supervision.
[SAVE] [✕] [☐] [▣] [🔲] [✕]

ABERDEEN

◆◆◆ Best Western Pinehurst Motor Inn
(910) 944-2367. **Call for rates.** 1500 Sandhills Blvd. From jct of US 15-501 on US 1, 0.3 mi s. Ext corridors. **Pets:** Supervision.

◆ Motel 6–1234
(910) 944-5633. **$39-$55.** 1408 Sand Hills Blvd. From jct US 15-501 on US 1, 0.3 mi s. Ext corridors. **Pets:** No service, supervision, crate.

ASHEVILLE

◆◆◆ Best Inns of America
(828) 298-4000. **$43-$63.** 1435 Tunnel Rd. I-40 exit 55. Int corridors. **Pets:** Small, other. No service, supervision, crate.

◆◆◆ Comfort Inn River Ridge
(828) 298-9141. **$79-$109.** 800 Fairview Rd. I-240 exit 8, jct I-40 and US 74; above River Ridge Market Place. Int corridors. **Pets:** Supervision.

◆◆ Days Inn Asheville Mall
(828) 254-4311. **$55-$75.** 199 Tunnel Rd. I-240 exit 6, 0.5 mi e on US 70. Int corridors. **Pets:** No service, supervision, crate.

◆◆ Days Inn-East
(828) 298-5140. **$50-$95.** 1500 Tunnel Rd. I-40 exit 55. Ext corridors. **Pets:** $4 daily fee/pet. Designated rooms, supervision.

◆◆ Econo Lodge-Tunnel Road
(828) 254-9521. **$65-$90, 3 days notice.** 190 Tunnel Rd. I-240 exit 6, 0.5 mi e on SR 70. Ext corridors. **Pets:** Medium. No service, supervision, crate.

◆◆◆ Holiday Inn-Asheville Mall
(828) 252-4000. **$69-$99.** 201 Tunnel Rd. I-240 exit 6, 0.5 mi e. Ext corridors. **Pets:** Medium. $15 daily fee/pet. Designated rooms, no service, supervision, crate.

◆◆ Holiday Inn East/Blue Ridge Pkwy
(828) 298-5611. **$59-$109.** 1450 Tunnel Rd. I-40 exit 55. Int corridors. **Pets:** Medium, other. Supervision.

◆ Motel 6–1134
(828) 299-3040. **$37-$53.** 1415 Tunnel Rd. I-40 exit 55. Ext corridors. **Pets:** Medium, other. No service, supervision, crate.

◆◆ Red Roof Inn-West
(828) 667-9803. **$47-$91.** 16 Crowell Rd. I-40 exit 44, just n on US 19 and 23, just w on old Haywood Rd, just s. Ext corridors. **Pets:** Small. No service, supervision, crate.

◆◆◆ Super 8 East
(828) 298-7952. **$49-$89, 7 days notice.** 1329 Tunnel Rd. I-40 exit 55, 0.3 mi w. Ext corridors. **Pets:** Other. $10 one-time fee/pet. No service, supervision, crate.

BANNER ELK

◆◆◆ Banner Elk Inn Bed & Breakfast
(828) 898-6223. **$85-$130, 30 days notice.** 407 Main St E. Jct SR 184 and 194, 0.3 mi n on SR 194. Int corridors. **Pets:** Large. Supervision.

BREVARD

◆◆◆ Hampton Inn-Brevard
(828) 883-4800. **$99-$119, 3 days notice.** 800 Forest Gate Ctr. From downtown 3.8 mi e on US 64, just e on SR 280, adjoins east end of Forest Gate Shopping Ctr. Int corridors. **Pets:** No service, supervision, crate.

AAA ◆ Sunset Motel **M** ☙
(828) 884-9106. **$44-$70.** 415 S Broad St. Just s on US 64W. Ext corridors. **Pets:** Other. $5 daily fee/room. Designated rooms, no service, supervision, crate.

[SAVE] [S🐾] [✕] [📋]

BURLINGTON

◆◆ Comfort Inn **M**
(336) 227-3681. **$62-$93.** 978 Plantation Dr. I-85 and I-40 exit 145, just n and then 0.3 mi w on service road. Ext corridors. **Pets:** Supervision.

[ASK] [✕] [📋] [💻] [🖨]

AAA ◆◆ Motel 6–1257 **M**
(336) 226-1325. **$37-$48.** 2155 Hanford Rd. I-85 and I-40 exit 145, just s and then just w. Ext corridors. **Pets:** No service, supervision, crate.

[S🐾] [✕] [🔊] [🖥] [🖨] [CTV]

CARY

◆◆◆ Candlewood Suites **A** ☙
(919) 468-4222. **$119.** 1020 Buck Jones Rd. I-40 exit 293, 0.3 mi sw on US 1 and 64W, just w, then 0.5 mi n. Int corridors. **Pets:** Other. Supervision.

[ASK] [✕] [🔊] [🖥] [📋] [💻]

AAA ◆◆◆ La Quinta Inn & Suites **M** ☙
(919) 851-2850. **$79-$119.** 191 Crescent Commons. US 1 and 64 exit 98A, 0.5 mi e on Tryon Rd, just n. Int corridors. **Pets:** Other. Supervision.

[SAVE] [✕] [🔊] [🖥] [🖨] [📋] [💻] [🖨]

AAA ◆◆ Red Roof Inn **M** ☙
(919) 469-3400. **$45-$65.** 1800 Walnut St. I-40 exit 293, 0.3 mi sw on US 1 and 64W; at Cary-Walnut St exit, just e. Int corridors. **Pets:** Small. Supervision.

[SAVE] [✕] [🔊] [🖥] [📋] [CTV]

CHAPEL HILL

AAA ◆◆◆◆ The Siena Hotel **MI** ☙
(919) 929-4000. **$165-$165.** 1505 E Franklin St. I-40 exit 270, 2 mi s on US 15/501. Int corridors. **Pets:** Other. $50 one-time fee/room. No service, supervision, crate.

[SAVE] [✕] [🔊] [📋]

Charlotte Metropolitan Area

CHARLOTTE

AAA ◆◆◆ AmeriSuites **M**
(704) 522-8400. **$99-$109.** 7900 Forest Point Blvd. Southbound, just e of I-77, exit 3; northbound, just e of exit 2, I-77, follow Arrowood Rd signs. Int corridors. **Pets:** Supervision.

[SAVE] [✕] [🔊] [🖥] [🖨] [📋] [💻] [🖨]

AAA ◆◆ Best Western Luxbury Inn **M** ☙
(704) 596-9229. **$59-$66, 30 days notice.** 4904 I-85N Service Rd. I-85 exit 41, just e to service road, 0.3 mi s. Int corridors. **Pets:** Small, dogs only. Supervision.

[SAVE] [✕] [📋] [💻] [CTV]

AAA ◆◆◆ Clarion Hotel **H** ☙
(704) 523-1400. **$59-$149.** 321 Woodlawn Rd. I-77 exit 6B, just w. Int corridors. **Pets:** Medium, other. $10 daily fee/room, $25 one-time fee/room. No service, supervision, crate.

[SAVE] [✕] [🔊] [🖥] [🖨] [📋] [💻] [🍴] [🖨]

AAA ◆◆◆ Comfort Inn Carowinds **M**
(704) 339-0574. **$79-$99.** Off I-77 exit 90; at Carowinds. Int corridors. **Pets:** Medium. Supervision.

[SAVE] [✕] [🔊] [📋] [🖨]

AAA ◆◆◆ Comfort Inn-Executive Park **M** ☙
(704) 525-2626. **$59-$149, 3 days notice.** 5822 Westpark Dr. I-77 exit 5, (Tyvola Rd). Int corridors. **Pets:** Medium. $10 daily fee/pet, $25 one-time fee/pet. No service, supervision, crate.

[SAVE] [S🐾] [✕] [🔊] [🖥] [🖨] [📋] [🖨] [CTV]

◆◆ Days Inn Charlotte South/Carowinds **M**
(803) 548-8000. **Call for rates.** 3482 Carowinds Blvd. Exit 90, off I-77 (Carowinds Blvd). Ext corridors. **Pets:** Designated rooms, no service, supervision, crate.

[✕] [🖨]

◆◆◆ Drury Inn & Suites **M** ☙
(704) 593-0700. **$79-$99.** 415 W W T Harris Blvd. I-85 exit 45A, just e. Int corridors. **Pets:** Medium, other. Designated rooms, no service, supervision, crate.

[✕] [🔊] [🖥] [🖨] [📋] [🖨]

AAA ◆◆◆ Hilton Charlotte Executive Park **H**
(704) 527-8000. **$79-$86.** 5624 Westpark Dr. I-77 exit 5 (Tyvola Rd), just e, then just s. Int corridors. **Pets:** Medium. Designated rooms, no service, supervision, crate.

[SAVE] [S🐾] [✕] [🔊] [🖥] [🖨] [📋] [💻] [🍴] [🖨] [CTV]

◆◆◆ Holiday Inn at University Executive
Park **MI** ☙
(704) 547-0999. **$94-$129.** 8520 University Executive Park Dr. I-77 exit 45A, 0.3 mi e. Int corridors. **Pets:** Medium, other. $25 one-time fee/room. Designated rooms, no service, supervision, crate.

[ASK] [✕] [🔥] [🖨] [📋] [🍴] [🖨]

AAA ◆◆◆ La Quinta Inn-Airport **M**
(704) 393-5306. **$49-$79.** 3100 I-85 S Service Rd. I-85 exit 33, just w and then just n. Ext/int corridors. **Pets:** Medium. Designated rooms, no service, supervision, crate.

[SAVE] [✕] [🔥] [🔊] [🖨] [📋] [🖨]

⬥⬥⬥ La Quinta Inn & Suites-Charlotte Coliseum 🅜 ❀

(704) 523-5599. **$69-$99.** 4900 S Tryon St. I-77 exit 6B, 0.3 mi w. Int corridors. **Pets:** Small. Designated rooms, no service, supervision, crate.

SAVE ⊠ ⛉ ⟊ ⟋ ⊟ ⬛ ⌖

⬥⬥⬥ La Quinta South 🅜 ❀

(704) 522-7110. **$39-$69.** 7900 Nations Ford Rd. Just e of I-77 and Nations Ford Rd, exit 4. Ext/int corridors. **Pets:** Small. Designated rooms, no service, supervision, crate.

SAVE ⊠ ⛉ ⟊ ⊟ ⬛ ⌖

⬥⬥ Quality Inn & Suites-Crown Point 🅜

(704) 845-2810. **$86-$96.** 2501 Sardis Rd N. 10.5 mi se of I-277 on US 74 E Independence Blvd; in the Crown Point Park. 2 mi w of jct SR 51 and US 74. Int corridors. **Pets:** Small. No service, supervision, crate.

SAVE S⚫ ⊠ ⟊ ⊟ ⬛ CTV

⬥⬥ Red Roof Inn-Airport 🅜 ❀

(704) 392-2316. **$46-$73.** 3300 I-85S Service Rd. I-85 exit 33, just w, then just s. Ext corridors. **Pets:** Small. Supervision.

SAVE ⊠ ⛉ ⟊

⬥⬥ Red Roof Inn Coliseum 🅜

(704) 529-1020. **$41-$68.** 131 Red Roof Dr. Just e of I-77 and Nations Ford Rd, exit 4. Ext corridors. **Pets:** Small. Designated rooms, no service, supervision, crate.

SAVE ⊠ ⛉ ⟊ CTV

⬥⬥⬥ Residence Inn by Marriott 🅐

(704) 547-1122. **$119-$139.** 8503 N Tryon St. I-85 exit 45A; 0.3 mi e, then just s. Ext corridors. **Pets:** Medium. Designated rooms, no service, supervision, crate.

A$K ⊠ ⛉ ⟊ ⌖ ⊠

⬥⬥⬥ Residence Inn by Marriott-Tyvola Executive Park 🅐 ❀

(704) 527-8110. **$129-$139.** 5816 Westpark Dr. I-77 exit 5 (Tyvola Rd), just e, then 0.4 mi s. Ext corridors. **Pets:** Medium, other. $10 daily fee/room. Supervision.

A$K ⊠ ⛉ ⟋ ⊟ ⬛ ⌖ ⊠

⬥⬥⬥ Sheraton Airport Plaza Hotel 🅗

(704) 392-1200. **$85-$85.** 3315 I-85S at Billy Graham Pkwy. I-85 exit 33, just e. Int corridors. **Pets:** Supervision.

S⚫ ⊠ ⛉ ⟊ ⊟ ⬛ ⍓ ⌖

⬥⬥ Sleep Inn 🅜 ❀

(704) 549-4544. **$68-$105, 7 days notice.** 8525 N Tryon St. 0.3 mi e on W T Harris Blvd from I-85, exit 45A, then just s on US 29. Int corridors. **Pets:** Other. $10 daily fee/room, $25 one-time fee/room. Designated rooms, no service, supervision, crate.

SAVE S⚫ ⊠ ⛉ ⟊ ⟋ ⊟ ⬛ ⌖ CTV

CORNELIUS

⬥⬥⬥ Holiday Inn Lake Norman 🅜🅘

(704) 892-9120. **$79-$79.** 19901 Holiday Ln. I-77 exit 28, just e. Ext corridors. **Pets:** Supervision.

⊠ ⛉ ⟊ ⊟ ⬛ ⍓ ⌖

❀ **END METROPOLITAN AREA** ❀

CHEROKEE

⬥⬥ Pioneer Motel 🅜 ❀

(828) 497-2435. **$58-$78, 3 days notice.** 0.8 mi w on US 19S. Ext corridors. **Pets:** Small, dogs only. $10 one-time fee/pet. Designated rooms, supervision.

SAVE S⚫ ⊠ ⊟ ⬛ ⌖ ⊠

DORTCHES

⬥⬥⬥ Holiday Inn Dortches 🅜🅘

(252) 937-6300. **$55, 3 days notice.** 5350 Dortches Blvd. I-95 exit 141, sw via service road. Ext corridors. **Pets:** Small. No service, supervision, crate.

SAVE S⚫ ⊠ ⟊ ⊟ ⬛ ⍓ ⌖

DURHAM

⬥⬥ Best Western Skyland Inn 🅜🅘 ❀

(919) 383-2508. **$52-$72.** 5400 US 70W. I-85 exit 170, 0.3 mi e on US 70 and just n. Ext corridors. **Pets:** Other. $5 one-time fee/pet. Supervision.

SAVE S⚫ ⊠ ⊟ ⬛ ⌖ ⊠

⬥⬥ Carolina Duke Motor Inn 🅜 ❀

(919) 286-0771. **$45-$57.** 2517 Guess Rd. I-85 exit 175, just e. Ext corridors. **Pets:** Medium, other. $5 daily fee/pet. Designated rooms, supervision.

SAVE ⊠ ⟋ ⊟ ⌖ CTV

⬥⬥⬥ Comfort Inn University 🅜 ❀

(919) 490-4949. **$69-$88.** 3508 Mount Moriah Rd. I-40 exit 270, just n on US 15-501, just e. Int corridors. **Pets:** Supervision.

SAVE S⚫ ⊠ ⛉ ⟊ ⊟ ⬛ ⌖

⬥⬥ Homestead Village Guest Studios 🅜 ❀

(919) 544-9991. **Call for rates.** 4515 NC Hwy 55. I-40 exit 278, just s. Ext corridors. **Pets:** Medium. $75 one-time fee/room. No service, supervision, crate.

⊠ ⛉ ⟊ ⟋ ⊟ ⬛

⬥⬥⬥ La Quinta Inn & Suites 🅜 ❀

(919) 401-9660. **$79-$109.** 4414 Chapel Hill Blvd. I-40 exit 270, 1.7 mi n on US 501. Int corridors. **Pets:** Small, other. No service, supervision, crate.

SAVE ⊠ ⛉ ⟊ ⟋ ⊟ ⬛ ⌖ CTV

⬥⬥ Red Roof Inn Chapel Hill 🅜

(919) 489-9421. **$51-$78.** 5623 Chapel Hill Blvd. Exit 270, off I-40; at jct US 15-501, just s of I-40 via service road. Ext corridors. **Pets:** No service, supervision, crate.

SAVE ⊠ ⟋ ⊟ ⬛ CTV

⬥⬥⬥ Wellesley Inn & Suites 🅜

(919) 998-0400. **$89-$129** (no credit cards). 4919 S Miami Blvd. I-40 exit 281, just s. Int corridors. **Pets:** Medium. Designated rooms, no service, supervision, crate.

SAVE S⚫ ⊠ ⛉ ⟊ ⟋ ⊟ ⬛ ⌖

ELIZABETH CITY

◆◆◆ Hampton Inn Ⓜ ❀
(252) 333-1800. **$61-$73, 3 days notice.** 402 Halstead Blvd. At Halstead Blvd and US 17 (bypass) jct. Int corridors. **Pets:** Medium, other. Supervision.

Ⓐ$Ⓚ ⊠ ⓑ ⓐ ⓔ ⓗ ⓛ ⓢ

FAYETTEVILLE

⊕ ◆◆◆ Best Western of Fayetteville Ⓜ ❀
(910) 438-0748. **$49-$87.** 1902 Cedar Creek Rd. I-95 exit 49, just w. Ext corridors. **Pets:** Other. Supervision.

Ⓢ̅ᴠ̅ᴇ̅ Ⓢ̅Ⓐ ⊠ ⓝ ⓗ ⓛ ⓢ

⊕ ◆◆◆ Comfort Inn I-95 Ⓜ ❀
(910) 323-8333. **$60-$75.** 1957 Cedar Creek Rd. I-95 exit 49, just w. Ext corridors. **Pets:** Small, other. No service, supervision, crate.

Ⓢ̅ᴠ̅ᴇ̅ Ⓢ̅Ⓐ ⊠ ⓐ ⓗ ⓛ ⓢ

◆◆◆ Holiday Inn Bordeaux Ⓜ
(910) 323-0111. **$71-$80.** 1707 Owen Dr. Jct I-95 business route and US 301, 2.3 mi w; from I-95 exit 40, southbound exit 56. Ext/int corridors. **Pets:** Small. No service, supervision, crate.

Ⓐ$Ⓚ Ⓢ̅Ⓐ ⊠ ⓐ ⓗ ⓛ ⓗ ⓢ

FRANKLIN

◆◆ Colonial Inn Ⓜ
(828) 524-6600. **$45-$70, 3 days notice.** 3157 Georgia Rd. 2.4 mi s on US 23/441 from US 441 bypass. Ext corridors. **Pets:** Medium. Designated rooms, supervision.

Ⓐ$Ⓚ Ⓢ̅Ⓐ ⊠ ⓔ ⓗ ⓛ ⓢ

◆◆ Days Inn-Franklin Ⓜ ❀
(828) 524-6491. **$84-$95, 3 days notice.** 1320 E Main St. Just nw on US 441 business route, at jct US 23 and 441 bypass. Ext corridors. **Pets:** Medium. $15 daily fee/room. No service, supervision, crate.

Ⓐ$Ⓚ ⊠ ⓗ ⓢ ⓧ

◆◆ Microtel Ⓜ ❀
(828) 349-9000. **$50-$60.** 81 Allman Dr. 0.4 mi s on US 23/441 from jct US 441 bypass. Int corridors. **Pets:** Small. $20 one-time fee/room. Designated rooms, no service, supervision, crate.

Ⓐ$Ⓚ Ⓢ̅Ⓐ ⊠ ⓔ ⓗ ⓛ

⊕ ◆◆ Mountainside Vacation Lodging Ⓐ ❀
(828) 524-6209. **$55-$70.** 8356 Sylva Rd. 4.8 mi n on US 441 and 23. Ext corridors. **Pets:** Medium. $25 deposit/room, $5 daily fee/room. No service, supervision, crate.

ⓗ ⓛ ⓩ

FUQUAY VARINA

◆◆ Comfort Inn Ⓜ ❀
(919) 557-9000. **$63-$68.** 7616 Purfoy Rd. 1 mi n on US 401 from jct SR 55, just e. Int corridors. **Pets:** Medium. $25 one-time fee/pet. No service, supervision, crate.

Ⓐ$Ⓚ Ⓢ̅Ⓐ ⊠ ⓔ ⓗ ⓢ

GARNER

◆◆◆ Hampton Inn Garner Ⓜ ❀
(919) 772-6500. **Call for rates.** 110 Drexmere St. 0.5 mi e on US 70 form jct US 401; behind IHOP restaurant. Int corridors. **Pets:** Designated rooms, no service, supervision, crate.

⊠ ⓑ ⓔ ⓗ ⓛ ⓢ ⓒ̅ᴛ̅ᴠ̅

GASTONIA

⊕ ◆◆ Motel 6–1281 Ⓜ
(704) 868-4900. **$36-$52.** 1721 Broadcast St. I-85 exit 17, just w, then just s. Ext corridors. **Pets:** No service, supervision, crate.

⊠ ⓑ ⓐ ⓔ ⓢ ⓒ̅ᴛ̅ᴠ̅

GOLDSBORO

⊕ ◆◆◆ Best Western Goldsboro Inn Ⓜ❶ ❀
(919) 735-7911. **$57-$65.** 801 US 70E bypass. 2 mi n on US 70E bypass Williams St exit; follow service road. Ext corridors. **Pets:** Medium, dogs only. $15 one-time fee/room. Supervision.

Ⓢ̅ᴠ̅ᴇ̅ ⊠ ⓗ ⓛ ⓗ ⓢ

GREENSBORO

◆◆ Biltmore Greensboro Hotel Ⓗ ❀
(336) 272-3474. **$85-$120, 30 days notice.** 111 W Washington St. Just s of town center on Elm St, then just w. Int corridors. **Pets:** No service, supervision, crate.

Ⓐ$Ⓚ ⊠ ⓗ

◆◆◆ Drury Inn & Suites Ⓜ
(336) 856-9696. **$75-$95.** 3220 High Point Rd. I-40 exit 217, just s. Int corridors. **Pets:** Medium. No service, supervision, crate.

⊠ ⓑ ⓐ ⓔ ⓗ ⓛ ⓢ

⊕ ◆◆ Red Roof Inn Greensboro-Airport Ⓜ
(336) 271-2636. **$41-$68.** 615 Regional Rd S. I-40 exit 210, just s on SR 68 via service road. Ext corridors. **Pets:** Supervision.

Ⓢ̅ᴠ̅ᴇ̅ ⊠ ⓐ ⓒ̅ᴛ̅ᴠ̅

◆◆◆ Residence Inn by Marriott Ⓐ
(336) 294-8600. **Call for rates.** 2000 Veasley St. I-40, 0.3 mi s, then 0.4 mi w. Ext corridors. **Pets:** Medium. Supervision.

⊠ ⓐ ⓗ ⓛ ⓢ ⓧ

HAVELOCK

◆◆ Days Inn Ⓜ ❀
(252) 447-1122. **$50-$65.** 1220 E Main St. 0.5 mi s on US 17. Int corridors. **Pets:** Medium, other. Designated rooms, supervision.

Ⓐ$Ⓚ ⊠ ⓗ ⓢ

HENDERSONVILLE

⊕ ◆◆◆ Comfort Inn Ⓜ ❀
(828) 693-8800. **$50-$95.** 206 Mitchell Dr. I-26 exit 18 B, just w. Ext corridors. **Pets:** Small. $10 one-time fee/room. No service, supervision, crate.

Ⓢ̅ᴠ̅ᴇ̅ Ⓢ̅Ⓐ ⊠ ⓗ ⓛ ⓢ

(AAA) ◆◆◆ **Quality Inn & Suites** 🅼🅸
(828) 692-7231. **$69-$199.** 201 Sugarloaf Rd. I-26 exit 18A. Ext/int corridors. **Pets:** Small. Designated rooms, no service, supervision, crate.

[SAVE] [✕] [📶] [💻] [🍴] [🏊] [✕]

HICKORY

(AAA) ◆◆ **Red Roof Inn Hickory** 🅼 ✿
(828) 323-1500. **$47-$61.** 1184 Lenoir Rhyne Blvd. I-40 exit 125, just n. Ext corridors. **Pets:** Medium, other. Supervision.

[SAVE] [✕] [🐾] [CTV]

HIGH POINT

(AAA) ◆◆ **Ramada Inn & Conference Center** 🅼🅸
(336) 886-7011. **$75-$265.** 236 S Main St. Town center; 1.5 mi n of Business Rt I-85, US 29 and 70. Int corridors. **Pets:** No service, supervision, crate.

[SAVE] [🔊] [✕] [🐾] [📶] [💻] [🍴] [🏊] [CTV]

HIGHLANDS

(AAA) ◆◆ **Mountain High Motel** 🅼
(828) 526-2790. **$79-$120, 3 days notice.** 200 Main St. Downtown. Ext corridors. **Pets:** Small. Supervision.

[SAVE] [✕] [📶] [💻]

KENLY

◆◆ **Best Western Inn** 🅼
(919) 284-3800. **$45-$100, 3 days notice.** 843 Johnson Pkwy. I-95 exit 106, just w and then just s. Ext corridors. **Pets:** Supervision.

[ASK] [✕] [🐾] [🏊]

KINSTON

◆◆◆ **Hampton Inn** 🅼
(252) 523-1400. **$58-$60, 60 days notice.** 1382 Hwy 258 S. Just s on US 258 from jct US 70 (bypass). Int corridors. **Pets:** No service, supervision, crate.

[ASK] [✕] [🐾] [🐾] [📶] [💻] [🏊]

LAURINBURG

◆◆◆ **Hampton Inn** 🅼 ✿
(910) 277-1516. **Call for rates.** 115 Hampton Cir. At jct US 15 and 401 bypass. Int corridors. **Pets:** Medium, other. Supervision.

[✕] [🐾] [💺] [📶] [💻] [🏊]

LENOIR

◆◆◆ **Ramada Limited** 🅼
(828) 758-4403. **$40-$89.** 142 Wilkesboro Blvd SE. Just e on US 64 from jct US 321. Ext corridors. **Pets:** Designated rooms, no service, supervision, crate.

[ASK] [🔊] [✕] [🐾] [🐾] [💻] [🏊]

LINCOLNTON

◆◆ **Days Inn** 🅼 ✿
(704) 735-8271. **Call for rates.** 614 Clark Dr. US 321 exit 24; 1 mi w on SR 150. Int corridors. **Pets:** Small. $10 daily fee/room. No service, supervision, crate.

[ASK] [✕] [📶] [💻] [🏊]

LUMBERTON

(AAA) ◆◆◆ **Best Western Lumberton** 🅼 ✿
(910) 618-9799. **$55.** 201 Jackson Ct. I-95 exit 22, just e. Ext corridors. **Pets:** Small, other. $10 daily fee/pet. No service, supervision, crate.

[SAVE] [🔊] [✕] [💺] [💺] [📶] [🏊]

◆◆◆ **Comfort Suites** 🅼 ✿
(910) 739-8800. **$80-$105.** 215 Wintergreen Dr. I-95 exit 22, just e, then just n. Int corridors. **Pets:** Medium, other. $50 deposit/room. Designated rooms, supervision.

[ASK] [🔊] [✕] [🐾] [📶] [💻] [🏊]

(AAA) ◆◆◆ **Super 8 Motel** 🅼
(910) 671-4444. **$45-$85.** 150 Jackson Ct. I-95 exit 22, just e. Ext corridors. **Pets:** Designated rooms, no service, supervision, crate.

[SAVE] [✕] [💺] [💺] [📶] [🏊]

MAGGIE VALLEY

◆ **Applecover Inn Motel** 🅼 ✿
(828) 926-9100. **$35-$80, 3 days notice.** 4077 Soco Rd. On US 19, 4.5 mi w from jct US 276. Ext corridors. **Pets:** $30 deposit/room, $10 one-time fee/room. Designated rooms, no service, supervision, crate.

[✕] [📶]

MORRISVILLE

◆◆◆ **Baymont Inn & Suites-Raleigh Airport** 🅼
(919) 481-3600. **$59-$66.** 1001 Aerial Center Pkwy. Eastbound I-40 exit 284A, 0.3 mi s; westbound I-40 exit 284, 0.3 mi s; in Aerial Center Park. Int corridors. **Pets:** Small. Supervision.

[✕] [🐾] [🐾] [📶] [💻] [CTV]

(AAA) ◆◆◆ **La Quinta Inn & Suites-Airport** 🅼
(919) 461-1771. **$59-$119.** 1001 Hospitality Ct. Eastbound I-40, exit 284A 0.3 mi s; westbound I-40, exit 284, 0.3 mi s; in Aerial Center Park. Int corridors. **Pets:** Supervision.

[SAVE] [✕] [💺] [🐾] [💺] [📶] [💻] [🏊] [CTV]

MURPHY

(AAA) ◆◆◆ **Best Western of Murphy** 🅼
(828) 837-3060. **$69-$99, 3 days notice.** 1522 Andrews Rd. US 74, 19 and SR 129, exit Andrews Rd. Ext corridors. **Pets:** Medium. No service, supervision, crate.

[SAVE] [✕] [📶] [🏊]

◆◆◆ **Comfort Inn** 🅼 ✿
(828) 837-8030. **$59-$115.** 754 Hwy 64 W. On US 64 W, 19 S, 74 W and 129 S. Ext corridors. **Pets:** $30 deposit/room. Supervision.

[ASK] [🔊] [✕] [📶] [💻] [🏊]

NEW BERN

◆◆◆ **Sheraton Grand Hotel** 🅷
(252) 638-3585. **$95-$120.** 1 Bicentennial Park. 3 mi e of US 17 and 70 Bypass; 0.5 mi n of E Front St exit off US 70 Bypass. Int corridors. **Pets:** Small. Designated rooms, no service, supervision, crate.

[ASK] [🔊] [✕] [🐾] [🐾] [📶] [💻] [🍴] [🏊] [✕] [CTV]

OUTER BANKS METROPOLITAN AREA

NAGS HEAD

◆ Vivianna Motel M ❀
(252) 441-7409. **Call for rates, 3 days notice.** 6905 Virginia Dare Tr. On NC 12 beach road at milepost 15.9. Ext corridors. **Pets:** Other. $5 daily fee/pet. No service, supervision, crate.

OCRACOKE

◆◆ The Anchorage Inn M ❀
(252) 928-1101. **$114-$125, 3 days notice.** Just n on SR 12 from Cedar Island Ferry, on south end of island. Ext corridors. **Pets:** Other. $10 daily fee/room. Designated rooms, no service, supervision, crate.

❀ END METROPOLITAN AREA ❀

RAEFORD

◆◆ Days Inn M ❀
(910) 904-1050. **$49-$150, 7 days notice.** 115 N US Hwy 401 Bypass. On US 401, just s of jct SR 211 and US 401. Ext corridors. **Pets:** Small. $4 daily fee/pet. Designated rooms, no service, supervision, crate.

RALEIGH

◆◆◆ AmeriSuites M
(919) 877-9997. **$79-$99.** 3301 Wake Forest Rd. I-440 exit 10, just n, then just w. Int corridors. **Pets:** Small. No service, supervision, crate.

◆◆◆ Fairfield Inn-Crabtree M
(919) 881-9800. **$49-$94** (no credit cards). 2201 Summit Park Ln. I-440 exit 7 eastbound, just n; then just e on Blue Ridge Rd, just n. Int corridors. **Pets:** Medium. Designated rooms, no service, supervision, crate.

◆◆◆ Holiday Inn-Crabtree M
(919) 782-8600. **$89-$89.** 4100 Glenwood Ave. I-440 beltline, exit 7B. Int corridors. **Pets:** Medium. No service, supervision, crate.

◆◆◆ Homestead Village Guest Studios M ❀
(919) 981-7353. **Call for rates.** 3531 Wake Forest Rd. I-440 exit 10, 0.5 mi n. Ext corridors. **Pets:** Medium, other. $75 one-time fee/pet. Supervision.

◆◆◆ La Quinta Inn & Suites M
(919) 785-0071. **$79-$129.** 2211 Summit Park Ln. I-440 exit 7B, just n to Blue Ridge Rd, then just e. Int corridors. **Pets:** Medium. No service, supervision, crate.

◆◆ Red Roof Inn-North M ❀
(919) 878-9310. **$39-$89.** 3201 Wake Forest Rd. I-440 exit 10, just n, then just w; enter behind Denny's. Ext corridors. **Pets:** Small. $25 deposit/room. Designated rooms, no service, supervision, crate.

◆◆ Red Roof Inn Raleigh M
(919) 231-0200. **$53-$78.** 3520 Maitland Dr. I-440 exit 13B; opposite Tower Shopping Plaza. Ext corridors. **Pets:** Medium. Supervision.

◆◆ Red Roof Inn-South M ❀
(919) 833-6005. **$64-$89.** 1813 S Saunders St. I-40 exit 298B, just n on US 401 and 70. Int corridors. **Pets:** Very small, other. Supervision.

◆◆◆ Residence Inn by Marriott A
(919) 878-6100. **Call for rates.** 1000 Navaho Dr. I-440 exit 10, just n, then sw. Ext corridors. **Pets:** Supervision.

◆◆ Sleep Inn M ❀
(919) 755-6005. **$50-$70.** 2617 Appliance Ct. I-440 exit 11B, just n on US 1N. Int corridors. **Pets:** Medium. $10 daily fee/room. Supervision.

ROANOKE RAPIDS

◆◆ Motel 6–1278 M ❀
(252) 537-5252. **$38-$54.** 1911 Julian R Allsbrook Hwy. I-95 exit 173; just w on US 158. Int corridors. **Pets:** Medium, other. Supervision.

ROCKY MOUNT

◆ Days Inn/Rocky Mount-Gold Rock M
(252) 446-0621. **$46-$72.** 6970 NC 4. I-95 exit 145, just e. Ext corridors. **Pets:** Designated rooms, supervision.

◆◆◆ Holiday Inn Rocky Mount M
(252) 937-6888. **$84-$94, 5 days notice.** 651 Winstead Ave. Exit 138 off I-95, 1 mi e on US 64, Winstead Ave extension exit, adjacent to Gateway Convention Center. Int corridors. **Pets:** Small. No service, supervision, crate.

◆ Howard Johnson Inn M ❀
(252) 977-9595. **$45-$80.** 7568 NC 48. I-95 exit 145, just w. Int corridors. **Pets:** Small. $5 daily fee/pet, $5 one-time fee/pet. No service, supervision, crate.

[AAA] ◆◆ **Quality Inn & Suites** [M] 🐾
(252) 977-0101. **$46-$76.** I-95 exit 145, just e. Int corridors. **Pets:** Other. $10 one-time fee/room. No service, supervision, crate.
[SAVE] 🚭 🚪 🍴 🏊

[AAA] ◆◆◆ **Red Roof Inn** [M]
(252) 984-0907. **$36-$63.** 1370 Weslyan Blvd. 1.5 mi n on US 301 from jct US 64 (Bypass). Int corridors. **Pets:** Medium. Designated rooms, no service, supervision, crate.
[SAVE] 🚭 👂 🚿 🚪 🏊

SALISBURY

[AAA] ◆◆ **Days Inn** [M] 🐾
(704) 633-4211. **$41-$90.** 1810 Lutheran Synod Dr. I-85 exit 75, just w. Ext corridors. **Pets:** $6 daily fee/pet, $6 one-time fee/pet. Designated rooms, no service, supervision, crate.
[SAVE] 🚭 👂 🚪 🏊

◆◆◆ **Hampton Inn** [M]
(704) 637-8000. **Call for rates.** 1001 Klumac Rd. I-85 exit 75, just w. Int corridors. **Pets:** Medium. Supervision.
🚭 👂 🚪 💻 🏊

SANFORD

[AAA] ◆◆ **Palomino Motel** [M]
(919) 776-7531. **$40-$44.** 1508 Westover Dr. 2.5 mi s on US 1, 15 and 501 bypass. Ext corridors. **Pets:** Designated rooms, no service, supervision, crate.
[SAVE] 🚭 ♿ 🚿 🚪 💻 🍴 🏊 🏋

SMITHFIELD

[AAA] ◆◆ **Super 8 Motel** [M] 🐾
(919) 989-8988. **$51-$63.** 735 Industrial Park Dr. I-95 exit 95, just w on US 70, then just n. Int corridors. **Pets:** Medium. $4 daily fee/room. Designated rooms, no service, supervision, crate.
[SAVE] 🚭 ♿ 👂 🚿 🚪 🏊 [CTV]

STATESVILLE

◆◆◆ **Hampton Inn Statesville** [M] 🐾
(704) 878-2721. **Call for rates.** 715 Sullivan Rd. I-40 exit 151, just s. Ext corridors. **Pets:** Medium, other. Supervision.
🚭 👂 💻

[AAA] ◆◆ **Red Roof Inn** [M] 🐾
(704) 878-2051. **$42-$57.** 1508 E Broad St. I-77 at Broad St, exit 50. Ext corridors. **Pets:** Other. Supervision.
[SAVE] 🚭 👂

[AAA] ◆◆ **Super 8 Motel** [M] 🐾
(704) 878-9888. **$46-$120, 7 days notice.** 1125 Greenland Dr. I-77 exit 49A, just e. Ext/int corridors. **Pets:** Small, dogs only. $5 daily fee/pet. No service, supervision, crate.
[SAVE] [SD] 🚭 👂

WADESBORO

◆◆ **Days Inn** [M]
(704) 694-7070. **$48-$100.** 209 E Caswell St. 0.5 mi e on US 74. Ext corridors. **Pets:** Small. No service, supervision, crate.
[ASK] 🚭 🚪 🏊

WASHINGTON

[AAA] ◆◆ **Econo Lodge** [M] 🐾
(252) 946-7781. **$35-$58.** 1220 W 15th. 1.3 mi n on US 17 at jct US 264. Ext corridors. **Pets:** Small. $5 daily fee/room. No service, supervision, crate.
[SAVE] 🚭 👂 🚪

WELDON

[AAA] ◆◆ **Days Inn** [M] 🐾
(252) 536-4867. **$45-$55, 3 days notice.** 1611 Roanoke Rapids Rd. I-95 exit 173, just e on US 158. Ext corridors. **Pets:** $5 daily fee/pet, $5 one-time fee/pet. Designated rooms, supervision.
[SAVE] [SD] 🚭 👂 🚪 🏊

WILLIAMSTON

◆◆◆ **Comfort Inn** [M] 🐾
(252) 792-8400. **$55-$64.** 100 E Blvd. At jct US 64 and 17 bypass. Int corridors. **Pets:** Medium, other. Supervision.
[ASK] 🚭 🚶 👂 💻 [CTV]

◆◆◆ **Holiday Inn** [M] 🐾
(252) 792-3184. **$59-$69.** 101 E Blvd. Jct Hwys 64 and 17. Ext/int corridors. **Pets:** Medium, other. Designated rooms, supervision.
[ASK] 🚭 👂 💻 🍴 🏊 [CTV]

WILMINGTON

[AAA] ◆◆◆ **Comfort Inn Executive Center** [M]
(910) 791-4841. **$75-$100.** 151 S College Rd. Just s on SR 132 from jct US 17. Int corridors. **Pets:** Designated rooms, supervision.
[SAVE] 🚭 👂 🚪 💻 🏊

WINSTON SALEM

[AAA] ◆◆◆ **Augustus T Zevely Inn** [BB]
(336) 748-9299. **$80-$125.** 803 S Main. In Old Salem Historical District. Ext/int corridors. **Pets:** Medium. Supervision.
[SAVE] 🚭 🚪

◆◆◆ **Residence Inn by Marriott** [A] 🐾
(336) 759-0777. **$114-$114.** 7835 N Point Blvd. US 52N exit 115B, 2 mi s on University Pkwy, just e. Ext corridors. **Pets:** $150 one-time fee/room. Supervision.
[ASK] [SD] 🚭 👂 🚪 💻 🏊 🏋 [CTV]

◆◆ **Salem Inn** [M]
(336) 725-8561. **$54-$96.** 127 S Cherry St. I-40 (Business), westbound exit 5D, just s; eastbound exit 5C, just s. Ext corridors. **Pets:** Medium. Designated rooms, supervision.
[ASK] 🚭 🚪 💻 🏊 [CTV]

WRIGHTSVILLE BEACH

[AAA] ◆◆ **Waterway Lodge** [M] 🐾
(910) 256-3771. **$110-$170.** 7246 Wrightsville Ave. From SR 132 and US 76, 4.7 mi e, just before the causeway. Ext corridors. **Pets:** Other. $15 daily fee/room. Supervision.
[SAVE] 🚭 🚪 🏊 🏋

NORTH DAKOTA

BISMARCK

◆◆ Best Western Doublewood Inn M ❀
(701) 258-7000. **$54-$69.** 1400 E Interchange Ave. Just s of I-94, exit 159, US 83. Int corridors. **Pets:** Other. $25 deposit/room. Supervision.
ASK S× × ♪ ✦ ■ ■ ¶ ≈

◆◆◆ Comfort Inn M
(701) 223-1911. **$44-$62.** 1030 Interstate Ave. I-94, exit 159 (US 83), 0.3 mi nw. Int corridors. **Pets:** Small. Designated rooms, no service, supervision, crate.
SAVE × ♪ ✦ ■ ≈

◆◆ Expressway Inn M ❀
(701) 222-2900. **$42-$54.** 200 Bismarck Expwy. Jct I-94 business loop and S 3rd St; opposite Kirkwood Mall. Int corridors. **Pets:** $5 one-time fee/room. Designated rooms, no service, supervision, crate.
ASK S× × ♪ ♪ ■ ■ ≈ ×

◆◆◆ Holiday Inn Hotel Bismarck H ❀
(701) 255-6000. **$59-$59.** 605 E Broadway. Center (Sixth and Broadway). Int corridors. **Pets:** Other. Supervision.
× ♪ ♪ ■ ■ ¶ ≈

◆◆◆ Kelly Inn M ❀
(701) 223-8001. **$51-$66.** 1800 N 12 St. On US 83, 0.3 mi s of jct I-94, exit 159. Int corridors. **Pets:** Other. No service, supervision, crate.
SAVE S× × ♪ ♪ ✦ ■ ■ ¶ ≈

◆◆◆ Radisson Inn Bismarck M
(701) 258-7700. **$64-$64.** 800 S 3rd St. Just s of jct I-94 business loop and S 3rd St; opposite Kirkwood Mall. Int corridors. **Pets:** Medium. No service, supervision, crate.
SAVE S× × ♪ ♪ ✦ ■ ■ ¶ ≈

◆◆ Select Inn M ❀
(701) 223-8060. **$34-$50.** 1505 Interchange Ave. I-94 and US 83, exit 159, just s of jct. Int corridors. **Pets:** Other. $25 deposit/room. No service, supervision, crate.
SAVE S× × ♪ ♪ ■

◆ Super 8 Motel M
(701) 255-1314. **$40-$59.** 1124 E Capitol Ave. I-94, exit 159, 0.3 mi s of jct, on US 83. Int corridors. **Pets:** No service, supervision, crate.
× ♪ ■

BOWMAN

◆ Budget Host 4U Motel M ❀
(701) 523-3243. **$28-$36.** 704 Hwy 12W. US 12 and 85, midway between 85 N and 85 S. Ext corridors. **Pets:** Other. Designated rooms, supervision.
× ■

◆◆ North Winds Lodge M ❀
(701) 523-5641. **$37-$47.** 503 Hwy 85 S. Just s of US 12, on US 85. Ext corridors. **Pets:** Other. $2 daily fee/pet. Designated rooms, no service, supervision, crate.
S× × ■ ■ ≈

CARRINGTON

◆◆ Chieftain Conference Center M ❀
(701) 652-3131. **$40-$85.** 60 4th Ave S. 0.5 mi e on US 52 and 281, just s of jct SR 200. Ext/int corridors. **Pets:** Small. $5 one-time fee/room. Designated rooms, no service, supervision, crate.
ASK S× × ¶

◆◆ Super 8 Motel M ❀
(701) 652-3982. **$40-$81.** 101 4th Ave S. 0.5 mi e on US 52 and 281, just s of jct SR 200. Int corridors. **Pets:** $5 daily fee/pet. No service, supervision, crate.
ASK S× ×

DEVILS LAKE

◆◆◆ Comfort Inn M
(701) 662-6760. **$50-$70.** 215 Hwy 2 E. Jct US 2 and SR 20. Int corridors. **Pets:** No service, supervision, crate.
ASK S× × ♪ ♪ ■ ■ ≈

◆◆ Days Inn Devils Lake M ❀
(701) 662-5161. **$49-$56, 7 days notice.** Hwy 20 S. On SR 20, just s of jct US 2. Ext corridors. **Pets:** $3 daily fee/pet. No service, supervision, crate.
SAVE S× × ■

◆ Trails West Motel M ❀
(701) 662-5011. **$34-$40.** Hwy 2 W. 0.8 mi sw on US 2. Int corridors. **Pets:** $5 one-time fee/pet. No service, supervision, crate.
SAVE S× ×

DICKINSON

◆◆◆ AmericInn Motel & Suites of Dickinson M ❀
(701) 225-1400. **$66-$78.** 229 15th St W. I-94, exit 61, just ne. Int corridors. **Pets:** Other. Designated rooms, no service, supervision, crate.
ASK S× × ♪ ♪ ✦ ■ ■ ≈

◆◆ Best Western Badlands Inn M ❀
(701) 225-9510. **$45-$65.** 71 Museum Dr.. Just se of jct SR 22 and I-94, exit 61. Int corridors. **Pets:** Medium. $50 deposit/room. Designated rooms, no service, supervision, crate.
SAVE S× × ■ ■ ≈

◆◆ **Comfort Inn** 🅜 🐾
(701) 264-7300. **$40-$69.** 493 Elk Dr. Just nw of jct SR 22 and I-94, exit 61. Int corridors. **Pets:** Other. Supervision.
🅐🅢🅚 ⊠ 🏠 📶 ⌨ 🍴 💻 🛋 🐾

◆◆◆ **Hartfiel Inn** 🅑🅑 🐾
(701) 225-6710. **$59-$69.** 509 3rd Ave W. On SR 22, downtown, 0.8 mi s from I-94, exit 61. Int corridors. **Pets:** Small, dogs only. No service, supervision, crate.
⊠ 💻

⊕ ◆ **Oasis Motel** 🅜 🐾
(701) 225-6703. **$40-$65.** 1000 W Villard St. I-94, exit 59, 1.8 mi e on I-94 Business Loop. Ext/int corridors. **Pets:** Medium. $25 deposit/room. Designated rooms, no service, supervision, crate.
🅢🅐🅥🅔 🕤 ⊠ 🍴 💻 🛋

FARGO

⊕ ◆◆ **Airport/Dome Days Inn &**
Suites 🅜 🐾
(701) 232-0000. **$54-$74.** 1507 19th Ave N. I-29, exit 67, 1.2 mi ne. Int corridors. **Pets:** Other. $15 deposit/room. Designated rooms, no service, supervision, crate.
🅢🅐🅥🅔 ⊠ 📶 ⌨ 🍴 💻 🛋

⊕ ◆◆◆ **Americinn Motel** 🅜 🐾
(701) 234-9946. **$54-$69.** 1423 35th St SW. I-29, exit 64 (13th Ave S), just se. Int corridors. **Pets:** Other. $50 deposit/ room. Designated rooms, no service, supervision, crate.
🅢🅐🅥🅔 🕤 ⊠ 📶 ⌨ 🍴

◆◆ **Best Western Doublewood Inn** 🅜🅘 🐾
(701) 235-3333. **$173.** 3333 13th Ave S. 0.3 mi e of I-29, exit 64 (13th Ave S). Int corridors. **Pets:** Other. Supervision.
🅐🅢🅚 🕤 ⊠ 🏠 📶 ⌨ 🍴 💻 🍴 🛋

⊕ ◆◆◆ **Best Western Kelly Inn** 🅜🅘 🐾
(701) 282-2143. **$59-$75.** 3800 Main Ave. I-29, exit 65 (Main Ave), just w. Int corridors. **Pets:** Medium. Designated rooms, no service, supervision, crate.
🅢🅐🅥🅔 🕤 ⊠ 📶 ⌨ 🍴 💻 🍴 🛋

◆◆◆ **Comfort Inn East** 🅜 🐾
(701) 280-9666. **$59-$89.** 1407 35th St S. Se of I-29, exit 64 (13th Ave S). **Pets:** Other. $5 one-time fee/room. Designated rooms, supervision.
🅐🅢🅚 🕤 ⊠ 📶 🍴 💻 🛋

◆◆◆ **Comfort Suites** 🅜
(701) 237-5911. **$64-$99.** 1415 35th St S. I-29, exit 64, just se (13th Ave S). Int corridors. **Pets:** Large. Designated rooms, no service, supervision, crate.
🅐🅢🅚 🕤 ⊠ 🏠 📶 ⌨ 🍴

⊕ ◆◆◆ **Country Suites By Carlson** 🅜 🐾
(701) 234-0565. **$67-$149.** 3316 13th Ave S. I-29, exit 64, 0.3 mi e. Int corridors. **Pets:** Other. $100 deposit/room. No service, supervision, crate.
🅢🅐🅥🅔 🕤 ⊠ 🍴 💻 🛋

◆◆ **Econo Lodge of Fargo** 🅜 🐾
(701) 232-3412. **$42-$64.** 1401 35th St S. I-29, exit 64 (13th Ave S), just se. Int corridors. **Pets:** Other. Designated rooms, no service, supervision, crate.
🅐🅢🅚 🕤 ⊠ 📶 ⌨ 💻

◆◆ **Expressway Inn** 🅜🅘
(701) 235-3141. **$43-$59.** 1340 21 Ave S. I-94, exit 351. Ext/int corridors. **Pets:** Designated rooms, supervision.
🅐🅢🅚 ⊠ 🏠 📶 ⌨ 🍴 💻 🍴 🛋

⊕ ◆◆ **Flying J Inn** 🅜
(701) 282-8473. **$38-$58.** 3150 39th St S. I-29, exit 62, just w. Int corridors. **Pets:** No service, supervision, crate.
🅢🅐🅥🅔 🕤 ⊠

◆◆◆ **Holiday Inn** 🅜🅘 🐾
(701) 282-2700. **$125.** 3803 13th Ave S. I-29, exit 64 (13th Ave S), just nw. Int corridors. **Pets:** Large, other. No service, supervision, crate.
🅐🅢🅚 🕤 ⊠ 🏠 📶 ⌨ 🍴 💻 🍴 🛋

◆◆◆ **Holiday Inn Express Fargo** 🅜
(701) 282-2000. **Call for rates.** 1040 40th St S. I-29, exit 64 (13th Ave S), just nw. Int corridors. **Pets:** Medium. Designated rooms, supervision.
⊠ 🏠 ⌨ 💻 🛋

⊕ ◆◆◆ **Kelly Inn 13th Avenue** 🅜 🐾
(701) 277-8821. **$54-$89.** 4207 13th Ave SW. I-29, exit 64 (13th Ave S), just w. Ext/int corridors. **Pets:** Small. No service, supervision, crate.
🅢🅐🅥🅔 🕤 ⊠ 🏠 📶 ⌨ 🍴 💻 🛋

⊕ ◆ **Motel 75** 🅜 🐾
(701) 282-1321. **$35-$48.** 3402 14th Ave S. Se jct of I-29 and 13th Ave, exit 64. Int corridors. **Pets:** Designated rooms, supervision.
🅢🅐🅥🅔 🕤 ⊠

⊕ ◆◆◆ **Radisson Hotel Fargo** 🅷 🐾
(701) 232-7363. **$79-$109.** 201 5th St N. Downtown; corner of 2nd Ave N and 5th St N. Int corridors. **Pets:** Small. $25 deposit/room. Designated rooms, no service, supervision, crate.
🅢🅐🅥🅔 🕤 ⊠ 🖐 📶 ⌨ 💻 🍴

⊕ ◆◆◆ **Ramada Plaza Suites & Conference**
Center 🅷 🐾
(701) 277-9000. **Call for rates.** 1635 42nd St SW. I-29, exit 64 (13th Ave S), 0.4 mi sw, then left. Int corridors. **Pets:** Small, dogs only. $50 deposit/room. Designated rooms, no service, supervision, crate.
🅢🅐🅥🅔 ⊠ 🖐 📶 ⌨ 🍴 💻 🍴 🛋

◆◆ **Red Roof Inn** 🅜
(701) 282-9100. **$40-$55.** 901 38th St SW. I-29, exit 64 (13th Ave S), just nw. Int corridors. **Pets:** Medium. Designated rooms, supervision.
🅐🅢🅚 🕤 ⊠ ⌨

⊕ ◆ **Select Inn** 🅜 🐾
(701) 282-6300. **$31-$49.** 1025 38th St SW. I-29, exit 64 (13th Ave S), just nw. Int corridors. **Pets:** Other. $25 deposit/room. Designated rooms, no service, supervision, crate.
🅢🅐🅥🅔 🕤 ⊠ ⌨ 🍴

◆◆ **Sleep Inn** 🅜
(701) 281-8240. **$59-$69.** 1921 44 St SW. I-94, exit 348 (45th St), ne jct. Int corridors. **Pets:** Medium. No service, supervision, crate.
🅐🅢🅚 ⊠ 🏠 ⌨ 💻 🛋

◆◆ **Super 8 Motel** ⓜ ☙
(701) 232-9202. **$36-$92.** 3518 Interstate Blvd. I-29, exit 64 (13th Ave), just n on e frontage road. Int corridors. **Pets:** Other. $3 daily fee/room. Supervision.

ⒶⓈⓀ ⊠ 🛢 🖵 🕿

GRAND FORKS

◆◆ **Best Western Town House** ⓜ
(701) 746-5411. **$55-$85.** 710 1st Ave N. Downtown; 1st Ave N and DeMers Ave (3 mi e of I-29, exit 140). Int corridors. **Pets:** Designated rooms, supervision.

ⒶⓈⓀ Ⓢ⊠ ⊠ 🅐 🛢 🖵 🕎 🕿 ⊠

◆◆◆ **Comfort Inn** ⓜ ☙
(701) 775-7503. **$54-$89.** 3251 30th Ave S. I-29, exit 138, 0.5 mi e. Int corridors. **Pets:** Large, other. Designated rooms, no service, supervision, crate.

ⒶⓈⓀ Ⓢ⊠ ⊠ 🛢 🕿

◆◆ **Days Inn** ⓜ ☙
(701) 775-0060. **$49-$89.** 3101 34th St S. I-29, exit 138, 0.5 mi e. Int corridors. **Pets:** Other. Designated rooms, no service, supervision, crate.

ⒶⓈⓀ Ⓢ⊠ ⊠ 🛢 🕿

◆◆ **Econo Lodge** ⓜ ☙
(701) 746-6666. **$44-$56.** 900 N 43 St. Just se of jct US 2 and I-29, exit 141 (Gateway Dr). Int corridors. **Pets:** Medium. No service, supervision, crate.

ⒶⓈⓀ Ⓢ⊠ ⊠ 🛢 🖵

◆◆◆ **Holiday Inn Grand Forks** ⓜ ☙
(701) 772-7131. **$62-$64.** 1210 N 43rd St. US 2, just e of jct I-29, exit 141 (Gateway Dr). Ext/int corridors. **Pets:** Designated rooms, no service, supervision, crate.

ⒶⓈⓀ Ⓢ⊠ ⊠ 🅐 🛢 🖵 🕎 🕿 ⊠

◆◆ **Rodeway Inn** ⓜ
(701) 795-9960. **$45-$55.** 4001 Gateway Dr. US 2, 0.3 mi e of I-29, exit 141 (Gateway Dr). Int corridors. **Pets:** Small. No service, supervision, crate.

ⒶⓈⓀ Ⓢ⊠ ⊠ 🖵

⑭ ◆ **Select Inn** ⓜ ☙
(701) 775-0555. **$30-$45.** 1000 N 42nd St. Jct US 2 and I-29, exit 141 (Gateway Dr), just se. Int corridors. **Pets:** Other. $25 deposit/room, $5 daily fee/pet, $5 one-time fee/pet. Designated rooms, no service, supervision, crate.

Ⓢ⒜ⓥⒺ Ⓢ⊠ ⊠

◆◆ **Westward Ho Motel** ⓜ ☙
(701) 775-5341. **$40-$61.** US 2 W. US 2, 0.8 mi e of I-29, exit 141 (Gateway Dr). Ext corridors. **Pets:** Supervision.

ⒶⓈⓀ Ⓢ⊠ ⊠ 🛢 🖵 🕎 🕿 ⊠

JAMESTOWN

◆◆◆ **Comfort Inn** ⓜ ☙
(701) 252-7125. **$59-$89.** 811 20 St SW. I-94, exit 258, just n, then w. Int corridors. **Pets:** Other. Designated rooms, no service, supervision, crate.

ⒶⓈⓀ Ⓢ⊠ ⊠ 🛢 🕿

⑭ ◆ **Ranch House Motel** ⓜ ☙
(701) 252-0222. **$35-$45.** 408 Business Loop W. 0.8 mi n on US 281 from jct I-94, exit 258. Ext/int corridors. **Pets:** $5 daily fee/pet. Designated rooms, no service, supervision, crate.

⊠ 🕿

MANDAN

◆◆◆ **Best Western Seven Seas Inn & Conference Center** ⓜ ☙
(701) 663-7401. **$51-$60.** 2611 Old Red Tr. I-94, exit 152, just nw. Int corridors. **Pets:** Other. $10 deposit/room. Supervision.

ⒶⓈⓀ Ⓢ⊠ ⊠ 🅐 🅕 🛢 🖵 🕎 🕿

MINOT

⑭ ◆◆◆ **Best Western International Inn** ⓜ
(701) 852-3161. **$56-$75.** 1505 N Broadway. 1.5 mi n on US 83. Int corridors. **Pets:** No service, supervision, crate.

ⓈⓐⓥⒺ Ⓢ⊠ ⊠ 🅐 🅕 🛢 🕎 🕿

⑭ ◆◆◆ **Best Western Kelly Inn** ⓜ ☙
(701) 852-4300. **$54-$89.** 1510 26th Ave SW. US 2 and 52 bypass at 16th St SW; adjacent to Dakota Square Mall. Ext/int corridors. **Pets:** Other. Designated rooms, no service, supervision, crate.

ⓈⓐⓥⒺ Ⓢ⊠ ⊠ 🛢 🕿

⑭ ◆◆ **Comfort Inn** ⓜ ☙
(701) 852-2201. **$48-$58, 7 days notice.** 1515 22nd Ave SW. US 2 and 52 bypass, at 16th St SW; adjacent to Dakota Square Mall. Int corridors. **Pets:** Other. No service, supervision, crate.

ⓈⓐⓥⒺ Ⓢ⊠ ⊠ 🅐 🕿

⑭ ◆◆ **Dakota Inn** ⓜ ☙
(701) 838-2700. **$33-$54.** 2401 US 2 & 52 bypass. Jct US 83, 1 mi w. Int corridors. **Pets:** Small, other. Designated rooms, no service, supervision, crate.

ⓈⓐⓥⒺ Ⓢ⊠ ⊠ 🅐 🕿

⑭ ◆ **Days Inn** ⓜ
(701) 852-3646. **$40-$56.** 2100 4th St SW. Just n of jct SR 83, Hwy 2 and 52 bypass. Int corridors. **Pets:** Medium. Supervision.

ⓈⓐⓥⒺ Ⓢ⊠ ⊠ 🅐 🅕 🛢 🖵 🕿

◆◆◆ **Holiday Inn Riverside Minot** ⓜ ☙
(701) 852-2504. **$55-$89.** 2200 Burdick Expwy E. 1.3 mi e on US 2 business route (Burdick Expwy E). Int corridors. **Pets:** Small, dogs only. No service, supervision, crate.

ⒶⓈⓀ Ⓢ⊠ ⊠ 🅐 🖵 🕎 🕿

⑭ ◆◆ **Select Inn** ⓜ ☙
(701) 852-3411. **$30-$46.** 225 22nd Ave NW. 2 mi n on US 83. Int corridors. **Pets:** Other. $25 deposit/room. No service, supervision, crate.

ⓈⓐⓥⒺ Ⓢ⊠ ⊠ 🅕 🛢 🖵

NEW TOWN

⑭ ◆◆ **4 Bears Lodge** ⓜ ☙
(701) 627-4018. **$55-$55.** SR 23 W. 4 mi w on SR 23. Int corridors. **Pets:** $10 deposit/room. Supervision.

ⓈⓐⓥⒺ Ⓢ⊠ ⊠ 🕎

VALLEY CITY

AAA ◆◆ Wagon Wheel Inn & Suites M 🐾
(701) 845-5333. **$38-$52.** 455 Winter Show Rd. I-94, exit 292, just ne. Ext/int corridors. **Pets:** Small, dogs only. Designated rooms, no service, supervision, crate.

SAVE

WAHPETON

◆◆ Comfort Inn M 🐾
(701) 642-1115. **$49-$79.** 209 13th St S. SR 13, 0.3 mi e of jct SR 210 bypass. Int corridors. **Pets:** Other. Designated rooms, no service, supervision, crate.

A$K

◆◆◆ Holiday Inn Express M 🐾
(701) 642-5000. **$54-$61, 3 days notice.** 1800 Two Ten Dr. 1 mi n on SR 210 bypass. Int corridors. **Pets:** Large, other. No service, supervision, crate.

A$K

WASHBURN

◆◆ ScotWood Motel M
(701) 462-8191. **$35-$46.** 1323 Frontage Rd. US 83, 1 mi s of jct SR 200. Int corridors. **Pets:** Supervision.

WATFORD CITY

AAA ◆ McKenzie Inn M 🐾
(701) 842-3980. **$29-$37.** 120 SW 3rd St. US 85, in town. Ext corridors. **Pets:** Designated rooms, no service, supervision, crate.

SAVE

WEST FARGO

AAA ◆◆ West Fargo Days Inn M 🐾
(701) 281-0000. **$52-$72.** 525 Main Ave E. I-29, exit 65, 2.3 mi w. Int corridors. **Pets:** Other. $15 deposit/room. Designated rooms, no service, supervision, crate.

SAVE CTV

WILLISTON

◆◆ El Rancho Motor Hotel MI 🐾
(701) 572-6321. **$42-$52.** 1623 2nd Ave W. US 2 and 85 N bypass, 1 mi n. Ext/int corridors. **Pets:** Designated rooms, supervision.

A$K

◆◆ Super 8 Motel M
(701) 572-8371. **$43-$48, 7 days notice.** 2324 2nd Ave W. 1.3 mi n on US 2 and 85 bypass. Int corridors. **Pets:** Small. Designated rooms, no service, supervision, crate.

A$K

OHIO

CITY INDEX

AKRON

🆀 ◆ Days Inn Akron South/Airport M 🐾
(330) 644-1204. **$55-$80.** 3237 S Arlington Rd. I-77, exit 120, jct Arlington Rd. Ext corridors. **Pets:** $5 daily fee/pet, $5 one-time fee/pet. No service, supervision, crate.
SAVE S🄳 ✕ 🅪

🆀 ◆◆◆ Holiday Inn Express Akron M 🐾
(330) 644-7126. **$89-$139.** 2940 Chenoweth Rd. I-77, exit 120, jct Arlington Rd. Int corridors. **Pets:** Other. Supervision.
SAVE S🄳 ✕ 🄺 🄳 🄳 🅪

🆀 ◆◆ Red Roof Inn-Akron South M
(330) 644-7748. **$47-$60.** 2939 S Arlington Rd. I-77, exit 120 at jct Arlington Rd. **Pets:** Small. Designated rooms, supervision.
SAVE ✕

ASHLAND

🆀 ◆◆ Days Inn-Ashland M 🐾
(419) 289-0101. **$45-$65.** 1423 SR 1575. I-71, exit 186, just w. Ext corridors. **Pets:** Other. $25 deposit/pet. Supervision.
SAVE S🄳 ✕ 🄳 🄳 🅪

ASHTABULA

🆀 ◆ Cedars Motel M 🐾
(440) 992-5406. **$45-$70.** 2015 W Prospect Rd. 3 mi w on US 20 from jct SR 11. Ext corridors. **Pets:** Other. $5 daily fee/pet, $5 one-time fee/pet. No service, supervision, crate.
SAVE S🄳 ✕

🆀 ◆ Ho Hum Motel M 🐾
(440) 969-1136. **$40-$65.** 3801 N Ridge West. I-90, exit 223, 3 mi n on SR 45, 1 mi e on SR 20. **Pets:** Other. $5 daily fee/pet, $5 one-time fee/pet. No service, supervision, crate.
✕

AURORA

◆◆◆ The Aurora Inn 🆑 🐾
(330) 562-6121. **$165-$195, 3 days notice.** 30 E Garfield Rd. Jct SR 82 and 306. Int corridors. **Pets:** Medium, other. $50 deposit/pet. No service, supervision, crate.
A🅂🄺 S🄳 ✕ 🄳 🄳 🄷 🅪 ✕ 🄲🄸🅅

AUSTINTOWN

🆀 ◆◆ Best Western Meander Inn 🄼 🐾
(330) 544-2378. **$65-$90.** 870 N Canfield-Niles Rd. I-80, exit 223, 0.3 mi s on SR 46. Int corridors. **Pets:** $6 daily fee/pet. Designated rooms, no service, supervision, crate.
SAVE ✕ 🄳 🄳 🄳 🄷 🅪

⨀ ◆◆ Motel 6–4066 M ❖
(330) 793-9305. **$50-$60.** 5461 Seventy Six Dr. I-80, exit 223, 0.4 mi s on SR 46. Ext corridors. **Pets:** Small. Designated rooms, no service, supervision, crate.
SAVE S X

BELLEFONTAINE

◆◆◆ Holiday Inn Bellefontaine M
(937) 593-8515. **Call for rates.** 1134 N Main St. Jct US 33 and SR 68. Ext/int corridors. **Pets:** Supervision.
X ⬛ 🍴 🔁

BOARDMAN

⨀ ◆◆ Days Inn M ❖
(330) 758-2371. **$49-$80, 7 days notice.** 8392 Market St. I-76, exit 16, 1.8 mi n on SR 7. Ext corridors. **Pets:** Other. $5 daily fee/pet. Designated rooms, supervision.
SAVE S X 🔁

⨀ ◆◆ Economy Inn M ❖
(330) 549-3224. **$45-$85.** 10145 Market St. I-76, exit 16, 0.3 mi n on SR 7. Ext/int corridors. **Pets:** Medium. $5 daily fee/pet, $5 one-time fee/pet. No service, supervision, crate.
SAVE S X

◆◆ Microtel Inn Youngstown M
(330) 758-1816. **Call for rates.** 7393 South Ave. 0.3 mi w of jct I-680 and US 224, 0.3 mi s. Int corridors. **Pets:** Medium. Supervision.
X 🔁

⨀ ◆◆◆ Super 8 Motel M ❖
(330) 549-2187. **$49-$80, 7 days notice.** 10076 Market St. I-76, exit 16, 0.3 mi n on SR 7. Ext/int corridors. **Pets:** $5 daily fee/pet. Designated rooms, supervision.
SAVE S X 🔁

BROOKVILLE

⨀ ◆◆ Days Inn Brookville M
(937) 833-4003. **$60-$70, 7 days notice.** 100 Parkview Dr. I-70, exit 21. Ext corridors. **Pets:** No service, supervision, crate.
SAVE S X 🔁

CAMBRIDGE

◆◆ Best Western Cambridge M ❖
(740) 439-3581. **$49-$79, 7 days notice.** 1945 Southgate Pkwy. SR 209, 0.3 mi n of jct I-70, exit 178. Ext corridors. **Pets:** Supervision.
ASK S X 🔁 🍴 ⬛ 🔁

◆◆ Budget Host Deer Creek Motel M ❖
(740) 432-6391. **$33-$65.** 2321 Southgate Pkwy. I-70, exit 178, just n on SR 209. Ext corridors. **Pets:** Dogs only. $5 one-time fee/room. Designated rooms, no service, supervision, crate.
ASK S X 🔁

⨀ ◆ Budget Inn M ❖
(740) 432-2304. **$30-$50.** 6405 Glenn Hwy. On US 22 and 40, just n of I-70, exit 176, e on US 40. **Pets:** Small. $10 deposit/room, $5 daily fee/room, $5 one-time fee/room. Designated rooms, no service, supervision, crate.
SAVE S X

⨀ ◆◆◆ Comfort Inn M ❖
(740) 435-3200. **$84-$109.** 2327 Southgate Pkwy. I-70, exit 178, just n. Int corridors. **Pets:** Very small, other. $10 one-time fee/room. Designated rooms, supervision.
SAVE X 🔁 🍴 ⬛ 🔁

◆◆◆ Holiday Inn Cambridge/Salt Fork
      Area M ❖
(740) 432-7313. **$99, 3 days notice.** 2248 Southgate Pkwy. On SR 209, just n of jct I-70, exit 178. Int corridors. **Pets:** Other. Designated rooms, no service, supervision, crate.
ASK S X 🔁 🍴 ⬛ 🍴 🔁

CANTON

⨀ ◆◆◆ Best Suites of America M
(330) 499-1011. **$70-$88.** 4914 Everhard Rd. I-77, exit 109, 1 mi w. Int corridors. **Pets:** Supervision.
SAVE S X 🔁 🍴 ⬛ 🔁

◆ Parke Suites A
(330) 494-2233. **$80-$90.** 4285 Everhart Rd NW. Just w on Everhart Rd at jct I-77, exit 109 southbound; exit 109A northbound. Ext corridors. **Pets:** Supervision.
ASK S X 🔁 🍴 ⬛ 🔁

⨀ ◆◆ Red Roof Inn M ❖
(330) 499-1970. **$46-$73.** 5353 Inn Circle Ct NW. I-77, exit 109, just w on Everhard Rd. Ext corridors. **Pets:** Supervision.
SAVE X 🔁 CTV

◆◆◆ Residence Inn By Marriott A ❖
(330) 493-0004. **$129-$179.** 5325 Broadmoor Cir NW. I-77, exit 109, 0.5 mi e on Everhard Rd. Int corridors. **Pets:** Medium. $150 one-time fee/room. No service, supervision, crate.
ASK X 🔁 🍴 ⬛ 🔁 X

CHILLICOTHE

⨀ ◆◆◆ Christopher Inn M ❖
(740) 774-6835. **$59-$129.** 30 N Plaza Blvd. US 35, Bridge St exit. Int corridors. **Pets:** Other. Supervision.
SAVE S X 🔁 🍴 ⬛ 🔁

⨀ ◆◆◆ Comfort Inn M
(740) 775-3500. **$60-$90.** 20 N Plaza. At jct US 35 and Business Rt US 23. Int corridors. **Pets:** Supervision.
SAVE S X 🔁 🍴 ⬛ 🔁

⨀ ◆ Country Hearth Inn M ❖
(740) 775-2500. **$48-$85.** 1135 E Main St. Jct US 35 and 50. Ext/int corridors. **Pets:** $25 deposit/room. No service, supervision, crate.
SAVE S X 🔁 ⬛ 🔁

◆ Days Inn Chillicothe M
(740) 775-7000. **$52-$56, 3 days notice.** 1250 N Bridge St. US 35, Bridge St exit, 0.8 mi n. Ext/int corridors. **Pets:** Small. No service, supervision, crate.
ASK S X 🔁 ⬛ 🍴 🔁

CINCINNATI METROPOLITAN AREA

BATAVIA

**▲▲▲ ◆◆◆ Holiday Inn-Cincinnati
Eastgate** M ❀
(513) 752-4400. **$109-$119.** 4501 Eastgate Blvd. I-275, exit
63B (SR 32), to Eastgate Mall exit. Int corridors.
Pets: Small, dogs only. No service, supervision, crate.
[SAVE] 🔊 ⊠ 🎵 ▭ 🍴 ▧

BLUE ASH

▲▲▲ ◆◆◆ AmeriSuites at Blue Ash M ❀
(513) 489-3666. **$89-$129.** 11435 Reed-Hartman Hwy.
I-275, exit 47, 0.8 mi s. Int corridors. **Pets:** Small, other.
Supervision.
[SAVE] ⊠ 🏠 🔋 ▭ ▧

▲▲▲ ◆◆◆ MainStay Suites-Blue Ash M ❀
(513) 985-9992. **$95.** 4630 Creek Rd. I-275, exit 47, 2.3 mi
s on Reed-Hartman Hwy, just e. Int corridors.
Pets: Medium, other. $75 deposit/room, $5 daily fee/room.
Designated rooms, no service, supervision, crate.
[SAVE] 🔊 ⊠ 🎵 🗝 🔋 ▭ ▧

▲▲▲ ◆◆ Red Roof Inn Northeast (Blue Ash) M
(513) 793-8811. **$63-$92.** 5900 Pfeiffer Rd. Jct Pfeiffer Rd
and I-71, exit 15. Ext corridors. **Pets:** No service, supervision, crate.
[SAVE] ⊠ 🏠 🔋

**◆◆◆ Residence Inn by Marriott-Blue
Ash** M ❀
(513) 530-5060. **$169.** 11401 Reed-Hartman Hwy. I-275,
exit 47, 1 mi s. Ext corridors. **Pets:** Other. $95 one-time
fee/room. Supervision.
[ASK] 🔊 ⊠ 🏠 🎵 🔋 ▭ ▧ 🗙

CHERRY GROVE

▲▲▲ ◆ Motel 6–1092 M ❀
(513) 752-2262. **$40-$71.** 3960 Nine Mile Rd. I-275, exit 65,
0.4 mi e. Ext corridors. **Pets:** Small, other. No service,
supervision, crate.
🔊 ⊠ 🗝 ▧ [CTV]

▲▲▲ ◆◆ Red Roof Inn Cincinnati East M ❀
(513) 528-2741. **$66-$80.** 4035 Mt Carmel-Tobasco Rd.
I-275, exit 65. Ext corridors. **Pets:** Medium, other. No service, supervision, crate.
[SAVE] ⊠

CINCINNATI

◆◆◆ Garfield Suites Hotel ⬛
(513) 421-3355. **$199-$399.** 2 Garfield Pl. At corner Vine
and 8th sts. Int corridors. **Pets:** No service, supervision,
crate.
[ASK] ⊠ 🎵 🔋 ▭ 🍴

◆◆◆ Hampton Inn-Cincinnati Eastgate M
(513) 752-8584. **$69-$99.** 858 Eastgate North Dr. I-275, exit
63B (SR 32). Int corridors. **Pets:** Small. Designated rooms,
no service, supervision, crate.
[ASK] 🔊 ⊠ 🎵 🗝 ▭ ▧

▲▲▲ ◆◆◆ Holiday Inn-Downtown M ❀
(513) 241-8660. **$71-$71.** 800 W 8th St. I-75, exit 1G,
entrance on 8th St. Int corridors. **Pets:** Small, other. $25
one-time fee/room. No service, supervision, crate.
[SAVE] 🔊 ⊠ 🖐 🎵 🗝 ▭ 🍴 ▧

FOREST PARK

▲▲▲ ◆◆◆ AmeriSuites M
(513) 825-9035. **$79-$119.** 12001 Chase Plaza Dr. I-275,
exit 39, just s, then just w. Int corridors. **Pets:** No service,
supervision, crate.
[SAVE] 🔊 ⊠ 🎵 🔋 ▭ ▧

MASON

**◆◆◆ Baymont Inn & Suites-Cincinnati
Northeast** M
(513) 459-1111. **$97-$102.** 9918 Escort Dr. I-71, exit 19
(Fields-Ertel Rd), just w, then just s. Int corridors.
Pets: Medium. Designated rooms, no service, supervision,
crate.
🔊 ⊠ 🎵 🗝 🔋 ▭ ▧

▲▲▲ ◆◆ Holiday Inn Express Kings Island M
(513) 398-8075. **$109-$169.** 5589 Kings Mills Rd. I-71, exit
25, just w and then just s. Ext corridors. **Pets:** Designated
rooms, supervision.
[SAVE] 🔊 ⊠ 🏠 🎵 🔋 ▭ ▧ 🗙

▲▲▲ ◆◆ Quality Inn-Kings Island M
(513) 398-8015. **$59-$109.** 9845 Escort Dr. Jct I-71, exit 19,
just w. Int corridors. **Pets:** Designated rooms, supervision.
[SAVE] 🔊 ⊠ ▭ 🍴 ▧

MIDDLETOWN

**◆◆◆ The Manchester Inn & Conference
Center** 🅗 ❀
(513) 422-5481. **$68-$140.** 1027 Manchester Ave. Just w of
SR 4 and 73, at Middletown Civic Center. Int corridors.
Pets: Large. No service, supervision, crate.
[ASK] 🔊 ⊠ 🔋 ▭

▲▲▲ ◆◆ Ramada Inn Middletown M ❀
(513) 424-1201. **$69.** 6147 W SR 122. I-75, exit 32, just e.
Int corridors. **Pets:** Small, other. Supervision.
[SAVE] 🔊 ⊠ 🎵 🔋 ▭ ▧

◆ Super 8 Motel M ❀
(513) 422-4888. **$48-$78.** 3553 Commerce Dr. Jct I-75, exit
32, just e, then just n. Int corridors. **Pets:** Other. Supervision.
[ASK] 🔊 ⊠ 🔋

NORWOOD

◆◆ Howard Johnson East M
(513) 631-8500. **$65-$85.** 5410 Ridge Ave. I-71, exit 8
southbound; exit 8B northbound, 4 mi nw. Int corridors.
Pets: Supervision.
[ASK] 🔊 ⊠ 🔋 ▭ ▧

◆◆◆ **Quality Hotel & Suites Central** 🅷
(513) 351-6000. **$95-$95.** 4747 Montgomery Rd. I-71, exit 7, 1 mi w on SR 562 to Montgomery Rd exit, just w and just s; from I-75, exit 7, 1.5 mi e on SR 562 at Montgomery Rd exit. Int corridors. **Pets:** Small. No service, supervision, crate.
(ASK) (S🖥) ⊠ 🛋 🚪 🖵 🕋

(AAA) ◆◆ **Red Roof Inn Cincinnati Central**
       (Norwood) 🅼
(513) 531-6589. **$50-$65.** 5300 Kennedy Dr. I-71, southbound exit 8; northbound exit 8B. Ext corridors. **Pets:** Supervision.
(SAVE) ⊠ (CTV)

SHARONVILLE

◆◆ **Days Inn Cincinnati/Sharonville** 🅼 ☼
(513) 554-1400. **$41-$140, 3 days notice.** 11775 Lebanon Rd. I-275, exit 46, just s. Ext/int corridors. **Pets:** No service, supervision, crate.
(ASK) (S🖥) ⊠ 🚪 🖵 🕋 (CTV)

◆◆◆ **Homewood Suites-Cincinnati**
       North 🅰 ☼
(513) 772-8888. **$103-$103.** 2670 E Kemper Rd. Jct Mosteller Rd and I-275, exit 44. Int corridors. **Pets:** Very small, other. $8 daily fee/pet. Supervision.
(ASK) (S🖥) ⊠ 🚪 🖵 🕋 ⊠

(AAA) ◆◆ **The Preston Hotel** 🅼🅸
(513) 771-0700. **$79-$109, 3 days notice.** 2235 Sharon Rd. I-75, exit 15, just e. Ext/int corridors. **Pets:** Small. No service, supervision, crate.
(SAVE) (S🖥) ⊠ 🗞 🖘 🚪 🖵 🍴 🕋 ⊠

(AAA) ◆◆◆ **Radisson Hotel Cincinnati** 🅷 ☼
(513) 772-1720. **$99-$159.** 11320 Chester Rd. I-75, exit 15, 0.3 mi w on Sharon Rd, 0.5 mi n. Int corridors. **Pets:** Medium, other. $50 deposit/room. No service, supervision, crate.
(SAVE) ⊠ 🗞 🖘 🚪 🖵 🍴 🕋

(AAA) ◆◆ **Red Roof Inn Chester Rd** 🅼
(513) 771-5141. **$50-$76.** 11345 Chester Rd. I-75, exit 15, 0.3 mi w on Sharon Rd, 0.5 mi n. Ext corridors. **Pets:** Small. No service, supervision, crate.
(SAVE) ⊠ 🖘 🗞 🖘 🚪

(AAA) ◆◆ **Red Roof Inn-Sharon Road** 🅼
(513) 771-5552. **$60-$75.** 2301 E Sharon Rd. I-75, exit 15, just e. Ext corridors. **Pets:** Supervision.
(SAVE) ⊠ 🗞 🚪

◆◆◆ **Residence Inn by Marriott** 🅰 ☼
(513) 771-2525. **$119-$119.** 11689 Chester Rd. I-75, exit 15, 0.3 mi w on Sharon Rd, 1 mi n. Ext corridors. **Pets:** Medium, other. $90 one-time fee/room. No service, supervision, crate.
(ASK) (S🖥) ⊠ 🖘 🚪 🖵 🕋 ⊠

◆◆◆ **Woodfield Suites** 🅼
(513) 771-0300. **$99-$189.** 11029 Dowlin Dr. I-75, exit 15, just e. Int corridors. **Pets:** Small. Supervision.
(ASK) (S🖥) ⊠ 🛋 🗞 🖘 🚪 🖵 🕋 ⊠

SPRINGDALE

◆◆ **Baymont Inn & Suites Cincinnati**
     North 🅼 ☼
(513) 671-2300. **$65-$65.** 12150 Springfield Pike. I-275, exit 41, just s. Int corridors. **Pets:** Other. $50 deposit/pet. Supervision.
(S🖥) ⊠ 🗞 🚪 🖵

◆◆◆ **Best Western Springdale Hotel & Conference**
       Centre 🅼
(513) 671-6600. **$69-$129.** 11911 Sheraton Ln. I-275, exit 41, just n on SR 4. Int corridors. **Pets:** Supervision.
(ASK) (S🖥) ⊠ 🖵 🍴 🕋

◆◆ **Howard Johnson Cincinnati North** 🅼 ☼
(513) 825-3129. **$50-$87.** 400 Glensprings Dr. I-275, exit 41, just s. Int corridors. **Pets:** Other. Supervision.
(ASK) (S🖥) ⊠ 🚪 🖵 🕋

WILMINGTON

◆◆◆ **Holiday Inn Express** 🅼 ☼
(937) 382-5858. **$74-$125.** 155 Holiday Dr. 1.6 mi e on US 22. Int corridors. **Pets:** Medium. Supervision.
(ASK) (S🖥) ⊠ 🛋 🗞 🖘 🚪 🖵 🕋

☼   **END METROPOLITAN AREA**   ☼

CLEVELAND METROPOLITAN AREA

BEACHWOOD

◆◆◆ **Residence Inn by Marriot**
       Cleveland-Beachwood 🅰 ☼
(216) 831-3030. **$169-$299.** 3628 Park East Dr. Jct US 422 and I-271, Chagrin Blvd exit, just w. Int corridors. **Pets:** Other. $250 one-time fee/room. No service, supervision, crate.
(ASK) (S🖥) ⊠ 🛋 🗞 🖘 🚪 🖵 🕋 ⊠

CLEVELAND

◆◆◆ **Baymont Inn & Suites**
       Cleveland/Airport 🅼
(216) 251-8500. **$68-$80.** 4222 W 150th St. Jct I-71 and 150th St. Int corridors. **Pets:** Designated rooms, supervision.
(S🖥) ⊠ 🗞 🚪 🖵

(AAA) ◆◆◆ Cleveland Airport Marriott 🅷 ❀
(216) 252-5333. **$89-$164.** 4277 W 150th St. I-71 at 150th
St, exit 240. Int corridors. **Pets:** $50 one-time fee/room.
Supervision.

[SAVE] [⊠] [🐾] [🔥] [🖵] [🍴] [☕]

◆◆ Radisson Hotel at
Gateway-Cleveland 🅷 ❀
(216) 377-9000. **$129-$139.** 651 Huron Rd. N side of
Jacob's Field. Int corridors. **Pets:** Very small. Designated
rooms, supervision.

[⊠] [🐾] [🖵] [🍴] [CTV]

(AAA) ◆◆◆◆ The Ritz Carlton,
Cleveland 🅷 ❀
(216) 623-1300. **$199-$279.** 1515 W 3rd St. In Tower City
Center. Int corridors. **Pets:** Small. $30 daily fee/room.
Supervision.

[⊠] [🐾] [☕]

INDEPENDENCE

(AAA) ◆◆◆ Amerisuites 🅼
(216) 328-1060. **$114-$134.** 6025 Jefferson Dr. Jct I-77 and
Rockside Rd, just w to W Creek Rd, just n. Int corridors.
Pets: Supervision.

[SAVE] [S🔥] [⊠] [🐾] [🔥] [🖵] [☕]

◆◆ Baymont Inn & Suites-Cleveland
(Independence) 🅼
(216) 447-1133. **$75-$87.** 6161 Quarry Ln. Jct I-77 and
Rockside Rd, just e. Int corridors. **Pets:** Small. No service,
supervision, crate.

[S🔥] [⊠] [🐾] [🔥] [🖵]

(AAA) ◆◆◆ Hilton Cleveland South 🅼 ❀
(216) 447-1300. **$109-$109.** 6200 Quarry Ln. Jct I-77 and
Rockside Rd. Int corridors. **Pets:** Very small. Supervision.

[SAVE] [⊠] [🔥] [🖵] [🍴] [☕]

(AAA) ◆◆ Red Roof Inn 🅼
(216) 447-0030. **$72-$100.** 6020 Quarry Ln. Jct I-77 and
Rockside Rd, just e. Ext corridors. **Pets:** No service, supervision, crate.

[SAVE] [⊠] [🐾] [🖐]

◆◆◆ Residence Inn 🅼 ❀
(216) 520-1450. **$129-$159.** 5101 W Creek Rd. Jct I-77
and Rockside Rd, just w to W Creek Rd, just n. Ext corridors. **Pets:** Medium, other. $200 one-time fee/room. Super-
vision.

[ASK] [S🔥] [⊠] [🐾] [🖐] [🔥] [🖵] [☕] [⊠]

MAYFIELD HEIGHTS

◆◆ Baymont Inn & Suites-Cleveland NE 🅼 ❀
(440) 442-8400. **$70-$82.** 1421 Golden Gate Blvd. 0.3 mi w
off US 322 from jct I-271, Mayfield exit. Int corridors.
Pets: Other. Designated rooms, no service, supervision,
crate.

[S🔥] [⊠] [🐾] [🔥] [🖵] [CTV]

MIDDLEBURG HEIGHTS

(AAA) ◆◆◆ Comfort Inn-Cleveland
Airport 🅼 ❀
(440) 234-3131. **$79-$129.** 17550 Rosbough Dr. I-71, exit
235, w 0.3 mi to Engle Rd, then 0.3 mi n. Int corridors.
Pets: $25 one-time fee/room. Designated rooms, supervi-
sion.

[SAVE] [S🔥] [⊠] [🔥] [🖵] [☕] [CTV]

(AAA) ◆ Motel 6-1111 🅼 ❀
(440) 234-0990. **$52-$64.** 7219 Engle Rd. I-71, exit 235,
just w on Bagley Rd. Ext corridors. **Pets:** Small, other. No
service, supervision, crate.

[⊠] [🐾] [CTV]

(AAA) ◆◆ Red Roof Inn-Middleburg
Heights 🅼 ❀
(440) 243-2441. **$68-$83.** 17555 Bagley Rd. I-71, exit 235,
just w. Ext/int corridors. **Pets:** Medium, other. No service,
supervision, crate.

[SAVE] [⊠] [CTV]

◆◆◆ Residence Inn by Marriott 🅰 ❀
(440) 234-6688. **$98-$125.** 17525 Rosbough Dr. I-71, exit
235, just w on Bagley Rd, just n on Engle Rd. Ext/int
corridors. **Pets:** Small, other. $250 one-time fee/room. Des-
ignated rooms, no service, supervision, crate.

[ASK] [⊠] [🐾] [🔥] [🖵] [☕] [⊠]

NORTH OLMSTED

◆◆ Homestead Village Guest Studios 🅼 ❀
(440) 777-8585. **$59-$74** (no credit cards). 24851 Country
Club Blvd. I-480, exit 6B, 0.3 mi n on SR 252. Ext corridors.
Pets: Other. $75 one-time fee/room. Supervision.

[ASK] [⊠] [🐾] [🔥] [🖵] [CTV]

STRONGSVILLE

(AAA) ◆◆ Red Roof Inn-Strongsville 🅼 ❀
(440) 238-0170. **$52-$61.** 15385 Royalton Rd. I-71, exit
231A, just e on SR 82, 1 mi s of turnpike, exit 161. Ext
corridors. **Pets:** Small. No service, supervision, crate.

[SAVE] [⊠] [🐾] [CTV]

WESTLAKE

(AAA) ◆◆ Red Roof Inn-Westlake 🅼 ❀
(440) 892-7920. **$70-$93.** 29595 Clemens Rd. I-90, exit
156. Ext corridors. **Pets:** Small, other. Designated rooms,
no service, supervision, crate.

[SAVE] [⊠] [🐾] [🔥] [CTV]

◆◆◆ Residence Inn by Marriott 🅰 ❀
(440) 892-2254. **$119-$159.** 30100 Clemens Rd. I-90, exit
156, just n. Ext corridors. **Pets:** Other. $200 one-time fee/
room. Supervision.

[ASK] [⊠] [🐾] [🖐] [🔥] [🖵] [☕] [⊠]

❀ **END METROPOLITAN AREA** ❀

COLUMBUS METROPOLITAN AREA

CIRCLEVILLE

◆ Knights Inn M
(740) 474-6006. **$40-$55.** 23897 US 23S. 1.5 mi s on US 23. Ext corridors. **Pets:** No service, supervision, crate.

[ASK] [S🐾] [✕] [🔒] [💻]

COLUMBUS

◍ ◆◆◆ AmeriSuites M
(614) 846-4355. **$79-$114.** 7490 Vantage Dr. Just n of jct I-270, exit 23, and US 23 N. Int corridors. **Pets:** Medium. Supervision.

[SAVE] [S🐾] [✕] [🔒] [🌊] [🔒] [💻] [🎒]

◍ ◆◆ Best Western University Inn M ❀
(614) 261-7141. **$55-$75.** 3232 Olentangy River Rd. SR 315, N Broadway exit, 0.3 mi s. Int corridors. **Pets:** $5 daily fee/pet. No service, supervision, crate.

[SAVE] [S🐾] [✕] [🔒] [💻] [🎒]

◍ ◆◆◆ Columbus Marriott North H
(614) 885-1885. **$79-$179.** 6500 Doubletree Ave. I-71, exit 117, 0.3 mi w on SR 161, 0.8 mi on Busch Blvd to Kingsmill Pkwy. Int corridors. **Pets:** Supervision.

[SAVE] [S🐾] [✕] [🔒] [🌊] [🗝] [🔒] [💻] [🍴] [🎒]

◍ ◆◆ Days Inn Fairgrounds M
(614) 299-4300. **$50-$65.** 1700 Clara St. I-71, exit 111, just w. Ext corridors. **Pets:** Supervision.

[SAVE] [S🐾] [✕] [🔒] [💻]

◆◆◆ Doubletree Guest Suites H ❀
(614) 228-4600. **$89-$144.** 50 S Front St. Corner of Front and State sts, just n. Int corridors. **Pets:** Small. $50 one-time fee/room. No service, supervision, crate.

[ASK] [S🐾] [✕] [🌊] [🔒] [💻] [🍴]

◍ ◆◆◆ Hawthorn Suites Ltd M
(614) 853-6199. **$139, 3 days notice.** 5505 Keim Cir. I-70, exit 91B, just n on Renner Rd. Int corridors. **Pets:** Large. Supervision.

[SAVE] [S🐾] [✕] [🔒] [🗝] [🔒] [💻] [🎒]

◍ ◆◆◆ Holiday Inn City Center MI
(614) 221-3281. **$89-$119, 3 days notice.** 175 E Town St. At 4th and E Town St. Int corridors. **Pets:** Designated rooms, no service, supervision, crate.

[SAVE] [S🐾] [✕] [🔒] [🌊] [🗝] [💻] [🍴] [🎒]

◆◆◆ Holiday Inn-Columbus Airport MI
(614) 237-6360. **$97-$107, 7 days notice.** 750 Stelzer Rd. 0.8 mi s of Port Columbus International Airport entrance. Int corridors. **Pets:** Medium. No service, supervision, crate.

[ASK] [✕] [🌊] [🔒] [💻] [🍴] [🎒]

◍ ◆◆◆ Holiday Inn-Columbus/Worthington Area MI ❀
(614) 885-3334. **$109.** 175 Hutchinson Ave. I-270, exit 23, just n of jct with US 23 N. Int corridors. **Pets:** Other. No service, supervision, crate.

[SAVE] [✕] [🔒] [🌊] [🔒] [💻] [🍴] [✕]

◆◆◆ Holiday Inn East I-70 H ❀
(614) 868-1380. **$79-$79.** 4560 Hilton Corporate Dr. I-70, exit 107 (Hamilton Rd). Int corridors. **Pets:** Supervision.

[ASK] [S🐾] [✕] [🔒] [🗝] [🔒] [💻] [🍴] [🎒] [✕]

◍ ◆◆◆ Holiday Inn on the Lane H
(614) 294-4848. **$119, 3 days notice.** 328 W Lane Ave. 0.5 mi e of SR 315, Lane Ave exit; opposite Ohio State University. Int corridors. **Pets:** Designated rooms, supervision.

[SAVE] [✕] [🔒] [🌊] [🔒] [💻] [🍴] [🎒] [✕]

◍ ◆◆◆ Homewood Suites M ❀
(614) 785-0001. **$109.** 115 Hutchinson Ave. I-270, exit 23, just ne. Int corridors. **Pets:** Other. $10 daily fee/room. Supervision.

[SAVE] [✕] [🌊] [🔒] [💻] [🎒] [✕]

◍ ◆◆ Knights Inn-Columbus East M ❀
(614) 864-0600. **$50-$89.** 4320 Groves Rd. I-70, exit 107, just s. Ext corridors. **Pets:** $35 deposit/room. No service, supervision, crate.

[SAVE] [S🐾] [✕] [🔒]

◆ Microtel Inn-North M
(614) 436-0556. **$64, 5 days notice.** 7500 Vantage Dr. Just n of jct I-270 (exit 23) and US 23 N. Int corridors. **Pets:** Designated rooms, supervision.

[✕] [🔒]

◍ ◆◆ Red Roof Inn Columbus North M
(614) 846-8520. **$54-$86.** 750 Morse Rd. I-71, exit 116. Ext corridors. **Pets:** Supervision.

[SAVE] [✕] [🔒] [🗝]

◍ ◆◆ Red Roof Inn-OSU M
(614) 267-9941. **$60-$88.** 441 Ackerman Rd. Off SR 315, 0.3 mi e from Ackerman Rd exit. Ext corridors. **Pets:** Supervision.

[SAVE] [✕]

◍ ◆◆ Red Roof Inn-West M ❀
(614) 878-9245. **$48-$74.** 5001 Renner Rd. I-70, exit 91 eastbound; exit 91B westbound (Rome-Hilliard Rd exit). Ext corridors. **Pets:** Other. No service, supervision, crate.

[SAVE] [✕] [🔒] [🗝]

◆◆◆ Residence Inn by Marriott-Columbus East ▲
(614) 864-8844. **$109, 5 days notice.** 2084 S Hamilton Rd. Just s off Hamilton Rd from jct I-70, exit 107. Ext corridors. **Pets:** No service, supervision, crate.

[ASK] [S🐾] [✕] [🔒] [🗝] [🔒] [💻] [🎒] [✕]

◆◆◆ The Residence Inn by Marriott-Columbus North ▲
(614) 431-1819. **Call for rates.** 6191 W Zumstein Dr. I-71, exit 117, 0.3 mi w on SR 161, 0.4 mi n on Busch Blvd, Shapter Mediterranean and Zumstein Dr. Ext corridors. **Pets:** No service, supervision, crate.

[✕] [🔒] [🗝] [💻] [🎒] [✕]

◆◆◆ Sheraton Suites Columbus H
(614) 436-0004. **Call for rates.** 201 Hutchinson Ave. I-270, exit 23, just ne. Int corridors. **Pets:** Medium. Supervision.

[✕] [🔒] [🌊] [🗝] [🔒] [💻] [🍴] [🎒]

(AAA) ◆◆◆ The University Plaza Hotel & Conference Center M
(614) 267-7461. **$80-$90.** 3110 Olentangy River Rd. 0.5 mi s of N Broadway, exit off SR 315. Int corridors. **Pets:** Designated rooms, no service, supervision, crate.
[SAVE] [S🐾] [✕] [🛎] [▥] [¶¶] [🍽]

(AAA) ◆◆◆ Wellesley Inn & Suites M 🐾
(614) 431-5522. **$69-$109.** 8555 Lyra Dr. I-71, exit 121, just w on Polaris Pkwy. Int corridors. **Pets:** $100 deposit/room. No service, supervision, crate.
[SAVE] [S🐾] [✕] [♿] [🐾] [🛎] [▥] [🍽]

(AAA) ◆◆◆◆ The Westin Great Southern Columbus H 🐾
(614) 228-3800. **$99-$155, 3 days notice.** 310 S High St. Corner of Main and High sts. Int corridors. **Pets:** Small, other. $100 deposit/room. No service, supervision, crate.
[SAVE] [✕] [🐾] [🐾] [▥] [¶¶]

DUBLIN

◆◆ Baymont Inn & Suites-Columbus (Dublin) M 🐾
(614) 792-8300. **$70-$75.** 6145 Park Center Cir. I-270, exit 15 (Tuttle Crossing), just e. Int corridors. **Pets:** Small. Designated rooms, supervision.
[S🐾] [✕] [🏠] [🐾] [🛎] [▥]

(AAA) ◆◆◆ Columbus Marriott Northwest M 🐾
(614) 791-1000. **$99-$159.** 5605 Paul Blazer Memorial Pkwy. I-270, exit 15. Int corridors. **Pets:** Very small. No service, supervision, crate.
[SAVE] [S🐾] [✕] [♿] [🐾] [🐾] [🛎] [▥] [¶¶] [🍽]

(AAA) ◆◆ Red Roof Inn-Dublin M
(614) 764-3993. **$57-$82.** 5125 Post Rd. Just e of jct SR 161, US 33 and I-270, exit 17A. Ext corridors. **Pets:** No service, supervision, crate.
[SAVE] [✕] [🏠]

◆◆◆ Residence Inn by Marriott A
(614) 791-0403. **$99-$119.** 435 Metro Place S. I-270, exit 17A, 0.5 mi s on Frantz Rd. Ext/int corridors. **Pets:** Designated rooms, supervision.
[ASK] [S🐾] [✕] [🏠] [🐾] [🛎] [▥] [🍽] [❌]

◆◆◆ Woodfin Suites Hotel A
(614) 766-7762. **$99-$150.** 4130 Tuller Rd. Sawmill Rd via Dublin Center Dr, 0.3 mi s of I-270, exit 20. Ext corridors. **Pets:** Medium. No service, supervision, crate.
[ASK] [S🐾] [✕] [🐾] [🛎] [▥] [🍽]

◆◆◆ Wyndham Dublin Hotel M 🐾
(614) 764-2200. **$129.** 600 Metro Place N. I-270, exit 17A. Int corridors. **Pets:** Medium. $50 one-time fee/room. No service, supervision, crate.
[ASK] [S🐾] [✕] [🛎] [▥] [¶¶] [🍽]

GROVE CITY

(AAA) ◆◆◆ Best Western Executive Inn M 🐾
(614) 875-7770. **$55-$65.** 4026 Jackpot Rd. I-71, exit 100 (Stringtown Rd), just e. Ext corridors. **Pets:** Small, dogs only. $9 one-time fee/pet. Designated rooms, supervision.
[SAVE] [S🐾] [✕] [🛎] [🍽]

(AAA) ◆◆ Red Roof Inn-South Columbus M 🐾
(614) 875-8543. **$57-$84.** 1900 Stringtown Rd. I-71, exit 100, just w. Ext corridors. **Pets:** Small. No service, supervision, crate.
[SAVE] [✕] [🐾]

HEATH

◆◆ Holiday Inn of Newark/Heath M
(740) 522-1165. **Call for rates.** 733 Hebron Rd. I-70, exit 129B, 7 mi n on SR 79. Ext corridors. **Pets:** Designated rooms, no service, supervision, crate.
[ASK] [✕] [🛎] [▥] [¶¶] [🍽]

HILLIARD

◆◆◆ Homewood Suites Columbus/Hillard M
(614) 529-4100. **$129.** 3841 Park Mill Run Dr. I-270, exit 13 southbound; exit 13A northbound. Int corridors. **Pets:** Medium. Designated rooms, supervision.
[ASK] [S🐾] [✕] [♿] [🐾] [🐾] [🛎] [▥] [🍽]

LANCASTER

(AAA) ◆◆◆ Hampton Inn Lancaster M 🐾
(740) 654-2999. **$71-$77.** 2041 Schorrway Dr. 3 mi nw on US 33. Int corridors. **Pets:** Medium, other. Supervision.
[SAVE] [S🐾] [✕] [🐾] [🛎] [▥] [🍽]

(AAA) ◆◆ Lancaster Best Western M 🐾
(740) 653-3040. **$57-$94.** 1858 N Memorial Dr. 2 mi nw on US 33. Ext/int corridors. **Pets:** Small. $5 one-time fee/room. No service, supervision, crate.
[SAVE] [S🐾] [✕] [🛎] [▥] [¶¶] [🍽] [❌]

MARYSVILLE

(AAA) ◆◆ Days Inn Marysville M 🐾
(937) 644-8821. **$69-$69, 7 days notice.** 16510 Square Dr. Just e of US 36, exit off US 33. Ext corridors. **Pets:** Small, other. $10 one-time fee/pet. Designated rooms, supervision.
[SAVE] [S🐾] [✕] [🛎] [▥]

◆ Super 8 Motel M 🐾
(614) 873-4100. **$45-$78.** 10220 US 42. US 42 at jct US 33. Ext/int corridors. **Pets:** $5 daily fee/pet. Supervision.
[S🐾] [✕]

NEWARK

◆◆◆ Cherry Valley Lodge M
(740) 788-1200. **$159-$169.** 2299 Cherry Valley Rd. 3.5 mi w on SR 16, then 0.3 mi s. Int corridors. **Pets:** Small. Designated rooms, no service, supervision, crate.
[ASK] [S🐾] [✕] [🏠] [🐾] [🛎] [▥] [¶¶] [🍽] [❌]

REYNOLDSBURG

(AAA) ◆◆ Best Western Inn East Airport M 🐾
(614) 864-1280. **$59-$73.** 2100 Brice Rd. I-70, eastbound exit 110B; westbound exit 110, just n. Int corridors. **Pets:** Designated rooms, supervision.
[SAVE] [S🐾] [✕] [🐾] [¶¶] [🍽]

◆◆◆ La Quinta Inn M 🐾
(614) 866-6456. **$65-$85.** 2447 Brice Rd. I-70, exit 110B eastbound; exit 110 westbound, 0.3 mi n. Int corridors. **Pets:** Small. No service, supervision, crate.
[ASK] [✕] [🛎] [▥] [🍽]

◆◆ **Red Roof Inn-East** **M**
(614) 864-3683. **$56-$78.** 2449 Brice Rd. At Brice Rd exit of
I-70, eastbound exit 110B; westbound exit 110. Ext corridors. **Pets:** Small. No service, supervision, crate.
SAVE ⊠ 🖼

WESTERVILLE

◆ **Knights Inn-Columbus/Westerville** **M**
(614) 890-0426. **$49-$99.** 32 Heatherdown Dr. I-270, exit
29, 0.3 mi n on SR 3. Ext corridors. **Pets:** No service,
supervision, crate.
ASK S⊘ ⊠ 🖥 💻 ⤢

⊛ **END METROPOLITAN AREA** ⊛

DAYTON

◆◆◆ **Crowne Plaza-Dayton** **H**
(937) 224-0800. **$129, 30 days notice.** 33 E Fifth St.
Downtown, opposite Dayton Convention Center, Fifth and
Jefferson sts. Int corridors. **Pets:** Designated rooms, super-
vision.
ASK S⊘ ⊠ 🖥 💻 🍴 ⤢

◆◆◆ **Dayton Marriott Hotel** **H**
(937) 223-1000. **$79-$119.** 1414 S Patterson Blvd. 1 mi e
of I-75, Edwin C Moses Blvd exit. Int corridors.
Pets: Medium. No service, supervision, crate.
⊠ ⊘ 🖥 💻 🍴 ⤢ ⊠

◆◆ **Howard Johnson Express Inn** **M** ⊛
(937) 454-0550. **$60-$100.** 7575 Poe Rd. I-75, exit 60,
northbound n on Poe Rd; southbound n on Miller Ln, then n
on Little York Rd to Poe Rd. Int corridors. **Pets:** Medium.
$50 deposit/room. Supervision.
ASK S⊘ ⊠ ⊘ 🖥 💻 ⤢

 ◆ **Motel 6–603** **M**
(937) 898-3606. **$36-$56.** 7130 Miller Ln. I-75, exit 60 (Little
York Rd). Ext corridors. **Pets:** Medium. No service, supervision, crate.
S⊘ ⊠ 🖼 ⤢

◆◆ **Ramada Inn-North** **MI** ⊛
(937) 890-9500. **$60-$80.** 4079 Little York Rd. Jct I-75, exit
60, 0.5 mi s of jct I-70. Ext/int corridors. **Pets:** Medium,
other. Designated rooms, supervision.
ASK S⊘ ⊠ ⊘ 🖥 💻 🍴 ⤢ ⊠

 ◆◆ **Red Roof Inn-North** **M** ⊛
(937) 898-1054. **$46-$72.** 7370 Miller Ln. On Little York Rd
at jct I-75, exit 60, 0.5 mi s of jct I-70. Ext corridors.
Pets: Other. Supervision.
SAVE ⊠ ⊘ 🖼 🖥 CTV

◆◆◆ **Residence Inn by Marriott-Dayton North** **A**
(937) 898-7764. **$140.** 7070 Poe Ave. At jct I-75, exit 60.
Ext corridors. **Pets:** No service, supervision, crate.
ASK S⊘ ⊠ ⊘ 🖼 🖥 💻 ⤢ ⊠

DOVER

◆ **Knights Inn** **M** ⊛
(330) 364-7724. **$40-$85, 7 days notice.** 889 Commercial
Pkwy. I-77, exit 83, just e. Ext corridors. **Pets:** Other. $5
one-time fee/pet. No service, supervision, crate.
ASK S⊘ ⊠ ⊘ ⤢

WORTHINGTON

 ◆◆◆ **Clarion Hotel Worthington** **MI** ⊛
(614) 436-0700. **$85-$95.** 7007 N High St. I-270, exit 23,
0.3 mi s on US 23. Int corridors. **Pets:** $10 daily fee/room,
$25 one-time fee/room. No service, supervision, crate.
SAVE S⊘ ⊠ 🖐 ⊘ 🖼 🖥 💻 🍴 ⤢

 ◆◆ **Red Roof Inn-Worthington** **M** ⊛
(614) 846-3001. **$65-$81.** 7474 N High St. Just n of jct US
23 N and I-270, exit 23. Ext corridors. **Pets:** Medium, other.
No service, supervision, crate.
SAVE ⊠ 🖼

EATON

◆◆ **Econo Lodge** **M**
(937) 456-5959. **$36-$60, 3 days notice.** 6161 Rt 127 N.
US 127, at jct I-70, exit 10. Ext corridors. **Pets:** No service,
supervision, crate.
ASK S⊘ ⊠ 🖼 🖥

ELYRIA

◆◆◆ **Comfort Inn** **M** ⊛
(440) 324-7676. **$80-$108.** 739 Leona St. Ohio Tpke, exit
145, 0.3 mi n on SR 57, 0.3 mi w on Griswald. Int corridors.
Pets: Small. $8 daily fee/pet, $8 one-time fee/pet. Designated rooms, no service, supervision, crate.
ASK S⊘ ⊠ 🖼

◆◆◆ **Super 8 Motel** **MI** ⊛
(440) 323-7488. **$54-$104.** 910 Lorain Blvd. On SR 57, 0.5
mi s of I-80, exit 8. Int corridors. **Pets:** Other. $10 one-time
fee/room. Designated rooms, supervision.
ASK S⊘ ⊠ 🖼 💻 🍴 ⤢

ENGLEWOOD

 ◆◆◆ **Holiday Inn-Dayton Northwest
Airport** **MI**
(937) 832-1234. **$99.** 10 Rockridge Rd. Jct I-70, exit 29. Int
corridors. **Pets:** No service, supervision, crate.
S⊘ ⊠ 🖼 🖥 💻 🍴 ⤢

FAIRBORN

 ◆◆◆ **Homewood Suites** **A**
(937) 429-0600. **$119-$139.** 2750 Presidential Dr. Jct Fair-
field Rd and I-675, exit 17. Ext/int corridors. **Pets:** Designated rooms, supervision.
SAVE S⊘ ⊠ ⊘ 🖼 🖥 💻 ⤢ ⊠

 ◆◆ **Red Roof Inn-Fairborn** **M**
(937) 426-6116. **$59-$86.** 2580 Colonel Glenn Hwy. Jct
Fairfield Rd and I-675, exit 17. Ext corridors. **Pets:** Small.
Supervision.
SAVE ⊠ ⊘ 🖼 CTV

FAIRLAWN

◆ **Akron Super 8 Motel** Ⓜ
(330) 666-8887. **$35-$110.** 79 Rothrock Rd. Jct I-77 and
SR 18, exit 137A. Int corridors. **Pets:** Small. No service,
supervision, crate.

Ⓐ🆂🆇⛛🔲💻

◆◆◆ **Best Western Inn & Suites** Ⓜ
(330) 670-0888. **$89-$999.** 160 W Montross Ave. I-77, exit
137B, just w. Int corridors. **Pets:** Small. No service, supervision, crate.

Ⓐ🆂🆇⛛🔲💻📺

◆◆◆ **Hampton Inn** Ⓜ
(330) 666-7361. **$85-$105.** 80 Springside Dr. Jct SR 18 and
I-77, exit 137A. Int corridors. **Pets:** No service, supervision,
crate.

Ⓐ🆂🆇⛛🔲💻

⟐⟐ ◆◆ **Red Roof Inn Akron North** Ⓜ
(330) 666-0566. **$61-$81.** 99 Rothrock Rd. Jct I-77 and SR
18, exit 137A. Ext corridors. **Pets:** Supervision.

🆂🆇⛛📺

◆◆◆ **The Residence Inn by Marriott** Ⓐ
(330) 666-4811. **$143.** 120 W Montrose Ave. I-77, exit
137B, just w. Ext corridors. **Pets:** Supervision.

Ⓐ🆂🆇🔲💻📺🆇

FINDLAY

⟐⟐ ◆◆ **Econo Lodge** Ⓜ 🐾
(419) 422-0154. **$35-$70.** 316 Emma St. Jct SR 12 and
I-75, exit 157. Ext corridors. **Pets:** Very small. $10 daily
fee/pet, $10 one-time fee/pet. No service, supervision,
crate.

🆂🆇🔲

⟐⟐ ◆◆◆ **Hawthorn Suites Ltd** Ⓜ
(419) 425-9696. **$89.** 2355 Tiffin Ave. 3 mi e on US 224. Int
corridors. **Pets:** Medium. Supervision.

🆂🆇⛛🔲💻📺

◆ **Ramada Inn** Ⓜ
(419) 423-8212. **Call for rates.** 820 Trenton Ave. Jct I-75
and US 224, exit 159. Ext corridors. **Pets:** Designated
rooms, supervision.

🆇⛛💻📺📺

⟐⟐ ◆◆ **Rodeway Inn** Ⓜ 🐾
(419) 424-1133. **$34-$64.** 1901 Broad Ave. 0.5 mi e at Jct
I-75 and US 224, exit 159. Ext corridors. **Pets:** Other. $10
one-time fee/pet. Supervision.

🆂🆇🔲📺

◆◆ **Super 8 Motel-Findlay** Ⓜ
(419) 422-8863. **$38-$52.** 1600 Fox St. I-75, exit 159, just
e. Int corridors. **Pets:** No service, supervision, crate.

🆂🆇⛛🔲

FOSTORIA

⟐⟐ ◆◆ **Days Inn** Ⓜ 🐾
(419) 435-6511. **$50-$66.** 601 Findlay St. SR 12, 1 mi w of
SR 23. Ext corridors. **Pets:** Small, other. Designated rooms,
supervision.

🆂🆇🆇💻

FREDERICKTOWN

◆◆◆ **Heartland Country Resort** 🆔 🐾
(419) 768-9300. **$80-$175, 7 days notice.** 2994 Township
Rd 190. I-71, exit 151, 2 mi e on SR 95, 2 mi s on SR 314,
1 mi e on SR 179. Int corridors. **Pets:** Other. $15 daily
fee/room. Designated rooms, supervision.

Ⓐ🆇🔲💻📺🆇📺

FREMONT

⟐⟐⟐ ◆ **Fremont Turnpike Motel** Ⓜ 🐾
(419) 332-6489. **$46-$80.** 520 E CR 89. Ohio Tpke, exit 91,
0.5 mi s on SR 53. Ext corridors. **Pets:** Small. $6 deposit/
pet, $6 daily fee/pet, $6 one-time fee/pet. No service, supervision, crate.

🆂🆇

◆◆◆ **Holiday Inn-Fremont/Port Clinton Turnpike**
      Exit 91 Ⓜ
(419) 334-2682. **Call for rates.** 3422 Port Clinton Rd. SR
53, at jct Ohio Tpke, exit 91. Int corridors. **Pets:** Medium.
No service, supervision, crate.

🆇🔲💻📺📺🆇

GALION

◆ **Hometown Inn** Ⓜ 🐾
(419) 468-9909. **$50-$140.** 172 N Portland Way. 1 mi w on
SR 598, n of jct SR 309/61/19. Ext/int corridors.
Pets: Other. $20 deposit/pet, $10 daily fee/room, $10 one-
time fee/pet. No service, supervision, crate.

Ⓐ🆂🆇🔲

GALLIPOLIS

⟐⟐⟐ ◆◆ **William Ann Motel** Ⓜ
(740) 446-3373. **$40-$45.** 918 2nd Ave. 0.8 mi n on SR 7.
Ext corridors. **Pets:** No service, supervision, crate.

🆂🆇🔲

GREENVILLE

⟐⟐⟐ ◆◆◆ **Greenville Inn** Ⓜ
(937) 548-3613. **$55-$100.** 851 E Martin. 0.3 mi w on SR
571, from jct US 127 and 36. Int corridors. **Pets:** Designated rooms, supervision.

🆂🆇🆇⛛🔲💻

HAMILTON

◆◆◆ **The Hamiltonian Hotel** 🅷 🐾
(513) 896-6200. **$91.** 1 Riverfront Plaza. Just off High St,
on Front St. Int corridors. **Pets:** $25 deposit/room. Supervi-
sion.

Ⓐ🆂🆇⛛🔲💻📺

HOLLAND

⟐⟐⟐ ◆◆ **Cross Country Inn** Ⓜ
(419) 866-6565. **$41-$55.** 1201 E Mall Dr. I-475, exit 8, just
w on SR 2; behind mall. Ext corridors. **Pets:** Medium. No
service, supervision, crate.

🆂🆇🆇⛛📺📺

◆◆ Red Roof Inn Toledo/Holland M
(419) 866-5512. **$47-$58.** 1214 Corporate Dr. I-475, exit 8, just e on SR 2, then just n on Holland-Sylvania Rd. Ext corridors. **Pets:** No service, supervision, crate.
[SAVE] [✕] [🐾] [🖥] [CTV]

◆◆◆ Residence Inn by Marriott A ❀
(419) 867-9555. **$159.** 6101 Trust Dr. I-475, exit 8, e to Holland/Sylvania Rd, just n. Ext corridors. **Pets:** $10 daily fee/room, $50 one-time fee/room. Designated rooms, no service, supervision, crate.
[ASK] [S🐾] [✕] [🐾] [🖥] [💻] [🔊] [✕]

HUBER HEIGHTS

◆◆ Travelodge M
(937) 236-9361. **$55-$70, 7 days notice.** 7911 Brandt Pike. SR 201, s of jct I-70, exit 38. Ext/int corridors. **Pets:** No service, supervision, crate.
[ASK] [S🐾] [✕] [🖥] [💻] [🔊]

HURON

◆ Plantation Motel M ❀
(419) 433-4790. **$59-$88, 3 days notice.** 2815 E Cleveland Rd. 3 mi e on US 6. Ext corridors. **Pets:** Other. $7 daily fee/pet, $7 one-time fee/pet. No service, supervision, crate.
[✕] [🖥] [💻] [🔊]

JACKSON

◆ Knights Inn M ❀
(740) 286-2135. **$40-$54.** 404 Chillicothe St. 0.7 mi n on Business Rt US 35. Ext corridors. **Pets:** $20 deposit/pet. No service, supervision, crate.
[ASK] [S🐾] [✕] [🖥]

KENT

◆◆◆ Holiday Inn-Akron/Kent M ❀
(330) 678-0101. **$98-$98.** 4363 SR 43. Jct I-76 and SR 43, exit 33. Ext corridors. **Pets:** Medium. $50 deposit/room. Supervision.
[SAVE] [S🐾] [✕] [🖥] [💻] [🍴] [🔊]

LIMA

◆ Days Inn M
(419) 227-6515. **$40-$75, 7 days notice.** 1250 Neubrecht Rd. I-75, exit 127, 0.5 mi nw. Ext/int corridors. **Pets:** Small. No service, supervision, crate.
[SAVE] [S🐾] [✕] [🖥] [🔊] [✕]

◆◆ Econo Lodge M ❀
(419) 222-0596. **$44-$49.** 1201 Neubrecht Rd. On SR 81, w of jct I-75, exit 127B (northbound); exit 127 (southbound). Ext/int corridors. **Pets:** $5 daily fee/pet. No service, supervision, crate.
[SAVE] [S🐾] [✕] [🖥] [💻] [🍴] [🔊] [✕]

◆◆◆ Holiday Inn Lima M ❀
(419) 222-0004. **$112-$112.** 1920 Roschman Ave. Jct SR 117, 309 and I-75, exit 125A. Int corridors. **Pets:** Small, other. Designated rooms, no service, supervision, crate.
[ASK] [S🐾] [✕] [🐾] [💻] [🍴] [🔊]

◆◆ Knights Inn M
(419) 331-9215. **$40-$60.** 2285 N Eastown Rd. 4.5 mi w of jct I-75; on SR 309, West of Lima Mall. Ext corridors. **Pets:** No service, supervision, crate.
[SAVE] [S🐾] [✕] [🖥] [🔊]

◆ Motel 6–586 M
(419) 228-0456. **$40-$56.** 1800 Harding Hwy. SR 117 and 309, e of jct I-75, exit 125. Ext corridors. **Pets:** Designated rooms, no service, supervision, crate.
[S🐾] [✕] [🖥] [CTV]

LISBON

◆◆◆ Days Inn Lisbon M ❀
(330) 420-0001. **$65-$75.** 40952 SR 154. Exit SR 154 off SR 11, just w. Int corridors. **Pets:** Other. $10 daily fee/pet. Supervision.
[✕] [🐾] [🖥] [💻] [🔊] [CTV]

LOGAN

◆ Shawnee Inn M ❀
(740) 385-5674. **$45-$55, 3 days notice.** 30916 Lake Logan Rd. SR 664, just s of US 33. Ext corridors. **Pets:** Small. Designated rooms, no service, supervision, crate.
[SAVE] [S🐾] [✕]

MACEDONIA

◆◆◆ Baymont Inn & Suites-Cleveland (Macedonia) M ❀
(330) 468-5400. **$101-$111.** 268 E Highland Rd. Jct I-271 and SR 8, 3 mi n of Ohio Tpk, exit 180. Int corridors. **Pets:** Small, other. $50 deposit/room. Designated rooms, supervision.
[S🐾] [✕] [🐾] [🐾] [🖥] [🖥] [💻] [🔊] [CTV]

◆ Knights Inn-Cleveland/Macedonia M ❀
(330) 467-1981. **$52-$72.** 240 E Highland Rd. Jct I-271 and SR 8; 3 mi n of I-80, exit 180. Ext corridors. **Pets:** Designated rooms, no service, supervision, crate.
[SAVE] [S🐾] [✕] [🖥] [💻] [🔊]

MANSFIELD

◆◆◆ Baymont Inn & Suites-Mansfield M
(419) 774-0005. **$60-$65.** 120 Stander Ave. Jct I-71 and SR 13, exit 169. Int corridors. **Pets:** Medium. Designated rooms, no service, supervision, crate.
[S🐾] [✕] [🐾] [🐾] [🖥] [🖥] [💻] [🔊]

◆ Best Western Mansfield Inn M
(419) 589-2200. **$69, 3 days notice.** 880 Laver Rd. I-71, exit 176, 1.5 mi w on US 30. Ext corridors. **Pets:** Medium. No service, supervision, crate.
[ASK] [S🐾] [✕] [🐾] [🖥] [💻] [🍴] [🔊]

◆◆◆ Comfort Inn M
(419) 529-1000. **$66-$85.** 500 N Trimble Rd. Jct US 30 and Trimble Rd. Int corridors. **Pets:** Designated rooms, no service, supervision, crate.
[SAVE] [S🐾] [✕] [🐾] [🖥] [💻] [🔊]

⚑ ◆◆ **EconoLodge** **M** ❀
(419) 589-3333. **$46-$60.** 1017 Koogle Rd. Off US 30, e of jct I-71, exit 176. Int corridors. **Pets:** $6 daily fee/pet, $6 one-time fee/pet. No service, supervision, crate.
[SAVE] [S🔒] [✕] [🖥] [💻] [🖼]

◆◆◆ **Hampton Inn** **M** ❀
(419) 747-5353. **$63-$71.** 1051 N Lexington Springmill Rd. Jct US 30 and Lexington Springmill Rd, south side. Int corridors. **Pets:** Small. Designated rooms, supervision.
[ASK] [S🔒] [✕] [🔊] [🖥] [🖼]

⚑ ◆ **Knights Inn** **M** ❀
(419) 529-2100. **$50-$100.** 555 N Trimble Rd. Jct US 30 and Trimble Rd. Ext corridors. **Pets:** $20 deposit/room. No service, supervision, crate.
[SAVE] [S🔒] [✕] [🔊] [🖥] [💻] [🖼]

◆◆ **Super 8 Motel** **M** ❀
(419) 756-8875. **$47-$62.** 2425 Interstate Cir. Jct SR 13 and I-71, exit 169. Int corridors. **Pets:** Other. $50 deposit/room. Designated rooms, supervision.
[ASK] [S🔒] [✕] [🔊] [🖥] [💻]

⚑ ◆ **Villager Lodge** **H**
(419) 522-7275. **$38-$53.** 191 Park Ave W. 3 blks w of downtown. Int corridors. **Pets:** Supervision.
[SAVE] [S🔒] [✕] [🖥]

MARIETTA

◆◆ **Econo Lodge** **M** ❀
(740) 374-8481. **$48-$65, 30 days notice.** 702 Pike St. At jct SR 7 and I-77, exit 1. Ext corridors. **Pets:** Other. $5 daily fee/room. Designated rooms, supervision.
[ASK] [S🔒] [✕] [💻] [🖼]

⚑ ◆◆ **Knights Inn** **M** ❀
(740) 373-7373. **$40-$75.** 506 Pike St. Jct I-77 and SR 7, exit 1. Ext corridors. **Pets:** Other. $5 daily fee/pet, $5 one-time fee/pet. Supervision.
[SAVE] [S🔒] [✕] [🖥] [🖼]

◆◆ **Super 8 Motel-Marietta** **M** ❀
(740) 374-8888. **$44-$63.** 46 Acme St. I-77, exit 1, just w. Int corridors. **Pets:** Supervision.
[ASK] [S🔒] [✕] [🔊] [🖥]

MARION

◆◆◆ **Marion Comfort Inn** **M** ❀
(740) 389-5552. **$66-$96.** 256 James Way. At jct SR 95 and US 23. Int corridors. **Pets:** Other. $10 one-time fee/room. Supervision.
[ASK] [S🔒] [✕] [🔊] [🌡] [🖥] [💻] [🖼]

MASSILLON

◆◆ **Super 8 Motel-Massillon** **M** ❀
(330) 837-8880. **$56-$62.** 242 Lincolnway W. Downtown. Int corridors. **Pets:** Small, other. $50 deposit/room. No service, supervision, crate.
[✕] [🖥]

MAUMEE

◆◆◆ **Country Inn & Suites By Carlson** **M** ❀
(419) 893-8576. **$71-$86.** 541 W Dussel Dr. From I-475 and US 23, exit 6, just e. Int corridors. **Pets:** Other. Supervision.
[ASK] [S🔒] [✕] [🔊] [🌡] [🖥] [💻] [🖼]

⚑ ◆◆ **Days Inn Toledo/Maumee** **M**
(419) 893-9960. **$60-$85.** 150 Dussel Dr. I-80/90 (Ohio Tpke), exit 4 and US 20, just s; from I-475, exit 6, 2 mi e. Ext corridors. **Pets:** No service, supervision, crate.
[SAVE] [✕] [🔊] [🖥] [💻] [🖼]

◆◆◆ **Homewood Suites Hotel** **A** ❀
(419) 897-0980. **Call for rates.** 1410 Arrowhead Rd. I-475, exit 6, just e. Int corridors. **Pets:** Small, other. $10 daily fee/room, $100 one-time fee/room. Supervision.
[✕] [🔊] [🖥] [💻] [🖼] [✕]

⚑ ◆ **Knights Inn-Toledo West** **M** ❀
(419) 865-1380. **$44-$90.** 1520 S Holland-Sylvania Rd. I-475, exit 8, just e on SR 2. Ext corridors. **Pets:** Designated rooms, no service, supervision, crate.
[SAVE] [S🔒] [✕] [🖥] [🖼]

⚑ ◆◆ **Red Roof Inn-Maumee** **M** ❀
(419) 893-0292. **$46-$64.** 1570 S Reynolds Rd. On US 20 and 23, just s of Ohio Tpke, exit 59. Ext/int corridors. **Pets:** Supervision.
[SAVE] [✕] [🔊] [🌡] [🖥] [CTV]

MIAMISBURG

◆◆◆ **Homewood Suites Hotel-Dayton Mall** **A** ❀
(937) 432-0000. **$135.** 3100 Contemporary Ln. SR 725 and I-75, exit 44, just e; in Prestige Plaza Complex. Int corridors. **Pets:** Other. $200 deposit/room, $5 daily fee/room, $50 one-time fee/pet. No service, supervision, crate.
[ASK] [S🔒] [✕] [🔊] [🌡] [🖥] [💻] [🖼]

⚑ ◆◆ **Red Roof Inn-South** **M** ❀
(937) 866-0705. **$57-$80.** 222 Byers Rd. Jct SR 725 and I-75, exit 44. Ext corridors. **Pets:** Small. Supervision.
[SAVE] [✕] [🔊] [🌡] [CTV]

◆◆◆ **Residence Inn by Marriott-Dayton South** **A**
(937) 434-7881. **$125.** 155 Prestige Pl. I-75, exit 44. Ext corridors. **Pets:** Supervision.
[ASK] [S🔒] [✕] [🌡] [🖥] [💻] [🖼] [✕]

MILAN

◆◆ **Motel 6-4016** **M** ❀
(419) 499-8001. **$75-$155, 3 days notice.** 11406 US 250 N. I-80/90 (Ohio Tpke), exit 118, 1.5 mi n on US 250. Int corridors. **Pets:** Small, other. No service, supervision, crate.
[ASK] [S🔒] [✕] [🌡] [🖼] [CTV]

MONTPELIER

◆◆ **Holiday Inn** **MI** ❀
(419) 485-5555. **$99-$169.** 13508 SR 15. SR 15, s of Ohio Tpke, exit 13. Int corridors. **Pets:** Large, other. Supervision.
[ASK] [S🔒] [✕] [🔊] [💻] [🍴] [🖼]

MORAINE

◆◆ Super 8 Motel–Moraine ⓜ ❖
(937) 298-0380. **$47-$86.** 2450 Dryden Rd. Jct Dryden Rd and I-75, exit 50A. Ext corridors. **Pets:** Small, other. $10 deposit/room. No service, supervision, crate.
(A$K) (S/D) (✕) (☎)

MOUNT GILEAD

⚠ ◆◆ Knights Inn ⓜ ❖
(419) 946-6010. **$42-$55.** 5898 SR 95. I-71, exit 151, then 0.3 mi w. Ext corridors. **Pets:** Dogs only. $15 deposit/room. Designated rooms, no service, supervision, crate.
(SAVE) (S/D) (✕) (☎) (CTV)

MOUNT VERNON

⚠ ◆◆◆ The Dan Emmett House
Hotel ⓜ ❖
(614) 392-6886. **$54-$85.** 150 Howard St. Just s on SR 13, just e. Int corridors. **Pets:** Other. $10 daily fee/room. Supervision.
(SAVE) (S/D) (✕) (☎) (☎) (☎) (☎) (☎)

◆◆◆ Holiday Inn Express ⓜ ❖
(740) 392-1900. **$68-$74.** 11555 Upper Gilchrist Rd. 3 mi e on US 36. Int corridors. **Pets:** Other. Designated rooms, supervision.
(A$K) (S/D) (✕) (☎) (☎) (☎) (☎) (☎)

NAPOLEON

◆◆ Quality Inn ⓜ
(419) 592-5010. **Call for rates.** 2395 N Scott St. Jct US 6 and 24 bypass, exit 108. Int corridors. **Pets:** Large. Supervision.
(✕) (☎) (☎) (☎) (☎)

NEW PARIS

◆ Golden Inn ⓜ ❖
(937) 437-0722. **$35-$50.** 8868 Rt 40 W. I-70, exit 156B, 1 mi ne. Ext corridors. **Pets:** Supervision.
(A$K) (✕) (☎)

NEW PHILADELPHIA

⚠ ◆◆◆ Holiday Inn-New Philadelphia/
Dover ⓜ ❖
(330) 339-7731. **$89-$125.** 131 Bluebell Dr SW. I-77, exit 81, 0.4 mi e on SR 39. Ext corridors. **Pets:** $15 one-time fee/pet. Supervision.
(SAVE) (S/D) (✕) (☎) (☎) (☎) (☎)

⚠ ◆ Motel 6–254 ⓜ
(330) 339-6446. **$40-$56.** 181 Bluebell Dr SW. I-77, exit 81, 0.4 mi e on SR 39. Ext corridors. **Pets:** Medium. No service, supervision, crate.
(S/D) (✕) (☎) (☎)

⚠ ◆◆◆ Schoenbrunn Inn by
Christopher ⓜ ❖
(330) 339-4334. **$79-$130, 7 days notice.** 1186 W High Ave. I-77, exit 81, 0.6 mi e on SR 39. Int corridors. **Pets:** $10 one-time fee/room. Supervision.
(SAVE) (S/D) (✕) (☎) (☎) (☎) (☎) (☎)

NEWTON FALLS

⚠ ◆ Rodeway Inn ⓜ
(330) 872-0988. **$35-$110.** 4248 SR 5. I-80, exit 209, just w on SR 5. Ext corridors. **Pets:** No service, supervision, crate.
(SAVE) (S/D) (✕) (CTV)

NORTH CANTON

◆◆◆ Holiday Inn-North Canton ⓜ ❖
(330) 494-2770. **$89-$169.** 4520 Everhard Rd NW. I-77, exit 109 southbound, exit 109A northbound, then 0.5 mi w. Int corridors. **Pets:** Small. No service, supervision, crate.
(A$K) (S/D) (✕) (☎) (☎) (☎) (☎) (☎)

⚠ ◆◆ Super 8 Motel Canton North ⓜ ❖
(330) 492-5030. **$50-$70.** 3950 Convenience Cir NW. I-77 S, exit 109, 0.3 mi e on Everhard, 0.3 mi s on Whipple; I-77 N, exit 109A, 0.3 mi s on Whipple. Ext corridors. **Pets:** Other. $5 daily fee/pet, $5 one-time fee/pet. No service, supervision, crate.
(SAVE) (S/D) (✕) (☎) (☎) (☎)

NORTH LIMA

⚠ ◆ Rodeway Inn ⓜ ❖
(330) 549-3988. **$49-$69.** 10650 Market St. I-76, exit 16, 0.3 mi s on SR 7. Ext corridors. **Pets:** Medium. $5 daily fee/pet, $5 one-time fee/pet. No service, supervision, crate.
(SAVE) (✕) (☎) (☎)

NORWALK

◆◆ Econo Lodge ⓜ ❖
(419) 668-5656. **$58-$118, 3 days notice.** 342 Milan Ave. 3 mi n on SR 250; 6 mi s of I-80/90, on SR 250. Ext corridors. **Pets:** Other. $30 deposit/pet. No service, supervision, crate.
(A$K) (S/D) (✕) (☎) (☎) (☎)

OBERLIN

◆◆ Oberlin Inn ⓜ ❖
(440) 775-1111. **$81-$141.** 7 N Main St. Center, on SR 58; at College and Main sts. Ext/int corridors. **Pets:** Small. Designated rooms, no service, supervision, crate.
(A$K) (S/D) (✕) (☎) (☎) (☎)

OREGON

⚠ ◆◆◆ Comfort Inn East ⓜ ❖
(419) 691-8911. **$56-$60.** 2930 Navarre Ave. I-280, exit 7 (Oregon), 0.5 mi e on Rt 2 (Navarre Ave). Int corridors. **Pets:** Other. Designated rooms, supervision.
(SAVE) (S/D) (✕) (☎) (☎) (☎) (☎)

ORRVILLE

◆◆ Royal Star Inn ⓜ
(330) 683-7827. **$58-$70.** 11980 Lincoln Way E. Jct US 30 and SR 57. Int corridors. **Pets:** Supervision.
(A$K) (✕) (☎) (☎)

PERRYSBURG

◆◆◆ Baymont Inn & Suites-Toledo
(Perrysburg) **M** ❀
(419) 872-0000. **$65-$72.** 1154 Professional Drive. I-75, exit 193, just w. Int corridors. **Pets:** Small, other. Designated rooms, supervision.
🔣 ⊗ 🔣 🔣 🔣 🔣 🔣 (CTV)

🅐🅐🅐 ◆◆ Howard Johnson Inn Toledo
South **M**
(419) 837-5245. **$37-$55, 7 days notice.** I-280 & Hanley Rd. Ohio Tpke, exit 71 to I-280, exit 1B. Ext/int corridors. **Pets:** Other. Supervision.
⊗ 🔣 🔣 🔣 🔣 🔣 (CTV)

🅐🅐🅐 ◆ Red Carpet Inn **M** ❀
(419) 872-2902. **$35-$50.** 26054 N Dixie Hwy. Jct I-475 and SR 25, exit 2. Ext corridors. **Pets:** $5 one-time fee/room. Supervision.
(SAVE) 🔣 ⊗ 🔣

PIQUA

◆◆◆ Ramada Limited **M** ❀
(937) 615-0140. **$66-$87.** 950 E Ash St. Jct SR 36 and I-75, exit 82, just w. Int corridors. **Pets:** Dogs only. $50 deposit/room. Supervision.
(ASK) 🔣 🔣 🔣 🔣 🔣

POLAND

🅐🅐🅐 ◆◆ Red Roof Inn **M** ❀
(330) 758-1999. **$49-$66.** 1051 Tiffany South. Jct I-680 and US 224, just w. Int corridors. **Pets:** Medium. No service, supervision, crate.
(SAVE) ⊗ 🔣 🔣 🔣 🔣

◆◆◆ Residence Inn **M** ❀
(330) 726-1747. **$169.** 7396 Tiffany South. Jct I-680 and US 224, just w. Int corridors. **Pets:** $200 one-time fee/room. No service, supervision, crate.
(ASK) 🔣 ⊗ 🔣 🔣 🔣 🔣 🔣 ⊗

PORT CLINTON

🅐🅐🅐 ◆◆ Country Hearth Inn **M** ❀
(419) 732-2111. **$60-$160.** 1815 E Perry St. 1.2 mi e on SR 163, w of jct SR 2. Ext/int corridors. **Pets:** Other. $50 deposit/room. Designated rooms, supervision.
(SAVE) 🔣 ⊗ 🔣 🔣 🔣

PORTSMOUTH

🅐🅐🅐 ◆◆ Best Western of Portsmouth **M** ❀
(740) 354-2851. **$54-$66, 3 days notice.** 3762 US Hwy 23 N. 4.5 mi n on US 23. Ext corridors. **Pets:** Other. $5 daily fee/room. Supervision.
(SAVE) 🔣 ⊗ 🔣 🔣 🔣 🔣 🔣

🅐🅐🅐 ◆◆ Ramada Inn **M** ❀
(740) 354-7711. **$62-$82, 5 days notice.** 711 2nd St. US 23, just w of US Grant Bridge. Ext/int corridors. **Pets:** Medium. Supervision.
(SAVE) 🔣 ⊗ 🔣 🔣 🔣 🔣 🔣

RICHFIELD

🅐🅐🅐 ◆◆◆ Holiday Inn-Richfield **M**
(330) 659-6151. **$89-$119, 3 days notice.** 4742 Brecksville Rd. Ohio Tpke, exit 173, just s. Int corridors. **Pets:** Medium. No service, supervision, crate.
(SAVE) 🔣 ⊗ 🔣 🔣 🔣 🔣 🔣 ⊗ (CTV)

RIO GRANDE

◆ College Hill Motel **M** ❀
(740) 245-5326. **$34-$43.** 10987 State Rt 588. Rio Grande exit off US 35. Ext corridors. **Pets:** No service, supervision, crate.
(ASK) 🔣 ⊗

SANDUSKY

◆◆◆ Clarion Inn Sandusky **M**
(419) 625-6280. **$100-$150, 3 days notice.** 1119 Sandusky Mall Blvd. 1.5 mi n of SR 2 on SR 250; in Sandusky Mall. Int corridors. **Pets:** No service, supervision, crate.
(ASK) 🔣 ⊗ 🔣 🔣 🔣 🔣 🔣 (CTV)

◆ Cornado Motel **M**
(419) 625-2954. **Call for rates.** 4319 Venice Rd. 1 mi e of SR 2 on US 6(Venice Rd). Ext corridors. **Pets:** Designated rooms, supervision.
⊗ 🔣

🅐🅐🅐 ◆◆◆ Radisson Harbour Inn **H** ❀
(419) 627-2500. **$139-$229, 3 days notice.** 2001 Cleveland Rd. Just n off US 250 and 10 mi n off Ohio Tpke. Int corridors. **Pets:** Other. Supervision.
(SAVE) 🔣 ⊗ 🔣 🔣 🔣 🔣 🔣 ⊗

SEVILLE

◆◆ Super 8 Motel-Seville **M**
(330) 769-8880. **$49-$77.** 6116 Speedway Dr. Jct SR 224 and Lake Rd. Int corridors. **Pets:** Small. Supervision.
(ASK) 🔣 ⊗ 🔣 🔣

SIDNEY

🅐🅐🅐 ◆◆ Days Inn **M** ❀
(937) 492-1104. **$45-$55.** 420 Folkerth Ave. SR 47, at jct I-75, exit 92. Ext corridors. **Pets:** Small. $5 daily fee/pet. Designated rooms, no service, supervision, crate.
(SAVE) 🔣 ⊗ 🔣 🔣 ⊗

🅐🅐🅐 ◆◆◆ Holiday Inn **M** ❀
(937) 492-1131. **$69-$79.** 400 Folkerth Ave. Off SR 47, w of jct I-75, exit 92. Int corridors. **Pets:** Small. No service, supervision, crate.
(SAVE) 🔣 ⊗ 🔣 🔣 🔣 🔣

SPRINGFIELD

🅐🅐🅐 ◆ Knights Inn **M** ❀
(937) 325-8721. **$50-$60, 3 days notice.** 2207 W Main St. From exit 47 or 52B off I-70, just e of US 68 on US 40. Ext corridors. **Pets:** $10 daily fee/room. No service, supervision, crate.
(SAVE) 🔣 ⊗ 🔣 🔣

ØØ ◆◆ **Ramada Limited** Ⓜ
(937) 328-0123. **$59-$74, 30 days notice.** 319 E Leffel Ln.
I-70, exit 54, just n. Int corridors. **Pets:** Designated rooms,
supervision.
⟨SAVE⟩ ⟨✕⟩ ⟨🐾⟩ ⟨🛏⟩ ⟨💻⟩ ⟨🍽⟩

ST. CLAIRSVILLE

ØØ ◆◆ **Knights Inn-St.**
        Clairsville/Wheeling Ⓜ ✿
(740) 695-5038. **$46-$69, 7 days notice.** 51260 National
Rd. On US 40; 0.5 mi ne of I-70, exit 218. Ext corridors.
Pets: $5 daily fee/room. No service, supervision, crate.
⟨SAVE⟩ ⟨S⟩ ⟨✕⟩ ⟨🐾⟩ ⟨🍽⟩

ØØ ◆◆ **Red Roof Inn** Ⓜ ✿
(740) 695-4057. **$51-$73.** 68301 Red Roof Ln. I-70, exit
218. Ext corridors. **Pets:** Other. Supervision.
⟨SAVE⟩ ⟨✕⟩ ⟨🐾⟩ ⟨🛏⟩

STEUBENVILLE

ØØ ◆◆◆ **Holiday Inn** Ⓜ ✿
(740) 282-0901. **$71-$71, 3 days notice.** 1401 University
Blvd. Jct US 22 and SR 7, 1 mi sw. Ext/int corridors.
Pets: No service, supervision, crate.
⟨SAVE⟩ ⟨S⟩ ⟨✕⟩ ⟨🐾⟩ ⟨✦⟩ ⟨🛏⟩ ⟨💻⟩ ⟨🍴⟩ ⟨🍽⟩

STOW

ØØ ◆ **Stow Inn** Ⓜ ✿
(330) 688-3508. **$60-$85.** 4601 Darrow Rd. 2 mi n on SR
91. Int corridors. **Pets:** No service, supervision, crate.
⟨SAVE⟩ ⟨S⟩ ⟨✕⟩ ⟨🛏⟩

TOLEDO

ØØ ◆◆◆ **Clarion Hotel Westgate** Ⓜ
(419) 535-7070. **$71-$79.** 3536 Secor Rd. I-475, exit 17,
just s. Int corridors. **Pets:** Supervision.
⟨SAVE⟩ ⟨S⟩ ⟨✕⟩ ⟨🐾⟩ ⟨🛏⟩ ⟨💻⟩ ⟨🍴⟩ ⟨🍽⟩ ⟨✕⟩

ØØ ◆◆ **Comfort Inn-North** Ⓜ ✿
(419) 476-0170. **$59-$80.** 445 E Alexis Rd. 2 mi w on
Alexis Rd from jct I-75. Int corridors. **Pets:** Small. $25
deposit/room. Designated rooms, no service, supervision,
crate.
⟨SAVE⟩ ⟨S⟩ ⟨✕⟩ ⟨🐾⟩ ⟨🛏⟩

ØØ ◆◆ **Comfort Inn Westgate** Ⓜ
(419) 531-2666. **$62-$62.** 3560 Secor Rd. I-475, exit 17,
just s. Int corridors. **Pets:** Medium. No service, supervision,
crate.
⟨SAVE⟩ ⟨S⟩ ⟨✕⟩ ⟨🐾⟩ ⟨✕⟩

ØØ ◆ **Crown Inn** Ⓜ ✿
(419) 473-1485. **$47-$60.** 1727 W Alexis Rd. On SR 184,
4.3 mi w of I-75, exit 210, 5 mi e of US 23, Sylvania exit.
Ext corridors. **Pets:** Other. $40 deposit/room, $6 daily fee/
pet. Designated rooms, no service, supervision, crate.
⟨SAVE⟩ ⟨S⟩ ⟨✕⟩ ⟨🍽⟩

ØØ ◆ **Econo Lodge** Ⓜ
(419) 381-8765. **Call for rates.** 2429 S Reynolds Rd.
I-80/90 (Ohio Tpke), exit 59, just n on US 20. Int corridors.
Pets: Very small. No service, supervision, crate.
⟨SAVE⟩ ⟨✕⟩ ⟨💻⟩

◆ **Quality Hotel** Ⓜ
(419) 381-8765. **$59-$99.** 2429 S Reynolds Rd. I-80/90
(Ohio Tpke), exit 59, just n on US 20. Int corridors.
Pets: Designated rooms, no service, supervision, crate.
⟨ASK⟩ ⟨S⟩ ⟨✕⟩ ⟨🐾⟩ ⟨🛏⟩ ⟨💻⟩ ⟨🍽⟩

ØØ ◆◆ **Red Roof Inn Secor** Ⓜ
(419) 536-0118. **$47-$62.** 3530 Executive Pkwy. I-475, exit
17, 0.5 mi s on Secor. Ext corridors. **Pets:** Designated
rooms, no service, supervision, crate.
⟨SAVE⟩ ⟨✕⟩ ⟨🐾⟩ ⟨🛏⟩ ⟨CTV⟩

TROY

◆◆◆ **Holiday Inn Express Hotel &**
         Suites Ⓜ ✿
(937) 332-1700. **$94.** 60 Troy Town Dr. I-75, exit 74, just w
on SR 41. Int corridors. **Pets:** Medium. No service, supervision, crate.
⟨ASK⟩ ⟨S⟩ ⟨✕⟩ ⟨🐾⟩ ⟨✦⟩ ⟨🛏⟩ ⟨💻⟩ ⟨🍽⟩

◆◆ **Knights Inn Troy** Ⓜ ✿
(937) 339-1515. **$40-$50.** 30 Troy Town Dr. I-75, exit 74,
just w on SR 41. Ext corridors. **Pets:** Other. Supervision.
⟨ASK⟩ ⟨S⟩ ⟨✕⟩ ⟨🛏⟩ ⟨💻⟩

◆◆ **Quality Inn & Suites** Ⓜ ✿
(937) 335-0021. **$69-$109, 3 days notice.** 1375 SR 55 W.
I-75, exit 73, just e. Ext corridors. **Pets:** Small. $10 one-time
fee/pet. No service, supervision, crate.
⟨ASK⟩ ⟨S⟩ ⟨✕⟩ ⟨🛏⟩ ⟨💻⟩ ⟨🍽⟩

◆◆◆ **Residence Inn By Marriott** Ⓐ ✿
(937) 440-9303. **$71-$104.** 87 Troy Town Dr. I-75, exit 74,
just w on SR 41. Int corridors. **Pets:** Other. $250 one-time
fee/room. Supervision.
⟨ASK⟩ ⟨S⟩ ⟨✕⟩ ⟨🐾⟩ ⟨✦⟩ ⟨🛏⟩ ⟨💻⟩ ⟨🍽⟩ ⟨✕⟩

TWINSBURG

◆◆ **Twinsburg Super 8 Motel** Ⓜ ✿
(330) 425-2889. **$63-$69.** 8848 Twins Hills Dr. Jct I-480 and
SR 82. Int corridors. **Pets:** Medium, other. No service,
supervision, crate.
⟨ASK⟩ ⟨S⟩ ⟨✕⟩

VANDALIA

ØØ ◆◆ **Park Inn International-Dayton Airport** Ⓜ
(937) 898-8321. **$50-$90.** 75 Corporate Center Dr. Across
from Dayton International Airport; off National Rd. Ext corridors. **Pets:** Supervision.
⟨SAVE⟩ ⟨S⟩ ⟨✕⟩ ⟨🛏⟩ ⟨💻⟩ ⟨🍽⟩

VERMILION

◆◆◆ **Holiday Inn Express** Ⓜ ✿
(440) 967-8770. **$99-$129, 3 days notice.** 2417 SR 60. Jct
SR 60 and 2. Int corridors. **Pets:** Medium, other. $40
deposit/room. No service, supervision, crate.
⟨ASK⟩ ⟨S⟩ ⟨✕⟩ ⟨🐾⟩ ⟨✦⟩ ⟨🛏⟩ ⟨🍽⟩ ⟨CTV⟩

WAPAKONETA

ØØ ◆◆◆ **Best Western Wapakoneta** Ⓜ ✿
(419) 738-8181. **$65-$85.** 1510 Saturn. On I-75 business
loop at jct I-75, exit 111. Int corridors. **Pets:** Other. $10
one-time fee/room. No service, supervision, crate.
⟨SAVE⟩ ⟨S⟩ ⟨✕⟩ ⟨🐾⟩ ⟨🛏⟩ ⟨💻⟩ ⟨🍽⟩

◆◆ **Super** 8 Motel-Wapakoneta Ⓜ
(419) 738-8810. **Call for rates, 3 days notice.** 1011 Lunar Dr. I-75 business loop at jct I-75, exit 111. Ext/int corridors. **Pets:** Small. Supervision.

⊠ 🔋 🖵

WARREN

ⒶⒶⒶ ◆◆◆ Best Western Downtown Motor Inn Ⓜ ☙
(330) 392-2515. **$55-$69.** 777 Mahoning Ave. 0.3 mi n of Courthouse Sq. Ext corridors. **Pets:** Other. No service, supervision, crate.

[SAVE] 🔋 ⊠ ▥ 🔋 🖾

WASHINGTON COURT HOUSE

ⒶⒶⒶ ◆ Knights Inn Ⓜ ☙
(740) 335-9133. **$46-$62.** 1820 Columbus Ave. 1.5 mi n on US 62 and SR 3. Ext corridors. **Pets:** Medium. Supervision.

[SAVE] 🔋 ⊠ 🔋

WAUSEON

ⒶⒶⒶ ◆◆◆ Best Western Del Mar Ⓜ ☙
(419) 335-1565. **$68-$79, 3 days notice.** 8319 SR 108. Ohio Tpke, exit 34. Ext corridors. **Pets:** Medium. $17 one-time fee/pet. No service, supervision, crate.

[SAVE] 🔋 ⊠ ▥ ▦ 🔋 🖵 🖾 ⊠

WHEELERSBURG

◆◆◆ Comfort Inn Ⓜ ☙
(740) 574-1046. **$98.** 8226 Ohio River Rd. US 52, Wheelersburg exit. Int corridors. **Pets:** Small. $25 deposit/room. No service, supervision, crate.

[ASK] 🔋 ⊠ ▦ 🖾

WILLOUGHBY

ⒶⒶⒶ ◆◆ Cleveland/Willoughby Travelodge Ⓜ ☙
(440) 585-1900. **$59-$79.** 34600 Maplegrove Rd. I-90, exit 189, just n on SR 91. Ext/int corridors. **Pets:** Other. $25 one-time fee/room. No service, supervision, crate.

[SAVE] 🔋 ⊠ ▥ 🔋 🖵 🖾

XENIA

◆◆ Best Western Regency Inn Ⓜ
(937) 372-9954. **Call for rates.** 600 Little Main St. 1 mi w on West Main St. Ext corridors. **Pets:** Designated rooms, no service, supervision, crate.

⊠ 🔋

YOUNGSTOWN

◆ Days Inn-North Ⓜ ☙
(330) 759-3410. **$100-$110.** 1610 Motor Inn Dr. I-80, exit 229, just s. Ext corridors. **Pets:** Small, other. $10 daily fee/room. Supervision.

[ASK] 🔋 ⊠ 🔋 🖾

ZANESVILLE

◆◆ Best Western Town House Ⓜ ☙
(740) 452-4511. **$65-$80.** 135 N 7th St. I-70, exit 155, on SR 60 via signs. Ext corridors. **Pets:** Large, other. $10 one-time fee/room. Designated rooms, supervision.

[ASK] 🔋 ⊠ ▥ 🔋 🖵

ⒶⒶⒶ ◆◆◆ Comfort Inn Ⓜ ☙
(740) 454-4144. **$75-$105.** 500 Monroe St. I-70 westbound, exit 155; eastbound 7th St exit, e on Elberon to light, just n on Underwood. Int corridors. **Pets:** Large, other. $10 one-time fee/room. Designated rooms, supervision.

[SAVE] 🔋 ⊠ ▥ ▦ 🔋 🖵 🖾

◆◆◆ Holiday Inn Conference Center Ⓜ ☙
(740) 453-0771. **$74-$109.** 4645 E Pike. On US 22 and 40 at jct I-70, exit 160. Int corridors. **Pets:** Designated rooms, no service, supervision, crate.

[ASK] 🔋 ⊠ ▥ ▦ 🔋 🖵 🍴 🖾

ⒶⒶⒶ ◆◆◆ Red Roof Inn Ⓜ ☙
(740) 453-6300. **$60-$100.** 4929 E Pike. I-70, exit 160, just s. Int corridors. **Pets:** Other. $10 one-time fee/room. Designated rooms, supervision.

[SAVE] 🔋 ⊠ ▦ ▦ 🖾

◆◆ Super 8 Motel-Zanesville Ⓜ ☙
(740) 455-3124. **$59-$80, 7 days notice.** 2440 National Rd. I-70, exit 152, just n on SR 40 (National Rd). Int corridors. **Pets:** Other. No service, supervision, crate.

[ASK] 🔋 ⊠ ▥ 🔋

AFTON

◆◆ Grand Lake Country Inn M ❀
(918) 257-8313. $29-$49. I-44, exit 302, 0.8 mi s to jct US 59, 60 and 69. Ext corridors. **Pets:** $5 deposit/room, $5 daily fee/room, $5 one-time fee/room. No service, supervision, crate.
ASK S▯ X ▯ ▯

ALTUS

⚠ ◆◆◆ Best Western Altus M ❀
(580) 482-9300. $54-$64. 2804 N Main St. 2 mi n on US 283. Ext corridors. **Pets:** Supervision.
SAVE S▯ X ▯ ▯ ▯

⚠ ◆ Days Inn M ❀
(580) 477-2300. $36-$44, 7 days notice. 3202 N Main St. 2.3 mi n on US 283. Ext corridors. **Pets:** Other. No service, supervision, crate.
SAVE S▯ X ▯

ARDMORE

⚠ ◆◆◆ Best Western Ardmore Inn M
(580) 223-7525. $50-$56. 6 Holiday Dr. I-35, exit 31A, just ne. Int corridors. **Pets:** Designated rooms, supervision.
SAVE S▯ X ▯

◆◆◆ Holiday Inn M ❀
(580) 223-7130. $69-$69. 2705 Holiday Dr. I-35, exit 31A, just e on SR 199. Ext corridors. **Pets:** Supervision.
ASK X ▯ ▯ ▯ ▯ ▯ X

◆◆ Super 8 Motel M ❀
(580) 223-2201. $34-$41, 7 days notice. 2120 Hwy 142 W. I-35, exit 33, 0.3 mi e. Int corridors. **Pets:** Medium, other. $5 daily fee/pet. Designated rooms, no service, supervision, crate.
ASK S▯ X ▯

BARTLESVILLE

◆◆ Holiday Inn M ❀
(918) 333-8320. $55-$76. 1410 SE Washington Blvd. On US 75, 0.3 mi n of jct US 60 E, 0.5 mi s of jct US 60 W. Int corridors. **Pets:** Small. $25 deposit/room. No service, supervision, crate.
ASK S▯ X ▯ ▯ ▯ ▯

◆◆ Super 8 M ❀
(918) 335-1122. $43-$47, 3 days notice. 211 SE Washington Blvd. On US 75, 0.7 mi n of jct US 60 and 75. Ext/int corridors. **Pets:** Other. Designated rooms, no service, supervision, crate.
ASK S▯ X ▯ ▯

BLACKWELL

⚠ ◆◆◆ Comfort Inn M
(580) 363-7000. $60-$68. 1201 N 44th St. Off I-35, exit 222. Int corridors. **Pets:** Supervision.
SAVE S▯ X ▯ ▯ ▯

⚠ ◆ Days Inn M ❀
(580) 363-2911. $37-$49, 7 days notice. 4302 W Doolin. Off I-35, exit 222. Ext corridors. **Pets:** Small. $5 daily fee/pet. No service, supervision, crate.
SAVE S▯ X ▯ ▯

CHECOTAH

⚠ ◆◆ Best Western La Donna Inn M ❀
(918) 473-2376. $44-$54. SR 150 & I-40. I-40, exit 259, 7 mi w. Ext corridors. **Pets:** Other. $5 daily fee/pet. Designated rooms, supervision.
SAVE S▯ X ▯

◆◆ Days Inn of Eufaula M ❀
(918) 689-3999. $55-$70. Hwy 69 & 150. Us 69, exit SR 150, just w. Ext corridors. **Pets:** Other. $5 daily fee/pet. Supervision.
ASK X

CHEROKEE

◆◆ Cherokee Inn 🅼 🐾
(580) 596-2828. **$57-$60.** 1720 S Grand. Jct US 64 and SR 58, 6.8 mi n. Ext corridors. **Pets:** Other. No service, supervision, crate.

ASK ✕ 🔊 💻

CHICKASHA

🆂 **◆◆ Best Western Inn** 🅼
(405) 224-4890. **$50-$65, 30 days notice.** 2101 S 4th St. I-44 (HE Bailey Tpke), exit 80, US 815, just n. Ext/int corridors. **Pets:** Medium. No service, supervision, crate.

SAVE 🆂 ✕ 🔋 🍴 🖼

CLINTON

🆂 **◆◆◆ Best Western Trade Winds Courtyard Inn** 🅼
(580) 323-2610. **$44-$95, 5 days notice.** 2128 Gary Blvd. Off I-40, exit 65, just n. Ext corridors. **Pets:** Small. No service, supervision, crate.

SAVE 🆂 ✕ 🔋 🍴 🖼

DUNCAN

◆ Heritage Inn 🅼
(580) 252-5612. **$30-$43.** 1515 S Hwy 81. 0.4 mi s of jct SR 7 and US 81. Ext corridors. **Pets:** Designated rooms, supervision.

✕ 🔋

DURANT

◆◆◆ Comfort Inn & Suites of Durant 🅼 🐾
(580) 924-8881. **$69-$94.** 2112 W Main St. US 75/69, exit US 70, just e. Int corridors. **Pets:** Other. $10 one-time fee/room. No service, supervision, crate.

ASK 🆂 ✕ 🔊 🖨 🔋 💻 🖼

ELK CITY

🆂 **◆◆ Best Western Elk City Inn** 🅼 🐾
(580) 225-2331. **$45-$65.** 2015 W 3rd St. Eastbound I-40, exit 32, 5 mi e I-40 Business Loop; westbound I-40, exit 41, 5 mi w I-40 Business Loop. Ext corridors. **Pets:** Medium. Designated rooms, no service, supervision, crate.

SAVE 🆂 ✕ 🖼

🆂 **◆ Budget Host Inn** 🅼 🐾
(580) 225-1811. **$30-$65.** 2000 W 3rd St. On US 66 (Business I-40), 1 mi w of center. Ext corridors. **Pets:** Very small, other. No service, supervision, crate.

SAVE 🆂 ✕

◆◆ Days Inn Elk City 🅼 🐾
(580) 225-9210. **$40-$50.** 1100 Hwy 34. Off I-40, exit 41. Ext corridors. **Pets:** Other. $5 daily fee/pet, $5 one-time fee/pet. Supervision.

ASK 🆂 ✕ 🔋 🖼

◆◆ Econo Lodge 🅼
(580) 225-5120. **Call for rates.** 108 Meadow Ridge. I-40, exit 38, 0.3 mi s. Ext corridors. **Pets:** No service, supervision, crate.

✕ 🔋 💻

◆◆ Elk City Travelodge 🅼 🐾
(580) 243-0150. **$30-$45.** 301 Sleepy Hollow Ct. I-40, exit 41. Ext corridors. **Pets:** Other. Designated rooms, no service, supervision, crate.

ASK 🆂 ✕ 🔋 💻

🆂 **◆◆◆ Holiday Inn** 🅼 🐾
(580) 225-6637. **$55-$65.** 101 Meadow Ridge Dr. I-40, exit 38, on SR 6. Ext/int corridors. **Pets:** Medium, other. Designated rooms, no service, supervision, crate.

SAVE 🆂 ✕ 🔊 🔋 💻 🍴 🖼 ✕

◆◆ Quality Inn 🅼 🐾
(580) 225-8140. **$45-$60.** 102 B J Hughes Access Rd. Off I-40, exit 38. Ext corridors. **Pets:** Medium. $5 daily fee/pet, $5 one-time fee/pet. No service, supervision, crate.

ASK 🆂 ✕ 💻 🖼

◆◆◆ Ramada Inn 🅼 🐾
(580) 225-0305. **$48-$51, 30 days notice.** 2500 S Main St. Off I-40, exit 38. Ext corridors. **Pets:** Medium. $5 daily fee/room. No service, supervision, crate.

✕ 🔋 💻 🍴 🖼

ENID

◆◆◆ Best Western Inn of Enid 🅼 🐾
(580) 242-7110. **$50-$59.** 2818 S VanBuren St. Jct US 412 and 81, 1.7 mi s on US 81. Int corridors. **Pets:** Medium. $5 daily fee/pet. No service, supervision, crate.

ASK 🆂 ✕ 🔋 🍴 🖼

◆◆◆ Comfort Inn 🅼
(580) 234-1200. **$62-$80, 7 days notice.** 210 N Van Buren. 0.7 mi n on US 81. Ext/int corridors. **Pets:** Small. Supervision.

ASK 🆂 ✕ 🔋 🖼

◆◆ Days Inn 🅼 🐾
(580) 234-0080. **$46-$51, 7 days notice.** 200 N Van Buren. 0.7 mi n on US 81. Ext corridors. **Pets:** Small. $20 deposit/room. Designated rooms, no service, supervision, crate.

ASK 🆂 ✕ 🔋

GUYMON

🆂 **◆◆ Ambassador Inn** 🅼 🐾
(580) 338-5555. **$60.** Hwy 64 N at 21st. 1.5 mi n on US 64 and SR 136. Ext corridors. **Pets:** Other. No service, supervision, crate.

SAVE 🆂 ✕ 🍴 🖼

◆◆◆ Best Western Townsman Inn 🅼
(580) 338-6556. **$51-$75.** 212 NE Hwy 54. 0.8 mi se on US 54. Ext corridors. **Pets:** Small. No service, supervision, crate.

ASK 🆂 ✕ 🔋 💻 🖼

🆂 **◆◆ Econo Lodge** 🅼 🐾
(580) 338-5431. **$37-$60.** 923 Hwy 54 E. On US 54 E, just s of jct US 64. Ext corridors. **Pets:** Very small, other. $5 daily fee/room, $5 one-time fee/room. Designated rooms, no service, supervision, crate.

SAVE 🆂 ✕

◆◆ Guymon Super 8 🅼 🐾
(580) 338-0507. **$47-$50.** 1201 Hwy 54 NE. Jct US 54 and 64. Int corridors. **Pets:** Other. No service, supervision, crate.

ASK 🆂 ✕ 🏠 🖨 🔋

HENRYETTA

(AAA) ◆◆ Gateway Inn M ❀
(918) 652-4448. **$32-$38.** Hwy 75 & Trudgeon St. 0.5 mi n of I-40, exit 240B. Ext/int corridors. **Pets:** Medium. $25 deposit/room. No service, supervision, crate.

SAVE S6 ✕ 🛈 ⌂

KETCHUM

◆◆ Summerside Inn Bed & Breakfast BB ❀
(918) 782-3301. **$150** (no credit cards). 7 Summerside. Jct Hwy 85 and Main St, 5 mi s. Ext/int corridors. **Pets:** Small, dogs only. $25 one-time fee/pet. Designated rooms, supervision.

✕ 🛈 ⌂ ✕

LAWTON

◆◆◆ Holiday Inn M
(580) 353-1682. **$54-$54.** 3134 Cache Rd. 2.5 mi w of I-44, US 277 and 281. Ext corridors. **Pets:** Medium. Designated rooms, supervision.

ASK S6 ✕ 🖫 🛈 ⌂ 🍴 ⌂

◆◆ Howard Johnson Hotel M
(580) 353-0200. **$63-$78.** 1125 E Gore Blvd. I-44, exit 37. Ext/int corridors. **Pets:** Supervision.

ASK S6 ✕ 🖫 🛈 ⌂ 🍴 ⌂ ✕

(AAA) ◆◆ Ramada Inn M ❀
(580) 355-7155. **$48-$56.** 601 NW 2nd St. On I-44, US 277 and 281; just s of jct US 62 W; I-44 exit 39B southbound, exit 37 northbound. Ext/int corridors. **Pets:** Medium. $15 daily fee/pet. Designated rooms, no service, supervision, crate.

SAVE S6 ✕ ⌂ 🍴 ⌂

(AAA) ◆◆ Super 8-Sandpiper Inn M ❀
(580) 353-0310. **$42-$64, 7 days notice.** 2202 NW US Hwy 277. On I-44 US 277 and 281, I-44 exit 40A. Ext corridors. **Pets:** Medium. $25 deposit/pet, $7 daily fee/pet. Designated rooms, supervision.

SAVE ✕ 🛈 ⌂

LOCUST GROVE

◆◆◆ Holiday Inn Express Hotel & Suites M ❀
(918) 479-8082. **$75-$105.** 106 Holiday Ln. US 412 (Cherokee Tpke) & Hwy 82, just nw. Int corridors. **Pets:** Small, dogs only. $10 daily fee/pet. Supervision.

✕ 🖫 🛈 ⌂ ⌂

MCALESTER

◆◆◆ Best Western Inn of McAlester M
(918) 426-0115. **$49-$64.** 1215 George Nigh Expwy. 6 mi s on US 69 bypass, 3 mi n of Indian Nation Tpke. Ext corridors. **Pets:** Medium. Designated rooms, supervision.

ASK S6 ✕ 🗐 🛈 ⌂ 🍴 ⌂

◆◆ Days Inn M
(918) 426-5050. **Call for rates.** 1217 S George Nigh Expwy. 6 mi s on US 69 bypass, 3 mi n of Indian Nation Tpke. Ext/int corridors. **Pets:** Small. Supervision.

✕ 🗐 🖫 🛈 ⌂ 🍴 ⌂

◆◆ Super 8 Motel M
(918) 426-5400. **$45-$65.** 2400 S Main. 1.8 mi s on US 69 business route, 2.5 mi n of Indian Nation Tpke. Ext corridors. **Pets:** Designated rooms, no service, supervision, crate.

ASK ✕ 🛈 ⌂

MUSKOGEE

(AAA) ◆◆ Days Inn M ❀
(918) 683-3911. **$50-$55, 5 days notice.** 900 S 32nd St. 3 mi s on US 64 and 69. Ext corridors. **Pets:** Very small. $5 daily fee/pet, $5 one-time fee/pet. No service, supervision, crate.

SAVE S6 ✕ 🛈 ⌂ ⌂

(AAA) ◆◆ Muskogee Inn M ❀
(918) 683-6551. **$46-$51.** 2360 E Shawnee. At e jct US 62 and SR 16. Ext corridors. **Pets:** Medium. $10 daily fee/pet. No service, supervision, crate.

SAVE S6 ✕ 🍴 ⌂

◆◆ Travelodge M
(918) 683-2951. **$49-$55, 7 days notice.** 534 S 32nd St. 2 mi w on US 64 and 69. Ext/int corridors. **Pets:** Medium. Designated rooms, no service, supervision, crate.

ASK S6 ✕ 🛈 ⌂ ⌂

◯KLAHOMA CITY METROPOLITAN AREA

DEL CITY

◆◆◆ La Quinta Inn-East M ❀
(405) 672-0067. **$62-$79.** 5501 Tinker Diagonal Rd. I-40, exit 156A Sooner Rd. Ext/int corridors. **Pets:** Other. No service, supervision, crate.

ASK ✕ 🏠 🗐 🖫 🛈 ⌂ ⌂

EDMOND

◆◆ Broadway Suites M ❀
(405) 341-6068. **$75-$75, 3 days notice.** 1305 S Broadway Ave. Just n of jct Broadway Ave and S 15th St. Ext corridors. **Pets:** Small, other. $50 deposit/pet, $25 one-time fee/pet. No service, supervision, crate.

ASK S6 ✕ 🛈 ⌂

◆◆◆ Ramada Plaza Hotel 🅷 ❀
(405) 341-3577. **$62-$62.** 930 E 2nd St. From I-35, exit
141, 2.3 mi w. Int corridors. **Pets:** Small, other. $25 deposit/
pet. No service, supervision, crate.

[ASK] [S🐾] [✕] [🐾] [🔲] [💻] [🍴] [🖼]

EL RENO

🆔 ◆◆◆ Best Western Hensley's 🅜 ❀
(405) 262-6490. **$44-$57.** 2701 S Country Club Rd. I-40,
exit 123, just s. Ext corridors. **Pets:** Other. $25 deposit/
room. Designated rooms, no service, supervision, crate.

[SAVE] [S🐾] [✕] [🐾] [🔲] [🖼]

🆔 ◆◆ Days Inn 🅜 ❀
(405) 262-8720. **$38-$52.** 2712 S Country Club Rd. I-40,
exit 123, just s. Ext corridors. **Pets:** Medium, other. $5
one-time fee/room. Designated rooms, no service, supervision, crate.

[SAVE] [S🐾] [✕] [🔲]

🆔 ◆◆ Super 8 Motel 🅜 ❀
(405) 262-8240. **$41-$70.** 2820 Hwy 81S. I-40, exit 125,
just nw. Ext corridors. **Pets:** Medium. $20 deposit/room. No
service, supervision, crate.

[SAVE] [S🐾] [✕] [🖼]

GUTHRIE

🆔 ◆◆ Best Western Territorial Inn 🅼 ❀
(405) 282-8831. **$55-$73.** 2323 Territorial Tr. Off I-35, exit
157, just sw. Int corridors. **Pets:** Small. Designated rooms,
no service, supervision, crate.

[SAVE] [S🐾] [✕] [🐾] [💻] [🖼]

MOORE

🆔 ◆◆ Super 8 Motel Moore 🅼
(405) 794-4030. **$44-$71, 4 days notice.** 1520 N Service
Rd. I-35, exit 118 (12th St). Ext corridors. **Pets:** No service,
supervision, crate.

[SAVE] [S🐾] [✕] [🔲]

NORMAN

🆔 ◆◆ Econo Lodge 🅜 ❀
(405) 364-5554. **$47-$62.** 100 SW 26th Dr. I-35, exit Main
St (109), just se. Ext corridors. **Pets:** Small. $10 deposit/
pet, $5 daily fee/pet, $5 one-time fee/pet. No service, supervision, crate.

[SAVE] [S🐾] [✕] [💻]

◆◆◆ La Quinta Inn & Suites 🅜
(405) 579-4000. **$69-$85.** 930 Ed Noble Dr. I-35, exit 108B
(Lindsey), just nw. Int corridors. **Pets:** Small. No service,
supervision, crate.

[ASK] [✕] [🐾] [🐾] [🔲] [💻] [🖼]

◆◆◆ The Residence Inn by Marriott 🅰 ❀
(405) 366-0900. **$89-$109, 5 days notice.** 2681 Jefferson
St. I-35, exit 108A, SR 9 E, then s following signs. Ext
corridors. **Pets:** Small, other. $75 one-time fee/room. Super-
vision.

[✕] [🐾] [🖼] [✕]

OKLAHOMA CITY

🆔 ◆◆◆ AmeriSuites Oklahoma
City-Airport 🅜
(405) 682-3900. **$115-$125.** 1818 S Meridian Ave. From
I-40, exit 145 (Meridian Ave), then 1 mi s. Int corridors.
Pets: Very small. No service, supervision, crate.

[SAVE] [S🐾] [✕] [🐾] [🐾] [🐾] [🔲] [💻] [🖼]

🆔 ◆◆◆ AmeriSuites (Oklahoma City/Quail
Springs) 🅜 ❀
(405) 749-1595. **$80-$107** (no credit cards). 3201 W
Memorial Rd. SR 74 (Hefner Pkwy), Memorial Rd exit, 1.1
mi e on Service Rd to May, 0.4 mi w on N Service Rd. Int
corridors. **Pets:** Small. No service, supervision, crate.

[SAVE] [S🐾] [✕] [🐾] [🔲] [💻] [🖼]

🆔 ◆◆◆ Best Western Saddleback
Inn 🅼 ❀
(405) 947-7000. **$65-$86.** 4300 SW 3rd St. I-40, exit 145
(Meridian Ave), just ne. Ext/int corridors. **Pets:** Small. $25
deposit/room. Supervision.

[SAVE] [S🐾] [✕] [🐾] [🔲] [💻] [🍴] [🖼]

🆔 ◆◆ Best Western Trade Winds Central
Inn 🅼
(405) 235-4531. **$50-$70.** 1800 E Reno. Off I-35, exit 127,
then just w. Ext corridors. **Pets:** Medium. No service, supervision, crate.

[SAVE] [S🐾] [✕] [🐾] [🔲] [🍴] [🖼]

◆◆◆ Clarion Meridian Hotel and Convention
Center 🅜 ❀
(405) 942-8511. **$79-$94.** 737 S Meridian Ave. I-40, exit
145 (Meridian Ave), then just s. Ext/int corridors.
Pets: Small, other. No service, supervision, crate.

[ASK] [✕] [🐾] [🐾] [🐾] [🔲] [💻] [🍴] [🖼]

◆◆ Comfort Inn Historic Route 66 🅜 ❀
(405) 947-0038. **$49-$55.** 4017 NW 39th Expwy. 1.5 mi w
of I-44 and US 66 (exit 123B Bethany). Ext corridors.
Pets: Designated rooms, no service, supervision, crate.

[ASK] [S🐾] [✕] [🐾] [💻] [🖼]

◆◆◆ Comfort Inn North 🅜 ❀
(405) 478-7282. **$65-$70.** 4625 NE 120th. I-35, exit 137
(122nd St), just sw. Int corridors. **Pets:** Medium. $5 daily
fee/pet. Designated rooms, no service, supervision, crate.

[ASK] [S🐾] [✕] [🐾] [🔲] [💻] [🖼]

🆔 ◆◆◆ Days Inn North 🅜
(405) 478-2554. **$55-$85.** 12013 N I-35 Service Rd. I-35,
exit 137, just sw. Ext/int corridors. **Pets:** No service, supervision, crate.

[SAVE] [S🐾] [✕] [🔲] [💻] [🖼]

🆔 ◆◆ Days Inn Northwest 🅼 ❀
(405) 946-0741. **$40-$50.** 2801 NW 39th St. I-44, exit 124
(May Ave). Ext corridors. **Pets:** Medium. $25 deposit/room.
Designated rooms, supervision.

[SAVE] [S🐾] [✕] [🐾] [🔲] [💻] [🍴] [🖼]

◆◆◆ Embassy Suites 🅷
(405) 682-6000. **$99-$139.** 1815 S Meridian Ave. From
I-40, exit 145 (Meridian Ave), then 1 mi s. Int corridors.
Pets: Supervision.

[ASK] [S🐾] [✕] [🐾] [🔲] [💻] [🍴] [🖼]

♦♦♦ Hawthorn Suites Limited 🅼
(405) 840-1440. **$75-$75, 5 days notice.** 1600 Northwest Expwy. Just e of I-44 exit. Ext/int corridors. **Pets:** Designated rooms, no service, supervision, crate.
[ASK] [S♦] [✕] [♿] [▣] [🛏] [🍴] [☞]

♠♠♠ Hilton Northwest 🅷 ❀
(405) 848-4811. **$69-$154.** 2945 Northwest Expwy. 8.5 mi nw on SR 3A and 74. Ext/int corridors. **Pets:** Small. $15 one-time fee/pet. Designated rooms, supervision.
[SAVE] [S♦] [✕] [♿] [♿] [▣] [🛏] [🍴] [☞]

♦♦♦ Holiday Inn Express 🅼
(405) 528-7563. **$65-$79, 3 days notice.** 5405 N Lincoln Blvd. I-44, exit 128, just sw. Int corridors. **Pets:** Medium. Designated rooms, no service, supervision, crate.
[ASK] [S♦] [✕] [♿] [☞]

♦♦♦ Holiday Inn Oklahoma City Airport 🅼
(405) 685-4000. **$82-$82.** 2101 S Meridian Ave. I-40, exit 145 (Meridian Ave), 1.3 mi s. Ext/int corridors. **Pets:** Designated rooms, no service, supervision, crate.
[ASK] [S♦] [✕] [♿] [♿] [▣] [🛏] [🍴] [☞]

♠♠♠ Howard Johnson Express Inn 🅼 ❀
(405) 943-9841. **$47-$51.** 400 S Meridian Ave. Off I-40, exit 145 (Meridian Ave), just n. Int corridors. **Pets:** Medium, other. $6 daily fee/room. No service, supervision, crate.
[SAVE] [S♦] [✕] [♿] [♿] [▣] [🛏] [☞]

♦♦ Howard Johnson Express Inn 🅼 ❀
(405) 677-0551. **$39-$46, 3 days notice.** 1629 S Prospect St. I-35, exit 125D (SE 15th St). Ext corridors. **Pets:** $25 deposit/room. Designated rooms, no service, supervision, crate.
[ASK] [S♦] [✕] [▣] [☞]

♦♦♦ La Quinta Inn & Suites 🅼
(405) 773-5575. **$109, 3 days notice.** 4829 Northwest Expwy. Jct SR 74 & 3, 2.4 mi w. Int corridors. **Pets:** Designated rooms, supervision.
[ASK] [S♦] [✕] [♿] [♿] [▣] [🛏] [☞]

♦♦♦ La Quinta Inn-South 🅼
(405) 631-8661. **$59-$79.** 8315 I-35S. Off I-35, exit 121A (82nd St). Ext corridors. **Pets:** No service, supervision, crate.
[ASK] [✕] [♿] [▣] [🛏] [☞]

♦♦♦ La Quinta Oklahoma City Airport 🅼 ❀
(405) 942-0040. **$69-$89.** 800 S Meridian Ave. Off I-40, exit 145 (Meridian Ave). Ext/int corridors. **Pets:** Other. Supervision.
[ASK] [✕] [♿] [▣] [🛏] [🍴] [☞]

♦♦ Microtel Inn and Suites 🅼
(405) 942-0011. **$45-$60.** 624 S MacArthur. I-40, MacArthur exit, just s. Int corridors. **Pets:** No service, supervision, crate.
[ASK] [S♦] [✕] [▣] [🛏] [☞]

♠♠ Motel 6 Airport-116 🅼
(405) 946-6662. **$38-$54.** 820 S Meridian Ave. Off I-40, exit 145 (Meridian Ave), just se. Ext corridors. **Pets:** Supervision.
[S♦] [✕] [♿] [♿] [☞]

♠♠ Motel 6-1182 🅼
(405) 478-4030. **$32-$51.** 12121 NE Expwy. I-35, exit 137 (122nd St), just sw. Ext corridors. **Pets:** Supervision.
[S♦] [✕] [♿] [♿] [☞]

♠♠ Motel 6 West-1128 🅼
(405) 947-6550. **$43-$58.** 4200 I-40 W. Off I-40, exit 145 (Meridian Ave), just e on S Frontage Rd. Ext/int corridors. **Pets:** Small. Supervision.
[S♦] [✕] [♿] [☞]

♦♦♦ Oklahoma City Marriott 🅷 ❀
(405) 842-6633. **$119-$129.** 3233 NW Expwy. On SR 3A at jct NW Expwy and Independence Ave; just e of SR 74 or 0.3 mi e of I 44, exit 125C. Int corridors. **Pets:** Small. Supervision.
[✕] [♿] [♿] [♿] [▣] [🛏] [🍴] [☞]

♠♠ Quality Inn 🅼 🐾
(405) 632-6666. **$58-$62.** 7800 C.A. Henderson Blvd. Off I-240, exit 2A, just s. Ext corridors. **Pets:** Small, dogs only. $10 one-time fee/pet. No service, supervision, crate.
[SAVE] [S♦] [✕] [▣] [🛏] [☞]

♦♦ Quality Inn-North 🅼
(405) 478-0400. **$45-$45.** 12001 N I-35 Service Rd. I-35, exit 137 (122nd St), just sw. Ext corridors. **Pets:** Medium. Designated rooms, no service, supervision, crate.
[ASK] [✕] [♿] [♿] [▣] [🛏] [☞] [✕]

♦♦ Quality Inn-West 🅼
(405) 943-2393. **$50-$60, 5 days notice.** 720 S MacArthur Rd. I-40, exit 144 (MacArthur Rd), just se. Ext corridors. **Pets:** Medium. Designated rooms, no service, supervision, crate.
[ASK] [S♦] [✕] [♿] [▣] [🛏] [☞]

♦ Ramada Inn Northwest 🅼
(405) 947-2351. **Call for rates.** 3535 NW 39th Expwy. I-44, exit 123B (Bethany). Ext/int corridors. **Pets:** Small. No service, supervision, crate.
[✕] [▣] [🛏] [🍴] [☞]

♠♠ Ramada Limited Airport-East 🅼
(405) 682-2211. **$49-$55.** 7400 S May Ave. I-240, exit 1-B (May Ave), just se. Ext corridors. **Pets:** No service, supervision, crate.
[SAVE] [S♦] [✕] [♿] [▣] [🛏] [☞]

♦♦♦ Residence Inn by Marriott-West 🅰 ❀
(405) 942-4500. **$122.** 4361 W Reno Ave. 0.3 mi n of I-40, exit 145 (Meridian Ave), then e. Ext corridors. **Pets:** Small, other. $75 one-time fee/pet. No service, supervision, crate.
[ASK] [S♦] [✕] [♿] [▣] [🛏] [☞] [✕]

♠♠ Travelodge Fifth Season Hotel 🅼 ❀
(405) 843-5558. **$66-$89.** 6200 N Robinson. Off I-235, just sw of 63rd St exit; 0.3 mi n of I-44 Broadway Ext, I-235 exit. Ext/int corridors. **Pets:** $50 deposit/room. Supervision.
[SAVE] [S♦] [✕] [▣] [🛏] [🍴] [☞]

♦♦♦♦ The Waterford Marriott 🅷 ❀
(405) 848-4782. **$139-$195.** 6300 Waterford Blvd. 3 mi w of jct US 77 and 63rd St. Int corridors. **Pets:** Very small, dogs only. Supervision.
[ASK] [S♦] [✕] [♿] [▣] [🛏] [🍴] [☞]

PURCELL

AAA ◆◆ **Econo Lodge** M1 ❀
(405) 527-5603. **$40-$55.** 2500 Hwy 74 S. I-35, exit 91, just w. Ext corridors. **Pets:** Small. $5 daily fee/pet. No service, supervision, crate.
[SAVE] [S6] [X] [icon] [icon]

SHAWNEE

AAA ◆◆ **Best Western Cinderella Motor Inn** M1 ❀
(405) 273-7010. **$49-$72.** 623 Kickapoo Spur. 2.5 mi s of I-40, exit 185; 0.3 mi w on US 270. Ext/int corridors. **Pets:** Other. Designated rooms, supervision.
[SAVE] [S6] [X] [icon] [icon] [icon] [icon] [icon]

◆◆◆ **Hampton Inn** M ❀
(405) 275-1540. **$55-$61.** 4851 N Kickapoo. I-40, exit 185, just se. Int corridors. **Pets:** Other. Supervision.
[ASK] [X] [icon] [icon] [icon] [icon] [icon]

AAA ◆◆ **Motel 6–1236** M
(405) 275-5310. **Call for rates.** 4981 N Harrison. Jct I-40 and SR 18, Shawnee Meeka exit. Int corridors. **Pets:** Small. Supervision.
[X] [icon] [icon] [icon]

◆◆◆ **Ramada Inn** M1 ❀
(405) 275-4404. **$58-$75, 7 days notice.** 4900 N Harrison. I-40, exit 186, just n. Ext/int corridors. **Pets:** Small. $25 deposit/pet. Designated rooms, no service, supervision, crate.
[ASK] [S6] [X] [icon] [icon] [icon] [icon] [icon]

YUKON

AAA ◆◆ **Comfort Inn-West** M
(405) 324-1000. **$52-$70.** 321 N Mustang Rd. I-40, Mustang Rd exit 138, just n. Ext corridors. **Pets:** Designated rooms, no service, supervision, crate.
[SAVE] [S6] [X] [icon] [icon]

❀ **END METROPOLITAN AREA** ❀

PAULS VALLEY

AAA ◆◆ **Amish Inn Motel** M ❀
(405) 238-7545. **$26-$36.** 3101 W Grant Ave. I-35, exit 72, just e on SR 19. Ext corridors. **Pets:** No service, supervision, crate.

PERRY

AAA ◆◆ **Best Western Cherokee Strip Motel** M1
(580) 336-2218. **$129-$159, 30 days notice.** I-35 & US 77. E of I-35, exit 185. Ext corridors. **Pets:** Medium. Designated rooms, supervision.

PONCA CITY

◆◆ **Holiday Inn Ponca City** M1 ❀
(580) 762-8311. **$62-$108, 3 days notice.** 2215 N 14th St. 2.8 mi n on US 77. Ext corridors. **Pets:** Small. $25 deposit/room. Designated rooms, no service, supervision, crate.
[ASK] [S6] [X] [icon] [icon] [icon] [icon] [icon]

PRYOR

◆◆ **Days Inn of Pryor** M ❀
(918) 825-7600. **$42-$68.** Hwy 69 S. 3.2 mi s on US 69. Ext corridors. **Pets:** Other. $5 daily fee/pet, $5 one-time fee/pet. No service, supervision, crate.
[ASK] [S6] [X] [icon] [icon] [icon] [icon]

ROLAND

◆◆◆ **Days Inn of Roland** M ❀
(918) 427-1000. **Call for rates.** 207 Cherokee Blvd. I-40, exit 325. Int corridors. **Pets:** Medium. $10 daily fee/pet. No service, supervision, crate.

SALLISAW

AAA ◆◆◆ **Best Western Blue Ribbon Motor Inn** M1 ❀
(918) 775-6294. **$40-$50.** 706 S Kerr Blvd (US 59). I-40, exit 308 (US 59), just n. Ext/int corridors. **Pets:** Other. $5 one-time fee/room. Supervision.
[SAVE] [S6] [X] [icon] [icon] [icon]

◆◆ **Days Inn** M ❀
(918) 775-4406. **$34-$50.** 1700 W Cherokee St. I-40, exit 308, 1.1 mi n, just w. Ext corridors. **Pets:** Other. $10 daily fee/pet, $10 one-time fee/pet. No service, supervision, crate.
[ASK] [S6] [X] [icon] [icon]

AAA ◆◆ **Super 8 Motel** M ❀
(918) 775-8900. **$37-$45.** 924 S Kerr Blvd (US 59). I-40, exit 308 (US 59), just n. Ext/int corridors. **Pets:** $5 one-time fee/room. Supervision.
[SAVE] [S6] [X] [icon] [icon] [icon] [icon] [icon]

SAVANNA

◆ **Travelodge** M ❀
(918) 548-3506. **$32-$68, 5 days notice.** Hwy 69 & Panola. On US 69, 2 mi sw of Indian Nation Tpke. Ext corridors. **Pets:** Other. No service, supervision, crate.
[ASK] [S6] [X] [icon]

STILLWATER

AAA ◆◆ **Best Western Stillwater** M1 ❀
(405) 377-7010. **$65-$90.** 600 E McElroy. 1 mi n on Hwy 177 (Perkins Rd). Int corridors. **Pets:** Small. Supervision.
[SAVE] [S6] [X] [icon] [icon] [icon] [icon] [icon]

◆◆◆ **Holiday Inn** M1
(405) 372-0800. **Call for rates.** 2515 W 6th Ave. 1.8 mi w on SR 51. Ext/int corridors. **Pets:** Small. No service, supervision, crate.

TAHLEQUAH

(AAA) ◆◆ **Budget Host Tahlequah Motor
    Lodge** Ⓜ
(918) 456-2350. **$49-$60, 3 days notice.** 2501 S Musko-gee. 2 mi s on US 62 and SR 10. Ext corridors.
Pets: Small. Supervision.
[SAVE] [S⊘] [✕] [🛏] [🍴] [🐾]

◆◆ **Oak Hill Motel Suites** Ⓜ ❀
(918) 458-1200. **$51-$70, 7 days notice.** 2600 S Musko-gee. 2 mi s on US 62 and SR 10. Ext corridors.
Pets: Medium, other. $25 deposit/room. Supervision.
[S⊘] [✕] [🛏] [💻] [🍴] [🐾]

Tulsa Metropolitan Area

BROKEN ARROW

(AAA) ◆ **Econo Lodge** Ⓜ
(918) 258-6617. **$55-$61.** 1401 N Elm Pl. Just s of Broken Arrow Expwy (US 64 and SR 51), exit 161st Ave. Int corri-dors. **Pets:** No service, supervision, crate.
[SAVE] [S⊘] [✕] [🛏] [💻]

◆◆ **Holiday Inn-South** Ⓜ
(918) 258-7085. **$66-$84.** 2600 N Aspen. At jct Broken Arrow Expwy (SR 51) and 145th St exit. Int corridors.
Pets: Designated rooms, supervision.
[A$K] [S⊘] [✕] [🐕] [🛏] [💻] [🐾]

CATOOSA

(AAA) ◆◆ **Super 8** Ⓜ
(918) 266-7000. **$33-$60.** 19250 Timbercrest Cir. I-44, exit 193rd East Ave, just nw. Ext corridors. **Pets:** Very small. No service, supervision, crate.
[SAVE] [S⊘] [✕] [🐕] [🐾]

CLAREMORE

(AAA) ◆◆ **Claremore Motor Inn** Ⓜ ❀
(918) 342-4545. **$33-$42.** 1709 N Lynn Riggs. Ext corridors.
Pets: Small. $25 deposit/room. Designated rooms, no serv-ice, supervision, crate.
[SAVE] [S⊘] [✕] [🛏]

◆◆◆ **Days Inn Claremore** Ⓜ ❀
(918) 343-3297. **$50-$75.** 1720 S Lynn Riggs. On US 66, 2 mi s. Int corridors. **Pets:** Other. $10 daily fee/pet. Desig-nated rooms, no service, supervision, crate.
[A$K] [S⊘] [✕] [🐕] [🛏] [💻] [🐾]

(AAA) ◆ **Motel Claremore** Ⓜ ❀
(918) 341-3254. **$39-$47.** 812 E Will Rogers Blvd. On SR 20; 0.5 mi w of Will Rogers Tpke. Ext corridors.
Pets: Small, dogs only. No service, supervision, crate.
[✕]

GLENPOOL

(AAA) ◆◆ **Best Western Glenpool Inn** Ⓜ ❀
(918) 322-5201. **$49-$99, 7 days notice.** 14831 S Casper St. 9.5 mi s on US 75 from jct I-44. Ext corridors.
Pets: Small. No service, supervision, crate.
[SAVE] [S⊘] [✕] [🛏] [💻] [🐾]

SAND SPRINGS

(AAA) ◆◆◆ **Best Western Sand Springs Inn &
    Suites** Ⓜ ❀
(918) 245-4999. **$65-$75, 5 days notice.** 211 South Lake Dr. Off SR 51, US 64 and 412, exit 81st W Ave, just sw. Ext/int corridors. **Pets:** $10 daily fee/room, $10 one-time fee/room. No service, supervision, crate.
[SAVE] [S⊘] [✕] [🐕] [🛏] [💻] [🐾]

SAPULPA

◆ **Sapulpa Super 8** Ⓜ ❀
(918) 227-3300. **$38-$52.** 1505 New Sapulpa Rd. 0.5 mi e on SR 66. Int corridors. **Pets:** Designated rooms, no serv-ice, supervision, crate.
[A$K] [S⊘] [✕] [🐕] [🛏] [🐾]

TULSA

(AAA) ◆◆◆ **AmeriSuites-Tulsa Hyde Park** Ⓜ
(918) 491-4010. **$109-$139.** 7037 S Zurich Ave. I-44, exit 229 (Yale Ave), 3 mi s to 71st St, just e. Int corridors.
Pets: Supervision.
[SAVE] [S⊘] [✕] [🐕] [🐕] [🐾] [🛏] [💻] [🐾]

◆◆◆ **Baymont Inn & Suites** Ⓜ
(918) 488-8777. **$55-$61.** 4530 E Skelly Dr.. I-44, exit 229 (Yale Ave), just s, then w. Int corridors. **Pets:** Medium.
Designated rooms, no service, supervision, crate.
[S⊘] [✕] [🐕] [🐾] [🛏] [💻] [🐾]

(AAA) ◆◆◆ **Best Western Trade Winds Central
    Inn** Ⓜ ❀
(918) 749-5561. **$66-$71.** 3141 E Skelly Dr. I-44, exit 228 (Harvard Ave), on nw frontage road. Ext/int corridors.
Pets: Very small. No service, supervision, crate.
[SAVE] [S⊘] [✕] [🐕] [🛏] [💻] [🍴] [🐾]

(AAA) ◆ **Days Inn-West** Ⓜ ❀
(918) 446-1561. **$39-$49, 8 days notice.** 5525 W Skelly Dr.
I-44 E, exit 222B, just w on s service road; I-44 W, exit 222A, just e on s service road. Ext/int corridors.
Pets: Other. $8 daily fee/pet. No service, supervision, crate.
[SAVE] [S⊘] [✕] [🛏] [🍴] [🐾]

◆◆◆ **Doubletree Hotel At Warren Place** Ⓗ ❀
(918) 495-1000. **$164-$164, 3 days notice.** 6110 S Yale Ave. I-44, exit 229 (Yale Ave), 1 mi s. Int corridors.
Pets: $25 one-time fee/room. No service, supervision, crate.
[A$K] [S⊘] [✕] [🐕] [🛏] [💻] [🍴] [🐾] [✕]

♦♦♦ Doubletree Hotel Downtown Tulsa 🅷 ❀
(918) 587-8000. **$100.** 616 W 7th St. 7th St and Houston. Int corridors. **Pets:** Small. $25 deposit/room, $25 one-time fee/room. No service, supervision, crate.

🆂🅰🆅🅴 🆂 ⊠ 🗐 🖬 💻 🍴 🕿

♦♦♦ GuestHouse Suites Plus 🅰 ❀
(918) 664-7241. **$120.** 8181 E 41st St. Broken Arrow Expwy, Memorial Dr exit, 1 mi s, then just e. Ext corridors. **Pets:** Other. $8 daily fee/pet. No service, supervision, crate.

🅰🆂🅺 🆂 ⊠ 🗐 🖬 💻 🕿 ⊠

♦♦♦ Holiday Inn Select 🅼 ❀
(918) 622-7000. **$79-$114.** 5000 E Skelly Dr. I-44 and SR 66, exit 229 (Yale Ave) on south frontage road. Ext/int corridors. **Pets:** Small. $25 one-time fee/room. No service, supervision, crate.

🅰🆂🅺 🆂 ⊠ 🗐 🖬 💻 🍴 🕿

♦♦♦ Holiday Inn-Tulsa East Airport 🅼
(918) 437-7660. **$96-$116, 3 days notice.** 1010 N Garnett Rd. I-244, exit 14 (Garnett Rd). Int corridors. **Pets:** Designated rooms, supervision.

🅰🆂🅺 🆂 ⊠ 🗐 🖋 🍴 🕿 ⊠

♦♦♦ La Quinta Inn Airport 🅼 ❀
(918) 836-3931. **$62-$82.** 35 N Sheridan Rd. I-244, exit 11, (Sheridan Rd). Ext corridors. **Pets:** Small, other. Designated rooms, no service, supervision, crate.

🅰🆂🅺 ⊠ 🗐 🖬 🕿

♦♦♦ La Quinta Inn 41st St 🅼 ❀
(918) 665-0220. **$62-$79.** 10829 E 41st St. US 169, E 41st St exit. Ext corridors. **Pets:** Small. Designated rooms, no service, supervision, crate.

🅰🆂🅺 ⊠ 🗐 🖬 💻

♦♦♦ La Quinta Inn-Tulsa South 🅼
(918) 254-1626. **$59-$79.** 12525 E 52nd St S. Broken Arrow Expwy (SR 51), 129th and 51st sts exit. Ext corridors. **Pets:** Designated rooms, no service, supervision, crate.

🅰🆂🅺 ⊠ 🗐 🖬 💻 🕿

♦♦ Ramada Inn 🅼
(918) 743-9811. **$71-$71, 7 days notice.** 3131 E 51st. I-44, exit 228 (Harvard Ave), just sw. Ext/int corridors. **Pets:** Very small. Designated rooms, no service, supervision, crate.

🆂🅰🆅🅴 🆂 ⊠ 🗐 🖬 💻 🕿

♦♦♦ Sheraton Tulsa Hotel 🅷
(918) 627-5000. **$119-$160.** 10918 E 41st St. Jct US 169 and 41st St, just e. Int corridors. **Pets:** Medium. No service, supervision, crate.

🆂🅰🆅🅴 🆂 ⊠ ♿ 🗐 🖋 🖬 💻 🍴 🕿

❀ **END METROPOLITAN AREA** ❀

WEATHERFORD

♦♦♦ Best Western Mark Motor Hotel 🅼 ❀
(580) 772-3325. **$45-$59.** 525 E Main St. Westbound I-40, exit 82, 0.3 mi w; eastbound I-40, exit 80A, 0.3 mi e. Ext corridors. **Pets:** Small, other. Designated rooms, no service, supervision, crate.

🆂🅰🆅🅴 🆂 ⊠ 🖋 🖬 💻 🕿

WOODWARD

♦♦♦ Northwest Inn 🅼 ❀
(580) 256-7600. **$54-$71.** Hwy 270 S & 1st St. 1 mi s on US 183, 270, SR 3 and 34. Ext/int corridors. **Pets:** Other. $10 one-time fee/room. No service, supervision, crate.

🅰🆂🅺 🆂 ⊠ 🖬 🍴 🕿

♦ Red Country Inn 🅼 ❀
(580) 254-9147. **$30-$39.** 2314 8th St. 0.4 mi s on US 183, 270, SR 3 and 34. Ext corridors. **Pets:** Other. $5 deposit/pet. No service, supervision, crate.

🅰🆂🅺 🆂 ⊠ 🖬 🕿

♦♦ Wayfarer Inn 🅼
(580) 256-5553. **$35-$44.** 2901 Williams Ave. 0.8 mi s on US 183, 270, SR 3 and 34. Ext corridors. **Pets:** Very small. No service, supervision, crate.

🅰🆂🅺 🆂 ⊠ 🖬 💻 🕿 ⊠

ALBANY

♦♦♦ Best Inn & Suites M ❀
(541) 928-5050. **$69-$95.** 1100 Price Rd SE. I-5 exit 233, just e and just n. Int corridors. **Pets:** Medium, other. $100 deposit/room. Supervision.
SAVE 🆂 ✕ 🛗 🔧 🍴 💻 🌐

♦♦♦ Best Western Pony Soldier Inn M ❀
(541) 928-6322. **$82-$88.** 315 Airport Rd SE. I-5 southbound exit 234B; northbound exit 234, just w and just s. Ext corridors. **Pets:** Medium, other. No service, supervision, crate.
SAVE 🆂 ✕ 🍴 💻 🌐

♦♦ Hawthorn Inn & Suites M
(541) 928-0921. **$82-$95.** 251 Airport Rd SE. I-5, southbound exit 234B; northbound exit 234, just w. Int corridors. **Pets:** No service, supervision, crate.
SAVE 🆂 ✕ 🚭 🍴 💻 🌐

ASHLAND

♦♦♦ Best Western Bard's Inn M
(541) 482-0049. **$95-$144.** 132 N Main St. Just n on SR 99 (N Main) from Downtown Plaza. Ext/int corridors. **Pets:** Small. Designated rooms, no service, supervision, crate.
✕ 🔧 🍴 💻 🌐

♦♦♦ Best Western Windsor Inn M
(541) 488-2330. **$85-$94.** 2520 Ashland St. I-5 exit 14, just e. Ext corridors. **Pets:** Supervision.
✕ 🚭 🍴 💻 🌐

♦♦ Hawthorn Inn & Suites M
(541) 482-6932. **$89-$119.** 434 Valley View Rd. I-5 exit 19, just w. Int corridors. **Pets:** Small. Designated rooms, supervision.
SAVE 🆂 ✕ 🚭 🍴 💻 🌐

♦♦ Knights Inn Motel M 🐾
(541) 482-5111. **$58-$66, 3 days notice.** 2359 Hwy 66. I-5 exit 14, just w. Ext corridors. **Pets:** Small. $50 deposit/room, $10 daily fee/pet. Designated rooms, supervision.
✕ 🍴 🌐

♦♦ Rodeway Inn M
(541) 482-2641. **$78-$88, 3 days notice.** 1193 Siskiyou Blvd. I-5 exit 14, 1.1 mi w on SR 66, just n on US 99. Ext corridors. **Pets:** Small. Designated rooms, no service, supervision, crate.
✕ 🚭 🍴 💻 🌐

♦♦♦ Windmill Inn of Ashland M
(541) 482-8310. **$99-$119.** 2525 Ashland St. I-5 exit 14, just e. Int corridors. **Pets:** Supervision.
SAVE 🆂 ✕ 🛗 🔧 🍴 🌐 ✕

ASTORIA

♦♦ Crest Motel M ❀
(503) 325-3141. **$73-$96.** 5366 Leif Erickson Dr. 4 mi e of Astoria Bridge on US 30. Ext corridors. **Pets:** Other. Supervision.
✕ 🍴 💻 🍽

♦♦ Red Lion Inn MI 🐾
(503) 325-7373. **$54-$84.** 400 Industry St. Just w of Astoria Bridge on US 30, just n on Basin St (Caution: do not turn onto Astoria-Megler Bridge). Ext corridors. **Pets:** Medium, other. $10 one-time fee/room. No service, supervision, crate.
SAVE 🆂 ✕ 🚭 🍴 💻 🍴 🍽

BAKER CITY

♦♦♦ Geiser Grand Hotel H ❀
(541) 523-1889. **$79-$199.** 1996 Main St. I-84 exit 304, downtown. Int corridors. **Pets:** Dogs only. $75 deposit/room, $10 daily fee/pet. Supervision.
🆂 ✕ 🔧 🍴

④④ ◆◆ **Quality Inn** M ✿
(541) 523-2242. **$54-$65.** 810 Campbell. I-84 exit 304, just s. Ext corridors. **Pets:** Large, other. $5 daily fee/pet. Designated rooms, no service, supervision, crate.

SAVE S⚙ ✕ ⯑ ➡

◆◆ **Welcome Inn** M ✿
(541) 523-3431. **$47-$63.** 175 Campbell St. Ext corridors. **Pets:** Very small, dogs only. $5 daily fee/pet. Designated rooms, supervision.

ASK S⚙ ✕ ➡

BANDON

④④ ◆◆ **Driftwood Motel** M ✿
(541) 347-9022. **$55-$80.** 460 Hwy 101. Center on US 101. Ext corridors. **Pets:** Dogs only. $10 deposit/pet, $5 daily fee/pet. Designated rooms, supervision.

✕ ⯑ ➡ ⯑

BEND

④④ ◆◆ **Best Inn & Suites** M ✿
(541) 388-2227. **$59-$99.** 61200 S Hwy 97. 3 mi s on US 97 from jct US 20 E. Int corridors. **Pets:** Other. Designated rooms, supervision.

SAVE S⚙ ✕ ⯑ ⯑ ➡ ⯑

④④ ◆◆ **Best Western Inn & Suites of Bend** M ✿
(541) 382-1515. **$59-$89.** 721 NE 3rd. On US 97, just s of jct US 20. Ext corridors. **Pets:** $5 daily fee/pet. Designated rooms, supervision.

SAVE S⚙ ✕ ⯑ ➡ ⯑

④④ ◆◆ **Econo Lodge** M ✿
(541) 318-0848. **$55-$95.** 20600 Grandview Ave. 2.8 mi n on US 97 from jct US 20 W. Int corridors. **Pets:** Small. $7 daily fee/room. Designated rooms, no service, supervision, crate.

SAVE S⚙ ✕ ⯑ ⯑ ⯑ ➡ ⯑

④④ ◆◆◆ **Hampton Inn** M ✿
(541) 388-4114. **$69-$99.** 15 NE Butler Market Rd. 1.5 mi n on US 97 from jct of US 20 E. Ext corridors. **Pets:** Other. Supervision.

S⚙ ✕ ➡ ⯑

④④ ◆◆◆ **Holiday Inn Express Hotel & Suites** M
(541) 317-8500. **$80-$89.** 20615 Grandview Dr. 2.8 mi n on US 97 from jct of US 20 W. Int corridors. **Pets:** Medium. No service, supervision, crate.

SAVE S⚙ ✕ ⯑ ⯑ ⯑ ⯑ ➡ ⯑

④④ ◆◆ **Red Lion Inn/North** M
(541) 382-7011. **$64-$69.** 1415 NE 3rd St. US 97, just n of jct US 20. Ext corridors. **Pets:** Designated rooms, no service, supervision, crate.

SAVE S⚙ ✕ ⯑ ⯑ ⯑ ➡ ⯑ ⯑

④④ ◆◆ **Red Lion Inn/South** M
(541) 382-8384. **$84-$89.** 849 NE 3rd St. US 97, just s of jct US 20. Ext corridors. **Pets:** Designated rooms, supervision.

SAVE S⚙ ✕ ⯑ ⯑ ⯑ ➡ ⯑

④④ ◆◆◆ **The Riverhouse Resort** M ✿
(541) 389-3111. **$79-$109.** 3075 N Hwy 97. 1.5 mi n on US 97 from jct US 20 E. Ext/int corridors. **Pets:** Other. Designated rooms, no service, supervision, crate.

✕ ⯑ ⯑ ⯑ ➡ ⯑ ⯑ ✕

◆◆◆ **Shilo Suites Hotel** M
(541) 389-9600. **$89-$199.** 3105 O B Riley Rd. 1.5 mi n on US 97 from jct US 20 E. Ext corridors. **Pets:** No service, supervision, crate.

ASK S⚙ ✕ ⯑ ⯑ ➡ ⯑ ⯑

◆◆ **Sleep Inn** M
(541) 330-0050. **$54-$74.** 600 NE Bellevue. On US 20 E, 2 mi e of jct US 97. Int corridors. **Pets:** Designated rooms, supervision.

ASK S⚙ ✕ ⯑ ⯑ ⯑ ⯑

BOARDMAN

④④ ◆◆ **Econo Lodge** M ✿
(541) 481-2375. **$44-$79.** 105 SW Front St. I-84 exit 164, just s. Ext corridors. **Pets:** Other. Designated rooms, supervision.

SAVE S⚙ ✕ ⯑ ➡ ⯑

BROOKINGS

④④ ◆◆◆ **Best Western Beachfront Inn** M ✿
(541) 469-7779. **$79-$109.** 16008 Boat Basin Rd. S end on US 101, 0.8 mi w on Lower Harbor Rd. Ext corridors. **Pets:** Large, other. $5 daily fee/pet. Designated rooms, supervision.

✕ ⯑ ⯑ ⯑ ⯑ ➡ ⯑ ✕ ⯑

④④ ◆ **Westward Motel** M
(541) 469-7471. **$38-$59, 3 days notice.** 1026 Chetco Ave. N end on US 101. Ext corridors. **Pets:** Supervision.
✕ ⯑

BURNS

④④ ◆◆ **Best Inn** M ✿
(541) 573-1700. **$53-$67.** 999 Oregon Ave. 1 mi w on US 395/20 from jct of SR 78. Ext/int corridors. **Pets:** Medium. $20 deposit/room, $5 one-time fee/pet. Designated rooms, no service, supervision, crate.

SAVE S⚙ ✕ ⯑ ⯑

④④ ◆◆ **Ponderosa Motel** M ✿
(541) 573-2047. **$43-$68.** 577 W Monroe. Just w on US 395/20 from jct of SR 78. Ext corridors. **Pets:** Medium, other. Designated rooms, supervision.

SAVE S⚙ ✕ ⯑ ⯑

CANNON BEACH

④④ ◆◆ **Cannon Beach Ecola Creek Lodge** M
(503) 436-2776. **$99-$120, 3 days notice.** 208 5th St. 0.3 mi w of US 101 via north exit to Ecola State Park. Ext corridors. **Pets:** Supervision.
✕ ⯑ ⯑ ⯑ ⯑

◆◆◆ **Hallmark Resort at Cannon Beach** M
(503) 436-1566. **Call for rates.** 1400 S Hemlock. US 101 exit Sunset Blvd, just s. Ext corridors. **Pets:** Supervision.
ASK ✕ ⯑ ⯑ ⯑ ⯑ ⯑

◆◆ Haystack Resort Motel M
(503) 436-1577. **$119-$189, 3 days notice.** 3339 S Hemlock. Just w of US 101, exit Tolovana Park. Ext corridors. **Pets:** $5 daily fee/pet, $5 one-time fee/pet. Designated rooms, supervision.

◆◆◆ Surfsand Resort M
(503) 436-2274. **$129-$319, 3 days notice.** Ocean Front & Gower. US 101, 2nd Cannon Beach exit; downtown at Oceanfront and Gower. Ext corridors. **Pets:** Other. $10 daily fee/pet. Designated rooms, supervision.

◆◆ Tolovana Inn CO
(503) 436-2211. **$68-$150, 3 days notice.** 3400 S Hemlock. 2 mi s, off US 101 Beach Loop. Ext corridors. **Pets:** Other. $10 daily fee/pet. No service, supervision, crate.

CASCADE LOCKS

◆◆◆ Best Western Columbia River Inn M
(541) 374-8777. **$89-$119.** 735 WaNaPa St. I-84 exit 44. Int corridors. **Pets:** Medium. Designated rooms, supervision.

COOS BAY

◆◆◆ Best Western Holiday Motel M
(541) 269-5111. **$73-$98.** 411 N Bayshore Dr. Just n of downtown on US 101. Ext/int corridors. **Pets:** Designated rooms, supervision.

◆◆◆ Edgewater Inn M
(541) 267-0423. **$85-$99.** 275 E Johnson St. Just s of downtown on US 101, then e. Ext/int corridors. **Pets:** Small. $8 one-time fee/pet. Designated rooms, no service, supervision, crate.

◆◆ Motel 6-1244 M
(541) 267-7171. **$52-$68.** 1445 Bayshore Dr. 0.6 mi n of downtown on US 101. Ext corridors. **Pets:** Other. Supervision.

◆◆◆ Red Lion Inn M
(541) 267-4141. **$89-$99.** 1313 N Bayshore Dr. 0.5 mi n of downtown on US 101. Ext corridors. **Pets:** Medium. Designated rooms, supervision.

COQUILLE

◆ Myrtle Lane Motel M
(541) 396-2102. **$34-$39.** 787 N Central Blvd. 0.4 mi n on N Central Blvd from SR 42. Ext corridors. **Pets:** Medium. Designated rooms, supervision.

CORVALLIS

◆◆ Motel Orleans M
(541) 758-9125. **$48-$64.** 935 NW Garfield. 1.5 mi n on 9th St. Int corridors. **Pets:** $100 deposit/pet. No service, supervision, crate.

◆◆ Shanico Inn M
(541) 754-7474. **$58-$80, 7 days notice.** 1113 NW 9th St. 1.3 mi n. Int corridors. **Pets:** Other. $5 daily fee/pet. Designated rooms, no service, supervision, crate.

◆◆ Super 8 Motel M
(541) 758-8088. **$50-$90.** 407 NW Second St. On US 20, just n jct SR 34. Int corridors. **Pets:** Other. $25 deposit/room. No service, supervision, crate.

COTTAGE GROVE

◆◆ Best Western Village Green Resort M
(541) 942-2491. **$59-$89, 3 days notice.** 725 Row River Rd. I-5 exit 174, just e. Ext corridors. **Pets:** Medium. Designated rooms, supervision.

◆◆ Comfort Inn M
(541) 942-9747. **$59-$79.** 845 Gateway Blvd. I-5 exit 174, just w. Ext corridors. **Pets:** Small. No service, supervision, crate.

◆◆◆ Holiday Inn Express M
(541) 942-1000. **$110-$110.** 1601 Gateway Blvd. I-5 exit 174, just w. Int corridors. **Pets:** Small. $10 daily fee/pet. Designated rooms, no service, supervision, crate.

CRESCENT

◆◆ Woodsman Country Lodge M
(541) 433-2710. **$35-$41.** 136740 Hwy 97 N. Center, on US 97. Ext corridors. **Pets:** Medium. $5 daily fee/room. Designated rooms, no service, supervision, crate.

CRESWELL

◆ Motel Orleans M
(541) 895-3341. **$35-$55.** 345 E Oregon. I-5, exit 182, just w. Ext corridors. **Pets:** No service, supervision, crate.

DALLAS

◆◆◆ Best Western Dallas Inn & Suites M
(503) 623-6000. **$59-$79.** 250 Orchard Dr. SR 223, just n. Int corridors. **Pets:** Small. $10 daily fee/pet. Designated rooms, no service, supervision, crate.

DEPOE BAY

⏹ ◆◆ Crown Pacific Inn 🅜 ✻
(541) 765-7773. **$70-$88.** 50 NE Bechill St. Center. Ext/int corridors. **Pets:** $5 daily fee/pet. No service, supervision, crate.
[SAVE] [S⚡] [✕] [🔧] [💻] [⚿]

ENTERPRISE

◆◆◆ Ponderosa Motel 🅜 ✻
(541) 426-3186. **$54-$64.** 102 E Greenwood St. Downtown, town center across from City Hall. Ext corridors. **Pets:** Medium, dogs only. $5 daily fee/pet. No service, supervision, crate.
[ASK] [S⚡] [✕] [🔧] [💻]

⏹ ◆◆ Wilderness Inn 🅜 ✻
(541) 426-4535. **$49-$59.** 301 W North St. Corner NW 2nd. Ext corridors. **Pets:** Medium, dogs only. $5 daily fee/pet. No service, supervision, crate.
[SAVE] [S⚡] [✕] [🔧] [💻]

EUGENE

⏹ ◆◆◆ Best Western Greentree Inn 🅜🅸 ✻
(541) 485-2727. **$64-$86.** 1759 Franklin Blvd. I-5 southbound exit 194B to I-105, then University of Oregon route; northbound I-5 exit 192, 1.2 mi w. Int corridors. **Pets:** Other. $25 deposit/pet. Designated rooms, supervision.
[SAVE] [✕] [🔧] [🍴] [⚿]

⏹ ◆◆◆ Best Western New Oregon Motel 🅜 ✻
(541) 683-3669. **$64-$86.** 1655 Franklin Blvd. I-5 southbound exit 194B to I-105, then U or Oregon Route; I-5 northbound exit 192, 1.3 mi w. Ext/int corridors. **Pets:** $25 deposit/pet. Supervision.
[SAVE] [✕] [🎵] [🔧] [⚿] [✕]

⏹ ◆◆ Campus Inn 🅜 ✻
(541) 343-3376. **$58-$72, 3 days notice.** 390 E Broadway. I-5 exit 194B, 1.3 mi w on I-105 exit 2, 1.5 mi s (follow U of O signs). Ext corridors. **Pets:** Dogs only. Supervision.
[SAVE] [S⚡] [✕] [🔧] [💻]

⏹ ◆◆◆ Eugene Hilton 🅗 ✻
(541) 342-2000. **$120-$180.** 66 E 6th & Oak sts. City Center at 6th and Oak sts. Int corridors. **Pets:** $25 one-time fee/room. Supervision.
[SAVE] [✕] [🎵] [🔧] [💻] [🍴] [⚿]

⏹ ◆ Motel 6–36 🅜 ✻
(541) 687-2395. **$44-$60.** 3690 Glenwood Dr. I-5 exit 191, just w then just s on feeder road. Ext corridors. **Pets:** Other. Supervision.
[S⚡] [✕] [🎰] [🗝] [⚿] [CTV]

⏹ ◆◆ Quality Inn & Suites 🅜
(541) 342-1243. **$65-$100.** 2121 Franklin Blvd. I-5 northbound exit 192, just w; southbound exit 194B, follow U of O signs. Ext corridors. **Pets:** No service, supervision, crate.
[SAVE] [S⚡] [✕] [🔧] [💻] [⚿]

⏹ ◆◆ Ramada Inn-Eugene 🅜🅸 ✻
(541) 342-5181. **$68-$100, 5 days notice.** 225 Coburg Rd. I-5 exit 194B, just w on I-105, exit Coburg Rd, then just n. Ext/int corridors. **Pets:** Small. $15 daily fee/room. No service, supervision, crate.
[SAVE] [S⚡] [✕] [🎵] [🗝] [🔧] [💻] [🍴] [⚿]

⏹ ◆◆ Red Lion Inn 🅜🅸 ✻
(541) 342-5201. **$54-$72.** 205 Coburg Rd. I-5 exit 194B, just w on I-105 exit Coburg Rd and just n. Ext corridors. **Pets:** Other. No service, supervision, crate.
[SAVE] [S⚡] [✕] [🎵] [🗝] [🔧] [💻] [🍴] [⚿]

⏹ ◆◆ Travelodge 🅜 ✻
(541) 342-6383. **$65-$75.** 1859 Franklin Blvd. I-5 northbound, exit 192, 1 mi w; southbound exit 194B, to I-105, exit University of Oregon route. Ext/int corridors. **Pets:** Other. No service, supervision, crate.
[SAVE] [S⚡] [✕] [💻]

◆◆◆ The Valley River Inn 🅜🅸 ✻
(541) 687-0123. **$150-$230.** 1000 Valley River Way. I-5 exit 194B, 1 mi w on I-105, Santa Clara exit, follow the Valley River Center signs. Int corridors. **Pets:** Other. Supervision.
[ASK] [S⚡] [✕] [🎵] [🗝] [🔧] [💻] [🍴] [⚿] [✕]

FLORENCE

⏹ ◆ Lighthouse Inn 🅜 ✻
(541) 997-3221. **$65-$75.** 155 Hwy 101. 0.5 mi s on US 101 from jct SR 126. Ext/int corridors. **Pets:** Small, other. $10 daily fee/pet. Designated rooms, supervision.
[SAVE] [S⚡] [✕] [⚿]

⏹ ◆ Money Saver Motel 🅜 ✻
(541) 997-7131. **$59-$69.** 170 Hwy 101. 0.5 mi s on US 101 from jct SR 126. Ext corridors. **Pets:** Small. Supervision.
[SAVE] [✕] [⚿]

⏹ ◆ Oceanbreeze Motel 🅜 ✻
(541) 997-2642. **$60-$83.** 85165 Hwy 101 S. 2 mi s on US 101 from jct of SR 126. Ext corridors. **Pets:** Small, dogs only. $7 one-time fee/pet. No service, supervision, crate.
[SAVE] [S⚡] [✕] [🔧] [💻] [⚿]

⏹ ◆◆ Park Motel 🅜 ✻
(541) 997-2634. **$49-$85.** 85034 Hwy 101 S. 2.2 mi s on US 101 from jct of SR 126. Ext corridors. **Pets:** $6 daily fee/pet. No service, supervision, crate.
[SAVE] [S⚡] [✕] [🔧] [⚿]

GEARHART

⏹ ◆◆ Gearhart By The Sea Resort 🅒🅞 ✻
(503) 738-8331. **$126-$178, 3 days notice.** 1157 N Marion. 1 mi w off US 101 via city center exit (Pacific Way). Ext corridors. **Pets:** Dogs only. $10 daily fee/room, $10 one-time fee/room. Supervision.
[SAVE] [S⚡] [✕] [🔧] [⚿] [⚿]

GLENEDEN BEACH

⚑ ◆◆◆◆ **The Westin Salishan Lodge & Golf Resort** **R** ❀
(541) 764-2371. **$249-$249, 5 days notice.** 7760 Hwy 101 N. Center; just e of US 101. Ext corridors. **Pets:** Other. $25 one-time fee/room. Supervision.

🅂🄰🅅🄴 🆂🄳 ⊠ 🄐 🄴 🖳 🍴 🏊 ⊠ 🎵

GLIDE

◆◆ **Steelhead Run B & B and Fine Art Gallery** **BB** ❀
(541) 496-0563. **$65-$105, 7 days notice.** 23049 N Umpqua (Hwy 138). On SR 138, 18 mi e of Rosebury at MM 20. Ext/int corridors. **Pets:** Other. $10 daily fee/room. Designated rooms, supervision.

🄰🅂🄺 🆂🄳 ⊠ ⊠ 🄲🅃🅅

GOLD BEACH

⚑ ◆◆◆ **Best Western Inn of The Beachcomber** **M** ❀
(541) 247-6691. **$89-$105.** 29266 Ellensburg Ave. S end on US 101. Ext/int corridors. **Pets:** Very small. Designated rooms, no service, supervision, crate.

🅂🄰🅅🄴 🆂🄳 ⊠ 🖥 🖳 🏊

⚑ ◆◆ **Econo Lodge Gold Beach** **M** ❀
(541) 247-6606. **$60-$99.** 29171 Ellensburg Ave. S end on US 101. Ext corridors. **Pets:** Medium. $5 deposit/pet, $5 one-time fee/pet. No service, supervision, crate.

🅂🄰🅅🄴 🆂🄳 ⊠ 🖥 🖳 🎵

⚑ ◆◆ **Ireland's Rustic Lodges** **C** ❀
(541) 247-7718. **$50-$70.** 29330 S Ellensburg. Center; on US 101. Ext corridors. **Pets:** Other. $5 daily fee/pet. Supervision.

⊠ 🖥 🖳 ⊠ 🎵 📠

⚑ ◆◆ **Jot's Resort** **MI** ❀
(541) 247-6676. **$85-$135.** 94360 Wedderburn Loop. W of US 101 at n end of Rogue River Bridge. Ext corridors. **Pets:** Other. Supervision.

🅂🄰🅅🄴 ⊠ 🖥 🖳 🍴 🏊 ⊠ 🎵

◆◆ **Motel 6–4047** **M** ❀
(541) 247-4533. **Call for rates.** 94433 Jerry's Flat Rd. N end of US 101. Ext corridors. **Pets:** Other. No service, supervision, crate.

⊠ 🖥 🎵

◆◆ **Sand 'n Sea Motel** **M**
(541) 247-6658. **$59-$89.** 29362 Ellensburg Ave. On US 101. Ext corridors. **Pets:** Small. No service, supervision, crate.

🄰🅂🄺 🆂🄳 ⊠ 🖥 🖳 ⊠ 🎵

◆◆ **Shore Cliff Inn** **M**
(541) 247-7091. **$60-$75.** 29346 Ellensburg Ave. On US 101. Ext corridors. **Pets:** No service, supervision, crate.

⊠ 🖥 🖳 🎵

GOVERNMENT CAMP

◆◆◆ **Mt. Hood Inn** **M** ❀
(503) 272-3205. **$134-$164, 4 days notice.** 87450 E Government Camp Loop. 0.5 mi w of center. Int corridors. **Pets:** Dogs only. $5 daily fee/pet. No service, supervision, crate.

🄰🅂🄺 🆂🄳 ⊠ 🄐 🖥 🖳 🎵 🄲🅃🅅

GRANTS PASS

⚑ ◆◆ **Best Western Grants Pass Inn** **M** ❀
(541) 476-1117. **$73-$83.** 111 NE Agness Ave. I-5 exit 55, just w. Ext corridors. **Pets:** Small, other. $5 one-time fee/pet. Designated rooms, no service, supervision, crate.

🅂🄰🅅🄴 🆂🄳 ⊠ 🖾 🖥 🖳 🏊

⚑ ◆◆◆ **Best Western Inn at the Rogue** **M** ❀
(541) 582-2200. **$85-$105.** 8959 Rogue River Hwy. 7 mi s, just w of I-5, exit 48. Int corridors. **Pets:** Small, other. $30 deposit/room, $10 daily fee/pet, $10 one-time fee/pet. No service, supervision, crate.

🅂🄰🅅🄴 🆂🄳 ⊠ 🖥 🏊

⚑ ◆◆◆ **Hawthorn Inn & Suites** **M** ❀
(541) 472-1808. **$64-$88.** 243 NE Morgan Lane. I-5, exit 58, just s on SR 99, then just e and just n on SR 99, then just e. Int corridors. **Pets:** Other. Designated rooms, no service, supervision, crate.

🅂🄰🅅🄴 🆂🄳 ⊠ ♿ 🖾 🖥 🖳 🏊

⚑ ◆◆◆ **Holiday Inn Express** **M** ❀
(541) 471-6144. **$83-$93.** 105 NE Agness Ave. I-5, exit 55, just w. Int corridors. **Pets:** Small, other. $5 one-time fee/pet. Designated rooms, no service, supervision, crate.

🅂🄰🅅🄴 🆂🄳 ⊠ 🖿 🖾 🖥 🖳

⚑ ◆ **Motel 6–253** **M**
(541) 474-1331. **$45-$61.** 1800 NE 7th St. I-5 exit 58, 0.4 mi s (southbound SR 99). Ext corridors. **Pets:** Large. No service, supervision, crate.

🆂🄳 ⊠ ♿ 🖾 🖥

⚑ ◆◆ **Redwood Motel** **M** ❀
(541) 476-0878. **$58-$92.** 815 NE 6th St. 1.3 mi sw of I-5, exit 58 (on SR 99). Ext corridors. **Pets:** Small. $10 one-time fee/pet. No service, supervision, crate.

🅂🄰🅅🄴 🆂🄳 ⊠ 🖿 🖾 🖥 🏊 ⊠

⚑ ◆◆ **Riverside Inn** **MI**
(541) 476-6873. **$65-$350.** 971 SE 6th St. 2.5 mi sw of I-5, exit 58, (southbound SR 99). Ext corridors. **Pets:** Very small. Designated rooms, no service, supervision, crate.

🅂🄰🅅🄴 🆂🄳 ⊠ 🖥 🖳 🍴 🏊

⚑ ◆◆ **Shilo Inn** **MI**
(541) 479-8391. **$49-$109.** 1880 NW Sixth St. Just s of I-5, exit 58 (southbound SR 99). Int corridors. **Pets:** Supervision.

🅂🄰🅅🄴 🆂🄳 ⊠ 🖾 🖥 🖳 🏊

⚑ ◆◆ **Travelodge** **M** ❀
(541) 479-6611. **$50-$62.** 1950 NW Vine St. Just s of I-5, exit 58 (southbound SR 99). Ext corridors. **Pets:** Small, dogs only. $5 daily fee/pet. Designated rooms, no service, supervision, crate.

🅂🄰🅅🄴 🆂🄳 ⊠ 🖥 🖳 🏊

HERMISTON

AAA ◆◆◆ **Oxford Suites M** ❀
(541) 564-8000. **$69-$109.** 1050 N First. 0.3 mi n on US 395. Int corridors. **Pets:** Medium, other. $20 one-time fee/pet. Designated rooms, no service, supervision, crate.
[SAVE] [S] [X] [🐾] [✒] [🖥] [🖼]

HOOD RIVER

AAA ◆◆◆ **Best Western Hood River Inn MI** ❀
(541) 386-2200. **$79-$119.** 1108 E Marina Way. I-84 exit 64, just n, then just e. Int corridors. **Pets:** Dogs only. $12 daily fee/room. No service, supervision, crate.
[SAVE] [S] [X] [🛏] [🐾] [🖥] [🖼] [🍴] [🖼] [🏊]

◆◆ **Meredith Motel M** ❀
(541) 386-1515. **$49-$75.** 4300 Westcliff Dr. Just n and 0.8 mi w of I-84, exit 62. Ext corridors. **Pets:** Dogs only. $10 one-time fee/room. No service, supervision, crate.
[X] [🖥]

AAA ◆◆ **Vagabond Lodge M** ❀
(541) 386-2992. **$44-$73.** 4070 Westcliff Dr. Just n and just w of I-84 exit 62. Ext corridors. **Pets:** Medium. Designated rooms, no service, supervision, crate.
[X] [🖥] [🖼]

JACKSONVILLE

◆◆ **The Stage Lodge M**
(541) 899-3953. **$68-$75, 3 days notice.** 830 N 5th. 0.3 mi ne on SR 238 (N 5th). Ext corridors. **Pets:** Medium. Supervision.
[X] [✒] [🖥] [🖼]

JOHN DAY

AAA ◆◆ **Best Western John Day Inn M** ❀
(541) 575-1700. **$58-$105, 5 days notice.** 315 W Main St. Just w on US 395 and 26. Ext corridors. **Pets:** Other. $5 daily fee/pet. Designated rooms, supervision.
[SAVE] [S] [X] [🐾] [🖥] [🖼] [🏊]

AAA ◆ **Dreamers Lodge M** ❀
(541) 575-0526. **$44-$64.** 144 N Canyon Blvd. Just n of jct US 26 and 395. Ext corridors. **Pets:** Other. No service, supervision, crate.
[X] [🖥] [🖼]

KLAMATH FALLS

AAA ◆◆ **Best Western Klamath Inn M** ❀
(541) 882-1200. **$80-$125.** 4061 S 6th St. Just w on 6th St (SR 140) from jct of SR 140E/39S and SR 39N/US 97 business route. Ext corridors. **Pets:** Other. Designated rooms, no service, supervision, crate.
[SAVE] [S] [X] [🐾] [🖥] [🖼] [🏊]

AAA ◆ **Motel 6-226 M** ❀
(541) 884-2110. **$45-$61.** 5136 S 6th St. 0.5 mi e on SR 140E from jct of SR 39/US 97 business route. Ext corridors. **Pets:** Small. Supervision.
[S] [X] [🛏] [✒] [🏊] [CTV]

AAA ◆ **Oregon Motel 8 M**
(541) 883-3431. **$44-$48.** 5225 Hwy 97 N. 3 mi n on US 97. Ext corridors. **Pets:** Supervision.
[SAVE] [X] [🖥] [🖼] [🏊]

AAA ◆◆ **Quality Inn M** ❀
(541) 882-4666. **$53-$62.** 100 Main St. Just e of US 97, city center exit. Ext corridors. **Pets:** Small, other. $50 deposit/room. No service, supervision, crate.
[SAVE] [S] [X] [🛏] [✒] [🖥] [🖼] [🏊]

AAA ◆◆ **Red Lion Inn MI** ❀
(541) 882-8864. **$59-$64.** 3612 S 6th St. 0.3 mi w on 6th St (SR 140) from jct of SR 140E/39S, SR 39N/US 97 business route. Ext corridors. **Pets:** Other. $20 deposit/room. Supervision.
[SAVE] [S] [X] [🛏] [🐾] [✒] [🖥] [🖼] [🍴] [🏊]

◆◆◆ **Shilo Suites Hotel MI**
(541) 885-7980. **$89-$125.** 2500 Almond St. N end of US 97. Int corridors. **Pets:** No service, supervision, crate.
[ASK] [S] [X] [♿] [🐾] [✒] [🖥] [🖼] [🍴] [🏊]

LA GRANDE

AAA ◆◆ **Howard Johnson Inn M** ❀
(541) 963-7195. **$67-$87.** 2612 Island Ave. On SR 82; just e of I-84, exit 261. Ext/int corridors. **Pets:** Other. $10 one-time fee/room. Supervision.
[SAVE] [S] [X] [🐾] [🖥] [🖼] [🏊]

LA PINE

◆◆◆ **Best Western Newberry Station M**
(541) 536-5130. **$55-$155.** 16515 Reed Rd. N end of town, just off SR 97. Int corridors. **Pets:** Small. No service, supervision, crate.
[ASK] [S] [X] [🛏] [✒] [🖥] [🖼] [🏊]

LAKEVIEW

AAA ◆◆◆ **Best Western Skyline Motor Lodge M** ❀
(541) 947-2194. **$70-$90.** 414 N G St. At jct US 395 and SR 140. Ext corridors. **Pets:** Small. $20 deposit/room. Designated rooms, no service, supervision, crate.
[SAVE] [S] [X] [🐾] [🖥] [🖼] [🏊]

LINCOLN CITY

AAA ◆◆ **Coho Inn M** ❀
(541) 994-3684. **$109-$134.** 1635 NW Harbor. Just w of US 101, exit N 17th St. Ext corridors. **Pets:** Small. $7 daily fee/pet. Designated rooms, no service, supervision, crate.
[X] [🖥] [🖼] [🎬]

AAA ◆◆ **Lincoln City Inn M**
(541) 996-4400. **$59-$99.** 1091 SE 1st St. On US 101, at D River. Int corridors. **Pets:** Small, supervision.
[SAVE] [S] [X] [🛏] [✒] [🖥]

AAA ◆◆◆ **The O'dysius Hotel M** ❀
(541) 994-4121. **$145-$179, 5 days notice.** 120 NW Inlet Cir. Center at D River on US 101. Int corridors. **Pets:** Small. $10 daily fee/pet. Designated rooms, no service, supervision, crate.
[SAVE] [S] [X] [🖥] [🖼] [🎬]

◆◆ **Shilo Oceanfront Resort MI** ❀
(541) 994-3655. **$49-$259.** 1501 NW 40th Pl. N side, just w of US 101, exit NW 40th. Ext/int corridors. **Pets:** $10 daily fee/pet. Supervision.
[ASK] [S] [X] [♿] [✒] [🖥] [🖼] [🍴] [🏊]

MADRAS

(AAA) ◆◆ Best Western Rama Inn M 🐾
(541) 475-6141. **$59-$99.** 12 SW 4th St. Downtown on US 97/US 26 southbound. Ext corridors. **Pets:** Other. $10 one-time fee/room. Designated rooms, supervision.
[SAVE] [S🐾] [✕] [🐾] [🛏] [💻] [🍽]

MEDFORD

(AAA) ◆◆ Best Inn & Suites M
(541) 773-8266. **$49-$65.** 1015 S Riverside Ave. I-5 exit 27, 0.4 mi w and just n (northbound SR 99). Ext corridors. **Pets:** No service, supervision, crate.
[SAVE] [S🐾] [✕] [🐾] [🛏] [💻] [🍽]

(AAA) ◆◆◆ Best Western Horizon Inn M
(541) 779-5085. **$84-$84.** 1154 E Barnett Rd. I-5 exit 27, just e. Ext corridors. **Pets:** Medium. Designated rooms, no service, supervision, crate.
[SAVE] [S🐾] [✕] [🐾] [🛏] [💻] [🍽]

(AAA) ◆◆◆ Best Western Pony Soldier Inn M
(541) 779-2011. **$82-$88.** 2340 Crater Lake Hwy. I-5 exit 30, just e on SR 62. Ext corridors. **Pets:** Small. No service, supervision, crate.
[SAVE] [S🐾] [✕] [🐾] [🛏] [💻] [🍽]

(AAA) ◆ Cedar Lodge Motor Inn M 🐾
(541) 773-7361. **$40-$53.** 518 N Riverside Ave. I-5 exit 27, 0.5 mi w then 1.2 mi n (SR 99). Ext corridors. **Pets:** Small. $20 deposit/room. Designated rooms, no service, supervision, crate.
[SAVE] [S🐾] [✕] [🛏] [🍽]

(AAA) ◆◆ Motel 6-Medford North–739 M
(541) 779-0550. **$48-$64.** 2400 Biddle Rd. I-5 exit 30, just e and just n. Ext corridors. **Pets:** Small. No service, supervision, crate.
[S🐾] [✕] [🐾] [🐾] [🍽] [CTV]

(AAA) ◆ Motel 6-Medford South–89 M
(541) 773-4290. **Call for rates.** 950 Alba Dr. I-5 exit 27, just e, then just n. Ext corridors. **Pets:** Supervision.
[✕] [🐾] [🍽] [CTV]

(AAA) ◆◆◆ Pear Tree Motel M 🐾
(541) 535-4445. **$65-$73.** 300 Pear Tree Ln. I-5 exit 24, just s on frontage road. Ext corridors. **Pets:** Medium, other. $10 one-time fee/pet. No service, supervision, crate.
[SAVE] [S🐾] [✕] [🍽]

◆◆◆ Red Lion Hotel M
(541) 779-5811. **$79-$79.** 200 N Riverside Ave. I-5 exit 27, 0.5 mi w on SR 99, 0.5 mi n, 1 mi n. Ext corridors. **Pets:** Medium. Designated rooms, no service, supervision, crate.
[✕] [🐾] [🐾] [💻] [🍽] [🍽]

(AAA) ◆◆ Reston Hotel M 🐾
(541) 779-3141. **$69-$130, 7 days notice.** 2300 Crater Lake Hwy. I-5 exit 30, just e, just s on Biddle. Int corridors. **Pets:** Medium, dogs only. $20 one-time fee/pet. Designated rooms, no service, supervision, crate.
[SAVE] [S🐾] [✕] [🛏] [💻] [🍽] [🍽]

◆◆ Shilo Inn M 🐾
(541) 770-5151. **$45-$99.** 2111 Biddle Rd. I-5 exit 30, just e and then just s. Int corridors. **Pets:** Other. $10 daily fee/pet. No service, supervision, crate.
[A$K] [S🐾] [✕] [🛏] [💻]

(AAA) ◆◆◆ Windmill Inn of Medford M 🐾
(541) 779-0050. **$84-$84.** 1950 Biddle Rd. I-5 exit 30, just e then just s. Int corridors. **Pets:** Other. Supervision.
[SAVE] [S🐾] [✕] [🐾] [🐾] [🛏] [🍽] [✕]

MYRTLE POINT

(AAA) ◆ Myrtle Trees Motel M 🐾
(541) 572-5811. **$36-$45.** 1010 8th St (Hwy 42). 0.5 mi e on SR 42. Ext corridors. **Pets:** Small. $5 daily fee/pet, $5 one-time fee/pet. Designated rooms, no service, supervision, crate.
[✕] [🛏] [🍿]

NEWBERG

(AAA) ◆◆◆ Shilo Inn M
(503) 537-0303. **$65-$89.** 501 Sitka Ave. On US 99 W. Int corridors. **Pets:** No service, supervision, crate.
[SAVE] [S🐾] [✕] [🐾] [🛏] [💻] [🍽]

NEWPORT

(AAA) ◆◆◆ Hallmark Resort M
(541) 265-2600. **$129-$239.** 744 SW Elizabeth St. 0.7 mi s on US 101 from jct US 20, just w on SW Bay St. Ext corridors. **Pets:** Medium. Designated rooms, no service, supervision, crate.
[SAVE] [S🐾] [✕] [🐾] [🐾] [🐾] [🛏] [💻] [🍴] [🍽] [✕] [🍿]

(AAA) ◆◆◆ Holiday Inn Newport at Agate Beach H 🐾
(541) 265-9411. **$119-$149.** 3019 N Coast Hwy. 1.5 mi n on US 101 from jct US 20. Int corridors. **Pets:** Other. $10 one-time fee/room. Designated rooms, no service, supervision, crate.
[SAVE] [S🐾] [✕] [🛏] [💻] [🍴] [🍽] [🍿]

◆◆◆ Shilo Oceanfront Resort M 🐾
(541) 265-7701. **$99-$159.** 536 SW Elizabeth St. 0.5 mi s on US 101 from jct US 20, just w on SW Falls St. Ext/int corridors. **Pets:** Other. $10 daily fee/pet. No service, supervision, crate.
[A$K] [S🐾] [✕] [🐾] [🛏] [💻] [🍴] [🍽] [🍿]

(AAA) ◆◆ Val-U Inn M 🐾
(541) 265-6203. **$69-$79.** 531 SW Fall St. 0.5 mi s on US 101 from jct US 20, just w. Int corridors. **Pets:** Dogs only. $5 daily fee/pet. Supervision.
[SAVE] [S🐾] [✕] [🛏] [🍿]

(AAA) ◆◆ Whaler Motel M 🐾
(541) 265-9261. **$95-$139.** 155 SW Elizabeth St. Just s on US 101 from jct US 20, just w on SW 2nd. Ext corridors. **Pets:** Small, dogs only. Designated rooms, no service, supervision, crate.
[SAVE] [S🐾] [✕] [🐾] [🐾] [🐾] [🛏] [💻] [🍽] [🍿]

OAKRIDGE

(AAA) ◆◆ Best Western Oakridge Inn M ☙
(541) 782-2212. **$55-$76.** 47433 Hwy 58. West end on SR 58. Ext corridors. **Pets:** Small. $5 one-time fee/room. No service, supervision, crate.

[SAVE] [S🌙] [✕] [🏠] [🖉] [🛏] [🖵] [🖼]

ONTARIO

(AAA) ◆◆◆ Best Western Inn & Suites M ☙
(541) 889-2600. **$49-$165.** 251 Goodfellow St. I-84 exit 376, just e. Int corridors. **Pets:** Medium, dogs only. $50 deposit/pet. Designated rooms, no service, supervision, crate.

[✕] [🛏] [🖵] [🖼]

(AAA) ◆◆ Carlile Motel M ☙
(541) 889-8658. **$37-$65.** 589 N Oregon St (SR 201). Eastbound I-84 exit 374, 1.5 mi se (Business SR 30 & 201); westbound I-84 exit 376A, 0.7 mi w on E Idaho, just n. Ext corridors. **Pets:** Small. $5 daily fee/pet. No service, supervision, crate.

[SAVE] [S🌙] [✕] [🛏] [🖵]

(AAA) ◆◆◆ Holiday Inn–Ontario, OR M！ ☙
(541) 889-8621. **$72-$77.** 1249 Tapadera Ave. On US 30, jct I-84 exit 376, just e. Int corridors. **Pets:** Other. $10 one-time fee/room. No service, supervision, crate.

[SAVE] [S🌙] [✕] [🏠] [🐾] [🖉] [🛏] [🖵] [🍴] [🖼]

(AAA) ◆ Holiday Motel M！ ☙
(541) 889-9188. **$36-$46.** 615 E Idaho. I-84 exit 376, just w. Ext corridors. **Pets:** Other. Supervision.

[SAVE] [S🌙] [✕] [🍴] [🖼]

(AAA) ◆ Stockman's Motel M ☙
(541) 889-4446. **$35-$50.** 81 SW 1st St. From I-84 exit 376, 0.9 mi w just off US 30 business. Ext corridors. **Pets:** Medium, dogs only. $10 deposit/pet. Designated rooms, supervision.

[SAVE] [✕] [🛏]

(AAA) ◆◆ Super 8 Motel M ☙
(541) 889-8282. **$53-$115.** 266 Goodfellow St. I-84 exit 376, just e. Int corridors. **Pets:** Small, dogs only. $20 deposit/room. Designated rooms, no service, supervision, crate.

[SAVE] [S🌙] [✕] [🐾] [🛏] [🖼]

PACIFIC CITY

(AAA) ◆◆◆ Inn at Cape Kiwanda M ☙
(503) 965-7001. **$149-$159.** 33105 Cape Kiwanda Dr. Just w on Pacific Ave, 1 mi n. Ext corridors. **Pets:** Other. $10 daily fee/pet. Designated rooms, supervision.

[SAVE] [S🌙] [✕] [♿] [🛏] [🖵] [🖊]

PENDLETON

(AAA) ◆ Chaparral Motel M ☙
(541) 276-8654. **$37-$57.** 620 SW Tutuilla Rd. Off I-84 exit 209, just s on US 395. Ext corridors. **Pets:** Small, dogs only. $5 daily fee/pet. Designated rooms, no service, supervision, crate.

[S🌙] [✕] [🛏] [🖵]

◆◆◆ Holiday Inn Express M ☙
(541) 966-6520. **Call for rates.** 600 SE Nye. I-84 exit 210, just se. Int corridors. **Pets:** $30 deposit/room, $10 one-time fee/room. Designated rooms, supervision.

[✕] [🖉] [🛏] [🖼]

◆◆◆ Oxford Suites M ☙
(541) 276-6000. **$79-$119.** 2400 SW Court Pl. Off I-84, exit 209, nw corner, just n on US 395. Int corridors. **Pets:** Small, other. $15 one-time fee/room. Designated rooms, no service, supervision, crate.

[✕] [♿] [🐾] [🖉] [🛏] [🖼]

(AAA) ◆◆ Red Lion Hotel M！ ☙
(541) 276-6111. **$59-$59.** 304 SE Nye Ave. I-84 exit 210. Ext/int corridors. **Pets:** Other. $20 deposit/room. No service, supervision, crate.

[SAVE] [S🌙] [✕] [🖉] [🖵] [🍴] [🖼]

◆◆ Super 8 Motel M ☙
(541) 276-8881. **Call for rates.** 601 SE Nye Ave. I-84 exit 210. Int corridors. **Pets:** Other. $10 deposit/room, $10 daily fee/room. Supervision.

[ASK] [✕] [🛏] [🖼]

(AAA) ◆◆ Travelodge M ☙
(541) 276-7531. **$49-$69.** 411 SW Dorion Ave. From I-84 exit 209, just w of town center on corner SW 4th St, SW Dorian across from City Hall. Ext corridors. **Pets:** $10 daily fee/room, $10 one-time fee/pet. No service, supervision, crate.

[SAVE] [S🌙] [✕] [🛏] [🖵]

◆◆ Wildhorse Resort Hotel M
(541) 276-0355. **$63-$140.** 72779 Hwy 331. 6 mi e, 0.6 mi n of I-84 exit 216. Int corridors. **Pets:** Supervision.

[ASK] [S🌙] [✕] [🖉] [🛏] [🖵] [🖼] [✕]

PORT ORFORD

(AAA) ◆ Sea Crest Motel M ☙
(541) 332-3040. **$52-$71.** 44 Hwy 101. 1 mi s on US 101. Ext corridors. **Pets:** Small. $5 daily fee/pet. Designated rooms, no service, supervision, crate.

[SAVE] [✕] [🛏] [🖵] [🖊]

PORTLAND METROPOLITAN AREA

BEAVERTON

(AAA) ◆◆◆ Greenwood Inn M！ ☙
(503) 643-7444. **$89-$109.** 10700 SW Allen Blvd. Just e of SR 217, exit Allen Blvd. Ext/int corridors. **Pets:** $20 one-time fee/pet. Designated rooms, supervision.

[SAVE] [S🌙] [✕] [🖉] [🛏] [🖵] [🍴] [🖼]

◆◆ Homestead Village Guest Studios M ☙
(503) 690-3600. **$59-$94.** 875 SW 158th Ave. US 26 exit 65, just s, then 1.1 mi e. Ext corridors. **Pets:** Medium. $75 one-time fee/room. Designated rooms, no service, supervision, crate.

[ASK] [S🌙] [✕] [♿] [🖉] [🛏] [🖵]

⊕ ◆◆ Ramada Inn Beaverton 🅼 🐾
(503) 643-9100. **$90-$110.** 13455 SW Canyon Rd. 1 mi w of SR 217, exit Canyon Rd (SR 8). Int corridors. **Pets:** Other. $5 daily fee/pet. No service, supervision, crate.
🆂🆅🅴 ⬛ ✕ ⬛ ⬛ ⬛ 🔄

◆◆ Shilo Inn-Portland/Beaverton 🅼 🐾
(503) 297-2551. **$79-$189.** 9900 SW Canyon Rd. SR 217, exit Canyon Rd/Beaverton Hillsdale Hwy, take feeder road, 0.3 mi e on SR 8 (Canyon Rd). Int corridors. **Pets:** Other. $7 daily fee/pet. Supervision.
🅰🆂🅺 ⬛ ✕ ⬛ ⬛ ⬛ ⬛ 🍴 🔄

CLACKAMAS

⊕ ◆◆ Clackamas Inn 🅼 🐾
(503) 650-5340. **$59-$99.** 16010 SE 82nd Dr. Just e of I-205 southbound exit 12A; northbound exit 12 (SR 212). Int corridors. **Pets:** Small, dogs only. $5 daily fee/pet. Designated rooms, no service, supervision, crate.
⬛ ✕ ⬛ ⬛ 🔄

GRESHAM

◆◆◆ Briarwood Inn 🅼 🐾
(503) 907-1777. **$69-$129.** 2752 NE Hogan Dr. I-84 exit 16, 1.7 mi s on NE 238th Dr/Hogan Dr. Ext corridors. **Pets:** Small. $10 daily fee/pet. Designated rooms, no service, supervision, crate.
🅰🆂🅺 ✕ ⬛ ⬛ ⬛ ⬛ ⬛ 🍴 🔄

⊕ ◆◆◆ Hawthorn Inn & Suites 🅼 🐾
(503) 492-4000. **$75-$96.** 2323 NE 181 Ave. Just e of I-84 exit 13. Int corridors. **Pets:** Other. No service, supervision, crate.
🆂🆅🅴 ⬛ ✕ ⬛ ⬛ ⬛ ⬛ 🔄

⊕ ◆◆ Travelers Inn & Suites 🅼 🐾
(503) 661-5100. **$49-$59.** 121 NE 181st Ave. I-84 exit 13, 1.3 mi s. Int corridors. **Pets:** Small, other. $50 deposit/room, $10 daily fee/pet. Designated rooms, supervision.
🆂🆅🅴 ⬛ ✕ ⬛

HILLSBORO

⊕ ◆◆◆ Best Western Cavanaughs Hillsboro 🅼 🐾
(503) 648-3500. **$90-$110.** 3500 NE Cornell Rd. US 26 exit 62, 1.1 mi s on Cornelius Pass Rd, 2.5 mi w; opposite Hillsboro Airport. Int corridors. **Pets:** $75 deposit/room, $5 daily fee/pet. Supervision.
🆂🆅🅴 ⬛ ✕ ⬛ ⬛ ⬛ 🍴 🔄

⊕ ◆◆◆ Candlewood Suites 🅼
(503) 681-2121. **$69-$118.** 3133 NE Shute Rd. US 26 exit 61, 1.2 mi s. Int corridors. **Pets:** No service, supervision, crate.
🆂🆅🅴 ⬛ ✕ ⬛ ⬛ ⬛

◆◆◆ Residence Inn by Marriott Portland West 🅰 🐾
(503) 531-3200. **$169.** 18855 NW Tanasbourne Dr. Just s of US 26 exit 64. Ext/int corridors. **Pets:** Dogs only. $10 daily fee/pet. Supervision.
🅰🆂🅺 ⬛ ✕ ⬛ ⬛ ⬛ ⬛ ⬛ 🔄 ✕

⊕ ◆◆◆ Wellesley Inn & Suites 🅼 🐾
(503) 439-0706. **$74-$94.** 19311 NW Cornell Rd. US 26, exit 64, 0.5 mi s on 185th, 0.4 mi w. Int corridors. **Pets:** Small. $50 daily fee/room, $5 one-time fee/room. Supervision.
🆂🆅🅴 ⬛ ✕ ⬛ ⬛ ⬛ ⬛ 🔄

KING CITY

⊕ ◆◆◆ Best Western Northwind Inn & Suites 🅼 🐾
(503) 431-2100. **$79-$89.** 16105 SW Pacific Hwy. I-5, exit 292 (SR 217), just nw on SR 217, exit SR 99 W, 2.5 mi s on SR 99 W. Int corridors. **Pets:** Small. $20 one-time fee/room. No service, supervision, crate.
🆂🆅🅴 ⬛ ✕ ⬛ ⬛ ⬛ ⬛ ⬛ 🔄

LAKE OSWEGO

⊕ ◆◆◆ Crowne Plaza 🅷 🐾
(503) 624-8400. **$159-$159.** 14811 Kruse Oaks Dr. Just e of I-5 exit 292. Int corridors. **Pets:** Medium, other. Supervision.
🆂🆅🅴 ⬛ ✕ ⬛ ⬛ ⬛ ⬛ ⬛ 🍴 🔄 ✕

◆◆◆ Residence Inn by Marriott-Portland South 🅰 🐾
(503) 684-2603. **$145-$165.** 15200 SW Bangy Rd. I-5 exit 292, just e and 0.3 mi s. Ext corridors. **Pets:** Other. $10 daily fee/pet. Supervision.
🅰🆂🅺 ⬛ ✕ ⬛ ⬛ 🔄

MILWAUKIE

⊕ ◆◆ Econo Lodge Suites Inn 🅼 🐾
(503) 654-2222. **$59-$79.** 17330 SE McLoughlin Blvd. I-205 exit 9, 2.3 mi n on SR 99 E (McLoughlin). Ext corridors. **Pets:** Other. Supervision.
🆂🆅🅴 ✕ ⬛ ⬛ ⬛ ⬛ 🔄

OREGON CITY

⊕ ◆◆ Rivershore Hotel 🅼 🐾
(503) 655-7141. **$72-$84, 3 days notice.** 1900 Clackamette Dr. Just n of I-205, exit 9. Int corridors. **Pets:** Other. $5 daily fee/pet. Supervision.
🆂🆅🅴 ⬛ ✕ ⬛ ⬛ ⬛ 🍴 🔄

PORTLAND

⊕ ◆◆◆◆ The Benson Hotel 🅷 🐾
(503) 228-2000. **$190-$190.** 309 SW Broadway. Downtown at SW Broadway and Oak. Int corridors. **Pets:** Other. $50 one-time fee/room. Designated rooms, supervision.
🆂🆅🅴 ⬛ ✕ ⬛ ⬛ ⬛ 🍴

⊕ ◆◆◆ Best Western Imperial Hotel 🅷 🐾
(503) 228-7221. **$110-$135.** 400 SW Broadway. Downtown at SW Broadway and Stark. Int corridors. **Pets:** Medium, other. $10 one-time fee/room. Supervision.
⬛ ✕ ⬛ ⬛ ⬛

⚫ ◆◆ Best Western Inn at the Convention Center Ⓜ
(503) 233-6331. **$75-$110.** 420 NE Holladay. I-5 exit 302A, just e on Weidler and just s on Martin Luther King Blvd. Int corridors. **Pets:** Large. Supervision.

SAVE ⬚ ⬚ ⬚ ⬚ ⬚

⚫ ◆◆◆ Best Western Inn at the Meadows Ⓜ ♣
(503) 286-9600. **$89-$99.** 1215 N Hayden Meadows Dr. Just e of I-5 exit 306B. Int corridors. **Pets:** $20 daily fee/room. No service, supervision, crate.

SAVE ⬚ ⬚ ⬚ ⬚ ⬚

◆◆◆ Doubletree Hotel-Columbia River Ⓜ
(503) 283-2111. **$89-$89.** 1401 N Hayden Island Dr. I-5 exit 308, just w on Hayden Island Dr at Jantzen Beach. Int corridors. **Pets:** No service, supervision, crate.

ASK ⬚ ⬚ ⬚ ⬚ ⬚ ⬚ ⬚ ⬚ ⬚

◆◆◆ Doubletree Hotel-Jantzen Beach Ⓜ ♣
(503) 283-4466. **$89-$89.** 909 N Hayden Island Dr. I-5 exit 308, just e on Hayden Island Dr at Jantzen Beach. Int corridors. **Pets:** Small. $35 one-time fee/pet. No service, supervision, crate.

ASK ⬚ ⬚ ⬚ ⬚ ⬚ ⬚ ⬚ ⬚ ⬚

⚫ ◆◆◆ DoubleTree Hotel-Lloyd Center Ⓗ
(503) 281-6111. **$175.** 1000 NE Multnomah St. I-5 exit 302A, just e and just s on 9th, just e on Multnomah; I-84 westbound, Lloyd Center exit. Int corridors. **Pets:** Large. Supervision.

⬚ ⬚ ⬚ ⬚ ⬚ ⬚ ⬚

⚫ ◆◆◆ Doubletree Hotel Portland Downtown Ⓜ ♣
(503) 221-0450. **$79-$109.** 310 SW Lincoln. I-5 to I-405, 4th Ave exit, just n, then just e. Ext/int corridors. **Pets:** Large, other. $25 deposit/room. Supervision.

⬚ ⬚ ⬚ ⬚ ⬚ ⬚ ⬚ ⬚

⚫ ◆◆◆◆ 5TH Avenue Suites Hotel Ⓗ
(503) 222-0001. **$150-$180.** 506 SW Washington. Downtown at SW 5th Ave and Washington. Int corridors. **Pets:** Medium. No service, supervision, crate.

SAVE ⬚ ⬚ ⬚ ⬚ ⬚ ⬚

⚫ ◆◆◆ Hawthorn Inn & Suites Ⓜ
(503) 497-9044. **$81-$105** (no credit cards). 4319 NW Yeon. Northbound, 2.5 mi w of jct I-405 exit 3 on US 30; southbound 2.5 mi w of jct I-405 exit 302B on US 30. Int corridors. **Pets:** Supervision.

SAVE ⬚ ⬚ ⬚ ⬚ ⬚ ⬚ ⬚

⚫ ◆◆◆◆ The Heathman Hotel Ⓗ
(503) 241-4100. **$200-$210.** 1001 SW Broadway. Downtown at SW Broadway and Salmon. Int corridors. **Pets:** Supervision.

SAVE ⬚ ⬚ ⬚ ⬚ ⬚

⚫ ◆◆◆ Hotel Vintage Plaza Ⓗ ♣
(503) 228-1212. **$160-$190.** 422 SW Broadway. Downtown at Broadway and Washington. Int corridors. **Pets:** Supervision.

SAVE ⬚ ⬚ ⬚

⚫ ◆◆ Howard Johnson Airport Hotel Ⓜ
(503) 255-6722. **$60-$85.** 7101 NE 82nd Ave. I-205 northbound, exit 24A to Airport Way, w to 82nd Ave, 0.3 mi s; southbound, exit 24 to Airport Way, w to 82nd Ave, 0.3 mi s. Ext/int corridors. **Pets:** Supervision.

SAVE ⬚ ⬚ ⬚ ⬚ ⬚ ⬚

⚫ ◆◆ Mallory Hotel Ⓗ ♣
(503) 223-6311. **$85-$150.** 729 SW 15th. At SW 15th and Yamhill; I-5 to I-405, northbound Salmon St exit; southbound Couch-Burnside exit. Int corridors. **Pets:** Other. $10 one-time fee/room. Supervision.

⬚ ⬚ ⬚ ⬚ ⬚

◆◆ The Mark Spencer Hotel Ⓐ ♣
(503) 224-3293. **$85-$140.** 409 SW 11th Ave. Downtown. Int corridors. **Pets:** Other. $200 deposit/room. Designated rooms, supervision.

⬚ ⬚ ⬚

◆◆ Oxford Suites Ⓜ ♣
(503) 283-3030. **$79-$189, 3 days notice.** 12226 N Jantzen Dr. I-5 exit 308, just e on Hayden Island Dr at Jantzen Beach. Int corridors. **Pets:** Medium, other. $15 one-time fee/pet. No service, supervision, crate.

ASK ⬚ ⬚ ⬚ ⬚ ⬚

◆◆◆ Portland Marriott Downtown Ⓗ
(503) 226-7600. **Call for rates.** 1401 SW Naito Pkwy. Downtown, between Columbia and Clay. Int corridors. **Pets:** No service, supervision, crate.

⬚ ⬚ ⬚ ⬚ ⬚ ⬚ ⬚ ⬚

⚫ ◆◆ Quality Inn Portland Airport Ⓜ ♣
(503) 256-4111. **$69-$79.** 8247 NE Sandy Blvd. I-84 exit 5, 1.5 mi n on 82nd Ave. Ext/int corridors. **Pets:** Small. $15 one-time fee/room. Supervision.

SAVE ⬚ ⬚ ⬚ ⬚ ⬚

◆◆◆ Residence Inn by Marriott-Lloyd Center Ⓐ ♣
(503) 288-1400. **Call for rates.** 1710 NE Multnomah. I-5 exit 302A, 1.3 mi e on Weidler St, just s on 15th Ave; I-84 westbound, Lloyd Center exit 1, just n on 13th St, then just e. Ext corridors. **Pets:** Other. $10 daily fee/room, $50 one-time fee/room. No service, supervision, crate.

⬚ ⬚ ⬚ ⬚ ⬚ ⬚ ⬚

⚫ ◆◆◆ RiverPlace Hotel Ⓗ ♣
(503) 228-3233. **$219-$279.** 1510 SW Harbor Way. Downtown at Naito Pkwy (formerly Front Ave) and SW Harbor Way on the Williamette River water front. Int corridors. **Pets:** Other. $100 one-time fee/pet. Designated rooms, no service, supervision, crate.

SAVE ⬚ ⬚ ⬚ ⬚ ⬚ ⬚ ⬚

⚫ ◆ Travelodge Convention Center Ⓜ
(503) 231-7665. **$71-$109.** 1506 NE 2nd Ave. I-5 exit 302, just e, then just s. Int corridors. **Pets:** Designated rooms, supervision.

SAVE ⬚ ⬚ ⬚ ⬚

⚫ ◆ Travelodge Portland Airport Ⓜ ♣
(503) 255-1400. **$59-$109.** 9727 NE Sandy Blvd. I-205 exit 23A, just e. Ext corridors. **Pets:** Other. $10 daily fee/pet, $10 one-time fee/pet. Designated rooms, supervision.

SAVE ⬚ ⬚ ⬚ ⬚ ⬚ ⬚

⚫⚫ ◆◆ Travelodge Suites Portland Ⓜ ❀
(503) 788-9394. **$75-$84.** 7740 SE Powell Blvd. I-205 exit
19, 1 mi w. Ext/int corridors. **Pets:** Small, dogs only. $10
daily fee/room. No service, supervision, crate.
Ⓢ Ⓢ ⊗ 🛑 💻

TIGARD

⚫⚫ ◆◆ Best Western Sherwood Inn Ⓜ
(503) 620-2980. **$64-$84.** 15700 SW Upper Boones Ferry
Rd. Just w of I-5 exit 291. Int corridors. **Pets:** Designated
rooms, supervision.
Ⓢ Ⓢ ⊗ 🛑 🍴 ⊗

⚫⚫ ◆◆◆ Embassy Suites Hotel-Portland
Washington Square Ⓗ ❀
(503) 644-4000. **$109-$159.** 9000 SW Washington Square
Rd. SR 217, exit Progress/Scholls Ferry Rd, just e, then just
s on Hall. Int corridors. **Pets:** Medium, other. Designated
rooms, no service, supervision, crate.
Ⓢ Ⓢ ⊗ 🔒 📶 🖊 🛑 💻 🍴 ⊗

◆◆ Homestead Village Guest Studios Ⓜ
(503) 670-0555. **$58-$63.** 13009 SW 68th Pkwy. SR 217,
exit 72nd St, just ne, just se on Hampton St, then just s. Ext
corridors. **Pets:** Supervision.
ⒶⓈⓀ ⊗ 🖊 🛑 💻

◆◆ Shilo Inn-Tigard/Washington Square Ⓜ ❀
(503) 620-4320. **$65-$109.** 10830 SW Greenburg Rd. Just
w of jct SR 217, exit Greenburg Rd. Int corridors.
Pets: Medium. $10 daily fee/pet. Supervision.
ⒶⓈⓀ Ⓢ ⊗ 🖊 🛑 💻

TROUTDALE

⚫⚫ ◆ Motel 6-Portland East–407 Ⓜ
(503) 665-2254. **$40-$56.** 1610 NW Frontage Rd. I-84 exit
17, on s frontage road. Ext corridors. **Pets:** Small. Designated rooms, no service, supervision, crate.
Ⓢ ⊗ ♿ 🖊 🛑 ⊗ 📺

⚫⚫ ◆◆◆ Phoenix Inn Ⓜ ❀
(503) 669-6500. **$66-$79.** 477 NW Phoenix Dr. I-84 exit 17,
on s frontage road. Int corridors. **Pets:** $10 daily fee/room.
Designated rooms, no service, supervision, crate.
Ⓢ Ⓢ ⊗ 🔒 📶 🛑 💻 ⊗

TUALATIN

⚫⚫ ◆◆◆ The Sweetbrier Inn Ⓜ ❀
(503) 692-5800. **$75-$115.** 7125 SW Nyberg Rd. I-5 exit
289, just e. Ext/int corridors. **Pets:** $100 deposit/room. No
service, supervision, crate.
Ⓢ Ⓢ ⊗ ♿ 📶 🖊 🛑 💻 🍴 ⊗ ⊗

WILSONVILLE

⚫⚫ ◆◆ Best Inn & Suites Ⓜ
(503) 682-3184. **$43-$61.** 8815 SW Sun Pl. I-5 exit 286,
just e. Int corridors. **Pets:** Medium. Supervision.
Ⓢ Ⓢ ⊗ 🛑 ⊗

⚫⚫ ◆◆ Comfort Inn Ⓜ
(503) 682-9000. **$64-$130, 3 days notice.** 8855 SW Citizens Dr. I-5 exit 283, just e and just n on Town Center Loop
West. Ext/int corridors. **Pets:** $3 daily fee/pet. Supervision.
Ⓢ Ⓢ ⊗ 📶 🖊 🛑 ⊗

⚫⚫ ◆◆◆ Holiday Inn Select-Portland South Ⓜ
(503) 682-2211. **$71-$81.** 25425 SW 95th Ave. Just w of
I-5, exit 286. Int corridors. **Pets:** Supervision.
Ⓢ Ⓢ ⊗ 🔒 📶 🛑 💻 🍴 ⊗

PROSPECT

◆◆ Prospect Historical Hotel-Motel & Dinner
House Ⓜ ❀
(541) 560-3664. **$70-$130.** 391 Mill Creek Dr. Off SR 62,
center of town. Ext/int corridors. **Pets:** Other. Supervision.
⊗ 🛑 💻 🍴 ⊗

REDMOND

⚫⚫ ◆◆ Motel 6 Redmond Ⓜ ❀
(541) 923-2100. **$40-$60.** 2247 S Hwy 97. 1 mi s on US 97
from jct of SR 126 W. Int corridors. **Pets:** Medium. No
service, supervision, crate.
Ⓢ ⊗ ♿ 📶 🖊

⚫⚫ ◆◆ Redmond Inn Ⓜ ❀
(541) 548-1091. **$55-$65.** 1545 Hwy 97S. 0.5 mi s on US
97 from jct of SR 126W. Ext corridors. **Pets:** Other. $5 daily
fee/pet. No service, supervision, crate.
Ⓢ Ⓢ ⊗ 🛑 💻 ⊗

REEDSPORT

⚫⚫ ◆ Anchor Bay Inn Ⓜ ❀
(541) 271-2149. **$43-$67.** 1821 Winchester Ave (Hwy 101).
On US 101, 0.8 mi s of jct SR 38. Ext corridors. **Pets:** $5
daily fee/pet. No service, supervision, crate.
Ⓢ Ⓢ ⊗ 🛑 ⊗

⚫⚫ ◆◆◆ Best Western Salbasgeon Inn Ⓜ
(541) 271-4831. **$73-$125.** 1400 Highway Ave 101. Just s
on US 101 from jct of SR 38. Ext corridors. **Pets:** Large. No
service, supervision, crate.
Ⓢ Ⓢ ⊗ 🛑 ⊗

⚫⚫ ◆ Economy Inn Ⓜ ❀
(541) 271-3671. **$35-$75.** 1593 Highway Ave 101. Center;
on US 101. Ext corridors. **Pets:** Medium, dogs only. $3
daily fee/pet, $3 one-time fee/pet. Supervision.
Ⓢ Ⓢ ⊗ 🛑 ⊗ ⊗

🏵 ◆◆ **Salbasgeon Inn of the Umpqua** Ⓜ
(541) 271-2025. **$68-$93, 24 days notice.** 45209 Hwy 38. 7.3 mi e on SR 38 from jct US 101. Ext corridors. **Pets:** No service, supervision, crate.
[SAVE] [S🔅] [✕] 🛗 [▣] [✕] [K̂]

ROCKAWAY BEACH

🏵 ◆◆ **Sea Treasures Inn** Ⓜ ❧
(503) 355-8220. **$50-$80.** 301 N Miller St. Center at jct 3rd Ave N. Ext corridors. **Pets:** Other. $5 one-time fee/pet. Designated rooms, no service, supervision, crate.
[SAVE] [✕] 🛗 [▣] [K̂]

🏵 ◆ **Silver Sands Motel** Ⓜ ❧
(503) 355-2206. **$136.** 215 S Pacific. Just w of US 101, off S 2nd Ave. Ext corridors. **Pets:** Dogs only. $5 one-time fee/pet. Designated rooms, supervision.
[SAVE] [✕] [⛱] 🛗 [▣] [☲] [✕] [K̂]

🏵 ◆◆ **Tradewinds Motel** Ⓜ
(503) 355-2112. **$55-$95.** 523 N Pacific St. Just w of US 101, off N 6th Ave. Ext corridors. **Pets:** No service, supervision, crate.
[✕] 🛗 [▣] [K̂]

ROSEBURG

🏵 ◆◆ **Best Inns** Ⓜ
(541) 673-5561. **$49-$69.** 427 NW Garden Valley Blvd. Just e of I-5, exit 125. Ext corridors. **Pets:** Small. No service, supervision, crate.
[SAVE] [S🔅] [✕] [🎲] [⛱] 🛗 [▣] [☲]

🏵 ◆◆ **Best Western Garden Villa**
   Motel Ⓜ ❧
(541) 672-1601. **$71-$91.** 760 NW Garden Valley Blvd. Just w of I-5 exit 125. Ext corridors. **Pets:** Other. $20 deposit/pet. Designated rooms, no service, supervision, crate.
[SAVE] [S🔅] [✕] [🎲] [⛱] 🛗 [▣] [☲]

🏵 ◆◆◆ **Holiday Inn Express** Ⓜ ❧
(541) 673-7517. **$89-$105.** 375 W Harvard Blvd. Just e of I-5, exit 124. Ext/int corridors. **Pets:** $5 daily fee/room. Supervision.
[SAVE] [S🔅] [✕] [🎲] [⛱] 🛗 [▣] [☲]

◆◆ **Howard Johnson Express Inn** Ⓜ ❧
(541) 673-5082. **$52-$68, 3 days notice.** 978 NE Stephen St. I-5 exit 125, 0.6 mi e on Garden Valley Blvd, 0.4 mi s. Ext corridors. **Pets:** Small, dogs only. $7 daily fee/pet, $7 one-time fee/pet. No service, supervision, crate.
[✕] 🛗 [▣]

🏵 ◆ **Shady Oaks Motel** Ⓜ ❧
(541) 672-2608. **$37-$46, 3 days notice.** 2954 Old Hwy 99 S. I-5 exit 120, 0.5 mi n. Ext corridors. **Pets:** Supervision.
[SAVE] [✕]

🏵 ◆◆◆ **Windmill Inn of Roseburg** Ⓜ ❧
(541) 673-0901. **$80-$86.** 1450 NW Mulholland Dr. Just e of I-5, exit 125. Int corridors. **Pets:** Other. Supervision.
[SAVE] [S🔅] [✕] 🛗 [☲] [✕]

SALEM

🏵 ◆ **Cozzzy Inn** Ⓜ
(503) 588-5423. **$39-$49.** 1875 Fisher Rd NE. I-5 exit 256, e on Market, n on Lancaster, w on Sunnyview, then s. Int corridors. **Pets:** Small. Designated rooms, no service, supervision, crate.
[SAVE] [S🔅] [✕] [⛱] 🛗 [▣]

🏵 ◆◆ **Motel 6–1343** Ⓜ
(503) 371-8024. **$39-$55.** 1401 Hawthorne Ave NE. I-5 exit 256, just w, then just s. Ext corridors. **Pets:** Small. No service, supervision, crate.
[S🔅] [⛱] [☲] [CTV]

🏵 ◆◆◆ **Phoenix Inn-South** Ⓜ ❧
(503) 588-9220. **$69-$89.** 4370 Commercial SE. I-5 exit 252, 1.5 mi w on Kuebler Rd, 0.7 mi n. Int corridors. **Pets:** Other. $10 daily fee/room. Designated rooms, supervision.
[SAVE] [S🔅] [✕] [🎰] [🎲] 🛗 [▣] [☲]

🏵 ◆◆◆ **Quality Inn** Ⓜ❧
(503) 370-7888. **$82-$105.** 3301 Market St NE. Just w of I-5, exit 256. Int corridors. **Pets:** Other. Supervision.
[SAVE] [S🔅] [✕] [⛱] 🛗 [▣] [🍴] [☲]

◆◆◆ **Travelodge Salem Capital** Ⓜ ❧
(503) 581-2466. **$84.** 1555 State St. 0.5 mi e of capital. Ext corridors. **Pets:** Other. $10 one-time fee/room. No service, supervision, crate.
[ASK] [S🔅] [✕] [🎰] [⛱] 🛗 [▣] [☲]

SANDY

🏵 ◆◆◆ **Best Western Sandy Inn** Ⓜ ❧
(503) 668-7100. **$59-$78.** 37465 Hwy 26. On US 26; w side of town. Int corridors. **Pets:** Dogs only. $10 daily fee/pet. No service, supervision, crate.
[SAVE] [S🔅] [✕] [🎰] 🛗 [☲]

SEASIDE

🏵 ◆◆◆ **Best Western Ocean View**
   Resort Ⓜ❧
(503) 738-3334. **$149-$210.** 414 N Prom. US 101 exit 1st Ave, just w, just n on Necanicum, just w on 4th. Ext/int corridors. **Pets:** Small, other. $15 daily fee/room. Designated rooms, supervision.
[SAVE] [S🔅] [✕] [⛱] 🛗 [▣] [☲] [K̂]

🏵 ◆◆◆ **Comfort Inn Boardwalk** Ⓜ ❧
(503) 738-3011. **$94-$137.** 545 Broadway. Just w of US 101, exit Ave A. Ext/int corridors. **Pets:** $7 daily fee/room, $7 one-time fee/room. Designated rooms, supervision.
[SAVE] [S🔅] [✕] [🎰] [🎲] [⛱] 🛗 [▣] [☲]

◆◆ **Motel 6–4062** Ⓜ ❧
(503) 738-6269. **$59-$69.** 2369 S Holladay Dr. South side on US 101. Int corridors. **Pets:** Small, other. Designated rooms, no service, supervision, crate.
[ASK] [✕] [♿] [⛱] 🛗

🏵 ◆◆ **Seaside Convention Center Inn** Ⓜ ❧
(503) 738-9581. **$99-$109, 3 days notice.** 441 Second Ave. US 101, exit 1st Ave, 0.4 mi w. Ext/int corridors. **Pets:** Medium. $5 daily fee/pet. Designated rooms, no service, supervision, crate.
[SAVE] [S🔅] [✕] [⛱] 🛗 [▣] [☲]

◆◆ **Shilo Inn-Seaside East** [M] ❖
(503) 738-0549. **$45-$125.** 900 S Holladay. US 101 exit Ave G, just w, then just s. Ext/int corridors. **Pets:** Other. $10 daily fee/pet. Supervision.

[ASK] [S☐] [✕] [🏠] [🛏] [🖵] [🕿]

SHADY COVE

🅐 ◆◆◆ **The Edgewater Inn on the Rogue River** [M] ❖
(541) 878-3171. **$74-$109, 7 days notice.** 7800 Rogue River Dr. Off SR 62. Ext corridors. **Pets:** Other. $7 daily fee/pet, $7 one-time fee/room. Supervision.

[SAVE] [S☐] [✕] [🖉] [🛏] [🖵] [🕿]

SISTERS

🅐 ◆◆◆ **Best Western Ponderosa Lodge** [M] ❖
(541) 549-1234. **$84-$84.** 500 Hwy 20 W. West end of town, just w on US 20 from jct of SR 242. Ext corridors. **Pets:** Large, other. $10 daily fee/pet. Designated rooms, no service, supervision, crate.

[SAVE] [S☐] [✕] [🖉] [🛏] [🖵] [🕿]

🅐 ◆◆ **Comfort Inn at Sisters** [M] ❖
(541) 549-7829. **$89-$109.** 540 Hwy 20 W. West end of town, just w on US 20 from jct of SR 242. Ext corridors. **Pets:** Other. Designated rooms, supervision.

[SAVE] [✕] [🏠] [🖉] [🛏] [🖵] [🕿]

SPRINGFIELD

◆◆◆ **Comfort Suites Eugene/Springfield** [M] ❖
(541) 746-5359. **$88-$100, 7 days notice.** 969 Kruse Way. Just e of I-5, exit 195A. Int corridors. **Pets:** Other. $20 daily fee/room. Designated rooms, supervision.

[ASK] [S☐] [✕] [🖉] [🛏] [🖵] [🕿]

🅐 ◆◆ **Doubletree Hotel/Eugene-Springfield** [MI] ❖
(541) 726-8181. **$74-$130.** 3280 Gateway St. I-5 exit 195A, just e, then just s. Ext/int corridors. **Pets:** Other. $10 daily fee/room. Supervision.

[SAVE] [S☐] [✕] [🖉] [🖉] [🛏] [🖵] [🍴] [🕿] [✕]

🅐 ◆ **Motel 6** [M] ❖
(541) 741-1105. **$38-$54.** 3752 International Court. I-5 exit 195A, just e and just n on Gateway St. Ext corridors. **Pets:** Small. No service, supervision, crate.

[S☐] [✕] [🖉] [🖉] [🕿] [CTV]

◆◆ **Shilo Inn-Eugene/Springfield** [MI]
(541) 747-0332. **$59-$109.** 3350 Gateway St. I-5 exit 195A, just e, then just s. Int corridors. **Pets:** Supervision.

[ASK] [S☐] [✕] [🖉] [🛏] [🍴] [🕿]

🅐 ◆◆ **Village Inn** [MI] ❖
(541) 747-4546. **$56-$72.** 1875 Mohawk Blvd. I-5 exit 194A, 2.5 mi e on SR 126, just n. Ext corridors. **Pets:** Medium, other. Designated rooms, supervision.

[SAVE] [S☐] [✕] [🛏] [🍴] [🕿]

ST. HELENS

🅐 ◆◆ **Best Western Oak Meadows Inn** [M] ❖
(503) 397-3000. **$79-$89.** 585 S Columbia River Hwy. S end of town on US 30. Int corridors. **Pets:** Other. $15 one-time fee/room. No service, supervision, crate.

[SAVE] [S☐] [✕] [🖉] [🛏] [🕿]

SUTHERLIN

🅐 ◆◆ **Pennywise Motel** [M] ❖
(541) 459-1424. **$64-$69.** 150 Myrtle St. Just e of I-5 exit 136. Ext corridors. **Pets:** $5 daily fee/pet. Supervision.

[SAVE] [S☐] [✕] [🛏] [🖵] [🕿]

SWEET HOME

🅐 ◆ **Sweet Home Inn** [M] ❖
(541) 367-5137. **$45-$65, 3 days notice.** 805 Long St. W side of town, just s of US 20. Ext corridors. **Pets:** Medium, dogs only. $20 deposit/pet, $10 one-time fee/pet. No service, supervision, crate.

[SAVE] [S☐] [✕] [🛏]

THE DALLES

🅐 ◆◆ **Best Western River City Inn** [M]
(541) 296-9107. **$69-$89.** 112 W Second. Just s of I-84 eastbound exit 84, westbound exit 85. Ext/int corridors. **Pets:** No service, supervision, crate.

[SAVE] [S☐] [✕] [🛏] [🕿]

🅐 ◆◆ **Days Inn** [M] ❖
(541) 296-1191. **$55-$65.** 2500 W 6th. Just s of I-84, eastbound exit 83; westbound exit 84. Int corridors. **Pets:** Small. $10 daily fee/pet. Supervision.

[SAVE] [✕] [🛏] [🕿]

🅐 ◆◆◆ **Lone Pine Motel** [M]
(541) 298-2800. **$59-$109, 30 days notice.** 351 Lone Pine Dr. Just n of I-84, exit 87. Int corridors. **Pets:** Supervision.

[SAVE] [S☐] [✕] [🛏] [🕿] [CTV]

🅐 ◆◆◆ **Quality Inn, Columbia River Gorge** [MI] ❖
(541) 298-5161. **$49-$95.** 2114 W 6th. Just s of I-84 eastbound exit 83; westbound exit 84. Ext corridors. **Pets:** Other. $10 daily fee/pet. Supervision.

[SAVE] [S☐] [✕] [🖉] [🖉] [🛏] [🖵] [🍴] [🕿]

◆◆ **Shilo Inn** [MI] ❖
(541) 298-5502. **$69-$129.** 3223 Bret Clodfelter Way. Just n of I-84, exit 87. Int corridors. **Pets:** Other. $10 daily fee/room. No service, supervision, crate.

[ASK] [S☐] [✕] [🛏] [🖵] [🍴] [🕿]

TILLAMOOK

◆◆◆ **Shilo Inn** [MI] ❖
(503) 842-7971. **$59-$135.** 2515 N Main. 1 mi n on US 101. Int corridors. **Pets:** Other. $10 daily fee/room. No service, supervision, crate.

[ASK] [S☐] [✕] [🏠] [🖉] [🛏] [🖵] [🍴] [🕿]

◆ **Western Royal Inn** 🅼
(503) 842-8844. **Call for rates.** 1125 N Main Ave. 0.5 mi n on US 101. Ext corridors. **Pets:** Small. Designated rooms, supervision.
(ASK) (X) (■)

WALDPORT

🆎 ◆◆ **Alsea Manor Motel** 🅼 🐾
(541) 563-3249. **$49-$65, 3 days notice.** 190 SW Arrow (US 101). Just s on US 101 from SR 34; downtown. Ext corridors. **Pets:** Small, dogs only. $5 daily fee/room. Designated rooms, supervision.
(SAVE) (X) (K)

WARRENTON

◆◆◆ **Shilo Inn** 🅼🅸 🐾
(503) 861-2181. **$65-$189.** 1609 E Harbor Dr. On US 26/101, near w end of Young's Bay Bridge. Int corridors. **Pets:** Other. $10 daily fee/pet. No service, supervision, crate.
(ASK) (S/D) (X) (■) (▣) (♨) (≈)

WOODBURN

🆎 ◆◆◆ **Best Western Woodburn** 🅼 🐾
(503) 982-6515. **$63.** 2887 Newberg Hwy. Just e of I-5 exit 271. Int corridors. **Pets:** Other. $10 one-time fee/room. Designated rooms, supervision.
(SAVE) (S/D) (X) (♿) (K) (■) (▣) (≈)

🆎 ◆◆ **Hawthorn Inn & Suites** 🅼 🐾
(503) 982-1727. **$75-$125.** 120 NE Arney Rd. I-5 exit 271, just w. Int corridors. **Pets:** $5 daily fee/room. No service, supervision, crate.
(SAVE) (X) (▣) (≈) (X)

YACHATS

🆎 ◆◆◆ **The Adobe Resort** 🅼🅸
(541) 547-3141. **Call for rates.** 1555 Hwy 101. 0.5 mi n on US 101. Int corridors. **Pets:** Small. Designated rooms, supervision.
(SAVE) (X) (🗲) (K) (■) (▣) (♨) (K)

🆎 ◆◆ **Fireside Motel** 🅼 🐾
(541) 547-3636. **$65-$120.** 1881 Hwy 101 N. 0.6 mi n on US 101. Ext corridors. **Pets:** $7 daily fee/pet. Supervision.
(SAVE) (S/D) (X) (■) (▣) (K)

🆎 ◆◆ **Shamrock Lodgettes** 🅲
(541) 547-3312. **$75-$118, 3 days notice.** 105 Hwy 101 S. Just s on US 101. Ext corridors. **Pets:** Supervision.
(SAVE) (X) (■) (▣) (K)

CITY INDEX

ABBOTTSTOWN

The Inn at the Altland House 🐾
(717) 259-9535. **$89-$89.** Center Sq Rt 30. Jct US 30 and SR 194. Int corridors. **Pets:** Medium. Supervision.

ALLENTOWN

Allenwood Motel 🐾
(610) 395-3707. **$40-$45.** 1058 Hausman Rd. 0.5 mi e on US 22 from Pennsylvania Tpke, exit 33, 0.8 mi s on SR 309, w on Tilghman St to light, 0.8 mi n on Hausman Rd to dead end. Ext corridors. **Pets:** No service, supervision, crate.

Days Inn Conference Center 🐾
(610) 395-3731. **$65-$150.** 1151 Bulldog Dr. Pennsylvania Tpke (I-476), exit 33, 0.5 mi e on US 22, 0.6 mi n on SR 309 via Bulldog Dr access road. Ext/int corridors. **Pets:** Other. $15 daily fee/room. Designated rooms, no service, supervision, crate.

Holiday Inn Express 🐾
(610) 435-7880. **Call for rates.** 1715 Plaza Ln. US 22, 15th St exit, just n. Int corridors. **Pets:** Other. $10 daily fee/room, $10 one-time fee/room. Supervision.

◆◆ **Howard Johnson Inn & Suites** Ⓜ ❀
(610) 439-4000. **$39-$139.** 3220 Hamilton Blvd. I-78, exit Hamilton Blvd, 1.5 mi n on US 222. Int corridors. **Pets:** Other. $10 daily fee/room. Supervision.
ⒶⓈⓀ Ⓢ Ⓧ Ⓛ Ⓐ Ⓔ Ⓑ Ⓛ Ⓐ

🅐🅐🅐 ◆◆ **Microtel Inn** Ⓜ ❀
(610) 266-9070. **$55-$65, 7 days notice.** 1880 Steelstone Rd. At Airport Rd S exit of US 22. Int corridors. **Pets:** Small, other. Supervision.
Ⓢ Ⓢ Ⓧ Ⓐ Ⓐ Ⓔ Ⓑ

🅐🅐🅐 ◆◆ **Red Roof Inn** Ⓜ
(610) 264-5404. **$61-$98.** 1846 Catasauqua Rd. Just s of US 22, exit Airport Rd S. Ext corridors. **Pets:** Medium. No service, supervision, crate.
Ⓢ Ⓧ Ⓐ Ⓐ Ⓑ

◆◆◆ **Sheraton Inn-Jetport** Ⓜ❶
(610) 266-1000. **$139-$169.** 3400 Airport Rd. On SR 987 N (Airport Rd), 0.5 mi n of jct SR 22. Int corridors. **Pets:** Medium. Supervision.
ⒶⓈⓀ Ⓢ Ⓧ Ⓐ Ⓑ Ⓛ Ⓣ Ⓐ

ALTOONA

◆◆◆ **Hampton Inn-Altoona/Pennsylvania** Ⓜ
(814) 941-3500. **$84-$89.** 180 Charlotte Dr. Just w of I-99/US 220, exit Plank Rd. Int corridors. **Pets:** Medium. No service, supervision, crate.
Ⓧ Ⓛ Ⓔ Ⓑ Ⓛ Ⓐ

🅐🅐🅐 ◆◆ **Motel 6-1415** Ⓜ ❀
(814) 946-7601. **$42-$60.** 1500 Sterling St. Just n of I-99/US 220, exit Plank Rd. Ext corridors. **Pets:** Small, other. No service, supervision, crate.
Ⓢ Ⓧ Ⓛ Ⓔ Ⓐ

◆◆ **Super 8 Motel Altoona** Ⓜ❶
(814) 942-5350. **$49-$60.** 3535 Fairway Dr. Just w of I-99/US 220, exit Frankstown Rd. Int corridors. **Pets:** Medium. Supervision.
ⒶⓈⓀ Ⓢ Ⓧ Ⓐ Ⓑ

ALUM BANK

🅐🅐🅐 ◆ **West Vu Inn** Ⓜ
(814) 839-2632. **$32-$45.** 4158 Quaker Valley Rd. On SR 56, just e of jct SR 96. Ext corridors. **Pets:** No service, supervision, crate.
Ⓢ Ⓧ Ⓑ

BARKEYVILLE

◆◆ **Days Inn** Ⓜ ❀
(814) 786-7901. **Call for rates.** I-80, exit 3, just n on SR 8. Ext corridors. **Pets:** Other. Supervision.
Ⓧ

BEDFORD

🅐🅐🅐 ◆◆◆ **Best Western Bedford Inn** Ⓜ❶ ❀
(814) 623-9006. **$48-$69.** 4517 Business Rt 220 N. I-70/76 (Pennsylvania Tpke), exit 11, 0.3 mi n. Ext corridors. **Pets:** Small. $50 deposit/room, $10 one-time fee/room. Designated rooms, no service, supervision, crate.
Ⓢ Ⓢ Ⓧ Ⓑ Ⓣ Ⓐ

🅐🅐🅐 ◆◆ **Budget Host Midway Inn** Ⓜ ❀
(814) 623-8107. **$35-$65, 3 days notice.** 4378 Business Rt 220 N. I-70/76 (Pennsylvania Tpke), exit 11, just n. Ext corridors. **Pets:** Other. $5 daily fee/pet. Designated rooms, no service, supervision, crate.
Ⓢ Ⓢ Ⓧ Ⓑ Ⓐ

🅐🅐🅐 ◆◆ **Janey Lynn Motel** Ⓜ ❀
(814) 623-9515. **$29-$75, 3 days notice.** 3567 Business Rt 220. I-70/76 (Pennsylvania Tpke), exit 11, 1.4 mi s on US 220 business route. Ext corridors. **Pets:** Small. $5 daily fee/pet, $5 one-time fee/pet. Designated rooms, no service, supervision, crate.
Ⓢ Ⓢ Ⓧ Ⓑ

🅐🅐🅐 ◆◆ **Motel Town House** Ⓜ
(814) 623-5138. **$32-$65.** 200 S Richard St. I-70/76 (Pennsylvania Tpke), exit 11, 2.5 mi s on US 220 business route. Ext corridors. **Pets:** Small. No service, supervision, crate.
Ⓢ Ⓢ Ⓧ Ⓑ

🅐🅐🅐 ◆◆◆ **Quality Inn Bedford** Ⓜ❶ ❀
(814) 623-5188. **$60-$72, 3 days notice.** 4407 Business Rt 220 N. I-70/76 (Pennsylvania Tpke), exit 11, just n. Ext/int corridors. **Pets:** Large. $5 daily fee/room. Designated rooms, no service, supervision, crate.
Ⓢ Ⓢ Ⓧ Ⓑ Ⓛ Ⓐ

BENTON

◆◆◆ **The Red Poppy Bed & Breakfast** Ⓑ❶ ❀
(570) 925-5823. **$55-$85, 7 days notice.** RR 2, Box 82. 0.5 mi n on SR 487 from n jct with SR 239. Int corridors. **Pets:** Dogs only. No service, supervision, crate.
Ⓧ Ⓑ Ⓚ Ⓩ

BETHEL

🅐🅐🅐 ◆◆◆ **Comfort Inn-Bethel/Midway** Ⓜ ❀
(717) 933-8888. **$62-$73.** 41 Diner Dr. I-78, exit 5. Int corridors. **Pets:** Other. $10 daily fee/pet. Supervision.
Ⓢ Ⓢ Ⓧ Ⓛ Ⓔ Ⓑ Ⓛ Ⓐ

BETHLEHEM

🅐🅐🅐 ◆◆◆ **Comfort Inn** Ⓜ ❀
(610) 865-6300. **$71-$110, 7 days notice.** 3191 Highfield Dr. Just s of US 22, exit SR 191. Ext/int corridors. **Pets:** Other. $10 daily fee/pet. No service, supervision, crate.
Ⓢ Ⓧ Ⓐ Ⓑ Ⓛ

◆◆◆ **Holiday Inn Hotel & Conference Center** Ⓜ❶
(610) 866-5800. **$99-$109.** US 22 & 512. Off US 22, Center St and SR 512 exit. Ext/int corridors. **Pets:** No service, supervision, crate.
Ⓧ Ⓐ Ⓐ Ⓔ Ⓑ Ⓛ Ⓣ Ⓐ Ⓧ

◆◆◆ **Residence Inn by Marriott** Ⓐ ❀
(610) 317-2662. **$120-$120.** 2180 Motel Dr. 0.8 mi se off US 22, Airport Rd S exit on Catasauqua Rd. Int corridors. **Pets:** Other. $6 daily fee/pet, $100 one-time fee/room. No service, supervision, crate.
ⒶⓈⓀ Ⓢ Ⓧ Ⓐ Ⓑ Ⓛ Ⓐ Ⓧ

BLOOMSBURG

✦✦ Econo Lodge at Bloomsburg M ❀
(570) 387-0490. **$50-$85, 3 days notice.** 189 Columbia Mall Dr. I-80, exit 34, on SR 42. Int corridors. **Pets:** Other. $10 one-time fee/room. Designated rooms, no service, supervision, crate.
SAVE S⬠ ⊠ ⬠ ⬠ ⬠

✦✦✦ The Inn at Turkey Hill CI ❀
(570) 387-1500. **$90-$98.** 991 Central Rd. I-80 westbound, exit 35A; eastbound, exit 35, just s. Ext/int corridors. **Pets:** Other. $15 one-time fee/room. Supervision.
⊠ ⬠ ⬠

BLUE MOUNTAIN

✦✦ Kenmar Motel M ❀
(717) 423-5915. **$45-$65.** 17788 Cumberland Hwy. I-76 (Pennsylvania Tpke), exit 15, just e on SR 997N. Ext corridors. **Pets:** Dogs only. Designated rooms, no service, supervision, crate.
SAVE S⬠ ⊠ ⬠ ⬠ CTV

BOYERTOWN

✦ Mel-Dor Motel M
(610) 367-2626. **$45-$49.** 1 Spring Garden Dr. 1 mi n of Boyertown at New Berlinville exit off SR 100. Ext corridors. **Pets:** Large. Designated rooms, supervision.
⊠ ⬠

BRADFORD

✦✦✦✦ Glendorn-A Lodge in the Country CI ❀
(814) 362-6511. **$375-$675, 30 days notice.** 1032 W Corydon. Main and Corydon, follow W Corydon 4.3 mi w to signs. Ext/int corridors. **Pets:** Other. $75 daily fee/pet. Designated rooms, no service, supervision, crate.
⬠ ⬠ ⬠ ⬠ ⊠ CTV

BREEZEWOOD

✦✦✦ Breezewood Ramada Inn M ❀
(814) 735-4005. **$49-$79.** Jct I-70 & Rt 30. I-70/76 (Pennsylvania Tpke), exit 12, just e on US 30. Int corridors. **Pets:** Other. Supervision.
SAVE S⬠ ⊠ ⬠ ⬠ ⬠ ⊠

✦✦ Comfort Inn of Breezewood M
(814) 735-2200. **$50-$75.** 16550 Lincoln Hwy. I-70/76 (Pennsylvania Tpke), exit 12, just e. Int corridors. **Pets:** Supervision.
SAVE S⬠ ⊠ ⬠ ⬠ ⬠

✦ Wiltshire Motel M ❀
(814) 735-4361. **$33-$46.** 140 S Breezewood Rd. I-70/76 (Pennsylvania Tpke), exit 12, just w on US 30 at jct SR 126. Ext corridors. **Pets:** Small. Supervision.
SAVE S⬠ ⊠ ⬠

BROOKVILLE

✦ Budget Host Gold Eagle Inn M ❀
(814) 849-7344. **$35-$50.** 250 W Main St. I-80, exit 13, 0.5 mi s on SR 36. Ext corridors. **Pets:** No service, supervision, crate.
⊠ ⬠ ⬠

✦✦ Holiday Inn Express M
(814) 849-8381. **$59-$79.** 235 Allegheny Blvd. I-80, exit 13, just s on SR 36. Int corridors. **Pets:** Designated rooms, no service, supervision, crate.
SAVE S⬠ ⊠

✦✦ Super 8 Motel M ❀
(814) 849-8840. **$46-$62.** 251 Allegheny Blvd. I-80, exit 13, just n on SR 36. Int corridors. **Pets:** Medium. Designated rooms, no service, supervision, crate.
ASK S⬠ ⊠ ⬠

CAMP HILL

✦✦✦ Radisson Penn Harris Hotel & Convention Center M ❀
(717) 763-7117. **$79.** 1150 Camp Hill By-Pass. Jct US 11, 15 and Erford Rd. Ext/int corridors. **Pets:** Small, dogs only. $25 one-time fee/room. Designated rooms, no service, supervision, crate.
ASK S⬠ ⊠ ⬠ ⬠ ⬠ ⬠ ⬠ ⬠ ⊠

CARLISLE

✦✦ Clarion Hotel and Convention Center H
(717) 243-1717. **$79-$99.** 1700 Harrisburg Pike. 0.4 mi n of jct I-81, exit 17 southbound or exit 17A northbound; 1.2 mi n of I-76 (Pennsylvania Tpke), exit 16. Int corridors. **Pets:** Small. Designated rooms, supervision.
SAVE S⬠ ⊠ ⬠ ⬠ ⬠ ⊠ ⊠

✦✦✦ Comfort Suites Hotel M ❀
(717) 960-1000. **$74-$149.** 10 S Hanover St. Downtown; just s of "square". Int corridors. **Pets:** Medium, other. No service, supervision, crate.
ASK S⬠ ⊠ ⬠ ⬠ ⬠ ⬠ ⬠

✦✦✦ Days Inn Carlisle M ❀
(717) 258-4147. **$65-$99.** 101 Alexander Spring Rd. I-81, exit 13, just se. Int corridors. **Pets:** $6 daily fee/pet. Designated rooms, no service, supervision, crate.
SAVE ⊠ ⬠ ⬠ ⬠ ⬠

✦✦ Econo Lodge M ❀
(717) 249-7775. **$42-$85.** 1460 Harrisburg Pike. On US 11 at jct I-81, exit 17; I-76 (Pennsylvania Tpke), 0.8 mi n from exit 16. Ext corridors. **Pets:** Other. $5 daily fee/pet. Designated rooms, supervision.
ASK S⬠ ⊠ ⬠ ⊠

✦✦✦ Holiday Inn Carlisle M ❀
(717) 245-2400. **$89-$99.** 1450 Harrisburg Pike. Just se of I-81, exit 17; 0.8 mi n of I-76 (Pennsylvania Tpke), exit 16. Int corridors. **Pets:** $10 daily fee/pet, $10 one-time fee/pet. Supervision.
ASK S⬠ ⊠ ⬠ ⬠ ⬠ ⬠ ⊠

✦✦ Motel 6-1297 M ❀
(717) 249-7622. **$36-$66.** 1153 Harrisburg Pike. Just s of I-76 (Pennsylvania Tpke), exit 16. Ext corridors. **Pets:** Small, other. Supervision.
⊠ ⬠ ⬠ ⬠ ⬠

⬤ ◆◆◆ Quality Inn Carlisle Ⓜ ☆
(717) 243-6000. **$68-$129, 7 days notice.** 1255 Harrisburg Pike. US 11 at jct I-81, exit 17; 0.8 mi n of I-76 (Pennsylvania Tpke), exit 16. Int corridors. **Pets:** No service, supervision, crate.
SAVE S⊘ ☒ ⬓ 🖥 🐾

⬤ ◆ Rodeway Inn Ⓜ ☆
(717) 249-2800. **$49-$85, 7 days notice.** 1239 Harrisburg Pike. 0.8 mi n of I-76 (Pennsylvania Tpke), exit 16; 0.3 mi s of jct I-81, exit 17. Ext corridors. **Pets:** Small. $5 daily fee/pet, $5 one-time fee/pet. Designated rooms, no service, supervision, crate.
SAVE S⊘ ☒ ⬓ 🖥 🐾

◆◆ Sleep Inn Carlisle Ⓜ
(717) 249-8863. **$60-$125, 3 days notice.** 5 E Garland Dr. I-81 N, exit 14, just ne; I-81 S, exit 14 E. Int corridors. **Pets:** Small. Designated rooms, no service, supervision, crate.
ASK S⊘ ☒ ♿ ⬓ 🖥 🐾

◆◆ Super 8 Motel Ⓜ
(717) 245-9898. **Call for rates.** 100 Alexander Spring Rd. Just se of I-81, exit 13. Int corridors. **Pets:** No service, supervision, crate.
ASK ☒ ⌂ ⬓

⬤ ◆◆ Travelodge Ⓜ
(717) 243-8585. **$45-$85, 3 days notice.** 1252 Harrisburg Pike. Jct I-81, exit 17 and US 11, 1 mi n of I-76 (Pennsylvania Tpke), exit 16; on US 11. Ext/int corridors. **Pets:** Supervision.
SAVE S⊘ ☒ 🖥

CHAMBERSBURG

◆◆◆ Comfort Inn-Chambersburg Ⓜ ☆
(717) 263-6655. **Call for rates.** 3301 Black Gap Rd. I-81, exit 8, just e, then just s on SR 997. Int corridors. **Pets:** Medium, other. $25 deposit/pet. Designated rooms, no service, supervision, crate.
ASK ☒ ⬓ 🖥 🐾

⬤ ◆◆ Days Inn Ⓜ ☆
(717) 263-1288. **$60-$78.** 30 Falling Spring Rd. I-81, exit 6, just e on US 30. Int corridors. **Pets:** Small, other. $5 daily fee/pet. Supervision.
SAVE S⊘ ☒ ⬓

⬤ ◆◆ Econo Lodge Ⓜ ☆
(717) 264-8005. **$47-$55.** 1110 Sheller Ave. I-81, exit 5, just w on SR 316. Int corridors. **Pets:** Other. $10 one-time fee/pet. No service, supervision, crate.
SAVE S⊘ ☒ ⬓ 🖥

⬤ ◆◆ Quality Inn & Suites Ⓜ
(717) 263-3400. **$65-$125.** 1095 Wayne Ave. I-81, exit 5, just w on SR 316. Ext/int corridors. **Pets:** No service, supervision, crate.
SAVE S⊘ ☒ ⬓ 🖥 🍴 🐾

CLARION

◆◆◆ Holiday Inn Ⓜ ☆
(814) 226-8850. **$95.** Rt 68 & I-80. I-80, exit 9, 0.5 mi n. Int corridors. **Pets:** $10 deposit/room. No service, supervision, crate.
☒ ⌂ ⬓ 🖥 🍴 🐾 ⊠

◆◆ Super 8 Ⓜ ☆
(814) 226-4550. **$55-$90.** Hwy 68. I-80, exit 9, just n. Ext corridors. **Pets:** Other. No service, supervision, crate.
ASK S⊘ ☒ ⬓ 🖥 🐾

CLARKS SUMMIT

⬤ ◆◆◆ Ramada Plaza Hotel Ⓜ ☆
(570) 586-2730. **$79-$98.** 820 Northern Blvd. On US 6 and 11, 0.3 mi w of I-476 (Pennsylvania Tpke), exit 39 and I-81, exit 58. Int corridors. **Pets:** $50 deposit/pet. Supervision.
SAVE S⊘ ☒ ⬓ 🖥 🍴 🐾

CLEARFIELD

⬤ ◆◆ Best Western Motor Inn Ⓜ ☆
(814) 765-2441. **$56-$69, 5 days notice.** Rt 879. I-80, exit 19, 0.4 mi ne. Int corridors. **Pets:** Designated rooms, supervision.
SAVE S⊘ ☒ 🍴 🐾

⬤ ◆ Budget Inn Ⓜ ☆
(814) 765-2639. **$27-$42.** Rt 322 E. I-80, exit 19, 1.5 mi sw on SR 879, 1.2 mi e. Ext/int corridors. **Pets:** Designated rooms, no service, supervision, crate.
SAVE S⊘ ☒ ⬓

◆◆◆ Comfort Inn Clearfield Ⓜ ☆
(814) 768-6400. **$75-$115.** Industrial Park Rd. Just s of I-80, exit 19. Int corridors. **Pets:** Medium, other. Supervision.
ASK S⊘ ☒ ⌂ ⬓ 🐾

⬤ ◆ Rodeway Inn Ⓜ
(814) 765-7587. **$39-$65.** US 322 E. I-80, exit 19, 1.5 mi sw on SR 879, 1.3 mi e. Ext corridors. **Pets:** No service, supervision, crate.
SAVE S⊘ ☒ 🖥

◆◆ Super 8 Motel-Clearfield Ⓜ ☆
(814) 768-7580. **Call for rates.** Rt 879. Just s of I-80, exit 19. Int corridors. **Pets:** Supervision.
ASK ☒ ♿ ⬓

DICKSON CITY

⬤ ◆◆ Quality Hotel Ⓗ ☆
(570) 383-9979. **$65-$95.** 1946 Scranton-Carbondale Hwy. I-81, exit 57A, 2 mi e on US 6; from Pennsylvania Tpke Northeast Extension, Clarks Summit exit, 4.5 mi e on US 6. Int corridors. **Pets:** Medium, other. $20 one-time fee/room. Designated rooms, no service, supervision, crate.
SAVE S⊘ ☒ ⬓ 🖥 🍴 🐾

DOUGLASSVILLE

◆◆ Econo Lodge Ⓜ ☆
(610) 385-3016. **$49-$85, 3 days notice.** 387 Ben Franklin Hwy. On Rt 422. From Pottstown 422 W 10 mi, from Reading 422 E 10 mi. Ext corridors. **Pets:** Large, other. $12 daily fee/pet. No service, supervision, crate.
ASK S⊘ ☒ 🖥 ⬓ 🖥

DU BOIS

◆◆◆ Holiday Inn Ⓜ ❀
(814) 371-5100. **$75-$75.** US 219 & I-80. I-80, exit 16, just s. Int corridors. **Pets:** Medium. Designated rooms, supervision.

A$K S⬚ ✕ ⬚ ⬚ ⬚ ⬚ ❙❙

DUNMORE

⬚ ◆◆ Days Inn Ⓜ
(570) 348-6101. **$50-$57.** 1226 O'Neil Hwy. Jct SR 347 and I-81, exit 55A. Int corridors. **Pets:** Supervision.

SAVE S⬚ ✕ ⬚ ⬚

◆◆◆ Holiday Inn-Scranton East Ⓜ
(570) 343-4771. **$135.** 200 Tigue St. I-380/84, exit 1 (Tigue St), 0.3 mi e of jct I-81. Ext/int corridors. **Pets:** Medium. No service, supervision, crate.

A$K S⬚ ✕ ⬚ ⬚ ❙❙ ⬚

◆◆ Super Budget Inn Ⓜ
(570) 346-8782. **$42-$95.** 1027 O'Neill Hwy. On SR 347 N, 0.3 mi n of I-81, exit 55 (Throop exit). Ext corridors. **Pets:** Very small. No service, supervision, crate.

A$K S⬚ ✕ ⬚

DUPONT

◆◆◆ Holiday Inn Express Ⓜ ❀
(570) 654-3300. **Call for rates.** 30 Concorde Dr. Just e of I-81, exit 49A. Int corridors. **Pets:** Small, other. $15 deposit/room, $15 one-time fee/room. Designated rooms, supervision.

✕ ⬚ ⬚ ⬚ ⬚ ⬚ ❙❙ ⬚

EASTON

⬚ ◆◆◆ Best Western Easton Inn Ⓜ
(610) 253-9131. **$75-$130.** 185 S Third St. US 22, 4th St (SR 611) exit, just e to 3rd St, 0.5 mi s; I-78, exit 22, 1 mi n following signs. Int corridors. **Pets:** No service, supervision, crate.

SAVE S⬚ ✕ ⬚ ⬚

◆◆ Days Inn Ⓜ ❀
(610) 253-0546. **$63-$90, 7 days notice.** 2555 Nazareth Rd. US 22, exit 25th St, just e on N Service Rd. Int corridors. **Pets:** Other. $5 daily fee/pet. No service, supervision, crate.

A$K S⬚ ✕ ⬚

EBENSBURG

◆◆◆ Comfort Inn Ⓜ ❀
(814) 472-6100. **$56-$75.** 111 Cook Rd. Just e on US 22 from jct of US 219. Int corridors. **Pets:** $25 deposit/pet, $6 daily fee/pet. No service, supervision, crate.

A$K S⬚ ✕ ⬚ ⬚ ⬚ ⬚

EDINBORO

⬚ ◆ Ramada Inn Ⓜ ❀
(814) 734-5650. **$80-$100.** SR 6 N. I-79, exit 38, 2 mi e. Int corridors. **Pets:** $15 one-time fee/room. No service, supervision, crate.

SAVE S⬚ ✕ ⬚ ⬚ ❙❙ ⬚ ✕

ERIE

◆◆◆ Days Inn Ⓜ ❀
(814) 868-8521. **$70-$100.** 7415 Schultz Rd. I-90, exit 7, just n. Int corridors. **Pets:** $5 daily fee/room, $5 one-time fee/room. Designated rooms, supervision.

A$K S⬚ ✕ ⬚ ⬚ ⬚

◆◆ Microtel Erie Ⓜ
(814) 864-1010. **$37-$75, 3 days notice.** 8100 Peach St. I-90, exit 6, just s. Int corridors. **Pets:** Supervision.

✕ ⬚ ⬚

◆◆ Motel 6 Ⓜ ❀
(814) 864-4811. **$60-$100.** 7575 Peach St. I-90, exit 6, just n. Int corridors. **Pets:** Medium, other. Supervision.

A$K S⬚ ✕ ⬚ ⬚

◆◆ Quality Inn & Suites Ⓜ ❀
(814) 864-4911. **$79-$109.** 8040 Perry Hwy. I-90, exit 7, just s. Ext/int corridors. **Pets:** Medium. No service, supervision, crate.

A$K S⬚ ✕ ⬚ ⬚ ❙❙ ⬚ CTV

⬚ ◆◆ Red Roof Inn Ⓜ ❀
(814) 868-5246. **$60-$107.** 7865 Perry Hwy. I-90, exit 7, just n. Ext/int corridors. **Pets:** Other. Supervision.

SAVE ✕ CTV

⬚ ◆◆ Super 8 Motel Ⓜ
(814) 864-9200. **$69-$99.** 8040 Perry Hwy. I-90, exit 7, just s. Ext/int corridors. **Pets:** Supervision.

SAVE S⬚ ✕ ⬚ ⬚ CTV

ERWINNA

◆◆◆ Golden Pheasant Inn ⒸⒾ ❀
(610) 294-9595. **$75-$145, 21 days notice.** 763 River Rd. On SR 32, 0.5 mi n of jct of Dark Hollow Rd. Ext/int corridors. **Pets:** Small, other. $20 daily fee/room. Designated rooms, no service, supervision, crate.

✕ ⬚ ⬚ ✕

FAYETTEVILLE

⬚ ◆ Rite Spot Motel Ⓜ ❀
(717) 352-2144. **$41-$47.** 5651 Lincoln Way E. On US 30, 1 mi w of jct SR 997. Ext corridors. **Pets:** Small. $3 daily fee/pet. No service, supervision, crate.

✕ ⬚ ❙❙

FOGELSVILLE

◆ Cloverleaf Motel Ⓜ ❀
(610) 395-3367. **$40-$50.** 327 Star Rd. On SR 100, s of US 22, left first traffic light and immediate left on service road, at end of service road. Ext corridors. **Pets:** Small. No service, supervision, crate.

✕ ⬚ ⬚

◆◆◆ Comfort Inn-Allentown Ⓜ
(610) 391-0344. **$120, 3 days notice.** I-78, exit 14B, just n SR 100. Int corridors. **Pets:** Medium. No service, supervision, crate.

A$K S⬚ ✕ ⬚ ⬚ ⬚

AAA ◆◆◆ Holiday Inn Conference
Center **M** ❀
(610) 391-1000. **$139-$149.** 7736 Adrienne Dr. 0.3 mi s of
jct I-78, exit 14A and SR 100 S. Int corridors. **Pets:** $10
one-time fee/room. Designbated rooms, supervision.
[SAVE] [S♦] [X] [♠] [♫] [■] [▬] [♦] [≈]

FRACKVILLE

AAA ◆◆ Econo Lodge **M** ❀
(570) 874-3838. **$30-$80.** 501 S Middle St. On SR 61 N,
exit 36W off I-81. Ext corridors. **Pets:** Other. $5 daily fee/
pet, $5 one-time fee/pet. Supervision.
[SAVE] [S♦] [X] [▬]

AAA ◆◆ Granny's Budget Host Inn &
Restaurant **M** ❀
(570) 874-0408. **$38-$48, 5 days notice.** 115 W Coal St.
I-81, exit 36W, 0.3 mi nw on SR 61, 0.3 mi n on Altamont
Blvd. Ext/int corridors. **Pets:** Other. $25 deposit/room.
Supervision.
[S♦] [X] [♫]

FRANKLIN

AAA ◆◆ The Inn At Franklin **M** ❀
(814) 437-3031. **$60-$80.** 1411 Liberty St. Center; on US
62 and SR 8. Int corridors. **Pets:** Small. $10 one-time fee/
pet. Designated rooms, no service, supervision, crate.
[SAVE] [S♦] [X] [■] [▬] [♫]

FRYSTOWN

◆ Motel of Frystown **M** ❀
(717) 933-4613. **$35-$45.** 90 Fort Motel Dr. Jct I-78 and SR
645, exit 2, just e on service road. Ext corridors.
Pets: Other. No service, supervision, crate.
[X] [CTV]

GALETON

AAA ◆ Pine Log Motel **M** ❀
(814) 435-6400. **$50-$75, 4 days notice.** 5156 US Rt 6 W.
9 mi w on US 6 W. Ext corridors. **Pets:** No service, supervision, crate.
[SAVE] [X] [■] [X] [♨] [CTV] [✆]

GETTYSBURG

AAA ◆◆ Best Inn **M** ❀
(717) 334-1188. **$62-$90.** 301 Steinwehr Ave. 1 mi s on US
15 business route, just s of jct SR 134. Ext/int corridors.
Pets: Medium, other. No service, supervision, crate.
[SAVE] [S♦] [X] [■] [≈]

◆ Heritage Motor Lodge **M** ❀
(717) 334-9281. **$81-$99, 30 days notice.** 613 Baltimore
St. Just sw on SR 97 from jct US 15 business route. Ext/int
corridors. **Pets:** Medium, other. $10 daily fee/pet, $10 one-
time fee/pet. Supervision.
[ASK] [S♦] [X] [♨]

◆◆◆ Holiday Inn-Battlefield **M** ❀
(717) 334-6211. **$98-$200.** 516 Baltimore St. At jct US 15
business route and SR 97. Ext corridors. **Pets:** Other.
Supervision.
[ASK] [S♦] [X] [♨] [■] [▬] [♫] [≈]

GRANTVILLE

◆◆◆ Holiday Inn Harrisburg-Hershey Area,
I-81 **M** ❀
(717) 469-0661. **$199.** 604 Station Rd. I-81, exit 28. Int
corridors. **Pets:** Other. Supervision.
[ASK] [S♦] [X] [♠] [♫] [♨] [■] [▬] [♫] [≈]

HARRISBURG

AAA ◆◆◆ Baymont Inn **M** ❀
(717) 540-9339. **$60-$80.** 200 N Mountain Rd. I-81, exit
26A northbound; exit 26 southbound. Int corridors.
Pets: Other. Supervision.
[SAVE] [S♦] [X] [♫] [■] [▬]

◆◆ Baymont Inn & Suites-Harrisburg
Airport **M** ❀
(717) 939-8000. **$64-$71.** 990 Eisenhower Blvd. Just se of
I-283, exit 1; Pennsylvania Tpke, exit 19, 1 mi n. Int corridors. **Pets:** Small, other. Designated rooms, no service,
supervision, crate.
[S♦] [X] [♫] [■] [▬]

AAA ◆◆ Best Western Capital Plaza **M** ❀
(717) 545-9089. **$61-$83.** 150 Nationwide Dr. I-81, exit 24,
just n. Ext/int corridors. **Pets:** Other. No service, supervision, crate.
[SAVE] [S♦] [X] [♫] [■]

AAA ◆◆◆ Best Western
Harrisburg/Hershey **M** ❀
(717) 652-7180. **$75-$89.** 300 N Mountain Rd. I-81, exit
26B northbound; exit 26 southbound. Int corridors.
Pets: Large, other. No service, supervision, crate.
[SAVE] [S♦] [X] [♫] [■]

◆◆◆ Comfort Inn **M** ❀
(717) 540-8400. **$99-$139.** 7744 Linglestown Rd. I-81, exit
27, 0.5 mi w. Int corridors. **Pets:** $15 one-time fee/pet.
Supervision.
[ASK] [S♦] [X] [♫] [♨] [■] [▬] [≈]

◆◆◆ Comfort Inn East **M** ❀
(717) 561-8100. **$79-$109.** 4021 Union Deposit Rd. I-83,
exit 29, just w. Int corridors. **Pets:** Medium, other. Supervision.
[ASK] [S♦] [X] [♫] [■] [▬] [≈]

AAA ◆◆◆ Comfort Inn Riverfront **M** ❀
(717) 233-1611. **$89-$139.** 525 S Front St. Center; 0.5 mi n
of I-83, exit 23. Ext/int corridors. **Pets:** Small, other. $10
daily fee/pet. No service, supervision, crate.
[SAVE] [S♦] [X] [♫] [♨] [■] [♫] [≈]

◆◆ Days Inn-Harrisburg Airport **M** ❀
(717) 939-4147. **$59-$99.** I-76, exit 19; I-283, exit 2 W
(Highspire). Ext corridors. **Pets:** Dogs only. No service,
supervision, crate.
[ASK] [S♦] [X] [♫] [■] [▬] [≈]

AAA ◆◆ Howard Johnson
Harrisburg/Hershey **M**
(717) 564-6300. **$79-$99.** 473 Eisenhower Blvd. 0.7 mi n
on Eisenhower Blvd from jct I-283, exit 1. Int corridors.
Pets: Small. No service, supervision, crate.
[SAVE] [S♦] [X] [■] [▬] [≈]

(AAA) ◆◆ **Red Roof Inn-North** M ❀
(717) 657-1445. **$49-$71.** 400 Corporate Cir. I-81, exit 24, just n on Progress Ave. Ext/int corridors. **Pets:** Other. Supervision.
SAVE ✕ 🗐 🕭

(AAA) ◆◆ **Red Roof Inn-South** M
(717) 939-1331. **$56-$76.** 950 Eisenhower Blvd. I-283, exit 1, just e. Ext/int corridors. **Pets:** Large. No service, supervision, crate.
SAVE ✕ 🗐 🕭 CTV

◆◆◆ **Residence Inn by Marriott Harrisburg-Hershey** A ❀
(717) 561-1900. **$139-$179.** 4480 Lewis Rd. Just e on US 322 from jct I-83, exit Penhar Dr. Ext corridors. **Pets:** $5 daily fee/pet, $50 one-time fee/pet. Supervision.
ASK S6 ✕ 🗐 🖥 🔌 🏠

◆◆ **Super 8 Motel-North** MI
(717) 233-5891. **$60-$75.** 4125 N Front St. I-81, exit 22, 0.8 mi n. Ext corridors. **Pets:** Supervision.
ASK S6 ✕ 🖥 🍴 🏠

(AAA) ◆◆ **Travelodge** M
(717) 564-3876. **$40-$75.** 631 S Eisenhower Blvd. I-283, exit 1 and SR 441, 0.5 mi n. Ext corridors. **Pets:** Medium. Supervision.
SAVE S6 ✕ 🖥

◆◆◆ **Wyndham Garden Hotel** MI ❀
(717) 558-9500. **$129.** 765 Eisenhower Blvd. Just w of I-283, exit 1. Int corridors. **Pets:** Small. $25 deposit/pet. No service, supervision, crate.
ASK S6 ✕ 🗐 🖥 🔌 🍴 🏠

HAZLETON

(AAA) ◆◆ **Best Western Genetti Motor Lodge** M ❀
(570) 454-2494. **$59-$109.** 32nd & N Church St. 2 mi n on SR 309; 6 mi s on SR 309; from I-80, exit 39. Ext/int corridors. **Pets:** Large, other. Designated rooms, supervision.
SAVE S6 ✕ 🗐 🖥 🏠 ✕

(AAA) ◆ **Hazleton Motor Inn** M
(570) 459-1451. **$38-$42.** 615 E Broad St. 0.5 mi e on SR 93. Int corridors. **Pets:** Designated rooms, supervision.
SAVE ✕ 🖥

◆◆◆ **Ramada Inn Hazleton** MI ❀
(570) 455-2061. **$69-$99, 30 days notice.** 2 mi n on SR 309; 6 mi s on SR 309 from I-80, exit 39; from I-81, exit 41, 0.5 mi s on SR 93, 1 mi e on Airport Rd, 0.7 mi s. Ext corridors. **Pets:** $10 daily fee/pet, $10 one-time fee/pet. No service, supervision, crate.
ASK S6 ✕ 🗐 🖥 🍴 🏠

HERMITAGE

◆◆ **Holiday Inn-Sharon/Hermitage** MI ❀
(724) 981-1530. **$86.** 3200 S Hermitage Rd. I-80, exit 1 N, just n on SR 18. Int corridors. **Pets:** Small. Designated rooms, no service, supervision, crate.
ASK S6 ✕ 🖥 🖥 🍴 🏠

HERSHEY

◆◆◆ **Hampton Inn & Suites** M
(717) 533-8400. **$169-$249.** 749 E Chocolate Ave. 0.9 mi e on US 422. Int corridors. **Pets:** No service, supervision, crate.
ASK S6 ✕ 🔌 🗐 🕭 🖥 🖥 🏠

(AAA) ◆◆◆ **Holiday Inn Express of Hershey** M
(717) 583-0500. **$149-$189.** Just nw of Jct US 322, 422 and SR 39. Int corridors. **Pets:** Large. No service, supervision, crate.
SAVE S6 ✕ 🔌 🗐 🕭 🖥 🖥 🏠

HUNTINGDON

◆◆ **Huntingdon Motor Inn** M
(814) 643-1133. **$39-$59.** Motor Inn Rd. On US 22 at jct SR 26. Ext corridors. **Pets:** Small. Designated rooms, no service, supervision, crate.
✕ 🗐 🖥 🖥

INDIANA

◆◆◆ **Best Western University Inn** M ❀
(724) 349-9620. **$58-$88.** 1545 Wayne Ave. 0.6 mi n of US 422, exit Wayne Ave. Int corridors. **Pets:** $15 one-time fee/room. Supervision.
✕ 🖥 🏠

◆◆ **Charbert Farm Bed and Breakfast** BB
(724) 726-8264. **$55-$95, 7 days notice.** 2439 Laurel Rd. Sw of Indiana; 1.3 mi w on SR 6056 from jct SR 286, 1.1 mi w on J. George's Rd, just n. Int corridors. **Pets:** Supervision.
ASK S6 ✕ ✕ 🔌 CTV

◆◆◆ **Comfort Inn Indiana** M ❀
(724) 465-7000. **Call for rates.** 1350 Indian Springs Rd. 0.7 mi e of US 422, exit Oakland Ave. Int corridors. **Pets:** Small. $25 deposit/room. No service, supervision, crate.
✕ 🔥 🕭 🏠

◆◆◆ **Holiday Inn Holidome** MI ❀
(724) 463-3561. **$59-$89, 60 days notice.** 1395 Wayne Ave. 1 mi n of US 422, exit Wayne Ave. Ext/int corridors. **Pets:** Medium. Supervision.
ASK S6 ✕ 🕭 🖥 🖥 🍴 🏠 ✕

◆◆ **Super 8 Motel** M ❀
(724) 349-4600. **$42-$46, 5 days notice.** 111 Plaza Dr. US 422, exit SR 286, just n; turn into South Town Plaza. Int corridors. **Pets:** Small. Designated rooms, no service, supervision, crate.
ASK S6 ✕ 🔌 🕭 🖥

JONESTOWN

◆◆◆ **Days Inn Lebanon/Lickdale** M ❀
(717) 865-4064. **$68-$88, 5 days notice.** 3 Everest Ln. I-81, exit 30. Int corridors. **Pets:** Medium. $10 daily fee/pet. Supervision.
ASK S6 ✕ 🕭 🖥 🖥

KANE

⊕ ◆ Kane View Motel M ❖
(814) 837-8600. **$38-$52.** Rt 6. 1 mi e. Ext corridors.
Pets: Other. $3 daily fee/pet. Designated rooms, supervision.
[SAVE] [S&] [X] [X] [K]

KITTANNING

◆◆◆ Comfort Inn M ❖
(724) 543-5200. **$65-$85.** 422 W Belmont. SR 28, exit 19A.
Int corridors. **Pets:** Medium. $25 deposit/room. No service, supervision, crate.
[ASK] [S&] [X] [⚹] [🛏] [💻] [🍽]

⊕ ◆ Rodeway Inn Kittanning M ❖
(724) 543-1100. **$50-$58.** US 422 E. E of jct US 422 and SR 66 and 28. Ext corridors. **Pets:** Small, dogs only. $26 deposit/pet, $10 one-time fee/room. Designated rooms, no service, supervision, crate.
[SAVE] [S&] [X] [🛏] [💻]

KUTZTOWN

⊕ ◆◆ Campus Inn M ❖
(610) 683-8721. **$50-$70, 3 days notice.** 15080 Kutztown Rd. US 222, Kutztown/Virginsville exit, 1 mi e. Ext corridors.
Pets: Small. No service, supervision, crate.
[SAVE] [S&] [X] [🛏] [🍽]

⊕ ◆◆ Lincoln Motel M ❖
(610) 683-3456. **$45-$70, 3 days notice.** Main St. US 222, Kutztown/Virginsville exit. Ext corridors. **Pets:** Medium, other. $5 daily fee/room. No service, supervision, crate.
[SAVE] [S&] [X]

LAMAR

◆◆ The Comfort Inn of Lamar M ❖
(570) 726-4901. **Call for rates.** I-80, exit 25, just n on SR 64. Int corridors. **Pets:** Other. $5 daily fee/room. No service, supervision, crate.
[X] [🛏] [🍽] [🍽] [X]

LAUREL HIGHLANDS METROPOLITAN AREA

CHALK HILL

⊕ ◆◆ The Lodge at Chalk Hill M ❖
(724) 438-8880. **$65-$84.** Just w on US 40. Ext corridors.
Pets: Other. $10 daily fee/pet. Designated rooms, supervision.
[X] [🛏] [X] [CTV]

JOHNSTOWN

⊕ ◆◆◆ Comfort Inn & Suites M ❖
(814) 266-3678. **$55-$66.** 455 Theatre Dr. Just e of US 219, exit Elton (SR 756). Int corridors. **Pets:** $6 daily fee/pet. No service, supervision, crate.
[SAVE] [S&] [X] [⚹] [🐾] [🛏] [💻] [🍽]

◆◆◆ Holiday Inn Downtown H
(814) 535-7777. **$84.** 250 Market St. Downtown; corner Market and Vine sts. Int corridors. **Pets:** Small. Designated rooms, no service, supervision, crate.
[ASK] [S&] [X] [⚹] [🛏] [💻] [🍽] [🍽]

◆◆◆ Holiday Inn Express Johnstown M ❖
(814) 266-8789. **$64-$79.** 1440 Scalp Ave. Just e of US 219, exit Windber (SR 56 E). Int corridors. **Pets:** Medium, other. Supervision.
[S&] [X] [⚹] [⚹] [🛏] [💻]

◆◆ Motel 6–4018 M ❖
(814) 536-1114. **$51-$63.** 430 Napoleon Pl. Downtown; at jct of SR 271 and 403. Int corridors. **Pets:** Other. No service, supervision, crate.
[S&] [X] [♿] [⚹]

◆◆ Sleep Inn M ❖
(814) 262-9292. **$44-$50.** 453 Theatre Dr. Just e of US 219, exit Elton (SR 756). Int corridors. **Pets:** Other. $8 daily fee/pet. Supervision.
[ASK] [S&] [X] [⚹] [🐾] [♿] [🛏] [💻]

◆◆ Super 8 Motel Johnstown M ❖
(814) 535-5600. **Call for rates.** 627 Solomon Run Rd. US 219, exit Galleria Dr, just w. Int corridors. **Pets:** Other. Supervision.
[X] [⚹] [🛏]

LIGONIER

⊕ ◆◆◆ Lady of the Lake Bed & Breakfast BB ❖
(724) 238-6955. **$85-$135.** 157 Rt 30 E. Just w of jct SR 711. Ext/int corridors. **Pets:** Medium, dogs only. $50 deposit/room, $10 one-time fee/pet. No service, supervision, crate.
[SAVE] [X] [🍽] [X] [🍽]

NEW STANTON

⊕ ◆◆ Ramada Inn MI ❖
(724) 925-6755. **$58-$105.** 110 N Main St/Byers Ave. I-70, exit 26B westbound; exit 26A eastbound, just ne; 0.2 mi w of I-76 (Pennsylvania Tpke), exit 8. Int corridors.
Pets: Small, dogs only. $10 daily fee/room. Designated rooms, supervision.
[SAVE] [S&] [X] [🛏] [🍽] [🍽]

SOMERSET

⊕ ◆◆◆ Best Western Executive Inn M
(814) 445-3996. **$45-$95.** 165 Water Works Rd. I-70/76 (Pennsylvania Tpke), exit 10, just e. Int corridors.
Pets: Designated rooms, supervision.
[SAVE] [S&] [X] [⚹]

⊕ ◆◆ Budget Host Inn M ❖
(814) 445-7988. **$28-$75.** 799 N Center Ave. I-70/76 (Pennsylvania Tpke), exit 10, 0.3 mi s. Ext corridors. **Pets:** Other. $5 daily fee/pet. Designated rooms, supervision.
[SAVE] [S&] [X] [🛏]

(AAA) ◆◆ **The Budget Inn** **M**
(814) 443-6441. **$20-$55.** 736 N Center Ave. I-70/76 (Pennsylvania Tpke), exit 10, 0.4 mi s. Ext corridors. **Pets:** Medium. Supervision.
(SAVE) (✕) (▤)

◆◆ **Days Inn-Somerset** **M** ❀
(814) 445-9200. **$44-$85.** 220 Water Works Rd. I-70/76 (Pennsylvania Tpke), exit 10, just e. Ext corridors. **Pets:** Small, other. $25 deposit/room. Supervision.
(ASK) (S♦) (✕) ·

(AAA) ◆◆ **Dollar Inn** **M** ❀
(814) 445-2977. **$25-$60, 4 days notice.** 1146 N Center Ave. I-70/76 (Pennsylvania Tpke), exit 10, just e via Water Works Rd, then just n on SR 601, at top of hill. Ext corridors. **Pets:** $10 deposit/pet, $5 daily fee/pet, $5 one-time fee/pet. Designated rooms, no service, supervision, crate.
(SAVE) (S♦) (✕) (▤)

(AAA) ◆◆◆ **Holiday Inn** **M**
(814) 445-9611. **$69-$109, 5 days notice.** 202 Harmon St. I-70/76 (Pennsylvania Tpke), exit 10, just s. Int corridors. **Pets:** Medium. No service, supervision, crate.
(SAVE) (S♦) (✕) (♫) (▤) (▣) (▥) (🍴) (🌊)

◆◆◆ **The Inn at Georgian Place** **BB** ❀
(814) 443-1043. **$95-$185, 7 days notice.** 800 Georgian Place Dr. I-70/76 (Pennsylvania Tpke), exit 10, just e via Water Works Rd, then 0.5 mi n on SR 601; at Horizon Outlet Center. Int corridors. **Pets:** Small. No service, supervision, crate.
(ASK) (S♦) (✕) (🍴)

◆◆ **Knights Inn** **M**
(814) 445-8933. **Call for rates.** 585 Ramada Rd. I-70/76 (Pennsylvania Tpke), exit 10, just s. Ext corridors. **Pets:** Medium. Designated rooms, no service, supervision, crate.
(✕) (▤) (▣) (🌊)

(AAA) ◆◆◆ **Ramada Inn** **MI** ❀
(814) 443-4646. **$54-$94.** Exit 10 PA Turnpike. I-70/76 (Pennsylvania Tpke), exit 10, just s. Int corridors. **Pets:** Medium. No service, supervision, crate.
(SAVE) (S♦) (✕) (▤) (▣) (🍴) (🌊)

UNIONTOWN

◆◆◆ **Holiday Inn** **MI** ❀
(724) 437-2816. **$99.** 700 W Main St. 1.8 mi w on US 40. Int corridors. **Pets:** Medium, other. No service, supervision, crate.
(ASK) (S♦) (✕) (▣) (🍴) (🌊) (✕)

❀ **END METROPOLITAN AREA** ❀

LEWISBURG

(AAA) ◆◆ **Days Inn-Lewisburg** **M** ❀
(570) 523-1171. **$61-$135.** US Rt 15. 0.5 mi n of jct SR 45. Ext corridors. **Pets:** Other. No service, supervision, crate.
(SAVE) (S♦) (✕) (▤) (▣) (🌊)

LOCK HAVEN

(AAA) ◆◆ **Best Western-Lock Haven** **M** ❀
(570) 748-3297. **$65-$99, 4 days notice.** 101 E Walnut St. Just e on E Walnut St from jct US 220, SR 120 W exit. Int corridors. **Pets:** $5 one-time fee/pet. No service, supervision, crate.
(S♦) (✕) (▤)

MANSFIELD

(AAA) ◆◆◆ **Comfort Inn** **M** ❀
(570) 662-3000. **$77-$170.** 300 Gateway Dr. Jct US 15 and 6. Int corridors. **Pets:** Other. Supervision.
(SAVE) (S♦) (✕)

(AAA) ◆◆ **Mansfield Inn** **M** ❀
(570) 662-2136. **$50-$75.** 26 S Main St. Just s on Business Rt 15 from jct Rt 6. Ext corridors. **Pets:** $6 daily fee/pet. No service, supervision, crate.
(SAVE) (S♦) (✕) (▣)

(AAA) ◆ **West's Deluxe Motel** **M** ❀
(570) 659-5141. **$36-$50.** Rt 15. 3.5 mi s. Ext corridors. **Pets:** Supervision.
(SAVE) (S♦) (✕) (▤) (▣) (🍴) (🌊)

MEADVILLE

(AAA) ◆◆ **Days Inn** **MI**
(814) 337-4264. **$56-$86.** 18360 Conneaut Lake Rd. I-79, exit 36A, just e on US 322. Int corridors. **Pets:** Small. Designated rooms, no service, supervision, crate.
(SAVE) (S♦) (✕) (▤) (🍴) (🌊)

◆◆ **Motel 6** **M** ❀
(814) 724-6366. **$55-$100.** 11237 Shaw Ave. I-79, exit 36A, just e on US 322. Int corridors. **Pets:** Medium, other. Supervision.
(ASK) (S♦) (✕) (🐾) (▤)

◆◆ **Super 8 Motel** **M** ❀
(814) 333-8883. **Call for rates.** 845 Conneaut Lake Rd. I-79, exit 36B, just w on US 322. Ext/int corridors. **Pets:** Small, other. No service, supervision, crate.
(✕) (▤)

MECHANICSBURG

◆◆◆ Holiday Inn Harrisburg-West  ❦
(717) 697-0321. **$99-$99, 3 days notice.** 5401 Carlisle
Pike. Just w on Carlisle Pike from jct of Carlisle Pike and
US 11. Ext corridors. **Pets:** Medium, other. $50 deposit/
room, $10 one-time fee/pet. No service, supervision, crate.

ASK S☻ ☒ ☎ ➠ ⑪ ➿ ☒

MERCER

🅐🅐🅐 ◆◆◆ Howard Johnson Lodge M
(724) 748-3030. **$74-$81.** 835 Perry Hwy. I-80, exit 2, on
US 19. Int corridors. **Pets:** Medium. Supervision.

SAVE S☻ ☒ ⚘ ☎ ➠ ⑪ ➿ ☒

MIFFLINVILLE

◆◆ Super 8 Motel M ❦
(570) 759-6778. **$66-$66.** 3rd St. I-80, exit 37, just n on SR
339. Ext corridors. **Pets:** Other. $20 deposit/room. No serv-
ice, supervision, crate.

ASK S☻ ☒

MILESBURG

◆◆◆ Holiday Inn M ❦
(814) 355-7521. **$75-$90, 7 days notice.** Rt 150. 0.4 mi n
of jct I-80, exit 23. Int corridors. **Pets:** Medium, other.
Supervision.

ASK S☻ ☒ ⚘ ☒ ☒ ➠ ⑪ ➿

MONTROSE

🅐🅐🅐 ◆◆ Ridge House BB ❦
(570) 278-4933. **$35-$55** (no credit cards). 6 Ridge St. I-81,
exit 67, 0.5 mi w on SR 492, 1 mi s on US 11, 8 mi w on
SR 706. Int corridors. **Pets:** Other. Supervision.

SAVE ☒ AC CTV ☎

MORGANTOWN

🅐🅐🅐 ◆◆◆ Holiday Inn M ❦
(610) 286-3000. **$89-$109.** 230 Cherry St (SR 10). Just s of
exit 22 off Pennsylvania Tpke and SR 10. Int corridors.
Pets: Other. $50 deposit/room. Supervision.

SAVE S☻ ☒ ⚘ ☎ ➠ ⑪ ➿

NEW CASTLE

🅐🅐🅐 ◆◆◆ Comfort Inn M ❦
(724) 658-7700. **$68-$128.** 1740 New Butler Rd. 1 mi e on
US 422 from jct SR 65, 1 mi w on US 422 business route.
Int corridors. **Pets:** Small, dogs only. $6 daily fee/pet, $20
one-time fee/room. Designated rooms, no service, supervision, crate.

SAVE ☒ ☎ ➠ CTV

NEW COLUMBIA

🅐🅐🅐 ◆◆◆ New Columbia Comfort Inn M ❦
(570) 568-8000. **$67-$77, 7 days notice.** I-80, exit 30A, US
15/New Columbia exit. Int corridors. **Pets:** Other. Supervision.

SAVE S☻ ☒ ⚘ ☎ ⑪ ➿

NEW CUMBERLAND

🅐🅐🅐 ◆◆ Days Inn–Harrisburg South M ❦
(717) 774-4156. **$55-$105.** 353 Lewisberry Rd. Just ne of
I-83, exit 18, 0.5 mi s of I-76 (Pennsylvania Tpke), exit 18.
Int corridors. **Pets:** Dogs only. $15 daily fee/room. No serv-
ice, supervision, crate.

SAVE ☒ ☎ ➠ ⑪ ➿ ☒

🅐🅐🅐 ◆◆◆ Harrisburg Holiday Inn Hotel &
Conference Center M
(717) 774-2721. **$129-$159.** 148 Sheraton Dr. Just e of
I-83, exit 18A; just n of I-76 (Pennsylvania Tpke), exit 18. Int
corridors. **Pets:** Medium. Designated rooms, no service,
supervision, crate.

SAVE S☻ ☒ ☒ ☎ ➠ ⑪ ➿

OIL CITY

🅐🅐🅐 ◆◆ Holiday Inn M ❦
(814) 677-1221. **$74-$100.** 1 Seneca St. Downtown. Ext/int
corridors. **Pets:** $25 deposit/room, $5 daily fee/room.
Supervision.

SAVE S☻ ☒ ☎ ➠ ⑪ ➿

PENNSYLVANIA DUTCH COUNTRY METROPOLITAN AREA

ADAMSTOWN

🅐🅐🅐 ◆◆ Black Forest Inn M ❦
(717) 484-4801. **$43-$119.** 500 Lancaster Ave. On SR 272;
2.8 mi n of I-76 (Pennsylvania Tpke), exit 21. Ext corridors.
Pets: Other. Designated rooms, no service, supervision,
crate.

☒ ☎ ➿

DENVER

🅐🅐🅐 ◆◆ Black Horse Lodge and Suites M ❦
(717) 336-7563. **$79-$119, 7 days notice.** 2180 N Reading
Rd. I-76 (Pennsylvania Tpke), exit 21, 1 mi w to SR 272,
then 0.3 mi n. Ext/int corridors. **Pets:** $10 daily fee/pet.
Designated rooms, no service, supervision, crate.

SAVE S☻ ☒ ☎ ➠ ➿ ☒

(AAA) ◆◆◆ Comfort Inn [M] ❀
(717) 336-4649. **$80-$119, 3 days notice.** 2015 N Reading Rd. I-76 (Pennsylvania Tpke), exit 21, 1 mi w to SR 272, then just s. Int corridors. **Pets:** Medium, dogs only. $25 one-time fee/room. Designated rooms, no service, supervision, crate.
[SAVE] [S$] [✕] [▭]

EPHRATA

(AAA) ◆◆◆ Historic Smithton Country Inn [BB]
(717) 733-6094. **$65-$175.** 900 W Main St. On US 322, just w of jct SR 272. Int corridors. **Pets:** No service, supervision, crate.
[✕] [🔲] [CTV]

LANCASTER

◆◆◆ Best Western Eden Resort Inn & Conference Center [MI] ❀
(717) 569-6444. **$40-$169.** 222 Eden Rd. At jct US 30 and SR 272 (Oregon Pike). Ext/int corridors. **Pets:** Small. Supervision.
[ASK] [S$] [✕] [🔲] [🔲] [▭] [❙❙] [🖼] [🖾]

(AAA) ◆◆◆ Comfort Inn-Sherwood Knoll [MI] ❀
(717) 898-2431. **$76-$106.** 500 Centerville Rd. 5 mi w on US 30, at Centerville exit. Int corridors. **Pets:** Medium. $6 daily fee/pet. Designated rooms, no service, supervision, crate.
[SAVE] [S$] [✕] [🔲] [▭] [❙❙] [🖼]

(AAA) ◆◆ Hotel Brunswick [H]
(717) 397-4801. **$89-$109.** Chestnut & Queen sts. Center. Int corridors. **Pets:** No service, supervision, crate.
[SAVE] [S$] [✕] [🔲] [🔲] [▭] [❙❙] [🖼]

◆◆◆ Lancaster Host Hotel & Conference Center [R] ❀
(717) 299-5500. **$139-$159.** 2300 Lincoln Hwy E. 5 mi e on US 30. Int corridors. **Pets:** Medium. $50 deposit/room. No service, supervision, crate.
[ASK] [S$] [✕] [🔲] [🔲] [▭] [❙❙] [🖼] [🖾]

(AAA) ◆◆ Travel Inn [M] ❀
(717) 299-8971. **$69-$79, 7 days notice.** 2151 Lincoln Hwy E. 4.5 mi e on US 30. Ext/int corridors. **Pets:** Dogs only. $7 daily fee/pet, $10 one-time fee/pet. Designated rooms, no service, supervision, crate.
[SAVE] [S$] [✕] [🖼]

MANHEIM

(AAA) ◆ Rodeway Inn-Penns Woods [M] ❀
(717) 665-2755. **$54-$58.** 2931 Lebanon Rd. I-76 (Pennsylvania Tpke), exit 20, just s on SR 72. Ext corridors. **Pets:** Small. $10 one-time fee/pet. Designated rooms, no service, supervision, crate.
[SAVE] [S$] [✕] [🖼]

NEW HOLLAND

(AAA) ◆ The Hollander Motel [M] ❀
(717) 354-4377. **$52-$65, 3 days notice.** 320 E Main St. Just e on SR 23. Ext corridors. **Pets:** $5 one-time fee/room. Supervision.
[SAVE] [✕]

STRASBURG

(AAA) ◆◆◆ Historic Strasburg Inn [CI] ❀
(717) 687-7691. **$139-$159.** One Historic Dr. 0.5 mi n on SR 896, 2.5 mi s of US 30. Ext/int corridors. **Pets:** Medium, dogs only. $25 deposit/room, $15 daily fee/room. Designated rooms, supervision.
[✕] [🔲] [▭] [❙❙] [🖼] [🖾]

❀ **END METROPOLITAN AREA** ❀

PHILADELPHIA METROPOLITAN AREA

BENSALEM

◆◆◆ Comfort Inn [M]
(215) 245-0100. **$109-$119.** 3660 Street Rd. Just se on SR 132 from jct US 1. Ext/int corridors. **Pets:** No service, supervision, crate.
[ASK] [S$] [✕] [🔲] [🔲] [▭]

◆◆◆ Holiday Inn-Philadelphia Northeast [MI] ❀
(215) 638-1500. **$119.** 3499 Street Rd. On SR 132, just se of jct US 1. Ext/int corridors. **Pets:** Medium, other. $50 deposit/room. No service, supervision, crate.
[ASK] [S$] [✕] [🔲] [🔲] [▭] [❙❙] [🖼]

BERWYN

◆◆◆ Residence Inn by Marriott [A]
(610) 640-9494. **Call for rates.** 600 W Swedesford Rd. From US 202 Devon exit, then 1 mi s on SR 252 (Swedesford Rd). Ext corridors. **Pets:** Supervision.
[✕] [🔲] [▭] [🖼] [🖾]

CHADDS FORD

(AAA) ◆◆◆ Brandywine River Hotel [M] ❀
(610) 388-1200. **$125-$169.** 2 mi w of US 202, at jct US 1 and SR 100. Int corridors. **Pets:** Small, dogs only. $20 daily fee/pet. Designated rooms, no service, supervision, crate.
[SAVE] [S$] [✕] [🔲] [🔲] [▭]

ESSINGTON

◆◆◆ Comfort Inn Airport ⛿ 🐾
(610) 521-9800. **$88-$150, 7 days notice.** 53 Industrial Hwy. On SR 291, just s of jct SR 420, 0.3 mi s of I-95, Essington exit (SR 420). Int corridors. **Pets:** Small. $10 daily fee/pet. Designated rooms, no service, supervision, crate.

(ASK) (S🐾) (✕) (🐾) (⛿) (💻)

◆◆◆ Ramada Inn-Philadelphia International Airport 🅷
(610) 521-9600. **$95-$105.** 76 Industrial Hwy. I-95 exit 9A, 0.5 mi w on SR 291. Int corridors. **Pets:** No service, supervision, crate.

(ASK) (S🐾) (✕) (🐾) (⛿) (💻) (🍽) (🛋)

🆎 ◆◆ Red Roof Inn-Airport ⛿ 🐾
(610) 521-5090. **$78-$95.** 49 Industrial Hwy. SR 291, just s of jct SR 420; 0.3 mi se of I-95, exit 9A, Essington SR 420. Ext corridors. **Pets:** Small. No service, supervision, crate.

(SAVE) (✕) (🐾)

EXTON

◆◆◆ Holiday Inn Express ⛿
(610) 524-9000. **Call for rates.** 120 N Pottstown Pike. Jct Business US 30 and SR 100, 3 mi s of Pennsylvania Tpke, exit 23. Int corridors. **Pets:** Medium. Supervision.

(✕) (🐾) (🐾) (⛿) (💻) (🛋)

HORSHAM

◆◆◆ Homestead Village Guest Studios ⛿ 🐾
(215) 956-9966. **Call for rates.** 537 Dresher Rd. Pennsylvania Tpke, exit 27, 1.5 mi n on SR 611, just w on Horsham Rd, then 0.5 mi s. Int corridors. **Pets:** Medium, other. $125 one-time fee/room. No service, supervision, crate.

(✕) (🐾) (🐾) (🐾) (⛿) (💻)

◆◆◆ Horsham Days Inn ⛿ 🐾
(215) 674-2500. **$89-$109.** 245 Easton Rd. On SR 611 N, exit 27 off Pennsylvania Tpke, 1 mi n on SR 611 (Easton Rd). Int corridors. **Pets:** $10 deposit/pet. No service, supervision, crate.

(ASK) (✕) (🐾) (🐾) (⛿) (💻)

◆◆◆ Residence Inn by Marriott-Willow Grove 🅰 🐾
(215) 443-7330. **Call for rates.** 3 Walnut Grove Dr. Pennsylvania Tpke, exit 27, 1 mi n on SR 611, 1.3 mi w on Dresher Rd. Ext corridors. **Pets:** Small, other. $150 deposit/room, $150 one-time fee/room. No service, supervision, crate.

(ASK) (✕) (🐾) (🐾) (⛿) (💻) (🛋) (✕)

KING OF PRUSSIA

◆◆◆ Homestead Village Guest Studios ⛿
(610) 962-9000. **Call for rates.** 400 American Ave. Pennsylvania Tpke, exit 24, I-76, exit 25 (Mall Blvd), 1.3 mi n on SR 363 (N Gulph Rd), 1 mi ne on 1st Ave. Int corridors. **Pets:** Medium. No service, supervision, crate.

(✕) (🐾) (🐾) (🐾) (⛿) (💻)

KINTNERSVILLE

◆◆◆ Lightfarm 🅱🅱
(610) 847-3276. **$79-$150, 7 days notice.** 2042 Berger Rd. 0.5 mi ne on Berger Rd from SR 412. Int corridors. **Pets:** Supervision.

(ASK) (✕) (🐾) (🐟)

KULPSVILLE

◆◆◆ Holiday Inn-Kulpsville ⛿ 🐾
(215) 368-3800. **$85-$100, 7 days notice.** 1750 Sumneytown Pike. Pennsylvania Tpke, Northeast Extension I-476, exit 31. Int corridors. **Pets:** Other. Designated rooms, no service, supervision, crate.

(✕) (⛿) (💻) (🍽) (🛋)

LANGHORNE

🆎 ◆◆ Red Roof Inn-Oxford Valley ⛿
(215) 750-6200. **$101-$121.** 3100 Cabot Blvd W. Just e of I-95, exit 29A; off US 1 N, 0.5 mi n of Sesame Place. Ext corridors. **Pets:** Supervision.

(SAVE) (✕) (🐾)

LEVITTOWN

🆎 ◆◆ Comfort Inn Levittown/Bristol ⛿ 🐾
(215) 547-5000. **$80-$90, 3 days notice.** 6401 Bristol Pk. 0.4 mi n, Pennsylvania Tpke, exit 29. Int corridors. **Pets:** Small, other. Supervision.

(SAVE) (S🐾) (✕) (⛿)

LIONVILLE

◆◆◆ Hampton Inn ⛿ 🐾
(610) 363-5555. **$83-$109.** 4 N Pottstown Pike. Jct SR 113 and 100; 0.5 mi s of Pennsylvania Tpke, exit 23. Int corridors. **Pets:** Other. No service, supervision, crate.

(ASK) (✕) (🐾) (🐾) (⛿) (💻) (🛋)

MALVERN

◆◆◆ Homewood Suites Hotel 🅰
(610) 296-3500. **$95-$149.** 12 E Swedesford Rd. Just w of US 202, SR 29 N exit; opposite Great Valley Corporate Center. Int corridors. **Pets:** No service, supervision, crate.

(ASK) (S🐾) (✕) (🐾) (🐾) (🐾) (⛿) (💻) (🛋)

NEW HOPE

◆◆◆ Aaron Burr House Inn & Conference Center 🅱🅱 🐾
(215) 862-2343. **$90-$255.** 80 W Bridge St (SR 179). 0.5 mi w of SR 32, at W Bridge and Chestnut sts. Int corridors. **Pets:** Dogs only. $25 daily fee/pet. No service, supervision, crate.

(ASK) (S🐾) (✕)

◆◆◆ Best Western New Hope Inn ⛿ 🐾
(215) 862-5221. **$89-$149.** 6426 Lower York Rd. 2 mi s on US 202, 1 mi w of jct SR 179. Ext corridors. **Pets:** Small. $20 daily fee/room. Designated rooms, supervision.

(ASK) (S🐾) (✕) (🐾) (🍽) (🛋) (✕)

▲▲▲ ◆◆◆ **The Fox & Hound Bed & Breakfast of New Hope** 🅱🅱 ❀
(215) 862-5082. **$70-$170.** 246 W Bridge St. 0.5 mi s on SR 179. Ext/int corridors. **Pets:** Small. $25 deposit/pet. Designated rooms, no service, supervision, crate.
⊠ 🄲🅃🅅 🄐

▲▲▲ ◆◆ **New Hope Motel In The Woods** Ⓜ ❀
(215) 862-2800. **$59-$109.** 400 W Bridge St. 1 mi s on SR 179, e of jct US 202. Ext corridors. **Pets:** Medium. $25 one-time fee/pet. Designated rooms, no service, supervision, crate.
🆂🅰🆅🅴 🆂🄐 ⊠ 🄱 🄐

▲▲▲ ◆◆◆ **The Wedgwood Inn of New Hope** 🅱🅱 ❀
(215) 862-2520. **$90-$265.** 111 W Bridge St (SR 179). 0.5 mi w of SR 32. Ext/int corridors. **Pets:** Dogs only. $20 daily fee/pet. No service, supervision, crate.
🆂🅰🆅🅴 🆂🄐 ⊠ 🄱 🄯

PHILADELPHIA

▲▲▲ ◆◆ **Best Western Center City Hotel** Ⓜ ❀
(215) 568-8300. **$109-$139.** 501 N 22nd St. Just n of Benjamin Franklin Pkwy. Int corridors. **Pets:** Small, other. $10 daily fee/pet, $10 one-time fee/pet. Supervision.
🆂🅰🆅🅴 🆂🄐 ⊠ 🄐 🄱 🍴 🄐

▲▲▲ ◆◆◆ **Best Western Independence Park Inn** 🄷 ❀
(215) 922-4443. **$140-$190.** 235 Chestnut St. In Independence Park Historic District; between 2nd and 3rd sts. Int corridors. **Pets:** Small, other. $50 one-time fee/room. Supervision.
🆂🅰🆅🅴 🆂🄐 ⊠ 🄐 🄱

◆◆◆ **Crowne Plaza Philadelphia Center City** 🄷 ❀
(215) 561-7500. **$139-$229.** 1800 Market St. Downtown; between 18th and 19th sts. Int corridors. **Pets:** Other. $100 deposit/pet, $30 one-time fee/room. No service, supervision, crate.
⊠ 🄐 🄐 🄱 🄯 🍴 🄐

▲▲▲ ◆◆◆◆◆ **Four Seasons Hotel** 🄷
(215) 963-1500. **$320-$425.** 1 Logan Sq. At corner 18th and Benjamin Franklin Pkwy. Int corridors. **Pets:** Medium. Designated rooms, no service, supervision, crate.
⊠ 🄐 🄐 🄐 🄱 🄯 🄐

▲▲▲ ◆◆◆ **Hawthorn Suites Philadelphia at the Convention Center** 🄷 ❀
(215) 829-8300. **$149-$159.** 1100 Vine St. Downtown; 11th and Vine sts. Int corridors. **Pets:** $100 deposit/room. No service, supervision, crate.
🆂🅰🆅🅴 🆂🄐 ⊠ 🄐 🄐 🄱 🄯

▲▲▲ ◆◆◆ **1011 Clinton** 🅱🅱 ❀
(215) 923-8144. **$135-$200.** 1011 Clinton St. Downtown; between Spruce and Pine sts and 10th and 11th sts. Int corridors. **Pets:** Dogs only. Designated rooms, supervision.
🆂🅰🆅🅴 🆂🄐 ⊠ 🄱 🄯

▲▲▲ ◆◆◆◆ **Park Hyatt Philadelphia at the Bellevue** 🄷
(215) 893-1234. **$240-$265.** 1415 Chancellor Ct. On Broad St, between Walnut and Locust sts; in Park Hyatt Philadelphia at the Bellevue. Int corridors. **Pets:** Small. Supervision.
🆂🅰🆅🅴 ⊠ 🄯 🄱 🄐 ⊠

◆◆◆ **Philadelphia Airport Marriott** 🄷 ❀
(215) 492-9000. **$199-$235.** 1 Arrivals Rd. Jct I-95 and SR 291, exit 10. Int corridors. **Pets:** Small, other. Supervision.
🆂🄐 ⊠ 🄒 🄯 🄔 🄱 🄯 🍴 🄐

◆◆◆ **Philadelphia Airport Residence Inn** Ⓜ ❀
(215) 492-1611. **$199.** 4630 Island Ave. I-95, exit 11 northbound; exit 13 southbound, 0.3 mi e on SR 291. Ext/int corridors. **Pets:** Large. $100 one-time fee/room. No service, supervision, crate.
🄰🆂🄺 🆂🄐 ⊠ 🄐 🄔 🄱 🄯 🄐 ⊠

◆◆◆ **Philadelphia Marriott** 🄷 ❀
(215) 625-2900. **Call for rates.** 1201 Market St. Downtown; adjacent Convention Center. Int corridors. **Pets:** Dogs only. $100 one-time fee/pet. No service, supervision, crate.
⊠ 🄯 🄔 🄱 🄯 🍴 🄐

▲▲▲ ◆◆◆◆◆ **The Rittenhouse Hotel and Condominium Residences** 🄷 ❀
(215) 546-9000. **$335-$360.** 210 W Rittenhouse Sq. Int corridors. **Pets:** Other. Supervision.
⊠ 🄯 🍴 🄐

◆◆◆ **Warwick Hotel and Towers** 🄷
(215) 735-6000. **$169-$289, 7 days notice.** 1701 Locust St. Jct 17th and Locust sts. Int corridors. **Pets:** Supervision.
🄰🆂🄺 🆂🄐 ⊠ 🄯 🄯 🍴

POTTSTOWN

◆◆◆ **Comfort Inn** Ⓜ ❀
(610) 326-5000. **$79-$89.** 99 Robinson St. On SR 100, 1 mi n of jct US 422. Int corridors. **Pets:** Other. $25 deposit/room. Supervision.
🄰🆂🄺 🆂🄐 ⊠ 🄯 🄱 🄯 🄐

▲▲▲ ◆◆ **Days Inn** Ⓜ ❀
(610) 970-1101. **$43-$54.** 29 High St. Just off SR 663, 0.5 mi e of jct SR 100. Ext corridors. **Pets:** Other. $10 daily fee/pet, $10 one-time fee/pet. Designated rooms, no service, supervision, crate.
🆂🅰🆅🅴 🆂🄐 ⊠ 🄱

◆◆◆ **Holiday Inn Express** Ⓜ ❀
(610) 327-3300. **$65-$65.** 1600 Industrial Hwy. Jct US 422 and Armand Hammer Blvd exit. Int corridors. **Pets:** Medium, other. Supervision.
🄰🆂🄺 🆂🄐 ⊠ 🄐 🄯 🄱 🄯 🄐

QUAKERTOWN

▲▲▲ ◆◆ **Quakertown Rodeway Inn** Ⓜ ❀
(215) 536-7600. **$59-$79.** 1920 SR 663. Just e of I-476 Pennsylvania Tpke, Northeast Extention, exit 32. Ext corridors. **Pets:** $9 daily fee/pet, $9 one-time fee/pet. No service, supervision, crate.
🆂🅰🆅🅴 🆂🄐 ⊠ 🄱 🄯

TREVOSE

AAA ◆◆ **Red Roof Inn** Ⓜ
(215) 244-9422. **$56-$88.** 3100 Lincoln Hwy. On US 1; Pennsylvania Tpke, exit 28, 0.5 mi s. Ext corridors. **Pets:** Medium. Designated rooms, supervision.
SAVE ⓧ 🕯 📶

WEST CHESTER

◆◆ **Microtel Inn & Suites** Ⓜ
(610) 738-9111. **Call for rates.** 500 Willowbrook Ln. Just se of US 202, Matlack Rd exit. Int corridors. **Pets:** Medium. Supervision.
ⓧ ♿ 📶 🛢 🛎 💻

❀ END METROPOLITAN AREA ❀

PHILIPSBURG

◆◆ **Harbor Inn** Ⓜ🅸 ❖
(814) 342-0250. **$51-$61, 7 days notice.** Rt 322 & 53. At jct US 322 and SR 53 N. Int corridors. **Pets:** Designated rooms, no service, supervision, crate.
ASK ⓧ 🍴

AAA ◆ **Main Liner Motel** Ⓜ ❖
(814) 342-2004. **$31-$55.** US 322. 1 mi w of jct SR 53 N. Ext corridors. **Pets:** Medium. $6 daily fee/room, $6 one-time fee/room. No service, supervision, crate.
SAVE 📶 ⓧ 🛢

PINE GROVE

◆◆ **Comfort Inn** Ⓜ ❖
(570) 345-8031. **$49-$149.** US 443 at I-81, exit 31. Int corridors. **Pets:** Other. No service, supervision, crate.
ASK ⓧ 🕯 📶 💻 🌐

AAA ◆◆ **Econo Lodge** Ⓜ ❖
(570) 345-4099. **$40-$70.** I-81, exit 31, just e on SR 443. Ext/int corridors. **Pets:** Other. $5 daily fee/pet. Designated rooms, supervision.
SAVE 📶 ⓧ 📶 💻

PITTSBURGH METROPOLITAN AREA

BEAVER FALLS

◆◆◆ **Holiday Inn** Ⓜ🅸 ❖
(724) 846-3700. **$89-$89.** 7195 Eastwood Rd. I-76, exit 2, just n. Int corridors. **Pets:** Other. Designated rooms, no service, supervision, crate.
ASK 📶 ⓧ 📶 🛢 💻 🍴 🌐 ⓧ

BETHEL PARK

◆◆◆ **Holiday Inn Pittsburgh South** Ⓜ🅸 ❖
(412) 833-5300. **$82-$120.** 164 Ft Couch Rd. 1 mi n on US 19, opposite South Hills Village Mall. Int corridors. **Pets:** Small. $20 deposit/room. Supervision.
ASK ⓧ 📶 🛢 💻 🍴 🌐

BRADDOCK HILLS

AAA ◆◆◆ **Holiday Inn Parkway East** Ⓜ🅸
(412) 247-2700. **$73.** 915 Brinton Rd. 0.3 mi n of I-376, exit 11, SR 8. Int corridors. **Pets:** Designated rooms, no service, supervision, crate.
SAVE 📶 ⓧ 📶 🛢 💻 🍴 🌐

BRIDGEVILLE

AAA ◆◆ **Knights Inn-Pittsburgh/Bridgeville** Ⓜ ❖
(412) 221-8110. **$45-$50.** 111 Hickory Grade Rd. I-79, exit 11. Ext corridors. **Pets:** Small. $5 daily fee/pet. Designated rooms, no service, supervision, crate.
SAVE 📶 ⓧ 📶 📶 🛢 💻 🌐

BUTLER

◆◆◆ **Comfort Inn** Ⓜ ❖
(724) 287-7177. **$64-$94.** 1 Comfort Ln. 4 mi s on SR 8. Int corridors. **Pets:** Large, other. Designated rooms, no service, supervision, crate.
ASK 📶 ⓧ 📶 🛢 💻 🌐

◆ **Days Inn** Ⓜ🅸 ❖
(724) 287-6761. **$59-$89.** 139 Pittsburgh Rd. 2 mi s on SR 8. Ext/int corridors. **Pets:** Other. $25 deposit/pet. Supervision.
ASK 📶 ⓧ 🛢 💻 🍴 🌐

◆◆ **Super 8 Motel** Ⓜ ❖
(724) 287-8888. **$46-$51.** 138 Pittsburgh/SR 8. 2 mi s on SR 8. Int corridors. **Pets:** Medium. $20 deposit/room, $5 daily fee/room. No service, supervision, crate.
ASK 📶 ⓧ 🛢

CORAOPOLIS

AAA ◆◆◆ **Embassy Suites-Pittsburgh International Airport** 🄷
(412) 269-9070. **$119-$169.** 550 Cherrington Pkwy. From SR 60 Coraopolis/Sewickley exit, just e to Cherrington Pkwy. Int corridors. **Pets:** Supervision.
SAVE 📶 ⓧ 📶 📶 🛢 💻 🍴 🌐

◆◆◆ **Hampton Inn Hotel Airport** Ⓜ ❖
(412) 264-0020. **$74-$84.** 1420 Beers School Rd. 0.5 mi n of Business Rt 60. Int corridors. **Pets:** Medium. Designated rooms, no service, supervision, crate.
ⓧ 📶 💻

ⓐ ◆◆◆ Holiday Inn-Pittsburgh Airport 🅷 ❀
(412) 262-3600. **$119-$135.** 1406 Beers School Rd. 1 mi n of Business Rt 60. Int corridors. **Pets:** $50 deposit/room. Supervision.
🆂🅰🆅🅴 ⬛ ⬛ ⬛ ⬛ ⬛ ⬛ ⬛

◆◆◆ La Quinta Inn-Airport 🅼 ❀
(412) 269-0400. **$62-$75.** 1433 Beers School Rd. 1 mi n of Business Rt 60. Int corridors. **Pets:** Supervision.
🅰🆂🅺 ⬛ ⬛ ⬛ ⬛

ⓐ ◆◆ Motel 6 Airport–1285 🅼
(412) 269-0990. **$38-$54.** 1170 Thorn Run Rd. Business Rt 60 to Coraopolis/Sewickley exit to Thorn Run Rd. Int corridors. **Pets:** Small. Supervision.
⬛ ⬛ ⬛ ⬛

◆◆ Pittsburgh Airport Super 8 Motel 🅼
(412) 264-7888. **Call for rates.** 1465 Beers School Rd. 1 mi n of Business Rt 60. Int corridors. **Pets:** No service, supervision, crate.
⬛ ⬛ ⬛

ⓐ ◆◆ Red Roof Inn Pittsburgh Airport 🅼
(412) 264-5678. **$50-$70.** 1454 Beers School Rd. 0.5 mi n of Business Rt 60. Ext corridors. **Pets:** Medium. Supervision.
🆂🅰🆅🅴 ⬛

CRAFTON

◆ Days Inn 🅼 ❀
(412) 922-0120. **Call for rates.** 100 Kisow Dr. I-79 N, exit 16; from I-79 S, exit 16B. Ext corridors. **Pets:** Medium. $10 daily fee/room. Supervision.
🅰🆂🅺 ⬛ ⬛ ⬛

DELMONT

◆◆ Super 8 Motel 🅼
(724) 468-4888. **Call for rates.** 180 Sheffield Dr. On SR 66, just s of US 22. Int corridors. **Pets:** Large. Supervision.
⬛ ⬛ ⬛

GIBSONIA

◆◆ Comfort Inn Gibsonia 🅼
(724) 444-8700. **$51-$61.** 5137 Rt 8. I-76 Tpke, exit 4, just n. Ext corridors. **Pets:** Small. Designated rooms, no service, supervision, crate.
🅰🆂🅺 ⬛ ⬛ ⬛

GREEN TREE

◆◆◆ Hampton Inn Hotel Green Tree 🅼 ❀
(412) 922-0100. **$75.** 555 Hampton Inn Dr. I-279, US 22 and 30, exit 4, 1 mi nw via Mansfield Ave. Int corridors. **Pets:** Designated rooms, no service, supervision, crate.
🅰🆂🅺 ⬛ ⬛ ⬛ ⬛

ⓐ ◆◆◆ Hawthorn Suites 🅰 ❀
(412) 279-6300. **$99-$149, 7 days notice.** 700 Mansfield Ave. I-279, US 22 and 30, exit 4, 1.5 mi nw via Mansfield Ave. Ext corridors. **Pets:** Other. $15 daily fee/room. Supervision.
🆂🅰🆅🅴 ⬛ ⬛ ⬛ ⬛ ⬛ ⬛ ⬛

ⓐ ◆◆◆ Holiday Inn-Pittsburgh Central (Green Tree) 🅼 ❀
(412) 922-8100. **$129-$134.** 401 Holiday Dr. I-279, US 22 and 30, exit 4, 1 mi nw via Mansfield Ave. Int corridors. **Pets:** No service, supervision, crate.
🆂🅰🆅🅴 ⬛ ⬛ ⬛ ⬛ ⬛ ⬛ ⬛

◆◆◆ The Radisson Hotel Green Tree/Pittsburgh 🅷
(412) 922-8400. **$99-$159.** 101 Marriott Dr. I-279, US 22 and 30; exit 4, 1.1 mi nw via Mansfield Ave. Int corridors. **Pets:** Very small. Supervision.
🅰🆂🅺 🆂 ⬛ ⬛ ⬛ ⬛ ⬛ ⬛ ⬛ ⬛

MONROEVILLE

◆◆ Days Inn-Monroeville 🅼 ❀
(412) 856-1610. **Call for rates.** 2727 Mosside Blvd. Exit 6 off I-76 (Pennsylvania Tpke), exit 16A off I-376, 1 mi s on SR 48. Ext corridors. **Pets:** Medium, dogs only. $5 daily fee/pet. Supervision.
⬛ ⬛

◆◆◆ Hampton Inn Monroeville/Pittsburgh 🅼 ❀
(412) 380-4000. **$99-$109.** 3000 Mosside Blvd. I-76 (Pennsylvania Tpke), exit 6; I-376, exit 16A, 0.3 mi s on SR 48. Int corridors. **Pets:** Small, other. No service, supervision, crate.
🅰🆂🅺 ⬛ ⬛ ⬛ ⬛ ⬛ ⬛

ⓐ ◆◆◆ Holiday Inn 🅼 ❀
(412) 372-1022. **$139.** 2750 Mosside Blvd. Exit 6 off I-76 (Pennsylvania Tpke), exit 16A off I-376, 0.4 mi s on SR 48. Int corridors. **Pets:** Other. No service, supervision, crate.
🆂🅰🆅🅴 🆂 ⬛ ⬛ ⬛ ⬛ ⬛ ⬛

ⓐ ◆◆ Red Roof Inn-Monroeville 🅼 ❀
(412) 856-4738. **$56-$79.** 2729 Mosside Blvd. Exit 6 off I-76 (Pennsylvania Tpke), exit 16A off I-376, 0.8 mi s on SR 48. Ext corridors. **Pets:** Other. Supervision.
🆂🅰🆅🅴 ⬛ ⬛ ⬛

◆◆ Super 8 Motel Pittsburgh/Monroeville 🅼 ❀
(724) 733-8008. **$49-$55, 3 days notice.** 1807 Rt 286. I-76, exit 6 or I-376, exit 7, 3 mi e on SR 22 E, then 2 mi n. Int corridors. **Pets:** Other. $25 deposit/room, $5 daily fee/room, $5 one-time fee/room. No service, supervision, crate.
🅰🆂🅺 🆂 ⬛ ⬛

MOON RUN

ⓐ ◆◆◆ AmeriSuites Pittsburgh Airport 🅼
(412) 494-0202. **$115-$115.** 6011 Campbells Run Rd. I-279 S, Moon Run exit, just w. Int corridors. **Pets:** Very small. No service, supervision, crate.
🆂🅰🆅🅴 🆂 ⬛ ⬛ ⬛ ⬛ ⬛ ⬛ ⬛

◆◆ Comfort Inn-Pittsburgh Airport 🅼
(412) 787-2600. **$53-$93.** 7011 Old Steubenville Pike. On US 22 and 30, at jct SR 60; 4 mi w of I-279 and 79. Ext/int corridors. **Pets:** Large. Designated rooms, supervision.
🅰🆂🅺 🆂 ⬛ ⬛ ⬛ ⬛ ⬛

(AAA) ◆◆ MainStay Suites Pittsburgh Airport M ❖
(412) 490-7343. **$79-$109.** 1000 Summit Park Dr. SR 60, Montour Run exit 2, just w on Cliff Mine Rd, just s. Int corridors. **Pets:** Medium. $100 deposit/pet, $10 daily fee/pet. No service, supervision, crate.
SAVE 🔲 ✕ 🔲 🔲 CTV

◆◆◆ Pittsburgh Airport Marriott H
(412) 788-8800. **Call for rates.** 777 Aten Rd. SR 60 at Montour Run, exit 2. Int corridors. **Pets:** Small. No service, supervision, crate.
✕ 🔲 🔲 🔲 🔲

(AAA) ◆◆ Red Roof Inn South Airport M
(412) 787-7870. **$54-$78.** 6404 Steubenville Pike. I-179, exit 16 B, 3.2 mi w on SR 60. Ext/int corridors. **Pets:** No service, supervision, crate.
SAVE ✕ 🔲 🔲 🔲

◆◆◆ Residence Inn-Pittsburgh Airport M ❖
(412) 787-3300. **$149-$149.** 1500 Park Lane Dr. SR 60, exit 2 (Montour Run Rd), just w on Cliff Mine Dr to Summit Park Dr, just s to Park Lane Dr, then just e. Int corridors. **Pets:** Other. $150 one-time fee/room. Supervision.
ASK 🔲 ✕ 🔲 🔲 🔲 🔲 🔲 ✕

◆◆◆ Wyndham Garden Hotel-Pittsburgh Airport M
(724) 695-0002. **$109.** 1 Wyndham Cir. Business Rt 60 at Montour Run exit. Int corridors. **Pets:** Designated rooms, no service, supervision, crate.
ASK 🔲 ✕ 🔲 🔲 🔲 🔲 🔲 🔲

NEW KENSINGTON

◆◆ Clarion Hotel M ❖
(724) 335-9171. **$64-$90, 3 days notice.** 300 Tarentum Bridge Rd. On SR 366; 1.5 mi s of SR 28, exit 14, at s end of Tarentum Bridge. Int corridors. **Pets:** No service, supervision, crate.
ASK 🔲 ✕ 🔲 🔲 🔲 🔲 🔲

PITTSBURGH

◆◆ Best Western University Center M
(412) 683-6100. **$77-$97.** 3401 Blvd of the Allies. Just w of jct Bates St. Int corridors. **Pets:** Designated rooms, supervision.
ASK 🔲 ✕ 🔲 🔲 🔲 🔲 🔲

◆◆◆ Doubletree Hotel Pittsburgh H ❖
(412) 281-3700. **$159-$199.** 1000 Penn Ave. At Liberty Center, adjacent to convention center. Int corridors. **Pets:** Other. Supervision.
✕ 🔲 🔲 🔲 🔲 🔲

◆◆◆ Hampton Inn-University Center M
(412) 681-1000. **$99-$119.** 3315 Hamlet St. At jct Blvd of the Allies. Int corridors. **Pets:** Medium. No service, supervision, crate.
ASK 🔲 ✕ 🔲 🔲 🔲

◆◆◆ Hilton Pittsburgh H ❖
(412) 391-4600. **$99-$179.** Gateway Center. In Gateway Center on Commonwealth, opposite Point State Park. Int corridors. **Pets:** Small, dogs only. Designated rooms, no service, supervision, crate.
ASK 🔲 ✕ 🔲 🔲 🔲 🔲

(AAA) ◆◆◆ Holiday Inn Pittsburgh North Hills M ❖
(412) 366-5200. **$85-$95.** 4859 McKnight Rd. 7 mi n; adjacent and behind North Hills Village Mall. Int corridors. **Pets:** Small. $25 deposit/room. Designated rooms, no service, supervision, crate.
SAVE 🔲 ✕ 🔲 🔲 🔲 🔲 🔲 🔲

◆◆◆ Holiday Inn Select University Center M ❖
(412) 682-6200. **$135-$135.** 100 Lytton Ave. Just nw of 5th Ave. Int corridors. **Pets:** $50 deposit/room. No service, supervision, crate.
✕ 🔲 🔲 🔲 🔲 🔲

◆◆◆ Westin William Penn H ❖
(412) 281-7100. **Call for rates.** 530 William Penn Pl. Jct 6th and William Penn. Int corridors. **Pets:** $50 deposit/room. Designated rooms, no service, supervision, crate.
✕ 🔲 🔲 🔲

WARRENDALE

(AAA) ◆◆◆ AmeriSuites Pittsburgh/Cranberry M ❖
(724) 779-7900. **$75-$125.** 136 Emeryville Dr. I-76 and 79 at SR 19. Int corridors. **Pets:** Very small. Supervision.
SAVE 🔲 ✕ 🔲 🔲 🔲 🔲 🔲

◆◆ Days Inn Warrendale M ❖
(724) 772-2700. **$62-$138, 7 days notice.** 924 Sheraton Dr. Exit 25 off I-79, US 19N; Tpk I-76 exit 3, 0.5 mi s on US 19. Int corridors. **Pets:** Small, other. $100 deposit/room. Supervision.
ASK 🔲 ✕ 🔲 🔲

◆◆◆ Holiday Inn Express M ❖
(724) 772-1000. **$74-$79.** 20003 Route 19. Jct SR 19 and Tpke. Int corridors. **Pets:** Small. No service, supervision, crate.
ASK 🔲 ✕ 🔲 🔲

(AAA) ◆◆ Red Roof Inn-Cranberry M
(724) 776-5670. **$55-$76.** 20009 Rt 19. I-76 and I-79 at SR 19. Ext corridors. **Pets:** Medium. No service, supervision, crate.
SAVE ✕ 🔲

WASHINGTON

(AAA) ◆◆◆ Holiday Inn-Meadow Lands M
(724) 222-6200. **$95-$95.** 340 Race Track Rd. I-79 N, exit 8B (Race Track Rd), 0.5 mi e; I-79 S, exit 8 (Meadow Lands), 1.5 mi e. Int corridors. **Pets:** Medium. No service, supervision, crate.
SAVE 🔲 ✕ 🔲 🔲 🔲 🔲 🔲 🔲

(AAA) ◆◆ Motel 6–1283 M
(724) 223-8040. **$38-$54.** 1283 Motel 6 Dr. I-70, exit 7A, 0.5 mi s on US 19. Ext corridors. **Pets:** Small. No service, supervision, crate.
⟨SD⟩ ⟨X⟩ ⟨cat⟩ ⟨≈⟩

(AAA) ◆◆ Red Roof Inn M
(724) 228-5750. **$50-$69.** 1399 W Chestnut St. I-70, exit 4, just e on US 40. Ext/int corridors. **Pets:** Small. Supervision.
⟨SAVE⟩ ⟨X⟩ ⟨cat⟩ ⟨H⟩

❀   **END METROPOLITAN AREA**   ❀

PITTSTON

(AAA) ◆◆ Knights Inn-Scranton/Pittston M ❀
(570) 654-6020. **$35-$46.** 310 SR 315. Just s on SR 315 from I-81, northbound exit 48, southbound exit 48A, and Pennslyvania Tpke NE Extension exit 37. Ext corridors. **Pets:** Medium, other. No service, supervision, crate.
⟨SAVE⟩ ⟨SD⟩ ⟨X⟩ ⟨H⟩

POCONO MOUNTAINS
METROPOLITAN AREA

BARTONSVILLE

◆◆◆ Holiday Inn MI ❀
(570) 424-6100. **Call for rates.** Rt 611 & I-80. I-80, exit 46B, just n. Int corridors. **Pets:** Other. No service, supervision, crate.
⟨X⟩ ⟨🐾⟩ ⟨H⟩ ⟨💻⟩ ⟨❖⟩ ⟨≈⟩

BLAKESLEE

(AAA) ◆◆◆ Blue Berry Mountain Inn BB ❀
(570) 646-7144. **$90-$135, 90 days notice.** Edmund Dr. I-80, exit 43, 3.5 mi n on SR 115, just ne on Thomas Rd, then to the end of Edmund Dr. Int corridors. **Pets:** Other. $50 deposit/room. Designated rooms, no service, supervision, crate.
⟨SAVE⟩ ⟨X⟩ ⟨H⟩ ⟨💻⟩ ⟨≈⟩ ⟨X⟩ ⟨Z⟩

EAST STROUDSBURG

(AAA) ◆◆◆ Budget Motel MI ❀
(570) 424-5451. **$45-$80.** I-80, exit 51. At jct I-80 exit 51, just se on Greentree Rd. Ext/int corridors. **Pets:** Other. $20 deposit/room. Designated rooms, supervision.
⟨X⟩ ⟨H⟩ ⟨❖⟩

◆◆ Super 8 Motel M ❀
(570) 424-7411. **$62-$82.** 340 Green Tree Dr. I-80, exit 51, just se. Int corridors. **Pets:** Small. $25 deposit/room. Designated rooms, no service, supervision, crate.
⟨ASK⟩ ⟨SD⟩ ⟨X⟩ ⟨cat⟩ ⟨H⟩

HAMLIN

(AAA) ◆◆◆ Comfort Inn M ❀
(570) 689-4148. **$79-$109.** SR 191. I-84, exit 5, just n. Int corridors. **Pets:** Other. $5 daily fee/pet. No service, supervision, crate.
⟨SAVE⟩ ⟨SD⟩ ⟨X⟩ ⟨H⟩ ⟨💻⟩

HAWLEY

(AAA) ◆◆ The Falls Port Inn & Restaurant CI ❀
(570) 226-2600. **$75-$100.** 330 Main Ave. At Main Ave (US 6) and Church St. Int corridors. **Pets:** Medium. $20 daily fee/room. No service, supervision, crate.
⟨SAVE⟩ ⟨X⟩ ⟨❖⟩ ⟨Z⟩

LAKE HARMONY

(AAA) ◆◆ Days Inn & Suites M ❀
(570) 443-0391. **$65-$95.** I-80, exit 42 and Pennsylvania Tpke (I-476) exit 35, 2.8 mi e on SR 940. Ext corridors. **Pets:** Small. $5 daily fee/pet. No service, supervision, crate.
⟨SAVE⟩ ⟨SD⟩ ⟨X⟩ ⟨🐾⟩ ⟨H⟩ ⟨💻⟩

(AAA) ◆◆◆ Ramada Inn-Pocono MI ❀
(570) 443-8471. **$90-$110, 3 days notice.** On SR 940, 0.5 mi e of I-80, exit 42 and turnpike exit 35. Int corridors. **Pets:** $50 deposit/room. Supervision.
⟨SAVE⟩ ⟨SD⟩ ⟨X⟩ ⟨🐾⟩ ⟨cat⟩ ⟨H⟩ ⟨💻⟩ ⟨❖⟩ ⟨≈⟩ ⟨X⟩

MARSHALLS CREEK

(AAA) ◆ Value Inn M
(570) 588-1100. **$49-$109.** 5219 Milford Rd. On US 209, 7.2 mi n of I-80, exit 52. Ext/int corridors. **Pets:** Large. Supervision.
⟨SAVE⟩ ⟨SD⟩ ⟨X⟩ ⟨H⟩ ⟨≈⟩ ⟨X⟩ ⟨Z⟩

MATAMORAS

(AAA) ◆◆◆ Best Western Inn at Hunt's Landing MI ❀
(570) 491-2400. **$62-$119.** 120 Rt 6 & 209. At jct I-84, exit 11. Int corridors. **Pets:** No service, supervision, crate.
⟨SAVE⟩ ⟨SD⟩ ⟨X⟩ ⟨🐾⟩ ⟨H⟩ ⟨💻⟩ ⟨❖⟩ ⟨≈⟩ ⟨X⟩

MILFORD

AAA ◆◆◆ Cliff Park Inn & Golf Course **CI**
(570) 296-6491. **$90-$175, 5 days notice.** 155 Cliff Park Rd. I-84, exit 10, 2 mi e on US 6, just s on 7th St, 1.5 mi w on SR 2001, then 0.5 mi s. Int corridors. **Pets:** Designated rooms, supervision.
SAVE ⊠ 🛈 ⊠

AAA ◆ Milford Motel **M**
(570) 296-6411. **$50-$80, 3 days notice.** 591 Rt 6 & 209. 0.7 mi e on SR 6 E and SR 209 N. Ext corridors. **Pets:** Supervision.
SAVE S⊘ ⊠ 🛈 ⌂ ⊠

AAA ◆◆ Myer Motel **C** ❀
(570) 296-7223. **$50-$88.** 600 Rt 6 & 209. 0.5 mi ne on US 6 and 209. Ext corridors. **Pets:** $20 deposit/room. Designated rooms, no service, supervision, crate.
SAVE S⊘ ⊠ 🛈

AAA ◆◆ Red Carpet Inn-Milford **M** ❀
(570) 296-9444. **$55-$99, 3 days notice.** 240 Rt 6. Just s of I-84, exit 10. Ext corridors. **Pets:** Medium. $5 daily fee/pet. Designated rooms, no service, supervision, crate.
SAVE S⊘ ⊠

AAA ◆ Tourist Village Motel **M**
(570) 491-4414. **$48-$78.** Pike US 6 & 209. I-84, exit 11, 1 mi s. Ext corridors. **Pets:** Supervision.
SAVE S⊘ ⊠ 🛈 ⚌

❀ **END METROPOLITAN AREA** ❀

PUNXSUTAWNEY

◆◆ Pantall Hotel **H** ❀
(814) 938-6600. **$59-$103.** 135 E Mahoning St. Downtown; on US 119 and SR 36, just across the park from "Punxsutawney Phil". Int corridors. **Pets:** Medium. $100 deposit/room. Designated rooms, supervision.
⊠ 🍴

READING

AAA ◆◆◆ Best Western Dutch Colony Inn & Suites **M** ❀
(610) 779-2345. **$78-$108, 3 days notice.** 4635 Perkiomen Ave. On US 422, 0.3 mi e of jct US 422 business route. Ext/int corridors. **Pets:** Small, other. $5 daily fee/pet. Designated rooms, no service, supervision, crate.
SAVE S⊘ ⊠ ⚲ 🛈 ⚌ 🍴 ⌂ ⊠

◆◆ Econo Lodge **M** ❀
(610) 378-1145. **$42-$68.** 2310 Fraver Dr. Just off US 222 business route (5th St), s of Warren St bypass (SR 12 E). Ext corridors. **Pets:** Small, dogs only. Designated rooms, supervision.
ASK S⊘ ⊠ ⚌

SELINSGROVE

AAA ◆◆ Comfort Inn **M** ❀
(570) 374-8880. **$69-$99.** 710 S US Hwy 11 & 15. Just n of jct US 522. Int corridors. **Pets:** Other. $10 one-time fee/room. Supervision.
SAVE S⊘ ⊠

SHAMOKIN DAM

AAA ◆◆◆ Hampton Inn **M** ❀
(570) 743-2223. **$70-$80.** 3 Stettler Ave. On US 11 and 15, 1 mi s of jct SR 61. Int corridors. **Pets:** Other. $25 one-time fee/room. No service, supervision, crate.
SAVE S⊘ ⊠ 🏠 ⚴ 🛈 ⚌ ⌂

SHARTLESVILLE

AAA ◆ Dutch Motel **M** ❀
(610) 488-1479. **$32-$47.** 1 Motel Dr. Nw of Shartlesville exit (exit 8) off I-78 and US 22. Ext corridors. **Pets:** Dogs only. $3 daily fee/pet, $3 one-time fee/pet. No service, supervision, crate.
SAVE ⊠

SHICKSHINNY

◆◆ The Blue Heron Bed & Breakfast **BB**
(570) 864-3740. **$60-$90** (no credit cards), 7 days notice. RR 2, Box 2212. 6.2 mi n on SR 239 from jct Rt 11, 2 mi n on CR 4016. Int corridors. **Pets:** Supervision.
⊠ ⚴ 📺

SLIPPERY ROCK

◆ Evening Star Motel **M**
(724) 794-3211. **$40-$49.** 915 New Castle Rd. On SR 108, 0.5 mi e of I-79, exit 30. Ext corridors. **Pets:** No service, supervision, crate.
⊠ ⚌

SOUTH WILLIAMSPORT

AAA ◆◆ Ridgemont Motel **M** ❀
(570) 321-5300. **$33-$37.** 637 US 15. 1.2 mi s on US 15. Ext corridors. **Pets:** Designated rooms, no service, supervision, crate.
⊠ 🛈

ST. MARYS

◆◆◆ Comfort Inn **M** ❀
(814) 834-2030. **$55-$55.** 976 S St. Marys Rd. S end of town on SR 255. Int corridors. **Pets:** Other. Supervision.
ASK S⊘ ⊠ ⚲ ⚴ 🛈 ⌂

STATE COLLEGE

♦♦ Autoport Motel 🅼 ❀
(814) 237-7666. **$65-$75.** 1405 S Atherton St. On US 322 business route, 1.4 mi e of jct SR 26. Ext/int corridors. **Pets:** $10 daily fee/pet. No service, supervision, crate.

[SAVE] [S🖥] [✕] [💻] [🍴] [🛎]

♦♦ Brewmeister's Motel 🅼 ❀
(814) 238-0015. **$40-$70.** 2070 Cato Ave. On SR 26, 2.6 mi s of jct US 322 business route. Ext corridors. **Pets:** Other. $7 daily fee/pet. No service, supervision, crate.

[ASK] [S🖥] [✕] [🖱] [🔒]

♦♦♦ Days Inn Penn State 🅷 ❀
(814) 238-8454. **$59-$90.** 240 S Pugh St. Downtown; just e of SR 26 northbound, 0.4 mi n of jct US 322 business route. Int corridors. **Pets:** Small. $10 daily fee/pet. No service, supervision, crate.

[SAVE] [S🖥] [✕] [🖱] [🔒] [🍴] [🛎]

♦♦ Motel 6 State College 🅼 ❀
(814) 234-1600. **$53-$70.** 1274 N Atherton St. US 322 business route, 1 mi w of jct SR 26. Int corridors. **Pets:** Small, other. No service, supervision, crate.

[✕] [♿] [🖱] [🔒]

♦♦♦ Ramada Inn-State College 🅼 ❀
(814) 238-3001. **$95-$175.** 1450 S Atherton St. On US 322 business route, 1.4 mi e of jct SR 26. Ext/int corridors. **Pets:** Other. $10 daily fee/room. Designated rooms, no service, supervision, crate.

[ASK] [S🖥] [✕] [💻] [🍴] [🛎]

WARREN

♦♦♦ Holiday Inn of Warren 🅼 ❀
(814) 726-3000. **$79-$79.** 210 Ludlow St. 1.5 mi w on US 6; at Ludlow St exit. Int corridors. **Pets:** Very small. No service, supervision, crate.

[SAVE] [S🖥] [✕] [🖱] [🔒] [💻] [🍴] [🛎]

♦♦ Warren Super 8 Motel 🅼
(814) 723-8881. **$50-$62, 7 days notice.** 204 Struthers St. 1.5 mi w on US 6, at Ludlow St exit, s on Allegheny. Ext/int corridors. **Pets:** Small. No service, supervision, crate.

[ASK] [S🖥] [✕] [🔒]

WAYNESBORO

♦♦ Best Western Waynesboro 🅼
(717) 762-9113. **$53-$72, 3 days notice.** 239 W Main St. 0.5 mi w on SR 16. Ext corridors. **Pets:** Small. Supervision.

[SAVE] [S🖥] [✕] [🔒] [🍴]

WAYNESBURG

♦♦♦ Comfort Inn 🅼 ❀
(724) 627-3700. **$59-$79.** 100 Comfort Ln. I-79, exit 3, just e. Int corridors. **Pets:** Medium. No service, supervision, crate.

[ASK] [S🖥] [✕] [🖱] [🔒] [🔒] [💻]

♦♦ Econo Lodge 🅼
(724) 627-5544. **$40-$77.** 350 Miller Ln. Jct I-79, exit 3, just w. Ext corridors. **Pets:** Medium. No service, supervision, crate.

[ASK] [S🖥] [✕] [🔒] [💻]

♦♦ Super 8 Motel-Waynesburg 🅼
(724) 627-8880. **Call for rates.** 80 Miller Ln. Jct I-79, exit 3, just w. Int corridors. **Pets:** Medium. No service, supervision, crate.

[✕] [🔒] [💻]

WELLSBORO

♦♦♦ Canyon Motel 🅼 ❀
(570) 724-1681. **$30-$52.** 18 East Ave. Just e on US 6 and SR 660. Ext/int corridors. **Pets:** Designated rooms, no service, supervision, crate.

[✕] [🔒] [🔒] [💻] [🛎] [✕]

♦ Colton Point Motel 🅼 ❀
(570) 724-2155. **$30-$55, 7 days notice.** 13 mi w on US 6 from jct Rt 287. Ext/int corridors. **Pets:** Other. $5 one-time fee/pet. No service, supervision, crate.

[SAVE] [S🖥] [✕] [🍴] [✕] [🅰] [✕]

WEST HAZLETON

♦♦♦ Comfort Inn-West Hazleton 🅼 ❀
(570) 455-9300. **$85-$119.** SR 93 & Kiwanis Blvd. 0.3 mi se of I-81, exit 41; 3.8 mi se of I-80, exit 38. Int corridors. **Pets:** Other. Supervision.

[SAVE] [S🖥] [✕] [🖱] [🔒] [💻] [🍴]

♦♦♦ Forest Hill Inn 🅼 ❀
(570) 459-2730. **$47-$52.** Rt 93. On SR 93, 0.3 mi se of I-81, exit 41; 3.8 mi se of I-80, exit 38. Ext corridors. **Pets:** Other. No service, supervision, crate.

[SAVE] [S🖥] [✕]

WEST MIDDLESEX

♦♦♦ Radisson Hotel Sharon 🅼 ❀
(724) 528-2501. **$90-$110.** Rt 18 & I-80. I-80, exit 1 N, just s on SR 18. Int corridors. **Pets:** Very small. Supervision.

[ASK] [S🖥] [✕] [🖱] [🔒] [🔒] [💻] [🍴] [🛎]

♦♦ Shenango Valley Comfort Inn 🅼 ❀
(724) 342-7200. **Call for rates.** SR 18 & Wilson Rd. I-80, exit 1N, just n. Int corridors. **Pets:** $10 one-time fee/room. No service, supervision, crate.

[✕] [🔒] [🛎] [CTV]

WILKES BARRE

♦♦♦ Best Western Genetti Hotel & Convention Center 🅷
(570) 823-6152. **$59-$89.** 77 E Market St. At Market and Washington sts. Int corridors. **Pets:** No service, supervision, crate.

[SAVE] [S🖥] [✕] [🔒] [🍴] [🛎]

♦♦ Days Inn 🅼 ❀
(570) 826-0111. **$52-$59.** 760 Kidder St. I-81, exit 47B, then exit 1, Rt 309 S business, just w; Pennsylvania Tkpe, exit 36, Rt 115 N, exit 1. Int corridors. **Pets:** Other. $5 daily fee/pet. Supervision.

[SAVE] [S🖥] [✕] [🔒]

◆◆◆ Hampton Inn Wilkes-Barre at Cross Creek Pointe M ❀

(570) 825-3838. **$58-$75.** 1063 Hwy 315. 0.3 mi n of jct I-81, exit 47B. Int corridors. **Pets:** Small. No service, supervision, crate.

ASK S⊘ ✕ 🐾 ▭

◆◆◆ Holiday Inn MI ❀

(570) 824-8901. **$84-$84.** 880 Kidder St. I-81, exit 47B, then exit 1 off expwy, 0.5 mi w. Ext corridors. **Pets:** Other. Supervision.

ASK S⊘ ✕ ♿ ♿ ▤ ▭ 🍴 ➣

◆◆ Red Roof Inn M

(570) 829-6422. **$46-$78.** 1035 Hwy 315. At jct SR 115, 0.7 mi w of I-81, exit 1 on to SR 315. Ext corridors. **Pets:** Medium. Supervision.

SAVE ✕ ▤

WILLIAMSPORT

◆◆◆ Genetti Hotel & Suites H ❀

(570) 326-6600. **$95-$175.** 200 W Fourth St. Downtown, at W Fourth and William sts. Int corridors. **Pets:** Dogs only. Supervision.

SAVE S⊘ ✕ ▤ 🍴 ➣

◆◆ Holiday Inn-Williamsport MI ❀

(570) 326-1981. **$79.** 1840 E Third St. Jct I-180 and US 220, Faxon St exit, just e on Third St eastbound, 1 mi w of Third St exit westbound. Ext corridors. **Pets:** Medium. No service, supervision, crate.

ASK S⊘ ✕ ▤ ▭ 🍴 ➣

◆◆◆ Radisson Hotel Williamsport H ❀

(570) 327-8231. **$79-$79.** 100 Pine St. Downtown, at jct US 220 and SR 15S. Int corridors. **Pets:** Small. No service, supervision, crate.

ASK S⊘ ✕ ▤ ▭ 🍴 ➣

WIND GAP

◆◆ Travel Inn of Wind Gap M

(610) 863-4146. **$45-$90.** 499 E Moorestown Rd. On SR 512, e of jct SR 33, Bath exit. Ext corridors. **Pets:** Supervision.

SAVE S⊘ ✕ ▤

WYOMISSING

◆◆◆ Clarion/Inn at Reading MI ❀

(610) 372-7811. **$89-$139.** 1040 Park Rd. US 422, Papermill Rd exit, 0.5 mi s, then just s on Spring St to Park Rd. Int corridors. **Pets:** Small. $50 deposit/room. Designated rooms, no service, supervision, crate.

SAVE S⊘ ✕ 🐾 ▤ ▭ 🍴 ➣ ✕

◆◆ Econo Lodge M

(610) 378-5105. **$49-$89.** 635 Spring St. Just off US 422, Papermill Rd exit. Int corridors. **Pets:** Small. Supervision.

SAVE S⊘ ✕ 🐾 ▤ ▭

◆◆◆ Sheraton Berkshire Hotel H ❀

(610) 376-3811. **$89-$199.** 1741 W Papermill Rd. From US 422, exit Papermill Rd, opposite Berkshire Mall. Int corridors. **Pets:** Medium, other. Supervision.

ASK S⊘ ✕ 🐾 ▤ ▭ 🍴 ➣ ✕

◆◆◆ Wellesley Inn & Suites M ❀

(610) 374-1500. **$55-$129.** 910 Woodland Ave. US 422 W, Papermill Rd exit, just e. Int corridors. **Pets:** Other. $5 daily fee/pet. Designated rooms, no service, supervision, crate.

SAVE S⊘ ✕ 🐾 🐾 ▤ ▭

WYSOX

◆◆◆ Comfort Inn M ❀

(570) 265-5691. **$72-$100.** US 6. Center. Int corridors. **Pets:** Other. $10 one-time fee/room. No service, supervision, crate.

ASK S⊘ ✕ 🐾 ▤ ➣

YORK

◆◆◆ Holiday Inn Holidome & Conference Center MI ❀

(717) 846-9500. **$102-$102.** 2000 Loucks Rd. I-83 northbound, exit 9 W, 2.5 mi w on US 30, just n on SR 74; I-83 southbound, exit 10, 0.5 mi s on SR 181, 2.2 mi w on US 30, just n. Int corridors. **Pets:** Other. No service, supervision, crate.

ASK S⊘ ✕ 🐾 ♿ ▭ 🍴 ➣ ✕

◆◆ Red Roof Inn M

(717) 843-8181. **$50-$68.** 323 Arsenal Rd. I-83, exit 9E, just e on US 30. Ext corridors. **Pets:** Small. No service, supervision, crate.

SAVE ✕

◆◆ Super 8 Motel M ❀

(717) 852-8686. **$48-$76.** 40 Arsenal Rd. I-83 northbound, exit 9W, 0.3 mi w on US 30; I-83 southbound, exit 10, 0.5 mi s on SR 181 to US 30. Int corridors. **Pets:** Other. $5 daily fee/room. Designated rooms, supervision.

ASK S⊘ ✕ ▤

RHODE ISLAND

MIDDLETOWN

 ◆ **The Bay Willows Inn** Ⓜ
(401) 847-8400. **$39-$169, 3 days notice.** 1225 Aquidneck Ave. SR 138A, at jct of SR 138 (E Main Rd). Ext corridors. **Pets:** Medium. Supervision.

⊠ 🅗

 ◆◆ **Howard Johnson Inn-Newport** Ⓜ 🐾
(401) 849-2000. **$99-$179.** 351 W Main Rd. On SR 114, 0.3 mi s of jct SR 138. Int corridors. **Pets:** Other. Designated rooms, supervision.

⟨SAVE⟩ ⟨S⟩ ⊠ 🅗 ▱ 🖾 ⊠ ⟨CTV⟩

 ◆ **SeaView Inn** Ⓜ 🐾
(401) 846-5000. **$59-$189, 3 days notice.** 240 Aquidneck Ave. SR 138A at jct SR 214. Ext corridors. **Pets:** $25 deposit/room, $10 daily fee/room. Supervision.

⊠ 🅗 ▱ ⊠

 ◆◆ **Travel Lodge** Ⓜ
(401) 849-4700. **$40-$160.** 1185 W Main Rd. SR 114, 1.1 mi n of jct SR 138. Ext/int corridors. **Pets:** Designated rooms, no service, supervision, crate.

⟨SAVE⟩ ⟨S⟩ ⊠

NEWPORT

 ◆ **Motel 6–1219** Ⓜ 🐾
(401) 848-0600. **$60-$76.** 249 J T Connell Hwy. 0.3 mi nw of Newport Bridge; near Newport Mall. Int corridors. **Pets:** Small, other. No service, supervision, crate.

⟨S⟩ ⊠ 🖾 🖾 ⟨CTV⟩

PORTSMOUTH

 ◆◆ **Founder's Brook Motel & Suites** Ⓧ 🐾
(401) 683-1244. **$69-$149, 3 days notice.** 314 Boyd's Ln. On SR 138 at jct SR 24, Mt Hope Bridge exit. Ext corridors. **Pets:** $20 one-time fee/room. Designated rooms, no service, supervision, crate.

⟨SAVE⟩ ⟨S⟩ ⊠ 🅗 ▱

PROVIDENCE

 ◆◆◆◆ **The Westin Providence** 🅗
(401) 598-8000. **$265-$315.** One W Exchange St. Downtown; I-95, exit 22. Int corridors. **Pets:** Supervision.

⟨SAVE⟩ ⟨S⟩ ⊠ ⟨⟩ 🖾 🖾 ▱ ⟨⟩ 🖾

SOUTH KINGSTOWN

◆◆◆ **The Kings' Rose Bed & Breakfast Inn** ⟨BB⟩ 🐾
(401) 783-5222. **$80-$145** (no credit cards). 1747 Mooresfield Rd. SR 138, 10.5 mi e of I-95, exit 3A, 3.3 mi w of US 1. Int corridors. **Pets:** Supervision.

⊠ ⊠ 🅘

WARWICK

◆◆ **Comfort Inn-Airport** Ⓜ
(401) 732-0470. **$99-$149.** 1940 Post Rd. On US 1; from I-95 airport exit 13 and Post Rd N. Int corridors. **Pets:** Supervision.

⟨ASK⟩ ⟨S⟩ ⊠ 🅗

◆◆◆ **Crowne Plaza Hotel** 🅗 🐾
(401) 732-6000. **$199-$209, 3 days notice.** 801 Greenwich Ave. SR 5, 0.3 mi e of I-95, exit 12A southbound; exit 12 northbound. Int corridors. **Pets:** Small. $50 deposit/room. No service, supervision, crate.

⟨ASK⟩ ⟨S⟩ ⊠ ⟨⟩ 🖾 🅗 ⟨⟩ 🖾

 ◆◆◆ **MainStay Suites, Warwick** Ⓜ
(401) 732-6667. **$120.** 268 Metro Center Blvd. I-95, exit 12, 0.4 mi e on SR 113, 0.4 mi n on SR 5, then 0.4 mi e. Int corridors. **Pets:** Medium. Designated rooms, no service, supervision, crate.

⟨SAVE⟩ ⟨S⟩ ⊠ 🖾 ⟨⟩ 🅗 ▱ ⊠

◆◆ **Master Hosts Inn** Ⓜ
(401) 737-7400. **$69-$160.** 2138 Post Rd. US 1, from I-95, airport exit 13 and Post Rd N. Int corridors. **Pets:** Designated rooms, no service, supervision, crate.

⟨ASK⟩ ⟨S⟩ ⊠ 🅗

◆◆◆ **Residence Inn by Marriott** Ⓐ 🐾
(401) 737-7100. **$143-$170.** 500 Kilvert St. I-95, exit 13 (TF Green Airport), to Jefferson Blvd, 0.3 mi n on Jefferson Blvd, then 0.5 mi w. Ext corridors. **Pets:** $25 one-time fee/room. No service, supervision, crate.

⟨ASK⟩ ⟨S⟩ ⊠ ⟨⟩ ▱ 🖾 ⊠

◆◆◆ **Sheraton Providence Airport Hotel** 🅗
(401) 738-4000. **$125-$250.** 1850 Post Rd. On US 1, from I-95 airport exit 13 and Post Rd N. Int corridors. **Pets:** Medium. Supervision.

⟨ASK⟩ ⟨S⟩ ⊠ ⟨⟩ 🅗 ▱ ⟨⟩ 🖾

SOUTH CAROLINA

CITY INDEX

AIKEN

◆◆ Comfort Inn & Suites M
(803) 641-1100. **$44-$64.** 3608 Richland Ave W. 2.3 mi w on US 1 and 78. Ext corridors. **Pets:** No service, supervision, crate.

◆◆ Days Inn-Downtown M ❄
(803) 649-5524. **$38-$45, 7 days notice.** 1204 Richland Ave W. 0.5 mi w on US 1 and 78. Ext corridors. **Pets:** Small. $10 daily fee/pet. No service, supervision, crate.

◆◆◆ Holiday Inn Express M ❄
(803) 648-0999. **$75.** 155 Colony Pkwy. US 78 and 1, 2 mi s on SR 19 off Whiskey/SR 19. Ext corridors. **Pets:** Medium, other. $25 one-time fee/room. No service, supervision, crate.

◆◆ Town & Country Inn BB ❄
(803) 642-0270. **$60-$95.** 2340 Sizemore Cir. From US 1 downtown, 4.5 mi s on SR 19, just w. Int corridors. **Pets:** Other. $50 deposit/room. Supervision.

ANDERSON

◆◆ Days Inn M ❄
(864) 375-0375. **Call for rates.** 1007 Smith Mill Rd. I-85 exit 19A, US 76, se corner. Ext corridors. **Pets:** Small. $7 daily fee/pet. No service, supervision, crate.

◆◆◆ Holiday Inn Express M ❄
(864) 231-0231. **$89, 3 days notice.** 103 Anderson Business Park. I-85 and SR 81, exit 27. Int corridors. **Pets:** Very small, dogs only. $50 deposit/room. No service, supervision, crate.

◆◆◆ La Quinta Inn M
(864) 225-3721. **$49-$79.** 3430 Clemson Blvd. I-85 exit 19A, 2.5 mi s. Ext corridors. **Pets:** Small. Supervision.

◆◆◆ Quality Inn-Anderson M
(864) 226-1000. **$62-$68, 3 days notice.** 3509 Clemson Blvd. I-85 exit 19A, 2 mi s. Int corridors. **Pets:** Supervision.

BEAUFORT

◆◆ Days Inn-Port Royal M ❄
(843) 524-1551. **Call for rates.** 1660 Ribaut Rd. 4 mi s on US 21, then 0.5 mi on SR 802 W. Ext corridors. **Pets:** $20 one-time fee/pet. Designated rooms, no service, supervision, crate.

◆◆◆ Holiday Inn of Beaufort M
(843) 524-2144. **Call for rates.** 2001 Boundary St. 2.5 mi nw on US 21 at Lovejoy St. Ext corridors. **Pets:** Supervision.

◆◆◆ Howard Johnson Express Inn M
(843) 524-6020. **$65-$80.** 3651 Trask Pkwy. US 21, 1.3 mi n of SR 170. Int corridors. **Pets:** Small. Supervision.

CAMDEN

◆◆◆ Colony Inn M ❄
(803) 432-5508. **$49-$55.** 2020 W DeKalb St. 1 mi w on US 1 and 601. Ext corridors. **Pets:** Small. $10 one-time fee/room. No service, supervision, crate.

◆◆ Lord Camden Inn BB ❄
(803) 713-9050. **$70-$110** (no credit cards), 5 days notice. 1502 Broad St. 0.5 mi n of US 1/521 on US 521. Int corridors. **Pets:** Other. $10 daily fee/room. Supervision.

CHARLESTON METROPOLITAN AREA

CHARLESTON

◆◆◆ Best Western Inn [M]
(843) 571-6100. **$89-$139.** 1540 Savannah Hwy. US 17, 2.5 mi w of Ashley River Bridge. Ext corridors. **Pets:** Supervision.

[ASK] [S☾] [✕] [🛏] [🖼]

◆◆◆ Doubletree Guest Suites [M]
(843) 577-2644. **$139-$269.** 181 Church St. At N Market and Church sts. Int corridors. **Pets:** Medium. Designated rooms, no service, supervision, crate.

[ASK] [✕] [☾] [🛏] [▣]

⚑ ◆◆◆ Holiday Inn-Riverview [M] ✿
(843) 556-7100. **$99-$145.** 301 Savannah Hwy. 1.8 mi w on US 17, s of bridge. Int corridors. **Pets:** Other. Supervision.

[SAVE] [✕] [▣] [🍴] [🖼]

◆◆◆ Indigo Inn [BB] ✿
(843) 577-5900. **$140-$235.** 1 Maiden Ln. Corner Meeting and Pinckney sts. Ext corridors. **Pets:** Other. $20 daily fee/pet. Supervision.

[✕] [☾]

⚑ ◆◆◆ Sheraton Charleston Hotel [H] ✿
(843) 723-3000. **$127-$152.** 170 Lockwood Dr. 1 mi n on US 17 S. Int corridors. **Pets:** Small. $50 deposit/room. Designated rooms, supervision.

[SAVE] [✕] [🛏] [▣] [🍴] [🖼]

◆◆◆ Town & Country Inn & Conference Center [M]
(843) 571-1000. **$69-$119.** 2008 Savannah Hwy. On US 17; 3.5 mi n of Ashley River Bridge. Ext corridors. **Pets:** Supervision.

[✕] [▣] [🍴] [🖼] [✕]

MOUNT PLEASANT

◆◆◆ Comfort Inn East [M] ✿
(843) 884-5853. **$69-$139.** 310 Hwy 17 bypass. On US 17; just e of Cooper River Bridge. Ext corridors. **Pets:** Small, dogs only. $10 one-time fee/room. Supervision.

[ASK] [✕] [▣] [🖼]

⚑ ◆◆ Red Roof Inn #242 [M] ✿
(843) 884-1411. **$53-$107.** 301 Johnnie Dodds Blvd. On US 17; just e of Cooper River Bridge. Ext corridors. **Pets:** Medium, other. Supervision.

[SAVE] [✕] [☾] [☾] [🛏] [🖼]

NORTH CHARLESTON

◆◆ Charleston Super 8 Motel [M] ✿
(843) 572-2228. **$50-$60.** 2311 Ashley-Phosphate Rd. I-26 exit 209. Ext corridors. **Pets:** Large. Supervision.

[ASK] [✕] [🖼]

◆◆ Comfort Inn Coliseum [M] ✿
(843) 554-6485. **$40-$99.** 5055 N Arco Ln. Jct I-26 and Montague Ave, exit 213, 3.8 mi from airport via Montague Ave. Ext corridors. **Pets:** Small, other. $6 daily fee/pet. No service, supervision, crate.

[ASK] [✕] [☾] [🛏] [▣] [🖼]

⚑ ◆◆◆ La Quinta Inn [M]
(843) 797-8181. **$59-$95.** 2499 La Quinta Ln. Nw on I-26, exit 209. Ext corridors. **Pets:** Small. No service, supervision, crate.

[SAVE] [✕] [☾] [☾] [🛏] [▣] [🖼]

⚑ ◆◆ Red Roof Inn [M]
(843) 572-9100. **$48-$58.** 7480 Northwoods Blvd. I-26 exit 209. Ext corridors. **Pets:** No service, supervision, crate.

[SAVE] [✕] [☾] [🛏]

SUMMERVILLE

◆◆◆ Holiday Inn Express-Charleston/Summerville [M] ✿
(843) 875-3300. **$99.** 120 Holiday Inn Dr. I-26 at jct US 17A, exit 199A. Int corridors. **Pets:** Medium. Supervision.

[✕] [☾] [🛏] [▣] [🖼]

✿ END METROPOLITAN AREA ✿

CHERAW

⚑ ◆◆ Days Inn–Cheraw [M] ✿
(843) 537-5554. **$40-$125, 3 days notice.** 820 Market St. Jct US 9, 52 and 1. Ext corridors. **Pets:** Other. $5 daily fee/pet, $5 one-time fee/pet. Supervision.

[SAVE] [S☾] [✕] [🛏] [▣] [🖼]

⚑ ◆◆ Inn Cheraw [M]
(843) 537-2011. **$40-$42.** 321 Second St. Downtown on US 1/52 and SR 9. Ext corridors. **Pets:** Supervision.

[SAVE] [S☾] [✕] [🛏] [▣]

CLEMSON

◆◆◆ Comfort Inn-Clemson [M] ✿
(864) 653-3600. **$49-$199.** 1305 Tiger Blvd. At jct US 76 and SR 123. Int corridors. **Pets:** Supervision.

[ASK] [S☾] [✕] [☾] [🛏] [▣] [🖼]

◆◆ Holiday Inn [M] ✿
(864) 654-4450. **$65-$99, 3 days notice.** 894 Tiger Blvd. 1 mi e on US 76, 123 and SR 28. Ext corridors. **Pets:** Medium. Supervision.

[ASK] [S☾] [✕] [🛏] [▣] [🍴] [🖼] [✕]

CLINTON

⊕ ◆◆ Comfort Inn Ⓜ ❀
(864) 833-5558. **$48-$60.** 12785 Hwy 56 N. N of I-26, exit 52. Ext corridors. **Pets:** Small. $10 daily fee/pet. Designated rooms, supervision.
[SAVE] [✕] [🐾] [🖥] [🖵] [🖎]

⊕ ◆◆ Days Inn Ⓜ ❀
(864) 833-6600. **$48-$55.** 12374 Hwy 56 N. I-26 exit 52. Ext corridors. **Pets:** Small, other. $10 daily fee/room, $10 one-time fee/pet. Supervision.
[SAVE] [✕] [🖵] [🖎]

⊕ ◆◆ Ramada Inn Ⓜ
(864) 833-4900. **$59-$89.** I-26 and SR 56, exit 52. Ext corridors. **Pets:** Medium. Designated rooms, no service, supervision, crate.
[SAVE] [S🖵] [✕] [🐾] [🖵] [🍽] [🖎]

COLUMBIA

⊕ ◆◆◆ AmeriSuites Ⓜ
(803) 736-6666. **$99, 6 days notice.** 7525 Two Notch Rd. US 1 at jct I-20, exit 74. Int corridors. **Pets:** Designated rooms, no service, supervision, crate.
[SAVE] [✕] [🐾] [🖥] [🖵] [🖎]

◆◆ Baymont Inn & Suites-Columbia East Ⓜ
(803) 736-6400. **$50-$56.** 1538 Horseshoe Dr. On US 1 (Two Notch Rd) at jct I-20, exit 74. Int corridors. **Pets:** Medium. Designated rooms, no service, supervision, crate.
[✕] [🖵] [🖵] [🖎]

◆◆◆ Baymont Inn & Suites-Columbia West Ⓜ ❀
(803) 798-3222. **$46-$46.** 911 Bush River Rd. Jct I-26 and Bush River Rd (exit 108). Int corridors. **Pets:** Medium. $50 deposit/room. Supervision.
[✕] [🖵] [🖵] [🖎]

◆◆◆ Holiday Inn-Coliseum at USC Ⓗ ❀
(803) 799-7800. **$99-$113.** 630 Assembly St. 0.5 mi s on US 21, 176, 321 and SR 215. Int corridors. **Pets:** Small. No service, supervision, crate.
[ASK] [✕] [🐾] [🖵] [🖵] [🍽] [🖎]

◆◆◆ Holiday Inn-Northeast Ⓜ
(803) 736-3000. **Call for rates.** 7510 Two Notch Rd. On US 1 (Two Notch Rd) at jct I-20, exit 74. Int corridors. **Pets:** Small. Designated rooms, supervision.
[ASK] [✕] [🖵] [🖵] [🍽] [🖎]

⊕ ◆◆◆ La Quinta Inn Ⓜ ❀
(803) 798-9590. **$49-$79.** 1335 Garner Ln. Jct I-20 and US 176, exit 65. Ext corridors. **Pets:** Small, other. No service, supervision, crate.
[SAVE] [✕] [🖵] [🖵] [🖎]

⊕ ◆◆ Motel 6-1404 Ⓜ ❀
(803) 798-9210. **$37-$53.** 1776 Burning Tree Rd. I-26 exit 106 and St Andrews Rd. Ext corridors. **Pets:** Small, other. No service, supervision, crate.
[✕] [🖎]

⊕ ◆◆◆ Ramada Plaza Hotel Ⓜ ❀
(803) 736-5600. **$79-$94.** 8105 Two Notch Rd. On US 1 and I-77, 0.5 mi from I-20, exit 74. Int corridors. **Pets:** Small. $50 deposit/room. Supervision.
[SAVE] [✕] [🖵] [🖵] [🍽] [🖎]

⊕ ◆◆ Red Roof Inn-East Ⓜ
(803) 736-0850. **$50-$64.** 7580 Two Notch Rd. On US 1 (Two Notch Rd) at jct I-20, exit 74. Ext corridors. **Pets:** Small. No service, supervision, crate.
[SAVE] [✕]

⊕ ◆◆ Red Roof Inn-West Ⓜ
(803) 798-9220. **$37-$64.** 10 Berryhill Rd. I-26 and St Andrews Rd, westbound exit 106A; eastbound exit 106. Ext corridors. **Pets:** No service, supervision, crate.
[SAVE] [✕] [CTV]

◆◆◆ Residence Inn by Marriott Ⓜ ❀
(803) 779-7000. **$130.** 150 Stoneridge Dr. 0.6 mi ne of I-126, exit Greystone Blvd. Ext corridors. **Pets:** Other. $10 daily fee/room. Designated rooms, supervision.
[ASK] [✕] [🐾] [🖵] [🖵] [🖎] [✕]

⊕ ◆◆◆ Sheraton Hotel & Conference Center Ⓗ
(803) 731-0300. **$135-$155.** 2100 Bush River Rd. Jct I-20 and Bush River Rd, exit 63. Int corridors. **Pets:** Supervision.
[SAVE] [S🖵] [✕] [🖵] [🖵] [🍽] [🖎]

⊕ ◆◆ Super 8 Motel Ⓜ
(803) 796-4833. **$40-$65, 3 days notice.** 2516 Augusta Rd. Jct I-26 and US 1, exit 111B. Ext/int corridors. **Pets:** Medium. Supervision.
[SAVE] [✕] [🖵] [🖎] [CTV]

⊕ ◆◆ Travelodge Columbia West Ⓜ
(803) 798-9665. **$55-$65.** 2210 Bush River Rd. At jct I-20, exit 63. Ext/int corridors. **Pets:** Medium. Designated rooms, no service, supervision, crate.
[SAVE] [S🖵] [✕] [🖵] [🖵] [🖎]

DILLON

⊕ ◆◆◆ Comfort Inn Ⓜ ❀
(843) 774-4137. **$53-$75.** 810 Radford Blvd. On SR 9, at jct I-95 exit 193. Ext corridors. **Pets:** Very small. No service, supervision, crate.
[SAVE] [✕] [🖵] [🖎]

⊕ ◆◆ Super 8 Motel Ⓜ ❀
(843) 774-4161. **$40-$99, 30 days notice.** 1203 Radford Blvd. I-95 exit 193 and SR 9. Ext corridors. **Pets:** Small. $5 daily fee/pet, $5 one-time fee/pet. No service, supervision, crate.
[SAVE] [✕] [🖵] [🖎]

EASLEY

◆◆ Days Inn Ⓜ
(864) 859-9902. **$48-$125.** 121 Days Inn Dr. On US 123 bypass; 0.5 mi e of jct SR 93. Ext corridors. **Pets:** Medium. No service, supervision, crate.
[ASK] [S🖵] [✕] [🐾] [🖵] [🖵] [🖎]

FLORENCE

Days Inn South ◆ ❖
(843) 665-8550. **$35-$54, 5 days notice.** 3783 W Palmetto St. I-95 exit 157, 0.4 mi e on US 76. Ext corridors. **Pets:** Small. $6 daily fee/pet. Supervision.

Econo Lodge ◆◆
(843) 665-8558. **$45-$60, 7 days notice.** 1811 W Lucas St. On US 52; just s of jct I-95, exit 164. Ext corridors. **Pets:** Small. Designated rooms, supervision.

Howard Johnson Express ◆◆◆ ❖
(843) 664-9494. **$57-$145.** 3821 Bancroft Rd. I-95 exit 157, 0.4 mi e on US 76. Ext corridors. **Pets:** $10 one-time fee/room. Designated rooms, supervision.

Motel 6–1250 ◆◆
(843) 667-6100. **$35-$51.** 1834 W Lucas St. I-95 exit 164, just e on US 52. Ext corridors. **Pets:** No service, supervision, crate.

Park Inn International ◆◆
(843) 662-9421. **$36-$44.** 831 S Irby St. 1.3 mi s on US 301 and 52. Ext corridors. **Pets:** Small. No service, supervision, crate.

Quality Inn/I-95 ◆ ❖
(843) 669-1715. **$40-$50.** 3024 TV Rd. I-95 exit 169, 0.3 mi w. Ext corridors. **Pets:** Large, other. $5 daily fee/room. No service, supervision, crate.

Ramada Inn ◆◆◆ ❖
(843) 669-4241. **$79-$79, 30 days notice.** 2038 W Lucas St. On US 52; at jct I-95, exit 164. Ext/int corridors. **Pets:** Other. Designated rooms, no service, supervision, crate.

Red Roof Inn ◆◆ ❖
(843) 678-9000. **$40-$72.** 2690 David McLeod Blvd. I-95 exit 160A, 0.4 mi e I-20 business spur. Ext corridors. **Pets:** Other. Supervision.

Thunderbird Motor Inn ◆◆
(843) 669-1611. **$36-$44.** 2004 W Lucas. I-95 exit 164, just w. Ext corridors. **Pets:** Designated rooms, no service, supervision, crate.

Young's Plantation Inn ◆◆ ❖
(843) 669-4171. **$29-$33, 3 days notice.** US 76 & I-95. I-95 exit 157, just w on US 76. Ext corridors. **Pets:** Other. $4 daily fee/pet. Supervision.

GAFFNEY

Comfort Inn ◆◆ ❖
(864) 487-4200. **$65-$95, 30 days notice.** 143 Corona Dr. Jct I-85 and SR 11, exit 92. Ext corridors. **Pets:** Other. $10 one-time fee/room. Supervision.

Days Inn ◆◆ ❖
(864) 489-7172. **Call for rates.** 136 Peachoid Rd. I-85 SR 11, exit 92. Ext corridors. **Pets:** Other. $8 one-time fee/pet. Supervision.

GREENVILLE

AmeriSuites Greenville ◆◆◆
(864) 232-3000. **$79-$125** (no credit cards). 40 W Orchard Park Dr. I-385 at Haywood Rd, exit 39. Int corridors. **Pets:** Small. No service, supervision, crate.

Comfort Inn Executive Center ◆◆◆ ❖
(864) 271-0060. **$59-$64.** 540 N Pleasantburg Dr. I-385 exit 40B. Ext corridors. **Pets:** Medium. No service, supervision, crate.

Crowne Plaza-Greenville ◆◆◆ ❖
(864) 297-6300. **$59-$149.** 851 Congaree Rd. On I-385 at jct Roper Mountain Rd, exit 37. Int corridors. **Pets:** Other. $100 one-time fee/room. Supervision.

Days Inn ◆◆ ❖
(864) 288-6221. **$55-$89, 3 days notice.** 831 Congaree Rd. 0.4 mi sw of I-385, exit 37. Int corridors. **Pets:** $15 one-time fee/room. No service, supervision, crate.

GuestHouse Suites Plus ◆◆◆
(864) 297-0099. **$108-$108.** 48 McPrice Ct. Off I-385 at Haywood Rd, exit 39. Ext corridors. **Pets:** Supervision.

Holiday Inn I-85 ◆◆◆
(864) 277-8921. **$84-$84.** 4295 Augusta Rd. I-85 exit 45A. Int corridors. **Pets:** Medium. No service, supervision, crate.

Howard Johnson Lodge & Suites ◆◆
(864) 288-6900. **Call for rates.** 2756 Laurens Rd. Just n of I-85, exit 48B. Int corridors. **Pets:** No service, supervision, crate.

La Quinta Inn ◆◆◆ ❖
(864) 297-3500. **$49-$79.** 31 Old Country Rd. On SR 146 at jct I-85, exit 51 Woodruff Rd. Ext corridors. **Pets:** Small, other. No service, supervision, crate.

Microtel Inn Greenville ◆◆ ❖
(864) 297-7866. **$52-$62, 7 days notice.** 20 Interstate Court. At jct I-85, exit 54 and Pelham Rd. Int corridors. **Pets:** $10 deposit/room. Supervision.

▲▲▲ The Phoenix, Greenville's Inn Ⓜ 🐾
(864) 233-4651. **$65-$130, 3 days notice.** 246 N Pleasant-burg Dr. On SR 291; 0.5 mi s of jct I-385. Ext corridors. **Pets:** Other. No service, supervision, crate.
[SAVE] [✕] [🖉] [🖥] [🖳] [🎧]

▲▲ Ramada Limited Ⓜ 🐾
(864) 277-3734. **$46-$46.** 1314 S Pleasantburg Dr. 0.5 mi n of I-85, exit 45B, on SR 291. Ext corridors. **Pets:** Other. $25 deposit/room. Supervision.
[ASK] [S🖉] [✕] [🖥] [🎧]

▲▲ Red Roof Inn Ⓜ
(864) 297-4458. **$46-$58.** 2801 Laurens Rd. On s frontage road, just s of I-85, exit 48A. Ext corridors. **Pets:** Medium. No service, supervision, crate.
[SAVE] [✕] [🖍]

GREER

▲▲▲ Comfort Suites–Greenville Ⓜ 🐾
(864) 213-9331. **$69-$89.** 2681 Dry Pocket Rd. From jct I-85 exit 54, 0.4 mi on The Parkway, 0.2 mi on Parkway Rd East. Int corridors. **Pets:** Medium. $25 daily fee/pet. Desig-nated rooms, no service, supervision, crate.
[SAVE] [S🖉] [✕] [🖉] [🖒] [🖥] [🖳] [🎧]

▲▲▲ MainStay Suites-Greenville Ⓜ 🐾
(864) 987-5566. **$49-$89.** 2671 Dry Pocket Rd. From jct I-85 exit 54, 0.4 mi on The Parkway, 0.2 mi on parkway Rd East. Int corridors. **Pets:** Medium, other. $50 deposit/pet, $5 daily fee/pet. No service, supervision, crate.
[SAVE] [S🖉] [✕] [🖥] [🖳] [🎧]

HARDEEVILLE

▲▲▲ Holiday Inn Express Ⓜ
(843) 784-2221. **$75-$75, 30 days notice.** I-95 exit 5 and US 17N, 0.8 mi n on US 17. Ext corridors. **Pets:** Small. Designated rooms, no service, supervision, crate.
[SAVE] [✕] [🖉] [🖒] [🖥] [🎧]

HILTON HEAD ISLAND

▲▲ Bayshore of Hilton Head Ⓒ🅾
(843) 842-9494. **$500-$6000, 60 days notice.** 81 Pope Ave, Heritage Plaza. Hwy 278 to Pope Ave; in the rear of Heritage Plaza above the Swiss Cookery Restaurant. Ext corridors. **Pets:** Small. Designated rooms, no service, supervision, crate.
[SAVE] [✕] [🖥] [🖳] [🎧] [✕]

▲▲▲ Comfort Inn & Suites Ⓜ🄸 🐾
(843) 842-6662. **$60-$159.** 2 Tanglewood Dr. Via US 278E to Sea Pines Cir, 0.3 mi n via Pope Ave and S Forest Beach Dr. Int corridors. **Pets:** Medium. $10 daily fee/room, $25 one-time fee/pet. No service, supervision, crate.
[SAVE] [✕] [🖉] [🖥] [🖳] [🍽] [🎧] [✕]

▲▲▲ Quality Inn & Suites of Hilton Head Island Ⓜ
(843) 681-3655. **Call for rates.** 200 Museum St. On US 278, just e of Island Bridge on n side of road. Ext corridors. **Pets:** Supervision.
[ASK] [✕] [🖉] [🖥] [🖳] [🎧] [✕]

▲▲ Red Roof Inn-Hilton Head Ⓜ
(843) 686-6808. **$66-$87.** 5 Regency Pkwy. On US 278; between Shipyard Plantation and Palmetto Dunes. Ext corridors. **Pets:** Medium. Supervision.
[SAVE] [✕] [🖉] [🖥] [🎧]

LANDRUM

▲▲▲ The Red Horse Inn Ⓒ 🐾
(864) 895-4968. **$105-$125, 7 days notice.** 310 N Camp-bell Rd. 1 mi w on SR 11 from jct SR 14, 1 mi s on Tugaloo Rd to N Campbell Rd. Ext corridors. **Pets:** Small. $50 deposit/pet. Designated rooms, no service, supervision, crate.
[ASK] [✕] [🖥] [🖳] [✕] [CTV]

LEXINGTON

▲▲ Ramada Limited Ⓜ 🐾
(803) 356-6533. **$50-$60, 3 days notice.** 1015 S Lake Dr. From I-20 exit 55 at jct of I-20 and SR 6. Ext corridors. **Pets:** Small, other. Supervision.
[SAVE] [S🖉] [✕] [🖒] [🖍] [🖥] [🖳] [🎧]

LUGOFF

▲▲▲ Ramada Limited Ⓜ
(803) 438-1807. **$48-$65** (no credit cards). 542 Hwy 601 S. I-20 exit 92, 0.5 mi w. Ext corridors. **Pets:** Medium. No service, supervision, crate.
[ASK] [S🖉] [✕] [🎧]

MANNING

▲▲ Comfort Inn Ⓜ 🐾
(803) 473-7550. **$48-$70, 7 days notice.** Hwy 261 & I-95. Jct I-95 and SR 261, exit 119. Ext corridors. **Pets:** Other. Supervision.
[SAVE] [✕] [🎧]

▲▲ Days Inn of Manning Ⓜ 🐾
(803) 473-2913. **$44-$74.** Rt 5 Box 448. From I-95 exit 115. Ext/int corridors. **Pets:** Other. $5 daily fee/pet, $5 one-time fee/pet. Designated rooms, no service, supervision, crate.
[SAVE] [✕] [🖥] [🎧]

NEWBERRY

▲▲ Best Western Newberry Inn Ⓜ 🐾
(803) 276-5850. **$40-$50.** 11701 S Carolina Hwy 34. On SR 34 at jct I-26, exit 74. Ext corridors. **Pets:** Small, other. $5 daily fee/room. No service, supervision, crate.
[✕] [🖥] [🎧] [✕]

ORANGEBURG

▲▲▲ Quality Inn & Suites Ⓜ🄸 🐾
(803) 531-4600. **$60-$74.** 1415 John C Calhoun Dr. 0.8 mi w on US 301 and 601. Ext corridors. **Pets:** Small. $10 daily fee/pet, $10 one-time fee/pet. No service, supervision, crate.
[ASK] [✕] [🖍] [🖉] [🖥] [🖳] [🍽] [🎧]

POINT SOUTH

◆◆◆ Holiday Inn Express Point
South/Yemassee M ❧
(843) 726-9400. **$69–$69.** 40 Frampton Dr. I-95 exit 33 and US 17. Int corridors. **Pets:** $10 one-time fee/room. Supervision.

[ASK] [✕] [🏠] [✍] [🍴] [💻] [🐾]

RICHBURG

◆◆ Days Inn M
(803) 789-5555. **$31–$65.** 3217 Lancaster Hwy. I-77 exit 65 and SR 9, just s. Ext corridors. **Pets:** Large. Supervision.

[ASK] [✕] [🍴] [🐾]

🆗 ◆◆ Super 8 Motel M ❧
(803) 789-7888. **$44–$79, 7 days notice.** 3085 Lancester Hwy. I-77 exit 65 and SR 9 N. Ext corridors. **Pets:** Small, other. $3 daily fee/pet. No service, supervision, crate.

[SAVE] [✕] [🍴] [🐾]

RIDGELAND

🆗 ◆◆◆ Comfort Inn M ❧
(843) 726-2121. **$45–$86.** Hwy 336–I-95. I-95 and US 278 exit 21. Ext/int corridors. **Pets:** Small, other. Supervision.

[SAVE] [✕] [🔇] [🍴] [🐾]

ROCK HILL

🆗 ◆◆◆ Best Western Inn MI ❧
(803) 329-1330. **$60–$72, 30 days notice.** 1106 N Anderson Rd. I-77 exit 82B, 0.6 mi w on US 21 to US 21 bypass. Int corridors. **Pets:** Small. $10 daily fee/pet. No service, supervision, crate.

[SAVE] [✕] [🍴] [💻] [🍴] [🐾]

◆◆◆ The Book & the Spindle BB ❧
(803) 328-1913. **$65–$85, 7 days notice.** 626 Oakland Ave. From I-77 exit 82B, 3.5 mi s on US 21; opposite Winthrop University. Int corridors. **Pets:** Small, other. No service, supervision, crate.

[✕] [💻] [🔇]

◆◆◆ Holiday Inn MI ❧
(803) 329-1122. **$74–$89.** 2640 N Cherry Rd. I-77 exit 82A. Int corridors. **Pets:** Other. $15 one-time fee/room. Supervision.

[ASK] [✕] [🔇] [🍴] [💻] [🍴] [🐾]

SANTEE

🆗 ◆◆◆ Comfort Inn M ❧
(803) 854-3221. **$60–$125.** 265 Britain St. I-95 exit 98 and SR 6. Ext corridors. **Pets:** $10 one-time fee/room. Supervision.

[SAVE] [✕] [🍴] [💻] [🐾]

◆◆ Days Inn M ❧
(803) 854-2175. **$45–$74.** 9078 Old Hwy 6. At jct I-95 and SR 6, exit 98. Ext corridors. **Pets:** Other. $6 daily fee/pet. Supervision.

[ASK] [✕] [🔇] [🍴] [🐾] [✕]

🆗 ◆◆◆ Ramada Inn MI ❧
(803) 854-2191. **$58.** 123 Mall Dr. On SR 6 at jct I-95, exit 98. Ext corridors. **Pets:** Other. Supervision.

[SAVE] [S🔇] [✕] [💻] [🍴] [🐾] [✕]

◆◆ Super 8 Motel M
(803) 854-3456. **$29–$31, 5 days notice.** 9125 Old Hwy 6. Off jct I-95, exit 98; 0.3 mi e on SR 6. Ext corridors. **Pets:** Small. Supervision.

[ASK] [S🔇] [✕] [🐾]

SPARTANBURG

🆗 ◆◆◆ The Quality Hotel & Conference
Center MI ❧
(864) 503-0780. **$59–$69.** 7136 Asheville Hwy. At jct Business I-85 and Hearon Cir, exit 4. Int corridors. **Pets:** Small. Designated rooms, supervision.

[SAVE] [✕] [🍴] [💻] [🍴] [🐾]

🆗 ◆◆◆ Ramada Inn MI ❧
(864) 576-5220. **$66–$76, 3 days notice.** 200 International Dr. Jct I-26 exit 19 and Business I-85, exit 2C from Business I-85. Ext/int corridors. **Pets:** Medium, other. $25 one-time fee/room. Supervision.

[SAVE] [S🔇] [✕] [🔇] [✍] [🍴] [💻] [🍴] [🐾]

ST. GEORGE

◆◆ Comfort Inn M ❧
(843) 563-4180. **$50–$55.** 139 Motel Dr. Jct I-95 and US 78, exit 77. Ext corridors. **Pets:** $15 one-time fee/pet. Supervision.

[ASK] [S🔇] [✕] [🔇] [💻] [🐾]

🆗 ◆ Economy Inn of America M ❧
(843) 563-4195. **$30–$60.** 5971 W Jim Bilton Blvd. On US 78 at jct I-95, exit 77. Ext corridors. **Pets:** Small. $10 deposit/room, $3 daily fee/pet. Designated rooms, no service, supervision, crate.

[SAVE] [S🔇] [✕] [🐾]

◆◆◆ Holiday Inn-St George MI ❧
(843) 563-4581. **$70–$95.** 6014 W Jim Bilton Blvd. At jct I-95 and US 78, exit 77. Ext corridors. **Pets:** Supervision.

[ASK] [S🔇] [✕] [✍] [💻] [🍴] [🐾]

🆗 ◆ St. George Economy Motel M ❧
(843) 563-2360. **$27–$45.** 125 Motel Dr. On US 78 at jct I-95, exit 77. Ext corridors. **Pets:** Small. Supervision.

[SAVE] [✕] [🐾]

🆗 ◆◆ Super 8 Motel M
(843) 563-5551. **$37–$41.** 114 Winningham Rd. On US 78 at jct 95, exit 77. Ext corridors. **Pets:** Supervision.

[SAVE] [✕] [🐾]

SUMTER

◆◆◆ Magnolia House BB ❧
(803) 775-6694. **$75–$85, 3 days notice.** 230 Church St. US 521/US 378 N Washington St, w on Calhoun, then right. Int corridors. **Pets:** Designated rooms, no service, supervision, crate.

[✕]

🆗 ◆◆◆ Ramada Inn MI ❧
(803) 775-2323. **$59–$89.** 226 N Washington St. 0.5 mi n on US 76 and 521 business route. Ext corridors. **Pets:** Small. $100 deposit/room. Supervision.

[SAVE] [✕] [🔇] [🍴] [💻] [🍴] [🐾] [✕]

THE GRAND STRAND METROPOLITAN AREA

MYRTLE BEACH

AAA ◆◆ **El Dorado Motel** M ❀
(843) 626-3559. **$59-$69, 21 days notice.** 2800 S Ocean Blvd. 28th Ave S and S Ocean Blvd. Ext corridors. **Pets:** Small, dogs only. $50 deposit/room, $10 daily fee/pet, $10 one-time fee/pet. No service, supervision, crate.
SAVE 🛏 🐾

AAA ◆◆◆ **La Quinta Inn & Suites** M ❀
(843) 916-8801. **$85-$159.** 1261 21st Ave N. Just e of US Bypass 17, 1.4 mi n of US 501. Int corridors. **Pets:** Small. Supervision.
SAVE ⊠ ♿ 📋 🐾 🛏 🖥 🐾

AAA ◆◆ **St. John's Inn** M ❀
(843) 449-5251. **$79-$105, 8 days notice.** 6803 N Ocean Blvd. 68th Ave N and N Ocean Blvd. Ext corridors. **Pets:** Medium, dogs only. $50 deposit/room, $10 daily fee/pet. Designated rooms, supervision.
SAVE 🆘 ⊠ 🛏 🍴 🐾

AAA ◆◆ **The Sea Mist Resort** R
(843) 448-1551. **$68-$295, 7 days notice.** 1200 S Ocean Blvd. 1.5 mi s, 12th Ave S and S Ocean Blvd. Ext/int corridors. **Pets:** Designated rooms, no service, supervision, crate.
⊠ 📋 🛏 🍴 🐾 ⊠

❀ END METROPOLITAN AREA ❀

TRAVELERS REST

AAA ◆◆ **Sleep Inn** M ❀
(864) 834-7040. **$48-$70.** 110 Hawkins Rd. From Hwy 25 at Hawkins Rd exit. Int corridors. **Pets:** Medium, other. $25 deposit/pet. No service, supervision, crate.
SAVE 🆘 ⊠ ♿ 📋 🍴 🛏 🖥 🐾

UNION

AAA ◆◆◆ **Comfort Inn** M ❀
(864) 427-5060. **$50-$65.** 315 N Duncan Bypass, Hwy 176. On US 176 and SR 215. Int corridors. **Pets:** Small. $25 deposit/pet, $10 daily fee/pet. Designated rooms, no service, supervision, crate.
SAVE 🆘 ⊠ 🍴 🖥 🛏 🖥 🐾

WALTERBORO

AAA ◆◆ **Best Western of Walterboro** M ❀
(843) 538-3600. **$45-$75.** 1428 Sniders Hwy. Jct I-95 and SR 63, exit 53. Ext corridors. **Pets:** Small. $5 daily fee/pet. Designated rooms, no service, supervision, crate.
SAVE 🆘 ⊠ 🐾

AAA ◆◆ **Econo Lodge** M ❀
(843) 538-3830. **$40-$65.** 1145 Sniders Hwy. I-95 exit 53. Ext corridors. **Pets:** Medium, other. Designated rooms, no service, supervision, crate.
SAVE ⊠ 🖥

AAA ◆◆◆ **Holiday Inn** M ❀
(843) 538-5473. **$75-$75.** 1286 Snider's Hwy. At jct I-95 and SR 63, exit 53. Ext corridors. **Pets:** Medium. $10 one-time fee/room. Designated rooms, no service, supervision, crate.
SAVE 🆘 ⊠ 📋 🖥 🖥 🍴 🐾

AAA ◆ **Rice Planters Inn** M ❀
(843) 538-8964. **$25-$40.** I-95 & SR 63. Jct I-95 and SR 63, exit 53. Ext corridors. **Pets:** Small. Supervision.
SAVE ⊠ 🐾

AAA ◆◆ **Super 8 Motel** M
(843) 538-5383. **$37-$55.** 1972 Bells Hwy. On Hwy 64 at jct I-95, exit 57. Ext corridors. **Pets:** Medium. Supervision.
SAVE ⊠ 🐾

AAA ◆ **Thunderbird Inn** M
(843) 538-2503. **$25-$36.** Jct I-95 and SR 63, exit 53. Ext corridors. **Pets:** Supervision.
SAVE 🆘 ⊠

WEST COLUMBIA

◆◆ **Holiday Inn Columbia Airport** M ❀
(803) 794-9440. **$80.** 500 Chris Dr. On US 1 at jct I-26; exit 111B. Ext corridors. **Pets:** Medium, other. $100 deposit/room, $25 one-time fee/room. Designated rooms, no service, supervision, crate.
ASK 🆘 ⊠ 📋 🛏 🖥 🍴 🐾 ⊠

AAA ◆◆◆ **Ramada Inn West** M ❀
(803) 796-2700. **$65-$75.** 114 McSwain Dr. At jct I-26 and US 378, exit 110. Ext/int corridors. **Pets:** Small. $25 one-time fee/room. Designated rooms, no service, supervision, crate.
SAVE ⊠ 🛏 🍴 🐾 ⊠

WINNSBORO

AAA ◆◆ **Days Inn** M ❀
(803) 635-1447. **$36-$54, 8 days notice.** 1894 US Hwy 321 Bypass. At jct SR 34 and 213; from jct I-77 6 mi w on SR 34. Ext corridors. **Pets:** Small. $5 daily fee/pet, $5 one-time fee/pet. Designated rooms, no service, supervision, crate.
SAVE ⊠ 🛏 🖥 🐾

SOUTH DAKOTA

CITY INDEX

ABERDEEN

◆◆ **Aberdeen East Super 8 Motel** Ⓜ ❖
(605) 229-5005. **$45-$55, 7 days notice.** 2405 6th Ave SE.
1.8 mi e on US 12. **Pets:** Large, other. Designated rooms,
no service, supervision, crate.

◆◆ **Aberdeen North Super 8 Motel** Ⓜ ❖
(605) 226-2288. **$45-$55, 7 days notice.** 770 NW Hwy
281. 1.5 mi nw on US 281. **Int** corridors. **Pets:** Other.
Designated rooms, no service, supervision, crate.

◆ **Aberdeen West Super 8 Motel** Ⓜ ❖
(605) 225-1711. **$38-$48, 7 days notice.** 714 S Hwy 281.
Jct US 12 and 281. Int corridors. **Pets:** Large, other. Designated rooms, no service, supervision, crate.

◆◆◆ **Best Western Ramkota Hotel** Ⓜ
(605) 229-4040. **$61-$85.** 1400 8th Ave NW. 1.5 mi nw on
US 281. Ext/int corridors. **Pets:** Supervision.

⍟ ◆ **Breeze-Inn Motel** Ⓜ
(605) 225-4222. **$29-$38.** 1216 6th Ave SW. 1 mi w on US
12/281. Ext corridors. **Pets:** Supervision.

⍟ ◆◆◆ **Comfort Inn** Ⓜ
(605) 226-0097. **$52-$57.** 2923 6th Ave SE. 2 mi e on US
12. Int corridors. **Pets:** Medium. No service, supervision,
crate.

⍟ ◆◆ **Ramada Inn** Ⓜ ❖
(605) 225-3600. **$61-$69.** 2727 6th Ave SE. 2 mi e on US
12. Ext/int corridors. **Pets:** Other. Supervision.

◆ **The White House Inn** Ⓜ
(605) 225-5000. **Call for rates.** 500 6th Ave SW. 0.5 mi w
on US 12 and 281. Int corridors. **Pets:** Small. Designated
rooms, supervision.

BADLANDS NATIONAL PARK

⍟ ◆ **Cedar Pass Lodge** Ⓒ ❖
(605) 433-5460. **$41-$45.** 1 Cedar St. On SR 240, at Visitor's Center, 8 mi s from I-90, exit 131. Ext corridors.
Pets: No service, supervision, crate.

BELLE FOURCHE

⍟ ◆ **Ace Motel** Ⓜ ❖
(605) 892-2612. **$25-$48.** 109 6th Ave. 0.5 mi n via US 85,
just e, just s of 212 bypass. Ext corridors. **Pets:** Medium. $4
one-time fee/pet. Designated rooms, no service, supervision, crate.

⍟ ◆ **Lariat Motel** Ⓜ ❖
(605) 892-2601. **$39-$42.** 1033 Elkhorn. 0.8 mi e of US 85
on Business 212 (State St). Ext corridors. **Pets:** Large,
other. $3 daily fee/room. No service, supervision, crate.

◆ **Super 8 Motel** Ⓜ
(605) 892-3361. **$60-$85, 7 days notice.** 501 National St.
Just e of US 85, s side of town. Int corridors. **Pets:** No
service, supervision, crate.

BRANDON

◆◆◆ **Holiday Inn Express of Brandon** Ⓜ ❖
(605) 582-2901. **$95, 3 days notice.** 1105 N Split Rock
Blvd. Just s of I-90, exit 406. Int corridors. **Pets:** Other. $10
one-time fee/room. No service, supervision, crate.

BROOKINGS

◆◆◆ **Brookings Super 8 Motel** Ⓜ
(605) 692-6920. **$45-$61, 30 days notice.** 3034 Lefevre Dr.
I-29, exit 132, just e. Int corridors. **Pets:** Medium. No service, supervision, crate.

⍟ ◆◆ **Staurolite Inn & Suites** Ⓜ ❖
(605) 692-9421. **$44-$67.** 2515 E 6th St. I-29, exit 132.
Ext/int corridors. **Pets:** Other. Designated rooms, no service, supervision, crate.

BUFFALO

◆ **Tipperary Lodge** Ⓜ ❄
(605) 375-3721. **$32-$36.** 604 First St W. 0.5 mi n on US 85, turn at sign. Int corridors. **Pets:** Small. Supervision. ⊠

CANISTOTA

🆔 ◆◆ **Best Western U-Bar Motel** Ⓜ
(605) 296-3466. **$42-$68.** 130 Ash St. I-90, exit 368, 6 mi s, follow signs. Ext corridors. **Pets:** Large. Supervision.
SAVE Ⓢ ⊠ 🖥 🖨

CHAMBERLAIN

🆔 ◆ **Alewel's Lake Shore Motel** Ⓜ ❄
(605) 734-5566. **Call for rates.** 115 N River St. Just n of US 16 bridge (the northernmost bridge). Ext corridors. **Pets:** Small. No service, supervision, crate.
SAVE ⊠ ⊠

🆔 ◆ **Bel Aire Motel** Ⓜ
(605) 734-5595. **$35-$64.** 312 E King St. Downtown on US 16 and I-90 business loop, exit 263 and 265. Ext/int corridors. **Pets:** No service, supervision, crate.
SAVE Ⓢ ⊠

🆔 ◆◆◆ **Cedar Shore Resort** Ⓡ ❄
(605) 734-6376. **$79-$139.** 101 Geo Mickelson Shoreline Dr. I-90, exit 260, 2.5 mi e on Business 90, 1 mi ne on Mickelson county road following signs. Int corridors. **Pets:** $10 daily fee/pet. No service, supervision, crate.
SAVE Ⓢ ⊠ 🐾 📶 🖥 🖨 🐾 ⊠

◆◆ **Days Inn of Oacoma** Ⓜ
(605) 734-4100. **Call for rates.** Just n of I-90, exit 260. Int corridors. **Pets:** Very small. No service, supervision, crate.
⊠ 🐾

🆔 ◆◆◆ **Oasis Inn** Ⓜ ❄
(605) 734-6061. **$57-$83.** W Hwy 16. 0.4 mi e of I-90, exit 260, on US 16 and I-90 business loop. Ext/int corridors. **Pets:** No service, supervision, crate.
SAVE Ⓢ ⊠ 🏠 📶 🖥 ⊠

CUSTER

🆔 ◆ **American Presidents Cabins, Campgrounds & Resort** Ⓒ ❄
(605) 673-3373. **$49-$77, 3 days notice.** Hwy 16 A. 1 mi e on US Alt 16. Ext corridors. **Pets:** No service, supervision, crate.
Ⓢ ⊠ 🖥 🐾 ⊠ 🖂

🆔 ◆◆◆ **Bavarian Inn Motel** Ⓜ
(605) 673-2802. **$72-$95, 3 days notice.** 1000 N Fifth St. 1 mi n on US 16 and 385. Ext/int corridors. **Pets:** Designated rooms, no service, supervision, crate.
⊠ 🖥 🖨 🐾 ⊠

🆔 ◆◆ **Chief Motel** Ⓜ ❄
(605) 673-2318. **$59-$87.** 120 Mt Rushmore Rd. Just w on US 16. Ext corridors. **Pets:** Medium. $5 daily fee/pet. Designated rooms, supervision.
⊠ 🐾

🆔 ◆ **The Roost Resort** Ⓒ ❄
(605) 673-2326. **$56-$68, 7 days notice.** US 16 A. 2 mi e on US Alt 16. Ext corridors. **Pets:** $20 deposit/room. No service, supervision, crate.
🖥 🖨 ⊠ 🖂

DAKOTA DUNES

🆔 ◆◆◆ **Country Inn & Suites By Carlson** Ⓜ
(605) 232-3500. **$71-$77.** 151 Tower Rd. Just w of I-29, exit 1. Int corridors. **Pets:** Medium. Supervision.
SAVE Ⓢ ⊠ 🏠 📶 🖥 🖨 🍴 🐾

DEADWOOD

🆔 ◆ **Budget Host Jackpot Inn** Ⓜ ❄
(605) 578-7791. **$59-$70.** US Hwy 385. 0.3 mi s of jct US 385 and 85. Int corridors. **Pets:** Small, dogs only. $10 daily fee/pet. No service, supervision, crate.
SAVE Ⓢ ⊠

🆔 ◆◆◆ **Days Inn at Deadwood Gulch Resort** Ⓜ ❄
(605) 578-1294. **$99-$145, 30 days notice.** 12 Timm Ln. 0.7 mi s on US 85 S. Ext/int corridors. **Pets:** $10 one-time fee/room. Supervision.
SAVE Ⓢ ⊠ 🍴 🐾 ⊠

🆔 ◆◆ **First Gold Hotel** Ⓜ ❄
(605) 578-9777. **$99-$139.** 270 Main St. 0.7 mi n on US 85. Ext/int corridors. **Pets:** Dogs only. $50 deposit/room. Designated rooms, no service, supervision, crate.
SAVE Ⓢ ⊠ 🖥 🖨 🍴

FAITH

◆◆ **Prairie Vista Inn** Ⓜ ❄
(605) 967-2343. **$49-$65.** Hwy 212. On US 212, at e city edge. Int corridors. **Pets:** Small. $50 deposit/room. No service, supervision, crate.
ASK Ⓢ ⊠ 🖥

FAULKTON

◆◆ **Super 8 Motel** Ⓜ
(605) 598-4567. **Call for rates.** 700 Main St. Center on US 212. Int corridors. **Pets:** Designated rooms, supervision.
⊠ 🖥

FORT PIERRE

🆔 ◆ **Fort Pierre Motel** Ⓜ ❄
(605) 223-3111. **$36-$48, 3 days notice.** 211 S First St. On US 83, 1.2 mi s of jct US 14. Ext corridors. **Pets:** Other. No service, supervision, crate.
SAVE Ⓢ ⊠ 🖥

◆◆◆ **Holiday Inn Express Hotel & Suites** Ⓜ ❄
(605) 223-9045. **$63-$63.** 110 E Stanley Rd. ON US 83, just s of jct US 14 and 34. Int corridors. **Pets:** Small, dogs only. $20 deposit/pet. Designated rooms, supervision.
ASK Ⓢ ⊠ 🏠 📶 🖥 🖥 🖨 🐾

FREEMAN

◆◆ Super 8 Motel
(605) 925-4888. **$47-$51.** 1019 S Hwy 81. Just s on US 81. Int corridors. **Pets:** Medium, dogs only. $50 deposit/pet, $4 daily fee/pet. Designated rooms, supervision.

HILL CITY

◆◆◆ Best Western Golden Spike Inn
(605) 574-2577. **$49-$127.** 106 Main St. Just n on US 16/385. Ext/int corridors. **Pets:** Other. Supervision.

◆◆ Lantern Inn Motel
(605) 574-2582. **$68-$92, 3 days notice.** 131 Main St. On n side of town, on US 16/385. Ext corridors. **Pets:** Small. $6 one-time fee/room. Designated rooms, no service, supervision, crate.

◆◆◆ The Lodge at Palmer Gulch
(605) 574-2525. **$105-$128.** 12620 SR 244. 5 mi w of Mt Rushmore. Int corridors. **Pets:** Other. No service, supervision, crate.

HOT SPRINGS

◆◆◆ Comfort Inn
(605) 745-7378. **$109-$149.** 737 S 6th St. 0.5 mi se off US 18 and 385. Int corridors. **Pets:** Small. Designated rooms, no service, supervision, crate.

◆◆ Hot Springs Super 8 Motel
(605) 745-3888. **$73-$91.** 800 Mammoth St. Hwy 18 truck bypass. Int corridors. **Pets:** $25 deposit/room. Designated rooms, supervision.

◆◆ Inn at Battle Mountain
(605) 745-3182. **$89-$89.** 402 Battle Mountain Ave. 1 mi n on US 385. Ext corridors. **Pets:** Medium. Designated rooms, no service, supervision, crate.

HURON

◆◆◆ Best Western of Huron
(605) 352-2000. **$70, 5 days notice.** 2000 Dakota Ave. 1.3 mi s on SR 37. Ext/int corridors. **Pets:** No service, supervision, crate.

◆◆◆ Holiday Inn Express
(605) 352-6655. **Call for rates.** 100 21st St SW. 1.3 mi s on SR 37. Ext/int corridors. **Pets:** $25 deposit/room, $25 one-time fee/room. No service, supervision, crate.

INTERIOR

◆ Badlands Budget Host Motel
(605) 433-5335. **$45-$50.** At jct SR 44 and 377, 2 mi s of Badlands National Park. Ext corridors. **Pets:** Designated rooms, supervision.

KADOKA

◆◆ Best Western H & H El Centro Motel
(605) 837-2287. **$62-$94.** 105 E Hwy 16. 1.5 mi w on I-90 business route, exit 150, 1.3 mi e from exit 150. Ext corridors. **Pets:** Other. Designated rooms, supervision.

◆ Dakota Inn
(605) 837-2151. **$40-$70.** I-90, exit 150. Ext corridors. **Pets:** Medium, other. $5 one-time fee/room. Designated rooms, no service, supervision, crate.

◆ Hill Top Motel
(605) 837-2216. **$45-$70.** E 225 Hwy 16. I-90, between exits 150 and 152, 0.3 mi s. Int corridors. **Pets:** Large, other. $5 one-time fee/room. Designated rooms, no service, supervision, crate.

◆ West Motel
(605) 837-2427. **$36-$60, 3 days notice.** 306 Hwy 16 W. I-90, exit 150, 1 mi e on I-90 business route. Ext corridors. **Pets:** Medium, other. $3 daily fee/room. No service, supervision, crate.

KEYSTONE

◆◆ Bed and Breakfast Inn
(605) 666-4490. **$75-$80.** 208 1st St. On SR 40, just e of US 16A jct. Ext corridors. **Pets:** Medium, other. $5 daily fee/pet. Supervision.

◆◆ Best Western Four Presidents Motel
(605) 666-4472. **$84-$94.** Hwy 16A. On US 16A, downtown. Ext/int corridors. **Pets:** Small, dogs only. $10 daily fee/pet. No service, supervision, crate.

◆◆◆ The First Lady Inn
(605) 666-4990. **$89-$99.** 702 Hwy 16A. On US 16A, w side of town. Ext/int corridors. **Pets:** Medium. No service, supervision, crate.

◆◆◆ Kelly Inn
(605) 666-4483. **$89-$99.** 320 Old Cemetary Rd. S on US 16A to Tramway, then just e. Ext/int corridors. **Pets:** No service, supervision, crate.

◆◆ **Mt Rushmore's White House Resort** 🅼 ❀
(605) 666-4917. **$55-$125, 3 days notice.** 115 Swanzey St. Jct US 16A and SR 40. Ext/int corridors. **Pets:** Medium, other. $10 daily fee/pet. Designated rooms, no service, supervision, crate.

🆂🅺 🆂🕖 ✖ 🅐 🅔 ❚ 🔲 🔄

◆◆ **Powder House Lodge** 🆇 ❀
(605) 666-4646. **$53-$135.** Hwy 16A. 1.5 mi n. Ext corridors. **Pets:** $6 daily fee/pet. No service, supervision, crate.

❚ 🔲 🔄 ✖

LEAD

🆔 ◆◆◆ **B W Golden Hills Resort & Convention Center** 🅷 ❀
(605) 584-1800. **$49-$119, 3 days notice.** 900 Miners Ave. Center; US 85 and 14A. Int corridors. **Pets:** Other. Supervision.

🆂🕖 ✖ 🅐 🄰 ❚ 🍴 🔄

🆔 ◆◆ **White House Inn** 🅼
(605) 584-2000. **$40-$115.** 395 Glendale Dr. 0.3 mi n on US 14A. Int corridors. **Pets:** No service, supervision, crate.

🆂🅰 🆂🕖 ✖ 🅐 🄰 🅔 ❚ 🔲

MADISON

◆ **Lake Park Motel** 🅼
(605) 256-3524. **$40-$52, 4 days notice.** 1515 NW 2nd St. 1 mi w on US 81 and SR 34. Ext corridors. **Pets:** Small. No service, supervision, crate.

🆂🅺 🆂🕖 ✖ ❚ 🔄

MILBANK

🆔 ◆ **Manor Motel** 🅼
(605) 432-4527. **$39-$49.** 1105 E 4th Ave. 0.8 mi e on US 12. Ext corridors. **Pets:** Supervision.

🆂🅰 🆂🕖 ✖ ❚ 🔄

MITCHELL

🆔 ◆ **Econo Lodge** 🅼
(605) 996-6647. **$49-$75.** 1313 S Ohlman. 0.5 mi n of I-90, exit 330. Int corridors. **Pets:** No service, supervision, crate.

🆂🅰 ✖ 🔲

◆◆◆ **Holiday Inn** 🅼
(605) 996-6501. **$100-$110.** 1525 W Havens St. 0.5 mi n of I-90, exit 330. Ext/int corridors. **Pets:** Small. No service, supervision, crate.

🆂🅺 🆂🕖 ✖ 🅐 🄰 🔲 🍴 🔄 ✖

MOBRIDGE

🆔 ◆◆ **Wrangler Motor Inn** 🅼 ❀
(605) 845-3641. **$51-$71.** 820 W Grand Crossing. 0.5 mi w on US 12. Ext/int corridors. **Pets:** Dogs only. No service, supervision, crate.

🆂🅰 🆂🕖 ✖ 🅔 🍴 🔄

MURDO

🆔 ◆◆ **Best Western Graham's** 🅼
(605) 669-2441. **$44-$79.** 301 W 5th. On I-90 business loop, 0.5 mi w of jct US 83; I-90, exit 191 and 192. Ext corridors. **Pets:** Designated rooms, no service, supervision, crate.

🆂🕖 ✖ 🔄 ✖

NORTH SIOUX CITY

◆◆ **Econo Lodge** 🅼 ❀
(605) 232-9600. **Call for rates.** 110 Sodrac Dr. I-29, exit 2. Int corridors. **Pets:** $10 one-time fee/room. Designated rooms, no service, supervision, crate.

✖ 🅔 ❚ 🔲

◆◆ **Hampton Inn** 🅼 ❀
(605) 232-9739. **$65-$80.** 101 S Sodrac Dr. I-29, exit 2. Int corridors. **Pets:** Medium. $20 daily fee/room. No service, supervision, crate.

🆂🅰 🆂🕖 ✖ 🅐 ❚ 🔲 🔄

◆◆ **Super 8 Motel** 🅼 ❀
(605) 232-4716. **$48-$116, 7 days notice.** 1300 River Dr. Just w of I-29, exit 2. Int corridors. **Pets:** Other. $10 one-time fee/pet. Designated rooms, no service, supervision, crate.

🆂🅺 🆂🕖 ✖ ❚

PICKSTOWN

🆔 ◆◆ **Fort Randall Inn** 🅼 ❀
(605) 487-7801. **$40-$57.** Hwy 18 & 281. Just e of the dam, on US 18/281. Ext corridors. **Pets:** Supervision.

🆂🅰 🆂🕖 ✖ ❚

PIEDMONT

🆔 ◆◆ **Elk Creek Resort & Lodge** 🅼
(605) 787-4884. **$99-$109.** Elk Creek Rd. 1 mi e of I-90, exit 46. Ext corridors. **Pets:** No service, supervision, crate.

🆂🅰 🆂🕖 ✖ ❚ 🔲 🔄 ✖ 📺

PIERRE

◆◆ **Best Western Kings Inn** 🅼 ❀
(605) 224-5951. **$49-$70.** 220 S Pierre St. Downtown; on US 14 and 83. Ext/int corridors. **Pets:** Large. $5 daily fee/room, $5 one-time fee/room. Supervision.

🆂🅺 ✖ ❚ 🔲 🍴

◆◆◆ **Best Western Ramkota Hotel** 🅼 ❀
(605) 224-6877. **$67-$80.** 920 W Sioux. 1 mi w on US 14 and 83. Ext/int corridors. **Pets:** Other. No service, supervision, crate.

🆂🅺 🆂🕖 ✖ 🅐 🄰 🅔 ❚ 🔲 🍴 🔄

🆔 ◆ **Budget Host Inn/State Motel** 🅼 ❀
(605) 224-5896. **$38-$50, 7 days notice.** 640 N Euclid Ave. 0.5 mi n on US 14 and 83. Ext corridors. **Pets:** Dogs only. No service, supervision, crate.

✖ ❚ 🔄

◆◆◆ Comfort Inn Ⓜ ❀
(605) 224-0377. **$65-$75.** 410 W Sioux Ave. Just w on US 14, 83 and 34. Int corridors. **Pets:** Small, other. $10 daily fee/pet, $10 one-time fee/pet. No service, supervision, crate.
(ASK) (S✿) (✕) (🐾) (🍴) (🛎) (🖥) (🍽)

◆◆ Days Inn Ⓜ
(605) 224-0411. **$50-$65.** 520 W Sioux Ave. On US 14, 83 and 34, just w. Int corridors. **Pets:** Supervision.
(ASK) (S✿) (✕) (🐾) (🍴) (🛎) (🖥)

ⒶⒶⒶ ◆◆◆ Governor's Inn Ⓜ ❀
(605) 224-4200. **$53-$75, 7 days notice.** 700 W Sioux Ave. On US 14, 83 and 34, just w. Ext/int corridors. **Pets:** Other. $10 one-time fee/room. Designated rooms, no service, supervision, crate.
(SAVE) (S✿) (✕) (🐾) (🍴) (🛎) (🖥) (🍽)

◆◆ Kelly Inn Ⓜ ❀
(605) 224-4140. **$47-$62.** 713 W Sioux. 1 mi w on US 14/83. Int corridors. **Pets:** Large, other. No service, supervision, crate.
(ASK) (S✿) (✕) (🍴)

◆◆ Super 8 Motel Ⓜ ❀
(605) 224-1617. **$41-$58, 30 days notice.** 320 W Sioux. Just w on US 14, 83 and 34. **Pets:** Medium. No service, supervision, crate.
(ASK) (✕) (🍴)

PLANKINTON

◆◆ Super 8 Motel Ⓜ
(605) 942-7722. **$65-$80.** 801 S Main St. Just n of I-90, exit 308. Int corridors. **Pets:** No service, supervision, crate.
(ASK) (S✿) (✕)

RAPID CITY

ⒶⒶⒶ ◆◆◆ Alex Johnson Hotel 🄷 ❀
(605) 342-1210. **$125-$135, 3 days notice.** 523 6th St. Downtown; I-90, exit 57, s on I-190, left at Omaha. Int corridors. **Pets:** Supervision.
(SAVE) (S✿) (✕) (🐾) (🛎)

ⒶⒶⒶ ◆ Big Sky Motel Ⓜ
(605) 348-3200. **$43-$48.** 4080 Tower Rd. 3 mi s on US 16, 0.3 mi n on Skyline Dr; take service road off US 16. Ext corridors. **Pets:** Medium. Supervision.
(✕) (✕) (CTV) (🛒)

◆◆ Econo Lodge of Rapid City Ⓜ
(605) 342-6400. **$250.** 625 E Disk Dr. I-90, exit 59, just ne. Ext/int corridors. **Pets:** Small. No service, supervision, crate.
(ASK) (S✿) (✕) (🛎) (🖥) (🍽)

ⒶⒶⒶ ◆◆ Fair Value Inn Ⓜ ❀
(605) 342-8118. **$55-$65.** 1607 LaCrosse St. I-90, exit 59, 0.3 mi s. Ext corridors. **Pets:** Very small, dogs only. Designated rooms, no service, supervision, crate.
(✕)

◆◆ Foothills Inn Ⓜ
(605) 348-5640. **Call for rates.** 1625 N LaCrosse St. Just s of I-90, exit 59. Int corridors. **Pets:** Medium. Designated rooms, no service, supervision, crate.
(ASK) (✕) (🛎) (🍽)

ⒶⒶⒶ ◆◆ Gold Star Motel Ⓜ
(605) 341-7051. **$55-$68.** 801 E North. 2 mi ne on I-90 business loop, exit 59 or 60. Ext corridors. **Pets:** Small. Designated rooms, no service, supervision, crate.
(SAVE) (S✿) (✕)

◆◆◆ Holiday Inn Express Ⓜ
(605) 341-9300. **Call for rates.** 750 Cathedral Dr. 1.4 mi s on US 16; just e. Int corridors. **Pets:** Small. Designated rooms, no service, supervision, crate.
(✕) (✿) (🐾) (🍴) (🛎) (🖥) (🍽)

◆◆◆ Holiday Inn Express Hotel & Suites, I-90 Ⓜ ❀
(605) 355-9090. **$250.** 645 E Disk Dr. I-90, exit 59, just ne. Int corridors. **Pets:** Other. Designated rooms, supervision.
(ASK) (S✿) (✕) (🐾) (🍴) (🛎) (🖥) (🍽)

ⒶⒶⒶ ◆ Motel 6–352 Ⓜ ❀
(605) 343-3687. **$70-$86.** 620 E Latrobe St. Se corner of I-90, exit 59 (La Crosse St). Ext corridors. **Pets:** Small. No service, supervision, crate.
(S✿) (✕) (🍴) (🍽) (CTV)

◆◆ Quality Inn Ⓜ
(605) 342-3322. **Call for rates.** 1902 LaCrosse St. I-90, exit 59, just s. Ext/int corridors. **Pets:** Supervision.
(✕) (🐾) (🛎) (🖥) (🍴) (🍽)

◆◆◆ Ramada Inn Rapid City Ⓜ ❀
(605) 342-1300. **$100-$150, 7 days notice.** 1721 N La Crosse St. Just s of I-90, exit 59. Int corridors. **Pets:** $25 one-time fee/room. No service, supervision, crate.
(ASK) (S✿) (✕) (🐾) (🛎) (🖥) (🍽)

ⒶⒶⒶ ◆◆ Rodeway Inn Ⓜ ❀
(605) 342-1303. **$95-$159.** 2208 Mt Rushmoore Rd. 1 mi s on US 16. Ext corridors. **Pets:** Designated rooms, supervision.
(SAVE) (S✿) (✕) (🛎) (🖥) (🍴) (🍽)

◆◆◆ Rushmore Plaza Holiday Inn 🄷 ❀
(605) 348-4000. **Call for rates.** 505 N Fifth St. I-90, exit 58, 1.3 mi s on Haines; adjacent to Civic Center. Int corridors. **Pets:** Medium, other. Designated rooms, no service, supervision, crate.
(✕) (✿) (🐾) (🍴) (🛎) (🖥) (🍴) (🍽)

◆◆ Super 8 Motel Ⓜ
(605) 348-8070. **$80-$140, 30 days notice.** 2124 LaCrosse St. Just n of I-90, exit 59. Int corridors. **Pets:** Medium. No service, supervision, crate.
(ASK) (S✿) (✕) (🐾) (🐾) (🍴) (🛎)

ⒶⒶⒶ ◆◆ Thrifty Motor Inn Ⓜ ❀
(605) 342-0551. **$55-$65.** 1303 La Crosse St. 0.5 mi s of I-90, exit 59. Ext corridors. **Pets:** Very small, dogs only. No service, supervision, crate.
(✕) (🛎)

ROCKERVILLE

◆ Rockerville Trading Post & Motel Ⓜ ❀
(605) 341-4880. **$45-$75, 3 days notice.** 13525 Main St. Center. Ext corridors. **Pets:** Other. $5 daily fee/pet. Designated rooms, supervision.
(S✿) (✕) (🖥) (🍽) (CTV)

SIOUX FALLS

◆◆◆ Baymont Inn M ❀
(605) 362-0835. **$62-$106.** 3200 Meadow Ave. Just w of I-29, exit 77 (41st St). Int corridors. **Pets:** Medium, other. Designated rooms, no service, supervision, crate.

ASK Sb X ⌂ 🛏 🖥 🖨 💻 🐾

◆◆◆ Best Western Ramkota Hotel MI ❀
(605) 336-0650. **$89-$109.** 2400 N Louise Ave. Just e of jct I-29, exit 81 (Airport/Russell St). Ext/int corridors. **Pets:** No service, supervision, crate.

ASK Sb X 🔒 🛏 🖥 🖨 💻 🍴 🐾 ⊠

◆◆ Comfort Inn North M ❀
(605) 331-4490. **$55-$89.** 5100 N Cliff Ave. 0.3 mi s of I-90, exit 399. Int corridors. **Pets:** Other. $10 daily fee/pet. Supervision.

ASK Sb X ⌂ 🛏 🖨 💻 🐾

◆◆ Comfort Inn South M
(605) 361-2822. **$55-$89.** 3216 S Carolyn Ave. Just ne of I-29, exit 77 (41st St). Int corridors. **Pets:** Large. Designated rooms, no service, supervision, crate.

ASK Sb X 🛏 🖨 💻 🐾

◆◆◆ Comfort Suites M
(605) 362-9711. **$65-$99.** 3208 S Carolyn Ave. Just ne of I-29, exit 77 (41st St). Int corridors. **Pets:** Medium. Designated rooms, no service, supervision, crate.

ASK Sb X 🛏 🖨 💻 🐾

◆◆ Days Inn Airport M ❀
(605) 331-5959. **$50-$100.** 5001 N Cliff Ave. Just s of I-90, exit 399 (N Cliff Ave). Int corridors. **Pets:** Other. $8 daily fee/room. No service, supervision, crate.

ASK Sb X ⌂ 🛏 🖨 💻

◆ Exel Inn of Sioux Falls M ❀
(605) 331-5800. **$37-$62.** 1300 W Russell St. 1.2 mi e from I-29, exit 81 (Airport/Russell St). Int corridors. **Pets:** Small, other. Designated rooms, no service, supervision, crate.

Sb X 🛏 💻

◆◆◆ Kelly Inn M ❀
(605) 338-6242. **$62-$79.** 3101 W Russell St. Just e of jct I-29, exit 81 (Airport/Russell St). Ext/int corridors. **Pets:** Other. Supervision.

ASK Sb X 🛏 🖨 💻 ⊠

◆◆◆ MainStay Suites M
(605) 361-2626. **$79-$109.** 4545 W Homefield Dr. I-29, exit 78 (26th), just w. Int corridors. **Pets:** Small. Supervision.

ASK Sb X ⌂ 🛏 🖨 💻 🐾

◆◆ Ramada Limited M ❀
(605) 330-0000. **$65-$85.** 407 S Lyons Ave. Just e of I-29, exit 79 (12th St). Int corridors. **Pets:** Other. $15 deposit/room. Designated rooms, no service, supervision, crate.

SAVE Sb X ⌂ 🛏 🖨 💻 🐾

◆◆◆ Residence Inn by Marriott ▲ ❀
(605) 361-2202. **$119-$217.** 4509 W Empire Pl. 0.5 mi se of I-29, exit 77 (41st St); in sw corner of Empire Mall. Int corridors. **Pets:** Medium, other. $5 daily fee/pet, $25 one-time fee/room. No service, supervision, crate.

ASK Sb X ⌂ 🛏 🖨 🛏 💻 🐾 ⊠

◆ Select Inn M
(605) 361-1864. **$33-$47.** 3500 S Gateway Blvd. Just w of I-29, exit 77 (41st St). Int corridors. **Pets:** Very small. Designated rooms, no service, supervision, crate.

SAVE Sb X 🖨 💻

◆◆ Sleep Inn M ❀
(605) 339-3992. **$65-$75.** 1500 N Kiwanis Ave. I-29, exit 81, 0.7 mi e on Russell St. Int corridors. **Pets:** Medium, other. Supervision.

ASK Sb X 🔒 🛏 🖨 🐾

SPEARFISH

◆◆ Best Western Downtown Spearfish M ❀
(605) 642-4676. **$75-$85.** 346 W Kansas. Downtown; follow signs off Main St. Ext corridors. **Pets:** Dogs only. Designated rooms, no service, supervision, crate.

SAVE Sb X 🛏 💻 🐾

◆◆ Country Hearth Inn of Spearfish MI ❀
(605) 642-8105. **$65-$75.** 323 S 27th St. Just s of I-90, exit 14. Int corridors. **Pets:** Small. $5 daily fee/room. No service, supervision, crate.

SAVE Sb X 🛏 🍴 🐾

◆◆◆ Holiday Inn Hotel & Convention Center MI ❀
(605) 642-4683. **$90-$90.** Just n of I-90, exit 14. Ext/int corridors. **Pets:** Other. $10 one-time fee/pet. No service, supervision, crate.

SAVE Sb X ⌂ 🛏 🖨 🛏 💻 🍴 🐾

◆◆ Kelly Inn M ❀
(605) 642-7795. **$75-$99.** 540 E Jackson. Just s of I-90, exit 12. Ext/int corridors. **Pets:** Small, other. Designated rooms, no service, supervision, crate.

SAVE Sb X ⌂

◆ Royal Rest Motel M ❀
(605) 642-3842. **$40-$50.** 444 Main St. Downtown; on US 14/85. Ext corridors. **Pets:** Medium. Designated rooms, no service, supervision, crate.

X 🐾

STURGIS

◆◆ Best Western of Sturgis MI ❀
(605) 347-3604. **$69-$94.** 2431 S Junction Ave. I-90, exit 32. Ext/int corridors. **Pets:** Medium. Designated rooms, supervision.

SAVE X 🛏 🍴 🐾

◆◆◆ Days Inn M ❀
(605) 347-3027. **$65-$105, 7 days notice.** I-90, exit 30, jct US 14A. Ext/int corridors. **Pets:** Medium. $25 deposit/room, $5 one-time fee/room. No service, supervision, crate.

ASK Sb X 🛏

VERMILLION

◆◆ Comfort Inn 🅜 🐾

(605) 624-8333. **$42-$72.** 701 W Cherry St. Business SR 50, 7.5 mi w of I-29, exit 26. Int corridors. **Pets:** Medium. $10 daily fee/pet. Designated rooms, no service, supervision, crate.

ASK S X 🖉 🗎 🖵 🕿

WALL

◆◆◆ Best Western Plains Motel 🅜

(605) 279-2145. **$69-$109.** 712 Glenn St. Just n of I-90, exit 110. Ext corridors. **Pets:** Designated rooms, no service, supervision, crate.

S X 🖵 🕿

◆◆ Econo Lodge 🅜 🐾

(605) 279-2121. **$79-$139.** 804 Glenn St. Just nw of I-90, exit 110. Ext corridors. **Pets:** Other. $20 deposit/pet. Designated rooms, no service, supervision, crate.

SAVE S X 🗎 🖵 🕿

◆ Kings Inn Motel 🅜

(605) 279-2178. **$63-$75.** 608 Main St. Downtown. Ext corridors. **Pets:** Large. No service, supervision, crate.

SAVE S X

WATERTOWN

◆◆ Best Western Ramkota Inn 🅜 🐾

(605) 886-8011. **$54-$69.** 1901 9th Ave SW. US 212, 4 mi w of I-29, exit 177. Int corridors. **Pets:** No service, supervision, crate.

ASK S X 🖉 🖉 🗎 🖵 🕪 🕿

◆◆◆ Comfort Inn 🅜 🐾

(605) 886-3010. **$59-$89.** 800 35th St Cir. Jct US 212 and I-29, exit 177. Ext/int corridors. **Pets:** $10 one-time fee/room. Designated rooms, no service, supervision, crate.

SAVE S X 🖄 🖉 🖉 🗎 🖵 🕿

◆◆◆ Country Inn & Suites By Carlson 🅜 🐾

(605) 886-8900. **$59-$125, 7 days notice.** 3400 8th Ave SE. I-29, exit 177, just w. Int corridors. **Pets:** Small. $20 one-time fee/room. Designated rooms, no service, supervision, crate.

SAVE S X 🖄 🖉 🖉 🗎 🖵 🕿

◆◆ Stone's Inn 🅜 🐾

(605) 882-3630. **$40-$53.** 3900 9th Ave SE. Just e of I-29, exit 177. Int corridors. **Pets:** Other. $10 one-time fee/pet. Designated rooms, no service, supervision, crate.

SAVE S X 🖉

◆◆ Travelers Inn 🅜 🐾

(605) 882-2243. **$39-$50, 7 days notice.** 920 14th St SE. 1.5 mi w of I-29, exit 177, then just s. Int corridors. **Pets:** Medium, other. $6 daily fee/pet. Designated rooms, no service, supervision, crate.

SAVE S X 🖉 🗎

WINNER

◆ Buffalo Trail Motel 🅜

(605) 842-2212. **$111-$120.** W Hwy 18 & 44. 1 mi w on US 18 and SR 44. Ext corridors. **Pets:** Small. No service, supervision, crate.

SAVE S X 🖵 🕿

YANKTON

◆◆◆ Best Western Kelly Inn-Yankton 🅜 🐾

(605) 665-2906. **$89-$119.** 1607 Hwy 50 E. 1 mi e on US 50. Ext/int corridors. **Pets:** Medium, other. Designated rooms, no service, supervision, crate.

ASK S X 🖄 🖉 🖉 🗎 🖵 🕪 🕿 🖾

◆◆ Comfort Inn 🅜

(605) 665-8053. **$56-$85.** 2118 Broadway. US 81, 1.7 mi n. Int corridors. **Pets:** Supervision.

ASK S X 🖵

◆◆ Days Inn 🅜 🐾

(605) 665-8717. **$45-$65.** 2410 Broadway. US 81, 1.8 mi n. Int corridors. **Pets:** Small, dogs only. $10 deposit/pet. No service, supervision, crate.

ASK S X

◆◆ Lewis & Clark Resort 🆁

(605) 665-2680. **$84-$199, 30 days notice.** 43496 Lake Shore Dr. 4 mi w on SR 52; in Lewis and Clark State Park, turn into park, just w of Marina. Ext corridors. **Pets:** Small. Designated rooms, no service, supervision, crate.

ASK X 🖉 🗎 🖵 🕿 🖾 🖾

TENNESSEE

CITY INDEX

ALCOA

⚑ ◆◆◆ MainStay Suites M ✿
(865) 379-7799. **$99-$150.** 361 Fountainview Cir. US 129 and SR 35, just e. Int corridors. **Pets:** Small. $5 daily fee/room, $100 one-time fee/room. Designated rooms, no service, supervision, crate.

ATHENS

◆◆ Ramada Inn M
(423) 745-1212. **$55-$83.** 115 CR 247. Jct I-75 and Mt Verd, exit 52. Ext corridors. **Pets:** Medium. No service, supervision, crate.

BOLIVAR

⚑ ◆ The Bolivar Inn M
(901) 658-3372. **$25-$45, 7 days notice.** 626 W Market St. Downtown at jct US 64 and SR 18. Ext corridors. **Pets:** Small. Supervision.

◆◆ Super 8 Motel M
(901) 658-7888. **$50-$60, 7 days notice.** 916 W Market St. US 64 at jct of SR 18. Ext corridors. **Pets:** Medium. No service, supervision, crate.

BRENTWOOD

⚑ ◆◆◆ AmeriSuites M
(615) 661-9477. **$118.** 202 Summit View Dr. I-65, exit 74A. Int corridors. **Pets:** Small. Designated rooms, no service, supervision, crate.

◆◆◆ Baymont Inn M
(615) 376-4666. **$65-$74.** 108 Westpark Dr. I-65, exit 74B, 1.5 mi w. Int corridors. **Pets:** No service, supervision, crate.

◆◆◆ Hilton Suites Brentwood H
(615) 370-0111. **$115-$189.** 9000 Overlook Blvd. I-65, exit 74B, 0.5 mi s on US 31, e on Church St. Int corridors. **Pets:** Large. No service, supervision, crate.

⚑ ◆◆◆ MainStay Suites-Brentwood M ✿
(615) 371-8477. **$72-$82.** 107 Brentwood Blvd. I-65, exit 74B. Int corridors. **Pets:** Small. $5 daily fee/pet, $100 one-time fee/pet. Supervision.

◆◆◆ Residence Inn Brentwood A
(615) 371-0100. **$89-$116, 7 days notice.** 206 Ward Cir. Sw of I-65, Brentwood exit 74B; 0.3 mi s on Franklin Pike (31S), 0.5 mi w on Maryland Way. Ext/int corridors. **Pets:** Small. No service, supervision, crate.

BRISTOL

⚑ ◆◆◆ Best Western Inn M ✿
(423) 968-1101. **$58-$69.** 111 Holiday Dr. I-81, exit 74B, just w. Ext corridors. **Pets:** No service, supervision, crate.

BROWNSVILLE

⚑ ◆◆ Days Inn M ✿
(901) 772-3297. **$55-$70.** 2530 Anderson Ave. I-40, exit 56. Ext corridors. **Pets:** Small. $6 daily fee/pet. No service, supervision, crate.

BUFFALO

⚑ ◆◆ Super 8 Motel M
(931) 296-2432. **$35-$47.** 15470 Hwy 13 S. I-40, exit 143. Ext corridors. **Pets:** Very small. No service, supervision, crate.

CAMDEN

◆◆◆ GuestHouse Inn M ☙
(901) 584-2222. **$50-$64.** 170 Hwy 641 N. US 641, 0.4 mi n from US 70 (business). Ext corridors. **Pets:** Other. Supervision.

(ASK) (S🐾) (✕) (🖅) (🖼)

CARYVILLE

◆ Budget Host Inn M ☙
(423) 562-9595. **$27-$36.** 115 Woods Ave. I-75, exit 134, just nw. Ext corridors. **Pets:** $6 daily fee/room, $6 one-time fee/room. Designated rooms, no service, supervision, crate.

(S🐾) (✕)

◆◆ Super 8 Motel of Caryville M ☙
(423) 562-8476. **$45-$55, 3 days notice.** 200 John McGhee Blvd. I-75, exit 134, just e then just w on CR 116. Ext corridors. **Pets:** $5 daily fee/room. Designated rooms, supervision.

(ASK) (S🐾) (✕) (🗐) (🖼)

CHATTANOOGA

◆◆◆ Baymont Inn and Suites M
(423) 821-1090. **Call for rates.** 3540 Cummings Hwy. I-24, exit 174, just s. Int corridors. **Pets:** Small. Designated rooms, no service, supervision, crate.

(✕) (🖾) (🖅) (🖼)

◆◆◆ Best Inn M
(423) 894-5454. **$52-$68, 4 days notice.** 7717 Lee Hwy. I-75, exit 7 southbound; exit 7B northbound, 6.5 mi n of jct I-24. Ext corridors. **Pets:** Supervision.

(ASK) (S🐾) (✕) (🗐) (🖅) (🖼)

◆◆◆ Best Western Royal Inn M ☙
(423) 821-6840. **$60-$85.** 3644 Cummings Hwy. 5.5 mi w on I-24, exit 174; jct US 64, 41 and 72. Ext corridors. **Pets:** Very small. $5 daily fee/pet. Supervision.

(SAVE) (S🐾) (✕) (🖅) (🖼)

◆◆ Chattanooga/Aquarium Super 8 Motel M
(423) 821-8880. **$49-$75.** 20 Birmingham Hwy. I-24, exit 174. Int corridors. **Pets:** Supervision.

(ASK) (S🐾) (✕) (🖅)

◆◆ Days Inn-Lookout Mountain Tiftonia West M ☙
(423) 821-6044. **$43-$70, 3 days notice.** 3801 Cummings Hwy. 5.5 mi w on I-24, exit 174, jct US 64, 41 and 72. Ext corridors. **Pets:** $7 daily fee/pet, $7 one-time fee/pet. Designated rooms, no service, supervision, crate.

(SAVE) (S🐾) (✕) (🗐) (🖅) (🖼)

◆◆◆ Holiday Inn Express M
(423) 490-8560. **$79-$96, 30 days notice.** 7024 McCutcheon Rd. I-75, exit 5 (Shallowford), 0.5 mi w. Int corridors. **Pets:** Designated rooms, no service, supervision, crate.

(SAVE) (S🐾) (✕) (🖾) (🖅) (🖼)

◆◆◆ Holiday Inn I-75 Airport M
(423) 855-2898. **$79-$96, 30 days notice.** 2345 Shallowford Village Dr. I-75, exit 5, 0.3 mi w to Shallowford Village Dr, n 0.3 mi. Ext/int corridors. **Pets:** Designated rooms, no service, supervision, crate.

(SAVE) (S🐾) (✕) (🖅) (🖼) (🍴) (🖼)

◆◆ Kings Lodge Motel M ☙
(423) 698-8944. **$40-$50, 7 days notice.** 2400 Westside Dr. 3.5 mi se on US 41 and 76; just se of I-24, exit 181 westbound; exit 181A eastbound. Ext/int corridors. **Pets:** Very small, other. $5 deposit/pet. No service, supervision, crate.

(SAVE) (S🐾) (✕) (🖅) (🖾) (🖼)

◆◆◆ La Quinta Inn M
(423) 855-0011. **$65-$89.** 7015 Shallowford Rd. I-75, exit 5 (Shallowford), 0.5 mi. Ext corridors. **Pets:** Small. No service, supervision, crate.

(SAVE) (✕) (🗐) (🖾) (🖅) (🖾) (🖼)

◆◆ MainStay Suites-Chattanooga M
(423) 485-9424. **$70-$80.** 7030 Amin Dr. I-75 and Shallowford Rd, exit 5, just w. Int corridors. **Pets:** Supervision.

(ASK) (S🐾) (✕) (🖅) (🖾)

◆◆ Microtel Inn-Chattanooga M ☙
(423) 510-0761. **Call for rates.** 7014 McCutcheon Rd. I-75, exit 5, 0.5 w to Shallowford Village Dr, 0.5 mi n, just w. Int corridors. **Pets:** $25 deposit/room, $5 daily fee/pet. Designated rooms, supervision.

(✕) (🖾) (🖅)

◆◆ Quality Inn Downtown M
(423) 622-8353. **$57-$90, 5 days notice.** 2000 E 23rd St. I-24, exit 181, just n on 4th St, just w. Ext corridors. **Pets:** Small. Supervision.

(SAVE) (S🐾) (✕) (🖅) (🖾) (🍴) (🖼)

◆◆ Red Roof Inn-Chattanooga M
(423) 899-0143. **$50-$65.** 7014 Shallowford Rd. I-75, exit 5 (Shallowford Rd). Ext corridors. **Pets:** Supervision.

(SAVE) (✕)

CLARKSVILLE

◆◆ Comfort Inn South M
(931) 358-2020. **$40-$65.** 1112 SR 76. I-24, exit 11. Ext corridors. **Pets:** Supervision.

(SAVE) (S🐾) (✕) (🖅) (🖼)

◆◆ Days Inn of Clarksville M ☙
(931) 358-3194. **$45-$55.** 1100 Hwy 76 Connector Rd. I-24, exit 11. Ext corridors. **Pets:** Small. $5 daily fee/room, $5 one-time fee/room. No service, supervision, crate.

(ASK) (S🐾) (✕) (🖅) (🖼)

◆◆◆ Holiday Inn-I-24 M ☙
(931) 648-4848. **$63-$69.** 3095 Wilma Rudolph Blvd. I-24, exit 4. Ext corridors. **Pets:** Other. Supervision.

(ASK) (S🐾) (✕) (🖅) (🖾) (🍴) (🖼) (🖾)

◆◆ Ramada Limited M ☙
(931) 552-0098. **$35-$60.** 3100 Wilma Rudolph Blvd. I-24, exit 4. Ext corridors. **Pets:** $30 deposit/pet. Designated rooms, no service, supervision, crate.

(ASK) (S🐾) (✕) (🖅) (🖼)

◆◆ Travelodge M
(931) 645-1400. **$48, 5 days notice.** 3075 Wilma Rudolph Blvd. I-24, exit 4. Int corridors. **Pets:** Medium. Designated rooms, no service, supervision, crate.

(ASK) (S🐾) (✕) (🖅) (🖾) (🍴) (🖼)

CLEVELAND

◆◆◆ Baymont Inn & Suites M
(423) 339-1000. **$70-$70.** 107 Interstate Dr NW. Jct I-75 and SR 60, exit 25. Int corridors. **Pets:** No service, supervision, crate.

[ASK] [S⊘] [✕] [🛢] [💻] [🖼]

⏣ ◆◆◆ Best Western Cleveland Inn M
(423) 472-5566. **$45-$75, 7 days notice.** 156 James Asbury Dr. Jct I-75 and Paul Huff Hwy, exit 27. Ext corridors. **Pets:** No service, supervision, crate.

[SAVE] [S⊘] [✕] [🗝] [🛢] [💻] [🖼]

◆ Colonial Inn Motel M ❀
(423) 472-6845. **$22-$32, 3 days notice.** 1555 25th St. Jct I-75 and SR 60, exit 25, 0.3 mi e. Ext corridors. **Pets:** Very small. $5 deposit/pet. No service, supervision, crate.

[✕] [🖼]

⏣ ◆◆◆ Comfort Inn M
(423) 478-5265. **$45-$75, 7 days notice.** 153 James Asbury Dr. I-75, exit 27, w 0.5 mi. Ext/int corridors. **Pets:** Supervision.

[SAVE] [S⊘] [✕] [💻] [🖼]

◆◆◆ Holiday Inn MI ❀
(423) 472-1504. **$110.** 2400 Executive Park Dr. Jct I-75 and SR 60, exit 25. Ext/int corridors. **Pets:** Medium. No service, supervision, crate.

[ASK] [S⊘] [✕] [🎱] [🛢] [💻] [🍴] [🖼]

⏣ ◆◆ Quality Inn-Chalet M
(423) 476-8511. **$54-$64.** 2595 Georgetown Rd. On SR 60 at jct I-75, exit 25. Ext corridors. **Pets:** Supervision.

[SAVE] [S⊘] [✕] [🗝] [🛢] [💻] [🍴] [🖼]

⏣ ◆◆ Super 8 Motel M ❀
(423) 476-5555. **$50-$65.** 163 Bernham Dr. I-75, exit 27. Ext/int corridors. **Pets:** Other. Supervision.

[SAVE] [S⊘] [✕] [🗝] [🛢] [💻] [🖼]

CLINTON

◆◆ Clinton Super 8 Motel M
(865) 457-0565. **$49-$55.** 2317 Andersonville Hwy. I-75, exit 122, w 0.5 mi. Int corridors. **Pets:** No service, supervision, crate.

[ASK] [S⊘] [✕] [🎱] [🌀] [🖼]

COLLEGE GROVE

◆◆◆◆ Peacock Hill Country Inn BB
(615) 368-7727. **$125-$225, 3 days notice.** 6994 Giles Hill Rd. I-65, exit 65, 1.5 mi e to Arno Rd, 14 mi s to Giles Hill Rd, 3 mi w. Int corridors. **Pets:** No service, supervision, crate.

[✕] [🛢] [💻] [CTV] [✎]

COLUMBIA

⏣ ◆◆◆ Econo Lodge M ❀
(931) 381-1410. **$50-$55, 5 days notice.** 1548 Bear Creek Pike. I-65, exit 46. Ext corridors. **Pets:** Small, other. $5 one-time fee/pet. No service, supervision, crate.

[SAVE] [S⊘] [✕] [💻]

⏣ ◆◆ James K Polk Motel M
(931) 388-4913. **$35-$40.** 1111 Nashville Hwy. I-65, exit 46, 7 mi w, just n on US 31. Ext corridors. **Pets:** Medium. Supervision.

[SAVE] [S⊘] [✕] [🛢] [🖼]

◆◆◆ Ramada Inn MI
(931) 388-2720. **$48-$53.** 1208 Nashville Hwy. US 31, n 2 mi. Ext corridors. **Pets:** Small. No service, supervision, crate.

[ASK] [S⊘] [✕] [🛢] [💻] [🍴] [🖼]

COOKEVILLE

⏣ ◆◆ Alpine Lodge & Suites M ❀
(931) 526-3333. **$38-$54.** 2021 E Spring St. I-40, exit 290, just s. Int corridors. **Pets:** Medium, other. $5 daily fee/room, $5 one-time fee/room. Designated rooms, no service, supervision, crate.

[SAVE] [S⊘] [✕] [🌀] [🛢] [💻] [🖼]

⏣ ◆◆◆ Best Western Thunderbird Motel M ❀
(931) 526-7115. **$39-$65.** 900 S Jefferson. I-40, exit 287. Ext corridors. **Pets:** Other. Supervision.

[SAVE] [S⊘] [✕] [🎱] [🗝] [🛢] [🖼]

◆◆ Days Inn M ❀
(931) 528-1511. **Call for rates.** 1292 Bunker Hill Rd. I-40, exit 287. Ext corridors. **Pets:** $5 one-time fee/room. Designated rooms, no service, supervision, crate.

[ASK] [✕] [🛢] [🖼]

⏣ ◆◆◆ Econolodge M ❀
(931) 528-1040. **$50-$65.** 1100 S Jefferson Ave. I-40, exit 287. Ext corridors. **Pets:** Other. $5 daily fee/pet. Supervision.

[SAVE] [S⊘] [✕] [🛢] [💻] [🖼]

◆◆◆ Hampton Inn M ❀
(931) 520-1117. **$60-$75, 7 days notice.** 1025 Interstate Dr. I-40, exit 287, 0.5 mi n. Ext corridors. **Pets:** Other. Supervision.

[✕] [🎱] [🌀] [🗝] [🛢] [🖼]

◆◆◆ Holiday Inn MI
(931) 526-7125. **$58-$78.** 970 S Jefferson. I-40, exit 287. Ext/int corridors. **Pets:** Medium. Supervision.

[S⊘] [✕] [🎱] [🛢] [💻] [🍴] [🖼]

CORNERSVILLE

⏣ ◆◆ Econo Lodge M ❀
(931) 293-2111. **$50-$55.** 3731 Pulaski Hwy. I-65 and US 31A, exit 22. Ext corridors. **Pets:** Very small, dogs only. $5 daily fee/pet, $5 one-time fee/pet. Designated rooms, no service, supervision, crate.

[SAVE] [S⊘] [✕] [🖼] [CTV]

CROSSVILLE

◆◆ Ramada Inn MI
(931) 484-7581. **$50-$72, 7 days notice.** 4083 Hwy 127 N. I-40, exit 317, just n. Ext corridors. **Pets:** No service, supervision, crate.

[✕] [💻] [🍴] [🖼]

CUMBERLAND GAP

◆◆ **Cumberland Gap Inn** Ⓜ
(423) 869-9172. **$65-$75.** 630 Brooklyn St. 58 E, exit Cumberland Gap to town, 1.5 mi, just s. Ext corridors. **Pets:** Small. No service, supervision, crate.
(A$K) (S⬦) (✕) (🛏) (🖵) (🕿)

◆◆◆ **Ramada Inn of Cumberland Gap** Ⓜ⎮ ☙
(423) 869-3631. **$65-$71, 7 days notice.** Hwy 58. Just n from US 58, just e of US 25 E. Int corridors. **Pets:** $25 one-time fee/room. Supervision.
(A$K) (S⬦) (✕) (🛏) (🍽) (🕿)

DANDRIDGE

◆◆◆ **Mountain Harbor Inn** Ⓒ⎮ ☙
(865) 397-3345. **$60-$95, 21 days notice.** 1199 Hwy 139. I-40, exit 412, 2 mi s to US 139, 1 mi e. Ext corridors. **Pets:** Other. $10 daily fee/pet. No service, supervision, crate.
(✕) (🛏) (🖵) (🍽) (✕) (🗭)

◆◆◆ **Tennessee Mountain Inn** Ⓜ ☙
(865) 397-9437. **$40-$100.** 531 Patriot Dr. I-40, exit 417, n side of jct SR 92. Ext corridors. **Pets:** Medium, other. Designated rooms, no service, supervision, crate.
(✕) (🕿) (CTV)

DAYTON

⏣ ◆◆◆ **Best Western Dayton** Ⓜ⎮ ☙
(423) 775-6560. **$55-$80.** 7835 Rhea County Hwy. 1 mi n on US 27. Ext corridors. **Pets:** Medium, other. $25 deposit/pet, $3 daily fee/pet. No service, supervision, crate.
(SAVE) (S⬦) (✕) (🛏) (🖵) (🍽) (🕿)

⏣ ◆◆ **Days Inn** Ⓜ ☙
(423) 775-9718. **$45-$75.** 3914 Rhea County Hwy. 1 mi s on US 27. Ext corridors. **Pets:** Other. $4 daily fee/room, $4 one-time fee/pet. No service, supervision, crate.
(SAVE) (S⬦) (✕) (🛏)

DICKSON

◆◆ **Comfort Inn** Ⓜ ☙
(615) 446-2423. **$46-$65.** 2325 Hwy 46 S. I-40, exit 172. Ext corridors. **Pets:** Small. $5 daily fee/pet. No service, supervision, crate.
(A$K) (✕) (🗭) (🛏) (🕿)

⏣ ◆◆ **Econo Lodge** Ⓜ ☙
(615) 446-0541. **$39-$60.** 2338 Hwy 46. I-40, exit 172. Ext corridors. **Pets:** Small, dogs only. $5 daily fee/pet. No service, supervision, crate.
(SAVE) (S⬦) (✕) (🗭) (🖵) (🕿)

⏣ ◆◆ **Holiday Inn** Ⓜ ☙
(615) 446-9081. **$59-$74.** 2420 Hwy 46S. I-40, exit 172. Ext corridors. **Pets:** Other. Supervision.
(SAVE) (S⬦) (✕) (🗭) (🛏) (🖵) (🍽) (🕿)

◆◆ **Super 8 Motel** Ⓜ ☙
(615) 446-1923. **$46-$69.** 150 Suzanne Dr. I-40, exit 172. Int corridors. **Pets:** Small. $5 daily fee/pet, $5 one-time fee/pet. No service, supervision, crate.
(A$K) (S⬦) (✕) (🛏) (🕿)

EAST RIDGE

◆◆ **Best Western Airport Inn** Ⓜ ☙
(423) 894-1860. **$45-$75, 3 days notice.** 6650 Ringgold Rd. I-75, exit 1. Ext/int corridors. **Pets:** Small. No service, supervision, crate.
(A$K) (S⬦) (✕) (🕿)

⏣ ◆◆◆ **Howard Johnson Plaza Hotel** Ⓜ⎮ ☙
(423) 892-8100. **$65-$65.** 6700 Ringgold Rd. 8.5 mi se on US 41 and 76, jct I-75, exit 1 (East Ridge). Int corridors. **Pets:** Other. Supervision.
(SAVE) (S⬦) (✕) (🛏) (🖵) (🍽) (🕿)

⏣ ◆◆◆ **Ramada Inn South** Ⓜ⎮ ☙
(423) 894-6110. **$40-$46, 5 days notice.** 6639 Capehart Ln. I-75, exit 1 (Ringgold Rd), 0.3 mi e. Ext/int corridors. **Pets:** $6 daily fee/room, $6 one-time fee/room. Designated rooms, no service, supervision, crate.
(SAVE) (S⬦) (✕) (🛏) (🖵) (🍽) (🕿) (✕)

FARRAGUT

◆◆◆ **Baymont Inn-Knoxville** Ⓜ ☙
(865) 671-1010. **$65-$80.** 11341 Campbell Lakes. I-40 and I-75, exit 373 (Campbell Station Rd). Int corridors. **Pets:** Other. Designated rooms, supervision.
(A$K) (S⬦) (✕) (🖐) (🏋) (🛏) (🖵) (🕿)

⏣ ◆◆◆ **Super 8** Ⓜ
(865) 675-5566. **$46-$79.** 11748 Snyder Rd. I-40 and I-75, exit 373, just ne. Ext corridors. **Pets:** Supervision.
(SAVE) (S⬦) (✕) (🖐) (🏋) (🛏) (🕿)

FAYETTEVILLE

◆◆◆ **Best Western-Fayetteville Inn** Ⓜ⎮
(931) 433-0100. **$53-$59, 7 days notice.** 3021 Thornton Taylor Pkwy. 0.7 mi e of US 431, on US 64 and 321 bypass. Ext corridors. **Pets:** No service, supervision, crate.
(A$K) (S⬦) (✕) (🛏) (🍽) (🕿)

FRANKLIN

⏣ ◆◆◆ **AmeriSuites** Ⓜ
(615) 771-8900. **$79-$99.** 650 Bakers Bridge Ave. I-65, exit 69 (Gallerria Blvd), 0.5 mi s, just e. Int corridors. **Pets:** Small. No service, supervision, crate.
(SAVE) (S⬦) (✕) (🖐) (🏋) (🎳) (🛏) (🖵) (🕿)

◆◆ **Baymont Inn & Suites-Nashville South** Ⓜ
(615) 791-7700. **$60-$65.** 4207 Franklin Commons Ct. I-65, exit 65. Int corridors. **Pets:** Supervision.
(S⬦) (✕) (🖐) (🏋) (🎳) (🛏) (🖵) (🕿)

⏣ ◆◆ **Best Western Franklin Inn** Ⓜ⎮ ☙
(615) 790-0570. **$65-$75.** 1308 Murfreesboro Rd. I-65 (SR 96), exit 65, just w. Ext corridors. **Pets:** Small. No service, supervision, crate.
(SAVE) (S⬦) (✕) (🛏) (🖵) (🕿)

⏣ ◆◆◆ **Comfort Inn** Ⓜ ☙
(615) 791-6675. **$60-$105, 6 days notice.** 4206 Franklin Commons Ct. I-65, exit 65, just w. Ext corridors. **Pets:** Very small, other. $10 daily fee/pet. Supervision.
(SAVE) (S⬦) (✕) (🛏) (🖵) (🕿)

(AAA) ◆◆◆ Days Inn M ❀
(615) 790-1140. **$59-$75, 31 days notice.** 4217 S
Carothers Rd. I-65, exit 65, just e. Ext corridors.
Pets: Other. $5 daily fee/pet. No service, supervision, crate.
[SAVE] [S$] [✕] [🛏] [🖥]

◆◆◆ Namaste Acres Country Ranch Inn BB ❀
(615) 791-0333. **$75-$85, 5 days notice.** 5436 Leipers
Creek. SR 96, 5 mi w, SR 46, 6 mi sw, 1.9 mi s. Int
corridors. **Pets:** Large, other. Designated rooms, no service,
supervision, crate.
[✕] [🛏] [🖥] [CTV]

◆◆ Super 8 M ❀
(615) 794-7591. **$53-$85.** 1307 Murfreesboro Rd. I-65, exit
65, just w. Ext corridors. **Pets:** Small. Supervision.
[ASK] [S$] [✕] [🗖] [🛏] [🖥] [🖥]

GATLINBURG

(AAA) ◆◆ Highland Motor Inn M ❀
(865) 436-4110. **$50-$88.** 131 Parkway. US 441, just n of
traffic light 1. Ext corridors. **Pets:** Other. $25 deposit/room,
$5 daily fee/pet. Supervision.
[SAVE] [S$] [✕] [🛏] [🖥]

◆◆◆ Holiday Inn Sunspree Resort M ❀
(865) 436-9201. **$79-$139.** 520 Airport Rd. US 441, 1 mi e
at traffic light 8. Ext/int corridors. **Pets:** Other. Supervision.
[ASK] [S$] [✕] [🖐] [🗖] [🖥] [🛏] [🖥] [🍴] [🖥] [🖥]

(AAA) ◆◆ Microtel-Gatlinburg M ❀
(865) 436-0107. **$59-$94, 7 days notice.** 211 Airport Rd.
US 441, traffic light 8, just e. Int corridors. **Pets:** Small,
other. Supervision.
[SAVE] [S$] [✕] [🖐] [🖥] [🖥]

(AAA) ◆◆ River Terrace Resort & Convention
Center M ❀
(865) 436-5161. **$59-$109, 3 days notice.** 240 River Rd.
Sw of US 441 and traffic light 5. Ext/int corridors. **Pets:** $50
deposit/room. Supervision.
[SAVE] [✕] [🛏] [🖥] [🍴] [🖥] [🖥]

GREENEVILLE

(AAA) ◆◆◆ The General Morgan Inn & Conference
Center H ❀
(423) 787-1000. **$89-$109.** 111 N Main St. Center of town,
US 11 E business, then n. Int corridors. **Pets:** Small. No
service, supervision, crate.
[SAVE] [S$] [✕] [🛏] [🍴]

HARRIMAN

◆◆ Best Western Sundancer Motor
Lodge M ❀
(865) 882-6200. **$42-$59.** 120 Childs Rd. I-40, exit 347, just
n. Ext corridors. **Pets:** Small. $5 daily fee/room. Supervision.
[S$] [✕]

◆◆◆ Holiday Inn Express M ❀
(865) 882-5340. **$59-$69.** 1845 S Roane St. I-40 exit 347,
just s. Ext corridors. **Pets:** Other. No service, supervision,
crate.
[ASK] [S$] [✕] [🗖] [🖥] [🛏] [🖥]

(AAA) ◆◆ Super 8 Motel M ❀
(865) 882-6600. **$36-$49.** 1867 S Roane St. I-40 exit 347,
0.3 mi s on US 27/SR 61. Ext corridors. **Pets:** Small, dogs
only. $5 deposit/pet, $5 daily fee/pet, $5 one-time fee/pet.
Designated rooms, no service, supervision, crate.
[SAVE] [S$] [✕] [🛏] [🖥]

HUNTSVILLE

◆◆◆ Holiday Inn Express-Big South Fork M
(423) 663-4100. **$62-$69, 3 days notice.** 11597 Scott Hwy.
SR 63 and 27, just n. Ext corridors. **Pets:** Supervision.
[ASK] [S$] [✕] [🗖] [🖥]

HURRICANE MILLS

(AAA) ◆◆◆ Holiday Inn Express M
(931) 296-2999. **$54-$65.** 15368 Hwy 13 S. I-40, exit 143,
just ne. Int corridors. **Pets:** Small. Designated rooms, no
service, supervision, crate.
[SAVE] [S$] [✕] [🗖] [🗖] [🛏] [🖥]

JACKSON

(AAA) ◆◆◆ AmeriHost Inn-Jackson M ❀
(901) 661-9995. **$69-$79.** 465 Vann Dr. I-40, exit 82B (US
45), 1 mi e via Vann Dr. Int corridors. **Pets:** Other. Supervision.
[SAVE] [S$] [✕] [🗖] [🖥] [🛏] [🖥] [🖥]

◆◆ Baymont Inn & Suites M ❀
(901) 664-1800. **$49-$54.** 2370 N Highland Ave. I-40, exit
82A. Int corridors. **Pets:** Small, other. $50 deposit/room.
Supervision.
[S$] [✕] [🛏] [🖥] [🖥]

(AAA) ◆◆◆ Best Western Old Hickory
Inn M ❀
(901) 668-4222. **$44-$69.** 1849 Hwy 45 bypass. I-40, exit
80A, 0.3 mi s. **Pets:** Small, other. Designated
rooms, no service, supervision, crate.
[SAVE] [S$] [✕] [🛏] [🍴] [🖥]

◆◆ Days Inn M
(901) 668-3444. **$40-$55.** 1919 US 45 bypass. I-40, exit
80A, just s. Ext corridors. **Pets:** Small. No service, supervision, crate.
[ASK] [✕] [🖥]

◆◆ Days Inn-West M ❀
(901) 668-4840. **$39-$55, 5 days notice.** 2239 Hollywood
Dr. I-40, exit 79. Ext corridors. **Pets:** Dogs only. Designated
rooms, supervision.
[ASK] [S$] [✕] [🛏] [🖥]

◆◆◆ Garden Plaza Hotel M
(901) 664-6900. **$79-$109.** 1770 Hwy 45 bypass. I-40, exit
80A, 0.5 mi s. Int corridors. **Pets:** Supervision.
[ASK] [S$] [✕] [🗖] [🛏] [🖥] [🖥] [🍴] [🖥]

(AAA) ◆ Travelers Motel M ❀
(901) 668-0542. **$26-$60.** 2247 N Highland Ave. I-40, exit
82A, 1 mi s. Ext corridors. **Pets:** Other. Supervision.
[SAVE] [S$] [✕] [🛏]

JELLICO

◆◆ Best Western Holiday Plaza Motel 🅜
(423) 784-7241. **$38-$80.** 133 Holiday Dr. I-75, exit 160, just w. Ext corridors. **Pets:** Medium. Supervision.

(ASK) (S&) (X) (≋)

◆◆ Days Inn 🅜 🐾
(423) 784-7200. **$46-$51.** US 25 W. I-75 exit 160, just w. Ext corridors. **Pets:** Small. $5 daily fee/room. Designated rooms, no service, supervision, crate.

(ASK) (X) (¶) (≋)

JOHNSON CITY

◆◆◆ Comfort Inn 🅜
(423) 928-9600. **$49-$145, 3 days notice.** 1900 S Roan St. I-181, exit 31, just n on US 321. Ext corridors. **Pets:** Supervision.

(ASK) (S&) (X) (🛏) (🖥) (≋)

🆔 ◆ Days Inn 🅜
(423) 282-2211. **$50-$50, 3 days notice.** 2312 Browns Mill Rd. I-181, exit 35B northbound; exit 35 southbound, just s and just e. Ext corridors. **Pets:** Small. Designated rooms, supervision.

(SAVE) (X) (🛏) (≋) (CTV)

◆◆◆ Holiday Inn-Johnson City 🅜 🐾
(423) 282-4611. **$81-$87.** 101 W Springbrook Dr. I-181, northbound exit 35B; southbound exit 35, just s. Int corridors. **Pets:** Other. $25 deposit/pet. Supervision.

(ASK) (S&) (X) (🗝) (🛏) (🖥) (¶) (≋)

🆔 ◆◆ Red Roof Inn-Johnson City 🅜
(423) 282-3040. **$47-$74.** 210 Broyles Dr. I-181, exit 35B northbound; exit 35 southbound, 0.5 mi s, then just w. Ext corridors. **Pets:** Large. No service, supervision, crate.

(SAVE) (X) (🗝) (CTV)

◆◆ Super 8 Motel 🅜 🐾
(423) 282-8818. **$44-$49, 7 days notice.** 108 Wesley St. I-181, exit 35A northbound; exit 35 southbound, just n to Springbrook Dr, just e. Int corridors. **Pets:** Supervision.

(ASK) (S&) (X) (🗝) (🛏)

KIMBALL

🆔 ◆◆ Days Inn Kimball 🅜
(423) 837-7933. **$46-$58, 7 days notice.** 130 Main St. I-24, exit 152 (US 72). Ext corridors. **Pets:** Supervision.

(SAVE) (S&) (X) (≋)

KINGSPORT

🆔 ◆◆◆ La Quinta Inn-Kingsport 🅜
(423) 323-0500. **$55-$79.** 10150 Airport Pkwy. I-81, exit 63, just e. Int corridors. **Pets:** Designated rooms, no service, supervision, crate.

(SAVE) (X) (♿) (🗝) (🐾) (🛏) (🖥) (≋)

◆◆ Microtel 🅜
(423) 378-9220. **$34-$54.** 1708 E Stone Dr. 3.5 mi e on US 11, w at jct SR 93. Int corridors. **Pets:** Medium. Designated rooms, supervision.

(ASK) (S&) (X) (♿) (🐾) (🛏)

KINGSTON

🆔 ◆◆ Days Inn 🅜 🐾
(865) 376-2069. **$38-$81.** 495 Gallaher Rd. I-40, exit 356. Ext corridors. **Pets:** Other. $5 daily fee/room, $5 one-time fee/pet. No service, supervision, crate.

(SAVE) (S&) (X) (🗝) (🛏) (≋)

KINGSTON SPRINGS

◆◆ Best Western Harpeth Inn 🅜
(615) 952-3961. **$65-$100, 3 days notice.** 116 Luy Ben Hills Rd. I-40, exit 188, just n. Ext corridors. **Pets:** Medium. Designated rooms, supervision.

(X) (🗝) (≋)

🆔 ◆◆ Econo Lodge 🅜
(615) 952-2900. **$45-$75.** 123 Luy Ben Hills Rd. I-40, exit 188. Ext corridors. **Pets:** Designated rooms, supervision.

(SAVE) (S&) (X) (🖥) (≋)

◆◆ Scottish Inn 🅜
(615) 952-3115. **Call for rates.** 116 Luy Ben Hills Rd. I-40, exit 188. Ext corridors. **Pets:** Medium. No service, supervision, crate.

(X)

KNOXVILLE

🆔 ◆◆ Best Western 🅜 🐾
(865) 688-3141. **$50-$114, 3 days notice.** 118 Merchant Dr. I-75, exit 108 (Merchant Dr). Ext/int corridors. **Pets:** Medium. $25 one-time fee/pet. Designated rooms, supervision.

(SAVE) (S&) (X) (🗝) (🛏) (🖥) (≋)

🆔 ◆◆ Best Western West 🅜 🐾
(865) 675-7666. **$45-$70.** 500 Lovell Rd. I-40 and I-75, exit 374, just n. Ext corridors. **Pets:** Other. $10 daily fee/pet. No service, supervision, crate.

(SAVE) (S&) (X) (🛏) (≋)

◆◆◆ Days Inn Conference Center 🅜
(865) 687-5800. **$69-$89.** 5335 Central Ave Pike. I-75, exit 108 (Merchant Dr). Int corridors. **Pets:** Medium. Supervision.

(ASK) (S&) (X) (🛏) (🖥) (≋)

◆◆ Days Inn West 🅜
(865) 966-5801. **$46-$76.** 326 Lovell Rd. I-40 and I-75, exit 374. Ext corridors. **Pets:** Small. Supervision.

(ASK) (S&) (X) (🗝) (🛏) (🖥) (≋)

◆◆◆ Hampton Inn-Knoxville West at Cedar Bluff 🅜 🐾
(865) 693-1101. **$74-$84, 30 days notice.** 9128 Executive Park Blvd. I-40 and I-75 (Cedar Bluff Rd), exit 378. Ext/int corridors. **Pets:** Medium, other. Designated rooms, supervision.

(X) (♿) (🗝) (🖥) (🖥) (≋)

◆◆◆ Hilton Knoxville Downtown 🅗
(865) 523-2300. **$84-$84, 3 days notice.** 501 W Church Ave. I-40, exit 388, 0.7 mi s on US 441, then just e; at Locust St. Int corridors. **Pets:** Large. Supervision.

(ASK) (X) (🔥) (🗝) (🛏) (🖥) (¶) (≋)

◆◆◆ **Holiday Inn-Central/Papermill Road** Ⓜ️ 🐾
(865) 584-3911. **$99-$189, 3 days notice.** 1315 Kirby Rd. I-40 and I-75, exit 383 (Papermill Rd). Int corridors. **Pets:** Large. $20 one-time fee/room. No service, supervision, crate.

🅰🆂🅺 💷 ✖️ 🎛 🎵 🔋 💻 🍴 🛍

◆◆ **Howard Jonson's Plaza** Ⓜ️
(865) 693-8111. **$59-$109.** 7621 Kingston Pike. I-40, exit 380 (West Hills). Int corridors. **Pets:** No service, supervision, crate.

🅰🆂🅺 💷 ✖️ 🎛 🔋 💻 🍴 🛍

🅰🅰🅰 ◆◆◆ **Hyatt Regency Knoxville** Ⓗ 🐾
(865) 637-1234. **$99-$124.** 500 Hill Ave SE. I-40, exit 388A, 0.5 mi s on James White Pkwy; adjacent to Civic Coliseum. Int corridors. **Pets:** Small, other. $35 one-time fee/room. Supervision.

💷 ✖️ 🎛 🎞 🔋 💻 🍴 🛍 ✖️

🅰🅰🅰 ◆◆◆ **La Quinta Inn** Ⓜ️
(865) 687-8989. **$55-$75.** 5634 Merchant Center Blvd. Nw of I-75, exit 108 (Merchant Dr), 0.5 mi w to Merchant Center Blvd, 0.5 mi n. Int corridors. **Pets:** Small. Designated rooms, supervision.

💷 ✖️ 🎛 🎞 🎞 🔋 💻 🛍

🅰🅰🅰 ◆◆◆ **La Quinta Inn** Ⓜ️ 🐾
(865) 690-9777. **$55-$75.** 258 Peters Rd N. I-40 and I-75, exit 378 (Cedar Bluff). Ext corridors. **Pets:** Medium, other. Supervision.

💷 ✖️ 🎛 🎞 🔋 💻 🛍

🅰🅰🅰 ◆◆◆ **Masters Manor Inn** 🅱🅱 🐾
(865) 219-9888. **$100-$200.** 1909 Cedar Ln. I-75, exit 108, 2 mi e. Int corridors. **Pets:** Medium. $25 deposit/room. Designated rooms, no service, supervision, crate.

💷 ✖️

◆◆ **Microtel** Ⓜ️ 🐾
(865) 531-8041. **Call for rates.** 309 N Peters Rd. I-40, exit 378, 0.5 mi s, just w. Int corridors. **Pets:** Medium, other. $25 deposit/room, $10 one-time fee/room. Designated rooms, supervision.

✖️ 🎞 🎞

🅰🅰🅰 ◆◆ **Motel 6-1252** Ⓜ️
(865) 675-7200. **$35-$51.** 402 Lovell Rd. I-40 and I-75, exit 374. Ext corridors. **Pets:** Small. No service, supervision, crate.

💷 ✖️ 🎞 🎞 🛍 🅒🅣🅥

🅰🅰🅰 ◆◆ **Quality Inn North** Ⓜ️ 🐾
(865) 689-6600. **$69-$89.** 6712 Central Ave Pike. I-75, exit 110 (Calahan Dr). Ext/int corridors. **Pets:** Other. $50 one-time fee/pet. Designated rooms, supervision.

💷 💷 ✖️ 💻 🍴 🛍

🅰🅰🅰 ◆◆◆ **Radisson Summit Hill** Ⓗ
(865) 522-2600. **$79-$99.** 401 Summit Hill Dr. I-40, exit 388, just w. Int corridors. **Pets:** Supervision.

💷 💷 ✖️ 🎞 🎞 🔋 💻 🍴 🛍

🅰🅰🅰 ◆◆ **Ramada Limited** Ⓜ️ 🐾
(865) 546-7271. **$49-$89.** 722 Brake Bill Rd. I-40, exit 398 (Strawberry Plains); just n. Ext corridors. **Pets:** Small, other. $20 deposit/room. Designated rooms, no service, supervision, crate.

💷 💷 ✖️ 🎞 🔋 💻 🛍

🅰🅰🅰 ◆◆ **Red Roof Inn-North** Ⓜ️
(865) 689-7100. **$34-$55.** 5640 Merchant Center Blvd. Nw of I-75, exit 108 (Merchant Dr). Ext corridors. **Pets:** Medium. Designated rooms, no service, supervision, crate.

💷 ✖️ 🎞

🅰🅰🅰 ◆◆ **Red Roof Inn-West** Ⓜ️
(865) 691-1664. **$36-$70.** 209 Advantage Pl. I-40 and I-75, exit 378, just sw. Ext corridors. **Pets:** Supervision.

💷 ✖️ 🎛 🎞 🔋 🅒🅣🅥

◆◆ **Sleep Inn** Ⓜ️ 🐾
(865) 531-5900. **$65-$95.** 214 Prosperity Dr. I-40/I-75, exit 378 eastbound; exit 378B westbound, 0.5 mi n to Executive Park Dr, 1.5 mi e. Int corridors. **Pets:** $10 daily fee/room. No service, supervision, crate.

🅰🆂🅺 💷 ✖️ ♿ 🎞 🔋 🛍

◆◆ **Super 8 Motel-Knoxville** Ⓜ️
(865) 584-8511. **$40-$70, 30 days notice.** 6200 Papermill Rd. I-40, exit 383, 0.3 mi e (Papermill Rd). Ext corridors. **Pets:** Small. No service, supervision, crate.

✖️ 🎛 🎞 🔋 💻 🛍

LAKE CITY

🅰🅰🅰 ◆◆ **The Lamb's Inn** Ⓜ️ 🐾
(865) 426-2171. **$29-$53.** 620 N Main. I-75, exit 129. Ext corridors. **Pets:** No service, supervision, crate.

💷 ✖️ 🛍

LAWRENCEBURG

◆◆ **Best Western Villa Inn** Ⓜ️ 🐾
(931) 762-4448. **$69.** 2126 N Locust Ave. On US 43, 2.2 mi n of jct US 64. Ext corridors. **Pets:** Designated rooms, no service, supervision, crate.

🅰🆂🅺 💷 ✖️ 🔋 💻 🛍

LEBANON

◆◆◆ **Best Western Executive Inn** Ⓜ️
(615) 444-0505. **$69-$74.** 631 S Cumberland St. I-40, exit 238, 0.5 mi n. Ext/int corridors. **Pets:** Supervision.

🅰🆂🅺 ✖️ 🔋 💻 🛍

🅰🅰🅰 ◆◆ **Comfort Inn** Ⓜ️ 🐾
(615) 444-1001. **$55-$55.** 829 S Cumberland St. I-40, exit 238. Ext corridors. **Pets:** Small, other. $5 daily fee/pet. Designated rooms, supervision.

💷 💷 ✖️ 🔋 🛍

◆◆ **Days Inn** Ⓜ️
(615) 444-5635. **$35-$52.** 914 Murfreesboro Rd. I-40, exit 238. Ext corridors. **Pets:** Small. No service, supervision, crate.

🅰🆂🅺 💷 ✖️ 🔋 🛍

◆◆◆ **Hampton Inn** Ⓜ️ 🐾
(615) 444-7400. **$69-$84, 3 days notice.** 704 S Cumberland St. I-40, exit 238. Ext corridors. **Pets:** Small. $50 deposit/room, $10 daily fee/room, $10 one-time fee/room. Designated rooms, no service, supervision, crate.

🅰🆂🅺 ✖️ 🎛 🎞 🔋 💻 🛍

◆◆ **Super 8 Motel** Ⓜ
(615) 444-5637. **$32-$48.** 914 Murfreesboro Rd. I-40, exit 238. Ext corridors. **Pets:** No service, supervision, crate.
(ASK) (S) (✕) (🗄) (🖼)

LOUDON

⬛ ◆◆◆ **Holiday Inn Express** Ⓜ 🐾
(865) 458-5668. **$79-$89.** 12452 Hwy 72N. I-75, exit 72. Ext corridors. **Pets:** Small. Supervision.
(S) (✕) (🏠) (🎞) (🖥) (🖼)

⬛ ◆◆ **Knights Inn** Ⓜ 🐾
(865) 458-5855. **$40-$60, 7 days notice.** 15100 Hwy 72. I-75, exit 72. Ext corridors. **Pets:** Medium. $3 daily fee/pet. Designated rooms, no service, supervision, crate.
(S) (S) (✕) (🗄) (🖼)

MANCHESTER

◆◆ **Days Inn** Ⓜ
(931) 728-6023. **Call for rates.** 890 Interstate Dr. Just e of I-24, exit 110. Ext corridors. **Pets:** Small. Supervision.
(✕) (🗄) (🖼)

⬛ ◆ **Scottish Inn** Ⓜ 🐾
(931) 728-0506. **$29-$69.** 2457 Hillsboro Blvd. I-24, exit 114, just e. Ext corridors. **Pets:** $5 daily fee/pet, $5 one-time fee/pet. Supervision.
(S) (S) (✕) (🗄) (🖼)

⬛ ◆◆ **Super 8 Motel** Ⓜ
(931) 728-9720. **$45-$65, 7 days notice.** 2430 Hillsboro Hwy. Just e of I-24, exit 114, on US 41. Ext corridors. **Pets:** Small. No service, supervision, crate.
(S) (S) (✕) (🗄) (🖼)

MCMINNVILLE

⬛ ◆◆◆ **Best Western McMinnville Inn** Ⓜ 🐾
(931) 473-7338. **$33-$65, 3 days notice.** 2545 Sparta Hwy. US 70S bypass, from I-24 exit 111, n on SR 55 to US 70S bypass. Ext corridors. **Pets:** Small. $7 daily fee/room. Designated rooms, no service, supervision, crate.
(S) (S) (✕) (🗄) (🖥) (🖼)

◆◆◆ **Shoneys Inn** Ⓜ 🐾
(931) 473-4446. **$48-$79.** 508 Sunnyside Heights. US 70S bypass, from I-24 exit 111, n on SR 55 to US 70S bypass. Int corridors. **Pets:** Supervision.
(ASK) (S) (✕) (🗄) (🖥) (🖼)

MEMPHIS METROPOLITAN AREA

COLLIERVILLE

⬛ ◆◆◆ **Comfort Inn** Ⓜ 🐾
(901) 853-1235. **$70-$88.** 1230 W Poplar. 2.5 mi w on Hwy 57 and 72. Ext corridors. **Pets:** Small, other. $25 one-time fee/room. No service, supervision, crate.
(S) (S) (✕) (🎞) (🗄) (🖼)

CORDOVA

⬛ ◆◆◆ **Best Suites of America-Memphis** Ⓜ
(901) 386-4600. **$70-$125, 7 days notice.** 8166 Varnavas Dr. I-40, exit 16, 0.3 mi s on Germantown Rd. Int corridors. **Pets:** Supervision.
(S) (S) (✕) (🐾) (🗄) (🖥) (🖼)

COVINGTON

⬛ ◆◆ **Best Western Inn** Ⓜ 🐾
(901) 476-8561. **$45-$55.** 873 Hwy 51 N. 0.8 mi n on US 51 N. Ext corridors. **Pets:** Small. $25 deposit/room. No service, supervision, crate.
(S) (S) (✕) (🎞) (🗄) (🖼)

GERMANTOWN

⬛ ◆◆ **Best Inns of America-Memphis** Ⓜ 🐾
(901) 757-7800. **$50-$88, 7 days notice.** 7787 Wolf River Blvd. I-40, exit 16, 5 mi s on Germantown Pkwy to Wolf River Blvd. Int corridors. **Pets:** Small. No service, supervision, crate.
(S) (S) (✕) (🏠) (🐾) (🗄) (🖥) (🖼)

◆◆◆ **Homewood Suites Germantown** Ⓜ 🐾
(901) 751-2500. **$129.** 7855 Wolf River Pkwy. I-40, exit 16, 5.8 mi s on CR 177 at jct of Germantown and Wolf River Pkwys. Int corridors. **Pets:** Small. $100 one-time fee/room. No service, supervision, crate.
(ASK) (S) (✕) (🐾) (🗄) (🖥) (🖼) (✕)

LAKELAND

◆◆ **Days Inn** Ⓜ 🐾
(901) 388-7120. **$55-$75, 7 days notice.** 9822 Huff & Puff Rd. I-40, exit 20. Ext corridors. **Pets:** Small. Supervision.
(ASK) (S) (✕) (🐾) (🖼) (🦮)

⬛ ◆◆ **Super 8 Motel** Ⓜ 🐾
(901) 372-4575. **$49-$69.** 9779 Huff & Puff Rd. I-40, exit 20. Ext corridors. **Pets:** Medium, dogs only. $10 daily fee/pet, $10 one-time fee/pet. No service, supervision, crate.
(S) (S) (✕) (🗄) (🖼)

MEMPHIS

⬛ ◆◆◆ **Amerisuites Memphis/Cordova** Ⓜ 🐾
(901) 371-0010. **$119-$139.** 7905 Giacosa Pl. I-40, exit 16, just n on Germantown Rd, just w. Int corridors. **Pets:** Very small, other. $50 one-time fee/room. Supervision.
(S) (S) (✕) (🦽) (🎞) (🐾) (🗄) (🖥) (🖼)

AmeriSuites Primacy Parkway M
(901) 680-9700. **$89-$99.** 1220 Primacy Pkwy. I-240, exit 15 (Poplar Ave), 0.3 mi e to Ridgeway Rd, just s. Int corridors. **Pets:** Small. No service, supervision, crate.

Baymont Inn & Suites-Memphis Airport M
(901) 396-5411. **$61-$66.** 3005 Millbranch Rd. Just s of I-240, exit 24 (Millbranch Rd). Int corridors. **Pets:** Medium. Designated rooms, no service, supervision, crate.

Baymont Inn & Suites-Memphis East M
(901) 377-2233. **$64-$72.** 6020 Shelby Oaks Dr. I-40, exit 12, just n. Int corridors. **Pets:** Medium. Designated rooms, no service, supervision, crate.

Comfort Inn Airport/Graceland M
(901) 345-3344. **$65-$96, 4 days notice.** 1581 E Brook Rd. I-55, exit 5A (Brook Rd), 0.3 mi e. Ext corridors. **Pets:** $10 one-time fee/pet. No service, supervision, crate.

Drury Inn-Memphis M
(901) 373-8200. **$71-$90.** 1556 Sycamore View. I-40, exit 12, just n. Int corridors. **Pets:** Small. Supervision.

Hampton Inn Walnut Grove M
(901) 747-3700. **$73-$89.** 33 Humphreys Center Dr. I-240, exit 13 (Walnut Grove E), just e, adjacent to Humphreys Center and Baptist East Memorial Hospital. Int corridors. **Pets:** Medium. Designated rooms, supervision.

Holiday Inn Express Northeast M
(901) 685-0704. **$55-$55, 3 days notice.** 5225 Summer Ave. I-240, exit 12A (Summer Ave E). Ext corridors. **Pets:** Designated rooms, no service, supervision, crate.

Holiday Inn-Medical Center H
(901) 278-4100. **Call for rates.** 1837 Union Ave. I-240, exit 30, (Union Ave) 1.3 mi e, Madison exit 29 southbound. Int corridors. **Pets:** Small. Designated rooms, no service, supervision, crate.

Holiday Inn Memphis East MI
(901) 682-7881. **$109-$159.** 5795 Poplar Ave. I-240, exit 15 (Poplar Ave) e. Int corridors. **Pets:** Supervision.

La Quinta Inn-Airport M
(901) 396-1000. **$59-$79.** 2745 Airways Blvd. I-240, exit 23B, Airways Blvd 0.5 mi s. Ext corridors. **Pets:** Designated rooms, no service, supervision, crate.

La Quinta Inn & Suites M
(901) 374-0330. **$69-$99.** 1236 Primacy Pkwy. I-240, exit 15 (Poplar Ave), 0.3 mi e to Ridgeway Rd, then just s. Int corridors. **Pets:** Small, other. No service, supervision, crate.

La Quinta Inn-East M
(901) 382-2323. **$65-$82.** 6068 Macon Cove. I-40, exit 12, just s. Ext corridors. **Pets:** Medium. Supervision.

La Quinta Inn-Medical Center M
(901) 526-1050. **$69-$89.** 42 S Camilla St. Jct I-240 and Union Ave W, exit 30, southbound exit 30 (Madison). Ext corridors. **Pets:** Small. No service, supervision, crate.

Marriott Residence Inn A
(901) 685-9595. **$139, 7 days notice.** 6141 Old Poplar Pike. I-240, exit 15 (Poplar Ave E), 0.5 mi e. Ext/int corridors. **Pets:** Supervision.

Memphis Inn East M
(901) 373-9898. **$39-$59, 30 days notice.** 6050 Macon Cove. I-40, exit 12, just s. Ext corridors. **Pets:** No service, supervision, crate.

The Memphis Marriott H
(901) 362-6200. **$139-$174.** 2625 Thousand Oaks Blvd. I-240, exit 18 (Perkins), 0.5 mi s, then e on American Way. Int corridors. **Pets:** Other. Supervision.

Motel 6-459 M
(901) 382-8572. **$42-$58.** 1321 Sycamore View. I-40 exit 12. Ext corridors. **Pets:** Small, other. Supervision.

Quality Inn Suites M
(901) 388-1300. **$50-$105, 7 days notice.** 1541 Sycamore View. I-40, exit 12, just n. Ext/int corridors. **Pets:** Small. Designated rooms, no service, supervision, crate.

Red Roof Inn-East M
(901) 388-6111. **$46-$64.** 6055 Shelby Oaks Dr. I-40, exit 12, just n. Ext corridors. **Pets:** Large, other. Supervision.

Red Roof Inn Medical Center M
(901) 528-0650. **$54-$70.** 210 S Pauline St. I-240N, Union Ave W exit 30, I-240S Madison Ave exit 30. Ext corridors. **Pets:** $5 daily fee/room. No service, supervision, crate.

Red Roof Inn-South M
(901) 363-2335. **$46-$72.** 3875 American Way. I-240, exit 20A (Getwell Rd) eastbound; I-240, exit 20 westbound. Ext corridors. **Pets:** Medium. Supervision.

Wellesley Inn & Suites M
(901) 380-1525. **$66-$66.** 2520 Horizon Lake Dr. I-40, exit 16B (Germantown Rd), just n, just w. Int corridors. **Pets:** Small. $100 deposit/room, $50 one-time fee/room. No service, supervision, crate.

MILLINGTON

◆◆ Best Western Inn M
(901) 587-2222. $54-$65. 7726 Hwy 51 N. 0.3 mi s on US
51 N. Ext corridors. Pets: Medium. Designated rooms, no
service, supervision, crate.

[ASK] [S&] [X] [♪] [♦] [♦] [♦]

(AAA) ◆◆ Magnolia Inn M ✿
(901) 873-4400. $46-$50, 7 days notice. 8193 Hwy 51 N.
0.3 mi n on US 51. Ext corridors. Pets: Small, other. Supervision.

[SAVE] [S&] [X] [♦] [♦] [♦]

✿ END METROPOLITAN AREA ✿

MORRISTOWN

(AAA) ◆◆ Days Inn M ✿
(423) 587-2200. $39-$52. 2512 E Andrew Johnson Hwy.
I-81, exit 8 (25E); 6 mi n, exit 2B (Greenville-Morristown
exit). Ext corridors. Pets: Small, other. $10 deposit/room.
Designated rooms, supervision.

[SAVE] [S&] [X] [♦]

(AAA) ◆◆◆ Ramada Inn MI ✿
(423) 587-2400. $62-$62. 5435 S Davy Crockett Pkwy. I-81,
exit 8, just n. Int corridors. Pets: Medium, other. No service,
supervision, crate.

[SAVE] [S&] [X] [♦] [♦] [♦] [♦]

◆◆ Super 8 Motel M ✿
(423) 318-8888. $43-$60. 5400 S Davey Crockett. I-81, exit
8, just n. Int corridors. Pets: Other. $9 daily fee/pet. Desig-
nated rooms, supervision.

[X] [♦] [♦]

MURFREESBORO

◆◆◆ Baymont Inn & Suites M ✿
(615) 890-1006. $66-$116. 2135 S Church St. I-24 exit 81B.
Int corridors. Pets: Medium. $50 deposit/pet. No service,
supervision, crate.

[ASK] [S&] [X] [♦] [♦] [♦] [♦]

(AAA) ◆◆ Best Western Chaffin Inn M ✿
(615) 895-3818. $65-$85. 168 Chaffin Pl. I-24, exit 78B (SR
96). Ext corridors. Pets: $8 daily fee/pet, $8 one-time fee/
pet. Designated rooms, no service, supervision, crate.

[S&] [X] [♦] [♦]

(AAA) ◆◆◆ Holiday Inn Holidome MI ✿
(615) 896-2420. $69-$89. 2227 Old Fort Pkwy. I-24, exit
78B. Ext/int corridors. Pets: Large. Designated rooms, no
service, supervision, crate.

[SAVE] [S&] [X] [♪] [♦] [♦] [♦] [♦]

(AAA) ◆◆ Howard Johnson Lodge M ✿
(615) 896-5522. $30-$85. 2424 S Church St. I-24, exit 81A.
Int corridors. Pets: Small. $5 daily fee/pet. Supervision.

[SAVE] [S&] [X] [♦] [♦] [♦] [♦]

(AAA) ◆◆ Quality Inn M
(615) 848-9030. $49-$99, 3 days notice. 118 Westgate
Blvd. I-24, exit 81A. Int corridors. Pets: No service, supervision, crate.

[SAVE] [S&] [X] [♦] [♦] [♦]

(AAA) ◆◆ Ramada Limited M ✿
(615) 896-5080. $40-$100. 1855 S Church St. I-24, exit 81,
just e. Int corridors. Pets: $10 daily fee/pet, $10 one-time
fee/pet. Supervision.

[SAVE] [S&] [X] [♦]

(AAA) ◆◆◆ Shoney's Inn M ✿
(615) 896-6030. $51-$69. 1954 S Church St. I-24, exit 81,
just e. Ext corridors. Pets: Supervision.

[SAVE] [S&] [X] [♪] [♪] [♦] [♦] [♦]

NASHVILLE METROPOLITAN AREA

GOODLETTSVILLE

◆◆◆ Baymont Inn & Suites North M ✿
(615) 851-1891. $55-$120. 120 Cartwright Ct. I-65, exit 97
(Long Hollow Pike), just w. Int corridors. Pets: Small. Designated rooms, supervision.

[S&] [X] [♦] [♪] [♦] [♦] [♦] [♦]

◆ Econo Lodge Rivergate M ✿
(615) 859-4988. $60-$100, 5 days notice. 320 Long Hollow Pike. I-65, exit 97 (Long Hollow Pike), 0.5 mi e. Ext
corridors. Pets: Small. $10 deposit/pet. Designated rooms,
no service, supervision, crate.

[ASK] [S&] [X] [♪] [♪] [♦] [♦] [♦] [CTV]

(AAA) ◆◆ Red Roof Inn-Nashville North M
(615) 859-2537. $40-$77. 110 Northgate Dr. I-65, exit 97
(Long Hollow Pike), 0.5 mi e. Ext corridors. Pets: Medium.
Supervision.

[SAVE] [X] [♪]

HERMITAGE

(AAA) ◆ Hermitage Inn M ✿
(615) 883-7444. $48-$73. 4144 Lebanon Rd. 2 mi n on Old
Hickory Blvd from I-40, exit 221, just e on US 70. Ext
corridors. Pets: Other. Supervision.

[SAVE] [S&] [X] [♦]

◆◆ Ramada Limited M
(615) 889-8940. $55-$70. 5770 Old Hickory Blvd. I-40, exit
221. Ext corridors. Pets: Designated rooms, no service,
supervision, crate.

[X] [♦] [♦] [CTV]

NASHVILLE

AAA ◆◆◆ AmeriSuites M
(615) 872-0422. **$99-$129.** 220 Rudy's Circle Dr. 6 mi ne, Briley Pkwy, exit 12; to Music Valley Dr, left 0.3 mi. Int corridors. **Pets:** Supervision.
[SAVE] [S6] [X] [ft] [B] [▭] [∼]

◆◆ Baymont Inn & Suites-Nashville Airport M ✿
(615) 885-3100. **$66-$74.** 531 Donelson Pike. I-40, exit 216C (Donelson Pike), 0.3 mi n. Int corridors. **Pets:** Small. $50 deposit/room. Designated rooms, no service, supervision, crate.
[S6] [X] [∅] [B] [▭] [∼]

AAA ◆◆◆ Best Suites of America M
(615) 391-3919. **Call for rates.** 2521 Elm Hill Pike. I-40, exit 215, 1 mi n on Briley Pkwy, exit 7; 1 mi e. Int corridors. **Pets:** Supervision.
[SAVE] [X] [∅] [B] [▭] [∼]

AAA ◆◆ Best Western Calumet Inn M ✿
(615) 889-9199. **$95, 7 days notice.** 701 Stewarts Ferry Pike. I-40, exit 219 (Stewarts Ferry Pike). Ext corridors. **Pets:** Small, other. $10 daily fee/room. Supervision.
[SAVE] [S6] [X] [B] [▭] [∼]

◆◆ Days Inn Bell Road M
(615) 731-7800. **$59-$85.** 510 Collins Park Dr. I-24, exit 59 (Bell Rd). Ext corridors. **Pets:** Supervision.
[ASK] [S6] [X] [∅] [∐] [∼]

◆◆◆ Drury Inn South M
(615) 834-7170. **$60-$80.** 341 Harding Pl. I-24, exit 56 (Harding Pl). Ext corridors. **Pets:** Supervision.
[X] [ft] [∅] [B] [▭] [∼]

AAA ◆◆ Econo Lodge M
(615) 226-9805. **$30-$90.** 2403 Brick Church Pike. I-65, exit 87 (Trinity Ln), just nw. Ext corridors. **Pets:** Small. No service, supervision, crate.
[SAVE] [S6] [X]

◆◆◆ Embassy Suites H ✿
(615) 871-0033. **$139-$139, 3 days notice.** 10 Century Blvd. I-40E, to Briley Pkwy N, exit Elm Hill Pk, 0.3 mi e to McGavock Pike, 0.3 mi s to Century Blvd, 0.3 mi w. Int corridors. **Pets:** Small, other. $50 one-time fee/room. No service, supervision, crate.
[ASK] [S6] [X] [⅍] [☒] [B] [▭] [∐] [∼]

◆◆ GuestHouse Inn M
(615) 329-1000. **$65-$85.** 1909 Hayes St. I-40, Church St exit, 1 mi w to 19th, just s. Int corridors. **Pets:** Small. Supervision.
[ASK] [S6] [X] [∅] [B] [▭]

◆◆◆ Hampton Inn Briley Parkway M ✿
(615) 871-0222. **$77-$95.** 2350 Elm Hill Pike. I-40, exit 215B, Briley Pkwy to exit 7, Elm Hill Pike. Ext corridors. **Pets:** Small, other. No service, supervision, crate.
[X] [ft] [∅] [▭] [∼]

AAA ◆◆ Holiday Inn Express M
(615) 889-0086. **$80-$99, 30 days notice.** 2516 Music Valley Dr. I-40, exit 215, 4 mi n; or I-65, exit 90, Magavock exit off Briley Pkwy. Int corridors. **Pets:** Medium. Designated rooms, no service, supervision, crate.
[SAVE] [S6] [X] [B] [∼]

AAA ◆◆◆ Holiday Inn Express M ✿
(615) 226-4600. **$61.** 2401 Brick Church Pike. I-65, exit 87B (Trinity Ln), just nw. Int corridors. **Pets:** Supervision.
[SAVE] [X] [∅] [∼]

◆◆◆ Holiday Inn Select Opryland/Airport MI
(615) 883-9770. **$69-$139, 3 days notice.** 2200 Elm Hill Pike. I-40 exit 215B, 0.5 mi n at jct Briley Pkwy and Elm Hill Pike. Int corridors. **Pets:** Large. Supervision.
[ASK] [S6] [X] [⅍] [∅] [☒] [B] [▭] [∐] [∼]

◆◆◆ Holiday Inn Select-Vanderbilt MI
(615) 327-4707. **$129-$179, 3 days notice.** 2613 W End Ave. I-40E, exit 209B w on Broadway, I-40W exit 209A, w on Broadway. Int corridors. **Pets:** Very small. Designated rooms, no service, supervision, crate.
[ASK] [S6] [X] [ft] [∅] [B] [▭] [∐] [∼]

AAA ◆◆◆ Holiday Inn-The Crossings M
(615) 731-2361. **$79-$86.** 201 Crossings Pl. I-24, exit 60, 0.5 mi e. Int corridors. **Pets:** Medium. No service, supervision, crate.
[SAVE] [S6] [X] [⅍] [∅] [☒] [▭] [∐] [∼]

◆◆◆ Homestead Village Guest Studios M ✿
(615) 316-9020. **$65-$100.** 727 McGavock Pike. I-40, exit 219, 0.5 n on Elm Hill Pk, exit 7, just e. Ext corridors. **Pets:** $75 one-time fee/pet. Supervision.
[X] [⅍] [∅] [B] [▭]

◆◆ Howard Johnson Motor Lodge-West M ✿
(615) 352-7080. **$48-$68.** 6834 Charlotte Pike. I-40, exit 201, 0.4 mi e on US 70. Int corridors. **Pets:** Other. Supervision.
[ASK] [S6] [X] [B] [∼]

AAA ◆◆◆ La Quinta Inn-Metro Center M
(615) 259-2130. **$59-$82.** 2001 Metro Center Blvd. I-265 exit 1, just n. Ext corridors. **Pets:** Small. No service, supervision, crate.
[SAVE] [X] [∅] [▭] [∼]

AAA ◆◆◆ La Quinta Inn Nashville Airport M
(615) 885-3000. **$69-$85.** 2345 Atrium Way. Briley Pkwy to exit 7, Elm Hill Pike, e to Atrium Way, then 0.3 mi n. Int corridors. **Pets:** Small. Designated rooms, supervision.
[SAVE] [X] [⅍] [∅] [B] [▭] [∼]

AAA ◆◆◆ La Quinta Inn-South M ✿
(615) 834-6900. **$55-$82.** 4311 Sidco Dr. I-65, exit 78A southbound; exit 78 northbound (Harding Pl). Ext corridors. **Pets:** Medium, other. Supervision.
[SAVE] [X] [ft] [▭] [∼]

AAA ◆◆◆◆ Loews Vanderbilt Plaza Hotel H ✿
(615) 320-1700. **$119-$159.** 2100 W End Ave. 1.3 mi w. Int corridors. **Pets:** Medium. Designated rooms, no service, supervision, crate.
[SAVE] [S6] [X] [∅] [☒] [B] [▭] [∐]

◆ Motel 6–156 **M**
(615) 333-9933. **$33-$55.** 95 Wallace Rd. I-24, exit 56 (Harding Rd). Ext corridors. **Pets:** Small. No service, supervision, crate.
⬚⬚⬚

◆◆ Pear Tree Inn South **M**
(615) 834-4242. **$45-$65.** 343 Harding Pl. I-24, exit 56 (Harding Pl). Ext corridors. **Pets:** Small. No service, supervision, crate.
⬚⬚⬚

◆◆ Quality Inn & Suites **M** ❀
(615) 226-9560. **$65-$70.** 2306 Brick Church Pike. I-65, exit 87 (Trinity Ln), just nw. Ext corridors. **Pets:** Very small. Designated rooms, no service, supervision, crate.
⬚⬚⬚⬚⬚⬚⬚

◆◆ The Quarters Motor Inn **M**
(615) 731-5990. **$50-$85.** 1100 Bell Rd. I-24, exit 59 (Bell Rd), just w. Ext corridors. **Pets:** Supervision.
⬚⬚⬚⬚

◆◆ Ramada Inn Southeast at Hickory Hollow Mall **M**
(615) 731-8540. **$49-$89, 7 days notice.** 1001 Bell Rd. I-24, exit 59(Bell Rd). Int corridors. **Pets:** Very small. Designated rooms, no service, supervision, crate.
⬚⬚⬚⬚⬚⬚⬚⬚⬚

◆◆ Red Roof Inn Airport **M**
(615) 872-0735. **$46-$68.** 510 Claridge Dr. I-40, exit 216C (Donaldson Pike), 0.3 mi n. Ext corridors. **Pets:** Medium. Supervision.
⬚⬚⬚⬚

◆◆ Red Roof Inns **M** ❀
(615) 889-0090. **$59-$70, 7 days notice.** 2460 Music Valley Dr. I-40, exit 215, 4 mi n, Magavock exit off Briley Pkwy. Int corridors. **Pets:** Small. Supervision.
⬚⬚⬚⬚

◆◆ Red Roof Inn South **M** ❀
(615) 832-0093. **$46-$68.** 4271 Sidco Dr. I-65, exit 78A southbound; exit 78 northbound. Ext corridors. **Pets:** Small, other. Supervision.
⬚⬚⬚⬚

◆◆◆◆ Sheraton Music City Hotel **H** ❀
(615) 885-2200. **$99-$99.** 777 McGavock Pike. I-40, exit 215B, 1 mi n to Elm Hill Pike, 0.5 mi e, then s. Int corridors. **Pets:** Other. $50 deposit/room. No service, supervision, crate.
⬚⬚⬚⬚⬚⬚⬚⬚⬚

◆◆◆ Shoney's Inn-of Music Valley **M** ❀
(615) 885-4030. **$98-$133.** 2420 Music Valley Dr. Briley Pkwy, exit 12B, 0.3 mi w, 0.3 mi n. Int corridors. **Pets:** Other. $100 deposit/pet. Designated rooms, supervision.
⬚⬚⬚⬚⬚⬚

◆◆◆ Shoney's Inn Of Nashville **M**
(615) 255-9977. **$65-$72, 3 days notice.** 1501 Demonbraun St. I-40/265, exit 209B. Ext corridors. **Pets:** Supervision.
⬚⬚⬚⬚

◆◆ Super 8 Motel **M**
(615) 356-0888. **$50-$60.** 412 Robertson Rd. I-40, exit 204. Int corridors. **Pets:** Designated rooms, no service, supervision, crate.
⬚⬚⬚⬚⬚

◆◆◆ Union Station, A Wyndham Grand Heritage Hotel **H** ❀
(615) 726-1001. **$169.** 1001 Broadway. I-40, exit 209, just ne. Int corridors. **Pets:** Small. $25 deposit/room. Designated rooms, no service, supervision, crate.
⬚⬚⬚⬚⬚⬚

◆◆◆ The Westin Hermitage Nashville **H** ❀
(615) 244-3121. **$139-$189.** 231 6th Ave N. Center. Int corridors. **Pets:** Other. $100 deposit/room. No service, supervision, crate.
⬚⬚⬚⬚⬚

◆◆◆ Wyndham Garden Hotel **MI** ❀
(615) 889-9090. **$115.** 1112 Airport Center Dr. I-40, exit 216C (Donaldson Pike N). Int corridors. **Pets:** Supervision.
⬚⬚⬚⬚⬚⬚⬚⬚⬚

❀ **END METROPOLITAN AREA** ❀

NEWPORT

◆◆◆ Best Western Newport Inn **M** ❀
(423) 623-8713. **$48-$139.** 1015 Cosby Hwy. I-40, exit 435, just w. Ext corridors. **Pets:** Supervision.
⬚⬚⬚⬚⬚⬚⬚

◆◆ Comfort Inn **M** ❀
(423) 623-5355. **$48-$159.** 1149 Smokey Mountain Ln. I-40, exit 432B. Int corridors. **Pets:** Small. $10 daily fee/pet, $10 one-time fee/pet. No service, supervision, crate.
⬚⬚⬚⬚⬚⬚⬚

◆◆◆ Holiday Inn **MI** ❀
(423) 623-8622. **$90.** 1010 Cosby Hwy. I-40, exit 435. Ext/int corridors. **Pets:** Other. Supervision.
⬚⬚⬚⬚⬚⬚⬚

◆◆ Motel 6–4090 **M** ❀
(423) 623-1850. **$37-$53.** 255 Heritage Blvd. I-40 exit 435 just n, turn right. Int corridors. **Pets:** Medium, other. No service, supervision, crate.
⬚⬚⬚⬚⬚

◆◆ Relax Inn **M** ❀
(423) 625-1521. **$24-$85.** 1148 W Hwy 25-70. I-40, exit 432B. Ext corridors. **Pets:** $4 deposit/pet. No service, supervision, crate.
⬚⬚⬚⬚

OAK RIDGE

◆◆◆ **Comfort Inn** Ⓜ ❖
(865) 481-8200. **$69-$89.** 433 S Rutgers Ave. 0.9 mi se of
SR 95 on SR 62. Int corridors. **Pets:** Large, other. No
service, supervision, crate.
(ASK) (So) (X) (🛏) (💻) (🍽) (🔜)

◆◆ **Days Inn** Ⓜ ❖
(865) 483-5615. **$49-$59, 7 days notice.** 206 S Illinois Ave.
0.5 mi se of SR 95 on SR 62. Ext corridors. **Pets:** Other. $3
daily fee/room. Supervision.
(ASK) (So) (X) (🛏) (🔜) (X)

◆◆◆ **Garden Plaza Hotel** Ⓗ ❖
(865) 481-2468. **$79-$99.** 215 S Illinois Ave. 0.3 mi se of
SR 95 on SR 62; adj to American Science and Energy
Museum. Int corridors. **Pets:** Small. No service, supervision,
crate.
(ASK) (So) (X) (🛏) (💻) (🍽) (🔜)

◆◆ **Super 8 Motel** Ⓜ ❖
(865) 483-1200. **$44-$69.** 1590 Oak Ridge Tpke. Jct of US
95 and 62. Ext corridors. **Pets:** Other. $5 daily fee/pet, $5
one-time fee/pet. No service, supervision, crate.
(ASK) (So) (X) (🛏) (🔜)

ONEIDA

🅰🅰🅰 ◆ **The Galloway Inn** Ⓜ ❖
(423) 569-8835. **$28-$36.** 299 Galloway Dr. 2 mi s on US
27. Ext corridors. **Pets:** Other. Supervision.
(SAVE) (So) (X) (🛏)

OOLTEWAH

◆ **Super 8 Motel** Ⓜ ❖
(423) 238-5951. **Call for rates.** 5111 Hunter Rd. Jct US 11,
64 and I-75, exit 11. Ext corridors. **Pets:** Very small. $10
deposit/pet, $5 daily fee/pet, $5 one-time fee/pet. Supervision.
(X) (🔜)

PARIS

◆◆ **Best Western Travelers Inn** Ⓜ
(901) 642-8881. **$40-$52.** 1297 E Wood St. 1 mi ne on US
79. Ext corridors. **Pets:** Supervision.
(X) (🛏) (🔜)

PIGEON FORGE

🅰🅰🅰 ◆◆◆ **Baymont Inn** Ⓜ ❖
(865) 428-7305. **$60-$100, 3 days notice.** 2179 Parkway. 2
mi n on US 441. Int corridors. **Pets:** Other. Supervision.
(SAVE) (So) (X) (🏠) (🔒) (🛏) (🔜)

🅰🅰🅰 ◆◆ **Grand Resort Hotel & Convention**
Center Ⓜ ❖
(865) 453-1000. **$70-$130.** 3171 N Parkway. US 441. Ext/
int corridors. **Pets:** Very small. $10 daily fee/room. No serv-
ice, supervision, crate.
(SAVE) (So) (X) (🛏) (🍽) (🔜) (X)

◆◆◆ **Holiday Inn Resort** Ⓜ ❖
(865) 428-2700. **Call for rates.** 3230 Parkway. Just w of
US 441. Int corridors. **Pets:** Medium, other. No service,
supervision, crate.
(ASK) (X) (🔒) (🛏) (💻) (🍽) (🔜)

🅰🅰🅰 ◆◆ **Microtel** Ⓜ ❖
(865) 429-0150. **$59-$94, 7 days notice.** 202 Emert St. US
441, just w between traffic light 7 and 8. Int corridors.
Pets: Other. Supervision.
(SAVE) (So) (X) (🛏) (🔜)

POWELL

◆◆◆ **Baymont Inn** Ⓜ ❖
(865) 947-7500. **$59-$80.** 7534 Conner Rd. I-75, exit 112
(Emory Rd), just e. Int corridors. **Pets:** Medium. $50
deposit/room. Designated rooms, no service, supervision,
crate.
(ASK) (So) (X) (♿) (🔒) (🛏) (💻) (🔜)

🅰🅰🅰 ◆◆ **Comfort Inn** Ⓜ
(865) 938-5500. **$69-$89.** 323 E Emory Rd. I-75 N, exit
112. Ext corridors. **Pets:** No service, supervision, crate.
(SAVE) (So) (X) (🛏) (💻) (🔜)

PULASKI

🅰🅰🅰 ◆◆ **Super 8 Motel** Ⓜ ❖
(931) 363-4501. **$39-$70.** 2400 Hwy 64 E. I-65, exit 14, just
e. Ext corridors. **Pets:** Medium, other. $5 daily fee/pet, $5
one-time fee/pet. No service, supervision, crate.
(SAVE) (So) (X) (🛏) (🔜) (CTV)

SEVIERVILLE

🅰🅰🅰 ◆◆◆ **Best Western Dumplin Valley**
Inn Ⓜ ❖
(865) 933-3467. **$45-$90.** 3426 Winfield Dunn Pkwy. I-40,
exit 407, 0.3 mi s. Ext corridors. **Pets:** Medium. $10 daily
fee/pet. Supervision.
(SAVE) (So) (X) (🔒) (🛏) (🔜)

◆◆◆ **High Valley Rentals** Ⓒ ❖
(865) 428-0608. **$85-$95** (no credit cards), 7 days notice.
630 Thomas Loop Rd. 10.6 mi n on US 411, 1.3 mi se on
Thomas Crossroads to second entrance Thomas Rd, 1.5
mi w. Ext corridors. **Pets:** Medium. $150 deposit/room, $40
one-time fee/pet. No service, supervision, crate.
(🛏) (💻) (CTV)

SHELBYVILLE

◆◆ **Super 8 Motel** Ⓜ ❖
(931) 684-6050. **$49-$60.** 317 N Cannon Blvd. 0.5 mi n on
US 231 business route. Ext corridors. **Pets:** Small, dogs
only. $10 daily fee/room. No service, supervision, crate.
(ASK) (So) (X) (🛏) (🔜)

SMYRNA

◆◆◆ **Days Inn** Ⓜ ❖
(615) 355-6161. **$55-$75, 3 days notice.** 1300 Plaza Dr.
I-24, exit 66, 2 mi ne. Ext corridors. **Pets:** Dogs only. $7
daily fee/pet, $7 one-time fee/pet. Designated rooms, no
service, supervision, crate.
(ASK) (So) (X) (🛏) (🔜)

SPRINGFIELD

[AAA] ◆◆◆ **Best Western Springfield** [M]
(615) 384-1234. **$54-$89.** 2001 Memorial Blvd. SR 41 and 431, 0.8 mi s. Ext corridors. **Pets:** Supervision.

[SAVE] [S/D] 🚭 👂 🧊 ☕ 🏊

SWEETWATER

[AAA] ◆◆◆ **Best Western Sweetwater Inn** [MI] 🐾
(423) 337-3541. **$65-$85.** 1421 Murray's Chapel Rd. Just w of I-75, exit 60. Ext/int corridors. **Pets:** Very small. No service, supervision, crate.

[SAVE] [S/D] 🚭 🧊 ☕ 🍴 🏊 [CTV]

[AAA] ◆◆ **Comfort Inn West** [M] 🐾
(423) 337-3353. **$40-$75.** 248 Hwy 68. I-75, exit 60. Ext/int corridors. **Pets:** Small, other. $5 daily fee/pet. No service, supervision, crate.

[SAVE] [S/D] 🚭 🧊 🏊

[AAA] ◆◆ **Days Inn** [M] 🐾
(423) 337-4200. **$39-$65, 3 days notice.** 229 Hwy 68. I-75, exit 60. Ext corridors. **Pets:** Large, other. $5 one-time fee/room. Supervision.

[SAVE] [S/D] 🚭 🧊 🏊

WHITE HOUSE

[AAA] ◆◆ **Days Inn Whitehouse** [M] 🐾
(615) 672-3746. **$39-$75, 3 days notice.** 1009 Hwy 76. I-65, exit 108, just w. Ext corridors. **Pets:** Small. $5 daily fee/pet. Designated rooms, no service, supervision, crate.

[SAVE] [S/D] 🚭 🧊 🏊

◆◆◆ **Holiday Inn Express** [M]
(615) 672-7200. **$54-$65.** 354 Hester Ln. I-65, exit 108, just e. Ext corridors. **Pets:** Medium. No service, supervision, crate.

[A$K] [S/D] 🚭 🚶 ♿ 🧊 🏊

WHITE PINE

◆◆ **Days Inn** [M]
(865) 674-2573. **$51-$129.** 3670 Roy Messer Hwy. I-81, exit 4. Ext corridors. **Pets:** Medium. No service, supervision, crate.

[A$K] [S/D] 🚭 🧊

CITY INDEX

ABILENE

◆◆ Antilley Inn
(915) 695-3330. **$33-$38.** 6550 S Hwy 83. Sw from I-20, exit 290 westbound, 10 mi s on Loop 322 to SR 83/84 and Antilley exit; I-20, exit 279 eastbound, 3 mi e to SR 83/84, 7 mi sw. Ext corridors. **Pets:** Medium, other. $10 daily fee/pet. No service, supervision, crate.

◆◆◆ Best Western Mall South
(915) 695-1262. **$61-$68.** 3950 Ridgemont Dr. Just s of US 83 and 84, Ridgemont Dr exit. Ext corridors. **Pets:** Supervision.

◆◆ Budget Host Colonial Inn
(915) 677-2683. **$42-$50, 3 days notice.** 3210 Pine St. Jct I-20 and US 83 business route, exit 286A. Ext/int corridors. **Pets:** Medium. $5 daily fee/pet, $5 one-time fee/pet. Supervision.

◆◆◆ Clarion Hotel & Conference Center
(915) 695-2150. **$64-$75, 3 days notice.** 5403 S 1st St. I-20, 1.7 mi s on US 83/84 (277S) to S 1st St exit. Int corridors. **Pets:** Other. $25 one-time fee/room. Supervision.

◆◆ Econo Lodge 🅼 ☂
(915) 673-5424. **$35-$50.** 1633 W Stamford. S Frontage Rd off I-20 and US 80, exit 285 eastbound; exit 286A westbound. Ext corridors. **Pets:** Small. Designated rooms, no service, supervision, crate.
[SAVE] [S6] [X] [▤]

◆◆◆ Embassy Suites Hotel 🅼
(915) 698-1234. **$91-$96.** 4250 Ridgemont Dr. 0.3 mi s of US 83 and 84, Ridgemont Dr exit; adjacent to Mall of Abilene. Ext/int corridors. **Pets:** No service, supervision, crate.
[ASK] [S6] [X] [▤] [▤] [↑↑] [▱]

◆◆ Executive Inn 🅼
(915) 677-2200. **$35-$55.** 1650 I-20 E. I-20, exit 288. Ext corridors. **Pets:** Small. No service, supervision, crate.
[ASK] [S6] [X] [▤] [▱]

◆◆◆ Hampton Inn 🅼
(915) 695-0044. **$55-$61.** 3917 Ridgemont Dr. I-20, exit 283A, 5 mi s to Curry Ln exit. Int corridors. **Pets:** Small. Supervision.
[X] [↗] [↙] [▤] [▤] [▱]

◆◆◆ Holiday Inn Express 🅼
(915) 673-5271. **$55-$70, 5 days notice.** 1625 SR 351. Jct SR 351 and I-20, exit 288. Ext corridors. **Pets:** Medium. No service, supervision, crate.
[ASK] [S6] [X] [↙] [↗] [▤] [▤] [▱]

◆◆◆ La Quinta Inn-Abilene 🅼
(915) 676-1676. **$65-$85.** 3501 W Lake Rd. I-20 at jct FM 600, exit 286C. Ext corridors. **Pets:** Supervision.
[SAVE] [X] [↙] [▤] [▱]

◆◆◆ Quality Inn 🅼
(915) 676-0222. **$59-$64.** 505 Pine St. Downtown. Ext corridors. **Pets:** No service, supervision, crate.
[SAVE] [S6] [X] [▤] [↑↑] [▱]

◆◆ Ramada Inn 🅼
(915) 695-7700. **$52-$57.** 3450 S Clack St. 5 mi sw on US 83 and 84, Southwest Dr exit. Int corridors. **Pets:** Supervision.
[ASK] [S6] [X] [▤] [▤] [↑↑] [▱]

◆◆ Super 8 Motel 🅼
(915) 673-5251. **$43-$55, 7 days notice.** 1525 E I-20. I-20, exit 288. Ext corridors. **Pets:** Supervision.
[ASK] [S6] [X] [▤] [▱]

ALPINE

◆◆◆ Ramada Limited 🅼 ☂
(915) 837-1100. **$70-$85.** 2800 W Hwy 90. 2 mi n on Hwy 90. Int corridors. **Pets:** $20 deposit/pet. No service, supervision, crate.
[SAVE] [S6] [X] [↙] [↗] [↙] [▤] [▤]

ALVIN

◆◆ Country Hearth Inn 🅼
(281) 331-0335. **$52-$62.** 1588 S Hwy 35 bypass. Hwy 35 bypass, 0.5 mi sw of SR 6. Ext corridors. **Pets:** Supervision.
[SAVE] [S6] [X] [▤] [▤] [▱]

AMARILLO

◆◆ Amarillo East Travelodge 🅼 ☂
(806) 372-8171. **$36-$52.** 3205 I-40E at Tee Anchor Blvd. I-40, exit 72B (Grand) eastbound to N Frontage Rd, 0.5 mi w; exit 72A (Tee Anchor Blvd) westbound, just w on N Frontage Rd. Int corridors. **Pets:** $10 one-time fee/room. No service, supervision, crate.
[X] [▤] [▤] [↑↑] [▱]

◆◆◆ Amarillo Residence Inn 🅼 ☂
(806) 354-2978. **$189, 7 days notice.** 6700 Interstate 40 West. I-40, exit 66 (Bell St); 0.5 mi w on n frontage road. Int corridors. **Pets:** Other. $10 daily fee/room, $50 one-time fee/room. Supervision.
[ASK] [S6] [X] [↙] [↗] [↙] [▤] [▱] [X]

◆◆◆ Amarillo West Travelodge 🅼
(806) 353-3541. **$50-$59.** 2035 Paramount Blvd. I-40, exit 68A (Paramount Blvd), just s. Ext corridors. **Pets:** Supervision.
[SAVE] [S6] [X] [↗] [▤] [▱]

◆◆◆ Best Western Amarillo Inn 🅼 ☂
(806) 358-7861. **$69-$89.** 1610 Coulter Dr. I-40, exit 65 (Coulter Dr), 0.6 mi n, adjacent to Amarillo Medical Center. Ext/int corridors. **Pets:** Small. $10 one-time fee/room. No service, supervision, crate.
[SAVE] [S6] [X] [↙] [▤] [▤] [↑↑] [▱]

◆◆◆ Best Western Santa Fe Inn 🅼
(806) 372-1885. **$75-$85.** 4600 I-40 E. I-40, exit 73 (Eastern St) eastbound; exit 73 (Bolton St) westbound, U-turn on S Frontage Rd. Int corridors. **Pets:** Small. No service, supervision, crate.
[SAVE] [S6] [X] [▱]

◆◆ The Big Texan Motel 🅼
(806) 372-5000. **$40-$55.** 7701 I-40E. I-40, exit 75 (Lakeside Dr), 0.3 mi w on n frontage road. Ext corridors. **Pets:** Large. Designated rooms, supervision.
[SAVE] [S6] [X] [▱]

◆◆◆ Hampton Inn 🅼 ☂
(806) 372-1425. **$69-$99.** 1700 I-40E. I-40, exit 71 (Ross-Osage), S Frontage Rd. Int corridors. **Pets:** Supervision.
[SAVE] [X] [↗] [▤] [▤] [▱]

◆◆◆ HomeGate Studios & Suites 🅼
(806) 358-7943. **$99-$109.** 6800 I-40 W. I-40, exit 66 (Bell St), 0.5 mi w on N Frontage Rd. Ext corridors. **Pets:** Designated rooms, no service, supervision, crate.
[SAVE] [S6] [X] [↗] [▤] [▤] [▱]

◆◆◆ La Quinta Inn-Amarillo-Medical Center 🅼 ☂
(806) 352-6311. **$69-$89.** 2108 S Coulter St. I-40W, exit 65 (Coulter Dr); just n. Ext corridors. **Pets:** Small, other. Supervision.
[SAVE] [X] [↑] [↗] [▤] [▤]

◆◆◆ La Quinta Inn East-Amarillo 🅼 ☂
(806) 373-7486. **$69-$89.** 1708 I-40E. I-40, exit 71 (Ross-Osage). Ext/int corridors. **Pets:** Other. No service, supervision, crate.
[SAVE] [X] [↗] [▤] [▱]

◆◆ **Motel 6 Central** Ⓜ ❀
(806) 355-6554. **$33-$46.** 2032 Paramount Blvd. I-40, exit 68A (Paramount Blvd), just nw. Ext corridors. **Pets:** Very small, dogs only. No service, supervision, crate.
⊠ 🎦 🗃 🖾 CTV

🅐🅐🅐 ◆◆◆ **Quality Inn & Suites** Ⓜ ❀
(806) 335-1561. **$79-$109, 7 days notice.** 1803 Lakeside Dr. Jct I-40 and US 287, exit 75 (Lakeside Dr). Ext/int corridors. **Pets:** Other. $5 daily fee/pet, $5 one-time fee/pet. Designated rooms, no service, supervision, crate.
SAVE 🖾 ⊠ ♿ 🎦 🗃 🖵 🖾

◆◆ **Radisson Inn Amarillo Airport** Ⓜ
(806) 373-3303. **$104-$124.** 7909 I-40 E. I-40, exit 75 (Lakeside Dr); just nw. Int corridors. **Pets:** Designated rooms, no service, supervision, crate.
ASK 🖾 ⊠ 🎦 🗃 🖵 🍴 🖾

◆◆◆ **Ramada Inn East Amarillo** Ⓜ ❀
(806) 379-6555. **Call for rates.** 2501 I-40 East. I-40, exit 72A (Nelson St); N Frontage Rd. Ext/int corridors. **Pets:** $10 one-time fee/room. No service, supervision, crate.
ASK ⊠ 🗃 🖵 🍴 🖾

🅐🅐🅐 ◆◆ **Sleep Inn Amarillo** Ⓜ ❀
(806) 372-6200. **$55-$89.** 2401 I-40 E. I-40, exit 72A (Nelson); 0.3 mi w on N Frontage Rd. Int corridors. **Pets:** Small. $10 daily fee/pet, $10 one-time fee/pet. No service, supervision, crate.
SAVE 🖾 ⊠ ♿ 🎦 🗃 🗃 🖵 🖾

ANGLETON

🅐🅐🅐 ◆ **Country Hearth Inn** Ⓜ
(409) 849-2465. **$50-$63.** 1235 N Velasco. 1 mi n of SR 35 on SR 288 business route. Ext corridors. **Pets:** Supervision.
SAVE 🖾 ⊠ 🗃 🖵 🖾

ANTHONY

🅐🅐🅐 ◆◆◆ **Super 8 El Paso West-Anthony** Ⓜ ❀
(915) 886-2888. **$41-$49.** 100 Park North Dr. I-10, exit zero. Ext corridors. **Pets:** Small. $10 daily fee/room. No service, supervision, crate.
SAVE 🖾 ⊠ ♿ 🎦 🗃

ARLINGTON

◆◆ **Baymont Inn & Suites Arlington** Ⓜ ❀
(817) 633-2400. **$76-$86.** 2401 Diplomacy Dr. SR 360 0.5 mi s of jct I-30, exit 30; off SR 360 Six Flags Dr exit northbound; off SR 360 Ave H/Lamar Blvd exit southbound. Int corridors. **Pets:** Medium, dogs only. $50 deposit/room. No service, supervision, crate.
🖾 ⊠ 🗃 🖵 🖾

◆◆ **Days Inn Airport Six Flags/Ball Park** Ⓜ
(817) 649-8881. **$59.** 1195 N Watson Rd. 4.3 mi n on SR 360; 0.5 mi n of I-30, Six Flags Dr exit. Ext corridors. **Pets:** Small. No service, supervision, crate.
ASK 🖾 ⊠ 🗃 🖾

🅐🅐🅐 ◆◆ **Days Inn Ballpark at Arlington/Six Flags** Ⓜ
(817) 261-8444. **$66-$95.** 910 N Collins St. 1.5 mi ne on SR 157; 1 mi s jct I-30, Collins St/SR 157, exit 28. Ext corridors. **Pets:** Small. No service, supervision, crate.
SAVE 🖾 ⊠ 🗃 🖾

◆◆◆ **Hawthorn Suites Hotel** Ⓜ
(817) 640-1188. **$110-$120.** 2401 Brookhollow Plaza Dr. 4.5 mi ne, just w of SR 360; 0.3 mi nw of I-30, exit 30 (SR 360 Six Flags Dr). Ext corridors. **Pets:** Designated rooms, supervision.
ASK 🖾 ⊠ 🎦 🗃 🖵 🖾 ⊠

◆◆ **Homestead Village** Ⓜ ❀
(817) 465-8500. **Call for rates.** 1980 W Pleasant Ridge Rd. I-20 at Cooper St exit, 0.3 mi n, then w. Int corridors. **Pets:** Small, other. $75 one-time fee/pet. Supervision.
⊠ 🗃

◆◆ **Homestead Village Guest Studios** Ⓜ
(817) 633-7588. **$40-$45.** 1221 N Watson Rd. Jct US 360 at Ave K/Brown Blvd exit. Ext corridors. **Pets:** No service, supervision, crate.
⊠ 🎦 🗃 🖵

🅐🅐🅐 ◆◆ **Howard Johnson Hotel, Conference Centre and Fitness Complex** Ⓜ
(817) 633-4000. **$64-$79, 7 days notice.** 117 S Watson Rd. Jct SR 360 and Abrams Rd. Int corridors. **Pets:** Medium. No service, supervision, crate.
SAVE 🖾 ⊠ 🗃 🖵 🍴 🖾

◆◆◆ **La Quinta Inn & Suites South Arlington** Ⓜ
(817) 467-7756. **$99-$109.** 4001 Scott's Legacy. I-20 at Matlock Rd exit. Int corridors. **Pets:** Medium. No service, supervision, crate.
ASK ⊠ 🎦 🗃 🖵 🖾

◆◆◆ **La Quinta Inn-Arlington-Conference Center** Ⓜ ❀
(817) 640-4142. **$79-$109.** 825 N Watson Rd. SR 360, just s of jct I-30, exit 30; off SR 360, Six Flags Dr exit northbound; off SR 360, Ave H/Lamar Blvd exit southbound. Ext corridors. **Pets:** Small, other. Supervision.
ASK ⊠ 🎦 🗃 🖵 🖾 ⊠

🅐🅐🅐 ◆ **Motel 6–122** Ⓜ ❀
(817) 649-0147. **$42-$58.** 2626 E Randol Mill Rd. Jct SR 360 and Randol Mill Rd. Ext corridors. **Pets:** Small. Supervision.
🖾 ⊠ 🖾

🅐🅐🅐 ◆◆ **Park Inn Limited** Ⓜ ❀
(817) 860-2323. **$50-$60.** 703 Benge Dr. I-30, 2 mi s on Cooper St exit 27, just w. Ext corridors. **Pets:** Very small, dogs only. $15 one-time fee/room. Designated rooms, no service, supervision, crate.
SAVE 🖾 ⊠ 🗃 🖾

◆◆ **Rodeway Inn-Arlington** Ⓜ
(817) 461-1122. **Call for rates.** 2001 E Copeland Rd. 3.3 mi ne off I-30, exit 30 (SR 360); 0.5 mi w on s service road. Ext corridors. **Pets:** Large. Supervision.
⊠ 🗃 🖾

Sleep Inn Arlington M
(817) 649-1010. **$69-$95.** 750 Six Flags Dr. I-30, exit 30 (SR 360), 0.5 mi w. Int corridors. **Pets:** Medium. Designated rooms, supervision.

ATLANTA

The Butler's Inn M
(903) 796-8235. **$38-$65.** 1100 W Main St. US 59, just n on jct SR 77. Ext corridors. **Pets:** Medium. Supervision.

AUSTIN

Amerisuites Arboretum M
(512) 231-8491. **$89-$135.** 3612 Tudor Blvd. US 183 n to SR 360 exit, 0.4 mi to Stonelake St then 0.4 mi s. Int corridors. **Pets:** Very small. No service, supervision, crate.

Austin Marriott at the Capitol H
(512) 478-1111. **$225-$225.** 701 E 11th St. 0.3 mi e on 11th St, at I-35. Int corridors. **Pets:** Small. Supervision.

Baymont Inn & Suites Austin North M
(512) 246-2800. **$67-$72.** 150 Parker Dr. I-35 exit 250 (SR 1325), 0.4 mi s on southbound Frontage Rd. Int corridors. **Pets:** Medium, other. $50 deposit/room. No service, supervision, crate.

Best Western Atrium North M
(512) 339-7311. **$69-$79.** 7928 Gessner Dr. I-35 exit 240A, w on N SR 183 frontage road 0.4 mi. Int corridors. **Pets:** Medium. Supervision.

Clarion Inn & Suites M
(512) 444-0561. **$55-$65.** 2200 I-35S. S off I-35, US 81 and 290, exit 232A (Oltorf Blvd). Int corridors. **Pets:** Other. $50 deposit/room. Designated rooms, supervision.

Days Inn University-Downtown M
(512) 478-1631. **$59-$99.** 3105 N IH-35. I-35 at 32nd St, exit 236A (from lower level). Ext corridors. **Pets:** Other. $8 one-time fee/room. No service, supervision, crate.

Doubletree Guest Suites-Austin H
(512) 478-7000. **$109-$179.** 303 W 15th St. Center. Int corridors. **Pets:** Medium. No service, supervision, crate.

Doubletree Hotel H
(512) 454-3737. **$99-$119.** 6505 IH-35N. 4.8 mi ne off I-35, US 81 and 183, exit 238B (US 290) southbound; exit 239 (St John's Ave) northbound. Int corridors. **Pets:** Small. $25 deposit/room. No service, supervision, crate.

Drury Inn & Suites-North M
(512) 467-9500. **$68-$92.** 6711 IH-35N. Ne off I-35, exit 239 (St John's Ave); 0.5 mi n of jct US 290 on northbound Frontage Rd. Int corridors. **Pets:** Other. Supervision.

Drury Inn Austin-Highland Mall M
(512) 454-1144. **$67-$91.** 919 E Koenig Ln. Sw off I-35, Hwy 290E, exit 238B. Int corridors. **Pets:** Small, other. No service, supervision, crate.

Exel Inn Of Austin M
(512) 462-9201. **$42-$79.** 2711 IH-35S. S off I-35, US 81 and 290, on E Access Rd, exit 232A (Oltorf St) northbound; exit 231 (Woodward Ave) southbound. Int corridors. **Pets:** Supervision.

Four Points Hotel by Sheraton MI
(512) 836-8520. **$103-$122.** 7800 I-35N. Nw off I-35 at jct US 183, exit 240A. Int corridors. **Pets:** Medium. No service, supervision, crate.

Four Seasons Hotel H
(512) 478-4500. **$260-$350.** 98 San Jacinto Blvd. Downtown, bordering Town Lake. Int corridors. **Pets:** Medium. Designated rooms, supervision.

Habitat Suites Hotel M
(512) 467-6000. **$127-$137.** 500 Highland Mall Blvd. Nw off I-35, exit 238B; just w on SR 2222 to Airport Blvd, 0.6 mi n to Highland Mall Blvd, 0.4 mi e. Ext corridors. **Pets:** Medium. $50 one-time fee/room. Designated rooms, no service, supervision, crate.

Hawthorn Suites Austin Central M
(512) 459-3335. **$129-$159.** 935 La Posada Dr. Ne off I-35, exit 239 (St John's Ave). Ext corridors. **Pets:** Medium. Supervision.

Hawthorn Suites-Austin South M
(512) 440-7722. **$98-$108.** 4020 I-35S. S off I-35, US 81 and 290, just n jct SR 71, exit 231 (Woodward St) northbound; exit 230B (Ben White Blvd) southbound. Ext corridors. **Pets:** Supervision.

Hawthorn Suites Northwest M
(512) 343-0008. **$89-$209.** 8888 Tallwood Dr. 10.8 mi nw; just sw of jct US 183 and Loop 1. Ext corridors. **Pets:** Small, other. $50 one-time fee/pet. No service, supervision, crate.

Hilton Austin North & Towers H
(512) 451-5757. **$95-$190.** 6000 Middle Fiskville Rd. Just w of jct I-35 and US 290, just n. Int corridors. **Pets:** Supervision.

AAA ◆◆◆ **Holiday Inn-Airport/Highland Mall** **M**
(512) 459-4251. **$50-$60.** 6911 IH-35N. 5.3 mi ne off I-35, exit 239 (St John's Ave) northbound; exit 238B (US 290 and FM 2222) southbound. Ext corridors. **Pets:** Designated rooms, supervision.

SAVE ⊠ 🔂 🔒 🖭 🍴 🖼

AAA ◆◆◆ **Holiday Inn Airport South** **M**
(512) 448-2444. **$89-$89.** 3401 I-35S. S off I-35, US 71 and 290, exit 231 (Woodward St) southbound; exit 230 (Ben White Blvd) northbound. Int corridors. **Pets:** Designated rooms, supervision.

SAVE 🔂 ⊠ 🔂 🔒 🖭 🍴 🖼 ⊠

◆◆◆ **Holiday Inn Northwest Plaza** **M**
(512) 343-0888. **$119.** 8901 Business Park Dr. 10.8 mi n at jct US 183 and Loop 1 (Mopac). Ext corridors. **Pets:** No service, supervision, crate.

ASK 🔂 ⊠ 🔂 🔒 🖭 🍴 🖼

◆◆◆ **Holiday Inn-Town Lake** **H** 🐾
(512) 472-8211. **$99-$149.** 20 N IH-35. I-35, exit 233. Int corridors. **Pets:** Small. $100 deposit/room, $25 one-time fee/room. Supervision.

ASK 🔂 ⊠ 🔂 🖭 🍴 🖼

◆◆◆ **Homestead Guest Studios-Austin/Downtown/**
Town Lake **M**
(512) 476-1818. **Call for rates.** 507 S First St. I-35 exit Ceasar Chavez, 1.8 mi w, 0.5 mi s. Int corridors. **Pets:** No service, supervision, crate.

⊠ 🔂 🔖 🔒 🖭

◆◆ **Homestead Village** **M** 🐾
(512) 458-5453. **Call for rates.** 937 Camino La Costa. Jct I-35 & US 290, just n on E Frontage Rd. Ext corridors. **Pets:** Medium. $75 one-time fee/room. No service, supervision, crate.

⊠ 🔂 🔒 🖭

◆◆ **Homestead Village Guest**
Studios-Northwest **M** 🐾
(512) 258-3556. **Call for rates.** 11901 Pavillon Blvd. US 183; exit Oak Knoll westbound, exit Duval/Balcones Woods eastbound; on eastbound Frontage Rd. Ext corridors. **Pets:** Small, other. $75 one-time fee/room. Supervision.

⊠ 🔖 🔒 🖭

◆◆◆ **La Quinta Capitol** **M**
(512) 476-1166. **$89-$109.** 300 E 11 St. Downtown; just e of State Capitol Building. Ext corridors. **Pets:** Supervision.

ASK ⊠ 🔂 🔒 🖭 🖼

◆◆◆ **La Quinta Inn & Suites-Austin North**
Mopac **M** 🐾
(512) 832-2121. **$79-$109.** 11901 N Mopac Expwy. US 183 1 mi n on Mopac to Duval exit. Int corridors. **Pets:** Small. No service, supervision, crate.

ASK ⊠ 🔊 🔂 🔒 🖭 🖼

◆◆◆ **La Quinta Inn-Ben White** **M**
(512) 443-1774. **$69-$85.** 4200 I-35S. S off I-35 and US 81; just s of jct US 290 and SR 71, exit 230B (Ben White Blvd) southbound; exit 230 northbound. Ext corridors. **Pets:** Small. No service, supervision, crate.

ASK ⊠ 🔒 🖭 🖼

◆◆◆ **La Quinta Inn-Highland Mall-Airport** **M**
(512) 459-4381. **$69-$85.** 5812 I-35N. 4.5 mi ne off I-35, US 79, 81 and 290, exit 238A. Ext corridors. **Pets:** Designated rooms, supervision.

ASK ⊠ 🔒 🖭 🖼

◆◆◆ **La Quinta Inn-North** **M**
(512) 452-9401. **$69-$89.** 7100 I-35N. Ne off I-35 and US 81; exit 239 (St John's Ave). Ext corridors. **Pets:** Small. Supervision.

ASK ⊠ 🔂 🔒 🖭 🖼

◆◆◆ **La Quinta Inn Oltorf** **M**
(512) 447-6661. **$79-$99.** 1603 E Oltorf Blvd. S off I-35, exit 232A (Oltorf Blvd). Ext corridors. **Pets:** Very small. No service, supervision, crate.

ASK ⊠ 🔒 🖭 🖼

◆◆◆ **La Quinta Inns & Suites-Austin**
(Airport) **M**
(512) 386-6800. **Call for rates.** 7625 E Ben White Blvd. I-35, exit 230B, 3 mi e. Int corridors. **Pets:** Small. Designated rooms, no service, supervision, crate.

⊠ 🔖 🔒 🖭 🖼

◆◆◆ **La Quinta SW** **M** 🐾
(512) 899-3000. **$89-$119.** 4525 Gaines Ranch Loop. 0.5 mi n of SR 71 on Loop 1 (Mopac). Int corridors. **Pets:** Small. Supervision.

⊠ 🔊 🔒 🖭 🖼

AAA ◆◆ **Motel 6 Airport–1118** **M**
(512) 467-9111. **$44-$60.** 5330 I-35N. I-35, exit 238B (51 St); s on Frontage Rd 1 mi; n on I-35, exit 238B (US 290); 0.3 mi n on Frontage Rd under I-35 and 0.3 mi on W Frontage Rd. Ext corridors. **Pets:** Small. Supervision.

🔂 ⊠ 🔖 🖼

AAA ◆◆ **Motel 6 Austin North–360** **M**
(512) 339-6161. **$40-$56.** 9420 N I-35. I-35, exit 240 (Rundberg St). Ext corridors. **Pets:** Very small. Supervision.

🔂 ⊠ 🔖 🖼

AAA ◆◆ **Motel 6 South–113** **M**
(512) 444-5882. **$42-$58.** 2707 I-35 S S. S off I-35, exit 231 (Woodward) southbound; exit 232A (Oltorf Blvd) northbound. Ext corridors. **Pets:** Very small. Supervision.

🔂 ⊠ 🔂 🔖 🖼

◆◆ **Ramada Inn South** **M**
(512) 447-0151. **$50-$86.** 1212 W Ben White Blvd. I-35, 2 mi w, exit 230 (Ben White Blvd); to Congress Ave, westbound access road. Int corridors. **Pets:** Small. Supervision.

ASK 🔊 ⊠ 🔂 🍴 🖼

◆◆ **Ramada Limited** **M**
(512) 451-7001. **$65-$75.** 5526 I-35N. 3.5 mi ne off I-35; exit 238B northbound, exit 238A southbound. Ext corridors. **Pets:** No service, supervision, crate.

ASK 🔊 ⊠ 🔂 🔒 🖭 🖼

AAA ◆◆◆ **Red Lion Hotel Austin Airport** **H**
(512) 323-5466. **$79-$99.** 6121 I-35N. Ne off I-35, US 81 and 290, US 290 exit 238B. Int corridors. **Pets:** Designated rooms, supervision.

🔊 ⊠ 🔂 🔒 🖭 🍴 🖼

⬤⬤ ◆◆ Red Roof Inn Austin North Ⓜ ✿
(512) 835-2200. **$46-$66.** 8210 IH-35N. 6.8 mi n on I-35, US 79 and 81; northbound Rundberg Ln exit 241; southbound US 83 exit 240A. Ext corridors. **Pets:** Small. Supervision.

🅂🅰🅅🄴 ⊠ 🖼

⬤⬤ ◆◆ Red Roof Inn-Austin South Ⓜ
(512) 448-0091. **$40-$50.** 4701 S Regional Hwy I-35. I-35 southbound exit 230B (Ben White Blvd), northbound exit 229 (Stassney Rd) on northbound frontage road. Int corridors. **Pets:** Medium. Supervision.

🅂🅰🅅🄴 ⊠ 🛋 🖼

⬤⬤ ◆◆◆ Renaissance Austin Hotel Ⓗ ✿
(512) 343-2626. **$179-$217.** 9721 Arboretum Blvd. 8.5 mi nw; 0.3 mi sw of jct US 183 and SR 360. Int corridors. **Pets:** Very small. $50 deposit/room. Supervision.

🅂🅰🅅🄴 🅂🄳 ⊠ 🌀 🗌 🛋 🖳 🍽 🖼

◆◆◆ Residence Inn Austin South Ⓜ
(512) 912-1100. **$99-$149.** 4537 S I-35. S off I-35; Stassney Rd exit southbound; exit 230 (Ben White Blvd) northbound. Int corridors. **Pets:** Designated rooms, supervision.

🄰🅂🄺 🅂🄳 ⊠ 🌀 🖼

◆◆◆ Residence Inn by Marriott-Austin Northwest Ⓜ
(512) 502-8200. **$139-$169.** 3713 Tudor Blvd. Nw on US 183, to Loop 360 exit. Int corridors. **Pets:** Supervision.

🄰🅂🄺 🅂🄳 ⊠ 🌀 🛋 🖳 🖼

◆◆◆ Sheraton Austin Hotel Ⓗ
(512) 480-8181. **Call for rates.** 500 N IH-35. I-35, 6th and 12th sts, exit 234C northbound; 8th and 3rd sts, exit 234B southbound. Int corridors. **Pets:** No service, supervision, crate.

⊠ 🌀 🛋 🖳 🍽 🖼

⬤⬤ ◆◆ Super 8 at Highland Mall Ⓜ
(512) 467-8163. **$39-$74.** 6000 Middle Fiskville Rd. Just w jct I-35 and US 290 on US 290, just n. Int corridors. **Pets:** No service, supervision, crate.

🅂🅰🅅🄴 🅂🄳 ⊠ 🌀

⬤⬤ ◆◆ Super 8 Central Ⓜ
(512) 472-8331. **$52-$79, 3 days notice.** 1201 N I-35. I-35 at 12th St, exit 234C. Ext corridors. **Pets:** Medium. No service, supervision, crate.

🅂🅰🅅🄴 🅂🄳 ⊠ 🖼

⬤⬤ ◆◆ Wellesley Inn & Suites Ⓜ ✿
(512) 219-6500. **$89-$107.** 12424 Research Blvd. US 183 exit Oak Knoll, on eastbound Frontage Rd. Int corridors. **Pets:** Small, other. No service, supervision, crate.

🅂🅰🅅🄴 🅂🄳 ⊠ 🌀 🗌 🛋 🖳 🖼

⬤⬤ ◆◆◆ Wellesley Inn & Suites Ⓜ
(512) 339-6005. **$79-$149.** 8221 N I-H 35. I-35 northbound exit 241 (Rutherford/Rundberg Lanes); southbound exit 240A (N SR 183), on northbound frontage road. Int corridors. **Pets:** Small. No service, supervision, crate.

🅂🅰🅅🄴 🅂🄳 ⊠ 🛋 🖳 🖼

⬤⬤ ◆ Wellesley Inn & Suites Ⓜ
(512) 326-0100. **$75-$115, 3 days notice.** 1001 S IH-35. I-35 exit 233 (Riverside/Townlake), just e. Int corridors. **Pets:** Supervision.

🅂🅰🅅🄴 🅂🄳 ⊠ 🗌 🛋 🖳 🖼

BANDERA

⬤⬤ ◆◆ Bandera Lodge Ⓜ
(830) 796-3093. **$55-$73.** 700 Hwy 16S. 1 mi s on Hwy 16; 7 mi s of jct Hwy 173. Ext corridors. **Pets:** Supervision.

🅂🅰🅅🄴 🅂🄳 ⊠ 🛋 🍽 🖼

BEAUMONT

⬤⬤ ◆◆◆ Best Western Beaumont Inn Ⓜ
(409) 898-8150. **$55-$71.** 2155 N 11th St. Just n of jct I-10, exit 853B (11th St). Ext corridors. **Pets:** Small. Supervision.

🅂🅰🅅🄴 🅂🄳 ⊠ 🗌 🛋 🖳 🖼

⬤⬤ ◆◆ Best Western Jefferson Inn Ⓜ
(409) 842-0037. **$55-$71.** 1610 I-10S. Westbound service road; 0.5 mi s of jct US 90; I-10, exit 851 (College St). Ext corridors. **Pets:** Small. No service, supervision, crate.

🅂🅰🅅🄴 🅂🄳 ⊠ 🌀 🛋 🖳 🖼

⬤⬤ ◆◆ Hilton Beaumont Ⓗ
(409) 842-3600. **$79-$159.** 2355 I-10S. Eastbound service road at jct I-10 and US 69, 96 and 287; I-10, exit 850 (Washington Blvd). Int corridors. **Pets:** Small. Supervision.

🅂🅰🅅🄴 🅂🄳 ⊠ 🌀 🗌 🛋 🖳 🍽 🖼

◆◆◆ Holiday Inn Beaumont Plaza Ⓗ ✿
(409) 842-5995. **$95-$125.** 3950 I-10S. Jct I-10, exit 848 (Walden Rd); 0.8 mi sw of jct US 69/96 and 287. Int corridors. **Pets:** $10 daily fee/pet. No service, supervision, crate.

🄰🅂🄺 🅂🄳 ⊠ 🌀 🗌 🛋 🖳 🍽 🖼

⬤⬤ ◆◆◆ Holiday Inn I-10 Midtown Ⓜ
(409) 892-2222. **$70-$100.** 2095 N 11th St. Just n of jct I-10, exit 853B (11th St). Int corridors. **Pets:** Small. No service, supervision, crate.

🅂🅰🅅🄴 🅂🄳 ⊠ 🌀 🗌 🛋 🖳 🍽 🖼

⬤⬤ ◆◆◆ La Quinta Inn-Beaumont Ⓜ
(409) 838-9991. **$59-$76.** 220 I-10N. Eastbound service road; I-10, exit 852B (Calder Ave) eastbound, exit 852A (Laurel Ave) westbound. Ext corridors. **Pets:** Small. Supervision.

🅂🅰🅅🄴 ⊠ 🌀 🗌 🛋 🖳 🖼

BEDFORD

◆◆◆ La Quinta Inn-Bedford Ⓜ ✿
(817) 267-5200. **$59-$79.** 1450 Airport Frwy. SR 121 and 183, 0.3 mi e of jct Bedford Rd/Forest Ridge Dr exit. Ext corridors. **Pets:** Small. No service, supervision, crate.

🄰🅂🄺 ⊠ 🌀 🖳 🖼

◆◆ MainStay Suites Ⓜ
(817) 318-5000. **Call for rates.** 2301 Plaza Pkwy. US 183, Central exit, just n, then just e. Int corridors. **Pets:** Supervision.

⊠ 🛋

BEEVILLE

◆◆ Beeville Days Inn Ⓜ ✿
(361) 358-4000. **$52-$65.** 400 US 181S Bypass, Box 1748. 0.3 mi s of jct US 59 and 181. Ext corridors. **Pets:** Other. Supervision.

🄰🅂🄺 🅂🄳 ⊠ 🛋 🖼

BELTON

◆◆ **Best Western River Forest Motel** 🅼
(254) 939-5711. **Call for rates.** PO Box 504. Jct FM 93 and I-35, US 81 and 190, exit 294B (6th St). Ext corridors. **Pets:** Medium. No service, supervision, crate.

🅐🅐🅐 ◆◆ **Budget Host Inn** 🅼 🐾
(254) 939-0744. **$39-$55, 7 days notice.** 1520 S I-35. I-35, exit 292 southbound; exit 293A northbound. Ext corridors. **Pets:** Other. No service, supervision, crate.

BIG SPRING

🅐🅐🅐 ◆◆ **Best Western Big Spring** 🅼 🐾
(915) 267-1601. **$44-$54.** 700 W I-20 St. Just n of jct I-20 and US 87, exit 177. Ext corridors. **Pets:** Other. Supervision.

🅐🅐🅐 ◆◆ **Comfort Inn** 🅼
(915) 267-4553. **$45-$60.** 2900 E I-20. I-20, exit 179. Ext corridors. **Pets:** Small. Supervision.

🆂🅰🆅🅴 🆂 ✕ 🅱 🖵 🖾

BOERNE

🅐🅐🅐 ◆◆ **Best Western Texas Country Inn** 🅼
(830) 249-9791. **$59-$90.** 35150 IH-10. 0.3 mi w of jct I-10 at US 46. Ext corridors. **Pets:** Small. Supervision.

BONHAM

🅐🅐🅐 ◆◆ **Days Inn** 🅼 🐾
(903) 583-3121. **$45-$50.** 1515 Old Ector Rd. US 82 at w jct of SR 121. Ext corridors. **Pets:** Very small. Designated rooms, no service, supervision, crate.

BORGER

◆◆ **Nendels Inn** 🅼 🐾
(806) 273-9556. **$29-$51, 7 days notice.** 100 Bulldog Blvd. Jct US 207 and SR 136. Ext corridors. **Pets:** No service, supervision, crate.

🅰🆂🅺 🆂 ✕ ⚙ 🖵 🖾

BOWIE

🅐🅐🅐 ◆◆ **Days Inn** 🅼 🐾
(940) 872-5426. **$42-$65, 3 days notice.** Hwy 59 & 287. 1 mi s on US 287 jct SR 59. Ext corridors. **Pets:** $5 daily fee/pet, $5 one-time fee/pet. Designated rooms, no service, supervision, crate.

🅐🅐🅐 ◆ **Park's Inn** 🅼 🐾
(940) 872-1111. **$30-$41.** 708 W Wise St. US 287, exit SR 81 northbound; exit SR 174 southbound, 2 mi s. Ext corridors. **Pets:** $5 daily fee/pet, $5 one-time fee/pet. Designated rooms, no service, supervision, crate.

🆂🅰🆅🅴 🆂 ✕ 🅱 🖾

BRADY

🅐🅐🅐 ◆◆ **Best Western Brady Inn** 🅼 🐾
(915) 597-3997. **$40-$75.** 2200 S Bridge St. 1 mi s on US 87 and SR 377. Ext corridors. **Pets:** Small, dogs only. No service, supervision, crate.

🆂🅰🆅🅴 🆂 ✕ 🅱 🖵 🖾

🅐🅐🅐 ◆◆ **Days Inn–Brady** 🅼 🐾
(915) 597-0789. **$36-$95.** 2108 S Bridge St. 1.5 mi s on US 87 and 377 at jct US 190. Ext corridors. **Pets:** Other. Supervision.

🆂🅰🆅🅴 🆂 ✕ 🅱 🖾

BRENHAM

◆◆◆ **Best Western Inn of Brenham** 🅼🅸
(409) 251-7791. **$54-$74, 3 days notice.** 1503 Highway 290 E. 0.7 mi w of jct US 290 E and SR 577 eastbound; westbound 1.3 mi e jct SR 36 and US 290. Ext corridors. **Pets:** Small. Designated rooms, no service, supervision, crate.

🅰🆂🅺 🆂 ✕ 🅱 🖵 🍴 🖾

BROWNSVILLE

◆◆◆ **Four Points Hotel by Sheraton** 🅼🅸
(956) 547-1500. **$89-$109.** 3777 N Expwy. US 77 and 83, McAllen Rd exit, 0.5 mi s on W Frontage Rd. Int corridors. **Pets:** No service, supervision, crate.

🅰🆂🅺 🆂 ✕ ⚙ 🅱 🖵 🍴 🖾

BROWNWOOD

◆◆ **Best Western Brownwood Inn** 🅼
(915) 646-3511. **$49-$65.** 410 E Commerce. 0.3 mi ne of traffic circle; on US 67, 84 and 377. Ext corridors. **Pets:** Supervision.

🅰🆂🅺 🆂 ✕ ⚙ 🅱 🖵 🖾

◆ **Gold Key Inn** 🅼🅸
(915) 646-2551. **Call for rates.** 515 E Commerce St. 0.8 mi n on SR 377. Ext corridors. **Pets:** Small. Supervision.

✕ 🅱 🖵 🍴 🖾

BURLESON

🅐🅐🅐 ◆◆◆ **Comfort Suites** 🅼
(817) 426-6666. **$71-$85.** 321 S Burleson Blvd. I-35 at Renfro St, exit 36. Int corridors. **Pets:** Designated rooms, supervision.

🆂🅰🆅🅴 🆂 🅱 🖵 🖾

🅐🅐🅐 ◆◆ **Days Inn** 🅼 🐾
(817) 447-1111. **$59-$69.** 329 S Burleson Blvd. I-35, exit 36 (Renfro St) westbound; 0.5 mi s jct Spur 50 and FM 3391, on e frontage road. Ext corridors. **Pets:** $10 daily fee/pet. No service, supervision, crate.

🆂🅰🆅🅴 🆂 ✕ 🅱

CANTON

🅐🅐🅐 ◆◆ **Best Western Canton Inn** 🅼 🐾
(903) 567-6591. **$57-$69.** 2251 N Trade Days Blvd. Jct I-20 and SR 19, exit 527. Ext corridors. **Pets:** Small, other. $10 daily fee/pet. No service, supervision, crate.

🆂🅰🆅🅴 🆂 ✕ 🅱 🖾

◆◆ Days Inn of Canton 🅼 🐾
(903) 567-6588. **$42-$110, 3 days notice.** 109 S I-20. I-20, exit 527. Ext corridors. **Pets:** Other. $6 daily fee/pet, $6 one-time fee/pet. No service, supervision, crate.
(A$K) (S&) (X) (🖪) (🗺)

CHILDRESS

🆎 ◆◆◆ Best Western Childress 🅼 🐾
(940) 937-6353. **$47-$52, 7 days notice.** 1805 Ave F NW. 1.5 mi w on US 287. Ext corridors. **Pets:** Small, dogs only. Designated rooms, no service, supervision, crate.
(SAVE) (S&) (X) (🖪) (💻) (🗺)

🆎 ◆◆◆ Comfort Inn 🅼 🐾
(940) 937-6363. **$69-$84.** 1804 Ave F NW. 1.5 mi w on US 287. Ext corridors. **Pets:** Medium. $5 daily fee/pet. Supervision.
(SAVE) (S&) (X) (🐾) (🗋) (🖪) (💻) (🗺)

🆎 ◆◆ Econo Lodge 🅼🅸 🐾
(940) 937-3695. **$38-$65.** 1612 Ave F NW Hwy 287. 1.3 mi w on US 287. Ext corridors. **Pets:** Other. $5 one-time fee/pet. No service, supervision, crate.
(SAVE) (S&) (X) (💻) (🗺)

CISCO

◆◆ Best Western Inn Cisco 🅼 🐾
(254) 442-3735. **$54-$64, 3 days notice.** 1898 Hwy 206 W. I-20, exit 330. Ext corridors. **Pets:** Very small. $10 daily fee/pet. No service, supervision, crate.
(X) (💻) (🗺)

CLARENDON

🆎 ◆◆ Western Skies Motel 🅼 🐾
(806) 874-3501. **$35-$45.** 800 W 2nd St. 0.5 mi nw on US 287 and SR 70. Ext corridors. **Pets:** Small, dogs only. Designated rooms, no service, supervision, crate.
(X) (🖪) (🗺) (X)

CLAUDE

🆎 ◆ L A Motel 🅼🅸 🐾
(806) 226-4981. **$28-$45, 7 days notice.** 200 E 1st St. 0.3 mi s on US 287. Ext corridors. **Pets:** Small. $25 deposit/room. Designated rooms, supervision.
(SAVE) (S&) (X) (🍴)

CLEBURNE

◆◆ Budget Host Sagamar Inn 🅼
(817) 556-3631. **$44-$60.** 2107 N Main. 2 mi n on SR 174. Ext corridors. **Pets:** Designated rooms, no service, supervision, crate.
(A$K) (S&) (X) (🖪) (🗺)

🆎 ◆◆ Days Inn 🅼
(817) 645-8836. **$50-$70, 4 days notice.** 101 N Ridgeway Dr. 1 mi w on US 67. Ext corridors. **Pets:** Designated rooms, supervision.
(SAVE) (S&) (X) (🖪) (💻) (🗺)

CLUTE

🆎 ◆◆◆ La Quinta Inn 🅼 🐾
(409) 265-7461. **$55-$82.** 1126 Hwy 332W. 3.5 mi e jct SR 288 and 332. Ext corridors. **Pets:** Small, other. No service, supervision, crate.
(SAVE) (X) (🐾) (🖪) (💻) (🗺)

COLDSPRING

🆎 ◆◆ San Jacinto Inn 🅼 🐾
(409) 653-3008. **$40-$43.** 13815 Hwy 150 W. 1.5 mi w on SR 150 W. Ext corridors. **Pets:** $10 one-time fee/pet. Supervision.
(S&) (X) (🖪)

COLLEGE STATION

◆◆ Holiday Inn-College Station 🅼
(409) 693-1736. **Call for rates.** 1503 S Texas Ave. 1.3 mi s of jct SR 60 on SR 6 business route. Int corridors. **Pets:** Small. Supervision.
(X) (🐾) (🖪) (💻) (🍴) (🗺)

🆎 ◆◆◆ La Quinta Inn 🅼
(409) 696-7777. **$69-$89.** 607 Texas Ave. Just s jct SR 60/6 business route to Live Oak St, just e. Ext corridors. **Pets:** Small. No service, supervision, crate.
(SAVE) (X) (🖪) (💻) (🗺)

◆◆ Manor House Inn 🅼
(409) 764-9540. **$65-$76.** 2504 Texas Ave S. 2.4 mi s jct SR 60/6 business route on SR 6 business route. Ext corridors. **Pets:** Small. Supervision.
(A$K) (S&) (X) (🖪) (💻) (🗺)

◆◆ Ramada Inn 🅼🅸 🐾
(409) 693-9891. **$69-$125, 3 days notice.** 1502 Texas Ave S. 1.3 mi s of jct SR 60 on SR 6 business route. Int corridors. **Pets:** Small. $10 daily fee/pet, $10 one-time fee/pet. No service, supervision, crate.
(A$K) (S&) (X) (🖪) (🍴) (🗺)

COLORADO CITY

🆎 ◆◆ Villa Inn 🅼 🐾
(915) 728-5217. **$32-$44.** 2310 Hickory St. Just s of I-20, exit 216. Ext/int corridors. **Pets:** Medium. $10 deposit/room, $10 one-time fee/pet. No service, supervision, crate.
(SAVE) (S&) (X) (🗺)

COLUMBUS

◆◆ Columbus Inn 🅼 🐾
(409) 732-5723. **$50-$65.** 2208 Hwy 71. Jct I-10 and SR 71, exit 696 (Hwy 71). Ext corridors. **Pets:** Other. $10 one-time fee/room. Designated rooms, no service, supervision, crate.
(A$K) (S&) (X) (🐾) (🖪) (💻) (🗺)

CONWAY

🆎 ◆◆ Budget Host S & S Motor Inn 🅼🅸 🐾
(806) 537-5111. **$35-$40, 3 days notice.** I-40 & SR 207. Jct I-40 and SR 207, 0.3 mi w on s access road. Ext corridors. **Pets:** Small. $20 deposit/pet. No service, supervision, crate.
(SAVE) (S&) (X) (🍴) (CTV)

CORPUS CHRISTI

◆◆ **Bayfront Inn** Ⓜ
(361) 883-7271. **Call for rates.** 601 N Shoreline Blvd. Just n, across from bay. Ext corridors. **Pets:** Very small. No service, supervision, crate.

Ⓧ 🗲 🖾

🅰🅰🅰 ◆◆◆ **Best Western Garden Inn** Ⓜ
(361) 241-6675. **$64-$99.** 11217 IH-37. I-37, exit 11B (Violet Rd). Ext corridors. **Pets:** No service, supervision, crate.

🆂🅰🆅🅴 🆂🄳 Ⓧ 🗲 🖵 🖾 Ⓧ

🅰🅰🅰 ◆◆◆ **Christy Estate Suites** 🅰 🐾
(361) 854-1091. **$129-$189.** 3942 Holly Rd. 0.5 mi s of SR 358, Weber Rd exit. Ext/int corridors. **Pets:** Medium. $300 deposit/pet, $45 one-time fee/room. Supervision.

🆂🅰🆅🅴 🆂🄳 Ⓧ 🗲 🖵 🖾

◆◆◆ **Corpus Christi Omni Bayfront** 🄷 🐾
(361) 887-1600. **$128-$175.** 900 N Shoreline. In town across from bay. Int corridors. **Pets:** Small. Supervision.

🄰🆂🄺 🆂🄳 Ⓧ 🛏 🗲 🍴 🖾 Ⓧ

🅰🅰🅰 ◆◆ **Days Inn** Ⓜ 🐾
(361) 888-8599. **$62-$62.** 901 Navigation Blvd. Jct Navigation Blvd and I-37, exit 3A. Ext corridors. **Pets:** Small. $10 daily fee/room. Designated rooms, supervision.

🆂🅰🆅🅴 Ⓧ 🗟 🗲 🖵 🍴 🖾

◆◆◆ **Drury Inn** Ⓜ 🐾
(361) 289-8200. **$59-$77.** 2021 N Padre Island Dr. Just s of jct I-37 on SR 358 at Leopard St. Int corridors. **Pets:** Small. Designated rooms, no service, supervision, crate.

Ⓧ 🗟 🗲 🖵 🖾

◆◆◆ **Hampton Inn Airport North** Ⓜ
(361) 289-5861. **Call for rates.** 5501 I-37. I-37 at Navigation St (exit 3A). Int corridors. **Pets:** Supervision.

🄰🆂🄺 Ⓧ 🗲 🖵 🍴 🖾

🅰🅰🅰 ◆◆◆ **Holiday Inn-Emerald Beach** Ⓜ 🐾
(361) 883-5731. **$140.** 1102 S Shoreline Blvd. 1.5 mi s on bay. Ext/int corridors. **Pets:** Medium. Supervision.

🆂🅰🆅🅴 🆂🄳 Ⓧ 🛏 🗟 🗲 🖵 🍴 🖾 Ⓧ

🅰🅰🅰 ◆◆◆ **Holiday Inn-Padre Island Drive** 🄷 🐾
(361) 289-5100. **$89-$99.** 5549 Leopard St. 5.5 mi w at jct SR 358 and Leopard St. Int corridors. **Pets:** Other. $100 deposit/room. Supervision.

🆂🅰🆅🅴 🆂🄳 Ⓧ 🗒 🗲 🖵 🍴 🖾

◆◆◆ **Holiday Inn Sun Spree Corpus Christi Gulf Beach Resort** 🄷
(361) 949-8041. **$129-$199.** 15202 Windward Dr. Park Rd 22, jct Whitecap Blvd, just e. Int corridors. **Pets:** Small. Designated rooms, supervision.

🄰🆂🄺 🆂🄳 Ⓧ 🛏 🗲 🖵 🍴 🖾 Ⓧ

🅰🅰🅰 ◆◆◆ **La Quinta Inn-Corpus Christi-North** Ⓜ
(361) 888-5721. **$69-$89.** 5155 I-37N. 0.3 mi w off I-37, exit 3A (Navigation Blvd). Ext corridors. **Pets:** Designated rooms, supervision.

🆂🅰🆅🅴 Ⓧ 🗟 🗲 🖾

🅰🅰🅰 ◆◆◆ **La Quinta Inn-South** Ⓜ
(361) 991-5730. **$79-$99.** 6225 S Padre Island Dr. 7.5 mi se off SR 358 Expwy, Airline Rd exit. Ext corridors. **Pets:** Small. No service, supervision, crate.

🆂🅰🆅🅴 Ⓧ 🗟 🗲 🖾

🅰🅰🅰 ◆◆ **Motel 6 Lantana–231** Ⓜ 🐾
(361) 289-9397. **$33-$49.** 845 Lantana St. I-37 at Lantana St (exit 4B). Ext corridors. **Pets:** Small, other. No service, supervision, crate.

🆂🄳 Ⓧ 🗲 🖾

🅰🅰🅰 ◆◆ **Motel 6 SPI Drive–413** Ⓜ
(361) 991-8858. **$42-$68.** 8202 S Padre Island Dr. South Padre Island Ave at Paul Jones St. Ext corridors. **Pets:** Small. No service, supervision, crate.

🆂🄳 Ⓧ 🗲 🖾

🅰🅰🅰 ◆◆ **Red Roof Inn Corpus Christi Airport** Ⓜ 🐾
(361) 289-6925. **$40-$53.** 6301 I-37. I-37, exit 5 (Corn Products Rd), southbound access road. Ext corridors. **Pets:** Small. No service, supervision, crate.

🆂🅰🆅🅴 Ⓧ 🗲 🖾

◆◆ **Surfside Condominium Apartments** 🅰
(361) 949-8128. **$110-$120, 3 days notice.** 15005 Windward Dr. Park 22 on N Padre Island Dr, jct Whitecap Blvd, just e. Ext corridors. **Pets:** Small. Supervision.

🄰🆂🄺 Ⓧ 🗲 🖵 🖾

🅰🅰🅰 ◆◆◆ **Travelodge Airport** Ⓜ
(361) 289-5666. **$60-$60.** 910 Corn Products Rd. I-37, exit 5 (Corn Products Rd); 0.3 mi w. Int corridors. **Pets:** Designated rooms, supervision.

🆂🅰🆅🅴 🆂🄳 Ⓧ 🗲 🖵 🍴 🖾 Ⓧ

DALHART

🅰🅰🅰 ◆ **Budget Inn** Ⓜ 🐾
(806) 244-4557. **$39-$59.** 415 Liberal St. US 54, just e of US 87 and 385. Ext corridors. **Pets:** Very small. $25 deposit/pet. Designated rooms, no service, supervision, crate.

🆂🅰🆅🅴 🆂🄳 Ⓧ 🗲

🅰🅰🅰 ◆◆ **Comfort Inn** Ⓜ
(806) 249-8585. **$60-$80.** Hwy 54 E. 0.5 mi e on US 54. Ext corridors. **Pets:** Supervision.

🆂🅰🆅🅴 🆂🄳 Ⓧ 🗲 🖵 🖾

🅰🅰🅰 ◆ **Sands Motel** Ⓜ 🐾
(806) 244-4568. **$34-$59.** 301 Liberal St. US 54, just e of US 87 and 385. Ext corridors. **Pets:** Very small, dogs only. No service, supervision, crate.

🆂🅰🆅🅴 🆂🄳 Ⓧ 🗲 🖾

DALLAS METROPOLITAN AREA

ADDISON

◆◆◆ Crowne Plaza North
Dallas/Addison 🅷 ✿
(972) 980-8877. **$69-$119.** 14315 Midway Rd. 0.8 mi s of jct Beltline and Midway rds. Int corridors. **Pets:** $100 deposit/room, $25 one-time fee/room. No service, supervision, crate.

(ASK) ⊠ ⛨ ⧉ 🛏 💷 ⊞ 🖼

◆◆◆ Hampton Inn-Addison 🅼
(972) 991-2800. **$80-$100, 7 days notice.** 4505 Beltway Dr. 0.3 mi se of jct Midway and Beltline rds. Int corridors. **Pets:** Supervision.

(ASK) 🆘 ⊠ ⛨ ⧉ 💷 🖼 ⊠

◆◆◆ Homewood Suites-Addison 🅼 ✿
(972) 788-1342. **$139-$139, 21 days notice.** 4451 Beltline Rd. 15 mi n in Addison. Ext corridors. **Pets:** Other. $75 one-time fee/pet. No service, supervision, crate.

⊠ ⛨ ⧉ 🛏 💷 🖼

◆◆◆ La Quinta Inn & Suites-Dallas Addison 🅼
(972) 404-0004. **$99-$109.** 14925 Landmark Blvd. Dallas Tollway, 0.3 mi w on Beltline Rd to Landmark Blvd, just s. Int corridors. **Pets:** Very small. No service, supervision, crate.

(ASK) ⊠ ⛨ ⧉ 🛏 💷 🖼

ⓐⓐⓐ ◆◆ Motel 6 Addison–1125 🅼
(972) 386-4577. **$46-$61.** 4325 Beltline Rd. Just e of jct Midway and Beltline rds. Ext corridors. **Pets:** No service, supervision, crate.

🆘 ⊠ ⧉ 🖼

◆◆ Ramada Limited 🅼
(972) 233-2525. **Call for rates.** 4151 Beltway Dr. 0.3 mi s of jct Beltline Rd and Beltway Dr. Ext corridors. **Pets:** Small. Supervision.

⊠ 🛏 💷 🖼

CARROLLTON

ⓐⓐⓐ ◆◆ Red Roof Inn-Carrollton 🅼 ✿
(972) 245-1700. **$36-$61.** 1720 S Broadway. Nw off I-35E and US 77, exit 442 (Valwood Pkwy). Ext corridors. **Pets:** Supervision.

(SAVE) ⊠ (CTV)

DALLAS

ⓐⓐⓐ ◆◆◆ AmeriSuites-West End 🅼
(214) 999-0500. **$98-$152.** 1907 N Lamar St. I-35, Commerce St exit, just e, then just n. Int corridors. **Pets:** Supervision.

(SAVE) 🆘 ⊠ ⧉ 🛏 🖼

◆◆◆ Bristol House Residential Suites 🅼
(972) 391-0000. **$69-$99.** 7880 Alpha Rd. I-635 Coit Rd, exit 19B, 0.3 mi n, then just w. Int corridors. **Pets:** Medium. Designated rooms, no service, supervision, crate.

(ASK) ⊠ ⛭ 🛏 💷 🖼

◆◆◆ Crowne Plaza Market Center 🅷
(214) 630-8500. **$69-$119.** 7050 Stemmons Frwy. I-35E, at jct SR 114 and 183; exit 433C (Mockingbird Ln) northbound, SR 356 exit 433A (Irving Blvd) southbound. Int corridors. **Pets:** Medium. Supervision.

(ASK) ⊠ ⛨ 🛏 💷 ⊞ 🖼

◆◆◆ Crowne Plaza Suites-Dallas 🅷
(972) 233-7600. **$69-$129.** 7800 Alpha Rd. Just n of I-635, 0.3 mi nw of jct I-635 and US 75; exit 19C (Coit Rd) eastbound; exit 19B (Coit Rd) westbound. Int corridors. **Pets:** Supervision.

(ASK) ⊠ ⧉ ⛭ 🛏 💷 ⊞ 🖼

◆◆ Days Inn 🅼
(972) 224-3196. **$50-$60.** 8312 S Lancaster Rd. I-20, exit 470 (Lancaster Rd). Ext corridors. **Pets:** Small. No service, supervision, crate.

🆘 ⊠ 🛏 🖼

ⓐⓐⓐ ◆◆ Days Inn Central 🅼 ✿
(214) 827-6080. **$60-$99.** 4150 N Central Exwy. N off US 75, exit 4 (Fitzhugh). Ext corridors. **Pets:** Small, dogs only. Supervision.

(SAVE) 🆘 ⊠ 🖼

◆◆◆ Doubletree Hotel at Campbell
Centre 🅷 ✿
(214) 691-8700. **$120-$134.** 8250 N Central Expwy. N off US 75, exit 13 (Caruth-Haven). Int corridors. **Pets:** Small, other. Supervision.

(ASK) 🆘 ⊠ ⧉ 🛏 💷 ⊞ ⊠

◆◆ Drury Inn-Dallas North 🅼
(972) 484-3330. **$62-$82.** 2421 Walnut Hill Ln. Nw off I-35E and US 77, exit 438 (Walnut Hill Ln). Int corridors. **Pets:** Supervision.

⊠ ⧉ 🛏 💷 🖼

◆◆◆ Embassy Suites Hotel-Dallas/Park
Central 🅷 ✿
(972) 234-3300. **$160-$160.** 13131 N Central Expwy. N off US 75, just n of I-635, 0.8 mi s of jct Midpark Rd; exit 22 (Midpark Rd) northbound; exit 21 (service road) southbound. Int corridors. **Pets:** Small. $25 one-time fee/pet. Supervision.

🆘 ⊠ ⧉ ⛭ 🛏 💷 ⊞ 🖼 ⊠

◆◆◆ Hampton Inn Dallas Downtown/West
End 🅼
(214) 742-5678. **$69-$89.** 1015 Elm St. Downtown near Historic West End District. Int corridors. **Pets:** Medium. Supervision.

⊠ 💷 🖼

◆◆◆ The Harvey Hotel-Dallas 🅷
(972) 960-7000. **$59-$85.** 7815 LBJ Frwy at Coit Rd. I-635, 0.3 mi w of jct US 75; exit 19C (Coit Rd) eastbound, exit 19B westbound. Int corridors. **Pets:** No service, supervision, crate.

⊠ ⧉ 🛏 💷 ⊞ 🖼

◆◆◆ **Hawthorn Suites Hotel-Dallas** Ⓜ ❀
(214) 688-1010. **$135-$155.** 7900 Brookriver Dr. Nw off I-35E and US 77, exit 433C (Mockingbird Ln) northbound; exit 433B southbound, just se. Ext corridors. **Pets:** Small. $100 deposit/pet, $50 one-time fee/pet. Designated rooms, no service, supervision, crate.
ASK 🔊 ✕ 🔥 🗐 🖥 🖨 ⊜

◆◆◆ **Holiday Inn Express-Love Field** Ⓜ
(214) 350-5577. **$69.** 2370 W Northwest Hwy. I-35, NW Hwy exit; 0.8 mi e. Int corridors. **Pets:** Supervision.
✕ 🗐 🖨 ⊜

◆◆ **Homestead Village** Ⓜ ❀
(214) 342-5400. **Call for rates.** 9801 Adela Ct. I-635 at Stillman/Adela, exit 16. Ext corridors. **Pets:** $75 one-time fee/room. Supervision.
✕ 🖨 🖥

◆◆◆ **Homewood Suites** Ⓜ
(972) 437-6966. **$89-$109, 7 days notice.** 9169 Markville Dr. I-635 exit 18A (Greenville Ave S). Int corridors. **Pets:** No service, supervision, crate.
ASK 🔊 ✕ 🗐 🐾 🖨 🖥 ⊜ ✕

Ⓐ ◆◆◆◆ **Hotel St. Germain** Ⓖ
(214) 871-2516. **$265-$650, 7 days notice.** 2516 Maple Ave. 0.3 mi n of Woodall Rogers Pkwy, Pearl St exit. Int corridors. **Pets:** Designated rooms, no service, supervision, crate.
🍴

◆◆◆ **La Quinta Inn-Dallas** Ⓜ ❀
(972) 234-1016. **$59-$79.** 13685 N Central Expwy. US 75 N, exit 22 (Midpark Rd). Ext corridors. **Pets:** Small. No service, supervision, crate.
ASK ✕ 🗐 🖨 ⊜

◆◆◆ **La Quinta Inn-Dallas-City Place** Ⓜ
(214) 821-4220. **$69-$89.** 4440 N Central Expwy. N off US 75; exit 5 (Henerson-Knox) northbound, exit 4 (Fitzhugh) southbound. Ext corridors. **Pets:** Medium. No service, supervision, crate.
ASK ✕ 🗐 🖥 ⊜

◆◆◆ **La Quinta Inn-Dallas-East** Ⓜ
(214) 324-3731. **$69-$89.** 8303 East R L Thornton Frwy. E off I-30, US 67 and 80; exit 51 (Jim Miller); 0.8 mi w of jct Loop 12. Ext corridors. **Pets:** Medium. Supervision.
ASK ✕ ⊜

◆◆◆ **La Quinta Inn-Dallas-Northpark** Ⓜ
(214) 361-8200. **$69-$89.** 10001 N Central Expwy. N off US 75, exit 18 (Meadow Rd). Ext corridors. **Pets:** Medium. Supervision.
ASK ✕ 🗐 🖨 🖥 ⊜

◆◆◆ **La Quinta Inn-Dallas-Regal Row** Ⓜ
(214) 630-5701. **$59-$79.** 1625 Regal Row. Nw off I-35E and US 77, exit 434B (Regal Row). Ext corridors. **Pets:** Supervision.
ASK ✕ 🗐 🐾 🖥 ⊜

Ⓐ ◆◆◆ **Le Meridien Dallas** Ⓗ
(214) 979-9000. **$129-$188.** 650 N Pearl St. 0.3 mi w of Central Expwy; in Plaza of The Americas Complex. Int corridors. **Pets:** Small. No service, supervision, crate.
SAVE 🔊 ✕ 🗐 🐾 🖨 🍴 ✕

Ⓐ ◆◆◆◆◆ **The Mansion On Turtle Creek** Ⓗ
(214) 559-2100. **$360-$490.** 2821 Turtle Creek Blvd. 2 mi nw, entrance on Gillespie St. Int corridors. **Pets:** Large. Supervision.
✕ 🖨 🍴 ⊜

Ⓐ ◆◆ **Motel 6 Forest Lane–1119** Ⓜ
(972) 484-9111. **$40-$56.** 2660 Forest Ln. I-635, exit 26 (Josey Lane); 0.5 mi s to Forest Lane, just w. Ext corridors. **Pets:** No service, supervision, crate.
🔊 ✕ ⊜ CTV

◆◆◆ **Quality Suites** Ⓜ
(214) 904-9955. **$79-$89, 7 days notice.** 2380 West Northwest Hwy. I-35, Northwest Hwy exit; 0.8 mi e. Int corridors. **Pets:** Small. Designated rooms, no service, supervision, crate.
ASK 🔊 ✕ ⊜

◆◆◆ **Radisson Hotel & Suites Dallas** Ⓗ ❀
(214) 351-4477. **$89.** 2330 W Northwest Hwy. Nw off I-35E and US 77 at jct Loop 12, exit 436. Int corridors. **Pets:** $25 deposit/pet, $25 one-time fee/pet. Designated rooms, supervision.
ASK 🔊 ✕ 🗐 🖨 🖥 🍴 ⊜

◆◆◆ **Radisson-Mockingbird** Ⓗ
(214) 634-8850. **$77, 7 days notice.** 1893 W Mockingbird Ln. 4.8 mi nw; 0.3 mi e of I-35E, Mockingbird Ln exit. Int corridors. **Pets:** Medium. No service, supervision, crate.
ASK 🔊 ✕ 🖨 🖥 🍴 ⊜ ✕

Ⓐ ◆◆ **Red Roof Inn-Dallas East** Ⓜ ❀
(214) 388-8741. **$41-$61.** 8108 E R L Thornton Frwy. I-30, US 67 and 80, exit 51 (Jim Miller Rd); 0.8 mi w of jct Loop 12. Ext corridors. **Pets:** Small, other. Supervision.
SAVE ✕ 🗐

Ⓐ ◆◆ **Red Roof Inn-Market Center** Ⓜ
(214) 638-5151. **$46-$59.** 1550 Empire Central Dr. Nw 0.3 mi e off I-35E and US 77, exit 434A (Empire Central). Ext corridors. **Pets:** Designated rooms, no service, supervision, crate.
SAVE ✕ 🗐

Ⓐ ◆◆ **Red Roof Inn-Northwest** Ⓜ ❀
(972) 506-8100. **$45-$58.** 10335 Gardner Rd. Just sw jct Loop 12 (Northwest Hwy) and Spur 348; 0.8 mi w of I-35E and US 77, exit 436. Ext corridors. **Pets:** Small, other. No service, supervision, crate.
SAVE ✕ 🗐

◆◆◆ **Residence Inn by Marriott at Central-Northpark** Ⓐ ❀
(214) 750-8220. **$121-$121.** 10333 N Central Expwy. N on US 75; exit 18 (Meadow Rd) northbound, exit 19 (Royal Ln) southbound. Ext corridors. **Pets:** Small, other. $100 one-time fee/pet. No service, supervision, crate.
ASK 🔊 ✕ 🗐 ⊜ ✕

◆◆◆ **Residence Inn by Marriott-Dallas Market Center** Ⓜ
(214) 631-2472. **$129.** 6950 N Stemmons Frwy. Nw off I-35E and US 77 at jct SR 114 and 183; exit 433C (Mockingbird Ln) northbound, SR 356 (Irving Blvd) exit 433A southbound. Ext corridors. **Pets:** No service, supervision, crate.
ASK 🔊 ✕ 🗐 🖨 🖥 ⊜ ✕

◆◆◆ The Residence Inn By Marriott-Dallas-North Central 🅰 ❀

(972) 669-0478. **$103-$113.** 13636 Goldmark Dr. N 0.5 mi n of jct I-635 and US 75, exit 22 (Midpark Rd). Ext/int corridors. **Pets:** Other. $60 deposit/pet, $60 one-time fee/ pet. No service, supervision, crate.

❌ 🏧 💻 📶

◆◆◆ Sheraton Dallas Brookhollow Hotel 🅷 ❀

(214) 630-7000. **$77, 7 days notice.** 1241 W Mockingbird Ln. Just nw of jct I-35E and W Mockingbird Ln. Int corridors. **Pets:** Small. Supervision.

🅰🆂🄺 🆂 ❌ 🕸 🛏 💻 🍴 📶

◆◆◆◆ The Westin Hotel, Galleria Dallas 🅷 ❀

(972) 934-9494. **$249-$249.** 13340 Dallas Pkwy. Just n of jct I-635 and N Dallas Pkwy; in Galleria Center. Int corridors. **Pets:** Small, other. No service, supervision, crate.

❌ 🔜 🕸 🛏 💻 🍴 📶 ❎

DENTON

⚛ ◆◆ Exel Inn of Denton 🅼 ❀

(940) 383-1471. **$39-$64.** 4211 I-35E North. Just n jct US 380 and I-35, exit 469. Int corridors. **Pets:** Small. Designated rooms, no service, supervision, crate.

🆂 ❌ 🕸 💻 📶

⚛ ◆◆◆ La Quinta Inn-Denton 🅼 ❀

(940) 387-5840. **$69-$89.** 700 Fort Worth Dr. Just n of I-35E, exit 465B (Fort Worth Dr). Ext corridors. **Pets:** Medium. No service, supervision, crate.

🆂🅰🆅🅴 ❌ 🕸 🛏 💻 📶

◆◆◆ Radisson Hotel Denton & Eagle Point Golf Club 🅼

(940) 565-8499. **$99-$99.** 2211 I-35E North. 2.5 mi sw, off I-35E and US 77, exit 466B (Ave D). Int corridors. **Pets:** Supervision.

🅰🆂🄺 🆂 ❌ 🛏 💻 🍴 📶 ❎

DESOTO

⚛ ◆◆ Red Roof Inn Dallas/DeSoto 🅼

(972) 224-7100. **$38-$42.** 1401 N Beckley. I-35 at Wintergreen Rd, exit 416. Ext corridors. **Pets:** No service, supervision, crate.

🆂🅰🆅🅴 ❌ 🛏

DUNCANVILLE

⚛ ◆◆◆ Hampton Inn-Dallas/Southwest 🅼 ❀

(972) 298-4747. **$59-$64.** 4154 Preferred Place. 1 mi w of US 67; just e of jct I-20 and Crokrell Hill Rd, exit 463. Ext corridors. **Pets:** Small. $15 one-time fee/room. Designated rooms, supervision.

🆂🅰🆅🅴 ❌ 🕸 🛏 💻 📶

◆◆ Holiday Inn-Dallas Southwest 🅼

(972) 298-8911. **$71-$71.** 711 E Camp Wisdom Rd. 2 mi w of US 67; 0.3 mi w of jct I-20 and Cockrell Hill Rd, exit 463. Ext corridors. **Pets:** Designated rooms, supervision.

🅰🆂🄺 🆂 ❌ 🕸 🛏 💻 🍴 📶

FARMERS BRANCH

◆◆ Best Western Dallas North 🅼

(972) 241-8521. **$49-$99, 30 days notice.** 13333 N Stemmons Frwy. 0.5 mi n of I-635 on I-35E, exit at Valwood 442; located on w side service road. Ext corridors. **Pets:** Small. Designated rooms, supervision.

🅰🆂🄺 🆂 ❌ 🛏 💻 🍴 📶

⚛ ◆◆◆ Days Inn–North Dallas 🅼 ❀

(972) 488-0800. **$59-$69.** 13313 Stemmons Frwy. I-35 at Valley View Ln, exit 441. Int corridors. **Pets:** Medium. $25 deposit/pet. Designated rooms, no service, supervision, crate.

🆂🅰🆅🅴 🆂 ❌ 🛏 📶

⚛ ◆◆ Econo Lodge Dallas Airport North 🅼 ❀

(972) 243-5500. **$46-$46.** 2275 Valley View Ln. I-35E, exit 441 (Valley View); 0.3 mi w. Ext corridors. **Pets:** Small, other. $10 deposit/room. Designated rooms, no service, supervision, crate.

🆂🅰🆅🅴 ❌ 🛏 📶

◆◆◆ La Quinta Inn-Dallas-Northwest-Farmers Branch 🅼 ❀

(972) 620-7333. **$59-$79.** 13235 Stemmons Frwy N. Nw off I-35E and US 77; 0.5 mi n of jct I-635, exit 441 (Valley View Ln). Ext corridors. **Pets:** Small. No service, supervision, crate.

🅰🆂🄺 ❌ 🕸 📶

GARLAND

◆◆ Days Inn-Dallas/Garland 🅼 ❀

(972) 226-7621. **Call for rates.** 6222 Belt Line Rd. E off I-30 and US 67 Belt Line Rd exit. Ext corridors. **Pets:** Small. $10 one-time fee/pet. No service, supervision, crate.

🅰🆂🄺 ❌ 📶

⚛ ◆◆◆ La Quinta Inn-Dallas-LBJ Northeast-Garland 🅼 ❀

(972) 271-7581. **$55-$75.** 12721 I-635. Ne off I-635, exit 11B (Northwest Hwy). Ext corridors. **Pets:** Other. Supervision.

🆂🅰🆅🅴 ❌ 🕸 🔜 🛏 💻 📶

⚛ ◆◆ Red Roof Inn Hotel & Conference Center 🅼

(972) 686-0202. **$36-$64.** 13700 LBJ Frwy. I-635 at Centerville Rd, exit 11A. Int corridors. **Pets:** Supervision.

🆂🅰🆅🅴 ❌ 🛏 💻 🍴 📶

GRAND PRAIRIE

◆◆◆ Hampton Inn Arlington/DFW Airport Area 🅼

(972) 988-8989. **$89-$89.** 2050 N Hwy 360. 6 mi ne on SR 360 (Watson Rd), Green Oaks Blvd/Carrier Pkwy exit. Int corridors. **Pets:** Supervision.

🅰🆂🄺 🆂 ❌ 🕸 🛏 📶

◆◆◆ La Quinta Inn-Dallas-Grand Prairie (Six Flags) 🅼

(972) 641-3021. **$75-$95.** 1410 NW 19th St. Jct I-30 and 19th St, exit 32. Ext corridors. **Pets:** Designated rooms, no service, supervision, crate.

🅰🆂🄺 ❌ 🔜 🕸 🛏 💻 📶

 ◆◆ **Motel 6–446** M ❀
(972) 642-9424. **$40-$61.** 406 E Safari Blvd. I-30, Beltline Rd exit; just n to Safari Blvd, just w. Ext corridors. **Pets:** Very small, other. Supervision.

S M ✕ 🖙 (CTV)

GREENVILLE

 ◆◆ **Gold Key Inn** M
(903) 454-7000. **$69-$69.** 1215 E I-30. Just e of jct I-30 and US 69, exit 94B. Int corridors. **Pets:** Medium. No service, supervision, crate.

SAVE S ✕ 🖙 🖙 🖙

IRVING

 ◆◆◆ **AmeriSuites Las Colinas** M
(972) 910-0302. **$139-$139.** 333 W John W Carpenter Frwy. SR 114 at Hidden Ridge exit. Int corridors. **Pets:** Very small. No service, supervision, crate.

SAVE S ✕ 🖙 🖙 🖙 🖙

 ◆◆ **Comfort Inn DFW Airport** M ❀
(972) 929-0066. **$59-$99.** 8205 Esters Rd. Nw off SR 114. Int corridors. **Pets:** Small. $15 daily fee/pet, $25 one-time fee/pet. No service, supervision, crate.

SAVE S ✕ 🖙 🖙 🖙 🖙

◆◆ **Drury Inn-DFW Airport** M
(972) 986-1200. **$72-$90.** 4210 W Airport Frwy. SR 183, Esters Rd exit on south access road. Int corridors. **Pets:** Supervision.

✕ 🖙 🖙 🖙 🖙

 ◆◆◆◆ **Four Seasons Resort & Club** R
(972) 717-0700. **$315-$425.** 4150 N MacArthur Blvd. Se off SR 114, 1.5 mi s of MacArthur Blvd exit. Int corridors. **Pets:** Designated rooms, no service, supervision, crate.

✕ 🖙 🖙 🖙 🖙 🖙 🖙

◆◆◆ **Hampton Inn-DFW Airport** M
(972) 986-3606. **$72-$90.** 4340 W Airport Frwy. SR 183, Valley View exit on south access road. Int corridors. **Pets:** Supervision.

✕ 🖙 🖙 🖙 🖙 🖙

◆◆◆ **Harvey Hotel-DFW Airport** H
(972) 929-4500. **$59-$119.** 4545 W John Carpenter Frwy. Nw off SR 114, Esters Rd exit. Int corridors. **Pets:** Supervision.

ASK ✕ 🖙 🖙 🖙 🖙 🖙

◆◆◆ **Harvey Suites-DFW Airport** M
(972) 929-4499. **$59-$89.** 4550 W John Carpenter Frwy. Int corridors. **Pets:** Medium. Supervision.

ASK ✕ 🖙 🖙 🖙 🖙 🖙

◆◆◆ **Homewood Suites Las Colinas** M
(972) 556-0665. **Call for rates.** 4300 Wingren Rd. Nw off SR 114; O'Connor Rd/Wingren Rd exit eastbound, Rochelle Rd exit westbound. Ext corridors. **Pets:** No service, supervision, crate.

✕ 🖙 🖙

◆◆◆ **La Quinta Inn-DFW Airport-South** M ❀
(972) 252-6546. **$59-$79.** 4105 W Airport Frwy. 3 mi nw of Irving off SR 183, Esters Rd exit; on north access road. Ext corridors. **Pets:** Very small. $20 deposit/room. No service, supervision, crate.

ASK ✕ 🖙 🖙 🖙 🖙

 ◆◆ **Motel 6–1274** M
(972) 915-3993. **$42-$58.** 7800 Heathrow Dr. Nw off SR 114, Freeport Pkwy exit. Int corridors. **Pets:** Very small. No service, supervision, crate.

S ✕ 🖙

 ◆◆ **Red Roof Inn/DFW Airport North** M
(972) 929-0020. **$53-$92.** 8150 Esters Blvd. Nw off SR 114. Ext corridors. **Pets:** Medium. Supervision.

SAVE ✕ 🖙 🖙

 ◆◆ **Red Roof Inn/DFW Airport South** M ❀
(972) 570-7500. **$49-$64.** 2611 W Airport Frwy. SR 183 at Story Rd exit. Int corridors. **Pets:** Designated rooms, no service, supervision, crate.

SAVE ✕ 🖙

◆◆◆ **Residence Inn By Marriott at Las Colinas** M
(972) 580-7773. **Call for rates.** 950 W Walnut Hill Ln. Nw off SR 114, 0.8 mi w of jct Walnut Hill Ln. Ext corridors. **Pets:** No service, supervision, crate.

✕ 🖙 🖙 🖙 🖙 🖙 ✕

◆◆◆ **Sheraton Grand Hotel** H
(972) 929-8400. **$118-$118.** Hwy 114 & Esters Blvd. Nw off SR 114, Esters Rd exit. Int corridors. **Pets:** Medium. No service, supervision, crate.

ASK S ✕ 🖙 🖙 🖙 🖙 🖙

 ◆◆ **Wellesley Inn & Suites** M ❀
(972) 790-1950. **$59-$99.** 3950 W Airport Frwy. SR 183 at Esters Rd exit on south access road. Ext corridors. **Pets:** Very small. $100 one-time fee/pet. Designated rooms, no service, supervision, crate.

SAVE S ✕ 🖙 🖙 🖙

◆◆◆ **Wilson World Hotel-DFW Airport South** M ❀
(972) 513-0800. **$89-$119.** 4600 W Airport Frwy. 3.3 nw off SR 183, Valley View exit. Int corridors. **Pets:** Medium. Supervision.

ASK S ✕ 🖙 🖙 🖙 🖙

LEWISVILLE

◆◆◆ **Comfort Suites** M
(972) 315-6464. **$75-$80.** 755 A Vista Ridge Mall Dr. I-35 at Round Grove Rd, exit 448A. Int corridors. **Pets:** Medium. Designated rooms, no service, supervision, crate.

S ✕ 🖙 🖙

◆◆◆ **Holiday Inn Express** M
(972) 434-1000. **$79-$99.** 200 N Stemmons Frwy. I-35E, at jct FM 1171, exit 452 (Main St). Ext corridors. **Pets:** Supervision.

ASK S ✕ 🖙 🖙 🖙 🖙

◆◆◆ **La Quinta Inn-Dallas-Lewisville** Ⓜ ❀
(972) 221-7525. **$59-$79.** 1657 S Stemmons Frwy. 1 mi se on I-35E, exit 449 (Corporate Dr). Ext corridors. **Pets:** Other. Supervision.
(ASK) ✕ 🗾 🗄 💻 🐾

◆◆ **Motel 6** Ⓜ
(972) 436-5008. **Call for rates.** 1705 Lakepointe Dr. I-35 exit 449 Corporate Dr. Int corridors. **Pets:** Small. No service, supervision, crate.
✕

◆◆◆ **Residence Inn** Ⓜ
(972) 315-3777. **$120-$130, 7 days notice.** 755 C Vista Ridge Blvd. I-35 at Round Grove Rd, exit 448A. Int corridors. **Pets:** Medium. No service, supervision, crate.
(ASK) (S🐾) ✕ 🗄 💻 🐾

MCKINNEY

🅐🅐🅐 ◆◆ **Days Inn McKinney** Ⓜ ❀
(972) 548-8888. **$60-$75.** 2104 N Central Expwy. US 75, 0.5 mi n jct US 380, exit 41. Ext corridors. **Pets:** No service, supervision, crate.
(SAVE) (S🐾) ✕ 🗄 🐾

MIDLOTHIAN

🅐🅐🅐 ◆◆◆ **Best Western Midlothian Inn** Ⓜ ❀
(972) 775-1891. **$55-$69, 3 days notice.** 220 N Hwy 67. 1 mi w on US 67; just n of jct US 287. Ext corridors. **Pets:** Other. $25 deposit/room. Supervision.
(SAVE) (S🐾) ✕ 🐾

PLANO

🅐🅐🅐 ◆◆◆ **AmeriSuites** Ⓜ
(972) 378-3997. **$109-$119.** 3100 Dallas Pkwy. N on Dallas Pkwy to W Park exit. Int corridors. **Pets:** Medium. Designated rooms, no service, supervision, crate.
(SAVE) (S🐾) ✕ 🏠 🗄 💻 🐾

◆◆◆ **Best Western Park Suites Hotel** Ⓜ
(972) 578-2243. **$85-$120.** 640 Park Blvd E. Just e of US 75; 0.3 mi ne of FM 544, exit 29A. Int corridors. **Pets:** Small. Supervision.
(ASK) (S🐾) ✕ 🗄 💻 🐾

◆◆ **Comfort Inn** Ⓜ
(972) 424-5568. **$55-$110.** 621 Central Pkwy E. Just e of US 75; 0.3 mi ne of FM 544, exit 29A. Int corridors. **Pets:** Designated rooms, supervision.
(ASK) (S🐾) ✕ 🗄 💻 🐾

🅐🅐🅐 ◆◆◆ **Hampton Inn Plano** Ⓜ ❀
(972) 519-1000. **$74-$104.** 4901 Old Shepherd Pl. I-635, exit 21 (Preston Rd), 6 mi n, just e. Int corridors. **Pets:** $15 one-time fee/room. Supervision.
(SAVE) (S🐾) ✕ 🗾 🗄 💻 🐾

◆◆◆ **The Harvey Hotel-Plano** Ⓗ
(972) 578-8555. **$59-$85.** 1600 N Central Expwy. US 75, just n of jct FM 544; exit 29 southbound, exit 29 Whitsitt Pkwy (15th St) northbound. Int corridors. **Pets:** No service, supervision, crate.
(ASK) ✕ 🏠 🗾 🗄 💻 🍴 🐾

◆◆◆ **Holiday Inn-Plano** Ⓜ
(972) 881-1881. **$69-$89.** 700 Central Pkwy E. Just e of US 75; 0.3 mi ne of jct FM 544, exit 29A. Ext corridors. **Pets:** No service, supervision, crate.
(ASK) ✕ 🗾 🍴 🐾

◆◆◆ **Homewood Suites Plano** Ⓜ ❀
(972) 758-8800. **Call for rates.** 4705 Old Shepherd Pl. I-635, exit 21 (Preston Rd); 6 mi n to Old Shepherd Pl, just e. Ext corridors. **Pets:** Medium, other. $75 one-time fee/pet. Supervision.
✕ 🗾 🗄 💻 🐾

◆◆◆ **La Quinta Inn & Suites-West Plano** Ⓜ ❀
(972) 599-0700. **$69-$89.** 4800 W Plano Pkwy. Jct Plano Pkwy and SR 259 (Preston Rd). Int corridors. **Pets:** Small. Designated rooms, no service, supervision, crate.
(ASK) ✕ 🗾 🗄 💻 🐾

◆◆◆ **La Quinta Inn-Dallas-Plano** Ⓜ
(972) 423-1300. **$65-$85.** 1820 N Central Expwy. US 7S, 0.3 mi n of jct FM 544, exit 29A. **Pets:** Small. No service, supervision, crate.
(ASK) ✕ 🗾 🗄 💻 🐾

🅐🅐🅐 ◆◆◆ **MainStay Suites** Ⓜ ❀
(972) 596-9966. **$60-$100.** 4709 W Plano Pkwy. Jct Plano Pkwy and SR 289 (Preston Rd). Int corridors. **Pets:** Medium. $10 daily fee/room, $25 one-time fee/room. No service, supervision, crate.
(SAVE) (S🐾) ✕ 🗾 🗄 💻 🐾

🅐🅐🅐 ◆◆ **Motel 6–1121** Ⓜ
(972) 578-1626. **$39-$61.** 2550 N Central Expwy. 1 mi n on US 75 Park Blvd, exit 29A. Ext corridors. **Pets:** Small. Supervision.
(S🐾) ✕ 🐾

🅐🅐🅐 ◆◆ **Red Roof Inn Dallas-Plano** Ⓜ ❀
(972) 881-8191. **$44-$61.** 301 Ruisseau Dr. SR 75 at Parker Rd exit 30, 0.5 mi w to Premier, then just n. Int corridors. **Pets:** Small, other. Designated rooms, no service, supervision, crate.
(SAVE) ✕ 🗄 💻

🅐🅐🅐 ◆◆ **Sleep Inn Plano** Ⓜ ❀
(972) 867-1111. **$60-$75, 7 days notice.** 4801 W Plano Pkwy. Jct Plano Pkwy and SR 289 (Preston Rd). Ext corridors. **Pets:** Small. $10 daily fee/room, $25 one-time fee/room. No service, supervision, crate.
(SAVE) (S🐾) ✕ 🐾

🅐🅐🅐 ◆◆◆ **Wellesley Inn & Suites** Ⓜ
(972) 378-9978. **$79-$109.** 2900 Dallas Pkwy. Dallas Pkwy northbound at Park Blvd exit; southbound exit Parker Blvd. Int corridors. **Pets:** Supervision.
(SAVE) (S🐾) ✕ 🏠 🗄 💻 🐾

RICHARDSON

🅐🅐🅐 ◆◆◆ **The Clarion Hotel Richardson** Ⓗ
(972) 644-4000. **$95-$155.** 1981 N Central Expwy. 1.8 mi n on US 75, at jct SR 5 exit 26 (Campbell Rd). Int corridors. **Pets:** Small. Designated rooms, supervision.
(SAVE) (S🐾) ✕ 🏠 🗾 🗄 💻 🍴 🐾

◆◆◆ Hampton Inn **M**
(972) 234-5400. **Call for rates.** 1577 Gateway Blvd. 1.8 mi n on US 75 at Campbell Rd, exit 26; 0.4 mi w to Gateway, just s. Int corridors. **Pets:** Small. No service, supervision, crate.

⊠ 🏠 💻 🍽

◆◆◆ Hawthorn Suites Hotel-Richardson **M** ❀
(972) 669-1000. **$149.** 250 Muncipal Drive. 1.8 mi n off US 75, from exit 26 (Campbell Rd); 1.3 mi w to Gateway, just s. Ext corridors. **Pets:** $5 daily fee/pet, $50 one-time fee/room. Supervision.

A$K Sб ⊠ ✍ 🏠 💻 🍽 ⊠

◆◆ Sleep Inn **M** ❀
(972) 470-9440. **Call for rates.** 2458 N Central Expwy. N on US 75; exit 27A (Renner Rd) northbound; exit 26 southbound. Int corridors. **Pets:** Small, other. No service, supervision, crate.

⊠ 🏠

◆◆◆ Wyndham Garden Hotel **MI** ❀
(972) 479-0500. **$109.** 901 E Campbell Rd. US 75 Campbell Rd, exit 26; just e. Int corridors. **Pets:** Medium. $30 one-time fee/pet. Supervision.

A$K Sб ⊠ 🏠 ✍ 🏠 💻 🍴 🍽

ROCKWALL

◆◆ Super 8 Motel **M**
(972) 722-9922. **Call for rates.** 1130 I-30. I-30, exit 69 westbound; exit 68 eastbound, on N Frontage Rd. Ext corridors. **Pets:** Small. Supervision.

⊠ 🏠 🍽

❀ **END METROPOLITAN AREA** ❀

DECATUR

🐾 ◆◆ Best Western Inn **M**
(940) 627-5982. **$53-$65, 7 days notice.** 1801 S Hwy 287. US 287. Ext corridors. **Pets:** No service, supervision, crate.

S$VE ⊠ 🏠 💻 🍽

🐾 ◆◆◆ Comfort Inn **M**
(940) 627-6919. **$49-$95.** 1709 Hwy 287 S. Ext corridors. **Pets:** No service, supervision, crate.

S$VE Sб ⊠ 🏠 💻 🍽

DEL RIO

🐾 ◆◆◆ Best Western Inn of Del Rio **M** ❀
(830) 775-7511. **$79-$99.** 810 Ave F. 0.8 mi nw on US 90, 277 and 377. Ext corridors. **Pets:** Other. $5 daily fee/pet. Designated rooms, supervision.

S$VE Sб ⊠ 🏠 💻 🍽

🐾 ◆◆ Days Inn and Suites **M** ❀
(830) 775-0585. **$43-$175.** 3808 Ave F. 3.5 mi nw on US 90. Ext corridors. **Pets:** Medium, other. $5 daily fee/room. No service, supervision, crate.

S$VE Sб ⊠ 🏠 💻 🍽

TERRELL

🐾 ◆◆ Best Western-La Piedra Inn **M** ❀
(972) 563-2676. **$45-$65.** 309 IH-20E. Jct I-20 and SR 34, exit 501. Ext corridors. **Pets:** Small, other. $5 one-time fee/room. Designated rooms, no service, supervision, crate.

S$VE Sб ⊠ 🏠 🍽

◆◆ Super 8 Motel **M** ❀
(972) 563-1511. **$50-$65.** 1705 Hwy 34 S. Jct I-20 and SR 34, exit 501. Ext corridors. **Pets:** Other. $5 daily fee/pet, $5 one-time fee/pet. No service, supervision, crate.

A$K Sб ⊠ 🍽

WAXAHACHIE

🐾 ◆◆ Best Western **M**
(972) 937-4202. **$52-$68, 7 days notice.** 200 N I-35E. I-35E and US 287 business route; 1.8 mi s of jct US 287, exit 401B. Ext corridors. **Pets:** Small. Supervision.

S$VE ⊠ 🏠 💻 🍽

◆◆◆ Holiday Inn Express **M** ❀
(830) 775-2933. **$42-$62, 7 days notice.** 3616 Ave F. 3.2 mi nw on US 90. Ext/int corridors. **Pets:** $10 one-time fee/pet. No service, supervision, crate.

A$K Sб ⊠ 📱 🏠 💻 🍽

🐾 ◆◆◆ La Quinta Inns-Del Rio **M**
(830) 775-7591. **$59-$79.** 2005 Avenue F. 1.8 mi nw on US 90, 277 and 377. Ext/int corridors. **Pets:** Small. Designated rooms, no service, supervision, crate.

S$VE ⊠ 💻 🍽

🐾 ◆◆◆ Ramada Inn **MI** ❀
(830) 775-1511. **$65-$90.** 2101 Ave F. 1.8 mi nw on US 90, 277 and 377. Ext/int corridors. **Pets:** Small, other. Designated rooms, no service, supervision, crate.

S$VE Sб ⊠ 🏠 💻 🍴 🍽 ⊠

DENISON

◆◆ Ramada Inn **MI**
(903) 465-6800. **$35-$55.** 1600 Eisenhower Pkwy. US 75 exit Texoma (northbound), exit US 69 (southbound). Ext corridors. **Pets:** Very small. Designated rooms, no service, supervision, crate.

A$K Sб ⊠ 🏠 💻 🍴 🍽

DUMAS

Econo Lodge M
(806) 935-9098. **$35-$95.** 1719 S Dumas Ave. US 287, 2 mi s of SR 152 jct US 87. Int corridors. **Pets:** Medium. $3 daily fee/pet, $3 one-time fee/pet. No service, supervision, crate.

Kona Kai Dumas Inn Motel M
(806) 935-6441. **$67-$80, 3 days notice.** 1712 S Dumas Ave. US Hwy 287, 1.5 mi s from jct US 87 and SR 152. Ext/int corridors. **Pets:** Medium. $20 deposit/room. Designated rooms, no service, supervision, crate.

EAGLE PASS

Best Western M
(830) 758-1234. **$72-$84.** 1923 Loop 431. US 57, jct Loop 431. Ext corridors. **Pets:** Small. Supervision.

La Quinta Inn-Eagle Pass M
(830) 773-7000. **$59-$79.** 2525 Main St E. US 57 and 277 at jct Loop 431. Ext corridors. **Pets:** Small. No service, supervision, crate.

Super 8 Motel M
(830) 773-9531. **$50-$60.** 2150 N Hwy 277. 4 mi n on US 277. Ext corridors. **Pets:** Medium. Supervision.

EARLY

Post Oak Inn M
(915) 643-5621. **$40-$50.** 606 Early Blvd. SR 377. Ext corridors. **Pets:** No service, supervision, crate.

EASTLAND

The Eastland BB
(254) 629-8397. **$65-$85.** 112 N Lamar St. I-20, exit 343, 1.5 mi n to Lamar St, just e. Int corridors. **Pets:** Supervision.

Econo Lodge of Eastland M
(254) 629-3324. **$38-$43.** 2001 I-20W. S service road at I-20, exit 343. Ext corridors. **Pets:** Small. No service, supervision, crate.

Ramada Inn M
(254) 629-2655. **$45-$65.** 2501 I-20 East. S service road at I-20, exit 343. Ext corridors. **Pets:** Supervision.

Super 8 Motel & RV Park M
(254) 629-3336. **$40-$48.** 3900 I-20E. N service road at I-20, exit 343. Ext corridors. **Pets:** No service, supervision, crate.

EL PASO

Baymont Inn & Suites El Paso East M
(915) 591-3300. **$46-$53.** 7944 Gateway Blvd E. I-10, exit 28B. Int corridors. **Pets:** Medium. Designated rooms, no service, supervision, crate.

Baymont Inn & Suites-El Paso West M
(915) 585-2999. **$45-$52.** 7620 N Mesa St. I-10, exit 11(Mesa St). Int corridors. **Pets:** $50 deposit/room. Designated rooms, supervision.

Best Western Airport Inn M
(915) 779-7700. **$50-$56.** 7144 Gateway E. I-10, exit 26 (Hawkins Blvd). Ext corridors. **Pets:** Very small. Designated rooms, no service, supervision, crate.

Best Western Sunland Park Inn M
(915) 587-4900. **$49-$69.** 1045 Sunland Park Dr. I-10, exit 13, 0.2 mi s. Ext corridors. **Pets:** Designated rooms, no service, supervision, crate.

Camino Real Hotel H
(915) 534-3000. **$95-$110.** 101 S El Paso St. Center. Int corridors. **Pets:** Very small, dogs only. $100 deposit/room, $25 one-time fee/room. No service, supervision, crate.

Chase Suites by Woodfin A
(915) 772-8000. **$79-$170.** 6791 Montana St. I-10, Airways Blvd exit, 1 mi n. Ext corridors. **Pets:** Small. Supervision.

Comfort Inn Airport M
(915) 594-9111. **$59-$79, 30 days notice.** 900 N Yarbrough St. I-10, Yarbrough St exit, just s. Ext corridors. **Pets:** Small. $25 deposit/room. No service, supervision, crate.

Comfort Inn West M
(915) 845-1906. **$45-$62.** 7651 N Mesa St. I-10, exit 11 (Mesa St). Int corridors. **Pets:** Medium. $5 daily fee/pet. No service, supervision, crate.

Comfort Suites M
(915) 587-5300. **$65-$80.** 949 Sunland Park Dr. I-10 exit 13. Int corridors. **Pets:** Dogs only. $15 one-time fee/room. Supervision.

Econo Lodge M
(915) 778-3311. **$45-$60.** 6363 Montana St. 6 mi e on US 62 and 180. Ext corridors. **Pets:** Medium. $10 one-time fee/pet. No service, supervision, crate.

El Paso Airport Hilton M
(915) 778-4241. **$114-$114.** 2027 Airway Blvd. I-10 exit 25, 1.3 mi n. Int corridors. **Pets:** $200 deposit/room. No service, supervision, crate.

◆◆◆ **El Paso Marriott Hotel** 🅷 🐾
(915) 779-3300. **$124-$154.** 1600 Airway Blvd. I-10, Airway Blvd exit, 1 mi n. Int corridors. **Pets:** Small. Supervision.
ⒶⓈⓀ 🆂🔟 ⊠ 🔽 📝 🔒 💻 🍴 ⊿

◆◆◆ **Embassy Suites Hotel** 🅷 🐾
(915) 779-6222. **Call for rates.** 6100 Gateway E. I-10, exit 24B (Geronimo St). Int corridors. **Pets:** Small. $50 one-time fee/room. No service, supervision, crate.
⊠ 📝 📝 🔒 💻 ⊿

◆◆◆ **Howard Johnson Inn** Ⓜ 🐾
(915) 591-9471. **$57-$72.** 8887 Gateway W. I-10, exit 26 (Hawkins Blvd). Int corridors. **Pets:** No service, supervision, crate.
ⒶⓈⓀ 🆂🔟 ⊠ 🔒 💻 🍴 ⊿

◆◆◆ **La Quinta Inn-El Paso-Airport** Ⓜ
(915) 778-9321. **$59-$79.** 6140 Gateway Blvd E. I-10, exit 24B. Ext corridors. **Pets:** Designated rooms, supervision.
ⒶⓈⓀ ⊠ 📝 🔒 💻 ⊿

◆◆◆ **La Quinta Inn-El Paso-Cielo Vista** Ⓜ 🐾
(915) 593-8400. **$69-$89.** 9125 Gateway W. I-10, exit 28B westbound; exit 27 eastbound. Ext corridors. **Pets:** Other. Supervision.
⊠ 📝 🔒 💻 ⊿

◆◆◆ **La Quinta Inn-El Paso-Lomaland** Ⓜ
(915) 591-2244. **$55-$75.** 11033 Gateway Blvd W. I-10, exit 29 eastbound; exit 30 westbound, 1 mi w. Ext corridors. **Pets:** Medium. Supervision.
ⒶⓈⓀ ⊠ 🔽 📝 📝 🔒 💻 ⊿

◆◆◆ **La Quinta Inn-El Paso-West** Ⓜ 🐾
(915) 833-2522. **$55-$75.** 7550 Remcon Cir. I-10, exit 11 (Mesa St). Ext corridors. **Pets:** Medium, other. No service, supervision, crate.
ⒶⓈⓀ ⊠ 📝 📝 🔒 💻 ⊿

◆◆◆ **Quality Inn** Ⓜ 🐾
(915) 778-6611. **$43-$75.** 6201 Gateway Blvd W. I-10, Geronimo St exit. Ext corridors. **Pets:** Other. No service, supervision, crate.
ⒶⓈⓀ 🆂🔟 ⊠ 🔼 📝 🔒 💻 🍴 ⊿

🆬 ◆◆◆ **Red Roof Inn West** Ⓜ
(915) 587-9977. **$45-$56.** 7530 Remcon Circle. I-10, exit 11 (Mesa St). Ext/int corridors. **Pets:** Small. Supervision.
🆂🅰🆅🅴 ⊠ 🔽 📝 📝 ⊿

◆◆ **Sleep Inn** Ⓜ 🐾
(915) 585-7577. **$55-$70.** 953 Sunland Park Dr. I-10 exit 13. Int corridors. **Pets:** Other. $15 one-time fee/room. Supervision.
ⒶⓈⓀ 🆂🔟 ⊠ 🔒 💻 ⊿

EULESS

◆◆◆ **La Quinta Inn-DFW Airport West-Euless** Ⓜ
(817) 540-0233. **$65-$85.** 1001 W Airport Frwy. SR 183, just e of FM 157, Industrial Blvd exit. Ext corridors. **Pets:** No service, supervision, crate.
ⒶⓈⓀ ⊠ 📝 🔒 💻 ⊿

🆬 ◆◆◆ **Ramada Inn DFW West** Ⓜ
(817) 283-2400. **$55-$130.** 2155 W Airport Frwy. SR 183, just e of jct SR 121; Westpark Way exit eastbound, Murphy Dr exit westbound. Int corridors. **Pets:** No service, supervision, crate.
🆂🅰🆅🅴 🆂🔟 ⊠ 📝 🔒 💻 🍴 ⊿

FORT HANCOCK

🆬 ◆◆ **Fort Hancock Motel** Ⓜ
(915) 769-3981. **$38-$52.** 1425 Knox Ave. I-10, exit 72. Ext corridors. **Pets:** Medium. No service, supervision, crate.
⊠ ⊿

FORT STOCKTON

◆◆◆ **Atrium West Inn** Ⓜ 🐾
(915) 336-6666. **Call for rates.** 1305 N Hwy 285. Just s of I-10, exit 257. Ext corridors. **Pets:** Medium. No service, supervision, crate.
ⒶⓈⓀ ⊠ 🔒 ⊿

🆬 ◆◆◆ **Best Western Swiss Clock Inn** Ⓜ 🐾
(915) 336-8521. **$52-$70, 3 days notice.** 3201 W Dickinson Blvd. I-10, exit 256, 0.5 mi e. Ext corridors. **Pets:** Small, other. Supervision.
🆂🅰🆅🅴 🆂🔟 ⊠ 🍴 ⊿

🆬 ◆◆◆ **Comfort Inn of Fort Stockton** Ⓜ
(915) 336-8531. **$52-$56, 7 days notice.** 3200 W Dickinson Blvd. I-10, exit 256. Int corridors. **Pets:** No service, supervision, crate.
🆂🅰🆅🅴 🆂🔟 ⊠ 🔒 🍴 ⊿

🆬 ◆◆◆ **Days Inn** Ⓜ
(915) 336-7500. **$46-$56.** 1408 N US Hwy 285. I-10, exit 257. Ext corridors. **Pets:** Very small. Supervision.
🆂🅰🆅🅴 🆂🔟 ⊠ 🔒 ⊿

🆬 ◆◆◆ **Holiday Inn Express** Ⓜ 🐾
(915) 336-5955. **$53-$69.** 1308 N US Hwy 285. Just s of I-10, exit 257. **Pets:** Small. $50 deposit/room. Designated rooms, no service, supervision, crate.
🆂🅰🆅🅴 🆂🔟 ⊠ 🔒 ⊿

🆬 ◆◆◆ **La Quinta Inn-Fort Stockton** Ⓜ
(915) 336-9781. **$49-$69.** 2601 I-10W. I-10, exit 257. Ext corridors. **Pets:** Designated rooms, supervision.
🆂🅰🆅🅴 ⊠ 📝 🔒 💻 🍴 ⊿

◆◆ **Super 8 Motel** Ⓜ 🐾
(915) 336-9711. **$42-$50.** 800 E Dickinson Blvd. W on I-10, exit 261; e on I-10, exit 256. Ext corridors. **Pets:** $8 one-time fee/pet. Designated rooms, no service, supervision, crate.
ⒶⓈⓀ 🆂🔟 ⊠ 🔒 💻 ⊿

FORT WORTH

🆬 ◆◆◆ **AmeriSuites Fort Worth City View** Ⓜ
(817) 361-9797. **$89-$114.** 5900 City View Blvd. I-20 exit 231 (Bryant Irvin Rd). Int corridors. **Pets:** Very small. No service, supervision, crate.
🆂🅰🆅🅴 🆂🔟 ⊠ 🔒 💻 ⊿

◆◆◆ Best Western Inn M ❖
(817) 847-8484. **Call for rates.** 6700 Fossil Bluff Dr. I-35 at Webster Center Blvd exit 58. Int corridors. **Pets:** Small. $5 daily fee/pet. No service, supervision, crate.

⊠ 🖥 💻 🕿

⚠ ◆◆ Best Western West Branch Inn M ❖
(817) 244-7444. **$50-$72.** 7301 W Frwy. 7.5 mi w at jct I-30 and SR 183, exit 7B. Ext corridors. **Pets:** $25 deposit/room. No service, supervision, crate.

SAVE 🖬 ⊠ 🖥 🕿

◆◆ Hampton Inn Fort Worth-West M ❖
(817) 560-4180. **$69-$74, 3 days notice.** 2700 Cherry Ln. 7.5 mi w, just s of I-30, exit 7A (Cherry Ln). Ext corridors. **Pets:** Large. No service, supervision, crate.

ASK 🖬 ⊠ 💻 🕿

⚠ ◆◆ Holiday Inn South Conference
Center MI
(817) 293-3088. **$69-$85.** 100 Altamesa E Blvd. 7.5 mi s of I-30 on I-35 W at exit 44. Int corridors. **Pets:** No service, supervision, crate.

SAVE 🖬 ⊠ 🖉 🖥 💻 🍴 🕿

◆◆ Homestead Village M ❖
(817) 338-4808. **$70.** 1601 River Run. I-30, exit University Dr, 0.4 mi s to Old University Dr, just e. Ext corridors. **Pets:** Medium, other. $75 daily fee/room, $75 one-time fee/room. Supervision.

⊠ 🖥 💻

◆◆◆ La Quinta Inn & Suites-Fort Worth M ❖
(817) 222-2888. **$79-$99.** 4700 North Frwy. N on I-35 at Meacham Blvd, exit 56A. Int corridors. **Pets:** Small. Supervision.

ASK ⊠ 🖉 🖥 💻 🕿

◆◆◆ La Quinta Inn & Suites Fort Worth
Southwest M
(817) 370-2700. **$85-$105.** 4900 Bryant Irving Rd. I-20 at Bryant Irvin Road, exit 231, 0.3 mi s. Int corridors. **Pets:** No service, supervision, crate.

ASK ⊠ 🖉 🖥 💻 🕿

◆◆◆ La Quinta Inn-Fort Worth West M
(817) 246-5511. **$59-$69.** 7888 I-30 W. I-30 at Cherry Ln, exit 7A. Ext corridors. **Pets:** Small. No service, supervision, crate.

ASK ⊠ 🖉 💻 🕿

⚠ ◆◆ Motel 6 M
(817) 834-7361. **$38-$56.** 1236 Oakland Blvd. I-30 at Oakland Blvd exit 18. Ext corridors. **Pets:** Small. Supervision.

🖬 ⊠ 🕿

⚠ ◆◆ Motel 6 North–153 M
(817) 625-4359. **$38-$56.** 3271 I-35 W. I-35, at northbound exit 54C 33rd St; southbound Paffort St exit 54B. **Pets:** Small. No service, supervision, crate.

🖬 ⊠ 🕿

⚠ ◆◆ Motel 6 South M
(817) 293-8595. **$38-$56.** 6600 S Freeway. I-35 at Altamere Blvd exit 44. Ext corridors. **Pets:** Small. No service, supervision, crate.

🖬 ⊠ 🕿

◆◆ Ramada Inn-Midtown MI
(817) 336-9311. **Call for rates.** 1401 S University Dr. 2.3 mi sw, just s of I-30, University Dr exit. Ext corridors. **Pets:** Small. No service, supervision, crate.

ASK ⊠ 🖬 💻 🍴 🕿

◆◆◆ Residence Inn By Marriott Fort Worth-River
Plaza A
(817) 870-1011. **$110-$110.** 1701 S University Dr. 2.8 mi sw; 0.3 mi s of I-30, University Dr exit. Ext corridors. **Pets:** Small. Supervision.

ASK 🖬 ⊠ ♿ 🖉 🖥 💻 🕿 ⊠

◆◆◆◆ The Worthington Hotel H ❖
(817) 870-1000. **Call for rates.** 200 Main St. At Tandy Center. Int corridors. **Pets:** $200 deposit/room. Supervision.

⊠ 🖉 🖥 💻 🍴 🕿 ⊠

FREDERICKSBURG

⚠ ◆◆ Budget Host Deluxe Inn M
(830) 997-3344. **$34-$75, 4 days notice.** 901 E Main St. 0.5 mi e on US 290. Ext/int corridors. **Pets:** Designated rooms, no service, supervision, crate.

⊠ 🖥

⚠ ◆◆◆ Comfort Inn M ❖
(830) 997-9811. **$64-$89.** 908 S Adams St. 0.8 mi sw on SR 16; 0.8 mi sw jct US 87 and 290. Ext corridors. **Pets:** Supervision.

SAVE 🖬 ⊠ 🖉 🖥 💻 🕿 ⊠

⚠ ◆◆ Dietzel Motel M ❖
(830) 997-3330. **$35-$62.** 1141 W US 290. 1 mi w on US 290 at jct US 87. Ext corridors. **Pets:** Other. $5 daily fee/pet. Supervision.

⊠ 🕿 🈂

⚠ ◆ Sunset Inn M
(830) 997-9581. **$45-$52.** 900 S Adams St. 0.8 mi sw jct US 290 and SR 16 (S Adams St). Ext corridors. **Pets:** Small. Designated rooms, supervision.

SAVE 🖬 ⊠ 🖥 💻

FREEPORT

⚠ ◆◆ Country Hearth Inn M
(409) 239-1602. **$49-$61.** 1015 W 2nd. 0.5 mi e of SR 288. Ext corridors. **Pets:** Supervision.

SAVE 🖬 ⊠ 🖥 💻 🕿

FULTON

⚠ ◆◆◆ Best Western Inn by the Bay MI ❖
(361) 729-8351. **$58-$68.** 3902 N Hwy 35. SR 35, 0.5 mi n of jct Business Rt 35 and FM 3063. Ext corridors. **Pets:** Medium. Designated rooms, no service, supervision, crate.

SAVE 🖬 ⊠ 🖉 🖥 💻 🕿

GAINESVILLE

⚠ ◆ Budget Host Inn M ❖
(940) 665-2856. **$36-$42.** Rt 2, Box 120. I-35, northbound exit 499; southbound exit 498B. Ext corridors. **Pets:** Other. No service, supervision, crate.

SAVE 🖬 ⊠ 🖥

GALVESTON

♦♦♦ La Quinta Inn
(409) 763-1224. **$85-$149.** 1402 Seawall Blvd. Seawall Blvd at 14th St. Ext corridors. **Pets:** Designated rooms, supervision.

GEORGETOWN

♦♦♦ Comfort Inn 🅼 🐾
(512) 863-7504. **$54-$89.** 1005 Leander Rd. 1 mi s on I-35, exit 260. Ext corridors. **Pets:** $5 daily fee/pet, $5 one-time fee/pet. Supervision.

♦♦♦ La Quinta-Georgetown-Sun City 🅼 🐾
(512) 869-2541. **$69-$89.** 333 I-35 N. I-35, exit 264. Ext corridors. **Pets:** Other. Supervision.

GIDDINGS

♦♦ Best Western Classic Inn 🅼
(409) 542-7611. **$39-$53.** 3556 E Austin Rd. 2 mi e on US 290. Ext corridors. **Pets:** No service, supervision, crate.

GRANBURY

♦♦♦ Comfort Inn 🅼
(817) 573-2611. **$55-$150, 30 days notice.** 1201 Plaza Dr N. 2 mi e on US 377 bypass. Ext corridors. **Pets:** Medium. No service, supervision, crate.

♦♦ Days Inn of Granbury 🅼 🐾
(817) 573-2691. **$59-$99.** 1339 N Plaza Dr. 2 mi e on US 377 bypass. Ext corridors. **Pets:** Small. $20 one-time fee/pet. No service, supervision, crate.

♦♦ Plantation Inn on the Lake 🅼
(817) 573-8846. **$60-$75.** 1451 E Pearl St. 0.3 mi w of Business Rt 377 at jct US 377 bypass. Ext corridors. **Pets:** No service, supervision, crate.

HARLINGEN

♦♦ Best Western Harlingen Inn 🅼
(956) 425-7070. **Call for rates.** 6779 W Expwy 83. US 83, 2.3 mi w of jct US 77; at Stuart Place Rd exit. Ext corridors. **Pets:** Medium. Supervision.

♦♦♦ La Quinta Inn-Harlingen 🅼 🐾
(956) 428-6888. **$69-$89.** 1002 US 83 S Expwy. US 83 and 77 Expwy, M St exit. Ext corridors. **Pets:** Small. No service, crate.

HEARNE

♦♦ Oak Tree Inn 🅼 🐾
(409) 279-5599. **$54-$69.** 1051 N Market St. 0.6 mi s of jct US 79 & SR 6. Ext/int corridors. **Pets:** Small. $25 deposit/pet. No service, supervision, crate.

HENDERSON

♦♦ Best Western Inn of Henderson 🅼 🐾
(903) 657-9561. **$59-$79.** 1500 Hwy 259 S. 2 mi s on US 259. Ext/int corridors. **Pets:** Very small. $10 deposit/room, $10 one-time fee/room. Supervision.

HEREFORD

♦♦ Best Western Red Carpet Inn 🅼
(806) 364-0540. **Call for rates.** 830 W 1st St. Just w of jct US 385 and 60. Ext corridors. **Pets:** No service, supervision, crate.

HILLSBORO

♦♦ Best Western Hillsboro Inn 🅼 🐾
(254) 582-8465. **$52-$62.** 307 I-35. Jct I-35 and FM 286, exit 368A northbound; exit 368B southbound. Ext corridors. **Pets:** Small. Supervision.

HONDO

♦♦ Whitetail Lodge 🅼 🐾
(830) 426-3031. **$42-$55, 5 days notice.** US 90 at jct Hwy 173. Ext corridors. **Pets:** Dogs only. Designated rooms, no service, supervision, crate.

HOUSTON METROPOLITAN AREA

BAYTOWN

♦♦♦ Baymont Inn & Suites-Houston Baytown 🅼
(281) 421-7300. **$61-$66.** 5215 I-10 E. I-10, exit 792. Int corridors. **Pets:** Medium. Designated rooms, no service, supervision, crate.

♦♦♦ La Quinta Inn-Baytown 🅼 🐾
(281) 421-5566. **$55-$76.** 4911 I-10 E. I-10, exit 792 (Garth Rd). Ext corridors. **Pets:** Small, other. Supervision.

♦ Motel 6-1136 🅼
(281) 576-5777. **$37-$53.** 8911 Hwy 146. I-10, exit 797 (Hwy 146). Ext corridors. **Pets:** No service, supervision, crate.

◆◆ Quality Inn Baytown 📗

(281) 427-7481. **$55-$59.** 300 S Hwy 146 business. 5 mi sw of jct I-10 and SR 146, exit 797, 2.2 mi s on Business 146 (Alexander Rd). Ext corridors. **Pets:** Large. Supervision.

A$K ⊠ 🛇 🔲 🎬 🎐

CHANNELVIEW

◆◆ Best Western Houston East 📗 ☙

(281) 452-1000. **$40-$45, 7 days notice.** 15919 I-10 E. I-10, exit 783 westbound; exit 784 eastbound. Ext corridors. **Pets:** Small. $10 deposit/pet, $10 one-time fee/pet. Designated rooms, no service, supervision, crate.

A$K 🛇 ⊠ 🛇 🔲 🎐

CONROE

◆◆◆ Baymont Inn-Conroe 📗 ☙

(409) 539-5100. **$60-$65.** 1506 I-45. I-45, exit 85 (Gladstell St) northbound; exit 84 (Frazier St) southbound. Int corridors. **Pets:** Medium. $50 deposit/room. Designated rooms, no service, supervision, crate.

🛇 ⊠ 🖉 🖑 🛇 🔲 🎐

HOUSTON

◆◆◆ AmeriSuites 📗

(281) 820-6060. **$64-$159.** 300 Ronan Park Pl. Sam Houston Pkwy (Beltway 8), Imperial Valley exit, 0.8 mi w on frontage road; Hardy Toll exit, turn under Pkwy 1.2 mi w on w frontage road eastbound. Int corridors. **Pets:** Small. No service, supervision, crate.

SAVE 🛇 ⊠ 🗍 🖑 🛇 🔲 🎐

◆◆◆ Baymont Inn & Suites-Houston North 📗 ☙

(281) 875-2000. **$62.** 12701 North Frwy. I-45, exit 61 (Greens Rd). Int corridors. **Pets:** Small, other. $50 deposit/room. Designated rooms, no service, supervision, crate.

🛇 ⊠ 🖉 🖑 🛇 🔲 🎐

◆◆◆ Baymont Inn & Suites Houston Northwest 📗

(713) 680-8282. **$58-$64.** 11130 Northwest Frwy. I-45 N to I-610 N, then US 290 W, exit W 34th St, just ne. Int corridors. **Pets:** Supervision.

A$K 🛇 ⊠ 🖑 🛇 🔲 🎐

◆◆◆ Baymont Inn & Suites-Houston Southwest 📗

(713) 784-3838. **$57-$62.** 6790 Southwest Frwy. Southwest Frwy (US 59), Hillcroft and W Park exit eastbound; Hillcroft exit westbound. Int corridors. **Pets:** Medium. Designated rooms, no service, supervision, crate.

🛇 ⊠ 🖑 🛇 🔲 🎐

◆◆◆ Comfort Suites 📗 ☙

(713) 787-0004. **$89-$94.** 6221 Richmond Ave. US 59, exit Hillcroft, 1 mi n on Hillcroft to Richmond, 0.6 mi w. Int corridors. **Pets:** Medium, other. $25 one-time fee/room. No service, supervision, crate.

A$K 🛇 ⊠ 🖑 🛇 🔲 🎐

◆ Days Inn 📗

(713) 523-3777. **$54-$64.** 4640 S Main St. Between Richmond and Blodgett sts. Ext corridors. **Pets:** No service, supervision, crate.

A$K ⊠ 🛇 🔲 🎐

◆◆◆ Days Inn & Suites 📗 ☙

(713) 783-1400. **$63-$69.** 9041 Westheimer Rd. Just w of jct Fondrew. Ext corridors. **Pets:** Small. $25 one-time fee/room. Supervision.

A$K 🛇 ⊠ 🛇 🔲 🎐

◆ Days Inn-Houston North 📗 ☙

(281) 820-1500. **$43-$55.** 9025 North Frwy. N off I-45 and US 75, exit 57A (Gulf Bank Rd). Ext corridors. **Pets:** Other. $20 deposit/room. Supervision.

A$K 🛇 ⊠ 🎐

◆◆ Days Inn West 📗

(713) 467-4411. **$39-$54, 7 days notice.** 9535 Katy Frwy. I-10, exit 758A (Bunker Hill). Ext/int corridors. **Pets:** Medium. Designated rooms, supervision.

A$K 🛇 ⊠ 🖉 🛇 🔲 🎐

⚠ ◆◆◆ Doubletree Guest Suites 🏨

(713) 961-9000. **$169-$169.** 5353 Westheimer Rd. 0.8 mi w off I-610, exit 8C (Westheimer Rd) northbound; exit 9A (San Felipe/Westheimer rds) southbound. Int corridors. **Pets:** Small. No service, supervision, crate.

SAVE 🛇 ⊠ 🖉 🛇 🔲 🎬 🎐

⚠ ◆◆◆ Doubletree Hotel at Allen Center 🏨

(713) 759-0202. **$195-$235.** 400 Dallas St. Downtown at Dallas and Bagby sts. Int corridors. **Pets:** Small. No service, supervision, crate.

SAVE 🛇 ⊠ 🖉 🖑 🛇 🔲 🎬

◆◆◆ Drury Inn & Suites I-10 West 📗

(281) 558-7007. **$62-$78.** 1000 N Hwy 6. Just n on SR 6 from I-10, exit 751 (Addicks/Hwy 6). Int corridors. **Pets:** Small. Supervision.

⊠ 🖑 🛇 🔲 🎐

◆◆◆ Drury Inn & Suites-Near Galleria 📗

(713) 963-0700. **$83-$103.** 1615 W Loop S. N I-610, exit 9 (San Felipe Rd); northbound I-610, exit 9A (San Felipe Rd); e service road. Int corridors. **Pets:** Designated rooms, supervision.

⊠ 🗍 🖉 🖑 🛇 🔲 🎐

◆◆◆ Drury Inn-Houston Hobby Airport 📗 ☙

(713) 941-4300. **$65-$85.** 7902 Mosley Rd. Southbound Service Rd, I-45 at Airport Blvd and College Rd, exit 36. Int corridors. **Pets:** Small, other. Supervision.

⊠ 🗍 🖉 🔲 🎐

⚠ ◆◆◆◆ Four Seasons Hotel Houston 🏨 ☙

(713) 650-1300. **$260-$380.** 1300 Lamar St. Lamar St and Austin. Int corridors. **Pets:** Small, other. Supervision.

SAVE ⊠ 🖉 🖑 🛇 🔲 🎬 🎐

⚠ ◆◆ The Grant Motor Inn 📗 ☙

(713) 668-8000. **$42-$66, 3 days notice.** 8200 S Main St. Jct I-610, exit 2 (Main St), 1.4 mi ne. Ext corridors. **Pets:** Small, other. Supervision.

SAVE 🛇 ⊠ 🎐 ⊠

⚠ ◆◆◆ Hampton Inn I-10E 📗 ☙

(713) 673-4200. **$59-$79.** 828 Mercury Dr. 11 mi e on I-10 E, exit 776A (Mercury Dr). Int corridors. **Pets:** Small. $25 one-time fee/room. Supervision.

SAVE 🛇 ⊠ 🖉 🛇 🔲 🎐

◆◆ **Hawthorn Suites** 🅰 🐾
(713) 785-3415. **$139-$159.** 6910 Southwest Frwy. US 59 (Southwest Frwy), Hillcroft St exit. Ext corridors. **Pets:** Small. $25 deposit/pet, $5 daily fee/pet. No service, supervision, crate.

⟨ASK⟩ ⟨S⟩ ⟨✕⟩ ⟨🍴⟩ ⟨🖵⟩ ⟨🕭⟩ ⟨✕⟩

◆◆◆ **Holiday Inn Hotel and Suites** 🅷
(713) 681-5000. **$101-$121, 3 days notice.** 7787 Katy Frwy. I-10, exit 762 (Antoine Dr) westbound; exit 762 (Silber/Post Oak Rd) eastbound, on S Service Rd. Int corridors. **Pets:** Medium. Supervision.

⟨ASK⟩ ⟨S⟩ ⟨✕⟩ ⟨🐕⟩ ⟨✍⟩ ⟨🍴⟩ ⟨🖵⟩ ⟨🍴⟩ ⟨🕭⟩

🆎 ◆◆◆ **Holiday Inn Houston Intercontinental Airport** 🅷
(281) 449-2311. **$80-$150.** 15222 JFK Blvd. N Sam Houston Pkwy E and JFK Blvd intersection. Int corridors. **Pets:** Small. Supervision.

⟨SAVE⟩ ⟨S⟩ ⟨✕⟩ ⟨🐕⟩ ⟨✍⟩ ⟨🍴⟩ ⟨🖵⟩ ⟨🍴⟩ ⟨🕭⟩ ⟨✕⟩ ⟨CTV⟩

🆎 ◆◆◆ **Holiday Inn Select-Greenway Plaza** 🅷
(713) 523-8448. **$90-$160.** 2712 Southwest Frwy. US 59, Kirby Dr exit. Int corridors. **Pets:** Medium. No service, supervision, crate.

⟨SAVE⟩ ⟨S⟩ ⟨✕⟩ ⟨🐕⟩ ⟨✍⟩ ⟨🍴⟩ ⟨🖵⟩ ⟨🍴⟩ ⟨🕭⟩

🆎 ◆◆◆ **Holiday Inn Select-Houston West** 🅷
(281) 558-5580. **$96-$156.** 14703 Park Row. SR 6, just n of jct I-10, exit 751 (Addicks Rd). Int corridors. **Pets:** Small. Designated rooms, no service, supervision, crate.

⟨SAVE⟩ ⟨S⟩ ⟨✕⟩ ⟨🐕⟩ ⟨✍⟩ ⟨🍴⟩ ⟨🖵⟩ ⟨🍴⟩ ⟨🕭⟩

◆◆ **Homestead Village Guest Studios** 🅼 🐾
(713) 797-0000. **$50-$65.** 7979 Fannin St. I-160, exit 1B, 0.8 mi n. Ext corridors. **Pets:** Medium. $75 one-time fee/ room. Supervision.

⟨✕⟩ ⟨✍⟩ ⟨🍴⟩ ⟨🖵⟩

◆◆ **Homestead Village Guest Studios** 🅼
(713) 785-8550. **Call for rates.** 3030 W Sam Houston Pkwy. Sam Houston Pkwy (Beltway 8), Westheimer Rd exit. Ext corridors. **Pets:** Small. No service, supervision, crate.

⟨ASK⟩ ⟨✕⟩ ⟨🐕⟩ ⟨✍⟩ ⟨🍴⟩ ⟨🖵⟩

◆◆ **Homestead Village Guest Studios** 🅼
(713) 895-2900. **Call for rates.** 14255 Northwest Frwy. US 290, Fairbanks/N Houston Rd exit, just s to Jameel Rd, w to Rothway, just n. Ext corridors. **Pets:** Small. No service, supervision, crate.

⟨✕⟩ ⟨✍⟩ ⟨🍴⟩ ⟨🖵⟩

◆◆ **Homestead Village Guest Studios-Cypress Station** 🅼
(281) 580-2221. **$49-$54.** 220 Bammel-Westfield Rd. I-45, exit 66, southbound Frontage Rd, just s. Ext corridors. **Pets:** No service, supervision, crate.

⟨✕⟩ ⟨🐕⟩ ⟨✍⟩ ⟨🍴⟩ ⟨🖵⟩

◆◆◆ **Homestead Village Guest Studios Galleria** 🅼
(713) 960-9660. **Call for rates.** 2300 W Loop S. I-10 W to 610 Loop S, exit 9A (San Felipe/Westheimer) southbound; exit 9 (San Felipe) northbound. Int corridors. **Pets:** Supervision.

⟨ASK⟩ ⟨✕⟩ ⟨✍⟩ ⟨🍴⟩ ⟨🖵⟩

◆◆ **Homestead Village Guest Studios-Houston Hobby South** 🅼 🐾
(281) 929-5400. **$29-$59.** 12700 Featherwood. I-45, exit 33 (Fugua St), stay in right lane and cross over I-45 just e to Fugua St, just s. Ext corridors. **Pets:** Small, other. $75 one-time fee/room. Supervision.

⟨✕⟩ ⟨✍⟩ ⟨🍴⟩ ⟨🖵⟩

◆◆ **Homestead Village Guest Studios-Willowbrook** 🅼
(281) 397-9922. **$259.** 13223 Champions Center Dr. Jct SR 249 and FM 1960 W, 0.9 mi e to Champion Center Dr, just n to Champion Center Plaza, just w. Ext corridors. **Pets:** Small. No service, supervision, crate.

⟨✕⟩ ⟨🐕⟩ ⟨✍⟩ ⟨🍴⟩ ⟨🖵⟩

◆◆ **Homestead Village-Park 10** 🅼
(281) 579-6959. **Call for rates.** 1255 Hwy 6 N. SR 6, just n of jct I-10, exit 751 (Addicks Rd). Ext corridors. **Pets:** Supervision.

⟨✕⟩ ⟨✍⟩ ⟨🍴⟩ ⟨🖵⟩

◆◆◆ **Hotel Sofitel Houston** 🅷 🐾
(281) 445-9000. **$79-$109.** 425 N Sam Houston Pkwy E. Beltway 8 (Sam Houston Pkwy), westbound exit Imperial Valley; eastbound exit Hardy Toll Road, on westbound frontage road. Int corridors. **Pets:** Small. $250 deposit/room, $25 one-time fee/room. No service, supervision, crate.

⟨✕⟩ ⟨🍴⟩ ⟨🍴⟩ ⟨🕭⟩

◆◆◆ **Houston Marriott Medical Center Hotel** 🅷
(713) 796-0080. **$179.** 6580 Fannin St. Jct I-610, exit 2 (Main St), 2.5 mi ne to Holcombe St, 0.3 mi e. Int corridors. **Pets:** Designated rooms, supervision.

⟨ASK⟩ ⟨S⟩ ⟨✕⟩ ⟨🐕⟩ ⟨✍⟩ ⟨🍴⟩ ⟨🖵⟩ ⟨🍴⟩ ⟨🕭⟩

🆎 ◆◆◆ **Houston Marriott Westside** 🅷 🐾
(281) 558-8338. **$99-$164.** 13210 Katy Frwy. Just n of jct I-10, exit 753A (Eldridge St). Int corridors. **Pets:** Small. $25 one-time fee/room. No service, supervision, crate.

⟨SAVE⟩ ⟨S⟩ ⟨✕⟩ ⟨🍴⟩ ⟨🍴⟩ ⟨🕭⟩ ⟨✕⟩

◆◆ **Houston TownPlace Suites** 🅼
(281) 646-0058. **$59-$89.** 15155 Katy Frwy. I-10, exit 751, just s on SR 6 to Grisby Rd, then w. Int corridors. **Pets:** No service, supervision, crate.

⟨ASK⟩ ⟨S⟩ ⟨✕⟩ ⟨🍴⟩ ⟨🖵⟩ ⟨🕭⟩

◆◆◆ **La Quinta Inn & Suites** 🅼 🐾
(281) 219-2000. **$75-$115.** 15510 JFK Blvd. Beltway 8 (Sam Houston Pkwy), exit JFK Blvd/Vickery. Int corridors. **Pets:** Other. Supervision.

⟨ASK⟩ ⟨✕⟩ ⟨🐕⟩ ⟨✍⟩ ⟨🍴⟩ ⟨🖵⟩ ⟨🕭⟩

◆◆◆ **La Quinta Inn & Suites** 🅼
(281) 646-9200. **$59-$102.** 15225 Katy Frwy. I-10 (Katy Frwy), exit 748 (Barker-Cypress Rd) eastbound, 2.6 mi on eastbound service road; exit 751 (Hwy 6) westbound, just s to Grisby Rd, 0.5 mi w. Int corridors. **Pets:** No service, supervision, crate.

⟨ASK⟩ ⟨✕⟩ ⟨✍⟩ ⟨🍴⟩ ⟨🖵⟩ ⟨🕭⟩

◆◆◆ **La Quinta Inn-Brook Hollow** 🅼
(713) 688-2581. **$49-$66.** 11002 Northwest Frwy. Nw on US 290, Magnum-Dacoma exit. Ext corridors. **Pets:** Small. Designated rooms, supervision.

⟨ASK⟩ ⟨✕⟩ ⟨✍⟩ ⟨🍴⟩ ⟨🖵⟩ ⟨🕭⟩

◆◆◆ La Quinta Inn-Greenway Plaza Ⓜ
(713) 623-4750. **$59-$92.** 4015 Southwest Frwy. Sw off US 59 (Southwest Frwy), Weslayan exit. Ext/int corridors. **Pets:** Small. No service, supervision, crate.

Ⓐ$Ⓚ ☒ 🗐 🔌 🖬 🖵 🖾

◆◆◆ La Quinta Inn-Houston-Astrodome Ⓜ
(713) 668-8082. **$69-$109.** 9911 Buffalo Speedway. Just s of jct I-610, exit 2 (Buffalo Speedway/S Main St). Ext corridors. **Pets:** Small. Supervision.

Ⓐ$Ⓚ ☒ 🗐 🖬 🖵 🖾

◆◆◆ La Quinta Inn-Houston-Cy-Fair Ⓜ
(281) 469-4018. **$59-$84.** 13290 FM 1960 W. SR 6, w of jct US 290 and FM 1960. Ext corridors. **Pets:** Small. Supervision.

Ⓐ$Ⓚ ☒ 🗐 🖬 🖵 🖾

◆◆◆ La Quinta Inn-Houston East Ⓜ 🐾
(713) 453-5425. **$55-$84.** 11999 E Frwy. E off I-10, exit 778A (Federal Rd) eastbound; exit 776B (Holland Ave) westbound. Ext corridors. **Pets:** Small, other. No service, supervision, crate.

Ⓐ$Ⓚ ☒ 🗐 🔌 🖬 🖵 🖾

◆◆◆ La Quinta Inn Houston-Galleria Area Ⓜ 🐾
(713) 355-3440. **$69-$129.** 1625 W Loop S. I-610, northbound exit 9 (San Felipe); southbound exit 9A (San Felipe/Westheimer), on northbound Service Rd. Int corridors. **Pets:** Small. Supervision.

Ⓐ$Ⓚ ☒ 🖼 🗐 🔌 🖬 🖵 🖾

◆◆◆ La Quinta Inn-Houston-Gessner Ⓜ
(713) 772-3626. **$52-$76.** 8201 Southwest Frwy. Sw on US 59, Gessner St exit. Ext corridors. **Pets:** Small. No service, supervision, crate.

Ⓐ$Ⓚ ☒ 🗐 🔌 🖬 🖵 🖾

◆◆◆ La Quinta Inn-Houston-Hobby Airport Ⓜ
(713) 941-0900. **$59-$82.** 9902 Gulf Frwy. I-45S (Gulf Frwy), exit 36, Airport Blvd-College Ave. Ext/int corridors. **Pets:** Small. No service, supervision, crate.

Ⓐ$Ⓚ ☒ 🖼 🗐 🖬 🖵 🖾

◆◆◆ La Quinta Inn-Houston-I-45 North(Loop 1960) Ⓜ
(281) 444-7500. **$59-$79.** 17111 North Frwy. I-45, southbound service road; 0.4 mi s of jct FM 1960 and I-45, exit 66. Ext corridors. **Pets:** No service, supervision, crate.

Ⓐ$Ⓚ ☒ 🖬 🖵 🖾

◆◆◆ La Quinta Inn-Houston-Southwest Frwy/Bltwy 8 Ⓜ 🐾
(713) 270-9559. **$45-$79.** 10552 Southwest Frwy. Sw on US 59, 1 mi sw of Bissonnet St exit. Ext/int corridors. **Pets:** Small. No service, supervision, crate.

Ⓐ$Ⓚ ☒ 🗐 🖬 🖵 🖾

◆◆◆ La Quinta Inn-Houston Wilcrest Ⓜ 🐾
(713) 932-0808. **$59-$82.** 11113 Katy Frwy. I-10, exit 754 (Kirkwood Dr) westbound; exit 755 (Wilcrest Rd) eastbound, on eastbound service road. Ext corridors. **Pets:** Small, other. No service, supervision, crate.

Ⓐ$Ⓚ ☒ 🗐 🔌 🖬 🖵 🖾

◆◆◆ La Quinta Inn-Intercontinental Airport Ⓜ
(281) 447-6888. **$59-$89.** 6 N Belt E. I-45, at n jct Beltway 8 Intercontinental Airport, exit 60B. Ext corridors. **Pets:** Small. Designated rooms, supervision.

Ⓐ$Ⓚ ☒ 🖵 🖾

◆◆◆ La Quinta Inn-Wirt Rd Ⓜ 🐾
(713) 688-8941. **$59-$89.** 8017 Katy Frwy. W off I-10, exit 761A (Wirt Rd). Ext corridors. **Pets:** Small. No service, supervision, crate.

Ⓐ$Ⓚ ☒ 🗐 🔌 🖬 🖵 🖾

◆◆ The Lovett Inn ⒷⒷ 🐾
(713) 522-5224. **$85-$250, 3 days notice.** 501 Lovett Blvd. I-610, Westheimer Rd exit, 4.5 mi e to Montrose Blvd, s to Lovett Blvd, just e. Ext/int corridors. **Pets:** Other. Designated rooms, supervision.

☒ 🖬 🖵 🖾

ⒶⒶⒶ ◆◆◆ Marriott-West Loop-By The Galleria Ⓗ
(713) 960-0111. **$69-$159.** 1750 W Loop S. Just w of I-610, exit 9 northbound; exit 9A (San Felipe) southbound, entrance from San Felipe or service road. Int corridors. **Pets:** Designated rooms, no service, supervision, crate.

Ⓢ🄰🆅🄴 🖼 ☒ 🔌 🖬 🖵 🍴 🖾

ⒶⒶⒶ ◆ Motel 6–1140 Ⓜ
(713) 937-7056. **$40-$56.** 16884 Northwest Frwy. US 290 westbound exit Jones Rd; eastbound exit Senate Ave on westbound Frontage Rd. Ext corridors. **Pets:** No service, supervision, crate.

🖼 ☒ 🔌 🖬 🖾

ⒶⒶⒶ ◆◆ Motel 6–1401 Ⓜ
(713) 334-9188. **$46-$62.** 2900 W Sam Houston Pkwy S. Sam Houston Pkwy (Beltway 8), Westheimer Rd exit. Int corridors. **Pets:** Medium. No service, supervision, crate.

🖼 ☒ 🗐 🔌 🖾

ⒶⒶⒶ ◆ Motel 6–345 Ⓜ
(713) 778-0008. **$38-$54.** 9638 Plainfield Rd. US 59, exit Bissonnet, just nw to Plainfield Rd on W Frontage Rd. Ext corridors. **Pets:** Small. No service, supervision, crate.

🖼 ☒ 🗐 🔌 🖬 🖾

◆◆ Quality Inn-Intercontinental Airport Ⓜ🄸 🐾
(281) 446-9131. **$64-$89.** 6115 Will Clayton Pkwy. 1.5 mi w of US 59 (Eastex Frwy), Will Clayton Pkwy exit. Ext/int corridors. **Pets:** $15 one-time fee/room. Designated rooms, supervision.

Ⓐ$Ⓚ 🖼 ☒ 🗐 🔌 🍴 🖾 ☒

ⒶⒶⒶ ◆◆◆ Radisson Hotel & Conference Center Ⓗ 🐾
(713) 943-7979. **$124-$145.** 9100 Gulf Frwy. I-45 at Airport Blvd-College Rd, exit 36, on w service road. Int corridors. **Pets:** Small, other. $50 deposit/pet. No service, supervision, crate.

Ⓢ🄰🆅🄴 🖼 ☒ 🗐 🔌 🖬 🖵 🍴 🖾

◆◆ Radisson Suite Hotel Houston Ⓗ 🐾
(713) 796-1000. **$139-$139.** 1400 Old Spanish Tr. I-610, exit 2 (S Main St/Buffalo Speedway), 1.3 mi n to Old Spanish Tr, 0.3 mi e. Int corridors. **Pets:** Other. Supervision.

Ⓐ$Ⓚ 🖼 ☒ 🗐 🔌 🖬 🖵 🍴 🖾

⚛ ◆◆◆ Ramada Plaza Hotel 🅗
(713) 462-9977. **$79-$79.** 12801 Northwest Frwy. Nw on US 290, Hollister Rd exit, 0.7 mi e on S Service Rd. Ext/int corridors. **Pets:** Small. No service, supervision, crate.
🅢🅐🅥🄴 ⬛ 🖥 💻 🍴 🎨

**◆◆◆ Ramada Plaza Hotel Near the
Galleria** 🅜 ❀
(713) 688-2222. **$69-$79, 3 days notice.** 7611 Katy Frwy. I-10, exit 762 (Silber Rd). Int corridors. **Pets:** Small, other. $10 daily fee/pet. No service, supervision, crate.
🎨 🖥 💻 🍴 🎨

**◆◆◆ Red Lion Hotel Houston/Galleria
Area** 🅗 ❀
(713) 961-3000. **$80-$80.** 2525 W Loop S. Jct I-610, exit 9A (San Felipe/Westheimer) southbound; exit 8C (Westheimer Rd) northbound. Int corridors. **Pets:** Dogs only. $100 deposit/room, $25 one-time fee/room. Supervision.
🅢🅐🎨🅥🄴 ⬛ 🖥 💻 🍴 🎨

⚛ ◆◆ Red Roof Inn Hobby Airport 🅜
(713) 943-3300. **$36-$61.** 9005 Airport Blvd. Just w of I-45, exit 36 (Airport Blvd-College St). Int corridors. **Pets:** Supervision.
🅢🅐🅥🄴 🖥 🎨

⚛ ◆◆ Red Roof Inn Houston West 🅜 ❀
(281) 579-7200. **$38-$50.** 15701 Park Ten Place. I-10, exit 751 (Addicks Rd/Hwy 6), 0.8 mi on w frontage road. Ext/int corridors. **Pets:** Medium. No service, supervision, crate.
🅢🅐🎨🅥🄴 🖥

⚛ ◆◆ Red Roof Inns 🅜 ❀
(713) 785-9909. **$47-$63.** 2960 SW Sam Houston Pkwy. SW Sam Houston (Beltway 8), Westheimer Rd exit. Ext/int corridors. **Pets:** Other. Supervision.
🅢🅐🎨🅥🄴 🖥 🎨

⚛ ◆◆ Red Roof Inns 🅜
(713) 939-0800. **$36-$61.** 12929 Northwest Frwy. US 290, Hollister and Tidwell rds exit, on eastbound service road. Ext/int corridors. **Pets:** Supervision.
🅢🅐🎨🅥🄴 🖥 🎨

◆◆◆ Renaissance Houston Hotel 🅗
(713) 629-1200. **$169-$179.** 6 Greenway Plaza E. In Greenway Plaza complex at US 59 (Southwest Frwy), Buffalo Speedway exit. Int corridors. **Pets:** Small. Supervision.
🄰🅢🅚 🖥 🎨🅥🄴 🖥 💻 🍴 🎨

**◆◆◆ Residence Inn by
Marriott-Astrodome** 🅐 ❀
(713) 660-7993. **$89-$139.** 7710 S Main St. I-610, exit 2, S Main St/Buffalo Speedway, 1.5 mi n. Ext corridors. **Pets:** Small, other. $5 daily fee/pet, $50 one-time fee/room. No service, supervision, crate.
🎨 🖥 💻 🎨 🎨

◆◆◆ Residence Inn-Houston Clear Lake 🅐 ❀
(281) 486-2424. **$85-$124.** 525 Bay Area Blvd. 1.2 mi e of I-45 S, exit 26 (Bay Area Blvd). Ext/int corridors. **Pets:** Other. $6 daily fee/pet, $50 one-time fee/room. Supervision.
🄰🅢🅚 🖥 🎨🅥🄴 🖥 🖥 💻 🎨 🎨

**◆◆◆ Residence Inn Houston
Westchase** 🅜 ❀
(713) 974-5454. **$75-$109, 3 days notice.** 9965 Westheimer. Beltway 8 (Sam Houston Pkwy) exit Westheimer; 0.7 mi w on Westheimer to Elmside Dr, just n. Int corridors. **Pets:** Medium, other. $5 daily fee/pet, $50 one-time fee/room. No service, supervision, crate.
🄰🅢🅚 🖥 🎨 🅥🄴 🖥 💻 🎨 🎨

◆◆ Robin's Nest Bed & Breakfast Inn 🅱🅱
(713) 528-5821. **$75-$120, 3 days notice.** 4104 Greeley. US 59 (Southwest Frwy), Richmond Ave exit; just n. Int corridors. **Pets:** Very small. Supervision.
🖥 🎨 🖥

**⚛ ◆◆◆ Sheraton Houston Brook
Hollow** 🅗 ❀
(713) 688-0100. **$58-$89.** 3000 N Loop W. Just nw of jct I-610 and US 290 exit 13C (TC Jester) off I-610. Int corridors. **Pets:** $50 deposit/room. Supervision.
🖥 🎨 🅥🄴 🅥🄴 🖥 💻 🍴 🎨

⚛ ◆◆◆ Shoney's Inn & Suites 🅜
(281) 493-5626. **$75.** 12323 Katy Frwy. I-10, exit 753 (Dairy-Ashford Rd), on s service road. Int corridors. **Pets:** Supervision.
🅢🅐🅥🄴 🖥 🎨 🖥 💻 🎨

**⚛ ◆◆ Shoney's Inn and Suites Houston
Southwest** 🅜
(713) 776-2633. **$64-$105.** 6687 Southwest Frwy. US 59, n exit Hillcroft Ave/West Park Dr, then just 0.7 mi eastbound; Hillcroft exit westbound. Int corridors. **Pets:** Supervision.
🅢🅐🅥🄴 🖥 🎨 🖥 💻 🎨

**⚛ ◆◆◆ Shoney's Inn and
Suites-Northwest** 🅜
(713) 690-1493. **$55-$98.** 7887 W Tidwell Rd. US 290 W, W Tidwell exit, 0.3 mi on service road to W Tidwell Rd; on se corner of eastbound service road and W Tidwell Rd. Int corridors. **Pets:** Supervision.
🅢🅐🅥🄴 🖥 🎨 🖥 💻 🎨

**⚛ ◆◆ Shoney's Inn Houston
Astrodome** 🅜 ❀
(713) 799-2436. **$68-$93.** 2364 S Loop W. I-610, exit 1C (Kirby Dr). Int corridors. **Pets:** Other. $25 deposit/room. Supervision.
🅢🅐🅥🄴 🖥 🎨 🖥 💻 🎨

⚛ ◆◆ Super 8 Houston Nasa 🅜
(281) 333-5385. **$50-$125.** 18103 Kingsrow Ln. 1.5 mi e of I-45 and US 75, exit 25 (NASA/Alvin). Ext/int corridors. **Pets:** Small. No service, supervision, crate.
🅢🅐🅥🄴 🖥 🎨 🎨 🎨

KATY

⚛ ◆◆ Best Western-Houston West 🅜 ❀
(281) 392-9800. **$53-$67.** 22455 I-10 (Katy Frwy). I-10, exit 743 (Grand Pkwy), just e on eastbound Service Rd. Ext corridors. **Pets:** $7 daily fee/pet. No service, supervision, crate.
🅢🅐🅥🄴 🖥 🎨 🖥 💻 🎨

◆◆◆ **Ramada Limited-West Houston** Ⓜ
(281) 392-8700. **Call for rates.** 22025 I-10 W. I-10, exit 745 (Mason Rd), just s to Provencial Blvd, just w to Applewhite Dr, just n. Int corridors. **Pets:** No service, supervision, crate.

Ⓧ 🐾 📠 🍴 💻 🏊

LA PORTE

🅰🅰🅰 ◆◆◆ **La Quinta Inn-La Porte** Ⓜ
(281) 470-0760. **$59-$89.** 1105 Hwy 146 S. SR 146, Fairmont Pkwy exit, at jct SR 146 business route. Ext corridors. **Pets:** Small. No service, supervision, crate.

SAVE Ⓧ 🐾 🍴 💻 🏊

ROSENBERG

◆ **Best Western Sundowner Motor Inn** Ⓜ
(281) 342-6000. **Call for rates.** 28382 Southwest Frwy. 0.3 mi w of jct US 59 and SR 36. Ext corridors. **Pets:** Designated rooms, no service, supervision, crate.

Ⓧ 🏊

STAFFORD

◆◆ **Homestead Village Guest Studios** Ⓜ 🐾
(281) 240-6900. **$29-$50, 24 days notice.** 12827 Southwest Frwy. US 59, northbound exit US 90 and SR 41 alt following frontage rd; southbound exit Corporate Dr, following frontage rd. Ext corridors. **Pets:** Small. $75 one-time fee/room. No service, supervision, crate.

Ⓧ 📠 🍴 💻

◆◆◆ **La Quinta Inn-Stafford** Ⓜ 🐾
(281) 240-2300. **$65-$92.** 12727 Southwest Frwy. US 59 eastbound service road, Corporate Dr exit southbound; Airport Blvd/Kirkwood Rd exit northbound. Int corridors. **Pets:** Small, other. Supervision.

ASK Ⓧ 🐾 🍴 💻 🏊

◆◆ **Microtel Inn** Ⓜ 🐾
(281) 240-8100. **$48-$58, 7 days notice.** 4630 Techniplex Dr. US 59, exit Kirkwood Dr, just s to Techniplex Dr, just w. Int corridors. **Pets:** Medium, other. $25 one-time fee/room. No service, supervision, crate.

ASK 🛏 Ⓧ 🐾 📠 🍴

SUGAR LAND

◆◆◆ **Drury Inn & Suites** Ⓜ
(281) 277-9700. **$67-$87.** 13770 Southwest Frwy. Sw on US 59, Sugarland/Alternate 90/Spur 41 (Dairy Ashford/Sugarcreek Blvd) exit. Int corridors. **Pets:** No service, supervision, crate.

Ⓧ 📠 🍴 🍴 💻 🏊

🅰🅰🅰 ◆◆ **Shoney's Inn & Suites Houston-Sugar Land** Ⓜ
(281) 565-6655. **$56-$63.** 14444 Southwest Frwy. Sw on US 59, Stafford/Sugarland(Dairy Ashford/Sugar Creek Blvd) exit. Int corridors. **Pets:** Medium. Designated rooms, no service, supervision, crate.

SAVE 🛏 Ⓧ 🍴 💻 🏊

THE WOODLANDS

◆◆◆ **Drury Inn & Suites-Houston The Woodlands** Ⓜ 🐾
(281) 362-7222. **$69-$89.** 28099 I-45 N. W service road of I-45 and US 75, exit 78 southbound; exit 77 northbound. Int corridors. **Pets:** Other. Supervision.

Ⓧ 🐾 📠 🍴 🍴 💻 🏊

◆◆◆ **La Quinta Inn-Houston-Woodlands** Ⓜ
(281) 367-7722. **$65-$85.** 28673 I-45 N. I-45 and US 75, exit 78 southbound; exit 79 northbound. Ext corridors. **Pets:** Small. Designated rooms, no service, supervision, crate.

ASK Ⓧ 📠 🍴 💻 🏊

🅰🅰🅰 ◆◆ **Red Roof Inn Houston-Woodlands** Ⓜ 🐾
(281) 367-5040. **$40-$52.** 24903 I-45 N. 0.5 mi se off I-45, exit 73 (Rayford/Sawdust) northbound and southbound exit 74. Ext corridors. **Pets:** Small. No service, supervision, crate.

SAVE Ⓧ 🍴 🏊

◆◆◆ **The Woodlands Residence Inn** Ⓜ 🐾
(281) 292-3252. **$116.** 1040 Lake Front Cr. I-45, exit 78 southbound; exit 79 northbound, 0.8 mi s of jct I-45 and Research Forest, just w. Int corridors. **Pets:** Large. $10 daily fee/room, $75 one-time fee/room. Supervision.

ASK 🛏 Ⓧ 🍴 🍴 💻 🏊 Ⓧ

WEBSTER

◆ **Motel 6** Ⓜ 🐾
(281) 332-4581. **$40-$55.** 1001 W Nasa Rd 1. I-45, exit 25, just e. Ext corridors. **Pets:** Small, other. No service, supervision, crate.

ASK 🛏 Ⓧ 🍴 🍴 🏊 📺

🅰🅰🅰 ◆◆ **Wellesley Inn & Suites** Ⓜ
(281) 338-7711. **$99-$129.** 720 W Bay Area Blvd. I-45, exit 26 (Bay Area Blvd), just e. Int corridors. **Pets:** Supervision.

SAVE 🛏 Ⓧ 📠 🍴 🍴 💻 🏊

❀   **END METROPOLITAN AREA**   ❀

HUNTSVILLE

🅰🅰🅰 ◆◆◆ **La Quinta Inn-Huntsville** Ⓜ 🐾
(409) 295-6454. **$62-$79.** 124 I-45 N. I-45, exit 116. Ext corridors. **Pets:** Other. Supervision.

SAVE Ⓧ 📠 💻 🏊

HURST

🅰🅰🅰 ◆◆◆ **AmeriSuites Fort Worth/Hurst** Ⓜ 🐾
(817) 577-3003. **$70-$117.** 1601 Hurst Tower Center Dr. US 183, Pricinct Line Rd exit, just n to Hurst Town Center Dr, just w. Int corridors. **Pets:** Very small, dogs only. Designated rooms, no service, supervision, crate.

SAVE 🛏 Ⓧ 🍴 💻 🏊

JACKSBORO

◆ **Jacksboro Inn**
(940) 567-3751. **$34-$43.** 704 S Main. 1.5 mi se on US 281 and SR 199. Ext corridors. **Pets:** Other. $30 deposit/pet, $3 daily fee/pet. Designated rooms, no service, supervision, crate.

JASPER

◆◆◆ **Best Western Inn Of Jasper**
(409) 384-7767. **$48-$59.** 205 W Gibson. US 190 and SR 63, 0.5 mi w of jct US 96. Ext corridors. **Pets:** Very small. $4 daily fee/pet. No service, supervision, crate.

◆◆◆ **Holiday Inn Express**
(409) 384-8600. **Call for rates.** 2100 N Wheeler. US 96, 1.8 mi n of jct US 190. Ext corridors. **Pets:** Supervision.

◆ **Ramada Inn**
(409) 384-9021. **$46-$58.** 239 E Gibson (US 190). US 190 and SR 63, just w of jct US 96. Ext corridors. **Pets:** Supervision.

JEFFERSON

◆◆ **Best Western**
(903) 665-3983. **Call for rates.** 400 S Walcott. US 59, just s of jct SR 49. Ext corridors. **Pets:** Designated rooms, supervision.

JOHNSON CITY

◆◆ **Save Inn Motel**
(830) 868-4044. **$36-$60.** 107 Hwy 281 & 290 S. Jct US 281 at US 290. Ext corridors. **Pets:** Supervision.

JUNCTION

◆◆◆ **Days Inn**
(915) 446-3730. **Call for rates.** 111 S Martinez St. 0.3 mi s of I-10, exit 457. Ext corridors. **Pets:** Medium. $4 daily fee/pet. No service, supervision, crate.

◆ **The Hills Motel**
(915) 446-2567. **$32-$40, 3 days notice.** 1520 Main St. 1.3 mi s of I-10, exit 456, on US 377. Ext corridors. **Pets:** Designated rooms, no service, supervision, crate.

◆◆ **La Vista Motel**
(915) 446-2191. **$27-$36.** 2040 N Main St. 0.8 mi s of I-10, exit 456, on US 377. Ext corridors. **Pets:** Medium, other. No service, supervision, crate.

KERRVILLE

◆◆◆ **Best Western Sunday Inn**
(830) 896-1313. **$65-$100.** 2124 Sidney Baker St. IH-10, exit 508 (Hwy 16). Ext corridors. **Pets:** Small. Designated rooms, supervision.

◆ **Budget Inn**
(830) 896-8200. **$40-$60.** 1804 Sidney Baker St. SR 16, 0.5 mi s of jct I-10, exit 508. Ext corridors. **Pets:** No service, supervision, crate.

◆◆◆ **Holiday Inn Y. O. Ranch Hotel & Conference Center**
(830) 257-4440. **$101-$111.** 2033 Sidney Baker St. SR 16, 0.3 mi s jct I-10. Ext/int corridors. **Pets:** Medium. Designated rooms, no service, supervision, crate.

◆◆◆ **Inn of the Hills Conference Resort**
(830) 895-5000. **$65-$130.** 1001 Junction Hwy. 1.5 mi nw on SR 27, exit 505 from I-10. Ext corridors. **Pets:** Very small. $50 deposit/room. Designated rooms, no service, supervision, crate.

KILGORE

◆◆ **Days Inn**
(903) 983-2975. **$44-$58.** 3505 Hwy 259 N. I-20, exit 589, 1.2 mi s on US 259. Ext corridors. **Pets:** Other. Supervision.

KILLEEN

◆◆◆ **La Quinta Inn-Killeen**
(254) 526-8331. **$65-$85.** 1112 Fort Hood St. 1.3 mi sw on RM 439 at jct US 190. Ext corridors. **Pets:** Small. Designated rooms, no service, supervision, crate.

KINGSVILLE

◆◆◆ **Best Western Kingsville Inn**
(361) 595-5656. **$49-$64.** 2402 E King Ave. 1.5 mi e on US 77 bypass, opposite jct SR 141. Ext corridors. **Pets:** Small, dogs only. $5 daily fee/pet. Designated rooms, supervision.

◆◆◆ **Holiday Inn**
(361) 595-5753. **$49-$59.** 3430 Hwy 77S. 1.5 mi s on US 77; in the Get-N-Go Travel Center. Ext corridors. **Pets:** Medium. Supervision.

◆◆ **Howard Johnson**
(361) 592-6471. **$45-$59.** 105 US 77. 0.8 mi e on US 77. Ext corridors. **Pets:** Medium. Supervision.

LAGUNA VISTA

◆◆ Budget Host Inn M ❀
(956) 943-7866. **$40-$60.** 1411 E Hwy 100. 7 mi w on Hwy 100. Ext corridors. **Pets:** Small, dogs only. $20 one-time fee/pet. Designated rooms, no service, supervision, crate.
(ASK) (S) (X) (2)

LAJITAS

◆◆◆ Lajitas On The Rio Grande MI ❀
(915) 424-3471. **$60-$80.** 1 Main Pl. Center. Ext/int corridors. **Pets:** Other. No service, supervision, crate.
(X) (💻) (🍴) (2) (X)

LAKE JACKSON

◆ Best Western Lake Jackson Inn M ❀
(409) 297-3031. **$43-$43.** 915 Hwy 332. 3 mi e jct SR 288 and SR 332. Ext corridors. **Pets:** Medium, dogs only. $7 one-time fee/pet. No service, supervision, crate.
(SAVE) (X) (🖥) (💻) (2)

LAMESA

◆ Budget Host Inn M
(806) 872-2118. **$30-$41, 3 days notice.** 901 S Dallas Ave. Jct US 180, 0.7 mi s on US 87. Ext corridors. **Pets:** Supervision.
(SAVE) (S) (X) (🖥) (2)

◆◆ Shiloh Inn M
(806) 872-6721. **$37-$240.** 1707 Lubbock Hwy. 1 mi n on US 87 from jct US 180. Ext corridors. **Pets:** Supervision.
(ASK) (S) (X) (🖥) (2)

LAREDO

◆◆◆ Best Western Fiesta Inn M ❀
(956) 723-3603. **$62-$62.** 5240 San Bernardo. 2.8 mi n on US 81 and 83, just off I-35. Ext corridors. **Pets:** $50 deposit/room. No service, supervision, crate.
(ASK) (S) (X) (🖥) (2)

◆◆◆ Family Gardens Inn M ❀
(956) 723-5300. **$57-$64, 7 days notice.** 5830 San Bernardo. I-35 at San Bernardo exit. Ext/int corridors. **Pets:** Small. $20 deposit/room. Supervision.
(ASK) (S) (X) (🖥) (2) (X)

◆◆◆ Hampton Inn M ❀
(956) 717-8888. **$75-$81.** 7903 San Dario. I-35, exit 4. Int corridors. **Pets:** Small. $25 one-time fee/room. No service, supervision, crate.
(SAVE) (S) (X) (💻) (2)

◆◆◆ Holiday Inn Civic Center MI ❀
(956) 727-5800. **$89-$89.** 800 Garden St. 2.3 mi n on US 81 and 83; off I-35, exit US 59. Int corridors. **Pets:** Small, other. Designated rooms, no service, supervision, crate.
(ASK) (S) (X) (🎱) (🖥) (💻) (🍴) (2)

◆◆◆ La Quinta Inn-Laredo M
(956) 722-0511. **$69-$89.** 3610 Santa Ursula Ave. I-35 at ext US 59 (Houston, Freer). Ext corridors. **Pets:** No service, supervision, crate.
(SAVE) (X) (🖥) (💻) (2)

◆◆ Motel 6–1107 M
(956) 722-8133. **$40-$56.** 5920 San Bernardo Ave. I-35, exit 4. Ext/int corridors. **Pets:** Very small. Supervision.
(S) (X) (🖥) (2)

◆◆ Motel 6 South-142 M ❀
(956) 725-8187. **$39-$55.** 5310 San Bernardo. Just w of I-35 at Mann Rd exit. Ext corridors. **Pets:** Small, other. Supervision.
(S) (X)

◆◆ Red Roof Inn Laredo M
(956) 712-0733. **$41-$66.** 1006 W Calton Rd. 0.3 mi w jct I-35, exit 3A. Ext/int corridors. **Pets:** Medium. No service, supervision, crate.
(SAVE) (X) (🖥) (2)

LITTLEFIELD

◆ Crescent Park Motel M ❀
(806) 385-4464. **$35-$55.** 2000 Hall Ave. 0.3 mi n on SR 385, from jct US 84. Ext corridors. **Pets:** $5 daily fee/pet. Supervision.
(SAVE) (S) (X) (🖥)

LLANO

◆◆◆ Best Western M
(915) 247-4101. **$47-$72, 30 days notice.** 901 W Young St. 1 mi w on US 71 and SR 29. Ext corridors. **Pets:** Large. Designated rooms, no service, supervision, crate.
(SAVE) (S) (X) (🖥) (2)

LONGVIEW

◆◆◆ Comfort Suites M ❀
(903) 663-4991. **$64-$79.** 3307 N 4th St. Loop 281, just w of jct US 259. Int corridors. **Pets:** Small, other. Supervision.
(ASK) (S) (X) (🖥) (🖥) (💻) (2)

◆◆ Days Inn of Longview M ❀
(903) 758-1113. **$50-$65, 7 days notice.** 3103 Estes Pkwy. 0.3 mi n of I-20, exit 595. Ext/int corridors. **Pets:** Medium. $10 daily fee/pet, $10 one-time fee/pet. Designated rooms, no service, supervision, crate.
(SAVE) (S) (X) (🖥) (2)

◆◆◆ La Quinta Inn M ❀
(903) 757-3663. **$59-$79.** 502 S Access Rd. Jct Estes Pkwy and I-20, exit 595. Ext corridors. **Pets:** Small. No service, supervision, crate.
(SAVE) (X) (🖥) (💻) (2)

◆◆ Travelodge M
(903) 758-0711. **$38-$50, 7 days notice.** 3304 S Eastman Rd. I-20, exit 596, just ne. Ext corridors. **Pets:** Supervision.
(ASK) (S) (X) (🖥) (💻) (2)

LUBBOCK

◆◆ Days Inn Texas Tech M ❀
(806) 747-7111. **$45-$69.** 2401 4th St. I-27, exit 4 (4th St), 1.5 mi w. Ext corridors. **Pets:** Small, dogs only. No service, supervision, crate.
(ASK) (S) (X) (2)

◆◆◆ Four Points Sheraton Hotel 🅷 ❀
(806) 747-0171. **$80-$109.** 505 Ave Q. 1 mi nw on US 84. Int corridors. **Pets:** Small. $25 deposit/room. No service, supervision, crate.

🅰🆂🅺 🆂🄳 ⊗ 🄰 🄱 🔳 🍴 🏖

🆤 ◆◆◆ Holiday Inn Park Plaza 🅼 ❀
(806) 797-3241. **$86.** 3201 Loop 289 S. 5 mi s on Loop 289 at Indiana exit; S Frontage Rd. Ext/int corridors. **Pets:** Supervision.

🆂🅰🆅🄴 🆂🄳 ⊗ 🄱 🔳 🍴 🏖

◆◆ Howard Johnson 🅼 ❀
(806) 747-1671. **$35-$65, 7 days notice.** 4801 Ave Q. I-27, 50th St exit, 0.5 mi w to US 84 (Ave Q), just n. Ext corridors. **Pets:** $5 deposit/pet. Supervision.

🅰🆂🅺 🆂🄳 ⊗

◆◆ I-27 Super 8 Motel 🅼
(806) 762-8400. **$50-$80, 7 days notice.** 5410 I-27. 3.5 mi s on I-27, exit 1B southbound; U-turn at exit 1A (50th St) northbound. Int corridors. **Pets:** Supervision.

🅰🆂🅺 🆂🄳 ⊗ 🄱 🏖

🆤 ◆◆◆ La Quinta Inn-Lubbock-Civic
Center 🅼
(806) 763-9441. **$65-$85.** 601 Ave Q. 0.8 mi nw on US 84. Ext corridors. **Pets:** Small. No service, supervision, crate.

🆂🅰🆅🄴 ⊗ 🄰 🄱 🏖

◆◆ Lubbock Super 8 Motel 🅼
(806) 762-8726. **Call for rates, 5 days notice.** 501 Ave Q. 1 mi nw on US 84. Ext corridors. **Pets:** Very small. Supervision.

⊗ 🄱

◆◆◆ Ramada Inn Regency Hotel 🅼
(806) 745-2208. **$59-$148, 3 days notice.** 6624 I-27. 3.8 mi s on I-27 and US 87; just w of jct Loop 289, exit 1B southbound. Int corridors. **Pets:** Small. No service, supervision, crate.

🅰🆂🅺 🆂🄳 ⊗ 🄱 🔳 🍴 🏖

◆◆◆ Residence Inn by Marriott 🅰 ❀
(806) 745-1963. **$82-$82.** 2551 S Loop 289. Loop 289, 3 mi w of University exit, S Frontage Rd. Ext corridors. **Pets:** Other. $25 one-time fee/room. Supervision.

🅰🆂🅺 🆂🄳 ⊗ 🔳 🏖 ⊗

LUFKIN

🆤 ◆◆◆ La Quinta Inn-Lufkin 🅼 ❀
(409) 634-3351. **$59-$86.** 2119 S 1st St. US 59, Carriageway northbound, 0.3 mi s of jct S Loop 287 and US 59 business route. Ext corridors. **Pets:** Small, other. No service, supervision, crate.

🆂🅰🆅🄴 ⊗ 🄰 🄱 🔳 🏖

MARBLE FALLS

🆤 ◆◆◆ Best Western Marble Falls
Inn 🅼 ❀
(830) 693-5122. **$55-$82.** 1403 Hwy 281 N. 0.8 mi n on US 281. Ext corridors. **Pets:** Small. $20 deposit/room. Designated rooms, no service, supervision, crate.

🆂🅰🆅🄴 🆂🄳 ⊗ 🄱 🏖

MARSHALL

◆◆ Best Western 🅼 ❀
(903) 935-1941. **Call for rates.** 5555 E End Blvd S. I-20, exit 617, just n on US 59. Ext corridors. **Pets:** Small. $10 one-time fee/room. Designated rooms, supervision.

⊗ 🄱 🔳 🏖

🆤 ◆◆ Economy Inn Express 🅼 ❀
(903) 935-0707. **$45-$69, 3 days notice.** 5201 E End Blvd S. I-20, exit 617, just n on US 59. Ext corridors. **Pets:** Small. $10 deposit/room, $5 daily fee/room, $5 one-time fee/room. Designated rooms, no service, supervision, crate.

🆂🅰🆅🄴 🆂🄳 ⊗ 🄱 🏖

MCALLEN

◆◆◆ Drury Inn-McAllen 🅼 ❀
(956) 687-5100. **$69-$93.** 612 W Expwy 83. US 83 Expwy, 2nd St exit, nw frontage road. Int corridors. **Pets:** Small. Supervision.

⊗ 🄱 🔳 🏖

◆◆◆ Hampton Inn 🅼 ❀
(956) 682-4900. **$68-$93.** 300 W Expwy US 83. US 83 Expwy, 2nd St exit, nw frontage road. Int corridors. **Pets:** Small. No service, supervision, crate.

⊗ 🄱 🔳 🏖

◆◆◆ Holiday Inn Civic Center 🅼 ❀
(956) 686-2471. **Call for rates.** 200 Expwy 83 W. 2nd St exit off US 83 Expwy. Ext/int corridors. **Pets:** Other. Supervision.

🅰🆂🅺 ⊗ 🄰 🄱 🔳 🍴 🏖

🆤 ◆◆◆ La Quinta Inn-McAllen 🅼
(956) 687-1101. **$74-$86.** 1100 S 10th St. 1.5 mi s on SR 336; just n of jct US 83 Expwy. Ext corridors. **Pets:** Small. Designated rooms, no service, supervision, crate.

🆂🅰🆅🄴 🆂🄳 ⊗ 🄰 🄱 🔳 🏖

◆◆ Thrifty-Inn 🅼 ❀
(956) 631-6700. **$39-$65.** 620 W Expwy 83. US 83 Expwy, 2nd St exit, nw frontage road. Int corridors. **Pets:** Small. $20 deposit/room. Supervision.

⊗

MIDLAND

🆤 ◆◆ Best Western Midland 🅼 ❀
(915) 699-4144. **$49-$64, 3 days notice.** 3100 W Wall St. 2 mi w on I-20 business loop. Int corridors. **Pets:** $7 daily fee/pet, $7 one-time fee/pet. No service, supervision, crate.

🆂🅰🆅🄴 🆂🄳 ⊗ 🄱 🍴 🏖

◆◆◆ Hampton Inn-Midland 🅼
(915) 694-7774. **$55-$55.** 3904 W Wall St. I-20, exit 134, 1 mi n on Midkiff Rd, 0.3 mi w on Business Rt I-20. Ext/int corridors. **Pets:** Large. No service, supervision, crate.

🅰🆂🅺 🆂🄳 ⊗ 🔳 🏖

◆◆◆ Holiday Inn 🅼
(915) 697-3181. **$50-$63.** 4300 W Wall St. I-20, exit 134 (Midkiff Rd), 1 mi n to I-20 business loop, 0.7 mi w. Ext/int corridors. **Pets:** Small. Designated rooms, no service, supervision, crate.

🅰🆂🅺 🆂🄳 ⊗ 🄱 🔳 🍴 🏖

(AAA) ◆◆◆ La Quinta Inn-Midland **M** ❀
(915) 697-9900. **$55-$75.** 4130 W Wall St. I-20, exit 131,
0.9 mi n on SR 250 Loop to exit 1A; 1.2 mi e on I-20
business route. Ext corridors. **Pets:** Other. Supervision.
[SAVE] [✕] [♿] [🏠] [🖵] [🖼]

◆◆ Lexington Hotel Suites **M**
(915) 697-3155. **Call for rates.** 1003 S Midkiff Rd. I-20, exit
134, 1 mi n. Ext corridors. **Pets:** Designated rooms, no
service, supervision, crate.
[✕] [🏠] [🖵] [🖼]

(AAA) ◆◆◆ Midland Hilton & Towers **H** ❀
(915) 683-6131. **$69-$129.** 117 W Wall St. Downtown, Wall
and Loraine sts. Int corridors. **Pets:** Other. $50 deposit/pet.
No service, supervision, crate.
[SAVE] [S6] [✕] [🖉] [🖵] [🍴] [🖼]

MINERAL WELLS

(AAA) ◆ Budget Host Inn Mesa Motel **M**
(940) 325-3377. **$36-$52, 3 days notice.** 3601 E Hwy 180.
US 281, 1.5 mi e. Ext corridors. **Pets:** Small. Supervision.
[SAVE] [S6] [✕] [🏠] [🖼]

MONAHANS

(AAA) ◆◆ Best Western Colonial Inn **MI**
(915) 943-4345. **$39-$56.** 702 W I-20. Jct I-20 and SR 18,
exit 80. Ext/int corridors. **Pets:** Supervision.
[SAVE] [S6] [✕] [🏠] [🍴] [🖼]

MOUNT PLEASANT

(AAA) ◆◆◆ Best Western Inn & Suites **M** ❀
(903) 572-5051. **$65-$65.** 102 Burton St. I-30 and Business
Rt US 271, exit 162. Ext corridors. **Pets:** $6 daily fee/pet.
Designated rooms, no service, supervision, crate.
[SAVE] [S6] [✕] [🖉] [🏠] [🖵] [🖼]

(AAA) ◆◆ Days Inn & Suites **M** ❀
(903) 577-0152. **$50-$60.** 2501 W Ferguson. I-30, exit 160,
just s. Int corridors. **Pets:** Small, dogs only. $6 daily fee/pet.
Designated rooms, no service, supervision, crate.
[SAVE] [S6] [✕] [🏠] [🖵] [🖼]

◆◆ Holiday Inn **MI**
(903) 572-6611. **Call for rates.** 2502 W Ferguson Rd. I-30,
exit 160. Ext corridors. **Pets:** Small. No service, supervision,
crate.
[✕] [🏠] [🖵] [🍴] [🖼]

(AAA) ◆◆ Super 8 **M** ❀
(903) 572-9808. **$45-$69.** 204 Lakewood Dr. I-30, eastbound exit 162; westbound exit 162A. Ext corridors.
Pets: $5 daily fee/pet. No service, supervision, crate.
[SAVE] [S6] [✕] [🏠] [🖵] [🖼]

MOUNT VERNON

(AAA) ◆◆ Super 8 Motel of Mount Vernon **M** ❀
(903) 588-2882. **$42-$44.** 401 W I-30. I-30 at Hwy 37, exit
146. Ext corridors. **Pets:** $5 one-time fee/room. No service,
supervision, crate.
[SAVE] [S6] [✕] [🖉] [🏠]

NACOGDOCHES

(AAA) ◆◆◆ La Quinta Inn-Nacogdoches **M** ❀
(409) 560-5453. **$59-$86.** 3215 South St. US 59 at S jct
Loop 224 and US 59 business route. Ext corridors.
Pets: Small, other. No service, supervision, crate.
[SAVE] [✕] [🖉] [🏠] [🖵] [🖼]

NEW BOSTON

(AAA) ◆◆◆ Best Western Inn of New
Boston **M** ❀
(903) 628-6999. **$56-$59, 3 days notice.** 1024 N Center.
I-30 at jct SR 8, exit 201. Ext corridors. **Pets:** Small, other.
$20 deposit/room. No service, supervision, crate.
[SAVE] [S6] [✕] [🖉] [🏠] [🖼]

NOCONA

(AAA) ◆◆ Nocona Hills Motel and Resort **M** ❀
(940) 825-3161. **$32-$44.** 100 E Huron Circle. 7 mi ne from
US 82, 0.5 mi n on SR 103 to SR 1956, 6 mi e to SR 3301,
2 mi n. Ext corridors. **Pets:** Large, other. $5 daily fee/pet.
No service, supervision, crate.
[SAVE] [S6] [✕] [🏠] [🖵]

NORTH RICHLAND HILLS

◆◆ Homestead Village Guest Studios **M**
(817) 788-6000. **Call for rates.** 7450 NE Loop 820. Loop
820 at Holiday Ln, exit 21, 0.3 mi e on S Access Rd. Ext
corridors. **Pets:** No service, supervision, crate.
[✕] [🏠] [🖵]

◆◆◆ La Quinta Inn-Northeast **M**
(817) 485-2750. **$59-$69.** 7920 Bedford-Euless Rd. I-820, e
of SR 121, exit 22A (Grapevine). Ext corridors.
Pets: Medium. Supervision.
[ASK] [✕] [🖉] [🏠] [🖵] [🖼]

(AAA) ◆◆ Lexington Inn-DFW West **M**
(817) 656-8881. **$62-$74.** 8709 Airport Frwy. SR 121 and
183, 0.5 mi sw of FM 3029, Precinct Line Rd exit, 0.5 mi e
of I-820. Ext corridors. **Pets:** Small. Supervision.
[SAVE] [S6] [✕] [🏠] [🖼]

(AAA) ◆◆ Motel 6–1336 **M** ❀
(817) 485-3000. **$38-$54.** 7804 Bedford Euless Rd N. Loop
820, exit 26, just n to Bedford Euless Rd N, 5 mi n. Ext
corridors. **Pets:** Small, other. Supervision.
[S6] [✕] [🖼]

ODEM

(AAA) ◆◆ Days Inn-Odem **M**
(361) 368-2166. **$45-$90, 3 days notice.** 1505 Voss (US
77) Ave. US 77, 1 mi s of jct 631. Ext corridors. **Pets:** No
service, supervision, crate.
[SAVE] [S6] [✕] [🏠] [🖼]

ODESSA

◆◆ Best Western Garden Oasis **MI**
(915) 337-3006. **$58-$78, 7 days notice.** 110 W I-20. Jct
I-20 and US 385, exit 116. Ext/int corridors. **Pets:** Designated rooms, supervision.
[ASK] [S6] [✕] [🏠] [🍴] [🖼]

◆◆ Days Inn 🅼 ❀
(915) 335-8000. **$43-$49, 7 days notice.** 3075 E Business Loop 20. I-20, exit 121, 0.7 mi n on Loop 338, then 0.5 mi w. Int corridors. **Pets:** Other. Supervision.
A$K S🐾 ☒ 🖥 🌊

◆◆◆ Holiday Inn Hotel & Suites 🅼 ❀
(915) 362-2311. **$58-$68, 7 days notice.** 6201 E Business Hwy 80. I-20, exit 121, 0.8 mi n on Loop 338, then 1 mi e. Ext corridors. **Pets:** Other. No service, supervision, crate.
A$K S🐾 ☒ 🐾 🖥 🖳 🍴 🌊

🐾 ◆◆◆ La Quinta Inn-Odessa 🅼
(915) 333-2820. **$55-$75.** 5001 E Business Loop I-20. I-20, exit 121, 0.8 mi n on Loop 338, then just w. Ext corridors. **Pets:** Small. No service, supervision, crate.
SAVE ☒ 🖳 🌊

◆◆ Relax Inn 🅼
(915) 333-1486. **Call for rates.** 1518 S Grant. 1.5 mi s on I-20, exit 116. Ext corridors. **Pets:** Small. Supervision.
☒ 🖥

🐾 ◆ Villa West Inn 🅼 ❀
(915) 335-5055. **$24-$35.** 300 W Pool Road. I-20, exit 116, just w on Frontage Rd. Ext corridors. **Pets:** Small. $20 deposit/room. No service, supervision, crate.
SAVE S🐾 ☒ 🖥

ORANGE

◆◆◆ Holiday Inn Express 🅼 ❀
(409) 988-0110. **$50-$70.** 2900 I-10. I-10, 1 mi w of jct SR 87, exit 876 westbound; exit 877 eastbound, on westbound service road. Int corridors. **Pets:** Small. $20 deposit/room. Supervision.
A$K S🐾 ☒ 🐾 🖥 🖳 🌊

OZONA

🐾 ◆◆ Daystop 🅼 ❀
(915) 392-2631. **$38-$57.** 820 Loop 466 W. 0.5 mi w on US 290 business route. Ext corridors. **Pets:** Small. $5 daily fee/room, $5 one-time fee/room. Designated rooms, no service, supervision, crate.
SAVE S🐾 ☒

PALESTINE

🐾 ◆◆◆ Best Western Palestine Inn 🅼 ❀
(903) 723-4655. **$45-$70.** 1601 W Palestine Ave. 0.7 mi sw jct US 287/SR 19 on US 79. Ext corridors. **Pets:** Supervision.
SAVE S🐾 ☒ 🐾 🖥 🖳 🍴 🌊 ☒

PARIS

◆◆ Best Western Inn of Paris 🅼 ❀
(903) 785-5566. **$48-$58.** 3755 NE Loop 286. Jct US 82 and E Loop 286, just n. Ext corridors. **Pets:** Small. No service, supervision, crate.
A$K S🐾 ☒ 🐾 🖥 🌊

🐾 ◆◆ Comfort Inn 🅼
(903) 784-7481. **$60-$72, 3 days notice.** 3505 NE Loop 286. 0.5 mi n of jct US 82 and Loop E 286. Ext corridors. **Pets:** Supervision.
SAVE S🐾 ☒ 🖥 🖳 🌊

◆◆ Holiday Inn 🅼
(903) 785-5545. **$80-$91, 3 days notice.** 3560 NE Loop 286. Loop E 286, 0.3 mi n of jct US 82. Ext corridors. **Pets:** Small. No service, supervision, crate.
A$K S🐾 ☒ 🐾 🖥 🖳 🍴 🌊

PEARSALL

🐾 ◆◆ Executive Inn 🅼 ❀
(830) 334-3693. **$36-$50, 3 days notice.** 613 N Oak. 6 mi e of jct I-35 and Hwy 140, exit 104. Ext corridors. **Pets:** Supervision.
SAVE S🐾 ☒ 🖥 🖳

PECOS

🐾 ◆◆ Best Western Swiss Clock Inn 🅼 ❀
(915) 447-2215. **$44-$65.** 133 S Frontage Rd. 1 mi w of jct US 285 and I-20; 1 mi e of jct SR 17 and I-20, exit 40. Ext corridors. **Pets:** Small. Designated rooms, no service, supervision, crate.
SAVE S🐾 ☒ 🍴 🌊

🐾 ◆ Laura Lodge 🅼 ❀
(915) 445-4924. **$28-$40.** 1000 E Business 20. I-20 at US 28 S, exit 42 1 mi e to Business 20, just s. Ext corridors. **Pets:** Small. $35 daily fee/pet. Designated rooms, no service, supervision, crate.
SAVE S🐾 ☒ 🖥 🌊

◆◆ Quality Inn 🅼
(915) 445-5404. **$71-$101.** 4002 S Cedar St. Jct I-20 and US 285, exit 42. Int corridors. **Pets:** No service, supervision, crate.
A$K S🐾 ☒ 🖥 🍴 🌊

PHARR

🐾 ◆◆◆ Ramada Limited Suites 🅼
(956) 702-3330. **$50-$57.** 1130 E Expwy 83. Jct US 83 Expwy and exit I Rd. Ext corridors. **Pets:** Small. Designated rooms, no service, supervision, crate.
SAVE S🐾 ☒ 🐾 🖥 🖳 🌊

PLAINVIEW

🐾 ◆◆◆ Best Western Conestoga Inn 🅼
(806) 293-9454. **$50-$73.** 600 N I-27. Just s of US 70 on east access road to I-27 and US 87, exit 49. Ext corridors. **Pets:** Small. Designated rooms, no service, supervision, crate.
SAVE S🐾 ☒ 🐾 🖥 🖳 🌊

PORT ISABEL

🐾 ◆◆ Southwind Inn 🅼 ❀
(956) 943-3392. **$50-$120, 4 days notice.** 600 Davis St. Queen Isabella Cswy to Musina, then 3 blks n. Ext corridors. **Pets:** $5 one-time fee/pet. No service, supervision, crate.
SAVE ☒ 🖥 🖳 🌊

PORTLAND

◆◆◆ Comfort Inn M ❀
(361) 643-2222. **$59-$94.** 1703 N Hwy 181. US 181 W access road, northbound exit FM 3239; southbound exit Lang St. Ext corridors. **Pets:** Small. Designated rooms, no service, supervision, crate.

[ASK] [S] [X] [▤] [▣]

ROBSTOWN

◆◆ Days Inn M
(361) 387-9416. **$50-$95.** 320 Hwy 77 S. 1 mi s on US 77. Ext corridors. **Pets:** No service, supervision, crate.

[ASK] [S] [X] [▤] [▣]

ROCKDALE

◆◆ Regency Inn M
(512) 446-7555. **$44-$57.** 2 N Hwy 77/79. US 77 at jct US 79. Ext corridors. **Pets:** No service, supervision, crate.

[SAVE] [S] [X] [▤]

ROCKPORT

◆◆◆ Laguna Reef A ❀
(361) 729-1742. **$75-$250.** 1021 Water St. 0.5 mi s, just e of Business 35; entrance is on S Austin St. Ext corridors. **Pets:** Medium. $40 deposit/pet, $5 daily fee/pet. Supervision.

[SAVE] [S] [X] [▣] [X]

◆◆ The Village Inn M ❀
(361) 729-6370. **$48-$55.** 503 N Austin St. Just w of jct SR 35 and Business 35. Ext corridors. **Pets:** Other. $6 daily fee/pet. Designated rooms, no service, supervision, crate.

[SAVE] [S] [X] [▣]

ROUND ROCK

◆◆◆ La Quinta Inn-Austin-Round Rock M
(512) 255-6666. **$65-$85.** 2004 I-35 N. 0.8 mi n on I-35; US 79 exit 253A southbound, US 81 business route n and FM 3406, exit 254 northbound. Int corridors. **Pets:** Small. Designated rooms, no service, supervision, crate.

[ASK] [X] [⌂] [▤] [▣] [▣]

◆◆ Sleep Inn M ❀
(512) 310-1111. **$59-$79, 7 days notice.** 1990 I-35 N. I-35, exit 254. Int corridors. **Pets:** $25 one-time fee/room. No service, supervision, crate.

[SAVE] [S] [X] [▤] [▣] [▣]

SAN ANGELO

◆◆ Best Western Inn of the West M ❀
(915) 653-2995. **$49-$59.** 415 W Beauregard. Just w on US 67 business route at jct US 87 southbound. Int corridors. **Pets:** Small, other. Supervision.

[SAVE] [S] [X] [▤] [▣] [Y] [▣]

◆◆ Days Inn M ❀
(915) 658-6594. **$40-$51, 7 days notice.** 4613 S Jackson. 2.8 mi s on US 87 and 277. Ext corridors. **Pets:** Other. $10 deposit/room. No service, supervision, crate.

[SAVE] [S] [X] [▣]

◆◆◆ Holiday Inn H ❀
(915) 658-2828. **$99-$107.** 441 Rio Concho Dr. Just e of US 67, 87 and 277; adjacent to Convention Center. Int corridors. **Pets:** Other. Supervision.

[ASK] [S] [X] [✎] [▤] [▣] [Y] [▣]

◆◆ Inn of the Conchos M ❀
(915) 658-2811. **$59-$89.** 2021 N Bryant Blvd. 2 mi n on US 87. Ext corridors. **Pets:** Other. Supervision.

[SAVE] [S] [X] [▤] [▣]

◆◆◆ La Quinta Inn-San Angelo M ❀
(915) 949-0515. **$59-$79.** 2307 Loop 306. 4.5 mi sw on Loop 306, Knickerbocker Rd exit. Ext corridors. **Pets:** Other. Supervision.

[SAVE] [X] [✎] [▤] [▣] [▣]

SAN ANTONIO METROPOLITAN AREA

LIVE OAK

◆◆◆ La Quinta-Inn-San
Antonio-Toepperwein M ❀
(210) 657-5500. **$59-$79.** 12822 I-35 N. I-35 N, Toepperwein exit (172); I-35 S, Judson Rd exit (170B). Ext/int corridors. **Pets:** Small. Supervision.

[ASK] [X] [⌂] [▤] [▣] [▣]

NEW BRAUNFELS

◆◆ Holiday Inn M ❀
(830) 625-8017. **$99.** 1051 IH-35 E. I-35, exit 189. Ext corridors. **Pets:** $5 daily fee/room, $50 one-time fee/room. Supervision.

[ASK] [S] [X] [⌂] [▣] [Y] [▣] [X]

◆◆ Rodeway Inn M ❀
(830) 629-6991. **$79-$89, 5 days notice.** 1209 IH-35 E. I-35S, exit 189. Ext corridors. **Pets:** Small, other. No service, supervision, crate.

[SAVE] [X] [▤] [▣] [▣]

◆◆ Super 8 M ❀
(830) 629-1155. **$59-$95.** 510 Hwy 46 S. 0.3 mi e, I-35 jct Hwy 46 (exit 189). Ext corridors. **Pets:** Other. $5 daily fee/pet. No service, supervision, crate.

[SAVE] [S] [X] [▤] [▣]

SAN ANTONIO

⚫ ◆◆ Aloha Inn M
(210) 828-0933. **$40-$50.** 1435 Austin Hwy. 0.8 mi s jct I-410. Ext corridors. **Pets:** Medium. No service, supervision, crate.

🆂🅰🆅🅴 🆂💰 ⊠ 🐾 ⊠

⚫ ◆◆◆ AmeriSuites-San Antonio Airport M ❀
(210) 930-2333. **$95-$135.** 7615 Jones Maltsberger Rd. US 281, Jones Maltsberger Rd exit, inside Loop 410. Ext corridors. **Pets:** Supervision.

🆂🅰🆅🅴 🆂💰 ⊠ 👐 ⊿ 🎁 🔌 🖥 🍴

⚫ ◆◆◆ Arbor House Inn & Suites BB ❀
(210) 472-2005. **$95-$175, 3 days notice.** 540 S St Mary's St. Downtown near La Villita. **Pets:** Medium, other. $50 deposit/room. No service, supervision, crate.

🆂🅰🆅🅴 ⊠ 🔌 🖥

◆◆◆ Best Western Fiesta Inn M
(210) 697-9761. **Call for rates.** 13535 I H 10 W. I-10W, exit 557; I-10E, exit 558. **Pets:** Designated rooms, no service, supervision, crate.

⊠ 🔌 🔌 🖥

◆◆◆ Best Western Ingram Park Inn M ❀
(210) 520-8080. **Call for rates.** 6855 NW Loop 410. 0.3 mi w of jct Ingram Rd, exit 11. Ext corridors. **Pets:** Small, dogs only. $50 deposit/pet. No service, supervision, crate.

⊠ 🔌 🖥

⚫ ◆◆ Best Western Town House Airport M ❀
(210) 826-6311. **$49-$89.** 942 NE Loop 410. I-410, exit 22, just sw. Ext/int corridors. **Pets:** Small. $10 one-time fee/ room. No service, supervision, crate.

🆂🅰🆅🅴 🆂💰 ⊠ 🔌 🖥 🍴

⚫ ◆◆ Comfort Inn Airport M ❀
(210) 653-9110. **$64-$70.** 2635 NE Loop 410. Jct Loop 410 and Perrin-Beitel Rd. Ext/int corridors. **Pets:** Small, dogs only. Supervision.

🆂🅰🆅🅴 🆂💰 ⊠ 🖥 🍴

⚫ ◆◆◆ Comfort Inn Sea World M ❀
(210) 684-8606. **$55-$89, 3 days notice.** 4 Piano Pl. Loop 410, 0.5 mi e jct Evers Rd. Ext corridors. **Pets:** Small. Supervision.

🆂🅰🆅🅴 🆂💰 ⊠ 🍴

◆◆◆ Days Inn & Suites M ❀
(210) 696-7922. **$59-$109.** 11790 I-10 West. I-10, De Zavala exit 558. Ext corridors. **Pets:** Other. Supervision.

🅰🆂🅺 🆂💰 ⊠ 🔌 🖥 🍴

◆ Days Inn-Downtown Laredo St M ❀
(210) 271-3334. **$49-$129.** 1500 IH-35 S/IH-10. 1.5 mi s, off IH-35 S; US 813 and IH-10, Laredo St exit. Ext/int corridors. **Pets:** Small. $25 one-time fee/room. No service, supervision, crate.

🅰🆂🅺 ⊠ 🔌 🍴

◆◆ Days Inn Northeast M ❀
(210) 225-4521. **Call for rates.** 3443 I-35 N. 4.8 mi ne off I-35, exit 160 (Splash Town); circle back under bridge, coliseum exit. Ext corridors. **Pets:** $25 deposit/room. Supervision.

🅰🆂🅺 ⊠ 🔌 🖥 🍴

⚫ ◆◆◆ Days Inn Windcrest M ❀
(210) 650-9779. **$49-$74.** 9401 I-35 N. I-35 N, exit 167 (Randolf Blvd) southbound; exit 167 (Starlight Terrace) northbound. Ext corridors. **Pets:** Small. $10 one-time fee/ pet. No service, supervision, crate.

🆂🅰🆅🅴 🆂💰 ⊠ 🎁 🔌 🍴

◆◆◆ Drury Inn & Suites Airport M ❀
(210) 308-8100. **$68-$93.** 95 NE Loop 410. Jct Jones Maltsberger Rd at Loop 410, 1.8 mi w of airport. Int corridors. **Pets:** Medium. Supervision.

⊠ 🎁 🔌 🔌 🖥 🍴

◆◆◆ Drury Inn Northeast M
(210) 494-1144. **$54-$81.** 8300 IH-35 N. I-35, Walzem Rd exit. Ext/int corridors. **Pets:** Small. No service, supervision, crate.

⊠ 🎁 🔌 🖥 🍴

◆◆◆ Executive Guesthouse Hotel M
(210) 494-7600. **$85-$95, 3 days notice.** 12828 US Hwy 281 N. 2 mi n of airport on US 281 Expwy, Bitters Rd exit, off US 281. Int corridors. **Pets:** Supervision.

🅰🆂🅺 🆂💰 ⊠ ⊿ 🔌 🖥 🍴

◆◆◆ Hampton Inn-Airport M ❀
(210) 366-1800. **$70-$92.** 8818 Jones Maltsberger Rd. Loop 410, airport exit. Int corridors. **Pets:** Supervision.

⊠ ⊿ 🖥 🍴

◆◆◆ Hawthorn Suites A ❀
(210) 561-9660. **$79-$79.** 4041 Bluemel Rd. 12 mi nw, 0.3 mi w jct Wurzbach Rd at I-10. Ext corridors. **Pets:** Medium, other. $5 daily fee/pet, $50 one-time fee/pet. No service, supervision, crate.

⊠ 🍴

⚫ ◆◆◆ Hawthorn Suites Ltd Airport M
(210) 599-4204. **$70-$70.** 2383 NE Loop 410. Loop 410 W access road at Starcrest exit. Ext corridors. **Pets:** Small. Supervision.

🆂🅰🆅🅴 ⊠ 🎁 🔌 🔌 🖥 🍴 ⊠

◆◆◆ Hawthorn Suites Riverwalk M
(210) 527-1900. **$98-$98.** 830 N St Marys St. Downtown on St Marys St, just n of Navarro St. **Pets:** Supervision.

🅰🆂🅺 🆂💰 ⊠ 🔌 🖥 🍴 🍴

◆◆◆◆ Hilton Palacio del Rio H ❀
(210) 222-1400. **$169-$219.** 200 S Alamo St. Adjacent to Convention Center, overlooking Hemisfair Plaza and San Antonio River. Int corridors. **Pets:** Medium, other. No service, supervision, crate.

⊠ 🎁 🔌 🖥 🍴 🍴

⚫ ◆◆◆ Holiday Inn Crockett Hotel H ❀
(210) 225-6500. **$89-$109, 30 days notice.** 320 Bonham St. Center across from the Alamo. Ext/int corridors. **Pets:** Very small. $50 one-time fee/pet. Designated rooms, no service, supervision, crate.

🆂🅰🆅🅴 🆂💰 ⊠ 🔌 🖥 🍴 🍴

◆◆◆ Holiday Inn-Downtown-Market Square M
(210) 225-3211. **$139.** 318 W Durango St. I-35, Durango St exit. Int corridors. **Pets:** Medium. $100 deposit/room, $25 one-time fee/room. No service, supervision, crate.

◆◆◆ Holiday Inn Express M ❀
(210) 599-0999. **Call for rates.** 11939 N IH-35. On I-35 southbound access road, 0.5 mi s Judson Rd exit. Ext corridors. **Pets:** Medium. $10 one-time fee/pet. No service, supervision, crate.

◆◆◆ Holiday Inn Express-Airport M ❀
(210) 308-6700. **$69-$94.** 91 NE Loop 410. N Jones Maltsberger Rd at Loop 410. Int corridors. **Pets:** Small. No service, supervision, crate.

◆◆ Holiday Inn-Northeast M ❀
(210) 226-4361. **$69-$99, 7 days notice.** 3855 I-35 N. I-35, Binz-Englemann Rd exit. Ext corridors. **Pets:** Small, other. $25 deposit/room. No service, supervision, crate.

◆◆◆ Holiday Inn Riverwalk H
(210) 224-2500. **$116-$143.** 217 N St. Mary's St. By the San Antonio River; from Houston St, s on St. Mary's St. Int corridors. **Pets:** Small. No service, supervision, crate.

◆◆◆ Holiday Inn Select H ❀
(210) 349-9900. **$99-$125.** 77 NE Loop 410. On Loop 410 westbound access road. Int corridors. **Pets:** Other. $100 deposit/room, $25 one-time fee/pet. Supervision.

❀❀ ◆◆ HomeGate Studios & Suites M
(210) 342-4800. **$79-$89.** 11221 San Pedro Ave. US 281 N Nakoma exit on w frontage road. Ext corridors. **Pets:** Small. Supervision.

◆◆ Homestead Village Guest Studios M ❀
(210) 349-3100. **$40-$55.** 7719 Louis Pasteur Ct. Loop 410, 1.5 mi w on Fredericksburg Rd to Louis Pasteur. Ext corridors. **Pets:** Small. $75 one-time fee/room. Supervision.

◆◆ Homestead Village Guest Studios M ❀
(210) 491-9009. **$50-$70.** 1015 Central Pkwy S. Loop 410, w mi w on US 287. Ext corridors. **Pets:** Other. $75 one-time fee/room. Supervision.

◆◆ Homestead Village Six Flags M
(210) 691-0121. **Call for rates.** 11802 I H 10 W. On I-10 eastbound access road, exit De Zavala. Ext corridors. **Pets:** Small. Supervision.

◆◆ Howard Johnson Downtown East M ❀
(210) 229-9220. **$30-$109, 7 days notice.** 2755 I-35 N. I-35 exit 159B (Walters Ave). Ext corridors. **Pets:** Small. $15 one-time fee/room. No service, supervision, crate.

◆◆◆ Howard Johnson Fiesta M ❀
(210) 558-7152. **$59-$69.** 13279 I-H 10 W. Nw I-10, exit 558, on westbound access road, located 4 mi from Fiesta Texas. Ext corridors. **Pets:** Medium, other. $25 deposit/room. Supervision.

❀❀ ◆◆ Knights Inn Windsor Park M ❀
(210) 646-6336. **$44-$59.** 6370 IH-35 N. Just off Loop 410/I-35, Rittiman Rd exit. Ext corridors. **Pets:** Small. $10 one-time fee/pet. Supervision.

❀❀ ◆◆◆ La Mansion del Rio H
(210) 518-1000. **$199-$339.** 112 College St. Just s on the riverwalk. Ext/int corridors. **Pets:** Medium. No service, supervision, crate.

◆◆◆ La Quinta Inn-Convention Center M
(210) 222-9181. **$89-$119.** 1001 E Commerce St. 0.5 mi ne opposite Hemisfair site, within walking of the Alamo. Ext/int corridors. **Pets:** Medium. No service, supervision, crate.

◆◆◆ La Quinta Inn Market Square M
(210) 271-0001. **$79-$109.** 900 Dolorosa. I-10 E or I-35 S, W Houston-Commerce exit, 0.5 mi sw. Ext corridors. **Pets:** Supervision.

◆◆◆ La Quinta Inn-San Antonio-Airport East M
(210) 828-0781. **$79-$89.** 333 NE Loop 410. Loop 410, airport exit. Ext/int corridors. **Pets:** Small. No service, supervision, crate.

◆◆◆ La Quinta Inn-San Antonio-Airport West M
(210) 342-4291. **$79-$89.** 219 NE Loop 410. Loop 410, airport exit. Ext corridors. **Pets:** Small. No service, supervision, crate.

◆◆◆ La Quinta Inn-San Antonio-Ingram Park M
(210) 680-8883. **$79-$99.** 7134 NW Loop 410. Exit 10 (Culebra Rd), off W Loop 410. Ext corridors. **Pets:** Medium. No service, supervision, crate.

◆◆◆ La Quinta Inn-San Antonio-Lackland M
(210) 674-3200. **$69-$89.** 6511 Military Dr W. Sw jct of US 90 and Military Dr W. Ext corridors. **Pets:** Small. Designated rooms, no service, supervision, crate.

◆◆◆ La Quinta Inn-San Antonio-Vance Jackson M ❀
(210) 734-7931. **$59-$99.** 5922 NW Expwy. Just e of jct I-10 and West Ave, Vance Jackson Rd exit. Ext corridors. **Pets:** Small. Supervision.

◆◆◆ La Quinta Inn-San Antonio-Windsor Park M
(210) 653-6619. **$59-$79.** 6410 I-35 N. 8.5 mi ne, on I-35 N access road between Rittiman and Eisenhauer rds, exit Rittiman Rd. Ext corridors. **Pets:** Supervision.

◆◆◆ La Quinta Inn-San Antonio-Wurzbach [M]
(210) 593-0338. **$79-$99.** 9542 I-10 W. Nw I-10, just s of jct I-10 and Wurzbach Rd. Ext corridors. **Pets:** Small. Supervision.
[A$K] [⊠] [🗎] [▣] [🌊]

[AAA] ◆◆◆◆ Marriott Rivercenter [H]
(210) 223-1000. **$209-$259.** 101 Bowie St. Corner Bowie and Commerce sts. Int corridors. **Pets:** Very small. Designated rooms, no service, supervision, crate.
[SAVE] [S⬆] [⊠] [▣] [🍴] [🌊]

[AAA] ◆◆◆◆ Marriott Riverwalk [H]
(210) 224-4555. **$209-$259.** 711 E Riverwalk. Opposite Convention Center and Hemisfair Plaza. Int corridors. **Pets:** Small. No service, supervision, crate.
[SAVE] [S⬆] [⊠] [🔊] [✦] [🗎] [▣] [🌊]

◆◆◆ Monarch House Bed & Breakfast [BB]
(210) 733-3939. **$55-$115, 7 days notice.** 128 W Mistletoe. E of I-281, exit Mulberry. Int corridors. **Pets:** Small. Supervision.
[A$K] [S⬆] [⊠] [🗎] [▣]

[AAA] ◆ Motel 6–183 [M]
(210) 333-1850. **$37-$53.** 138 N W W White Rd. I-10, exit 580 (W W White Rd). Ext corridors. **Pets:** Very small. Supervision.
[S⬆] [⊠] [🌊]

[AAA] ◆◆ Motel 6–1122 [M]
(210) 225-1111. **$50-$71.** 211 N Pecos St. I-10 W/I-35 S, exit 155B. Ext corridors. **Pets:** Very small. Supervision.
[S⬆] [⊠] [✦] [🌊]

[AAA] ◆ Motel 6–134 [M]
(210) 650-4419. **$33-$51.** 9503 I-35 N. I-35, exit 167A (Randolf Blvd) southbound; exit 167 (Starlight Terrace) northbound. Ext corridors. **Pets:** Very small. Supervision.
[S⬆] [⊠] [🌊]

[AAA] ◆ Motel 6–1208 [M] ✿
(210) 697-0731. **$48-$64.** 16500 I-10 W. I-10, exit 555 (Cantera Pkwy) westbound; exit 556B eastbound. Ext corridors. **Pets:** Small, other. Supervision.
[S⬆] [⊠] [🔊] [✦] [🌊]

[AAA] ◆ Motel 6–651 [M] ✿
(210) 673-9020. **$42-$58.** 2185 SW Loop 410. I-410 Loop, exit 7 (Marbach Rd) to 410 Frontage Rd SW. Ext corridors. **Pets:** Small, other. Designated rooms, no service, supervision, crate.
[S⬆] [⊠] [🔊] [✦] [🌊] [CTV]

◆◆◆ Pear Tree Inn Airport [M]
(210) 366-9300. **$53-$80.** 143 NE Loop 410. Loop 410W. Int corridors. **Pets:** Small. No service, supervision, crate.
[⊠] [🗎] [🌊]

[AAA] ◆◆◆◆ Plaza San Antonio, A Marriott Hotel [H] ✿
(210) 229-1000. **$244-$264.** 555 S Alamo St. Opposite Convention Center and Hemisfair Plaza. Int corridors. **Pets:** Small, dogs only. Supervision.
[SAVE] [S⬆] [⊠] [✦] [🔊] [▣] [🌊] [✕]

◆◆◆ Quality Inn and Suites [M] ✿
(210) 359-7200. **$79-$99.** 222 S W W White Rd. On W W White Rd, 0.4 mi s I-10 exit W W White (exit 580). Ext corridors. **Pets:** $25 deposit/room, $5 daily fee/room, $5 one-time fee/room. No service, supervision, crate.
[A$K] [S⬆] [⊠] [🗎] [▣]

[AAA] ◆◆ Quality Inn Northwest [M] ✿
(210) 736-1900. **$49-$69.** 6023 NW IH-10 W. Jct I-10 and Vance Jackson Rd. Ext corridors. **Pets:** Very small. $25 one-time fee/pet. No service, supervision, crate.
[SAVE] [S⬆] [⊠] [🗎] [▣] [🌊]

◆◆ Radford Inn [M]
(210) 690-5500. **Call for rates.** 13575 I-H 10 W. I-10, exit 557. Ext corridors. **Pets:** Medium. No service, supervision, crate.
[A$K] [✦] [🗎] [🌊]

[AAA] ◆◆ Red Roof Inn-San Antonio Airport [M] ✿
(210) 340-4055. **$48-$73.** 333 Wolfe Rd. N US 281, Isom Rd exit. Ext/int corridors. **Pets:** Supervision.
[SAVE] [⊠] [⬆] [🔊]

[AAA] ◆◆ Red Roof Inn San Antonio (Alamo Downs) [M]
(210) 509-3434. **$46-$66.** 6880 NW Loop 410. NW Loop 410 at Alamo Downs Pkwy. Ext/int corridors. **Pets:** No service, supervision, crate.
[SAVE] [⊠] [🏠] [✦] [🌊]

[AAA] ◆◆◆ Red Roof Inn San Antonio (Downtown) [M] ✿
(210) 229-9973. **$70-$90.** 1011 E Houston St. I-37, northbound exit 141; southbound exit 141B. Int corridors. **Pets:** No service, supervision, crate.
[SAVE] [⊠] [🗎] [🌊]

◆◆◆ Residence Inn by Marriott [A] ✿
(210) 231-6000. **$89-$219.** 628 S Santa Rosa. 0.5 mi e jct I-35 and Durango St. Ext corridors. **Pets:** Other. $5 daily fee/room, $50 one-time fee/room. Supervision.
[A$K] [S⬆] [⊠] [✦] [▣] [🌊] [✕]

◆◆◆ Residence Inn San Antonio-Airport [M]
(210) 805-8118. **Call for rates.** 1014 NW Look 410. On Loop 410 eastbound access road, exit Broadway St. Ext corridors. **Pets:** Small. Designated rooms, supervision.
[⊠] [✦] [▣] [🍴] [🌊] [✕]

◆◆ Rodeway Inn-Crossroads [M]
(210) 734-7111. **Call for rates.** 6804 Northwest Expwy. I-10, 0.3 mi s of Loop 410, Crossroads exit. Ext corridors. **Pets:** Small. No service, supervision, crate.
[A$K] [⊠] [▣] [🌊]

[AAA] ◆◆ Rodeway Inn-Six Flags [M] ✿
(210) 698-3991. **$58-$99.** 19793 I-10 W. Nw I-10, exit 554 (Camp Bullis Rd). Ext corridors. **Pets:** Small. $50 deposit/room. No service, supervision, crate.
[SAVE] [S⬆] [⊠] [🗎] [▣] [🌊]

♦♦♦ San Antonio Airport Hilton & Conference Center 🅗 ❀
(210) 340-6060. **$121-$159.** 611 NW Loop 410. Jct Loop 410, US 281 N (San Pedro Ave) exit. Int corridors. **Pets:** Small, other. No service, supervision, crate.
🆂🅰🆅🅴 ⊠ 🗗 🖉 🖥 💻 🍴 🐾 ⊠

♦♦ Super 8 Motel Downtown North 🅼 ❀
(210) 227-8888. **$42-$88.** 3617 N PanAm Expwy. I-35, exit 160. Ext corridors. **Pets:** Medium. $50 deposit/pet. No service, supervision, crate.
🅰🆂🅺 🆂🐾 ⊠ 🏠 🖥 🐾

♦♦ Super 8 Motel of San Antonio Airport 🅼 ❀
(210) 637-1033. **$35-$85.** 11027 IH-35 N. IH-35 S, exit 168 (Weidner Rd). Int corridors. **Pets:** Large, other. $25 deposit/room. Designated rooms, supervision.
🅰🆂🅺 🆂🐾 ⊠ 🐾

♦♦ Super 8 Motel-Six Flags Fiesta 🅼 ❀
(210) 696-6916. **$54-$94.** 5319 Casa Bella. I-10, De Zavala Rd exit. Int corridors. **Pets:** $5 daily fee/pet. No service, supervision, crate.
🆂🅰🆅🅴 🆂🐾 ⊠ 🖉 🐾

SEGUIN

♦♦ Best Western of Seguin 🅼
(830) 379-9631. **$69-$89, 7 days notice.** 1603 IH-10 & Hwy 46. Jct I-10 and SR 46, exit 607. Ext corridors. **Pets:** Small. No service, supervision, crate.
🆂🅰🆅🅴 ⊠ 🐾

♦♦♦ Holiday Inn Seguin 🅼🅸 ❀
(830) 372-0860. **$78-$92, 3 days notice.** 2950 N 123 Bypass. On SR 123 at jct I-10, exit 610. Ext corridors. **Pets:** Small. $25 deposit/room. No service, supervision, crate.
🆂🐾 ⊠ 🗗 🖉 🖥 💻 🍴 🐾

♦♦ Super 8 Motel of Seguin 🅼
(830) 379-6888. **Call for rates.** 1525 N Hwy 46. Jct I-10 at SR 46, exit 607. Int corridors. **Pets:** Small. No service, supervision, crate.
🅰🆂🅺 ⊠ 🖥

UNIVERSAL CITY

♦♦♦ Clarion Suites Hotel 🅼
(210) 655-9491. **$69-$149, 3 days notice.** 13101 E Loop, 1604N. 1604 at Pat Booker Rd; 0.8 mi e of I-35. Ext corridors. **Pets:** Supervision.
🆂🅰🆅🅴 🆂🐾 ⊠ 🖉 🐾

❀ **End Metropolitan Area** ❀

SAN MARCOS

♦♦♦ AmeriHost Inn-San Marcos 🅼 ❀
(512) 392-6800. **$67-$77.** 4210 I-35 S. I-35 exit 200 (Center Point Rd), southbound Frontage Rd. Int corridors. **Pets:** Small. Supervision.
🆂🅰🆅🅴 🆂🐾 ⊠ 🖉 🖥 💻 🐾

♦♦♦ Comfort Inn 🅼
(512) 396-5665. **$50-$80.** 1611 IH-35 N. I-35, exit 206. Ext corridors. **Pets:** Small. No service, supervision, crate.
🆂🅰🆅🅴 ⊠ 🖥 🐾

♦♦ Days Inn 🅼 ❀
(512) 353-5050. **$40-$95.** 1005 IH-35 N. Just s of jct I-35, 80 at exit 205 or 204B. Ext corridors. **Pets:** Small. $25 deposit/room. Designated rooms, no service, supervision, crate.
🆂🅰🆅🅴 🆂🐾 ⊠ 🖥 🐾

♦♦ Howard Johnson 🅼🅸
(512) 353-8011. **Call for rates.** 1635 Aquarena Springs Dr. 2.5 mi n at jct I-35 and Loop 82, exit 206. Ext corridors. **Pets:** Small. No service, supervision, crate.
⊠ 🗗 💻 🐾

♦♦♦ La Quinta Inn-San Marcos 🅼
(512) 392-8800. **$69-$99.** 1619 IH-35 N. Jct IH-35, exit 206. Ext corridors. **Pets:** Medium. Designated rooms, no service, supervision, crate.
🆂🅰🆅🅴 ⊠ ♿ 🗗 🖉 🖥 🐾

SANDERSON

♦ Desert Air Motel 🅼
(915) 345-2572. **$30-$39.** 0.5 mi w on US 90, just e of jct US 285. Ext corridors. **Pets:** Medium. No service, supervision, crate.
🆂🅰🆅🅴 🆂🐾 🖥

SEMINOLE

♦♦ Raymond Motor Inn 🅼 ❀
(915) 758-3653. **$37-$45.** 301 W Ave A. 0.3 mi w on US 62 and 180. Ext corridors. **Pets:** $5 daily fee/pet, $5 one-time fee/pet. Supervision.
🆂🅰🆅🅴 🆂🐾 ⊠ 🖥

♦♦ Seminole Inn 🅼 ❀
(915) 758-9881. **$40-$45.** 2200 Hobbs Hwy. 1.5 mi w on US 62 and 180. Ext corridors. **Pets:** Medium, other. $5 daily fee/pet. No service, supervision, crate.
🆂🅰🆅🅴 🆂🐾 ⊠ 🖥 🐾

SHAMROCK

♦♦♦ Best Western Irish Inn 🅼🅸 ❀
(806) 256-2106. **$49-$69.** 301 I-40E. I-40, exit 163, 0.3 mi e on n service road. Ext/int corridors. **Pets:** Other. Designated rooms, supervision.
🆂🅰🆅🅴 🆂🐾 ⊠ 🗗 🖥 💻 🍴 🐾

♦♦ Econo Lodge 🅼 ❀
(806) 256-2111. **$35-$60.** 1006 E 12th St. I-40, exit 164 westbound, exit 161 or 163 eastbound; just e of US 83. Ext corridors. **Pets:** Small. $5 one-time fee/room. Designated rooms, no service, supervision, crate.
🆂🅰🆅🅴 🆂🐾 ⊠ 💻 🐾

🔺 ◆ The Western Motel Ⓜ 🐾
(806) 256-3244. **$35-$55.** 104 E 12th St. Business I-40 and US 83. Ext corridors. **Pets:** Small. $5 one-time fee/room. Supervision.
[SAVE] [S🐾] [✕] [🍴]

SHERMAN

🔺 ◆◆◆ La Quinta Inn & Suites
Sherman Ⓜ 🐾
(903) 870-1122. **$69-$89.** 2912 US 75 N. US 75, exit 63, jct US 82, just sw. Int corridors. **Pets:** Other. Designated rooms, supervision.
[SAVE] [✕] [⌨] [🛗] [💻] [📶]

🔺 ◆◆ Super 8 Motel Ⓜ 🐾
(903) 868-9325. **$40-$50.** 111 E Hwy 1417. 3 mi s on US 75, exit 56. Int corridors. **Pets:** $5 daily fee/pet, $5 one-time fee/pet. Supervision.
[SAVE] [✕]

SNYDER

🔺 ◆◆ Purple Sage Motel Ⓜ 🐾
(915) 573-5491. **$44-$63.** 1501 E Coliseum. 2.5 mi se on US 180. Ext corridors. **Pets:** Other. Supervision.
[SAVE] [S🐾] [✕] [🛗] [💻] [📶]

◆◆ Willow Park Inn Ⓜ
(915) 573-1961. **Call for rates.** 1137 E Hwy 180. 3.8 mi s on US 180 at jct US 84. Int corridors. **Pets:** Small. Designated rooms, no service, supervision, crate.
[✕] [🛗] [💻] [📶]

SONORA

🔺 ◆◆ Days Inn Ⓜ 🐾
(915) 387-3516. **$40-$60.** 1312 N Service Rd. Just n of I-10, exit 400, on US 277. Ext corridors. **Pets:** Small, other. $2 daily fee/pet, $2 one-time fee/pet. No service, supervision, crate.
[SAVE] [S🐾] [✕] [💻] [🍴] [📶]

🔺 ◆◆ Holiday Host Motel Ⓜ 🐾
(915) 387-2532. **$31-$39.** 127 Loop 467E (Hwy 290E). Exit 404, 3 mi w on Loop 467 westbound; exit 399, 3 mi, e on Loop 467 eastbound. Ext corridors. **Pets:** $5 deposit/pet. Supervision.
[✕] [📶]

🔺 ◆ Twin Oaks Motel Ⓜ 🐾
(915) 387-2551. **$35-$52.** 907 N Crockett Ave. I-10, exit 400 westbound, exit 399 0.6 mi, 0.3 mi s on Hwy 277. Ext corridors. **Pets:** Small. $10 one-time fee/room. Designated rooms, no service, supervision, crate.
[SAVE] [✕]

SOUTH PADRE ISLAND

◆◆ Bahia Mar Resort Ⓜ 🐾
(956) 761-1343. **$165-$170, 3 days notice.** 6300 Padre Blvd. 3.5 mi n of Queen Isabella Cswy. Ext/int corridors. **Pets:** Very small. $35 one-time fee/pet. Supervision.
[ASK] [S🐾] [✕] [🏊] [🛗] [💻] [🍴] [📶] [✕]

🔺 ◆◆ Best Western Fiesta Isles Ⓜ 🐾
(956) 761-4913. **$99-$199.** 5701 Padre Blvd. 3 mi n of Queen Isabella Cswy. Ext corridors. **Pets:** Medium, other. $25 deposit/room. Supervision.
[SAVE] [S🐾] [✕] [🛗] [💻] [📶] [✕]

◆◆ Days Inn Ⓜ
(956) 761-7831. **Call for rates.** 3913 Padre Blvd. 3.5 mi n of Queen Isabella Cswy. Ext corridors. **Pets:** Designated rooms, no service, supervision, crate.
[✕] [🛗] [📶]

◆◆ The Tiki Apartment Hotel 🄰 🐾
(956) 761-2694. **$115-$235, 7 days notice.** 6608 Padre Blvd. 3.8 mi n of Queen Isabella Cswy. Ext corridors. **Pets:** Small. $2 daily fee/pet. Designated rooms, supervision.
[ASK] [S🐾] [🛗] [📶] [✕]

STEPHENVILLE

◆◆◆ Holiday Inn Stephenville Ⓜ 🐾
(254) 968-5256. **$62-$98, 7 days notice.** 2865 W Washington St. 1.5 mi s on SR 377. Ext corridors. **Pets:** Other. $50 deposit/room. No service, supervision, crate.
[ASK] [S🐾] [✕] [🛗] [💻] [🍴] [📶]

◆◆ Texan Inn Ⓜ
(254) 968-5448, **7 days notice.** 3030 W Washington. 3 mi sw on US 67 and 377. Ext corridors. **Pets:** Small. No service, supervision, crate.
[✕] [💻]

SULPHUR SPRINGS

◆◆◆ Best Western Trail Dust Inn Ⓜ
(903) 885-7515. **$54-$99, 3 days notice.** 1521 Shannon Rd. Jct I-30 and Loop 301, exit 127. Ext/int corridors. **Pets:** Small. Designated rooms, no service, supervision, crate.
[S🐾] [✕] [⌨] [🛗] [💻] [📶]

◆◆◆ Holiday Inn Ⓜ 🐾
(903) 885-0562. **$59-$69, 3 days notice.** 1495 E Industrial Dr. I-30, exit 127. Int corridors. **Pets:** Small. Designated rooms, supervision.
[ASK] [S🐾] [✕] [🛗] [💻] [🍴] [📶]

SWEETWATER

◆◆◆ Mulberry Mansion 🄱🄱
(915) 235-3811. **$65-$225.** 1400 Sam Houston St. 0.3 mi n off I-20, exit 244. Int corridors. **Pets:** Very small. Supervision.
[ASK] [S🐾]

🔺 ◆◆ Ranch House Motel &
Restaurant Ⓜ 🐾
(915) 236-6341. **$37-$57.** 301 SW Georgia Ave. I-20, just w of jct SR 70 on s access road, exit 244. Ext corridors. **Pets:** Medium. Designated rooms, no service, supervision, crate.
[✕] [🍴] [📶]

TAYLOR

◆◆ Regency Inn **M**
(512) 352-2666. **$40-$49.** 2007 N Main. N on SR 95. Int corridors. **Pets:** No service, supervision, crate.

ASK SO X H

TEMPLE

AAA ◆◆◆ Best Western-Inn at Scott & White **MI** ❀
(254) 778-5511. **$56-$72, 3 days notice.** 2625 S 31st St. 3 mi sw on FM 1741, 0.3 mi ne jct Loop 363, US 190 and SR 36. Ext corridors. **Pets:** No service, supervision, crate.

SAVE SO X ℱ H ▣ ⊤⊥ ᗡ

AAA ◆◆◆ La Quinta Inn-Temple **M**
(254) 771-2980. **$65-$85.** 1604 W Barton Ave. SR 53, just e, jct I-35 and US 81, exit 301. Ext corridors. **Pets:** Designated rooms, no service, supervision, crate.

SAVE X H ᗡ

AAA ◆ Motel 6–257 **M**
(254) 778-0272. **$34-$50.** 1100 N General Bruce Dr. I-35, exit 302 (Nugent Ave); just s on access, follow signs. Ext corridors. **Pets:** Small. Supervision.

SO X ᗡ

AAA ◆ Stratford House Inn **M** ❀
(254) 771-1495. **$43-$58.** 1602 N General Bruce Dr. I-35 at Nugent Ave, exit 302. Ext corridors. **Pets:** Medium. $20 deposit/room, $5 daily fee/pet, $5 one-time fee/pet. No service, supervision, crate.

SAVE SO X H ᗡ

TERLINGUA

AAA ◆◆ Big Bend Motor Inn **M**
(915) 371-2218. **$65-$77, 7 days notice.** SR 118, 2 mi from entrance of Big Bend National Park. Ext corridors. **Pets:** Supervision.

X H ▣ ᗡ

TEXARKANA

AAA ◆◆ Best Western Northgate Inn **MI**
(903) 793-6565. **$46-$55, 30 days notice.** 400 W 53rd St. I-30, exit 223B, on NW Frontage Rd. Int corridors. **Pets:** Small. Designated rooms, no service, supervision, crate.

SAVE SO X H ▣ ⊤⊥ ᗡ ⊠

◆◆ Four Points Hotel Sheraton Texarkana **H**
(903) 792-3222. **Call for rates.** 5301 N State Line Ave. I-30 at State Line, exit 223B. Int corridors. **Pets:** Supervision.

ℱ H ▣ ᗡ

◆◆◆ Holiday Inn Express **M** ❀
(903) 792-3366. **$69-$69.** 5401 N State Line Ave. US 71, 0.3 mi n of jct I-30, exit 223B. Int corridors. **Pets:** Small. $100 deposit/room, $25 one-time fee/room. No service, supervision, crate.

ASK SO X H ▣ ᗡ

AAA ◆◆◆ La Quinta Inn-Texarkana **M**
(903) 794-1900. **$59-$79.** 5201 State Line Ave. I-30, exit 223A, sw of jct US 59 and 71. Ext corridors. **Pets:** No service, supervision, crate.

SAVE X H ▣ ᗡ

AAA ◆◆ Motel 6–201 **M**
(903) 793-1413. **$30-$41.** 1924 Hampton Rd. I-30 at Summerhill Rd, exit 222. Ext corridors. **Pets:** Small. No service, supervision, crate.

X ᗡ

TEXAS CITY

AAA ◆◆◆ La Quinta Inn **M**
(409) 948-3101. **$49-$79.** 1121 Hwy 146N. Jct SR 146S and FM 1764; 5 mi se of I-45, exit 16 southbound; exit 15 northbound. Ext corridors. **Pets:** No service, supervision, crate.

SAVE X ℱ H ▣ ᗡ

THREE RIVERS

◆◆ Nolan Ryan's Bass Inn **M** ❀
(361) 786-3521. **Call for rates.** State Hwy 72, 7.5 mi w of jct US 281; adjacent to Choke Canyon Lake. Ext corridors. **Pets:** Other. Supervision.

X H ᗡ

TULIA

◆◆◆ Select Inn of Tulia **M** ❀
(806) 995-3248. **$50-$58.** Rt 1, Box 60. Jct I-27 and exit 74. Ext corridors. **Pets:** Small, other. $5 daily fee/pet. Designated rooms, supervision.

ASK SO X ℱ ▣ ᗡ

TYLER

AAA ◆◆ Best Western Inn & Suites **M** ❀
(903) 595-2681. **$44-$79.** 2828 W NW Loop 323. Jct US 69 N and Loop 323. Ext corridors. **Pets:** Medium, other. $10 daily fee/pet. Supervision.

SAVE SO X H ▣ ᗡ

◆◆ Econo Lodge **M** ❀
(903) 531-9513. **$39-$69.** 2739 W NW Loop 323. At jct US 69 N and Loop 323. Ext corridors. **Pets:** Very small, other. $10 one-time fee/room. No service, supervision, crate.

ASK SO X H

◆◆◆ Holiday Inn-Southeast Crossing **MI**
(903) 593-3600. **$79-$79.** 3310 Troup Hwy. 3.5 mi se on SR 110, 0.3 mi n of jct E Loop 323. Ext corridors. **Pets:** Small. Designated rooms, supervision.

ASK SO X ⅋ H ▣ ⊤⊥ ᗡ

AAA ◆◆◆ La Quinta Inn **M**
(903) 561-2223. **$62-$92.** 1601 W SW Loop 323. 1 mi w of S US 69 on W Loop 323. Ext corridors. **Pets:** Small. No service, supervision, crate.

SAVE X ℱ ▣ ᗡ

AAA ◆ Motel 6–165 **M**
(903) 595-6691. **$30-$34.** 3236 Gentry Pkwy. I-20 exit 556 SR 69 7 mi s. Ext corridors. **Pets:** Small. No service, supervision, crate.

X ᗡ

◆◆◆ Residence Inn by Marriott **A** ❀
(903) 595-5188. **$72-$125.** 3303 Troup Hwy. 3.5 mi se on SR 110, 0.3 mi n of jct E Loop 323. Ext corridors. **Pets:** Medium. $50 one-time fee/pet. Supervision.

ASK SO X H ▣ ᗡ ⊠

◆◆◆ **Sheraton Tyler Hotel** Ⓜ 🐾
(903) 561-5800. **$87-$99.** 5701 S Broadway. 5 mi s on US 69. Int corridors. **Pets:** Small. $25 one-time fee/room. Supervision.
(ASK) 🆂 ⊗ 🎦 🖥 💻 🍴 🍽

UVALDE

◆◆ **Best Western Continental Inn** Ⓜ
(830) 278-5671. **$42-$57.** 701 E Main St. 0.5 mi e on US 90. Ext corridors. **Pets:** Small. No service, supervision, crate.
(ASK) 🆂 ⊗ 🖥 🍽 ⊗

◆◆ **Holiday Inn** Ⓜ 🐾
(830) 278-4511. **$60-$75.** 920 E Main St. 0.5 mi e on US 90. Ext corridors. **Pets:** $50 deposit/room. Supervision.
(ASK) 🆂 ⊗ 🖥 💻 🍴 🍽

VAN HORN

🄰🄰🄰 ◆◆◆ **Best Western Inn of Van Horn** Ⓜ
(915) 283-2410. **$39-$89, 3 days notice.** 1705 W Broadway. 1 mi w on US 80; 0.3 mi e of I-10, exit 138. Ext corridors. **Pets:** Small. No service, supervision, crate.
(SAVE) 🆂 ⊗ 🖥 💻 🍽

🄰🄰🄰 ◆◆◆ **Best Western American Inn** Ⓜ 🐾
(915) 283-2030. **$42-$70.** 1309 W Broadway. 1 mi e of I-10, exit 138; 1 mi w of US 90, I-10, exit 140A. Ext corridors. **Pets:** Other. Supervision.
(SAVE) 🆂 ⊗ 🎦 🖥 🍽

🄰🄰🄰 ◆ **Economy Inn** Ⓜ 🐾
(915) 283-2754. **$25-$38.** 1500 W Broadway St. US 80, 0.5 mi e of jct I-10, exit 138. Ext corridors. **Pets:** Medium, other. Supervision.
(SAVE) 🆂 ⊗ 🖥

🄰🄰🄰 ◆◆◆ **Holiday Inn Express** Ⓜ 🐾
(915) 283-7444. **$54-$64.** 1905 SW Frontage Rd. I-10, exit 138 (Golf Course Dr). Ext corridors. **Pets:** Small, other. Supervision.
(SAVE) 🆂 ⊗ 🎣 🎦 🖥 🍽

🄰🄰🄰 ◆ **Motel 6–4024** Ⓜ 🐾
(915) 283-2992. **$35-$41.** 1805 W Broadway St. I-10, exit 138 (Golf Course Dr). Ext corridors. **Pets:** Small. Supervision.
(SAVE) 🆂 ⊗ 🍽

🄰🄰🄰 ◆◆ **Ramada Inn** Ⓜ 🐾
(915) 283-2780. **$48-$68.** 200 Golf Course Dr. I-10 and Golf Course Dr, exit 138. Int corridors. **Pets:** Small. $5 daily fee/pet, $5 one-time fee/pet. Designated rooms, no service, supervision, crate.
(SAVE) 🆂 ⊗ 🖥 🍽

🄰🄰🄰 ◆◆◆ **Van Horn Super 8** Ⓜ
(915) 283-2282. **$38-$42, 3 days notice.** 1807 E Service Rd. I-10, exit 138 (Golf Course Dr). Ext corridors. **Pets:** Small. Supervision.
(SAVE) 🆂 ⊗ 🐾 🖥

VEGA

🄰🄰🄰 ◆◆ **Best Western Country Inn** Ⓜ 🐾
(806) 267-2131. **$49-$69.** 1800 W Vega Blvd. 0.5 mi w on US 40 business loop. Ext corridors. **Pets:** Supervision.
(SAVE) 🆂 ⊗ 💻 🍴 🍽

VERNON

◆◆ **Best Western Village Inn** Ⓜ 🐾
(940) 552-5417. **$46-$54, 7 days notice.** 1615 Expwy. 0.5 mi n on US 287, just e on jct US 183, Main St exit. Ext corridors. **Pets:** Small. $5 one-time fee/pet. Supervision.
⊗ 🖥 💻 🍽

🄰🄰🄰 ◆◆ **Days Inn Vernon** Ⓜ 🐾
(940) 552-9982. **$38-$47.** 3110 Frontage Rd. 0.3 mi w on US 287 at Bentley St exit. Ext corridors. **Pets:** Supervision.
(SAVE) 🆂 ⊗ 🖥 🍽

🄰🄰🄰 ◆◆ **Econo Lodge** Ⓜ
(940) 553-3384. **$30-$60.** 4100 Hwy 287 NW. 1 mi nw on SR 287 at jct SR 70. Ext corridors. **Pets:** Small. Designated rooms, no service, supervision, crate.
(SAVE) 🆂 ⊗ 🖥 💻 🍽

◆◆ **Greentree Inn** Ⓜ 🐾
(940) 552-5421. **$39-$39.** 3029 Morton St. 1 mi n on US 287 and Bently St exit. Ext corridors. **Pets:** Small. $5 daily fee/pet. Designated rooms, supervision.
(ASK) 🆂 ⊗ 🍽

◆◆ **Super 8 Motel** Ⓜ
(940) 552-9321. **Call for rates.** 1829 Expwy Hwy 287. 0.5 mi nw on US 287, Main St exit. Ext corridors. **Pets:** Small. No service, supervision, crate.
⊗ 🖥

🄰🄰🄰 ◆ **Western Motel** Ⓜ 🐾
(940) 552-2531. **$25-$40.** 715 Wilbarger St. 0.8 mi e on US 70, 183 and 287 business rts. Ext corridors. **Pets:** Medium. $5 deposit/room. No service, supervision, crate.
(SAVE) 🆂 ⊗ 💻 🍽 ⊗

VICTORIA

◆◆◆ **Comfort Inn** Ⓜ
(361) 574-9393. **$61-$75.** 1906 Houston Hwy. 3.5 mi ne on US 59. Ext corridors. **Pets:** Medium. Designated rooms, no service, supervision, crate.
(ASK) 🆂 ⊗ 🖥 💻 🍽

◆◆◆ **Hampton Inn** Ⓜ
(361) 578-2030. **Call for rates.** 3112 E Houston Hwy (Bus Rt 59). 2 mi ne on US 59. Ext corridors. **Pets:** Small. No service, supervision, crate.
(ASK) ⊗ 💻 🍽

◆◆◆ **Holiday Inn Holidome** Ⓜ
(361) 575-0251. **$63-$145, 7 days notice.** 2705 E Houston Hwy (Bus Rt 59). 2.5 mi ne on US 59. Ext/int corridors. **Pets:** Supervision.
⊗ 🖥 💻 🍴 🍽

🄰🄰🄰 ◆◆◆ **La Quinta Inn-Victoria** Ⓜ 🐾
(361) 572-3585. **$59-$79.** 7603 N Navarro (US 77) St. 4 mi n on US 77 at jct Loop 463. Ext corridors. **Pets:** Medium, other. No service, supervision, crate.
(SAVE) ⊗ 🎦 🖥 💻 🍽

◆◆ Ramada Inn
(361) 578-2723. **$59-$69, 7 days notice.** 3901 E Houston Hwy (Bus Rt 59). Hwy 59 business route, 2.3 mi ne of jct US 77. Ext corridors. **Pets:** No service, supervision, crate.

ASK ⬛ ⬛ ⬛ ⬛ ⬛

WACO

AAA ◆◆◆ Best Western Old Main
Lodge  ❖
(254) 753-0316. **$58-$71.** I-35 & 4th St. I-35 and US 81, exit 335A (4th-5th St). Ext corridors. **Pets:** Small. No service, supervision, crate.

SAVE ⬛ ⬛ ⬛ ⬛ ⬛

AAA ◆◆◆ Best Western Waco Mall
(254) 776-3194. **$54-$70.** 6624 Hwy 84W. 5 mi s on US 84; 0.3 mi w of jct SR 6 and Loop 340. Ext corridors. **Pets:** Supervision.

SAVE ⬛ ⬛ ⬛ ⬛ ⬛

AAA ◆◆ Days Inn
(254) 799-8585. **$59-$75.** 1504 I-35. N off I-35 at exit 338B (Behrens Circle). Ext corridors. **Pets:** Medium. No service, supervision, crate.

SAVE ⬛ ⬛ ⬛ ⬛ ⬛

◆◆◆ Holiday Inn-Waco I-35
(254) 753-0261. **$72-$72.** 1001 Martin Luther King Blvd. N off I-35, exit 335C (Lake Brazos Dr). Int corridors. **Pets:** Supervision.

ASK ⬛ ⬛ ⬛ ⬛ ⬛ ⬛ ⬛

AAA ◆◆◆ La Quinta Inn-Waco
(254) 752-9741. **$79-$99.** 1110 S 9th St. E off I-35; exit 334 (17th St) southbound, exit 334A (18th St) northbound. Ext corridors. **Pets:** Very small. No service, supervision, crate.

SAVE ⬛ ⬛ ⬛ ⬛

◆◆◆ Waco Hilton Inn  ❖
(254) 754-8484. **$79-$89.** 113 S University Parks Dr. 1.5 mi n, adjacent to convention center. Int corridors. **Pets:** Dogs only. Supervision.

ASK ⬛ ⬛ ⬛ ⬛ ⬛ ⬛ ⬛ ⬛

◆◆◆ Waco Residence Inn
(254) 714-1386. **Call for rates.** 501 University Park Dr. I-35 at University Park exit 330B, 0.3 mi w. Int corridors. **Pets:** No service, supervision, crate.

⬛ ⬛ ⬛ ⬛

WEATHERFORD

◆◆ Best Western Santa Fe Inn  ❖
(817) 594-7401. **$54-$69, 7 days notice.** 1927 Santa Fe Dr. FM 2552, 0.3 mi nw of jct I-20, exit 409 (Clear Lake Rd). Ext corridors. **Pets:** $10 daily fee/pet. Supervision.

ASK ⬛ ⬛ ⬛ ⬛

AAA ◆◆◆ Comfort Inn  ❖
(817) 599-8683. **$50-$95.** 809 Palo Pinto St. 0.8 mi w of Courthouse on US 80 and 180. Ext corridors. **Pets:** Other. Supervision.

SAVE ⬛ ⬛ ⬛ ⬛

WELLINGTON

◆ Cherokee Inn & Restaurant
(806) 447-2508. **$28-$37.** 1105 Houston. US 83. Ext corridors. **Pets:** Very small. No service, supervision, crate.

ASK ⬛ ⬛ ⬛

WESLACO

AAA ◆◆◆ Best Western Palm Aire Motor Inn &
Suites  ❖
(956) 969-2411. **$50-$95.** 415 S International Blvd. US 83 at International Blvd exit. Ext corridors. **Pets:** Medium. Supervision.

SAVE ⬛ ⬛ ⬛ ⬛ ⬛ ⬛ ⬛ ⬛

◆◆◆ Holiday Inn Express  ❖
(956) 969-9920. **$89-$110.** 1702 E Expwy 83. US 83 exit Airport Dr. Ext corridors. **Pets:** Small. No service, supervision, crate.

ASK ⬛ ⬛ ⬛ ⬛ ⬛

WEST COLUMBIA

AAA ◆◆ Country Hearth Inn  ❖
(409) 345-2399. **$50-$62, 7 days notice.** 714 Columbia (Hwy 36). Dr. Jct Hwy 35 and 36 at Columbia Dr. Ext corridors. **Pets:** Small. No service, supervision, crate.

SAVE ⬛ ⬛ ⬛ ⬛ ⬛

WESTLAKE

◆◆◆ Dallas-Fort Worth Marriott Solana
(817) 430-3848. **$79-$179.** 5 Village Cir. SR 114, Kirkwood Blvd exit. Int corridors. **Pets:** Designated rooms, no service, supervision, crate.

⬛ ⬛ ⬛ ⬛ ⬛ ⬛

WHARTON

AAA ◆◆ Country Hearth Inn
(409) 532-1152. **$45-$57.** 1808 FM 102. 0.5 mi se of Hwy 59. Ext corridors. **Pets:** Designated rooms, supervision.

SAVE ⬛ ⬛ ⬛ ⬛ ⬛

WICHITA FALLS

AAA ◆◆ Best Western Towne Crest Inn
(940) 322-1182. **$37-$42.** 1601 8th St. 0.8 mi w, just w of US 82, 281 and 287 southbound. Ext corridors. **Pets:** Designated rooms, no service, supervision, crate.

SAVE ⬛ ⬛

◆◆◆ Comfort Inn  ❖
(940) 322-2477. **$57-$75.** 1750 Maurine St. 2.8 mi nw off I-44, US 277 and 287, exit 2 (Maurine St), just e. Int corridors. **Pets:** Other. $10 deposit/room, $10 one-time fee/room. Supervision.

ASK ⬛ ⬛ ⬛ ⬛

◆◆ Days Inn
(940) 723-5541. **Call for rates.** 1211 Central Expwy. 3 mi nw off I-44, US 277, 281 and 287, exit 2 (Maurine St). Ext corridors. **Pets:** Small. No service, supervision, crate.

⬛ ⬛ ⬛

◆◆ **Econo Lodge** Ⓜ ❀
(940) 761-1889. **$55-$70.** 1700 5th St. On I-44 and US 287 at Abilene exit. Ext corridors. **Pets:** Large, other. $7 one-time fee/pet. No service, supervision, crate.
🅰️🆂🏧 Ⓢ❌ 🔋 📺 ⌂

🅰🅰🅰 ◆◆◆ **La Quinta Inn-Wichita Falls** Ⓜ ❀
(940) 322-6971. **$59-$79.** 1128 Central Frwy N. 2.8 mi nw off I-44, US 277, 281 and 287, exit 2 (Maurine St). Ext corridors. **Pets:** Other. Supervision.
🆂🅰🆅🅴 ❌ 🐾 🔋 ⌂

🅰🅰🅰 ◆◆ **Motel 6** Ⓜ ❀
(940) 322-8817. **$39-$46, 4 days notice.** 1812 Maurine St. 2.8 mi nw off I-44, US 277 and 287, exit 2. Ext corridors. **Pets:** Small, other. No service, supervision, crate.
Ⓢ❌ ⌂

ZAPATA

🅰🅰🅰 ◆◆◆ **Best Western Inn by the Lake** Ⓜ🅸 ❀
(956) 765-8403. **$54-$61.** 0.5 mi se on US 83. Int corridors. **Pets:** Medium, other. $20 deposit/room. Designated rooms, supervision.
🆂🅰🆅🅴 Ⓢ❌ 🔋 ⌂

UTAH

CITY INDEX

AMERICAN FORK

◆◆◆ Quality Inn & Suites 🅼
(801) 763-8383. $49-$69. 712 S Utah Valley Dr. I-15, exit 279; in Utah Valley Business Park. Int corridors. Pets: Supervision.
[ASK] [S₀] [✕] [🐾] [🅱] [🖥] [🖼]

BEAVER

◆◆◆ Best Western Butch Cassidy Inn 🅼 ❀
(435) 438-2438. $59-$69. 161 S Main St. E of I-15, exit 109 or 112. Ext corridors. Pets: Medium, other. No service, supervision, crate.
[ASK] [S₀] [✕] [🍴] [🖼]

🆔 ◆◆◆ Best Western Paradise Inn 🅼🅸 ❀
(435) 438-2455. $53-$73. 1451 N 300 West. E of I-15, exit 112. Ext corridors. Pets: Medium. Supervision.
[SAVE] [S₀] [✕] [🍴] [🖼]

🆔 ◆◆ DeLano Motel 🅼 ❀
(435) 438-2418. $36-$45, 7 days notice. 480 N Main St. E of I-15, exit 109 or 112. Ext corridors. Pets: $5 daily fee/room, $10 one-time fee/room. Supervision.
[✕] [🅱]

BICKNELL

🆔 ◆◆ Aquarius Motel and Restaurant 🅼🅸 ❀
(435) 425-3835. $30-$45. 240 W Main St. SR 24, 9 mi w of Capitol Reef National Park. Ext/int corridors. Pets: Other. $25 deposit/room, $5 daily fee/room. Supervision.
[✕] [🅱] [🍴]

BLANDING

🆔 ◆◆◆ Best Western Gateway Inn 🅼
(435) 678-2278. Call for rates. 88 E Center. E side on US 191. Ext corridors. Pets: Medium. No service, supervision, crate.
[SAVE] [S₀] [✕] [🖼]

🆔 ◆◆ Four Corners Inn 🅼 ❀
(435) 678-3257. $50-$60. 131 E Center St. Just e off US 191. Ext corridors. Pets: Other. Supervision.
[SAVE] [S₀] [✕] [🅱]

BLUFF

🆔 ◆ Kokopelli Inn 🅼 ❀
(435) 672-2322. $50-$50. Hwy 191. Hwy 191. Int corridors. Pets: Small. $10 daily fee/pet. No service, supervision, crate.
[✕]

🆔 ◆◆ Recapture Lodge 🅼 ❀
(435) 672-2281. $44-$56. 220 E Main St. US 191. Ext corridors. Pets: Other. No service, supervision, crate.
[SAVE] [✕] [🐾] [🅱] [🖼] [✕] [🅰🅲] [CTV] [🗲]

BOULDER

◆◆◆ Boulder Mountain Lodge 🅼🅸 ❀
(435) 335-7460. $79-$149. 20 N Highway 12. Jct SR 12 and Burr Trail. Ext/int corridors. Pets: Other. $9 daily fee/pet. Designated rooms, supervision.
[✕] [🅱] [🖥] [🍴] [CTV]

BRIGHAM CITY

◆◆◆ Crystal Inn 🅼🅸 ❀
(435) 723-0440. $55-$69. 480 Westland Dr. Exit 364, 1 mi e of I-15. Int corridors. Pets: Medium, other. $20 deposit/room. Designated rooms, no service, supervision, crate.
[✕] [🐾] [🐾] [🅱] [🖼]

🆔 ◆◆ Howard Johnson Inn 🅼 ❀
(435) 723-8511. $48-$58. 1167 S Main St. US 89, 91, 2 mi e of I-15 and I-84, Logan and Brigham City exit 364. Ext corridors. Pets: Other. No service, supervision, crate.
[SAVE] [S₀] [✕] [🐾] [🅱] [🖥] [🖼]

BRYCE

♦♦♦ Best Western Ruby's Inn Ⓜ ❀
(435) 834-5341. **$90-$105.** UT Hwy 63. SR 63, 1 mi s of SR 12, 1 mi n of Bryce Canyon N P entrance. Ext/int corridors. **Pets:** $100 deposit/room. No service, supervision, crate.
🆂 ⊠ ♿ 🕸 🎱 🍴 💻 🍴 🎨 ⊠

♦♦ Bryce Canyon Resorts Ⓜ�I ❀
(435) 834-5351. **$65-$75.** 13500 E Hwy 12. Jct of Hwy 12 and 63. Ext corridors. **Pets:** $20 deposit/room, $5 daily fee/room. No service, supervision, crate.
⊠ 🍴 💻 🍴 🎨

♦ Bryce Junction Inn Ⓜ
(435) 676-2221. **$39-$70.** 3068 E Hwy 12. On Hwy 12. Int corridors. **Pets:** No service, supervision, crate.
🆂 ⊠ 🍴

♦♦ Bryce View Lodge Ⓜ ❀
(435) 834-5180. **$55-$65.** UT Hwy 63. Ext corridors. **Pets:** $100 deposit/room. No service, supervision, crate.
🆂 ⊠ 🍴 💻

♦♦ Harolds Place Cabins Ⓒ
(435) 676-2350. **$60-$60.** 3066 Hwy 12. Ext corridors. **Pets:** Supervision.
🅰🆂🅺 🆂 ⊠ 💻 🌀

CANNONVILLE

♦♦ Grand Staircase Inn Ⓜ
(435) 679-8400. **$55-$79.** 105 N Kodachrome Dr. Center of town. Ext/int corridors. **Pets:** Medium. No service, supervision, crate.
🆂 🆂 ⊠ 🖍 🄲🅃🅅

CEDAR CITY

♦♦ Cedar Rest Motel Ⓜ
(435) 586-9471. **$30-$55.** 479 S Main. Ext corridors. **Pets:** Supervision.
🆂 🆂 ⊠

♦♦ Comfort Inn Ⓜ ❀
(435) 586-2082. **$64-$92.** 250 N 1100 West. Just e of I-15 Central exit 59. Ext corridors. **Pets:** Designated rooms, no service, supervision, crate.
🅰🆂🅺 🆂 ⊠ 🕸 🍴 💻 🎨

♦♦♦ Days Inn Ⓜ
(435) 867-8877. **$55-$89.** 1204 S Main. I-15, exit 57, 0.4 mi e. Ext corridors. **Pets:** Medium. No service, supervision, crate.
🆂 🆂 ⊠ 🕸 🖍 🍴 🎨

♦♦♦ Holiday Inn-Convention Ctr Ⓜ�I ❀
(435) 586-8888. **$72-$89, 30 days notice.** 1575 W 200 North. Just w of I-15, exit 59. Ext/int corridors. **Pets:** Other. $25 deposit/room. Designated rooms, no service, supervision, crate.
🅰🆂🅺 🆂 ⊠ 🕸 🍴 💻 🍴 🎨

♦♦ Motel 6 of Cedar City–4041 Ⓜ
(435) 586-9200. **$40-$54.** 1620 W 200 N. Just w of I-15 at exit 59. Int corridors. **Pets:** No service, supervision, crate.
⊠ 🕸 🖍

♦♦ Rodeway Inn Ⓜ ❀
(435) 586-9916. **$62-$76, 3 days notice.** 281 S Main St. E of I-15, exit 57. Ext corridors. **Pets:** No service, supervision, crate.
🆂 🆂 ⊠ 💻 🎨 ⊠

♦♦ Super 8 Motel Ⓜ ❀
(435) 586-8880. **$50-$57, 7 days notice.** 145 N 1550 W. W of I-15, exit 59. Int corridors. **Pets:** Other. $5 one-time fee/pet. No service, supervision, crate.
🅰🆂🅺 🆂 ⊠ ♿ 🕸 🖍 🍴

♦♦♦ Travelodge Ⓜ ❀
(435) 586-7435. **$52-$79.** 2555 N Main St. I-15, exit 62. Ext corridors. **Pets:** Small. $10 daily fee/pet. No service, supervision, crate.
🆂 🆂 ⊠ 🍴 💻 🎨

♦ Valu-Inn Ⓜ
(435) 586-9114. **$25-$50.** 344 S Main St. E of I-15, exit 57. Ext corridors. **Pets:** Supervision.
🆂 🆂 ⊠ 🍴

CIRCLEVILLE

♦♦♦ Butch Cassidy's Hideout Ⓜ ❀
(435) 577-2008. **$48-$52.** 339 S Hwy 89. S end of town. Ext corridors. **Pets:** Very small. $50 deposit/room. No service, supervision, crate.
🅰🆂🅺 🆂 ⊠ 🍴

CLEARFIELD

♦♦ Clearfield Super 8 Ⓜ ❀
(801) 825-8000. **$40-$65.** 572 N Main. W of I-15, exit 338. Int corridors. **Pets:** Other. $20 deposit/room. Supervision.
⊠ 🕸 🖍 🍴

DELTA

♦♦♦ Best Western Motor Inn Ⓜ ❀
(435) 864-3882. **$41-$63.** 527 E Topaz Blvd. US 6, at jct US 50. Ext corridors. **Pets:** $10 deposit/room. Designated rooms, no service, supervision, crate.
🆂 ⊠ 🍴 🎨

DUCK CREEK VILLAGE

♦♦ Duck Creek Village Inn Ⓜ
(435) 682-2565. **$49-$64.** Hwy 14. 30 mi e of Cedar City on Hwy 14. Ext corridors. **Pets:** Small. No service, supervision, crate.
⊠ 🍴 🎟 🌀

♦♦ The Inn at Cedar Mountain Ⓜ
(435) 682-2378. **$79-$90.** 31 mi e of Cedar City in Cedar Mountain Village; 11 mi w of US 89; 0.3 mi s of SR 14, via Cedar Mt Rd. Ext corridors. **Pets:** Medium. Supervision.
🅰🆂🅺 🆂 🍴 💻 ⊠ 🎟 🄲🅃🅅 🌀

♦♦ Pinewoods Resort 🅇
(435) 682-2512. **$79-$90.** 121 Duck Greek Ridge Rd. Just s of SR 14 via Cedar Mt Rd, 31 mi e of Cedar City in Cedar Mountain Village; 10 mi w of jct US 89. Ext/int corridors. **Pets:** Designated rooms, no service, supervision, crate.
🅰🆂🅺 🆂 ⊠ 🍴 💻 ⊠ 🎟 🌀

ESCALANTE

◆◆ **Rainbow Country Bed & Breakfast Inn** 🅱🅱 ❀
(435) 826-4567. **$50-$65, 3 days notice.** 586 E 300 S. Just off SR 12. Int corridors. **Pets:** No service, supervision, crate.
🆂🅺 🆂🅾 ⊠ 🄰🄲 🄲🅃🅅 ⊠

FILLMORE

🆂 ◆◆◆ **Best Western Paradise Inn** 🅼 ❀
(435) 743-6895. **$51-$71.** 905 N Main. I-15, exit 167, just e. Ext corridors. **Pets:** Medium. Supervision.
🆂🅰🆅🅴 🆂🅾 ⊠ 🄳 🍴 🅰 ⊠

◆ **Fillmore Motel** 🅼
(435) 743-5454. **$32-$43.** 61 N Main St. E of I-15; exits 163 or 167. Ext corridors. **Pets:** No service, supervision, crate.
🆂🅺 🆂🅾 ⊠ 🄳

FRY CANYON

🆂 ◆◆ **Fry Canyon Lodge** 🅼 ❀
(435) 259-5334. **$74-$89.** Hwy 95. 22 mi w of Natural Bridges National Monument at MM 71, Hwy 95. Ext corridors. **Pets:** $10 daily fee/pet. No service, supervision, crate.
🆂🅰🆅🅴 ⊠ 🍴 🄰🄲 🄲🅃🅅 ⊠

GREEN RIVER

🆂 ◆ **Motel 6** 🅼
(435) 564-3436. **$46-$61.** 946 E Main. Ext corridors. **Pets:** Medium. No service, supervision, crate.
⊠ 🄲 🄳 🅰

🆂 ◆◆◆ **Super 8 Motel** 🅼
(435) 564-8888. **$60-$65, 21 days notice.** 1248 E Main. I-70, exit 162. Int corridors. **Pets:** No service, supervision, crate.
🆂🅰🆅🅴 🆂🅾 ⊠ 🄿 🄲 🄳 🅰

HATCH

🆂 ◆◆ **Riverside Motel** 🅼 ❀
(435) 735-4223. **$42-$50, 3 days notice.** 594 US Hwy 89. 1 mi n on US 89; at the Riverside Campground. Ext corridors. **Pets:** Small, other. $200 deposit/room, $5 one-time fee/pet. Designated rooms, no service, supervision, crate.
🆂🅾 ⊠ 🄳 🍴 ⊠ 🄲🅃🅅 ⊠

HEBER CITY

🆂 ◆◆ **National 9 High Country Inn** 🅼
(435) 654-0201. **Call for rates.** 1000 S Main. On US 40E. Ext corridors. **Pets:** No service, supervision, crate.
🆂🅰🆅🅴 ⊠ 🄳 🅰

🆂 ◆◆ **Swiss Alps Inn** 🅼 ❀
(435) 654-0722. **$40-$65.** 167 S Main. Ext corridors. **Pets:** Other. No service, supervision, crate.
🆂🅾 ⊠ 🄳 🅰 ⊠

HURRICANE

◆◆ **Best Western Weston Lamplighter** 🅼
(435) 635-4647. **$47-$169.** 280 W State. Just w on SR 9. Ext corridors. **Pets:** Supervision.
🆂🅺 🆂🅾 ⊠ 🄳 🄳 🅰

◆◆◆ **Motel 6–4050** 🅼
(435) 635-4010. **$49-$89.** 650 W State. Just w on SR 9. Ext corridors. **Pets:** Medium. Supervision.
🆂🅺 ⊠ 🄳 🄳 🅰

◆◆ **Westons Inn** 🅼
(435) 635-0808. **Call for rates.** 65 S 700 W. Just s of SR 9. Ext corridors. **Pets:** Small. Designated rooms, supervision.
⊠ 🄲 🄳 🄳 🅰

KANAB

🆂 ◆◆ **Aikens Lodge National 9** 🅼 ❀
(435) 644-2625. **$38-$51.** 79 W Center St. US 89. Ext corridors. **Pets:** Small, dogs only. $10 one-time fee/pet. No service, supervision, crate.
⊠ 🄲 🅰

🆂 ◆ **Bob-Bon Inn** 🅼
(435) 644-5094. **$40-$57.** 236 Hwy 89 N. On US 89. Ext corridors. **Pets:** Medium. Designated rooms, no service, supervision, crate.
⊠ 🄳

◆ **Color Country Inn** 🅼
(435) 644-2164. **$35-$40.** 1550 S US 89A. 1.5 mi s on US 89A. Int corridors. **Pets:** Small. No service, supervision, crate.
🆂🅺 🆂🅾 ⊠

🆂 ◆ **Four Seasons Motel & Restaurant** 🅼 ❀
(435) 644-2635. **$65-$74.** 36 N 300 W. Ext corridors. **Pets:** Small. $20 deposit/room. No service, supervision, crate.
🆂🅰🆅🅴 🆂🅾 ⊠ 🄳 🍴 🅰

◆◆◆ **Holiday Inn Express** 🅼
(435) 644-8888. **$80-$89.** 815 E Hwy 89. Just e on US 89. Int corridors. **Pets:** Supervision.
🆂🅺 🆂🅾 ⊠ 🄲 🄳 🄳 🅰 ⊠

🆂 ◆ **Kanab Mission Motel** 🅼 ❀
(435) 644-5373. **$42-$52.** 386 E 300 S. Int corridors. **Pets:** Dogs only. No service, supervision, crate.
🆂🅰🆅🅴 🆂🅾 ⊠ 🄲🅃🅅

🆂 ◆◆ **K Motel** 🅼
(435) 644-2611. **$37-$59.** 300 S 100 E. Jct of US 89 and 89A. Ext corridors. **Pets:** Supervision.
🆂🅾 ⊠ 🄳 🅰

◆◆ **Parry Lodge** 🅼 ❀
(435) 644-2601. **$48-$75.** 89 E Center St. Center, on US 89, corner of 100 E. Ext/int corridors. **Pets:** Medium, other. $20 deposit/room, $5 daily fee/pet. Designated rooms, supervision.
🆂🅺 🆂🅾 ⊠ 🄳 🄳 🍴 🅰

🆂 ◆◆ **Quail Park Lodge** 🅼
(435) 644-5094. **$32-$52, 3 days notice.** 125 Hwy 89 N. US 89. Ext corridors. **Pets:** Small. No service, supervision, crate.
⊠ 🄳 🅰

◆◆◆ **Shilo Inn** 🅼
(435) 644-2562. **$49-$149.** 296 West 100 North. On US 89. Int corridors. **Pets:** No service, supervision, crate.
🆂🅺 🆂🅾 ⊠ 🄿 🄳 🄳 🅰

(AAA) ◆ Sun N Sand Motel M ☼
(435) 644-5050. **$34-$48.** 347 S 100 E. Jct Hwy 89 and 89A. Ext corridors. **Pets:** Large, other. $10 deposit/room, $5 one-time fee/room. Designated rooms, no service, supervision, crate.

(S⊘) (✕) (🔊) (☎) (🐾)

(AAA) ◆◆ Treasure Trail M
(435) 644-2687. **$40-$58.** 150 W Center St. Center of downtown. Ext corridors. **Pets:** Small. No service, supervision, crate.

(S⊘) (✕) (🔊) (☎)

LAKE POWELL

◆◆◆ Defiance House-Bullfrog Marina M⊡
(435) 684-3000. **$124-$124.** Bullfrog Marina. 70 mi s of Hanksville and 44 mi s off Hwy 95; on Hwy 276. Int corridors. **Pets:** No service, supervision, crate.

(✕) (💻) (🍴) (🐾)

LAYTON

(AAA) ◆◆◆ Comfort Inn M ☼
(801) 544-5577. **$48-$75.** 877 N 400 W. E of I-15 exit 334. Int corridors. **Pets:** Very small, dogs only. Supervision.

(SAVE) (S⊘) (✕) (🔊) (☎) (💻) (🐾)

◆◆◆ Hampton Inn M
(801) 775-8800. **$79-$89.** 1700 N Woodland Park D. I-15, exit 335, 0.3 mi se. Int corridors. **Pets:** No service, supervision, crate.

(ASK) (✕) (🔊) (☎) (💻) (🐾)

◆◆◆ Holiday Inn Express M ☼
(801) 773-3773. **$75-$105.** 1695 Woodland Park Dr. I-15, exit 335, 0.25 mi se. Int corridors. **Pets:** Medium. No service, supervision, crate.

(ASK) (S⊘) (✕) (🔊) (☎) (💻) (🐾)

◆◆◆ La Quinta Inn M
(801) 776-6700. **$65-$85.** 1965 N 1200 West. 1 blk e of I-15 exit 335; corner Antelope Dr and Angel Rd. Int corridors. **Pets:** Designated rooms, no service, supervision, crate.

(ASK) (✕) (🔊) (☎) (💻) (🐾)

◆◆◆ Towne Place Suites M
(801) 779-2422. **Call for rates.** 1743 Woodland Park Blvd. I-15, exit 335, 0.3 mi se. Int corridors. **Pets:** Small. No service, supervision, crate.

(✕) (🔊) (☎) (💻) (🐾)

LEHI

(AAA) ◆◆◆ Best Western Timpanogos Inn M ☼
(801) 768-1400. **$63-$84.** 195 S 850 E. I-15 at exit 282, sw side. Int corridors. **Pets:** Other. $20 deposit/room, $5 daily fee/room. Designated rooms, no service, supervision, crate.

(SAVE) (S⊘) (✕) (🔊) (☎) (💻) (🐾)

(AAA) ◆◆ Motel 6–1405 M ☼
(801) 768-2668. **$42-$48.** 210 S 1200 E. I-15, exit 282, just e. Int corridors. **Pets:** Small, other. No service, supervision, crate.

(✕) (🔊) (☎) (🐾) (CTV)

◆◆◆ Super 8 M ☼
(801) 766-8800. **$60-$79.** 125 S 850 E. I-15, exit 282 sw side. Int corridors. **Pets:** $50 deposit/room. No service, supervision, crate.

(ASK) (S⊘) (✕) (🔊) (☎) (🐾)

LOGAN

(AAA) ◆◆◆ Best Western Weston Inn M ☼
(435) 752-5700. **$49-$69, 7 days notice.** 250 N Main. US 89 and 91. Ext corridors. **Pets:** Small. $5 daily fee/room. No service, supervision, crate.

(SAVE) (S⊘) (✕) (🔊) (☎) (💻) (🐾)

◆◆ Logan Days Inn M
(435) 753-5623. **Call for rates.** 364 S Main. US 89 and 91. Ext corridors. **Pets:** No service, supervision, crate.

(✕) (💻) (☎) (💻) (🐾)

MEXICAN HAT

(AAA) ◆◆ San Juan Inn M ☼
(435) 683-2220. **$68-$70.** Hwy 163 & San Juan River. On US 163. Ext corridors. **Pets:** Dogs only. Supervision.

(SAVE) (S⊘) (✕) (☎) (🍴) (🐾)

MOAB

(AAA) ◆◆ Apache Motel M ☼
(435) 259-5727. **$39-$85.** 166 S 400 East. Just e off US 191. Ext corridors. **Pets:** Medium. $25 deposit/room. No service, supervision, crate.

(✕) (☎) (🐾)

(AAA) ◆◆◆ Best Western Greenwell Inn M⊡ ☼
(435) 259-6151. **$45-$129.** 105 S Main St. US 191 at 100 S. Ext corridors. **Pets:** Small. $100 deposit/room. Designated rooms, no service, supervision, crate.

(SAVE) (✕) (🔊) (☎) (🍴) (🐾)

(AAA) ◆◆◆ Big Horn Lodge M ☼
(435) 259-6171. **$75-$80.** 550 S Main St. S end of town. Ext corridors. **Pets:** $5 daily fee/pet. No service, supervision, crate.

(SAVE) (S⊘) (✕) (☎) (💻) (🍴) (🐾)

◆◆ Bowen Motel M
(435) 259-7132. **$65-$75.** 169 N Main St. Ext corridors. **Pets:** Medium. No service, supervision, crate.

(✕) (☎) (🐾)

(AAA) ◆◆◆ Cedar Breaks Condos CO ☼
(435) 259-7830. **$90-$130, 7 days notice.** 50 E Center St. Just s off US 191. Ext corridors. **Pets:** No service, supervision, crate.

(✕) (☎) (💻) (🐾)

◆◆◆ Comfort Suites M
(435) 259-5252. **$89-$109.** 800 S Main St. Int corridors. **Pets:** Designated rooms, supervision.

(ASK) (S⊘) (✕) (🔊) (☎) (💻) (🐾)

(AAA) ◆◆◆ The Gonzo Inn M ☼
(435) 259-2515. **$120-$153.** 100 W 200 S. Downtown. Ext/int corridors. **Pets:** Other. $25 one-time fee/room. No service, supervision, crate.

(S⊘) (✕) (🔊) (☎) (💻) (🐾)

◆ Kokopelli Lodge 🅜 ❀
(435) 259-7615. **$54-$67, 7 days notice.** 725 100 E. Downtown. Ext corridors. **Pets:** Other. $5 daily fee/pet, $5 one-time fee/pet. No service, supervision, crate.
(SAVE) (X) (🖥) (💻)

◆◆◆ Moab Valley Inn 🅜 ❀
(435) 259-4419. **$80-$135.** 711 S Main St. S 1 mi on Hwy 191. Int corridors. **Pets:** Designated rooms, supervision.
(A$K) (S🖥) (X) (♿) (🖥) (💻) (🍽)

◆◆ Red Rock Lodge 🅜
(435) 259-5431. **$55-$65.** 51 N 100 W. Just w of Main. Ext/int corridors. **Pets:** No service, supervision, crate.
(SAVE) (S🖥) (X) (🖥) (💻)

◆◆ Red Stone Inn 🅜 ❀
(435) 259-3500. **$65-$70.** 535 S Main St. Int corridors. **Pets:** Other. $5 daily fee/pet. Designated rooms, no service, supervision, crate.
(SAVE) (S🖥) (X) (🖥) (💻)

◆◆ Rustic Inn 🅜 ❀
(435) 259-6177. **$45-$70.** 120 E 100 S. Ext corridors. **Pets:** Other. $5 daily fee/room. No service, supervision, crate.
(X) (🖥) (💻) (🍽)

◆◆ Sleep Inn 🅜 ❀
(435) 259-4655. **$70-$95.** 1051 S Main. S end of town. Int corridors. **Pets:** Designated rooms, supervision.
(A$K) (S🖥) (X) (♿) (🚭) (🖥) (💻) (🍽)

◆◆ The Virginian Motel 🅜 ❀
(435) 259-5951. **$53-$74.** 70 E 200 S. Just e of US 191. Ext corridors. **Pets:** Other. $10 daily fee/pet, $10 one-time fee/pet. No service, supervision, crate.
(SAVE) (S🖥) (X) (🖥) (💻)

MOUNT CARMEL JUNCTION

◆◆◆ Best Western Thunderbird Resort 🅜 ❀
(435) 648-2203. **$79-$93.** Jct US Hwy 89 & 9. Jct US 89 and 9. Ext corridors. **Pets:** Small. Designated rooms, supervision.
(S🖥) (X) (🍽) (🍽) (🍽)

◆◆ Golden Hills Motel 🅜 ❀
(435) 648-2268. **$40-$43.** US 89, jct SR 9. Ext/int corridors. **Pets:** Medium. No service, supervision, crate.
(SAVE) (X) (🍽) (🍽) (CTV)

NEPHI

◆◆ Best Western Paradise Inn 🅜
(435) 623-0624. **$51-$71.** 1025 S Main St. I-15, exit 222, 0.5 mi n. Ext corridors. **Pets:** Medium. No service, supervision, crate.
(SAVE) (S🖥) (X) (🖥) (🍽) (🍽)

◆◆ Motel 6 🅜
(435) 623-0666. **$43-$49.** 2195 S Main. S of I-15, exit 222. Int corridors. **Pets:** Supervision.
(A$K) (X) (🍽)

◆◆ Safari Motel 🅜 ❀
(435) 623-1071. **$32-$42.** 413 S Main St. 3 mi nw of I-15 exit 222. Ext corridors. **Pets:** Medium. $3 daily fee/pet, $3 one-time fee/pet. No service, supervision, crate.
(X) (🖥) (🍽)

OGDEN

◆◆◆ Best Rest Inn 🅜 ❀
(801) 393-8644. **$66-$66, 7 days notice.** 1206 W 21st St. Adjacent to and E of I-15, exit 346. Ext/int corridors. **Pets:** $20 deposit/room.
(A$K) (S🖥) (X) (🚭) (♿) (🖥) (🍽) (🍽)

◆◆◆ Best Western High Country Inn 🅜 ❀
(801) 394-9474. **$53-$69.** 1335 W 12th St. 12th St off-ramp, e of exit 347, I-15. Ext corridors. **Pets:** Other. $25 deposit/room. Supervision.
(SAVE) (S🖥) (X) (🚭) (🖥) (💻) (🍽) (🍽)

◆◆◆ Comfort Suites of Ogden 🅗
(801) 621-2545. **$83-$88.** 1150 W 2150 S. Adj to I-15 at exit 346E. Int corridors. **Pets:** Medium. Designated rooms, no service, supervision, crate.
(A$K) (S🖥) (X) (🚭) (♿) (🖥) (💻) (🍽) (🍽) (X)

◆◆◆ Historic Radisson Suite Hotel-Ogden 🅗 ❀
(801) 627-1900. **$119-$159, 3 days notice.** 2510 Washington Blvd. E of I-15, exit 344, 30th St, 2 mi ne via 31st St and Washington Blvd. Ext/int corridors. **Pets:** Medium. $50 deposit/pet. No service, supervision, crate.
(SAVE) (S🖥) (X) (🚭) (🖥) (💻) (🍽)

◆◆ Sleep Inn of Ogden 🅜
(801) 731-6500. **Call for rates.** 1155 S 1700 West. Exit 347, w of I-15. Int corridors. **Pets:** No service, supervision, crate.
(X) (🚭) (♿) (🖥) (💻) (🍽)

◆◆ Super 8 Motel 🅜 ❀
(801) 731-7100. **$40-$47.** 1508 W 2100 South. W of and adjacent to I-15, exit 346. Int corridors. **Pets:** Other. $20 deposit/room. Supervision.
(A$K) (S🖥) (X) (🚭) (♿)

◆◆ Western Colony Inn 🅜 ❀
(801) 627-1332. **$42-$49.** 234 24th St. City center. Ext corridors. **Pets:** Other. $20 deposit/room. Supervision.
(SAVE) (S🖥) (X) (🖥)

OREM

◆◆◆ Best Inn & Suites 🅜 ❀
(801) 235-9555. **$49-$89.** 1100 W 780 N. I-15 e side, exit 275. Int corridors. **Pets:** Medium. Designated rooms, supervision.
(SAVE) (S🖥) (X) (🚭) (♿) (🖥) (💻) (🍽)

◆◆◆ La Quinta Inn & Suites 🅜 ❀
(801) 226-0440. **$75-$95.** 521 W University Pkwy. I-15, exit 272 to 12th St, s 1 mi e. Int corridors. **Pets:** Small, other. $50 deposit/room. Designated rooms, no service, supervision, crate.
(A$K) (X) (🚭) (♿) (🖥) (💻) (🍽)

PANGUITCH

◆ Adobe Sands Motel M 🐾
(435) 676-8874. **$28-$54.** 390 N Main. Ext corridors.
Pets: Small. $20 deposit/room. No service, supervision,
crate.

PARK CITY
[SAVE] [S] [X]

◆◆ Color Country Motel M
(435) 676-2386. **$36-$52.** 526 N Main. On US 89. Ext
corridors. **Pets:** Supervision.
[X] [≈]

◆◆ Horizon Motel M 🐾
(435) 676-2651. **$50-$70.** 730 N Main. US 89. Ext corridors. **Pets:** Very small, dogs only. $10 one-time fee/room.
No service, supervision, crate.
[X] [B] [▣] [X]

◆ Marianna Inn Motel M
(435) 676-8844. **$35-$75.** 699 N Main St. On SR 89. Ext
corridors. **Pets:** Very small. Designated rooms, no service,
supervision, crate.
[SAVE] [X] [▣]

PARK CITY

◆◆◆ Best Western Landmark Inn MI 🐾
(435) 649-7300. **$139-$169, 21 days notice.** 6560 N Landmark Dr. Adjacent to I-80, at exit 145, 5 mi N of Park City.
Int corridors. **Pets:** Other. $25 deposit/room. Designated
rooms, supervision.
[SAVE] [S] [X] [♪] [B] [▣] [≈]

**◆◆◆ Holiday Inn Express Hotel &
Suites** M 🐾
(435) 658-1600. **$164-$210, 30 days notice.** 1501 W Ute
Blvd. I-80, exit 145, 5 mi n of Park City. Int corridors.
Pets: Other. $50 deposit/room. No service, supervision,
crate.
[ASK] [S] [X] [♪] [⌨] [B] [▣] [≈]

◆◆◆ Radisson Park City MI
(435) 649-5000. **$199-$219, 30 days notice.** 2121 Park
Ave. N end of town, I-80 at Kimball Juntion exit. Int corridors. **Pets:** Small. Supervision.
[SAVE] [S] [X] [♪] [B] [▣] [Ⅱ] [≈]

PAROWAN

**◆◆◆ Best Western Swiss Village
Inn** M 🐾
(435) 477-3391. **$54-$69, 3 days notice.** 580 N Main St.
Just e of I-15 exit 78. Ext corridors. **Pets:** Other. $5 daily
fee/pet, $5 one-time fee/pet. No service, supervision, crate.
[SAVE] [S] [X] [▣] [Ⅱ] [≈]

◆◆◆ Days Inn M 🐾
(435) 477-3326. **$42-$70.** 625 West 200 South. 1.5 mi e of
I-15, exit 75. Ext corridors. **Pets:** Medium, other. $10 daily
fee/pet. Supervision.
[SAVE] [S] [X] [B] [≈]

PAYSON

◆◆◆ Comfort Inn M 🐾
(801) 465-4861. **$66-$105.** 830 N Main. Just e of I-15 exit
254. Int corridors. **Pets:** $20 deposit/room. No service,
supervision, crate.
[ASK] [S] [X] [♪] [B] [▣] [≈]

PRICE

◆◆ Budget Host Inn M 🐾
(435) 637-2424. **$37-$44.** 145 N Carbonville Rd. E of and
adjacent to US 6, exit 240. Ext corridors. **Pets:** Very small,
dogs only. $5 daily fee/pet, $5 one-time fee/pet. No service,
supervision, crate.
[SAVE] [S] [X] [B] [≈]

◆◆ Greenwell Inn & Convention Center M
(435) 637-3520. **$39-$56.** 655 E Main. Ext/int corridors.
Pets: Very small. No service, supervision, crate.
[ASK] [S] [X] [B] [Ⅱ] [≈]

◆◆ National 9-Price River Inn M
(435) 637-7000. **$34-$49.** 641 W Price River Dr. US 6 exit
240 West Price. Ext/int corridors. **Pets:** Medium. Designated rooms, no service, supervision, crate.
[ASK] [S] [X] [B] [▣] [X]

PROVO

◆◆◆ Best Inn & Suites M 🐾
(801) 374-6020. **$65-$90.** 1555 Canyon Rd. 3.5 mi e of I-15
exit 272. Ext/int corridors. **Pets:** Small, other. $25 deposit/
room, $10 one-time fee/room. Supervision.
[SAVE] [S] [X] [♪] [B] [≈]

◆ Colony Inn Suites-National 9 M 🐾
(801) 374-6800. **$39-$59.** 1380 S University Ave. E of I-15,
exit 266. Ext corridors. **Pets:** Small. $25 deposit/pet, $5
daily fee/pet. Designated rooms, supervision.
[SAVE] [S] [X] [B] [≈]

◆◆◆ Days Inn M
(801) 375-8600. **$54-$74.** 1675 N 200W. 3.5 mi e of I-15
exit, 272; at Village Green Square. Ext corridors. **Pets:** Very
small. No service, supervision, crate.
[ASK] [S] [X] [♪] [⌨] [B] [▣] [≈]

◆◆◆ Hampton Inn M 🐾
(801) 377-6396. **$89, 3 days notice.** 1511 S 40 E. E of
I-15, exit 266. Int corridors. **Pets:** $7 one-time fee/pet. No
service, supervision, crate.
[ASK] [S] [X] [♪] [⌨] [B] [▣] [≈]

◆◆◆ Residence Inn by Marriott M 🐾
(801) 374-1000. **$79-$99.** 252 W 2230 N. From I-15, exit
272, 3.1 mi e via University Pkwy. Int corridors. **Pets:** Small.
$150 one-time fee/room. Supervision.
[ASK] [S] [X] [🐕] [♪] [⌨] [B] [▣] [≈] [X]

◆◆ Sleep Inn M 🐾
(801) 377-6597. **$45-$89.** 1505 S 40 E. E of I-15, exit 266.
Int corridors. **Pets:** Other. $7 one-time fee/room. Supervi-
sion.
[ASK] [S] [X] [♪] [⌨] [B] [▣]

▲▲▲ ◆◆ Uptown Motel Ⓜ ✿
(801) 373-8248. **$28-$70.** 469 W Center St. E of I-15, exit 268. Ext corridors. **Pets:** Medium, other. $4 daily fee/pet. Designated rooms, no service, supervision, crate.
[SAVE] [✕] [🛏] [⌂]

RICHFIELD

◆◆◆ Best Western AppleTree Inn Ⓜ
(435) 896-5481. **$69-$69.** 145 S Main St. US 89; s of I-70, exits 37 or 40. Ext corridors. **Pets:** Medium. Designated rooms, no service, supervision, crate.
[✕] [🛏] [⌂]

▲▲▲ ◆◆◆ Budget Host Nights Inn Ⓜ ✿
(435) 896-8228. **$38-$49.** 69 S Main St. S of I-70, exit 37 or 40, on US 89. Ext corridors. **Pets:** Other. Designated rooms, no service, supervision, crate.
[SAVE] [S] [✕] [🛏] [⌂]

▲▲▲ ◆ New West Motel Ⓜ ✿
(435) 896-4076. **$33-$41.** 447 S Main St. S of I-70, exits 37 or 40, on US 89. Ext corridors. **Pets:** $5 one-time fee/pet. Designated rooms, no service, supervision, crate.
[SAVE] [S] [✕]

▲▲▲ ◆◆ Romanico Inn Ⓜ
(435) 896-8471. **$34-$45.** 1170 S Main St. S of I-70, exit 37. Ext corridors. **Pets:** Medium. Designated rooms, supervision.
[SAVE] [S] [✕] [🛏]

ROOSEVELT

▲▲▲ ◆◆ Frontier Motel Ⓜ ✿
(435) 722-2201. **$36-$55.** 75 S 200 E. US 40. Ext corridors. **Pets:** Dogs only. No service, supervision, crate.
[✕] [🛏] [🍴] [⌂]

SALINA

▲▲▲ ◆◆ I.M.A. Henry's Hideway Ⓜ ✿
(435) 529-7467. **$48-$60.** 60 N State St. Center; 2.5 mi n of I-70, exit 54, on US 89. Ext corridors. **Pets:** Other. $20 deposit/room. Designated rooms, supervision.
[SAVE] [S] [✕] [🛏] [⌂]

◆ Ranch Motel Ⓜ
(435) 529-7789. **$33-$42.** 80 N State. ON US 89 near town center. Ext/int corridors. **Pets:** Medium. No service, supervision, crate.
[ASK] [S] [✕] [🛏]

◆◆ Scenic Hills Budget Host Ⓜ ✿
(435) 529-7483. **$42-$55.** 75 E 1500 S. I-70, exit 54, 1 blk. Ext corridors. **Pets:** Other. $6 daily fee/pet. Supervision.
[✕] [🛏] [⌂]

SALT LAKE CITY METROPOLITAN AREA

DRAPER

◆◆ Ramada Ltd Ⓜ ✿
(801) 571-1122. **$45-$75.** 12605 S Minuteman Dr. I-15 at exit 294, s 0.3 mi on Frontage Rd. Int corridors. **Pets:** Small. $20 deposit/room, $5 one-time fee/room. No service, supervision, crate.
[ASK] [S] [✕] [⌂] [⌂] [🛏] [💻]

MIDVALE

▲▲▲ ◆◆◆ Best Western Executive Inn Ⓜ
(801) 566-4141. **$69-$99.** 280 W 7200 South. State St w, 0.8 mi on 72nd so. Int corridors. **Pets:** Medium. No service, supervision, crate.
[SAVE] [S] [✕] [⌂] [🛏] [💻] [⌂]

▲▲▲ ◆◆◆ Discovery Inn Ⓜ ✿
(801) 561-2256. **$57-$69.** 380 W 7200 South. State St w, 0.8 mi on 72nd s. Ext corridors. **Pets:** Small. Supervision.
[SAVE] [S] [✕] [⌂] [🛏] [💻] [⌂]

◆◆◆ Homewood Suites Ⓗ ✿
(801) 561-5999. **$107-$116.** 844 E N Union Ave. State st e 1 mi via 72nd s and Fort Union Blvd. Int corridors. **Pets:** Small. $75 one-time fee/room. Supervision.
[ASK] [S] [✕] [⌂] [⌂] [⌂] [🛏] [💻] [⌂] [✕]

◆◆◆ La Quinta Inn Ⓜ
(801) 566-3291. **$65-$85.** 530 Catalpa Rd. E of I-15, exit 301. Int corridors. **Pets:** Medium. Designated rooms, supervision.
[ASK] [✕] [⌂] [⌂] [🛏] [💻] [⌂]

MURRAY

◆◆ Homestead Village Ft. Union Ⓜ ✿
(801) 685-2102. **$59-$84.** 975 E 6600 S. I-215 at exit 7 n on 900 e 0.5 mi. Ext corridors. **Pets:** Small. $150 deposit/pet, $11 daily fee/pet, $75 one-time fee/pet. Supervision.
[✕] [⌂] [⌂] [🛏] [💻]

▲▲▲ ◆◆◆ Quality Inn-Midvalley Ⓜ ✿
(801) 268-2533. **$60-$90.** 4465 Century Dr. W from State St 0.8 mi on 4500 s. Int corridors. **Pets:** Small, other. $25 deposit/room, $5 daily fee/pet. No service, supervision, crate.
[SAVE] [S] [✕] [⌂] [🛏] [💻] [⌂]

▲▲▲ ◆◆◆ Reston Hotel Ⓜ ✿
(801) 264-1054. **$61-$65.** 5335 College Dr. I-15 exit 303 w 0.3 mi. Int corridors. **Pets:** Other. $30 one-time fee/room. Supervision.
[S] [✕] [⌂] [🛏] [🍴] [⌂]

NORTH SALT LAKE

▲▲▲ ◆◆◆ Best Western Cotton Tree Ⓜ ✿
(801) 292-7666. **$69-$79.** 1030 N 400E. Exit I-15 #318, 10 mi n of city. Int corridors. **Pets:** Small. $25 deposit/room. Designated rooms, supervision.
[SAVE] [S] [✕] [⌂] [🛏] [💻] [⌂]

SALT LAKE CITY

◆◆ Alpine Executive Suites
(801) 533-8184. **$99-$149, 30 days notice.** 150 S 900 E. Cross sts 200 s and 900 e. Ext/int corridors. **Pets:** Dogs only. $300 deposit/pet. Designated rooms, no service, supervision, crate.

◆◆◆ Best Inn & Suites
(801) 355-4567. **$60-$65.** 1009 S Main St. Cross streets S 10th and Main. Ext/int corridors. **Pets:** Medium, other. $100 deposit/pet. Designated rooms, no service, supervision, crate.

◆◆◆ Best Western Salt Lake Plaza
(801) 521-0130. **$99-$119, 3 days notice.** 122 W So Temple. Downtown w of Temple Sq. Int corridors. **Pets:** Small. Designated rooms, no service, supervision, crate.

◆◆◆ Chase Suite Hotel
(801) 532-5511. **$135-$135.** 765 East 400 S. Ext corridors. **Pets:** Medium, other. $150 deposit/room, $5 daily fee/pet. Supervision.

◆◆◆ Comfort Inn-Salt Lake City International Airport
(801) 537-7444. **$77-$97.** 200 N Admiral Byrd Rd. I-80 exit 113N, E Amelia Earhart, 0.3 mi s. Int corridors. **Pets:** Small. $25 deposit/room. No service, supervision, crate.

◆◆◆ Days Inn-Salt Lake City Airport
(801) 539-8538. **$63-$89.** 1900W N Temple. W of Temple 59, 2.5 mi on n Temple. Int corridors. **Pets:** Other. $20 deposit/room. Designated rooms, no service, supervision, crate.

◆◆◆ Doubletree Hotel Salt Lake City
(801) 328-2000. **$79-$169.** 255 S W Temple. Int corridors. **Pets:** Medium. No service, supervision, crate.

◆◆ Econo Lodge
(801) 363-0062. **$49-$69.** 715 W N Temple. W from Temple Sq 2 mi on n Temple. Ext corridors. **Pets:** Medium. $30 deposit/room, supervision, supervision.

◆◆◆ Hilton Salt Lake City
(801) 532-3344. **$89-$99.** 150 W 5th S. At 200 W. Int corridors. **Pets:** Other. $50 one-time fee/room. Designated rooms, no service, supervision, crate.

◆◆ Homestead Village Redwood
(801) 269-9292. **$59-$79.** 5683 S Redwood Rd. I-215 at exit 13 n 0.5 mi. Ext corridors. **Pets:** Small. $75 deposit/pet, $75 one-time fee/pet. Supervision.

◆◆ Homestead Village-Sugarhouse
(801) 474-0771. **$54-$69.** 1220 E 2100 S. Cross sts 1300 E and 2100 S Sugarhouse. Ext corridors. **Pets:** Small. $15 daily fee/room, $75 one-time fee/room. Designated rooms, supervision.

◆◆◆ Hotel Monaco
(801) 595-0000. **$139-$149.** 15 W 200 S. Downtown, cross sts 200 S and Main. Int corridors. **Pets:** No service, supervision, crate.

◆◆◆ Howard Johnson Express Inn
(801) 521-3450. **$59-$89.** 121 N 300 W. At North Temple. Ext/int corridors. **Pets:** Small. No service, supervision, crate.

◆◆◆ La Quinta Inn & Suites Salt Lake City Airport
(801) 366-4444. **$85-$105.** 4905 W Wiley Post Way. I-80, exit 114, 0.3 mi nw. Int corridors. **Pets:** Designated rooms, supervision.

◆◆ Microtel Inn & Suites
(801) 236-2800. **$45-$60.** 61 N Tommy Thompson Rd. I-80, exit 114, n on Wright Brothers Dr following signs. Int corridors. **Pets:** Small. $25 deposit/room. No service, supervision, crate.

◆◆◆ Quality Inn-City Center
(801) 521-2930. **$49-$104.** 154 W 600 S. Between 100-200 W. Ext/int corridors. **Pets:** No service, supervision, crate.

◆◆ Ramada Inn Downtown
(801) 364-5200. **$59-$59.** 230 W 600 S. Ext/int corridors. **Pets:** Medium. Supervision.

◆◆ Red Brick Inn
(801) 322-4917. **$60-$120, 7 days notice.** 1030 E 100S. E side of town, cross street McClelland. Int corridors. **Pets:** Small, dogs only. Supervision.

◆◆◆ Residence Inn by Marriott at The Cottonwoods
(801) 453-0430. **Call for rates.** 6425 S 3000 E. I-215S, exit 6200 S, 0.3 mi se to 3000 E. Int corridors. **Pets:** Small. No service, supervision, crate.

◆◆ Salt Lake City Centre Travelodge
(801) 531-7100. **Call for rates.** 524 S West Temple. Ext corridors. **Pets:** Medium. No service, supervision, crate.

◆ Salt Lake Travelodge At Temple Square
(801) 533-8200. **$49-$85.** 144 W N Temple. 1/2 blk n of Genealogical Library. Ext/int corridors. **Pets:** Other. No service, supervision, crate.

♦♦ The Skyline Inn M ❀
(801) 582-5350. **$57-$69.** 2475 E 1700 S. E off Foothill Dr, at 1700 s. Ext corridors. **Pets:** Supervision.

♦♦ Sugar House Village-All Suites Inn M ❀
(801) 486-9976. **$69-$129, 3 days notice.** 1339 E 2100 S. Cross street 1400 E. Ext/int corridors. **Pets:** Small. Supervision.

♦♦♦ Super 8 Airport M ❀
(801) 533-8878. **$65-$73.** 223 N Jimmy Doolittle Rd. I-80, exit 113. Int corridors. **Pets:** $50 deposit/room. Supervision.

♦♦ Super 8 Motel M ❀
(801) 534-0808. **$40-$53, 3 days notice.** 616 S 200 West. Int corridors. **Pets:** $50 deposit/room. Designated rooms, no service, supervision, crate.

SANDY

♦♦♦ Best Western Cottontree Inn M ❀
(801) 523-8484. **$69-$79.** 10695 S Automall Dr. I-15, exit 297 e 0.3 mi. Int corridors. **Pets:** Small, dogs only. $10 one-time fee/room. Designated rooms, no service, supervision, crate.

♦♦♦ Comfort Inn M
(801) 255-4919. **$54-$76.** 8955 S 255 West. W from State St, 0.5 mio n 90th so. Int corridors. **Pets:** Medium. Designated rooms, no service, supervision, crate.

♦♦♦ Quality Inn & Suites M ❀
(801) 495-1317. **$70-$80.** 10680 S Automall Dr. I-15, exit 297, e 0.3 mi. Int corridors. **Pets:** Medium, other. $10 daily fee/pet. No service, supervision, crate.

♦♦♦ Residence Inn M
(801) 561-5005. **Call for rates.** 270 W 10000 S. W from Stare St, 0.3 mi on 1000 s. Int corridors. **Pets:** Small. No service, supervision, crate.

♦♦♦ Sandy-Hampton Inn M
(801) 571-0800. **Call for rates.** 10690 S Holiday Park Dr. I-15 exit 297E. Int corridors. **Pets:** Supervision.

♦♦♦ Super 8 Motel-South Jordan M ❀
(801) 553-8888. **$59-$64.** 10722 S 300 W. State st W, 1 mi on 106th to Frontage Rd. Int corridors. **Pets:** Small. $50 deposit/room. Designated rooms, no service, supervision, crate.

SOUTH SALT LAKE

♦♦♦ Days Inn-Central M
(801) 486-8780. **$49-$75.** 315 W 3300 South. W from State St, 0.3 mi. Ext corridors. **Pets:** Supervision.

WEST VALLEY

♦♦ Parkway Suites M ❀
(801) 977-0800. **$40-$99.** 3580 W Parkway Blvd. Cross streets 2700 s and 3600 w. Ext corridors. **Pets:** Medium. $100 deposit/room. Designated rooms, supervision.

♦♦ Sleep Inn M ❀
(801) 975-1888. **$55-$155.** 3440 S 2200 W. I-215, exit 18. Int corridors. **Pets:** Small. $10 deposit/room. Designated rooms, no service, supervision, crate.

WEST VALLEY CITY

♦♦♦ Baymont Inn & Suites-Salt Lake City M ❀
(801) 886-1300. **$66-$71.** 2229 W City Center Ct. I-215, exit 18; 0.3 mi e. Int corridors. **Pets:** Medium. $50 deposit/room. Designated rooms, no service, supervision, crate.

♦♦♦ Hawthorn Inn & Suites M
(801) 954-9292. **$80.** 3540 S 2200 W. I-215 e side, exit 18. Int corridors. **Pets:** Small. No service, supervision, crate.

❀ **END METROPOLITAN AREA** ❀

SPANISH FORK

♦♦♦ Western Inn M ❀
(801) 798-9400. **$55-$65.** 632 Kirby Ln. 0.5 mi e of I-15 at exit 261. Int corridors. **Pets:** Other. $10 one-time fee/room. Supervision.

SPRINGDALE

♦♦♦ Best Western Zion Park Inn M ❀
(435) 772-3200. **$83-$97.** 1215 Zion Park Blvd. 2 mi s of park entrance. Int corridors. **Pets:** Medium. $25 one-time fee/room. Designated rooms, no service, supervision, crate.

♦♦♦ Canyon Ranch Motel C
(435) 772-3357. **$58-$88.** 668 Zion Park Blvd. SR 9, just s of South Gate to Zion N P. Ext corridors. **Pets:** Small. Supervision.

♦♦♦ Driftwood Lodge M ❀
(435) 772-3262. **$72-$102.** 1515 Zion Park Blvd. SR 9, 2 mi s of south gate to Zion N.P.. Ext corridors. **Pets:** No service, supervision, crate.

Flanigan's Inn & Cafe  **M**
(435) 772-3244. **$79-$99.** 428 Zion Park Blvd. Just s of South Gate to Zion N P. Ext corridors. **Pets:** Medium, other. $25 one-time fee/room. No service, supervision, crate.

SPRINGVILLE

Best Western Cottontree Inn M
(801) 489-3641. **$64-$88, 7 days notice.** 1455 N 1750 W. E of I-15 exit 265, just s of Provo. Int corridors. **Pets:** Small, other. $15 deposit/room, $5 one-time fee/room. No service, supervision, crate.

Days Inn M
(801) 491-0300. **$39-$59.** 520 S 2000 W. From I-15 at exit 263. Int corridors. **Pets:** Supervision.

ST. GEORGE

Ambasador Inn M
(435) 673-7900. **$40-$70.** 1481 S Sunland Dr. I-15, exit 6. Int corridors. **Pets:** Other. $25 deposit/room, $10 daily fee/room. Designated rooms, supervision.

An Olde Penny Farthing BB
(435) 673-7755. **$45-$95, 3 days notice.** 278 N 100 W. Historical district. Int corridors. **Pets:** No service, supervision, crate.

Atkin's Singletree Inn M
(435) 673-6161. **$58-$72.** 260 E St. George Blvd. 1.5 mi w of I-15, exit 8. Ext corridors. **Pets:** Medium. $5 daily fee/room, $5 one-time fee/room. No service, supervision, crate.

The Bluffs Motel M
(435) 628-6699. **$39-$89.** 1140 S Bluff. W of I-15, Bluff St exit 6. Ext corridors. **Pets:** Very small. $15 daily fee/pet, $15 one-time fee/pet. Designated rooms, no service, supervision, crate.

Budget Inn & Suites M
(435) 673-6661. **Call for rates.** 1221 S Main St. W of I-15, Bluff St, exit 6. Ext corridors. **Pets:** Supervision.

The Coyote Inn at Green Valley Spa R
(435) 628-8060. **$500-$900.** 1871 W Canyon View Dr. From Bluff at S Main, 4 mi sw via Hilton Dr to Tonaquint Dr, to Dixie Dr to Canyon View Dr. Ext corridors. **Pets:** Medium, other. $300 deposit/room, $25 daily fee/room. Supervision.

Days Inn & Thunderbird Art Gallery M
(435) 673-6123. **$46-$76.** 150 N 1000 E. Just w of I-15 exit 8, St George Blvd. Ext corridors. **Pets:** Small, other. $20 deposit/room, $5 one-time fee/room. No service, supervision, crate.

Econolodge M
(435) 673-4861. **$35-$49.** 460 E St George Blvd. Downtown; cross sts 500 E and St George Blvd. Ext corridors. **Pets:** No service, supervision, crate.

Holiday Inn/Holidome M
(435) 628-4235. **$69-$109, 3 days notice.** 850 S Bluff St. Just w of I-15, Bluff St exit 6. Ext/int corridors. **Pets:** Small. Supervision.

Sheraton Four Points Hotel M
(435) 628-0463. **$94-$104.** 1450 S Hilton Dr. Just w of I-15, Bluff St exit 6. Int corridors. **Pets:** Medium. Designated rooms, supervision.

Super 8 Motel M
(435) 628-4251. **Call for rates.** 915 S Bluff. W of I-15, Bluff St exit 6. Int corridors. **Pets:** No service, supervision, crate.

Travelodge East M
(435) 673-4621. **$36-$99, 3 days notice.** 175 N 1000 East. Just w of I-15, St George Blvd exit 8. Ext corridors. **Pets:** $5 daily fee/pet. No service, supervision, crate.

TORREY

Cactus Hill Motel M
(435) 425-3578. **$38-$45, 3 days notice.** 830 S 1000 E. 5 mi s of Sr 24, 5 mi w of SR 12, exit Teasdale; 13 mi w of Capitol Reef National Park, 2 mi se of Town Center. Ext corridors. **Pets:** Small, dogs only. $25 deposit/room. Designated rooms, supervision.

TREMONTON

Marble Motel M
(435) 257-3524. **$35-$45.** 116 N Tremont St. I-15 and 84 N, exit 379, 3.5 mi via Cross Roads Blvd and Main; I-15 S, exit 383 2.5 mi via 1000 N and Main. Ext corridors. **Pets:** No service, supervision, crate.

Sandman Motel M
(435) 257-7149. **$42-$50.** 585 W Main. I-15 and I-84, Tremonton exit 383. Ext corridors. **Pets:** Medium, other. $20 deposit/pet. No service, supervision, crate.

TROPIC

Dougs Country Inn Motel M
(435) 679-8600. **$50-$50.** 141 N Main St. Center; on US 12. Int corridors. **Pets:** Medium, other. $10 one-time fee/pet. No service, supervision, crate.

World Host Bryce Valley Inn M
(435) 679-8811. **$57-$74.** 200 North & Main Sts. SR 12; 10 mi e of Bryce Canyon Park. Ext/int corridors. **Pets:** Other. $15 one-time fee/pet. No service, supervision, crate.

VERNAL

◆◆ Econolodge M
(435) 789-2000. **$51-$60.** 311 E Main St. Ext corridors.
Pets: Small. Supervision.
[ASK] [S̶ō] [✕] [🛏] [💻] [🍽]

◆◆ Rodeway Inn M ☼
(435) 789-8172. **$48-$60.** 590 W Main St. US 40. Ext corridors. **Pets:** Medium, other. $5 one-time fee/pet. No service, supervision, crate.
[ASK] [S̶ō] [✕] [🛏] [💻]

◆ Sage Motel & Restaurant MI ☼
(435) 789-1442. **Call for rates.** 54 W Main. Center. Ext corridors. **Pets:** Other. $5 daily fee/pet. Designated rooms, supervision.
[✕] [🛏] [🍽]

◆◆ Super 8 Motel M ☼
(435) 789-4326. **$50-$65.** 1624 W Hwy 40. W end of town. Int corridors. **Pets:** Small, other. Supervision.
[ASK] [S̶ō] [✕] [🍽]

WELLINGTON

◆◆ National 9 Inn MI
(435) 637-7980. **$34-$49.** 50 S 700 E. US 6. Ext/int corridors. **Pets:** Medium. Supervision.
[ASK] [S̶ō] [✕] [🛏] [🍽] [💻]

WENDOVER

AAA ◆◆◆ Days Inn of Wendover M ☼
(435) 665-2215. **$39-$79.** 685 E Wendover Blvd. In town; exit I-80 via Utah 2. Int corridors. **Pets:** Other. $5 daily fee/room. Supervision.
[SAVE] [✕] [🖉] [🛏] [💻]

◆◆◆ State Line Inn M
(435) 665-2226. **Call for rates.** 295 E Wendover Blvd. In town; exit 2, I-80. Ext/int corridors. **Pets:** No service, supervision, crate.
[✕] [💻]

CITY INDEX

BARRE

The Hollow Inn & Motel [M] ❀
(802) 479-9313. **$95-$105.** 278 S Main St. SR 14, 1 mi s of jct US 302; I-89, exit 6, 4.3 mi e on SR 63, 0.7 mi n on SR 14. Ext/int corridors. **Pets:** $10 daily fee/room. Designated rooms, supervision.

BENNINGTON

◆ **Apple Valley Inn & Cafe** [MI] ❀
(802) 442-6588. **$59-$79.** Rt 7. 2 mi s on US 7. Ext/int corridors. **Pets:** Supervision.

◆◆ **Bennington Motor Inn** [M] ❀
(802) 442-5479. **$78-$86.** 143 W Main St, (SR 9). 0.3 mi w on SR 9 from jct US 7. Ext corridors. **Pets:** Small. $15 daily fee/room. Designated rooms, supervision.

◆◆◆ **Darling Kelly's Motel** [M] ❀
(802) 442-2322. **$79-$85, 3 days notice.** 357 US 7 S. 1.3 mi s. Ext corridors. **Pets:** Dogs only. Designated rooms, no service, supervision, crate.

◆◆◆ **Fife 'N Drum Motel** [M]
(802) 442-4074. **$72-$98, 3 days notice.** US 7. 1.5 mi s on US 7 from jct of SR 9. Ext corridors. **Pets:** Supervision.

◆◆ **Knotty Pine Motel** [M] ❀
(802) 442-5487. **$70-$84.** 130 Northside Dr. Jct SR 9, 1.2 mi n on US 7, then just n on Historic SR 7A. Ext corridors. **Pets:** Other. Supervision.

◆ **Pleasant Valley Motel** [C] ❀
(802) 442-6222. **$40-$48.** Pleasant Valley Rd. 3.8 mi w on SR 9, 0.3 mi s. Ext corridors. **Pets:** Other. Supervision.

◆◆ **South Gate Motel** [M] ❀
(802) 447-7525. **$54-$89, 3 days notice.** US 7 S. 1.5 mi s. Ext corridors. **Pets:** $6 daily fee/pet, $6 one-time fee/pet. Designated rooms, supervision.

BRADFORD

◆◆ **Bradford Motel** [M] ❀
(802) 222-4467. **$48-$58, 7 days notice.** Rt 5. I-91, exit 16, 0.8 mi n. Ext corridors. **Pets:** No service, supervision, crate.

BRATTLEBORO

◆◆ **Colonial Motel & Spa** [MI] ❀
(802) 257-7733. **$60-$95.** 889 Putney (US 5) Rd. I-91, exit 3, 0.5 mi s on US 5. Ext corridors. **Pets:** $10 daily fee/room. Supervision.

CAVENDISH

◆◆◆ **Cavendish Pointe Hotel** [MI]
(802) 226-7688. **$139-$209.** SR 103. At jct SR 103 and 131. Int corridors. **Pets:** No service, supervision, crate.

COLCHESTER

◆◆◆ **Hampton Inn Hotel & Conference Center** [MI]
(802) 655-6177. **$99-$109.** 8 Mountain View Dr. I-89, exit 16. Int corridors. **Pets:** Supervision.

◆◆ **Motel 6–1407** [M] ❀
(802) 654-6860. **$38-$51.** 74 South Park Dr. I-89, exit 16, just e. Int corridors. **Pets:** Other. No service, supervision, crate.

CRAFTSBURY COMMON

◆◆◆ **The Inn on the Common** [CI] ❀
(802) 586-9619. **$245-$290.** Main St. Center of village. Int corridors. **Pets:** Other. $15 one-time fee/pet. Supervision.

ESSEX JUNCTION

◆◆◆ **The Wilson Inn** [M] ❀
(802) 879-1515. **$94-$134.** 10 Kellogg Rd. I-89, exit 15, 2.1 mi e on Rt 15, 0.5 mi n on Susie Wilson Rd, just w. Int corridors. **Pets:** Small. $10 daily fee/room. Designated rooms, supervision.

FAIRLEE

◆◆ Silver Maple Lodge & Cottages 🅱🅱 ❀
(802) 333-4326. **$52-$86.** 520 US 5 S. I-91, exit 15, 0.5 mi
s. Ext/int corridors. **Pets:** Other. Designated rooms, supervision.
🆂 ⊠ 🖥 💻 ⊠ 📺 🇿

JEFFERSONVILLE

🆂🆂🆂 ◆◆ Deer Run Motor Inn Ⓜ ❀
(802) 644-8866. **$55-$80.** 80 Deer Run Loop. 0.5 mi e on
SR 15. Ext/int corridors. **Pets:** $8 daily fee/pet, $8 one-time
fee/pet. No service, supervision, crate.
🆂 ⊠ 🖥 💻 🇿

KILLINGTON

🆂🆂🆂 ◆◆ Butternut on the Mountain Ⓜ
(802) 422-2000. **$65-$250, 30 days notice.** Killington &
Weathervane Rd. 1 mi s on Killington access road from US
4. Ext/int corridors. **Pets:** Designated rooms, no service,
supervision, crate.
⊠ 🖥 🇷 🇿

🆂🆂🆂 ◆◆◆ The Cascades Lodge Ⓜ ❀
(802) 422-3731. **$99-$199, 21 days notice.** 58 Old Mill Rd.
3.5 mi off Rt 4 on Killington Rd. Int corridors. **Pets:** Other.
$10 daily fee/room, $25 one-time fee/room. Designated
rooms, supervision.
🆂🅰🆅🅴 🆂 ⊠ 🇷 🖥 💻 🇿 ⊠

🆂🆂🆂 ◆◆ Val Roc Motel Ⓜ
(802) 422-3881. **$64-$120.** 8006 US 4. 0.3 mi w of jct SR
100 S. Ext/int corridors. **Pets:** Designated rooms, supervision.
🆂🅰🆅🅴 🆂 ⊠ 🖥 💻 🇿 ⊠

LUDLOW

🆂🆂🆂 ◆◆◆ Happy Trails Motel Ⓜ ❀
(802) 228-8888. **$100-$200.** 321 Rt 103 S. On SR 103, 1.6
mi e of jct SR 100. Ext/int corridors. **Pets:** Small, dogs only.
$10 daily fee/pet. No service, supervision, crate.
🆂🅰🆅🅴 🆂 ⊠ 🖥 💻

🆂🆂🆂 ◆◆◆ Timber Inn Motel Ⓜ
(802) 228-8666. **$59-$149.** 112 Rt 103S. 1 mi e on SR 103.
Ext corridors. **Pets:** Designated rooms, supervision.
⊠ 🖥 💻 🇿 ⊠

MENDON

◆◆◆ Cortina Inn and Resort Ⓜ ❀
(802) 773-3333. **$104-$199.** 103 US 4. US 4, 3 mi w of jct
SR 100 N. Int corridors. **Pets:** Other. $5 daily fee/pet. No
service, supervision, crate.
🅰🆂🅺 ⊠ 🇷 🖥 🇷 🇿 ⊠

🆂🆂🆂 ◆◆ Econo Lodge-Pico Ⓜ ❀
(802) 773-6644. **$56-$98, 7 days notice.** 51 US 4. US 4,
5.3 mi e of jct US 7. Int corridors. **Pets:** Medium, other. No
service, supervision, crate.
🆂🅰🆅🅴 🆂 ⊠ 💻 🇿

◆ Edelweiss Motel & Chalets Ⓜ ❀
(802) 775-5577. **$54-$115.** 119 Rt 4. US 4, 3 mi w of jct SR
100 N. Ext corridors. **Pets:** Other. $5 daily fee/pet, $5 one-
time fee/pet. Designated rooms, supervision.
🅰🆂🅺 🆂 ⊠ 🖥 💻 🇿

🆂🆂🆂 ◆◆◆ Mendon Mountainview Resort
             Lodge Ⓜ
(802) 773-4311. **$39-$139.** US 4. 6 mi e of jct US 7. Int
corridors. **Pets:** Supervision.
🆂🅰🆅🅴 🆂 ⊠ 🇷 🇿 ⊠

◆◆◆ Red Clover Inn 🇨🇮 ❀
(802) 775-2290. **$185-$450.** 7 Woodward Rd. 0.5 mi s of
US 4 on Woodward Rd, 5.3 mi e of jct US 7. Ext/int
corridors. **Pets:** Dogs only. $10 daily fee/pet, $10 one-time
fee/pet. Designated rooms, no service, supervision, crate.
⊠ 🇿 🇿

MIDDLEBURY

🆂🆂🆂 ◆◆◆ The Middlebury Inn 🇨🇮 ❀
(802) 388-4961. **$76-$355, 3 days notice.** 14 Court
Square. Center; on US 7. Ext/int corridors. **Pets:** Other. $6
daily fee/room. Supervision.
🆂🅰🆅🅴 🆂 ⊠ 🇷 🇷 🖥 💻 🇷

NEWFANE

◆◆◆ Four Columns Inn 🇨🇮
(802) 365-7713. **$140-$280.** 21 West St. Center; just w of
SR 30. Int corridors. **Pets:** Designated rooms, no service,
supervision, crate.
⊠ 🇿 ⊠ 📺

NEWPORT

🆂🆂🆂 ◆◆ Inn at the Hill Ⓜ
(802) 334-6748. **$75-$95.** 1724 E Main St. Ext/int corridors.
Pets: Supervision.
🆂🅰🆅🅴 🆂 ⊠ 🖥 ⊠

NORTH HERO

🆂🆂🆂 ◆◆ Shore Acres Inn Ⓜ ❀
(802) 372-8722. **$90-$139.** 237 Shore Acres Dr. 0.5 mi s on
US 2. Ext corridors. **Pets:** $5 daily fee/pet. No service,
supervision, crate.
⊠ 🖥 ⊠ 🇿

NORTH SPRINGFIELD

◆◆ The Abby Lyn Motel Ⓜ
(802) 886-2223. **$60-$75.** I-91, exit 7, 7 mi n on SR 106 at
jct SR 10. Ext corridors. **Pets:** Large. No service, supervision, crate.
🅰🆂🅺 🆂 ⊠ 🖥

PERU

◆◆ Johnny Seesaw's 🇱 ❀
(802) 824-5533. **$75-$200.** SR 11. 2.5 mi e on SR 11 from
jct of SR 30 and 11. Ext/int corridors. **Pets:** Medium, other.
$10 daily fee/pet. Designated rooms, no service, supervi-
sion, crate.
🖥 🇷 🇿 ⊠ 🇽 📺

PUTNEY

⊕ ◆◆◆ The Putney Inn **M** ✿
(802) 387-5517. **$98-$158.** 57 Putney Landing Rd. I-91, exit 4 norhtbound; exit 4 southbound, just n, then e. Ext corridors. **Pets:** Other. $10 daily fee/pet. Supervision.
[SAVE] [✕]

RUTLAND

⊕ ◆◆◆ The Best Western Inn &
Suites **M** ✿
(802) 773-3200. **$69-$139.** 3 mi e on US 4. Ext corridors. **Pets:** Other. $5 daily fee/pet, $25 one-time fee/pet. No service, supervision, crate.
[SAVE] [S6] [✕] [▣] [☎] [✕]

◆◆ Econo Lodge **M**
(802) 773-2784. **$49-$139, 30 days notice.** 238 S Main St. US 7, 2 mi s of jct US 4 E. Ext corridors. **Pets:** Medium. Supervision.
[ASK] [S6] [✕] [✆] [▣]

⊕ ◆◆ Green Mont Motel **M** ✿
(802) 775-2575. **$57-$110.** 138 N Main St. US 7, 0.5 mi n of jct US 4 E. Ext corridors. **Pets:** Small. $25 deposit/pet, $10 daily fee/pet, $10 one-time fee/pet. Designated rooms, no service, supervision, crate.
[SAVE] [S6] [✕] [✆] [☎]

⊕ ◆◆◆ Holiday Inn **M** ✿
(802) 775-1911. **$140-$218.** 476 US 7 S. 2.4 mi s on US 7 from US 4 W; 0.4 mi n, US 7 from US 4 E. Int corridors. **Pets:** $10 daily fee/room. No service, supervision, crate.
[SAVE] [S6] [✕] [✆] [▣] [▯] [☎]

◆◆ Howard Johnson **M** ✿
(802) 775-4303. **$109-$159.** 401 S Rt 7. 2.3 mi s on US 7. Int corridors. **Pets:** Small. No service, supervision, crate.
[ASK] [S6] [✕] [✇] [✆] [▣] [☎]

⊕ ◆◆◆ Ramada Limited of Rutland **M** ✿
(802) 773-3361. **$69-$151, 21 days notice.** 253 S Main St, US 7. 2 mi s on US 7. Ext/int corridors. **Pets:** Medium. No service, supervision, crate.
[SAVE] [S6] [✕] [▣] [☎]

⊕ ◆◆ Royal Motel **M** ✿
(802) 773-9176. **$37-$109, 7 days notice.** 115 Woodstock Ave. US 4 (Woodstock Ave), 0.5 mi e of jct US 7. Ext/int corridors. **Pets:** $5 daily fee/pet, $5 one-time fee/pet. No service, supervision, crate.
[SAVE] [S6] [✕] [✆] [☎]

SHAFTSBURY

◆◆ Hillbrook Motel **M** ✿
(802) 447-7201. **Call for rates.** Historic SR 7A. 1.8 mi n on Historic SR 7A from country store; set back from hwy. Ext corridors. **Pets:** Other. Designated rooms, no service, supervision, crate.
[✕] [✆] [☎] [☏]

⊕ ◆ Serenity Motel **C** ✿
(802) 442-6490. **$55-$80.** 4379 Rt 7A. 3.3 mi n on Historic SR 7A from SR 67. Ext corridors. **Pets:** Other. No service, supervision, crate.
[SAVE] [S6] [✆]

SOUTH BURLINGTON

⊕ ◆◆ Anchorage Inn **M** ✿
(802) 863-7000. **$68-$100.** 108 Dorset St. I-89, exit 14 E, 0.3 mi e. Int corridors. **Pets:** Dogs only. $50 deposit/pet. Designated rooms, supervision.
[SAVE] [✕] [✆] [☎]

⊕ ◆◆◆ Best Western Windjammer Inn &
Conference Center **M** ✿
(802) 863-1125. **$89-$179, 30 days notice.** 1076 Williston Rd. 1.3 mi e on US 2; 0.3 mi e of I-89, exit 14 E. Int corridors. **Pets:** Large, other. $5 daily fee/pet. Designated rooms, no service, supervision, crate.
[SAVE] [S6] [✕] [✇] [✈] [✆] [▣] [☎] [✕]

⊕ ◆◆◆ Clarion Hotel and Conference
Center **M** ✿
(802) 658-0250. **$159-$159.** 1117 Williston Rd. Just e on US 2 at jct I-89, exit 14 E. Int corridors. **Pets:** $50 deposit/room. No service, supervision, crate.
[SAVE] [S6] [✕] [✇] [✆] [▣] [☎]

⊕ ◆◆◆ Holiday Inn Burlington **M** ✿
(802) 863-6363. **$115-$146.** 1068 Williston Rd. Just off I-89, exit 14 E. Int corridors. **Pets:** Medium. $10 one-time fee/room. Supervision.
[SAVE] [S6] [✕] [✇] [▣] [▯] [☎]

◆◆◆ Sheraton-Burlington Hotel & Conference
Center **H** ✿
(802) 865-6600. **$200-$240.** 870 Williston Rd. US 2 at jct I-89, exit 14 W. Int corridors. **Pets:** Small. $100 deposit/room. No service, supervision, crate.
[ASK] [S6] [✕] [✇] [✆] [▣] [▯] [☎]

⊕ ◆◆ Town & Country Motel **M**
(802) 862-5786. **$65-$95.** 490 Shelburne Rd. 1.8 mi s on US 7; just n of jct I-189. Ext corridors. **Pets:** No service, supervision, crate.
[✆]

SOUTH WOODSTOCK

◆◆◆ Kedron Valley Inn **C** ✿
(802) 457-1473. **$186-$309, 7 days notice.** Rt 106. 5 mi s on SR 106. Ext/int corridors. **Pets:** Other. Supervision.
[✆] [▣] [✕] [CTV] [☏]

SPRINGFIELD

◆◆◆ Holiday Inn Express **M**
(802) 885-4516. **$99.** 818 Charlestown Rd. Jct I-91 and US 5, exit 7. Int corridors. **Pets:** Large. No service, supervision, crate.
[ASK] [S6] [✕] [✆] [▣] [☎]

ST. ALBANS

⊕ ◆◆ Econo Lodge **M**
(802) 524-5956. **$70-$95.** 287 S Main St. I-89, exit 19, 0.5 mi s on Rt 7. Ext/int corridors. **Pets:** Small. No service, supervision, crate.
[SAVE] [S6] [✕] [✆] [▣]

ST. JOHNSBURY

AAA ◆ **Aime's Motel** **M** ❀
(802) 748-3194. **$55-$70.** 46 VT Rt 18. US 2 at jct SR 18; 0.5 mi n of jct I-93, exit 1. Ext corridors. **Pets:** Other. Supervision.

◆◆◆ **Fairbanks Inn** **M** ❀
(802) 748-5666. **$95-$125.** 401 Western Ave. US 2; 1 mi e of jct I-91, exit 21. Ext corridors. **Pets:** Other. $5 daily fee/pet. Designated rooms, supervision.
⊠ 🖥 📺 📬

◆◆ **Holiday Motel** **M** ❀
(802) 748-8192. **$45-$95.** 222 Hastings St. Jct US 5 and Alt 5. Ext corridors. **Pets:** Dogs only. $10 daily fee/pet. Designated rooms, no service, supervision, crate.
⊠ 📬

STOWE

AAA ◆◆ **Andersen Lodge-An Austrian Inn** **CI** ❀
(802) 253-7336. **$78-$178.** 3430 Mountain Rd. SR 108, 3.5 mi nw of jct SR 100. Int corridors. **Pets:** Small, dogs only. $10 daily fee/room. No service, supervision, crate.
SAVE S⊠ 🖥 📺 🍴 📬 ⊠ CTV

AAA ◆◆ **Commodores Inn** **MI** ❀
(802) 253-7131. **$78-$248, 30 days notice.** 823 Main St. SR 100, 0.8 mi s of jct SR 108. Int corridors. **Pets:** Other. $10 one-time fee/room. Supervision.
SAVE S⊠ ⊠ 🖥 📺 🍴 📬 ⊠

AAA ◆◆◆ **Green Mountain Inn** **CI**
(802) 253-7301. **$89-$199.** 18 S Main St. Center; on SR 100 at jct SR 108. Ext/int corridors. **Pets:** No service, supervision, crate.
S⊠ ⊠ 🖥 📺 🍴 📬

AAA ◆◆ **Hob Knob Inn** **MI**
(802) 253-8549. **$85-$95.** 2364 Mountain Rd. SR 108, 2.5 mi w of jct SR 100. Ext/int corridors. **Pets:** Designated rooms, supervision.
SAVE S⊠ ⊠ 🖥 📺 🍴 📬

AAA ◆◆◆ **Honeywood Country Lodge** **M** ❀
(802) 253-4124. **$109-$169.** 4527 Mountain Rd. SR 108, 4.5 mi w of jct SR 100. Ext corridors. **Pets:** Dogs only. $10 daily fee/pet, $10 one-time fee/pet. Designated rooms, no service, supervision, crate.
SAVE S⊠ ⊠ 🖥 📬 ⊠

AAA ◆◆ **Innsbruck Inn at Stowe** **M**
(802) 253-8582. **$69-$154.** 4361 Mountain Rd. SR 108, 4.5 mi w of jct SR 100. Ext/int corridors. **Pets:** Medium. No service, supervision, crate.
SAVE S⊠ ⊠ 🖥 📺 📬 ⊠

AAA ◆◆◆◆ **The Mountain Road Resort** **M**
(802) 253-4566. **$90-$225.** 1007 Mountain Rd. SR 108, 1 mi w of jct SR 100. Ext corridors. **Pets:** Small. Designated rooms, supervision.
SAVE S⊠ ⊠ 🖥 📺 📬 ⊠

◆◆◆ **Notch Brook Condominiums** **X**
(802) 253-4882. **$49-$99.** 1229 Notch Brook Rd. Jct SR 100, 5.3 mi w on SR 108, 1.3 mi n. Ext corridors. **Pets:** No service, supervision, crate.
⊠ 📺 📬 ⊠ 🐾

AAA ◆◆ **Season's Pass Inn** **M** ❀
(802) 253-7244. **$62-$105.** 613 S Main St. SR 100, 0.5 mi s of jct SR 108. Ext corridors. **Pets:** Dogs only. Supervision.
SAVE S⊠ ⊠ 🖥 📬 📬

AAA ◆◆ **Ten Acres Lodge** **X**
(802) 253-7638. **$200-$260.** 14 Barrows Rd. From jct SR 100, 2.1 mi w on SR 108, 0.5 mi s on Luce Hill Rd. Ext/int corridors. **Pets:** Small. Designated rooms, no service, supervision, crate.
⊠ 🖥 📺 📬 ⊠

AAA ◆◆◆ **Topnotch at Stowe Resort & Spa** **R**
(802) 253-8585. **$230-$900.** 4000 Mountain Rd. SR 108, 4 mi w of jct SR 100. Ext/int corridors. **Pets:** Small. Designated rooms, supervision.
SAVE ⊠ 🖥 📺 🍴 📬 ⊠

SUNDERLAND

AAA ◆◆◆ **Arcady at the Sunderland Motor Lodge** **M** ❀
(802) 362-1176. **$70-$130.** 2249 Rt 7A. 6.3 mi s of jct SR 11. Ext corridors. **Pets:** $10 daily fee/room. No service, supervision, crate.
SAVE ⊠ 📺 📬 ⊠

SWANTON

AAA ◆ **Blue Ford Motel** **M** ❀
(802) 868-4147. **$35-$75, 3 days notice.** 325 N River St. I-89, exit 21, 3.3 mi w on Rt 78. Ext corridors. **Pets:** Medium, dogs only. $10 one-time fee/room. Designated rooms, no service, supervision, crate.
⊠ 🖥 📬

WARREN

AAA ◆◆ **PowderHound Inn & Condominiums** **X** ❀
(802) 496-5100. **$80-$145.** 203 Powderhound Rd. SR 100, 0.3 mi s of jct Sugarbush Access Rd. Ext corridors. **Pets:** Other. $5 daily fee/pet. Supervision.
🖥 📺 🍴 📬 ⊠ 🐾

AAA ◆◆ **The Sugar Lodge** **M** ❀
(802) 583-3300. **$79-$99.** Sugarbush Access Rd. Jct SR 100, 2 mi w on Sugarbush Access Rd. Int corridors. **Pets:** Dogs only. $10 one-time fee/pet. Designated rooms, no service, supervision, crate.
SAVE S⊠ ⊠ 🐾

WATERBURY

AAA ◆◆◆ **Holiday Inn of Waterbury-Stowe** **MI** ❀
(802) 244-7822. **$139-$179, 3 days notice.** 45 Blush Hill Rd. SR 100; just nw of jct I-89, exit 10. Int corridors. **Pets:** $35 deposit/room. Designated rooms, no service, supervision, crate.
SAVE S⊠ ⊠ 🕸 🖥 📺 🍴 📬 ⊠

◆◆ The Old Stagecoach Inn BB ❀
(802) 244-5056. **$55-$200.** 18 N Main St. SR 100, 0.5 mi se of jct I-89, exit 10. Int corridors. **Pets:** Medium. $10 daily fee/pet. Supervision.
SAVE ⊠ 🔋 ⑪

WEST BRATTLEBORO

◆ Molly Stark Motel M ❀
(802) 254-2440. **$48-$80.** Rt 9. On SR 9, 3.3 mi w of jct I-91 exit 2. Ext corridors. **Pets:** Large. $5 one-time fee/pet. No service, supervision, crate.
⊠ 🔋

WEST DOVER

 ◆◆◆ Snow Goose Inn BB ❀
(802) 464-3984. **$105-$300.** 259 Rt 100. 1 mi n on SR 100. Int corridors. **Pets:** Other. $20 daily fee/pet. Designated rooms, supervision.
SAVE 🄂 ⊠ 🔋 🆉

WESTMORE

 ◆◆ WilloughVale Inn on Lake Willoughby CI
(802) 525-4123. **$108-$219.** 793 Rt 5A. On Lake Willoughby. Int corridors. **Pets:** Small. Designated rooms, no service, supervision, crate.
🄂 ⊠ 🔋 🖥 ⑪ 🅇 CTV 🆉

WHITE RIVER JUNCTION

 ◆◆◆ Best Western at the Junction M ❀
(802) 295-3015. **$99-$139.** Rt 5. On US 5, at jct I-89 and I-91. Int corridors. **Pets:** Medium. $7 one-time fee/room. Designated rooms, supervision.
SAVE 🄂 ⊠ 🔋 🖥 🖼 🅇

 ◆◆ Ramada Inn-White River Junction MI ❀
(802) 295-3000. **$135-$165.** Holiday Dr. Jct I-89 and I-91, just e. Int corridors. **Pets:** $50 deposit/room. Designated rooms, no service, supervision, crate.
SAVE 🄂 ⊠ 🔋 🖥 ⑪ 🖼 🅇

WILLISTON

◆◆◆ Residence Inn by Marriott A
(802) 878-2001. **Call for rates.** 35 Hurricane Ln. SR 2A; just s of I-89, exit 12. Ext corridors. **Pets:** No service, supervision, crate.
⊠ 🛀 🔋 🖥 🖼 🅇

WOODSTOCK

 ◆◆ Braeside Motel M
(802) 457-1366. **$88-$108.** Rt 4 E. 1 mi e on US 4. Ext corridors. **Pets:** Designated rooms, supervision.
⊠ 🔋 🖼

 ◆◆◆ The Winslow House BB ❀
(802) 457-1820. **$95-$150.** 492 Woodstock Rd (Rt 14). 1.8 mi w on US 4. Int corridors. **Pets:** No service, supervision, crate.
⊠ 🔋

Virginia

CITY INDEX

ABINGDON

AAA ◆◆ Comfort Inn Abingdon **M** ❀
(540) 676-2222. **$66-$200.** 170 Jonesboro Rd. I-81, exit 14. Int corridors. **Pets:** Very small, other. $50 deposit/room. Supervision.

ALTAVISTA

AAA ◆◆◆ Comfort Suites Hotel **M** ❀
(804) 369-4000. **$66-$89.** 1558 Main St. US 29 business route, US 29 exit. Int corridors. **Pets:** Medium, other. Designated rooms, supervision.

APPOMATTOX

AAA ◆ Budget Inn **M** ❀
(804) 352-7451. **$40-$50.** 714 W Confederate Blvd. Center; US 460 business route. Ext corridors. **Pets:** Small. Designated rooms, no service, supervision, crate.
[SAVE] ⨉ 🛏

BEDFORD

AAA ◆◆ Best Western Terrace House Inn **M** ❀
(540) 586-8286. **$47-$64.** 921 Blue Ridge Ave. 1.5 mi w on US 221 and 460. Ext corridors. **Pets:** Very small. $5 one-time fee/room. Designated rooms, no service, supervision, crate.
[SAVE] 🛏 ⨉ 🛏 🖵 🍽 🛬

BIG STONE GAP

AAA ◆ Country Inn Motel **M** ❀
(540) 523-0374. **$42-$48.** 627 Gilley Ave. US 23, 1 mi w on US 23 Business and US 58 A. Ext corridors. **Pets:** Small, dogs only. $2 daily fee/pet. No service, supervision, crate.
[SAVE] ⨉ 🛏

BLACKSBURG

AAA ◆◆◆ Best Western Red Lion Inn **M**
(540) 552-7770. **$64-$92, 7 days notice.** 900 Plantation Rd. 1.7 mi w on SR 685; jct US 460 bypass and Prices Fork Rd. Ext corridors. **Pets:** Small. No service, supervision, crate.
[SAVE] 🛏 ⨉ 🍽 🛬 ⨉

AAA ◆◆◆ Comfort Inn **M** ❀
(540) 951-1500. **$65-$145.** 3705 S Main St. 3.5 mi s on US 460, jct US 460 bypass. Int corridors. **Pets:** Other. No service, supervision, crate.
[SAVE] 🛏 ⨉ 🖵 🛬

◆◆◆ **Four Points Hotel by
	Sheraton-Blacksburg** Ⓜ
(540) 552-7001. **$89-$149.** 900 Prices Fork Rd. 0.7 mi e on Prices Fork Rd (SR 412) from jct 460 bypass. Int corridors. **Pets:** Supervision.

ASK Ⓢ ✕ ⊟ ⚏ ⑪ ⌚ ✕

BLAND

◆ **Big Walker Motel** Ⓜ
(540) 688-3331. **$34-$48.** I-77, exit 52, just e on top of hill. Ext corridors. **Pets:** Small. Supervision.

✕ ✕

BRISTOL

◆ **Econo Lodge** Ⓜ
(540) 466-2112. **$35-$80.** 912 Commonwealth Ave. 1.5 mi e of I-81, exit 3. Ext corridors. **Pets:** Medium. Supervision.

ASK Ⓢ ✕ ⊟ ⚏

⠀ ◆◆◆ **Holiday Inn Hotel & Suites** Ⓗ ❀
(540) 466-4100. **$90-$90.** 3005 Linden Dr. I-81, exit 7. Int corridors. **Pets:** Other. No service, supervision, crate.

SAVE Ⓢ ✕ ⌂ ⊟ ⚏ ⑪ ⌚

⠀ ◆◆◆ **La Quinta Inn** Ⓜ
(540) 669-9353. **$49-$69.** 1014 Old Airport Rd. I-81, exit 7. Ext corridors. **Pets:** Small. No service, supervision, crate.

SAVE ✕ ⌂ ⊟ ⚏ ⌚

◆◆ **Super 8 Motel** Ⓜ
(540) 466-8800. **$65-$95, 7 days notice.** 2139 Lee Hwy. I-81, exit 5. Int corridors. **Pets:** Small. No service, supervision, crate.

Ⓢ ✕ ⊟

BUENA VISTA

⠀ ◆ **Buena Vista Motel** Ⓜ
(540) 261-2138. **$36-$59.** 447 E 29th St. I-81, exit 188A; 4.3 mi e on US 60; 0.4 mi w of Blue Ridge Pkwy. Ext corridors. **Pets:** Supervision.

SAVE Ⓢ ✕ ⊟ ⑪

CHAMPLAIN

⠀ ◆◆◆ **Linden House Bed & Breakfast
	Plantation** Ⓑ
(804) 443-1170. **$95-$95, 7 days notice.** 11770 Tidewater Tr. US 17, west side; 0.6 mi s of CR 631. Ext/int corridors. **Pets:** Small. Supervision.

✕ ⊟ ✕ ⑩ ☎

CHARLOTTESVILLE

⠀ ◆◆ **Best Western-Mount Vernon** Ⓜ ❀
(804) 296-5501. **$8-$68.** 1613 Emmet St. US 29, just n of jct US 250 bypass. Ext corridors. **Pets:** Other. No service, supervision, crate.

SAVE Ⓢ ✕ ⊟ ⚏ ⌚

⠀ ◆◆◆ **Comfort Inn** Ⓜ ❀
(804) 293-6188. **$75-$88.** 1807 Emmet St. Just n on US 29 from jct US 250 bypass. Int corridors. **Pets:** Other. $10 one-time fee/room. Designated rooms, supervision.

SAVE Ⓢ ✕ ✎ ⊟ ⚏ ⌚

◆◆◆ **Days Inn University Area** Ⓜ ❀
(804) 293-9111. **$60-$90, 7 days notice.** 1600 Emmet St. US 29, just n of jct US 250 bypass. Ext corridors. **Pets:** $10 daily fee/pet. Supervision.

ASK Ⓢ ✕ ⊟ ⚏ ⑪ ⌚

◆◆◆ **Quality Inn-University Area** Ⓜ ❀
(804) 971-3746. **$55-$85, 7 days notice.** 1600 Emmet St. US 29, just n of jct US 250 bypass, just e on Holiday Dr. Ext corridors. **Pets:** $10 daily fee/pet. Supervision.

ASK Ⓢ ✕ ⊟ ⚏

◆ **University Econo Lodge** Ⓜ
(804) 296-2104. **$45-$90.** 400 Emmet St. 1 mi s on US 29 business route from jct US 250 bypass. Ext corridors. **Pets:** Supervision.

ASK Ⓢ ✕ ⊟ ⚏ ⌚

CHRISTIANSBURG

⠀ ◆◆ **Econo Lodge** Ⓜ ❀
(540) 382-6161. **$45-$85.** 2430 Roanoke St. I-81, exit 118, just w on US 11/460. Ext corridors. **Pets:** Small, dogs only. $5 daily fee/pet, $5 one-time fee/pet. Designated rooms, no service, supervision, crate.

SAVE Ⓢ ✕ ⊟ ⚏ ⌚

◆◆ **Super 8 Motel-Christiansburg West** Ⓜ ❀
(540) 382-5813. **$48-$84.** 55 Laurel St NE. I-81, exit 118; 1 mi w on US 11/460, then 3.5 mi nw on US 460 bypass; at jct SR 114. Int corridors. **Pets:** Medium, other. No service, supervision, crate.

ASK Ⓢ ✕ ⊟

COLLINSVILLE

◆◆◆ **Dutch Inn** Ⓜ
(540) 647-3721. **$62-$80.** 2360 Virginia Ave. Jct US 58, 3 mi n on US 220 business route. Ext corridors. **Pets:** No service, supervision, crate.

ASK Ⓢ ✕ ⊟ ⚏ ⑪ ⌚

⠀ ◆◆ **Knights Inn** Ⓜ ❀
(540) 647-3716. **$44-$52.** 2357 Virginia Ave. 3 mi n on US 220 business route from jct US 58. Ext corridors. **Pets:** Small. $20 deposit/room. Designated rooms, supervision.

SAVE Ⓢ ✕ ⊟ ⌚

COLONIAL BEACH

⠀ ◆◆ **Days Inn** Ⓜ ❀
(804) 224-0404. **$70-$96, 3 days notice.** 30 Colonial Ave. SR 205, 0.5 mi e of jct SR 205. Ext/int corridors. **Pets:** Small. $10 daily fee/room. Designated rooms, no service, supervision, crate.

SAVE Ⓢ ✕ ⊟ ⌚ ✕

COVINGTON

◆◆◆ **Best Western Mountain View** Ⓜ
(540) 962-4951. **$70-$90.** 820 E Madison St. I-64, exit 16; just n. Ext corridors. **Pets:** Medium. Designated rooms, no service, supervision, crate.

ASK Ⓢ ✕ ⊟ ⚏ ⑪ ⌚

◆◆◆ **Comfort Inn** Ⓜ ❀
(540) 962-2141. **$63-$72.** 203 Interstate Dr. I-64, exit 16; just sw. Int corridors. **Pets:** Other. $10 one-time fee/pet. No service, supervision, crate.

(ASK) (S🅰) (✕) (⬛) (💻) (❙❙) (🕮)

◆◆ **Knights Inn** Ⓜ
(540) 962-7600. **$53-$73.** 908 Valley Ridge Rd. I-64, exit 16; just ne. Ext corridors. **Pets:** No service, supervision, crate.

(ASK) (S🅰) (✕) (⬛) (💻)

CULPEPER

⚠⚠⚠ ◆◆ **Comfort Inn** Ⓜ ❀
(540) 825-4900. **$75-$81, 7 days notice.** 890 Willis Ln. 2 mi s on US 29 business route, at jct US 29, just e. Ext corridors. **Pets:** Other. $15 one-time fee/room. Designated rooms, no service, supervision, crate.

(SAVE) (S🅰) (✕) (🕮) (⬛) (💻) (🕮)

◆◆◆ **Holiday Inn** Ⓜⓘ ❀
(540) 825-1253. **$99, 3 days notice.** 791 James Madison Rd S. 2 mi s on US 29 business route, at jct US 29. Ext corridors. **Pets:** Large. Supervision.

(ASK) (S🅰) (✕) (🕮) (⬛) (💻) (🕮)

DISTRICT OF COLUMBIA METROPOLITAN AREA

ALEXANDRIA

◆◆ **Alexandria Suites Hotel** Ⓐ ❀
(703) 370-1000. **$99-$119.** 420 N Van Dorn St. I-395 exit 3A, 0.3 mi e on SR 236 to S Van Dorn St, then 0.5 mi n. Int corridors. **Pets:** Large, other. $100 one-time fee/room. Supervision.

(ASK) (S🅰) (✕) (🖋) (⬛) (💻) (🕮)

◆ **Days Inn-Alexandria** Ⓜ
(703) 354-4950. **$66-$85.** 110 S Bragg St. I-395 at SR 236W, exit 3B. Ext corridors. **Pets:** Supervision.

(ASK) (S🅰) (✕) (🕮) (🕮) (CTV)

⚠⚠⚠ ◆◆◆ **Doubletree Guest Suites-Alexandria** Ⓐ ❀
(703) 370-9600. **$119-$159.** 100 S Reynolds St. 0.8 mi e of jct I-395, SR 236E, exit 3A (Duke St), just s. Int corridors. **Pets:** Large, other. $10 daily fee/room. Supervision.

(SAVE) (✕) (🕮) (🕮) (🖋) (⬛) (💻) (❙❙)

◆◆◆ **Executive Club Suites** Ⓐ ❀
(703) 739-2582. **$110-$130, 7 days notice.** 610 Bashford Ln. Jct George Washington Memorial Pkwy. Int corridors. **Pets:** Other. $250 deposit/pet, $50 one-time fee/pet. Supervision.

(ASK) (S🅰) (⬛) (💻) (🕮)

⚠⚠⚠ ◆◆◆ **Hilton Alexandria Mark Center** Ⓗ
(703) 845-1010. **$119-$239.** 5000 Seminary Rd. I-395, exit 4 (Seminary Rd), just w. Int corridors. **Pets:** Small. Supervision.

(SAVE) (S🅰) (✕) (🕮) (🕮) (⬛) (💻) (❙❙) (🕮) (✕)

DALEVILLE

⚠⚠⚠ ◆◆◆ **Best Western-Coachman Inn Roanoke/Daleville** Ⓜ ❀
(540) 992-1234. **$58-$72.** 235 Roanoke Rd. I-81, exit 150B; just nw on US 220. Ext corridors. **Pets:** Small. $10 daily fee/pet. Designated rooms, supervision.

(SAVE) (S🅰) (✕) (🕮) (⬛) (💻) (🕮)

DANVILLE

⚠⚠⚠ ◆◆◆ **Stratford Inn** Ⓜⓘ ❀
(804) 793-2500. **$61-$75, 7 days notice.** 2500 Riverside Dr. US 58, just e of jct US 29 business. Ext corridors. **Pets:** Other. Supervision.

(SAVE) (S🅰) (✕) (🕮) (🖋) (⬛) (💻) (🕮)

◆◆ **Holiday Inn Eisenhower Metro** Ⓜⓘ ❀
(703) 960-3400. **$99-$139.** 2460 Eisenhower Ave. Jct Telegraph Rd (SR 214N) and I-95/I-495; exit 2 s and westbound, exit 2B n and eastbound; immediate e onto Pershing Ave, then s on Stovall St. Int corridors. **Pets:** Medium. $30 deposit/room. Supervision.

(ASK) (S🅰) (✕) (🕮) (⬛) (❙❙) (🕮)

⚠⚠⚠ ◆◆◆ **Holiday Inn Select-Old Town** Ⓗ ❀
(703) 549-6080. **$161-$171.** 480 King St. In Old Town on SR 7; between S Pitt & S Royal sts; just w of City Hall. Int corridors. **Pets:** Other. No service, supervision, crate.

(SAVE) (S🅰) (✕) (🕮) (💻) (❙❙) (🕮) (✕)

◆◆ **Homestead Village-Alexandria** Ⓜ
(703) 329-3399. **$89-$94.** 200 Blue Stone Rd. I-95/495, exit 3A (Eisenhower Ave Connector), just n to Eisenhower Ave, then 1.2 mi e. Int corridors. **Pets:** Small. Supervision.

(✕) (🕮) (🖋) (⬛)

⚠⚠⚠ ◆◆◆ **Radisson Hotel Old Town Alexandria** Ⓗ
(703) 683-6000. **$89-$89.** 901 N Fairfax St. In Old Town area; between First St and Montgomery. Int corridors. **Pets:** Large. Supervision.

(SAVE) (✕) (🕮) (⬛) (💻) (❙❙) (🕮)

⚠⚠⚠ ◆◆ **Red Roof Inn-Alexandria** Ⓜ ❀
(703) 960-5200. **$75-$91.** 5975 Richmond Hwy. US 1, 0.5 mi s of jct I-95/I-495, exit 1A (Capital Beltway). Ext corridors. **Pets:** Small. Supervision.

(SAVE) (S🅰) (✕) (CTV)

◆◆◆ Sheraton Suites Alexandria 🅗 ☙
(703) 836-4700. **$139-$155.** 801 N St. Asaph St. In Old Town; just e of Washington St. Int corridors. **Pets:** Small, dogs only. Supervision.

ARLINGTON

◆◆ Best Western Key Bridge 🅜 ☙
(703) 522-0400. **$129-$169.** 1850 N Fort Myer Dr. In Rosslyn Area; just sw of Key Bridge; from I-66, exit 73. Int corridors. **Pets:** $25 one-time fee/room. Designated rooms, no service, supervision, crate.

◆◆ Executive Club Suites-Arlington 🅐
(703) 522-2582. **$110.** 108 S Courthouse Rd. Just s off Washington Blvd; From I-395 exit 8A, 1 mi w. Ext corridors. **Pets:** No service, supervision, crate.

◆◆◆ Holiday Inn Rosslyn 🅗 ☙
(703) 807-2000. **$120-$120.** 1900 N Fort Myer Dr. From I-66, exit 73, just sw of Key Bridge; in Rosslyn area. Int corridors. **Pets:** Very small, other. Supervision.

◆◆◆ Quality Hotel Courthouse Plaza 🅗 ☙
(703) 524-4000. **$79-$179.** 1200 N Courthouse Road. 1.5 mi sw of Theodore Roosevelt Bridge on US 50. Ext/int corridors. **Pets:** Medium, other. $10 daily fee/room, $25 one-time fee/room. Designated rooms, no service, supervision, crate.

◆◆ Quality Inn-Iwo Jima 🅜 ☙
(703) 524-5000. **$90-$109.** 1501 Arlington Blvd. 1 mi w of Theodore Roosevelt Bridge on US 50. Ext/int corridors. **Pets:** Other. $10 daily fee/room. Designated rooms, supervision.

CHANTILLY

◆◆ Homestead Village Guest Studios Dulles South-Chantilly 🅜 ☙
(703) 263-3361. **$89-$134.** 4504 Brookfield Corporate Dr. Off SR 28, 3 mi n of I-66, exit 53; 1 mi s of jct US 28 and 50. Ext corridors. **Pets:** Medium, other. $75 one-time fee/pet. Supervision.

DUMFRIES

◆◆◆ Holiday Inn Express-Dumfries 🅜
(703) 221-1141. **$65-$85.** 17133 Dumfries Rd. I-95, exit 152, just w on SR 234 N. Ext/int corridors. **Pets:** Medium. Supervision.

FAIRFAX

◆◆◆ Comfort Inn University Center 🅜
(703) 591-5900. **$139.** 11180 Main St. US 50, 0.8 mi se of jct I-66, exit 57A, 0.5 mi nw of jct US 29. Int corridors. **Pets:** Very small. Supervision.

◆◆◆ Holiday Inn-Fair Oaks 🅜
(703) 352-2525. **$134.** 11787 Lee Jackson Memorial Hwy. US 50 at jct I-66, exit 57B; adjacent to Fair Oaks Mall. Int corridors. **Pets:** Supervision.

◆◆ Homestead Village Guest Studios-Fair Oaks 🅜 ☙
(703) 273-3444. **$75-$105.** 12104 Monument Dr. I-66, exit 57B, 0.8 mi w on US 50, then 0.3 mi s on SR 620 (West Ox Rd), just se. Ext corridors. **Pets:** Small. $75 one-time fee/pet. No service, supervision, crate.

◆◆ Wellesley Inn & Suites 🅜
(703) 359-2888. **$80-$155.** 10327 Lee Hwy. US 29/50 and I-66, exit 60, 0.7 mi s on SR 123, 0.3 mi e on US 29/50. Int corridors. **Pets:** Medium. No service, supervision, crate.

HERNDON

◆◆◆ Hilton Washington Dulles Airport 🅗
(703) 478-2900. **$95-$167.** 13869 Park Center Rd. SR 267 (Dulles Toll Rd), exit 9; 3 mi s on SR 28. Int corridors. **Pets:** Small. Supervision.

◆◆◆ Holiday Inn Express–Herndon 🅜
(703) 478-9777. **$104.** 485 Elden St. 0.3 mi e on SR 606. Int corridors. **Pets:** Supervision.

◆◆◆ Residence Inn by Marriott-Herndon/Reston 🅜
(703) 435-0044. **Call for rates.** 315 Elden St. 0.5 mi e on SR 606. Int corridors. **Pets:** Medium. Supervision.

◆◆◆ Summerfield Suites Hotel 🅜
(703) 713-6800. **$99-$178.** 13700 Coppermine Rd. SR 267 (Dulles Toll Rd), exit 10; 0.7 mi s on Centerville Rd, 0.4 mi w. Ext corridors. **Pets:** Large. No service, supervision, crate.

LEESBURG

◆◆◆ Holiday Inn at Carradoc Hall 🅜 ☙
(703) 771-9200. **$109-$159.** 1500 E Market St. 2 mi e on SR 7. Int corridors. **Pets:** Medium. $75 deposit/room. Designated rooms, no service, supervision, crate.

LORTON

◆◆◆ Comfort Inn Gunston Corner 🅜 ☙
(703) 643-3100. **$69-$129, 3 days notice.** 8180 Silverbrook Rd. I-95, exit 163, just w. Int corridors. **Pets:** Small, other. $25 one-time fee/room. Designated rooms, no service, supervision, crate.

MANASSAS

AAA ◆◆◆ **Best Western Battlefield Inn** Ⓜ️ ❖
(703) 361-8000. **$59-$105.** 10820 Balls Ford Rd. I-66; exit 47A westbound, exit 47 eastbound; just s on SR 234, then w. Ext corridors. **Pets:** Very small, dogs only. $10 daily fee/pet. No service, supervision, crate.

〔SAVE〕 〔S🔒〕 〔✕〕 〔🛏〕 〔¶〕 〔🏊〕

AAA ◆◆ **Red Roof Inn-Manassas** Ⓜ️ ❖
(703) 335-9333. **$55-$82.** 10610 Automotive Dr. I-66 exit 47 eastbound, exit 47A westbound; just s on SR 234, just e on Balls Ford Rd. Ext corridors. **Pets:** No service, supervision, crate.

〔SAVE〕 〔✕〕 〔🌙〕

MCLEAN

AAA ◆◆◆ **Best Western Tysons Westpark Hotel** Ⓗ ❖
(703) 734-2800. **$79-$149.** 8401 Westpark Dr. SR 7, 1.3 mi w of I-495; exit 10 southbound, exit 10B northbound; 0.3 mi w of jct SR 123. Int corridors. **Pets:** Other. No service, supervision, crate.

〔SAVE〕 〔S🔒〕 〔✕〕 〔👤〕 〔🛏〕 〔¶〕 〔🏊〕

◆◆◆ **Hilton McLean Tysons Corner** Ⓗ ❖
(703) 847-5000. **Call for rates.** 7920 Jones Branch Dr. I-495, exit 11B; 0.3 mi sw on SR 123, just nw on Tyson's Blvd, 0.4 mi ne on Galleria/Westpark Dr, just s. Int corridors. **Pets:** Small. $50 one-time fee/room. No service, supervision, crate.

〔ASK〕 〔✕〕 〔🏠〕 〔🌙〕 〔🛏〕 〔💻〕 〔¶〕 〔🏊〕 〔✕〕

SPRINGFIELD

◆◆◆ **Comfort Inn Springfield** Ⓜ️ ❖
(703) 922-9000. **$89-$129.** 6560 Loisdale Ct. Jct I-95 and SR 644E, exit 169A; 0.7 mi s of jct I-395 and I-495; adjacent to Springfield Mall. Int corridors. **Pets:** Other. No service, supervision, crate.

〔ASK〕 〔S🔒〕 〔✕〕 〔🌙〕 〔👤〕 〔🛏〕

◆◆◆ **Hampton Inn** Ⓜ️ ❖
(703) 924-9444. **$89-$129.** 6550 Loisdale Ct. Jct I-95 and SR 644E, exit 169A; 0.6 mi s of jct I-395 and I-495; adjacent to Springfield Mall. Int corridors. **Pets:** Small. Designated rooms, no service, supervision, crate.

〔ASK〕 〔S🔒〕 〔✕〕 〔🏠〕 〔🌙〕 〔👤〕 〔🛏〕 〔💻〕 〔🏊〕

STERLING

AAA ◆◆◆ **Hampton Inn Washington-Dulles Airport** Ⓜ️ ❖
(703) 471-8300. **$59-$115.** 45440 Holiday Dr. SR 28, 1.8 mi n of Dulles Toll Rd (SR 267), exit 9B. Ext corridors. **Pets:** Small, other. $10 one-time fee/room. Designated rooms, supervision.

〔SAVE〕 〔S🔒〕 〔✕〕 〔🌙〕 〔🛏〕 〔💻〕

◆◆◆ **Holiday Inn Washington Dulles International Airport** Ⓜ️
(703) 471-7411. **$189.** 1000 Sully Rd. SR 28, 1.8 mi n of Dulles Toll Rd (SR 267), exit 9B. Ext/int corridors. **Pets:** Very small. Supervision.

〔ASK〕 〔S🔒〕 〔✕〕 〔👤〕 〔🛏〕 〔💻〕 〔¶〕 〔🏊〕

◆◆◆ **Homestead Village Guest Studios** Ⓜ️
(703) 904-7575. **Call for rates.** 45350 Catalina Ct. SR 267 (Dulles Toll Rd), exit 9B, 0.8 mi n on SR 28, then just w on SR 606. Ext corridors. **Pets:** Small. Supervision.

〔✕〕 〔♿〕 〔🛏〕 〔💻〕

◆◆◆ **Towne Place Suites by Marriott** Ⓜ️
(703) 707-2017. **$89-$99.** 22744 Holiday Park Dr. SR 267 (Dulles Toll Rd) exit 9B, 1.8 mi n on SR 28, then just ne. Int corridors. **Pets:** Medium. No service, supervision, crate.

〔ASK〕 〔S🔒〕 〔✕〕 〔👤〕 〔♿〕 〔🛏〕 〔💻〕 〔🏊〕

TRIANGLE

◆◆◆ **Ramada Inn-Quantico** Ⓜ️ ❖
(703) 221-1181. **$59-$75.** 4316 Inn St. I-95, exit 150, just e. Int corridors. **Pets:** Medium. $10 daily fee/room. Designated rooms, no service, supervision, crate.

〔ASK〕 〔S🔒〕 〔✕〕 〔🛏〕 〔¶〕 〔🏊〕

VIENNA

◆◆◆ **Residence Inn by Marriott-Tysons Corner** Ⓐ
(703) 893-0120. **$179-$249.** 8616 Westwood Center Dr. SR 7, just s on Westwood Center Dr; from I-495, exit 10 southbound, exit 10B northbound; 1.9 mi w on SR 7. Ext corridors. **Pets:** Supervision.

〔ASK〕 〔S🔒〕 〔✕〕 〔🛏〕 〔💻〕 〔🏊〕 〔✕〕

WOODBRIDGE

◆◆◆ **Days Inn Potomac Mills** Ⓜ️ ❖
(703) 494-4433. **$64-$94.** 14619 Potomac Mills Rd. I-95 exit 156, 0.5 mi w. Int corridors. **Pets:** Other. Designated rooms, no service, supervision, crate.

〔ASK〕 〔✕〕 〔🛏〕 〔💻〕 〔🏊〕

AAA ◆◆ **Quality Inn** Ⓜ️ ❖
(703) 494-0300. **$44-$90.** 1109 Horner Rd. I-95, exit 161 southbound; 1.5 mi s on US 1, just n on SR 123, then just s, exit 160A northbound, 0.5 mi s on SR 123, then just e. Int corridors. **Pets:** Other. $10 daily fee/room. Supervision.

〔SAVE〕 〔S🔒〕 〔✕〕 〔🌙〕 〔🛏〕 〔💻〕 〔🏊〕

❖ **END METROPOLITAN AREA** ❖

EMPORIA

⊕⊕ ◆◆◆ Best Western Emporia Ⓜ ☸
(804) 634-3200. **$55-$75.** 1100 W Atlantic St. I-95, exit 11B, US 58, just w. Ext corridors. **Pets:** Other. $10 one-time fee/room. Supervision.

[SAVE] [S♨] [✕] [✎] [🛏] [🏊]

⊕⊕ ◆◆◆ Comfort Inn Ⓜ ☸
(804) 348-3282. **$45-$69.** 1411 Skippers Rd. Jct I-95, exit 8 and US 301. Ext corridors. **Pets:** Medium. $10 one-time fee/room. Designated rooms, no service, supervision, crate.

[SAVE] [S♨] [✕] [🛏] [🍽] [🏊]

◆◆ Days Inn-Emporia Ⓜ
(804) 634-9481. **$53-$83.** 921 W Atlantic St. Jct I-95 and US 58, exit 11B. Ext corridors. **Pets:** Designated rooms, no service, supervision, crate.

[ASK] [S♨] [✕] [🛏] [🏊] [✕]

⊕⊕ ◆◆◆ Hampton Inn Ⓜ ☸
(804) 634-9200. **$60-$75.** 1207 W Atlantic St. I-95 and US 58 W, exit 11B. Ext corridors. **Pets:** Other. Supervision.

[SAVE] [S♨] [✕] [🐾] [🛏] [🍽] [🏊]

◆◆ Holiday Inn Ⓜ ☸
(804) 634-4191. **$70-$70.** 311 Florida Ave. Jct I-95 and US 58 E, exit 11A. Ext/int corridors. **Pets:** Other. Supervision.

[ASK] [S♨] [✕] [🐾] [🍽] [🛏] [🏊] [✕]

◆ Knights Inn Ⓜ ☸
(804) 535-8535. **$30-$64.** 3173 Sussex Dr. I-95, exit 17, 0.5 mi s on US 301. Ext corridors. **Pets:** Small, dogs only. No service, supervision, crate.

[ASK] [S♨] [✕] [🏊]

⊕⊕ ◆ Reste' Motel Ⓜ
(804) 535-8505. **$30-$50.** 3190 Sussex Dr. I-95, exit 17, 0.5 mi s on US 301. Ext corridors. **Pets:** Designated rooms, supervision.

[SAVE] [S♨] [✕] [🛏] [🏊] [✕]

FANCY GAP

◆◆ Cascade Mountain Inn Ⓜ
(540) 728-2300. **$50-$85.** 96 Cascade Tr. 0.3 mi n on Blue Ridge Pkwy from jct US 52, 1.3 mi e on SR 608. Ext corridors. **Pets:** Small. Supervision.

[ASK] [✕] [🍽] [✕] [CTV] [🏊]

⊕⊕ ◆◆ Doe Run Lodge Ⓒ ☸
(540) 398-2212. **$109-$275, 3 days notice.** Milepost 189. Milepost 189.5 on Blue Ridge Pkwy; 10 mi n from US 52 (parkway entrance). Ext corridors. **Pets:** Other. $25 one-time fee/room. Designated rooms, supervision.

[SAVE] [S♨] [✕] [🛏] [🍽] [🍽] [🏊] [✕] [CTV]

FRANKLIN

◆◆ Best Western Franklin Inn Ⓜ
(757) 562-4100. **$49-$55.** 1467 Carrsville Hwy. 1 mi e on US 258 N and 58 E business route. Ext corridors. **Pets:** Supervision.

[ASK] [✕] [🛏] [🍽] [🏊]

◆◆◆ Days Inn Ⓜ ☸
(757) 562-2225. **$60-$80.** 1660 Armory Dr. Jct US 58 bypass and SR 671. Ext corridors. **Pets:** Other. $5 deposit/room, $5 daily fee/room, $5 one-time fee/room. No service, supervision, crate.

[ASK] [S♨] [✕] [🛏] [🏊]

FREDERICKSBURG

⊕⊕ ◆◆◆ Best Western Central Park Ⓜ ☸
(540) 786-7404. **$46-$62.** 3000 Plank Rd. SR 3 at jct I-95, exit 130B; adjacent to Spotsylvania Mall. Ext corridors. **Pets:** Small. Supervision.

[SAVE] [S♨] [✕] [🐾] [🛏]

⊕⊕ ◆◆◆ Best Western Fredericksburg Ⓜ ☸
(540) 371-5050. **$50-$69.** 2205 William St. SR 3, 0.3 mi e of jct I-95, exit 130A. Ext corridors. **Pets:** Very small. Designated rooms, no service, supervision, crate.

[SAVE] [S♨] [✕] [🐾] [🛏] [🏊]

◆◆ Days Inn Fredericksburg South Ⓜ
(540) 898-6800. **$50-$55.** 5316 Jefferson Davis Hwy. US 1, just n of I-95, exit 126A. Ext corridors. **Pets:** Small. No service, supervision, crate.

[ASK] [S♨] [✕] [🛏] [🏊] [✕]

⊕⊕ ◆◆◆ Dunning Mills Suites Ⓧ ☸
(540) 373-1256. **$53-$73.** 2305 C Jefferson Davis Hwy. I-95, exit 126, US 1, 3 mi n. Ext corridors. **Pets:** Other. $200 deposit/room, $5 daily fee/pet. No service, supervision, crate.

[SAVE] [S♨] [🛏] [🏊]

⊕⊕ ◆◆◆ Hampton Inn Ⓜ
(540) 371-0330. **$62-$86.** 2310 William St. I-95 and SR 3 E, exit 130A. Ext corridors. **Pets:** Supervision.

[SAVE] [S♨] [✕] [🛏] [🍽] [🏊]

⊕⊕ ◆◆◆ Holiday Inn-Fredericksburg North Ⓜ ☸
(540) 371-5550. **$67-$82.** 564 Warrenton Rd. US 17 at jct I-95, exit 133 (Falmouth-Warrenton). Ext corridors. **Pets:** Other. Supervision.

[SAVE] [S♨] [✕] [🛏] [🍽] [🏊]

◆◆◆ Holiday Inn Fredericksburg South Ⓜ ☸
(540) 898-1102. **$75-$85.** 5324 Jefferson Davis Hwy. Jct I-95 and US 1, exit 126 southbound; exit 126A northbound, 0.3 mi n. Ext/int corridors. **Pets:** Very small. Designated rooms, supervision.

[ASK] [S♨] [✕] [🛏] [🍽] [🏊]

⊕⊕ ◆◆◆ Holiday Inn Select Fredericksburg Ⓗ ☸
(540) 786-8321. **$89-$89.** 2801 Plank Rd. SR 3 at jct I-95, exit 130B. Int corridors. **Pets:** Medium. $150 deposit/room, $25 one-time fee/room. Designated rooms, no service, supervision, crate.

[S♨] [✕] [🐾] [🛏] [🍽] [🍽] [🏊] [✕]

⊕⊕ ◆◆ Howard Johnson Ⓜ ☸
(540) 898-1800. **$75-$85, 7 days notice.** 5327 Jefferson Davis Hwy. US 1 at jct I-95, exit 126 (Massaponax). Int corridors. **Pets:** Other. No service, supervision, crate.

[SAVE] [S♨] [✕] [✎] [🛏] [🍽] [🏊]

⊕ ◆◆◆ Quality Inn Fredericksburg MI ❀
(540) 373-0000. **$65-$85.** 543 Warrenton Rd. US 17 at jct I-95, exit 133 (Falmouth-Warrenton). Ext corridors. **Pets:** Other. $8 daily fee/pet. Supervision.
[SAVE] ⊠ ⊡ ⑪ ⊜ ⊠

⊕ ◆◆◆ Ramada Inn MI ❀
(540) 786-8361. **$50-$65.** 2802 Plank Rd. SR 3 at jct I-95, exit 130B. Ext corridors. **Pets:** Medium, other. $25 deposit/pet. No service, supervision, crate.
[SAVE] [S∅] ⊠ ⊟ ⑪ ⊜

FRONT ROYAL

⊕ ◆◆ Bluemont Inn MI
(540) 635-9447. **$45-$65.** 1525 N Shenandoah Ave. I 66, exit 6, 1.8 mi s on US 340/522. Ext corridors. **Pets:** Designated rooms, no service, supervision, crate.
[SAVE] [S∅] ⊠ ⊟

⊕ ◆ Budget Inn MI ❀
(540) 635-2196. **$35-$75.** 1122 N Royal Ave. I-66, exit 6, 2.2 mi s on US 340/US 522 and SR 55. Ext corridors. **Pets:** $5 daily fee/pet. No service, supervision, crate.
[SAVE] [S∅] ⊠ ⊟

⊕ ◆ Relax Inn MI ❀
(540) 635-4101. **$29-$65, 3 days notice.** 1801 Shenandoah Ave. I-66, exit 6, 1.5 mi s on US 340/522. Ext corridors. **Pets:** Other. $5 daily fee/pet, $5 one-time fee/pet. Designated rooms, supervision.
[SAVE] [S∅] ⊠ ⊜

HAMPTON ROADS METROPOLITAN AREA

CHESAPEAKE

⊕ ◆ Motel 6–1258 MI
(757) 420-2976. **$42-$58.** 701 Woodlake Dr. I-64, exit 289A (Greenbrier Pkwy), just n. Ext corridors. **Pets:** Designated rooms, no service, supervision, crate.
[S∅] ⊠ ⓐ [CTV]

⊕ ◆◆ Red Roof Inn MI
(757) 523-0123. **$54-$67.** 724 Woodlake Dr. I-64, exit 289A (Greenbrier Pkwy), just n to Woodlake Dr, just e. Ext corridors. **Pets:** Supervision.
[SAVE] ⊠ ⊟ [CTV]

◆◆ Super 8 Motel MI ❀
(757) 686-8888. **$52-$66, 7 days notice.** 3216 Churchland Blvd. I-664, exit 9B, SR 17, 1 mi s. Int corridors. **Pets:** Other. Supervision.
[ASK] [S∅] ⊠ ⓕ ⊟

◆◆◆ TownePlace Suites By Marriott MI
(757) 523-5004. **$79-$109.** 2000 Old Greenbriar Rd. I-64, exit 298A (Greenbrier Pkwy), just n. Int corridors. **Pets:** Supervision.
[ASK] [S∅] ⊠ ⓖ ⓐ ⓔ ⊟ ⊜

⊕ ◆◆ Wellesley Inn & Suites MI ❀
(757) 366-0100. **$60-$170.** 1750 Sara Dr. I-64, exit 289A (Greenbrier Pkwy), n to Woodlake Dr, 2 blks e. Int corridors. **Pets:** Other. Designated rooms, supervision.
[SAVE] [S∅] ⊠ ⓖ ⓔ ⊟ ⊡ ⊜

⊕ ◆◆ Scottish Inn MI
(540) 636-6168. **$39-$79.** 533 S Royal Ave. I-66, exit 6, 3.8 mi s on US 340, at jct SR 55. Ext corridors. **Pets:** No service, supervision, crate.
[SAVE] [S∅] ⊠ ⊟

◆◆ Super 8 Motel MI
(540) 636-4888. **Call for rates.** 111 South St. I-66, exit 6, 3.8 mi s on US 340, then just e on SR 55. Int corridors. **Pets:** Supervision.
⊠ ⊟

⊕ ◆ Twi-Lite Motel MI ❀
(540) 635-4148. **$59-$85.** 53 W 14th St. I-66, exit 6, 2.3 mi s on US 340/522. Ext corridors. **Pets:** Small, dogs only. $10 deposit/pet, $4 daily fee/pet. Designated rooms, no service, supervision, crate.
[SAVE] [S∅] ⊠ ⊟ ⊜

GREENVILLE

⊕ ◆◆ Hessian Econo Lodge MI ❀
(540) 337-1231. **$45-$75.** Jct US 11/340. I-81 exit 213, 0.3 mi e. Ext corridors. **Pets:** $6 daily fee/room. Designated rooms, supervision.
[SAVE] [S∅] ⊠ ⊟ ⊡ ⊜ ⊠

HAMPTON

◆ Arrow Inn MI
(757) 865-0300. **$46-$67.** 7 Semple Farm Rd. I-64, exit 261B eastbound; exit 262B westbound, US 134N (Magruder Blvd), 2 mi n. Ext corridors. **Pets:** No service, supervision, crate.
[ASK] ⊠ ⊟

◆◆◆ Candlewood Suites MI
(757) 766-8976. **$89.** 401 Butler Farm Rd. From I-64 eastbound exit 261B/Hampton Rds Center Pkwy; westbound exit 261 (Magruder Blvd), then n. Int corridors. **Pets:** Designated rooms, no service, supervision, crate.
[ASK] ⊠ ⓔ ⊟

◆◆ Days Inn-Hampton MI
(757) 826-4810. **$49-$90.** 1918 Coliseum Dr. I-64, exit 263B (Mercury Blvd and Coliseum Dr). Ext corridors. **Pets:** No service, supervision, crate.
[ASK] [S∅] ⊠ ⓖ ⊟ ⑪ ⊜

◆◆◆ Hampton Inn MI ❀
(757) 838-8484. **$74-$89, 3 days notice.** 1813 W Mercury Blvd. I-64, exit 263B, Mercury Blvd at jct SR 58. Int corridors. **Pets:** Small. No service, supervision, crate.
[ASK] [S∅] ⊠ ⓖ ⊟ ⊡

◆◆◆ Holiday Inn MI
(757) 838-0200. **$99-$129, 3 days notice.** 1815 W Mercury Blvd. I-64, exit 263B, adjacent to coliseum. Ext/int corridors. **Pets:** Designated rooms, supervision.
[ASK] [S∅] ⊠ ⓕ ⓖ ⊟ ⊡ ⑪ ⊜

△△△ ◆◆◆ La Quinta Inn **M**
(757) 827-8680. **$69-$89.** 2138 W Mercury Blvd. Just s of jct I-64 and Mercury Blvd/US 258, exit 263A. Ext/int corridors. **Pets:** Small. Designated rooms, no service, supervision, crate.

⟦SAVE⟧ ⟦⟧ ⟦⟧ ⟦⟧ ⟦⟧ ⟦⟧ ⟦⟧ ⟦⟧

△△△ ◆◆◆ Quality Inn & Suites Conference
Center **H**
(757) 838-5011. **$89-$129.** 1809 W Mercury Blvd. I-64, exit 263B (Mercury Blvd/US 258 N), at jct SR 58. Int corridors. **Pets:** Designated rooms, supervision.

⟦SAVE⟧ ⟦⟧ ⟦⟧ ⟦⟧ ⟦⟧ ⟦⟧ ⟦⟧ ⟦⟧ ⟦⟧

△△△ ◆◆ Red Roof Inn **M** 🐾
(757) 838-1870. **$41-$91.** 1925 Coliseum Dr. I-64, exit 263B (Mercury Blvd and Coliseum Dr). Ext corridors. **Pets:** Other. Supervision.

⟦SAVE⟧ ⟦⟧ ⟦⟧

NEWPORT NEWS

◆◆◆ Comfort Inn **M** 🐾
(757) 249-0200. **$89-$99.** 12330 Jefferson Ave. I-64, exit 255A, just s on Clarie Ln (mall parking lot). Int corridors. **Pets:** Other. No service, supervision, crate.

⟦ASK⟧ ⟦⟧ ⟦⟧ ⟦⟧ ⟦⟧ ⟦⟧ ⟦⟧ ⟦⟧

△△△ ◆◆ Days Inn **M** 🐾
(757) 874-0201. **$53-$65.** 14747 Warwick Blvd. I-64, exit 250A (SR 105); Ft Eustis Blvd S, 2.5 mi to US 60E, Warwick Blvd on US 60. Ext corridors. **Pets:** Other. $5 daily fee/pet, $5 one-time fee/pet. No service, supervision, crate.

⟦SAVE⟧ ⟦⟧ ⟦⟧ ⟦⟧ ⟦⟧

△△△ ◆◆◆ Days Inn-Oyster Point **M** 🐾
(757) 873-6700. **$85-$100, 3 days notice.** 11829 Fishing Point Dr. I-64, exit 255A (Jefferson Ave), 2.5 mi s to Thimble Shoals Dr E, 1 blk to property. Int corridors. **Pets:** Other. $10 daily fee/pet. Supervision.

⟦SAVE⟧ ⟦⟧ ⟦⟧ ⟦⟧ ⟦⟧ ⟦⟧ ⟦⟧

△△△ ◆◆ Host Inn **M** 🐾
(757) 599-3303. **$40-$77.** 985 J Clyde Morris Blvd. I-64, exit 258B, 0.8 mi w. Ext corridors. **Pets:** Small. $6 daily fee/pet. Designated rooms, no service, supervision, crate.

⟦⟧ ⟦⟧ ⟦⟧

△△△ ◆◆◆ Ramada Inn **MI**
(757) 599-4460. **$65-$69.** 950 J Clyde Morris Blvd. US 17, at jct I-64, exit 258B. Ext/int corridors. **Pets:** No service, supervision, crate.

⟦SAVE⟧ ⟦⟧ ⟦⟧ ⟦⟧ ⟦⟧ ⟦⟧ ⟦⟧ ⟦⟧

◆◆◆ TownePlace Suites by Marriott **A** 🐾
(757) 874-8884. **Call for rates.** 200 Cybernetics Way. From I-64, exit 256B, Victory Blvd, e to Kiln Creek Pkwy to Cybernetics Way. Int corridors. **Pets:** Other. $10 daily fee/pet. Supervision.

⟦⟧ ⟦⟧ ⟦⟧ ⟦⟧ ⟦⟧

NORFOLK

△△△ ◆◆ Days Inn Marina **M** 🐾
(757) 583-4521. **$85-$95, 3 days notice.** 1631 Bayville St. I-64, exit 272; at e end of Hampton Roads Bridge Tunnel. Ext corridors. **Pets:** Small, other. $15 one-time fee/pet. No service, supervision, crate.

⟦SAVE⟧ ⟦⟧ ⟦⟧ ⟦⟧ ⟦⟧ ⟦⟧

◆ Econo Lodge Airport **M** 🐾
(757) 855-3116. **$55-$128.** 3343 N Military Hwy. From I-64, exit 281 (SR 165) Military Hwy, just n. Ext corridors. **Pets:** Small. $25 deposit/pet. Designated rooms, supervision, sion.

⟦ASK⟧ ⟦⟧ ⟦⟧ ⟦⟧ ⟦⟧

◆◆ James Madison Hotel, a Sterling
Hotel **H** 🐾
(757) 622-6682. **$99-$139.** 345 Granby St. Downtown at jct w/Freemason St. Int corridors. **Pets:** Small, other. $20 one-time fee/pet. Supervision.

⟦ASK⟧ ⟦⟧ ⟦⟧ ⟦⟧ ⟦⟧ ⟦⟧

◆◆◆ Norfolk Waterside Marriott Hotel **H**
(757) 627-4200. **$139-$139, 3 days notice.** 235 E Main St. Center; corner Main St and Atlantic. Int corridors. **Pets:** No service, supervision, crate.

⟦ASK⟧ ⟦⟧ ⟦⟧ ⟦⟧ ⟦⟧ ⟦⟧ ⟦⟧

△△△ ◆◆ Quality Inn-Lake Wright **MI**
(757) 461-6251. **$79-$99, 3 days notice.** 6280 Northampton Blvd. US 13; 0.5 mi e of jct I-64, exit 282 (Norfolk International Airport), then 0.5 mi w. Ext corridors. **Pets:** Designated rooms, supervision.

⟦SAVE⟧ ⟦⟧ ⟦⟧ ⟦⟧ ⟦⟧ ⟦⟧ ⟦⟧ ⟦⟧

◆◆◆ Radisson Hotel Downtown Norfolk **H** 🐾
(757) 627-5555. **$119-$119, 7 days notice.** 700 Monticello Ave. Downtown at Brambleton Ave & St Pauls Blvd across form Scope. Int corridors. **Pets:** Small. $25 deposit/room. No service, supervision, crate.

⟦ASK⟧ ⟦⟧ ⟦⟧ ⟦⟧ ⟦⟧ ⟦⟧ ⟦⟧ ⟦⟧ ⟦⟧

PORTSMOUTH

◆◆◆ Holiday Inn-Olde Towne
Portsmouth **MI** 🐾
(757) 393-2573. **$92-$113.** 8 Crawford Pkwy. At Green St. Int corridors. **Pets:** Supervision.

⟦ASK⟧ ⟦⟧ ⟦⟧ ⟦⟧ ⟦⟧ ⟦⟧ ⟦⟧ ⟦⟧

VIRGINIA BEACH

△△△ ◆◆◆ Clarion Hotel Pembroke Corporate
Center **H** 🐾
(757) 473-1700. **$109-$159.** 4453 Bonney Rd. SR 44 (Expressway), exit 3B (Independence Blvd), 0.5 mi se. Int corridors. **Pets:** Small, other. $35 deposit/room, $10 daily fee/room. No service, supervision, crate.

⟦SAVE⟧ ⟦⟧ ⟦⟧ ⟦⟧ ⟦⟧ ⟦⟧

△△△ ◆◆◆ Days Inn Oceanfront **MI** 🐾
(757) 428-7233. **$145-$225, 3 days notice.** Atlantic Ave at 32nd St. Just n of jct Atlantic Ave and Laskin Rd (SR 58). Int corridors. **Pets:** Other. $15 daily fee/pet. Designated rooms, no service, supervision, crate.

⟦SAVE⟧ ⟦⟧ ⟦⟧ ⟦⟧ ⟦⟧ ⟦⟧

△△△ ◆ Flagship Motel **M** 🐾
(757) 425-6422. **$60-$175.** 512 Atlantic Ave. Atlantic Ave and 6th St. Ext corridors. **Pets:** Other. Supervision.

⟦⟧ ⟦⟧ ⟦⟧

△△△ ◆◆◆ La Quinta Inn **M** 🐾
(757) 497-6620. **$75-$102.** 192 Newtown Rd. I-64, exit 284B, to SR 44, Newtown Rd S exit. Int corridors. **Pets:** Small, other. Supervision.

⟦SAVE⟧ ⟦⟧ ⟦⟧ ⟦⟧ ⟦⟧ ⟦⟧

[AAA] ◆◆ **Ocean Holiday Hotel** [M]
(757) 425-6920. **$95-$195, 3 days notice.** 2417 Atlantic Ave. Atlantic Ave and 25th St. Int corridors. **Pets:** Supervision.
🚭 ▣ 🏊 ⊗

[AAA] ◆◆◆ **Ramada Inn Airport** [MI] 🐾
(757) 464-9351. **$62-$92, 7 days notice.** 5725 Northampton Blvd. US 13, 1 mi n of jct I-64, exit 282; 2.5 mi n of Norfolk International Airport. Ext corridors. **Pets:** Medium, other. $25 one-time fee/pet. No service, supervision, crate.
[SAVE] [SD] 🚭 ▣ 📺 🍴 🏊

[AAA] ◆◆ **Red Roof Inn-Virginia Beach** [M]
(757) 490-0225. **$60-$75.** 196 Ballard Ct. 0.5 mi e of jct I-64 and SR 44/I-264, just s and just e on Greenwich; Newtown Rd exit westbound, SR 44; Newtown Rd S exit eastbound. Ext corridors. **Pets:** Small. Designated rooms, no service, supervision, crate.
[SAVE] 🚭 ▣ 🏊

[AAA] ◆◆ **The Thunderbird Motor Lodge** [MI] 🐾
(757) 428-3024. **$65-$135, 3 days notice.** 3410 Atlantic Ave. 1.2 mi n of SR 44, at Atlantic Ave and 35th St. Ext/int corridors. **Pets:** Small. $10 daily fee/pet. No service, supervision, crate.
🚭 ▣ 🍴 🏊 ⊗

◆◆◆ **TownePlace Suites By Marriott** [A] 🐾
(757) 490-9367. **$64-$119.** 5757 Cleveland St. I-64, exit 284B to SR 44, Newtown Rd N exit to Cleveland St. Int corridors. **Pets:** Other. $75 deposit/room, $10 daily fee/room. Supervision.
[ASK] [SD] 🚭 ♿ 🚿 ▣ 🏊

🐾 **END METROPOLITAN AREA** 🐾

HARRISONBURG

[AAA] ◆◆◆ **Comfort Inn** [M]
(540) 433-6066. **$72-$92.** 1440 E Market St. I-81, exit 247A, just e. Int corridors. **Pets:** Supervision.
[SAVE] [SD] 🚭 🦻 🚿 ▣ 📺 🏊

◆◆ **Days Inn Harrisonburg** [M] 🐾
(540) 433-9353. **$45-$90.** 1131 Forest Hill Rd. I-81, exit 245, just e. Int corridors. **Pets:** Other. $5 one-time fee/room. Supervision.
[ASK] [SD] 🚭 ▣ 📺 🏊

[AAA] ◆◆ **Howard Johnson Inn** [MI] 🐾
(540) 434-6771. **$45-$70.** 605 Port Republic Rd. I-81, exit 245, just e. Ext/int corridors. **Pets:** No service, supervision, crate.
[SAVE] [SD] 🚭 ▣ 📺 🍴 🏊

[AAA] ◆◆ **Ramada Inn** [MI] 🐾
(540) 434-9981. **$45-$85.** 1 Pleasant Valley Rd. I-81, exit 243, just w, then just n on US 11. Ext corridors. **Pets:** Very small, other. $10 one-time fee/room. Supervision.
[SAVE] [SD] 🚭 🦻 ▣ 📺 🍴 🏊

[AAA] ◆ **Rockingham Motel** [M]
(540) 433-2538. **$33-$39.** 4035 S Main St. I-81, exit 243, just w to US 11, then 0.7 mi s. Ext corridors. **Pets:** No service, supervision, crate.
[SAVE] [SD] 🚭 ▣ ⊗

◆◆◆ **Sheraton Four Points Hotel** [H]
(540) 433-2521. **$99-$109.** 1400 E Market St. I-81, exit 247A, just e on US 33. Int corridors. **Pets:** No service, supervision, crate.
[ASK] [SD] 🚭 🦻 🚿 ▣ 📺 🍴 🏊

[AAA] ◆◆ **Super 8 Motel** [M] 🐾
(540) 433-8888. **$47-$55.** 3330 S Main St. I-81, exit 243, just e, then just s on US 11. Int corridors. **Pets:** Small. No service, supervision, crate.
[SAVE] [SD] 🚭 ▣

[AAA] ◆◆ **Village Inn** [MI] 🐾
(540) 434-7355. **$50-$60.** 4979 South Valley Pike. I-81, exit 240, 0.6 mi w on SR 257, then 1.5 mi n on US 11; exit 243, just w to US 11, then 1.7 mi s.. Ext corridors. **Pets:** Other. $5 daily fee/pet. No service, supervision, crate.
🚭 ▣ 📺 🏊 ⊗

HILLSVILLE

[AAA] ◆◆ **Best Western Four Seasons South** [M] 🐾
(540) 728-4136. **$53-$69.** 57 Airport Rd. I-77, exit 14, just w on US 58 and 221. Ext corridors. **Pets:** Very small. $10 daily fee/pet, $10 one-time fee/pet. No service, supervision, crate.
[SAVE] [SD] 🚭 🦻

[AAA] ◆◆◆ **Holiday Inn Express** [M] 🐾
(540) 728-2120. **$69-$150, 7 days notice.** 85 Airport Rd. I-77, exit 14, just w on US 58 and 221. Ext corridors. **Pets:** Medium, other. $10 daily fee/pet. No service, supervision, crate.
[SAVE] [SD] 🚭 ♿ 🚿 ▣ 🏊

HOPEWELL

◆◆◆ **Comfort Inn** [MI] 🐾
(804) 452-0022. **$55-$85.** 5380 Oaklawn Blvd. SR 36, just w of I-295, exit 9B. Int corridors. **Pets:** Other. $20 one-time fee/room. No service, supervision, crate.
[ASK] [SD] 🚭 ▣ 📺 🍴 🏊

HOT SPRINGS

◆◆ **Roseloe Motel** [M] 🐾
(540) 839-5373. **$38-$55.** 590 US 220 N. 3 mi n on US 220. Ext corridors. **Pets:** Other. Supervision.
🚭 ▣ 📺

IRVINGTON

◆◆◆ The Tides Inn 🆁 ❀
(804) 438-5000. **Call for rates, 7 days notice.** 480 King Carter Dr. 0.3 mi w of CR 200. Ext/int corridors. **Pets:** Other. $10 daily fee/room. Designated rooms, no service, supervision, crate.

🔀 📶 🛗 💻 🍽 🗺 ⊠

◆◆◆ Tides Lodge 🆁 ❀
(804) 438-5000. **Call for rates.** #1 St Andrews Ln. 1 mi nw on SR 200, 1.8 mi w via CR 646 follow signs. Int corridors. **Pets:** Other. $10 daily fee/room. Designated rooms, no service, supervision, crate.

🔀 📶 🛗 💻 🍽 ⊠

KEYSVILLE

◆◆ Sheldon's Motel 🄼 ❀
(804) 736-8434. **$38-$55.** 1450 Four Locust Hwy. 1.3 mi n on US 15 and 360 business route. Ext corridors. **Pets:** Other. Supervision.

SAVE 📶 🔀 🛗 🍽

LEXINGTON

◆◆◆ Best Western Inn at Hunt Ridge 🄼 ❀
(540) 464-1500. **$80-$89.** 25 Willow Springs Rd. I-64, exit 55, just n on US 11 to SR 39, then just w; from I-81, exit 191, 0.6 mi w. Int corridors. **Pets:** Small. Designated rooms, no service, supervision, crate.

SAVE 🔀 ♿ 📶 🐾 🛗 💻 🍽 🗺

◆◆◆ Comfort Inn-Virginia Horse Center 🄼 ❀
(540) 463-7311. **$50-$85.** 62 Comfort Way. I-64 exit 55, just s on US 11; from I-81 exit 191, 0.6 mi w. Int corridors. **Pets:** Medium, other. Designated rooms, supervision.

SAVE 🔀 🛗 💻 🗺

◆◆ Days Inn Keydet General 🄼 ❀
(540) 463-2143. **$48-$70.** 325 W Midland Tr. I-81, exit 188B, US 60 W 4.5 mi; from I-64, exit 50, 5 mi e on US 60. Ext/int corridors. **Pets:** Other. $5 daily fee/pet. No service, supervision, crate.

SAVE 📶 🔀 🛗

◆◆ Econo Lodge 🄼 ❀
(540) 463-7371. **$38-$75.** I-64 & US 11. I-64 exit 55, just s on US 11; from I-81 exit 191, 0.6 mi w. Ext corridors. **Pets:** $7 daily fee/pet. Designated rooms, supervision.

SAVE 📶 🔀 💻

◆◆◆ Holiday Inn Express 🄼 ❀
(540) 463-7351. **$65-$104.** Rt 11 N & & I-64. I-64 exit 55, just s on US 11; from I-81 exit 191, 1.6 mi w. Ext corridors. **Pets:** Medium, other. Designated rooms, no service, supervision, crate.

SAVE 📶 🔀 🐾 💻

◆◆ Howard Johnson Inn 🄼
(540) 463-9181. **$60-$75, 7 days notice.** 2836 N Lee Hwy. I-81, exit 195, just s on US 11. Int corridors. **Pets:** Designated rooms, supervision.

SAVE 📶 🔀 🐾 🛗 💻 🍽 🗺

◆◆ Ramada Inn Lexington 🄼 ❀
(540) 463-6400. **$52-$68.** 2814 N Lee Hwy. I-81, exit 195, just sw on US 11. Int corridors. **Pets:** $5 daily fee/pet, $5 one-time fee/pet. No service, supervision, crate.

SAVE 📶 🔀 🐾 🐾 🍽 🗺

LURAY

◆◆◆ Best Western Intown of Luray 🄼 ❀
(540) 743-6511. **$69-$95.** 410 W Main St. 0.3 mi w on US 211 business route. Ext corridors. **Pets:** $20 daily fee/pet. Designated rooms, no service, supervision, crate.

📶 🔀 🛗 🍽 🗺 ⊠

LYNCHBURG

◆◆◆ Comfort Inn 🄼 ❀
(540) 847-9041. **$67-$87.** 3125 Albert Lankford Dr. 2.5 mi s on US 29 Expwy, exit 7 (Odd Fellows Rd). Int corridors. **Pets:** Other. Designated rooms, no service, supervision, crate.

SAVE 📶 🔀 🛗 💻 🍽 🗺

◆◆◆ Holiday Inn Select 🄷
(804) 528-2500. **$71.** 601 Main St. Center; Main St downtown exit 1, off US 29 Expwy. Int corridors. **Pets:** Small. Supervision.

SAVE 🔀 🛗 💻 🍽 🗺

MARION

◆◆◆ Best Western-Marion 🄼
(540) 783-3193. **$60-$73.** 1424 N Main St. I-81, exit 47, 0.3 mi sw on US 11. Ext corridors. **Pets:** Designated rooms, no service, supervision, crate.

SAVE 📶 🔀 🐾 🛗 💻 🍽 🗺

◆◆ Econo Lodge 🄼
(540) 783-6031. **$54-$69.** 1426 N Main St. I-81, exit 47, 0.3 mi sw on US 11. Ext corridors. **Pets:** Medium. No service, supervision, crate.

ASK 📶 🔀 🐾 🛗 💻

◆ Virginia House Motor Inn 🄼 ❀
(540) 783-5112. **$44-$49, 7 days notice.** 1419 N Main St. I-81, exit 47, 0.3 mi sw on US 11. Ext corridors. **Pets:** Small. $5 one-time fee/pet. No service, supervision, crate.

ASK 📶 🔀 🗺

MARTINSVILLE

◆◆ Best Lodge 🄼 ❀
(540) 647-3941. **$40-$65.** 1985 Virginia Ave. 2.5 mi n on US 220 business route, from jct US 58. Ext corridors. **Pets:** Small. $7 daily fee/pet, $7 one-time fee/pet. Designated rooms, no service, supervision, crate.

SAVE 📶 🔀 🛗 💻

◆◆◆ Best Western Martinsville Inn 🄼 ❀
(540) 632-5611. **$55-$85.** US 220 business S. 2.3 mi n on US 220 business route, from jct US 58. Ext corridors. **Pets:** Supervision.

📶 🔀 🛗 💻 🍽 🗺

◆◆ **Super 8 Motel** Ⓜ
(540) 666-8888. **Call for rates.** 1044 N Memorial Blvd. 1.5 mi n on US 220 business route, from jct US 58. Int corridors. **Pets:** Supervision.

⊠ 🛢

MAX MEADOWS

🅐 ◆◆◆ **Super 8 Motel** Ⓜ
(540) 637-4027. **$56-$140, 7 days notice.** I-77 and I-81 exit 80, just w. Int corridors. **Pets:** Medium. Supervision.

ⓈAVE 🖠 ⊠ 🖑 🖐 🛢 🖾

MINT SPRING

◆◆ **Armstrong Family Motel & Restaurant** Ⓜ ❧
(540) 337-2611. **$48-$48.** I-81, exit 217, just w on SR 654. Ext corridors. **Pets:** Other. Supervision.

🅐🅢🅚 ⊠ 🍴 🖾

◆◆ **Days Inn** Ⓜ ❧
(540) 337-3031. **$59-$119.** I-81, exit 217, just e on SR 654. Ext corridors. **Pets:** Other. $5 daily fee/room. Supervision.

🅐🅢🅚 🖠 ⊠ 🖉 🖐 🖾

MOUNT JACKSON

🅐 ◆◆◆ **Best Western-Mt. Jackson** Ⓜ ❧
(540) 477-2911. **$60-$85, 3 days notice.** 250 Conickville Rd. I-81, exit 273, just e. Ext corridors. **Pets:** Other. $6 daily fee/room. Designated rooms, supervision.

ⓈAVE 🖠 ⊠ 🍴 🖾 🖾

◆◆◆ **The Widow Kip's** 🅱🅱 ❧
(540) 477-2400. **$100, 5 days notice.** 355 Orchard Dr. I-81, exit 273, 1.5 mi s on US 11, just w on SR 263, then just sw on SR 698. Int corridors. **Pets:** Other. $5 daily fee/pet, $5 one-time fee/pet. Designated rooms, no service, supervision, crate.

🅐🅢🅚 🖠 ⊠ 🛢 🖾 🖾 🗹

NASSAWADOX

🅐 ◆ **Anchor Motel** Ⓜ
(757) 442-6363. **$60-$77, 7 days notice.** 7120 Lankford Hwy. Just n on US 13. Ext corridors. **Pets:** Supervision.

ⓈAVE ⊠ 🛢

NATURAL BRIDGE

🅐 ◆◆ **Budget Inn** Ⓜ
(540) 291-2896. **$32-$68, 7 days notice.** 4331 S Lee Hwy. I-81, exit 180 northbound, 1 mi nw on US 11; exit 180B southbound, just w. Ext corridors. **Pets:** Small. Designated rooms, no service, supervision, crate.

ⓈAVE 🖠 ⊠ 🛢

NEW CHURCH

◆◆◆ **The Garden & The Sea Inn** 🅲🅸
(757) 824-0672. **$75-$175.** 4188 Nelson Rd. Rt 13, 0.3 mi n, just w on Rt 710 (Nelson Rd). Int corridors. **Pets:** Medium. Supervision.

🅐🅢🅚 ⊠ 🛢 🗹

NEW MARKET

🅐 ◆ **Budget Inn** Ⓜ ❧
(540) 740-3105. **$29-$65, 3 days notice.** 2192 Old Valley Pike. I-81, exit 264, 1 mi n on US 11. Ext corridors. **Pets:** Small. $100 deposit/pet, $5 daily fee/pet, $5 one-time fee/pet. Designated rooms, no service, supervision, crate.

ⓈAVE 🖠 ⊠ 🛢 🖾

NORTON

◆◆ **Holiday Inn Norton** Ⓜ🅸 ❧
(540) 679-7000. **$79-$115.** 551 Hwy 58E. Jct US 58 and 23. Int corridors. **Pets:** Other. No service, supervision, crate.

🅐🅢🅚 🖠 ⊠ 🖉 🛢 🖭 🍴 🖾

PETERSBURG

🅐 ◆◆ **Best Western of Petersburg** Ⓜ🅸 ❧
(804) 733-1776. **$45-$106.** 405 E Washington St. I-95, exit 52 southbound, exit 50D northbound; I-85, exit 69. Ext corridors. **Pets:** Medium. $5 daily fee/pet. Designated rooms, supervision.

ⓈAVE 🖠 ⊠ 🖉 🛢 🖭 🍴 🖾

🅐 ◆◆◆ **Comfort Inn** Ⓜ ❧
(804) 732-2900. **$50-$90.** 11974 S Crater Rd. Jct I-95 and US 301, exit 45. Ext corridors. **Pets:** Small. No service, supervision, crate.

ⓈAVE 🖠 ⊠ 🛢 🖭 🖾

🅐 ◆◆◆ **Days Inn** Ⓜ🅸 ❧
(804) 733-4400. **$57-$79.** 12208 S Crater Rd. I-95, exit 45 (US 301). Ext corridors. **Pets:** $7 daily fee/pet. Supervision.

ⓈAVE 🖠 ⊠ 🖉 🛢 🖭 🖾 🖾

🅐 ◆◆◆ **The High Street Inn** 🅱🅱
(804) 733-0505. **$75-$110, 5 days notice.** 405 High St. In Olde Towne Historic District; I-95, exit 52, 0.5 mi on Washington St, just n on Market St, just w. Int corridors. **Pets:** No service, supervision, crate.

ⓈAVE ⊠ 🛢

🅐 ◆◆◆ **Quality Inn-Steven Kent** Ⓜ🅸 ❧
(804) 733-0600. **$50-$70.** 12205 S Crater Rd. 6 mi s on I-95 at jct US 301, exit 45. Ext/int corridors. **Pets:** Other. $5 daily fee/pet. Designated rooms, supervision.

ⓈAVE 🖠 ⊠ 🖉 🛢 🖭 🖾 🖾

🅐 ◆◆ **Ramada Inn** Ⓜ🅸 ❧
(804) 733-0730. **$43-$70.** 501 E Washington St. Jct I-95 and Washington St, exit 50D northbound; exit 52 southbound. Ext/int corridors. **Pets:** Small. Designated rooms, no service, supervision, crate.

ⓈAVE ⊠ 🖉 🛢 🖭 🍴 🖾

RADFORD

◆◆◆ **The Alleghany Inn** 🅲🅸
(540) 731-4466. **$65-$95, 7 days notice.** 1123 Grove Ave. I-81, exit 109, 4.4 mi w on SR 177, just s. Ext/int corridors. **Pets:** Supervision.

🅐🅢🅚 🖠 ⊠ 🛢 🖭

⚑⚑⚑ ◆◆◆ **Best Western Radford Inn** Ⓜ **❀**
(540) 639-3000. **$69-$89.** 1501 Tyler Ave. I-81, exit 109, 2.7 mi nw on SR 177. Int corridors. **Pets:** Small, other. $40 deposit/room, $10 one-time fee/room. Designated rooms, no service, supervision, crate.
[SAVE] [S⊘] [✕] [🔒] [▢] [▯] [🍽] [🏊]

⚑⚑⚑ ◆ **Dogwood Lodge** Ⓜ **❀**
(540) 639-9338. **$30-$38.** 7073 Lee Hwy, US 11. 2.5 mi sw on US 11, just n of jct SR 741. Ext corridors. **Pets:** Other. $5 daily fee/room. Supervision.
[SAVE]

RAPHINE

◆◆ **Days Inn-Shenandoah Valley** Ⓜ **❀**
(540) 377-2604. **$54-$99.** 584 Oakland Cr. I-81, exit 205, just sw. Int corridors. **Pets:** Medium, other. $5 one-time fee/pet. Supervision.
[ASK] [✕] [🏊] [CTV]

RICHMOND METROPOLITAN AREA

CARMEL CHURCH

◆◆ **Days Inn-Carmel Church/Kings Dominion** Ⓜ **❀**
(804) 448-2011. **$65-$99.** 24320 Rogers Clark Blvd. Jct I-95 and SR 207, exit 104 (Carmel Church Rd). Ext corridors. **Pets:** Large, other. $5 daily fee/pet. No service, supervision, crate.
[ASK] [S⊘] [✕] [🔒] [🔒] [▯] [🏊] [✕]

◆◆ **Ramada Inn-Carmel Church** Ⓜ **❀**
(804) 448-2828. **$69-$89, 3 days notice.** 23500 Welcome Way Dr. At jct SR 207 and I-95, exit 104. Int corridors. **Pets:** Small, other. $10 one-time fee/room. Supervision.
[ASK] [S⊘] [✕] [🖉] [🖋] [🔒] [▢] [🍽] [🏊] [CTV]

CHESTER

◆◆ **Days Inn-Chester** Ⓜ **❀**
(804) 748-5871. **$58-$89.** 2410 W Hundred Rd. I-95, exit 61B (SR 10), 0.8 mi w. Ext/int corridors. **Pets:** Other. $6 daily fee/pet. Supervision.
[ASK] [S⊘] [✕] [🔒] [🔒] [🏊] [✕]

⚑⚑⚑ ◆◆ **Howard Johnson Hotel-Chester** Ⓜ **❀**
(804) 748-6321. **$68-$85.** 2401 W Hundred Rd. Just e of jct SR 10 and I-95, exit 61B. Int corridors. **Pets:** Small, other. $50 deposit/room. Supervision.
[SAVE] [S⊘] [✕] [🖉] [🔒] [▢] [🍽] [🏊]

GLEN ALLEN

◆◆◆ **Homestead Village-Innsbrook** Ⓜ **❀**
(804) 747-8898. **$59-$99.** 10961 W Broad St. I-64, exit 178B, just e US 250 (W Broad St), just s on Cox Rd. Ext corridors. **Pets:** Medium. $75 one-time fee/room. No service, supervision, crate.
[✕] [🖉] [🖋] [🔒]

◆◆◆ **Homewood Suites Hotel Richmond West End** Ⓜ
(804) 217-8000. **Call for rates.** 4100 Innslake Dr. From I-64, exit 178B, just e on W Broad St and Cox Rd, just n. Int corridors. **Pets:** Supervision.
[✕] [🖋] [🖉] [🖋] [🔒] [▢] [🏊]

◆◆◆ **Residence Inn by Marriott** 🅰 **❀**
(804) 762-9852. **$114-$179.** 3940 Westerre Pkwy. Just s of jct W Broad St and Westerre Pkwy; from I-64 exit 178B, 0.5 mi e. Int corridors. **Pets:** Other. $150 one-time fee/room. Supervision.
[S⊘] [✕] [🖋] [🔒] [▢] [🏊] [✕]

◆◆◆ **Towne Place Suites by Marriott** 🄷 **❀**
(804) 747-5253. **Call for rates.** 4231 Park Place Ct. From I-64, exit 178B, just e on W Broad St to Cox Rd, just n to Innslake Dr. Int corridors. **Pets:** Other. $65 one-time fee/room. Supervision.
[✕] [🖋] [🔒] [🏊]

RICHMOND

⚑⚑⚑ ◆◆◆ **AmeriSuites Richmond Arboretum** Ⓜ **❀**
(804) 560-1566. **$67-$129.** 201 Arboretum Pl. Jct Powhite Pkwy (US 195) and Midlothian Tpk (US 60), just w enter at the Arboretum Pl. Int corridors. **Pets:** Small. $5 daily fee/pet. Designated rooms, no service, supervision, crate.
[SAVE] [S⊘] [✕] [🔒] [🖉] [🖋] [🔒] [▢] [🏊]

◆◆ **Best Western** Ⓜ
(804) 275-7891. **$49-$89.** 7007 W Broad St. US 250, just w of jct I-64, exit 183C westbound; exit 183 eastbound. Int corridors. **Pets:** Small. Supervision.
[ASK] [S⊘] [✕] [🔒] [🏊]

◆◆◆ **Days Inn-Richmond/Broad St** Ⓜ **❀**
(804) 282-3300. **$57-$93.** 2100 Dickens Rd. I-64, exit 183B westbound; exit 183 eastbound, 0.3 mi e on W Broad St. Int corridors. **Pets:** Medium, other. $6 one-time fee/pet. No service, supervision, crate.
[ASK] [S⊘] [✕] [🖉] [🔒] [▢] [🏊]

⚑⚑⚑ ◆◆◆ **Holiday Inn-Bells Road** Ⓜ
(804) 275-7891. **$49-$109.** 4303 Commerce Rd. I-95, exit 69 (Bells Rd), just n. Int corridors. **Pets:** Very small. Designated rooms, no service, supervision, crate.
[SAVE] [S⊘] [✕] [🖉] [🔒] [▢] [🍽] [🏊] [CTV]

⚑⚑⚑ ◆◆◆ **Holiday Inn Central** Ⓜ **❀**
(804) 359-9441. **$89-$119, 3 days notice.** 3207 N Boulevard. I-64 and I-95, exit 78 (N Blvd). Ext/int corridors. **Pets:** Small. $30 deposit/room. Designated rooms, no service, supervision, crate.
[SAVE] [S⊘] [✕] [🖉] [🔒] [▢] [🍽] [🏊]

◆◆◆ **Homestead Village Guest Studios-Richmond/Midlothian** Ⓜ
(804) 272-1800. **$49.** 241 Arboretum Pl. From jct Powhite Pkwy (US 76) and Midlothian Tpke (US 60), just w, enter at the Arboretum Pl. Int corridors. **Pets:** Small. Supervision.
[✕] [🖉] [🖋] [🔒]

⚅ ◆◆◆◆◆ The Jefferson Hotel 🅷 ❀
(804) 788-8000. **$150-$265.** Franklin & Adams sts. Center. Int corridors. **Pets:** Large. $25 one-time fee/room. No service, supervision, crate.
[SAVE] [✕] [🐾] [📶] [📺] [🍽] [🔲]

⚅ ◆◆◆ La Quinta Inn 🅼
(804) 745-7100. **$45-$59.** 6910 Midlothian Tpk. US 60 E, Chippenham Pkwy exit; on Midlothian Tpk (US 60). Ext corridors. **Pets:** Supervision.
[SAVE] [✕] [🛏] [🐾] [📶] [📺] [🔲]

⚅ ◆◆◆ Quality Inn West 🅼
(804) 346-0000. **$54-$74.** 8008 W Broad St. 1.5 mi w of jct I-64, exit 183C westbound; exit 183 eastbound (Broad St). Int corridors. **Pets:** Small. Designated rooms, supervision.
[SAVE] [✕] [⚅] [📶] [📺] [🔲]

⚅ ◆◆ Red Roof Inn-Chippenham 🅼 ❀
(804) 745-0600. **$56-$82.** 100 Greshamwood Pl. US 60 and SR 150, US 60 E (Middlothian Tpk) off Chippenham Pkwy; behind Steak and Ale. Ext corridors. **Pets:** Small, other. Supervision.
[SAVE] [✕] [CTV]

⚅ ◆◆ Red Roof Inn-Richmond South 🅼
(804) 271-7240. **$49-$81.** 4350 Commerce Rd. I-95, exit 69 (Bells Rd). Ext corridors. **Pets:** Medium. Supervision.
[SAVE] [✕] [📶] [CTV]

◆◆◆ Residence Inn by Marriott ☒
(804) 285-8200. **Call for rates.** 2121 Dickens Rd. 0.3 mi e of jct I-64, exit 183B, just n of US 60 (Broad St). Ext corridors. **Pets:** Small. Supervision.
[ASK] [✕] [🐾] [📶] [📶] [📶] [☒]

◆◆ Richmond Hotel & Conference Center 🅼 ❀
(804) 285-9951. **$89-$139, 3 days notice.** 6531 W Broad St. Just e of I-64, exit 183B eastbound. Int corridors. **Pets:** $20 one-time fee/pet. Supervision.
[ASK] [💲] [✕] [📶] [📶] [🍽] [🔲]

SANDSTON

◆ Days Inn-Richmond Airport 🅼
(804) 222-2041. **$50-$86.** 5500 Williamsburg Rd. I-64, exit 197A, 0.3 mi s to Williamsburg Rd, 0.5 mi e. Ext corridors. **Pets:** Medium. No service, supervision, crate.
[ASK] [💲] [✕] [🐾] [⚅] [📶] [🍽] [🔲]

◆◆◆ Holiday Inn-Airport 🅼 ❀
(804) 222-6450. **$89-$139, 7 days notice.** 5203 Williamsburg Rd. I-64, exit 195, 1.5 mi s to Williamsburg Rd, just e. Ext/int corridors. **Pets:** Small. $25 one-time fee/room. No service, supervision, crate.
[ASK] [💲] [✕] [⚅] [🔲] [🍽] [🔲]

⚅ ◆◆ Microtel Inn & Suites 🅼 ❀
(804) 737-3322. **$50-$75.** 6000 Audubon Dr. I-64, exit 197A, just s. Int corridors. **Pets:** No service, supervision, crate.
[SAVE] [💲] [✕] [♿] [🐾] [⚅] [📶] [🔲]

──── ❀ **END METROPOLITAN AREA** ❀ ────

ROANOKE

⚅ ◆◆◆ Clarion Hotel Roanoke Airport 🅷 ❀
(540) 362-4500. **$69-$139.** 2727 Ferndale Dr NW. I-581 exit 3W, just w to Ordway Dr, then 0.6 mi n via service road. Int corridors. **Pets:** Medium. $10 daily fee/pet, $25 one-time fee/pet. No service, supervision, crate.
[SAVE] [💲] [✕] [🐾] [⚅] [📶] [🔲] [🍽] [🔲] [☒]

◆◆ Days Inn Civic Center 🅼 ❀
(540) 342-4551. **$60-$100, 72 days notice.** 535 Orange Ave. I-581, exit 4E, just e on US 460. Ext/int corridors. **Pets:** Medium, other. $25 deposit/room. Supervision.
[ASK] [✕] [📶] [🔲] [☒] [CTV]

◆◆◆ Holiday Inn Hotel Tanglewood 🅷 ❀
(540) 774-4400. **$69-$75, 3 days notice.** 4468 Starkey Rd. I-581 (US 220), Franklin Rd/Salem exit, 0.8 mi n on SR 419. Int corridors. **Pets:** Small. Supervision.
[✕] [🐾] [📶] [🔲] [🍽] [🔲]

⚅ ◆◆ Howard Johnson Express Inn 🅼
(540) 344-0981. **$50-$70.** 320 Kimball Ave NE. I-581, exit 4E northbound; exit 5 southbound, just e, then 0.7 mi s on Williamson, then just e. Int corridors. **Pets:** Medium. Supervision.
[SAVE] [💲] [✕] [📶] [🔲] [🔲]

◆◆◆ Ramada Limited Airport 🅼
(540) 563-2871. **$48-$54.** 6520 Thirlane Rd. I-581, exit 25, just s on SR 117, just w on SR 626. Ext corridors. **Pets:** Supervision.
[💲] [✕] [📶] [🔲] [🔲]

⚅ ◆◆◆ Roanoke AmeriSuites at Valley View 🅼
(540) 366-4700. **$69-$119.** 5040 Valley View Blvd. I-581, exit 3E (Hershberger Rd), just e, then just s via shopping center exit. Int corridors. **Pets:** Small. No service, supervision, crate.
[SAVE] [💲] [✕] [♿] [🐾] [⚅] [📶] [🔲] [🔲]

⚅ ◆ Roanoker Motor Lodge 🅼
(540) 362-3344. **$33-$47.** 7645 Williamson Rd. I-81, exit 146, 1 mi se on SR 115, n on US 11. Ext corridors. **Pets:** No service, supervision, crate.
[SAVE] [💲] [✕] [🔲]

◆◆ Super 8 Motel 🅼
(540) 563-8888. **$48-$54.** 6616 Thirlane Rd. I-581 exit 2S, s on SR 117 (Peters Creek Rd), just w. Int corridors. **Pets:** Supervision.
[ASK] [💲] [✕] [📶]

◆◆ **Villager Lodge** **M**
(540) 265-7600. **$35-$60.** 6510 Thirlane Rd. I-581, exit 25, just s on SR 117, just w on SR 626. Ext corridors. **Pets:** Supervision.

🅰🆂🅺 🆂 ⊠ 🖼 🖥

◆◆◆ **Wyndham Roanoke** **H**
(540) 563-9300. **$69-$229.** 2801 Hershberger Rd NW. I-581, exit 3W, just w to Ordway Dr, just n via service road. Int corridors. **Pets:** Supervision.

🅰🆂🅺 🆂 ⊠ 🖼 🖥 🍽 🛰 ⊠

ROCKY MOUNT

🄰🄰🄰 ◆◆ **Franklin Motel** **M** ❖
(540) 483-9962. **$33-$50.** 20281 Virgil H Goode Hwy. 6.5 mi n on US 220. Ext corridors. **Pets:** Very small, dogs only. $10 deposit/pet, $10 one-time fee/pet. Designated rooms, no service, supervision, crate.

🆂🅰🆅🅴 🆂 ⊠ 🖼

RUTHER GLEN

◆◆◆ **Holiday Inn Express-Carmel Church** **M**
(804) 448-2608. **Call for rates.** 24011 Ruther Glen Rd. I-95, exit 104, just e on SR 207. Ext corridors. **Pets:** Medium. Supervision.

⊠ 🖼 🖥 🛰

◆◆◆ **Howard Johnson Express Inn** **M** ❖
(804) 448-2499. **$85-$85.** 23786 Rogers Clark Blvd. I-95, exit 104, just e on SR 112. Ext corridors. **Pets:** Small, other. $10 daily fee/room, $10 one-time fee/room. No service, supervision, crate.

🅰🆂🅺 🆂 ⊠ 🖼 🖥 🖥

SALEM

◆◆◆ **Baymont Inn Roanoke-Salem** **M** ❖
(540) 562-2717. **$50-$80, 3 days notice.** 140 Sheraton Dr. I-81 exit 141, 0.5 mi se on SR 419. Int corridors. **Pets:** Small. $20 deposit/room. Designated rooms, no service, supervision, crate.

🅰🆂🅺 🆂 ⊠ 🖼 🖥 🛰

🄰🄰🄰 ◆ **Blue Jay Budget Host Inn** **M** ❖
(540) 380-2080. **$38-$65, 3 days notice.** 5399 W Main St. I-81, exit 132, just e, then 0.3 mi n on US 11/460. Ext corridors. **Pets:** Medium. $5 daily fee/pet, $5 one-time fee/pet. Designated rooms, no service, supervision, crate.

🆂🅰🆅🅴 🆂 ⊠ 🖼 🛰

🄰🄰🄰 ◆◆◆ **Holiday Inn** **M** ❖
(540) 389-7061. **$59-$89, 7 days notice.** 1671 Skyview Rd. I-81, exit 137, just w on SR 112, then just n. Ext corridors. **Pets:** Medium. No service, supervision, crate.

🆂🅰🆅🅴 🆂 ⊠ 🖼 🖥 🖥 🍽 🛰

🄰🄰🄰 ◆◆ **Knights Inn-Roanoke/Salem** **M** ❖
(540) 389-0280. **$39-$55.** 301 Wildwood Rd. I-81, exit 137, just e on SR 112. Ext corridors. **Pets:** Other. No service, supervision, crate.

🆂🅰🆅🅴 🆂 ⊠ 🖼

🄰🄰🄰 ◆◆◆ **Quality Inn Roanoke/Salem** **M** ❖
(540) 562-1912. **$52-$78.** 179 Sheraton Dr. I-81, exit 141, 0.4 mi e on SR 419. Int corridors. **Pets:** Very small. $6 one-time fee/room. Designated rooms, no service, supervision, crate.

🆂🅰🆅🅴 🆂 ⊠ 🖼 🖥 🍽 🛰 ⊠

SCOTTSVILLE

◆◆◆ **High Meadows Vineyard & Mountain Sunset Inn** **CI** ❖
(804) 286-2218. **$85-$285.** High Meadows Ln. I-64, exit 121, SR 20, 17 mi s, 1 mi n. Int corridors. **Pets:** $20 deposit/pet, $20 one-time fee/pet. Designated rooms, supervision.

🅰🆂🅺 ⊠ 🖼 🖥 🍽 ⊠ 🆂🆃🆅 🕿

SOUTH BOSTON

◆◆◆ **Best Western Howard House Inn** **MI**
(804) 572-4311. **$60-$88, 3 days notice.** 2001 Seymour Dr. 1 mi e on US 360, from jct US 58, 501 and 360. Ext corridors. **Pets:** Designated rooms, supervision.

🅰🆂🅺 🆂 ⊠ 🖼 🍽 🛰

◆◆ **Super 8 Motel** **M** ❖
(804) 572-8868. **$54-$64.** 1040 Bill Tuck Hwy. Just e on US 59, from jct US 501. Int corridors. **Pets:** Other. No service, supervision, crate.

🅰🆂🅺 🆂 ⊠ 🖼

SOUTH HILL

◆◆◆ **Best Western South Hill** **MI** ❖
(804) 447-3123. **$56-$80.** 911 E Atlantic St. US 58, just w of jct I-85, exit 12. Ext corridors. **Pets:** Small. No service, supervision, crate.

🅰🆂🅺 🆂 ⊠ 🖼 🖥 🍽 🛰

🄰🄰🄰 ◆◆ **Econo Lodge** **M** ❖
(804) 447-7116. **$40-$75, 3 days notice.** 623 Atlantic St. 0.5 mi w of I-85, exit 12, on US 58. Ext corridors. **Pets:** Other. $5 one-time fee/room. No service, supervision, crate.

🆂🅰🆅🅴 🆂 ⊠ 🖼 🖥

STAUNTON

◆◆◆ **Ashton Country House** **BB** ❖
(540) 885-7819. **$65-$125, 7 days notice.** 1205 Middlebrook Ave. I-81, exit 222, 2.2 mi w on US 250, 0.3 mi s on Greenville Ave, 0.3 mi w on Hampton St to Middlebrook, then 1 mi s. Int corridors. **Pets:** Other. $10 daily fee/room. Designated rooms, supervision.

🅰🆂🅺 🆂 ⊠ 🕿

🄰🄰🄰 ◆◆◆ **Comfort Inn** **M** ❖
(540) 886-5000. **$65-$85.** 1302 Richmond Ave. I-81, exit 222, just w on US 250. Int corridors. **Pets:** Small. $10 daily fee/room. Designated rooms, no service, supervision, crate.

🆂🅰🆅🅴 🆂 ⊠ 🖼 🖥 🖥 🛰

🄰🄰🄰 ◆◆ **Econo Lodge Staunton** **M** ❖
(540) 885-5158. **$54-$78, 7 days notice.** 1031 Richmond Ave. I-81, exit 222, 0.7 mi w on US 250. Ext/int corridors. **Pets:** Other. Supervision.

🆂🅰🆅🅴 🆂 ⊠ 🖼 🖥

◆◆◆ Quality Inn-Staunton 🅼 ❀
(540) 248-5111. **$59-$89.** 96 Baker Ln. I-81, exit 225, just e on SR 275 (Woodrow Wilson Pkwy). Ext corridors. **Pets:** $6 daily fee/room, $6 one-time fee/room. No service, supervision, crate.

SAVE 🖾 ✕ 🖥 💻 🏊

◆◆ Sleep Inn 🅼 ❀
(540) 887-6500. **$59-$94.** 222 Jefferson Hwy. I-81, exit 222, just e on US 250. Int corridors. **Pets:** Other. Designated rooms, no service, supervision, crate.

SAVE 🖾 ✕ 🖾 💻

◆◆ Super 8 Motel 🅼 ❀
(540) 886-2888. **$54-$78, 7 days notice.** 1015 Richmond Rd. I-81, exit 222, 1.2 mi w on US 250. Int corridors. **Pets:** Other. Supervision.

SAVE 🖾 ✕ 🖥

STEPHENS CITY

◆◆◆ Comfort Inn-Stephens City 🅼 ❀
(540) 869-6500. **$65-$70.** 167 Town Run Ln. I-81, exit 307, just se. Int corridors. **Pets:** $10 daily fee/pet. No service, supervision, crate.

SAVE 🖾 ✕ 🖾 🖥 💻 🏊

STRASBURG

◆◆◆ Hotel Strasburg 🅲🅸
(540) 465-9191. **$79-$89.** 213 Holliday St. I-81, exit 298, 2.2 mi s on US 11, just s. Int corridors. **Pets:** Small. Designated rooms, supervision.

SAVE 🖾 ✕

THORNBURG

◆◆◆ Holiday Inn Express 🅼 ❀
(540) 582-1097. **$69-$89.** 6409 Dan Bell Ln. Jct I-95 and SR 606, exit 118. Ext corridors. **Pets:** Small. $10 daily fee/pet, $10 one-time fee/pet. No service, supervision, crate.

ASK 🖾 ✕ 🖾 🖾 🖥 🏊

TROUTVILLE

◆◆◆ Comfort Inn Troutville 🅼 ❀
(540) 992-5600. **$67-$88.** 2654 Lee Hwy S. I-81, exit 150A, then just s on US 11. Int corridors. **Pets:** Other. Supervision.

SAVE ✕ 🖥 💻 🏊

◆ Daystop Roanoke 🅼🅸
(540) 992-3100. **$49-$75.** US 220. I-81, exit 150A, just e on US 220; at jct US 11. Ext corridors. **Pets:** No service, supervision, crate.

ASK 🖾 ✕

◆◆ Travelodge Roanoke North 🅼 ❀
(540) 992-6700. **$55-$65.** 2444 Lee Hwy S. I-81, exit 150A, just e, then just s on US 11. Ext corridors. **Pets:** $6 one-time fee/pet. No service, supervision, crate.

SAVE 🖾 ✕ 🖥 💻 🏊 ✕

VERONA

◆◆◆ Ramada Limited 🅼 ❀
(540) 248-8981. **$55-$75, 30 days notice.** 70 Lodge Ln. I-81, exit 227, just w, then just n. Ext corridors. **Pets:** Medium. $5 daily fee/pet. Designated rooms, no service, supervision, crate.

ASK 🖾 ✕ 💻 🏊

WARRENTON

◆◆◆ Comfort Inn 🅼 ❀
(540) 349-8900. **$65-$79.** 7379 Comfort Inn Dr. 1.5 mi n on US 15/29, on service road. Ext/int corridors. **Pets:** $10 daily fee/pet. Designated rooms, no service, supervision, crate.

SAVE 🖾 ✕ 🖥 💻 🏊

◆◆◆ Hampton Inn 🅼 ❀
(540) 349-4200. **$63-$79.** 501 Blackwell Rd. 1 mi n on US 29 business route and 211. Ext corridors. **Pets:** No service, supervision, crate.

SAVE 🖾 ✕ 🖾 🖾 🖥 💻 🏊

◆◆ Howard Johnson Inn 🅼 ❀
(540) 347-4141. **$45-$85.** 6 Broadview Ave. US 17/29 business route, jct US 211 W. Int corridors. **Pets:** Very small, dogs only. $10 deposit/pet, $10 one-time fee/room. Designated rooms, no service, supervision, crate.

SAVE 🖾 ✕ 🖥 💻 🏊

WARSAW

◆◆◆ Best Western Warsaw 🅼 ❀
(804) 333-1700. **$54-$68.** 4522 Richmond Rd. US 360, just w of town. Int corridors. **Pets:** Small, other. $10 daily fee/pet, $10 one-time fee/pet. No service, supervision, crate.

ASK 🖾 ✕ 🖥 🏊

WAYNESBORO

◆◆ Comfort Inn Waynesboro 🅼
(540) 942-1171. **$53-$73, 7 days notice.** 640 W Broad St. I-64, exit 96, 3 mi w on SR 624; at jct US 250 and 340. Ext/int corridors. **Pets:** Very small. Designated rooms, no service, supervision, crate.

ASK 🖾 ✕ 🖾 🖥 💻 🏊

◆◆ Super 8 Motel 🅼 ❀
(540) 943-3888. **Call for rates.** 2045 Rosser Ave. I-64, exit 94, n on US 340 to Lew DeWitt Blvd, just w to Apple Tree Ln. Int corridors. **Pets:** Medium, other. Supervision.

✕ 🖾 🖥

WILLIAMSBURG, JAMESTOWN & YORKTOWN METROPOLITAN AREA

CHARLES CITY

◆ **River's Rest Motel & Marina** Ⓜ ❀
(804) 829-2753. **$49-$69.** 9100 Willcox Neck Rd. From SR 5, 10 mi n on SR 615, just w on SR 623. Ext corridors. **Pets:** Other. Designated rooms, supervision.
ⒶⓈⓀ ⓈⒹ 🍴 ⊠ ⒸⓉⓋ ☎

LIGHTFOOT

🆎🅰🅰 ◆◆ **Econo Lodge-Pottery** Ⓜ
(757) 564-3341. **$30-$130.** 7051 Richmond Rd. I-64, exit 231A, 1 mi s on SR 607, 2.4 mi e on US 60. Ext corridors. **Pets:** Small. Designated rooms, no service, supervision, crate.
ⓈⒶⱽⒺ ⊠ 🖨

WILLIAMSBURG

🆎🅰🅰 ◆◆◆ **Best Western Colonial Capitol Inn** Ⓜ ❀
(757) 253-1222. **$89-$109, 3 days notice.** 111 Penniman Rd. Just n of jct US 60 and SR 5/SR 31. Int corridors. **Pets:** Other. $5 daily fee/room. Supervision.
ⓈⒶⱽⒺ ⓈⒹ ⊠ 🔥 🔥 🖥 🖨 🖥 ⊠

🆎🅰🅰 ◆◆◆ **Best Western Patrick Henry Inn** Ⓗ ❀
(757) 229-9540. **$109-$119, 3 days notice.** 249 E York St NW. E on US 60 at jct SR 5 and 31, 1 blk from Colonial Williamsburg. Int corridors. **Pets:** Medium. Supervision.
ⓈⒶⱽⒺ ⓈⒹ ⊠ 🔥 🔥 🖥 🍴 🖨 ⊠

🆎🅰🅰 ◆◆ **Best Western Williamsburg** Ⓜ
(757) 229-3003. **$89-$119, 3 days notice.** 7411 Pocahantas Tr. 2 mi e on US 60 at jct SR 199. Ext corridors. **Pets:** Small. Supervision.
ⓈⒶⱽⒺ ⓈⒹ ⊠ 🔥 🔥 🖥 🍴 🖨 ⊠

🆎🅰🅰 ◆◆◆ **Best Western Williamsburg Westpark Hotel** Ⓜ ❀
(757) 229-1134. **$69-$99.** 1600 Richmond Rd. Jct US 60/Richmond Rd and SR 612/Ironbound Rd. Ext/int corridors. **Pets:** No service, supervision, crate.
ⓈⒶⱽⒺ ⓈⒹ ⊠ 🖥 🖥 🍴 🖨

🆎🅰🅰 ◆◆◆ **Heritage Inn** Ⓜ ❀
(757) 229-6220. **$80-$80, 3 days notice.** 1324 Richmond Rd. Just e of jct Richmond and Bypass rds (US 60). Ext corridors. **Pets:** Other. Supervision.
ⓈⒶⱽⒺ ⓈⒹ ⊠ 🖨

🆎🅰🅰 ◆◆◆ **Holiday Inn Patriot** Ⓜ ❀
(757) 565-2600. **$79-$129.** 3032 Richmond Rd. I-64, exit 234, s on 646 to US 60 then, 2 mi e. Int corridors. **Pets:** Medium. $75 deposit/room, $10 daily fee/pet. Supervision.
ⓈⒶⱽⒺ ⓈⒹ ⊠ 🖊 🖥 🖥 🍴 🖨 ⊠

◆◆◆ **The Inn at 802** 🅱🅱 ❀
(757) 564-0845. **$125-$145, 7 days notice.** 802 Jamestown Rd. Jct W SR 199, 1 mi ne of SR 31 and 5. Int corridors. **Pets:** Other. Supervision.
ⒶⓈⓀ ⊠ ☎

🆎🅰🅰 ◆◆ **Quarterpath Inn** Ⓜ
(757) 220-0960. **$65-$85.** 620 York St. US 60 E, 0.5 mi se of jct SR 5. Ext corridors. **Pets:** Medium. Supervision.
ⓈⒶⱽⒺ ⓈⒹ ⊠ 🖥 🖨

🆎🅰🅰 ◆◆◆ **Ramada Inn Historic** Ⓜ
(757) 220-1410. **$79-$114.** 500 Merrimac Tr. Jct SR 143 and 162, 0.8 mi e of US 60. Int corridors. **Pets:** No service, supervision, crate.
ⓈⒶⱽⒺ ⓈⒹ ⊠ 🔥 🖥 🖥 🍴 🖨

❀ END METROPOLITAN AREA ❀

WINCHESTER

◆◆◆ **Baymont Inn & Suites-Winchester** Ⓜ
(540) 678-0800. **$59-$64.** 800 Millwood Ave. I-81, exit 313 northbound; 313B southbound, just nw on US 50/17/522. Int corridors. **Pets:** Large. No service, supervision, crate.
ⓈⒹ ⊠ 🔥 🖊 🖥 🖥

🆎🅰🅰 ◆◆◆ **Best Western Lee-Jackson Motor Inn** Ⓜ
(540) 662-4154. **$53-$58.** 711 Millwood Ave. I-81, exit 313 northbound; 313B southbound, just nw on US 50/522/17. Ext corridors. **Pets:** Medium. Supervision.
ⓈⒶⱽⒺ ⊠ 🖥 🖥 🍴 🖨

🆎🅰🅰 ◆◆ **Days Inn** Ⓜ ❀
(540) 667-1200. **$46-$69.** 2951 Valley Ave. I-81, exit 310, just w, then 1.8 mi n on US 11. Ext corridors. **Pets:** Medium. $6 daily fee/pet. Supervision.
ⓈⒶⱽⒺ ⓈⒹ ⊠ 🖥 🍴 🖨

◆ **Mohawk Motel** Ⓜ ❀
(540) 667-1410. **$34-$38.** 2754 Northwestern Pike. I-81, exit 317, 3 mi s on SR 37, 1.7 mi w on US 50. Ext corridors. **Pets:** Other. $5 one-time fee/pet. Designated rooms, supervision.
ⒶⓈⓀ ⓈⒹ ⊠

🆎🅰🅰 ◆◆ **Quality Inn East** Ⓜ ❀
(540) 667-2250. **$62-$75.** 603 Millwood Ave. I-81, exit 313 northbound; exit 313B southbound, 0.5 mi nw on US 50/522/17. Ext corridors. **Pets:** Other. $7 daily fee/pet. Supervision.
ⓈⒶⱽⒺ ⓈⒹ ⊠ 🖥 🖥 🖨

AAA ◆ **Tourist City Motel** **M** ❀
(540) 662-9011. **$29-$38, 5 days notice.** 214 Millwood Ave.
I-81, exit 313 northbound; exit 313B southbound, 1 mi nw
on US 50/522. Ext corridors. **Pets:** $4 daily fee/pet, $4
one-time fee/pet. Designated rooms, no service, supervision, crate.

SAVE **S** **X** **◻**

AAA ◆◆◆ **Travelodge of Winchester** **M** ❀
(540) 665-0685. **$53-$71, 7 days notice.** 160 Front Royal
Pike. I-81, exit 313 northbound; exit 313A southbound, just
s on US 522. Int corridors. **Pets:** Other. $5 one-time fee/
room. Supervision.

SAVE **S** **X** **◻** **◻** **◻** **◻**

WOODSTOCK

AAA ◆ **Budget Host Inn** **M** ❀
(540) 459-4086. **$36-$48.** 1290 S Main St. I-81, exit 283,
0.8 mi se on SR 42, then 0.6 mi s on US 11. Ext corridors.
Pets: No service, supervision, crate.

SAVE **S** **X** **◻**

WYTHEVILLE

AAA ◆◆ **Days Inn** **M** ❀
(540) 228-5500. **$45-$75, 3 days notice.** 150 Malin Dr.
I-81, exit 73, just w. Ext corridors. **Pets:** Small. $5 daily
fee/pet. No service, supervision, crate.

SAVE **X** **◻**

◆◆ **Econo Lodge** **M** ❀
(540) 228-5517. **$35-$90.** 1160 E Main St. I-81, exit 73, 0.8
mi w. Ext corridors. **Pets:** Medium. $10 one-time fee/room.
Supervision.

ASK **S** **X** **◻** **◻** **◻**

AAA ◆◆◆ **Holiday Inn** **MI** ❀
(540) 228-5483. **$89.** 1800 E Main St. I-81, exit 73, just w.
Ext/int corridors. **Pets:** Other. Supervision.

SAVE **S** **X** **◻** **◻** **◻** **◻** **◻** **CTV**

AAA ◆◆ **Ramada Inn** **MI** ❀
(540) 228-6000. **$50-$85, 7 days notice.** 955 Peppers
Ferry Rd. I-77, exit 41, just w. Ext corridors. **Pets:** Other.
Supervision.

SAVE **S** **X** **◻** **◻** **◻** **◻**

AAA ◆◆ **Red Carpet Inn** **M** ❀
(540) 228-5525. **$45-$115, 7 days notice.** 280 Lithia Rd.
I-81, exit 73, just w. Ext corridors. **Pets:** Medium. $10 daily
fee/pet. No service, supervision, crate.

SAVE **S** **X**

◆◆ **Super 8 Motel** **M**
(540) 228-6620. **Call for rates.** 130 Nye Cir. I-77, exit 41,
just e. Ext corridors. **Pets:** Small. No service, supervision,
crate.

ASK **X** **◻** **◻**

AAA ◆◆ **Wytheville Inn** **M** ❀
(540) 228-7300. **$59-$79.** 355 Nye Rd. I-77, exit 41, just e.
Int corridors. **Pets:** $6 daily fee/room. Supervision.

SAVE **S** **X** **◻** **◻** **◻**

WASHINGTON

CITY INDEX

ABERDEEN

⊕⊕⊕ ◆◆ Olympic Inn M
(360) 533-4200. **$45-$95.** 616 W Heron St. Downtown, 0.5 mi w. Ext corridors. **Pets:** Supervision.
[SAVE] [S6] [✕] [🔒] [Ⓚ]

⊕⊕⊕ ◆◆ Red Lion Inn M ☼
(360) 532-5210. **$99-$99.** 521 W Wishkah. 0.5 mi w on US 101 N. Ext corridors. **Pets:** Other. Supervision.
[SAVE] [S6] [✕] [🔒] [✍] [🔒] [💻]

ANACORTES

⊕⊕⊕ ◆◆ Anacortes Inn M
(360) 293-3153. **$65-$70, 5 days notice.** 3006 Commercial Ave. SR 20, 1.8 mi s. Ext corridors. **Pets:** No service, supervision, crate.
[SAVE] [S6] [✕] [🔒] [💻] [🏊]

⊕⊕⊕ ◆◆◆ Fidalgo Country Inn M ☼
(360) 293-3494. **$79-$169.** 7645 SR 20. Jct of SR 20. Ext/int corridors. **Pets:** Medium. $20 daily fee/pet. Supervision.
[SAVE] [S6] [✕] [🔒] [✍] [🔒] [💻] [🏊]

⊕⊕⊕ ◆◆ Ship Harbor Inn M
(360) 293-5177. **$50-$105.** 5316 Ferry Terminal Rd. 0.3 mi s of ferry landing. Ext corridors. **Pets:** No service, supervision, crate.
[SAVE] [S6] [✕] [🔒] [💻] [✕] [Ⓚ]

BELFAIR

⊕⊕⊕ ◆◆ Belfair Motel M 🐾
(360) 275-4485. **$50-$60.** NE 23322 Hwy 3. Downtown. Ext corridors. **Pets:** $10 one-time fee/pet. No service, supervision, crate.
[SAVE] [S6] [✕] [🔒] [💻]

BELLINGHAM

⊕⊕⊕ ◆◆◆ Best Western Lakeway Inn 🅷 🐾
(360) 671-1011. **$69-$119, 3 days notice.** 714 Lakeway Dr. I-5 exit 253, just e. Int corridors. **Pets:** Small. $5 daily fee/room. No service, supervision, crate.
[SAVE] [S6] [✕] [✍] [🔒] [💻] [🍴] [🏊]

⊕⊕⊕ ◆◆ Coachman Inn M 🐾
(360) 671-9000. **$45-$70.** 120 N Samish Way. I-5 exit 252, 0.5 mi w. Int corridors. **Pets:** Medium, other. $10 daily fee/pet. Supervision.
[SAVE] [S6] [✕] [🔒] [🏊]

⊕⊕⊕ ◆◆◆ Days Inn M 🐾
(360) 671-6200. **$59-$79.** 125 E Kellogg Rd. I-5 exit 256, 1 mi n on Meridian St. Int corridors. **Pets:** Medium. $7 daily fee/pet. Supervision.
[SAVE] [S6] [✕] [🔒] [💻] [🏊]

◆◆◆ Holiday Inn Express-Bellingham M
(360) 671-4800. **$75-$85.** 4160 Guide Meridian. I-5 exit 256A, 0.7 mi e. Int corridors. **Pets:** Large. Designated rooms, supervision.
[ASK] [S6] [✕] [♿] [✍] [📺] [🔒] [💻] [🏊]

◆◆ Motel 6-44 Ⓜ
(360) 671-4494. **$42-$58.** 3701 Byron Ave. I-5 exit 252, just n. Ext corridors. **Pets:** Small. No service, supervision, crate.

◆◆◆ Quality Inn Baron Suites Ⓜ ❀
(360) 647-8000. **$74-$114.** 100 E Kellogg Rd. I-5 exit 256, 1 mi ne via Guide Meridian St. Ext/int corridors. **Pets:** Other. $25 one-time fee/room. Designated rooms, no service, supervision, crate.

◆◆ Rodeway Inn Ⓜ
(360) 738-6000. **$40-$95.** 3710 Meridian St. I-5 exit 256, just w. Int corridors. **Pets:** No service, supervision, crate.

◆ Shangri-La Downtown Motel Ⓜ
(360) 733-7050. **$38-$48.** 611 E Holly St. I-5 exit 253 Lakeway exit (0.3 mi nw from exit). Ext corridors. **Pets:** Medium. Supervision.

◆◆ Travel House Inn Ⓜ ❀
(360) 671-4600. **$44-$60, 7 days notice.** 3750 Meridian St. I-5 exit 256A, just w. Ext corridors. **Pets:** Medium. $10 deposit/room, $10 one-time fee/room. Supervision.

◆◆ Val-U Inn Ⓜ ❀
(360) 671-9600. **$50-$84.** 805 Lakeway Dr. I-5 exit 253, just e. Int corridors. **Pets:** Dogs only. $5 daily fee/pet. Designated rooms, no service, supervision, crate.

BLAINE

◆◆◆◆ Resort Semiahmoo Ⓡ ❀
(360) 371-2000. **Call for rates.** 9565 Semiahmoo Pkwy. 10 mi w of I-5, exit 270 on Semiahmoo Spit. Int corridors. **Pets:** $50 one-time fee/room. Designated rooms, supervision.

BREMERTON

◆◆◆ Best Western Bremerton Inn Ⓜ
(360) 405-1111. **$71-$169, 7 days notice.** 4303 Kitsap Way. 3.5 mi w of ferry terminal; SR 3, Kitsap Way exit, 0.5 mi e. Ext corridors. **Pets:** Medium. Supervision.

◆◆ Dunes Motel Ⓜ
(360) 377-0093. **$45-$65, 7 days notice.** 3400 11th St. 2 mi w of ferry terminal; SR 3, Kitsap Way exit, 1 mi e. Ext corridors. **Pets:** Medium. Designated rooms, no service, supervision, crate.

◆◆◆ Flagship Inn Ⓜ ❀
(360) 479-6566. **$59-$99.** 4320 Kitsap Way. 3.5 mi w of ferry terminal; SR 3, Kitsap Way exit, 0.5 mi e. Int corridors. **Pets:** $6 daily fee/pet. Designated rooms, supervision.

◆◆◆ Mid Way Inn Ⓜ
(360) 479-2909. **$59-$74.** 2909 Wheaton Way. SR 303, 2 mi n, Wheaton Way in East Bremerton. Int corridors. **Pets:** Small. Designated rooms, no service, supervision, crate.

◆◆ Oyster Bay Inn Ⓜ❶ ❀
(360) 377-5510. **$69-$80.** 4412 Kitsap Way. 3.8 mi w of ferry terminal; SR 3, Kitsap Way exit, 0.5 mi e. Int corridors. **Pets:** Small. $20 one-time fee/room. No service, supervision, crate.

BUCKLEY

◆◆◆ Mt View Inn Ⓜ ❀
(360) 829-1100. **$58-$68.** 29405 Hwy 410 E. On SR 410 at jct of SR 165. Int corridors. **Pets:** Other. $10 one-time fee/room. Designated rooms, no service, supervision, crate.

CASHMERE

◆◆◆ Village Inn Motel Ⓜ ❀
(509) 782-3522. **$37-$65, 7 days notice.** 229 Cottage Ave. Downtown on US 2-97 business route. Ext corridors. **Pets:** Small. $5 daily fee/pet. No service, supervision, crate.

CASTLE ROCK

◆◆◆ Timberland Inn & Suites Ⓜ
(360) 274-6002. **$59-$75.** 1271 Mt St Helens Way. I-5 exit 49, just e. Ext corridors. **Pets:** Medium. Supervision.

CENTRALIA

◆◆ Centralia Travelodge Ⓜ ❀
(360) 736-9344. **$60-$70.** 1325 Lakeshore Dr. I-5 exit 81, just nw. Ext corridors. **Pets:** Dogs only. $5 deposit/room, $5 daily fee/room, $5 one-time fee/room. Designated rooms, no service, supervision, crate.

◆ Motel 6-394 Ⓜ
(360) 330-2057. **$35-$56.** 1310 Belmont Ave. I-5 exit 82, 0.6 mi nw. Ext corridors. **Pets:** Small. No service, supervision, crate.

CHEHALIS

◆◆ Relax Inn Ⓜ
(360) 748-8608. **$35-$75.** 550 SW Parkland Dr. I-5 exit 76 (13th St), just e. Ext corridors. **Pets:** Small. No service, supervision, crate.

CHELAN

◆◆◆ Best Western Lakeside Lodge
(509) 682-4396. **$129-$229, 7 days notice.** W 2312 Woodin Ave. W end of town. Ext corridors. **Pets:** Small, other. $10 daily fee/pet, $10 one-time fee/pet. Designated rooms, no service, supervision, crate.

CHEWELAH

◆◆ Nordlig Motel
(509) 935-6704. **$44-$50.** 101 W Grant St. N edge of town on US 395. Ext corridors. **Pets:** Other. $5 one-time fee/room. No service, supervision, crate.

CLE ELUM

◆◆ Cle Elum Travelers Inn
(509) 674-5535. **$34-$100.** 1001 E 1st St. I-90 exit 85, 1 mi w on SR 903. Ext/int corridors. **Pets:** Other. $5 daily fee/pet. No service, supervision, crate.

◆◆ Stewart Lodge
(509) 674-4548. **$51-$73.** 805 W First St. I-90 exit 84 eastbound, just n; I-90 exit 84 westbound, 0.6 mi w. Ext corridors. **Pets:** Other. $5 one-time fee/pet. No service, supervision, crate.

◆◆ Timber Lodge Inn
(509) 674-5966. **$50-$75.** 301 W First St. I-90 exit 84 eastbound, 1 mi ne; I-90 exit 84 westbound, just w. Ext/int corridors. **Pets:** No service, supervision, crate.

◆ Wind Blew Inn
(509) 674-2294. **$43-$53.** 811 Hwy 970. I-90 exit 85, just w. Ext corridors. **Pets:** Small. No service, supervision, crate.

COULEE DAM

◆◆ Coulee House Motel
(509) 633-1101. **$64-$84.** 110 Roosevelt Way. Just e of river bridge. Ext corridors. **Pets:** Other. $15 daily fee/pet, $15 one-time fee/pet. No service, supervision, crate.

COUPEVILLE

◆◆◆ The Victorian Bed & Breakfast
(360) 678-5305. **$65-$100, 7 days notice.** 602 N Main St. Downtown; 0.3 mi n of jct SR 20. Ext/int corridors. **Pets:** Medium. $100 deposit/room, $10 one-time fee/room. Supervision.

DAYTON

◆◆◆ The Weinhard Hotel
(509) 382-4032. **$70-$125.** 235 E Main St. Downtown. Int corridors. **Pets:** Designated rooms, no service, supervision, crate.

EAST WENATCHEE

◆◆◆ Cedars Inn, East Wenatchee
(509) 886-8000. **$64-$87.** 80 Ninth St NE. Just e of SR 28. Int corridors. **Pets:** $6 daily fee/room. Supervision.

ELLENSBURG

◆◆ Best Western Ellensburg Inn
(509) 925-9801. **$63-$78.** 1700 Canyon Rd. I-90 exit 109, just n. Int corridors. **Pets:** Medium. $20 deposit/room. Supervision.

◆◆◆ Ellensburg Comfort Inn
(509) 925-7037. **$77-$141.** 1722 Canyon Rd. I-90 exit 109. Int corridors. **Pets:** Large. $10 one-time fee/room. Supervision.

◆◆ I-90 Inn Motel
(509) 925-9844. **$46-$68.** 1390 Dollar Way Rd. Just n of I-90 exit 106. Ext corridors. **Pets:** Small. Supervision.

◆◆ Nites Inn
(509) 962-9600. **$45-$53.** 1200 S Ruby. 0.5 mi n of I-90, exit 109. Ext corridors. **Pets:** Other. $10 one-time fee/room. Supervision.

ENUMCLAW

◆◆◆ Best Western Park Center Hotel
(360) 825-4490. **$75-$75, 7 days notice.** 1000 Griffin Ave. Downtown. Ext corridors. **Pets:** Other. $10 one-time fee/pet. No service, supervision, crate.

FERNDALE

◆◆◆ Executive Inn Express
(360) 380-4600. **$99-$99.** 5370 Barrett Rd. I-5 exit 262, 1 mi s. Ext/int corridors. **Pets:** $25 one-time fee/pet. Designated rooms, supervision.

FORKS

◆◆ Forks Motel
(360) 374-6243. **$50-$90.** 351 Forks Ave S. Just s on US 101. Ext corridors. **Pets:** Medium. $10 daily fee/pet. No service, supervision, crate.

◆◆ **Manitou Lodge** 🅱🅱 ❀
(360) 374-6295. **$90-$120, 5 days notice.** 813 Kilmer Rd.
8 mi sw on SR 110 (Lapush Rd), 1 mi w on Mora Rd, then
1 mi n. Ext/int corridors. **Pets:** Other. $10 daily fee/room.
Designated rooms, supervision.

⊠ 🖥 💻 ⊠ 🕱 🖵 🗷

◆◆ **Miller Tree Inn Bed & Breakfast** 🅱🅱 ❀
(360) 374-6806. **$55-$125, 4 days notice.** 654 E Division.
Downtown, 0.3 mi e of US 101. Ext/int corridors. **Pets:** $10
daily fee/pet. Designated rooms, no service, supervision,
crate.

⊠ 🖥 💻 🕱 🗷

FREELAND

◆◆ **Harbour Inn Motel** Ⓜ ❀
(360) 331-6900. **$58-$88.** 1606 Main St. Just e of SR 525.
Ext corridors. **Pets:** Other. $6 daily fee/pet. Designated
rooms, no service, supervision, crate.

⊠ 🖥 💻 🕱

GOLDENDALE

🆊 ◆◆ **Ponderosa Motel** Ⓜ ❀
(509) 773-5842. **$40-$55.** 775 E Broadway St. 0.5 mi w off
US 97, Klickitat and Goldendale (SR 142) exit. Ext corridors. **Pets:** Medium. $7 daily fee/room, $12 one-time fee/
room. Designated rooms, no service, supervision, crate.

⊠ 🖥 💻

KELSO

🆊 ◆◆◆ **Best Western Aladdin** Ⓜ ❀
(360) 425-9660. **$72-$97.** 310 Long Ave. W end Cowlitz
Bridge. Int corridors. **Pets:** $5 daily fee/pet, $5 one-time
fee/pet. Supervision.

🆂🅰🆅🅴 🆂🔟 ⊠ 🖥 🆒

🆊 ◆◆◆ **GuestHouse Inn & Suites** Ⓜ ❀
(360) 414-5953. **$130.** 501 Three Rivers Dr. I-5 exit 39, 0.3
mi w on Allen St, then 0.3 mi s. Int corridors. **Pets:** Small.
$10 daily fee/room. Supervision.

🆂🔟 ⊠ 🗷 🆒 🖥 💻 🆒

🆊 ◆ **Motel 6–43** Ⓜ ❀
(360) 425-3229. **$44-$60.** 106 Minor Rd. I-5 exit 39, 0.3 mi
ne. Ext corridors. **Pets:** Other. Supervision.

🆂🔟 ⊠ 🆒 🆒 🖵

◆◆◆ **Red Lion Hotel Kelso/Longview** Ⓜ
(360) 636-4400. **$84-$134.** 510 Kelso Dr. I-5 exit 39, 0.3 mi
se. Int corridors. **Pets:** Small. No service, supervision, crate.

🅰$🅺 🆂🔟 ⊠ 🗷 🆒 🖥 💻 🔢 🆒

KENNEWICK

🆊 ◆◆◆ **Best Western Kennewick Inn** Ⓜ
(509) 586-1332. **$69-$79.** 4001 W 27th St. 0.8 mi n of I-82
exit 113. Int corridors. **Pets:** Medium. No service, supervision, crate.

🆂🅰🆅🅴 🆂🔟 ⊠ 🆒 🖥 💻 🆒

🆊 ◆◆◆ **Cavanaughs At Columbia Center** Ⓜ
(509) 783-0611. **$109-$119.** 1101 N Columbia Center Blvd.
0.5 mi s on Columbia Center Blvd from SR 240. Int corridors. **Pets:** Small. No service, supervision, crate.

🆂🅰🆅🅴 🆂🔟 ⊠ 🕔 🖥 💻 🔢

◆◆◆ **Clearwater Inn** Ⓜ ❀
(509) 735-2242. **$59-$59.** 5616 W Clearwater Ave. 1.9 mi w
on Clearwater Ave from US 395. Int corridors. **Pets:** Small.
$6 daily fee/pet. Designated rooms, no service, supervision,
crate.

🅰$🅺 🆂🔟 ⊠ 🗷 🆒 🖥

◆◆◆ **Comfort Inn** Ⓜ
(509) 783-8396. **$56-$56.** 7801 W Quinault Ave. 0.5 mi s
on Columbia Center Blvd from SR 240. Int corridors.
Pets: Medium. Designated rooms, no service, supervision,
crate.

🅰$🅺 ⊠ 🗷 🆒 🖥 💻 🆒

🆊 ◆◆◆ **Hawthorn Inn & Suites** Ⓜ ❀
(509) 736-3326. **$79-$93, 7 days notice.** 4220 W 27th Pl.
0.8 mi n of I-82, exit 113 (US 395). Int corridors.
Pets: Large. $50 deposit/room. Designated rooms, no serv-
ice, supervision, crate.

🆂🅰🆅🅴 🆂🔟 ⊠ 🕔 🆒 🖥 💻 🆒

◆◆ **Kennewick Super 8** Ⓜ ❀
(509) 736-6888. **$50, 7 days notice.** 626 Columbia Center
Blvd. 1.1 mi s of SR 240. Int corridors. **Pets:** $25 deposit/
room. No service, supervision, crate.

🅰$🅺 🆂🔟 ⊠ 🕔 🗷 🆒 🖥 🆒

🆊 ◆◆ **Ramada Inn Clover Island** Ⓜ
(509) 586-0541. **$80-$110.** 435 Clover Island. US 395 Port
of Kennewick exit, 1 mi e on Columbia Dr, just n on Washington St. Int corridors. **Pets:** Medium. No service, supervision, crate.

🆂🅰🆅🅴 🆂🔟 ⊠ 🖥 💻 🔢 🆒

◆◆ **Tapadera Inn** Ⓜ ❀
(509) 783-6191. **Call for rates.** 300A N Ely St. On US 395
at jct of Clearwater St. Ext corridors. **Pets:** $5 one-time
fee/room. No service, supervision, crate.

🅰$🅺 ⊠ 🖥 🆒

LA CONNER

🆊 ◆◆◆ **La Conner Country Inn** Ⓜ ❀
(360) 466-3101. **$95-$120.** 107 S 2nd St. Downtown; at
2nd and Morris sts. Ext/int corridors. **Pets:** Other. $25 one-
time fee/room. Supervision.

🆂🅰🆅🅴 🆂🔟 ⊠ 🆒 💻 🕱

LEAVENWORTH

🆊 ◆◆◆ **Alpen Inn** Ⓜ ❀
(509) 548-4326. **$49-$109.** 405 W Hwy 2. W end. Ext
corridors. **Pets:** Other. $50 deposit/room, $12 daily fee/pet.
Designated rooms, no service, supervision, crate.

🆂🅰🆅🅴 🆂🔟 ⊠ 🖥 🆒

🆊 ◆◆◆ **Der Ritterhof Motor Inn** Ⓜ ❀
(509) 548-5845. **$80-$100, 3 days notice.** 190 Hwy 2. 0.3
mi w on US 2. Ext corridors. **Pets:** Dogs only. $10 daily
fee/pet. Supervision.

🆂🅰🆅🅴 ⊠ 🗷 🖥 💻 🕱

🆊 ◆◆ **The Evergreen Inn** Ⓜ ❀
(509) 548-5515. **$45-$95.** 1117 Front St. US 2, just s. Ext/
int corridors. **Pets:** $10 daily fee/pet. No service, supervi-
sion, crate.

🆂🅰🆅🅴 🆂🔟 ⊠ 🖥 💻

AAA ◆◆◆ Obertal Motor Inn M
(509) 548-5204. **$69-$109.** 922 Commercial St. Off Hwy 2, center of city. Ext corridors. **Pets:** No service, supervision, crate.
[SAVE] [S&] [⊠] [☰] [▣]

◆◆ River's Edge Motel M
(509) 548-7612. **$62-$77, 7 days notice.** 8401 Hwy 2. 3.5 mi e on US 2. Ext corridors. **Pets:** Small. No service, supervision, crate.
[⊠] [☰] [▣] [🖼] [⊠]

AAA ◆◆◆ Rodeway Inn & Suites M 🐾
(509) 548-7992. **$59-$119.** 185 Hwy 2. 0.3 mi w on US 2. Ext corridors. **Pets:** $12 daily fee/pet. Designated rooms, no service, supervision, crate.
[SAVE] [S&] [⊠] [🖉] [☰] [▣] [🖼]

◆◆ Tyrolean Ritz Hotel M 🐾
(509) 548-5455. **$68-$100, 7 days notice.** 633 Front St. Center of town. Ext/int corridors. **Pets:** Large. $20 deposit/pet, $10 one-time fee/pet. No service, supervision, crate.
[ASK] [S&] [⊠] [☰] [▣] [🍴]

LONG BEACH

AAA ◆◆ Anchorage Cottages C 🐾
(360) 642-2351. **$59-$103, 7 days notice.** 2209 Boulevard N. Just w of SR 103. Ext corridors. **Pets:** $6 daily fee/pet. Supervision.
[⊠] [☰] [▣] [⊠] [🖉] [🖉]

AAA ◆◆ Edgewater Inn MI 🐾
(360) 642-2311. **$94.** 409 10th St SW. Just w of SR 103. Ext/int corridors. **Pets:** Medium, other. $8 daily fee/pet. Supervision.
[SAVE] [S&] [⊠] [🖉] [☰] [▣] [🖉]

AAA ◆◆ Our Place at the Beach M 🐾
(360) 642-3793. **$49-$80.** 1309 South Blvd. S end of town. Ext corridors. **Pets:** Medium, other. $5 daily fee/pet. No service, supervision, crate.
[SAVE] [S&] [⊠] [☰] [▣] [🖉]

AAA ◆◆ Shaman Motel M 🐾
(360) 642-3714. **$79-$89.** 115 3rd St SW. Downtown. Ext corridors. **Pets:** Other. $5 one-time fee/pet. Supervision.
[SAVE] [⊠] [☰] [▣] [🖼] [🖉]

LONGVIEW

◆◆◆ Holiday Inn Express of Longview M 🐾
(360) 414-1000. **$79-$160.** 723 7th Ave. I-5 exit 36, 3 mi w on SR 432. Int corridors. **Pets:** Other. $15 one-time fee/room. Designated rooms, no service, supervision, crate.
[ASK] [S&] [⊠] [♿] [🖉] [🖉] [☰] [▣] [🖼]

AAA ◆◆ Hudson Manor Inn M 🐾
(360) 425-1100. **$38-$46, 5 days notice.** 1616 Hudson St. Downtown. Ext corridors. **Pets:** Other. $25 deposit/pet. Designated rooms, no service, supervision, crate.
[SAVE] [S&] [⊠] [☰]

AAA ◆ The Townhouse Motel M 🐾
(360) 423-7200. **$36-$50.** 744 Washington Way. Downtown. Ext corridors. **Pets:** $5 one-time fee/pet. Supervision.
[SAVE] [S&] [⊠] [☰] [🖼]

LYNDEN

◆◆ Windmill Inn Motel, Inc M
(360) 354-3424. **$45-$62, 3 days notice.** 8022 Guide Meridian Rd. On SR 539, just s of jct Birch Bay-Lynden Rd. Ext corridors. **Pets:** Small. Designated rooms, no service, supervision, crate.
[ASK] [S&] [⊠] [☰]

MOCLIPS

◆◆ Hi Tide Ocean Beach Resort CO 🐾
(360) 276-4142. **$95-$169.** 4890 Railroad Ave. SR 109, 0.8 mi nw on beach at 6th and Railroad sts. Ext corridors. **Pets:** Medium, dogs only. $10 daily fee/pet, $10 one-time fee/pet. Designated rooms, no service, supervision, crate.
[ASK] [⊠] [☰] [▣] [🖉] [🖉]

◆◆ Ocean Crest Resort M 🐾
(360) 276-4465. **$60-$175, 7 days notice.** 4651 SR 109 N. S edge of town. Ext corridors. **Pets:** Other. $50 deposit/room, $13 daily fee/pet. No service, supervision, crate.
[ASK] [S&] [⊠] [🖉] [☰] [▣] [🍴] [🖼] [⊠] [🖉]

MORTON

AAA ◆◆◆ The Seasons Motel M
(360) 496-6835. **$50-$70.** 200 Westlake. At jct SR 7 and US 12. Ext corridors. **Pets:** No service, supervision, crate.
[⊠]

MOSES LAKE

AAA ◆◆◆ Best Western Hallmark Inn MI 🐾
(509) 765-9211. **$84-$99.** 3000 Marina Dr. I-90 exit 176. Int corridors. **Pets:** Medium. Supervision.
[SAVE] [S&] [⊠] [☰] [▣] [🍴] [⊠]

◆◆◆ Holiday Inn Express M 🐾
(509) 766-2000. **$79-$95.** 1745 E Kittleson. I-90 exit 179. Int corridors. **Pets:** Designated rooms, supervision.
[ASK] [S&] [⊠] [🏠] [🖉] [☰] [▣] [🖼]

AAA ◆ Moses Lake Travelodge M 🐾
(509) 765-8631. **$49-$89.** 316 S Pioneer Way. Downtown on Business Loop 90. Ext corridors. **Pets:** Medium, dogs only. $5 one-time fee/room. Supervision.
[SAVE] [S&] [⊠] [☰] [▣]

◆◆◆ Shilo Inn M
(509) 765-9317. **$69-$99.** 1819 E Kittleson. I-90 exit 179. Int corridors. **Pets:** Small. Designated rooms, no service, supervision, crate.
[ASK] [S&] [⊠] [🖉] [☰] [▣] [🖼]

MOUNT VERNON

AAA ◆◆ Best Western College Way Inn M
(360) 424-4287. **Call for rates.** 300 W College Way. I-5 exit 227, just w. Ext corridors. **Pets:** No service, supervision, crate.
[SAVE] [⊠] [🖉] [☰] [▣] [🖼]

△△△ ◆◆◆ Best Western Cotton Tree Inn & Convention Center M ☺
(360) 428-5678. **$60-$90.** 2300 Market. I-5, exit 227, 0.3 mi e on College Way, then 0.5 mi n on Riverside Dr. Int corridors. **Pets:** Small, dogs only. $10 one-time fee/room. Designated rooms, no service, supervision, crate.
SAVE 🐾 ✕ 👤 🐾 🍴 💻 ⛱

△△△ ◆◆◆ Comfort Inn-Mount Vernon M ☺
(360) 428-7020. **$69-$89, 30 days notice.** 1910 Freeway Dr. I-5 exit 227, just w on College Way, then just n. Ext corridors. **Pets:** Other. $10 daily fee/room. Designated rooms, no service, supervision, crate.
SAVE 🐾 ✕ 🍴 💻 ⛱

◆◆ Days Inn, Mt Vernon M ☺
(360) 424-4141. **$60-$70.** 2009 Riverside Dr. I-5 exit 227, 0.5 mi e on College Way, just n. Int corridors. **Pets:** Other. $5 daily fee/room. No service, supervision, crate.
ASK 🐾 ✕ 🍴 🍴 ⛱

OAK HARBOR

△△△ ◆◆ Acorn Motor Inn M ☺
(360) 675-6646. **$52-$78.** 31530 SR 20. On SR 20 at jct 300th Ave W (SE Barrington Dr). Int corridors. **Pets:** Other. $10 daily fee/room. No service, supervision, crate.
SAVE 🐾 ✕ 🍴

△△△ ◆◆◆ Best Western Harbor Plaza M
(360) 679-4567. **$109-$119.** 33175 SR 20. Just n on SR 20. Int corridors. **Pets:** Designated rooms, supervision.
SAVE 🐾 ✕ 👤 🐾 🍴 💻 ⛱

OCEAN PARK

△△△ ◆ Ocean Park Resort M ☺
(360) 665-4585. **$65-$90.** 25904 R St. In town; just e of SR 103. Ext corridors. **Pets:** Small. $7 daily fee/pet. Supervision.
SAVE 🐾 🍴 💻 ⛱ ✕ 🐾 ☎

OCEAN SHORES

△△△ ◆◆◆ Grey Gull CO
(360) 289-3381. **$120-$325.** 651 Ocean Shores Blvd SW. Just s of Shores Mall. Ext corridors. **Pets:** Designated rooms, no service, supervision, crate.
SAVE 🐾 ✕ 🍴 💻 ⛱ 🐾

△△△ ◆◆◆ The Nautilus CO ☺
(360) 289-2722. **$80-$135.** 835 Ocean Shores Blvd N. N end of town. Ext corridors. **Pets:** Dogs only. $20 one-time fee/pet. Supervision.
SAVE ✕ 🍴 💻 🐾

△△△ ◆◆◆ The Polynesian Condominium Resort CO ☺
(360) 289-3361. **$89-$119.** 615 Ocean Shores Blvd. Just s of Shores Mall. Ext/int corridors. **Pets:** Other. $15 daily fee/pet. Designated rooms, no service, supervision, crate.
SAVE 🐾 ✕ 🐾 🍴 💻 🍴 ⛱ ✕ 🐾

OKANOGAN

△△△ ◆◆ Ponderosa Motor Lodge M ☺
(509) 422-0400. **$39-$45.** 1034 S 2nd Ave. 0.3 mi n on SR 215 from jct SR 20. Ext corridors. **Pets:** Other. Designated rooms, no service, supervision, crate.
SAVE ✕ 🍴 💻 ⛱

OLYMPIA

△△△ ◆◆ Best Western Aladdin Motor Inn M ☺
(360) 352-7200. **$72-$125.** 900 Capitol Way. I-5 northbound exit 105; southbound exit 105A, 0.4 mi w on 14th St, 0.5 mi n. Int corridors. **Pets:** Small. $5 daily fee/pet. Designated rooms, no service, supervision, crate.
SAVE 🐾 ✕ 🐾 ⚐ 🍴 🍴 ⛱

△△△ ◆◆◆ Cavanaughs at Capitol Lake M ☺
(360) 943-4000. **$108-$118.** 2300 Evergreen Park Dr SW. I-5 exit 104, 0.5 mi nw, via US 101 and Cooper Point Rd exit n; in Morris Business Park. Int corridors. **Pets:** Small, dogs only. $100 deposit/room, $35 one-time fee/room. No service, supervision, crate.
SAVE 🐾 ✕ 🍴 💻 🍴

OLYMPIC NATIONAL PARK

◆ Log Cabin Resort L ☺
(360) 928-3325. **$75-$120.** 3183 E Beach Rd. 3.3 mi nw of US 101 mm 232; on Lake Crescent at Piedmont Recreation Area. Ext corridors. **Pets:** Other. Designated rooms, supervision.
✕ 🍴 💻 🍴 ✕ AC CTV ☎

OMAK

△△△ ◆ Leisure Village Motel M
(509) 826-4442. **$36-$47.** 630 Okoma Dr. SR 97 exit 215, 1 mi w. Ext corridors. **Pets:** Small. Supervision.
SAVE 🐾 ✕ 🍴 💻 ⛱

△△△ ◆◆ Motel Nicholas M ☺
(509) 826-4611. **$37-$46.** 527 E Grape Ave. 0.8 mi n on SR 215 business route, 0.3 mi w of US 97 on n exit to Omak. Ext corridors. **Pets:** Dogs only. $4 daily fee/pet, $4 one-time fee/pet. Designated rooms, supervision.
SAVE 🐾 ✕ 🍴 ⛱

△△△ ◆◆◆ Omak Inn M ☺
(509) 826-3822. **$53-$58.** 912 Koala Dr. On US 97, just n of Riverside Dr. Int corridors. **Pets:** Small. $10 one-time fee/room. No service, supervision, crate.
SAVE 🐾 ✕ 🍴 ⛱

OTHELLO

△△△ ◆◆◆ Best Western Lincoln Inn M ☺
(509) 488-5671. **$49-$109.** 1020 E Cedar St. Just off Main St at 10th and Cedar. Int corridors. **Pets:** Dogs only. $10 daily fee/pet. Designated rooms, no service, supervision, crate.
SAVE 🐾 ✕ 🍴 ⛱

PACIFIC BEACH

♦♦ Sandpiper Beach Resort CO ☼
(360) 276-4580. **$55-$195.** 4159 SR 109. 1.8 mi s. Ext corridors. **Pets:** Other. $10 daily fee/pet. Supervision.
SAVE ⊟ 🖵 ⊠ 🕱 CTV 🕿

PACKWOOD

♦ Woodland Motel M ☼
(360) 494-6766. **$40-$50.** 11890 US 12. 4.5 mi w on Hwy 12. Ext corridors. **Pets:** Other. Supervision.
SAVE S⊘ ⊠ ⊟ 🖵 🕿

PASCO

♦♦♦ DoubleTree Hotel Pasco MI
(509) 547-0701. **$89-$109.** 2525 N 20th Ave. N of I-182 exit 12B. Int corridors. **Pets:** Small. No service, supervision, crate.
ASK ⊠ 🕭 🕱 🕱 ⊟ 🖵 🍴 🕿

PORT ANGELES

♦♦ Flagstone Motel M
(360) 457-9494. **$52-$68.** 415 E First St. On US 101 eastbound, between Peabody and Vine sts. Ext corridors. **Pets:** No service, supervision, crate.
⊠ ⊟ 🕿 🕱

♦♦♦ Maple Rose Inn Bed & Breakfast BB
(360) 457-7673. **$79-$157, 7 days notice.** 112 Reservoir Rd. 203 mi s of ferry terminal; from US 101, 0.6 mi s on Lincoln, 0.5 mi w on 8th St, 1.1 mi s on Pine St, just w. Ext/int corridors. **Pets:** Very small. Supervision.
ASK S⊘ ⊠ ⊟ 🖵 🕱

♦ The Pond Motel M ☼
(360) 452-8422. **$25-$50.** 1425 W US 101. 2 mi w. Ext corridors. **Pets:** $10 daily fee/pet. Designated rooms, no service, supervision, crate.
SAVE ⊠ ⊟ 🖵 🕱 🕿

♦♦ Portside Inn M ☼
(360) 452-4015. **$79-$99.** 1510 E Front St. Front St at Alder, e end. Ext corridors. **Pets:** Small. $25 deposit/room. Supervision.
SAVE S⊘ ⊠ ⊟ 🕿

♦♦♦ Red Lion Hotel Port Angeles MI ☼
(360) 452-9215. **$95-$139.** 221 N Lincoln St. On US 101 westbound, at the ferry landing. Ext/int corridors. **Pets:** $35 deposit/room. Supervision.
⊠ 🕱 🕱 ⊟ 🖵 🍴

♦♦ Riviera Inn M ☼
(360) 417-3955. **$49-$77, 3 days notice.** 535 E Front St. Downtown on US 101 W. Ext corridors. **Pets:** $10 daily fee/pet. Designated rooms, no service, supervision, crate.
SAVE S⊘ ⊠ ⊟ 🖵 🕱

PORT ORCHARD

♦♦♦ GuestHouse Inn M ☼
(360) 895-7818. **$84-$99.** 220 Bravo Terrace. SR 16 Sedgwick exit, just e. Int corridors. **Pets:** Small, other. $10 daily fee/room. Supervision.
S⊘ ⊠ 🕱 🕱 ⊟ 🖵 🕿

PORT TOWNSEND

♦♦♦ Bishop Victorian Guest Suites H
(360) 385-6122. **$94-$199, 3 days notice.** 714 Washington St. Corner of Washington and Quincy sts. Int corridors. **Pets:** Designated rooms, no service, supervision, crate.
SAVE S⊘ ⊠ ⊟ 🕱

♦♦♦ Harborside Inn M
(360) 385-7909. **$72-$102.** 330 Benedict St. Just e of SR 20. Ext corridors. **Pets:** Supervision.
⊠ ⊟ 🖵 🕿 🕱

♦♦ Palace Hotel H ☼
(360) 385-0773. **$69-$159.** 1004 Water St. Downtown. Int corridors. **Pets:** $20 one-time fee/room. Designated rooms, supervision.
SAVE S⊘ ⊠ ⊟ 🖵 🕱 🕿

♦♦ Port Townsend Inn M
(360) 385-2211. **$68-$175.** 2020 Washington St. 0.5 mi s on SR 20. Ext corridors. **Pets:** Supervision.
⊠ 🕭 🕱 ⊟ 🖵 🕿 🕱

♦♦♦ The Swan Hotel H
(360) 385-1718. **$115-$250, 3 days notice.** 222 Monroe St. Downtown. Ext corridors. **Pets:** Designated rooms, no service, supervision, crate.
SAVE S⊘ ⊠ ⊟ 🖵 🕱

♦ The Water Street Hotel H
(360) 385-5467. **$50-$120.** 635 Water St. Downtown historic district; cross street Quincy. Int corridors. **Pets:** Designated rooms, no service, supervision, crate.
SAVE S⊘ ⊠ ⊟ 🖵 🍴 🕱 🕿

PORTLAND METROPOLITAN AREA

VANCOUVER

♦♦ Best Inn & Suites M ☼
(360) 256-7044. **$62-$75.** 221 NE Chkalov Dr. I-205 exit 28 (Mill Plain), just ne. Ext corridors. **Pets:** $15 one-time fee/room. No service, supervision, crate.
SAVE S⊘ ⊠ ⊟ 🖵 🕿

♦♦♦ Best Inn & Suites M ☼
(360) 696-0516. **$68-$82.** 7001 NE Hwy 99. I-5 exit 4, 0.8 mi se. Ext/int corridors. **Pets:** Other. $5 daily fee/room. Designated rooms, no service, supervision, crate.
SAVE S⊘ ⊠ 🕱 ⊟ 🖵 🕿

◆◆◆ Best Western Ferryman's Inn M ❀
(360) 574-2151. **$54-$68.** 7901 NE 6th Ave. I-5 exit 4, just nw. Ext/int corridors. **Pets:** Other. $3 daily fee/pet. Supervision.

(ASK) (S⬝) (✕) (⬝) (⬝)

◆◆◆ Homewood Suites Hotel A ❀
(360) 750-1100. **Call for rates.** 701 SE Columbia Shores Blvd. Hwy 14 exit 1, just s. Ext/int corridors. **Pets:** Other. $10 daily fee/pet, $5 one-time fee/pet. Supervision.

(✕) (⬝) (⬝) (⬝) (⬝) (✕)

◆◆◆ Red Lion Hotel at the Quay M
(360) 694-8341. **$89-$89.** 100 Columbia St. 0.5 mi s on dock at foot of Columbia St. Int corridors. **Pets:** Supervision.

(SAVE) (S⬝) (✕) (⬝) (⬝) (⬝) (⬝) (⬝) (⬝) (⬝) (✕)

◆◆◆ Residence Inn Vancouver A ❀
(360) 253-4800. **$139-$189.** 8005 NE Parkway Dr. From jct I-205 and SR 500, 0.5 mi w on SR 500 to Thurston Way, just n to NE Parkway Dr, then just w. Ext corridors. **Pets:** Other. $10 daily fee/pet. Supervision.

(ASK) (S⬝) (✕) (⬝) (⬝) (⬝) (⬝) (⬝) (✕)

❀ **END METROPOLITAN AREA** ❀

POULSBO

◆◆ Poulsbo Inn M ❀
(360) 779-3921. **$70-$99.** 18680 Hwy 305. SR 3, 1 mi e on SR 305. Ext corridors. **Pets:** Medium, other. $10 daily fee/pet. Designated rooms, no service, supervision, crate.

(SAVE) (S⬝) (✕) (⬝) (⬝) (⬝) (✕)

PROSSER

◆◆◆ Best Western Prosser Inn M ❀
(509) 786-7977. **$69-$99.** 225 Merlot Dr. Just s of I-82, exit 80. Int corridors. **Pets:** Medium, dogs only. $10 one-time fee/pet. Supervision.

(ASK) (✕) (⬝) (⬝) (⬝) (⬝)

PULLMAN

◆◆ American Travel Inn M ❀
(509) 334-3500. **$47-$64.** 515 S Grand. Just s on US 195 business route from jct SR 270. Ext corridors. **Pets:** Small, dogs only. Designated rooms, supervision.

(SAVE) (S⬝) (✕) (⬝) (⬝)

◆◆◆ Hawthorn Inn & Suites M
(509) 332-0928. **$72-$119.** 928 NW Olsen St. 1.6 mi e on SR 270 from US 195. Int corridors. **Pets:** Designated rooms, supervision.

(SAVE) (S⬝) (✕) (⬝) (⬝) (⬝) (⬝) (⬝) (⬝)

◆◆◆ Holiday Inn Express Hotel & Suites M ❀
(509) 334-4437. **$79-$109.** SE 1190 Bishop Blvd. 1 mi e on SR 270, from jct of US 195 business route, 0.5 mi s. Int corridors. **Pets:** Supervision.

(ASK) (S⬝) (✕) (⬝) (⬝) (⬝) (⬝) (⬝) (⬝) (✕)

◆◆◆ Shilo Inn-Downtown Vancouver M ❀
(360) 696-0411. **$65-$95.** 401 E 13th St. I-5, Mill Plain exit, just w, then s on D St. Int corridors. **Pets:** Other. $10 daily fee/pet. No service, supervision, crate.

(SAVE) (S⬝) (✕) (⬝) (⬝) (⬝)

◆◆ Shilo Inn-Hazel Dell/Vancouver M ❀
(360) 573-0511. **$59-$99.** 13206 Hwy 99. I-5 exit 7, just e; I-205 exit 36, just w. Int corridors. **Pets:** Other. $10 daily fee/room. No service, supervision, crate.

(ASK) (S⬝) (✕) (⬝) (⬝) (⬝)

◆◆◆ Quality Inn Paradise Creek M ❀
(509) 332-0500. **$64-$84.** 1400 SE Bishop Blvd. 1 mi e on SR 270, from jct of US 195 business route, just s. Int corridors. **Pets:** Other. Supervision.

(SAVE) (S⬝) (✕) (⬝) (⬝) (⬝) (⬝)

RAYMOND

◆ Maunu's Mountcastle Motel M
(360) 942-5571. **$40-$55, 5 days notice.** 524 3rd St. US 101, City Center exit, just w. Ext corridors. **Pets:** Medium. Supervision.

(SAVE) (S⬝) (⬝) (K⬝)

RICHLAND

◆◆◆ Best Western Tower Inn & Conference Center M ❀
(509) 946-4121. **$79-$109.** 1515 George Washington Way. 2.5 mi n of I-182 exit 5B. Int corridors. **Pets:** $25 one-time fee/room. Supervision.

(ASK) (S⬝) (✕) (⬝) (⬝) (⬝) (⬝) (⬝) (⬝)

◆◆ Red Lion Hotel Richland Hanford House M ❀
(509) 946-7611. **$55-$65.** 802 George Washington Way. I-182 exit 5B, 1.3 mi n, on SR 240 business route. Ext/int corridors. **Pets:** Other. No service, supervision, crate.

(ASK) (S⬝) (✕) (⬝) (⬝) (⬝) (⬝)

◆◆◆ Shilo Conference Hotel M ❀
(509) 946-4661. **$69-$199.** 50 Comstock St. I-182 exit 5B, 0.5 mi n. Int corridors. **Pets:** Other. $10 daily fee/room. No service, supervision, crate.

(ASK) (S⬝) (✕) (⬝) (⬝) (⬝) (⬝) (⬝) (✕)

RIMROCK

◆ **Game Ridge Motel-Lodge** Ⓜ ☙
(509) 672-2212. **$39-$115, 7 days notice.** 27350 US Hwy 12. Ext corridors. **Pets:** $10 daily fee/pet. Supervision.
🆎 🆑 ⊠ 🔒 💻 ⊠ 🎟 ☎

RITZVILLE

🆙 ◆◆◆ **Best Inn & Suites** Ⓜ ☙
(509) 659-1007. **$59-$89.** 1513 Smitty's Blvd. I-90 exit 221, just n. Int corridors. **Pets:** Other. No service, supervision, crate.
🆂🅰🆅🅴 🆑 ⊠ 🎵 🔒 💻 🔙

🆙 ◆◆ **Colwell Motor Inn** Ⓜ ☙
(509) 659-1620. **$44-$62.** 501 W 1st Ave. I-90 exit 220, 0.9 mi n. Ext corridors. **Pets:** Other. $25 deposit/room, $5 daily fee/pet, $5 one-time fee/pet. No service, supervision, crate.
🆂🅰🆅🅴 🆑 ⊠ 🔒 💻 🔙

SAN JUAN ISLANDS METROPOLITAN AREA

FRIDAY HARBOR

◆◆ **Halvorsen House Bed & Breakfast** 🅱🅱 ☙
(360) 378-2707. **$104-$155.** 216 Halvorsen Rd. In Friday Harbor, 2 mi sw on Tucker Ave, 0.5 mi w. Ext/int corridors. **Pets:** Supervision.
🆎 🆑 ⊠ 🔒 💻 🎟 📺

🆙 ◆◆ **The Inn At Friday Harbor** Ⓜ ☙
(360) 378-4000. **$145-$195, 3 days notice.** 410 Spring St. In Friday Harbor, 0.5 mi w of ferry dock. Ext corridors. **Pets:** $50 deposit/room. Designated rooms, no service, supervision, crate.
🆑 ⊠ 🎮 🔒 💻 🔙

☙ END METROPOLITAN AREA ☙

SEATTLE METROPOLITAN AREA

ARLINGTON

🆙 ◆◆ **Arlington Motor Inn** Ⓜ
(360) 652-9595. **$47-$59.** 2214 SR 530. I-5 exit 208, just ne. Ext corridors. **Pets:** Supervision.
🆂🅰🆅🅴 ⊠ 🔒 📺

◆◆ **Crossroads Inn** Ⓜ
(360) 403-7222. **$59-$120, 3 days notice.** 5200 172nd St NE. I-5 at exit 206, 1 mi ne. Int corridors. **Pets:** Small. Designated rooms, no service, supervision, crate.
🆎 🆑 ⊠ 🔒

◆ **Smokey Point Motor Inn** Ⓜ ☙
(360) 659-8561. **$45-$50.** 17329 Smokey Point Dr. I-5 exit 206 just ne; adjoining the Smokey Point Shopping Center. Ext corridors. **Pets:** Small, other. $8 daily fee/pet. Supervision.
🆎 🆑 ⊠ 🔒 💻 🔙

AUBURN

🆙 ◆◆◆ **Auburn Howard Johnson Inn** Ⓜ ☙
(253) 939-5950. **$72-$85.** 1521 D St NE. SR 167, exit (15th St nw) just e. Ext corridors. **Pets:** $10 daily fee/room. Supervision.
🆂🅰🆅🅴 🆑 ⊠ 🎵 🔒 💻 🔙

◆◆ **Microtel Inn & Suites** Ⓜ
(253) 833-7171. **$50-$87.** Nine 16th St NW. SR 167 exit (15th St), 0.3 mi e. Int corridors. **Pets:** Very small. Designated rooms, supervision.
🆎 🆑 ⊠ 🎐 🎵 🎮 🔒 💻

🆙 ◆ **Nendels Valu Inn** Ⓜ ☙
(253) 833-8007. **$45-$65.** 102 15th St NE. SR 167 exit (15th St NW), just e. Int corridors. **Pets:** Very small, other. $50 deposit/pet, $10 one-time fee/pet. No service, supervision, crate.
🆂🅰🆅🅴 ⊠ 🔒

🆙 ◆◆◆ **Val-U Inn** Ⓜ ☙
(253) 735-9600. **$54-$89.** 9 14th St NW. SR 167, exit (15th St NW), just e. Int corridors. **Pets:** Small, dogs only. $5 daily fee/pet, $5 one-time fee/pet. No service, supervision, crate.
🆂🅰🆅🅴 🆑 ⊠ 🎮 🔒

BELLEVUE

◆◆◆ **Candlewood Suites Hotel** Ⓜ ☙
(425) 373-1212. **$135.** 15805 SE 37th St. I-90 eastbound exit 11A; westbound exit 11, 0.9 mi se on s frontage road. Int corridors. **Pets:** Large, other. $10 daily fee/pet, $5 one-time fee/room. Supervision.
🆎 ⊠ 🎵 🎮 🔒 💻 ⊠

◆◆◆ **Doubletree Hotel-Bellevue Center** Ⓜ🅸 ☙
(425) 455-1515. **$139-$150.** 818 112th Ave NE. I-405 exit 13B, 0.3 mi nw. Ext/int corridors. **Pets:** Small, other. $20 one-time fee/room. No service, supervision, crate.
🆎 🆑 ⊠ 🎵 🔒 💻 🍴 🔙

◆◆ **Homestead Village Guest Studios-Bellevue Factoria** Ⓜ
(425) 865-8680. **$89-$94.** 3700 132nd Ave SE. I-90 W exit 11, I-90 E exit 10B. Ext corridors. **Pets:** Supervision.
🆎 ⊠ 🎵 🎮 🔒 💻

◆◆ Homestead Village Guest
    Studios-Redmond
(425) 885-6675. **$89-$109.** 15805 NE 28th St. SR 520 exit 148th Ave NE (south), just e on 24th St, just ne on Bel-Red Rd, just n on 156th Ave, just e. Ext corridors. **Pets:** Medium. Designated rooms, no service, supervision, crate.

❌ 🐾 ♿ 🛄 💻

◆◆◆ The Residence Inn By Marriott Seattle
    East 🅰 🐾
(425) 882-1222. **$139-$189.** 14455 NE 29th Pl. From I-405 at SR 520 exit, n at 148th N exit to 29th Pl. Ext corridors. **Pets:** Other. $50 one-time fee/pet. Supervision.

(ASK) 🆓 ❌ 🐾 🛄 💻 ➰ ❌

🇦 ◆◆◆ WestCoast Bellevue Hotel
(425) 455-9444. **$104-$135.** 625 116th Ave NE. I-405 exit 13B, 0.3 mi se. Ext/int corridors. **Pets:** Supervision.

(SAVE) 🆓 ❌ ♿ 🐾 ♿ 🛄 💻 🍴 ➰

BOTHELL

◆◆◆ Residence Inn by Marriott Seattle
    NE 🅰 🐾
(425) 485-3030. **$108-$162.** 11920 NE 195th St. I-405, exit 24, just e. Ext corridors. **Pets:** Large. $5 daily fee/pet, $50 one-time fee/room. No service, supervision, crate.

(ASK) 🆓 ❌ 🐾 🛄 💻 ➰ ❌

EDMONDS

🇦 ◆◆◆ Edmonds Harbor Inn  🐾
(425) 771-5021. **$79-$109.** 130 W Dayton St. Just s at Port of Edmonds; in Harbor Square Shopping Center. Int corridors. **Pets:** Small, other. $10 daily fee/pet. Designated rooms, supervision.

(SAVE) 🆓 ❌ 🐾 🛄 💻

🇦 ◆◆ K & E Motor Inn 🅼 🐾
(425) 778-2181. **$49-$64, 3 days notice.** 23921 Hwy 99. I-5 exit 177, 1 mi w, 0.3 mi n of jct SR 99 and 104. Ext corridors. **Pets:** Small, other. $20 deposit/pet, $5 daily fee/pet. No service, supervision, crate.

(SAVE) 🆓 ❌ 🛄 💻

EVERETT

🇦 ◆◆ Everett Travelodge 🅼 🐾
(425) 259-6141. **$49-$89.** 3030 Broadway. At Broadway and Pacific Ave; I-5 N exit 193, then 0.5 mi w on Pacific Ave; I-5 S exit 194, then 0.7 mi w on Everett Ave and 0.4 mi s. Ext corridors. **Pets:** $5 one-time fee/room. No service, supervision, crate.

(SAVE) 🆓 ❌ 🛄 💻

🇦 ◆◆◆ Holiday Inn Hotel & Conference Center
    Seattle/Everett 🅼 🐾
(425) 337-2900. **$79-$79.** 101 128th St SE. I-5 exit 186, just e. Int corridors. **Pets:** Other. $50 deposit/room, $50 one-time fee/room. Designated rooms, no service, supervision, crate.

(SAVE) 🆓 ❌ 🐾 🛄 💻 🍴 ➰

FEDERAL WAY

🇦 ◆◆◆ Best Western Federal Way
    Executel 🅼 🐾
(253) 941-6000. **$129-$149.** 31611 20th Ave S. I-5 exit 143, 0.5 mi w (0.3 mi n of S 20th across from Sea-Tac Mall). Int corridors. **Pets:** Large, other. $20 one-time fee/room. Supervision.

(SAVE) 🆓 ❌ 🐾 🛄 💻 🍴 ➰

◆◆◆ Federal Way Comfort Inn 🅼 🐾
(253) 529-0101. **$89-$99, 7 days notice.** 31622 Pacific Hwy S. I-5 exit 143, 0.5 mi nw. Int corridors. **Pets:** $50 one-time fee/room. No service, supervision, crate.

(ASK) 🆓 ❌ 🐾 🛄 💻 ➰

FIFE

🇦 ◆◆◆ Best Western Executive Inn 🅼 🐾
(253) 922-0080. **$84-$135, 7 days notice.** 5700 Pacific Hwy E. I-5 exit 137, just ne. Int corridors. **Pets:** $25 one-time fee/room. Supervision.

(SAVE) 🆓 ❌ 🐾 🛄 💻 🍴 ➰

🇦 ◆◆◆ Comfort Inn 🅼 🐾
(253) 926-2301. **$59-$89.** 5601 Pacific Hwy E. I-5 exit 137, just e. Ext corridors. **Pets:** $15 one-time fee/room. Designated rooms, no service, supervision, crate.

(SAVE) 🆓 ❌ 🛄

🇦 ◆◆ Days Inn 🅼
(253) 922-3500. **$45-$90.** 3021 Pacific Hwy E. I-5 S exit 136; I-5 N exit 136B, just nw. Int corridors. **Pets:** Designated rooms, no service, supervision, crate.

(SAVE) 🆓 ❌ 🛄 💻 ➰

🇦 ◆◆◆ Royal Coachman Inn 🅼 🐾
(253) 922-2500. **$69-$81.** 5805 Pacific Hwy E. I-5 exit 137, just ne. Int corridors. **Pets:** $25 deposit/room. No service, supervision, crate.

(SAVE) 🆓 ❌ 🛄 💻 🍴

GIG HARBOR

🇦 ◆◆◆ Best Western Wesley Inn 🅼 🐾
(253) 858-9690. **$169, 24 days notice.** 6575 Kimball Dr. SR 16, City Center exit, just e on Pioneer Way, 0.3 mi s. Int corridors. **Pets:** Other. $10 daily fee/pet. Designated rooms, no service, supervision, crate.

(SAVE) 🆓 ❌ 🐸 ♿ 🛄 💻

🇦 ◆◆◆ The Inn at Gig Harbor 🅷 🐾
(253) 858-1111. **$105-$115.** 3211 56th St NW. SR 16, Olympic Dr exit, just w on Olympic Dr, 0.4 mi n on Fosduck Rd. Int corridors. **Pets:** Other. $5 daily fee/room, $15 one-time fee/room. No service, supervision, crate.

(SAVE) ❌ ♿ ♿ 🛄 💻 🍴

ISSAQUAH

🇦 ◆ Motel 6–295 🅼
(425) 392-8405. **$56-$72.** 1885 15th Place NW. I-90 exit 15, 0.3 mi n on Renton Issaquah Rd, just w on NW Sammamish Rd. Ext corridors. **Pets:** Small. No service, supervision, crate.

🆓 ❌ ♿ ➰

KENT

▲▲▲ ◆◆◆ Best Inn & Suites M
(253) 520-6670. **$89-$149, 4 days notice.** 25100 74th Ave
S. I-5 exit 149 (Willis St, Des Moines), 2.5 mi se via SR 516
to 74th Ave. Int corridors. **Pets:** Medium. Designated
rooms, no service, supervision, crate.

[SAVE] [S🐾] [✕] [🖉] [🗲] [🛏] [💻] [🕾] [✕]

◆◆ Days Inn South Seattle/Kent M 🐾
(253) 854-1950. **$79-$98.** 1711 W Meeker St. I-5 exit 149,
2.3 mi se via SR 516 to Meeker St. Int corridors.
Pets: Small. $10 one-time fee/pet. Designated rooms, no
service, supervision, crate.

[ASK] [S🐾] [✕] [🛏] [💻]

▲▲▲ ◆◆◆ Howard Johnson Inn M
(253) 852-7224. **$69-$129.** 1233 N Central. SR 167 84th
Ave exit. Ext corridors. **Pets:** Supervision.

[SAVE] [S🐾] [✕] [🛏] [💻] [🕾]

▲▲▲ ◆◆ Val U Inn M 🐾
(253) 872-5525. **$69-$89.** 22420 84th Ave S. SR 167 exit
(84th Ave S), just n. Int corridors. **Pets:** Dogs only. $5 daily
fee/pet. No service, supervision, crate.

[SAVE] [S🐾] [✕] [🛏]

KIRKLAND

▲▲▲ ◆◆◆ Best Western Kirkland Inn M 🐾
(425) 822-2300. **$86-$97, 7 days notice.** 12223 NE 116th
St. Just e of I-405, northbound exit 20A; southbound exit
20; in Totem Lake area. Ext corridors. **Pets:** Small. $50
deposit/room. Designated rooms, no service, supervision,
crate.

[SAVE] [S🐾] [✕] [🗲] [🛏] [💻] [🕾]

◆◆◆ La Quinta Inn M 🐾
(425) 828-6585. **$99-$119.** 10530 NE Northup Way. From
I-405 exit SR 520W to 108th St exit, s on 108th St, then w.
Int corridors. **Pets:** Other. Supervision.

[ASK] [✕] [🖉] [🗲] [🛏] [💻]

▲▲▲ ◆ Motel 6–687 M 🐾
(425) 821-5618. **$58-$74.** 12010 120th Pl NE. I-405 N exit
20B; I-405 S exit 20, just se. Ext corridors. **Pets:** Small,
other. No service, supervision, crate.

[S🐾] [✕] [🖉] [🗲] [🕾]

**▲▲▲ ◆◆◆◆ The Woodmark Hotel on Lake
Washington H 🐾**
(425) 822-3700. **$155-$165.** 1200 Carillon Point. At Carillon
Point on Lake Washington Blvd; 1 mi n of SR 520. Int
corridors. **Pets:** Very small. Supervision.

[SAVE] [S🐾] [✕] [🖉] [💻] [✕]

LAKEWOOD

**▲▲▲ ◆◆◆ Best Western Lakewood Motor
Inn M 🐾**
(253) 584-2212. **$65-$110.** 6125 Motor Ave SW. I-5 exit
125, 2 mi nw via Bridgeport to Gravelly Lake Dr, just left.
Ext corridors. **Pets:** Medium, dogs only. $6 daily fee/pet.
Supervision.

[SAVE] [S🐾] [✕] [🖉] [🛏] [💻]

▲▲▲ ◆◆ Quality Inn M
(253) 588-5241. **$56-$71.** 9920 S Tacoma Way. I-5 exit
127, 0.3 mi nw. Ext corridors. **Pets:** Supervision.

[SAVE] [S🐾] [✕] [🛏] [💻]

LYNNWOOD

**▲▲▲ ◆◆◆ Best Western Seattle North
Lynnwood M**
(425) 775-7447. **$79-$89.** 4300 200th St SW. I-5 N exit
181A, just w; I-5 S exit 181, 0.5 mi sw via 196th St and
40th Ave. Int corridors. **Pets:** Medium. Designated rooms,
no service, supervision, crate.

[SAVE] [S🐾] [✕] [🛏] [💻] [🕾]

**◆◆◆ The Residence Inn by Marriott-Seattle
North ▲ 🐾**
(425) 771-1100. **$210.** 18200 Alderwood Mall Pkwy. I-5 exit
183, just w on 164th St SW, 1.5 mi se on 28th St W; just n
of Alderwood Mall Shopping Center. Ext corridors.
Pets: Other. $10 daily fee/pet. Supervision.

[ASK] [S🐾] [✕] [🖉] [🛏] [💻] [🕾] [✕]

◆◆◆ Silver Cloud Inn at Lynnwood M 🐾
(425) 775-7600. **$72-$107.** 19332 36th Ave W. I-5 S exit
181, just w; I-5 N exit 181B, 0.8 mi ne via 200th St SW,
then n on 196th St SW near Alderwood Mall. Int corridors.
Pets: Other. Supervision.

[ASK] [S🐾] [✕] [🖉] [🗲] [🛏] [💻] [🕾]

MARYSVILLE

▲▲▲ ◆◆ The Village Motor Inn M 🐾
(360) 659-0005. **$60-$65.** 235 Beach Ave. I-5 exit 199, just
se. Int corridors. **Pets:** Small. $12 daily fee/pet. No service,
supervision, crate.

[SAVE] [S🐾] [🛏] [💻]

MONROE

▲▲▲ ◆◆◆ Best Western Baron Inn M 🐾
(360) 794-3111. **$49-$99.** 19233 Hwy 2. W end of town. Int
corridors. **Pets:** Other. $25 one-time fee/room. Supervision.

[SAVE] [S🐾] [✕] [🗲] [🛏] [🕾]

MOUNTLAKE TERRACE

**◆◆ Homestead Village Guest Studios-North
Seattle M 🐾**
(425) 771-3139. **$59-$64.** 6017 244th St SW. I-5 exit 177,
just nw. Ext corridors. **Pets:** Other. $75 one-time fee/room.
Supervision.

[ASK] [✕] [🔒] [🖉] [🗲] [🛏] [💻]

PUYALLUP

◆ Northwest Motor Inn Inc. M 🐾
(253) 841-2600. **$60-$73.** 1409 S Meridian St. 0.3 mi s of
Meridian exit off SR 512. Ext corridors. **Pets:** Other. $5
daily fee/pet. No service, supervision, crate.

[ASK] [S🐾] [✕] [🛏]

SEA TAC

⚫ ◆ Airport Plaza Hotel Ⓜ ❖
(206) 433-0400. **$60-$65.** 18601 International Blvd S. On SR 99. Int corridors. **Pets:** Small. $15 daily fee/pet, $15 one-time fee/pet. Designated rooms, no service, supervision, crate.
Ⓢⓐⓥⓔ Ⓢ⊘ ☒ 🔋 🍽

◆◆◆ Clarion Hotel Ⓜ ❖
(206) 242-0200. **$89-$109.** 3000 S 176th St. I-5, exit 152, 0.7 mi w to International, 1 mi n to 176th St. Int corridors. **Pets:** Supervision.
ⒶⓈⓀ Ⓢ⊘ 🔒 🔋 💻 🍽 ☞

⚫ ◆◆◆ Doubletree Hotel Seattle Airport Ⓜ ❖
(206) 246-8600. **$69-$119.** 18740 International Blvd. On SR 99. Int corridors. **Pets:** No service, supervision, crate.
Ⓢⓐⓥⓔ ☒ 🔌 🛢 🔋 💻 🍽 ☞

⚫ ◆◆◆ Hilton Seattle Airport Ⓜ
(206) 244-4800. **$169-$169, 3 days notice.** 17620 International Blvd. On SR 99. Int corridors. **Pets:** Small. No service, supervision, crate.
Ⓢⓐⓥⓔ Ⓢ⊘ ☒ 🔌 🛢 🔋 💻 🍽 ☞

⚫ ◆◆◆ Holiday Inn Sea-Tac 🅷 ❖
(206) 248-1000. **$129-$159.** 17338 International Blvd. On SR 99. Int corridors. **Pets:** Small. $25 daily fee/room. No service, supervision, crate.
Ⓢⓐⓥⓔ Ⓢ⊘ ☒ 🔒 🔌 🔋 💻 🍽 ☞

◆◆◆ La Quinta Inn-Sea Tac Intl Ⓜ
(206) 241-5211. **$89-$109.** 2824 S 188th St. Int corridors. **Pets:** Large. Designated rooms, no service, supervision, crate.
ⒶⓈⓀ ☒ 🔌 🔋 💻 ☞

⚫ ◆ Motel 6-90 Ⓜ
(206) 241-1648. **$47-$63.** 18900 47th Ave S. I-5 exit 152, just sw. Int corridors. **Pets:** Supervision.
Ⓢ⊘ ☒ 🔌 🔌 ☞

⚫ ◆◆ Motel 6-1332 Ⓜ ❖
(206) 246-4101. **$50-$66.** 16500 International Blvd. 1 mi n of airport entrance. Ext corridors. **Pets:** Very small. Supervision.
Ⓢ⊘ ☒ 🔌

⚫ ◆◆◆ Seattle Marriott Sea-Tac Airport 🅷
(206) 241-2000. **$183-$183.** 3201 S 176th St. Just e of SR 99. Int corridors. **Pets:** Medium. Designated rooms, no service, supervision, crate.
☒ 🔌 🔌 🔋 💻 ☞

SEATTLE

⚫ ◆◆◆◆ The Alexis Hotel 🅷 ❖
(206) 624-4844. **$230-$250.** 1007 First Ave. Corner of Madison and First Ave. Int corridors. **Pets:** Large, other. Supervision.
Ⓢⓐⓥⓔ Ⓢ⊘ ☒ 🔌 🔌 💻 ☒

⚫ ◆◆◆ Cavanaughs on Fifth Avenue 🅷 ❖
(206) 971-8000. **$245-$260.** 1415 W 5th Ave. Downtown, between Pike and Union. Int corridors. **Pets:** Small. $75 deposit/room. No service, supervision, crate.
Ⓢⓐⓥⓔ Ⓢ⊘ ☒ 🔌 🔌 💻 🍽

⚫ ◆◆◆◆ Four Seasons Olympic Hotel 🅷 ❖
(206) 621-1700. **$295-$365.** 411 University St. Int corridors. **Pets:** Small, other. Supervision.
Ⓢⓐⓥⓔ ☒ 🔌 🔌 🔋 🍽 ☞

⚫ ◆◆◆ Hawthorn Inn & Suites Ⓜ ❖
(206) 624-6820. **$110-$185.** 2224 8th Ave. Downtown, at 8th Ave and Blanchard. Int corridors. **Pets:** Other. $50 one-time fee/room. Supervision.
Ⓢⓐⓥⓔ Ⓢ⊘ ☒ 🔌 🔋 💻

⚫ ◆◆◆◆ Hotel Monaco 🅷 ❖
(206) 621-1770. **$230-$240.** 1101 Fourth Ave. Downtown, corner of 4th Ave and Spring St. Int corridors. **Pets:** Other. No service, supervision, crate.
Ⓢⓐⓥⓔ Ⓢ⊘ ☒ 🔌 💻

⚫ ◆ Motel 6-736 Ⓜ
(206) 824-9902. **$48-$68.** 20651 Military Rd. I-5 exit 151, just s. Ext corridors. **Pets:** Medium. Designated rooms, no service, supervision, crate.
Ⓢ⊘ ☒ 🔌 🔌 ☞

⚫ ◆◆◆ Ramada Inn Seattle at Northgate Ⓜ ❖
(206) 365-0700. **$109-$109.** 2140 N Northgate Way. I-5, exit 173, just w. Ext corridors. **Pets:** Other. Supervision.
Ⓢⓐⓥⓔ Ⓢ⊘ ☒ 🔌 🔋 💻 ☞

◆◆◆ Residence Inn by Marriott Seattle Downtown 🅰
(206) 624-6000. **$115-$300.** 800 Fairview Ave N. I-5 exit 767 (Mercer St), to s end of Lake Union. Int corridors. **Pets:** Large. No service, supervision, crate.
☒ 🔌 🔋 💻 ☞

⚫ ◆◆◆ Travelodge by the Space Needle Ⓜ ❖
(206) 441-7878. **$119-$159.** 200 6th Ave N. I-5 exit 166, 1 mi w, just w of SR 99. Int corridors. **Pets:** Medium, dogs only. $5 daily fee/room. No service, supervision, crate.
Ⓢⓐⓥⓔ Ⓢ⊘ ☒ 🔌 🔋 💻 ☞

⚫ ◆◆ Vagabond Inn by the Space Needle Ⓜ
(206) 441-0400. **$90-$98.** 325 Aurora N. SR 99. Ext/int corridors. **Pets:** Small. Supervision.
Ⓢⓐⓥⓔ Ⓢ⊘ ☒ 🔋 💻 ☞

⚫ ◆◆◆◆ The Westin Seattle 🅷 ❖
(206) 728-1000. **$149-$179.** 1900 5th Ave. Int corridors. **Pets:** Small, dogs only. $250 deposit/room. No service, supervision, crate.
Ⓢⓐⓥⓔ ☒ 🔌 🔌 🔌 🔋 💻 🍽 ☞

SNOQUALMIE

⚫ ◆◆◆◆ Salish Lodge & Spa 🅛 ❖
(425) 888-2556. **$229-$389, 5 days notice.** 6501 Railroad Ave SE. I-90 exit 27 eastbound, 5 mi ne, via North Bend Way, Meadowbrook Way and SR 202; I-90 exit 31 westbound, 7 mi nw via SR 202. Int corridors. **Pets:** Medium. $50 one-time fee/room. Designated rooms, no service, supervision, crate.
Ⓢⓐⓥⓔ ☒ 🔌 💻 ☒

SUMNER

◆◆ **Sumner Motor Inn** Ⓜ ❖
(253) 863-3250. **$50-$66.** 15506 E Main St. Center. Ext corridors. **Pets:** $10 one-time fee/pet. Supervision.
🅰🅢🅚 🆂🅾 ⓧ 🆗

TACOMA

🅐🅐🅐 ◆◆◆ **Best Western Tacoma Inn** Ⓜ❗ ❖
(253) 535-2880. **$69-$97, 7 days notice.** 8726 S Hosmer St. I-5 N exit 128, just se; I-5 S exit 129, just e on 72nd St, 1.2 mi s. Ext corridors. **Pets:** Other. $20 one-time fee/room. Supervision.
🆂🅰🆅🅴 🆂🅾 ⓧ 🕙 🐾 🆗 🔲 🍴 ⓧ

🅐🅐🅐 ◆◆◆ **Days Inn Tacoma** Ⓜ
(253) 475-5900. **$69-$80.** 6802 Tacoma Mall Blvd. I-5 exit 129, 0.3 mi nw. Int corridors. **Pets:** Very small. Designated rooms, no service, supervision, crate.
🆂🅰🆅🅴 🆂🅾 ⓧ 🆗 🔲

◆◆◆ **La Quinta Inn** Ⓜ❗ ❖
(253) 383-0146. **$89-$109.** 1425 E 27th St. I-5 S exit 135; I-5 N exit 134, just n. Int corridors. **Pets:** Small, other. Supervision.
🅰🅢🅚 ⓧ 🕙 🆗 🔲 🍴 🐾

🅐🅐🅐 ◆ **Motel 6–735** Ⓜ ❖
(253) 473-7100. **$48-$68.** 1811 S 76th St. I-5 N exit 129, just e on 72nd St, just s on Hosmer St; I-5 S exit 129, just e on 74th St to 72nd St. Ext corridors. **Pets:** Small, other. No service, supervision, crate.
🆂🅾 ⓧ 🕙 🐾 🐾

🅐🅐🅐 ◆◆◆ **Sheraton Tacoma Hotel** 🅷 ❖
(253) 572-3200. **$120-$146.** 1320 Broadway Plaza. Downtown, I-5 exit 133 to I-705 N (city center), A St exit, left on 11th, then left. Int corridors. **Pets:** Small, other. $250 deposit/room. No service, supervision, crate.
🆂🅰🆅🅴 🆂🅾 ⓧ 🕙 🆗 🔲 🍴

◆◆◆ **Shilo Inn** Ⓜ
(253) 475-4020. **$79-$109.** 7414 S Hosmer St. I-5 exit 129, just se. Int corridors. **Pets:** Medium. No service, supervision, crate.
🅰🅢🅚 🆂🅾 ⓧ 🐾 🆗 🔲 🐾

TUKWILA

◆◆ **Homestead Village Guest Studios-Southcenter** Ⓜ
(425) 235-7160. **Call for rates.** 15635 W Valley Hwy. I-405 exit 1, just s. Ext corridors. **Pets:** Medium. Designated rooms, no service, supervision, crate.
ⓧ 🕎 🕙 🐾 🆗 🔲

◆◆◆ **Homewood Suites** 🅷 ❖
(206) 433-8000. **$129-$199.** 6955 Fort Dent Way. I-405 at exit 1N. Ext/int corridors. **Pets:** Other. $20 daily fee/pet. No service, supervision, crate.
🆂🅾 ⓧ 🕙 🆗 🔲 🐾 ⓧ

◆◆◆ **Residence Inn by Marriott-Seattle South** 🄰
(425) 226-5500. **Call for rates.** 16201 W Valley Hwy. I-405 exit 1, just s across from Boeing Longacre Park. Ext corridors. **Pets:** Large. Supervision.
ⓧ 🕙 🆗 🔲 🐾 ⓧ

VASHON

◆◆ **The Swallow's Nest Guest Cottages** 🅲 ❖
(206) 463-2646. **$75-$180.** 6030 SW 248th St. Se section of the island near Pt Robinson. Ext corridors. **Pets:** Other. $10 daily fee/pet. Designated rooms, no service, supervision, crate.
ⓧ 🆗 🔲 🕎 🅲🆃🆅

❖ END METROPOLITAN AREA ❖

SEDRO WOOLLEY

🅐🅐🅐 ◆◆◆ **Three Rivers Inn** Ⓜ❗
(360) 855-2626. **$63-$77.** 210 Ball St. On SR 20; just w of jct SR 9 N. Ext corridors. **Pets:** Designated rooms, no service, supervision, crate.
ⓧ 🆗 🔲 🍴 🐾

SEQUIM

🅐🅐🅐 ◆◆◆ **Best Western Sequim Bay Lodge** Ⓜ ❖
(360) 683-0691. **$81-$91.** 268522 US 101. 3.2 mi se of town. Ext corridors. **Pets:** Other. $10 daily fee/pet. Designated rooms, supervision.
🆂🅰🆅🅴 🆂🅾 ⓧ 🕙 🆗 🔲 🐾

🅐🅐🅐 ◆◆ **Coffel's Sundowner Motel** Ⓜ
(360) 683-5532. **$69-$79.** 364 W Washington St. Center. Ext corridors. **Pets:** Designated rooms, supervision.
🆂🅰🆅🅴 🆂🅾 ⓧ 🆗

🅐🅐🅐 ◆◆ **Econo Lodge** Ⓜ ❖
(360) 683-7113. **$69-$125.** 801 E Washington St. E end of downtown. Int corridors. **Pets:** Other. $6 daily fee/pet. Supervision.
🆂🅰🆅🅴 ⓧ 🕙 🆗 🐾

◆ **Groveland Cottage** 🅱🅱
(360) 683-3565. **Call for rates, 3 days notice.** 4861 Sequim-Dungeness Way. 5 mi n via Sequim Ave and Sequim-Dungeness Way. Ext/int corridors. **Pets:** Medium. Supervision.
ⓧ 🆗 🔲 🕎

◆◆◆ **Juan de Fuca Cottages** 🅲 ❖
(360) 683-4433. **$125-$130, 7 days notice.** 182 Marine Dr. 7 mi n; via Sequim Ave and E Anderson Rd. Ext corridors. **Pets:** Small, dogs only. No service, supervision, crate.
ⓧ 🆗 🔲 ⓧ 🕎 🆉

SHELTON

AAA ◆◆ **Shelton Inn** **M**
(360) 426-4468. **$48-$68.** 628 Railroad Ave. 0.4 mi w of SR 3. Ext corridors. **Pets:** Medium. Supervision.
[SAVE] [S] [X] [B] [⬛] [🅰]

AAA ◆◆ **Super 8 Motel of Shelton** **M**
(360) 426-1654. **$51-$61.** 2943 Northview Circle. US 101, exit Wallace-Kneeland Blvd, just e. Int corridors. **Pets:** Small. No service, supervision, crate.
[X] [B] [⬛]

SILVERDALE

◆◆ **Cimarron Motel** **M** ❀
(360) 692-7777. **$56-$66.** 9734 NW Silverdale Way. Downtown. Int corridors. **Pets:** Small, other. $10 deposit/room, $10 one-time fee/room. Supervision.
[ASK] [S] [X] [B] [⬛]

SKYKOMISH

AAA ◆◆ **SkyRiver Inn** **M** ❀
(360) 677-2261. **$65-$100.** 333 River Dr E. 16 mi w of Stevens Pass on US 2, s end of Skykomish River Bridge. Ext/int corridors. **Pets:** Other. $3 daily fee/pet. Supervision.
[SAVE] [B] [⬛] [X]

SNOQUALMIE PASS

AAA ◆◆◆ **Best Western Summitt Inn** **MI** ❀
(425) 434-6300. **$79-$199.** 603 SR 906. I-90 E, exit 52, 0.3 mi e on SR 906; I-90 W exit 53, 0.3 mi w. Int corridors. **Pets:** Medium, other. $10 one-time fee/room. Designated rooms, supervision.
[SAVE] [S] [X] [B] [⬛] [🍴] [🅰]

SOAP LAKE

◆◆◆ **Notaras Lodge** **M**
(509) 246-0462. **$58-$65, 3 days notice.** 236 E Main. Just w of SR 17. Ext corridors. **Pets:** Medium. No service, supervision, crate.
[X] [B] [X]

SOUTH BEND

◆◆◆ **The Russell House** **BB**
(360) 875-6487. **$60-$200, 7 days notice.** 902 E Water St. 0.5 mi s on Harrison. Int corridors. **Pets:** Designated rooms, supervision.
[ASK] [S] [X] [🎇]

SPOKANE

◆◆ **Alpine Motel and RV Park** **M**
(509) 928-2700. **$50-$60.** 18815 E Cataldo. I-90 exit 293, just n. Ext corridors. **Pets:** Supervision.
[X] [🎇] [🅰] [X]

AAA ◆◆ **Apple Tree Inn** **M** ❀
(509) 466-3020. **$50-$55.** 9508 N Division St. Jct of US 2 and 395, just n. Ext/int corridors. **Pets:** Medium, dogs only. $25 deposit/room. Designated rooms, no service, supervision, crate.
[SAVE] [S] [X] [B] [🅰] [CTV]

AAA ◆◆ **Best Inn & Suites** **M**
(509) 535-7185. **$49-$89.** 6309 E Broadway. Just w of I-90 exit 286. Ext/int corridors. **Pets:** Small. Designated rooms, no service, supervision, crate.
[SAVE] [S] [X] [B] [⬛] [🅰]

◆◆◆ **Best Western Peppertree Airport Inn** **M** ❀
(509) 624-4655. **$65-$150.** 3711 S Geiger Blvd. Just n of I-90, exit 276. Int corridors. **Pets:** Medium. Supervision.
[ASK] [S] [X] [🅑] [🎇] [B] [⬛] [🅰]

◆◆◆ **Best Western Pheasant Hill** **M** ❀
(509) 926-7432. **$65-$95.** 12415 E Mission. I-90 exit 289, just se. Int corridors. **Pets:** Other. $20 deposit/room. Designated rooms, supervision.
[X] [🎇] [B] [⬛] [🅰]

AAA ◆◆ **Best Western Thunderbird Inn** **MI** ❀
(509) 747-2011. **$65-$75.** 120 W 3rd Ave. I-90 exit 281, just n, then just w on 2nd Ave. Ext corridors. **Pets:** Very small, dogs only. $10 daily fee/pet. No service, supervision, crate.
[SAVE] [S] [X] [🎇] [B] [⬛] [🅰]

AAA ◆◆◆ **Best Western Trade Winds North** **M** ❀
(509) 326-5500. **$69-$89, 7 days notice.** 3033 N Division. 2.3 mi n on US 2 and 395 from jct I-90, exit 281. Ext/int corridors. **Pets:** Small, other. $50 deposit/room. Designated rooms, no service, supervision, crate.
[SAVE] [S] [X] [🅰]

AAA ◆◆ **Cavanaughs Fourth-Avenue** **MI** ❀
(509) 838-6101. **$69-$99.** 110 E 4th Ave. Downtown, I-90 exit 281, just e on Frontage Rd (eastbound) or just n on Division, just w on 2nd, just s on Browne and just e on Frontage Rd (westbound). Int corridors. **Pets:** Other. Supervision.
[SAVE] [S] [X] [B] [⬛] [🍴] [🅰]

AAA ◆◆◆ **Cavanaughs Ridpath Hotel** **H**
(509) 838-2711. **$105-$135.** 515 W Sprague Ave. Downtown. Int corridors. **Pets:** Small. Designated rooms, no service, supervision, crate.
[SAVE] [S] [X] [🅑] [B] [⬛] [🍴] [🅰]

AAA ◆◆◆ **Cavanaughs River Inn** **MI** ❀
(509) 326-5577. **$89-$126, 7 days notice.** N 700 Division St. 0.8 mi n of I-90, exit 281. Int corridors. **Pets:** Other. No service, supervision, crate.
[SAVE] [S] [X] [B] [⬛] [🍴] [🅰] [X]

AAA ◆◆ **Days Inn Spokane** **MI** ❀
(509) 747-2021. **$50-$65.** 4212 W Sunset Blvd. I-90, eastbound exit 277A, 1 mi on Garden Spring Rd; westbound exit 277, just n on Rustle. Ext corridors. **Pets:** Other. $10 one-time fee/room. Designated rooms, supervision.
[SAVE] [S] [X] [B] [🍴] [🅰]

AAA ◆◆◆ **Doubletree Hotel Spokane City Center** **H**
(509) 455-9600. **$79-$109.** 322 N Spokane Falls Court. I-90 exit 281, just n (downtown). Int corridors. **Pets:** Small. No service, supervision, crate.
[SAVE] [X] [🅑] [B] [⬛] [🍴] [🅰]

(AAA) ◆◆ Doubletree Hotel Spokane Valley H ❖
(509) 924-9000. **$79-$109.** 1100 N Sullivan Rd. I-90 exit 291, just s. Int corridors. **Pets:** Small. $50 deposit/room. Designated rooms, no service, supervision, crate.
SAVE ✕ 🐾 🖬 💻 🍴 🖼

◆◆◆ Hampton Inn Spokane M ❖
(509) 747-1100. **$74-$93, 3 days notice.** 2010 S Assembly Rd. I-90; eastbound exit 277A, 1 mi on Garden Springs Rd; westbound exit 277, just n on Rustle, just w on Sunset Blvd. Int corridors. **Pets:** Small. $20 one-time fee/room. Designated rooms, supervision.
✕ 🐾 🐾 🖬 💻 🍴 🖼

(AAA) ◆◆◆ Hawthorn Inn & Suites M
(509) 893-0955. **$69-$79.** 3808 N Sullivan Rd. 1.3 mi n of I-90, exit 291. Int corridors. **Pets:** Small. Designated rooms, no service, supervision, crate.
SAVE 🐾 🐾 🐾 🖬 💻 🖼

(AAA) ◆◆ Howard Johnson Inn M ❖
(509) 838-6630. **$60-$75.** 211 S Division St. Just n of I-90 exit 281 (Division). Int corridors. **Pets:** Medium. $25 deposit/room, $10 daily fee/pet. Designated rooms, no service, supervision, crate.
SAVE 🐾 ✕ 🖬 💻

◆◆◆ Quality Inn Oakwood M ❖
(509) 467-4900. **$69-$89.** 7919 N Division St. I-90 exit 281, 8 mi n. Int corridors. **Pets:** Small. $20 one-time fee/pet. Designated rooms, no service, supervision, crate.
ASK 🐾 ✕ 🐾 🐾 🖬 💻 🖼

◆◆◆ Quality Inn Valley Suites M
(509) 928-5218. **$79-$91.** 8923 E Mission. I-90 exit 287. Int corridors. **Pets:** Small. Designated rooms, no service, supervision, crate.
ASK 🐾 ✕ 🐾 🐾 🐾 🖬 💻 🖼

◆◆◆ Ramada Inn Airport M ❖
(509) 838-5211. **$83-$97.** Airport Rd. I-90, eastbound exit 277B; westbound exit 277, 3.4 mi n. Int corridors. **Pets:** Medium. Supervision.
ASK 🐾 ✕ 🐾 🖬 💻 🍴 🖼 ✕

◆◆◆ Ramada Inn & Suites M ❖
(509) 468-4201. **$59-$89.** 9601 N Newport Hwy. Just n on Newport Hwy (US 2) from jct of US 2 and 395. Int corridors. **Pets:** Medium, other. $25 deposit/room, $25 one-time fee/room. Designated rooms, supervision.
ASK 🐾 ✕ 🐾 🐾 🖬 🖼

◆◆ Ramada Limited M ❖
(509) 838-8504. **$44-$64.** S 123 Post. I-90 exit 280B, just n on Lincoln St, just e, then just s. Ext corridors. **Pets:** $5 daily fee/pet. No service, supervision, crate.
ASK 🐾 ✕ 🐾 🖬

(AAA) ◆ Shangri-La Motel M ❖
(509) 747-2066. **$47-$49.** 2922 W Government Way. I-90 eastbound exit 277A; westbound exit 277, Garden Springs Rd to Sunset Blvd, 1 mi e to Government Way, just n to Hartson. Ext corridors. **Pets:** Medium, dogs only. No service, supervision, crate.
SAVE 🐾 ✕ 🖬 💻 🖼 ✕

◆◆◆ Shilo Hotel M ❖
(509) 535-9000. **$79-$119.** 923 E 3rd Ave. Just n of I-90, exit 281, 0.7 mi e. Int corridors. **Pets:** $10 deposit/room. Supervision.
ASK 🐾 ✕ 🐾 🖬 💻 🍴 🖼

(AAA) ◆◆ The Spokane House Hotel H ❖
(509) 838-1471. **$64-$69.** 4301 W Sunset Blvd. I-90 E exit 277A, 1 mi n on Gaden Springs Rd; I-90 W exit 277, just n on Rustle. Int corridors. **Pets:** Supervision.
SAVE 🐾 ✕ 🖬 💻 🍴 🖼

◆◆ Super 8 Motel M ❖
(509) 928-4888. **$54-$76.** N 2020 Argonne Rd. Just n of I-90, exit 287. Int corridors. **Pets:** Other. $25 deposit/room. Designated rooms, no service, supervision, crate.
ASK 🐾 ✕

◆◆ Super 8 West M
(509) 838-8800. **$49-$79.** 11102 W Westbow Blvd. Just s of I-90, exit 272. Int corridors. **Pets:** Small. Designated rooms, supervision.
ASK 🐾 ✕ 🖬 🖼

(AAA) ◆◆ Trade Winds Motel M ❖
(509) 838-2091. **$50-$70.** 907 W 3rd Ave. Eastbound exit 280 off I-90, e on 3rd; westbound exit 280B. Int corridors. **Pets:** Other. $25 deposit/room. No service, supervision, crate.
SAVE 🐾 ✕ 🖬 💻 🖼

◆◆◆ Travelodge M ❖
(509) 623-9727. **$83-$83.** W 33 Spokane Falls Blvd. I-90 exit 281, 0.5 mi n on Division, just w on Trent. Int corridors. **Pets:** Other. $10 deposit/room, $10 one-time fee/room. Supervision.
ASK 🐾 ✕ 🐾 🐾 🖬 💻

SULTAN

(AAA) ◆◆ Dutch Cup Motel M ❖
(360) 793-2215. **$57-$70, 7 days notice.** 918 Main St. US 2 and Main St. Ext corridors. **Pets:** Medium, other. $7 daily fee/room. No service, supervision, crate.
SAVE 🐾 ✕ 🖬

SUNNYSIDE

◆◆ Rodeway Inn M ❖
(509) 837-5781. **$69-$84.** 3209 Picard Pl. I-82 exit 69, just n. Int corridors. **Pets:** Other. $45 deposit/room, $11 one-time fee/pet. Designated rooms, supervision.
ASK 🐾 ✕ 🖬 🖼

TOPPENISH

(AAA) ◆◆◆ Toppenish Inn Motel M
(509) 865-7444. **$60-$68.** 515 S Elm St. 3.1 mi e of I-82 exit 50 (jct of US 97 and SR 22). Int corridors. **Pets:** No service, supervision, crate.
SAVE 🐾 ✕ 🐾 🖬 🖼

TUMWATER

(AAA) ◆◆◆ Best Western Tumwater Inn M ❖
(360) 956-1235. **$70-$83.** 5188 Capitol Blvd. I-5 exit 102, just e. Int corridors. **Pets:** Other. $5 daily fee/room. Supervision.
SAVE 🐾 ✕ 🐾 🖬

(AAA) ◆◆◆ **GuestHouse Inn & Suites** M ❀
(360) 943-5040. **$78-$135.** 1600 74th Ave SW. I-5 exit 101, just e. Int corridors. **Pets:** Small. $10 daily fee/room. Supervision.

⬛⬛⬛⬛⬛⬛⬛⬛

(AAA) ◆ **Motel 6–77** M
(360) 754-7320. **$40-$56.** 400 W Lee St. I-5 exit 102, just e on Trosper Rd, just s on Capital Blvd, then just w. Ext corridors. **Pets:** Supervision.

⬛⬛⬛⬛

TWISP

(AAA) ◆◆ **Idle-A-While Motel** M ❀
(509) 997-3222. **$45-$72, 4 days notice.** 505 N Hwy 20. Just n of town. Ext corridors. **Pets:** Dogs only. $4 daily fee/pet. No service, supervision, crate.

⬛⬛⬛⬛⬛

UNION GAP

(AAA) ◆◆◆ **Quality Inn-Yakima Valley** M
(509) 248-6924. **$49-$99.** 12 E Valley Mall Blvd. I-82 exit 36, just s. Ext corridors. **Pets:** No service, supervision, crate.

⬛⬛⬛⬛⬛⬛⬛⬛

WALLA WALLA

(AAA) ◆◆◆ **Best Western Walla Walla Suites Inn** M
(509) 525-4700. **$79-$115.** 7 E Oak St. US 12 exit 2nd Ave, just s. Int corridors. **Pets:** Designated rooms, no service, supervision, crate.

⬛⬛⬛⬛⬛⬛⬛⬛

(AAA) ◆◆◆ **Hawthorn Inn & Suites** M
(509) 525-2522. **$69-$109.** 520 N 2nd St. US 12 exit 2nd St, just s. Int corridors. **Pets:** No service, supervision, crate.

⬛⬛⬛⬛⬛⬛

(AAA) ◆◆ **Howard Johnson Express Inn** M ❀
(509) 529-4360. **$74-$124.** 325 E Main. US 12, 2nd Ave exit, 0.5 mi s just e. Ext/int corridors. **Pets:** Medium. Designated rooms, no service, supervision, crate.

⬛⬛⬛⬛⬛⬛

◆◆ **Walla Walla Super 8** M ❀
(509) 525-8800. **$52-$68.** 2315 Eastgate St N. US 12 Wilbur exit, just s. Int corridors. **Pets:** Other. $25 deposit/room. No service, supervision, crate.

⬛⬛⬛⬛⬛⬛⬛⬛

(AAA) ◆◆ **Walla Walla Travelodge** M ❀
(509) 529-4940. **$48-$75.** 421 E Main. US 12, 2nd Ave exit, 0.5 mi s, just e. Ext/int corridors. **Pets:** Medium, dogs only. $5 daily fee/pet, $5 one-time fee/pet. No service, supervision, crate.

⬛⬛⬛⬛⬛⬛

WENATCHEE

◆◆ **Avenue Motel** M ❀
(509) 663-7161. **Call for rates.** 720 N Wenatchee Ave. On US 2 business loop; just nw of downtown. Ext/int corridors. **Pets:** Designated rooms, supervision.

⬛⬛⬛⬛

(AAA) ◆◆◆ **Columbia River Comfort Inn** M ❀
(509) 662-1700. **$80-$90.** 815 N Wenatchee Ave. Downtown. Int corridors. **Pets:** Medium, other. $15 one-time fee/room. No service, supervision, crate.

⬛⬛⬛⬛⬛⬛

(AAA) ◆◆◆ **Hawthorn Inn & Suites** M
(509) 664-6565. **$64-$99, 3 days notice.** 1905 N Wenatchee Ave. W end of town. Int corridors. **Pets:** Small. Designated rooms, supervision.

⬛⬛⬛⬛⬛⬛⬛⬛

(AAA) ◆◆ **Orchard Inn** M ❀
(509) 662-3443. **$49-$77.** 1401 N Miller St. 1.5 mi n on US 2. Int corridors. **Pets:** $10 one-time fee/room. No service, supervision, crate.

⬛⬛⬛⬛⬛⬛

◆◆ **Red Lion Hotel Wenatchee** M ❀
(509) 663-0711. **$79-$89.** 1225 N Wenatchee Ave. Just nw of downtown. Int corridors. **Pets:** Small. $75 deposit/room. No service, supervision, crate.

⬛⬛⬛⬛⬛⬛⬛⬛

◆◆◆ **WestCoast Wenatchee Center Hotel** M ❀
(509) 662-1234. **$79-$89.** 201 N Wenatchee Ave. Downtown. Int corridors. **Pets:** Other. $50 deposit/room. Supervision.

⬛⬛⬛⬛⬛⬛

WESTPORT

◆◆ **Mariners Cove Inn** M
(360) 268-0531. **$49-$60, 7 days notice.** 303 Ocean St. Downtown. Ext corridors. **Pets:** Small. No service, supervision, crate.

⬛⬛⬛⬛⬛

WHITE SALMON

◆◆ **Inn of the White Salmon** BB
(509) 493-2335. **Call for rates, 3 days notice.** 172 W Jewett. Downtown on SR 141. Int corridors. **Pets:** Supervision.

⬛

WINTHROP

(AAA) ◆◆◆ **Best Western Cascade Inn** M ❀
(509) 996-3100. **$67-$150.** 960 Hwy 20. 0.8 mi e. Ext corridors. **Pets:** Other. $10 daily fee/pet. Supervision.

⬛⬛⬛⬛⬛

◆◆◆ **RiverRun Inn** M ❀
(509) 996-2173. **$60-$89, 3 days notice.** 27 Rader Rd. 0.5 mi w of town, just s of SR 20. Ext/int corridors. **Pets:** Medium, dogs only. $10 daily fee/pet. No service, supervision, crate.

⬛⬛⬛⬛⬛⬛⬛⬛

◆◆ **The Virginian Resort** M ❀
(509) 996-2535. **$75-$95.** 808 N Cascade Hwy. E end of town, on SR 20. Ext corridors. **Pets:** Other. $5 daily fee/pet. No service, supervision, crate.

⬛⬛⬛⬛⬛

AAA ◆◆ **Winthrop Inn** **M** ❀
(509) 996-2217. **$60-$85.** 960 Hwy 20. 0.8 mi e. Int corridors. **Pets:** Dogs only. $7 daily fee/pet. No service, supervision, crate.

[SAVE] [X] [🗐] [🖻] [X]

WOODLAND

AAA ◆◆◆ **Lewis River Inn** **M** ❀
(360) 225-6257. **$48-$71.** 1100 Lewis River Rd. I-5 exit 21, just e. Ext corridors. **Pets:** Small, other. $6 daily fee/pet, $6 one-time fee/pet. Designated rooms, no service, supervision, crate.

[SAVE] [X] [🗐] [🖻]

AAA ◆ **Scandia Motel** **M** ❀
(360) 225-8006. **$32-$42.** 1123 Hoffman St. I-5 exit 21, just nw. Ext corridors. **Pets:** $6 deposit/pet. No service, supervision, crate.

[SAVE] [X] [🗐]

AAA ◆◆◆ **Woodlander Inn** **M** ❀
(360) 225-6548. **$47-$55.** 1500 Atlantic St. I-5 exit 21, just ne. Ext corridors. **Pets:** Medium, other. No service, supervision, crate.

[SAVE] [X] [🗐] [🖻]

YAKIMA

◆◆◆ **Best Western Peppertree Yakima Inn** **M**
(509) 453-8898. **$65-$125.** 1614 N 1st St. Just s of I-82, exit 31. Int corridors. **Pets:** Supervision.

[ASK] [S$] [X] [🗝] [🗐] [🖻]

◆◆◆ **Cavanaugh's at Yakima Center** **M**
(509) 248-5900. **$72-$91.** 607 E Yakima Ave. 0.8 mi s of I-82, exit 33 (westbound) and 33B (eastbound). Ext/int corridors. **Pets:** No service, supervision, crate.

[ASK] [S$] [X] [🎵] [🗐] [🍴]

◆◆◆ **Cavanaugh's Gateway Hotel** **M** ❀
(509) 452-6511. **$72-$91.** 9 N 9th St. Just s of I-82, exit 33 (westbound) or 33B (eastbound). Int corridors. **Pets:** Large, other. $15 one-time fee/room. Designated rooms, no service, supervision, crate.

[ASK] [S$] [X] [🗐] [🖻] [🍴] [🖻]

AAA ◆◆◆ **Comfort Suites-Yakima** **M** ❀
(509) 249-1900. **$94-$104.** 3702 Fruitvale Blvd. US 12 exit (40th Ave), just s. Int corridors. **Pets:** Supervision.

[SAVE] [S$] [X] [🗐] [🖻] [🖻]

◆◆ **Doubletree Inn-Yakima Valley** **M** ❀
(509) 248-7850. **$59-$59.** 1507 N 1st St. I-82 exit 31, 0.5 mi s. Int corridors. **Pets:** Other. $20 deposit/room. No service, supervision, crate.

[X] [🍸] [🗝] [🗐] [🖻] [🍴] [🖻] [X]

AAA ◆◆◆ **Holiday Inn Express** **M** ❀
(509) 249-1000. **$74-$98.** 1001 E A St. Int corridors. **Pets:** Small. $6 one-time fee/room. Designated rooms, no service, supervision, crate.

[SAVE] [S$] [X] [🎵] [🗝] [🗐] [🖻] [🖻] [CTV]

◆◆◆ **Oxford Suites** **M**
(509) 457-9000. **$75-$105.** 1701 Terrace Heights Dr. On I-82 at Yakima Ave westbound exit 33; eastbound exit 33B. Int corridors. **Pets:** Medium. No service, supervision, crate.

[ASK] [S$] [X] [🗝] [🗐] [🖻] [X]

AAA ◆◆◆ **Red Lion Inn** **M** ❀
(509) 453-0391. **$49-$69.** 818 N 1st St. I-82 exit 31, 1.2 mi s. Ext corridors. **Pets:** Other. No service, supervision, crate.

[SAVE] [S$] [X] [🗝] [🗐] [🖻] [🖻]

AAA ◆◆ **Sun Country Inn** **M** ❀
(509) 248-5650. **$48-$58, 5 days notice.** 1700 N 1st St. Just s of I-82, exit 31. Ext corridors. **Pets:** $5 daily fee/room. No service, supervision, crate.

[SAVE] [S$] [X] [🗐] [🖻]

ZILLAH

◆◆◆ **Comfort Inn** **M**
(509) 829-3399. **$76-$130.** 911 Vintage Valley Pkwy. I-82, exit 52, just n. Int corridors. **Pets:** No service, supervision, crate.

[ASK] [S$] [X] [🎵] [🍸] [🗐] [🖻]

WEST VIRGINIA

CITY INDEX

BARBOURSVILLE

◆◆◆ **Barboursville Comfort Inn**
(304) 733-2122. **$53-$150.** 249 Mall Rd. I-64, exit 20, 0.4 mi n. Int corridors. **Pets:** $25 one-time fee/room. Supervision.

🔳 🔳 🔳 🔳 🔳 🔳 🔳

BECKLEY

🔺 ◆◆ **Best Western Four Seasons Inn** 🅼 ❀
(304) 252-0671. **$45-$80.** 1939 Harper Rd. I-64/77, exit 44, just e on SR 3. Ext/int corridors. **Pets:** Small. $5 one-time fee/room. Supervision.

🔳 🔳 🔳 🔳

◆◆ **Comfort Inn** 🅼 ❀
(304) 255-2161. **$61-$90.** 1909 Harper Rd. I-64/77, exit 44, 0.3 mi e on SR 3. Ext/int corridors. **Pets:** Other. $10 deposit/room. Supervision.

🔳 🔳 🔳 🔳 🔳 🔳

🔺 ◆◆◆ **Country Inn & Suites By Carlson** 🅼 ❀
(304) 252-5100. **$75-$85.** 2120 Harper Rd. I-77, exit 44, just w on SR 3. Int corridors. **Pets:** Other. Designated rooms, supervision.

🔳 🔳 🔳 🔳 🔳 🔳 🔳 🔳

BLUEFIELD

◆◆ **Econo Lodge Cumberland Road** 🅼
(304) 327-8171. **$35-$70.** 3400 Cumberland Rd. I-77, exit 1, 3.8 mi nw via US 52/460, 0.4 mi n on US 52. Ext corridors. **Pets:** Small. Designated rooms, no service, supervision, crate.

🔳 🔳 🔳 🔳 🔳

◆◆◆ **Holiday Inn-On The Hill** 🅼🅸 ❀
(304) 325-6170. **$100.** US 460. I-77, exit 1, 3.8 mi nw via US 52/460. Int corridors. **Pets:** Small. Designated rooms, no service, supervision, crate.

🔳 🔳 🔳 🔳 🔳 🔳 🔳

🔺 ◆◆ **Ramada Inn-East River Mountain** 🅼🅸
(304) 325-5421. **$67-$77, 3 days notice.** 3175 E Cumberland Rd. I-77, exit 1, 3.8 mi nw via US 52/460, then 0.7 mi n on US 52. Ext corridors. **Pets:** Medium. Designated rooms, no service, supervision, crate.

🔳 🔳 🔳 🔳 🔳 🔳 🔳

BRIDGEPORT

🔺 ◆◆◆ **Holiday Inn Clarksburg-Bridgeport** 🅼🅸 ❀
(304) 842-5411. **$79-$90, 30 days notice.** 100 Lodgeville Rd. I-79, exit 119, just e on US 50. Int corridors. **Pets:** Other. Supervision.

🔳 🔳 🔳 🔳 🔳 🔳 🔳 🔳 🔳

◆◆ **Knights Inn-Clarksburg** 🅼 ❀
(304) 842-7115. **$42-$80.** 1235 W Main St. I-79, exit 119, 0.3 mi e on US 50. Ext corridors. **Pets:** Other. Supervision.

🔳 🔳 🔳 🔳 🔳

◆◆ **Sleep Inn** 🅼
(304) 842-1919. **$59-$99.** 115 Tolley Dr. I-79, exit 119, just e on US 50. Int corridors. **Pets:** No service, supervision, crate.

🔳 🔳 🔳 🔳 🔳

CHAPMANVILLE

🔺 ◆◆ **Rodeway Inn** 🅼 ❀
(304) 855-7182. **$45-$85.** Rt 10/119. Just s on SR 10, from jct US 119. Ext/int corridors. **Pets:** Very small. $5 daily fee/pet, $5 one-time fee/pet. Supervision.

🔳 🔳 🔳 🔳 🔳

CHARLESTON

◆◆ **Days Inn** 🅼
(304) 925-1010. **$45-$55, 7 days notice.** 6400 MacCorkle Ave SE. I-77, exit 95, just s on SR 61. Int corridors. **Pets:** Designated rooms, no service, supervision, crate.

🔳 🔳 🔳 🔳 🔳 🔳 🔳

◆◆◆ **Holiday Inn Civic Center** 🅷 ❀
(304) 345-0600. **$99.** 100 Civic Center Dr. I-64, eastbound exit 58B; westbound exit 58C, just s. Int corridors. **Pets:** No service, supervision, crate.

🔳 🔳 🔳 🔳 🔳 🔳

◆◆◆ **Holiday Inn Downtown Charleston House** 🅷 ❀
(304) 344-4092. **$99-$99, 3 days notice.** 600 Kanawha Blvd E. I-64, exit 58B eastbound; exit 58C westbound, Virginia St to corner Laidley and Kanawha; or I-64/77, exit 97, 4.5 mi w on US 60 (Kanawha Blvd). Int corridors. **Pets:** Medium, other. Supervision.

🔳 🔳 🔳 🔳 🔳 🔳 🔳 🔳 🔳

⚑ ◆◆ Red Roof Inn-Kanawha City Ⓜ
(304) 925-6953. **$43-$67.** 6305 SE MacCorkle Ave. I-77, exit 95, just s on SR 61. Ext corridors. **Pets:** Small. No service, supervision, crate.
🆂🅰🆅🅴 ⊠

DAVIS

⚑ ◆◆◆ Deerfield Village Resort-Canaan Valley Ⓒ 🐾
(304) 866-4698. **$140-$140.** Cortland Ln. 7 mi s on SR 32. Ext corridors. **Pets:** Medium, other. $50 one-time fee/room. Designated rooms, no service, supervision, crate.
🆂🅳 ⊠ 🈁 🖵 🍽 🈁 ⊠ 🇰

ELKINS

◆◆ Econo Lodge Ⓜ
(304) 636-5311. **$40-$70.** US 33 E. 1 mi e on US 33. Ext/int corridors. **Pets:** Small. Supervision.
🅰🆂🅺 ⊠ 🈁 🈁

◆◆ Elkins Days Inn Ⓜ 🐾
(304) 637-4667. **$53-$74.** 1200 Harrison Ave. 1 mi w on US 33/250/SR 92. Int corridors. **Pets:** $5 daily fee/pet. Supervision.
🅰🆂🅺 🆂🅳 ⊠ 🈁 🈁 🖵 🍽

FAIRMONT

⚑ ◆◆ Days Inn Ⓜ 🐾
(304) 366-5995. **$44-$56.** 228 Middletown Rd. I-79, exit 132, just se on US 250, then just s. Ext corridors. **Pets:** Medium. $10 one-time fee/pet. No service, supervision, crate.
🆂🅰🆅🅴 🆂🅳 ⊠ 🈁 🖵 🍽

⚑ ◆◆◆ Holiday Inn Ⓜ 🐾
(304) 366-5500. **$72-$109.** 930 E Grafton Rd. I-79, exit 137, just e. Int corridors. **Pets:** Small. Designated rooms, no service, supervision, crate.
🆂🅰🆅🅴 🆂🅳 ⊠ 🈁 🈁 🈁 🖵 🍽 🈁

⚑ ◆◆ Red Roof Inn Ⓜ 🐾
(304) 366-6800. **$45-$61.** 50 Middletown Rd. I-79, exit 132, 0.3 mi s on US 250, just w, then just s. Ext corridors. **Pets:** Medium. Supervision.
🆂🅰🆅🅴 ⊠ 🈁 🈁

◆◆ Super 8 Motel Ⓜ 🐾
(304) 363-1488. **Call for rates.** 2208 Pleasant Valley Rd. I-79, exit 133, just e. Int corridors. **Pets:** Small, dogs only. Designated rooms, supervision.
⊠ 🈁

FAYETTEVILLE

◆◆◆ White Horse Bed & Breakfast Ⓑ🅱
(304) 574-1400. **$70-$110, 7 days notice.** 120 Fayette Ave. US 19, 0.4 mi e on Court St, just n. Ext/int corridors. **Pets:** Medium. No service, supervision, crate.
🅰🆂🅺 🆂🅳 ⊠ 🇰 🇨🇹🇻 🈁

HUNTINGTON

◆◆◆ Days Inn Ⓜ 🐾
(304) 733-4477. **$50-$64.** 5196 US Rt 60. I-64, exit 15, just s. Ext corridors. **Pets:** Very small. $100 deposit/room. Designated rooms, supervision.
🅰🆂🅺 🆂🅳 ⊠ 🈁 🖵 🈁

◆◆◆ Holiday Inn Hotel & Suites Ⓜ🅸
(304) 523-8880. **$89-$95, 3 days notice.** 800 Third Ave. I-64, exit 11, 3 mi n on SR 10, then 0.9 mi w. Int corridors. **Pets:** No service, supervision, crate.
🅰🆂🅺 🆂🅳 ⊠ 🈁 🈁 🈁 🈁 🖵 🍽 🈁

⚑ ◆◆ Red Roof Inn Ⓜ
(304) 733-3737. **$47-$74.** 5190 US Rt 60 E. I-64, exit 15, just s. Ext corridors. **Pets:** Supervision.
🆂🅰🆅🅴 ⊠ 🈁

HURRICANE

⚑ ◆◆ Ramada Limited Ⓜ
(304) 562-3346. **$52-$52.** 419 Hurricane Creek Rd. Jct I-64, exit 34. Ext corridors. **Pets:** No service, supervision, crate.
🆂🅰🆅🅴 🆂🅳 ⊠ 🈁 🈁

JANE LEW

⚑ ◆◆ Wilderness Plantation Inn & Restaurant Ⓜ🅸 🐾
(304) 884-7806. **$46-$63.** Rt 7 Berlin Rd. I-79, exit 105, just e then 0.3 mi s. Ext corridors. **Pets:** $6 daily fee/pet. Supervision.
🆂🅰🆅🅴 ⊠ 🈁 🍽 🈁

KEYSER

⚑ ◆◆ Keyser Econo Lodge Ⓜ
(304) 788-0913. **$55-$85.** Rt 220 S. 2.3 mi s on US 220. Int corridors. **Pets:** Other. No service, supervision, crate.
🆂🅰🆅🅴 🆂🅳 ⊠ 🈁 🖵

LEWISBURG

⚑ ◆◆ Brier Inn Ⓜ🅸 🐾
(304) 645-7722. **$46-$51.** 540 N Jefferson St. I-64, exit 169, just s on US 219. Ext corridors. **Pets:** Other. $10 one-time fee/pet. Designated rooms, supervision.
🆂🅰🆅🅴 🆂🅳 ⊠ 🈁 🍽 🈁

⚑ ◆ Budget Host Fort Savannah Inn Ⓜ🅸 🐾
(304) 645-3055. **$34-$75.** 204 N Jefferson St. I-64, exit 169, 1.3 mi s on US 219. Ext/int corridors. **Pets:** Very small. $5 one-time fee/pet. Designated rooms, no service, supervision, crate.
🆂🅰🆅🅴 🆂🅳 ⊠ 🍽 🈁

⚑ ◆◆ Days Inn Ⓜ
(304) 645-2345. **$48-$110.** 635 N Jefferson St. I-64, exit 169, 0.3 mi n on US 219. Ext corridors. **Pets:** Very small. Designated rooms, supervision, crate.
🆂🅰🆅🅴 🆂🅳 ⊠

◆◆ Super 8 Motel Ⓜ 🐾
(304) 647-3188. **$48-$84.** 550 N Jefferson St. I-64, exit 169, just s on US 219. Int corridors. **Pets:** Other. $10 deposit/pet. Supervision.
🅰🆂🅺 🆂🅳 ⊠ 🈁 🈁

MARTINSBURG

◆◆◆ Days Inn Shenandoah Ⓜ ☀
(304) 263-1800. **$59-$69.** 209 Viking Way. I-81, exit 13, just e on W King St (CR 15). Ext/int corridors. **Pets:** Other. Supervision.
⬛⬛⬛⬛⬛

◆◆ Econo Lodge Ⓜ ☀
(304) 274-2181. **$44-$52.** Rt 2, Box 208N. I-81, exit 20, just e. Ext/int corridors. **Pets:** Other. Supervision.
⬛⬛⬛⬛⬛⬛

◆ Economy Inn Ⓜ ☀
(304) 267-2994. **$32-$40.** 1193 Winchester (US 11S). I-81, exit 12, 0.3 mi e on SR 45, 0.3 mi s on US 11. Ext corridors. **Pets:** Very small, other. $500 deposit/room. Designated rooms, no service, supervision, crate.
⬛⬛⬛⬛

◆◆◆ Hampton Inn Ⓜ ☀
(304) 267-2900. **$59-$75.** 975 Foxcroft Ave. I-81, exit 12, just e on SR 45, then just n. Int corridors. **Pets:** Other. No service, supervision, crate.
⬛⬛⬛⬛⬛⬛⬛⬛

◆◆◆ Holiday Inn Martinsburg Ⓜ ☀
(304) 267-5500. **$69-$89.** 301 Foxcroft Ave. I-81, exit 13, just e on w King St (CR 15). Int corridors. **Pets:** Other. Supervision.
⬛⬛⬛⬛⬛⬛⬛⬛⬛

◆◆ Knights Inn Ⓜ
(304) 267-2211. **$45-$70, 7 days notice.** 1599 Edwin Miller Blvd. I-81, exit 16E, 0.4 mi e on SR 9. Ext corridors. **Pets:** No service, supervision, crate.
⬛⬛⬛⬛

◆◆ Martinsburg Travelodge Ⓜ ☀
(304) 263-8811. **$65-$75.** 1700 Edwin Miller Blvd. I-81 exit 16E, just e. Ext/int corridors. **Pets:** $15 daily fee/room. Supervision.
⬛⬛⬛⬛⬛⬛⬛

◆ Relax Inn Ⓜ ☀
(304) 263-0831. **$28-$59, 3 days notice.** 1022 Winchester (US 11 N) Ave. I-81, exit 12, 0.3 mi e on SR 45, then just n on US 11. Ext corridors. **Pets:** Small. $5 daily fee/pet, $5 one-time fee/pet. No service, supervision, crate.
⬛⬛⬛⬛⬛

◆ Scottish Inns Ⓜ ☀
(304) 267-2935. **$32-$50.** 1024 Winchester Ave US 11. I-81, exit 12, 0.3 mi e on SR 45, just n on US 11. Ext corridors. **Pets:** Dogs only. $5 daily fee/pet, $5 one-time fee/pet. Designated rooms, no service, supervision, crate.
⬛⬛⬛⬛⬛

MORGANTOWN

◆◆ Ramada Inn Ⓜ ☀
(304) 296-3431. **$75-$115, 3 days notice.** US Rt 119, I-68 & I-79. I-68, exit 1, 0.3 mi n. Int corridors. **Pets:** Other. $12 daily fee/room. Supervision.
⬛⬛⬛⬛⬛⬛⬛

NITRO

◆◆ Best Western Motor Inn Ⓜ ☀
(304) 755-8341. **$60-$75.** 4115 1st Ave. I-64, exit 45, 0.5 mi e on SR 25. Ext corridors. **Pets:** Small. $10 daily fee/pet. Designated rooms, supervision.
⬛⬛⬛⬛⬛

PARKERSBURG

◆ Expressway Motor Inn Ⓜ ☀
(304) 485-1851. **$38-$50.** 6333 Emerson Ave. I-77, exit 179, 0.4 mi sw on SR 68. Ext corridors. **Pets:** Other. $3 daily fee/pet. Supervision.
⬛⬛⬛⬛

◆◆ Red Roof Inn Ⓜ
(304) 485-1741. **$50-$66.** 3714 E 7th St. I-77, exit 176, just w on US 50. Ext corridors. **Pets:** Supervision.
⬛⬛⬛

PHILIPPI

◆◆ Philippi Super 8 Motel Ⓜ ☀
(304) 457-5888. **$64-$70, 3 days notice.** Rt 2, Box 155. 2.5 mi s on US 250. Int corridors. **Pets:** No service, supervision, crate.
⬛⬛⬛⬛⬛⬛

PRINCETON

◆◆◆ Days Inn Ⓜ
(304) 425-8100. **$55-$65.** 347 Meadowfield Ln. I-77, exit 9, 0.3 mi w on US 460, just s on Ambrose Ln, then just e. Ext corridors. **Pets:** Supervision.
⬛⬛⬛⬛⬛⬛⬛

◆◆◆ Ramada Limited Ⓜ
(304) 425-8711. **$43-$68, 5 days notice.** 1115 Oakvale Rd. I-77, exit 9, just w then just ne via service rd. Int corridors. **Pets:** Supervision.
⬛⬛⬛⬛⬛⬛

◆◆ Sleep Inn Ⓜ ☀
(304) 431-2800. **$45-$100.** 1015 Oakvale Rd. I-77, exit 9, just w on US 460, then just n via service road. Int corridors. **Pets:** Small, other. No service, supervision, crate.
⬛⬛⬛⬛⬛⬛⬛⬛

◆◆ Town-N-Country Motel Ⓜ ☀
(304) 425-8156. **$33-$55.** 805 Oakvale Rd. I-77, exit 9, 0.3 mi w on US 460. Ext corridors. **Pets:** Very small. $5 one-time fee/pet. Designated rooms, supervision.
⬛⬛⬛⬛

RIPLEY

◆◆ Ripley Super 8 Motel Ⓜ ☀
(304) 372-8880. **Call for rates.** 102 Duke Dr. I-77, exit 138, just e on SR 33. Int corridors. **Pets:** Small, other. No service, supervision, crate.
⬛⬛⬛⬛

SOUTH CHARLESTON

◆◆ Microtel Inn Ⓜ ☀
(304) 744-4900. **$40-$55.** 600 2nd Ave. I-64, exit 56, just ne. Int corridors. **Pets:** Other. Supervision.

⬛⬛⬛

◆◆◆ **Ramada Plaza Hotel Charleston** 🅜 ❀
(304) 744-4641. **$99-$140.** 400 Second Ave. I-64, exit 56, just nw. Int corridors. **Pets:** Medium, other. $50 deposit/room, $10 daily fee/room. Supervision.
(ASK) (S6) (✕) (🗊) (🔳) (🔲) (🍴) (🔄)

🆔 ◆◆ **Red Roof Inn-S Charleston** 🅜 ❀
(304) 744-1500. **$49-$84.** 4006 MacCorkle Ave SW. I-64, exit 54. Ext corridors. **Pets:** Small. Supervision.
(SAVE) (✕) (🗊) (🔳)

ST. ALBANS

◆◆ **Days Inn** 🅜 ❀
(304) 766-6231. **$40-$58, 7 days notice.** 6210 MacCorkle Ave SW. I-64, exit 54, 3.2 mi w on US 60. Ext corridors. **Pets:** Small, other. $50 deposit/room. Designated rooms, no service, supervision, crate.
(ASK) (S6) (✕) (🔳) (🔲) (🍴) (🔄) (✕)

STAR CITY

◆◆ **Econo Lodge Coliseum** 🅜 ❀
(304) 599-8181. **$66-$66, 7 days notice.** 3506 Mononga-hela Blvd. I-79, exit 155, 1.4 mi s on US 19/SR 7. Ext corridors. **Pets:** Other. No service, supervision, crate.
(ASK) (S6) (✕) (🔳) (🔲)

🆔 ◆◆◆ **Holiday Inn** 🅜 ❀
(304) 599-1680. **$79-$89, 30 days notice.** 1400 Saratoga Ave. I-79, exit 155, 1.7 mi s on US 119/SR 7. Ext corridors. **Pets:** Large, other. $10 daily fee/room. Supervision.
(SAVE) (S6) (✕) (🏠) (🗊) (🔳) (🔲) (🍴) (🔄)

SUMMERSVILLE

🆔 ◆◆ **Best Western Summersville Lake Motor Lodge** 🅜 ❀
(304) 872-6900. **$45-$54, 7 days notice.** 1203 S Broad St. US 19 and Broad St; 0.6 mi s of jct SR 39. Ext corridors. **Pets:** No service, supervision, crate.
(SAVE) (S6) (✕) (🔳)

🆔 ◆◆◆ **Comfort Inn** 🅜 ❀
(304) 872-6500. **$50-$119.** 903 Industrial Dr N. US 19, 1.9 mi n of jct SR 39. Int corridors. **Pets:** Other. $5 daily fee/pet, $5 one-time fee/pet. Designated rooms, no service, supervision, crate.
(SAVE) (S6) (✕) (🗊) (🔳) (🔲) (🔄) (✕)

🆔 ◆◆ **Sleep Inn of Summersville** 🅜 ❀
(304) 872-4500. **$45-$81, 7 days notice.** 701 Professional Park Dr. US 19, 1.7 mi n of jct SR 39; at Northside Plaza. Int corridors. **Pets:** Small. $5 daily fee/pet. Designated rooms, no service, supervision, crate.
(SAVE) (S6) (✕) (🗊) (🏠) (🔳) (🔲) (🔄)

TEAYS

🆔 ◆◆ **Red Roof Inn** 🅜 ❀
(304) 757-6392. **$54-$64.** SR 34 & I-64. I-64, exit 39, just n on SR 34, just e on Putnam Village Rd; behind Liberty Square Shopping Center. Ext corridors. **Pets:** Small. Super-vision.
(SAVE) (✕) (🏠) (🔳)

TRIADELPHIA

🆔 ◆◆◆ **Holiday Inn Express Wheeling East** 🅜 ❀
(304) 547-1380. **$53-$63.** Jct I-70, exit 11 (Dallas Pike). Int corridors. **Pets:** Medium. $10 daily fee/pet. Designated rooms, no service, supervision, crate.
(SAVE) (S6) (✕) (🗊) (🔲) (🔄)

WEIRTON

◆◆◆ **Best Western Inn-Weirton** 🅜
(304) 723-5522. **$79-$139, 3 days notice.** 350 Three Springs Dr. 4.5 mi e on US 22, Three Springs Dr exit. Int corridors. **Pets:** Small. Supervision.
(ASK) (S6) (✕) (🗊) (🔳) (🍴) (🔄)

WESTON

🆔 ◆◆◆ **Comfort Inn** 🅜
(304) 269-7000. **$59-$69.** I-79 & Rt 33 E. I-79, exit 99, just e on US 33. Ext corridors. **Pets:** Supervision.
(SAVE) (S6) (✕) (🗊) (🏠) (🔲) (🍴) (🔄)

Wisconsin

CITY INDEX

ALGOMA

[AAA] ◆◆ **Algoma Beach Motel & Condos** [X] 🐾
(920) 487-2828. **$70-$219, 3 days notice.** 1500 Lake St. 0.4 mi s on SR 42. Ext/int corridors. **Pets:** Medium, other. $10 daily fee/pet. Designated rooms, no service, supervision, crate.
[SAVE] [S/D] ☒ ▣ 📺 ✂

◆◆ **Scenic Shore Inn** [M] 🐾
(920) 487-3214. **$44-$54, 3 days notice.** 2221 Lake St. 0.8 mi s on SR 42. Ext corridors. **Pets:** Small, dogs only. Designated rooms, no service, supervision, crate.
☒ ▣ 📺 ✂

APPLETON

◆◆ **Baymont Inn-Appleton** [M]
(920) 734-6070. **$54-$71.** 3920 W College Ave. US 41, exit 137 (SR 125), just e. Ext/int corridors. **Pets:** Medium. Designated rooms, no service, supervision, crate.
[S/D] ☒ ▣ 📺 🏊 ✂

[AAA] ◆◆◆ **Best Western Midway Hotel** [MI] 🐾
(920) 731-4141. **$89-$119.** 3033 W College Ave. US 41, exit 137 (SR 125), 0.5 mi e. Int corridors. **Pets:** Other. $10 daily fee/room, $10 one-time fee/room. Designated rooms, supervision.
[SAVE] [S/D] ☒ 👂 ▣ 📺 🍴 🏊

◆◆◆ **Comfort Suites Comfort Dome** [M] 🐾
(920) 730-3800. **$89-$140.** 3809 W Wisconsin Ave. US 41, exit 138 (Wisconsin Ave), just e. Int corridors. **Pets:** Other. Supervision.
[A$K] [S/D] ☒ 👂 ▣ 📺 🏊

◆◆◆ **Country Inn & Suites By Carlson** [M] 🐾
(920) 830-3240. **$72-$92.** 355 Fox River Dr. US 41, exit 137 (SR 125), just nw. Int corridors. **Pets:** Medium, other. Designated rooms, no service, supervision, crate.
[A$K] [S/D] ☒ ♿ ▣ 📺 🏊

[AAA] ◆◆ **Exel Inn of Appleton** [M] 🐾
(920) 733-5551. **$40-$66.** 210 N Westhill Blvd. US 41, exit 137 (SR 125), just e. Int corridors. **Pets:** Small, other. Designated rooms, no service, supervision, crate.
[S/D] ☒ ▣ 📺

◆◆ **Ramada Inn** [MI]
(920) 735-2733. **Call for rates.** 200 N Perkins St. US 41, exit 137 (SR 125), 1.5 mi e. Int corridors. **Pets:** Designated rooms, no service, supervision, crate.
[A$K] ☒ 👂 ▣ 📺 🏊

◆◆◆ **Residence Inn** [A] 🐾
(920) 954-0570. **$76-$116.** 310 Metro Dr. US 41, exit 137 (W SR 125), just nw on Mall Dr. Int corridors. **Pets:** Other. $10 daily fee/room, $25 one-time fee/room. Supervision.
[A$K] [S/D] ☒ 👂 ♿ ▣ 📺 🏊 ✂

◆ **Roadstar Inn** [M] 🐾
(920) 731-5271. **$37-$85.** 3623 W College Ave. US 41, exit 137 (SR 125), just e. Int corridors. **Pets:** $50 deposit/room. Designated rooms, no service, supervision, crate.
[A$K] [S/D] ☒ ▣

◆◆◆ **Woodfield Suites** [MI] 🐾
(920) 734-7777. **$82-$180.** 3730 W College Ave. US 41, exit 137 (SR 125), just e. Int corridors. **Pets:** Small. $50 deposit/room, $10 daily fee/room. No service, supervision, crate.
[A$K] [S/D] ☒ ▣ 📺 🏊

ARCADIA

◆ **RKD Motel** M
(608) 323-3338. **$35-$55.** 915 E Main ST. On SR 95, 0.6 mi w jct SR 93. Ext corridors. **Pets:** Supervision.
⊠ 🛅 🖳

ASHLAND

🅐 ◆◆◆ **AmericInn Motel & Suites** M 🐾
(715) 682-9950. **$68-$140.** 3009 Lakeshore Dr E. On US 2, 0.6 mi n. Int corridors. **Pets:** Other. $50 deposit/room, $6 one-time fee/room. Designated rooms, no service, supervision, crate.
[SAVE] [S🐾] ⊠ 🦽 🛅 🖳 🍽

🅐 ◆◆ **Anderson's Chequamegon Motel** M 🐾
(715) 682-4658. **$39-$59.** 2200 W Lakeshore Dr. 1.8 mi w on US 2 and SR 13. Ext corridors. **Pets:** Small. $25 deposit/pet. Designated rooms, no service, supervision, crate.
[SAVE] ⊠ 🛅 🖳 🐾

🅐 ◆ **Ashland Motel** M 🐾
(715) 682-5503. **$34-$73.** 2300 W Lake Shore Dr. 2 mi w on US 2, 63 and SR 13. Ext corridors. **Pets:** Other. $5 one-time fee/pet. Designated rooms, no service, supervision, crate.
[SAVE] [S🐾] ⊠

🅐 ◆◆ **Lake Aire Inn** M 🐾
(715) 682-4551. **$45-$95.** 101 E Lake Shore Dr. US 2 and Hwy 13. Ext/int corridors. **Pets:** $25 deposit/room. Supervision.
⊠ 🛅

◆◆ **Super 8 Motel** M
(715) 682-9377. **$47-$91.** 1610 W Lakeshore Dr. On US 2, at 16th Ave. Int corridors. **Pets:** No service, supervision, crate.
[S🐾] ⊠ 🦽 🦽 🍽

BARABOO

🅐 ◆ **Spinning Wheel Motel** M
(608) 356-3933. **$53-$69, 3 days notice.** 809 8th St. On SR 33, 2 mi e of jct US 12. Ext corridors. **Pets:** Small. Designated rooms, no service, supervision, crate.
[SAVE] [S🐾] ⊠ 🛅

BEAVER DAM

◆◆ **Super 8 Motel** M 🐾
(920) 887-8880. **$46-$58.** 711 Park Ave. US 151, exit 132 (SR 33), just w. Int corridors. **Pets:** Medium. $50 deposit/pet. Designated rooms, no service, supervision, crate.
[ASK] [S🐾] ⊠ 🦮

BELOIT

◆◆ **Comfort Inn of Beloit** M 🐾
(608) 362-2666. **$49-$89.** 2786 Milwaukee Rd. I-90, exit 185A, just w (jct I-43 and SR 81). Int corridors. **Pets:** Other. Designated rooms, no service, supervision, crate.
[ASK] [S🐾] ⊠ 🦮 🛅 🖳 🍽

◆◆ **Super 8 Motel** M
(608) 365-8680. **$47-$56.** 3002 Milwaukee Rd. I-90, exit 185A, (jct I-43 and SR 81) just w. Int corridors. **Pets:** Supervision.
[ASK] [S🐾] ⊠ 🛖 🛅

BLACK RIVER FALLS

🅐 ◆◆ **Best Western-Arrowhead Lodge** MI 🐾
(715) 284-9471. **$59-$99.** 600 Oasis Rd. I-94, exit 116, at jct SR 54. Int corridors. **Pets:** Other. No service, supervision, crate.
[SAVE] [S🐾] ⊠ 🦮 🦽 🛅 🖳 🍽 🍽 ⊠

🅐 ◆◆ **Days Inn** M 🐾
(715) 284-4333. **$61-$81.** 919 Hwy 54 E. I-94, exit 116, just w. Int corridors. **Pets:** Small, other. Designated rooms, supervision.
[SAVE] [S🐾] ⊠ 🦽 🛅 🖳 🍽

BOULDER JUNCTION

◆◆◆ **White Birch Village** R
(715) 385-2182. **$642-$1019** (no credit cards), 30 days notice. 8746 Hwy K E. On CR K, 8 mi se. Ext corridors. **Pets:** Small. No service, supervision, crate.
🛅 🖳 ⊠ 📺 🕿

CABLE

🅐 ◆◆◆ **Lakewoods Resort** R 🐾
(715) 794-2561. **$70-$500, 30 days notice.** 8.5 mi e on CR M. Ext/int corridors. **Pets:** Dogs only. $50 one-time fee/pet. Designated rooms, no service, supervision, crate.
[SAVE] ⊠ 🛅 🖳 🍽 🍽 ⊠

CAMERON

◆◆ **Viking Motel** M 🐾
(715) 458-2111. **$40-$65.** 201 S 1st St. On US 8 and CR SS, at jct CR W. Ext corridors. **Pets:** Other. Supervision.
⊠ 🖳

CAMP DOUGLAS

◆◆ **K & K Motel** M 🐾
(608) 427-3100. **$45-$60.** 219 Hwy 12 & 16. I-90/94, exit 55, just s. Ext corridors. **Pets:** Small. $5 one-time fee/pet. No service, supervision, crate.
[ASK] [S🐾] ⊠ 🛅

CHIPPEWA FALLS

◆◆ **AmericInn Motel & Suites** M 🐾
(715) 723-5711. **$60-$76.** 11 W South Ave. 2 mi s on SR 124, access via CR J. Int corridors. **Pets:** Large. $25 deposit/pet. No service, supervision, crate.
[ASK] [S🐾] ⊠ 🦮 🦽 🛅 🖳 🍽

🅐 ◆◆ **Indianhead Motel** M 🐾
(715) 723-9171. **$42-$48.** 501 Summit Ave. 1 mi s on SR 124, beside Chippewa Mall. Ext corridors. **Pets:** Very small. $5 daily fee/pet, $5 one-time fee/pet. No service, supervision, crate.
[SAVE] [S🐾] ⊠ 🛅

◆◆◆ Park Inn International-Chippewa Falls M ✿

(715) 723-2281. **$72-$92.** 1009 W Park Ave. Jct SR 124 and CR J. Ext/int corridors. **Pets:** Other. $10 daily fee/pet. Supervision.

[SAVE] [S$] [X] [B] [P] [TI] [≋]

CRIVITZ

◆◆ Shaffer Park Motel M

(715) 854-2186. **$64-$70.** N 7217 Shaffer Rd. 5 mi w on CR W. Ext corridors. **Pets:** Supervision.

[ASK] [S$] [B] [P] [TI] [≋] [X] [CTV] [Z]

DE FOREST

◆◆◆ Holiday Inn Express M ✿

(608) 846-8686. **$69-$99.** 7184 Morrisonville Rd. I-90/94 exit 126, just e on CR V. Int corridors. **Pets:** Medium, other. No service, supervision, crate.

[ASK] [S$] [X] [✎] [✐] [B] [P] [≋]

DODGEVILLE

◆◆◆ Best Western Quiet House & Suites M ✿

(608) 935-7739. **$83-$113.** 1130 N Johns St. On US 18, just e of jct SR 23. Int corridors. **Pets:** Other. $15 daily fee/pet. Designated rooms, no service, supervision, crate.

[SAVE] [S$] [X] [✎] [✐] [B] [≋]

◆ Pine Ridge Motel M

(608) 935-3386. **$39-$55.** 405 Hwy YZ. On CR YZ, 0.5 mi o of jct SR 23. Ext corridors. **Pets:** Small. No service, supervision, crate.

[SAVE] [S$] [X] [CTV]

◆◆ Super 8 Motel of Dodgeville M ✿

(608) 935-3888. **$73-$83.** 1308 Johns St. Just n of US 18. Int corridors. **Pets:** $50 deposit/room. No service, supervision, crate.

[ASK] [S$] [X] [B]

Door County Metropolitan Area

BAILEYS HARBOR

◆◆ Baker's Sunset Motel & Cottages M ✿

(920) 839-2218. **$70-$85.** 8404 Hwy 57. 1 mi n on SR 57. Ext corridors. **Pets:** $40 deposit/room, $8 daily fee/pet. No service, supervision, crate.

[S$] [X] [B] [P] [X] [AC] [CTV] [Z]

FISH CREEK

◆◆ Julie's Park Cafe & Motel M ✿

(920) 868-2999. **$75-$82.** 4020 Hwy 42. 0.3 mi n on SR 42. Ext corridors. **Pets:** Other. $15 daily fee/pet. Designated rooms, no service, supervision, crate.

[X] [B] [TI] [Z]

GILLS ROCK

◆◆◆ Harbor House Inn BB ✿

(920) 854-5196. **$60-$159, 21 days notice.** 12666 SR 42. Center on SR 42. Ext/int corridors. **Pets:** $10 daily fee/ room. Supervision.

[X] [B] [P] [X] [CTV] [Z]

◆ Maple Grove Motel M ✿

(920) 854-2587. **$45-$70.** 809 State Road 42. 0.3 mi e on SR 42, 1.5 mi w of car ferry. Ext corridors. **Pets:** Dogs only. $5 daily fee/pet. Designated rooms, no service, supervision, crate.

[X] [P] [CTV] [Z]

SISTER BAY

◆◆ Edge of Town Motel M ✿

(920) 854-2012. **$58-$65.** 11092 Hwy 42. 1.5 mi n on SR 42. Ext corridors. **Pets:** Small. $8 daily fee/pet, $8 one-time fee/pet. No service, supervision, crate.

[X] [B] [Z]

STURGEON BAY

◆ Chal-A Motel M ✿

(920) 743-6788. **$49-$59.** 3910 SR 42 & 57. 3 mi n of Sturgeon Bay Bridges on Hwy 42 and 57. Ext corridors. **Pets:** Small. Supervision.

[X]

◆◆ Comfort Inn M

(920) 743-7846. **$69-$99.** 923 Green Bay Rd. At jct SR 42/57 and CR S. Int corridors. **Pets:** Supervision.

[ASK] [S$] [X] [B] [P] [≋]

✿ End Metropolitan Area ✿

EAGLE RIVER

◆◆◆ Days Inn M ✿

(715) 479-5151. **$70-$92.** 844 Hwy 45 N. 0.5 mi n on US 45. Int corridors. **Pets:** Medium, other. Designated rooms, supervision.

[SAVE] [S$] [X] [✐] [B] [P] [≋]

◆ The Edgewater Inn & Resort M ✿

(715) 479-4011. **$40-$70, 30 days notice.** 5054 Hwy 70 W. 1 mi w on SR 70. Ext corridors. **Pets:** Other. $10 one-time fee/room. No service, supervision, crate.

[ASK] [S$] [X] [B] [P] [X]

◆◆ White Eagle Motel **M**
(715) 479-4426. **Call for rates, 7 days notice.** 4948 Hwy 70 W. 0.8 mi w on SR 70. Ext corridors. **Pets:** Designated rooms, no service, crate.

(ASK) ⊠ 🖬 🖾 ⊠ 🖉

EAU CLAIRE

⊛ ◆◆◆ AmericInn Motel & Suites **M** 🐾
(715) 874-4900. **$59-$79.** 6200 Texaco Dr. I-94, exit 59, at jct US 12. Int corridors. **Pets:** Other. No service, supervision, crate.

(SAVE) 🖪 ⊠ 🖫 🖬 🖵 🖾

⊛ ◆◆ Antlers Motel **M**
(715) 834-5313. **$38-$65.** 2245 S Hastings Way. Jct US 12 and 53. Ext corridors. **Pets:** Very small. No service, supervision, crate.

⊠ 🖾

◆◆ Best Western White House Inn **M** 🐾
(715) 832-8356. **$49-$125.** 1828 S Hastings Way. 1.3 mi n of jct SR 12 on US 53. Int corridors. **Pets:** Dogs only. $25 deposit/room, $10 one-time fee/room. Designated rooms, no service, supervision, crate.

(ASK) 🖪 ⊠ 🖉 🖬 🖾

◆◆ Comfort Inn **M** 🐾
(715) 833-9798. **$54-$99.** 3117 Craig Rd. I-94, exit 65, 1.3 mi n on SR 37, just s of jct US 12. Int corridors. **Pets:** $10 daily fee/room. Designated rooms, supervision.

(ASK) 🖪 ⊠ 🖬 🖵 🖾

◆◆◆ Country Inn & Suites By Carlson **M**
(715) 832-7289. **$69-$99.** 3614 Gateway Dr. I-94, exit 70, 0.8 mi n on US 50, just ne on CR AA. Int corridors. **Pets:** Supervision.

(ASK) 🖪 ⊠ 🖫 🖉 🖬 🖵 🖾

⊛ ◆◆ Days Inn-West **M** 🐾
(715) 874-5550. **$55-$70.** 6319 Truax Ln. I-94, exit 59, at jct US 12. Int corridors. **Pets:** $25 deposit/room. Designated rooms, no service, supervision, crate.

(SAVE) ⊠ 🖉 🖬 🖵 🖾

⊛ ◆◆◆ Econo Lodge **M** 🐾
(715) 833-8818. **$59-$79.** 4608 Royal Dr. I-94, exit 68, just n on SR 93, just w on Golf Rd, then just s. Int corridors. **Pets:** No service, supervision, crate.

(SAVE) 🖪 ⊠ 🖬 🖵

⊛ ◆◆ Exel Inn of Eau Claire **M**
(715) 834-3193. **$39-$65.** 2305 Craig Rd. I-94, exit 65, 1.3 mi n on SR 37, just w of jct US 12. Int corridors. **Pets:** Small. Designated rooms, no service, supervision, crate.

🖪 ⊠ 🖬 🖵

⊛ ◆◆ Holiday Inn Campus Area **M** 🐾
(715) 835-2211. **$70-$85.** 2703 Craig Rd. I-94, exit 65, 1.3 mi n on SR 37, just w of jct US 12. Int corridors. **Pets:** Other. $15 one-time fee/room. Designated rooms, no service, supervision, crate.

(SAVE) 🖪 ⊠ 🖬 🖵 🍴 🖾

⊛ ◆◆◆ Holiday Inn Convention Center **H** 🐾
(715) 835-6121. **$64-$84.** 205 S Barstow St. Center; S Barstow at Gibson St. Int corridors. **Pets:** Designated rooms, no service, supervision, crate.

(SAVE) 🖪 ⊠ 🖉 🖬 🖵 🍴 🖾

⊛ ◆ Maple Manor Motel **M** 🐾
(715) 834-2618. **$35-$45.** 2507 S Hastings Way. I-94, exit 70, 3 mi n on US 53, exit US 12 (Claremont Ave), just se. Ext corridors. **Pets:** No service, supervision, crate.

(SAVE) 🖪 ⊠ 🖬 🖵 🍴

⊛ ◆◆◆ Park Inn & Suites International **M** 🐾
(715) 838-9989. **$59-$149.** 3340 Mondovi Rd. I-94, exit 65, then just n. Int corridors. **Pets:** $10 daily fee/room. Designated rooms, supervision.

(SAVE) 🖪 ⊠ 🖬 🖵 🖾

⊛ ◆◆ Quality Inn **M** 🐾
(715) 834-6611. **$59-$139.** 809 W Clairemont Ave. I-94, exit 65, 1.3 mi n on SR 37, just e of jct US 12. Ext/int corridors. **Pets:** Other. $10 one-time fee/room. No service, supervision, crate.

(SAVE) 🖪 ⊠ 🖉 🖫 🖬 🖵 🍴 🖾

◆◆◆ Ramada Inn & Conference Center **M** 🐾
(715) 834-3181. **$58-$68, 30 days notice.** 1202 W Clairemont Ave. I-94, exit 65, 1.3 mi n on SR 37, just w of jct US 12. Int corridors. **Pets:** Other. $25 one-time fee/room. Designated rooms, supervision.

(ASK) 🖪 ⊠ 🖉 🖫 🖬 🖵 🍴 🖾

EDGERTON

◆◆◆ Comfort Inn **M** 🐾
(608) 884-2118. **$69-$93.** 11102 Goede. I-90, exit 163, just e. Int corridors. **Pets:** Small. $25 deposit/room. Designated rooms, no service, supervision, crate.

(ASK) 🖪 ⊠ 🖫 🖬 🖵 🖾

FENNIMORE

⊛ ◆◆ Fenmore Hills Motel **M** 🐾
(608) 822-3281. **$52-$66.** 5814 Hwy 18 W. 2.4 mi w on US 18. Int corridors. **Pets:** No service, supervision, crate.

(SAVE) 🖪 ⊠ 🖬 (CTV)

FOND DU LAC

◆◆◆ Baymont Inn & Suites **M**
(920) 921-4000. **$55-$250.** 77 Holiday Ln. Sw of jct US 41 and 151. Int corridors. **Pets:** Small. Designated rooms, supervision.

(ASK) 🖪 ⊠ 🖬 🖵 🖾

◆◆◆ Holiday Inn **M** 🐾
(920) 923-1440. **$120-$140, 3 days notice.** 625 W Rolling Meadows Dr. On US 151, just sw of jct US 41. Int corridors. **Pets:** Medium. $150 deposit/room. Designated rooms, no service, supervision, crate.

(ASK) 🖪 ⊠ 🖫 🖬 🖵 🍴 🖾

(AAA) ◆ **Northway Motel M** ❀
(920) 921-7975. **$50-$70, 7 days notice.** 301 S Pioneer Rd. From US 41 exit US 151, just e, then 0.8 mi n on CR VV; or exit SR 23, 1 mi s on CR VV. Ext corridors. **Pets:** $15 deposit/pet, $5 one-time fee/pet. No service, supervision, crate.
SAVE **S** **X** **☎** **💻**

◆◆ **Super 8 Motel M** ❀
(920) 922-1088. **$51-$61, 30 days notice.** 391 N Pioneer Rd. Just n of jct of US 41 and SR 23, on e frontage road (CR VV). Int corridors. **Pets:** $15 one-time fee/pet. Designated rooms, no service, supervision, crate.
ASK **S** **X** **✒** **☎**

GRANTSBURG

(AAA) ◆◆ **Wood River Motel M**
(715) 463-2541. **$42-$48.** 703 W SR 70. 1 mi w of jct SR 70 and SR 87. Ext corridors. **Pets:** No service, supervision, crate.
SAVE **S** **X** **☎**

GREEN BAY

(AAA) ◆◆◆ **AmericInn M** ❀
(920) 434-9790. **$75-$95.** 2032 Velp Ave. US 41, exit 170, 0.3 mi w. Int corridors. **Pets:** Medium. $25 deposit/room. Supervision.
SAVE **S** **X** **☎** **✦** **☎** **🏊**

(AAA) ◆ **A-1 Tower Motel M** ❀
(920) 468-1242. **$45-$90, 3 days notice.** 2625 Humboldt Rd. I-43, exit 185, just w on University, then just se on CR N. Ext corridors. **Pets:** $25 deposit/room. No service, supervision, crate.
SAVE **S** **X** **☎**

◆◆ **Baymont Inn M** ❀
(920) 494-7887. **$63-$88, 6 days notice.** 2840 S Oneida St. US 41, exit 164 (Oneida St), just e. Int corridors. **Pets:** Very small. $50 deposit/room. No service, supervision, crate.
ASK **S** **X** **☎** **💻**

(AAA) ◆◆ **Bay Motel M** ❀
(920) 494-3441. **$39-$70, 3 days notice.** 1301 S Military Ave. US 41, exit 167 (Lombardi Ave), 0.4 mi e to Marlee, 0.6 mi n. Ext corridors. **Pets:** $5 daily fee/pet. Designated rooms, no service, supervision, crate.
SAVE **S** **X** **☎**

(AAA) ◆◆◆ **Best Western Washington St Inn & Conference Center M**
(920) 437-8771. **$75-$129, 3 days notice.** 321 S Washington St. Downtown, on e side of Fox River, just s of Walnut St (SR 29). Int corridors. **Pets:** Supervision.
SAVE **S** **X** **✒** **☎** **💻** **🍴** **🏊** **🚫**

(AAA) ◆◆ **Days Inn-City Center M** ❀
(920) 435-4484. **$65-$105, 3 days notice.** 406 N Washington St. Downtown, adjacent to the Port Plaza Mall. Int corridors. **Pets:** $7 daily fee/pet. Designated rooms, supervision.
SAVE **S** **X** **✒** **☎** **💻** **🏊**

(AAA) ◆◆ **Exel Inn of Green Bay M** ❀
(920) 499-3599. **$50-$75.** 2870 Ramada Way. US 41, exit 164 (Oneida St), just e. Int corridors. **Pets:** Small, other. Designated rooms, no service, supervision, crate.
S **X** **💻**

◆◆◆ **Holiday Inn City Centre Downtown M** ❀
(920) 437-5900. **$92-$119.** 200 Main St. Downtown, opposite Port Plaza Mall. Int corridors. **Pets:** $25 deposit/room. Supervision.
ASK **S** **X** **✦** **✒** **✦** **☎** **💻** **🍴** **🏊**

◆◆◆ **Residence Inn by Marriott A**
(920) 435-2222. **$159-$159.** 335 W St Joseph St. SR 172, exit Riverside Dr, 1.1 mi n on SR 57, then just e. Ext corridors. **Pets:** Medium. Designated rooms, no service, supervision, crate.
ASK **X** **☎** **💻** **🏊** **🚫**

(AAA) ◆◆ **Super 8 Motel M** ❀
(920) 494-2042. **$60-$77, 3 days notice.** 2868 S Oneida St. US 41, exit 164 (Oneida St), just e. Int corridors. **Pets:** Other. $25 deposit/room. No service, supervision, crate.
SAVE **S** **X** **✒** **☎**

HAYWARD

(AAA) ◆◆◆ **AmericInn Motel M** ❀
(715) 634-2700. **$52-$160.** 15601 US Hwy 63. Just n jct US 63 and 77. Int corridors. **Pets:** $50 deposit/pet, $6 daily fee/pet. Designated rooms, no service, supervision, crate.
SAVE **S** **X** **✦** **☎** **💻** **🏊**

(AAA) ◆◆◆ **Best Western Northern Pine Inn M** ❀
(715) 634-4959. **$69-$79, 3 days notice.** 9966 N Hwy 27. 1.3 mi s on SR 27. Ext/int corridors. **Pets:** $5 daily fee/pet, $5 one-time fee/pet. No service, supervision, crate.
S **X** **☎** **💻** **🏊**

◆◆◆ **Comfort Suites M** ❀
(715) 634-0700. **$69-$139** (no credit cards). 15586 Country Road B. 0.5 mi s of jct SR 27. Int corridors. **Pets:** $25 deposit/room. Designated rooms, no service, supervision, crate.
ASK **S** **X** **✦** **✦** **☎** **💻** **🏊** **🚫**

(AAA) ◆◆◆ **Ross' Teal Lake Lodge and Teal Wing Golf Club R** ❀
(715) 462-3631. **Call for rates, 21 days notice.** 12425 N Ross Rd. 21 mi e on SR 77, 1 mi n. Ext corridors. **Pets:** Other. $5 daily fee/pet. Supervision.
X **☎** **💻** **🍴** **🏊** **🚫** **🏌** **📺** **✈**

(AAA) ◆◆ **Super 8 Motel M** ❀
(715) 634-2646. **$52-$75, 3 days notice.** 10444 N SR 27. On SR 27, 0.3 mi s. Ext/int corridors. **Pets:** Other. Supervision.
SAVE **X** **🏊**

HUDSON

◆◆◆ **Comfort Inn M**
(715) 386-6355. **Call for rates.** 811 Dominion Dr. I-94, exit 2, 1 mi w on frontage road (Crestview Dr). Int corridors. **Pets:** No service, supervision, crate.
X **☎** **💻** **🏊**

◆ Royal Inn **M**
(715) 386-2366. **$40-$70, 3 days notice.** 1509 Coulee Rd. I-94, exit 2, 1 mi w on Frontage Rd. Ext corridors. **Pets:** Medium. Designated rooms, no service, supervision, crate.
[S⊘] [✕] [🛏]

 ◆◆◆ Super 8 Motel of Hudson **M** �
(715) 386-8800. **$68-$88.** 808 Dominion Dr. I-94, exit 2, 1 mi w on Frontage Rd (Crestview Dr). Int corridors. **Pets:** $50 deposit/room. Designated rooms, supervision.
[SAVE] [S⊘] [✕] [🛏] [💻] [🍴]

HURLEY

◆◆ Days Inn of Hurley M 🐾
(715) 561-3500. **$59-$76.** 850 10th Ave N. S of jct US 2 and 51. Int corridors. **Pets:** Medium. Designated rooms, supervision.
[SAVE] [S⊘] [✕] [🛏] [💻] [🍴]

◆◆ Ramada Inn MI
(715) 561-3030. **$50-$95.** 1000 10th Ave. S of jct US 2 and 51. Int corridors. **Pets:** No service, supervision, crate.
[ASK] [S⊘] [✕] [🍴] [🍴]

JANESVILLE

◆◆◆ Baymont Inns & Suites M 🐾
(608) 758-4545. **$70.** 616 Midland Rd. I-90, exit 175B, just e (SR 11). Int corridors. **Pets:** $10 daily fee/room. Supervision.
[ASK] [S⊘] [✕] [🛏] [🗝] [🛏] [💻] [🍴]

◆◆ Best Western Janesville MI
(608) 756-4511. **$59-$89.** 3900 Milton Ave. I-90, exit 171A (SR 26) just e. Int corridors. **Pets:** Small. No service, supervision, crate.
[SAVE] [S⊘] [✕] [🛏] [💻] [🍴] [🍴]

◆◆ Microtel Inn M 🐾
(608) 752-3121. **$39-$56.** 3121 Wellington Pl. I-90, exit 171C, just e. Int corridors. **Pets:** Small. $10 one-time fee/room. No service, supervision, crate.
[SAVE] [✕] [🗝] [🗝] [🛏]

◆ Motel 6–214 M 🐾
(608) 756-1742. **$35-$51.** 3907 Milton Ave. I-90, exit 171A, just e (SR 26). Ext corridors. **Pets:** Medium, other. No service, supervision, crate.
[S⊘] [✕] [🗝]

◆ Select Inn M 🐾
(608) 754-0251. **$38-$52.** 3520 Milton Ave. I-90, exit 171A (SR 26), just sw. Int corridors. **Pets:** Other. $25 deposit/room. No service, supervision, crate.
[SAVE] [S⊘] [✕] [🛏] [💻]

JEFFERSON

◆◆◆ Rodeway Inn M 🐾
(920) 674-4404. **Call for rates.** 1456 S Ryan Ave. On SR 26, 1.2 mi s of jct US 18. Int corridors. **Pets:** Small, other. $50 deposit/pet, $10 daily fee/pet, $10 one-time fee/pet. Designated rooms, no service, supervision, crate.
[ASK] [✕] [🗝] [🗝] [🛏] [💻] [🍴]

JOHNSON CREEK

◆◆◆ Days Inn-Johnson Creek M 🐾
(920) 699-8000. **$52-$77.** W4545 Linmar Ln. I-94, exit 267 (SR 26), just ne. Int corridors. **Pets:** Medium. $50 deposit/room, $5 daily fee/room. No service, supervision, crate.
[ASK] [S⊘] [✕] [🗝] [🛏] [💻] [🍴]

KENOSHA

◆◆ Baymont Inn-Kenosha M
(262) 857-7911. **$69-$76.** 7540 118th Ave. I-94, exit 344, just e on SR 50. Int corridors. **Pets:** Designated rooms, no service, supervision, crate.
[S⊘] [✕] [💻]

◆◆◆ Holiday Inn Express M 🐾
(262) 658-3281. **$89-$110.** 5125 6th Ave. Downtown, just ne of jct SR 32 & 158. Int corridors. **Pets:** Small. $25 deposit/pet. No service, supervision, crate.
[ASK] [S⊘] [✕] [🗝] [🛏] [💻]

LA CROSSE

◆ Eagle Bluff Motel M
(608) 781-7381. **$39-$55.** 2344 St Rd 16. I-90, exit 5, 2 mi s on SR 16W. Ext corridors. **Pets:** Medium. No service, supervision, crate.
[ASK] [S⊘] [✕] [🛏]

◆◆ Exel Inn of La Crosse M 🐾
(608) 781-0400. **$39-$70.** 2150 Rose St. I-90, exit 3, 0.8 mi s. Int corridors. **Pets:** Small, other. Designated rooms, no service, supervision, crate.
[S⊘] [✕] [🛏] [💻]

◆◆◆ The Radisson Hotel La Crosse H 🐾
(608) 784-6680. **$115-$135.** 200 Harborview Plaza. Downtown; just w of US 53. Int corridors. **Pets:** $25 deposit/room. No service, supervision, crate.
[SAVE] [S⊘] [✕] [🗝] [🛏] [💻] [🍴] [🍴]

◆◆ Super 8 of La Crosse M 🐾
(608) 781-8880. **$69-$85.** 1625 Rose St. I-90, exit 3, 1.2 mi s on US 53. Int corridors. **Pets:** Other. $10 daily fee/pet. Designated rooms, no service, supervision, crate.
[ASK] [S⊘] [✕] [🛏] [💻] [🍴]

LADYSMITH

◆◆◆ Best Western El Rancho Motel MI
(715) 532-6666. **Call for rates.** 8500 W Flambeau Ave. On SR 27, 1 mi n. Ext/int corridors. **Pets:** Supervision.
[SAVE] [✕]

LAKE GENEVA

◆◆◆ T C Smith Historic Inn Bed & Breakfast BB 🐾
(262) 248-1097. **$125-$365, 30 days notice.** 865 Main St. Center on SR 50. Int corridors. **Pets:** Dogs only. No service, supervision, crate.
[ASK] [S⊘] [✕] [✕]

LAND O'LAKES

◆◆◆ Sunrise Lodge 🄲 ❀
(715) 547-3684. **$65-$144, 3 days notice.** 5894 W Shore Dr. 2 mi s on US 45, 3 mi e on CR E, then 1 mi n. Ext corridors. **Pets:** Other. Supervision.
🄰🄺 🅂🄳 🄴 🄻 🅃🄸 ⌧ 🄺 🄲🅃🅅 ☒

LUCK

⊕ ◆◆ Luck Country Inn 🄼🄸 ❀
(715) 472-2000. **$51-$71.** 10 Robertson St. At jct SR 35 and 48. Int corridors. **Pets:** Other. Designated rooms, no service, supervision, crate.
🅂🄰🅅🄴 🅂🄳 ⌧ 🄴 🄻 ☒

MADISON

◆◆◆ Baymont Inn & Suites 🄼 ❀
(608) 831-7711. **$83-$105.** 8102 Excelsior Dr. US 12 and 14, exit 253 (Old Sauk Rd), then just nw. Int corridors. **Pets:** Other. Supervision.
🄰🄺 🅂🄳 ⌧ 🄴 🄻 ☒

◆◆ Best Western West Towne Suites 🄼
(608) 833-4200. **$99-$149, 4 days notice.** 650 Grand Canyon Dr. US 12 and 14, exit 255 (Gammon Rd), just e on Odana Rd, then just sw. Int corridors. **Pets:** Small. Designated rooms, supervision.
🄰🄺 🅂🄳 ⌧ 🄲 🄴 🄻

◆◆◆ The Collins House Bed & Breakfast 🄱🄱 ❀
(608) 255-4230. **$85-$160.** 704 E Gorham St. 0.5 mi e of the Capitol Square. Int corridors. **Pets:** No service, supervision, crate.
⌧ 🄴

◆◆◆ Comfort Suites 🄼 ❀
(608) 836-3033. **$89-$199.** 1253 John Q Hammonds Dr. US 12 and 14, exit 252 (Greenway Blvd) then just sw. Int corridors. **Pets:** Other. Supervision.
🄰🄺 🅂🄳 ⌧ 🄲 🄴 🄻 ☒

⊕ ◆◆◆ Crowne Plaza 🄷 ❀
(608) 244-4703. **$79-$159.** 4402 E Washington Ave. I-90/94, exit 135A, 0.4 mi w. Int corridors. **Pets:** $123 deposit/room. Designated rooms, supervision.
🅂🄰🅅🄴 🅂🄳 ⌧ 🄹 🄴 🄻 🄸 ☒

◆◆ Days Inn-Madison Southeast 🄼
(608) 223-1800. **$75-$96, 5 days notice.** 4402 E Broadway Service Rd. US 12 and 18, exit 266 (US 51), just n. Int corridors. **Pets:** No service, supervision, crate.
🄰🄺 🅂🄳 ⌧ 🄲 🄴 🄻 ☒

⊕ ◆◆◆ East Towne Suites 🄼 ❀
(608) 244-2020. **$66-$84, 30 days notice.** 4801 Annamark Dr. I-90/94, exit 135A, just w on US 151. Int corridors. **Pets:** Other. $20 deposit/room. No service, supervision, crate.
🅂🄰🅅🄴 🅂🄳 ⌧ 🄹 🄴 ☒

⊕ ◆ Edgewood Motel 🄼 ❀
(608) 222-8601. **$39-$52.** 101 W Broadway. US 12 and 18, exit 265 (Monona Dr), just nw. Ext corridors. **Pets:** Other. Supervision.
🄴 🄻

⊕ ◆◆ Exel Inn of Madison 🄼
(608) 241-3861. **$42-$75.** 4202 E Towne Blvd. I-90/94, exit 135A, 0.5 mi w on US 151. Int corridors. **Pets:** Small. Designated rooms, no service, supervision, crate.
🅂🄳 ⌧ 🄴 🄻

⊕ ◆◆◆ Holiday Inn Express 🄼
(608) 255-7400. **$74-$99.** 722 John Nolen Dr. US 12 and 18, exit 263 (John Nolen Dr), then just ne. Int corridors. **Pets:** Small. Designated rooms, supervision.
🅂🄰🅅🄴 🅂🄳 ⌧ 🄹 🄲 🄴 🄻 ☒

⊕ ◆◆ Ivy Inn Hotel & Restaurant 🄼🄸
(608) 233-9717. **$68-$78.** 2355 University Ave. 2.3 mi nw. Int corridors. **Pets:** Designated rooms, supervision.
🅂🄰🅅🄴 🅂🄳 ⌧ 🄲 🄴 🄻

⊕ ◆◆ Red Roof Inn-Madison 🄼
(608) 241-1787. **$53-$72.** 4830 Hayes Rd. I-90/94, exit 135A, just w on US 151. Ext corridors. **Pets:** Small. Supervision.
🅂🄰🅅🄴 ⌧ 🄹

◆◆◆ Residence Inn 🄰 ❀
(608) 244-5047. **$129.** 4862 Hayes Rd. I-90/94, exit 135A, just w on US 151. Int corridors. **Pets:** $100 one-time fee/room. Designated rooms, no service, supervision, crate.
🄰🄺 🅂🄳 ⌧ 🄹 🄲 🄴 🄻 ☒ ☒

◆◆◆ Residence Inn By Marriott-Madison West 🄰 ❀
(608) 833-8333. **$160.** 501 D'Onofrio Dr. US 12 and 14, exit 254 (Mineral Point Rd) 0.4 mi e, then just s. Ext corridors. **Pets:** Other. $5 daily fee/pet, $100 one-time fee/room. Designated rooms, no service, supervision, crate.
🄰🄺 🅂🄳 ⌧ 🄹 🄴 🄻 ☒ ☒

⊕ ◆ Select Inn 🄼 ❀
(608) 249-1815. **$44-$56.** 4845 Hayes Rd. I-90/94, exit 135A, just w on US 151. Int corridors. **Pets:** Other. $25 deposit/pet. Designated rooms, no service, supervision, crate.
🅂🄰🅅🄴 🅂🄳 ⌧ 🄲 🄴

◆◆◆ Super 8 Motel 🄼 ❀
(608) 258-8882. **$64-$76.** 1602 W Beltline Hwy. US 12 and 18, exit 260B, just w on n frontage road. Int corridors. **Pets:** Other. $50 deposit/pet. No service, supervision, crate.
🄰🄺 🅂🄳 ⌧ 🄲 🄴 ☒

◆◆ West Towne Road Star 🄼 ❀
(608) 274-6900. **$44-$76.** 6900 Seybold Rd. US 12 and 14, exit 255 (Gammon Rd), just se. Int corridors. **Pets:** Medium. $50 deposit/room. Supervision.
🄰🄺 🅂🄳 ⌧ 🄴

⊕ ◆◆◆ Wingate Inn 🄼 ❀
(608) 224-1500. **$75-$95.** 3510 Mill Pond Rd. I-90, exit 142B. Int corridors. **Pets:** Other. $25 one-time fee/room. No service, supervision, crate.
🅂🄰🅅🄴 🅂🄳 ⌧ 🄲 🄴 🄻 ☒

◆◆◆ Woodfield Suites 🄼 ❀
(608) 245-0123. **$90-$165.** 5217 E Terrace Dr. US 151, exit 98B (American Pkwy), then just sw. Int corridors. **Pets:** $50 deposit/pet, $10 one-time fee/pet. Designated rooms, supervision.
🄰🄺 ⌧ 🄷 🄹 🄲 🄴 🄻 ☒

MANITOWOC

◆◆ Comfort Inn ⓜ 🐾
(920) 683-0220. **$84-$99.** 2200 S 44th St. I-43, exit 149, just e. Int corridors. **Pets:** Other. No service, supervision, crate.

🅰🆂🅺 🆂 ✖ 🛆 🖵

◆◆◆ Holiday Inn ⓜ
(920) 682-6000. **$140-$160.** 4601 Calumet Ave. I-43, exit 149, just e. Int corridors. **Pets:** Designated rooms, supervision.

🅰🆂🅺 🆂 ✖ 🛆 🖵 🍽 ⌂ ✖

⚙ ◆◆◆ Inn on Maritime Bay ⓜ 🐾
(920) 682-7000. **$95-$115.** 101 Maritime Dr. Just e of US 10 on lakefront. Int corridors. **Pets:** $25 one-time fee/room. Designated rooms, supervision.

✖ 🛆 🖵 🍽 ⌂

◆◆ Super 8 Motel ⓜ 🐾
(920) 684-7841. **$45-$65.** 4004 Calumet Ave. I-43, exit 149, 0.8 mi e. Int corridors. **Pets:** $4 daily fee/pet, $4 one-time fee/pet. Designated rooms, supervision.

🅰🆂🅺 🆂 ✖ ✎

MAUSTON

◆◆◆ Country Inn By Carlson ⓜ 🐾
(608) 847-5959. **$75-$96.** 1001 SR 82. I-90/94, exit 69. Int corridors. **Pets:** Other. $5 one-time fee/room. Supervision.

🅰🆂🅺 🆂 ✖ 🛆 🖵 ⌂

◆◆ Super 8 Motel ⓜ 🐾
(608) 847-2300. **$72-$81.** 1001A Hwy 82 E. I-90/94, exit 69. Int corridors. **Pets:** Other. $5 daily fee/pet. Designated rooms, no service, supervision, crate.

🅰🆂🅺 🆂 ✖ 🛆 🖵 ⌂

MEDFORD

◆◆ AmericInn of Medford ⓜ 🐾
(715) 748-2330. **$60-$100.** 435 S 8th St. 0.5 mi s of jct SR 64 on SR 13. Int corridors. **Pets:** Dogs only. Supervision.

🅰🆂🅺 🆂 ✖ ✎ 🛆 🖵 ⌂

MENOMONIE

⚙ ◆◆ Best Western Holiday Manor Motel ⓜ 🐾
(715) 235-9651. **$49-$89, 3 days notice.** 1815 N Broadway. I-94, exit 41, just sw. Ext/int corridors. **Pets:** Medium. $10 one-time fee/room. Designated rooms, no service, supervision, crate.

🆂🅰🆅🅴 🆂 ✖ 🛆 🖵 ⌂

◆◆ Bolo Country Inn ⓜ
(715) 235-5596. **$55-$85, 7 days notice.** 207 Pine Ave W. I-94, exit 41, 0.3 mi s, then just w. Ext corridors. **Pets:** Small. No service, supervision, crate.

🆂 ✖ 🍽

MERCER

⚙ ◆◆ Pine Noel Resort Ⓡ 🐾
(715) 476-2539. **$440-$490** (no credit cards), 30 days notice. 3307 Goettsche Rd. 0.3 mi s on US 51, just e on Clinic St, just se on Martha Lake Rd, 0.4 mi ne to the end of Goettsche Rd. Ext corridors. **Pets:** Medium, other. $25 deposit/pet. Supervision.

🛆 🖵 ✖ 🎣 ✂

MERRILL

⚙ ◆◆◆ Super 8 Motel ⓜ 🐾
(715) 536-6880. **$55-$62, 3 days notice.** 3209 E Main St. I-39 and US 51, exit 208, 0.5 mi w on SR 64. Int corridors. **Pets:** Other. $25 deposit/room. No service, supervision, crate.

🆂🅰🆅🅴 🆂 ✖ ♿ ✎ 🛆 ⌂

MILWAUKEE METROPOLITAN AREA

BROOKFIELD

◆◆◆ Homestead Guest Studios Ⓐ
(262) 782-9300. **$59-$79.** 325 N Brookfield Rd. I-94, exit 297, 1.1 mi e on US 18, just e. Int corridors. **Pets:** Small. Supervision.

🅰🆂🅺 🆂 ✖ ✎ ✎ 🛆 🖵

DELAFIELD

◆◆◆ Baymont Inn & Suites-Milwaukee (Delafield) ⓜ 🐾
(262) 646-8500. **$74-$93.** 2801 Kettle Ct W. I-94, exit 287, just s on SR 83, then just e. Int corridors. **Pets:** Medium, other. $50 deposit/pet. Designated rooms, no service, supervision, crate.

🆂 ✖ 🎣 ✎ ✎ 🛆 🖵

◆◆◆ Holiday Inn Express ⓜ
(262) 646-7077. **$89-$109.** 3030 Golf Rd. I-94, exit 287, just n, then just e. Int corridors. **Pets:** Designated rooms, no service, supervision, crate.

🅰🆂🅺 🆂 ✖ 🎣 ✎ 🛆 🖵 ⌂

GERMANTOWN

◆◆◆ Holiday Inn Express Milwaukee NW-Germantown ⓜ 🐾
(262) 255-1100. **$109.** W 177 N9675 Riversbend Ln. US 41 and 45, exit CR Q Country Line Rd, then just w. Int corridors. **Pets:** Small, other. Designated rooms, no service, supervision, crate.

🅰🆂🅺 🆂 ✖ ♿ ✎ 🛆 🖵 ⌂

◆◆ Super 8

Motel-Germantown/Milwaukee
(262) 255-0880. **Call for rates.** N96 W17490 County Line Rd. US 41 and 45, exit CR Q County Line Rd, then just w. Int corridors. **Pets:** Other. $50 deposit/room. Supervision.

GLENDALE

◆◆ **Baymont Inn-Milwaukee NE**
(414) 964-8484. **$66-$93.** 5110 N Port Washington Rd. I-43 N, exit 77A, just e on Hampton Ave, then 0.5 mi n; I-43 S, exit 78A, just e on Silver Spring Dr, just s. Int corridors. **Pets:** Medium, other. $50 deposit/room. Designated rooms, supervision.

◆◆ **Exel Inn of Milwaukee Northeast**
(414) 961-7272. **$47-$76.** 5485 N Port Washington Rd. I-43, exit 78A (Silver Spring), just e, then just s. Int corridors. **Pets:** Supervision.

◆◆◆ **Residence Inn by Marriott**
(414) 352-0070. **Call for rates.** 7275 N Port Washington Rd. I-43, exit 80 (Good Hope Rd), just e. Ext corridors. **Pets:** Small. No service, supervision, crate.

◆◆◆ **Woodfield Suites**
(414) 962-6767. **$90-$145, 3 days notice.** 5423 N Port Washington Rd. I-43, exit 78A (Silver Springs Rd). Int corridors. **Pets:** $50 deposit/room. Supervision.

MEQUON

◆◆◆ **Best Western Quiet House & Suites**
(262) 241-3677. **$101-$200.** 10330 N Port Washington Rd. I-43, exit 85, just w on SR 167, 1 mi s on CR W. Int corridors. **Pets:** Medium, other. $15 daily fee/pet. No service, supervision, crate.

◆◆ **Breeze Inn to the Chalet Motel**
(262) 241-4510. **$59-$85.** 10401 N Port Washington Rd. I-43, exit 85, just w on SR 167, 0.9 mi s on CR W. Ext corridors. **Pets:** Medium, other. $7 daily fee/room. Designated rooms, supervision.

MILWAUKEE

◆◆ **Baymont Inn & Suites-Milwaukee NW**
(414) 535-1300. **$75-$93.** 5442 N Lovers Lane Rd. US 45, exit 46 (Silver Spring Rd), just e. Int corridors. **Pets:** Small, other. Designated rooms, no service, supervision, crate.

◆◆◆ **Best Western Inn Towne**
(414) 224-8400. **$89-$119.** 710 N Old World 3rd St. At corner of Wisconsin Ave and N Old World 3rd St. Int corridors. **Pets:** Medium. No service, supervision, crate.

◆◆ **The Executive Inn**
(414) 342-0000. **$69-$109.** 2301 W Wisconsin Ave. Corner of W Wisconsin Ave and N 23rd St. Int corridors. **Pets:** $75 deposit/room. No service, supervision, crate.

◆◆ **Super 8-Milwaukee Airport**
(414) 481-8488. **$66-$92.** 5253 S Howell Ave. I-94, exit 318 (Airport), 1.1 mi e, then just n of SR 38. Int corridors. **Pets:** Other.

OAK CREEK

◆◆◆ **Baymont Inn & Suites-Milwaukee South**
(414) 762-2266. **$70-$87.** 7141 S 13th St. I-94, exit 320, just e on Rawson Ave (CR BB). Int corridors. **Pets:** Medium, other. $50 deposit/room. Designated rooms, supervision.

◆◆ **Exel Inn of Milwaukee South**
(414) 764-1776. **$45-$75.** 1201 W College Ave. I-94, exit 319 (CR ZZ), just e. Int corridors. **Pets:** Small, other. Designated rooms, no service, supervision, crate.

◆◆ **Knights Inn-Milwaukee**
(414) 761-3807. **Call for rates.** 9420 S 20th St. I-94, exit 322 (SR 100), just nw. Ext corridors. **Pets:** Medium. Designated rooms, no service, supervision, crate.

◆◆ **Red Roof Inn-Milwaukee**
(414) 764-3500. **$49-$70.** 6360 S 13th St. I-94, exit 319, just e on College Ave (CR ZZ). Ext corridors. **Pets:** No service, supervision, crate.

PORT WASHINGTON

◆◆ **Best Western Harborside**
(262) 284-9461. **$79-$199, 30 days notice.** 135 E Grand Ave. I-43, exit 96, 2 mi e on SR 33, then 1.5 mi e on SR 32 N; at waterfront. Int corridors. **Pets:** Small. Designated rooms, no service, supervision, crate.

WAUKESHA

◆◆◆ **Exel Grand Hotel**
(262) 524-9300. **$62-$86.** 2840 N Grandview Blvd. I-94, exit 293, just s on CR T. Int corridors. **Pets:** Designated rooms, supervision.

◆◆ **Select Inn**
(262) 786-6015. **$46-$70.** 2510 Plaza Ct. I-94, exit 297, just w on CR JJ, Bluemound Rd. Int corridors. **Pets:** Medium. $25 deposit/pet. Designated rooms, no service, supervision, crate.

◆◆ Super 8 **M**
(262) 785-1590. **Call for rates.** 2501 Plaza Ct. I-94, exit 297, just w on US 18, then n on Kossow Rd. Ext corridors. **Pets:** Medium. No service, supervision, crate.

⊠ 🕭 🔋 🖵

WAUWATOSA

(AAA) ◆◆ Exel Inn of Milwaukee West **M** ❀
(414) 257-0140. **$47-$80.** 115 N Mayfair Rd. I-94, exit 304B, just n on SR 100. Int corridors. **Pets:** Small, other. Designated rooms, no service, supervision, crate.

S🔒 ⊠ 🔋 🖵

❀ **END METROPOLITAN AREA** ❀

MINERAL POINT

◆◆◆ Comfort Inn **M** ❀
(608) 987-4747. **$59-$89.** 1345 Business Park Rd. On US 151, 0.6 mi n of jct SR 23 and 39. Int corridors. **Pets:** Medium. $25 deposit/room. Designated rooms, no service, supervision, crate.

ASK **S🔒** ⊠ 🔋 🖵 📶

MINOCQUA

(AAA) ◆◆◆ AmericInn of Minocqua **M**
(715) 356-3730. **$85-$163.** 700 Hwy 51. Downtown; on US 51. Int corridors. **Pets:** Medium. Supervision.

SAVE **S🔒** ⊠ 🐾 🔋 🖵 📶

◆◆ Best Western Lakeview Motor Lodge **M** ❀
(715) 356-5208. **$78-$116.** 311 E Park Ave. N end of US 51 bridge. Ext/int corridors. **Pets:** Other. $8 daily fee/pet. Supervision.

ASK **S🔒** ⊠ 🔋 🖵 ⊠

◆◆◆ Comfort Inn **M**
(715) 358-2588. **$53-$90.** 8729 Hwy 51 N. At jct SR 70 W. Int corridors. **Pets:** Supervision.

ASK ⊠ 🔋 🖵 📶

(AAA) ◆◆ Super 8 Motel **M**
(715) 356-9541. **$65-$75.** 8730 Hwy 51 N. At jct SR 70 W. Ext/int corridors. **Pets:** Designated rooms, no service, supervision, crate.

SAVE **S🔒** ⊠ 🔋 🖵

MONONA

(AAA) ◆◆◆ Country Inn & Suites By
  Carlson **M** ❀
(608) 221-0055. **$79-$111.** 400 River Pl. US 12 and 18, exit 265 (Monona Dr), just nw. Int corridors. **Pets:** Supervision.

SAVE **S🔒** ⊠ 🛗 🔋 🖵 📶

MOSINEE

(AAA) ◆◆◆ AmeriHost Inn-Mosinee **M** ❀
(715) 693-9000. **$65-$75.** 400 Orbiting Dr. I-39 and US 51, exit 179 SR 153, just sw. Int corridors. **Pets:** Small. Supervision.

SAVE **S🔒** ⊠ 🕭 🛗 🔋 🖵 📶

◆◆◆ Holiday Inn Hotel & Suites **MI** ❀
(715) 355-1111. **$80-$180.** 1000 Imperial Ave. I-39 and US 51, exit 185 (US Business 51), just se. Int corridors. **Pets:** Medium. $10 daily fee/room. Designated rooms, no service, supervision, crate.

ASK **S🔒** ⊠ 🕭 🛗 🔋 🖵 🍴 📶

NEW GLARUS

◆ Swiss-Aire Motel **M**
(608) 527-2138. **$61-$105.** 1200 SR 69. 0.3 mi s on SR 39 and 69. Ext/int corridors. **Pets:** No service, supervision, crate.

ASK **S🔒** ⊠ 📶

NEW LISBON

(AAA) ◆◆ Edge O' the Wood Motel **M** ❀
(608) 562-3705. **$37-$55.** W 7396 Frontage Rd. I-90/94, exit 61 (SR 80), just e on n frontage road. Ext corridors. **Pets:** Designated rooms, no service, supervision, crate.

SAVE **S🔒** ⊠ 🔋 📶 ⊠

(AAA) ◆◆ Travelodge of New Lisbon **M**
(608) 562-5141. **$55-$90.** 1700 E Bridge St. I-90/94, exit 61 (SR 80). Int corridors. **Pets:** Designated rooms, no service, supervision, crate.

SAVE **S🔒** ⊠ 🛗 🔋 🖵 📶

NEW RICHMOND

◆◆◆ AmericInn Motel **M** ❀
(715) 246-3993. **$53-$81.** 1020 S Knowles Ave. 0.5 mi s on SR 65, jct SR 64. Int corridors. **Pets:** $25 deposit/room. No service, supervision, crate.

ASK ⊠ 🛗 🔋 🖵 📶

ONALASKA

◆◆◆ Baymont Inn & Suites **M** ❀
(608) 783-7191. **$69-$79.** 5377 N Kinney Coulee Rd. I-90, exit 5 (SR 16), just ne. Int corridors. **Pets:** Medium. Designated rooms, no service, supervision, crate.

ASK **S🔒** ⊠ 🕭 🛗 🔋 🖵 📶

◆◆◆ Comfort Inn **M** ❀
(608) 781-7500. **$69-$109.** 1223 Crossing Meadows Dr. I-90, exit 4, just s on US 157. Int corridors. **Pets:** Small. Designated rooms, no service, supervision, crate.

ASK **S🔒** ⊠ 🕭 🔋 🖵 📶

◆◆ Microtel Inn **M** ❀
(608) 783-0833. **$45-$67.** 3240 N Kinney Coulee Rd. I-90, exit 5, just ne. Int corridors. **Pets:** Other. $5 daily fee/room. Supervision.

ASK **S🔒** ⊠ 🛗 🔋

OSHKOSH

◆◆ Baymont Inn-Oshkosh **M**
(920) 233-4190. **$60-$77.** 1950 Omro Rd. US 41, exit 119, at jct SR 21. Int corridors. **Pets:** Small. No service, supervision, crate.

S🔒 ⊠ 🖵

◆◆◆ Holiday Inn Express Hotel &
Suites 🅜 ❀
(920) 303-1300. **$109, 3 days notice.** 2251 Westowne Ave.
US 41, exit 119, 0.4 mi sw from jct SR 21. Int corridors.
Pets: Other. Designated rooms, no service, supervision,
crate.

🅰🅢🅚 🆂🗙 🔳 🗃 🔳 🖭 🖾

🅐🅐🅐 ◆◆◆ Oshkosh Park Plaza International Hotel
and Convention Center 🅗 ❀
(920) 231-5000. **$109-$145.** 1 N Main St. Downtown, on
shore of Fox River. Int corridors. **Pets:** Very small, other.
$25 deposit/room. No service, supervision, crate.

🆂🅰🆅🅴 🆂🗙 🗃 🗃 🖭 🍴 🖾

◆◆ Super 8 Motel 🅜 ❀
(920) 426-2885. **Call for rates.** 1581 W South Park Ave.
US 41, exit 116, 0.4 mi e on SR 44, adjacent to airport. Int
corridors. **Pets:** Medium, other. Supervision.

🅰🅢🅚 🗙 🗃 🗃 🖭

OSSEO

◆ Budget Host Ten-Seven Inn 🅜
(715) 597-3114. **$35-$60.** 12554 Gunderson Rd. I-94, exit
88, just e. Ext corridors. **Pets:** Small. Designated rooms, no
service, supervision, crate.

🅰🅢🅚 🆂🗙 🗙

PARK FALLS

◆◆ Northway Motor Lodge 🅜 ❀
(715) 762-2406. **Call for rates.** Hwy 13 S. Just s on SR 13.
Ext/int corridors. **Pets:** Other. $8 daily fee/pet, $8 one-time
fee/pet. Designated rooms, no service, supervision, crate.

🅰🅢🅚 🗙 🖾 🖾

🅐🅐🅐 ◆◆ Super 8 Motel Park Falls 🅜
(715) 762-3383. **$50-$70.** 1212 Hwy 13S. Just s on SR 13.
Int corridors. **Pets:** No service, supervision, crate.

🆂🅰🆅🅴 🗙

PEMBINE

◆ Grand Motel 🅜 ❀
(715) 324-5417. **$30-$50.** W 18379 Hwy 141. At jct US 141
and US 8 W. Ext corridors. **Pets:** Supervision.

🗙 🗃 🖭

PHILLIPS

◆◆ Timber Inn Motel 🅜 ❀
(715) 339-3071. **$43-$49.** 606 N Lake. 0.5 mi n on SR 13.
Ext corridors. **Pets:** Other. Supervision.

🅰🅢🅚 🆂🗙 🗃

PLATTEVILLE

◆◆◆ Mound View Inn 🅜
(608) 348-9518. **$40-$65, 3 days notice.** 1755 E Hwy 151.
On US 151, 2 mi n of jct SR 80/81 N. Int corridors.
Pets: Supervision.

🗙 🗃 🖾

PLOVER

🅐🅐🅐 ◆◆ Elizabeth Inn 🅜 ❀
(715) 341-4414. **$44-$64.** 5246 Harding Ave. I-39, exit 151
(SR 54), just ne. Int corridors. **Pets:** Dogs only. $10 daily
fee/room. Designated rooms, no service, supervision, crate.

🆂🅰🆅🅴 🆂🗙 🗃 🗃 🖾 🖾

PRAIRIE DU CHIEN

🅐🅐🅐 ◆◆◆ Best Western Quiet House &
Suites 🅜
(608) 326-4777. **$83-$150.** Hwy 18 & 35 S. On US 18, 1.9
mi e of jct SR 27 N. Ext/int corridors. **Pets:** Supervision.

🆂🅰🆅🅴 🆂🗙 🗃 🖭 🖾

◆◆ Delta Motel 🅜
(608) 326-4951. **$37-$69.** 1733 1/2 S Marquette Rd. On US
18 1.6 mi e of jct SR 27 N. Ext corridors. **Pets:** Small.
Designated rooms, no service, supervision, crate.

🗃 🖭

◆ Prairie Motel 🅜 ❀
(608) 326-6461. **Call for rates.** 1616 S Marquette Rd. On
US 18, 1.5 mi e of jct SR 27 N. Ext corridors. **Pets:** Small.
No service, supervision, crate.

🗙 🗃 🖭 🖾 🖾

🅐🅐🅐 ◆◆ Super 8 Motel 🅜 ❀
(608) 326-8777. **$60-$84.** Rt 2 Box 426. On US 18, 1.9 mi
e of jct SR 27 N. Ext/int corridors. **Pets:** $15 one-time
fee/room. No service, supervision, crate.

🆂🅰🆅🅴 🆂🗙 🗃

PRENTICE

◆◆ Countryside Motel 🅜 ❀
(715) 428-2333. **$38-$50.** W5370 Granberg Rd. Jct US 8
and SR 13, just se. Int corridors. **Pets:** Other. $10 daily
fee/pet. Designated rooms, supervision.

🗙

RACINE

🅐🅐🅐 ◆◆ Knights Inn 🅜 ❀
(262) 886-6667. **$60-$95.** 1149 Oakes Rd. I-94, exit 333,
4.5 mi e on SR 20. Ext corridors. **Pets:** No service, supervision, crate.

🆂🅰🆅🅴 🆂🗙 🗃 🗃 🖭

◆◆◆ Racine Marriott Hotel 🅗 ❀
(262) 886-6100. **$150.** 7111 Washington Ave. I-94, exit 333,
4.5 mi e on SR 20. Int corridors. **Pets:** Small. $30 deposit/
room. No service, supervision, crate.

🅰🅢🅚 🆂🗙 🖾 🗃 🖭 🍴 🖾

◆◆ Super 8-Racine 🅜
(262) 884-0486. **$55-$95.** 7141 Kinzie Ave. I-94, exit 333,
4.5 mi e on SR 20. Int corridors. **Pets:** Small. No service,
supervision, crate.

🅰🅢🅚 🆂🗙 🗙 🗃 🗃

REEDSBURG

◆◆ Best Value Copper Springs Motel M ❀
(608) 524-4312. **$39-$58, 3 days notice.** E7278 Hwy 23 & 33. 2 mi e on SR 23 and 33. Ext corridors. **Pets:** $20 deposit/pet. Designated rooms, no service, supervision, crate.

SAVE SD X ▯ ▭

◆◆◆ Comfort Inn-Reedsburg M ❀
(608) 524-8535. **$80-$98.** 2115 E Main St. 1.5 mi e on SR 23 and 33. Int corridors. **Pets:** Small, other. Designated rooms, no service, supervision, crate.

ASK SD X ▭ ▨

RHINELANDER

◆◆◆ AmericInn M ❀
(715) 369-9600. **$58-$71.** 648 W Kemp St. On Business Rt US 8, 0.3 mi e of jct SR 47. Int corridors. **Pets:** Designated rooms, supervision.

ASK SD X ▨ ▨ ▯ ▨ ▨

◆◆ Claridge Motor Inn, Best Western M ❀
(715) 362-7100. **$64-$99.** 70 N Stevens St. Downtown; on SR 17. Int corridors. **Pets:** Other. $5 daily fee/room. Supervision.

SAVE SD X ▯ ▭ ▯ ▨

◆◆◆ Comfort Inn M ❀
(715) 369-1100. **Call for rates.** 1490 Lincoln St. On Business Rt US 8, 2.6 mi e of jct SR 47. Int corridors. **Pets:** $25 deposit/room. Supervision.

X ▯ ▭ ▨

◆◆◆ Holiday Acres Resort ☒
(715) 369-1500. **$79-$104.** 4060 S Shore Dr. 4.5 mi e on US Business Rt 8, 2.3 mi n on W Lake George Rd. Ext/int corridors. **Pets:** Supervision.

SAVE X ▯ ▭ ▨ ▨

◆◆ Holiday Inn M ❀
(715) 369-3600. **$69-$69.** 668 W Kemp St. On Business Rt US 8, 0.3 mi e of jct SR 47. Int corridors. **Pets:** Medium. $25 one-time fee/room. Supervision.

ASK SD X ▨ ▭ ▯ ▨

◆◆ Kafka's Resort ☒ ❀
(715) 369-2929. **$650-$650** (no credit cards), 30 days notice. 4281 W Lake George Rd. 4.5 mi e on US Business 8, 0.5 mi n. Ext corridors. **Pets:** No service, supervision, crate.

▯ ▭ ▨ ▨ ▨

RICE LAKE

◆◆ Currier's Lakeview Resort Motel M ❀
(715) 234-7474. **$47-$85, 7 days notice.** 2010 E Sawyer St. 1.5 mi n on CR SS from jct CR O, 1 mi e and n on CRC. Ext/int corridors. **Pets:** Other. Supervision.

SAVE X ▯ ▭ ▨

◆◆ Super 8 Motel M
(715) 234-6956. **Call for rates.** 2401 S Main St. 0.3 mi n on CR SS from jct CR O S. Int corridors. **Pets:** Medium. Supervision.

X

RICHLAND CENTER

◆◆ Super 8 Motel-Richland Center M
(608) 647-8988. **Call for rates.** 100 Foundry Dr. 0.9 mi e on US 14. Int corridors. **Pets:** Supervision.

ASK X ▯ ▭ ▨

◆◆ White House Travelodge M
(608) 647-8869. **$55-$80.** 1450 Veterans Dr. 0.5 mi e on US 14. Int corridors. **Pets:** Small. Supervision.

ASK SD X ▯ ▭ ▯ ▨

RIVER FALLS

◆◆ Super 8 Motel M ❀
(715) 425-8388. **$68-$88.** 1207 St Croix St. On SR 65, 0.5 mi w jct SR 35. Int corridors. **Pets:** Other. Supervision.

ASK SD X ▯ ▨

SHAWANO

◆◆ Shawano Super 8 Motel M ❀
(715) 526-6688. **$49-$75.** 211 Waukechon St. 1.2 mi on SR 29. Int corridors. **Pets:** Other. $25 deposit/room. Designated rooms, supervision.

ASK X ▨ ▯

SHEBOYGAN

◆◆◆ AmericInn Motel & Suites M ❀
(920) 208-8130. **$75-$135.** 3664 S Taylor Dr. I-43, exit 123, just e. Int corridors. **Pets:** $50 deposit/room, $7 daily fee/ pet. Designated rooms, supervision.

SAVE X ▨ ▯ ▭ ▨

◆◆ Baymont Inn-Sheboygan M ❀
(920) 457-2321. **$59-$76.** 2932 Kohler Memorial Dr. 1 mi e of I-43, exit 126, on SR 23. Int corridors. **Pets:** Medium, other. No service, supervision, crate.

SD X ▨ ▭

◆◆ Comfort Inn M
(920) 457-7724. **$58-$81.** 4332 N 40th St. I-43, exit 128, 0.3 mi e on Business Rt 42. Int corridors. **Pets:** Small. No service, supervision, crate.

ASK X ▨ ▯ ▭ ▨

◆ Super 8 Motel M ❀
(920) 458-8080. **$49-$59.** 3402 Wilgus Rd. I-43, exit 126, just ne. Int corridors. **Pets:** Dogs only. $10 daily fee/room. Supervision.

ASK SD X

SHELL LAKE

◆◆ Aqua Vista Resort Motel M
(715) 468-2256. **$45-$69.** 412 E CR B. On US 63 at jct CR B, 0.3 mi n. Ext corridors. **Pets:** Designated rooms, no service, supervision, crate.

X ▯ ▨

SIREN

◆ Pine Wood Motel Ⓜ ❀
(715) 349-5225. **$29-$52.** 23862 Hwy 35 S. On SR 35; 0.3 mi s of jct SR 70 W and CR B. Ext corridors. **Pets:** Medium, dogs only. No service, supervision, crate.
[SAVE] [✕] [🛏] [CTV]

SPARTA

◆◆◆ Country Inn By Carlson Ⓜ
(608) 269-3110. **$71-$119.** 737 Avon Rd. I-90, exit 25, on SR 27. Int corridors. **Pets:** No service, supervision, crate.
[SAVE] [⛊] [✕] [🛏] [🛏] [💻] [🌊]

◆◆◆ Super 8 Sparta Ⓜ ❀
(608) 269-8489. **$61-$76.** 716 Avon Rd. I-90, exit 25, just n on SR 27. Int corridors. **Pets:** Medium. $5 daily fee/pet. No service, supervision, crate.
[ASK] [✕] [🛏] [💻] [🌊]

SPOONER

◆◆◆ American Heritage Inn Ⓜ ❀
(715) 635-9770. **$55-$94.** 101 Maple St. Jct Hwy 63 and 70, 1 mi w of Hwy 53. Int corridors. **Pets:** Small. Designated rooms, no service, supervision, crate.
[SAVE] [⛊] [✕] [🛏] [💻] [🌊]

◆◆ Country House Lodging and RV Park Ⓜ ❀
(715) 635-8721. **$42-$79.** 717 S River St, Hwy 63. 0.5 mi s of jct SR 70. Ext/int corridors. **Pets:** Medium. $5 daily fee/pet. Designated rooms, no service, supervision, crate.
[✕] [💻] [🌊]

ST. GERMAIN

◆◆ North Woods Rest Motel Ⓜ
(715) 479-8770. **$37-$47, 3 days notice.** 8083 Hwy 70 E. 0.8 mi e on SR 70. Ext corridors. **Pets:** No service, supervision, crate.
[🛏] [💻]

STEVENS POINT

◆◆◆ Baymont Inn & Suites-Stevens Point Ⓜ ❀
(715) 344-1900. **$57-$62.** 4917 Main St. 2 mi e on US 10 or w of jct I-39, US 51 and 10, exit 158. Int corridors. **Pets:** Medium. $50 deposit/room. Designated rooms, supervision.
[⛊] [✕] [🎵] [🛏] [💻] [🌊]

◆◆◆ Holiday Inn Ⓜ ❀
(715) 341-1340. **$99-$119.** 1501 N Point Dr. 1.5 mi n on US 51 business route; 0.5 mi s of I-39 and US 51 business route, exit 161. Int corridors. **Pets:** Small. $25 one-time fee/room. Designated rooms, no service, supervision, crate.
[SAVE] [⛊] [✕] [🎵] [🛡] [🛏] [💻] [🍴] [🌊]

◆◆ Point Motel Ⓜ ❀
(715) 344-8312. **$36-$52, 3 days notice.** 209 Division St. 0.6 mi n on US 51 business route. Ext corridors. **Pets:** $6 daily fee/pet, $6 one-time fee/pet. No service, supervision, crate.
[ASK] [⛊] [✕] [🛏]

◆ Traveler Motel Ⓜ ❀
(715) 344-6455. **$30-$44.** 3350 Church St. 1.8 mi s on US 51 business route from jct US 10. Ext corridors. **Pets:** Very small, dogs only. Designated rooms, supervision.
[SAVE] [⛊] [✕] [🛏] [💻]

STURTEVANT

◆◆◆ Holiday Inn Express-Racine Ⓜ ❀
(262) 884-0200. **$74-$94.** 13339 Hospitality Ct. I-94, exit 333, just e on SR 20. Int corridors. **Pets:** Small. Designated rooms, supervision.
[SAVE] [⛊] [✕] [🛡] [🎵] [🖥] [🛏] [💻] [🌊]

SUN PRAIRIE

◆◆◆ AmeriHost Inn-Sun Prairie Ⓜ
(608) 834-9889. **$65-$90, 3 days notice.** 105 Business Park Dr. US 151, exit 103 (CR N), then just n. Int corridors. **Pets:** Small. No service, supervision, crate.
[SAVE] [⛊] [✕] [🖥] [🛏] [💻] [🌊]

◆◆ McGovern's Motel & Suites Ⓜ
(608) 837-7321. **$42-$80.** 820 W Main St. US 151, exit 101, 1.5 mi ne on US 151 business route. Ext corridors. **Pets:** Supervision.
[SAVE] [⛊] [✕] [🛏] [💻] [🍴]

SUPERIOR

◆◆◆ Best Western Bay Walk Inn Ⓜ
(715) 392-7600. **$55-$99.** 1405 Susquehanna Ave. 1 mi w on US 2 and Belknap St from jct SR 35. Int corridors. **Pets:** Supervision.
[ASK] [⛊] [✕] [🛏] [🌊]

◆◆ Best Western Bridgeview Motor Inn Ⓜ
(715) 392-8174. **$65-$110.** 415 Hammond Ave. 0.8 mi n on Hammond Ave. Int corridors. **Pets:** Medium. Designated rooms, no service, supervision, crate.
[SAVE] [⛊] [✕] [🛏] [💻] [🌊]

◆◆ Driftwood Inn Ⓜ
(715) 398-6661. **$30-$75.** 2200 E 2nd St. 3.3 mi se on US 2/53. Ext corridors. **Pets:** Small. Designated rooms, no service, supervision, crate.
[SAVE] [✕] [🛏] [💻]

◆◆ Prime Rate Inn Ⓜ ❀
(715) 392-4783. **$99-$139.** 110 Harborview Pkwy. Just n of jct US 2 W and US 53 N, 1.8 mi ne. Ext/int corridors. **Pets:** $50 deposit/room, $10 daily fee/pet. No service, supervision, crate.
[✕] [🌊]

◆ Stockade Motel Ⓜ
(715) 398-3585. **$24-$75, 7 days notice.** 1610 E 2nd St. On US 2/53, 2.8 mi se. Ext corridors. **Pets:** No service, supervision, crate.
[✕] [💻]

◆◆ Superior Inn Ⓜ ❀
(715) 394-7706. **$75-$119.** 525 Hammond Ave. 0.8 mi n on Hammond Ave. Int corridors. **Pets:** Dogs only. Designated rooms, no service, supervision, crate.
[SAVE] [⛊] [✕] [🛏] [🌊]

TOMAH

◆◆◆ AmericInn Ⓜ ❀
(608) 372-4100. **$70-$85.** 750 Vandervort St. I-94, exit 143, just e on SR 21. Int corridors. **Pets:** Other. $50 deposit/room. Designated rooms, no service, supervision, crate.

Ⓐ🆂🅺 🆂🔟 ⊠ ⟳ ✎ 🗄 🖥 🌊

◆◆ Brentwood Inn Ⓜ
(608) 372-4500. **$50-$75.** 24318 Gopher Ave. I-90, exit 41 (SR 131). Ext corridors. **Pets:** Designated rooms, supervision.

Ⓐ🆂🅺 🆂🔟 ⊠ 🗄

⚠ ◆◆ Budget Host DayBreak Motel Ⓜ
(608) 372-5946. **$55-$65.** 215 E Clifton. On US 12 and SR 16; 1.5 mi n of I-90, exit 43; 3.5 mi s of I-94, exit 143. Ext corridors. **Pets:** No service, supervision, crate.

🆂🅰🆅🅴 🆂🔟 ⊠ 🗄

◆◆ Cranberry Suites Ⓜ ❀
(608) 374-2801. **$77-$100.** 319 Wittig Rd. I-94, exit 143, just w on SR 21. Int corridors. **Pets:** Small. $5 daily fee/room. No service, supervision, crate.

Ⓐ🆂🅺 🆂🔟 ⊠ 🗄 🖥

◆◆ Econo Lodge Ⓜ ❀
(608) 372-9100. **$57-$90.** 2005 N Superior Ave. I-94, exit 143, just w on SR 21. Ext/int corridors. **Pets:** Other. $5 daily fee/pet. Supervision.

Ⓐ🆂🅺 🆂🔟 ⊠ ⟳ 🗄 🖥 🌊

◆◆◆ Holiday Inn Ⓜ�’ ❀
(608) 372-3211. **$69-$69.** 1017 E McCoy Blvd. I-94, exit 143, just e on SR 21. Int corridors. **Pets:** Supervision.

Ⓐ🆂🅺 ⊠ 🗄 🖥 🍴

⚠ ◆◆ Lark Inn Ⓜ ❀
(608) 372-5981. **$49-$74.** 229 N Superior Ave. I-94, exit 143, 1.5 mi s on US 12; I-90, exit 41, 2 mi n on US 12. Ext/int corridors. **Pets:** Small. $6 daily fee/pet. Supervision.

🆂🅰🆅🅴 ⊠ 🗄 🖥 🍴

⚠ ◆ Park Motel Ⓜ ❀
(608) 372-4655. **$42-$62.** 1515 Kilbourne Ave. On US 12, 1.5 mi n of I-90, exit 43; 3.5 mi s of I-94, exit 143. Ext corridors. **Pets:** Other. No service, supervision, crate.

🆂🅰🆅🅴 🆂🔟 ⊠ ⟳

◆◆ Super 8 Motel Ⓜ
(608) 372-3901. **$50-$79.** 1008 E McCoy Blvd. I-94, exit 143, just n on SR 21. Int corridors. **Pets:** Designated rooms, no service, supervision, crate.

Ⓐ🆂🅺 ⊠ ✎ 🗄 🖥

◆◆◆ Tomah Comfort Inn Ⓜ
(608) 372-6600. **$64-$99.** 305 Wittig Rd. I-94, exit 143, just w on SR 21. Int corridors. **Pets:** Designated rooms, supervision.

Ⓐ🆂🅺 🆂🔟 ⊠ ⟳ 🗄 🖥 🌊

TOMAHAWK

◆◆ Super 8 Motel-Tomahawk Ⓜ ❀
(715) 453-5210. **$55-$79.** 108 W Mohawk Dr. On US 51 business route, just n of downtown. Int corridors. **Pets:** Other. $25 deposit/room. Supervision.

Ⓐ🆂🅺 🆂🔟 ⊠ ✎ 🗄 🌊

TWO RIVERS

◆◆ Village Inn-Motel & Suites Ⓜ�’ ❀
(920) 794-8818. **$50-$175, 48 days notice.** 3310 Memorial Dr. 2 mi s on SR 42. Ext/int corridors. **Pets:** Medium, other. $10 one-time fee/room. Designated rooms, no service, supervision, crate.

⊠ 🗄 🖥 🍴 🌊 ⊠

VERONA

◆◆◆ Rodeway Inn Ⓜ
(608) 848-7829. **$60-$109.** 131 Horizon Dr. US 18 and 151, southbound exit 94; northbound exit 89, just n of US Business Rt 18 and 151. Int corridors. **Pets:** Small. Designated rooms, no service, supervision, crate.

Ⓐ🆂🅺 🆂🔟 ⊠ 🗄 🖥 🌊

VIROQUA

⚠ ◆◆ Doucette's Hickory Hill Motel Ⓜ ❀
(608) 637-3104. **$40-$65.** Rt 4, Hwy 14. 1.8 mi se on US 14, SR 27 and 82. Ext corridors. **Pets:** Supervision.

🆂🅰🆅🅴 🆂🔟 ⊠ 🗄 🌊

WASHBURN

⚠ ◆◆ Redwood Motel & Chalets Ⓜ ❀
(715) 373-5512. **$50-$75.** 26 W Bayfield St. On SR 13. Ext/int corridors. **Pets:** Other. $3 daily fee/pet, $3 one-time fee/pet. Supervision.

🆂🅰🆅🅴 🆂🔟 🗄 🖥

◆◆ Super 8 Motel Ⓜ ❀
(715) 373-5671. **$70-$90, 5 days notice.** From SR 13, just e on 2nd Ave. Int corridors. **Pets:** Other. $25 deposit/room. Supervision.

Ⓐ🆂🅺 🆂🔟 ⊠

WATERTOWN

◆◆◆ Holiday Inn Express Ⓜ ❀
(920) 262-1910. **$80-$99.** 101 Aviation Way. On SR 26, 1.5 mi s of jct SR 19. Int corridors. **Pets:** Medium, other. $50 deposit/room. No service, supervision, crate.

Ⓐ🆂🅺 ⊠ ✎ 🗄 🖥 🌊

◆◆ Super 8 Motel Ⓜ
(920) 261-1188. **$54-$84.** 1730 S Church St. On SR 26, 1.5 mi s of jct SR 19. Int corridors. **Pets:** Supervision.

Ⓐ🆂🅺 🆂🔟 ⊠ 🗄 🖥 🌊

WAUPACA

⚠ ◆◆◆ Baymont Inn & Suites Ⓜ ❀
(715) 258-9212. **$75-$119.** 110 Grand Seasons Dr. At jct US 10 and SR 54. Int corridors. **Pets:** Medium, other. No service, supervision, crate.

🆂🅰🆅🅴 🆂🔟 ⊠ ⟳ ✎ 🗄 🖥 🌊

WAUPUN

◆◆◆ AmericInn-Waupun Ⓜ ❀
(920) 324-2500. **$53-$80.** 5 Gateway Dr. US 151, exit 146 (SR 49), just nw. Int corridors. **Pets:** $25 deposit/room. No service, supervision, crate.

⊠ 🏠 ✎ 🗄 🖥 🌊

◆◆ Inn Town Motel M ❀
(920) 324-4211. **$35-$51.** 27 S State St. US 151, exit 146 (SR 49), then 1.3 mi w. Ext corridors. **Pets:** Dogs only. $7 daily fee/room. Designated rooms, no service, supervision, crate.
SAVE ✕ 🔌 💻

WAUSAU

◆◆ Baymont Inn-Wausau M ❀
(715) 842-0421. **$54-$66.** 1910 Stewart Ave. I-39 and US 51, exit 192, just e. Int corridors. **Pets:** Medium, other. $50 deposit/room. Designated rooms, no service, supervision, crate.
🌅 ✕ 🐾 🔌 💻 ☕

◆◆◆ Best Western Midway Hotel M ❀
(715) 842-1616. **$75-$95, 7 days notice.** 2901 Martin Ave. I-39 and US 51, exit 190 (CR NN) just sw. Int corridors. **Pets:** Supervision.
SAVE 🌅 ✕ 🐾 🔌 💻 🍴 ☕ ✕

◆◆ Exel Inn of Wausau M
(715) 842-0641. **$39-$65.** 116 S 17th Ave. I-39 and US 51, exit 192, just e. Int corridors. **Pets:** Small. Designated rooms, no service, supervision, crate.
🌅 ✕ 🔌 💻

◆◆ Rib Mountain Inn M
(715) 848-2802. **$70-$76, 21 days notice.** 2900 Rib Mountain Way. I-39 and US 51, exit 190 (CR NN), 1 mi w. Int corridors. **Pets:** No service, supervision, crate.
🔌 💻 ✕

◆◆ Super 8 Motel M
(715) 848-2888. **$48-$65.** 2006 Stewart Ave W. I-39 and US 51, exit 192, just e. Int corridors. **Pets:** Small. No service, supervision, crate.
ASK 🌅 ✕ 🐾 🗝 💻 ☕

WAUTOMA

◆◆ Super 8 Lodge M ❀
(920) 787-4811. **$58-$93.** Hwy 21 & 73 E. 1.5 mi e on SR 21 and 73. Int corridors. **Pets:** Other. $25 deposit/room. No service, supervision, crate.
SAVE 🌅 ✕ 🔌 ☕

WEST SALEM

◆◆◆ AmericInn M ❀
(608) 786-3340. **$80-$100.** 125 Buol Rd. I-90, exit 12, just sw on CR C. Int corridors. **Pets:** Other. No service, supervision, crate.
ASK 🌅 ✕ 🗝 🔌 💻 ☕

WESTBY

◆◆ Central Express Inn M
(608) 634-2950. **$45-$50.** US Hwy 14 at SR 27. 0.5 mi n on US 14. Int corridors. **Pets:** Very small. Supervision.
🌅 ✕ 🔌 💻 🍴

WINDSOR

◆◆◆ Days Inn M ❀
(608) 846-7473. **$89-$110.** 6311 Rostad Dr. I-90/94, exit 131 (SR 19). Int corridors. **Pets:** Other. $50 deposit/room, $8 one-time fee/pet. Supervision.
ASK 🌅 ✕ 🗝 🔌 💻 ☕

◆◆ Super 8 Motel-Windsor/North Madison M ❀
(608) 846-3971. **$50-$75.** 4506 Lake Cir. I-90/94, exit 131 (SR 19). Int corridors. **Pets:** $20 deposit/room, $5 daily fee/pet, $5 one-time fee/pet. Designated rooms, no service, supervision, crate.
SAVE 🌅 ✕ 🔌 💻

WISCONSIN DELLS

◆◆ Baker's Sunset Bay Resort M ❀
(608) 254-8406. **$95-$140.** 921 Canyon Rd. I-90/94, exit 92, 0.5 mi w on US 12, right on E Adams St, right on Canyon Rd, 0.8 mi on left. Ext/int corridors. **Pets:** Medium, dogs only. $10 daily fee/room, $10 one-time fee/room. Designated rooms, no service, supervision, crate.
SAVE 🌅 ✕ 🔌 💻 ☕ ✕

◆ Bridge View Motel M ❀
(608) 254-6114. **$55-$88, 3 days notice.** 1020 River Rd. Center, just n of SR 13 (Broadway). Ext corridors. **Pets:** Small. $50 deposit/room, $10 daily fee/pet. Designated rooms, no service, supervision, crate.
SAVE ✕ 🔌 ☕ ✕

◆◆ Super 8 Motel M ❀
(608) 254-6464. **$57-$88.** 800 Co Hwy H. I-90/94, exit 87, just e. Int corridors. **Pets:** Other. No service, supervision, crate.
ASK ✕ 🐾 💻 ☕

WISCONSIN RAPIDS

◆◆ Best Western Rapids Motor Inn M ❀
(715) 423-3211. **$48-$70, 3 days notice.** 911 Huntington Ave. 0.5 mi s on SR 13 from jct SR 54. Int corridors. **Pets:** Designated rooms, no service, supervision, crate.
SAVE 🌅 ✕ 🔌

◆ Camelot Motel M
(715) 325-5111. **$34-$48.** 9210 Hwy 13S. On SR 13, just n of jct SR 73 S. Ext corridors. **Pets:** Medium. No service, supervision, crate.
🔌 💻 ☕

◆◆ Econo Lodge M ❀
(715) 423-7000. **$40-$60, 30 days notice.** 3300 8th St S. 1.8 mi s on SR 13 from jct SR 54. Ext/int corridors. **Pets:** Very small, dogs only. $25 deposit/pet. Designated rooms, no service, supervision, crate.
ASK 🌅 ✕ 🔌 💻 🍴

◆◆◆ Hotel Mead M
(715) 423-1500. **$83-$99.** 451 E Grand Ave. 0.5 mi n on SR 54 from jct SR 13, just w. Int corridors. **Pets:** Supervision.
SAVE ✕ 🐾 🗝 🔌 💻 ☕

◆◆ Super 8 Motel M ❀
(715) 423-8080. **$49-$59.** 3410 8th St S. 1.9 mi s on SR 13 from jct SR 54 W. Int corridors. **Pets:** Medium. $10 one-time fee/room. No service, supervision, crate.
ASK 🌅 ✕ 🐾 🔌

AFTON

🛇🛇🛇 ◆◆◆ Best Western Hi Country Inn Ⓜ

(307) 886-3856. **$75-$140.** 689 S Washington. 0.8 mi s on US 89. Ext corridors. **Pets:** Small. No service, supervision, crate.

◆◆ Mountain Inn Ⓜ 🐾

(307) 886-3156. **$47-$72.** 83542 Hwy 89. 1.5 mi s on US 89. Ext corridors. **Pets:** Small, dogs only. $5 daily fee/pet. No service, supervision, crate.

ALPINE

🛇🛇🛇 ◆◆ Royal Resort at Snake River Canyon Ⓜ 🐾

(307) 654-7545. **$70-$80.** 50 W US Hwy 26. Jct US 26 and 89. Int corridors. **Pets:** Small. $5 daily fee/pet. Designated rooms, no service, supervision, crate.

SAVE ✕ 🛗 ✂ ⊠

BUFFALO

🛇🛇🛇 ◆ Arrowhead Motel Ⓜ 🐾

(307) 684-9453. **$32-$60.** 749 Fort St. Jct US 16, 87 and Business Loop 75, 0.6 mi w. Ext corridors. **Pets:** Other. $5 daily fee/pet. No service, supervision, crate.

✕ 🛗

🛇🛇🛇 ◆ Canyon Motel Ⓜ 🐾

(307) 684-2957. **$36-$55.** 997 Fort St. Jct US 16/87/ Business Loop 25, 0.9 mi w on US 16. Ext corridors. **Pets:** Other. $3 daily fee/room. Supervision.

SAVE ✕ 🛗

◆◆◆ Comfort Inn Ⓜ

(307) 684-9564. **$105-$115.** 65 Hwy 16 E. US 16, just e of I-25, exit 299, 1.3 mi w of I-90, exit 58. Ext/int corridors. **Pets:** Supervision.

ASK S🔊 ✕

◆◆ Crossroads Inn Ⓜ▮

(307) 684-2256. **$45-$94.** 75 N Bypass Rd. From I-90, exit 56B, then I-25 exit 299, just w on US 16. Ext/int corridors. **Pets:** Supervision.

ASK S🔊 ✕ ▣ ¶ ✂

🛇🛇🛇 ◆◆ Super 8 Motel of Buffalo Ⓜ 🐾

(307) 684-2531. **$69-$75.** 655 E Hart St. Just w of I-25, exit 299, on US 16, 1.3 mi w of I-90, exit 58. Int corridors. **Pets:** Large, other. $5 daily fee/pet. Designated rooms, no service, supervision, crate.

SAVE S🔊 ✕ ⊠

🛇🛇🛇 ◆◆ Wyoming Motel Ⓜ 🐾

(307) 684-5505. **$62-$88.** 610 E Hart St. US 16, just w of I-25, exit 299, 1.3 mi w of I-90, exit 58. Ext corridors. **Pets:** Designated rooms, supervision.

✕ 🛗 ▣ ⊠

🛇🛇🛇 ◆◆ Z-Bar Motel IMA Ⓒ 🐾

(307) 684-5535. **$48-$63, 30 days notice.** 626 Fort St. Jct US 16, 87 and Business Loop 25, 0.5 mi w on US 16. Ext corridors. **Pets:** Other. $4 daily fee/pet. No service, supervision, crate.

SAVE S🔊 ✕ 🛗

CASPER

🛇🛇🛇 ◆◆ Best Western Casper Ⓜ 🐾

(307) 234-3541. **$54-$84.** 2325 E Yellowstone Hwy. Just s of I-25, exit 186, just s on Beverly, then e. Ext/int corridors. **Pets:** $8 daily fee/room. Designated rooms, no service, supervision, crate.

SAVE ✕ 🛗 ✂

◆◆ Casper Days Inn Ⓜ 🐾

(307) 234-1159. **$57-$67.** 301 East E St. I-25, exit 188A (Center St). Int corridors. **Pets:** Other. No service, supervision, crate.

ASK S🔊 ✕ 🛗 ▣ ✂

◆◆ Econo Lodge Ⓜ 🐾

(307) 266-2400. **$51-$63.** 821 N Poplar St. N of I-25, exit 188B (SR 220). Ext/int corridors. **Pets:** Other. Designated rooms, no service, supervision, crate.

ASK S🔊 ✕ ♿

◆◆◆ Hampton Inn Ⓜ▮ 🐾

(307) 235-6668. **$75-$95, 7 days notice.** 400 West F St. Just n of I-25, between exits 188A and 188B. Int corridors. **Pets:** Other. $10 daily fee/pet. No service, supervision, crate.

◆◆◆ Holiday Inn M ❀
(307) 235-2531. **$79-$129.** 300 West F St. Just n of I-25, between exits 188A and 188B. Int corridors. **Pets:** Medium, other. $50 deposit/room. Supervision.
SAVE S⬤ ✕ ⬤ ⬤ ⬤ ⬤ ⬤ ⬤ ⬤

◆ National 9 Inn Showboat M
(307) 235-2711. **$39-$56.** 100 West F St. Just n of I-25, exit 188A (Center St). Int corridors. **Pets:** Medium. Supervision.
SAVE ✕ ⬤

◆◆ Parkway Plaza Hotel & Convention Centre H ❀
(307) 235-1777. **$55-$55.** 123 West E St. Just s of I-25, exit 188A (Center St). Ext/int corridors. **Pets:** Other. $25 deposit/room. Supervision.
SAVE S⬤ ✕ ⬤ ⬤ ⬤ ⬤ ⬤ ⬤

◆◆◆ Radisson Hotel Casper H
(307) 266-6000. **$85.** 800 N Poplar St. N of I-25, exit 188B (SR 220). Int corridors. **Pets:** Small. No service, supervision, crate.
SAVE S⬤ ✕ ⬤ ⬤ ⬤ ⬤ ⬤ ⬤

◆◆ Super 8 Motel M ❀
(307) 266-3480. **$53-$69.** 3838 Cy Ave. 3 mi sw, on SR 220. Int corridors. **Pets:** Other. $3 one-time fee/room. Designated rooms, no service, supervision, crate.
ASK S⬤ ✕ ⬤

◆ Westridge Motel M ❀
(307) 234-8911. **$35-$49.** 955 Cy Ave. I-25, S Poplar St exit, 1 mi sw on SR 220. Ext corridors. **Pets:** Other. $7 one-time fee/pet. Designated rooms, no service, supervision, crate.
SAVE S⬤ ✕ ⬤

CHEYENNE

◆◆◆ A Drummond's Ranch Bed & Breakfast BB ❀
(307) 634-6042. **$65-$175.** 399 Happy Jack Rd. I-25N, exit 10B, 22.4 mi w on SR 210 (Happy Jack Rd), s on private road. Ext/int corridors. **Pets:** Other. $10 daily fee/room. Designated rooms, no service, supervision, crate.
✕ ⬤ ⬤ ⬤ ⬤ ⬤

◆◆◆ Best Western Hitching Post Inn M ❀
(307) 638-3301. **$89-$129.** 1700 W Lincolnway. 1 mi w on I-80 business loop and US 30, 1 mi e of jct I-25 and I-80, W Lincolnway exit. Ext/int corridors. **Pets:** Other. No service, supervision, crate.
SAVE S⬤ ✕ ⬤ ⬤ ⬤ ⬤ ⬤ ⬤ ⬤

◆◆ Comfort Inn M ❀
(307) 638-7202. **$69-$84, 30 days notice.** 2245 Etchepare Dr. I-25, exit 7 (College Dr), 1 mi s of I-80; at Flying J Plaza. Int corridors. **Pets:** $20 deposit/pet. No service, supervision, crate.
ASK S⬤ ✕ ⬤ ⬤ ⬤

◆◆ Days Inn Cheyenne M ❀
(307) 778-8877. **$69-$84.** 2360 W Lincolnway. 1.5 mi w on I-80 business loop and US 30 at jct I-25. Int corridors. **Pets:** Other. $25 deposit/pet. No service, supervision, crate.
ASK S⬤ ✕ ⬤ ⬤ ⬤

◆ Fleetwood Motel M ❀
(307) 638-8908. **$40-$50.** 3800 E Lincolnway. I-80, exit 364, n on College Dr (SR 212). Ext corridors. **Pets:** Small. $3 daily fee/pet. No service, supervision, crate.
SAVE S⬤ ✕ ⬤

◆◆◆ La Quinta Inn M ❀
(307) 632-7117. **$75-$95.** 2410 W Lincolnway. 2 mi w on I-80 business loop and US 30 at jct I-25. Int corridors. **Pets:** Medium, other. No service, supervision, crate.
ASK S⬤ ✕ ⬤ ⬤ ⬤ ⬤ ⬤

◆◆ Lincoln Court M ❀
(307) 638-3302. **$55-$85.** 1720 W Lincolnway. 1 mi w on I-80 business loop and US 30; 1 mi e of jct I-25 and I-80, W Lincolnway exit. Ext/int corridors. **Pets:** Other. No service, supervision, crate.
SAVE S⬤ ✕ ⬤ ⬤ ✕

◆◆ Porch Swing Bed & Breakfast BB ❀
(307) 778-7182. **$50-$80.** 712 E 20th St. Downtown. Int corridors. **Pets:** Supervision.
✕ ⬤ CTV

◆◆◆ Windy Hills Guest House BB ❀
(307) 632-6423. **$70-$168.** 393 Happy Jack Rd. I-25, exit 10B, then 22.4 mi w on SR 210 (Happy Jack Rd), 1 mi s on private dirt road, 23 mi e of Laramie. Ext corridors. **Pets:** $25 deposit/pet. No service, supervision, crate.
ASK S⬤ ✕ ⬤ ⬤ ✕ ⬤

CHUGWATER

◆◆ Chugwater Super 8 M
(307) 422-3248. **$55-$64, 30 days notice.** 100 Buffalo Dr. Just ne of I-25, exit 54. Int corridors. **Pets:** Small. Designated rooms, supervision.
ASK S⬤ ✕ ⬤ ⬤

CODY

◆◆ Best Western Sunrise Motor Inn M ❀
(307) 587-5566. **$79-$97.** 1407 8th St. 0.8 mi w on US 14/16/20. Ext corridors. **Pets:** Small, dogs only. No service, supervision, crate.
ASK ✕ ⬤

◆◆◆ Best Western Sunset Motor Inn M ❀
(307) 587-4265. **$85-$119.** 1601 8th St. 0.8 mi w on US 14/16/20. Ext/int corridors. **Pets:** Small, other. Designated rooms, no service, supervision, crate.
SAVE S⬤ ✕ ⬤ ⬤ ⬤ ✕

◆ Big Bear Motel M
(307) 587-3117. **$70-$70.** 139 W Yellowstone Hwy. 2 mi w on US 14/16/20, from city center. Ext corridors. **Pets:** Supervision.
S⬤ ✕ ⬤ ⬤

◆◆ Cody Super 8 Motel M ❀
(307) 527-6214. **$85-$135.** 730 Yellowstone Rd. 0.5 mi w of downtown on Hwy 14/16. Int corridors. **Pets:** Supervision.
ASK S⬤ ✕ ⬤ ⬤ ⬤

⚠ ◆◆◆ Kelly Inn of Cody M �★
(307) 527-5505. **$92-$112.** 2513 Greybull Hwy. 1.5 mi e on US 14, 16 and 20. Ext/int corridors. **Pets:** Other. No service, supervision, crate.
SAVE S☐ ☒ ☐

⚠ ◆◆ Parkway Inn M �★
(307) 587-4208. **$88-$98.** 720 Yellowstone Hwy. 1.4 mi w on US 14/16/20. Ext corridors. **Pets:** Small, dogs only. No service, supervision, crate.
SAVE ☒ ☜

⚠ ◆◆ Skyline Motor Inn M
(307) 587-4201. **$48-$62.** 1919 17th St. 0.8 mi e on US 14/16/20 and SR 120. Ext corridors. **Pets:** Medium. No service, supervision, crate.
☒ ☜ ☒

DOUGLAS

⚠ ◆ Alpine Inn M
(307) 358-4780. **$40-$60.** 2310 E Richards St. I-25, exit 135. Ext corridors. **Pets:** Very small. Designated rooms, no service, supervision, crate.
SAVE ☒

⚠ ◆◆◆ Best Western Douglas Inn & Conference Center M �★
(307) 358-9790. **$69-$89.** 1450 Riverbend Dr. I-25, exit 140. Int corridors. **Pets:** Other. $25 deposit/room. Designated rooms, supervision.
SAVE S☐ ☒ ☜

DUBOIS

◆◆ Bald Mountain Inn M �★
(307) 455-2844. **$38-$70, 7 days notice.** 1349 W Ramshorn St. 1.6 mi w on US 26 and 287. Ext corridors. **Pets:** Medium, dogs only. $5 daily fee/pet. Designated rooms, no service, supervision, crate.
☒ ☐ ☐ ☒ ☒

⚠ ◆ Black Bear Country Inn M �★
(307) 455-2344. **$30-$60.** 505 N Ramshorn. 0.5 mi w on US 26 and 287. Ext corridors. **Pets:** Dogs only. $3 daily fee/pet, $3 one-time fee/pet. Supervision.
SAVE S☐ ☒ ☐ ☒ ☒

⚠ ◆◆ Branding Iron Inn C �★
(307) 455-2893. **$48-$53, 3 days notice.** 401 W Ramshorn. 0.3 mi w on US 26 and 287. Ext corridors. **Pets:** Other. $50 deposit/room. Supervision.
SAVE S☐ ☒ ☐ ☒

⚠ ◆◆◆ Chinook Winds Mt Lodge M
(307) 455-2987. **$40-$120.** 640 S First St. 0.8 mi s on US 26 and 287. Ext corridors. **Pets:** Small. Supervision.
SAVE S☐ ☒ ☐ ☒ ☒

⚠ ◆◆ Pinnacle Buttes Lodge & Campground M
(307) 455-2506. **$50-$160, 3 days notice.** 3577 US Hwy 26W. 20 mi w on US 26 and 287; in Shoshone National Forest. Ext corridors. **Pets:** No service, supervision, crate.
SAVE ☐ ☐ ☜ ☒ ☒ ☒

◆◆ Riverside Inn M �★
(307) 455-2337. **$30-$50.** 5810 US Hwy 26. 2.7 mi e of town center. Ext corridors. **Pets:** Dogs only. $5 one-time fee/pet. No service, supervision, crate.
☐ ☐ ☒ ☐ ☒

⚠ ◆◆◆ Stagecoach Motor Inn M �★
(307) 455-2303. **$38-$64.** 103 Ramshorn. Center; on US 26 and 287. Ext corridors. **Pets:** Medium. $5 daily fee/pet, $5 one-time fee/pet. Designated rooms, no service, supervision, crate.
SAVE ☒ ☐ ☐ ☐ ☜ ☒ ☒

EVANSTON

⚠ ◆◆ Days Inn Evanston M �★
(307) 789-2220. **$55-$60, 5 days notice.** 339 Wasatch Rd. Just n of I-80, exit 3 (Harrison Rd n to Wasatch Rd). Int corridors. **Pets:** Supervision.
SAVE S☐ ☒ ☐ ☐ ☐

◆ Evanston Super 8 Motel M ☆
(307) 789-7510. **Call for rates.** 70 Bear River Dr. I-80, exit 6, 1.4 mi w. Int corridors. **Pets:** Other. $25 deposit/room. No service, supervision, crate.
☒

⚠ ◆◆ Prairie Inn M
(307) 789-2920. **$35-$60.** 264 Bear River Dr. 0.3 mi n of I-80, exit 6. Ext/int corridors. **Pets:** No service, supervision, crate.
☒

EVANSVILLE

◆◆◆ Casper Comfort Inn M ☆
(307) 235-3038. **$66-$80.** 480 Lathrop Rd. Just n of I-25, exit 185. Int corridors. **Pets:** Other. Designated rooms, no service, supervision, crate.
ASK S☐ ☒ ☐ ☒ ☐ ☐ ☜

⚠ ◆◆ Shilo Inn-Casper/Evansville M ☆
(307) 237-1335. **$49-$99.** I-25 & Curtis Rd. Just n of I-25, exit 185 (East Casper). Int corridors. **Pets:** $7 daily fee/pet. Designated rooms, supervision.
SAVE S☐ ☒ ☐ ☐ ☐ ☜

GILLETTE

◆◆◆ Holiday Inn of Gillette M
(307) 686-3000. **$125.** 2009 S Douglas Hwy 59. Just se of I-90, exit 126. Ext/int corridors. **Pets:** Very small. Designated rooms, no service, supervision, crate.
ASK S☐ ☒ ☐ ☐ ☐ ☐ ☜ ☒

GLENROCK

⚠ ◆◆ All American Inn M ☆
(307) 436-2772. **$29-$39.** 500 W Aspen St. I-25, exit 165, 2.4 mi n. Ext corridors. **Pets:** Small. $20 deposit/room. Designated rooms, supervision.
SAVE ☒ ☐

GRAND TETON NATIONAL PARK

⦾⦾ ◆◆◆ Flagg Ranch Village M ❀
(307) 543-2861. **$131-$140.** Hwy 89 and US 191, 2 mi s of Yellowstone National Park s entrance, 5 mi n of Grand Teton National park n entrance. Ext corridors. **Pets:** Other. $5 daily fee/pet. Supervision.

⊠ 🛏 🐾 🗲 🖵 🍴 ⊠ 🐾 CTV

⦾⦾ ◆ Hatchet Resort M ❀
(307) 543-2413. **$90-$180.** 7.5 mi e, on US 26 and 287, from Moran Jct. Ext corridors. **Pets:** Medium, other. Supervision.

SAVE ⊠ 🍴 ⊠ 🐾 CTV 🗲

◆◆◆ Jackson Lake Lodge H ❀
(307) 543-2811. **$115-$198.** 5 mi nw of Moran, jct US 89 and 287. Ext/int corridors. **Pets:** Dogs only. Designated rooms, supervision.

⊠ 🛏 🐾 🗲 🖵 🍴 🍽 ⊠ 🐾 CTV

GREEN RIVER

◆◆ Oak Tree Inn M ❀
(307) 875-3500. **$55-$60.** 1170 W Flaming Gorge Way. I-80, exit 89. Ext/int corridors. **Pets:** $5 daily fee/pet. Supervision.

ASK S🐾 ⊠ 🛏 🐾 🗲 🖬 🍴 🐾

⦾⦾ ◆◆ Super 8 Motel Green River M ❀
(307) 875-9330. **$42-$56.** 280 W Flaming Gorge Way. Just w on US 30 and I-80 business loop. Int corridors. **Pets:** Other. $25 deposit/room. No service, supervision, crate.

SAVE S🐾 ⊠

GREYBULL

◆ Antler Motel M
(307) 765-4404. **$40-$53.** 1116 N 6th St. 0.8 mi w on US 14/16/20. Ext corridors. **Pets:** No service, supervision, crate.

ASK S🐾 ⊠ 🖬 🖵 🐾

⦾⦾ ◆ Sage Motel M
(307) 765-4443. **$36-$48.** 1009 N 6th St. 0.8 mi nw on US 14/16/20. Ext corridors. **Pets:** No service, supervision, crate.

SAVE S🐾 ⊠ 🖬

⦾⦾ ◆◆ Yellowstone Motel M ❀
(307) 765-4456. **$50-$65, 3 days notice.** 247 Greybull Ave. 0.4 mi e on US 14. Ext corridors. **Pets:** Other. $10 deposit/room. No service, supervision, crate.

SAVE S🐾 ⊠ 🖬 🖵 🍽 🐾

GUERNSEY

◆◆ The Bunkhouse Motel M
(307) 836-2356. **Call for rates.** 350 W Whalen. Just w on US 26. Ext corridors. **Pets:** No service, supervision, crate.

ASK ⊠ 🖬

HULETT

⦾⦾ ◆ Hulett Motel M ❀
(307) 467-5220. **$45-$60.** 202 Main St. SR 24 at n end of town. Ext corridors. **Pets:** Medium. Supervision.

⊠

JACKSON

⦾⦾ ◆ Motel 6 of Jackson Hole–328 M
(307) 733-1620. **$76-$92.** 600 S Hwy 89. Jct US 26/89/189, then s, 0.4 mi e on US 89. Ext corridors. **Pets:** Small. No service, supervision, crate.

S🐾 ⊠ 🐾 🐾 🗲 🐾

⦾⦾ ◆◆ Painted Buffalo Inn M ❀
(307) 733-4340. **$95-$139.** PO Box 2547. Just w of town square. Ext corridors. **Pets:** Small, other. $10 one-time fee/pet. No service, supervision, crate.

SAVE S🐾 ⊠ 🖬 🍴 🐾

⦾⦾ ◆◆◆ Quality 49'er Inn and Suites M ❀
(307) 733-7550. **$84-$200.** 330 W Pearl St. Just w and just s of town square. Ext/int corridors. **Pets:** Designated rooms, no service, supervision, crate.

SAVE ⊠ 🐾 🗲 🖬 🖵 🍴

⦾⦾ ◆◆◆ Red Lion/Wyoming Inn M
(307) 734-0035. **$189-$259, 3 days notice.** 930 W Broadway. 0.5 mi s on US 26/89/191. Int corridors. **Pets:** Large. No service, supervision, crate.

SAVE S🐾 ⊠ 🐾 🗲 🖬 🖵

⦾⦾ ◆◆◆ Snow King Resort X ❀
(307) 733-5200. **$200-$430, 3 days notice.** 400 E Snow King Ave. Just se of town square. Int corridors. **Pets:** Other. $50 deposit/room, $50 one-time fee/room. Designated rooms, supervision.

SAVE S🐾 ⊠ 🖬 🖵 🍴 🍽 ⊠

LANDER

⦾⦾ ◆ Holiday Lodge National 9 M ❀
(307) 332-2511. **$37-$47.** 210 McFarlane Dr. S on US 287 at jct SR 789. Ext corridors. **Pets:** Other. $5 daily fee/pet. No service, supervision, crate.

⊠ 🖬

◆◆◆ Piece of Cake Bed & Breakfast BB ❀
(307) 332-7608. **$70-$90.** 2343 Baldwin Creek Rd. 4.8 mi sw on Baldwin Creek Rd, off US 287 at n side of town. Ext/int corridors. **Pets:** Designated rooms, supervision.

⊠ 🖬 🖵 ⊠ 🐾 CTV 🗲

⦾⦾ ◆◆◆ Pronghorn Lodge M ❀
(307) 332-3940. **$56-$74.** 150 E Main St. Just n on US 287 at jct SR 789. Ext corridors. **Pets:** Medium. $10 daily fee/room, $10 one-time fee/room. Designated rooms, no service, supervision, crate.

S🐾 ⊠ 🐾 🗲 🖬 🍴

⦾⦾ ◆ Silver Spur Motel M
(307) 332-5189. **$40-$90.** 1240 Main St. 1.5 mi w on US 287 and SR 789. Ext corridors. **Pets:** No service, supervision, crate.

SAVE S🐾 ⊠ 🖬 🖵 🍽

LARAMIE

⦾⦾ ◆◆ Best Western Foster's Country Inn M ❀
(307) 742-8371. **$52-$73.** 1561 Snowy Range Rd. I-80, exit 311 (Snowy Range Rd). Ext corridors. **Pets:** $5 daily fee/pet. No service, supervision, crate.

SAVE S🐾 ⊠ 🖬 🍴 🍽

(AAA) ◆◆ Best Western Gas Lite M
(307) 742-6616. **$45-$85.** 960 N 3rd St. I-81, exit 313, 1.7 mi n. Ext corridors. **Pets:** Supervision.
[SAVE] [X] [≋]

(AAA) ◆◆ 1st Inn Gold MI ☀
(307) 742-3721. **$78-$91, 7 days notice.** 421 Boswell. Just n of I-80, exit 313 (3rd St). Ext/int corridors. **Pets:** Very small. $5 one-time fee/pet. Designated rooms, no service, supervision, crate.
[SAVE] [S0] [X] [Ⲧ] [≋]

◆◆◆ Holiday Inn of Laramie MI
(307) 742-6611. **$85-$107.** 2313 Soldier Springs. I-80, exit 313 (3rd St). Ext/int corridors. **Pets:** Designated rooms, no service, supervision, crate.
[ASK] [S0] [X] [≋] [≋] [Ⲧ] [≋]

(AAA) ◆◆ Sunset Inn M ☀
(307) 742-3741. **$46-$62.** 1104 S 3rd St. 0.3 mi n of I-80, exit 313 (3rd St). Ext corridors. **Pets:** Medium. $50 deposit/room. Designated rooms, no service, supervision, crate.
[SAVE] [S0] [X] [≋] [≋]

(AAA) ◆◆ Travelodge Downtown M ☀
(307) 742-6671. **$60-$75.** 165 N 3rd St. Just n on I-80 business loop (exit 313), US 30 and 287. Ext corridors. **Pets:** Other. $50 deposit/room. Designated rooms, no service, supervision, crate.
[SAVE] [S0] [X] [≋]

LOVELL

◆ Cattlemen Motel M
(307) 548-2296. **$38-$52.** 470 Montana Ave. Center; US 310 (Main St), just s. Ext corridors. **Pets:** Supervision.
[ASK] [S0] [X]

(AAA) ◆◆ Horseshoe Bend Motel M
(307) 548-2221. **$36-$50.** 375 E Main St. 0.3 mi e on US 14A and 310. Ext/int corridors. **Pets:** Designated rooms, supervision.
[SAVE] [S0] [X] [≋] [≋]

LUSK

◆ Town House Motel M ☀
(307) 334-2376. **$32-$64, 3 days notice.** 525 S Main St. In town, on US 20 and 85. Ext corridors. **Pets:** Medium, other. $5 daily fee/pet. Supervision.
[S0] [X] [≋]

(AAA) ◆◆ Trail Motel M ☀
(307) 334-2530. **$52-$62, 7 days notice.** 305 W 8th St. 0.3 mi sw on US 20; just w of US 85. Ext corridors. **Pets:** Small. $10 daily fee/room. Designated rooms, no service, supervision, crate.
[SAVE] [S0] [X] [≋] [X]

NEWCASTLE

◆ Auto Inn Motel M ☀
(307) 746-2734. **$40-$64.** 2503 W Main St. W end of town on US 16. Ext corridors. **Pets:** Other. $6 daily fee/pet. Designated rooms, supervision.
[ASK] [S0] [X]

(AAA) ◆◆ Pines Motel M ☀
(307) 746-4334. **$42-$75.** 248 E Wentworth St. Downtown; e on Wentworth St off SR 16, at blue "motels" sign. Ext corridors. **Pets:** Medium, other. No service, supervision, crate.
[SAVE] [S0] [X] [≋] [≋]

(AAA) ◆ Sage Motel M
(307) 746-2724. **$36-$58** (no credit cards), 3 days notice. 1227 S Summit Ave. 0.3 mi s of jct US 16 and 85, just w. Ext corridors. **Pets:** Medium. Supervision.
[SAVE] [S0]

PAINTER

◆ Hunter Peak Ranch RA
(307) 587-3711. **$90-$120, 30 days notice.** 4027 Crandall Rd. WY 296, 5 mi s of US 212; 40 mi n of WY 120. Ext corridors. **Pets:** Medium. Supervision.
[X] [≋] [Ⲧ] [X] [AC] [CTV] [Z]

PINEDALE

(AAA) ◆◆◆ Best Western Pinedale Inn M ☀
(307) 367-6869. **$60-$110, 30 days notice.** 850 W Pine St. 0.5 mi n on US 191. Int corridors. **Pets:** Other. No service, supervision, crate.
[SAVE] [S0] [X] [≋] [≋]

(AAA) ◆◆ Sun Dance Motel M ☀
(307) 367-4336. **$35-$65.** 148 E Pine St. US 191; in city center. Ext corridors. **Pets:** No service, supervision, crate.
[X] [≋] [AC]

◆◆◆ Window on the Winds B & B BB ☀
(307) 367-2600. **$60-$95, 7 days notice.** 10151 US 191. 2 mi n on US 191. Int corridors. **Pets:** Other. Supervision.
[X] [≋] [≋] [AC]

POWELL

◆◆ Best Western Kings Inn MI ☀
(307) 754-5117. **$68-$76, 30 days notice.** 777 E 2nd St. 0.3 mi e on US 14A. Ext corridors. **Pets:** Small, other. Designated rooms, no service, supervision, crate.
[ASK] [S0] [X] [≋] [≋] [Ⲧ] [≋]

RANCHESTER

(AAA) ◆ Ranchester Western Motel M
(307) 655-2212. **$45-$65.** 350 Dayton St. US 14. Ext corridors. **Pets:** Supervision.
[X]

RAWLINS

(AAA) ◆◆◆ Best Western CottonTree Inn MI ☀
(307) 324-2737. **$69-$89.** 2221 W Spruce St. 1.5 mi w on I-80 and US 30 business loop, 0.3 mi e of I-80, exit 211 (Spruce St). Ext/int corridors. **Pets:** Medium, other. $25 deposit/room. Designated rooms, no service, supervision, crate.
[SAVE] [S0] [X] [≋] [≋] [≋] [≋]

(AAA) ◆◆ Sleep Inn M ☀
(307) 328-1732. **$59-$71.** 1400 Higley Blvd. I-80, exit 214 (Higley Blvd). Int corridors. **Pets:** Other. Designated rooms, no service, supervision, crate.
[SAVE] [S0] [X] [≋] [≋]

RIVERTON

◆◆ Days Inn 🅜 🐾
(307) 856-9677. **$50-$70.** 909 W Main St. 0.5 mi nw on US 26. Ext corridors. **Pets:** Medium. $5 daily fee/pet, $5 one-time fee/pet. No service, supervision, crate.

🅐🅢🅚 🅢🅓 ⊠ 🄴 🄱

◆◆ Sundowner Station 🅜 🐾
(307) 856-6503. **$50-$65.** 1616 N Federal Blvd. 1.4 mi ne on US 26 and SR 789. Int corridors. **Pets:** Other. $25 deposit/room. Supervision.

🅢🅓 ⊠ 🍴

◆◆ Super 8 Motel 🅜 🐾
(307) 857-2400. **$47-$62.** 1040 N Federal Blvd. 1 mi ne on US 26 and SR 789. Int corridors. **Pets:** Other. $5 daily fee/pet, $5 one-time fee/pet. Supervision.

🅐🅢🅚 🅢🅓 ⊠ 🄱

◆ Thunderbird Motel 🅜
(307) 856-9201. **$36-$46.** 302 E Fremont. Downtown; just n of US 26. Ext corridors. **Pets:** No service, supervision, crate.

🅢🅐🅥🅔 🅢🅓 ⊠ 🄱

ROCK SPRINGS

◆◆◆ Comfort Inn 🅜 🐾
(307) 382-9490. **$56-$68.** 1670 Sunset Dr. 0.3 mi s of I-80, exit 102 (Dewar Dr), just w. Ext corridors. **Pets:** Medium. $10 daily fee/room, $10 one-time fee/room. No service, supervision, crate.

🅢🅐🅥🅔 🅢🅓 ⊠ ♿ 🄲 🄻 🄰 ⊠

◆◆ Econo Lodge 🅜 🐾
(307) 382-4217. **$45-$68.** 1635 N Elk St. Just n of I-80, exit 104 (Elk St). Ext corridors. **Pets:** Medium. $5 daily fee/pet. No service, supervision, crate.

🅐🅢🅚 🅢🅓 ⊠ 🄻 🍴 🄰

◆◆◆ Holiday Inn 🅜 🐾
(307) 382-9200. **$68-$79, 7 days notice.** 1675 Sunset Dr. 0.3 mi sw of I-80, exit 102 (Dewar Dr). Ext/int corridors. **Pets:** Other. $10 one-time fee/room. Designated rooms, supervision.

🅢🅐🅥🅔 🅢🅓 ⊠ 🏃 🄯 🄲 🄻 🄰

◆◆ The Inn At Rock Springs 🅜 🐾
(307) 362-9600. **$44-$80, 3 days notice.** 2518 Foothill Blvd. I-80 at Dewar Dr, exit 102. Int corridors. **Pets:** Other. $15 deposit/room. Supervision.

🅢🅓 ⊠ 🄱 🍴 🄰

◆ Motel 6–395 🅜
(307) 362-1850. **$40-$56.** 2615 Commercial Way. I-80, exit 102 (Dewar Dr), n to Foothills Blvd, just e. Ext corridors. **Pets:** Small. No service, supervision, crate.

🅢🅓 ⊠ ♿ 🄲 🄰

◆◆◆ Ramada Limited 🅜 🐾
(307) 362-1770. **$50-$75.** 2717 Dewar Dr. Just n of I-80, exit 102 (Dewar Dr). Int corridors. **Pets:** Small. $5 daily fee/pet. Supervision.

🅐🅢🅚 🅢🅓 ⊠ 🄯 🄱 🄻 🄰

◆◆ Rock Springs Days Inn 🅜 🐾
(307) 362-5646. **$51-$60.** 1545 Elk St. Just s of I-80, exit 104 (Elk St). Ext corridors. **Pets:** Other. Designated rooms, supervision.

🅢🅐🅥🅔 🅢🅓 ⊠ 🄲 🄱 🄻 🄰

◆◆ Rodeway Inn 🅜 🐾
(307) 362-6673. **$44-$74.** 1004 Dewar Dr. I-80 business loop, 1.3 mi se of I-80, exit 102 (Dewar Dr). Ext corridors. **Pets:** Other. $5 one-time fee/room. Designated rooms, no service, supervision, crate.

🅢🅐🅥🅔 🅢🅓 ⊠ 🄱 🄻

◆ Springs Motel 🅜
(307) 362-6683. **$40-$50.** 1525 9th St. I-80, exit 107, 0.3 mi w. Ext corridors. **Pets:** Small. Designated rooms, no service, supervision, crate.

🅢🅐🅥🅔 ⊠

SARATOGA

◆◆ Hacienda Motel 🅜 🐾
(307) 326-5751. **$54-$74, 7 days notice.** 1116 S 1st St. 0.5 mi s on SR 130; adjacent to airport. Int corridors. **Pets:** $10 daily fee/pet, $10 one-time fee/pet. Designated rooms, supervision.

🅐🅢🅚 🅢🅓 ⊠ 🄱

SHERIDAN

◆◆ Best Western Sheridan Center 🅜 🐾
(307) 674-7421. **$70-$90.** 612 N Main St. I-90, exit 20, 1.7 mi s. Ext/int corridors. **Pets:** Medium. $15 one-time fee/room. Designated rooms, no service, supervision, crate.

🅐🅢🅚 🅢🅓 ⊠ 🄳 🄻 🍴 🄰

◆ Guest House Motel 🅜 🐾
(307) 674-7496. **$45-$55.** 2007 N Main St. 0.7 mi s from I-90, exit 20; on I-90 business loop. Ext corridors. **Pets:** $5 one-time fee/pet. Designated rooms, no service, supervision, crate.

🅢🅐🅥🅔 🅢🅓 ⊠ 🄱 🄻

◆◆◆ Holiday Inn 🅜 🐾
(307) 672-8931. **$72-$114.** 1809 Sugarland Dr. 0.3 mi nw of I-90, exit 25. Int corridors. **Pets:** Other. $50 deposit/room. No service, supervision, crate.

🅢🅐🅥🅔 ⊠ 🄳 🄱 🄻 🍴 🄰 ⊠

◆ Rock Trim Motel LLC 🅜 🐾
(307) 672-2464. **$40-$60.** 449 Coffeen Ave. I-90, exit 25, w to Coffeen Ave, 1.3 mi n. Ext corridors. **Pets:** Other. $5 daily fee/room. No service, supervision, crate.

🅢🅐🅥🅔 ⊠ 🄱 🄻

SUNDANCE

◆ Bear Lodge Motel 🅜 🐾
(307) 283-1611. **$48-$64.** 218 Cleveland Ave. I-90 business loop and US 14. Ext corridors. **Pets:** Medium. $4 daily fee/pet. No service, supervision, crate.

🅢🅐🅥🅔 🅢🅓 ⊠

◆◆◆ Best Western Inn at
Sundance **M** ☀
(307) 283-2800. **$64-$109.** 2719 E Cleveland. I-90, exit 189, just n, then just w on I-90 business loop. Int corridors. **Pets:** Medium. $25 deposit/room, $5 one-time fee/room. No service, supervision, crate.
[SAVE] [X] [≈]

 ◆◆ Sundance Mountain Inn **M** ☀
(307) 283-3737. **$59-$99.** 26 SR 585. I-90, exit 187, 0.4 mi n on SR 585. Ext corridors. **Pets:** Medium. $25 deposit/pet, $5 one-time fee/room. No service, supervision, crate.
[SAVE] [S⌀] [X] [▣] [≈]

TETON VILLAGE

◆◆ Sassy Moose Inn of Jackson Hole **BB**
(307) 733-1277. **$129-$149, 30 days notice.** 3859 Miles Rd. 2 mi n on SR 390 from jct SR 22, 5 mi s from Teton Village, 6 mi nw from Jackson. Int corridors. **Pets:** Supervision.
[X] [K]

THERMOPOLIS

◆◆◆ Holiday Inn of the Waters **M** ☀
(307) 864-3131. **$68-$110.** 115 E Park St. In Hot Springs State Park. Ext/int corridors. **Pets:** Other. $30 deposit/pet. Supervision.
[ASK] [X] [⌀] [▣] [¶] [≈] [X]

TORRINGTON

◆◆ Kings Inn **M**
(307) 532-4011. **$65-$85.** 1555 Main St. Downtown; on US 85. Int corridors. **Pets:** Designated rooms, no service, supervision, crate.
[SAVE] [X] [▤] [▣] [¶] [≈]

◆◆ Maverick Motel **M** ☀
(307) 532-4064. **$36-$38.** US 26 W. 1.5 mi w on US 26 and 85. Ext corridors. **Pets:** $5 one-time fee/room. No service, supervision, crate.
[SAVE] [S⌀] [X] [▤]

WAPITI

◆◆◆ Elephant Head Lodge **C** ☀
(307) 587-3980. **$75-$110, 30 days notice.** 1170 E Yellowstone Hwy. 19.8 mi w on US 14/16/20. Ext corridors. **Pets:** Other. Supervision.
[SAVE] [S⌀] [X] [▤] [¶] [X] [K] [CTV] [☎]

◆◆ Goff Creek Lodge **C**
(307) 587-3753. **$95-$115, 30 days notice.** 995 E Yellowstone Hwy. 21.4 mi w on US 14/16/20. Ext corridors. **Pets:** Medium. No service, supervision, crate.
[SAVE] [S⌀] [X] [▤] [▣] [¶] [X] [K] [CTV] [☎]

◆◆ Shoshone Lodge **C**
(307) 587-4044. **$99-$189, 45 days notice.** 349 Yellowstone Hwy. 28 mi w on US 14/16/20. Ext corridors. **Pets:** Medium. No service, supervision, crate.
[SAVE] [S⌀] [X] [▤] [X] [K] [CTV] [☎]

◆◆ Wise Choice Inn **M** ☀
(307) 587-5004. **$50-$70.** 2908 Yellowstone Hwy. 2.8 mi w on US 14/16/20. Ext corridors. **Pets:** Other. $3 daily fee/pet. Designated rooms, no service, supervision, crate.
[SAVE] [S⌀] [X] [X] [CTV] [☎]

WHEATLAND

◆◆◆ Best Western Torchlite Motor
Inn **M** ☀
(307) 322-4070. **$75-$80.** 1809 N 16th St. I-25, between exits 78 and 80, on frontage road. Ext corridors. **Pets:** Other. $25 deposit/pet. No service, supervision, crate.
[SAVE] [S⌀] [X] [▤] [¶] [≈]

◆ Motel West Winds **M**
(307) 322-2705. **Call for rates.** 1756 South Rd. 1 mi n of I-25, exit 78. Ext corridors. **Pets:** Designated rooms, no service, supervision, crate.
[X]

◆◆ Vimbo's Motel **M** ☀
(307) 322-3842. **$69-$77.** 203 16th St. 0.3 mi n from I-25, exit 78. Ext/int corridors. **Pets:** Medium. Designated rooms, supervision.
[SAVE] [X]

WORLAND

◆◆ Best Western Settlers Inn **M** ☀
(307) 347-8201. **$42-$58.** 2200 Big Horn Ave. 1 mi e on US 16. Int corridors. **Pets:** Supervision.
[SAVE] [S⌀] [X] [▤] [▣]

◆◆◆ Comfort Inn of Worland **M** ☀
(307) 347-9898. **$59-$99.** 100 N Road 11. On US 16, 1.4 mi e. Int corridors. **Pets:** Medium. $10 daily fee/pet. No service, supervision, crate.
[ASK] [S⌀] [X] [⌖] [▤] [▣] [≈]

◆◆ Days Inn **M** ☀
(307) 347-4251. **$48-$68.** 500 N 10th St. 0.5 mi n on US 20. Ext corridors. **Pets:** Very small. $50 deposit/pet, $5 daily fee/pet, $5 one-time fee/pet. No service, supervision, crate.
[SAVE] [S⌀] [X] [▤]

◆◆ Super 8 Motel **M**
(307) 347-9236. **$42-$55.** 2500 Big Horn Ave. US 16, 0.9 mi e. Int corridors. **Pets:** No service, supervision, crate.
[ASK] [S⌀] [X] [▤]

Canada

ALBERTA

ATHABASCA

(AA) ◆◆◆ **Best Western Athabasca Inn** MI
(780) 675-2294. **$89-$119.** 5211 41 Ave. 1 km s on Hwy 2.
Int corridors. **Pets:** Medium. Designated rooms, no service,
supervision, crate.
SAVE S☉ ✕ ⊟ ⊡ ⑪

BANFF

(AA) ◆◆◆ **Banff Ptarmigan Inn** MI
(403) 762-2207. **$178-$208, 3 days notice.** 337 Banff Ave.
Sw of Moose St. Int corridors. **Pets:** Small. No service,
supervision, crate.
SAVE S☉ ✕ ⊡ ⑪ ✕ ♘

(AA) ◆◆◆ **Banff Rocky Mountain Resort** ⊠ ♧
(403) 762-5531. **$140-$290, 3 days notice.** 1029 Banff
Ave. Banff Ave at Tunnel Mountain Rd, just s of Trans
Canada Hwy 1. Ext corridors. **Pets:** $15 daily fee/room.
Designated rooms, no service, supervision, crate.
S☉ ✕ ⊟ ⊡ ⑪ ⌂ ✕ ♘

(AA) ◆◆◆ **Best Western Siding 29 Lodge** M
(403) 762-5575. **$85-$195.** 453 Marten St. 1.3 km ne off
Banff Ave. Int corridors. **Pets:** Medium. No service, supervision, crate.
SAVE S☉ ✕ ⊟ ⌂ ♘

(AA) ◆◆◆◆ **Canadian Pacific Banff Springs**
Hotel ⧠
(403) 762-2211. **$317-$499, 3 days notice.** 405 Spray Ave.
Just s on Banff Ave over bridge, 0.5 km e. Int corridors.
Pets: Very small. No service, supervision, crate.
✕ ⚕ ⊟ ⊡ ⑪ ⌂ ✕

◆◆◆ **Castle Mountain Village** ⧠ ♧
(403) 762-3868. **$330.** 32 km w on Hwy 1, at Castle jct, 1
km ne on Hwy 1A (Bow Valley Pkwy). Ext corridors.
Pets: Other. $20 one-time fee/pet. No service, supervision,
crate.
⊟ ⊡ ✕ ♘ ⑪ ✕

◆◆ **Johnston Canyon Resort** ⧠ ♧
(403) 762-2971. **$109-$245.** Hwy 1A. 24 km nw on Hwy 1A
(Bow Valley Pkwy) at Johnston Canyon. Ext corridors.
Pets: Other. No service, supervision, crate.
✕ ⊟ ⊡ ⑪ ✕ ♘ ⑪ ✕

(AA) ◆◆◆ **Red Carpet Motor Inn** M ♧
(403) 762-4184. **$75-$160.** 425 Banff Ave. 1 km ne. Ext/int
corridors. **Pets:** Medium. No service, supervision, crate.
✕ ⊟ ⊡

BROOKS

◆◆◆ **The Douglas Country Inn** ⧠
(403) 362-2873. **Call for rates.** On Hwy 873, 6.5 km n of jct
Trans Canada Hwy 1. Int corridors. **Pets:** Small. Supervision.
✕ ⑪ ⑪ ✕

◆◆ **Heritage Inn** MI
(403) 362-6666. **$78-$88.** 1303 2nd St W. On Hwy 873, 0.8
km s jct Trans Canada Hwy 1. Int corridors. **Pets:** Small.
No service, supervision, crate.
A$K ✕ ⊟ ⊡ ⑪

◆◆ **Super 8 Motel-Brooks** M
(403) 362-8000. **$65-$68.** 1240 Cassils Rd E. From Trans
Canada Hwy (Hwy 1), 0.3 km sw on SR 542 (E Brooks
exit). Int corridors. **Pets:** Small. Supervision.
A$K S☉ ✕ ⌂ ⊟

CALGARY METROPOLITAN AREA

AIRDRIE

(AA) ◆◆ **Super 8 Motel-Airdrie** M
(403) 948-4188. **$90-$90.** 815 E Lake Blvd. Hwy #2 Airdrie
(east) exit, 0.8 km e on Hwy 587 e, then 1.8 km s. Int
corridors. **Pets:** Supervision.
SAVE S☉ ✕ ⊟

CALGARY

(AA) ◆◆◆ **Best Western Hospitality Inn** MI
(403) 278-5050. **$115-$190, 7 days notice.** 135 Southland
Dr SE. On Hwy 2 (Macleod Tr), corner of Southland Dr. Int
corridors. **Pets:** Designated rooms, no service, supervision,
crate.
SAVE S☉ ✕ ⊟ ⊡ ⑪ ⌂

(CAA) ◆◆◆ **Best Western Suites**
Downtown 🅷 ❄
(403) 228-6900. **$110-$145, 3 days notice.** 1330 8th St SW. Corner of 8th St and 13th Ave SW. Int corridors. **Pets:** Other. Supervision.
SAVE S❄ ✕ 🛄 ▣

(CAA) ◆◆◆ **Best Western Village Park Inn** 🅼
(403) 289-0241. **$129-$149.** 1804 Crowchild Tr NW. Just ne of jct Trans Canada Hwy 1 and Crowchild Tr; in Motel Village. Int corridors. **Pets:** Designated rooms, supervision.
SAVE S❄ ✕ 🛄 ▣ 🍴 🍽

(CAA) ◆◆◆ **Blackfoot Inn** 🅼 ❄
(403) 252-2253. **$125-$165, 3 days notice.** 5940 Blackfoot Tr SE. At 58th Ave SE; access to property from 58th Ave only. Int corridors. **Pets:** Other. Designated rooms, supervision.
SAVE S❄ ✕ 🍴 ▣ 🍴 🍽

(CAA) ◆◆◆ **Calgary Westways Guest**
House 🅱🅱 ❄
(403) 229-1758. **$70-$105, 7 days notice.** 216 25th Ave SW. 1.7 km s on MacLeod Tr S, 0.5 km w. Int corridors. **Pets:** $5 daily fee/room. Supervision.
SAVE ✕

(CAA) ◆◆◆ **Carriage House Inn** 🅼 ❄
(403) 253-1101. **$129-$139.** 9030 Macleod Tr S. On Hwy 2, corner of 90th Ave SW. Int corridors. **Pets:** Other. $5 daily fee/room, $5 one-time fee/room. Designated rooms, supervision.
SAVE S❄ ✕ 🛄 ▣ 🍴 🍽

(CAA) ◆◆◆ **The Coast Plaza Hotel** 🅼 ❄
(403) 248-8888. **$165-$175.** 1316 33rd St NE. Just s of jct 16th Ave (Trans Canada Hwy 1) and 36th St NE, just w on 12th Ave NE, adjacent to Franklin Mall. Int corridors. **Pets:** Other. $20 one-time fee/room. No service, supervision, crate.
SAVE S❄ ✕ 🏠 🛄 ▣ 🍴 🍽

(CAA) ◆◆ **Days Inn-Calgary West** 🅼 ❄
(403) 289-1961. **$95-$120.** 1818 16th Ave NW. 5.2 km nw on Trans Canada Hwy 1. Int corridors. **Pets:** Medium. $25 deposit/pet. Designated rooms, no service, supervision, crate.
SAVE S❄ ✕ ▣ 🍴 🍽

◆◆◆ **Delta Bow Valley** 🅷 ❄
(403) 266-1980. **$170-$170.** 209 4th Ave SE. 1st St SE and 4th Ave SE. Int corridors. **Pets:** No service, supervision, crate.
✕ ▣ 🍴 🍽

(CAA) ◆ **Elbow River Inn & Casino** 🅼 ❄
(403) 269-6771. **$59-$109, 3 days notice.** 1919 Macleod Tr SE. Jct Macleod Tr and 1st St SE; opposite Stampede Park. Int corridors. **Pets:** No service, supervision, crate.
S❄ ✕ ▣ 🍴 ✕ 🎰

(CAA) ◆◆◆ **Greenwood Inn Hotels** 🅼
(403) 250-8855. **$129-$159, 30 days notice.** 3515 26th ST NE. From Barlow Tr N, just e on 32nd Ave NE, then just n. Int corridors. **Pets:** Designated rooms, no service, supervision, crate.
SAVE ✕ 🍴 🛄 ▣ 🍴 🍽

◆◆◆ **Holiday Inn Calgary Airport** 🅼 ❄
(403) 230-1999. **$114-$145.** 1250 McKinnon Dr NE. 1 km e of jct Deerfoot Tr (Hwy 2) and 16th Ave NE (Trans Canada Hwy 1). Int corridors. **Pets:** Other. $10 one-time fee/room. No service, supervision, crate.
✕ ▣ 🍴 🍽

(CAA) ◆◆◆ **Holiday Inn Calgary**
Downtown 🅷 ❄
(403) 266-4611. **$179-$209.** 119 12th Ave SW. Centre, at 1st St SW. Int corridors. **Pets:** Very small. $20 one-time fee/room. Designated rooms, no service, supervision, crate.
SAVE S❄ ✕ 🍴 🍴 🛄 ▣ 🍴 🍽

(CAA) ◆◆◆ **Holiday Inn Express University** 🅼
(403) 289-6600. **$110-$180, 3 days notice.** 2227 Banff Tr NW. 16 Ave (Trans Canada Hwy 1) and Banff Tr NW; in Motel Village. Int corridors. **Pets:** Medium. Designated rooms, supervision.
SAVE ✕ 🍴 🍴 🛄 ▣

◆◆◆◆ **The Palliser Fairmont Hotel & Resort** 🅷
(403) 262-1234. **$175-$269.** 133 9th Ave SW. 9th Ave SW at 1st St SW. Int corridors. **Pets:** No service, supervision, crate.
✕ ▣ 🍴 🍽

(CAA) ◆◆ **Quality Hotel & Conference**
Centre 🅼 ❄
(403) 243-5531. **$89-$119.** 3828 Macleod Tr S. Corner of Macleod Tr and 38th Ave SE. Int corridors. **Pets:** Medium, other. $10 daily fee/pet. Designated rooms, no service, supervision, crate.
SAVE S❄ ✕ ▣ 🍴 🍽

(CAA) ◆◆◆ **Radisson Hotel Calgary**
Airport 🅼 ❄
(403) 291-4666. **$99-$139.** 2120 16th Ave NE. 0.5 km e of jct Trans Canada Hwy 1 and 16th Ave NE and Hwy 2. Int corridors. **Pets:** $35 deposit/room. No service, supervision, crate.
SAVE ✕ 🏠 ▣ 🍴 🍽

(CAA) ◆◆◆ **Ramada Crowchild Inn** 🅼
(403) 288-5353. **$130-$150.** 5353 Crowchild Tr NW. Crowchild Tr at 53rd St NW. Int corridors. **Pets:** No service, supervision, crate.
SAVE S❄ ✕ ▣ 🍴 🍽

(CAA) ◆◆◆ **Ramada Hotel Downtown** 🅷 ❄
(403) 263-7600. **$119-$225, 3 days notice.** 708 8th Ave SW. At 6th St. Int corridors. **Pets:** Small. Designated rooms, no service, supervision, crate.
SAVE S❄ ✕ 🛄 ▣ 🍴 🍽

(CAA) ◆◆ **Super 8 Motel Calgary Airport** 🅼 ❄
(403) 291-9888. **$90-$159.** 3030 Barlow Tr NE. Corner of 32nd Ave and Barlow Tr NE. Int corridors. **Pets:** Dogs only. $10 daily fee/room. No service, supervision, crate.
SAVE S❄ ✕

(CAA) ◆◆ **Super 8 Motel Northwest** 🅼 ❄
(403) 289-9211. **$70-$150.** 1904 Crowchild Tr NW. In Motel Village; just n of jct Trans Canada Hwy 1 and Crowchild Tr. Ext corridors. **Pets:** Small, dogs only. $50 deposit/pet, $10 daily fee/pet. Designated rooms, no service, supervision, crate.
SAVE S❄ ✕ ▣ 🍽

◆◆◆◆ The Westin Calgary 🅷 ✿
(403) 266-1611. **$160-$425.** 320 4th Ave SW. Corner of 4th
Ave and 3rd St. Int corridors. **Pets:** No service, supervision,
crate.

[S🐾] [✕] [🔥] [💻] [🍴] [🏊]

COCHRANE

◆◆◆ Bow River Inn 🅼 ✿
(403) 932-7900. **$79-$99.** 3 Westside Dr. Hwy 1A, 1 km sw
on Hwy 22. Ext corridors. **Pets:** No service, supervision,
crate.

[ASK] [✕] [🔌] [💻]

OKOTOKS

◆◆ Okotoks Country Inn 🅼
(403) 938-1999. **$62-$97, 3 days notice.** 59 River Side
Gate. On Hwy 2A (Northridge Dr), ne of Sheep River. Int
corridors. **Pets:** No service, supervision, crate.

[S🐾] [✕] [🔌]

◆ **END METROPOLITAN AREA** ◆

CANMORE

◆◆◆ Banff Boundary Lodge 🆒 ✿
(403) 678-9555. **$99-$229, 3 days notice.** 1000 Harvie
Heights Rd. Just e of Banff National Park east gate, parallel
to Hwy 1, Harvie Heights exit. Ext corridors. **Pets:** Small.
$10 daily fee/pet, $10 one-time fee/pet. Supervision.

[SAVE] [S🐾] [✕] [🔌] [💻] [🎿]

◆◆◆ Quality Resort-Chateau Canmore 🆇 ✿
(403) 678-6699. **$109-$165.** 1720 Bow Valley Tr. 4.8 km e
of Banff National Park gate, on Hwy 1A. Ext/int corridors.
Pets: $10 daily fee/room. Designated rooms, supervision.

[ASK] [✕] [🔌] [💻] [🍴] [🏊] [🐾]

◆◆◆ Radisson Hotel & Conference
Centre 🅼🅸 ✿
(403) 678-3625. **$189-$189.** 511 Bow Valley Tr. 6 km e of
Banff National Park gate, on Hwy 1A via Canmore exit
from Trans Canada Hwy 1. Ext/int corridors. **Pets:** Small,
other. $10 one-time fee/pet. Designated rooms, supervision.

[SAVE] [S🐾] [✕] [💻] [🍴] [🏊] [🐾]

◆◆ Rundle Mountain Motel and
Gasthaus 🅼🅸 ✿
(403) 678-5322. **$93-$125.** 1723 Bow Valley Tr. 4.8 km e of
Banff National Park East gate, on Hwy 1A, adjacent to
Trans Canada Hwy 1. Ext corridors. **Pets:** Other. $7 daily
fee/pet. Designated rooms, no service, supervision, crate.

[SAVE] [✕] [💻] [🍴] [🏊] [🐾] [🎿]

◆◆ Rundle Ridge Chalets 🅲 ✿
(403) 678-5387. **$99-$144.** 1100 Harvie Heights Rd. 1 km e
of Banff National Park East gate on Trans Canada Hwy 1,
Harvie Heights exit. Ext corridors. **Pets:** Medium. $10 daily
fee/pet. Designated rooms, supervision.

[✕] [🔌] [🐾] [🎿] [📷]

STRATHMORE

◆◆◆ Best Western Strathmore Inn 🅼 ✿
(403) 934-5777. **$70-$140, 21 days notice.** 550 Hwy 1.
Centre; on Trans Canada Hwy 1, jct SR 817. Int corridors.
Pets: $40 deposit/room. Designated rooms, supervision.

[SAVE] [S🐾] [✕] [🔌] [🏊]

◆◆ Super 8 Motel 🅼 ✿
(403) 934-1808. **Call for rates.** 450 Westlake Rd. Just n on
SR 817. Ext/int corridors. **Pets:** Other. $5 one-time fee/pet.
Designated rooms, no service, supervision, crate.

[✕] [🔌] [💻]

◆ The Stockade Log Cabins 🅲
(403) 678-5212. **$68-$110.** 1050 Harvie Heights Rd. 1 km e
of Banff National Park East gate on Trans Canada Hwy 1;
Harvie Heights exit. Ext corridors. **Pets:** Medium. Designated rooms, no service, supervision, crate.

[SAVE] [S🐾] [✕] [🔌] [💻] [🎿] [📷]

CARDSTON

◆◆ Flamingo Motel 🅼
(403) 653-3952. **$57-$75.** 848 Main St S. 1 km s on Hwy 2,
just s of Remington Carriage Ctr. Ext corridors.
Pets: Supervision.

[ASK] [S🐾] [✕] [🔌] [💻] [🏊] [🐾]

CLARESHOLM

◆◆ Bluebird Motel 🅼 ✿
(403) 625-3395. **$59-$79.** 5505 1st St W. 0.5 km n on Hwy
2. Ext corridors. **Pets:** Other. Designated rooms, no service,
supervision, crate.

[ASK] [S🐾] [✕] [🔌] [💻]

COLD LAKE

◆◆ New Frontier Motel 🅼
(780) 639-3030. **$38-$80.** 1002 8th Ave. In centre of town,
on Hwy 28. Ext corridors. **Pets:** No service, supervision,
crate.

[SAVE] [S🐾] [✕] [🔌]

DEAD MAN'S FLATS

◆◆ **Pigeon Mountain Motel** Ⓜ
(403) 678-5756. **$70-$85, 3 days notice.** 250 1st Ave. On Trans Canada Hwy 1; at Dead Man's Flats Service Centre. Ext corridors. **Pets:** Medium. No service, supervision, crate.
Ⓧ 💻 Ⓐ Ⓒ

DIDSBURY

◆◆ **Super 8 Motel-Didsbury** Ⓜ 🐾
(403) 335-8088. **$62-$67.** 1714 20th Ave. Just e, 7.7 km w of Hwy 2, exit Didsbury. Int corridors. **Pets:** Other. Designated rooms, supervision.
Ⓐ Ⓢ Ⓧ Ⓗ

EDMONTON METROPOLITAN AREA

EDMONTON

◆◆ **Alberta Place Suite Hotel** Ⓐ 🐾
(780) 423-1565. **$71-$90, 7 days notice.** 10049 103rd St. Just s of Jasper Ave. Int corridors. **Pets:** Other. Designated rooms, supervision.
Ⓐ Ⓢ Ⓧ 💻 Ⓐ

◆◆ **Argyll Plaza Hotel** Ⓜ 🐾
(780) 438-5876. **$65-$69.** 9933 63rd Ave. 63rd Ave at 99th St. Int corridors. **Pets:** Other. $5 daily fee/room. No service, supervision, crate.
Ⓐ Ⓢ Ⓧ Ⓗ 💻

◆◆◆ **Best Western Cedar Park Inn** Ⓜ 🐾
(780) 434-7411. **$89-$109.** 5116 Calgary Tr Northbound. Calgary Tr at 51st Ave. Int corridors. **Pets:** Medium, other. $25 deposit/pet. No service, supervision, crate.
Ⓢ Ⓢ Ⓧ 💻 Ⓣ Ⓐ

◆◆ **Chateau Louis Hotel & Conference Centre** Ⓜ
(780) 452-7770. **$79-$99.** 11727 Kingsway. On Kingsway and 117th St. Int corridors. **Pets:** Small. Designated rooms, no service, supervision, crate.
Ⓢ Ⓧ Ⓗ 💻 Ⓣ

◆◆ **Comfort Inn** Ⓜ 🐾
(780) 484-4415. **$83-$99, 3 days notice.** 17610 100th Ave. On 100th Ave at 176th St. Int corridors. **Pets:** Large. No service, supervision, crate.
Ⓐ Ⓢ Ⓧ Ⓗ

◆◆◆ **Crowne Plaza-Chateau Lacombe** Ⓗ 🐾
(780) 428-6611. **$99-$139.** 10111 Bellamy Hill. At jct 101st St, MacDonald Dr and Bellamy Hill. Int corridors. **Pets:** Medium, other. No service, supervision, crate.
Ⓢ Ⓢ Ⓧ Ⓕ 💻 Ⓣ

◆◆◆ **Delta Edmonton Centre Suite Hotel** Ⓗ 🐾
(780) 429-3900. **$94-$124.** 10222 102nd St. 102nd St at 103rd Ave. Int corridors. **Pets:** Designated rooms, supervision.
Ⓐ Ⓢ Ⓧ Ⓗ 💻 Ⓣ

◆◆◆ **Delta Edmonton South Hotel and Conference Centre** Ⓗ 🐾
(780) 434-6415. **$84-$109.** 4404 Calgary Tr. At jct Calgary Tr (Hwy 2) and Whitemud Frwy. Int corridors. **Pets:** Small. $20 one-time fee/pet. Designated rooms, no service, supervision, crate.
Ⓢ Ⓧ Ⓗ 💻 Ⓣ Ⓐ

◆◆ **Edmonton Inn** Ⓜ
(780) 454-9521. **$65-$65.** 11830 Kingsway Ave. 4 km nw on Kingsway Ave at 119th St. Int corridors. **Pets:** No service, supervision, crate.
Ⓐ Ⓢ Ⓧ 💻 Ⓣ

◆◆◆ **Holiday Inn Convention Centre** Ⓜ
(780) 468-5400. **$89-$89.** 4520 76th Ave. From Hwy 14, just s via 50th St exit, then just e. Int corridors. **Pets:** Supervision.
Ⓢ Ⓢ Ⓧ 💻 Ⓣ Ⓐ

◆◆◆ **Holiday Inn Express Hotel & Suites** Ⓜ 🐾
(780) 483-4000. **$89-$174.** 10017 179A St. On 100th Ave, just w of 178th St. Int corridors. **Pets:** Medium. $15 daily fee/room. Supervision.
Ⓢ Ⓢ Ⓧ Ⓕ 💻 Ⓐ

◆◆◆ **Holiday Inn The Palace** Ⓜ 🐾
(780) 438-1222. **$89-$89.** 4235 Calgary Tr N. Just s of Whitemud Dr. Int corridors. **Pets:** $50 deposit/room, $10 daily fee/pet. Designated rooms, no service, supervision, crate.
Ⓢ Ⓢ Ⓧ Ⓗ 💻 Ⓣ

◆◆◆◆ **Hotel Macdonald** Ⓗ 🐾
(780) 424-5181. **$179.** 10065 100th St. Just s of Jasper Ave. Int corridors. **Pets:** Medium, other. $20 daily fee/room. Supervision.
Ⓧ Ⓕ 💻 Ⓐ

◆◆◆ **The Mayfield Inn & Suites, Edmonton** Ⓗ 🐾
(780) 484-0821. **$99-$139.** 16615 109th Ave. 1.6 km n of jct Hwy 2 and 16A on Mayfield Rd. Int corridors. **Pets:** Small. $15 daily fee/room. Supervision.
Ⓢ Ⓧ Ⓗ 💻 Ⓣ Ⓐ Ⓧ

◆◆◆ **Ramada Inn and Conference Centre** Ⓜ 🐾
(780) 454-5454. **$65-$65.** 11834 Kingsway Ave. 4 km nw on Kingsway Ave at 119th St. Int corridors. **Pets:** Small, other. $10 daily fee/room. Designated rooms, no service, supervision, crate.
Ⓐ Ⓢ Ⓧ 💻 Ⓣ

◆◆ **Travelodge Beverly Crest** Ⓜ 🐾
(780) 474-0456. **$73-$79.** 3414 118th Ave. 8 km e of Capilano Dr, 1 km s from W Hwy 16 (Yellowhead Tr) on Victoria Tr exit. Int corridors. **Pets:** Medium. No service, supervision, crate.
Ⓢ Ⓢ Ⓧ Ⓗ 💻 Ⓣ

◆◆◆◆ **The Westin Edmonton** [H]
(780) 426-3636. **$240-$270.** 10135 100th St. 101A Ave at 100th St. Int corridors. **Pets:** Designated rooms, supervision.
☒ 👂 📺 🏊

FORT SASKATCHEWAN

◆◆◆ **Best Western Fort Inn and Suites** [MI] 🐾
(780) 998-7888. **$99-$109.** 10115 88th Ave. Just e of Hwy 15/21 and 101st St. Int corridors. **Pets:** Small. $150 deposit/room. No service, supervision, crate.
[A$K] [SD] ☒ 🏋 ▤ 📺 🍴

SHERWOOD PARK

[CAA] ◆◆◆ **First Canada Inns** [MI] 🐾
(780) 464-1000. **$69-$99.** 26 Strathmoor Dr. Just sw of Hwy 16, Broadmoor Blvd exit. Int corridors. **Pets:** Medium. $100 deposit/room. Designated rooms, no service, supervision, crate.
[SAVE] [SD] ☒ 🍴

[CAA] ◆◆ **Franklin's Inn** [MI] 🐾
(780) 467-1234. **$75-$91.** 2016 Sherwood Dr. At Granada Blvd. Int corridors. **Pets:** Medium. $100 deposit/room, $5 daily fee/pet. Designated rooms, no service, supervision, crate.
[SAVE] [SD] ☒ ▤ 📺 🍴

[CAA] ◆◆◆ **Ramada Limited-Edmonton East/ Sherwood Park** [M] 🐾
(780) 467-6727. **$89-$99.** 30 Broadway Blvd. From Hwy 14, 1.5 km e on Baseline Rd, 0.4 km n on Broadmoor Rd; from Hwy 16, 2.5 km s via Broadmoor Rd exit. Int corridors. **Pets:** Medium. $10 daily fee/room. Designated rooms, supervision.
[SAVE] [SD] ☒ 🏋 ▤ 📺

STONY PLAIN

[CAA] ◆◆◆ **Ramada Inn & Suites** [MI] 🐾
(780) 963-0222. **$61-$125.** 3301 43rd Ave. 2 km e on Hwy 16A. Ext/int corridors. **Pets:** Other. $4 daily fee/pet. Designated rooms, supervision.
[SAVE] [SD] ☒ ▤ 📺 🍴 🏊

[CAA] ◆◆ **Stony Motor Inn** [MI] 🐾
(780) 963-3444. **$49-$81.** 4620 48th St. From Hwy 16A, 0.8 km s on SR 779 (Stony Plain exit). Int corridors. **Pets:** Other. $3 daily fee/pet. Designated rooms, supervision.
[SAVE] [SD] ☒ ▤ 📺 🍴

🐾 **END METROPOLITAN AREA** 🐾

EDSON

◆◆◆ **Best Western High Road Inn** [MI]
(780) 712-2378. **$109-$134.** 300 52nd St. Center; on 2nd Ave. Int corridors. **Pets:** Small. Supervision.
☒ ▤ 📺 🍴 🏊

FORT MACLEOD

[CAA] ◆◆ **Sunset Motel** [M]
(403) 553-4448. **$50-$70.** 104 Hwy 3W. 1 km w on Hwy 2 and 3. Ext corridors. **Pets:** Supervision.
[SAVE] [SD] ☒ ▤

GRANDE PRAIRIE

◆◆◆ **Service Plus Inns and Suites** [M] 🐾
(780) 538-3900. **$74-$99.** 10810 107th A Ave. 2.2 km w on Hwy 2, just n (adjacent to casino). Int corridors. **Pets:** Medium. $10 one-time fee/pet. No service, supervision, crate.
☒ ♿ ▤ 📺 🏊

◆◆ **Stanford Inn** [MI] 🐾
(780) 539-5678. **$60-$75.** 11401 100 Ave. 2.8 km w on Hwy 2. Ext/int corridors. **Pets:** Other. $5 daily fee/pet. Supervision.
[A$K] [SD] ☒ ▤ 📺 🍴

HINTON

[CAA] ◆◆ **Crestwood Hotel** [MI]
(780) 865-4001. **$89-$99.** 678 Carmichael Ln. 1 km w on Hwy 16. Int corridors. **Pets:** Medium. Supervision.
[SAVE] [SD] ☒ 📺 🍴 🏊

[CAA] ◆◆◆ **Holiday Inn** [MI] 🐾
(780) 865-3321. **$89-$109.** 393 Gregg Ave. 0.5 km w on Hwy 16. Int corridors. **Pets:** Small. $50 deposit/room. Designated rooms, no service, supervision, crate.
[SAVE] [SD] ☒ ▤ 📺 🍴 🏊

◆◆ **Super 8 Motel** [M] 🐾
(780) 817-2228. **$90-$105.** 284 Smith St. 1.6 km e on Hwy 16. Int corridors. **Pets:** Medium, other. $10 daily fee/room. Designated rooms, no service, supervision, crate.
☒ 🏋 ▤ 🏊

JASPER

◆◆◆ **Jasper Inn** [MI] 🐾
(780) 852-4461. **Call for rates.** 98 Geikie St. 1.2 km ne at Geikie and Bonhomme sts. Ext/int corridors. **Pets:** $10 one-time fee/pet. Designated rooms, supervision.
☒ ▤ 📺 🍴 🏊 [AC]

◆◆◆◆ **Jasper Park Lodge** [R] 🐾
(780) 852-3301. **$344-$517, 3 days notice.** Lodge Rd. 4.8 km ne via Hwy 16; 3.2 km se off hwy via Maligne Rd, follow signs for lodge. Ext corridors. **Pets:** $30 daily fee/pet. Supervision.
☒ ♿ ▤ 📺 🍴 🏊 🎾 [AC]

[CAA] ◆◆◆ **Lobstick Lodge** [MI] 🐾
(780) 852-4431. **$196-$220.** 94 Geikie St. 1.2 km ne at Geikie and Juniper sts. Int corridors. **Pets:** Designated rooms, supervision.
☒ ▤ 📺 🍴 🏊 [AC]

(CAA) ◆◆ **Marmot Lodge** **M** ❀
(780) 852-4471. **$179-$225.** 86 Connaught Dr. 1.6 km ne.
Ext corridors. **Pets:** Designated rooms, supervision.

⊠ 🖪 🖵 ▥

◆◆◆ **Patricia Lake Bungalows** **C** ❀
(780) 852-3560. **$72-$170, 7 days notice.** Pyramid Lake
Rd. 4.8 km nw via Pyramid Lake Rd. Ext corridors.
Pets: Small, dogs only. Designated rooms, no service,
supervision, crate.

⊠ 🖪 🖵 ▨ ▥ 🖵 ▨

(CAA) ◆◆ **Sunwapta Falls Resort** **M** ❀
(780) 852-4852. **$159-$159.** Hwy 93. 55 km s on Hwy 93
(Icefields Pkwy). Ext corridors. **Pets:** $10 one-time fee/
room. Designated rooms, supervision.

⊠ 🖪 🖵 ▥ ▨ ▥ 🖵 ▨

(CAA) ◆◆ **Tekarra Lodge** **C** ❀
(780) 852-3058. **$139-$199, 7 days notice.** Hwy 93 A.
From jct Hwy 93 and 16, 1.4 km s on Hwy 93, 1.2 km ne.
Ext/int corridors. **Pets:** $10 daily fee/room. Designated
rooms, no service, supervision, crate.

SAVE S❀ ⊠ 🖪 ▥ ▨ ▥ 🖵 ▨

KANANASKIS

◆◆◆ **Delta Lodge at Kananaskis** **R** ❀
(403) 591-7711. **$197-$287, 3 days notice.** Kanasaskis Village. From Trans Canada Hwy 1, 23.5 km s on Hwy 40
(Kananaskis Tr), then 3 km on Kananaskis Village access
road, follow signs. Int corridors. **Pets:** Small, other. $100
one-time fee/pet. Designated rooms, supervision.

⊠ ▨ 🖵 ▥ ▨ ▥ 🖵 ▥

LAKE LOUISE

◆◆◆◆ **Canadian Pacific Chateau Lake
Louise** **R**
(403) 522-3511. **$185-$475, 3 days notice.** 111 Lake Louise Dr. 3 km up the hill from the village. Int corridors.
Pets: Medium. Designated rooms, no service, supervision,
crate.

ASK S❀ ⊠ 🖵 ▥ ▨ ▨ ▥

LETHBRIDGE

(CAA) ◆◆ **Days Inn Lethbridge** **M**
(403) 327-6000. **$55-$68.** 100 3rd Ave S. Centre; corner of
3rd Ave and Scenic Dr. Ext corridors. **Pets:** Large. Designated rooms, supervision.

SAVE S❀ ⊠ 🖪 🖵

(CAA) ◆◆◆ **Lethbridge Lodge** **M** ❀
(403) 328-1123. **$109-$119.** 320 Scenic Dr. Centre; Scenic
Dr at 4th Ave S. Int corridors. **Pets:** Other. $10 daily fee/pet.
Designated rooms, no service, supervision.

SAVE ⊠ 🖵 ▥ ▨

(CAA) ◆◆ **Pepper Tree Inn** **M**
(403) 328-4436. **$60-$88, 3 days notice.** 1142 Mayor
Magrath Dr. 3.2 km se on Hwy 4 and 5 (Mayor Magrath
Dr). Ext corridors. **Pets:** Medium. Designated rooms, no
service, supervision, crate.

SAVE S❀ ⊠ 🖪 ▨

(CAA) ◆◆◆ **Quality Inn** **M** ❀
(403) 328-6636. **$67-$75, 7 days notice.** 1030 Mayor
Magrath Dr. 3.2 km se on Hwy 4 and 5 (Mayor Magrath Dr)
at 10th Ave S. Ext/int corridors. **Pets:** Small. $5 one-time
fee/room. Designated rooms, no service, supervision, crate.

SAVE S❀ ⊠ 🖵 ▨

◆◆ **Super 8 Lodge** **M** ❀
(403) 329-0100. **$66-$80, 7 days notice.** 2210 7th Ave S.
2.4 km se on Hwy 4 and 5 (Mayor Magrath Dr) at 7th Ave
S. Ext corridors. **Pets:** No service, supervision, crate.

ASK S❀ ⊠ 🖪 🖵 ▥ ▨ ▨

LLOYDMINSTER

(CAA) ◆◆ **Tropical Inn** **M** ❀
(780) 875-7000. **$58-$190.** 5621 44 St. Jct Hwy 17 and 16,
1 km w. Ext/int corridors. **Pets:** Small. No service, supervision, crate.

SAVE S❀ ⊠ 🖪 🖵 ▥ ▨

◆◆ **Wayside Inn** **M** ❀
(780) 875-4404. **$67-$92.** 5411 44th St. 0.8 km w on Hwy
16 from jct Hwy 17. Int corridors. **Pets:** Small. $5 daily
fee/pet, $5 one-time fee/pet. Designated rooms, no service,
supervision, crate.

ASK S❀ ⊠ 🖪 🖵 ▥ ▨

◆◆ **West Harvest Inn** **M**
(780) 875-6113. **$69-$74.** 5620 44th St. From jct Hwy 17
and 16, 1 km w. Ext/int corridors. **Pets:** Designated rooms,
supervision.

ASK S❀ ⊠ 🖪 🖵 ▥ ▨

MEDICINE HAT

◆◆◆ **Best Western Inn** **M**
(403) 527-3700. **$69-$199.** 722 Redcliff Dr. On Trans
Canada Hwy 1; 0.4 km w of jct Hwy 3 access 7th St SW.
Ext/int corridors. **Pets:** Small. Supervision.

ASK S❀ ⊠ ▥ 🖪 🖵 ▨

(CAA) ◆◆◆ **Imperial Inn** **M** ❀
(403) 527-8811. **$59-$74.** 3282 13th Ave SE. 3.6 km se;
opposite Southview Shopping Mall; just n off Trans Canada
Hwy 1. Ext/int corridors. **Pets:** Other. $5 daily fee/room, $5
one-time fee/room. Designated rooms, supervision.

SAVE S❀ ⊠ 🖪 🖵 ▥ ▨

◆◆◆ **Medicine Hat Lodge Hotel & Convention
Centre** **H** ❀
(403) 529-2222. **$89-$169.** 1051 Ross Glen Dr SE. E end
approach to city on Trans Canada Hwy 1, at jct Dunmore
Rd. Int corridors. **Pets:** Designated rooms, supervision.

ASK S❀ ⊠ 🖪 🖵 ▥ ▨ ▨

◆ **Ranchmen Motel** **M** ❀
(403) 527-2263. **$34-$38.** 1617 Bomford Crescent SW. On
Trans Canada Hwy 1 at 16th St SW. Ext corridors.
Pets: Small. Designated rooms, no service, supervision,
crate.

⊠ 🖪 🖵 ▨

◆◆ **Super 8 Motel** Ⓜ ☆
(403) 528-8888. **$61-$91.** 1280 Trans Canada Way SE. Trans Canada Way at 13 Ave SE; just n off Trans Canada Hwy 1. Ext/int corridors. **Pets:** Other. $5 daily fee/room. Designated rooms, no service, supervision, crate.
🄰🅂🄺 🆂 ⊠ 🔥 🄳 🖼

🄒🄐 ◆◆◆ **Travelodge/Travelodge Medicine
                    Hat** Ⓜ ☆
(403) 527-2275. **$90-$105.** 1100 Redcliff Dr SW. 2.8 km sw on Trans Canada Hwy 1 at jct Hwy 3. Ext/int corridors. **Pets:** Medium. No service, supervision, crate.
🆂🅰🆅🅴 ⊠ 🔥 🄳 🍴 🖼

NISKU

🄒🄐 ◆◆◆ **The International Inn** Ⓜ ☆
(780) 955-3001. **$115-$125.** 501 11th Ave. 30 km s; from Hwy 2, exit Edmonton International Airport/Nisku Business Park (10th Ave), 0.8 km e. Int corridors. **Pets:** Medium. No service, supervision, crate.
🆂🅰🆅🅴 🆂 ⊠ 🔥 🄳 🍴

◆◆ **Nisku Inn and Conference Centre** Ⓜ
(780) 955-7744. **$85-$85.** 1103 4th St. 30 km s; from Hwy 2, exit Edmonton International Airport/Nisku Business Park (10th Ave), 0.5 km e. Int corridors. **Pets:** No service, supervision, crate.
🄰🅂🄺 🆂 ⊠ 🔥 🄳 🍴 🖼

PEACE RIVER

🄒🄐 ◆◆ **Traveller's Motor Hotel** Ⓜ ☆
(780) 624-3621. **$49-$62.** 9510 100th St. Just off Hwy 2 southbound; town center exit. Ext/int corridors. **Pets:** Designated rooms, no service, supervision, crate.
🆂🅰🆅🅴 🆂 ⊠ 🔥 🔥 🄳 🍴

PINCHER CREEK

◆◆ **Heritage Inn** Ⓜ ☆
(403) 627-5000. **$68-$78, 7 days notice.** 919 Waterton Ave (Hwy 6). SR 3, 4.7 km s on SR 6. Int corridors. **Pets:** Other. Designated rooms, no service, supervision, crate.
🄰🅂🄺 🆂 ⊠ 🔥 🄳 🍴

◆◆ **Super 8 Motel-Pincher Creek** Ⓜ
(403) 627-5671. **$63-$69.** 1307 Freebarn Ave. SR 3, 2.6 km s on SR 6. Int corridors. **Pets:** Medium. No service, supervision, crate.
🄰🅂🄺 🆂 ⊠ 🔥

RED DEER

🄒🄐 ◆◆◆ **Holiday Inn Express-Red
                    Deer** Ⓜ ☆
(403) 343-2112. **$89-$99.** 2803 50th Ave. 1.8 km e on Hwy 2A (Gaetz Ave). Int corridors. **Pets:** Small. $10 daily fee/pet. Designated rooms, no service, supervision, crate.
🆂🅰🆅🅴 🆂 🔥 🄳 🖼

◆◆◆ **Holiday Inn Red Deer** Ⓜ ☆
(403) 342-6567. **$89-$89, 24 days notice.** 6500 67th St. 3.2 km nw; 0.8 km e of Hwy 2, 67th St exit. Int corridors. **Pets:** Small. No service, supervision, crate.
🄰🅂🄺 🆂 ⊠ 🔥 🄳 🍴

◆◆◆ **Service Plus Inns and Suites** Ⓜ ☆
(403) 342-4445. **$89-$104.** 6853 66th St. 3.6 km nw, 0.5 km e of Hwy 2, 67th St exit. Int corridors. **Pets:** Medium. Designated rooms, no service, supervision, crate.
🄰🅂🄺 🆂 ⊠ 🔥 🄳 🖼

🄒🄐 ◆◆ **Travelodge Red Deer** Ⓜ ☆
(403) 346-2011. **Call for rates.** 2807 50th Ave. 1.8 km e on Hwy 2A (Gaetz Ave). Ext/int corridors. **Pets:** $50 deposit/room. Designated rooms, no service, supervision, crate.
🆂🅰🆅🅴 ⊠ 🔥 🄳 🍴 🖼

TABER

◆◆ **Heritage Inn** Ⓜ
(403) 223-4424. **$70-$79.** 4830 46th Ave. 1 km e of jct Hwy 3 and 36 S, on Hwy 3. Int corridors. **Pets:** Designated rooms, no service, supervision, crate.
🄰🅂🄺 ⊠ 🔥 🄳 🍴

VALLEYVIEW

◆ **Raven Motor Inn** Ⓜ ☆
(780) 524-3383. **$58-$75.** 4606 50th St. Jct Hwy 49 and 43. Ext corridors. **Pets:** Medium. Designated rooms, no service, supervision, crate.
🄰🅂🄺 🆂 ⊠ 🔥 🄳 🖼 ⊠

WATERTON PARK

🄒🄐 ◆◆ **Bayshore Inn** Ⓜ ☆
(403) 859-2211. **$129-$139.** 111 Waterton Ave. Centre. Ext corridors. **Pets:** Medium. Designated rooms, supervision.
⊠ 🔥 🄳 🍴 ⊠ 🄰🄲 🄲🅃🅅

🄒🄐 ◆◆◆ **The Lodge at Waterton Lakes** Ⓡ ☆
(403) 859-2151. **$145-$175.** 101 Clematis Ave. Centre. Ext/int corridors. **Pets:** $15 daily fee/room. Designated rooms, no service, supervision, crate.
🆂🅰🆅🅴 🆂 🔥 🔥 🄳 🍴 🖼 ⊠ 🄲🅃🅅

WESTLOCK

◆ **Highway Motor Inn** Ⓜ
(780) 349-3138. **Call for rates.** East Service Rd, Hwy 44. 0.3 km n jct Hwy 44 and 18. Ext/int corridors. **Pets:** Supervision.
⊠ 🔥 🄳

WETASKIWIN

◆◆ **Super 8 Motel** Ⓜ
(780) 361-3808. **$69-$69.** 3820 56th St. On Hwy 2A, just s of jct Hwy 13W. Ext/int corridors. **Pets:** Very small. Designated rooms, supervision.
🄰🅂🄺 🆂 ⊠ 🔥

◆◆ **Wayside Inn** Ⓜ ☆
(780) 352-6681. **$65-$65.** 4103 56 St. Just n of Hwy 13W, on Hwy 2A. Int corridors. **Pets:** $25 deposit/room. Designated rooms, no service, supervision, crate.
🄰🅂🄺 🆂 ⊠ 🄳 🍴

WHITECOURT

◆◆ **Quality Inn** 🅼 ❀
(780) 778-5477. **$75-$95.** 5420 47th Ave. On Hwy 43, 0.5
kn e of Hwy 32. Int corridors. **Pets:** Medium. Designated
rooms, supervision.
🅰🆂🅺 🆂🅳 ✉ 🔲 🖵 🍽

100 MILE HOUSE

◆◆ 100 Mile House Super 8 Ⓜ
(250) 395-8888. **$77-$88.** 989 Alder Ave. 1 km s on Hwy 97. Ext corridors. **Pets:** Designated rooms, supervision.
ASK Ⓢ ⊠ 🖥 💻

Ⓐ ◆◆◆ Red Coach Inn Ⓜ❶
(250) 395-2266. **$79-$85.** 170 Cariboo Hwy N. On Hwy 97, on the n end of town. Ext/int corridors. **Pets:** Small. Supervision.
SAVE Ⓢ ⊠ 🏠 💻 🍴 🏊

ABBOTSFORD

◆ Alpine Motor Inn Ⓜ ❖
(604) 859-3171. **$69-$96.** 32111 Marshall Rd. Trans Canada Hwy 1 exit 87, Clearbrook Rd. Ext/int corridors. **Pets:** $10 one-time fee/room. Supervision.
ASK Ⓢ ⊠ 🖥 💻 🏊

Ⓐ ◆◆◆ Holiday Inn Express Ⓜ ❖
(604) 859-6211. **$79-$109.** 2073 Clearbrook Rd. Trans Canada Hwy 1, exit 87. Ext/int corridors. **Pets:** Other. $10 daily fee/pet. No service, supervision, crate.
SAVE ⊠ 🏠 🖥 💻 🍴 🏊

◆◆◆ Ramada Inn-Abbotsford Ⓜ ❖
(604) 870-1050. **$89-$119.** 36035 N Parallel Rd. Trans Canada Hwy 1 exit 95, Whatcom Rd. Int corridors. **Pets:** Other. $10 daily fee/pet. Designated rooms, no service, supervision, crate.
ASK Ⓢ ⊠ ♿ 🔧 💻 🍴 🏊

◆◆ Welcome Inn Abbotsford Ⓜ
(604) 853-1141. **$45-$80.** 1881 Sumas Way. Trans Canada Hwy 1, exit 92 Town Centre, just n on Hwy 11. Ext corridors. **Pets:** Medium. No service, supervision, crate.
ASK Ⓢ ⊠ 🖥 💻 🏊

BARRIERE

Ⓐ ◆◆ Mountain Springs Motel Ⓜ ❖
(250) 672-0090. **$47-$58.** 4253 Yellowhead Hwy. 1 km s on Hwy 5 (Yellowhead Hwy). Ext corridors. **Pets:** Medium, dogs only. $5 daily fee/pet. No service, supervision, crate.
SAVE Ⓢ ⊠ 🖥 💻 🍴 🎥

BLUE RIVER

Ⓐ ◆◆ Glacier Mountain Lodge Ⓜ ❖
(250) 673-2393. **$70-$95.** Hwy 5 & Shell Rd. On Hwy (Yellowhead Hwy) at Shell Rd, follow signs. Int corridors. **Pets:** Other. $7 daily fee/pet. Designated rooms, supervision.
SAVE ⊠

◆◆◆ Mike Wiegele Helicopter Skiing Ⓡ ❖
(250) 673-8381. **$145-$395, 3 days notice.** Harrwood Dr. On Hwy 5 (Yellowhead Hwy) at Harrwood Dr, follow signs. Ext corridors. **Pets:** $25 daily fee/room. No service, supervision, crate.
ASK Ⓢ ⊠ 🖥 💻 🍴 🎥 🐾 CTV

BOSWELL

◆◆ Destiny Bay Resort Ⓒ
(250) 223-8234. **$130-$220.** 11935 Hwy 3A. 45 km n of Creston, 34 km s of Kootenay Lake ferry dock. Ext corridors. **Pets:** Supervision.
🖥 💻 🍴 🎥 🐾 CTV 🎵

◆◆ Mountain Shores Resort & Marina Ⓜ
(250) 223-8258. **Call for rates.** 13485 Hwy 3A. 9 km n; 25.6 km s of Kootenay Lake ferry dock. **Pets:** Medium. Designated rooms, supervision.
⊠ 🖥 💻 🏊 🎥 🐾 CTV 🎵

CACHE CREEK

CAA ◆◆ **Bonaparte Motel** **M** ❀
(250) 457-9693. **$55-$85.** 1395 Hwy 97 N. On Hwy 97; 1 km n of jct Trans Canada Hwy 1. Ext corridors. **Pets:** Other. $10 daily fee/pet, $10 one-time fee/pet. Designated rooms, no service, supervision, crate.
⊠ 🖥 ➔

CAA ◆ **Tumbleweed Motel** **M** ❀
(250) 457-6522. **$55-$75.** On Trans Canada Hwy 1; just e of jct Hwy 97. Ext corridors. **Pets:** Supervision.
SAVE S🔊 ⊠ 🖥

CAMPBELL RIVER

CAA ◆◆◆ **Best Western Austrian Chalet** **M** ❀
(250) 923-4231. **$89-$160.** 462 S Island Hwy. 3.2 km s on Hwy 19. Ext/int corridors. **Pets:** Medium, other. $6 daily fee/pet. Designated rooms, no service, supervision, crate.
SAVE S🔊 ⊠ 🖥 💻 ➔ ⊠ 🎾

◆ **Campbell River Lodge Fishing & Adventure Resort** **M** ❀
(250) 287-7446. **$69-$84, 3 days notice.** 1760 Island Hwy. On Hwy 19, nw of downtown, across from Redwood St.. Ext/int corridors. **Pets:** Other. $6 daily fee/pet. Supervision.
ASK S🔊 ⊠ 🖥 ❘❘ 🎾

◆◆ **Campbell River Super 8** **M** ❀
(250) 286-6622. **$78-$91.** 340 S Island Hwy. 3 km s on Hwy 19. Int corridors. **Pets:** Medium, dogs only. Supervision.
S🔊 ⊠ 🏠 🖥 ➔

CHASE

◆◆ **Chase Country Inn Motel** **M** ❀
(250) 679-3333. **$60-$76.** 576 Coburn St. Trans Canada Hwy 1 and Coburn St. Ext corridors. **Pets:** Medium. $50 deposit/pet, $5 daily fee/pet. No service, supervision, crate.
⊠ 🖥

CAA ◆◆◆ **Quaaout Lodge Resort** **L** ❀
(250) 679-3090. **$125-$175.** Trans Canada Hwy 1, exit Squilax Bridge, then Little Shuswap Rd 2.5 km w. Int corridors. **Pets:** Medium. $50 deposit/pet, $10 daily fee/pet. Designated rooms, no service, supervision, crate.
SAVE S🔊 ⊠ 🏠 🖥 💻 ❘❘ ➔ ⊠ CTV

CHEMAINUS

◆◆ **Fuller Lake Motel** **M**
(250) 246-3282. **$60-$85.** 9300 Trans Canada Hwy. On Trans Canada Hwy 1 and Henry Rd. Ext corridors. **Pets:** Medium. No service, supervision, crate.
⊠ 🖥 🎾

CHRISTINA LAKE

CAA ◆ **New Horizon Motel** **M**
(250) 447-9312. **$65-$90, 7 days notice.** 2037 Hwy 3. Just e on Hwy 3. Ext corridors. **Pets:** Designated rooms, no service, supervision, crate.
SAVE ⊠ 🖥 💻

CLEARWATER

CAA ◆ **Jasper Way Inn** **M**
(250) 674-3345. **$45-$90.** 57 E Old N Thompson Hwy. 1 km w on Old N Thompson Hwy just off Hwy 5 (Yellowhead Hwy). Ext corridors. **Pets:** Designated rooms, supervision.
⊠ 🖥 ⊠

COURTENAY

CAA ◆◆◆ **Best Western Collingwood Inn** **M** ❀
(250) 338-1464. **$82-$92, 3 days notice.** 1675 Cliffe Ave. 1 km s on Island Hwy 19. Ext corridors. **Pets:** Medium, other. $8 daily fee/pet. Designated rooms, supervision.
S🔊 ⊠ 💻 ❘❘ 🎾

◆ **The Coast Westerly Hotel** **M** ❀
(250) 338-7741. **$79-$104, 30 days notice.** 1590 Cliffe Ave. 1 km s on Island Hwy 19. Int corridors. **Pets:** Other. $200 deposit/room, $10 daily fee/pet. No service, supervision, crate.
S🔊 ⊠ 🖥 💻 ❘❘ ➔

◆◆ **Kingfisher Oceanside Resort & Spa** **M**
(250) 338-1323. **$104-$275.** 4330 S Island Hwy. 8 km s on Island Hwy 19. Ext corridors. **Pets:** Supervision.
ASK S🔊 ⊠ 🖥 💻 ❘❘ ➔ ⊠ 🎾

CAA ◆ **Travelodge Courtenay** **M** ❀
(250) 334-4491. **$70-$77.** 2605 S Island Hwy. 1.8 km s of downtown, on Island Hwy 19, adjacent Driftwood mall. Ext corridors. **Pets:** Other. $50 deposit/room. Designated rooms, supervision.
SAVE S🔊 ⊠ 💻 ➔ 🎾

CRANBROOK

◆◆ **Heritage Inn of the South** **M**
(250) 489-4301. **$85-$94, 30 days notice.** 803 Cranbrook St N. Centre; Hwy 3 and 95. Int corridors. **Pets:** Designated rooms, supervision.
S🔊 ⊠ 🖥 💻 ❘❘ ➔

CAA ◆◆◆ **Model A Inn** **M** ❀
(250) 489-4600. **$75-$150.** 1908 Cranbrook St N. 2.5 km n on Hwy 3 and 95. Ext corridors. **Pets:** Small. $5 daily fee/pet. No service, supervision, crate.
SAVE S🔊 ⊠ 🖥 💻

CAA ◆ **Ponderosa Motel** **M** ❀
(250) 426-6114. **$40-$60.** 500 Van Horne St S. 2.5 km w on Hwy 3. Ext corridors. **Pets:** Small, other. No service, supervision, crate.
SAVE S🔊 ⊠ 🖥 💻

◆◆ **Super 8 Motel** **M**
(250) 489-8028. **$80-$94.** 2370 Cranbrook St N. Just w of jct Hwy 93 and 95, corner of 30th Ave. Int corridors. **Pets:** Medium. Designated rooms, supervision.
ASK S🔊 ⊠ 🏠

CRESTON

◆ **City Centre Motel** **M**
(250) 428-2257. **$36-$55, 3 days notice.** 220 15th Ave N. Just n of Hwy 3. Ext corridors. **Pets:** Medium. No service, supervision, crate.
ASK S🔊 ⊠ 🖥

◆ **Downtowner Motor Inn** [M] 🐾
(250) 428-2238. **$40-$58.** 1218 Canyon St. Corner of 12th Ave N. Int corridors. **Pets:** Medium, other. $4 daily fee/pet. Supervision.
[SD] ⊠ ▣

[CAA] ◆◆ **Sunset Motel** [M]
(250) 428-2229. **$48-$58.** 2705 Canyon St. 1 km e on Hwy 3. Ext corridors. **Pets:** Small. Designated rooms, no service, supervision, crate.
⊠ ▣ 🖥 🏊

DAWSON CREEK

[CAA] ◆◆ **The George Dawson Inn** [MI] 🐾
(250) 782-9151. **$65-$80.** 11705-8th St. 2 km s on Hwy 2. Int corridors. **Pets:** Medium. $50 deposit/room. No service, supervision, crate.
[SAVE] [SD] ⊠ ▣ 🍴

[CAA] ◆◆◆ **Trail Inn** [M] 🐾
(250) 782-8595. **$64-$87.** 1748 Alaska Ave. Jct Alaska and Hart (97 N) hwys. Ext corridors. **Pets:** Medium. $6 daily fee/pet. Designated rooms, no service, supervision, crate.
⊠ ▣ 🖥

DUNCAN

[CAA] ◆◆◆ **Best Western Cowichan Valley Inn** [MI]
(250) 748-2722. **$89-$105.** 6474 Trans Canada Hwy. 3 km n on Trans Canada Hwy 1. Int corridors. **Pets:** No service, supervision, crate.
[SAVE] [SD] ⊠ ▣ 🖥 🍴 🏊

[CAA] ◆◆ **Days Inn Duncan** [MI] 🐾
(250) 748-0661. **$59-$94.** 5325 Trans Canada Hwy. 1.5 km s on Trans Canada Hwy 1. Int corridors. **Pets:** Other. $10 one-time fee/room. Supervision.
[SAVE] [SD] ⊠ ▣ 🖥 🍴 [AC]

◆◆ **Falcon Nest Motel** [M] 🐾
(250) 748-8188. **$54-$67.** 5867 Trans Canada Hwy 1. 1.5 km n on Trans Canada Hwy 1. Ext corridors. **Pets:** Small, dogs only. $5 daily fee/pet, $5 one-time fee/pet. Designated rooms, no service, supervision, crate.
[A$K] [SD] ⊠ ▣ 🖥 🏊

◆◆ **Silver Bridge Inn & Conference Centre** [MI] 🐾
(250) 748-4311. **$59-$84.** 140 Trans Canada Hwy. Just n of the Silver Bridge. Ext corridors. **Pets:** Other. $10 daily fee/pet. Supervision.
[A$K] [SD] ⊠ ▣ 🖥 🍴

ENDERBY

[CAA] ◆ **Howard Johnson Fortunes Landing** [MI] 🐾
(250) 838-6825. **$59-$69, 4 days notice.** 1510 George St. 1 km n on Hwy 97A. Ext corridors. **Pets:** Other. $5 one-time fee/room. Supervision.
[SAVE] [SD] ⊠ 🖥 🍴 🏊

FERNIE

[CAA] ◆◆ **Cedar Lodge** [MI]
(250) 423-4622. **$61-$125.** 1101 7th Ave. On Hwy 3; 1 km e of W Bridge. Int corridors. **Pets:** No service, supervision, crate.
[SAVE] [SD] ⊠ ▣ 🖥 🍴 🏊

[CAA] ◆◆◆ **Park Place Lodge** [MI]
(250) 423-6871. **$80-$179.** 742 Hwy 3. At 7th St. Int corridors. **Pets:** Medium. Designated rooms, supervision.
[SAVE] [SD] ⊠ ▣ 🖥 🍴 🏊 ✂

◆◆ **Super 8 Motel-Fernie** [M]
(250) 423-6788. **Call for rates.** 2021 Hwy 3. 1.5 km w on Hwy 3. Int corridors. **Pets:** Medium. Designated rooms, no service, supervision, crate.
⊠

FIELD

◆◆ **Kicking Horse Lodge** [L] 🐾
(250) 343-6303. **$118-$162, 7 days notice.** 100 Centre St. Centre. Ext corridors. **Pets:** Small, other. $10 daily fee/pet, $10 one-time fee/pet. No service, supervision, crate.
⊠ 🖥 🍴 ✂ [AC] ☎

FORT ST. JOHN

[CAA] ◆◆◆ **Best Western Coachman Inn** [M] 🐾
(250) 787-0651. **$84-$89.** 8540 Alaska Rd. 2 km s on Hwy 97. Int corridors. **Pets:** Small, dogs only. $15 daily fee/pet. Designated rooms, supervision.
[SAVE] [SD] ⊠ ▣ 🖥 🍴

◆◆◆ **Ramada Limited** [M]
(250) 787-0779. **$89-$107.** 10103 98 Ave. Centre, corner 100th St. **Pets:** No service, supervision, crate.
[A$K] [SD] ⊠ ♿ ♿ ▣ 🖥 🍴

GIBSONS

[CAA] ◆◆◆ **Cedars Inn** [M] 🐾
(604) 886-3008. **$74-$83.** 895 Sunshine Coast Hwy. Hwy 101 and Shaw Rd opposite Sunnycrest Mall; 6 km n from ferry terminal. Ext/int corridors. **Pets:** Medium. $10 daily fee/pet. Designated rooms, supervision.
[SAVE] [SD] ⊠ ▣ 🖥 🍴 🏊

GOLDEN

[CAA] ◆◆◆ **Best Western Mountain View Inn** [M]
(250) 344-2333. **$140-$190.** 1024 11th St N. On Hwy 1; s service road 0.7 km w of jct Hwy 95 and Trans Canada Hwy 1. Int corridors. **Pets:** Supervision.
[SD] ⊠ ▣ 🖥 🏊

[CAA] ◆◆ **Golden Rim Motor Inn** [MI] 🐾
(250) 344-2216. **$90-$100, 3 days notice.** 1416 Golden View Rd. 1.5 km e on Hwy 1 from jct Hwy 95. Ext corridors. **Pets:** Medium. $6 one-time fee/pet. Designated rooms, no service, supervision, crate.
[SAVE] ⊠ ▣ 🍴 🏊

(CAA) ◆◆◆ **Hillside Lodge & Chalets** 🅇
(250) 344-7281. **$90-$115, 5 days notice.** 1740 Seward Frontage Rd. 15 km w on Hwy 1, follow signs n of hwy. Ext corridors. **Pets:** Medium. Designated rooms, no service, supervision, crate.
⊗ 🔋 💻 ⊗ 🔑 🖵 ☎

GRAND FORKS

◆ **Imperial Motel** 🅜
(250) 442-8236. **$55-$65.** 7389 Riverside Dr. Downtown, corner of Hwy 3. Ext corridors. **Pets:** Medium. Designated rooms, no service, supervision, crate.
🅰🆂🅺 🆂 ⊗ 🔋 💻

(CAA) ◆◆ **Western Traveller** 🅜
(250) 442-5566. **$55-$70.** 1591 Central Ave. W end of town on Hwy 3. Ext corridors. **Pets:** Medium. Designated rooms, supervision.
🆂🅰🆅🅴 🆂 ⊗ 🔋

GULF ISLANDS METROPOLITAN AREA

QUADRA ISLAND

(CAA) ◆◆ **Taku Resort** 🅇
(250) 285-3031. **$99-$225, 30 days notice.** 616 Taku Rd. From Campbell River ferry terminal, 8 km n on West Rd, then just w on Heriot Bay Rd, follow signs to Heriot Bay. Ext corridors. **Pets:** Small. Designated rooms, no service, supervision, crate.
⊗ 🔋 💻 ⊗ 🔑 🖵 ☎

SALTSPRING ISLAND

◆◆ **Seabreeze Inn** 🅜 🐾
(250) 537-4145. **$89-$99, 4 days notice.** 101 Bittancourt Rd. 1 km s on Fulford-Ganges Rd, from Ganges.. Ext corridors. **Pets:** Medium, other. Designated rooms, no service, supervision, crate.
🅰🆂🅺 ⊗ 💻 🔑

🐾 END METROPOLITAN AREA 🐾

HARRISON HOT SPRINGS

(CAA) ◆◆◆ **Harrison Hot Springs Resort** 🅇 🐾
(604) 796-2244. **$149-$179, 7 days notice.** 100 Esplanade Ave. Just w on lakefront. Int corridors. **Pets:** No service, supervision, crate.
🆂 ⊗ 🍴 🖼 ⊗

(CAA) ◆◆◆ **Quality Hotel** 🅜 🐾
(604) 796-5555. **$89-$159.** 190 Lillooet Ave. Corner of Hwy 9 (Hot Springs Rd) and Lillooet Ave. Int corridors. **Pets:** Medium, other. $10 daily fee/pet. Designated rooms, supervision.
🆂🅰🆅🅴 ⊗ 🔋 💻

HOPE

(CAA) ◆◆ **Alpine Motel** 🅜
(604) 869-9931. **$64-$72.** 505 Old Hope-Princeton Way. Westbound from Hwy 5 exit 173; eastbound from Hwy 5 ext 170, just n from lights. Ext corridors. **Pets:** Designated rooms, no service, supervision, crate.
🆂🅰🆅🅴 🆂 ⊗ 🔋 💻

(CAA) ◆◆ **Inn-Towne Motel** 🅜 🐾
(604) 869-7276. **$54-$110, 7 days notice.** 510 Trans-Canada Hwy. From Hwy 5, exit 170, 1 km n to downtown; near the s end of the Fraser River Bridge.. Ext corridors. **Pets:** $3 daily fee/pet, $3 one-time fee/pet. No service, supervision, crate.
🆂🅰🆅🅴 🆂 ⊗ 🔋 🖼

(CAA) ◆◆◆ **Quality Inn** 🅜
(604) 869-9951. **$76-$86.** 350 Old Hope Princeton Way. Westbound from Hwy 5 exit 173; eastbound from Hwy 5 exit 170, just n from lights. Int corridors. **Pets:** Medium. Designated rooms, supervision.
🆂🅰🆅🅴 🆂 ⊗ 🔥 🔋 💻 🖼

(CAA) ◆ **Swiss Chalets** 🅲 🐾
(604) 869-9020. **$55-$65, 5 days notice.** 456 Trans-Canada Hwy. From Hwy 5, exit 170, 1 km n to downtown, near the s end of the Fraser River Bridge.. Ext corridors. **Pets:** Very small, dogs only. $10 one-time fee/room. Designated rooms, no service, supervision, crate.
🆂🅰🆅🅴 🆂 ⊗

◆ **Windsor Motel** 🅜
(604) 869-9944. **Call for rates.** 778 3rd Ave. From Hwy 5, exit 170 downtown; 3rd Ave at Wallace St. Int corridors. **Pets:** Medium. Designated rooms, no service, supervision, crate.
⊗ 💻

KAMLOOPS

(CAA) ◆◆ **A Super View Motel** 🅜 🐾
(250) 374-8100. **$58-$85.** 1200 Rogers Way. Trans Canada Hwy 1 exit 368, then just n. Ext corridors. **Pets:** $5 daily fee/room, $5 one-time fee/room. Supervision.
🆂🅰🆅🅴 🆂 ⊗ 🔋 💻 🖼

(CAA) ◆ **Casa Marquis Motor Inn** 🅜 🐾
(250) 372-7761. **$49-$65.** 530 Columbia St. Just n of the corner of 5th Ave and Columbia St downtown; via City Centre. Ext corridors. **Pets:** Small, dogs only. $5 daily fee/pet. Supervision.
🆂🅰🆅🅴 🆂 ⊗ 🔋 💻

◆◆◆ **Courtesy Motel** Ⓜ 🐾
(250) 372-8533. **$58-$77.** 1773 Trans Canada Hwy E. 2.4 km e on Trans Canada Hwy 1, s side of service access road. Ext corridors. **Pets:** Medium, other. $5 daily fee/pet. Designated rooms, supervision.

🆂⒟ ☒ 🏠 🛏 💻 🍽

◆◆ **Days Inn** Ⓜ 🐾
(250) 374-5911. **$84-$109.** 1285 Trans Canada Hwy W. Trans Canada Hwy 1 exit 368, just s. Int corridors. **Pets:** Medium. $10 daily fee/room. Designated rooms, no service, supervision, crate.

🅰🆂🅺 ☒ 🛏 💻 🍽 🍽

◆◆ **Dream Lodge** Ⓜ 🐾
(250) 314-9889. **$70-$90.** 1855 Rogers Pl. Trans Canada Hwy 1, exit 368 then just n. Int corridors. **Pets:** $5 daily fee/pet. No service, supervision, crate.

🅰🆂🅺 🆂⒟ ☒ 🛏 💻 🍽

🅒🅐🅐 ◆ **Fountain Motel** Ⓜ 🐾
(250) 374-4451. **$52-$68, 3 days notice.** 506 Columbia St. Corner of 5th Ave and Columbia St downtown; via City Centre. Ext corridors. **Pets:** Other. $3 daily fee/pet. Supervision.

🆂🅰🆅🅴 🆂⒟ ☒ 🛏

🅒🅐🅐 ◆◆ **Grandview Motel** Ⓜ 🐾
(250) 372-1312. **$66-$81.** 463 Grandview Terr. Trans Canada Hwy 1, exit 369 2 km n on Columbia St, or exit 370 Summit Dr to Columbia St, via City Centre Rt. Ext corridors. **Pets:** Small. $5 daily fee/pet. No service, supervision, crate.

🆂🅰🆅🅴 🆂⒟ ☒ 🛏 💻

🅒🅐🅐 ◆◆◆ **Hospitality Inn** Ⓜ 🐾
(250) 374-4164. **$72-$84.** 500 W Columbia St. Trans Canada Hwy 1, eastbound exit 369 2 km n on Columbia St; westbound exit 370 Summit Dr to Columbia St, via City Centre Rt. Ext corridors. **Pets:** Medium. $10 one-time fee/room. Designated rooms, supervision.

🆂🅰🆅🅴 ☒ 🛏 💻 🍽 🍽

◆◆ **Kamloops Super 8 Motel** Ⓜ
(250) 374-8688. **$80-$90.** 1521 Hugh Allan Dr. Trans Canada Hwy 1 exit 367 Pacific Way. Int corridors. **Pets:** Small. Supervision.

🆂⒟ ☒ 🏠

🅒🅐🅐 ◆◆ **Kamloops Travelodge** Ⓜ 🐾
(250) 372-8202. **$76-$99.** 430 Columbia St. Corner of 4th Ave and Columbia St downtown; via City Centre. Ext corridors. **Pets:** Other. $10 daily fee/room, $10 one-time fee/room. Designated rooms, supervision.

🆂🅰🆅🅴 🆂⒟ ☒ 💻 🍽 🍽

🅒🅐🅐 ◆ **Lamplighter Motel** Ⓜ 🐾
(250) 372-3386. **$40-$70.** 1901 Trans Canada Hwy E. 3.2 km e on Trans Canada Hwy 1, s side of service access road. Ext corridors. **Pets:** Medium. $5 deposit/pet, $5 daily fee/pet. No service, supervision, crate.

🆂🅰🆅🅴 🆂⒟ ☒ 🛏

◆◆ **Ranchland Motel** Ⓜ
(250) 828-8787. **$38-$63.** 2357 Trans-Canada Hwy E. 4.5 km e on Trans Canada Hwy 1 exit River Rd, then just w along service access road. Ext corridors. **Pets:** Medium. Designated rooms, no service, supervision, crate.

🅰🆂🅺 🆂⒟ ☒ 🏠 🛏 💻

🅒🅐🅐 ◆◆◆ **Stay'n Save Inns** Ⓜ 🐾
(250) 374-8877. **$109-$129.** 1325 Columbia St W. Trans Canada Hwy 1, exit 369 Columbia St at Notre Dame Dr; or Summit Dr, exit 370 at Notre Dame Dr. Ext corridors. **Pets:** $10 one-time fee/room. Designated rooms, supervision.

🆂🅰🆅🅴 🆂⒟ ☒ 🏠 🛏 💻 🍽

◆◆ **The Thompson Hotel & Conference Centre** Ⓜ 🐾
(250) 374-1999. **$82-$118.** 650 Victoria St. Downtown, at 6th Ave. Int corridors. **Pets:** Small. Supervision.

🅰🆂🅺 🆂⒟ ☒ 🛏 💻 🍽 🍽

🅒🅐🅐 ◆ **Thrift Inn** Ⓜ
(250) 374-2488. **$37-$50.** 2459 Trans Canada Hwy E. 4.8 km e on Trans Canada Hwy 1, just e of jct River Rd along service access road, follow signs. Ext corridors. **Pets:** Medium. Designated rooms, no service, supervision, crate.

☒ 🍽

KELOWNA

🅒🅐🅐 ◆◆◆ **Best Western Inn-Kelowna** Ⓜ 🐾
(250) 860-1212. **$119-$159.** 2402 Hwy 97 N. 1 km s of jct Hwy 33 and 97 N, corner of Leckie Rd. Ext/int corridors. **Pets:** Small, other. Designated rooms, no service, supervision, crate.

🆂🅰🆅🅴 🆂⒟ ☒ 🎮 🛏 💻 🍽 🍽 ☒

🅒🅐🅐 ◆◆ **Big White Motor Lodge** Ⓜ 🐾
(250) 860-3982. **$83-$106.** 1891 Parkinson Way. From Hwy 97 N (Harvey Ave) just w on Spall Rd, follow signs. Ext corridors. **Pets:** $10 daily fee/room. Designated rooms, supervision.

🆂🅰🆅🅴 ☒ 🛏 🍽

🅒🅐🅐 ◆◆ **Pandosy Inn** Ⓜ
(250) 762-5858. **Call for rates, 7 days notice.** 3327 Lakeshore Rd. From Hwy 97 N, 3 km s on Pandosy St which becomes Lakeshore Rd.. Ext corridors. **Pets:** Very small. Designated rooms, no service, supervision, crate.

☒ 💻 🍽

◆◆ **Ramada Lodge Hotel** Ⓜ 🐾
(250) 860-9711. **Call for rates.** 2170 Harvey Ave. Hwy 97 N (Harvey Ave) at Dilworth Dr. Ext/int corridors. **Pets:** $10 daily fee/pet. No service, supervision, crate.

🅰🆂🅺 ☒ 💻 🍽 🍽

◆ **Safari Inn** Ⓜ
(250) 860-8122. **$59-$69, 3 days notice.** 1651 Powick Rd. Just s of Hwy 97 N and jct Hwy 33, behind National/Tilden Rental car. Ext corridors. **Pets:** Small. Designated rooms, no service, supervision, crate.

🅰🆂🅺 🆂⒟ ☒ 🛏 🍽

🅒🅐🅐 ◆◆◆ **Siesta Motor Inn** Ⓜ 🐾
(250) 763-5013. **$89-$118, 7 days notice.** 3152 Lakeshore Rd. Hwy 97 N, 2.8 km s on Pandosy St which becomes Lakeshore Rd. Ext corridors. **Pets:** Small, dogs only. Designated rooms, no service, supervision, crate.

☒ 🛏 💻 🍽 ☒

Ⓐ ◆◆◆ **Stay'n Save Inn** Ⓜ
(250) 862-8888. **$109-$129.** 1140 Harvey Ave. Corner of Hwy 97 N and Gordon Dr. Ext corridors. **Pets:** Medium. Designated rooms, no service, supervision, crate.

🅂🅰🅅🄴 Ⓢ ✕ 🎣 🔋 🖵 🍴 🏊

◆ **Town & Country Motel** Ⓜ 🐾
(250) 860-7121. **$70-$90.** 2629 Hwy 97 N. 0.5 km n on Hwy 97 N and jct Hwy 33. Ext corridors. **Pets:** Small. $5 daily fee/pet. No service, supervision, crate.

✕ 🐾 🔋 🖵 🏊

KIMBERLEY

◆◆ **Quality Inn** Ⓜ 🐾
(250) 427-2266. **$65-$95, 7 days notice.** 300 Wallinger Ave. Centre. Int corridors. **Pets:** Small. $5 one-time fee/ room. Designated rooms, no service, supervision, crate.

🄰🅂🄺 Ⓢ ✕ 🔋 🖵 🍴

LADYSMITH

◆ **Seaview Marine Resort** Ⓒ
(250) 245-3768. **$60-$70.** 11111 Chemainus Rd. 2.5 km s on Trans Canada Hwy 1, 3 km se. Ext corridors. **Pets:** Small. No service, supervision, crate.

✕ 🔋 🖵 🎷 ☎

LOGAN LAKE

◆ **Logan Lake Lodge** Ⓜ 🐾
(250) 523-9466. **$55-$69, 7 days notice.** 111 Chartrand Ave. Centre of Meadow Creek Rd and Chartrand Cresent. Int corridors. **Pets:** Medium, other. $10 daily fee/pet. Designated rooms, supervision.

🄰🅂🄺 Ⓢ ✕ 🖵 🍴 🎷

MADEIRA PARK

◆◆ **Sunshine Coast Resort** Ⓒ 🐾
(604) 883-9177. **$110-$120, 7 days notice.** 12695 Sunshine Coast Hwy 101. Just n of Madeira Park Rd, watch for signs. Int corridors. **Pets:** $10 daily fee/room. No service, supervision, crate.

✕ 🔋 🖵 🎷 🎷 ☎

MANNING PARK

Ⓐ ◆◆ **Manning Park Resort** 🄻 🐾
(250) 840-8822. **$109-$139.** Hwy 3. Crowsnest Hwy 3, midway between Hope and Princeton. Ext/int corridors. **Pets:** Other. $3 daily fee/room. Designated rooms, supervision.

Ⓢ ✕ 🔋 🖵 🍴 🎷 🎷 🄲🅃🅅 ☎

MCBRIDE

Ⓐ ◆◆ **North Country Lodge** Ⓜ 🐾
(250) 569-0001. **$54-$99.** 868 N Frontage Rd. Just w of village main exit, on Hwy 16, n service road. Ext corridors. **Pets:** Medium. Supervision.

✕ 🔋 🖵 🍴 🎷 🄲🅃🅅

MERRITT

Ⓐ ◆◆ **Merritt Motor Inn** Ⓜ
(250) 378-9422. **$60-$70.** 3561 Voght St. Hwy 5 exit 290, just w. Ext corridors. **Pets:** Designated rooms, supervision.

🅂🅰🅅🄴 Ⓢ ✕ 🔋 🍴 🏊

Ⓐ ◆◆ **Merritt Travelodge** Ⓜ
(250) 378-8830. **$65-$69.** 3581 Vought St. Hwy 5, exit 290, then just w. Int corridors. **Pets:** Small. Designated rooms, no service, supervision, crate.

🅂🅰🅅🄴 Ⓢ ✕ 🔋 🖵 🍴 🏊

NAKUSP

◆◆ **The Selkirk Inn** Ⓜ 🐾
(250) 265-3666. **$50-$62.** 210 W 6th Ave. Just n. Int corridors. **Pets:** Small. $8 daily fee/pet. Designated rooms, supervision.

✕ 🔋 🖵 🎷

NANAIMO

Ⓐ ◆◆ **Harbourview Days Inn** Ⓜ 🐾
(250) 754-8171. **$68-$78.** 809 Island Hwy S. 2 km s on Island Hwy 1. Int corridors. **Pets:** Small. $7 daily fee/room. Designated rooms, no service, supervision, crate.

🅂🅰🅅🄴 Ⓢ ✕ 🔋 🖵 🍴 🏊

Ⓐ ◆◆ **Travelodge Nanaimo** Ⓜ 🐾
(250) 754-6355. **$78-$95.** 96 Terminal Ave N. At jct Hwy 19A and 1, access from either hwy. Int corridors. **Pets:** Small, other. $3 daily fee/room. Designated rooms, supervision.

🅂🅰🅅🄴 Ⓢ ✕ 🔋 🖵

NARAMATA

Ⓐ ◆◆ **The Village Motel** Ⓜ
(250) 496-5535. **$59-$86.** 244 Robinson Dr. 14 km n on Naramata Rd from Penticton. Ext corridors. **Pets:** Designated rooms, supervision.

🅂🅰🅅🄴 Ⓢ ✕ 🔋 🖵 🎷 🎷 ☎

NELSON

Ⓐ ◆◆◆ **Best Western Baker Street Inn** Ⓜ
(250) 352-3525. **$129.** 153 Baker St. At jct Hwy 6 and 3A, at Baker St. Int corridors. **Pets:** Medium. No service, supervision, crate.

🅂🅰🅅🄴 ✕ 🎣 🔋 🖵 🍴

OLIVER

◆ **Southwind Inn** Ⓜ 🐾
(250) 498-3442. **$79-$95.** 1.2 km s on Hwy 97. Int corridors. **Pets:** Other. Designated rooms, no service, supervision, crate.

🄰🅂🄺 Ⓢ ✕ 🔋 🖵 🍴 🏊

OSOYOOS

Ⓐ ◆◆ **Westridge Motor Inn** Ⓜ
(250) 495-7322. **$75-$110, 3 days notice.** 9913 Hwy 3. At jct Hwy 3 and 97. Ext corridors. **Pets:** Designated rooms, supervision.

🅂🅰🅅🄴 Ⓢ ✕ 🔋 🖵 🏊

PARKSVILLE

◈◈ ◆◆◆ Best Western Bayside Inn Ⓜ ✿
(250) 248-8333. **$129-$169, 3 days notice.** 240 Dogwood St. Island Hwy 19 N Parksville exit, 8 km n on Hwy 19A. Int corridors. **Pets:** Medium, other. $10 daily fee/room. Supervision.

[SAVE] [S🐾] [✕] [🏠] [🛏] [💻] [🍴] [🐾] [✕]

◆◆◆ The Oceanside Inn Ⓜ ✿
(250) 248-2232. **$99-$159.** 424 W Island Hwy. Island Hwy 19 N, Parksville exit, 8 km n on Hwy 19A. Int corridors. **Pets:** Other. $10 daily fee/pet. Designated rooms, no service, supervision, crate.

[ASK] [S🐾] [✕] [🏠] [💻] [🛏]

◈◈ ◆◆◆ Tigh Na Mara Resort Hotel ⓧ ✿
(250) 248-2072. **$109-$209, 30 days notice.** 1095 E Island Hwy. Island Hwy 19 N Parksville exit, 2 km n on Hwy 19A. Ext corridors. **Pets:** Other. $2 daily fee/pet. Designated rooms, no service, supervision, crate.

[✕] [🛏] [💻] [🛏] [✕] [🐾]

◈◈ ◆◆ V.I.P. Motel Ⓜ ✿
(250) 248-3244. **$82-$93.** 414 W Island Hwy. Island Hwy 19 N Parksville exit, 6.5 km n on Hwy 19A. Ext corridors. **Pets:** $10 daily fee/room. No service, supervision, crate.

[SAVE] [S🐾] [✕] [🛏] [💻] [🐾]

PARSON

◆◆ Timber Inn-Chalet & Restaurant ⓒ ✿
(250) 348-2228. **$75-$125, 3 days notice.** 3483 Hwy 95. 34 km s of Golden on Hwy 95; 0.5 km s of general store/post office. Follow signs. Int corridors. **Pets:** Dogs only. $5 daily fee/pet, $5 one-time fee/pet. Supervision.

[✕] [🍴] [✕] [🐾] [CTV] [🖊]

PEACHLAND

◆◆ Hatheume Lake Resort ⓒ
(250) 767-2642. **$110-$140.** PO Box 490. 42 km w on 97C, exit Sunset Main Rd, follow signs 26 km on Bear Creek Rd. Ext corridors. **Pets:** No service, supervision, crate.

[✕] [🛏] [✕] [🐾] [CTV] [🖊]

PENTICTON

◈◈ ◆◆ Golden Sands Resort Ⓜ
(250) 492-4210. **$80-$90.** 1028 Lakeshore Dr W. Riverside Dr and Lakeshore Dr W. Ext corridors. **Pets:** Designated rooms, no service, supervision, crate.

[SAVE] [S🐾] [✕] [🛏] [🛏] [✕]

◈◈ ◆◆◆ Penticton Lakeside Resort & Conference
Centre ⓗ ✿
(250) 493-8221. **$137-$155.** 21 Lakeshore Dr W. Main St at Lakeshore Dr W. Int corridors. **Pets:** Medium. $20 one-time fee/room. Supervision.

[SAVE] [✕] [🛏] [💻] [🍴] [🛏] [✕]

◆◆ Penticton Slumber Lodge Ⓜ ✿
(250) 492-4008. **$88-$106.** 274 Lakeshore Dr W. From Hwy 97, n on Riverside Dr, 1.5 km e. Ext corridors. **Pets:** Other. $10 daily fee/pet. Designated rooms, supervision.

[ASK] [S🐾] [✕] [🛏] [💻] [🍴] [🛏]

◈◈ ◆◆◆ Ramada Courtyard Inn & Suites Ⓜ
(250) 492-8926. **Call for rates.** 1050 Eckhardt Ave W. 1.2 km w on Hwy 97. Ext corridors. **Pets:** Small. Supervision.

[SAVE] [✕] [🛏] [💻] [🍴] [🛏] [✕]

◈◈ ◆◆ Spanish Villa Resort Ⓜ
(250) 492-2922. **$58-$120, 7 days notice.** 890 Lakeshore Dr W. Corner Power St and Lakeshore Dr W. Ext corridors. **Pets:** Medium. No service, supervision, crate.

[SAVE] [✕] [🛏] [💻] [🛏] [✕]

◆◆ Waterfront Inn Ⓜ ✿
(250) 492-8228. **$58-$95, 30 days notice.** 3688 Parkview St. Hwy 97 to Channel Pkwy and Skaha Lake Rd, then just ne to Lee Ave; adjacent to Skaha Park. Ext corridors. **Pets:** Small, other. $3 daily fee/pet. Designated rooms, no service, supervision, crate.

[✕] [🛏]

PORT ALBERNI

◆◆ Coast Hospitality Inn Ⓜ ✿
(250) 723-8111. **$125-$140, 3 days notice.** 3835 Redford St. 3.2 km sw of jct Hwy 4 via City Centre/Port Alberni South Rt. Int corridors. **Pets:** Other. $25 deposit/room. No service, supervision, crate.

[ASK] [S🐾] [✕] [💻] [🍴]

◆ Timberlodge & RV Campground Ⓜ ✿
(250) 723-9415. **Call for rates.** 5 km e on Hwy 4; at jct City Centre/Port Alberni South Rt. Ext corridors. **Pets:** $10 daily fee/room, $10 one-time fee/room. Designated rooms, supervision.

[ASK] [✕] [🛏] [💻] [🍴] [🛏] [🖊]

PORT HARDY

◈◈ ◆ Pioneer Inn Ⓜ ✿
(250) 949-7271. **$82-$104, 7 days notice.** 4965 Byng Rd. 1 km w off Island Hwy 19 on Byng Rd.. Ext corridors. **Pets:** Other. Designated rooms, no service, supervision, crate.

[SAVE] [✕] [🛏] [💻] [🍴] [✕] [🖊]

PRINCE GEORGE

◈◈ ◆ Connaught Motor Inn Ⓜ ✿
(250) 562-4441. **$63-$77.** 1550 Victoria St. Corner of Victoria (Hwy 16) and Patricia Blvd, s end of downtown core. Ext corridors. **Pets:** Other. $6 daily fee/pet. Designated rooms, no service, supervision, crate.

[SAVE] [S🐾] [✕] [🛏] [🍴] [🛏]

PRINCE RUPERT

◈◈ ◆◆ Aleeda Motel Ⓜ ✿
(250) 627-1367. **$58-$76.** 900 3rd Ave W. Corner of 3rd Ave W and 8th St. Int corridors. **Pets:** Other. $6 daily fee/room. No service, supervision, crate.

[S🐾] [✕] [🛏] [🖊]

PRINCETON

◈◈ ◆◆◆ Best Western Princeton Inn Ⓜ ✿
(250) 295-3537. **$89-$139.** 169 Hwy 3. On Hwy 3, town centre. Ext corridors. **Pets:** Very small. $50 deposit/room, $10 daily fee/pet, $10 one-time fee/pet. Designated rooms, no service, supervision, crate.

[SAVE] [S🐾] [✕] [🛏] [🛏]

QUALICUM BEACH

◆◆ **Old Dutch Inn (By The Sea) M ❖**
(250) 752-6914. **$79-$109.** 2690 Island Hwy W. From Hwy 19, exit Qualicum Beach/Port Alberni, 4 km on Memorial Ave at jct Hwy 19A. Int corridors. **Pets:** Small. $10 daily fee/pet. Supervision.

⊠ 🖥 💻 🍴 🚲 🐾

QUESNEL

◆◆ **Talisman Inn M ❖**
(250) 992-7247. **$55-$81.** 753 Front St. 1 km n of Carson Ave, on Hwy 97. Int corridors. **Pets:** Other. Designated rooms, no service, supervision, crate.

⊠ 🖥 💻

RADIUM HOT SPRINGS

◆◆ **Cedar Motel M ❖**
(250) 347-9463. **$52-$72.** 7593 Main St W. Off Hwy 93 and 95, 0.3 km s of jct Hwy 93, on service road (Main St). Ext corridors. **Pets:** Medium. $5 daily fee/pet. Designated rooms, no service, supervision, crate.

SAVE S⊘ ⊠ 🖥

◆◆ **The Chalet Europe M ❖**
(250) 347-9305. **$95-$125, 7 days notice.** 5063 Madsen Rd. Just e of jct Hwy 93 and 95, 1 km off Hwy 93 up the hill. Ext corridors. **Pets:** $10 daily fee/pet. Designated rooms, no service, supervision, crate.

⊠ 🖥 🐾 🎾 ✍

◆◆ **Lido Motel M ❖**
(250) 347-9533. **$44-$68.** 4876 McKay St. Hwy 93 and 95 S, Stanley St w to Main St W, then s. Ext corridors. **Pets:** $2 daily fee/pet. Designated rooms, no service, supervision, crate.

⊠ 🖥 💻 ✍

◆◆◆ **Sunrise Suite Motel A**
(250) 347-0008. **$75-$135, 4 days notice.** 7371 Prospector Ave. From jct Hwy 93/95, 0.7 km n on Hwy 95, just sw. Ext corridors. **Pets:** Small. No service, supervision, crate.

⊠ 💻 🐾 🎾

◆◆ **Sunset Motel M**
(250) 347-9863. **$42-$80.** 4883 McKay St. Hwy 93 and 95 S, w to service road (Main St) and just s. Ext corridors. **Pets:** No service, supervision, crate.

SAVE S⊘ ⊠ 🖥 ✍

REVELSTOKE

◆◆◆ **Best Western Wayside Inn M ❖**
(250) 837-6161. **$99-$139.** 1901 LaForme Blvd. N side of Trans Canada Hwy 1, at intersection nearest east end of Columbia River Bridge. Ext/int corridors. **Pets:** Other. Designated rooms, supervision.

SAVE S⊘ ⊠ 🐾 🖥 💻 🍴 🚲

◆◆◆ **The Regent Inn M**
(250) 837-2107. **$99-$179.** 112 1st St E. 2 km s from Trans Canada Hwy 1; at Victoria Rd in historic downtown adjacent to Grizzly Plaza. Int corridors. **Pets:** Designated rooms, no service, supervision, crate.

SAVE S⊘ ⊠

◆ **Swiss Chalet Motel M**
(250) 837-4650. **$49-$75.** 1101 Victoria Rd. 0.9 km s from Hwy 1. Ext/int corridors. **Pets:** Small. No service, supervision, crate.

⊠ 🖥 💻 🍴

ROSSLAND

◆ **Swiss Alps Inn M ❖**
(250) 362-7364. **$49-$69, 60 days notice.** 1199 Nancy Green Hwy. 1 km w on Hwy 3B, at jct of Hwy 22. Ext corridors. **Pets:** $5 daily fee/pet. Designated rooms, supervision.

SAVE S⊘ ⊠ 🖥 🍴 ⊠

SALMON ARM

◆◆◆ **The Coast Shuswap Lodge M ❖**
(250) 832-7081. **$130-$140.** 200 Trans Canada Hwy W. 1 km w on Trans Canada Hwy 1. Int corridors. **Pets:** Other. Supervision.

SAVE S⊘ ⊠ 💻 🍴 🚲

◆◆ **Super 8 Motel M**
(250) 832-8812. **Call for rates.** 2901 10th Ave NE. 1 km e on Trans Canada Hwy 1. Int corridors. **Pets:** Supervision.

⊠ 🏠

◆◆ **Travelodge-Salmon Arm M ❖**
(250) 832-9721. **$75-$92.** 2401 Trans Canada Hwy W. 3 km w on Trans Canada Hwy 1. Ext corridors. **Pets:** Medium. $5 daily fee/pet. No service, supervision, crate.

SAVE ⊠ 🏠 🖥 💻 🚲

SAVONA

◆◆◆ **Lakeside Country Inn M ❖**
(250) 373-2528. **$89-$139.** 7001 Savona Access Rd. Trans Canada Hwy 1, exit Savona, along the Business Frontage Rd. Ext corridors. **Pets:** Supervision.

⊠ 🖥 💻 🍴 ⊠ 🎾

SECHELT

◆ **Bella Beach Motor Inn M**
(604) 885-7191. **Call for rates.** 4748 Hwy 101. 5 km s on Hwy 101. Ext corridors. **Pets:** No service, supervision, crate.

⊠ 🖥 💻 🍴 🎾

SICAMOUS

◆◆ **Sicamous Super 8 Motel M ❖**
(250) 836-4988. **$87-$118.** 1122 Riverside Ave. Trans Canada Hwy 1, s on Hwy 97A, then just w on Main St to traffic circle, then just s. Ext corridors. **Pets:** Other. No service, supervision, crate.

S⊘ ⊠ 🏠 🖥

SILVERTON

◆◆ **William Hunter Cabins C ❖**
(250) 358-2844. **$75-$98.** 303 Lake Ave. Centre. Ext corridors. **Pets:** Other. No service, supervision, crate.

ASK S⊘ ⊠ 🖥 💻 🎾 CTV

SMITHERS

🏨 ◆◆ Aspen Motor Inn Ⓜ ❀
(250) 847-4551. **$71-$77.** 4628 Yellowhead Hwy. 1.5 km w on Hwy 16. Ext corridors. **Pets:** Small. $5 daily fee/pet. Designated rooms, no service, supervision, crate.
(SAVE) (S) (X) (⬛) (💻) (🍴) (🏊)

SUMMERLAND

◆◆ Summerland Motel Ⓜ ❀
(250) 494-4444. **$89-$99.** 2107 Tait St. 5 km s on Hwy 97. Ext corridors. **Pets:** Very small, dogs only. $10 daily fee/pet. No service, supervision, crate.
(X) (⬛) (🏊)

TERRACE

◆◆◆ Best Western Terrace Inn and Conference Centre Ⓜ ❀
(250) 635-0083. **$69-$109.** 4553 Greig Ave. Hwy 16 just e on Greig Ave, follow City Centre signs. Int corridors. **Pets:** Small. $10 daily fee/pet. Designated rooms, supervision.
(ASK) (X) (💻) (🍴)

🏨 ◆◆◆ Coast Inn of the West Ⓜ ❀
(250) 638-8141. **$75-$115.** 4620 Lakelse Ave. Hwy 16 to City Centre, 0.5 km e to Emerson, just n. Int corridors. **Pets:** Small, other. No service, supervision, crate.
(SAVE) (X) (💻) (🍴)

TOFINO

◆◆◆ Crystal Cove Beach Resort Ⓒ ❀
(250) 725-4213. **$180-$230.** 1165 Cedarwood Pl. 4.5 km s on Hwy 4. Ext corridors. **Pets:** $15 one-time fee/room. Supervision.
(X) (⬛) (X) (Ⓐ) (CTV) (Ⓩ)

🏨 ◆◆◆◆ Wickaninnish Inn Ⓛ
(250) 725-3100. **$300-$400, 7 days notice.** Osprey Ln at Chesterman Bch. 4.3 km e on Hwy 4. Int corridors. **Pets:** Small. Designated rooms, no service, supervision, crate.
(SAVE) (X) (🏠) (💻) (🍴) (X) (Ⓐ)

VALEMOUNT

◆◆ Best Western Canadian Lodge Ⓜ
(250) 566-8222. **Call for rates.** 1501 5th Ave. Just e of Hwy 5 (Yellowhead). Ext corridors. **Pets:** Small. Supervision.
(X) (⬛) (CTV)

VANCOUVER METROPOLITAN AREA

BURNABY

◆◆◆ Lake City Motor Inn Ⓜ ❀
(604) 294-5331. **$87-$102.** 5415 Lougheed Hwy. Boundary Rd, 3 km e on Lougheed Hwy at Holdom Ave, entrance on n side of hwy. Ext corridors. **Pets:** Small. $5 daily fee/pet. No service, supervision, crate.
(X) (⬛) (🏊)

🏨 ◆◆◆ Stay'n Save Inn Vancouver Burnaby Ⓜ ❀
(604) 473-5000. **$114-$134.** 3777 Henning Dr. Trans Canada Hwy 1 exit 28 Grandview Hwy, just n on Boundary Rd. Ext corridors. **Pets:** Small. Designated rooms, no service, supervision, crate.
(SAVE) (X) (♿) (✎) (⬛) (💻) (🍴)

CHILLIWACK

🏨 ◆◆ Best Western Rainbow Country Inn Ⓜ ❀
(604) 795-3828. **$99-$109.** 43971 Industrial Way. Trans Canada Hwy 1 exit 116, Lickman Rd. Int corridors. **Pets:** Small. $10 daily fee/pet. No service, supervision, crate.
(SAVE) (S) (X) (⬛) (💻) (🍴) (🏊)

🏨 ◆◆ Chilliwack Travelodge Ⓜ ❀
(604) 792-4240. **$69-$75, 3 days notice.** 45466 Yale Rd W. Trans Canada Hwy 1, eastbound exit 119B; westbound exit 119A, then just n. Int corridors. **Pets:** $5 one-time fee/pet. No service, supervision, crate.
(SAVE) (S) (X) (⬛) (💻) (🍴) (🏊)

◆◆ Comfort Inn Ⓜ ❀
(604) 858-0636. **$69-$105.** 45405 Luckakuck Way. Trans Canada Hwy 1 eastbound exit 119A; westbound exit 119B, s on Vedder Rd, then 1 km w. Int corridors. **Pets:** Small, other. Designated rooms, no service, supervision, crate.
(ASK) (S) (X) (🏠)

🏨 ◆◆◆ Holiday Inn Chilliwack-Downtown Ⓜ ❀
(604) 795-4788. **$85-$119.** 45920 1st Ave. Trans Canada Hwy 1 eastbound exit 119B; westbound exit 119A, 3 km n, then just w. Int corridors. **Pets:** $10 daily fee/room. Designated rooms, no service, supervision, crate.
(SAVE) (S) (X) (🏠) (⬛) (💻) (🍴) (🏊)

🏨 ◆ Rainbow Motor Inn Ⓜ ❀
(604) 792-6412. **$59-$69.** 45620 Yale Rd W. Trans Canada Hwy 1, eastbound exit 119B; westbound exit 119A, then 1 km n. Ext corridors. **Pets:** Medium. $2 daily fee/pet. Supervision.
(SAVE) (S) (X) (⬛) (💻)

DELTA

🏨 ◆◆◆ Best Western Tsawwassen Inn Ⓜ ❀
(604) 943-8221. **$119-$129.** 1665 56th St. Hwy 99, exit 28 Tsawwassen Ferries, then 8 km w on Hwy 17; only 5 km from the Island Ferry Terminal. Int corridors. **Pets:** Other. Designated rooms, no service, supervision, crate.
(SAVE) (S) (X) (⬛) (💻) (🍴) (🏊)

⊛ ◆◆ **Delta Town & Country Inn** Ⓜ ❀
(604) 946-4404. **$95-$125.** 6005 Hwy 17 at Hwy 99. Hwy 99 at jct Hwy 17, exit 28 Ladner/Tsawwassen Ferries; 12 km ne on Hwy 17 of Tsawwassen-Victoria Ferry terminal. Int corridors. **Pets:** Small, other. Supervision.
SAVE ⊠ ▣ ⑪ ⌲ ⊠

LANGLEY

⊛ ◆◆◆ **Holiday Inn Express Hotel &**
    Suites Ⓜ ❀
(604) 882-2000. **$89-$107.** 8750 204th St. Trans Canada Hwy 1, exit 58 (Langey City/200th St), 1 km e on 200th St. Int corridors. **Pets:** Medium, other. $10 daily fee/room. Designated rooms, no service, supervision, crate.
SAVE Sᴅ ⊠ ♿ ⌖ ❏ ▣ ⌲

⊛ ◆ **Travelodge-Langley Motor Inn** Ⓜ ❀
(604) 533-4431. **$59-$84.** 21653 Fraser Hwy. Trans Canada Hwy 1 exit 58, (200th St/Langley City), 5 km s, 2.5 km e on Hwy 10, then 1.5 km e. Ext corridors. **Pets:** Medium, dogs only. $25 deposit/pet, $10 daily fee/pet. Designated rooms, no service, supervision, crate.
SAVE Sᴅ ⊠ ❏ ▣

⊛ ◆◆ **Westward Inn** Ⓜ ❀
(604) 534-9238. **$62-$72.** 19650 Fraser Hwy. Trans Canada Hwy 1, exit 58 (200th St/Langley City), 5 km s on 200th St, 1 km w on Hwy 10, then just w. Ext corridors. **Pets:** Other. $4 daily fee/pet. No service, supervision, crate.
SAVE Sᴅ ⊠ ❏

MAPLE RIDGE

◆ **Travelodge Maple Ridge** Ⓜ ❀
(604) 467-1511. **$69-$129.** 21650 Lougheed Hwy. 2 km w on Lougheed Hwy (Hwy 7) from downtown Maple Ridge. Int corridors. **Pets:** Medium. $50 deposit/room, $10 daily fee/room. No service, supervision, crate.
Sᴅ ⊠ ❏ ▣

MISSION

⊛ ◆◆◆ **Best Western Mission City**
    Lodge Ⓜ ❀
(604) 820-5500. **$85-$95.** 32281 Lougheed Hwy. Just w of Hwy 11, corner of Lougheed Hwy (7) and Hurd St. Int corridors. **Pets:** Small. $10 daily fee/room. Designated rooms, no service, supervision, crate.
SAVE Sᴅ ⊠ ♿ ⌖ ❏ ▣ ⑪ ⌲

PORT COQUITLAM

⊛ ◆◆◆ **Best Western Poco Inn & Suites** Ⓜ
(604) 941-6216. **$99-$169.** 1545 Lougheed Hwy. 3.5 km e of Coquitlam on Lougheed Hwy (Hwy 7). Ext/int corridors. **Pets:** Small. Designated rooms, no service, supervision, crate.
Sᴅ ⊠ ⌖ ❏ ▣ ⑪

RICHMOND

⊛ ◆◆ **Best Western Richmond Inn Hotel &**
    Convention Center Ⓜ ❀
(604) 273-7878. **$139-$265.** 7551 Westminster Hwy. Corner of Minoru Rd and Westminster Hwy. Int corridors. **Pets:** Medium. Designated rooms, no service, supervision, crate.
SAVE Sᴅ ⊠ ⌖ ❏ ▣ ⑪ ⌲ ⊠

⊛ ◆◆◆ **Comfort Inn-Airport** Ⓜ ❀
(604) 278-5161. **$110-$130.** 3031 #3 Rd & Sea Island Way. From Hwy 99 N exit 39 to Airport; from Hwy 99 S, Bridgeport Rd exit to Airport. Int corridors. **Pets:** Other. $10 one-time fee/pet. Designated rooms, no service, supervision, crate.
SAVE Sᴅ ⊠ ▣ ⑪ ⌲

◆◆◆ **Delta Pacific Resort and Conference**
    Centre Ⓗ ❀
(604) 278-9611. **$155-$155.** 10251 St. Edwards Dr. From Vancouver, southbound via Hwy 99 exit 39 Richmond; northbound via Hwy 99 exit 39 Bridgeport. Int corridors. **Pets:** Other. $30 one-time fee/room. Supervision.
⊠ ⌖ ▣ ⑪ ⌲ ⊠

◆◆◆ **Delta Vancouver Airport** Ⓗ
(604) 278-1241. **$155-$155.** 3500 Cessna Dr. Corner of Russ Baker Way and Cessna Rd, near the Moray Bridge. Int corridors. **Pets:** Designated rooms, supervision.
Sᴅ ⊠ ▣ ⑪ ⌲ ⊠

⊛ ◆◆◆◆ **Radisson President Hotel &**
    Suites Ⓗ ❀
(604) 276-8181. **$260-$290.** 8181 Cambie Rd. Corner of #3 and Cambie rds. Int corridors. **Pets:** Other. Supervision.
Sᴅ ⊠ ⌖ ❏ ▣ ⑪ ⌲

⊛ ◆◆ **Ramada Inn Vancouver Airport** Ⓜ ❀
(604) 207-9000. **$132-$152.** 7188 Westminster Hwy. Corner of Alderbridge Way and Westminster Hwy. Int corridors. **Pets:** Medium. $50 deposit/room. No service, supervision, crate.
SAVE Sᴅ ⊠ ⌖ ❏ ▣

⊛ ◆◆◆ **Stay'n Save Inns** Ⓜ ❀
(604) 273-3311. **$114-$134.** 10551 St Edwards Dr. Hwy 99 N, exit 39 (Bridgeport/Airport) to St Edwards Dr; Hwy 99 S, exit 39A (Richmond/Airport). Ext corridors. **Pets:** Medium, other. Designated rooms, supervision.
SAVE Sᴅ ⊠ ♿ ❏ ▣ ⑪

◆◆◆ **Vancouver Airport Marriott** Ⓗ ❀
(604) 276-2112. **$149-$165.** 7571 Westminster Hwy. Corner of Minoru Rd and Westminster Hwy. Int corridors. **Pets:** Dogs only. Supervision.
Sᴅ ⊠ ⌖ ❏ ▣ ⑪ ⌲

SURREY

⊛ ◆◆◆ **Days Hotel-Surrey Centre** Ⓜ ❀
(604) 588-9511. **$110-$116.** 9850 King George Hwy. Jct Fraser Hwy (1A) and Hwy 99A (King George Hwy). Int corridors. **Pets:** Other. $5 daily fee/pet. Designated rooms, no service, supervision, crate.
SAVE Sᴅ ⊠ ▣ ⑪ ⌲

Ⓐ ◆◆◆ **Ramada Limited**
Surrey-Langley 🅜 ❧
(604) 576-8388. **$113-$113.** 19225 Hwy 10. Trans Canada Hwy 1 exit 58, 5 km s on 200th St, then 2 km w on Hwy 10, corner of 192nd St and Hwy 10.. Int corridors. **Pets:** $10 daily fee/pet. No service, supervision, crate.
🆂🅰🆅🅴 🆂🐾 ⊠ 🦽 🅘 🅟 🅵 🛏 🏨 🍴 🖼

Ⓐ ◆◆◆ **Sheraton Guildford Hotel**
Surrey 🅷 ❧
(604) 582-9288. **$119-$179.** 15269 104th Ave. Trans Canada Hwy 1 E, exit 48, 1 km s on 152 St, then just e; Trans Canada Hwy 1 W, exit 50, then just w. Int corridors. **Pets:** Small. $50 one-time fee/room. Designated rooms, supervision.
🆂🐾 ⊠ 🅟 🍴 🖼

VANCOUVER

Ⓐ ◆◆◆ **Best Western Sands** 🅜 ❧
(604) 682-1831. **$159-$199.** 1755 Davie St. Davie at Denman St. Int corridors. **Pets:** Dogs only. $15 daily fee/room. Supervision.
🆂🅰🆅🅴 🆂🐾 ⊠ 🅟 🍴

Ⓐ ◆◆ **Bosman's Motor Hotel** 🅜 ❧
(604) 682-3171. **$109-$125.** 1060 Howe St. Just s of Nelson St. Int corridors. **Pets:** Supervision.
🆂🅰🆅🅴 🆂🐾 ⊠ 🍴 🖼

◆◆◆◆ **Canadian Pacific Hotel**
Vancouver 🅷 ❧
(604) 684-3131. **$299-$299.** 900 W Georgia St. Corner of Burrard at W Georgia St, enter from Hornby St. Int corridors. **Pets:** $20 daily fee/pet. Designated rooms, no service, supervision, crate.
🅰🆂🅺 🆂🐾 ⊠ 🅟 🅵 🅟 🍴 🖼

◆◆◆◆ **Canadian Pacific Waterfront Centre**
Hotel 🅷 ❧
(604) 691-1991. **$299-$299.** 900 Canada Place Way. Opposite Canada Pl at Waterfront; motor entrance use Howe St. Int corridors. **Pets:** $25 one-time fee/room. Supervision.
🅰🆂🅺 🆂🐾 ⊠ 🅟 🅟 🍴 🖼

◆◆◆ **Crowne Plaza Hotel Georgia** 🅷 ❧
(604) 682-5566. **$299-$349.** 801 W Georgia St. Corner W Georgia and Howe sts. Int corridors. **Pets:** Small. No service, supervision, crate.
🅰🆂🅺 🆂🐾 ⊠ 🅟 🅟 🍴

◆◆◆ **Delta Vancouver Suites** 🅷 ❧
(604) 689-8188. **$215-$215.** 550 W Hastings St. Corner of Seymour and W Hastings. Int corridors. **Pets:** Small. Designated rooms, no service, supervision, crate.
⊠ 🅟 🅟 🍴 🖼

Ⓐ ◆◆◆◆◆ **Four Seasons Hotel**
Vancouver 🅷 ❧
(604) 689-9333. **$420-$480.** 791 W Georgia St. Howe at W Georgia St. Int corridors. **Pets:** Small. Supervision.
🆂🅰🆅🅴 ⊠ 🍴 🖼 ⊠

◆◆◆ **The Georgian Court Hotel** 🅷 ❧
(604) 682-5555. **$185-$260.** 773 Beatty St. Robson at Beatty St. Int corridors. **Pets:** $20 one-time fee/room. No service, supervision, crate.
⊠ 🅟 🍴

Ⓐ ◆◆◆ **Granville Island Hotel** 🅷
(604) 683-7373. **$209-$219.** 1253 Johnston St. Granville Island below bridge, follow well marked signs. Int corridors. **Pets:** Designated rooms, supervision.
🆂🅰🆅🅴 🆂🐾 ⊠ 🅟 🍴

Ⓐ ◆◆◆ **Holiday Inn Hotel & Suites Vancouver**
Downtown 🅷
(604) 684-2151. **$169-$199.** 1110 Howe St. Corner of Helmcken and Howe sts. Int corridors. **Pets:** Supervision.
🆂🅰🆅🅴 🆂🐾 ⊠ 🅟 🅟 🍴 🖼

Ⓐ ◆◆ **Holiday Inn-Vancouver Centre** 🅷 ❧
(604) 879-0511. **$169-$209.** 711 W Broadway. Between Heather and Willow sts. Int corridors. **Pets:** Medium, other. Designated rooms, supervision.
🆂🐾 ⊠ 🅟 🅟 🍴 🖼

◆ **The London Guard Motel** 🅜
(604) 430-4646. **$60-$70.** 2227 Kingsway. 6.8 km se on Hwy 1A and 99A (Kingsway). Ext corridors. **Pets:** No service, supervision, crate.
⊠ 🅟 🅺

Ⓐ ◆◆◆◆ **Metropolitan Hotel** 🅷 ❧
(604) 687-1122. **$335-$395.** 645 Howe St. Between Georgia and Dunsmuir sts. Int corridors. **Pets:** Medium. Supervision.
🆂🅰🆅🅴 🆂🐾 ⊠ 🅟 🅟 🍴 🖼 ⊠

Ⓐ ◆◆◆ **Pacific Palisades Hotel** 🅷 ❧
(604) 688-0461. **$350-$450.** 1277 Robson St. Robson at Jarvis St. Int corridors. **Pets:** No service, supervision, crate.
🆂🅰🆅🅴 🆂🐾 ⊠ 🅟 🅰 🅟 🍴 🖼 ⊠

Ⓐ ◆◆◆◆◆ **The Pan Pacific Hotel**
Vancouver 🅷
(604) 662-8111. **$445-$525.** 999 Canada Pl. At Canada Pl, motor entrance off Howe St. Int corridors. **Pets:** Small. No service, supervision, crate.
🆂🅰🆅🅴 🆂🐾 ⊠ 🅟 🍴 🖼 ⊠

◆◆ **Quality Hotel-Inn at False Creek** 🅷
(604) 682-0229. **$149-$229.** 1335 Howe St. N end of Granville St Bridge, Drake at Howe St. Int corridors. **Pets:** Supervision.
🅰🆂🅺 🆂🐾 ⊠ 🦽 🅵 🅟 🍴 🖼

◆◆◆ **Renaissance Vancouver Hotel**
Harbourside 🅷 ❧
(604) 689-9211. **$266-$266.** 1133 W Hastings St. W Hastings at Thurlow. Int corridors. **Pets:** $100 deposit/room. Supervision.
🆂🐾 ⊠ 🅟 🅟 🍴 🖼

Ⓐ ◆◆◆ **Residence Inn by Marriott,**
Vancouver 🅷
(604) 688-1234. **$199-$235.** 1234 Hornby St. Corner of Hornby and Davie sts. Int corridors. **Pets:** Small. Designated rooms, supervision.
🆂🅰🆅🅴 🆂🐾 ⊠ 🅟 🅵 🅟 🍴 🖼

◆◆ Sylvia Hotel 🅼 ❀
(604) 681-9321. **$85-$125.** 1154 Gilford St. Beach Ave at Guilford St, across from English Bay. Int corridors. **Pets:** Small. Supervision.
🍴 🐾

㉿ ◆◆ 2400 Motel 🅼 ❀
(604) 434-2464. **$71-$105.** 2400 Kingsway. 7.2 km se on Hwy 1A and 99A (Kingsway). Ext corridors. **Pets:** $4 daily fee/pet. Designated rooms, no service, supervision, crate.
✖ 🐾

❀ END METROPOLITAN AREA ❀

VERNON

㉿ ◆◆◆ Best Western Vernon Lodge & Conference Centre 🅼 ❀
(250) 545-3385. **$99-$129.** 3914 32nd St. 1.5 km n on Hwy 97. Int corridors. **Pets:** Dogs only. $10 daily fee/pet. Designated rooms, no service, supervision, crate.
SAVE 🐾 ✖ 🔋 🖥 🍴 🐾

㉿ ◆◆ Best Western Villager Motor Inn 🅼 ❀
(250) 549-2224. **$73-$109.** 5121 26th St. 2.5 km n; across Village Green Mall. Ext/int corridors. **Pets:** Supervision.
🐾 ✖ 🔋 🖥 🐾

㉿ ◆◆ Comfort Inn 🅼 ❀
(250) 542-4434. **$84-$99.** 4204 32nd St N. 1 km n on Hwy 97 (32nd St) at corner of 43rd Ave. Int corridors. **Pets:** $10 daily fee/room. Designated rooms, no service, supervision, crate.
SAVE 🐾 ✖ 🐾

◆◆ The Maria Rose Bed & Breakfast 🅱🅱 ❀
(250) 549-4773. **$45-$80.** 8083 Aspen Rd. 9.5 km e on Silver Star Rd, follow the Silver Star Resort signs. Ext corridors. **Pets:** Medium. $5 daily fee/pet. No service, supervision, crate.
✖ 🔋 🖥 🐾 📺 🔋

㉿ ◆ Schell Motel 🅼
(250) 545-1351. **$50-$77, 4 days notice.** 2810 35th St. Centre; corner 35th St and 30th Ave. Ext corridors. **Pets:** Designated rooms, no service, supervision, crate.
🐾 ✖ 🔋 🐾

◆◆ Vernon Travelodge 🅼
(250) 545-2161. **$59-$84.** 3000 28th Ave. Hwy 97 (32nd St), just e on 28th Ave, near Polson Park. Ext corridors. **Pets:** No service, supervision, crate.
ASK 🐾 ✖ 🔋 🖥 🐾

VICTORIA METROPOLITAN AREA

MALAHAT

㉿ ◆◆ Malahat Bungalows Motel 🅲 ❀
(250) 478-3011. **$62-$125, 3 days notice.** On Trans Canada Hwy 1 (Malahat Dr), 26 km n of Victoria. Ext corridors. **Pets:** Medium, other. $50 deposit/room, $8 daily fee/pet, $8 one-time fee/pet. Designated rooms, no service, supervision, crate.
SAVE 🐾 🔋 🐾 ✖ 🗡 🔋

SAANICHTON

◆◆ Quality Inn Waddling Dog 🅼 ❀
(250) 652-1146. **$99-$129.** 2476 Mt Newton Crossroad. Corner of Hwy 17 and Mt Newton Crossroad. Int corridors. **Pets:** $10 daily fee/pet. Supervision.
ASK 🐾 ✖ 🖥 🍴

◆◆ Super 8 Victoria/Saanichton 🅼 ❀
(250) 652-6888. **$90-$100.** 2477 Mt Newton Crossroad. Just e of Hwy 17. Int corridors. **Pets:** Other. Supervision.
🐾 ✖ 🔋 🔋

SIDNEY

㉿ ◆◆◆ Best Western Emerald Isle Motor Inn 🅼 ❀
(250) 656-4441. **$119-$169.** 2306 Beacon Ave. Just e of Hwy 17 on Beacon Ave, exit Sidney; 5 km s of Swartz Bay Ferry. Int corridors. **Pets:** Medium, other. $25 one-time fee/room. Designated rooms, no service, supervision, crate.
SAVE 🐾 ✖ 🔋 🖥 🍴

㉿ ◆◆◆ Cedarwood Inn & Suites 🅼 ❀
(250) 656-5551. **$99-$190.** 9522 Lochside Dr. From Hwy 17, just e on McTavish Rd, then 1.4 km n on Lochside Dr. Ext corridors. **Pets:** Small, dogs only. $10 daily fee/pet. No service, supervision, crate.
SAVE ✖ 🔋 🖥 🗡

㉿ ◆◆ Victoria Airport Travelodge Sidney 🅼 ❀
(250) 656-1176. **$115-$165.** 2280 Beacon Ave. Just e of Hwy 17; 5 km s of Swartz Bay Ferry. Int corridors. **Pets:** Other. Designated rooms, supervision.
SAVE 🐾 ✖ 🖥 🐾 🗡

SOOKE

㉿ ◆◆ Ocean Wilderness Country Inn 🅱🅱 ❀
(250) 646-2116. **$90-$180.** 109 W Coast Rd. 14 km w on Hwy 14. Ext/int corridors. **Pets:** $10 daily fee/room. No service, supervision, crate.
SAVE ✖ 🔋 🗡 📺 🔋

㉿ ◆◆◆ Sooke Harbour House 🅲🅸
(250) 642-3421. **$280-$512.** 1528 Whiffen Spit Rd. 2 km w on Hwy 14. Ext/int corridors. **Pets:** Supervision.
SAVE ✖ ♿ 🛏 🔋 🖥 🍴 🗡 📺

VICTORIA

⊕ ◆◆◆ Admiral Motel M ☆
(250) 388-6267. **$169-$195.** 257 Belleville St. Corner of Belleville and Quebec sts. Ext corridors. **Pets:** Other. $10 daily fee/room. Designated rooms, no service, supervision, crate.

[SAVE] [S♦] [✕] [🛏] [💻]

⊕ ◆◆ Blue Ridge Inns M ☆
(250) 388-4345. **$84-$94.** 3110 Douglas St. 3.5 km n. Ext corridors. **Pets:** Small. Designated rooms, no service, supervision, crate.

[SAVE] [✕] [🛏] [💻] [🍴] [🏊] [Ⅺ]

⊕ ◆◆ Dashwood Seaside Manor Ⅺ ☆
(250) 385-5517. **$185-$385.** 1 Cook St. 1 km e of Douglas St on Dallas Rd. Int corridors. **Pets:** Medium, dogs only. $25 daily fee/pet. Designated rooms, supervision.

[SAVE] [S♦] [✕] [🛏] [💻] [Ⅺ] [✎]

⊕ ◆ Dutchman Inn M ☆
(250) 386-7557. **$75-$105.** 2828 Rock Bay Ave. From Douglas St, just w, Gorge Rd & Rock Bay Ave. Ext corridors. **Pets:** Small, dogs only. $10 one-time fee/room. Supervision.

[SAVE] [✕] [🛏] [💻] [Ⅺ]

◆◆◆◆ The Empress H ☆
(250) 384-8111. **$89-$314.** 721 Government St. Government at Wharf St, just n of the Parliament buildings. Int corridors. **Pets:** $50 deposit/room. Designated rooms, no service, supervision, crate.

[✕] [⌂] [✎] [🛏] [💻] [🍴] [🏊] [Ⅺ]

⊕ ◆◆ Executive House Hotel H ☆
(250) 388-5111. **$145-$175.** 777 Douglas St. At Burdett St. Int corridors. **Pets:** Medium, other. $15 daily fee/pet. Designated rooms, supervision.

[SAVE] [S♦] [✕] [🛏] [💻] [🍴] [Ⅺ]

⊕ ◆◆◆ Harbour Towers Hotel H ☆
(250) 385-2405. **$139-$239.** 345 Quebec St. Between Osweyo and Pendray Sts. Int corridors. **Pets:** Medium. $50 deposit/room. Designated rooms, no service, supervision, crate.

[SAVE] [✕] [⌂] [💻] [🍴] [🏊] [Ⅺ]

⊕ ◆◆◆ Ocean Pointe Resort Hotel &
Spa H ☆
(250) 360-2999. **$159-$409.** 45 Songhees Rd. Just w of Johnson St Bridge, Esquimalt at Tyee rds. Int corridors. **Pets:** No service, supervision, crate.

[SAVE] [✕] [⌂] [🛏] [💻] [🍴] [🏊] [✕]

⊕ ◆◆ Oxford Castle Inn M ☆
(250) 388-6431. **$88-$138.** 133 Gorge Rd E. From Douglas St, 2 km w. Int corridors. **Pets:** Very small, dogs only. $100 deposit/pet, $15 daily fee/pet. Designated rooms, no service, supervision, crate.

[SAVE] [S♦] [✕] [🛏] [💻] [🏊] [Ⅺ]

⊕ ◆◆ Robin Hood Motel M ☆
(250) 388-4302. **$57-$81.** 136 Gorge Rd E. From Douglas St, 2.4 km w. Ext corridors. **Pets:** Dogs only. $5 daily fee/pet. Designated rooms, no service, supervision, crate.

[SAVE] [S♦] [✕] [🛏] [💻] [Ⅺ]

◆◆◆ Ryan's Bed & Breakfast BB
(250) 389-0012. **$135-$185, 7 days notice.** 224 Superior St. Between Montreal and Oswego sts.. Int corridors. **Pets:** Supervision.

[ASK] [✕] [Ⅺ] [✎]

⊕ ◆ Shamrock Motel A ☆
(250) 385-8768. **$89-$119.** 675 Superior St. Douglas and Superior Sts. Ext corridors. **Pets:** Small, dogs only. $5 daily fee/pet. Designated rooms, no service, supervision, crate.

[SAVE] [S♦] [✕] [🛏] [💻] [Ⅺ]

⊕ ◆◆◆ Stay'n Save Inn M ☆
(250) 475-7500. **$114-$134.** 3233 Maple St. 3 km n on Blanshard (Hwy 17); corner of Blanchard and Cloverdale Ave. Ext corridors. **Pets:** Designated rooms, supervision.

[SAVE] [S♦] [✕] [⌂] [🛏]

⊕ ◆ Tally Ho Motor Inn MI ☆
(250) 386-6141. **$89-$99.** 3020 Douglas St. 2.4 km n on Douglas St (Hwy 1), just s of Finlayson St. Int corridors. **Pets:** Other. No service, supervision, crate.

[SAVE] [S♦] [✕] [💻] [🍴] [🏊]

⊕ ◆ Traveller's Inn-In Town M
(250) 978-1000. **$70-$90.** 3025 Douglas St. 2.4 km n on Douglas St (Hwy 1), just s of Finlayson St. Ext corridors. **Pets:** Supervision.

[SAVE] [✕] [🛏] [Ⅺ]

☆ **END METROPOLITAN AREA** ☆

WESTBANK

◆◆◆ Holiday Inn M
(250) 768-8879. **$109, 7 days notice.** 2569 Dobbin Rd. 4 km n of Coquihalla connector on Hwy 97. Int corridors. **Pets:** Designated rooms, supervision.

[✕] [🛏] [💻] [🍴] [🏊]

WHISTLER

◆◆◆◆ Canadian Pacific Chateau Whistler
Resort H
(604) 938-8000. **$349-$449, 45 days notice.** 4599 Chateau Blvd. From Hwy 99, 1 km e on Lorimer Rd, then just w on Blackcomb Way. Int corridors. **Pets:** Medium. No service, supervision, crate.

[ASK] [S♦] [✕] [⌂] [💻] [🍴] [🏊] [✕]

(AA) ◆◆◆ **Delta Whistler Resort** **H** ☙
(604) 932-1982. **$229-$229, 30 days notice.** 4050 Whistler Way. From Hwy 99, follow Whistler Way. Int corridors. **Pets:** Other. Supervision.

[SAVE] ☒ ☎ ▣ ⑪ ⌨ ☒

(AA) ◆◆◆ **Delta Whistler Village Suites** **H**
(604) 905-3987. **$315-$469.** 4308 Main St. From Hwy 99, just e on Village Gate Blvd, then just n on Northlands Blvd, just e. Int corridors. **Pets:** Small. Designated rooms, supervision.

[SAVE] [S/b] ☒ ⌂ ☎ ▣ ⑪ ⌨ ☒

(AA) ◆◆ **Edgewater Lodge** **L** ☙
(604) 932-0688. **$105-$199.** 8841 Hwy 99. 4 km n of Whistler Village via Hwy 99, e on Alpine Way. Ext corridors. **Pets:** Dogs only. $100 deposit/room, $20 daily fee/room. No service, supervision, crate.

[SAVE] ☒ ⑪ ☒ ⒦

◆◆◆ **Residence Inn by Marriott** **CO** ☙
(604) 905-3400. **$199-$450.** 4899 Painted Cliff Rd. From Hwy 99, 1 km e on Lorimer Rd (Upper Village), just se on Blackcomb Way, then just w. Int corridors. **Pets:** Other. $20 daily fee/room. Designated rooms, supervision.

[ASK] ☒ ☎ ▣ ⌨ ⒦

(AA) ◆◆◆ **Summit Lodge** **H** ☙
(604) 932-2778. **$315-$435, 30 days notice.** 4359 Main St. From Hwy 99, just n on Village Gate Rd, then just w on Northland Blvd. Int corridors. **Pets:** Small, dogs only. $30 daily fee/room. Designated rooms, no service, supervision, crate.

[SAVE] [S/b] ☒ ▣ ⑪ ⌨

(AA) ◆◆ **Tantalus Resort Condominium Lodge** **CO** ☙
(604) 932-4146. **$165-$310, 30 days notice.** 4200 Whistler Way. Jct Hwy 99 & Whistler Way. Int corridors. **Pets:** Other. Designated rooms, supervision.

[SAVE] ☒ ☎ ⌨ ☒ ⒦

WILLIAMS LAKE

(AA) ◆◆ **Drummond Lodge Motel** **M** ☙
(250) 392-5334. **$65-$82.** 1405 Cariboo Hwy. 1 km s on Hwy 97. Ext corridors. **Pets:** $5 one-time fee/pet. Designated rooms, no service, supervision, crate.

☒ ☎

◆◆ **Williams Lake Super 8 Motel** **M** ☙
(250) 398-8884. **$65-$89.** 1712 Broadway Ave S. 2 km s on Hwy 97. Int corridors. **Pets:** Medium. $35 deposit/pet. Designated rooms, no service, supervision, crate.

[ASK] [S/b] ☒ ⌂ ☎

YALE

◆ **Fort Yale Motel** **M**
(604) 863-2216. **$44-$54.** 31265 Trans Canada Hwy. On Trans Canada Hwy 1, just n of main set of lights. Ext corridors. **Pets:** Medium. Designated rooms, no service, supervision, crate.

☒ ☎ ▣ ⒵

BRANDON

◆◆◆ Comfort Inn M ❀
(204) 727-6232. **$64-$93.** 925 Middleton Ave. Northside Trans Canada service road, between Hwy 10 N and 10 S, just e of MacDonalds Restaurant. Int corridors. **Pets:** Other. Designated rooms, no service, supervision, crate.

(ASK) (S0) (X) (f) (B) (Q)

(CAA) ◆ Rodeway Inn Motel M ❀
(204) 728-7230. **$49-$63.** 300 18th St N. 3.2 km s of Trans Canada Hwy 1, on Hwy 10 S. Ext/int corridors. **Pets:** Small. $3 daily fee/room, $3 one-time fee/room. Designated rooms, no service, supervision, crate.

(SAVE) (X) (B)

◆◆ Royal Oak Inn MI
(204) 728-5775. **$86-$106.** 3130 Victoria Ave. 5 km s of Trans Canada Hwy 1; 1.4 km w of jct Hwy 10 (18th St) and Hwy 1A (Victoria Ave). Int corridors. **Pets:** Small. No service, supervision, crate.

(ASK) (X) (B) (Y) (Q)

◆◆ Super 8 Motel Brandon M ❀
(204) 729-8024. **Call for rates.** 1570 Highland Ave. On Hwy 1, s service road, just e of Hwy 10. Int corridors. **Pets:** Other. Designated rooms, no service, supervision, crate.

(X) (f) (Q)

(CAA) ◆◆◆ Victoria Inn MI ❀
(204) 725-1532. **$75-$106.** 3550 Victoria Ave. 5 km s of Trans Canada Hwy 1; 1.8 km w of jct Hwy 10 (18th St) and Hwy 1A (Victoria Ave). Int corridors. **Pets:** Other. $5 daily fee/room. Designated rooms, supervision.

(SAVE) (S0) (X) (B) (B) (Y) (Q)

CHURCHILL

◆◆ Polar Inn M ❀
(204) 675-8878. **$90-$110.** 15 Franklin St. Centre. Ext corridors. **Pets:** $50 deposit/room. No service, supervision, crate.

(ASK) (X) (B) (B) (K)

DAUPHIN

◆◆ Rodeway Inn Motel MI
(204) 638-5102. **$56-$105.** Hwy 5 & 10 S. 2.4 km s on Hwy 5A and 10A (Main St). Ext/int corridors. **Pets:** Designated rooms, no service, supervision, crate.

(ASK) (S0) (X) (B) (Y) (Q)

FLIN FLON

(CAA) ◆◆ Victoria Inn North MI ❀
(204) 687-7555. **$66-$82.** 10 Hwy N. 6 km s, from jct Hwy 10 and 10A, just w. Int corridors. **Pets:** Other. $5 daily fee/room. Supervision.

(SAVE) (X) (B) (Y) (Q)

GIMLI

(CAA) ◆◆◆ Lakeview Resort MI ❀
(204) 642-8565. **$67-$105.** 10 Centre St. 0.8 km e of jct Hwy 9. Int corridors. **Pets:** Very small. Designated rooms, no service, supervision, crate.

(SAVE) (S0) (X) (B) (B) (Y) (Q) (X)

HECLA VILLAGE

◆◆ Solmundson Gesta Hus BB ❀
(204) 279-2088. **$55-$75.** On Hwy 8 in Hecla Village, in Hecla Provincial Park. Int corridors. **Pets:** Small. No service, supervision, crate.

(ASK) (S0) (X) (X) (K) (CTV) (☎)

NEEPAWA

◆◆ Neepawa Super 8 Motel M ❀
(204) 476-8888. **Call for rates.** 160 Main St W. Hwy 16, just w of jct Rt 5. Int corridors. **Pets:** Other. Designated rooms, no service, supervision, crate.

(X) (Q)

PORTAGE LA PRAIRIE

◆ Manitobah Inn MI ❀
(204) 857-9791. **Call for rates.** S side service road on Trans Canada Hwy 1 by-pass. Int corridors. **Pets:** No service, supervision, crate.

(X) (Y) (Q) (X) (CTV)

◆◆ Westgate Inn Motel M ❀
(204) 239-5200. **$39-$49.** 1010 Saskatchewan Ave E. 1 km e on Trans Canada Hwy 1A. Ext corridors. **Pets:** Designated rooms, supervision.

(S0) (X) (CTV)

RUSSELL

ⒶⒶ ◆◆ **The Russell Inn Hotel & Conference Center** Ⓜ ❖
(204) 773-2186. **$80-$80.** 1.2 km se on Hwy 16 and 83. Ext/int corridors. **Pets:** Other. Supervision.
[SAVE] [S🔊] [✕] [🖥] [💻] [🍴]

THE PAS

ⒶⒶ ◆◆◆ **Kikiwak Inn** Ⓜ ❖
(204) 623-1800. **$93-$93.** Hwy 10 N. 0.6 km n on Hwy 10. Int corridors. **Pets:** Designated rooms, no service, supervision, crate.
[SAVE] [S🔊] [✕] [🏠] [💻] [🍴] [≋]

ⒶⒶ ◆◆ **Wescana Inn** Ⓜ
(204) 623-5446. **$75-$79.** 439 Fischer Ave. Just s on Hwy 10. Ext/int corridors. **Pets:** Supervision.
[SAVE] [S🔊] [✕] [🖥] [💻]

THOMPSON

ⒶⒶ ◆◆◆ **Country Inn & Suites By Carlson** Ⓜ
(204) 778-8879. **$84-$104.** 70 Thompson Dr N. Just w of Hwy 6 on Thompson Dr N at Quartz St. Int corridors. **Pets:** Supervision.
[SAVE] [S🔊] [✕] [💻] [≋]

WINKLER

◆◆ **Winkler Inn** Ⓜ ❖
(204) 325-4381. **$65-$89.** 851 Main St N. Center, Main St and Hwy 14. Int corridors. **Pets:** Small. $6 daily fee/pet. Designated rooms, no service, supervision, crate.
[✕] [💻] [🍴] [≋]

WINNIPEG

ⒶⒶ ◆◆ **Best Western Carlton Inn** Ⓜ ❖
(204) 942-0881. **$65-$80.** 220 Carlton St. Just s off Metro Rt 85 (Portage Ave); opposite Convention Centre. Int corridors. **Pets:** Other. No service, supervision, crate.
[SAVE] [S🔊] [✕] [🍴] [≋]

◆◆◆ **Canadian Pacific The Lombard** 🏨 ❖
(204) 957-1350. **$99-$149.** 2 Lombard Pl. Just e of corner Portage Ave and Main St. Int corridors. **Pets:** Other. $50 daily fee/room. No service, supervision, crate.
[✕] [🔊] [🖥] [💻] [🍴] [≋]

ⒶⒶ ◆◆ **Canad Inns Express Fort Garry** Ⓜ ❖
(204) 269-6955. **$60-$80.** 1792 Pembina Hwy. Pembina Hwy at Adamar Rd. Ext/int corridors. **Pets:** Medium. Supervision.
[SAVE] [S🔊] [✕] [🖥] [💻] [🍴]

ⒶⒶ ◆◆ **Canad Inns Windsor Park** Ⓜ ❖
(204) 253-2641. **$67-$77.** 1034 Elizabeth Rd. Elizabeth Rd at Lagimodiere Blvd. Int corridors. **Pets:** Small, dogs only. Supervision.
[SAVE] [S🔊] [✕] [🖥] [💻] [🍴] [≋]

◆◆◆ **Comfort Inn** Ⓜ ❖
(204) 269-7390. **$70-$103.** 3109 Pembina Hwy. Just n of jct Perimeter Hwy 100 and 75. Int corridors. **Pets:** Small. Designated rooms, supervision.
[A$K] [S🔊] [✕] [🖥]

◆◆◆ **Comfort Inn** Ⓜ ❖
(204) 783-5627. **$75-$100.** 1770 Sargent Ave. At Sargent Ave and King Edward St. Int corridors. **Pets:** Other. Designated rooms, supervision.
[A$K] [S🔊] [✕] [🏠] [🖥] [💻]

ⒶⒶ ◆◆◆ **Country Inn & Suites By Carlson** Ⓜ ❖
(204) 783-6900. **$85-$95, 7 days notice.** 730 King Edward St. Just s of jct Wellington Ave. Int corridors. **Pets:** Other. $25 deposit/room. Supervision.
[SAVE] [S🔊] [✕] [🏠] [🖥] [💻]

ⒶⒶ ◆◆◆ **Crowne Plaza Winnipeg Downtown** 🏨 ❖
(204) 942-0551. **$89-$169.** 350 St Mary Ave. St Mary Ave at Hargrave St; adjacent to Convention Centre. Int corridors. **Pets:** Other. No service, supervision, crate.
[SAVE] [✕] [🏠] [🖥] [💻] [🍴] [≋]

ⒶⒶ ◆ **Gordon Downtowner Motor Hotel** Ⓜ
(204) 943-5581. **$60-$73.** 330 Kennedy St. Kennedy St at Ellice Ave. Int corridors. **Pets:** Supervision.
[SAVE] [S🔊] [🖥] [🍴]

ⒶⒶ ◆◆◆ **Holiday Inn Winnipeg South** 🏨 ❖
(204) 452-4747. **$95-$95.** 1330 Pembina Hwy. At McGillivray Blvd. Int corridors. **Pets:** Other. Designated rooms, supervision.
[SAVE] [✕] [🖥] [💻] [🍴] [≋]

ⒶⒶ ◆◆ **International Inn-Best Western** Ⓜ
(204) 786-4801. **$92-$150.** 1808 Wellington Ave. Wellington Ave at Berry St. Int corridors. **Pets:** No service, supervision, crate.
[SAVE] [S🔊] [✕] [🍴] [≋]

ⒶⒶ ◆◆◆ **Place Louis Riel All-Suite Hotel** 🏨 ❖
(204) 947-6961. **$90-$110.** 190 Smith St. Smith St at St Mary Ave. Int corridors. **Pets:** Large. $25 deposit/room. Designated rooms, no service, supervision, crate.
[SAVE] [S🔊] [✕] [🏠] [💻] [🍴]

ⒶⒶ ◆◆◆ **Quality Inn** Ⓜ
(204) 453-8247. **$60-$90.** 635 Pembina Hwy. Pembina Hwy at Grand Ave. Int corridors. **Pets:** Supervision.
[SAVE] [S🔊] [✕] [🖥] [💻] [🍴]

◆◆◆ **Radisson Hotel Winnipeg Downtown** 🏨 ❖
(204) 956-0410. **$179-$194.** 288 Portage Ave. Portage Ave at Smith St. Int corridors. **Pets:** Large. No service, supervision, crate.
[A$K] [S🔊] [✕] [💻] [🍴] [≋]

◆◆◆ **Ramada Marlborough Hotel** 🅷
(204) 942-6411. **$62-$62.** 331 Smith St. Just n off Metro Rt 85 (Portage Ave). Int corridors. **Pets:** No service, supervision, crate.
Ⓐ$Ⓚ 🆂 ⊠ 🍴 🖵 〽

◆ **Twin Pillars Bed & Breakfast** 🅱🅱 🐾
(204) 284-7590. **$40-$52** (no credit cards). 235 Oakwood Ave. 0.6 km e of Osborne St. Int corridors. **Pets:** Dogs only. $35 deposit/room. Designated rooms, supervision.
Ⓐ$Ⓚ ⊠

◆◆ **Viscount Gort Hotel** 🅼
(204) 775-0451. **$82-$150.** 1670 Portage Ave. Portage Ave at Rt 90. Int corridors. **Pets:** No service, supervision, crate.
Ⓐ$Ⓚ 🆂 ⊠ 🍴 🖵 〽 🏠

NEW BRUNSWICK

CITY INDEX

BATHURST

◆◆◆ Atlantic Host Hotel  ❀
(506) 548-3335. **$75-$95.** 1450 Vanier Blvd. On Hwy 11 at jct Vanier Blvd, exit 310. Int corridors. **Pets:** Small. Designated rooms, no service, supervision, crate.
⊠ 🖥 🕿 ⊠

◆◆ Comfort Inn ❀
(506) 547-8000. **$67-$91.** 1170 St Peter's Ave. 3.4 km n on Rt 134 (St Peter's Ave). Int corridors. **Pets:** Other. No service, supervision, crate.
ASK 🖥 ⊠

CAA **◆◆◆ Country Inn & Suites By Carlson** M
(506) 548-4949. **$66-$94.** 777 St Peter's Ave. 3 km n on Rt 134 (St Peter's Ave). Int corridors. **Pets:** No service, supervision, crate.
SAVE 🖥 ⊠ 📶 🖥 🖥

CAA **◆◆◆ Keddy's Le Chateau Bathurst** MI
(506) 546-6691. **$59-$94.** 80 Main St. Centre on Hwy 134 and 7. Ext/int corridors. **Pets:** Medium. Supervision.
SAVE 🖥 ⊠ 🖥 🍴 🕿

CAMPBELLTON

CAA **◆◆ Comfort Inn** M ❀
(506) 753-4121. **$88-$108.** 111 Val D'amour Rd. 1 km e of Hwy 11, at exit 415; on Sugarloaf St W. Ext/int corridors. **Pets:** Other. Supervision.
SAVE 🖥 ⊠ 🖥 🖥

COCAGNE

◆◆ Cocagne Motel M ❀
(506) 576-6657. **$50-$75.** Hwy 11, exit 15, 1 km n on Rt 535. Ext corridors. **Pets:** Small. No service, supervision, crate.
🖥 ꭓ

EDMUNDSTON

◆◆ Comfort Inn M ❀
(506) 739-8361. **$104-$112.** 5 Bateman Ave. Nw quadrant off Herbert Blvd and Trans Canada Hwy. Int corridors. **Pets:** Designated rooms, supervision.
ASK 🖥 ⊠ 🖥

FLORENCEVILLE

CAA **◆◆ Florenceville Motor Inn** MI
(506) 392-6053. **$67-$107, 5 days notice.** 239 Burnham Rd. 0.5 km s on Trans Canada Hwy 2. Ext/int corridors. **Pets:** Supervision.
SAVE 🖥 ⊠ 🍴 🕿 CTV

FREDERICTON

◆◆ Carriage House Inn BB ❀
(506) 452-9924. **$70-$85.** 230 University Ave. Centre. Int corridors. **Pets:** Small. Designated rooms, supervision.
⊠

◆◆ Comfort Inn M ❀
(506) 453-0800. **$95-$115.** 255 Prospect St W. Trans Canada Hwy 2, eastbound exit 289 (Hanwell Rd); westbound exit 291 (Smythe St). Int corridors. **Pets:** Medium. Designated rooms, supervision.
ASK 🖥 ⊠ 🖥 🖥

CAA **◆◆◆ Country Inn & Suites By Carlson** M ❀
(506) 459-0035. **$92-$116.** 665 Prospect St. Trans Canada Hwy 2, exit 289 (Hanwell St), 0.4 km e. Int corridors. **Pets:** Small. $50 deposit/room, $4 daily fee/pet. Designated rooms, supervision.
SAVE 🖥 ⊠ 🖥 🖥

◆◆◆ Holiday Inn Fredericton MI ❀
(506) 363-5111. **$99-$119.** 35 Mactaquac Rd. Trans Canada Hwy 2, exit 274, 18 km w of Fredericton. Ext/int corridors. **Pets:** Designated rooms, supervision.
ASK 🖥 ⊠ 📶 🖥 🖥 🕿 ⊠

◆◆ Howard Johnson Hotel MI ❀
(506) 460-5500. **$99-$136.** On Trans Canada Hwy 2, n end of Princess Margaret Bridge. Int corridors. **Pets:** Designated rooms, supervision.
ASK 🖥 ⊠ 🖥 🖥 🍴 🕿 ⊠ 🖧

◆◆ Keddy's Inn MI
(506) 454-4461. **Call for rates.** 368 Forest Hill Rd. 1.6 km se on Trans Canada Hwy 2 at Forest Hill exit 295. Ext/int corridors. **Pets:** Medium. No service, supervision, crate.
ASK ⊠ 🖥 🖥 🍴 🕿 ⊠

CAA **◆◆◆ Lord Beaverbrook Hotel** H
(506) 455-3371. **$90-$120.** 659 Queen St. Centre. Int corridors. **Pets:** Medium. No service, supervision, crate.
SAVE 🖥 ⊠ 🖥 🍴 🕿

GRAND FALLS

◆◆ Auberge Pres-du-Lac Inn MI ❀
(506) 473-1300. **$80-$100, 7 days notice.** 4 km w on Trans Canada Hwy 2. Ext/int corridors. **Pets:** Very small. No service, supervision, crate.
🖥 ⊠ 🍴 🕿 ⊠

MIRAMICHI

◆◆ Comfort Inn 🅼 ❄
(506) 622-1215. **$76-$98.** 201 Edward St. 1 km w on Rt 8. Int corridors. **Pets:** No service, supervision, crate.

ASK ✕

ⒸⒶ ◆◆◆ Country Inn & Suites By Carlson 🅼 ❄
(506) 627-1999. **$71-$101, 7 days notice.** 333 King George Hwy. 1.8 km w on Rt 8. Int corridors. **Pets:** Small. $50 deposit/room. Designated rooms, supervision.

SAVE ✕ ✕ 🔒 ✕

◆◆◆ Rodd Miramichi River-A Rodd Signature Hotel 🅼 ❄
(506) 773-3111. **$84-$134.** 1809 Water St. Hwy 11, exit 120, 0.6 km e. Int corridors. **Pets:** $10 one-time fee/room. Designated rooms, supervision.

ASK ✕ ✕ ✕ 🔒 ✕ ✕ ✕

MONCTON

◆◆ Beacon Light Motel 🅼 ❄
(506) 384-1734. **$60-$85.** 1062 Mountain Rd. From Trans Canada Hwy 2, exit 492 Mapleton Rd, 2.8 km to Rt 126 (Mountain Rd), just s. Ext/int corridors. **Pets:** Medium. Supervision.

✕ 🔒 ✕ ✕

ⒸⒶ ◆◆◆ Brunswick Hotel 🄷 ❄
(506) 854-6340. **$89-$116.** 1005 Main St. Highfield and Main sts. Int corridors. **Pets:** $100 deposit/room. Supervision.

SAVE ✕ ✕ ✕ ✕ ✕

◆◆ Colonial Inns 🅼
(506) 382-3395. **$61-$69.** 42 Highfield St. Centre. Ext/int corridors. **Pets:** Small. No service, supervision, crate.

ASK ✕ ✕ 🔒 ✕ ✕

◆◆ Comfort Inn 🅼 ❄
(506) 859-6868. **$82-$140.** 20 Maplewood Dr. Trans Canada Hwy 2, exit 496A onto Hwy 115 S, left on Rt 134 E (Lewisville Rd). Int corridors. **Pets:** No service, supervision, crate.

ASK ✕ ✕ ✕

◆◆ Comfort Inn 🅼 ❄
(506) 384-3175. **$90-$99.** 2495 Mountain Rd. Trans Canada Hwy 2, eastbound exit 488A; westbound exit 488B. Int corridors. **Pets:** Other. No service, supervision, crate.

ASK ✕ ✕ 🔒 ✕

ⒸⒶ ◆◆◆ Country Inn & Suites By Carlson 🅼 ❄
(506) 852-7000. **$90-$130.** 2475 Mountain Rd. Trans Canada Hwy 2, eastbound exit 488A; westbound exit 488B. Int corridors. **Pets:** Small. $10 one-time fee/pet. Designated rooms, no service, supervision, crate.

SAVE ✕ ✕ 🔒 ✕

◆◆◆ Holiday Inn Express 🅼
(506) 384-1050. **Call for rates.** Trans Canada Hwy 2, eastbound exit 488A; westbound exit 488B. Ext/int corridors. **Pets:** No service, supervision, crate.

ASK ✕ ✕ ✕ ✕

ⒸⒶ ◆◆ Keddy's Inn 🅼
(506) 854-2210. **$75-$95, 3 days notice.** 1510 Shediac Rd. Jct Trans Canada Hwy 2 and Shediac Rd (Rt 134S), Lakeville exit 502. Ext/int corridors. **Pets:** Medium. Supervision.

SAVE ✕ ✕ ✕ ✕ ✕ ✕

ⒸⒶ ◆◆◆ Nor-West Motel 🅼 ❄
(506) 384-1222. **$80-$105.** 1325 Mountain Rd. Trans Canada Hwy 2, exit 488A eastbound; 488B westbound, 5.2 km se on Rt 126; opposite Moncton Shopping Mall. Ext/int corridors. **Pets:** No service, supervision, crate.

SAVE ✕ ✕

◆◆ Rodd Park House Inn 🅼
(506) 382-1664. **$84-$130.** 434 Main St. 1 km e on Hwy 6. Ext/int corridors. **Pets:** No service, supervision, crate.

ASK ✕ ✕ ✕ ✕ ✕

SACKVILLE

ⒸⒶ ◆◆◆ Marshlands Inn 🄲 ❄
(506) 536-0170. **$69-$89.** 55 Bridge St. Centre on Hwy 106. Int corridors. **Pets:** Designated rooms, no service, supervision, crate.

SAVE ✕ 🄰🄲

SAINT JOHN

◆ Colonial Inns 🅼
(506) 652-3000. **Call for rates.** 175 City Rd. Adjacent to Hwy 1, exit 112. Ext/int corridors. **Pets:** Small. Supervision.

ASK ✕ 🔒 ✕ ✕

◆◆ Comfort Inn 🅼
(506) 674-1873. **$75-$110.** 1155 Fairville Blvd. Hwy 1, westbound exit 4; eastbound exit 107, left turn to Fairville Blvd. Int corridors. **Pets:** Very small. No service, supervision, crate.

ASK ✕ ✕ ✕

ⒸⒶ ◆◆◆ Country Inn & Suites By Carlson 🅼 ❄
(506) 635-0400. **$95-$135.** 1011 Fairville Blvd. Hwy 1 eastbound exit 107B, left on Catherwood Dr, left at lights. Int corridors. **Pets:** Other. $50 deposit/room. Designated rooms, supervision.

SAVE ✕ ✕ 🔒 ✕

ⒸⒶ ◆◆◆ Delta Brunswick 🄷 ❄
(506) 648-1981. **$127-$127.** 39 King St. Centre; atop Brunswick Square Mall with connecting skywalk to Market Square. Int corridors. **Pets:** Medium. $50 deposit/room. Designated rooms, no service, supervision, crate.

✕ ✕ ✕ ✕ ✕

◆◆ Fort Howe Hotel 🄷
(506) 657-7320. **Call for rates.** 10 Portland St at Main St. 1 km w on Hwy 1; n end Chesley Dr exit off Harbour Bridge. Int corridors. **Pets:** Medium. No service, supervision, crate.

ASK ✕ ✕ ✕ ✕

◆◆ Howard Johnson Hotel 🅼 ❄
(506) 642-2622. **$115-$125.** 400 Main St/Chesley Dr. 1 km w on Hwy 1; n end Chesley Dr exit off Harbour Bridge. Int corridors. **Pets:** No service, supervision, crate.

ASK ✕ ✕ 🔒 ✕ ✕ ✕

◆ **Island View Motel** Ⓜ ☸
(506) 672-1381. **$55-$85.** 1726 Manawagonish Rd. 1.8 km w on Rt 100. Ext corridors. **Pets:** Small. $100 deposit/room, $15 one-time fee/room. Designated rooms, no service, supervision, crate.
🆂 ⊠ � ⲕ

ⒸⒶ ◆ **Regent Motel** Ⓜ
(506) 672-8273. **$45-$48, 3 days notice.** 2121 Ocean West Way. Hwy 1 E, exit 99, 2.4 km e on Rt 100; Hwy 1 W, exit 101 onto exit 96 w, 0.5 km w on Rt 100. Ext corridors. **Pets:** Designated rooms, supervision.
🆂 🅷 ⊠ ⓚ ⓩ

◆◆◆ **Saint John Hilton** Ⓗ ☸
(506) 693-8484. **$144-$214.** 1 Market Square. At Market Square. Int corridors. **Pets:** Very small. No service, supervision, crate.
Ⓐ⑄ⓚ ⊠ ⬛ �

◆◆◆ **Shadow Lawn Inn** Ⓒ ☸
(506) 847-7539. **$99-$165, 3 days notice.** 3180 Rothesay Rd. Hwy 1 eastbound, exit 125B, westbound exit 125A; follow signs for Rothesay and Rt 100, 1.6 km left on Old Hampton Rd (Rt 100), then left onto Rt 100. Int corridors. **Pets:** Supervision.
⊠ 🅷 ⬛ ⓣ

ST LEONARD

ⒸⒶ ◆◆ **Daigle's Motel** Ⓜ
(506) 423-6351. **$62-$79.** 68 rue DuPont. On Hwy 17; 1 km s of Trans Canada Hwy 2, exit 58. Ext corridors. **Pets:** Designated rooms, supervision.
🆂 🆂 ⊠ �

ST. ANDREWS

◆◆◆ **Canadian Pacific The Algonquin** Ⓗ ☸
(506) 529-8823. **$75-$149, 3 days notice.** 184 Adolphus St. Off Hwy 127. Int corridors. **Pets:** Other. Designated rooms, supervision.
⊠ 🅷 ⬛ ⓣ � ⓧ

ST. GEORGE

ⒸⒶ ◆◆◆ **Granite Town Hotel & Country Inn** Ⓜ ☸
(506) 755-6415. **$69-$99.** 79 Main St. From Hwy 1, westbound exit 43, 3 km w. Int corridors. **Pets:** $10 daily fee/room. Designated rooms, supervision.
🆂 ⊠ ⓣ

◆◆ **Lake Digdeguash Four Season Chalets** Ⓒ
(506) 755-2737. **$205-$545** (no credit cards), 30 days notice. 9 km w on Rt 760 from jct Hwy 1 to entry road, 1.5 km e on gravel entry road. Ext corridors. **Pets:** No service, supervision, crate.
⬛ ⓧ ⓚ ⓒⓣⓥ ⓩ

ST. STEPHEN

◆◆ **Loon Bay Lodge** Ⓛ
(506) 466-1240. **$100-$125, 7 days notice.** 10 km n on Rt 3, 21 km n on Rt 745; last 4 km is gravel. Ext/int corridors. **Pets:** Designated rooms, no service, supervision, crate.
Ⓐ⑄ⓚ ⊠ ⓣ ⓧ ⓚ ⓒⓣⓥ ⓩ

ⒸⒶ ◆ **St. Stephen Inn** Ⓜ ☸
(506) 466-1814. **$60-$75.** 99 King St. Centre on Hwy 1. Ext/int corridors. **Pets:** $10 daily fee/room. Designated rooms, supervision.
🆂 🆂 ⊠

SUSSEX

◆◆ **Econo Lodge** Ⓜ ☸
(506) 433-2220. **$65-$100.** 1015 Main St. Centre. Ext corridors. **Pets:** Small. $10 daily fee/pet. Designated rooms, no service, supervision, crate.
Ⓐ⑄ⓚ ⊠

◆◆ **Pine Cone Motel** Ⓜ
(506) 433-3958. **$50-$60.** From Trans Canada Hwy 2, exit 418, 2 km e on Hwy 114 toward Penobquis. Ext corridors. **Pets:** Small. No service, supervision, crate.
⊠ ⓒⓣⓥ ⓩ

ⒸⒶ ◆◆◆ **Quality Inn Fairway** Ⓜ ☸
(506) 433-3470. **$44-$135.** On Trans Canada Hwy 2 at jct Hwy 1. Ext/int corridors. **Pets:** Small. $10 daily fee/pet. Designated rooms, no service, supervision, crate.
🆂 🆂 ⊠ ⬛ �

WOODSTOCK

◆◆ **Auberge Wandlyn Inn** Ⓜ ☸
(506) 328-8876. **$62-$83, 7 days notice.** 4.8 km w on Trans Canada Hwy 2, exit 191B (Houlton Rd) at jct Hwy 95. Ext/int corridors. **Pets:** Other. Supervision.
Ⓐ⑄ⓚ 🆂 ⊠ �

◆◆ **Panorama Motel** Ⓜ
(506) 328-3315. **$59-$99, 7 days notice.** Trans Canada Hwy 2, exit 191B. Ext/int corridors. **Pets:** Small. Designated rooms, no service, supervision, crate.
⊠ ⓣ � ⓧ

ⒸⒶ ◆ **Stiles Motel Hill View** Ⓜ
(506) 328-6671. **$60-$80.** 827 Main St. Centre, 1.2 km n on Hwy 103. Ext corridors. **Pets:** Supervision.
🆂 🆂 ⊠ ⓣ

YOUNGS COVE ROAD

ⒸⒶ ◆ **McCready's Motel** Ⓜ
(506) 362-2916. **$44-$55.** Young's Cove Rd. Centre, 36.8 km nw of Sussex on Trans Canada Hwy 2. Ext corridors. **Pets:** Medium. No service, supervision, crate.
ⓣ ⓚ ⓒⓣⓥ ⓩ

NEWFOUNDLAND AND LABRADOR

CITY INDEX

CORNER BROOK

◆◆ Comfort Inn **MI**
(709) 639-1980. **Call for rates, 30 days notice.** 41 Maple Valley Rd. Trans Canada Hwy 1, exit 5 eastbound; exit 6 westbound, via Confederation Ave. Int corridors. **Pets:** Designated rooms, supervision.

◆◆◆ Holiday Inn **MI** 🐾
(709) 634-5381. **$85-$85.** 48 West St. Centre. Int corridors. **Pets:** Other. Supervision.

GANDER

◆◆ Albatross Hotel **MI** 🐾
(709) 256-3956. **$69-$150.** On Trans Canada Hwy 1. Ext/int corridors. **Pets:** Designated rooms, supervision.

◆◆ Comfort Inn **MI**
(709) 256-3535. **$74-$89, 7 days notice.** 112 Trans Canada Hwy 1. Centre. Ext/int corridors. **Pets:** Small. Designated rooms, no service, supervision, crate.

◆◆ Hotel Gander **MI** 🐾
(709) 256-3931. **$129-$139.** 100 Trans Canada Hwy. Centre. Int corridors. **Pets:** Other. Supervision.

◆◆ Sinbad's Hotel & Suites **MI** 🐾
(709) 651-2678. **$69-$150.** Bennett Dr. Centre. Ext corridors. **Pets:** Other. Supervision.

GRAND FALLS

◆◆ Mount Peyton Motor Hotel **MI**
(709) 489-2251. **Call for rates.** 214 Lincoln Rd. 1 km ne on Trans Canada Hwy 1. Ext/int corridors. **Pets:** Medium. No service, supervision, crate.

ST. JOHN'S

◆◆ The Battery Hotel & Suites **MI** 🐾
(709) 576-0040. **$92-$92, 30 days notice.** 100 Signal Hill Rd. 1.6 km e. Int corridors. **Pets:** Other. Supervision.

◆◆ Best Western Travellers Inn, St. John's **MI**
(709) 722-5540. **$80-$80.** 199 Kenmount Rd. 4.8 km w on Trans Canada Hwy 1. Ext/int corridors. **Pets:** Medium. No service, supervision, crate.

CAA ◆◆◆◆ Delta St John's **H** 🐾
(709) 739-6404. **$145-$145.** 120 New Gower St. Centre. Int corridors. **Pets:** Other. No service, supervision, crate.

◆◆◆ Holiday Inn-St. John's **MI** 🐾
(709) 722-0506. **$107-$107.** 180 Portugal Cove Rd. 2.4 km n on Portugal Cove Rd; at jct Prince Phillip Dr. Ext/int corridors. **Pets:** Medium. No service, supervision, crate.

◆◆◆ Quality Hotel **H** 🐾
(709) 754-7788. **$99-$119.** 2 Hill O-Chips. Centre. Cavendish Sq. Int corridors. **Pets:** Supervision.

STEPHENVILLE

◆◆◆ Holiday Inn **MI** 🐾
(709) 643-6666. **$120-$128.** 44 Queen St. Centre. Int corridors. **Pets:** Medium, other. No service, supervision, crate.

AMHERST

◆◆ Auberge Wandlyn Inn
(902) 667-3331. **$85-$105.** 1 km w on Trans Canada Hwy 104, exit 3; at Victoria St. Ext/int corridors. **Pets:** Other. Designated rooms, no service, supervision, crate.

◆◆ Comfort Inn
(902) 667-0404. **$107-$120.** 143 Albion St S. 1.5 km n on Hwy 2 from Trans Canada Hwy 104, exit 4. Int corridors. **Pets:** Other. Supervision.

ANTIGONISH

◆◆ Maritime Inn Antigonish
(902) 863-4001. **$8-$120.** 158 Main St. Centre. Ext/int corridors. **Pets:** Supervision.

AULDS COVE

◆◆ Cove Motel & Mariner Dining Room
(902) 747-2700. **$78-$86.** 1 km off Hwy 104, 3 km w of Canso Cswy. Ext corridors. **Pets:** Small. Supervision.

BADDECK

◆◆ McIntyre's Housekeeping Cottages
(902) 295-1133. **$86-$117, 4 days notice.** 8908 Hwy 105. 5 km w on Trans Canada Hwy 105. Ext corridors. **Pets:** $5 daily fee/pet. Supervision.

◆◆◆ Silver Dart Lodge
(902) 295-2340. **$92-$128, 3 days notice.** 259 Hwy 205. Off Trans Canada Hwy 105, exit 8, 1 km e on Shore Rd, Rt 205. Ext/int corridors. **Pets:** Medium, dogs only. No service, supervision, crate.

BEDFORD

◆ Esquire Motel
(902) 835-3367. **$74-$80.** 771 Bedford Hwy. From Hwy 102, exit 4A, 5.3 km e on Rt 2 (Bedford Hwy). Ext corridors. **Pets:** Other. No service, supervision, crate.

◆ Travelers Motel
(902) 835-3394. **$69-$79.** 773 Bedford Hwy. From Hwy 102, exit 4A, 5.3 km e on Rt 2 (Bedford Hwy). Ext corridors. **Pets:** Small. Designated rooms, no service, supervision, crate.

BLACK POINT

◆ Grand View Motel
(902) 857-9776. **$49-$65.** Hwy 3. Hwy 103, westbound exit 5; eastbound exit 6 to Rt 3, 9 km e. Ext corridors. **Pets:** Small, other. $25 one-time fee/pet. Supervision.

BRIDGETOWN

◆◆ Bridgetown Motor Inn
(902) 665-4403. **$62-$69.** 396 Granville St. Hwy 101, exit 20, 1 km w on Rt 1. Ext corridors. **Pets:** Other. Supervision.

BRIDGEWATER

◆◆ Auberge Wandlyn Inn
(902) 543-7131. **$89-$99.** 50 North St. 1 km e on Hwy 325; adjacent to South Shore Shopping Mall; Hwy 103, exit 12 to North St. Int corridors. **Pets:** Supervision.

◆◆ Comfort Inn
(902) 543-1498. **$76-$116.** 49 North St. From Hwy 103, exit 12, 1.7 km s on Rt 10. Int corridors. **Pets:** Other. Supervision.

CHESTER

◆ Windjammer Motel
(902) 275-3567. **$44-$65.** 4070 Rt 3. 1 km w on Rt 3. Ext corridors. **Pets:** Other. Designated rooms, supervision.

CHETICAMP

◆◆ Cabot Trail Sea & Golf Chalets
(902) 224-1777. **$129-$129, 7 days notice.** 71 Fraser Doucet Ln. Centre. Ext corridors. **Pets:** Medium. $5 daily fee/room. No service, supervision, crate.

◆◆ Laurie's Motor Inn ⓂⅠ
(902) 224-2400. **Call for rates, 7 days notice.** 15456 Main St. 1 km n, 7.2 km sw of West Gate Cape Breton Highlands National Park on the Cabot Tr. Ext/int corridors. **Pets:** Designated rooms, supervision.

ASK ✕ 🛏 💻 ✕ AC

CHURCH POINT

◆◆ Le Manoir Samson Inn ⓂⅠ ☙
(902) 769-2526. **$65-$77, 5 days notice.** 1768 Rt 1. Centre on Hwy 1. Ext corridors. **Pets:** Designated rooms, no service, supervision, crate.

ASK S✆ ✕ 🛏 💻 AC

DARTMOUTH

ⓇⒶ ◆◆ Best Western Mic Mac Hotel ⓂⅠ ☙
(902) 469-5850. **$69-$119.** 313 Prince Albert Rd. S exit of Micmac Jct, Hwy 7, 18 and 111. Int corridors. **Pets:** Designated rooms, supervision.

SAVE S✆ ✕ 💻 🍴

◆◆ Comfort Inn ⓂⅠ ☙
(902) 463-9900. **$108-$126, 3 days notice.** 456 Windmill Rd. Rt 111, Shannon Park exit. Int corridors. **Pets:** Small, other. Designated rooms, supervision.

ASK S✆ ✕ 💻

ⓇⒶ ◆◆◆ Country Inn & Suites By
        Carlson ⓂⅠ ☙
(902) 465-4000. **$76-$108, 7 days notice.** 101 Yorkshire Ave. Rt 111, Shannon Park exit. Int corridors. **Pets:** Small. $75 deposit/pet, $8 daily fee/pet. Designated rooms, no service, supervision, crate.

SAVE S✆ ✕

◆◆ Future Inns ⓂⅠ ☙
(902) 465-6555. **$81-$90.** 20 Highfield Park Dr. From Murray Mackay Bridge, 1.2 km n on Hwy 111, exit 3 Burnside Dr. Int corridors. **Pets:** Other. Supervision.

✕ 🛏 🍴

ⓇⒶ ◆◆◆ Holiday Inn-Harbourview 🅗
(902) 463-1100. **$120-$150.** 99 Wyse Rd. Adjacent to Angus L MacDonald Bridge at Wyse Rd. Int corridors. **Pets:** Supervision.

SAVE S✆ ✕ 🛏 💻 🍴 🏊

◆◆ Keddy's Dartmouth Inn ⓂⅠ
(902) 469-0331. **Call for rates.** 9 Braemar Dr. S exit of Micmac Jct, Hwy 7, 18 and 111. Ext/int corridors. **Pets:** Small. Designated rooms, no service, supervision, crate.

ASK ✕ 💻 🍴

ⓇⒶ ◆◆◆ Park Place Ramada Plaza
        Hotel 🅗 ☙
(902) 468-8888. **$119-$260.** 240 Brownlow Ave. From Murray Mackay Bridge, 1.2 km n on Hwy 111, exit 3 Burnside Dr; in Park Place Centre. Int corridors. **Pets:** Small. $50 deposit/pet. Designated rooms, no service, supervision, crate.

SAVE S✆ ✕ 🏠 💻 🍴 🏊

DIGBY

ⓇⒶ ◆◆ Admiral Digby Inn ⓂⅠ ☙
(902) 245-2531. **$89-$135.** 441 Shore Rd. Hwy 101, exit 26, 2.5 km n following St John Ferry signs, 5 km w on Victoria Rd, follow signs; 1 km e of ferry terminal. Ext corridors. **Pets:** Small. No service, supervision, crate.

✕ 🛏 🏊

DINGWALL

◆◆ Markland Coastal Resort ☒ ☙
(902) 383-2246. **Call for rates, 7 days notice.** 802 Dingwall Rd. Follow signs marked "Resort" to end of winding road. Ext corridors. **Pets:** Supervision.

✕ 🛏 💻 🍴 🏊 ✕ AC CTV

HALIFAX

◆◆ Auberge Wandlyn Inn ⓂⅠ
(902) 443-0416. **$79-$99.** 50 Bedford Hwy. 5.2 km w on Rt 2 Bedford Hwy. Ext/int corridors. **Pets:** Supervision.

S✆ ✕ 💻

◆◆ Chebucto Inn ⓂⅠ
(902) 453-4330. **$105-$145.** 6151 Lady Hammond Rd. From jct Hwy 111 and Rt 2, 0.7 km e. Ext corridors. **Pets:** Small. Designated rooms, no service, supervision, crate.

ASK ✕ 🍴

◆◆◆ Citadel Halifax Hotel 🅗 ☙
(902) 422-1391. **$129-$139.** 1960 Brunswick St. Centre. Int corridors. **Pets:** Designated rooms, supervision.

ASK ✕ 🛏 💻 🍴 🏊

ⓇⒶ ◆◆◆ Delta Barrington 🅗 ☙
(902) 429-7410. **$132-$132.** 1875 Barrington St. Centre. Int corridors. **Pets:** Small. No service, supervision, crate.

✕ 💻 🍴 🏊

◆◆◆◆ Delta Halifax 🅗 ☙
(902) 425-6700. **$135-$155.** 1990 Barrington St. In Scotia Square; corner Cogswell and Barrington sts. Int corridors. **Pets:** Designated rooms, no service, supervision, crate.

✕ 🛏 💻 🍴 🏊

ⓇⒶ ◆◆ Econo Lodge ⓂⅠ ☙
(902) 443-0303. **$79-$119.** 560 Bedford Hwy. 9.6 km w on Rt 2, Bedford Hwy. Int corridors. **Pets:** No service, supervision, crate.

SAVE S✆ ✕ 🏊

◆ Halifax TraveLodge Ⓜ
(902) 443-1576. **Call for rates.** 374 Bedford Hwy. 8 km w on Rt 2, Bedford Hwy, 1 km e of Birch Cove-Kearney Lake exit off Bicentennial Dr. Ext corridors. **Pets:** Small. Designated rooms, no service, supervision, crate.

✕ 🛏 💻

◆◆◆ Holiday Inn Express ⓂⅠ ☙
(902) 445-1100. **$129-$159.** 133 Kearney Lake Rd. Hwy 102, exit 2. Int corridors. **Pets:** Small. Designated rooms, no service, supervision, crate.

ASK S✆ ✕ 🏠 ✕ 💻 🏊

◆◆◆ **Holiday Inn Select-Halifax Centre** 🅷 🐾
(902) 423-1161. **$154-$169.** 1980 Robie St. At jct Quinpool and Robie sts. Int corridors. **Pets:** Very small. No service, supervision, crate.

Ⓐ🆂🅺 🆂🔴 ✕ 🖥 🍴 🕿

Ⓐ ◆◆ **Keddy's Halifax Hotel** 🅼 🐾
(902) 477-5611. **$75-$84.** 20 St. Margaret's Bay Rd. On Hwy 3, 1 km w of Armdale Traffic Circle. Ext/int corridors. **Pets:** Medium. Designated rooms, no service, supervision, crate.

🆂🅰🆅🅴 🆂🔴 ✕ 🖥 🍴 🕿

Ⓐ ◆◆◆ **The Prince George Hotel** 🅷 🐾
(902) 425-1986. **$149-$209, 3 days notice.** 1725 Market St. Centre; direct access to World Trade Centre. Int corridors. **Pets:** Other. Supervision.

🆂🅰🆅🅴 🆂🔴 ✕ 🏠 🖥 🍴 🕿

Ⓐ ◆◆◆◆ **The Sheraton Halifax Hotel** 🅷 🐾
(902) 421-1700. **$225-$257.** 1919 Upper Water St. Centre, adjacent to historic properties. Int corridors. **Pets:** Supervision.

🆂🅰🆅🅴 🆂🔴 ✕ 🖥 🖥 🍴 🕿

◆◆◆ **The Westin Nova Scotian** 🅷 🐾
(902) 421-1000. **$149-$239.** 1181 Hollis St. Centre. Int corridors. **Pets:** Supervision.

Ⓐ🆂🅺 🆂🔴 ✕ 🖥 🍴 🕿 ✕

INGONISH BEACH

Ⓐ ◆◆◆ **Keltic Lodge** 🆇
(902) 285-2880. **$208-$298, 3 days notice.** Middle Head Peninsula. 2 km from East Gate Cape Breton Highlands National Park entrance, off Cabot Tr main hwy. Ext/int corridors. **Pets:** Designated rooms, no service, supervision, crate.

✕ 🖥 🍴 🕿 ✕

KENTVILLE

Ⓐ ◆ **Allen's Motel** 🅼
(902) 678-2683. **$50-$50.** 384 Park St. From Hwy 101, exit 14, 3 km e on Rt 1. Ext corridors. **Pets:** Supervision.

🆂🅰🆅🅴 🆂🔴 ✕ 🅺 🕿

◆◆ **Auberge Wandlyn Inn** 🅼 🐾
(902) 678-8311. **$78-$83, 30 days notice.** 3230 Hwy 1. Hwy 101, exit 14 Coldbrook. Ext/int corridors. **Pets:** Other. Supervision.

🆂🔴 ✕ 🖥 🖥 🍴 🕿 ✕

Ⓐ ◆ **Sun Valley Motel** 🅼 🐾
(902) 678-7368. **$45-$60.** 905 Park St. 3.2 km w on Rt 1; from Hwy 101 exit 14, 0.8 km e on Rt 1. Ext corridors. **Pets:** Other. Designated rooms, no service, supervision, crate.

🆂🅰🆅🅴 🆂🔴 ✕ ✕ 🅺 🕿

LISCOMB

Ⓐ ◆◆◆ **Liscombe Lodge** 🆇 🐾
(902) 779-2307. **$119-$129, 3 days notice.** Guysborough County. On Hwy 7. Ext/int corridors. **Pets:** Designated rooms, supervision.

✕ 🖥 🖥 🕿 ✕ 🅺

LUNENBURG

◆◆◆ **Boscawen Inn** 🅲🅸
(902) 634-3325. **$90-$130.** 150 Cumberland St. Centre. Int corridors. **Pets:** No service, supervision, crate.

🍴 🅺 🕿

◆◆ **Homeport Motel & Inn** 🅼
(902) 634-8234. **$70-$160.** 167 Victoria Rd. 1 km w on Rt 3. Ext corridors. **Pets:** Small. No service, supervision, crate.

✕ 🖥 🖥

MAHONE BAY

◆◆◆ **Bayview Pines Country Inn** 🅱🅱 🐾
(902) 624-9970. **$70-$75.** 678 Oakland Rd Indian Point. Hwy 103, exit 10, 2 km w on Rt 3 to Kedy's Landing, 6 km e of Mahone Bay. Ext/int corridors. **Pets:** Designated rooms, no service, supervision, crate.

🖥 🖥 ✕ 🅺 🕿

◆◆◆ **The Manse at Mahone Bay Country Inn** 🅱🅱
(902) 624-1121. **$85-$105.** 88 Orchard St. Centre, just off harbour. Ext/int corridors. **Pets:** No service, supervision, crate.

✕ ✕ 🅺 🕿

MARGAREE VALLEY

◆◆ **The Normaway Inn** 🆇
(902) 248-2987. **Call for rates, 7 days notice.** 691 Egypt Rd. 3.2 km e on Egypt Rd from jct Cabot Tr. Ext/int corridors. **Pets:** Medium. Designated rooms, no service, supervision, crate.

✕ 🍴 ✕ 🅺 🅲🆃🆅 🕿

MAVILLETTE

◆◆ **Cape View Motel & Cottages** 🅼
(902) 645-2258. **$50-$61.** Centre on Rt 1, 32 km ne of Yarmouth. Ext corridors. **Pets:** Supervision.

✕ 🖥 ✕ 🅺 🕿

NEW GLASGOW

◆◆ **Comfort Inn** 🅼
(902) 755-6450. **$68-$114.** 740 Westville Rd. On Hwy 289, just e of jct Trans Canada Hwy 104, exit 23; opposite shopping mall. Int corridors. **Pets:** Small. Designated rooms, supervision.

Ⓐ🆂🅺 🆂🔴 ✕ 🖥

Ⓐ ◆◆◆ **Country Inn & Suites By
Carlson** 🅼 🐾
(902) 928-1333. **$85-$113.** 700 Westville Rd. On Hwy 289, just e of jct Trans Canada Hwy 104, exit 23; opposite shopping mall. Int corridors. **Pets:** Small. $50 deposit/room. Designated rooms, supervision.

🆂🅰🆅🅴 🆂🔴 ✕ 🖥

NORTH SYDNEY

Ⓐ ◆◆ **Clansman Motel** 🅼 🐾
(902) 794-7226. **$69-$99.** From Hwy 125, exit 2, just e on King St. Ext/int corridors. **Pets:** Other. Supervision.

🆂🅰🆅🅴 🆂🔴 ✕ 🖥 🕿

PORT HASTINGS

⬦⬦ Keddy's Inn M ⬅
(902) 625-0460. **$70-$84.** E of Canso Cswy on Trans
Canada Hwy 105 rotary; entrance through n side of church.
Ext/int corridors. **Pets:** Medium. No service, supervision,
crate.

SAVE S X 🖥 💻 🍴

⬦⬦ MacPuffin Motel M
(902) 625-0621. **$74-$84.** 1.6 km n on Hwy 4, 1.6 km s of
Canso Cswy. Ext corridors. **Pets:** Medium. Supervision.

X 🍴 🔁

⬦ Skye Lodge M ⬅
(902) 625-1300. **$66-$86.** At jct of Hwy 105, Rt 104 and 19.
Ext/int corridors. **Pets:** Supervision.

SAVE S X 🖥 💻

PORT HAWKESBURY

⬦⬦ Maritime Inn Port Hawkesbury M
(902) 625-0320. **$75-$98.** 717 Reeves St. 6.4 km e of
Canso Cswy on Hwy 4; opposite shopping centre. Ext/int
corridors. **Pets:** Medium. No service, supervision, crate.

X 💻 🔁

SCOTSBURN

⬦⬦⬦ Stonehame Chalets C ⬅
(902) 485-3468. **$105-$149.** From Trans Canada Hwy 104,
exit 20, 9 km e following signs; last 2 km gravel. 12 km
from Pictou. Ext corridors. **Pets:** Other. Supervision.

X 🖥 💻 X X Z

SHELBURNE

⬦⬦ MacKenzie's Motel & Cottages M
(902) 875-2842. **$60-$75.** 260 Water St. Hwy 103, exit 26,
1.5 km e on Rt 3. Ext corridors. **Pets:** Small. No service,
supervision, crate.

X 💻 🔁

SMITHS COVE

⬦⬦ Hedley House M
(902) 245-2500. **Call for rates.** RR 1. From Hwy 101 E,
exit 25; Hwy 101 W, exit 24. Ext corridors. **Pets:** Medium.
Designated rooms, no service, supervision, crate.

X 🖥 💻 X X Z

⬦⬦ Mountain Gap Inn X ⬅
(902) 245-5841. **$70-$105, 3 days notice.** Hwy 101, eastbound exit 25; westbound exit 24, on Rt 1. Ext corridors.
Pets: Other. Supervision.

SAVE S X 🖥 💻 🍴 🔁 X X

SYDNEY

⬦⬦ Comfort Inn M ⬅
(902) 562-0200. **$101-$128.** 368 Kings Rd. On Hwy 4, 3.5
km e of jct Hwy 125, exit 6E. Ext corridors. **Pets:** Other. No
service, supervision, crate.

ASK S X 💻

⬦⬦⬦ Days Inn Sydney M ⬅
(902) 539-6750. **$109-$129.** 480 Kings Rd. On Hwy 4, 2.8
km e of jct Hwy 125, exit 6E. Int corridors. **Pets:** Other. No
service, supervision, crate.

SAVE S X 💻

⬦⬦⬦ Delta Sydney H
(902) 562-7500. **$119-$119.** 300 Esplanade. Centre; on
Hwy 4, 5.5 km e of jct Hwy 125, exit 6E. Int corridors.
Pets: Supervision.

S X 💻 🍴 🔁

SYDNEY MINES

⬦⬦⬦ Gowrie House Country Inn CI
(902) 544-1050. **$109-$295.** 139 Shore Rd. From Hwy 105,
exit 21, 3 km n on Rt 305. Ext/int corridors. **Pets:** Medium.
Supervision.

ASK X 🖥 💻 🍴

TRURO

**⬦⬦⬦ Best Western Glengarry Trade & Convention
    Centre** M
(902) 893-4311. **$95-$110.** 150 Willow St. 1 km se on Hwy
2. Ext/int corridors. **Pets:** Small. Designated rooms, no
service, supervision, crate.

ASK S X 💻 🔁

⬦⬦ Comfort Inn M ⬅
(902) 893-0330. **$82-$98.** 12 Meadow Dr. Trans Canada
Hwy 102, exit 14. Int corridors. **Pets:** Other. Designated
rooms, supervision.

ASK S X 💻

⬦⬦ Keddy's Inn M
(902) 895-1651. **$70-$91.** 437 Prince St. Centre. Ext/int
corridors. **Pets:** Designated rooms, no service, supervision,
crate.

SAVE S X 🖥 💻 🍴 🔁

⬦ Palliser Resort M ⬅
(902) 893-8951. **$39-$59, 5 days notice.** Tidal Bore Rd. Off
Hwy 102, exit 14, 3.2 km s of Trans Canada Hwy, exit 15.
Ext corridors. **Pets:** Supervision.

X X Z

WESTERN SHORE

⬦⬦ Oak Island Inn & Marina M ⬅
(902) 627-2600. **$115-$129.** 55 Vaughn Rd. From Hwy 103,
exit 9 or 10, follow signs on Rt 3, 10 km e of Mahone Bay..
Int corridors. **Pets:** Other. Supervision.

SAVE X 🖥 💻 🍴 🔁 X

WHITE POINT

⬦⬦ White Point Beach Resort X ⬅
(902) 354-2711. **$130-$150, 3 days notice.** White Point
Beach. Hwy 103, exit 20A, 9 km w on Rt 3. Ext/int corridors. **Pets:** Supervision.

X 🖥 💻 🍴 🔁 X

YARMOUTH

CAA ◆◆ **Best Western Mermaid Motel** M 🐾
(902) 742-7821. **$99-$140, 7 days notice.** 545 Main St. On Hwy 1 at jct Hwy 3. Ext corridors. **Pets:** Small. Designated rooms, no service, supervision, crate.
SAVE S/D ✕ ☕ 🏊 AC

◆◆ **Capri Motel** M 🐾
(902) 742-7168. **$99-$120, 7 days notice.** 8-12 Herbert St. 1.6 km n on Hwy 1. Ext corridors. **Pets:** Small. Designated rooms, no service, supervision, crate.
A$K S/D ✕ 🚪

◆◆ **Comfort Inn** M
(902) 742-1119. **$70-$115.** 96 Starrs Rd. At jct Hwy 101 E and Rt 3. Int corridors. **Pets:** No service, supervision, crate.
A$K S/D ✕ ☕

CAA ◆ **Lakelawn Motel** M
(902) 742-3588. **$59-$74.** 641 Main St. 1 km n on Hwy 1. Ext/int corridors. **Pets:** No service, supervision, crate.
SAVE ✕ AC ☎

◆◆ **Rodd Colony Harbour Inn** MI 🐾
(902) 742-9194. **$85-$102.** 6 Forrest St. At ferry terminal. Int corridors. **Pets:** Medium. No service, supervision, crate.
A$K S/D ✕ 🚪 ☕ 🍴 AC

◆◆◆ **Rodd Grand Yarmouth-A Rodd Signature Hotel** H
(902) 742-2446. **$90-$150.** 417 Main St. Near centre. Int corridors. **Pets:** Supervision.
A$K S/D ✕ ☕ 🍴 🏊 AC

CITY INDEX

BANCROFT

(AAA) ◆◆ **Best Western Sword Motor Inn** **MI** 🐾
(613) 332-2474. **$79-$99, 3 days notice.** 146 Hastings St. Centre; on Hwy 62 N. Ext/int corridors. **Pets:** Small. No service, supervision, crate.
SAVE Sᴆ ✕ 🛢 💻 ⃝ ⃝ ✕

BARRIE

◆◆◆ **Holiday Inn Barrie** **MI**
(705) 728-6191. **$129-$145.** 20 Fairview Rd. 1.6 km s at jct Hwy 400 and 27, exit 94 (Essa Rd). Int corridors. **Pets:** Supervision.
ASK Sᴆ ✕ ⃝ 💻 ⃝ ✕

◆◆◆ **Travelodge Barrie** **M** 🐾
(705) 734-9500. **$99-$115.** 55 Hart Dr. From Hwy 400, exit 96A S (Dunlop St). Int corridors. **Pets:** Supervision.
ASK Sᴆ ✕ 🛢 💻 ⃝ ⃝

BARRY'S BAY

◆◆ **Mountain View Motel** **M** 🐾
(613) 756-2757. **$65-$75.** 4 km e on Hwy 60. Ext corridors. **Pets:** Other. No service, supervision, crate.
✕ 🛢 💻 ✕ CTV

BAYFIELD

(AAA) ◆◆◆◆ **The Little Inn of Bayfield** **CI**
(519) 565-2611. **$85-$345, 3 days notice.** Main St. From Hwy 21, exit Main St, at jct Catherine. Int corridors. **Pets:** Supervision.
SAVE Sᴆ ✕

BELLEVILLE

(AAA) ◆◆◆ **Best Western Belleville** **M** 🐾
(613) 969-1112. **$88-$108.** 387 N Front St. Hwy 401, exit 543A, 0.5 km s on N Front St (Hwy 62). Int corridors. **Pets:** Medium, other. Designated rooms, no service, supervision, crate.
SAVE Sᴆ ✕ 🛢 💻 ⃝

◆◆ **Comfort Inn** **M** 🐾
(613) 966-7703. **$89-$119.** 200 N Park St. Hwy 401, exit 543A, 1 km s on N Front St (Hwy 62). Int corridors. **Pets:** Medium. Designated rooms, no service, supervision, crate.
ASK Sᴆ ✕ 🛢 💻

◆◆◆ **Ramada Inn on the Bay** **H**
(613) 968-3411. **$120-$145, 30 days notice.** 11 Bay Bridge Rd. 0.5 km s of Hwy 2, on E Zwick Island Park. Int corridors. **Pets:** Designated rooms, no service, supervision, crate.
ASK Sᴆ ✕ 💻 ⃝ ⃝ ✕

BLENHEIM

(AAA) ◆ **Queen's Motel** **M** 🐾
(519) 676-5477. **$40-$65.** 1.2 km w on Hwy 3 (Talbot Trail). Ext corridors. **Pets:** Other. No service, supervision, crate.
SAVE Sᴆ ✕ 🛢 CTV

BRACEBRIDGE

(AAA) ◆◆ **Bellwood Motel** **M** 🐾
(705) 645-4424. **$58-$88.** 133 Manitoba St. Corner of Ida and Manitoba sts. Ext corridors. **Pets:** Other. $25 deposit/ room. Designated rooms, no service, supervision, crate.
SAVE ✕ 🛢

(QA) ◆◆◆ Islander Inn **M** ❖
(705) 645-2235. **$79-$129.** 320 Taylor Rd (42). Hwy 11, exit
Taylor Rd (42), 1 km w. Ext corridors. **Pets:** Small. No
service, supervision, crate.
⊠ 🖥 🔳 ⊠

BRAMPTON

◆◆◆ Comfort Inn **M**
(905) 452-0600. **$104-$119.** 5 Rutherford Rd S. From Hwy
401, exit 410N, 11 km to Hwy 7 E (Queen St), 1 km w. Int
corridors. **Pets:** No service, supervision, crate.
(ASK) 🔳 ⊠ 🖥 🔳

◆◆◆ Holiday Inn Select **H**
(905) 792-9900. **$185-$225.** 30 Peel Centre Dr. Hwy 410 N,
exit 7 (Queen St), 2 km e. Int corridors. **Pets:** Small. No
service, supervision, crate.
(ASK) 🔳 ⊠ 🖥 🔳 🔳 🔳

BRANTFORD

◆◆◆ Comfort Inn **M** ❖
(519) 753-3100. **$89-$149.** 58 King George Rd. Just s of jct
Hwy 403 and 24. Int corridors. **Pets:** Very small, other. No
service, supervision, crate.
(ASK) ⊠ 🔳 🔳

◆◆◆ Days Inn **M** ❖
(519) 759-2700. **$80-$90, 7 days notice.** 460 Fairview Dr.
0.8 km n of Hwy 403; Wayne Gretzky Pkwy. Int corridors.
Pets: Other. Supervision.
(ASK) 🔳 ⊠ 🖥 🔳 🔳

BRIGHTON

◆ Presquile Beach Motel **M** ❖
(613) 475-1010. **$44-$66.** 243 Main St W. Hwy 401, exit
509, 4 km s on Hwy 30, 1 km w on Hwy 2. Ext corridors.
Pets: Other. No service, supervision, crate.
🖥 🔳 (CTV) 🔳

BURLINGTON

◆◆ Comfort Inn **M** ❖
(905) 639-1700. **$88-$128.** 3290 S Service Rd. Westbound
on QEW, exit Walker's Line s to Harvester Rd, w to S
Service Rd; eastbound on QEW, exit Guelph Line Rd s to
Harvester Rd, e to S Service Rd. Int corridors. **Pets:** Other.
Supervision.
(ASK) 🔳 ⊠ 🖥 🔳

◆◆◆ Holiday Inn Burlington **H** ❖
(905) 639-4443. **$110-$160.** 3063 S Service Rd. From
QEW, exit s on Guelph Line Rd to Service Rd. Int corridors.
Pets: Small. $50 deposit/room. Supervision.
(ASK) 🔳 ⊠ 🖥 🔳 🔳 🔳

(QA) ◆◆ Town & Country Motel **M** ❖
(905) 634-2383. **$45-$60, 4 days notice.** 517 Plains Rd E.
QEW, exit Plains Rd, Hwy 2 W. Ext corridors.
Pets: Medium. Supervision.
(SAVE) 🔳 🖥 🔳

CAMBRIDGE

(QA) ◆◆ Gateway Inn **M** ❖
(519) 622-1070. **$68-$150.** 650 Hespeler Rd. Hwy 401, exit
282, 0.5 km s. Int corridors. **Pets:** Dogs only. Designated
rooms, no service, supervision, crate.
(SAVE) 🔳 ⊠ 🖥 🔳 🔳

◆◆◆ Holiday Inn-Cambridge **M**
(519) 658-4601. **$116-$130.** 200 Holiday Inn Dr. Hwy 401,
exit 282, n to Groh Ave. Int corridors. **Pets:** Supervision.
⊠ 🔳 🔳 🔳 🔳

(QA) ◆◆◆◆ Langdon Hall Country House Hotel &
Spa **CI** ❖
(519) 740-2100. **$229-$325, 7 days notice.** RR 33. From
Hwy 401, exit 275, Homer Watson Blvd (Fountain St) 1 km
s to Blair Rd, follow signs 1 km to Langdon Dr. Ext/int
corridors. **Pets:** $50 one-time fee/room. Supervision.
🔳 ⊠

CHAPLEAU

◆ Riverside Motel **M** ❖
(705) 864-0440. **$60-$75.** 116 Cherry St. Ne section of
town, corner Grey and Cherry sts; on Chapleau River. Ext
corridors. **Pets:** Other. $50 deposit/room. Designated
rooms, supervision.
(ASK) 🔳 ⊠ 🖥 🔳 🔳

CHATHAM

(QA) ◆◆◆ Comfort Inn **M** ❖
(519) 352-5500. **$62-$116.** 1100 Richmond St. From Hwy
401, exit 81, Bloomfield Rd, 5 km n to Richmond St (Hwy
2). Int corridors. **Pets:** Medium, other. No service, supervision, crate.
(SAVE) 🔳 ⊠ 🖥 🔳

◆◆◆ Luxury Inn **M**
(519) 354-3366. **Call for rates.** 25 Michener Rd. From Hwy
401, exit 90 to Hwy 40, 6.5 km n to Communications Rd,
1.6 km to Hwy 2, 1.8 km w on Hwy 2; jct Hwy 2 and
Michener Rd. Int corridors. **Pets:** Small. Designated rooms,
no service, supervision, crate.
⊠ 🖥 🔳

CHATSWORTH

◆◆ Key Motel **M**
(519) 794-2350. **$65-$70.** On Hwy 6 and 10. Ext/int corridors. **Pets:** Medium. Supervision.
⊠ 🖥 🔳 ⊠ (CTV)

COBOURG

(QA) ◆◆◆ Best Western Cobourg Inn and
Convention Centre **M** ❖
(905) 372-2105. **$120-$160, 5 days notice.** 930 Burnham
St. From Hwy 401, exit 472 (Burnham St). Int corridors.
Pets: Other. No service, supervision, crate.
(SAVE) 🔳 ⊠ 🖥 🔳 🔳

CORNWALL

(AA) ◆◆◆ **Best Western Parkway Inn & Conference
Centre** Ⓜ️ ❖
(613) 932-0451. **$109-$149.** 1515 Vincent Massey Dr. From
Brookdale Ave w on Vincent Massey Dr (Hwy 2). Int corri-
dors. **Pets:** Supervision.
〔SAVE〕〔Ｓ🔘〕〔✕〕〔💻〕〔¶〕〔🖼️〕〔✕〕

◆◆ **Holiday Inn Express** Ⓜ️ ❖
(613) 937-0111. **$96-$110.** 1625 Vincent Massey Dr. From
Brookdale Ave w on Vincent Massy Dr (Hwy 2). Int corridors. **Pets:** Other. Designated rooms, supervision.
〔ASK〕〔Ｓ🔘〕〔✕〕〔🔒〕〔💻〕

(AA) ◆◆◆ **Ramada Inn & Conference
Centre** Ⓜ️ ❖
(613) 933-8000. **$95-$155.** 805 Brookdale Ave. 4 km s from
Hwy 401, exit 789. Int corridors. **Pets:** Small. Designated
rooms, supervision.
〔SAVE〕〔Ｓ🔘〕〔✕〕〔🔒〕〔💻〕〔¶〕〔🖼️〕〔✕〕

DRYDEN

(AA) ◆◆◆ **Best Western Motor Inn** Ⓜ️ ❖
(807) 223-3201. **$60-$98.** 349 Government Rd. On Hwy 17.
Ext/int corridors. **Pets:** Other. Designated rooms, no service, supervision, crate.
〔SAVE〕〔Ｓ🔘〕〔✕〕〔🔒〕〔💻〕〔¶〕〔🖼️〕

◆◆◆ **Comfort Inn** Ⓜ️ ❖
(807) 223-3893. **$76-$90.** 522 Government Rd. On Hwy 17.
Int corridors. **Pets:** Other. Designated rooms, no service,
supervision, crate.
〔ASK〕〔Ｓ🔘〕〔✕〕〔💻〕

ELLIOT LAKE

◆◆ **Dunlop Lake Lodge** Ⓜ️
(705) 848-8090. **$52-$65, 3 days notice.** 75 Dunlop Lake
Rd. Hwy 17, 38.8 km n on Hwy 108, 0.8 km w following
signs. Int corridors. **Pets:** Designated rooms, no service,
supervision, crate.
〔ASK〕〔Ｓ🔘〕〔✕〕〔¶〕〔✕〕〔🐾〕〔CTV〕

EMSDALE

(AA) ◆◆◆ **Fern Glen Inn** 〔BB〕 ❖
(705) 636-1391. **$60-$70.** RR 1. From Hwy 11, follow Fern
Glen Rd 7 km w, following signs. Int corridors.
Pets: Medium, other. Supervision.
〔✕〕〔💻〕〔✕〕〔🐾〕〔CTV〕〔☎〕

FONTHILL

◆ **Hipwell's Motel** Ⓜ️ ❖
(905) 892-3588. **$63.** 299 Regional Rd 20. 1.6 km w on
Regional Rd 20 from town centre. Ext corridors.
Pets: Other. $4 daily fee/pet. No service, supervision, crate.
〔✕〕〔🔒〕〔¶〕〔🖼️〕〔✕〕〔CTV〕

FORT ERIE

◆◆ **Comfort Inn** Ⓜ️
(905) 871-8500. **$80-$139.** 1 Hospitality Dr. Just off Walden
Blvd and QEW. Int corridors. **Pets:** Medium. Supervision.
〔ASK〕〔Ｓ🔘〕〔✕〕〔💻〕

GANANOQUE

(AA) ◆◆◆ **Country Squire Resort** Ⓜ️ ❖
(613) 382-3511. **$99-$199.** 715 King St E. On Hwy 401, exit
647 eastbound; exit 648 westbound, 1 km w on Hwy 2
(King St). Ext/int corridors. **Pets:** Small, other. Supervision.
〔SAVE〕〔Ｓ🔘〕〔✕〕〔🔒〕〔💻〕〔¶〕〔🖼️〕〔✕〕

GUELPH

(AA) ◆◆◆ **Best Western Emerald Inn** Ⓜ️
(519) 836-1331. **$109-$156.** 106 Carden St. On Carden St,
just e of Wydham. Int corridors. **Pets:** Medium. Designated
rooms, no service, supervision, crate.
〔SAVE〕〔Ｓ🔘〕〔✕〕〔🔒〕〔💻〕〔¶〕

◆◆◆ **Comfort Inn** Ⓜ️
(519) 763-1900. **$95-$105, 5 days notice.** 480 Silvercreek
Pkwy. At jct Hwy 6 and 7 (Woodlawn Rd). Int corridors.
Pets: Medium. No service, supervision, crate.
〔ASK〕〔Ｓ🔘〕〔✕〕〔🔒〕〔💻〕

◆◆◆ **Holiday Inn-Guelph** Ⓜ️ ❖
(519) 836-0231. **$129-$170.** 601 Scottsdale Dr. At jct Hwy 6
N and Stone Rd E; 8 km n of jct Hwy 401. Int corridors.
Pets: Other. Supervision.
〔ASK〕〔Ｓ🔘〕〔✕〕〔🔒〕〔💻〕〔¶〕〔🖼️〕〔✕〕

(AA) ◆◆ **Super 8 Motel-Guelph** Ⓜ️
(519) 836-5850. **$80-$1000.** 281 Woodlawn Rd W. At jct
Hwy 6 and 7. Ext/int corridors. **Pets:** Medium. Designated
rooms, no service, supervision, crate.
〔SAVE〕〔Ｓ🔘〕〔✕〕〔🔒〕〔💻〕〔¶〕

HAMILTON

◆◆◆ **Ramada Plaza Hotel** 〔Ｈ〕
(905) 528-3451. **$69-$129.** 150 King St E. At corner of
Catherine St S. Int corridors. **Pets:** Supervision.
〔ASK〕〔Ｓ🔘〕〔✕〕〔🔒〕〔💻〕〔¶〕〔🖼️〕

(AA) ◆◆◆◆ **Sheraton Hamilton** 〔Ｈ〕
(905) 529-5515. **$225-$255.** 116 King St W. Downtown at
Jackson Square shopping centre; on Hwy 6 and 8 westbound. Int corridors. **Pets:** Medium. Supervision.
〔SAVE〕〔✕〕〔🔒〕〔💻〕〔¶〕〔🖼️〕

HILTON BEACH

◆◆ **Hilton Harbour Resort** Ⓜ️ ❖
(705) 246-0063. **Call for rates.** 3117 Marks St. In Hilton
Beach; Hwy 17 to Hwy 548, follow signs. Ext corridors.
Pets: Small, dogs only. No service, supervision, crate.
〔✕〕〔🔒〕〔💻〕〔✕〕〔🐾〕

HUNTSVILLE

◆◆◆ **Comfort Inn** Ⓜ️ ❖
(705) 789-1701. **$98-$120.** 86 King William St. At jct Hwy
60. Int corridors. **Pets:** Other. Supervision.
〔ASK〕〔Ｓ🔘〕〔✕〕〔🔒〕〔💻〕

(AA) ◆◆ **Highland Court** Ⓜ️
(705) 789-4424. **$54-$85.** 208 W Main St. On Muskoka Rd
3; 0.5 km e of jct Hwy 11. Ext corridors. **Pets:** Supervision.
〔SAVE〕〔Ｓ🔘〕〔✕〕〔🔒〕

◆◆ **Tulip Motor Inn** Ⓜ ❀
(705) 789-4001. **$69-$98.** 1661 Muskoka Rd 3 N. At jct of Hwy 11 and Muskoka Rd 3 N. Ext corridors. **Pets:** Other. No service, supervision, crate.

⊠ 🔒 ⊠

INGERSOLL

◆◆◆ **Travelodge Ingersoll** Ⓜ
(519) 425-1100. **$68-$91.** 20 Samnah Crescent. From Hwy 401, exit 216 (Culloden Rd). Int corridors. **Pets:** Supervision.

🅰🆂🅺 🆂🔟 ⊠ 🔒 ▣ 🍴 ⌂

IRON BRIDGE

🅰🅰 ◆ **Red Top Motor Inn** Ⓜ ❀
(705) 843-2100. **$38-$64.** Hwy 17. 0.5 km w on Hwy 17. Ext corridors. **Pets:** Other. Supervision.

🆂🅰🆅🅴 🆂🔟 ⊠ 🍴 ⌂ ⊠ 🄲🅃🅅

JORDAN

🅰🅰 ◆◆ **Best Western Beacon Harborside Resort & Conference Centre** Ⓜ ❀
(905) 562-4155. **$129-$199, 30 days notice.** 2793 Beacon Blvd. QEW, exit 57. Int corridors. **Pets:** Other. Supervision.

🆂🅰🆅🅴 🆂🔟 ⊠ 🔒 ▣ 🍴 ⌂ ⊠ 🄲🅃🅅

KAPUSKASING

◆◆ **Comfort Inn** Ⓜ
(705) 335-8583. **$79-$97.** 172 Government Rd E. On Hwy 11, corner Burnell Rd. Int corridors. **Pets:** Medium. Supervision.

🅰🆂🅺 🆂🔟 ⊠ 🔒 ▣

KENORA

◆◆◆ **Best Western Lakeside Inn & Convention Centre** Ⓜ
(807) 468-5521. **$99-$124.** 470 First Ave S. Centre. Int corridors. **Pets:** Designated rooms, supervision.

🅰🆂🅺 🆂🔟 ⊠ ▣ ⌂ ⊠

◆◆ **Comfort Inn** Ⓜ ❀
(807) 468-8845. **$72-$84.** 1230 Hwy 17 E. 1.5 km e on Hwy 17. Int corridors. **Pets:** Medium. Designated rooms, supervision.

🅰🆂🅺 ⊠ ▣

🅰🅰 ◆◆ **Whispering Pines Motel** Ⓜ
(807) 548-4025. **$54-$67.** 5 km w of jct Hwy 17 and 71, on Hwy 17; or 15 km e on Hwy 17 from Kenora Centre. Ext corridors. **Pets:** Designated rooms, no service, supervision, crate.

🆂🅰🆅🅴 ⊠ 🔒 ▣ 🄲🅃🅅 🖉

KINGSTON

◆◆◆ **Comfort Inn** Ⓜ
(613) 546-9500. **$95-$125.** 55 Warne Crescent. Hwy 401, exit 617, Division St; 0.5 km s to Dalton Ave. Int corridors. **Pets:** Medium. Supervision.

🅰🆂🅺 🆂🔟 ⊠ 🔒 ▣

🅰🅰 ◆◆ **The Executive Motel** Ⓜ ❀
(613) 549-1620. **$56-$78, 3 days notice.** 794 Hwy 2 E. Hwy 401, exit 623, 8 km s, 2 km e Hwy 2. Ext corridors. **Pets:** Small. $6 one-time fee/room. Designated rooms, no service, supervision, crate.

🆂🅰🆅🅴 ⊠ 🔒 ⌂

◆◆◆ **Holiday Inn Kingston Waterfront** 🄷 ❀
(613) 549-8400. **$160-$190.** 1 Princess St. Centre, corner Ontario St. Int corridors. **Pets:** Other. Designated rooms, no service, supervision, crate.

🅰🆂🅺 🆂🔟 ⊠ 🔒 ▣ 🍴 ⌂

◆◆ **The North Nook Bed & Breakfast** 🄱🄱 ❀
(613) 547-8061. **$105-$135.** 83 Earl St. Between Wellington and Bagot sts. Int corridors. **Pets:** Medium, dogs only. $20 daily fee/pet, $20 one-time fee/pet. No service, supervision, crate.

⊠ 🖉

🅰🅰 ◆◆◆ **Peachtree Inn** Ⓜ ❀
(613) 546-4411. **$100-$110, 7 days notice.** 1187 Princess St. Hwy 401, exit 615, 4 km sw. Int corridors. **Pets:** Designated rooms, no service, supervision, crate.

🆂🅰🆅🅴 🆂🔟 ⊠ 🔒 ▣

KIRKLAND LAKE

◆◆ **Comfort Inn** Ⓜ ❀
(705) 567-4909. **$80-$110.** 455 Government Rd W. On Rt 66, 12.8 km e of Rt 11, just w of town centre. Int corridors. **Pets:** Other. Designated rooms, supervision.

🅰🆂🅺 🆂🔟 ⊠ 🔒 ▣

KITCHENER

◆◆ **Aram's "Roots and Wings"** 🄱🄱 ❀
(519) 743-4557. **$55-$95.** 11 Sunbridge Crescent. Hwy 86 N, exit University E, 1 km to Bridge St, 0.5 km s to Bridal Trail, then directly e. Int corridors. **Pets:** Other. Supervision.

⊠ 🔒 ⌂ ⊠

◆◆◆ **Comfort Inn** Ⓜ ❀
(519) 894-3500. **$83-$125.** 2899 King St E. Jct Weber St, Fairway Rd and Hwy 8; 5.6 km n of Hwy 401 via Hwy 8 and Weber St. Int corridors. **Pets:** Medium. No service, supervision, crate.

🅰🆂🅺 🆂🔟 ⊠ 🔒 ▣

◆◆ **The Conestoga Howard Johnson Hotel** Ⓜ
(519) 893-1234. **$79-$129.** 1333 Weber St E. 6.4 km w of Hwy 401, exit 278 to Kitchener, on Hwy 8 W, exit Weber St W. Ext/int corridors. **Pets:** Supervision.

🅰🆂🅺 🆂🔟 ⊠ 🔒 ▣ 🍴 ⌂

🅰🅰 ◆◆◆ **Four Points Hotel Sheraton** 🄷
(519) 744-4141. **$140-$165.** 105 King St E. Downtown; opposite Kitchener Farmer's Market, corner of King and Benton sts. Int corridors. **Pets:** Supervision.

🆂🅰🆅🅴 🆂🔟 ⊠ 🔒 ▣ 🍴 ⌂ ⊠

◆◆◆ **Holiday Inn-Kitchener** Ⓜ
(519) 893-1211. **$116-$135.** 30 Fairway Rd S. 5.6 km w off Hwy 401, exit 278 via Hwy 8W to Weber St exit, just e on King St. Int corridors. **Pets:** Supervision.

⊠ 🔒 ▣ 🍴 ⌂ ⊠

◆◆◆ **Radisson Hotel Kitchener** M ☙
(519) 849-9500. **$109-$119.** 2960 King St E. 6 km w of
Hwy 401, exit 35 on Hwy 8 W Weber St exit. Int corridors.
Pets: Supervision.

⊠ 🯁 💻 🍴 🛋

CAA ◆◆ **Rodeway Suites Conestoga** M
(519) 895-2272. **$65-$75.** 55 New Dundee Rd. Directly n of
jct Hwy 401 and Homer Watson Blvd (exit 275). Int corridors. **Pets:** No service, supervision, crate.

SAVE S⊡ ⊠ 🯁 💻

LEAMINGTON

◆◆◆ **Comfort Inn** M ☙
(519) 326-9071. **$86-$108.** 279 Erie St. Directly s of jct Hwy
3 and Erie St; on direct route to Point Pelee National Park.
Int corridors. **Pets:** Small. Designated rooms, no service,
supervision, crate.

ASK S⊡ ⊠

LONDON

CAA ◆◆◆ **Best Western Lamplighter
Inn** M ☙
(519) 681-7151. **$105-$159.** 591 Wellington Rd S. 3.7 km n
off Hwy 401, exit 186. Ext/int corridors. **Pets:** Medium, dogs
only. No service, supervision, crate.

SAVE S⊡ ⊠ 🯁 💻 🍴 🛋

◆◆ **Comfort Hotel** M
(519) 661-0233. **$75-$135.** 374 Dundas St. Between Waterloo and Colburne. Int corridors. **Pets:** No service, supervision, crate.

ASK S⊡ ⊠ 🯁 💻

◆◆◆ **Comfort Inn** M ☙
(519) 685-9300. **$80-$170.** 1156 Wellington Rd. N off Hwy
401, exit 186B. Int corridors. **Pets:** Other. Designated
rooms, no service, supervision, crate.

ASK S⊡ ⊠ 💻

◆◆◆◆ **Delta London Armouries** H ☙
(519) 679-6111. **$129-$129.** 325 Dundas St. On Hwy 2. Int
corridors. **Pets:** Small, other. No service, supervision, crate.

⊠ 💻 🍴 🛋 ⊠

◆◆◆ **Quality Suites** M ☙
(519) 680-1024. **$115-$165.** 1120 Dearness Dr. From Hwy
401, exit 186B, Wellington Rd N, 1.6 km to Dearness Dr. Int
corridors. **Pets:** No service, supervision, crate.

ASK S⊡ ⊠ 💻

CAA ◆◆◆ **StationPark All Suite Hotel** H
(519) 642-4444. **$145-$145.** 242 Pall Mall St. From Hwy
401, exit Wellington Rd N, 9 km to Pall Mall St (jct Wellington Rd and Pall Mall St). Int corridors. **Pets:** No service,
supervision, crate.

SAVE S⊡ ⊠ 💻 🍴

MARATHON

CAA ◆◆ **Peninsula Inn** M ☙
(807) 229-0651. **$60-$78, 3 days notice.** On Hwy 17, 2.4
km w of jct Hwy 626. Ext corridors. **Pets:** Small. No service,
supervision, crate.

SAVE S⊡ ⊠

MISSISSAUGA

◆◆◆ **Comfort Inn** M
(905) 624-6900. **$95-$123.** 1500 Matheson Blvd. Hwy 401,
exit Dixie Rd, then s. Int corridors. **Pets:** Small. No service,
supervision, crate.

ASK S⊡ ⊠ 🯁 💻 🍴

CAA ◆◆◆◆ **Delta Meadowvale Resort and
Conference Centre** H
(905) 821-1981. **$89-$209.** 6750 Mississauga Rd. S of jct
Hwy 401W and Mississauga Rd, exit 336. Int corridors.
Pets: Supervision.

SAVE ⊠ 🯁 💻 🍴 🛋 ⊠

CAA ◆◆◆ **Four Points Hotel Sheraton Toronto
Airport** H
(905) 624-1144. **$129-$149.** 5444 Dixie Rd. 1 km s of jct
Hwy 401 and Dixie Rd. Int corridors. **Pets:** Small. Supervision.

SAVE ⊠ 🯁 💻 🍴 🛋 ⊠

◆◆◆ **Holiday Inn Toronto West** M ☙
(905) 890-5700. **$105-$132, 30 days notice.** 100 Britannia
Rd E. Jct Hwy 401 and 10; from Hwy 401, exit 10S to
Britannia Rd E. Int corridors. **Pets:** Small. Designated
rooms, supervision.

⊠ 🯁 💻 🍴

CAA ◆◆◆ **Novotel Hotel Mississauga** H ☙
(905) 896-1000. **$134-$134.** 3670 Hurontario St. On Hwy
10 at Burnhamthorpe Rd; from Hwy 401, exit Hwy 10 S, 5
km. Int corridors. **Pets:** Medium, other. $15 daily fee/room.
No service, supervision, crate.

SAVE ⊠ 🍴 🛋 ⊠

CAA ◆◆◆ **Radisson Hotel
Toronto-Mississauga** H ☙
(905) 858-2424. **$98-$145, 30 days notice.** 2501 Argentia
Rd. Sw of Hwy 401 and Mississauga Rd, corner Derry and
Argentia rds. Ext/int corridors. **Pets:** Small. Designated
rooms, no service, supervision, crate.

⊠ 🯁 💻 🍴 🛋

◆◆◆ **Sandalwood Hotel & Suites** M
(905) 238-9600. **$134-$134.** 5050 Orbitor Dr. From Eglinton
Ave and Renforth Dr, 2.3 km w on Eglinton Ave. Int corridors. **Pets:** Designated rooms, supervision.

ASK S⊡ ⊠ 🯁 💻

CAA ◆◆◆◆ **Sheraton Gateway Hotel In Toronto
International Airport** H ☙
(905) 672-7000. **$197-$227.** Box 3000. Int corridors.
Pets: Small. No service, supervision, crate.

SAVE ⊠ 🯂 💻 🍴 🛋

◆◆◆ **Toronto Airport Hilton** H
(905) 677-9900. **$169-$169.** 5875 Airport Rd. From Hwy
401, exit Dixon Rd, 3.5 km w; 1 km from Toronto Pearson
International Airport. Int corridors. **Pets:** Supervision.

ASK ⊠ 💻 🍴 🛋

MONETVILLE

◆◆ **Memquisit Lodge Inc** 🄲 🐾
(705) 898-2355. **$75-$168.** 20.8 km ne on w arm of Lake Nipissing on Hwy 64 and Memquisit Lodge Rd, or 36.8 km sw off Hwy 17 on Hwy 64. Ext corridors. **Pets:** Other. Supervision.
Ⓐ🅂�🄐 🅂🄳 🄴 🍴 ⊠ 🄰🄲 🄲🅃🅅 🄩

MOUNT HOPE

◆◆◆ **Mount Hope/Hamilton Airport Super 8
    Motel** 🄼
(905) 679-3355. **$70-$90, 7 days notice.** 2975 Homestead Dr. At jct Hwy 6S and Homestead Dr. Int corridors. **Pets:** No service, supervision, crate.
Ⓐ🅂🄚 🅂🄳 ⊠ 🄴

NIAGARA FALLS METROPOLITAN AREA

NIAGARA FALLS

ⓒ🄰🄰 ◆◆ **Best Western Fallsview Motor
    Hotel** 🄼🄸 🐾
(905) 356-0551. **$129-$249, 3 days notice.** 5551 Murray St. Just n on Murray St from jct Niagara Pkwy. Ext/int corridors. **Pets:** No service, supervision, crate.
🅂🄰🅅🄴 🅂🄳 ⊠ 🍴 🄬 ⊠ 🄲🅃🅅

ⓒ🄰🄰 ◆◆ **Camelot Inn** 🄼 🐾
(905) 354-3754. **$49-$229.** 5640 Stanley Ave. Just n of Hwy 20, n on Stanley Ave; just s of Hwy 420. Ext corridors. **Pets:** Medium, other. No service, supervision, crate.
🅂🄰🅅🄴 🅂🄳 ⊠ 🄴 🄬 🄩

◆ **Glengate Motel** 🄼
(905) 357-1333. **$50-$130, 3 days notice.** 5534 Stanley Ave. Just.s of Hwy 420 and Stanley Ave. Ext corridors. **Pets:** No service, supervision, crate.
Ⓐ🅂🄚 🅂🄳 ⊠ 🄴 🄬

ⓒ🄰🄰 ◆◆◆ **Holiday Inn-By The Falls** 🄼🄸 🐾
(905) 356-1333. **$115-$255.** 5339 Murray Hill at Buchanan Ave. Just w from the falls on Murray St; adjacent to Skylon Tower. Int corridors. **Pets:** Supervision.
🅂🄰🅅🄴 🅂🄳 ⊠ 🍴 🄬

ⓒ🄰🄰 ◆ **Inn On The Niagara Parkway** 🄼
(905) 295-4371. **$69-$189.** 7857 Niagara River Pkwy. 2 km s of Horseshoe Falls. Ext corridors. **Pets:** Medium. No service, supervision, crate.
🅂🄳 ⊠ 🄬 🄲🅃🅅

ⓒ🄰🄰 ◆◆ **Niagara Parkway Court Motel** 🄼 🐾
(905) 295-3331. **$49-$149.** 3708 Main St. 2.5 km s of the falls on the Niagara Pkwy. Ext corridors. **Pets:** Large. $15 daily fee/room. Designated rooms, supervision.
🅂🄰🅅🄴 🅂🄳 ⊠ 🄴 🄬 🄩

ⓒ🄰🄰 ◆◆◆ **Peninsula Inn & Resort** 🄷 🐾
(905) 354-8812. **$109-$199.** 7373 Niagara Square Dr. QEW, exit McLeod Rd, just w. Int corridors. **Pets:** Very small. $10 daily fee/room. No service, supervision, crate.
🅂🄰🅅🄴 🅂🄳 ⊠ 🄴 🄬 🍴 🄬

NEWMARKET

◆◆ **Comfort Inn** 🄼 🐾
(905) 895-3355. **$80-$135.** 1230 Journey's End Cir. From Hwy 404, exit Davis Dr. Int corridors. **Pets:** No service, supervision, crate.
Ⓐ🅂🄚 🅂🄳 ⊠ 🄴 🄬

ⓒ🄰🄰 ◆◆ **Stanley Motor Inn** 🄼 🐾
(905) 358-9238. **$65-$150.** 6220 Stanley Ave. 2 blks from the falls, w of Skylon Tower. Ext corridors. **Pets:** Small. $20 deposit/room, $10 daily fee/pet, $10 one-time fee/pet. No service, supervision, crate.
🅂🄰🅅🄴 ⊠ 🄴 🄬 🄩

◆◆ **Thriftlodge** 🄼
(905) 358-6243. **$80-$220.** 6000 Stanley Ave. 1.3 km w on Hwy 20, just s. Ext/int corridors. **Pets:** Supervision.
Ⓐ🅂🄚 🅂🄳 ⊠ 🄴 🄬

NIAGARA ON THE LAKE

◆◆◆ **Gate House Hotel** 🄲🄸
(905) 468-3263. **Call for rates, 7 days notice.** 142 Queen St. At jct Gate. Int corridors. **Pets:** Medium. Designated rooms, no service, supervision, crate.

ST. CATHARINES

ⓒ🄰🄰 ◆◆◆ **Comfort Inn** 🄼🄸 🐾
(905) 687-8890. **$109-$189.** 2 Dunlop Dr. QEW, exit 46 (Lake St), between Lake and Geneva sts. Int corridors. **Pets:** Other. No service, supervision, crate.
🅂🄰🅅🄴 ⊠ 🄍 🄴 🄬 🍴

◆◆ **Holiday Inn St Catharines** 🄼🄸
(905) 934-8000. **$152-$152.** 2 N Service Rd. Just e of QEW, Lake St exit. Int corridors. **Pets:** Medium. Supervision.
Ⓐ🅂🄚 🅂🄳 ⊠ 🄴 🄬 🍴 🄬

ⓒ🄰🄰 ◆◆ **Howard Johnson Hotel & Conference
    Centre** 🄼🄸 🐾
(905) 934-5400. **$89-$199.** 89 Meadowvale Dr. Jct QEW and Lake St. Int corridors. **Pets:** Medium. $5 daily fee/room. Designated rooms, no service, supervision, crate.
🅂🄰🅅🄴 🅂🄳 ⊠ 🄴 🄬 🍴 🄬 ⊠

ⓒ🄰🄰 ◆◆ **Ramada Parkway Inn and Conference
    Centre** 🄼🄸 🐾
(905) 688-2324. **$110-$200.** 327 Ontario St. 0.8 km s of jct QEW and Ontario St, exit 47. Int corridors. **Pets:** No service, supervision, crate.
🅂🄰🅅🄴 🅂🄳 ⊠ 🄴 🄬 🍴 🄬

THOROLD

◆◆◆ Niagara Suites Hotel Ⓜ ❀
(905) 984-8484. **$179-$259.** 3530 Schmon Pkwy. Hwy 406, exit St. David's Rd W. Int corridors. **Pets:** No service, supervision, crate.
(ASK) (S🅿) (✕) (🛏) (💻) (🍽) (🏊)

WELLAND

◆◆ Comfort Inn Ⓜ ❀
(905) 732-4811. **$85-$100.** 870 Niagara St. 2.5 km n. Int corridors. **Pets:** Designated rooms, no service, supervision, crate.
(ASK) (S🅿) (✕) (🛏) (💻)

❀   END METROPOLITAN AREA   ❀

NORTH BAY

Ⓒ **◆◆◆ Best Western North Bay** Ⓜ ❀
(705) 474-5800. **$99-$199.** 700 Lakeshore Dr. On Hwy 11B, 4 km n of jct Hwy 11, Lakeshore Dr exit. Int corridors. **Pets:** Other. Supervision.
(SAVE) (S🅿) (✕) (🛏) (💻) (🍽) (🏊)

◆◆◆ Comfort Inn Ⓜ
(705) 494-9444. **$93-$103.** 676 Lakeshore Dr. On Hwy 11B (Lakeshore Dr), 4 km n of jct Hwy 11. Int corridors. **Pets:** No service, supervision, crate.
(ASK) (✕) (💻)

◆◆◆ Comfort Inn Ⓜ
(705) 476-5400. **$89-$140.** 1200 O'Brien St. 3 km e on Hwy 11 and 17 bypass at O'Brien St exit. Int corridors. **Pets:** Small. Designated rooms, no service, supervision, crate.
(ASK) (S🅿) (✕) (💻)

◆◆◆ Travelodge North Bay Ⓜ ❀
(705) 495-1133. **$103-$130.** 1525 Seymour St. At jct Hwy 11, 17 and Seymour St. Int corridors. **Pets:** Other. No service, supervision, crate.
(ASK) (S🅿) (✕) (🛏) (💻) (🏊)

OAKVILLE

Ⓒ **◆◆◆ Quality Hotel & Suites-Oakville** Ⓜ
(905) 847-6667. **$129-$149.** 754 Bronte Rd. QEW, exit 111, Bronte Rd (Hwy 25), 0.4 km s. Int corridors. **Pets:** No service, supervision, crate.
(SAVE) (S🅿) (✕) (🛏) (🍽) (🏊)

ORILLIA

◆◆◆ Comfort Inn Ⓜ ❀
(705) 327-7744. **$99-$126.** 75 Progress Dr (RR #1). Corner of Progress Dr and Memorial Ave; from Hwy 11 N, exit 8, on Memorial Ave. Int corridors. **Pets:** Small. No service, supervision, crate.
(ASK) (S🅿) (✕) (🛏) (💻)

Ⓒ **◆◆ Econolodge** Ⓜ ❀
(705) 326-3554. **$60-$120.** 265 Memorial Ave. 0.5 km n of Hwy 12. Int corridors. **Pets:** Supervision.
(SAVE) (S🅿) (✕) (🛏) (💻)

OSHAWA

◆◆◆ Comfort Inn Ⓜ ❀
(905) 434-5000. **$124-$154.** 605 Bloor St W. Hwy 401, exit 416 (Park Rd), s to Bloor St, 0.8 km w. Int corridors. **Pets:** $100 deposit/room. Supervision.
(ASK) (S🅿) (✕) (🛏) (💻)

Ⓒ **◆◆ Oshawa Travelodge** Ⓜ
(905) 436-9500. **$125-$160.** 940 Champlain Ave. Hwy 401, exit 412, Thickson Rd N. Int corridors. **Pets:** Medium. Designated rooms, no service, supervision, crate.
(SAVE) (S🅿) (✕) (🛏) (💻) (🏊)

OTTAWA METROPOLITAN AREA

GLOUCESTER

◆◆ Comfort Inn Ⓜ ❀
(613) 744-2900. **$87-$116.** 1252 Michael St. Hwy 417, exit 115, St Laurent Blvd n to Lemieux St. Int corridors. **Pets:** Medium. Designated rooms, no service, supervision, crate.
(ASK) (S🅿) (✕) (💻)

Ⓒ **◆◆ Travelodge** Ⓜ ❀
(613) 745-1133. **$109.** 1486 Innes Rd. Hwy 417, exit 112 (Innes Rd), just e. Int corridors. **Pets:** Medium. Designated rooms, supervision.
(✕) (🛏) (💻) (🍽) (🏊)

NEPEAN

Ⓒ **◆◆ Monterey Inn Resort** Ⓜ ❀
(613) 226-5813. **$87-$105.** 0.5 km s of Hunt Club Rd. Ext corridors. **Pets:** $15 daily fee/pet. Designated rooms, no service, supervision, crate.
(SAVE) (✕) (🛏) (💻) (🍽) (🏊) (✕)

◆◆ Rideau Heights Motor Inn Ⓜ ❀
(613) 226-4152. **$86-$96.** 72 Rideau Heights Dr. Hwy 16 0.5 km n of Hunt Club Rd. Ext corridors. **Pets:** Small, other. $50 deposit/pet, $10 daily fee/pet. Designated rooms, no service, supervision, crate
(S🅿) (✕) (🛏)

OTTAWA

Albert House Inn [BB]
(613) 236-4479. **$76-$116.** 478 Albert St. Between Bay St and Bronson Ave. Int corridors. **Pets:** Dogs only. $5 daily fee/room. Supervision.

Days Inn-Downtown (Ottawa) [M]
(613) 789-5555. **$95-$125.** 319 Rideau St. Between Nelson St and King Edward Ave. Ext/int corridors. **Pets:** Designated rooms, no service, supervision, crate.

Delta Ottawa Hotel and Suites [H]
(613) 238-6000. **$149-$149.** 361 Queen St. Corner Lyon St. Int corridors. **Pets:** Small. Supervision.

Les Suites Hotel Ottawa [A]
(613) 232-2000. **$195-$230.** 130 Besserer St. Between Nicholas and Waller sts. Int corridors. **Pets:** Designated rooms, supervision.

Lord Elgin Hotel [H]
(613) 235-3333. **$106-$160.** 100 Elgin St. Between Laurier Ave and Slater St, opposite National Arts Centre. Int corridors. **Pets:** Supervision.

Novotel Ottawa Hotel [H]
(613) 230-3033. **$165-$165.** 33 Nicholas St. Corner Daly Ave. Int corridors. **Pets:** Medium. No service, supervision, crate.

Ottawa Marriott [H]
(613) 238-1122. **$199-$199.** 100 Kent St. Corner Queen St. Int corridors. **Pets:** Small. No service, supervision, crate.

Quality Hotel [M]
(613) 789-7511. **$130-$165.** 290 Rideau St. Corner King Edward Ave. Int corridors. **Pets:** No service, supervision, crate.

Ramada Hotel & Suites [H]
(613) 238-1331. **$91-$101.** 111 Cooper St. Corner Cartier St. Int corridors. **Pets:** Designated rooms, no service, supervision, crate.

Sheraton Ottawa Hotel [H]
(613) 238-1500. **$140-$140.** 150 Albert St. Corner O'Connor St. Int corridors. **Pets:** Small. No service, supervision, crate.

Southway Inn [M]
(613) 737-0811. **$92-$118, 3 days notice.** 2431 Bank St. On Hwy 31, corner of Hunt Club Rd. Int corridors. **Pets:** Other. $5 daily fee/pet. No service, supervision, crate.

Webb's Motel [M]
(613) 728-1881. **$70-$90.** 1705 Carling Ave. 0.5 km n on Maitland Ave from jct Hwy 417, exit 126, then 0.5 km e. Ext/int corridors. **Pets:** Supervision.

The Westin, Ottawa [H]
(613) 560-7000. **$149-$195.** 11 Colonel By Dr. Corner Rideau St, adjacent to Rideau Centre Complex. Int corridors. **Pets:** Small, other. No service, supervision, crate.

❀ END METROPOLITAN AREA ❀

OWEN SOUND

Comfort Inn [M]
(519) 371-5500. **$87-$127.** 955 9th Ave E. Jct Hwy 6/10/21/26. Int corridors. **Pets:** Designated rooms, supervision.

Crystal Motel [M]
(519) 372-2929. **$65-$100.** 672 10th St W. 2.2 km w on 10th St W (Hwy 6 and 21) from jct Hwy 6, 26 and 10. Ext corridors. **Pets:** Medium. Supervision.

Owen Sound Motor Inn [M]
(519) 371-3011. **$69-$125.** 485 9th Ave E. From jct Hwy 6/10/26/21; follow Hwy 6 and 10 1 km s. Int corridors. **Pets:** Supervision.

Travelodge [M]
(519) 371-9297. **Call for rates.** 880 10th St E. At jct of Hwy 6/10/21/26. Int corridors. **Pets:** Medium. Designated rooms, no service, supervision, crate.

PARRY SOUND

Comfort Inn [M]
(705) 746-6221. **$95-$105.** 120 Bowes St. Jct Hwy 69 and Bowes St. Int corridors. **Pets:** Medium. Designated rooms, no service, supervision, crate.

Jolly Roger Inn [M]
(705) 378-2461. **$89-$105, 3 days notice.** Hwy 69. 10 km s of Parry Sound Centre. Ext/int corridors. **Pets:** Designated rooms, no service, supervision, crate.

Sunny Point Cottages & Inn [X]
(705) 378-2505. **$650-$1722, 30 days notice.** Rosseau Rd. 16 km s on Trans Canada Hwy 69 to Blackstone and Crane Lake Rd, then 6 km w following signs. Ext corridors. **Pets:** Designated rooms, supervision.

PEMBROKE

◆◆ **Best Western Pembroke Inn & Conference Centre** Ⓜ ❀
(613) 735-0131. **$98-$128.** One International Dr. At jct of Hwy 17 and 41. Int corridors. **Pets:** Medium. $10 one-time fee/room. Designated rooms, no service, supervision, crate.

(ASK) (S◯) (✕) (📱) (💻) (♨) (🍴) (🛏) (✕) (CTV)

◆◆ **Colonial Fireside Inn** Ⓜ ❀
(613) 732-3623. **$45-$78.** 1350 Pembroke St W. 5 km n on Forest Lea Rd from jct Hwy 17, then just e. Ext corridors. **Pets:** Medium. $5 daily fee/pet, $5 one-time fee/pet. Designated rooms, no service, supervision, crate.

(✕) (📱) (💻) (🛏)

(CAA) ◆◆ **Comfort Inn** Ⓜ ❀
(613) 735-1057. **$65-$75.** 959 Pembroke St E. 1.8 km e of town centre on Old Hwy 17. Int corridors. **Pets:** Medium. No service, supervision, crate.

(SAVE) (S◯) (✕) (📱)

PETERBOROUGH

(CAA) ◆◆◆ **Comfort Inn** Ⓜ
(705) 740-7000. **$105-$135.** 1209 Lansdowne St W. On Lansdowne St, 0.6 km w of jct Hwy 28. Int corridors. **Pets:** Designated rooms, supervision.

(SAVE) (S◯) (✕) (📱) (💻) (🍴) (🛏)

◆◆◆ **Holiday Inn Peterborough Waterfront** Ⓜ ❀
(705) 743-1144. **$109-$136.** 150 George St N. From Charlotte and George (clock tower), 1 km s. Int corridors. **Pets:** No service, supervision, crate.

(✕) (📱) (💻) (🍴) (🛏) (✕)

◆◆ **King Bethune House** BB ❀
(705) 743-4101. **$75-$155, 4 days notice.** 270 King St. From Charlotte and George (Clock Tower) s on George to King St, then w. Int corridors. **Pets:** Other. $10 daily fee/pet. Supervision.

(✕) (📱) (✕)

(CAA) ◆◆ **Quality Inn** Ⓜ
(705) 748-6801. **$95-$125.** 1074 Lansdowne St W. On Lansdowne; 3 km from jct Hwy 115 and bypass. Int corridors. **Pets:** Supervision.

(SAVE) (S◯) (✕) (💻)

◆◆ **Robyn's Motel** Ⓜ
(705) 745-3225. **Call for rates.** 1136 Hwy 7E. On Hwy 7, 2.5 km e of Television Rd. Ext corridors. **Pets:** No service, supervision, crate.

(✕) (📱) (CTV)

PICKERING

◆◆ **Comfort Inn** Ⓜ ❀
(905) 831-6200. **$125-$145.** 533 Kingston Rd. Hwy 401, exit 394 N (White's Rd), to Hwy 2, 0.5 km w. Int corridors. **Pets:** Designated rooms, supervision.

(ASK) (S◯) (✕) (📱) (💻)

PLANTAGENET

◆◆ **Motel De Champlain** Ⓜ
(613) 673-5220. **$65-$78.** 200 Hwy 17. On Hwy 17 at jct CR 9. Ext/int corridors. **Pets:** Medium. Supervision.

(ASK) (S◯) (✕) (📱) (🍴)

PORT HOPE

◆◆ **The Carlyle Inn** Ⓗ ❀
(905) 885-8686. **$89-$169, 3 days notice.** 86 John St. At jct of Augusta, just s of Hwy 2. Int corridors. **Pets:** Medium. Supervision.

(✕) (📱) (🍴)

(CAA) ◆◆◆ **Comfort Inn** Ⓜ ❀
(905) 885-7000. **$105-$135, 7 days notice.** At jct Hwy 401 and 28, exit 464. Int corridors. **Pets:** Very small. Designated rooms, no service, supervision, crate.

(SAVE) (S◯) (✕) (📱) (💻)

◆◆◆ **The Hill & Dale Manor** BB
(905) 885-8686. **$89-$169, 3 days notice.** 47 Pine St S. Just s of Hwy 2. Int corridors. **Pets:** Very small. Designated rooms, no service, supervision, crate.

(✕)

PROVIDENCE BAY

(CAA) ◆ **Huron Sands Motel** Ⓜ ❀
(705) 377-4616. **$65-$73, 3 days notice.** 5216 Hwy 551 General Delivery. Centre, on Hwy 551; 27.2 km w of South Baymouth, via 10th Side Rd, following signs. Ext corridors. **Pets:** Other. No service, supervision, crate.

(📱) (✕) (🌀)

RICHARDS LANDING

◆ **The Clansmen Motel** Ⓜ ❀
(705) 246-2581. **$45-$65.** In Richards Landing; Hwy 548, just e. Ext corridors. **Pets:** Medium. Supervision.

(S◯) (✕) (📱) (💻) (✕) (🎿) (🌀)

ROSSPORT

◆◆ **The Willows Inn Bed & Breakfast** BB
(807) 824-3389. **$65-$125.** 1 Main St. Centre. Int corridors. **Pets:** Designated rooms, no service, supervision, crate.

(✕) (🎿) (CTV)

SARNIA

(CAA) ◆◆ **Best Western Guildwood Inn** Ⓜ ❀
(519) 337-7577. **$70-$75, 3 days notice.** 1400 Venetian Blvd. 1 km e of Bluewater Bridge. Ext/int corridors. **Pets:** Other. Supervision.

(SAVE) (S◯) (✕) (📱) (💻) (🍴) (🛏) (✕)

(CAA) ◆◆◆ **The Drawbridge Inn** Ⓜ
(519) 337-7571. **$100-$100.** 283 N Christina St. 1.5 km s of Hwy 402, Christina St exit. Int corridors. **Pets:** Small. Supervision.

(SAVE) (S◯) (✕) (📱) (💻) (🍴) (🛏)

◆◆◆ **Holiday Inn-Sarnia** Ⓜ
(519) 336-4130. **$114.** 1498 Venetian Blvd. E of Bluewater Bridge. Int corridors. **Pets:** Designated rooms, supervision.

(✕) (📱) (💻) (🍴) (🛏) (✕)

SAULT STE. MARIE

◆◆ Ambassador Motel M ❀
(705) 759-6199. **$59-$84.** 1275 Great Northern Rd. 6.4 km n on Hwy 17. Ext corridors. **Pets:** Medium. $5 daily fee/pet. Designated rooms, no service, supervision, crate.
⊠ 🖥 💻 ⌦ ⊠

(CAA) ◆ Bel-Air Motel M ❀
(705) 945-7950. **$50-$75.** 398 Pim St. 2 km n on Hwy 17B. Ext corridors. **Pets:** Medium. $25 deposit/room, $5 daily fee/room, $5 one-time fee/room. No service, supervision, crate.
SAVE S🔒 ⊠ 🖥

◆◆ Comfort Inn M ❀
(705) 759-8000. **$96-$109.** 333 Great Northern Rd. 3.6 km n on Hwy 17B. Ext/int corridors. **Pets:** Other. Designated rooms, supervision.
ASK S🔒 ⊠ 🖥 💻 ⊠

◆◆◆ Glenview Vacation Cottages C
(705) 759-3436. **$89-$120, 5 days notice.** 2611 Great Northern Rd. 9.6 km n on Hwy 17. Ext corridors. **Pets:** Small. Designated rooms, no service, supervision, crate.
⊠ 🖥 ⌦ ⊠

◆◆◆ Holiday Inn M ❀
(705) 949-0611. **$143-$180.** 208 St. Marys River Dr. On the waterfront, behind Station Mall. Int corridors. **Pets:** No service, supervision, crate.
ASK S🔒 ⊠ 🖥 💻 🍽 ⌦ ⊠

(CAA) ◆ Northlander Motel M ❀
(705) 254-6452. **$50-$77.** 243 Great Northern Rd. 3 km n on Hwy 17B. Ext corridors. **Pets:** Other. No service, supervision, crate.
SAVE ⊠ 🖥

◆◆ Ramada Inn M
(705) 942-2500. **$89-$119, 5 days notice.** 229 Great Northern Rd. 3 km n on Hwy 17B. Int corridors. **Pets:** Designated rooms, no service, supervision, crate.
ASK S🔒 ⊠ 🖥 💻 🍽 ⌦ ⊠

◆ Satelite Motel M ❀
(705) 759-2897. **$50-$95, 3 days notice.** 248 Great Northern Rd. 3 km n on Hwy 17B. Ext corridors. **Pets:** Medium, other. Supervision.
⊠ 🖥

(CAA) ◆◆◆ Travelodge Suites M ❀
(705) 759-1400. **$105-$120.** 332 Bay St. Opposite Station Mall. Int corridors. **Pets:** Supervision.
SAVE S🔒 ⊠ 🖥 💻

SIMCOE

◆◆◆ Comfort Inn M
(519) 426-2611. **$80-$100.** 85 The Queensway E. 0.5 km e on Hwy 3. Int corridors. **Pets:** Medium. No service, supervision, crate.
ASK S🔒 ⊠ 🖥

ST. THOMAS

◆◆◆ Comfort Inn M ❀
(519) 633-4082. **$69-$85.** 100 Centennial Ave. 6.5 km e on Hwy 3. Int corridors. **Pets:** Medium. $50 deposit/pet. No service, supervision, crate.
ASK ⊠ 🖥 💻

SUDBURY

◆◆ Comfort Inn M ❀
(705) 522-1101. **$100-$130.** 2171 Regent St S. 5 km s on Hwy 46. Int corridors. **Pets:** Other. No service, supervision, crate.
ASK S🔒 ⊠ 💻

◆◆ Comfort Inn M ❀
(705) 560-4502. **$80-$120, 7 days notice.** 440 Second Ave N. The Kingsway at Second Ave. Int corridors. **Pets:** Medium, other. Designated rooms, no service, supervision, crate.
ASK S🔒 ⊠ 🖿

◆◆ Ramada Inn Sudbury H ❀
(705) 675-1123. **$109-$135.** 85 St. Anne Rd. Centre; St Anne Rd and Notre Dame Ave. Int corridors. **Pets:** No service, supervision, crate.
ASK S🔒 ⊠ 🖥 💻 🍽 ⌦

(CAA) ◆◆ Travelodge Hotel Sudbury M ❀
(705) 522-1100. **$100-$112.** 1401 Paris St. 1.5 km n of jct Hwy 69. Int corridors. **Pets:** Other. Designated rooms, supervision.
SAVE S🔒 ⊠ 🖥 💻 🍽 ⌦

THESSALON

(CAA) ◆ Carolyn Beach Motel M ❀
(705) 842-3330. **$60-$783.** One Lakeside Dr. Just w on Hwy 17, at jct Hwy 17B. Ext corridors. **Pets:** Supervision.
SAVE S🔒 ⊠ 🖥 💻 🍽 ⊠ 🐾

THUNDER BAY

(CAA) ◆◆◆ Best Western Nor'Wester Resort Hotel M ❀
(807) 473-9123. **$99-$119.** 2080 Hwy 61. 9.2 km sw of jct Hwy 11, 17 and 61 at Loch Lomond Rd. Int corridors. **Pets:** Designated rooms, no service, supervision, crate.
SAVE S🔒 ⊠ 🖥 💻 🍽 ⌦ ⊠

◆◆◆ Comfort Inn M ❀
(807) 475-3155. **$110-$140, 5 days notice.** 660 W Arthur St. Jct Hwy 11, 17 and 61, just e. Int corridors. **Pets:** Other. Designated rooms, supervision.
ASK S🔒 ⊠ 💻

◆ Pinebrook Bed & Breakfast BB
(807) 683-6114. **$45-$75.** 134 Mitchell Rd. 4.3 km n on Hwy 527, follow signs on dirt road for 1.8 km. Int corridors. **Pets:** Very small. No service, supervision, crate.
⊠ ⊠ 🐾 CTV 🖨

◆ Ritz Motel M
(807) 623-8189. **$64-$70.** 2600 Arthur St E. Jct Hwy 11, 17 and 61, 2 km e. Ext corridors. **Pets:** Designated rooms, no service, supervision, crate.
S🔒 ⊠ 🖥

(CAA) ◆◆ **Super 8 Motel** M ✿
(807) 344-2612. **$64-$74.** 439 Memorial Ave. 2.4 km s of North Metro area, on Hwy 17B and 11B.. Int corridors. **Pets:** Medium, other. Designated rooms, no service, supervision, crate.
[SAVE] [S🐾] [✕]

TILLSONBURG

(CAA) ◆◆◆ **Super 8 Motel-Tillsonburg** MI ✿
(519) 842-7366. **$85-$99.** 92 Simcoe St. Jct Hwy 19, directly e. Int corridors. **Pets:** No service, supervision, crate.
[SAVE] [S🐾] [✕] [🛏] [💻] [🍽]

TIMMINS

◆◆ **Comfort Inn by Journey's End** M ✿
(705) 264-9474. **$75-$93.** 939 Algonquin Blvd E. Hwy 101, 0.5 km e of Rt 655. Int corridors. **Pets:** Medium. Supervision.
[A$K] [S🐾] [✕] [💻]

TORONTO METROPOLITAN AREA

DOWNSVIEW

(CAA) ◆◆◆ **Montecassino Hotel and Banquet Halls** MI
(416) 630-8100. **$119-$149.** 3710 Chesswood Dr. On Chesswood Dr at Sheppard Ave. Int corridors. **Pets:** Supervision.
[SAVE] [S🐾] [✕] [🛏] [💻] [🍽]

MARKHAM

◆◆◆ **Comfort Inn** M ✿
(905) 477-6077. **$79-$107.** 8330 Woodbine Ave. From Hwy 401, exit 375, 9 km n (Hwy 404) exit e on Hwy 7, then s. Int corridors. **Pets:** Other. $10 one-time fee/room. Designated rooms, supervision.
[A$K] [S🐾] [✕] [🛏] [💻]

RICHMOND HILL

(CAA) ◆◆◆ **Best Western Parkway Inn-Toronto North** M
(905) 881-2600. **$129-$129.** 600 Hwy 7 E. From jct Hwy 401 and Don Valley Pkwy, exit 375, Don Valley Pkwy (Hwy 404), 8 km n to jct Hwy 7, 1 km w. Int corridors. **Pets:** No service, supervision, crate.
[SAVE] [✕] [🛏] [💻] [🛎] [✕]

TORONTO

◆◆◆ **Canadian Pacific SkyDome Hotel** H
(416) 341-7100. **Call for rates.** 1 Blue Jays Way. Int corridors. **Pets:** Medium. No service, supervision, crate.
[A$K] [✕] [🛏] [💻] [🍽] [🛎] [✕]

(CAA) ◆◆ **Carlingview Airport Inn** MI ✿
(416) 675-3303. **$105-$115.** 221 Carlingview Dr. QEW, exit Hwy 427 N to Dixon Rd E, 1 km to Carlingview Dr, then directly s. Ext/int corridors. **Pets:** Small, dogs only. $50 deposit/room. Designated rooms, no service, supervision, crate.
[SAVE] [S🐾] [✕] [🍽] [🛎]

◆◆ **Comfort Inn** MI ✿
(416) 736-4700. **$129-$139, 7 days notice.** 66 Norfinch Dr. From Hwy 400, exit Finch Ave E, then n. Int corridors. **Pets:** Supervision.
[A$K] [S🐾] [✕] [🛏] [💻] [🍽]

(CAA) ◆◆ **Comfort Inn** M
(416) 269-7400. **$80-$165, 7 days notice.** 3306 Kingston Rd. 5.2 km s of Hwy 401, exit 60 (Markham Rd), to Hwy 2 (Kingston Rd), just 1 km w. Int corridors. **Pets:** No service, supervision, crate.
[SAVE] [S🐾] [✕] [🛏] [💻]

◆◆ **Days Inn-Toronto Downtown** H
(416) 977-6655. **$155-$155, 7 days notice.** 30 Carlton St. Adjacent to Maple Leaf Gardens. Int corridors. **Pets:** Small. Supervision.
[A$K] [S🐾] [✕] [🛏] [💻] [🍽] [🛎]

(CAA) ◆◆◆◆ **Delta Chelsea** H
(416) 595-1975. **$180-$200.** 33 Gerrard St W. W of Yonge St, just s of College St. Int corridors. **Pets:** Designated rooms, supervision.
[SAVE] [✕] [🛏] [💻] [🍽] [🛎] [✕]

(CAA) ◆◆◆ **Delta Toronto Airport** H ✿
(416) 675-6100. **$129-$169.** 801 Dixon Rd W. At jct Hwy 27 N and Dixon Rd W. Int corridors. **Pets:** Medium, other. $50 deposit/room. No service, supervision, crate.
[SAVE] [S🐾] [✕] [🍽] [🛎]

(CAA) ◆◆◆◆ **Delta Toronto East** H ✿
(416) 299-1500. **$179-$179.** 2035 Kennedy Rd. Just ne of jct Hwy 401 and Kennedy Rd, exit 379. Int corridors. **Pets:** Other. $30 daily fee/room. Designated rooms, no service, supervision, crate.
[SAVE] [✕] [🛏] [💻] [🍽] [🛎] [✕]

(CAA) ◆◆◆◆ **Four Seasons Hotel** H ✿
(416) 964-0411. **$345-$570.** 21 Avenue Rd. Corner Avenue Rd and Cumberland Ave. Int corridors. **Pets:** Medium, other. No service, supervision, crate.
[S🐾] [✕] [🛏] [💻] [🍽] [🛎] [✕]

◆◆◆◆ **Hilton Toronto** H
(416) 869-3456. **Call for rates.** 145 Richmond St W. At jct of University Ave. Int corridors. **Pets:** Designated rooms, no service, supervision, crate.
[✕] [🛏] [🍽] [🛎]

◆◆◆ **Holiday Inn Express Toronto-North York** M
(416) 665-3500. **$109-$149.** 30 Norfinch Dr. From Hwy 400, exit Finch Ave E to Norfinch Dr. Int corridors. **Pets:** No service, supervision, crate.
[A$K] [✕] [💻]

◆◆◆ Holiday Inn On King 🅷 🐾
(416) 599-4000. **$219-$259, 7 days notice.** 370 King St W. Jct King and Peter sts. Int corridors. **Pets:** Supervision.
🅰🆂🅺 🆂 ✕ 🖥 💻 🍴 🛥

◆◆◆◆ Hotel Inter-Continental Toronto 🅷
(416) 960-5200. **$365-$465.** 220 Bloor St W. Just w of Avenue Rd (University Ave). Int corridors. **Pets:** No service, supervision, crate.
🅰🆂🅺 🆂 ✕ 🖥 💻 🍴 🛥

Ⓐ ◆◆◆ International Plaza Hotel & Conference
  Centre 🅷 🐾
(416) 244-1711. **$109-$238.** 655 Dixon Rd. At jct of Hwy 27 N; directly w of jct Hwy 401. Int corridors. **Pets:** Large, other. No service, supervision, crate.
🆂🅰🆅🅴 🆂 ✕ 💻 🍴 🛥

Ⓐ ◆◆◆◆ Le Royal Meridien King Edward
  Hotel 🅷
(416) 863-3131. **$350-$395.** 37 King St E. Just e of Yonge. Int corridors. **Pets:** No service, supervision, crate.
🆂🅰🆅🅴 🆂 ✕ 🖥

Ⓐ ◆◆◆◆ Metropolitan Hotel 🅷
(416) 977-5000. **$199-$310.** 108 Chestnut St. Directly s of Dundas St. Int corridors. **Pets:** Small. No service, supervision, crate.
🆂🅰🆅🅴 ✕ 🖥 🍴 🛥

Ⓐ ◆◆◆ Novotel North York Hotel 🅷
(416) 733-2929. **$219-$219.** 3 Park Home Ave. From Hwy 401, Yonge St exit, 2 km n on Yonge, just w. Int corridors. **Pets:** No service, supervision, crate.
🆂🅰🆅🅴 🆂 ✕ 🖥 🍴 🛥

Ⓐ ◆◆◆ Novotel-Toronto Airport 🅷 🐾
(416) 798-9800. **$175-$175.** 135 Carlingview Dr. Hwy 427, exit Dixon Rd, 0.6 km w to Carlingview Dr, 0.9 km s. Int corridors. **Pets:** Small. No service, supervision, crate.
🆂🅰🆅🅴 ✕ 🍴 🛥

Ⓐ ◆◆◆ Novotel Toronto Centre 🅷 🐾
(416) 367-8900. **$220-$240.** 45 The Esplanade. Just ne of Gardiner Expwy via Yonge St. Int corridors. **Pets:** $20 daily fee/pet. No service, supervision, crate.
🆂 ✕ 🍴 🛥

Ⓐ ◆◆◆◆ Park Hyatt Toronto 🅷
(416) 925-1234. **$251-$380.** 4 Avenue Rd. Corner of Bloor. Int corridors. **Pets:** Medium. Supervision.
🆂🅰🆅🅴 ✕ 🍴

Ⓐ ◆◆◆ Quality Hotel 🅼 🐾
(416) 968-0010. **$140-$200.** 280 Bloor St W. Just w of St George. Int corridors. **Pets:** No service, supervision, crate.
🆂🅰🆅🅴 🆂 ✕ 💻 🍴

◆◆◆ Quality Hotel & Suites Toronto Airport
  East 🅼
(416) 240-9090. **$149-$210, 30 days notice.** 2180 Islington Ave. Hwy 401, exit 356. Int corridors. **Pets:** No service, supervision, crate.
🅰🆂🅺 🆂 ✕ 🖥 💻 🍴

Ⓐ ◆◆◆ Quality Hotel Downtown 🅼
(416) 367-5555. **$139-$189, 5 days notice.** 111 Lombard St. W side of Jarvis St between Adelaide and Lombard sts; 1 km n off Gardiner Expwy at Jarvis St exit. Int corridors. **Pets:** Medium. Supervision.
🆂🅰🆅🅴 🆂 ✕ 🖥 💻

Ⓐ ◆◆◆ Quality Suites 🅼 🐾
(416) 674-8442. **$180-$210, 3 days notice.** 262 Carlingview Dr. 1 km w of jct Hwy 27 N and Dixon Rd. Int corridors. **Pets:** Medium, other. No service, supervision, crate.
🆂🅰🆅🅴 🆂 ✕ 💻 🍴

Ⓐ ◆◆◆ Radisson Plaza Hotel Admiral
  Toronto-Harbourfront 🅷 🐾
(416) 203-3333. **$169-$169.** 249 Queen's Quay W. QEW E to Gardiner Expwy, exit Bay St S to Queen's Quay W. Int corridors. **Pets:** Small, dogs only. No service, supervision, crate.
✕ 🍴 🛥

◆◆◆ Radisson Suite Hotel Toronto
  Airport 🅷 🐾
(416) 242-7400. **$149-$179, 7 days notice.** 640 Dixon Rd. Directly e of jct Dixon Rd and Hwy 27; 0.3 km w of jct Hwy 401 and Dixon Rd. Int corridors. **Pets:** Other. No service, supervision, crate.
🅰🆂🅺 ✕ 💻 🍴

◆◆◆◆ Royal York-Canadian Pacific Hotels 🅷
(416) 368-2511. **$189-$369.** 100 Front St W. Opposite Union Station; entrance on Wellington St; from QEW/Gardiner Expwy, exit n on York or Bay sts. Int corridors. **Pets:** Small. Supervision.
🅰🆂🅺 🆂 ✕ 🅰 🖥 💻 🍴 🛥

Ⓐ ◆◆◆ Toronto Colony Hotel 🅷
(416) 977-0707. **$159-$159.** 89 Chestnut St. Adjacent to City Hall. Int corridors. **Pets:** Small. Supervision.
🆂🅰🆅🅴 ✕ 🖥 💻 🍴 🛥

Ⓐ ◆◆ Travelodge Hotel Dixon Road (Toronto
  Airport) 🅼 🐾
(416) 674-2222. **$96-$106.** 925 Dixon Rd. At corner Carlingview and Dixon rds. Int corridors. **Pets:** Medium. Designated rooms, no service, supervision, crate.
🆂🅰🆅🅴 🆂 ✕ 💻 🍴 🛥

◆◆ Travelodge Toronto East 🅼 🐾
(416) 299-9500. **$109-$149.** 20 Milner Business Ct. Jct Hwy 401 and Markham Rd, just n on Markham Rd. Int corridors. **Pets:** Medium, other. Supervision.
🅰🆂🅺 🆂 ✕ 🖥 💻 🍴 🛥

◆◆ Travelodge Toronto North (North
  York) 🅼 🐾
(416) 663-9500. **$80-$130.** 50 Norfinch Dr. From Hwy 400, exit Finch Ave E to Norfinch Dr. Int corridors. **Pets:** Small. Supervision.
🅰🆂🅺 🆂 ✕ 🖥 💻 🍴 🛥

(AA) ◆◆◆ Valhalla Inn-Toronto **H**
(416) 239-2391. **$125-$135.** 1 Valhalla Inn Rd. 17.6 km w on e side of Hwy 427; 3.2 kms s of Hwy 401 via Hwy 427, exit Burnhamthorpe Rd, just e then s on East Mall. Int corridors. **Pets:** Medium. No service, supervision, crate.

SAVE Sб ✕ ⬜ �][⌂

(AA) ◆◆◆◆ The Westin Harbour Castle **H** ❀
(416) 869-1600. **$169-$299.** One Harbour Square. Foot of Bay St on shore of Lake Ontario. Int corridors. **Pets:** Small. Supervision.

✕ ⬜ ⏫ ⌂ ✕

❀ **END METROPOLITAN AREA** ❀

TRENTON

◆◆◆ Comfort Inn **M** ❀
(613) 965-6660. **$76-$117.** 68 Monogram Pl. Hwy 401, exit 526 (Glen Miller Rd S). Int corridors. **Pets:** Medium, other. Designated rooms, supervision.

A$K Sб ✕ ⌂ ⬜

◆◆◆ Holiday Inn Trenton **MI** ❀
(613) 394-4855. **$120.** 99 Glen Miller Rd. Hwy 401, exit 526. Int corridors. **Pets:** Other. Designated rooms, supervision.

A$K Sб ✕ ⬛ ⬜ ⏫ ⌂ ✕

TWEED

◆ Park Place Motel **M** ❀
(613) 478-3134. **$42-$50.** 43 Victoria St. On Hwy 37, 0.5 km s of centre. Ext corridors. **Pets:** Supervision.

⬛

WALLACEBURG

◆◆ Super 8 Motel **M**
(519) 627-0781. **$60-$74.** 76 McNaughton Ave. On Hwy 40 (McNaughton Ave) on south side of town. Int corridors. **Pets:** Small. Supervision.

A$K Sб ✕ ⬛

WASAGA BEACH

◆◆ Bon Air Motel **M**
(705) 429-6364. **$50-$99, 30 days notice.** 268 Main St. Hwy 92, directly n on Main St. Ext corridors. **Pets:** No service, supervision, crate.

⬛ ⬜ ✕ ⏸

◆◆ Kingsbridge Inn **M**
(705) 429-6364. **$75-$125, 30 days notice.** 268 Main St. From Hwy 92, directly n on Main St. Ext corridors. **Pets:** No service, supervision, crate.

⬛ ⬜ ✕ ⏸

WATERLOO

◆◆◆ Comfort Inn **MI** ❀
(519) 747-9400. **$80-$125.** 190 Weber St N. E side off Weber St, 0.3 km s of University Ave (Hwy 86). Int corridors. **Pets:** Other. No service, supervision, crate.

A$K Sб ✕ ⬛ ⬜ ⏫

◆◆◆ Waterloo Inn **MI** ❀
(519) 884-0220. **$115-$125.** 475 King St N. 3 km n on King St, at jct Hwy 86. Int corridors. **Pets:** $5 one-time fee/pet. Designated rooms, no service, supervision, crate.

✕ ⬛ ⬜ ⏫ ⌂

WAWA

(AA) ◆ Kinniwabi Pines Motel/Cottages **M**
(705) 856-7302. **$48-$61.** On Hwy 17, 5.3 km s of jct Hwy 101. Ext corridors. **Pets:** Designated rooms, no service, supervision, crate.

SAVE ✕ ⬛ ⬜ ✕ ℳ

◆◆ Parkway Motel **M** ❀
(705) 856-7020. **$48-$55.** On Hwy 17, 4 km s of jct Hwy 101. Ext corridors. **Pets:** Medium, dogs only. Supervision.

⬛ ⬜ ✕ ℳ

◆◆ Sportsman's Motel **M** ❀
(705) 856-2272. **$55-$65.** 45 Mission Rd. Hwy 101, 2.4 km e of jct Hwy 17. Ext corridors. **Pets:** Medium. $10 one-time fee/room. Designated rooms, supervision.

Sб ✕ ⬛ ⬜ ℳ

(AA) ◆ Wawa Northern Lights Motel **MI** ❀
(705) 856-1900. **$49-$54.** Hwy 17 N. On Hwy 17, 8 km n of jct Hwy 101. Ext corridors. **Pets:** Other. No service, supervision, crate.

SAVE Sб ✕ ⬛ ⏫ ✕ ℳ CTV

WHITBY

◆◆◆ Quality Suites **M** ❀
(905) 432-8800. **$150.** 1700 Champlain Ave. Hwy 401, exit 412 (Thickson Rd), 0.5 km n to Champlain, just 1 km e. Int corridors. **Pets:** Other. Supervision.

A$K ✕ ⬜

WHITEFISH FALLS

(AA) ◆◆◆ The Island Lodge **L** ❀
(705) 285-4343. **$82-$148** (no credit cards), 30 days notice. Box 87. Parking and dock just w of Hwy 6. Phone for boat at Espanola or Little Current. Ext corridors. **Pets:** $9 daily fee/pet, $30 one-time fee/room. Supervision.

SAVE ⬛ ⬜ ⏫ ✕ ℳ CTV ⏸

WINDSOR

◆◆◆ Comfort Inn **M**
(519) 966-7800. **$102-$120.** 2955 Dougall Ave. 5.3 km s on Hwy 3B, off Hwy 401 via Tunnel exit. Int corridors. **Pets:** Supervision.

A$K Sб ✕ ⬛ ⬜

◆◆◆ Hilton Windsor **H** ❀
(519) 973-5555. **$139-$229.** 277 Riverside Dr W. 1 km w of Detroit-Windsor Tunnel; 1 km e of Ambassador Bridge. Int corridors. **Pets:** Small. No service, supervision, crate.

A$K ✕ ⬜ ⏫ ⌂

◆◆◆ **The Holiday Inn Select Windsor** 🅷
(519) 966-1200. **$129-$159.** 1855 Huron Church Rd. Jct Huron Church and Malden rds; 1.5 km n of EC Row Expwy. Int corridors. **Pets:** Small. Designated rooms, supervision.
ⓢ S X 🅗 💻 🍽 🖼

◆◆ **Ivy Rose Motor Inn** 🅼
(519) 966-1700. **$60-$140.** 2885 Howard Ave. 4.8 km s; just n of Devonshire Shopping Mall. Ext corridors. **Pets:** Small. Supervision.
ⓢ S X 🅗 🍽 🖼 ⊠

◆◆◆ **Quality Suites** 🅼
(519) 977-9707. **$149-$399.** 250 Dougall Ave. Downtown; jct Dougall Ave and Chatham St. Int corridors. **Pets:** Supervision.
ⒶⓈⓀ ⊠ 💻 🍽

◆◆◆ **Radisson Riverfront Hotel** 🅷 ☙
(519) 977-9777. **$109-$129.** 333 Riverside Dr W. 1 km w of Detroit-Windsor Tunnel, 1 km e of Ambassador Bridge. Int corridors. **Pets:** Small, other. No service, supervision, crate.
ⒶⓈⓀ S X 💻 🍽 🖼

WOODSTOCK

◆◆◆ **Quality Inn** 🅼 ☙
(519) 537-5586. **$85-$112.** 580 Bruin Blvd. Just n and w of Hwy 59; Hwy 401, exit 232. Int corridors. **Pets:** Medium. No service, supervision, crate.
ⓢ S X 🅗 💻 🍽 🖼

◆◆ **Super 8 Motel** 🅼
(519) 421-4588. **$81-$125.** 560 Norwich Ave. Directly n of jct Hwy 401 and Hwy 59 (exit 232). Int corridors. **Pets:** Supervision.
ⓢ S X 🅗

WYOMING

◆◆ **Country View Motel and RV-Park Camping Resort** 🅼 ☙
(519) 845-3394. **$39-$54.** Hwy 22. Hwy 402, exit 25, Hwy 21 1 km s to Hwy 22, then directly e. Ext corridors. **Pets:** Small. $50 deposit/room, $10 daily fee/room. No service, supervision, crate.
X 🅗 🖼 ⊠ ⒸⓉⓋ

PRINCE EDWARD ISLAND

CAVENDISH

◆◆ **Bay Vista Motor Inn** M 🐾
(902) 963-2225. **$83-$87.** RR1. 4.8 km w on Rt 6 from jct Rt 13. Ext corridors. **Pets:** Small. Designated rooms, no service, supervision, crate.
⊠ 🖘 ⊠ CTV ☎

CAA ◆◆◆ **Cavendish Bosom Buddies Cottages** C 🐾
(902) 963-3449. **$150-$185.** RR1. Jct Rt 6 and 13, 0.6 km e on Rt 6. Ext corridors. **Pets:** Designated rooms, no service, supervision, crate.
SAVE S⬛ ⊠ 🖫 ⊠ 🐾 ☎

CAA ◆◆◆ **Cavendish Maples Cottages** C
(902) 963-2818. **$112-$230.** Jct Rt 6 and 13, 2.5 km w on Rt 6. Ext corridors. **Pets:** Designated rooms, no service, supervision, crate.
SAVE 🖫 🖘 ⊠ 🐾 ☎

CHARLOTTETOWN

◆◆ **Best Western Charlottetown** MI 🐾
(902) 892-2461. **$149-$174, 30 days notice.** 238 Grafton St. Centre. Int corridors. **Pets:** Medium, other. Designated rooms, supervision.
ASK S⬛ ⊠ 🦽 🗦 🦽 🖫 🖳 🍴 🖘

◆◆ **Comfort Inn** M 🐾
(902) 566-4424. **$97-$117.** 112 Trans Canada Hwy. On Trans Canada Hwy 1, 4.5 km w. Int corridors. **Pets:** Small. Designated rooms, no service, supervision, crate.
ASK S⬛ ⊠ 🖳

CAA ◆◆◆ **Delta Prince Edward Hotel** H
(902) 566-2222. **$159-$269.** 18 Queen St. Centre. Int corridors. **Pets:** Medium. Designated rooms, supervision.
SAVE S⬛ ⊠ 🖳 🍴 🖘

CAA ◆◆◆ **Holiday Inn Express** M 🐾
(902) 892-1201. **$149-$149.** 4.8 km w on Trans Canada Hwy 1. Int corridors. **Pets:** Other. No service, supervision, crate.
SAVE S⬛ ⊠ 🦽 🗦 🖫 🖳 🖘

◆◆ **Quality Inn On the Hill** MI 🐾
(902) 894-8572. **$122-$133.** 150 Euston St. Centre. Int corridors. **Pets:** Medium. Supervision.
ASK S⬛ ⊠ 🖫 🖳 🍴

◆◆◆ **Rodd Charlottetown-A Rodd Signature Hotel** H 🐾
(902) 894-7371. **$132-$180.** Kent & Pownal sts. Centre. Int corridors. **Pets:** $10 daily fee/room. Designated rooms, supervision.
ASK S⬛ ⊠ 🖫 🖳 🍴 🖘

◆◆ **Rodd Confederation Inn & Suites** MI
(902) 892-2481. **$83-$121.** 4 km w on Trans Canada Hwy 1. Ext/int corridors. **Pets:** Designated rooms, supervision.
ASK S⬛ ⊠ 🖫 🖳 🍴 🖘

◆◆ **Rodd Royalty Inn & Conference Center** MI
(902) 894-8566. **$92-$145.** 4 km w on Trans Canada Hwy 1. Ext/int corridors. **Pets:** Designated rooms, supervision.
ASK S⬛ ⊠ 🖫 🖳 🍴 🖘

CORNWALL

CAA ◆◆ **Sunny King Motel** M 🐾
(902) 566-2209. **$66-$116, 3 days notice.** Centre on Hwy 1. Ext corridors. **Pets:** Other. $25 deposit/room. Designated rooms, no service, supervision, crate.
SAVE S⬛ ⊠ 🖘 ⊠ 🐾

MONTAGUE

◆◆◆ **Rodd Marina Inn & Suites** M 🐾
(902) 838-4075. **$104-$134.** 115 Sackville St. Centre. Int corridors. **Pets:** Medium, other. $10 daily fee/room. Designated rooms, no service, supervision, crate.
ASK S⬛ ⊠ 🖫 🖳

NORTH RUSTICO

CAA ◆ **St. Lawrence Motel** M 🐾
(902) 963-2053. **$60-$90, 7 days notice.** In PEI National Park on Gulf Shore Rd. Ext corridors. **Pets:** Medium, other. No service, supervision, crate.
⊠ 🖫 ⊠ 🐾 ☎

ROSENEATH

◆◆◆ **Rodd Brudenell River-A Rodd Signature Resort** X
(902) 652-2332. **$99-$399, 3 days notice.** Jct Rt 4 and 3, 5.5 km e on Rt 3, Brudenell River Provincial Park. Ext/int corridors. **Pets:** Supervision.
ASK S⬛ ⊠ 🖫 🖳 🍴 🖘 ⊠

STRATFORD

CAA ◆◆◆ **Anne's Ocean View Haven Bed & Breakfast** BB
(902) 569-4644. **$95-$185** (no credit cards). Kinloch Rd. Hwy 1, 2 km w. Ext/int corridors. **Pets:** Designated rooms, no service, supervision, crate.
⊠ 🖫 🐾 ☎

SUMMERSIDE

(AAA) ◆◆◆ Quality Inn Garden of the
Gulf **M** 🐾
(902) 436-2295. **$119-$129.** 618 Water St. 1.6 km e on
Hwy 11. Ext/int corridors. **Pets:** Designated rooms, supervision.
[SAVE] [S🅐] [✕] [🛢] [🖥] [🍽] [✕]

WOODSTOCK

◆◆ Rodd Mill River-A Rodd Signature Hotel **M**
(902) 859-3555. **$73-$161, 3 days notice.** On Rt 136, just
e of jct Rt 2; in Mill River Provincial Park. Int corridors.
Pets: Designated rooms, supervision.
[ASK] [S🅐] [✕] [🍽] [🍴] [✕] [CTV]

AYLMER

(AA) ◆◆◆ Chateau Cartier Resort R
(819) 778-0000. **$169-$249, 30 days notice.** 1170 chemin Aylmer. On Hwy 148, 1 km w of Champlain Bridge. Int corridors. **Pets:** Small. No service, supervision, crate.
⊞ ⊠ ⊟ ⊡ ⊟ ⊞ ⊠

BAIE-COMEAU

◆◆ Comfort Inn M
(418) 589-8252. **$73-$82.** 745 boul Lafleche. On Rt 138. Int corridors. **Pets:** Supervision.
⊞ ⊠ ⊟

BAIE-ST-PAUL

◆◆ Hotel Baie-Saint-Paul M
(418) 435-3683. **$80-$99.** 911 boul Mgr Laval. On Rt 138. Int corridors. **Pets:** Designated rooms, no service, supervision, crate.
⊠ ⊠ ⊟ ⊡ ⊟ ⊠

BERTHIERVILLE

◆◆ Days Inn Berthierville M
(450) 836-1621. **Call for rates.** 760 Gadoury. Hwy 40, exit 144. Int corridors. **Pets:** Medium. Designated rooms, supervision.
⊠ ⊟ ⊡

CHICOUTIMI

◆◆ Comfort Inn M
(418) 693-8686. **$76-$84.** 1595 boul Talbot. 2.8 km n from jct Rt 170. Int corridors. **Pets:** Small, other. No service, supervision, crate.
⊞ ⊠ ⊟ ⊡

◆◆ Le Nouvel Hotel La Sagueneenne M
(418) 545-8326. **Call for rates.** 250 des Sagueneens. Just w of jct Rt 175 (boul Talbot). Int corridors. **Pets:** Small. $200 deposit/room. No service, supervision, crate.
⊠ ⊡ ⊟ ⊠

DRUMMONDVILLE

◆◆ Comfort Inn M
(819) 477-4000. **$65-$105.** 1055 rue Hains. 0.5 km s on boul St-Joseph from jct Hwy 20, exit 177; then just w on rue Hains. Int corridors. **Pets:** Other. No service, supervision, crate.
⊞ ⊠ ⊠ ⊟ ⊡

GASPE

(AA) ◆◆ Motel Adams M
(418) 368-2244. **$69-$89.** 20 rue Adams. Centre, corner rue Jacques Cartier. Ext/int corridors. **Pets:** Small. No service, supervision, crate.
⊠ ⊠ ⊟ ⊟

GATINEAU

(AA) ◆◆ Comfort Inn M
(819) 243-6010. **$85-$140.** 630 boul La Gappe. 2 km e from jct Hwy 50, exit 140. Int corridors. **Pets:** Small. No service, supervision, crate.
⊞ ⊠ ⊠ ⊡

GRANBY

◆◆ Hotel Le Castel M
(450) 378-9071. **$70-$80.** 901 rue Principale. On Rt 112, 1 km e of jct Rt 139; from Hwy 10, exit 68. Int corridors. **Pets:** Supervision.
⊞ ⊠ ⊠ ⊟ ⊡ ⊟ ⊠

LA MALBAIE POINTE AU PIC

◆◆◆ Le Manoir Richelieu R
(418) 665-3703. **$199-$299, 7 days notice.** 181 rue Richelieu. 1 km s of Rt 362. Int corridors. **Pets:** Supervision.
⊞ ⊠ ⊠ ⊟ ⊡ ⊟ ⊠ ⊠

LA POCATIERE

◆◆ Motel Le Pocatois M
(418) 856-1688. **$59-$75.** 235 Rt 132. 0.8 km s of jct Hwy 20, exit 439. Int corridors. **Pets:** Small. No service, supervision, crate.
⊞ ⊠ ⊠ ⊟

LAC-BROME (KNOWLTON)

(CAA) ◆◆◆ **Auberge Lakeview Inn** [CI] ❀
(450) 243-6183. **$120-$210.** 50 rue Victoria. Centre. Int corridors. **Pets:** Supervision.
[SAVE] [✕] [❚❚] [≈]

LENNOXVILLE

(CAA) ◆ **La Paysanne Motel** [MI] ❀
(819) 569-5585. **$56-$74.** 42 rue Queen. On Rt 143. Ext/int corridors. **Pets:** Other. Supervision.
[SAVE] [SD] [❚❚] [≈]

LOUISEVILLE

◆◆ **Gite du Carrefour and Maison Historique J.L.L. Hamelin** [BB] ❀
(819) 228-4932. **$45-$55** (no credit cards). 11 ave St-Laurent ouest. Centre, on Rt 138. Int corridors. **Pets:** Small. No service, supervision, crate.
[✕] [AC] [CTV] [∅]

MATANE

(CAA) ◆ **Motel La Marina** [MI] ❀
(418) 562-3234. **$42-$82, 7 days notice.** 1032 ave du Phare Ouest. On Rt 132. Ext corridors. **Pets:** Dogs only. Supervision.
[❚] [❚❚] [≈] [AC]

◆◆ **Quality Inn Inter-Rives Matane** [MI] ❀
(418) 562-6433. **$85-$125.** 1550 ave du Phare Ouest. On Rt 132. Ext/int corridors. **Pets:** Medium, other. Supervision.
[ASK] [SD] [✕] [❚] [▣] [❚❚] [≈] [✕]

MONTEBELLO

◆◆◆◆ **Le Chateau Montebello** [R] ❀
(819) 423-6341. **$165-$185.** 392 rue Notre-Dame. On Rt 148. Int corridors. **Pets:** Medium. $30 daily fee/room, $30 one-time fee/room. No service, supervision, crate.
[ASK] [✕] [❚] [▣] [❚❚] [≈] [✕]

MONTREAL METROPOLITAN AREA

BOUCHERVILLE

◆◆ **Comfort Inn** [M]
(450) 641-2880. **$90-$100.** 96 boul de Mortagne. At jct Hwy 20, exit 92. Int corridors. **Pets:** Large. Designated rooms, no service, supervision, crate.
[✕] [▣]

BROSSARD

◆◆ **Comfort Inn** [M] ❀
(450) 678-9350. **$71-$100.** 7863 boul Taschereau. On Rt 134, 1.5 km w of jct Hwy 10, boul Taschereau Ouest exit. Int corridors. **Pets:** Designated rooms, no service, supervision, crate.
[ASK] [SD] [✕] [❚]

DORVAL

◆◆ **Comfort Inn** [M] ❀
(514) 636-3391. **$105-$145.** 340 ave Michel-Jasmin. Hwy 520 eastbound, exit 2; westbound, exit 1, 0.3 km along service road to ave Marshall, follow to ave Michel-Jasmin. Int corridors. **Pets:** Medium. Designated rooms, supervision.
[ASK] [SD] [✕]

(CAA) ◆◆ **Travelodge Dorval Airport** [M] ❀
(514) 631-4537. **$90-$105, 7 days notice.** 1010 chemin Herron. Hwy 20 westbound exit 54, just s on boul Fenelon to ave Dumont, follow to chemin Herron; eastbound exit 54, 1.7 km along service road. Int corridors. **Pets:** Other. No service, supervision, crate.
[SAVE] [SD] [✕] [❚] [▣]

LAVAL

(CAA) ◆◆ **Comfort Inn** [MI] ❀
(450) 686-0600. **$92-$150.** 2055 Autoroute des Laurentides. Hwy 15, exit 8, e on boul St-Martin, 0.7 km n on boul Le Corbusier, w on boul Tessier. Int corridors. **Pets:** Small. Designated rooms, no service, supervision, crate.
[SAVE] [SD] [✕] [❚] [❚❚]

◆◆◆ **Hotel President Laval** [H]
(450) 682-2225. **$150-$200.** 2225 Autoroute des Laurentides. Hwy 15, exit 10. Int corridors. **Pets:** Medium. No service, supervision, crate.
[ASK] [SD] [✕] [▣] [❚❚] [≈]

◆◆◆ **Hotel Travelodge Laval** [MI]
(450) 682-9000. **$175-$175.** 2900 boul Le Carrefour. Hwy 15, exit 10, following signs to boul Le Carrefour. Int corridors. **Pets:** Large. Designated rooms, no service, supervision, crate.
[ASK] [SD] [✕] [❚] [▣] [❚❚] [≈]

(CAA) ◆◆◆ **Quality Suites** [M] ❀
(450) 686-6777. **$108-$185.** 2035 Autoroute des Laurentides. Hwy 15, exit 8, e on boul St-Martin, 0.7 km n on boul Le Corbusier, w on boul Tessier. Int corridors. **Pets:** Small. Designated rooms, no service, supervision, crate.
[SAVE] [SD] [✕]

LONGUEUIL

◆◆ **Days Inn Longueuil** [MI] ❀
(450) 677-8911. **$72-$92.** 2800 boul Marie-Victorin. From Hwy 20/Rt 132 eastbound, exit 15E following signs for boul Marie-Victorin est; from Hwy 20 westbound, exit 90. Int corridors. **Pets:** No service, supervision, crate.
[ASK] [SD] [✕] [▣] [❚❚]

◆◆◆ **Holiday Inn Montreal-Longueuil** [H] ❀
(450) 646-8100. **$95-$139.** 900 rue St-Charles est. Rt 132/Hwy 20, exit 11, to boul Rolland Therrien. Int corridors. **Pets:** Very small. $75 one-time fee/room. No service, supervision, crate.
[ASK] [SD] [✕] [▣] [❚❚] [≈]

MONTREAL

(CAA) ◆◆◆ **Best Western Europa Downtown** [H]
(514) 866-6492. **$99-$309.** 1240 rue Drummond. Between rue Ste-Catherine and boul Rene Levesque. Int corridors. **Pets:** Designated rooms, no service, supervision, crate.
[SAVE] [SD] [✕] [❚] [▣] [❚❚]

(CAA) ◆◆◆ **Chateau Versailles Hotel** H
(514) 933-3611. **$255-$295, 7 days notice.** 1659 rue Sherbrooke Ouest. Corner rue St-Mathieu. Int corridors. **Pets:** No service, supervision, crate.
SAVE ✕ ▭

◆◆◆ **Crowne Plaza Metro Centre** H
(514) 842-8581. **$129-$159.** 505 rue Sherbrooke est. Between rue Berri and St-Hubert. Int corridors. **Pets:** Medium. No service, supervision, crate.
✕ ▭ ¶¶ ⌂

(CAA) ◆◆◆ **Delta Montreal** H
(514) 286-1986. **$149-$189.** 475 ave President-Kennedy. Corner rue City Councillor. Int corridors. **Pets:** Supervision.
SAVE ✕ ▤ ▭ ¶¶ ⌂

(CAA) ◆◆◆◆ **Hilton Montreal**
            Bonaventure H ❖
(514) 878-2332. **$195-$195.** 1 Place Bonaventure. Corner Mansfield and de la Gauchetiere. Int corridors. **Pets:** Small. $50 deposit/room. Designated rooms, no service, supervision, crate.
SAVE ✕ ▭ ¶¶ ⌂

(CAA) ◆◆ **Holiday Inn Montreal-Midtown** H ❖
(514) 842-6111. **$109-$169.** 420 rue Sherbrooke Ouest. Between City Councillors and de Bleury. Int corridors. **Pets:** Medium. $50 deposit/room. No service, supervision, crate.
SAVE S▫ ✕ ▤ ▭ ¶¶ ⌂

◆◆ **Hotel Auberge Universel Montreal** H ❖
(514) 253-3365. **$80-$90.** 5000 rue Sherbrooke est. Corner rue Viau; just e of Olympic Stadium. Int corridors. **Pets:** Small. No service, supervision, crate.
✕ ▤ ¶¶ ⌂

◆◆◆◆ **Hotel Inter-Continental Montreal** H
(514) 987-9900. **$340.** 360 rue St-Antoine ouest. In Old Montreal, corner rue St-Pierre. Int corridors. **Pets:** Supervision.
ASK S▫ ✕ ▭ ¶¶ ⌂

◆◆ **Hotel Lord Berri** H ❖
(514) 845-9236. **$169-$189, 5 days notice.** 1199 rue Berri. Between boul Rene Levesque and rue Ste-Catherine. Int corridors. **Pets:** Very small, other. No service, supervision, crate.
ASK S▫ ✕ ▤ ¶¶

(CAA) ◆◆◆◆ **Hotel Omni Montreal** H ❖
(514) 284-1110. **$199-$475.** 1050 Sherbrooke Ouest. Corner rue Peel. Int corridors. **Pets:** Other. Supervision.
SAVE ✕ ▤ ¶¶ ⌂

(CAA) ◆◆◆ **Hotel Tour Versailles** H
(514) 933-8111. **$179-$214, 7 days notice.** 1808 rue Sherbrooke ouest. Corner rue St-Mathieu. Int corridors. **Pets:** Large. Designated rooms, no service, supervision, crate.
SAVE ✕ ▤ ▭

◆ **Hotel Travelodge Montreal Centre** MI ❖
(514) 874-9090. **$89-$99, 30 days notice.** 50 boul Rene-Levesque Ouest. Between rue St-Urbain and St-Laurent. Int corridors. **Pets:** Small. $10 daily fee/pet. No service, supervision, crate.
✕ ▭

(CAA) ◆◆◆ **Le Centre Sheraton** H ❖
(514) 878-2000. **$169-$169.** 1201 boul Rene-Levesque Ouest. Between rue Drummond and Stanley. Int corridors. **Pets:** Medium. No service, supervision, crate.
SAVE ✕ ▭ ¶¶ ⌂

◆◆◆◆ **Loews Hotel Vogue** H ❖
(514) 285-5555. **$430-$430.** 1425 rue de la Montagne. Between rue Ste-Catherine and boul de Maisonneuve. Int corridors. **Pets:** Small. No service, supervision, crate.
ASK ✕ ▤ ▭

◆◆◆ **Marriott Residence Inn-Montreal** MI ❖
(514) 982-6064. **$125-$375.** 2045 rue Peel. Between rue Sherbrooke and boul de Maisonneuve. Int corridors. **Pets:** Medium, other. $10 daily fee/room, $250 one-time fee/room. No service, supervision, crate.
ASK S▫ ✕ ▭ ⌂

(CAA) ◆◆◆ **Novotel Montreal Centre** H
(514) 861-6000. **$129-$300.** 1180 rue de la Montagne. Between rue Ste-Catherine and boul Rene-Levesque. Int corridors. **Pets:** Medium. Designated rooms, supervision.
SAVE ✕ ¶¶

(CAA) ◆◆◆ **Quality Hotel** MI ❖
(514) 849-1413. **$115-$200.** 3440 ave du Parc. Between rue Sherbrooke and Milton. Int corridors. **Pets:** Designated rooms, no service, supervision, crate.
SAVE ✕ ▤ ▭ ¶¶

◆◆◆ **Renaissance Hotel du Parc** H ❖
(514) 288-6666. **$169-$250.** 3625 ave du Parc. Corner rue Prince-Arthur. Int corridors. **Pets:** No service, supervision, crate.
ASK S▫ ✕ ▤ ▭ ¶¶ ⌂ ✕

◆◆◆ **Sheraton Four Points Montreal** H ❖
(514) 842-3961. **$125-$125.** 475 rue Sherbrooke Ouest. Between rue Durocher and Aylmer. Int corridors. **Pets:** Small. Supervision.
ASK ✕ ▤ ▭ ¶¶

POINTE-CLAIRE

◆◆ **Comfort Inn** MI ❖
(514) 697-6210. **$125-$165.** 700 boul St-Jean. 0.3 km s on boul St-Jean from jct Hwy 40, exit 52. Int corridors. **Pets:** Large, other. Designated rooms, no service, supervision, crate.
ASK S▫ ✕ ▭

◆◆◆ **Holiday Inn Montreal Pointe-Claire** H ❖
(514) 697-7110. **$125-$165.** 6700 route Transcanadienne. At jct Hwy 40, exit 52 (southside service road). Int corridors. **Pets:** No service, supervision, crate.
ASK S▫ ✕ ▭ ¶¶ ⌂

◆◆◆ **Quality Suites** MI ❖
(514) 426-5060. **$135-$215.** 6300 Trans Canada Hwy. Hwy 40, exit 52, southside service road. westbound, follow signs for boul St-Jean sud and Hwy 40 est to get onto southside service road. Int corridors. **Pets:** Designated rooms, no service, supervision, crate.
ASK S▫ ✕ ▭ ¶¶

ST-LAURENT

◆◆ **Holiday Inn Montreal Aeroport** M ❄
(514) 739-3391. **$89-$100.** 6500 Cote de Liesse. Eastbound Hwy 520 exit 5, on southside service road; westbound exit 5 to rue Ness, following signs for rue Hickmore
and Hwy 520 E. Ext/int corridors. **Pets:** Other. Supervision.
ASK S X ⌂ ▤ ▣ ⎰ ⊠

CAA ◆◆◆ **Quality Hotel Dorval** M ❄
(514) 731-7821. **$145-$195.** 7700 Cote de Liesse. Eastbound Hwy 520 exit 4, on southside service road; westbound exit 4 (Montee-de-liesse). Int corridors. **Pets:** Small.
No service, supervision, crate.
SAVE S X ▣ ⎰ ⊠

❄ **END METROPOLITAN AREA** ❄

NEW RICHMOND

CAA ◆◆ **Hotel Motel Francis** M ❄
(418) 392-4485. **$75-$94.** 210 Pardiac. Just s of Rt 132.
Ext/int corridors. **Pets:** Very small, dogs only. $30 deposit/
pet. Supervision.
SAVE S X ▣ ⎰ ⊠ ⊠ 𝓚

PASPEBIAC

CAA ◆ **Motel Carol** M ❄
(418) 752-3158. **$59-$69.** 127 boul Gerard D Levesque CP
1035. On Rt 132, in town centre. Ext corridors. **Pets:** Other.
$25 deposit/pet, $19 daily fee/pet. Supervision.
S ▤ 𝓚 ☎

PERCE

◆ **Au Pic de l'Aurore** C ❄
(418) 782-2166. **$57-$109, 7 days notice.** 1 Rt 132. 2 km
e on Rt 132. Ext corridors. **Pets:** Supervision.
⊠ ▤ ▣ 𝓚

◆◆ **Bonaventure Pavillon Cote Surprise** M ❄
(418) 782-2166. **$68-$123, 7 days notice.** 367 Rt 132. On
Rt 132. Ext/int corridors. **Pets:** Supervision.
⊠ ▤ ▣ ⎰ 𝓚

◆◆ **Hotel Motel Manoir de Perce** M ❄
(418) 782-2022. **$55-$118, 5 days notice.** 212 Rt 132.
Centre. Ext/int corridors. **Pets:** Supervision.
S ⊠ ⎰ ⊠ 𝓚

PINE HILL

CAA ◆◆◆◆ **Hotel du Lac Carling** R ❄
(450) 533-9211. **$200-$750.** 2255 Rt 327 nord. 5 km n on
Rt 327. Int corridors. **Pets:** Small. No service, supervision,
crate.
SAVE S X ▤ ▣ ⎰ ⊠

QUEBEC METROPOLITAN AREA

BEAUPORT

◆◆ **Comfort Inn** M ❄
(418) 666-1226. **$68-$120.** 240 boul Ste-Anne. At jct Hwy
440, exit Francois-De-Laval. Int corridors. **Pets:** Designated
rooms, no service, supervision, crate.
ASK ⊠ ▣

L'ANCIENNE LORETTE

◆◆ **Comfort Inn** M
(418) 872-5900. **$85-$99.** 1255 boul Duplessis. At jct boul
Duplessis and Wilfrid-Hamel (Rt 138). Int corridors.
Pets: Supervision.
ASK ⊠ ▣

LEVIS

CAA ◆◆ **Comfort Inn** M ❄
(418) 835-5605. **$80-$150.** 10 du Vallon est. Hwy 20, exit
325 S eastbound; exit 325 westbound. Int corridors.
Pets: Small. No service, supervision, crate.
SAVE S X ▤ ▣

QUEBEC

◆◆ **Chateau Grande-Allee** H
(418) 647-4433. **$79-$249.** 601 Grande-Allee e. Corner de
la Chevrotiere. Int corridors. **Pets:** Designated rooms, no
service, supervision, crate.
ASK ⊠

CAA ◆◆◆ **Hilton Quebec** H ❄
(418) 647-2411. **$159-$205.** 1100 boul Rene-Levesque E.
Corner of ave Dufferin. Int corridors. **Pets:** Small. Designated rooms, no service, supervision, crate.
SAVE ⊠ ▤ ▣ ⎰ ⊠

CAA ◆◆ **Hotel Chateau Bellevue** M ❄
(418) 692-2573. **$99-$199.** 16 rue de La Porte. In old Quebec, corner ave Ste-Genevieve. Int corridors. **Pets:** No
service, supervision, crate.
▤

CAA ◆◆◆ **Hotel Chateau Laurier** H ❄
(418) 522-8108. **$109-$329.** 1220 George V W. Corner
Grande Allee est. Int corridors. **Pets:** Supervision.
⊠ ⎰

CAA ◆◆◆ **Hotel Le Manoir LaFayette** H
(418) 522-2652. **$99-$259.** 661 rue Grande Allee Est.
Between rue d'Artigny and de la Chevrotiere. Int corridors.
Pets: Small. Designated rooms, supervision.
⊠ ▤ ⎰

◆◆◆ **Hotel Quality Suites Quebec** M ❄
(418) 622-4244. **$99-$150, 7 days notice.** 1600 rue Bou-
vier. Hwy 40, exit 312 N (Pierre Bertrand nord) 2 km w of jct
Rt 358. Int corridors. **Pets:** Other. No service, supervision,
crate.
ASK S X ▣

Ⓐ ◆◆ **L'Hotel du Vieux Quebec** 🅷 ❀
(418) 692-1850. **$129-$239.** 1190 rue St-Jean. In Old Quebec, corner rue de l'Hotel-Dieu. Int corridors. **Pets:** No service, supervision, crate.
[SAVE] ⊠ 🖥 [🍴]

Ⓐ ◆◆◆◆ **Loews Le Concorde** 🅷 ❀
(418) 647-2222. **$160-$270.** 1225 Place Montcalm. Corner of Grande Allee est. Int corridors. **Pets:** No service, supervision, crate.
[SAVE] [S☉] ⊠ 🖥 [▣] [🍴] [⌂]

STE-FOY

◆◆ **Comfort Inn** 🅼
(418) 872-5038. **$83-$97, 7 days notice.** 7320 boul Wilfrid-Hamel. On Hwy 138, 1.5 km w of boul Duplessis. Int corridors. **Pets:** Designated rooms, supervision.
[A$K] [S☉] ⊠ 🖥 [▣]

◆◆◆ **Holiday Inn Quebec Sainte-Foy** 🅼🅸 ❀
(418) 653-4901. **$109-$109.** 3125 boul Hochelaga. Autoroute 73, exit 136, Hochelaga ouest. Int corridors. **Pets:** Designated rooms, no service, supervision, crate.
⊠ 🖥 [▣] [⌂] [⊠]

Ⓐ ◆◆◆ **Motel L'Abitation** 🅼 ❀
(418) 653-7267. **$89-$130, 3 days notice.** 2828 boul Laurier. 1.5 km e of jct Hwy 73, exit 136. Ext corridors. **Pets:** Medium. No service, supervision, crate.
[SAVE] ⊠ 🖥 [▣] [⌂]

Ⓐ ◆◆ **Motel Oncle Sam** 🅼 ❀
(418) 872-1488. **$55-$99.** 7025 boul Wilfrid-Hamel. On Hwy 138 at jct boul Duplessis. Ext corridors. **Pets:** Other. Designated rooms, no service, supervision, crate.
[SAVE] ⊠ 🖥 [⌂]

❀ END METROPOLITAN AREA ❀

RIMOUSKI

◆◆ **Comfort Inn** 🅼 ❀
(418) 724-2500. **$85-$105.** 455 boul St-Germain Ouest. On Rt 132. Int corridors. **Pets:** Other. Supervision.
[A$K] [S☉] ⊠ 🖥 [▣]

◆◆ **Hotel L'Empress** 🅼🅸 ❀
(418) 723-6944. **$55-$69.** 360 Montee Industrielle. Hwy 20 eastbound until it ends, then 2.4 km n. Int corridors. **Pets:** Supervision.
[A$K] [S☉] ⊠ 🖥 [🍴] [⊠]

RIVIERE-DU-LOUP

◆◆ **Comfort Inn** 🅼 ❀
(418) 867-4162. **$98-$160.** 85 boul Cartier. Just s on boul Cartier from jct Hwy 20, exit 507. Int corridors. **Pets:** Other. Designated rooms, supervision.
[A$K] [S☉] ⊠

Ⓐ ◆◆ **Days Inn-Riviere-du-Loup** 🅼 ❀
(418) 862-6354. **$85-$135.** 182 rue Fraser. On Rt 132. Ext corridors. **Pets:** $10 daily fee/room. Supervision.
[SAVE] ⊠ 🖥 [▣] [⌂]

ROBERVAL

Ⓐ ◆◆◆ **Hotel Chateau Roberval** 🅷
(418) 275-7511. **$74-$160.** 1225 boul St-Dominique. Centre on Hwy 169. Int corridors. **Pets:** Designated rooms, no service, supervision, crate.
⊠ 🖥 [▣] [🍴] [⌂] [⊠]

ROCK FOREST

◆◆ **Comfort Inn** 🅼
(819) 564-4400. **$68-$86.** 4295 boul Bourque. On Rt 112, 1.5 km w of jct Hwy 410, exit 4. Int corridors. **Pets:** Supervision.
[A$K] [S☉] [⊠]

ROUYN NORANDA

◆◆ **Comfort Inn** 🅼
(819) 797-1313. **$67-$77.** 1295 rue Lariviere. On Rt 117, 4 km s from town centre. Int corridors. **Pets:** No service, supervision, crate.
[A$K] [S☉] ⊠ [▣]

SALABERRY DE VALLEYFIELD

◆◆◆ **Hotel Valleyfield by Delta** 🅷 ❀
(450) 373-1990. **$87-$87.** 40 ave du Centenaire. Center, corner rue St-Laurent. Int corridors. **Pets:** Medium. No service, supervision, crate.
⊠ 🖥 [▣] [🍴] [⌂]

SEPT ILES

◆◆ **Comfort Inn** 🅼 ❀
(418) 968-6005. **$71-$85.** 854 boul Laure. 4.5 km w on Rt 138. Int corridors. **Pets:** Small. No service, supervision, crate.
[A$K] [S☉] ⊠ 🖥

SHAWINIGAN

◆◆ **Auberge Escapade** 🅼
(819) 539-6911. **$54-$54.** 3383 rue Garnier. Hwy 55, exit 217. Int corridors. **Pets:** Medium. No service, supervision, crate.
⊠ 🖥 [🍴] [⊠]

SHAWINIGAN SUD

◆ **Motel Safari** 🅼
(819) 536-2664. **$60-$75.** 4500 12e Ave. On Rt 157. Ext/int corridors. **Pets:** Medium. Designated rooms, no service, supervision, crate.
[A$K] [S☉] 🖥 [⊠]

SHERBROOKE

◆◆◆ Delta Sherbrooke Hotel and Conference Centre [H]
(819) 822-1989. **$79-$89.** 2685 rue King Ouest. On Rt 112, 1 km e of jct Hwy 410, exit 4-E. Int corridors. **Pets:** Large. Designated rooms, supervision.
☒ ☕ 🍴 🏊

◆◆ Motel La Reserve [M]
(819) 566-6464. **Call for rates.** 4235 rue King ouest. On Rt 112, 1 km w of jct Hwy 410, exit 4-O. Ext/int corridors. **Pets:** Small. Designated rooms, no service, supervision, crate.
☒ ▣ ☕ 🏊

ST-ANTOINE-DE-TILLY

◆◆◆ Manoir de Tilly [CI] 🐾
(418) 886-2407. **$106-$135.** 3854 chemin de Tilly. Centre; 8.5 km n on Rt 273 from jct Hwy 20, exit 291. Int corridors. **Pets:** Other. Supervision.

ST-FAUSTIN-LAC-CARRE

◆ Motel sur la Colline [M] 🐾
(819) 688-2102. **$75-$75.** 357 Rt 117. On Rt 117, 4 km n of exit for city. Ext/int corridors. **Pets:** Designated rooms, no service, supervision, crate.
[A$K] [S/D] ▣ ☕ 🏊

ST-FELICIEN

[CAA] ◆◆◆ Hotel du Jardin [H]
(418) 679-8422. **$99-$150.** 1400 boul du Jardin. On Hwy 167. Int corridors. **Pets:** Medium. Designated rooms, no service, supervision, crate.
[SAVE] [S/D] ☒ ▣ 🍴 🏊 🎾

ST-HYACINTHE

[CAA] ◆◆ Hotel Gouverneur St-Hyacinthe [H] 🐾
(450) 774-3810. **$150-$160.** 1200 Johnson. Just e on Gauvin St from Laframboise Blvd from Hwy 20, exit 130S. Ext/int corridors. **Pets:** Small. Designated rooms, no service, supervision, crate.
[SAVE] [S/D] ☒ ▣ ☕ 🍴 🏊 🎾

ST-JEAN-PORT-JOLI

◆ Auberge du Faubourg [MI] 🐾
(418) 598-6455. **$49-$92, 7 days notice.** 280 ave de Gaspe Ouest. 2.4 km w on Rt 132 from jct Rt 204; Hwy 20, exit 414. Ext corridors. **Pets:** No service, supervision, crate.
[A$K] [S/D] ▣ 🍴 🏊 [AC]

ST-JEAN-SUR-RICHELIEU

◆◆ Comfort Inn [M]
(450) 359-4466. **$69-$109.** 700 rue Gadbois. At jct Hwy 35, exit 9, e on rue Pierre-Caisse. Int corridors. **Pets:** No service, supervision, crate.
[A$K] ☒ ▣ 🏊

◆◆ Hotel Gouverneur St-Jean-sur-Richelieu [H]
(450) 348-7376. **Call for rates.** 725 boul du Seminaire nord. At jct Hwy 35, exit 7. Int corridors. **Pets:** Supervision.
☒ ▣ ☕ 🍴 🏊

STE-AGATHE-NORD

◆◆ Auberge de la Sauvagine [CI]
(819) 326-7673. **Call for rates.** 1592 Rt 329 nord. Hwy 15, exit 89, 2 km n on Rt 329. Int corridors. **Pets:** Designated rooms, no service, supervision, crate.
☕ 🍴 🏊 🎾

STE-ANNE-DES-MONTS

[CAA] ◆◆ Motel Beaurivage [M]
(418) 763-2291. **$55-$75, 5 days notice.** 245 1 ere ave ouest. Just off Rt 132. Ext/int corridors. **Pets:** Designated rooms, supervision.
[SAVE] ☒ ▣ ☕ 🎾 [AC]

STE-MARTHE

◆◆◆ Auberge des Gallant [CI] 🐾
(450) 459-4241. **$89-$189.** 1171 chemin St-Henri. 8.5 km w on chemin St-Henri from jct Hwy 201. Int corridors. **Pets:** Large, other. $25 one-time fee/room. Designated rooms, supervision.
☒ ☕ 🏊 🎾

THETFORD MINES

◆◆ Comfort Inn [M] 🐾
(418) 338-0171. **$73-$83.** 123 boul Smith S. On Rt 112. Int corridors. **Pets:** Other. Designated rooms, no service, supervision, crate.
[A$K] [S/D] ☒ ▣

TRACY

◆◆ Hotel Le Dauphin [M]
(450) 743-2791. **$55-$97.** 8200 rue Industrielle. Hwy 30, exit 181 (boul de la Mairie). Int corridors. **Pets:** Large. Supervision.
▣

TROIS-RIVIERES

◆◆◆ Delta Trois-Rivieres Hotel and Conference Centre [H] 🐾
(819) 376-1991. **$78-$78.** 1620 rue Notre-Dame. Centre, corner rue St-Roch. Int corridors. **Pets:** No service, supervision, crate.
☒ ☕ 🍴 🏊

TROIS-RIVIERES-OUEST

◆◆ Comfort Inn [M]
(819) 371-3566. **$79-$98, 20 days notice.** 6255 rue Corbeil. Hwy 55, exit 183 (boul Jean XXIII), 2 km n of Laviolette Bridge. Int corridors. **Pets:** Supervision.
[A$K] [S/D] ☒ ▣ ☕

VAL-D'OR

◆◆ Comfort Inn [M] 🐾
(819) 825-9360. **$85-$93.** 1665 3 ieme ave. 3.9 km w of jct Rt 117. Int corridors. **Pets:** Other. Supervision.
[A$K] [S/D] ☒

SASKATCHEWAN

CARONPORT

(AA) ◆◆◆ The Pilgrim Inn M ❖
(306) 756-5002. $65-$65. 310 College Dr. Jct Main Access; on Trans Canada Hwy 1. Int corridors. **Pets:** Other. No service, supervision, crate.
SAVE S⊘ ✕ ✕

ELBOW

◆ Lakeview Lodge Motel M ❖
(306) 854-4444. $48-$53. 447 Saskatchewan St. Off Hwy 19, 1 km w. Ext corridors. **Pets:** Other. $10 deposit/room. Designated rooms, supervision.
✕ 🛢 ▣ 🍴

FOAM LAKE

◆ La Vista Motel M ❖
(306) 272-3341. $45-$50. Jct Hwy 16 & 310. On Hwy 16. Int corridors. **Pets:** No service, supervision, crate.
ASK S⊘ ✕ 🛢 ▣

KINDERSLEY

◆◆ Best Western Westridge Motor Inn MI
(306) 463-4687. $54-$72. 100 12 Ave NW. Jct of Hwy 7 and 21. Ext/int corridors. **Pets:** No service, supervision, crate.
✕ ▣ 🍴

LLOYDMINSTER

(AA) ◆◆ Imperial 400 Lloydminster MI
(306) 825-4400. $66-$79. 4320 44 St. From jct Hwy 17 and 16, 1.2 km e on Hwy 16. Ext/int corridors. **Pets:** Small. Designated rooms, no service, supervision, crate.
SAVE S⊘ ✕ 🛢 ▣ 🍴 🏊

MOOSE JAW

◆◆ Heritage Inn MI ❖
(306) 693-7550. $77-$150. 1590 Main St N. 1.5 km s of jct Trans Canada Hwy 1 and 2; access from Hwy 2 via Thatcher Dr. Int corridors. **Pets:** Other. $25 deposit/room. Supervision.
ASK ✕ 🛢 ▣ 🍴 🏊

(AA) ◆◆ Prairie Oasis Motel M ❖
(306) 693-8888. $48-$60. 955 Thatcher Dr E. Just s of jct Hwy 1 (Trans Canada Hwy) and Thatcher Dr. Ext corridors. **Pets:** Other. Designated rooms, no service, supervision, crate.
✕ ▣ 🏊 ✕

◆◆ Super 8 Motel-Moose Jaw M
(306) 692-8888. **Call for rates.** 1706 Main St N. 1.5 km s of jct Trans Canada Hwy 1 and 2; access from Hwy 2 via Thatcher Dr. Int corridors. **Pets:** Small. Designated rooms, no service, supervision, crate.
✕ 🐾

NORTH BATTLEFORD

◆ Super 8 Motel M
(306) 446-8888. $59-$75. 1006 Hwy 16 Bypass. 0.5 km nw of jct Hwy 16. Int corridors. **Pets:** Small. Supervision.
ASK S⊘ ✕ 🛢 CTV

◆◆ Tropical Inn MI
(306) 446-4700. $59-$69. 1001 Hwy 16 bypass. Corner of Battleford Rd and Hwy 16 bypass. Int corridors. **Pets:** Small. No service, supervision, crate.
✕ 🛢 ▣ 🍴 🏊

PRINCE ALBERT

◆◆ Comfort Inn M ❖
(306) 763-4466. $72-$88. 3863 2nd Ave W. 2.3 km s at jct Hwy 2 and Marquis Rd. Int corridors. **Pets:** Other. No service, supervision, crate.
ASK S⊘ ✕ 🐾

(AA) ◆ Imperial 400 Prince Albert MI ❖
(306) 764-6881. $66-$79. 3580 2nd Ave W. 2.1 km s at jct Hwy 2 and Marquis Rd. Ext/int corridors. **Pets:** Other. Designated rooms, supervision.
SAVE S⊘ ✕ 🛢 ▣ 🍴 🏊

◆◆ Travelodge Prince Albert MI
(306) 764-6441. $77-$87. 3551 2nd Ave W. 2.2 km s at jct Hwy 2 and Marquis Rd. Ext/int corridors. **Pets:** No service, supervision, crate.
ASK S⊘ ✕ 🛢 ▣ 🍴 🏊

REGINA

◆◆ Chelton Suites Hotel H
(306) 569-4600. **Call for rates.** 1907 11th Ave. Centre, corner Rose St. Int corridors. **Pets:** Small. No service, supervision, crate.
ASK ✕ 🛢 ▣ 🍴

◆◆◆ Comfort Inn M ❖
(306) 789-5522. $77-$85. 3221 East Eastgate Dr. Off Trans Canada Hwy 1, 2 km e of Ring Rd at eastern approach to Regina. Int corridors. **Pets:** Other. No service, supervision, crate.
ASK S⊘ ✕ ▣

(AA) ◆◆◆ Country Inn & Suites By Carlson M
(306) 789-9117. $63-$99, 3 days notice. 3321 E Eastgate Bay. Off Trans Canada Hwy 1, 2 km e of Ring Rd at eastern approach to city. Int corridors. **Pets:** No service, supervision, crate.
SAVE S⊘ ✕ 🐾 🛢 ▣